CONTEMPORARY POETS

Contemporary Writers of the English Language

Contemporary Poets

Contemporary Novelists
(including short story writers)

Contemporary Dramatists

CONTEMPORARY
POETS

SECOND EDITION

WITH A PREFACE BY
C. DAY LEWIS

EDITOR
JAMES VINSON

ASSOCIATE EDITOR
D. L. KIRKPATRICK

ST. JAMES PRESS
LONDON

ST. MARTIN'S PRESS
NEW YORK

CONTENTS

PREFACE
to the first edition

I have been asked to say something, by way of a preface, about what the writing and reading of poetry have meant to me in my own life. Writing it, which I did copiously from 14 or 15, must presently become either a way of life or a pleasant occasional pastime. For me it became the former: in my teens I wanted nothing so much as to be a Poet, and I firmly believed that I would never be capable of doing anything but write poetry: this is a good start, since it concentrates any powers one may have and sets up a strong initial momentum. Art cannot be a substitute for religion; but the habit of poetry has something in common with the habit of prayer – through it we search the unknown and search our own heart, to praise and to understand; we submit ourselves to a discipline which is partly a discipline of meditation and partly one of craft, of making language adapt itself to the conveying of states of mind incommunicable in any other way. The meditation and the craft are interfused, for his craft is the poet's mode of meditation.

Since words are what he works in, the young poet should always be extending his knowledge of them and of the way other poets have used them. He should read a page or two of the dictionary every day, as a priest reads his breviary. I wish I had done so myself. The colour, configuration, connotations of a single word may be the seed of a poem. Equally, he will read the work of poets living and dead, to learn what poetry is and gradually to understand how difficult it is to write a good poem. At school I read poetry because I wanted to be different, a one-man élite – it was a kind of social protest – Swinburne, Masefield, the early Yeats, and I was also attracted to Virgil, Wordsworth, Keats and Tennyson. What drew me – a raw dreamy, provincial boy – was the sound of words, the shapes of lyric writing, the sense that I was on the brink of a glorious mystery, and my own feeling for nature reflected back and as it were justified by the poems of other men.

Just as in early manhood one makes the most lasting friendships, so one receives the strongest impressions from poetry: though I have admired many poets since my Oxford days, it is the ones I read there to whom I most often return: the later Yeats, Owen, Frost, Emily Dickinson, Hardy, the Meredith of *Modern Love*, Pope, the Metaphysicals. I was fortunate in getting to know a number of coaevals who wrote poetry. I was no less fortunate in being susceptible to their enthusiasms but not overwhelmed by them: Donne and Eliot were two of these; but, making nothing of them at first, I put them aside and was able to return to them later when I was ripe for them.

Most poets' reading is a desultory affair, not a diligent and orderly course of "required reading." The books he requires are those of poets who, at any given stage of his life, can offer him encouragement, new ways of approaching poetry and new technical possibilities which present both a challenge and a way in to some new phase of his own work. This is the meaning of tradition, the right use of influences. A mediating power.

I was also lucky to be one of a group (it was never consciously a "movement") of young men who came from not dissimilar environments and responded keenly to one another's work and to the weather of the times. A considerable momentum is set up when a group of poets is pulling in roughly the same direction: but the degree of the momentum cannot be gauged until each of the group has cast off from the others and is pursuing an individual course. That course is unpredictable. With certain poets – I am not one of them – hindsight reveals a continuity of development: my own work, though I can see its obsessive and recurrent themes, appears to me a hand-to-mouth affair – a seizing upon any subject which comes my way and trying to make something of it. "Making something" of a subject means the deepening of its implications: but if one carries the deepening beyond what the subject will allow, the poem gets out of its depth and becomes an incoherent, echoing void filled with empty poeticisms.

One thing I have begun to learn from the reading and writing of poetry is level – the level at which a given poem should work. If we take such dissimilar objects as the writings of the Caroline poets and Clough's *Amours de Voyage*, we see how delicately these poets have adjusted their treatment to the weight of theme their verse can bear, never tempted into profundities where their subject would go astray and be lost. As we do not always want to be reading Shakespeare or Dante, so we should not always be pining to write the great poem. When I was young, I wished to write a better poem than Auden; later, I wanted each poem I was writing to be my best: now, I want to write another poem.

In the writing, I have always been so captivated by the charms and possibilities of more-or-less strict verse form that I very seldom have attempted the larger liberties of "free verse." It is as difficult to handle as the Protestant conscience – only a few poets in England and America have produced a first-class body of work in this medium. It may be that the poetry of the future will more and more be written in this formless form: we are told it enables the poem to be truly "organic" – whatever that may mean. But for me the endless fascination of verse, of organising a poem in metre and rhyme, outweighs any advantage that could be gained from the free way of writing. Form is not something a poet imposes on a poem: it is worked out by him in collaboration with the growing poem – its needs and nuances – as the meaning of that poem little by little becomes clear to him. I believe every artist is required to make coherent patterns out of chaos, not to reproduce it.

Nevertheless, one cannot have read poetry for fifty years, even in the specialised way poets read, without knowing that time and again the value of the great technical innovators has gone unrecognised by their contemporaries. The innovation of free verse as we know it, dating only from Whitman, is still resisted – if only by reactionary poets like myself. But so long as its practitioners can communicate in a memorable as well as a novel way, their work will justify itself: new forms will be seen to have emerged from behind the apparent formlessness, and the core of the poetic tradition be felt beneath a multiplicity of seemingly heterodox and even anarchic poems.

The present volume, which contains material about some thousand living poets from all over the world who write in English, is more than a handbook of information, less than a definitive roll of honour. We cannot tell how many of these names will survive through their work even beyond their own lifetime: 10%? 1%? Nevertheless, the book does honour to poetry, and provides a mass of information. It offers the serious reader a conspectus of respresentative writers from many countries, and so encourages him to extend his curiosity and broaden his reading. More important still, the book is a witness to the remarkable diversity of talents, the vigour and the inventiveness which poetry can command, even in a bitter, bewildering age when its sources are muddied or obstructed, "under conditions that seem unpropitious."

C. DAY LEWIS

EDITOR'S NOTE

The selection of poets included in this book is based upon the recommendations of the advisers listed on page xiii.

The entry for each poet included consists of a biography, a full bibliography, a comment by the poet on his verse if he chose to make one, and a signed critical essay on his work.

Only those critical studies recommended by the entrant have been listed. British and United States editions of all books have been listed; other editions are listed only if they are the first editions.

An appendix of entries has been included for some nineteen poets who have died since 1950 but whose reputations are essentially contemporary. Preceding the list of poetry anthologies are notes on recent poetry movements.

We would like to thank the entrants and contributors for their patience and cooperation in helping us compile this book.

ADVISERS

Donald Allen
James Bertram
Earle Birney
Edward Brathwaite
Hayden Carruth
John Robert Colombo
John Cotton
James A. Emanuel
G. S. Fraser
Donald Hall
Thomas Kinsella
Maurice Lindsay
Edward Lucie-Smith

Roland Mathias
Ralph J. Mills, Jr.
John Montague
William Plomer
Arthur Ravenscroft
Howard Sergeant
Martin Seymour-Smith
A. J. M. Smith
C. K. Stead
Douglas Stewart
Allen Tate
Anthony Thwaite

CONTRIBUTORS

Abdul Majid Bin Nabi Baksh
Duane Ackerson
Fleur Adcock
Michael André
Jane Augustine
Houston A. Baker, Jr.
Roger Baker
Bruce Beaver
D. R. Beeton
Charles G. Bell
Carol Bergé
Bernard Bergonzi
James Bertram
Harold Bloom
Robert Bly
Carl Bode
Elmer Borklund
Corrine Bostic
Robert Boyers
Gaynor F. Bradish
Edward Brathwaite
Alan Brownjohn
George Bruce
Joseph Bruchac
Jim Burns
Don Byrd
Edward Callan
Rivers Carew
Hayden Carruth
Charles Causley
D. D. C. Chambers
Samuel Charters
Richard Church
Alan Clark

Austin Clarke
Anne Cluysenaar
Arthur A. Cohen
John Robert Colombo
William Cookson
John R. Cooley
Seamus Cooney
John Cotton
Richard Damashek
Aneirin Talfan Davies
Anthony Delius
Peter Desy
Babette Deutsch
R. H. W. Dillard
Dale Doepke
Max Dorsinville
Louis Dudek
Douglas Dunn
Clifford Dyment
Terry Eagleton
Gavin Ewart
Nissim Ezekiel
Lloyd Fernando
Ian Fletcher
Carol Francis
G. S. Fraser
Norman Friedman
Robin Fulton
Norman T. Gates
Edward B. Germain
S. R. Gilbert
Michael Gnarowski
Alvin Greenberg
Thom Gunn

Ralph Gustafson
Donald Hall
Rodney Hall
Ruth Harnett
David M. Heaton
Geof Hewitt
William Heyen
Douglas Hill
Philip Hobsbaum
Jacqueline Hoefer
Daniel Hoffman
A. D. Hope
Theodore R. Hudson
Charles L. James
Louis James
Elizabeth Jennings
Eldred D. Jones
Glyn Jones
Nancy Keesing
Burton Kendle
Brendan Kennelly
Thomas Kinsella
James Korges
Richard Kostelanetz
Stanley W. Lindberg
Carl Lindner
Maurice Lindsay
Edward Lucie-Smith
Glenna Luschei
Norman MacCaig
Roy Macnab
Gerard Malanga
Roland Mathias
William Matthews
John Matthias
E. L. Mayo
George McElroy
David Meltzer
Ralph J. Mills, Jr.
Shankar Mokashi-Punekar
Charles Molesworth
John Montague
Edwin Morgan
Gerald Morgan
Norman Moser
Meenakshi Mukherjee
Rosalie Murphy
S. Nagarajan
Rudy Nelson
John Newlove
Leslie Norris
Robert Nye
William Oxley
Jerry Paris
Joseph Parisi

Derek Parker
E. Pereira
Lenrie Peters
Kirsten Holst Petersen
William Plomer
Peter Porter
John Press
Dudley Randall
Julia Randall
David Ray
J. C. Reid
John M. Reilly
Colin Rickards
Alan Roddick
J. P. W. Rogers
Gordon Rohlehr
Lawrence Russ
Anna Rutherford
Andreas Schroeder
Alexander Scott
Howard Sergeant
Martin Seymour-Smith
Thomas W. Shapcott
David Shapiro
Alan R. Shucard
Jon Silkin
Joan Murray Simpson
Robin Skelton
A. J. M. Smith
Kendrick Smithyman
M. K. Spears
Radcliffe Squires
William Stafford
Donald Barlow Stauffer
C. K. Stead
Carol Simpson Stern
Holly Stevens
Joan Stevens
Anne Stevenson
Douglas Stewart
Mark Strand
Lucien Stryk
Rosemary Sullivan
William Sylvester
Julian Symons
Henry Taylor
Myron Taylor
Arthur Terry
Derick S. Thomson
Edwin Thumboo
Anthony Thwaite
Anne Tibble
Saundra Towns
John Tripp
Michael True

Constantine Trypanis
Roland Turner
John Van Domelen
Mark Van Doren
Milton Van Sickle
James Vinson
Diane Wakoski
William Walsh

Lewis Warsh
James Whitehead
John Stuart Williams
Joseph Wilson
George Woodcock
Judith Wright
Leopoldo Y. Yabes

CONTEMPORARY
POETS

Dannie Abse
Chinua Achebe
Milton Acorn
Léonie Adams
Fleur Adcock
Rewi Alley
A. Alvarez
Kingsley Amis
A. R. Ammons
Michael Anania
Patrick Anderson
Carlos A. Angeles
John Ashbery
Margaret Atwood
Alvin Aubert
W. H. Auden
Margaret Avison
Kofi Awooner

Howard Baker
Gavin Bantock
Douglas Barbour
George Barker
Gene Baro
Taner Baybars
Bruce Beaver
Samuel Beckett
John Beecher
Patricia Beer
Henry Beissel
Ben Belitt
Charles G. Bell
Martin Bell
Marvin Bell
Frances Bellerby
Michael Benedikt
Louise Bennett
Asa Benveniste
Anne Beresford
Stephen Berg
Carol Bergé
Bill Berkson
Daniel Berrigan
Ted Berrigan
Francis Berry
Wendell Berry
James Bertolino
John Betjeman
Earle Birney
Elizabeth Bishop
Bill Bissett
D. M. Black

Thomas Blackburn
Robin Blaser
John Blight
Edmund Blunden
Robert Bly
Charles Boer
Alan Bold
Martin Booth
Philip Booth
Keith Bosley
Ronald Bottrall
George Bowering
Edgar Bowers
Kay Boyle
John Brandi
Edward Brathwaite
Richard Brautigan
Ray Bremser
Kwesi Brew
Elizabeth Brewster
Alan Brilliant
John Malcolm Brinnin
Edwin Brock
David Bromige
Gwendolyn Brooks
James Broughton
George Mackay Brown
Wayne Brown
Michael Dennis Browne
Alan Brownjohn
Michael Brownstein
George Bruce
Dennis Brutus
Tom Buchan
George Buchanan
Vincent Buckley
Charles Bukowski
Michael Bullock
Basil Bunting
William Burford
Kenneth Burke
Jim Burns
Stanley Burnshaw
Guy Butler

Alistair Campbell
David Campbell
Donald Campbell
Paul Carroll
Hayden Carruth
Martin Carter
Michael Casey

Charles Causley
Joseph Ceravolo
Syl Cheyney-Coker
John Ciardi
John Pepper Clark
Leonard Clark
Tom Clark
Austin Clarke
Jack Clemo
Lucille Clifton
Sydney Clouts
Anne Cluysenaar
Bob Cobbing
Frederick Cogswell
Leonard Cohen
Barry Cole
Elliott Coleman
Laurence Collinson
Frank Collymore
John Robert Colombo
Alex Comfort
Stewart Conn
Tony Connor
Robert Conquest
Anthony Conran
Stanley Cook
Clark Coolidge
Jane Cooper
Stanley Cooperman
Hilary Corke
Cid Corman
Sam Cornish
John William Corrington
Gregory Corso
John Cotton
Henri Coulette
Jeni Couzyn
Malcolm Cowley
Louis Coxe
Robert Creeley
Judson Crews
Kevin Crossley-Holland
Helen B. Cruickshank
Victor Hernández Cruz
Marcus Cumberlege
J. V. Cunningham
Allen Curnow
R. N. Currey

Peter Dale
Ruth Dallas
Robert Dana
Roy Daniells
D. K. Das
Kamala Das

Donald Davie
Peter Davison
Bruce Dawe
Paul Dehn
Anthony Delius
Ricaredo Demetillo
James Den Boer
Babette Deutsch
James Dickey
R. P. Dickey
William Dickey
Patric Dickinson
R. H. W. Dillard
Diane di Prima
Rosemary Dobson
Ed Dorn
Basil Dowling
Charles Doyle
Louis Dudek
Alan Dugan
Robert Duncan
Ronald Duncan
Douglas Dunn
Lawrence Durrell
Geoffrey Dutton
Bob Dylan

Charles Edward Eaton
Richard Eberhart
Michael Echeruo
George Economou
Russell Edson
Larry Eigner
George P. Elliott
Kenward Elmslie
James A. Emanuel
William Empson
Paul Engle
Maurice English
D. J. Enright
Theodore Enslin
Clayton Eshleman
Federico Espino
Abbie Huston Evans
Mari Evans
Gloria Evans Davies
Ronald Everson
William Everson
Gavin Ewart
Nissim Ezekiel

Ruth Fainlight
John Fairfax
Colin Falck
Padraic Fallon

Elaine Feinstein
Irving Feldman
James Fenton
Lawrence Ferlinghetti
Thomas Hornsby Ferril
Doug Fetherling
Edward Field
John Figueroa
Robert Finch
Donald Finkel
Ian Hamilton Finlay
Joan Finnigan
Roy Fisher
Robert Fitzgerald
Robert D. FitzGerald
Ian Fletcher
Charles Henri Ford
R. A. D. Ford
Gene Fowler
Janet Frame
Robert Francis
G. S. Fraser
Christopher Fry
John Fuller
Roy Fuller
Robin Fulton

Vi Gale
Isabella Stewart Gardner
Robert Garioch
Raymond Garlick
George Garrett
David Gascoyne
Karen Gershon
Brewster Ghiselin
Zulfikar Ghose
Monk Gibbon
Ruth Gilbert
David Gill
Allen Ginsberg
Nikki Giovanni
Robert Gittings
John Glassco
Duncan Glen
Denis Glover
Louise Glück
Michael Gnarowski
Denis Goacher
Patricia Goedicke
Giles Gordon
Phyllis Gotlieb
Henry Graham
W. S. Graham
Robert Graves
Jonathan Greene

Arthur Gregor
Horace Gregory
Bryn Griffiths
Geoffrey Grigson
Frederick Grubb
Peter Gruffydd
Barbara Guest
Harry Guest
Charles Gullans
Thom Gunn
Ralph Gustafson
Ramon Guthrie
Don Gutteridge

John Haines
Donald Hall
J. C. Hall
Rodney Hall
Michael Hamburger
Ian Hamilton
Christopher Hampton
Kenneth O. Hanson
Pauline Hanson
Michael S. Harper
Wilson Harris
Jim Harrison
Keith Harrison
Tony Harrison
David Harsent
Michael Hartnett
William Hart-Smith
Gwen Harwood
Lee Harwood
Robert Hayden
H. R. Hays
Samuel Hazo
Seamus Heaney
John Heath-Stubbs
Anthony Hecht
David Helwig
Hamish Henderson
A. L. Hendriks
Adrian Henri
Rayner Heppenstall
Calvin C. Hernton
Geof Hewitt
John Hewitt
Norman Hidden
Charles Higham
Geoffrey Hill
Daryl Hine
Jack Hirschman
George Hitchcock
Philip Hobsbaum
Sandra Hochman

Daniel Hoffman
David Holbrook
Molly Holden
John Hollander
Anselm Hollo
John Holloway
Edwin Honig
Jeremy Hooker
A. D. Hope
Michael Horovitz
Katherine Hoskins
Sylvester Houédard
Richard Howard
Anthony Howell
Barbara Howes
Harry Howith
Andrew Hoyem
Alejandrino Hufana
Robert Huff
Glyn Hughes
Ted Hughes
Richard Hugo
Sam Hunt
Pearce Hutchinson
Daniel Huws

David Ignatow
Kenneth Irby
Kevin Ireland
Valentin Iremonger

Alan Jackson
Paul Jacob
Josephine Jacobsen
David Jaffin
Peter Jay
Elizabeth Jennings
Judson Jerome
B. S. Johnson
Louis Johnson
Ronald Johnson
George Johnston
George Jonas
Brian Jones
D. G. Jones
David Jones
Evan Jones
Glyn Jones
LeRoi Jones
Erica Jong
M. K. Joseph
Donald Justice

Chester Kallman
Lenore Kandel

P. J. Kavanagh
Lionel Kearns
Richard Kell
Robert Kelly
X. J. Kennedy
Brendan Kennelly
Milton Kessler
Keorapetse Kgositsile
Galway Kinnell
Thomas Kinsella
James Kirkup
Carolyn Kizer
Etheridge Knight
John Knoepfle
Bill Knott
Kenneth Koch
James Koller
Bernard Kops
Mary Norbert Körte
Richard Kostelanetz
Maxine Kumin
Stanley Kunitz
Joanne Kyger

P. Lal
Philip Lamantia
Joseph Langland
Philip Larkin
Richmond Lattimore
James Laughlin
Irving Layton
Dennis Lee
Don L. Lee
Laurie Lee
Owen Leeming
Geoffrey Lehmann
John Lehmann
Tom Leonard
Douglas LePan
Laurence Lerner
Kenneth Leslie
Christopher Levenson
Denise Levertov
Peter Levi
Philip Levine
John L'Heureux
Laurence Lieberman
Lyn Lifshin
Maurice Lindsay
Lou Lipsitz
Dorothy Livesay
Douglas Livingstone
Taban lo Liyong
Liz Lochhead
Ronald Loewinsohn

John Logan
Christopher Logue
Michael Longley
Audre Lorde
Edward Lowbury
Robert Lowell
Walter Lowenfels
Edward Lucie-Smith

Lewis MacAdams
George MacBeth
Norman MacCaig
Hugh MacDiarmid
Gwendolyn MacEwen
Alastair Mackie
Alasdair Maclean
Archibald MacLeish
Joseph Macleod
Jackson Mac Low
Roy Macnab
Jay Macpherson
Barry MacSweeney
Charles Madge
Derek Mahon
Clarence Major
Eli Mandel
Bill Manhire
John Manifold
Jack Marshall
Harold Massingham
William H. Matchett
Roland Mathias
William Matthews
Seymour Mayne
E. L. Mayo
James McAuley
James J. McAuley
Michael McClure
Ronald McCuaig
Nan McDonald
Roger McDonald
David McFadden
Roy McFadden
Phyllis McGinley
Roger McGough
Thomas McGrath
Tom McKeown
Anthony McNeill
George McWhirter
Matthew Mead
David Meltzer
William Meredith
James Merrill
W. S. Merwin
Bert Meyers

Robert Mezey
James Michie
Christopher Middleton
Josephine Miles
Vassar Miller
Eric Millward
Ewart Milne
Adrian Mitchell
David Mitchell
John Moat
Shankar Mokashi-Punekar
John Mole
John Montague
Nicholas Moore
Dom Moraes
Edwin Morgan
Frederick Morgan
Pete Morgan
Robert Morgan
Howard Moss
Stanley Moss
Oswald Mtshali
Ian Mudie
Paul Muldoon
Richard Murphy
Les A. Murray
Susan Musgrave

Vladimir Nabokov
Pritish Nandy
Leonard Nathan
Adèle Naudé
Larry Neal
Howard Nemerov
John Newlove
bpNichol
Louise Townsend Nicholl
Norman Nicholson
John Frederick Nims
Leslie Norris
Harold Norse
Kathleen Nott
Alden Nowlan
Jeff Nuttall
Robert Nye

Philip Oakes
Ned O'Gorman
Desmond O'Grady
John Okai
Gabriel Okara
Elder Olson
Michael Ondaatje
George Oppen
Joel Oppenheimer

Gil Orlovitz
John Ormond
Vincent O'Sullivan
Rochelle Owens
William Oxley

Robert Pack
Ron Padgett
P. K. Page
Thomas Parkinson
Betty Parvin
Brian Patten
Raymond R. Patterson
Basil Payne
Okot p'Bitek
Grace Perry
Lenrie Peters
Donald Petersen
Paul Petrie
W. H. Petty
Tom Pickard
Marge Piercy
William Pillin
Christopher Pilling
Kenneth Pitchford
Ruth Pitter
Allen Planz
William Plomer
Hal Porter
Peter Porter
Craig Powell
F. T. Prince
Frederic Prokosch
J. H. Prynne
A. G. Prys-Jones
John Pudney
Sally Purcell
A. W. Purdy

Kathleen Raine
Carl Rakosi
A. K. Ramanujan
Paul Ramsey
Dudley Randall
Julia Randall
Margaret Randall
John Crowe Ransom
Tom Raworth
David Ray.
James Reaney
Peter Redgrove
Henry Reed
Ishmael Reed
F. D. Reeve
James Reeves

Alastair Reid
Kenneth Rexroth
Charles Reznikoff
Adrienne Rich
I. A. Richards
Edgell Rickword
Alan Riddell
Laura Riding
Anne Ridler
Roland Robinson
Jeremy Robson
Paul Roche
Alan Roddick
Carolyn M. Rodgers
Edouard Roditi
Alan Rook
William Pitt Root
Raymond Roseliep
Joseph Rosenblatt
M. L. Rosenthal
Alan Ross
Jerome Rothenberg
David Rowbotham
J. R. Rowland
A. L. Rowse
Larry Rubin
Muriel Rukeyser
Peter Russell
Vern Rutsala

Sonia Sanchez
Ed Sanders
Stephen Sandy
Aram Saroyan
May Sarton
Teo Savory
Vernon Scannell
James Schevill
Michael Schmidt
Dennis Schmitz
Andreas Schroeder
James Schuyler
Armand Schwerner
Alexander Scott
F. R. Scott
Tom Scott
E. J. Scovell
James Scully
Peter Scupham
Frederick Seidel
Howard Sergeant
Anne Sexton
A. J. Seymour
Martin Seymour-Smith
Thomas W. Shapcott

David Shapiro
Harvey Shapiro
Karl Shapiro
Richard Shelton
Judith Johnson Sherwin
Glen Siebrasse
Eli Siegel
Jon Silkin
Alan Sillitoe
Charles Simic
James Simmons
Louis Simpson
R. A. Simpson
Keith Sinclair
L. E. Sissman
C. H. Sisson
Sacheverell Sitwell
Robin Skelton
Knute Skinner
David Slavitt
A. J. M. Smith
Iain Crichton Smith
John Smith
Ken Smith
Michael Smith
Sydney Goodsir Smith
Vivian Smith
William Jay Smith
Kendrick Smithyman
W. D. Snodgrass
Gary Snyder
Mary Ellen Solt
Gilbert Sorrentino
Raymond Souster
Wole Soyinka
Muriel Spark
Charles Spear
Stephen Spender
Radcliffe Squires
William Stafford
Jon Stallworthy
Ann Stanford
George Stanley
George Starbuck
C. K. Stead
Stephen Stepanchev
Alan Stephens
Meic Stephens
Peter Stevens
Anne Stevenson
Douglas Stewart
Harold Stewart
Adrien Stoutenberg
Randolph Stow
Mark Strand

Lucien Stryk
Dabney Stuart
Hollis Summers
Robert Sward
May Swenson

John Tagliabue
Nathaniel Tarn
Allen Tate
James Tate
Colin Thiele
D. M. Thomas
R. S. Thomas
Derick Thomson
Anthony Thwaite
Edith Tiempo
Terence Tiller
Richard Tillinghast
Ruthven Todd
Charles Tomlinson
Rosemary Tonks
Emmanuel Torres
Shirley Toulson
Philip Toynbee
Sydney Tremayne
John Tripp
Constantine Trypanis
Lewis Turco
Gael Turnbull
W. Price Turner
Hone Tuwhare

Louis Untermeyer
John Updike
Constance Urdang

Jean Valentine
Mona Van Duyn
Monika Varma
Robert Vas Dias
Peter Viereck
José Garcia Villa
R. G. Vliet

Miriam Waddington
David Wagoner
John Wain
Diane Wakoski
Derek Walcott
Anne Waldman
Margaret Walker
Ted Walker
Christopher Wallace-Crabbe
Chad Walsh
William Wantling

Francis Warner
Rex Warner
Robert Penn Warren
Lewis Warsh
Robert Watson
Roderick Watson
Wilfred Watson
Francis Webb
Harry Webb
Phyllis Webb
Richard Weber
Ian Wedde
Theodore Weiss
Daniel Weissbort
James Welch
Anne Welsh
David Wevill
Philip Whalen
John Hall Wheelock
Peter Whigham
Laurence Whistler
Thomas Whitbread
Ivan White
Kenneth White
James Whitehead
Ruth Whitman
Reed Whittemore
John Wieners
Richard Wilbur
Peter Wild
Nancy Willard

C. K. Williams
Emmett Williams
Gwyn Williams
Herbert Williams
Hugo Williams
John Stuart Williams
Jonathan Williams
Miller Williams
Margaret Willy
Keith Wilson
Sheila Wingfield
Hubert Witheford
Wong May
Wong Phui Nam
George Woodcock
John Woods
David Wright
James Wright
Judith Wright

J. Michael Yates
Al Young
David Young
Douglas Young
Ian Young

Marya Zaturenska
Paul Zimmer
Harriet Zinnes
Louis Zukofsky
Lotte Zurndorfer

APPENDIX

James K. Baxter
John Berryman
C. Day Lewis
Jean Garrigue
Langston Hughes
Randall Jarrell
Patrick Kavanagh
Louis MacNeice
Frank O'Hara
Christopher Okigbo

Charles Olson
Kenneth Patchen
Sylvia Plath
Theodore Roethke
Delmore Schwartz
Burns Singer
Stevie Smith
Dylan Thomas
Vernon Watkins

ABSE, Dannie. Welsh. Born in Cardiff, Glamorgan, 22 September 1923. Educated at St. Illyd's College, Cardiff; University of South Wales and Monmouthshire, Cardiff; King's College, London; Westminster Hospital, London; qualified as physician, M.R.C.S., L.R.C.P. Served in the Royal Air Force, rising to the rank of Squadron Leader. Married Joan Mercer in 1951; has three children. Poet in Residence, Princeton University, New Jersey, 1973–74. Recipient: Foyle Award, 1960; Welsh Arts Council award, 1971. Agent: (drama) Margery Vosper Ltd., 53a Shaftesbury Avenue, London W.1; (literary) Anthony Shiel Associates Ltd., 52 Floral Street, London W.C.2. Address: 85 Hodford Road, London N.W.11, England.

PUBLICATIONS

Verse

After Every Green Thing. London, Hutchinson, 1949.
Walking under Water. London, Hutchinson, 1952.
Tenants of the House. London, Hutchinson, 1957; New York, Criterion Books, 1958.
Poems, Golders Green. London, Hutchinson, 1962.
Dannie Abse: A Selection. London, Studio Vista, 1963.
A Small Desperation. London, Hutchinson, 1968.
Demo. Frensham, Surrey, Sceptre Press, 1969.
Selected Poems. London, Hutchinson, and New York, Oxford University Press, 1970.
Corgi Modern Poets in Focus 4, with others, edited by Jeremy Robson. London, Corgi, 1972.
Funland and Other Poems. London, Hutchinson, and New York, Oxford University Press, 1973.

Recording: *Poets of Wales,* Argo, 1972.

Plays

Fire in Heaven (produced London, 1948). London, Hutchinson, 1956; revised version, as *Is the House Shut?* (produced London, 1964); revised version, as *In the Cage,* included in *Three Questor Plays,* 1967.
Hands Around the Wall (produced London, 1950).
House of Cowards (produced London, 1960). Included in *Three Questor Plays,* 1967; in *Twelve Great Plays,* edited by Leonard F. Dean, New York, Harcourt Brace, 1970.
The Eccentric (produced London, 1961). London, Evans, 1961.
Gone (produced London, 1962). Included in *Three Questor Plays,* 1967.
The Joker (produced London, 1962).
Three Questor Plays (includes *House of Cowards, Gone, In the Cage*). London, Scorpion Press, 1967.
The Dogs of Pavlov (produced London, 1969; New York, 1974). London, Vallentine Mitchell, 1973.
The Courting of Essie Glass, in *The Jewish Quarterly* (London), 1972.

Radio Plays: *Conform or Die,* 1957; *No Telegrams, No Thunder,* 1962; *You Can't Say Hello to Anybody,* 1964; *A Small Explosion,* 1964.

Novels

Ash on a Young Man's Sleeve. London, Hutchinson, 1954; New York,
Criterion Books, 1955.
Some Corner of an English Field. London, Hutchinson, 1956; New York,
Criterion Books, 1957.
O. Jones, O. Jones. London, Hutchinson, 1970.

Other

Medicine on Trial. London, Aldus Books, 1967; New York, Crown, 1969.
A Poet in the Family: An Autobiography. London, Hutchinson, 1974.

Editor, with Howard Sergeant, *Mavericks.* London, Editions Poetry and
Poverty, 1957.
Editor, *European Verse.* London, Studio Vista, 1964.
Editor, *Corgi Modern Poets in Focus 1, 3, 5.* London, Corgi, 1971–73.
Editor, *Thirteen Poets.* London, Poetry Book Society, 1973.
Editor, *Poetry Dimensions 2.* London, Robson Books, 1974.

Critical Studies: Interviews in *Poetry Book Society Bulletin* (London), Summer 1962,
Jewish Quarterly (London), Winter 1962–63, and *Flame* (Wivenhoe, Essex) March
1967; by the author in *The Listener* (London), 21 March 1967; by Roland Mathias, in
Anglo-Welsh Review (Quarry Bank, Worcestershire), Winter 1967.

*   *   *

After Every Green Thing, Dannie Abse's first book of poems, was declamatory,
full of an eloquence natural to his gifted Jewish family background. His elder
brother Leo, still and for many years M.P. for Pontypool, often spoke from a
soap-box in Llandaff Fields and Dannie himself, a combative Socialist in a Catholic
school, saw poetry as a generalised exposition of ideals and experiences, in which
repetition and rhetoric were dominant features. When he became a medical student,
first at Cardiff and then in London, the back pages of his notebooks were always
"noisy with poems." This first work, notwithstanding its eloquent verbosity and
the "publicness" of its poetic attitude (extended by Dannie's early practice in
reading poetry to an audience), is attractive even when flawed, and his second
book, *Walking under Water,* with its rejection of naivete and its much greater formal
control, is at first sight a disappointment. But behind the new discipline, in which a
variable refrain is often used to indicate the steps of the poetic argument and in
which symbols as well as words are rigorously organised, the successes of the
future were being prepared.

With *Tenants of the House* Dannie Abse emerged as a poet of undoubted significance. In this volume his hortatory intention is provided with a satisfactory vehicle
and an understood destination. Briefly, an extended symbolic concept, itself the
main or entire structure of the individual poem, uses the existing knowledge of the
reader to make the narrative line or the poetic argument absolutely clear, enabling
even the uninitiate among readers to "get at" the second level of meaning. Thus
"Social Revolution in England" overtly presents a picture of a bewildered aristocratic household emptied by the bailiffs. His fondness for refrain, too, brought Abse
at this stage to the discovery of a rhythmic structure which would carry the

message of the poem just as well as an understood "picture." The nursery-rhyme basis of "The Trial" –

> I'll sum up, the severe Judge moans
> showing the white of his knucklebones

– provides an area of unconscious suggestion in which the "meaning" is far more easily grasped.

Always remarkable for the sensitivity and honesty of his search for poetic experience, Dannie Abse, in his next volume, *Poems, Golders Green,* moved back to quieter and more personal country. This collection was perhaps less uniformly successful than its predecessor, but it contains some halfdozen very fine poems, amongst which "Return to Cardiff" (most of all for the scrupulousness of its "point") is outstanding:

> Unable to define anything I can hardly speak
> and still I love the place for what I wanted it to be
> as much as for what it unashamedly is
> now for me, a city of strangers, alien and bleak.

A Small Desperation is as remarkable for the width of its interest as for the variety of its formal treatment. Dannie Abse has now entirely "gritted down" his original eloquence: his vocational knowledge of medicine has provided him with more than one poetic breakthrough: and his self-criticism, amused as well as searching, gives him an approach to the "condition of man" which is as little limited as are his moods. Honesty can place him, for instance, at a poetic distance from Vietnam:

> Later, I walk back to the hotel thinking:
> wherever women crouch beside their dead,
> as Hecuba did, as Andromache,
> motionless as sculpture till they raise their head,
> with mouths wildly open to howl and curse,
> now they call that cloud not Helen, no,
> but a thousand names and each one still untrue.

In Dannie Abse's work now one finds not an entrenched position and a deliberate rhetoric, but a not-yet-defeated optimism and an anxious sensitivity, to people as to events. He is an entirely contemporary as well as important poet.

– Roland Mathias

————————

ACHEBE, Chinua. Nigerian. Born in Ogidi, 16 November 1930. Educated at Government College, Umuahia, 1944–47; University College, Ibadan, 1948–53, B.A. (London) 1953. Married Christie Okoli in 1961; has four children. Talks Producer, Lagos, 1954–57, Controller, Enugu, 1958–61, and Director, Lagos, 1961–66, Nigerian Broadcasting Corporation. Chairman, Citadel Books Ltd., Enugu, 1967. Visiting Professor, University of Massachusetts, Amherst, 1972–73. Since 1967,

Senior Research Fellow, University of Nigeria, Nsukka. Since 1970, Director of Heinemann Educational Books (Nigeria) Ltd., and Nwankwo-Ifejika and Company (Publishers) Ltd., Enugu. Since 1971, Editor of *Okike*, a Nigerian journal of new writing. Member, University of Lagos Council, 1966; Chairman, Society of Nigerian Authors, 1966. Recipient: Margaret Wrong Memorial Prize, 1959; Nigerian National Trophy, 1960; Rockefeller Fellowship, 1960; UNESCO Fellowship, 1963; Jock Campbell Award, *New Statesman*, 1965; Commonwealth Poetry Prize, 1972. Address: Institute of African Studies, University of Nigeria, Nsukka, Nigeria.

PUBLICATIONS

Verse

Beware Soul-Brother and Other Poems. Enugu, Nigeria, Nwankwo-Ifejika, 1971; New York, Doubleday, 1972; revised edition, London, Heinemann, 1972.
Christmas in Biafra and Other Poems. New York, Doubleday, 1973.

Novels

Things Fall Apart. London, Heinemann, 1958; New York, McDowell Obolensky, 1959.
No Longer at Ease. London, Heinemann, 1960; New York, Obolensky, 1961.
Arrow of God. London, Heinemann, 1964; New York, Day, 1967.
A Man of the People. London, Heinemann, and New York, Day, 1966.

Short Stories

The Sacrificial Egg and Other Short Stories. Onitsha, Nigeria, Etudo, 1962.
Girls at War and Other Stories. London, Heinemann, and New York, Doubleday, 1972.

Other

Chike and the River (juvenile). London and New York, Cambridge University Press, 1966.
How the Leopard Got His Claws (juvenile). Enugu, Nigeria, Nwankwo-Ifejika, 1972; New York, Third Press, 1973.

Editor, *The Insider: Stories of War and Peace from Nigeria.* Chatham, New Jersey, Chatham Bookseller, 1971.

Bibliography: in *Africana Library Journal* (New York), Spring 1970.

Critical Studies: *Chinua Achebe* by Arthur Ravenscroft, London, Longman, 1969; *Chinua Achebe* by David Carroll, New York, Twayne, 1970.

*   *   *

With the publication of *Christmas in Biafra*, Chinua Achebe showed the kind of mature and sensitive voice which might make his book the kind of landmark in African writing which his first novel, *Things Fall Apart*, was fourteen years earlier.

Coming out of the incredible tragedy of a civil war, the poems show remarkable restraint, their language simple and careful, yet never lacking in depth. Their imagery, as in the first few lines of ''After a War,'' is exact and intense:

> After a war life catches
> desperately at passing
> hints of normalcy like
> vines entwining a hollow
> twig . . .

Many of the poems make use of biting irony, as in ''Christmas in Biafra'' where the seasonal music broadcast over the radio bears messages of ''pure transcendental hate'' and the starving mothers and children stare mutely at a manger where Jesus lies ''plump-looking and rose-cheeked.''

Not all of the poems are about the Biafran conflict, for Achebe ranges from personal statements to far-reaching satirical comments on Western foreign policy as in ''He Loves Me; He Loves Me Not'':

> Harold Wilson he loves
> me he gave me
> a gun in my time
> of need to shoot
> my rebellious brother . . .

but Achebe's subject matter, as in his other writings, is rooted in the confused landscape of post-colonial Africa, where rotten politics and international deals affect the lives of people who still follow traditional paths. One of his best poems, ''Beware, Soul Brother,'' which begins

> We are the men of soul
> men of song we measure out
> our joys and agonies
> too, our long, long passion week
> in paces of the dance

is a reminder to the African reader of his connection with the earth and warns against those ''lying in wait leaden-footed, tone deaf / passionate only for the deep entrails / of our soil . . .,'' yet it is also a poem for all human beings who remember

> where a man's
> foot must return whatever beauties
> it may weave in air, where
> it must return for safety
> and renewal of strength. . . .

– Joseph Bruchac

ACORN, Milton. Canadian. Born in Charlottetown, Prince Edward Island, in 1923.

PUBLICATIONS

Verse

In Love and Anger. Privately printed, 1957.
The Brain's the Target. Toronto, Ryerson Press, 1960.
Against a League of Liars. Toronto, Hawkshead Press, 1960.
Jawbreakers. Toronto, Contact Press, 1963.
I've Tasted My Blood: Poems 1956 to 1968, edited by Al Purdy. Toronto, Ryerson Press, 1969.
I Shout Love and Shaving Off His Beard. Toronto Village Book Store Press, 1971.
More Poems for People. Toronto, NC Press, 1972.

*   *   *

Milton Acorn, after serving in the Canadian armed forces in World War II, gravitated to Montreal where he settled in the 1950's. Here, he published his first book, and, with two other writers, the poet Al Purdy and the poet/novelist Gwen MacEwen (whom he later married) he edited the little magazine, *Moment* (1960–1962). Acorn moved to Toronto in the early 1960's, and established himself as a figure of some prominence in the freer and less "established" sectors of that city's literary life. One of the first "public" poets and readers on the coffee house poetry reading scene in Canada in the 1950's, Acorn used to frequent and was variously associated with some of the great coffee houses of the period: *viz.* L'Echourie, El Cortijo, The Place, The Bohemian Embassy. He was honoured in a dramatic but genuine gesture by Canadian poets who presented him with the first Canadian Poets' Award in May of 1970 as an act of defiance and reproach aimed at the Governor General's Awards Committee which, with an American academic on its panel, had given the annual award to George Bowering and Gwendolyn MacEwen.

Milton Acorn is a poet of realistic statement and strong political feelings. A carpenter by training, he sees himself as a workingman's poet, and has taken a strong left-wing and nationalist stance. He says: "I have called myself many things; but I guess the one that sticks best is 'revolutionary poet' – that is 'revolutionary' in the political sense, not the poetic sense." From the outset, Acorn has written a poetry of direct, almost commonplace rhetoric, relying on hard, driving rhythms, and a near-palpable physicality of image. In scanning his own performance, Acorn has suggested that: "My own poetry, from 1956 on, has been built around the voice. I originally patterned the voice rhythm of my poems around that of the most intelligent (because the best-travelled and the best-read) of workers at that time – the merchant seamen."

Acorn's full range extends appreciably beyond the poetry of social and socialist concerns. He has a fine sense of locale which is revealed in his better poems which have to do with Maritime Canada; a certain lyrical bent which slides easily into his own peculiar kind of introspectiveness and poetic home-spun. Cragginess, a cragginess of mind and spirit, is Acorn's best quality:

> Since I'm Island-born home's as precise
> as if a mumbly old carpenter,
> shoulder-straps crossed wrong,
> laid it out,
> refigured to the last three-eighths of a shingle.

– Michael Gnarowski

ADAMS, Léonie. American. Born in Brooklyn, New York, 9 December 1899. Educated at Girls' High School; Barnard College, New York, B.A. (magna cum laude) 1922 (Phi Beta Kappa). Married the writer William Troy in 1933 (died, 1961). Bookshop Assistant, Best and Company, New York, 1922–23; Research Secretary, Yale University Law School, New Haven, Connecticut, 1923–24; Editorial Assistant, Wilson Publishing Company, New York, 1924; English Teacher, Hamilton Institute for Girls, New York, 1925; Editorial Assistant, Metropolitan Museum of Art, New York, 1926–28; Instructor, Washington Square College, New York, 1930–32; Instructor, Sarah Lawrence College, Bronxville, New York, 1933–34; Instructor, Bennington College, Vermont, 1935–37, 1941–45; Lecturer, New Jersey College for Women, New Brunswick, 1946–48; Lecturer, Columbia University, New York, 1947–68; Consultant in Poetry, 1948–49, and Fellow in American Letters, 1949–55, Library of Congress, Washington, D.C.; Lecturer, New School for Social Research, New York, 1952–53; Fulbright Professor, France, 1955–56; Visiting Professor, Trinity College, Hartford, Connecticut, Summer 1960; Visiting Professor, University of Washington, Seattle, 1960, 1968–69; Visiting Professor, Purdue University, Lafayette, Indiana, 1971–72. Recipient: Guggenheim Fellowship, 1928, 1929; National Institute of Arts and Letters grant, 1949; Harriet Monroe Poetry Award, 1954; Shelley Memorial Award, 1955; Bolligen Prize, 1955; Academy of American Poets Fellowship, 1959; National Endowment for the Arts grant, 1966; Brandeis University Creative Arts Award, 1968. D.Litt.: New Jersey College for Women, 1950. Secretary, National Institute of Arts and Letters, 1959–61. Address: Candlewood Mountain, R.R.2, New Milford, Connecticut 06776, U.S.A.

PUBLICATIONS

Verse

Those Not Elect. New York, McBride, 1925.
High Falcon and Other Poems. New York, Day, 1929.
This Measure. New York, Knopf, 1935.
Poems: A Selection. New York, Funk and Wagnalls, 1954.

Other

Editor, and translator with others, *Lyrics of François Villon.* Croton Falls, New York, Limited Editions Club, 1933.

Manuscript Collection: Beinecke Library, Yale University, New Haven, Connecticut.

Critical Studies: by Eda Low Walton, in *The Nation* (New York), 1930; "Three Younger Poets" by Louis Untermeyer, in *The English Journal* (Champaign, Illinois), 1932; *Poetry in Our Time* by Babette Deutsch, New York, Holt, 1952, revised edition, 1963.

Léonie Adams comments:

Lyric Poetry, in largely traditional forms. At formative period influenced by Elizabethan, early Romantic and, through Yeats largely, Symbolist poetry.

My work has been described sometimes as "metaphysical" and sometimes as "romantic." It is perhaps some sort of fusion. Though its images are largely from nature (and tradition of Nature), I have tended in my better work toward a contemplative lyric articulated by some sort of speech music. To find my "figurative language" in the natural scene was less a literary habit I think than one absorbed from my mother, in whom the traditional American experience of nature remained unbroken by her translation from rural Maryland to the city. It was only thus I could catch and keep the tune. As for other and larger modes I could admire, and (hopefully) possess, their use by others.

*   *   *

The poetry of Léonie Adams is very traditional: the poet's imagery derives from careful observations of beauty in nature. Her diction is strongly reminiscent of the Romantics: possibly to accommodate rhyme, normal sentence structure is often ignored:

> Never, being damned, see paradise.
> The heart will sweeten at its look;
> Nor hell was known, till paradise
> Our senses shook.
>   – "Those Not Elect"

At times, this device is bothersome, and combined with the heavy emphasis on traditional, romantic subjects, results in archaic textures:

> Birds are of passage now,
> Else-wending; where
> (Songless, soon gone of late)
> They night among us,
> No tone now upon grass
> Downcast from hedge or grove
> With goldening day invites.
>   – "Words for the Raker of Leaves"

In counterpoint, the best of Miss Adams's work incorporates traditional concerns with a contemporary vision. The reader has been lulled by her lyrics (which are varied enough rhythmically that their lulling is accomplished by subject, not tedious sing-song). "Ghost Tree" begins as a typically romantic ode: "Oh beech, unbind your yellow leaf, for deep / The honeyed time lies sleeping, and lead shade / Seals up the eyelids of its golden sleep." Suddenly, the poet abandons the multi-syllabic adjectives and allows the scene to describe its own potential:

> And here is only the cold scream of the fox,
> Only the huntsman following on the hound;
> While your quaint-plumaged,
> The bird that your green summer boughs lapped round,
> Bends south its soft bright breast.

These poems are meticulously crafted. Nowhere does the reader feel that the poet has abandoned her poem in favor of a digressive second look at the subject. This single-mindedness sometimes results in an almost too-predictable unity to Miss Adams's work, but the energy with which she welds her vision to her art provides an oasis for those who thirst after a time when the poem was a song of life, neither contradictory nor simple.

– Geof Hewitt

ADCOCK, Fleur. British. Born in Papakura, New Zealand, 10 February 1934; emigrated to the United Kingdom in 1963. Educated in England, 1939–47; Wellington Girls' College and Victoria University of Wellington, New Zealand, M.A. (honours) in classics. Divorced; has two children. Temporary Assistant Lecturer in Classics, University of Otago, New Zealand, 1958. Held library posts at the University of Otago, 1959–61, and at Turnbull Library, Wellington, 1962. Since 1963, Assistant Librarian, Foreign and Commonwealth Office Library, London. Recipient: Festival of Wellington Prize, 1961; New Zealand State Library Fund Award, 1964; Buckland Award, 1967; Jessie MacKay Award, 1968, 1972. Address: 14 Lincoln Road, London N2 9DL, England.

PUBLICATIONS

Verse

The Eye of the Hurricane. Wellington, Reed, 1964.
Tigers. London, Oxford University Press, 1967.
High Tide in the Garden. London, Oxford University Press, 1971.
Corgi Modern Poets in Focus 5, with others, edited by Dannie Abse. London, Corgi, 1973.
The Scenic Route. London, Oxford University Press, 1974.

Critical Study: Introduction by Dannie Abse to *Corgi Modern Poets in Focus 5*, 1973.

Fleur Adcock comments:

I can't give a code of my poetic practice or a set of rules by which I have operated; I can only point to certain tendencies and outline an attitude. Poetry is a search for ways of communication; it must be conducted with openness, flexibility, and a constant readiness to listen. The content of my poems is the content of those parts of my life which are directly experienced: relationships with people or places; images and insights which have presented themselves sharply from whatever source, conscious or subconscious; the investigation of certain ideas. The voice has to be my own and has to carry the weight of whatever I want to say and whatever in addition the poem may want to say for me. Therefore I take care to be honest, not to use tricks or masks or to act as a ventriloquist. For this reason my language tends to be plain, syntactically conventional, and, I hope, accessible.

My verse forms are relatively traditional (traditions alter). In general they have moved away from strict classical patterns in the direction of greater freedom – as is

19

usual with most artists learning a trade. It takes courage, however, to leave all props behind, to cast oneself, like Matisse, upon pure space. I still await that confidence. In the meantime I continue to learn; and sometimes find it fruitful to return to a rigid metrical form as a discipline and for a different kind of exploration.

I write primarily for the printed page, not for performance (regarding poetry readings as the trailer, not the movie). But because the sound of words is central to the experiencing of a poem I read my work aloud as it develops and try to remove anything which is clumsy or unacceptable to the ear. As for the eye, the patterns of lines in type don't particularly interest me; words, not their shape on the page, are what matter. If one is fortunate their destination, like their origin, will be as voices speaking in the mind.

*   *   *

An inherited interest in psychology (shared professionally by her parents and her sister Marilyn Duckworth, who writes psychological novels), sharpened by early classical studies, gives more depth and edge to the verses of Fleur Adcock than is commonly found among women poets. She has expressed her admiration for the work of Yeats, Graves and Auden – "who, like the best of the Elizabethan and seventeenth century poets, have written in strict verse-forms with no loss of grace, passion or precision. I find understatement generally more telling than rhetorical exaggeration . . ." (*Recent Poetry in New Zealand,* edited by Charles Doyle, Auckland, Collins, 1965, p. 18). Her first book of verse, *The Eye of the Hurricane,* shows throughout this compactness of form, crispness of phrase, and skilful selection of detail, in short. poems which do not neglect the natural surface of things, but constantly turn inward to explore or illuminate the clash of deeply-involved personal relationships. Fleur Adcock's mind is always her own, sometimes startingly so. She can write chilling idiosyncratic variations on scraps of old myth or folklore; a later expanded collection, *Tigers,* contains poems which make very effective imaginative use of animal symbolism. Since 1963 she has lived in London with her young son, and her work shows even less New Zealand colouring than formerly. It is Fleur Adcock's special distinction – writing with unusual candour as wife, lover, or mother-to-child – to avoid any trace of cosiness or sentimentality: in her poetry she is always alert, feline, and formidably self-possessed – suggesting a kind of anti-romantic George Sand of another age, or a more worldly Christina Rossetti.

– James Bertram

ALLEY, Rewi. New Zealander. Born in Springfield, Canterbury, 2 December 1897. Educated at Christchurch Boys High School. Served in the New Zealand Expeditionary Force during World War I: Military Medal. Sheep farmer, 1920–26. Has lived in China since 1926: Factory Inspector, Shanghai, 1927–38, then active in Gung Ho Cooperatives Movement; Director of Baillie Industrial School, Sandan, 1941–45; later New Zealand representative for the Asian and Pacific Peace Liaison Committee. D.Litt.: Victoria University of Wellington, 1971. Agent: P. J. Alley, 70 Clyde Road, Christchurch 4, New Zealand. Address: 1 Yung Ke Road, Peking, China.

PUBLICATIONS

Verse

Gung Ho: Poems, edited by H. Winston Rhodes.   Christchurch, Caxton Press, 1948.
Leaves from a Sandan Notebook (includes prose), edited by H. Winston Rhodes.   Christchurch, Caxton Press, 1950.
This Is China Today: Poems, edited by H. Winston Rhodes.   Christchurch, Rewi Alley Aid Group, 1951.
Fragments of Living Peking and Other Poems, edited by H. Winston Rhodes.   Christchurch, New Zealand Peace Council, 1955.
Beyond the Withered Oak Ten Thousand Saplings Grow: Poems, edited by H. Winston Rhodes.   Christchurch, Caxton Press, 1962.
Who Is the Enemy? Poems.   Peking, New World Press, 1964.
The Mistake: Poems.   Peking, New World Press, 1965.
For the Children of the Whole World.   New York, Far East Reporter, 1966.
In Southeast Asia Today: The United States, Vietnam, China: Four Poems.   New York, Far East Reporter, 1966.
What Is Sin? Poems.   Christchurch, Caxton Press, 1967.
Twenty-Five Poems of Protest.   Christchurch, Caxton Press, 1968.
Upsurge: Asia and the Pacific: Poems.   Christchurch, Caxton Press, 1969.
73-Man to Be: Poems.   Christchurch, Caxton Press, 1970.
Winds of Change.   Christchurch, Caxton Press, 1972.
Poems for Aotea Roa.   Auckland, New Zealand China Society, 1972.
Hills of Blue.   Christchurch, Caxton Press, 1974.

Other

The Chinese Industrial Cooperatives.   Chungking, China Information Publishing Company, 1940.
Two Years of Indusco.   Hong Kong, Chinese Industrial Cooperatives, 1940.
Yo Banfa! (We Have a Way!), edited by Shirley Barton.   Peking, China Monthly Review, 1952.
The People Have Strength: Sequel to "Yo Banfa!"   Peking, privately printed, 1954.
Man Against Flood: A Story of the 1954 Flood on the Yangtse and of the Reconstruction That Followed It.   Peking, New World Press, 1956.
Spring in Vietnam: A Diary of a Journey.   Christchurch, Raven Press, 1956.
Land of the Morning Calm: A Diary of Summer Days in Korea.   Christchurch, Raven Press, 1956.
Buffalo Boys of Vietnam.   Hanoi, Foreign Languages Publishing House, 1956.
Journey to Outer Mongolia: A Diary with Poems.   Christchurch, Caxton Press, 1957.
Human China: A Diary with Poems.   Christchurch, New Zealand Peace Council, 1957.
Peking Opera: An Introduction Through Pictures.   Peking, New World Press, 1957.
Children of the Dawn: Stories of Asian Peasant Children.   Peking, New World Press, 1957.
Stories out of China.   Peking, New World Press, 1958.
Sandan: An Adventure in Creative Education.   Christchurch, Caxton Press, 1959.
Towards a People's Japan.   Christchurch, Caxton Press, 1960.

China's Hinterland in the Leap Forward. Peking, New World Press, 1961.
3 Conferences at Cairo, New Delhi, and Bandung. . . . Christchurch, Caxton Press, 1961.
Land and Folk in Kiangsi: A Chinese Province in 1961. Peking, New World Press, 1962.
Amongst Hills and Streams of Yunan in the Fall of 1962. Peking, New World Press, 1963.
Our Seven – Their Five: A Fragment from the Story of Gung Ho. Peking, New World Press, 1963.
Co-operative Management, with Shou Tseng Meng. New Delhi, National Co-operative Union of India, 1964.
In the Spirit of Hunghu: A Story of Hupeh Today. Peking, New World Press, 1966.
Fruition: The Story of George Alwin Hogg. Christchurch, Caxton Press, 1967.
Oceania. Christchurch, Caxton Press, 1971.
Chinese Children: A Book of Photographs. Christchurch, Caxton Press, 1972.
The Prisoners. Christchurch, Caxton Press, 1973.
The Rebels. Christchurch, Caxton Press, 1973.
Travels in China 1966–1971. Peking, New World Press, 1973.
A Highway and an Old Chinese Doctor. Christchurch, Caxton Press, 1973.

Translator, *Peace Through the Ages: Translations from the Poets of China.* Peking, 1954.
Translator, *The People Speak Out: Translations of Poems and Songs of the People of China.* Peking, 1954.
Translator, *Lament of the Soldier's Wife,* by Dang-Tran-Con. Hanoi, Foreign Languages Publishing House, 1956.
Translator, *The People Sing: More Translations of Poems and Songs of the People of China.* Peking, 1958.
Translator, *Poems of Revolt: Some Chinese Voices from the Last Century.* Peking, New World Press, 1962.
Translator, *Selected Poems,* by Tu Fu. Peking, Foreign Languages Press, 1962.
Translator, *Not a Dog: An Ancient Thai Ballad.* Peking, New World Press, 1962.
Translator, *The Eighteen Laments,* by Yen Ts'ai. Peking, New World Press, 1963.

*   *   *

Rewi Alley's verse (whether in his own spasmodic lyrics, or in translations from the Chinese) is the by-product of an intensely active life as a pioneer social worker, organiser of industrial co-operatives, and propagandist of the Chinese Revolution. No westerner has been so intimately linked with the struggles of the Chinese people since 1927 as this stocky New Zealander who has tramped the hills and fields of every province, and now lives as an honoured sage in the old Legation Quarter of Peking.

Alley has the broad vision of a poet, with few of the niceties of the craft. A self-made writer, he is far more concerned with content than with form, and can turn out political verses that are mere lists of slogans. But when he is writing directly about people and places, things seen and done, his warm human sympathy and creative response to experience find their own natural eloquence.

His free-verse jottings (generally made on the spot, and seldom revised) chart with vivid immediacy the landscape, the lives, and the longings of ordinary people confronting war, revolution and social change. More recently, he has written as vividly of scenes and people in his native New Zealand. Because of his unrivalled familiarity with the Chinese vernacular and terrain, and his historical understanding, his translations from classical and modern Chinese poetry have a force and vigour seldom achieved by more academic scholars.

In verse as in prose, Alley can be very uneven. Yet when passionate conviction touches his superb firsthand material into imaginative life, he becomes a direct popular writer (in eastern or western traditions) of a very high order indeed.

– James Bertram

———————

ALVAREZ, A(lfred). British. Born in London, 5 August 1929. Educated at Oundle School, Northamptonshire; Corpus Christi College, Oxford (Senior Research Scholar, 1952–53, 1954–55), B.A. 1952, M.A. 1956; Princeton University, New Jersey (Proctor Visiting Fellow, 1953–54). Married Ursula Barr in 1956 (marriage dissolved, 1961), one son; Anne Adams, 1966, one son and one daughter. Gauss Lecturer, Princeton University, 1957–58; Visiting Professor, Brandeis University, Waltham, Massachusetts, 1960, and State University of New York, Buffalo, 1966. Editor, *Journal of Education*, 1957; Drama Critic, *New Statesman*, London, 1958–60. Since 1956, Advisory Poetry Editor, *The Observer*, London, and since 1965, Advisory Editor, Penguin Modern European Poets in Translation. Recipient: Rockefeller Fellowship, 1955; D. H. Lawrence Fellowship, 1958; Vachel Lindsay Prize (*Poetry*, Chicago), 1961. Address: c/o The Observer, 160 Queen Victoria Street, London E.C.4, England.

PUBLICATIONS

Verse

(*Poems*). Oxford, Fantasy Press, 1952.
The End of It. Privately printed, 1958.
Twelve Poems. London, The Review, 1968.
Lost. London, Turret Books, 1968.
Penguin Modern Poets 18, with Roy Fuller and Anthony Thwaite. London, Penguin, 1970.
Apparition. Brisbane, University of Queensland Press, 1971.
The Legacy. London, Poem-of-the-Month Club, 1972.

Play

Screenplay: *The Anarchist*, 1969.

Novel

Hers. London, Weidenfeld and Nicolson, 1974; New York, Random House, 1975.

Other

The Shaping Spirit: Studies in Modern English and American Poets. London,
   Chatto and Windus, 1958; as *Stewards of Excellence: Studies in Modern English*
   and American Poets, New York, Scribner, 1958.
The School of Donne. London, Chatto and Windus, 1961; New York, Pantheon
   Books, 1962.
Under Pressure: The Artist and Society: Eastern Europe and the U.S.A. London,
   Penguin, 1965.
Beyond All This Fiddle: Essays 1955–1967. London, Allen Lane, 1968; New
   York, Random House, 1969.
The Savage God: A Study of Suicide. London, Weidenfeld and Nicolson, 1971;
   New York, Random House, 1972.
Beckett. London, Fontana, and New York, Viking Press, 1973.

Editor, *The New Poetry: An Anthology.* London, Penguin, 1962; revised edition, 1966.

*   *   *

A. Alvarez has published very little poetry – his output is barely enough to fill a
standard slim volume. One gets the feeling that his production was inhibited by the
fact that he was, for some years, the most celebrated critic of contemporary verse
in England, and also, through his Penguin collection *The New Poetry*, a most
influential anthologist. It was he who denounced the "gentility principle," and
proclaimed the merits of Confessional Verse – especially that written by two
Americans, Robert Lowell and Sylvia Plath. One might expect Alvarez's own
poems to show very visible signs of Lowell's influence in particular, but this is not
the case. What is admirable about them is a restraint which seems to spring from
the sources – Augustan verse and the work of William Empson – which also
inspired the poets of the Movement, but with small trace of Movement mannerisms. Characteristically, the poems proceed by means of direct statements:

> The same wrist lies along my cheek;
> My fingers touch it. The same head on my chest
> Stirs. My arms round the same body;
> And I feel the dead arms stir.
> My fingers in the same dead hair.
> The same belly, dead thighs stir.

There is enough individuality here to make one wish that Alvarez had been more
prolific.

– Edward Lucie-Smith

AMIS, Kingsley (William).   British.   Born in London, 16 April 1922. Educated at
City of London School; St. John's College, Oxford, M.A. Served in the Royal
Corps of Signals, 1942–45. Married Hilary Ann Bardwell in 1948 (marriage dis-
solved, 1965); the novelist Elizabeth Jane Howard, 1965; has three children. Lect-
urer in English, University College, Swansea, Wales, 1949–61; Fellow in English,
Peterhouse, Cambridge, 1961–63. Visiting Fellow in Creative Writing, Princeton
University, New Jersey, 1958–59; Visiting Professor, Vanderbilt University, Nash-
ville, Tennessee, 1967. Recipient: Maugham Award, 1955. Agent: A. D. Peters, 10
Buckingham Street, London W.C.2, England.

PUBLICATIONS

Verse

Bright November.   London, Fortune Press, 1947.
A Frame of Mind.   Reading, Berkshire, University of Reading School of Art,
  1953.
A Case of Samples: Poems 1946–1956.   London, Gollancz, 1956; New York,
  Harcourt Brace, 1957.
The Evans Country.   Oxford, Fantasy Press, 1962.
Penguin Modern Poets 2, with Dom Moraes and Peter Porter.   London, Pen-
  guin, 1962.
A Look round the Estate: Poems 1957–1967.   London, Cape, 1967; New York,
  Harcourt Brace, 1968.

Recordings: Kingsley Amis Reading His Own Poems, Listen, 1962; Poems, with
Thomas Blackburn, Jupiter, 1962.

Plays

Radio Play: Something Strange, 1962.

Television Plays: A Question about Hell, 1964; The Importance of Being Harry,
1971.

Novels

Lucky Jim.   London, Gollancz, and New York, Doubleday, 1954.
That Uncertain Feeling.   London, Gollancz, 1955; New York, Harcourt Brace,
  1956.
I Like It Here.   London, Gollancz, and New York, Harcourt Brace, 1958.
Take a Girl like You.   London, Gollancz, 1960; New York, Harcourt Brace,
  1961.
One Fat Englishman.   London, Gollancz, 1963; New York, Harcourt Brace,
  1964.
The Egyptologists, with Robert Conquest.   London, Cape, 1965; New York,
  Random House, 1966.
The Anti-Death League.   London, Gollancz, and New York, Harcourt Brace,
  1966.
Colonel Sun: A James Bond Adventure (as Robert Markham).   London, Cape,
  and New York, Harper, 1968.
I Want It Now.   London, Cape, 1968; New York, Harcourt Brace, 1969.
The Green Man.   London, Cape, 1969; New York, Harcourt Brace, 1970.
Girl, 20.   London, Cape, 1971.
The Riverside Villas Murder.   London, Cape, and New York, Harcourt Brace,
  1973.
Ending Up.   London, Cape, and New York, Harcourt Brace, 1974.

Short Stories

My Enemy's Enemy.   London, Gollancz, 1962; New York, Harcourt Brace,
  1963.
Penguin Modern Stories 11, with others.   London, Penguin, 1972.
Dear Illusion.   London, Covent Garden Press, 1972.

Other

Socialism and the Intellectuals. London, Fabian Society, 1957.
New Maps of Hell: A Survey of Science Fiction. New York, Harcourt Brace,
  1960; London, Gollancz, 1961.
The James Bond Dossier. London, Cape, and New York, New American
  Library, 1965.
Lucky Jim's Politics. London, Conservative Political Centre, 1968.
What Became of Jane Austen? and Other Essays. London, Cape, 1970; New
  York, Harcourt Brace, 1971.
On Drink. London, Cape, 1972; New York, Harcourt Brace, 1973.
Kipling and His World. London, Thames and Hudson, 1974.

Editor, with James Michie, *Oxford Poetry 1949.* Oxford, Blackwell, 1949.
Editor, with Robert Conquest, *Spectrum: A Science Fiction Anthology.* London,
  Gollancz, 1961; New York, Harcourt Brace, 1962. (and later volumes.)
Editor, *Selected Short Stories of G. K. Chesterton.* London, Faber, 1972.
Editor, *Tennyson.* London, Penguin, 1973.

Manuscript Collection: State University of New York, Buffalo.

Kingsley Amis comments:

I used to be lumped into the "Movement" of the 1950's. No doubt I have, or
had, something in common with some of the other poets lumped into it.

*   *   *

Although Kingsley Amis's most celebrated work is his fiction, he began as a
poet, continues to write and publish poems, and is unambiguously convinced that
poetry is a higher form of art. His first book (*Bright November*) was decent but
quite unremarkable, though it included one poem – "Beowulf" – which he has
reprinted and which sits happily enough with his later work. The first clearly
Amisian poems appeared in *A Frame of Mind*, most of the contents of which were
collected in *A Case of Samples: Poems 1946–1956.* There is a good deal of variety
here, both in form and content, and some evidence of well-learned and well-
digested influence from Auden, Graves, and Amis's own admired contemporary,
Philip Larkin. The plain-man stance is apparent, with a distrust of extremes and a
reliance on disabused commonsense; but this is managed with more gravity, more
mutedly, than in the novels. "Against Romanticism" sets the tone well, in its
steady-eyed wish for a landscape

> not parched or soured by frantic suns
>   Doubling the commands of a rout of gods,
> Nor trampled by the havering unicorn;
>   Let the sky be clean of officious birds
> Punctiliously flying on the left;
>   Let there be a path leading out of sight,
> And at its other end a temperate zone:
>   Woods devoid of beasts, roads that please the foot.

The novelist of *Lucky Jim* and its successors is more recognizable in *A Look round the Estate: Poems 1957–1967*, particularly in the sequence of coarse and comical vignettes, "The Evans Country," with its sly and almost admiring delineation of Dai Evans, South Walian hypocrite and lecher. "What about you?" – the question with which both the opening and closing poems end – is a clear invitation not to cast the first stone at Dai before having a good look at oneself.

The love poems are less individual, and in fact the hand of Graves is too obvious in them. In general, though, the later poems seem intelligent, witty, concentrated, and essentially light by-products of the impulse that has made the Amis novels. They compare favourably with Larkin's rather similar lighter poems (such as "Naturally the Foundation Will Bear Your Expenses"), but with one early exception (the poem "Masters," which was first published in 1949), Amis has never approached the measured grandeur of Larkin's best work.

– Anthony Thwaite

AMMONS, A(rchie) R(andolph). American. Born in Whiteville, North Carolina, 18 February 1926. Educated at Wake Forest College, North Carolina, B.A. 1949; University of California, Berkeley, 1950–52. Served in the United States Naval Reserve, 1944–46. Married Phyllis Plumbo in 1949; has one child. Principal, Hatteras Elementary School, North Carolina, 1949–50. Executive Vice-President, Friedrich and Dimmock, Inc., Mellville, New Jersey, 1952–62. Since 1964, Member of the Faculty, Associate Professor, 1969–71, since 1971, Professor of English, and since 1973, Goldwin Smith Professor of English, Cornell University, Ithaca, New York. Poetry Editor, *Nation*, New York, 1963. Recipient: Bread Loaf Writers Conference Scholarship, 1961; Guggenheim Fellowship, 1966; American Academy of Arts and Letters Travelling Fellowship, 1967; National Endowment for the Arts grant, 1969; Levinson Prize (*Poetry*, Chicago), 1970; National Book Award, 1973. D.Litt.: Wake Forest University, 1972; University of North Carolina, Chapel Hill, 1973. Address: Department of English, Cornell University, Ithaca, New York 14850, U.S.A.

PUBLICATIONS

Verse

Ommateum, with Doxology. Philadelphia, Dorrance, 1955.
Expressions of Sea Level. Columbus, Ohio State University Press, 1964.
Corsons Inlet: A Book of Poems. Ithaca, New York, Cornell University Press, 1965.
Tape for the Turn of the Year. Ithaca, New York, Cornell University Press, 1965.
Northfield Poems. Ithaca, New York, Cornell University Press, 1966.
Selected Poems. Ithaca, New York, Cornell University Press, 1968.
Uplands. New York, Norton, 1970.

Briefings: Poems Small and Easy.   New York, Norton, 1971.
Collected Poems 1951–1971.   New York, Norton, 1972.
Sphere: The Form of a Motion.   New York, Norton, 1974.

Critical Studies: "A Poem Is a Walk" by the author, in *Epoch* (Ithaca, New York), Fall 1968; "A. R. Ammons: When You Consider the Radiance" by Harold Bloom, in *The Ringers in the Tower*, Chicago, University of Chicago Press, 1971; "A. R. Ammons Issue" of *Diacritics* (Ithaca, New York), 1974.

                          *   *   *

   A. R. Ammons is an American Romantic in the tradition of Emerson and Whitman. He is committed to free and open forms, to the amassing of the exact details experience provides rather than the extrusion therefrom of any *a priori* order. His favorite subject is the relation of man to nature as perceived by a solitary wanderer along the beaches and rural fields of New Jersey, where Ammons grew up. Because of the cumulative nature of his technique, Ammons's work shows to best advantage in poems of some magnitude. Perhaps the best, and best known, of these is the title poem from *Corsons Inlet*, in which, describing a walk along a tidal stream, he says,

        I was released from forms,
        from the perpendiculars,
        straight lines, blocks, boxes, binds
        of thought
        into the hues, shadings, rises, flowing bends and blends of sight. . . .

Mr. Ammons here as elsewhere accepts only what is possible to a sensibility attuned to the immediacy of experience, for he admits that

            Scope eludes my grasp, that there is no finality of vision,
            that I have perceived nothing completely,
            that tomorrow a new walk is a new walk.

   Another kind of poem characteristic of Ammons is the brief metaphysical fable, in which there are surprising colloquies between an interlocutor and mountains, winds, or trees:

                    So it came time
                    for me to cede myself
                    and I chose
                    the wind
                    to be delivered to.
                    The wind was glad
                    and said it needed all
                    the body
                    it could get
                    to show its motions with. . . .
                            – "Mansion"

The philosophical implications in these poems are explicit in "What This Mode of Motion Said," a meditation upon permanence and change phrased as a cadenza on Emerson's poem "Brahma."

Ammons's *Collected Poems* was chosen for the National Book Award in 1973. Not included in this compendious volume is his book-length *Tape for the Turn of the Year,* a free-flowing, imaginative journal composed in very short lines, written on a roll of adding-machine tape. The combination here of memory, introspection, and observation, rendered in an ever-changing musical phrasing, is impressive. Ammons's work is consistent in its experimentation with open forms and its celebration of the oneness of living processes and the identity of man with nature.

– Daniel Hoffman

ANANIA, Michael. American. Born in Omaha, Nebraska, 5 August 1939. Educated at the University of Nebraska, at Lincoln, 1957–58, at Omaha, B.A. 1961; State University of New York, Buffalo, Ph.D. 1969. Married Joanne Oliver in 1960. Bibliographer, Lockwood Library, State University of New York, Buffalo, 1963–64; Instructor in English, State University of New York, Fredonia, 1964–65, and Northwestern University, Evanston, Illinois, 1965–68. Instructor, 1968–70, and since 1970, Assistant Professor of English, University of Illinois, Chicago. Poetry Editor, *Audit,* 1963–64, and Co-Editor, *Audit/Poetry,* 1963–67, Buffalo. Since 1968, Literary Editor, Swallow Press, Chicago; since 1971, Member, Board of Directors, and since 1972, Member, Executive Committee, Coordinating Council of Literary Magazines. Recipient: Swallow Press New Poetry Series Award, 1970. Address: Department of English, University of Illinois at Chicago Circle, Chicago, Illinois 60680, U.S.A.

PUBLICATIONS

Verse

The Color of Dust. Chicago, Swallow Press, 1970.

Other

Editor, *New Poetry Anthology I* and *II.* Chicago, Swallow Press, 1969, 1972.

*   *   *

In *The Color of Dust,* Michael Anania traces his passage from the timeless to the contemporary, from small-town life by the Missouri River to a state of mind questioning national myths and the consequences of war. By evoking a sense of the land and people, and by recognizing the permanence and the regenerative powers of the river, he demonstrates how identity stems from the knitting together of person and place ("We are not confused, / we do not lose our place"). But self-definition may be accomplished only one moment at a time and periods of doubt inevitably occur ("Am I a songster or a dealer?"). So, too, in his calling, the poet attempts to capture and maintain, thereby creating his own dilemma; the writing of a poem means the wresting of something from its organic context. But it is the nature of the creator to utter his vision and, in doing so, to preserve what he perceives. Time and again the poet must confront the realization that all things change; in Robert Creeley's words, "Everything is water / if you look long enough." Anania's attempts to preserve the inter-relatedness of experience may be seen metaphorically in "The Fall" and dramatically in his war pieces. In the latter, he presents the survivors – those men with fragments of mind and those who suffer physical decay. Here Anania successfully weaves a living tapestry as he reveals the tragic operation of causality in human lives. Time goes on and man improves – his weapons; he progresses from shrapnel to napalm. The American hero, manifestation of national power, propagated by the media, wears

> the satin cape
> the big red S
> meaning, after all, better than.

Superman's cool efficiency and superior strength symbolize the power of a machine-driven culture. The country has progressed so well, technologically, that astronauts, at ease in their capsule-laboratory, high above the earth,

> . . . serve as princes of progress
> through stability, demonstrating
> the nation's fitness to rule,
> ever-reclining, by touch and tell.

– Carl Lindner

ANDERSON, Patrick (John MacAllister). British (at one time Canadian). Born in Ashtead, Surrey, 4 August 1915. Educated at Sherborne School, Dorset; Worcester College, Oxford, B.A., M.A.; Columbia University, New York, M.A. Co-Founder, *Preview* magazine, Montreal. Assistant Professor, McGill University, Montreal, 1948–50; Lecturer, University of Malaya, Kuala Lumpur, 1950–52; Lecturer, Dudley Training College, Worcestershire, 1954–57. Since 1957, Member of the English Department, since 1967, Principal Lecturer, and since 1968, Head of Department, Trent Park College of Education, Barnet, Hertfordshire. Recipient: Commonwealth Fellowship, 1938; Harriet Monroe Memorial Prize (*Poetry,* Chicago), 1946. Address: Field House, Gosfield Lake, Halstead, Essex, England.

PUBLICATIONS

Verse

Poems (juvenilia). Privately printed, 1929.
On This Side Nothing (juvenilia). Privately printed, 1932.
A Tent for April: Poems. Montreal, First Statement Press, 1945.

The White Centre. Toronto, Ryerson Press, 1946.
The Colour as Naked. Toronto, McClelland and Stewart, 1953.

Other

Snake Wine: A Singapore Episode. London, Chatto and Windus, 1955.
Search Me: Autobiography: The Black Country, Canada, and Spain: London, Chatto and Windus, 1957.
First Steps in Greece. London, Chatto and Windus, 1958.
Finding Out about the Athenians. London, Muller, 1961.
The Character Ball: Chapters of Autobiography. London, Chatto and Windus, 1963.
Dolphin Days: A Writer's Notebook of Mediterranean Pleasures. London, Gollancz, 1963; New York, Dutton, 1964.
The Smile of Apollo: A Literary Companion to Greek Travel. London, Chatto and Windus, 1964.
Over the Alps: Reflections on Travel and Travel Writing with Special Reference to the Grand Tours of Boswell, Beckford, and Byron. London, Hart Davis, 1969.
Foxed; or, Life in the Country. London, Chatto and Windus, 1972.

Editor, with Alistair Sutherland, *Eros: An Anthology of Friendship.* London, Blond, 1961; as *Eros: An Anthology of Male Friendship*, New York, Citadel Press, 1963.

Critical Studies: by John Sutherland, in *Northern Review* (Montreal), 1951; "Montreal Poets of the Forties" by Wynne Francis, in *A Choice of Critics*, London, Oxford University Press, 1966; "Patrick Anderson and the Critics" by C. X. Ringrose, in *Canadian Literature* (Vancouver), Winter 1970; "A Poet Past and Future" by the author, in *Canadian Literature* (Vancouver), Spring 1973.

Patrick Anderson comments:

I returned to poetry in my early fifties after a long period of autobiography, travel writing and literary journalism. For some fifteen years I applied what is I suppose an incorrigibly "poetic" temperament and style almost exclusively to prose.

I wrote most of my published poetry during the ten years I spent in Canada. In the relative isolation of Canada, with the temptations of a seemingly "heroic" and "national" task (to bring things alive for the "first time" and to promote a perhaps wonderfully "new" response) I wallowed fairly happily in the wake of other people's masterpieces, and of distant schools and attitudes; my hope was to create the big work which would assimilate and reinterpret so much of Europe. (I was considered a European influence, and some thought this sinister, over-elegant, or mannered, or corrupt.) I expect my main contribution was not my neo-Marxist politics but (1) a love of words and word-play and (2) a sensuous praising of the physical world. A lot of frustrated sex got sublimated this way.

Poetry terrifies me. I think of the pages and pages of revision, the concentration needed, the sheer hard work. And the way words in poetry sit on the page, exposing their nakedness only to start endless entanglements: naked words reaching out in all directions, with their dynamism, their explosiveness, their famous ambiguity. And then, as often as not, suddenly going all flat.

I have little confidence about poetry, which has always been to me the hardest thing, and which I sometimes actively dislike because of the muddle between suggestiveness and meaning, emotion and statement. (I have lectured on it for so long, and more now than ever before, and yet I wonder whether I enjoy Eliot to a greater degree at this moment, when I am supposed to "understand" him, than I did when I read him in a late-night drunken haze before falling asleep at Oxford.)

I often thought that I'd conned editors into accepting my work: couldn't they see how derivative it was, scarcely mine at all? On the other hand, if a piece does come off, isn't it just as far from being "my" work, "my" property? I'm the grubby, disorganised caretaker at the base of the monument.

Of recent years I've been (roughly) a poet writing in prose. Much of my prose has been a self-exploration. I want to tell people what it feels like to be alive in the hope that my life experiences will spill over into, or reflect, theirs. In prose it's like giving somebody a present in a parcel, and opening it for them. You explain, you qualify, you direct attention, you engage them with tone. "Then there's this, which by the way . . . And I wonder what you'll think of this." There is some sweetness of relationship. You don't risk too much. You hesitate, smile, turn to undo a different tissue. Above all you have time. But a poem is the pebble or flower pressed by the child into the stranger's hand. And the pebble is naked, immediate, enigmatic, astonishing. The directness goes beyond the niceties of relationship.

Having just begun to do some poems again, I don't very much want to read most of my old, generally Canadian, stuff. I'd like to let words alone, so that they could flower the way they wanted to, with just the emotion to give them some nourishment, but of course the tug of "meaning" comes in; and the memory of something someone else has done, and a patterning of "form" which leads the words this way and that (and perhaps reduces them, leads them by the nose) and there is the exasperating range of choices.

Some years ago I put some of this into verse:

POEM AS BIRD

This side the enormous trust of poetry
the irritable passion like a bird
whose gift is to be feathered on a cry
or sigh itself into the lucid wood,
pecks intellectual bars and fouls a word
until a tortured dryness fills my eye
and is the parrot of my solitude.
If I should let it go, it will not be
myself, but like the nightingale express
(or the vulgar cuckoo) all things to all people
and turn on me its savagery of success,
and when I say "You lie, for all your song"
insuperably impose its separation.

For, breathing it, it amputates my breath –
becomes a casual watchword to the young
and tiptoes like an angel from a death.

*   *   *

Although he spent only ten years in Canada, Patrick Anderson's timing was excellent. He arrived in Montreal when poets like A. J. M. Smith, F. R. Scott, and P. K. Page were finally coming to terms with Eliot and Auden. By the time he left,

32

the modernist movement had been established for good. As an editor he was a founder of *Preview* which, merged with *First Statement*, turned into *Northern Review*, a general literary magazine and a precursor of *The Tamarack Review*.

Patrick Anderson's three collections of poetry – *A Tent for April*, *The White Centre*, *The Colour as Naked* – can be read with pleasure, although a period flavour predominates. The poems suggest a wide reading in Eliot and Auden and especially Dylan Thomas. Anderson was able to combine a rhetorical flow with an ability to mint memorable phrases and arresting metaphors. He has been called, perhaps unkindly, "a kind of tea-drinking Dylan Thomas."

Anderson's theme is a social one: the self-alienating tendencies of a mechanistic society. His work shows an eagerness to become a participant in all that surrounds him, and this has led him to write about the country itself. A particularly ambitious work is "Poem on Canada" from *The White Centre* which documents the history and geography of Canada in anecdotal and evocative terms. "I am the wind that wants a flag," he writes, but he concludes that the country is "a cold kingdom."

A great deal of information is conveyed in Patrick Anderson's poetry. There is a documentary turn to his mind, and he responded to the topography and life of the country he found himself living in. This sense of involvement and his eye for telling details have helped Anderson immeasurably in his new career – as the author of travel books about faraway and often exotic places.

– John Robert Colombo

ANGELES, Carlos A. Filipino. Born in Tacloban City, Philippines, 25 May 1921. Educated at the University of the Philippines, Diliman, Quezon City. Married to Concepcion Reynoso; has seven children. Chief of Bureau, International News Service, Manila, 1948–58. Philippine Presidential Press Assistant, 1958–59. Since 1959, Public Relations Manager, Pan American World Airways, Manila. Recipient: United States State Department grant, 1958; Philippine Cultural Heritage Award, 1964; Palanca Memorial Award, 1964. Address: 141 Pinatubo Street, Mandaluyong, Rizal, Philippines; or, Post Office Box 172, Manila, Philippines.

PUBLICATIONS

Verse

A Stun of Jewels. Manila, Alberto S. Florentino, 1963.

Critical Study: Introduction by Leonard Casper to *A Stun of Jewels,* 1963.

*   *   *

Carlos A. Angeles' reputation depends on a volume of his collected poems, *A Stun of Jewels*, and a number of other pieces which have been anthologised. His poetry attaches value to everyday commonplace experiences but the banality is deceptive. "Highway," for example, operates at different levels; the description of the winding road is a search for truth; its being couched in the terminology of the chase makes it a metaphor of the quest for sexual fulfilment while the intensity of the quest is responsible for the success of his best poetic pieces. His quartet "Poems for My Psychiatrist's Future Reference" takes its origin in trivial incidents but goes on to trace a pattern of specific human emotions. His other poems develop similarly. Each explores a central idea through concrete images. In "Landscape" the sun becomes an eye; in "The Eye," the eye is likened to the sun; and each by piercing the centre of reality becomes the stronghold of reality. Actually, Angeles does not plumb the depths of his subject. He presents not the realised experience but the experience itself moving towards definition. It is the immediacy distilled by this "poetry-in-progress" that makes Angeles' poems such pleasing pieces.

– Abdul Majid bin Nabi Baksh

ANTONINUS, Brother.   See **EVERSON, William O.**

ASHBERY, John (Lawrence).   American.   Born in Rochester, New York, 28 July 1927. Educated at Deerfield Academy, Massachusetts; Harvard University, Cambridge, Massachusetts (Member of the Editorial Board, *The Harvard Advocate*), B.A. in English 1949; Columbia University, New York, M.A. in English 1951; New York University, 1957–58. Copywriter, Oxford University Press, New York, 1951–54, and McGraw-Hill Book Company, New York, 1954–55. Art Critic, European Edition of *New York Herald Tribune*, Paris, 1960–65, and *Art International*, Lugano, Switzerland, 1961–64. Editor, *Locus Solus* magazine, Lans-en-Vercors, France, 1960–62; Editor, *Art and Literature*, Paris, 1963–64; Paris Correspondent, 1964–65, and Executive Editor, 1965–72, *Art News*, New York. Recipient: Fulbright Fellowship, 1955, 1956; Yale Series of Younger Poets Award, 1956; Poets Foundation grant, 1960, 1964; Ingram Merrill Foundation grant, 1962, 1972; Harriet Monroe Memorial Prize, 1963, and Union League Civic and Arts Foundation Prize, 1966 (*Poetry*, Chicago); Guggenheim Fellowship, 1967, 1973; National Endowment for the Arts grant, 1968, 1969; National Institute of Arts and Letters award, 1969; Shelley Memorial Award, 1973. Agent: Georges Borchardt Inc., 145 East 52nd Street, New York, New York 10022. Address: 360 West 22nd Street, New York, New York 10011, U.S.A.

PUBLICATIONS

Verse

Turandot and Other Poems.   New York, Tibor de Nagy, 1953.
Some Trees.   New Haven, Connecticut, Yale University Press, 1956.

The Poems. New York, Tiber Press, 1960.
The Tennis Court Oath: A Book of Poems. Middletown, Connecticut, Wesleyan University Press, 1962.
Rivers and Mountains. New York, Holt Rinehart, 1966.
Selected Poems. London, Cape, 1967.
Sunrise in Suburbia. New York, Phoenix Book Shop, 1968.
Three Madrigals. New York, Poet's Press, 1968.
Fragment. Los Angeles, Black Sparrow Press, 1969.
The Double Dream of Spring. New York, Dutton, 1970.
The New Spirit. New York, Boke Press, 1970.
Penguin Modern Poets 19, with Lee Harwood and Tom Raworth. London, Penguin, 1971.
Three Poems. New York, Viking Press, 1972.
The Vermont Journal. Los Angeles, Black Sparrow Press, 1975.

Plays

The Heroes (produced New York, 1952). Published in *Artists' Theatre,* edited by Herbert Machiz, New York, Grove Press, 1960.
The Compromise (produced Cambridge, Massachusetts, 1956). Published in *The Hasty Papers,* New York, Alfred Leslie, 1960.
The Philosopher, in *Art and Literature 2* (Paris), 1964.

Novel

A Nest of Ninnies, with James Schuyler. New York, Dutton, 1969.

Other

Editor, with others, *American Literary Anthology 1.* New York, Farrar Straus, 1968.
Editor, *Penguin Modern Poets 24.* London, Penguin, 1973.
Editor, *Muck Arbour,* by Bruce Marcus. Chicago, O'Hara, 1974.

Translator, *Melville,* by Jean-Jacques Mayoux. New York, Grove Press, 1960.
Translator, *Alberto Giacometti,* by Jacques Dupin. Paris, Maeght, 1963.

Bibliography: *A Bibliography of John Ashbery,* by David K. S. Kermani, New York, Phoenix Book Shop, 1974.

Critical Studies: "Speeding Hackney Cabriolet" by Howard Wamsley, in *Poetry* (Chicago), December 1966; *Alone with America* by Richard Howard, New York, Atheneum, 1969; "Urgent Masks: An Introduction to John Ashbery's Poetry" by David Shapiro, in *Field 5* (Oberlin, Ohio), Fall 1971; "Poetry and Public Experience" by Stephen Donadio, in *Commentary* (New York), February 1973; "John Ashbery: The Charity of the Hard Moments" by Harold Bloom, in *Salmagundi* (Satatoga Springs, New York), Spring-Summer 1973; *Rose, Where Did You Get That Red?* by Kenneth Koch, New York, Random House, 1973; *American Free Verse: The Modern Revolution in Poetry* by Walter Sutton, New York, New Directions, 1973; "Very Different Cats" by Robert Mazzocco, in *New York Review of Books,* 13 December 1973.

Theatrical Activities:

Actor: **Play** – *City Junket*, by Kenward Elmslie, New York, 1974.

John Ashbery comments:

There are no themes or subjects in the usual sense, except the very broad one of
an individual consciousness confronting or confronted by a world of external
phenomena. The work is a very complex but, I hope, clear and concrete transcript
of the impressions left by these phenomena on that consciousness. The outlook is
Romantic. Original sources were Auden, Stevens, Perse, Roussel, Hölderlin, some
folk and epic poetry and much American and English poetry of the 1930's and
'40's; I am not sure to what extent these are apparent today. Characteristic devices
are ellipses, frequent changes of tone, voice (that is, the narrator's voice), point of
view, to give an impression of flux. I use verse forms only rarely.

*   *   *

John Ashbery is an experimental poet, and he has not been afraid to run one of
the chief risks of the avant-garde artist – obscurity. Only in his case, it is an
obscurity so dense as to be all but impenetrable. His volume *The Tennis Court
Oath* exemplifies at least three causes of this unintelligibility: an apparent lack of
connection between word and word, phrase and phrase; an extremely allusive way
of referring to unexplained people and situations; and an almost total lack of
structural development as the poem unfolds. Gertrude Stein, Pound, Eliot, Joyce,
Cummings, and Stevens, all at once and together, seem to be outdone by such a
poem as "America," for example, which begins:

> Piling upward
> the fact the stars
> In America the office hid
> archives in his
> stall. . . .

Whether taken by parts or on the whole, such poems are all subject and no
predicate. "America" continues:

> Arm along the rail
> We were parked
> Millions of us
> The accident was terrible.

There is some syntax here, but neither the action nor the meaning is yet clear, for
there is no way of knowing who "We" are, or what the accident was. The poem
has five numbered sections, and we are still in the first of the two paragraphs of
the first section. We read in the second paragraph:

> The person
> Horror – the morsels of his choice
> Rebuked to me I
> – in the apartment
> the pebble we in the bed.

Nothing in the first paragraph prepared for this, just as nothing here follows from it.

This effect might be that of an arbitrary pointillism of words, phrases, and images, or it might be that of a whimsical automatic writing. We can try to rearrange it logically, or just let the mind drift along passively, or look at it associatively. If we try the first approach, such writing will certainly defeat the mind; if we try the second, it will surely slip through the consciousness as water through a sieve; if we try the third, such density will exhaust even the effort to piece out clusters of symbols. Obscure poetry can be interesting reading if it has other attractions – vivid juxtapositions, brilliant images, a strong but graceful style, suggestions of profound meanings, and a hint of yielding ultimately to concentrated study – but one looks in vain for any of these alleviations in Ashbery.

With two kinds of exceptions: *some* poems do mercifully have an appearance of syntax, such as "They Dream Only of America," "Thoughts of a Young Girl," and "Two Sonnets"; others contain elements of a Pop-Art wit that is quite entertaining, as in "Europe," or "Idaho." Otherwise, his work is quite frustrating. If the experimental poet aims at greater freshness, originality, and immediacy, he must at the same time exert such control as is needed to transform his raw material into art. Avoidance of form means avoidance of meaning, and where so very little is intelligible, very little is effective.

—Norman Friedman

ATWOOD, Margaret (Eleanor). Canadian. Born in Ottawa, Ontario, Canada, 18 November 1939. Educated at Victoria College, University of Toronto, B.A., 1961; Radcliffe College, Cambridge, Massachusetts, A.M. 1962; Harvard University, Cambridge, Massachusetts. Lecturer in English, University of British Columbia, Vancouver, 1964–65; Instructor in English, Sir George Williams University, Montreal, 1967–68. Recipient: E. J. Pratt Medal, 1961; President's Medal, University of Western Ontario, 1966; Governor-General's Award, 1967; Centennial Commission prize, 1967; Union League Civic and Arts Foundation Prize (*Poetry*, Chicago), 1969. Lives in Ontario. Address: c/o Oxford University Press, 70 Wynford Drive, Don Mills, Ontario, Canada.

PUBLICATIONS

Verse

Double Persephone. Toronto, Hawkshead Press, 1961.
The Circle Game. Bloomfield Hills, Michigan, Cranbrook Academy of Art, 1964; revised edition, Toronto, Contact Press, 1966.
Talismans for Children. Bloomfield Hills, Michigan, Cranbrook Academy of Art, 1965.
Kaleidoscopes: Baroque. Bloomfield Hills, Michigan, Cranbrook Academy of Art, 1965.
Speeches for Doctor Frankenstein. Bloomfield Hills, Michigan, Cranbrook Academy of Art, 1966.

The Animals in That Country. Toronto, Oxford University Press, 1968;
Boston, Little Brown, 1969.
Five Modern Canadian Poets, with others, edited by Eli Mandel. Toronto,
Holt Rinehart, 1970.
The Journals of Susanna Moodie: Poems. Toronto, Oxford University Press,
1970.
Procedures for Underground. Toronto, Oxford University Press, and Boston,
Little Brown, 1970.
Power Politics. Toronto, House of Anansi, 1971; New York, Harper, 1973.
You Are Happy. New York, Harper, 1974.

Novels

The Edible Woman. Toronto, McClelland and Stewart, London, Deutsch, and
Boston, Little Brown, 1969.
Surfacing. Toronto, McClelland and Stewart, 1972; London, Deutsch, and
New York, Simon and Schuster, 1973.

Other

Survival: A Thematic Guide to Canadian Literature. Toronto, House of
Anansi, 1972.

Manuscript Collection: University of Toronto.

Margaret Atwood comments:

I feel that the task of criticising my poetry is best left to others (i.e., critics) and
would much rather have it take place after I am dead. If at all.

*   *   *

The year 1967 marked the Centennial of Canada and the poetic coming-of-age of
an astonishingly assured young writer, Margaret Atwood. During the festive year
not only did she receive the Governor-General's Award for Poetry for her first
book, *The Circle Game,* but she also won first prize from the Centennial Commission for a group of poems that would later appear in her second book, *The Animals
in That Country.*

Perhaps because her work is cool and controlled on the surface but turbulent and
involved underneath she has been called a "quiet Mata Hari." Like a beautiful
spy, Margaret Atwood wages a constant tug-of-war with the world. Objects and
other people menace her until she is able to impose her psychological patterns upon
them. The poems in *The Circle Game* are replete with "I," "me," and "my," and
rich in the perceptual games that poets play in the sixties. Between her striking
imagination and the real world stands a woman's temperament which delights in
oblique observations, oddities of response, a sense of incongruity, and a delight in
psychological paradox. One pleasure of her early work is her graceful and humorous approach to herself: "That small black speck / travelling towards the horizon /
at almost the speed of light / is me."

The more recent poems in *The Animals in That Country* are more dramatic in subject matter. She writes knowingly about landladies, giant tortoises, Frankenstein, the Boston Strangler, and even about the menace of "A Night in the Royal Ontario Museum." She is particularly concerned with organising her world and with defining those things that "refused to name themselves," but her main concern remains retaining a tenuous hold on her own identity: "I have to keep / insisting on solidity."

Margaret Atwood began as a protegée of Jay Macpherson and a student in the mythopoeic school associated with the literary critic Northrop Frye. But she has brought to this a contemporary style when writing about psychological paradoxes and mild identity crises. Her poems sometimes come close to Confessional Verse, but they also have an interesting and impersonal dramatic strain, especially when writing about the geography and history of Canada – "a new land cleaned of geometries," "progressive insanities of a pioneer."

—John Robert Colombo

AUBERT, Alvin. American. Born in Lutcher, Louisiana, 12 March 1930. Educated at Southern University, Baton Rouge, Louisiana, B.A. 1959; University of Michigan, Ann Arbor (Woodrow Wilson Fellow), A.M. 1960. Married to Bernadine Tenant; has two daughters. Instructor, 1960–62, Assistant Professor, 1962–65, Associate Professor of English, 1965–70, Southern University; Visiting Professor of English, University of Oregon, Eugene, Summer 1970. Since 1970, Associate Professor of English, State University of New York, Fredonia. Editor, *Obsidian* magazine, Fredonia, New York. Recipient: Bread Loaf Fellowship, 1968: National Endowment for the Arts grant, 1973. Address: 10 George's Place, Fredonia, New York 14063, U.S.A.

PUBLICATIONS

Verse

Against the Blues. Detroit, Broadside Press, 1972.

Critical Studies: by J. B., in *Kliatt* (West Newton, Massachusetts), November 1972; James Shokoff, in the *Buffalo Courier-Express*, 8 June 1973.

Alvin Aubert comments:

A poem is a verification (in every sense of the word) of experience in thought and feeling, but mostly the latter, for feeling is the means by which essential experience is transmitted. If the feeling is "right" the intellectual content is "right" also, which is to say that in the poem that works there takes place a mutual verification of thought by feeling, feeling by thought. From another perspective, a successful poem embodies an ordering of external data (experience), a forming of it to facilitate a significant connection of externals and internals, the data out there and the data in the (yes) soul. I am an Afro-American, one who is lately. very much aware of his roots in that somewhat unique region of the U.S., south Louisiana, with its French influence. But I am above all an Afro-American of African descent, and the two terms constitute a reality far beyond their sum. Thus, there is no question as to the source of that experience which verifies, as well as finds its verification in, a poem of mine. As for my thematic concerns, I concur with James Shokoff's assessment: "His themes are death, the shapes of the past, the terror of existence, and the pain of endurance, yet [hopefully] the poems are neither depressing nor pessimistic."

*   *   *

The title of Alvin Aubert's first book of poetry, *Against the Blues*, suggests the significance of his verse. First, the poet's consciousness evidently counters the familiar portrayal in country blues of the sad world where an uncertainty of personal career epitomizes the effects of the coercive social milieu inhabited by blacks. For example, "Nat Turner in the Clearing." earliest of the poems in composition, presents Turner's reflection upon the sudden end of his divinely inspired revolt. Plans and hopes are as ashes from the cooking fire where his band has feasted less than an hour before; yet, Aubert sees in the metaphoric possibilities of the consuming fire a concrete image of historical continuity and so has Turner refuse despair and see that in the breath he expends giving the dying fire one last glow a source of future inspiration for a dark child who will, in time, pass that way again.

Departure from the outlook of traditional blues, however, is in no sense a repudiation. After all, Aubert's volume begins with an invocation of Bessie Smith, his own Gloriana. Rather his poetic title indicates that the poems are to be heard, rather than read, as foreground played against the background of recalled folk sources. Aubert elucidates the esthetic basis of his practice in "Black American Poetry: Its Language and the Folk Tradition" (*Black Academy Review*, Spring/Summer 1972) where he argues that the essence of continuity in black poetry consists in increasingly sophisticated approximations of folk sources by literary poets.

In Aubert's own verse such approximation is at once apparent in "Uncle Bill" or "De Profundis" where the syntactic compression, double negatives, nearly identical rhymes, and unexpected climaxes activate memories of the oral games fundamental to Black English.

Seeing his task as negotiating a relationship between his community and his own literary imagination, Aubert can perceive soulful grace in the movements of an anonymous child playing with a hula hoop ("Black Girl") or the subtle evidence of exploitive race relations in an ordinary event ("Economics"). The poem most successfully uniting esthetic purpose and unique sensibility, though, must be "Death in the Family," which tells of an aged domestic worker's taste for newspaper accounts of crime. Beginning as biography of an uncle, the poem is soon animated by the folk practice of an improvised "toast," but the invention within it comes not from tradition but from Aubert's completion of the story in an epic-sized and witty conflict.

Less rhetorical than the work of his contemporaries, Aubert's poems show that the basis for a new, black esthetic lies in a sensibility attuned as his is to the essential language of black living.

—John M. Reilly

AUDEN, W(ystan) H(ugh). American. Born in York, England, 21 February 1907; emigrated to the United States in 1938; naturalized, 1946. Educated at St. Edmund's School, Grayshott, Surrey: Gresham's School, Holt, Norfolk; Christ Church (exhibitioner), Oxford, 1925–28. Served for the Loyalists in the Spanish Civil War; with the Strategic Bombing Survey of the United States Army in Germany during World War II. Married Erika Mann in 1935. Schoolmaster, Larchfield Academy, Helensburgh, Scotland, and Downs School, Colwall, near Malvern, Worcestershire, 1930–35. Co-Founder of the Group Theatre, 1932; worked with the G.P.O. Film Unit, 1935. Travelled extensively in the 1930's, in Europe, Iceland, and China. Taught at St. Mark's School, Southborough, Massachusetts, 1939–40; American Writers League School, 1939; New School for Social Research, New York, 1940–41, 1946–47; University of Michigan, Ann Arbor, 1941–42; Swarthmore College, Pennsylvania, 1942–45; Bryn Mawr College, Pennsylvania, 1943–45; Bennington College, Vermont, 1946; Barnard College, New York, 1947; Neilson Research Professor, Smith College, Northampton, Massachusetts, 1953; Professor of Poetry, Oxford University, 1956–61. Editor, Yale Series of Younger Poets, 1947–62. Member of the Editorial Board, *Decision* magazine, 1940–41, and *Delos* magazine, 1968; The Readers' Subscription book club, 1951–59, and The Mid-Century Book Club, 1959–62. Recipient: King's Gold Medal for Poetry, 1936; Guggenheim Fellowship, 1942; American Academy of Arts and Letters Award of Merit Medal, 1945, Gold Medal, 1968; Pulitzer prize, 1948; Bollingen Prize, 1954; National Book Award, 1956; Feltrinelli Prize, 1957; Guinness Award, 1959; Poetry Society of America's Droutskoy Gold Medal, 1959; National Endowment for the Arts grant, 1966; National Book Committee's National Medal for Literature, 1967. D.Litt.: Swarthmore College, 1964. Member, American Academy of Arts and Letters, 1954; Honorary Student, Christ Church, Oxford, 1962, and since 1972, in residence. Address: c/o Faber and Faber Ltd., 3 Queen Square, London W.C.1, England. *Died 28 September 1973.*

PUBLICATIONS

Verse

Poems. N.p, S.H.S. (Stephen Spender), 1928.
Poems. London, Faber, 1930; revised edition, 1933.
The Orators: An English Study. London, Faber, 1932; revised edition, 1934, 1966; New York, Random House, 1967.
Poem. Bryn Mawr, Pennsylvania, Frederic Prokosch, 1933.
Two Poems. Bryn Mawr, Pennsylvania, Frederic Prokosch, 1934.
Poems (includes *The Orators* and *The Dance of Death*). New York, Random House, 1934.
Our Hunting Fathers. London, Frederic Prokosch, 1935.
Sonnet. London, Frederic Prokosch, 1935.
Look, Stranger! London, Faber, 1936; as *On This Island*, New York, Random House, 1937.
Spain. London, Faber, 1937.
Letters from Iceland, with Louis MacNeice. London, Faber, and New York, Random House, 1937.
Selected Poems. London, Faber, 1938.
Journey to a War, with Christopher Isherwood. London, Faber, and New York, Random House, 1939.

Ephithalamion Commemorating the Marriage of Giuseppe Antonio Borghese and Elisabeth Mann. New York, privately printed, 1939.

Another Time: Poems (includes *Spain*). New York, Random House, and London, Faber, 1940.

Some Poems. London, Faber, 1940.

The Double Man. New York, Random House, 1941; as *New Year Letter*, London, Faber, 1941.

Three Songs for St. Cecilia's Day. New York, privately printed, 1941.

For the Time Being. New York, Random House, 1944; London, Faber, 1945.

The Collected Poetry of W. H. Auden. New York, Random House, 1945.

Litany and Anthem for St. Matthew's Day. Northampton, St. Matthew's, 1946.

The Age of Anxiety: A Baroque Eclogue (produced New York, 1954). New York, Random House, 1947; London, Faber, 1948.

Collected Shorter Poems 1930–1944. London, Faber, 1950.

Nones. New York, Random House, 1951; London, Faber, 1952.

Mountains. London, Faber, 1954.

The Shield of Achilles. New York, Random House, and London, Faber, 1955.

The Old Man's Road. New York, Voyages Press, 1956.

Reflections on a Forest. Greencastle, Indiana, DePauw University, 1957.

Goodbye to the Mezzogiorno (bilingual edition). Milan, All'Insegno del Pesce d'Oro, 1958.

W. H. Auden: A Selection by the Author. London, Penguin-Faber, 1958; as *Selected Poetry*, New York, Modern Library, 1959.

Homage to Clio. New York, Random House, and London, Faber, 1960.

W. H. Auden: A Selection, edited by Richard Hoggart. London, Hutchinson, 1961.

Elegy for J. F. K., music by Igor Stravinsky. New York, Boosey and Hawkes, 1964.

The Common Life (in German, translated by Dieter Leisegang). Darmstadt, J. G. Bläschke Verlag, 1964.

The Cave of Making (in German, translated by Dieter Leisegang). Darmstadt, J. G. Bläschke Verlag, 1965.

Half-Way. Cambridge, Massachusetts, Lowell-Adams House Printers, 1965.

About the House. New York, Random House, 1965; London, Faber, 1966.

The Twelve, music by William Walton. London, Oxford University Press, 1966.

Marginalia. Cambridge, Massachusetts, Ibex Press, 1966.

Collected Shorter Poems, 1927–1957. London, Faber, 1966; New York, Random House, 1967.

River Profile. Cambridge, Massachusetts, Laurence Scott, 1967.

Selected Poems. London, Faber, 1968.

Collected Longer Poems. London, Faber, 1968; New York, Random House, 1969.

Two Songs. New York, Phoenix Book Shop, 1968.

A New Year Greeting, with *The Dance of the Solids*, by John Updike. New York, Scientific American, 1969.

City Without Walls and Other Poems. London, Faber, 1969; New York, Random House, 1970.

Natural Linguistics. London, Poem-of-the-Month Club, 1970.

Academic Graffiti. London, Faber, 1971; New York, Random House, 1972.

Epistle to a Godson and Other Poems. London, Faber, and New York, Random House, 1972.

Auden/Moore: Poems and Lithographs, edited by John Russell. London, British Museum, 1974.

Poems, lithographs by Henry Moore, edited by Vera Lindsay. London, Petersburg Press, 1974.
Thank You Fog: Last poems.   London, Faber, 1974.

Recordings: *Reading His Own Poems*, Harvard Vocarium, 1941; *Reading from His Works*, Caedmon, 1954; *Auden*, Argo, 1960; *Selected Poems*, Spoken Arts, 1968.

Plays

The Dance of Death (produced London, 1934; as *Come Out into the Sun*, produced Poughkeepsie, New York, 1935; as *The Dance of Death*, produced New York, 1936).   London, Faber, 1933; in *Poems*, 1934.
The Dog Beneath the Skin; or, Where is Francis?, with Christopher Isherwood (produced London, 1936; revised version, produced New York, 1947).   London, Faber, and New York, Random House, 1937.
No More Peace! A Thoughtful Comedy, with Edward Crankshaw, adaptation of the play by Ernst Toller (produced London, 1936; New York, 1937).   New York, Farrar and Rinehart, and London, Lane, 1937.
The Ascent of F6, with Christopher Isherwood (produced London, 1937; New York, 1939).   London, Faber, 1936; revised edition, New York, Random House, and Faber, 1937.
On the Frontier, with Christopher Isherwood (produced Cambridge, 1938; London, 1939).   London, Faber, 1938; New York, Random House, 1939.
The Dark Valley (broadcast, 1940).   Published in *Best Broadcasts of 1939–40*, edited by Max Wylie, New York, Whittlesey House, and London, McGraw Hill, 1940.
John Bunyan, music by Benjamin Britten (produced New York, 1941).
The Duchess of Malfi, music by Benjamin Britten, adaptation of the play by John Webster (produced New York, 1946).
The Knights of the Round Table, adaptation of the work by Jean Cocteau (broadcast, 1951; produced Salisbury, Wiltshire, 1954).   Published in *The Infernal Machine and Other Plays*, by Jean Cocteau, New York, New Directions, 1963.
The Rake's Progress, with Chester Kallman, music by Igor Stravinsky (produced Venice, 1951; New York, 1953; London, 1962).   London and New York, Boosey and Hawkes, 1951.
Delia; or, A Masque of Night, with Chester Kallman (libretto), in *Botteghe Oscure XII* (Rome), 1953.
The Punch Revue (lyrics only) (produced London, 1955).
The Magic Flute, with Chester Kallman, adaptation of the libretto by Schikaneder and Giesecke, music by Mozart (televised, 1956).   New York, Random House, 1956; London, Faber, 1957.
The Play of Daniel (narration only) (produced New York, 1958; London, 1960).   Editor, with Noah Greenberg, New York, Oxford University Press, 1959; London, Oxford University Press, 1960.
The Seven Deadly Sins of the Lower Middle Class, with Chester Kallman, adaptation of the work by Brecht, music by Kurt Weill (produced New York, 1959; Edinburgh and London, 1961).   Published in *Tulane Drama Review* (New Orleans), September 1961.
Don Giovanni, with Chester Kallman, adaptation of the libretto by Lorenzo da Ponte, music by Mozart (televised, 1960).   New York and London, Schirmer, 1961.

The Caucasian Chalk Circle (lyrics only), with James and Tania Stern, adaptation of the play by Brecht (produced London, 1962). Published in *Plays*, London, Methuen, 1960.

Elegy for Young Lovers, with Chester Kallman, music by Hans Werner Henze (produced Stuttgart and Glyndebourne, Sussex, 1961). Mainz, B. Schotts Söhne, 1961.

Arcifanfarlo, King of Fools; or, It's Always Too Late to Learn, with Chester Kallman, adaptation of the libretto by Goldoni, music by Dittersdorf (produced New York, 1965).

Die Bassariden (The Bassarids), with Chester Kallman, music by Hans Werner Henze (produced Salzburg, 1966; Santa Fe, New Mexico, 1968; London, 1974). Mainz, B. Schotts Söhne, 1966.

Moralities: Three Scenic Plays from Fables by Aesop, music by Hans Werner Henze. Mainz, B. Schotts Söhne, 1969.

The Ballad of Barnaby, music by Wykeham Rise School Students realized by Charles Turner (produced New York, 1970).

The Entertainment of the Senses, with Chester Kallman, music by John Gardner (produced London, 1974). Published in *Thank You Fog*, 1974.

Radio Writing: *Hadrian's Wall*, 1937 (U.K.); *The Dark Valley*, 1940 (U.S.A.); *The Rocking-Horse Winner*, with James Stern, 1941 (U.S.A.); *The Knights of the Round Table*, 1951 (U.K.).

Television Writing: *The Magic Flute*, 1956 (U.S.A.); *Don Giovanni*, 1960 (U.S.A.).

Other

Education Today – and Tomorrow, with T. C. Worsley. London, Hogarth Press, 1939.

The Intent of the Critic, with others, edited by Donald A. Stauffer. Princeton, New Jersey, Princeton University Press, 1941.

Poets at Work: Essays Based on the Modern Poetry Collection at the Lockwood Memorial Library, University of Buffalo, with others, edited by Charles D. Abbott. New York, Harcourt Brace, 1948.

The Enchafèd Flood; or, The Romantic Iconography of the Sea. New York, Random House, 1950; London, Faber, 1951.

Making, Knowing and Judging. Oxford, Clarendon Press, 1956.

The Dyer's Hand and Other Essays. New York, Random House, 1962; London, Faber, 1963.

Louis MacNeice: A Memorial Lecture. London, Faber, 1963.

Selected Essays. London, Faber, 1964.

Worte und Noten: Rede zur Eröffnung der Salzburger Festspiele 1968. Salzburg, Festungsverlag, 1968.

Secondary Worlds. London, Faber, and New York, Random House, 1969.

A Certain World: A Commonplace Book. New York, Viking Press, 1970; London, Faber, 1971.

Forewords and Afterwords (essays), edited by Edward Mendelson. New York, Viking Press, and London, Faber, 1973.

Editor, with Charles Plumb, *Oxford Poetry 1926*. Oxford, Blackwell, 1926.
Editor, with C. Day-Lewis, *Oxford Poetry 1927*. Oxford, Blackwell, 1927.
Editor, with John Garrett, *The Poet's Tongue: An Anthology*. London, G. Bell, 2 vols., 1935.

Editor, *The Oxford Book of Light Verse*. Oxford, Clarendon Press, 1938.

Editor, *A Selection from the Poems of Alfred, Lord Tennyson*. New York, Doubleday, 1944; as *Tennyson: An Introduction and a Selection*, London, Phoenix House, 1946.

Editor, *The American Scene, Together with Three Essays from "Portraits of Places,"* by Henry James. New York, Scribner, 1946.

Editor, *Slick But Not Streamlined: Poems and Short Pieces*, by John Betjeman. New York, Doubleday, 1947.

Editor, *The Portable Greek Reader*. New York, Viking Press, 1948.

Editor, with Norman Holmes Pearson, *Poets of the English Language*. New York, Viking Press, 5 vols., 1950; London, Eyre and Spottiswoode, 5 vols., 1952.

Editor, *Selected Prose and Poetry*, by Edgar Allan Poe. New York, Rinehart, 1950.

Editor, *The Living Thoughts of Kierkegaard*. New York, McKay, 1952; as *Kierkegaard*, London, Cassell, 1955.

Editor, with Marianne Moore and Karl Shapiro, *Riverside Poetry 1953: Poems by Students in Colleges and Universities in New York City*. New York, Association Press, 1953.

Editor, with Chester Kallman and Noah Greenberg, *An Elizabethan Song Book: Lute Songs, Madrigals and Rounds*. New York, Doubleday, 1955; London, Faber, 1957.

Editor, *The Faber Book of Modern American Verse*. London, Faber, 1956; as *The Criterion Book of Modern American Verse*, New York, Criterion Books, 1956.

Editor, *Selected Writings of Sydney Smith*. New York, Farrar Straus, 1956; London, Faber, 1957.

Editor, *Van Gogh: A Self-Portrait: Letters Revealing His Life as a Painter*. Greenwich, Connecticut, New York Graphic Society, and London, Thames and Hudson, 1961.

Editor, with Louis Kronenberger, *The Viking Book of Aphorisms: A Personal Selection*. New York, Viking Press, 1962; as *The Faber Book of Aphorisms*, London, Faber, 1964.

Editor, *A Choice of De La Mare's Verse*. London, Faber, 1963.

Editor, *The Pied Piper and Other Fairy Tales*, by Joseph Jacobs. New York, Macmillan, and London, Collier Macmillan, 1963.

Editor, *Selected Poems*, by Louis MacNeice. London, Faber, 1964.

Editor, with John Lawler, *To Nevill Coghill from Friends*. London, Faber, 1966.

Editor, *Selected Poetry and Prose*, by George Gordon, Lord Byron. New York, New American Library, 1966; London, New English Library, 1967.

Editor, *Nineteenth Century British Minor Poets*. New York, Delacorte Press, 1966; as *Nineteenth Century Minor Poets*, London, Faber, 1967.

Editor, *G. K. Chesterton: A Selection from his Non-Fiction Prose*. London, Faber, 1970.

Editor, *A Choice of Dryden's Verse*. London, Faber, 1973.

Editor, *George Herbert*. London, Penguin, 1973.

Editor, *Selected Songs of Thomas Campion*. London, Bodley Head, 1974.

Translator, "On Poetry," in *Two Addresses*, by St.-John Perse. New York, Viking Press, 1961.

Translator, with Elizabeth Mayer, *Italian Journey 1786–1788*, by Goethe. London, Collins, and New York, Pantheon Books, 1962.

Translator, with Leif Sjöberg, *Markings*, by Dag Hammarskjöld. New York, Knopf, and London, Faber, 1964.

Translator, with Paul B. Taylor, *Völupsá: The Song of the Sybil*, with an Icelandic Text edited by Peter H. Salus and Paul B. Taylor. Iowa City, Windhover Press, 1968.

Translator, *The Elder Edda: A Selection.* London, Faber, and New York, Random House, 1969.

Translator, with Elizabeth Mayer and Louise Bogan, *The Sorrows of Young Werther, and Novella*, by Goethe. New York, Random House, 1973.

Bibliography: *W. H. Auden: A Bibliography: 1924–1969*, by B. C. Bloomfield and Edward Mendelson, Charlottesville, University Press of Virginia, 1972.

*   *   *

Such titles as "greatest living poet" are more appropriate to publishers' blurbs than to serious criticism. Nevertheless, they sometimes accurately designate a real and generally acknowledged pre-eminence. At Yeats's death the successor was clearly T. S. Eliot; that W. H. Auden inherited the title from Eliot was perhaps less immediately obvious, but in retrospect hardly open to dispute.

For more than four decades, Auden has taken seriously – but never solemnly – his responsibilities as man of letters. He has been, throughout his career, one of the most consistently interesting and intelligent book reviewers of our times, and has revealed himself (apparently with some reluctance) as a critic of major stature with the publication of *The Dyer's Hand.* He has felt it to be his duty to interpret the times, to diagnose the ills of society and to deal with intellectual and moral problems of public concern. This feeling, together with his own prodigal gifts, has made his poetry sometimes bewildering in its variety; for the need to express the deeply personal world of the dream and the unconscious has been equally apparent. In recent years, however, Auden has ordered the world of his poetry and made it easier of access: He has collected his poems, revised them, and presented them chronologically in two volumes, one of shorter and one of longer poems. At about the same time, he has begun at last to get his due from the critics, who, instead of complaining of the multiplicity of his work, now tend to attempt the definition of its unity.

As one looks over the *Collected Shorter Poems* and *Collected Longer Poems* (which constitute all of the poetry Auden wishes to preserve), one's primary impression is of generous abundance: entertainment, instruction, intellectual challenge and excitement, and aesthetic pleasures ranging from the simplest to the most complex. There are limericks, clerihews, ribald epigrams; many kinds of songs, ballads, musical pieces; but also poems dealing with the basic intellectual and moral issues of our time, and attempts at all the major genres, from ode and elegy to verse essay and quasi-drama, as well as sonnet sequences. There are also numerous genres that Auden seems to have invented, such as the short story, critical essay, or biography compressed into a sonnet, the verse oratorio, the "commentary" in the form of a play-after-a-play, the mock-pastoral "baroque eclogue," and so on. There is, of course, a dazzling display of metrical virtuosity.

Auden is thus a very different kind of poet from Eliot, for example, He has no intention of restricting poetry to its quintessential function, its purest and most intense manifestations. Instead, he is a very impure poet indeed, copious, facile, and versatile, even mixing prose with his verse. Unblushingly, he undertakes to instruct and entertain; he writes occasional poems on events public and private, and adopts the personae of earlier poets from Langland to Byron. At the same time, he is one of the most inward and subjective of poets (especially in the early verse), and his poems, taken individually, are often obscure; taken together, however, they create a cosmos, a poetic universe with its repeated symbolic properties, from landscape to typical characters and recurrent situations. Thus he unites traditional and "modern" qualities; if he masquerades as a Victorian Sage, we may be sure that the favorite role of lunatic clergyman is not far off.

In temperament and in quality of imagination as well as in interests, Auden is in some respects more like a scientist than like other modern poets. His knowledge of biology and psychology is extensive and current, and he is widely read in anthropology, sociology, geology, and other sciences. A certain tough-mindedness, a detachment, sometimes a remoteness, are manifest in his attitude; he often views human life from a great distance, concerning himself with the differences between man and the other animals and between man and the rest of nature, or with man in the vast perspective of geological or biological time. Often his imagination tends to generalize, like that of a scientist: he frames hypotheses and patterns into which specific instances may be placed. But this tendency is balanced by what some critics have called the Dickensian quality of his imagination, vividly concrete and specific, and by the compassion, tolerance, and sympathy for "ordinary" people and things that have grown more and more marked in his verse. The tendency is balanced also by his preoccupation with the supernatural, apparent not only in the religious aspect of the verse (which was present from the beginning) but also in the later denial of the "magical" function of poetry and the definitions of it as embodying "sacred awe."

There is no space here to do more than indicate briefly the stages into which Auden's career may be divided. The first includes the early poems from 1927, when Auden was still an undergraduate, through *The Orators* in 1932. The "charade" "Paid on Both Sides" reveals the imperfectly fused but still fascinating mixture of Icelandic sagas, Anglo-Saxon poetry, revolutionary politics, psychological theory, and public school behavior that lies behind these poems. The second period, 1933–1938, is that in which Auden was the hero of the Left; it includes *Look, Stranger!*, the plays written with Isherwood, the trip to Iceland with MacNeice described in *Letters from Iceland*, the trip to Spain during the Civil War, and the trip to China with Isherwood recorded in *Journey to a War*, after which both decided to move to the United States. The third period (1939–1947) begins with that move; it includes the volume *Another Time*, containing some of Auden's best songs and topical poems, *The Double Man*, which describes the spiritual and intellectual developments that led to Auden's return to the Anglican church in 1940, and the *Collected Poetry* of 1945. It also contains all of Auden's long poems: *New Year Letter*, the long epistle in couplets, the Christmas oratorio *For the Time Being*, the quasi-dramatic commentary on *The Tempest*, *The Sea and the Mirror* (the two latter published in a separate volume, 1944), and the "baroque eclogue" *The Age of Anxiety*, with which the period ends. The beliefs and attitudes that are basic to all of Auden's writing after 1940 are defined in the last three of these works in a manner that seems, retrospectively, almost programmatic: religious in *For the Time Being*, aesthetic in *The Sea and the Mirror*, and social-psychological in *The Age of Anxiety*. In technique, *For the Time Being* is external and objective, *The Age of Anxiety* internal and subjective, and *The Sea and the Mirror* intermediate. Auden has written no long poems since, and certainly one reason would appear to be that the three works together make a kind of triptych, a completed achievement. The fourth period begins in 1948, when Auden began spending summers in Ischia; in compiling the *Collected Shorter Poems* he considered it as ending in 1957, when he transferred his summer residence from Ischia to Austria. But since Auden confessed frankly that he was terminating the volume at 1957 largely as a matter of convenience, simply because that gave him enough poems for a large volume, and since no major change is discernible in the poetry, we may consider the fourth period as still continuing. (Most poets are divided, like Gaul, into three parts; we should not divide Auden into more than four unless it is really necessary.) In this last period Auden's principal volumes are *The Shield of Achilles*, *Homage to Clio*, and *About the House*. His only long works are the groups of poems in sequences or cycles in these volumes, such as "Bucolics" or "Horae Canonicae," poems in various forms arranged according to an external pattern (canonical hours, types of landscape) and dealing with a common theme. Much of his time goes into the writing, with Chester Kallman, of opera libretti; it may be said, without exaggeration, that they have rehabilitated the art of the libretto. Of these the best known are *The Rake's Progress*, for Stravinsky, and *Elegy for Young Lovers* and *The Bassarids*, for Hans Werner Henze. An increasing amount of time is spent, also, on editing and on translating, tasks that Auden performs with unfailing intelligence, care, and zest. No falling off in energy is manifest.

Much used to be made by hostile critics of Auden's changes of belief and attitude in the thirties, from a psychological to a quasi-Marxist orientation, thence to a liberal humanism, and thence to Christianity at the end of the decade. With the passage of time, such criticism has come to seem dated: now that thirty years have passed without significant change, it is hardly plausible to represent Auden as a man of rapidly shifting beliefs. As one looks back from this distance, it is clear that the principal changes were confined to one brief period in the late thirties, that they were all in the same direction, and that, once the commitment to Christianity had been fully made, the only changes were mere shifts of emphasis.

Criticism of Auden has more recently been concerned with the question of defining the qualities that are central to his work, and this is an enterprise that seems likely to continue for some time. Few critics have taken so radical a position as Auden himself (who dropped "Spain 1937" and "September 1, 1939" from *Collected Shorter Poems*). But he has been described in recent books as primarily a satirist and anti-romantic and as centrally concerned with the dilemma of divided consciousness. A religious poet who is also a clown, a virtuoso who is incorrigibly didactic, a satirist who is also a musician and lyricist, is hard to sum up; and there will be many other descriptions.

In Auden's recent volume, *About the House*, the basic theme is rededication to poetry and a redefinition of the poet's role. Perhaps the best rendering of it is in "The Cave of Making," which is also an elegy for Louis MacNeice. (This poem is part of a sequence based on Auden's house near Kirchstetten, called "Thanksgiving for a Habitat"; there is a poem for each room in the house, including cellar and attic, and this is the one for the study.) The contemporary poet, Auden dares to suggest, has much to be thankful for: if his audience is small, it is more expert than ever before, and his work cannot, like music or painting, be "turned into/background noise for study/or hung as a status trophy by rising executives"; poetry still "insists upon/being read or ignored." Auden aligns himself with Goethe, who, unlike the "Francophile/gaggle of pure songsters," wished that poetry were Truth; he would, he confesses, like to become "a minor Atlantic Goethe." As sage, however, Goethean or Horatian, Auden takes his role with appropriate lightness; "On the Circuit," about his experiences on a lecture tour of the U.S., is one of his finest pieces of light verse, and "The Maker" is a kind of archetypal portrait of the artist in basic and primitive terms as gifted craftsman. In 1964, Auden wrote that he finds the element of " 'theatre,' of exaggerated gesture and fuss, of indifference to the naked truth," in much "serious" poetry increasingly revolting. He would like his reader to be conscious primarily of the poem's truth, and to secure this effect is "prepared to sacrifice a great many poetic pleasures." His aim is "a style which shall combine the drab sober truthfulness of prose with a poetic uniqueness of expression. . . ." "Whatever else it may or may not be, I want every poem I write to be a hymn in praise of the English language. . . ."

In "Auden at Sixty" (*The Atlantic*, July 1967) John Hollander described Auden as "an uncrowned laureate" who "has spoken not for national affairs or victories, but on events and crises in the world of the moral imagination." And on the same occasion Robert Lowell said (in *Shenandoah*, Winter 1967):

> Auden's work and career are like no one else's, and have helped us all. He has been very responsible and ambitious in his poetry and criticism, constantly writing deeply on the big subjects, and yet keeping something wayward, eccentric, idiosyncratic, charming, and his own. Much hard, ingenious, correct toil has gone into inconspicuous things: introductions, anthologies, and translations . . . I am most grateful for three or four supreme things: the sad Anglo-Saxon alliteration of his beginnings, his prophecies that seemed the closest voice to our disaster, then the marvel-lous crackle of his light verse and broadside forms, . . . and finally for a kind of formal poem that combines a breezy baroque grandeur with a sophisticated Horatian simplicity. Last winter, John Crowe Ransom said to me that we had made an even exchange, when we lost Eliot to England, and later gained Auden. Both poets have been kind to the lands of their exile, and brought gifts the natives could never have conceived of.

—M. K. Spears

AVISON, Margaret (Kirkland). Canadian. Born in Galt, Ontario, 23 April 1918. Educated at the University of Toronto, B.A. 1940. Recipient: Guggenheim Fellow-ship, 1956; Governor-General's Award, 1961. Address: 17 Lascelles Boulevard, Apartment 108, Toronto M4V 2B6, Ontario, Canada.

PUBLICATIONS

Verse

Winter Sun. Toronto, University of Toronto Press, and London, Routledge, 1960.
The Dumbfounding. New York, Norton, 1966.

Other

The Research Compendium, with Albert Rose. Toronto, University of Toronto Press, 1964.

*   *   *

Although her poems have been appearing in literary magazines and anthologies since the early forties, Margaret Avison did not publish a volume until 1960, when *Winter Sun* appeared, to be followed in 1966 by *The Dumbfounding*. With these, the reputation she had already acquired among a small group of critical readers as an original and significant modern poet was confirmed by an almost universal sanction.

Miss Avison's originality lies partly in the stylistic and organizational boldness with which she gives expression to an extraordinary sensibility. This is first and most strikingly a visual one. Her poetry "begins (and often ends)," wrote the critic Milton Wilson, "with the perceptive eye." Problems of focus, structure, and design – intellectual, emotional, and moral – are everywhere at the heart of her early poems and persist with an added congruence into the later. Such titles as "Geo-metaphysics," "Perspective," and "Meeting Together of Poles and Latitudes" are indicative of this preoccupation. Her perceptive eye, however, is also a contempla-tive eye, metaphysical as well as physical, and it is not the eye alone that is made the instrument of critical awareness but the organs of the more intimate senses of smell, taste, and touch as well.

There are some literary affinities here perhaps, a hint occasionally of Wallace Stevens or Marianne Moore, of Herbert or Hopkins, but they are of little signifi-cance when set against the gnarled syntax and conglomerate diction she has forged out for herself. No single adjective is adequate to describe her diction: it is erudite, complex, archaic, simple, modern – an amalgam of the scientific and philosophical with the familiar and the new, a high style and a low, pillaged and put to work. Her poems come to terms with a reality that is heterogeneous and explosive. They set up a constant tension between a grainy local foreground and an eternal circumambiance of space and time.

In her second book Miss Avison goes beyond perception and philosophy into a pure Christian poetry that brings something of the grace and humility of George Herbert easily and naturally into the modern world and into her own personal experience. "The Word," "The Dumbfounding," "Person, or a Hymn on and to the Holy Ghost," "Searching and Sounding," and the remarkable dramatic dialogue "A Story" are acts of submission and worship as well as poems. They are the result of a precisely dated mystical experience. I believe they have a validity as firm as the religious poetry of Hopkins or Eliot.

—A. J. M. Smith

AWOONER, Kofi. Ghanaian. Born in Wheta, 13 March 1935. Educated at the University of Ghana, Accra, B.A. 1960; University of London (Longmans Fellow, 1967–68), M.A. 1968. Married; has three children. Research Fellow, Institute of African Studies, Legon, 1960–64; Director, Ghana Ministry of Information Film Corporation, 1964–67. Since 1968, Poet-in-Residence, State University of New York, Stony Brook. Visiting Professor, University of Texas, Austin, 1972–73. Past Editor, *Okyeame,* Accra, and Past Co-Editor, *Black Orpheus,* Ibadan. Recipient: Gurrey Prize, 1959. Address: c/o Loretta Barrett, Doubleday Publishing Company, 277 Park Avenue, New York, New York 10017, U.S.A.

PUBLICATIONS

Verse

Rediscovery and Other Poems. Ibadan, Nigeria, Mbari, and Evanston, Illinois, Northwestern University Press, 1964.

Night of My Blood. New York, Doubleday, 1971.
Ride Me, Memory. Greenfield Center, New York, Greenfield Review Press,
   1973.

Plays

   Ancestral Power, and *Lament,* in *Short African Plays,* edited by Cosmo
   Pieterse. London, Heinemann, 1972.

Novel

   This Earth, My Brother: An Allegorical Tale of Africa. London, Heinemann,
   1970; New York, Doubleday, 1971.

Other

   Editor, with George Adali-Martty, *Messages: Poems from Ghana.* London,
   Heinemann, 1970; New York, Humanities Press, 1971.

Kofi Awooner comments:

   Traditional oral poetry of the Ewes with its emphasis on lyricism, the chant,
repetition of lines, symbolism and imagery transfused into English through the
secondary influence of Pound, Dylan Thomas, etc.

                          *   *   *

   Educated almost exclusively in Africa, Kofi Awoonor has been less influenced by
the poetic traditions of Britain and America than many of his African contemporaries, though his work makes it obvious that he has read widely and he does not
hesitate to use biblical references and echoes where he deems it necessary to his
purpose. From the beginning of his poetic career, Awoonor made it his aim to write
poetry in which genuine African experiences are communicated, in a language which
owes something to the African vernaculars, even when writing in English (and he
also writes in Ewe, his native tongue). So that when he says "In our beginnings lies
our journey's end" ("Salvation"), the phrase is appropriate to the poem and the
reader appreciates that the thought has not been taken over from Eliot, but derived
from the actual experience of the Ghanaian poet; he has arrived at the same
destination as Eliot from a completely different direction. He has, in fact, perceived
the significance and value – both for his own writing as well as that of other poets –
of the rich oral and folk traditions of Africa, and has experimented, not always
successfully, with them in his poetry. Where other poets, and especially those
educated in Britain and America, have felt alienated and have experienced an acute
sense of conflict between the imposed values of western society and those of Africa,
so that it became incumbent on them to emphasise their "African-ness," Awoonor
has been able to be his natural self, without shouting the odds about Africa, to go on
writing quite unperturbed by the conflicts around him (or so it might seem from his
work). The title of his volume *Rediscovery* has implications at two levels – firstly, it
celebrates the need to rediscover the African traditions of thought and way of life,

which entails a knowledge of both the past and the present; secondly, it expresses the urge of the poet himself towards self-identification in terms of his own environment. At both levels he draws freely upon ideas and imagery from African rituals and ceremonies – sacrificial offerings, altars, bitter herbs, drums, purification rites, etc., abound in his work, to merge occasionally with specifically Christian images (as in "That Which Flesh Is Heir to") – and by a technique he describes as "transliteration of thoughts" introduces literally translated vernacular expressions and coinages into his English, which adds both freshness and meaning to his work. Although several of the poems in *Rediscovery* have been much anthologised, Awoonor has made rapid progress in the development of an individual style since the publication of his first volume. Amongst later poems are "Songs of Sorrow," based on an Anlo dirge, "The Sea Eats the Land at Home" and, one of his most ambitious and best-sustained efforts to date, the long poem entitled "I Heard a Bird Cry."

—Howard Sergeant

BAKER, Howard (Wilson). American. Born in Philadelphia, Pennsylvania, 5 April 1905. Educated at Whittier College, California, B.A. 1927; Stanford University, California, M.A. 1929; Sorbonne, Paris, 1929–31; University of California, Berkeley (Phelan Fellowship, 1933–35), Ph.D. 1937 (Phi Beta Kappa). Married the novelist Dorothy Dodds in 1931 (died, 1968); Virginia De Camp Beattie, 1969; has two daughters. Briggs-Copeland Instructor, Harvard University, Cambridge, Massachusetts, 1937–43; Visiting Professor, University of California, Berkeley, 1958–59, Davis, 1963–66. Founding Member, The Barn Theatre, Porterville, California. Olive and orange grower: Director, Lindsay Ripe Olive Company, Lindsay, California, 1956–57; President of the Board of Directors, Grand View Heights Citrus Association, 1962–73, and Tulare-Kern Citrus Exchange, 1969–73; Member, Citrus Advisory Board of California. Recipient: Guggenheim Fellowship, 1944. Agent: Lucille Sullivan, R.R.2, Box 171, West Brattelboro, Vermont 05301. Address: Route 1, Box 11, Terra Bella, California 93270, U.S.A.

PUBLICATIONS

Verse

    A Letter from the Country and other Poems. New York, New Directions, 1941.
    Ode to the Sea and Other Poems. Denver, Swallow, 1966.

    Recording: *Ode to the Sea,* Library of Congress, 1949.

Plays

    Trio, with Dorothy Baker (produced New York, 1944).
    The Ninth Day, with Dorothy Baker (televised, 1957; produced Dublin, 1962). Dixon, California, Proscenium Press, 1967.

    Television Play: *The Ninth Day,* 1957.

Novel

Orange Valley. New York, Coward McCann, 1931.

Other

Introduction to Tragedy: A Study in the Development of Dramatic Form. Baton Rouge, Louisiana State University Press, 1939.

Critical Study: by William Van O'Connor, in *Poetry* (Chicago), January 1967.

Howard Baker comments:

Since our poetry begins with Homer, if you are going to be a poet, the best place to begin, ideally, is in the Epics and the Hymns. For me, living in the country in California, though the ideal was always present, the fulfillment was far beyond my capacities. But this was for the best, possibly, because, with a little digging into the poetry of Homer, the farm and the farm workshop, the seasons for hunting and fishing, and the astonishing sights that were to be met in the mountains and on the beaches, and in the crowded places where men congregate, became more freshly Homeric, I think, than the unvaried application to the Homeric text could have made them. The natural unavoidable impact of the past on the present, and the present on the past, with no forced applications of the one on the other, is good for poets, and I would imagine for everyone. The ideal to be strived for is the scope of the Renaissance Man; and of the pre-Renaissance, pre-Socratic viewer of many races and many cities.

May I restate all this by quoting from the title poem in *A Letter from the Country*?

> Be much hedged in. Rehearse the ancient ways
> Till to your strong windbreak on wholesome days,
>   Timid, to fright still uninured,
>   Comes Amaryllis, reassured;
>
> Comes softly, briar-scratched, with tangled hair
> Leading those others who wait and shyly state –
>   Masters who fled the savage wave,
>   Returned unkempt from their high cave.
>
> Then lean your head to their slow syllables:
> Whispering deep seas beneath the fleeting gulls:
>   The torch of Hecuba, the birth,
>   Ruined Ilium fading into earth. . . .

*   *   *

Among the pungent footnotes to Yvor Winters' important essay, "Problems for the Modern Critic of Literature," is the famous second, referring to one of Winters' best students, a poet and scholar who, after teaching at Harvard for three years became disgusted with academic politics and wastefulness of Departmental Life. The unnamed talented poet withdrew from the Academy, having decided there is

53

more profit (and more intellectual honesty) in raising olives and oranges in a California valley. The unnamed subject of that footnote was Howard Baker. Recently Baker agreed to leave his orchards, giving a few lectures at a California university. He has also published recently some essays on classical subjects, essays which are stimulating and well as being learned. Since he does not have to "publish or perish," he publishes only what he thinks worthy of print. His standards tend to be higher than those of the academic marketplace.

Baker's "Advice to a Man Who Lost a Dog" (in a difficult stanza form) may remind readers of Winters' celebrated "Elegy on a Young Airedale Bitch Lost Some Years Since in the Salt-Marsh." Unfortunately Baker's poem is almost unknown; here is one of the seven stanzas:

> Think, when you hunt him on the windy brow
> Where the lean settler led his shaggy cow
> And questioning yielded to the tranquil plow,
>   That that fine poise bequeathed alone
>   A cellar overgrown.

And of course, neither poem is about a dead dog at all. The sonnet "Dr. Johnson" is one of Baker's best poems, tragically concluding: "We are all Boswells harkening the worms." The intelligence and the prosodic brilliance which inform his best poems make them models of their kind. At times, in the lesser poems, the irony may be easy; but there is scarcely a fault in "Pont Neuf." That poems about response to a public statue have become almost "set piece" now should not dull our response to Baker's poem, an almost perfect example of the kind. Other poems one wishes more people knew are "Quiet Folk," "The Passing Generation," and, despite Winters' objections to its associational technique, the long "Ode to the Sea":

> Conserving sea! To what auroral plains
> Have you consigned the meaning of the names
>   Augustine, Abelard,
>   Aquinas, Bede, Bernard?
> Permanent, Lossless, undiminished Sea,
> Change is the law of your stability!

Although Baker's poems tend to be passed over by anthologists who favor more showy pieces, his poems will remain a delight and an instruction to discriminating readers.

—James Korges

BANTOCK, Gavin (Marcus August). British. Born in Barnt Green, near Birmingham, Warwickshire, 4 July 1939. Educated at King's Norton Grammar School; New College, Oxford, M.A. (honours) in English Language and Literature 1964. Head of English department in various private secondary schools in England. Since 1969, Lecturer in English, Reitaku University, Kashiwa-shi, Chiba-ken, Japan. Recipient: Richard Hillary Memorial Prize, 1964; Alice Hunt Bartlett Prize 1966; Eric Gregory Award, 1969. Agent: Peter Jay, 69 King George Street, London S.E.10. Address: The Grey Cottage, 36 Bittell Road, Barnt Green, near Birmingham, England.

PUBLICATIONS

Verse

Christ: A Poem in Twenty-Six Parts.   Oxford, Donald Parsons, 1965.
Juggernaut.   London, Anvil Press Poetry, 1968.
A New Thing Breathing.   London, Anvil Press Poetry, 1969.
Anhaga.   London, Anvil Press Poetry, 1970.
Gleeman.   Cardiff, Second Aeon Publications, 1972.
Eirenikon.   London, Anvil Press Poetry, 1973.

Play

The Last of the Kings: Frederick the Great (produced Edinburgh, 1968).

Gavin Bantock comments:

Themes and subjects: In *Christ* – Jesus as a man suffering human emotions and human love – a tragic, yet optimistic, interpretation of the Gospel Christ.

In middle-length poems, ''Hiroshima,'' ''Juggernaut,'' ''Ichor,'' and ''Person'' – examination of the human predicament, in a world of intense suffering where there is no God, except violence and destruction, and where life is lived only in the present with no possible planned future. Condemnation of narrow-minded and blindly orthodox people.

Eirenikon is an attack on all those crying for peace, and on this rotten western, capitalistic society – of which the U.S.A. is the chief culprit. All the evils of modern society originate in the U.S.A.

Verse forms etc.: Usually disciplined free verse, based on somewhat elevated speech rhythms; perhaps too much rhetorical usage; trying to eliminate this. (Much early practice in iambic English verse forms.)

Main sources and influences: Anglo-Saxon (I've made numerous translations), The Bible, Ezra Pound, Dylan Thomas, Ted Hughes. *Other strong interests:* Beethoven, Einstein, Astronomy, Dictators, Pipe-organs.

My chief aims are to expose the short-comings of people who live narrow lives, who are unconscious of the strength of simplicity and of the practical wisdom of the much-damned attitude of loving-kindness. My attitude to such people is ruthless when they will not listen and sympathetic when they cannot listen. I have great admiration for people with strong wills and powers of endurance; I despise idleness and escapism and irresponsible action in human affairs.

Artistically, I am trying to keep modern poetry steady in strength and efficiency of words used, in logical forms and order and in importance of subject. Too much poetry today is formless, trivial, arbitrary, small-minded, and does not make use of words or images designed to *develop* the language – too much of the language of modern poetry is dead and dull.

I believe writing poetry is a skilled craft, and must be learned. Too many people write lines of verse without ever making poetry.

I am trying to make a distinction between the versifying of hippies and layabouts and the making of good poetry by dedicated poets. The public seem to be confused about the values of both.

*   *   *

Gavin Bantock's poetry has always been unfashionably rhetorical; his imagination centres on moral and often religious themes. His long poem *Christ*, which won both the Richard Hillary and Alice Hunt Bartlett awards, has many passages of considerable power; but those who found its rhetoric distasteful will not have been comforted by his more recent poetry. *Juggernaut*, *Anhaga*, and *Eirenikon*, written after a long stay in Japan, continue to use language forcefully, making points often by devices (such as repetition) used today by few poets of standing. But Bantock's irony never deserts him, and is sharp and bitter enough to give his verse considerable muscle even when its form seems a little heavy:

> Rejoice and be exceeding glad for great is your reward
> surely his goodness and mercy shall grant you
> a cup of tea and a biscuit in the interval.

One of the difficulties facing Bantock as a communicator is that his poems are long (*Christ* has some 7,000 lines), though extremely dense, when his rhetoric is under proper control. A further refinement of his technique will no doubt bring him within range of readers who at present find his poetry somewhat unapproachable, and indeed will do that poetry no harm. The passages one remembers are those furthest from bellowing:

> And the last dragon on its back coiled in divine agony
> offers its silken belly to sword or feather-duster and lies there
> dying of uncontrollable laughter and a surfeit of greenhorn spells.

—Derek Parker

BARAKA, Imamu Amiri. See **JONES, LeRoi.**

BARBOUR, Douglas. Canadian. Born in Winnipeg, Manitoba, 21 March 1940. Educated at Acadia University, Wolfville, Nova Scotia, B.A. in English 1962; Dalhousie University, Halifax, Nova Scotia, M.A. in English 1964; Queen's University, Kingston, Ontario (Canada Council Doctoral grant, 1967–68). Married Sharon Barbour in 1966. Editor, *Quarry* magazine, Kingston, Ontario, for three years. Since 1969, Assistant Professor, University of Alberta, Edmonton. Address: 10808 75th Avenue, Edmonton, Alberta T6E 1K2, Canada.

PUBLICATIONS

Verse

Land Fall. Montreal, Delta Canada, 1971.
A Poem As Long As the Highway. Kingston, Ontario, Quarry Press, 1971.

White.   Fredericton, New Brunswick, Fiddlehead, 1972.
Songbook..   Vancouver, Talonbooks, 1973.
He & She &.   Ottawa, Golden Dog Press, 1974.

Douglas Barbour comments:

My poetry has moved from an attempt to articulate the outer landscape in the best words I could find to the varying attempt to articulate the inner landscape that *is* both the best words I can find at any single moment of writing and me and my friends, our relations as those words can landscape them.

I feel that rime, in all its guises, that rhythm (that "absolute rhythm" of which Ezra Pound wrote), that *sound:* these are what poetry is about, and it goes about playing, most seriously, with these and with the many multifaceted relationships such games explore.

To explore, anything, that is the great game of making poems. I try.

*   *   *

Douglas Barbour is one of the younger generation of poets who emerged in the later 1960's, and whose work is distinguished by open if intensely self-contained forms, and a new eclecticism as far as related or absorbed influences are concerned. Not directly descended from any one of the three major movements in contemporary Canadian poetry, he has combined an awareness of the speaking voice in the poem with a somewhat more tenacious reliance on form, albeit open form, which in its turn is more disciplined than the compositional openness of the "field" theorists. In his first slim collection, *Land Fall,* Barbour moved between examples of prefigured concreteness and what one reviewer described as his "mindscapes." In his second volume the process of the poem became dependent on the physical tracings of a cross-country journey in which geography buttressed perception, and the act of travelling issued its summons to the imagination. *Songbook,* Barbour's fourth book, is a collection of lyrical jottings which, by virtue of being part impression and part reminiscence, strikes one as somewhat less imaginatively secure, although it has fine moments in which the sensuous and the personal is challenged by the unpunctuated austerities of lower-case statement, and the lonely sharpness of mind-images.

—Michael Gnarowski

BARKER, George (Granville).   British.   Born in Loughton, Essex, 26 February 1913. Educated at Marlborough Road School, Chelsea, London; Regent Street Polytechnic, London; "principally for 2 years by Jesuit Fathers." Married Elspeth Langlands in 1964; has "many children, the latest a son Roderick, the eldest a daughter Georgina." Lived in the United States, 1940–43, and in Rome, 1960–65. Professor of English Literature, Imperial Tohoku University, Sendai, Japan, 1939–41; Visiting Professor, New York State University, Buffalo, 1965–66; Arts Fellow, York University, 1966–67; Visiting Professor, University of Wisconsin, Madison, 1971–72. Patron of the Poetry Society, Oxford University, 1953. Recipient: Royal Society of Literature bursary, 1950; Guinness prize, 1962; Levinson Prize (*Poetry*, Chicago), 1965; Borestone Mountain Poetry Prize, 1967; Arts Council bursary, 1968. Address: Bintry House, Itteringham, Aylsham, Norfolk, England.

PUBLICATIONS

Verse

Thirty Preliminary Poems. London, Parton Press, 1933.
Poems. London, Faber, 1935.
Calamiterror. London, Faber, 1937.
Elegy on Spain. London, Parton Press, 1939.
Lament and Triumph. London, Faber, 1940.
Selected Poems. New York, Macmillan, 1941.
Sacred and Secular Elegies. New York, New Directions, 1943.
Eros in Dogma. London, Faber, 1944.
Love Poems. New York, Dial Press, 1947.
The True Confession of George Barker. London, Fore Publications, 1950; augmented edition, New York, New American Library, 1964; London, MacGibbon and Kee, 1965.
News of the World. London, Faber, 1950.
A Vision of Beasts and Gods. London, Faber, 1954.
Collected Poems, 1930–1955. London, Faber, 1957; New York, Criterion, 1958.
The View from a Blind I. London, Faber, 1962.
Penguin Modern Poets 3, with Charles Causley and Martin Bell. London, Penguin, 1962.
Collected Poems, 1930–1965. New York, October House, 1965.
Dreams of a Summer Night. London, Faber, 1966.
The Golden Chains. London, Faber, 1968.
At Thurgarton Church. London, Trigram Press, 1969.
Runes and Rhymes and Tunes and Chimes (for children). London, Faber, 1969.
What Is Mercy and a Voice. London, Poem-of-the-Month Club, 1970.
To Aylsham Fair (for children). London, Faber, 1970.
The Alphabetical Zoo (for children). London, Faber, 1970.
Poems of Places and People. London, Faber, 1971.
III Hallucination Poems. New York, Helikon Press, 1972.
In Memory of David Archer. London, Faber, 1973.

Plays

Two Plays (The Seraphim and In the Shade of the Old Apple Tree). London, Faber, 1958.

Radio Plays: The Seraphim, 1956; Oriel O'Hanlon (published as In the Shade of the Old Apple Tree), 1957.

Novels

Alanna Autumnal. London, Wishart, 1933.
Janus (two novellena). London, Faber, 1935.
The Dead Seagull. London, Lehmann, 1950; New York, Farrar Straus, 1951.

Other

Essays. London, MacGibbon and Kee, 1970.

Editor, *Idylls of the King and a Selection of Poems*, by Alfred, Lord Tennyson. New York, Doubleday, 1961.

Manuscript Collections: University of Texas, Austin; Lockwood Memorial Library, State University of New York, Buffalo; Berg Collection, New York Public Library.

Critical Studies: "A Prolegomena to George Barker" by Patrick W. Swift, in *X* (London), 1960; *English Poetry 1900–1950* by C. H. Sisson, London, Hart Davis, 1971; *Homage to George Barker on His 60th Birthday*, edited by John Heath-Stubbs and Martin Green, London, Martin Brian and O'Keeffe, 1973.

                              *   *   *

During his poetic career, George Barker's reputation has perhaps suffered on two counts. First, he emerged as a poet at the same time as Dylan Thomas, and at almost exactly the same age. From the beginning they were often linked by critics as being in some sense "romantic," as poets of personal concern and extravagant gesture, somehow seen in opposition to the supposedly more social concerns of Auden, Spender and MacNeice. And though the essays in Francis Scarfe's *Auden and After* (a book which gives a fair picture of critical orthodoxies in the early 1940's) give equal prominence to Barker and Thomas, Thomas's later reputation, particularly after his death, seems to have obscured Barker's. Second, the anti-romantic tide in the mid-1950's turned against Barker, making him seem a period figure and wrongly lumping him indiscriminately with the New Apocalyptics and the wholly inflated tone which was taken to be the mark of the bad old wartime days.

In fact Barker's development has been much more interesting than this. There is an awkward Miltonic grandeur about some of the early work in *Thirty Preliminary Poems* and *Poems*, expressed in flowing and serpentine syntax, and a heady rhetoric which was given a more extended outing in his long poem *Calamiterror*. But the first fully achieved books are *Lament and Triumph* and *Eros in Dogma*, particularly in those poems (such as "Allegory of the Adolescent and the Adult," "Resolution of Dependence," and the much-anthologised "To My Mother") which show an effort of concentration on some external object or narrative.

With *News of the World*, there begins a relaxation of tone and a greater linguistic simplicity which Barker has continued through his later books. His themes were by this time established: elegies, both particular and general; the furies and betrayals of love; celebration and disgust. All reached their most concentrated, ambitious and notorious expression in *The True Confession of George Barker*, a long poem in which Barker seemed to take a baleful delight in trying on the various masks

(Villon and Baudelaire, for example) of a damned, despairing but nevertheless jaunty creature:

> I know only that the heart
>   Doubting every real thing else
> Does not doubt the voice that tells
>   Us that we suffer. The hard part
> At the dead centre of the soul
>   Is an age of frozen grief
> No vernal equinox of relief
>   Can mitigate, and no love console.

The View from a Blind I shows two more recent manners, in his sardonic or satirical ballads (such as "The Ballad of Yucca Flats" and "Scottish Bards and an English Reviewer"), and in the limpid and sometimes even conversational "Roman Poems." The heavy rhetorical tread of the early poems has been replaced by something much more spontaneous and lyrical, though equally copious – and sometimes, even now, prolix, as in parts of the recent loosely-connected sequence of quatrains in *The Golden Chains*. Barker's faults of verbal absurdity and self-indulgence are plain for all to see, but the compensations of energy and eloquence have not sufficiently been noticed.

—Anthony Thwaite

—————————

BARO, Gene.   American.   Born in New York City, in 1924.

PUBLICATIONS

Verse

Northwind and Other Poems.   New York, Scribner, 1959.
A View of Water.   Leeds, Northern House, 1965.
Claes Oldenberg and Gene Baro.   New York, Wittenborn, 1968.

Other

Editor, *Beat Poets.*   London, Vista Books, 1961.
Editor, *Famous American Poems.*   London, Vista Books, 1962.
Editor, *After Appomattox: The Image of the South in Its Fiction 1865–1900.*   New York, Corinth Books, 1963.
Editor, *Modern American Stories.*   London, Faber, 1963.

*   *   *

A distinction increasingly being made in criticism is that between history and myth, between facts in related sequence, and the concept behind "events"; between distinct occurrences in sequence, and the everlasting moment that erases the lineal idea of time. The first attitude is Judaic, and the second belongs to the Greeks. If we say Yeats fits more readily into the second of these, it can be seen that to conceptualize with passion involves elegance; and if we consider these two as inseparable, then passionate elegance is that Yeatsian mode which best describes Gene Baro's work. Narrative does not concern Baro. It is the timeless, fixed moment, the moment in which all the strands implied by narrative are brought into intense, significant conjunction, with which Baro is concerned. This Byzantine preoccupation produces at its best a sense of both permanence and hazard. The images (and it is essentially an image-orientated position) strike into the senses creating the illusion of permanence by their intense isolate quality. At the same time, this sense of isolation suggests vulnerability, lack of physical connection and support – from the world. Thus it is not accidental that Baro's creatures are often seen in postures of duress, and suffering. The preoccupation perhaps chooses the mode of expression. In "Sebastian":

> Focus of eyes, focus of arrows:
> this is the plot the body demanded,
> young captain and hero.
> . . . Yet of all this the increment
> is death, the gift but an infant
> corruptible and triumphant.

And again in "The Laundresses":

> Plunging their arms in steam,
> as martyrs take hold of their fires, . . .
> the laundresses mightily
> hunch at buckets and tubs,
> heave and lunge.

Assuming that some must bear suffering, and many more inflict it, taking for granted the desire for purification as fundamental, Baro can concern himself with the intensity and elegance with which all this is rendered. The position is traditional, concerned as it is with detail only as it subscribes to the lasting moment, and as it perfects an area previously worked and defined by other poets.

—Jon Silkin

BAYBARS, Taner. British. Born in Nicosia, Cyprus, 18 June 1936. Educated privately, and at the Turkish Lycée, Nicosia. Married to Kristin Baybars; has one daughter. Since 1956, Member of the Staff, and since 1972, Head of the Overseas Reviews Scheme, British Council, London. Address: 69 Onslow Gardens, London N10 3JY, England.

Publications

Verse

> *Mendilin Ucunakiler* (in Turkish).   Nicosia, Cyprus, Çardak Yayinevi, 1953.
> *To Catch a Falling Man.* Lowestoft, Suffolk, Scorpion Press, 1963.

Novel

> *A Trap for the Burglar.* London, Peter Owen, 1965.

Other

> *Plucked in a Far-Off Land: Images in Self Biography.* London, Gollancz, 1970.

> Editor, with Osman Türkay, *Modern Turkish Poetry.* London, Modern Poetry in Translation, 1971.

> Translator, *Selected Poems of Nazim Hikmet.* London, Cape, 1967; New York, Humanities Press, 1968.
> Translator, *The Moscow Symphony and Other Poems,* by Nazim Hikmet. London, Rapp and Whiting, 1970; Chicago, Swallow Press, 1971.
> Translator, *The Day Before Tomorrow,* by Nazim Hikmet. Oxford, Carcanet Press, 1972.

Critical Studies: "Voice Production" by Frederick Grubb, in *Poetry Review* (London), 1964; "Bigger Than Both of Us" by Bernard Share, in *Irish Times* (Dublin), 12 June 1965; *The Poet Speaks* by Peter Orr, London, Routledge, 1966; "Plucked Untimely" by Raymond Gardner, in *The Guardian* (London), 19 May 1970.

Taner Baybars comments:

   I try to express experiences without turning them into "stories"; I try to select images which should convey something without verbal stuffing – to be able to say more by leaving quite a lot out of the poem. Themes: human relationships, fears and the significant aspect of the commonplace; scientific mysticism. Influenced by prose writers more than by poets.

*   *   *

   Taner Baybars is a Cypriot whose first book of poems, written in Turkish, was published in Nicosia in 1953. Coming to England twelve years later with the intention of studying Law (though he soon gave up the the idea), he decided to stay in London and has adopted English as his literary language with quite remarkable effect. If Baybars experienced any difficulties in writing his poems in a second language, he certainly has enjoyed an advantage over his British contemporaries in that he has remained free of group pressures and influences, and has never shown the slightest inclination to follow prevailing fashions in diction or subject. He has always been inimitably Taner Baybars and his poems are quite unlike anyone else's. In his *To Catch a Falling Man* the poems are arranged in chronological order so that it is possible to trace his development throughout the volume. The earliest poems seem to reflect a simplicity or clarity of vision combined with an unusually sophisticated outlook, supported by a creative mind that enables him to evoke the scene described in such phrases as "the coquettish wind perambulating in the wheels" (of a bicycle) or "the waves unkiss the cliff." If his themes are taken from everyday life – the demolition of an old house, taking barbitone for sleep, the end of a concert, or a key in a lock – he somehow contrives to surround them with an almost sinister atmosphere, as in his poem about a computer, "The Oracle":

> the problem is fed in, the drone irregularly
> distends, no answer is laid. We grow old and visit
> every day the clean, compact brain and wait.

In his later work the simplicity of his earlier style seems to be giving way to a search for the unexpected, for what goes on below the surface of human existence, for the motives beneath the conversation, for the realities underlying appearances, without losing the directness of his approach.

—Howard Sergeant

BEAVER, Bruce (Victor). Australian. Born in Sydney, New South Wales. 14 February 1928. Educated at Manly Public School and Sydney Boys' High School. Married to Brenda Beaver. Lived in New Zealand, 1958–62. Currently, Free-lance Journalist. Recipient: *Poetry Magazine* Award, Sydney, 1963; Commonwealth Literary Fellowship, 1967; Captain Cook Bi-Centenary Prize, 1970; Grace Leven Prize, 1970; Poetry Society of Australia Award, 1970. Address: 14 Malvern Avenue, Manly, New South Wales 2095, Australia.

PUBLICATIONS

Verse

Under the Bridge: Poems. Sydney, Beaujon Press, 1961.
Seawall and Shoreline: Poems. Sydney, South Head Press, 1964.
Open at Random: Poems. Sydney, South Head Press, 1967.
Letters to Live Poets: Poems. Sydney, South Head Press, 1969.

Novels

The Hot Spring. Sydney, Horvitz, 1965.
You Can't Come Back. Adelaide, Rigby, 1966.

Critical Studies: *New Impulses in Australian Poetry*, edited by Thomas Shapcott and Rodney Hall, Brisbane, University of Queensland Press, 1968; "New Australian Poetry" by James Tulip, in *Southerly* (Sydney), 1970; *Poets on Record 7*, Brisbane, University of Queensland Press, 1972.

*   *   *

Something of a maverick among Australian poets, Bruce Beaver is an original and idiosyncratic writer whose reputation has grown with the appearance of each new book. A first collection of poems, *Under the Bridge*, was published in 1961 to some critical acclaim and not a little grumbling. Though his work was said to be colourful and lively in its descriptions of landscapes and regional settings, the human element touched on throughout was vaguely eccentric and even in part perverse; it certainly does not have the dryly humorous to openly heroic characterisation that appeals to so many Australian poets.

In his second book he consolidated the thematic development of 20th century man in and sometimes versus a landscape. In "A View from the Bridge-rail" and "Letters from Sydney" he stressed the relative brevity and existential pressures of human life, setting these against a Heraclitean background of flux and fusion in the book's title poem "Seawall and Shoreline." An impressive sequence entitled "Harbour Sonnets" describes with a lyrical fervour the landscape near his home at Manly, N.S.W.

The same attachment, almost obsessional, to an intimate landscape is seen in the opening pages of his third book, somewhat diffidently entitled *Open at Random*, in poems such as "Excursion" and "Remembering." Again the critics were divided in their estimates of this non-conforming talent. Some found the characterisation too splenetic, others remarked on the apparent opacity of some of the verses, yet the book has had its share of praise and an elder poet of stature, R. D. Fitzgerald, has stated that he considers one of the poems, "The Killers," as among the best poems written in Australia.

—Staff of *Poetry Australia*

BECKETT, Samuel (Barclay). Irish. Born near Dublin, 13 April 1906. Educated at Portora Royal School, County Fermanagh; Trinity College, Dublin, B.A. in French and Italian 1927, M.A. 1931. Worked at the Irish Red Cross Hospital, St. Lô, France, 1945. Married Suzanne Dechevaux-Dumesnil in 1948. Lecturer in English, Ecole Normale Supérieure, Paris, 1928–30; Lecturer in French, Trinity College, Dublin, 1930–32. Closely associated with James Joyce in Paris in the late 1920's and the 1930's. Settled in Paris in 1938, and has written chiefly in French since 1945; translates his own work into English. Recipient: *Evening Standard* award, for drama, 1955; Obie Award, for drama, 1958, 1960, 1962, 1964; Italia Prize, 1959; International Publishers Prize, 1961; Prix Filmcritice, 1965; Tours Film Prize, 1966; Nobel Prize for Literature, 1969. D.Litt.: Dublin University, 1959. Address: c/o Editions de Minuit, 7 rue Bernard-Palissy, Paris 6, France.

PUBLICATIONS

Verse

    Whoroscope.   Paris, Hours Press, 1930.
    Echo's Bones and Other Precipitates.   Paris, Europa Press, 1935.
    Gedichte (collected poems in English and French, with German translations).
        Wiesbaden, Limes Verlag, 1959.
    Poems in English.   London, John Calder, 1961; New York, Grove Press, 1963.

Plays

    Le Kid, with Georges Pelorson (produced Dublin, 1931).
    En Attendant Godot (produced Paris, 1953).   Paris, Editions de Minuit, 1952;
        translated by the author as *Waiting for Godot: Tragicomedy* (produced
        London, 1955; Miami and New York, 1956), New York, Grove Press, 1954;
        London, Faber, 1956.
    Fin de Partie; Suivi de Acte sans Paroles (produced London, 1957).   Paris,
        Editions de Minuit, 1957; translated by the author as *Endgame: A Play in
        One Act; Followed by Act Without Words: A Mime for One Player*
        (*Endgame*, produced New York and London, 1958; *Act Without Words*,
        produced New York, 1960), New York, Grove Press, and London, Faber,
        1958.
    All That Fall (broadcast, 1957).   New York, Grove Press, 1957; as *All That
        Fall: A Play for Radio*, London, Faber, 1957.
    Krapp's Last Tape (produced London, 1958; New York, 1960).   Included in
        Krapp's Last Tape and Embers, 1959; in *Krapp's Last Tape and Other
        Dramatic Pieces*, 1960.
    Embers (broadcast, 1959).   Included in *Krapp's Last Tape and Embers*, 1959;
        in *Krapp's Last Tape and Other Dramatic Pieces*, 1960.
    Krapp's Last Tape and Embers.   London, Faber, 1959.
    Act Without Words II (produced New York, 1959; London, 1960).   Included
        in *Krapp's Last Tape and Other Dramatic Pieces*, 1960; in *Eh Joe and Other
        Writings*, 1967.
    Krapp's Last Tape and Other Dramatic Pieces (includes *All That Fall, Em-
        bers, Act Without Words I* and *II*).   New York, Grove Press, 1960.
    Happy Days (produced New York, 1961; London, 1962).   New York, Grove
        Press, 1961; London, Faber, 1962.
    Words and Music (broadcast, 1962).   Included in *Play and Two Short Pieces
        for Radio*, 1964; in *Cascando and Other Short Dramatic Pieces*, 1968.
    Cascando (broadcast, in French, 1963).   Paris, Editions de Minuit, 1963;
        translated by the author as *Cascando: A Radio Piece for Music and Voice*
        (broadcast, 1964), included in *Play and Two Short Pieces for Radio*, 1964; in
        Cascando and Other Short Dramatic Pieces, 1968.
    Play (produced Ulm-Donau, 1963; New York and London, 1964).   Included in
        Play and Two Short Pieces for Radio, 1964; in *Cascando and Other Short
        Dramatic Pieces*, 1968.
    Play and Two Short Pieces for Radio (includes *Words and Music* and
        Cascando).   London, Faber, 1964.
    Eh Joe (televised, 1966).   Included in *Eh Joe and Other Writings*, 1967; in
        Cascando and Other Short Dramatic Pieces, 1968.
    Come and Go: Dramaticule (produced Paris, 1966; Dublin, 1968; London,
        1970).   London, Calder and Boyars, 1967; in *Cascando and Other Short
        Dramatic Pieces*, 1968.

Eh Joe and Other Writings (includes *Act Without Words II* and *Film*). London, Faber, 1967.
Cascando and Other Short Dramatic Pieces (includes *Words and Music, Eh Joe, Play, Come and Go, Film*). New York, Grove Press, 1968.
Film. New York, Grove Press, 1969; London, Faber, 1971.
Breath (produced Oxford, 1970). Included in *Breath and Other Shorts*, 1971.
Beckett 3 (includes *Come and Go, Cascando, Play*) (produced London, 1970).
Breath and Other Shorts (includes *Come and Go, Act Without Words I and II*, and the prose piece *From an Abandoned Work*). London, Faber, 1971.
Not I (produced New York, 1972; London, 1973). London, Faber, 1973; in *First Love and Other Shorts*, 1974.

Screenplay: *Film*, 1965.

Radio Plays: *All That Fall*, 1957; *Embers*, 1959; *The Old Tune*, 1960; *Words and Music*, 1962; *Cascando*, 1963.

Television Play: *Eh Joe*, 1966.

Novels

Murphy. London, Routledge, 1938; New York, Grove Press, 1957.
Molloy. Paris, Editions de Minuit, 1951; translated by the author and Patrick Bowles, Paris, Olympia Press, and New York, Grove Press, 1955; London, John Calder, 1959.
Malone meurt. Paris, Editions de Minuit, 1951; translated by the author as *Malone Dies*, New York, Grove Press, 1956; London, John Calder, 1958.
L'Innommable. Paris, Editions de Minuit, 1953; translated by the author as *The Unnamable*, New York, Grove Press, 1958; London, John Calder, 1959.
Watt (written in English). Paris, Olympia Press, 1953; New York, Grove Press, 1959; London, John Calder, 1963.
Comment C'Est. Paris, Editions de Minuit, 1961; translated by the author as *How It Is*, New York, Grove Press, and London, John Calder, 1964.
Mercier et Camier. Paris, Editions de Minuit, 1970.

Short Stories and Texts

More Pricks Than Kicks. London, Chatto and Windus, 1934; New York, Grove Press, 1970.
Nouvelles et Textes pour Rien. Paris, Editions de Minuit, 1955; translated by the author as *Stories and Texts for Nothing*, New York, Grove Press, 1967; included in *No's Knife*, 1967.
From an Abandoned Work. London, Faber, 1958.
Imagination morte imaginez. Paris, Editions de Minuit, 1965; translated by the author as *Imagination Dead Imagine*, London, Calder and Boyars, 1965.
Assez. Paris, Editions de Minuit, 1966; translated by the author as *Enough*, in *No's Knife*, 1967.
Bing. Paris, Editions de Minuit, 1966; translated by the author as *Ping*, in *No's Knife*, 1967.
Têtes-Mortes (includes *D'Un Ouvrage Abandonné, Assez, Bing, Imagination morte imaginez*). Paris, Editions de Minuit, 1967; translated by the author, in *No's Knife*, 1967.

No's Knife: Selected Shorter Prose, 1945–1966 (includes *Stories and Texts for Nothing, From an Abandoned Work, Imagination Dead Imagine, Enough, Ping*). London, Calder and Boyars, 1967.

L'Issue. Paris, Georges Visat, 1968.

Sans. Paris, Editions de Minuit, 1969; translated by the author as *Lessness,* London, Calder and Boyars, 1971.

Premier Amour. Paris, Editions de Minuit, 1970; translated by the author as *First Love,* London, Calder and Boyars, 1973.

Le Dépeupleur. Paris, Editions de Minuit, 1971; translated by the author as *The Lost Ones,* London, Calder and Boyars, 1972.

The North. London, Enitharmon Press, 1973.

First Love and Other Shorts. New York, Grove Press, 1974.

Other

"Dante . . . Bruno . Vico . . Joyce," in *Our Exagmination round His Factification for Incamination of Work in Progress.* Paris, Shakespeare and Company, 1929; London, Faber, 1936; New York, New Directions, 1939.

Proust. London, Chatto and Windus, 1931; New York, Grove Press, 1957; with *Three Dialogues with Georges Duthuit,* London, John Calder, 1965.

Bram van Welde, with others. Paris, Georges Fall, 1958; translated by the author and Olive Classe, New York, Grove Press, 1960.

A Samuel Beckett Reader. London, Calder and Boyars, 1967.

Translator, *Anthology of Mexican Poetry,* edited by Octavio Paz. Bloomington, Indiana University Press, 1958; London, Thames and Hudson, 1959.

Translator, *The Old Tune,* by Robert Pinget. Paris, Editions de Minuit, 1960; in *Three Plays,* by Robert Pinget, New York, Hill and Wang, 1966; in *Plays,* London, Calder and Boyars, 1966.

Manuscript Collections: University of Texas, Austin; Ohio State University, Columbus; Washington University, St. Louis, Missouri; Dartmouth College, Hanover, New Hampshire.

Bibliography: *Samuel Beckett: His Work and His Critics: An Essay in Bibliography* by Raymond Felderman and John Fletcher, Berkeley, University of California Press, 1970 (through 1966).

Theatrical Activities:

Director: **Plays** – *Come and Go,* Paris, 1966; *Endgame,* Berlin, 1967; *Krapp's Last Tape,* Berlin, 1969; *Krapp's Last Tape and Act Without Words,* Paris, 1970; *Happy Days,* Berlin, 1971. **Television** – *Eh Joe,* 1966 (Germany).

*   *   *

Samuel Beckett published two very short volumes of verse in his youth, each with minority presses, *Whoroscope* (Hours Press), and *Echo's Bones* (Europa Press). They attracted no critical attention at all and when in 1962 he was a very famous writer indeed, and John Calder brought out the bulk of these early poems as *Poems in English*, so far as I know I was the only reviewer to write about them, and that briefly and anonymously. They are, indeed, minor poems as Joyce's are, but, like Joyce's poems at their best (and like those plays of Beckett's, *All That Fall* and *Embers*, for instance, which were not translated from Beckett's French but written directly in English – Irish English – for radio), they express the author's intimate feelings with a certain concentration and they have a rooted feeling, a local lovingness, they offer some intimate clues to Beckett's bitterness. It is impossible for anybody to be as chillingly negative in verse, consistently, as Beckett is in prose. He is a great master of prose and, like Joyce, only a rather small and precious master in verse, and very much in the Irish tradition of the glumps, or melodious subjective gloom. In verse, unlike prose, the writer has to expose, or give away, the intimate hurts of the inner heart. And these, for Beckett as for most people, are the hurts of lost or rejected love, and the self-disgust, or the self-despisal, that goes with rejection:

> the churn of stale words in the heart again
> love love love thud of the old plunger
> pestling the unalterable
> whey of words

The metaphor is from butter-making and one seems to smell the stale milk smells of a dairy. The Anglo-Irish aspirate *w* where the English do not and in standard English "whey of words" becomes "way of words." *Plunger* and *pestling* and *unalterable*, like *churn*, suggest a mechanical, desperate, barren sexuality. But the most moving short poem in the book is one of a set on Dieppe, written first in French, and then in very traditional Irish English, echoing Synge and Lady Gregory, in Kiltartan or *Playboy of the Western World* language, one might say:

> I would like my love to die
> and the rain to be falling on the graveyard
> and on me walking the streets
> mourning the first and last to love me.

These four lines have lasted in my memory with a hurting poignancy. I spoke of them, when I wrote my too brief review, as expressing "the quiet persistence of loving self-hurt, the innocent, exorbitant, childish bitterness preserved and hardened in manhood and used to claw down the world."

—G. S. Fraser

BEECHER, John. American. Born in New York City, 22 January 1904. Educated at Virginia Military Institute, Lexington, 1919–20; Cornell University, Ithaca, New York, 1921–24; University of Alabama, University, 1924–25, A.B. 1925; Harvard University, Cambridge, Massachusetts, 1926–27; University of Paris, 1928; University of Wisconsin, Madison, 1929–30, M.A. 1930; University of North Carolina, Chapel Hill, 1933–34. Served in the United States Maritime Service during World War II: Combat Medal. Married Barbara Marie Scholz in 1955; has five children. Chemist, 1918–19, Steel Worker, 1920–21, 1923–24, and Open Hearth Metallurgist, 1928–29, U.S. Steel Corporation, Birmingham, Alabama. Instructor in

English, Dartmouth College, Hanover, New Hampshire, 1927, and University of Wisconsin, 1929–33. United States government administrator, in the South, New York, and New England, 1934–43. Director, Displaced Persons Program, UNRRA, Stuttgart, Germany, 1945. Chief, National Institute of Social Relations Editorial Section, Washington, D.C., 1946–47. Assistant Professor of Sociology, San Francisco State College, 1948–50. Rancher and Fine Press Operator, Sebastopol, California, 1951–58. Lecturer in English, Arizona State University, Tempe, 1959–61; Poet-in-Residence, University of Santa Clara, California, 1963–65; Visiting Professor, Miles College, Birmingham, Alabama, 1966–67; Poet-in-Residence, North Shore Community College, Beverly, Massachusetts, 1969–71; Campus Visitor, Association of American Colleges Arts Program, New York, 1969–72; Poet-in-Residence, Saint John's University, Collegeville, Minnesota, 1970; Poet-in-Residence, Assumption College, Worcester, Massachusetts, 1971. Since 1973, Visiting Scholar, Duke University, Durham, North Carolina. Correspondent and Staff Writer, San Francisco *Chronicle*, Birmingham *Age-Herald* and *News, New York Post*, 1943; Associate Editor, *Ramparts Magazine*, San Francisco, 1959–63. Recipient: Ford Fellowship, 1951. L.H.D.: Illinois College, Jacksonville, 1948. Address: P.O. Box 2521, Durham, North Carolina 27705, U.S.A.

PUBLICATIONS

Verse

And I Will Be Heard.   New York, Twice a Year Press, 1940.
Here I Stand.   New York, Twice a Year Press, 1941.
Land of the Free: A Portfolio of Poems on the State of the Union. Oakland, California, Morning Star Press, 1956.
Observe the Time: An Everyday Tragedy in Verse.   San Francisco, Morning Star Press, 1956.
Just Peanuts.   San Francisco, Morning Star Press, 1957.
Inquest.   San Francisco, Morning Star Press, 1957.
Moloch.   San Francisco, Morning Star Press, 1957.
In Egypt Land.   Scottsdale, Arizona, Rampart Press, 1960.
Homage to a Subversive.   Scottsdale, Arizona, Rampart Press, 1961.
Phantom City.   Scottsdale, Arizona, Rampart Press, 1961.
Report to the Stockholders and Other Poems, 1932–1962.   New York, Monthly Review Press, 1962.
Undesirables.   Phoenix, Rampart Press, 1962.
Bestride the Narrow World.   Phoenix, Rampart Press, 1963.
Conformity Means Death.   Phoenix, Rampart Press, 1963.
On Acquiring a Cistercian Breviary.   Phoenix, Rampart Press, 1963.
Yours in the Bonds.   Phoenix, Rampart Press, 1963.
An Air That Kills.   Phoenix, Rampart Press, 1963.
A Humble Petition to the President of Harvard.   Phoenix, Rampart Press, 1963.
Undesirables (collection).   Lanham, Maryland, Goosetree Press, 1964.
To Live and Die in Dixie and Other Poems.   Birmingham, Red Mountain Editions, 1966.
Hear the Wind Blow! Poems of Protest and Prophecy.   New York, International Publishers, 1968.
Collected Poems. New York, Macmillan, 1974.

Recording: *To Live and Die in Dixie*, Folkways, 1968.

Other

All Brave Sailors: The Story of the S.S. Booker T. Washington. New York,
Fischer, 1945.

Complete Works and Papers published on microfilm by Microfilming Corporation of America, New York, 1973.

Bibliography: "Homage to a Crusader: John Beecher and His Rampart Press in
Arizona" by James S. Fraser, in *Arizona Librarian* (Tempe), Winter 1967.

Critical Studies: "The Poetry of John Beecher" by Leslie Woolf Hedley, in
Mainstream (New York), September 1962; "If I Forget Thee, O Birmingham" by
Cornelia Jessey, in *Way* (San Francisco), April 1967; Introduction by Maxwell
Geismar to *Hear the Wind Blow!*, 1968; "Hear the Wind Blow!" by Donald
Demarest, in *Way* (San Francisco), March 1969; "America's Poetic Voice of
Protest" by Edgar Battle, in *Irish Independent* (Dublin), 15 July 1970; "Here I
Stand" by Clayton Barbeau, in *San Francisco Magazine*, April 1973.

John Beecher comments:

I am known principally as a poet of social protest. My very earliest published
work, which appeared in the Twenties, dealt with the injustice I encountered when
I worked 12-hour shifts in the steel mills of Alabama as a youth of 16. My heritage
may also have influenced me. I am descended from Abolitionists and social
reformers. Harriet Beecher Stowe was a great-great aunt. In the Thirties I was
involved with the poor – the unemployed city workers, sharecrop farmers and
uprooted migrants, disadvantaged blacks and chicanos, Jews barred from jobs
because of their religion. After the great war for freedom was over I refused to
sign an unconstitutional "loyalty" oath and was blacklisted myself, becoming a
rancher when my profession as a college teacher was closed to me. All these
experiences have made me the kind of poet I am. Fortunately I lived through it all
and find today that even my work of the Twenties and Thirties meets with a better
response and deeper understanding than when I first wrote it. But I am not a poet
of the Twenties and Thirties primarily. I am a poet also of the Forties, Fifties,
Sixties and Seventies. I have been writing poems for 50 years now. My *Collected
Poems* will I hope show the continuity. My autobiography is to follow.

                    *   *   *

John Beecher is the stuff of legends: his abolitionist heritage (Henry Ward
Beecher and Harriet Beecher Stowe), his personal history of protest, and especially
his poems, have attracted an enthusiastic audience. The poems chronicle the
desperation and tragedy of the poor, and the crimes of man to men from the
Thirties into the present.
Beecher's poems are not "literary" but stress an incantatory voice of preacher
or prophecy; the narratives are expansive and (unfortunately) timeless, but his
heroes and sympathies remain individual: there is an epic quality and effort in, for
example, "In Egypt Land."

Beecher's view of nature and man is Romantic while society is starkly and brutally political. Overlying the poems is a heavy and *credible* shadow of physical danger; within the poems a frustration, as tactile as that of Steinbeck's famous *The Grapes of Wrath*, threatens to explode.

Beecher concentrates on three topics: laborers (steelworkers, especially), blacks (farmers and the civil rights movement), and political liberty. Although recent poems are occasionally weakened by a discomforting note of self-righteousness ("A Commemorative Ode," "A Humble Petition . . ."), the poet deals with a history which textbooks have failed to present and still are trying to accomplish, too slowly Beecher knows ("After Eighty Years"). Even though his anger occasionally overwhelms his vision, and a prose rhetoric covers some poems with preachment, it is always to Beecher's credit as a poet – and as a "radical" and human – that he at least makes us seriously wonder if such passion may not be as good as inevitable. In these poems the enemy is immediate, obvious, physical and simple. There is little of the subtle maneuvering and abstraction one has come to associate with much of the "protest" art of the middle class in America. This is direct rage: Beecher's poems are of the uneducated poor who do not deal in abstractions, but suffer the immediate danger of the "foremen" and the "agents" of abstractions.

—Joseph Wilson

————————————

BEER, Patricia. British. Born in Exmouth, Devon, 4 November 1924. Educated at Exmouth Grammar School; Exeter University, B.A. (honours) in English (London); St. Hugh's College, Oxford, B.Litt. Married to the architect Damien Parsons. Lecturer in English, University of Padua, 1946–48, British Institute, Rome, 1948, and Ministero Areonautica, Rome, 1950–53; Senior Lecturer in English, Goldsmiths' College, London, 1962–68. Address: 1 Lutton Terrace, Flask Walk, London N.W.3, England.

PUBLICATIONS

Verse

Loss of the Magyar and Other Poems. London, Longman, 1959.
The Survivors. London, Longman, 1963.
Just Like the Resurrection. London, Macmillan, and Chester Springs, Pennsylvania, Dufour, 1967.
The Estuary. London, Macmillan, 1971.
Spanish Balcony. London, Poem-of-the-Month Club, 1973.

Other

Mrs. Beer's House (autobiography). London, Macmillan, 1968.
An Introduction to the Metaphysical Poets. London, Macmillan, 1972.

Editor, with Ted Hughes and Vernon Scannell, *New Poems 1962.* London, Hutchinson, 1962.

Patricia Beer comments:

In my opinion my verse has changed radically since the publication of *Loss of the Magyar* in 1959. I do not repudiate my early work but I am now aiming at something quite different. I am trying to break away from the limitations imposed by traditional metres and have been turning increasingly to free verse and syllabics. I am also aiming at using less obvious metaphor.

The writing of my autobiography has influenced my work in two ways: the intensive use of prose has made me try for greater precision in my poetry; and since the publication of the autobiography I have felt able to deal poetically with subjects of a more overtly personal nature. I am not speaking in terms of confessional poetry because that is a mode which, though I respect it, is not for me. But I find I have less need to present my themes objectively by the use of, for example, legend.

The poets whom, currently, I most admire are Yeats, Robert Lowell, Ted Hughes.

                              *   *   *

Patricia Beer's poems may seem at first glance to have something literary and secondhand about them, in that many of them are pegged to romantic myths, legends, historical anecdotes; and literariness of this sort is rightly distrusted. But what is remarkable is that, starting out from such received themes, and using repeatedly such words as "love," "blood," "joy," "grief," "bone," "gold," she transcends the derivative and the tiresomely plangent. She is neatly eloquent, with a fine control of syntax and structure.

The most ambitious poem in her first book was the title one, "The Loss of the Magyar," a sequence of eight pieces, varied in form, on the sinking of the small Devon ship of which her great-grandfather was Master and in which all the crew was drowned. "The Loss of the Magyar" showed from the start that Patricia Beer could handle plain stuff plainly (the second and third sections, for example) as well as the more heightened rhetoric of the close. Another good poem in this book, and one which gains from its close circumstantial detail, is "The Fifth Sense."

Birth and death – again, common themes but seldom handled by Miss Breer as if they were commonplace – are the substance of the poems in *The Survivors.* "Gynaecological Ward," "Life Story," "New Year," "Next of Kin," "Out of Season," and most notably "Death of a Nun," are all good poems drawing on these two great facts. Here and there (as in *Loss of the Magyar*) there are chant-like cadences that remind one uncomfortably of Yeats, but more generally there is a freshness and individuality in her measures, well demonstrated in "The Gorilla," which takes the creature in his cage in the zoo and ends:

> And yet my human fantasy
> Imagines in him wrath at more
> Than being trapped, involuntary
> Anger at his successors' dullness
> Who do not understand his wholeness,
>
> As if some black prophetic rage
> At the mistaking of his nature
> Had gripped him from an early age
> With knowledge that through all his future
> People would talk before his cage
> Clothed and upright, would turn and pass
> Saying how like a man he was.

Patricia Beer's book *Just Like the Resurrection* shows no startling development, but she now seems more prepared to risk lack of resonance for a more glancing effect, using a looser line and sometimes syllabics. There is more room in these poems for the casual, the trivial and the whimsical; and though the danger, of course, is *mere* whimsy (as in "Foam: Cut to Any Size"), she shows that she can handle an odd insight with economy and wit, as in the nine-line poem "Scratch-path."

—Anthony Thwaite

BEISSEL, Henry (Eric). Canadian. Born in Cologne, Germany, 12 April 1929; emigrated to Canada in 1951. Educated at the University of Cologne, 1950–51; University College, London, 1951; University of Toronto (Epstein Award, 1958; Davidson Prize, 1959), B.A. 1958, M.A. 1960. Packer, salesman, and clerk, in Canada, 1951–54; free-lance writer and film-maker, Canadian Broadcasting Corporation, 1954–58. Lecturer, University of Munich, 1960–62; University of Alberta, Edmonton, 1962–64; University of the West Indies, Trinidad, 1964–66. Since 1966, Associate Professor of English, Sir George Williams University, Montreal. Since 1963, Editor, *Edge* magazine, Montreal. Recipient: Canada Council grant, 1967, 1968, 1969, 1971, 1973. Address: 4158 Oxford Avenue, Montreal H4A 2Y4, Quebec, Canada.

PUBLICATIONS

Verse

Witness the Heart. Toronto, Green Willow Press, 1963.
New Wings for Icarus: A Poem in Four Parts. Toronto, Coach House Press, 1966.
The World Is a Rainbow (for children), music by W. Bottenberg. Toronto, Canadian Music Centre, 1969.
Face on the Dark: Poems. Toronto, New Press, 1970.
Quays of Sadness. Montreal, Delta Press, 1973.

Plays

The Curve, adaptation of a play by Tancred Dorst (produced Edmonton, 1963).
Mister Skinflint: A Marionette Play (produced Montreal, 1969; London, 1971).
A Trumpet for Nap, adaptation of a play by Tancred Dorst (produced London, 1970). Toronto, Playwrights Co-op, 1973.
Inook and the Sun (produced Stratford, Ontario, 1973). Toronto, Playwrights Co-op, 1974.

Other

Introduction to Spain (filmstrip and text). London, Common Ground, 1955.

Translator, *The Price of Morning: Selected Poems*, by Walter Bauer. Vancouver, Prism International Press, 1968.

Henry Beissel quotes an editorial from *Edge* (Montreal), Winter 1967–68:

It is as the supreme power of humanization that I celebrate poetry here. These reflections are no more than a gesture to invite to the celebration. On the one hand the poet as shepherd of language: if Heidegger is right that "language is the house of Being," then the poet is keeper of all that is holy in our world. Even on a less exalted plane, his office as purifier, to use Valéry's phrase, of "the dialect of the tribe" invests him with vast and varied responsibilities. An individual or a nation or a civilization is precisely as shallow or profound, rich or poor, corrupt or pure as its language. And it is easy to see that today, with the immense vested interests in the degradation and falsification of language in the series of numberless forms of political, commercial, religious and academic cupidity, the poet's task is of especial importance.

On the other hand the poet as myth-maker: all art, as Yeats said, is founded upon personal vision, and myth is the embodiment of man's vision of himself and his world. It is this vision that distinguishes man from all other forms of being. And here too, in a time like ours determined to pervert the individual and to obscure all true vision, the poet's task is of especial magnitude.

Not many poets today would wish to talk about poetry in this way. There are of course other ways, some equally valid, others faddish. The present Canadian poetry scene abounds with faddists. But fads pass. The tragic-comic face of the poet is an expression of the high seriousness that true poetry is never without. And that remains.

Auschwitz, Hiroshima and Vietnam, computers, hydrogen bombs and technocracy – these are phases of dehumanization. A long and dark night is falling upon the world. In this world-night the poet, according to Heidegger, expresses what is holy. But whether in search of holiness or wholeness, the poet wandering about in the growing darkness cuts an incongruous figure. When vacating the Oxford Chair of Poetry some years ago, W. H. Auden said that he thought there was something "absurd and comical" about a Chair of Poetry in our time, but that the University of Oxford had good reason to be proud of it. Absurd and comical poetry may well be these days, but it is also increasingly becoming the only way in which we can remain human. Perhaps there is something absurd and comical about being human.

*   *   *

Henry Beissel is a poet whose considerable interest in drama is readily apparent in his work. He is immensely conscious of the poet's role, both in the practice of his art and in relation to the society in which he finds himself. This consciousness has found expression in various acts of protest or strong social comment which should be linked to Beissel's views on poetry which he has made known at poetry readings and in his editorial in *Edge 7* (Winter 1967–68). He has summarised his own and the poet's function in the following excerpt: "On the other hand the poet as myth-maker: all art, as Yeats said, is founded upon personal vision, and myth is the embodiment of man's vision of himself and his world. It is this vision that distinguishes man from all other forms of being. And here too, in a time like ours determined to pervert the individual and to obscure all true vision, the poet's task is of especial magnitude." Beissel's first, noteworthy statement is contained in *New Wings for Icarus*, a book-length poem in four parts in which his personal vision works to telescope time and experience in what is, on occasion, a critical but generally affirming comment on the human process: ". . . to render us human / for the one night in which we bloom." *Face on the Dark* is a more personal and more intimately considered collection of poems. Again, there is something of the conscious poetic *persona* operating in the verse, and there is a good deal of drawing on travel as an ordering experience. Social comment crops up in one or two rather tense poems. Otherwise, the line has become longer, the poems, structurally more complex.

As a more recent development, Beissel has shifted his energy into drama, and he is presently at work on a children's play. His translation of the German poems of Walter Bauer was widely and favourably reviewed.

—Michael Gnarowski

BELITT, Ben. American. Born in New York City, 2 May 1911. Educated at the University of Virginia, Charlottesville, B.A. 1932 (Phi Beta Kappa), M.A. 1934, 1934–36. Served in the United States Infantry, 1942–44; Editor-Scenarist, Signal Corps Photographic Center Combat Film Section, 1945–46. Assistant Literary Editor, *The Nation*, New York, 1937–38. Since 1938, Member of the English Department, and currently Professor of literature and languages, Bennington College, Vermont. Taught at Mills College, Oakland, California, 1939, and Connecticut College, New London, 1948–49. Recipient: Shelley Memorial Award, 1937; Guggenheim Fellowship, 1945; Oscar Blumenthal Award, 1957, and Union League Civic and Arts Foundation prize, 1960 (*Poetry*, Chicago); Brandeis University Creative Arts Award, 1962; National Institute of Arts and Letters award, 1965; National Endowment for the Arts grant, 1967. Address: Department of English, Bennington College, Bennington, Vermont 05201, U.S.A.

PUBLICATIONS

Verse

The Five-Fold Mesh. New York, Knopf, 1938.
Wilderness Stair. New York, Grove Press, 1955.
The Enemy Joy: New and Selected Poems. Chicago, University of Chicago Press, 1964.
Nowhere But Light: Poems 1964–1969. Chicago, University of Chicago Press, 1970.

Other

Editor and Translator, *Poet in New York: Federico García Lorca.* New York, Grove Press, 1955; London, Thames and Hudson, 1956.
Editor and Translator, *Selected Poems of Pablo Neruda.* New York, Grove Press, 1961.
Editor and Translator, *Juan de Mairena and Poems from the Apocryphal Songbooks.* Berkeley, University of California Press, 1963.
Editor and Translator, *Selected Poems of Rafael Alberti.* Berkeley, University of California Press, 1966.
Editor and Translator, *A New Decade: Poems 1958–67*, by Pablo Neruda. New York, Grove Press, 1969.
Editor and Translator, *Splendor and Death of Joaquín Murieta*, by Pablo Neruda. New York, Farrar Straus, 1972; London, Alcove Press, 1973.

Editor and Translator, *New Poems, 1968–1970*, by Pablo Neruda.   New York.
Grove Press, 1973.
Editor and Translator, *Poems of Five Decades: 1925–1970*, by Pablo
Neruda.   New York, Grove Press, 1974.

Translator, *Four Poems by Rimbaud: The Problem of Translation.*   Denver,
Swallow, 1947; London, Sylvan Press, 1948.
Translator, with others, *Cántico: Selections*, by Jorge Guillén.   Boston, Little
Brown, 1965.
Translator, *Poems from Canto General*, by Pablo Neruda.   New York, Racolin
Press, 1968.
Translator, with others, *Selected Poems 1923–1967*, by Jorge Luis
Borges.   New York, Delacorte Press, 1972.
Translator, *A la pintura*, by Rafael Alberti.   West Islip, New York, Universal
Art Editions, 1972.

Bibliography: "Ben Belitt Issue" of *Voyages* (Washington, D.C.), Fall 1967.

Manuscript Collections: University of Virginia Library, Charlottesville; State University of New York Library, Buffalo; Boston University Library.

Critical Studies: "In Search of the American Scene" by the author, in *Poets on Poetry*, edited by Howard Nemerov, New York, Basic Books, 1965; "The Fascination of What's Difficult" by Howard Nemerov, in *Reflexions on Poetry and Poetics*, New Brunswick, New Jersey, Rutgers University Press, 1972; "Antipodal Man: An Interview with Ben Belitt" by Joan Hutton, in *Quadrille* (Bennington, Vermont), Spring 1973; "A Wild Severity: The Poetry of Ben Belitt" by Joan Hutton, in *Salmagundi* (Saratoga Springs, New York), April 1973; "Confronting Nullity: The Poetry of Ben Belitt" by Robert Boyers, in *Sewanee Review* (Tennessee), Fall 1973.

Ben Belitt quotes from "In Passing," in *Voyages* (Washington, D.C.), Fall 1967:

Perhaps the best way of accounting for my purposes as a poet at the present time is to say that I intend more poems. I can add to that an increased sense of wonder with regard to the forms, sounds, dimensions, and subjects my poems may take in the future; for more than ever I realize that the whole realm of *subject* – the occasions which produce poems, or which are created by poems – needs to be extended, imagined, wondered at. In the past, I have been preoccupied with the factor of *place* – *real* places lived in, with their genius for crystallizing experience, testing identity, specifying – as the source of the poet's opportunity: the "world's body" as an inalienable aspect of his subject. In this belief, I have kept my geography mobile – exchanged Vermont for Block Island or New Mexico, New Mexico for Old Mexico, Granada for Florence, the Alhambra for the Uffizi, the new world for the old: all in the hope of reassembling my identity in the "place" which matters to me most – some new poem I will inhabit for myself or leave as a trust for whomsoever it may concern. For this reason, I suppose, I have come to look upon poetry as a series of "departures," arranged my books in colors and areas like a map-maker, found no substitute for the specificities of the substantive world.
I shall go on doing so; but after ten years, Vermont and Mexico (between which most of my poems have been recently strewn) are not half heterogeneous enough.

They have, however, helped me to keep antipodal, pointed my head two ways, allowed me to walk under and over my subject, wrenched my inner ear. A collateral aspect of my concern for place, over the years, has been a concern for the *language* of the place, domestic or exotic – English, Spanish, Italian, French – as well as its spirit; and a further consequence for poetry has been my concern for the translation of that language. It is this kind of deployment and displacement which has brought me to the translation into English of selected works from Federico García Lorca, Antonio Machado, Pablo Neruda, Borges, Jorge Guillén, Rafael Alberti, Arthur Rimbaud, and incidental lyrics by Montale, Quasimodo, Valéry, as well as to certain prosodic and textural reverberations which have helped to translate me to myself.

I am curious about matters which lie suspended between myself and the world outside me. I would like to search for a subject at the heart of the poetic function itself for which there is perhaps no given "place," on the Augustinian hunch that "place there is none: we go backward and forward, and there is no place." I long to live on the "invisible edge" of Things, to write poems which coincide exactly with the time that induced them, and thereby create a subject which is *time's* – uniquely time's – and thus gives the spirit a further dimension to move in.

*   *   *

Ben Belitt extends and enriches a tradition in which the eccentric particular flourishes, and in which the line between will and fancy, on the one hand, and responsible imagination, on the other, is consistently challenged, though rarely obscured. We experience in reading Belitt's verse "the fascination of what's difficult," to borrow the title of Howard Nemerov's 1964 essay on Belitt; but what is difficult in Belitt seems also necessary, if not perfectly inevitable. That is to say, the texture of Belitt's verse is characteristically dense in a way that compels strict attention to details even as those details beckon towards others which seem not so much predicated by their earlier counterparts as waywardly implied. We are not tempted, really, to stop at particular images for very long, for we believe the poet knows just where he is going and where he can confidently take us, and we feel we ought somehow to let ourselves be guided. We learn gradually to anticipate not the inevitable but the relevant particular, the word or image that surprises us by revealing a significant pattern we had not expected but had only minimally apprehended. Rarely in Belitt does the extravagant detail disturb the reader's developing or retrospective experience of the poem as a whole. Always the function of the vivid metaphor, the strange idiom, the rare and chiselled phrase, is to enlarge the context of the poem, or to clothe an abstraction in the flesh of an unmistakable object. Verbal feeling, an at least partial reliance on the sound and texture of words in themselves, does not in Belitt vie with sense, with the content of the poem, for, as in Stevens, the processes of the poem's composition are very largely what the poem deals in. What we value above anything else in our experience of the poetry of a Belitt is the pleasure of making our way through the obliquities of syntax and imagery and diction, for we recognize throughout that the obliquity is no evasive stratagem contrived to throw us off the trail of meaning, whatever that may be. We accept in reading this sort of work that poetry evokes a complex state of consciousness of which ideas and reductive meanings are a very limited part. Probably it is useful to say that certain poets require to be read only by a certain kind of reader, to be confronted by an intelligence to whom the idea of an equilibrium perilously approached and maintained continues to be beautiful.

Belitt is determined through his work to live in the spirit, and to make it possible for his readers at least temporarily to do so. This is a very special sort of thing in Belitt, for Belitt's is no moral vision, no saintly pursuit, no trance-like reduction of self to a still-point stripped of instinct and content with waiting for some ultimate deliverance. For Belitt, to live in the spirit is nothing less than the conception of a poetic idiom so finely modulated that it constitutes a system of notations far removed from practical language. This is in no way to suggest that the raw materials with which the poet works are to be discounted, or tolerated only so that they may be transformed. What Belitt loves are the things *and* the transformative urgency he must at once yield to and control. What we wonder at in reading Belitt is that he transmutes his raw materials, the stuff of reality as we generally acknowledge it, as completely as the grape is transmuted in its conversion to a fine wine, and yet the original elements remain. In fact, they are felt with greater force and clarity than they were before their translation into the specifically poetic medium.

Associated with all this is Belitt's marvellous evocation of dream-like longings without the accompanying fuzziness of patently poetical dream states. Occasionally the mind is made to boggle a bit before it can get at the sense of a poem, but such disorientation as a reader may experience has more to do with the laxness of conventional discourse than with the excessive rigors of Belitt's. The late R. P. Blackmur once wrote of Stevens that his "ambiguity is that of a substance so dense with being, that it resists paraphrase and can be truly perceived only in the form of words in which it was given." It is what one feels compelled to say of whatever seems inscrutable or at least resistant to paraphrase in Belitt. In his work, possibility is evoked by means of that tenuous equilibrium which the words of a language conspire at once to establish and to unsettle. In his power to make us wonder at the extraordinary things poetry can do, Belitt is truly one of our greatest modern masters.

—Robert Boyers

BELL, Charles G(reenleaf). American. Born in Greenville, Mississippi, 31 October 1916. Educated at the University of Virginia, Charlottesville, B.A. 1936; Oxford University (Rhodes Scholar, 1936–38), B.A. 1938, B.Litt. 1939, M.A. 1966. Married Mildred Cheatham Winfree in 1939 (divorced, 1949), three daughters; Diana Mason, 1949, two daughters. Instructor in English, Blackburn College, Carlinville, Illinois, 1939–40; Instructor and Assistant Professor of English, Iowa State College, Ames, 1940–45; Assistant professor of English, Princeton University, New Jersey, 1945–49; Assistant Professor of Humanities, University of Chicago, 1949–56; Tutor, Saint John's College, Annapolis, Maryland, 1956–67. Since 1967, Tutor, Saint John's College, Santa Fe, New Mexico. Guest Professor, University of Frankfurt, 1952; Guest Professor and Director of the Honors Program, University of Puerto Rico, Mayaguez, 1955–56; Fulbright Professor, in art and philosophy, Technische Hochschule, Munich, 1958–59; Poet-in-Residence, University of Rochester, New York, Spring 1967; Guest Professor, in philosophy, State University of New York, Old Westbury, Spring 1970. Recipient: Rockefeller Fellowship, 1948; Ford Fellowship, 1952. Address: 1260 Canyon Road, Santa Fe, New Mexico 87501, U.S.A.

PUBLICATIONS

Verse

> *Songs for a New America.* Bloomington, Indiana University Press, 1953;
> revised edition, Dunwoody, Georgia, Norman S. Berg, 1966.
> *Delta Return.* Bloomington, Indiana University Press, 1956; revised edition,
> Dunwoody, Georgia, Norman S. Berg, 1969.

Novels

> *The Married Land.* Boston, Houghton Mifflin, 1962.
> *The Half Gods.* Boston, Houghton Mifflin, 1968.

Manuscript Collection: Boston University.

Critical Study: "A Poet of Re-Attachment" by Galway Kinnell, in *Modern Age* (Chicago), Summer 1958.

Charles G. Bell comments:

My style grew out of the older tradition: Wordsworth, Blake, Milton, then the Elizabethans, then Middle English, then Dante in Italian, Goethe and Hölderlin in German, all memorized *in extenso*; I never read any moderns until after my own manner was more or less formed. My preoccupation from the first was philosophic and discursive, aimed at a long poem, or at the shorter formed poem of controlled statement and apocalyptic intimation.

From Stringfellow Barr at Virginia I took (1934) the challenge of cyclical history, which drove me to study great books, language, and the arts, and which put me in my earliest published poems (1938–9) on more or less the same ground of meaning that Yeats had occupied in his last, though I was not aware of that at the time. My treatment of the cyclical theme had two distinct phases, from the war years and after: as I have written in the preface of the revised edition of *Songs for a New America*:

> It was a temptation to arrange the pieces chronologically. For they reflect
> ten years' struggle with notions of life and death in history, which, in an
> age like ours, one did not have to read Spengler to be haunted by; and
> they run the gamut from Augustinian despair of time and search for faith,
> to romantic affirmation of the moment in which it seemed our greatness to
> burn.

My second book, *Delta Return*, attempted an organic manifold of self and world, based on the play of polarities, a dialectic of symbolic forces, light-dark, east-west, north-south, earth-water, etc. As I wrote in the foreword to the revised edition:

> These poems arose from a trip I made in June of 1953 to visit my mother
> in my home town of Greenville, Mississippi. I had sent off my first book,
> in which the title poem, "Songs for a New America," celebrated the
> tragic daring of the flight west. Here that Promethean theme yields to the

water-death and ebbing of the motion south and home. Though, as with
other underworld journeys, what is sought is not death simply, but some
ambivalent, regenerative sign.

In the last years, having deflected some of the larger urge into my novels (which
in a sense are vastly expanded prose poems), I have been refining a purer verse
concentrate – though it remains philosophical:

MAN

Two, subconscious of each
Other, one waking
While the other sleeps.

To reach out and touch
The double above our waking,
The One, who sleeps.

*   *   *

The best poems in Charles G. Bell's first collection, *Songs for a New America*,
are accomplished and attractive enough to make readers regret that there has been
no new volume since 1956. Cast in a variety of traditional metrical patterns, the
Songs are essentially lyrical and meditative responses to the problem of change, the
loss of past forms and sanctions, and the crude excesses of technology and
"progress." Looking down from a plane in cross-continental flight Bell wonders
(as Chicago fades from view)

is this curse of earth and air
And water, this rearward ugliness the cost
Of every embodied dream and act of power?

"We build as we destroy," he reflects at first, "consummately," a people "involved in the doom / Of shifting things, knowing no permanent goods." The
controlling metaphor of one of the most effective poems, "These Winter Dunes,"
is that of a sensitive man watching the endless movement of the sand:

If there are strangers still coming to this great land,
Tell them out of pity, and make it plain,
Not to love what they find; or if love surprise
(As we are weak), let it be of a special kind,
Quick and evasive; for here all things will change
Before the fruit can ripen on the vine.

But Bell's final conclusions are far from being tragic, or even much more than
sadly nostalgic for the old civilities and an unspoiled countryside. Change means
challenge and the possibility of new growth (the precedent, after all, seems to be
on our side):

> The impossible future holds
> No more impossible miracle than we own
> Here in this present – out of the fall and rain
> Of energy, building of atoms and cells,
> Desperate chances of reptiles, mammals and men,
> This present we have won, unbelievable,
> This gift, this now.
> The property of spirit
> Is transcendence. We have much to transcend.

The later poems in this volume depart, quite literally, from America, with their fond picture-postcard recollections of Como, Königstein, Le Havre and other places cherished by the cultivated tourist. There are a few experiments with dramatic monologues, but whatever the scene or poetic mode, the refrain is always the same: "Life is a wave that moves by breaking." The sum of wisdom is acceptance – not only acceptance of change but the joyful anticipation of what change may offer. The truly wise man is like the skillful rider: "Perceptive spirit rides with loosened rein."

The freshness of the *Songs* is largely absent from the poems in *Delta Return*, at least in part because Bell has forced his themes into an obsessively rigid pattern of three five-part cantos, divided into five subsections, each in turn divided into five five-line iambic pentameter stanzas, irregularly rhymed. The occasion for the cycle is Bell's return from the energetic, constructive "North" to his home town, Greenville, Mississippi – a symbolic "ebbing to passivity, a dissolving." The motion is neither sentimental, however, nor regressive: the journey is that of the eternal return, the descent into one's past necessary for renewal and reëmergence. The dialectic is modish but not inherently unpoetic. Bell's problem is not so much his model as the extreme unevenness of his diction, which ranges from rhetorical posturing to banal flatness, and his forcing of personal experience to take on the weight of impersonal, mythic significance.

—Elmer Borklund

BELL, Martin. British. Born in Southampton, Hampshire, 2 February 1918. Educated at Taunton's School, Southampton; University of Southampton, B.A. (honours) in English. Lieutenant Corporal, then Acting Sergeant, Royal Engineers, 1939–46. Twice married; has two daughters. Member of the Communist Party, 1935–39. Taught in London schools, 1956–67. Founder-Member of The Group and involved in its reincarnation as the Writers Workshop. Opera Critic, *Queen* magazine, London, 1966. Gregory Fellow, Leeds University, 1967–69. Since 1968, part-time Lecturer, Leeds College of Art. Recipient: Arts Council bursary, 1964, and travel grant, 1968. Address: 3 Moorland Avenue, Leeds 6, Yorkshire, England.

Publications

Verse

> *Penguin Modern Poets 3*, with George Barker and Charles Causley.   London,
>   Penguin, 1962.
> *Collected Poems 1937–1966.*   London, Macmillan, and New York, St. Martin's
>   Press, 1967.
> *Letters from Cyprus* (includes prose).   London, Macmillan, 1970.

Martin Bell comments:

Major themes: don't know. Characteristic subjects: clowns, masks, educational institutions, the army, dead friends, live friends, love, alcohol, cats, nightmares, money. Usual verse forms: various. General sources and influences: usual modern poets in English, especially W. H. Auden. American poets: Stevens, Pound, Eliot, Ransom. French poets: I have translated poems from Baudelaire, Corbière, Laforgue, Rimbaud, Eluard, Ponge. Characteristic stylistic devices: modulation of tone.

*   *   *

In Martin Bell, as in Gavin Ewart, the spirit of the thirties achieved a belated apotheosis. Bell's first hardcover book was also his *Collected Poems* and in these hundred pages is crystallised thirty years' concentration on the difficult art of turning the vernacular into the grand style. Bell is perhaps the most accomplished performer with the colloquial voice writing poetry in Britain today. What gives his poems their resonance is the width and depth of his reading. He knows French poetry and not just the French poetry that everybody knows. His knowledge of English and American poetry is considerable. He weaves the literature of the past into his work in the manner of Eliot – few of his poems are without their subtly integrated quotations. But he has an epigrammatic way with references – a few lines suit him better than an exegesis. Here is his summing-up of the often-bruited Bach v. Belsen polarity of Germany:

> Cultivated Signals types
> During the campaign in Italy
> Used to tune sets in
> To German stations
> . . . (Our chief culture-martyr
> Was Glenn Miller)
> The Tedeschi certainly bought
> Their magic bullets.

Bell's thirties' inheritance is not politics but a characteristic love of the social machinery of life. If you crossed Louis MacNeice with Mass Observation and added the strangeness of Philip O'Connor, you would have someone a little like Bell. His best poems, "To Celebrate Eddie Cantor," "Ode to Groucho," "Headmaster, Modern Style," "Reasons for Refusal," "Letter to a Friend," "High St., Southampton" and "Techniques for Détente," although written in the fifties are candidates for an ideal issue of *New Verse*. Two poems, "Ode to Himself" and "Ode to Psycho-Analysis," combine the style of confessional writing with the public stance of the pindaric. In the sixties, Bell invented the persona of *Don Senilio* to cover his retreat into middle age. The Senilio poems introduce a dark dandyism, which is the most perfectly constructed of all his masks. These recent poems show more strongly than ever that Bell is an observer of his fellow-men on whom nothing is lost. They also reveal him as a coiner of famous last words. His translations of Laforgue, Corbière, Rimbaud and Nerval have not been surpassed by anybody.

—Peter Porter

BELL, Marvin (Hartley). American. Born in New York City, 3 August 1937. Educated at Alfred University, New York, B.A. 1958; Syracuse University, New York, 1958; University of Chicago, M.A. 1961; University of Iowa, Iowa City, M.F.A. 1963. Served as a Foreign Military Training Officer in the United States Army, 1963–65. Married Mary Mammosser in 1958; Dorothy Murphy, 1961; has two sons. Visiting Lecturer, 1965, Assistant Professor, 1966–69, and since 1969, Associate Professor of English, University of Iowa. Visiting Professor, Oregon State University, Corvallis, Summer 1969, and Goddard College, Plainfield, Vermont, Summer 1972. Editor, *Statements* magazine, 1959–64; Poetry Editor, *North American Review*, Mount Vernon, Iowa, 1964–69, and *Iowa Review*, 1969–71. Recipient: Lamont Poetry Selection Award, 1969; Bess Hokin Prize (*Poetry*, Chicago), 1969; Emily Clark Balch Prize (*Virginia Quarterly Review*), 1970. Address: Writers Workshop, University of Iowa, Iowa City, Iowa 52242, U.S.A.

PUBLICATIONS

Verse

Things We Dreamt We Died For. Iowa City, Stone Wall Press, 1966.
Poems for Nathan and Saul. Mount Vernon, Iowa, Hillside Press, 1966.
A Probable Volume of Dreams: Poems. New York, Atheneum, 1969.
The Escape into You: A Sequence. New York, Atheneum, 1971.
Woo Havoc. Somerville, Massachusetts, Barn Dream Press, 1971.
Residue of Song. New York, Atheneum, 1974.

Other

Editor, *Iowa Workshop Poets 1963.* Iowa City, Statements-Midwest Magazine, 1963.

Critical Study: "The Poetry of Marvin Bell" by Peter Elfed Lewis, in *Stand* (Newcastle upon Tyne), xiii, 4, 1972.

*   *   *

For *A Probable Volume of Dreams*, his first full-length collection of poems, Marvin Bell drew heavily on his own early experience as a Jew, the son of a Jew. Bell's approach, for which the reader is prepared at the outset by Yiddish proverbs ("Sleep faster, we need the pillows") is easy, almost too smooth. The poems, like a stand-up comedian, come close to naming some essential areas of experience: they sober up just long enough to provide serious relief before the earnest frown fades back to be replaced by smiles. The throwaway line undercuts the poem, and a tension is created between Bell the poet and Bell the entertainer, as in the last half of "A Poor Jew":

> Either way, he looks forward
> to an inevitable fixing-up –
> that settling of his mind and body
> amid great welcome –
> but at great expense.
> And he goes about getting fixed
> to afford it. Love is
> alright, genes
> are to be expected, also
> toys, games, plans and fate
> are worth looking into.
> But with money in your pocket,
> you are wise and you are
> handsome and you sing well too.

In some of these poems, the play of language, a proliferation of puns, threaten to obscure any real feeling other than mild amusement, and the end result is that they seem too consciously crafted, too pat:

> Finally, I am clearing out
> by marking down.
> And I am for hire,
> who cannot keep Father's
> glass front firm . . .
>
> —"In Memory of H. G. Grand"

Bell's sense of humor has wrought one of literature's finest beginnings for a marriage poem:

> It is customary to conceive
> of the bride in white,
> dressed to merit pleasure
> and holier than thou.
>
> —Section 1 of "A Bride in White"

The same volume contains "Toward Certain Divorce," where Bell encounters squarely all that is serious and doubting and searching:

> I am afraid I have only the casual prophecy
> and not the life of the word, that energy,
> within me, though I have sworn to seek it.
> Swear to me, that you leave to seek it too.

The Escape into You, Bell's most recent book, carries out the promise of his earlier meditational poems. A sequence of 54 18-line poems, the book confronts identity less obliquely than *A Probable Volume*, with bigger belly laughs and greater moments of despair. The form curiously loosens the language and these poems have a wonderful mixture of the colloquial and the formal:

> The death of the father is my shepherd
> he maketh me three versions of wanting.
> He giveth back my shadow; he restores.
> He pays out and pays out the darkness.
> How much does it cost to keep silence?

> —"The Children"

Bell knows the ultimate identity of absurdity and pathos, but *The Escape into You* does not accept or write off such wisdom, but comes instead to war it.

He is a funny man, but unlike most, his wit wakens the reader an hour overdue with the nagging memory of a euphoric giggle. Wondering, "did he mean something else by that . . .?" the reader goes back to the poem and learns that just behind the smile, the seemingly easy language, the quick laugh, is something deeper, a challenge far greater:

> "The Pornographic But Serious History"

> of myself, begging your pardon, as a
> young man, quick to draw arms, quick
> to take a fence for daggers toward my
> heart, quick to shoot from the hip,
> fast to let fly in all directions
> as if to injure fatally the unsettled

> just recognized in myself, which is why
> in the end I take myself for example
> though what the new critic says isn't proof
> and the thin line is shifting again
> between comic and tragic, body and spirit,
> and the wife doesn't know her husband.

> Not to fill up with history but no ideas,
> not to merely *see* life and think it images,
> not to think morality a bad medicine
> does the husband offer his boyhood to his
> wife's mouth, the words are a white balm,
> the self heated to the temper of its time.

> —Geof Hewitt

BELLERBY, Frances. British. "Born and brought up in Bristol. Strong strain of Welsh blood (mother's father). After many childhood visits to Cornwall, gravitated back there to various parts again and again in adult life, finally living there consistently for 12 years. Deep influence on poetry. Now lives in Devon and thinks about Cornwall." Address: Upsteps, Goveton, Kingsbridge, Devon, England.

Publications

Verse

> *Plash Mill: Poems.* London, Davies, 1946.
> *The Brightening Cloud and Other Poems.* London, Davies, 1949.
> *The Stone Angel and the Stone Man: Poems.* Plymouth, Devon, Ted Williams, 1958.
> *The Sheltering Water and Other Poems.* Gillingham, Kent, ARC Publications, 1970.
> *Selected Poems,* edited by Charles Causley. London, Enitharmon Press, 1971.
> *The First-Known and Other Poems.* London, Enitharmon Press, 1974.

Novel

> *Hath the Rain a Father?* London, Davies, 1946.

Short Stories

> *Come to an End and Other Stories.* London, Methuen, 1939.
> *The Acorn and the Cup with Other Stories.* London, Davies, 1948.
> *A Breathless Child and Other Stories.* London, Collins, 1952.

Francis Bellerby comments:

Main (i.e. all-inclusive) influences: my mother; the 1914-18 War; East Cornwall. Poetry was a part of my inner life at three, perhaps earlier. Not that my mother tried to "impart a love of poetry" (as if one could!) but, simply, we were in natural sympathy about the matter and we both knew this. I was making up poems from four onwards, perhaps earlier, but seldom spoke of them or showed them, except later for School Magazine work, for they were a part of my inner life – which in a child has no connection with speech. But of course my mother "Knew." And when I was eight I made, in dead secret, a "book" of my poems, to give to her in dead secret. I must mention also her beautiful reading of poetry (women do not usually read poetry well, I think, being too inclined to *con expressione*); and that she would at my hungry demand read me sometimes the same poem day after day after day until I felt I could live without it, or by reading it to myself. As for that War – I came to it a child, without an inkling that public affairs could touch my own world. I emerged – still at school – with the personnel of my childhood entirely altered. Poetry, Pantheism, Athletics, were my refuge, my release, my nourishment. Because of them I dared to study death.

Poetry, then, from three to thirty. Then – it left me. Seeped away, unregretted. For some years I'd been working on Short Stories. They now took over. I seldom even read poetry. Cause? Unknown, though I have imprecise ideas, a mixture of mysticism and psychology.

Eleven years later poetry returned with no warning, no encouragement, and for no known or surmised reason. Suddenly. Late one autumn night. When I was alone, of course. Thick-walled whitewashed room, old cottage by stream, away from roads, under the edge of the moor, East Cornwall. Wrote down a poem suddenly, three more in next few days. Poetry has never left again since then.

And so, having begun at four I was in my forties when I first thought of trying to get poetry published. And that was only because, to my surprise, the agent who dealt with my short stories sold those first four poems at once. Then everything stepped up. The fair success of a novel resulted in the publication of two collections of poems, and a book of short stories (my second).

Some years later, after the publication of a third book, I perceived that short stories used up power which my poetry needed.

Perhaps I can't judge the development of my poetry since first publication. It seems to me to have developed in snatches – one individual poem suddenly as it were jumping ahead, showing me the way. I dislike the tone of some of the poems I wrote in the early excitement of poetry's return. Too poetic. Too soft. Sometimes, alas, even moral-drawing. But others, a few, were and are a lesson to me. I'd heard accurately. (I've not lacked *seeing*. It has been *hearing* that I've too often blurred or partly faked.)

At least now I know more clearly what I'm meant to do. Vision, yes. But then, good secretaryship: to hear, and write down, accurately. Not in emotional words but in the *right* words. And never myself to point out a moral, precept, theory. In fact, since I *discover* by the writing down of poems (and by the reading and re-reading of poems), it's certainly not my job to force moral-drawing onto them.

One more thing: never, in childhood or youth, did I say or think "I am going to be a poet." A poetry reputation at school from the age of 10 onwards (I did not go to school until I was nine) brought me no nearer such an impossible thought. For to me A Poet was next to God. To *write poetry* was a different matter. It could no more have occurred to me that I should ever live without writing poetry than that I should ever live without drawing in and letting out breath.

This initial attitude has cast so long an influence that it is only quite recently that I have mastered the hesitation, the instinctive withdrawing, if ever I have to say "I'm a poet."

*   *   *

By its very quietness, the poetry of Frances Bellerby has the gift of creating a kind of stillness around it. Having lived for many years with an illness involving severe pain and recurrent nearness to death, she is more keenly aware than most of eternal reality shining through appearances, and prizes more dearly the natural world and all its intricate marvels. In one poem she says: "Then fire burned my body to a clear shell," and there is in her work the profundity that only deeply felt and ultimate experience can give.

Her use of words is subtle and fresh, and her style, like that of all true originals, has a timeless quality. Though her first book was published in 1946 and her latest in 1974 the writing seems all of a piece. Her lines move with assurance, never trudging in dull rhythms; her rhymes come so naturally that they take their places almost un-noticed.

As well as the springs of quiet homage always welling up in her work, there is a sense of mystery, of some visitation always freshly expected, a suggestion of the numinous just over the hill, just beyond the opening door. Indeed, the opening door or window is a recurring image.

She never over-writes. There is a tautness, a discipline in her writing, as if her experiences have honed away all self-indulgence, and in spite of hardship there is never a hint of self-pity.

Her eye is quick, her ear delicate, her work refined in the most complete sense of the word. At the deepest level there is nearly always a metaphysical content in her poetry, as if she has heard "news from another country" and has come back to speak of it with knowledge and longing.

—Joan Murray Simpson

BENEDIKT, Michael. American. Born in New York City, 26 May 1937. Educated at New York University, B.A. 1956; Columbia University, New York, M.A. 1961. Served in the United States Army, 1958–59. Married Marianne Benedikt in 1962. Associate Editor, Horizon Press, publishers, 1959–61; New York Correspondent, *Art International*, Lugano, 1965–67. Associate Editor, *Art News* magazine, New York, 1963–72. Instructor in Language and Literature, Bennington College, Vermont, 1968–69; Poet in Residence, Sarah Lawrence College, Bronxville, New York, 1969–73. Since 1973, Associate Professor of Arts and Humanities, Hampshire College, Amherst, Massachusetts. Since 1974, Poetry Editor, *Paris Review*, Paris and New York. Recipient: Bess Hokin Prize (*Poetry*, Chicago), 1968; Guggenheim Fellowship, 1969; National Endowment for the Arts grant, 1969. Address: 315 West 98th Street, New York, New York 10025, U.S.A.

PUBLICATIONS

Verse

Serenade in Six Pieces. Huntington, Connecticut, privately printed, 1958.
Changes. Detroit, The New Fresno, 1961.
8 Poems. New York, privately printed, 1966.
The Body. Middletown, Connecticut, Wesleyan University Press, 1968.
Sky. Middletown, Connecticut, Wesleyan University Press, 1970.
Mole Notes. Middletown, Connecticut, Wesleyan University Press, 1971.

Recording: *Today's Poets 5*, Folkways, 1968.

Plays

The Vaseline Photographer (produced New York, 1965).
The Orgy Bureau, in *Chelsea* (New York), 1968.
Box (produced New York, 1970).

Other

Editor, with George E. Wellwarth, *Modern French Theatre: The Avant-Garde, Dada, and Surrealism.* New York, Dutton, 1964; as *Modern French Plays: An Anthology from Jarry to Ionesco*, London, Faber, 1965.
Editor, with George E. Wellwarth, *Postwar German Theatre: An Anthology of Plays.* New York, Dutton, 1967; London, Macmillan, 1968.
Editor and Translator, *Ring Around the World: The Selected Poems of Jean L'Anselme.* London, Rapp and Whiting, 1967; Denver, Swallow, 1968.

Editor, *Theatre Experiment: New American Plays.* New York, Doubleday, 1967.

Editor, with George E. Wellwarth, *Modern Spanish Theatre: An Anthology of Plays.* New York, Dutton, 1968.

Editor, *Surrealism.* Boston, Little Brown, 1970.

Editor, *22 Poems of Robert Desnos.* Santa Cruz, California, Kayak Books, 1971.

Editor, *25 Poems of Paul Eluard.* Ithaca, New York, Lillabulero Press, 1974.

Translator, with others, *Medieval Age.* New York, Dell, 1963.

Author of music, cinema, art, and literary criticism in magazines and anthologies.

Michael Benedikt comments:

Major theme is probably the relationship of matter and spirit; sometimes the sensual and the "pure." General sources and influences: the French Symbolists and Surrealists until about 1966; most recently, the English romantic poets. Stylistically, I am interested in the treatment of "difficult" subjects with clarity, since their reality *is* very clear (at least to me). I am probably as much influenced by contemporary painting, sculpture, and theatre as I am by any movement in poetry. Lately, I have become interested in the possibilities of the poem in prose as well as verse.

*   *   *

In an American time when moralism is out of style (except when apologizing for the war), Michael Benedikt is a moralist. *The Body,* Benedikt's first book-length collection, contains work that ranges from surreal fables (an example, "The Ambitious Lump," reminds me of my father's favorite book – an anthology of pieces from the defunct *St. Nicholas Magazine*) to direct statement. In "A Room," the poet watches from a window the "transactions of perverts. Yes! they are more generous than they / are ever credited with being; but oh! they have no love!" "The Ambitious Lump" tells of Geoffrey, whose success somehow depended on the lump be received as a child when papa hit him with a frying pan. The lump grows as Geoffrey advances professionally:

> When Geoffrey took over the presidency of the large
> construction corporation
> He was at last a total cripple.
> The lump had risen up day after day
> And one evening had taken its ultimate revenge

Finally,

> Only the lump could elevate him any further
>
> When I visited Buenos Aires recently
> I noticed Geoffrey on top of Sugar Leaf Mountain.
> He was standing there ten thousand feet above the sea level
> Hitting himself over the head

One of Benedikt's greatest strengths is his ability to assume more than one voice. "Mr. Rainman," a favorite of mine, has no less than three voices, all the narrator's. The poet shifts gracefully from his own diction to that of a child to that of an older man. The poem, in turn, is factual, romantic, and finally meditational. In most of Benedikt's work, such shifts of diction or attention provide delightful surprises. "The Cities" opens with an old "experimental chemist" who dies of a "desperate unrequited love" for his assistant. The title has set us up for a different kind of poem; after twelve lines devoted almost·entirely to the chemist, the poem takes another turn. "Phyllis's life was changed by the event. / No sooner has she attended Georg's / Funeral, than she abandoned her old ways." The poem moves, with Phyllis, home to Peoria, where her parents eventually complain:

> you seem more hip
> Now and very unlikely to stay
>
> More than an unhappy few months more here.
> Why don't you get out and leave now?

Benedikt's poems are pop or romantic and often, quite successfully, both at the same time. The imagery, in keeping with the title of his book, is frequently visceral, as in "Gemini Emblem":

> And I had this picture in my mind of carrying around my lungs as if they
> were valises I was trying to smuggle through customs, perhaps as if to slip
> my heart through my mind.

Occasionally, as in "A Beloved Head," such imagery is almost too strong: the poem does not need such constant jacking up, and the density of these images works as a distraction. Chiefly because of this density and Benedikt's happy penchant for drastic shifting, the poems in *The Body* need, as well as deserve, close reading.

—Geof Hewitt

BENNETT, Louise. Jamaican. Educated at primary and secondary schools in Jamaica; Royal Academy of Dramatic Art, London (British Council Scholarship). Worked with the BBC (West Indies Section) as resident artist, 1945–46 and 1950–53, and with repertory companies in Coventry, Huddersfield, and Amersham. Returned to Jamaica, 1955. Drama Specialist with the Jamaica Social Welfare Commission, 1955–60; Lecturer in drama and Jamaican folklore, Extra-Mural Department, University of the West Indies, Kingston, 1959–61. Represented Jamaica at the Royal Commonwealth Arts Festival in Britain, 1965. Has lectured in the United States and the United Kingdom on Jamaican music and folklore. Recipient: Silver Musgrave Medal of the Institute of Jamaica. M.B.E. (Member, Order of the British Empire). Address: Enfield House, Gordon Town, St. Andrew, Jamaica.

PUBLICATIONS

Verse

Dialect Verses. Kingston, Gleaner Company, 1940.
Jamaican Dialect Verses. Kingston, Gleaner Company, 1942; expanded version, Kingston, Pioneer Press, 1951.
Jamaican Humour in Dialect. Kingston, Gleaner Company, 1943.
Miss Lulu Sez. Kingston, Gleaner Company, 1948.
Anancy Stories and Dialect Verse, with others. Kingston, Pioneer Press, 1950.
Laugh with Louise: A Potpourri of Jamaican Folklore, Stories, Songs, Verses. Kingston, Bennett City Printery, 1960.
Jamaica Labrish. Kingston, Sangster's Book Stores, 1966.

Recordings: *Jamaican Folk Songs*, Folkways, 1954; *Jamaican Singing Games*, Folkways, 1954; *West Indies Festival of Arts*, Cook, 1958; *Miss Lou's Views*, Federal, 1967; *Listen to Louise*, Federal, 1968.

Critical Study: Introduction by Rex Nettlefold, to *Jamaica Labrish*, 1968.

Louise Bennett comments:

I have been described as a "poet of utterance performing multiple roles as entertainer, as a valid literary figure and as a documenter of aspects of Jamaican life, thought, and feeling." I would not disagree with this.

*   *   *

Louise Bennett is to Jamaica what the calypsonian The Mighty Sparrow is to Trinidad and Tobago: an articulate voice of the people, a political commentator, a satirist, and, in many ways, a social historian. The difference between them is the difference between the traditional Trinidadian calypso and the traditional Jamaican mento. The calypso, however, when set down in the cold light of print, loses its sparkle and its inflections and becomes dull and often meaningless, because it has lost its music. The mento, on the other hand, can be understood and enjoyed merely from the printed page.

The "West Indian English" which is in common use, and in which Miss Bennett works, is gradually being recognised by anthropologists and linguistic specialists as a language with its own grammar, syntax and rules, rather than as a mere dialect. "English," the Barbadian poet and novelist George Lamming has said, "is a West Indian language." "West Indian English" – called Creole in some islands, Patois in others (especially those which have been, for periods in their history, French) – has enabled Louise Bennett to get many points across in pithy phrases which would have taken a whole paragraph to say in dictionary terms. It has the kind of racy flavour which suits her style, and she has been quick to use, too, some of the words and phrases in common daily use which go back to the standard English of Elizabethan and Cromwellian times.

Louise Bennett's researches have rescued from oblivion, often from extinction, a number of the island's folk songs, stories and sayings, and her stage productions have put Jamaican vernacular before large audiences.

There is a mass of her writing scattered about, very largely in Jamaica's Newspapers and magazines over the years, and much of it was collected into a book entitled *Jamaica Labrish* (a dialect word meaning chatter or gossip) in 1966.

No subject has been sacred from her fancy and biting wit. She has tackled the changing city, the war, Jamaican history, politics, middle-class attitudes, immigration and many other things, and no poet in Jamaica has a better understanding of the island and its people.

—Colin Rickards

BENVENISTE, Asa. British. Born in New York City, 25 August 1925; emigrated to England in 1950, became British subject in 1965. Educated at James Monroe High School, New York; New School for Social Research, New York, B.A. 1948; Sorbonne, Paris, 1950. Served as a Radio Operator in the United States Army Infantry, 1943–46. Married Pip Walker in 1949; has three stepsons. Researcher, Jewish News Agency, New York, 1947; Co-Editor, *Zero Quarterly*, Paris, Tangier, and London, 1948–56; Correspondent, *Nugget Magazine*, London, 1956–57; Copy Editor, Doubleday and Company, publishers, New York, 1957–58; Senior Art Editor, Paul Hamlyn Ltd., publishers, London, 1959–61; Senior Editor, Studio Vista Ltd., publishers, London, 1961–63. Since 1965, Staff Member, and currently Executive Editor, Trigram Press Ltd., London. Address: Blue Tile House, Stibbard, Fakenham, Norfolk, England.

Publications

Verse

Poems of the Mouth. London, Trigram Press, 1966.
A Word in Your Season: A Portfolio of Six Seriagraphs, with Jack Hirschman. London, Trigram Press, 1967.
Count Three. Berkeley, California, Maya, 1969.
The Atoz Formula. London, Trigram Press, 1969.
Free Semantic No. 2. London, Wallrich Books, 1970.
Umbrella. London, Wallrich Books, 1972.
Time Being, with Ray Di Palma and Tom Raworth. London, Blue Chair, 1972.
Blockmakers Black. London, Steam Press, 1973.
Certainly Metaphysics. London, Blue Chair, 1973.
It's the Same Old Feeling Again. London, Trigram Press, 1973.
Edge. London, Joe DiMaggio Press, 1974.

Plays

Radio Plays: *Tangier for the Traveller*, 1956; *Piano Forte*, 1957.

Other

Autotypography: A Book of Design Priorities.   London, Latimer New Dimensions, 1974.

Manuscript Collection: Washington University, St. Louis.

Critical Study: "Great Rejoicing" by Anselm Hollo, in *Ambit 41* (London), 1969.

Asa Benveniste comments:

Environmentalists will agree: describe the situation and you describe yourself. It's become clearer that poets mainly function within two areas: descriptive clarity or language. Most English poets fall within the former range ("Breakfast in the morning, then how do I compare with everyone else's corn flakes"). I can see how this might have a narrowing effect on the employment of language – and usually does, all around us. You can tell from the first line what the last line will read like. It's that prelude to tedium: To Thine Own Self Be True. Good enough for my aunt, good enough for me. Housman, Tennyson, after all, *are* good poets.

The second kind of work verges on the hysterical. Logic, clarity, description, narration, connecting links, have to make it as best they can, so long as they don't interfere with the *other* exercise, the possibility of hitting psychic accuracy and the sheer pleasure of two words coming together for the first time ever, and miraculously. For example: Robert Fludd, John Clare, Blake, Novalis, Zukofsky. Language for itself, and then its by-products like meaning, truth, perspicacity, play, pleasure, secret rejoicing. But it's dense material to work with, and anyone who argues publicly in favor of it, is bound to lose.

*   *   *

Asa Benveniste writes with light. Illuminated poems. Clear, subtle, lucid. I often imagine that even his punctuation marks become prisms on the page.

He is able to verify the mystical vision and tradition in poems often as simple as breath – and that's the essence of their power and immediacy. He is able to give added dimension to the real and enhance commonplace objects with mystery. Conversely he makes real and accessible the remote symbols of the Kabbalah and gives them face and form.

Tradition tells us that the great secrets and mysteries exist beyond the book and can only be exchanged from teacher to disciple through speech. Much of the available literature demonstrates the difficulty of verbalizing the inner journey and its unfolding, and of balancing the visible with the invisible and delineating the continual interplay between these two realities.

Therefore, Asa Benveniste's two books of poetry – *Poems of the Mouth* and *The Atoz Formula* – must be considered as valuable guides to the creative use of the process. They are sparks and must be cherished for their clarity.

Each volume develops possibilities inherent in a given mystical realm. *Poems of the Mouth* expands a proposition in the *Sefer Yetsira*, a primary Kabbalist textbook. *The Atoz Formula* explores the Hebrew Alphabet and the metaphorical/meta-actual progression of symbols enclosed within the cards of the Tarot.

It must also be noted that Asa Benveniste is an imaginative and elegant printer. The books he has issued from the Trigram Press are of consistently high quality.

—David Meltzer

BERESFORD, Anne. British. Born in Redhill, Surrey, 10 September 1929. Educated privately, and at Central School of Speech Training and Dramatic Art, London. Married Michael Hamburger, *q.v.*, in 1951 (divorced, 1970); remarried Michael Hamburger, 1974; has three children. Former stage actress and BBC broadcaster. Teacher at the Poetry Workshop, Cockpit Theatre, London, 1971–73. Since 1969, drama teacher, Wimbledon High School; since 1970, extra-mural teacher of drama and elocution, London. Address: 3a Half Moon Lane, London S.E. 24, England.

PUBLICATIONS

Verse

   Walking Without Moving. London, Turret Books, 1967.
   The Lair. London, Rapp and Whiting, 1968.
   Footsteps in Snow. London, Agenda Editions, 1972.
   Modern Fairy Tale. Rushden, Northamptonshire, Sceptre Press, 1972.
   The Courtship. Brighton, Unicorn Bookshop, 1972.

Plays

   Radio Plays: *Struck by Apollo*, with Michael Hamburger, 1965; *The Villa*, 1968.

Critical Studies: review by Christopher Levenson, in *Queen's Quarterly* (Kingston, Ontario), September 1971; review in *Times Literary Supplement* (London), 13 October 1972.

Anne Beresford comments:

It becomes increasingly difficult for me to talk about my poems. As far as possible I try to express, simply, feelings and experiences of people; nobody can change the world but they might be able to change themselves; only by a confrontation with oneself can any change be made. What I hope to achieve in my writing is an open-mindedness and a wider understanding of how and why we live.

*   *   *

Ezra Pound wrote: "Our life is, in so far as it is worth living, made up in great part of things indefinite, impalpable; and it is precisely because the arts present us these things that we – humanity – cannot get on without the arts" (*Selected Prose*, London, Faber, 1973, p. 33). Much of the subtlety of Anne Beresford's poetry stems from her attempts to define moments and states of mind of this nature – those aspects of consciousness and daily life which are most impatient of words. Anne Beresford's "Heimweh" is short enough to give in its entirety:

> a thrush sings
> every evening
> in the ash tree
>
> it has been singing
> for as long
> as I can remember
> only then
> the tree was probably
> an oak
>
> the song
> aches and aches
> in the green light
> if I knew
> where it was
> I would go
> home

Anne Beresford seldom overstates, but is reticent and elliptical. This gives her work an impersonal quality which is rare. At its best her writing expresses an imagination (*not* fancy) unlike that of any other contemporary poet. This is connected, in a strange way, with humour and satire. Her irony succeeds because it is not obvious.

A fault present in some poems is a tenuousness of rhythm, where the emotions don't seem strong enough to generate sufficient rhythmic energy. But this is sometimes offset by a clarity and simplicity of imagery which evoke much, particularly if these poems are lived with rather than read quickly:

> outside, high on the mountains
> is the great plain with wild flowers
> wild flowers and air so fresh
> one's head goes light.

> —from "Eurydice"

At times the imagery is menacing:

> You have come to a tower of slate
> crumbling into grey sky.
> Don't climb, not there. . . .

> —from "Half-Way"

This is not poetry which strives for immediate effect; hence a first reading often misses how much meaning her usually very simple words contain.

Anne Beresford uses dream and myth to express states of mind which are real, never as ornament or literary device. Her most recent work makes use of dramatic monologue and shows an historical consciousness which raises her poetry above that of contemporary writers of the short poem who seem to be incapable of embodying subjects other than the personal and the incidentals of everyday life. I shall close these notes by quoting "Nicodemus" in full:

> Keeping a sense of proportion
> lip service to what is considered correct
> I have brought what is needed to bury the dead.
> Once again I come to you by night.
> This time to take away all visible proof of my understanding.
> In secret I have applied myself
> to seek out wisdom
> to know what is before my face –
> the inside and the outside are reversed
> that which is
> has become that which is not –
> displaced, troubled
> I live naked in a house that is not my own
> and the five trees of Paradise evade me.

—William Cookson

BERG, Stephen. American. Born in Philadelphia, Pennsylvania, 2 August 1934. Educated at the University of Pennsylvania, Philadelphia; Boston University; University of Iowa, Iowa City, B.A. 1959; University of Indiana, Bloomington. Married Millie Lane in 1959; has two daughters. Formerly, Instructor in English, Temple University, Philadelphia. Currently, Assistant Professor, Philadelphia College of Art. Poetry Editor, *Saturday Evening Post*, Philadelphia, 1961–62; Editor, with Stephen Parker and Rhoda Schwartz, *The American Poetry Review*, Philadelphia. Recipient: Rockefeller-Centro Mexicano de Escritores grant, 1959–61; National Translation Center grant, 1969; Frank O'Hara Prize (*Poetry*, Chicago), 1970; Guggenheim Fellowship, 1974. Address: 715 Pine Street, Philadelphia, Pennsylvania 19106, U.S.A.

PUBLICATIONS

Verse

> *Berg Goodman Mezey: Poems.* Philadelphia, New Ventures Press, 1957.
> *Bearing Weapons: Poems.* Iowa City, Cummington Press, 1963.
> *The Queen's Triangle: A Romance.* West Branch, Iowa, Cummington Press, 1970.
> *The Daughters: Poems.* Indianapolis, Bobbs Merrill, 1971.
> *Grieve Like This.* New York, Grossman, 1974.

Other

> Editor, with Robert Mezey, *Naked Poetry: Recent American Poetry in Open Forms*, and *Naked Poetry 2*.   Indianapolis, Bobbs Merrill, 1969, 1974.
> Editor, with S. J. Marks, *Between People*.   Chicago, Scott Foresman, 1972.
> Editor, with S. J. Marks, *Doing the Unknown*.   New York, Dell, 1974.

> Translator, with others, *Cántico: Selections*, by Jorge Guillén.   Boston, Little Brown, 1965.
> Translator, *Nothing in the Word* (Aztec verse).   New York, Grossman, 1972.
> Translator, with others, *Clouded Sky*, by Miklos Radnoti.   New York, Harper, 1973.

Manuscript Collection: Mugar Memorial Library, Boston University.

Stephen Berg comments:

Non-theoretical: all comments on my work – such as the introductions to *Nothing in the Word*, *Clouded Sky*, and *Grieve Like This* – are random and apply only to the particular books and poems in question. Some remarks in the essay "Hands and Feet," the introduction to *Between People*, and an essay on French Poetry in *Poetry* (Chicago), May 1970, may shed some light.

*   *   *

Many of the poems in Stephen Berg's large collection (his most complete one to date), *The Daughters*, break forth with an almost breathless fury of speech, the expression of an agonized, compassionate mind and sensibility confronting the bitter realities of modern existence:

> We, the dooms, your future, the bloody fire
> between places, dancers on the corpses of who,
> we eat what there is. Are you
> sitting at a table? Is there food? Us,
> the zero washing itself, bones entering the floor,
> leaves zigzagging down through silt, through farms
> in the lone face of a mirror.

Berg appears to write with the example of such poets as Neruda, Vallejo, Patchen, among others, behind him. Like them he strives for a language and imagery that will encompass the irony, fatality, and suffering of a life everywhere overshadowed by mortality, a life unredeemed and unaccounted for either by reason or by any known God. In this endeavour Berg often stretches words and syntax to their extreme limits; frequently his means of progression – more evident, naturally, in his longer pieces, where there are greater space and freedom – are elliptical and associative rather than logical or merely sequential. Sometimes his poems surge and lash out seemingly uncontrollably; yet this is never the case, I think, for a strong, inventive imagination operates constantly, drawing together disparate details, linking objects and bodies, love and death. pain and anger, until the reader feels himself inside a poetic universe which lights up his own sense of the world with sudden, vivid and terrible lightning strokes of vision. To be sure,

Berg's poetry has at times its lapses, excesses, and repetitions, but these are minor in comparison with the ambitiousness and force of what he attempts, and recent, as yet uncollected poems, show a calmer, more reflective side to his writing. Berg is an energetic and highly talented poet, translator, and editor of whom considerable accomplishment may be expected. "I can go anywhere, I can let go forever / and live in the middle of fire, in silence. . . ."

—Ralph J. Mills, Jr.

BERGÉ, Carol. American. Born in New York City, 4 October 1928. Educated at New York University, 1946–52; New School for Social Research, New York, 1952–54. Has one son, Peter. Editorial assistant, Syndicate Publications, Simon and Schuster, publishers, *Forbes* magazine, and Hart Publishing Company, New York, 1950–54; Assistant to the President, Pendray Public Relations, New York, 1955. Member of the Board of Directors, COSMEP, 1971–73. Since 1971, Editor, *Center* magazine. Free-lance editor, lecturer, poetry reader, and tutor. Recipient: Mac-Dowell Fellowship, 1971, 1973, 1974; New York State Council on the Arts grant, for editing, 1971, for fiction, 1974. Agent: Charles Neighbors, 240 Waverly Place, New York, New York 10014. Address: Box 698, Woodstock, New York 12498, U.S.A.

PUBLICATIONS

Verse

> *Four Young Lady Poets*, with others, edited by LeRoi Jones. New York, Totem-Corinth, 1962.
> *The Vulnerable Island.* Cleveland, Renegade Press, 1964.
> *Lumina.* Cleveland, Flowers Press, 1965.
> *Poems Made of Skin.* Toronto, Weed/Flower Press, 1968.
> *Circles, As in the Eye.* New Mexico, Desert Review Press, 1968.
> *An American Romance, The Alan Poems, A Journal.* Los Angeles, Black Sparrow Press, 1969.
> *The Chambers.* Aylesford Priory, Kent, Aylesford Review Press, 1969.
> *From a Soft Angle: Poems about Women.* Indianapolis, Bobbs Merrill, 1972.

Novel

> *Acts of Love.* Indianapolis, Bobbs Merrill, 1973.

Short Stories

> *The Unfolding, Part 1.* New York, Theo Press, 1969.
> *A Couple Called Moebius.* Indianapolis, Bobbs Merrill, 1972.

Other

> *The Vancouver Report: A Report and Discussion of the Poetry Seminar at the University of British Columbia.* New York, Peace Eye, 1964.
> *A Chronograph of the Poets: A History of the "Deux Mégots Poets" from 1959–1965.* New York, Island Press, 1965.

Manuscript Collection: University of Texas, Austin.

Critical Studies: by Hayden Carruth, in *Hudson Review* (New York), 1969; Howard McCord, in *Measure* (Pullman, Washington), 1970; Ishmael Reed, in Washington, D.C., *Post*, 1973.

Carol Bergé comments:

I worked in poetry through 1968 and had been moving more and more into prose as the Big Challenge since 1965. With the publication of the 190-page collection, *From a Soft Angle*, in 1972, a book that encompasses work from 1959 through 1971, I feel the work in that field is wrapped up, and am working almost solely in prose now. The book of stories, *A Couple Called Moebius*, has been well-received and reviewed and I'm content to be represented by the stories therein. The novel *Acts of Love* is as well-made as I can achieve at this time: it operates on at least three levels: that of a sociological/historical novel, that of a description of contemporary life, and that of an interesting and occasionally amusing fiction. It was a joy to write, I am now working on a third novel (the first novel, unpublished, needs revision); this one is concerned with the alternatives offered to Singles, a subdivision of which I have been a part for a long time. I hope to be as good a writer as Isak Dinesen, as Kobo Abe, as Jacov Lind, as Margaret Mitchell, as lady Murasaki. There is no separating the life from the work. These days, I will write perhaps one poem every two months or so; therefore, I no longer feel I can be classified as a poet, but as a novelist.

*   *   *

Female intensities, of wit, of lust, tenderness, the intelligence of the body, its groping, the ravage and despair, and all in language as varied as the weather, formalities of basic talk, spontaneous yet out of much reading, responding, looking: this is Carol Bergé's poetry. But foremost and always female, in her own voice or in dozens of personae, the terrible endlessness of sexual need, loving, hating, fighting, forgiving:

> The women breast to breast across empty
> across lava-strewn bitter plains
> facing lidless eyes of the majestic surgeons
> who demand they empty their wombs
> of the quintuplet dolls shaped like "husband"
> Women offering full teats to
> men with infant faces who drink with mouths
> the violet of sleep or of healed circumcision

And so on and on, the hurt imagination putting out, but not sloganizing or attitudinizing – at least not much. And then the nuances of observance of self:

> these days
> when you draw back
> as I reach for you
> it is an old wound you rip
> open . . .

Bergé can be, and often is, talkative. Her poems sometimes seem put together from random images, broken by unlikely shifts of tone and texture, with little attempt at lyric unity. But her talk is intelligent, tough, urbane, and original, which is more than can be said for a good deal of poetry. And when she breaks through her talk into genuine poems of her own, they are moving and lucid, and they show a degree of maturity that most writing by other self-conscious female poets today cannot approach.

—Hayden Carruth

BERKSON, Bill. American. Born in New York City, 30 August 1939. Educated at Brown University, Providence, Rhode Island, 1957–59; New School for Social Research, New York (Dylan Thomas Memorial Award, 1959); Columbia University, New York, 1959–60. Editorial Associate, *Portfolio and Art News Annual*, New York, 1960–63; Associate Producer, *Art-New York* series, WNDT-TV, New York, 1964–65; taught at the New School for Social Research, 1964–69; Guest Editor, Museum of Modern Art, New York, 1965–69; Editor, *Best and Company* magazine, 1969; Teaching Fellow, Ezra Stiles College, Yale University, New Haven, Connecticut, 1969–70. Since 1972, Editor, *Big Sky* magazine and Big Sky Books, Bolinas, California. Recipient: Poets Foundation grant, 1968; Coordinating Council of Literary Magazines grant, 1973. Address: Box 272, Bolinas, California 94924, U.S.A.

PUBLICATIONS

Verse

Saturday Night: Poems 1960–61. New York, Tibor de Nagy Editions, 1961.
Shining Leaves. New York, Angel Hair Books, 1969.
Two Serious Poems and One Other, with Larry Fagin. Bolinas, California, Big Sky Books, 1972.
Recent Visitors. New York, Angel Hair Books, 1973.
Ants. Berkeley, California, Arif Press, 1974.
Quiet World. San Francisco, Grape Press, 1974.
Hymns of St. Bridget, with Frank O'Hara. New York, Boke Press, 1974.

Other

Editor, *In Memory of My Feelings*, by Frank O'Hara. New York, Museum of
Modern Art, 1967.
Editor, with Irving Sandler, *Alex Katz*. New York, Praeger, 1971.

Manuscript Collection: University of Connecticut, Storrs.

*   *   *

Bill Berkson is first a cosmopolitan poet, a Manhattan *boulevardier*. Not Nick
Kenny. Try Cafavy or Frank O'Hara. Or sometimes even Apollinaire.
Elegant as Fred Astaire.
Intelligent, astute, wide-ranged. He maintains a city-dweller's constant curiosity
for all forms of culture.
A serious reader, accurate listener, authoritative (cautious) witness to paintings
& sculpture. Well-grounded.
His only collection to date is *Shining Leaves* and it's composed of work done
primarily in 1967–1968. As all first books it serves as map for work to come. What
will be added onto or subtracted is in plain view.
Some of the poems are casual as speech. Often wry, occasionally self-effacing,
sometimes a bit stiff, the poems are miraculously never pretentious – a ritual flaw
of most first books.
No stance beyond the telling of gathered information. No overt opinions. Infer
judgement rather than dish it out. That's the grace of cosmopolites.
Painterly poems as well. Sometimes using words as textures, surfaces, energies
placed on a page.
Another aspect of his creative considerations is revealed in *The Big Sky*, a
magazine he has edited since 1972. It is a model review of well-placed poetry,
prose and graphics.
Like many others he has left the East for the West and lives in Bolinas, a village
in Marin County in Northern California. (There *is* a difference between the North
and South in California.)
His poetry is taking on a different shape. More compressed. Direct takes on
essence, specific moments. Also indicated is a philosophical concern with meaning
and the duplicity of language.

—David Meltzer

BERRIGAN, Daniel J., S.J. American. Born in Minnesota, 9 May 1921. Edu-
cated at Weston (Jesuit) Seminary, Massachusetts; ordained Roman Catholic priest,
1952. Taught French and philosophy, Brooklyn Preparatory School, New York,
1954–57; Professor of New Testament Studies, LeMoyne College, Syracuse, New
York, 1957–63; Director of United Christian Work, Cornell University, Ithaca,
New York, 1967–68. Jailed for anti-war activities, 1968. Recipient: Lamont Poetry
Selection Award, 1957; Thomas More Association Medal, 1970; Melcher Book
Award, 1971. Address: 99 Claremont Avenue, New York, New York 10027,
U.S.A.

PUBLICATIONS

Verse

> *Time Without Numbers.* New York, Macmillan, 1957.
> *Encounters.* Cleveland, World, 1960.
> *The World for Wedding Ring: Poems.* New York, Macmillan, 1962.
> *No One Walks Waters.* New York, Macmillan, 1966.
> *False Gods, Real Men: New Poems.* New York, Macmillan, 1966.
> *Love, Love at the End: Parables, Prayers, and Meditations.* New York, Macmillan, 1968.
> *Night Flight to Hanoi: War Diary with 11 Poems.* New York, Macmillan, 1968.
> *Crime Trial.* Boston, Impressions Workshop, 1970.
> *Trial Poems*, with Thomas Lewis. Boston, Beacon Press, 1970.
> *Selected and New Poems.* New York, Doubleday, 1973.
> *Prison Poems.* Greensboro, North Carolina, Unicorn Press, 1973.
> *Prison Poems.* New York, Viking Press, 1974.

Play

> *The Trial of the Catonsville Nine* (produced New York and London, 1971). Boston, Beacon Press, 1970.

Other

> *The Bride: Essays in the Church.* New York, Macmillan, 1959.
> *The Bow in the Clouds: Man's Covenant with God.* New York, Coward McCann, and London, Burns and Oates, 1961.
> *They Call Us Dead Men: Reflections on Life and Conscience.* New York, Macmillan, 1966.
> *Consequences: Truth and . . .* New York, Macmillan, and London, Collier Macmillan, 1967.
> *Go from Here: A Prison Diary* (includes verse). San Francisco, Open Space, 1968.
> *No Bars to Manhood.* New York, Doubleday, 1970.
> *The Dark Night of Resistance.* New York, Doubleday, 1971.
> *The Geography of Faith: Conversations Between Daniel Berrigan, When Underground, and Robert Coles.* Boston, Beacon Press, 1971.
> *Absurd Convictions, Modest Hopes: Conversations after Prison with Lee Lockwood.* New York, Random House, 1972.
> *American Is Hard to Find.* New York, Doubleday, 1972; London, SPCK, 1973.
> *Jesus Christ.* New York, Doubleday, 1973.
> *Lights On in the House of the Dead: A Prison Diary.* New York, Doubleday, 1974.

*   *   *

In spite of his Jesuit training there is little in Daniel Berrigan's poetry to remind one of so conspicuously available a model as Gerard Manley Hopkins. Reading the *Imprimaturs* and the *Nihil Obstats* on the early volumes is surprising to the reader who has come to Berrigan from his later work where such marks of orthodoxy are so conspicuously absent, perhaps even unavailable. Hopkins was probably too abstractly theological to be a model for Dan Berrigan's taste. Berrigan's early poems have more the feel of 17th-century English devotional verse. His references to Simone Weil suggest an indebtedness to her favorite poet among the English writers – George Herbert. The early volumes brought quick success to Berrigan as a poet:

> Style
> envelops a flower like its odor;
> bestows on radiant air
> the spontaneous word that greets and makes a king.

An early poem addressed to Wallace Stevens interestingly accepts the techniques but repudiates the metaphysics that was a part of the Stevens' aesthetic:

> Awakening
> When I grew appalled by love
> and promised nothing, but stood, a sick man
> first time on feeble knees
> peering at walls and weather
> like the feeble minded –
> the strange outdoors, the house of strangers –
> there, there was a beginning.

But even the early poems were dedicated to Dorothy Day, the quiet figure so central to the life of radical Catholicism in America – *beata pauperes spiritu* and *beata pacifici* they intone in their dedications, and Berrigan was to take the words seriously.

His opposition to the Vietnam War led him to found Clergy and Laymen Concerned about Vietnam when he returned to the U.S. This ecumenical action so enraged Cardinal Spellman that he exiled Berrigan to South America, a move that proved so unpopular that the Cardinal was quickly forced to rescind the action. But the tour through South America – the response to the appalling poverty he saw there – brought him back to the U.S. a convinced religious radical. *Consequences: Truth and . . .* is the record of his spiritual and political development during that period.

A post as professor of religion and poetry at Cornell University did not dampen his growing involvement with his brother Philip in active opposition to the war. Pouring blood on draft files led on to the burning of draft files in Catonsville, Maryland. As he turned increasingly to direct action, he also turned to prose. His poetry was used to focus his personal reaction to the events he experienced. In *Night Flight to Hanoi* he wrote of holding one child saved from bombing:

> Children in the Shelter
> Imagine; three of them.
> As though survival
> were a rat's word,
> and a rat's end
> waited there at the end
> And I must have
> in the century's boneyard

heft of flesh and bone in my arms
I picked up the littlest
a boy, his face
breaded with rice (his sister calmly feeding him
as we climbed down)
In my arms fathered
in a moment's grace, the messiah
of all my tears. I bore, reborn
a Hiroshima child from hell.

The Trial of the Catonsville Nine brought Berrigan to world-wide attention, and his prison journals were among the eloquent publications of the last years of the 1960's. *The Dark Night of Resistance,* published in that period, illustrated the growing influence on Berrigan of St. John of the Cross. Read in the 1950's by poets influenced by the religious revival of that period, one has a sense that Berrigan came to understand him in the late 1960's. He found St. John of the Cross in his prison experience a model to be lived rather than a style to be imitated.

Berrigan remains a Roman Catholic and a Jesuit. He is less active in writing poetry now, and more active in building a society that can be honestly celebrated in poetry. Despite the serious moral and political issues he forced through his personal involvement, there remains throughout his poetry a sustained joyousness – a marked characteristic of all his work.

—Myron Taylor

BERRIGAN, Ted (Edmund J. Berrigan, Jr.). American. Born in Providence, Rhode Island, 15 November 1934. Educated at the University of Tulsa, Oklahoma, B.A. 1959, M.A. 1962. Served in the United States Army, 1954–57. Married to Sandra Alper; has two children. Editor of "*C*" magazine and "*C*" Press, New York. Taught in the Poetry Workshop at the St. Marks Arts Project, New York, 1966–67; Visiting Lecturer, University of Iowa, Iowa City, 1968–1969. Recipient: Poetry Foundation Award, 1964. Address: 911 West Diversey Parkway, Chicago, Illinois 60614, U.S.A.

PUBLICATIONS

Verse

The Sonnets. New York, "*C*" Press, 1964.
Many Happy Returns to Dick Gallup. New York, Angel Hair Books, 1967.
Bean Spasms, with Ron Padgett. New York, Kulchur Press, 1967.
Some Thing, with Joe Brainard and Ron Padgett. Privately printed, n.d.
Living with Christ. New York, Boke Books, n.d.
Many Happy Returns: Poems. New York, Corinth Books, 1969.
Fragment for Jim Brodey. London, Cape Goliard Press, 1969.

In the Early Morning Rain. London, Cape Goliard Press, 1970; New York, Grossman, 1971.
Back in Boston Again, with Tom Clark and Ron Padgett. Philadelphia, Telegraph Books, 1972.

Plays

Seventeen: Collected Plays, with Ron Padgett. New York, "C" Press, 1965.

Ted Berrigan comments:

> I'm a sophisticated American
> Primitive. I make up each
> poem (i.e. "verse form") as
> it arrives by putting
> things where they have to go
> tho I sometimes vary this by putting
> things where they don't have to go.
>
> My influences are obvious and I put
> them in too, just like
> everybody else does.

*   * *   *

> Thus I, red faced and romping in the wind
> Whirl thru mad Manhattan dressed in books
> – "Sonnet LXXV"

When I first read Ted Berrigan's *The Sonnets* in the early sixties I was attracted to what now seems the easiest and most accessible way to get to this work – the repetition of lines, the threads or motifs which run through the poems creating a narrative one can follow like guidelines along a road one is not quite familiar with. These guidelines seem like billboard signs now, with Ted sitting alongside, smiling a detached smile as he watches the world file past. It took me awhile, and several readings of *The Sonnets,* to realize that it was possible to write the word "I" in a poem and then stand back, get away from the truth – a true description of what is really happening which is itself interesting but might be boring – and still come out with a line that was true to yourself, your own voice. A great deal of the pleasure I get from reading *The Sonnets* comes from the involvement I'm forced to feel with what is going on in the poems, how they've been put together, what the sources are behind many of the lines, why those sources were chosen, and how they connect to the basic pattern of the poem as a whole. Instinct, and voice (the feeling that the way you are saving what you are saying is right), and knowledge – how to write about what you know without consciously considering you know anything – are a few of the characteristics of this work I admire. It is also a very inspiring series of poems, in a spiritual sense, due I think to the poet's attitude towards himself, his friends, strangers, and most of all, poetry in general. It's a very healthy attitude, filled with insight which ceases to be psychological when the poet recognizes his own sanity. *The Sonnets* may or may not have been written with that in mind but for me the insights, i.e. new meanings, occur not out of a feeling of self-analysis but out of the breakdown of the normal way of studying oneself, language and feeling. If *The Sonnets* is a "literary" work, it's because the poet makes use of literature not to impress but because, as a poet, that's what poets deal with, that's what a good deal of their lives are all about. Instead of merely digesting literature one should accept what one reads for what one gets out of it, for the pleasure one receives as the person, the "I" who is reading. Berrigan's system of values, his judgement and taste, his hardness balanced by a generosity which allows him to write about himself because that's his way of giving, and his concepts about poetry which are often obscured by the actual results of the theories themselves – the poems as theories – make *The Sonnets* one of the few works of the last ten years that is both formidable and readable, and great.

– Lewis Warsh

BERRY, Francis. British. Born in Ipoh, Malaya, 23 March 1915. Educated at Hereford Cathedral School; Dean Close School; University of London, B.A. 1949; University of Exeter, M.A. 1960. Served in the British Army, 1939–46. Married Nancy Melloney Graham in 1947 (died); Patricia Thomson, 1970; has one daughter and one son. Articled clerk, 1931. Assistant Lecturer, Lecturer, Senior Lecturer, Reader, and Professor of English, University of Sheffield, 1947–70. Since 1970, Professor of English, Royal Holloway College, University of London, Egham, Surrey. Visiting Lecturer, Carleton College, Northfield, Minnesota, 1951–52, and University of the West Indies, Jamaica, 1957; British Council Lecturer in India, 1966–67; Visiting Lecturer in Germany, 1972. Fellow, Royal Society of Literature, 1969. Address: Department of English, Royal Holloway College, University of London, Egham, Surrey, England.

PUBLICATIONS

Verse

> *Gospel of Fire.* London, Elkin Mathews, 1933.
> *Snake in the Moon.* London, Williams and Norgate, 1936.
> *The Iron Christ: A Poem.* London, Williams and Norgate, 1938.
> *Fall of a Tower and Other Poems.* London, Fortune Press, 1943.
> *Murdock and Other Poems.* London, Dakers, 1947.
> *The Galloping Centaur: Poems 1933–1951.* London, Methuen, 1952.
> *Morant Bay and Other Poems.* London, Routledge, 1961.
> *Ghosts of Greenland: Poems.* London, Routledge, 1966.

Plays

> Radio Plays: *Illnesses and Ghosts at the West Settlement*, 1965; *The Sirens*, 1966; *The Near Singing Dome*, 1971.

Other

> *Herbert Read.* London, Longman, 1953; revised edition, 1961.
> *Poets' Grammar: Person, Time and Mood in Poetry.* London, Routledge, 1958;
> Westport, Connecticut, Greenwood Press, 1974.
> *Poetry and the Physical Voice.* London, Routledge, and New York, Oxford
> University Press, 1962.
> *The Shakespearean Inset: Word and Picture.* London, Routledge, 1965; New
> York, Theatre Arts Books, 1966; revised edition, Carbondale, Southern Illi-
> nois University Press, 1971.
> *John Masefield: The Narrative Poet.* Sheffield, University of Sheffield, 1968.
> *Thoughts on Poetic Time.* Abingdon-on-Thames, Berkshire, Abbey Press, 1972.

> Editor, *Essays and Studies.* London, Murray, 1969.

Manuscript Collections: Lockwood Memorial Library, University of Buffalo, New
York; Sheffield Public Library.

Critical Study: "Francis Berry" by G. Wilson Knight, in *Neglected Powers*, London, Routledge, 1971.

Francis Berry comments:

Have been deeply enchanted by geography – the Mediterranean, the West Indies,
Greenland – for the settings it supplies for human actions. Strongest emotion used
to be fear in its varieties, especially around sunset or in the night. But even strong
noontide sunlight provoked anxiety. Cruelty figures in early poems because I am
frightened of cruelty. Have felt responsive to other times as well as other places:
so history and myths are also poetic preoccupations. I believe the dead might still
care, and would not hurt them. It is a gratification to have written any poem that I
think is good enough, but the long poem, narrative or dramatic, of lively structure,
compact, of varied rhythm, and vivid images, is what I would most delight in
making: its making would sustain the maker day after day during its making and
render tolerable the return of first consciousness each morning.

*   *   *

Francis Berry is a master of the long poem, and his finest work is in that genre.
Because of this, he has been under-represented in magazines and anthologies and
his reputation has yet to match the opinion which such critics as G. Wilson Knight
and Donald Davie have formed of his work.

The Iron Christ tells of a statue made from the guns of the frontier fortresses of
Chile and Argentina and the attempt to erect this on the highest point of the Andes
as a symbol of peace. The struggle up the mountain is rendered graphically:

> The driver turns his face, his arm to throttle
> Levering steam, but, with a cursing, spin
> The driving-wheels, skidding upon raw rails,
> Circuiting vainly, then grab, heel over rods,
> Pistons pant, valves hiss, wheels grip, groan, grab . . .

Fall of a Tower shows a town dominated and overshadowed by a church, and the attempt of a man, Edmund, to blow that church up:

> Struts straddle; West Front
> Walks apart, begins ungainly waddle,
> Collapses on its face; brick and mortar
> Flee yelling from their stocks . . .

Murdock chronicles the unending affray of two ghostly brothers:

> We of this Village know our heavy Wood
> Haunted by Brothers in their furious Mood.
> Two Brothers, locked and pledged to nightly Duel,
> Fight under Trees, hidden at fullest Moon.
> Though dumb, their Blows do toss upon the Gale;
> Their Groans disturb us at our Murdock fires;
> Their sobs are heard through Falls of Autumn Rain . . .

Morant Bay deals with a negro uprising in Jamaica, put down ruthlessly by Governor Eyre in 1865. The exotic coloration is instantly compelling:

> . . . On the other side of the ravine
> Rises the opposing flank of another spur,
> Its sandstone swooned from the blurs of that sun,
> Dotted with thorned scrub, roots bedded in stone,
> On which the red spider darts or the lizard waits
> Before his next scurry with a sobbing throat . . .

Equally compelling are the different voices that interweave the narration. One thinks of the diatribe which emanates from the black Deacon Bogle. He denounces the governor and is echoed by the impassioned responses of his congregation:

> "Der he be
> In dat King's House, an' he eat" –
> *In dat King's House, an' he eat.*
> "He eat fishes an' he eat meat,"
> *He eat fishes an' he eat meat,*
> *War-o, heavy war-o . . .*

Because he uses the voices of his protagonists, Mr. Berry is able to enter into their characters and see all sides of this question – Eyre, courageous but bigoted; the coloured Gordon, intelligent and envious; Deacon Bogle, personification of the superstitious blacks. What is so impressive about this poem upon a vexed subject – race hatred – is that it does not take sides. Instead, it seeks to understand the difficulty of a situation. In many ways, *Morant Bay* is a great Catholic poem. It seems the massacre at Morant Bay in terms of original sin, an obeah

> Whose magic undergoes all manner of transfer
> But cannot be cast out.

In *Illnesses and Ghosts at the West Settlement*, Mr. Berry's recreation of voices takes a further step and enters a new terrain. This is the Greenland colonized at the end of the first millenium A.D. by Erik the Red. Plague strikes down the little settlement, smashing the sanctions that govern even this primitive society. The remnant of people staying there becomes demoralized. The whole poem is couched in terms of a recollection by the various ghosts hovering above the colony where they suffered so dreadfully a thousand years ago. Erik's daughter-in-law, Gudrid, is the central character. Her voice comes across the centuries in characteristically tentative metres, recreating a woman's agony in the face of male intransigence:

> Illnesses and ghosts.
> You founded Greenland. I've seen enough of your Greenland
> And I want the sun for a while, husband or no husband.
> I want the sun because I am so cold, you know I am so cold,
> That I could hear that particular sound again
> Oh, I am so old
> Before I am hardly girl. Dear Father, Father-in-law, help me . . .

It is questionable whether any contemporary poet can show so great a range of technique and subject-matter. And the characteristically exotic settings are a means of staging a penetration into the motives behind human affection and human action. The story doesn't end with Greenland, however. Francis Berry's most recent major work, not yet published, was broadcast in the summer of 1971. It concerns Shah Jehan who built the Taj Mahal in memory of his wife. Here is the voice of another woman: the dead Mumtaz accusing her husband of wishing her dead in order to erect his immemorial dome:

> I died because you wanted me to die.
> Or thought you did . . . Sometimes. For I could read
> That silent thought in the way you looked
> At me . . . sometimes. It made me sad – for you,
> Because I surmised you would be desolate
> And helpless . . . I gone. And that you would regret
> That thought you had allowed me to discern . . .
> Sometimes . . . though you should have not . . .

This is a sparser, more austere verse than we are used to from Mr. Berry. And indeed *The Near Singing Dome* may still be part of a work in progress. The reputation of the man who wrote this, and *Illnesses and Ghosts, Morant Bay, Murdock, Fall of a Tower* and *The Iron Christ,* may continue to grow slowly, as great reputations will. But the admirers of Francis Berry believe that his work will certainly endure.

– Philip Hobsbaum

BERRY, Wendell (Erdman). American. Born in Henry County, Kentucky, 5 August 1934. Educated at the University of Kentucky, Lexington, A.B., M.A. Married Tanya Amyx in 1957; has one daughter and one son. Since 1964, Member of the English Department, University of Kentucky. Recipient: Guggenheim Fellowship, 1951; Rockefeller Fellowship, 1965; Bess Hokin Prize (*Poetry,* Chicago), 1967; National Endowment for the Arts grant, 1969. Address: Port Royal, Kentucky 40058, U.S.A.

PUBLICATIONS

Verse

> *November Twenty-Six, Nineteen Hundred Sixty-Three.* New York, Braziller, 1964.
> *The Broken Ground: Poems.* New York, Harcourt Brace, 1964; London, Cape, 1966.
> *Openings: Poems.* New York, Harcourt Brace, 1969.
> *Findings.* Iowa City, Prairie Press, 1969.

Novels

> *Nathan Coulter.* Boston, Houghton Mifflin, 1960.
> *A Place on Earth.* New York, Harcourt Brace, 1967.
> *The Hidden Wound.* Boston, Houghton Mifflin, 1970.

Other

> *The Long-Legged House* (essays). New York, Harcourt Brace, 1969.
> *Farming: A Hand Book.* New York, Harcourt Brace, 1970.
> *The Unforeseen Wilderness: An Essay on Kentucky's Red River Gorge.* Lexington, University Press of Kentucky, 1971.
> *A Continuous Harmony: Essays Cultural and Agricultural.* New York, Harcourt Brace, 1972.
> *The Memory of Old Jack.* New York, Harcourt Brace, 1974.

*   *   *

The decisive event in Wendell Berry's poetry, and very likely in his life as well, was his decision, after several youthful years spent in New York City, to return to his native region, the hill country of northern Kentucky. It was no casual decision, but a determination to abjure modern commercial society and to recover instead the values of his ancestors in the scenes of his own childhood. He settled on a small farm that had once been part of his family's holdings. Since then he has worked as a farmer, and as a teacher, writer, and lecturer too, but with the primary emphasis on turning his farm into a self-sustaining enterprise by using principles of tillage retrieved from the time before the inception of industrial agriculture. As a writer he has striven to impart his sense of the relationship between social, cultural, and religious values on one hand and the processes of nature on the other. By varied means, ranging from fantasy to technical discussions of agricultural problems, he has sought to restore an understanding of mankind's creative relationship to the land, often in terms of explicit sexual–vegetative imagery. Many of his poems, novels, and essays have become touchstones for the youthful counter-culture which sprang up in the U.S. during the 1960's, especially that part of it which dropped out of urban society and turned to rural living.

Whatever else he is, Berry is a poet first of all, however. One sees in his poems the most forceful parts of his argument. Recently he has begun to experiment with poems in rhyme and meter, but in most of his work he has been associated with the free-form poets of his generation. In general his poems fall into two kinds: long-line poems that approximate very loosely to blank verse, and short-line poems in acutely toned and measured phrasings, influenced by the work of Denise Levertov. In both modes his voice is distinctly his own, however, compounded partly from the native speech of Kentucky, partly from suggestions of biblical syntax and rhetoric, and partly from the general American tradition of "transcendental" nature writing, as found in the works of John Woolman, Thoreau, John Muir, and many others. His greatest distinction, in both poetry and prose, is his ability to reduce complex cultural materials to simple, easily flowing language that has about it an air of both gentleness and precision. If we take *pastoral* to mean, not the Renaissance convention, but a mode of pre-classical, syncretic vision, then Berry's poems are pastoral in the fullest sense of the term.

All these qualities are evident in "The Current," a poem which is both characteristic and good:

> Having once put his hand into the ground,
> seeding there what he hopes will outlast him,
> a man has made a marriage with his place,
> and if he leaves it his flesh will ache to go back.
> His hand has given up its birdlife in the air.
> It has reached into the dark like a root
> and begun to wake, quick and mortal, in timelessness,
> a flickering sap coursing upward into his head
> so that he sees the old tribespeople bend
> in the sun, digging with sticks, the forest opening
> to receive their hills of corn, squash, and beans,
> their lodges and graves, and closing again.
> He is made their descendant, what they left
> in the earth rising into him like a seasonal juice.
> And he sees the bearers of his own blood arriving,
> the forest burrowing into the earth as they come,
> their hands gathering the stones up into walls,
> and relaxing, the stones crawling back into the ground
> to lie still under the black wheels of machines.
> The current flowing to him through the earth
> flows past him, and he sees one descended from him,
> a young man who has reached into the ground,
> his hand held in the dark as by a hand.

– Hayden Carruth

BERTOLINO, James. American. Born in Hurley, Wisconsin, 4 October 1942. Educated at the University of Wisconsin, Stevens Point, Madison, and Oshkosh, B.S. in English and art, 1970; Washington State University, Pullman, 1970–71; Cornell University, Ithaca, New York, 1971–73, M.F.A., 1973. Married the artist Lois Behling in 1966. Teaching Assistant, Washington State University, 1970–71; Teaching Assistant, 1971–73, and Lecturer in Creative Writing, 1973–74, Cornell University. Editor, *Abraxas* magazine and Abraxas Press, Madison, Wisconsin, and Ithaca, New York, 1968–72; Editor, Stone Marrow Press, Ithaca, New York, 1970–72; Assistant Editor, *Epoch* magazine, Ithaca, New York, 1971–73. Recipient:

Book-of-the-Month Club Award, 1970; Coordinating Council of Literary Magazines grant, 1970; YM-YWHA Poetry Center Discovery Award, 1972; National Endowment for the Arts grant, 1974. Address: Department of English, Cornell University, Ithaca, New York 14850, U.S.A.

PUBLICATIONS

Verse

Day of Change. Milwaukee, Gunrunner Press, 1968.
Drool. Madison, Wisconsin, Quixote Press, 1968.
Mr. Nobody. Marshall, Minnesota, Ox Head Press, 1969.
Ceremony: A Poem. Milwaukee, Morgan Press, 1969.
Maize: A Poem. Madison, Wisconsin, Abraxas Press, 1969.
Stone Marrow. Madison, Wisconsin, Anachoreta Press–Abraxas Press, 1969.
Becoming Human: Poems. Oshkosh, Wisconsin, Road Runner Press, 1970.
The Interim Handout. Ithaca, New York, privately printed, 1972.
Employed. Ithaca, New York, Ithaca House, 1972.
Edging Through. Berkeley, California, Serendipity Books, 1972.
Soft Rock. Tacoma, Washington, Charas Press, 1973.
Making Space for Our Living. Orangeburg, South Carolina, Peaceweed Press, 1973.

Other

Editor, *Quixote: Northwest Poets.* Madison, Wisconsin, Quixote Press, 1968.
Editor, *The Abraxas/Five Anthology.* Ithaca, New York, Abraxas Press, 1972.
Editor, "Young Poets Issue" of *Stone Drum* (Huntsville, Texas), Fall-Winter 1973.

Manuscript Collection: Murphy Library, University of Wisconsin, La Crosse.

Critical Studies: "Three Good Prospects" by James Naiden, in *Granite* (Hanover, New Hampshire), Autumn 1972; "Observations on a Book of Poetry" by Steven Granger, in *Seizure* (Eugene, Oregon), Fall-Winter 1972; "Employed" by Ripley Schemm, in *Bartleby's Review 2* (Machias, Maine), 1973.

James Bertolino comments:

My recent work in poetry, 1971–73, has been characterized by each poem being a series of rapidly accelerating images which, though often discordant, are forced to cohere due to the speed at which the reader is propelled through them. The poems, then, when experienced properly by the reader, become something akin to psychic depth-charges. That is, though they "meaningfully" cohere under the pressure of their lyric-kinetic structures, once they've been driven through the protective walls of the psyche, they explode like fragmentation bombs, the disparate images like pieces of shrapnel lodging in the most sensitive areas.

I know this sounds rather brutal, but clearly the poems aren't "nice," and aren't satisfied with titillating the surface-level pre-conception of many readers of poems. My work in *Granite* (numbers 4, 5, and 6) is indicative of this phase of my work.

*　　　*　　　*

Poised precariously between innocence and wisdom, James Bertolino's poems may run the risk of being taken for the expression of an artless naivete. Actually, there is no doodling with abstractions, no aimless stream-of-consciousness in his work. Here everything is pared to the quick, every syllable functional. Consider in these lines from "The Old Clearing" –

> a gentle force
> the morning draws me here
> place I've never off dusty road
> under carefully the
> barbed-wire
> miles from how I've walked here

– how "carefully" suggests the physical movements of the sleepwalker with the obstruction, and "barbed-wire" the persistence of the real. No line of Bertolino's has more than six words in it, most only three. And although he never makes use of formal meter, not syllable count but *stress* (as in W. C. Williams) is the secret of all his rhythmic effects.

Each poem, moreover, is not so much a picture (as in Pound, H.D., etc.) as it is an *event*. In a series of images embracing all the senses including the kinesthetic *something happens*. Perhaps it is Bertolino's verbal parsimony that makes us realize how terrible and precise a single word standing alone (but drawing strength from a sparse context) can be. For instance:

> a green Mack truck
> (with no trailer)
> bore down upon a preoccupied
> wren
> & before the feathers
> had settled,
> three sparrows &
> the rest
> of the wrens
> were singing again.

One notices the assonantal "en" melody which makes the poem end in song (and yet this is free verse!) and how the single word "wren" upon the page becomes the bird itself, and how the Mack truck's having no trailer gives a kind of factual authenticity to the event. So in "Design" two sharp details lead us to a startling recognition:

> Worms hole
> flower petals
> with composition
>
> the sun
> free
> below.

There is a lot of joy in these poems, joy in nature and joy in love, a surprising circumstance perhaps in view of the times in which we live. But the second section of *Employed,* entitled "The Executrix of Weirds" is Bertolino's descent into Hell, and his emergence from it. Here his imagery at times brings us close to nausea, and we no longer doubt, if we had before, the presence of evil in the world. Yet in these poems too we find the same precise workmanship, beauty of form, control.

Intensity is the norm in these poems, each of which seems to be an event encapsulated out of time. Furthermore, Bertolino knows exactly what he is doing. In a recent interview (in *The Outer Circle 4,* Fall 1973), Bertolino remarked:

> I think I've always had an impulse toward condensation, making a poem very tight and clear and small, and, by the same token, emphasizing or zeroing in on the essential small details of an experience . . . a concern with finding . . . where the spaces between objects and details are that open up into something else, the larger experience.

> – E. L. Mayo

BETJEMAN, John. British. Born in Highgate, London, 1906. Educated at Marlborough; Magdalen College, Oxford. Served as Press Attaché, Dublin, 1941–42; in the Admiralty, 1943. Married Penelope Valentine Hester in 1933; has one son and one daughter. Book reviewer, *Daily Herald,* London; radio and television speaker. Columnist ("City and Suburban"), *Spectator,* London, 1954–58. Founder, Victorian Society. Member, Royal Fine Art Commission; Governor, Pusey House (Church of England). Recipient: Heinemann Award, 1949; Foyle Poetry Prize, 1955, 1959; Loines Award (USA), 1956; Duff Cooper Memorial Prize, 1958; Queen's Gold Medal for Poetry, 1960; Companion of Literature, Royal Society of Literature, 1968. LL.D.: Aberdeen University; D.Litt.: Oxford, Reading and Birmingham universities. Honorary Associate, Royal Institute of British Architects. Honorary Member, American Academy of Arts and Letters, 1973. C.B.E. (Companion, Order of the British Empire), 1960; Knighted, 1969. Named Poet Laureate, 1972. Address: 29 Radnor Walk, London, S.W.3, England.

PUBLICATIONS

Verse

> *Mount Zion; or, In Touch with the Infinite.* London, James Press, 1931.
> *Continual Dew: A Little Book of Bourgeois Verse.* London, Murray, 1937.
> *Sir John Piers* (as Epsilon). Mullingar, Ireland, Westmeath Examiner, 1938.
> *Old Lights for New Chancels: Verses Topographical and Amatory.* London, Murray, 1940.
> *New Bats in Old Belfries: Poems.* London, Murray, 1945.
> *Slick But Not Streamlined: Poems and Short Pieces,* edited by W. H. Auden. New York, Doubleday, 1947.
> *Selected Poems,* edited by John Sparrow. London, Murray, 1948.
> *A Few Late Chrysanthemums.* London, Murray, 1954.

Poems in the Porch.   London, SPCK, 1954.

Collected Poems, edited by the Earl of Birkenhead.   London, Murray, 1958; Boston, Houghton Mifflin, 1959; revised edition, 1962, 1972.

Poems.   London, Hulton, 1959.

Summoned by Bells (verse autobiography).   London, Murray, and Boston, Houghton Mifflin, 1960.

A Ring of Bells, edited by Irene Slade.   London, Murray, 1962; Boston, Houghton Middlin, 1963.

High and Low.   London, Murray, 1966; Boston, Houghton Mifflin, 1967.

Six Betjeman Songs, music by Mervyn Horder.   London, Turret Books, 1967.

A Wembley Lad, and The Crem.   London, Poem-of-the-Month Club, 1971.

A Nip in the Air.   London, Murray, 1974.

Recording: *John Betjeman Reading His Own Poems,* Argo, 1961.

Play

Television Documentaries: *The Stained Glass at Fairford,* 1955; *Pity about the Abbey,* with Stewart Farver, 1965.

Other

Ghastly Good Taste; or, A Depressing Story of the Rise and Fall of English Architecture.   London, Chapman and Hall, 1933; revised edition, 1970.

Devon.   London, Architectural Press, 1936.

An Oxford University Chest: Comprising a Description of the Present State of the Town and University of Oxford, with an Itinerary Arranged Alphabetically.   London, J. Miles, 1938.

Antiquarian Prekudice.   London, Hogarth Press, 1939.

Vintage London.   London, Collins, 1942.

English Cities and Small Towns.   London, Collins, 1943.

John Piper.   London, Penguin, 1944.

Murray's Buckinghamshire Architectural Guide, with John Piper.   London, Murray, 1948.

Murray's Berkshire Architectural Guide, with John Piper.   London, Murray, 1949.

Murray's Shropshire Architectural Guide, with John Piper.   London, Murray, 1951.

First and Last Loves (essay on architecture).   London, Murray, 1952.

The English Town in the Last Hundred Years.   Cambridge, University Press, 1956.

Collins Guide to English Parish Churches, Including the Isle of Man.   London, Collins, 1958; as *An American's Guide to English Parish Churches,* New York, McDowell Obolensky, 1959; revised edition, as *Collins Pocket Guide to English Parish Churches,* Collins, 2 vols., 1968.

Ground Plan to Skyline (as Richard M. Farren).   London, Newman Neame, 1960.

English Churches, with Basil Clarke.   London, Studio Vista, 1964.

Cornwall.   London, Faber, 1965.

The City of London Churches.   London, Pitkin Pictorials, 1965.

London's Historic Railway Stations.   London, Murray, 1972.

A Pictorial History of English Architecture.   London, Murray, and New York, Macmillan, 1972.

West Country Churches.   London, Society of SS. Peter and Paul, 1973.

Editor, *Cornwall Illustrated: In a Series of Views of Castles, Seats of the Nobility, Mines, Picturesque Scenery, Towns, Public Buildings, Churches, Antiquities, Etc.* London Architectural Press, 1934.

Editor, *A Pickwick Portrait Gallery, from the Pens of Divers Admirers.* London, Chapman and Hall, and New York, Scribner, 1936.

Editor, with Geoffrey Taylor, *English, Scottish, and Welsh Landscape, 1700–ca. 1860* (verse anthology). London, Muller, 1944.

Editor, with Geoffrey Taylor, *English Love Poems.* London, Faber, 1957.

Editor, *Altar and Pew: Church of England Verses.* London, Hulton, 1959.

Editor, with Sir Charles Tennyson, *A Hundred Sonnets,* by Charles Tennyson Turner. London, Hart Davis, 1960.

Editor, with Winifred Hindley, *A Wealth of Poetry.* Oxford, Blackwell, 1963.

Editor, *Victorian and Edwardian London from Old Photographs.* London, Batsford, 1968; New York, Viking Press, 1969.

Editor, with J. S. Gray, *Victorian and Edwardian Brighton from Old Photographs.* London, Batsford, 1972.

Editor, with A. L. Rowse, *Victorian and Edwardian Cornwall from Old Photographs.* London, Batsford, 1974.

*   *   *

John Betjeman is of the same generation as W. H. Auden, a contemporary at Oxford, but his name has never been bracketed with those of other poets as that of a partner in some real or supposed school or movement. He has affinities with certain other poets of his time but it would be hard to name a single one of them who could speak of Isaac Watts, Dyer, or Mickle as "easily among my favourites," or even of Praed and Hood, still less of John Mason Neale. His taste for certain lesser poets of the 18th and 19th centuries, as well as for such great ones as Tennyson and Hardy, is partly, he has said, topographical. He admires in them particularly their ability "to catch the atmosphere of places and times," which can be seen as one of his own chief aims and successes.

No English poet of his generation seems to have been more deeply enchanted by the atmosphere of places known in childhood. Betjeman's impressionability in the North London suburb where his well-to-do and conventional parents brought him up, and on the North Cornish coast to which he was taken in summertime, was so intense that in his poetry he is able to recall these places with a precision of detail hardly to be matched among poets of English life in the early part of this century.

His lifelong love-affair with Edwardian England (in many ways the last period of Victorian England) has included old churches, old railways, old gaslit streets, old country-towns, old dons, and old invalids; it has also given him a distaste for much of what is supposed to represent progress. Narrow judgments may write him off as a backward-looking sentimentalist, too traditional in his interests and beliefs, and in his forms, rhythm, and diction, to be taken seriously as a poet in the 1960's; but poetry is not invalidated by retrospection, and one of the things he has done better than anybody else is to give form in poetry to the affectionate sadness inherent in all those old enough and feeling enough to have known happiness in an England now only vestigial, after two World Wars and political, economic, social, and technological revolutions.

One effect of Betjeman's poetry has been so to heighten general consciousness of what excites his own admiration that it has done much to cause a revolution (or should one say a counter-revolution?) in English taste. Manifestations, particularly in church architecture, of Victorian and Edwardian religious faith, fantasy, art, and craftsmanship, formerly taken for granted, condemned as ugly aberrations, or simply ignored, are now far better appreciated and understood. He is much more than "the Laureate of the suburbs and the Gothic Revival." Among the conspicuous qualities of his work are humanity, euphony, and a playful wit. No doubt among the main causes of his popularity, these qualities are not always discernible in contemporary poetry. What is more, they do not always appear appreciable by certain of the newer species of academic pedants and prigs, who parade their limitations and prejudices in literary journalism, but whose hack work, or hatchet work, is seldom heeded or even seen by the "common reader" of poetry. Whether from envy of the poet or a feeling of intellectual superiority towards his admirers, they seem to regard his popularity (enlarged and strengthened by his later career in television) as a serious weakness. As for his playfulness and wit, these things always disconcert earnest dogmatists, who wrongly suppose them incompatible with gravity.

The appeal of Betjemin's poetry is no doubt greater to older than to younger readers, if only because in it he shows himself moved by memories, scenes, associations and beliefs less familiar and less poignant to later generations than his own. There is nothing international about him except his humanity. He has not shown any concern with or even consciousness of world-wide revolutionary tendencies, intellectual fashions, the atomic danger, space travel, or Chairman Mao. Why should he?

Betjeman's poetic technique has shown no signs of being open to American influences, or to fashionable trends or doctrines. Lecturing in 1968, Roy Fuller, a poet only a few years younger than Betjeman, spoke of "the need to break away from the tyranny of the iambic line." One can suppose that this phrase would astonish Betjeman, who, never having felt any such tyranny, could feel no need to break away from it. His use of iambics suggests that he finds them not only traditional but idiomatically natural for the utterance of an English poet. In his long autobiographical poem, *Summoned by Bells,* he has used blank verse, with rhymed interludes, so effectively and skilfully that it is impossible to imagine how any other metre could have suited his purpose.

Summoning bells, like the sound of the sea, are often and variously to be heard in his poems. When he was a boy, church bells in England, as I myself remember, used to ring louder and longer than they do now, and almost everywhere. To some the sound of them was and is melancholy, vexing, and anachronistic, but Betjeman's poems show that they have never rung in vain for him. His interest in churches is not merely aesthetic; he is in fact a religious poet, a practising member of the Church of England, whose poetry shows him to be a believer in the reality of evil, in the need for self-questioning, in prayer, grace, hope, and charity – a charity which means giving not merely alms but one's imagination and, if need be, one's whole self.

Betjeman is at times a satirical poet, and can be found attacking cruelty, want of imagination, and (as in his "In Westminster Abbey") a combination of stupidity and hypocrisy with racial, social, and personal self-complacency. The people in his poems tend to be old and sad and helpless, or young and vigorous in a breezy way (like Joan Hunter Dunn), or falsely genteel and emptily materialistic, accepters of cheap shoddiness and up-to-date cant, given to reckless driving and low standards of taste and manners. There are an exceptional gentleness and good nature in his affection for "ordinary," marginal people and in his understanding of, for example, the deceased secretary of a golf club, lonely business girls in Camden Town, or a Platonist bank-clerk. That he is not self-important appears from certain poems about humiliating moments in his own life; and his ironic wit is inseparable from his humour, which can turn into the joviality of old-fashioned song, as in a piece like his "A Shropshire Lad." That is one of the "tales in verse" included by John Sparrow in Betjeman's *Selected Poems.* Another, "Sir John Piers," is both the most concentrated expression of Betjeman's recurrent response to the "ruins and rain" of Ireland and one of his most dramatic poems. In these "tales," and indeed throughout his work, there is a dramatic, novelistic element.

In *Summoned by Bells* the character drawing of his father and mother brings them freshly to life, and the self-portrait in the same poem is no less lifelike. Betjeman has always felt vividly, and conveyed vividly, the stimulus of the particular. He is as little given to general statements or vague rhetoric as to trendiness. His acute sensibility to the past has prevented his being recognized as an innovator: his themes are in fact as curiously his own as his orchestration of detail, his fluency, and his honesty. A few low-voltage passages in his work are perhaps the result of an over-simplification of thought. He is at his best in unravelling the complexities of a vanished or vanishing England to which he seems, unmistakably, devotedly, and sadly, to be saying good-bye.

– William Plomer

BIRNEY, Earle. Canadian. Born in Calgary, Alberta, 13 May 1904. Educated at the University of British Columbia, Vancouver, B.A. 1926; University of Toronto, M.A. 1927, Ph.D. 1936; University of California, Berkeley, 1927–30; Queen Mary College, London, 1934–35. Served in the Canadian Army, in the reserves 1940–41, and on active duty 1942–45: Major-in-Charge, Personnel Selection, Belgium and Holland, 1944–45. Married Esther Bull in 1940; has one child. Instructor in English, University of Utah, Salt Lake City, 1930–34; Lecturer, later Assistant Professor of English, University of Toronto, 1936–42; Supervisor, European Foreign Language Broadcasts, Radio Canada, Montreal, 1945–46; Professor of Medieval English Literature, 1946–63, and Professor and Chairman of the Department of Creative Writing, 1963–65, University of British Columbia; Writer-in-Residence, University of Toronto, 1965–67, and University of Waterloo, Ontario, 1967–68; Regents Professor in Creative Writing, University of California, Irvine, 1968. Since 1968, free-lance Writer and Lecturer. Literary Editor, *Canadian Forum,* Toronto, 1936–40; Editor, *Canadian Poetry Magazine,* Edmonton, 1946–48; Editor, *Prism International,* Vancouver, 1964–65; Advisory Editor, *New: American and Canadian Poetry,* Trumansburg, New York, 1966–70. Recipient: Governor-General's Award, 1943, 1946; Stephen Leacock Medal, 1950; Borestone Mountain Poetry Award, 1951; Canadian Government Overseas Fellowship, 1953, Service Medal, 1970; Lorne Pierce Medal, 1953; President's Medal, University of Western Ontario, 1954; Nuffield Fellowship, 1958; Canada Council Senior Arts Fellowship, 1962, Medal, 1968, Special Fellowship, 1968, and Travel Award, 1971. LL.D.: University of Alberta, Edmonton, 1965. Fellow, Royal Society of Canada, 1954. Address: c/o McClelland and Stewart, 25 Hollinger Road, Toronto, Ontario M43 3G2, Canada.

PUBLICATIONS

Verse

David. Toronto, Ryerson Press, 1942.
Now Is Time. Toronto, Ryerson Press, 1945.
Strait of Anian. Toronto, Ryerson Press, 1948.
Trial of a City. Toronto, Ryerson Press, 1952.
Ice Cod Bell or Stone. Toronto, McClelland and Stewart, 1962.

Near False Creek Mouth. Toronto, McClelland and Stewart, 1964.
Selected Poems 1940–1966. Toronto, McClelland and Stewart, 1966.
Memory No Servant. Trumansburg, New York, New Books, 1968.
Poems of Earle Birney. Toronto, McClelland and Stewart, 1969.
Pnomes, Jukollages and Other Stunzas. Toronto, Gronk Press, 1969.
Rag and Bone Shop. Toronto, McClelland and Stewart, 1971.
Five Modern Canadian Poets, with others, edited by Eli Mandel. Toronto, Holt
    Rinehart, 1970.
Four Parts Sand: Concrete Poems, with others. Ottawa, Oberon Press, 1972.
Bear on the Delhi Road. London, Chatto and Windus, 1973.
What's So Big about Green? Toronto, McClelland and Stewart, 1973.
Collected Poems. Toronto, McClelland and Stewart, 2 vols., 1974.

Recordings: *David,* 1964; *Earle Birney Reads His Poems,* Barnet, 1970; *Birney,*
Ontario Institute for Studies in Education, 1971.

Play

The Damnation of Vancouver: A Comedy in Seven Episodes (broadcast,
    1952). Included in *Trial of a City,* 1952; revised version (produced Seattle,
    1957), in *Selected Poems,* 1966.

Radio Play: *The Damnation of Vancouver,* 1952.

Novels

Turvey: A Military Picaresque. Toronto, McClelland and Stewart, 1949; Lon-
    don and New York, Abelard Schuman, 1959.
Down the Long Table. Toronto, McClelland and Stewart, 1955; London, Abe-
    lard Schuman, 1959.

Other

The Creative Writer. Toronto, CBC Publications, 1966.
The Cow Jumped over the Moon: The Writing and Reading of Poetry. Toronto,
    Holt Rinehart, 1972.

Editor, *Twentieth Century Canadian Poetry.* Toronto, Ryerson Press, 1953.
Editor, *Record of Service in the Second World War.* Vancouver, University of
    British Columbia, 1955.
Editor, with others, *New Voices.* Vancouver, Dent, 1956.
Editor, *Selected Poems of Malcolm Lowry.* San Francisco, City Lights Books,
    1962.
Editor, with Margerie Lowry, *Lunar Caustic,* by Malcolm Lowry. New York,
    Grossman, 1963; London, Cape, 1968.

Bibliography: in *West Coast Review* (Burnaby, British Columbia), October 1970.

Manuscript Collection: University of Toronto Library.

Critical Studies: by Paul West, in *Canadian Literature* (Vancouver), Summer 1962; "Poet Without a Muse" by Milton Wilson, in *Canadian Literature* (Vancouver), Autumn 1966; *Earle Birney* by Richard Robillard, Toronto, McClelland and Stewart, 1971; *Earle Birney*, edited by Bruce Nesbitt, Toronto, McGraw Hill Ryerson, 1974.

Earle Birney comments:

(1970) In recent years I have been successively influenced by Beat, Projectivist and Concretist poetry, and I hope to remain responsive – but eclectic – in relation to contemporary change and experimentation. I believe that poetry is both an oral entertainment and a visual notation. I write in free form tending towards the "concrete" and mixed media.

I write out of compulsion to talk to another man within me, an intermittent madman who finds unpredictable emblems of the Whole in the trivia of my experience, and haunts me with them until I have found a spell of words and rhythms to exorcise these ghosts and, for the moment, appease him. For me, the hauntings and the exorcizings are happenings so intense as to be beyond pleasure or pain – ends in themselves. But I go on to publish some of the result because I believe that my poems are the best proof I can print of my Humanness, signals out of the loneliness into which all of us are born, and in which we die, affirmations of kinship with all the other wayfarers.

(1974) Over the last 30 years I have tried to develop an ability to read my own poetry effectively, and I have sought audiences wherever there was a knowledge of the English language. In Canada I have many times toured the universities and colleges from Vancouver Island to Newfoundland, and have also read to students in high schools, and to audiences in art galleries and public libraries. With the help of Canada Council grants I have sounded my work and that of other living Canadians in most of the universities of Australia and New Zealand, Chile, Peru, Mexico, the University of the West Indies, and about 30 universities in the U.S.A. I have also read in Japan, Hong Kong, Singapore, Malaya, India, Tanzania, Kenya, Nigeria, Ghana, Sierra Leone, Gambia, and at the University of Bordeaux. In 1971 I gave readings in Dublin and in the chief cities of Great Britain, especially to workingclass groups and in public houses.

*   *   *

Earle Birney's first book of verse, *David,* was published in 1942, when he was already 38, and he came into prominence in the Canadian literary world as one of the generation of the Forties which greatly enriched the Canadian voice that began to speak in the Twenties and Thirties through the work of Pratt, Smith, Klein and Scott. Birney, however, was not a late starter; he had been writing poems since the Twenties, and one of the influences that permanently affected his writing was the political radicalism of the Thirties. His academic speciality, Old and Middle English poetry, has also deeply influenced his choice of form and language, while an acute consciousness of the physical environment, bred in a childhood lived in the Rockies, has given a peculiarly topographical nature to a great deal of his poetry.

One characteristic of Birney as a poet is his disinclination to be definite. Many of his books contain poems that have appeared in earlier volumes, but one sees, on reading them, that they have been changed, time and again, in the same way as Birney's intimate friend, Malcolm Lowry, constantly revised his novels. One can relate this tendency to Birney's predilection for parody. Both are forms of criticism – the first of his own work, and the second of poetic modes in general, and it is essentially as a critical poet that one must see Birney, for the stylistic criticism embodied in the form of his poems is matched by the social and moral criticism embodied in the content, which cannot be under-estimated, for Birney is a deliberate and sharply intellectual poet. His one dramatic poem, "The Damnation of Vancouver," is a strong criticism of contemporary Canadian life. His poems on the United States, and pieces like "Canada: Case History," are, from various viewpoints, criticisms of the society in which, unavoidably but not entirely willingly, he lives; his poems of South America and Asia – for Birney is a great poetic traveller – are criticisms of other ways of life.

One is aware, all the time, of a man observing and reflecting on his own and other worlds; yet what we see is not merely the observed but also the observer. For Birney projects, through a voice, a personality, and a very idiosyncratic one. The voice often takes on – and especially in his American poems – an emphatic jerkiness, almost spasmodic, which affects the visual shape of the poem as much as its sound when read. In other poems, and particularly those of recent years, the voice slows, broadening its flow, taking the narrative pace necessary for the content, as in his Mexican and Asian poems and in the best of his Vancouver poems, "November Walk near False Creek Mouth." Here the verse walks on lanky paces, though the steps still break, and the tone is at times almost whimsically laconic. One is aware all the time of an irritable vitality, at times joyful but more often impatient, and impelling that search for brotherhood, for the lost links between persons and peoples, that becomes – with the need for wandering which is its other aspect – the great theme of Birney's later poems (and perhaps not only his later, if we remember the end of "Mappemounde" in 1945 – "Adread in that mere we drift to map's end").

Experience always, but seen in its moral dimension, is the content of Birney's poems, and the most congenial are those, contained particularly in his collections *Ice Cod Bell or Stone* and *Near False Creek Mouth*, in which he combines his topographical flair with his sense of history and his power of conveying the immediacy of present experience.

– George Woodcock

BISHOP, Elizabeth. American. Born in Worcester, Massachusetts, 8 February 1911. Educated at Vassar College, Poughkeepsie, New York, A.B. 1934. Lived in Brazil for 16 years. Consultant in Poetry, Library of Congress, 1949–50. Poet-in-Residence, University of Washington, Seattle, 1966, 1973. Since 1970, Lecturer in English, Harvard University, Cambridge, Massachusetts. Recipient: Houghton Mifflin Fellowship, 1944; Guggenheim Fellowship, 1947; National Institute of Arts and Letters grant, 1951; Shelley Memorial Award, 1953; Pulitzer Prize, 1956; *Partisan Review* Fellowship, 1956; Amy Lowell Traveling Fellowship, 1957; Chapelbrook Fellowship, 1962; Academy of American Poets Fellowship, 1964; Rockefeller Fellowship, 1967; Ingram Merrill Foundation grant, 1969; National Book Award, 1970. LL.D.: Smith College, Northampton, Massachusetts, 1968; Rutgers University, New Brunswick, New Jersey, 1972; Brown University, Providence, Rhode Island, 1972. Chancellor, Academy of American Poets, 1966; Member, National Institute of Arts and Letters. Order of Rio Branco (Brazil), 1971. Address: c/o Farrar Straus and Giroux, 19 Union Square West, New York, New York 10003, U.S.A.

PUBLICATIONS

Verse

North and South.   Boston, Houghton Mifflin, 1946.
Poems: North and South – A Cold Spring.   Boston, Houghton Mifflin, 1955.
Poems.   London, Chatto and Windus, 1956.
Questions of Travel.   New York, Farrar Straus, 1965.
Selected Poems.   London, Chatto and Windus, 1967.
The Ballad of the Burglar of Babylon.   New York, Farrar Straus, 1968.
The Complete Poems.   New York, Farrar Straus, 1969; London, Chatto and
    Windus, 1970.

Other

Brazil, with the Editors of Life.   New York, Time, 1962.

Editor and Translator, *Anthology of Contemporary Brazilian Poetry,* volume
    1.   Middletown, Connecticut, Wesleyan University Press, 1972.

Translator, *The Diary of Helena Morley.*   New York, Farrar Straus, 1957;
    London, Gollancz, 1958.

Critical Study: *Poetry and the Age* by Randall Jarrell, New York, Knopf, 1953.

Elizabeth Bishop comments:

My "personal statements" are, I hope, in my poems – naturally I hope there is
still much more to be said, and better said than I have been able to manage so far.

*   *   *

"The Map," the poem with which Elizabeth Bishop's first book opens, is characteristic of her work in several respects. Among these are the precision of the
concrete detail, the deft handling of language and cadence, the echoing parallel-
isms, the seemingly casual rhymes, the quiet humor and suggestive fantasy. Enlarging the associations that we have with maps, the poem subtly reminds us of the
ways in which we apprehend the world not reduced to an abstraction. Such pieces
as "The Imaginary Iceberg" and "Little Exercise" differ from each other as they
do from "The Map" in structure and texture, the one announcing that "Icebergs
behoove the soul / (Both being self-made from elements not visible)," the other
ostensibly about a storm, which, for all its savagery, barely disturbs the man
"sleeping in the bottom of a row-boat / tied to a mangrove root or the pile of a
bridge." Both can be read as relating to courage. "The Fish" is meaningful
because of its evocative matter-of-factness, which culminates in an apotheosis of
the virtue by which we must live.
    If Miss Bishop is as keen a moralist as her late friend, Marianne Moore, she is
even more playful than that witty woman. Coleridge would have called her fanciful,
as when she plots the gyrations of a dainty mechanical toy or considers sleeping on

122

the ceiling. She is also imaginative in a large way. Her imaginings may have been nourished in part by the exoticism of the scene that she not seldom offers us. But what her books add up to is that they put us in the presence of a woman with a strong grasp on reality, and that for her this combines poverty and abundance, food for fantasy, for entertainment, and for grieving sympathy, the rough and the smooth, the dark and the bright, the sweet, the bitter, the salty, of our common experience, which, by examining it closely, she makes uncommon.

– Babette Deutsch

BISSETT, Bill. Canadian. Born in Halifax, Nova Scotia, 23 November 1939. Since 1962, Editor and Printer, Blewointmentpress, Vancouver. Artist: One-Man Show, Vancouver Art Gallery, 1972. Recipient: Canada Council grant, 1967, 1968, 1972, bursary and travel grant, 1971. Address: Box 8870, Station Bentall, Vancouver 5, British Columbia, Canada.

PUBLICATIONS

Verse

Th jinx ship nd othr trips: pomes-drawings-collage. Vancouver, Very Stone House, 1966.
we sleep inside each other all (with drawings). Toronto, Ganglia Press, 1966.
Fires in th Tempul (with drawings). Vancouver, Very Stone House, 1967.
where is miss florence riddle. Toronto, Luv Press, 1967.
what poetiks. Vancouver, Blewointmentpress, 1967.
(th) Gossamer Bed Pan. Vancouver, Blewointmentpress, 1967.
Lebanon Voices. Toronto, Weed/Flower Press, 1967.
Of th Land/Divine Service Poems. Toronto, Weed/Flower Press, 1968.
Awake in the Red Desert! Vancouver, Talonbooks, 1968.
Killer Whale. Vancouver, See Hear Productions, 1969.
Sunday Work? Vancouver, Blewointmentpress–Intermedia Press, 1969.
Liberating Skies. Vancouver, Blewointmentpress, 1969.
The Lost Angel Mining Co. Vancouver, Blewointmentpress, 1969.
S th Story I to. Vancouver, Blewointmentpress, 1970.
Th Outlaw. Vancouver, Blewointmentpress, 1970.
blew trewz. Vancouver, Blewointmentpress, 1970.
Nobody Owns th Earth. Toronto, House of Anansi, 1971.
air 6. Vancouver, Air, 1971.
Tuff Shit Love Pomes. Windsor, Ontario, Bandit/Black Moss Press, 1971.
dragon fly. Toronto, Weed/Flower Press, 1971.
Rush what fukin thery. Vancouver, Blewointmentpress, 1971.
Four Parts Sand: Concrete Poems, with others. Ottawa, Oberon Press, 1972.
th Ice bag. Vancouver, Blewointmentpress, 1972.
pomes for yoshi. Vancouver, Blewointmentpress, 1972.
drifting into war. Vancouver, Talonbooks, 1972.
air 10–11–12. Vancouver, Air, 1972.

Pass th Food, Release th Spirit Book.   Vancouver, Talonbooks, 1973.
th first sufi line.   Vancouver, Blewointmentpress, 1973.
Vancouver Mainland Ice & Cold Storage.   London, Writers Forum, 1973.
Living with th vishyun.   Vancouver, New Star Books, 1974.
what.   Vancouver, Blewointmentpress, 1974.
drawings.   Vancouver, Blewointmentpress, 1974.
Medicine my mouths on fire.   Ottawa, Oberon Press, 1974.
space travl.   Vancouver, Air, 1974.
yu can eat it at th opening.   Vancouver, Blewointmentpress, 1974.

Plays

Television Documentaries: *In search of innocence,* 1963; *Strange grey day this,* 1964; *Poets of the 60's,* 1967.

Other

Illustrator, *The Circus in the Boy's Eye,* by Jim Brown.   Vancouver, Very Stone House, 1966.

Critical Study: "The Typography of bill bissett" by bpNichol, in *we sleep inside each other all,* 1966.

Bill Bissett comments:

poet and painter: abt equal time nd involvment, been merging th fields for sum time now, since abt '62 nd previous with concrete poetry, which i early got into with lance farrell, allowing th words to act visually on th page, was aware of such effects before i cud accept th use of say grammatical thot in writing as such appeard too limiting to th singularly amazing development of th person.
spelling – mainly phonetic
syntax – mainly expressive or musical rather than grammatic
visual form – apprehension of th spirit shape of th pome rather than stanzaic nd rectangular
major theme – search for harmony within th communal self thru sharing (dig Robin Hood), end to war thereby – good luck
characteristic stylistic device – elipse
favorite poet – mick jagger
general source – there is only one, nd th variation that spawnd th fingrs of night woven grace. issue (romanticism or elevation, i don't feel th I, i.e. ME writes but that i transcribe indications of flow mused spheres sound), from a hoop

                                    *   *   *

I like Bill Bissett's poetry when it's most woolly. He admits he can't spell or write right: "the way is clear, the free hard path, no correct spelling, no grammar rules":

              dew yu linger on the far side of the dream

Puns seem to replace meter:

> hes closin all the doors then iul open them yer all stond

Drugs seem to replace vision. The language is dialect, what's known around here as
the Southwestern Ontario Rock 'n Roll Accent. Stupidity, almost, is faked, as in
Chaucer, adding a little, as in Chaucer, to the difficulty of the dialect of speeding
speech:

> did yu blow cock eat cunt make a good
> business deal and still relate were yu are
> yu happy were yu good just once did yu today
> have an existential moment in no time were yu
> normal today did yu screw society but found
> sum innocent outlets like no one knew or evry
> one knew did yu buy sum orange pop sticks green
> ones did yu have a treat and were clean were yu
> a dirty outlet for a while managin at th same
> time to find pleasure in nature and read a thot
> conditionin book by a provocative author did. . . .

Bissett asks a lot of questions. His monologues are unpunctuated but best when
interrogatory. It's exuberant. It's genuinely written by someone who is outside
himself, making rapid connections. Perhaps calling popsicles pop sticks is a trifle
cutesy. Bissett draws, writes narrative, political and concrete poetry and chants.
But there is sadness, still interrogatory:

> why just when my body nd souls startin to fit
> sum they rip it all up mother i was happy
> in sum of those open spaces why hard times
> again did yu catch me foolin with th images
> now how can i carry any once cross this
>
> swamp ium sinkin in th deep mud myself

Hopkins? There is a religious aspect, drugs seem a mere polite excuse for vision.
Analogously, Warhol's starting to look like Burroughs, and gets sadder, and sadder,
and lines form. It's not poetry, those lines. Bissett wears a mask in his poetry; the
art in a man's face, the lines, are not fictive, which is why I wish I knew Bissett
personally. Still, Burroughs and Warhol are distant from Bissett. Bissett's *Nobody
Owns th Earth* values the earth, love and country. Did I say cliché? Not really, just
downhome talk. Smart people, like Chaucer, know the difference between cliché
and proverb; Canadians are a young people like Chaucer's English were. Nevertheless, I prefer New Yorkers, and wonder if it is precisely the provinciality of
Canada that pushes Bissett beyond sadness into heavy hopelessness:

> there is
> nothing
> to hope
>
> th candul
> yu lit it
> is going
>
> there is
> nothing
> to hope

shut out
the wind
flame

there is
nothing
to hope

a sea of
skulls in
th harbor

These lines are from a chant in which Bissett turns from a benign "mother" to give
some orders to "flame." Bissett's assertive mood is heavy. When he stops asking
and hoping, he starts hinting at an apocalypse. Of course, that hinting is itself a
hoping, the hope for an end.

– Michael André

BLACK, D(avid) M(acleod).   Scottish.   Born in Wynberg, South Africa, 8 November 1941. Educated at Edinburgh University, M.A. in philosophy 1966; University
of Lancaster, M.A. in religious studies. Recipient: Scottish Arts Council prize,
1968, and publication award, 1969; Arts Council of Great Britain bursary, 1968.
Lives in London.

PUBLICATIONS

Verse

Rocklestrakes.   London, Outposts Publications, 1960.
From the Mountains.   London, Outposts Publications, 1963.
Theory of Diet.   London, Turret Books, 1966.
With Decorum.   Lowestoft, Suffolk, Scorpion Press, 1967.
A Dozen Short Poems.   London, Turret Books, 1968.
Penguin Modern Poets 11, with Peter Redgrove and D. M. Thomas.   London,
    Penguin, 1968.
The Educators: Poems.   London, Barrie and Rockliff–Cresset Press, 1969.
The Old Hag.   Preston, Lancashire, Akros, 1972.
The Happy Crow.   Edinburgh, Lines Review Editions, 1974.

Critical Study: "The World of D. M. Black" by John Herdman, in *Scottish
International 13* (Edinburgh), February 1971.

D. M. Black comments:

My verse is currently undergoing a lot of change, and I can't say too much that'll
be at all useful. What I've published so far has been mainly a kind of surrealist-ish

narrative poetry; I'm now moving from that to a simpler and more daylit subject-matter which (hopefully) will be seen to be a move from concern primarily with effects to concern primarily with some such question as "how to live in the world as it is." But I think that at bottom that was always the concern. Let the change be symbolized by the fact that I am descending from the heights of my initials, and shall publish in future under the name of David Black.

*   *   *

The 1960's saw a revived interest in surrealism, and no doubt D. M. Black's poetry reflects this, but it is a surrealism of a modified type, laced by side-shrieks from George MacBeth's poetry of cruelty, tinged by science-fiction and mythmaking, and peppered by the place-names of a hallucinatory Edinburgh. The heady mixture was poured into a flat, deadpan, jerkily enjambed free verse which at moments of stress could take off into lyrical humours and mild, almost pop horror. Long exotic narratives like *Theory of Diet,* "Without Equipment," and "The Rite of Spring," which refuse to come into clear focus, present nightmare explorations of cannibal islands, dwarfs speaking dwarf language, a prince whose mother is devoured by ants. Among the shorter poems, violent and extraordinary fantasies are more successfully related to a ruling idea: in "My Species" it is artificial insemination, in "The Educators" it is the generation gap, in "The Fury Was on Me" it is the transforming power of anger, in "The Eighth Day" it is the revenge of fruitfulness on asceticism. In some of the most attractive poems, fantasy shades off towards reality: "Leith Docks" and "The Red Judge" with their evocation of the dramatic northernness and Calvinist tensions of Edinburgh, *With Decorum* celebrating the mysterious sense of renewal in death like a 28-line *Finnegans Wake,* "Clarity" turning a track-suited lout into a dancer. A poet still young and in process of change, but clearly talented and spirited:

> Open the
> windows, Jock! My
> beauties, my
> noble horses – yoked in
> pairs, white horses, drawing my great
> hearse, galloping and
> frolicking over the cropped turf.

– Edwin Morgan

BLACKBURN, Thomas (Eliel Fenwick). British. Born in Hensingham, Cumberland, 10 February 1916. Educated at Durham University, Honours degree in English. Principal Lecturer in English, College of St. Mark and St. John, Chelsea, London. Recipient: Eric Gregory Fellowship, 1964–66. Fellow, Royal Society of Literature. Address: 4 Luttrell Avenue, London S.W.15, England.

PUBLICATIONS

Verse

The Outer Darkness.   Aldington, Kent, Hand and Flower Press, 1951.
The Holy Stone.   Aldington, Kent, Hand and Flower Press, 1954.
In the Fire.   London, Putnam, 1956.
The Next Word.   London, Putnam, 1958.
A Smell of Burning.   London, Putnam, 1961; New York, Morrow, 1962.
A Breathing Space: Poems.   London, Putnam, and Chester Springs, Pennsylvania, Dufour, 1964.
The Fourth Man: Poems.   London, MacGibbon and Kee, 1971.
The Feast of the Wolf.   London, MacGibbon and Kee, 1971.
Corgi Modern Poets in Focus 2, edited by Jeremy Robson.   London, Corgi, 1971.

Recording: *Poems,* with Kingsley Amis, Jupiter, 1962.

Play

The Judas Tree: A Musical Drama of Judas Iscariot, music by Peter Dickinson (produced London, 1965).   London, Novello, 1965.

Other

The Price of an Eye (criticism).   London, Longman, 1961; Westport, Connecticut, Greenwood Press, 1974.
Robert Browning: A Study of His Poetry.   London, Eyre and Spottiswoode, 1967.
A Clip of Steel: A Picaresque Autobiography.   London, MacGibbon and Kee, 1969.

Editor, with Philip A. Wayne, *The Middle School Book of Verse.*   London, Harrap, 1955.
Editor, with C. Day Lewis and Kathleen Nott, *New Poems 1957.*   London, Joseph, 1957.
Editor, *45–60: An Anthology of English Poetry, 1945–60.*   London, Putnam, 1960.
Editor, *Presenting Poetry: A Handbook for English Teachers.*   London, Methuen, 1966.
Editor, *Gift of Tongues: A Selection from the Work of Fourteen 20th Century Poets.*   London, Nelson, 1967.

Critical Study: *Rule and Energy* by John Press, London, Oxford University Press, 1962.

*   *   *

Considered retrospectively, Thomas Blackburn's poetry represents what Roy Fuller once well described as a "relentless" probing "of his own psyche." The influence of Yeats was over-apparent in his first four books, but this has recently vanished; violence and energy, expressed until recently in strongly traditional forms, have been a consistent element. His intention has always been – as he put it in a note on *A Breathing Space* – to evoke in the reader "a quality of thought or feeling which has value," and so to write, "to some extent," "his biography." By "value" Blackburn means "emotional and archetypal validity," and by "biography" he means not a conventional series of events but, rather, the Jungian process of spiritual integration called "individuation." Not in any sense an orthodoxly religious man, Blackburn even now may nevertheless only be approached as an intensely religious poet, whose aim is to make a new, existential sense out of outworn mythical and Christian symbols. "The Veil," an early poem from *The Holy Stone*, announces this programme, to which – despite many changes of emphasis and procedure – he has remained consistent. Here "The Word" is seen as defeated, but still valid and powerful:

> So the two hemispheres were thrust apart
> By a great darkness of the Temple Veil,
> Her mystic numerals forsook the heart
> And the exhausted centuries grew pale.
> But, "Through the bondage of the temple veil"
> Still rips the lightning of God's finger-nail;
> Oh, seven dead candles; the High Priest in tears!

In later and much more integrated poems Blackburn has continued to employ religious imagery – as in "Hospital for Defectives," where, in describing four defectives working silently in a turnip field, he says:

> And yet between the four of them
> No word is ever said.
> Because the yeast was not put in
> Which makes the human bread.

And he asks the "Lord of the Images" what it is that he can say of the spectacle of the "unleavened man" who did not cry out under "the warder's blows."

But a newer and an altogether sharper manner has distinguished Blackburn's most recent poetry, from which the rhetorical influence of Yeats has been purged; it is more colloquial, conversational, and its rhythms are freer. This was first seen in the memorable "A Small Keen Wind," which described the miseries of a marriage in the process of breaking up with remarkable directness – and entirely without the rhetoric that lay rather heavily over the earlier poems. In his most considerable recent poem, "Teaching Wordsworth," Blackburn has maintained his directness and his eschewal of metrical regularity, but has retained his earlier mysticism:

> As he drew and dwindled into a worse
> End of life (as regards verse).
> My conclusion is: must words do violence
> To what he said. Listen to silence.

– Martin Seymour-Smith

BLASER, Robin. American. Born in Denver, Colorado, 18 May 1925. Educated at the University of California, Berkeley, B.A., M.A., M.L.S. Librarian, Harvard University Library, Cambridge, Massachusetts, 1955–59, California Historical Society, 1960, and San Francisco State College Library, 1961–65. Co-Founder, *Measure,* Boston, 1957. Currently, University Lecturer in Poetry, Simon Fraser University, Burnaby, British Columbia. Recipient: Poetry Society Award, New York, 1965; National Endowment for the Arts grant, 1968. Lives in Vancouver, British Columbia, Canada.

PUBLICATIONS

Verse

    The Moth Poem. San Francisco, Open Space, 1964.
    Les Chimères (versions of Gérard de Nerval). San Francisco, Open Space, 1965.
    Cups. San Francisco, Four Seasons Foundation, 1968.

Robin Blaser comments:

I have had two great companions in poetry, Jack Spicer and Robert Duncan. And there is a real debt to Charles Olson.

I have insisted in my work upon a poetry which in its imagery is cosmological. I have tried to include, take in, and bring over in the content of that work images of those worlds to which one is given the possibility of entrance.

I am interested in a particular kind of narrative – what Jack Spicer and I agreed to call in our own work the serial poem – this is a narrative which refuses to adopt an imposed story line, and completes itself only in the sequence of poems, if, in fact, a reader insists upon a definition of completion which is separate from the poems themselves. The poem tends to act as a sequence of energies which run out when so much of a tale is told. I like to describe this in Ovidian terms, as a *carmen perpetuum*, a continuous song, in which the fragmented subject matter is only apparently disconnected. I believe a poet must reveal a mythology which is as elemental as air, earth, fire, and water; and that the authors who count take responsibility for a map of those worlds that is addressed to companions of the earth, the world, and the spirit.

*   *   *

Literature misses a lot of things. Of course, people miss a lot of literature. They missed Robin Blaser. He's an unknown classic – some of the people in this book are classic unknowns, so that's a small and utter difference.

But literature does miss a lot of things. Robin Blaser, besides an audience, missed the future. I'm talking about his style, about:

above

This poem is doubtless something archaic, something free versey, and something symbolic, not something "avant-garde." I have not yet looked at the poem you have looked at, above. This poem was selected at random by pointing my finger at a passage in a random Blaser book.

Dear Mr. Blaser, Why don't you answer your mail? Here you see an example of the truth of the aleatory mode. Are you at all familiar with this? I am a great fan of yours. I worry, though, that you imagine you write perfectly – but perfect writing is not marred by insensitive attitudes, and is more adventurous than yours.

Still, Blaser has written some superb poems. Here is Poem 8 from *Cups*:

There is no salutation. The
harvesters with gunny sacks
bend picking up jade stones

(Sure that Amor would appear
in sleep. Director. Guide.)

Secret borrowings fit into their hands.

Cold on the tongue
White flecks on the water.

These jade pebbles are true green
when wet.

On the seventh night, the branches parted.
                    The other replied,
How photographic. Amor doesn't appear
on demand. He's more like a snake skin.
If he fits, he lets you in
or sheds your body against the rocks.

                    I slept in a fort.
My bed pushed up against the log
enclosure. At 3:00 his ankles pressed
against each side of my head.
When I woke crying for help
he rose near the kitchen door
dressed as a hunter.

                    The other replied,
Amor born like a cup trembles
at the lip. Superstitions fit
into your hands.

Thou has returned to thy house.

                    The other replied,

Torn loose from the eaves,
the blood trembles at the lips.

Nine fetters on thy feet
Nine crossings of the street

Nine suppers where they meet
Nine words of loss repeat
this and that

Nine hunters cross the field
Nine lovers yield
their right of way

Two came fighting out of the dark.

– Michael André

———————————

BLIGHT, John.   Australian.   Born in Unley, South Australia, 30 July 1913. Educated to secondary school level; qualified in accountancy. Married to Madeline
D'Arcy Irvine; has two daughters. Worked as a clerk, orchardist and swagman, and
later as a public servant. Retired as secretary to a sawmilling company. Member,
The Timber Inquiry Commission, 1949–50. Recipient: Meyer Award, 1965. Address:
34 Greenway Street, The Grange, Brisbane, Queensland, Australia.

PUBLICATIONS

Verse

The Old Pianist.   Sydney, Dymock's Book Arcade, 1945.
The Two Suns Met: Poems.   Sydney, Edwards and Shaw, 1954.
A Beachcomber's Diary: Ninety Sea Sonnets.   Sydney, Angus and Robertson,
    1964.
My Beachcombing Days: Ninety Sea Sonnets.   Sydney, Angus and Robertson,
    1968.

Critical Study: *Preoccupations in Australian Poetry* by Judith Wright, Melbourne and
London, Oxford University Press, 1965.

John Blight comments:

I have written published poetry for over thirty years. In that time I have written
as I would speak, with the difference that when I write a poem my vision is
naturally heightened by aftersight, and my speech, therefore, becomes more
intense. The poem pronounces with certitude upon an aspect of life. The success of
the poem is relative to the acuteness of the vision.

Goethe comes closest for me in his definition of poetry – a criticism of life. If
you are looking for theme in my poetry, take heed of Goethe's definition. I like to
examine closely this quality of matter – life. It is simple then to become intense and
excited about it – to become poetical.

Over the last decade I have deliberately chosen the sonnet as the vehicle for my
poetry. I have adapted it to suit my purpose, not deeming it relevant to conform to
Elizabethan or Wordsworthian patterns. I have striven to use it allegorically rather
than lyrically.

It has benefited my work by avoidance of the abstract, in concentrating illumination of the subject, holding it before one for a brief space of time like life itself.

*   *   *

John Blight's contribution to Australian poetry is no doubt minor compared with, say, the scope of A. D. Hope or Robert D. FitzGerald; but it is nevertheless solid, distinctive and, very likely, durable. When he began writing in the 1940's his themes and forms were variable. He wrote quite memorably, in a modern style, on such elements of outback mythology as "Camp Fever" (the quarrels that develop between men camped in isolation) and "The Hurricane Lantern" that had lit so many lonely tents. He composed a poem of some length on one of the outback explorers, in the mode that had been established by Kenneth Slessor, FitzGerald and Francis Webb; and, turning to the sea, wrote in smooth flowing witty style a fantasy about becalmed sailors who, if they jumped overboard to drown themselves, bumped their heads on their own reflections.

But after these preliminary explorations he was very soon to settle into the style, form and theme that he has made distinctively his own: and for the best part of thirty years he has devoted himself to the single occupation of writing sonnets about the sea. Most of *The Two Suns Met*, the whole of *A Beachcomber's Diary* and the whole of *My Beachcombing Days* consist of these sea-sonnets; and these, though extensive enough, are only a selection from the hundreds more he has written on his one theme.

But this description of his poetry is misleading. Though one uses the term "sonnet" for convenience and because basically that is what his poems are, he has his own interpretation of the form and his own peculiar rugged use of language, writing so freely that each sonnet is different from the next. They are closer in style to the sonnets of Hopkins than to the Shakespearean mode but show no direct influence and seem just his own natural utterance. And if, again, one says that he writes on a single theme, it must be remembered that the sea, as are his poems, is teeming with variety. It is the source of life, the cradle of evolution, the home of the strange, the macabre, the ferocious and the beautiful; and it is John Blight's purpose to record and ponder these weird forms of life, probing into them for such intimations of immortality as they may reveal.

Any one of his poems is typical of the rest. I choose at random, to illustrate the queer bluntness of his style, the queer creatures he writes about, and the restless probing of his mind, a couple of lines from a sonnet called "The Cunjevoi" – the cunjevoi, also known as the "sea-squirt," is a half-vegetable, half-animal creature that, after a brief period of free swimming as a fish or animal, attaches itself head-first to a rock in the surf and becomes (possibly) a vegetable:

> What does his thinking then? How has this squirt out-thought
> The stresses of the ocean, whose thinking's set at nought?

Though John Blight is represented in most standard Australian anthologies, the best place to read his poetry is in his own books, where his style and rare, odd, thoughtful personality get a chance to establish themselves.

– Douglas Stewart

BLUNDEN, Edmund (Charles). British. Born in London, 1 November 1896. Educated at Cleave's Grammar School, Yalding, Kent; Christ's Hospital; Queen's College, Oxford, M.A. Served with The Southdowns, Royal Sussex Regiment, 1916–19: Military Cross. Married Claire Margaret Poynting in 1945; has four daughters. Professor of English Literature, University of Tokyo, 1924–27; Fellow and Tutor in English Literature, Merton College, Oxford, 1931–43. Staff Member, Oxford Senior Training Corps, 1940–44; Member of the UK Liaison Mission, Tokyo, 1948–50. Professor of English Literature, University of Hong Kong, 1953–64, and since 1964, Professor Emeritus. Clark Lecturer, Cambridge University, 1932; Professor of Poetry, Oxford University, 1966–68. Recipient: Hawthornden Prize, 1922; Benson Medal, 1932, and Companion of Literature, Royal Society of Literature; Queen's Gold Medal for Poetry, 1956; Midsummer Prize, Corporation of London, 1970. Litt.D.: Leeds and Leicester universities. C.B.E. (Companion, Order of the British Empire), 1951; Order of the Rising Sun, 3rd Class (Japan), 1963. Address: Hall Mill, Long Melford, Suffolk, England. *Died 20 January 1974.*

PUBLICATIONS

Verse

Poems, 1913 and 1914. Horsham, Sussex, privately printed, 1914.
Poems, Translated from the French, July 1913–January 1914. Horsham, Sussex, privately printed, 1914.
The Barn, with Certain Other Poems. Uckfield, Sussex, privately printed, 1916.
Three Poems. Uckfield, Sussex, privately printed, 1916.
The Harbingers: Poems. Uckfield, Sussex, privately printed, 1916.
Pastorals: A Book of Verses. London, Erskine Macdonald, 1916.
The Waggoner and Other Poems. London, Sidgwick and Jackson, 1920.
The Shepherd and Other Poems of Peace and War. London, Cobden Sanderson, and New York, Knopf, 1922.
Old Homes: A Poem. Clare, Suffolk, W. T. Ward, 1922.
Dead Letters: Poems. Privately printed, 1922.
To Nature: New Poems. London, Beaumont Press, 1923.
Masks of Time: A New Collection of Poems, Principally Meditative. London, Beaumont Press, 1925.
English Poems. London, Cobden Sanderson, 1925; New York, Knopf, 1926.
(Poems). London, Benn, 1925.
Retreat. London, Cobden Sanderson, and New York, Doubleday, 1928.
Winter Nights: A Reminiscence. London, Faber, 1928.
Near and Far: New Poems. London, Cobden Sanderson, 1929; New York, Harper, 1930.
The Poems of Edmund Blunden. London, Cobden Sanderson, 1930.
A Summer's Fancy. London, Beaumont Press, 1930.
The Weathercock/La Girouette, 1917. London, Ulysses Bookshop, 1931.
Constantia and Francis: An Autumn Evening. Edinburgh, privately printed, 1931.
To Themis: Poems on Famous Trials, with Other Pieces. London, Beaumont Press, 1931.
In Summer: The Rotunda of the Bishop of Derry. London, privately printed, 1931.
Japanese Garland. London, Beaumont Press, 1932.

Halfway House: 'A Miscellany of New Poems. London, Cobden Sanderson, 1932.

Choice or Chance: New Poems. London, Cobden Sanderson, 1934.

Verses: To H.R.H. The Duke of Windsor. Oxford, Alden Press, 1936.

An Elegy and Other Poems. London, Cobden Sanderson, 1937.

On Several Occasions, by a Fellow of Merton College. London, Corvinus Press, 1938.

Poems, 1930–1940. London, Macmillan, 1940.

Shells by a Stream: New Poems. London, Macmillan, 1944.

After the Bombing and Other Poems. London, Macmillan, 1949.

Eastward: A Selection of Verses Original and Translated. Tokyo, Sone Sakai Nishizaki and Oshima, 1950.

Edmund Blunden: A Selection of His Poetry and Prose, edited by Kenneth Hopkins. London, Hart Davis, 1950.

Records of Friendship: Occasional and Epistolary Poems Written During Visits to Kyushu, edited by T. Nakayama. Fukuoka, Kyushu University, 1950.

Verses on Behalf of the University of Hong Kong in Honour of the Vice-Chancellor Dr. L. T. Ride's Marriage with Miss Violet May Witchell on 12 November 1954. Hong Kong, University of Hong Kong, 1954.

Poems of Many Years. London, Collins, 1957.

A Hong Kong House. London, Poetry Book Society, 1959.

A Hong Kong House: Poems 1951–1961. London, Collins, 1962.

Guest of Thomas Hardy. Beaminster, Dorset, J. Stevens Cox, 1964.

Eleven Poems. Cambridge, Golden Head Press, 1965.

A Selection of the Shorter Poems. Long Melford, Suffolk, Restoration Fund Committee, 1966.

Poems on Japan, Hitherto Uncollected and Mostly Unprinted, edited by T. Saito. Tokyo, 1967.

The Midnight Skaters: Poems for Young Readers, edited by C. Day Lewis. London, Bodley Head, 1968.

A Selection from the Poems of Edmund Blunden, edited by Jim White. Long Melford, Suffolk, Restoration Fund Committee, 1969.

Play

The Dede of Pittie: Dramatic Scenes Reflecting the History of Christ's Hospital and Offered in Celebration of the Quatercentenary (produced London, 1953). Privately printed, 1953.

Other

The Appreciation of Literary Prose: Being One of the Special Courses of the Art of Life. London, 1921.

The Bonaventura: A Random Journal of an Atlantic Holiday. London, Cobden Sanderson, 1922.

Christ's Hospital: A Restrospect. London, Christophers, 1923.

More Footnotes to Literary History: Essays on Keats and Clare. Tokyo, Kenkyusha, 1926.

On the Poems of Henry Vaughan: Characteristics and Imitations, with His Principal Latin Poems Carefully Translated into English Verse. London, Cobden Sanderson, 1927.

Undertones of War. London, Cobden Sanderson, 1928; revised edition, 1930.

135

Leigh Hunt's "Examiner" Examined. . . .   London, Cobden Sanderson, 1928.
Nature in Literature.   London, Hogarth Press, 1929.
Leigh Hunt: A Biography.   London, Cobden Sanderson, 1930.
De Bello Germanico: A Fragment of Trench History.   Hawstead, Suffolk, 1930.
Votive Tablets: Studies Chiefly Appreciative of English Authors and Books.   London, Cobden Sanderson, 1931.
Fall In, Ghosts: An Essay on a Battalion Reunion.   London, White Owl Press, 1932.
The Face of England: In a Series of Occasional Sketches.   London, Longman, 1932.
We'll Shift Our Ground; or, Two on a Tour, with Sylvia Norman.   London, Cobden Sanderson, 1933.
Charles Lamb and His Contemporaries.   Cambridge, University Press, 1933.
The Mind's Eye: Essays.   London, Cape, 1934.
Edward Gibbon and His Age.   Bristol, privately printed, 1935; Folcroft, Pennsylvania, Folcroft Editions, 1974.
Keats's Publisher: A Memoir of John Taylor, 1781-1864.   London, Cape, 1936; Clifton, New Jersey, A. M. Kelley, 1974.
English Villages.   London, Collins, 1941.
Thomas Hardy.   London, Macmillan, 1941.
Cricket Country.   London, Collins, 1944.
Shelley: A Life Story.   London, Collins, 1946.
Sons of Light: A Series of Lectures on English Writers.   Tokyo, Tuttle, 1949.
Poetry and Science and Other Lectures.   Osaka, Osaka Kyoiku-Tosho Kabushiki-Kaisha, 1949.
Favourite Studies in English Literature.   Tokyo, Hokuseido Press, 1950.
Influential Books.   Tokyo, Hokuseido Press, 1950.
Reprinted Papers: Partly Concerning Some English Romantic Poets.   Tokyo, Kenkyusha, 1950.
Chaucer to "B.V.": With an Additional Paper on Herman Melville.   Tokyo, Kenkyusha, 1950.
Hamlet and Other Studies.   Tokyo, Yuhodo, 1950.
A Wanderer in Japan: Sketches and Reflections in Prose and Verse (bilingual edition).   Tokyo, Asahi Shimbun Sha, 1950.
John Keats.   London, Longman, 1950, revised edition, 1954, 1966.
Essayists in the Romantic Period, edited by I. Nishizaki.   Tokyo, 1952.
Charles Lamb.   London, Longman, 1954.
Addresses on General Subjects Connected with English Literature.   Tokyo, Kenkyusha, 1955.
Shakespeare and Hardy: Short Studies of Characteristic English Authors.   Tokyo, Kenkyusha, 1956.
War Poets, 1914-1918.   London, Longman, 1958.
Three Young Poets: Critical Sketches of Byron, Shelley, and Keats.   Tokyo, Kenkyusha, 1959.
A Wessex Worthy: Thomas Russell.   Beaminster, Dorset, Toucan Press, 1960.
English Scientists as Men of Letters.   Hong Kong, University of Hong Kong, 1961.
A Corscambe Inhabitant.   Beaminster, Dorset, Toucan Press, 1963.
William Crowe, 1745-1829.   Beaminster, Dorset, Toucan Press, 1963.
A Brief Guide to the Great Church of the Holy Trinity, Long Melford.   Ipswich, Anglian Magazine, 1965.
John Clare: Beginner's Luck.   Wateringbury, Kent, Bridge Books, 1972.

Editor, *John Clare: Poems Chiefly from Manuscript.*   London, Cobden Sanderson, 1920.

Editor, *A Song to David with Other Poems,* by Christopher Smart. London, Cobden Sanderson, 1924.

Editor, *Shelley and Keats, As They Struck Their Contemporaries.* London, Beaumont, 1925; Folcroft, Pennsylvania, Folcroft Editions, 1974.

Editor, with B. Brady, *Selected Poems,* by Bret Harte. Tokyo, 1926.

Editor, *A Hundred English Poems from the Elizabethan Age to the Victorian.* Tokyo, Kenkyusha, 1927; revised edition, 1949.

Editor, *Great Short Stories of the War.* London, Eyre and Spottiswoode, 1930.

Editor, *The Poems of Wilfred Owen.* London, Chatto and Windus, 1931.

Editor, with E. L. Griggs, *Coleridge: Studies by Several Hands on the Hundredth Anniversary of His Death.* London, Constable, 1934.

Editor, *Hymns for the Amusement of Children,* by Christopher Smart. Oxford, Blackwell, 1947.

Editor, with others, *The Christ's Hospital Book.* London, Hamish Hamilton, 1953.

Editor, *Poems, Principally Selected from Unpublished Manuscripts,* by Ivor Gurney. London, Hutchinson, 1954.

Editor, *Selected Poems of Shelley.* London, Collins, 1954.

Editor, *Selected Poems of Keats.* London, Collins, 1955.

Editor, *Selected Poems of Tennyson.* London, Heinemann, 1960.

Editor, with Bernard Mellor, *Wayside Poems of the Early Seventeenth Century.* London, Oxford University Press, 1963.

Editor, with Bernard Mellor, *Wayside Poems of the Early Eighteenth Century.* London, Oxford University Press, 1964.

Editor, with Bernard Mellor, *Wayside Sonnets, 1750–1850.* Hong Kong, University of Hong Kong Press, 1970.

Bibliography: "A Blunden Bibliography" by Takeshi Saito, in *Today's Japan 5* (Tokyo), March–April 1960.

*   *   *

I think no poet writing today has a closer association with the secret, shy self of England than has Edmund Blunden. How can one best describe his peculiar quality? You know the faint twitter of a hedge-sparrow on a silent winter afternoon: a little, wistful piercing-sweet note that is unlocatable? That is Blunden's voice. You know the grey-veiled umbers and dying reds in a frozen clot of mouldering leaves: you know the acrid but hopeful scent of those leaves at the thaw? Such are the colour and the savour of Blunden's verse.

Again, he has his summer moods; the deep-throated nightingale singing through a hot honey-suckle-smothered midnight, the moon bosomed on the heavy trees, and a planet or two dropping gouts of cold fire as though the heavens were bleeding ecstasy. All these qualities inspire Blunden's slow-moving verse, giving a subconscious background, a chorus of the senses, to his deliberate thought.

I do not suggest, however, that his thought – the self-seen and conscious part of him – is not original. Indeed, he has had his unique experience of life; trials and setbacks, war years, exile in the Far East; and he interprets them in his own way.

What is that way? First, he has an unusually quick-darting vision, bright and bird-like. He picks out shy, odd things, the minutest happenings, the most shadowy of moods, and peers at them by the light of his fierce curiosity. What he discovers

there is always related by him to the huge stock of memoried scenes and deeds and
moods stored in his mind; a mind that harbours also, for useful comparisons, a
cache of book-treasures, the glories of other poets whose work is a part of our
English scenery and atmosphere, and whose genius haunts our lanes and cottages,
like swallows at nightfall.

In consequence, his ideas are always de-personalised by the time he has finished
this subtle manipulation. He seems to hide his feeling behind his thought, and to
deprecate, in almost an agony of shyness, the direct form of appeal between himself
and his reader. You approach him by the paths of scholarship, and unless you
know the road, with its rich scenes of local history, custom and language, you
never get near him or his meaning.

When you do approach, and can penetrate that façade, you find a being of simple
mood and impulse; a creature eloquent with faith and that rare quality, joy. Joy is
the mainspring of his life and art, joy childlike, that takes the knocks and accidents
of life wonderingly, and refuses to be disillusioned, even by the nightmare
memories of his wartime experience in the mud and trenches of Flanders, during
the 1914–1918 war. He goes back always to those wide-eyed moods of childhood,
where the innocent mind moves like a prophet toward the future. In the following
poem he deals deliberately with this mood, and you will notice, in the last line,
what goal he reaches, and what company he keeps:

> Deed and event of prouder stature
> Dare not always overshade
> The first fresh buddings of our nature;
> Their hidden colour does not fade.
>
> We well may quit our laboured action
> At some sweet call to early loves,
> And find the jewel of self-contraction
> Like saints in rocks and springs and groves.
>
> Win back the world when true Aurora
> Dawned a goddess, not an hour!
> Think, have you caught the smile of Flora
> Since your own life was a young flower?
>
> And Love, even Love, has dropped her lilies
> On the hot high-road; once she knew
> How columbines and daffadillies
> Created her own sun and dew.
>
> Return; how stands that man enchanted
> Who, after seas and mountains crossed,
> Finds his old threshold, so long scanted,
> With not a rose or robin lost!
>
> The wise, from passion now retreating
> To the hamlets of the mind,
> In every glance have claimed the greeting
> Of spirits infinitely kind.

– Richard Church

BLY, Robert (Elwood). American. Born in Madison, Minnesota, 23 December 1926. Educated at St. Olaf College, Northfield, Minnesota, 1946–47; Harvard University, Cambridge, Massachusetts, B.A. (magna cum laude) 1950; University of Iowa, Iowa City, M.A. 1956. Served in the United States Navy, 1944–46. Married Carolyn McLean in 1955; has four children, Mary, Bridget, Noah, and Micah. "I earn my living giving readings at American colleges and universities, and translating." Founding-Editor, since 1958, *The Fifties* magazine (later *The Sixties* and *The Seventies*), and The Fifties Press (later The Sixties and The Seventies Press), Madison, Minnesota. Recipient: Fulbright Fellowship, 1956; Amy Lowell Traveling Fellowship, 1964; Guggenheim Fellowship, 1964; National Institute of Arts and Letters grant, 1965; Rockefeller Fellowship, 1967; National Book Award, 1968. Address: Odin House, Madison, Minnesota 56256, U.S.A.

PUBLICATIONS

Verse

Silence in the Snowy Fields: Poems. Middletown, Connecticut, Wesleyan University Press, 1962; London, Cape, 1967.
The Light Around the Body: Poems. New York, Harper, 1967; London, Rapp and Whiting, 1968.
Chrysanthemums. Menomenie, Wisconsin, Ox Head Press, 1967.
Ducks. Menomenie, Wisconsin, Ox Head Press, 1968.
The Morning Glory: Another Thing That Will Never Be My Friend: Twelve Prose Poems. San Francisco, Kayak Books, 1969; revised edition, 1970.
The Teeth Mother Naked at Last. San Francisco, City Lights Books, 1970.
Poems for Tennessee, with William E. Stafford and William Matthews. Martin, Tennessee Poetry Press, 1971.
Water under the Earth. Rushden, Northamptonshire, Sceptre Press, 1972.
Jumping Out of Bed. Barre, Massachusetts, Barre, 1973.
Sleepers Joining Hands. New York, Harper, 1973.
Old Man Rubbing His Eyes. Santa Barbara, California, Unicorn Press, 1974.
Point Reyes Poems. San Francisco, Mudra, 1974.

Recording: *Today's Poets 5,* with others, Folkways.

Other

A Broadsheet Against the New York Times Book Review. Madison, Minnesota, Sixties Press, 1961.
The Lion's Tail and Eyes: Poems Written Out of Laziness and Silence, with James Wright and William Duffy. Madison, Minnesota, Sixties Press, 1962.
Leaping Poetry. Boston, Beacon Press, 1973.

Editor, with David Ray, *A Poetry Reading Against the Vietnam War.* Madison, Minnesota, American Writers Against the Vietnam War, 1966.
Editor, *The Sea and the Honeycomb: A Book of Poems.* Madison, Minnesota, Sixties Press, 1966.
Editor, *Forty Poems Touching on Recent American History.* Boston, Beacon Press, 1970.

139

Translator, *Reptiles and Amphibians of the World*, by Hans Hvass. New York, Grosset and Dunlap, 1960.

Translator, with James Wright, *Twenty Poems of Georg Trakl*. Madison, Minnesota, Sixties Press, 1961.

Translator, *The Story of Gösta Berling*, by Selma Lagerlof. New York, New American Library, 1962.

Translator, with James Wright and John Knoepfle, *Twenty Poems of César Vallejo*. Madison, Minnesota, Sixties Press, 1962.

Translator, with Eric Sellin and Thomas Buckman, *Three Poems*, by Thomas Tranströmer. Lawrence, Kansas, T. Williams, 1966.

Translator, *Hunger*, by Knut Hamsun. New York, Farrar Straus, 1967; London, Duckworth, 1974.

Translator, with Christina Paulston, *I Do Best Alone at Night*, by Gunnar Ekelöf. Washington, D.C., Charioteer Press, 1967.

Translator, with Christina Paulston, *Late Arrival on Earth: Selected Poems of Gunnar Ekelöf*. London, Rapp and Carroll, 1967.

Translator, with others, *Selected Poems*, by Yvan Goll. San Francisco, Kayak Books, 1968.

Translator, with James Wright, *Twenty Poems of Pablo Neruda*. Madison, Minnesota, Sixties Press, and London, Rapp and Whiting, 1968.

Translator, *Forty Poems of Juan Ramón Jiménez*. Madison, Minnesota, Sixties Press, 1969.

Translator, *Ten Poems*, by Issa Kobayashi. Privately printed, 1969.

Translator, with James Wright and John Knoepfle, *Neruda and Vallejo: Selected Poems*. Boston, Beacon Press, 1971.

Translator, *Twenty Poems of Tomas Tranströmer*. Madison, Minnesota, Seventies Press, 1971.

Translator, *The Fish in the Sea Is Not Thirsty: Versions of Kabir*. Ithaca, New York, Lillabulero Press, 1971.

Translator, *Night Vision*, by Tomas Tranströmer. Ithaca, New York, Lillabulero Press, 1971; London, London Magazine Editions, 1972.

Translator, *The First Ten Sonnets to Orpheus*, by Rainer Maria Rilke. San Francisco, Zephyrus Image Magazine, 1972.

Translator, *Lorca and Jiménez: Selected Poems*. Boston, Beacon Press, 1973.

Translator, *Martinson, Ekelöf, Tranströmer: Selected Poems*. Boston, Beacon Press, 1973.

Translator, *Basho*. San Francisco, Mudra, 1974.

Bibliography: Robert Bly Checklist by Sandy Dorbin, in *Schist 1* (Willimantie, Connecticut), Fall 1973.

Critical Studies: *Alone with America* by Richard Howard, New York, Atheneum, 1969; "The Emotive Imagination: A New Departure in American Poetry" by Ronald Moran and George Lensing, in *Southern Review* (Baton Rouge, Louisiana), 1971; *The Inner War: Forms and Themes in Recent American Poetry*, Philadelphia, Fortress Press, 1972; "Robert Bly Alive in Darkness" by Anthony Libby, in *Iowa Review* (Iowa City), Summer 1972; "Robert Bly: Radical Poet" by Michael D. True, in *Win* (Rifton, New York), 15 January 1973.

*   *   *

Robert Bly has been a leading figure in a revolt against rhetoric – a rebellion that is a taking up of the Imagist revolution betrayed, a reassertion of much of the good sense Pound brought to poetry – but also a movement which has in it much that is perfectly new. The new is found in a pure form in Bly's work and is echoed in the works of other poets (e.g., James Wright, Louis Simpson, Donald Hall), whose work reveals Bly's radical and transfiguring influence. Numerous younger poets have also been dramatically and decisively influenced by Bly (e.g., John Haines); and Bly's doctrine of the "underground image" and his admiration for the poetry of other languages which he believes (as Pound did) to be more suited to poetry, are characteristic concerns of his followers.

The key to Bly's aesthetic can be found in his writings on other poets. "The poems of Georg Trakl have a magnificent silence in them," Bly wrote. "It is very rare that he himself talks – for the most part he allows the images to speak for him. Most of the images, anyway, are images of silent things." Bly admires the renunciation of rhetoric; the orthodoxy represented by poets like Allen Tate suffers attack almost by implication in his deliberately stripped work. In his criticism Bly has mercilessly attacked that school of poetry led by Robert Lowell (though a friend and colleague in his work against the Vietnam war) and followed up in such Lowell disciples as Anne Sexton and Frederick Seidel. Often, indeed, Bly's doctrinaire denunciation of overly personal poets, poets who violate his notion of what the true poet essentially is (candid, happy – though hurt by the world's weight, mystical) long ago carried him into violations of New Critic standards for compassion in criticism, a *noli me tangere* protecting the poet's personality. Bly strongly resisted the appeals of Randall Jarrell's work during that poet's lifetime (though they are concerned with some of the same problems, e.g., the lives of inner selves), and his attack in *The Sixties* of James Dickey is a classic in the denunciation of a poet by a contemporary. And yet, Bly is able, in his work, to transcend his involvement in literary battles, and to achieve a purity and simplicity rare in English poetry, burdened as it is by an essentially unpoetic syntax (according to Bly):

> There has been a light snow.
> Dark car tracks move in out of the darkness.
> I stare at the train window marked with soft dust.
> I have awakened at Missoula, Montana, utterly happy.

Such a poem is stripped, and yet an excitement is built fiercely into it, to flare up in the reader's memory; a singing takes itself up: the poem returns the reader to its subjects; it is a poetry of excitement primarily about a certain kind of life and vision to which the poem directs attention rather than stealing attention from that experience. The poet makes no attempt to incorporate the great world of objects into his poem, to replace them; he takes them for granted, as universals, and simply reminds the reader, returning him – away from the page – to his own life. Although all poets take into themselves parts of the exterior world ("introject" them) and put them back in a rearrangement, Bly narrowly limits the choice of celebrant realities; the work is mannered, aflame with simple, or at least quiet, intensity – and expresses a deeply moral judgement about what life and poetry should be. The poet who rejoices at solitude, nature, the sullen beauty of the provinces and of American history cannot – as advocate of that vision – be a poet who celebrates smog, hypochondria, and insanity, glamorizing Miltown, dizzy with admiration for his own sophistication. For Bly – as a visionary – the words of his poems are real, and he is in the most curious sense sponsor of their life and reality – they *are* old Pontiacs and expressways, ditches, cornrows, abandoned barns that remind him of ships, streetlamps, small towns, bathtubs, mailboxes, the hand of a beloved: a poem is a chosen world. And so this work turns from the tortured self of so much modern poetry to the transcending, mystical self; it is a canon of epiphany, celebrant of names and landscapes – a poetry of images either outside the self or celebrating the self's capacity to respond to an outer world. As might be expected, this work, like that of many mystics, is heavily burdened with a sense of death, and is comparatively opaque, in terms of the author's personal experiences.

All this was most true of his first book, *Silence in the Snowy Fields,* which acquired myriad imitators. Bly had left out of that book earlier poems on the ascension of J. P. Morgan, with Morgan dominating the gutted land and the twisted tin of Shell signs, and many other poems of darker tone – as if they violated a rule – poems of dolor and grime. Bly was fascinated in these poems by robber barons, by the sadness of a plundered land, by the corruption of American presidents, but as if committed to public optimism, he excised them. In his second book, *The Light Around the Body* (which was given the National Book Award for 1968), Bly admits to a heavier melancholy, and the imagery becomes notably more complex and often, as if distorted by pain, surreal. It is as if he'd tried to avoid a war with society, but found it inescapable:

> A cathedral: I see
> Starving men, weakened, leaning
> On their knees. But the bells ring anyway,
> Sending out over the planted fields
> A vegetation, sound waves with long leaves.

The titles of these poems echo the shift: "Smothered by the World," "In Danger from the Outer World," "Counting Small-Boned Bodies," "Listening to President Kennedy Lie about the Cuban Invasion," "Those Being Eaten by America," "Driving Through Minnesota During the Hanoi Bombings" –

> Let's count the bodies over again.
> If we could only make the bodies smaller,
> The size of skulls,
> We could make a whole plain white with skulls in the moonlight!
> If we could only make the bodies smaller,
> Maybe we could get
> A whole year's kill in front of us on a desk!
> If we could only make the bodies smaller,
> We could fit
> A body into a finger-ring, for a keepsake forever.

This volume contains many poems written against the Vietnam war; in 1966, Bly gave a reading at Reed College in Portland, Oregeon, and used the occasion to launch a group which called itself American Writers Against the Vietnam War. Bly became one of the most effective of the anti-war intellectuals; like a politician he took his cause into the streets, joined public protests and marches to Washington.

Whatever he does, Robert Bly projects his unique personality vividly onto American cultural life; he has left a deep mark, and the assessment of his influence will long be a controversy for the future.

– David Ray

BOER, Charles. American. Born in Cleveland, Ohio, 25 June 1939. Educated at Western Reserve University, Cleveland, 1957–61, A.B. 1961; University of Florence (Fulbright Fellow), 1961–62; Harvard University, Cambridge, Massachusetts

(Woodrow Wilson Fellow, 1962–63); State University of New York, Buffalo, 1963–66, Ph.D. in comparative literature 1967. Assistant Professor, 1966–70, and since 1970 Associate Professor of English and Comparative Literature, University of Connecticut, Storrs. Recipient: Swallow Press New Poetry Series Award, 1969. Address: Box 69, Pomfret Center, Connecticut 06258, U.S.A.

PUBLICATIONS

Verse

The Odes.   Chicago, Swallow Press, 1969.
Varmint Q: An Epic Poem on the Life of William Clarke Quantrill.   Chicago, Swallow Press, 1972.

Other

Charles Olson in Connecticut (biography).   Chicago, Swallow Press, 1975.

Editor, with George Butterick, The Maximus Poems of Charles Olson, Volume Three.   New York, Grossman, 1974.

Translator, The Homeric Hymns.   Chicago, Swallow Press, 1971.
Translator, The Bacchae of Euripides, in An Anthology of Greek Tragedy.   Indianapolis, Bobbs Merrill, 1972.

*   *   *

Classicist Charles Boer puts the ancient forms of ode and epic, now largely fallen into disuse, in the service of perennial themes of war, love, and loss, but with a contemporary mood. Predominantly serious in tone, his score of irregular odes follow English tradition in variety but favor fragmentary colloquialism in grammatical structure. In apostrophes to sea nymphs, movie stars, a Wagnerian soprano, in scenes of wartime Europe and a nameless French river, classical allusions resonate within the matrix of the modern idiom. Unhampered by frequent punctuation, run-on lines drive a sometimes breathless lyric, while ambiguity and repetition give phrase and verse an oracular air, though at the price of dissipating force by frequently choppy caesurae and by strained and jerky syntax. Eschewing the confessional mode, Boer's lines lack the precision and polish of Allen Tate's and the charm of Frank O'Hara's. Individual images – petals and the four elements, especially fiery sun and timeless ocean, are his favorites – strike vividly, but the impression is often blunted by a nebulous context or a too-sudden shift of subject. Classical metaphor can control by maintaining distance, but it can also mask the personal. When the difficult or obscure is avoided, and the poet speaks directly, as in "The Water Ode," his voice is more affecting.

Varmint Q., "an epic poem on the life of William Clarke Quantrill," mocks epic conventions with wry humor but fits more comfortably with picaresque fiction. The history and myth of Q., alias Charley Hart, alias Capt. Quantrill, of the "peculiar eyes" are told through poetry interlarded with the sometimes semi-literate narratives and letters of his accomplices and antagonists, forming a novelistic composite of contrasting points-of-view. Boer sets the ironic tone with "An Invocation to

John Greenleaf Whittier As an Aside" and with a genealogy of Q.'s fraudulent, forging kin (incidentally having Mary Quantrill snatch from the "old gray head" of Barbara Frietchie, Whittier's heroine, the honor of saving the flag at Frederick). In contrast to Whittier's high-toned narratives, Boer portrays the violent career of a juvenile delinquent whose sadistic tendencies held him in good stead as Indian-fighter, Civil War guerilla, and tutor of Cole Younger and the James Boys. Q.'s own letters to his mother reveal a poetic sensibility, unfortunately belied by ox-theft, gambling, attempted and successful murder, among other things. Having fun with folklore, Boer plays ironic counterpoint throughout by recounting conflicting reports of Q.'s treacherous exploits (for example, he helps the Underground Rail-road steal slaves to freedom then sells them back, after setting up the massacre of the Abolitionists) and by adding a descant of asides and rhetorical questions. Spurred on by his adulterous muse, Annie Walker (invoked under her other name, A. Slaughter), Q.'s odyssey surveys the deadly life of the Western underworld, in which the scoundrel-hero can and does take both sides. Even the epic "game" is disreputable, a horse race in which Q.'s filthy steed wins by a mile, and a ruse. In his final madness, Q. offers as a hecatomb the massacre and burning of Lawrence, Kansas, and he dreams of assassinating Lincoln. Ill-omened and too late for that, he dies ingloriously, but not without the poet's reflections on the demise of the wild West by urbanization and on the making of an American myth.

– Joseph Parisi

BOLD, Alan (Norman). Scottish. Born in Edinburgh, 20 April 1943. Educated at Broughton Secondary School, Edinburgh; Edinburgh University (travelling scholar-ship in fine art, 1964), 1961–65. Married Alice Howell in 1963; has one daughter. Editor, *Gambit*, 1963, 1965, *Extra Verse*, and *Rocket*, 1965–66, all in Edinburgh. Member of the Editorial Staff, *Times Educational Supplement*, London, 1966–67. Recipient: Scottish Arts Council bursary, 1967, 1974. Address: 19 Gayfield Square, Edinburgh EH1 3NX, Scotland.

PUBLICATIONS

Verse

Society Inebrious. Edinburgh, Mowat Hamilton, 1965.
The Voyage, adaptation of a poem by Baudelaire. Edinburgh, M. Macdonald, 1966.
To Find the New. London, Chatto and Windus-Hogarth Press, 1967; Middle-town, Connecticut, Wesleyan University Press, 1968.
A Perpetual Motion Machine. London, Chatto and Windus-Hogarth Press, and Middletown, Connecticut, Wesleyan University Press, 1969.
Penguin Modern Poets 15, with Edward Brathwaite and Edwin Morgan. Lon-don, Penguin, 1969.
The State of the Nation. London, Chatto and Windus-Hogarth Press, and Middletown, Connecticut, Wesleyan University Press, 1969.

He Will Be Greatly Missed: A Poem. London, Turret Books, 1971.
The Auld Symie. Preston, Lancashire, Akros, 1971.
A Century of People. London, Academy Editions, 1971.
A Pint of Bitter. London, Chatto and Windus-Hogarth Press, and Middletown, Connecticut, Wesleyan University Press, 1971.
A Lunar Event: A Poem and a Drawing. Richmond, Surrey, Keepsake Press, 1973.

Short Stories

The Hammer and the Thistle, with David Morrison. Wick, Caithness Books, 1974.

Other

Art and Action: A Lecture. London, Peter Moran, 1965.
Bonnie Prince Charlie. London, Pitkin Pictorials, 1973.
Robert Burns. London, Pitkin Pictorials, 1973.

Editor, *The Penguin Book of Socialist Verse.* London, Penguin, 1970.
Editor, *The Cambridge Book of English Verse.* Cambridge, University Press, 1974.

Critical Study: "Poet in Search of a Public" by Philip Oakes, in *Sunday Times* (London), 8 February 1970.

Alan Bold comments:

(1970) I am mainly concerned in my poems to explore the insights made available to modern man through scientific research and political change. However, I do not limit myself to one type of poem such as the discursive epic or the short satirical poem. I believe that modern poetry should be judged by the same rigorous standards we apply to the literature of the past and consequently I have made it my business to equip myself with the full range of poetic forms. In this way I am able to emphasise thematic unity by the use of formal variety. Most modern poetry is timid, pretentious, incompetent and inadequate. I would like to see instead of the present fashions – confessional verse, concrete poetry &c. – a poetry of precision which tested the authenticity of its emotion against the observable world of fact. I want poetry to be more ambitious than the novel and the play and to win a new mass audience. And I would like to contribute to this process.

(1974) When I look at my statement in the 1970 edition it seems to suggest that poetry is simply a mechanical process of perfecting a technique and then applying it to all and sundry subjects. I now see that technical expertise is but a beginning and that it can never be fully attained, as each *real* poem demands its own particular technical as well as emotional solution. Thus my poetry has become more experimental (using the word in its scientific sense as the exploration of possibilities, not its lit. crit. sense) and more personal as I feel less inclined to pontificate on the world and more sure of my own feelings. Not that I intend to produce a self-pitying form of versified pessimism but I am now more likely to create a poem in and through personally meaningful language whereas before I would think of something to say and then execute it in poetry. I still feel contemporary English poetry (and that includes Scottish poetry in English, of course) is inadequate: a safety-first response to life in timid and academically acceptable phraseology. I want to write poems that have a life of their own and that reflect life in general and not books or other men's styles. Probably the most significant recent development in my books has been my entry into the visual field. In 1972 I had six exhibitions: of etchings, drawings, paintings and Illuminated Poems. These Illuminated Poems are a combination of original manuscript and watercolour illustration.

*   *   *

The political instinct has too often betrayed poets, and has rarely found fortunate expression in verse; Alan Bold shows some courage in his constant use of his art as a political weapon. Unlike Adrian Mitchell, perhaps the best known contemporary political polemicist in verse, Bold makes use of conventional poetic style, and even appears somewhat reactionary in his poetic diction: like many Marxists, he deeply suspects modern experiments in poetry, art and music. In his own work, he is led by this attitude, at worst, to extremely prosaic passages of verse, in which the socialist "message" appears not only boldly but baldly; and the pitfalls more often than not avoided by his hero Hugh MacDiarmid can trip him up. Even at his best – say, in "June 1967 at Buchenwald" – old-fashioned stylistic tricks (notably dull repetion, alliteration, the expected rather than the inevitable phrase) tend to stifle the raw emotion which generated the piece, and can still be felt beneath the surface, not alas with sufficient force to make the poetry truly memorable. But the very drabness of the writing can have an atmosphere of its own; if it lacks the elegance which surely must be an attribute of conventional form if it is to be effective, it also lacks the pretentiousness which more experimental verse provokes in poets. Bold, feeling that "Words are fallible. They cannot do / More than hint at torment," may yet find the confidence which, with a little broadening of his style, could bring out to the full a talent which as yet has on the whole failed to convince.

– Derek Parker

BOOTH, Martin. British. Born in Lancashire, 7 September 1944. Educated at King George V School, Hong Kong; Trent Park College of Education, Barnet, Hertfordshire. Founder, 1968, The Sceptre Press, Frensham, Surrey, later Rushden, Northamptonshire. Since 1971, Editor, Fuller d'Arch Smith, publishers, London. Schoolmaster Fellow, St. Peter's College, Oxford, 1973. Since 1968, Member of the Executive Council, Poetry Society, London. Regular Contributor, *Tribune* and *The Teacher*, London. Recipient: Guinness Award, 1970; Gregory Award, 1971; York International Poetry Festival prize, 1973. Address: Fuller d'Arch Smith, Publishers Ltd., 60 Oxford Street, London W1A 4WD, England.

PUBLICATIONS

Verse

Paper Pennies and Other Poems.   Hong Kong, privately printed, 1967.
Supplication to the Himalayas.   Frensham, Surrey, Sceptre Press, 1968.
In the Yenan Caves.   Frensham, Surrey, Sceptre Press, 1969.
The Borrowed Gull: After Virginia Woolf.   Frensham, Surrey, Sceptre Press, 1970.
A Winnowing of Silence.   Richmond, Surrey, Keepsake Press, 1971.
The Crying Embers.   London, Fuller d'Arch Smith, 1971.
Pilgrims and Petitions.   Birmingham, Aquila, 1972.
On the Death of Archbishop Broix.   Cardiff, Second Aeon, 1972.
Nature Study.   St. Ives, Cornwall, Poetry St. Ives, 1972.
Teller.   London, Poet and Printer, 1972.
Coronis.   Jersey, Channel Islands, Andium Press, 1973.
Spawning the Os.   London, Quarto Books, 1974.
Yogh.   Denver, Ally Press, 1974.
Brevities.   New Rochelle, New York, Elizabeth Press, 1974.
Snath.   London, Oasis Books, 1975.

Other

White Bat (juvenile).   London, Macmillan, 1974.
The Poetry of Aleister Crowley.   London, BBC, 1974.

Editor, *Unpublished Poems and Drafts of J. E. Flecker.*   Richmond, Surrey, Keepsake Press, 1971.
Editor, with George MacBeth, *The Book of Cats.*   London, Secker and Warburg, 1975.

Critical Studies: in *Malahat Review* (Victoria, British Columbia), Summer 1972; in *Second Aeon 15* (Cardiff), Summer 1972.

Martin Booth comments:

Martin Booth is an imagist: his work is concerned with imagery and symbolism and with an attempt to place self in the context of the personal world.

                    *   *   *

One of the difficulties in writing an interim report on the work of Martin Booth (and since he is developing so rapidly it can only be an interim report) is that he has written so much and not all his work has been published in collected form. Prior to his first collected volume, *The Crying Embers*, at least half a dozen booklets and pamphlet collections of his work had appeared, and at least two have been published since. Fortunately, his most accomplished poetry is to be found in *Coronis* which contains poems written between 1971 and 1973.

From the start Martin Booth had a fine command of language and an ear for rhythm and music. In many of his early poems, however, he was inclined to leave too much to the reader. Despite his remarkable descriptive and lyrical talent, many of his early pieces seemed like extracts from a longer sequence, so that read in isolation, they failed to make the impact they might have done if related one to the next. Characters would suddenly be introduced as "he" or "she" without a hint of their background or relevance to the theme. One must exclude from this comment such admirable poems as "Cathedral Starlings," "Hunt," "The Black Cranes" and "Dismissal at the Building of the Tower of Babel." With the publication of *The Crying Embers* his intention became a good deal clearer and it was possible to discern the unity of his work, which drew substantially on dream imagery. The best thing in this volume is "Orbis Picture," a series of emblem poems based upon woodcuts from Comenius's pedagogical work published in Nuremberg in 1658. Although largely descriptive, the significant details have been selected to recreate the atmosphere of the printshop; each section is as stark and clearly defined as the woodcut concerned and the language is perfectly controlled. In 1971 Booth won a Gregory Award on the strength of his achievements. *Coronis*, divided into three sections and containing his ambitious long poem "On the Death of Archdeacon Broix," shows the distance he has travelled and confirms the promise of his early work. Martin Booth is one of the most interesting of the younger poets writing today and clearly possesses rich potentiality.

– Howard Sergeant

BOOTH, Philip. American. Born in Hanover, New Hampshire, 8 October 1925. Educated at Dartmouth College, Hanover, A.B. 1948; Columbia University, New York, M.A. 1949. Served in the United States Army Air Force, 1944–45. Married Margaret Tillman in 1946; has three daughters. Instructor, Bowdoin College, Maine, 1949–50; Assistant to the Director of Admissions, 1950–51, and Instructor, 1954, Dartmouth College; Assistant Professor, Wellesley College, Massachusetts, 1954–61. Associate Professor, 1961–65, and since 1965, Professor of English and Poet-in-Residence, Syracuse University, New York. Taught at the University of New Hampshire Writers Conference, Durham, 1955; Spencer Memorial Lecturer, Bryn Mawr College, Pennsylvania, 1959; taught at Tufts University Poetry Workshop, Medford, Massachusetts, 1960, 1961. Phi Beta Kappa Poet, Columbia University, 1962. Recipient: Bess Hokin Prize (*Poetry*, Chicago), 1955; Lamont Poetry Selection Award, 1956; *Saturday Review* prize, 1957; Guggenheim Fellowship, 1958, 1965; Emily Clark Balch Prize (*Virginia Quarterly Review*), 1964; National Institute of Arts and Letters grant, 1967; Rockefeller Fellowship, 1968; Theodore Roethke Prize (*Poetry Northwest*), 1970. D.Litt.: Colby College, Waterville, Maine, 1968. Address: North Eagle Village Road, Manlius, New York 13104, U.S.A.

PUBLICATIONS

Verse

Letter from a Distant Land. New York, Viking Press, 1957.
The Islanders. New York, Viking Press, 1961.

North by East.   Boston, Impressions Workshop, 1966.
Weathers and Edges.   New York, Viking Press, 1966.
Margins: A Sequence of New and Selected Poems.   New York, Viking Press, 1970.

Recording: *Today's Poets 4*, with others, Folkways.

Other

Editor, *The Dark Island.*   Lunenberg, Vermont, Stinehour Press, 1960.
Editor, *Syracuse Poems, 1965, 1970, and 1973.*   Syracuse, New York, Syracuse University Department of English, 1965, 1970, 1973.

Manuscript Collections: State University of New York, Buffalo; University of Texas, Austin; Dartmouth College, Hanover, New Hampshire.

*   *   *

Beginning in the 1950's with somewhat formal poems, then moving toward freer but still concise, controlled statements, Philip Booth has made himself the poet of the Maine coast:

> Crouched hard on granite,
> facing a weathered sea,
> I breathe as slow as rock.

It is his home, important to him not simply as home – place of sea and stone, gull and bellbuoy, weather and poor washed towns – but as the edge of land, the margin. Again and again he returns to the idea of man at the brink of the sea:

> The late fog, lifting.
> A first wind, risen.
> The long tide, at ebb.
>
> And cast off finally,
> into that routine hope,
> the fishboats: going out.

Booth's poems, even the long ones, are laconic in manner, suggesting the speech of Maine; suggesting, too, the hard-bitten quality of mind that casts off into a "routine hope." His fishermen and coastal farmers, who carry the Yankee tradition into the machine age, are skeptics, despairers, silent sufferers, intensely human – alive in their particularities of speech and culture; and the wry poems which celebrate them, Booth's elegies of the verge, have won a distinct place in the varied literature of New England.

– Hayden Carruth

BOSLEY, Keith. British. Born in the Thames Valley, 16 September 1937. Educated at Borlase School, Marlow, Buckinghamshire, 1949–56; the universities of Reading, Paris, and Caen, 1956–60, B.A. (honours) in French 1960. Married Helen Sava in 1962; has two children. Since 1961, Announcer, Scriptwriter, Producer, and Studio Manager, BBC External Services, London. Address: 108 Upton Road, Slough SL1 2AW, England.

Publications

Verse

Russia's Other Poets (translations). London, Longman, 1968; as Russia's Underground Poets, New York, Praeger, 1969.
An Idiom of Night, translations from Pierre Jean Jouve. London, Rapp and Whiting, 1968.
The Possibility of Angels: Poems. London, Macmillan, 1969.
The War Wife: Vietnamese Poetry (translations). London, Allison and Busby, 1972.
And I Dance: Poems Original and Translated. London, Angus and Robertson, 1972.
Snake Charm. London, Menard Press, 1972.
The Song of Aino. High Wycombe, Buckinghamshire, Moonbird Publications, 1973.

Other

Tales from the Long Lakes: Finnish Legends from the Kalevala. London, Gollancz, 1966; as The Devil's Horse: Tales from the Kalevala, New York, Pantheon Books, 1971.

Keith Bosley comments:

Since the publishers of my first collection accepted then rejected its successor, my work – in spite of constant efforts to place it elsewhere – has been unobtainable in book form; furthermore, most editors of magazines (not to mention radio producers) prefer to use their friends' work – as someone said, with friends like that who needs poets: it seems to me therefore rather unreal to make a statement about my work, beyond declaring that it exists and even advances. That first collection, which like all my books was warmly received, is now far behind me; the mass of work done since has crystallised into two manuscripts, and I am now deeply into something different – a single large structure which should keep me out of mischief for quite a while and from which I occasionally read for the amusement of my fellow creatures. When I am not writing my own poems I like writing other people's: translation is an integral part of my kind of poet's job, along with an active involvement in linguistics and music.

*   *   *

Keith Bosley is a poet of considerable charm, much technical ability and with a certain amount to say. At his best, he achieves a tender lyricism rare in this violent age, as in "The Smoke":

> Summer persists.
>   The smoke
> from that squat chimney climbs
> into a perfect sky
> this still October, trees
> hang yellow against blue
> longing for leaf fall. . . .

Again, at his best, Mr. Bosley can manage a clear plot-line better than most of his contemporaries. This is true of "The Unknown Language" where the speaker mysteriously picks up on the 16 metre band of his radio the tongue of the ancient Incas. It is true also of "Haunted" – a poem about a mad grandmother sniped at by imaginary soldiers who go away after her (real) death. Most of all, perhaps, the argument commands attention in "Wind at Midnight":

> The night I was away you said the wind
> vaulted the horizon, tore overland
> snatched at the trees and stole their dark green sleep
> fingered the river and set it gasping
>
> and then walked to our house, quite quietly
> to where you lay alone . . .

The wind behaves like an interloper, howling to get in, sighing when excluded, going away as disappointed as a man. Then

> Tonight we are together. Listen: your
> horizon, land, trees, river move. I stand
> shut in my tomb or kennel at the door
> real and whimpering as any wind.

Mr. Bosley's original work has learned a good deal from his translations. There are a good many of them. This from Ranetsu, for example:

> The house is locked up:
> around a paper lantern
> the bats are dancing.

And Mr. Bosley, more than any translator I have come across, makes us feel the genius of Ranetsu's master, Basho. If in his original works Mr. Bosley has a tendency to fall into the faux-naif, he compensates for this absence of matter by rendering into English verse poets as different as the Japanese masters of haiku and that very European elegist, Lorca. So, in our age of violence, Mr. Bosley is among the distinguished practitioners of a civilized art: translation.

– Philip Hobsbaum

BOTTRALL, (Francis James) Ronald. British. Born in Camborne, Cornwall, 2 September 1906. Educated at Redruth County School; Pembroke College, Cambridge (Foundress' Scholar; Charles Oldham Shakespeare Scholar, 1927), M.A. (honours); Princeton University, New Jersey (Commonwealth Fund Fellowship, 1931–33). Married Margaret Florence Saumarez Smith in 1934 (marriage dissolved, 1954), has one son; Margot Pamela Samuel, 1954. Lector in English, University of Helsingfors, Finland, 1929–31; Johore Professor of English Language and Literature, Raffles College, Singapore, 1933–37; Assistant Director and Professor of English, British Institute, Florence, 1937–38; Secretary, School of Oriental and African Studies, London University, 1939–45. With the Air Ministry, 1940–41. British Council Representative in Sweden, 1941; Italy, 1945; Brazil, 1954; Greece, 1957; Japan (and Cultural Counsellor, Tokyo), 1959–61. Chief, Fellowships and Training Branch, Food and Agricultural Organization of the United Nations, Rome, 1963–65. Recipient: Coronation Medal, 1953; Syracuse International Poetry Prize, 1954. Fellow, Royal Society of Literature, 1955. Grand Officer of the Order of Merit, Italy, 1973. C.B.E. (Commander, Order of the British Empire), 1949. Knight of the Order of St. John of Jerusalem, 1972. Address: Via IV Fontane, 00184 Rome, Italy.

PUBLICATIONS

Verse

The Loosening and Other Poems. Cambridge, Gordon Fraser The Minority Press, 1931.
Festivals of Fire. London, Faber, 1934.
The Turning Path. London, Arthur Barker, 1939.
Farewell and Welcome: Poems. London, Editions Poetry, 1945.
Selected Poems. London, Editions Poetry, 1946.
The Palisades of Fear: Poems. London, Editions Poetry, 1949.
Adam Unparadised. London, Derek Verschoyle, 1954.
The Collected Poems of Ronald Bottrall. London, Sidgwick and Jackson, 1961.
Day and Night. London, London Magazine Editions, 1973.
Poems 1955–1973. London, Anvil Press Poetry, 1974.

Other

Rome. London, Joseph, and Cleveland, World, 1968.

Editor, with Gunnar Ekelöf, Dikter, by T. S. Eliot. Stockholm, Albert Bonniers Förlag, 1942.
Editor, with Margaret Bottrall, The Zephyr Book of English Verse. Stockholm, Zephyr Books, 1945.
Editor, with Margaret Bottrall, Collected English Verse. London, Sidgwick and Jackson, 1946.

Essays on Byron, Pound, and others published in periodicals and anthologies.

Manuscript Collections: State University of New York, Buffalo; University of Texas, Austin; British Museum, London.

Ronald Bottrall comments:

At the beginning one has plenty of thematic material but only after trial and error can one use it effectively. In mid-career things coalesce and clarify and when situations present themselves one has the technique and experience to deal with them to the best of one's ability. In later years the technical skill is still there, but the situations are harder to grasp and transmute into poetry. My imagery derives from my early years in Cornwall in the country and by the sea. Later from my extensive travels. The greatest influence on my early poetry was Ezra Pound's *Hugh Selwyn Mauberley*. In the course of my work I have used a great many metrical forms, including, from 1946–49, syllabic verse. An ability to make use of metrical forms is most important for a poet.

*   *   *

(1970) Ronald Bottrall's reputation as a poet has suffered a great deal through his being tipped off, in the early 1930's, by Dr. F. R. Leavis as the most rangingly intelligent of the younger poets at that time. His early poetry owes a great deal to the example of Ezra Pound, on whose early *Cantos* he wrote a most acute critical study in *Scrutiny*, and, having spent most of his life in such diverse places as Scandinavia, Italy and Brazil, working for the British Council, he is like Pound a cosmopolitan and multi-lingual poet, full of oblique allusions; he is like Pound also in his learning: in the BBC volume of translations from Dante's *Inferno* his opening ones were perhaps the best. These preoccupations and also perhaps a tendency to write too rapidly and fluently made him seem apart from the mainstream of British verse in the 1930's. And when, at the end of the 1940's, younger poets like John Wain rediscovered the equally learned and obscure poetry of Bottrall's Cambridge friend and contemporary, William Empson, they did not rediscover Bottrall.

Yet a selection of his best poems would be an impressive volume. Always very much in the thick of the world of cultural poses and pretensions, he has a gift for satirising this, in an oblique way, borrowed from Pound's *Hugh Selwyn Mauberley*, that includes a great deal of self-satire. But he has also a directly lyrical gift, for modulation and phrasing. In spite of his Cambridge connections, he was much admired by Dame Edith Sitwell, and the free, loose rhythmical movement of many of his later poems has something in common with her work. A certain roughness, hastiness, or impatience of workmanship flaws many of his later poems; a natural fluency makes it hard for him to eliminate and condense. Nor is there any final philosophy of life in his poetry except that of the sceptical, disabused, but always eager and curious spectator and critic of life, an urbane cynic coupled with a lyrical celebrator. One of his best poems is on the primitive painter, Arnold Wallis, like himself a Cornishman, like himself of working-class origin. Bottrall was to move on from such origins to explore all the splendours of the world. But it may be that it is a certain wistfulness for a lost simplicity and innocence that gives his over-abundant, always accomplished but always uneven verse its most poignant moments.

(1974) Since I wrote the above, Bottrall, at sixty-seven, has had an extraordinary new burst of creativity. This began with a group of short poems, which occurred to him just as he was waking in the morning, and then were immediately written down. They have a quality of condensed mysteriousness. He has also written his longest poem to date, *Talking to the Ceiling*, an extremely vivid, loving and Chaucerianly humorous evocation of his Cornish childhood and his father, sixty years ago. It is a poet's late assertion of the sacredness of roots, the strength of family ties, and the richness of life, a kind of counterblast to *The Waste Land*. These poems, which I have been privileged to see in the process of composition, are now being published, along with a number of other new ones. In bulk they'are almost equivalent to his earlier *Collected Poems* and they have a new serenity, simplicity, and directness. Bottrall's intelligence and skill had been highly praised in the 1930's by F. R. Leavis, in the 1940's by Edith Sitwell, and in the 1960's by Charles Tomlinson. Three such different critics, two of them poets – and very different poets – cannot, between them, have been entirely wrong. This late flowering should restore Bottrall to a central position in the poetic scene.

– G. S. Fraser

BOWERING, George. Canadian. Born in Keremeos, British Columbia, 1 December 1938. Educated at Victoria College, British Columbia; University of British Columbia, Vancouver, B.A. 1960, M.A. 1963; University of Western Ontario, London. Served in the Royal Canadian Air Force, 1954–57. Married Angela Luoma in 1962; Thea Claire Bowering, 1971. Has worked for the British Columbia Forest Service and for the Federal Department of Agriculture. Assistant Professor, University of Calgary, Alberta, 1963–66; Writer-in-Residence, 1967–68, and Assistant Professor of English, 1968–72, Sir George Williams University, Montreal. Since 1972, Associate Professor of English, Simon Fraser University, Burnaby, British Columbia. Editor, *Imago* magazine, Vancouver. Recipient: Canada Council grant, 1968, 1971; Governor-General's Award, 1969. Agent: Susan Lands, 235 Metcalfe Avenue, Apartment 207, Montreal 6, Quebec. Address: 2499 West 37th Avenue, Vancouver 13, British Columbia, Canada.

PUBLICATIONS

Verse

Sticks and Stones. Vancouver, Tishbooks, 1963.
Points on the Grid. Toronto, Contact Press, 1964.
The Man in the Yellow Boots. Mexico City, El Corno Emplumado, 1965.
The Silver Wire. Kingston, Ontario, Quarry Press, 1966.
Baseball. Toronto, Coach House Press, 1967.
Two Police Poems. Vancouver, Talonbooks, 1968.
Rocky Mountain Foot: A Lyric, A Memoir. Toronto, McClelland and Stewart, 1968.
The Gangs of Kosmos. Toronto, House of Anansi, 1969.
Sitting in Mexico. Montreal, Imago, 1970.
George, Vancouver: A Discovery Poem. Toronto, Weed/Flower Press, 1970.
Geneve. Toronto, Coach House Press, 1971.
Touch: Selected Poems 1960–1970. Toronto, McClelland and Stewart, 1971.
The Sensible. Toronto, Massasauga Editions, 1972.
Layers. Toronto, Weed/Flower Press, 1973.
In the Flesh. Toronto, McClelland and Stewart, 1974.

Plays

A *Home for Heroes*, in *Prism International* (Vancouver), 1962.

Television Play: *What Does Eddie Williams Want?*, 1965.

Novel

Mirror on the Floor. Toronto, McClelland and Stewart, 1967.

Short Stories

Flycatcher. Ottawa, Oberon Press, 1974.

Other

How I Hear "Howl". Montreal, Sir George Williams University, 1968.
Al Purdy. Toronto, Copp Clarke, 1970.
Autobiology. Vancouver, Vancouver Writing Series, 1971.
Curious. Toronto Coach House Press, 1974.

Editor, *Vibrations: Poems of Youth*. Toronto, Gage, 1970.
Editor, *The Story So Far*. Toronto, Coach House Press, 1971.

Manuscript Collection: Douglas Library, Queen's University, Kingston, Ontario.

Critical Study: Introduction by the author to *Touch: Selected Poems*, 1971.

George Bowering comments:

I don't think that I will make a "personal statement introducing my work" because I don't write personal poetry. In fact when personal poetry gets to be confessional poetry I turn it off & reach for the baseball scores. I'll share with you what I wrote as notes 2 days ago: The snowball appears in hell every morning at seven. Dr Babel contends about the word's form, striking its prepared strings endlessly, a pleasure moving rings outward thru the universe. All sentences are to be served. You've tried it & tried it & it cant be done, you cannot close your ear – i.e. literature must be thought, now. Your knee oh class equal poet will like use a simile because he hates ambiguity. The snowball says it: all sentences are imperative.

*   *   *

"I was all those things that other poets always are on the dust jackets before they became poets." George Bowering's boast must be true, for his work is immensely various and the poet himself seems at times a powder-keg of energy. Wondering what Bowering will publish next is almost a pastime in Canadian poetry circles.

Bowering's work is terribly uneven, however, and irritatingly bad when it is poor. The virtues and vices are both found in *Touch: Selected Poems 1960–1970*, which includes poems from his earlier books, including *Rocky Mountain Foot* for which he received the Governor-General's Award in 1969. This last book is the first that groups poems thematically rather than chronologically, for as he explained, "Now nearly all I work on are books themselves."

A few of the vices include his misspelled words; his endless egotism; his philistinism; his ultra-radical chic. Some of his virtues are a vivid sense of space and time; a lyricism that is capable of sprouting wings; a happy-go-lucky sensibility (when not radicalized); an instant sympathy for the oppressed. It could be said his work has more tone than taste.

"Emphasis is on voice," Bowering wrote, and his poetry does have a decided cadence, a nonchalance of its own, and a quickness that is characteristic and enjoyable. Perhaps the spirit of his work can best be caught in a poem like "Grandfather" which begins:

> Grandfather
>   Jabez Harry Bowering
> strode across the Canadian prairie
> hacking down trees
>   & building churches
> delivering personal baptist sermons in them
> leading Holy holy holy lord god almighty songs in them.

The poem does not conclude so much as end:

> Till he died the day before his eighty fifth birthday
> in a Catholic hospital of sheets white as his hair.

The need to create a personal mythology is here, as it is in Whitman's verse, and Bowering's poems all seem interconnected in some vast Life of the Western Canadian Poet.

Perhaps Hugh MacCallum best summed Bowering's work up when he wrote: "The speaker in these poems achieves at times an almost bardic simplicity of manner that allows him to revel in the ordinary, the commonplace, the self-evident. But there is also a kind of wonder at the fullness and assertiveness of phenomena. Energy is the thing that arouses the poet's imagination – energy in landscape, man, or woman."

– John Robert Colombo

BOWERS, Edgar. American. Born in Rome, Georgia, 2 March 1924. Educated at the University of North Carolina, Chapel Hill, B.A. 1947; Stanford University, California, M.A. 1949, Ph.D. 1953. Served in the United States Army, 1943–46. Instructor, Duke University, Durham, North Carolina, 1952–55; Assistant Professor, Harpur College, Binghamton, New York, 1955–58. Since 1958, Member of the

English Department, and currently Professor of English, University of California, Santa Barbara, Recipient: Swallow Press New Poetry Series Award, 1955; Guggenheim Fellowship, 1958; *Sewanee Review* Fellowship; Fulbright Fellowship; Edward F. Jones Foundation Fellowship; University of California Institute of Creative Arts Fellowship. Address: 1502 Miramar Beach, Santa Barbara, California 93101, U.S.A.

PUBLICATIONS

Verse

The Form of Loss. Denver, Swallow, 1956.
Five American Poets, with others, edited by Ted Hughes and Thom Gunn. London, Faber, 1963.
The Astronomers. Denver, Swallow, 1965.
Living Together: New and Selected Poems. Boston, Godine Press, 1973.
Paroxisms: A Guide to the Isms. New York, New Directions, 1974.

Critical Study: *Forms of Discovery* by Yvor Winters, Denver, Swallow, 1967.

*   *   *

Sometimes a major poet may be ignored by the majority of readers, so that he must content himself with fit audience, though few. Sometimes a major poet may seem less "important" than more public figures, for instance, poets who disturb political conventions or march on the Pentagon, or who titillate the public with confessional songs and sonnets. No matter how worthy their causes or how honest their confessions, poets must be judged by their poems, not their activities or biographies. Edgar Bowers has not sought publicity, nor has he achieved notoriety. He has not written in the modish confessional manner of divorce, madness, and self-advertisement. He has simply written some of the great poems of our time. One needs to read his work slowly and carefully; his poems are worth taking the time to understand.

Bowers' powerful treatment of themes of deception and honesty, of shadow and lucidity, of loss and form can be found in his earliest poems; but his depth and range have grown, with no diminution of his prosodic mastery. A chief characteristic of his poems, as Yvor Winters pointed out, is that "sensory perception and its significance are simultaneous." This is especially true of "Autumn Shade," a sequence of ten poems that ends *The Astronomers* and that Winters mistakenly slighted. The sequence begins with a sense of destiny which amounts almost to predestination, a sense that appears in other poems by Bowers:

> Now, toward his destined passion there, the strong,
> Vivid young man, reluctant, may return
> From suffering in his own experience
> To lie down in the darkness.

The young man wakes, he works, he sleeps again; but the first poem ends with a chilling image: "The snake / Does as it must, and sinks into the cold." In another poem the young man lights a fire as the night grows cold:

157

>   Gently
> A dead soprano sings Mozart and Bach.
> I drink bourbon, then go to bed, and sleep
> In the Promethean heat of summer's essence.

This is pentameter so subtle in modulation that one may miss a good deal of the technical virtuosity which makes the apparently colloquial notation of actions possible. So much is packed into the subdued, suggestive style that one may overlook the complexity of life and of emotional response to sensations being presented: perception and significance are simultaneous, statement and meaning coincide. The young man of the sequence is aware that the things "I have desired / Evade me, and the lucid majesty / That warmed the dull barbarian to life. / So I lie here, left with self-consciousness." One of Winters' mistakes in reading the sequence seems to have been a confusion of "self-consciousness" with solipsism. Within the sequence, the young man's books, his old neighbor who drives through rain and snow, the recollection of Hercules (though the young man does not try for the great task), and of his own father (a form of loss), and his view out the window of a Cherokee trail ("I see it, when I look up from the page"), all indicate the reality of the external world. The density of reference suggests the presence of the past, and the complexity of a man's perceptions. The young man is trying in this dark night, during these seasons of the soul, to understand his own past and thus his present. His old neighbor's driving in snow recalls to him his own driving in war:

> Was this our wisdom, simply, in a chance
> In danger, to be mastered by a task,
> Like groping round a chair, through a door, to bed?

Not many poets in the language could have written those lines. The verbal precision evokes deep resonance of response. His firm control, his stylistic brilliance permit Bowers a potentially dangerous ending for the sequence: it would be trite, after this night of darkness and cold to have the sunlight transform the room, so that even shadows become "substantial light." But like all masters, Bowers takes the potentially trite and makes it hugely moving. The man of the sequence survives:

>   I stay
> Almost as I have been, intact, aware,
> Alive, though proud and cautious, even afraid.

This ending is indicative of one of Bowers' strengths, as man and as poet: his refusal to be deceived, his almost desperate honesty.

The dramatic monologue "The Prince" is a major examination of what we term "German war guilt"; in it, familial relations become the vehicle for a poetic rendering of moral relations:

>   My son, who was the heir
> To every hope and trust, grew out of caring
> Into the form of loss as I had done,
> And then betrayed me who betrayed him first.

Likewise, in another fine poem, "From J. Hayden to Constanze Mozart (1791)," a verse letter expressing grief becomes a meditation on the rare fusion of mind and body, sense and reason that Mozart's music embodies: "Aslant at his clavier, with careful ease, / To bring one last enigma to the norm, / Intelligence perfecting the mute keys." These poems, along with "Amor vincit omnia" (the greatest poem on the theme of the Magi since Yeats's), "The Mountain Cemetery," and "The

Astronomers of Mont Blanc" are part of the enduring body of work that distinguishes Edgar Bowers' books. One can return to these poems as one returns to
Campion, Donne, or Landor: to clear one's sense of language. For in Bowers we
have a poet at once exact and exciting in his use of language. The word always fits
the sense; and the sense never exceeds what language is capable of doing:
"Whereof we cannot speak, thereof we must be silent."

– James Korges

BOYLE, Kay. American. Born in St. Paul, Minnesota, 19 February 1903. Edu-
cated at the Cincinnati Conservatory of Music; Ohio Mechanics Institute, 1917–19.
Married Richard Brault in 1923 (divorced); Laurence Vail, 1931 (divorced); Baron
Joseph von Franckenstein (died, 1963); has six children. Lived in Europe for 30
years. Foreign Correspondent, *The New Yorker* magazine, 1946–53. Professor of
English, San Francisco State College, 1963–72. Lecturer, New School for Social
Research, New York, 1962; Fellow, Wesleyan University, Middletown, Connecticut, 1963; Director, New York Writers Conference, Wagner College, New York,
1964; Fellow, Radcliffe Institute for Independent Study, Cambridge, Massachusetts, 1964–65; Writer-in-Residence, University of Massachusetts, Amherst,
1967, and Hollins College, Virginia, 1970–71. Recipient: Guggenheim Fellowship,
1934, 1961; O. Henry Award, for short story, 1935, 1941. D.Litt.: Columbia College, Chicago, 1971. Member, National Institute of Arts and Letters. Address: c/o
A. Watkins Inc., 77 Park Avenue, New York, New York 10016, U.S.A.

PUBLICATIONS

Verse

A Glad Day. New York, New Directions, 1938.
American Citizen: Naturalized in Leadville, Colorado. New York, Simon and
    Schuster, 1944.
Collected Poems. New York, Knopf, 1962.
Testament for My Students. New York, Doubleday, 1970.

Novels

Plagued by the Nightingale. New York, Smith, and London, Cape, 1931.
Year Before Last. New York, Smith, and London, Faber, 1932.
Gentlemen, I Address You Privately. New York, Smith, 1933; London, Faber,
    1934.
My Next Bride. New York, Harcourt Brace, 1934; London, Faber, 1935.
Death of a Man. New York, Harcourt Brace, and London, Faber, 1936.
Monday Night. New York, Harcourt Brace, and London, Faber, 1938.

Primer for Combat. New York, Simon and Schuster, 1942; London, Faber, 1943.
Avalanche. New York, Simon and Schuster, and London, Faber, 1944.
A Frenchman Must Die. New York, Simon and Schuster, and London, Faber, 1946.
1939. New York, Simon and Schuster, and London, Faber, 1948.
His Human Majesty. New York, McGraw Hill, 1949; London, Faber, 1950.
The Seagull on the Step. New York, Knopf, and London, Faber, 1955.
Generation Without Farewell. New York, Knopf, 1960.
The Underground Woman. New York, Doubleday, 1975.

Short Stories

Short Stories. Paris, Black Sun Press, 1929.
Wedding Day and Other Stories. New York, Smith, 1930; London, Faber, 1932.
The First Lover and Other Stories. New York, Random House, 1933; London, Faber, 1937.
The White Horses of Vienna and Other Stories. New York, Harcourt Brace, 1936; London, Faber, 1937.
The Crazy Hunter: Three Short Novels. New York, Harcourt Brace, 1940; as *The Crazy Hunter and Other Stories,* London, Faber, 1940.
Thirty Stories. New York, Simon and Schuster, 1946; London, Faber, 1948.
The Smoking Mountain: Stories of Post War Germany. New York, McGraw Hill, 1951; London, Faber, 1952.
Three Short Novels. Boston, Beacon Press, 1958.
Nothing Ever Breaks Except the Heart. New York, Doubleday, 1966.

Other

The Youngest Camel (juvenile). Boston, Little Brown, and London, Faber, 1939; revised edition, New York, Harper, 1959; Faber, 1960.
Breaking the Silence: Why a Mother Tells Her Son about the Nazi Era. New York, Institute of Human Relations Press-American Jewish Committee, 1962.
Pinky: The Cat Who Liked to Sleep (juvenile). New York, Crowell Collier, 1966.
Pinky in Persia (juvenile). New York, Crowell Collier, 1968.
Being Geniuses Together, with Robert McAlmon. New York, Doubleday, 1968; London, Joseph, 1970.
The Long Walk at San Francisco State and Other Essays. New York, Grove Press, 1970.

Editor, with others, *365 Days.* New York, Harcourt Brace, and London, Cape, 1936.
Editor, *The Autobiography of Emanuel Carnevali.* New York, Horizon Press, 1967.
Editor, *Enough of Dying! An Anthology of Peace Writings.* New York, Dell, 1972.

Translator, *Don Juan,* by Joseph Delteil. New York, Smith, 1931.
Translator, *Mr. Knife, Miss Fork,* by R. Crevel. Paris, Black Sun Press, 1931.
Translator, *Devil in the Flesh,* by Raymond Radiguet. New York, Smith, 1932; London, Grey Walls Press, 1949.

Acted as ghost-writer for the books *Relations and Complications: Being the Recollections of H. H. the Dayang Muda of Sarawak*, by Gladys Palmer Brooke, London, Lane, 1929, and *Yellow Dusk*, by Bettina Bedwell, London, Hurst and Blackett, 1937.

Manuscript Collection: Morris Library, Southern Illinois University Library, Carbondale.

Kay Boyle comments:

Although I have published over twenty books of short stories and novels, I consider myself primarily a poet.

[My poetry] is extremely personal in motivation and deals in the main with social and political problems. I have been influenced by William Carlos Williams, D. H. Lawrence, James Joyce, and Padraic Colum.

*   *   *

Kay Boyle has been an important novelist, short story writer, and poet since the expatriate generation of the 1920's, and her fiction and poetry have enriched one another. Perhaps the distinguishing formal characteristic of her poetry has been her emphasis upon the implied narrative occasion of most lyric poems. In her work this narrative framework, which incites the lyric response, has been handled in contrasting ways. In certain poems, and these extend throughout her career, the story-telling elements are deliberately made obvious to the point that the poems contain passages of both prose and verse, with the prose usually presenting more factual material and the verse intensifying it to poetic significance. The complex, macabre, and splendid "A Complaint for Mary and Marcel" is an arresting variation of this technique. The opposite method is also used. In these poems the narrative or plot elements are withheld but assumed, and the poems have the mysterious immediacy of overheard conversation. The poems, also characteristic of her work throughout, give an up-to-date, "coded" quality to her writing and seem to anticipate the work of such recent poets as James Merrill.

In content Miss Boyle's poems, taken as a whole, expand the personal emotion of private relationships toward a strong communal and political consciousness, with an accompanying stress upon the social role of the artist. Over the years she has focused her sensibilities and quiet outrage upon political injustice, from the victims of the Fascists to the problems of American students in the 1960's. But her point of view was and remains positive. There is a strong emphasis upon youth and death in her poetry, but her frequent use of images of nature, and the importance of spring and renewal in her work, point to a kind of informed Shelleyean optimism and place her in the mainstream of American romanticism. If her poetry is sometimes more effusive than current taste prefers, Kay Boyle represents nevertheless the testament of a committed artist to an active belief in the possibilities of a heightened human identity, which has been after all the great and underlying theme of poetry since its beginning.

– Gaynor F. Bradish

BRANDI, John. American. Born in Los Angeles, California, 5 November 1943. Educated at California State College, Northridge, B.F.A. 1965. Married Gioia Tama de Brandi in 1968; has two children. Member, Peace Corps, South America, 1965–68. Has exhibited paintings in the United States and Mexico. Recipient: *Portland State Review* Prize, for prose, 1971. Address: Box 356, Guadalupita, New Mexico 87722, U.S.A.

PUBLICATIONS

Verse

Poem Afternoon in a Square of Guadalajara. San Francisco, Maya Press, 1970.
Emptylots: Poems of Venice and LA. Bolinas, California, Nail Press, 1971.
Field Notes from Alaska. Bolinas, California, Nail Press, 1971.
Firebook. Virgin River, Utah, Smoky the Bear Press, 1974.

Short Stories

Desde Alla. Bolinas, California, Tree Books, 1971.
One Week of Mornings at Dry Creek. Santa Barbara, California, Christopher's Press, 1971.
Y Aun Hay Mas, Dreams and Explorations: New and Old Mexico. Santa Barbara, California, Christopher's Press, 1972.
Narrowgauge to Riobamba. Santa Barbara, California, Christopher's Press, 1973.

Other

San Francisco Lastday Homebound Hangover Highway Blues. Guadalupita, New Mexico, Nail Press, 1973.
A Partial Exploration of Palo Flechado Canyon. Guadalupita, New Mexico, Nail Press, 1973.
The Phoenix Gas Slam. Guadalupita, New Mexico, Nail Press, 1974.

Critical Study: by Moritz Thomsen, in the *San Francisco Chronicle,* April 1972.

John Brandi comments:

I am a poet, painter, and woodsman at heart, and support my family by carpentry jobs. I am concerned with the dream state, and subconscious as it operates in the wakened portion of reality. What I am talking about with my brush and crayons, my ink and pen, is that ghost, that shadow, of a man, a planet, a river, etc., which is somehow offset from its readily perceived image. I'm looking for that fragment of a world engulfed by dawn, by twilight, where landscape meets dreamscape. I want to bring back home that separate galaxy and show it off as a postcard from some place no longer on the map.

Desde Alla and *Narrowgauge to Riobamba* are two books akin to two separately painted panels translating the one-same diorama, that of isolated hamlets in the inter-mountain basins of the remote Andes where I spent a few years living with Quechua-speaking peasants.

Whenever I journey, I travel in two separate vehicles. One over the physical landscape, the other within the meta-physical. My writing and painting link the two spheres, migrating back and forth between inner and outer geographies.

That's what my books are about. They're geography books. Earth primers.

*   *   *

John Brandi ("born LA 1943 / first drawings at the age of four / . . . art folklore anthro scuba & taxidermy / BFA 1965 U of Cal Northridge / . . . 'rural community worker' Peace Corps 1966–68 Ecuador / Highland Andes Quechua Indian serfs & agrarian reform . . . Machu Picchu Mexico Chicago Dads Rootbeer Houston Yukon . . .") a native California hybrid seer, dreamer, wanderer, clown, chthonic tap-dancer, poet.

Artist and artisan.

A rare concoction like Blaise Cendrars or Vachel Lindsay or Henry Miller or Kerouac or John's *compadre* Dr. Jo-Mo (Fred Marchman) – writers whose works defy description or category and can only be understood by engagement with their writings.

Brandi is directed by a prolific creative energy which finds expression in a diversity of forms and sources. Gardener, herbalist. Built a house for himself and his lovely Argentine wife Gioia and their children Giovanna and Joaquin Coyote in New Mexico which is an amazement to be inside of or outside of. From an archaic hand-crank mimeograph machine (Rotary Neostyle Hand Mimeo) he produces enchanting books of poems, journals and lore which he often illustrates and then hand-colors. He keeps an illuminated journal whose water-color explorations of external and internal realities seem blessed by Blake and George Herriman. Shrine-maker, magician and chanter of on-the-spot drones and hymns that have been known to charm or alarm owls, racoons and frogs. Translator, journalist, outlaw scholar, iconographer. Woodsman, apprentice shaman, travel-logger.

Like many US gypsy artists he belongs everywhere and nowhere and maintains a fist-shaking citizen's rage against state and institutionalisms. He and his wife are resourceful and they manage to live from the land, growing the food they eat, bartering works and services for extras such as fuel for their kerosene lamps and fabrics for Gioia to transfer into raiment that seems to step out of John's fanciful drawings.

A major collection of his work is in the process of being assembled and will appear in the near future. This book, dealing primarily with his responses and experience as a Peace Corps worker, will make John Brandi's writings available to a larger audience who should, if I'm not mistaken, find his work irresistible.

– David Meltzer

BRATHWAITE, L. Edward. Barbadian. Born in Bridgetown, Barbados, 11 May 1930. Educated at Harrison College, Barbados; Pembroke College, Cambridge (Barbados Scholar), 1950–54, B.A. (honours) in history 1953, Cert.Ed. 1954; University

of Sussex, Falmer, 1965–68, D.Phil. 1968. Married Doris Monica Welcome in 1960;
has one son, Michael Kwesi. Education Officer, Ministry of Education, Ghana,
1955–62; Tutor, University of the West Indies Extra Mural Department, St. Lucia,
1962–63. Lecturer, 1963–72, and since 1972, Senior Lecturer in History, University
of the West Indies, Kingston. Plebiscite Officer in the Trans-Volta Togoland,
United Nations, 1956–57. Founding Secretary, 1966, Caribbean Artists Movement.
Since 1970, Editor, *Savacou* magazine, Mona. Recipient: Arts Council of Great
Britain bursary, 1967; Camden Arts Festival prize, London, 1967; Cholmondeley
Award, 1970; Guggenheim Fellowship, 1972; City of Nairobi Fellowship, 1972;
Bussa Award, 1973. Address: Department of History, University of the West
Indies, Mona, Kingston 7, Jamaica.

PUBLICATIONS

Verse

> *Rights of Passage.*   London, Oxford University Press, 1967.
> *Masks.*   London, Oxford University Press, 1968.
> *Islands.*   London, Oxford University Press, 1969.
> *Penguin Modern Poets 15,* with Alan Bold and Edwin Morgan.   London, Pen-
>   guin, 1969.
> *Panda No. 349.*   London, Royal Institute for the Blind, 1969.
> *The Arrivants: A New World Trilogy* (includes *Rights of Passage, Masks,
>   Islands*).   London, Oxford University Press, 1973.

> Recordings: *The Poet Speaks 10,* Argo, 1968; *Rights of Passage,* Argo, 1969.
> *Masks,* Argo, 1972; *Islands,* Argo, 1973.

Plays

> *Four Plays for Primary Schools* (produced Saltpond, Ghana, 1961–62).   London,
>   Longman, 1964.
> *Odale's Choice* (produced Saltpond and Accra, Ghana, 1962).   London, Evans,
>   1967.

Others

> *The People Who Came, 1–3* (textbooks).   London, Longman, 1968, 1969, 1972.
> *Folk Culture of the Slaves in Jamaica.*   London, New Beacon Books, 1970.
> *The Development of Creole Society in Jamaica.*   Oxford, Clarendon Press, 1971.
> *Caribbean Man in Space and Time.*   Mona, Jamaica, Savacou Publications,
>   1974.
> *Contradictory Omens: Cultural Diversity and Integration in the Caribbean.*   Mona,
>   Jamaica, Savacou Publications, 1974.

> Editor, *Iouanaloa: Recent Writing from St. Lucia.*   Castries, University of West
>   Indies Department of Extra-Mural Studies, 1963.

Bibliography: in *Savacou Bibliographical Series 2* (Mona, Jamaica), 1973.

Critical Studies: "The Poetry of Edward Brathwaite" by Jean D'Costa, in *Jamaica Journal* (Kingston), September 1968; *The Chosen Tongue* by Gerald Moore, London, Longman, 1969; "Brathwaite's Song of Dispossession" by K. E. Senanu, in *Universitas* (Accra), March 1969; "The Poetry of Edward Brathwaite" by Damian Grant, in *Critical Quarterly* (London), Summer 1970; "Dimensions of Song" by Anne Walmsley, in *Bim 51* (Bridgetown, Barbados), July-December 1970; "Three Caribbean Poets" by Maria K. Mootry, in *Pan-Africanist*, ii, 1, 1971; "This Broken Ground" by Mervyn Morris, in *New World Quarterly* (Kingston), v, 3. 1971; "Islands" by Gordon Rohlehr, in *Caribbean Studies* (Rio Piedras, Puerto Rico), January 1971; "Walcott versus Brathwaite" by Patricia Ismond, in *Caribbean Quarterly 17* (Kingston), September-December 1971; "A Study of Some Ancestral Elements in Brathwaite's Trilogy" by Samuel Asein, in *African Studies Association of the West Indies Bulletin 4* (Mona, Jamaica), December 1971; "Edward Brathwaite y el neoafricanismo antillano" by G. R. Coulthard, in *Cuadernos Americanos* (Mexico City), September-October 1972; "Odomankoma Kyerema se: A Study of Masks" by Maureen Warner, in *Caribbean Quarterly* (Kingston), June 1973.

Edward Brathwaite comments:

the texture and life-style of peoples: seen as dialectic of motion: history as achievement: failure: equilibrium / catastrophe
in this context we might try to understand the new world of the caribbean (the new world and the caribbean): what explosions occurred to create the symbolic fragments of continent: el dorado: lost atlantis: prospero's drowned island etc.
what caused the death of the amerindians: the holocaust of slavery: the birth of tom and caliban
in terms of my weltanschaung: my culture-view: it all began with the fall of the roman empire: this imperial achievement had created an equilibrium of material / spirit: metropole / province: law / chaos: which made possible a definition of values
with the decline and fall of rome: flux appeared: movements of magic into the metropole: custon replaced statute: gargoyle replaced statue
the vikings moved in fron the north: the goths, huns, magyars came on from the east: the crescent of islam curved north: african and aztec civilizations began to prophesy disaster
christianity (the holy roman empire) attempted to restore / retain the equilibrium but it was impossible: there were too many alternatives: there was mohamet: there were magi: there was the new science of copernicus, the natural philosophers, the medical school at salerno. there was a choice: galilee or galileo: emperor or pope: priest or politician
and then money became the centre of this shattered universe: market, bourg, bourse: commerce, ship, merchant, bank: middle class, taxes, nations, mercantilism: travel to new lands: control of new markets: the shift of authority outwards: supported by bullet and bible: but no prayer: but purse: not custom anymore, but curse
marco polo overland to china: the portuguese by stepping stone to africa: columbus to san salvador
moctezuma collapsed: chichen itza defeated: geronimo doomed: saskatchewa: mohican: esquimo and ewe whale-worshippers: timbucto, kumasi, ile-ife, benin city, zimbabwe
caribs moving towards malaria and syphilis: cherokees moving towards the horse, the weston rifle, the waggon train: ibo and naga to slave ships: zulus towards the locomotive tank: masai towards the jumbo jet, caliban to new york, paris, london town.

so that here in the caribbean we have people without (apparent) root: values of
whip, of bomb, of bottle: the culture of materialism, not equilibrium
food, flesh, house, harbour: not stone, demon, wilderness, space: extermination of
the arawaks
first 10, then 20
first 20, then 200
first 200 then 200,000 africans: slaves, lukumi, tears
200,000: 300,000: 400,000: a million: tears, tears, lukumi
1 million: 2 million: 3 million: 4 million: materialism building hotels, plantation
houses
10 million: 20 million: lukumi: lukumi: tears
30 million: 40 million: 50 million: we could go on counting: men: money: materialism: tears: tears: lukumi
the spaniards drained the lake of mexico away: the modern city sited in the dust
bowl
where are the bison of the prairies: leviathan of the pacific indians
where are those 50 million africans: without tongue, without mother, without god
can you expect us to establish houses here?
to build a nation here? where
will the old men feed their flocks?
where will we make our markets? (Masks, p. 21)
the history of catastrophe requires such a literature to hold a broken mirror up to
broken nature.

*   *   *

Edward Brathwaite's poetry has been extensively published in *Bim,* a Caribbean
journal, but it was with *Rights of Passage* that he achieved international recognition.
This long poem, the first of a trilogy, is an attempt to review the situation of the
black man in the Third World by appreciating what he has been able to create in
spite of centuries of exile.

The deracinated black has many faces. He is the pathetic Uncle Tom; the
dilettante who loses self and soul by acting out the role prescribed him in the white
world; the Rastafarian, prophet and pariah of Jamaican society, consumed by a
smouldering blend of love, despair, anger and hope for Apocalypse; the faceless
arriviste in his concrete and steel palace; Barbadian villagers gossiping about the
World War, an erupting volcano and the unexplainable sickness of the time; and
finally an archetypal Noah, father of Ham and grandfather of all travelling blacks,
who dreams of a new green day.

In technique, *Rights of Passage* suggests new dimensions for West-Indian Poetry. It
is the first sustained attempt to appropriate West Indian cadences and musical
rhythms for the purposes of poetry. More than this, Brathwaite tries, with fair and
sometimes marked success, to achieve the poetic equivalent of the worksong, blues,
jazz, calypso and Jamaican Ska. His aim is not to do in verse something much
better done in music, but to bring out the musical potential of words in the
rhythmic combinations suggested by various musical forms of the black.

Masks, the second poem in the trilogy, is an epic poem about the lost kingdoms of
Africa, and is essentially elegiac and grave in tone, where *Rights of Passage* was
cool, blue, detached and quietly ironic. In *Masks,* Brathwaite, who has lived in
Ghana, seeks reasons why the tribes disintegrated, and concludes that the African
too is guilty for what occurred. This makes him appreciate his own cultural
orphanage – "Whose brother now am I?" – and the futility of a sentimental
self-identification with Africa – "all beginnings end in this ghetto."

But *Masks,* like *Rights,* seeks positives, and asks what did the African create in spite of all; how did he transcend the eternal circle of journey, arrival, disaster and further journey. Brathwaite sees the dance as a form in which the African constantly reaffirms his unity with the earth and sky, and finds a self by abandoning his mask.

The tribal drum is the central symbol of *Masks.* Its very making is steeped in ritual, and intimations of sacrifice and redemption. "The goat must be killed and its skin stretched" before the drum releases its music. The history of the tribe is contained in the making of the drum. Like the drum the tribe's music, its rhythm, the inner essence of its life, will be released only after suffering and long acquaintance with death. *Masks* constantly shifts from meditation and prayer, to journey and exile, and returns to the dance, symbol of transcendence.

– Gordon Rohlehr

BRAUTIGAN, Richard. American. Born in Tacoma, Washington, 30 January 1933. Recipient: National Endowment for the Arts grant, 1968. Address: c/o Simon and Schuster Inc., 630 Fifth Avenue, New York, New York 10020, U.S.A.

PUBLICATIONS

Verse

The Return of the Rivers.   San Francisco, Inferno Press, 1957.
The Galilee Hitch-Hiker.   San Francisco, White Rabbit Press, 1958.
The Octopus Frontier.   San Francisco, Carp Press, 1960.
The Pill Versus the Springhill Mine Disaster (Poems 1957–1968).   San Francisco, Four Seasons Foundation, 1968; London, Cape, 1971.
Rommel Drives On Deep into Egypt.   New York, Dell, 1970.

Novels

In Watermelon Sugar.   San Francisco, Four Seasons Foundation, 1964; London, Cape, 1970.
A Confederate General from Big Sur.   New York, Grove Press, 1965; London, Cape, 1971.
Trout Fishing in America.   San Francisco, Four Seasons Foundation, 1967; London, Cape, 1970.
The Abortion: An Historical Romance 1966.   New York, Simon and Schuster, 1971.
The Hawkins Monster: A Gothic Western.   New York, Simon and Schuster, and London, Cape, 1974.

Short Stories

Revenge of the Lawn: Stories 1962–1970.   New York, Simon and Schuster, 1971; London, Cape, 1972.

*   *   *

The Pill Versus the Springhill Mine Disaster, his first collection of poems, confirmed for Richard Brautigan in poetry the same place *Trout Fishing in America* had won him in fiction. His work, characterized by spare form and cool reserve, is extremely popular on American college campuses, and he rates with Hesse and Tolkein as an underground literary favorite.

Brautigan's poems, like epitaphs, tell more about what's under them that about the man who carved the words. His work is popular, but not because of the easy sentimentality that distinguishes the poetry of other commercially successful "poets." In comparison to other best-sellers, Brautigan's books are refreshing; his poems have true intelligence, the dash of impeccable inspiration–imagination:

> When you take your pill
> it's like a mine disaster.
> I think of all the people
> lost inside of you.

That is the title poem in its entirety. We see the precision with which the mason has cut the words. His imagery is sharp and beautifully rendered, and when connected to something of consequence, especially memorable: he describes himself and a harbor "that does not know / where your body ends / and my body begins":

> Fish swim between our ribs
> and sea gulls cry like mirrors
> to our blood.
>
> > – from "The Harbor"

That final stanza, with its continued identity-suggestion of the mirrors, and the internal-tactile association of fish in the ribs, completes the suggestion of the poet's unity with his environment. The poem thus becomes a whole realization, a wonderfully understated acid trip.

Brautigan's second collection of poems, *Rommel Drives On Deep into Egypt,* continues in the same vein, but fewer poems strike such moments of brilliance. The title poem is as flashy as "The Pill . . . ," but significantly, it suggests a lighter view of consequence, reflective of the entire collection:

> Rommel is dead.
> His army has joined the quicksand legions
> of history where battle is always
> a metal echo saluting a rusty shadow.
> His tanks are gone.
> How's your ass?

This sort of vision is enticing because it suggests the ultimate powerlessness of the military. But it is not, I'm afraid, of much value to us of this world which can be powdered instantly by any of many frustrated generals. At times Brautigan's offhandedness becomes annoying, which I believe is ultimately less harmful than the seduction also occurring in *Rommel Drives On*. Four pages of the book are blank, except for titles at the top of the page: the first, on page two, works, but thereafter the joke begins to pale. Here are the four "poems," complete with titles, squeezed into less space than they claim in the book: "A 48-Year-Old-Burglar from San Diego"; "1891–1944"; "8 Millimeter (mm)"; " '88' Poems."

His cleverness, at this point, seems to work against him. Reading *Rommel Drives On,* I feel less and less that he is writing for me, an individual reader; more and more the poems seem aimed at an audience of semi-literate flower children. And I envision them thinking: this stuff's not deep enough.

Another possibility is that Brautigan's immersion in absurdity will not last forever, and that the flash will ignite a greater warmth. One cannot question his imaginative ability, nor the unpretentiousness of those poems consisting of more than a title. At the same time, one wishes that he would come to poetry with more commitment than that of a story teller anxious to dump his less-promising thoughts.

– Geof Hewitt

BREMSER, Ray. American. Born in Jersey City, New Jersey, 22 February 1934. Served in the United States Air Force. Married Bonnie Frazer in 1959; has one child. Served prison sentences for armed robbery, parole violation, and bail jumping.

PUBLICATIONS

Verse

Poems of Madness. New York, Paper Book Gallery, 1965.
Angel: The Work of One Night in the Dark, Solitary Confinement, New Jersey State Prison, Trenton. New York, Tompkins Square Press, 1967.
Drive Suite: An Essay on Composition, Materials, Reference, Etc. San Francisco, Nova Broadcast Press, 1968.
Beau Fleuve. Buffalo, New York, Intrepid Press, 1972.

*   *   *

The best of Ray Bremser's poetry is a celebration of life as it is lived by some of the denizens of our 20th Century cities, a wild, swinging (in the jazz sense) discourse on the ups and downs, and the joys and sorrows, of the streets and apartments and prisons which – in Bremser's case, at least – form such an integral part of the total experience. And it's fitting that the language of the poems is often as chaotic and colourful as the subject-matter, as varied and sometimes shocking as Bremser's own activities.

It is language which is the key factor in the poems, and it can move within a single stanza from a knowing patter redolent of street corners and jazz cellars and prison cells to an articulate imagery which displays a highly-developed awareness of the impact of the pure sound of words. And it is always rhythmic. It would not be absurd to suggest that Bremser's work is best read to a background of fast-moving jazz records.

In suggesting that his main attribute is a penchant for lively language one doesn't wish to play down his knowledge, unpolished and fragmentary though it may often be. He was once described as an "American primitive," and it is an accurate summing-up of his general position. One sees him as wandering through the city, occasionally involved in its quick pleasures, and then again capable of grassroots flashes of insight which highlight the pain and corruption also to be found there.

True, Bremser has certain basic faults. He can be tasteless, and his verbal trickiness can lead to passages which, rhythmic though they are, have little of substance in them. One accepts them in the context of the poems, just as one accepts tawdry advertisements found in parts of a city, but there is nothing to be learned from them. They are, to be fair, a part of the whole scene, but one moves on to more profitable things. Bremser's lapses should be ignored, if possible, and his less-frenetic expressions studied with care. When he succeeds he offers a personal view of life which, despite its limitations, is often more accurate and honest than that proposed by poets with seemingly-superior techniques.

– Jim Burns

BREW, O. H. Kwesi. Ghanaian. Born in Cape Coast, Ghana in 1928. Educated at schools in Cape Coast, Kumasi, Tamale and Accra; University College of the Gold Coast (now the University of Ghana). Entered the Administrative Service in 1953; Government Agent at Keta for nearly two years, then Assistant Secretary in the Public Service Commission. Now in the Ghana Foreign Service: has been Ambassador for Ghana to England, France, India, Germany, the U.S.S.R., and Mexico. Currently, Ambassador to Senegal. Recipient: British Council Prize. Address: c/o Foreign Office, Accra, Ghana.

PUBLICATIONS

Verse

The Shadows of Laughter: Poems.   London, Longman, 1968.
Pergamon Poets 2: Poetry from Africa, with others, edited by Howard Sergeant. Oxford, Pergamon Press, 1968.

Play

Screenplay: The Harvest.

*   *   *

Kwesi Brew has a much wider range, both of subject and style, than most of his African contemporaries, and over the years he has developed a voice inherently his own. He has written poems about childbirth ("Gamelli's Arm Has Broken into Buds"), childhood memories, youthful indiscretions, and middle-age reflections ("The Middle of the River"), as well as some of the most tender love poems to come out of Africa ("Flower and Fragrance," "The Two Finds," "The Mesh," etc.). Ghanaian folk song and customs are intricately woven into the tapestry of his poetry and since Brew has exceptional descriptive gifts the Ghanaian landscape and idiom come suddenly to life for non-African readers when he makes use of them, as he frequently does as a background element. If he has written about such specifically traditional subjects as ancestor-worship ("Ancestral Faces") and the passing of the fighting tribes ("Questions of Our Time"), he has not hesitated to deal with a recent event of great significance for his country – the downfall of President Nkrumah – in a poem entitled "A Sandal on the Head." In this fascinating poem, which appeared in *Outposts* shortly after the event it celebrates, Brew maintained a careful distance from his subject by employing an objective correlative appropriate to the situation in the Ghanaian custom of touching the head of a chief with one of his own sandals to declare him "de-stooled." "Ghost Dance," "The Master of the Common Crowd," "The Secrets of the Tribe," "A Plea for Mercy," "The Harvest of Our Life," and many other poems draw strongly upon the African way of life and present the conflict between old and new, between tribal instinct and national aspiration, and between the regional and the universal.

– Howard Sergeant

BREWSTER, Elizabeth (Winifred). Canadian. Born in Chipman, New Brunswick, 26 August 1922. Educated at the University of New Brunswick, Fredericton, B.A. 1946; Radcliffe College, Cambridge, Massachusetts, M.A. 1947; University of Toronto (Pratt Gold Medal and Prize, 1953), B.L.S. 1953; Indiana University, Bloomington, Ph.D. 1962. Cataloguer, Carleton University Library, Ottawa, 1953–57, and Indiana University Library, 1957–58; Member of the English Department, Victoria University, British Columbia, 1960–61; Reference Librarian, Mount Allison University Library, Sackville, New Brunswick, 1961–65; Cataloguer, New Brunswick Legislative Library, Fredericton, 1965–68, and University of Alberta Library, Edmonton, 1968–72; Visiting Assistant Professor of English, University of Alberta, 1970–71. Since 1972, Assistant Professor of English, University of Saskatchewan, Saskatoon. Recipient: Canada Council award, 1971. Address: Department of English, University of Saskatchewan, Saskatoon, Saskatchewan, Canada.

PUBLICATIONS

Verse

East Coast. Toronto, Ryerson Press, 1951.
Lillooet. Toronto, Ryerson Press, 1954.
Roads and Other Poems. Toronto, Ryerson Press, 1957.

Five New Brunswick Poets, with others, edited by Fred Cogswell.   Fredericton, New Brunswick, Fiddlehead, 1962.
Passage of Summer: Selected Poems.   Toronto, Ryerson Press, 1969.
Sunrise North.   Toronto, Clarke Irwin, 1972.
In Search of Eros.   Toronto, Clarke Irwin, 1974.

Novel

The Sisters.   Ottawa, Oberon Press, 1974.

Critical Study: "The Poetry of Elizabeth Brewster" by Desmond Pacey, in *Ariel* (Calgary, Alberta), July 1973.

*   *   *

"I have written poems principally to come to a better understanding of myself, my world, and other people," Elizabeth Brewster has explained. Her work does dramatize (again in her own words) "the struggle to lead a human rational life in a world which is increasingly inhuman and irrational."

This credo applies particularly to *Passage of Summer: Selected Poems*, which brings together the best poems of the New Brunswick-born writer's earlier collections. These poems are sometimes slight and always sentimental, celebrating as they do life in "one of its gentler moods" (as Miss Brewster wrote on one occasion). The poet's early memories are brought to life and given an overall structure in "Lillooet," a poem about a Maritime village written in twenty pages of rhyming couplets. The poem concludes:

> No matter where I live, my neighbour still
> Will be Miss Ruby Mullins or Peter Hill.

It is a moving experience to read "Lillooet," but it is not a particularly memorable work.

The poems of Miss Brewster's more recent book, *Sunrise North*, are less concerned with the past and more focused on the present and the future. They display to advantage a new facet of the poet's personality: a delightful, rather pixie-like, sense of humour. There is a poem called "Munchausen in Alberta" which ends: "That's the only time / I was ever a fire-eater." And in "Gold Man" she concludes: "Next time I am born / I intend to come / from a different country."

The forms of the new poems are all free and flowing, rather in the manner of Raymond Souster. They are Souster-ish, too, in that the lyric spirit takes off imaginatively from an anecdote or an incongruity observed by the poet. The poems are quiet but somewhat fanciful, as if the author has been freed to some extent from her earlier credo ("human *rational* life") and may now explore less rational realms of desire and imagination.

One does not expect Miss Brewster to turn into a Confessional poet, but she has become a truly contemporary poet. She is beginning to write more out of her personality, and it is interesting to note the last line of "Advice to the Fearful Self": "If necessary, scream." One wonders whether or not she will.

– John Robert Colombo

BRILLIANT, Alan. American. Born in St. Louis, Missouri, 22 May 1936. Educated at Columbia University, New York, B.A. 1959. Married Teo Savory, *q.v.*, in 1958. Publisher, *Pan* magazine, New York, 1956–58, and *Bread* magazine, Mexico, 1959. Since 1966, Co-Founding Director, with Teo Savory, Univorn Press, Santa Barbara, California, later Greensboro, North Carolina. Address: Unicorn Press, P.O. Box 3307, Greensboro, North Carolina 27402, U.S.A.

PUBLICATIONS

Verse

At Trial. Santa Barbara, California, Unicorn Press, 1969.
Searching for Signs. Santa Barbara, California, Unicorn Press, 1969.
Journeyman. Santa Barbara, California, Unicorn Press, 1970.

Other

Translator, *Selected Poems of Garcia Lorca.* Santa Barbara, California, Unicorn Press, 1969.

*   *   *

Alan Brilliant has published a collection of his poems, *Journeyman*, and has many translations to his credit including poems by Federico Garcia Lorca. I think of him, though, as a master craftsman first and a writer second. To see him in his essence, I believe you have to hold a Unicorn book in your hand.

The Unicorn Press, now located in Greensboro, North Carolina, is distinguished by the core of monastic souls who aid in its printing and gain satisfaction through the production of hand-crafted books rather than in actual money. Not only have there been poetry readings in the history of the press but also vigils and demonstrations against the Vietnamese war and repeated printings of *The Cry of Vietnam*.

– Glenna Luschei

––––––––––

BRINNIN, John Malcolm. American. Born in Halifax, Nova Scotia, Canada, 13 September 1916. Educated at the University of Michigan, Ann Arbor, B.A. 1941; Harvard University, Cambridge, Massachusetts, 1941–42. Associate Editor, Dodd Mead, publishers, New York, 1948–50. Taught at Vassar College, Poughkeepsie, New York, 1942–47, and at the University of Connecticut, Storrs, 1951–62. Director, YM-YWHA Poetry Center, New York, 1949–56. State Department Lecturer and Delegate in Europe in 1954, 1956 and 1961. Since 1961, Professor of English, Boston University. Recipient: Levinson Prize (*Poetry*, Chicago), 1943; Poetry Society of America Gold Medal, 1955; National Institute of Arts and Letters grant, 1968. Address: Duxbury, Massachusetts 02332, U.S.A.

PUBLICATIONS

Verse

> The Garden Is Political.   New York, Macmillan, 1942.
> The Lincoln Lyrics.   New York, New Directions, 1942.
> No Arch, No Triumph.   New York, Knopf, 1945.
> The Sorrows of Cold Stone: Poems 1940–1950.   New York, Dodd Mead, 1951.
> The Selected Poems of John Malcolm Brinnin.   Boston, Little Brown, and London, Weidenfeld and Nicolson, 1963.
> Skin Diving in the Virgins and Other Poems.   New York, Delacorte Press, 1970; London, Macmillan, 1974.

Other

> Dylan Thomas in America: An Intimate Journal.   Boston, Little Brown, 1955; London, Dent, 1956.
> The Third Rose: Gertrude Stein and Her World.   Boston, Little Brown, 1959; London, Weidenfeld and Nicolson, 1960.
> William Carlos Williams: A Critical Study.   Minneapolis, University of Minnesota Press, 1961.
> Arthur: The Dolphin Who Didn't See Venice (juvenile).   Boston, Little Brown, 1961.
> William Carlos Williams.   Minneapolis, University of Minnesota Press, 1963.
> Dylan.   New York, Random House, 1964.
> The Sway of the Grand Saloon: A Social History of the North Atlantic.   New York, Delacorte Press, 1971.

> Editor, with Kimon Friar, Modern Poetry: American and British.   New York, Appleton Century Crofts, 1951.
> Editor, A Casebook on Dylan Thomas.   New York, Crowell, 1960.
> Editor, Poems, by Emily Dickinson.   New York, Dell, 1960.
> Editor, with Bill Read, The Modern Poets: An American-British Anthology.   New York, McGraw Hill, 1963; revised edition, 1970.
> Editor, Selected Operas and Plays of Gertrude Stein.   Pittsburgh, University of Pittsburgh Press, 1970.
> Editor, with Bill Read, Twentieth Century Poetry, American and British (1900–1970): An American-British Anthology.   New York, McGraw Hill, 1971.

Critical Study: by the author, in Poets on Poetry, edited by Howard Nemerov, New York, Basic Books, 1965.

*   *   *

It is obvious enough that the surface of John Malcolm Brinnin's verse has caught something of the tone of both Dylan Thomas and of Theodore Roethke; but this has tended to mislead readers – especially at that level of discussion which, while it doesn't reach print, makes or mars reputations – from his own qualities. I doubt if he is a poet much actually read except in anthologies; and this is unjust. For, unlike Thomas (who was not an intellectual at all), and in a manner totally different from Roethke's, Brinnin works very hard, and with persistent intelligence, to control his verbally excited surface. This amounts to a method – not to an excess – and it is a method that is instructive. Whether it is entirely successful is another matter; but poetry, at much cost to the individual poet, thrives on failure. Brinnin is consistently interesting and serious: his poetry deserves to be better known than his famous *Dylan Thomas in America*, and this is not the case.

Brinnin is infinitely better educated than Thomas (which does sometimes add an unnecessary dimension of literary rhetoric to his work, but also gives it greater coherence) and less violently self-centred than Roethke. A better clue to the nature of his work, however, is to be found in his admiration of, and fine translation from, the poetry of the gifted Ecuadorian Jorge Carrera Andrade – who was one of the favourite poets of William Carlos Williams, on whom Brinnin has written a book. Andrade, who employed surrealism but was not a surrealist, learned much from the early poetry of Francis Jammes, and one of Brinnin's qualities is the possession of a Jammesian gentleness and melancholy. He thus has two distinct styles (his capacity for pastiche is a third that is avowedly less serious): the Bardic-religious, with overtones of Thomas, of which "The Worm in the Whirling Cross" is the most representative example, and a more pellucid, direct and humorous manner. There is no doubt that the latter comes more naturally to him; but the former is (and understandably) more ambitious. Thus, the language of "The Worm in the Whirling Cross" cannot quite match up to its highly complex content, and even falls back on Hopkins (a surprising fault in a poet already mature):

> No further, fathering logos, withering son,
> Shall I my sense for want of grace confess,
> But vouch this matter of decaying green
> That with a shark's-tooth grin
> Hinges the rooftree of my dwelling place. . . .

He is more effective, and in fact as profound, when he is less ambitious, as in "Architect, Logician," the little poem about a snail:

> Architect, logician, how well the snail
> Narrates his tenuous predicament!
> . . . .
> Each hauls his house; the trick's to live in it.

Brinnin's ultimate problem as a poet is the introduction of himself – as any kind of entity other than a literary one – into the work: he seems not to exist in his poems, to evade the quality of his own feeling. This strategy sometimes does, of course, reveal the poetic personality, and one may point to him as a composer of very superior literary artifacts. But poetry requires something more, and here Brinnin (so far) has only shown himself in a few, and too widely dispersed, lines.

– Martin Seymour-Smith

BROCK, Edwin. British. Born in London, 19 October 1927. Educated at state primary and grammar schools. Served in the Royal Navy, 1945–47. Married Patricia Brock in 1959 (marriage dissolved, 1964); Elizabeth Brock, 1964; has three children. Editorial Assistant, Stonhill and Gillis, London, 1947–51; Police Constable, Metropolitan Police, London, 1951–59; Advertising Writer, Mather and Crowther,

1959–63, J. Walter Thompson, 1963–64, and Masius Wynne-Williams, 1964, all London; Creative Group Head, S. H. Benson, London, 1964–72. Since 1972, Free-lance Writer, Ogilvy Benson and Mather, London. Since 1960, Poetry Editor, *Ambit* magazine, London. Agent: David Higham Associates Ltd., 5–8 Lower John Street, Golden Square, London W1R 4HA. Address: 13 Finch Way, The Street, Brundall, Norfolk, England.

PUBLICATIONS

Verse

An Attempt at Exorcism.   London, Scorpion Press, 1959.
A Family Affair: Two Sonnet Sequences.   London, Scorpion Press, 1960.
With Love from Judas.   Lowestoft, Suffolk, Scorpion Press, 1963.
Penguin Modern Poets 8, with Geoffrey Hill and Stevie Smith.   London, Penguin, 1966.
Fred's Primer: A Little Girl's Guide to the World Around Her.   London, Macmillan, 1969.
A Cold Day at the Zoo.   London, Rapp and Whiting, 1970.
Invisibility Is the Art of Survival: Selected Poems.   New York, New Directions, 1972.
The Portraits and the Poses.   London, Secker and Warburg, and New York, New Directions, 1973.
Paroxisms.   New York, New Directions, 1974.
I Never Saw It Lit.   Santa Barbara, California, Capra Press, 1974.

Plays

Radio Play: *Night Duty on Eleven Beat*, 1960.

Television Play: *The Little White God*, 1964.

Novel

The Little White God.   London, Hutchison, 1962.

Manuscript Collection: State University of New York, Buffalo.

Critical Studies: *The New Poets* by M. L. Rosenthal, New York, Oxford University Press, 1967; Introduction by Alan Pryce-Jones to *Invisibility Is the Art of Survival*, 1972.

Edwin Brock comments:

One of the more embarrassing chores foisted by publishers upon their writers is that of writing the autobiographical note for the book's jacket; writing an introduction to one's work runs it a very close second. On one such jacket-note I said recently that I have spent the years since 1927 waiting for something to happen, and that poetry is the nearest thing to an activity I have yet found. This statement was not as flip as it sounds: I believe that most activity is an attempt to define oneself in one way or another: for me poetry, and only poetry, has provided this self-defining act. With such an attitude, it was inevitable that my early poetry would be autobiographical; and, indeed, there is still an autobiographical core to most of my writing. But self-examination is an open-ended process: there comes a point at which if one is to "make" or define oneself, one has first to make or define a Maker. It is this which provided the content of most of my recent work. "Consequently I rejoice, having to construct something / Upon which to rejoice," said the maestro, and this seems, to me, to be a role of the artist. If this sounds a self-centred, non-communicating attitude for a writer, I would add that it is only when the process of defining/making/constructing results in something which has an objective "shareable" reality that it becomes exciting – both for the writer and the reader.

So far, critics have traced the following influences in my work: Dylan Thomas, Robert Graves, Philip Larkin, Edmund Blunden, Ted Hughes, Thomas Hardy, and William Blake. To find a common factor in that lot, you have to be . . . another critic!

*   *   *

The style of Edwin Brock's poetry is very much that of the man, so a public reading by Brock is revealing in the way that few other poets' readings are. Although his poems are always well made, Brock's technique is closer to the extemporised or projective method of some Americans than to the iambic and syllabic norms usual in England. He has been classified as a confessional poet, but he is so only in the religious sense. His first collection was entitled *An Attempt at Exorcism,* and Brock has remained faithful to the personal view revealed there. He recalls the past half as a fallen Christian and half as a worldly masochist, so that lyricism and harshness are accommodated in the same work.

Marriage is the home base of his poetry. In his first book, he celebrated its quotidian order – life among the parks and responsibilities of South London. But his domestic scenes were always likely to be surprised by the magical levitations of love and childhood. His most important book to date, *With Love from Judas,* is the obverse of *An Attempt at Exorcism* and is his report from the destruction of his marriage. In "A Last Poem to My Wife," he daringly identifies her perishable love with the death of God: the poem ends:

> Soon you will return to your belief in witches,
> but there will be no need to burn you:
> nobody may live long with the cancer of a dying god.
>
> I shall place pennies on your eyes, and call
> the creature up from your open mouth –
> and ask permission for your body to be in consecrated ground.

Brock's personal experience of the minutiae of the fallen world (he has worked in the police and in advertising) gives strength to his underlying mysticism. Recently, he has developed successfully a talent for writing on public issues. He brings great authenticity to this, owing to his habit of particularising and referring back to his own experience. One of his finest poems of this order is "Song of the Battery Hen." Brock identifies himself with the poor sedated birds in their pens:

> I have the same orange-
> red comb, yellow beak and auburn
> feathers, but as the door opens and you
> hear above the electric fan a kind of
> one-word wail, I am the one
> who sounds loudest in my head.

The poem ends with these desolate lines:

> God made us all quite differently,
> and blessed us with this expensive home.

Although couched in popular form, Brock's recent poetry is among the most intensely felt of its time.

– Peter Porter

BROMIGE, David (Mansfield). Canadian. Born in London, England, 22 October 1935. Educated at Haberdashers' Aske's School for Boys, London; University of British Columbia, Vancouver, B.A. 1962; University of California, Berkeley (Woodrow Wilson Fellow, 1962–63; Poet Laureate Competition prize, 1964; Phelan Award, 1968), M.A. 1964. Married Ann Livingston in 1957 (divorced, 1961); Joan Peacock, 1961 (divorced, 1970), one son; Sherril Jaffe, 1970. Dairy farm worker, 1950–53; mental hospital attendant, 1954–55; elementary school teacher, in England, 1957–58, and in British Columbia, 1959–62; free-lance reviewer, Canadian Broadcasting Corporation, 1960–62; Instructor in English, University of British Columbia, Summer 1964. Teaching Assistant, 1965–69, and Instructor in English, 1969–70, University of California, Berkeley. Since 1970, Assistant Professor of English, California State College, Sonoma. Editor, *Raven* magazine, 1960–62; Poetry Editor, *Northwest Review*, Eugene, Oregon, 1963–64; Editor, *R.C. Lion*, Berkeley, 1966–67. Recipient: Canadian Broadcasting Corporation prize, 1961; KVOS-TV prize, for play, 1962; Canada Council grant, 1965, 1966, and bursary, 1971; National Endowment for the Arts grant, 1969. Address: 880 First Street, Sebastopol, California 95472, U.S.A.

PUBLICATIONS

Verse

The Gathering. Buffalo, New York, Sunbooks, 1965.
Please, Like Me. Los Angeles, Black Sparrow Press, 1968.
The Ends of the Earth. Los Angeles, Black Sparrow Press, 1968.

The Quivering Roadway. Berkeley, California, Archangel Press, 1969.
In His Image. Berkeley, California, Twybyl Press, 1970.
Threads. Los Angeles, Black Sparrow Press, 1971.
The Fact So of Itself. Los Angeles, Black Sparrow Press, 1971.
They Are Eyes. San Francisco, Panjundrum Press, 1972.
Birds of the West. Toronto, Coachhouse Press, 1973.
Tight Corners and What's Around Them. Los Angeles, Black Sparrow Press, 1974.
Ten Years in the Making. Vancouver, New Star Books, 1974.

Plays

Radio and Television Plays: *Palace of Laments,* 1957; *The Medals,* 1959; *The Cobalt Poet,* 1960; *Save What You Can,* 1961.

Short Stories

Three Stories. Los Angeles, Black Sparrow Press, 1973.

David Bromige comments:

Primary among my associations in the field of poetry is the work of Robert Creeley, Charles Olson, and Robert Duncan – particularly Duncan – and therefore those poets they draw on, and those who share certain terms of the poem with the three named. But I use whatever I can, I can see, wherever.

I would sooner not state what, to my mind, are my major themes, preferring to leave that up to the reader. Again, he will be the best judge of my so-called stylistic devices – though I would draw attention to the note at the end of my book *The Ends of the Earth.* I have no usual verse forms, although no doubt patterns are apparent; certainly I love rime as passionately as I deplore (unless that *is* the concern of the specific poem) a mindless regularity of meter.

I am not interested in poetry as vehicle for ideas but rather as speech arising from dumb desire and passion and arousing further word clusters until constellations emerge I had previously no knowledge were within me. Nor, in a sense, were they: speaking, we enter a Speech, and though we may think we sit each in his aloneness, yet the words which then enter bear news of others; I was not born with that vocabulary, nor were those who, reading my poems, make of them something more than I could ever plan to give. In the instant when I had assumed I had understood certain linguistic and philosophical arguments intended to destroy faith in language – "we must all be talking about a different place," one recent poet put it – I found their flaw. Seekers after "the truth" who, in order to keep clear their minds, would dismiss much that is imagination's creation, choose not to see the prior act of their own imaginations which have created so singular a notion of the truth.

I believe a poet is one both by birth and nurture; I don't believe that everyone can be a poet; nor can I see why anyone should *want* to be. There are obsessions which weigh less heavily and constantly upon a life. This is no request for gratitude. One is what one is and is used accordingly. However, there are poets who, because they wrote, and published, have enabled me to go on living; that is enough for me.

*   *   *

179

David Bromige's work comes out of Black Mountain via the Vancouver nexus of poets around the magazine *Tish*. His dissertation (in progress) is on Duncan and Creeley, but already in his first book, *The Gathering*, he had written some of the best Creeley criticism I know – criticism in the form of poems which elucidate Creeley's techniques by intelligent adaptation. There was more to the book than this, of course – among other things the first workings in an area of subject matter he has continued to mine, personal erotic-psychological experience, and long narrative-based poems which have also continued. Less elusively than many of Creeley's, Bromige's poems too, even when they do subsume a narrative element, always locate their action on the page, not in some anterior "real" world. Always, too, they have more than one kind of interest: feeling, tone, music, logopoeia, and (a particular strength of his) a rapidly eliding muscular syntax which keeps pace with the mind's play rather than imposing too neat an order on a linguistic end-product. The results are invigorating and delightful. I wish I could quote several poems to show his range – from *The Gathering*: "She Rose Up Singing" for its lovely music, "We Could Get a Drink" for its energetic use of an Olson-like open structure, and "The Sign" for its humor; from *The Ends of the Earth*: "A Call" and "Forgets Five" as short and long examples of his convincing dream poems, and "A Kind Numbness" for its tender and traditional imagery (interestingly – and oddly – comparable to Larkin's "At Grass"); and from *Threads*: "For –" with its erotic tribute to the muse-goddess. And many others. Space being limited, here is one short piece to give a glimpse of his wit:

> "I can see arguments for both sides"
> how impressive this intelligence
> where will its weight be placed –
> in this scale here
> in that scale here . . .

– Seamus Cooney

BROOKS, Gwendolyn. American. Born in Topeka, Kansas, 17 June 1917. Educated at Wilson Junior College, Chicago, graduated 1936. Married Henry Blakely in 1939; has two.children. Publicity Director, NAACP Youth Council, Chicago, in the 1930's. Taught at Northeastern Illinois State College, Chicago, Columbia College, Chicago, and Elmhurst College, Illinois. Distinguished Professor of the Arts, City College, City University of New York, 1971. Editor, *The Black Position* magazine. Recipient: Guggenheim Fellowship, 1946, 1947; National Institute of Arts and Letters grant, 1946; Eunice Tietjens Memorial Prize (*Poetry*, Chicago), 1949; Pulitzer Prize, 1950; Anisfield-Wolf Award, 1968. L.H.D.: Columbia College, 1964; D.Litt.: Lake Forest College, Chicago, 1965; Brown University, Providence, Rhode Island, 1974. Poet Laureate of Illinois, 1969. Address: 7248 South Evans Avenue, Chicago, Illinois 60619, U.S.A.

PUBLICATIONS

Verse

A Street in Bronzeville. New York, Harper, 1945.
Annie Allen. New York, Harper, 1949.
Bronzeville Boys and Girls. New York, Harper, 1956.
The Bean Eaters (verse for children). New York, Harper, 1960.
Selected Poems. New York, Harper, 1963.
In the Time of Detachment, In the Time of Cold. Springfield, Illinois, Civil War Centennial Commission of Illinois, 1965.
In the Mecca: Poems. New York, Harper, 1968.
For Illinois 1968: A Sequecentennial Poem. Chicago, Illinois Sesquecentennial Commission, 1968.
Riot. Detroit, Broadside Press, 1969.
The Wall. Detroit, Broadside Press, n.d.
Family Pictures. Detroit, Broadside Press, 1970.
Aloneness. Detroit, Broadside Press, 1971.

Novel

Maud Martha. New York, Harper, 1953.

Other

A Portion of That Field, with others. Urbana, University of Illinois Press, 1967.
The World of Gwendolyn Brooks (miscellany). New York, Harper, 1971.
Report from Part One: An Autobiography. Detroit, Broadside Press, 1972.

Editor, *A Broadside Treasury.* Detroit, Broadside Press, 1971.
Editor, *Jump Bad: A New Chicago Anthology.* Detroit, Broadside Press, 1971.

*   *   *

Gwendolyn Brooks, whose poetry has earned her Guggenheim fellowships and the Pulitzer Prize for Poetry is one of America's most imaginative and accomplished poets. Her work paints and sings the songs and griefs of Chicago, largely of those who have been made to feel: "The fact that we are black is our ultimate reality." But she makes the minority's reality the world's reality. "The Bean Eaters," like a Cezanne or a Van Gogh, achieves a real universality. "The Woman-hood" is alive with a parent's suffering wonder for those "who are adjudged the leastwise of the land / Who are my sweetest lepers, who demand / No velvet . . . ." asking the terrible and difficult question "What shall I give my children?", how "ratify my little halves who bear / Across an autumn freezing everywhere"? She writes of the envy of the mistreated for the rich:

> We say ourselves fortunate to be driving by today.
> That we may look at them, in their gardens where
> The summer ripeness rots. But not raggedly.
> Even the leaves fall down in lovelier patterns here.
> And the refuse, the refuse is a neat brilliancy.

In "A Lovely Love" and "To Be in Love" she has written with sweet power of love's desperation, and she is familiar in other poems with its cruelties. Clearly, her work derives its strength from a sense of values that can be defended: she does not distort with the emotional rhetoric of euphemism or sentimentality, nor does she become shrill in her hatreds. One feels that her lines make people, streets, and songs come alive without advertising them – even when she deals, as in "A Catch of Shy Fish" and "Gay Chaps at the Bar," with subjects that invite standard distortions.

For all this, and more, she has received some praise. "Anyone who has a real heart-hunger for poetry ought to know Gwendolyn Brooks. She is original. Her imagery is startling," Marjorie Holmes has truthfully written, and Paul Engle has noted that "she marvellously balances between the merely savage and the merely sentimental. Her eye is candid, as aware of the gay sun as it is of the malevolent midnight. . . ." But there is a quality in her language that has not really been noted, a deeper, more imaginative penetration with the word, rare in America, recalling Stevens. And, as with Stevens, the ingenuity thrives with satire. In "The Lovers of the Poor" Gwendolyn Brooks uses language powerfully to treat what is, of course, more complicated than hypocrisy. The ladies turn at last away from the smells and real rats of the Ghetto, hoping to find

> Some serious sooty half-unhappy home! –
> Where loathe-love likelier may be invested.
> Keeping their scented bodies in the center
> Of the hall as they walk down the hysterical hall,
> They allow their lovely skirts to graze no wall,
> Are off at what they manage of a canter,
> And, resuming all the clues of what they were,
> Try to avoid inhaling the laden air.

Only the close investigation of her choice of individual words reveals the full genius here, not merely the talent of a protest poet, the achievement of a Pulitzer Prize, but much more. She has been faithful to life as well as to poetry, an art that so often strays far from life. And her power so far exceeds that of many who are riding high on a kind of critical combine run away with itself that it is necessary to direct the reader to her work. She writes with the empty eye Yeats commended, accepting life's flatness and rejecting its phony miracles, finding real ones where they are neglected and despised. She is, in short, one of the most *objective* poets writing in the United States. We feel, after reading her work, that we know where the hearts are breaking, where the tears are falling, and we know our own short-comings in not going to relieve that misery. The poet seems to know hers too, and can only advise: "Conduct your blooming in the noise and whip of the whirlwind."

– David Ray

BROUGHTON, James (Richard). American. Born in Modesto, California, 10 November 1913. Educated at Stanford University, California, B.A.; New School for Social Research, New York. Married to Suzanna Broughton; has two children, Serena and Orion. Worked in the merchant marine. Lecturer, San Francisco State College, and San Francisco Art Institute. Director, Farallone Films. Recipient: Phelan Award, 1948; Avon Foundation grant, 1968; Guggenheim Fellowship, 1970, 1973; film awards in Edinburgh, 1953, Cannes, 1954, and Oberhausen, 1968. Address: P.O. Box 183, Mill Valley, California 94941, U.S.A.

PUBLICATIONS

Verse

Songs for Certain Children. San Francisco, Adrian Wilson, 1947.
The Playground. San Francisco, Centaur Press, 1949.
The Ballad of Mad Jenny. San Francisco, Centaur Press, 1950.
Musical Chairs: A Songbook for Anxious Children. San Francisco, Centaur Press, 1950.
An Almanac for Amorists. Paris, Olympia Press, 1954; New York, Grove Press, 1955.
True and False Unicorn. New York, Grove Press, 1957.
The Water Circle: A Poem of Celebration. San Francisco, Pterodactyl Press, 1965.
Tidings. San Francisco, Pterodactyl Press, 1967.
Look In Look Out. Eugene, Oregon, Toad Press, 1968.
High Kukus. Highlands, North Carolina, Jargon, 1969.
A Long Undressing: Collected Poems 1949–1969. Highlands, North Carolina, Jargon, 1971.

Recording: The Bard and the Harper, MEA, 1965.

Plays

A Love for Lionel (produced New York, 1944).
Summer Fury (produced Palo Alto, California, 1945). Published in The Best One-Act Plays of 1945, edited by Margaret Mayorga, New York, Dodd Mead, 1946.
Burning Questions (produced San Francisco, 1958).
The Last Word. Boston, Baker, 1958.
The Rites of Women (produced San Francisco, 1959).
Bedlam; or, America the Beautiful Mother (produced Waterford, Connecticut, 1969).

Other plays: The Condemned Playground, 1946; How Pleasant It Is to Have Money, 1964.

Films: The Potted Psalm, 1946; Mother's Day, 1948; Adventures of Jimmy, 1950; Four in the Afternoon, 1951; Loony Tom the Happy Lover, 1951; The Pleasure Garden, 1953; The Bed, 1968; Nuptiae, 1969; The Golden Positions, 1970; This Is It, 1971; Dreamwood, 1972; High Kukus, 1973; Testament, 1974.

Other

The Right Playmate. London, Hart Davis, and New York, Farrar Straus, 1952; revised edition, San Francisco, Pterodactyl Press, 1964.

James Broughton comments:

Although I have done as much work in theater and cinema forms as I have in pure verse, I consider myself first and foremost a poet, for all my work is motivated by a poet's view and attitude. I have been associated with various San Francisco groups since 1949, but I do not belong to any school of poetry.

The greatest influences upon my poetry: Bach, Blake, Mother Goose, Shakespeare, Stravinsky, Yeats, Joyce, Firbank, Stein, and folk song.

Fellow poets who have personally taught me the most: Auden, Cummings, Robert Duncan, Dylan Thomas.

Poetry is a search for essence, becomes an essence, remains an essential.

The poet has to allow everything to happen to him, or he can make nothing happen. The poet has to let go in order to hold on.

A poet is in the service of something larger than his personal life, his craft, or his published works. Poetry is an act of love, it asks no rewards.

To live poetically is more important than to write good poems.

Poetry may be a criticism of life, as Arnold said, but life triumphs over all criticism.

Poetry is a quest for liberation. But it must be limited in order to be liberated. A poem is a uniqueness defined by its limitations.

A poem is a stone, a wind, a glass of water, a fire on the plain.

Writing the poem is not difficult except that the poet must know and must now know what he is doing. Poets are both more irrational and more conscious than other human beings.

Without joy there is no wonder, and without wonder there is no magic, and without magic there is no poem.

A book of poems is a seed catalogue, a tarot pack, a package of dynamite, a menu for gourmets, a field of stars, a map of the sea floor.

A poem can be about anything if it is not about anything but itself.

Poetry is always both sense and nonsense: the sense in nonsense, and the nonsense of sense.

There is an enormous difference between art and self-expression.

Poetry is a confessional, but it is also an altar. It is a vessel of transformation, it is the host and the communion cup. But it is also the fly on the windowpane.

Poetry is impersonal about the personal, personal about the non-personal, and personally transpersonal.

A poem is, was, and will be. It is of the present only if it is connected to the past and to the future. A contemporary poem needs some fragrance of the ancient, an echo of the primordial, a taste of the everlasting: otherwise it has no parents nor progeny.

A poem can be what it always is when it can become what it already was. "Attain the inevitable!"

Poets are defined by businessmen, as everything is defined by its opposite. And opposites always need each other, else there is no wholeness nor texture.

In school time learn, in love time sing, in wisdom ripen. Allness is ripe.

> Do you ever hear it?
> Do you know
>   what your voice is
> Listen!   always singing?
>
>   It sings
>   (like everything)
> as if no song
>   were ever sung before like
> It   this
>   is the song you have been singing
>   all your life.

*   *   *

James Broughton has always been considered a San Francisco poet, though as he says himself he has ranged over the world both as traveler and as artist. In the years after the second World War – during what was called the San Francisco poetry renaissance – he and, among many others, Kenneth Rexroth and Weldon Kees, were at the center of San Francisco's creative life, and his plays and films were as widely known as his poetry. He approaches life with a sensitive, often outraged humanism that expresses itself in poems that are sometimes angry and hard, dense and difficult, but with a surface simplicity that leads the eye into the poem, even when there is no sureness as to where it's being led. He is brought up against the cruel reality of the modern world time and time again. "Did you ever try embracing a hangman?" he asks in one poem. At best he allows himself a bare, dangerous optimism. You can almost feel him walking a grim, trembling tight rope when he lets himself hope:

> I stopped where I stepped, sleep I dared not,
> I waited awake – then was banged overside
> by shepherd that grew utter beast on a cord.

Often his imagery centers on innocent animals, as often on the death and corruption of the body and the flesh. It is poetry of emotional thrusts and hard questioning, that always comes back again to his anger at the ferocity of the world around him, because it is love that he wants to return to. Wherever he begins, whatever he forces himself, and us, to look at, he returns again and again to the place he has described as

> where the birth and the death and the life are one
> and the last word I speak is Love.

– Samuel Charters

BROWN, George Mackay. British. Born in Stromness, Orkney, Scotland, 17 October 1921. Educated at Stromness Academy; Newbattle Abbey College; Edinburgh University, M.A. 1960. Recipient: Arts Council Award, 1966; Society of Authors Travel Award, 1968; Scottish Arts Council Literature Prize, 1969, and award, 1971; Katherine Mansfield Menton Short Story Prize, 1971. O.B.E. (Officer, Order of the British Empire), 1974. Address: 3 Mayburn Court, Stromness, Orkney, Scotland.

PUBLICATIONS

Verse

The Storm. Orkney, Orkney Press, 1954.
Loaves and Fishes. London, Hogarth Press, 1959.
The Year of the Whale. London, Hogarth Press, 1965.
The Five Voyages of Arnor. Falkland, Fife, K. D. Duval, 1966.
Twelve Poems. Belfast, Festival Publications, 1968.

Fishermen with Ploughs: A Poem Cycle. London, Hogarth Press, 1971.
New and Selected Poems. London, Hogarth Press, 1971.
Lifeboat and Other Poems. Crediton, Devon, Gilbertson, 1971.
Penguin Modern Poets 21, with Iain Crichton Smith and Norman MacCaig. London, Penguin, 1972.
Poems New and Selected. New York, Harcourt Brace, 1973.

Plays

Witch (produced Edinburgh, 1969). Included in *A Calendar of Love,* 1967.
A Spell for Green Corn (broadcast, 1967; produced Edinburgh, 1970). London, Hogarth Press, 1970.
Loom of Light (produced Kirkwall, 1972).

Radio Play: *A Spell for Green Corn,* 1967.

Television Plays: Three Stories from *A Time to Keep,* 1969; *Orkney,* 1971.

Novels

Greenvoe. London, Hogarth Press, 1972; New York, Harcourt Brace, 1973.
Magnus. London, Hogarth Press, 1973.

Short Stories

A Calendar of Love. London, Hogarth Press, 1967; New York, Harcourt Brace, 1968.
A Time to Keep. London, Hogarth Press, 1969; New York, Harcourt Brace, 1970.
Hawkfall and Other Stories. London, Hogarth Press, 1974.
The Two Fiddlers (juvenile). London, Chatto and Windus, 1974.

Other

An Orkney Tapestry. London, Gollancz, 1969.

Manuscript Collections: Scottish National Library, Edinburgh; Edinburgh University.

George Mackay Brown comments:

Themes: mainly religious (birth, love, death, resurrection, ceremonies of fishing and agriculture). Verse forms: traditional stanza forms, sonnets, ballads, *vers libre,* prose poems, runes, choruses, etc. Sources and influences: Norse sagas, The Bible, Catholic rituals and ceremonies.

*   *   *

Born and bred in the Orkney Islands, where he still lives, and a convert (since 1961) to Catholicism, George Mackay Brown has always expressed in his work, both verse and prose, his insight into the communal customs and the individual characters of the Orkney people, and his appreciation of the significance and power of religious myth and symbol. In his first book, *The Storm*, these themes are treated separately – in "Orcadians," a sequence of character-sketches written in a free verse which sometimes fails to avoid the prosaic in its attempt to achieve vernacular simplicity, and in "Saint Magnus on Egilsay," where the measured blank verse and the images of arrested action show the influence of Edwin Muir – while in many of the best of his later poems he contrives to combine them and thereby to enhance both. At the same time, his voice has become unmistakably his own, without the echoes of Yeatsian lyricism or Muirish mythologising or Dylan Thomas organ-intoning which mar the earlier work, although he often achieves a singing directness not unworthy of Yeats, a legendary richness not inferior to Muir, and a verbal resonance not less remarkable than Thomas.

While most of his poems are intensely local, he neither sees nor presents his characters as provincial oddities – as queer fish in an island backwater – but always as individual souls enshrined in the flesh of Orkney fishermen and farmers, and the implications of their dreams and deeds, pursuits and passions, have width as well as depth of relevance. Again, his fascination with Orkney's patron saint, Magnus, martyred in the 12th century, has led to a concern with the whole of island history and a consequent enrichment of his work through the interplay of past and present. His themes, perhaps inevitably with a religious poet living in a small community in close contact with the fields and the fishing-grounds, are the fundamental ones of work and worship, growth and decay, death by land and water, the interweaving of love and lust between man and woman, and, under and above, and through them all, the divine mercy. His emotional range is considerable, not only from poem to poem but also within a single creation, moving from religious ecstasy to wry realisation of human weakness in "Our Lady of the Waves," from melancholy acceptance of the inevitability of death to grateful appreciation of the inexhaustible richness of life in "The Year of the Whale." Many of the poems are dramatic, and such is the writer's sensitivity to the feelings of others that he can speak through the mouth of Harald, the agnostic ale-drinking shepherd, with as much sympathetic understanding as when he wears the mask of a medieval abbot, while "Ikey on the People of Hellya" is as comically revealing about the character of the speaker, a thieving tramp, as about those of the people whom he plunders. Mackay Brown's style, at its best, is superbly simple, combining conciseness with clarity in phrases which are both functional and fine.

His most recent work, however, makes demands which some readers may be unable to meet. In the "New Poems" section of *Poems New and Selected*, while the scene occasionally lies beyond Orkney, the balance between past and present which is a notable feature of his earlier collections has swung decisively towards the historical, and many of the poems seem to emanate from a kind of medieval religious dream, beautiful and delicate, but remote from any actuality experienced by the contemporary reader, while others express a Viking paganism equally distant from present feeling. His "poem cycle" *Fishermen with Ploughs*, presenting a mythical "history" of Orkney, shows that the other balance in his work, between ritual and reality, is also in danger of tipping over into what begins to appear as an almost-obsessive concern with the mystical. Until now, because of his comprehension of everyday individuals and events, Mackay Brown has retained the imaginative sympathy of non-Catholic readers, even when denied their intellectual assent, but such sympathy may wane if his work continues to be increasingly concerned with ritualism. Yet the best of his new poems, even when they spring from the same old ground (or ancient ocean) as their predecessors, are written with as much cunning of evocation as ever.

– Alexander Scott

BROWN, Wayne. Trinidadian. Born in Trinidad, 18 July 1944. Educated at the University of the West Indies, Kingston, Jamaica, 1965–68, B.A. (honours) in English 1968. Married Megan Hopkyn-Rees in 1968. Staff Journalist, 1963–65, Art Critic, 1970–71, *Trinidad Guardian*; Schoolteacher, Jamaica, 1969, Trinidad, 1970–71. Recipient: Jamaican Independence Festival Poetry Prize, 1968; Commonwealth Poetry Prize, 1972. Address: Whitehill End, Green Lane, Ockham, Woking, Surrey, England.

PUBLICATIONS

Verse

On the Coast. London, Deutsch, 1972.

Critical Studies: "Coming to Terms with Major Issues of Modern West Indies" by Lee Johnson, *Trinidad Sunday Guardian*, 25 February 1973; "In Cold Rage," in the *Times Literary Supplement* (London), 4 May 1973; "Marine Depths" by John Carey, in *London Magazine*, June 1973; "Below the Surface" by Mervyn Morris, in the *Sunday Gleaner* (Kingston, Jamaica), 16 September 1973.

*   *   *

Wayne Brown is outstanding amongst West Indian poets, even considered in the context of so good an anthology as Andrew Salkey's *Breaklight*. Brown's *On the Coast* confirms the impression that he is capable of sophisticated and powerful original statements, as in the remarkable "Soul on Ice" with its flow of un-Jamaican imagery and unexplained, but totally communicative, exclamations: an assured, moving projection of personal, local dilemmas into terms that can form the objective correlative for quite other pressures and yet, of course, by that very fact, make real to the reader experiences he may never know more directly. Brown is already a poet who can use his art as a means of, in Solzhenitsyn's words, performing "the miracle of overcoming man's characteristic weakness of learning only by his own experience, so that the experience of others passes him by."

– Anne Cluysenaar

BROWNE, Michael Dennis. British. Born in Walton-on-Thames, Surrey, 28 May 1940. Educated at St. George's College, Weybridge, Surrey; Hull University, 1958–62, B.A. (honours) in French and Swedish 1962; Oxford University, 1962–63, Cert. Ed. 1963; University of Iowa, Iowa City (Fulbright Scholar, 1965), 1965–67, M.A. in English 1967. Visiting Lecturer in Creative Writing, University of Iowa, 1967–68; Adjunct Assistant Professor, Columbia University, New York, 1968–69;

Member of the English Department, Bennington College, Vermont, 1969–71. Since 1971, Assistant Professor, University of Minnesota, Minneapolis. Recipient: Hallmark Prize, 1967. Address: Department of English, University of Minnesota, Minneapolis, Minnesota 55455, U.S.A.

PUBLICATIONS

Verse

The Wife of Winter.   London, Rapp and Whiting, and New York, Scribner, 1970.
The Sun Fetcher.   1974.

Plays

How the Stars Were Made (cantata for children), music by David Lord (produced Farnham, Surrey, 1967).   London, Chester, 1967.
The Wife of Winter (song cycle), music by David Lord (produced Aldeburgh, Suffolk, 1968).   London, Universal Editions, 1968.
The Sea Journey (cantata for children), music by David Lord (produced Farnham, Surrey, 1969).   London, Universal Editions, 1969.
Nonsongs, music by David Lord.   London, Universal Editions, n.d.

Michael Dennis Browne comments:

Since my first book, I have become very interested in material very dangerous and pretentious, and maybe also essential, for a young writer to approach. Writers like Jung (always), Erich Neumann, Joseph Campbell. I am finally reading The Golden Bough. . . . I come to this material by way of my dreams, which have presented me with images of such power I have had to follow them out into contexts much larger than my own individual life. I hope that I will always write poems which are lyrical, vivid, and happy; I want also to find forms, find the music, for the deeper motions I find beginning to move in myself. I hope, as does any poet who plans to grow, to be able to make larger and more visionary discoveries and statements in my work. But I love clarity in poetry and hope to keep my work, in the best sense, clear. I am also beginning to write fables, children's stories, where there are few rhetorical comforts, and all that is required of the writer is invention!
Finally, I am excited by the landscapes I am beginning to see. Whether or not I can reach them, I do not know.

*   *   *

Michael Dennis Browne is a poet of hard, surprising images. The clarity and suddenness of imagery make real the dreams that fill The Wife of Winter: the order of reality is successfully inverted and the crazy world of the dream is the real, the normal, and not at all nightmarish.

Browne's voice affirms with a kind of joy – although there is a sardonic edge to the war poems and the Michael Morley sequence; he dreams and sings in face and spite of some nameless, abstract things which underlie the world of the poems:

> And you can forget the poems
> that have run away from you in horror
> like headless birds in the dark
> you have not quite killed,
>
> because in this house and place
> there are good fresh ghosts,
> there are small & near ones here.

The poems are not preoccupied with traditional "themes" and grand ideas ("The Terrible Christmas"), but focus on the naming of things to create his world. He praises a woman, because

> When the king of ideas advanced through the wood
> you fed him an image and he went away.

Another woman, the speaker of the excellent title sequence, the "Wife of Winter," finds that waking and the morning are

> Dark. A new dark. I am dropped
> from the high claw of a dream. Fox
>
> retrieves me, wolf waits.
> Who is the owl with wings of snow?
> And where is my eagle now?
> He is not here, my lady they cry.

Browne leaps past prose with recurring, angry eagles, apples, Fox, snow, images which may attain the symbolic in much the same way that Roethke – one of Browne's strongest influences – created symbols. Browne has learned much from Roethke. It is readily apparent in his rhythms and the song-like quality of many of his poems, even in an occasional image, but Browne's own voice remains clear.

– Joseph Wilson

BROWNJOHN, Alan (Charles). British. Born in Catford, London, 28 July 1931. Educated at Brownhill Road School, London; Brockley County School, London; Merton College, Oxford, 1950–53, B.A. 1953, M.A. 1961. Married Shirley Toulson, *q.v.*, in 1960 (divorced, 1969), has one son; Sandra Willingham, 1972. Wandsworth Borough Councillor, London, 1962–65. Labour Party Parliamentary Candidate, Richmond, Surrey, 1964. Since 1965, Senior Lecturer in English, Battersea College of Education, London. Since 1968, Poetry Critic, *New Statesman*, London. Member, Arts Council Literature Panel, 1968–72. Address: 2 Belsize Park, London N.W.3, England.

PUBLICATIONS

Verse

Travellers Alone. Liverpool, Heron Press, 1954.
The Railings. London, Digby Press, 1961.
The Lions' Mouths. London, Macmillan, and Chester Springs, Pennsylvania, Dufour, 1967.
Oswin's Word (libretto for children). London, BBC Publications, 1967.
Woman Reading Aloud. Oxford, Sycamore Press, 1969.
Being a Garoon. Frensham, Surrey, Sceptre Press, 1969.
Sandgrains on a Tray: Poems. London, Macmillan, and Chester Springs, Pennsylvania, Dufour, 1969.
Penguin Modern Poets 14, with Michael Hamburger and Charles Tomlinson. London, Penguin, 1969.
A Day by Indirections. Frensham, Surrey, Sceptre Press, 1969.
Brownjohn's Beasts (for children). London, Macmillan, and New York, Scribner, 1970.
Synopsis. Frensham, Surrey, Sceptre Press, 1970.
Frateretto Calling. Frensham, Surrey, Sceptre Press, 1970.
Transformation Scene. London, Poem-of-the-Month Club, 1971.
An Equivalent. Rushden, Northamptonshire, Sceptre Press, 1971.
Warrior's Career. London, Macmillan, 1972.

Other

To Clear the River (novel for children, as John Berrington). London, Heinemann, 1964.
The Little Red Bus Book. London, Inter-Action, 1972.

Editor, *First I Say This: A Selection of Poems for Reading Aloud.* London, Hutchinson, 1969.
Editor, with Seamus Heaney and Jon Stallworthy, *New Poems 1970-1971.* London, Hutchinson, 1971.

Manuscript Collection: Manor House Library (Lewisham Public Library), London.

Critical Studies: Review by Peter Porter, in *London Magazine,* October 1969; *The Society of the Poem* by Jonathan Raban, London, Harrap, 1971; by Roger Garfitt, in *British Poetry since 1960,* edited by Michael Schmidt and Grevel Lindop, Oxford, Carcanet Press, 1972.

Alan Brownjohn comments:

In consulting with Peter Digby Smith, the publisher of my first hardback volume of verse, *The Railings,* I evolved for the dust-jacket the simple statement "Poems concerned with love, politics, culture, time."

I think this still defines the themes of my verse, with one or other of these four dominant at different moments. But they all, of course, intersect and interrelate: states of politics or culture affect the values of love; love and time constantly stare at one another, amused, shame-faced or fatalistic; time watches politics rise to honourable humane achievement, or decline into vanity.

I've come to some recent conclusions about the language, tone and temperament of my poetry which critics might confirm; or contradict. Although I am quietly, but very seriously, atheist, socialist and internationalist, it's the English-ness of what I write that strikes me most as I look back at it – the use of language, the attitudes rehearsed, the codes of honour and styles of reticence employed. I don't feel like making apology for this, because I greatly admire certain English puritan values and feel that English rationalism, democracy and humanity would be our best post-imperial contribution to the world at large; the vehicle for transmission of these values being the English language.

Every poet would like to feel he was writing for, communicating to, the world; and if I ever succeed in doing that, in any thing at all, I'd like to feel it was in the above terms, and transmitting the above values. "The world," incidentally, is not the European Economic Community.

*   *   *

Though the subject matter of Alan Brownjohn's poetry ranges widely, taking in such traditional themes as love and childhood, it is the expression of his concern for social issues that marks his poetry out as specially his own. A recent poem, "Knightsbridge Display Window," ends:

> Sometimes perhaps we'll get
> A commonwealth of sense, and not with guns.

The poem aims, Brownjohn tells us in an explanatory piece in the magazine *Ambit*, "at a kind of cheerful democratic puritanism." An ideal not without a degree of paradox; but that may well be in the nature of all ideals. In his first collection *The Railings* Brownjohn's concern can be seen from the beginning as very much a poet's concern:

> Don't look for hunger or disease before
> You blame a country. Stop and listen, now,
> For the unquestioned currency of talk
> Its people handle.
>   – from "Whose Highest Dreams"

A standpoint from which a society is to be judged by the quality of life it reflects. In his second collection *The Lions' Mouths* this concern is pursued, and we find that while it is compassionate it is, nevertheless, allied to an uncompromising critical faculty. "Why shouldn't they do as they like?" asks the "Fool-libertarian voice" in the poem "A Hairdressers." "No," the poet replies, "I can't wish I were as liberal as that."

In all Brownjohn's poetry there is the same sharp mind probing and enquiring. The poem "For a Journey" explores the significance of what at first seems an unlikely subject, the naming of country fields: "Topfield," "Third field," and the like, to conclude:

> Who knows what could become of you where
> No one has understood the place with names?

Indeed, this need for Brownjohn to analyse is reflected in the language he uses. On occasion it can become as complex as the line of thought he pursues:

> It is with metaphor
> We can assuage, abolish and
> Create. I will apologise
> With metaphors:

he writes in "Apology for Blasphemy," and the tendency is for such poetry to become too abstract both in content and form. Yet in *Sandgrains on a Tray,* Brownjohn's third collection, we find him successfully combating this, and developing a clarity and directness which give an added strength and purpose to his work. These poems pursue his social themes via those "creatures" of the urban landscape: a television set left on in a shop window, a major road, or abandoned motor cars. It is very much a territory Brownjohn is making his own, where these objects are related to their surroundings and then to us. The poem "A202" is a good example of this where he concludes:

> It only means well in the worst of ways
> How much of love is much less compromised?

In his latest collection, *Warrior's Career*, poems such as "Ode to Centre Point" and "A Politician" see him making his points much more directly, and a new, more personal, element is to be observed emerging in the section of love poems this volume contains. Brownjohn is clearly one of our best social poets; he is also a continually developing one.

– John Cotton

BROWNSTEIN, Michael. American. Born in Philadelphia, Pennsylvania, 25 August 1943. Educated at Antioch College, Yellow Springs, Ohio; New School for Social Research, New York. Recipient: Poets' Foundation Grant, 1966; Fulbright Scholarship, 1967; Frank O'Hara Award, 1969. Address: 33 St. Mark's Place, New York, New York 10003, U.S.A.

PUBLICATIONS

Verse

Behind the Wheel. New York, "C" Press, 1967.
Highway to the Sky. New York, Columbia University Press, 1969.
Three American Tantrums. New York, Angel Hair Books, 1970.

Novel

Country Cousins. New York, Braziller, 1974.

Short Stories

Brainstorms: Stories. Indianapolis, Bobbs Merrill, 1971.

*   *   *

Highway to the Sky, Michael Brownstein's first collection, is cryptic, elliptical, ironic, witty, occasionally symbolic or surreal; it's also inbred and a bit smart-assed. "Genius," he says, is "to eat and mumble in peace." His poems about poetry are not the usual jejune praise:

> Life is beautiful.   However
>
> The only truly human, American expressions
>   of its staggering rich moments
>   (two baby bulldogs in open window, 3:17 a.m.)
> Aren't really forms of expression like language, but
>
> The only truly human, American expressions
>   of its staggering rich moments
>   (two baby tomatoes in open window, 3:17 a.m.)
> Aren't really forms of expression like language, but
>
> Parallels manifesting themselves right alongside
> Those moments, like music.

Brownstein is his most brilliant when he concentrates on what something represents or, that horrid word, "symbolizes." "The method must be purest meat, and no symbolic dressing," Ginsberg says, speaking for many of his generation. In his usual weird tone, Brownstein deadpans agreement with this Beat and Black Mountain formula:

> A naturalist witnessing the scene begins to weep
> for joy. A small child of either sex joins him:
>   it's a tableau, simple and real.
>   No "symbols," no straining after a meaning
> that wasn't there in the beginning, obvious to all,
>   before the first walrus appeared . . .

His assent is mitigated by that last line and the gratuitously bizarre and generalized "small child of either sex." Brownstein's second book, in fact, consists of prose poems of mythic, symbolic and even (cf. Empson) ambiguous import. "The Overcoat," for instance, contrasts the political and sexual implications of a preference for overcoats over t-shirts. In "Who Knows Where the Time Goes" a mythy figure of magic asks the persona of the poem more and more curious questions till finally the persona wearily indicates he's merely a Bowery bum giving a good rap for his dime. The stone outlaw seems tougher and more impassive than the other outlaws in his gang till it transpires, finally, that he is a literal statue. Brownstein's recent work in fiction suggests that though he struck a tone in poetry, for its blossoming he needs the larger forms of prose.

– Michael André

BRUCE, George. British. Born in Fraserburgh, Aberdeenshire, Scotland, 10 March 1909. Educated at Fraserburgh Academy; Aberdeen University, M.A. (honours) in English. Married Elizabeth Duncan in 1935; has one son, David, and one daughter, Marjorie. Taught English and history, Dundee High School, 1933–46. General Programmes Producer, Aberdeen, 1946–56, and since 1956, Documentary Talks Producer, BBC, Edinburgh. Recipient: Scottish Arts Council award, 1968, 1971. Address: 25 Warriston Crescent, Edinburgh 3, Scotland.

PUBLICATIONS

Verse

Sea Talk. Glasgow, Maclellan, 1944.
Selected Poems. Edinburgh, Oliver and Boyd, 1947.
Landscapes and Figures: A Selection of Poems. Preston, Lancashire, Akros, 1967.
The Collected Poems of George Bruce. Edinburgh, Edinburgh University Press, 1970.

Play

To Scotland, With Rhubarb (produced Edinburgh, 1965).

Other

Scottish Sculpture, with T. S. Halliday. Dundee, Findlay, 1946.
Anne Redpath. Edinburgh, Edinburgh University Press, 1974.

Editor, The Exiled Heart: Poems 1941–1956, by Maurice Lindsay. London, Hale, 1957.
Editor, with Edwin Morgan and Maurice Lindsay, Scottish Poetry One to Six. Edinburgh, Edinburgh University Press, 1966–72.
Editor, The Scottish Literary Revival: An Anthology of Twentieth Century Poetry. London, Collier Macmillan, and New York, Macmillan, 1968.

Manuscript Collections: State University of New York, Buffalo; National Library of Scotland, Edinburgh.

Critical Studies: The Scottish Tradition in Literature by Kurt Wittig, Edinburgh, Oliver and Boyd, 1958; The Scots Literary Tradition by John Spiers, London, Faber, 1962.

George Bruce comments:

I belong, I suppose, to the current Scottish Literary Revival, though I believe I owe nothing in style to any of my Scottish contemporaries. I have learned the craft of verse especially from Ezra Pound.

From about 1941 to 1953 the main subject-matter was life in a sea town and the environment of that life. The approach was definitive rather than descriptive: I was concerned to establish the extraordinary nature of the case, that people continued to believe in life and to make a particular thing of it in circumstances that might have warranted despair; but then should one not despair in any case of human life which is, *ipso facto,* precariously placed between light and dark.

I came to this subject when the war seemed to confirm by its explicit outrage on human dignity the evidence of␣Eliot's *The Waste Land.* In these circumstances I found myself – for I did not seek to do so – making a statement in verse about the establishing of life on a minimal basis. I noted the fishermen whose lives were almost continuously threatened by the life giving and killing element from which they drew their livelihood. To their adaptation to, and acceptance of, their situation they added an ␣apparently unreasonable belief in a personal God. I could not identify myself with their attitudes, nor with them. But in looking with particularity at them the sense of a separate existence came home at a time when the word "object' was almost meaningless to me. I had found an "objective correlative."

I proceeded to apply a craft of verse that I had learned from Ezra Pound, particularly from *Mauberley,* with, as far as I could, clinical exactness. Just as much of my country was mere rock so my language should be, so the rhythms short and vigorous. When I applied my ear to what I had written I found the tone and accent and articulation of the words and sentences related more closely to the manner of speech of the community in which I had been brought up (and to some extent continued about me, for I believe there is a tendency in educated Scottish speech, in English, to certain general characteristics) than to the implied accent of Pound or to the speech of Southern England. A strong emphasis on consonants and a high articulation is characteristic. In my more successful poems of this period I think these elements are present. This was a point of beginning. All my poems were in English.

Then I became increasingly interested in the idea of order. That aspect of nature I knew best, and the irregular characteristics of growth itself threatened order. My poem about St. Andrews, "A Gateway to the Sea," is written as an exposition on the order of a mediaeval town which embodies theological concepts of order in its structure, an order that is threatened by men and by the ravages of the sea. This interest is subordinated in several poems to a rejoicing in the irregularity and variety of creation. It is easy enough to accept that variety as one looks back in history; it is more difficult to accept when the force of life expresses itself in what appears to be brashness and vulgarity. This is the main concern of my poem *Landscapes and Figures.*

As my poetic interests widened I came to use a longer line but to incorporate short lines for incantatory or dramatic purposes. Recently I have included Scots in my poems as the voice of a *persona,* using the same brief rhythms as I did many years ago in English.

*   *   *

The term "regional poet" can either mean a minor writer who celebrates his locality with a certain amount of enthusiasm and charm, or a writer who uses the sights and smells and sounds of his native district as imaginative material for containing problems and predicaments that· are humanity's. It is in this second, good sense, that George Bruce is the poet of the North Eást of Scotland, with its cold farm-lands, its rugged cliffscapes, and its dour and tenacious fishermen.

That tenacity, that necessary continuing belief in life at its basic food-winning level during the early years of the second World War, inspired some of the poems in Bruce's first book, *Sea Talk.* His technique he learned to some extent from Eliot, though principally from Pound, especially *Mauberley*. But the tone and timbre of the application of that technique are very much his own, relating to those durable qualities among which he had been brought up. "Just as much of my country was mere rock," the poet has explained, "so my language should be, so the rhythms short and vigorous." Comparing the graciousness which allowed Gothic spires to flourish in wind-swept Balbec and Finistère with the granite knuckle-thrust where the Buchan fisherman has his being, Bruce exclaims:

> To defend life thus and so to grace it
> What art! but you, my friend, know nothing of this,
> Merely the fog, more often the east wind
> That scours the sand from the shore,
> Bequeathing it to the sheep pasture,
> Whipping the dust from fields,
> Disclosing the stone ribs of earth –
> The frame that for ever presses back the roots of corn
> In the shallow soil. This wind,
> Driving over your roof,
> Twists the sycamore's branches
> Till its dwarf fingers shoot west,
> Outspread on bare country, lying wide.
> Erect against the element
> House and kirk and your flint face.

Just as the relentless action of wind and waves has shaped his coastline, so pat generations have moulded his North East character:

> This which I write now
> Was written years ago
> Before my birth
> In the features of my father.
>
> It was stamped
> In the rock formations
> West of my hometown.
> Not I write
>
> But perhaps, William Bruce,
> Cooper. . . .

The poet's words become

> . . . the paint
> Smeared upon
> The inarticulate.

Against this backcloth of the elements, Bruce sets the hero, determinedly going about his business, doing what needs to be done:

> The short man waves his hand,
> Half turns, and then makes off.
> He is going to the country. . . .

Such experiences, as Kurt Wittig has remarked, spring from specific moments of the poet's personal life, and are "explained in very personal symbols (such as the curtain half way up the stairs) and seen in flashes of very personal and momentary observation.''

Perhaps because of the role of impresario to other poets which Bruce's post as a BBC Producer has imposed on him, he has published all too little. Twenty-three years lie between *Sea Talk* and *Landscape and Figures*. By the second collection, the range and power of the verse has deepened. There is still the hero, ''a man of inconsequent build,'' his

> Odyssey the trains between
> Two ends of telephone . . .

He is still

> . . . the small man
> With broad pale brow lined deep as if the pen
> Held tight in hand had pressed its ink
> In strokes.

There are also clear, objective recollections of the details of childhood, as in the much-praised ''Tom.'' In one part of this sequence, ''Tom on the Beach,'' the poet asks himself:

> How many years since with sure heart
> And prophesy of success
> Warmed in it
> Did I look with delight on the little fish,
>
> Start with happiness, the warm sun on me?
> Now the waters spread horizonwards,
> Great skies meet them,
> I brood upon uncompleted tasks.

Now Bruce occasionally uses Scots, though usually only for special colloquial effects in the counterpart of his verse's rugged music. Henry Moore's sculpture, the impact of distant wars through the television screen and the experience of an Italian sojourn have given him new thematic material. When eventually a fuller collection of Bruce's work is published, though there will undoubtedly be surprises and fresh riches discovered, I doubt if anything will surpass ''A Gateway to the Sea,'' his elegy for the changelessness of change. The ''gateway'' leads to ruined St. Andrew's Cathedral, where once there was living gossip:

> . . . Caesar's politics.
> And he who was drunk last night;
> Rings, diamants, snuff boxes, warships,
> Also the less worthy garments of worthy men!

Here once:

> The European sun knew these streets
> O Jesu parvule; Christus Victus: Christus Victor.
> The bells singing from their towers, the waters
> Whispering to the waters, the air tolling
> To the air – the faith, the faith, the faith.

But:

> All that was long ago. The lights
> Are out, the town is sunk in sleep . . .

198

And yet:

> Under the touch the guardian stone remains
> Holding memory reproving desire, securing hope
> In the stop of water, in the lull of night.
> Before dawn kindles a new day.

I know of no other "regional" poet whose treatment of the oldest and most Universal theme of all is as powerfully affecting as Bruce's in this poem. The voice is Scottish, but the words are warmed into poetry by a European mind.

– Maurice Lindsay

BRUTUS, Dennis (Vincent).   British (South African).   Born in Salisbury, Rhodesia, 28 November 1924. Educated in South Africa at Paterson High School; Fort Hare University, Alice, B.A. in English 1947; Witwatersrand University, Johannesburg, 1963–64. Married May Jaggers in 1950; has eight children. High school teacher and journalist for 14 years. Served 18 months in Robben Island Prison, for opposition to apartheid, 1964–65. Left South Africa in 1966. Director, Campaign for Release of South African Political Prisoners, London, 1966–71; Staff Member, International Defence and Aid Fund, London, 1966–71. Visiting Professor, University of Denver, 1970. Since 1971, Professor of English, Northwestern University, Evanston, Illinois. Visiting Professor, University of Texas, Austin, 1974–75. Since 1959, Secretary, South African Sports Association; since 1963, President, South African Non-Racial Olympic Committee; since 1972, Chairman, International Campaign Against Racism in Sport. Recipient: Mbari Prize, 1962. Address: 18 Hilton Avenue, London N.12, England; or, 1501 Gaston Avenue, Austin, Texas 78703, U.S.A.

PUBLICATIONS

Verse

Sirens, Knuckles, Boots: Poems.   Ibadan, Mbari, 1963; Evanston, Illinois, Northwestern University Press, 1964.
Letters to Martha and Other Poems from a South African Prison.   London, Heinemann, 1968.
The Denver Poems.   Denver, University of Denver, 1969.
Poems from Algiers.   Austin, University of Texas, 1970.
Thoughts Abroad (as John Bruin).   Del Valle, Texas, Troubadour Press, 1971.
A Simple Lust: Collected Poems of South African Jail and Exile.   London, Heinemann, and New York, Hill and Wang, 1973.

Manuscript Collection: Northwestern University Library, Evanston, Illinois.

Critical Studies: Introduction to African Literature by Ulli Beier, Evanston, Illinois, Northwestern University Press, 1967; Who's Who in African Literature by Janheinz Jahn, Tübingen, Germany, Horst Erdman Verlag, 1972; African Authors by Herdeck, Washington, D.C., Black Orpheus Press, 1973; The Black Mind by O. R. Dathorne, Minneapolis, University of Minnesota Press, 1974.

Dennis Brutus comments:

A lyrical poet: "protest" elements are only incidental, as features of the South African scene obtrude. Favourite poets: John Donne, Wallace Stevens. Others: Browning, Hopkins, Eliot, Pound, Patchen, Rexroth, Lowell.

*   *   *

It is hardly surprising that the earliest poetry of Dennis Brutus should be marked by expressions of anger, bitterness and frustration, and that the images employed in his poems should be taken direct from his South African environment:

> investigating searchlights rake
> our naked unprotected contours . . .
>
> under jackboots our bones and spirits crunch . . .
>
> police cars cockroach through the tunnelled streets . . .

Brutus has, in fact, been criticized on this score by some West African critics, but surely it is understandable that a young poet in his situation, living in a police state and constantly harassed by the authorities for his anti-apartheid activities, should feel the need to express himself in such direct terms, rather than through the medium of a polite literary language acceptable to those who have not shared his experience. To know his poetry is to know the man. As he said in a speech at a conference held in Stockholm in 1967, "I am not concerned with how a man expresses his involvement: I am desperately concerned that he should."

Brutus was born of South African parents in Rhodesia. After graduating from Fort Hare University College he took up a teaching post at Port Elizabeth; but, as President of the South African Non-Racial Olympic Committee, his protests against racialism in sport and his campaign for the exclusion of South Africa from the Olympic Games soon brought him into conflict with the authorities and he was barred from teaching. He was arrested in 1963 and escaped while still on bail, and though he possessed a Rhodesian passport, the Portuguese Secret Police in Mozambique handed him over to the South African Security Police. He was shot down while attempting to escape again and on recovery was sentenced to eighteen months hard labour at the notorious Robben Island. His first book, *Sirens, Knuckles, Boots*, was published by Mbari while he was in prison. He wrote the poems of his second book, *Letters to Martha*, after his release from prison but during the period in which he was not allowed to write anything of a publishable nature, so that his poems had to be devised as "letters" to his sister-in-law. He would be a curious poet indeed if this experience was not reflected in his work.

Nevertheless, if Dennis Brutus has expressed his rage at times his craftsmanship has been apparent from the beginning. In "Erosion: Transkei" he uses the subject – the erosion of the land – as an objective correlative and describes his own feelings, so that the poem has meanings at more than one level. Examples of his method of interweaving image and idea can be found in poem after poem, and he frequently deploys language in a new and significant way. Take, for instance, the poem "This Sun on This Rubble":

> – sun-stripped perhaps, our bones may later sing
> or spell out some malignant nemesis
> Sharpevilled to spearpoints for revenging
> but now our pride-dumped mouths are wide
> in wordless supplication
> – are grateful for the least relief from pain
> – like this sun on this debris after rain.

The coinage here, "Sharpevilled," is more than a clever gimmick, and in its context, "Sharpevilled to spearpoints for revenging" is extremely apt, adding tremendous power to what is being said. In other poems he writes of "Saracened arrest," "quixoting," etc. But there is always anger beneath the surface of the poem, finding its way even into the most tender of his love poems:

> we found a poignant edge to tenderness,

> and, sharper than our strain, the passion
> against our land's disfigurement and tension;
> hate gouged out deeper levels for our passion –

> a common hate enriched our love and us.

One third of the poems in *Letters to Martha* are directly concerned with his prison experience and these poems tend, on that account, to be somewhat restricted in range and tone. If there is "the sense of challenge of confrontation, vague heroism mixed with self-pity," there is more often fear, humiliation, and the sense of vulnerability. But in the rest of the volume there is a wide variety of mood and subject. "The Mob" describes a crowd of whites who attacked those protesting against the Sabotage Bill. There are landscapes and seascapes, poems written on a train journey and in flight over the Atlantic. "Blood River Day" deals ironically with the annual celebration of the Battle of Blood River (1838) in which the Boers commemorate their triumph over the black Africans in their trek northwards from British control:

> Each year on this day
> they drum the earth with their boots
> and growl incantations
> to evoke the smell of blood
> for which they hungrily sniff the air . . .

Finally, there is the long "Our Aims Our Dreams Our Destinations," in which the poet agonises over the human condition and questions his own religious faith:

> Can we find hope
> in thinking that our pain
> refines us of our evil dross,
> prepares us for a splendid destiny?

> or in a fellow-link
> a shared enterprise
> the splendid Gethsemane
> which must purchase redemption for the world
> and by our agony
> pay debts to buy
> the pardon for the world. . . .

> > > – Howard Sergeant

BUCHAN, Tom (Thomas Buchanan Buchan). Scottish. Born in Glasgow, 19 June 1931. Educated at Jordanhill College School; Balfron High School; Aberdeen

Grammar School; University of Glasgow, 1947–53, M.A. (honours) in English 1953. Married Emma Chapman in 1962; has three children. Teacher, Denny High School, Stirlingshire, 1953–56; Lecturer in English, University of Madras, India, 1957–58; Warden, Community House, Glasgow, 1958–59; Teacher, Irvine Royal Academy, 1963–65; Senior Lecturer in English and Drama, Clydebank Technical College, Glasgow, 1967–70. Since 1970, Free-lance Writer. Partner, Poni Press, Offshore Theatre Company, and Arts Projects, all in Edinburgh. Recipient: Scottish Arts Council award, 1969, and bursary, 1971. Address: 10 Pittville Street, Edinburgh EH15 2BY, Scotland.

PUBLICATIONS

Verse

Ikons. Madras, Tambaram Press, 1958.
Dolphins at Cochin: Poems. London, Barrie and Rockliff-Cresset Press, and New York, Hill and Wang, 1969.
Exorcism. Glasgow, Midnight Press, 1972.
Poems 1969–1972. Edinburgh, Poni Press, 1972.

Plays

Tell Charlie Thanks for the Truss (produced Edinburgh, 1972).
The Great Northern Welly Boot Show, lyrics by Billy Connolly (produced Glasgow and London, 1972).
Knox and Mary (produced Edinburgh, 1972).

Novel

Makes You Feel Great. Edinburgh, Poni Press, 1971.

Tom Buchan comments:

Considered chronologically, my poetry shows a steady progression from traditional forms, through traditional forms used in unconventional ways, to open verse. In poetry, I am rapidly approaching what seems to be a formal impasse, and my writing in this medium is becoming increasingly fragmented. I hope that beyond this impasse lies new forms appropriate to our times.

Partly because of this, I am developing my work as writer/director/actor in the theatre, and am presently engaged also in writing fiction and multi-media entertainments.

My early work was political and polemical. My most recent work is difficult to categorize – "spiritual," "religious," "metaphysical" or "mystical" would be too precious a description – but I am pressing on with my own inner development and at the same time trying to make a combination which anyone could enjoy.

*   *   *

Tom Buchan's poetry shows a distinctive and consistent development from his first collection, *Dolphins at Cochin,* to his most recent *Poems 1969–1972.* His distinction, in the first instance, is in his making a true aesthetic response to machine imagery of the twentieth century. He in no way indulges this response, but it provides the cutting edge to his satire. Thus he depicts "The White Hunter" in *Dolphins at Cochin:*

> The white hunter in his newly laundered outfit
> emerges from the acacias hung about with guns,
> compasses, bandoliers, belts, charms, binoculars,
> Polaroid sun-specs, cameras and a shockproof watch.

The more vividly the equipment displays itself the greater the doubt cast on the reality of the person encased in it. Buchan's effects are immediate; their impact is decisive. "The Everlasting Astronauts" begins:

> These dead astronauts cannot decay –
> they bounce on the quilted walls of their tin grave
> and very gently collide with polythene balloons
> full of used mouthwash, excrements and foodscraps.

The hallucinatory effect of the floating bodies is captured, but the emphasis is on doubt as to the values of the achievement of modern man. The nausea suggested in the last line of the quatrain becomes in Buchan's second collection a more important factor in a book which exhibits passionate indignation, disgust and contempt at the hypocrisy and callousness of officials in power in modern society. The achievement is in the creation of a nightmare world inhabited by politicians who seem to be caricatures of actual persons. These creations induce belief. They are seen as we know them projected on screens of the cinema and television. He presents "Mister Nixon President" thus:

> announces the U.S. invasion of Cambodia
> (Cambodia) on TV and sincerely his sincere right eye
> fixes the poor old silent US majority
> with Operation Total Myopic Solemnity.

The observation is cruel, comic and with some truth in it. Buchan's stated "subversive" intention does not limit him to satirising capitalist politicians. In the same poem he hits off Brezhnev:

> meanwhile dateline moss-cow Comrade Leonid
> Nebuchadnezzar Brezhnev in a weird soft hat
> reviews the latest lumpen May Day
> parade with a stiff diminutive wave
> reminiscent of our own dear Queen . . . .

The poet undermines the reader's sense of the truth of the observation by injecting into his text such references as CUT and CAM 2, reminding him that for him these are shadows on a screen. He uses the idea of our seeing the object through a camera lens to a more subtle and profound purpose in his very fine poem, "The Flaming Man," in which we seem to witness the death of a man by burning napalm in slow motion.

Indignation in this poem gives way to compassion. This is Buchan at his best. Occasionally he resorts to political campaigning and to an indulgence in nausea, which characteristics manifest themselves in a strident rhetoric. But for the greater part Buchan's rhetoric gives a sinewy strength to his verse.

– George Bruce

BUCHANAN, George (Henry Perrott). British. Born in Kilwaughter, County Antrim, Northern Ireland, 9 January 1904. Educated at Campbell College and Queens University, Belfast. Served in the Royal Air Force Coastal Command, 1940–45. Married Mary Corn in 1938 (marriage dissolved, 1945); Noel Beasley, 1949 (died, 1951); the Hon. Janet Margesson, 1952 (died, 1968); has two daughters, Florence and Emily. Reviewer for the *Times Literary Supplement*, London, 1928–40; on the editorial staff, *The Times*, London, 1930–35; Columnist and Drama Critic, *News Chronicle*, London, 1935–38. Chairman, Town and Country Development Committee, Northern Ireland, 1949–53. Since 1954, Member of the Executive Council of the European Society of Culture, Venice. Address: 27 Ashley Gardens, London S.W.1, England.

PUBLICATIONS

Verse

Bodily Responses. London, Gaberbocchus, 1958.
Conversation with Strangers. London, Gaberbocchus, 1961.
Annotations. Oxford, Carcanet Press, 1970.
Minute-Book of a City. Oxford, Carcanet Press, 1972.

Plays

Dance Night (produced London, 1934). London, French, 1935.
A Trip to the Castle (produced London, 1960).
Tresper Revolution (produced London, 1961).
War Song (produced London, 1965).

Novels

A London Story. London, Constable, 1935; New York, Dutton, 1936.
Rose Forbes: The Biography of an Unknown Woman (part 1). London, Constable, 1937.
Entanglement. London, Constable, 1938; New York, Appleton Century, 1939.
The Soldier and the Girl. London, Heinemann, 1940.
Rose Forbes (parts 1 and 2). London, Faber, 1950.
A Place to Live. London, Faber, 1952.
Naked Reason. New York, Holt Rinehart, 1971.

Other

> *Passage Through the Present: Chiefly Notes from a Journal.* London, Constable, 1932; New York, Dutton, 1933.
> *Words for Tonight: A Notebook.* London, Constable, 1936.
> *Green Seacoast* (autobiography). London, Gaberbocchus, 1959; New York, Red Dust, 1968.
> *Morning Papers* (autobiography). London, Gaberbocchus, 1965.

George Buchanan comments:

The book titles suggest preoccupations: passage through the present, bodily responses, conversation with strangers – mainly to do with the role of the imagination in submerged mass-life in a city ("I am in the poem, not the poem in me"). Which implies also a permanent revolutionary intention. ("Perhaps poetry is / our desires expressed as laws. / We desire what is absolutely necessary. / . . . The next line may be the next line.")

The Russian Formalists saw that writers often took a subliterary genre and turned it to literature (e.g. Pushkin and the *vers de société*). We may take the subliterary genre of intelligent conversation and turn it, if we can, to poetic speech.

*   *   *

George Buchanan is a quirky, eccentric poet: a man with something quite specifically different to say, and with a different way of saying it. In his earlier small volumes, such as *Bodily Responses* and *Conversation with Strangers*, the footnotes are larger and better (in the sense of being epigramatically provocative) than the poems, which are both lightweight and themselves prosy. This is partly because he tended towards the use of a line whose length he was not adept at handling: the genuinely epigrammatic effect of his footnotes is lost in arhythmic drag:

> Sneering at the sheer number of others is a drug for
> self-cultivators
> Who are also (they won't believe it) particles of the
> mass.
> All of us are; and are filled with that million-made
> blaze.

The footnotes are those of a very odd-man-out indeed: a man whose intelligence is refreshingly angled to the stream of fashion. Much more of this emerges in the recent poetry of *Minute-Book of a City* (no footnotes), in the poems of which form plays an important part in the creation of tension, leading to a sharper and more effective wit – as in "Anger":

> Cut out feeling (they say) yet often
> policy is the expression of a bad temper:
> when feeling's excluded, anger is the exception.
> We're at the mercy of official tempers.
> Irritable statesmen set the tone.
> Would well-intentioned villagers
> form a milder Cabinet,
> or would their rural eyes flash
> in ultra defiance even more animal?

– Martin Seymour-Smith

BUCKLEY, Vincent (Thomas). Australian. Born in Victoria, 8 July 1925. Educated at St. Patrick's (Jesuit) College, East Melbourne; University of Melbourne, B.A., M.A.; Cambridge University. Married; has two daughters. Lockie Fellow, 1958–60, Reader, 1960–67, and since 1967, Professor of English, University of Melbourne. Formerly, Member of the Editorial Board, *Prospect* magazine. Recipient: Australian Literature Society Gold Medal, 1959; Meyer Award, 1967. Lives in Melbourne.

PUBLICATIONS

Verse

The World's Flesh. Melbourne, Cheshire, 1954.
Masters in Israel: Poems. Sydney, Angus and Robertson, 1961.
Arcady and Other Places: Poems. Melbourne, Melbourne University Press, and
  London, Cambridge University Press, 1966.

Other

Essays in Poetry, Mainly Australian. Melbourne, Melbourne University Press,
  1957.
*Poetry and Morality: Studies in the Criticism of Matthew Arnold, T. S. Eliot, and
  F. R. Leavis.* London, Chatto and Windus, 1959.
Henry Handel Richardson. Melbourne, Lansdowne Press, 1961.
Poetry and the Sacred. London, Chatto and Windus, and New York, Barnes
  and Noble, 1968.

Editor, *The Incarnation in the University: Studies in the University
  Apostolate.* Melbourne, University Catholic Federation of Australia, 1955;
  London, International Movement of Catholic Students, and Chicago, Young
  Christian Students, 1957.
Editor, *Australian Poetry 1958.* Sydney, Angus and Robertson, 1958.
Editor, *The Campion Paintings,* by Leonard French. Melbourne, Gayflower
  Press, 1962.
Editor, *Eight by Eight.* Brisbane, Jacaranda Press, 1963.

Vincent Buckley comments:

My chief tendency might be described as romantic.

*   *   *

Vincent Buckley's career as a poet has gone hand in glove with that of a critic;
each of his three books of poems has been preceded or followed by a volume of
critical writings. In his criticism as in his poetry he has sought to enunciate a
particular ethos: that of Christian humanism. In his first book of poems, *The
World's Flesh,* marred by a besetting fault of rhetorical slackness, this talented
writer linked his questing forbears with Quiros' search for the southern continent in

the sequence "Land of No Fathers." In both subsequent books, *Masters in Israel* and *Arcady and Other Places*, he has modified the prophetic tone and shown his family, especially his father, in a plainer spoken yet truer light as in "Father and Son" and the moving sequence "Stroke."

The longest poem in his second book was a commemorative piece entitled "In Time of the Hungarian Martyrdom." Again, though deeply felt, a tendency towards rhetorical phrasing and religious mystification left many critics in two minds as to the overall quality of such protest. In comparison both "Impromptu for Francis Webb" and "To Praise a Wife" sustained with forceful clarity their subjects of an afflicted friend and an admirable marriage.

Probably the most important poetry he has written in recent years is to be found in the sequence "Eleven Political Poems" included in his third book. These muscular, witty poems are concerned more with man as a socio-religious rather than as a political being and keep direct references to the murk and savagery of power politics to a minimum. Indeed, in a recent article their author has admitted the original title of the sequence was "Eleven Anti-Political Poems."

One of the most impressive aspects of Vincent Buckley's art is his ability to engage himself fully yet unsentimentally in a portrayal of the most intimate and harrowing of all human relationships where love and death face each other at the borderline of human experience. This is seen at its best in the above mentioned "Stroke" sequence and in "Versions from Catullus," a group of eight poems. In the latter, though taken from classical antiquity, these poems of love and mortal loss are given a new lease of poetic life in Vincent Buckley's luminous translations.

– Bruce Beaver

BUKOWSKI, Charles. American. Born in Andernach, Germany, 16 August 1920; emigrated to the United States in 1922. Attended Los Angeles City College, 1939–41. Divorced; has one child. Formerly, Editor, *Harlequin*, Wheeler, Texas, then Los Angeles, and *Laugh Literary* and *Man the Humping Guns*, both in Los Angeles. Columnist ("Notes of a Dirty Old Man"). *Open City*, Los Angeles, then *Los Angeles Free Press*. Recipient: Loujon Press award. Lives in Los Angeles. Address: c/o Black Sparrow Press, P.O. Box 26469, Los Angeles, California 90026, U.S.A.

PUBLICATIONS

Verse

Flower, Fist and Bestial Wail. Eureka, California, Hearse Press, 1959.
Longshot Poems for Broke Players. New York, 7 Poets Press, 1961.
Run with the Hunted. Chicago, Midwest, 1962.
Poems and Drawings. Crescent City, Florida, Epos, 1962.
It Catches My Heart in Its Hand: New and Selected Poems, 1955–1963. New Orleans, Loujon Press, 1963.
Cold Dogs in the Courtyard. Chicago, Chicago Literary Times, 1965.
Crucifix in a Deathhand: New Poems, 1963–65. New Orleans, Loujon Press, 1965.
The Genius of the Crowd. Cleveland, 7 Flowers Press, 1966.
True Story. Los Angeles, Black Sparrow Press, 1966.
On Going Out to Get the Mail. Los Angeles, Black Sparrow Press, 1966.

To Kiss the Worms Goodnight. Los Angeles, Black Sparrow Press, 1966.
The Girls. Los Angeles, Black Sparrow Press, 1966.
The Flower Lover. Los Angeles, Black Sparrow Press, 1966.
2 by Bukowski. Los Angeles, Black Sparrow Press, 1967.
The Curtains Are Waving. Los Angeles, Black Sparrow Press, 1967.
At Terror Street and Agony Way. Los Angeles, Black Sparrow Press, 1968.
Poems Written Before Jumping Out of an 8-Story Window. Berkeley, California, Litmus, 1968.
If We Take. . . . Los Angeles, Black Sparrow Press, 1969.
The Days Run Away Like Wild Horses over the Hills. Los Angeles, Black Sparrow Press, 1969.
Penguin Modern Poets 13, with Philip Lamantia and Harold Norse. London, Penguin, 1969.
Another Academy. Los Angeles, Black Sparrow Press, 1970.
Fire Station. Santa Barbara, California, Capricorn Press, 1970.
Mockingbird Wish Me Luck. Los Angeles, Black Sparrow Press, 1972.
Me and Your Sometimes Love Poems. Los Angeles, Kisskill Press, 1972.
While the Music Played. Los Angeles, Black Sparrow Press, 1973.

Novel

Post Office. Los Angeles, Black Sparrow Press, 1971; London, London Magazine Editions, 1974.

Short Stories

Notes of a Dirty Old Man. North Hollywood, California, Essex House, 1969.
Erections, Ejaculations, Exhibitions and General Tales of Ordinary Madness. San Francisco, City Lights Books, 1972.
South of No North. Los Angeles, Black Sparrow Press, 1973.
Life and Death in the Charity Ward. London, London Magazine Editions, 1974.
Burning in Water, Drowning in Flames: Stories. Los Angeles, Black Sparrow Press, 1974.

Other

Confessions of a Man Insane Enough to Live with Beasts. Bensenville, Illinois, Mimeo Press, 1965.
All the Assholes in the World and Mine. Bensenville, Illinois, Open Skull Press, 1966.

Illustrator, *Six Poets.* Ellensburg, Washington, Vagabond Press, 1973.

Bibliography: *A Bibliography of Charles Bukowski* by Sanford Dorbin, Los Angeles, Black Sparrow Press, 1969.

Manuscript Collection: University of Santa Barbara, California.

*   *   *

When, around the bend of the Fifities, an almost aging prose-fiction writer emerged from a ten-year bout with bottles and bar-rooms and burst into flame, the prophecy of a San Francisco journalist-poet had come true: There was indeed, a need for a "crude disheveled kind of poetry." The man was Charles Bukowski. "Poetry is going into the streets, into the whorehouses, into the sky . . . into the whiskeybottle. The fraud is over –" says Bukowski, in *Ole*'s "monster-review" edition (no. 7).

For this new giant, poetry is just "too fine / and lacks the coarseness / of gamble" (from "The Last Round"). This is no poetic image: Bukowski prides himself on his horse-playing abilities. Here is a poet who is obviously at one with the experiences in his poems, a crucial point when you think of most other poets. To this day, he drinks and brawls as wildly as ever, and as far as I know, still plays the horses. His tough-guy image, however, is only partly true; in person, he is most generous and trusting. If he belongs to any school, it'd be the School of Funk!

His best poems aren't word-games. In rough-hewn, gasping and gaping lines he wraps his guts around a tree, then calmly walks off. You can call it protest poetry, you can call it some of the most hilarious sado-masochistic satiric plunges poetry ever saw. Sometimes it's both. For at least a decade he's been ripping out the likes of

> . . . not enough water to save the burning
> birds   and *they* are telling me now:
>   FLAME! FLAME! FLAME!
> as old trains move through the
> deserts
> as the schoolboys dream of laborless
> love
>   the birds BURN and
>   die before me
>   they
> fly away done
> leaving the grass for what's left of the
> worms . . .
>   – from "Singing Is Fire"

Few poets manage such complete release with anything like Bukowski's ferocity. Why? The risks are too great. His work has the power of "forcing the hidden psychopath in us back to reality," says a midwest poet-editor in *The Outsider*'s famous Bukowski celebration-issue (no. 3). Joe Friedman, once editor of the fine magazine *Venture*, adds that his laughter is often meant to be offensive, "*offensive* to connote attack, an impertinent zany attack on death, for . . . he is keenly sensitive to the innermost innards of being alive." This rings well. It can also be, with only slight modification, said of the foremost of his many imitators, among whom Doug Blazek is the best and most original.

It is, of course, possible to point to several poets Bukowski is fond of and roughly similar to – Jeffers, Pound and Ginsberg, whom he kids: "the Whitman-esque prophet rantings of the later Ginsberg." Strange, since these two poets are perhaps his closest spiritual companions, although in Bukowski there is no hint of homosexuality. Certainly, many of his long rambling prose-poems can only be called Whitmanesques. Here, too, no double-dealing: He owns up to the outrageous badness of a considerable number of these poems. It might help to remember Neruda's concept of Impure Poetry, Henry Miller's analogy of the supreme imper-fection of both art *and* life, or Jackson Pollock's approach to painting. One rather famous poet-editor (who also spans both decades) still finds Bukowski's main contribution to be in his prose. Well, if you call *all* his poems prosepoems, a small measure of truth might be lurking somewhere here; but it is just this kind of hokum or petty professional jealousy that so turns Bukowski (and me) off the "literary scene" here and in England. Long after, I feel, the pretty, precious verses of 90 per cent of the name poets of 20th century U.S. and British poetry have ceased to have interest to anyone but the narrowest of scholars, lines like these will still clearly stand out – for their flamelike intensity and searing honesty:

> some day I will walk into a cage with a bear
> look at Him, light a cigarette
> and He will sit down and cry,
> 40 billion people watching without sound
> as the sky turns upside down and
> splits the backbone
> open
> > – from "Like a Flyswatter"

> – Norman Moser

BULLOCK, Michael (Hale).   British.   Born in London, 19 April 1918. Educated at Stowe School, Buckinghamshire; Hornsey College of Art, London. Married Charlotte Schneller in 1941; has two children. Chairman, Translators Association, London, 1964–67. McGuffey Visiting Professor of English, Ohio University, Athens, 1968. Since 1969, Associate Professor of Creative Writing, University of British Columbia, Vancouver. Founding Editor, *Expression* magazine, London; Member of the Editorial Board, *Canadian Fiction Magazine*, Vancouver; since 1972, Editor-in-Chief, *Prism International* magazine, Vancouver. Recipient: Schlegel-Tieck Translation Prize, 1966. Agent: International Copyrite Bureau, 28 Charing Cross Road, London W.1, England. Address: 3836 West 18th Avenue, Vancouver, British Columbia V6S 1B5, Canada.

Publications

Verse

> *Transmutations* (as Michael Hale).   London, Favil Press, 1938.
> *Sunday Is a Day of Incest: Poems.*   London and New York, Abelard Schuman, 1961.
> *World Without Beginning, Amen!* London, Favil Press, 1963.
> *Zwei Stimmen in Meinem Mund* (bilingual edition, translated by Hedwig Rohde).   Andernach, Germany, Atelier Verlag, 1967.
> *A Savage Darkness.*   Vancouver, Sono Nis Press, 1969.
> *Black Wings White Dead.*   London, Fuller d'Arch Smith, 1973.

Plays

Andorra, adaptation of the play by Max Frisch (produced New York, 1963;
London, 1964). New York, Hill and Wang, 1962.
Nicht Nach Hong Kong (produced Andernach, Germany, and London, 1966);
translated by the author as Not to Hong Kong (produced London, 1972).
Published in Dialogue and Dialectic, Guelph, Ontario, Alive Press, 1973.
The Island Abode of Bliss (produced Vancouver, 1972).

Radio Play: Mäntelspiel, 1966 (Germany).

Short Stories

Sixteen Stories as They Happened. Vancouver, Sono Nis Press, 1969.
Green Beginning Black Ending. Vancouver, Sono Nis Press, 1971.
Randolph Cranstone and the Pursuing River. Vancouver, Raven Press, 1974.

Other

Translator, with Jerome Ch'ên, Poems of Solitude. London and New York,
Abelard Schuman, 1961.
Translator, The Tales of Hoffman. London, New English Library, 1962; New
York, Ungar, 1963.
Translator, with Jerome Ch'ên, Mao and the Chinese Revolution, With 37 Poems
by Mao Tse-Tung. London, Oxford University Press, 1965.
Translator, The Stage and Creative Arts. Greenwich, Connecticut, New York
Graphic Society, 1969.
Translator, Foreign Bodies, by Karl Krolow. Athens, Ohio University Press,
1969.
Translator, Invisible Hands, by Karl Krolow. London, Cape Goliard Press,
and New York, Grossman, 1969.
Translator, with Jagna Boraks, Astrologer in the Underground, by Andrzej Bus-
za. Athens, Ohio University Press, 1971.

Other translations include novels and plays by Max Frisch and over 130 other
titles from French and German.

Critical Studies: by John Ditsky, in Canadian Forum (Toronto), February 1971;
Richard Hopkins, in British Columbia Library Quarterly (Victoria), January 1972;
"Light on a Dark Wood" by John Reid, in Canadian Literature (Vancouver),
Autumn 1972; interview with Richard Hopkins, in British Columbia Library Quarterly
(Victoria), June 1973.

Michael Bullock comments:

I consider myself a surrealist, or at least a neo-surrealist, in that I base my work
upon the free play of the imagination without, however, sacrificing clarity of
expression. I seek to use vivid and striking imagery to convey states of mind and
emotion and to create an autonomous world freed from the restrictions and limitations of everyday existence. This world and the means I use to give it form remain

the same whether I am writing verse, prose or drama. I believe that my writing in all three genres can with almost equal right be described as poetry. All of it is a vehement rejection of realism. I like to hope that there is some truth in the comment of a reviewer who wrote that my fables "bear witness to one of the most wildly imaginative minds ever to reach the printed page" and in Anaïs Nin's description of my work as "a liberating expansion of what is reality." The two remarks together sum up what I am trying to do.

*   *   *

In a poem taken from *A Savage Darkness*, which might easily stand as his personal manifesto, Michael Bullock explains:

> The real surrounds me
> with its barbed wire entanglements
> Leaping upwards I clutch at a cloud
> and stuff it into my head
>
> In a blue haze
> figures emerge
> and drift
> in an endless floating dance
>
> Women with streaming hair
> fall downwards
> holding burning flowers
> Flocks of eyes fly around gazing
> and flapping their lids
>
> Stretched out
> on the cloud in my mind
> I wait for the approach
> of the ultimate dream . . .
>   – from "Escape"

The poem continues, but the most important catch-phrase has occurred: "the ultimate dream." For Michael Bullock is a Surrealist, an almost orthodox one in fact, and both his poetry and his prose insist entirely on the freedom, the total possibility which is the dream – both as a source and as mode. Bullock's poems are associative, fantastical, alogical; they leap and swirl to the arabesques of the imagination like a free-form dance. Through his writings Bullock re-enacts creation according to his own laws, according to a triumphantly lyrical, non-lineal progression both in time and space:

> Out of the air I draw the memory of a bird.
> Out of the earth I draw the memory of a tree.
> From the memory of the bird
> and the memory of the tree
> I make the memory of a poem
> that weighs lighter than air
> and floats away without wind . . .

The result is that Bullock's poetry almost always departs from unexpected places and arrives at unfamiliar destinations. And the means by which it gets there is, needless to say, no less unpredictable.

– Andreas Schroeder

BUNTING, Basil. British. Born in Scotswood on Tyne, Northumberland, 1 March 1900. Educated at a Quaker public school; London School of Economics. Jailed as a conscientious objector during World War I. Married Marian Culver in 1930; Sima Alladadian, 1948; has two children. Assistant Editor, *Transatlantic Review*, Paris, in the 1920's; Music Critic, *The Outlook*, London; lived in Italy and the United States in the 1930's; Persian Correspondent for *The Times*, London, after World War II; Sub-Editor, Newcastle *Morning Chronicle*, for 12 years. Taught at the University of California, Santa Barbara; Poetry Fellow, universities of Durham and Newcastle, 1968–70; taught at the universities of British Columbia, Vancouver, Binghamton, New York, and Victoria, British Columbia. Since 1972, President, The Poetry Society, London. Recipient: Levinson Prize (*Poetry*, Chicago), 1966; Arts Council bursary, 1966. D.Litt.: Newcastle, 1971. Address: Shadingfield, Wylam, Northumberland, England.

PUBLICATIONS

Verse

Redimiculum Matellarum.   Milan, Grafica Moderna, 1930.
Poems 1950.   Galveston, Texas, Cleaners' Press, 1950.
First Book of Odes.   London, Fulcrum Press, 1965.
Loquitur.   London, Fulcrum Press, 1965.
The Spoils: A Poem.   Newcastle-upon-Tyne, The Morden Tower Book Room, 1965.
Ode II/2.   London, Fulcrum Press, 1965.
Briggflatts.   London, Fulcrum Press, 1966.
Two Poems.   Santa Barbara, California, Unicorn Press, 1967.
What the Chairman Told Tom.   Cambridge, Massachusetts, Pym Randall Press, 1967.
Collected Poems.   London, Fulcrum Press, 1968.
Descant on Rawley's Madrigal (Conversations with Jonathan Williams).   Lexington, Kentucky, Gnomon Press, 1968.

Basil Bunting comments:

Minor poet, not conspicuously dishonest.

*   *   *

The rediscovery of Basil Bunting's work was one of the really notable events to occur in British poetry during the nineteen-sixties. In a sense, British readers could not be blamed for their ignorance of what Bunting had written, as his work first appeared in a limited edition printed in Milan (1930), and subsequently in a larger collection published in Texas (1950) when the poet himself was living in Persia.

There was also the fact that Bunting, as a poet, belonged obstinately to the tradition of the twenties, while his work began to appear more or less simultaneously with that of the "new men" of the following decade: Auden, MacNeice, Spender and Day Lewis. Bunting has acknowledged that the profoundest influence on him, exerted by contemporary writers, was that of Ezra Pound and Louis Zukofsky. He knew Pound well in the Rapallo years, and the *Guide to Kulchur* is dedicated jointly to him and to Zukofsky, "strugglers in the desert."

Pound's example certainly had its effect on the more important of Bunting's early poems, such as "Villon" and "Chomei at Toyama," but these are by no means imitations. They have, for one thing, a certain obstinate Englishness, a close-knit organisation which is alien to Pound. One notable feature of both these poems is the uncertainty of the precise boundary between the "persona" adopted, and the poet himself. Section II of "Villon," for example, contains a number of obvious allusions to Bunting's sufferings when imprisoned as a conscientious objector during the First World War. Another characteristic which seems equally striking is the "musical" quality which both possess, not only from line to line (Bunting has an exquisite ear) but as structures. Bunting has acknowledged the influence of music on his work by labelling a whole group of his poems "Sonatas," "Villon" among them.

Bunting's finest work is probably that which he has published in recent years, notably *Briggflatts*, the long poem which established his reputation among young readers. Cyril Connolly described it as "the finest long poem to have been published in England since *Four Quartets*." *Briggflatts* is another "sonata," but one which is also subtitled "an autobiography." It is, in fact, the poem where Bunting works most directly with the material supplied to him by his own life. No-one who has seen Bunting's acknowledged list of masters – they include Wordsworth, Dante, Horace, Wyatt, Malherbe, Villon, Whitman, Spenser and the Persian poet Ferdosi – would expect an open, easy, confessional work. Bunting knits together the historical and the personal – Welsh bards, the music of Monteverdi, Viking kings in York, the Northumbrian landscape – with the poet's own first experience of love. Few English poems are so dense with both personal and historical alusion; few have such a lyric sweetness. Perhaps the only comparison which comes to mind is Milton's *Lycidas*. It is not unapt, because *Briggflatts*, too, is an elegy – but for the poet's own life:

> Sirius glows in the wind. Sparks on ripples
> mark his line, lures for spent fish.
>
> Fifty years a letter unanswered;
> a visit postponed for fifty years.
>
> She has been with me fifty years.
>
> Starlight quivers. I had day enough.
> For love uninterrupted night.

– Edward Lucie-Smith

BURFORD, William (Skelly). American. Born in Shreveport, Louisiana, 20 February 1927. Educated at Amherst College, Massachusetts (Glasscock Memorial Award, Mount Holyoke College, 1949), B.A. (magna cum laude) 1949 (Phi Beta Kappa); the Sorbonne, Paris, 1951–52 (Fulbright Scholar); Johns Hopkins University, Baltimore, M.A. 1956, Ph.D. 1966. Served in the United States Army, 1945. Married Lola Egan in 1956; has three daughters. Assistant to the President, Richardson Refining Company, Texas City, 1949–50. Instructor in English, Southern Methodist University, Dallas, 1950–51, 1952–54, and John Hopkins University, 1955–58; Assistant Professor, 1958–64, and Associate Professor of English, 1964–65, University of Texas, Austin; Associate Professor of Humanities, University of Montana, Missoula, 1966–68; Professor of English, Texas Christian University, Fort Worth, Texas, 1968–72. Since 1972, teacher in the National Endowment for the Arts Poetry-in-the-Schools Program. Poet-in-Residence, Evergreen State College, Olympia, Washington, 1974. Recipient: Walt Whitman Memorial Award, 1962. Address: 3000 West Gambrell, Fort Worth, Texas 76133, U.S.A.

PUBLICATIONS

Verse

Man Now. Dallas, Southern Methodist University Press, 1954.
Faccia della Terra/Face of the Earth (bilingual edition). Bologna, Libreria Antiquaria Palmaverde, 1960.
A World. Austin, University of Texas Press, 1962.
A Beginning: Poems. New York, Norton, 1966.
Gymnos. N.p., Four Mountains Press, 1973.

Other

Editor and Translator, with Christopher Middleton, *The Poet's Vocation: Selections from the Letters of Hölderlin, Rimbaud, and Hart Crane.* Austin, University of Texas Press, 1967.
Editor and Translator, with Jean Autret, *On Reading*, by Marcel Proust. New York, Macmillan, and London, Souvenir Press, 1972.

Critical Studies: Review by David Ignatow, in *The New York Times*, 6 January 1967; by the author, in *The Nation* (New York), 7 and 14 February 1972.

William Burford comments:

Poetry, at least as I have learned to want to write it, is a way of giving reality and even courage to the life a man senses within himself, and which he knows, by living among other men, is their chief possession also. The poetry which seems to me the most admirable is characterized by a certain firm delicacy, a style which at once both moves and instructs the sense of life in us. If a man writes poems for any length of time, he learns how much experience of both life and art is required to achieve this style, how few men have been masters of it, and these few seemingly by some grace of nature or intelligence or artistic perception, that cannot be willed by himself into his own possession but only perhaps gradually approached if he has a view of the goal.

*   *   *

In scenes of childhood innocence, in cities of youthful pleasure lurk recurring forms of terror, loneliness, and melancholy. A childish game destroys a harmless life. A boy, frightened by his nurse's disfigured face, marks his fate with clocks ticking the hours of a father's absence. A father bids his son remove annoying sparrows which return in nightmare as birds of prey. In sunlit Paris the youth denies the phantom of himself. He finds Venice "sunk to a sewer." In Amsterdam an old man tells him: "To live is to persist." The poet sees with the eyes of the painter; indeed, paintings become subjects for some of his strongest lines. The once-benevolent surgeon's scalpel stabs the brain that was a world. The sensuous face of the sexless monk mocks the artist. Stones arranged like human bones spell out station-names in fields lying in ashes. Images of frost, marble waves, slivers of glass quickly etch vignettes made even more poignant by the poet's delicate, controlling hand. Yet William Burford's incisive, sombre scenes do not depress but comfort and enlighten; for usually a calm instilled by oblique and muted Christian symbolism pervades and promises hope, which in later poems finds fruition in the loving presence of a sleeping wife and awkward grace of an adolescent son.

Burford seeks to capture "that moment fatal in our lives" by asking: "Where does one go for love these days?" This probing for the fundamental gives his poetry a continuity of theme and purpose (and several early poems reappear, revised, in later volumes); he traces the private world of child and youth as it opens to the social consciousness of maturity. But early he learned that passion is "aged to a patience." He cried, "My name is man, and I am dumb from pain." "In an ironic age," he discovers, "reasonable men" are hospitable to the Devil they do not believe in; judges behind their tinted glass are still "hypnotizing existence." Solipsistic man thinks his body is the world, "And so a final philosophy." The perfect young dancer thinks himself immortal, though destruction waits in the wings. The poet, too, has "measureless privacy," but he turns his penetrating eye upon the ephemeral and finds the "self is strong, unisolated, / And from its birth forms bonds throughout all." Unlike the windy, undisciplined, but fashionable voices decrying a fractured world in despair, Burford depicts in short, polished verse a destructive universe still capable of meaning through humanity and faith.

– Joseph Parisi

BURKE, Kenneth (Duva). American. Born in Pittsburgh, Pennsylvania, 5 May 1897. Educated at Peabody High School, Pittsburgh; Ohio State University, Columbus, 1916–17; Columbia University, New York, 1917–18. Married Lily Mary Batterham in 1919 (divorced); Elizabeth Batterham, 1933; has five children. Research Worker, Laura Spelman Rockefeller Memorial, New York, 1926–27. Music Critic, *Dial*, New York, 1927–29, and *The Nation*, New York, 1934–35. Editor, Bureau of Social Hygiene, New York, 1928–29. Lecturer, New School for Social Research, New York, 1937; University of Chicago, 1938, 1949–50; Bennington College, Vermont, 1943–61; Princeton University, New Jersey, 1949; Kenyon College, Gambier,

Ohio, 1950; Indiana University, Bloomington, 1953, 1958; Drew University, Madison, New Jersey, 1962, 1964; Pennsylvania State University, University Park, 1963; Regents Professor, University of California at Santa Barbara, 1964–65; Lecturer, Central Washington State University, Ellensburg, 1966; Harvard University, Cambridge, Massachusetts, 1967–68; Washington University, St. Louis, 1970–71. Recipient: *Dial* Award, 1928; Guggenheim Fellowship, 1935; National Institute of Arts and Letters grant, 1946; Princeton Institute for Advanced Study Fellowship, 1949; Stanford University Center for Advanced Study in the Behavioral Sciences Fellowship, 1957; Rockefeller grant, 1966; Brandeis University Creative Arts Award, 1967; National Endowment for the Arts grant, 1968 D.Litt.: Bennington College, 1966; Rutgers University, New Brunswick, New Jersey; Dartmouth College, Hanover, New Hampshire. Member, American Academy of Arts and Letters; American Academy of Arts and Sciences. Address: R. D. 2, Andover, New Jersey 07821, U.S.A.

PUBLICATIONS

Verse

> *Book of Moments: Poems 1915–1954.* Los Altos, California, Hermes, 1955.
> *Collected Poems 1915–1967.* Berkeley, University of California Press, and London, Cambridge University Press, 1968.

Novel

> *Towards a Better Life: Being a Series of Epistles or Declarations.* New York, Harcourt Brace, 1932; revised edition, Berkeley, University of California Press, and London, Cambridge University Press, 1966.

Short Stories

> *The White Oxen and Other Stories.* New York, Boni, 1924.
> *The Complete White Oxen: Collected Shorter Fiction.* Berkeley, University of California Press, 1968.

Other

> *Counter-Statement.* New York, Harcourt Brace, 1931; revised edition, Berkeley, University of California Press, and London, Cambridge University Press, 1968.
> *Permanence and Change: An Anatomy of Purpose.* New York, New Republic, 1935; revised edition, Los Altos, California, Hermes, 1954.
> *Attitudes Towards History.* New York, New Republic, 2 vols., 1937; revised edition, Los Altos, California, Hermes, 1959.
> *The Philosophy of Literary Forms: Studies in Symbolic Action.* Baton Rouge, Louisiana State University Press, 1941; revised edition, New York, Random House, 1957; London, Peter Smith, 1959.
> *A Grammar of Motives.* New York, Prentice Hall, 1945; London, Dobson, 1947.

A Rhetoric of Motives.   New York, Prentice Hall, 1950; London, Bailey Brothers and Swinfen, 1955.

The Rhetoric of Religion: Studies in Logology.   Boston, Beacon Press, 1961.

Perspective by Incongruity, edited by Stanley Edgar Hyman.   Bloomington, Indiana University Press, 1964.

Terms for Order, edited by Stanley Edgar Hyman.   Bloomington, Indiana University Press, 1964.

Language as Symbolic Action: Essays on Life, Literature and Method.   Berkeley, University of California Press, and London, Cambridge University Press, 1966.

Translator, *Death in Venice,* by Thomas Mann.   New York, Knopf, 1925.

Translator, *Genius and Character,* by Emil Ludwig.   New York, Harcourt Brace, 1927; London, Cape, 1930.

Translator, *Saint Paul,* by Emile Baumann.   New York, Harcourt Brace, 1929.

Kenneth Burke comments:

In calling my theory of language as symbolic action "Dramatistic" (as contrasted with "Scientistic") I have in mind a distinction that boils down to this: A "Scientistic" approach centers in "It is/it is not"; a "Dramatistic" approach centers in "Do/don't." My aim is to develop a theory of language in general, with emphasis upon its application to specific texts.

*   *   *

My favorite among Kenneth Burke's *Collected Poems 1915–1967* is a 17-page poem in 5 parts entitled "Tossing on Floodtides of Sinkership: A Diaristic Fragment." Driving across the country, the speaker floats on a turbulent sea of memories, reflections, and feelings – the dangers of traffic, the power of the machine, pollution, reactions to America's face and fate, politics, Vietnam, his own inner conflicts – but concludes with the stubborn persistence of spring and the sunrise. Now Burke writes most frequently about our public life, but what I find distinctive in this poem is the way in which the public is seen in terms of the personal, for not only do the larger issues arise naturally and dramatically out of the particular situation, but they are also seen *in relation* to the speaker and his own turmoil. He sees the destructiveness of highspeed autos in political terms – the easy manipulation of such vicarious power may tend to make us docile citizens – and he feels the fascination of his own suicidal urge to spin off the road as well. He sees the deterioration of the land, and he senses a connection with his own desolation: "half experimental animal, / half control group. / I am mine own disease." And when he comes to the Vietnam issue, he not only vents his indignation – "Cook them with napalm in the name of freedom / tear up their way of life" – he also confronts his own hesitation – "Gad! I couldn't tell them that!" – and concludes this section (IV) with the wry admission that "To be safe in striking at the powerful / make sure that your blows are powerless."

It is not, alas, always thus. Too often his poems are simply public statements without either tension or intensity. Excellent critic that he is, Burke offers a Foreword and various explanatory prose excursions, whose gist is that, contrary to our common assumptions, prose is more subtle, conditional, and qualified than lyric poetry. Criticism, he says in "Extraduction from What?," is "moderate in tone and at least theoretically charitable. . . . The very attempt to be circumspect in criticism could make one, by rebound, at least *wish* for *some* verse in 'the style of a news broadcast blasting forth pellets. . . ." And therein lies the problem, for the very life of the lyric depends upon its stemming from and embodying a sense of personal urgency, it seems to me, and if you would write the unqualified sort, as E.E. Cummings does, for example, your sense of self must be intense, accepting, intuitive, passionate, and transcendent, so that when it confronts the troublesome public world it will do so on the basis of inner confidence. Yet, in "Extraduction," he speaks of "my morbid Selph, lost among the monsters of machinery and politics." And in his admiring elegy on Cummings, he takes pleasure in opining that Cummings had more brains than he admitted to – "you secretly, like the scholastics' God, / an intellectual" – as if to say that Cummings' mysticism was less than whole-hearted.

An instructive contrast to the Vietnam section of "Tossing" is found in another, shorter poem on the same subject, "The Great Debate," which is in this "news broadcast" style, and which concludes:

> But time is running out.
> Where we but increase our forces
> the enemy escalates.
>
> Give us an honorable peace
> And we'll stop
> Our dishonorable war.
>
> (There's shouting in the streets – and I wanna go home)

There is irony here, of course, but it is still, as is the rest of the poem, rather flat, and the final line is an ineffectual attempt to supply a dramatic base, for it is a deliberately forlorn gesture and is simply stuck on at the end – quite different in function and effect from the similar conclusion of Cummings' "pity this busy monster, manunkind": "listen: there's a hell / of a good universe next door; let's go."

One would think, then, that Burke would be more at home in writing the qualified sort of lyric, as in "Tossing," in which the sense of personal urgency arises from tension, conflict, intelligence, consideration, and self-confrontation, and one recalls Yeats's sobering remark that we make rhetoric out of our quarrel with others, but poetry out of our quarrel with ourselves. But Burke's poetic self is just as tenuous when confronting itself as the public world, betraying its uncertainties and avoidances in a wobbly style which skitters from the melodic to the prosaic, and touches doggerel, slang, nonsense, and puns along the way. And self-knowledge rarely gets in touch either with the possibility that the public is an extension of ourselves or that it becomes internalized and sticks within as a part of ourselves.

It is this awareness which surfaces but seldom in Burke's poetry, and when it does it finds its only acknowledged symptom in insomnia. Nevertheless, in six successive lyrics entitled "On a Photo of Himself," "Self-Portrait," "Know Thyself," "Now I Lay Me," "On the Reflexive," and "Personality Problem," the speaker presents himself with gentleness, wit, and frankness as sleepless and aging:

> One-third insomnia
> One-third art
> One-third The Man
> With the Cardiac Heart. . . .
>
> I'm flunking my Required Course
> In Advanced Burkology.
>   – from "Know Thyself"

This is less powerful than "half experimental animal, etc.," but it is effective in its own way. And he can on occasion combine self-study with social criticism, as in "Photo," which concludes:

> Bring on your bombs, your bugs, and the trick chemicals,
> Get this damned business done
>
> But in the interim
> Curse me for a not-yet-housebroken cur
> And rub my nose in filthy lucre.

And "L'Auberge" is a lovely counterpart, in its depiction of a respite at an inn while traveling, to the similar concluding section of Part I of "Tossing," but it drives even deeper into the recesses of the self. Here and throughout he appears as an engaged and engaging poet indeed, more moderate and charitable than he seems to think he is. I could only wish that he did not feel his poetry represented an escape from his more brilliant and arduous critical work.

– Norman Friedman

BURNS, Jim. British. Born in Preston, Lancashire, 19 February 1936. Educated at local schools. Served in the British Army, 1954–57. Divorced; has two sons. Editor, *Move* magazine, Preston, 1964–68. Since 1964, regular contributor, *Tribune*, London. Address: 7 Ryelands Crescent, Larches Estate, Preston, Lancashire, England.

PUBLICATIONS

Verse

Some Poems. New York, Crank Books, 1965.
Some More Poems. Cambridge, R Books, 1966.
My Sad Story and Other Poems. Chatham, Kent, New Voice, 1967.
The Store of Things. Manchester, Phoenix Pamphlet Poets Press, 1969.
A Single Flower. Jersey, Channel Islands, Andium Press, 1972.
Leben in Preston. Cologne, Palmenpresse, 1973.

Other

Cells: Prose Pieces. Lincoln, Grosseteste Press, 1967.
Saloon Bar: 3 Jim Burns Stories. London, Ferry Press, 1967.
Types: Prose Pieces and Poems. Cardiff, Second Aeon Publications, 1970.

Literary and jazz articles published in periodicals and collections.

Critical Studies: "The American Influence" by the author, in *New Society* (London), 7 December 1967; "Exit to Preston" by Raymond Gardner, in *The Guardian* (London), 10 August 1972; "A Poet in His Northern Corner" by Bel Mooney, in *Daily Telegraph Magazine* (London), 2 March 1973.

Jim Burns comments:

(1970) I suppose my main subject-matter tends towards the "domestic," i.e., that which I know best and experience personally. Brevity and wit are attributes I admire in a poet and I think (or hope) that some of this comes in some of my own work.

My main influences have been contemporary American and English poets, and some translations from the Chinese and Japanese. I like the directness in these latter. If asked to single out one poet whose work I particularly like and find stimulating I would name Kenneth Rexroth.

I have a deep feeling that the most significant ideas can be expressed in direct and clear language, and that the unusual and significant are in the obvious.

The reader may also get an idea of my leanings from the opinions expressed in the articles I have contributed (since 1964) to *Tribune* on little-magazines and related publications.

(1974) In the past three or four years, my poetry has, I think, tended to diversify, both in form and content. I still like brevity and wit, but have found that, in order to deal with matters outside the domestic concerns my poems once related to, I've had to become perhaps more discursive. In a sense, as the subject-matter widens, so do the forms I use. The lines tend to be longer, the rhythm less precise. Interestingly enough, however, I find that when I do revert to "domestic" concerns the form tightens again.

*   *   *

If one had to find a single word to describe Jim Burns' poems it would be "anecdotal." Each poem tells a story and the tone adopted is that of the raconteur where the impetus relies more on the narrative flow and the ultimate making of a point than on language or rhythm as such. What informs each story is the persona adopted, that of the wryly candid man who, though beguiled by the romantic, is never taken in by it; whether it be romantic love:

> Better to make love in bed, turn
> your back afterwards. Sleep easy
> > – from "The Way It Is"

or the pretentiousness of romantic politics:

> The left wing intellectuals
> had fought the Paris Commune, the
> General Strike, the Spartacist uprising
> and the Spanish Civil War all over
> again and would have sung the Red Flag
> had they known the words or tune.
> Instead, they ordered another round
> and the landlord rubbed his hands
> and then called time. For everyone
> > – from "Meanwhile"

Indeed, it seems to be Burns' mission to gently deflate the phoney and the ostentatious; gently because he too knows the temptations and has some sympathy with those who succumb. For this reason the language used avoids the "high flown" to the point of flatness; Burns' sense of rhythm and the narrative flow carrying the poems on. Nevertheless, the truth must out.

> Is a man any less a poet
> because he stays at home
> with his wife and children

he asks in "A Single Flower." Poetry stands or falls by what is on the page; it is irrelevant if the author washes himself, sleeps with his sister or has two heads, if he is an arch bishop or an arch-Villon:

> I once slept out all night
> with the homeless, and although
> it taught me pity
> it did not teach me poetry.

And he is right; though there are some who will not forgive him for that! But self-depreciatory, honest and always caring as he is, one cannot help liking the man behind the poems.

– John Cotton

BURNSHAW, Stanley. American. Born in New York City, 20 June 1906. Educated at Columbia University, New York, 1924; University of Pittsburgh, B.A. 1925; University of Poitiers, 1927; University of Paris, 1927–28; Cornell University, Ithaca, New York, M.A. 1933. Married Madeline Burnshaw in 1934 (divorced); Lydia Powsner, 1942; has one daughter, Valerie, and two stepchildren, Amy and David. Advertising Assistant, Blaw-Knox Company, Blawnox, Pennsylvania, 1925–27; Advertising Manager, The Hecht Company, New York, 1928–32; Co-Editor and Drama Critic, *The New Masses*, New York, 1934–36; Editor-in-Chief, The Cordon Company, publishers, New York, 1937–39; President and Editor-in-Chief, Dryden Press, New York, 1939–58; Vice-President, 1958–66, and Consultant to the President, 1966–68, Holt, Rinehart and Winston Inc., publishers, New York. Lecturer, New York University, 1958–62. Founding Editor (and hand setter), *Poetry Folio* magazine, and Folio Press, Pittsburgh, 1926–29. Contributing Editor, *Modern Quarterly*, 1932–33, and *Theatre Workshop* magazine, 1935–38. Director, American Institute of Graphic Arts, 1960–61. Recipient: National Institute of Arts and Letters award, 1971. Address: Lamberts Cove, Martha's Vineyard, Massachusetts 02568, U.S.A.

PUBLICATIONS

Verse

Poems. Pittsburgh, Folio Press, 1927.
The Great Dark Love. New York, privately printed, 1932.

The Iron Land: A Narrative.   Philadelphia, Centaur Press, 1936.
The Revolt of the Cats in Paradise: A Children's Book for Adults.   Gaylordsville,
   Connecticut, Crow Hill Press, 1945.
Early and Late Testament.   New York, Dial Press, 1952.
Caged in an Animal's Mind.   New York, Holt Rinehart, 1963.
The Hero of Silence.   Lugano, Switzerland, privately printed, 1965.
In the Terrified Radiance.   New York, Braziller, 1972.

Play

The Bridge (in verse).   New York, Dryden Press, 1945.

Novel

The Sunless Sea.   London, Davies, 1948; New York, Dial Press, 1949.

Other

A Short History of the Wheel Age.   Pittsburgh, Folio Press, 1928.
André Spire and His Poetry: Two Essays and Forty Translations.   Philadelphia,
   Centaur Press, 1933.
*The Seamless Web: Language-Thinking, Creature-Knowledge, Art-
   Experience.*   New York, Braziller, and London, Allen Lane, 1970.

Editor, *Two New Yorkers* (Kruse lithographs and Kreymborg poems).   New
   York, Bruce Humphries, 1938.
Editor, with others, *The Poem Itself: 45 Modern Poets in a New
   Presentation.*   New York, Holt Rinehart, 1960; London, Penguin, 1964.
Editor, with T. Carmi and Ezra Spicehandler, *The Modern Hebrew Poem Itself:
   From the Beginnings to the Present: Sixty-Nine Poems in a New
   Presentation.*   New York, Holt Rinehart, 1960.
Editor, *Varieties of Literary Experience: Eighteen Essays in World
   Literature.*   New York, New York University Press, 1962; London, Peter
   Owen, 1963.

Critical Studies: "The Great Dark Love" by André Spire, in *Mercure de France*
(Paris), 1 December 1933; "The Poem Itself" by Lionel Trilling, in *The Mid-Century*
(New York), August 1960; "On Translating Poetry" by Herbert Read, in *Poetry*
(Chicago), April 1961; "The Poet Is Always Present" by Germaine Brée, in *The
American Scholar* (Washington, D.C.), Summer 1970; "In the Terrified Radiance"
by James Dickey, in *New York Times Book Review*, 24 September 1972.

Stanley Burnshaw comments:

Poetry is the expression of the creator's total organism – or, as I say at the
beginning of *The Seamless Web*:

Poetry begins with the body and ends with the body. Even Mallarmé's
symbols of abstract essence lead back to the bones, flesh, and nerves. My

approach, then, is "physiological," yet it issues from a vantage point difference from Vico's when he said that all words originated in the eyes, the arms, and the other organs from which they were grown into analogies. My concern is rather with the type of creature-mind developed by the evolutionary shock which gave birth to what we have named self-consciousness. So far as we know, such biological change failed to arise in any other living creature. So far as we can tell, no other species, dead or alive, produced or produces the language-thinking of poetry. We are engaged, then, with a unique phenomenon issuing from a unique physiology which seems to function no differently from that of other animals – in a life-sustaining activity based on continuous interchange between organism and environment.

Poetry begins with the body and ends with the body – *The Seamless Web* pursues and confronts the implications of this statement from three different vantage points: 1) Language-Thinkings, 2) Creature-Knowledge, 3) Art-Experience. The Third (Art-Experience) offers the clearest introduction to my poetry, especially for the reader who has at hand a copy of my *Caged in an Animal's Mind*: there are numerous references to the pages in that volume of my poems.

*   *   *

Writing of man's struggle through science and technology to master Nature, and the culmination of that struggle in the discovery and use of atomic power, Stanley Burnshaw says: "The war against Nature had been confidently waged and won; and we post-moderns, of 1945-and-after, breathe the spirit of a different epoch, and we have a different terror on our minds: Now that man is victorious, how shall he stay alive?"

This question is a recurring one in his poems, as death, love, and life wage unceasing war, observed by a coal-hard intellect striving relentlessly to illuminate the world, "this eden," through a sense of its kinship with the world of nature. In his forty-year-long poetry-writing career, Burnshaw has remained contemporary, and in his view of the urgency of confronting man's imminent self-annihilation through the destruction of nature he is in agreement with many poets younger than himself. His latest collection, *In the Terrified Radiance*, gives us those parts of his earlier work he wants us to remember, and his *oeuvre* is made to seem remarkably of a piece. From the beginning, he has filled his lyrics with stones, flames, wind, trees, singing, and blood – an imagery suggestive at times of Robinson Jeffers and at others of Theodore Roethke; in all of them, however, Burnshaw is distinctively (if somewhat monotonously and humorlessly) himself.

In his dense, hard-surfaced poems one encounters a harsh, relentless, and totally committed intelligence fronting with mind and senses the inexorable facts of death and life. The effect is a seamless web (to borrow the title of his book about the physiological origins of the creative act) of images of storm, fire, growth, destruction, and the nourishment of creativity by the forces that destroy. These are not simply poems about the "good that comes from evil" or of the cyclical quality of nature; there is something much more elemental in their feeling of primordial unity. Burnshaw, in a paradox of cerebral style and physiological message – what he refers to as creature-knowledge – seems a solemn shaman preserving his intellectual detachment whilst in an ecstasy of sympathy with the tides of being.

– Donald Barlow Stauffer

BUTLER, (Frederick) Guy. South African. Born in Cradock, Cape Province, 21 January 1918. Educated at local high school; Rhodes University, Grahamstown, M.A. 1939; Brasenose College, Oxford, M.A. 1947. Served in World War II in the Middle East, Italy, and the United Kingdom. Married; has four children. Taught at the University of Witwatersrand, Johannesburg, 1948–50. Currently, Professor of English at Rhodes University, Grahamstown, South Africa. Editor, with Ruth Harnett, *New Coin* magazine, Grahamstown. D.Litt.: University of Natal, Durban, 1968. Address: Department of English, Rhodes University, Grahamstown, South Africa.

PUBLICATIONS

Verse

Stranger to Europe. Cape Town, Balkema, 1952; augmented edition, 1960.
South of the Zambezi: Poems from South Africa. London, Abelard Schuman, 1966.
On First Seeing Florence. Grahamstown, South Africa, New Coin-Rhodes University, 1968.

Plays

The Dam (produced Cape Town, 1953). Cape Town, Balkema, 1953.
The Dove Returns (produced Cape Town, 1956). Cape Town, Balkema, and London, Fortune Press, 1956.
Take Root or Die (produced Grahamstown, 1966). Cape Town, Balkema, 1970.
Cape Charade (produced Cape Town, 1968). Cape Town, Balkema, 1968.

Other

An Aspect of Tragedy. Grahamstown, Rhodes University, 1953.
The Republic of the Arts. Johannesburg, Witwatersrand University Press, 1964.

Editor, *A Book of South African Verse.* London, Oxford University Press, 1959.
Editor, *When Boys Were Men.* Cape Town, Oxford University Press, 1969.
Editor, *The 1820 Settlers.* Cape Town, Human and Rousseau, 1974.

Manuscript Collection: Thomas Pringle Collection for English in Africa, Rhodes University, Grahamstown.

Guy Butler comments:

Much of my poetry – but by no means all – is generated by the European-African encounter as experienced by someone of European descent, who feels himself to belong to Africa. I am, I think, a product of the old, almost forgotten Eastern Cape Frontier tradition, with its strong liberal and missionary admixture. The nature of the frontier has changed and spread, until all articulate men, but particularly artists, are frontiersmen and/or interpreters. English, as the chosen language of literature of millions of Blacks, has a great and exciting future in Africa; and I've made it my life's business to encourage its creative use in this corner of the world.

*   *   *

Guy Butler's work is a sustained endeavour to distinguish and reconcile the two strains of Europe and Africa – chiefly, but not merely, the southern part of the continent; to record and interpret the local scene; to find appropriate media – vocabulary, imagery, forms – through which to discover and express something of the African essence and primitive consciousness; to establish an African mythology and archetypes (Livingstone, Camoens, the last Trekker); to acclimatize as far as possible "the Grecian and Mediaeval dream." Orpheus has an "African incarnation" ("Myths"), Apollo must come to "cross the tangled scrub, the uncouth ways" ("Home Thoughts") and join the Dionysian dance.

Africa almost becomes an image for a state of mind in which the poet's imagination tries to find dwelling and the human being strives to come to terms with himself, a testing ground for his beliefs and values. The inescapable preoccupation of the modern artist, to find his place in his world, is, for the English poet in Africa, sensitive to European history, art and thought, perhaps more dramatically evident than for his British counterpart. The struggle to articulate, clarify, harmonize and balance contending forces, and be true to experience, informs Butler's poetry with tension and some anguish, and lifts it above trivialities. Circumstances tempt the South African writer to exploit rather than explore his material, to be self-conscious or self-pitying, to address too limited a home audience, to slide into fashionable political or literary cant. Butler rarely succumbs.

T. S. Eliot observes of the genuine poet that "his strict duty is to his *language*, first to preserve, and second to extend and improve." Butler's responsible and experimental use of language is grounded in such an awareness of literary tradition. This leads him to genres other than the ubiquitous meditative lyric – ballad, song, sonnet, elegy, narrative, metaphysical debate, in a variety of measures; and particularly the long poem where he shows a not inconsiderable architectonic skill. Besides verse drama, there is the seemingly casual free verse anecdote ("Sweet-Water") and the formal symphonic poem in fairly elaborate stanzas ("Bronze Heads"). With an understanding of neoclassic decorum, he uses a range of styles, language prismatic or transparent, speaking voice or singing robes. Sometimes regarded as an old-fashioned versifier playing safe, he is in fact often taking risks, with rhyme, intricate verse and image patterns, colloquialisms, cliché, plain statement or rhetorically splendid utterance. The long poem "On First Seeing Florence" is a complex structure of varied styles, rhythms and images which eloquently presents a moment of vision.

Because of this readiness to undertake the hazardous and difficult, this range, breadth, and technical skill, and because he has something to say, Butler is possibly the most considerable poet now writing in South Africa. Others may reach greater heights in individual poems; few can present a body of work which has such a wholeness, complexity, variety and approachableness. Nor is his appeal merely local, though certain poems will have a particular poignancy for his countrymen. A lyric like "Stranger to Europe," a meditation like "Myths," will be read wherever poetry is recognised.

– Ruth Harnett

CAMPBELL, Alistair (Te Ariki). New Zealander. Born in Rarotonga, Cook Islands, 25 June 1925; emigrated to New Zealand in 1933. Educated at Otago Boys' High School, Dunedin; Victoria University of Wellington, B.A. in Latin and English. Married Fleur Adcock, *q.v.* (divorced), two sons; Meg Anderson, 1958, three children. Editor, Department of Education School Publications Branch, Wellington, 1955–72. Since 1972, Senior Editor, New Zealand Council for Educational Research, Wellington. Address: 4 Rawhiti Road, Pukerua Bay, Wellington, New Zealand.

PUBLICATIONS

Verse

> *Mine Eyes Dazzle: Poems 1947–49.* Christchurch, Pegasus Press, 1951; revised
>   edition, 1956.
> *Sanctuary of Spirits.* Wellington, Victoria University-Wai-te-ata Press, 1967.
> *Wild Honey.* London, Oxford University Press, 1964.
> *Blue Rain: Poems.* Wellington, Wei-te-ata Press, 1967.
> *Drinking Horn.* Paremata, Bottle Press, 1971.
> *Walk the Black Path.* Paremata, Bottle Press, 1971.
> *Kapiti: Selected Poems, 1947–71.* Christchurch, Pegasus Press, 1972.

> Recording: *The Return and Elegy*, KIWI.

Plays

> *When the Bough Breaks* (produced Wellington, 1970). Wellington, Downstage,
>   1970.

> Radio Plays: *The Homecoming, The Proprietor, The Suicide, The Wairau Incident.*

> Television Documentary: *Island of Spirits*, 1973.

Other

> *The Fruit Farm* (juvenile). Wellington, School Publications Branch, 1953.
> *The Happy Summer* (juvenile). Christchurch, Whitcombe and Tombs, 1961.
> *New Zealand: A Book for Children.* Wellington, School Publications Branch,
>   1967.
> *Maori Legends.* Wellington, Seven Seas, 1969.

Critical Studies: by James Bertram, in *Comment* (Wellington), January-February 1965; "Alistair Campbell's *Mine Eyes Dazzle*: An Anatomy of Success" by David Gunby, in *Landfall* (Christchurch), March 1969.

Alistair Campbell comments:

Primarily a lyric poet, my main themes are love, death, loss, solitude – in fact, the perennial themes. My early verse, written in a variety of regular verse forms, shows the influence of such poets as Tennyson, Yeats, Pound, and Edward Thomas. More recently, Latin-American and Spanish poets, among others, have shown me how to write with a new freedom and spontaneity.

*   *   *

Alistair Campbell, of mixed Scottish and Polynesian descent, first became known as a poet in the late nineteen-forties, when he was a member of a literary group in Wellington associated with the sophisticated, avowedly "internationalist" periodical *Arachne* (others in the group included Erik Schwimmer, W. H. Oliver, and Hubert Witheford). Like R. A. K. Mason before him, Campbell had read classics at the university and shows a strong formal interest in rhetoric, but the immediate impact of his early work was almost extravagantly romantic. His "Elegy" for a friend killed in the Southern Alps – a lyrical sequence filled with Yeatsian echoes but vibrant with youthful feeling – was given a fine Schubertian setting by the composer Douglas Lilburn, and formed the centrepiece of a collection (*Mine Eyes Dazzle*) which ran through three editions in his own country. Another sequence (originally linked under the title "The Cromwell Gorge") concluded with the mysterious incantatory poem "The Return," where the "plant gods, tree gods" of the dreamlike Pacific Island setting ignore "the drowned Dionysus, sand in his eyes and mouth": this poem too has prompted a highly original "sound image" by Lilburn. *Sanctuary of Spirits* recreates dramatically something of the legend of the bloodthirsty Maori chief Te Rauparaha. This plangent work, with a number of poems of emotional crisis showing naked feeling and compressed power of statement, was drawn on for the English collection *Wild Honey. Blue Rain* contains further lyrics torn from private anguish; Campbell *can* write coolly, with wit and satirical precision, but this is rare. His chief stimulus seems to be the wound, and his best poems embrace bitter love, or death.

– James Bertram

CAMPBELL; David. Australian. Born in Ellerslie, Adelong, New South Wales, 16 July 1915. Educated at King's School, Parramatta; Jesus College, Cambridge, B.A. Served in the Royal Australian Air Force during World War II: Distinguished Flying Cross and Bar. Married Bonnie Lawrence in 1940; has two sons and a daughter. Address: The Run, Queanbeyan, New South Wales 2620, Australia.

PUBLICATIONS

Verse

Speak with the Sun. London, Chatto and Windus, 1949.
The Miracle of Mullion Hill: Poems. Sydney, Angus and Robertson, 1956.
Poems. Sydney, Edwards and Shaw, 1962.

Selected Poems 1942–1968.   Sydney, Angus and Robertson, 1968.
The Branch of Dodona and Other Poems.   Sydney, Angus and Robertson, 1970.
Selected Poems 1942–1970.   Sydney, Angus and Robertson, 1973.
Starting from Central Station.   Sydney, Angus and Robertson, 1973.
Devils' Rock.   Sydney, Angus and Robertson, 1974.

Short Stories

Evening under Lamplight.   Sydney, Angus and Robertson, 1959.

Other

Editor, *Australian Poetry 1966.*   Sydney, Angus and Robertson, 1966.
Editor, *Modern Australian Poetry.*   Melbourne, Sun Books, 1970.

Critical Study: "David Campbell, Selected Poems 1942–1968" by Leonie Kramer, in *Southerly* (Sydney), 1969.

*   *   *

Though there is considerable variety in his poetry, ranging from light-hearted sophisticated satires of city life such as "The Golden Cow" to the love lyrics which were published for the first time in his *Selected Poems 1942–1968*, David Campbell is best known in Australia as the poet of the Monaro. This is the district where he lives, having for its centre the national capital, Canberra. It is a beautiful, unspoilt countryside of sheep and cattle stations, rising from the low rolling hills near Canberra – patrolled by flocks of the white cockatoos and the hawks with which, as an ex-airman and a descendant of Highland chieftains, Campbell has always shown some affinity – to the granite uplands of the Snowy Mountains. Since World War II, when he served with the R.A.A.F. in the South Pacific and was awarded the D.F.C. and bar, Campbell has farmed two properties in the Monaro and in both places, while leading the apparently carefree life of the Australian landowner, he went in for an intensive programme of pasture improvement. Where there had been one blade of grass, there were two; where there had been kangaroo-grass or tussock, there were subterranean clover and phalaris.

These facts, though they may look a little agricultural and irrelevant, are in truth highly relevant to his poetry, for it is based on care and love: care for the right word and the pure melody; love for the small flowers and creatures of the earth:

> Alone the pallid cuckoo now
> Fills his clear bottles in the dew:
> Four five six seven – climb with him!
> And eight brings morning to the brim . . .

for his own sheep and lambs:

> But in the evening light the lambs
> Forget their hillward-munching dams;
> To cuckoo-pipes their dances start
> And fill and overflow the heart . . .

for the land itself:

> Sweet rain, bless our windy farm,
> Sweeping round in skirts of storm
> While these marble acres lie
> Open to an empty sky . . .

and for the people of the Monaro seen in a variety of moods from the comic ballad of "Jack Spring" to the archetypal figure of Peter Quinn

> Who, from the pools of Dairyman,
> Has learned the dreamer's power
> To shut up mountains in his mind
> As the seed holds the flower.

Campbell himself of course has this same "dreamer's power"; and ultimately his creatures of the Monaro, while cherished for their own sakes, become symbols of some principle of joy infusing and indeed creating the universe: a magpie sings in the moonlight

> And to the heartbeats of the light
> Now from the deepness of the glade
> Well up the bubbles of delight:
> Of such stuff the stars were made.

– Douglas Stewart

CAMPBELL, Donald. Scottish. Born in Wick, Caithness, 25 February 1940. Educated at Boroughmuir Senior Secondary School, Edinburgh. Married Jean Fairgrieve in 1966; has one son. Writer-in-Residence, Edinburgh Education Department, 1974–75. Recipient: Scottish Arts Council bursary, 1973. Address: 53 Viewforth, Edinburgh, Scotland.

Publications

Verse

Poems. Preston, Lancashire, Akros, 1971.
Rhymes 'n Reasons. Edinburgh, Reprographia, 1972.

Critical Studies: "The Progress of Scots" by John Herdman, in *Akros* (Preston, Lancashire), 1972; "The MacDiarmid Makars" by Alexander Scott, in *Akros* (Preston, Lancashire), 1972.

Donald Campbell comments:

The bulk of my work is written in Scots – that is to say, in the language which is, to a greater or lesser extent, the language of the greater part of the Scottish people. Now, this in itself probably requires a great deal of explanation – but, without going into a mass of detail, I will be as brief as possible. Most people who know little of Scots poetry appear to assume that Scots is a language (like English or Spanish) which died out years ago and that the work of the Modern Scots poets is no more than a sentimental attempt to revive or re-create it. This is not the case. Scots has never been subject to formal documentation like most other modern languages and survives for two reasons (a) its proximity to English (most English speakers can, with little difficulty, learn to read and understand Scots) and (b) because it has been sustained for over seven centuries by its own distinctive literary tradition. It is within this tradition that I appear to work. The advantages for a poet who is working in Scots (and who can work in Scots) are that he is not restricted by so many "rules of language" and that, although there is a great deal of poetry in our tradition, there are vast uncharted areas of poetic possibility that have never been explored. For instance, although we have had many poets who have written what you might call poems of "direct statement," not much work has been done with the use of images in Scots. We have had many great formal craftsmen (Dunbar, Henrysoun, Fergusson, etc.) but very few who can handle free verse.

My work as a poet does not start and end with Scots however. That is only the tool. I have no concise aims (poets should never have aims) but what I am against *as a man* is the erection of barriers among men. This may seem paradoxical unless you realise that Standard English is a great barrier in Scotland. The inability to speak "correct" English often prevents our people from realising their full potential – and I am naturally against that not simply because they are Scottish but because they are human beings. I want to help exorcise the shame of having for your most natural speech a language which is not recognised as an official language but is, as often as not, not recognised as a language at all. I think all this shows in my poems.

My influences have been mostly foreign – the main ones being the Russian, Mayakovsky, the Frenchman, Jacques Prévert, and the English poet, Gerard Manley Hopkins. Scots poets who have influenced me have been Hugh MacDiarmid, Sydney Goodsir Smith, Robert Garioch, and, most important of all, both the Alexander Scotts – the medieval love poet from Dalkeith and the modern poet and dramatist from Aberdeen. I am also a great admirer of the artistry and language of Norman MacCaig.

*   *   *

In Donald Campbell's first pamphlet, *Poems*, all the verse was in Scots, and its energy and contemporary concern suggested better work to come when those qualities were combined with greater self-criticism and technical care. This combination has been achieved in a majority of the poems in *Rhymes 'n Reasons*. The characteristic Scottish expression of tenderness through the medium of a darkly-ironical apparent callousness is a difficult mode to master, but Campbell brings it off with fine panache in "Vietnam on My Mind," while in another political – or anti-political – poem, "Bangla Desh," he accomplishes the even trickier feat of expressing sympathy through its seeming denial. This command of ambiguity finds a subject in itself in "Ye Say 'Glass,' " and enables a love-poem, "You're the Warst," to end a series of amusing paradoxes by becoming a savage hate-poem too. Yet Campbell is also capable of restraint, and the quietness of "At a Party" is fairly appropriate to its desolate theme of two lovers failing to meet. His few poems in English, sharing the human sympathy expressed in such Scots work as "Keelie" and "Communion at Dunkirk," have a nice delicacy of under-emphasis.

– Alexander Scott

CARROLL, Paul American. Born in Chicago, Illinois, 15 July 1927. Educated at the University of Chicago, M.A. in English 1952. Served in the United States Naval Reserve, 1945–46. Married Inara Birnbaum in 1964 (divorced, 1973); has one son, Luke. Poetry Editor, *Chicago Review*, 1957–59; Editor, *Big Table Magazine*, Chicago, 1959–61; Editor, Big Table Books, Follett Publishing Company, Chicago, 1966–71. Visiting Professor of English, University of Iowa, Iowa City, 1966–67. Since 1968, Professor of English and Chairman of The Program for Writers, University of Illinois, Chicago. Poet-in-Residence, Barnford College, Yale University, New Haven, Connecticut, Spring 1969. Address: Department of English, University of Illinois at Chicago Circle, Chicago, Illinois 60680, U.S.A.

PUBLICATIONS

Verse

Odes. Chicago, Follett, 1968.
The Luke Poems. Chicago, Follett, 1971.

Other

The Poem in Its Skin. Chicago, Follett, 1968.

Editor, *The Edward Dahlberg Reader.* New York, New Directions, 1966.
Editor, *The Young American Poets.* Chicago, Follett, 1968.

Paul Carroll comments:

I can't imagine life without poetry.

*   *   *

Paul Carroll's esthetic understanding abruptly flowered in three volumes of 1968–69. *The Poem in Its Skin* analyzed ten poems by, to Carroll's eyes, the ten leading American poets. *The Young American Poets*, an anthology of 54 poets, encouraged and further directed young poets. *Odes*, Carroll's own selected poems, promulgates in verse the same sensibility and fashions as the essays and anthology.

In the essay on James Wright in *The Poem in Its Skin*, Carroll characterizes Wright's poem as a hip or "impure" homage to Po Chu-i. Similar homage is a motive in Carroll's own odes, though Carroll offers homage not to past poets like Trakl or Po Chu-i but to leading contemporaries like Dickey, Ginsberg, Logan, Wright, and, especially, Neruda. *Odes* owes its title and certain techniques to Neruda's *Odas Elementales*; Carroll acknowledges this explicitly by offering an "Ode to Neruda." "Ode on My 40th Birthday," the opening poem, reworks the theme of Dickey's "Heaven of Animals," a poem Carroll analyzed in *The Poem in Its Skin*. Dickey typically divides life between predator and prey, and reconciles them in a "ritual" hunt. Carroll, spiritually a Catholic, finds a Saint Francis who succumbs less to ritual than "role," becoming, briefly, the glint-toothed, priestly predator:

> Francis free finally to be
> the timber wolf he's feared in dreams
> because its teeth and fur are yours
> slaughters the lamb for the feast reciting
> the prayer at the top of his voice.

Some lines later Carroll dextrously invokes Dickey's antithesis, the Buddhist Allen Ginsberg:

> Do you dance
> on your own body throughout eternity
> as your new lover Allen Ginsberg says?

Carroll's earliest poems depend, significantly, on the literally Catholic and allusive manner of Lowell's *Lord Weary's Castle*. An "Ode to Claes Oldenburg" alerts us that the "impure poem" – a poem, celebrated in Carroll's criticism, which is markedly contemporaneous – derives from Pop art. Carroll's musical odes appeal to the kindly, well-dressed mandarin-about-town.

– Michael André

CARRUTH, Hayden. American. Born in Waterbury, Connecticut, 3 August 1921. Educated at the University of North Carolina, Chapel Hill, B.A. 1943; University of Chicago, M.A. 1947. Served in the United States Army Air Force during World War II. Married Sara Anderson in 1943; Eleanore Ray, 1952; Rose Marie Dorn, 1961; has two children. Editor, *Poetry*, Chicago, 1949–50; Associate Editor, University of Chicago Press, 1950–51, and Intercultural Publications Inc., New York, 1952–53. Currently, Member of the Editorial Board, *Hudson Review*, New York, and Poet-in-Residence, Johnson State College, Vermont. Recipient: Bess Hokin Prize, 1954, Vachel Lindsay Prize, 1956, Levinson Prize, Eunice Tietjens Memorial Prize, and Morton Dauwen Zabel Prize, 1968 (*Poetry*, Chicago); Harriet Monroe Award, 1960; Bollingen Fellowship, 1963; Carl Sandburg Prize, 1963; Emily Clark Balch Prize (*Virginia Quarterly Review*), 1964; Guggenheim Fellowship, 1965; National Endowment for the Arts grant, 1966, 1968, 1974. Address: Crow's Mark, Johnson, Vermont 05656, U.S.A.

PUBLICATIONS

Verse

The Crow and the Heart, 1946–1959. New York, Macmillan, 1959.
Journey to a Known Place. New York, New Directions, 1961.
The Norfolk Poems, 1 June to 1 September 1961. Iowa City, Prairie Press, 1962.
North Winter. Iowa City, Prairie Press, 1964.
Nothing for Tigers: Poems 1959–1964. New York, Macmillan, 1965.
Contra Mortem. Johnson, Vermont, Crow's Mark Press, 1967.
For You: Poems. New York, New Directions, 1970; London, Chatto and Windus, 1972.
The Clay Hill Anthology. Iowa City, Prairie Press, 1970.
From Snow and Rock, From Chaos. New York, New Directions, and London, Chatto and Windus, 1973.
Dark World. Santa Cruz, California, Kayak Books, 1974.
The Bloomingdale Papers. Athens, University of Georgia Press, 1974.

Other

Appendix A. New York, Macmillan, 1963.
After "The Stranger": Imaginary Dialogues with Camus. New York, Macmillan, 1965.

Editor, with James Laughlin, *A New Directions Reader.* New York, New Directions, 1964.
Editor, *The Voice That Is Great Within Us: American Poetry of the Twentieth Century.* New York, Bantam, 1970.
Editor, *The Bird/Poem Book: Poems on the Wild Birds of North America.* New York, McCall, 1970.

*   *   *

Hayden Carruth has a rather special reputation in American letters for versatility and prolificness. In addition to much verse, he has written fiction, a book on Albert Camus and, in strong learned prose, many reviews, tough though essentially fair. As poet, his most impressive work is in the sustained meditation, *Journey to a Known Place*, unquestionably one of finest longish efforts in contemporary poetry, at times breath-taking in its lyrical flights:

> And there were open places where I found
> Other journeyers, resting or climbing, strangers,
> Sweet eyes once cracked in the torturing cold;
> And some few I saw known to me, and one was
> A woman I had once married, now like a soft ash
> Inly aglow, rippling the violet of mind's smile
> Like the concentricities of a woodland pool.

Like amplitude, richness is found elsewhere in the poet's work, yet it is particularly in the long stretch, when his vision can gather intensity, that he seems most himself. Here is another brief passage from *Journey*:

And we came at last to the park where the city opened
Round an emblazoned zone and the light, liquescent
And shimmering, seemed a golden-roseate intensity,
Seemed a fountain ascending, whose returning flow
Made the sunfire's cascade, swirling and vaporing.

In his volumes of shorter works, which contain a fairly high average of fully
realized pieces, Carruth is never less than himself, and in one, *The Norfolk Poems*,
there is an extraordinary piece on Eichmann, notable, considering where most
public poems take us, for an absolute honesty of response, even at moments fury:

But let his ears never, never be shut,
And let young voices read to him, name by name,
From the rolls of all those people whom he has shut
Into the horrible beds, and let his name
Forever and ever be the word for hate. . . .

It is perhaps in the poet's moving "Asylum" poems, collected in his first volume,
The Crow and the Heart, that he shows himself capable of achieving the same level
of intensity to be found invariably in his long poems. "The Asylum" is a 13-part
sequence of beautifully controlled pieces which pierce one with the finality of their
anguish, calling to mind the heartbreaking John Clare. Here is the conclusion of
one of the strongest poems in the sequence:

We lived. The aftersilence fell.
For which word mattered, pity or shame? The roots
Try my breast-cage. My bone
Gleams in the rot. I know you, sir! What bruits
This cry from many a dolmen stone?
Murther! I'm human. Come then, jacket me.
A flawed mind's falling. But say, what page is blown
By the furrowing wind over a black, black sea?

Hayden Carruth is a deeply intelligent, sometimes troubled but always lucid
writer whose works, notably the long meditations, represent an indisputable and –
happily – increasingly honored achievement in American poetry.

– Lucien Stryk

CARTER, Martin (Wylde). Guyanan. Born in Georgetown, British Guiana, now
Guyana, in 1927. Educated at Queen's College, Georgetown. Worked as a clerk in
the Civil Service for four years: forced to resign as a result of his political
activities. Currently, representative for Guyana at the United Nations.

PUBLICATIONS

Verse

The Hill of Fire Glows Red. Georgetown, Miniature Poets, 1951.
To a Dead Slave. Privately printed, 1951.

The Kind Eagle.   Privately printed, 1952.
The Hidden Man.   Privately printed, 1952.
Poems of Resistance from British Guiana.   London, Lawrence and Wishart, 1954.

*   *   *

Apart from contributions in the now defunct Guyanese journal, *Kyk-over-al*, the main significant body of Martin Carter's work is to be found in *Poems of Resistance* (1954) and "Jail Me Quickly," five poems first published in 1964 by the *New World Fortnightly.*

Carter's specific concern is with politics, political revolution and colonial oppression. *Poems of Resistance* was written when the poet was placed in detention for his political views in 1953. "Jail Me Quickly" are direct responses to the political crisis in Guyana in 1962, when the Guyanese Constitution, under Dr. Cheddi Jagan, was suspended by the British Government and British troops were moved in to uphold "law and order" in the country:

> were some who ran one way.
> were some who ran another way.
> were some who did not run at all.
> were some who will not run again.
> and I was with them all,
> when the sun and streets exploded,
> and a city of clerks
> turned a city of men!
> – "Black Friday 1962"

This is Carter's hope – that the individual man may become an aware and fully rounded person, despite the horrors and failures of his colonial past:

> I come from the nigger yard of yesterday
> leaping from the oppressor's hate
> and the scorn of myself;
> from the agony of the dark hut in the shadow
> and the hurt of things . . .
> – "I Come from the Nigger Yard"

But Carter's poetry reveals little *substantial* awareness of the past. He asserts that he will "turn to the histories of men and the lives of the peoples"; but unlike his older contemporary, A. J. Seymour, he has produced no work of reconstruction. Because of this shallow soil of heritage, Carter, poet of the revolution, has really only himself and the revolution and a hope for the future to sustain his vision:

> The sharp knife of dawn glitters in my hand
> but how bare is everything – tall tall tree
> infinite air, the unrelaxing tension of the world
> and only hope, hope only, the kind eagle soars and wheels in flight.
> – "The Knife of Dawn"

What is more fully realized in his poetry is an apprehension of terror (here he reminds us of Yeats), of hopelessness and futility:

> And I have seen some creatures rise from holes,
> and claw a triumph like a citizen,
> and reign until the tide!
> – "Black Friday"

But this hopelessness and terror and futility are transformed through Martin Carter's energy of image and metaphor into a triumph of the writer's art; the elevation of a single mind against the world:

> The long streets of night move up and down
> baring the thighs of a woman
> and the cavern of generation.
> The beating drum returns and dies away
> the bearded men fall down and go to sleep
> the cocks of dawn stand up and crow like bugles.
> — "University of Hunger"

And again:

> O it was the heart like this tiny star near to the sorrows
> straining against the whole world and the long twilight
> spark of man's dream conquering the night
> moving in darkness stubborn and fierce
> till leaves of sunset change from green to blue
> and shadows grow like giants everywhere.
> — "I Come from the Nigger Yard"

— Edward Brathwaite

CASEY, Michael. American. Born in Lowell, Massachusetts, in 1947. Educated at Lowell Technological Institute, B.S. 1968; State University of New York, Buffalo, M.A. 1973. Served in the United States Army. Research Assistant, State University of New York, Buffalo, 1972–73; Guest Editor, *Rapport*, Buffalo, Summer 1973. Since 1972, Editorial Adviser, Alice James Press, Cambridge, Massachusetts. Recipient: Yale Series of Younger Poets Award, 1971. Address: c/o Yale University Press, 92a Yale Station, New Haven, Connecticut 06520, U.S.A.

PUBLICATIONS

Verse

Obscenities. New Haven, Connecticut, Yale University Press, 1972.
On Scales. Buffalo, New York, Lockwood Memorial Library, 1972.
My Youngest That Tall. Buffalo, New York, Slow Loris Press, 1972.
my brother-in-law and me. Cambridge, Massachusetts, Pomegranate Press, 1974.

Critical Study: by A. Poulin, Jr., in *Modern Poetry Studies* (Buffalo, New York), iii, 4, 1972.

*   *   *

Any critical statement on the poetry of Michael Casey must be drawn from his single collection, *Obscenities*, and must therefore be qualified – despite its having won the Yale Series of Younger Poets award. It is a slim book, well received by most critics and definitely showing promise; it also, however, shows Casey operating within a relatively narrow range, both technically and thematically.

Obscenities is a product of the war in Vietnam: "a kind of anti-poetry," Stanley Kunitz asserts in the Foreword, "that befits a kind of war empty of any kind of glory." Avoiding all traditional rhetorical stances toward war, Casey presents a series of short anecdotes about army life and the war in Vietnam as seen from his somewhat peripheral position as a military policeman. These anecdotes are related with economy and with maximum use of crude but authentic G.I. slang. They are witty, often ironic, occasionally moving or disturbing. And they entertain.

At his best (e.g., in "Learning" and "On What the Army Does to Heads") Casey goes far beyond mere entertainment, of course, transcending surface simplicity and moving toward ambiances that resonate, reward. But all too many of these poems are already time-bound; in his attempt to avoid cant, he simply adopts a different but equally limiting argot. After a while his poems tend to sound alike, gimmicky, almost formulaic; and like most pop art, many fail to invite or sustain subsequent readings.

Despite these reservations, one senses that Michael Casey is a poet worth watching in the future. His first volume shows clear potential and some fine moments within its limited boundaries. As one of the youngest poets ever to win the Yale award, Michael Casey has time on his side. One hopes that he can find new strategies to mature beyond this successful beginning.

– Stanley W. Lindberg

CAUSLEY, Charles (Stanley). British. Born in Launceston, Cornwall, 24 August 1917. Educated at Launceston National School; Horwell Grammar School; Launceston College; Peterborough Training College. Served in the Royal Navy, 1940–46. Since 1947, taught in Cornwall. Honorary Visiting Fellow in Poetry, University of Exeter, 1973–74. Literary Editor of BBC radio magazines, *Apollo in the West* and *Signature*, 1953–56. Member of the Arts Council Poetry (later Literature) Panel, 1962–66. Vice-President, West Country Writers' Association; Vice-President. The Poetry Society, London. Recipient: Society of Authors travelling scholarship, 1954, 1966; Queen's Gold Medal for Poetry, 1967; Cholmondeley Award, 1971. Fellow, Royal Society of Literature, 1958. Agent: David Higham Associates Ltd., 5–8 Lower John Street, Golden Square, London W1R 3PE. Address: 2 Cyprus Well, Launceston, Cornwall, England.

PUBLICATIONS

Verse

Farewell, Aggie Weston.   Aldington, Kent, Hand and Flower Press, 1951.
Survivor's Leave.   Aldington, Kent, Hand and Flower Press, 1953.
Union Street: Poems.   London, Hart Davis, 1957; Boston, Houghton Mifflin, 1958.

The Ballad of Charlotte Dymond. Dartington Hall, Devon, privately printed, 1958.
Johnny Alleluia: Poems. London, Hart Davis, 1961.
Penguin Modern Poets 3, with George Barker and Martin Bell. London, Penguin, 1962.
Ballad of the Bread Man. London, Macmillan, 1968.
Underneath the Water: Poems. London, Macmillan, 1968.
Figure of 8: Narrative Poems. London, Macmillan, 1969.
Figgie Hobbin: Poems for Children. London, Macmillan, 1970; New York, Walker, 1973.
Pergamon Poets 10, with Laurie Lee, edited by Evan Owen. Oxford, Pergamon Press, 1970.
Timothy Winters, music by Wallace Southam. London, Turret Books, 1970.
The Tail of the Trinosaur (for children). Leicester, Brockhampton Press, 1973.
As I Went Down Zig Zag (for children). London, Warne, 1974.
Six Women. Richmond, Surrey, Keepsake Press, 1974.
Collected Poems, 1951–1975. London, Macmillan, and Boston, Godine Press, 1975.
The Animals' Carol. London, Macmillan, 1975.

Recordings: *Here Today 1*, Jupiter; *The Poet Speaks 8*, Argo; British Council tapes, 1960, 1966, 1968.

Plays

Runaway. London, Curwen, 1936.
The Conquering Hero. London, Curwen, and New York, Schirmer, 1937.
Benedict. London, Muller, 1938.
How Pleasant to Know Mrs. Lear. London, Muller, 1948.

Short Stories

Hands to Dance. London, Carroll and Nicholson, 1951.
Their Heads Made of Gold (for children). London, Macmillan, 1975.

Other

Editor, *Peninsula: An Anthology of Verse from the West-Country.* London, Macdonald, 1957.
Editor, *Dawn and Dusk: Poems of Our Time.* Leicester, Brockhampton Press, 1962; New York, Watts, 1963.
Editor, *Rising Early: Story Poems and Ballads of the 20th Century.* Leicester, Brockhampton Press, 1964; as *Modern Ballads and Story Poems*, New York, Watts, 1965.
Editor, *Modern Folk Ballads.* London, Studio Vista, 1966.
Editor, *In the Music I Hear: Poems by Children.* Gillingham, Kent, ARC Press, 1970.
Editor, *Oats and Beans and Barley: Poems by Children.* Gillingham, Kent, ARC Press, 1971.
Editor, *Selected Poems*, by Frances Bellerby. London, Enitharmon Press, 1971.
Editor, *The Puffin Book of Magic Verse.* London, Penguin, 1974.

Manuscript Collections: State University of New York, Buffalo; University of Exeter Library, Devon.

Critical Studies: *Poetry Today 1957–60* by Elizabeth Jennings, London, Longman, 1961; "Of Tigers and Trees" by John Pett, in *The Guardian* (London), 15 January 1965; *Poets of the 1939–1945 War* by R. N. Currey, London, Longman, 1967; "Charles Causley Talks to Peter Orr", on British Council Tape Recording 1390, 1968; "Haiku in the Park" by Norman Hidden, in *The Times Educational Supplement* (London), 17 November 1972; *Poetry Today 1960–73* by Anthony Thwaite, London, Longman, 1973.

*   *   *

Charles Causley's poems are not the sort of work that would readily attract the adjective "pioneer": most of them are, or seem to be, utterly traditional. Yet Causley's handling of ballad and lyrical forms, and his jaunty, vivid, humorous way with language, seem – in a way not often acknowledged – to lie behind much of the "pop" poetry of the late 1960's: a poetry intended to be spoken aloud, to be grasped immediately and cheerfully by a mass audience.

Causley was writing such poems before many of his debtors were born. *Farewell, Aggie Weston* and *Survivor's Leave* contain work which could easily fit into his recent book, *Underneath the Water*; and their simple ballad rhythms, their hyperbolic images and their spry blending of old and new imagery could sit comfortably in such a collection as *Love Love Love* – though they are considerably better written and more intelligent:

> I saw a shot-down angel in the park
> His marble blood sluicing the dyke of death,
> A sailing tree firing its brown sea-mark
> Where he now wintered for his wounded breath.

These early poems also remind one sometimes of Roy Campbell, but they lack the often oppressive (and aggressive) personality of Campbell. In fact, a legitimate charge against much of Causley's work up until *Underneath the Water* would be that it is too blandly and automatically anonymous, a voice without a man behind it: an attractive but rather irrelevant voice. There was also a feeling that sombre and complex subjects were being prettified and over-simplified, as in "Recruiting Drive":

> Down in the enemy country
> Under the enemy tree
> There lies a lad whose heart has gone bad
> Waiting for me, for me.

All these are justifiable objections, but they do not take in the whole of Causley, by any means. From the beginning, he could break away from lilting measures and gaudy diction when it suited him, as in "Chief Petty Officer," which is an excellent comic sketch in free verse, and – in a more traditional mode – he could be weighty, as in "I Am the Great Sun." More impressively, *Underneath the Water* contains poems drawing more closely from the personal and the circumstantial, with the old lyrical sweetness but with new depths: for example, "Conducting a Children's Choir":

I bait the snapping breath, curled claw, the deep
And delicate tongue that lends no man its aid.
The children their unsmiling kingdoms keep,
And I walk with them, and I am afraid.

Causley's wartime experiences in the Navy, the mundane stuff of his childhood
and present life as a teacher, are handled with a brisk attention to real detail. Yet
the "folk" properties and the oral narrative characteristics are still there as plainly
and successfully as ever, in "By St. Thomas Water," "Reservoir Street," "In
Coventry," "Lord Sycamore" and "Ballad of the Bread Man." These poems are
not artless: what Roy Campbell wrote of Causley several years ago is still true:
"The poems have an apparent freshness and spontaneity about them which, with
their fine finish, could never have been attained without the most careful work and
subtle refinement." His work has an initial availability (often to children as well as
to adults) which, unlike that of some more recent popular poets, bears re-hearing
and re-reading: the rhythms and images work their way into the memory, and earn
their keep there.

– Anthony Thwaite

CERAVOLO, Joseph. American. Born in New York City, 22 April 1934. Edu-
cated at City College of New York, B.C.E. 1959. Has three children. Junior
Engineer, New York State Department of Public Works, New York City, 1959–60;
Design Engineer, Jersey Testing Laboratories, Newark, New Jersey, 1961–64, and
Porter and Ripa Associates Inc., Newark, New Jersey, 1964–69; Principal Engineer,
Town of Bloomfield, New Jersey, 1969–71; Design Engineer, Purcel Associates,
East Orange, New Jersey, 1971–72, and Engelhard Enterprises, South Plainfield,
New Jersey, 1972. Since 1972, Hydraulic Engineer, Porter and Ripa Associates
Inc., Morristown, New Jersey. Recipient: Poets Foundation Award, 1962, 1963,
1965, 1967; National Endowment for the Arts grant, 1966, 1972; Frank O'Hara
Award, 1968. Address: 65 Spruce Street, Bloomfield, New Jersey 07003, U.S.A.

PUBLICATIONS

Verse

Fits of Dawn. New York, "C" Press, 1965.
Wild Flowers Out of Gas. New York, Tibor de Nagy Gallery, 1967.
Spring in This World of Poor Mutts. New York, Columbia University Press,
   1968.

Critical Study: by Robert Cohen, in *Poetry* (Chicago), 1969.

*   *   *

Joseph Ceravolo's poetry has neither the madcap inventiveness of Frank O'Hara nor the sustained, albeit frustrating, dandyism of John Ashbery, though whatever interest it does possess lies in the shadow of these two prominent figures. It is work that is weakly imitative of an already eclectic mode, and as such often bores the reader who persists, or vanishes before anyone who glances through looking for humor or recognition. In the transvaluation of all values left in the wake of surrealism, and the stochastic aesthetic of Jackson Pollock and John Cage, such boredom and vapidity stand as "natural" consequences. In certain poets adept at this method, these disvalues can even be a challenge, but when talent, verve, and expressiveness are absent, the result drags very badly:

> I'm tired
> I'm going to bed.
> I'm tired. Look for me
> I will wake up
> And kiss me
> Whether I wake up
> or not.
> I'm tired
> When the birds stop
> I will wake up or not.
> The windows are open.

This is an entire poem, called "Noise Outside," and it survives only by its staggering inconsequence. Ceravolo easily masters the ephemeral, and his true domain is the egotistical mundane ("Since this tripod of despair is / here alone. I am with you / forever. / The rag in the tree is still there" – a complete poem called "Tripod"). Most of the poems are brief, though some are extended through a sort of pastiche reminiscent less of William Burroughs than Ted Berrigan.

Being the first poet to win the Frank O'Hara Award for Poetry, given somewhat incongruously by Columbia University Press, Ceravolo might be seen to signal the demise of the much (self-) publicized New York School. Ceravolo's humor has far too little buoyancy to keep even a slight poem afloat, and seldom does any turn of image or juxtaposition really startle. Occasionally a phrase demonstrates sensibility ("Love speeds in, struggle / in beautied temptations"), but just as often the sensibility is left completely alone to flirt with banality ("the small breath / of the insect / is like a breeze / before rain"). In many instances, he falls back on the vocative, and the poems sound like calls of distress, or very secular prayers. It is difficult to say whether Ceravolo is afraid of larger significance, mistrusts it, chooses to avoid it as misleading, or is simply bored by it. In any case he avoids it utterly, but with little adroitness. Auden's remark that finally we praise an avant-garde poem because one of our friends has written it must explain how this poetry can be called, both in truth and truest camp, "award-winning."

– Charles Molesworth

CHEYNEY-COKER, Syl. Sierra Leonean. Born in Freetown, 28 June 1945. Educated at the University of Oregon, Eugene; University of California, Los Angeles; University of Wisconsin, Madison. Has been a drummer, radio producer, factory worker and dock worker. Journalist, Eugene, Oregon, 1968–69; Teaching Assistant, University of Wisconsin, 1971. Recipient: Ford grant, 1970. Lives in Freetown.

PUBLICATIONS

Verse

Concerto for an Exile.   London, Heinemann, and New York, Africana, 1972.
The Graveyard Also Has Teeth.   London, New Beacon, 1974.

Syl Cheyney-Coker comments:

I hold the terrible distinction of being the only poet from my country who has published a sizeable volume of poems. I say terrible not in the pejorative sense but from a feeling of painful awareness that before my appearance, my country was a ghetto of silence.

A popular awareness of self and the creation of different modes of expression of our social and cultural needs seem to me to be the immediate task of the Sierra Leonean writer. We are a strange people; our history, language and culture are not to be confused with those of other English-speaking Africans.

The admixture of English philanthropy and African exotica that has produced and shaped the Sierra Leonean Creole is for me the makeup of any genuine Sierra Leonean Literature.

My "Afro-Saxon" heritage has meant a lot for me as I summarize my passion and I hope it will convey something of the strangeness of my people to the reader.

                    *   *   *

The question of ancestry is a central concern in the writing of many Third World poets. In the poems of Syl Cheyney-Coker, especially those collected in his book Concerto for an Exile, this concern becomes a fixation, his

          . . . Creole ancestry
          which gave me my negralised head
          all my polluted streams

providing the impulse for poems which, in the extravagance and precise violence of their imagery, match some of the best writing of Vallejo and U'Tamsi, two poets whom Cheyney-Coker acknowledges as influences.

There are also definite echoes of the Negritude school and the poems of David Diop. The "Africa, my Africa" of Diop's poems has, however, been narrowed down to a specific nation, Sierra Leone, the land of freed slaves where a patois language, Creole and a Western influenced capital, Freetown, are ironic heritages of the colonial era:

          In my country the Creoles drink only
          Black and White with long sorrows
          hanging from their colonial faces . . .

Cheyney-Coker's poems are cries of bitter agony and bright illumination at one and the same time. They present the picture – as in "Agony of the Dark Child" or in "Misery of the Convert" with its lines:

> I was a king before they nailed you on the cross
> converted I read ten lies in your silly commandments
> to honour you my Christ
> when you have deprived me of my race . . .

– of a nation and a poet tortured by a culture and a religion imposed upon them, a nation and a poet who may find salvation through defiance.

Painful is a word which can be readily applied to much of Syl Cheyney-Coker's writing, just as another word – truthful – can also be applied to the same poems. He attempts, through a wrenching examination of personal and national histories, to create a new vision, a more honest world. In his poem "Guinea," written on the unsuccessful invasion of that nation by Portuguese mercenaries, he defines his role:

> I am not the renegade
> who has forsàken your shores
> I am not the vampire
> gnawing at your heart
> to feed capitalist banks
> I am your poet
> writing No to the world.

– Joseph Bruchac

CIARDI, John (Anthony). American. Born in Boston, Massachusetts, 24 June 1916. Educated at Bates College, Lewiston, Maine, 1934–36; Tufts College, Medford, Massachusetts, A.M. (magna cum laude) 1938 (Phi Beta Kappa); University of Michigan, Ann Arbor (Hopwood Award, 1939), 1939. Served in the United States Army Air Force, 1942–45: Air Medal, Oak Leaf Cluster. Married Myra Judith Hostetter in 1946; has three children. Instructor, University of Kansas City, Missouri, 1940–42; Briggs Copeland Instructor in English, 1946–48, and Assistant Professor, 1948–53, Harvard University, Cambridge, Massachusetts; Lecturer, 1953–54, Associate Professor, 1954–56, and Professor of English, 1956–61, Rutgers University, New Brunswick, New Jersey; Lecturer, 1947–73, and Director, 1956–72, Bread Loaf Writers Conference, Vermont. Editor, Twayne Publishers, New York, 1949; Lecturer, Salzburg Seminar in American Studies, 1951; Poetry Editor, *Saturday Review*, New York, 1956–73; Host, *Accent* program, CBS-TV, 1961–62. Since 1973, Contributing Editor, *World Magazine*, New York. Recipient: Oscar Blumenthal Prize, 1943, Eunice Tietjens Memorial Prize, 1944, Levinson Prize, 1946, and Harriet Monroe Memorial Prize, 1955 (*Poetry*, Chicago); New England Poetry Club Golden Rose, 1948; American Academy in Rome Fellowship, 1956; Boys' Clubs of America Junior Book Award, 1962. D.Litt.: Tufts College, 1960; Ohio Wesleyan University, Delaware, 1971; Washington University, St. Louis, 1971; Hum.D.: Wayne University, Detroit, 1963; LL.D.: Ursinus College, Collegeville, Pennsylvania, 1964; D.L.H.: Kalamazoo College, Michigan, 1964;

Bates College, 1970. Member, National Institute of Arts and Letters, and American Academy of Arts and Sciences. Address: 359 Middlesex Avenue, Metuchen, New Jersey 08840, U.S.A.

PUBLICATIONS

Verse

> *Homeward to America.* New York, Holt, 1940.
> *Other Skies.* Boston, Little Brown, 1947.
> *Live Another Day: Poems.* New York, Twayne, 1949.
> *From Time to Time.* New York, Twayne, 1951.
> *As If: Poems New and Selected.* New Brunswick, New Jersey, Rutgers University Press, 1955.
> *I Marry You: A Sheaf of Love Poems.* New Brunswick, New Jersey, Rutgers University Press, 1958.
> *39 Poems.* New Brunswick, New Jersey, Rutgers University Press, 1959.
> *In the Stoneworks,* New Brunswick, New Jersey, Rutgers University Press, 1961.
> *In Fact.* New Brunswick, New Jersey, Rutgers University Press, 1962.
> *Person to Person.* New Brunswick, New Jersey, Rutgers University Press, 1964.
> *The Strangest Everything.* New Brunswick, New Jersey, Rutgers University Press, 1966.
> *An Alphabestiary: Twenty-Six Poems.* Philadelphia, Lippincott, 1967.
> *A Genesis: 15 Poems.* New York, Touchstone Publications, 1967.
> *The Achievement of John Ciardi: A Comprehensive Selection of His Poems with a Critical Introduction,* edited by Miller Williams. Chicago, Scott Foresman, 1969.
> *Lives of X.* New Brunswick, New Jersey, Rutgers University Press, 1972.
> *The Little That Is All.* New Brunswick, New Jersey, Rutgers University Press, 1974.

Recording: *As If,* Folkways.

Other

> *The Reason for the Pelican* (verse for children). Philadelphia, Lippincott, 1959.
> *Scrappy the Pup* (juvenile). Philadelphia, Lippincott, 1960.
> *I Met a Man* (verse for children). Boston, Houghton Mifflin, 1961.
> *The Man Who Sang the Sillies* (verse for children). Philadelphia, Lippincott, 1961.
> *You Read to Me, I'll Read to You* (verse for children). Philadelphia, Lippincott, 1962.
> *The Wish-Tree* (juvenile). New York, Crowell Collier, 1962.
> *Dialogue with an Audience.* Philadelphia, Lippincott, 1963.
> *Poetry: A Closer Look,* with James M. Reid and Laurence Perrine. New York, Harcourt Brace, 1963.
> *John J. Plenty and Fiddler Dan: A New Fable of the Grasshopper and the Ant* (verse for children). Philadelphia, Lippincott, 1963.
> *You Know Who* (juvenile). Philadelphia, Lippincott, 1964.

The King Who Saved Himself from Being Saved (verse for children). Philadelphia, Lippincott, 1965.
The Monster Den; or, Look What Happened at My House – and to It (verse for children). Philadelphia, Lippincott, 1966.
Someone Could Win a Polar Bear (verse for children). Philadelphia, Lippincott, 1970.
Manner of Speaking (*Saturday Review* columns). New Brunswick, New Jersey, Rutgers University Press, 1972.
Fast and Slow (verse for children). Boston, Houghton Mifflin, 1975.

Editor, *Mid-Century American Poets.* New York, Twayne, 1950.
Editor, *How Does a Poem Mean?* Boston, Houghton Mifflin, 1960.

Translator, *The Inferno,* by Dante. New Brunswick, New Jersey, Rutgers University Press, 1954.
Translator, *The Purgatorio,* by Dante. New York, New American Library, 1961.
Translator, *The Paradiso,* by Dante. New York, New American Library, 1970.

Bibliography: *John Ciardi: A Bibliography,* by William White, Detroit, Wayne State University Press, 1959.

John Ciardi comments:

Poetry, for me, finds voices, but the aim should not be an idiosyncratic single voice immediately recognizable as the voice of a given man (style as signature). Something of that sort is bound to happen as a man learns to write into himself; there will be some of the lub-dub of his own heart if the writing lives at all. I take that personalization to be essential and inevitable but secondary. The ideal accomplishment of a poem may be put as *homo fecit*. A man did it, and any man may say it of himself as one of the voices of his humanity, of his humanity quickened to itself.

*   *   *

John Ciardi's poetic strength lies in the diversity and the fluency of his work. Few poets of his generation can have produced more, but, unlike many prolific writers, he gives us the feeling that to be fertile is part of his poetic personality; that he is always ready to attempt something new. Critics have frequently pointed to the strongly personal note in his work; some of them indeed have criticised it for being too personal. It is certainly difficult to envisage the poems apart from the writer of them; they are the exuberant expression of Ciardi's delight in the world, the interest which his own life affords him. It is his good fortune to have an extremely direct and unselfconscious access to his own psyche.
These virtues are to some extent balanced by corresponding weaknesses. Ciardi is eclectic, and at moments seems not to have entirely absorbed his influences. In particular, one catches the echoes, in his earlier work, of British poets such as W. H. Auden and Dylan Thomas. Individual poems often seem to go on a bit too long; the author's exuberance and delight in words outrun the reader's patience. As a result, one seldon remembers individual poems, but rather a personality and a tone of voice which can be found throughout Ciardi's poetry.

The command of tone is important, however, because it gives us a clue as to the reasons for Ciardi's vast popularity as a reader of his own work. As a poet, he seems to communicate very directly to his audience. For him, more than for most poets, poetry is speech, a means of linking one man to another. Ciardi's numerous books of verse provide us with a singularly complete and endearing self-portrait.

– Edward Lucie-Smith

CLARK, John Pepper. Nigerian. Born in Kiagbolo, 6 April 1935. Educated at Warri Government College, Ughelli, 1948–54; Ibadan University, 1955–60, B.A. (honours) in English 1960; Princeton University, New Jersey (Parvin Fellowship), 1962–63; Ibadan University (Institute of African Studies Research Fellowship, 1961–64). Married; has one daughter. Nigerian Government Information Officer, 1960–61; Head of Features and Editorial Writer, *Daily Express,* Lagos, 1961–62. Founding-Editor, *The Horn* magazine, Ibadan. Since 1964, Lecturer in English, University of Lagos. Founding Member, Society of Nigerian Authors. Agent: Curtis Brown Ltd., 13 King Street, London W.C.2, England. Address: Department of English, University of Lagos, Lagos, Nigeria.

PUBLICATIONS

Verse

> *Poems.* Ibadan, Mbari, 1962.
> *A Reed in the Tide: A Selection of Poems.* London, Longman, 1965; New York, Humanities Press, 1970.
> *Casualties: Poems 1966–1968.* London, Longman, and New York, Africana, 1970.

Plays

> *Song of a Goat* (produced Ibadan, 1961; London, 1965). Ibadan, Mbari, 1961; in *Three Plays,* 1964.
> *Three Plays: Song of a Goat, The Raft, The Masquerade.* London, Oxford University Press, 1964.
> *The Masquerade* (produced London, 1965). Included in *Three Plays,* 1964.
> *The Raft* (broadcast, 1966). Included in *Three Plays,* 1964.
> *Ozidi.* Ibadan, London, and New York, Oxford University Press, 1966.

> Screenplays: *The Ozidi of Atazi* (documentary); *The Ghost Town* (documentary).

> Radio Play: *The Raft,* 1966.

Other

America, Their America.   London, Deutsch-Heinemann, 1964; New York, Africana, 1969.

Example of Shakespeare: Critical Essays on African Literature.   New York, Africana, 1970.

*   *   *

At a time when the question "Has Africa a culture?" was being asked again and again, John Pepper Clark emerged as one of a group of talented Nigerian writers who answered in the indisputable affirmative and did much to improve the image of the African personality abroad. He has remained a pioneer of the new African expression, coping as best he might with the problem of the two cultures. As he suggests in a personal note to one of his books, he feels himself "mulatto" in mind, coming as he does from a Nigerian stock from which he has never quite felt severed, but educated in the English language and tradition.

Pepper Clark's poems are wide ranging in subject matter and display an incisive intelligence and wit. Out of his European and African experiences he strives to evolve a third. Thus many of his symbols and images are Nigerian, and though unobtrusive in their use require some knowledge on the reader's part of their sources. Such is the agility of the poet's mind that his images shift like "quicksilver flakes and flecks." His political statements are laced in proverbs, his nature poems as in "Girl Bathing" are rich in aesthetic insight, but always buried in the traditional myths and symbols of his own people.

Pepper Clark's technique is personal and dictated by the sense of the poem he is creating, but his facility with language and compression of rhythms sometimes make his poems clipped and abrupt. Here is a writer who has the makings of a significant poet by any standards, whose depth is greater than his breadth, and whose poetry demands that we re-read it with greater application when we think we have understood it,

– Lenri Peters

CLARK, Leonard. British. Born in St. Peter Port, Guernsey, 1 August 1905. Educated at Monmouth School; Normal College, Bangor, Caernarvonshire, Cert.Ed. 1930. Served in the Devon Regiment of the Home Guard, 1940–43. Married Jane Callow in 1954; has two children. Taught in Gloucestershire and London, 1922–28, 1930–36; Inspector of Schools, 1936–70. Since 1970, Editor, Longmans Poetry Library series (64 titles). Member of the Arts Council Literature Panel, 1965–69. Freeman of the City of London, 1965. Fellow, Royal Society of Literature, 1953. Knight of the Order of St. Sylvester, 1970. O.B.E. (Officer, Order of the British Empire), 1966. Address: 50 Cholmeley Crescent, London N6 5HA, England.

PUBLICATIONS

Verse

Poems. London, Fortune Press, 1940.
Passage to the Pole and Other Poems. London, Fortune Press, 1944.
Rhandanim. Leeds, Salamander Press, 1945.
The Mirror and Other Poems. London, Allen Wingate, 1948.
XII Poems. Birmingham, City of Birmingham School of Printing, 1948.
English Morning and Other Poems. London, Hutchinson, 1953.
Selected Poems, 1940–1957. London, Hutchinson, 1958.
Daybreak: A First Book of Poems for Children. London, Hart Davis, 1963.
The Year Round: A Second Book of Poems for Children. London, Hart Davis,
    1966.
Fields and Territories. London, Turret Books, 1967.
Good Company: Poems for Children. London, Dobson, 1968.
Near and Far: Poems for Children. London, Hamlyn, 1968.
Here and There: Poems for Children. London, Hamlyn, 1969.
Walking with Trees. London, Enitharmon Press, 1970.
Every Voice. Guildford, Surrey, Words Press, 1971.
All Along Down Along: A Book of Stories in Verse. London, Longman, 1971.
Secret as Toads: Poems for Children. London, Chatto and Windus, 1972.
Singing in the Streets: Poems for Christmas. London, Dobson, 1972.
The Broad Atlantic: Poems for Children. London, Dobson, 1974.
Four Seasons: Poems for Children. London, Dobson, 1974.
The Hearing Heart: Poems. London, Enitharmon Press, 1974.

Other

Alfred Williams: His Life and Works. Oxford, Blackwell, 1945; New York, A.
    M. Kelly, 1969.
Ideas in Poetry. Birmingham, City of Birmingham School of Printing, 1947.
*Sark Discovered: Prospect of an Island: Being a Literary and Pictorial Record of the
    Island of Sark.* London, Dent, 1956; revised edition, London, Dobson, 1971.
Walter de la Mare: A Checklist. Cambridge, University Press, 1956.
Walter de la Mare. London, Bodley Head, 1960; New York, H. Z. Walck,
    1961.
Green Wood: A Gloucestershire Childhood. London, Parrish, 1962.
Andrew Young. London, Longman, 1964.
When They Were Children (juvenile). London, Parrish, and New York, Roy,
    1964.
A Fool in the Forest (autobiography). London, Dobson, 1965.
Robert Andrew Tells a Story (juvenile). London, Arnold, 1965.
Robert Andrew and Tiffy (juvenile). London, Arnold, 1965.
Robert Andrew by the Sea (juvenile). London, Arnold, 1965.
Robert Andrew and the Holy Family (juvenile). London, Arnold, 1965.
Robert Andrew and the Red Indian Chief (juvenile). London, Arnold, 1966.
Robert Andrew and Skippy (juvenile). London, Arnold, 1966.
Robert Andrew in the Country (juvenile). London, Arnold, 1966.
Prospect of Highgate and Hampstead. London, Highgate Press, 1967.
Grateful Caliban (autobiography). London, Dobson, 1967.
The Tale of Prince Igor. London, Dobson, 1975.

Editor, *The Magic Kingdom: An Anthology of Verse for Seniors.*   London, Elkin Mathews and Marrot, 1937.

Editor, *The Open Door: Anthology of Verse for Juniors.*   London, Elkin Mathews and Marrot, 1937.

Editor, *The Kingdom of the Mind: Essays and Addresses by Albert Mansbridge, 1903–1937.*   London, Dent, 1944.

Editor, *Andrew Young: Prospect of a Poet: Essays and Tributes by Fourteen Writers.*   London, Hart Davis, 1957.

Editor, *Quiet as Moss: Thirty Six Poems,* by Andrew Young.   London, Hart Davis, 1959.

Editor, *The Collected Poems of Andrew Young.*   London, Hart Davis, 1960.

Editor, *Drums and Trumpets: Poetry for the Youngest.*   London, Bodley Head, 1962; Chester Springs, Pennsylvania, Dufour, 1963.

Editor, *Common Ground: An Anthology for the Young.*   London, Faber, 1964.

Editor, *Selected Poems by John Clare, 1793–1864.*   Leeds, Arnold, 1964.

Editor, *All Things New: An Anthology.*   London, Constable, 1965; Chester Springs, Pennsylvania, Dufour, 1968.

Editor, *Following the Sun: Poems by Children.*   London, Odhams, 1967.

Editor, *Flute and Cymbals: Poetry for the Young.*   London, Bodley Head, 1968; New York, Crowell, 1969.

Editor, with others, *The Complete Poems of Walter de la Mare.*   London, Faber, 1969.

Editor, *Sound of Battle.*   Oxford, Pergamon Press, 1969.

Editor, *Poems by Children.*   London, Studio Vista, 1970.

Editor, *The Complete Poems of Andrew Young.*   London, Secker and Warburg, 1973.

Editor, *Poems of Ivor Gurney, 1890–1937.*   London, Chatto and Windus, 1973.

Leonard Clark comments:

I have been described as a "Neo-Blake Imagist" and as "of the company of Traherne and Clare." But my themes are nature (whether in town or country), religion, childhood, and love. I have tried most verse forms, but my more recent work is of its own day – unrhyming but strong and subtle thythmic and sound effects. I have been influenced by Edward Thomas, de la Mare, Hardy, Andrew Young and by some of my younger contemporaries. I have been trying to master the English language for forty years, developing slowly, with my best work still to come. I have tried to keep a sense of wonder and my belief in a few eternal values, forgetting the unhappier aspects of living. I believe I have a special gift for writing poetry for the young and am seeking to develop this by greater insight, and technical power. I am essentially a countryman, wherever I happen to live, with a strong feeling for history and music.

*   *   *

Leonard Clark is one of those poets who, familiar with the experience in versification of the past half-century, and to some extent profiting by this, remains at heart a Georgian poet, with many of the virtues of that school and few of its vices. He is primarily a nature poet, who began by writing poems celebrating the English landscape ("Forest Pools," "High Beeches," "Abyss"); as time has passed, his poems have become more personal, more mystical, but if anything simpler in expression. Both in those verses written specifically for children and in others, his language is perfectly straightforward – sometimes seeming almost too simplistic, remaining one (as in "Men as Trees") of Victorian hymns. But when, as in "Golden Eagle," he combines a deeply personal vision with a sharply observant eye, the result is a poem which is memorable. Technically, Clark uses often a loose form within which he can move easily; very occasionally in early poems the apparently deliberate use of somewhat archaic language can jar. But in his latest work he uses a sure ear to make carefully judged effects which round his poems off into well-shaped wholes, only now and then betraying their subjects by seeming oversmooth. The body of his work shows a mind moving within certain bounds, but surveying the ground completely and thoroughly. Few poets have been so successful in restricting their themes so deftly, in order to avoid over-reaching themselves.

– Derek Parker

———————————

CLARK, Tom. American. Born in Chicago, Illinois, 1 March 1941. Educated at the University of Michigan, Ann Arbor (Hopwood Prize, 1963), B.A. 1963; Cambridge and Essex universities (Fulbright Fellow, 1963–65). Married Angelica Heinegg in 1968; has one child. Since 1963, Poetry Editor, *Paris Review*, New York and Paris. Instructor in American Poetry, University of Essex, Wivenhoe, 1966–67. Recipient: Bess Hokin Prize, 1966, and George Dillon Memorial Prize, 1968 (*Poetry,* Chicago); National Endowment for the Arts grant, 1966, 1968; Poets Foundation Award, 1967; Rockefeller Fellowship, 1968. Address: Box 6, Cherry Road, Bolinas, California 94924, U.S.A.

PUBLICATIONS

Verse

Airplanes. Brightlingsea, Essex, Once Press, 1966.
The Sand Burg: Poems. London, Ferry Press, 1966.
Bunn, with Ron Padgett. New York, Angel Hair Books, 1968.
Stones. New York, Harper, 1969.
Air. New York, Harper, 1970.
Green. Los Angeles, Black Sparrow Press, 1971.
John's Heart. London, Cape Goliard Press, and New York, Grossman, 1972.
Back in Boston Again, with Ted Berrigan and Ron Padgett. Philadelphia, Telegraph Books, 1972.
Smack. Los Angeles, Black Sparrow Press, 1972.
Blue. Los Angeles, Black Sparrow Press, 1974.

Play

The Emperor of the Animals. London, Goliard Press, 1967.

*   *   *

Most of Tom Clark's poems are written in stanzas or as blocks of lines, with not very much space in between. The fact that the poems look traditional is misleading, though Clark's knowledge of how poems are made, how to create works out of the sources in his environment, is one of many attributes placing him among the most interesting poets writing today. This knowledge, or knowhow, at once his greatest strength, at other times becomes an obstacle between himself and his ability to express himself clearly. His poems are very fast, which compensates for the lack of space, speed giving air and rhythm to the density which in turn barrels through with a sense of assurance becoming joy.

Most of the poems in Tom Clark's book *Stones* were written, I would guess, between 1964 and 1967, when the poet became interested in language at the risk of inciting the irrational qualities of his intelligence. Letting go of all restrictions as to what goes into the poem while retaining the ability to make everything come out right – that "technique" which as a word doesn't really seem fitting – his work from this period, while always lyrical, becomes slightly feverish, never hard, as serious as it is speculative and witty. While dealing with the physical world, the objects and people that comprise his experience, his interest extends to the possibilities of what happens to that experience when you write about it. When the rhythm that impels him to write enters his head, it sets into motion a very complicated sense apparatus which, opening outwards, releases a tremendous amount of energy. I'm not sure that's what actually happens, but it often seems necessary to empty one's head of all points of reference and arrive at a new, clear picture of where one is, before writing.

Clark's poems have a way of becoming nostalgic, almost as a bonus alongside everything else that is there. In "Superballs," the opening poen in *Stones,* the poet's attitude shifts from intense speculation about the past to the more casual, gentle vibrations given off by the last few lines:

> You say
> Her body is limp not plastic
> Your heart is missing from it
> You replace your heart in your breast and go on your way.

In his more recent work the frenetic pace has slowed down a bit with the emphasis now on feeling and mood, paralleling the shift from city life to the serenity of a more natural environment. The concern with beauty remains, however, as the basis for most of Tom Clark's poetry. Re-reading works like "You," "Doors," "The Lake," "Poem (Like Musical Instruments)," and "The Top of the World," I think that the darker, more intense side of his poetry – a side which does exist and is the reason for the "literary" quality of many of the poems – functions as a wall the poet must get through in order to create beauty, and that the willingness to try – in Tom Clark's poetry – is already there.

– Lewis Warsh

CLARKE, Austin. Irish. Born in Dublin, 9 May 1896. Educated at Belvedere College, Dublin; University College, Dublin, M.A. Married to Nora Walker; has three children. Lecturer in English, University College, Dublin, 1917–21. Assistant

Editor, *Argosy*, London, 1929. Chairman, Dublin Verse Speaking Society, and Lyric Theatre Company. President, Irish P.E.N., 1939–42, 1946–49. Recipient: Tailteann Games National Award, 1932; Denis Devlin Memorial Award, 1964; Arts Council Special Poetry Prize, 1964; Irish Academy of Letters Gregory Medal, 1968. D.Litt.: Trinity College, Dublin, 1966. Founding Member, 1932, and President, 1952–54, Irish Academy of Letters. Address. Bridge House, Templeogue, Dublin 14, Ireland. *Died 19 March 1974.*

PUBLICATIONS

Verse

The Vengeance of Fionn. Dublin, Maunsel, 1917.
The Fires of Bäal. Dublin, Maunsel and Roberts, 1921.
The Sword of the West. Dublin, Maunsel and Roberts, 1921.
The Cattledrive in Connaught and Other Poems. London, Allen and Unwin, 1925.
Pilgrimage and Other Poems. London, Allen and Unwin, 1929; New York, Farrar and Rinehart, 1930.
The Collected Poems of Austin Clarke. Dublin, Orwell Press, 1936.
Night and Morning. Dublin, Orwell Press, 1938.
Ancient Lights. Privately printed, 1955.
Too Great a Vine: Poems and Satires. Dublin, Bridge Press, 1957.
The Horse-Eaters: Poems and Satires. Dublin, Bridge Press, 1960.
Collected Later Poems. Dublin, Dolmen Press, 1961.
Forget-Me-Not. Dublin, Dolmen Press, 1962.
Six Irish Poets, with others, edited by Robin Skelton. London, Oxford University Press, 1962.
Flight to Africa and Other Poems. Dublin, Dolmen Press, 1963.
Poems: A Selection, with Tony Connor and Charles Tomlinson. London, Oxford University Press, 1964.
Mnemosyne Lay in Dust. Dublin, Dolmen Press, and London, Oxford University Press, 1966.
Old-Fashioned Pilgrimage and Other Poems. Dublin, Dolmen Press, London, Oxford University Press, and Chester Springs, Pennsylvania, Dufour, 1967.
The Echo at Coole and Other Poems. Dublin, Dolmen Press, and Chester Springs, Pennsylvania, Dufour, 1968.
A Sermon on Swift and Other Poems. Dublin, Bridge Press, 1968.
Orphide. Privately printed, 1970.
Tiresias: A Poem. Dublin, Bridge Press, 1971.
The Wooing of Becfola (After the Irish). London, Poem-of-the-Month Club, 1973.
Collected Poems, edited by Liam Miller. Dublin, Dolmen Press, and London and New York, Oxford University Press, 1974.

Plays

The Son of Learning (produced Cambridge, 1927). London, Allen and Unwin, 1927.
The Flame (produced Edinburgh, 1932; Dublin, 1941). London, Allen and Unwin, 1930.

Sister Eucharia (produced Dublin, 1941). Dublin, Orwell Press, 1941.
Black Fast (produced Dublin, 1941). Dublin, Orwell Press, 1941.
As the Crow Flies (broadcast, 1942). Dublin, Bridge Press, and London, Williams and Norgate, 1943.
The Kiss (produced Dublin, 1942). Included in *The Viscount of Blarney and Other Plays*, 1944.
The Plot Is Ready (produced Dublin, 1943). Included in *The Viscount of Blarney and Other Plays*, 1944.
The Viscount of Blarney (produced Dublin, 1944). Included in *The Viscount of Blarney and Other Plays*, 1944.
The Viscount of Blarney and Other Plays (includes *The Kiss* and *The Plot Is Ready*). Dublin, Bridge Press, and London, Williams and Norgate, 1944.
The Second Kiss (produced Dublin, 1946). Dublin, Bridge Press, 1946.
The Plot Succeeds (produced Dublin, 1950). Dublin, Bridge Press, 1950.
The Moment Next to Nothing (produced Dublin, 1958). Dublin, Bridge Press, 1953.
Collected Plays. Dublin, Dolmen Press, 1963.
The Student from Salamanca (produced Dublin, 1966). Included in *Two Interludes*, 1968.
Two Interludes Adapted from Cervantes: The Student from Salamanca and The Silent Lover. Dublin, Dolmen Press, 1968.
The Impuritans. Dublin, Dolmen Press, and London, Oxford University Press, 1973.

Novels

The Bright Temptations: A Romance. London, Allen and Unwin, and New York, Morrow, 1932.
The Singing Men at Cashel. London, Allen and Unwin, 1936.
The Sun Dances at Easter. London, Andrew Melrose, 1952.

Other

First Visit to England and Other Memories. Dublin, Bridge Press, 1945.
Poetry in Modern Ireland. Dublin, Three Candles Press, 1951; revised edition, 1962; Folcroft, Pennsylvania, Folcroft Editions, 1974.
Twice round the Black Church: Early Memories of Ireland and England. London, Routledge, 1962.
A Penny in the Clouds: More Memories of Ireland and England. London, Routledge, 1968.
The Celtic Twilight and the Nineties. Dublin, Dolmen Press, 1969.

Editor, *The Poems of Joseph Campbell.* Dublin, Allen Figgis, 1963.

Austin Clarke comments:

Later work mostly on social subjects here and elsewhere. Rhyme being exhausted, I have used, as far as possible in English, the prosodic internal assonantal patterns of Gaelic poetry. In recent years, I have used *rime riche,* or homonyms, a device which has been avoided in English verse.

*   *   *

Novels, verse-plays, narrative and lyric verse make up Austin Clarke's varied output. It is the product of a long and devoted career, whose main features are the mixed influence of Yeats, a pre-occupation with the Catholic Church in Ireland and a humanitarian rage. Though much of Clarke's middle life was spent in England, there was clearly never any likelihood that he would mix into the English scene as, say, Louis MacNeice did. His work is affected at every point by the fact of his being an Irish writer.

The early narrative poems were inspired by the narrative poems of the Irish poet, Samuel Ferguson, a generation earlier; their themes are mainly from Irish mythology. His novels are on medieval matters – schoolmen and saints and temptation – that have relevance in Ireland still. (All were banned by the Irish Censorship Board on publication.) His earlier lyric poems are very much concerned with Ireland's landscape and religion; his, later poems, which bring to full development the latent sensuality of all his writing, come more and more closely into focus on the social and religious irritants in Irish society.

Clarke appears to value his verse-plays as highly as his verse, but there is little doubt that a judgment on his work must hinge on the poems, particularly the later poems. Here, his work falls into two quite distinct periods: the early poems, culminating in *Pilgrimage* (1929), and – after what can now be seen as a transitional book, *Night and Morning,* in 1938 – the later poems, in a prolific series from *Ancient Lights* to *Tiresias.* As might be expected, the poetry written after the break differs greatly from that before it. It is more forthright and partisan in its concerns; it operates more intensely on a narrower front; it is sharper in tone and diction, bristling with particularities of time and place. Perhaps because of the break, it is also highly idiosyncratic. For a full appreciation of many of the later poems, it is useful to have a great deal of specific local knowledge, but the lack of it is not often a real obstacle to understanding – any more than it is with Robert Lowell. As the poems accumulated, in tiny private editions, it became evident that a perfectly integral world was under investigation, in which – despite the unusually minute scale – the proportions of reality were more or less preserved.

The new poems up to 1961, with *Pilgrimage* and *Night and Morning* both long out of print, were published as *Later Poems* by the Dolmen Press, Dublin. The generally favourable reception of this book was accompanied, outside of Ireland, by a mild surprise that a talent of this force had managed to stay underground. In the sudden warmth, Clarke produced a quantity of new and exciting verse in "a continual, voluptuous state of mind during which the various pieces arrived with . . . joyful ease . . . ." These are the poems of *Flight to Africa,* almost certainly Clarke's best book: their subjects range with great energy over intimate autobiography, anti-clerical anecdote, topographical description, energetic translations of eighteenth-century Irish songs, satire (straight and allegorical), blue jokes and genre pieces. At least one of these, "Martha Blake at Fifty-One," stands out, idiosyncracies and all, as a major poem by any standard.

Clarke, over 70, continues to pour out new poems. Not all of them add to his stature, but the supremacy of *Flight to Africa* should not lessen our gratitude for them. And one must be careful not to make final statements. His recent collection, *A Sermon on Swift* (another virtually secret pamphlet), contains some wicked and sensuous verse ranking with his best.

– Thomas Kinsella

CLEMO, Jack (Reginald John Clemo). British. Born in St. Austell, Cornwall, 11 March 1916. Educated at Trethosa Village School. Married Ruth Grace Peaty in

1968. "A dreamer and social misfit, I had already spent five years as an unemploy-able hermit mystic before partial deafness increased my isolation." · Recipient: Atlantic Award, Birmingham University, 1948; Arts Council Festival Prize, 1951; Civil List pension, 1961, supplemented in 1966 and 1969. Address: Goonamarris, St. Stephen's, St. Austell, Cornwall, England.

PUBLICATIONS

Verse

The Clay Verge.   London, Chatto and Windus, 1951.
The Map of Clay.   London, Methuen, 1961; Richmond, Virginia, John Knox Press, 1968.
Penguin Modern Poets 6, with Edward Lucie-Smith and George MacBeth.   Lon-don, Penguin, 1964.
Cactus on Carmel: Poems.   London, Methuen, 1967.
The Echoing Tip.   London, Methuen, 1971.
Broad Autumn.   London, Methuen, 1975.

Novel

Wilding Graft.   London, Chatto and Windus, and New York, Macmillan, 1948.

Other

Confession of a Rebel (autobiography).   London, Chatto and Windus, 1949.
The Invading Gospel (theology).   London, Bles, 1958; revised edition, London, Morgan Marshall and Scott, 1972; Old Tappan, New Jersey, Fleming Revell, 1973.

Critical Study: *Rule and Energy* by John Press, London, Oxford University Press, 1963.

Jack Clemo comments:

(1970) I intended to be chiefly a prose writer, but the loss of my sight in 1955 forced me to restrict myself to composing verse.

Apart from a few poems describing the Cornish clay district, my poetry reflects various phases of Christianity as an experience of personal conversion. Its main themes are the Christian view of "fallen nature," the sacrament of marriage, and the place of suffering in the achievement of true happiness. There are also some fierce Barthian strictures on religious humanism, and a realistic Evangelical optim-ism akin to Browning's. My first two collections of verse were chiefly odes in the Francis Thompson vein, though grimmer and bleaker because I used the imagery of clay-mining. In my later work, I have developed a more modern imagist technique with sprung rhythm and a minimum of rhyme; the symbols are more frequently drawn from nature, and I show a deep affinity with primitive Catholic visionaries like Bernadette. This, however, does not involve any discarding of my earlier creed or my taste for stark aesthetic patterns. I write entirely on spiritual inspiration and do not consciously choose either the subject or the style of my poems. My erotic mysticism, though it answers D. H. Lawrence, was spontaneously evolved under the pressure of my emotional crises. Incidents from my own life are often depicted in my verse, and the range is widened by dramatic monologues and tributes to various writers, saints and preachers. I think that my three collections make a fairly complete statement of my philosophy, but the physical handicaps of my mature years have restricted my output and are too often dragged in by critics to explain my beliefs and attitudes which I had already adopted while unhandicapped.

*   *   *

The root of Jack Clemo's poetry is in the tension between nature and divine grace. The surface of much of his work is as uncompromisingly scabbed and scarred as the particular mid-Cornish landscape in which he has lived all his life: a farming land torn apart by the advances of a vast china-clay industry. It is a landscape that mirrors the personal situation of a poet who has suffered intermittent attacks of blindness from early childhood, became deaf at about the age of twenty, and has now been blind since 1955.

The poetry is set against this "landscape of purgation" or "crab country." The mood is fiercely isolationist, often exultant at the apparent defeat of the forces of natural life. Clemo's work, all the same, has often been too easily labelled that of a "blind poet." It is important to remember that everything up to the last five poems in *The Map of Clay* was written while he was still sighted. With *Cactus on Carmel*, and as his visual memory of the clay-world faded, Clemo imaginatively drove deeper within himself for inspiration; the poems here are wider-ranging in theme, less personal, more abstract.

Like Browning, Clemo sees the poet in the rôle of priest and lover. The basic, romanticised Calvinism is self-evident. Clemo accepts the doctrine of Election: that before being hauled up into heaven, he who wears the badge of salvation will be hunted down by God and severely tested. But such trials are more than a test of his general faith in God. Clemo sees them also as a test of his faith in his "Election" for marriage, which took place in October, 1968. In a prefatory note to *The Echoing Tip*, Clemo declared, "While I was climbing towards the peak I wrote chiefly about the peak, the various thrills of the ascent, and the rather complicated map (showing mystical and theological routes) on which I relied. Now from the summit I can evoke a much wider spiritual landscape."

Certainly, in this latest volume, the tone of his verse has undergone a subtle sea-change:

> Elect for marriage – I sang
> That stubborn theme through three decades
> Of hunger, mirage, avalanche:
> When nature made hopes blanch,
> A text like a clay-bed tang,
> Like the bride's own breath, stirred in the shades.
> — "Wedding Eve"

The parallel with nature – apparently dead, yet slowly insinuating itself into the abandoned clay-dumps until they finally flower again – is clear. Clemo, one of the finest landscape poets of his generation, has made this area of Cornwall unassailably his own. The landscape remains frightening; often one of industrial horror.

257

Through Jack Clemo's powerful and unique vision, we may now also see it in personal terms of purest poetry.

– Charles Causley

CLIFTON, Lucille. Afro-American. Born in Depew, New York, 27 June 1936. Educated at Howard University, Washington, D.C., 1953–55. Married Fred J. Clifton in 1958; has six children. Formerly, Visiting Writer, Columbia University School of the Arts, New York. Since 1971, Poet-in-Residence, Coppin State College, Baltimore. Recipient: YM-YWHA Poetry Center Discovery Award, 1969; National Endowment for the Arts grant, 1969. Agent: M. Marlow, Curtis Brown Ltd., 60 East 56th Street, New York, New York 10022. Address: 2605 Talbot Road, Baltimore, Maryland 21216, U.S.A.

PUBLICATIONS

Verse

    Good Times. New York, Random House, 1969.
    Good News about the Earth. New York, Random House, 1972.
    An Ordinary Woman. New York, Random House, 1974.

Other

    Some of the Days of Everett Anderson (juvenile). New York, Holt Rinehart, 1970.
    The Black B C's (juvenile). New York, Dutton, 1970.
    Everett Anderson's Christmas Coming (juvenile). New York, Holt Rinehart, 1972.
    All Us Come cross the Water (juvenile). New York, Holt Rinehart, 1973.
    Don't You Remember (juvenile). New York, Dutton, 1974.
    Everett Anderson's Year (juvenile). New York, Holt Rinehart, 1974.
    The Times They Used to Be (juvenile). New York, Holt Rinehart, 1974.

Lucille Clifton comments:

I am a black woman poet, and I sound like one.

*   *   *

Two things are apparent in the poetry of Lucille Clifton – that she is Black and that she is a woman. Her Blackness becomes evident mainly in her themes and insights. Characteristically, in "after Kent State" she writes, "white ways are / the way of death / come into the / Black / and live," and in an untitled poem she states, "listen children / . . . we have never hated black / . . . always / all ways / . . . we have always loved each other / . . . pass it on." Seeing with clarity the bitterness, ugliness, and adversity wrought by racism, she nevertheless is constructive and optimistic. There is celebration, affirmation, of Black life in her poems. Her Black perception also manifests itself in the heroes that she poetically portrays, such as Fred Clifton (her husband), Little Richard, Angela Davis, and in her creative reactions to biblical personnages and events in the "Some Jesus" section of her *Good News about the Earth.*

Mrs. Clifton's femininity is revealed by her dignity and poise and by her themes. Poems such as "the lost baby poem," about an aborted baby, and "Mary," an empathetic depiction of the Virgin Mary, could have been written only by a lady. Her womanly sensitivity, however, is not one of weak softness, protected reclusion, cloying sentimentality, or shielded vision. For example, in "Admonitions" she says, "girls / first time a white man / opens his fly / like a good thing / we'll just laugh."

Lucille Clifton's poems are short, graceful, incisive, usually with pointed conclusions which sometimes come to the reader as a re-reaction. Her lines, usually short, are sinewy, lithe. Her diction is plain; she only occasionally employs so-called Black grammar or dialect. Her characterizations are precise and economical. She uses both poetic indirection and flat statement effectively, employs understated or subtle metaphorical language skillfully.

– Theodore R. Hudson

CLOUTS, Sydney (David). South African. Born in Cape Town, 10 January 1926. Educated at South African College School; University of Cape Town, B.A. Married; has three sons. Since 1969, Research Fellow of the Institute of the Study of English in Africa. Recipient: Olive Schreiner Award, 1968; Ingrid Jonker Prize, 1968. Address: c/o Rhodes University, Grahamstown, South Africa.

PUBLICATIONS

Verse

One Life. Cape Town, Purnell, 1966.

*　　*　　*

I believe Sydney Clouts to be a truly great poet, this in spite of the fact that he is not a "name" even in his own country and he has written only one volume, *One Life.* There is an inevitability about his best poems that resists analysis. Yet to me there is nothing cold about his sheerness, nothing hard in his brillancy. His talent is almost heathen – in his wish simply to *be* – as the pebble he describes in "Of Thomas Traherne" is heathen. "Heathen" here has an unaffected self-possession:

> Obscure vermilion heats the dim pebble I hold.
> . . . I have read firm poems of God.
> Good friend, you perceived bright angels.
> This heathen bit of world lies warm in my palm.

His quality is immediately apprehended in his crystalline imagery, but it is often best seen in the quieter shades of his perception: "firm poems" – this economical phrasing is neither too delicate nor too confident; a sure balance has been kept by a gift that knows itself. Traherne's "Contentments," and their opposite – the sense of communion with, and separation from, the spirit moving in nature – are evident in Clouts's own work, though here they are transmuted into the paradox of his succinct imagery, and, in particular, his unforgettable closing lines. The concluding

> and the sea came by
> the breaking sea came by

in "After the Poem" conveys a sense of existence outside life, and yet the poet, by identifying his perception, defines the wonder of being and its important connection with consciousness.

Clouts can be quite dazzling, as in the following stanzas from "Prince Henry the Navigator":

> Through the leafy Lisbon trees I heard
> the frogless ocean whiten wild as flutes.
>
> . . . silent I prayed, my task began
> I cross the deliberate gulf of man

or quietly eloquent, as in his address to "Marge" in "The Sleeper":

> When you awake
> gesture will waken
> to decisive things.
> Asleep, you have taken
> motion and tenderly laid it within,
> deeply within you.

But both in dazzling imagery and quiet attitude the fusion of honesty and affection (with Clouts one hesitates to use so ostentatious a word as "love") makes for his inviolable quality.

The poet is highly aware of the excitements and grandeurs of Africa, particularly of the Cape of Good Hope. We see this in "Prince Henry the Navigator" and in "After the Poem." In "The Discovery" his link between Portugal and Africa is poetically forged:

> Rounding the Cape, the sodden
> wooden grumble of the wheel.

Here the prosaic touch, the low-toned "grumble," counterpoints the splendour of its context.

Clouts is also aware of the tragic divisions of his country, for example in the two "Roy Kloof" poems, where a boy of mixed origin, of confusing pride and shame, cries out:

> My country has given me flint for a soul.

The readily discernible complexities of Roy Kloof's condition would lead to the far more impenetrable human condition indicated by a piece such as "Within," which in the striking power of its closing lines shows the verbal "purity" I have been trying to characterize:

> flat is the world you'd find:
> a row of wooden rooftops
> that can easily topple
> and bring the heart down
> and bring down the mind.

It is not only in this kind of imagery that his exploration of the human condition signals itself. In "The Game" at one level – and a very real level – he takes part in the child's game of hide and seek, but the closing lines give the clue to another dimension:

> I'll find myself as well,
> hidden where truth has eyes.

The finally undissectible sheerness of his texture indicates why it is necessary for him to write poetry and not anything else, a necessity that shares humility with greatness. In him we are induced to believe that sheerness explains and seeks generosity amidst the overwhelming conditions of existence:

> Flowers are toppling
> the earth burbles blood.
> O scholars of Mercy
> interpret the flood!

– D. R. Beeton

CLUYSENAAR, Anne. Irish. Born in Brussels, Belgium, 15 March 1936. Educated at Trinity College, Dublin (Vice-Chancellor's Prize, 1956); Manchester University. Reader to the writer Percy Lubbock for one year. Taught at Lancaster University; Huddersfield Polytechnic, 1972–73. Since 1973, Member of the Department of Language and Literature, University of Birmingham. Address: Department of Language and Literature, The University, Birmingham 15, England.

PUBLICATIONS

Verse

A Fan of Shadows. Manchester, David Findley Press, 1967.
Nodes. Dublin, Dolmen Press, 1969.

Other

Introduction to Literary Stylistics: A Discussion of Dominant Structure in Verse and Prose. London, Batsford, 1974.

*   *   *

As a reviewer of contemporary poetry, in, for instance, her regular contributions to the quarterly *Stand,* Anne Cluysenaar combines both an exacting attention to detail and an ability to extract thought-provoking generalisations. To date, the incisiveness with which she can discuss other people's poetry is absent from her own not very bountiful work. In one sense her careful, rather genteel poems may appear to be incidental to her general literary activities as a critic and academic, but it is clear that the themes pursued in her poetry are important to her and relate to the pressures of personal experience. Perhaps those very pressures – absent when dealing with other people's poetry – explain the lack of incisiveness: a poem for example which refers to "the authority of a trained imagination" must be prepared to exhibit such authority, not simply refer to it. Abstractions such as "the olive-branch of my peace," "the Sea / Of time," or "the circular flow of life's river" hardly show much authority. And the rather staid generalisations act as another distancing factor: "Trying to do too much more than exist / Soon all life is stopped at the source." Even the similes and metaphors, though frequently handled with delicacy, have a static thought-out effect: e.g., of a swallow – "with sharp wings / Cupped at the fountains of the air." Yet take a short piece like "Owl":

> In my fingers, in their naked heat,
> the tiny body shrinks its blood,
> flicks the saucered eye-feathers.
> Along the pale rims of the eyes
> flecks of dry blood, like the intimate stippling
> on the vagina of a wild flower.

This is static too, and miniature, but achieved: if we can imagine this kind of precision applied to the personal experience which so far appears to be held at arm's length, we can see a possible and useful line of development.

– Robin Fulton

COBBING, Bob. British. Born in Enfield, Middlesex, 30 July 1920. Married; has five children. Formerly, teacher and bookshop manager. Publisher, Writers Forum, London. Editor, *Kroklok* magazine, London. Performer with the abAna group. Chairman, Association of Little Presses, and Association of Little Magazines; Past Member of the Poetry Society General Council and Executive. Recipient: C. Day Lewis Fellowship, Goldsmiths' College, London, 1973. Address: 262 Randolph Avenue, London W.9, England.

Publications

Verse

Massacre of the Innocents, with John Rowan.   London, Writers Forum, 1963.
Sound Poems: An ABC in Sound.   London, Writers Forum, 1965.
Eyearun.   London, Writers Forum, 1966.
Chamber Music.   Stuttgart, Editions Hansjörg Mayer, 1967.
Kurrirrurriri.   London, Writers Forum, 1967.
SO: Six Sound Poems.   London, Writers Forum, 1968.
Octo: Visual Poems.   London, Writers Forum, 1969.
Whisper Piece.   London, Writers Forum, 1969.
Why Shiva Has Ten Arms.   London, Writers Forum, 1969.
Whississippi.   London, Writers Forum, 1969.
Etcetera: A New Collection of Found and Sound Poems.   Cardiff, Vertigo, 1970.
Kwatz.   Gillingham, Kent, ARC Publications, 1970.
Sonic Icons.   London, Writers Forum, 1970.
Kris Kringles Kesmes Korals.   Cardiff and London, Vertigo-Writers Forum, 1970.
Three Poems for Voice and Movement.   London, Writers Forum, 1971.
Konkrete Canticle.   London, Covent Garden Press, 1971.
Beethoven Today.   London, Covent Garden Press, 1971.
Spearhead.   London, Writers Forum, 1971.
Five Visual Poems.   London, Writers Forum, 1971.
The Judith Poem.   London, Writers Forum, 1971.
Poster No. 2.   London, Judith Walker Posters, 1971.
Songsignals.   Cardiff, Second Aeon Publications, 1972.
Tomatomato.   Kettering, Northamptonshire, All-In, 1972.
15 Shakespeare-Kaku.   London, Writers Forum, 1972.
Trigram.   London, Writers Forum, 1972.
E colony.   London, Writers Forum, 1973.
Circa 73–74.   London, Writers Forum, 1973.
Alphapitasuite.   London, Writers Forum, 1973.
In Any Language.   London, Writers Forum, 1973.
The Five Vowels.   London, Writers Forum, 1974.

Recordings: *An ABC in Sound*, with Ernst Jandl, Writers Forum, 1965; *Chamber Music*, Swedish Radio-Fylkingen, 1968; *Whississippi*, Swedish Radio-Fylkingen, 1969; *Marvo Moves Natter* and *Spontaneous Appealinair Contemprate Apollinaire*, Ou Magazine, 1969; *Variations on a Theme of Tan*, Stedelijk Museum, Amsterdam, 1970; *As Easy*, Swedish Radio-Fylkingen, 1971; *Ga(il s)o(ng), Suesequence, Poem for Voice and Mandoline and Poem for Gillian, Hymn to the Sacred Mushroom*, Arts Council of Great Britain, 1971; *Experiments in Disintegrating Sound*, Arts Council of Great Britain, 1972; *Khrajrej*, Opus Magazine, 1973; *E colony*, Typewriter Magazine, 1973.

Other

Editor, *Gloup and Woup: A Folio of English Concrete Poetry.*   Todmorden, Lancashire, Arc Publications, 1974.

Critical Studies: by Dom Sylvester Houédard, in "Bob Cobbing Issue," *Extra Verse 17* (London), 1966; by Eric Mottram, in *Second Aeon 16–17* (Cardiff), 1973; *Bob Cobbing and "Writers Forum,"* Sunderland, Ceolfrith Press, 1974.

Bob Cobbing comments:

My earlier poems "might seem to be conventionally linear; but their urge is towards stabilized diagram, intemized pieces of information in a spatial lay-out which is, in fact, the syntax" (Eric Mottram). In later poems, the dance of letters, half-letters, syllables and words on the page is score for "a ballet of the speech organs" (Victor Shklovsky). In still later poems, the scores are for instrumental as well as vocal poetry; for a ballet of the whole body and not just the voice.

I have been described as "a lettriste, thirty years out of date" (François Dufrêne), and it is true that I value lettriste principles, but not solely. My work derives equally from Joyce, Stein and the Kerouac of "Old Angel Midnight"; from François Dufrêne's post-lettriste cri-rythmes and the vocal micro-particles of Henri Chopin. This leads Dom Sylvester Houédard to note the range of my personal scale (a) from eye to ear, (b) from most to least abstract.

At present I am working on single-voice poems; multi-voiced poems; poems based on words; poems not using words or even letters; poems for electronic treatment on tape; poems for "voice as instrument and instruments as speaking voices" (*Time Out* magazine, concerning the group abAna with which I perform); poems as scores for dance or drama, invitations to act out an event in space, sound and choreography.

"History points to an origin that poetry and music share in the dance that seems to be a part of the make-up of homo sapiens and needs no more justification or conscious control than breathing" (Basil Bunting). This attitude is worth exploring again and means both a going back and a going forward.

*   *   *

The claim that Bob Cobbing is the leading British exponent of Sound Poetry is not an unreasonable one. Certainly he has been an indefatigable worker and propagandist in this country for that international flowering of abstract poetry which has been a distinctive phenomenon in the last two decades. The steady flow of publications from his Writers Forum Press; the exhibitions he has organised; and his recent magazine *Kroklok,* which on completion intends to present a comprehensive anthology of sound and concrete poetry, are all part of an energetic campaign to put such poetry on the British map.

The projected *Kroklok* anthology underlines one of the difficulties Cobbing and his fellow concrete and sound poets have to encounter. By its very nature such work does not offer itself for publication in the usual way. For this reason we find Cobbing's poems in folders, on cards and cut-outs, and in the case of sound poems the gramophone record is clearly the only possible medium for wide dissemination. But recording is expensive and it was only in 1972 that Cobbing and some of his fellow sound poets were able to produce, with the aid of the Arts Council, *Experiments in Disintegrating Language* and *Konkrete Canticle,* the first British sound poetry L.P.

It was W. H. Auden, when once describing his method of composition, who said, in essence, that unless he abandoned some of his poems he would never cease revising them. In a contrary way Bob Cobbing subscribes to such a view, in that far from abandoning his poems he is to be seen constantly revising them or, to put it better perhaps, constantly producing new versions of them. Thus one of the more successful of his visual poems, "Are Your Children Safe in the Sea?," is to be found in many versions. The copy I have before me at the moment is a folded card "triptych" described as "one of several eye interpretations of the poem." The poem itself is a five lined verbal poem of which *Extra Verse 17,* for example, contains another and completely different visual interpretation. "Wowromwrormm

(Worm)," an attempt to balance the appeal between eye and ear using Apollinaire's "Rain" as a jumping off point, is another poem to be found in various versions on cards, folders or in books. Other visual poems are described as "typographic interpretations of sound poems" where Cobbing keeps worrying a theme into a variety of mediums.

The sound poems themselves are often composed directly onto tape recorders and then interpreted or re-interpreted by use of superimposition, play-back and other electronic recording techniques. Here Cobbing's technical skill is undeniable, and often his sound poems, such as "Tan Tandinanan," with their almost obsessive repetition, can be seen to be paralleled in the Mantras. Another relationship might be that concrete poetry is to the visual arts as sound poetry is to music. Though I imagine Bob Cobbing might see that as too facile a formula.

But is it poetry? A question often asked, and the title of one side of the recent sound-poem L.P., *Experiments in Disintegrating Language*, tends to beg such a question. Indeed, Bob Cobbing and I publicly debated this very subject one evening at the Poetry Society. If we accept the validity of what Cobbing is doing we could still deny that it is poetry and categorize it instead as one of the visual arts or music. The telling argument against abstraction in general is to me, a poet working in a traditionally verbal medium, that it can be seen as an attempt to dehumanize the arts, and at a time when concern is expressed over the dehumanizing effects of an increasing technology, the increased urbanization of mass society and of the growth of bureaucratic organizations, it would seem unfortunate, to say the least of it, for such a movement to be encouraged by the practitioners of arts the very purpose of which should be to celebrate, explore and defend the human condition. To this the answer is given that the more the artist abstracts the less he becomes mimetic, descriptive and consequently deceptive, and the more his art becomes concretely truthful and, it follows, of human value. Bob Cobbing himself says he is working towards "a new abstract entity – the re-amalgamation of poetry with music and dance," an attempt to transcend intellect which will "reunite poetry with music."

The argument can be seen as that between those who feel language is one of the essential instruments with which to probe reality and the truth underlying it, and those who feel it to be a hindrance. It is interesting here to note how in many of Cobbing's typographical interpretations the degree of overprinting could be seen as an urge to obliterate the word, and yet in contradiction to this an element of the verbal is always retained however fragmented. I suppose, ultimately, the answer here must be of the "proof of the pudding" kind: by their fruits you will know them.

But if one refuses, as one should, to accept the frontiers of art as inviolable, and acknowledges the valuable contribution of past experimentation in the arts, then one must but recognize the pioneering work of Bob Cobbing and his colleagues. A renewed attention to the visual and aural qualities of poetry could well be a "spin off" from which we will all benefit.

– John Cotton

COGSWELL, Frederick (William). Canadian. Born in East Centreville, New Brunswick, 8 November 1917. Educated at the University of New Brunswick, Fredericton, B.A. 1949, M.A. 1950; University of Edinburgh, Ph.D. 1952. Served in the Canadian Army, 1940–45. Married Margaret Hynes in 1944; has two daughters.

Assistant Professor, 1952–57, Associate Professor, 1957–61, and since 1961, Professor of English, University of New Brunswick. Editor, *Fiddlehead* magazine, 1952–66, and *Humanities Association Bulletin*, 1967–72, both in Fredericton. Since 1960, Editor, Fiddlehead Poetry Books, Fredericton. Recipient: Nuffield Fellowship, 1959, Canada Council Fellowship, 1966. Address: 769 Reid Street, Fredericton, New Brunswick, Canada.

PUBLICATIONS

Verse

> *The Stunted Strong.*   Fredericton, New Brunswick, Fiddlehead, 1955.
> *The Haloed Tree.*   Toronto, Ryerson Press, 1956.
> *Descent from Eden.*   Toronto, Ryerson Press, 1959.
> *Lost Dimension.*   London, Outposts Publications, 1960.
> *Five New Brunswick Poets,* with others, edited by Frederick Cogswell.   Fredricton, New Brunswick, Fiddlehead, 1962.
> *Star-People.*   Fredericton, New Brunswick, Fiddlehead, 1968.
> *Immortal Plowman.*   Fredericton, New Brunswick, Fiddlehead, 1969.
> *In Praise of Chastity.*   Fredricton, New Brunswick, Chapbooks, 1970.
> *The Chains of Liliput.*   Fredericton, New Brunswick, Fiddlehead, 1971.
> *The House Without a Door.*   Fredricton, New Brunswick, Fiddlehead, 1973.

Other

> Editor, *A Canadian Anthology.*   Fredericton, New Brunswick, Fiddlehead, 1960.
> Editor, *Five New Brunswick Poets.*   Fredricton, New Brunswick, Fiddlehead, 1962.
> Editor, with Robert Tweedie and S. W. MacNutt, and contributor, *The Arts in New Brunswick.*   Fredericton, University of New Brunswick Press, 1966.
> Editor, with Thelma Reid Lower, *The Enchanted Land: Canadian Poetry for Young Readers.*   Toronto, Gage, 1967.
>
> Translator, *One Hundred Poems of Modern Quebec.*   Fredricton, New Brunswick, Fiddlehead, 1970.
> Translator, *A Second Hundred Poems of Modern Quebec.*   Fredericton, New Brunswick, Fiddlehead, 1971.
> Translator, *Confrontation,* by G. Lapointe.   Fredericton, New Brunswick, Fiddlehead, 1973.

Frederick Cogswell comments:

My poetry is a response, as a rule, to direct personal experience. It finds its own form instinctively out of the various forms which I have encountered either traditional or modern. It is marked by directness, economy, sincerity, and the avoidance of long words.

*   *   *

"It is marked by directness, economy, sincerity, and the avoidance of long words." This is not a critic dissecting Frederick Cogswell's verse, but the poet himself discussing his own work. The statement displays all the characteristic self-deprecation of the poet. For many years Cogswell has tirelessly served the interests of fellow writers, as a teacher of English, as the publisher of *The Fiddlehead*, the best magazine of poetry in the Maritimes, and now as the publisher of Fiddlehead Poetry Books, a seemingly endless stream of chapbooks devoted in the main to the work of new young poets.

All along Cogswell has been publishing a rivulet, if not a stream, of booklets of brief poems. His first publication, *The Stunted Strong*, is a series of arresting vignettes dramatizing the negative aspects of life in the small communities that make up Atlantic Canada; the collection had a decided influence on the early work of Alden Nowlan and was widely read across the country. The early phase of biographical and autobiographical poems ended in the publication of *Descent from Eden*, a kind of selected poems. Since then the poems have been elliptical and epigrammatic as well as lyric, as two recent publications, *The Chains of Liliput* and *The House Without a Door*, demonstrate.

"It was the chains of Liliput / Taught Gulliver he was a giant," Cogswell explains. The poet cannot resist a too-easy parody called "Spiv's Innisfree" which begins: "I will arise and go to a pub in Piccadilly / And six quick ones will I down there, of Scotch and soda made." His strengths are shown in this verse from "Unhappy Clown":

> I smile and I sing,
> And I laugh like a king
> For the same reason as you,
> To be part of the show.

One is always aware, reading a Cogswell poem, that the poet is aware of writing it. Sometimes the poet is able to make this work to his – and the reader's – advantage, as it does in this sincere poem "In Defence of Rosaries":

> and God whose stillness
> speaks as loud as noise
> will understand
> my private prayer

> – John Robert Colombo

COHEN, Leonard (Norman). Canadian. Born in Montreal, Quebec, 21 September 1934. Educated at McGill University, Montreal, B.A. 1955; Columbia University, New York. Composer and Singer: has given concerts in Canada, the United States and Europe. Recipient: McGill University Literary Award, 1956; Canada Council Award, 1960; Quebec Literary Award, 1964. D.L.: Dalhousie University, Halifax, Nova Scotia, 1971. Lives in Montreal and Greece. Address: c/o Martin J. Machat, 1501 Broadway, 30th Floor, New York, New York 10036, U.S.A.

Publications

Verse

Let Us Compare Mythologies. Montreal, Contact Press, 1956.
The Spice-Box of Earth. Toronto, McClelland and Stewart, 1961; New York,
    Viking Press, 1965; London, Cape, 1971.
Flowers for Hitler. Toronto, McClelland and Stewart, 1964.
Parasites of Heaven. Toronto, McClelland and Stewart, 1966.
Selected Poems, 1956–1968. Toronto, McClelland and Stewart, and New York,
    Viking Press, 1968; London, Cape, 1969.
Leonard Cohen's Song Book. New York, Collier, 1969.
Five Modern Canadian Poets, with others, edited by Eli Mandel. Toronto, Holt
    Rinehart, 1970.
The Energy of Slaves. Toronto, McClelland and Stewart, New York, Viking
    Press, and London, Cape, 1972.

Recordings: The Songs of Leonard Cohen, Columbia, 1968; Songs from a Room,
Columbia, 1969; Songs of Love and Hate, Columbia, 1971; Live Songs, Columbia, 1973; New Skin for the Old Ceremony, Columbia, 1974.

Plays

The Next Step (produced London, 1972).
Sisters of Mercy: A Journey into the Words and Music of Leonard Cohen (produced
    Niagara-on-the-Lake, Ontario, 1973).

Novels

The Favorite Game. New York, Viking Press, and London, Secker and War-
    burg, 1963.
Beautiful Losers. Toronto, McClelland and Stewart, and New York, Viking
    Press, 1966; London, Cape, 1970.

Critical Study: Leonard Cohen by Michael Ondaatje, Toronto, McClelland and
Stewart, 1970.

*   *   *

The figures of Leonard Cohen's poems rise like figures in Chagall, transformed
from the ordinary, surprised into a world of visionary experience. Out of the junk
of the everyday – "the garbage and the flowers" – the magical world of the
imaginative is created. There is a strong sense in which his poetry is a prodigious
search of experience for the exit from the ordinary. But it is not always violently
so. Some of the earlier lyrics – "Go by Brooks," for instance – have a simple
lyricism that is also intense. Occasionally, it slopes off into a wry humour that is
characteristic of him; more often its apparent Emily Dickinson simplicities conceal
a toughness and a danger for which only the ballad form is adequate. And it is in
the ballads that his greatest strength lies. The concentration of the imagery and the

force of the rhyme give a telling intensity to the surrealist experiences of his imagination – an intensity that becomes at times almost gnomic:

> History is a needle
> for putting men asleep
> anointed with the poison
> of all they want to keep.

Certain themes continue to pre-occupy Cohen as certain images haunt his imagination. His search is for the sensual heaven of "The Sisters of Mercy," not the skeletal world of the ideal, the astringent dead world of "I Have Not Lingered in European Monasteries." Indeed, his religion is the rejection of the suffering ascetic – "I disdain God's suffering. / Men command sufficient pain" – for a priapic world in which the liturgical celebrations are the extreme of physical – a "constant love / and passion without flesh" – that is not a bloodless mysticism but the apogee of the physical, almost like "high." But even in the physical world his fear of entrapment by the deadly females of such poems as "The Unicorn Tapestries" or "I Long to Hold Some Lady" is strong. They become in his poetic fabric the creatures – associated with doctors, rabbis, and priests – of the liturgy of death. "The Story of Isaac" lurks behind the sacrificial metaphors to which he recurs. What is most telling in this balladic pre-occupation with the undefined horror is Cohen's recognition of it not as external to himself, but part of his own psyche. Dachau is everyday Montreal; the amatory is also the murderous "tasting blood on your tongue / does not shock me." So the poetry (of *Flowers for Hitler* especially) is exculpatory, and the desire to escape from the "ape with angel glands" the more intense.

In his most recent poetry there is a sense of imminence. The partisan's retreat is more embattled even than "the small oasis where we lie" of his earlier love poems. His concern with freedom, his feeliing of the "incomparable sense of loss" to which he refers in "Queen Victoria and Me," is more than a nostalgia for a lost land of freedom and the spirit. It is a matter of skirmishes in the hills "on the side of the ghost and the king," a matter of escaping from the horrific city whose terrors are also the terrors of "the armies marching still" towards the war that must surely come.

Cohen's voice is most sympathetic and most telling, not in his escapes from the horror and the junk into the fashionable "pot" world of despair, but in his celebrations of the poet's capacity not only to hold out against the faceless butchers but to make acclaim of "orange peels, / cans, discarded guts." The Prophets and *The Song of Songs* inform this voice. Its celebration is of a beauty, entirely human, that prevails over "the clubfoot crowds." Its affirmation is that not only all poets but "all men will be sailors."

– D. D. C. Chambers

COLE, Barry. British. Born in Woking, Surrey, 13 November 1936. Served in the Royal Air Force for two years. Married Rita Linihan in 1958; has three children. Worked in the Central Office of Information, London, 1965–70. Northern Arts Fellow in Literature, universities of Newcastle upon Tyne and Durham,

1970–72. Address: c/o Jonathan Clowes Ltd., 20 New Cavendish Street, London W.1., England.

PUBLICATIONS

Verse

> *Blood Ties.* London, Turret Books, 1967.
> *Ulysses in the Town of Coloured Glass.* London, Turret Books, 1968.
> *Moonsearch.* London, Methuen, 1968.
> *The Visitors.* London, Methuen, 1970.
> *Vanessa in the City.* London, Trigram Press, 1971.
> *Pathetic Fallacies.* London, Eyre Methuen, 1973.

Novels

> *A Run Across the Island.* London, Methuen, 1968.
> *Joseph Winter's Patronage.* London, Methuen, 1969.
> *The Search for Rita.* London, Methuen, 1970.
> *The Giver.* London, Methuen, 1971.
> *Doctor Fielder's Common Sense.* London, Methuen, 1972.

Barry Cole comments:

The subjects of my poems are myself, love, my wife; the world I know I see and the world I think I see. My verse forms are neither traditional nor *avant garde,* but of my own time at any given moment. Sometimes they rhyme, sometimes they don't, but I try for precision, brevity and clarity. The poems aim at wit and intelligence, though they may hit none or any of these. Their sources are my own felt and thought experiences and those of sympathetic antecedents and contemporaries. Influences are few and unrecognizable.

*   *   *

Barry Cole has, in recent years, been a prolific novelist. The novels have an instantly recognisable atmosphere – one of strangeness rooted in the ordinary, as if a different order, with totally different rules, subsumed the mundane world we see, and manifested itself unexpectedly at moments of crisis. The atmosphere in Cole's most interesting poems is exactly the same as that which we discover in the novels – they are, in fact, capsule versions of the stories he tells in prose. The thing that counts is the total image; not the individual line. Quoted in fragments, the poetry often seems flat. It is only when we read the poem through as a narrative that we see what the poet's purpose is.

– Edward Lucie-Smith

COLEMAN, Elliott.   American.   Born in Binghamton, New York, 26 September 1906.   Educated at Wheaton College, Illinois, B.A. 1926; Princeton Theological Seminary, New Jersey; General Theological Seminary, New York; St. Stephen's House, Oxford.   Ordained to the Diaconate of the Episcopal Church, 1942.   Master, Asheville School, North Carolina, 1928–40.   Worked for Henry Holt and Company, publishers, 1943, and Doubleday and Company, publishers, 1944, both in New York.   Since 1945, Member of the English Department, currently Professor of English and Director of the Writing Seminars, Johns Hopkins University, Baltimore.   Address: Department of English, Johns Hopkins University, Baltimore, Maryland 21218, U.S.A.

PUBLICATIONS

Verse

The Poems of Elliott Coleman.   New York, Dutton, 1936.
An American in Augustland.   Chapel Hill, University of North Carolina Press, 1940.
Pearl Harbor.   Privately printed, 1942.
27 Night Sonnets.   Milan and New York, New Directions, 1949.
A Glass Darkly: New Sonnets.   Baltimore, Contemporary Poetry, 1952.
33 Night Sonnets.   Baltimore, Contemporary Poetry, 1955.
Sonetti (bilingual edition, translated by Alfredo Rizzardi).   Bologna, Italy, Libreria Antiquaria Palmaverde, 1959.
Mockingbirds at Fort McHenry.   Pamplona, Spain, Atlantis Editions, 1963.
Broken Death.   Baltimore, Linden Press, 1964.
Rose Demonics: 1936–1966.   Baltimore, Linden Press, 1967.
One Hundred Poems.   Chapel Hill, North Carolina, Tinker Press, 1972.
The Tangerine Birds.   Baltimore, Harbor House, 1973.
In the Canyon.   Baltimore, Bay Press, 1974.

Other

The Golden Angel: Papers on Proust.   New York and Sacramento, Coley Taylor–Academy Guild, 1954.

Editor, *Lectures in Criticism.*   New York, Pantheon Books, 1949.
Editor, *Poems of Byron, Keats and Shelley.*   New York, Doubleday, 1968.

Translator, with the author, *Studies in Human Time,* by Georges Poulet.   Baltimore, Johns Hopkins University Press, 1956.
Translator (unrhymed portions only), *The Mad Poet,* by Pierre Emmanuel.   Baltimore, Contemporary Poetry, 1956.
Translator, with the author, *The Interior Distance,* by Georges Poulet.   Baltimore, Johns Hopkins University Press, 1959.
Translator, with the author, *Towns of This World,* by Alfredo Rizzardi.   Baltimore, Contemporary Poetry, 1962.
Translator, with the author and Mrs. Carley Dawson, *The Metamorphoses of the Circle,* by Georges Poulet.   Baltimore, Johns Hopkins University Press, 1967.

Elliott Coleman comments:

Very few of the earliest poems – influenced by Virgil, Shelley, Wordsworth, Browning, Brooke and Hardy – are worth saving.

In a middle period, two books of sonnets experimented impetuously with the Shakespearean form.

Later work – *Mockingbirds at Fort McHenry, Rose Demonics* – was in large part a taking of fragmentary dictation from the pre-conscious.

The latest stuff, a reflective series of Proses, is the most strangely imagined of all.

Intention: Hoping never to write anything else that is boring, not just now concerned about writing anything else at all, I still should pray for a few more interesting catches, early in the morning.

*   *   *

Elliott Coleman is one of the most neglected poets in America. His chief works are either long out of print or are privately printed; the anthologists have over-looked him; and he is principally known as a translator (of Poulet) and essayist (on Proust and others). Only A. R. Ammons has spoken out boldly enough for his poems: "Elliott Coleman's poems search out the deeper elements of mind that are at once sharp reality and vision. It is as if – in rejecting the control of his experience by archetypes – he has discovered the elements of which archetypes are made, without any loss to their luminosity and suggestiveness. Because of this, poems that derive from particular experience generalize spontaneously into a community of insight and feeling. The total body of Mr. Coleman's work represents one of the supreme poetic achievements of our time." One could look to any of Elliott Coleman's volumes to authenticate Ammons's statement. His "Sonnets on the Roman Light" are an exercise in painting, in mixing streets, classes, sights, occupations, as only light does:

> The sweating roadworker wears it into the night.
> Each flower holds the pollen of its rust.
> From street or height the marvel can be viewed,
> Owing to latitude, and longitude.

In *Mockingbirds at Fort McHenry* Coleman indulges a private wit, a metaphysical devotion to name-punning, a sense of the painfully elliptical, that have no doubt lost him readers, even in the age of Eliot. Coleman has never sought popular approval; and in his "New York Sonnets" he evidently understood, and accepted with laconic good humor, what his work would suffer:

> The languge flashes. Summer is washed away.
> The lover at last in love, the beach and primer
> Of the blue world open to the open day,
> Learns what he knew: to laugh at the right places:
> Child and man. *But most is labor and grief,*
> *The dark, the fright, the Hallowe'en false faces,*
> *The accuser by day, and, in the night, the thief!*

Like many others, he waits the recognition that is due him, that has perhaps been stolen by the noisier.

It is often clear in Coleman's work that he is total (or nearly total) victim to the image with which experience afflicts:

> To see the dark life,
> The death in black angles.
> The name of it, 506,
> *Night and Roses*
>   – from his poem for John Kennedy

One senses in Coleman the mark of the really great artist – that he is genuinely lost in his impressions, that he begs relief from the sufferings they impose by shaping his poems ("after the beauties / abstractions / what a relief"). Luckily, Elliott Coleman's humor ("tell it alight") lightens a heavy difficult sensibility ("holy adorment / tenseless / eternal"). The mingled world of his images can be heard clearly in his poem on "Joyce's Grave":

> The whole cool hill faces away
> From lake, from town, and from the pain of looking.
> Haystacks sweeten across the road.
> Children march past these open gates
> To the tickets and turnstiles of the Zoo,
> Right for flamingos,
> Left for the blazing zebras.

It is a world of heavy insight, relieved by color and broad humor, by a duty to the art object and a responsibility to nature.

– David Ray

COLLINSON, Laurence (Henry).   British.   Born in Leeds, Yorkshire, 7 September 1925. Educated at various Australian primary schools; Brisbane State High School; Dalby High School, Queensland; University of Queensland, Brisbane; Julian Ashton Art School, Sydney; Mercer House, Melbourne, teaching diploma 1955. Freelance radio, magazine and newspaper writer until 1954; English and Maths teacher in Victoria secondary schools, 1956–61; Editor, *The Educational Magazine,* Melbourne, teachers' journal of the Victorian Education Department, 1961–64. Also acted, directed and wrote for various Australian little theatres up to 1956. Sub-Editor, IPC Magazines Ltd., London, 1965–73. Recipient: Society of Australian Authors prize, London, 1969; Australian Council of the Arts special grant and fellowship, 1973. Agent: Margery Vosper Ltd., Suite 8, 26 Charing Cross Road, London WC2H 0DG. Address: 97 Edgwarebury Lane, Edgware, Middlesex HA8 8NA, England.

PUBLICATIONS

Verse

Poet's Dozen.   Melbourne, privately printed, 1952.
The Moods of Love.   Melbourne, Overland, 1957.
Who Is Wheeling Grandma?   Melbourne, Overland, 1967.

Plays

> *Friday Night at the Schrammers'* (produced Brisbane, 1949). Published in *Australian One-Act Plays, Book 2,* edited by Greg Branson, Adelaide, Rigby, 1962.
> *No Sugar for George* (produced Brisbane, 1949).
> *The Zelda Trio* (produced Melbourne, 1961; London, 1974).
> *A Slice of Birthday Cake* (broadcast, 1963). Published in *Eight Short Plays,* Melbourne, Nelson, 1965.
> *The Wangaratta Bunyip,* in *Plays for Young Players,* edited by Colin Thiele and Greg Branson. Adelaide, Rigby, 1970.

Screenplays: two *Export Action* series documentaries, 1964.

Radio Plays: *A Slice of Birthday Cake,* 1963 (Australia); *The Slob on Friday,* 1969 (Canada).

Television Plays: *Uneasy Paradise,* 1963 (Australia); *Nude with Violin,* 1964 (Australia); *The Audition,* 1964 (Australia); *The Moods of Love,* 1964 (Australia); *Number Thirty Approximately,* 1968 (U.K.); *Loving Israel,* 1968 (U.K.); *The Girl from Upstairs,* 1971 (U.K.).

Novel

> *Cupid's Crescent.* London, Grandma Press, 1973.

Laurence Collinson comments:

I write poems only when compelled to by some kind of "inner necessity." The impulse may derive from a subjective emotion or an external situation: my two primary subjects in 30 years of writing have been physical love and the self-deception that pervades our personal and social lives. Once the "poetic" idea comes into my consciousness, I try my best to shape the poem according to the needs of the subject and my desire to communicate pleasurably – formal pleasure being essential whether the subject is tragic or comic or something in between. I still adhere to the pronouncement of one of my high-school English teachers that the principal elements of a poem are its music and imagery. So many "avant-garde," "concrete," or otherwise "experimental" poems that I read seem to be merely exercises that a "proper poet" discards on his way to a final draft. The freedom from technique that many "contemporary" poets demand in order to allow themselves full self-expression seems to me unrewarding for both writer and reader: I believe with other Marxists that "freedom is the recognition of necessity," and the limitations imposed on a subject by the use of even the simplest of traditional forms create an infinitely more complex, gratifying, and precious object than the wildest expressionist verses. When I read the work of other poets, what delights and moves me more than anything else is to come across an astonishing and absolutely right image and to feel also that the poet has set down an experience in such a way that I can recognise and share it with him totally. And this is what I would like other readers to find in my own poetry.

*   *   *

Laurence Collinson was born in England, but with his family moved to Australia when he was very young. Education, outlook and basic perceptions are, therefore, influenced by Australia, and Collinson identifies himself with that country. Almost all his published verse first appeared in Australian magazines and anthologies and his two major collections were published by the Melbourne publisher Overland. This identification is not, however, jingoistic in any sense – Collinson claims he feels no urge to assert any specific Australian-ness. Some poets have driven powerful (and some bathetic) work out of the landscape and names of Australia; Collinson only allows a precise sense of place to emerge when it is necessary to the wider movement of a poem. Most of his work could have been written anywhere where the English language is spoken and respected.

Collinson's first collection of poems, *The Moods of Love*, was published in 1957 when he was already well-known as one of the more important younger poets working in Australia. Critics were sharply divided in their reactions, mostly (seen at this distance) on trivial issues. But one thing does emerge from that response, and which is relevant to any consideration of Collinson's poetry, is that many critics were made uneasy by the strong social/political comment implicit in much of the verse. At the time of the volume's publication, Collinson wrote about "a world duped and doped by commercialism, dulled by education (such as we know it), broken by war and oppression. . . ." His work is never didactic on these themes; but neat, observed pieces such as "Suburban Party" and "The Clerk's Prayer" make their points through satire and a sardonic wit. The sonnet sequence that gives the book its title explores, often with great intensity, the responsiveness of one human being to the contact of love. The tone is often deceptively conversational ("I think I love you all the ways there are") which serves only to underscore the personal involvement and technical control of the work.

The second major volume, *Who Is Wheeling Grandma?*, was published in 1967. A sense of political commitment is still present in some poems, notably in "Aspects of Modern Education," a sequence subtitled "Double Standards in Search of a Schoolboy." The overall feel is darker, however, and "the lover drowns as dreams capsize." The poems are generally shorter, and tighter. Collinson has always been a highly disciplined writer; he believes that shape and form are as important as content, and his very concise imagery and perfectly balanced lines do, indeed, give a great deal of pleasure.

– Roger Baker

COLLYMORE, Frank (Appleton). British (West Indian). Born in Barbados, 7 January 1893. Educated at Combermere School, Barbados, 1903–09. Married Gwendolyn Hutchinson in 1917; Ellice Lorna Honychurch, 1947; has four daughters. Teacher, 1910–49, 1958–63, and Deputy Headmaster, 1949–58, Combermere School. Editor, *Bim* magazine, Bridgetown, Barbados, 1943–73. Amateur actor. M.A.: University of the West Indies, Kingston, 1968. O.B.E. (Officer, Order of the British Empire), 1958. Address: Woodville, Chelsea Road, St. Michael, Barbados, West Indies.

PUBLICATIONS

Verse

Thirty Poems.   Bridgetown, Barbados, Advocate Company, 1944.
Beneath the Casuarinas.   Bridgetown, Barbados, Advocate Company, 1945.
Flotsam.   Bridgetown, Barbados, Advocate Company, 1948.
A Dozen Short Poems.   Georgetown, Guyana, Miniature Poets, 1952.
Collected Poems.   Bridgetown, Barbados, Advocate Company, 1959.
Rhymed Ruminations on the Fauna of Barbados.   Bridgetown, Barbados, Advocate Company, 1969.
Selected Poems.   Bridgetown, Barbados, Coles Printery, 1971.

Other

Notes for a Glossary of Words and Phrases of Barbadian Dialect.   Bridgetown, Barbados, Advocate Company, 1953; revised edition, 1957, 1965, 1970.

Frank Collymore comments:

I had always enjoyed the reading of poetry and had on several occasions tried to write verse unsuccessfully. In the early forties, I happened to be living alone, and the reading of the poetry of Day Lewis, W. H. Auden, and Louis MacNeice seemed to act as stimuli to whatever dormant muse may have been awaiting expression. During the forties and early fifties I wrote continuously – I suppose well over 200 poems – and encouraged by some friends, I ventured to have them published.

I am afraid that since that period my muse has forsaken me, although I have from time to time written some light verse.

*   *   *

Frank Collymore has so far published four books of poems: *Thirty Poems, Beneath the Casuarinas, Flotsam* and *Collected Poems.* A selection of his light verse, *Rhymed Ruminations on the Fauna of Barbados,* appeared in 1969, and another selection in 1971. He is essentially a "Nature" poet, "Georgian" in mode. His themes are landscape, love, beauty, mutability, reflections on an empire of the mind in which man's perceptions were once whole:

> All that our mortal hands have wrought
> Upon time's wide and fleeting range
> Enjoy but brief integrity,
> Soon suffer change.
>
> Even the temple that we rear
> To love, so proud against the sky,
> May not prevail o'er transience,
> For love must die.
>   – "Mutability"

But though he is very conscious of the fragility of things, Frank Collymore is not a sentimentalizer. His perception of love and beauty is often fixed within tight, exact images; and his landscapes are often fully realized. The sea, for example, is "crisscrossed with stillness" in lines which use the overtly ordinary "lazylapping," "windruffed" and "aglitter" in a combination which produces effects more memorable and accurate than might, on the surface, be expected:

> Always, always, the encroaching sea,
> Eternal, lazylapping, crisscrossed with stillness;
> Or windruffed, aglitter with gold; and the surf
> Waist-high for children, or horses for Titans . . .
> > – "Hymn to the Sea"

In "Blue Agave," from *Flotsam*, this language takes on the hard, harsh, barren quality of the seaside plant:

> Perched between stones, rooted in rock;
> Thriving in drought and seablast . . .
>
> The bunched fingers spiked, at first
> Resentful, now drooping as fountains drip
> . . .; reptilian leaves armoured
> Against the unknown foe . . .
>
> Avid the pronged claws, the idle
> Teeth; and the uncoiling leaves, stark
> And impervious as shark's hide, bear
> The imprint of tooth and claw upon them . . .
>
> Armoured against forgotten fate
> They score the low horizon . . .

No other West Indian poet, not even Derek Walcott in *The Castaway*, has captured the desolation of the windward Caribbean coasts as precisely and as symbolically as Collymore in this poem. And as the West Indian archipelago is a fragment of a continent, and our history a fragment of a lost and possible whole, so Collymore's sensibility perceives the splinters:

> Words – words are the poem,
> The incalculable flotsam;
> That which bore them vanished beneath
> The hurrying drift of time.
>
> How shall they speak, how tell
> Of the ship and the lost crew?
> Each plank a splinter,
> Each splinter enough for memory?
> > – "Words Are the Poem"

This sense of fragment, of ruin, the loss of something that was once beautiful, receives its fullest social expression in "Old Windmill":

> . . . Once she was the focused joy
> Of the countryside, her mighty sails unfurled:
>
> Queen of the trades, a good ship manned
> By her pressed crews to ride the surge and swell
> Of the blue days . . .
>
> Then there was singing, there was laughter, delight
> In her life's blood . . .
>
> Desolate now; only the empty eyes
> Forever framed within the past . . .
> > Under windswept skies
> The sloven tractors shamble to the factory.

But to properly appreciate the achievement of Frank Collymore, one must read him alongside the "older" generation of West Indian poets – Tom Redcam, Claude McKay, Clare McFarlane, and those others who appear in *A Treasury of Jamaican Poetry* (1949). His "Blue Agave" (above) must be compared with, say, McKay's "Spanish Needle":

> Lovely, dainty Spanish Needle
> > With your yellow flower and white,
> Dew-bedecked and softly sleeping,
> > Do you think of me tonight?

The differences are devastating. The point is that Collymore transcends the verse of his "Georgian" contemporaries. While they attempted to "sing" like Tennyson, he was learning from the discoveries of T. S. Eliot. He is the great poet of the West Indian transition. He is not yet concerned with social reality, however. His poem "The Windmill" looks back to a golden time before mechanization, but gives no hint, except in "pressed crews," of the plantation system of which it is also a symbol. This failure to come to terms with this central area of West Indian experience is perhaps responsible for a certain lack of development in his poetry. One feels that, with his talents, he has consciously limited himself. On the other hand, he transforms an apparently everyday world which the poets of the "revolution" have often forgotten or have had little time for. More surely than most of his contemporaries of both generations, he can move from

> Are you loved?
> > Weep; for the doll may never return
> The kisses its mother
> > Bestows . . .
> > > – "Chanson Triste"

to

> See how nicely his tie sits underneath his collar . . .
> > You can always tell an educated man if you know where to look.
> See, he takes his hat off when the band is playing
> > The National Anthem! That man's no bloody fool:
> He owns three houses and a drugstore in Porkmarket;
> > He has learnt to use both edges of the Golden Rule.
> > > – "Voici la plume de mon oncle"

> – Edward Brathwaite

COLOMBO, John Robert. Canadian. Born in Kitchener, Ontario, 24 March 1936. Educated at Waterloo College, Ontario, 1956–57; University College, University of Toronto, B.A. 1959, 1959–60. Editorial Assistant, University of Toronto Press, 1959–60; Assistant Editor, Ryerson Press, 1960–63. Since 1964, Senior Advisory Editor, McClelland and Stewart, Toronto. Former Editor, *The Montrealer* and *Exchange.* Since 1959, Managing Editor, *Tamarack Review,* Toronto, and since 1970, Advising Editor, *Performing Arts* magazine, Toronto. Occasional Instructor, York University, Toronto. Former Member, Canada Council Arts Advisory Panel. Guest of the U.S.S.R. Writers Union, 1971. Recipient: Canada Council grant, 1967, 1971; Centennial Medal, 1967. Address: 42 Dell Park Avenue, Toronto M6B 2T6, Ontario, Canada.

PUBLICATIONS

Verse

Fragments. Kitchener, Ontario, privately printed, 1957.
Variations. Kitchener, Ontario, Hawkshead Press, 1958.
This Citadel in Time. Kitchener, Ontario, privately printed, 1958.
This Studied Self. Kitchener, Ontario, Hawkshead Press, 1958.
Poems and Other Poems. Toronto, Hawkshead Press, 1959.
Lines for the Last Day. Toronto, Hawkshead Press, 1960.
The Mackenzie Poems. Toronto, Swan, 1965.
The Great Wall of China: An Entertainment. Montreal, Delta Canada, 1966.
Abracadabra. Toronto, McClelland and Stewart, 1967.
Miraculous Montages. Toronto, Heine, 1967.
John Toronto: New Poems by Dr. Strachan, Found by John Robert Colombo. Ottawa, Oberon Press, 1969.
Neo Poems. Vancouver, Sono Nis Press, 1970.
The Great San Francisco Earthquake and Fire. Fredericton, New Brunswick, Fiddlehead, 1971.
Praise Poems and Leonardo's Lists. Toronto, Weed/Flower Press, 1972.
Translations from the English. Toronto, Peter Martin Associates, 1974.
The Sad Truths. Toronto, Peter Martin Associates, 1974.

Other

Editor, *The Varsity Chapbook.* Toronto, Ryerson Press, 1959.
Editor, with Jacques Godbout, *Poésie 64/Poetry 64.* Toronto and Montreal, Ryerson Press-Editions du Jour, 1963.
Editor, with Raymond Souster, *Shapes and Sounds: Poems of W. W. E. Ross.* Toronto, Longman, 1968.
Editor, *How Do I Love Thee: Sixty Poems of Canada (and Quebec). . . .* Edmonton, Hurtig, 1970.
Editor, *New Directions in Canadian Poetry.* Toronto, Holt Rinehart, 1970.
Editor, *Rhymes and Reasons.* Toronto, Holt Rinehart, 1971.
Editor, *Colombo's Canadian Quotations.* Edmonton, Alberta, Hurtig, 1974.

Translator, *From Zero to One.* Vancouver, Sono Nis Press, 1973.

Manuscript Collection: Mills Memorial Library, McMaster University, Hamilton, Ontario.

Critical Studies: by Northrop Frye, in *University of Toronto Review*, July 1959; by Alfred Purdy, in Toronto *Globe and Mail*, 4 June 1966; by George Woodcock, in *Canadian Literature* (Vancouver), Summer 1966; by Louis Dudek, in Montreal *Gazette*, 22 October 1966; by Miriam Waddington, in Toronto *Globe and Mail*, 18 March 1967; by Hugh MacCallum, in *University of Toronto Review*, July 1967 and July 1968.

John Robert Colombo comments:

Poetry can be written in the language of song, which is verse, or in the language of speech, which is prose. In my original poems, and especially in my found poetry, I am exploring the rhythms of the poem-as-prose. I prefer the authentic effect of prose to the artifice of a poem. I want the reader or listener to be so startled by the poem he will regard the world itself as a work of art – as a Great Collage. Favourite writers include Jorge Luis Borges, Nicanor Parra, Rainer Maria Rilke, Wallace Stevens, Francis Ponge, Constantine Cavafy, Jozsef Attila, Miroslav Holub, Zbigniew Herbert, etc. They are always with me.

*   *   *

The appearance of John Robert Colombo's *Abracadabra* in 1967 marked a welcome return by him to a poetry whose resonances were familiar and whose values were less stridently asserted – closer to the central human experience. To use his own lines: "What is immensely important here is life itself: man / feeding on the world." It is that affirmation that one finds celebrated in the *Abracadabra* volume – the more than cerebral apprehension of terror in "There is No Way Out," for instance.

Not all his celebrations are as fortunate, however. "The hot wells of your flowing kidneys" must surely be classed among the great lines of "unredeemed poetry." And the preciocity incumbent upon a sustained attention to works of art bespeaks, and is exacerbated by, the leaden "relevances" of a naive and isolated provincialism often present in his work.

This feeling of the provincially claustrophobic is present in *The Mackenzie Poems*. There is a sense in which these pieces of "found poetry" or "redeemed prose" are made to assume the mantle of a Canadian Gettysburg, and they (even as prose) will not stand the strain. If there is something sympathetic and attractive in the firebrand character of Mackenzie's life it is not an attractiveness that his prose conveys. Ultimately the factiousness becomes tedious, and, worse, the limitations of Mackenzie's imagination ("System is everything") work at variance to the larger mundo of poetry.

Coleridge said that the power of poetry "reveals itself in the balance or reconciliation of opposite or discordant qualities; . . . a more than usual state of emotion, with more than usual order." The emotion in these poems, unfortunately, is scarcely ever above the pedestrian. This is not the politically visionary stuff of Blake or Milton, or even Pope. At its best it is Felix Holt. And when the order is "more than usual" it is so because the prose itself has a rhetorical (e.g., Ciceronian) structure that encourages the transformation into poetry.

No such structure underlies the private and public letters of Bishop Strachan – the raw material of Colombo's next volume *New Poems by Dr. Strachan*. Strachan and Mackenzie were adversaries in the early polity of Upper Canada – Strachan as resolutely Church of England establishment as Mackenzie was non-conformist radical. *New Poems* was announced as a book that "tells the other half of the story," but one wonders, remembering Arnold's observations on the turgid flatulence of Victorian Toronto society, whether "the story" was worth the candle – let alone two volumes of poetry.

Something of the deadness of Strachan's position (let alone the issues) is conveyed in the "poem" "Universal Corruption": "I am still the same Tory / that you knew me to be / forty years ago." This is a man who can refer to the magnificent wilderness, still unspoiled, as "a dismal wood." Even Mr. Casaubon in all his dullness was not arrayed so drably as this. Minds as lapidary as Strachan's are not creative of great prose, let alone poetry. Even in his private reflections we have the sense of a man dead at the centre – the complacent (and complaisant) voice of orotund establishment, feeding its piety with goose dinners and Addisonian maxims, assured that the business of religion is in dispensing the unquestionable intellectual and moral superiority of the British nation.

The reader has a similar sense of weighty indigestion in *The Great Wall of China* but there the weariness comes from a weight of accumulated statistic and observation, lightened only occasionally by such magical poems as "The Legendary Mound of Ch'in." For there the felicities are of the realm of the lyrical imagination as the pleasures of "Arabesque" (another poem in the sequence, taken from Maugham) are the rhetorical enchantments of a high order of descriptive prose.

In *Neo Poems'* again one has the sense of a notebook full of possible poems, never quite realised. Many if not most are collections of para-Haiku, at their best finely descriptive: "the sea drifts into France" or "The mind has / a tongue in both its cheeks." But Colombo is not alone among Canadian poets in allowing the gnomic to become merely the cute. "I want to scribble passionate marginalia all through the Book of Life" is too close to Rod McKuen for comfort of mind.

Part of Colombo's problem here is a distinctively Canadian one – a rather adolescent stridency that tends to a chauvinism that is both personal and national. (Often they tend to become confused.) Quoting with approval Symons's "it is not natural to be what is called 'natural' any longer," the poet assumes the role of exile-in-one's-own-country and exalts the sententious and truistic to the level of the profound. We are offered "In all literature, the traditional must expose the actual" as if that statement (piece of poetry?) meant something.

This is a pity, for Colombo is a good poet and a fine wit – a poet who has yet to find a medium appropriate to his sensibility. For ultimately it is not his "found poetry" but his "made poetry" that has the greater stature. And it is in this mode that (as he says of Wyeth) "a detail becomes a dimension" because the imaginative life that sustains it is not fortuitous or ideologically strident but integral and creative, and affirmative of life at its highest pitch.

– D. D. C. Chambers

COMFORT, Alex(ander). British. Born in London, 10 February 1920. Educated at Highgate School, London; Trinity College, Cambridge, M.B., B.Ch. 1944, M.A. 1945; The London Hospital, D.C.H. 1945; Ph..D. (biochemistry) 1949, D.Sc. (gerontology) 1963; Member of the Royal College of Surgeons; Licentiate of the

Royal College of Physicians. Editor, *Lyra, New Roads,* and *Poetry Folios,* in the early 1940's. House Physician, The London Hospital, 1944; Resident Medical Officer, Royal Waterloo Hospital, London, 1944–45. Lecturer in Physiology, 1945–51, Honorary Research Associate, Department of Zoology, since 1951, Director of the Medical Research Group on the Biology of Ageing, 1966–70, and since 1970, Director of Research in Gerontology, University College, London. President, British Society for Research on Ageing, 1967. Recipient: Ciba Foundation Prize, 1958, Karger Memorial Prize in Gerontology, 1969.

PUBLICATIONS

Verse

> *France and Other Poems.*   London, Favil Press, 1941.
> *Three New Poets,* with Roy McFadden and Ian Seraillier.   London, Grey Walls Press, 1942.
> *A Wreath for the Living.*   London, Routledge, 1942.
> *Elegies.*   London, Routledge, 1944.
> *The Song of Lazarus.*   Barnet, Hertfordshire, Poetry Folios, and New York, Viking Press, 1945.
> *The Signal to Engage.*   London, Routledge, 1946.
> *And All But He Departed.*   London, Routledge, 1951.
> *Haste to the Wedding.*   London, Eyre and Spottiswoode, 1962; Chester Springs, Pennsylvania, Dufour, 1964.
> *Coming Together: Poems Chiefly about Women.*   New York, Crown, 1975.

Plays

> *Into Egypt: A Miracle Play.*   London, Grey Walls Press, 1942.
> *Cities of the Plain: A Democratic Melodrama.*   London, Grey Walls Press, 1943.

Television Play: *The Great Agrippa,* 1968.

Novels

> *The Silver River: Being the Diary of a Schoolboy in the South Atlantic.*   London, Chapman and Hall, 1937.
> *No Such Liberty.*   London, Chapman and Hall, 1941.
> *The Almond Tree: A Legend.*   London, Chapman and Hall, 1942.
> *The Powerhouse.*   London, Routledge, 1944; New York, Viking Press, 1945.
> *On This Side Nothing.*   London, Routledge, 1948; New York, Viking Press, 1949.
> *A Giant's Strength.*   London, Routledge, 1952.
> *Come Out to Play.*   London, Eyre and Spottiswoode, 1961.

Short Stories

> *Letters from an Outpost.*   London, Routledge, 1947.

Other

Art and Social Responsibility: Lectures on the Ideology of Romanticism. London, Grey Walls Press, 1947.

The Novel and Our Time. Letchworth, Hertfordshire, Phoenix House, and Denver, Swallow, 1948.

Barbarism and Sexual Freedom: Six Lectures on the Sociology of Sex from the Standpoint of Anarchism. London, Freedom Press, 1948.

First Year Physiological Techniques. London and New York, Staples Press, 1948.

The Pattern of the Future. London, Routledge, and New York, Macmillan, 1949.

Authority and Delinquency in the Modern State: A Criminological Approach to the Problem of Power. London, Routledge, 1950.

Sexual Behaviour in Society. London, Duckworth, and New York, Viking Press, 1950; revised edition, Duckworth, 1963; as *Sex in Society*, New York, Citadel Press, 1966.

The Biology of Senescence. London, Routledge, and New York, Rinehart, 1956; revised edition, Routledge, 1964; as *Aging: The Biology of Senescence*, New York, Holt Rinehart, 1964.

Darwin and the Naked Lady: Discursive Essays on Biology and Art. London, Routledge, 1961; New York, Braziller, 1962.

The Process of Ageing. London, Weidenfeld and Nicolson, 1965.

The Nature of Human Nature. New York, Harper, 1965; as *Nature and Human Nature*, London, Weidenfeld and Nicolson, 1966.

The Anxiety Makers: Some Curious Preoccupations of the Medical Profession. London, Nelson, 1967.

The Joy of Sex: A Gourmet's Guide to Love Making. New York, Crown, and London, Quartet, 1973.

More Joy: A Beautiful Lovemaking Sequel to "The Joy of Sex." New York, Crown, 1974.

Editor, with John Bayliss, *New Road 1944: New Directions in European Art and Letters.* London, Grey Walls Press, 1944.

Editor, *History of Erotic Art, I.* London, Weidenfeld and Nicolson, and New York, Putnam, 1969.

Translator, with Allan Ross Macdougall, *The Triumph of Death*, by C. F. Ramuz. London, Routledge, 1946.

Translator, *Koka Shastra.* London, Allen and Unwin, 1964; New York, Stein and Day, 1965.

Bibliography: "Alexander Comfort: A Bibliography in Progress" by D. Callaghan, in *West Coast Review* (Burnaby, British Columbia), 1969.

Critical Studies: *The Freedom of Poetry* by Derek Stanford, London, Falcon Press, 1947; "The Scientific Humanism of Alex Comfort" by Wayne Burns, in *The Humanist* (London), November-December 1951; "The Anarchism of Alex Comfort" by John Ellerby, "Sex, Kicks and Comfort" by Charles Radcliffe, and "Alex Comfort's Art and Scope" by Harold Drasdo, all in *Anarchy* (London), November 1963.

* * *

Alex Comfort's best known poems are concerned with sexual love – with a sometimes tender, sometimes bawdy exploration of the sexual impulse in man and woman. If other poets have occasionally explored this area, Dr. Comfort is (apart from his contemporary, Gavin Ewart) the only poet who is known almost exclusively for it – partly no doubt because of his extrapoetic writing, often about sexual psychology and physiology, and partly through the continual anthologisation of his fine poem "For Ruth" ("There is a white mare that my love keeps / unridden in a hillside meadow . . .").

Comfort's earlier poems, owing much (as whose did not?) to Eliot, consisted often of meditations on death – not only on violent death in war (as in *Elegies*), but death seen lurking in the natural world of landscape: "The condemned cell of the woods lies round our doors, / the trees are bars, and barbs the bramble carries. . . ." His later war poems (in *The Signal to Engage*) were as bitter as those of Siegfried Sassoon, a generation earlier, who sometimes seems indeed to have been a direct influence (cf. "Song for the Heroes").

But it was later, within the last twenty years, that Dr. Comfort found the theme and the style, sometimes extrovert, sometimes interior, which was to enable him to write the poems in which he is seen at his most amusing, accomplished and wise. His range, within that theme, is considerable, from the lyrical to the epigrammatic ("Babies' and lovers' toes express / ecstacies of wantonness. / That's a language which we lose / with the trick of wearing shoes").

Comfort's technical range is not great, yet he does command a technique which enables him to make his points in a sinewy and terse language which only occasionally is marred by sentimentality. His anecdotes, often telling a short story which might have appealed to Maupassant (cf. "The Charmer"), are succinct, and if he turns his hand to a purpose-made piece, as in the epithalamion *Haste to the Wedding*, the note is never false and invariably lively.

His attitude to love, now increasingly shared by his younger readers, is celebrated in poetry like none that has been written since the Restoration: direct and uncompromising, a note of wholehearted enjoyment; he is tired of "the best pentameters," of "eloquence overdone": "That first act of our own / is still the best act left. Let's go to bed." Of course this means there are limitations: Dr. Comfort has never perhaps wholly recaptured the tenderness of "For Ruth." But many other poets have written single poems of considerable beauty; not so many have written, for instance, a complaining elegy on bed-manufacturers: "Surely the trade has one Stradivarius? / If not, I know why in Neolithic days / the Goddess was steatopygic. / For the meantime let us unroll the rug."

His later love poems succeed perhaps *because* they lack the painful intensity of longing that pierces the verse of poets both less happy as lovers amd more intent on their poetry. Comfort's verse celebrates, not mourns nor yearns. His words "serve to fill the space / between meeting and meeting – / this is the eloquent thing / that they are celebrating / and nothing that we write / myself or any other / matches the fine content / of what we do together."

– Derek Parker

CONN, Stewart. British. Born in Glasgow, Scotland, 5 November 1936. Educated at Kilmarnock Academy and Glasgow University. National Service: Royal Air Force. Married Judith Clarke in 1963. Since 1962, Radio Drama Producer, BBC, Glasgow. Since 1972, Literary Adviser, Edinburgh Royal Lyceum Theatre. Recipient: Gregory Award, 1963; Scottish Arts Council Prize and Publication

Award, 1968. Lives in Glasgow. Agent: Mrs. Nina Froud, Harvey Unna Ltd., 14 Beaumont Mews, Marylebone High Street, London W1N 4HE, England.

PUBLICATIONS

Verse

> *Thunder in the Air: Poems.* Preston, Lancashire, Akros, 1967.
> *The Chinese Tower.* Edinburgh, Macdonald, 1967.
> *Stoats in the Sunlight: Poems.* London, Hutchinson, 1968; as *Ambush and Other Poems*, New York, Macmillan, 1970.
> *Corgi Modern Poets in Focus 3*, with others, edited by Dannie Abse. London, Corgi, 1971.
> *An Ear to the Ground.* London, Hutchinson, 1972.

Plays

> *Break-Down* (produced Glasgow, 1961).
> *Birds in a Wilderness* (produced Edinburgh, 1964).
> *I Didn't Always Live Here* (produced Glasgow, 1967). Included in *The Aquarium, The Man in the Green Muffler, I Didn't Always Live Here*, 1974.
> *The King* (produced Edinburgh, 1967; London, 1972). Published in *New English Dramatists 14*, London, Penguin, 1970.
> *Broche* (produced Exeter, Devon, 1968).
> *Fancy Seeing You, Then*, in *Playbill Two*, edited by Alan Durband. London, Hutchinson, 1969.
> *Victims* (includes *The Sword, In Transit*, and *The Man in the Green Muffler*) (produced Edinburgh, 1970). *In Transit* published New York, Breakthrough Press, 1972; *The Man in the Green Muffler* included in *The Aquarium, The Man in the Green Muffler, I Didn't Always Live Here*, 1974.
> *The Burning* (produced Edinburgh, 1971). London, Calder and Boyars, 1972.
> *A Slight Touch of the Sun* (produced Edinburgh, 1972).
> *The Aquarium* (produced Edinburgh, 1973). Included in *The Aquarium, The Man in the Green Muffler, I Didn't Always Live Here*, 1974.

> Radio Plays: *Any Following Spring*, 1962; *Cadenza for Real*, 1963; *Song of the Clyde*, 1964; *The Canary Cage*, 1967.

> Television Play: *Wally Dugs Go in Pairs*, 1973.

Other

> Editor, *New Poems 1973–74.* London, Hutchinson, 1974.

Manuscript Collection: Scottish National Library, Edinburgh.

Critical Studies: Interview with James Aitchison in *Scottish Theatre* (Edinburgh), March 1969; introduction by Dannie Abse to *Corgi Modern Poets in Focus 3*, 1971; interview with Allen Wright in *The Scotsman* (Edinburgh), 30 October 1971.

Theatrical Activities:

Director: **Radio** – *Armstrong's Last Goodnight*, 1964; *The Anatomist*, 1965; *My Friend Mr. Leakey*, 1967; *Mr. Gillie*, 1967; *Happy Days Are Here Again*, 1967.

*   *   *

At this stage two poems alone, "Todd" and "Simon," both in *Stoats in the Sunlight*, are enough to secure Stewart Conn a special niche. The conviction and originality of the voice are established in the concentrated first two lines of "Todd":

My father's white uncle became
Arthritic and testamental in
Lyrical stages. . . .

The "white uncle," at once legendary in its suggestion, becomes almost immediately suffering actuality in "arthritic," before turning Old Testament prophet in "testamental," but the prophet's fires burn in his passion for horses; yet the horses themselves are "a primal extension of rock and soil," though equally they have "cracked hooves" and are fed on "bowls of porridge." The world of the stable is activated in sounds – "thundered nail" – and in smells – "his own horsey breath" – the uncle's breath, as horse and he are one. The success of the poem, and frequently in the poems that follow in the first of the two sections of the book, is in the sense of a compelling experience charging the words with a meaning that flows to-fro between the actual and the mythical.

In the second section the poems are more deliberately dramatic, and as the more conscious art of the playwright becomes evident so the feeling of inevitable development and impending eruption diminishes, and this despite evidence that the poet feels acutely the hazard of existence, and despite the direction seeming to be the true psychological one, after his identification with the energies of nature – and I include human nature. Yet a talent as distinguished as Conn's must go its own way. What has already been achieved in poems and plays is a distinctive contribution. The prospect is very interesting.

– George Bruce

CONNOR, Tony (John Anthony Augustus Connor). British. Born in Manchester, Lancashire, 16 March 1930. Left school at fourteen. Served as a tank driver in the 5th Royal Inniskilling Dragoon Guards, 1948–50. Married Frances Foad in 1961; has three children. Textile Designer, Manchester, 1944–60. Assistant in Liberal Studies, Bolton Technical College, 1961–64; Visiting Poet, Amherst College, Massachusetts, 1967–68. Visiting Poet and Lecturer, 1968–69, and since 1971, Professor of English, Wesleyan University, Middletown, Connecticut. Visiting Playwright, Oxford Playhouse, England, 1974–75. M.A.: Manchester University, 1968; Wesleyan University, 1971. Fellow, Royal Society of Literature. Address: 44 Brainerd Avenue, Middletown, Connecticut 06457, U.S.A.

PUBLICATIONS

Verse

With Love Somehow: Poems.   London, Oxford University Press, 1962.
Lodgers: Poems.   London, Oxford University Press, 1965.
Poems: A Selection, with Austin Clarke and Charles Tomlinson.   London and
    New York, Oxford University Press, 1964.
12 Secret Poems.   Manchester, MICA, 1965.
Kon in Springtime: Poems.   London, Oxford University Press, 1968.
In the Happy Valley: Poems.   London, Oxford University Press, 1971.
The Memoirs of Uncle Harry.   London, Oxford University Press, 1974.
Seven Last Poems from the Memoirs of Uncle Harry.   Newcastle upon Tyne,
    Northern House, 1974.

Recording: *Poems,* with Norman Nicholson, Argo, 1974.

Plays

Billy's Wonderful Kettle (produced Manchester, 1971).
*I Am Real and So Are You, A Visit from the Family, and Crewe Station at 2
    A.M.* (produced London, 1971).
The Last of the Feinsteins (produced London, 1972).
A Couple with a Cat (produced London, 1972).
Otto's Interview (produced London, 1973).
Crankenheim's Mixed-Up Monster (produced Oxford, 1974).

Other

Translator, with George Gomöri, *Love of the Scorching Wind,* by Laszlo Nagy.
    London, Oxford University Press, 1973.

Tony Connor comments:

There are no critical studies of Tony Connor's work, which has received scant
and condescending attention from English reviewers. In U.S.A., however, he is
considered "one of the poets now bringing new life to English verse" (M. L.
Rosenthal, *Saturday Review,* 1968) and "undoubtedly one of the best and most
authentic of recent British poets" (*Poetry,* January 1969).
His poetry is unacademic, independent and original and uses domestic themes
and imagery in a free-flowing, at times surrealistic, manner. The moral ambiguity of
Mr. Connor's apparent simplicities reminds one of Frost more than of any modern
English poet, and this, perhaps, helps to explain the fact that his reputation stands
higher in the United States than in his own country.

*   *   *

Tony Connor has established himself as one of the best of the numerous domestic poets now writing in England. Ordinary incidents of family life, the rubs of

marriage, even memories of National Service, supply him with material for poems which are usually strongly and logically constructed and economically if rather conventionally written. Recent attempts to extend his range, and to write more complex work, have been less successful. But his more characteristic poetry is often attractive – earthy, straightforward, convincingly truthful, and far less monotonous than the restricted subject matter might suggest.

– Edward Lucie-Smith

CONQUEST, (George) Robert (Acworth). British. Born in Great Malvern, Worcestershire, 15 July 1917. Educated at Winchester College, Hampshire; Magdalen College, Oxford, B.A. 1939, M.A. 1972; University of Grenoble, France. Served in the Oxfordshire and Buckinghamshire Light Infantry, 1939–46. Married Caroleen Macfarlane in 1964; has two children by a previous marriage. Member of the U.K. Diplomatic Service, 1946–56; Fellow, London School of Economics, 1956–58; Lecturer in English, State University of New York at Buffalo, 1959–60; Literary Editor, *The Spectator,* London, 1962–63; Senior Fellow, Columbia University, New York, 1964–65. Recipient: P.E.N. prize, 1945; Festival of Britain prize, 1951. Fellow, Royal Society of Literature, 1972. O.B.E. (Officer, Order of the British Empire), 1955. Address: 4 York Mansions, Prince of Wales Drive, London S.W.11, England.

PUBLICATIONS

Verse

> *Poems.* London, Macmillan, and New York, St. Martin's Press, 1955.
> *Between Mars and Venus.* London, Hutchinson, and New York, St. Martin's Press, 1962.
> *Arias from a Love Opera.* London, Macmillan, and New York, Macmillan, 1969.

Novels

> *A World of Difference.* London, Ward Lock, 1955; New York, Ballantine, 1964.
> *The Egyptologists,* with Kingsley Amis. London, Cape, 1965; New York, Random House, 1966.

Other

> *Common Sense about Russia.* London, Gollancz, and New York, Macmillan, 1960.
> *Courage of Genius: The Pasternak Affair.* London, Collins-Harvill, and Philadelphia, Lippincott, 1961.

Power and Policy in the U.S.S.R.   London, Macmillan, and New York, St.
Martin's Press, 1962.

Russia after Khrushchev.   London, Pall Mall Press, and New York, Praeger,
1965.

The Great Terror: Stalin's Purge of the Thirties.   London, Macmillan, and New
York, Macmillan, 1968.

The Nation Killers: The Soviet Deportation of Nationalities.   London, Macmillan,
and New York, Macmillan, 1970.

Lenin.   London, Fontana, and New York, Viking Press, 1972.

Editor, *New Lines I* and *II.*   London, Macmillan, 1956, 1963.

Editor, *Back to Life* (anthology).   London, Hutchinson, and New York, St.
Martin's Press, 1958.

Editor, with Kingsley Amis, *Spectrum: A Science Fiction Anthology.*   London,
Gollancz, 5 vols., 1961–66; New York, Harcourt Brace, 5 vols., 1962–67.

Editor, *Soviet Studies Series.*   London, Bodley Head, 8 vols., 1967–68; New
York, Praeger, 8 vols., 1968–69.

Editor, *Pyotr Yakir.*   London, Macmillan, 1972; New York, Coward McCann,
1973.

Editor, *The Robert Sheckley Omnibus.*   London, Gollancz, 1973.

Critical Studies: in *The Times Literary Supplement* (London), 30 May 1955; by D. J.
Enright, in *The Month* (London), May 1956; by John Holloway, in *Hudson Review*
(New York), xiv, 4, 1961; by Thom Gunn, in *The Spectator* (London), 4 May 1962.

Robert Conquest comments:

I suppose my main theme is the poet's relationship to the phenomenal universe –
in particular to landscape, women, art and war. Forms usually, though not always,
traditional. Sometimes straight lyric, more often with development of a train of
thought: an attempt to master, or transmit, a presented reality in intellectual and
emotive terms simultaneously. The vocabulary often runs to words – not specialist
ones – drawn from the technical, scientific and philosophical spheres, and media-
tised into the ordinary language.

Since all this is in principle a complex and difficult process, a strong effort goes
into keeping it as comprehensible as possible, avoidance of forced obscurities,
and provision of a rigorous guidance of sound and structure.

*   *   *

Although as a very young man in the late thirties Robert Conquest had contributed some Audenesque exercises to *Twentieth Century Verse,* he did not emerge as
a mature poet until his first collection, *Poems,* came out in 1955. A year later
Conquest edited *New Lines,* an anthology of the poets of the so-called "Movement," and his own poetry exhibited the favoured qualities of that school: exactness of form, intellectual structure, emphasis on empricism and common-sense
values, and a certain preoccupation with the nature of the poetic process. But
Conquest was distinguished from the other contributors to *New Lines* by the greater
range of his subject matter. He wrote love poems and poems about Eastern Europe
and the Mediterranean, and philosophical reflections on the nature of perception.
And in "The Landing in Deucalion" Conquest wrote the first of several poems

inspired by his abiding interest in science fiction. *Poems* was an enjoyable, even distinguished first collection. It presented the reader with an urbane and civilized mind, widely read and widely travelled, sympathetically curious about most forms of human activity. The poetic influences were from Auden and Robert Graves, but they were well assimilated, and Conquest's voice was highly personal, however much he employed the general idiom of the Movement. Formal precision was combined with delicacy of response, and though feeling was controlled it was unmistakably present. The qualities of Conquest's best poetry can be seen in his sonnet, "Guided Missiles Experimental Range," where he responds to a modern, technological subject with a precisely deployed classical reference. Here is the sestet:

> Stronger than lives, by empty purpose blinded,
> The only thought their circuits can endure is
> The target-hunting rigour of their flight;
>
> And by that loveless haste I am reminded
> Of Aeschylus' description of the Furies:
> *"O barren daughters of the fruitful night."*

If most of the poems in the book are in traditional metres and rhyme schemes, one of the finest, "Near Jakobslev," is in free verse, a beautifully rendered account of a sub-arctic landscape in summer.

Conquest's later poetry continues the subjects of his first book: love, landscapes, science fiction, poetry itself. But it is generally less rewarding; the precision of the verse has become a little mechanical, and the pressure of feeling to be contained is less immediate. There is a heavy reliance on certain recurring key words – "love," "poem," "girl" – and an air of self-imitation. Even so, the craftsmanship remains admirable at a time when the formal virtues that Conquest argued for and exhibited in the mid-fifties have been disregarded by many younger poets. And he remains capable of formidable feats of skill, as in his recent completion of two fragments of verse from a Housman manuscript, turning them into finished poems in the form and metre of Housman's drafts ("Two Housman Torsos," *Times Literary Supplement,* October 19, 1973). One regrets, though, that so gifted a poet has remained content with his own gifts, and developed them so little.

– Bernard Bergonzi

CONRAN, Anthony. British. Born in Kharghpur, India, 7 April 1931. Educated at University College of North Wales, Bangor, B.A. (honours) in English and philosophy, M.A. in English. Since 1957, Research Fellow and Tutor, University College of North Wales. Recipient: Welsh Arts Council award, 1960, and bursary, 1968. Address: 1 Frondirion, Glanrafon, Bangor, Caernarvonshire, Wales.

PUBLICATIONS

Verse

Formal Poems.   Llandybie, Carmarthenshire, Christopher Davies, 1960.
Metamorphoses.   Pembroke Dock, Pembrokeshire, Dock Leaves Press, 1961.

Icons (opus 6).   Bangor, privately printed, 1963.
Asymptotes (opus 7).   Denbigh, privately printed, 1963.
A String o Blethers (opus 8).   Bangor, privately printed, 1963.
Sequence of the Blue Flower.   Privately printed, 1963.
The Mountain.   Privately printed, 1963.
For the Marriage of Gerard and Linda.   Privately printed, 1963.
Stelae and Other Poems (opus 9).   Oxford, Clive Allison, 1965.
Guernica.   Denbigh, Gee and Son, 1966.
Collected Poems:
   Volume I (1951–58).   Oxford, Clive Allison, 1966.
   Volume II (1959–61).   Denbigh, Gee and Son, 1966.
   Volume III (1962–66).   Denbigh, Gee and Son, 1967.
   Volume IV (1967).   Denbigh, Gee and Son, 1968.
Claim, Claim, Claim: A Book of Poems.   Guildford, Surrey, Circle Press, 1969.
Spirit Level.   Llandybie, Carmarthenshire, Christopher Davies, 1974.
Poems 1951–67.   Bangor, Deiniol Press, 1974.

Other

   Editor and Translator, *The Penguin Book of Welsh Verse.*   London, Penguin, 1967.

Critical Study: by Gwyn Thomas, in *Poetry Wales* (Cardiff), Spring 1967.

Anthony Conran comments:

[I belong to] the Anglo-Welsh School of Hopkins, Dylan Thomas, and R. S. Thomas; and behind them the Welsh literary tradition of Taliesin and Cynddelw Brydydd Mawr.

I will try anything once. I write poems when people seem to want them; and the demands of what they want set me formal problems which I solve in my poems.

*   *   *

Anthony Conran is one of the foremost translators of Welsh poetry and has edited the *Penguin Book of Welsh Verse,* doing valuable work in bringing a number of masterpieces before a wider audience.

His own collected poems, *Spirit Level,* cover the years 1956–68, including a section of experiments in strict metre from Chinese, Japanese, Provençal, and Celtic, which are certainly different and partly successful. He also includes his "gift-poems" – pieces of praise, and celebrations of other people's marriages (given as presents on wedding-days) and the births of their children. Conran dedicates many of his poems to friends and writers, alive and dead. He says that the giving and receiving of gifts and odes formed the "central arch of Welsh civilisation," and he should know, because he is steeped in it. There are plenty of these poems in his volumes, following a groove of sentimentality, and leaving a slightly syrupy taste in the mouth.

Conran favours custom and ceremony, ritual, elegy, tradition, and the formal language-splash of Dylan Thomas, to whose memory he dedicates an earlier poem in which he employs Thomas compounds, like "womblight," "dreamdank," "out-wombward," "chapeldownunder" (which sounds a reference to an Australian church), "gift of gab devil" and "steepled town." Elsewhere, although originally a stranger and outsider to Wales who sank eagerly into its culture, he writes of his "Lineage":

> My lineage is kingly. Once, my fathers ruled
> The broad acres of an island sweet with grass
> And climbed the volcanic hills, through dingle
> Of birch and pinetree, scrubland where wild deer
> Picked out their path to the bald peak:
> There the visiting gods conversed, who came
> As friends to friends with the kings my fathers. . . .

And these lines to a Welsh potter:

> And the racks in your front-room shop
> No longer fill
> Quietly, quietly, with the cups and jugs
> Of your fingers' skill;
>
> And because now, though the potter's gone
> And the clay dries dead,
> We are glad that the love of a bride
> Has graced your bed –

Of Conran's erudition, stockpiled classical allusions, intermittent elegance and varied technical skill, one has no doubt, but these frequently run into the sand, or explode in trivial puffs of smoke which soon drift away. All that scholarly brilliance still has a whiff of the midnight-candle about it, as if plotted from an ivory-tower above a quadrangle. A measure of fustian also inhabits his work, loading some thin subject-matter that simply cannot carry the weight.

As a critic, he has a reputation for severity, often using a sledgehammer to crack a nut by bringing the considerable weapons of his armoury to bear on marginal work. He interpolates rare and precious words of praise into devastating, remorseless hatchet-jobs, which are often massacres disguised as reviews. He also has a weakness for fashionable psychology-based criticism, which occasionally leads him into a weird area of precipitate assumption, odd parallels and comparisons, and manufactured mysteries where none exist. It is a perilous area, which temptingly invites hasty surmise in the absence of evidence, and dramatic overstatement, as well as the inaccurate analysis of sexual imagery.

Conran's premier accomplishment as a translator ranges from Taliesin (late 6th century) to the excellent moderns, such as R. Williams Parry, Saunders Lewis, Gwenallt Jones, Euros Bowen, and Waldo Williams. He is adept at assessing what some mistakenly consider to be a minor and ancillary literature, about which no general opinion has previously been built up. His main purpose has been to make poetic sense, in English, of sometimes very difficult poems, and to this end he has stated that he often departed further from the literal meaning than would easily be justifiable were his purpose purely scholarly – though he has always attempted to be literal. In his extremely knowledgeable introduction to the Penguin selection, he also makes it clear that the special relationship which the Welsh-language "bard" has with his public is very different from the English poet's connection with his minority audience. The Welshman is something of a leader within his own community, often a national figure who appears at public functions and is constantly asked to give opinions on poetry, political matters, and even international affairs, knowing that many "influential" people are going to listen. As Anthony Conran adds: "No English poet has been able to do this since Tennyson."

– John Tripp

COOK, Stanley. British. Born in Austerfield, Yorkshire, 12 April 1922. Educated at Doncaster Grammar School, 1933–40; Christ Church, Oxford, 1940–44, B.A. in English language and literature 1943, M.A. 1948. Married Kathleen Mary Daly in 1947; has two daughters and one son. Assistant Master, Barrow-in-Furness Grammar School, 1944–48; Sixth Form English Master, Bury Grammar School, 1948–55; Senior English Master, Firth Park School, Sheffield, 1955–68. Since 1969, Lecturer in English, The Polytechnic, Huddersfield. Recipient: Hull Arts Centre-BBC Competition Prize, 1969; Cheltenham Festival Competition Prize, 1972. Address: 600 Barnsley Road, Sheffield S5 6UA, England.

Publications

Verse

Form Photograph. Stockport, Cheshire, Harry Chambers, 1971.
Signs of Life. Manchester, E. J. Morten, 1972.

Critical Studies: by Robert Nye, in *The Times* (London), 10 February 1972; *Critical Quarterly* (Manchester), Spring 1972; *The Teacher* (London), 3 March 1972; Colin Bulman, in *The Teacher* (London), 27 October 1972; "Signs of Life" in *The Times* (London), 14 December 1972; *Times Literary Supplement* (London), 17 August 1973.

Stanley Cook comments:

In 1972 I found myself being described, at 50, as a new poet. Had it not been for Harry Chambers (editor of both series in which my poetry has been published), I feel sure I should never have had a collection of my poems published, despite trying all the London publishers at least once and often two or three times. In the event, I found one of my poems being admired that had been written 25 years before it appeared in *Signs of Life.* In Yorkshire one is bred to accept such things, but I can't help thinking of other Northern writers who deserve a wider public and who will never, unless they are very lucky, get one. I myself will appear biased, but I feel that any impartial assessment of Harry Chambers' achievement as an editor would class it as remarkable.

My attitude to my poetry is expressed in the Introduction to *Form Photograph:*

You live with your subject matter for years; one day something puts it into your head to write about it. After that it is simply a case of stating accurately what you have observed. Of course you have observed inaccurately and the accurate recording of the distinctive inaccuracies of which you are unaware is the theme of your poems. There ought to be more in a poem than you are conscious of expressing and more than your reader is conscious of receiving.

As far as style is concerned, I hope the steelworker and his wife next door would never need a dictionary to read my poems. I like to feel, too, that I have been as practical and unsentimental with a poem as if I had farmed, smithed or carpentered it – that the rest of the family would think I had done some "real work" and had not let them down.

Arising out of my belief that a poet should work to be enjoyed as widely as possible and by the accident of my working mainly with intending teachers at Huddersfield Polytechnic and my wife's teaching Infants, I write poems for Infants (a neglected audience), in response to particular requests and for the BBC programme "for the very young," Poetry Corner. Most of my concrete poetry (though I try to achieve an adult standard) has children of this age range in mind and it is a great pleasure to go into Infant School and get children aged 6 to 8 to do their own concrete poems, some of which are better in some ways than anything adults can do.

*   *   *

For many years Stanley Cook was a schoolmaster in Sheffield. His two main themes are Yorkshire and education. The metre he characteristically uses is a roughened blank verse. This is conducive to the description of exact minutiae that make up his world. It has taken some years for his work to gain a hearing, for his qualities are not the obvious ones. His tone is subdued, his day overcast, his walks through depressed areas and neglected parks. Mr. Cook is at his best when his landscapes are equipped with figures. The murderer, Charles Peace, gives him a cue for black comedy; so does his mother's landlord. That other Sheffield poet, James Montgomery, merits only satire for his lack of an eye to the world about him – that Sheffield world of rain and railings which Mr. Cook observes with acquaintance and insight. The most moving poems are those about the author's family, especially those who had to endure the hungry thirties. The one about his father is, in middle age, also about himself:

> My body is buried, when I used to be my father,
> In the overspill from the village churchyard
> Into a field, where a single electrified wire
> Keeps back the cows but not the grass or flowers.
> Now he is I he waits for a worthwhile task
> In which to succeed, better than the water towers
> And colliery washers bulky as beer-drinkers
> He built as foreman. Pity everyone
> Who had, like him, to swim for it in the Thirties,
> Fully clothed in the nation's economy.
> Those days when he sat in his chair with nothing to smoke
> And dressed in his best suit weekly to draw the dole
> Pared people down to their character . . .

Read on. The verse is never as simple as it seems. Mr. Cook's voice inflects and turns with the independence of its native speech. Glamour, romance and melodrama are not his stock in trade: his power is in his redoubtable honesty. No critic can sum up Mr. Cook as well as he can himself:

> I promised myself this walk in a minor key
> Along the old canal dismissed from its trade . . .

– Philip Hobsbaum

COOLIDGE, Clark. American. Born in Providence, Rhode Island, 26 February 1939. Attended Brown University, Providence, 1956–58. Married to Susan Hopkins; has one daughter, Celia Elizabeth. Editor, *Joglars* magazine, Providence, 1964–66. Recipient: National Endowment for the Arts grant, 1966; New York Poets Foundation Award, 1968. Lives in Hancock, Massachusetts. Address: Box 224, New Lebanon, New York 12125, U.S.A.

PUBLICATIONS

Verse

Flag Flutter and U.S. Electric. New York, Lines Books, 1966.
(Poems). New York, Lines Books, 1967.
Ing. New York, Angel Hair Books, 1969.
Space. New York, Harper, 1970.
The So. New York, Boke Press, 1971.
Moroccan Variations. Bolinas, California, Big Sky Publications, 1971.
Clark Coolidge Issue of *Big Sky 3* (Bolinas, California), 1972.
Suite V. New York, Boke Press, 1973.
The Maintains. San Francisco, This Press, 1974.

Play

To Obtain the Value of the Cake Measure from Zero, with Tom Veitch. San Francisco, Pants Press, 1970.

Critical Studies: Interview in *This 4* (San Francisco), Spring 1973; "The New Poetries in America" by Richard Kostelanetz, in *The End of Intelligent Writing,* New York, Sheed and Ward, 1973.

Clark Coolidge comments:

The context of my works is the Tonality of Language (seen, heard, spoken, thought) itself, a tonality that centers itself in the constant flowage from meaning to meaning, and that sideslippage between meanings. All the books we shall perhaps never read again form a constant background of reference points. We are free now to delight in the Surface of Language, a surface as deep as the distance between (for instance) a noun (in the mind) (in a dictionary) and its object somewhere in the universe.

*   *   *

None of the younger experimental poets in America has been as various, intelligent and prolific as Clark Coolidge, who also edited one of the few genuinely avant-garde literary magazines of the sixties, *Joglars.* His opening book, *Flag Flutter and U.S. Electric,* collected his early forays into post-Ashberyan acoherence, where the poet tries to realize the semblance of literary coherence without resorting to such traditional organizing devices as meter, metaphor, exposition, symbolism, consistent allusion, declarative statements or autobiographical reference. (The key Ashbery work in this vein is "Europe," 1960, collected in *The Tennis Court Oath,* 1962.) In a theoretical statement contributed to Paul Carroll's anthology of *The Young American Poets* (1968), Coolidge wrote that "Words have a universe of qualities other than those of descriptive relation: Hardness, Density, Sound-Shape, Vector-Force, & Degrees of Transparency/Opacity," and his earlier poems revealed rather exceptional linguistic sensitivities, esspecially regarding the selection and placement of words. The intelligence informing his creative processes is radically poetic, precisely because it is *not* prosaic.

In his subsequent work Coolidge pursued not just varieties of acoherence, but reductionism, joining Kenneth Gangemi and Robert Lax among America's superior minimal poets. In the back sections of Coolidge's fullest retrospective, *Space,* are several especially severe examples, such as the untitled poem, beginning "by a I" which contains individually isolated words, none more than two letters long, that are scattered across the space of a single page (which has so far been Coolidge's primary compositional unit). These words are nonetheless related to each other – not only in terms of diction and corresponding length (both visually and verbally), but spatial proximity; for if the individual words were arranged in another way, both the poem and the reading experience would be different. It should also be noted that Coolidge's work extends radically the Olsonian traditions both of "composition by field," as opposed to lines, and of emphasizing syllable, rather than rhyme and meter.

Like all genuinely experimental artists, Coolidge accepted the challenge of an inevitable next step, extending his delicate reductionist techniques into two of the most remarkable long poems of the past decade: "AD," originally published in *Ing* and then reprinted in *Space*; and *Suite V,* which appeared as a booklet in 1973, although it was initially composed several years before. "AD" begins in the familiar Coolidgean way, with stanzas of superficially unrelated lines, but the poetic material is progressively reduced over twenty pages (thereby recapitulating Coolidge's own poetic development, in a kind of formalist autobiography) until the poem's final pages contain just vertically ordered fragments of words. *Suite V* is yet more outrageously spartan, containing nothing more than pairs of three-letter words in their plural forms, with one four-letter word at the top and the other at the bottom of otherwise blank pages.

Coolidge has scattered his writings through numerous periodicals and anthologies, as well as small-press booklets, and much of his work remains unpublished. The best introduction to his excellences is not *Space,* which also suffers from ineptly tiny typography, but the third issue of *Big Sky,* a periodical edited by Bill Berkson. The poetry collected there is far more various and, for that reason, more indicative of Coolidge's experimental temper. It is my considered opinion that he is the most extraordinary American poet of our mutual generation.

– Richard Kostelanetz

COOPER, Jane (Marvel). American. Born in Atlantic City, New Jersey, 9 October 1924. Educated at Vassar College, Poughkeepsie, New York, 1942–44; University of Wisconsin, Madison, B.A. 1946; University of Iowa, Iowa City, M.A. 1954. Since 1950, Member of the English Department, Sarah Lawrence College,

Bronxville, New York. Recipient: Yaddo grant, 1958, 1967, 1968; Guggenheim Fellowships, 1960; MacDowell Colony grant, 1965; Lamont Poetry Selection Award, 1968; National Endowment for the Arts grant, 1969; Ingram Merrill Foundation grant, 1971. Address: Department of English, Sarah Lawrence College, Bronxville, New York 10708, U.S.A.

PUBLICATIONS

Verse

The Weather of Six Mornings. New York, Macmillan, 1969.
Maps and Windows. New York, Macmillan, 1974.

Jane Cooper comments:

My earliest poems (largely unpublished) were heavily metrical. I thought of writing a book of war poems from the point of view of a woman, a non-combatant. What concerned me was what could survive in the way of an individual feeling, or moral life, in a world at war. There is no longer a specific war in most of the poems I write now, but there is the same conviction that we live in a very stripped-down landscape. At the same time joy, if not happiness, is important. Many of my poems have to do with deaths; others with love, the life of the physical world in and around us, and above all with the possibility of writing, of speaking out.

Poetry is a kind of non-abstract musical composition. In my latest work, I am interested in a more open American speech line and in the activity that goes on between lines and even words of a poem, almost more than in what is "said." Pasternak is an influence, in his emphasis on the poem happening *now*. The long poem has always been a challenge. I like trying sequences of shorter poems, almost apparently unrelated; what is their effect on one another? I want to get more fluidity into single pieces now; the self is variable, places change and disappear. I should like to write city poems – another version of life fragmented as if by war.

*   *   *

Jane Cooper's first volume of poems represents her creative efforts over a period exceeding ten years. Although she has no radical experiments in form, her poems demonstrate a versatility ranging from highly patterned to spare, free verse. And though her images are seldom vivid or startling, she employs them, most notably images of weather, with precision and appropriateness.

Most of her poems, and her best, are drawn from the intimate reserves of her own experience: memories of her childhood, of her mother, her loves, her encounters with death, and most effectively her moments of loss, regret, and loneliness. Cooper's poems seldom function as a single, unambiguous perception of an experience. Her poems, as she says in "A Letter for Philo Buck," leave "the tongue unraveling sweets from sours." Many poems seem balanced between emotional polarities of release and joy (the ecstasy of "Morning on the St. John's") and restraint and resignation (the advice in "A Little Vesper" to "bed with what

297

we are"). A poem recalling the childhood rapture of collecting butterflies is entitled "Practicing for Death"; and one of her most successful poems, "Obligations," images the speaker and her lover "wrapped in the afternoon / As in a chrysalis of silken light" awaking reluctantly to "the long war, and shared reality, / And death and all we came here to evade."

The inescapable reality of time and change and memory seems increasingly to concern Jane Cooper. "Once you leave the landing," she says in "Leaving Water Hyacinths," "Your whole life after will be sailing back."

– Dale Doepke

————————

COOPERMAN, Stanley. Canadian. Born in New York City, 22 October 1929. Educated at New York University, B.A. 1951, 1952–55; Indiana University, Bloomington (Lilly Fellow, 1959, University Fellow, 1961), Ph.D. 1962. Married Ruth Doernberg in 1952 (marriage dissolved); Charlotte Alexander, 1960 (marriage dissolved); Jenifer L. Svendsen, 1962, has one daughter. Journalist and Freelance Writer, 1951–55; Assistant Professor, University of Oregon, Eugene, 1961–63, and Hofstra University, Hempstead, Long Island, New York, 1963–65. Since 1965, Associate Professor, then Professor of English, Simon Fraser University, Burnaby, British Columbia. Recipient: Fulbright Award, 1960; Canada Council Fellowship, 1967. Address: 4527 Marineview Crescent, North Vancouver, British Columbia, Canada.

PUBLICATIONS

Verse

The Day of the Parrot and Other Poems.   Lincoln, University of Nebraska Press, 1968.
The Owl Behind the Door.   Toronto, McClelland and Stewart, 1968.
Cappelbaum's Dance.   Lincoln, University of Nebraska Press, 1970.
Cannibals.   Ottawa, Oberon Press, 1972.

Other

Review Notes and Study Guide to Steinbeck.   New York, Monarch Press, 1964.
Review Notes and Study Guide to Hemingway's "A Farewell to Arms," "The Sun Also Rises," "For Whom the Bell Tolls" and "The Old Man and the Sea."   New York, Monarch Press, 1964.
Hemingway's "The Old Man and the Sea": A Critical Commentary.   New York, Monarch Press, 1965; revised edition, with Murray H. Cohen, New York. Barrister Publishing Company, 1966.
F. Scott Fitzgerald's "The Great Gatsby": A Critical Commentary.   New York, Monarch Press, 1965.

F. Scott Fitzgerald's "Tender Is the Night" and "This Side of Paradise": A Critical Commentary. New York, Monarch Press, 1965.
Hemingway's "For Whom the Bell Tolls": A Critical Commentary. New York, Barrister Publishing Company, 1966.
World War I and the American Novel. Baltimore, Johns Hopkins Press, 1967.
The Novels of Philip Roth: A Critical Commentary. New York, Simon and Schuster, 1974.

Critical Studies: in *Mosaic* (Winnipeg), 1967; *The Nation* (New York), 24 June 1968; *Minnesota Review* (St. Paul), 1968; *Prairie Schooner* (Lincoln, Nebraska), Fall 1969; *Concerning Poetry* (Bellingham, Washington), Fall 1969; *Virginia Quarterly Review* (Charlottesville), Winter 1969; *Trace* (Hollywood and London), Autumn 1970; *Canadian Literature* (Vancouver), 1971; *Quarry* (Kingston, Ontario), Winter 1971; *Dalhousie Review* (Halifax, Nova Scotia), 1973; *Toronto Globe*, 17 February 1973.

Stanley Cooperman comments:

In a moment of irritation with the moral pharmacists who always seem to be nagging, nagging, nagging other people into fixed prescriptions for Virtue, I once wrote that poems are "real; as real as mountains, trees, supermarkets, polar bears, wars, bridges, flowers, sewer pipes, apples, or the socks you wear inside your shoes." What I meant by this bit of hyperbole is simple enough: the fact that the poet is, by the very nature of his art, committed to real human action. His action needs no "defense" because poetry is a basic means for defending human language, and therefore human value, against emotional and intellectual mush.

It is through poetry that the old and crippling dualisms between body and mind, flesh and spirit, are reconciled – and more: they are made to dance. But the dance is not with the feet only, nor with hand-me-down political proclamations. The dance of poetry is a rhythm that forces us to think with our skin and feel with our brains: the poem is a catalyst for scepticism and faith, love and hate, form and chaos, hope and despair. And sometimes it is all of these things at once.

The result, of course, is that many people become furious with poetry, especially the evangelicals of monolithic Salvation. Either they demand that the poet Think Right Thoughts, or they attempt to bully him into not thinking at all. Two ends of the spectrum: the philosophic guardians, or the slush-bucket exotics. And both, alas, are all too well represented at universities, especially American and Canadian universities, which have – as still a third method of un-fleshing the reality of poetry – re-introduced hand-me-down psychiatric formuli. As a ready-packaged set of legitimizing platitudes, psychology has in recent years developed into a major method of non-reading: "scientific" psychological critics apply their borrowed dogmas to (or on?) poetry with elephantine solemnity.

About my own work specifically: I resist all rules, and distrust all Laws – especially Laws revealed by dogmatists or their fleas. This does not mean that I equate poetry with anarchy. Because a poem is action, it – like other forms of action – necessarily involves discipline, energy, and purpose. The most successful poems are those in which all three elements are fused to form meaning: meaning fleshed into perception, perception at once abstract and particular ("the incandescence of the intellect").

Some critics have defined my poetry as "surrealist." They are wrong – or rather, they are not right enough. Surrealism for me is an instrument, not an end. Effects themselves are cheap and easy to achieve. What the poem *does* with its effects – with its energy of image-and-language – creates the action it becomes.

And this action for me is both lyrical and moral – that is, critical. Fleshed in the pyrotechnics of language, there must finally be the *argument* – the "Old Jacob's Eye" of judgment and witness. But again, this cannot be predicted – nor can it be prescribed. And always, it seems to me, the artist is both within and outside the particularities from which he works. He refuses to "stop talking" for any cause or reason whatsoever; and – perhaps most important – he refuses to stop *looking*.

As a poet, of course, I "look" with the instrument of language – a flawed instrument, at best, and one which requires an infinite variety of images, masques, and associations. But this "surrealism" is device, not substance.

*   *   *

Stanley Cooperman's creation is one which is magical and fantastic, explosively imagistic, often brutal and always startling. And his dance through it – as poet or *persona* – sums up its most singular characteristic: energy, "the energy / to grab you by the roots of your breath / and shake crazy dreams / from your glands." Curiously juxtaposed, surrealistic, often synaesthetic images are spat at the reader, as in the eating and spewing imagery of *Cannibals,* or swirled around him in a nightmarish miasma that is the more terrible and effective for its apparent control. Even the more personal, love poems (although displaying a delicacy and romanticism that should accompany the lyrical) are charged with energy and filled with adverbs of suddeness, urgency and stress.

Typical of all the poems, too, is a Swiftian interest in the anatomically grotesque and defecatory; many of the images bursting around the reader are of garbage and glands, apes, hair and blood. And yet in its fast pace, the pop art collage neither forces nor allows any lingering in the repellent and, besides, the images are very often so bizarre as to transcend the puerile: "My head rolls on my shoulders / like a bladder / filled / with possible jokes, / and I pratfall in all directions."

Recurrent also are unanswered questions, especially in the earlier poems of *The Owl Behind the Door.* These questions, often concerning the identity or significance of a fantasy figure created in the poem ("Apparition on the Second Narrows Bridge") and used as a poetic device, prompt an extensive use of definition, also as device. In poems such as "Three Mouths of God," and "Masada," Cooperman builds upon a series of definition stanzas to a final, thematic synthesis. In the early poems this synthesis is often only a frustrating further question; in the later poems it is generally a more satisfying glimpse at a solution. Rarely, however, can Cooperman be faulted for transparency. Like E. E. Cummings, whom he often resembles in vision if not in typography, Cooperman creates a new, poetic world peopled like Chagall's and dictated by little or no causality; if the reader begins to understand it is not because he is told but because he enters this world and "finds all the places / where he was taught / never / to be found."

That Cooperman sees his function as poet to be the conjuring of passports to this world is clear in his poems on the art of poetry, and in his assertion that "to have poemed / is a kind of loving. . . ."

This direct relation of poet and lover is closely paralleled by Cooperman's association of the outcast poet with the outcast Jew. He is careful, however, not to extend this relationship until his poetic world of love and awareness becomes simply a Jewish heaven. Cooperman is neither xenophobic nor childish and his poetry, though rich in Jewish imagery and sentiment, creates an eclectic universe which mixes but stands outside traditional philosophical and moral systems. As a result, it is easy for the gentile reader to forceably identify with the Western Jew who starkly confronts the Holy Land in the "Masada" series and with him to discover something shattering and real about race and homecoming.

Poems such as "Masada" are, in fact, more accessible despite their Jewish patina than are certain of the more literary pieces. The creation of a personal iconography is a difficult task and, at times, Cooperman's fantasy universe collapses. At others, it simply becomes too esoteric to be comprehensible, so that in *The Owl Behind the Door,* for example, the conundrums sometimes remain just that. Fortunately, a development of control is clear in the series of publications to date. *Cappelbaum's Dance* attempts a unity of all things that is not always acceptable and which justifies the charge that here Cooperman's iconography is a brilliant disguise for a fear of commitment. In *Cannibals,* however, the poet is much more sure, is wholly committed, and creates images with a correctness and appropriateness that occasionally startle in their nearness to perfection. In *Cannibals,* moreover, an affirmative power arises from the dialectic between love and "nothingness" which haunts all the poems (cf. "Greco's Mourning Song" and "Greco's Dance"), and this positivism functions with the forcefulness of the collection to make reading it simultaneously breathtaking and encouraging. In *Cannibals,* Stanley Cooperman dances with his characteristic energy through his own universe and with the understanding its twisted images give him shouts back "Yes: / yes to the world."

– S. R. Gilbert

CORKE, Hilary. British. Born in Malvern, Worcestershire, in 1921. Educated at Charterhouse; Christ Church, Oxford. Served in the Royal Artillery, 1941–45. Married to the poet Sylvia Bridges; has four children. Lecturer, Cairo University, two years, and the University of Edinburgh, four years. Since 1956, Free-lance Writer. Lives in Abinger Hammer, Surrey, England.

PUBLICATIONS

Verse

Epithalamium, The Nightfearers. West Worthing, Sussex, Fantasma, 1948.
Adam Awake. Palma de Mallorca, privately printed, 1961.
The Early Drowned and Other Poems. London, Secker and Warburg, 1961.

Other

Editor, with William Plomer and Anthony Thwaite, *New Poems 1961.* London, Hutchinson, 1961.

Translator, *Poems in the Rough,* by Paul Valéry. London, Routledge, 1969; New York, Pantheon Books, 1970.

*   *   *

301

Hilary Corke first became known as a literary critic who used his wit and verbal ingenuity to distinguish the real thing from the pretense. These talents and this interest, along with a power of lyric melody, are present in his poetry. Corke's early poems are often celebrations of sexual love. There is much ardor, and there is much enjoyment of the classics in English love poetry. In "Sleeping," for example, he presents his own version of Donne's intricate conceits. In "Oiseuse," he makes something of his own out of Eliot's "Fire Sermon" in *The Waste Land*. Corke's linguistic virtuosity appears also in his rich, sometimes witty, musical rhetoric. The wit often serves as a kind of check on the ardor with which the rhetoric praises love, but it is sometimes difficult to tell just how seriously that ardor is meant to be taken. One has the sense of a poet who has yet to find his own voice.

In the later poems, love is viewed from a perspective of loss and suffering, as Corke shifts his attention to experience that is, as in "The Evening Walk," at once personal and part of contemporary history:

> Have you noticed, by the way, it is growing chilly?
> That could be predicted. Are you done predicting?
> And we old. Let us speak of details.
>
> That, when you come down to it, is all.
> A question of region . . .

The region in question is England in the 1950's and early 1960's; it is also the particularity of the poet's own situation. A kind of imitation of earlier poets remains. Some of these poems – in their now often conversational qualities, their moral landscapes and their sense of the generally ominous – recall poetry written between the two World Wars by W. H. Auden. Others recall Yeats's attempt to create poetry out of his own situation in history. Yet the necessity in the face of pain and loss to define one's own bearings leads Corke in these later poems to speak with a modest, authoritative voice of his own.

– Jerry Paris

CORMAN, Cid (Sidney Corman). American. Born in Boston, Massachusetts, 29 June 1924. Educated at Boston Latin School; Tufts College, Medford, Massachusetts, B.A. 1945; University of Michigan, Ann Arbor (Hopwood Award, 1947), 1946–47; University of North Carolina, Chapel Hill, 1947; the Sorbonne, Paris, 1954–55. Married. Poetry Broadcaster, WMEX, Boston, 1949–51. Since 1951, Editor, *Origin* magazine and Origin Press, Kyoto, Japan. Recipient: Chapelbrook Foundation grant, 1967–69; National Endowment for the Arts grant, 1974. Address: Fukuoji-cho 82, Utano-ku, Kyoto 616, Japan.

PUBLICATIONS

Verse

subluna (juvenilia). Boston, privately printed, 1945.
Thanksgiving Eclogue. New York, Sparrow Press, 1954.

Ferrini and Others, with others.   Berlin, Gerhardt, 1955.
The Precisions.   New York, Sparrow Press, 1955.
The Responses.   Bari, Italy, Origin Press, 1956.
Stances and Distances.   Matera, Italy, Origin Press, 1957.
The Marches.   Florence, Origin Press, 1957.
A Table in Provence.   Kyoto, Origin Press, 1958.
The Descent from Daimonji.   Kyoto, Origin Press, 1959.
Clocked Stone.   Kyoto, Origin Press, 1959.
For Sure.   Kyoto, Origin Press, 1959.
For Instance.   Kyoto, Origin Press, 1960.
For Good.   Kyoto, Origin Press, 1961.
Sun Rock Man.   Kyoto, Origin Press, 1962; New York, New Directions, 1970.
In Good Time.   Kyoto, Origin Press, 1964.
In No Time.   Kyoto, privately printed, 1964.
All in All.   Kyoto, Origin Press, 1965.
Nonce.   New Rochelle, New York, Elizabeth Press, 1965.
For You.   Kyoto, Origin Press, 1966.
For Granted.   New Rochelle, New York, Elizabeth Press, 1966.
Stead.   New Rochelle, New York, Elizabeth Press, 1966.
Words for Each Other.   London, Rapp and Carroll, 1967.
& Without End.   New Rochelle, New York, Elizabeth Press, and London, Villiers Publications, 1968.
No Less.   New Rochelle, New York, Elizabeth Press, 1968.
Hearth.   Kyoto, Origin Press, 1968.
No More.   New Rochelle, New York, Elizabeth Press, 1969.
Plight.   New Rochelle, New York, Elizabeth Press, 1969.
Nigh.   New Rochelle, New York, Elizabeth Press, 1970.
Livingdying.   New York, New Directions, 1970.
Of the Breath of.   Berkeley, California, Maya, 1970.
For Keeps.   Kyoto, Origin Press, 1970.
For Now.   Kyoto, Origin Press, 1971.
Out and Out.   New Rochelle, New York, Elizabeth Press, 1972.
Be Quest.   New Rochelle, New York, Elizabeth Press, 1972.
A Language Without Words.   Saffron Walden, Essex, Byways 6, 1973.
So Far.   New Rochelle, New York, Elizabeth Press, 1973.
Poems: Thanks to Zuckerkandl.   Rushden, Northamptonshire, Sceptre Press, 1973.
Breathings.   Tokyo, Mushinsha, 1973.

Other

At: Bottom.   Bloomington, Indiana, Caterpillar, 1966.

Editor, *The Gist of "Origin": An Anthology.*   New York, Grossman, 1973.

Translator, *Cool Melon*, by Basho.   Kyoto, Origin Press, 1959.
Translator, *Cool Gong.*   Kyoto, Origin Press, 1959.
Translator, with Kamaike Susumu, *Selected Frogs*, by Shimpei Kusano. Kyoto, Origin Press, 1963.
Translator, *Back Roads to Far Towns*, by Basho.   Tokyo, Mushinsha, 1967.
Translator, with Kamaike Susumu, *Frogs and Others: Poems*, by Shimpei Kusano.   Tokyo, Mushinsha, 1968; New York, Grossman, 1969.
Translator, *Things*, by Francis Ponge.   Tokyo, Mushinsha, and New York, Grossman, 1971.

Translator, *Leaves of Hypnos,* by René Char.   Tokyo, Mushinsha, and New York, Grossman, 1973.
Translator, *Breathings,* by Philippe Jaccottet.   New York, Grossman, 1974.

Bibliography: by John Taggart, New Rochelle, New York, Elizabeth Press, 1975.

Manuscript Collections: University of Texas, Austin; Kent State University, Ohio; Indiana University, Bloomington; New York University; State University of New York, Buffalo.

Cid Corman comments:

My work has developed from the pioneer poetry of Pound-Williams-Stevens, but much also from contact with French poetry. No forms, but a strict sense of the sounded meaning of words, pauses, verses, etc., and the felt thought that poetry is. Brevity, immediacy, clarity. A poetry that makes the role of the critic pointless, needless. The ideal, always, to join that most human society of poets whose work is published under the title of ANON.

Poetry calls for anonymity. It appeals, in short, to the each in all and the all in each. Its particularity must become yours. Autobiography is implicit in anyone's work and may be taken for granted, but what has been realized and so set out as to be shared loses itself in the self that is found extended without end in song.

As the author has elsewhere put it: *If I have nothing to offer you in the face of death – in its stead – the ache behind every ache, the instant man knows, I have no claim as poet. My song must sing into you a little moment, stay in you what presence can muster – of sense more than meaning, of love more than sense, of giving the life given one with the same fulness that brought each forth, each to each from each, nothing left but the life that is going on.*

*   *   *

Cid Corman's poems are tight, reticent, and resonant. He has learned (from the Japanese principally, one assumes) how evocative the minimal registration of specifics can be, and he has combined with this his own life-long concern for the sound of poetry, syllable by syllable (Zukofsky is for him, as for Creeley, a measure of such possibilities). The result, both in the longer more discursive poems of *Sun Rock Man* or *& Without End* and in the short haiku-like poems of such books as *Nonce, Stead,* and *Nigh,* is a poetry of considerable grace and strength.

As one reads the early poems now, they seem to cry out for the compression of the later style. "First Farm North" from *The Precisions* begins: "I stood above at the bathroom window" and goes on, in leisurely anecdotal style, to evoke a mood by careful accumulation of detail, ending:

> The mirror was thawed into the scene
> and the brightness of the morning
> pressed a cool handful of water
> into my eyes and my pulse raced song.

Corman is already free of iambic regularity while retaining a sense of measure in these lines, but the poem, though charming, is diffuse. In other poems one notices 1950's elegance ("Leaves discuss the wind") consorting somewhat uneasily with touches of what has come to seem Corman's characteristic sensibility ("It takes all my time, and my father's, / to let life go").

Between such early work and the development seen in *Sun Rock Man* there intervenes the first stay in Japan and the translations from Bashō and others published in *Cool Gong* and *Cool Melon*. A gain in expressive means – shorter lines, barer statement, more fluid syntax – is seen throughout the 1962 book. Here is "The Gift":

> First night in a
> strange town to
> be going home
>
> passing a
> strange girl saying
> goodnight to me
>
> how night is
> when she says so
> suddenly good

The line breaks are like Creeley's, the syntax with its dangling participles and the canny deployment which gets the clinching phrase at the end owes something to Williams (cp. "Poem": "As the cat / climbed over . . .") and the syllabic grid (4–3–4; 3–4–4; 3–4–4) suggests Marianne Moore. But the poem is, in its feelings, wholly Corman's. And the entire book, its sum exceeding its parts as a tribute to a place and people – the Italian town where the poet spent a year teaching English – marks the emergence of Corman's mature voice.

In the next book, *For Instance*, one finds more specific oriental influences in content, tone, and technique. Number 7 reads:

> gong gone
> odor of cherry tolling
> eventide

Though a haiku translation, the juxtaposed verbless phrases evoking that mood of contemplative harmony with natural surroundings that one associates with Japanese poetry, this is nevertheless a western poem in its reliance on metaphor, assonance, and connotative language (who'd have thought it possible to rescue "eventide" for a modern poem?).

Corman's work has continued along the lines of the two books just mentioned. It cannot be denied that his emotional range is narrow and that his tone can verge on too easy a plangency, too self-indulgent an acquiescence in the drift towards dissolution. "The Mystery," for instance, from *In Good Time,* ends (speaking of swallows): "How each / pursues // each, / pursued / by a green sky / as the sun settles, // desperate / to let themselves / go, O / against night." Unfair, of course, to crowd it like that, but it may be agreed that the melodramatic "desperate" and the moaning "o" sounds produce too facile a pathos and distract attention from the things seen to the emoting observer. Contrast the restraint of a successful poem on roughly the same thing:

> Someone will
> sweep the fallen
> petals away
>
> away. I know,
> I know. Weight of
> red shadows.

Here the talking voice is never swamped and the tone plays against and makes more convincing the feelings that weigh on the speaker. Even more fully impersonal is the following, also from *Nonce:*

> The leaf that moved with the wind
> moves
> with the stream.

The energy is released by so simple a means as a change in tense. And the emotional effect is complex – transience is recognized but also cyclical renewal – and all is made to inhere in the thing seen, not worked up by the sensibility of the poet. When he writes like this, and he does it often enough for every book to be rewarding, Corman's is a voice that earns our careful attention.

– Seamus Cooney

CORNISH, Sam(uel James). American. Born in Baltimore, Maryland, 22 December 1935. Educated at Booker T. Washington High School, Baltimore. Served in the armed service, 1958–60. Married Jean Cornish in 1967. Former Editor of the Enoch Pratt Library publication *Chicory*, Baltimore. Currently, Editor, *Mimeo* magazine. Consultant in elementary-school teaching, Central Atlantic Regional Educational Laboratories Humanities Program. Recipient: National Endowment for the Arts grant, 1967, 1969. Address: 395 Broadway, Cambridge, Massachusetts 02114, U.S.A.

PUBLICATIONS

Verse

In This Corner: Sam Cornish and Verses. Baltimore, Fleming McAllister, 1961.
People under the Window. Baltimore, Sacco Publishers, 1962.
Generations. Baltimore, Beanbag Press, 1964.
Angles. Baltimore, Beanbag Press, 1965.
Winters. Cambridge, Massachusetts, San Souci Press, 1968.
Generations: Poem. Boston, Beacon Press, 1971.
Streets. Chicago, Third World Press, 1973.
Sometimes: Ten Poems. Cambridge, Massachusetts, Pym Randall Press, 1973.

Other

Your Hand in Mine. New York, Harcourt Brace, 1970.
Grandmother's Pictures (juvenile). Lenox, Massachusetts, Bookstore Press, 1974.

Editor, with Lucian W. Dixon, *Chicory: Young Voices from the Black Ghetto.* New York, Association Press, 1969.

Editor, with Hugh Fox, *The Living Underground: An Anthology of Contemporary American Poetry.* East Lansing, Michigan, Ghost Dance Press, 1969.

Critical Study: Introduction by Ron Schreiber to *Winters,* 1968.

Sam Cornish comments:

Most of my major themes are of urban life, the negro predicament here in the cities and my own family. I try to use a minimum of words to express the intended thought or feeling, with the effect of being starkly frank at times. Main verse form is unrhymed, free. Main influences – Lowell, T. S. Eliot, LeRoi Jones.

*   *   *

Sam Cornish's talent is steady and upwards and ongoing. He possesses a consistent tone, a wide range of subjects, and the ability to represent fully his feelings by evoking a sensual richness in which he can connect with the nature of himself in the body as the glyph of erotic metaphor. This is his strength. This is his power. His voice, his rhythm, his vision, and the particular ways of relating the disparate parts of existence – his existence – are also his meaning. He simply hears and sees what he hears. Thus the process *is* cyclical, even if it appears not to be, and incomprehensible to any ordinary explicatory methods. His poems are tight, conveying a tension that allows for the language to move outwards the identity of the poem into the world by being in the poem – centered, that is – in the body which *is* language. Therefore the poem does not slip inward, in any given instance, but unfolds its inner vision, as in the superb "Cape Cod," in which Cornish potently writes about emotion – a rare and precarious endeavor:

everything human
the marble steps the shapes
move
behind newspapers and wooden back yard
fences
are close to me

sometimes
this street where the boulevard
is the greyhound going
to new york

the police car on a dark summer
night
can be more fun
than kids water skiing and talking
of civil rights and europe

i cannot swim
tennis is the pretense in me
children still dance to water
from hydrants

cocktail hour
and talk is not the same
as a walk through the city
as yards of wooden chairs
and unfed children
who wonder what the second
language
is.

The precision is reached by the images and the tight rhythms and the intent of the voice – the poet's voice – in the poem that is speaking. The vision and tension tell us what *is* felt; what *is* felt is the subject of the poem: the poet's response in himself to class division and elitism through language that tragedy exists in any resolution of human encounter where alternatives are not acknowledged; where alternatives are not chosen; where all options are closed.

Sam Cornish creates a poetry out of language that is at once poerful in feeling, crisp and clear in diction, strong and tight in structure, and important in themes. His is a poetry of dignity. A poetry of purpose, though that purpose need not be a benefit to anyone except the poet. His work to date is but part of a growth toward further achievements.

– Gerard Malanga

CORRINGTON, John William. American. Born in Memphis, Tennessee, 28 October 1932. Educated at Centenary College, Shreveport, Louisiana, A.B. 1956; Rice University, Houston, M.A. 1958; University of Sussex, Falmer, D.Phil. 1964; Tulane University Law School, New Orleans. Married Joyce Elaine Hooper in 1959; has four children. Taught at Louisiana State University, Baton Rouge; Loyola University, New Orleans; University of California, Berkeley, 1968. Recipient: Charioteer Prize, 1962; National Endowment for the Arts grant, 1966. Address: 1724 Valence Street, New Orleans, Louisiana 70115, U.S.A.

PUBLICATIONS

Verse

Where We Are. Washington, D.C., Charioteer Press, 1962.
The Anatomy of Love and Other Poems. Fort Lauderdale, Florida, Roman Books, 1964.
Mr. Clean and Other Poems. San Francisco, Amber House Press, 1964.
Lines to the South and Other Poems. Baton Rouge, Louisiana State University Press, 1965.

Plays

Screenplays, with Joyce H. Corrington: *Richthofen or Brown*, 1970; *The Omega Man*, 1970; *Box Car Bertha*, 1972; *The Arena*, 1973; *Battle for the Planet of the Apes*, with Paul Dehn, 1973.

Television Play: *The Deadly Bees*, 1974.

Novels

And Wait for the Night. New York, Putnam, and London, Blond, 1964.
The Upper Hand. New York, Putnam, 1967; London, Blond, 1968.
The Bombardier. New York, Putnam, 1970.

Short Stories

The Lonesome Traveler and Other Stories. New York, Putnam, 1968.

Other

Editor, with Miller Williams, *Southern Writing in the Sixties.* Baton Rouge, Louisiana State University Press, 2 vols., 1966–67.

John William Corrington comments:

I am primarily a novelist. Poetry served me chiefly as a school in which to learn the intensive use of figurative language – as opposed to analytical and metaphysical language. My work in poetry gave me a far greater sensitivity to form and style than an apprenticeship in prose fiction would have produced.

The larger part of my work, looked at in retrospect, seems to be composed of brief dramatic monologues, narratives of an elliptical nature, more or less sly jokes, and textured obscenities – none of these taken to exclude the others.

Again, in retrospect, it would appear that I am something of a religious maniac, an overwhelming percentage of my poetry in one way or another dealing with theological matters. This mania would unnerve me if it were not for the fact that, in the twentieth century, a religious nut seems among the least objectionable kind, and of a certain antiquarian interest and value.

My chief influences seem to have been Browning, Auden, Cummings, Wallace Stevens and Lawrence Ferlinghetti. I would add the name of James Dickey, but that would be hubris. His work is too good to digest.

I have written chiefly fiction over the past four years, but hope to remember soon how to write a poem. Perhaps I am too wise to write poetry now. Or perhaps not.

*   *   *

The central drama of Christianity, recurring or perpetually present, dominates the characteristic Corrington poem. The "messianic sun" and a "bronzejawed noncom / his arm a clutter of / roman stripes" ("It Happens Every Spring") are the eternal antagonists. Military life is the most obvious image of commitment to death: in "Corps Commander at Anzio," the officer boasts ". . . Now they realize my map – carve projected / salients in flesh and iron, murder my / statistics into fact"; in "Lines to the South," a statue of General Sherman sits astride a pony "whose shoulders / withers / flank / shrink from their burden / ooze metallic shame / whose blind sculptured eyes / look southward with / brute sympathy –." "Prayers for a Mass in the Vernacular" explores the sources of this lethal dedication: fallen man, who worships a "chrome madonna," perverts meaning in the guise of creating it ("then we communicated"), and celebrates The Word "in other words." Distortion of meaning is also the theme of "The Anatomy of Love," a series of vignettes which test varieties of modern love by their approximation to "the same standard," presumably that of the crucifixion scenes that begin and end the poem. As usual, Corrington's language is precise, exciting, and his spare lines carry each episode to an appropriate, often shocking, climax. But as in the other ambitious long poems, "Prayers for a Mass in the Vernacular," and "Communique," "Anatomy" inadequately dramatizes its personae, in this instance characters articulating the obsessive power of profane love. Thus, the poem is more successful in satirizing these proponents of the secular than in sustaining a tension between them and the implicit spiritual criterion. "Communique," an eclectic poem in three parts (which reads like a more accessible version of Pound's *Cantos*), so skillfully fuses its Eliotesque "fragments" from history, literature, and folklore into a controlled and consistently ironical picture of the consequences of the loss of faith that it fails to generate a sense that the evil embodied in the archetypal "commander grinly" could accomplish its destructive ends. Despite Corrington's wonderful play on "absolutely" in a variety of sexual and military contexts, the poem creates no Paolo and Francesca to make sin a live option, and no Capaneus to suggest the temptation of defiant violence. Corrington is stronger with the cosmic aftermath of the failure of faith in "Pastoral," where a Japanese farmer feels "the breath of armageddon / on his neck," and sees "a brook leap into steam," and "the city being eaten by the sun."

Though he has not yet written his *Waste Land*, Corrington's wit and often dazzling imagery and word-play animate both his pervasive motifs and his straightforward love poems and Audenesque explorations of neurosis like "An Exemplary Fiction." Familiar themes of the perversion of meaning, the atrophy of love and attendant burgeoning of egoism, often in military guise, explode powerfully from the image of Lucifer "wrapped in a banner of pronouns" ("Lucifer Means Light"). In "The Portable Goya," the gnomic verse that simultaneously mocks and reinforces the picture of the artist become a "giltframed classic" epitomizes the ambition and daring of Corrington's own poetry:

> there is no art without risk
> as dr frankenstein
> wheezed dying to a
> village constable.

– Burton Kendle

CORSO, (Nunzio) Gregory. American. Born in New York City, 26 March 1930. Married Sally November in 1963; has two children. Manual laborer, 1950–51; Reporter, Los Angeles *Examiner*, 1951–52; merchant seaman, 1952–53. Member of the English Department, State University of New York, Buffalo, 1965–70. Recipient: Longview Foundation Award; Poetry Foundation Award. Address: c/o Phoenix Bookshop, 18 Cornelia Street, New York, New York 10014, U.S.A.

PUBLICATIONS

Verse

The Vestal Lady on Brattle and Other Poems. Cambridge, Massachusetts, Richard Brukenfeld, 1955.
Gasoline. San Francisco, City Lights Books, 1958.
Bomb. San Francisco, City Lights Books, 1958.
A Pulp Magazine for the Dead Generation: Poems, with Henk Marsman. Paris, Dead Language, 1959.
The Happy Birthday of Death. New York, New Directions, 1960.
Minutes to Go, with others. Paris, Two Cities Editions, 1960.
Long Live Man. New York, New Directions, 1962.
Selected Poems. London, Eyre and Spottiswoode, 1962.
Penguin Modern Poets 5, with Lawrence Ferlinghetti and Allen Ginsberg. London, Penguin, 1963.
The Mutation of the Spirit. New York, Death Press, 1964.
There Is Yet Time to Run Back Through Life and Expiate All That's Been Sadly Done. New York, New Directions, 1965.
10 Times a Poem. New York, Poets Press, 1967.
Elegiac Feelings American. New York, New Directions, 1970.

Plays

This Hung-Up Age (produced Cambridge, Massachusetts, 1955).
That Little Black Door on the Left, in *Pardon Me Sir, But Is My Eye Hurting Your Elbow?,* edited by Bob Booker and George Foster. New York, Geis, 1968.

Novel

The American Express. Paris, Olympia Press, 1961.

Other

The Minicab War (parodies), with Anselm Hollo and Tom Raworth. London, Matrix Press, 1961.

Editor, with Walter Höllerer, *Junge Amerikanische Lyrik.* Munich, Carl Hanser Verlag, 1961.

Gregory Corso comments:

[I am a] mental explorer, un-Faustian.
[My verse is] hopeful – naive – strange – sweet – soon smart – why not.

*   *   *

Gregory Corso first became widely known in the U.S. when, in 1956, his name was linked with those of Ginsberg, Kerouac, Snyder, and others in a group which became known as "the Beat poets." Like all such arbitrarily catalogued groups, this one dispersed soon after it was discovered; and it has become clear that Corso's is an individual voice which has relatively little to do with the voices of the other "Beats." It is a quieter, more introvert voice than Ginsberg's; more disciplined and intense than Kerouac's.

In his first collection, *The Vestal Lady on Brattle,* Corso had written mainly of humankind menaced – menaced by death, by nature, by society. His style was simple and traditional; at times, indeed, becoming almost pastiche:

> I climb and enter a fiery gathering of knights
> they unaware of my presence lay forth sheepskin plans
> and with mailcoated fingers trace my arrival . . .

But by 1958 and the next volume, *Gasoline,* the voice had become harder, more didactic, certainly more incantatory – almost Whitmanesque – doubtless under the influence of the other members of the Beat group, with whom Corso was regularly appearing at public readings. This louder tone of voice was accompanied, at times, by a weakening sentimentality:

> Your sound is faultless
> pure & round
> holy
> almost profound . . .

In *The Happy Birthday of Death* he seemed to recover his balance; his poetry reverted to a more natural, conversational idiom in some splendidly controlled and moving poems such as "Marriage," one of his best, and best-known, poems.

Corso's work since 1960 has occasionally been flippant, sometimes sentimental, but often successfully sardonic. The influences on his work have continued to be ill-digested; for instance, that of e. e. cummings:

> Bad nights of drink
> make bad days of sorry.

Not, perhaps, a very accomplished technician, he has made relatively few technical experiments; but the lack of superficial trickiness in his poetry has made him stand out among his immediate contemporaries. He has shared in the over-publicity which has dogged them, but only Ginsberg now seems more likely to survive as a lasting, insistent and memorable voice.

– Derek Parker

COTTON, John. British. Born in London, 7 March 1925. Graduate of London University, B.A. (honours). Served as an officer in the Royal Naval Commandos in the Far East during World War II. Married Peggy Cotton in 1948; has two sons. Since 1947, teacher, and since 1963, headmaster of a comprehensive school, Hertfordshire. Founder, with Ted Walker, and Editor, 1962–72, *Priapus* magazine. Since 1969, Editor, *The Private Library.* Since 1972, Chairman, The Poetry Society, London. Recipient: Arts Council award, 1971. Address: 37 Lombardy Drive, Berkhamsted, Hertfordshire HP4 2LQ, England.

PUBLICATIONS

Verse

Fourteen Poems. Berkhamsted, Hertfordshire, Priapus, 1967.
Outside the Gates of Eden and Other Poems. Bushey Heath, Hertfordshire, Taurus Press, 1969.
Ampurias. Berkhamsted, Hertfordshire, Priapus, 1969.
Old Movies and Other Poems. London, Chatto and Windus-Hogarth Press, 1971.
The Wilderness. Berkhamsted, Hertfordshire, Priapus, 1971.
Columbus on St. Dominica. Rushden, Northamptonshire, Sceptre Press, 1972.
A Sycamore Press Broadsheet. Oxford, Sycamore Press, 1973.
Kilroy Was Here. London, Chatto and Windus-Hogarth Press, 1974.

Critical Studies: in *Poetry Book Society Bulletin 69* (London), 1971; by Anne Cluyse-naar, in *Stand* (Newcastle-upon-Tyne), xiv, 1, 1972.

John Cotton comments:

The early poetry was concerned with the contrast between the world we imagine or wish it to be and the world as it is, and the attempt to maintain a balance between the two. Later work has been more concerned with attempting to create an order out of the plethora of disparate experiences to which we are subjected, and in order to find a meaning or purpose. This links, no doubt, with a subconscious fear of an anarchy of emotion and intellect and the consequent social disorder. While mutability – "All human things are subject to decay," Dryden – underlies all. An ordered decay which continually holds in question the vanity of human wishes.

*   *   *

John Cotton's writing presents a persistent, unspectacular search for consistency of awareness despite the complex conditions of human living:

> Innocence, as all things
> With man, has to be attained.

At once brisk and delicate in observation, his poems attempt balance and sanity in the face of an acute sense of the disparateness of experience (a sense which the quietness of his manner never exploits). So he may speculate on the social motives that lead the Romans to heave "great stones . . . into a wall" and find time to notice, by the side of the wall, "a hundred whitening snails" clustering "on a single stem to conserve moisture." The bringing together of these observations on different scales is, in Cotton, more than a device to relate man's attempt at order and life with nature's: it demonstrates a willingness to be comprehensive in his conception of order, and to reject idealism for a harder form of innocence, encompassing both the commonplace and the inevitable.

– Anne Cluysenaar

COULETTE, Henri. American. Born in Los Angeles, California, 11 November 1927. Educated at Los Angeles State College, B.A. 1952; University of Iowa, Iowa City, M.F.A. 1954, Ph.D. 1959. Served in the United States Army, 1945–46. Married Jacqueline Meredith in 1950. Lecturer, University of Iowa, 1957–59. Since 1959, Member of the English Department, and currently Professor of English, California State University, Los Angeles. Associate Editor, *Midland* magazine. Recipient: Lamont Poetry Selection Award, 1965; Phelan Award, 1966. Order of the Black Rose, Krakow, Poland, 1972. Address: 475 Madeline Drive, Padadena, California 91105, U.S.A.

PUBLICATIONS

Verse

> *The War of the Secret Agents.* New York, Scribner, 1966.
> *The Family Goldschmitt.* New York, Scribner, 1971.

Other

> Editor, with Paul Engle, *Midland: Twenty-Five Years of Fiction and Poetry Selected from Writing Workshops of the State University of Iowa.* New York, Random House, 1961.
> Editor, with Philip Levine, *Character and Crisis: A Contemporary Reader.* New York, McGraw Hill, 1966.
> Editor, *The Broken Lyre: Interviews with 14 Poets.* Washington, D.C., National Endowment for the Arts, 1971.

Henri Coulette comments:

I consider myself a *maker* rather than a *bard.* From this consideration, all else follows. I am interested in technique, and take pride in demonstrating it: in traditional meter, syllabics, accentuals. I like to think that I bear witness to my experience; i.e., that my subject matter is being me, here, now. I hope that I may rise above these limitations, but I have no illusions about being a spokesman for others, or of possessing the truth. Limitation is mystery, and I try to live with the excitements and discomforts thereof.

*   *   *

Henri Coulette, particularly in *The War of the Secret Agents,* displays a definite predilection for oddities, for people and things

> . . . like old streetcars buried at sea,
> In the wrong element, with no place to go.

He shows an allegiance and affection for things the world at large might consider neither proper, practical, nor valuable. He writes about an imagined fifth season, about neglected attic treasures, about a soldier who falls asleep during a mock battle and is killed when he falls from his truck, about "gentle kooks" and mild failures.

"The War of the Secret Agents" itself is about events surrounding a group of amateur agents for the Allies in World War II, about whom Coulette writes, "They will appeal to lovers of the absurd," being like "debutantes slumming on Skid Row." The 35-page poem, title-piece of the book for which Coulette was awarded the Lamont Poetry Selection Award, is wonderful. Written in a syllabic scheme appropriately odd (stanzas of 11–5–7–9–11–7), the poem captures the hypocrisy and duplicity of modern nations, and the lives of people trapped in their collectivist webs, dramatizing them with a kind of subtlety, humor, irony, and sympathy that runs contrary to present literary fashions. The language of the poem, if not fashionable, is thoroughly contemporary; Coulette has a marvelous ear for the natural speaking voice.

In *The Family Goldschmitt* Coulette has turned away from the matter and rhyme of his first book, but the poems still give the impression of being more formal than most recent poetry. The book, though it does contain fine poems, seems a drop-off from his first, with nothing that approaches "War of the Secret Agents" or the force of this short poem from the first book:

Robert Roger Coulette, Musician

He plays no more
Whose play was need,
The darkened score,
The broken reed.

– Lawrence Russ

COUZYN, Jeni. South African. Born in South Africa, 26 July 1942. Educated at the University of Natal, B.A. 1962, B.A. (honours) 1963. Drama Teacher, Rhodesia, 1964; Producer, African Music and Drama Association, Johannesburg, 1965; Teacher, Special School, London, 1966; Poetry Organiser and Gallery Attendant, Camden Arts Centre, London, 1967. Since 1968, Free-lance Poet. Recipient: Arts Council grant, 1971. Address: 17 Willow Road, London N.W.3, England.

PUBLICATIONS

Verse

Flying. London, Workshop Press, 1970.
Monkeys' Wedding. London, Cape, 1972.

Other

Editor, *Twelve to Twelve: Poems Commissioned for Poetry D-Day, Camden Arts Festival 1970.* London, Poets' Trust, 1970.

315

Jeni Couzyn comments:

I am interested in using symbol rather than image, and tend to write with as much clarity as I can. I am at times monosyllabic, and look for the shortest and simplest words I can find. I believe poetry should be "true" at the deepest possible level, and dislike the kind of poetry that appears to be complex on the surface, crammed with learned references and tricky images, but which finally has little to say.

I write in free verse, using rhythm and stress to underline meaning and to counterpoint the sense whenever I can. Similarly I use rhyme for surprise and emphasis rather than in any metrical pattern. I am particularly fond of imperfect rhymes, especially where the rhyming syllable falls on the unstressed part of the word.

I believe that poetry should be spoken, and read on the page only as a kind of specialised reference – as music is written to be played and listened to. Reviewers at this time in the history of poetry use the words "poetry circuit" as a dirty word, as though it were some kind of big roundabout that only the common and the simple people climbed aboard. The simply expressed but profound truth of a poem like Robert Frost's "Nothing Gold Can Stay" is what I most admire in poetry and most seek for. The criteria I use to judge my own work are: is it interesting; is it relevant to other people's lives; is it music; is it true in the deepest sense – in a lasting way. To the extent that these criteria are approached, I am pleased or displeased with a poem.

In sound I have been most influenced by Dylan Thomas – not so much in his technique as in his courage in defying the dry tradition of poetry he was born into.

That I am a poet in an age where the "unintellectual" (i.e., almost everybody) think of poetry as something they didn't like when they were at school, and the intellectual think it is something the masses should be excluded from, is sad for me. This age has too much reverence for poetry, and too little respect – for by the same token it is very difficult indeed to earn a living from poetry. Nor are poets considered valid members of the community – you will never see a panel set up to discuss drug usage, for example, or terrorism in Ireland, with a poet among the psychiatrists, students, businessmen, clergy and housewives being asked to give their view.

For me being a poet is a job rather than an activity. I feel I have a function in society, neither more nor less meaningful than any other simple job. I feel it is part of my work to make poetry more accessible to people who have had their rights withdrawn from them. Standing in the way of this are the poetry watchdogs who bark in the Sunday reviews, trying to preserve their sterile territory. Also it is necessary to overcome the apathy and ignorance of a whole society with a totally untrained ear and a profoundly sluggish imagination.

*   *   *

Jeni Couzyn's first book, *Flying,* came as a shock even to readers who thought they were sophisticated. Few of the poems had reached the usual magazines and anthologies since Miss Couzyn was known mainly for her appearances on the recital circuits. *Flying* contained reflections upon her South African background; descriptions of London's grey suburbia; dramatizations of love relationships and of mental stress. These last were at their best when the author expressed her internal conflicts through her fund of exotic imagery. For example, "The Farm" deals with what looks like a depressive illness, but it does so in terms almost of a child's holiday:

> On the farm there are two
> cows.
> And there are a lot of
> trees. They change their leaves
> whenever they like. When they change their leaves you
> know
> that it is autumn. The two cows have a calf and then you
> know
> that it is spring.
> You can take your cat with you to the farm or whatever
> you like. You can take your
> bicycle
> or your
> typewriter
> or all your books
> you can take whatever you like with you to the farm . . .

These patient monosyllables ratify a childlike acceptance of what becomes more abnormal the further the poem proceeds. And this conflict between the innocent and the sinister sets up an uneasy tension in the reader. Miss Couzyn can be a distinguished poet when she deploys her narrative gifts to project a parable of the mind's cliffs of fall.

But her second book, *Monkey's Wedding*, suffers from over-explicitness. Many of the attitudes are straight out of Women's Lib. The collection contains some powerful work; perhaps most notably ''The Babies,'' a painful poem about contraception and abortion. But the skin of fiction is stretched too thin over the agony. We are more conscious of outcry than of experience. One could wish that Miss Couzyn would approach her themes more circumspectly. Such emotion demands an objective correlative if it is not to seem shrill.

However, remarks such as these are based on the evidence of only two books. And already Miss Couzyn is among the best, as well as the most promising, younger poets of today.

– Philip Hobsbaum

COWLEY, Malcolm. American. Born in Belsano, Pennsylvania, 24 August 1898. Educated at Harvard University, Cambridge, Massachusetts (Editor, *The Advocate*, 1919), A.B. (cum laude) 1920 (Phi Beta Kappa); University of Montpellier, Diplome 1922. Served in the American Ambulance Service in France, 1917, and the United States Army, 1918; Office of Facts and Figures, Washington, D.C., 1942. Married Muriel Maurer in 1932; has one son, Robert. Associate Editor, *Broom* magazine, New York, 1923, and *Cessation*, Paris; Literary Editor, *New Republic*, New York, 1929–44. Visiting Professor: University of Washington, Seattle, 1950; Stanford University, California, 1956, 1959, 1960–61, 1965; University of Michigan, Ann Arbor, 1957; University of California, Berkeley, 1962; Cornell University, Ithaca, New York, 1964; University of Minnesota, Minneapolis, 1971; University of Warwick, England, 1973. Since 1948, Literary Adviser, The Viking Press, New York.

Director of the Yaddo Corporation. Recipient: Levinson Prize, 1927, and Harriet Monroe Memorial Prize, 1939 (*Poetry*, Chicago); National Institute of Arts and Letters grant, 1946; National Endowment for the Arts grant, 1967. Litt.D.: Franklin and Marshall College, Lancaster, Pennsylvania, 1961; Colby College, Waterville, Maine, 1962. President, 1956–59, 1962–65, National Institute of Arts and Letters; Member, American Academy of Arts and Letters; since 1968, Chancellor, American Academy of Arts and Letters. Address: Sherman, Connecticut 06784, U.S.A.

PUBLICATIONS

Verse

Blue Juniata: Poems. New York, Cape and Smith, 1929.
The Dry Season. New York, New Directions, 1941.
Blue Juniata: Collected Poems. New York, Viking Press, 1968.

Other

Exile's Return: A Narrative of Ideas. New York, Norton, 1934; London, Cape, 1935; revised edition, as *Exile's Return: A Literary Odyssey of the 1920's,* New York, Viking Press, 1951; London, Bodley Head, 1961.
The Literary Situation. New York, Viking Press, 1954.
Black Cargoes: A History of the Atlantic Slave Trade, 1518–1865, with Daniel P. Mannix. New York, Viking Press, 1962; London, Longman, 1963.
The Faulkner-Cowley File: Letters and Memories, 1944–1962. New York, Viking Press, and London, Chatto and Windus, 1966.
Think Back on Us: A Contemporary Chronicle of the 1930's, edited by Henry Dan Piper. Carbondale, Southern Illinois University Press, 1967.
A Many-Windowed House: Collected Essays on American Writers and American Writing. Carbondale, Southern Illinois University Press, 1970.
A Second Flowering: Works and Days of the Lost Generation. New York, Viking Press, and London, Deutsch, 1973.

Editor, *Adventures of an African Slaver: Being a True Account of the Life of Captain Theodore Canot,* by Brantz Mayer. London, Routledge, 1928.
Editor, *After the Genteel Tradition: American Writers since 1910.* New York, Norton, 1937; revised edition, Carbondale, Southern Illinois University Press, 1964.
Editor, with Bernard Smith, *Books That Changed Our Minds.* New York, Doubleday, 1940.
Editor, *The Portable Hemingway.* New York, Viking Press, 1944.
Editor, with Hannah Josephson, *Aragon: Poet of the French Resistance.* New York, Duell, 1945; as *Aragon: Poet of Resurgent France,* London, Pilot Press, 1946.
Editor, *The Portable Faulkner.* New York, Viking Press, 1946; revised edition, 1966; London, Chatto and Windus, 1967.
Editor, *The Portable Hawthorne.* New York, Viking Press, 1948; revised edition, 1969.
Editor, *The Complete Poetry and Prose of Walt Whitman.* New York, Pellegrini, 1948; as *The Works of Walt Whitman,* New York, Funk and Wagnalls, 1968.
Editor, *Stories,* by F. Scott Fitzgerald. New York, Scribner, 1951.

Editor, *Great Tales of the Deep South.* New York, Lion Library, 1955.

Editor, *Writers at Work: The "Paris Review" Interviews.* New York, Viking Press, and London, Secker and Warburg, 1958.

Editor, *Leaves of Grass, The First (1855) Edition,* by Walt Whitman. New York, Viking Press, 1959.

Editor, with Robert Cowley, *Fitzgerald and the Jazz Age.* New York, Scribner, 1966.

Editor, with Howard E. Hugo, *The Lessons of the Masters: An Anthology of the Novel from Cervantes to Hemingway.* New York, Scribner, 1971.

Translator, *On Board the Morning Star,* by Pierre MacOrlan. New York, Boni, 1924.

Translator, *Joan of Arc,* by Joseph Delteil. New York, Minton, 1926.

Translator, *Variety,* by Paul Valéry. New York, Harcourt Brace, 1927.

Translator, *Catherine-Paris,* by Marthe Lucie Bibesco. New York, Harcourt Brace, 1928.

Translator, *The Green Parrot,* by Marthe Lucie Bibesco. New York, Harcourt Brace, 1929.

Translator, *The Sacred Hill,* by Maurice Barrès. New York, Macauley, 1929.

Translator, *The Count's Ball,* by Raymond Radiguet. New York, Norton, 1929.

Translator, *Imaginary Interviews,* by André Gide. New York, Knopf, 1944.

Translator, with James R. Lawler, *Leonardo Poe Mallarmé,* by Paul Valéry. Princeton, New Jersey, Princeton University Press, 1972.

Bibliography: *Malcolm Cowley: A Checklist of His Writings,* by Diane U. Eisenberg, Carbondale, Southern Illinois University Press, 1975.

Manuscript Collection: Newberry Library, Chicago.

Critical Studies: Introduction by Henry Dan Piper to *A Many-Windowed House,* 1970; by Lewis P. Simpson, in *Sewanee Review* (Tennessee), Autumn 1974.

Malcolm Cowley comments:

I am sorry to record that my principal theme has been nostalgia: for the countryside where I was born, for the easier society in which I came to manhood, for the friends of my younger days. I try to make each poem an action complete in itself; to let it discover its own form, often by patient revision. I am more interested in sound than sight, in tonal qualities than in images. I believe that every successful poem is a charm or mantra in which every word has become unchangeable.

*   *   *

Malcolm Cowley's output as a poet has never been copious. Throughout a long and distinguished literary career he has been known primarily as a critic and historian of American literature rather than a poet. Nevertheless, *Blue Juniata,* the 1968 volume of collected poems, shows that Cowley's talents as a poet are real and unforced, however infrequently he may have exercised them. He sees his poems as expressions and illustrations of his personal and intellectual history, beginning in a

Pennsylvania childhood in the opening years of this century; an attachment to country life and the natural world is a recurring theme in his poetry. But as well as its personal dimension, Cowley's poetry also documents and crystallizes crucial moments in modern American history. Thus, "Chateau de Soupir: 1917" is a sharp recollection of the First World War; "Ezra Pound at the Hotel Jacob" recalls the expatriate Parisian literary life of the 1920's; "Tomorrow Morning" reflects the political passions of the 1930's and the impact of the Spanish Civil War. Most recently, "Here with the Long Grass Rippling" looks in passing at the Vietnam war.

Cowley's poetry is not dramatic or particularly vivid in its language. But it possesses the solid virtues of craftsmanship, urbanity, controlled lyricism, and exact observation of the physical world.

– Bernard Bergonzi

COXE, Louis (Osborne). American. Born in Manchester, New Hampshire, 15 April 1918. Educated at St. Paul's School, Concord, New Hampshire; Princeton University, New Jersey, B.A. 1940. Served in the United States Navy, 1942–46. Married Edith Winsor in 1946; has four children. Instructor, Princeton University, 1946; Briggs-Copeland Fellow, Harvard University, Cambridge, Massachusetts, 1948–49; Assistant Professor, then Associate Professor, University of Minnesota, Minneapolis, 1949–55. Professor of English, 1955–56, and since 1956, Pierce Professor of English, Bowdoin College, Brunswick, Maine. Fulbright Lecturer, Trinity College, Dublin, 1959–60. Recipient: Donaldson Award, for drama, 1952; *Sewanee Review* Fellowship, 1956; Brandeis University Creative Arts Award, 1960. Address: Department of English, Bowdoin College, Brunswick, Maine 04011, U.S.A.

PUBLICATIONS

Verse

The Sea Faring and Other Poems. New York, Holt, 1947.
The Second Man and Other Poems. Minneapolis, University of Minnesota Press, 1955.
The Wilderness and Other Poems. Minneapolis, University of Minnesota Press, 1958.
The Middle Passage. Chicago, University of Chicago Press, 1960.
The Last Hero and Other Poems. Nashville, Tennessee, Vanderbilt University Press, 1965.
Nikal Seyn, Decoration Day: A Poem and a Play. Nashville, Tennessee, Vanderbilt University Press, 1966.

Plays

Billy Budd, with Robert Chapman, adaptation of the story by Herman Melville (produced New York, 1951). Princeton, New Jersey, Princeton University Press, 1951; London, Heinemann, 1966; as The Good Sailor (produced London, 1956).

The General (produced Cambridge, Massachusetts, 1954).
The Witchfinders (produced Rochester, Minnesota, 1955; New York, 1958).

Other

Edwin Arlington Robinson.   Minneapolis, University of Minnesota Press, 1962.
Edwin Arlington Robinson: The Life of Poetry.   New York, Pegasus, 1969.

Editor, *Chaucer.*   New York, Dell, 1963.

*   *   *

The Sea Faring, the title of his first book, is also Louis Coxe's favorite theme. The sea acts not only as a setting for individual displays of courage and villainy but also as a powerful metaphor for the universal struggles endured in man's precarious moral voyages. The poet frames his astute observations with skilful verse forms, but several early and some later works suffer from a hypercerebral tone, overly technical terminology, and complex and constricting syntax; what might be music is muffled by a heavy academic pall, which also gives the impression of greater profundity than actually lies beneath the convoluted surface. Even here, however, the search for fundamentals, for the eternal designs behind the ephemeral, gives Coxe's lines their particular strength. The persona asks, "How shall he tell you: Mac, the war / Was rugged?" and answers through descriptions of strategic maneuvers and vignettes of warship personnel, for brief and vivid abstracts best convey the fearful order in the larger strife. Later, in the panoramic treatment of a disastrous naval battle, "The Strait," he commemorates the "Thousands who burned or drowned died to no end . . . far from imagined loves" at Pearl Harbor and in the South Pacific, and reveals the deadly artistry behind apparent chaos.

Coxe's sense of history – as a cyclic, usually violent, seldom redemptive process – underlines and unifies the several strands in his work. The harsh Colonial past is peopled by the likes of Hannah Dustin, who castrates and scalps her Indian rapist with his own knife; by Samuel Sewall, late witch-burner now obsessed with guilt and possessed by the Devil; by Thomas Jefferson, imposing his classical designs upon the treacherous wilderness that is the young country – and the heart of man. Salem and Boston send forth handsome sailing ships, whose "wrecks grow timber out of shale." The greed, destructiveness, and sexual perversion behind the Puritan facade of salty self-reliance is most brilliantly revealed in the long blank-verse narrative, *The Middle Passage*. A shrewd but seemingly innocent nineteen-year-old, Canot, soon commandeers *The Happy Delivery*, a slaveship disguised as a whaler, half outwits its crafty Yankee owners, but experiences a sea-change: the filthy but lucrative business exacts its toll, 300 blacks drowned and the loss of Canot's soul in an orgy of sadistic lust, drink, and drugs, culminating in grand theft and murder: "New Englanders don't damn / The easy way. . . ." But all is part of the pattern. The sins of the Forefathers breed the current misery of the cities: "We are strangers on the earth, / To one another, and lament a private loss." We are left with "separate lives inside, grown separate hells." "Progress" is merely repetition of original sin, a myth amounting to a moral stand-still.

Despite the seriousness of most of Coxe's verse, its effect is not gloomy. He has a gift for dramatic exposition. Even when the perhaps inexplicable motivations of the "heroes" of *The Middle Passage* and *Nikal Seyn* remain murky, we share the fascination of the limited and unreliable narrators with their flamboyant adventures. Poems celebrating nature, particularly flights of birds, rise with lyrical power. Several portraits strip historical personages to the core: Dean Swift, "Who studied hate lest pity turn him mad"; Ambrose Bierce, of whom Coxe asks, "Yet how can sworn enemy / of corruption rot / embalmed by hate?" Often poignant and witty, especially in "personal" poems dedicated to family and friends, Coxe's best lines give the satisfaction that comes when problems and paradoxes are subtly restated and elegantly shaped by art.

– Joseph Parisi

CREELEY, Robert (White). American. Born in Arlington, Massachusetts, 21 May 1926. Educated at Holderness School, Plymouth, New Hampshire; Harvard University, Cambridge, Massachusetts, 1943–46; Black Mountain College, North Carolina, B.A. 1955; University of New Mexico, Albuquerque, M.A. 1960. Served with the American Field Service in India and Burma, 1944–45. Married twice; has six children. Taught on a finca in Guatemala for two years; Instructor, Black Mountain College, Spring 1954, Fall 1955; Visiting Lecturer, 1961–62, and Lecturer, 1963–66, 1968–69, University of New Mexico; Lecturer, University of British Columbia, Vancouver, 1962–63. Visiting Professor, 1966–67, and since 1967, Professor of English, State University of New York, Buffalo. Visiting Professor, San Francisco State College, 1970–71. Operated the Divers Press, Palma de Mallorca, 1953–55. Editor, *Black Mountain Review,* North Carolina, 1954–57, and associated with *Wake, Golden Goose, Origin, Fragmente, Vou, Contact, CIV/n,* and *Merlin* magazines in the early 1950's, and other magazines subsequently. Recipient: Levinson Prize, 1960, Oscar Blumenthal Prize, 1964, and Union League Civic and Arts Foundation Prize, 1967 (*Poetry,* Chicago); D. H. Lawrence Fellowship, 1960; Guggenheim Fellowship, 1964, 1971; Rockefeller Fellowship, 1965. Lives in Bolinas, California. Address: Department of English, State University of New York, Buffalo, New York 14214, U.S.A.

PUBLICATIONS

Verse

Le Fou. Columbus, Ohio, Golden Goose Press, 1952.
The Kind of Act of. Palma, Mallorca, Divers Press, 1953.
The Immoral Proposition. Karlsruhe-Surlach, Germany, Jonathan Williams, 1953.
A Snarling Garland of Xmas Verses. Palma, Mallorca, Divers Press, 1954.
All That Is Lovely in Men. Asheville, North Carolina, Jonathan Williams, 1955.
Ferrini and Others, with others. Berlin, Gerhardt, 1955.
If You. San Francisco, Porpoise Bookshop, 1956; London, Lion and Unicorn Press, 1968.
The Whip. Worcester, Migrant Press, 1957.
A Form of Women. New York, Jargon Books-Corinth Books, 1959.
For Love: Poems 1950–1960. New York, Scribner, 1962.
Distance. Lawrence, Kansas, Terrence Williams, 1964.
Two Poems. San Francisco, Oyez, 1964.
Hi There! Urbana, Illinois, Finial Press, 1965.
Words. Rochester, Minnesota, Perishable Press, 1965.

About Women.   Los Angeles, Gemini, 1966.

Poems 1950–1965.   London, Calder and Boyars, 1966.

For Joel.   Madison, Wisconsin, Perishable Press, 1966.

A Sight.   London, Cape Goliard Press, 1967.

Words.   New York, Scribner, 1967.

Robert Creeley Reads (with recording).   London, Turret Books-Calder and Boyars, 1967.

The Finger.   Los Angeles, Black Sparrow Press, 1968.

5 Numbers.   New York, Poets Press, 1968.

The Charm: Early and Uncollected Poems.   Mount Horeb, Wisconsin, Perishable Press, 1968; London, Calder and Boyars, 1971.

The Boy.   Buffalo, New York, Gallery Upstairs Press, 1968.

Numbers.   Stuttgart and Dusseldorf, Edition Domberger-Galerie Schmela, 1968.

Divisions and Other Early Poems.   Mount Horeb, Wisconsin, Perishable Press, 1968.

Pieces.   Los Angeles, Black Sparrow Press, 1968.

Hero.   New York, Indianakatz, 1969.

A Wall.   New York and Stuttgart, Bouwerie Editions-Edition Domberger, 1969.

Mary's Fancy.   New York, Bouwerie Editions, 1970.

In London.   Bolinas, California, Angel Hair Books, 1970.

The Finger: Poems 1966–1969.   London, Calder and Boyars, 1970.

For Betsy and Tom.   Detroit, Alternative Press, 1970.

For Benny and Sabina.   New York, Samuel Charters, 1970.

As Now It Would Be Snow.   Los Angeles, Black Sparrow Press, 1970.

America.   Miami, Press of the Black Flag, 1970.

Christmas: May 10, 1970.   Buffalo, State University of New York at Buffalo Lockwood Memorial Library, 1970.

St. Martin's.   Los Angeles, Black Sparrow Press, 1971.

Sea.   San Francisco, Cranium Press, 1971.

1.2.3.4.5.6.7.8.9.0.   Berkeley, California, and San Francisco, Shambala-Mudra, 1971.

For the Graduation.   San Francisco, Cranium Press, 1971.

Change.   San Francisco, Hermes Free Press, 1972.

One Day after Another.   Detroit, Alternative Press, 1972.

A Day Book (includes prose).   New York, Scribner, 1972.

For My Mother.   Rushden, Northamptonshire, Sceptre Press, 1973.

Kitchen.   Chicago, Wine Press, 1973.

Sitting Here.   Storrs, University of Connecticut Library, 1974.

Thirty Things.   Los Angeles, Black Sparrow Press, 1974.

Recordings: *Today's Poets 3*, with others, Folkways; *Robert Creeley Reads*, Turret Books-Calder and Boyars, 1967.

Play

Listen (produced London, 1972).   Los Angeles, Black Sparrow Press, 1972.

Novel

The Island.   New York, Scribner, 1963; London, John Calder, 1964.

Short Stories

The Gold Diggers.   Palma, Mallorca, Divers Press, 1954.
Mister Blue.   Frankfurt, Insel, 1964.
The Gold Diggers and Other Stories.   London, John Calder, and New York, Scribner, 1965.

Other

An American Sense (essay).   London, Sigma, 1965(?).
Contexts of Poetry.   Buffalo, New York, Audit, 1968.
A Quick Graph: Collected Notes and Essays.   San Francisco, Four Seasons Foundation, 1970.
A Day Book.   Berlin, Graphis, 1970.
The Creative.   Los Angeles, Black Sparrow Press, 1973.
A Sense of Measure (essays).   London, Calder and Boyars, 1973.
Contexts of Poetry: Interviews 1961–71.   Bolinas, California, Four Seasons Foundation, 1973.
Inside Out: Notes on the Autobiographical Mode.   Los Angeles, Black Sparrow Press, 1974.

Editor, *Mayan Letters*, by Charles Olson.   Palma, Mallorca, Divers Press, 1953; London, Cape, and New York, Grossman, 1968.
Editor, with Donald Allen, *New American Story.*   New York, Grove Press, 1965.
Editor, *Selected Writings*, by Charles Olson.   New York, New Directions, 1966.
Editor, with Donald Allen, *The New Writing in the U.S.A.*   London, Penguin, 1967.
Editor, *Whitman.*   London, Penguin, 1973.

Bibliography: *Robert Creeley: An Inventory 1945–1970* by Mary Novik, Montreal, McGill-Queen's University Press, 1974.

Manuscript Collection: Washington University, St. Louis.

Critical Studies: Review by Robert Duncan, in *New Mexico Quarterly* (Albuquerque), xxxii, 3–4, 1962–63; "Introduction to Robert Creeley" by Charles Olson, in *Human Universe and Other Essays*, New York, Grove Press, 1967; Louis B. Martz, in *Yale Review* (New Haven, Connecticut), 1969; "Address and Posture in the Poetry of Robert Creeley" by Kenneth Cox, in *Cambridge Quarterly*, iv, 3, 1969; *Three Essays on Creeley* by Warren Tallman, Toronto, Coach House Press, 1973; "Robert Creeley's *For Love: Poems 1950–1960*" by Charles Olson, in *Additional Prose*, San Francisco, Four Seasons Foundation, 1974.

Robert Creeley comments:

I write to realize the world as one has come to live in it, thus to give testament. I write to move in *words*, a human delight. I write when no other act is possible.

*　　　*　　　*

Although he was one of the founders of the "Black Mountain movement" in American poetry, Robert Creeley was working in the direction of the movement well before the movement began, as the recent republication of his early poems makes clear. From the first, his native gifts combined a keen and affectionate regard for colloquial American speech with an austere sense of the supra-colloquial function of poetic language as such. In the mid-1950's, when he had already published a number of books, he joined the faculty at Black Mountain College in North Carolina, and while there helped to found and edit the *Black Mountain Review,* in which the writings of the new group were presented for the first time as a more or less cohesive force. There, too, his association with Charles Olson, the elder poet of the group, which had begun well before the period at Black Mountain, became particularly close. Creeley has performed important service in editing Olson's *Selected Writings* and *Mayan Letters,* a collection of Olson's communications to Creeley during a sojourn in Yucatan. Creeley himself has lived in New Mexico and Guatemala, and the emphasis both poets have placed upon New-World sources in their poetry, taken together with their formal statements of an anti-symbolist and anti-academic esthetic, has virtually revolutionized the attitudes of younger American poets toward their poetic materials in the 1950's and 1960's.

At the same time, Creeley's association with the movement should not obscure his own precisely articulated individuality. Unlike most other Black Mountain poets, Creeley has limited his production almost exclusively to short, self-contained lyrics, and has generally refused to admit social and political themes to his work, even during the recent period of revolutionary ferment in America. Both these predilections seem to have arisen from his feeling about the aspects of failure, structural and substantial, in such earlier works as Ezra Pound's *Cantos* and William Carlos Williams' *Paterson.* The result is that Creeley's poetry, taken as a whole, has a narrower range than that of Olson, for example, or Robert Duncan. Yet what it lacks in breadth it makes up in concentration: from its minutely explored base in personal, chiefly erotic experience, it extends by strategic verbal probings toward an achieved foothold in metaphysical and esthetic understanding.

At the simplest verbal level, Creeley is a superb technician. His emphasis on the poem as an objective structure, composed of objective parts, has made him the most acute student of words among modern poets. For him the poem is a thing, an adjunct of reality; words are the amorphous base matter which contains reality *in potentia.* Hence the evolution of Creeley's poetic technique has been a continual crisis of responsibility. To maintain strict probity in his relationship to existence the poet must continually seek the true, intrinsic, unique and self-sustaining form of each imaginative object as it emerges into being. The result in Creeley's best work is a kind of firm and unmistakable formalism, which nevertheless bears almost no relationship to the historically received formalisms of prior literature. His poems are self-completing gestures of tone, syntax, logic, image, measure and connotative feeling. They have at their best a beauty and sufficiency, and often a lightness and good humor, that are belied by any attempt, such as this, to talk about them.

Creeley's personal influence on other writers has been widespread. What was his individual manner has become a public property; one sees it everywhere in the work of younger poets. His writing has been studied with an intentness seldom accorded the works of living poets, and he himself is in great demand as a public reader and teacher. Recently for several years, he has been poet-in-residence at the University of Buffalo in Buffalo, New York, one of the principal centers of poetic activity in the U.S.

– Hayden Carruth

CREWS, Judson. American. Born in Waco, Texas, 30 June 1917. Educated at La Vega High School, Waco; Baylor University, Waco, A.B. 1941, M.A. in sociology and psychology 1944, graduate work in art, 1946; Kinzinger Field School of Art, Taos, New Mexico, 1947. Served in the United States Medical Corps, 1942–44. Married Mildred Tolbert in 1947; has two daughters. Graduate Assistant in Sociology, Baylor University, 1941–42. Consumer Market Researcher, Stewart Dougal and Associates, New York, 1948; Printer and Publisher, Taos *Star, El Crepusculo,* Taos *News,* 1948–66. Former Caseworker, El Paso County Child Welfare Unit, Texas; former Instructor in Sociology and Psychology, Wharton County Junior College, Texas. Intensive Care Unit Director, State Training School for Girls, Chillicothe, Missouri, 1973. Currently, Lecturer in Social Development Studies, University of Zambia, Lusaka. During the 1930's, 1940's, and 1950's, Editor, *Vers Libre, Taos, Motive, The Flying Fish, Suck-Egg Mule, The Deer and Dachshund, Poetry Taos,* and *The Naked Ear* magazines. Address: University of Zambia, P.O. Box 2379, Lusaka, Zambia.

PUBLICATIONS

Verse

Psalms for a Late Season. New Orleans, Iconograph Press, 1942.
No Is the Night. Taos, New Mexico, privately printed, 1949.
Come Curse the Moon. Ranches of Taos, New Mexico, privately printed, 1952 (?).
The Anatomy of Proserpine. Ranches of Taos, New Mexico, privately printed, 1955.
The Wrath Wrenched Splendor of Love. Ranches of Taos, New Mexico, privately printed, 1956.
The Heart in Naked Hunger. Ranches of Taos, New Mexico, Motive Book Shop, 1958.
To Wed Beneath the Sun. Privately printed, 1958 (?).
A Sheaf of Christmas Verse. Washington, D.C., Three Hands, n.d.
The Ogres Who Were His Henchmen. Eureka, California, Hearse Press, 1958.
Inwade to Barney Garth. Taos, New Mexico, Este Es Press, 1960.
The Feel of Sun and Air upon Her Body. Eureka, California, Hearse Press, 1960.
A Unicorn When Needs Be. Taos, New Mexico, Este Es Press, 1963.
Hermes Past the Hour. Taos, New Mexico, Este Es Press, 1963.
Selected Poems. Cleveland, Renegade Press, 1964.
You, Mark Antony, Navigator upon the Nile. Taos, New Mexico, privately printed, 1964.
Angels Fall, They Are Towers. Taos, New Mexico, Este Es Press, 1965.
Three on a Match, with Wendell B. Anderson and Cerise Farallon. Taos, New Mexico, privately printed, 1966.
The Stones of Konarak. Santa Fe, New Mexico, American Poets Press, 1966.

Other

The Southern Temper. Waco, Texas, Motive Book Shop, 1946.
Patocinio Barela: Taos Wood Carver, with Mildred Crews and Wendell B. Anderson. Taos, New Mexico, Taos Recordings and Publications, 1955; revised edition, 1962.

Manuscript Collections: University of Texas, Austin; University of California, Los Angeles; Yale University, New Haven, Connecticut.

Critical Studies: *A Critical Analysis of Poems by a Contemporary Poet of the Avant-Garde: Judson Crews*, by Wendell B. Anderson, Rindge, New Hampshire, Franklin Pierce College, unpublished thesis, 1969.

*   *   *

In the poetry of Judson Crews, the imagination of a man of the Southwestern United States comes into contact with the poetic innovations of Pound, Williams, Charles Olson and Wallace Stevens. Crews's response to these innovations is original and idiosyncratic. He is something of a primitive poet, doggedly pursuing his own way. Mostly short lyrics, his poems range from simple songs to abstract meditations. Verbal experiment is used both for its own sake and as a kind of exploration into the sources of creative life.

Often Crews begins a poem with a striking, sometimes strange phrase ("No wail it went the gladsome son"), and pursues its meanings through the use of language generated by similarity of sound or by a kind of verbal inventiveness ("he sought the wicked in the middle heart / night was lonelier than a restless wing"). Many poems are brief, often zany fables that reach towards mythic realities, towards dimly grasped terrors and possibilities of courage. Language is pushed to hyperbole, even to nonsense, for the sheer sake of celebration. It is true that at times the language is too "poetic" and that the poems at times move with rhythmical monotony and a kind of glibness. The lyric extravagance allows the inclusion of much that is banal. But beyond the affectation and excess are a rambunctious kind of humor and an eager, open sense of wonder.

This humor and this wonder seem rooted in the man himself and in his region. The young Crews, wrote Henry Miller, "reminded one, because of his shaggy beard and manner of speech, of a latter-day prophet." And there is something larger than ordinary life in the energy and constant power of invention present in Crews's poetic career. Certainly his imagination is indiscriminate; but it is also prolific. And he writes with a gusto that is rare in contemporary American poetry.

– Jerry Paris

CROSSLEY-HOLLAND, Kevin (John Williams). British. Born in Mursley, Buckinghamshire, 7 February 1941. Educated at Bryanston school; St. Edmund Hall, Oxford, B.A. (honours) in English language and literature. Married; has two sons by first marriage. Editor, Macmillan and Company, publishers, London, 1962–71. Gregory Fellow, University of Leeds, 1969–71. Talks Producer, BBC, London, 1972. Since 1972, Editorial Director, Victor Gollancz Ltd., publishers, London. Recipient: Arts Council award, for children's book, 1968. Agent: Deborah Rogers Literary Agency, 29 Goodge Street, London W.C.1, England.

PUBLICATIONS

Verse

On Approval. London, Outposts Publications, 1961.
My Son. London, Turret Books, 1966.
Alderney: The Nunnery. London, Turret Books, 1968.
Norfolk Poems. London, Academy Editions, 1970.
A Dream of a Meeting. Frensham, Surrey, Sceptre Press, 1970.
Confessional. Frensham, Surrey, Sceptre Press, 1970.
More Than I Am. London, Steam Press, 1971.
The Wake. Richmond, Surrey, Keepsake Press, 1972.
The Rain-Giver. London, Deutsch, 1972.

Other

Havelock the Dane (juvenile). London, Macmillan, 1964; New York, Dutton, 1965.
King Horn (juvenile). London, Macmillan, 1965; New York, Dutton, 1966.
The Green Children (juvenile). London, Macmillan, 1966; New York, Seabury, 1968.
The Callow Pit Coffer (juvenile). London, Macmillan, 1968; New York, Seabury, 1969.
Wordhoard (juvenile). London, Macmillan, and New York, Farrar Straus, .1969.
The Pedlar of Swaffham (juvenile). London, Macmillan, 1971; New York, Seabury, 1972.
Pieces of Land: Journeys to Eight Islands. London, Gollancz, 1972.
The Sea-Stranger (juvenile). London, Heinemann, 1973; New York, Seabury, 1974.
The Fire-Brother (juvenile). London, Macmillan, 1974.

Editor, *Winter's Tales for Children 3.* London, Macmillan, 1967.
Editor, *Running to Paradise: An Introductory Selection of the Poems of W. B. Yeats.* London, Macmillan, 1967; New York, Macmillan, 1968.
Editor, *Winter's Tales 14.* London, Macmillan, 1968.

Translator, *The Battle of Maldon and Other Old English Poems.* London, Macmillan, and New York, St. Martin's Press, 1965.
Translator, *Beowulf.* London, Macmillan, and New York, Farrar Straus, 1968.
Translator, *Storm and Other Old English Riddles.* London, Macmillan, and New York, Farrar Straus, 1970.

Kevin Crossley-Holland comments:

Marginally influenced by The Group; an admirer of the best of the "confessional" poets, who have certainly influenced me.

My poetry is concerned with the minutiae of day-to-day life, and with the relation of past to present, person to place (sometimes with a slightly surreal edge), rather than with social issues. Many of my poems are autobiographical, love poems and poems about the relationship of father and son; others celebrate the elements, especially water – I return again and again in my work to North Norfolk, a wide mysterious marshland that cuts men down to size. If this sounds pretentious, my poems are not so; in fact, they do not dare enough. I am under no delusions: if I write half a dozen really good poems in my life, I will have exploited my talent to the full. I make use of traditional forms and have been influenced (in my use of alliteration, for instance) by my love of Old English literature. Yeats too has certainly influenced me.

If the society reflected in Old English poetry now seems alien, many of its moods are wholly familiar, essentially English: an out-and-out heroism, a dogged refusal to surrender, a love of the sea, an enjoyment of melancholy, nostalgia. In translating it, my staple diet has been a non-syllabic four-stress line, controlled by light alliteration. There are plenty of cases, though, where I have not conformed to this pattern; my concern has been to echo rather than slavishly to imitate the originals. My diction inclines to the formal, though it certainly is less formal than that of the Anglo-Saxon poets; it seemed to me important at this time to achieve truly accessible versions of these poems, that eschewed the use of archaisms, inverted word orders, and all "poetic" language. I have not gone out of my way to avoid words that spring from Latin roots, but the emphasis has fallen naturally on words derived from Old English. My translations are, I believe, faithful by and large to the letter of the originals, but it is the mood I have been after. And if I have not caught anything of it, then I have not succeeded in my purpose.

*   *   *

Kevin Crossley-Holland's poetry seems to me a particularly successful example of the "middle style" written by many British poets of the post-war period. This style was basically the invention of the poets of the Movement, but subsequent practitioners have moved away from Movement tenets. They have been attracted, especially, by some of the better Georgians, notably Edward Thomas and Edmund Blunden. Blunden, in fact, supplies a happy comparison where Crossley-Holland is concerned. In both poets there are a natural decorousness and gentleness, a refusal to show off. The result can occasionally be dull, but it is always honest and often tender. In Crossley-Holland's case, the style is leavened by his interest in Anglo-Saxon poetry – he has made many translations from the Anglo-Saxon, including a new version of *Beowulf* and a selection of Anglo-Saxon riddles. Despite this affection for the heroic age, he is not a poet who willingly raises his voice. His tone can perhaps be represented by the brief poem, "A Plea," I quote here:

> This is the time to reduce the volume.
> Listen. You can still just walk
> In the diminishing peaceable-enough copse
> Through green light, amongst under-surfaces.
>
> It is time to do this. Take the leaf
> A singular oblique sunshaft lit
> And come back listening for difference.
> Sound not the screams but each distress.

– Edward Lucie-Smith

CRUICKSHANK, Helen B(urness). Scottish. Born in Montrose, Angus, 15 May 1886. Educated at Montrose Academy. Entered Civil Service 1903: worked for 10 years in London and 30 years in Edinburgh, retired, 1945, as Staff Officer, Department of Health for Scotland. Honorary Secretary, Scottish Centre of P.E.N. for seven years. Life member of Saltire Society and of Scottish Association for Speaking of Verse, and lay member of Society of Scottish Artists. Recipient: Scottish Arts Council Award, 1968. M.A.: Edinburgh University, 1970. Address: 4 Hillview Terrace, Corstorphine, Edinburgh 12, Scotland.

PUBLICATIONS

Verse

Up the Noran Water and Other Scots Poems. London, Methuen, 1934.
Sea Buckthorn. Dunfermline, Fife, Macpherson, 1954.
The Ponnage Pool. Edinburgh, M. Macdonald, 1968.
Collected Poems. Edinburgh, G. Gordon Wright, 1971.

Other

Editor, with Maurice Lindsay, Selected Poems of Marion Angus. Edinburgh, Serif Books, 1950.

Manuscript Collections: Edinburgh University Library; Scottish National Library, Edinburgh.

Critical Study: The Scottish Tradition in Literature by Kurt Wittig, Edinburgh, Oliver and Boyd, 1958.

* * *

For Hugh MacDiarmid's 75th birthday Helen B. Cruickshank wrote a poem including the line, "Ye've 'kept the pottie boilin' this lang time." The phrase applies even more appropriately to herself, for she has been writing poems – chiefly lyrical, in Scots and English – for more than sixty years, that have in them "the breath of hill and sea and bog." Especially in Scots, she has kept the kettle on the boil, relying on the Lowland Scots tongue as she heard it spoken about her. She began to write at a time when excessive devotion to sentiment in traditional Scots verse suggested that this mode had outlived its literary usefulness. But Helen B. Cruickshank's verse – and it is a poetry of feeling – keeps in touch with the actual world. In "Background," the first poem in her book The Ponnage Pool (published in 1968 for her 82nd birthday), a "bairn comin' hame frae schule" on a winter day is met with the words, "Bairn, your blue wi' cauld!" As in the poem to MacDiarmid, the commonplace Scots expression is integrated into the texture of the verse. This reliance on Scots idiom, people and place gives her lyrics an honest character, more important, I think, to their durability than the charm they possess by virtue of her musical ear. In "The Ponnage Pool," the last poem in the book of that name, she goes a step further. She identifies herself with her home-place:

> I am the deep o' the pule,
> The fish, the fisher

and in doing so the verse movement develops tensions appropriate to the idea.

This may also give a hint as to why Helen B. Cruickshank's belief in the continuity of Scots character and speech in no way inhibited her welcoming the experiments of MacDiarmid in verse and Lewis Grassic Gibbon in prose. Her contribution to Scottish Literature cannot, indeed, be assessed without taking into account her perceptive, often courageous, active encouragement of writers of the Scottish Literary Movement of this century.

– George Bruce

CRUZ, Victor Hernández. Puerto Rican. Born in Aguas Buenas, 6 February 1949; emigrated to the United States in 1954. Married; has one son. Formerly, Editor, *Umbra* magazine, New York. Since 1973, Instructor, San Francisco State University. Agent: Georges Borchardt Inc., 145 East 52nd Street, New York, New York 10022. Address: P.O. Box 40148, San Francisco, California 94140, U.S.A.

PUBLICATIONS

Verse

Papo Got His Gun. New York, Calle Once Publications, 1966.
Snaps: Poems. New York, Random House, 1969.
Mainland. New York, Random House, 1972.

Other

Editor, with Herbert Kohl, *Stuff: A Collection of Poems, Visions and Imaginative Happenings from Young Writers in Schools – Opened and Closed.* Cleveland, World, 1970.

Victor Hernández Cruz comments:

My life and work is to clear the smoke – to make things clear – America Vespucci is a strange place with some weird concepts about reality – it is very easy to be confused here. I write from an inner view – realizing that one first understands onself; because I write about myself from myself I write about people because I am. In words I try to make the Universe into the whole that it is – there is only one reality – interpreted many different ways. Many people don't know that they are alive. Words are magic and should not be treated lightly.

*   *   *

Some of Victor Hernández Cruz's poems exhibit the urgency of the new world poets to write stirring and highly motivated work. Others seem vehicles of the poetic-political meld to be read silently, or aloud, throughout the Third and transcending worlds. Such poetry demands validation of older new world ideals:

> when they stop poems
> in the mail & clap
> their hands or dance to
> them
> when women become pregnant
> by the side of poems
> the strangest sounds making
> the river go along.

Mr. Cruz was born in Puerto Rico. However, he grew up in New York City, and much of his work reflects a bilingual ease:

> thoughts in Spanish run through
> the mind
> the buildings seem broken English.

With a combination Latin/Anglo imagery he creates a tense warm lyricism:

> Que Pasa?
> Y los palos
> do not feel at home anymore La luna
> goes round the star dotted cielo? Let's watch
> In this part of Mexico
> Se habla inglish

The poetry of Cruz is filled with humorous, angry, brilliant imagery that makes him one of America's finest young poets.

– Corrine E. Bostic

CUMBERLEGE, Marcus (Crossley). British. Born in Antibes, France, 23 December 1938. Educated at Sherborne School, Dorset; St. John's College, Oxford, B.A. Married; has one daughter. Worked for the British Council in Lima, Peru, 1957–58, 1962–63; Advertising Executive, Ogilvy and Mather, London, 1964–68. Since 1968, English Language Teacher, Lycée International, St. Germain-en-Laye, France. Recipient: Eric Gregory Award, 1967. Address: Lycée International, 78 St. Germain-en-Laye, France.

PUBLICATIONS

Verse

Oases. London, Anvil Press Poetry, 1968.
Poems for Quena and Tabla. Oxford, Carcanet Press, 1970.
Running Towards a New Life. London, Anvil Press Poetry, 1973.
Hear the Wind Blow. London, Anvil Press Poetry, 1974.

Marcus Cumberlege comments:

Major Influences: César Vallejo, the French Symbolists, Garcia Lorca, Rilke, Eliot, Yeats.

Themes: (1) survival of "human beings" in urban society, compassion for the former while satirizing shortcomings of the latter; (2) automatic poetry attempting to situate the poet geographically and define his role as interpreter of mysteries; (3) original poetry in Spanish and French; translation from contemporary Latin American poets.

*   *   *

It might be said that during the last ten years Marcus Cumberlege has been intent upon developing an individual style, experimenting with words, ideas, forms, and the use of diction to obtain effects, and it is only recently that his own voice has begun to break through unmistakably. The result is that his recent collection *Running Towards a New Life*, since it covers a period of about ten years, gives the impression that his work is more uneven than, in fact, it is at the present time. In that sense it shows him at a disadvantage, except in the later poems. Sometimes the influences are a little too obvious in the earlier poems; one can recognise the Auden style and the Brian Patten style, for instance; but there is a calm assurance about the more recent poems. Nevertheless, whatever the style, Cumberlege has always written civilised verse, work that is witty, sophisticated, and rooted in European poetry, demonstrating a wide reading of classical and modern poetry. The polished couplets of his "Mural for the Country Residence of a Latin American President," with its deliberate connection with Eliot's "Prufrock" at the beginning, is still one of the best things he has ever done. His knowledge of technique is remarkable, but his most striking characteristic is a capacity for finding the startlingly apt image or metaphor; when he manages to combine these qualities with a driving theme, he can be quite superb. But having worked his way systematically through a long period of experimentation, Cumberlege is now reaping the benefit and will no doubt produce some first class poetry in the future. He has a firmer control of his material, is manipulating language in a more effective manner, and paying far more attention to precision in statement. The poem "There Are Days" shows his real potentiality.

– Howard Sergeant

CUNNINGHAM, J(ames) V(incent). American. Born in Cumberland, Maryland, 23 August 1911. Educated at St. Mary's College, Kansas, 1928; Stanford University, California, A.B. 1934, Ph.D. 1945. Married the poet Barbara Gibbs in 1937 (divorced, 1942); Dolora Gallagher, 1945 (divorced, 1949); Jessie MacGregor Campbell, 1950; has one daughter. Instructor, Stanford University, 1937–45; Assistant Professor, University of Hawaii, Honolulu, 1945–46, University of Chicago, 1946–52, and University of Virginia, Charlottesville, 1952–53. Since 1953, Professor of English, Brandeis University, Waltham, Massachusetts. Visiting Professor, Harvard University, Cambridge, Massachusetts, 1952; University of Washington, Seattle, 1956; Indiana University, Bloomington, 1961; University of California, Santa

Barbara, 1963. Recipient: Guggenheim Fellowship, 1959, 1967; National Institute of Arts and Letters grant, 1965; National Endowment for the Arts grant, 1966. Address: Department of English, Brandeis University, Waltham, Massachusetts 02154, U.S.A.

PUBLICATIONS

Verse

The Helmsman.   San Francisco, Colt Press, 1942.
The Judge Is Fury.   New York, Swallow Press-Morrow, 1947.
Doctor Drink: Poems.   Cummington, Massachusetts, Cummington Press, 1950.
Trivial, Vulgar and Exalted: Epigrams.   San Francisco, Poems in Folio, 1957.
The Exclusions of a Rhyme: Poems and Epigrams.   Denver, Swallow, 1960.
To What Strangers, What Welcome: A Sequence of Short Poems.   Denver, Swallow, 1964.
Some Salt: Poems and Epigrams . . .   Madison, Wisconsin, Perishable Press, 1967.
The Collected Poems and Epigrams of J. V. Cunningham.   Chicago, Swallow Press, and London, Faber, 1971.

Other

The Quest of the Opal: A Commentary on "The Helmsman."   Denver, Swallow, 1950.
Woe or Wonder: The Emotional Effect of Shakespearean Tragedy.   Denver, University of Denver Press, 1951.
Tradition and Poetic Structure: Essays in Literary History and Criticism.   Denver, Swallow, 1960.
The Journal of John Cardan: Together with The Quest of the Opal and The Problem of Form.   Denver, Swallow, 1964.
The Collected Essays of J. V. Cunningham.   Chicago, Swallow Press, 1974.

Editor, The Renaissance in England.   New York, Harcourt Brace, 1966.
Editor, The Problem of Style.   Greenwich, Connecticut, Fawcett, 1966.
Editor, In Shakespeare's Day.   Greenwich, Connecticut, Fawcett, 1970.

Bibliography: A Bibliography of the Published Writings of J. V. Cunningham by Charles Gullans, Los Angeles, University of California Library, 1973.

Critical Studies: The Poetry of J. V. Cunningham by Yvor Winters, Denver, Swallow, 1961; Connoiseurs of Chaos by Denis Donoghue, New York, Macmillan, 1965; "The Poetry of J. V. Cunningham" by Patrick Cosgrave, in Spectator (London) 23 October 1971; "The Collected Poems and Epigrams" by John Hollander, in New York Times Book Review, 21 November 1971.

*   *   *

In *The Quest of the Opal,* J. V. Cunningham has provided a commentary on his own verse which is so masterly that it is hard for any other critic to follow in his footsteps. The poet, for instance, is well aware of his own difference from most of his contemporaries, and, speaking in the third person, remarks: "Substantially, he viewed himself rather as a professional writer, however laconic, one to whom poetry was verse . . . Verse is a professional activity, social and objective, and its methods and standards are those of craftsmanship. It is a concern of the ordinary human self, and is on the whole within a man's power to do well or not. Its virtues are the civic virtues. If it lacks much, what it does have is ascertainable and can be judged."

Cunningham goes on to say that "the earlier verses in his book were nothing but constructions that offered to the reader certain schemes of experience, certain progressions of thought and feeling from the first line to the last. The later ones were direct statements of something he had to say, given form and definiteness by the technique of verse." Essentially, then, Cunningham tries to compress the complexities of experience into the simplicities of statement, without betraying the one or corrupting the other. The verse which results can seem, as he admits, difficult to many readers, but he contends that it does have a small and specific audience, and that his methods are, therefore, not merely wilful.

Writing which stands so much upon the defensive cannot expect to play a major role in the literature of its time, as Cunningham himself acknowledges. What he has done, however, is to supply a point of reference for his contemporaries, a dry rebuke to their worst extravagancies.

– Edward Lucie-Smith

CURNOW, Allen. New Zealander. Born in Timaru, 17 June 1911. Educated at Christchurch Boys' High School, 1924–28; University of New Zealand, Canterbury, 1929–30, Auckland, 1931–38, B.A. 1938; St. John's College (Anglican theological), Auckland, 1931–33. Married Elizabeth J. LeCren in 1936, has three children; married Jennifer Mary Tole, 1965. Cadet Journalist, *Sun,* Christchurch, 1929–30; Reporter and Sub-Editor, 1935–48, and Dramatic Critic, 1945–47, *The Press,* Christchurch; Member of the News and Sub-Editorial Staff, *News Chronicle,* London, 1949. Lecturer in English, 1951–66, and since 1967, Associate Professor of English, University of Auckland. Recipient: New Zealand State Literary Fund travel award, 1949; Carnegie grant, 1950; New Zealand University Research Committee grant, 1957, 1966; Jessie Mackay Memorial Prize, 1957, 1962; Institute of Contemporary Arts Fellowship, Washington, D.C., 1961; Whittall Fund award, Library of Congress, 1966. Litt.D.: University of Auckland, 1966. Address: 62 Tohunga Crescent, Parnell, Auckland 1, New Zealand.

PUBLICATIONS

Verse

Enemies: Poems 1934–1936. Christchurch, Caxton Press, 1937.
Not in Narrow Seas. Christchurch, Caxton Press, 1939.

Island and Time. Christchurch, Caxton Press, 1941.
Verses, 1941–1942 (as Whim-Wham). Christchurch, Caxton Press, 1942.
Sailing or Drowning. Wellington, Progressive Publishing Society, 1943.
Jack Without Magic. Christchurch, Caxton Press, 1946.
At Dead Low Water, and Sonnets. Christchurch, Caxton Press, 1949.
Poems 1947–1957. Wellington, Mermaid Press, 1957.
A Small Room with Large Windows: Selected Poems. Wellington and London, Oxford University Press, 1962.
Whim Wham Land (as Whim-Wham). Auckland, Blackwood and Janet Paul, 1967.
Trees, Effigies, Moving Objects: A Sequence of 18 Poems. Wellington, Catspaw Press, 1972.
An Abominable Temper and Other Poems. Wellington, Catspaw Press, 1973.
Collected Poems 1933–1973. Wellington, Reed, 1974.

Plays

The Axe: A Verse Tragedy (produced Christchurch, 1948). Christchurch, Caxton Press, 1949.
Moon Section (produced Auckland, 1959).
The Overseas Expert (broadcast, 1961). Included in *Four Plays*, 1972.
Doctor Pom (produced Auckland, 1964).
The Duke's Miracle (broadcast, 1967). Included in *Four Plays*, 1972.
Resident of Nowhere (broadcast, 1969). Included in *Four Plays*, 1972.
Four Plays (includes *The Axe*, *The Overseas Expert*, *The Duke's Miracle*, and *Resident of Nowhere*). Wellington, Reed, 1972.

Radio Plays: *The Overseas Expert*, 1961; *The Duke's Miracle*, 1967; *Resident of Nowhere*, 1969.

Other

Editor, *A Book of New Zealand Verse, 1923–1945*. Christchurch, Caxton Press, 1945; revised edition, 1951.
Editor, *The Penguin Book of New Zealand Verse*. London, Penguin, 1960.

Critical Study: "Allen Curnow's Poetry (Notes Towards a Criticism)" by C. K. Stead, in *Landfall* (Christchurch), March 1963.

Allen Curnow comments:

I don't know of any school I would care to belong to. New Zealand is difficult enough for me.

I don't know anything about "themes," "subjects," etc., only that "ocassions" for poems or plays crop up, as one feels a need (intermittently) to touch something, to check on its existence or one's own.

I don't know about influences either, but sometimes think of Yeats's dictum, "All that is personal soon rots; it must be packed in ice or salt. Ancient salt is best packing." This is bound to be misinterpreted. I would like to be a poet writing verse so radically old that it looks radically new. I would have to be a much better poet than I am.

Twenty years ago I wrote a good few poems "about" New Zealand, as much to find out what I was, as what it was. Worry about one's country is one of the major human worries; of course, one can think of "universality" and worry about that instead, but it's an arid ground for poetry. One learns to live with the oddity of one's country, like Byron's lame foot or Wallace Stevens's insurance company, and these "universal" poems record the learning-process. Poetry won't bear too much accidental stuff, but must have some. Warning: do not exceed the stated dose.

*   *   *

Allen Curnow has been a central figure – *the* central figure – in modern New Zealand poetry. His is a fine talent, but he has a double relevance to the discussion of his country's poetry. His *A Book of New Zealand Verse, 1923–1945*, a selection of poems supported by a long and impressive critical introduction, made apparent for the first time that New Zealand's modern poets had produced a body of work of sufficient quality, and with a flavour sufficiently distinct, to constitute the beginnings of a national tradition. The period of "colonial" literature was over – this was Curnow's point, demonstrated by the fact that poets were no longer romanticising their environment with an eye to, or with the eyes of, English readers, but coming to terms with it as it was in reality, and not least with its limitations. The old whimsies of the "Kowhai Gold" school had been replaced by wit, asperity, modernity and exactness of definition. Curnow's argument was further supported by a re-issue and enlargement of his anthology in 1951, and extended in his 1960 *Penguin Book of New Zealand Verse*.

This critical writing went hand in hand with the writing of his poetry, contributing to the development of his subject matter, which had always (however obscurely personal its origins) reached towards public statement. In the 1930's while still finding his voice, he wrote political and social satire. But his vision of his country was never simple, and his characteristic style as he found it in the forties was one of ironic complexity, brooding over one or another distinctly New Zealand scene or historical event, making its detail sharply present to the senses, yet working at it verbally until its particulars rendered up some broader significance. A sonnet in memory of a cousin killed in North Africa begins:

> Weeping for bones in Africa, I turn
> Our youth over like a dead bird in my hand.

By the end, however, the dead soldier has assumed, not heroic, but national proportions:

> But O if your blood's tongued it must recite

> South Island feats, those tall, snow-country tales
> Among incredulous Tunisian hills.

A recording of a Beethoven quartet becomes "Your 'innermost Beethoven' in the uttermost isles." The skeleton of the extinct moa "on iron crutches" in a South Island museum suggests a vision of the New Zealand poet:

> Not I, some child, born in a marvellous year,
> Will learn the trick of standing upright here.

Even at his most difficult, Curnow's gift for the dazzling phrase arrests and holds attention. Lines such as

> Small gods in shawls of bark, blind, numb, and deaf,
> But buoyant, eastward, in the blaze of surf

have the ring of major statement, even in isolation from the context that gives them meaning.

In his latest poems, most of them written in the mid-1950's, very different occasions, or "subjects," seem to have led Curnow consistently to the same preoccupation: the weighing of objective against subjective, real against ideal. In the real – in the present place and time – and in that alone our salvation, or more simply our satisfaction, lies. It is the pursuit of the ideal that will damn us. The message is not new – nor would it be interesting if it came as a "message." It is in the poetry not as abstraction but as a truth re-discovered in experience. The self is defined as it confronts what exists *out there:*

> A kingfisher's naked arc alight
> Upon a dead stick in the mud
> A scarlet geranium wild on a wet bank
> A man stepping it out in the near distance
> With a dog and a bag.

If James K. Baxter was New Zealand's most fluent and naturally eloquent poet, Allen Curnow is its most sophisticated, witty and complex. Few modern poets have such an array of skills as Curnow can draw upon when the moment permits him a poem.

– C. K. Stead

––––––––––

CURREY, R(alph) N(ixon). British. Born in Mafeking, South Africa, 14 December 1907. Educated in South Africa; Kingswood School, Bath; Wadham College, Oxford, 1927–30, M.A. (honours) in modern history 1930. War Service, 1941–46: Commissioned with the Royal Artillery, Staff Major after 1945, writing and editing Army Bureau of Current Affairs publications. Married the playwright Stella Martin Currey in 1932; has two sons. Senior English Master, 1946–72, and Senior Master for Arts Subjects, 1964–72, Royal Grammar School, Colchester, Essex. Since 1967, President of the Suffolk Poetry Society, Ipswich; since 1972, Member of the Eastern Arts Association Advisory Panel for Literature, Cambridge. Recipient: Viceroy's Prize, 1945; South African Poetry Prize, 1959. Fellow, Royal Society of Literature, 1970. Address: 3 Beverley Road, Colchester, Essex CO3 3NG, England.

PUBLICATIONS

Verse

Tiresias and Other Poems. London, Oxford University Press, 1940.
This Other Planet. London, Routledge, 1945.
Indian Landscape: A Book of Descriptive Poems. London, Routledge, 1947.
The Africa We Knew. Cape Town, David Philip, 1973.

Plays

Radio Plays: *Between Two Worlds*, 1948; *Early Morning in Vaaldorp*, 1961.

Other

Poets of the 1939–1945 War.   London, Longman, 1960; revised edition, 1967.

Editor, with R. V. Gibson, *Poems from India by Members of the Forces.*   Bombay, Oxford University Press, 1945; London, Oxford University Press, 1946.
Editor, *Letters and Other Writings of a Natal Sheriff: Thomas Phipson, 1815–1876.*   Cape   Town   and   London,   Oxford   University   Press, 1968.
Translator, *Formal Spring: French Renaissance Poems of Charles d'Orléans, Villon, Ronsard, du Bellay and Others.*   London, Oxford University Press, 1950.

Critical Studies: *A Critical Survey of South African Poetry in English* by G. M. Miller and Howard Sergeant, Cape Town, Balkema, 1957; by W. G. Saunders, in *South African Poetry: A Critical Anthology*, edited by D. R. Beeton and W. D. Maxwell-Mahon, Pretoria, University of South Africa Press, 1966.

R. N. Currey comments:

It takes a lifetime to discover what kind of poet one is. I appear to be an occasional poet, having written much more at some periods of my life than at others.

In the war I found myself placed, quite unprepared by any previous technical training, in a highly technical branch of warfare, in which destruction was carried out impersonally at a distance. I received from this experience an intense impression of what I take to be the likely warfare of the future, in which it will require a strong effort of imagination on the part of the killer to realize what he is doing. I wrote of this in *This Other Planet* and in *Between Two Worlds*, and am intrigued to find that some of the poems in which I tried to express my response to this are now being anthologized more often than the conventional war poems that found more favour at the time.

When I was posted to India, I found there, still going on, the Middle Ages I had read about when studying History at Oxford. Indians still went on pilgrimage, as people did in the England of Chaucer's time, and my anti-aircraft gunners, who had the same names as the gods in the Indian temples, belonged to the same pre-industrial world. The excitement of this theme is still with me, and I hope to write about it again. Translating French poems, of the Renaissance and Middle Ages, has also given me an entry into those pre-industrial times; and I am glad to find that these poems, too, have the vitality that gets them reprinted many years after first being published.

I have written other topographical poems about places of special importance to me. South Africa, where I spent my boyhood, and where I have a long family connexion, has underlined contrasts and aroused tensions of the sort that produce poetry. *The Africa We Knew* is a book of South African poems, most of which have been printed and broadcast both in England and in South Africa. I recently edited the letters of a great-grandfather who went to South Africa in 1849, and found much that called for a poetical rather than a historical treatment. This I hope to give it at some time.

I find that I have to go to a new country to discover the one in which I live, to move for a while into a different period in order to come to terms with the present. Both North Africa and the Western United States have given me new viewpoints from which to see the imperial world in which I grew up.

I have published poems, at different times in my life, in different countries, mainly in England, but also in the United States, India, South Africa and Ireland. For many years I have done my writing and broadcasting alongside teaching English and running an English Department at a grammar school, but have now retired to do more writing. There is a great deal that I want to do.

*   *   *

T. S. Eliot said of R. N. Currey that he was the best war-poet, in the precise sense of the word, that World War II produced. This was high praise since between 1939 and 1945 some very distinguished verse appeared in the little reviews and the numerous anthologies of the period. But the war poems, collected in his volume *This Other Planet*, reconsidered after nearly a quarter of a century, seem still to hold the essence of their period, in what was felt and thought by those who were the *dramatis personae* of "this damned unnatural sort of war," where so much was remote and impersonal. Like the enemy pilot:

> To us he is no more than a machine
> Shown on an instrument; what can he mean
> In human terms? – a man, somebody's son,
> Proud of his skill; compact of flesh and bone,
> Fragile as Icarus – and our desire
> To see that damned machine come down on fire.

It was as a war poet that Currey really established his reputation, and it is significant that he was chosen by the British Council to write their publication *Poets of the 1939–1945 War*. Nevertheless, it is largely as a South African poet that he has developed, finding his themes in, and feeding his imagination on, the physical Africa that he knew as a boy and on the history of men and things in that complicated but fascinating Eur-African world with its odd duality:

> Eating our Christmas pudding beneath the grace
> Of feminine willows on the vivid grass

or

> My father, all that tawny homeward run,
> Remembering snow as I remember sun.

Although Currey has lived most of his adult life in Britain, he goes home from time to time, and his long work, *Early Morning in Vaaldorp*, successfully broadcast by the BBC, is in a sense a tribute to his South African *oeuvres*, "which could not have been written if I had not come from a long South African tradition and spent most of my impressionable years there." North Africa, particularly Morocco, has been responsible for other impressive poems by Currey, who claims to be able to see the Southern Cross from both ends of the Dark Continent, a kind of unifying light in his work. India, too, where much of his war was spent, makes a further link in this chain of poetic topography.

Some of his most memorable poem, of love particularly, have a lyric poignancy that, devoid of any particular context of time or place, achieves a universality of appeal. Such is his beautifully constructed "Song," revealing how truth emerges only from the tug-of-war of contrasts:

> There is no joy in water apart from the sun,
> There is no beauty not emphasized by death,
> No meaning in home if exile were unknown;
> A man who lives in a thermostat lives beneath
> A bell of glass alone with the smell of death.

In such poems as these, Currey reveals himself as a poet of considerable artistry, taking infinite pains with his verse-making to derive the maximum impact from word or image, an observer of life or landscape with very particular vision.

– Roy Macnab

DALE, Peter (John). British. Born in Addlestone, Surrey, 21 August 1938. Educated at Strode's School, Egham, Surrey; St. Peter's College, Oxford, 1960–63, B.A. (honours) in English 1963. Married Pauline Strouvelle in 1963; has two children. English Master, 1965–71, and Head of English, 1971–72, Glastonbury High School, Sutton, Surrey. Since 1972, Head of English, Hinchley Wood School, Surrey. Since 1971, Associate Editor, *Agenda* magazine, London. Recipient: Arts Council bursary, 1969. Agent: David Higham Associates, 5–8 Lower John Street, Golden Square, London W1R 3PE. Address: 10 Selwood Road, Sutton, Surrey, England.

PUBLICATIONS

Verse

Nerve: Poems. Privately printed, 1959.
Walk from the House. Oxford, Fantasy Press, 1962.
The Storms. London, Macmillan, and Chester Springs, Pennsylvania, Dufour, 1968.
Mortal Fire. London, Macmillan, and Chester Springs, Pennsylvania, Dufour, 1970.
The Legacy and Other Poems of Francois Villon. London, Agenda Editions, 1971; revised edition, as *The Legacy, The Testament and Other Poems*, London, Macmillan, and New York, St. Martin's Press, 1973.
The Seasons of Cankam. London, Agenda Editions, 1974.

Critical Study: "Notes on the Poetry of Peter Dale" by William Cookson, in *Agenda* (London), viii, 3–4, 1970.

Peter Dale comments:

I cannot make a statement about my work which I have any confidence that I would still agree with by the time this volume is printed. It would be improper to try to guess what one's skills and learnings were and therefore impossible to say how they have developed, or will. At the moment I am experimenting with forms in *vers libre* but I cannot say how successfully or how long I shall continue with them. Rationalizing about one's work probably damages it by making one self-conscious the next time one has to write but this is not to say that poetry is entirely intuitive or instinctive; the creative and critical faculties are probably concurrent once at work. The poems will have to speak for themselves.

*   *   *

Peter Dale took as epigraph to his first hardback collection, *The Storms* (Macmillan, 1968), a line of William Blake, "The most sublime act is to set another before you." He is obsessed with two things in his poetry: the problem of suffering and the problem of "knowing" another person. The first is worked out in various poems based on jobs in hospitals; the second in love poems and friendship poems. In the most recent work these two themes fuse in poems about family life. His early booklet, *Walk from the House* (1962), criticizes the Christian view: "I would erect suffering into a belief. . . ." This idealisation is rejected and other poems in that book and *The Storms* set suffering sometimes savagely in its animal/human context. "Just Visiting" represents the human difficulties in attending the sick:

> And some of them have indolent golden hair.
> Over there a woman is dying, the line
> of used laughter hung in bands on the lean
> bones. And what you say I cannot hear.

In this context, the poetry is more and more concerned with the uselessness of compassion to alleviate pain, to "know" another's suffering. "Passing the Gates" and "Patient in a Ward" are two poems that analyse this.

The problem of knowing another person runs through the same books and is perhaps best summed up in the title poem "The Storms" that deals with a painter and writer who tried to "record" the same tree and their troubled friendship. The theme occurs more fully in "Having No Alternative" (*Agenda*, Spring 1969), part of Mr. Dale's third book, *Mortal Fire* (1970), where drug addiction strains a friendship to breaking point. The final poem in the sequence, "Thinking of Writing a Letter," ends with a sense of loneliness, distances and desolation which is deeply moving.

Old themes, but what is fresh is the obsessive power of the poems, their direct yet subtle unfolding of the situations. Peter Dale is a realist and portrays the world, recognisable and tragic. There are a hardness and honesty about his poetry which preclude sentimentality. Work which is rootedly personal and yet never runs the risk of embarrassing the reader is rare. What T. S. Eliot has called "private experience at its greatest intensity becoming universal" seems an appropriate description. Much of this power comes from the quiet, concealed control of technique. The central prosodic quality of these poems is freedom within form. The forms range from traditional stanzas like Chaucerians through experiments with various rhyme techniques to a free verse which is moving in its rhythm while owing little to

Pound, Eliot or Williams. And always there is the individual tone of a voice talking quietly with a great force of controlled emotion behind the words. I quote from "Unaddressed Letter":

> Now it is autumn . . . And rain . . . Big drops you can trace.
> I notice how one drop's enough to tear
> an amber leaf out of the brittle trees.
> I suppose much the same happened last year,
> but it is now I notice watching a caricature
> of your face talking to myself as I stare
> out of the window where the puddles stir.

Along with the range of forms goes a range of approach and tone. Mr. Dale can manage dramatic monologue with great variety: there is the detached irony of "Afternoon Operating List" – early version in *Walk from the House* – and the powerful involvement of "It Is Finished" (*Mortal Fire*). There are the humorous "Obtainable at All Good Herbalists," the quiet gratitude of "Dedication," and the Imagist concision of "Last Respects."

The straightforwardness and directness of the finest of Peter Dale's poems often veil a more subtle undercurrent to the feeling and the thought. They stand the acid tests that once read, they remain in the mind, and when reread, they do not bore, but gain in strength. The blurb of *The Storms* suggests that while the poems are haunting, there are no memorable lines. This is partly due to method; the shifting caesuras and constant overrunning of lines prevent this. But what is memorable is the clarity and delicacy of the imagery:

> and underwings extend wood-ember white.

or:

> Across the playing fields the amber leaves
> shine oldgold through the frost.

or:

> Your presence, love,
> like the underlight of trees
> within a wood.

Since *Mortal Fire* Dale has further widened his scope by translating almost the complete works of François Villon. This is a strict metrical translation which faithfully reproduces the rhyme schemes of the original – an incredibly difficult task in English. By this method, Dale has recreated the spirit of Villon with sometimes electric energy. He has written, in my opinion, the finest English Villon we are likely to get – certainly no other version has expressed with such power the humour, word-play and swift changes of tone of the French together with its elegiac lyricism. The difference between Dale's Villon and his own poetry is a good measure of the breadth and versatility of his writing. It's impossible to quote this translation adequately by a few lines, but perhaps some of its quality comes across in this stanza from *The Testament:*

> My days are swiftly spent like ends
> the weaver trims off at a stroke
> with a burning straw. A thread extends
> a bit too far beyond the yoke
> and goes up in a puff of smoke;
> says Job. So I no longer fear
> what twists and turns of fate provoke
> for death's the level of all things here.

343

Peter Dale has probably produced a greater variety and extent of work which will endure than other poets of his generation. Undeflected by fashions and influences, his poetry is instantly recognisable. The loudest voices soon grow hoarse.

– William Cookson

DALLAS, Ruth. New Zealander. Born in Invercargill, New Zealand, 29 September 1919. Recipient: New Zealand Literary Fund Achievement Award, 1962; Robert Burns Fellowship, University of Otago, 1968. Address: 448 Leith Street, Dunedin, New Zealand.

PUBLICATIONS

Verse

Country Road and Other Poems 1947–52. Christchurch, Caxton Press, 1953.
The Turning Wheel. Christchurch, Caxton Press, 1961.
Experiment in Form. Dunedin, Otago University Bibliography Room, 1964.
Day Book: Poems of a Year. Christchurch, Caxton Press, 1966.
Shadow Show: Poems. Christchurch, Caxton Press, 1968.

Other

The Children in the Bush (juvenile). London, Methuen, 1969.
Ragamuffin Scarecrow (juvenile). Dunedin, Otago University Bibliography Room, 1969.
A Dog Called Wig (juvenile). London, Methuen, 1970.
The Wild Boy in the Bush (juvenile). London, Methuen, 1971.
The Big Flood in the Bush (juvenile). London, Methuen, 1972.
The House on the Cliffs (juvenile). London, Methuen, 1975.

Critical Studies: by James Bertram in *Landfall 29* and *62* (Christchurch), March 1954 and June 1962.

Ruth Dallas comments:

I am sometimes rather frowningly called a "nature poet"; but I have never lived in a large city and been separated from the life of the earth and the coming up and going down of the sun in unpolluted skies; so I take my imagery where I find it. I have tried to keep in the forefront of my mind my position in space and time; I want never to forget that I am on a remote small planet in space, and never to forget that I am on it at present and must soon leave. And who is to say that I am to write 20th century poetry, or any other kind of poetry? It is chance that I was born in the 20th century and not the 10th, and chance that I was born in New Zealand and not Scandinavia or China. I care nothing for fashion in poetry and think a poem should be as free as one of the far-ranging seabirds I have watched by the hour flying in storm and calm about the coasts of New Zealand. A bird is not always flying; when it is still it is very still; but you know what it can do. Perhaps for this reason I have been attracted to the ancient meditative poems of the Chinese and Japanese, who used words with as much thought as they used the brush-strokes from which their poems are hardly separable. I, too, like to use words sparingly, and to make them carry as many overtones as possible, but all should seem spontaneous. A poem is a human utterance, like dance and song, or an involuntary cry. What would please me most would be to find that my poems appeared effortless, however hard I work on them. But if I fail, it is difficult to believe that it matters. Poetry runs in our veins, and over the centuries will flower now here, now there. If it does not come from my pen it will come from another's.

*   *   *

With *Country Road* Ruth Dallas was at once established (and typed) as a "nature-poet" of the Southland region – New Zealand's wilder "Lake District," with its small farms, lonely coasts, and dark brooding beech-forests. Her work seemed the instinctive and untutored expression of a talent reared in isolation, sensitive to the interplay of natural forces and the intimacies of a constricting domestic situation (she was early threatend with blindness, and long cared for an ailing mother: see "Beginnings," by Ruth Dallas, *Landfall 76*, December, 1965) and content to express these themes in mild and rather unadventurous lyrical forms. This was a respectable achievement, and such poems as "Milking Before Dawn," "Grandmother and Child," "The World's Centre," soon became stock New Zealand anthology pieces; thereafter her work was strangely neglected.

But The Turning Wheel revealed a much more restless and capacious mind, responding especially to the reconciling influences of Buddhism and oriental thought. Her "Letter to a Chinese Poet" (Po Chü-I) is an ambitious sequence in which local and personal material is assimilated into a cultural and metaphysical sunthesis of remarkable power and intensity, rivalled in scope (for a New Zealand woman poet) only by the best work of Ursula Bethell. Other poems in this volume, and in *Day Book*, show a persistent and dedicated interest in formal verse experiment: short, concentrated pieces in which language is distilled to a final clarity. Ruth Dallas is one of the most independent and "unfashionable" of New Zealand writers: she has cultivated chiefly her own eclectic tradition of "permanent" poetry; but the dedication of two of her volumes to Basil Dowling and Charles Brasch shows where her affinities lie. Her own purity of diction and clear singing note seem likely to preserve her work when much more aggressively modern verse is forgotten.

– James Bertram

DANA, Robert (Patrick). American. Born in Allston, Massachusetts, 2 June 1929. Educated at Drake University, Des Moines, Iowa, B.A. 1951; University of Iowa, Iowa City, M.A. 1953. Served as a radioman in the United States Navy, 1946–48. Has three children. Since 1953, Member of the English Department, currently Professor of English, Cornell College, Mt. Vernon, Iowa. Editor, Hillside Press, 1957–67, and *The North American Review*, 1964–68, Mt. Vernon, Iowa. Recipient: Danforth grant, 1959; Rinehart Foundation Fellowship, 1960; Ford-ACM grant, 1966. Address: 613 Second Avenue South, Mt. Vernon, Iowa 52314, U.S.A.

PUBLICATIONS

Verse

My Glass Brother and Other Poems. Iowa City, Stone Wall Press, 1957.
The Dark Flags of Waking. Iowa City, Qara Press, 1964.
Journeys from the Skin: A Poem in Two Parts. Iowa City, Hundred Pound Press, 1966.
Some Versions of Silence: Poems. New York, Norton, 1967.
The Power of the Visible. Chicago, Swallow Press, 1971.
The Watergate Elegy. Chicago, Wine Press, 1973.
Tryptych. Chicago, Wine Press, 1974.

Bibliography: *Voyages to the Inland Sea III*, edited by John Judson, La Crosse, University of Wisconsin Press, 1973.

Critical Study: "A World That Comes Apart like a Surprise" by Anselm Hollo, in *New Letters* (Kansas City, Missouri), Summer 1973.

Robert Dana comments:

I see myself as a poet – I don't believe in poets as prophets, or priests, or even as people of superior intelligence and feeling. Though I'm sure I once did and once in a while still do. Ultimately, I think, I believe what Auden and Cunningham have believed before me – that the poet's only magic is with words. He begins life with a natural gift for handling them and hearing them. He loves them for their sounds, their taste, their soft or their steel feel. And for their enduring strangeness. Each word has, for him, its own perfect story.

Much later, when the poet begins to develop a style, he comes to recognize that style is not just a way of saying things but a way of seeing things. And seeing them with the whole being at once. Poetry is felt thought, Eliot once said. And so it is. But being both at once, it is neither. A poem is an experience of a total kind in which the transitory in our existence passes into permanence.

*   *   *

Robert Dana crafts in irony the perishing world as it becomes part of his inner-life, charting this country's taste for concrete in images "Unlikely as Chicago," the American view of nature:

Pigs blister the hillside . . .
Morning may strike us anywhere.

Separate, but not separated from that, as in a never-consummated divorce, Dana looks for balance in another direction, towards the T'ang poets he translates or to

> The grace of simple food . . .
> . . . the table wooden as the loneliness of plain fact
>
> And bread for the moon
> the heart's small loaf.

Sometimes the tension between these worlds is manifest in his silences, sometimes it's in the "zag zag zag of sodium lamps / blue across the causeways," sometimes it's in the precision of an elegant image. His technical skill carries it through a range of modern poetic strategies.

In Pound's terms, Robert Dana is a master rather than an inventor, moving through a variety of techniques and images, frequently using them better than their originators. His first book contains a tense world, sparse, attenuated details of vivid intensity, controlled word-by-word, his technique at its best nearly equal to Creeley's at *his* best. Dana works primarily with resonances, articulate matter accusing itself across silences.

In his second book, the poetry becomes metamorphic, turns toward dreams:

> And I am driving into my own sleep
> of white chickens
> past barnyard harvests of junked cars
> the wind slumps through the empty eyes of cows.

The landscape begins to flash surrealistically, Los Angeles slumps into the ocean after nine days rain, Kennedy is assassinated again, "razors could not cut the rain from the glass." Without reveling in vatic zeal or surreal petulance, however, the poet

> . . . whistles under the true sky of his troubles
> walking slowly
> inside himself

realizing that regardless of the emotions that flood him, he gains only a measured wisdom:

> I see that I am what I always was
> that ordinary man on his front steps
> bewildered under the bright mess of the heavens
> by the fierce indecipherable language of its stars.

It is this balance, or candidness, that more and more characterizes Dana's recent poetry, with its growing breadth of concern, its remarkable sureness of technique: one learns to have confidence in this voice.

– Edward B. Germain

DANIELLS, Roy. Canadian. Born in London, England, 6 April 1902; emigrated to Canada in 1910. Educated at the University of British Columbia, Vancouver, B.A.

1930; University of Toronto, M.A. 1931, Ph.D. 1936. Married Laurenda Francis in 1948; has two children. Head of the Department of English, University of Manitoba, Winnipeg, 1937–46. Head of the Department of English, 1948–65, and since 1965, University Professor of English, University of British Columbia. Recipient: Lorne Pierce Medal, 1970. LL.D.: University of Toronto, 1964; Queen's University, Kingston, Ontario, 1964; D.Litt.: McMaster University, Hamilton, Ontario, 1970; University of Windsor, Ontario, 1971. President, Royal Society of Canada, 1970–71. Companion of the Order of Canada, 1972. Address: 1741 Allison Road, Vancouver V6T 1S7, British Columbia, Canada.

PUBLICATIONS

Verse

> *Deeper into the Forest.*   Toronto, McClelland and Stewart, 1948.
> *The Chequered Shade.*   Toronto, McClelland and Stewart, 1963.

Other

> *Milton, Mannerism and Baroque.*   Toronto, University of Toronto Press, 1963.
> *Alexander Mackenzie and the North West.*   London, Faber, and New York, Barnes and Noble, 1969.

> Editor, *A Serious and Pathetical Contemplation of the Mercies of God, in Several Most Devout and Sublime Thanksgivings for the Same. . .*, by Thomas Traherne.   Toronto, University of Toronto Press, 1941.
> Editor, with others, and contributor, *Literary History of Canada.*   Toronto, University of Toronto Press, 1965.

Roy Daniells comments:

Strongest influences have been religion, Canadian history and travel in Europe. Most poems are sonnets. The influence of Milton and Marvell is apparent.

*   *   *

Roy Daniells is a scholar and a critic, a Miltonist who has also written eloquently on the Canadian traveller Alexander Mackenzie, and this breadth of interest not only defines the quality of his humanism, but also reflects the apparent contradictions within his poetry. In poetry, as in scholarship, he appears at first to be a traditionalist, until one discovers that, just as his thought roves over whole Canadas of speculation, so his verse achieves, through the use of tried forms, that idiosyncratic quality which marks the work of all truly religious poets. His history of publication spans from the Forties to the Sixties, but he belongs to no school and is hard to place securely in any decade. His output has been small and slow – one book, *Deeper into the Forest*, published when he was 46, and a second, *The Chequered Shade*, published when he had just passed 60. *Deeper into the Forest* contained one memorable long poem in quatrains, "Farewell to Winnipeg," in which Daniells built, around the Canadian folk hero Louis Riel, an elaborate meditation on the world in his time, but most of his poems have been sonnets, and he has adapted this form to his own uses with a virtuosity rare among modern poets. Undoubtedly the best of his sonnets are those in *The Chequered Shade*; the form is traditional, but the way of speaking is contemporary, and the human predicament is seen within the frame and form with the eyes of a modern man. Particularly in the central sequence, based on texts from The Psalms and the New Testament, the agony of endurance that marks man's relationship to whatever is not himself is celebrated, often with an irradiating humour, always with a curiously irreverent reverence.

– George Woodcock

DAS, D(eb) K(umar). Indian. Born in Calcutta, 22 December 1935. Educated at St. Xavier's College, Calcutta University (Quinlan Medallist, 1955; Tata Fellowship, 1955), B.A. (honours) 1955; Queens' College, Cambridge, B.A. 1958, M.A. 1962. Management Staff, I.C.I., Calcutta, 1959–61; Teaching Assistant, University of Washington, Seattle, 1961–63; Instructor, then Superintendent, S.O.I.C., Seattle, 1967–70; Deputy Director, then Director of Research and Planning, State Board for Community College Education, Seattle, 1970–72. Since 1972, Director, United States National Utilization Project for post-secondary education, Seattle. Broadcaster, Viewpoint radio program, for two years. Paintings exhibited in India and the United States. Agent: P. Lal, c/o Writers Workshop, 162–92 Lake Gardens, Calcutta 45, India. Address: 3105½ Eastlake Avenue E., Seattle, Washington 98102, U.S.A.

PUBLICATIONS

Verse

    The Night Before Us: Poems. Calcutta, Writers Workshop, 1960.
    Through a Glass Darkly: Poems. Calcutta, Writers Workshop, 1965.
    The Eyes of Autumn: An Experiment in Poetry. Calcutta, Writers Workshop, 1968.
    The Four Labyrinths. Calcutta, Writers Workshop, 1969.
    The Fire Canto. Calcutta, Writers Workshop, 1971.

Other

    Navbharat Papers: A Political Programme for a New India. Seattle, San Vito Press, 1968.
    Freedom and Reality, Parts I to VI. Seattle, privately printed, 1968.
    The First Philosopher: Yājñavalka. Seattle, San Vito Press, 1971.
    The Agony of Arjun and Other Essays. Seattle, privately printed, 1971.
    Svatvavāda: Towards a Theory of Property, 2000 B.C.–1800 A.D.: An Essay in Three Parts. Privately printed, 1972.

An Essay on the Forms of Individualism. Seattle, SFSC Press, 1973.
What Final Frontier? or, The Future of Man in Space. Seattle, SFSC Press, 1973.
Beginnings of Human Thought: The Rig Vedas. Seattle, SFSC Press, 1973.

Translator, *Two Upaniśads: Iśa and Kena.* Calcutta, Writers Workshop, 1969.
Translator, *Sankarāchārya: A Discourse on the Real Nature of Self.* Calcutta, Writers Workshop, 1970.
Translator, *Jabala and Paingaba Upanisads.* Calcutta, Writers Workshop, 1974.

D. K. Das comments:

My interest is divided about equally between *writing* (in all forms), *painting* (have had several one-man exhibitions in India and U.S.A.), and *research/teaching* in mathematics/economics.

Conflict is a basic theme in my poetry; that between past and future, order and anarchy, passion and reason – with war as an extension of this contemporary human condition. My pre-suppositions are those of the *Bhagavad Gita*; by image as well as reference, I have tried to translate into contemporary terms its message that centrality, being, even meaning, can be found in the *heart* of conflict; the "eye of the storm," its still centre. Space exploration and technological images/themes appear frequently in my poetry, because of my search for modern metaphors, and a contemporary frame of reference. Other than Indian philosophy (especially Vedanta), the strongest influences on my work were undoubtedly T. S. Eliot and W. H. Auden; my mathematical training also influenced my language and "poetic logic"; Albert Camus' *Myth of Sisyphus* also entered many of my poetic intuitions. I am also experimenting with poetic form, trying to create small and large poetic formats capable of carrying poetic *as well as* metaphysical meaning.

*   *   *

Writer, poet, and economist, educated at St. Xavier's College and Cambridge, D. K. Das, in 1958, helped found Calcutta's Writers Workshop whose purpose was to discuss, encourage and publish Indo-English writing. Exceptionally, he often used traditional verse-forms – most successfully, blank verse, though rhyme sometimes adds irony or piquancy.

He acknowledges influences from Eliot, Auden, and Camus, but more basically the Bhagavat-Gita and Vedanta classics (he has translated upanisads, and Sankarācharyā's *A Discourse on the Real Nature of Self*). He uses his logical-mathematical training to organize poems as penetrations from conflicts and paradoxes into cores of central meaning – the "still point" at the heart of every storm. This may be sardonic – to improve the army computer, which, one factor missing, fire-bombs its own unit then duly notifies next-of-kin, he suggests creating "a special digit / for machine error's contradiction . . . / a voice that click-clacked error, to the last." More seriously, in "Descartes' God" God's "death" might logically prove Descartes did not exist – or was he wrong, for the wrong reasons, and so logically, right: "Man's mind was a parasite / In symbiosis with a word called God."

Words, like God, are matters of faith. Poets coin names to keep events whole, lest historians simplify them – yet in saying they "mean" feelings or facts, "we are only / crossing our fingers – / Praying that those three blind / movings / (words, feelings, facts) / Are moving Together, finitely."

The Fire Canto, Das's most successful attempt at· combining "poetic . . . [and] metaphysical meaning," finds Fire the primal substance, man's mind the "Fire of this forever universe," whose burning, "we being merely Fire-bearers must affirm; in order to be and to become Ourselves."

Das found it increasing hard to so affirm in India's "clockwork existence"; it had "too many anxious excuses for everything / Except the freedom of the firefly's search / . . . Truth repeated two hundred thousand times / until its words were only incantations." In 1968 he went to Seattle to teach economics and math to ghetto children. He continued to send to Writers Workshop poems, stories and translations, but – no doubt for this desertion – Pritish Nandy pointedly omitted him from his 1972 anthology of Indo-English poetry.

– George McElroy

DAS, Kamala. Pseudonym: Madhavikutty. Indian. Born in Malabar, South India, 31 March 1934. Privately educated. Married K. Madhava Das in 1949; has three sons. Recipient: P.E.N. Prize, 1964; Kerala Sahitya Academy Award, for fiction, 1969. Address: c/o K. Madhava Das, The Reserve Bank of India, Bombay 1, India.

PUBLICATIONS

Verse

Summer in Calcutta: Fifty Poems.   Delhi, Everest Press, 1965.
The Descendants.   Calcutta, Writers Workshop, 1967.
The Old Playhouse.   Madras, Longman, 1973.

Short Stories

Pathu Kathakal (Ten Stories), *Tharisunilam* (Fallow Fields), *Narachirukal Parakkumbol* (When the Bats Fly), *Ente Snehita Aruna* (My Friend Aruna), *Chuvanna Pavada* (The Red Skirt), *Thanuppu* (Cold), *Rajavinte Premabajanam* (The King's Beloved), *Premathinte Vilapa Kavyam* (Requiem for a Love), *Mathilukal* (Walls).   Trichur, Kerala, Current Books, 1953–72.

Other

Driksakshi Panna (Eyewitness) (juvenile).   Madras, Longman, 1973.

Critical Study: Review by John Bernard, in *Journal of Commonwealth Literature* (Leeds), 1967.

Kamala Das comments:

(1970) I began to write poetry with the ignoble aim of wooing a man. There is therefore a lot of love in my poems. I feel forced to be honest in my poetry. I have read very little poetry. I do not think that I have been influenced by any poet. I have liked to read Kalidasa. When I compose poetry, whispering the words to myself, my ear helps to discipline the verse. Afterwards, I count the syllables. I like poetry to be tidy and disciplined.

(1974) My grand-uncle is Nalapat Narayana Menon, the well-known poet–philosopher of Malabar. My mother is the well-known poetess Nalapat Balamani Amma. I belong to the matriarchal community of Nayars. Our ancestral house (Nalapat House) is more than 400 years old and contains valuable palm-leaf manuscripts like the *Varahasamhita, Susrutha Samhita,* and books of mantras.

As I have no degree to add to my name, my readers considered me in the beginning like a cripple. My writing was like the paintings done by "foot and mouth" painters or like the baskets made by the blind. I received some admiration, but the critics, well-known academicians, tore my writing to shreds. This only made my readers love me more. All I have wanted to do is to be real and honest to my readers.

*   *   *

Mrs. Kamala Das was widely noticed from the very start of her literary career because she was the first Indian woman writing in English to speak frankly about sex. It would be unfair to suggest that her verse had no other interest. On the contrary, it attracted by its spontaneity and freshness, its fiery tone, and its confession of intensely human suffering:

> I am a freak. It's only
> To save my face, I flaunt, at
> Times, a grand flamboyant lust.

As woman, as Indian, and as poet, Mrs. Das finds tyrannical roles thrust on her which she resists strongly. She could easily have been the spokesman of a generation, except that most of her dilemmas seem personal rather than social. And she is no craftsman. Her memorable statements are thrown out at random, preceded and followed by loose, careless images and muddled rhythms. Her poems are essentially formless. Their power derives from the inner urgency of her utterance, the pressure of her conflicts and the pathos of her helplessness. The indictment of Indian society implicit in some of her poems has a tragic resonance:

> When
> I asked for love, not knowing what else to ask
> For, he drew a youth of sixteen into the
> Bedroom and closed the door.

The improvised air of these lines is characteristic of Mrs. Das. Her intellectual interests are not very wide. The redemption of her poetry from its own limits is achieved by the elemental note she strikes from time to time, a note which is completely convincing and moving.

– Nissim Ezekiel

DAVIE, Donald (Alfred). British. Born in Barnsley, Yorkshire, 17 July 1922. Educated at Barnsley Grammar School; St. Catharine's College, Cambridge, B.A. 1947, M.A. 1949, Ph.D. 1951. Served in the Royal Navy, 1941–46. Married Doreen John in 1945; has three children. Lecturer in English, 1950–57, and Fellow of Trinity College, 1954–57, Dublin University; Lecturer in English, 1958–64, and Fellow of Gonville and Caius College, 1959–64, Cambridge University; Professor of English, 1964–68, and Pro-Vice-Chancellor, 1965–68, University of Essex, Wivenhoe. Since 1968, Professor of English, Stanford University, California. Visiting Professor, University of California, Santa Barbara, 1957–58; British Council Lecturer, Budapest, 1961; Elliston Lecturer, University of Cincinnati, 1963. Recipient: Guggenheim Fellowship, 1973. Honorary Fellow, St. Catharine's College, Cambridge, 1973; Fellow, American Academy of Arts and Sciences, 1973. Address: Department of English, Stanford University, Stanford, California 94305, U.S.A.

PUBLICATIONS

Verse

(Poems). Oxford, Fantasy Press, 1954.
Brides of Reason. Oxford, Fantasy Press, 1955.
A Winter Talent and Other Poems. London, Routledge, 1957.
The Forests of Lithuania, adapted from a poem by Adam Mickiewicz. Hessle, Yorkshire, Marvell Press, 1959.
A Sequence for Francis Parkman. Hessle, Yorkshire, Marvell Press, 1961.
New and Selected Poems. Middletown, Connecticut, Wesleyan University Press, 1961.
Events and Wisdoms: Poems 1957–1963. London, Routledge, 1964; Middletown, Connecticut, Wesleyan University Press, 1965.
Poems. London, Turret Books, 1969.
Essex Poems 1963–1967. London, Routledge, 1969.
Six Epistles to Eva Hesse. London, London Magazine Editions, 1970.
Collected Poems, 1950–1970. London, Routledge, and New York, Oxford University Press, 1972.
Orpheus. London, Poem-of-the-Month Club, 1974.
The Shires: Poems. London, Routledge, 1974.

Other

Purity of Diction in English Verse. London, Chatto and Windus, 1952; New York, Oxford University Press, 1953.
Articulate Energy: An Enquiry into the Syntax of English Poetry. London, Routledge, 1955; New York, Harcourt Brace, 1958.
The Heyday of Sir Walter Scott. London, Routledge, and New York, Barnes and Noble, 1961.
The Language of Science and the Language of Literature, 1700–1740. London, and New York, Sheed and Ward, 1963.
Ezra Pound: Poet as Sculptor. London, Routledge, and New York, Oxford University Press, 1964.
Thomas Hardy and British Poetry. New York, Oxford University Press, 1972; London, Routledge, 1973.
The Augustan Lyric. London, Heinemann, 1974.

Editor, *The Victims of Whiggery*, by George Loveless. Hobart, Tasmania, privately printed, 1946.

Editor, *The Late Augustans: Longer Poems of the Later Eighteenth Century.* London, Heinemann, and New York, Macmillan, 1958.

Editor, *Poems: Poetry Supplement.* London, Poetry Book Society, 1960.

Editor, *Poetics Poetyka.* Warsaw, Panstwowe Wydawn, 1961.

Editor, *Selected Poems of Wordsworth.* London, Harrap, 1962.

Editor, *Russian Literature and Modern English Fiction: A Collection of Critical Essays.* Chicago, University of Chicago Press, 1965.

Editor, with Angela Livingstone, *Pasternak.* London, Macmillan, 1969.

Editor, "Thomas Hardy Issue" of *Agenda* (London), Spring–Summer 1972.

Translator, *The Poems of Doctor Zhivago*, by Boris Pasternak. Manchester, Manchester University Press, and New York, Barnes and Noble, 1965.

Manuscript Collection: University of Essex, Wivenhoe.

Critical Studies: by Calvin Bedient, in *The Iowa Review* (Iowa City), 1971; "A Breakthrough into Spaciousness" by Donald Greene, in *Queen's Quarterly* (Kingston, Ontario), 1973.

*   *   *

There has been a tendency to regard Donald Davie's presence in the *New Lines* anthology as merely contingent, an accident of literary history. It is true that Davie never had some of the more disagreeable characteristics of the Movement – its cult of drabness and fear of any rich artistic effect, its pawky attitude towards experimentalism, its easygoing laodicean poses. On the other hand he shared some salient features of the New Line tone and manner. His earlier poems were verbally dense, almost cluttered in the Empson fashion with semantic collisions and tautly stretched grammar. "The Nonconformist" is lighter than most of the work represented in *A Winter Talent,* brisk social satire written in neat antithetical clauses. Its deft handling of paradox nevertheless relates directly to Davie's qualities at large, notably his command of stylised gesture in verse.

More important, *A Winter Talent* breathes in places a somewhat puzzled air. Davie reveals the same earnest desire to get facts and emotions straight which distinguishes Philip Larkin, in other ways a most dissimilar writer. The poems in this impressive collection range from the lyrically plangent "Time Passing Beloved" to the direct vocative address of *"Mens Sana,"* one of the author's first brushes with the Polish poet Mickiewicz. There are many poems of place, indicating a clash between the bleak asperities of Davie's West Riding birthplace and the softer Mediterranean landscape. This conflict is enacted in much of Davie's work, right up to the present. He is a man especially sensitive to lines, gradients, contours. A recurring image is "the shape of truth"; ungainly "Derbyshire Angles" prompt a reflection, rather in the manner of Wallace Stevens, on the commerce between visual reality and artistic expression. Slag, wasteland, moor often figure in these poems; Davie seems little interested in texture, and concentrates instead on bare geological form. His imagery is often sharply focused ("the dry detritus of an August hill") or, as in "Under St. Paul's," physical and fullbodied.

Three outstanding poems illustrate these tendencies. "Hearing Russian Spoken" rests on a half-submerged conceit on the word "broken" (as used in "broken English"). Again the question is the relation of the forms of language to states of feeling; full rhymes and naked abstract nouns are deployed with great boldness.

"Dream Forest" recounts a symbolic act of consecration, by which the poetic imagination is transformed to a kind of commemorative garden like Shenstone's Leasowes or the Elysian Fields at Stowe. The poet speaks of "a sculptor's logic," a recurring thread in his work. Finally, one of Davie's finest poems, "The Wind at Penistone," uses a flexible line and quiet sibilance to convey a sense of grudging nostalgia amid the gnarled Northern landscape. The poet can "hardly praise this clenched and muffled style" – of scenic beauty, of social living, of artistic presentation.

Davie has always been deeply concerned with style and grace, indeed with aesthetics in the old-fashioned sense. But his work is also deeply embedded in history and politics. Many of these interests come together in *The Forests of Lithuania*, his free version of Mickiewicz. After this pleasantly energetic and eclectic poem, Davie brought out *Events and Wisdoms*. This is a more ambitious collection than *A Winter Talent*, but not in my view more assured. A dedicatory poem indicates a move towards "a style less consummate"; the lesson is that "an art's / More noble office is to leave half-done." This was interpreted by some critics to mean a shift towards a more open and relaxed poetic, and indeed some of the new poems were organised less tightly. Davie seemed now occupied by the problem of tracing "the path of an energy through the mind" (as one of his critical books has it). To this end, he adopted a freer stophic patterns, endeavouring to press "the lately formless" into a newly emergent expressive form. But the slipshod muse is not for Davie, and some of the better poems were again graceful and finished productions – notably "Metals," "Low Lands" and even "A Battlefield," with its hints of the cautious depressive accuracy of the Movement. Elsewhere there were signs of facility ("Her blondness under the swimsuit fits / That sunbrowned girl like a tunic"), and occasional cloudy portentousness, as in "Life Encompassed." The last section of the book shows a switch to the confessional mode, not wholly successful in my view.

Donald Davie remains what he has always been: an adroit and widely accomplished poet, devoted to his calling as it is both art and craft. His greatest achievement has been perhaps to unite human and emotional warmth with a rigorous fidelity to the artistic conscience and a sensuous alertness of striking detective power.

– J. P. W. Rogers

DAVISON, Peter (Hubert). American. Born in New York City, 27 June 1928. Educated at the Fountain Valley School, Colorado Springs; Harvard University, Cambridge, Massachusetts, A.B. (magna cum laude) 1949 (Phi Beta Kappa); St. John's College, Cambridge (Fulbright Scholar), 1949–50. Served in the United States Army, 1951–53. Married Jane Truslow in 1959; has two children. Page in the United States Senate, 1944. Editor, Harcourt Brace, publishers, New York, 1950–51, 1953–55; Assistant to the Director, Harvard University Press, 1955–56. Associate Editor, 1956–59, Executive Editor, 1959–64, and since 1964, Director, Atlantic Monthly Press, Boston. Since 1972, Poetry Editor, *Atlantic Monthly*, Boston. Recipient: Yale Series of Younger Poets Award, 1964; National Institute of Arts and Letters award, 1972. Address: 11 Mellen Street, Cambridge, Massachusetts 02138, U.S.A.

PUBLICATIONS

Verse

> *The Breaking of the Day and Other Poems.* New Haven, Connecticut, Yale
> University Press, 1964.
> *The City and the Island: Poems.* New York, Atheneum, 1966.
> *Pretending to Be Asleep: Poems.* New York, Atheneum, 1970.
> *Dark Houses.* Cambridge, Massachusetts, Halty Ferguson, 1971.
> *Walking the Boundaries: Poems 1957–1974.* New York, Atheneum, and Lon-
> don, Secker and Warburg, 1974.

Other

> *Half-Remembered: A Personal History.* New York, Harper, 1973; London,
> Heinemann, 1974.

Manuscript Collection: Beinecke Library, Yale University, New Haven, Connecticut.

Critical Study: Foreword by Dudley Fitts to *The Breaking of the Day and Other
Poems,* 1964.

*   *   *

Most of Peter Davison's poetry has an even, gem-like quality that typifies
intelligent, academic verse. Davison's work, generously laden with mythical allusions, is often rhymed and carefully metered. At its best, the poetry illuminates a
moment or an observation from the poet's life without straining towards an
undeserved depth. In "Lunch at the Coq D'Or," Davison portrays a fancy restaurant where "Each noon at table tycoons crow / And flap their wings around each
other's shoulders." He is waiting for an associate, Purdy, who eventually "is
seated with his alibis":

> I know my man. Purdy's a hard-nosed man.
> Another round for us. It's good to work
> With such a man. "Purdy," I hear myself,
> "It's good to work with you." I raise
> My arm, feathery in the dimlight, and extend
> Until the end of it brushes his padded shoulder.
> "Purdy, how are you? How you doodle do?"

Here, Davison has included himself among the blamed by repeating the feather-
wing imagery of the tycoons and then his own arm of luncheon goodwill. The
humor of his concluding line emphasizes the nonsense encountered in daily business intercourse.

Too often, Davison lacks this detachment; he becomes merely a clever man with
a pen, rhyming when he should be working his guts in ink. His position is ambiguous: surely, "Conviction Means Loss of License" deals with a serious subject, but

Davison seems only to consider the fatal car crash of three brothers an opportunity to exercise his wit. And worse, he preaches in the sardonic manner of a radar cop:

> For they were faithful to the plan
> That nature must make way for man
>
> And fed their faith in this great cause
> By putting speed above the laws
> Designed to neither help nor hurt.
>
> Inertia rendered them inert.

In other poems, particularly "Intacta," (where he tells the familiar story of a seemingly virginal, but permissive girl) and "Winter Fear," which ends, "The weather tells of famine and defeat, / Of lying leaves and how we were betrayed / By spring. But winter never yet has won," he seems too pat. How, after all, does he know that the girl of "Intacta" is loose unless he's been in her pants? And, although it's true that winter "never yet has won," neither has any season (or condition of mind, the poem suggests to me) triumphed over winter. In short, Davison refuses to confess his own possible guilt or confusion.

These comments are perhaps unfairly negative, for there is much to admire in the body of Davison's work. "The Breaking of the Day," title poem of his first collection, is a perfect refutation of the criticisms I levy against the least successful poetry. Here, the poet takes the risk of baring himself to the reader, acknowledging his doubts: "I shall never know myself / Enough to know what things I half believe / And, half believing, only half deny." In a poem such as this, the fusion of craft and insight is fully realized, and Davison proves himself the poet of skill his reputation holds him to be.

Davison's *Dark Houses,* published in a limited edition in 1971, is a seven-part retrospective in verse on the life of his father, poet Edward Davison, whose presence is fully documented in Peter Davison's *Half-Remembered,* an autobiogrphy. *Dark Houses* is a very fine poem, crafted with a precision less and less evident among contemporary poets:

> And now his thirsty body
> Is part of the land at last, land of his children,
> Where the grey ungiving stone can always stand
> For fathers, thrusting up above the fields
> Not ever his own, though dearer than the land
> That gave him birth but never knew his name.

– Geof Hewitt

DAWE, (Donald) Bruce. Australian. Born in Geelong, Victoria, 15 February 1930. Educated at Northcote High School; Melbourne University; Queensland University, Brisbane; University of New England, Armidale, New South Wales, Litt.B. 1973. Served in the Royal Australian Air Force for nine years. Married

Gloria Desley; has four children. Worked as labourer, gardener, postman. Currently, Lecturer in Literature, Institute of Advanced Education, Darling Heights, Toowoomba. Recipient: Myer Prize, 1966, 1969; Ampol Arts Award, 1967. Address: 30 Cumming Street, Toowoomba, Queensland, Australia.

PUBLICATIONS

Verse

No Fixed Address. Melbourne, Cheshire, 1962.
A Need of Similar Name. Melbourne, Cheshire, 1965.
An Eye for a Tooth: Poems. Melbourne, Cheshire, 1968.
Beyond the Subdivision: Poems. Melbourne, Cheshire, 1969.
Heat-Wave. Melbourne, Sweeney Reed, 1970.
Condolences of the Season. Melbourne, Cheshire, 1971.
Bruce Dawe, edited by Basil Shaw. Melbourne, Cheshire, 1973.

Critical Studies: *The Man down the Street,* edited by Ian V. Hansen, Melbourne, V.A.T.E., 1972; *Times and Seasons: An Introduction to Bruce Dawe* by Basil Shaw, Melbourne, Cheshire, 1974.

Bruce Dawe comments:

The themes I deal with are the common ones of modern civilization, loneliness, old age, death, dictatorship, love. I like the dramatic monologue form, and use it in free, blank and rhymed verse-forms, attempting at the same time to capture something of the evanescence of contemporary idiom, which is far richer and more allusive than the stereotyped stone-the-crows popular concept of Australian speech would have people believe.

*　　　*　　　*

Bruce Dawe has been certainly the most central and pivotal poet in Australia during the decade of the 1960's. His work first appeared in Melbourne in the late 1950's and broke through to a wide audience with *No Fixed Address,* his first collection. *No Fixed Address* displayed a freshness and gaiety quite unusual in Australian literature at the time, and, more importantly, demonstrated a highly developed sense of local speech cadence and inflection. Bruce Dawe has always been concerned with the celebration of the maligned denizens of the great sprawl of outer suburbs that surround our cities. He views them with affection, sympathy and wit, and an ear attuned to natural speech rhythms that is more precise and more immediately convincing than that of any other poet. This perceptiveness is coupled with a brilliant feeling of language and, particularly, of image.

Dawe broke through to a whole new generation of Australian readers, and his popularity has been gained without any loss of integrity or style; indeed, because of the genuineness of his essential attitudes, such popularity is a natural aspect of his poetic justification. Over recent years, and in his later volumes, Bruce Dawe has been concerned with developing his initial vision and perceptions. He has been one of the few Australian poets who has found a convincing method of dealing with current political events and issues without loss of poetic validity. This is an area where Australian poetry has always been backward and undeveloped. In 1972 a selected volume *Condolences of the Season* offered readers a summary of Dawe's work. His later poems tend to employ a more elegiac cadence, but though the subject matter is often eclectic and wide flung, it would seem, still, that his contribution related primarily to the admission into the corpus of Australian poetry of an area of suburban reality and liveliness that had only been approached in the most awkward and uncomfortable way by his predecessors.

– Thomas W. Shapcott

DEHN, Paul (Edward). British. Born in Manchester, Lancashire, 5 November 1912. Educated at Shrewsbury School; Brasenose College, Oxford, B.A. in English. Served with the Special Operations Executive, 1939–45: Major. Film Critic, *Sunday Referee*, 1936–39, *Sunday Chronicle*, 1945–53, *News Chronicle*, 1954–60, *Daily Herald*, 1960–63, all in London. Regular Contributor to *Punch*, London, and the BBC programme *The Critics*. Former Councillor, Royal Society for the Protection of Birds. Recipient: Academy Award, 1952; Venice Award, for screenplay, 1952; Cheltenham Festival Poetry Prize, 1957; British Film Academy Award, 1958. Address: 19 Bramerton Street, London SW3 5JS, England.

PUBLICATIONS

Verse

The Day's Alarm. London, Hamish Hamilton, 1949.
Romantic Landscape: Poems. London, Hamish Hamilton, 1952.
Quake, Quake, Quake: A Leaden Treasury of English Verse (parodies). London, Hamish Hamilton, and New York, Simon and Schuster, 1961.
The Fern on the Rock: Collected Poems 1935–1965. London, Hamish Hamilton, 1965.

Plays

Sketches in *The Lyric Revue* (produced London, 1951).
Sketches in *Penny Plain* (produced London, 1952).
Sketches in *The Globe Revue* (produced London, 1952).
A Woman of No Importance, adaptation of the play by Oscar Wilde (produced London, 1953). London, Evans, 1954.
Sketches in *At the Lyric* (produced London, 1953).
Sketches in *Going to Town* (produced London, 1954).
A Dinner Engagement, music by Lennox Berkeley (produced Aldeburgh and London, 1954).
Sketches in *The Punch Revue* (produced London, 1955).

Joie de Vivre (lyrics only), adaptation by Terence Rattigan of his own play
    French Without Tears, music by Robert Stolz (produced London, 1960).
Virtue in Danger, adaptation of the play *The Relapse* by Vanbrugh, music by
    James Bernard (produced London, 1963; Ashland, Oregon, 1969).
The Bear, music by William Walton (produced Aldeburgh and London,
    1967). London, Oxford University Press, 1967.
Castaway, music by Lennox Berkeley (produced Aldeburgh and London,
    1967). London, Chester, 1967.

Screenplays: *Seven Days to Noon,* with James Bernard, 1951; *Waters of Time*
(documentary), 1952; *On Such a Night,* 1955; *Orders to Kill,* with George St.
George, 1958; *A Place for Gold* (documentary), 1960; *Goldfinger,* with Richard
Maibaum, 1964; *The Spy Who Came In from the Cold,* 1964; *The Deadly Affair,*
1965; *The Taming of the Shrew,* 1965; *The Night of the Generals,* with Joseph
Kessel, 1966; *Fragment of Fear,* 1970; *Beneath the Planet of the Apes,* 1970; *Escape
from the Planet of the Apes,* 1971; *Conquest of the Planet of the Apes,* 1972; *Battle for
the Planet of the Apes,* with John William and Joyce H. Corrington, 1973; *Murder
on the Orient Express,* 1974.

Other

For Love and Money (miscellany). London, Reinhardt, 1956; New York, Van-
    guard Press, 1957.
Cat's Cradle (juvenile), with Ron Spillman. New York, Doubleday, 1959.
Kittens on the Keys (juvenile), with Ron Spillman and Jack Ramsay. London,
    Longman, and New York, Doubleday, 1961.
Cat's Whiskers (juvenile), with Ron Spillman. London, Longman, and New
    York, Doubleday, 1963.

Paul Dehn comments:

A major theme, since World War II with its nuclear climax interrupted my 20's,
has been humanity's need to preserve the "innocent eye" of childhood if the world
is ever to achieve a peaceful old age. This theme is common to the "sick," satirical
parodies of *Quake, Quake, Quake:*

> Nuclear wind, when wilt thou blow
> That the small rain down can rain?
> Christ, that my love were in my arms
> And I had my arms again

and to the serious poetry of my other volumes:

> O yellow-hammered sun, my bird
> In paradise beyond the cage,
> Sing to the fossil mind, unscale
> The lizard eye of age.

Such a preoccupation would perhaps account for my chief influence: the lyric
poets of the 14th and 15th century, who wrote when English Poetry itself was still
young enough excitedly to proclaim the sea blue and the leaves green rather than
(jadedly) the foliage emerald and the main azure. Like them, I prefer to discipline

my frenzy (as my modern heroes Auden and Dylan Thomas do) within the confines of strict form.

*   *   *

"Look!" "Listen!" Paul Dehn's poetry frequently exhorts us to share the moment of creation:

> . . . when the mind
> Lay paper-white in a winter's peace
> And watched the printed bird-tracks
> Turn into words.
> – from "Ice on the Round Pond"

Often, Dehn's burgeoning metaphors suggest an enriching imagination which, paradoxically, equalizes all images:

> . . . a pony-footed wind
> Kicks on the cobbled water; and salt-spray
> Is tracer bullet, hailstone, falling star.
> – from "Hardangerfjord"

Only rarely, as in "Armistice," the best of Dehn's many war poems, do the translated images produce a violent fusion/disjunction which itself becomes meta-phoric:

> Be strong to remember, how the dead died, screaming;
> Gangrene was corn, and monuments went mad.

In Dehn's world, threatened by war and repressed by convention, love, appar-ently homosexual love, "must live silently" ("At the Dark Hour") until, ironically, war "Permits me to have loved them, who lack flesh" ("The Sweet War Man Is Dead"). Age is the chief enemy, whether for the questing pub-crawler in "Habi-tué" or the forsaken "swaggerer" in "Sailor's Song" (retitled "Trade" in *The Fern on the Rock*). The aging man's desperate recreation of his youthful self, a theme shaping a number of poems, works most powerfully in the straightforward language of "Narcissus":

> Lord, let there be a little rain, to furrow
> The pool's face and scatter
> My image on the morrow.
> Let there be but a little wind
> To ruffle this water.

Water dominates many poems, most often as the sea, beautiful, but sometimes mocking, always underlining man's alien situation:

> I am the fat-knuckled noisy diver
> But you are the quietest fish in the sea.
> – from "Lament for a Sailor"

An invariably fatal seducer of human visitors, the sea ". . . like a lover arches / Its ribs against his own" ("Sirens' Song").

Dehn's poems prophesying cosmic nuclear destruction or invoking universal

361

brotherhood lack the intensity of these lyrics on individual ageing and death. The
bitter parodies of *Quake, Quake, Quake,* which pervert traditional verse into appropriate adages for the atomic age, seem more repetitious than obessive and only
sporadically fuse the two levels into a complex evocation of man's enduring vanity:

> Cool, Britannia! beneath the nuclear wave
> While the bigger, bigger nations misbehave.

Except for the bitchy "Epitaph for a Columnist," Dehn's wit rarely supports a
whole poem. More often, a pun illuminates a serious context: the old man who
"sniffs his salad days" and the poet who shall remember "When thyme and tide
are wild no more" ("Kamiros, Rhodes").

Through more than thirty years of changing themes and concerns, the chief
virtue of Dehn's verse operates unchecked – a lucidity, strengthened by traditional
metrical and sound patterns and many allusions, that frequently glows with a low
but steady intensity: ". . . and the chair / Scraped to a sun-trap over cold stone"
("Spring '46"). This illumination, however muted, highlights that process of
experience becoming poetry which Dehn's best work both describes and embodies:

> . . . when I began to wrote, the link was forged
> In the flush of the setting sun which, once again

> Flooding my window, colours the final page.
>   "Romantic Landscape"

>   – Burton Kendle

DELIUS, Anthony (Ronald St. Martin). South African. Born in Simonstown, 11
June 1916. Educated at St. Aidan's College, Grahamstown; Rhodes University,
Grahamstown, B.A. 1938. Served in the South African Intelligence Corps, 1940–45.
Married in 1941; has two children. Staff Member, Port Elizabeth *Evening Post*,
1947–50; Parliamentary Correspondent, *Cape Times*, Cape Town, 1951–54, 1958–68.
Banned from the South Africa House of Assembly for his *Cape Times* political
commentary. Currently, Writer, BBC Africa Service, London. Former Co-Editor,
Standpunte, Cape Town. Since 1962, Member of the Editorial Board, *Contrast*
magazine, Cape Town. Address: Africa Service, British Broadcasting Corporation,
Bush House, London W.C.2, England.

PUBLICATIONS

Verse

> *An Unknown Border: Poems.* Cape Town, Balkema, 1954.
> *The Last Division.* Cape Town, Human and Rousseau, 1959.
> *A Corner of the World: Thirty-Four Poems.* Cape Town, Human and Rousseau,
>   1962.
> *Black South-Easter.* Grahamstown, New Coin, 1966.

Play

   The Fall: A Play about Rhodes.   Cape Town, Human and Rousseau, 1957.

Novel

   The Day Natal Took Off: A Satire.   Cape Town, Human and Rousseau, and
   London, Pall Mall Press, 1963.

Other

   The Young Traveller in South Africa.   London, Phoenix House, 1947; revised
   edition, 1959.
   The Long Way Round (travel in Africa).   Cape Town, Howard B. Timmins,
   1956.
   Upsurge in Africa.   Toronto, Canadian Institute of International Affairs, 1960.

                            *   *   *

Anthony Delius has described himself as one of the most indoctrinated of South
Africans, a misleading description, since it would imply an acceptance of current
socio-political attitudes in his country which would be the opposite of the truth.
What one can properly infer, however, is that of the poets of his country writing in
English he is probably the most consciously South African. It is an identification
with *A Corner of the World* – the title of his 1964 collection – that is his own but it
is more than a country, rather the Africam continent as a whole, many of his
poems reflecting his travels there. From his early poems, including the long,
impressive "Time in Africa" written during the Second World War, Delius has
shown himself fascinated by what living in Africa has accumulated over the centuries, seeing history as a continuous process working on his own contemporary
experience and on into the future like a prophecy.
In "Black South-Easter," probably the best long poem produced by a South
African, in a generation, Delius, twenty years after "Time in Africa," succeeded
in using history as a poet should, taking imagination as catalyst to produce a recipe
for the making of myth. The poet, struggling through the windy Cape night, is
confronted by historical ghosts, by symbolical figures of contemporary values, the
millionaire and the actress and by his own many-sidedness, his own "Indian file of
selves," while his mind and memory are swept dramatically on a course of their
own through a wider and deeper disorder of time and circumstance – for instance,
seeing the Fifteenth Century navigator Diaz thus:

                     His niche was the stern
                     Of a torpedoed tanker, cliff-hung
                     Like an opera box.

Here is a tremendously ambitious poem; that it succeeds is the measure of the
poet's power to use language to control a variety of influences working on the
imagination at the same time. If Delius has proved his staying power in attempting
the long distances (since *The Lusiads,* the Cape presents a surviving challenge to
South African poets to go for the big theme), yet his enduring reputation may well
lie among some of his short poems, such as the exquisite "The Gamblers," about

Cape Coloured fishermen, a popular anthology piece since it first appeared in *The New Yorker:*

> Day flips a golden coin – but they mock it.
> With calloused, careless hands they reach
> Deep down into the sea's capacious pocket
> And pile their silver counters on the beach.

"Deaf and Dumb School" is another poem beautifully conceived to express the poet's compassion:

> Silence like a shadow shows the room
> Of minds that make their signs and mouth their cries.

There is another kind of compassion, perhaps of the best kind, that which comes after very clear vision has stripped away from situations and people what humbug, false myth and sloth have accumulated about them. In this process satire acts like a paint-stripper, and Delius, as satirist, has long been active in the South African context. Though echoes of Roy Campbell sometimes interrupt originality, there are parts of *The Last Division* (1959) whose humour will preserve it long after the lampooned figures of politics have been forgotten.

– Roy Macnab

DEMETILLO, Ricaredo. Filipino. Born in Dumangas, Iloilo, 2 June 1920. Educated at Silliman University, Dumaguete City, A.B. in English; University of Iowa, Iowa City, M.F.A. in English and creative writing. Married to Angelita Demetillo; has four children. Assistant Professor, 1959–70, Chairman of the Department of Humanities, 1961–62, and since 1970, Associate Professor of Humanities, University of the Philippines, Diliman, Quezon City. Recipient: Rockefeller Fellowship, 1952; University of the Philippines Golden Jubilee Award; Philippines Republic Cultural Heritage Award, 1968. Address: T 1416, Area 14, University of the Philippines, Diliman, Quezon City, Philippines.

PUBLICATIONS

Verse

No Certain Weather: A Collection of Poetry. Quezon City, Guinhalinan Press, 1956.
La Via: A Spiritual Journey. Quezon City, Diliman Review, 1958.
Daedalus and Other Poems. Quezon City, Guinhalinan Press, 1961.
Barter in Panay. Quezon City, University of the Philippines Office of Research Coordination, 1961.
Masks and Signature. Quezon City, University of the Philippines Press, 1968.

The Scare-Crow Christ. Quezon City, Diliman Review, 1973.
The City and the Thread of Light. Quezon City, Diliman Review, 1974.
Lazarus, Troubadour. Quezon City, New Day, 1974.

Play

The Heart of Emptiness Is Black (produced Quezon City, 1973).

Other

The Authentic Voice of Poetry. Quezon City, University of the Philippines Office of Research Coordination, 1962.

Critical Studies: "The Wounded Diamond" by Leonard Casper, in *Bookmark* (Manila), 1964; by Leonard Casper, in *Solidarity Magazine* (Manila), 1968.

Ricaredo Demetillo comments:

(1970) My poetry has been much influenced by the New Criticism in America, but I don't belong to any "school."

My poetry has been concerned with the following major themes: the rebellion of the young against the conventional values of an overly repressive society; the modern journey of the individual from lostness to wholeness and fullest creativity; the rise and fall of civilization using the myth of Daedalus in ancient Crete to objectify and evoke the human condition; and the important position of the artists as the bearers and the creators of volumes necessary to the renewal of society. To project all these themes, I have used the lyric, the elegiac, the poetic essay, the epic, etc., with relatively good success. Always, I have been concerned with the human condition and also celebrated the hierarchy of light. Strongest influences: Homer, Dante, Baudelaire, Dylan Thomas, W. B. Yeats and Auden, not to mention myths of all sorts, including the Filipino ones.

(1974) My recent book, *The Scare-Crow Christ*, was written mostly during the troubled period of student activism in Manila and contains poems objectifying the poverty and the spiritual confusion of the time. One poem speaks of the indifference of the average man to the welfare of the "diminished, unfulfilled" man and asks: "Are you not Judas to this scare-crow Christ?"; still another one pays "tall tribute to the hardihood of man" that is able to survive the horrors of war (in Vietnam and elsewhere).

But these new poems are evocations, not propagandistic statements.

My forthcoming verse drama, *The Heart of Emptiness Is Black,* really a sort of sequel to *Barter in Panay,* deals centrally with the conflict between tribalism and emergent individualism, which may have relevance to the present situation of the Philippines under martial law. I chose the drama as a form so that I can be heard by the public, for poetry locally is mostly unheard and unread, if not dead.

The forthcoming *The City and Other Poems* objectifies or evokes the lostness of man in the modern city and the poet's search for any available meaning in the human condition today.

*   *   *

Ricaredo Demetillo is dedicated to overcoming modern man's bewilderment in a world of changing values. In *No Certain Weather,* he asserts his right to destroy traditional norms, "To breathe the ordered Word into psychic strife" ("Baudelaire"), in order to forge his own values. The iconoclastic wit of *La Via* is directed at the cant and humbug of society. Actually, the new order he envisions is unexcitingly obvious and reactionary. This becomes explicit in *Daedalus and Other Poems,* where his being "a part of one vast whole" ("Sonnet") causes joy. The self-concern is finally dispersed in *Barter in Panay,* a loose adaptation of the folk-odyssey *Maragtas* and the first Filipino epic in English. It suggests that life can be meaningful only through identification with the community.

Demetillo's language which throughout approximates to well-written prose reflects the enlarging of his vision. The stridency of such early images as "What cuckold's voice announced the crib of Christ . . .?" ("Baudelaire") is, however, progressively modulated; the serenity in *Daedalus,* of having been "a part of one vast whole" becomes more pronounced in *Barter in Panay* which has, in addition, the detachment and urbanity of the philosopher who has realised his quest. Demetillo's high place among Filipino poets is assured if his development is consistent.

– Abdul Majid bin Nabi Baksh

DEN BOER, James. American. Born in Sheboygan, Wisconsin, 21 August 1937. Educated at Calvin College, Grand Rapids, Michigan, A.B. 1960; University of California, Santa Barbara, M.A. 1969. Served in the United States Naval Reserve, 1955–63. Married Emily C. Williams in 1970; has one daughter (by previous marriage) and one son. Field Epidemiologist, New Jersey State Department of Health, Trenton, 1962–63; Writer and Editor, United States Public Health Service, Washington, D.C., 1963–67; Deputy Director, White House Conference on Children and Youth, Washington, D.C., 1970–71; Free-lance Consultant, Santa Barbara, 1972–73. Since 1973, Research Information Officer, University of California, Santa Barbara. Assistant Director, Unicorn Press, 1968–70, and Editor, *Spectrum,* Santa Barbara, 1969. Since 1966, Associate Editor, *Voyages* magazine, and since 1971, Editor-at-Large, *Black Box* magazine, Washington, D.C. Recipient: International Poetry Forum Award, 1967; National Endowment for the Arts grant, 1971; National Institute of Arts and Letters grant, 1971; Author's League of America grant, 1973; Carnegie Foundation grant, 1973. Address: 1804 Loma Street, Santa Barbara, California 93103, U.S.A.

PUBLICATIONS

Verse

Learning the Way. Pittsburgh, University of Pittsburgh Press, 1968.
Trying to Come Apart. Pittsburgh, University of Pittsburgh Press, 1971.
Nine Poems. Santa Barbara, California, Christopher's Books, 1972.

James Den Boer comments:

(1970) Bah – who knows what tomorrow's poems will be like; I don't want to be limiting. Poetic *ideals* are a different thing: I'd like my poems to look spare, be direct, colloquial when necessary, a touch surreal, compassionate, courageous, tender, magnamimous – one could go on – the language always fresh and energetic. Themes, subjects, sources probably would reduce to being the same for all poets – what one sees and feels; forms are what happens to happen on the page, and never are "usual."

(1974) I'm not given to placing my poetry within the boundaries of a "school" or particular group of American poets – in many ways, I've deliberately avoided such placing. My major concerns have been with the physical world: woods, water, trees, animals; but within that context it is the human response that matters most – how is it that we relate to the world, what place do we have in it, what succor can we give or take from it, what is our appropriate relationship to it? By "appropriate" I mean a relationship that is primarily non-destructive, that recognizes differences but celebrates congruence, that affords the most insight and the highest degree of transcendant experience. I am not an urban poet, to be most succinct, although that is not deliberate choice but a function of personal happenstance. As to form, I want my poems to be open, colloquial, organic; in the past year or so I have been attempting to write poems that will hold real trees and animals and at the same time deal with ideas – that is, ideas as real as trees and animals. My reading is largely in the life sciences and philosophy; that kind of knowledge brackets my work, however spontaneously or emotionally the poems are triggered.

*   *   *

James Den Boer's two books, *Learning The Way* and *Trying To Come Apart*, present evidence for the emergence of an important talent. In both books, Den Boer draws heavily on autobiographical material, and displays a rare ability to look at his life without flinching.

As the title of *Learning The Way* hints, the poems in this book, Den Boer's first, comprise a sort of itinerary of places and events from the first thirty years of the poet's life. In fact, the book can almost be read as an episodic autobiographical novel, though the episodes are poems, and none of the events seems fabricated; Den Boer writes with the assurance of having lived through every one, and done so from the skin down to wherever genuine poems are born. The experiences form the poems instead of being embedded and half-concealed in poems like pebbles in conglomerate. This nakedness, even more apparent in dealing with the more harrowing experiences (marital breakup, for example) that form *Trying to Come Apart*, is counterpointed by careful organization in this first book, from the first, and title poem, set in the childhood of the poet along Lake Michigam, where he plays at being an Indian, and "tested the limits / of my cunning in isolation," through to the last, "The Jar," in which he declares:

> I have been promised
> help, despite myself,
>
> and have seen
> in the depth of glaze
>
> all I lack – not of color
> but of depth –
>
> creator, there are many
> flaws. I cross the room
> to touch orange, centering.

"The Jar," in addition to expressing an assessment of his life and work at that moment, bringing to at least a temporary terminus the movement started in "Learning the Way," does several other things: "I cross the room / to touch orange, centering" also suggests, in terms of Den Boer's itinerary, his arrival in California, the destination suggested several poems earlier in "The Summons" ("I reach across / the continent, my hand touches California"). "Creator, there are many / flaws" could be an address to himself, an assessment of his book, or an address to God, a half-humorous reproach for creating a poet with all his human imperfections; actually, it's probably both, and in the light of the latter implication, Den Boer himself becomes the "one jar, thrown / on a stranger's wheel" and is, in centering the jar, centering on himself, trying to go deeper for the next journey, the new book.

That next book, *Trying to Come Apart*, does go deeper, especially in a long, powerful poem sequence, "Muttering," about the breakup of the poet and his wife. The book seems an attempt not so much to exorcise, or rationalize, the pain of such experiences, as to deal with it, honestly and openly. The line length of the poems, and the length of the poems themselves, tend to be longer than in the earlier book, and Den Boer tends to see the poems in more and longer sequences than in the first book. The over-all effect is choppier, more discontinuous, than in the first book, as even the title should suggest. The first section opens the book on a hopeful note: the couple, settling in the wilds, hoping for a new life, though this hope is shattered in the second section, "Muttering." The last two sections seem to be an attempt to cope with past experience, to heal and put it in perspective, by accepting the hurt and "trying to come apart." Necessarily, this book does not have the neat sense of design of the first, but there is the exciting sense here of a man not merely viewing his life as potential material for art, but attempting to use his art to heal his life. Den Boer's search is open-ended, without clear resolutions, as is that of most honest men. Those who realize the value lies in the journey, rather than its destination, will want to continue to travel with him in the future.

– Duane Ackerson

DEUTSCH, Babette. American. Born in New York City, 22 September 1895. Educated at Barnard College, New York, B.A. 1917. Married Avrahm Yarmolinsky in 1921; has two sons. Taught at the New School for Social Research, New York, 1933–35, and Columbia University, New York, 1944–71. Honorary Consultant to the Library of Congress, Washington, D.C., 1960–66. Recipient: *Nation* prize, 1926; Ford Foundation Prize, 1941; William Rose Benet Memorial Award, 1957. D.Litt.: Columbia University, 1946. Past Secretary, National Institute of Arts and Letters; Member, American Academy of Arts and Letters. Chancellor, Academy of American Poets. Address: 300 West 108th Street, New York, New York 10025, U.S.A.

PUBLICATIONS

Verse

Banners. New York, Doran, 1919.
Honey out of the Rock. New York and London, Appleton, 1925.
Fire for the Night. New York, Cape and Smith, 1930.
Epistle to Prometheus. New York, Cape and Smith, 1931.

One Part Love. New York, Oxford University Press, 1939.
Take Them, Stranger. New York, Holt, 1944.
Animal, Vegetable, Mineral. New York, Dutton, 1954.
Coming of Age: New and Selected Poems. Bloomington, Indiana University Press, 1959; London, Oxford University Press, 1960.
Collected Poems, 1919–1962. Bloomington, Indiana University Press, 1963.
The Collected Poems of Babette Deutsch. New York, Doubleday, 1969.

Novels

A Brittle Heaven. New York, Greenberg, 1926.
In Such a Night. New York, Day, and London, Secker, 1927.
Mask of Silenus: A Novel about Socrates. New York, Simon and Schuster, 1933.
Rogue's Legacy: A Novel about François Villon. New York, Coward McCann, 1942.

Other

Potable Gold: Some Notes on Poetry and This Age. New York, Norton, 1929.
This Modern Poetry. New York, Norton, 1935; London, Faber, 1936.
Heroes of the Kalevala, Finland's Saga. New York, Messner, 1940; London, Methuen, 1941.
Walt Whitman: Builder for America. New York, Messner, 1941.
It's a Secret! (juvenile). New York and London, Harper, 1941.
The Welcome (juvenile). New York, Harper, 1942.
The Reader's Shakespeare. New York, Messner, 1946.
Poetry in Our Time. New York, Holt, 1952; revised edition, New York, Doubleday, 1963.
Tales of Faraway Folk (juvenile), with Avrahm Yarmolinsky. New York, Harper, 1952.
Poetry Handbook: A Dictionary of Terms. New York, Funk and Wagnalls, 1957; London, Cape, 1958; revised edition, Funk and Wagnalls, 1962, 1969, 1974; Cape, 1965.
More Tales of Faraway Folk (juvenile), with Avrahm Yarmolinsky. New York, Harper, 1963.
I Often Wish (juvenile). New York, Funk and Wagnalls, 1966.

Editor, with Avrahm Yarmolinsky, and Translator, *Contemporary German Poetry*. New York, Harcourt Brace, 1923.
Editor, *Poems of Samuel Taylor Coleridge.* New York, Crowell, 1967.

Translator, with Avrahm Yarmolinsky, *The Twelve,* by Alexander Blok. New York, Heubsch, 1920.
Translator, *Modern Russian Poetry,* edited by Avrahm Yarmolinsky. New York, Harcourt Brace, 1921; London, Lane, 1923; revised edition, as *Russian Poetry,* New York, International Publishers, 1927.
Translator, *Crocodile,* by K. I. Chukovsky. Philadelphia, Lippincott, 1931.
Translator, *Poems from "The Book of Hours,"* by Rainer Maria Rilke. New York, New Directions, 1941; London, Vision, 1947; revised edition, New Directions, 1969.
Translator, *Eugene Onegin,* by Alexander Pushkin, edited by Avrahm Yarmolinsky. New York, Heritage Press, 1943; London, Penguin, 1965.

Translator, with Avrahm Yarmolinsky, *The Steel Flea*, by N. Leskov. New York, Harper, 1943; revised edition, 1964.

Translator (verse only), *Selected Writings of Boris Pasternak*. New York, New Directions, 1949.

Translator, *Jean sans Terre*, by Yvan Goll. New York and London, Yoseloff, 1958.

Translator, *Elegy of Ihpetonga*, by Ivan Goll. Kentfield, California, Allen Press, 1962.

Translator, *Two Centuries of Russian Verse*, edited by Avrahm Yarmolinsky. New York, Random House, 1966.

Translator, *There Comes a Time* (juvenile), by Elisabeth Borchers. New York, Doubleday, 1969.

Manuscript Collection: University of Buffalo.

Critical Study: "The Naked Voice" by George Garrett, in *Virginia Quarterly* (Charlottesville), Spring 1964.

Babette Deutsch comments:

The most "personal statement" concerning my work is in the poems themselves. My hope is (as I have written on poetry elsewhere) that my poems "realize an unusually comprehensive experience more intensely" or "realize an unusually intense, if sometimes trivial, experience more comprehensively."

*   *   *

Babette Deutsch, whose first book of poems appeared in 1919, has published eight more in the fifty years since then, along with novels, books for children, and critical works of commanding importance. She remains primarily a poet, and because her mind is of the very finest grain, and because the range of her interests is unlimited, she continues to occupy a high, unique place among her peers. She is one of the most intelligent poets who ever wrote, and one of the most toughly sensitive, with an unimpeachable seriousness which humor keeps always sweet. Her phrasing is brilliant and swift, but her chief charm is in the completeness with which she realizes and renders a subject. For example, "Lizard at Pompeii":

> Little finger of fiery green, it
> flickers over stone. Waits
> in a weed's shadow.
> Flashes emerald –
> is gone.
>
> Here once horror poured so hot, heavy, thick,
> everyone was dead before he was sick.
> Now here is no heat but the sun's
> on old stone treads;
> no motion but that rippling inch of whip:
> yours, you little live jewel, who slipped away
> into silence. Yet stay on to haunt memory,
> like those dead.

Or "History":

> History
> Coming too close
> Is monstrous, like a doll
> That is alive and bigger than the child
> Who tries to hold it.
> It is a clock that tolls the thirteenth hour.
> It is a theatre
> On fire.

Or "To the Moon, 1969":

> Now you have been reached, you are altered beyond belief –
> . . . a planet that men have, almost casually, cheapened.

Babette Deutsch has been valuable as a translator of Russian, German, and French poetry; and certainly she has been valuable as a critic; but her permanent gift to us is the pleasure we derive from the play of her mind over truths of the heart she has known how to make finally plain.

– Mark Van Doren

DICKEY, James (Lafayette). American. Born in Atlanta, Georgia, 2 February 1923. Educated at Clemson College, South Carolina, 1942; Vanderbilt University, Nashville, Tennessee, B.A. (magna cum laude) 1949 (Phi Beta Kappa), M.A. 1950. Served in the United States Army Air Force during World War II, and in the Air Force during the Korean War. Married Maxine Syerson in 1949; has two sons. Taught at Rice University, Houston, 1950, 1952–54, and the University of Florida, Gainesville, 1955–56; Poet-in-Residence, Reed College, Portland, Oregon, 1962–64, San Fernando Valley State College, Northridge, California, 1964–66, and the University of Wisconsin, Madison, 1966. Consultant in Poetry, Library of Congress, Washington, D.C., 1967–69. Since 1969, Professor of English and Writer-in-Residence, University of South Carolina, Columbia. Recipient: *Sewanee Review* Fellowship, 1954; Union League Civic and Arts Foundation Prize (*Poetry*, Chicago), 1958; Vachel Lindsay Prize, 1959; Longview Foundation Award, 1960; Guggenheim Fellowship, 1961; Melville Cane Award, 1966; National Book Award, 1966; National Institute of Arts and Letters grant, 1966. Address: 4620 Lelia's Court, Lake Katherine, Columbia, South Carolina 29206, U.S.A.

PUBLICATIONS

Verse

Into the Stone and Other Poems. New York, Scribner, 1960.
Drowning with Others: Poems. Middletown, Connecticut, Wesleyan University Press, 1962.

Helmets: Poems. Middletown, Connecticut, Wesleyan University Press, and London, Longman, 1964.

Two Poems of the Air. Portland, Oregon, Centicore Press, 1964.

Buckdancer's Choice. Middletown, Connecticut, Wesleyan University Press, 1965.

Poems 1957–1967. Middletown, Connecticut, Wesleyan University Press, and London, Rapp and Carroll, 1967.

The Achievement of James Dickey: A Comprehensive Selection of His Poems, with a Critical Introduction, edited by Laurence Lieberman. Chicago, Scott Foresman, 1968.

The Eye-Beaters, Blood, Victory, Madness, Buckhead and Mercy. New York, Doubleday, and London, Hamish Hamilton, 1970.

Recordings: *Poems,* Spoken Arts; *James Dickey Reads His Poetry,* Caedmon Tapes.

Play

Screenplay: *Deliverance,* 1972.

Novel

Deliverance. Boston, Houghton Mifflin, and London, Hamish Hamilton, 1970.

Other

The Suspect in Poetry. Madison, Minnesota, Sixties Press, 1964.

A Private Brinksmanship. Pasadena, California, Castle Press, 1965.

Spinning the Crystal Ball: Some Guesses at the Future of American Poetry. Washington, D.C., Library of Congress, 1967.

Metaphor as Pure Adventure: A Lecture. . . . Washington, D.C., Library of Congress, 1968.

Babel to Byzantium: Poets and Poetry Now. New York, Farrar Straus, 1968.

Self-Interviews, edited by Barbara and James Reiss. New York, Doubleday, 1970.

Sorties (essays). New York, Doubleday, 1971.

Exchanges . . .: Being in the Form of a Dialogue with Joseph Trumbull Stickney. Bloomfield Hills, Michigan, Bruccoli Clark Books, 1971.

Jericho: The South Beheld, paintings by Hubert Shuptrine. Birmingham, Alabama, Oxmoor House, 1974.

Translator, *Stolen Apples,* by Evgenii Evtushenko. New York, Doubleday, 1971; London, W. H. Allen, 1972.

Critical Study: Introduction by Laurence Lieberman to *The Achievement of James Dickey,* 1968.

Theatrical Activities:

Actor: **Film** – *Deliverance,* 1972.

James Dickey comments:

I like to think the major theme, if there is one, is continuity between the self and the world, and the various attempts by men to destroy this (wars, and so on: heavy industry and finance and the volume-turnover system). I try to say something about the individual's way, or ways, of protecting this sense of continuity in himself, or of his attempts to restore it. Much of my work deals with rivers, mountains, changes of weather, seas and the air. I am lately trying to move into a kind of poetry in which the exchanges between people – rather than between one person and, say, the landscape – will have more part.

*   *   *

The emergence and growth of James Dickey as a poet in a little more than a decade is a remarkable phenomenon, a testimony to his enormous drive and the extraordinary powers of his imagination. As if this accomplishment were not sufficient in itself, his collected reviews and essays on contemporary verse, *Babel to Byzantium*, clearly place him as one of the three or four excellent practical critics of poetry now functioning.

In his essay "The Poet Turns on Himself," Dickey has observed that he did not begin to write poems until the age of 24, and then with no particular knowledge of the various formal techniques available from the English poetic tradition. Instead, his concentration was upon "the individually imaginative or visionary quality" that might be attained in the effort to render with immediacy and force the most intense moments of experience. He came also to realize that his own life, its love affairs and deaths, its periods spent in two wars as a combat pilot, an inclination toward athletics and motorcycle riding in youth, a fascination with hunting animals using only bow and arrow, was the richest potential material for his art; and so Dickey has carried that life experience into poetry, but has so beautifully and amazingly transformed it through language, image, rhythm, through his seemingly endless imaginative resources and capacity for extending the range of his feelings, that to encounter one of his poems is to enter the realms of myth or dream. The universe of Dickey's poetry is charged with hidden energies; things exist in secret relation with one another; here everything is possible, for the imagination which brings these images to birth is both sophisticated and primitive, animistic. Not only that, but the individual or self in his poems continually manifests the ability to reach out and participate in the being of others: two boys in a tree house at night simply by their presence summon their dead brother to join them; the hunter senses within himself the existence of the animal he tracks; the shadows of people seated on a lighted screened porch are cast upon the surrounding grass of the yard inhabited by chirping night insects, and mysteriously these human shadows bring the souls of the people with them into the grass so that the two worlds of the living momentarily coalesce:

> Where the people are lying,
> Emitted by their own house
> So humanly that they become
> More than human, and enter the place
> Of small, blindly singing things,
> Seeming to rejoice
> Perpetually, without effort,
> Without knowing why
> Or how they do it.

More recently, Dickey has been exploring the possibilities of some longer poems, and while they still exemplify his strengths and vision, they tend at times to become wordy and diffuse. Though his writing is uniquely his own, Dickey stands in a line of poetic descent from Whitman and Roethke, both of whom he admires greatly, and perhaps has learned from Rilke and other modern European poets. Among contemporaries, his closest literary affinities are with Robert Bly, James Wright, Louis Simpson, and W. S. Merwin, though each poet bears his own distinctive manner, has his own particular interests.

– Ralph J. Mills, Jr.

DICKEY, R(obert) P(reston). American. Born in Flat River, Missouri, 24 September 1936. Educated at the University of Missouri, Columbia, B.A. 1968, M.A. 1969. Served in the United States Air Force, 1954–56. Married the poet Victoria McCabe in 1969; has one son. Instructor, University of Missouri, 1967–69. Since 1969, Assistant Professor, Southern Colorado State College, Pueblo. Since 1966, Founding Editor, *Poetry Bag Magazine.* Recipient: Swallow Press New Poetry Series Award, 1969. Address: 5420 North Grande, Tucson, Arizona, U.S.A.

PUBLICATIONS

Verse

Four Poets, with others. Pella, Iowa, C.U.I. Press, 1967.
Running Lucky. Chicago, Swallow Press, 1969.
Acting Immortal: Poems. Columbia, University of Missouri Press, 1970.
Concise Dictionary of Lead River, Mo. Taos, New Mexico, Black Bear Press, 1972.
The Basic Stuff of Poetry. Dubuque, Iowa, Kendall Hunt, 1972.
Life-Cycle of Seven Songs. Taos, New Mexico, Talmaneh Press, 1972.
McCabe Wants Chimes. Taos, New Mexico, Talmaneh Press, 1973.
The McCabes: A Family Sketch. Privately printed, 1973.
Drunk on a Greyhound. Shawnee Mission, Kansas, BkMk Press, 1973.
One Man in Pueblo. Privately printed, 1973.

Plays

This Is Our Living Room (produced Denver, 1971).
Concise Dictionary of Lead River, Mo., music by Carol Ann Plonkey (produced Pueblo, Colorado, 1973). Taos, New Mexico, Black Bear Press, 1973.

Critical Studies: Reviews in *Sou'wester* (Edwardsville, Illinois), Winter 1970, Winter 1971; *Times-Union* (Rochester, New York), 28 January 1970; *Contempora* (Atlanta), May–June 1970; *Choice* (Chicago), July–August 1970; *Library Journal* (New York), 1 October 1970, September 1972; *South Dakota Review* (Vermillion), Winter 1970–71; *Western Humanities Review* (Salt Lake City), Winter 1971; *December* (Western Springs, Illinois), xiii, 1–2, 1971; *Poetry* (Chicago), July 1971; *Western American Literature* (Fort Collins, Colorado), v, 1.

R. P. Dickey comments:

I consider myself primarily a poet. Roughly 75% of my poems are in the prose mode, 25% in the verse mode. I didn't plan it, but as I check out my books, it seems that I use rhyme in about 15% of my poems, for whatever that might be worth. I have written about thirty short stories and published exactly one; about fifty reviews and published all of them except one – the editor said it was "intemperate," which was what I had considered its central virtue. Several critical articles of mine have been published, but the less said on that the better. I tend to agree with the late Win Scott when he said, "Criticism is dead the minute it's written and buried the minute it's published." I completed my first novel after seven years of false starts and woeful ignorance of technique, in 1971. Called *Clarkey's Itinerary,* it's my *Inferno* of the times and so far (*circa,* March, 1973) hasn't found the proper publisher. It has done me for the prose end of the continuum for a while. One of these days I may write my *Purgatorio,* but just now I'm back into my true love, poetry, and working slowly on a new play. Plays, like public readings (I've given nearly 200 since 1966), are among other things, sobering; they get one in touch with a healthy objectivity of a kind we all need. Such activities can be rescue jobs from the narcissistic subjectivity and self-pity all of us wallow in, alas, too much of the time.

It seems that the peculiar quality of a poem, as such, resides in the tension which exists because on one level the poem is calling attention to itself, to itself as *language* formally organized, and on another level is directing the reader's attention away from itself, out of things and actual events, is pointing away from itself, is making itself into as transparent a medium as it can in order that the reader may see through it to the enduring truth and universals it points to with its marshalling of particulars. Something like that. I believe that whatever the truth is, it is both manifold and one, and that the medium of poetry exists in order to help get us in touch with it, to help us get with it. I believe that the truth – again, whatever it is in any final description – is not dependent nor any way reliant upon the observer, the poet. It is the poet's difficult job to get with *it*, as much as he can.

What makes poetry important as a body of knowledge is that nowhere else can a reader go to find out how people *really* feel about things; that makes poetry unique. The poet has a duty, a responsibility to what John Ciardi has called that "midnight man" of 100 years from now who will be rummaging through a shelf of books of poems trying to find some hard, clear, complex, honest help in answering the question of who he is. Saul Bellow or R. G. Collingwood, one of them said that art is a medicine for society's disease of stupidity, and of course sometimes medicine is hard to swallow or comes in the form of a bitter pill. The poet, like anyone trying to be worth his salt, looks for what is good; but he must record, not what he is looking for, but what he actually *finds*. It follows that simplism is the poet's main enemy as he makes his forms.

I like to extend myself and try longer things sometimes, but these days I find myself writing mostly short poems, meditative if not lyric, but more and more, influenced by Browning, dramatic instead of meditative. Pound and Yeats have been my major literary influences and I suspect continue to be so. (I am both bothered and embarrassed when thoughtless people say, of some poet or other, that he was "all right for his time, but is outdated now," etc., forgetting that they are talking about art as if it were journalism. The two profoundly wise aphorisms by Pound which they need to remember in this context are these: "Literature is news that stays news"; and, in art "All ages are contemporaneous.") I still like to experiment with traditional structures and rimes, slant-rimes mostly, but less and less. At the risk of souding hopelessly didactic, I agree with Rilke's archaic torso of Apollo that a great work of art tells you, among other things, that you must change your life. The best poems happen to you, you have to write them; but in between there is the necessary difficulty of keeping the pencil sharp for those infrequent good ones, by writing bad ones, Parnassian ones, practice ones, whatever, just to keep writing, to keep sane so you might be able to handle the next bout of inspiration or madness. And you read, and reread. I reread a lot in Ted Hughes, Larkin, Lowell, James Dickey, Leonard Cohen, Browning, Shakespeare, Dante, Pound, Yeats, Bellow, the King James Bible, and C. S. Lewis's non-fiction, among others.

*   *   *

The title poem to R. P. Dickey's first volume, "Running Lucky," exemplifies the tone of much of his poetry – ironic, self-mocking, and rebellious: "I run with shabby baggage, / a toy for some god that won't grow up. / And yet I feel I'm lucky." The extent of his luck is to have escaped being nailed "to that well-built cross / on which the stricken and hopeless hang."

Dickey's escape, always provisional, rests upon an allegiance to personal feelings and values as they are related to his surroundings (principally, the central Missouri area) and to the men and women who give significance to his life. Many of the poems, especially in the second volume, *Acting Immortal*, are about friends or dedicated to them. They speak persuasively for the belief that intimate contact is the foundation of living. In this regard, Dickey attaches special importance to sensory experience; some of his best poems record his delight with the human body and the experience of love.

He uses effectively natural speech rhythms, breath phrasing, short lines, expressive word positioning, and compressed syntax in the experimental tradition of Cummings, Williams, and more recently, the Projectivist poets. When least successful, the style is self-conscious and contrived; when most successful, the controlled casualness of his style reflects Dickey's theme of confronting life honestly and without pretense.

– Dale Doepke

DICKEY, William. American. Born in Bellingham, Washington, 15 December 1928. Educated at Reed College, Portland, Oregon, B.A. 1951 (Phi Beta Kappa); Harvard University, Cambridge, Massachusetts, M.A. 1955; University of Iowa, Iowa City, M.F.A. 1956; Jesus College, Oxford (Fulbright Scholar), 1959–60. Married Shirley Ann Marn in 1959 (divorced, 1972). Instructor, Cornell University, Ithaca, New York, 1956–59; Assistant Professor, Denison University, Granville,

Ohio, 1960–62. Since 1962, Member of the English Department, and currently Professor of English, California State University, San Francisco. Visiting Professor, University of Hawaii, Honolulu, Spring 1973. Formerly, Managing Editor, *Western Review,* and Editorial Assistant, *Civil War History.* Recipient: Yale Series of Younger Poets Award, 1959; Union League Civic and Arts Foundation Prize (*Poetry,* Chicago), 1962. Address: 121 Liberty Street, San Francisco, California 94110, U.S.A.

PUBLICATIONS

Verse

Of the Festivity.   New Haven, Connecticut, Yale University Press, 1959.
Interpreter's House.   Columbus, Ohio State University Press, 1963.
Rivers of the Pacific Northwest.   San Francisco, Twowindows Press, 1969.
More under Saturn.   Middletown, Connecticut, Wesleyan University Press, 1971.

William Dickey comments:

I am closest to various poets who studied at the Writers Workshop of the University of Iowa in the 1950's; but I don't know that it would be recognized as a school.

*   *   *

William Dickey's first book was W. H. Auden's last selection as editor of the Yale Younger Poets, and the older poet was clearly one of the chief influences on the then neophyte:

> And through the morns the ample ladies gather
> The ribbons of their lives and press them dear.
> They are intrinsic selves and need no other
> Posture to arrive and interfere.

Dickey's book overflows with the posturings of several selves, and often the several postures of the individual divided against himself. But such division is always controlled, always measured. The title poem of this volume is elaborately rhymed with simple words and concerns the speaker's inanition, his fear of the potential disruption of love, but it also reveals an awe of communication mingled with doubt of its efficacy ("And all the words my mouth has ever said / Will fail to tell us whether we live or die"). The poems are learned, but not to a fault, though too often they form a commentary on experience rather than a presentation of it. As such, the book stood at the end of a decade whose poetic idiom, replete with irony and balanced wit, it substantially epitomized.

His latest book, *More under Saturn,* differs radically from the first; an aesthetic of openness, of imaginative suddenness, has replaced the earlier, formalistic decorum. Now we have Macy's department store instead of Caesar's Gallic Wars, an almost surreal jangle of images in place of the structured rhetoric, and a coarse colloquial ear keeping measure, rather than the polished flow of iambs. Here is a poem, complete, called "The Instructor Has Not Followed the Lesson Plan Very Carefully":

> The motor grinds & won't catch.
> Nowhere worth going to: so the car thinks.
>
> And I think. Once there was punctuation
> worth listening to. I was used to that & I said:
>
> Here are all the commas you will use up in a normal life.
> The students bit at my wrists & ankles &
>
> A wild deer burst into the office & bled to death
> Kicking the files to mush.

The irony is still there, but now instead of bringing things into focus, it's employed to break open the closures of the poems, to celebrate madness rather than to contain neurotic stasis. The ampersand and the colon have replaced the comma, and, instead of assured articulation, we are offered, almost threatened with, insistent juxtapositions.

Dickey's startling development, or devolution if looked at from another angle, is symptomatic of changes in American poetry throughout the 1960's. As the Eliotic–Audenesque hegemony broke apart, the dominant idiom splintered, and many poets, certainly Dickey among them, were set adrift. His career is too heterogeneous to judge easily, and his main strengths at this point are his quiet responsiveness and his continued responsibility to use language to sharpen the contours of his experience. This may require release as well as concision for the moment. He is a poet in mid-stride, though obviously very capable of energetic movement.

– Charles Molesworth

DICKINSON, Patric (Thomas).   British.   Born in Nasirabad, India, 26 December 1914. Educated at St. Catharine's College, Cambridge (Crabtree Exhibitioner), B.A. (honours) in English and classics 1936. Served with the Artists' Rifles, 1939–40. Married the anthologist Sheila Shannon in 1947; has two children. Schoolmaster, 1936–39. Producer, 1942–45, and Poetry Editor, 1945–48, BBC, London. Since 1948, Free-lance Writer. Gresham Professor of Rhetoric, City University, London, 1964–67. Recipient: Atlantic Award, 1948; Cholmondeley Award, 1973. Address: 38 Church Square, Rye, Sussex, England.

PUBLICATIONS

Verse

The Seven Days of Jericho.   London, Dakers, 1944.
Theseus and the Minotaur and Poems.   London, Cape, 1946.

Stone in the Midst and Poems.   London, Methuen, 1948.
The Sailing Race and Other Poems.   London, Chatto and Windus, 1952.
The Scale of Things: Poems.   London, Chatto and Windus, 1955.
The World I See.   London, Chatto and Windus–Hogarth Press, 1960.
This Cold Universe: Poems.   London, Chatto and Windus–Hogarth Press, 1964.
Selected Poems.   London, Chatto and Windus, 1968.
More Than Time.   London, Chatto and Windus–Hogarth Press, 1970.
A Wintering Tree.   London, Chatto and Windus–Hogarth Press, 1973.

Plays

Theseus and the Minotaur (broadcast, 1945).   Included in *Theseus and the Minotaur and Poems,* 1946.
Stone in the Midst (produced London, 1949).   Included in *Stone in the Midst and Poems,* 1948.
Robinson, adaptation of a play by Jules Supervielle (produced London, 1953).
The Golden Touch (produced Wolverhampton, Staffordshire, 1959; London, 1960).
A Durable Fire (produced Canterbury, 1962; London, 1963).   London, Chatto and Windus, 1962.
Pseudolus, adaptation of the play by Plautus (produced Stoke on Trent, 1966).
Ode to St. Catharine, music by Bernard Rose (produced Cambridge, 1973).
Creation, music by Alan Ridout (produced Ely, 1973).
The Miller's Secret, music by Stephen Dodgson (produced Cookham, Berkshire, 1973).

Radio Plays: *Theseus and the Minotaur,* 1945; *The First Family,* 1960; *Wilfred Owen,* 1970; *The Pensive Prisoner,* 1970.

Television Play: *Lysistrata,* 1964.

Other

A Round of Golf Courses.   London, Evans, 1951.
The Good Minute: An Autobiographical Study.   London, Gollancz, 1965.

Editor, *Soldiers' Verse.*   London, Muller, 1945.
Editor, *Byron: Poems.*   London, Grey Walls Press, 1949.
Editor, with Erica Marx and J. C. Hall, *New Poems 1955.*   London, Joseph, 1955.
Editor, *Poetry Supplement.*   London, Poetry Book Society, 1958.
Editor, with Sheila Shannon, *Poems to Remember.*   London, Harvill Press, 1958.
Editor, with Sheila Shannon, *Poets' Choice: An Anthology of English Poetry from Spenser to the Present Day.*   London, Evans, 1967.
Editor, *C. Day Lewis: Selections from His Poetry.*   London, Chatto and Windus, 1967.

Translator, *Aristophanes Against War: Three Plays.*   London, Oxford University Press, 1957.
Translator, *The Aeneid of Virgil.*   New York, New American Library, 1961.
Translator, *The Complete Plays of Aristophanes.*   London, Oxford University Press, 2 vols., 1971.

Patric Dickinson comments:

Bias towards country subjects since I live in the country. No "usual" verse forms: a tendency to invention. General sources: English poetry from 1500. Influences in youth: Yeats, Frost, Edward Thomas, in particular. Stylistic devices: a continual attempt at greater honesty, clarity, and conciseness.

*   *   *

The poetry of Patric Dickinson is difficult to assess as a *corpus* because it is crossed obliquely by contradictory passions, of which two are dominant: tenderness of personal love with its close privacy and intimacy, and over against this a stormy, desperate outcrying rage against circumstances, both those that are tangible in the society around him, and those which roar through the tundra of his spirit. The general effect of his work, as one retreats from close reading to contemplate it in perspective, is that of a tempestuous solitude, as it were of a human figure fighting his way through a blizzard. Such an impression also conjures a concept of courage.

What sort of courage? It is engendered, I suspect, by the conflicts within his own nature, against which he struggles openly, at least in his verse. But it is controlled, and given shape, by an impressive discipline of classical learning, which gives concision to his verse, even when it is expressing an outcry as violent as that of Victor Hugo in his most romantic moods:

> O my love I am out of breath,
> I have come this second, now,
> To tell you about death.
> How long will the news keep?

It is this mood of desperation in a world made unpredictable not only by the climate of nature, but also by mankind, which causes this abnormally susceptible poet to suspect his own shadow. Chaucer's line "the smiler with the knife" might well be quoted as a subscription to Mr. Dickinson's muse. But the poetry inherent in his nature makes use even of this lack of trust in the goings-on of the universe. The very symbol of song, as he says,

> Out there, the nightingale
> In a cold hieroglyph
> Is prototypical,
> Yet melts into local life,
> Is the bird at fever pitch
> In the spring wood tonight.
> Both make the masterpiece
> Till who knows which is which?

The reader of his poetry is also puzzled, trying, with an earnestness which the work demands, to "know which is which," the pentrating tenderness of personal approach, or the wild outbursts, the violent gestures with which he thrusts the rest of the world away.

Certainly, the agony of mind which induces this second aspect of his poetry, a philosophy of negation, gives the dominant to his music. He is inspired, like Peer Gynt, to something that retreats from him. It is always hovering on the horizon, a tragic sun about to set. As an artist, he reaches out toward it, his verbal gesture urgent and compulsive, but he is driven back upon himself unsatisfied, least of all with his own work and capability.

The result is a body of work that is as disturbing as it is appealing. It has the authority of an intense sincerity re-enforced by a firm craftsmanship:

> Only be true, never
> Deceive with the cute lies
> That so easily outface you
> Shamefaced honesties.
> None but professional mutes
> Profit from nothings-said.
>
> Be understanding, listen,
> Always communicate:
> Losses fester on
> A tongue too reserved or tender;
> Praises that go unsung
> Squander their tunes in hatred.

– Richard Church

DILLARD, R(ichard) H(enry) W(ilde). American. Born in Roanoke, Virginia, 11 October 1937. Educated at Roanoke College, Salem, Virginia, 1955–58, B.A. 1958 (Phi Beta Kappa); University of Virginia, Charlottesville (Woodrow Wilson Fellowship, 1958–59; DuPont Fellowship, 1959-61), M.A. 1959, Ph.D. 1965. Married Annie Doak in 1965. Instructor in English, Roanoke College, Summer 1961, and University of Virginia, 1961–64. Assistant Professor, 1964–68, Associate Professor, 1968–74; since 1971, Chairman of the Graduate Program in Contemporary Literature and Creative Writing, and since 1974, Professor of English, Hollins College, Virginia. Since 1966, Contributing Editor, *The Hollins Critic*, Hollins College, Virginia; since 1973, Vice President, *The Film Journal*, New York. Recipient: Academy of American Poets Prize, 1961; Ford grant, 1972. Agent: Blanche C. Gregory, 2 Tudor City Place, New York, New York 10017. Address: Box 9671, Hollins College, Virginia 24020, U.S.A.

PUBLICATIONS

Verse

The Day I Stopped Dreaming about Barbara Steele and Other Poems. Chapel Hill, University of North Carolina Press, 1966.
News of the Nile. Chapel Hill, University of North Carolina Press, 1971.
After Borges. Baton Rouge, Louisiana State University Press, 1972.

Play

Screenplay: *Frankenstein Meets the Space Monster,* with George Garrett and John Rodenbeck, 1966.

Novel

The Book of Changes.   New York, Doubleday, 1974.

Other

    Editor, with Louis D. Rubin, Jr., *The Experience of America: A Book of Readings.*   New York, Macmillan, and London, Collier Macmillan, 1969.
    Editor, with George Garrett and John Rees Moore, *The Sounder Few: Essays from "The Hollins Critic."*   Athens, University of Georgia Press, 1971.

R. H. W. Dillard comments:

    Although I have thought a good deal about what I am doing in my poems, I don't know that I really am able to express the results of that thinking very clearly, except (I hope) in the poems themselves. Allow me, then, to offer in place of an introductory statement about my poetry, excerpts from two poems which might do the job.
    The first, from the poem "News of the Nile," is just a description of the source of my poems – experience in the broadest sense:

> All these things I have read and remembered,
> Witnessed, imagined, thought and written down. . . .

    The second, from the poem "Construction," may be a bit more helpful, for it is as close as I've come to an explicit esthetic statement, and it also makes explicit my central concern with the vital involvement of seeing and saying, of action and belief:

> To say as you see. To see as by stop-action,
> Clouds coil overhead, the passage of days,
>
> Trees bend by the side of the road
> Like tires on a curve, plants uncurl,
>
> How the world dissolves in the water of the eye:
> The illusion speed produces. The reality of speed.
>
> A result: to see as you say,
> As gravity may bend a ray of light.
>
> To say the earth's center is of fire:
> Life leaps from the soil like sun flares.
>
> To see the world made true,
> An art of rocks and stones and trees,
>
> Real materials in real space,
> *L'esthétique de la vitesse.*

*   *   *

Each of R. H. W. Dillard's three fine volumes is an important contribution to American poetry. The first, *The Day I Stopped Dreaming about Barbara Steele*, despite its echoes of Williams, Auden, Stevens, Ransom and Tate, is a highly sophisticated, humorous and unique representation of experience. The most traditionally formal of the three volumes, it is most impressive in its sardonic rendering of a wide range of "things." Mr. Dillard, fascinated by the power of his imagination, transforms into objects of beauty things – objects, emotions, experiences – that might otherwise be ephemeral or unnoticed. The wit in this volume does not diminish the sense of tragedy but as in Williams' "Pictures from Brueghel: Landscape with the Fall of Icarus," enlarges it by placing it in a comic context. At the same time it should be emphasized that the "thinginess" is definitely not that of the empiricist, realist or naturalist, but more that of the esthete.

News of the Nile, his second volume, is a further development of a distinctive voice. The See-er of visions of the imagination, intellectualized and witty, becomes autobiographical, personal, subjective, troubled. The models shift to Lowell and Roethke. Perhaps too much influenced by his study of horror movies, Mr. Dillard examines the perverse in human nature and experience – blood lust, cannibalism, the macabre. Poems such as "Night of the Living Dead," "Event; A Gathering; Vastation," "Act of Detection," studies of the predatory and bestial nature of man, revel in visions of horror. Other poems, much lighter, struggle in the poet's soul to deal honestly with the substance of his own time and place and his relationship to it.

Mr. Dillard's third volume, *After Borges,* represents a mature achievement. The title signals a profound experience with the work of the Argentine writer, Jorge Luis Borges. The shock of a recent discovery of evil of too many of the poems in *News of the Nile* has given way to the good humor and wit of the first volume. Poems such as "Round Ruby," "What Can You Say to Shoes," "Sweet Strawberries," and "Wings" express a new found and authentic joy in life, its triviality, absurdity, beauty and pathos. Others, such as "Limits," "The Other Tiger," "Argumentum Ornithologicum," and "Epilogue" which purport to be "after the Spanish of Jorge Luis Borges," are more serious and complex. At the base of these poems is an extreme solipsism. Thus "Epilogue" tells us of the poet who sets "out to shape a world," and finds at the end of his work a "face, wearing / And worn, warm as worn stone, / A face you know: your own." The tension in this and other poems is based on the conflict of ego struggling to see through, beyond, or around itself, its face, to another self or world which seems inaccessible. Perhaps most important about the direction of these latest poems is that, if his work is becoming more psychological and personal, it is also more conscious of the psyche in history. Mr. Dillard's discovery of Borges's labyrinth helped him to see himself in a deeper and richer, if more difficult, context.

– Richard Damashek

---

di PRIMA, Diane. American. Born in New York City, 6 August 1934. Attended Swarthmore College, Pennsylvania, 1950–51. Married Alan S. Marlowe in 1962; has three children. Contributing Editor, *Kulchur* magazine, New York, 1960–61; Editor, with LeRoi Jones, *Floating Bear* magazine, New York, 1961–69, and *Signal* magazine, New York, in the 1960's. Since 1964, Editor and Publisher, with Alan S.

Marlowe, Poets Press, New York. Recipient: National Endowment for the Arts grant, 1966. Address: Box 629, Point Reyes, California 94956, U.S.A.

PUBLICATIONS

Verse

> *This Kind of Bird Flies Backward.* New York, Totem Press, 1958.
> *The Monster.* New Haven, Connecticut, Penny Poems, 1961.
> *The New Handbook of Heaven.* San Francisco, Auerhahn Press, 1963.
> *Unless You Clock In.* Palo Alto, California, Patchen Cards, 1963.
> *Poets Vaudeville.* New York, Feed Folly Press, 1964.
> *Combination Theatre Poem and Birthday Poem for Ten People.* New York, Brownstone Press, 1965.
> *Poems for Freddie.* New York, Poets Press, 1966.
> *Haiku.* Topanga, California, Love Press, 1967.
> *Earthsong: Poems 1957–59,* edited by Alan S. Marlowe. New York, Poets Press, 1968.
> *Hotel Albert: Poems.* New York, Poets Press, 1968.
> *New Mexico Poem, June–July 1967.* New York, Roodenko, 1968.
> *The Star, The Child, The Light.* Privately printed, 1968.
> *Revolutionary Letters.* New York, Long Hair Books, 1969.
> *L.A. Odyssey.* New York, Poets Press, 1969.
> *New As. . . .* New York, privately printed, 1969.
> *Notes on a Summer Solstice.* Privately printed, 1969.
> *Kerhonkson Journal, 1966.* Berkeley, California, Oyez, 1971.
> *Prayer to the Mothers.* New York, privately printed, 1971.
> *So Fine.* Santa Barbara, California, Yes Press, 1971.
> *The Calculus of Letters.* San Francisco, privately printed, 1972.
> *Loba, Part I.* Santa Barbara, California, Capra Press, 1973.

Plays

> *Murder Cake* (produced New York, 1960).
> *Paideuma* (produced New York, 1960).
> *The Discomfort of a Russian Prince* (produced New York, 1961).
> *Like* (produced New York, 1964).

Novels

> *The Calculus of Variation.* New York, Poets Press, 1966.
> *Spring and Autumn Annuals.* San Francisco, Frontier Press, 1966.
> *Love on a Trampoline* (as Sybah Darrich). New York, Olympia Press, 1968.
> *Memoirs of a Beatnik.* New York, Olympia Press, 1969.

Short Stories

> *Dinners and Nightmares.* New York, Corinth Books, 1961; revised edition, 1974.

Other

Editor, *Various Fables from Various Places*. New York, Putnam, 1960.
Editor, *War Poems*. New York, Poets Press, 1968.
Editor, with LeRoi Jones, *The Floating Bear: A Newsletter, Numbers 1–37*. La Jolla, California, Laurence McGilvery, 1974.

Translator, *Seven Love Poems from the Middle Latin*. New York, Poets Press, 1965.

*   *   *

Diane di Prima's work is always worth reading.

It has the great value of being clear, compassionate, witty and intelligent. It's an impressive body of work that offers in its full range an absorbing blend of romance, reality, vision and practical detail.

In another sense her work also tells a history of the visible and invisible threads uniting U.S.A.'s "street" poets and artists during the past two decades. By "street" I mean the "other" culture – the culture existing beyond the university or corporation. A culture of strays, tribes, families and other so-called minorities who lead productive lives in opposition to middle-class standards of imagination. When I refer to "street" I mean a combination of cultures which has produced America's most vital art forms.

Her work is an uncompromising history of herself as self as woman as citizen as artist. From the early works in *This Kind of Bird Flies Backward* and *Earthsong*, to the in-progress exploration of archetype, *Loba*, di Prima's work retains a unity of purpose and is evidence of her continuously emerging consciousness and surety as an artist.

The work is diverse but there are no contradictions. The magical poems in *A New Handbook of Heaven* in no way betray the straightforward polemics of *Revolutionary Letters*; the lyric and tender *Kerhonkson Journal* complements the erotic vaudevilles in *Memoirs of a Beatnik*. In all the work there are a forthrightness and honesty. Whatever posture she takes always returns to source and source is the center her work spreads from in all its manifestations.

Her poems record survival with grace.

She is a witness who functions as poet also to give grace to give memory (to restore) those lives that did not endure.

Her poems are steps of a spiritual progression now resident in disciplines of Zen Buddhism.

But poetry is the discipline which gives silence voice.

Love letters and grocery lists.

The historic journey from New York City to California, the edge of America.

The poems tell this, the changes, the journey.

Thick soup made out of whatever is available. Carrot tops, barley, potatos, celery, daikon – whatever is at hand and all of it transformed via fusion of herbal alchemy.

– David Meltzer

DOBSON, Rosemary. Australian. Born in Sydney, New South Wales, 18 June 1920. Educated at Frensham, Mittagong, New South Wales; Sydney University. Married A. T. Bolton in 1951; has one daughter and two sons. Recipient: Sydney

Morning Herald prize, 1946; Myer Award, 1966. Address: 61 Stonehaven Crescent, Deakin, Canberra, ACT 2600, Australia.

PUBLICATIONS

Verse

In a Convex Mirror.   Sydney, Dymock's Book Arcade, 1944.
The Ship of Ice and Other Poems.   Sydney, Angus and Robertson, 1948.
Child with a Cockatoo and Other Poems.   Sydney, Angus and Robertson, 1955.
(Poems), selected and introduced by the author. Sydney, Angus and Robertson, 1963.
Cock Crow: Poems.   Sydney, Angus and Robertson, 1965.
Rosemary Dobson Reads from Her Own Work (with recording).   Brisbane, University of Queensland Press, 1970.
Collected Poems.   Sydney, Angus and Robertson, 1973.

Recording: *Rosemary Dobson Reads from Her Own Work*, University of Queensland Press, 1970.

Other

Focus on Ray Crooke.   Brisbane, University of Queensland Press, 1971.

Editor, *Australia, Land of Colour, Through the Eyes of Australian Painters.*   Sydney, Ure Smith, 1962.
Editor, *Songs for All Seasons: 100 Poems for Young People.*   Sydney, Angus and Robertson, 1967.

Critical Studies: "Rosemary Dobson: A Portrait in a Mirror" by A. D. Hope, in *Quadrant* (Sydney), July–August 1972; "The Poetry of Rosemary Dobson" by James McAuley, in *Australian Literary Studies* (Hobart), May 1973.

*   *   *

While still in her mid-twenties Rosemary Dobson achieved poetic fame as the author of a prize-winning poem, "The Ship of Ice." Conceived as a series of dramatic monologues in verse, this poem later became the title piece of her second collection. The best work in this book, however, is to be found in "The Devil and the Angel," a sequence of set pieces in which the protagonists of the title compete for the souls of an artist, a poet, a map-maker, a scarecrow, the biblical character Methuselah and a king.

Rosemary Dobson studied and taught art early in her career. This has provided her with a lasting source of inspiration, and a number of poems in her third book *Child with a Cockatoo* originated as meditations upon famous paintings. Her interest in art should be regarded, perhaps, as a secondary source, for, whatever the theme, each poem is concerned primarily with an aspect of reality which has enlarged her experience and engaged her imagination.

Cock Crow, probably her best book of verse to date, shows her as something more than a writer of exquisite taste and lyrical perception. A number of its poems explore a constant yet rarely documented problem of creativity, the overlapping of the rival roles of parent and artist. This is poignantly stated in the book's title poem, while another clear look at the frustration of the artist-domestic is taken in "Jack" in which the boxed nursery toy becomes a symbol of the trapped poet.

By now the rewriting of ancient myths has become a commonplace source of flagging poetic motivation. The versions of Hero and Leander and Europa in "Across the Straits" and "The Rape of Europa" are redeemed by the uniqueness of their settings, a big city office-block after hours and the Australian countryside, as well as in the crisp freshness of their writing. In one of her best poems of recent years Rosemary Dobson dispenses with the world of painters and mythology and tells in the starkly compelling stanzas of "Ghost Town: New England" of the country's essential aloofness to human aspirations.

– Bruce Beaver

DORN, Ed(ward Merton). American. Born in Villa Grove, Illinois, 2 April 1929. Educated at the University of Illinois, Urbana; Black Mountain College, North Carolina. Visiting Professor of American Literature (Fulbright Lecturer, 1965–66, 1966–67), University of Essex, Wivenhoe, 1965–68. Visiting Poet, University of Kansas, Lawrence, 1968–69. Taught at Idaho State University, Pocatello. Editor, *Wild Dog* magazine, in the mid-1960's. Member of the English Department, University of Essex, Wivenhoe, England, 1974–75. Recipient: National Endowment for the Arts grant, 1966, 1968; D. H. Lawrence Fellowship, 1969. Lives in San Francisco.

PUBLICATIONS

Verse

The Newly Fallen: Poems. New York, Totem Press, 1961.
Hand Up! New York, Totem Press, 1964.
From Gloucester Out. London, Matrix Press, 1964.
Idaho Out. London, Fulcrum Press, 1965.
Geography. London, Fulcrum Press, 1965.
The North Atlantic Turbine. London, Fulcrum Press, 1967.
Gunslinger, Book I. Los Angeles, Black Sparrow Press, 1968.
Gunslinger, Book II. Los Angeles, Black Sparrow Press, 1969.
Gunslinger, Books I and II. London, Fulcrum Press, 1969.
Twenty-Four Love Songs. San Francisco, Frontier Press, 1969.
The Midwest Is That Space Between the Buffalo Statler and the Lawrence Eldridge. Lawrence, Kansas, T. Williams, 1969.
The Cosmology of Finding Your Spot. Lawrence, Kansas, Cottonwood, 1969.
Songs: Set Two, A Short Count. West Newbury, Massachusetts, Frontier Press, 1970.
Spectrum Breakdown: A Microbook. LeRoy, New York, Athanor Books, 1971.
A Poem Called Alexander Hamilton. Lawrence, Kansas, Tansy-Peg Leg Press, 1971.

The Cycle.   West Newbury, Massachusetts, Frontier Press, 1971.
The Hamadryas Baboon at the Lincoln Park Zoo.   Chicago, Wine Press, 1972.
Gunslinger, Book III: The Winterbook Prologue to the Great Book IV Kornerstone.   West Newbury, Massachusetts, Frontier Press, 1972.
Recollections of Gran Apacheria.   San Francisco, Turtle Island Foundation, 1973.
Gunslinger, Books I, II, III, IV.   Berkeley, California, Bookpeople, 1975.
Collected Poems.   Bolinas, California, Grey Fox Press, 1975.

Recording: *Edward Dorn Reads from "The North Atlantic Turbine,"* Livingdiscs, 1967.

Short Stories

Some Business Recently Transacted in the White World.   West Newbury, Massachusetts, Frontier Press, 1971.

Other

What I See in the Maximus Poems.   Worcester, Migrant Press, 1960.
Prose 1, with Michael Rumaker and Warren Tallman.   San Francisco, Four Seasons Foundation, 1964.
The Rites of Passage: A Brief History.   Buffalo, New York, Frontier Press, 1965; revised edition, as *By the Sound*, Mount Vernon, Washington, Frontier Press, 1971.
The Shoshoneans: The People of the Basin-Plateau.   New York, Morrow, 1966.

Translator, with Gordon Brotherston, *Our Word: Guerilla Poems from Latin America.*   London, Cape Goliard Press, and New York, Grossman, 1968.
Translator, with Gordon Brotherston, *Tree Between Two Walls,* by José Emilio Pacheco.   Los Angeles, Black Sparrow Press, 1969.

Bibliography: "Ed Dorn: A Checklist" by George F. Butterick, in *Athanor* (Clarkson, New York), Winter 1973.

Critical Study: "An Interview with Edward Dorn," in *Contemporary Literature* (Madison, Wisconsin), xv, 3.

*   *   *

   Ed Dorn's work has been widely praised in both England and America. Russell Banks, writing in *Lillabulero,* has compared him, not invidiously, with Olson, Williams, and Pound. In England, A. Alvarez decided that Dorn has produced "a handful of beautifully pure and unaffected love-songs, and an intriguing long poem about a drive, 'Idaho Out,' in which cultural worry loses out to a kind of anarchic, footloose vitality and a feeling for the vast, frozen emptiness of the American West." Dorn's work reminds Alvarez of Hemingway, and it is true that Dorn is concerned with capturing idiomatic speech accurately; but he also indulges a kind of jam-pack jumbling of observations that is more the poetic counterpart of exuberant and excited writers like Thomas Wolfe. Dorn's recall of childhood, his feeling for places and writers, his political convictions, his tourism, all find their way, in cascades of energy, into his loose, straying verse – though it is only fair to say that there is, supposedly, some underlying structure based more or less on "projective verse" sympathies.

Dorn's reactions to England, where he has lived for some time, are particularly sensitive:

> As we go
> through Sussex, hills are round
> bellies are the downs
> pregnantly lovely
> the rounds of them, no towns
> the train passes
> shaking along the groove
> of the countryside.

He purports "to love / that, and retain an ear for / the atrocities of my own hemisphere," criticizing, with simplistic pessimism, almost everything about America:

> The thorn however
> remains, in the desert
> of american life, the thorn
> in the throat of our national hypocrisy.

And yet he is also sentimental at will about his land:

> And yes Fort Benton is lovely
> and quiet, I would gladly give it as a gift
> to a friend, and with pride, a place of marked indolence . . .

Indeed, at his best, Dorn is a sentimentalist for the American he denounces:

> Bitterly cold were the nights.
> The journeymen slept in the lots of filling stations
> and there were the interrupting lights
> of semis all night long as those beasts
> crept past or drew up to rest their motors
> or roared on.

And his *Gunslinger* must be built on these strong native feelings: it is an effort at building a comic epic on the Western, for Dorn finds there the archetypal characters and enthusiasms that reveal America. For painting and wit, the commendable:

> And why do you have a female horse
> Gunslinger? I asked. Don't move
> he replied
> the sun rests deliberately
> on the rim of the sierra.

This work also moves away from the Ego as center, which was getting to be a problem in long poems in which Dorn spoke as a seer; it is only to be hoped that he does not lose other qualities of his earlier work – exuberance, puritanical anger, authority about his enthusiasms.

– David Ray

DOWLING, Basil (Cairns). British. Born in Southbridge, Canterbury, New Zealand, 29 April 1910. Educated at St. Andrew's College; Canterbury University College, Christchurch, New Zealand, M.A.; Otago University, Dunedin; Cambridge University. Married to Margaret Wilson; has one son and two daughters. Librarian at Otago University, Dunedin, 1947–52; Assistant Master, Downside School, Surrey, England, 1952–54. Assistant Master, 1954–65, and, since 1965, Head of English Department, Raine's Foundation Grammar School, London. Recipient: Jessie Mackay Memorial Prize, New Zealand, 1954. Address: 12 Mill Road, Rye, Sussex, England.

PUBLICATIONS

Verse

    A Day's Journey.   Christchurch, Caxton Press, 1941.
    Signs and Wonders: Poems.   Christchurch, Caxton Press, 1944.
    Canterbury and Other Poems.   Christchurch, Caxton Press, 1949.
    Hatherley: Recollective Lyrics.   Dunedin, University of Otago Bibliography Room, 1968.
    A Little Gallery of Characters.   Christchurch, Nag's Head Press, 1971.
    Bedlam: A Mid-Century Satire.   Christchurch, Nag's Head Press, 1972.
    The Unreturning Native.   Christchurch, Nag's Head Press, 1973.

Manuscript Collections: State University of New York, Buffalo; Hocken Library, Otago University, Dunedin, New Zealand; Alexander Turnbull Library, Wellington, New Zealand.

Critical Study: *Recent Trends in New Zealand Poetry* by James K. Baxter, Christchurch, Caxton Press, 1951.

Basil Dowling comments:

[My poetry] has been said to be at its best when descriptive of the New Zealand landscape, more particularly that of Canterbury. Certainly, landscape, both for its own sake and as a background to human life and history, has been a main preoccupation, but many of my poems have had philosophical overtones, and perhaps something reminiscent of the English metaphysical poets of the seventeenth century. I have been influenced most, I should say, by Hardy, Edward Thomas, Robert Frost and Andrew Young, and to some extent by Wilfred Owen and Siegfried Sassoon. As for method and manner, I like metrical variety, lightness of touch even when the subject is serious and profound, and, most of all, precision and economy of statement.

*   *   *

Basil Dowling's poems are traditional in form, technically neat, and somewhat Georgian in their general flavour. The prevailing mode is New Zealand pastoral – contemplative description lit with verbal felicities – although there is an epigrammatic wryness in some of his shorter lyrics and his range extends also to the deservedly much-anthologized ballad "The Early Days."

Mr. Dowling was prolific in the nineteen-forties, coming into his full powers in *Canterbury and Other Poems,* but he has published relatively little since; he appears to have suffered a poetic amputation when he cut himself off from the South Island environment which so profoundly permeated his most vigorous work. His poems about the Canterbury landscape are full of crisp, accurate visual details, beautiful and often exultant descriptions of scenes and weathers, gentle pictures of birds, animals, trees. He is compassionate when he writes (more rarely) of people, and calm when he writes (even less frequently) about his personal life; but there is a deep pessimism underlying all but the most sunfilled of his poems. This becomes most intense in *Bedlam: A Mid-Century Satire,* written in 1958, in which the Christian philosophy of his earlier work has given way to gloomy fatalism.

In his recent book, *A Little Gallery of Characters,* he returns to his "holy land of childhood," a peopled place this time, to portray sympathetically or with half-wistful humour the more memorable acquaintances of his early youth.

– Fleur Adcock

DOYLE, Charles (Desmond). Pseudonym: **Mike Doyle.** British. Born in Birmingham, Warwickshire, 18 October 1928. Educated at Wellington Teachers College, New Zealand, Dip.Ed. 1955; Victoria University College, University of New Zealand (Macmillan Brown Prize, 1956), B.A. 1956, M.A. 1958; University of Auckland, Ph.D. Served in the Royal Navy. Married Doran Ross Smithells in 1959 (second marriage); has three sons and one daughter. Taught at the University of Auckland; Visiting Fellow, Yale University, New Haven, Connecticut (American Council of Learned Societies Fellowship), 1967–68. Currently, Associate Professor of English, and Director of the Division of American and Commonwealth Literature, University of Victoria, British Columbia. Editor, *Tuatara* magazine. Recipient: Jessie Mackay Memorial Prize, 1955; UNESCO Creative Artist Fellowship, 1958. Address: Department of English, University of Victoria, Victoria, British Columbia, Canada.

PUBLICATIONS

Verse

A Splinter of Glass: Poems 1951–55. Christchurch, Pegasus Press, 1956.
The Night Shift: Poems on Aspects of Love, with others. Wellington, Capricorn Press, 1957.
Distances: Poems 1956–61. Auckland, Paul's Book Arcade, 1963.
Messages for Herod. Auckland and London, Collins, 1965.

A Sense of Place: Poems.   Wellington, Wai-te-ata Press, 1965.
Earth Meditations: 2.   Auckland, Aldritt, 1968.
Noah.   Vancouver, Soft Press, 1970.
Earth Meditations.   Toronto, Coach House Press, 1971.
Abandoned Sofa.   Victoria, British Columbia, Soft Press, 1971.
Earthshot.   Exeter, Exeter Books, 1972.
Preparing for the Ark.   Toronto, Weed/Flower Press, 1973.
Going On.   Toronto, Seripress, 1974.

Other

Small Prophets and Quick Returns: Reflections on New Zealand Poetry.   Auckland,
    New Zealand Publishing Society, 1966.
R. A. K. Mason.   New York, Twayne, 1970.

Editor, *Recent Poetry in New Zealand.*   Auckland and London, Collins, 1965.

Manuscript Collection: Hocken Library, Otago University, Dunedin, New Zealand.

Critical Studies: *Aspects of New Zealand Poetry* by James K. Baxter, Christchurch,
Caxton Press, 1967; "Earth Meditations One to Five" in *Quarry* (Kingston,
Ontario), Summer 1972.

Charles Doyle comments:

   Much that is best in poetry today is attributable to the influence of Ezra Pound,
but there is too much "poetry" and a high proportion of the most experimental is
also the most pointless and boring. This is what I have learnt in the past five years,
as poet, critic and editor. Pound, and the Black Mountain group, have done a great
deal for poetry; but for myself I have been meditating on the possibilities of a more
formal, traditional means. I've yet to discover whether I have the capacity to move
back in that direction.

                              *   *   *

   The landscape which Mike Doyle inhabits is international, or, more to the point,
non-national. Although he has written Section One of *Earth Meditations* as a Canadian, and renounces his New Zealand "bone country" as "there no longer," he is
clearly a citizen more of Academe than of Canada. The poems are full (perhaps
overfull) of allusions to the subjective philosophers to Western thought and abound
with place names from various countries, with non-english lines and with onomatopoeic neologisms. He contradicts this Joycean intellectualism, however, by numerous references to personal friends who may have influenced Doyle but are
unknown to the reader. And, more seriously, his syntax contradicts the appealing,
almost Zen-like simplicity of his essential philosophy of acceptance: "To be one
self / fully / a love / a / (life like music)."
   Academic, too, is the format of *Abandoned Sofa*, a limited, illustrated edition, and
especially of *Earth Meditations* in which quotations from the French surrealist
painter René Magritte are expanded by Doyle in a collage of styles, including the
concrete and pop-artistic. The pity of the collection is that the original, fascinating

musings of Magritte remain more compelling in their epigrammatic simplicity than are Doyle's elaborations in the manner of the Black Mountain aesthetic. Largely projectivist in prosody, the poems are, as their title announces, meditations – propositions, theories, personal thoughts arranged in a catalogue that climaxes with the cry of vision, "Shekinah! Shekinah!" and then curiously presents a world-view that seems not to have benefited from the immediately preceding epiphany.

Nevertheless, the editor of *Tuatara* magazine is undeniably a skillful craftsman and an impressive, literary intellect. One would like to read poems by Doyle which were as painstakingly crafted, but appeared to be less so. Subsequent volumes, should they develop arguments as worthy as those of *Earth Meditations* in a less self-indulgently scholarly mode, will be very interesting collections, indeed.

– S. R. Gilbert

DRINAN, Adam. See **MACLEOD, Joseph (Todd Gordon).**

DUDEK, Louis. Canadian. Born in Montreal, Quebec, 6 February 1918. Educated at Montreal High School; McGill University, Montreal, B.A. 1939; Columbia University, New York, M.A. in history 1946, Ph.D. in English and comparative literature 1955. Instructor in English, City College of New York, 1946–51. Since 1951, Member of the English Department, and currently Greenshields Professor of English, McGill University. Associated with *First Statement* magazine, 1941–43; Editor, *Delta* magazine, 1957–66; former Publisher, Contact Press, Toronto, and Delta Canada Press, Montreal. Currently, Publisher, DC Books, Montreal. Director-at-Large, Canadian Council of Teachers of English. Member, Humanities Research Council of Canada. Recipient: Quebec Literary Award, 1968. Address: 5 Ingleside Avenue, Montreal 215, Quebec, Canada.

PUBLICATIONS

Verse

> *Unit of Five,* with others.   Toronto, Ryerson Press, 1944.
> *East of the City.*   Toronto, Ryerson Press, 1946.
> *The Searching Image.*   Toronto, Ryerson Press, 1952.
> *Cerberus,* with Irving Layton and Raymond Souster.   Toronto, Contact Press, 1952.
> *Twenty-Four Poems.*   Toronto, Contact Press, 1952.
> *Europe.*   Toronto, Laocoon Press, 1954.
> *The Transparent Sea.*   Toronto, Contact Press, 1956.
> *En México.*   Toronto, Contact Press, 1958.

Laughing Stalks.   Toronto, Contact Press, 1958.
Atlantis.   Montreal, Delta Canada, 1967.
Collected Poetry.   Montreal, Delta Canada, 1971.

Other

Literature and the Press: A History of Printing, Printed Media, and Their Relation to Literature.   Toronto, Ryerson Press-Contact Press, 1960.
The First Person in Literature.   Toronto, Canadian Broadcasting Corporation, 1967.

Editor, with Irving Layton, *Canadian Poems, 1850–1952.*   Toronto, Contact Press, 1952.
Editor, *Selected Poems,* by Raymond Souster.   Toronto, Contact Press, 1956.
Editor, *Poetry of Our Time: An Introduction to Twentieth Century Poetry, Including Modern Canadian Poetry.*   Toronto, Macmillan, 1966.
Editor, with Michael Gnarowski, *The Making of Modern Poetry in Canada: Essential Articles on Contemporary Canadian Poetry in English.*   Toronto, Ryerson Press, 1967.
Editor, *All Kinds of Everything.*   Toronto, Clarke Irwin, 1973.

Translator, *Montreal, Paris d'Amérique,* by Michel Regnier.   Montreal, 1961.

Critical Studies: "Louis Dudek as Man of Letters," in *Canadian Literature* (Vancouver), Autumn 1964; "Louis Dudek Issue" of *Yes 14* (Montreal); *The Oxford Anthology of Canadian Literature,* Toronto, Oxford University Press, 1973.

*   *   *

> I hate travel
> but all the poetry I've ever written
> seems to be about travel.

Louis Dudek was born in Montreal; lives in Montreal; always returns to the harbour of his birthright and local knowledge. And with all this adherence to place, to the environment which formed him and the context which identifies him, he is constant voyager. He is the true Balboa of Canada; eternally discovering his Pacifics with courage and resourcefulness and accumulation of stubborn wonder.

His outer life is witness to this. He is the instigator to farther horizons. He brings back his horizons to where he lives with others; teaching the young, instituting vehicles of expression, implementing starting-points. He is a professor of European literature and modern poetry at McGill University; he set up in type and launched ten years of excitement in his magazine *Delta*; helped found and keep alive for new books of poetry Contact Press, and his present Delta Press. His energy is witnessed in a hundred places.

His poetry is witness. The energy and driving aesthetic are put into his books for anyone to have; shaped, committing, intellectual and passionate, Nine volumes, starting way back a quarter of a century ago. He was written off by the pundits on his seventh, 15 years ago. What did they know? What does anyone know about a poet's timing? His genius is to stop the clocks. Dudek has always stopped clocks.

He stops them always at the present. For ten years he watched the hands turn; then stops us at the present again in his eighth book, *Atlantis.*

In *Atlantis* we have the accumulated wisdom and resolutions of the eternal voyager, this Canadian of regional placement shaping in poetry his Pacific. Cosmic regionalism the university tailors of literature call it, stitching on their labels. Dudek takes a trip and comes up with a contemporary epic; goes to Naples, Rome, Paris and London, and brings them back to Montreal. A Ulysses and his Ithaca. He is after what is worth, of the past for the illumination of the present. Others have poetically descended from Ezra Pound but none has practised Pound with more affinity and cogency than Dudek. What's more, his pound is his own weight:

> Today we passed over Atlantis,
>   which is our true home.
> We live in exile
> waiting for that world to come.

And what is Dudek's City of Dioce whose walls are seven of seven colours? First, and a first which makes the others of little matter, first: all-encompassing love, Walt Whitman's love, love that is human compassion – and love not left romantic. Dudek has sufficient knowledge of the negative that is everywhere, alas:

> The price is suffering,
>   it doesn't matter.
> "We've had it, Chiquita."
>   (The waste is frightening.)
> What does matter is the dawn,
> the nimbus, the brief light of love.
> Try standing in the sun for a minute once a day.

And there Dudek does stand, his minute in the sun, before the horrendous world innocent so that he can have wonder. He has the answer, this poet of Canada:

> Always everywhere
>   to treat everyone as a person
> worthy and serious, and vulnerable to love.

> – Ralph Gustafson

DUGAN, Alan. American. Born in Brooklyn, New York, 12 February 1923. Educated at Olivet College, Michigan; Mexico City College, B.A. 1951. Served in the United States Army Air Force during World War II. Married to Judith Shahn. Taught at Sarah Lawrence College, Bronxville, New York, 1967–71. Since 1971, Staff Member for Poetry, Fine Arts Work Center, Provincetown, Massachusetts. Recipient: Yale Series of Younger Poets Award, 1961; Pulitzer Prize, 1962; National Book Award, 1962; American Academy in Rome Fellowship, 1962; Guggenheim Fellowship, 1963, 1972; Rockefeller Fellowship, 1966; Levinson Prize (*Poetry*, Chicago), 1967. Address: Box 97, Truro, Massachusetts 02666, U.S.A.

PUBLICATIONS

Verse

General Prothalamion in Populous Times. New Haven, Connecticut, privately
   printed, 1961.
Poems. New Haven, Connecticut, Yale University Press, 1961.
Poems 2. New Haven, Connecticut, Yale University Press, 1963.
Poems 3. New Haven, Connecticut, Yale University Press, 1967.
Collected Poems. New Haven, Connecticut, Yale University Press, 1969; Lon-
   don, Faber, 1970.
Poems 4. Boston, Little Brown, 1974.

                              *   *   *

    Alan Dugan is a fine poet who has created a significant body of work while
cultivating a confining style and exercising his caustic intelligence on a relatively
narrow range of subjects. One does not get terribly excited about his work, but one
nevertheless returns to it with increasing regularity, for it successfully inhabits that
middle ground of experience which our best poets today seem to loathe to admit. In
Dugan, at least, if one is able to hope at all, he hopes to endure rather than to
triumph. If one feels trapped, he will strive not for ultimate freedon and total
independence, but for the sensation of freedom, temporary, imperfect, illusory.
Dugan's spirit is best expressed in the conditional, which is to say that nothing he
feels or thinks is very far removed from regret for what might have been. It has
been generally accepted that Dugan is something of a moralist, and I suppose it is
possible to go along with such a view if we understand a moralist to be someone
who experiences convulsive fits of nausea from time to time, whenever he remembers what he is and to what he has given his approval if only by means of
undisturbed acquiescence. Dugan's is an intensely private, almost a claustrophobic
vision, and his poems usually communicate small perceptions appropriate to the
lives of small people, so that we listen not because of any glittering eye, but
because we feel we should. The voice that apprehends us is as earnest as any we
might hope to encounter, and the combination of brittle surfaces and an underlying
warmth is relentlessly imposing.
    Dugan's poems have variety, but they might all be drawn together as a single
long poem. The same alert but static sensibility is operant in all of them, and the
speaker rarely indulges the sort of emotional extremism which might distinguish his
more inspired from his more characteristically quotidian utterances. Particulars in
the work are easily reducible to an elementary abstraction in which polarities are
anxiously opposed until, under the wry focus of Dugan's imagination, they somehow coalesce. Alternatives become merely matters of perspective, and the wise
man gradually learns that as between one choice and another, we had best avoid
choices altogether.
    The predictable, low-keyed humor, so often remarked upon by others, does little
to mitigate the stinging venom of self-contempt that courses through so much of
Dugan's work. His is a bitter eloquence. If the cadence is austere, it is rarely
impoverished, and the muscular flow of his terse diction is rarely purchased at the
expense of complexity. Dugan invites us to witness with him, without any redemptive qualification, the sordid spectacle of our common humiliation. It is a strangely
unimpassioned witnessing, but the amusement of ironic detachment has much to
recommend it, or so it would seem. What Dugan fears most is that neutrality which

predicts the death of the spirit, but more and more it appears to him that this is indeed his most authentic reality.

– Robert Boyers

DUNCAN, Robert (Edward). American. Born in Oakland, California, 7 January 1919. Educated at the University of California, Berkeley, 1936–38, 1948–50. Editor, *The Experimental Review*, 1938–40, *Phoenix*, and *The Berkeley Miscellany*, 1948–49, all in Berkeley. Lived in Mallorca, 1955–56. Taught at Black Mountain College, North Carolina, 1956; Assistant Director of the Poetry Center (Ford grant), 1956–57, and Lecturer in the Poetry Workshop, 1965, San Francisco State College; Lecturer, University of British Columbia, Vancouver, 1963. Recipient: Union League Civic and Arts Foundation Prize, 1957, Harriet Monroe Memorial Prize, 1960, and Levinson Prize, 1964 (*Poetry*, Chicago); Guggenheim Fellowship, 1963; National Endowment for the Arts grant, 1966 (two grants). Address: 3267 20th Street, San Francisco, California 94110, U.S.A.

PUBLICATIONS

Verse

Heavenly City, Earthly City. Berkeley, California, Bern Porter, 1947.
Poems 1948–1949. Berkeley, California, Berkeley Miscellany Editions, 1950.
Medieval Scenes. San Francisco, Centaur Press, 1950.
The Song of the Border-Guard. Black Mountain, North Carolina, Black Mountain College, 1952.
Caesar's Gate: Poems 1949–1950. Palma, Mallorca, Divers Press, 1955.
Letters. Highlands, North Carolina, Jargon, 1958.
Selected Poems. San Francisco, City Lights Books, 1959.
The Opening of the Field. New York, Grove Press, 1960; London, Cape, 1969.
Roots and Branches: Poems. New York, Scribner, 1964; London, Cape, 1970.
Writing, Writing: A Composition Book of Madison 1953, Stein Imitations. Albuquerque, New Mexico, Sumbooks, 1964.
Wine. Berkeley, California, Oyez, 1964.
Uprising. Berkeley, California, Oyez, 1965.
A Book of Resemblances: Poems 1950–1953. New Haven, Connecticut, Henry Wenning, 1966.
Of the War: Passages 22–27. Berkeley, California, Oyez, 1966.
The Year As Catches: First Poems 1939–1946. Berkeley, California, Oyez, 1966.
Fragments of a Disordered Devotion. San Francisco, Gnomon Press, 1966.
Epilogos. Los Angeles, Black Sparrow Press, 1967.
The Cat and the Blackbird. San Francisco, White Rabbit Press, 1967.
Christmas Present, Christmas Presence! Los Angeles, Black Sparrow Press, 1967.
Bending the Bow. New York, New Directions, 1968; London, Cape, 1971.

My Mother Would Be a Falconess. Berkeley, California, Oyez, 1968.
Names of People. Los Angeles, Black Sparrow Press, 1968.
The First Decade: Selected Poems 1940–1950. London, Fulcrum Press, 1968.
Derivations: Selected Poems 1950–1956. London, Fulcrum Press, 1968.
Play Time, Pseudo Stein. New York, Poets Press, 1969.
Achilles' Song. New York, Phoenix Book Shop, 1969.
Poetic Disturbances. San Francisco, Maya, 1970.
Bring It Up from the Dark. Berkeley, California, Cody's Books, 1970.
Tribunals: Passages 31–35. Los Angeles, Black Sparrow Press, 1970.
In Memoriam Wallace Stevens. Storrs, University of Connecticut, 1972.
The Truth and Life of Myrtle. Fremont, Michigan, Sumac Press, 1972.

Recording: *Letters,* Stream.

Plays

Faust Foutu (produced San Francisco, 1955; New York, 1959–60). Published
    as *Faust Foutu: Act One of Four Acts: A Comic Mask,* San Francisco, White
    Rabbit Press, 1958; complete edition, as *Faust Foutu: An Entertainment in
    Four Parts,* Stinson Beach, California, Enkidu Surrogate, 1960.
Medea at Kolchis: The Maiden Head (produced Black Mountain, North Carolina,
    1956). Berkeley, California, Oyez, 1965.

Other

The Artist's View. San Francisco, privately printed, 1952.
On Poetry (radio interview with Eugene Vance). New Haven, Connecticut,
    Yale University, 1964.
As Testimony: The Poem and the Scene. San Francisco, White Rabbit Press,
    1964.
The Sweetness and Greatness of Dante's "Divine Comedy," 1265–1965. San
    Francisco, Open Space, 1965.
Six Prose Pieces. Rochester, Michigan, Perishable Press, 1966.
"Robert Duncan Issue" of *Audit* (Buffalo), iv, 3, 1967.
The Truth and Life of Myth: An Essay in Essential Autobiography. New York,
    House of Books, 1968.
*65 Drawings: A Selections of 65 Drawings from One Drawing-Book:
    1952–1956.* Los Angeles, Black Sparrow Press, 1970.
Notes on Grossinger's "Solar Journal: Oecological Sections." Los Angeles,
    Black Sparrow Press, 1970.
An Interview with George Bowering and Robert Hogg, April 19, 1969. Toronto,
    Beaver Kosmos Folio, 1971.

*   *   *

Robert Duncan, born 1919 in Oakland, California, and still closely identified with
San Francisco, as well as with the Black Mountain group of the Fifties, has long
been building "a hut of words primitive to our nature," accepting and reflecting in
poems and journals of torrential associationism "the language in its natural disarray." In the section of Donald Allen's *The New American Poetry 1945–1960* in which
he discusses his aesthetics, Duncan writes: "I learned that the poem that might be
fantastic life, that might be insight into the real, was a rite. The poem was a ritual

referring to divine orders." Poetry for Duncan "is the story of the romance of forms. It involves for all of us numinous powers, quests and workings of the spirit, apprehensions of our share in history, reverence for our 'ancestors' in spirit." Duncan trusts "the figures as they emerge," has "faith that there is the wholeness of form." He freely acknowledges the sources of his forms, but in each case, for Duncan, form is transformation. Even what he calls "imitations of Gertrude Stein" are as original as anything in recent American poetry. It would not be easy to find words for Duncan's work: it is Orphic, sensual, numinous, transcendent – all words he uses at times as if working toward self-definition. Often too, his images are beautifully simple: "What I am picturing is a poetry spun out of an evening as a whole cloth spun out of a web of worn wool. And an out of the way – that ever lasting cottage in the deepest part of the forest of the tales told by a fire. What I am picturing is an old shawl worn, of no earthly importance, a poetry reduced again to its ashes, an evening entertainment of no great measure. Talk in a room we are going toward we were from. A secluded interrogation. . . ." Duncan's sense of time passing, of the fantastic which the image must catch, is obsessive: "This is a net, torn, thru which stars fall, / a largest residue — or wholeness, among leavings." One feels everywhere remarkable and serious play with words: "Reality, for the artist, is no more than a subject matter – a beastly head of hair." He finds the myth, the presence of the "promethean" or that "life of the spirit that involves fairies and Christs, saints and the present" everywhere, e.g., in tree rings, surrounded perhaps, by still other rings: "Encirclements of outcry. A silent band. That makes his audience uneasy. Out: land, house, cry; side, man. Outriders. She wrings out his shirk and hangs him to drive. The poems of correspondents reappear as outleafings of. Where there are rings of trees a forest appears. Wood whistlings and storms of green contagion spread: The ayre denser there. And these men are called woodsmen; subservient to the element: wood."

His most admired poems are musical and expansive, sometimes obscure; and always (as in "The Venice Poem") "a loosening of conventions and return to open form." Like Olson and Creeley he is concerned with the field, with the measure that emerges. "You have carried a branch of tomorrow into the room." In "A Poem Beginning with a Line by Pindar," he is concerned with "a survival of obsolete mode, there may have been old voices in the survival that directed the heart." Duncan confronts "Psyche's tasks –" creating "lilac blossoms of courage in daily act / striving to meet a natural measure." His language is so overpowering at times that the reader shares with the weeping and the coming near death that goes with the ecstacy of language, as Dante or Duncan follow a myth right into the depths of their hearts. Duncan recognizes that the finding of measure and image accepts no strict Instruction or formulization: "I work at the language as a spring of water works at the rock, to find a course, and so, blindly. In this I am not a maker of things, but, if maker, a maker of a way. For the way is itself. . . . And vast as the language is, it is no end but a resistance thru which a poem might move – as it flows or dances or puddles in time – making it up in its going along and yet going only as it breaks the resistance of the language." He respects the "pools, vacant energies below meaning, hidden to our purposes." In a poet so private, so often occult, it is not surprising that the reader too must make an effort. Images created in so nearly an autistic fashion, as they sometimes are by Duncan, offer a private world to share, and Duncan, like Whitman, often seems to despair of his reader . . . "across an emptiness of time I see you. I shall never reach you – between me and thee."

In fact, Duncan's autistic isolation and sense of occult privacy might be understood by many as a rejection of much of his potential audience. This judgment seems to me confirmed by Duncan's remark that for him the world of poetry is "a love cult." In any case, he has willfully limited his audience. According to Michael McClure, Duncan has vowed to publish nothing for several years. What might earlier have been seen as a truculent and angry rejection of that part of society that does not interest him, either socially or as an audience, can now be seen as an almost swooning retreat into privacy: for Duncan that privacy is perhaps the almost hallucinatory experiencing of poetry for itself, not for any such connection with an audience as Walt Whitman professed. Robert Duncan may well emerge as one of the chief literary curiosities of our age, one whose personal and aesthetic dramatics ultimately interest only an impassioned cult.

– David Ray

DUNCAN, Ronald (Frederick Henry). British. Born in Salisbury, Rhodesia, 6 August 1914. Educated in Switzerland and at Downing College, Cambridge, M.A. 1936. Married Rose Marie Theresa Hansom in 1941; has two children. Editor, *The Townsman,* London, 1938–46; Columnist ("Jan's Journal"), *Evening Standard,* London, 1946–56. Has farmed in Devon since 1939. Founder, Devon Festival of the Arts, Bideford, 1953; Co-Founder, English Stage Company at the Royal Court Theatre, London, 1955. Agents: David Higham Associates, 5–8 Lower John Street, Golden Square, London W.1; and Eric Glass Ltd., 28 Berkeley Square, London W.1. Address: Welcombe, Bideford, Devon, England.

PUBLICATIONS

Verse

Postcards to Pulchinella. London, Fortune Press, 1941.
The Mongrel and Other Poems. London, Faber, 1950.
The Solitudes. London, Faber, 1960.
Judas. London, Blond, 1960.
Unpopular Poems. London, Hart Davis, 1969.
Man, part 1. London, Rebel Press, 1970.
Man, part 2. Welcombe, Devon, Rebel Press, 1972.
Man, part 3. Welcombe, Devon, Rebel Press, 1972.
Man, parts 4 and 5. Welcombe, Devon, Rebel Press, 1974.

Plays

Birth (produced London, 1937).
The Dull Ass's Hoof (includes *The Unburied Dead; Pimp, Skunk and Profiteer; Ora Pro Nobis*). London, Fortune Press, 1940.
This Way to the Tomb: A Masque and Anti-Masque, music by Benjamin Britten (produced London, 1946; New York, 1961). London, Faber, 1946; New York, Theatre Arts, 1967.

The Eagle Has Two Heads, adaptation of a play by Jean Cocteau (produced
  London, 1946). London, Vision Press, and New York, Funk and Wagnalls,
  1948.
The Rape of Lucretia, music by Benjamin Britten, adaptation of a play by
  André Obey (produced Glyndebourne, Sussex, 1946). London, Boosey and
  Hawkes, 1946; augmented edition, London, Lane, 1948.
Amo Ergo Sum (cantata), music by Benjamin Britten (produced London, 1948).
The Typewriter, adaptation of a play by Jean Cocteau (produced London,
  1950). London, Dobson, 1948.
Stratton, music by Benjamin Britten (produced London, 1950). London,
  Faber, 1950.
St. Spiv (as *Nothing up My Sleeve,* produced London, 1950; revised version, as
  St. 'Orace, music by Jerry Wayne, produced London, 1964). Included in
  Collected Plays, 1971.
Our Lady's Tumbler, music by Arthur Oldham (produced Salisbury, Wiltshire,
  1951). London, Faber, 1951.
Don Juan (produced Bideford, Devon, 1953; London, 1956). London, Faber,
  1954.
The Death of Satan (produced Bideford, Devon, 1954; London, 1956; New
  York, 1960) London, Faber, 1955; in *Satan, Socialites, and Solly Gold; Three
  New Plays from England,* New York, Coward McCann, 1961.
A Man Named Judas, adaptation of a play by C. A. Puget and Pierre Bost
  (produced Edinburgh, 1956).
The Cardinal, with Hans Keuls, adaptation of a play by Harold Brett (produced
  Cambridge, 1957).
The Apollo de Bellac, adaptation of a play by Jean Giraudoux (produced
  London, 1957). London, French, 1958.
The Catalyst (produced London, 1958; revised version, as *Ménage à Trois,*
  produced London, 1963). London, Rebel Press, 1964; New York, Theatre
  Arts, 1967.
Christopher Sly, music by Thomas Eastwood (produced London, 1960).
Abelard and Heloise: A Correspondence for the Stage (produced London,
  1960). London, Faber, 1961.
The Rabbit Race, adaptation of a play by Martin Walser (produced Edinburgh,
  1963). Published in *Plays, vol. 1* by Martin Walser, London, Calder, 1963.
O-B-A-F-G$_S$R-N: *A Play in One Act in Stereophonic Sound* (produced Exeter,
  Devon, 1964). London, Rebel Press, 1964; New York, Theatre Arts, 1967.
The Trojan Women, adaptation of a play by Jean-Paul Sartre based on the play
  by Euripides (produced Edinburgh, 1967). London, Hamish Hamilton, and
  New York, Knopf, 1967.
The Seven Deadly Virtues: A Contemporary Immorality Play (produced London,
  1968). Included in *Collected Plays,* 1971.
The Gift (produced Exeter, Devon, 1968). Included in *Collected Plays,* 1971.
The Rehearsal (as *Still Life,* televised 1970). Included in *Collected Plays,* 1971.
Collected Plays (includes *This Way to the Tomb, St. Spiv, Our Lady's Tumbler,
  The Rehearsal, The Seven Deadly Virtues, O-B-A-F-G, The Gift*). London,
  Hart Davis, and New York, Theatre Arts, 1971.

Screenplay: *Girl on a Motorcycle,* 1969.

Television Plays: *The Portrait,* 1954; *The Janitor,* 1955; *Preface to America,* 1959;
Not All the Dead Are Buried, 1960; *The Rebel,* music by Thomas Eastwood,
1969; *Still Life,* 1970; *Mandala,* 1972.

Novels

The Last Adam.   London, Dobson, 1952.
Saint Spiv.   London, Dobson, 1961.

Short Stories

The Perfect Mistress and Other Stories.   London, Hart Davis, 1971.
A Kettle of Fish.   London, Hart Davis, 1971.

Other

The Complete Pacifist.   London, Boriswood, 1937.
The Rexist Party Manifesto (as the Bishop of Marsland).   London, Townsman, 1937.
Strategy in War (as Major-General Marsland).   London, Townsman, 1937.
Journal of a Husbandman.   London, Faber, 1944.
Home-Made Home (on architecture).   London, Faber, 1947.
Jan's Journal 1.   London, William Campion, 1949.
Tobacco Growing in England.   London, Faber, 1950.
The Blue Fox (newspaper articles).   London, Museum Press, 1951; New York, Oxford University Press, 1952.
Jan at the Blue Fox (newspaper articles).   London, Museum Press, 1952.
Where I Live.   London, Museum Press, 1953.
Jan's Journal 2.   London, Museum Press, 1954.
All Men Are Islands: An Autobiography.   London, Hart Davis, 1964.
Devon and Cornwall.   London, Batsford, and New York, Hastings House, 1966.
How to Make Enemies (autobiography).   London, Hart Davis, 1968.

Editor, *Songs and Satires of John Wilmot, 2nd Earl of Rochester.*   London, Forge Press, 1948.
Editor, *Selected Poems,* by Ben Jonson.   London, Grey Walls Press, 1949.
Editor, *Selected Writings of Mahatma Gandhi.*   London, Faber, and Boston, Beacon Press, 1951.
Editor, with the Countess of Harewood, *Classical Songs for Children.*   London, Blond, and New York, Potter, 1965.
Editor, with Marion Harewood, *The Penguin Book of Accompanied Songs.*   London, Penguin, 1973.

Translator, *Diary of a Film: La Belle et la Bête,* by Jean Cocteau.   London, Dobson, 1950.

Bibliography: in *Ronald Duncan* by Max Walter Haueter, London, Rebel Press, 1969.

Manuscript Collection: University of Texas, Austin.

Critical Study: *Ronald Duncan* by Max Walter Haueter, London, Rebel Press, 1969.

Theatrical Activities:

Director: **Play** – *Abelard and Heloise,* London, 1973.

*   *   *

Although there was a period when Ronald Duncan was so in fashion that his poems almost seemed pastiches ("Passion's no prince, / is the maimed mind's blindness"), he has, over thirty years, pursued his own course. His interest in music provoked (or resulted from?) verse forms which have always been disciplined, even when apparently at their loosest; and a strong note of sensuality has sometimes found a beautifully cool expression: "Oh Rose Marie if you make yourself / As naked and smooth as the moon / I will become the softest mist / And cover you." Some of the verse has worn badly (cf. the once much-admired libretto for Britten's *Rape of Lucretia);* but, in a harsher timbre, the love poems in *The Solitudes,* written in loneliness and despair, are almost totally successful, and perhaps represent Duncan at his most approachable. With *Judas,* Duncan turned to a longer form, and during the past ten years has concentrated on *Man,* a long poem tracing "emergent consciousness in man," having concluded that "90% of poetry is no more than a mating call. That may be sufficient for adolescents." *Man,* much concerned with science, is by no means an unapproachable poem; it has been insuffiently examined by critics, for it is in fact one of the more serious examples recently published of a sustained long poem, and has passages of great intensity. If the reader is forced to consider, in the end, whether Duncan has in fact chosen the right setting for his speculations, he has undeniably written an original long poem which is discernably an exploration of form as well as subject; and such truly exploratory verse in our time is rare.

– Derek Parker

DUNN, Douglas (Eaglesham). British. Born in Inchinnan, Renfrewshire, 23 October 1942. Educated at Renfrew High School; Camphill School, Paisley; Scottish School of Librarianship; University of Hull, 1966–69, B.A. in English 1969. Married Lesley Balfour Wallace in 1964. Library Assistant, Renfrew County Library, Paisley, 1959–62, and Andersonian Library, Glasgow, 1962–64; Assistant Librarian, Akron Public Library, Ohio, 1964–66; Librarian, Chemistry Department Library, University of Glasgow, 1966; Assistant Librarian, Brynmor Jones Library, University of Hull, 1969–71. Since 1971, Poetry Reviewer, *Encounter* magazine, London. Recipient: Eric Gregory Award, 1966; Scottish Arts Council award, 1970; Maugham Award, 1972. Address: c/o Faber and Faber Ltd., 3 Queen Square, London W.C.1, England.

PUBLICATIONS

Verse

Terry Street. London, Faber, 1969; New York, Chilmark Press, 1973.
Corgi Modern Poets in Focus 1, with others, edited by Dannie Abse. London, Corgi, 1971.

Backwaters.   London, The Review, 1971.
Night.   London, Poem-of-the-Month Club, 1971.
The Happier Life.   London, Faber, 1972.
Love or Nothing.   London, Faber, 1974.

Other

Editor, *New Poems 1972–73.*   London, Hutchinson, 1973.
Editor, "British Poetry Issue" of *Antaeus 12* (New York), 1973.
Editor, *A Choice of Byron's Verse.*   London, Faber, 1974.

Manuscript Collection: Brynmor Jones Library, University of Hull.

*   *   *

Douglas Dunn's first poems to appear in such anthologies as *Scottish Poetry* gave evidence of a talent for accurately-observed sensuous imagery as it reflects from the surface of things. The best section of his first book, *Terry Street*, related this talent to the setting and the way of life of a working-class street in Hull, as in "From the Night-Window":

> The night rattles with nightmares,
> Children cry in the close-packed houses,
> A man rots in his snoring.
> On quiet feet, policemen test doors.
> Footsteps become people under streetlamps.

Sometimes the effect of active engagement with the urban scene is got simply by a kind of cumulative cataloguing, redeemed from being a series of prose statements by a personal rhythmic tone:

> On the quiet street, Saturday night's fag-packets,
> Balls of fish and chip newspaper, bottles
> Placed neatly on window sills, beside cats.
>
> A street of oilstains and parked motorbikes,
> Wet confectionery wrappers becoming paste,
> Things doing nothing, ending, rejected.
>
> Revellers return tieless, or with hairdos deceased,
> From parties, paying taxis in the cold,
> Unsmiling in the fogs of deflated mirth.
>
> Neighbours in pyjamas watch them from upstairs,
> Chewing on pre-breakfast snacks,
> Waiting for kettles to boil, wives quit the lav.

To some extent this is Larkin without either the tension or the compassion. But since at any rate many Scots readers still applaud most loudly those among their poets who write of lonely places and aspects of dying peripheral cultures, any poet who tries to come to terms with the urban situation of the majority as successfully as does Dunn in *Terry Street* must be respected.

Unfortunately, having re-created in poetry's terms a mirror-image of this situation, albeit as an expatriate – yet one who, in "Ships," can still write evocatively of his native Clydeside:

> A fine rain attaches itself to the ship like skin.
> The lascars play poker, the Scottish mate looks
> At the last lights, one that is Ayrshire,
> Others on lonely rocks, or clubfooted peninsulas

– what does the poet do next? The *Terry Street* Room-at-the-Top Dunn becomes, in *The Happier Life,* his second volume, Life-at-the-Top Dunn: and all he seems to want to do is snipe and sneer at everything that comes within range of his cleverness, from "Ted Heath's Britain" (an image as meaningless and vague as "Harold Wilson's Britain" or "Lord Palmerston's Britain"), to Irish girls come to town in search of a fuller life, who can be bought for an hour for ten pounds ("essentially rural whores, essentially innocent"), sportsmen ("scum, they have fast cars and money"), and "the rising young executives." An attempt is made to deal with the problem of a cohesing tension by resorting either to rhyming couplets or to formal stanzas. Sicanus, Thucydides, Ceres, and other literary allusions, are also used to help out when the pressure of something to say is low.

I do not mean to suggest that *The Happier Life* is wholly without interest. Cleverness abounds, like the detailed, formal expression of the disgust of a poor young man who nevertheless remains the kept pimp of a rich older woman ("Morning Bedroom"); and the more direct final section of the poem "Fixed." But ultimately the overall impression is of a staleness as flat as a copy of last Sunday's *News of the World.* Dunn doesn't really like people much. Why? I suspect because in "Modern Love," he writes of an evening

> where we are alive
> In a domestic love, seemingly alone,
> All other lives worn down to trees and sunlight,
> Looking forward to a visit from the cat.

And in "A Faber Melancholy" (ugh!)

> A thorn has scored my writing hand.
> No one can now have Byron's love, or fry
> With Shelley in great company on the sand.
> To do is only to be like, or try,
>   And to achieve is only to be less
>   Than all these dead. There is no success.

There is: but it is not to be found through sneering envy, in denigrating the daily concerns of ordinary people, or by longing for large romantic gestures while sliding uncertainly over the surface of one's own self-pity.

– Maurice Lindsay

DURRELL, Lawrence (George). British. Born in Julundur, India, 27 February 1912. Educated at the College of St. Joseph, Darjeeling, India; St. Edmund's School, Canterbury, Kent. Married Nancy Myers in 1935 (divorced, 1947); Eve

Cohen, 1947 (divorced); Claude Durrell, 1961 (died, 1967); Ghislaine de Boysson, 1973; has two children. Has had many jobs, including jazz pianist (Blue Peter nightclub, London), automobile racer, and real estate agent. Lived in Corfu, 1934–40. Editor, with Henry Miller and Alfred Perles, *The Booster* (later *Delta*), Paris, 1937–39; Columnist, *Egyptian Gazette*, Cairo, 1941; Editor, with Robin Fedden and Bernard Spencer, *Personal Landscape*, Cairo, 1942–45; Special Correspondent in Cyprus for *The Economist*, London, 1953–55; Editor, *Cyprus Review*, Nicosia, 1954–55. Taught at the British Institute, Kalamata, Greece, 1940. Foreign Press Service Officer, British Information Office, Cairo, 1941–44; Press Attaché, British Information Office, Alexandria, 1944–45; Director of Public Relations for the Dodecanese Islands, Greece, 1946–47; Press Attaché, British Legation, Belgrade, 1949–52; Director of Public Relations for the British Government in Cyprus, 1954–56. Director of the British Council Institute, Cordoba, Argentina, 1947–48. Recipient: Duff Cooper Memorial Prize, 1957; Prix du Meilleur Livre Etranger, 1959. Fellow, Royal Society of Literature, 1954. Has lived in France since 1957. Address: c/o National and Grindlay's Bank, 13 St. James's Square, London S.W.1, England.

PUBLICATIONS

Verse

Quaint Fragment: Poems Written Between the Ages of Sixteen and Nineteen. London, Cecil Press, 1931.
Ten Poems. London, Caduseus Press, 1932.
Bromo Bombastes. London, Caduseus Press; 1933.
Transition: Poems. London, Caduseus Press, 1934.
Proems: An Anthology of Poems, with others. London, Fortune Press, 1938.
A Private Country. London, Faber, 1943.
Cities, Plains and People. London, Faber, 1946.
Zero, and Asylum in the Snow: Two Excursions into Reality. Rhodes, privately printed, 1946; New York, Circle Editions, 1947.
On Seeming to Presume. London, Faber, 1948.
Deus Loci. Ischia, Italy, Di Mato Vito, 1950.
Private Drafts. Nicosia, Cyprus, Proodos Press, 1955.
The Tree of Idleness and Other Poems. London, Faber, 1955.
Selected Poems. London, Faber, and New York, Grove Press, 1956.
Collected Poems. London, Faber, and New York, Dutton, 1960; revised edition, 1968.
Penguin Modern Poets 1, with Elizabeth Jennings and R. S. Thomas. London, Penguin, 1962.
Beccafico Le Becfigue (English, with French translation by F.-J. Temple). Montpellier, France, La Licorne, 1963.
La Descente du Styx (English, with French translation by F.-J. Temple). Montpellier, France, La Murène, 1964.
Selected Poems 1935–63. London, Faber, 1964.
The Ikons: New Poems. London, Faber, 1966; New York, Dutton, 1967.
The Red Limbo Lingo: A Poetry Notebook for 1968–1970. London, Faber, 1971.
On the Suchness of the Old Boy. London, Turret Books, 1972.
Vega and Other Poems. London, Faber, 1973.
Plant-Magic Man. Santa Barbara, California, 1973.

Plays

Sappho: A Play in Verse (produced Hamburg, 1959; Edinburgh, 1961; Evanston, Illinois, 1964). London, Faber, 1950; New York, Dutton, 1958.
Acte (produced Hamburg, 1961). London, Faber, 1965; New York, Dutton, 1966.
An Irish Faustus: A Morality in Nine Scenes (produced Sommerhausen, Germany, 1966). London, Faber, 1963; New York, Dutton, 1964.

Television Script: *The Lonely Roads*, 1971.

Recording: *Ulysses Come Back: Sketch for a Musical* (story, music and lyrics by Lawrence Durrell), 1971.

Novels

Pied Piper of Lovers. London, Cassell, 1935.
Panic Spring (as Charles Norden). London, Faber, and New York, Covici Friede, 1937.
The Black Book: An Agon. Paris, Obelisk Press, 1938; New York, Dutton, 1960; London, Faber, 1973.
Cefalû. London, Editions Poetry, 1947; as *The Dark Labyrinth*, New York, Ace, 1958.
White Eagles over Serbia. London, Faber, and New York, Criterion Books, 1957.
The Alexandria Quartet:
    Justine. London, Faber, and New York, Dutton, 1957.
    Balthazar. London, Faber, and New York, Dutton, 1958.
    Mountolive. London, Faber, 1958; New York, Dutton, 1959.
    Clea. London, Faber, and New York, Dutton, 1960.
The Revolt of Aphrodite. London, Faber, 1974.
    Tunc. London, Faber, and New York, Dutton, 1968.
    Nunquam. London, Faber, and New York, Dutton, 1970.
Monsieur; or, The Prince of Darkness. London, Faber, and New York, Viking Press, 1975.

Short Stories

Espirit de Corps: Sketches from Diplomatic Life. London, Faber, 1957; New York, Dutton, 1958.
Stiff Upper Lip: Life among the Diplomats. London, Faber, 1958; New York, Dutton, 1959.
Sauve Qui Peut. London, Faber, 1966; New York, Dutton, 1967.
The Best of Antrobus. London, Faber, 1974.

Other

Prospero's Cell: A Guide to the Landscape and Manners of the Island of Corcyra. London, Faber, 1945; New York, Dutton, 1960.
A Landmark Gone. Los Angeles, privately printed, 1949.
Key to Modern Poetry. London, Peter Nevill, 1952; as *A Key to Modern British Poetry,* Norman, University of Oklahoma Press, 1952.

407

Reflections on a Marine Venus: A Companion to the Landscape of Rhodes. London, Faber, 1953; New York, Dutton, 1960.

Bitter Lemons (on Cyprus). London, Faber, 1957; New York, Dutton, 1958.

Art and Outrage: A Correspondence about Henry Miller Between Alfred Perles and Lawrence Durrell, with an Intermission by Henry Miller. London, Putnam, 1959; New York, Dutton, 1960.

Lawrence Durrell and Henry Miller: A Private Correspondence, edited by George Wickes. New York, Dutton, and London, Faber, 1963.

Spirit of Place: Letters and Essays on Travel, edited by Alan G. Thomas. London, Faber, and New York, Dutton, 1969.

Le Grand Suppositoire (a taped biographical interview with Marc Alyn). Paris, Editions Pierre Belfond, 1972; as *The Big Supposer,* New York, Grove Press, 1974.

Editor, with others, *Personal Landscape: An Anthology of Exile.* London, Editions Poetry, 1945.

Editor, *A Henry Miller Reader.* New York, New Directions, 1959; as *The Best of Henry Miller,* London, Heinemann, 1960.

Editor, *New Poems, 1963: A P.E.N. Anthology of Contemporary Poetry.* London, Hutchinson, 1963.

Editor, *Lear's Corfu: An Anthology Drawn from the Painter's Letters.* Corfu, Corfu Travel, 1965.

Editor, *Wordsworth.* London, Penguin, 1973.

Translator, *Six Poems from the Greek of Sekilanos and Seferis.* Rhodes, privately printed, 1946.

Translator, with others, *The King of Asine and Other Poems,* by George Seferis. London, Lehmann, 1948.

Translator, *The Curious History of Pope Joan,* by Emmanuel Royidis. London, Verschoyle, 1954; revised edition, as *Pope Joan: A Personal Biography,* London, Deutsch, 1960; New York, Dutton, 1961.

Bibliography: by Alan G. Thomas, in *Lawrence Durrell: A Study* by G. S. Fraser, London, Faber, 1968.

Critical Studies: *The World of Lawrence Durrell,* edited by Harry T. Moore, Carbondale, Southern Illinois University Press, 1962; *Lawrence Durrell and the Alexandria Quartet* by Alan Warren Friedman, Norman, University of Oklahoma Press, 1970.

Lawrence Durrell comments:

If there is virtue in polixity and a protean temperament then I perhaps may claim a certain modest excellence for my prose and poetry. Always conscious that an artist has only one thing to say I have tried to say it in a number of different forms. Of course, one cannot always win, and some books may be better than others. But hasn't one the right to be judged by one's best work?

*   *   *

Lawrence Durrell's world fame is based on his series of novels of the 1950's, *The Alexandria Quartet,* but critics like Francis Hope, who dislike these and also the subterranean novel of the late 1930's, published in Paris, *The Black Book,* see his real achievement in his poems and in his three travel books, which have much of the quality of his poems, about Corfu before the Second World War, Rhodes during its post-war Allied occupation, and Cyprus during the troubles of the early 1950's. Those who feel that as a novelist Durrell is over-rated would probably say that in *The Alexandria Quartet* the set scenes, the landscapes, the evocations of local atmosphere are the work of a poet but that the handling of incident and character is excessively romantic, in a "story-book" sense. It is oddly true that the tone and diction of the poems are quieter, more subdued, much less boldly coloured than much of the prose of *The Alexandria Quarter* and *Tunc*: Durrell does not seem to be trying so hard, straining his resources so much, and it may be therefore that as a poet he is at his most convincing.

There is not much development in the poetry, and in his collected and selected poems Durrell rightly arranges the poems according to affinities of kind, tone, or subject-matter rather than in chronological order. Though he is very obviously a "modern" poet, he owes a great deal to two of his favourite poets of the nineteenth century, Landor and Browning. In short lyrics like "Water Music" he aims at, and often achieves, a Landorian perfection of form. Longer poems about characters or places have deliberately a certain Browningesque looseness or roughness of texture, and resemble Browning's dramatic monologues in setting great figures of the past, Byron, Horace, Rochefoucauld, in a perspective of ambiguous self-questioning; but more obviously than Browning, influenced perhaps by Browning's disciple Ezra Pound, Durrell is using such figures to express or sometimes to reject aspects of his own nature.

Poems about places, like the effective "Alexandria," written in war-time, similarly use a place and sometimes friends and enemies in a place to concretise a creative mood. The place becomes, as in the good little poem about the cold chaste beauty of the English West Country, "Bere Regis," a symbol for a whole complex of attitudes to be savoured, appreciated, perhaps finally to be relegated to the large category of attitudes which, for Durrell, are not finally adequate. Durrell is not an objective poet of landscape like his friend, that fine, neglected poet, Bernard Spencer, but a poet of what may be called moodscape.

A third category of poems is what Robert Graves calls "satires and grotesques": humorous and fantastic poems, but always in the end affectionate rather than sharply satirical, like "Uncebunke" or "The Ballad of the Good Lord Nelson." There are some poems like the early "Sonnet of Hamlet" or the later short "Nemea" where the main interest seems to be in the poetry of vocabulary, in surprising collocations or strange and beautiful echoings of words: such poems are perhaps the equivalent of what T. S. Eliot called "five-finger exercises."

The total impression that one derives from Durrell's poems is of a benign quietism, something like that of a humorous Chinese sage gazing on waterfalls from a hut on a mountain. Born in India, Durrell has always been deeply interested in Eastern thought, in what he calls the "expurgation" of the self, in the achievement of states of calm contemplation. This spiritual bent is expressed, however, in scene or anecdote, strange joke, or hushed and gentle lyric rather than in abstract or dogmatic terms. The sage is strangely married, also, to the literary dandy. Durrell's kind of poetry is today distinctly unfashionable; it is not confessional, it is not socially committed, its language and attitudes may seem excessively "literary." It never clamours for attention. Yet it has always pleased good critics and it will last.

– G. S. Fraser

DUTTON, Geoffrey (Piers Henry).   Australian.   Born in Anlaby, South Australia, 2
August 1922. Educated at Geelong Grammar School, Victoria, 1932–39; University
of Adelaide, 1940–41; Magdalen College, Oxford, 1946–49, B.A. 1949. Served as a
Flight Lieutenant in the Royal Australian Air Force, 1941–45. Married Ninette Trott
in 1944; has three children. Senior Lecturer in English, University of Adelaide,
1954–62; Visiting Lecturer in Australian Literature, University of Leeds, 1960;
Visiting Professor, Kansas State University, Manhattan, 1962. Editor, Penguin
Australia, Melbourne, 1961–65. Since 1965, Editorial Director of Sun Books Pty.
Ltd., Melbourne. Co-Founder, *Australian Letters,* Adelaide, 1957, and *Australian
Book Review,* Kensington Park, 1962. Member of the Australian Council for the
Arts, 1968–70, and Commonwealth Literary Fund Advisory Board, 1972–73. Since
1973, Member, Australian Literature Board. Address: Old Anlaby, Kapunda, South
Australia 5373, Australia.

PUBLICATIONS

Verse

Nightflight and Sunrise.   Melbourne, Reed and Harris, 1945.
Antipodes in Shoes.   Sydney, Edwards and Shaw, 1955.
Flowers and Fury.   Melbourne, Cheshire, 1963.
On My Island: Poems for Children.   Melbourne, Cheshire, 1967.
Poems Soft and Loud.   Melbourne, Cheshire, 1968.
Findings and Keepings.   Adelaide, Australian Letters, 1970.
New Poems to 1972.   Adelaide, Australian Letters, 1972.

Novels

The Mortal and the Marble.   London, Chapman and Hall, 1950.
Andy.   Sydney and London, Collins, 1968.
Tamara.   Sydney and London, Collins, 1970.

Other

A Long Way South (travel).   London, Chapman and Hall, 1953.
Africa in Black and White.   London, Chapman and Hall, 1956.
States of the Union (travel).   London, Chapman and Hall, 1958.
Founder of a City: The Life of William Light.   Melbourne, Cheshire, and Lon-
    don, Chapman and Hall, 1960.
Patrick White.   Melbourne, Lansdowne Press, 1961; London, Oxford Univer-
    sity Press, 1971.
Walt Whitman.   Edinburgh, Oliver and Boyd, 1961.
Paintings of S. T. Gill.   Adelaide, Rigby, 1962.
Russell Drysdale (art criticism).   London, Thames and Hudson, 1962.
Tisi and the Yabby (juvenile).   Sydney and London, Collins, 1965.
Seal Bay (juvenile).   Sydney and London, Collins, 1966.
*The Hero as Murderer: The Life of Edward John Eyre, Australian Explorer and
    Governor of Jamaica, 1815–1901.*   Melbourne, Cheshire, and London, Collins,
    1967.
Tisi and the Pageant (juvenile).   Adelaide, Rigby, 1968.

Australia's Last Explorer: Ernest Giles.   London, Faber, 1970.

Australia since the Camera: 1901–14.   Melbourne, Cheshire, 1971.

White on Black: The Australian Aborigine Portrayed in Art.   London, Macmillan, 1974.

Editor, *The Literature of Australia.*   Melbourne, Penguin, 1964; Baltimore, Penguin, 1965.

Editor, *Modern Australian Writing.*   London, Fontana, 1966.

Editor, with Max Harris, *The Vital Decade: 10 Years of Australian Art and Letters.*   Melbourne, Sun Books, 1968.

Translator, with Igor Mezhakoff-Koriakin, *Bratsk Station,* by Yevgeny Yevtushenko.   Melbourne, Sun Books, 1966; New York, Doubleday, 1967; London, Hart Davis, 1968.

Translator, with Igor Mezhakoff-Koriakin, *Fever,* by Bella Akhmadulina.   Melbourne, Sun Books, 1968; New York, Morrow, 1969; London, Peter Owen, 1970.

Geoffrey Dutton comments:

My poetry began in the turmoil of war, and the *Angry Penguins* period of modernism in Australia; my poetic thinking was heavily influenced by modern French and German as well as the English and American poetry. I was fortunate enough to be in close contact with a remarkable group of poets in Adelaide in the 1940's, which included Donald Kerr, Max Harris, and Paul Pfeiffer; both Kerr and Pfeiffer were killed in the R.A.A.F. during the war. In Melbourne in 1944 I shared my ideas with the poet Alister Kershaw and the painters Arthur Boyd and Sidney Nolan.

Six years in Oxford, London and France after the war, and friendship with Roy Campbell and Richard Aldington, made me work towards a greater clarity and technical control. My wandering life and return to Australia were reflected in my poems.

In the early 1960's I was much influenced towards attempting a more complex human response to my own country by studying Walt Whitman. In the late 1960's I met and travelled in Russia with the poet Yevgeny Yevtushenko, having with Igor Mezhakoff-Koriakin translated a large number of his poems; with Igor Mezhakoff-Koriakin I also translated Bella Akhmadulina's new poems, and met her on my visits to Russia in 1966 and 1967. In these visits I discovered the vast field of modern Russian poetry, and have learnt a great deal from the modern Russian poets about the relation between poetry and the modern world on both sides of the so-called iron curtain. Also the importance of rhyme and rhythm in Russian has helped shore up my technical beliefs in them at a time when regular rhyme and rhythm have been unpopular.

I think many of the poems which are nearest to what I had hoped they might be are to do with love; it is difficult to write anything about these.

I welcome what has been called the new nationalism in Australia, not for narrow pseudo-patriotic reasons, but because it may help give Australian poets confidence in welcoming the nourishment most good poets draw from the soil in which they grew.

*   *   *

Remarkable for its intrinsic light-heartedness, the poetry of Geoffrey Dutton has tended to be under-rated by most critics while a growing audience of appreciative readers testifies to its inherent qualities.

Despite the light-heartedness, this poet is capable of extended lyrical meditations of a uniquely beautiful nature. His best work to be found in poems such as "Abandoned Airstrip, Northern Territory" in which he recapitulates his memories as a flyer in the Second World War; "Night Fishing," a long nocturne celebrating the shared lives and joys of an Australian couple in love and experiencing the primal mateship of hunters alone in an eternally providing world; and "The Smallest Sprout," a poem written in memory of his mother in which his natural lyricism is enriched by elegiacal overtones.

His recent work has been spread evenly among suites and individual pieces descriptive of his travels in Russia – elsewhere his versions of Yevtushenko are noteworthy – and America, equally appreciative of the most positive as well as the negative aspects of both countries and the inhabitants, and in tart and pungent satires criticising and ridiculing the tasteless and the chauvinistic in modern Australia. His comments in verse on the Vietnamese war show him to be capable of clear-headed and compellingly written poems of protest, but it is in the longer autobiographical poem imbued with lyrical insights and quiet humour that this fine poet's best work is found.

— Bruce Beaver

DYLAN, Bob. American. Born Robert Zimmerman in Duluth, Minnesota, 24 May 1941. Educated at the University of Minnesota, Minneapolis, 1960. Married; has children. Composer and Performer: concert appearances in the United States, 1961–66, 1971, 1974, and in Europe and Australia, 1964–66. Recipient: Emergency Civil Liberties Committee Tom Paine Award, 1963. D.Mus.: Princeton University, New Jersey, 1970. Address: P.O. Box 264, Cooper Station, New York, New York 10003, U.S.A.

PUBLICATIONS

Verse

Tarantula. New York, Macmillan, 1966.
Approximately Complete Works. Amsterdam, De Bezige Bij-Thomas Rap, 1970.
Poem to Joanie. London, Aloes Press, 1972.
Words. London, Cape, 1973.
Writings and Drawings. New York, Knopf, and London, Cape, 1973.

Scores: The Bob Dylan Songbook, New York, Witmark, 1963; Songs for Voice and Guitar, New York, Witmark, 2 vols., 1968; Bob Dylan's Songs for Harmonica, New York, Witmark, 1968.

Recordings: *Bob Dylan Himself*, Columbia Records, 1962; *The Freewheelin' Bob Dylan*, Columbia Records, 1963; *The Times They Are A-Changin'*, Columbia Records, 1963; *Another Side of Bob Dylan*, Columbia Records, 1964; *Bringing It All Back Home*, Columbia Records, 1965; *Highway 61 Revisited*, Columbia Records, 1965; *Blonde on Blonde*, Columbia Records, 1966; *Bob Dylan's Greatest Hits*, Columbia Records, 1967; *John Wesley Harding*, Columbia Records, 1968; *Nashville Skyline*, Columbia Records, 1969; *Self Portrait*, Columbia Records, 1970; *New Morning*, Columbia Records, 1970; *More Bob Dylan Greatest Hits*, Columbia Records, 1971; *Dylan*, Columbia Records, 1974; *Planet Waves*, Island, 1974; *Before the Flood*, Asylum, 1974; incidental music for the film *Pat Garrett and Billy the Kid*, 1972.

Theatrical Activities

Actor: **Films** – *Don't Look Back*, 1965; *Eat the Document*, 1966; *Pat Garrett and Billy the Kid*, 1972.

*   *   *

With the recent publication of *Writings and Drawings* by Bob Dylan, readers have an opportunity to review, without the music, the lyrics of America's most influential mid-century songwriter. Dylan's historical significance is still too immediate to evaluate. His words and his music are a part of world culture unlike any other human being's have ever been. We weep for the strange obliterations of sensibility necessary before "Blowin' in the Wind" is first orchestrated without voice and second played on Muzac systems in airports from Duluth to Johannesburg. Here in the U.S., one cannot pull the words from the music and an assessment of the "poetry" is that it is song, as it was intended to be. If poetry, it would never have gone to Muzac – or South Africa.

I think Dylan, himself, has tried to sidestep the "poetry" question – I think of him as someone who is embarrassed by the invitations of poetry editors. Yet any perception of such an elusive media-favorite is bound to be speculative: I sometimes wonder that the same person wrote

> They're selling postcards of the hanging
> They're painting the passports brown
> The beauty parlor is filled with sailors
> The circus is in town

and

> So if you find someone that gives you all of her love,
> Take it to your heart, don't let it stray,
> For one thing that's certain,
> You will surely be a-hurtin',
> If you throw it all away.

Other Dylan songs, especially his early "message" songs, blended passion, conscience and history to waken a sleeping generation.

Dylan's poems are included in an 11-page chapter entitled "Some Other Kinds of

Songs,'' and reveal a more private introspection than his songs generally suggest. He writes of watching a man who is threatening to jump off the Brroklyn Bridge:

> i couldn't stay an' look at him
> because i suddenly realized that
> deep in my heart
> i really wanted
> t' see him jump

The narrative extends, as he pulls himself away from the gaping mob to walk the New York streets, haunted by curiosity:

> intellectual spiders
> weave down sixth avenue
> with colt forty-fives
> stickin' out of their
> belly buttons
> an' for the first time
> in my life
> i'm proud that
> i haven't read into
> any masterpiece books
> (an' why did i wanna see that
> poor soul so dead?)

Bob Dylan has fine narrative ability, and surely of no kind that would suggest he's "read into any masterpieces." It's all plain talk, strictly American, rendered with a sense of humor; and, as the book says, it is another kind of song:

> (in greece, a little old lady
> a worker lady
> looks at me
> rubs her chin
> an' by sign language asks
> how come i'm so unshaven
> "the sea is very beautiful here"

> i reply
> pointin' t' my chin.
> an' she believes me
> needs no other answer
> i strum the guitar
> she dances.

– Geof Hewitt

EATON, Charles Edward. American. Born in Winston-Salem, North Carolina, 25 June 1916. Educated at Duke University, Durham, North Carolina, 1932–33; University of North Carolina, Chapel Hill, 1933–36, B.A. 1936 (Phi Beta Kappa);

Princeton University, New Jersey, 1936–37; Harvard University, Cambridge, Massachusetts, 1938–40, M.A. in English 1940. Married Isabel Patterson in 1950. Instructor, Ruiz Gandia School, Poncé, Puerto Rico, 1937–38; Instructor in Creative Writing, University of Missouri, Columbia, 1940–42; Vice Consul, American Embassy, Rio de Janeiro, Brazil, 1942–46; Professor of Creative Writing, University of North Carolina, 1946–51. Free-lance Writer and Art Critic, and Organizer of Art Shows. Recipient: Bread Loaf Writers Conference Robert Frost Fellowship, 1941; Boulder, Colorado, Writers Conference Fellowship, 1942; Ridgely Torrence Memorial award, 1951; Gertrude Boatwright Harris Award, 1954; *Arizona Quarterly* Award, 1956; New England Poetry Club Golden Rose, 1972; O. Henry Award, for fiction, 1972; Alice Fay di Castagnola Award, 1974. Address: Merlin Stone, Woodbury, Connecticut 06798, U.S.A.

PUBLICATIONS

Verse

    The Bright Plain.   Chapel Hill, University of North Carolina Press, 1942.
    The Shadow of the Swimmer.   New York, Fine Editions Press, 1951.
    The Greenhouse in the Garden.   New York, Twayne, 1955.
    Countermoves.   New York and London, Abelard Schuman, 1962.
    On the Edge of the Knife.   New York and London, Abelard Schuman, 1969.

Play

    Sea Psalm (produced Chapel Hill, North Carolina, 1933).   Published in *North Carolina Drama*, Richmond, Virginia, Garrett and Massie, 1956.

Novel

    A Lady of Pleasure.   Lunenburg, Vermont, North Country Publishing Company, 1972.

Short Stories

    Write Me from Rio.   Winston-Salem, North Carolina, John F. Blair, 1959.
    The Girl from Ipanema.   Lunenburg, Vermont, North Country Publishing Company, 1972.

Other

    Charles and Isabel Eaton Collection of America Paintings.   Chapel Hill, University of North Carolina Art Department, 1970.
    Karl Knaths.   Washington, Connecticut, Shiver Mountain Press, 1971.
    Karl Knaths: Five Decades of Painting.   Washington, D.C., International Exhibitions Foundation, 1973.

Manuscript Collections: (Verse) State University of New York at Syracuse Library; (Prose) Mugar Memorial Library, Boston University.

Critical Studies: by Louis Untermeyer, in *Yale Review* (New Haven, Connecticut), Winter 1944; by Robert Hillyer, in *New York Times Book Review,* 22 July 1951; "The Poetry of Charles Edward Eaton" by W. W. Davidson, in *Georgia Review* (Athens), Spring 1956; by Gerard P. Meyer, in *Saturday Review* (New York), 31 March 1956; in *Booklist* (Chicago), 1 May 1956; by May Swenson, in *Poetry* (Chicago), March 1957; "The Greenhouse in the Garden" by William Carlos Williams, in *Arizona Quarterly* (Tucson), Spring 1957; by Wallace Fowlie, in *New York Times Book Review,* 12 May 1963; by John Engels, in *Poetry* (Chicago), September 1963; by F. C. Flint, in *Virginia Quarterly Review* (Charlottesville), Autumn, 1963; "Betwixt Tradition and Innovation" by Robert D. Spector, in *Saturday Review* (New York), 26 December 1970; "The Crisis of Regular Forms" by John T. Irwin, in *Sewanee Review* (Tennessee), Winter 1973.

Charles Edward Eaton comments:

Though I am resistant in general to definitions of poetry and poets as too limiting, if pressed, I might admit to being a modern formalist, but I should insist on the importance of the qualifying adjective. I compose in a number of verse forms, and write lyrical as well as dramatic poetry, but I do not lean on any poet of the past or present for technical inspiration. I believe that each poet must develop his own organic sense of form and adapt even the most conventional meter to his personal rhythm. For example, a number of my poems are written in triptychs, their long lines rhyming every other line, modulated in an entirely individual way. William Carlos Williams, in a study of my work, called this three line stanza an Americanization of *terza rima.* Perhaps he felt it was very American in its love of freedom and yet somewhat European in its formal allegiance. There is no doubt that I like poetry that is both vigorous and controlled.

In this respect, I think the best short statement about my work has been made by Robert D. Spector in *The Saturday Review:* "Charles Edward Eaton may not belong at all in the category of unconventional poets, and yet, it seems to me, his use of conventions becomes a very personal thing that removes him from tradition. . . . If Eaton's poetry, with its use of rhymed stanzas, appears superficially to belong to a formal tradition, his long, free lines and sometimes brutal imagery and diction, pushing his feelings to their limit, suggest otherwise. *On the Edge of the Knife* combines conventional and unconventional in such a way that it is finally the poet's own work. Perhaps, after all, that is the way of poetry. Whether bound to tradition or not, its value rests on the peculiar virtues of the poet."

I am in emphatic accord with any statement about my work which indicates that I believe in working powerfully and freely on one's own terms within the entire range of poetry. I am in no sense a reductionist, but have confidence in the fundamental richness of poetry and the surprise lurking in its possibilities. Form should be an energetic expression of the poet's own psychology not an artificial imposition, and the poem should convey some sense of the struggle which went into the formal achievement:

> I have a powerful nature in pursuit of pleasure,
> Peace, good will, and I do not share
> My time's contempt for passion balanced by strict measure.

An extension of what is involved in this position is given at the conclusion of "The Turkey":

> So the bird I know is like a gaudy catafalque.
> If you should carry a secret hump upon your back,
> You, too, would have a burdened and uncertain walk.
>
> This is what it is to spread an image in the sun –
> This is how we teach thick, precarious balance as if the land
>   moved like a ship
> And one set sail heavily, slowly, encumbered with imagination.

As to my subject matter, it is greatly influenced by where I am living and what I am doing at any given time. In this sense, it is always around me, and it moves forward with me as I go along. Almost every poem, hidden though it may be to the reader, has its *donnée* from some aspect of my experience. Landscape wherever I have lived (North Carolina, Puerto Rico, Brazil, Connecticut, etc.) comes strongly into my work, but I do not consider myself a nature poet. Animals and flowers are continuous with and contiguous to my interest in human beings, and are a constant motif in my work, but I am not interested in fauna or flora *per se,* and am in no sense a botanical or zoological poet. All of my subjects are finally a way of talking about people in the expanding enclave of interest and experience I have chosen to explore. I have been amused by one magazine editor's recognition of my predilection for "all things, great and small" in welcoming a new submission as another poem from "the Garden of Eaton."

Painting has been another seminal influence, and I have long enjoyed what John Singleton Copley called "the luxury of seeing." This interest is the specific motivation in such poems as "The Gallery," "The Museum," "Homage to the Infanta," and "Nocturne for Douanier Rousseau," among others, but it is a constantly underlying, energizing source. "Five Etudes for the Artist" (*Art International,* November 1972) is an extended statement of this pictorial dedication which has been noted by numerous artists, including the New England painter Karl Knaths who has commented at length on the "vital imaginative reality" of the visual qualities of the poems.

The intellectual content of my poetry and of its final outlook and credo has been greatly strengthened by the study of philosophy. Writing in the *New York Times* about *Countermoves,* Wallace Fowlie recognized this influence when he said: "Charles Eaton demonstrates an admirable technical control over the effects he wishes to make, and a clear awareness of at least one major function of poetry. This would be the art of questioning everything, and of questioning in particular the power of poetry."

Fowlie's acknowledgment of the power of sentiment as balancing the intellectual in the poetry is reflected in a line from my long poem, "Robert E. Lee: An Ode": "I believe in the world seen through a temperament." I am certain that it is always the task of the writer to give us his personal vision of reality. This means an uncommon dedication, a determination to keep the fine arts fine, a perpetual sense of renewal and reaffirmation. One must constantly ask oneself in times of discouragement: Who will do my particular kind of writing if I don't? Who will take care of my dreams when I am gone? In our dispersive time, it is not easy to keep a sense of personality and purpose, and, as a consequence, attention to the disciplines of character is equally important with ability. Probably more writers fail through lack of character than of ability. Morale is one of the essential fibres of a meaningful life. Cézanne reminded himself every morning to be *"Sur le motif!"* So must the poet.

*   *   *

Charles Edward Eaton's carefully composed and contrived poetry, employing traditional forms but with well-established innovations (assonance, dissonance, variation of metrical length), reflects his philosophical interests, which are mainly neo-Christian and Utopian. His intelligence and his awareness of the work of other poets are not in doubt. He is an intellectual poet, rewarding for the congruity and subtlety of his thinking. Only occasionally is he embarrassingly cultural, as in "Della Robbia in August," which begins "Luca, we are not eloquent / Enough to be profound / By being simple . . ." – a perfect example of an "I've been there and know" "holiday" poem – or unfortunate ("I mate with lilacs"). This is, with occasional exceptions, admirable verse, written with thought and effort. "Sea Trauma" represents him at his best; the opening lines read:

> In so much blue there is a loss of blue,
> A hope cast down as if abysses made
> A staircase in the sand look up at you,
> A ravaged saw of steps, a broken blade.

But even this is too educated: too responsible in an irresponsible world. The rhyming is forced: the unknown deeps of the mind play no part here, or in Eaton's other work, except as some quality respectfully alluded to. "A good poet," Robert Graves once said, "has to be a little mad." Eaton is everything but this. One can admire; but emotional response is difficult. "The Dream of the Whip" (from *The Greenhouse in the Garden*) shows most clearly that Eaton is aware of the irrational; but he has rationalised this awareness into decent "New Criticism" verse instead of surrendering to the surreal, to the mysterious energy of language itself. Of course a poet needs to transform his linguistic "givens" into some kind of coherence; but Eaton's academic clumsiness ("You, the animal felt for, not the man who felt, / Rushed on with brunt of force behind your plummet-trail") demonstrates an evasion of terror that, however humanly understandable, is poetically reprehensible. Poetry can no longer be merely neat – unless, in the light of our universal nightmare, the poet is able to give a convincing vision of the Kingdom of Heaven.

– Martin Seymour-Smith

EBERHART, Richard (Ghormley). American. Born in Austin, Minnesota, 5 April 1904. Educated at the University of Minnesota, Minneapolis, 1922–23; Dartmouth College, Hanover, New Hampshire, B.A. 1926; St. John's College, Cambridge, B.A. 1929, M.A. 1933; Harvard University, Cambridge, Massachusetts, 1932–33. Served in the United States Naval Reserve, 1942–46: Lieutenant Commander. Married Helen Butcher in 1941; has two children. Tutor to the son of King Prajadhipok of Siam, 1930–31. English Teacher, St. Mark's School, Southboro, Massachusetts, 1933–41, and Cambridge School, Kendal Green, Massachusetts, 1941–42. Assistant Manager to the Vice-President, Butcher Polish Company, Boston, 1946–52; now honorary Vice-President and Member of the Board of Directors. Visiting Professor, University of Washington, Seattle, 1952–53, 1967, 1972; Professor of English, University of Connecticut, Storrs, 1953–54; Visiting Professor, Wheaton College, Norton, Massachusetts, 1954–55; Resident Fellow and Gauss Lecturer, Princeton University, New Jersey, 1955–56. Professor of English and

Poet-in-Residence, 1956–68, Class of 1925 Professor, 1968–70, and since 1970, Professor Emeritus, Dartmouth College. Elliston Lecturer, University of Cincinnati, 1961. Founder, 1950, and First President, Poets' Theatre, Cambridge, Massachusetts; Member, 1955, and since 1964, Director, Yaddo Corporation. Phi Beta Kappa Poet, Tufts University, Medford, Massachusetts, 1941, Brown University, Providence, Rhode Island, 1957, Swarthmore College, Pennsylvania, 1963, Trinity College, Hartford, Connecticut, 1963, College of William and Mary, Williamsburg, Virginia, 1963, University of New Hampshire, Durham, 1964, and Harvard University, 1967. Consultant in Poetry, 1959–61, and Honorary Consultant in American Letters, 1963–69, Library of Congress, Washington, D.C. Recipient: Guarantor's Prize, 1946, and Harriet Monroe Memorial Prize, 1950 (*Poetry,* Chicago); New England Poetry Club Golden Rose, 1950; Shelley Memorial Award, 1952; Harriet Monroe Poetry Award, 1955; National Institute of Arts and Letters grant, 1955; Bollingen Prize, 1962; Pulitzer Prize, 1966; Academy of American Poets Fellowship, 1969. D.Litt.: Dartmouth College, 1954; Skidmore College, Saratoga, New York, 1966; College of Worcester, Ohio, 1969; Colgate University, Hamilton, New York, 1974. Since 1972, Honorary President, Poetry Society of America. Member, National Institute of Arts and Letters, 1960, and American Academy of Arts and Sciences, 1967. Address: 5 Webster Terrace, Hanover, New Hampshire 03755, U.S.A.

PUBLICATIONS

Verse

>   *A Bravery of Earth.*   London, Cape, 1930; New York, Cape and Smith, 1931.
>   *Reading the Spirit.*   London, Chatto and Windus, 1936; New York, Oxford University Press, 1937.
>   *Song and Idea.*   London, Chatto and Windus, 1940; New York, Oxford University Press, 1942.
>   *Poems, New and Selected.*   New York, New Directions, 1944.
>   *Burr Oaks.*   New York, Oxford University Press, and London, Chatto and Windus, 1947.
>   *Brotherhood of Men.*   Pawlet, Vermont, Banyan Press, 1949.
>   *An Herb Basket.*   Cummington, Massachusetts, Cummington Press, 1950.
>   *Selected Poems.*   New York, Oxford University Press, and London, Chatto and Windus, 1951.
>   *Undercliff: Poems 1946–1953.*   London, Chatto and Windus, 1953; New York, Oxford University Press, 1954.
>   *Great Praises.*   New York, Oxford University Press, and London, Chatto and Windus, 1957.
>   *The Oak: A Poem.*   Hanover, New Hampshire, Pine Tree Press, 1957.
>   *Collected Poems 1930–1960, Including 51 New Poems.*   New York, Oxford University Press, and London, Chatto and Windus, 1960.
>   *The Quarry: New Poems.*   New York, Oxford University Press, and London, Chatto and Windus, 1964.
>   *The Vastness and Indifference of the World.*   Milford, New Hampshire, Ferguson Press, 1965.
>   *Fishing for Snakes.*   Cambridge, Massachusetts, privately printed, 1965.
>   *Selected Poems 1930–1965.*   New York, New Directions, 1965.
>   *Thirty One Sonnets.*   New York, Eakins Press, 1967.
>   *Shifts of Being: Poems.*   New York, Oxford University Press, and London, Chatto and Windus, 1968.

The Achievement of Richard Eberhart: A Comprehensive Selection of His Poems,
  edited by Bernard F. Engle.   Chicago, Scott Foresman, 1968.
Three Poems.   Cambridge, Massachusetts, Pym Randall Press, 1968.
Fields of Grace.   New York, Oxford University Press, and London, Chatto and
  Windus, 1972.

Recording: *Richard Eberhart Reading His Own Poems,* Caedmon, 1966.

Plays

The Apparition (produced Cambridge, Massachusetts, 1951).   Included in
  Collected Verse Plays, 1962.
The Visionary Farms (produced Cambridge, Massachusetts, 1952).   Included in
  Collected Verse Plays, 1962.
Triptych (produced Chicago, 1955).   Included in *Collected Verse Plays,* 1962.
The Mad Musician, and Devils and Angels (produced Cambridge, Massachusetts,
  1962).   Included in *Collected Verse Plays,* 1962.
Collected Verse Plays (includes *Triptych, The Visionary Farms, The Apparition,
  The Mad Musician, Devils and Angels, Preamble I* and *II*).   Chapel Hill,
  University of North Carolina Press, 1962.
The Bride from Mantua, adaptation of a play by Lope de Vega (produced
  Hanover, New Hampshire, 1964).

Other

Editor, with Selden Rodman, *War and the Poet: An Anthology of Poetry
  Expressing Man's Attitude to War from Ancient Times to the Present.*   New
  York, Devin Adair, 1945.
Editor, . . . *Dartmouth Poems.*   Hanover, New Hampshire, Dartmouth
  Publications-Butcher Fund, 12 vols., 1958–59, 1962–71.

Critical Studies: "Richard Eberhart" by Ralph J. Mills, Jr., in *Contemporary
American Poetry,* New York, Random House, 1960; *Richard Eberhart* by Ralph J.
Mills, Jr., Minneapolis, University of Minnesota Press, 1966; Introduction by Ber-
nard F. Engle to *The Achievement of Richard Eberhart,* 1968; "The Cultivation of
Paradox: The War Poetry of Richard Eberhart" by Richard J. Fein, in *Forum*
(Muncie, Indiana), Spring 1969; *Richard Eberhart: The Progress of an American Poet*
by Joel Roache, New York, Oxford University Press, 1971; *Richard Eberhart* by
Bernard F. Engle, New York, Twayne, 1972; *Richard Eberhart* (film), directed by
Samuel Mandelbaum, New York, Tri-Pix, 1972; *Richard Eberhart* (film), directed by
Irving Broughton, Seattle, University of Washington, 1974.

Richard Eberhart comments:

My poetry celebrates life, which does not last long, and mankind, which is
temporal as well, through understanding and perception of my times, insofar as I
am able to create poems which may communicate values and meanings I can know.

*   *   *

The senior poet of the generation which followed Eliot, Pound, Stevens, and Williams, Richard Eberhart began his education in America but continued it at Cambridge, where I. A. Richards and F. R. Leavis were teaching and William Empson and Kathleen Raine also were students. Tennyson, he has said, was the first poet he read thoroughly; but later, at Cambridge, he was strongly influenced by Blake, Hopkins, and Wordsworth, each of whom left traces on his early writing while aiding him in finding his own "true voice of feeling." His initial book, *A Bravery of Earth*, composed, as Eberhart has admitted, "under the spell of Wordsworth," is an autobiographical narrative poem inspired by *The Prelude*. While it is very uneven and the author has retained only a few passages from it in his *Collected Poems*, these have remarkable lyric and dramatic qualities:

> This fevers me, this sun on green,
> On green grass glowing, this young spring.
> The secret hallowing is come,
> Regenerate sudden incarnation,
> Mystery made visible . . . .

Eberhart concludes his long poem, the chief theme of which is the turbulent, often painful but liberating transition from innocence to experience, by distinguishing three kinds of "awareness" he has arrived at successively – "mortality," "mentality," and "men's actions" – that are in fact prophetic of the continuing thematic interests of his poetry.

"Poetry," Eberhart has remarked, "is a confrontation of the whole being with reality. It is a basic struggle of the soul, the mind, and the body to comprehend life; to bring order to chaos or phenomena; and by will and insight to create communicable verbal forms for the pleasure of mankind" (*Poets on Poetry*, ed. Howard Nemerov). And with each new volume of poems he has demonstrated his adherence to that definition. His attachment to Wordsworth and Hopkins is accounted for in part by his own sharp eye for and sensitive response to the particulars of nature, the changing moods of weather and season. Yet if such details are valued for their own sake, they are also subjected to an intense imaginative scrutiny as the means by which the poet may apprehend a higher truth, attain to a realm of visionary or metaphysical knowledge that will provide a spiritual counterbalance to the certainty that "Life blows like the wind away." Many of his best-known poems from earlier collections such as "The Groundhog," "For a Lamb," "Rumination" face the harshness of death without discovering any spiritual resources to offset the bleak prospect of annihilation. Yet Eberhart's general view is not of this pessimistic order, is indeed religious and mystical, if heterodox; this latter aspect of his thought and feeling has emerged more obviously in recent books, though it is present from the start. In "Meditation One" he writes, "to God we have incontestably to go, / We have to announce him as we pale in flesh . . . ."

Eberhart's poems do not all begin as contemplations of the external world; a considerable number originate in some type of inward state: a dream, image, vision, or a complex idea, an intellectual paradox that reveals the strange inconsistencies of man's estate. The poet Philip Booth has shrewdly observed that Eberhart frequently proceeds deductively in a poem rather than inductively. Similarly, he can with tremendous power and authority assume the role of prophet or seer, one who sees through the follies and cruelties of mankind yet senses the larger enigmas underlying them. This role is nowhere put to more effective use than in certain of the justly famous war poems, "The Fury of Aerial Bombardment," for instance:

> You would think the fury of aerial bombardment
> Would rouse God to relent; the infinite spaces
> Are still silent. He looks on shock-pried faces.
> History, even, does not know what is meant.

You would feel that after so many centuries
God would give man to repent; yet he can kill
As Cain could, but with multitudinous will,
No farther advanced than in his ancient furies.

Quite a few, though by no means all, of Eberhart's later pieces belong to the
category he has called "Psyche" poetry, that is, poems of mature grace and
reflectiveness which tend to resolve themselves in an apprehension of spiritual
fulfillment or harmony; yet a recent collection, *Shifts of Being,* still shows an
unflagging interest in life's abundant and energetic manifestations. Believing in the
seizures of poetic inspiration, that poems are perhaps best when "born whole,"
Eberhart is by turns apocalyptic, meditative, and lyrical. At its best, his style is
bold, vigorous, idiosyncratic, and moves with rhythmical impulse; occasionally,
however, his approach to the poem leads to lapses in diction, careless composition.
But these are the risks taken for a poetry so unique and daring, so rich in vision, so
distinctly bearing the stamp of Eberhart's fertile, restless imagination.

– Ralph J. Mills, Jr.

ECHERUO, Michael (Joseph Chukwudalu). Nigerian. Born in Umunumo, Mbano
Division, 14 March 1937. Educated at Stella Maris College, Port Harcourt, 1950–54;
University College, Ibadan, 1955–60, B.A. (honours) 1960; Cornell University,
Ithaca, New York (Phi Beta Kappa), 1962–65, M.A. 1963; Ph.D. 1965. Married
Rose N. Echeruo in 1968; has four children. Lecturer, Nigerian College of Arts and
Technology, Enugu, 1960–61. Lecturer, 1961–70, Senior Lecturer, 1970–73, and
Professor, 1973–74, University of Nigeria, Nsukka. Since 1974, Professor of
English, University of Ibadan. Recipient: All-Africa Poetry Competition Prize,
1963. Address: Department of English, University of Ibadan, Ibadan, Nigeria.

PUBLICATIONS

Verse

Mortality: Poems. London, Longman, 1968.

Other

Joyce Cary and the Novel of Africa. London, Longman, 1973.

Editor, *Igbo Traditional Life, Literature, and Culture.* Austin, Texas, Conch
Publications, 1972.

*   *   *

Michael Echeruo, like his late countryman Christopher Okigbo, has forged, from
the crossroads experience of an African heritage and a "European" education,

poetry which is wide-ranging, deceptively simple and highly individual. Although the poems in his first volume *Mortality* often come out of his experiences as an M.A. and Doctoral student in the United States, they are still like trees with their roots deep in African soil, no matter how high their branches reach into a foreign sky. The return to Africa, whether physically or metaphorically, is implicit, as in the first poem in the book, "Debut":

> Have we not looked the whole world out,
>   searched the whole hearth out
>   till we saw the palm-nuts again
> by which we were to live?

It is, therefore, no accident that an entire section of his book is titled "Defections" and that he says in the poem "Harvest time":

> Village maidens
>   are the bearers of my harvest. . . .

Wit and irony also figure strongly in Echeuro's poetry, along with a sense of what it is to be an African poet in a foreign land:

> . . . like an unfeathered bird
> in their spring –
> white and spruce and clean –
> . . . like an unclassified gift
> to their museums
> where they spin out fine tall tales
> all day long
> amid the blistering flurries
> of their bleak December days.

Though his Nigeria figures strongly in his verse, Echeruo also ranges, capably, throughout Western literature, bringing in such diverse sources as the Bible, D. H. Lawrence, Joyce and St. John of the Cross. His poem "The Signature," which revolves around the figure of O'Brien (who seems to be an Irish priest like the Flannagan of Chris Okigbo's "Limits"), draws a picture of African ceremonies in conjunction with Catholic rites and draws the conclusion that

> The priests and elders of my past
> would love to see O'Brien's paradise.

There is one last quality about Echeruo's poetry which should be taken note of. Whether ironic or celebratory, whether a poem of love or a poem of satire, there is a current of lyricism which runs through all of Echeruo's verse, a lyricism which can be felt in these lines from his poem "Wedding," lines which speak of birth and stress again his ties to the soil:

> Tap roots beneath the giant
> speak like the gods
> and life comes
> like a spasm of light. . . .

> – Joseph Bruchac

ECONOMOU, George. American. Born in Great Falls, Montana, 24 September 1934. Educated at Colgate University, Hamilton, New York, A.B. 1956; Columbia University, New York, M.A. 1957, Ph.D. 1967. Married Rochelle Owens, *q.v.*, in 1962. Lecturer, Wagner College, New York, 1958–60. Since 1961, Member of the English Department, and currently Professor of English, Long Island University, Brooklyn, New York. Editor, *Chelsea Review*, New York, 1958–60; Editor, *Trobar*, New York, 1960–64. Address: 606 West 116th Street, New York, New York 10027, U.S.A.

PUBLICATIONS

Verse

> *The Georgics.* Los Angeles, Black Sparrow Press, 1968.
> *Landed Natures.* Los Angeles, Black Sparrow Press, 1969.
> *Poems for Self-Therapy.* Mount Horeb, Wisconsin, Perishable Press, 1972.

Other

> *The Goddess Natura in Medieval Literature.* Cambridge, Massachusetts, Harvard University Press, 1972.

Critical Study: Review by Harry Lewis, in *Mulch* (Amherst, New York), Spring 1972.

George Economou comments:

Major themes – Nature, the great one we live in and the small ones that are myself and those I love.

*   *   *

George Economou is most closely associated with poetry of the "deep image," and for a time co-edited, along with Robert and Joan Kelly, *Trobar,* the "deep image" poetry journal. Robert Kelly defined "deep image" as poetry filled with "intensity and immediacy," and "containing the primal gestures of language." First referred to in Jerome Rothenberg's *Poems for the Floating World* the "deep image" comes from dream, from the invisible pull and tug of life. It is a poetry charged with the rough, raw energy transmitted by direct and primal human actions. Most of these qualities are present in George Economou's poetry. His poems contain the facts and rituals of life close to the earth; earth rhythms and surprises animate it.

Economou's *The Goddess Natura in Medieval Literature* illuminates his frequent poetic reference to his muse and patron, the goddess Natura. She is the allegorical personification of nature in classic and medieval literature, and also an intermediary between man and God. Like Chaucer's "Nature" in *The Parliament of Fowls,* Economou's goddes presides over a harmonious landscape, and fruitfulness in love and romance. In "Prayer of a Natural Man" he asks Natura to set his heart high, to let him "be the sure handler / of every bird and snake it finds. . . ." Economou's poems are informal and conversational – the words of a poet who walks for his health, talks to himself, invokes muses and animal spirits. The poet's "secret life" in nature is everywhere present: "I am a magnificent animal . . ."; "I become wolf / I become wolf man. . . ." The first portion of *Landed Natures* is composed of eight "Georgics," and even though the landscape is the American West there are thematic connections with Virgil's *Georgics*. Economou, as earth husband, consoles the "poor earth we live off / nobody here loves you. . . ." He advises the shepherd in us to love our flock:

> caress them daily and be
> kind as you can,
> enter their dumb world
> without a word or thought.

There are qualities here reminiscent of the earth poems of Gary Snyder, and, to a lesser degree, of Galway Kinnell and James Dickey, but Economou is not at this point up to the calibre of such poets. Yet there is a compelling directness in these conversations between poet and reader. Earth guide, mystic traveler, George Economou speaks as one who has been to the territory and who, given a chance, will reveal some of nature's finest mysteries.

– John R. Cooley

EDSON, Russell. American. Born 9 April 1935. Educated at the Art Students League, New York; New School for Social Research, New York; Columbia University, New York; Black Mountain College, North Carolina. Married to Frances Edson. Recipient: Guggenheim Fellowship, 1974. Agent: George Borchardt Inc., 145 East 52nd Street, New York, New York 10022. Address: 149 Weed Avenue, Stamford, Connecticut, 06902, U.S.A.

PUBLICATIONS

Verse

Appearances: Fable and Drawings.   Stamford, Connecticut, Thing Press, 1961.
A Stone Is Nobody's: Fables and Drawings.   Stamford, Connecticut, Thing Press, 1961.
The Boundry (sic).   Stamford, Connecticut, Thing Press, 1964.
The Very Thing That Happens: Fables and Drawings.   New York, New Directions, 1964.
The Brain Kitchen: Writings and Woodcuts.   Stamford, Connecticut, Thing Press, 1965.
What a Man Can See.   Highlands, North Carolina, Jargon, 1969.
The Childhood of an Equestrian.   New York, Harper, 1973.
The Clam Theatre.   Middletown, Connecticut, Wesleyan University Press, 1973.

Plays

The Falling Sickness.   New York, New Directions, 1975.

425

Critical Studies: *A Prose Poem Anthology*, edited by Duane Ackerson, Pocatello, Idaho, Dragonfly Press, 1970; "Prose Poems" by William Matthews, in *New: American and Canadian Poetry 15* (Trumansburg, New York), 1971; "I Am Sure Happiness Is Not Too Far Away" by Thomas Meyer, in *Parnassus* (New York), ii, 1, 1974.

Russell Edson comments:

I write short prose pieces which are neither fiction nor reportage. Perhaps the Current popular term in America (although we certainly didn't originate it), *prose poem*, is vague enough to describe the blurred borders of my gross generality. But, as soon as I say this I want to shout that I refuse to write prose poems, that I want to write the work that is always in search of itself, in a form that is always building itself from the inside out.

In that I am more at home in my work than in describing it, I offer an example below, "A Chair":

> A chair has waited such a long time to be
> with its person. Through shadow and fly buzz
> and the floating dust it has waited such a
> long time to be with its person.
>   What it remembers of the forest it forgets,
> and dreams of a room where it waits – Of the
> cup and the ceiling – Of the animate one.

*   *   *

In an introduction to his first major book, *The Very Thing That Happens*, Denise Levertov says this of Russell Edson: "Russell Edson is one of those originals who appear out of the loneliness of a vast, thronged country to create a peculiar and defined world." Several books later, this impression of Edson's eccentric genius (as perhaps all true genius appears eccentric) remains as strong as ever. His is the world seen from all the frightening, and funny, perspectives adults so often forget to see, or choose to forget: worlds seen through the wrong end of the spyglass, or through the looking glass, where everything pursues a strange, relentless logic of its own. His soap bubble worlds refuse to pop, returning us, like the knowledge we have had a dream, to the reassuring; instead, the world they reflect comes apart in the face of dream logic. A man's hand is a white spider, and, driven by the necessity of such metamorphoses, suspends the man eventually from the ceiling by the spider webs it has woven. Edson's prose poetry is more carefully wedded to metaphor, and the pursuit of metaphor to its sometimes ludicrous, sometimes lovely ends, than most verse, as in "Antimatter," where Edson manages a fine blend of both:

> On the other side of a mirror there's an inverse world,
> where the insane go sane; where bones climb out of the earth
> and recede to the first slime of love.
>   And in the evening the sun is just rising.
>   Lovers cry because they are a day younger, and soon
> childhood robs them of their pleasure.
>   In such a world there is much sadness which, of course,
> is joy. . . .

Edson is also a playwright, and the earlier poems of *What a Man Can See* and *The Very Thing That Happens* are like miniature theatre-of-the-absurd plays, vignettes of family life in which everyone converses in shouts and parents pass on parental wisdom untouched by human thought. Though the humor touches on cartoons (Edson's father was a famous cartoonist) and the black humor of the absurd, there is an undercurrent of pathos reminiscent of Chekhov and O'Neill; these prose poems and fables constitute *A Long Day's Journey into Night* without the tedium.

Edson's range is considerable, from these exchanges to still-life portraits like "A Chair" ("A chair has waited such a long time to be with its person . . .") or beast fables tinged with melancholy, like "How a Cow Comes to Live with Long Eared Ones," in which an over-inquisitive cow is kidnapped by a rabid rabbit. Edson pulls such antics off, and creates a real slapstick tragedy, the sort of thing other American artists like Chaplin have been drawn to attempt. Sometimes, the moral explicitness we might expect from the traditional fable is there (though more often, as in "A Journey by Water," Edson creates a sort of anti-fable that satirizes didacticism), as in "A Lovely Man":

> A man is such a lovely man; he really is if you'll only
> look past him into the flower garden.
> Wait, shall he move so that you can look more fully
> into the garden?
> Shall he die and be put under the flower garden to nourish
> beauty and never to be in the way of it again?

The prevailing mood of many of these poems is melancholy, but it's a darkness defined by quick lightning streaks of humor, like a figure in a cubistic woodcut (which Edson's drawings in his various collections resemble) cracking a grin. Edson's prose poems tend to attack the false security and self satisfaction by which we too often live, to dismantle our umbrellas and let us see the storm that is always raging. They throw off just enough light to let us see that black sky overhead again.

– Duane Ackerson

EIGNER, Larry (Lawrence Joel Eigner). American. Born in Lynn, Massachusetts, 7 August 1927. Educated at home; Massachusetts Hospital School, Canton, 2 years; correspondence courses from University of Chicago. Palsied from birth. Address: 23 Bates Road, Swampscott, Massachusetts 01907, U.S.A.

PUBLICATIONS

Verse

From the Sustaining Air. Palma, Mallorca, Divers Press, 1953; augmented edition, Eugene, Oregon, Toad Press, 1967.
Look at the Park. Lynn, Massachusetts, privately printed, 1958.

On My Eyes: Poems. Highlands, North Carolina, Jargon, 1960.
The Music, The Rooms. Albuquerque, New Mexico, Desert Review Press, 1965.
The Memory of Yeats, Blake, DHL. London, Circle Press, 1965.
Six Poems. Portland, Oregon, Wine Press, 1967.
Another Time in Fragments. London, Fulcrum Press, 1967.
The- /Towards Autumn. Los Angeles, Black Sparrow Press, 1967.
Air the Trees. Los Angeles, Black Sparrow Press, 1967.
The Breath of Once Live Things, In the Field with Poe. Los Angeles, Black Sparrow Press, 1968.
A Line That May Be Cut. London, Circle Press, 1968.
Valleys, Branches. London, Big Venus, 1969.
Flat and Round. New York, Pierrepont Press, 1969.
Over and Over, Ends, As the Wind May Sound. Cambridge, Massachusetts, Restau Press, 1970.
Poem Nov. 1968. London, Tetrad Press, 1970.
Circuits: "A Microbook, A Microbook." LeRoy, New York, Athanor Press, 1971.
Looks Like Nothing, The Shadow Through Air. Guildford, Surrey, Circle Press, 1972.
What You Hear. London, Edible Magazine, 1972.
Selected Poems, edited by Samuel Charters and Andrea Wyatt. Berkeley, California, Oyez, 1972.
Words Touching Ground Under. Belmont, Massachusetts, Hellric Publications, 1972.
Shape Shadow Elements Move. Los Angeles, Black Sparrow Press, 1973.
Earth Birds. Guildford, Surrey, Circle Press, 1973.
Stirring Together or Far Away. Los Angeles, Black Sparrow Press, 1974.
Anything on Its Side. New Rochelle, New York, Elizabeth Press, 1974.

Play

Murder Talk: The Reception: Suggestions for a Play; Five Poems, Bed Never Self Made. Placitas, New Mexico, Duende, 1964.

Short Stories

Clouding. New York, Samuel Charters, 1968.
Farther North. New York, Samuel Charters, 1969.

Bibliography: *A Bibliography of Works by Larry Eigner, 1937–1969* by Andrea Wyatt, Berkeley, California, Oyez, 1970.

Manuscript Collection: Kenneth Spencer Research Library; University of Kansas, Lawrence.

*   *   *

For Larry Eigner the circumstances of his life have given a form and a shape to his poetry. He is a spastic, and his life has been spent in a glassed-in front porch of a frame house on a side street of a small Massachusetts town. Through the windows – and through the window of his bedroom – he follows the world of the seasons, the sky, the birds, the trees. There has been some travel – to visit his brothers in San Francisco and Missouri – and smaller trips into Boston or further along Cape Ann to see other poets. And despite the limits of his physical world he is part of the community of younger American poets through a wide and open correspondence, and continued reading of the books and magazines that pile up on his desk. He has always thought of himself as close to the poets who broke from the Anglo-Americam tradition, and there are clear elements of style from Williams, Olson, and Creeley in his poetry – though he doesn't work in the larger forms that characterize the work of Olson – or of Pound, another poet Eigner thinks of as a source. His prose pieces, which tie closely to the poetry and have their own distinct presence, have some correspondences to the Gertrude Stein of the *Autobiography*. The intense use of the immediate image is at the center of his work, and in poem after poem he has framed the physical world he sees through his windows. He can write a poem complete within a few words, so total is his glimpse of this world:

> the wind masses such birds
> green inside the tree

There is excitement in the poetry about his surroundings – fire engines go by, cars pass in the night, storms grip the trees, birds come, children play loudly – but a dominating theme in his evocation of this scene is a nostalgia at the impermanence of it,

> two big pigeons on the new roof
> below which he grew corn
>   ten years back, one year

a nostalgia that becomes sad, musing:

> But I grow old
> because I was too much a child

And even though much of his published work was written while he was still in his twenties and thirties he has had to spend too many hours in hospitals, and he is deeply conscious of the presence of death:

> once a man is born he has to die
>   and that is time

A poem that is often quoted:

> the knowledge of death, and now
> the knowledge of the stars
>
> there is one end
>
>   and the endless
> Room at the center
>   passage / in no time
> a rail thickets hills grass

But as often as the mood is subdued the poems more often have an open, direct optimism. They have also a lightness, a deftness, but with such care in their detail that he can make sudden emphases, sudden shifts of meaning with only a few words. He does not insist on his own presence in the work – there is an essential modesty in the poetry, as well as a large intelligence that he uses only to keep the elements of the poem in easy balance with each other. There is much of Eigner's work published, all of it with his distinctive voice and style. The longer poems of a few years ago have given way to short, almost haiku-like poems of recent collections, but this has not been an intentional shift in direction, only an intuitive strengthening and purifying of his line. The work will continue, and the new direction could as well be back to the longer poem. It is this strength of his response – the persistence of it – that will go on in the poetry. As he says:

> The fountain of youth is a poetry
> and whether we are one minute older
> the present always arrives.

– Samuel Charters

ELLIOTT, George P(aul). American. Born in Knightstown, Indiana, 16 June 1918. Educated at the University of California, Berkeley, A.B. 1939, M.A. 1941. Married Mary Emma Jeffress in 1941; has one child. Assistant Professor, St. Mary's College, California, 1947–55, 1962–63, Cornell University, Ithaca, New York, 1955–56, and Barnard College, New York, 1957–60; Lecturer, University of Iowa, Iowa City, 1960–61, and University of California, Berkeley, 1962. Since 1963, Professor of English, Syracuse University, New York. Since 1965, Member of the Corporation of Yaddo. Recipient: Albert Bender grant, 1951; Fund for the Advancement of Education Fellowship, 1953; *Hudson Review* Fellowship, 1956; Guggenheim Fellowship, 1961, 1970; D. H. Lawrence Fellowship, 1962; Ford Fellowship, for theatre, 1965; National Institute of Arts and Letters grant, 1969. Address: Department of English, Syracuse University, Syracuse, New York 13210, U.S.A.

PUBLICATIONS

Verse

> *Fever and Chills.* Iowa City, Stone Wall Press, 1961.
> *Fourteen Poems.* Lanham, Maryland, Goosetree Press, 1964.
> *From the Berkeley Hills.* New York, Harper, 1969.

Novels

> *Parktilden Village.* Boston, Beacon Press, 1958.
> *David Knudsen.* New York, Random House, 1962.
> *In the World.* New York, Viking Press, 1965.
> *Muriel.* New York, Dutton, 1972.

Short Stories

> *Among the Dangs.*   New York, Holt Rinehart, 1961; London, Secker and Warburg, 1962.
> *An Hour of Last Things and Other Stories.*   New York, Harper, 1968; London, Gollancz, 1969.

Other

> *A Piece of Lettuce: Personal Essays on Books, Beliefs, American Places and Growing Up in a Strange Country.*   New York, Random House, 1964.
> *Conversions: Literature and the Modernist Deviation* (essays).   New York, Dutton, 1971.

> Editor, *Fifteen Modern American Poets.*   New York, Rinehart, 1956; London, Peter Smith, 1963.
> Editor, *Types of Prose Fiction.*   New York, Random House, 1964.

Manuscript Collection: Washington University Library, St. Louis.

Critical Study: "Recurrences" by X. J. Kennedy, in *Nation* (New York), 30 March 1970.

George P. Elliott comments:

I function best as a narrative poet using syllabic verse. Usually I operate in the regions of lower rhetorical and prosodic intensity. I commonly employ verse as a way of heightening the story, the ideas, the imagined experience, rather than using these as material for pure poetry.

*   *   *

George P. Elliott has worked with alacrity in a variety of forms since he began writing poetry in 1942. Always sensitive to the depth effects of the aural, he has mastered rhymed, regular but unrhymed, and free verse alike. Highly controlled, his poems are very rarely self-conscious. His syntax is, however, occasionally convoluted so that while it suits psychological complexities it skirts the voice's natural timbre. He has achieved a subtle control of his line, displaying a consistent precision for letting enjambments carry a significant but not heavy burden of ambiguity and irony. His dramatic monologues and narrative poems spring from a compelling curiosity about the psychology of intense confrontations.

Elliott often juxtaposes life as we actually feel it with rational and scientific "truth," whether constituted by the facts of chromosomes or interstellar space. His tone can be quietly epiphanal when a common-place marvel of the natural or affectional order seizes his fancy. Thus he can ponder the Kingfisher and its mysterious origins: "What is the bow, blue arrow, that flashed you by?" And as regards a man's child, he remarks what the "rationalistic eye" of a camera never could: "Tosses of laughter, his daughter just turned from waving."

He records, also, the extreme feelings which come with the ruination of domestic peace, ranging from the mild and the torturing ambivalences of infidelities to the blank withdrawals of nervous collapse and schizophrenia. Pre-eminently, though, his poetry elaborates the vicissitudes of marital and romantic love and especially moments of enlightening if painful realization. In this sphere he is nowhere better than in "Three in the Morning," the adroit title of which complements its fine delineation of a woman's tormented relation to husband and lover and to her own ineffectual "will." It is likewise in this sphere that his imagery is so often poignantly evocative, as when, in "Seen Through a Doorway," the speaker glimpses within a sun-drenched room, "charged with powers of gold," a woman's "bite of melon poised / Chartreuse in a dazzling spoon."

– David M. Heaton

ELMSLIE, Kenward. American. Born in New York City, 27 April 1929. Educated at Harvard University, Cambridge, Massachusetts, B.A. 1950. Worked with the Karamu Inter-Racial Theatre, Cleveland. Art Critic, *Art News*, New York, 1966–67. Recipient: Ford grant, 1964; National Endowment for the Arts grant, 1966; Frank O'Hara Award, 1971. Address: 104 Greenwich Avenue, New York, New York 10011, U.S.A.

PUBLICATIONS

Verse

Pavilions. New York, Tibor de Nagy Gallery, 1961.
The Power Plant Poems. New York, "C" Press, 1967.
The Champ. Los Angeles, Black Sparrow Press, 1968.
Album. New York, Kulchur Press, 1969.
Circus Nerves. Los Angeles, Black Sparrow Press, 1971.
Motor Disturbance. New York, Columbia University Press, 1971.
Girl Machine. New York, Angel Hair Books, 1971.
Penguin Modern Poets 24, with Kenneth Koch and James Schuyler. London, Penguin, 1973.

Plays

Unpacking the Black Trunk, with James Schuyler (produced New York, 1965).
Lizzie Borden, music by Jack Beeson (produced New York, 1965). New York, Boosey and Hawkes, 1965.
Miss Julie, music by Ned Rorem (produced New York, 1965). New York, Boosey and Hawkes, 1965.
The Sweet Bye and Bye, music by Jack Beeson (produced Kansas City, 1973). New York, Boosey and Hawkes, 1966.

The Grass Harp, music by Claibe Richardson, adaptation of the novel by
  Truman Capote (produced New York, 1971).   New York, French, 1971.
City Junket (produced New York, 1974).   New York, Boke Press, 1972.
The Seagull, music by Thomas Pasatieri, adaptation of the play by Chekhov
  (produced Houston, 1974).

Novel

The Orchid Stories.   New York, Doubleday, 1973.

Other

The Baby Book.   New York, Boke Press, 1965.
The 1967 Gamebook Calendar.   New York, Boke Press, 1967.
Shiny Ride.   New York, Boke Press, 1972.

Critical Study: "Poetry and Public Experience" by Stephen Donadio, in
Commentary (New York), February 1973.

Kenward Elmslie comments:

Since about 1961, I've considered myself primarily a poet; before that I thought
of myself, and *was,* primarily a writer of lyrics for songs. I have continued to write
for the theatre, and have now completed a novel, but I feel most centred (as a
writer) when working on a poem. I am sometimes listed as a member of the New
York School of Poets, and I've been involved with Koch, Ashberry, and the late
Frank O'Hara, the "School's" founders, but the word "school" seems somehow
awfully serious.
  I haven't thought much about "major themes" etc. – I've tried to describe places
I've been, moods I've been in, people I've been close to. Some of my poems are
lectures, or appreciations, or gossip – I like some sort of stanza form to fit the
words into, but I don't go in for "formal" dum-dum-di-dum poems. I have written
one *sestina,* and enjoyed doing so. I've been influenced by, mainly, Koch, Ashberry, O'Hara, Wallace Stevens, James Schuyler, Jane Bowles, Joe Brainard, John
Latouche, Ron Padgett, Bert Brecht, Evelyn Waugh, Gogol, Kafka, S. J. Perelman,
W. C. Williams.

                    *   *   *

  Kenward Elmslie has reached a plateau, asking with Wittgenstein, "What, me
worry?" There is no discrepancy between what he means and what he says. He
means business about pleasure.
  In *Lizzie Borden,* an Elmslie libretto, Lizzie is denied money and freedom
(pleasure) by her father, so Lizzie gives the fellow forty-one whacks with an axe,
and Elmslie approves. In *The Seagull,* based on the Chekhov downer, Constantine
is denied love and respect by his mother and step-father figure and, in a typical
bourgeois confusion, commits not murder but suicide. In the musical *The Grass
Harp,* a spinster behaves unpleasantly, so her family goes to live in a treehouse.

Just what is so much fun? Spectacle, firstly. I see no spectacle, no panoramic imagination, in other members of the New York School (except in the prose of Harry Mathews).

In the lush, sly drama, *City Junket*, the family of a middle class bumpkin visits the New York metropolis of 1889. I acted in one production with Kenward, Anne Waldman, Joe Brainard and John Ashbery, and had occasion, as well, to view it. The audience was engulfed. Giant slides by Larry Rivers mapped rich verbal vistas which at once transfigure and travesty.

The texture of the writing ranges from delicate to concrete. He likes Hollywood and Scientific Americana. A Romantic stanza imitates, concretely, Busby Berkeley:

    what a life,   just falling in and out of
    what a life,   just falling in and out of
                        swimming pools
    xylophones   WANTED   xylophones
    WANTED   female singer   WANTED
    bigtime floorshow   bigtime floorshow
    bigtime floorshow   bigtime floorshow.

What else is fun? Elmslie will get into the act even in pastorals:

    Around here, all is simpler. Down the paths whistling minks
    rush unafraid. Too clumsy to shy at the beauty of bodies,
        they never pay for the damage they do – trampled mushrooms
    bruised raspberries. And the storms never pay for the damage *they* do.

The role is fatherly but in grander, surreal transformations, it becomes childlike. Beyond dreams, where do dreams begin? "Shirley Temple Surrounded by Lions" opens:

    In a world where kapok on a sidewalk looks like an "accident" –
    innards – would that freckles could enlarge, well, meaningfully,
        into kind of friendly brown kingdoms, all isolate,
    with a hero's route, feral glens,
        and a fountain where heroines cool their mouths.

It would be well to contrast this with the large scale of New York painting, the long poems of Olson and others, Manhattan skyscrapers, and of course Cinemascope.

– Michael André

EMANUEL, James A(ndrew, Sr.). American. Born in Alliance, Nebraska, 15 June 1921. Educated at Alliance High School, 1935–39; Howard University, Washington, D.C., 1946–50, B.A. (summa cum laude) 1950; Northwestern University, Evanston, Illinois, 1950–53, M.A. 1953; Columbia University, New York, 1953–62, Ph.D. 1962. Served in the 93rd Infantry Division, United States Army, 1944–46: Army Commendation Ribbon. Married Mattie Johnson in 1950; has one son. Canteen Steward, Civilian Conservation Corps, Wellington, Kansas, 1939–40; Elevator Operator, Des Moines, Iowa, 1940–41; Weighmaster, Rock Island, Illinois, 1941–42;

Confidential Secretary, Office of the Inspector General, United States War Department, Washington, D.C., 1942–44; Civilian Chief, Pre-Induction Section, Army and Air Force Induction Station, Chicago, 1951–53; Instructor, Harlem YWCA Business School, New York, 1954–56. Instructor, 1957–62, Assistant Professor, 1962–70, Associate Professor, 1970–72, and since 1972, Professor of English, City College of New York. Fulbright Professor of American Literature, University of Grenoble, France, 1968–69; Visiting Professor of English, University of Toulouse, France, 1971–73. Since 1971, General Editor, Broadside Press "Critics Series," Detroit. Recipient: Saxton Memorial Fellowship, 1965. Address: Department of English, City College of New York, Convent Avenue, New York, New York 10031, U.S.A.

PUBLICATIONS

Verse

The Treehouse and Other Poems.   Detroit, Broadside Press, 1968.
At Bay.   Detroit, Broadside Press, 1969.
Panther Man.   Detroit, Broadside Press. 1970.

Other

Langston Hughes.   New York, Twayne, 1967.
How I Write 2, with MacKinlay Kantor and Lawrence Osgood.   New York, Harcourt Brace, 1972.

Editor, with Theodore L. Gross, *Dark Symphony: Negro Literature in America.*   New York, Free Press, 1968.

Critical Studies: by Dudley Randall, in *Negro Digest* (Chicago), June 1968; *Publisher's Weekly* (New York), 21 October 1968; *San Francisco Sunday Examiner, and Chronicle,* 17 November 1968; *Christian Science Monitor* (Boston), 12 December 1968; James Cunningham, in *Negro Digest* (Chicago), January 1969; *Road Apple Review* (Oshkosh, Wisconsin), Winter 1971–72.

James A. Emanuel comments:

Some of the personal history, and many of the ideas, reflected in my poetry can be found in my contribution to the book *How I Write 2.* By now, writing poetry is my principal method of finding and expressing what life means. From the time that I began to write poetry steadily, in the late 1950's, the exacting labor and the large mysteries of that activity – usually carried on late at night – have centered upon vital, everyday matters. The categories into which my poems can be divided describe areas of experience and thought with which ordinary men are well acquainted (and I have wanted my poetry to be fundamentally clear to the largest possible audience): recurrent subjects are youth (centrally my son, James) and miscellaneous Black experience; other subjects include writers, anti-Semitism, blues, war, etc.; the lyrics continue philosophical, descriptive, and personal themes; the tone is usually serious, sometimes satirical, once in a while humorous; the form varies from strict sonnets to free verse that attempts to catch nuances of Black American speech patterns that might be heard on a Harlem street. My poetry runs roughly parallel to my life: a movement from the reflective traditional to the compressed tensions of the 1970's, with inevitably special emphasis on racism, but also with constantly interspersed lyrics that have little to do with our perilous decades. Thus I hope that my poetry, in its unplanned evolution and variety, attests the crucial, dual role of the Black poet: to struggle as embroiled man, but to reflect as clear Mind; to denude and expose as destroyer, yet to clothe and grace as creator; to live as Black and therefore made for the wide world, yet American and therefore made for the narrow cauldron that our nation has become.

My latest work, especially "The Toulouse Poems" and generally those written in and after 1972, might well suggest that three loves develop in my work: parental, racial, and romantic. These common passions are the staple of my poetry. Trying to fathom them and to transform them into art. I am content to be judged by that mass of readers who feel as strongly as they think and who are drawn to what I want increasingly to keep in my poetry: the bite and song of reality.

*   *   *

James A. Emanuel's sympathies are clear even without his statement in *Panther Man* that young people are "the only people whom I tend to respect as a group." Poems like "A Clown at Ten," "The Young Ones, Flip Side," "Fourteen," "Sixteen, Yeah," and "Fisherman" celebrate with an understanding smile the passion and energy of youth while they steer clear of Housmanian idolatry and pathos. Young adulthood is pain, punching, and confusion for the poet, the hopeful stage through which the world passes to confrontation. Behind it stretches the pre-lapsarian vista of childhood. The poet captures the antics of the bathtub sailor in "The Voyage of Jimmy Poo," a time of sterling memory in "I Wish I Had a Red Balloon," and the joy of answering children's questions in "For the 4th Grade, Prospect School: How I Became a Poet."

Manhood brings a different order: understanding, rebellion, militancy, anguish, and death. "Emmett Till," "Where Will Their Names Go Down," and "For Malcolm, U.S.A." pay tribute to the victims, while "Panther Man," "Animal Tricks," "Crossover: for RFK," and "Black Man, 13th Floor" speak in strident (sometimes black, idiomatic) tones of the growth of a generation of men who are rising to take control.

Surrounding and undergirding all stages, however, is the essential romantic humanism of the poet. "Nightmare" and "Christ, One Morning" let us know that all is in the hands of man; there is no God who can be trusted. And ceaselessly, Emanuel reaffirms the power of the imaginative intellect to scale the heights of its own treehouse and dream ("A Negro Author" and "The Treehouse"), or to bring the authoritarian assumptions of the world down with a wince ("Black Poet on the Firing Range"). Two new poems from Toulouse show a sweep and maturity that combine this essential vision with a firm formal mastery.

– Houston A. Baker, Jr.

EMPSON, William. British. Born in Yokefleet, East Yorkshire, 27 September 1906. Educated at Winchester College, Hampshire; Magdalene College, Cambridge, B.A. in mathematics 1929, M.A. 1935. Married Hester Henrietta Crouse in 1941;

has two children. Taught English Literature, Tokyo National University, 1931–34, and National University, Peking, 1937–39, 1947–52. Member of the Monitoring Service, 1940, and Chinese Editor, Far Eastern Section, 1941–46, BBC, London. Taught at Kenyon College, Gambier, Ohio, Summers 1948, 1950, 1954. Professor of English Literature, Sheffield University, 1953–71; since 1971, Emeritus Professor. Litt.D.: University of East Anglia, Norwich, 1968; Bristol University, 1971; Sheffield University, 1974. Address: Studio House, 1 Hampstead Hill Gardens, London N.W.3, England.

PUBLICATIONS

Verse

Letter IV. Cambridge, Heffer, 1929.
Poems. London, Chatto and Windus, 1935.
The Gathering Storm. London, Faber, 1940.
Collected Poems of William Empson. New York, Harcourt Brace, 1949; London, Chatto and Windus, 1955; revised edition, Harcourt Brace, 1961.

Recording: *Poems,* Listen, 1961.

Other

Seven Types of Ambiguity. London, Chatto and Windus, 1930; revised edition, 1947; New York, Noonday Press, 1955; revised edition, London, Penguin-Chatto and Windus, 1963.
Some Versions of Pastoral. London, Chatto and Windus, 1935; as *English Pastoral Poetry,* New York, Norton, 1938.
Shakespeare Survey, with George Garrett. London, Brendin, 1937.
The Structure of Complex Words. London, Chatto and Windus, and New York, New Directions, 1951.
Milton's God. London, Chatto and Windus, 1961; New York, New Directions, 1962; revised edition, Chatto and Windus, 1965.

Editor, *Outlook of Science,* by John Haldane. London, Routledge, 1935.
Editor, *Science and Well-Being,* by John Haldane. London, Routledge, 1935.
Editor, *Shakespeare's Poems.* New York, New American Library, 1969.
Editor, with David Pirie, *Coleridge's Verse: A Selection.* London, Faber, 1972; New York, Schocken Books, 1973.

Critical Studies: *William Empson: The Man and His Work,* edited by Roma Gill, London, Routledge, 1974.

William Empson comments:

(1974) Most of the poets who were starting to write around 1930 hoped to learn methods and techniques from the French Symbolists and also the seventeenth-century English Metaphysicals; but Mallarmé would consider it vulgar to argue, if

437

ever confronted with argufying in poetry, whereas Donne did it all the time. The young Eliot was large-minded and courageous, I still think, to write so much (in his prose) recommending Donne, a poet so very remote from his own practice; and I suppose he was merely being charitable or reassuring to his disciples when he told them they needn't actually bother about the arguments.

I imitated Donne only, which made me appear pointlessly gawky or half undressed; but I still think that the two methods cannot be combined – you cannot write both like Mallarmé and like Donne at the same time, or anyway not energetically enough. So, though grateful for the generous and sympathetic remarks of my old friend George Fraser, I cannot really feel pleased when he tells you at the end not to bother about the arguments. They are what the poetry is made out of, whether the result is good or bad.

*   *   *

William Empson's great reputation and influence as a poet are based mainly on his volume of 1935, *Poems,* and his volume of 1940, *The Gathering Storm.* The *Collected Poems* of 1955 contain only a few more short poems and a masque written mainly by Empson's students at Sheffield for a visit by the Queen to the university there, a masque to which Empson himself contributed only a few lines. The poems in the first volume reflect very much the influence of Donne, who remains Empson's favourite English poet. The style is terse, riddling and elliptical, there are many metaphors as in Donne from astronomy, biology, and the other natural sciences, the mood is one of witty desperation, or even despair; many of the poems are love poems, others are about the neutrality and indifference of the outer universe to man's predicament. Though the influence of Donne is the most obvious one, there is a touch, in the general attitude to life, of ironic defiance or slightly swaggering pessimism, that might recall A. E. Housman, who is also one of Empson's favourite poets. There is a sense of an intricate, witty, and deliberately puzzling form being imposed on a massive and almost unbearable personal unhappiness. With all the intricacy, there is an odd rough directness in the tone of voice.

The Gathering Storm, by contrast, is in the main a poem of public events and the public tone of voice. In the intervening years Empson had taught both in Japan and in China, at the time of the Japanese invasion of Manchuria. Fleeing, as he puts it in one of the finest poems in the volume, "Aubade," from the disorder and injustice of Europe, he had found in the Far East "only the same war on a stronger toe." Yet his very experience of violence had oddly strengthened him: "The heart of standing is we cannot fly." The poems suggested a deep trust in the fundamental, sane anti-Facism of the British people – when tested by the Hoare-Laval pact, for instance, the "thing has answered like a gong" – and in a combination of prudence and courage in facing Axis aggression. There is nothing of the rather naive belief of Auden (mocked at in "Just a Smack at Auden") either that Western civilization is automatically running to an end or that we shall have Utopia tomorrow. The voice has a tart and humorous authority. The tone suggests political poets of the Restoration, like Dryden, Rochester, or Marvell in his satires much more than Donne; there is a kind of bulldog sturdiness in it, and in a way it was appropriate that Churchill should choose the same title, *The Gathering Storm,* for his volume of memoirs about the 1930's. The tone of tense and intricate personal despair is replaced by one of humorous combative stoicism. Technically, what is notable is the use of forms like the *villanelle* involving the use of a refrain or repeated lines, in a way that gives a twist or change of emphasis at each repetition. There is also a very effective use of a deliberate colloquial flatness and terseness. Both the diction and the verse forms were borrowed extensively by the young "Movement" poets of the early 1950's, notably John Wain, who also, at the end of the 1940's, wrote the first proper appreciation of Empson's poetic achievement so far. But Edwin Muir noted that these young disciples tended to lack the element that transforms Empson's poetry, passion. The strength of the later Empsonian style is the sense that so much is held in reserve, so many fires are banked under: "You don't want madhouse and the whole thing there." For all their intelligence, and the brilliance of Empson's own prose notes on them, these poems, so unlike anybody else's, do not lend themselves to simple summary in terms of theme: irony and ambiguity, hurdles for the reader's intelligence, are everywhere. Donald Davie has suggested that Empson is predominantly a poet of *tone*, of tact and skill in channelling and modifying the reader's responses. A dominating personality certainly comes through, as it does also in his prose criticism: and a peculiar flavour, tart, fibrous, captivating, like that of a quince or a crab apple. What one remembers in the end of Empson perhaps is "a taste in the mind."

– G. S. Fraser

ENGLE, Paul (Hamilton). American. Born in Cedar Rapids, Iowa, 12 October 1908. Educated at Coe College, Cedar Rapids, B.A. 1931 (Phi Beta Kappa); University of Iowa, Iowa City, M.A. 1932; Columbia University, New York, 1932–33; Merton College, Oxford (Rhodes Scholar), B.A. 1936, M.A. 1939. Married to Hualing Nieh; has two daughters and three grandchildren. Director of the Creative Writing Program, 1937–65, since 1946, Professor of English, and since 1966, Director of the International Writing Program, University of Iowa. Member of the Advisory Commission on the Arts, and the National Council on the Arts. Recipient: Yale Series of Younger Poets Award, 1932; Guggenheim Fellowship, 1953; Lamont Poetry Selection Award, 1962; Rockefeller Fellowship; Ford Fellowship. D.Litt.: Coe College, 1946; LL.D.: Monmouth College, Illinois, 1949; L.H.D.: Iowa Wesleyan College, Mount Pleasant, 1956. Agent: William Morris Agency Inc., 1350 Avenue of the Americas, New York, New York 10019. Address: 1104 North Dubuque, Iowa City, Iowa 52240, U.S.A.

PUBLICATIONS

Verse

Worn Earth.   New Haven, Connecticut, Yale University Press, 1932.
American Song: A Book of Poems.   New York, Doubleday, 1934; London, Cape, 1935.
Break the Heart's Anger.   New York, Doubleday, and London, Cape, 1936.
Corn.   New York, Doubleday, 1939.
New Englanders.   Muscatine, Iowa, Prarie Press, 1940.
West of Midnight.   New York, Random House, 1941.
American Child.   Muscatine, Iowa, Prarie Press, 1944.
American Child: A Sonnet Sequence.   New York, Random House, 1945; revised

edition, as *American Child: Sonnets for My Daughter, with Thirty Six New Poems,* New York, Dial Press, 1956.
The Word of Love. New York, Random House, 1951.
Book and Child: Three Sonnets. Iowa City, Cummington Press, 1956.
Poems in Praise. New York, Random House, 1959.
Christmas Poems. Privately printed, 1962.
A Woman Unashamed and Other Poems. New York, Random House, 1965.
Embrace: Selected Love Poems. New York, Random House, 1969.

Plays

For the Iowa Dead, music by Philip Bezanson. Iowa City, State University of Iowa, 1956.
Golden Child, music by Philip Bezanson (televised, 1960). New York, Doubleday, 1962.

Novels

Always the Land. New York, Random House, 1941.
Golden Child. New York, Dutton, 1962.

Other

Robert Frost. Iowa City, State University of Iowa Library, 1959.
A Prarie Christmas. New York, Longman, 1960.
An Old-Fashioned Chrstmas. New York, Dial Press, 1964.
Who's Afraid? (juvenile). New York, Crowell Collier, 1963.

Editor, *Prize Stories: The O. Henry Awards.* New York, Doubleday, 6 vols., 1954–59.
Editor, with Warren Carrier, *Reading Modern Poetry.* Chicago, Scott Foresman, 1955; revised edition, 1968.
Editor, *Homage to Baudelaire, on the Centennial of "Les Fleurs du Mal," from the Poets at the State University of Iowa.* Iowa City, Cummington Press, 1957.
Editor, with Henri Coulette, *Midland: Twenty-Five Years of Fiction and Poetry from the Writing Workshops of the State University of Iowa,* and *Midland II.* New York, Random House, 1961, 1970.
Editor, with Joseph Langland, *Poet's Choice.* New York, Dial Press, 1962.
Editor, *On Creative Writing.* New York, Dutton, 1964.

Translator, with Hualing Nieh, *Poems of Mao Tse-Tung.* New York, Dell, 1972; London, Wildwood House, 1974.

Manuscript Collection: University of Iowa Library, Iowa City.

Paul Engle comments:

My poetry tries to find the most concentrated human feeling in the fewest words. It was a sprawling effort in the early years and has tightened up in the later years.

The poems about Edmund Blunden at Oxford University represent the struggle to absorb direct experience into direct language. Emotion without sentimentality, images containing the emotion as object. Rilke and Yeats the greatest influences.

*   *   *

Paul Engle has been a major figure in American poetry for thirty years and more. As a principal in the founding and development of the famous Writers Workshop at the University of Iowa, as a teacher and editor, he has been an important and encouraging influence for many young poets: several are important contemporary voices. Engle's current efforts are largely directed toward the development of a Translation Workshop, also at the University of Iowa.

As a poet, Engle's reputation is based on more than ten volumes published since 1932. It is perhaps not surprising to note that these contain consistently energetic poems of affirmation. It is an optimistic verse which frequently states its opposition to the modern voice of despair and makes use of so-called "American themes": *Corn*, and *A Prairie Christmas*, "Coney Island," "American Harvest." It is a verse which, like his titles, and even in the later volumes which reach outside of America for some subject matter, is direct and uncomplicated:

> Her spine curves like a C,
> But does it therefore beg
> For pity and despair
> Like Lautrec's crooked leg?
>
> No! For the food she grows
> That Tokyo may eat,
> Comes from determination
> Perfect and complete.

A poet of Engle's ability and temperament has apparently had to answer some hard questions: How is one to affirm in a world where despair is more obvious and cynicism seems safer? How do we have a popular poetry, of good taste, in a nation where the real has so often been merely vulgar?

Engle has proclaimed and praised with control and clear speech in each of his volumes. His subjects and attitudes are occasionally close to Whitman or Sandburg or Lindsay, but it would be wrong to say Engle sings or celebrates. The tone of his early poems is reminiscient of the Georgians and, in later volumes, several reviewers have noted that the poems are nostalgic although occasionally "worn" or "repetitive."

He is at his best when his verse is simplest:

> That was a shocking day
> When we watched, lying prone,
> The two trout sidle under
> The underwater stone . . .

And in "Pair":

> Nothing can live alone,
> Two are behind each birth.
> Every fallen stone
> Lies on the rock of earth.

> Never a single thing
> Has the whole power to be.
> Always the wind must bring
> Pollen from tree to tree.
>
> A man is how he stands,
> Thrust of foot in shoe.
> I am my own long hands
> And their live touch of you.

But in the eagerness to attack despair, too often there are lines which are prosaic or merely sentimental:

> There is a primitive old strength of heart
> Men have called courage and that we call guts,
> It bore the Crucifix and warped the wagons
> Of Boone's men westward through the frozen ruts . . .
>
> (1939)

> Abruptly in her black and grateful eyes
> The red firecrackers of her heart explode.
>
> (1965)

One of the excellences of contemporary poetry has been its recognition that there are moments of special emotion when the poet should be struck speechless, and his poem communicate that "silence between the words." It is the essayist or teacher who explains, or over-explains, and too often explains away, but the essayist or teacher is seeking a different, and predominantly intellectual, credibility.

Engle's technique has been markedly influenced by several poets: Shelley in the early volumes, Donne's use of paradox and metaphor, Eliot in several poems (e.g., "Harlem Airshaft"), Auden's Christmas oratorio, Frost, and his former teacher at Oxford, Edmund Blunden. Like Blunden he keeps a distance from the physical – and from his subjects – which is often as aristocratic as aesthetic. Engle's best poems for the contemporary ear are lyric and personal, avoiding strong masculine rhymes, similes, and deliberate iambics. "Kaarlo in Finland" is a sensitive sequence of "letters" around the "Russo-Finnish" war. The title sequence of *A Woman Unashamed* and "In a Bar near Shibuya Station, Tokyo" are good examples of his best work in which there is a striking delicacy:

> As if on a summer day, in the dazzle of noon,
> One snowflake fell on my astonished hand.

– Joseph Wilson

ENGLISH, Maurice. American. Born in Chicago, Illinois, 21 October 1909. Educated at Harvard University, Cambridge, Massachusetts, A.B. 1933 (Phi Beta Kappa). Married Fanita Blumberg in 1945; has two children. Free-lance Journalist in the United States and Europe, 1933–54; Editor-in-Chief, International Division,

NBC, 1941–43. Editor and Publisher, *Chicago Magazine*, 1954–58. Managing Editor, 1961–63, and Senior Editor, 1963–69, University of Chicago Press. Since 1969, Director, Temple University Press, Philadelphia. United States Delegate to Les Biennales Internationales de Poésie, Knokke-Le-Zoute, Belgium, 1965. Recipient: Fulbright Fellowship, 1966. Address: 2004 Spruce Street, Philadelphia, Pennsylvania 19103, U.S.A.

PUBLICATIONS

Verse

> *Midnight in the Century: Poems.* Park Forest, Illinois, Prairie School Press, 1964.
> *A Savaging of Roots.* Waterloo, Ontario, Pasdeloup Press, 1974.

Other

> Editor, *The Testament of Stone: Writings of Louis Sullivan.* Evanston, Illinois, Northwestern University Press, 1963.

> Translator, with others, *Selected Poems of Eugenio Montale.* New York, New Directions, 1967.

Critical Studies: by Ralph J. Mills, Jr., in *Tri-Quarterly* (Evanston, Illinois), Spring 1965; by Peter Michelson, in *Chicago Maroon Literary Supplement*, 1965.

Maurice English comments:

Peter Viereck once wrote that I was the "post-modern" poet who had most successfully assimilated lessons from such divergent sources as Eliot and Hart Crane; I hope he is right; I share in the universal debt to the French poets from Baudelaire on, and owe a particular one to Eugenio Montale, whose poetry I first read, with revivifying effect on my own, while learning Italian and (under the tutelage of the late Renato Poggioli) translating it into English.

My major themes and characteristic subjects are both indicated by the title of my book of poems *Midnight in the Century*. Nearly all the poems I most value have been compelled into existence; I have been essentially a medium for them.

*   *   *

Action/contemplation, passion/premeditation, impulse/custom, chaos/order, "all the fanged opposites," form the continuing theme and structure of Maurice English's poems. Though he perceives the dualities in his subjects, balance in the expression does not result: the latter halves of the oppositions usually dominate. He begins his volume with the apologia: "I have put on these masks to show you my face." But the reserved temperament permits only a filtered vision; the cautious persona emerges just on the brink of revelation. Not that the poet is cold (or coy); but he is, above all, controlled. The poems under the heading of a Social Security number invite autobiographical interpretation. The first, a précis of the standard saga of callow youth – education, travel (flight), return – ends in middle-aged repose with "fat decanter" and hope of son and daughter sharing the "rare flotsam of my joy." "Form Was the World" marks the passage from a boy's love of geometric perfection to a man's appreciation of natural spontaneity. "Thalassa" tells how a sea unseen is traded for life in an inland city, how preferred grace is denied in favor of "the El, the grassless yard." "I turned away a manic guide," he explains in "Acrophobia II," "To travel by the urge of brain and bone." But, weary of intellection, the "annihilating eye," and afraid of the "dangerous voyages" of the heart, he cries: "Blessed are those who do not understand." He comforts Narcissus: "You have no knowledge, and are therefore wise." This and other paradoxes are the logical products of a love of contrasts. Likewise, the cerebral poet expresses conflict and contradiction in parables, further reduced to a pithy "Epitaph" and witty "Biography," and still further compressed in clever aphorisms. His agile pen is honed to a cutting edge when he writes "Against Elders" or indicts with easy sarcasm a Pope who can forget Guernica as he blesses the Spanish generals.

Despite his strong voice, a sense of impotence breaks through, the feeling of inadequacy in "Healing sick passion with sick wit." This may explain his championing of men of daring and action, partisans and soldiers who fight the restraining forces. Hence, too, the engrossing fascination in "The House of Mirrors," a five-part dramatic poem depicting a murder-suicide in a cathouse from several perspectives. A news item introduces the question whether "*Pity, though meant to cure*" can prove a butchery. The supercilious newspaperman jokes as he phones in his report, oblivious to the agony of the victims, a tart plagued daily by brutish "tricks" and haunted nightly by dreams of childhood violation, and her would-be savior, the whorehouse pianist driven by paranoid fantasies to slay her and himself, thus releasing them from their separate demons. Confronting the internal conflicts and expressing the self-destructive dichotomies in our natures, lucidly and without sentimentality, the poet can evoke our sympathies. In the strength of honest lines he achieves his "hope to breed / A passion that is purpose and some power."

– Joseph Parisi

ENRIGHT, D(ennis) J(oseph). British. Born in Leamington, Warwickshire, 11 March 1920. Educated at Leamington College; Downing College, Cambridge, B.A. (honours) in English 1944, M.A. 1946; University of Alexandria, Egypt, D.Litt. 1949. Married Madeleine Harders in 1949; has one child. Lecturer in English, University of Alexandria, 1947–50; Extra-Mural Lecturer, Birmingham University, England, 1950–53; Visiting Professor, Konan University, Kobe, Japan, 1953–56; Gastdozent, Free University, West Berlin, 1956–57; British Council Professor of English, Chulalongkorn University, Bangkok, 1957–59; Professor of English, University of Singapore, 1960–70. Temporary Lecturer in English, University of Leeds, Yorkshire, 1970–71. Co-Editor of *Encounter* magazine, London, 1970–72. Editorial Advisor, 1971–73, and since 1973, Member, Board of Directors, Chatto and Windus, publishers, London. Recipient: Cholmondeley Award, 1974. Fellow, Royal Society of Literature, 1961. Address: Chatto and Windus Ltd., 40–42 William IV Street, London WC2N 4DF, England.

PUBLICATIONS

Verse

The Laughing Hyena and Other Poems. London, Routledge, 1953.
Bread Rather Than Blossoms. London, Secker and Warburg, 1956.
Some Men Are Brothers. London, Chatto and Windus, 1960.
Addictions. London, Chatto and Windus, 1962.
The Old Adam. London, Chatto and Windus, 1965.
Unlawful Assembly. London, Chatto and Windus, and Middletown, Connecticut, Wesleyan University Press, 1968.
Selected Poems. London, Chatto and Windus, 1969.
The Typewriter Revolution and Other Poems. New York, Library Press, 1971.
In the Basilica of the Annunciation. London, Poem-of-the-Month Club, 1971.
Daughters of Earth. London, Chatto and Windus, 1972.
Foreign Devils. London, Covent Garden Press, 1972.
The Terrible Shears: Scenes from a Twenties Childhood. London, Chatto and Windus, 1973; Middletown, Connecticut, Wesleyan University Press, 1974.
Rhymes Times Rhyme (for children). London, Chatto and Windus, 1974.

Novels

Academic Year. London, Secker and Warburg, 1955.
Heaven Knows Where. London, Secker and Warburg, 1957.
Insufficient Poppy. London, Chatto and Windus, 1960.
Figures of Speech. London, Heinemann, 1965.

Other

A Commentary on Goethe's "Faust". New York, New Directions, 1949.
The World of Dew: Aspects of Living Japan. London, Secker and Warburg, 1955; Chester Springs, Pennsylvania, Dufour, 1959.
Literature for Man's Sake: Critical Essays. Tokyo, Kenkyusha, 1955.
The Apothecary's Shop. London, Secker and Warburg, 1957; Chester Springs, Pennsylvania, Dufour, 1959.
Robert Graves and the Decline of Modernism (address). Singapore, Craftsman Press, 1960; Folcroft, Pennsylvania, Folcroft Editions, 1974.
Conspirators and Poets. London, Chatto and Windus, and Chester Springs, Pennsylvania, Dufour, 1966.
Memoirs of a Mendicant Professor. London, Chatto and Windus, 1969.
Shakespeare and the Students. London, Chatto and Windus, 1970; New York, Schocken Books, 1971.
Man Is an Onion: Essays and Reviews. London, Chatto and Windus, 1972; La Salle, Illinois, Library Press, 1973.

Editor, *Poetry of the 1950's: An Anthology of New English Verse.* Tokyo, Kenkyusha, 1955.
Editor, with Takamichi Ninomiya, *The Poetry of Living Japan.* London, Murray, and New York, Grove Press, 1957.
Editor, with E. de Chickera, *English Critical Texts: 16th Century to 20th Century.* London and New York, Oxford University Press, 1962.

Critical Study: *D. J. Enright: Poet of Humanism* by William Walsh, London, Cambridge University Press, 1974.

*   *   *

D. J. Enright is a poet whose work gives the impression of possessing very vividly the quality of currency. It has the air of registering this world at this moment and of rising out of, and being addressed to, our perplexities as they are now. Enright has an eye for the thematic possibilities of novel and distinctly contemporary tracts of experience. The events of the poet's life play an important part in a poetry which has a solidly objective character. He has worked as a university teacher in Germany, Egypt, Japan, Siam, India and Malaya, countries which expose the sensitive nerve of the modern world. As a teacher of a self-conscious generation he is in direct touch with people's intimately human concerns; as a post-imperial Englishman his human shape is unmuffled by the toga, his relationships undistorted by the hypocrisies of power or obedience. He writes in "Entrance Visa":

> We were the Descendancy. Hurt but not surprised.
> Atoning for our predecessors' every oath and sneer,
> We paid in poverty the rich men's debt.

The poet's glance, wry and original as it is, bent upon reality. The ambiguous and yet appealing relationships of the "sad and naughty persons" he is drawn to, their odd and slippery jobs, are fully and firmly established and with a minimum of descriptive reference. The poems are quite unpadded, and rest elegantly on nothing more than their own bones. Disciplined observation, we realise, can be a remarkably productive poetic instrument; it is, indeed, an important and neglected human power:

> The flame-tree shames us, one and all,
>   for what fit audience, though few, do we afford?

And to notice a thing with the poet's fine, unblurred particularity is to rescue it from falling into the refuse of life:

> If we do not observe, who will?
> Will anything observe or mourn for us?

The observation of the poet is not, of course, the neutrality of the mirror. It depends upon a particular attitude and carries a special tone. In Enright's case as with the most of these poets the attitude is pitying, the tone ironic:

> Only one subject to write about: pity.
> Self-pity: the only subject to avoid.
> How difficult to observe both conditions!

The pity is without the least taint of *de haut en bas*; it is a level, unfussy feeling, of which the impulse is seeing in another's plight an extension of one's own and recognising his nature within one's own self. It is an acknowledgment of the common thing in men: "And being common / Therefore something rare indeed." "Men are brothers," murmurs this voice, lucidly, lovingly – a simplicity which is immediately corrected to a more astringent, complicated comment, "Some men are brothers." The peculiar flavour of the poems comes from combining the mild (a favourite word of the poet), the mild taste of charity with the acrid one of "real cities, real houses, real time."

Enright is a poet with a bias towards light and intelligibility, with a gift for defining in the current, shabby language natural vivacities, with a delicate mastery of suppleness in tone, who treats a serious subject with a comedian's manner, and who celebrates in an individual and wholly contemporary voice the human virtues of hope and charity.

– William Walsh

ENSLIN, Theodore (Vernon). American. Born in Chester, Pennsylvania, 25 March 1925. Educated in public and private schools; studied composition with Nadia Boulanger. Remarried Alison Jose in 1969; has three children. Address: R.F.D. 1, Temple, Maine 04984, U.S.A.

PUBLICATIONS

Verse

The Work Proposed. Kyoto, Japan, Origin Press, 1958.
New Sharon's Prospect. Kyoto, Japan, Origin Press, 1962.
The Place Where I Am Standing. New Rochelle, New York, Elizabeth Press, 1964.
This Do (and The Talents). Mexico City, El Corno Emplumado, 1966.
New Sharon's Prospect and Journals. San Francisco, Coyote's Journal, 1966.
To Come To Have Become. New Rochelle, New York, Elizabeth Press, 1966.
The Four Temperaments. Privately printed, 1966.
Characters in Certain Places. Portland, Oregon, Prensa de Lagar–Wine Press, 1967.
The Diabelli Variations and Other Poems. Annandale-on-Hudson, New York, Matter Books, 1967.
2/30–6/31: Poems 1967. Cabot, Vermont, Stoveside Press, 1967.
Agreement and Back: Sequences. New Rochelle, New York, Elizabeth Press, 1969.
The Poems. New Rochelle, New York, Elizabeth Press, 1970.
Forms, Part One: The First Dimension. New Rochelle, New York, Elizabeth Press, 1970.
Views 1–7. Berkeley, California, Maya, 1970.
The Country of Our Consciousness. Berkeley, California, Sand Dollar, 1971.
Forms, Part Two. New Rochelle, New York, Elizabeth Press, 1971.
Forms, Part Three. New Rochelle, New York, Elizabeth Press, 1972.
Etudes. New Rochelle, New York, Elizabeth Press, 1972.
Views. New Rochelle, New York, Elizabeth Press, 1973.

Forms, Part Four. New Rochelle, New York, Elizabeth Press, 1973.
Sitio. Hanover, New Hampshire, Granite, 1973.
In the Keepers House. Dennis, Massachusetts, Salt Works Press, 1973.
With Light Reflected. Fremont, Michigan, Sumac Press, 1973.
The Swamp Fox. Dennis, Massachusetts, Salt Works Press, 1974.
The Mornings. Berkeley, California, Shaman/Drum, 1974.

Manuscript Collection: Fales Collection, New York University Libraries.

Critical Study: "The Frozen State" by the author, in *Elizabeth* (New Rochelle, New York), 1965.

Theodore Enslin comments:

I suppose I would classify as a "non-academic," and have been allied with those who broke with the "New Criticism" in the early fifties.

Perhaps, as Cid Corman once said, I write more "you" poems than anyone else now alive. My "themes" are what I find around me, and since I live in the country, this has sometimes led to thinking that I am in some way a "nature poet." I heartily disavow this. My poems are intensely introspective from which I attempt to produce the impersonality/personality which I feel necessary to any valid work of art. My formal structure is based on sound, and I feel that my musical training has shaped this more than anything else. The line breaks/stresses are indicated as a type of notation, something which concerns me, since I believe we have no adequate notation for poetry, and I conceive of any poem as requiring a performance. It should be read aloud. In ways, some important to me, and some to the work itself, I would say that Rilke, W. C. Williams, Thoreau, and latterly Louis Zukofsky, were influences. The rest must be said in the poems themselves.

*   *   *

Theodore Enslin's work became known in the pages of *Origin,* the seminal magazine edited by Cid Corman, who also published Enslin's first book. It's not surprising, then, to find a continuity between the work of the two men. Both write spare, quiet, post-Williams poems grounded in a shared respect for the otherness and autonomy of natural things and a distruct of the romantic ego. A basic premise is that sufficiently careful naming of phenomena can by itself energize attention. But Enslin is more diffuse than Corman. Many of his poems, read quickly, seem merely flat, no more than prose jottings. Reread, however, with due attention to the lineation and sound, the best of them take on a pondered weight and become meditations rather than mere statements. His method of condensing daily experience and observation into poems can be seen in the charming *New Sharon's Prospect,* which gives both the prose anecdotes and sketches and the poems which crystallize out of them. Enslin's work is filled with the places, people, and things of rural New England, where he lives. If at times it reminds you of a Frost landscape, it is free of Frost's often intrusive "personality." Others of his poems are more abstract notations of emotion or of the problematic relations of observer and external reality; this one is from *The Place Where I Am Standing*:

I turned once to the window
and once
to you
                not here.
I would have shown you
a world I see there,
but it would not have been your world.
It is better this way.
In absence, you come to the window,
look out on just those things
I have shown you.

Recently Enslin has published the first three of what are to be five volumes of *Forms,* a long open-structure poem, the product of "sixteen years of experiment and discovery" which he describes as "my apperception of art, of history, of experience, whatever any of it may have been worth, and no matter how limited." First acquaintance suggests that it is less rewarding than the short poems, but the interest of the latter is grounds enough for thinking the long work will deserve frequentation.

– Seamus Cooney

ESHLEMAN, Clayton. American. Born in Indianapolis, Indiana, 1 June 1935. Educated at Indiana University, Bloomington, 1953–61, B.A. in philosophy, M.A. in English. Married Barbara Novak in 1961 (divorced, 1967); Caryl Eshleman; has one son, Matthew, from first marriage. Instructor, University of Maryland Eastern Overseas Division, Japan, 1961–62; Instructor in English, Matsushita Electric Corporation, Osaka, Japan, 1962–64; lived in Peru, 1965; Instructor, New York University American Language Institute, 1966–68; Member of the School of Critical Studies, California Institute of the Arts, Valencia, 1970–72. Editor and Publisher, *Caterpillar* magazine, New York, 1967–70, and Sherman Oaks, California, 1970–73. Recipient: Union League Civic and Arts Foundation Prize (*Poetry,* Chicago), 1968; National Translation Center awards; National Endowment for the Arts grant, 1969; Coordinating Council of Literary Magazines grant, 1969, 1970, 1971. Address: 14211 Dickens Street, Sherman Oaks, California 91403, U.S.A.

PUBLICATIONS

Verse

Mexico and North. Tokyo, privately printed, 1962.
The Chavin Illumination. Lima, Peru, La Rama Florida, 1965.
Lachrymae Mateo: 3 Poems for Christmas 1966. New York, Caterpillar, 1966.
Walks. New York, Caterpillar, 1967.
The Crocus Bud. Reno, Nevada, Camels Coming, 1967.
Brother Stones. New York and Kyoto, Caterpillar, 1968.

Cantaloups and Splendour.   Los Angeles, Black Sparrow Press, 1968.
T'ai.   Cambridge, Massachusetts, Sans Souci Press, 1969.
The House of Okumura.   Toronto, Weed/Flower Press, 1969.
Indiana: Poems.   Los Angeles, Black Sparrow Press, 1969.
The House of Ibuki: A Poem, New York City, 14 March–30 Sept. 1967.   Fremont,
   Michigan, Sumac Press, 1969.
The Yellow River Record.   London, Big Venus, 1969.
A Pitchblende.   San Francisco, Maya, 1969.
The Wand.   Santa Barbara, California, Capricorn Press, 1971.
Bearings.   Santa Barbara, California, Capricorn Press, 1971.
Altars.   Los Angeles, Black Sparrow Press, 1971.
The Sanjo Bridge.   Los Angeles, Black Sparrow Press, 1972.
Coils.   Los Angeles, Black Sparrow Press, 1973.
Human Wedding.   Los Angeles, Black Sparrow Press, 1973.
*The Last Judgment: For Caryl Her Thirty-First Birthday, The End of Her
   Pain.*   Los Angeles, Plantin Press, 1973.

Other

Editor, *A Caterpillar Anthology: A Selection of Poetry and Prose from Caterpillar
   Magazine.*   New York, Doubleday, 1971.

Translator, *Residence on Earth,* by Pablo Neruda.   San Francisco, Amber
   House, 1962.
Translator, with Denis Kelly, *State of the Union,* by Aimé Césaire.   Blooming-
   ton, Indiana, Caterpillar, 1966.
Translator, *Poemas Humanos/Human Poems,* by César Vallejo.   New York,
   Grove Press, 1968; London, Cape, 1969.
Translator, with José Rubia Barcia, *Spain, Take This Cup from Me,* by César
   Vallejo.   New York, Grove Press, 1974.

Manuscript Collections: Lilly Library, Indiana University, Bloomington; Special
Collections Library, New York University.

Critical Studies: review by Hayden Carruth, in *New York Times Book Review,* 13
February 1972; Introduction by the author to *Coils,* 1973.

*   *   *

Clayton Eshleman is unusual among his contemporaries because he did not start
writing poetry until he was in college, whereas most poets are composing little
masterpieces to the rose bush or their puppies before they are seven and often have
written an entire body of work before they are 30. And part of the fascination of
Eshleman's poetry is its organic relationship to his life. He has created a poetry
which embodies the struggles of transformation from an insulated bourgeois business administration student from the Mid-West into a poet of raw and brutal
self-revelations.

Taking as his mentor William Blake, Eshleman has commenced a spiritual
journey, in an attempt to purge the clogging murky insulation of his early life and
create a poetry out of the new revealed personality. Eshleman is an archetypal
poet, looking for the everyman in his experiences, looking for the primal sources in

himself and trying to locate the self in poetry. His work is obsessively self-involved, filled with minute details of his personal observations, and almost cruelly willing to reveal every impression of the self in hopes that such bareness will finally discover the rich spirit of poet in each person.

His most powerful book to date, *Coils*, is a rare document combining his own sense of the mythic self with the autobiographical Clayton Eshleman from Indiana, U.S.A. His poems are filled with a sensuousness that transcends the most painful moments. His ability to describe the textures of a world seen as a thrillingly beautiful place, surface as magic moments which almost deny the purposes of the poems and yet give the poet precisely what he is looking for – the poetry of existence.

Eshleman's career as a poet has been intertwined with that of a magazine he founded and published, called *Caterpillar*. This magazine created a forum for Eshleman and his colleagues who write longer poems in open forms. The inspiration for this magazine (and for much of his work, Eshleman claims) was Cid Corman, an American editor who founded *Origin* magazine.

– Diane Wakoski

ESPINO, Federico (Licsi, Jr.). Filipino. Born in Pasig, Rizal, 10 April 1939. Educated at the University of Santo Tomas, Manila, B.A. in journalism 1959. Assistant Editor, *Mirror Magazine*, Manila, 1969–72. Recipient: Asia Foundation–Silliman University Fellowship, 1966; Palanca Memorial Award, 1967, 1969, 1972; *Free Press* Short Story prize, 1972; *Graphic* Short Story prize, 1972. Address: 178 Marcelo H. del Pilar, Pasig, Rizal, Philippines.

PUBLICATIONS

Verse

> *In Three Tongues: A Folio of Poems in Tagalog, English, and Spanish.* Quezon City, Bustamante Press, 1963.
> *Apocalypse in Ward 19 and Other Poems.* Quezon City, Journal Press, 1965.
> *The Shuddering Clavier.* Quezon City, Journal Press, 1965.
> *Sa Paanan ng parnaso.* Quezon City, Journal Press, 1965.
> *Toreng Bato, Kastilyong Pawid.* Quezon City, Journal Press, 1966.
> *Balalayka ni Pasternak at iba pang tula* (in Tagalog and English). Manila, Pioneer Press, 1967.
> *A Rapture of Distress.* Manila, Pioneer Press, 1968.
> *Alak na buhay, hinog na abo, phoenix na papel* (in Tagalog and English). Manila, Pioneer Press, 1968.
> *Dark Sutra.* Quezon City, Pioneer Press, 1969.
> *Burnt Alphabets: Poems in English, Tagalog, and Spanish.* Manila, Pioneer Press, 1969.

Dawn and Downsitting: Poems.   Quezon City, Pioneer Press, 1969.
Counterclockwise: Poems 1965–1969.   Quezon City, Bustamante Press, 1969.
A Manner of Seeing: A Folio of Poems.   Privately printed, 1970.
Caras y Caretas de Amor.   Quezon City, Bustamante Press, 1970.
The Winnowing Rhythm.   Quezon City, Bustamante Press, 1970.
Makinilya at lira, tuluyan at tula.   Manila, Pioneer Press, 1970.
Letters and Nocturnes.   Manila, Pioneer Press, 1973.

Short Stories

The Country of Sleep.   Quezon City, Bustamante Press, 1969.
Percussive Blood.   Manila, Pioneer Press, 1972.

Critical Study: "Philippine Poetry in English: Some Notes for Exploration" by Cirilo Bautista, in *Solidarity Magazine* (Manila), December 1970.

Federico Espino comments:

I have been compared to the French Symbolists though the affinity I have with them is only a matter of subject matter, not of form. I do not, however, believe in a Rimbaudian derangement of the senses or in the Baudelairean theory of correspondences and I eschew the celebration of neurosis, though in my stories I write about neurotic people. The psychological minorities interest me only in relation to a Cathólic frame of reference.

*   *   *

Federico Espino is not only an English language poet: he has the distinction of being the leading Filipino writer in Tagalog, which is the language of Manila and its environs, and which forms the basis of the artificial national language. Nothing that he has done in English verse is as good as the short stories collected in *The Country of Sleep*; but he shows signs of development. His English poetry is often too obviously derivative and self-consciously experimental, and he seems to have been over-influenced by his important compatriot José Garcia Villa (although Villa, strangely, is generally much disliked in his native country): various sorts of technical effects, often well-executed, tend to swallow up or diminish the content of his poems. He is at his best when his subject is the actual problem of poetic procedure, with which he is honestly and unpretentiously concerned. His use of Lowell and Stevens has been unproductive; but Guillén, with his sonorous, nostalgic toughness, has been a valuable influence. His difficulties may originate in his bilingualism: there is not really a large or appreciative audience for Tagalog writing, and it is natural enough that an author with a perfect command of English should turn to the latter language. The decision has been successful in the realm of short fiction; but one is bound to wonder if Espino's Tagalog poetry is not better than his English: more authentically his own.

– Martin Seymour-Smith

EVANS, Abbie Huston. American. Born in Lee, New Hampshire, 20 December 1881. Educated at Radcliffe College, Cambridge, Massachusetts, B.A. 1913 (Phi Beta Kappa); M.A. 1918. Member of the Staff, the Settlement Music School, Philadelphia, 1923–53. Recipient: Guarantor's Prize (*Poetry*, Chicago), 1931; Loines Memorial Award, 1960; New England Poetry Club Golden Rose, 1965. Litt.D.: Bowdoin College, Brunswick, Maine, 1961. Address: 404 North Walnut Street, Westchester, Pennsylvania 19380, U.S.A.

PUBLICATIONS

Verse

Outcrop. New York and London, Harper, 1928.
The Bright North. New York, Macmillan, 1938.
Fact of Crystal. New York, Harcourt Brace, 1961.
Collected Poems. Pittsburgh, University of Pittsburgh Press, 1970.

Other

Editor, with Florence S. Esdall, *The Poems of Jean Batchelor.* New York, Rockport Press, 1947.

Critical Study: *Quintet: Essays on Five American Women Poets* by George Brandon, The Hague, Mouton, 1967.

Abbie Huston Evans comments:

Most recent work reflecting increasingly contemporary discoveries in Natural Science.

*   *   *

Abbie Huston Evans is so reticent a poet – she published no book between *The Bright North* (1938), her second volume, and *Fact of Crystal* (1961) – that her name was scarcely known to readers of contemporary verse when she received the Loines Award for Poetry from the National Institute of Arts and Letters in 1960. Her *Collected Poems* appeared in 1970.

When Abbie Evans grew up in Camden, Maine, where her father was the Congregational minister, among her Sunday School pupils was a gifted girl named Edna St. Vincent Millay. While still at college Millay burst into print, but Miss Evans, who has said "Words have to ripen for me," did not publish until after her former student was famous. In her foreword to Miss Evans's first book, *Outcrop*, Millay wrote, "Read these poems too swiftly, or only once, and your heart may still be free of them. Read them again, with care, and they will lay their hands upon you."

Of her late-blooming poetry Miss Evans has said, "I must hold the record for slowness. . . . Three or four short things are my output." Her patience and persistence are rewarded when she writes lovingly of her heritage – her father had been a coal miner in Wales at the age of seven – and of the Maine mountains and the sea. Perhaps her father's life in the mines and her own experience after World War I as a social worker in a Colorado mining camp have made her so imaginatively responsive to rocks, to crystals, to geologic time. Miss Evans is that rare thing, a nature poet who does not sentimentalize her subjects but acknowledges their power, vastness, and mystery. Whether she writes of frost on the bunchberry or of rocks as old as the stars, her language, like a "fact of crystal," is "grappled into jewel."

For many years Miss Evans taught dancing, art, and dramatics at the Settlement Music School in Philadelphia. (Half of the members of the Philadelphia Orchestra are said to have been her students.) In these lines, published in her ninetieth year, Miss Evans has the grace, the courage, and the joy to say, "To a Poet Yet Unborn":

> No one but you can help us much. Subdue what blasts. Dare do it.
> Ride formlessness, word wordlessness. Be not aghast. Be poet.

– Daniel Hoffman

EVANS, Mari. American. Born in Toledo, Ohio. Attended the University of Toledo. Writer-in-Residence, Indiana University-Purdue University, Indianapolis; Northwestern University, Evanston, Illinois, 1972–73. Producer, Writer, and Director, The Black Experience television program, Indianapolis. Recipient: John Hay Whitney Fellowship, 1965; Woodrow Wilson Foundation grant, 1968. Address: c/o Doubleday & Co. Inc., 277 Park Avenue, New York, New York 10017, U.S.A.

PUBLICATIONS

Verse

Where Is All the Music? London, Paul Breman, 1968.
I Am a Black Woman. New York, Morrow, 1970.

Other

JD (juvenile). New York, Doubleday, 1973.
I Look at Me. Chicago, Third World Press, 1973.
Rap Stories. Chicago, Third World Press, 1973.

*   *   *

Though she was born during the Harlem Renaissance, Mari Evans' poetry reveals little of the inclination toward compromise with white values and forms that was cherished by most black intellectuals of that period. Quite the contrary, her work is informed by the uncompromising black pride that burgeoned in the 1960's, and she stands tall with Don Lee, Nikki Giovanni, Sonia Sanchez, and the resuscitated Gwendolyn Brooks as a powerful poetic proclaimer of the new black awareness.

That she is conscious of the change in black stance is demonstrated by the deliberate contrast she achieves between Countee Cullen's famous plaint of the mid-1920's "Yet Do I Marvel" and her "Who Can Be Born Black." Where Cullen constructs a Shakespearian sonnet replete with classical allusions to express his wonder at God's great capacity to create horror, the most amazing example of which is "To make a poet black, and bid him sing," she responds briefly and without apparent artifice:

> Who
> can be born black
> and not
> sing
> the wonder of it
> the joy
> the
> challenge
>
> Who
> can be born black
> and not exult!

Mari Evans, like the best of the new black poets, usually keeps close to the bone of black experience and frequently works through the rhythms of its speech and music. Hopefully a non-black will find that experience, as filtered through her poetry, a paradigm of the human condition, but it is clear that she is unconcerned about the feelings of those who are too opaque to find it so.

– Alan R. Shucard

EVANS DAVIES, Gloria. British. Born in Maesteg, Glamorgan, 17 April 1932. Educated at schools in Wales and Bristol. Recipient: Gulbenkian Foundation grant; Royal Literary Fund grant. Address: 25c High Street Superior, Brecon, South Wales, United Kingdom.

PUBLICATIONS

Verse

Words – For Blodwen.   London, Chatto and Windus, 1962.
Her Name Like the Hours.   London, Chatto and Windus, 1974.

*   *   *

Within Wales, the standing of Gloria Evans Davies as a poet is a strange one. Although she has published poems elsewhere, she has been largely unacknowledged in her own country, and her obvious accomplishment almost ignored. This may well be because she lives and writes – in the mountain township of Brecon – in some isolation from the main urban centres of Welsh life and culture, though it is also possible that her work has simply not appealed to the editors of certain magazines through the past few years.

In her second collection, *Her Name Like the Hours*, fresh, original images are drawn from the mountain and coastal landscape, comprising a number of sharp, visual details played off one against the other in rather curious sequences. She conveys clear impressions of sea, shore and hills with accuracy and precision, each line intense and concentrated in its effects. In one short poem, "West Wales Coast," she gives a feeling of both heat and weight, combining to produce a vision of time past:

> Waves are heavy with the deep,
> The heat scalds though the sun
> Is a pressed fern against its own light.
>
> Forests smell of sawdust,
> Villages crust with houses;
> A leaf turns to flame and to leaf again.

Gloria Evans Davies writes with an instinctive sense of rhythm, perhaps more like a musician, which she once wanted to become, than a conventional poet. The phrasing and structure link smoothly with the meaning – which is rarely obscure – as seen in such a poem as "Breconshire":

> Rain runs along the silver wire of dawn,
> And already the tourists on the Usk,
> Beacons and Llangorse lake;
> Trees show more scratches from cats
> Than leaves . . .
>
> Because of rain all week
> One is not crowded into a standstill
> Except by sheep in the town centre . . .
>
> Slate roofs turn mauve in a shower.

The basic unit of meaning in her poems is the image; an obvious example comes from an earlier, four-line poem, "Peace":

> The sun sets into a moon. Trees let birds in.
> Wish we could put a name to what peace can begin.
>
> The waves hunt Summer to the shore and defeat,
> Where down corridors of mist gun to gun we meet.

Here, after celebrating harmonious nature, the shock last line – against man's spoiling – pulls the reader up short. The fragility of peace, like an armed truce, is shattered by the destructive element in human relations.

Gloria Evans Davies's range may not be very wide, but her vision is deep, and her modest achievement distinctive. It is impressive because of a quality of authenticity ("hammering out a simplicity," as she says), and there can be little doubt – though recognition is still late in coming – as to her poetic merit.

– John Tripp

EVERSON, Ronald (Gilmour). Canadian. Born in Oshawa, Ontario, 18 November 1903. Educated at the University of Toronto, 1923–27, B.A. 1927; Upper Canada Law Society, 1927–30; called to the Ontario Bar 1930. Served with British Security Co-ordination, 1940–45. Married Lorna Jean Austin in 1931. Managing Director, 1936–47, and President, 1947–63, Johnston, Everson and Charlesworth Ltd., Toronto. Chairman, Communications-6 Inc., Montreal, 1964–66. Co-founding Director, Delta Canada Books, Montreal, 1960–63; Director, Ryerson Press, Toronto, 1960–65; Co-founder, League of Canadian Poets, 1966. Agent: Glen Siebrasse, 351 Gerald, Montreal 690. Address: 4920 Maisonneuve O., Suite 404, Montreal 215, Canada.

PUBLICATIONS

Verse

Three Dozen Poems. Montreal, Cambridge Press, 1927.
A Lattice for Momos. Toronto, Contact Press, 1958.
Blind Man's Holiday. Toronto, Ryerson Press, 1963.
Four Poems. Norwich, Vermont, American Letters Press, 1963.
Wrestle with an Angel. Montreal, Delta Canada, 1965.
Incident on Cote des Neiges. Amherst, Massachusetts, Green Knight Press, 1966.
Raby Head and Other Poems. Amherst, Massachusetts, Green Knight Press, 1967.
The Dark Is Not So Dark. Montreal and Santa Barbara, California, Delta Canada–Unicorn, 1969.
Selected Poems 1920–1970. Montreal, Delta Canada, 1970.

Bibliography: in *Salt* (Moose Jaw, Saskatchewan), Summer 1973.

Manuscript Collection: Public Archives of Canada, Ottawa.

Critical Studies: by Margaret Avison, in *Poetry* (Chicago), June 1959; by James Dickey, in *Sewanee Review* (Tennessee), Autumn 1960, and in *Poetry* (Chicago), February 1964; by Munro Beattie, in *Literary History of Canada*, Toronto, University of Toronto Press, 1965; by M. J. Sidnell, in *Canadian Forum* (Toronto), January

1966; by Robert Gibbs, in *Fiddlehead* (Fredericton, New Brunswick), April 1970; by Al Purdy, in *Quarry* (Kingston, Ontario), Spring, 1970; by Ralph Gustafson, in *Canadian Literature* (Vancouver), Summer 1971; by William Dickey, in *Hudson Review* (New York), April 1971; by Charles Molesworth, in *Poetry* (Chicago), May 1972.

*   *   *

"I admire poetry that risks going out beyond the end of thinking," Ronald Everson has written. Everson published his first book in 1927; his second appeared over thirty years later when he was fifty-four years old. But the Montreal poet has made up for lost time, for since then the former public-relations consultant has gained the admiration of James Dickey who perceptively noted that Everson "thinks of practicality as one of the greatest of the artistic virtues, and as underlying all real imagination."

After a reading of his *Selected Poems 1920–1970*, it is difficult not to see Everson as the perfect embodiment of his United Empire Loyalist ancestors. He is his own man, like the New England farmer. A true "U.E.L.," he retains a realistic approach to life without requiring the consolations of compromise or moral superiority. He seems to be an agnostic, but not an atheist, for he can write: "I do not know where we are / None knows where we are."

Everson is knowledgeable without being pedantic, shrewd without being cutting, worldly-wise without being sophisticated. He is a great traveller, yet his poems about the places he has been are neither anecdotal nor picturesque, and hence escape the label "travel poetry." Instead they are splendid and precise evocations, in the imagistic manner, of the associations that a modest and reasonable man would have in the presence of the unyielding world.

Everson's particular stamping ground is the Maritimes and rural Ontario, although he has written about other parts of Canada as well. In "Love Poem," he writes about having "given up on the salvation of mankind." Perhaps this accounts for his mellow outlook. In another poem, he meditates on "a field of Ontario Quaker graves." The poem comes to a magnificent conclusion:

> No new graves
> Congregation gone
> Religion gone
> They entered underground to lie unknown
> on their own plan
> I stare at the chance-taking dead.

– John Robert Colombo

EVERSON, William (Oliver). American. Born in Sacramento, California, 10 September 1912. Educated at Fresno State College, California, 1931, 1934–35. Conscientious objector during World War II: spent three and a half years in work camps in Oregon. Co-Founder, Untide Press, Waldport, Oregon. Dominican lay brother, 1951–69 (Brother Antoninus). Since 1971, Poet-in-Residence, Kresge College, University of California, Santa Cruz. Recipient: Guggenheim Fellowship, 1949. Address: 312 Swanton Road, Davenport, California 95017, U.S.A.

PUBLICATIONS

Verse (as William Everson)

These Are the Ravens.   San Leandro, California, Greater West Publishing Company, 1935.
San Joaquin.   Los Angeles, Ward Ritchie Press, 1939.
The Masculine Dead: Poems 1938–1940.   Prairie City, Illinois, James A. Decker, 1942.
Waldport Poems.   Waldport, Oregon, Untide Press, 1944.
War Elegies.   Waldport, Oregon, Untide Press, 1944.
Residual Years: Poems 1940–1941.   Waldport, Oregon, Untide Press, 1945.
Poems MCMXLII.   Waldport, Oregon, Untide Press, 1945.
The Residual Years: Poems 1934–1946.   New York, New Directions, 1948.
A Privacy of Speech: Ten Poems in Sequence.   Berkeley, California, Equinox Press, 1949.
Triptych for the Living.   Oakland, California, Seraphim Press, 1951.
There Will Be Harvest.   Berkeley, California, Albion Press, 1960.
The Year's Declension.   Berkeley, California, Albion Press, 1961.
The Blowing of the Seed.   New Haven, Connecticut, Henry W. Wenning, 1966.
Single Source: The Early Poems of William Everson, 1934–1940.   Berkeley, California, Oyez, 1966.
In the Fictive Wish.   Berkeley, California, Oyez, 1967.
The Springing of the Blade.   Reno, Nevada, Black Rock Press, 1968.
The Residual Years: Poems 1934–1948.   New York, New Directions, 1968.
Tendril in the Mesh.   Aromas, California, Cayucos Books, 1973.
Black Hills.   San Francisco, Didymus Press, 1973.
Man-Fate: The Swan Song of Brother Antoninus.   New York, New Directions, 1974.

Verse (as Brother Antoninus)

At the Edge.   Oakland, California, Albertus Magnus, 1958.
A Fragment for the Birth of God.   Oakland, California, Albertus Magnus, 1958.
An Age Insurgent.   San Francisco, Blackfriars, 1959.
The Crooked Lines of God: Poems 1949–1954.   Detroit, University of Detroit Press, 1959.
The Hazards of Holiness: Poems 1957–1960.   New York, Doubleday, 1962.
The Poet Is Dead: A Memorial for Robinson Jeffers.   San Francisco, Auerhahn Press, 1964.
The Rose of Solitude.   Berkeley, California, Oyez, 1964.
The Rose of Solitude (collection).   New York, Doubleday, 1967.
The Achievement of Brother Antoninus: A Comprehensive Selection of His Poems with a Critical Introduction, by William E. Stafford.   Chicago, Scott Foresman, 1967.
A Canticle to the Waterbirds.   Berkeley, California, Eizo, 1968.
The City Does Not Die.   Berkeley, California, Oyez, 1969.

The Last Crusade.   Berkeley, California, Oyez, 1969.
Who Is She That Looketh Forth as the Morning.   Santa Barbara, California,
    Capra Press, 1972.

Recording: *Savagery of Love*, Caedmon, 1968.

Other

The Dominican Brother: Province of the West.   San Francisco, privately printed,
    1967.
Robinson Jeffers: Fragments of an Older Fury.   Berkeley, California, Oyez, 1968.
If I Speak Truth: An Inter View-ing, with Jerry Burns.   San Francisco, Goliards
    Press, 1968.
Earth Poetry.   Berkeley, California, Oyez, 1971.

Editor, *Cawdor and Medea*, by Robinson Jeffers.   New York, New Directions,
    1970.
Editor, *Californians*, by Robinson Jeffers.   Aromas, California, Cayucos
    Books, 1971.
Editor, *The Alpine Christ*, by Robinson Jeffers.   Aromas, California, Cayucos
    Books, 1973.
Editor, *Tragedy Has Obligations*, by Robinson Jeffers.   Santa Cruz, California,
    Lime Kiln Press, 1973.
Editor, *Brides of the North Wind*, by Robinson Jeffers.   Aromas, California,
    Cayucos Books, 1974.

Manuscript Collections: (earlier work) William Andrews Clark Library, University
of California, Los Angeles; (middle period) Bancroft Library, University of California, Berkeley.

Critical Studies: *Assays* by Kenneth Rexroth, New York, New Directions, 1961;
Contemporary American Poetry by Ralph J. Mills, Jr., New York, Random House,
1965; Introduction by William J. Stafford to *The Achievement of Brother Antoninus*,
1967; Introduction by Kenneth Rexroth to *The Residual Years*, 1968; *Some
Poems/Poets* by Samuel Charters, Berkeley, California, Oyez, 1971; *The Inner War*
by Paul A. Lacey, Philadelphia, Fortress Press, 1972; *The Poet in America* by Albert
Gelpi, Boston, Heath, 1973.

William Everson comments:

(1970) I was born William Oliver Everson, the son of Louis Waldemar Everson,
an immigrant Norwegian musician and composer, and Francelia Marie Herber, a
Minnesota farm girl of German–Irish extraction who was twenty years his junior.
With an older sister and younger brother I grew up in the little town of Selma,
California, where our father was bandmaster. My mother had been born a Catholic,
but left that faith to marry my father; we children were brought up as Christian
Scientists. In adolescence I became an agnostic, but at Fresno State College, I
encountered the verse of Robinson Jeffers, whose mystical pantheism opened my
soul to the constitutive religious reality sustaining the cosmos, and I dropped out of
college to go back to the land and become a poet in my own right, to plant a
vineyard, commune with nature, and marry my highschool sweetheart.

In World War II I was drafted as a conscientious objector and spent three and a half years in the work camps of Oregon. At Waldport I headed a Fine Arts Program and helped establish the Untide Press, one of the few experimental presses of the war period. After release I migrated to San Francisco, joining the group of anarchists and poets around Kenneth Rexroth. I remarried, this time to the writer Mary Fabilli. Through her hands I encountered Catholicism, and we separated to enter the Roman Catholic Church in 1949. There followed a year on a Guggenheim Fellowship, and another year of troubled interior search; I served with the Catholic Worker movement in the Oakland slums, and resolved to leave the world to find my vocation as a monk, just as I had once left college to find my vocation as a poet.

Thus I became a Dominican lay brother in 1951, receiving the name of Brother Antoninus, and for seven years of monastic withdrawal disappeared from the literary scene. I re-emerged with the San Francisco Renaissance in the late fifties, identifying openly with the Beat Generation because it proclaimed against a triumphant American pragmatism the necessity for mystical vision, and because as a literary movement it launched a dionysian revolt against that pretentious highbrow formalism which, owing to the disassociation between the American poet and the American people, is always able to pass itself off as genuine tradition. Resuming publication, I used the detached freedom possible in monastic life to spend long periods on the poetry reading circuits, developing my own platform style based on oracular Beat intensity as befitting the prophetic mission of the poet, but embodying my own sense of the encounter which has, since Isaiah, constituted the archetype of religious awareness whenever a poet and his people confront.

I began as a nature poet with religious overtones but upon embracing Catholicism began to write a poetry of emphatic religious content etched against the immense backdrop of the American West. It is not surprising, then, that stylistically I favor a more rhetorical idiom than is currently fashionable. Rhetoric is the vehicle of consequence. That it can be faked does not dispense us from its essential use, for life is consequential, existence is infinitely consequential. The area of deepest consequence I believe to be the sexual exaltation and travail between man and woman, insofar as this encounter is the analogue of the exaltation and travail between man and God. I believe that the solution to the problem of violence is found only in the Cross, but I also believe that the poet alone can accommodate the violence of his age to the Cross. This for me constitutes his archetypal role as prophet to his time. It is his failure, and it is awesome, that sends the best minds of his generation in search of solutions where none can ever be found.

(1974) In 1969 I left the Dominican Order to marry Susanna Rickson, and spent two years with her and her infant son Jude at Stinson Beach, north of San Francisco. In 1971 I became Poet in Residence at Kresge College, University of California, Santa Cruz. My preoccupation with the Cross as solution to the mystery of violence, noted above, has not abated, but in the ecological crisis has shifted to the numen subsistent in Nature, as totem, or metaphor, in the encounter between man and God. Rational European theological speculation exhausted the human and divine aspects of the Incarnation. It remains now to recover the atavistic implications inherent in the flesh of Christ. Thus in the final phase of my life now opening I look for aboriginal modes of response to the fact of existence on this continent, and in my work will seek to recover the pertinence of Wilderness as purifier to the corrupt civilized dream.

*   *   *

Slowly, from various outposts he found during the 1940's, William Everson began to send out his own kind of direct, emphatic poems of social judgment.

461

Though he listed no church affiliation when he was held as a conscientious objector in work camps in Oregon and California during World War II, his writings – like those of Robinson Jeffers, who influenced him greatly – were always moral and principled, and serious; and by the time those poems came into general notice in the early 1950's William Everson had become Brother Antoninus, a Dominican lay brother, and one of the early and influential participants in the "San Francisco Group" of "Beat Poets."

In his career since that early seasoning, when he actually had to live outside American society and look at it long, Brother Antoninus has continued his measured assessment, in many periodicals and many books and many public readings. His language has taken on religious tonality but in a way to make ritual violently confront jagged experience. His progression has not been so much toward leaving the Robinson Jeffers non-human stance as it has been toward combining the brute world and the church. He hammers the language of religion into statements that create shock: bleak juxtapositions, stern assertions. In his most characteristic works, the landscapes and the creature-scapes of a rugged coastal region get yoked into a chant of judgment:

> Clack your beaks you cormorants and kittiwakes,
> North on those rock-croppings finger-jutted into the rough Pacific surge . . .
> Break wide your harsh and salt-encrusted beaks unmade for song
> And say a praise up to the Lord.
> > – *A Canticle to the Waterbirds*

> – William Stafford

EWART, Gavin (Buchanan). British. Born in London, 4 February 1916. Educated at Wellington College; Christ's College, Cambridge (Exhibitioner), B.A. (honours) in English 1936. Served in the Royal Artillery during World War II. Married; has two children. Worked for the British Council, 1946–52; advertising copywriter, 1952–71. Since 1971, Free-lance Writer. Recipient: Cholmondeley Award, 1971. Address: 57 Kenilworth Court, Lower Richmond Road, London S.W.15, England.

PUBLICATIONS

Verse

Poems and Songs. London, Fortune Press, 1939.
Londoners. London, Heinemann, 1964.
Throwaway Lines. Richmond, Surrey, Keepsake Press, 1964.
Two Children. Richmond, Surrey, Keepsake Press, 1966.
Pleasures of the Flesh. London, Alan Ross, 1966.
The Deceptive Grin of the Gravel Porters. London, Alan Ross, 1968.
Twelve Apostles. Belfast, Ulsterman Publications, 1970.
Folio, with others. Frensham, Surrey, Sceptre Press, 1971.

The Gavin Ewart Show. London, Trigram Press, 1971.
Venus. London, Poem-of-the-Month Club, 1972.
The Select Party. Richmond, Surrey, Keepsake Press, 1972.
Alphabet Soup. Oxford, Sycamore Press, 1972.
Penguin Modern Poets 25, with B. S. Johnson and Zulfikar Ghose. London,
Penguin, 1974.

Other

Editor, *Forty Years On: An Anthology of School Songs.* London, Sidgwick and
Jackson, 1964.

Manuscript Collections: National Library of Scotland, Edinburgh; University of
Texas, Austin.

Gavin Ewart comments:

Formal. Rhyming. More recently – experimental in vocabulary and form. Alliterative, Subjects mainly concerned with the pressures and pleasures of contemporary
urban life.
The "school" of Auden was from the start a major influence.

                            *   *   *

Gavin Ewart began precociously early. In 1933, at the age of seventeen, he was
contributing assured and witty poems to Geoffrey Grigson's *New Verse.* They
included "Phallus in Wonderland," a set of epigrams and short poems written in
skilful pastiche of Pound, Eliot, Auden and other contemporaries, and "Audenesque for an Initiation," which showed Ewart to be an early if critical admirer of the
dominating English poet of the thirties. As a young poet in the pre-war years Ewart
exhibited the social and political concerns of the age, though in a wryly individual
voice. What is striking about his subsequent career is that more than forty years
later Ewart is still writing in much the same way about similar subjects: the
occasional splendours and frequent absurdities of sex; himself, as *l'homme moyen
sensuel*; and the kaleidoscope surface of modern urban life. From the beginning
Ewart has been the master of a kind of writing that is poised between amusing light
verse and an authentic poetry of serious social comment or personal reflection.
When the poise fails he is inclined to fall into slack triviality on the one hand or
neat sentimentalities on the other. He has a good ear and can write memorable lines
and elegant lyrics. At the same time, he is rather complacently attached to his
favourite stylistic devices; having found that "kisses" makes an effective rhyme
for "cissies" in a poem published in 1937 he is still using the same rhymes in
poems in *The Gavin Ewart Show* in 1971.
    Thematically, too, there is variation rather than great development. In his earliest
poems Ewart treated sexual subjects with the characteristic bravado and anxiety of
adolescence. "Young Blondes: A Religious Poem" is a crisp and poignant instance
from the forties. In the sixties and seventies similar themes are presented with the
more urgent anxiety of middle-age, often rather tastelessly. If there is a new
element in Ewart's poetry it is a greater compassion that undercuts his characteristic tone of cool ironic comment on human folly. Increasingly his greatest irony is

directed at himself, as in "The Ewart Organization" or the delightful "2001: The Tennyson/Hardy Poem" which looks forward to a time when the poet will have outlived all his contemporaries. Here Ewart once more displays his skill as a writer of pastiche, this time of Thomas Hardy:

> Soon comes the day when the stream runs dry
> And the boat runs back as the tide is turning,
> The voice once strong no more than a sigh
> By the hearth where the fire is scarcely burning.
> Stiff in my chair like a children's guy,
> Simply because I have no seniors
> The literati will raise the cry:
>> Ewart's a genius!

Ewart preserves in a remarkably pure form the positive qualities of the poetry of the thirties: the wit, the formal skill, the willingness to combine comic means and serious ends, and, at his best, an attractive intellectual gaiety.

– Bernard Bergonzi

EZEKIEL, Nissim. Indian. Born in Bombay, 16 December 1924. Educated at the University of Bombay (Lagu Prize, 1947), 1941–47, M.A. 1947. Married Daisy Jacob in 1952; has two daughters and one son. Lecturer, Khalsa College, Bombay, 1947–48; Professor of English and Vice-Principal, Mithibai College, Bombay, 1961–72. Since 1972, Reader in American Literature, Bombay University. Visiting Professor, University of Leeds, 1964, and University of Chicago, 1967. Editor, *Quest* magazine, 1955–57; Associate Editor, *Imprint* magazine, 1961–67; Art Critic, *The Times of India,* Bombay, 1964–67. Lived in London, 1948–52. Recipient: Farfield Foundation travel grant, 1957. Address: The Retreat, Bellasis Road, Bombay 400008, India.

PUBLICATIONS

Verse

> *A Time to Change and Other Poems.* London, Fortune Press, 1952.
> *Sixty Poems.* Bombay, Strand Bookshop, 1953.
> *The Third.* Bombay, Strand Bookshop, 1958.
> *The Unfinished Man: Poems Written in 1959.* Calcutta, Writers Workshop, 1960.
> *The Exact Name: Poems 1960–1964.* Calcutta, Writers Workshop, 1965.
> *Pergamon Poets,* with others, edited by Howard Sergeant. Oxford, Pergamon Press, 1969.

Plays

> *Three Plays* (includes *Nalini, Marriage Poem, The Sleepwalkers*) (produced Bombay, 1969). Calcutta, Writers Workshop, 1969.

Other

> *The Actor: A Sad and Funny Story for Children of Most Ages.*   Bombay, India
> Book House, 1974.

> Editor, *A New Look at Communism.*   Bombay, Indian Committee for Cultural
> Freedom, 1963.
> Editor, *Indian Writers in Conference.*   Mysore, P.E.N. All India Writers Con-
> ference, 1964.
> Editor, *Writing in India.*   Lucknow, P.E.N. All India Writers Conference,
> 1965.
> Editor, *An Emerson Reader.*   Bombay, Popular Prakashan, 1965.
> Editor, *A Martin Luther King Reader.*   Bombay, Popular Prakashan, 1969.
> Editor, *All My Sons,* by Arthur Miller.   Madras, Oxford University Press,
> 1972.

Critical Studies: *The Poetry of Nissim Ezekiel*, by Meena Belliapa and Rajeev Tara-
nath, Calcutta, Writers Workshop, 1966; student edition of *The Unfinished Man*,
Calcutta, Writers Workshop, 1969; by Rajeev Taranath in *Quest 74* (Bombay)
January-February 1972; *Nissim Ezekiel: A Study* by Chetan Karnani, New Delhi,
Arnold-Heinemann, 1974; "Nissim Ezekiel Issue" of *Journal of South Asian
Literature* (Rochester, Michigan), September-December 1974.

Nissim Ezekiel comments:

I do not identify myself with any particular school of poetry. Labelled "Indo-
Anglian" or "Indo-English," i.e., an Indian poet writing in English, I accept the
label. I am satisfied at present to be included among the poets of the Commonwealth, but hope to be better known in the U.K. and U.S.A. as an *Indian* poet. I
consider myself a modernist but not avant-garde.

I have written in the traditional verse forms as well as in free verse. Major
influences: Pound, Eliot, Auden, MacNeice, Spender, Yeats and modern English
and American poetry in general. My latest poetry, 1966-73, is beyond all influences. Some of my recent poems are in Indian English. I have written "found"
poems on scientific subjects and several on newspaper reports and personal letters.
Major themes: love, personal integration, the Indian contemporary scene, modern
urban life, spiritual values. I aim at clarity above all, claim never to have written an
obscure poem. I like to make controlled, meaningful statements, avoiding extremes
of thought and expression.

*   *   *

In the foreword to *Sixty Poems* Nissim Ezekiel confesses that his main reason for
publishing the poems in the collection is that he has not the courage to destroy
them:

> There is in each line or phrase, an idea or image which helps me to
> maintain some sort of continuity in my life. If I could transcend the
> personal importance of these poems, I would not publish them . . . . [The
> present collection] does not claim to be poetry but it reveals a few small
> discoveries in the pursuit of poetry.

Mr. Ezekiel is thus a poet of scrupulous critical standards keen on the unremitting development of his craft. This is somewhat unusual in an Indian poet writing in English and even the failures of such a poet are worthy of consideration in discussing the possibilities of English poetry in India. Reading through his collections one has the impression of a keen desire to write on a variety of subjects in a variety of styles but the poems that usually succeed are those in which some comment (not necessarily profound or original) on a social or personal experience is given witty, ironical expression ("At the Hotel" in *The Third*, "In India" or "Night of the Scorpion" in *The Exact Name*). Mr. Ezekiel has attempted some poems of greater depth of reflection and feeling on the great themes of human experience, but these are not equally successful ("Philosophy," "Perspective" in *The Exact Name*, "Morning Prayer," "Marriage" in *The Unfinished Man*). The expression tends to get out of step with the essential simplicity of what he has to say. In spite of these lapses, Mr. Ezekiel is among the few Indian poets who have a sense of poetic rhythm, a sense of words, and a sense of vocation. His main difficulty seems to be the same as that of many other Indian poets writing in English – they have nothing much to say.

– S. Nagarajan

FAINLIGHT, Ruth. American. Born in New York City. Educated at schools in America and England. Address: 14 Ladbroke Terrace, London W.11, England.

PUBLICATIONS

Verse

A Forecast, A Fable. London, Outposts Publications, 1958.
Cages. London, Macmillan, 1966; Chester Springs, Pennsylvania, Dufour, 1967.
18 Poems from 1966. London, Turret Books, 1967.
To See the Matter Clearly and Other Poems. London, Macmillan, 1968; Chester Springs, Pennsylvania, Dufour, 1969.
Poems, with Alan Sillitoe and Ted Hughes. London, Rainbow Press, 1971.
The Region's Violence. London, Hutchinson, 1973.
21 Poems. London, Turret Books, 1973.

Play

All Citizens Are Soldiers, with Alan Sillitoe, adaptation of a play by Lope de Vega (produced London, 1967). London, Macmillan, and Chester Springs, Pennsylvania, Dufour, 1969.

Short Stories

> *Penguin Modern Stories 9,* with others.   London, Penguin, 1971.
> *Daylife and Nightlife.*   London, Deutsch, 1971.

*   *   *

Though married to Alan Sillitoe, the English novelist and poet, Ruth Fainlight is nevertheless American by birth. As such she is one of a small but distinguished group of American women poets, expatriated by marriage. The most famous number of this group is, of course, Sylvia Plath, with whom Ruth Fainlight was on close terms. Surprisingly, one has to hunt quite hard to find the Plath influence in Fainlight's poetry. Essentially, hers is a much quieter voice. Though it sometimes speaks of desperation, the despair is stubbornly combatted; if possible, the energies it generates are turned into something useful – an attitude well summed up in two lines from Ruth Fainlight's most recent collection: "The poem, though derived from suffering, does / Not describe its chill of death." On the whole, this poet does not as yet enjoy the reputation she deserves – partly because her development has been a gradual one; partly because she displays an uncomfortable honesty about aspects of character – aggressive impulses, for example – which many readers would prefer not to confront.

– Edward Lucie-Smith

FAIRFAX, John.   British.   Born in London, 9 November 1930. Educated at public school and by private tutors. Married; has two sons. Editor of *Nimbus* magazine in the early 1950's. School teacher, 1955–62. British Editor, *Panache* magazine, New York. Since 1967, Director, Phoenix Press, Newbury, Berkshire. Since 1968, Co-Founding Director, Arvon Foundation, Devon. Recipient: Society of Authors award; Art Council grant. Address: The Thatched Cottage, Hermitage, Newbury, Berkshire, England.

PUBLICATIONS

Verse

> *This I Say: Twelve Poems.*   Newbury, Berkshire, Phoenix Press, 1967.
> *The 5th Horseman of the Apocalypse.*   Newbury, Berkshire, Phoenix Press, 1969.
> *Double Image.*   London, Longman, 1972.

Other

Editor, *Listen to This: A Contemporary Anthology.* London, Longman, 1967.
Editor, *Stop and Listen: An Anthology of Thirteen Living Poets.* London, Longman, 1969.
Editor, *Frontier of Going: An Anthology of Space Poetry.* London, Panther, 1969.
Editor, *Horizons.* London, Arnold, 1971.

Critical Studies: by Graham Fawcett, in *Southern Arts Review* (Winchester, Hampshire), March and May 1970.

John Fairfax comments:

Two main themes (at present): one is the Space Odyssey and the other, countryside and animals. The two themes are compatible in my view. My style has been called "analogical." And I go along with this. Form tending to traditional although I write for the ear and voice rather than the eye. Rhythm is very important as I prefer my work to be read aloud.

*   *   *

John Fairfax's juxtaposition of space-age philosophy and rural concerns is an interesting one; but it has not too often manifested itself in his poems, whose general weakness is that they cannot sustain the reader's interest by rhythmical or linguistic means. His most ambitious and successful poem is the relatively long *The 5th Horseman of the Apocalypse*, which runs to over 600 short lines. One wonders if the author had Blok's extraordinary *The Twelve* in mind, even though its style has not influenced him. For here, too, his men "Hack through dead cities." In this poem as a whole, Fairfax has subsumed his dark theme under an imaginative language far more effective than anything found in his earlier poems; his handling of the short line is reasonably deft and sure:

> Four horsemen and hounds
> Belong to the crossed master
> Of hounds and horse.
> They are photographed by dazzling
> Kodacolours of a magnifying
> Eye which repeats
> The image into new birth
> Until nothing exists. . . .

This vision is sustained, and the ambiguous figure of the fifth horseman is introduced with proper dramatic effect. Furthermore, the performance of the poem does add a genuine, and not merely rhetorical, dimension to it.

– Martin Seymour-Smith

FALCK, Colin. British. Born in London, 14 July 1934. Educated at Christ's Hospital; Magdalen College, Oxford, B.A. in philosophy, politics and economics 1957, B.A. in philosophy, psychology and physiology 1959. Served in the British Army, 1952–54. Lecturer in Sociology, London School of Economics, 1961–62; part-time lecturer in literature, London and Hertfordshire, 1962–64. Since 1964, Lecturer in Humanities, Chelsea College, London. Associate Editor, *the Review*, Oxford and London, 1962–72. Agent: John Johnson, 51–54 Goschen Buildings, 12–13 Henrietta Street, London WC2E 8LF. Address: 16 St. Augustine's Road, London NW1 9RN, England.

PUBLICATIONS

Verse

The Garden in the Evening, adaptations of poems by Antonio Machado. Oxford, The Review, 1964.
Promises. London, The Review, 1969.
Backwards into the Smoke. Cheadle, Cheshire, Caracanet Press, 1973.

Other

Editor, with Ian Hamilton, *Poems since 1900.* London, Macdonald, 1974.

Colin Falck comments:

Writing a poem means persuading the semi-verbal impulses which start up at the back of one's mind under the pressure of some insistent emotion to arrange themselves poetically on the page. By doing this one discovers more about what the emotion was. The only test I can find for a poem's validity is that it should be moving – should generate the distinctive feeling or *frisson* (cf. Housman and others) which signals the presence of poetry. For me this has a lot to do with rhythm and sound-texture – but no analysis seems to take one very near to understanding what is really going on.

The poems I have written so far are quite short. I could wish they were longer, but the writing of short poems has been – for me – a bottleneck that has to be gone through. I would like to be able to get through it and to move on from poems of straightforward mood and atmosphere to poems which handle larger amounts of material and more public themes – but which handle them poetically, rather than merely versifying attitudes and opinions or stringing out a lot of images on one long idea (this may be some kind of reaction to the poetry which was prevalent in Britain during the 1950's). *Backwards into the Smoke* is a mood-sequence, to do with learning to accept life, learning where one's more negative and irrational impulses can lead, hoping to accept such impulses and remain dedicated to life and humanity. I would like, before very long, to be able to write poems which look more obviously adequate to such heavyweight preoccupations.

*   *   *

Colin Falck is one of a group of poets and critics associated during the nineteen-sixties with the English magazine, *The Review,* who made a deliberate attempt to revive Imagism as a poetic discipline and a mode of imaginative apprehension. Falck is an explicit theorist in criticism and he has argued that Imagism continues the essential insights of Romanticism: a poem, whatever else it does, must articulate the emotion of a particular moment as truthfully as possible. Falck's own poems present Imagist notations of encounters and places. They are calculatedly small-scale and, in a sense, insubstantial; sometimes they remain merely frail and even trivial, but at other times they achieve a haunting resonance with a very few words. In his love poems Falck is courageously vulnerable; where they succeed they are tremulously beautiful and where they fail they tumble into bathos. He is literally on firmer ground in his poems based on places, such as "Central Ohio," "End of the Summer Term at Christ's Hospital," "Box Hill" and "Lyme Regis Station." He is considerably influenced by modern Spanish poetry, and has published a set of exquisite translations of poems by Antonio Machado.

– Bernard Bergonzi

FALLON, Padraic. Irish. Born in Athenry, County Galway, 3 January 1905. Educated at Mt. St. Joseph's College, Roscrea, County Tipperary. Married Dorothea Maher in 1930; has six sons. Worked as Customs Official for forty years, mainly in Wexford; now retired. Member, Irish Academy of Letters. Address: Hill Cottage, Scilly, Kinsale, County Cork, Ireland. *Died 9 October 1974.*

PUBLICATIONS

Verse

Collected Poems.   Dublin, Dolmen Press, 1974.

Plays

The Seventh Step (produced Cork and Dublin, 1954).
Sweet Love till Morn (produced Cork and Dublin, 1971).

Radio Plays: *Diarmuid and Grainne*; *The Vision of Maconglinne*; *The Wooing of Etain*; *Deirdre's King*; *The Poplar*; *Steeple Jerkin*; *Outpost, or, Out on a Limb*; *Last and Final Appearance*; *The Third Bachelor*; *The Five Stations*; *At the Bridge Inn*; *Two Men with a Face*; *The Hags of Clough.*

Television Play: *The Shield of Steel*, 1966.

Short Story

Lighting Up Time.   Dublin, Orwell Press, 1938.

Other

Editor, *The Poems of Emily Lawless.*   Dublin, Dolmen Press, 1965.

Padraic Fallon comments:

My verse plays are not a mere extension of my poetry but an integral part of it. Indeed, my lyrics can be taken as the high points of, or as correlative to, the continuous drama that goes on in the psyche where worlds are meeting and where history is always of the present. The long poem is a form I haven't any great liking for, so I invent my own equivalent which is drama suitable for broadcasting on sound radio. In that I can relate the prose-verse vision of the poet to an inner unity.

*   *   *

It is impossible to write of music and do anything other than talk round about it. The experience cannot be conveyed except by the thing itself. To some extent this is also true of the work of Padraic Fallon. Furthermore, while I have never seen a bad poem from his pen, and all that he does has an urgent vitality of language, his work gains from being read in quantity.

As the Scottish shade of Burns fell so broadly over the surrounding ground that few plants beneath it could make much growing headway, so the shade of Yeats lies across the Irish literary scene. In his *Collected Poems* Fallon does go in for a bit of Yeatsing (and, indeed, also of Blind Raffertying!); but even these poems push their way beyond the circumference of the shadow, and, indeed, throw by contrast a new kind of colouring upon the nature and achievement of Yeats, as in "Yeats at Athenry Perhaps":

> But I'd never heard of him, the famous poet,
> Who lived as the crow flies fifteen miles away.
>
> Certainly he'd have touched us changing trains
> For Gort, have hours to idle, shared
> The silence of our small town shell;
> Maybe he passed me by
> In a narrow gutted street, an aimless
> Straying gentleman, and I
> The jerseyed fellow driving out the cows.

Like so many Irish poets, Fallon is heir not only to the vivid descriptive phrase characteristic of Gaelic, but also to its rhymes clashed against half-rhymes, and its internal assonances. The subject-matter he writes about is ostensibly the small townsman in close contact with the day-to-day activities of the surrounding countryside and the ways of men of the sea. But for him, the central concern is for the human condition; things as they are, or seem to be, touching off a sense of the wonder of human life. Of "The Christmas Vigil" he writes:

> I like things as they are,
> World as it is, the wonder just round the corner;
> And if at midnight
> All the clocks in the world meet to chime
>
> Over the world's newest child, this
> Will be the more spacious for happening in my sleep
> Where ends can meet in peace
> When the great harps sweep out upon the pediments
> And the wren waken with a tiny cheep.

The juxtaposition of the mythic angels' harping and the actual sound of one of the smallest of birds is typical of the kind of tautness which makes Fallon's poetry full of surprises.

His sense of the earth's fertility, and of the reflection of this in terms of human sexuality, is powerful, and gives his work strong earth roots, a sense of contact with what matters most, wholly missed by those who proffer descriptions of the mechanisms of sex or pretty surface images little better than conceits. Thus in "Mater Dei" he writes:

> Milk ran wild
> Across the heavens. Imperiously He
> Sipped at the delicate beakers she proffered him.
> How was she to know
> How huge a body she was, how she corrected
> The very tilt of the earth on its new course?

Even if many today feel that perhaps now the earth has taken yet another tilt, to me that image seems unforgettable.

A Scots fellow-practitioner of the craft inevitably falls back upon the luck of the Irish in still possessing a kind of English richly coloured by the overtones of spoken Gaelic (as, for rather different reasons, though to a lesser extent, also do American poets). But Fallon will have none of this:

> And wasn't I lucky, born with
> Boundaries floating, language still making
> Out of the broadlands where my fathers
> Tended their clouds of ewes?
>
> Bunkum, Dear P. The thing was gone, or
> Never was. And we were the leftovers,
> Lord-ridden and pulpit-thumped for all our wild
> Cudgels of Gaelic.

The poet's range is wide, his attention always focussed upon the human fundamentals: birth, love, the sometimes comic or ironic consequences of sexual attraction, and death. It is typical of the sheer megalopalian parochialness of English literary awareness and taste that Fallon's poetry – like that of many other poets of the so-called Celtic fringe – is almost unknown outside Ireland and America. His *Collected Poems,* which I have read in typescript but which should be available by the time this is being read, must surely adjust the compensatory balance.

Since Yeats, Fallon is the most continuously exciting poet to come out of Ireland, and a poet whose involvement is with life, and so ultimately neither subject to cliques and claques nor their fashions: a poet of affirmation. As he himself puts it:

> Man lives; Gods die:
> It is only the genuflection that survives.

                                                    – Maurice Lindsay

FEINSTEIN, Elaine. British. Born in Bootle, Lancashire, 24 October 1930. Educated at Wyggeston Grammar School, Leicester; Newnham College, Cambridge. Married Dr. Arnold Feinstein in 1956; has three sons. Editorial Staff Member, Cambridge University Press, 1960–62; Lecturer in English, Bishop's Stortford Training College, Hertfordshire, 1963–66; Assistant Lecturer in Literature, University of Essex, Wivenhoe, 1967–70. Recipient: Arts Council grant, 1970; Daisy Miller Award, for fiction, 1971. Agent: Olwyn Hughes, 100 Chetwynd Road, London, N.W.5. Address: c/o Hutchinson Publishing Group Ltd., 3 Fitzroy Square, London W.1, England.

PUBLICATIONS

Verse

    In a Green Eye. London, Goliard Press, 1966.
    The Magic Apple Tree. London, Hutchinson, 1971.
    At the Edge. Rushden, Northamptonshire, Sceptre Press, 1972.
    The Celebrants and Other Poems. London, Hutchinson, 1973.

Novels

    The Circle. London, Hutchinson, 1970.
    The Amberstone Exit. London, Hutchinson, 1972.
    The Glass Alembic. London, Hutchinson, 1973; as *The Crystal Garden*, New York, 1974.
    The Children of the Rose. London, Hutchinson, 1974.

Short Story

    Matters of Chance. London, Covent Garden Press, 1972.

Other

    Editor, *Selected Poems of John Clare.* London, University Tutorial Press, 1968.

    Translator, *The Selected Poems of Marina Tsvetayeva.* London, Oxford University Press, 1971.

Manuscript Collection: Cambridge University.

Critical Study: *British Poetry since 1960,* edited by Michael Schmidt and Grevel Lindop, Oxford, Carcanet Press, 1972.

Elaine Feinstein comments:

Even to try and place myself in the single context of British Poetry bewilders me. When I began writing in the early sixties I felt the influence of the Americans (Stevens and perhaps even Emily Dickinson as much as W. C. Williams); and I suppose the turning point in finding a voice of my own arose, paradoxically, from working on the translations of Marina Tsvetayeva and other modern Russian poets. And perhaps also from writing prose, which began at first as an extension of the poetic impulse, but (after four novels) works as a channel for the exploration of my humanist concerns, and leaves me freer now to take greater risks with language when I choose to write lyric poetry. Perhaps both experiences have encouraged me to write longer poems (such as the title poem of *The Celebrants*), and to find longer lines and new rhythms, as well as richer subject matter.

                              *   *   *

As is clear from her Tsvetayeva translations and from some of her prose fiction, Elaine Feinstein's attention to the details of her language (including syntax, rhythm, punctuation, spacing) is very pointed. This does not save her from the occasional mere idiosyncracy, nor, surprisingly, from frequent uncertainty over line-breaks. And now and then a poem will blur into abstraction towards the end as if it had not been given time to grow further on its own terms: compare for instance the endings of "Anniversary," "Out," and "In the Matter of Miracles" with the much sharper conclusions of poems like "West" or "Exile."

Yet her effects can be fresh and subtle, allowing her not just to describe but to re-enact her sense of being "open to the surprises of the season," as in "Sundance in Sawston," "In the Question of Survival," "The Magic Apple Tree," "Released," or "Our Vegetable Love Shall Grow," which latter begins:

> Shaking in white streetlight in
> a cold night wind, two luminous blue fangs
> push through the grass at the bus shelter:
> an early crocus, drawing colour from
> some hidden underfoot bulb.

Her similes too can be surprisingly active: "the chestnut, radiant as a moving tiger / the willow falling like water spilt. . . ."

Further, she can absorb into the essence of her poetry a degree of mature personal experience sometimes beyond the grasp of more overtly ambitious poets (a feature which singled out her contribution to Faber's *Poetry Introduction 1*). The fears, difficulties and joys may be unspectacular but they are the kind we all live with – the vulnerability of those close to us, as in "Bodies" or "Aubade for a Scientist," or the fluctuating securities and insecurities of marriage, as in "A Dream of Spinsterhood" or "Marriage." Those fluctuations in the latter are finely balanced:

> . . . any celibate
> could look for such retreat, for me
> it was a luxury to be insisted on
> in the sight of those grass overgrown dormitories
>
> We have taken our shape from the
> damage we do one another. . . .

– Robin Fulton

FELDMAN, Irving (Mordecai).   American.   Born in Brooklyn, New York, 22 September 1928. Educated at the City College of New York, B.S. 1950; Columbia University, New York, M.A. 1953. Married Carmen Alvarez in 1955; has one son. Taught at the University of Puerto Rico, Rio Piedras, 1954–56, University of Lyons, France, 1957–58, and Kenyon College, Gambier, Ohio, 1958–64. Since 1964, Professor of English, State University of New York, Buffalo. Recipient: Jewish Book Council of America Kovner Award, 1962; Ingram Merrill Foundation grant, 1963; National Institute of Arts and Letters grant, 1973; Guggenheim Fellowship, 1973. Address: 349 Berryman Drive, Buffalo, New York 14226, U.S.A.

PUBLICATIONS

Verse

> *Work and Days and Other Poems.*   Boston, Little Brown, and London, Deutsch, 1961.
> *The Pripet Marshes and Other Poems.*   New York, Viking Press, 1965.
> *Magic Papers and Other Poems.*   New York, Harper, 1970.
> *Lost Originals.*   New York, Holt Rinehart, 1972.

Critical Study: *Alone with America,* by Richard Howard, New York, Atheneum, 1970.

*   *   *

Irving Feldman has always been a Jewish poet, which is to say that his work has been typically marked by an ardent spirituality tending frequently toward verbal abstraction and vaguely detailed suffering. Like Randall Jarrell, he has had a strong feeling for dream-states, though without Jarrell's ear for and sensitivity to the language of dreams. Richard Howard has described his mature verse as "the expression of a full heart" committed to the examination of loss. This sense of loss, and of faith at odds with obvious circumstance, is so consistently and impressively felt in Feldman's work that one hesitates to demand particulars by way of substantiation. What we've lost, according to Feldman, is precisely those objects of faith which make us feel at home with our longings and comfortably warm, rather than a little queasy, in our affections.

In one of his early volumes, Feldman spoke of his desire to teach his fathers – the insulted and injured – of a Jewish past it is this poet's function to reclaim and repossess, "the light-hearted dance," but he is not authentically of the light-hearted. He is in fact endowed with much the same spirit that illuminates the work of others more fatally bound and defined by blood and tradition. Feldman is a singer of hope and modest suffering in the service of vision. What he aims at is the change of heart which is nothing so grand as those transformations of character or of the human condition which a great many American poets have taken as their burden. Feldman's change of heart is typically more modest, a desire not for light-heartedness which would be a function of absolute self-mastery or self-effacement, but for that temporary lightness which involves at once accommodation to things as they are and a refusal of slavish acquiescence. Feldman's work represents what is best in the contemporary Jewish tradition, which is a combination of earnestness, faithfulness in search of suitable objects, and lucidity.

Sometimes, Feldman seems more in perfect control of his materials than we'd expected, and we feel a little suspicious – we know, of course, that the poet must be in charge, must master the materials of his vision, but ordinarily we like to feel that the poet is also himself possessed in a way that might almost be thought subversive to the purposes of craftsmanship and routine orderliness or coherence. We want the communicated impression that the poet is deeply moved by his vision, that in his desire to manifest it he will allow it to develop a momentum of its own. In reading Feldman, we sometimes want to ask whether he is expressing a passing fancy or a more permanent intuition of things.

At his best, Feldman manages a tone that is sharply ironic and commiserating by turns, or that rings with a prophetic authority that distinguishes him from any of his contemporaries. Some of Feldman's poems are conceptually intricate and sustained in a remarkable way, replete with verbal felicities of great wit and variety. More surprising, Feldman is an accomplished poet whose work clearly reveals a whole range of borrowed cadences, in his recent work from the late Randall Jarrell. These cadences are an aspect of Feldman's gift for ventriloquism, his inclination towards dramatic utterance. Though Feldman has more and more come to speak in his own voice, this voice has remained various, the expression of alternating masks. In working through these masks, Feldman betrays nothing of that anxiety which so pollutes the exchanges between other poets – one thinks for example of the altogether more tense and problematic borrowings that characterize the relation between Roethke and Yeats. Feldman's poetry works through tension and uncertainties, rather than allowing them to fester. In so doing, Feldman manages a complex evocation of the contemplative urgency of the faithful heart.

– Robert Boyers

FENTON, James (Martin). British. Born in Lincoln, 25 April 1949. Educated at Durham Chorister School; Repton School; Magdalen College, Oxford (Newdigate Prize, 1968), B.A. 1970. Assistant Literary Editor, 1971, and Member, Editorial Staff, 1972–73, *New Statesman*, London. Recipient: Eric Gregory Award, 1973. Address: c/o New Statesman, 10 Great Turnstile, London W.C.1, England.

PUBLICATIONS

Verse

Our Western Furniture. Oxford, Sycamore Press, 1968.
Put Thou Thy Tears into My Bottle. Oxford, Sycamore Press, 1969.
Terminal Moraine. London, Secker and Warburg, 1972.

James Fenton comments:

Eclectic, serious, should go far.

*   *   *

Immediately, James Fenton's verse has two striking features. The first is his technical skill, for he already sees more virtue in the labours of craftsmanship than many other young poets are prepared to. In his first collection we can follow this through from his varied handling of the sonnet in "Our Western Furniture" (21 sonnets) to the consciously smart performance of "Open Letter to Richard Cross-man," with 25 stanzas rhyming abababcc. In the latter, even modesty is part of the smartness – "And I've failed even to twit / You in this style, by AUDEN out of BYRON."

The second feature is the considerable extent to which the substance of his poetry is detailed, factual and documented, as if his poetic function were primarily to fashion into verse the ideas and information culled by a voracious reader. Thus we have the biological material incorporated in "Frog" and "The Fruit-Grower in War-Time," and the reminiscences of the first Americans in Japan in "Our Wes-tern Furniture," the closing lines of which aptly describe his method: "we offer you an almost-fiction / Constructed on a grid of contradiction."

That poets should be willing to meet and utilise the multifarious information which is so accessible to the modern reader is vitally important for this is one of the ways in which poetry can prevent its confinement to a marginal role. An extreme instance of course is Hugh MacDiarmid, in whose work the numerous spoils from numerous worlds of knowledge are caught up in an impetuous imagina-tive driving-force. For Fenton, at the beginning of his career, the highly referential nature of his poetry may well serve as a prop, so it will be interesting to see how he uses his skills when he moves (if he does) into more difficult areas of personal commitment where the raw material is not, *a priori*, clear-cut.

– Robin Fulton

FERLINGHETTI, Lawrence.   American.   Born in Yonkers, New York, 24 March 1919. Educated at the University of North Carolina, Chapel Hill, A.B.; Columbia University, New York, M.A. 1948; the Sorbonne, Paris, Doctorat de l'Université 1951. Served in the Naval Reserve, 1941–45: Lieutenant-Commander. Married Selden Kirby Smith in 1951; has two children. Worked for *Time* magazine, New York, in the 1940's. Co-Founder, 1952, with Peter L. Martin, and since 1953, Owner and Editor-in-Chief, City Lights Books. Delegate, with Allen Ginsberg, to the Pan American Cultural Conference, University of Concepción, Chile, 1960. Address: City Lights Books, 1562 Grant Avenue, San Francisco, California 94133, U.S.A.

PUBLICATIONS

Verse

Pictures of the Gone World.   San Francisco, City Lights, 1955.
A Coney Island of the Mind.   New York, New Directions, 1958.

Tentative Description of a Dinner Given to Promote the Impeachment of President Eisenhower. San Francisco, Golden Mountain Press, 1958.

One Thousand Fearful Words for Fidel Castro. San Francisco, City Lights, 1961.

Berlin. San Francisco, Golden Mountain Press, 1961.

Starting from San Francisco: Poems. New York, New Directions, 1961; revised edition, 1967.

Penguin Modern Poets 5, with Allen Ginsberg and Gregory Corso. London, Penguin, 1963.

Where is Vietnam? San Francisco, City Lights, 1965.

To Fuck is to Love Again; Kyrie Eleison Kerista; or, The Situation in the West; Followed by a Holy Proposal. New York, Fuck You Press, 1965.

An Eye on the World: Selected Poems. London, MacGibbon and Kee, 1967.

After the Cry of the Birds. San Francisco, Dave Haslewood Books, 1967.

Moscow in the Wilderness, Segovia in the Snow. San Francisco, Beach Books, 1967.

The Secret Meaning of Things. New York, New Directions, 1969.

Tyrannus Nix? New York, New Directions, 1969.

Back Roads to Far Places. New York, New Directions, 1971.

Open Eye, Open Heart. New York, New Directions, 1973.

Recordings: *Poetry Readings in "The Cellar,"* with Kenneth Rexroth, Fantasy, 1958; *Tentative Description of a Dinner to Impeach President Eisenhower and Other Poems,* Fantasy, 1959; *Tyrannus Nix? and Assassination Raga,* Fantasy, 1971; *The World's Greatest Poets 1,* with Allen Ginsberg and Gregory Corso, CMS, 1971.

Plays

The Alligation (produced San Francisco, 1962; New York, 1970). Included in *Unfair Arguments with Existence,* 1963.

Unfair Arguments with Existence: Seven Plays for a New Theatre (includes *The Soldiers of No Country, Three Thousand Red Ants, The Alligation, The Victims of Amnesia, Motherlode, The Customs Collector in Baggy Pants, The Nose of Sisyphus*). New York, New Directions, 1963.

The Customs Collector in Baggy Pants (produced New York, 1964). Included in *Unfair Arguments with Existence,* 1963.

The Soldiers of No Country (produced London, 1969). Included in *Unfair Arguments with Existence,* 1963.

3 by Ferlinghetti: Three Thousand Red Ants, The Alligation, The Victims of Amnesia (produced New York, 1970) Included in *Unfair Arguments with Existence,* 1963.

Routines (includes 13 short pieces). New York, New Directions, 1964.

Novel

Her. New York, New Directions, 1960; London, MacGibbon and Kee, 1966.

Other

The Howl of the Censor, edited by J. W. Ehrlich. New York, Nourse, 1961.

The Mexican Night: Travel Journal. New York, New Directions, 1970.

Editor, *Beatitude Anthology.*   San Francisco, City Lights, 1960.
Editor, *City Lights Journal.*   San Francisco, City Lights, 4 vols., 1963–73.
Editor, *Hunk of Skin,* by Pablo Picasso.   San Francisco, City Lights, 1969.
Editor, *Panic Grass,* by Charles Upton.   San Francisco, City Lights, 1969.
Editor, *City Lights Anthology.*   San Francisco, City Lights, 1974.

Translator, *Selections from Paroles by Jacques Prévert.*   San Francisco, City
Lights, 1958; London, Penguin, 1963.

Manuscript Collection: Columbia University, New York.

*   *   *

Lawrence Ferlinghetti is one of the oldest members of the Beat Generation and
differs from those who were his immediate juniors by the emphasis he puts on
commitment: "the wiggy nihilism of the Beat Hipster, if carried to its natural
conclusion, actually means the death of the creative artist himself. While the
'non-commitment' of the artist is itself a suicidal and deluded variant of this same
nihilism."

In fact, what we seem to find in Ferlinghetti's work is an adaptation of the
methods and ideas of the French left-wing surrealism of the nineteen-thirties to the
rather different needs of American radical populism. Ferlinghetti is a poet who
speaks out; who protests, exclaims, exhorts. He has said that his work is written to
be read aloud, and that much of it is composed on a tape recorder. But it is not
simplistic work, as this description might suggest. The range of reference is very
wide, especially to painters, art movements, the heroes of the first phase of
modernism, etc. The poet is addressing a new audience, which has gradually
become as familiar with these references as he is himself. Ferlinghetti's enumera-
tions (a characteristic feature which, in his poetry, as in Allen Ginsberg's, seems to
be derived from Whitman) spread out before the reader or listener a shared cultural
landscape.

It might be said that Ferlinghetti's rhetoric is often too easy; that he and his
younger colleagues are busy preaching to the converted. His immense success with
audiences, however, demonstrates the need which his listeners feel for some point
of identification, for someone who has the courage to get up and say outloud the
thoughts which all are thinking.

– Edward Lucie-Smith

FERRIL, Thomas Hornsby.   American.   Born in Denver, Colorado, 25 February
1896. Educated at East Denver High School; Colorado College, Colorado Springs,
A.B. 1918. Served as an Officer in the Signal Corps Aviation Section, 1918.
Married Helen Drury Ray in 1921; has one daughter. Drama Critic, Denver *Times,*
1919–21; worked in motion picture advertising, 1921–26. Employed by the Great
Western Sugar Company in 1926: Editor, *Through the Leaves* and *The Sugar Press,*
1926–68. Since 1939, Editor and Publisher, with his wife, *The Rocky Mountain
Herald* weekly newspaper. Columnist ("Western Half-Acre"), *Harper's Magazine,*
New York. Associated with the Colorado University Writers Conference since its

inception, and other conferences. Recipient: Yale Series of Younger Poets Award, 1926; *Nation* prize, 1927; Oscar Blumenthal Prize (*Poetry,* Chicago), 1937; Denver *Post*-Central City Opera House Association Prize, 1958; Robert Frost Poetry Prize, 1960; Ridgely Torrence Prize, 1963. Honorary Degrees from Colorado College, Colorado University, Boulder, and Denver University. Honorary Member, Phi Beta Kappa, Denver University, 1955. Address: 2123 Downing Street, Denver, Colorado 80205, U.S.A.

Publications

Verse

> *High Passage.* New Haven, Connecticut, Yale University Press, 1926.
> *Westering.* New Haven, Connecticut, Yale University Press, 1934.
> *Trial by Time.* New York and London, Harper, 1944.
> *New and Selected Poems.* New York, Harper, 1952.
> *Words for Denver and Other Poems.* New York, Morrow, 1966.

Plays

> *. . . And Perhaps Happiness* (produced Central City, Colorado, 1958).
> *Ferril, Etc.* (produced Denver, 1972).

Musical Collaborations with Cecil Effinger performed and published.

Other

> *I Hate Thursday* (essays). New York and London, Harper, 1946.

> Editor, with Helen Ferril, *The Rocky Mountain Herald Reader.* New York, Morrow, 1966.

Manuscript Collection: Denver Public Library.

Critical Study: *The Poetry of Thomas Hornsby Ferril* by Robert Fulton Richards, Columbia University, New York, unpublished dissertation, 1960.

*   *   *

Thomas Hornsby Ferril for years has pursued a course somewhat apart from the mainstream of modern American poetry. He has been an individualist of the old stripe, eschewing all cliques and cults and academic auspices. The result is that his poetry took a long time finding a place among the works of his generation, though by now it is firmly established. For many years Ferril and his wife published the *Rocky Mountain Herald,* a weekly newspaper, far better edited than most, which celebrated the mountains of Colorado and adjoining regions. At the same time

Ferril himself became an amateur scholar of mountain folklore and culture, while he wrote his poems about life in the high country.

Ferril's characteristic poem is in slackened but recognizably traditional meter, incorporating the colloquial diction of his region. His characteristic theme is the speed of change in a frontier culture. In one of his best poems, "Waltz Against the Mountains," he writes:

> I was pulling hair from the trunk of a cottonwood tree
> The longhorn cattle rubbed when a sudden man
> Started tossing red-hot rivets up through the leaves,
> Scorching the amber varnish of the leaves.
> He made the red-hot rivets stick to the sky.

Anyone in western America knows that longhorn cattle haven't been raised in that region since the days of the frontier, seventy or eighty years ago. Yet now one of the greatest cities of America, Denver, sprawls against the mountainside, its skyscrapers lifting their lights toward the sky. The swiftness of time, the pathos of loss, the fear of impermanence, the courage of resistance – these are the typically western motifs of Ferril's poetry, bringing into clear relationship the frontier and the existentialist homeland of modern Europe.

– Hayden Carruth

FETHERLING, Doug. Canadian. Born in Ohio County, West Virginia, United States, 1 January 1947; emigrated to Canada in 1967; naturalized citizen. Left school at age 16. Worked as tree trimmer, bartender, reporter. Editor, House of Anansi Press, Toronto, 1968–69; Script Writer and Consultant, Canadian Broadcasting Corporation, Toronto, 1969–70; Book Page Editor, Toronto *Star*, 1973; Associate Editor, Books in Canada, Toronto, 1974. Recipient: Canada Council and Ontario Arts Council grants. Address: Box 367, Station F, Toronto, Ontario M4Y 2L8, Canada.

PUBLICATIONS

Verse

The United States of Heaven.   Toronto, House of Anansi, 1968.
My Experience in the War.   Toronto, Weed/Flower Press, 1970.
Our Man in Utopia.   Toronto, Macmillan, 1971.
Eleven Early Poems.   Toronto, Weed/Flower Press, 1972.
Cafe Terminus.   Toronto, Missing Link Press, 1973.
Achilles' Navel: Throbs, Laments and Vagaries.   Toronto, Press Porcepic, 1974.

Other

Hugh Garner.   Toronto, Forum House, 1972.

Editor, *Thumbprints: An Anthology of Hitchhiking Poems.*   Toronto, Peter Martin, 1969.

Editor, *A Caricature History of Canadian Politics.*   Toronto, Peter Martin, 1974.
Editor, *The Four Jameses*, by W. A. Deacon.   Toronto, Macmillan, 1974.

* . *   *

Doug Fetherling, the Toronto poet and cultural journalist, published his first collection of poems when he was twenty-one. *The United States of Heaven* was heavily influenced by "the greatest English language poet of all time, Allen Ginsberg, to whom this is dedicated." The poems, made up of discontinuous words and images, read like jottings taken down while descending the rings of some metropolitan inferno. A taste of the book as a whole can be conveyed by quoting a single line: "i fully expect to be dead be4 im 30."

Our Man in Utopia, the title of Fetherling's next major collection, conveys the notion that the poet is a correspondent, rather than a participant, right down to the device of calling the poems "Dispatch Number Two," "Dispatch Number Twenty-One," etc. The poet has a new beat now, an inner one, and he is not unduly concerned that

> Every thirteen minutes somewhere
> in this troubled world rioters
> are taking over the post office
> while we lie here relishing the
> night or cursing the morning.

The poet-correspondent is able to "sidestep all their / politics like puddles" and maintain "an involvement with more / than they have to offer." Here are poems, evocative and sensitive to the nuances of speech, that are as well-written as prose.

Fetherling's next – and most recent – collection is archly entitled *Achilles' Navel*. The archness extends to the subtitle (*Throbs, Laments and Vagaries*) and demonstrates the distance Fetherling has travelled from the "surrealist hell" (Raymond Souster's description of the world of his first book) to the more meditative world he now inhabits. The book opens on the macabre image of a child playing with a human skull and closes on an ironic love poem written "in the manner of Irving Layton." In between there are poems that show an awareness of history, of uncertain relationships, and of possibly difficult futures. Fetherling treats imaginatively the ghost of W. L. Mackenzie (a nineteenth-century revolutionary), the film actor Leslie Howard, and civilized values in a poem about a poet who is "au courant with emptiness." There is even a meditation on the passing years:

> Twice, for instance, while combing my hair,
> my hand has touched a bald spot I knew did not exist,
> and more than once an older face has sprung up
> in the mirror.

It is hard to believe this is the voice of a poet who is only twenty-seven, who fully expects "to be dead be4 im 30."

– John Robert Colombo

FIELD, Edward. American. Born in Brooklyn, New York, 7 June 1924. Attended New York University. Served in the United States Army Air Force, 1942–46. Lecturer, YM-YWHA Poetry Center, New York. Recipient: Lamont Poetry Selection Award, 1962; Guggenheim Fellowship, 1963. Address: Box 72, Village Post Office, New York, New York 10028, U.S.A.

PUBLICATIONS

Verse

Stand Up, Friend, With Me.   New York, Grove Press, 1963.
Variety Photoplays.   New York, Grove Press, 1967.

Other

Editor and Translator, *Eskimo Songs and Stories, Collected by Knud Rasmussen on the Fifth Thule Expedition.*   New York, Delacorte Press, 1973.

Critical Studies: Review by Robert Mazzocco, in *New York Review of Books*, 1967; by Richard Howard, in *Kenyon Review* (Gambier, Ohio), Fall 1968.

*   *   *

Edward Field's two books of poetry are wonderful: his first, *Stand Up, Friend, With Me*, won the Lamont Poetry Selection Award in 1962, and, like his more recent *Variety Photoplays*, sustains a tonal integrity without resorting to artificial forms. Field writes in a voice distinctly his own, distinctly "unpoetic," and wholly consistent throughout his poems. So, while many poets utilize their gift to portray a shifting, unpredictable personality, Field's intense concentration is on his subjects – and language is used as a plain extension of the poet's observation: no metaphoric technique imposed to beef up an "image":

> Hanukkah has its terrors as well as joys:
> Not that we have to dread an annual slaughter anymore
> with cossacks racing through Jewtown,
> but now it is preparation for the period of sorrow that follows
> when the Christians make a big fuss about Christmas
> forcing us to admit that they enjoy themselves sometimes.
> In other words it's not so bad to be a goy
> and maybe it would even be fun to have a foreskin again,
> risking infection, cheese, and the other well-known perils.
> – first stanza of "A Jew on Christmas"

Field is a master story-teller. Sexual candor, similar to, but more moderately expressed than Portnoy's, occasionally appears in admonition against parents' meddling with the natural expressions of their children. His experience is common, but how rarely does a poet turn his open memory to wet dreams and earlier sexual knowledge, without moralizing, without false nostalgia! The first stanza of "Playing in the Back Fields" establishes the situation with all the directness a child would use:

> All the kids of the block, Sonny, Totsy, me and my sisters,
> used to gather under the sumac bushes in the back fields,
> and sitting in a circle, pull down pants and bloomers,
> and stare and stare at each other:
> We called it dirty stuff.

Many of Field's best poems create a serio-comic situation whose humor somehow arises from the directness of his language, and the energy with which he zings into the topic. "Poem for the Left Hand" begins: "Cancer strikes and I lose my left hand: / My whole life has to be reorganized / Since I can no longer earn my living as a typist." The situation is mildly absurd, but believable; the poem ends with a surprising statement about freedom: "Knots are too difficult for one hand to be bothered with: / Now I cut them through and laugh for the liberation."

Field has written some of the most memorable opening lines in all contemporary poetry. His poems don't "warm up"; they plunge to their topic:

> Blessings on all the kids who improve the signs in the subways:
> They put a beard on the fashionable lady selling soap,
> Fix up her flat chest with the boobies of a chorus girl . . .
>
> – from "Graffiti"

Featured in *Variety Photoplays* are several "Old Movies," such as "Curse of the Cat Woman," "The Life of Joan Crawford," and "Frankenstein." In these, Field indulges his special interest in film (he wrote the narrative for *To Be Alive,* an award-winning documentary shown at the New York World's Fair) to recapture the old stories once again.

Field's two books contain some of the best poems published during the 1960's; I hope there will be more.

– Geof Hewitt

FIGUEROA, John (Joseph Maria). Jamaican. Born in Kingston, Jamaica, 4 August 1920. Educated at schools in Jamaica; Holy Cross College, Worcester, Massachusetts; London University; degrees: A.B., M.A., L.H.D. Married Dorothy Grace Murray Alexander; has four sons and three daughters. Teacher and Lecturer in the United States; Lecturer in English and Philosophy, University of London; Sports Reporter, 1946–60, and Broadcaster, BBC, London. Formerly, Dean, and currently, Professor of Education, University of the West Indies, Kingston. Recipient: British Council Scholarship, 1946; Carnegie Award, 1960; Guggenheim Fellowship, 1964. Address: Department of Education, University of the West Indies, Mona, Kingston 7, Jamaica.

PUBLICATIONS

Verse

> *Blue Mountain Peak.* Kingston, Gleaner Company, 1944.
> *Love Leaps Here.* Kingston, C. Tinling, 1962.

Other

> *Staffing and Examinations in Secondary Schools in the British Caribbean.* London, Evans, 1964.
> *Society, Schools and Progress in the West Indies.* Oxford, Pergamon Press, 1971.

> Editor, *Caribbean Voices: An Anthology of West Indian Poetry.* London, Evans, 2 vols., 1966, 1970; New York, Luce, 1973.

John Figueroa comments:

I hope that [my verse] is influenced by Horace and Virgil and Sappho as well as by our Jamaican speech rhythms and Trinidadian calypsoes. But I'm hardly the one to say. Once in the early days a well-known critic excused himself from commenting (in a broadcast) on the verse, on the grounds that it was "very religious." Perhaps he was being tactful.

*   *   *

John Figueroa is well-known throughout the Caribbean as poet, editor, critic and educationalist. However, both his volumes of poetry, *Blue Mountain Peak* and *Love Leaps Here*, were published locally so that his verse is not as widely known outside the West Indies as it ought to be.

Figueroa is certainly an original poet at his best and quite unlike any other West Indian poet. He is acutely aware of the physical world and responds to contrasts of one kind or another – contrasts of place, as in his "At Home the Green Remains," contrasts of colour, and even contrasts in modes of living. He constantly seems to be relating one thing to another, the known to the unfamiliar, darkness to light, and rough to smooth.

An eminent scholar, Figueroa has obviously read widely. His influences might be said to be partly environmental (i.e., Jamaican speech rhythms, Trinidadian calypsoes, etc.) and partly classical (Virgil, Sappho, and particularly Horace, a good deal of whose verse he has translated). Indeed, in his poetry there seems to be some kind of conflict between the two, so that the struggle to achieve a balance between the urge to express his own individual experience and the need for technical control, is not easily resolved. At times, the academic pressures seem to prevent him from speaking in his own voice.

John Figueroa has a wide range of styles and subjects, but his work falls into five broad categories: 1) reflective poems, 2) poems with a religious theme or insight, 3) poems arising out of experiences in other countries, 4) personal and anecdotal poems, and 5) translations. His greatest strength, however, lies in his reflective and philosophical poetry. In such poems as "On Hearing Dvorak's 'New World' Symphony," "Other Spheres," "Green Is the Colour of Hope," "The

485

Three Epiphanies," "From the Caribbean with Love," and "Columbus Lost," one finds significant utterance combined with unusual craftsmanship.

– Howard Sergeant

FINCH, Robert (Duer Claydon). Canadian. Born in Freeport, Long Island, New York, United States, 14 May 1900. Educated at the University of Toronto (Jardine Memorial Prize, 1924), B.A. 1925; the Sorbonne, Paris, 1928; studied music with Alberto Guerrero and Wanda Landowska. Painter: exhibitions in Toronto, Paris, New York. Professor of French, 1952–68, and since 1968, Professor Emeritus, University College, University of Toronto. Recipient: Governor General's Award, 1947, 1962; Lorne Pierce Medal, 1968. LL.D.: University of Toronto, 1973. Fellow, Royal Society of Canada, 1963. Address: Massey College, 4 Devonshire Place, Toronto 5, Ontario, Canada.

PUBLICATIONS

Verse

Poems. Toronto, Oxford University Press, 1946.
The Strength of the Hills. Toronto, McClelland and Stewart, 1948.
Acis in Oxford and Other Poems. Oxford, privately printed, 1959; Toronto, University of Toronto Press, 1961.
Dover Beach Revisited and Other Poems. Toronto, Macmillan, 1961.
Silverthorn Bush and Other Poems. Toronto, Macmillan, 1966.

Play

A Century Has Roots (produced Toronto, 1953). Toronto, Toronto University Press, 1953.

Other

The Sixth Sense: Individualism in French Poetry 1686–1760. Toronto, University of Toronto Press, 1966.

Editor, with Eugène Joliat, *French Individualist Poetry 1686–1760: An Anthology.* Toronto, University of Toronto Press, 1971.

*   *   *

Literary verse is infrequently attempted presently in Canada, that area of verse-making where the form commands the content, where the thought is sophisticate, the metaphor more cogent than daring. It is an area out of fashion, an area dangerous and difficult to achieve success in – dangerous since to fail is to leave the literary rather than the vital effect; difficult, for it demands that the formality become necessary to the communication.

Robert Finch dares the hazards of this kind of poetry and proves them surmountable. Amid the turbulence of the world, he dares to write sonnets; his adherence to grace of thought demands his formality. It is a poetry of pensive mood and sensitive craftsmanship. To read his books is to have walked, aware of the melancholy world outside, in a garden of Le Nostre.

Finch first found assertion long ago in that watershed of an anthology, *New Provinces*. His presentation then was as an Imagist when Imagism and the French Symbolists might not have existed as far as Canadian awareness was concerned:

> Lacks a blue buck bearing vermilion horns
> led by a groom in tightest daffodil?

Finch soon established himself with a poetry of precision and form and accurate detailed sensuousness. The definition is not surprising. Finch is a skilled musician, painter – and professor of French in Toronto. His eye is that of the painter:

> The dark green truck on the cement platform
> is explicit as a paradigm.
> Its wheels are four black cast-iron starfish . . .
> The truck holds eleven cakes of ice,
> each cake a different size and shape.
> Some look as though a weight had hit them.
> One, solid glass, has a core of sugar.
> They lean, a transitory Icehenge.

This imagist stasis is deceived into movement. The movement proceeds by paradox; the logic, by metaphor. He is as fond of variations as a musician is. His book *Dover Beach Revisisted and Other Poems* contains eleven variations on the theme of Matthew Arnold's poem. It witnesses the quality of his mind, a quiet perception of tides and time in a verse of intellectual lyricism. The passage of the seasons is everywhere evident. Reliance on the variations in weather to express mood and emotion is to admit the usual conventional dangers. Finch startles in his best poems of this kind by concurrent, spare intellectualism, a sophistication of taste and perception. The happy wind, the pensive trees

> have all gone and we are far away
> Where every season is a winter's day
> That comes and goes and always is the same

> Except that we, more than its atmosphere,
> Still know and feel and see and breathe and hear
> That wind, that grass, those trees, that eager stream.

Finch's poetry is a poetry of personality, seasoned, spare yet sensuous, astringent yet warm with humility and compassion. Its effect is that of a resolution in music, inevitable and

> Building with Euclidean grace.

– Ralph Gustafson

FINKEL, Donald. American. Born in New York City, 21 October 1929. Educated at Columbia University, New York, B.S. in philosophy 1952 (Phi Beta Kappa), M.A. in literature 1953. Married Constance Urdang, *q.v.*, in 1956; has three children. Instructor, University of Iowa, Iowa City, 1957–58, and Bard College, Annandale-on-Hudson, New York, 1958–60. Since 1960, Poet-in-Residence, Washington University, St. Louis. Visiting Lecturer, Bennington College, Vermont, 1966–67. Visited Antarctica, 1969–70, at invitation of National Science Foundation. Recipient: Helen Bullis Prize (*Poetry Northwest*), 1964; Guggenheim Fellowship, 1967; National Endowment for the Arts grant, 1969, 1973; Ingram Merrill Foundation grant, 1972; Theodore Roethke Memorial Prize, 1974. Address: 6943 Columbia Place, St. Louis, Missouri 63130, U.S.A.

PUBLICATIONS

Verse

The Clothing's New Emperor and Other Poems.   New York, Scribner, 1959.
Simeon: Poems.   New York, Atheneum, 1964.
A Joyful Noise: Poems.   New York, Atheneum, 1966.
Answer Back.   New York, Atheneum, 1968.
The Garbage Wars: Poems.   New York, Atheneum, 1970.
Adequate Earth.   New York, Atheneum, 1972.
A Mote in Heaven's Eye.   New York, Atheneum, 1975.

Play

The Jar (produced Boston, 1961).

Manuscript Collection: Washington University Library, St. Louis.

Critical Study: *Alone with America*, by Richard Howard, New York, Atheneum, 1969.

*   *   *

Donald Finkel is one of the most energetic and consistent of the American poets in mid-career. The range of his interest and involvements is very large, from "Reflections On Violence," one of the best pieces in *A Joyful Noise*, his third book, to surrealistic responses to pop art – "Three for Robert Rauschenberg" – in the same volume. He works best in the short lyric, or sequences, his style being somewhat too febrile to make the long poems fully accessible to him – though his one serious attempt at a sustained work, *Answer Back*, briefly discussed below, has its real felicities and triumphs.

The following piece from *A Joyful Noise*, "Hands," demonstrates well the manner in which he can invest the abstract with body and, while giving wit free range, come up with something wholly satisfying:

> The poem makes truth a little more disturbing,
> like a good bra, lifts it and holds it out
> in both hands. (In some of the flashier stores
> there's a model with the hands stitched on, in red or black.)
>
> Lately the world you wed, for want of such hands,
> sags in the bed beside you like a tired wife.
> For want of such hands, the face of the moon is bored,
> the tree does not stretch and yearn, nor the groin tighten.
>
> Devious or frank, in any case,
> the poem is calculated to arouse.
> Lean back and let its hands play freely on you:
> there comes a moment, lifted and aroused,
> when the two of you are equally beautiful.

The poet delights in word play – pun, paradox, double meaning – and the delight never seems to flag: there is little slackness. Occasionally, as perhaps the natural consequence of such gusto, there is slapstick, as in these lines from ''Convalescence'' in *A Joyful Noise:*

> I must drink a glass of kitchen every night
> before going to bed.
> I must get fat.

For the most part, however, the manner leads to real successes, as in the following from the same volume, ''Winter Nights,'' short enough to quote in full:

> Setting the crooked straight, and the straight crooked,
> speaking without speaking, being heard:
> winter nights, after a long day in the grave
> schoolyard, when I could be sailing
> a small yacht in Bermuda, or upstairs in bed,
> feeding grapes to my wife,
> I think about it until after midnight.

Answer Back, while not appearing to represent an inevitable direction for someone with Donald Finkel's gifts, has such fine passages and at least one fully satisfying section, ''Wow Shaft,'' that it should not be ignored by those interested in the come-back of the long poem. Full of extraordinary juxtapositions and dealing with the gamut, sex to politics, and fearing nothing, the poem accomplishes one thing certainly: it gives the reader a strong sense of the man behind it – his loves, fears, hates, hang-ups. Perhaps one should not expect more, perhaps purely as modern experiment it is as much a realization as one could want. The following is a specimen of the sharp writing throughout:

> The window is open! The counterweights
> clatter in their dry wells.
> The mountain squats, up to its shoulders in mist.
> Over the house the maple hunches like an ogre,
> dripping rain from his green beard.
> Sunflame the wind diffuses, morning, ghost-white,
> dank as a stone against my cheek.

– Lucien Stryk

FINLAY, Ian Hamilton. Scottish. Born in Nassau, Bahamas, 28 October 1925. Left school at 13. Married to Susan Finlay; has two children, Eck and Ailie. Concrete Poetry exhibited at Axiom Gallery, London, 1968, Scottish National Gallery of Modern Art, Edinburgh, 1972, and National Maritime Museum, Greenwich, 1973; Sundials: University of Kent, Canterbury, and in Biggar, Lanarkshire; Poems designed for Max Planck Institute, Stuttgart. Editor, *Poor. Old. Tired. Horse*, Dunsyre, Lanarkshire; Publisher, with Sue Finlay, Wild Hawthorn Press, Edinburgh, 1961–66, Easter Ross, 1966, and since 1969, Dunsyre, Lanarkshire. Recipient: Scottish Arts Council bursary, 1966, 1967, 1968; Atlantic-Richfield Award (USA), 1968. Address: Stonypath, Dunsyre, Lanarkshire, Scotland.

PUBLICATIONS

Verse

The Dancers Inherit the Party.   Worcester, Migrant Press, 1960.
Glasgow Beasts, an a Burd.   Edinburgh, Wild Hawthorn Press, 1961.
Concertina.   Edinburgh, Wild Hawthorn Press, 1962.
Rapel.   Edinburgh, Wild Hawthorn Press, 1963.
Canal Stripe Series 3 and 4.   Edinburgh, Wild Hawthorn Press, 1964.
Telegrams from My Windmill.   Edinburgh, Wild Hawthorn Press, 1964.
Ocean Stripe Series 2 and 3.   Edinburgh, Wild Hawthorn Press, 1965.
Cytherea.   Edinburgh, Wild Hawthorn Press, 1965.
Autumn Poem.   Edinburgh, Wild Hawthorn Press, 1966.
6 Small Pears for Eugen Gomringer.   Easter Ross, Wild Hawthorn Press, 1966.
6 Small Songs in 3's.   Easter Ross, Wild Hawthorn Press, 1966.
Tea-Leaves and Fishes.   Easter Ross, Wild Hawthorn Press, 1966.
Ocean Stripe Series 4.   Easter Ross, Wild Hawthorn Press, 1966.
4 Sails.   Easter Ross, Wild Hawthorn Press, 1966.
Headlines Eavelines.   Corsham, Wiltshire, Openings Press, 1967.
Stonechats.   Dunsyre, Lanarkshire, Wild Hawthorn Press, 1967.
Ocean Stripe Series 5.   Nottingham, Tarasque Press, 1967.
Canal Game.   London, Fulcrum Press, 1967.
The Collected Coaltown of Callange Tri-kai.   Newport, Monmouthshire, Screwpacket Press, 1968.
Air Letters.   Nottingham, Tarasque Press, 1968.
The Blue and The Brown Poems.   New York, Atlantic Richfield–Jargon Press, 1968.
3/3's.   Dunsyre, Lanarkshire, Wild Hawthorn Press, 1969.
A Boatyard.   Dunsyre, Lanarkshire, Wild Hawthorn Press, 1969.
Lanes.   Dunsyre, Lanarkshire, Wild Hawthorn Press, 1969.
Wave.   Dunsyre, Lanarkshire, Wild Hawthorn Press, 1969.
Rhymes for Lemons.   Dunsyre, Lanarkshire, Wild Hawthorn Press, 1970.
"Fishing News" News.   Dunsyre, Lanarkshire, Wild Hawthorn Press, 1970.
30 Signatures to Silver Catches.   Nottingham, Tarasque Press, 1971.
Poems to Hear and See.   New York, Macmillan, 1971.
A Sailor's Calendar.   New York, Something Else Press, 1971.
The Olsen Excerpts.   Göttingen, Verlag Udo Breger, 1971.
A Memory of Summer.   Dunsyre, Lanarkshire, Wild Hawthorn Press, 1971.
From "An Inland Garden."   Dunsyre, Lanarkshire, Wild Hawthorn Press, 1971.
Evening/Sail 2.   Dunsyre, Lanarkshire, Wild Hawthorn Press, 1971.

The Weed Boat Masters Ticket, Preliminary Text (Part Two). Dunsyre, Lanarkshire, Wild Hawthorn Press, 1971.
Sail/Sundial. Dunsyre, Lanarkshire, Wild Hawthorn Press, 1972.
Jibs. Dunsyre, Lanarkshire, Wild Hawthorn Press, 1972.
Honey by the Water. Los Angeles, Black Sparrow Press, 1973.
Butterflies. Dunsyre, Lanarkshire, Wild Hawthorn Press, 1973.
A Family. Dunsyre, Lanarkshire, Wild Hawthorn Press, 1973.
Exercise X. Dunsyre, Lanarkshire, Wild Hawthorn Press, 1974.

Cards and Folding Cards, Poem/Prints, etc. (all published by Wild Hawthorn Press unless otherwise noted): *Standing Poem 1, 2, 3*, 1963, 1965; *Poster Poem (Le Circus)*, 1964; *First Suprematist Standing Poem*, 1965; *Earthship*, 1965; *Summer Poem*, 1966; *Acrobats*, Nottingham, Tarasque Press, 1966; *Star/Steer* (poem/print), Nottingham, Tarasque Press, 1966, (card) Brighton, Festival Publications, 1967; *Sea-Poppy 1* (poem/print), Nottingham, Tarasque Press, 1966, (card) 1968; *Ajar*, 1967; *La Belle Hollandaise*, 1967; *Land/Sea*, 1967; *3 Blue Lemons*, 1967; *2 from the Yard of . . .* , 1967; *Arcady*, Nottingham, Tarasque Press, 1968; *Marine*, 1968; *Sea-Poppy 2* (poem/print and card), 1968; *The Land's Shadow*, 1968; *From "The Analects of 'Fishing News,' "* 1968; *From "The Illuminations of 'Fishing News,' "* 1969; *From "Ta Myoika of 'Fishing News,' "* 1969; *Net/Planet*, 1969; *Point-to-Point*, 1969; *4 Sails*, 1969; *Xmas Star*, 1969; *Poem/Print No. 11*, 1969; *Seams*, 1969; *After the Russian*, Corsham, Wiltshire, Openings Press, 1969; *Skylarks*, 1970; *Valses pour Piano*, 1970; *Arcadian Sundials*, 1970; *From "The Metamorphoses of 'Fishing News,' "* 1970; *A Waterlily Pool*, 1970; *Still Life with Lemons*, 1970; *Les Hirondelles,*, 1970; *A Patch . . .* , 1970; *Sheaves*, 1970; *A Use for Old Beehives*, 1970; *Xmas Rose*, 1970; *Evening/Sail*, 1970; *Catameringue*, 1970; *Poem/Print No. 14*, 1970; *The Little Seamstress*, 1970; *Homage to Mozart*, 1970; *Scottish Zulu,* 1970; *Errata*, 1970; *The Weed Boat Masters Ticket, Preliminary Text (Part One)*, Nottingham, Tarasque Press, 1970; *Boats of Letters*, 1970; *Zulu "Chieftain,"* 1971; *A Sea Street Anthology*, 1971; *Homage to Donald McGill*, 1971; *Flags*, 1971; *The Sign of the Nudge*, 1971; *The Harbour*, 1971; *The Old Nobby*, 1971; *Sail/Waves 1* and *2*, 1971; *I Saw Three Ships*, 1971; *Is There a Ship . . .* , 1971; *A Heart Shape*, 1971; *Birch-Bark*, 1971; *Daisies*, 1971; *Book-Flag*, 1971; *The Land's Shadow*, 1971; *Kite*, 1971; *Tree-Shells*, 1971; *Catches*, 1971; *Unicorn*, 1971; *Elegy for "Whimbrel" and "Petrel,"* Wilsden, Yorkshire, Sepia Press, 1971; *Xmas Morn*, 1971; *Glossary*, 1971; *Street Handout*, Sunderland, Ceolfrith Press, 1971; *Shenval Christmas Poem/Print*, 1971; *Sailing Barge Redwing*, 1971; *A Rock Rose*, 1971; *Archangel*, 1971; *Seashells*, 1971; *The Little Drummer Boy*, 1971; *Homage to Vuillard*, 1971; *Prinz Eugen*, 1972; *Sail Wholemeal*, 1972; *Homage to Modern Art*, 1972; *Illustrious*, 1972; *The Washington Fountain*, 1972; *Topiary Aircraft Carrier*, 1972; *Homage to E. A. Hornel*, 1972; *F1*, 1972; *The End . . .* , 1972; *Homage to Seurat*, 1972; *Homage to Walter Reekie's Ring Netters*, 1972; *Kite – Estuary Model*, 1972; *Iron Ship*, 1972; *Homage to Jonathan Williams*, 1972; *Blue/Water's/Bark*, 1972; *Spiral Binding*, 1972; *D1*, 1972; *The Sea's/Waves'/Sheaves*, 1972; *Der Tag*, 1972; *Christmas Card*, 1972; *Estuary Cupboards*, 1972; *Neck Tank*, 1973; *Arcadia*, 1973; *Trim Here*, 1973; *Mid-Pacific Elements*, 1973; *Bath Roundels*, 1973; *Mower Is Less*, 1973; *Homage to Pop Art*, 1973; *Tea-Card Series*, 1973; *Copyright*, 1973; *Stationary*, 1973; *Homage to Robert Lax*, 1974; *Silhouettes*, 1974.

Short Stories

The Sea-Bed and Other Stories. Edinburgh, Alna Press, 1958.

Manuscript Collection: Lilly Library, University of Indiana, Bloomington.

Critical Studies: "Ian Hamilton Finlay Issue" of *Extra Verse 15* (London), Spring 1965; by Bryan Robertson, in *Spectator* (London), 6 September 1968; *Ian Hamilton Finlay* by Stephen Bann, Edinburgh, Scottish National Gallery of Modern Art, 1972.

Ian Hamilton Finlay comments:

As a "concrete" poet I am interested in poetry as "the best words, in the best possible order" . . . *in the best materials,* i.e., such as glass or stone for interiors of gardens. I have been described as "the leading concrete poet now writing in English." But "concrete" has no meaning nowadays. What is concrete?

My verse is not a *single* thing since it has changed over the years. On the other hand, I have usually tried for the same ends – lucidity, clarity, a resolved complexity. I have used many forms, from traditional rhymed verse to poems designed as entire gardens (such as the poem I prepared for the American architect John Johansen). I consider that the seasons, nature, inland waterways, and oceans are proper themes for poetry. I do not expect poems to solve my problems. I do not believe in "the new man." Possibly A. Alvarez is the stupidest writer I have ever come across. I admire the poems of George Herbert. In the context of this time, it is not the job of poetry to "expand consciousness" but to offer a modest example of a decent sort of order.

*   *   *

Ian Hamilton Finlay's poetry has undergone a considerable evolution during the decade since it first began to appear, but the movements in that evolution are not random or (in the wrong sense) "experimental." The main driving-force behind his work may be called classical, if classicism implies a deliberate search for order, form, and economy, yet his classicism is accompanied by obviously romantic and playful elements. He indicated something of this in sub-titling his collection *Rapel* "10 fauve and suprematist poems." The fauve element preserves his work from frigidity, as the suprematist element preserves it from clutter and indulgence.

His first book, *The Dancers Inherit the Party,* contained short poems of much charm and humour, in traditional rhyming verse, about love, people, fishing, Orkney. The brevity of many of these poems was taken a step farther in his next two productions, *Glasgow Beasts* and *Concertina,* both of which had illustrations closely tied to the text. As well as the enhanced visual presentation, there was again a strong infusion of humour in both books.

The visual element, and the movement towards verbal economy, both predisposed Finlay to react with enthusiasm to the international development known as concrete poetry, which he learned about in 1962. Most of his work from *Rapel* (1963) onwards has been received and discussed under the "concrete" label, unsatisfactory and amorphous as that term has now become. Essentially it should signify (to quote the Brazilian Poets' "Pilot-Plan for Concrete Poetry" of 1958) a poetry that "begins by being aware of graphic space as structural agent" and is "against a poetry of expression, subjective and hedonistic." To Finlay, it was a poetry that would link back to the purity and harmony of artists like Malevich and Mondrian, and in general to those Constructivist ideals of half a century ago which had been sterilized by a new wave of expressionism. Painter as well as poet, he found no difficulty in seeing and accepting this formal extension of a verbal art into a visual domain; that many people do find it difficult he has had to admit. But whether his work is to be called "poetry" or something else, it will win over most unprejudiced eyes by its beauty and complete integrity.

"Little Calendar" could be quoted as representing his concrete approach at its most transparent:

april	light	light	light	light
may	light	trees	light	trees
june	trees	light	trees	light
july	trees	trees	trees	trees
august	trees'	light	trees'	light
september	lights	trees	lights	trees

But from this basis, which is still that of the poem printed on the page, Finlay evolved a range of ancillary conceptions of the poem: standing poems (printed on specially folded cards), poster poems, "kinetic" poems which release a serial meaning through the act of turning over the pages of a book, and three-dimensional poem-objects and poem-environments involving the use of metal or stone or glass and produced in cooperation with craftsmen in these materials. These meticulously designed and striking objects (especially successful are *Autumn Poem* and *Ocean Stripe 5* among the "kinetic" books, and "Wave/Rock" and "Seas/Ease" among the three-dimensional poems) have a characteristic distinction of using the simplest of means, and often a very Scottish and homely simplicity – rocks and water, boats and fishing-nets, canals and tugs, stars and potato-fields – to bring out patterns, harmonies, analogies, and meanings that transcend their strongly local and native roots.

– Edwin Morgan

FINNIGAN, Joan. Canadian. Born in Ottawa, Ontario, 25 November 1923. Educated at Carleton University, Ottawa; Queen's University, Kingston, Ontario, B.A. Widow of Charles Grant MacKenzie (died, 1965); has three children. Formerly, school teacher, and reporter for the Ottawa *Journal*. Since 1965, Free-lance Writer, for the National Film Board of Canada and the Canadian Broadcasting Corporation, Toronto. Recipient: Borestone Mountain Poetry Prize, 1959, 1961, 1963; Canada Council grant, 1965, 1967, 1968, 1969, 1973; Centennial Prize, 1967; President's Medal, University of Western Ontario, 1968; Etrog Award, for screenplay, 1969. Address: 17 Parkwood Place, Kingston, Ontario, Canada.

PUBLICATIONS

Verse

Through the Glass Darkly. Toronto, Ryerson Press, 1957.
A Dream of Lilies. Fredericton, New Brunswick, Fiddlehead, 1965.

Entrance to the Green-house.   Toronto, Ryerson Press, 1968.
It Was Warm and Sunny When We Set Out.   Toronto, Ryerson Press, 1970.
In the Brown Cottage on Loughborough Lake.   Toronto, CBC Learning Systems, 1970.
Celebrate This City.   Toronto, McClelland and Stewart, 1975.

Plays

Screenplays: *The Best Damn Fiddler from Calabogie to Kaladar,* 1969; *Godsend,* 1973.

Manuscript Collection: Queen's University, Kingston, Ontario.

Joan Finnigan comments:

Since I was seven I have been writing poetry. At forty I came to creative film-scripts and so began to write long poems. My poetry always veered towards the dramatic and my film-scripts are strongly poetic. The reason a creative film-script, done with integrity, is like a long poem is that both are condensations of intensity, a boiling down to the quintessence, a search for ultimate essence. I had matured enough to move from the short form – the poem – to the one requiring greater sustaining power – the screenplay – when the National Film Board of Canada began commissioning me to work for them.

*   *   *

That "poetry is not a turning loose of emotion but an escape from emotion" has become axiomatic in the criticism and the writing of modern poetry. Such a statement finds support in the general scientific and philosophic evolution of the age, and it informs the modern poetical canon's scepticism towards the perception of Nature as a paradigm for benevolent humanism or the articulation of traditional themes (love, birth, death, marriage) through the filter of sensibility removed from the conditioning factors of man-made environment. In Canada, this consciousness is central to the work of an E. J. Pratt and the poets of The McGill Movement, and it is emblematized in the wilderness-garden mythos of the Frye school of poets from D. G. Jones to Margaret Atwood. The rejection of facile romanticism at the core of Eliot's pronouncement was germane to the poetics initiated in the Twenties in Canada as a reaction against the nineteenth century Confederation Poets. At any rate, it is a commonplace now that the eternal verities can be improved by being expressed in diction and vision attuned to the age.

With these considerations in mind, it is no small surprise to encounter the poetry of Joan Finnigan celebrating a domestic world revolving around family life, the family cottage, the family friends, love and nature rendered in language free from sophistication. An openness toward self and others characterizes an outlook whose subjective correlative is the operations of benevolent Nature. The world is Edenic and pristine in her first three books, dominated by radiant colors and cheerful sounds controlled by the key symbol of the sun shining at the height of summer. There exudes a feeling of oneness with the elements culminating in transcendental intimations of immortality, no doubt sincerely felt by the poetess. Eve-like, but unlike Eve since her boundless innocence cannot precipitate any Fall of Man, she celebrates a garden whose paradisiacal emoluments she has no reason to suspect. To be sure, a few queries are raised ("Oh, who in all of heathendom, / Is half so sad as I?"), but they pose no threat of disruption to this Arcadia where no vital concerns are entertained.

Miss Finnigan's two favorite themes – love and nature – recur in her last books. The related feelings of nostalgia, flight of time, urbanophobia conveying an undercurrent of sweet melancholy are now accentuated with the intrusion of death. In *It Was Warm and Sunny When We Set Out*, the theme is, at first, embarrassingly stated – "And I think perpetually now of your dead HEART (for no one could get directions to that place, not even yourself) . . ." – in the not surprising ingenuous confessional style – "Who, who could ever believe our private murders or the possibility of this revenge?" – which the poetess delights in. It finds a more felicitous expression, however, in the contrasting use of symbols. The sun that hitherto glowed on a bountiful world presently reflects the destruction of the Covenant: it is blinding, bleeding, mocking, scorching. Though the diction falters – "If people really love one another, / snow, why do they die?" – one finds interesting, nonetheless, the substitution of the symbolic winter grip for the vision of warmth generated by summer. The intensity of personal suffering finally yields through visceral apprehension a sober consciousness structured by a lucid polarization of the universals in Miss Finnigan's last book, *In the Brown Cottage on Loughborough Lake*. In a book markedly contrasting with her early work, the weaving of alternating polarities (light and dark, summer and autumn, outer life and inner life, life and death, happiness and sorrow) germinates in the mature expression of pain endured, challenged and possibly conquered. Her beloved Nature is still there, as anthropomorphic as ever, the language is still mined with clichés, the world as restricted as usual. But this elegy, which can all too easily be assigned to the Wordsworthian canon, is quite moving in its expression of emotions barely recovering from the trauma of exposure to the existence of pain and cruelty. Even fractionally the poetess has been able to master and contain pain and bear witness to this control over emotion by finding a structure of objective correlatives, making this her best work to date. Maybe Eliot was not wrong after all.

– Max Dorsinville

FISHER, Roy. British. Born in Handsworth, Birmingham, Warwickshire, 11 June 1930. Educated at Wattville Road Elementary School; Handsworth Grammar School; Birmingham University, B.A., M.A. Married Barbara Venables in 1953; has two sons. Pianist with jazz groups since 1946. School and college teacher, 1953–63; Principal Lecturer and Head of the Department of English and Drama, Bordesley College of Education, Birmingham, 1963–71. Since 1971, Member of the Department of American Studies, University of Keele, Staffordshire. Recipient: Andrew Kelus Prize, 1970. Address: Department of American Studies, University of Keele, Keele, Staffordshire ST5 5BG, England.

495

PUBLICATIONS

Verse

City. Worcester, Migrant Press, 1961.
Ten Interiors with Various Figures. Nottingham, Tarasque Press, 1967.
The Memorial Fountain. Newcastle-upon-Tyne, Northern House, 1967.
Collected Poems 1968: The Ghost of a Paper Bag. London, Fulcrum Press, 1969.
Correspondence. London, Tetrad Press, 1970.
Matrix. London, Fulcrum Press, 1971.
Also There. London, Tetrad Press, 1972.
Bluebeard's Castle. Guildford, Surrey, Circle Press, 1972.

Other

Then Hallucinations: City 2. Worcester, Migrant Press, 1962.
The Ship's Orchestra (prose poem). London, Fulcrum Press, 1966.
Titles. Nottingham, Tarasque Press, 1969.
Metamorphoses (prose poems). London, Tetrad Press, 1971.
The Cut Pages (prose poems). London, Fulcrum Press, 1971.

Critical Studies: "Resonances and Speculations upon Reading Roy Fisher's City" by Gael Turnbull, in Kulchur 7 (New York), 1962; by Stuart Mills and Simon Cutts, in Tarasque 5 (Nottingham), 1967; "Roy Fisher's Work" by Eric Mottram, in Stand (Newcastle upon Tyne), xi, 1, 1969; "Roy Fisher: An Appreciation" in Thomas Hardy and British Poetry, by Donald Davie, New York, Oxford University Press, 1972, and London, Routledge, 1973; Preface by Jon Silkin to Poetry of the Committed Individual, London, Gollancz-Penguin, 1973.

*   *   *

Roy Fisher belongs to the group of poets who originally centred on the Migrant Press – one of the founder-imprints in the so-called "little press movement." He was in early and close contact with the American poets of the Black Mountain group, and thus in opposition to the prevailing poetic current of the 1950's in England. He is also and very consciously a "provincial" – he was not only born in Birmingham, but has lived and worked there all his life. The result of all this was that his work was until recently very little known in England. Fisher is by conviction a modernist – his little book The Ship's Orchestra is perhaps the most hermetic text to have been published in England in recent years. But he is not really a follower of Pound as his association with the Black Mountain might suggest. He once aptly described himself as "a 1920's Russian modernist," and his best work certainly has the force, the compression and the integrity of poets such as Blok and Mandelstam.

– Edward Lucie-Smith

FITZGERALD, Robert (Stuart). American. Born in Geneva, New York, 12 October 1910. Educated at Springfield High School, Illinois; Choate School, Wallingford, Connecticut; Harvard University, Cambridge, Massachusetts, 1929–31, 1932–33, A.B. 1933; Trinity College, Cambridge, 1931–32. Served in the United States Naval Reserve, 1943–46. Married Sarah Morgan in 1947; has six children. Reporter, New York *Herald-Tribune*, 1933–35; Staff Writer, *Time* magazine, 1936–40, 1941–43, 1946–49. Instructor, Sarah Lawrence College, Bronxville, New York, 1946–53, and Princeton University, New Jersey, 1950–52; Poetry Reviewer, *New Republic*, Washington, D.C., 1948–52. Lived in Italy, 1953–64. Visiting Professor, Notre Dame University, Indiana, 1957, University of Washington, Seattle, 1961, and Mount Holyoke College, South Hadley, Massachusetts, 1964. Since 1965, Boylston Professor of Rhetoric, Harvard University. Since 1951, Fellow, Indiana University School of Letters, Bloomington. Recipient: Midland Author's Prize (*Poetry*, Chicago), 1931; Guggenheim Fellowship, 1952, 1971; Shelley Memorial Award, 1956; National Institute of Arts and Letters grant, 1957; Ford grant, 1959; Bollingen Award, for translation, 1961; Bollingen Fellowship, 1965; National Endowment for the Arts grant, 1969, 1972; Ingram Merrill Foundation grant, 1973. D.Litt.: Holy Cross College, Worcester, Massachusetts, 1967. Member, National Institute of Arts and Letters, 1961; Member, American Academy of Arts and Sciences, 1962. Chancellor, Academy of American Poets, 1968. Address: 3 Warren House, Harvard University, Cambridge, Massachusetts 02138, U.S.A.

PUBLICATIONS

Verse

Poems. New York, Arrow Editions, 1935.
A Wreath for the Sea. New York, Arrow Editions, 1943.
In the Rose of Time: Poems 1931–1956. New York, New Directions, 1956.
Ombra di Primavera (bilingual edition). Milan, Edizioni del Triangolo, 1959.
Spring Shade: Poems 1931–1970. New York, New Directions, 1971.

Other

Editor, *The Aeneid of Virgil, Translated by John Dryden.* New York, Macmillan, 1965.
Editor, *The Collected Poems of James Agee.* Boston, Houghton Mifflin, 1968.
Editor, *The Collected Short Prose of James Agee.* Boston, Houghton Mifflin, 1968.
Editor, with Sally Fitzgerald, *Mystery and Manners: Occasional Prose,* by Flannery O'Connor. New York, Farrar Straus, 1969.

Translator, with Dudley Fitts, *Alcestis,* by Euripides. New York, Harcourt Brace, 1936.
Translator, with Dudley Fitts, *Antigone,* by Sophocles. New York, Harcourt Brace, 1939.
Translator, *Oedipus at Colonus,* by Sophocles. New York, Harcourt Brace, 1941; London, Faber, 1957.
Translator, with Dudley Fitts, *Oedipus Rex,* by Sophocles. New York, Harcourt Brace, 1949; London, Faber, 1950.

Translator, with Dudley Fitts, *The Oedipus Cycle.* New York, Harcourt Brace, 1958.

Translator, *Amphion, Semiramis,* and *The Narcissus Cantata,* in *Plays,* by Paul Valéry. New York, Pantheon Books, and London, Routledge, 1960.

Translator, *The Odyssey,* by Homer. New York, Doubleday, 1961; London, Heinemann, 1962.

Translator, *Chronique,* by St. John Perse. New York, Pantheon Books, 1961.

Translator, *Birds,* by St. John Perse. New York, Pantheon Books, 1965.

Translator, *Dante,* in *Two Addresses,* by St. John Perse. New York, Pantheon Books, 1966.

Translator, *Deathwatch on the Southside,* by Jorge Luis Borges. Cambridge, Massachusetts, Grolier Book Shop, 1968.

Translator, *The Little Passion: 37 Wood-cuts by Albrecht Dürer . . . with the Latin Poems of Benedictus Chelidonius . . . .* Verona, Italy, Officina Bodoni, 1971.

Translator, *The Iliad,* by Homer. New York, Doubleday, 1974.

Manuscript Collection: Houghton Library, Harvard University, Cambridge, Massachusetts.

Robert Fitzgerald comments:

I have been independent and trustful of my own powers. Poetry can be at least an elegance, at most a revelation, and I have worked as opportunity offered between these limits. Eliot was and remains a great touchstone and irritant. The Greek Masters have been before me often, and more lately so has Dante. I hold by constructive beauty, energy of language, depth of life.

*   *   *

Robert Fitzgerald's original poetry has probably not had the attention it deserves because (ironically) of his great distinction as a teacher and as a translator. Furthermore, as Donald Davidson wrote in reviewing his first book – one of, he claimed, "major" accent – Fitzgerald's "subject and form are minor."

As befits one of this century's finest translators of Greek in the English language, Fitzgerald's sense of form – best described as pliant rather than free – is highly developed. From the beginning his poems, whatever their scope, were word perfect, rhythmically impeccable. In an early poem "In This House," the enjambements already display a practised and craftsmanlike poet:

> In this house of the untidy lamp, a
> Man is leafing lexicons, his
> Limpid fingers in forgotten
> Brains. . . .
>
> Who dreamt he bedded with a whore
> 's face, body of a child. . . .

There is here already, too, a somewhat over-bookish, though never dry, quality, which has characterized all Fitzgerald's poetry. He is nothing if not a literary poet. However, and again in poetry of the first half of the Thirties, he anticipated many aspects of post-war poetry – aspects that were not to be confined to English poetry. Sometimes he is merely mannered (". . . Keenly / Clenching the eye push into bone wisp, see / How thick the shadow is, teems, is prodigious, / Stored with time . . .") but at others he is genuinely concerned with the interior of the mind – in a manner somewhat akin to that of the Swedish poet Ekelöf in his immediately post-surrealist "suicidal" phase of the mid-Thirties. Thus he could produce, before 1935, a line such as "Between dinner and death the crowds shadow the loom of steel" – and that this is "Park Avenue" (the title) does not diminish, but rather reinforces, the inner resonances.

Fitzgerald's post-war poetry became more rhetorical, more cultural (in the "American-in-Europe" sense), a little simpler: the poems are not perhaps as suggestive as the earlier, but the ear has remained as sure, and one is always in the presence of an elegant and educated sensibility. "The Painter" thus packs in much comment on its subject, and is as intellectually calculated as it is eloquent, as its opening stanza shows:

> On bluish inlets bristling
> Black in the tall north,
> Like violet ghosts risen
> The great fish swam forth,
> And hoary blooms and submarine
> Lightning in the cradling west
> Lent summer her vivid sheen
> For the deep eye's interest.

– Martin Seymour-Smith

FitzGERALD, Robert D(avid). Australian. Born in Hunters Hill, New South Wales, 22 February 1902. Educated at Sydney Grammar School; Sydney University, 1920–21; Fellow, Institution of Surveyors. Married Marjorie-Claire Harris in 1931; has four children. Surveyor, FitzGerald and Blair, 1926–30; Native Lands Commission Surveyor, Fiji, 1931–36; Municipal Surveyor, 1936–39; Surveyor, Australian Department of the Interior, 1939–65, now retired. Visiting Lecturer, University of Texas, Austin, 1963. Recipient: Australian Sesqui-Centenary Poetry Prize, 1938; Australian Literature Society Gold Medal, 1938; Grace Leven Prize, 1952, 1959, 1962; Fulbright grant, 1963; Encyclopedia Britannica Award, 1965. O.B.E. (Officer, Order of the British Empire), 1951. Address: 4 Prince Edward Parade, Hunters Hill, New South Wales 2110, Australia.

PUBLICATIONS

Verse

The Greater Apollo. Sydney, privately printed, 1927.
To Meet the Sun. Sydney, Angus and Robertson, 1929.
Moonlight Acre. Melbourne, Melbourne University Press, 1938.
Heemskerck Shoals. Melbourne, Mountainside Press, 1949.

Between Two Tides.   Sydney, Angus and Robertson, 1952.
This Night's Orbit: Verses.   Melbourne, Melbourne University Press, 1953.
The Wind at Your Door: A Poem.   Sydney, Talkarra Press, 1959.
Southmost Twelve.   Sydney, Angus and Robertson, 1962.
Of Some Country: 27 Poems.   Austin, University of Texas, 1963.
(Poems), selected and introduced by the author.   Sydney, Angus and Robert-
    son, 1963.
Forty Years' Poems.   Sydney, Angus and Robertson, 1965.

Other

The Elements of Poetry.   Brisbane, University of Queensland Press, 1963.

Editor, *Australian Poetry 1942.*   Sydney, Angus and Robertson, 1942.
Editor, *Selected Verse,* by Mary Gilmore.   Sydney and London, Angus and
    Robertson, 1948; revised edition, 1969.
Editor, *The Letters of Hugh McCrae.*   Sydney, Angus and Robertson, 1970.

Critical Studies: *Six Australian Poets* by T. Inglis Moore, Melbourne, Robertson and
Mullen, 1942; *Literature of Australia* edited by Geoffrey Dutton, Melbourne, Penguin, 1964; *Preoccupations in Australian Poetry* by Judith Wright, Melbourne, Oxford
University Press, 1965; *Robert D. FitzGerald* by A. Grove Day, New York, Twayne,
1973.

                         *   *   *

   The outstanding characteristics of Robert D. FitzGerald's poetry are his command of technique and, in Matthew Arnold's term, his "high seriousness." His
verse is plain, bare, without ornament and almost without adjectives, taking its life
from his vigorous individual speech rhythm and the controlled emotional intensity
of his thought; and his thought is concerned with Australia's national destiny in this
place

                       which lay, unleased,
            beneath its empty centuries and stars turning,
            . . . waking under his love;

with the aspiration that has taken mankind into far places and far thoughts and
achievements:

                the necessity in men, deep down, close cramped,
                not seen in their own hearts, for some attempt
                at being more than ordinary men,
                rising above themselves;

and ultimately, because both national destiny and worthwhile achievement depend
upon it, with human integrity:

Attitude matters: bearing. Action in the end
goes down the stream as motion, merges as such
with the whole of life and time; but islands stand:
dignity and distinction that attach
to the inmost being of us each.
It matters for man's private respect that still
face differs from face and will from will.

It is important how men looked and were.
Infirm, staggering a little as Hastings was,
his voice was steady as his eyes. Kneeling at the bar
(ruler but late of millions) had steeled his poise;
he fronted inescapable loss
and thrown, stinking malice and disrepute,
calmly, a plain man in a plain suit.

Though he has written many admirable short poems, from his early lyrical reflections on life and landscape set in Fiji (where he spent some years as a surveyor) to the more recent compact meditations in *Southmost Twelve,* his reputation rests chiefly on a number of medium-length and long poems. Among these, "The Hidden Bole" is a curious exploration of the banyan tree for the "hidden bole," the central principle hidden in the complexity of existence. "Essay on Memory," which won the poetry prize in the Australian sesqui-centenary competition, deals with the influence of the past in human history upon the present. "The Face of the Waters," unusually fluid in technique, is an extraordinary vision of the creation and perpetual recreation of the universe. *Between Two Tides,* a poem of book length, is an epic of tribal war in Tonga, by implication a commentary on power politics and corruption by power. And "Heemskerck Shoals" (about the navigator Abel Janszoon Tasman), "Fifth Day" (about the shorthand writer who recorded the trial of Warren Hastings), and "The Wind at Your Door" (about the convicts and their masters who were the first settlers of Australia) are poems of that middle length in which his powers of sustained thought and construction and the portrayal of character in action have reached their most impressive combination.

– Douglas Stewart

FLETCHER, Ian. British. Born in London, 22 August 1920. Educated at Dulwich College, London; Goldsmiths' College, University of London; University of Reading, Berkshire, Ph.D. 1965. Served in the Middle East in the Ministry of Information and Forces Broadcasting, 1942–46. Married Loraine Hollyman in 1965; has two children. Children's Librarian, Lewisham Borough Council, 1946–55. Since 1965, Reader in English Literature, University of Reading. Address: Faculty of Letters, The University, Whiteknights Park, Reading, Berkshire, England.

PUBLICATIONS

Verse

An Homily to Kenneth Topley.   Tripoli, privately printed, 1945.
Orisons, Picaresque and Metaphysical.   London, Editions Poetry, 1947.
The Lover's Martyrdom: Translations from the Italian of Dante, Guarini, Tasso, and
    Marino with Original Texts.   Oxford, Fantasy Press, 1957.
Motets: Twenty One Poems.   Reading, Berkshire, University of Reading, 1962.
The Milesian Intrusion: A Restoration Comedy Version of Iliad XIV.   Notting-
    ham, Byron Press, 1968.

Plays

A Passion Play.   Khartoum, Sudan Bookshop, 1943.
Get up What Stairs?, with Peter Myers (produced London, 1948).

Other

Partheneia Sacra.   Aldington, Kent, Hand and Flower Press, 1950.
Walter Pater.   London, Longman, 1959; revised edition, 1972.
A Catalogue of the Imagist Poets.   New York, J. H. Woolmer, 1966.
Beaumont and Fletcher.   London, Longman, 1967.
Swinburne.   London, Longman, 1972.

Editor, with G. S. Fraser, Springtime: An Anthology of Young Poets and
    Writers.   London, Peter Owen, 1953.
Editor, The Complete Poems of Lionel Johnson.   London, Unicorn Press, 1953.
Editor, Romantic Mythologies.   London, Routledge, and New York, Barnes and
    Noble, 1967.
Editor, Meredith Now.   London, Routledge, 1971.
Editor, Poems of Victor Plarr.   London, E. and J. Stevens, 1974.
Editor, Collected Poems of John Gray.   London, Cecil Woolf, 1974.

Manuscript Collections: University of Buffalo, New York; University of Kansas,
Lawrence; University of Reading, Berkshire.

Ian Fletcher comments:

Dualism; topographical and architectural topics; moderately strict verse forms.
Influence, Yeats; I like trying my hand at free translation. Syllabics need not apply.

*   *   *

Ian Fletcher was one of the most interesting poets to reach maturity during the
Forties, and some critics have expressed regret that he seems to have half-
abandoned his career – whether this is so or not, he has certainly published much
less in recent years. But some of this strongly-thewed and energetic later work

shows signs of a development towards a greater directness and increase in purely descriptive power. His early poems were highly involute, well-made, reflecting an intelligence engaged with problems of culture, often expressed in terms of the past, and with the significance of religious change. *The Maenad under the Cross*, the title of a projected volume that never appeared, aptly sums up his position. His best-known poem, "Adolescents in the Dusk" is the apogee of his earlier manner, and well illustrates his technical control, subtle use of metaphor, and the metaphysicality that underlies his pictorial imagination:

> About this time when dusk falls like a shutter
> Upon the decomposition of the time
> Eliding eye and day and surfaces and shapes,
> Whitening of faces like stoles in the twilight . . .
> When the gardens between the houses are rose –
> Encumbered with sidereal roses
> And the roads like gorges grey in the tired light of falling. . . .

The new poems are less involute, more confident, stronger in thrust – but they do not sacrifice the old subtlety. Fletcher was once a leading poet of his generation, and a serious one; it is to be hoped that current fashions will not obscure his earlier or his later achievement, and that he will be encouraged to put himself forward, once again, as the owner of a distinctive voice and manner.

– Martin Seymour-Smith

FORD, Charles Henri. American. Born in Hazlehurst, Mississippi, 10 February 1913. Lived in Paris in the 1920's. Editor, *Blues*, Columbus, Mississippi, 1929–30; *View*, New York, 1940–47. Photographer and Painter: One-Man Shows – Institute of Contemporary Arts, London, 1955; Galerie Marforen, Paris, 1956; Galerie du Dragon, Paris, 1957, 1958; Cordier and Ekstrom Gallery, New York, 1965; New York Cultural Center, 1975. Address: 1 West 72nd Street, New York, New York 10023, U.S.A.

PUBLICATIONS

Verse

A Pamphlet of Sonnets. Mallorca, Caravel Press, 1936.
The Garden of Disorder and Other Poems. New York, New Directions, and London, Europa, 1938.
ABC's. Prairie City, Illinois, Press of James A. Decker, 1940.
The Overturned Lake. Cincinnati, Little Man Press, 1941.
Poems for Painters. New York, View, 1945.
The Half-Thoughts, The Distances of Pain. New York, Gotham Bookmart, 1947.
Sleep in a Nest of Flames. New York, New Directions, 1949.

Spare Parts. New York, New View Books, 1966.
Silver Flower Coo. New York, Kulchur Press, 1968.
Flag of Ecstasy: Selected Poems, edited by Edward B. Germain. Los Angeles,
Black Sparrow Press, 1972.

Play

Screenplay: *Johnny Minotaur,* 1971.

Novel

The Young and Evil, with Parker Tyler. Paris, Obelisk Press, 1933.

Other

Editor and Translator, *Mirror for Baudelaire.* New York, New Directions,
1942.
Editor, *A Night with Jupiter and Other Fantastic Stories.* New York, New
Directions, 1945; London, Dobson, 1947.

Manuscript Collection: University of Texas, Austin.

Critical Studies: Introduction by William Carlos Williams to *The Garden of Disorder
and Other Poems,* 1938; Introduction by Edith Sitwell to *Sleep in a Nest of Flames,*
1949.

                            *   *   *

When he began publishing in 1929, Charles Henri Ford was unique: America's
surrealist poet. In retrospect, he is seminal. His first two books create American
surrealism. *Garden of Disorder* welds together radio jazz and iambic pentameter,
surrealist conceits and the sonnet form. *The Overturned Lake* shows Ford as
influenced by Whitman, Poe, and Mother Goose as by Breton, Reverdy, and
Eluard, employing a freer line and lyric forms. It demonstrates Ford's forte: the
surrealist image. In one poem, Ford transforms the day from a poem into a horse.
He turns the sky into an arm, a mouth, a man, a thief, and then into an enormous
face. The sun, he makes into a wound, a jewel, an equation, an eye, a tear. Night
is a ditch. All in eight lines, with obvious ease, and clarity.
    The "New York School" centered around Frank O'Hara and John Ashbery owes
something to these early surrealist lyrics. During World War II, Ford encouraged
young poets, like Philip Lamantia, in the pages of his influential surrealist magazine, *View* – the first literary magazine to publish Allen Ginsberg. Ford himself
began writing longer poems at this time, typically part dream or ghost-story, part
amoral allegory, filled with convulsive imagery and sexual themes. Often parts of
these poems are greater than their whole. The self-conscious mannerism implicit in
many of them surfaces in Ford's next two books, *Spare Parts* and *Silver Flower
Coo,* collage poems which are exercises in gratuitous eroticism. Another, far more

interesting series, written but not published during this period, are Ford's prose-poems and found-poetry, represented in the "Drawings" section of his selected poems.

Ford's best work lies predominantly with the rather narrow lyric form in his early books. Some of these poems, "Plaint," for example, are among the most evocative and moving short lyrics of our century. In most, Ford creates wonder, wit, and a sensuous beauty free from the predictable tropes and rapacious glibness of much surrealist-influenced poetry of the 1960's and 1970's.

                                                                                    – Edward B. Germain

---

FORD, R(obert) A(rthur) D(ouglass). Canadian. Born in Ottawa, Ontario, 8 January 1915. Educated at the University of Western Ontario, London, B.A. 1937; Cornell University, Ithaca, New York, M.A. 1940. Married Maria Thereza Gomes in 1946. Member of the History Department, Cornell University, 1938–40. Joined the Canadian Department of External Affairs, 1940: served in Rio de Janeiro, Moscow, and London, 1940–51; Head of the European Division, Ottawa, 1954–57; Ambassador to Columbia, 1957–58, to Yugoslavia, 1959–61, and to the United Arab Republic, 1961–63. Since 1964, Canadian Ambassador to the Soviet Union. Recipient: Governor-General's Medal, 1957. D.Litt.: University of Western Ontario, 1965. Companion of Order of Canada, 1971. Address: Canadian Embassy, Moscow, U.S.S.R.

PUBLICATIONS

Verse

A Window on the North. Toronto, Ryerson Press, 1956.
The Solitary City. Toronto, McClelland and Stewart, 1969.

*   *   *

The poetic canon of R. A. D. Ford is relatively small: two slender volumes (which include a number of translations). Although separated by thirteen years, his books share similar themes and techniques; one clear voice emerges. These are quiet, serious poems, lyric rather than dramatic, but always restrained. They explore around the edges of emotion, seldom taking risks. They offer little irony, less of the comic, very few surprises. And yet they are nearly all worth reading – consistently competent, sincere, quietly rewarding.

A sense of isolation pervades Ford's poems, whether in the loneliness of open spaces or the equally barren "landscape of the past." Also regularly present – especially in his first volume, A Window on the North – is an oppressive sense of the Cold, silently "smothering the world," pressing into rooms and lives, invading

The sanctity of man propped lone on
The plain edge of winter, not
Day but the dull half white dawn
Of the never-ending snow night . . . .

For the most part Ford's poetry is marked by clear statement and traditional meters. He sometimes employs rhyme effectively (as in "Avoiding Greece"), but usually when rhyme is present, too much else appears sacrificed to it. This intrusion of technique is, somewhat surprisingly, more common in *A Solitary City* than in his first book. Fortunately, he avoids rhyme in most of his poems, and the best of his later work demonstrates a growing freedon from form and a more successful, more believably earned realization of experience (as in "The Thieves of Love" and "How Doth the Solitary City Stand").

Ford's translations deserve special note, for they demonstrate both fidelity to the spirit of the originals and a view of Ford's abilities that remain hidden behind self-imposed restraints in much of his own poetry. The quality of the translations and adaptations appears consistently high, and the range of his interests (from the Russian of Pasternak, Akhmatova, Yessenin, and others, to Brazilian Portuguese, French, and Serbo-Croatian) is in itself inpressive. Together they reinforce the impression one has from Ford's own poems, that the deeply quiet, unpretentious voice of R. A. D. Ford is one worth hearing.

– Stanley W. Lindberg

FOWLER, Gene. American. Born in Oakland, California, 5 October 1931. High school education. Served in the United States Army, three years. Served five years in San Quentin Prison. Poet-in-Residence, University of Wisconsin, Milwaukee, Summer 1970. Recipient: National Endowment for the Arts grant, 1966, 1969, 1970. Address: 1321 19th Avenue, San Francisco, California 94122, U.S.A.

PUBLICATIONS

Verse

Field Studies.   El Cerrito, California, Dustbooks, 1965.
Quarter Tones.   Grande Ronde, Oregon, GRR Press, 1966.
Shaman Songs.   El Cerrito, California, Dustbooks, 1967.
Her Majesty's Ship.   Sacramento, California, Grande Ronde Press, 1969.
*Fires.   Berkeley, California, Thorp Springs Press, 1971.
Vivisection.   Berkeley, California, Thorp Springs Press, 1974.
Collected Poems, 1963–1973.   Berkeley, California, Thorp Springs Press, 1974.

Novel

Lady Scatterly's Lovers, edited by H. Allen Smith.   Secaucus, New Jersey, Lyle Stuart, 1973.

Critical Study: by James K. Bell, in *Eikon* (Ogunquit, Maine), i, 1, 1967.

Gene Fowler comments:

There are no "positions" for non-academic poets. Officially, I am illiterate. Not qualified to teach the use of language, existing literature or other such.

I am not and have never been a member of a school of poetry – though reviewers have tried to stuff me into one or another. I battle against such entities.

Whitman wrote critical analysis of his own work – but under other names. I've done what amounts to c. a. in letters. But, here, I'll say only what I believe I'm up to. I want to write poems that when recalled are confused with the reader's own experiences, not recalled – at first – as "something read" but as "something that happened." Fighting against myth perpetuated by both outlaws and academics that craft is the same thing as academic tone. I take the Orphic myth literally. Believe words can induce and manipulate perceptions. Intend, in my poems, to prove this.

*   *   *

Gene Fowler is a contemporary symbolist, a maker of surprising equations. In poems like "The Lover," these equations develop dramatically, become revelations; the body of the beloved is the earth. "The Words" is a little allegory about writing:

> I carry boulders across the day
> From the field to the ridge,
> And my back grows tired . . .
> I take a drop of sweat
> Onto my thumb,
> Watch the wind furrow its surface,
> Dream of a morning
> When my furrows will shape this field,
> When these rocks will form my house.
> Alone, with heavy arms,
> I listen through the night to older farms.

Unlike Creeley, who has a collection titled *Words*, Fowler finds writing a heavy labor. His rhythms, in poems like "Venus Returns to the Sea," are heavy (though that is not a literal deduction from a symbolic equation). What happens to words transmuted into poems? They grow hot, like coals or fires:

> i come upon stones
> in the wind shoved grasses
>
> they wait
> tensed
> curled in on themselves
>
> i reach out to touch
> sun warmed quiet and flame
> jumps to scorch my fingers.

Fowler's first major collection is called *Fires*. The symbols are systematically deployed. "Shaman Songs," collected in *Fires* (though mangled by the publisher), compares society to an Indian tribe and the poet to a neglected shaman. The songs rise above symbol and allegory to ritual and magic, as in "on taking coal from the fire in naked fingers":

The word
is in the hand.
Under the moon
in the hand.
At the head of the valley
in the hand.
It glows in the hand.
Here!
Look here
in the hand.
Look at the word
in the hand.
It glows.
A great translucence
in the hand.
Go thru the translucence
in the hand.
Into the world
in the hand.

– Michael André

FRAME, Janet. New Zealander. Born in Dunedin, 28 August 1924. Educated at Oamaru North School; Waitaki Girls' High School; Otago University Teachers Training College, Dunedin. Recipient: Church Memorial Award, 1951, 1954; New Zealand Literary Fund Award, 1960; New Zealand Scholarship in Letters, 1964; Robert Burns Fellowship, Otago University, 1965. Address: c/o Brandt and Brandt, 101 Park Avenue, New York, New York 10017, U.S.A.

PUBLICATIONS

Verse

The Pocket Mirror: Poems. New York, Braziller, and London, W. H. Allen, 1967.

Novels

Owls Do Cry. Christchurch, Pegasus Press, 1957; New York, Braziller, 1960; London, W. H. Allen, 1961.
Faces in the Water. Christchurch, Pegasus Press, and New York, Braziller, 1961; London, W. H. Allen, 1962.
The Edge of the Alphabet. Christchurch, Pegasus Press, New York, Braziller, and London, W. H. Allen, 1962.

Scented Gardens for the Blind. Christchurch, Pegasus Press, and London, W. H. Allen, 1963; New York, Braziller, 1964.

The Adaptable Man. Christchurch, Pegasus Press, New York, Braziller, and London, W. H. Allen, 1965.

A State of Siege. New York, Braziller, 1966; London, W. H. Allen, 1967.

The Rainbirds. London, W. H. Allen, 1968; as *Yellow Flowers in the Antipodean Room*, New York, Braziller, 1969.

Intensive Care. New York, Braziller, 1970; London, W. H. Allen, 1971.

Daughter Buffalo. New York, Braziller, 1972; London, W. H. Allen, 1973.

Short Stories

The Lagoon: Stories. Christchurch, Pegasus Press, 1951; revised edition, as *The Lagoon and Other Stories*, 1961.

The Reservoir: Stories and Sketches. New York, Braziller, 1963.

Snowman, Snowman: Fables and Fantasies. New York, Braziller, 1963.

The Reservoir and Other Stories. Christchurch, Pegasus Press, and London, W. H. Allen, 1966.

Other

Mona Minim and the Smell of the Sun (juvenile). New York, Braziller, 1969.

*   *   *

Janet Frame is best known as a novelist. She has published only one collection of poems – *The Pocket Mirror*. It has the appearance, not of a nervous slim volume of carefully selected, carefully worked samples of the writer's best, but of a file of poems, each hastily written and quickly forgotten, taken up and sent to the publisher without revision, perhaps to be rid of them. All their strengths and limitations depend on the casual indifference with which they have been written. Janet Frame is not indifferent to her subject matter but to the art of poetry itself. She is also immensely talented, endlessly inventive, fluent, and has a good ear. Her natural mode of thinking is not abstract but in images. So her poems are mostly "thoughts," "ideas," put down in the form of free verse. Their weakness is often that they are neither fish nor fowl – too abstract for the images to seem solid, hard, irreducible reality; and not rigorous enough to seem more than whimsical when considered as ideas. They are also a kind of verbal conjuring, the images conjured into being as an illustration of her thought rather than convincingly confronted in nature. Thus Miss Frame has primacy over Nature, which seems the wrong way about.

But Miss Frame has the enviable freedom of a talented writer not wholly committed to poetry. To compare her with another New Zealand woman poet, Fleur Adcock, is instructive. There can be no doubt that Miss Adcock's poems are better made – yet her work can seem crabbed and cramped when set alongside the novelist's casual fluency, which can afford so many misses and still score enough remarkable hits to make her presence as a poet felt.

– C. K. Stead

FRANCIS, Robert (Churchill). American. Born in Upland, Pennsylvania, 12 August 1901. Educated at Harvard University, Cambridge, Massachusetts, A.B. 1923, Ed.M. 1926. Phi Beta Kappa Poet, Tufts University, Medford, Massachusetts, 1955, and Harvard University, 1960. Recipient: Shelley Memorial Award, 1939; New England Poetry Club Golden Rose, 1942; American Academy in Rome Fellowship, 1957; Jennie Tane Award (*Massachusetts Review*), 1962; Amy Lowell Traveling Scholarship, 1967. L.H.D.: University of Massachusetts, Amherst, 1970. Address: Fort Juniper, 170 Market Hill Road, Amherst, Massachusetts 01002, U.S.A.

PUBLICATIONS

Verse

   Stand with Me Here. New York, Macmillan, 1936.
   Valhalla and Other Poems. New York, Macmillan, 1938.
   The Sound I Listened For. New York, Macmillan, 1944.
   The Face Against the Glass. Amherst, Massachusetts, privately printed, 1950.
   The Orb Weaver: Poems. Middletown, Connecticut, Wesleyan University
      Press, 1960.
   Come Out into the Sun: Poems New and Selected. Amherst, University of
      Massachusetts Press, 1965.
   Like Ghosts of Eagles. Amherst, University of Massachusetts Press, 1974.

   Recording: *Today's Poets 1*, with others, Folkways, 1967.

Novel

   We Fly Away. New York, Swallow-Morrow, 1948.

Other

   The Satirical Rogue on Poetry (essays). Amherst, University of Massachusetts
      Press, 1968.
   The Trouble with Francis: An Autobiography. Amherst, University of Massa-
      chusetts Press, 1971.
   Frost: A Time to Talk: Conversations and Indiscretions. Amherst, University of
      Massachusetts Press, 1972; London, Robson Books, 1973.

Critical Studies: "Constants Carried Forward: Naturalness in the Poetry of Robert Francis" by John Holmes, in *Massachusetts Review* (Amherst), Summer 1960; by Albert Stewart, in *Masterplots: 1967 Annual*, New York, Salem Press, 1967.

Robert Francis comments:

   Neither avant-garde nor traditional. Less and less dependence on accepted forms while stressing form itself, the forming of the poem. Early poems, quiet and brooding; later poems, more active and colorful. During the 60's some poems in a new technique I call "word-count." Still more recently poems that explore surface fragmentation to intensify impact of total poem.

                                    *   *   *

Robert Francis is a balanced poet, both in art and sensibility. Although his rhythms are variable, his rhyming flexible, his language fresh, and his world an out-of-doors and immediate universe, his poems are carefully structured, often too carefully structured. And, although his outlook is mature and in some ways profound, it is more placid and complacent than intense and compelling. Each poem is a serene process of unfolding rather than a shocking flash of revelation, suffering from a kind of overdevelopment which is caused by excessive explicitness in dealing with the material and drawing out its meaning. And this in turn, paradoxically, seems to be the effect of a certain limitation of insight, as if over-explicitness were a compensation for deficiency of vision and passionate involvement. He is objective and impersonal, not in the Shakespearian or Keatsian or Yeatsian or Eliotic senses, but rather in the sense of being simply an observer – acute, perceptive, witty, but with neither an anguished self that must wrestle with experience nor an empathy for the anguish of others.

The first section of *The Orb Weaver*, for example, deals largely with skill and the analogies the poet sees between various bodily skills and those of art. He writes about boys riding horses, baseball players, wrestlers, divers, swimmers, and so on. And his interest lies in the tension of balance that such skills must sustain between opposing forces. And yet, as in "Two Wrestlers," all is too perfectly balanced and worked out; he at once says too much and implies too little.

The second section is mainly about Nature – her fruits, her seasons, mountains, creatures, and so on. These are good poems, and they speak movingly of fulness. "Waxwings," for example, depends more for its effect on imagery and less on explanation than usual:

> Four Tao philosophers as cedar waxwings
> chat on a February berry-bush
> in sun, and I am one.

Section III is primarily concerned with the relation of people to Nature. "The Revelers" is one of the most effective, portraying crowds joyously enthralled by summer, and so is reminiscent of Stevens' "Sunday Morning" and "Credences of Summer," but it is, alas, almost entirely without the greater poet's depth and intensity.

The fourth section gets darker, dwelling more on the side of night and winter, and the stanza-patterns get more regular, perhaps as a sign of the need to control a deepening mood. "Three Darks Come Down Together" is quite good.

The fifth and final section is darker still, dealing with death, winter, and loss. Robert Frost is a strong influence, and this becomes most specific in the title poem, "The Orb Weaver," which is about a ghastly spider much like the one in Frost's "Design." A reading of Francis' conclusion, however, will not sustain the comparison:

> I have no quarrel with the spider
> But with the mind or mood that made her
> To thrive in nature and in man's nature.

"Two Bums Walk Out of Eden," though, is interesting, and "Cold," which describes a freeze, is excellent:

> Under the glaring and sardonic sun,
> Behind the icicles and double glass,
> I huddle, hoard, hold out, hold on, hold on.

– Norman Friedman

FRASER, G(eorge) S(utherland).   British.   Born in Glasgow, Scotland, 8 November 1915. Educated at Glasgow Academy; Aberdeen Grammar School; St. Andrews University, M.A. 1937. Served in the Middle East, 1939–45. Married Eileen Lucy Andrew in 1946; has two daughters and one son. Journalist, Aberdeen *Press and Journal*, 1937–39. Free-lance Journalist, 1946–59. Cultural Adviser to the UK Liaison Mission in Japan, 1950–51. Regular Reviewer and Leaderwriter, *Times Literary Supplement*, London. Reviewer, *New Statesman*, London, and "New Poetry" broadcaster on BBC radio, in the 1950's. Lecturer, 1959–63, and since 1964, Reader in Modern English Literature, University of Leicester. Visiting Professor, Rochester University, New York, 1963–64. Recipient: Hodder and Stoughton bursary, 1946. Address: 19 Guilford Road, Stoneygate, Leicester, England.

PUBLICATIONS

Verse

> *The Fatal Landscape and Other Poems.*   London, Editions Poetry, 1943.
> *Home Town Elegy.*   London, Editions Poetry, 1944.
> *The Traveller Has Regrets and Other Poems.*   London, Harvill Press-Editions Poetry, 1948.
> *Leaves Without a Tree.*   Tokyo, Hokuseido Press, 1956.
> *Conditions: Selected Recent Poetry.*   Nottingham, Byron Press, 1969.

Other

> *Vision of Scotland.*   London, Elek, 1948.
> *News from South America* (travel).   London, Harvill Press, 1949; New York, Library Publishers, 1952.
> *Post-War Trends in English Literature.*   Tokyo, Hokuseido Press, 1950.
> *The Modern Writer and His World.*   London, Verschoyle, 1953; New York, Criterion Books, 1955; revised edition, London, Deutsch, 1964; New York, Praeger, 1965.
> *W. B. Yeats.*   London, Longman, 1954; revised edition, 1962.
> *Scotland.*   London, Thames and Hudson, and New York, Studio Publications, 1955.
> *Dylan Thomas.*   London, Longman, 1957; revised edition, 1964.

Vision and Rhetoric: Studies in Modern Poetry. London, Faber, 1959; New York, Barnes and Noble, 1960.

Ezra Pound. Edinburgh, Oliver and Boyd, 1960; New York, Grove Press, 1961.

Lawrence Durrell: A Study. London, Faber, 1968; New York, Dutton, 1969.

Lawrence Durrell. London, Longman, 1970.

Metre, Rhythm, and Free Verse. London, Methuen, 1970.

Editor, with J. Waller, *The Collected Poems of Keith Douglas.* London, Editions Poetry, 1951; revised edition, with J. Waller and J. C. Hall, London, Faber, 1966; New York, Chilmark Press, 1967.

Editor, with Ian Fletcher, *Springtime: An Anthology of Young Poets and Writers.* London, Peter Owen, 1953.

Editor, *Poetry Now: An Anthology.* London, Faber, 1956.

Editor, *Selected Poems of Robert Burns.* London, Heinemann, and New York, Macmillan, 1960.

Editor, *Vaughan College Poems.* Leicester, University of Leicester, 1963.

Editor, with J. Waller and J. C. Hall, *Alamein to Zem Zem,* by Keith Douglas. London, Faber, 1966; New York, Chilmark Press, 1967.

Editor, with others, *Workshop 8* (London), 1969.

Translator, *The Dedicated Life in Poetry, and The Correspondence of Laurent de Cayeux,* by Patrice de la Tour du Pin. London, Harvill Press, 1948.

Translator, *The Mystery of Being,* by Gabriel Marcel. London, Harvill Press, 1950.

Translator, *Men Against Humanity,* by Gabriel Marcel. London, Harvill Press, 1952.

Translator, *Pascal: His Life and Works,* by Jean Mesnard. London, Harvill Press, 1952.

Translator, with E. de Mauny, *Béla Bartók,* by S. Moreux. London, Harvill Press, 1953.

Translator, with others, *Dante's Inferno.* London, BBC Publications, 1966.

Critical Studies: in *Times Literary Supplement* (London), 1944; *Poetry in Our Time* by Babette Deutsch, New York Doubleday, 1963.

G. S. Fraser comments:

[Poetry is] my main gift. But to earn a living I became first a literary journalist, then a university teacher, and now teaching, especially the teaching of poetry, has become as true a vocation as writing poetry. . . . Like many Scottish poets I am old-fashioned in my taste for strict metrics and explicit poetic statement.

I think my best poems have been, in a sense, "occasional," responses to particular scenes and situations (Egypt in the second World War) of a partly reflective, partly descriptive kind. The feelings tend to be subjective and personal and for that very reason I usually need a strict form and a clear pattern of statement. Lately I have become much more experimental, particularly in the use of unrhymed syllabic verse. I am very conscious of the poem as something to be read aloud, though not in an over-dramatic manner. I worry most about the true modulation of feeling in verse. I am a rather intermittent writer, never trying to "force" a poem. I think my productivity was cut down a great deal in the 1950's and after, first by reviewing much current verse, later by teaching students to appreciate great poetry: I have grown more and more fastidious about my own poems, though not in the least dispirited about the best of them. I have thought of myself as a rather forgotten poet, but have been pleased in recent years to find that many people know some of my poems and that students seem to respond to them.

*   *   *

G. S. Fraser first appeared in the rather strange company of the writers of that Second World War movement which called itself "The New Apocalypse." There was nothing remarkable about this association, since during the early 1940's the New Apocalyptics virtually dominated the poetry-magazine scene. Yet Fraser's work stood out from that of other members of the group by virtue of its elegant clarity, qualities appropriate to one on whom the influence of Yeats was apparent.

In his early work, much of it written while he was serving in the Middle East, he captured with great delicacy the innocent sensuousness of youth; the sharpness of its pangs, whether of joy or sorrow; above all, its evanesence. So, from Egypt, he remembers aspects of his native Aberdeen:

> I think of the glitter of granite and distances
> And against the blue air the lovely and bare trees,
> And slippery pavements spangled with delight
> Under the needles of a winter's night,
> And I remember the dances, with scarf and care,
> Strolling home in the cold with the silly refrain
> Of a tune by Cole Porter or Irving Berlin
> Warming a naughty memory up like gin,
> And Bunny and Sheila and Joyce and Rosemary
> Chattering on sofas or preparing tea,
> With delicate voices and their small white hands.
> This is the sorrow everyone understands
> More than Rostov's artillery . . . .

But it is also a sorrow which, in Fraser's case, related not only to the down on the cheeks of college-girls, but to Scotland and, in particular, to less pleasing qualities met with in his native city:

> Here, where the baby paddles in the gutter,
>   Here, in the slaty greyness and the gas,
> Here, where the women wear dark shawls and mutter
>   A hasty word as other women pass.
>
> Telling the secret, telling, clucking and tutting
>   Sighing, or saying that it served her right,
> The bitch! – the words and weather both are cutting
>   In Causewayend, on this November night.

Fraser became an expatriate, not only from his own country – a parting from the sense of people which he celebrates with the movingly beautiful lyric "The Traveller Has Regrets," a remarkable technical achievement in that it consists of one long, musical sentence – but, as everybody must, from the sharp edges of his youth.

His most recent volume, *Conditions,* widens his range to take in the philosophical preoccupations of middle life, the cynicism of ideals bent back upon themselves, as in "The Insane Philosophers" and "On the Persistence of Humanity." But it is these poems using his familiar technique of building up detail, layer upon layer, sometimes with the odd colloquial Byronic rhyme, conserving the whole ambience of an age-group, that he is at his most successful. One such poem is "For Tilly, Sick, with Love":

> People don't give such parties now. The young men
> > are
> Busy with social do-gooding or class
> > self-importance:
> More on the make than we were, if all were told.

Elegiac sadness is one of life's universal experiences. It has rarely been captured as gracefully or as gently as it is in one of the best of Fraser's later poems, "Autumnal Elegy":

> These are the words that moved us long ago
> And now like smiles through smoke in public-houses
> Can reassure us of a warmth we know.

They are the words, too, of a poet who a quarter of a century earlier made plain a standpoint, from which he has never departed, either in his criticism or in his poetry:

> What a race has is always crude and common,
> > And not the human or the personal:
> I would take sword up only for the human,
> > Not to revive the broken ghosts of Gael.

– Maurice Lindsay

FRY, Christopher. British. Born in Bristol, 18 December 1907. Educated at Bedford Modern School, 1918–26. Served in the Non-Combatant Corps, 1940–44. Married Phyllis Marjorie Hart in 1936; has one son. Teacher, Bedford Froebel Kindergarten, 1926–27; Actor and Office Worker, Citizen House, Bath, 1927; Schoolmaster, Hazelwood School, Limpsfield, Surrey, 1928–31; Secretary to H. Rodney Bennett, 1931–32; Founding Director, Tunbridge Wells Repertory Players, 1932–35; Lecturer and editor of schools magazine, Dr. Barnardo's Homes, 1934–39; Director, 1939–40, and Visiting Director, 1945–46, Oxford Playhouse; Visiting Director, 1946, and Staff Dramatist, 1947, Arts Theatre Club, London. Recipient: Shaw Prize Fund Award, 1948; Foyle Poetry Prize, 1951; New York Drama Critics Circle Award, 1951, 1952, 1956; Queen's Gold Medal for Poetry, 1962; Heinemann Award, 1962. Fellow, Royal Society of Literature. Agent: ACTAC Ltd., 16 Cadogan Lane, London S.W.1. Address: The Toft, East Dean, near Chichester, Sussex, England.

PUBLICATIONS

Plays

To Sea in a Sieve (as Christopher Harris) (produced Reading, 1935).

She Shall Have Music, with F. Eyton and M. Crick (produced London, 1935).

Open Door (produced London, 1936). Goldings, Hertfordshire, Printed by the Boys at the Press of Dr. Barnardo's Homes, n.d.

The Boy with a Cart: Cuthman, Saint of Sussex (produced Coleman's Hatch, Sussex, 1938; London, 1950; New York, 1953). London, Oxford University Press, 1939; New York, Oxford University Press, 1951.

The Tower (pageant; produced Tewkesbury, Gloucestershire, 1939).

Thursday's Child: A Pageant, music by Martin Shaw (produced London, 1939). London, Girls' Friendly Society, 1939.

A Phoenix Too Frequent (produced London, 1946; Cambridge, Massachusetts, 1948; New York, 1950). London, Hollis and Carter, 1946; New York, Oxford University Press, 1949.

The Firstborn (produced Edinburgh, 1948). Cambridge, University Press, 1946; New York, Oxford University Press, 1950; revised version (produced London, 1952; New York, 1958), London and New York, Oxford University Press, 1952, 1958.

The Lady's Not for Burning (produced London, 1948; New York, 1950). London and New York, Oxford University Press, 1949; revised version, 1950, 1958.

Thor, With Angels (produced Canterbury, 1948; Washington, D.C., 1950; London, 1952). Canterbury, H. J. Goulden, 1948; New York, Oxford University Press, 1949.

Venus Observed (produced London, 1950; New York, 1952). London and New York, Oxford University Press, 1950.

Ring round the Moon: A Charade with Music, adaptation of a play by Jean Anouilh (produced London and New York, 1950). London and New York, Oxford University Press, 1950.

A Sleep of Prisoners (produced Oxford, London and New York, 1951). London and New York, Oxford University Press, 1951.

The Dark Is Light Enough: A Winter Comedy (produced London, 1954; New York, 1955). London and New York, Oxford University Press, 1954.

The Lark, adaptation of a play by Jean Anouilh (produced London, 1955). London, Methuen, 1955; New York, Oxford University Press, 1956.

Tiger at the Gates, adaptation of a play by Jean Giraudoux (produced London and New York, 1955). London, Methuen, 1955; New York, Oxford University Press, 1956.

Duel of Angels, adaptation of a play by Jean Giraudoux (produced London, 1958; New York, 1960). London, Methuen, 1958; New York, Oxford University Press, 1959.

Curtmantle (produced Tilburg, Holland, 1961; London, 1962). London and New York, Oxford University Press, 1961.

Judith, adaptation of a play by Jean Giraudoux (produced London, 1962). London, Methuen, 1962.

The Bible: Original Screenplay, assisted by Jonathan Griffin. New York, Pocket Books, 1966.

Peer Gynt, adaptation of the play by Ibsen (produced Chichester, 1970). London and New York, Oxford University Press, 1970.

A Yard of Sun: A Summer Comedy (produced Nottingham and London, 1970). London and New York, Oxford University Press, 1970.

The Brontes of Haworth (televised, 1973). London, Davis Poynter, 2 vols., 1974.

Screenplays: *The Beggar's Opera,* 1953; *The Queen Is Crowned* (documentary), 1953; *Ben Hur,* 1959; *Barabbas,* 1962; *The Bible: In the Beginning,* 1966.

Radio Plays: for *Children's Hour* series, 1939–40.

Television Plays: *The Canary,* 1950; *The Tenant of Wildfell Hall,* 1968; *The Brontës of Haworth* (four plays), 1973.

Other

An *Experience of Critics,* with *The Approach to Dramatic Criticism* by W. A. Darlington and others. London, Perpetua Press, 1952; New York, Oxford University Press, 1953.
The Boat That Mooed (juvenile). New York, Macmillan, 1966.

Translator, *The Boy and the Magic,* by Colette. London, Dobson, 1964.

Bibliography: in *Tulane Drama Review* (New Orleans), March 1960.

Critical Studies: *Christopher Fry* by Derek Stanford, London, Longman, 1954; *The Drama of Comedy: Victim and Victor* by Nelson Vos, Richmond, Virginia, John Knox Press, 1965; *Creed and Drama* by W. M. Merchant, London, SPCK, 1965; *The Christian Tradition in Modern Verse Drama* by William V. Spanos, New Brunswick, New Jersey, Rutgers University Press, 1967; *Christopher Fry: A Critical Essay* by Stanley M. Wiersma, Grand Rapids, Michigan, Eerdmans, 1970.

Theatrical Activities:

Director: **Plays** – *How-Do, Princess?* by Ivor Novello, toured, 1936; *The Circle of Chalk* by James Laver, London, 1945; *The School for Scandal* by Sheridan, London, 1946; *A Phoenix Too Frequent,* Brighton, 1950; *The Lady's Not for Burning,* toured, 1971.

Actor: **Plays** – in repertory, Bath, 1937.

Christopher Fry comments:

Influences are difficult to pin-point. Certainly, as it must be with anyone of my generation, T. S. Eliot was a releasing factor. In the plays I have tried to work towards an end which I broadly expressed in a lecture: "No event is understandable in a prose sense alone. Its ultimate meaning (that is to say, the complete life of the event, seen in its eternal context) is a poetic meaning." I have tried to shape a verse form (a metrical system) which could contain both the "theatrical" elements (rhetoric, broad colours, etc.) and the rhythms and tone of the colloquial, which would work for the "artificial comedy," or the historical, or the conversation of the present time.

*   *   *

It was Christopher Fry (and, later, T. S. Eliot) who led the short revival of interest in the poetic drama during the decade or so after the second world war – an interest which now seems completely dead. *A Phoenix Too Frequent,* an imperfect sentimental farce, attracted some attention in 1946; and with *The Lady's Not for Burning* Fry captured the imagination of the critics, and of a potentially large audience. The most obviously brilliant of Fry's plays, it was fortunate in an impeccable production by John Gielgud, and a fine cast, headed by Pamela Brown, Claire Bloom, Richard Burton and Gielgud himself. Its amusing plot and the natural yet highly decorated language, finely characterised and supremely dramatic (Fry himself was for some time an actor), were a revelation after the dryness and aridity of the language of wartime drama. Over-succulent on the page, the verse (especially when delivered in the romantic style of acting still predominant in the late 1940's) seemed irresistible in performance.

But as Fry's technical assurance grew, so critical and public interest waned. *Venus Observed,* written for Laurence Olivier, was a critical and to some extent public failure; a graver comedy of autumn, its language was more disciplined and restrained, still often witty, but quieter and without the obvious verbal fireworks of its predecessor. In *A Sleep of Prisoners,* perhaps his most entirely successful piece, Fry turned to wholly serious matters, and most obviously to his perennial theme of "the growth of vision: the increased perception of what makes for life and what makes for death." Prisoners-of-war penned up in a Church explore each other's personalities in their dreams. It is a moving and totally realised poetic drama. *The Dark Is Light Enough,* a winter play based on Fabre's parable of the butterfly making its way through storm and profound darkness to arrive brightly inviolate at its destination, was written for Edith Evans and staged in 1954. It was disliked both by critics and by the public. Since its production Fry has concentrated for the most part on translation (from Anouilh and Giraudoux, for instance) and film scripting. He has, however, written a play which completes the quartet of plays of the seasons – a comedy of high summer.

His place in the theatre is perhaps ephemeral; he has been compared, damagingly, to the Victorian poetic dramatist Stephen Phillips, whose *Paolo and Francesca* seemed at the turn of the century to be a masterpiece, but is now almost totally forgotten. The comparison seems unfair; Fry is more accomplished both as poet and dramatist than Phillips. His language is, on the page, overblown, and seems lacking in muscle and discipline. But in performance it is always amusing and dramatically viable; and its sentiment is at worst harmlessly touching. It is strange now to remember that many critics found Fry "difficult" in the 1940's and 50's. Whatever he is, he is not that. Accused of over-writing ("Too many words!") Fry replied (in *An Experience of Critics,* 1952): "It means, I think, that I don't use the same words often enough; or else, or as well, that the words are an ornament on the meaning and not the meaning itself. That is certainly sometimes – perhaps often – true in the comedies, though almost as often I have meant the ornament to be, dramatically or comedically, an essential part of the meaning; and in my more sanguine moments I think the words are as exact to my purpose as I could make them at the time of writing."

Posterity may find this claim to be true. It is unlikely that he is in any sense a major writer, but within his own set limits Fry is a craftsman of considerable accomplishment, and where he is most successful, he is memorable.

– Derek Parker

FULLER, John (Leopold). British. Born in Ashford, Kent, 1 January 1937; son of Roy Fuller, *q.v.* Educated at St. Paul's School; New College, Oxford (Newdigate Prize, 1960), B.A. 1960, M.A. 1964, B.Litt. 1965. Married Cicely Prudence Martin in 1960; has three children. Visiting Lecturer, State University of New York, Buffalo, 1962–63; Assistant Lecturer, Manchester University, 1963–66. Since 1966, Fellow of Magdalen College, Oxford. Publisher, Sycamore Press, Oxford. Recipient: Richard Hillary Memorial Prize, 1961; Eric Gregory Award, 1965; Faber Memorial Prize, 1974. Address: 4 Benson Place, Oxford, England.

PUBLICATIONS

Verse

> *Fairground Music.* London, Chatto and Windus-Hogarth Press, 1961.
> *The Tree That Walked.* London, Chatto and Windus-Hogarth Press, 1967.
> *The Art of Love.* Oxford, The Review, 1968.
> *The Labours of Hercules: A Sonnet Sequence.* Manchester, Manchester Institute of Contemporary Arts, 1969.
> *Annotations of Giant's Town.* London, Poem-of-the-Month Club, 1970.
> *The Wreck.* London, Turret Books, 1970.
> *Cannibals and Missionaries.* London, Secker and Warburg, 1972.
> *Boys in a Pie.* London, Steam Press, 1972.
> *Hut Groups.* Hitchin, Hertfordshire, Cellar Press, 1973.
> *Penguin Modern Poets 22*, with Adrian Mitchell and Peter Levi. London, Penguin, 1973.
> *Epistles to Several Persons.* London, Secker and Warburg, 1973.
> *Poems and Epistles.* Boston, David R. Godine, 1974.
> *Squeaking Crust.* London, Chatto and Windus, 1974.

Plays

> *Herod Do Your Worst*, music by Bryan Kelly (produced Thame, Oxfordshire, 1967). London, Novello, 1968.
> *Three London Songs*, music by Bryan Kelly. London, Novello, 1969.
> *Half a Fortnight*, music by Bryan Kelly (produced Leicester, 1970).
> *The Spider Monkey Uncle King*, music by Bryan Kelly (produced Cookham, Berkshire, 1971).
> *Fox-Trot*, music by Bryan Kelly (produced Leicester, 1972).
> *The Queen in the Golden Tree*, music by Bryan Kelly (produced Edinburgh, 1974).

Other

> *A Reader's Guide to W. H. Auden.* London, Thames and Hudson, and New York, Farrar Straus, 1970.
> *The Sonnet.* London, Methuen, 1972.

> Editor, *Light Blue Dark Blue.* London, Macdonald, 1960.
> Editor, *Oxford Poetry 1960.* Oxford, Fantasy Press, 1960.
> Editor, *Poetry Supplement.* London, Poetry Book Society, 1962.

Editor, with Harold Pinter and Peter Redgrove, *New Poems 1967.* London, Hutchinson, 1968.
Editor, *Poetry Supplement.* London, Poetry Book Society, 1970.
Editor, *Nemo's Almanac.* Oxford, Sycamore Press, 3 vols., 1971–73.

*   *   *

In reviewing John Fuller's second book of poems, *The Tree That Walked,* Stephen Wall wrote, in a generally favourable review: "the poems . . . are oddly tangential to some of the central commonplaces of human feeling. The impression of a rooted reticence has something to do with the sense of powers not only excellently under control but also sometimes too tightly restrained." And Fuller himself has disparaged "powerful feelings and simplicity"; poetry, he feels, "must perform its moral function." From this, it is easy to infer that he is not a "confessional" or a lyrical poet. One or two of the poems collected in his first book, *Fairground Music,* do contain lines that can be (and by one critic have been) compared to Rupert Brooke; but this element has very carefully and deliberately been purged from the poems of his second volume.

Notwithstanding the "Georgian" element in his earliest poems – which is hardly unusual – Fuller is and always has been a markedly intellectual poet whose main source of literary inspiration is the eighteenth century. His first book was characterized by wit, playfulness, sophistication and by a tendency towards melodrama that sometimes seemed inconsistent with his anti-romanticism.

In the best poems of his second book, which reveals a considerable development of his talent, he has often succeeded in achieving a style that better suits his extremely cerebral content. One of his most admired and serious poems, "Hedge Tutor," combines one side of Marvell's anthropocentric genius with Augustan descriptive virtues in a manner that has not yet been seen in modern poetry. The subject is the Marvellian one of the relationship between people and landscape, and the restraint and elegance of its surface are beautifully achieved:

> Consulting the calendar of hedges
> Banked up higher than your head,
> We seem to share the surprise of walking
> Upon a riverbed. . . .
>
> . . . we lean to ourselves, and to
> These rituals that love condemns
> Us to, gathering until the hand
> Is hot with stems.

Fuller's virtues include intelligence, technical control and grace. His chief recurring fault is probably that where his subject is fantastic or frivolous his elegance tends to degenerate into a decadent rococo. But he remains an assured craftsman, in whose poetry learning is natural and never pretentious.

– Martin Seymour-Smith

FULLER, Roy (Broadbent). British. Born in Failsworth, Lancashire, 11 February 1912. Educated at private schools; qualified as a solicitor, 1933. Served in the Royal Navy, 1941–46; Lieutenant, Royal Naval Volunteer Reserve. Married Kathleen Smith in 1936; has one son, John Fuller, *q.v.* Assistant Solicitor, 1938–58, Solicitor, 1958–69, and since 1969, Director, Woolwich Equitable Building Society, London. Chairman of the Legal Advisory Panel, 1958–69, and since 1969, Vice-President, Building Societies Association. Since 1972, Governor, BBC. Chairman of the Poetry Book Society, London, 1960–68. Professor of Poetry, Oxford University, 1968–73. Recipient: Arts Council Poetry Award, 1959; Duff Cooper Memorial Prize, 1968; Queen's Gold Medal for Poetry, 1970. Fellow, Royal Society of Literature, 1958. C.B.E. (Companion, Order of the British Empire), 1969. Address: 37 Langton Way, London S.E.3, England.

PUBLICATIONS

Verse

Poems. London, Fortune Press, 1939.
The Middle of a War. London, Hogarth Press, 1942.
A Lost Season. London, Hogarth Press, 1944.
Epitaphs and Occasions. London, Lehmann, 1949.
Counterparts. London, Verschoyle, 1954.
Brutus's Orchard. London, Deutsch, 1957; New York, Macmillan, 1958.
Collected Poems, 1936–1961. London, Deutsch, and Chester Springs, Pennsylvania, Dufour, 1962.
Buff. London, Deutsch, and Chester Springs, Pennsylvania, Dufour, 1965.
New Poems. London, Deutsch, and Chester Springs, Pennsylvania, Dufour, 1968.
Pergamon Poets 1, with R. S. Thomas, edited by Evan Owen. Oxford, Pergamon Press, 1968.
Off Course. London, Turret Books, 1969.
Penguin Modern Poets 18, with A. Alvarez and Anthony Thwaite. London, Penguin, 1970.
To an Unknown Reader. London, Poem-of-the-Month Club, 1970.
Song Cycle from a Record Sleeve. Oxford, Sycamore Press, 1972.
Tiny Tears. London, Deutsch, 1973.
An Old War. Edinburgh, Tragara Press, 1974.

Novels

The Second Curtain. London, Verschoyle, 1953; New York, Macmillan, 1956.
Fantasy and Fugue. London, Verschoyle, 1954; New York, Macmillan, 1956.
Image of a Society. London, Deutsch, 1956; New York, Macmillan, 1958.
The Ruined Boys. London, Deutsch, 1959; as *That Distant Afternoon,* New York, Macmillan, 1959.
The Father's Comedy. London, Deutsch, 1961.
The Perfect Fool. London, Deutsch, 1963.
My Child, My Sister. London, Deutsch, 1965.
The Carnal Island. London, Deutsch, 1970.

Other

> *Savage Gold* (juvenile).   London, Lehmann, 1946.
> *With My Little Eye* (juvenile).   London, Lehmann, 1948; New York, Macmillan, 1957.
> *Catspaw* (juvenile).   London, Alan Ross, 1966.
> *Owls and Artificers: Oxford Lectures on Poetry.*   London, Deutsch, and La Salle, Illinois, Library Press, 1971.
> *Seen Grandpa Lately?* (juvenile verse).   London, Deutsch, 1972.
> *Professors and Gods: Last Oxford Lectures on Poetry.*   London, Deutsch, 1973; New York, St. Martin's Press, 1974.

> Editor, *Byron for Today.*   London, Porcupine Press, 1948.
> Editor, with Clifford Dyment and Montagu Slater, *New Poems 1952.*   London, Joseph, 1952.
> Editor, *Supplement of New Poetry.*   London, Poetry Book Society, 1964.

Manuscript Collections: State University of New York, Buffalo; British Museum, London.

Critical Study: "Private Images of Public Ills: The Poetry of Roy Fuller" by George Woodcock, in *Wascana Review* (Regina, Saskatchewan), iv, 2, 1970.

$$*\qquad *\qquad *$$

Roy Fuller's poetry falls into two fairly distinct parts: the work he produced up to roughly 1950, which was concerned chiefly with poetry as a means of illuminating truths about human beings as social animals, and the poetry written since that time which is more closely personal, more concerned with individual psychology than with social action, and technically much more experimental. He has written about this himself with admirable clarity, saying on his own early attitude:

> One can't emphasise too much the sense one had, during almost all this period, of poetry being as intimately connected with day-to-day life as economic forces and the actions of politicians.

This feeling did not long survive the war, and he has written of the difficulty he found in making poetry again out of civilian life, "difficulties that had already appeared when in the Navy I had exchanged a seat in the Petty Officers' Mess for a chair at the Admiralty." *Epitaphs and Occasions* may be regarded as the last work produced by the poet primarily concerned with the social animal, *Counterparts* as the first rather cautious step towards a different kind of poetry reflecting a changed approach. The five year gap between the two books is significant. In recent years Fuller has moved into various kinds of technical experiment including syllabics, about which again he writes with unusual directness and simplicity. Discussing their "apparent arbitrariness" he says that this is deceptive:

> Since one works in lines of an odd number of syllables one is working at what seems to be a logical extension of the problems of the normal metrical English line. Behind the 11-syllable line, for example, is the ghost of the iambic pentameter.

He suggests that syllabic metres are particularly suited to verse read aloud and adds that "a return to traditional metrics after a regimen of syllabics makes one conscious of the speech tones still possible in the older procedure."

These comments are not only of intrinsic interest, and relevant to Fuller's own poetical practice, but in their tone and weight they express the seriousness of his own approach to poetry. Such seriousness does not exclude wit, and this quality which joins his early and late work has been too little remarked by critics. It can be found in single phrases like "The edges of the country are fraying with // Too much use" about the British coastline under the pressure of German air raids, or in whole poems like the ironic "War Poet" about the "fertile lack of balance" in many poets. These are early works. The tone has become mordant in a poem like "Obituary of R. Fuller" which comes at the end of what has been defined here as his first period:

> Quite often he was heard to babble
> "Poets should be intelligible"
> Or "What determines human fate
> Is the class structure of the state"
> Or "Freud and Marx and Dickens found –
> And so do I – souls not profound."

In the later poems the wit is often a comment on middle age and illness. In "In Lambeth Palace Road," after visiting St. Thomas's Hospital, the poet sits in a tea shop, waits "for the gland / To dispose of the radioactive iodine" and reflects on the reasons why, suddenly, the springs of verse are flowing again. Why?

> It scarcely needed
> The shiny tentacles of the cardiograph
> Or the sting of the syringe's proboscis to release them.
> They would have been satisfied to observe a waitress
> Making sure of her lipstick before going off duty.

From this personal reflection the poem expands into a view of the contradictions between man's constant concern with gods and immortality and his individual triviality and weakness. In form and approach it is an admirable example of his later style.

Fuller is an intellectual poet, one who believes that "the criterion of success in poetry is brain power," and the progression in many of these recent poems is logical but complex. They start usually with something very concretely observed – a girl with fat legs reading Georgette Heyer, blackbirds and a squirrel lured on to a window sill, a disliked head seen at the next hotel table – and go on to general reflections about the nature of life, the importance of gods to men (they are seen as benevolent or magnificent, where in the early poems they might have been capitalist myths), a psychoanalytical interpretation of religion. Present critical opinion finds these allusive poems of much greater importance than his earlier work (cf. Kenneth Allott's view that nothing in the earlier books "really prepares us for the authority of the writing in *Brutus's Orchard* [1957]" and the reception of his *New Poems* [1968]), and this is a view that Fuller himself seems to share. It is possible to dissent from this opinion while admiring the ingenuity with which these later poems are written, and the sophisticated intelligence of their thought. Sometimes, as in the poem quoted, the shifts from one plane of reference to another seem fully justified, but in other poems they appear contrived. The early work shows a progression from confusion to directness, and in his two wartime volumes he found it possible to write straightforwardly and memorably about many aspects of a conscript's life, defending a harbour, waiting to be drafted, writing letters home. If his later work shows a much increased awareness of all kinds of human possibilities, it marks also a lessening of sensual intensity and the growth of a detachment that occasionally ends in a rather too distant comment on emotion rather than participation in it. The wartime and immediate postwar poems certainly represent an important part of his poetic achievement, and at present they are undervalued. What both aspects of his work share is a very rare and persistent devotion to poetry both as a craft and an art. There was a time when the kind of poetry he wrote was totally out of fashion and disregarded, but he was as little moved poetically by this as he has been by recent acknowledgements of his major importance among the English poets of his generation.

– Julian Symons

FULTON, Robin. Scottish. Born in the Isle of Arran, Scotland, 6 May 1937. Educated at Edinburgh University, M.A. 1959, Ph.D. 1972. Since 1967, Editor of *Lines Review,* Edinburgh. Recipient: Eric Gregory Award, 1966; Edinburgh University Writer's Fellowship, 1969–71; Arts Council bursary, 1972. Lives in Scandinavia.

PUBLICATIONS

Verse

A Matter of Definition.   Edinburgh, Giles Gordon, 1963.
Instances.   Edinburgh, M. Macdonald, 1967.
Inventories.   Thurso, Caithness Books, 1969.
The Spaces Between the Stones Is Where the Survivors Live.   New York, New Rivers Press, 1971.
Quarters.   West Linton, Peeblesshire, Castlelaw Press, 1971.
The Man with the Surbahar.   Edinburgh, M. Macdonald, 1971.
Tree Lines.   New York, New Rivers Press, 1973.

Other

Contemporary Scottish Poetry: Individuals and Context.   Edinburgh, M. Macdonald, 1974.

Editor, "Ten Scottish Poets," in Spirit (South Orange, New Jersey), Summer 1971.
Editor, Trio: New Poets from Edinburgh.   New York, New Rivers Press, 1971.

Translator, An Italian Quartet: Versions after Saba, Ungaretti, Montale, Quasimodo.   London, Alan Ross, 1966.
Translator, Blok's Twelve.   Preston, Lancashire, Akros, 1968.

Translator, *Selected Poems*, by Lars Gustafsson. New York, New Rivers
    Press, 1972.
Translator, *Selected Poems*, by Gunnar Harding. London, London Magazine
    Editions, 1973.
Translator, *Selected Poems*, by Tomas Tranströmer. London, Penguin, 1973.
Translator, with Anselm Hollo, *Paavo Haavikko and Tomas Tranströmer*.
    London, Penguin, 1974.
Translator, *Selected Poems*, by Osten Sjöstrand. Harrow, Middlesex, Oleander
    Press, 1975.

                    *   *   *

Robin Fulton is a delicate and fastidious poet. His craftsmanship does not show
itself in regular or conventional verse forms, but arises from the exacting objectives
of his art. In "A Lifework" he writes:

> to say what you mean is hazardous
> to sort out and plainly describe
> one mere subdivision
> of a minor species takes more
> than a homemade poet with a simple lens.

At his simplest he is, as he entitles a poem, "A Meticulous Observer," in which he
writes:

> he watched boys with almost pre-
> hensile feet on high walls
> where they risked their short lives
> for reasons no-one else would appreciate
>
> he watched girls with newly-shaped
> bodies advertising themselves
> without guile in the summery light
> and without needing a reason to guide them.

The detached tone is equable to the point of the poems becoming clinical studies.
The movement of the verse never reflects the shocks to life nor bodily sensations.
What the mind's eye sees is all important. He notes appearances, placing them
judiciously, as a means of discovering truths. He has created a flexible, exact art,
in which by subtle shifts of tone and viewpoint he exposes a mental condition. In
his poem, "forecast for a quiet night," he moves from witty talk to humane
concern, as these lines witness:

> by dawn too a generation of mice
> will have been snipped by a night-shift of owls
> working separately and almost in silence
>
> and the mild local disturbance behind the eyes
> of the invalid
> will have been noted only by the next of kin.

Fulton has made a means of inquisition which he uses gently, but by which he
may penetrate deeply. He is a humane intellectual, conscious of the burden of

525

being true to what he creates and examines. This is increasingly matter of consequence. The following lines are from "the survivors begin again" in his collection,
The Spaces Between the Stones:

> we huddle in our old-fashioned coats watching
> our thin smoke bend as the mist breathes
> and one of us points to a green mist in the trees –
> small leaves prick through the peeling rust
>
> soon our blades will be sharp enough to let blood.

– George Bruce

GALE, Vi. American. Born in Noret, Dala-Jarna, Sweden. Educated at the
University of Oregon, Eugene; Lewis and Clark College, Portland, Oregon; Portland State University; University of Colorado, Boulder. Married. Since 1962, Director, YWCA Writing Workshops and currently, conducting Community Program,
Portland. Writer-in-Residence, Eastern Oregon College, La Grande, Summer 1968,
and Clatsop Community College, Astoria, Oregon, Summer 1969. Recipient: Swallow Press New Poetry Series Award, 1958. Address: 11519 N.E. Prescott, Portland,
Oregon, 97220, U.S.A.

PUBLICATIONS

Verse

Several Houses. Denver, Swallow, 1959.
Love Always. Denver, Swallow, 1965.
Nineteen Ing Poems. Portland, Press-22, 1970.
Clouded Sea. Portland, Press-22, 1971.
Clearwater. Chicago, Swallow Press, 1974.

Critical Studies: Reviews by Dudley Fitts, in *Saturday Review* (New York), 1959,
and Bruce Berlind, in *Poetry* (Chicago), February 1960.

*   *   *

Vi Gale's poems since her 1959 collection, *Several Houses*, have, like much
American poetry moving from the rigid academic poetry so prevalent in the fifties

to the freer poetic climate of the sixties, become more relaxed, more conversational, and more interesting. This is especially true of one of her longer collections, *Love Always*, published by Alan Swallow, the publisher for the earlier collection as well. The latter book contains such effective poems as "Did You Hear?," "Orange," "Today, in the Obituaries," and "Pattern Pretty Much Established." Ms. Gale's poems are strongly autobiographical and personal, dealing frequently with her experiences, friends, and relatives. They risk – and sometimes succumb to – sentimentality. Unlike the poems mentioned above, some in *Love Always*, and *Nineteen Ing Poems*, an even more recent collection, finally fail ("Hunters" is one example of this) to draw potentially interesting material together; Ms. Gale is strongest when she sticks close, as she frequently does, to personal material, weakest when she fails to let the experience speak for itself, tacking on an unprepared-for leap into universality. The fine, homely and well-observed details of hunters' preparations for a plunge into the wilds are undercut in "Hunters," for example, by the last two lines ("Slow the fleeing deer. / Let these driven hunters kill what stalks us down"), as the entirety of "Don't Eat the Snow" is marred by the attempt to make it a protest against radiation pollution; in either case, we're much more able to respond to the personal death or injury, the boy drowned at the end of "Did You Hear?" (one of her most powerful poems), than to such generalizations. Ms. Gale is best in her personally observed and felt responses to people and nature (of which she is a keen and well-informed observer, like many good Northwest poets). The personal experience – two experiences, actually, nature the link – speaks evocatively and well for her in "Orange," from which the first and third stanza:

> Once the long season had us in its reach
> our miracles were few. On the Christmas Eve
> that an uncle came traveling, traveling on skis
> with the gift of an orange, my brother and I
> went wild in our marveling.
>
> Halfway around the world one later December
> on a day so mild that we'd sunned in Los Angeles,
> I reached easily into the boughs, into rich leaves;
> pulled out a childhood of long snow,
> the far sound of skis.

– Duane Ackerson

GARDNER, Isabella Stewart. American. Born in Newton, Massachusetts, 7 September 1915. Educated at Foxcroft School, Middleburg, Virginia, 1931–33; Leighton Rollins School of Acting, East Hampton, New York; Embassy School of Acting, London, 1937. Married Harold Van Virk in 1938, one daughter; Maurice Seymour, 1943 (divorced, 1947), one son; Robert H. McCormick III, 1947 (divorced, 1957); Allen Tate, *q.v.*, 1959 (divorced, 1966). Professional Actress; occasional reader for publishers. Associate Editor, with Karl Shapiro, *Poetry*, Chicago, 1952–56. Address: 1305 Foothill Road, Ojai, California 93023, U.S.A.

PUBLICATIONS

Verse

> *Birthdays from the Ocean.* Boston, Houghton Mifflin, 1955.
> *Un Altra Infanzia* (bilingual edition, translated by Alfredo Rizzardi). Bologna,
>   Libreria Antiquaria Palmaverde, 1959.
> *The Looking Glass: New Poems.* Chicago, University of Chicago Press, 1961.
> *West of Childhood: Poems 1950–1965.* Boston, Houghton Mifflin, 1965.

Manuscript Collection: Washington University, St. Louis.

Critical Studies: "The Celebration of Birthdays" by John Logan, in *Sewanee Review* (Tennessee), Winter 1956; *Contemporary American Poetry* by Ralph J. Mills, Jr., New York, Random House, 1965; *The Poem in Its Skin* by Paul Carroll, Chicago, Follett, 1968.

Isabella Stewart Gardner comments:

My poems celebrate and affirm life, but they are also elegiac. My central theme is the inter-personal failure of love, the failure of the I-Thou relationship. They are the poems of a poet who is woman first and poet second. My content determines my prosody. I use many verse forms including, recently, syllabic verse. My poems, while often romantic and erotic, are also often ironic. I am politically engaged but seldom write polemically.

*   *   *

The mature woman in the arts achieves the stature of Myth within the lifetime; but Isabella Stewart Gardner is the woman behind the myths: alive here, classic, modern, ageless, in rooms and at tables as real as flesh: tall, long-limbed, the strength and soft-edged energy flowing where she walks. Or sits, decidedly grace-ful, sorrel hair, natural colors, with live blossoms, geodes, shells arrayed to give information about her spirit . . . She chooses a certain blue-green, intense, and umbers, earth-colors that appear in the poems front-and-center, rather than as backdrop. . . . And always the flesh-tones, bright faces, her own, her children's, her friends' and her students' in a comforting ring . . . one is, as a poet, always alone. The warmth of friends and children and lovers near. But not in the making of the page. The solitary process. After which the faces reappear, conjured whole in the wrought words. . . .

Having begun the craft early; left it "because I was too facile" in her early teens; stopped reading (contemporary) poetry; leaned the talents into acting and followed this, in character parts where her shy stutter would be less liable to obtrude (and burrs and brogues: the devices), until the children were born. And back then into writing: "the courage and energy" entailed and finally faced.

So few books over the past fifteen years. Not a productive fountain: her work is edited before it reaches paper, then wrought and hewn to the precision, the *forms*, necessary. (This is a Virgo lady: who shapes with honor.) In a time where a thousand poets cry for notice, leafleting the world with accidental prosodies . . . "the challenge of form." Precision, gift for the gestures of language.

A woman, writing of the soft and tough consciousness. Love of earth's good presences (that angular sight into others' lives never achieved by the arrogant or the haughty), talk in the poems of the daughter, the son, their fathers; sweet, dark liturgies of loss; her voice's timbre unmistakable, on or off the page. A voice the color of her auburn hair. The Boston accent, "*Poet*," not poetess, said softly clearly hard, like quartzite formed.

Explains carefully (with *care*!) that she may pass the friends without acknowledging them if they are too far for her eyes to see clearly; nor can she recall names of the myriad friends and acquaintances of her years: stumbles for their names, not wishing to slur, and is SHY, thus with a fierce respect for your, and her, privacy of soul and motion. The word "discretion." How we choose chambers, and then shape them to fit: the friends today are rarely those of earlier years; the Setting a protection, that the poet may continue; and only part of it is "how," agreeing that the poet is the child who has no one to talk with: that gap is filled by the inner sounds of poetry (at first an interior dialogue). And the process brings it through and out, distills the voices, the clarity, brings vision in . . . Belle Gardner, as transmuter, witch, reading, listening, above all seeing as if the eyes, the ears, the skin itself were all tender antennae.

The eyes, as readers: voraciously, at first; then, not at all; now, when accomplished, selectively, solemnly, seldom. But always with care. Caring. Who will trouble to read all friends' poems and to give of time. As an editor of *Poetry*, reached out to a new poet with encouragement, though the poems were not accepted there, referred the woman to a Dylan Thomas anthology being done at Yale; twenty years later, this poet recalls Isabella Gardner as "someone I owe all of it to: my beginnings; a wonderfully kind, warm person; imagine, taking the trouble to send me a telegram about that anthology! – and soon, my poems appearing next to hers in it! I'd never even read my poems to anybody!" Spoken with respect and affection. . . .

Generous, in the life and in chance-taking: seeking, working with the voice of the self. "Not that oneself is better than another but that the self is all that the poet knows acutely, it is for him the burning glass and the prism."

And the modesty, before which must stand the "necessary nakedness" required of the poet: that risk of confrontation, of honesty. Of the assumption of the work, follow-through, development of a form visibly one's own, through the imperative solitary strengths . . . recognition of, absorption of, defiance of the possibilities for failure. A gambling-game, see her fine poem "Writing Poetry": "it's the gamblers wearing their own hides who shoot / the moon rocketing on unprotected feet to outer space . . ." for the sake of all men. This concern, with craft and with fellow-workers. She will quote those she admires for their desire for oneness with all men, *einfuhlung*, as Keats has it, or Unamuno, or the "failure of the love which is . . . recognition of one human being by another. Communication. The meeting, greeting, acknowledging, the outstretched hand, the asking and accepting voice, the eye that really looks and really sees, the democracy of universal vulnerability. . . ." This is the stance of the woman in her own rooms and spaces. She has succeeded in defining herself, and in the definition has succeeded in the communication of love.

– Carol Bergé

GARIOCH, Robert (Sutherland). Scottish. Born in Edinburgh, 9 May 1909. Educated at Royal High School, Edinburgh; University of Edinburgh, 1927–31, M.A. (honours) in English. Served in the Royal Signals, 1941–46; Prisoner of War, 1942–45. Married Margaret Sutherland in 1941; has two children. School master in Edinburgh, London, and Kent; now retired. Since 1965, Lexicographer, Dictionary of the Older Scottish Tongue, and Transcriber with the School of Scottish Studies. Writer-in-Residence, University of Edinburgh, 1971–73. Recipient: Sloan Prize, for verse in Scots, 1930; Scottish Arts Council Award, 1968. Address: 4 Nelson Street, Edinburgh 3, Scotland.

PUBLICATIONS

Verse

> *17 Poems for 6d: In Gaelic, Lowland Scots and English*, with Somhairle MacGhill-Eathain. Edinburgh, Chalmers Press, 1940.
> *Chuckies on the Cairn: Poems in Scots and English.* Edinburgh, Chalmers Press, 1949.
> *The Masque of Edinburgh.* Edinburgh, M. Macdonald, 1954.
> *Jephthah and the Baptist, Translatit frae Latin in Scots*, by George Buchanan. Edinburgh, Oliver and Boyd, 1959.
> *Selected Poems.* Edinburgh, M. Macdonald, 1966.
> *The Big Music.* Thurso, Caithness Books, 1971.
> *Doktor Faust in Rose Street.* Edinburgh, M. Macdonald-Lines Review, 1973.
> *Two Men and a Blanket.* Penicuik, Midlothian, Southside, 1974.

Other

> Editor, *Made in Scotland: An Anthology of Fourteen Scottish Poets.* Cheadle, Cheshire, Carcanet Press, 1974.

Manuscript Collection: National Library of Scotland, Edinburgh.

Robert Garioch comments:

In general, I am a Scottish writer belonging to the Lowlands, knowing no Gaelic, but aware that the Gaelic culture also is part of the Scottish environment. Accustomed in childhood to hearing more Scots than English spoken, I spoke school-English consciously as required; this is, or was then, a usual experience, and not injurious, except to those who try to cultivate a kind of West-end London accent, which can sound ludicrous and has given rise to many jokes. Like everyone else, I suffer more or less from belonging to a half-nation betrayed to and taken over by the English government of 1707. So there is a political reason for writing in Scots, but poetical reasons come first in poetry, I hope, and I write in English when it seems more suitable for reasons not always arguable, but possibly valid for all that.

*   *   *

The largest part of Robert Garioch's poetry, and certainly the best of it, is in Scots. He is one of the most fluent and convincing users of the Scottish tongue in recent literature, and much of the pleasure his work gives to a Scottish reader comes from the way in which he handles the language. But his genius is essentially comic and the enjoyment of his high spirits, of a satire that is never harsh but often very telling, easily communicates itself to readers and audiences outside Scotland. Like his beloved predecessor, Robert Fergusson of the eighteenth century, he is particularly a poet of Edinburgh, and this is seen both in extended entertainments like "Embro to the Ploy" (on the Edinburgh Festival) and *The Masque of Edinburgh* (a dramatic fantasy) and in the more tightly controlled and remarkable series of "Edinburgh Sonnets" where he tilts with laconic ingenuity and glorious rhymes against the bailies of the city, the local brands of casual violence, the anti-pleasures of northern religion, the enthusiasms of the avant-garde, and his own uneasy position as teacher, observer and bard. A play with a religious theme is eagerly argued over by its Saturday-night audience, but:

> It seemed discussion wad last out the nicht,
> hadna the poliss, sent by Mrs Grundy
> pitten us out at twelve. And they were richt!
> Wha daur debait religion on a Sunday?

The wry humour of a reticent autobiographer is glimpsed through fables like "The Percipient Swan" and "Sisyphus." The man of his time brooding on science and suffering shows (less successfully, but interestingly) in "The Muir" and "The Wire." The skill of the patient craftsman makes fine translations from Pindar and Belli and George Buchanan. Garioch is not a prolific poet, but an entertaining, perceptive and original one.

– Edwin Morgan

GARLICK, Raymond (Ernest). Welsh. Born in London, 21 September 1926. Educated at the University College of North Wales, Bangor, 1944–48, B.A. 1948. Married Elin Jane Hughes in 1948; has one son and one daughter. Taught in Wales, 1948–60, and the Netherlands, 1961–67. Senior Lecturer in English, 1967–72, and since 1972, Director of Welsh Studies and Principal Lecturer, Trinity College, Carmarthen. Founding Editor, *Dock Leaves* later *The Anglo-Welsh Review*, Pembroke Dock, 1949–60. Recipient: Welsh Arts Council Prize, 1969, 1973. Address: Hen Ysgoldy, Llansteffan, Carmarthen SA33 5HA, Wales.

PUBLICATIONS

Verse

Poems from the Mountain-House. London, Fortune Press, 1950.
Requiem for a Poet. Pembroke Dock, Dock Leaves Press, 1954.
Poems from Pembrokeshire. Pembroke Dock, Dock Leaves Press, 1954.

The Welsh-Speaking Sea.   Pembroke Dock, Dock Leaves Press, 1954.
Blaenau Observed.   Pembroke Dock, Dock Leaves Press, 1957.
Landscapes and Figures: Selected Poems 1949–63.   London, Merrythought Press, 1964.
A Sense of Europe: Collected Poems 1954–1968.   Llandysul, Cardiganshire, Gomer, 1968.
A Sense of Time.   Llandysul, Cardiganshire, Gomer, 1972.

Recording: *Poets of Wales* series, Argo.

Other

   An Introduction to Anglo-Welsh Literature.   Cardiff, University of Wales, 1970; revised edition, 1972.

   Editor, *Poetry from Wales.*   Brooklyn, New York, Poetry Book Magazine, 1954.

Bibliography: in *A Bibliography of Anglo-Welsh Literature, 1900–1965* by Brynmor Jones, Swansea, Library Association, 1970.

Manuscript Collection: National Library of Wales, Aberystwyth.

Critical Studies: "The Poetry of Raymond Garlick" by John Hill, in *The Anglo-Welsh Review* (Pembroke Dock), Summer 1972; statement by the author, in *Artists in Wales 2*, edited by Meic Stephens, Llandysul, Cardiganshire, Gomer, 1973.

Raymond Garlick comments:

   Major themes: Wales and Europe, non-violence, non-privilege. Interest in the stanza as a visual and aural pattern. General influence: Anglo-Welsh poetry from the sixteenth century on. Concern: precise communication.

                              *   *   *

   Raymond Garlick was born in London but was educated and has lived most of his life in Wales, which is a major source of his inspiration. In 1949 he founded *Dock Leaves,* later renamed *The Anglo-Welsh Review,* which he edited till 1960; it began mainly as a vehicle for Pembrokeshire writers, but quickly developed into a magazine of national interest. During the 1950's he published several important critical articles examining the writing of English poetry by Welshmen; he argued that from the late sixteenth century there is a tradition of Anglo-Welsh verse, and that some of the poets in this tradition did not deserve the neglect into which they had fallen (see *The Dublin Magazine,* Spring 1954, among others).
   Mr. Garlick's poetry has appeared in numerous periodicals and anthologies in addition to several collections. His best writing builds bridges between English and Welsh Wales (he has learnt to speak and read Welsh), between the Welsh past and present, and between Wales and Europe – seven years in Holland (1961–67)

impressed his work deeply. He has, too, an obsession with words and problems of communication and with verse-forms. His poetry is still growing in stature, in technical assurance and in ever-broadening realisation of the rewards and difficulties of being a Welshman and a European.

– Gerald Morgan

GARRETT, George (Palmer, Jr.). American. Born in Orlando, Florida, 11 June 1929. Educated at Sewanee Military Academy; The Hill School; Columbia University, New York, 1948–49; Princeton University, New Jersey, 1947–48, 1949–52, B.A. 1952, M.A. 1956. Served in the Field Artillery, United States Army, 1952–55. Married Susan Parrish Jackson in 1952; has three children. Assistant Professor, Wesleyan University, Middletown, Connecticut, 1957–60; Visiting Lecturer, Rice University, Houston, 1961–62; Associate Professor, University of Virginia, Charlottesville, 1962–67; Writer-in-Residence, Princeton University, 1964–65; Professor of English, Hollins College, Virginia, 1967–71; Professor of English and Writer-in-Residence, University of South Carolina, Columbia, 1971–73. President of Associated Writing Programs, 1971–73. United States Poetry Editor, *Transatlantic Review*, Rome (later London) and New York, 1958–71; Contemporary Poetry Series Editor, University of North Carolina Press, Chapel Hill, 1962–68; Co-Editor, *Hollins Critic*, Virginia, 1965–71. Since 1970, Contributing Editor, *Contempora*, Atlanta; since 1971, Assistant Editor, *The Film Journal*, Hollins College, Virginia; since 1972, Co-Editor, *Worksheet*, Columbia, South Carolina. Recipient: *Sewanee Review* Fellowship, 1958; American Academy in Rome Fellowship, 1958; Ford grant, in drama, 1960; National Endowment for the Arts grant, 1967; *Contempora* award, 1971; Guggenheim Fellowship, for fiction, 1974. Agent: Perry Knowlton, Curtis Brown Ltd., 60 East 56th Street, New York, New York 10022. Address: York Harbor, Maine 03911, U.S.A.

PUBLICATIONS

Verse

The Reverend Ghost: Poems. New York, Scribner, 1957.
The Sleeping Gypsy and Other Poems. Austin, University of Texas Press, 1958.
Abraham's Knife and Other Poems. Chapel Hill, University of North Carolina Press, 1961.
For a Bitter Season: New and Selected Poems. Columbia, University of Missouri Press, 1967.

Plays

Sir Slob and the Princess: A Play for Children. New York, French, 1962.
Garden Spot, U.S.A. (produced Houston, 1962).

Screenplays: *The Young Lovers,* 1964; *The Playground,* 1965; *Frankenstein Meets the Space Monster,* 1966.

Novels

The Finished Man. New York, Scribner, 1959; London, Eyre and Spottis-
woode, 1960.
Which Ones Are the Enemy? Boston, Little Brown, 1961; London, W. H.
Allen, 1962.
Do, Lord, Remember Me. New York, Doubleday, and London, Chapman and
Hall, 1965.
Death of the Fox. New York, Doubleday, 1971; London, Barrie and Jenkins,
1972.
Magic Striptease. New York, Doubleday, 1973.

Short Stories

King of the Mountain. New York, Scribner, 1958; London, Eyre and Spottis-
woode, 1959.
In the Briar Patch. Austin, University of Texas Press, 1961.
Cold Ground Was My Bed Last Night. Columbia, University of Missouri Press,
1964.
A Wreath for Garibaldi. London, Hart Davis, 1969.

Other

Editor, *New Writing from Virginia.* Charlottesville, Virginia, New Writing
Associates, 1963.
Editor, *The Girl in the Black Raincoat.* New York, Duell, 1966.
Editor, with W. R. Robinson, *Man and the Movies.* Baton Rouge, Louisiana
State University Press, 1967.
Editor, with R. H. W. Dillard and John Moore, *The Sounder Few: Essays from
"The Hollins Critic."* Athens, University of Georgia Press, 1971.
Editor, with O. B. Hardison, Jr., and Jane Gelfman, *Film Scripts One, Two,
Three* and *Four.* New York, Appleton Century Crofts, 1971–72.
Editor, with William Peden, *New Writing in South Carolina.* Columbia, Univer-
sity of South Carolina Press, 1971.
Editor, with John Graham, *Craft So Hard to Learn.* New York, Morrow, 1972.
Editor, with John Graham, *The Writer's Voice.* New York, Morrow, 1973.
Editor, with Virginia Walton, *Intro 5.* Charlottesville, University Press of
Virginia, 1974.
Editor, with Katherine Garrison Biddle, *The Botteghe Oscure Reader.* Middle-
town, Connecticut, Wesleyan University Press, 1974.
Editor, *Intro 6: Life As We Know It.* New York, Doubleday, 1974.

Bibliographies: in *Seven Princeton Poets,* Princeton, New Jersey, Princeton University Library, 1963; "George Garrett: A Checklist of His Writings" by R. H. W.
Dillard, in *Mill Mountain Review* (Roanoke, Virginia), Summer 1971.

Manuscript Collections: University of Virginia, Charlottesville; Wesleyan University, Middletown, Connecticut.

Critical Studies: "George Palmer Garrett, Jr." by James B. Meriwether, in *The Princeton University Library Chronicle* (New Jersey), xxv, 1, 1963; "The Poetry of George Garrett" by Henry Taylor, in *Latitudes* (Houston), ii, 2, 1968; "The Poetry of Garrett" by R. H. W. Dillard, in *Masterpieces of World Literature 6*, New York, Salem Press, 1968; "The Poetry of George Garrett" by Richard Moore, in *Mill Mountain Review* (Roanoke, Virginia), Summer 1971.

George Garrett comments:

All of my work in all forms, including the verse, is part and parcel of the same voice. I make no distinction in the voice, only the forms.

*   *   *

George Garrett's poetry shares much of the character of his fiction. His language is free and colloquial, but always strictly under control and serving the larger ends of his thought and feeling. He is personal without being confessional, and his vision is Christian without being pietistic. His work is composed upon a framework of contradictions, of polarities. The sinner who is a saint, the wounding truth that finds its only anodyne in a lie, the spirit trapped in the cage of flesh which discovers moral freedom in physical action, the cruel and painful joy (and mystery) of love – these are some of the enigmas upon which Garrett builds the lively textures of his poems.

The world of George Garrett's seeing and saying is a fallen one, a world of clenched fists and dark bruises where we all still suffer the consequences of Adam's fall in bone and flesh, and where we act out that fall again and again each passing day. His Salome describes that world in the important poem that bears her name:

> A bad marriage from the beginning,
> you say, a complete mismatch.
> Flesh and spirit wrestle
> and we call it love.
>
> We couple like dogs in heat.
> We shudder and are sundered.
> We pursue ourselves,
> sniffing, nose to tail
> a comic parade of appetites.
>
> That is the truth,
> but not the whole truth.
> Do me a little justice.
> I had a dream of purity
> and I have lived in the desert ever since.

In the desert, one holds to what he has (and what he had), learning like Adam and Eve after they were cast out of the garden "to lie a little and to live together." That learning is not always serious, and Garrett is capable of writing comic poems, some of which satirize our vice and folly and others of which celebrate our vital foolishness (particularly as it expresses itself in the relationships between men and women). But the tone and substance of his poetry are perhaps best expressed by the closing stanza of "For My Sons," a poem which figures importantly in the novel *Death of the Fox*:

Nothing of earned wisdom I can give you,
nothing save the old words like rock candy
to kill the taste of dust on the tongue.
Nothing stings like the serpent, no pain greater.
Bear it. If a bush should burn and cry out,
bow down. If a stranger wrestles, learn his name.
And if after long tossing and sickness you find
a continent, plant your flags, send forth a dove.
Rarely the fruit you reach for returns your love.

– R. H. W. Dillard

———————————

GASCOYNE, David (Emery). British. Born in Harrow, Middlesex, 10 October 1916. Educated at Salisbury Cathedral Choir School; Regent Street Polytechnic, London. Lived in France, 1937–39, 1954–65. Recipient: Rockefeller-Atlantic Award, 1949. Fellow, Royal Society of Literature, 1951. Address: 48 Oxford Street, Northwood, Cowes, Isle of Wight, United Kingdom.

PUBLICATIONS

Verse

Roman Balcony and Other Poems. London, Lincoln Williams, 1932.
Man's Life Is This Meat. London, Parton Press, 1936.
Hölderlin's Madness. London, Dent, 1938.
Poems 1937–1942. London, Editions Poetry, 1943.
A Vagrant and Other Poems. London, Lehmann, 1950.
Night Thoughts. London, Deutsch, and New York, Grove Press, 1956.
Collected Poems, edited by Robin Skelton. London, Oxford University Press-Deutsch, 1965.
Penguin Modern Poets 17, with Kathleen Raine and W. S. Graham. London, Penguin, 1970.
The Sun at Midnight: Notes on the Story of Civilisation Seen as the History of the Great Experimental Work of the Supreme Scientist. London, Enitharmon Press, 1970.
Collected Verse Translations, edited by Robin Skelton and Alan Clodd. London, Oxford University Press-Deutsch, 1970.

Play

The Hole in the Fourth Wall; or, Talk, Talk, Talk (produced London, 1950).

Novel

Opening Day. London, Cobden Sanderson, 1933.

Other

A Short Survey of Surrealism.   London, Cobden Sanderson, 1935.
Thomas Carlyle.   London, Longman, 1952.

Editor, *Outlaw of the Lowest Planet,* by Kenneth Patchen.   London, Grey Walls
   Press, 1946.

Translator, with Humphrey Jennings, *A Bunch of Carrots: Twenty Poems,* by
   Benjamin Peret.   London, Roger Roughton, 1936; revised edition, as *Remove
   Your Hat,* 1936.
Translator, *What Is Surrealism?,* by André Breton.   London, Faber, 1936.

Critical Studies: by Edwin Muir, in *The Observer* (London), December 1950;
"Poetry and Ideas II: David Gascoyne" by Anthony Cronin, in *London Magazine,*
July 1957; "The Restoration of Symbols" by Kathleen Raine, in *Every Changing
Shape,* London, Deutsch, 1961; "A Voice from the Darkness" by Gavin Ewart, in
London Magazine, November 1965; "David Gascoyne and the Prophetic Role" by
Kathleen Raine, in *Defending Ancient Springs,* London, Oxford University Press,
1967; *David Gascoyne: The Evolution of the Ideas of a Surrealist Poet* by Michel
Rémy, University of Nancy, unpublished thesis, 1968.

                            *   *   *

David Gascoyne began his literary career precociously early. Whilst still in his
teens he was an active propagandist for the Continental surrealist movement, and
was one of the few English poets to produce work in the surrealist manner that still
looked like genuine poetry. Gascoyne's surrealist apprenticeship gave him a feeling
for the arresting image, and for the way in which unexpectedly juxtaposed images
can produce a disturbing but memorable effect. In the late thirties and early
forties Gascoyne produced the major phase of his work; the poems he wrote at that
time were collected in his *Poems 1937–1942,* which remains one of the few distinguished collections of the decade. In these poems Gascoyne was preoccupied with
several recurring themes: a sense of personal anguish expressed in the terms of
existential philosophy, as in such poems as "Noctambules," "A War-Time Dawn"
and "The Gravel-Pit Field"; an awareness of a world first threatened by war and
then overwhelmed by it; and a deep interest in the central symbols of Christianity.
Gascoyne used these very effectively in a sequence of poems called "Miserere,"
though his interest in the Christian religion was that of a poetic mythologizer rather
than that of an orthodox believer. The opening of "Pieta" from this sequence
shows Gascoyne's ability to express intense feeling in vivid images, in a verse that
is mannered and yet at the same time highly controlled:

> Stark in the pasture on the skull-shaped hill,
> In swollen aura of disaster shrunken and
> Unsheltered by the ruin of the sky,
> Intensely concentrated in themselves the banded
> Saints abandoned kneel.

Elsewhere, in "Snow in Europe," which is dated "Christmas, 1938," Gascoyne
shows both his awareness of the pressures of history and his adroit handling of
images:

> The warring flags hang colourless a while;
> Now midnight's icy zero feigns a truce
> Between the signs and seasons, and fades out
> All shots and cries. But when the great thaw comes,
> How red shall be the melting snow, how loud the drums!

Gascoyne's post-war poetry is, by comparison, less intense and generally less interesting. *Night Thoughts*, a long semi-dramatic poem intended for radio, may have come across effectively in that medium, but is flat and diffuse on the page.

– Bernard Bergonzi

GERSHON, Karen. British. Born in Bielefeld, Germany, 29 August 1923; emigrated to England in 1938, to Israel in 1969. Married; has four children. Recipient: Arts Council bursary, 1967; *Jewish Chronicle* prize, 1967; President of Israel's grant, 1967; Pioneer Women Award, 1968. Lives in Jerusalem, Israel.

PUBLICATIONS

Verse

New Poets 1959, with Christopher Levenson and Iain Crichton Smith. London, Eyre and Spottiswoode, 1959.
Selected Poems. London, Gollancz, and New York, Harcourt Brace, 1966.
Legacies and Encounters: Poems 1966–1971. London, Gollancz, 1972.
My Daughters, My Sisters. London, Gollancz, 1974.

Other

Editor, *We Came as Children: A Collective Autobiography.* London, Gollancz, and New York, Harcourt Brace, 1966.
Editor, *Postscript: A Collective Account of the Lives of Jews in West Germany since the Second World War.* London, Gollancz, 1969.

Translator, *Obscene: The History of an Indignation,* by Ludwig Marcuse. London, MacGibbon and Kee, 1965.

Karen Gershon comments:

All my work is largely autobiographical; until now it has concerned mainly minority experiences (especially the holocaust). More recently, in family poems, I have begun writing about experiences shared by everybody. And I have extended my experimentation with counter-rhythm and free rhyme.

538

Being in a position rather like Conrad's, I long ago adapted to myself his saying: "And it is thus, with poignant grief in my heart, that I write [poems] to amuse the English." But now the moving force has ceased to be grief.

*   *   *

Karen Gershon was born in Germany, of Jewish parentage, and was one of the German Jewish children who were saved at the last moment from the Nazis. Her parents were left behind to die. Jewishness, the sense of exile, guilt for the past, the search for an identity in the changed circumstances of the present – these form the subject-matter of her poems. The search has been pursued in reality as well as in literature. At one time the poet went to Israel to live, but has now returned to England. Though there are occasions when she refers to herself as "exiled" in language, her poems belong very much to the English tradition. Wilfred Owen, in particular, has been an important influence. Her ideal is the plain style which has maximum emotional impact. Her work can be criticised, quite justly, for technical limitations – notably an over-use of jog-trot rhythms – and for a certain monotony of feeling, but she nevertheless remains, in my view, one of the few really interesting "confessional" poets to have flourished in England.

– Edward Lucie-Smith

GHISELIN, Brewster. American. Born in Webster Groves, Missouri, 13 June 1903. Educated at the University of California, Los Angeles, A.B. 1927; University of California, Berkeley, M.A. 1928, 1931–33; Oxford University, 1928–29. Married Olive F. Franks in 1929; has two sons. Instructor in English, University of Utah, Salt Lake City, 1929–31; Assistant in English, University of California, Berkeley, 1931–33. Instructor, 1934–38, Lecturer, 1938–39, Assistant Professor, 1939–46, Associate Professor, 1946–50, Director of the Writers' Conference, 1947–66, Professor of English, 1950–71, Distinguished Research Professor, 1967–68, and since 1971, Professor Emeritus, University of Utah. Poetry Editor, 1937–46, and Associate Editor, 1946–49, *Rocky Mountain Review*, later *Western Review*, Salt Lake City and Lawrence, Kansas. Recipient: Ford Fellowship, 1952; Ben and Abby Grey Foundation Award, 1965; National Institute of Arts and Letters grant, 1970; Oscar Blumenthal Prize (*Poetry*, Chicago), 1973. Address: Department of English, University of Utah, Salt Lake City, Utah 84112, U.S.A.

PUBLICATIONS

Verse

Against the Circle. New York, Dutton, 1946.
The Nets. New York, Dutton, 1955.

Images and Impressions, with Edward Lueders and Clarice Short. Salt Lake City, University of Utah Printmaking Department, 1969.
Country of the Minotaur. Salt Lake City, University of Utah Press, 1970.

Other

Writing. Washington, D.C., American Association of University Women, 1959.

Editor, *The Creative Process: A Symposium.* Berkeley, University of California Press, 1952.

Literary criticism and short stories published in periodicals and anthologies.

Manuscript Collection: Lockwood Memorial Library, State University of New York, Buffalo.

Critical Studies: *Spinning the Crystal Ball* by James Dickey, Washington, D.C., Library of Congress, 1967; "An Earthen Vessel" by William Ralston, in *Sewanee Review* (Tennessee), Summer 1969; by Radcliffe Squires, in *Concerning Poetry* (Bellingham, Washington), Fall 1970; by Kathleen Raine, in *Sewanee Review* (Tennessee), Spring 1971; by Samuel French Morse, in *Michigan Quarterly Review* (Ann Arbor), Fall 1971; by Henry Taylor, in *Masterplots: 1971 Annual,* New York, Salem Press, 1971; "The Long and Short of It" by Robert B. Shaw, in *Poetry* (Chicago), March 1972; "The Needle and the Garment" by X. J. Kennedy, in *Counter/Measures 3* (Bedford, Massachusetts), 1974.

Brewster Ghiselin comments:

Like almost every poet, I feel that my poetry can live only in being heard – that it must be given the body of life, as sensation of sound and of vibration and movement of the articulating voice. Though I have used a great variety of forms and measures, I have never written free verse. The measure I have most often found right is *accentual,* a strongly stressed and syllabically various flow that I first heard clearly when I read *Beowulf* in Old English, and turned to my own freer use, long before I read any of Gerard Manley Hopkins.

In my writing of poetry, all considerations of verse form arise from the fact that the shaping of verse is the shaping of breath – the breath of life in every sense. If a poet says that "The poetry does not matter," as T. S. Eliot did in one context, meaning, I suppose, that nothing matters except what has been called "the ground of being," he simply reminds me of the vast importance of poetry, which only through accord with that inexhaustible attains whatever life it has. In the degree that poetry is realization and communion, it is false to say that it does not matter:

> The poetry matters:
> Whom the wind scatters
> Breath makes one again.

My central subject is men's struggle for breath, for being and light. Under the universal necessity of change, which sweeps away all form, man can have integrity and wholeness only through ceaseless shaping and reshaping of himself and his course and of those perspectives of vision that direct it. What draws my interest most and gives me matter and theme is the passion of living creatures to transcend the limits that choke them, and to find and enjoy the limits that, each in changing succession, are the freeing form of a moment of breath.

*   *   *

Brewster Ghiselin's two early collections offered many poems whose parts were so polished that it was difficult to grasp the whole. The effect was that of Byzantine mosaics seen close, an effect of brilliant yet disparate atomies rather than of anatomy. Yet in his latest collection, *Country of the Minotaur,* the opposite is true. The parts are still burnished, but the confluence of a tidal rhythm, an audacious language, and important themes distances the poems, so that one sees their integrity and strength, as Yeats saw the integrity and strength of the lofty mosaics at Ravenna. This virtuous distance has come because Ghiselin has developed into one of the few poets today whose faith rests in universals. Because his quandaries are eternal they remain pure, for they remain unresolved. Because his passions are conceived as parallels of the passions of vast energies, like sea and land, they remain at peace; most at peace when most violent.

Passion and peace define the boundaries of his poems, and the field within the boundaries is that Nature which modern science has made both more heartless and more mysteriously beautiful than the Nature Wordsworth knew. It is a Nature that can only be understood as a broad order which barely superintends random movement, fluctuation. Except for St. John Perse I can think of no one who is so majestically at home in this nomadic drift-land. And in some ways Ghiselin is the better poet, for he varies his focus, and Perse does not.

– Radcliffe Squires

GHOSE, Zulfikar. British. Born in Sialkot, Pakistan, 13 March 1935. Educated at Keele University, England, B.A. in English and philosophy 1959. Married in 1964. Cricket Correspondent for *The Observer*, London, 1960–65. Teacher in London, 1963–69. Since 1969, Lecturer in English, University of Texas, Austin. Recipient: Arts Council of Great Britain bursary, 1967. Agent: Harold Matson Company Inc. 22 East 40th Street, New York, New York 10016. Address: Department of English, University of Texas, Austin, Texas 78712, U.S.A.

PUBLICATIONS

Verse

The Loss of India. London, Routledge, 1964.
Jets from Orange. London, Macmillan, and Chester Springs, Pennsylvania, Dufour, 1967.

The Violent West. London, Macmillan, 1972.
Penguin Modern Poets 25, with Gavin Ewart and B. S. Johnson. London,
  Penguin, 1974.

Novels

The Contradictions. London, Macmillan, 1966.
The Murder of Aziz Khan. London, Macmillan, 1967; New York, Day, 1969.
The Incredible Brazilian, Book I. London, Macmillan, and New York, Holt
  Rinehart, 1972.
The Beautiful Empire. London, Macmillan, 1974.

Short Stories

Statement Against Corpses, with B. S. Johnson. London, Constable, 1964.

Other

Confessions of a Native-Alien (autobiography). London, Routledge, 1965.

                              *   *   *

Born in Sialkot (now in Pakistan) and educated in Bombay, Zulfikar Ghose left
for England at the age of seventeen. The sense of alienation, which in many
modern writers is something internal and metaphorical, is for Ghose a living
predicament because he is literally the product of three countries and of at least
two cultures. The recurring themes of his first volume of poetry, *The Loss of India*,
were a search for roots and a need to belong somewhere – "from the grains of my
skin pluck out hairs to look for roots." Memories of his childhood in the then-India
figure largely in his matter even today. The pressing need to know that his roots
can be discovered in some point of time and space has shaped some of his finest
poetry. Speaking to his ancestors, he asks:

> But who were you? From where did you come?
> I feel my cheekbones, finger the sutures
> along my skull, massage away random
> conjectures, but look for you in myself as
> an exiled monarch rules a map for a kingdom.
> Oh fathers, I am afraid of mirrors.

This concern with the need to belong – even granting the conditions of his
obvious uprooting – might well become a retarding factor in Ghose's development
as a poet because it tends to turn most of his poems into an extension of his
personal life. His autobiographical work, *Confessions of a Native-Alien,* reveals to
readers an uncomfortably close correspondence between actual experiences of life
and their poetic counterparts. Yet this is his essential strength. It enables him to
explore the lost links of his existence and distil moments of significance through
the diverse backgrounds of landscape, physical as well as cultural. An unfailing
response to history and geography underlies Ghose's poems. Several deal with
subjects like the encounter between Shivaji and Afzal Khan, the decline of the

Moghul empire, the misfortunes of Humayun; others range over contours as different as the Himalayan heights and the tiger country of East Pakistan to lush Provençal farmland and Kew Bridge. Yet none of these poems is merely nostalgic or descriptive. There is an attempt in each case to relate an experience limited in time and space to something that transcends the near and the particular.

The poems of his more recent volume, *Jets from Orange*, show that even fifteen years after leaving his land of birth, the memories of hunger and pain, of dust and misery, will not be exorcised. April in England, with its rich honeysuckle and abundance of chestnuts, reminds him of the threat of famine in another land. But in several other poems – and not only in those set in France – there is indication that Ghose is exploring experiences which do not flow from his more familiar sources. The first person singular is occasionally in abeyance as this young poet stretches his muscles to test them for tasks that lie ahead.

So far an utter simplicity of statement has accompanied his genuinely felt but simple moments of joy or pain or regret or shame. Even in his recent attempts to impersonalise his experience and view it from a distance, he has not yet felt the need of oblique statement. Apart from recollections of boyhood, the theme which Ghose handles most effectively is that of love. In an age grown impervious to or suspicious about love as a literary subject, Ghose can surprise us with his freshness, especially in the way even his love for a woman is somehow related to his feeling for land.

Ghose's poetry deals with themes that are not new. But the poems move us because he expresses without pretence the unresolved conflict and the agony out of which poetry is born:

> I wrote poems
> that floated about me as a black gown
> around a priest, but could not write
> the poem I wore in my heart.
> Poems pain the body, at night
> they do not come off like a shirt.

– Meenakshi Mukherjee

GIBBON, (William) Monk. Irish. Born in Dublin 15 December 1896. Educated at St. Columba's College, Rathfarnham; Keble College, Oxford (Open History Exhibitioner); Dublin University, Ph.D. Served as an Officer in the Royal Army Service Corps, 1914–18. Taught at Chateau d'Oex, Switzerland; Oldfeld School, Swanage, Dorset; Clive House, Prestatyn; Aravon School, Bray, county Wicklow; Brook House, Monkstown, County Dublin. Tredegar Lecturer, Royal Society of Literature, 1952; Tagore Centenary Lecturer, Abbey Theatre, 1961. Recipient: Tailteann Games Silver Medal, 1928. Fellow, Royal Society of Literature, 1950. Member, 1960, and Vice-President, 1967, Irish Academy of Letters. Address: 24 Sandycove Road, Sandycove, County Dublin, Ireland.

PUBLICATIONS

Verse

The Tremulous String: Poems in Prose. Fair Oak, Hampshire, At the Sign of the
    Grayhound, 1926.
Wise Small Birds. Dublin, Cuala Press, 1926.
The Branch of Hawthorn Tree. London, Grayhound Press, 1927.
Within a Little Field. Dublin, Cuala Press, 1927.
For Daws to Peck At. London, Gollancz, and New York, Dodd Mead, 1929.
A Ballad. Winchester, Hampshire, Grayhound Press, 1930.
Now We'll Forget the Windy Hill. Dublin, Cuala Press, 1931.
Seventeen Sonnets. London, Joiner and Steele, 1932.
This Insubstantial Pageant: Collected Poems in Verse and Prose. London, Phoe-
    nix House and New York, Devin Adair, 1951.
The Velvet Bow and Other Poems. London, Hutchinson, 1972.

Other

The Seals (autobiography). London, Cape, 1935.
The Stapleton Children in Jersey. Bath, privately printed, 1938.
Mount Ida (autobiography). London, Cape, 1948.
The Red Shoes Ballet: A Critical Study. London, Saturn Press, and New York,
    Auvergne Publications, 1948.
Swiss Enchantment. London, Evans, 1950.
The Tales of Hoffman: A Study of the Film. London, Saturn Press, 1951.
An Intruder at the Ballet. London, Phoenix House, 1952.
Austria. London, Batsford, 1953.
In Search of Winter Sport. London, Evans, 1953.
Western Germany. London, Batsford, 1955.
The Rhine and Its Castles. London, Putnam, 1957; New York, Norton, 1958.
The Masterpiece and the Man: Yeats As I Knew Him. London, Hart Davis,
    1959.
Netta (biography of Henrietta Franklin). London, Routledge, 1960.
The Climate of Love (autobiography). London, Gollancz, 1961.
Inglorious Soldier (autobiography). London, Hutchinson, 1968.
The Brahms Waltz (autobiography). London, Hutchinson, 1970.

Editor, *The Living Torch: An Anthology of Prose by AE, Principally Drawn from
    "Irish Statesman."* London, Macmillan, 1937.
Editor, *Poems from the Irish,* by Douglas Hyde. Dublin, Allen Figgis, 1963.
Editor, *The Poems of Katherine Tynan.* Dublin, Allen Figgis, 1963.
Editor, *Thy Tears Might Cease,* by Michael Farrell. London, Hutchinson, and
    New York, Knopf, 1964.

Bibliography: *Monk Gibbon: A Bibliography* by Alan Denson, privately printed,
1967.

Critical Studies: "Metanoia" by Alan Denson, in *Irish Press* (Dublin), 8 July 1972;
"The Treason of Memory" by Eavan Boland, in *Irish Times* (Dublin), 5 August
1972.

Monk Gibbon comments:

A poet can be lucky enough to be borne along upon the contemporary tide, or it may happen to have set against him. Herbert Palmer described me in a review as "one of the most neglected of poets today whose work is 'of consequence." He meant that I was not "with it." My own view is that a poem, even when topical, should lie outside time. My earlier poetry is very simple, my later a good deal more complex; but I have had a few venerated readers who could take both sorts. It is hard not to be influenced by fashion, but I think that readers should be completely above all poetic snobbery. I am lost in admiration for Dylan Thomas's allusive "Fern Hill." But that doesn't prevent me thinking Housman and W. H. Davies superb poets. Poetic coteries fight hard for their own – which is laudable – and even harder against their opposites – which is contemptible.

I try in my verse to crystallise certain moments of vision, delight, or mere contemplation. I try quite often to embalm the past: I try to give an inkling of how profoundly our emotions can record, transmute or interpret the external world.

*   *   *

Compared to much present-day poetry, Monk Gibbon's inevitably appears old-fashioned. Though he has experimented successfully with free verse, by far the greater part of his poetry has been written in strict metrical forms. His diction and syntax make few concessions to modern colloquial usage and his subject-matter is rooted in an earlier tradition. The list of touchstones in "Ultimates" illustrates Monk Gibbon's traditional approach to his craft:

> All else passes
> These remain
> Sun's warmth,
> Wind, rain;
>
> Grass underfoot
> Cloud overhead,
> Birds in flight,
> Man's slow tread . . .

Throughout his career Monk Gibbon has remained detached from the mainstream of modern poetry, concentrating on his own exploration of traditional themes and on the preservation of an individual and distinctive voice. The theme to which he returns most often is the celebration of beauty, mainly as embodied in woman. It follows that a good deal of his output consists of love poems. These are generally tender and reflective, poems of admiration rather than of passionate involvement, though at times passion breaks through. "The Black Heart" presents a finely controlled statement of polarities in love:

> So all night long we spell
> Love's language slowly out,
> Who have forgotten that theft
> Ends always as great drouth.
>
> For theft is always loss –
> "Yet theft is ecstasy?"
> This, at the mouth of hell,
> My black heart says to me.

Monk Gibbon's pre-occupations are generally private rather than public, meta-physical rather than actual. Often there is a troubled awareness of the fragility of man's consciousness, floating for a while on a tide of sensation between dark and dark:

> My life is like a dream:
> I do not know
> How it began, nor yet
> How it will go.
>
> Out of the night a bird
> Has quickly flown
> Across the lighted room
> And now is gone
>
> Into the dark again
> From whence it came . . .

Monk Gibbon's poetry demonstrates only a modest degree of involvement with the Ireland of tradition or of the present day, although social and political comment does find a place in his later poetry. Some of the more recent poems and the collection of sonnets dating from 1932 show him technically at his most ambitious, but when he attempts to fill the larger or more difficult structures the inspiration is not always sufficient to meet the demands made upon it. He is generally most satisfying when writing economically and the finest of the simple lyrics from the earlier collections, *The Branch of the Hawthorn Tree* and *For Daws to Peck At* are still among his best.

– Rivers Carew

GILBERT, (Florence) Ruth. New Zealander. Born in Greytown, 26 March 1917. Educated at Hamilton High School; Otago School of Physiotherapy, Dunedin. Married to Dr. John Bennett Mackay; has two daughters and two sons. Formerly, Physiotherapist, Otago School of Physiotherapy. Recipient: Jessie Mackay Memorial Award, 1948, 1949, 1967. Address: 83 Donald Street, Karori, Wellington, New Zealand.

PUBLICATIONS

Verse

Lazarus and Other Poems. Wellington, Reed, 1949.
The Sunlit Hour. London, Allen and Unwin, 1955.
The Luthier. Wellington, Reed, 1966.

Manuscript Collection: Turnbull Library, Wellington.

*   *   *

Ruth Gilbert's talent is for the straightforward evocation of brief moments of emotion, particularly those of the child or the woman, within the tradition of the romantic lyric. For her, the poetry seems to lie more in the words themselves than in the experiences; she is willing to take over poetic resonances established by others, reshuffling them for her own purposes:

> How steeped in beauty these old names are:
> Saffron, Sandalwood, Cinnibar . . .

This is a Georgian attitude, resulting in low-pressure poems of simple statement. If she has a poetic ancestor, it is Walter de la Mare, who is close at hand in "Phobia," "Legendary Lady" and "Portrait."

Some of these moments of emotion are as imagined in the lives of others, particularly within Bible stories, where such figures as Joseph, Rachel and Lazarus are sympathetically probed. Some are personal to the poet, as "Sanatorium" and nearer to the bone, "Fall Out." Some are crystallised into small perfection, as in "Li Po," "Metamorphosis" and "The Trees of Corot."

Ruth Gilbert has made several attempts to increase her scale, by binding lyrics into a sequence. Of these the most successful is *The Luthier*, which, even if conventionally romantic in essence, has the merit of a more vigorous vocabulary, and more complex rhythms than she has commanded elsewhere.

At her best, she can set up quiet ripples – never disturbing ones – which take her meaning beyond the sensitive but unadventurous moment which she describes. Her later work, however, suggests a growing awareness of the forces to be tapped when the form has been hammered out by the pressure of the content and is not a mere relaxed rehandling of old worlds and shapes. There may therefore be different work ahead of her. But her natural place is with the Georgians.

– Joan Stevens

GILL, David (Lawrence William). British. Born in Chislehurst, Kent, 3 July 1934. Educated at Chislehurst and Sidcup Grammar School; University College, London, B.A. (honours) in German 1955, B.A. (honours) in English 1970; Birmingham University, Cert.Ed. 1959. Served in the Royal Signals, 1955–57. Married Irene Zuntz in 1958; has three children. Taught at Bedales School, Hampshire, 1960–62, Nyakasura School, Fort Portal, Uganda, 1962–64, and Magdalen College School, Oxford, 1965–71. Since 1971, Lecturer, Newland Park College of Education, Chalfont St. Giles, Buckinghamshire. Recipient: Birmingham *Post* Prize, 1959. Address: 33 Melbourne Road, High Wycombe, Buckinghamshire, England.

PUBLICATIONS

Verse

Men Without Evenings. London, Chatto and Windus-Hogarth Press, 1966; Middletown, Connecticut, Wesleyan University Press, 1967.
The Pagoda and Other Poems. London, Chatto and Windus-Hogarth Press, 1969; Middletown, Connecticut, Wesleyan University Press, 1970.
Peaches and Aperçus. London, Poet and Peasant Books, 1974.

David Gill comments:

I began writing verse as a schoolboy on chemistry labs, daffodils, gym masters, myself, love and other universal topics. A late developer, I wrote one good poem at university. The influences of my German reading – Rilke, Stefan George, as well as Welsh idols such as Dylan Thomas and Wilfred Owen – had a delayed action. Rilke's *Dinggedichte* plus a certain mistrust of the abstract brought home to me the importance of things at the centre of poems, visual things like roundabouts, pagodas, punch-and-judy shows, cartwheels, missiles.

In 1958 I became involved in the struggle against nuclear weapons, and, in poetry, in a parallel struggle to tame proud and angry feelings in a cage of words. At the same time (1959–62) I wanted to say quieter things about the Hampshire hangers and beech-forests near Selbourne, and became aware of the truth that poems are ways of stating the contrasts that bother the mind, the contrast of present and past:

> Bunches of angels hang from exploding branches
> Watching the aisles. Six hundred years below
> My son makes progress on the gothic floor,
> Ant-explorer, crawling to and fro
> Between the massive trees.
> — "On the Cathedral Floor"

Or the contrast of here and elsewhere in the world-village:

> This day as every day my clock-shod mind
> Has tramped to crises in the Timbuctoos,
> Tibets and Thailands of the headlined news,
> But only at such frontiers to find
> The vultures knife-eyed; victims small and blind.
> — "I Must Withdraw"

The shape of my verse has travelled from quatrains to more complex stanzas to a kind of free-verse, which at times goes near to prose. Preoccupations with people, politics, landscape, animals, dominate the collection of poems written in Uganda and entitled *Men Without Evenings*. Of these poems the *Guardian* critic Bernard Bergonzi wrote: "His poems are immersed in the colours, sounds, and smells of that country, but they have an intelligent moral dimension which makes them something more than touristic snapshot verse."

*   *   *

David Gill's poetry describes and comments but seldom enacts or explores. The range of subject-matter is considerable, attesting for instance to wide travel, but in a sense this very richness of his raw material draws attention to the relatively meagre use he makes of it poetically. For it *remains* subject-matter, safely beyond the reader's capacity for surprise. Whether the ostensible subject is political prisoners, children, historical figures or exotic landscapes, the ready adjective and the banal (if admirably sensible) observation screen us from any sense of discovery or presentness. Descriptions of animals for example have none of the inventive flair we would find in, say, Norman MacCaig's animals. And, more seriously, the effort to mould his verse into the shape he wants can sometimes blind him to a betrayal of a doubtless sincere feeling, as in the conclusion of "Beatrix Potter," or lines like these:

> Will you not think, you gentle theologians,
> of what has been expunged from these calm walks?
> The buddhist priests bleeding in burning pagodas,
> and clouds of helicopters hanging like hawks.

This may well mean no more than that Gill accepts a limited function for his poetry, but in the context of a survey such as this the point must be made. His own description of his writing, made with reference to the craft of a wheelwright, clarifies the issue:

> the bark of images is stripped to show
> the dead-straight grain of relevance behind,
> and soon the jobbing words begin the slow
>
> and careful fashioning of stalwart verse . . .

The imagination has a way, unfortunately, of eluding the most carefully fashioned invitations.

– Robin Fulton

GINSBERG, Allen. American. Born in Newark, New Jersey, 3 June 1926. Educated at Paterson High School, New Jersey; Columbia University, New York, B.A. 1948. Served in the Military Sea Transport Service. Married Peter Orlovsky in 1954. Associated with the Beat movement and the San Francisco Renaissance in the 1950's. Widely travelled; participated in many poetry readings and demonstrations. "Visited W. C. Williams, Basil Bunting, Ezra Pound, Jack Kerouac, W. S. Burroughs, Jean Genet, L. F. Céline, Henri Michaux, Louis Zukofsky, Giuseppe Ungaretti, Andrei Vosnosensky, and W. H. Auden." Recipient: Guggenheim Fellowship, 1965; National Endowment for the Arts grant, 1966; National Institute of Arts and Letters grant, 1969; National Book Award, 1974. Member, National Institute of Arts and Letters, 1973. Address: P.O. Box 582, Stuyvesant Station, New York, New York 10009, U.S.A.

PUBLICATIONS

Verse

Howl and Other Poems. San Francisco, City Lights Books, 1956.
Siesta in Xbalba and Return to the States. Privately printed, 1956.

549

Empty Mirror: Early Poems. New York, Totem Press-Corinth Books, 1961.
Kaddish and Other Poems, 1958–1960. San Francisco, City Lights Books, 1961.
Reality Sandwiches, 1953–60. San Francisco, City Lights Books, 1963.
Penguin Modern Poets 5, with Lawrence Ferlinghetti and Gregory Corso. London, Penguin, 1963.
The Change. London, Writers Forum, 1963.
Kral Majales. Berkeley, California, Oyez, 1965.
Prose Contribution to Cuban Revolution. Detroit, Artists Workshop, 1966.
Wichita Vortex Sutra. London, Peace News Poetry, 1966.
Housemans. San Francisco, Coyote Books, 1966.
T.V. Baby Poems. London, Cape Goliard Press, 1967; New York, Grossman, 1968.
Wales – A Visitation, July 29, 1967. London, Cape Goliard Press, 1968.
Scrap Leaves, Tasty Scribbles. New York, Poets Press, 1968.
The Heart Is a Clock. Buffalo, New York, Gallery Upstairs Press, 1968.
Message II. Buffalo, New York, Gallery Upstairs Press, and London, Ad Infinitum, 1968.
Planet News, 1961–1967. San Francisco, City Lights Books, 1968.
Airplane Dreams: Compositions from Journals. Toronto, House of Anansi, 1968; San Francisco, City Lights Books, 1969.
Ankor-Wat. London, Fulcrum Press, 1969.
For the Soul of the Planet Is Wakening. Santa Fe, Desert Review Press, 1970.
The Moments Return: A Poem. San Francisco, Grabhorn Hoyem, 1970.
Notes after an Evening with William Carlos Williams. New York, Charters, 1970.
Iron Horse. Toronto, Coach House Press, 1972.
The Fall of America: Poems of These States 1965–1971. San Francisco, City Lights Books, 1972.
The Gates of Wrath (Early Rhymed Poems 1948–1951). Bolinas, California, Grey Fox Press, 1972.

Recordings: *Howl and Other Poems,* Fantasy-Galaxy, 1959; *Kaddish,* Atlantic Verbum, 1966; *William Blake's Songs of Innocence and Experience Tuned by Allen Ginsberg,* MGM, 1970.

Plays

Don't Go Away Mad, in *Pardon Me, Sir, But Is My Eye Hurting Your Elbow?,* edited by Bob Booker and George Foster. New York, Geis, 1968.
Kaddish (produced New York, 1972). San Francisco, City Lights Books, 1973.

Other

The Yage Letters, with William S. Burroughs. San Francisco, City Lights Books, 1963.
Notes on an Interview with Allen Ginsberg, by Edward Lucie-Smith. London, Turret Books, 1965.
Indian Journals: March 1962-May 1963: Notebooks, Diary, Blank Pages, Writings. San Francisco, Dave Haselwood, 1970.
Interview with Allen Young. Bolinas, California, Grey Fox Press, 1974.
Allen Verbatim: Lectures on Poetry, Politics, Consciousness, edited by Gordon Ball. New York, McGraw Hill, 1974.

Bibliography: *A Bibliography of the Works of Allen Ginsberg* by George Dowden. San Francisco, City Lights Books, 1970.

Manuscript Collections: Columbia University, New York; University of Texas, Austin.

Critical Studies: *Allen Ginsberg in America* by Jane Kramer, New York, Random House, 1968; *Scenes Along the Road,* edited by Ann Charters, New York, Gotham Bookmart, 1971; *Allen Ginsberg in the 60's* by Eric Mottram, Brighton, Sussex, Unicorn Bookshop, 1972.

Allen Ginsberg comments:

(1970) Beat-Hip-Gnostic-Imagist.
Major themes: transformation of consciousness to include visionary gleam of planet-light in Eternity before death. Characteristic subject: my own body or imagistic body of planet. Usual forms and sources: Bible and Kit Smart, parallelism and litany. Sources in Whitman, Rimbaud, Shakespeare, Blake above all, Pound, Jack Kerouac, and W. C. Williams. Influenced by "Black Mountain" poets, Olson, Creeley, Duncan. Travels and music of Orient leading into Mantra chanting reflect back on poesy as prophetic Shamanistic Chaunt. I have achieved the introduction of the word *fuck* into texts inevitably studied by schoolboys.
(1974) A.D. 1973 studying poetics and meditation in the whispered transmission school of Mila Repa (12th century Tibetan Buddhist yogi-poet) with Rimpoche Chögyam Truagpahoma, also a poet; tendency of my poetry practice last 2 years has been toward natural minded improvisation, taking for granted that "first thought is best thought," an attitude necessary for the realization of spontaneous flow of rhymed lines; presently in U.S. black Blues form and wedded to traditional triple-chord (CFG or GCD etc.) Western Blues. This is outgrowth of a decade's monochord practice mantra-chanting, followed by several years tuning Blake's lyrics to actual song (restoring the words to song, so to speak).
The tradition of improvising poems on the spot in communal situations is I believe older than the written tradition and perhaps more distinguished – as in the work of Homer or the much more ancient oral epic tradition of Australian Aborigine Song Men with whom I've had some brief contact Spring 1972. In any case it may be appropriate to restore facility in the bardic improvised mourner in this over-civilized day and age when we are not sure that the supply of electric or paper will outlast the century, outlast our own lives. So as a conservation of viable poetries independent of material base (printed book) in case of, just in case of, historical necessity, and as outgrowth of Beat-hip-gnostic-imagistic spontaneous mind style, I am practicing improvised poetry.

*   *   *

A poet who has made himself a more bristling energetic and controversial public figure than any other poet of his time; a performer who can hold and entrance large audiences with the lengthiest of his visionary dithyrambs; the prophet and idol of an entire rebel generation – all these elements go to make up the complex and erratic talent that is Allen Ginsberg. He is so much the powerful public personality, that his poetry eludes the grasp of the critics: his detractors dismiss it out of hand, his admirers accept the message wholly, as something almost akin to spiritual revelation. Quiet, considered assessment of his stature and worth as a poet is thus comparatively rare.

What stands behind Ginsberg in the history of American poetry is fairly clear. He is the latest of that long line of American poets who have striven in poetry for a world view that embraces anything and everything in sight – and sought, at the same time, for a kind of vision that is essentially and fruitfully American. D. H. Lawrence distinguished between the American "palefaces," dependent on and reverential towards, the European tradition, and the "redskins," who sought to create an unashamed and unmistakeable American literature. Ginsberg joins Whitman, Crane, Sandburg and Jeffers in the "redskin" camp. His early poems (*Empty Mirror*) received the blessing of another great and resolutely American poet, the late William Carlos Williams. The book acknowledges this particular debt by including a poem actually entitled "Paterson" (after Williams); but already the young Ginsberg is turning towards that mode of blended social criticism and prophetic utterance which was to characterise almost all his later work: something very far from Williams' approachable, yet highly-wrought and crystalline poetry. "Hymn" clearly anticipates in method the kind of resounding mystical-rhetorical writing one finds in the latest Ginsberg verse.

Ginsberg's celebrity, and representativeness as the leading apostle of the "Beat Generation," began in the U.S.A. and abroad with the publication of *Howl* (1956). The shorter poems in the book celebrated or criticised the fabric of modern American civilisation in a way that combined a personal kind of rhetoric with an eye for evocative detail. But it was in the long title-poem that Ginsberg's philosophy found its clearest definition. "Howl" was an elegy, and a claim, on behalf of a whole generation of rebels and outcasts to whom contemporary American society – whether on the political, social or intellectual level – offered nothing. At times diffuse and gesturing, at times raw, moving and eloquent, *Howl* effectively concentrated the philosophy of a world of drop-outs previously only half-articulate in the tiny underground magazines and presses.

All the principal features of Ginsberg's work were present in "Howl": the observant lyricism, the seething topicality, the vast accumulations of images and references personal and public which he switched and mixed with heady rapidity, bringing together the idealistic, the mystical and the crudely repellent. It was – and remains – an essentially egocentric poetry, vigorously asserting Ginsberg's claim to be the voice of a transforming vision: he himself is always pre-eminently there at the centre of a stage on which most kinds of bizarre, libertarian, non-conforming experience are celebrated. And the precepts of the poetry have been lived in the public figure. Ginsberg has been the avowed and practising homosexual, drug-taker, Civil Rights campaigner, Zen Buddhist and anti-war demonstrator. If *Kaddish,* with its harrowing account of his mother's illness and death, amplified the personal legend, *Planet News*, with its long meditations on his travels, testified to Ginsberg's acceptance as an international public figure preaching revolution and living his own philosophy. The figure remains predominantly and resplendently there at the centre of the poetry in his most recent volume, characteristically titled *The Fall of America*; though there are signs, in some shorter and shorter-lined poems in particular, of an increasing preoccupation with personal ageing, the theme of his own mortality. New and uncollected poems – which he performs at public readings with all the old vigour and charisma – dwell increasingly on the fact of death with a sad, resigned lyricism.

Ginsberg's verse is rarely separated from the philosophy it enshrines and from the public performances he gives of it. But on the page it seems only too indulgent and incoherent, a wild, overreaching confusion of mystical visions, and personal and social references. Only in the shorter poems is a logical sequence of reasoning easily traceable. For the most part, the poetry is sprawling, formless and eccentric in print, smothering moments of real, haunting precision and genuine satirical power with inordinate length and diffuseness:

> can see new Fortune officers look like spies from 20
> floors below with their eyeglasses & gold skulls –
> silver teeth flashing up the shit-mouthed grin –
> weeping in their martinis! There is no secret to
> the success of the

> Six Billionaires that own all Time since the Gnostic
> revolt in Aegypto – they built the Sphinx to confuse
> my sex life, Who Fuckd the Void?

> Why are they starting that war all over again in Laos
> over Neutral Mind? Is the United States CIA army
> Legions overthrowing somebody like Angelica
> Balibanoff?

Only for those to whom order and coherence do not represent necessary or important qualities in poetry does this kind of writing, energetic and vigorously iconoclastic as it is, commend itself completely. If poetry in a time of confused and changing cultural conditions should finally become an art where the effectiveness of social gesture is held to be more important than the artifice and logic with which its statements are made, then Ginsberg's acceptance is assured.

– Alan Brownjohn

———————

GIOVANNI, Nikki. American. Born in Knoxville, Tennessee, 7 June 1943. Educated at Fisk University, Nashville, Tennessee, 1960–61, 1964–67, B.A. (honors) in history 1967; University of Pennsylvania School of Social Work, Philadelphia; Columbia University, New York. Has one son. Assistant Professor of Black Studies, Queens College, Flushing, New York, 1968; Associate Professor of English, Livingston College, Rutgers University, New Brunswick, New Jersey, 1968–70. Editorial Consultant, *Encore* magazine, Albuquerque, New Mexico. Recipient: Ford grant, 1968; National Endowment for the Arts grant, 1969. D.H.: Wilberforce University, Ohio, 1972. Agent: Eugene Winick, 5 West 45th Street, New York, New York 10022, U.S.A.

PUBLICATIONS

Verse

Black Judgement. Detroit, Broadside Press, 1968.
Black Feeling, Black Talk. Detroit, Broadside Press, 1968.
Re: Creation. Detroit, Broadside Press, 1970.

Black Feeling Black Talk/Black Judgement. New York, Morrow, 1970.
Poem of Angela Yvonne Davis. New York, TomNik Ltd., 1970.
My House. New York, Morrow, 1972.

Recordings: *Truth Is on Its Way*, Right On, 1971; *Like a Ripple on a Pond*, 1973.

Other

Spin a Soft Black Song (juvenile). New York, Hill and Wang, 1971.
*Gemini: An Extended Autobiographical Statement on My First Twenty-Five Years of
  Being a Black Poet.* Indianapolis, Bobbs Merrill, 1971.
Ego Tripping and Other Poems for Young Readers. Westport, Connecticut,
  Lawrence Hill, 1973.
A Dialogue: James Baldwin and Nikki Giovanni. Philadelphia, Lippincott, 1973.
*A Poetic Equation: Conversations Between Nikki Giovanni and Margaret
  Walker.* Washington, D.C., Howard University Press, 1974.

Editor, *Night Comes Softly* (anthology). New York, TomNik Ltd., 1970.

Manuscript Collection: Mugar Memorial Library, Boston University.

                    *   *   *

An American seer once said that each of us should inscribe the word "whim"
above our study door. He knew that words, recorded prophecies, injunctions are
double-edged swords, growing sharper through time, turning to rend the creator.
Listen to the poet's voice in 1968 asking "Nigger / Can you kill," and deriding
Wilmington for aspiring to be "coloredman-of-the-year." Hear her asking in "Reflection on April 4, 1968": "What can I, a poor Black woman, do to destroy
america?" So fierce, so talented and ironical, Nikki Giovanni turns the non-violent
corner, sweeps the country with vitriol dripping. The hortatory goddess urging the
young boys to play Mau Mau, the old men to follow revolutionary tides, and the
tight-pantsed Black men to understand her loneliness and desire. Black English is
her forte; she turns the humorous phrase and calls up moving echoes of hymns, the
Bible, rhythm and blues. If she, like Langston Hughes, can't hold them with
"Christ in Alabama," she will turn her audiences's heads with explicit sexual
imagery. And if they reject bitterness and hatred, there is time to assert: "Black
love is Black wealth." But a revolutionary ideology is sometimes monomaniac.
Yes, there can be no "Seduction" of the myopic ideologue.
   Where are you taking us, Nikki, with your cynical, crushing, sometimes clever
Black wit?
   The answer is surprising. After the apocalyptic horns and bells, beyond the
repudiation of bourgeois, childhood pretensions and Jack-and-Jill respectability
stands the happy girl-self of yesteryear. "Knoxville, Tennessee" and "Nikki-Rosa"
represent the essential self: girl from a motivating family, wanting all the things
every "universal" middle-class American desires. The nostalgia is sincere – and
definitive.
   Spring returns. The daughter of Lyndon Johnson, one of Nikki's chosen antagonists, hands her "the coloredwoman-of-the-year" award, and the poet tells *Jet*:
"People like things better if they're not screamed at." The latest volume, *My
House*, has the childhood reveries of *Spin a Soft Black Song* and the egotism of *Re:*

Creation. There are beautiful tree and sky poems, drawn – naturally – from Knox-ville's happy childhood. We know the fire and shouting are formulaic responses to an oppressive time. A wise man, Emerson.

– Houston A. Baker, Jr.

GITTINGS, Robert (William Victor). British. Born in Portsmouth, Hampshire, 1 February 1911. Educated at St. Edward's School, Oxford; Jesus College, Cambridge (Chancellor's Medal, 1931), B.A. 1933, M.A. 1936. Married Katharine Edith Cambell in 1934 (marriage dissolved); Joan Grenville Manton, 1939; has two sons and one daughter. Research Student and Research Fellow, 1933–38, and Supervisor in History, 1938–40, Jesus College, Cambridge. Producer and Scriptwriter, BBC, 1940–63. Visiting Professor, Vanderbilt University, Nashville, Tennessee, Summer 1966, Boston University, 1970, and University of Washington, Seattle, 1972, 1974. Recipient: Heinemann Award for non-fiction, 1955; Phoenix Trust Award, 1963; Smith Award, for non-fiction, 1969. Litt.D.: Cambridge University, 1970. Fellow, Royal Society of Literature. C.B.E. (Commander, Order of the British Empire), 1970. Address: Dodds, East Dean, Chichester, Sussex, England.

PUBLICATIONS

Verse

The Roman Road and Other Poems. London, Oxford University Press, 1932.
The Story of Psyche. Cambridge, University Press, 1936.
Wentworth Place: Poems. London, Heinemann, 1950.
Famous Meeting: Poems, Narrative and Lyric. London, Heinemann, 1953.
This Tower My Prison and Other Poems. London, Heinemann, 1961.
Matters of Love and Death. London, Heinemann, 1968.
American Journey: Twenty-Five Sonnets. London, Heinemann, 1972.

Plays

The Seven Sleepers (produced London, 1950).
The Makers of Violence. London, Heinemann, 1951.
Through a Glass, Lightly. London, Heinemann, 1952.
Man's Estate: A Play of Saint Richard of Chichester, in *Two Saints Plays,* edited by Leo Lehman. London, Heinemann, 1954.
Out of This Wood: A Country Sequence of Five Plays (includes *The Brontë Sisters, Our Clouded Hills, Parson Herrick's Parishioners, Thomas Tusser's Wife, William Cowper's Muse*). London, Heinemann, 1955.
Love's a Gamble: A Ballad Opera, music by Doris Gould. London, Oxford University Press, 1961.
This Tower My Prison (produced London, 1961). Included in *This Tower My Prison and Other Poems,* 1961.

555

Conflict at Canterbury: An Entertainment in Sound and Light (produced Canterbury, 1970). London, Heinemann, 1970.

Son et Lumière scripts: *This Tower My Prison*, 1961; *St. Paul's*, 1968; *Conflict at Canterbury*, 1970.

Radio Writing: Adaptations and Features, 1939–63, including *Famous Meetings* series, 1948–51.

Other

The Peach Blossom Forest and Other Chinese Legends, with Jo Manton. London, Oxford University Press, 1951.
John Keats: The Living Year, 21 September 1818 to 21 September 1819. London, Heinemann, and Cambridge, Massachusetts, Harvard University Press, 1954.
The Mask of Keats: A Study of Problems. London, Heinemann, and Cambridge, Massachusetts, Harvard University Press, 1956.
Windows on History, with Jo Manton. London, Hulton, 4 vols., 1959–61.
Shakespeare's Rival: A Study in Three Parts. London, Heinemann, 1960.
The Story of John Keats, with Jo Manton. London, Methuen, and New York, Dutton, 1962.
The Keats Inheritance. London, Heinemann, 1964; New York, Barnes and Noble, 1965.
Makers of the Twentieth Century, with Jo Manton. London, Hulton, 1966.
John Keats. London, Heinemann, and Boston, Little Brown, 1968.
The Odes of Keats and Their Earliest Known Manuscripts in Facsimile. London, Heinemann, and Kent, Ohio, Kent State University Press, 1970.

Editor, *The Living Shakespeare*. London, Heinemann, 1960; Greenwich, Connecticut, Fawcett, 1961.
Editor, with Evelyn Hardy, *Some Recollections*, by Emma Hardy. London, Oxford University Press, 1961.
Editor, *Selected Poems and Letters of John Keats*. London, Heinemann, and New York, Barnes and Noble, 1966.
Editor, *Omniana; or, Horae otiosiores*, by Robert Southey and Samuel Taylor Coleridge. London, Centaur Press, 1969.
Editor, *Letters of John Keats: A New Selection*. London, Oxford University Press, 1970.

Robert Gittings comments:

I have tried to use, so far as one ever consciously does, the best, or what seems to me best, of what is old and what is new.

Major themes are probably indicated by the title of my book of verse, *Matters of Love and Death*.

I do not feel I have fully achieved this, but am still trying.

Technically, I am interested in the use of verse for dramatic and narrative purposes, have written verse-plays and verse-scripts for Son et Lumière productions and for broadcasting.

*   *   *

There can be little doubt that Robert Gittings's reputation as a critic and, in particular, his study of John Keats, has overshadowed his attributes as a poet in his own right. In his earliest work he tended to write in an unfashionably traditional mode, though at any other period his poems would have attracted attention. Since then, however, he has produced several volumes of poetry and developed a personal style and approach, and it is high time that his poetic talents were properly recognised. In his narrative vein he is quite unlike any other poet, for most of his contemporaries have found it extremely difficult to write convincing narrative verse. Robert Gittings can and does – with a quite extraordinary flair. This is probably best demonstrated in *Famous Meeting* which contains nine narrative poems on such diverse subjects as the meeting between Wellington and Nelson, Livingstone, Boswell's ''London Journal,'' and a lost explorer in the Australian desert. His next volume, *This Tower My Prison,* takes its title from the dramatic monologue between Robert Carr, Earl of Somerset, and Frances Howard, on the murder of Sir Thomas Overbury and makes skilful use of the historic present.

Gittings's understanding of character and his dramatic gifts are to be discerned, once again, in the long poems included in his *Matters of Love and Death*: ''Antony and Cleopatra,'' ''The Secret Mistress,'' and ''By the Lake'' (a sequence on D. H. Lawrence and Frieda). Each of these volumes also contains a number of lyrics which, if assembled in a single collection, would be enough to establish a sound reputation for any poet. Amongst these are to be found such admirable poems as ''The Guillemot's Egg,'' ''Kilvert at Clyro,'' ''A Breath of Air,'' ''A Daughter,'' and ''The Middle-Aged Man.'' *American Journey* is a collection of 25 sonnets, all competently executed, inspired by a winter journey by air to America.

– Howard Sergeant

GLASSCO, John (Stinson). Canadian. Born in Montreal, Quebec, 15 December 1909. Educated at Selwyn House School, Montreal; Bishop's College School, Lennoxville, Quebec, 1923–24; Lower Canada College, Montreal, 1924–25; McGill University, Montreal, 1925–28. Married the dancer Elma von Colmar in 1963 (died, 1971); Marion McCormick, 1974. Councillor, 1948–52, and Mayor, 1952–54, Village of Foster, Quebec. Founder, 1951, and Honorary Chairman, 1964, Foster Horse Show. Recipient: Quebec Provincial Prize, 1961; Canada Council Senior Arts Fellowship, 1966; Governor-General's Award, 1972. Address: Jamaica Farm, Foster, Quebec, Canada.

PUBLICATIONS

Verse

Conan's Fig. Paris, transition, 1928.
The Deficit Made Flesh. Toronto, McClelland and Stewart, 1958.
A Point of Sky. Toronto, Oxford University Press, 1964.
Square Hardman (as George Colman). Waterloo, Quebec, Pastime Press, 1966.
Selected Poems. Toronto, Oxford University Press, 1971.
Montreal. Montreal, Delta Canada, 1973.

Novels

Contes en Crinoline (as Jean de Saint-Luc).   Paris, Gaucher, 1930.
Under the Hill (completion of the unfinished novel by Aubrey Beardsley). Paris, Olympia Press, 1959; London, New English Library, 1966; New York, Grove Press, 1967.
The English Governess (as Miles Underwood).   Paris, Olympia Press, 1960.
Harriet Marwood, Governess (published anonymously).   New York, Grove Press, 1967.
Fetish Girl (as Sylvia Bayer).   New York, Grove Press, 1972.
The Fatal Woman: 3 Novellas.   Toronto, House of Anansi, 1974.

Other

Memoirs of Montparnasse.   Toronto and New York, Oxford University Press, 1970.

Editor, *English Poetry in Quebec* (Proceedings of the Foster Poetry Conference). Montreal, McGill University Press, 1965.
Editor, *The Poetry of French Canada in Translation.*   Toronto, Oxford University Press, 1970.
Editor, *The Temple of Pederasty,* by Ihara Saikaku.   North Hollywood, California, Essex House, 1970.

Translator, *The Journal of Saint-Denys-Garneau.*   Toronto, McClelland and Stewart, 1962.
Translator, *Lot's Wife,* by Monique Bosco.   Toronto, McClelland and Stewart, 1974.

Manuscript Collection: McGill University Library, Montreal.

*   *   *

John Glassco is an elegiac poet in the classic tradition who has found a subject-matter for his philosophical and evocative verses in the rural life of the Eastern Townships of his native province of Quebec. A little pocket of country isolation, of run-down farms and stony pastures, is presented as symbolic of a kind of forlorn and heroic rejection of the mechanization and success-worship of the acquisitive society. In such poems as "The Entailed Farm," "The Rural Mail," or "Deserted Buildings under Shefford Mountain," the spirit of John Clare or Edward Thomas has been introduced into Canadian poetry.

Besides his eclogues and bucolic verses John Glassco has written witty and sophisticated poems of a personal and psychological nature which testify to the wide range of his experience and the eclecticism of his literary taste. The irony and stylistic elegance found in his prose *tour de force,* the completion of Aubrey Beardsley's unfinished *Under the Hill,* and in several *novellas* published by the Olympia Press, is seen also in metaphysical love poems like "A Devotion" and mordant satires like "Brummell at Calais," "Utrillo's World," or "The Screaming Child." In these poems, technically strict and carefully shaped, a modern consciousness that shares something of the allusive richness of Proust has found its most natural expression in a traditional style that manages to be at once local and universal. This is especially true of the three or four long philosophical meditations on death which give a peculiar distinction to the collection, *A Point of Sky*. They demonstrate clearly that the tradition of Matthew Arnold, Robert Bridges and E. A. Robinson is still capable of producing work that is personal, intense and thoroughly alive.

– A. J. M. Smith

GLEN, Duncan. Scottish. Born in Cambuslang, Lanark, 11 January 1933. Educated at West Coats School, Cambuslang, 1938–46; Rutherglen Academy, 1946–49; Heriot-Watt College, Edinburgh, 1950–53; Edinburgh College of Art, 1953–56. Served in the Royal Air Force, 1956–58. Married Margaret Eadie in 1957; has one daughter and one son. Typographic Designer, Her Majesty's Stationery Office, London, 1958–60; Lecturer in Typographic Design, Watford College of Technology, 1960–63; Editor, Robert Gibson and Sons Ltd., publishers, Glasgow, 1963–65. Since 1965, Senior Lecturer in Graphic Design, Preston Polytechnic, Lancashire. Editor, *Knowe*, Preston, 1971. Since 1965, Sole Owner, Akros Publications, and Editor, *Akros*, Penwortham, Preston. Associate, Society of Industrial Artists and Designers. Address: 14 Parklands Avenue, Penwortham, Preston, Lancashire PR1 0QL, England.

PUBLICATIONS

Verse

> *Stanes.* Kinglassie, Fife, Duncan Glen, 1966.
> *Idols: When Alexander Our King Was Dead.* Preston, Lancashire, Akros, 1967.
> *Kythings and Other Poems.* Thurso, Caithness Books, 1969.
> *Sunny Summer Sunday Afternoon in the Park?* Preston, Lancashire, Akros, 1969.
> *Unnerneath the Bed.* Preston, Lancashire, Akros, 1970.
> *In Appearances.* Preston, Lancashire, Akros, 1971.
> *Clydesdale: A Sequence o Poems.* Preston, Lancashire, Akros, 1971.
> *Feres.* Preston, Lancashire, Akros, 1971.
> *A Journey Past: A Sequence o Poems.* Preston, Lancashire, Akros, 1972.
> *A Cled Score: Poems.* Preston, Lancashire, Akros, 1974.

Other

> *Hugh MacDiarmid: Rebel Poet and Prophet, A Short Note on His Seventieth Birthday.* Hemel Hempstead, Hertfordshire, Drumalban Press, 1962.
> *Hugh MacDiarmid and the Scottish Renaissance.* Edinburgh, Chambers, 1964.
> *The Literary Masks of Hugh MacDiarmid.* Glasgow, Drumalban Press, 1964.
> *Scottish Poetry Now.* Preston, Lancashire, Akros, 1966.
> *An Afternoon with Hugh MacDiarmid.* Privately printed, 1969.
> *A Small Press and Hugh MacDiarmid: With a Checklist of Akros Publications, 1962-1970.* Preston, Lancashire, Akros, 1970.

559

The MacDiarmids: A Conversation Between Hugh MacDiarmid and Duncan Glen with Valda Grieve and Arthur Thompson. Preston, Lancashire, Akros, 1970.

The Individual and the Twentieth Century Scottish Literary Tradition. Preston, Lancashire, Akros, 1971.

A Bibliography of Scottish Poets from Stevenson to 1974. Preston, Lancashire, Akros, 1974.

Editor, *Poems Addressed to Hugh MacDiarmid and Presented to Him on His Seventy-Fifth Birthday.* Preston, Lancashire, Akros, 1967.

Editor, *Selected Essays of Hugh MacDiarmid.* London, Cape, 1969; Berkeley, University of California Press, 1970.

Editor, *The Akros Anthology of Scottish Poetry, 1965–1970.* Preston, Lancashire, Akros, 1970.

Editor, *Whither Scotland? A Prejudiced Look at the Future of a Nation.* London, Gollancz, 1971.

Editor, *Hugh MacDiarmid: A Critical Survey.* Edinburgh, Scottish Academic Press, 1972.

Critical Studies: by Paul Duncan, in *Sou' Wester* (Carbondale, Illinois), Summer 1970; Sam Adams, in *Anglo-Welsh Review* (Pembroke Dock, Wales), Autumn 1970; John C. Weston, in *Akros* (Preston, Lancashire), April 1971; Anne Cluysenaar, in *Stand* (Newcastle upon Tyne), xii, 4, 1971; "Meaning and Self" by Walter Perrie, in *Chapman* (Hamilton, Lanarkshire), Spring 1972; "The Progress of Scots" by John Herdman, in *Akros* (Preston, Lancashire), December 1972.

*   *   *

Duncan Glen belongs to that important community of Scottish writers who have developed a style in Scots (or Lallans – the fashionable term) on a prose base. Glen, one feels, or his people, might speak with the same calculated understatement or with the not unkindly irony of his poetry. His idiom allows him to sketch the picture of his dead father in his poem, "My Faither," with a sense of truth, respect and manliness. The poem begins:

> Staunin noo aside his bress-haunled coffin
> I mind him fine aside the black shinin range
> In his grey strippit troosers, galluses and nae collar
> For the flannel shirt. My faither.

> (Standing now beside his brass handled coffin
> I remember him well beside the black shining range
> In his grey striped trousers, braces and no collar
> For the flannel shirt. My father.)

This honest, modest achievement is characteristic of a deal of the rather better writing in Scots, but Glen goes beyond this in his finer poems. In the last verse of "My Faither" the writer looks down on the body, "laid oot in the best / Black suitin. . . ." This father ("My father") – he uses the English spelling – he does not know. The solid, known person becomes dramatically unknowable.

The domestic imagery in Scots is Glen's point of beginning. His poem "Progress" begins from naive statement, bouncing along like a nursery rhyme, but there is a remorseless logic in it. It proceeds thus:

> Is not nature wonderful
> We cam oot heid first – get a slap
> and oor mither toungue.

By the end one is aware Glen is applying a kind of Socratic dialogue to the argument. The bright tone darkens. He takes this development further in "Bacchae in Suburbia." Written in a homely Scots ("You are feart son?"), one hears, as it were, behind the words, the knock on the door that might mean death or torture, as it has done for many in Europe in our time.

So far the concentration and intensity achieved in the poems referred to have been rare. It may be that the diffuse verse written by Duncan Glen mainly in English has been due to time spent generously in publishing and editing known and unknown writers. This has been a very valuable service, but the cultivation of his own markedly individual talent may well be more rewarding to Scottish letters.

– George Bruce

GLOVER, Denis (James Matthews). New Zealander. Born in Dunedin, 10 December 1912. Educated at Auckland Grammar School; Christ's College; Canterbury University College, A.B. Served as an officer in the Royal Navy during World War II: Distinguished Service Cross. Married Mary Granville in 1936; Lyn Cameron, 1972; has one son (first marriage). Taught English at Canterbury University, 1936–38, and typography at the Technical Correspondence Institute, Christchurch. Founder, Caxton Press, Christchurch, 1936; joined Pegasus Press, 1953, and Wingfield Press, 1955. Formerly, journalist, *The Press*, Christchurch. Former President, New Zealand P.E.N., and Friends of the Turnbull Library, Wellington; Member of the Canterbury University Council, and of the New Zealand State Literary Fund Committee. Recipient: Jessie Mackay Award, 1960. Address: 3/231 The Terrace, Wellington, New Zealand.

PUBLICATIONS

Verse

Thistledown.   Christchurch, Caxton Club, 1935.
Six Easy Ways of Dodging Debt Collectors.   Christchurch, Caxton Press, 1936.
The Arraignment of Paris.   Christchurch, Caxton Press, 1937.
Thirteen Poems.   Christchurch, Caxton Press, 1939.
Cold Tongue.   Christchurch, Caxton Press, 1940.
Recent Poems, with others.   Christchurch, Caxton Press, 1941.
The Wind and the Sand: Poems 1934–44.   Christchurch, Caxton Press, 1945.
Summer Flowers.   Christchurch, Caxton Press, 1945.
Sings Harry and Other Poems.   Christchurch, Caxton Press, 1951.
Arawata Bill: A Sequence of Poems.   Christchurch, Pegasus Press, 1953.
Since Then.   Wellington, Mermaid Press, 1957.

Poetry Harbinger, with A. R. D. Fairburn.   Auckland, Pilgrim Press, 1958.
Enter Without Knocking: Selected Poems.   Christchurch, Pegasus Press, 1964;
   augmented edition, 1971.
Sharp Edge Up: Verses and Satires.   Auckland, Blackwood and Janet Paul,
   1968.
Myself When Young.   Christchurch, Nag's Head Press, 1970.
To a Particular Woman.   Christchurch, Nag's Head Press, 1970.
Diary to a Woman.   Wellington, Catspaw Press, 1971.

Plays

   Screenplays: *The Coaster,* 1951; *Nick Stimson,* with John Lang, 1972.

   Radio Play: *They Sometimes Float at Sea,* 1970.

Other

   A Clutch of Authors and a Clot.   Wellington, Wingfield Press, 1960.
   Hot Water Sailor.   Wellington, Reed, 1962.
   Denis Glover's Bedside Book.   Wellington, Reed, 1963.

   Editor, with Geoffrey Fairburn, *The Woman Problem and Other Prose,* by A. R.
      D. Fairburn.   Auckland, Blackwood and Janet Paul, 1967.

                          *   *   *

   Denis Glover was one of the group of New Zealand poets whose work began to
appear in the 1930's. He was also a printer, and his founding of the Caxton Press in
Christchurch established what has become a tradition of fine printing in New
Zealand, particularly in the production of editions of poetry. This is characteristic
of the boldness with which Glover and his friend Allen Curnow set out on their
poetic careers. Where there was no publisher for poetry they became publishers
themselves. Where there was no interest in poetry they created it. Where there was
no criticism they wrote it. In Glover's early poetry there is a double sense of
excitement: that which was in the air of the time everywhere; and that which
belongs peculiarly to a moment in New Zealand's literary history. There are many
echoes in his early work of the Auden group – both in his political beliefs and in his
technical innovations:

        Rolling along the roads on holiday wheels
        Now wonder at their construction, the infinite skill
        That planned the road to the gradient of the hill,
        The precision, the planning, the labour it all reveals.

        An unremembered legion of labourers did this . . . .

        These men we should honour above the managers of banks . . . .

But there was also a freshness in the writing that came from a consciousness that
he and his contemporaries in purely New Zealand terms were opening up territory
to poetry that had previously been closed to it; that they were turning their backs

not merely on Georgianism in the broadest sense, but on the local Georgianism that looked to England as "Home." Colonial versifying was over:

> I do not dream of Sussex downs
> Or quaint old England's quaint old towns:
> I think of what will yet be seen
> In Johnsonville and Geraldine.

Glover's collected poems would read like a handbook of good writing without containing anything that lays claim to being "major." Glover himself seldom appears and this is perhaps a limitation. The scene, the event, the "subject" are ruggedly presented to us, without a word wasted. But the poet who felt moved to write is withdrawn. Instead there is often a persona – his fictional "Harry," who sings in the windbreak; the historical figure of the prospector, "Arawata Bill"; or simply the voice of an observer who remains distinct from the poet because he is detached – sometimes irritable, sometimes preposterous, often funny, but never revealing himself fully.

Glover has written some of New Zealand's finest descriptive verse, and some of its most beautiful lyrics:

> Once the days were clear
> Like mountains in water,
> The mountains were always there
> And the mountain water . . .

And here is Glover the satirist, catching at once the flavour of New Zealand life and that of its literature, holding them both up to gentle ridicule:

> The Centennial Baths
> (Horace III, 13, O Fons Bandusiae)
>
> O municipal baths with your gleaming tiles,
> Most worthy I find you of praise,
> Of tribute worthy in a column of news.
>
> Tomorrow to you do I vow
> My virginal togs; in your coolness
> How brightly their colours will glow!
>
> In vain do the nor'-westers beat
> On your surface that offers delight
> To the weary, the restless crowd on the street.
>
> And you among noble baths will take station
> When I sing of the flagpole above your tiles
> And your waters loquacious with motion.

– C. K. Stead

GLÜCK, Louise (Elisabeth). American. Born in New York City, 22 April 1943. Attended Sarah Lawrence College, Bronxville, New York; Columbia University,

New York. Married Charles Hertz, Jr., in 1967 (divorced); has one son. Visiting Artist, Goddard College, Plainfield, Vermont, 1971–72; Visiting Lecturer, University of North Carolina, Greensboro, Spring 1973. Recipient: Academy of American Poets Prize, 1966; Rockefeller Fellowship, 1967; National Endowment for the Arts grant, 1969; Eunice Tietjens Memorial Prize (*Poetry*, Chicago), 1971. Lives in Vermont. Address: c/o Daniel Glück, 966 Northfield Road, Woodmere, New York 11598, U.S.A.

PUBLICATIONS

Verse

Firstborn. New York, New American Library, 1968; London, Anvil Press Poetry, 1969.
The House on Marshland. New York, Ecco Press, 1974.

*   *   *

Louise Glück is a younger poet whose work has given extraordinary promise of things to come. A consummately meticulous craftsman, she has tended to work with materials associated with the confessional tradition. Not strictly a confessionalist, though, she speaks in a variety of voices, creating a body of work that is painful and shocking, but without sufficient coherence always to justify the relentless evocations of violence that reverberate in so many of her pages. In a typical poem, images of corruption and decay are marshalled, but we do not know why they must have any connection with the people presented in the poem.

Echoes of other poets abound in Ms. Glück's work, but she nonetheless achieves a voice of her own, skillfully playing off of masters like Jarrell and Lowell and Kunitz. Through the deliberately partial assimilation of other poetic voices, in fact, Ms. Glück achieves a poise and serenity, in some of her work, which constitute a remarkable tribute to one so young. Given, as well, the poet's casual weaving of dense aural patterns, one cannot but wonder at her developing mastery.

Ms. Glück is a poet of few themes, but these she develops with a ferocity that borders on obsession. She appears to write best when she is least herself, when she writes out of contexts which are relatively unfamiliar to her own experience, and which she need not invest with the accouterments of melodrama or terror in order to make them striking. The poems are often extremely lean, several cultivating a stenographic bluntness which owes more to Alan Dugan than to any of the woman poets I can think of. The resemblance to Dugan is seen too in the many combinations of slang words and elaborate Latinisms. What informs Dugan's work, though, is a moral passion which is largely lacking in Ms. Glück. Instead we too often get melodrama, the forcing of images to yield more than they can or ought to yield. Situations are unambiguously awful, characters nothing but prototypes. Details accumulate as if by an energy of their own, but an energy in no way responsible to the shaping intelligence that presumably controls the poem. Hopefully Ms. Glück will turn more and more to cultivate the unusual capacity for playful compassion she demonstrates in her more successful poems.

– Robert Boyers

GNAROWSKI, Michael. Canadian. Born in Shanghai, China, 27 September 1934. Educated at McGill University, Montreal, B.A.; University of Montreal, M.A.; University of Ottawa, Ph.D. Married; has three children. Formerly, Associate Professor, and Coordinator of Canadian Studies, Sir George Williams University, Montreal. Currently, Professor of English, Carleton University, Ottawa. Editor, Critical Views on Canadian Writers series, McGraw Hill-Ryerson Press, Toronto; Editor, The Carleton Library, McClelland and Stewart, Toronto. Co-Editor, *Le Chien d'Or/The Golden Dog* magazine. Address: 15 Ossington Way, Ottawa, Ontario, Canada.

PUBLICATIONS

Verse

> *Postscript for St. James Street.* Montreal, Delta Canada, 1965.
> *The Gentlemen Are Also Lexicographers.* Montreal, Delta Canada, 1969.

Other

> *Contact 1952–1954: Being an Index to the Contents of "Contact," a Little Magazine edited by Raymond Souster . . . .* Montreal, Delta Canada, 1966.

> Editor, with Louis Dudek, *The Making of Modern Poetry in Canada: Essential Articles on Contemporary Canadian Poetry in English.* Toronto, Ryerson Press, 1967.
> Editor, *The Rising Village of Oliver Goldsmith: A New Edition.* Montreal, Delta Canada, 1968.
> Editor, *Archibald Lampman.* Toronto, Ryerson Press, 1970.
> Editor, *Selected Stories of Raymond Kneister.* Ottawa, University of Ottawa Press, 1972.

Michael Gnarowski comments:

Influenced by the "Montreal School" of Dudek, Layton, etc., and particularly by Wallace Stevens as the major external influence. Major themes, or, more accurately, major concerns could be said to be related to urban realism and the response of the individual to the complexity of modern business and its society.

*   *   *

Michael Gnarowski's poetry is deceptively modern, steeped in the technological urban world, in a search for humanist values denied relevance in an ecology of bankers, developers, brokers and other captains of the marketplace – the battering rams of material progress. The sensibility is attuned to the age, and, though the locus for reflection is specific, St. James Street is paradigmatic of the Wall Streets and the Bond Streets that rule over the quality of modern man's life. Gnarowski does not make concessions to the reader, using a tightly-controlled verbal medium, self-reflexive in tonality, imagery and symbolism. The structure is thematically consistent. The world of the city, concrete, physical, heavy with cement and mammoth steel and glass monuments to itself, weighs on its human architects and pillars as leaden and mute as their constructions blotting out the natural cycle whose destroyed wilderness has yielded a factory-made garden. The necessary counterpoise of a felt sensibility – be it the archetypal pioneer past or the reassuring atmosphere of an old Church, the free play of the senses or the recollection of the dream of immigrants who came to the New World in search of innocence and vitality – is evoked as a vision betrayed: "You'all must come and visit me / in my New World of small inventions / and turned away / dispensing such new wisdom / as gallonage of pumps / and tachometric spec of old machines." Always the vision is made poignant in the face of the irreconcilability of urban desolation and corporate anonymity. Loneliness, alienation prevail. Even in poems where the land is addressed, the image of virginal splendor and purity is deflated by its larger perception as a "white asylum." The wilderness is within as well as without.

Gnarowski functions evidently in the poetic tradition of the Eliot-Stevens-Williams school where verbal economy and self-reliance become their own structure of meaning. But in a number of poems, particularly in his second book of poetry, there lurk yearnings for the celebration of love, warmth and gentleness binding the poet to his fellowman. Deflected, they signal a possible flaw: the apparent indebtness of the poet's sensibility to the Fifties' "lonely crowd" mythos. The poet's strategy in the face of defeat is to seek refuge behind words whose increasing obscurity and gratuitousness ironically imply that the technology and the plasticity previously denounced now claim the poet as victim when language becomes sound or noise with no referential point. Admittedly, the irony can be at the expense of the reader. Gnarowski's second book may be a sign of artistic evolution when it is understood that the emblematic arrangement of typography is a conceit of "pure poetry" substituted for the early thematic order. Yet, the poet's original vision is that of a moralist subtly summoning the age to account for its failures and betrayals. As such, his last book leaves one unsatisfied; the more so when one of the greatest tragedies of our time, Vietnam, is suggested only as a sign of the ambient technological nightmare and not explored as a nexus of a general moral crisis.

The decade when Vietnam came to dominate our consciousness, the Sixties, saw the parallel emergence of a novel sense of self that spread across North America and Europe. Beyond its symbol in the revolution of the young, the temper of the Sixties affirmed the need to invade the wilderness and the africas within and without. New Forces were released, defiant rages vented, but a belief in the celebration of the Dionysian imperative was also expressed denying that despair was an inevitable and inescapable condition for technological man. This affirmation is belied in Gnarowski's refuge in "pure poetry," if not silence. Too bad.

– Max Dorsinville

GOACHER, Denis. British. Born in London, 9 June 1925. Has two children. Address: Dioné House, Wembworthy, Chulmleigh, North Devon, England.

PUBLICATIONS

Verse

> *The Marriage Rite,* with Peter Whigham.   Ditchling, Sussex, Ditchling Press,
> 1960.
> *Logbook.*   Kingswinford, Staffordshire, Grosseteste Review Books, 1972.
> *Transversions.*   Kingswinford, Staffordshire, Grosseteste Review Books, 1973.
> *Night of the 12th, 13th.*   Rushden, Northamptonshire, Sceptre Press, 1973.

Other

> Editor, *Soldier On* (autobiography of Colonel Sir Mike Ansell).   London, Peter
> Davies, 1973.

> Translator, *Inferno* (Cantos 29–31), by Dante.   London, BBC Publications,
> 1965.

Denis Goacher comments:

The rapidly increasing tendency of "poets" to give prose reductions of their poetic aims makes their function, as poets, increasingly preposterous.

For myself, the aim and aspiration can be entirely deduced from my published collections – to those who can *read.* Alas, that skill, like that of the wheelwright, the stonemason and the butcher, is now quite rare.

*   *   *

Denis Goacher's poems have a sense of style, and contain some freshly perceptive and original lines. He is elliptical, and it is clearly a problem to him as to how to preserve the sound of his own voice and yet to maintain the communicability he seeks. In the first three lines of "Dead Friends" –

> How many years?
> My capsule holds a smeary track
> signals pass

– he succeeds because of the resonances set up by the evocative second line, and the rhythmical assuredness. Elsewhere he does preserve his own way of speaking (and hearing), but at the expense of failing to achieve coherence. But the praise he has received from Basil Bunting and Herbert Read has been deserved: this is a positive and entirely honest response, and a voice (as Bunting has pleaded) that is original:

> I touched a buttercup petal fell
> not far
> saw the shrew dead on her back
> then blessed one foxglove gave my finger
> luck
> and heart's ease. . . .

– Martin Seymour-Smith

GOEDICKE, Patricia.   American.   Born in Boston, Massachusetts, 21 June 1931. Educated at Middlebury College, Vermont. B.A. 1953 (Phi Beta Kappa, 1952); Ohio University, Athens, M.A. 1963. Married Leonard Wallace Robinson in 1969. Editorial Assistant, Harcourt Brace and World, publishers, New York, 1953–54, and T. Y. Crowell, publishers, New York, 1955–56. Instructor in English, Ohio University, 1962–68, and Hunter College, New York, 1969–71. Co-Editor, *Page* magazine, Athens, Ohio, 1961–66. Recipient: National Endowment for the Arts grant, 1969. Address: Aptdo. 462, San Miguel de Allende, Guanajuato, Mexico.

PUBLICATIONS

Verse

Between Oceans.   New York, Harcourt Brace, 1968.

Critical Study: by Erica Jong, in *Back Door* (Athens, Ohio), Spring 1974.

Patricia Goedicke comments:

As the daughter of a psychiatrist, I have subjected myself to so much self-analysis that I prefer to confine any general analysis of my poetry to specific poems. People I have admired and learned from – some have influenced my poetry as such, some not – are W. H. Auden, Hollis Summers, Robert Frost, Dylan Thomas, William Carlos Williams, Robert Creeley, Charles Olson, Patricia Grean, Leonard Wallace Robinson, and many others. I try to tell the truth in my poetry as "memorably" as possible. Verse forms are free.

*   *   *

Patricia Goedicke writes relatively little, one assumes, her single book having included work fron a ten year period. Many of her poems are occasional, dealing with experiences of girlhood, love, marriage, death, while others are more like self-imposed literary exercises, often on themes from what Larkin calls "the myth kitty." The poems of the first kind show her at her weakest. They are marred by disconcerting coyness ("Yet my lord husband / Loves me, loves this dizzy daisy / Picking itself to pieces!") or pretentious solemnity ("To wake up in the night / Terrified, trembling, to think / Of Beowulf, and Christ, and Homer gone / Is natural . . .") and seem uncomfortably vulnerable. There are exceptions, however. Two longer poems, "Stranger in the House" (about the recurrent awareness of death from childhood on) and "At the River: For Nicholas" (about the death of a son), despite their unevenness, engage one's sympathies by their subject matter, and "The Thunder," on the same subject as "At the River," is all the better for touching on it indirectly. It speaks of having tape-recorded bird song while a storm approached, and ends:

> Now, on the playback,
> One of us having
> Lost his voice forever,
>
> Out of the balloon of silence,
> In a rumor of distant birds
>
> We do not ask for wisdom, we keep
> Listening to the thunder.

The poems of the second sort, many using personages from myth and fairy tale, are more frequently successful, perhaps because attempting less. "The Prodigal" shows the haunting presence within the young man of the family he has deserted. "Cassandra" evokes well the prophetic mood of terrified insight and powerlessness to communicate it to others. And the following poem, despite the triteness of "highways of the year" and the echo of Stevens' "The Emperor of Ice Cream" at the end, is charmingly effective in its concrete imagery and represents the writer at her best. It is called "Goldilocks":

> Between the bricks the warmth.
> Crumble of weeds. Clay. The honey husk of nuts.
>
> Sunshine after a bitter night.
> Like pots of herbs the odors cluster
>
> But the days are getting colder.
> Darkening along the highways of the year
>
> Oak leaves, arthritic, stiffen.
> The heel of morning hardens
>
> O but listen, call Goldilocks!
> Such a little jug of jelly, so sweet –
>
> Call the silly liar, one last time
> Let her display the whiteness of her feet.

> – Seamus Cooney

GORDON, Giles (Alexander Esme). British. Born in Edinburgh, 23 May 1940. Educated at Edinburgh Academy, 1948–57. Married Margaret Anna Eastoe in 1964; has two sons and one daughter. Advertising Executive, Secker and Warburg, publishers, London, 1962–63; Editor, Hutchinson Publishing Group, London, 1963–64, and Penguin Books, London, 1964–66; Editorial Director, Victor Gollancz, publishers, London, 1967–72. Since 1972, Partner, Anthony Sheil Associates, literary agents, London. Since 1971, Lecturer in Creative Writing, in London, for Tufts University, Medford, Massachusetts. C. Day Lewis Fellow in Writing, King's College, London, 1974–75. Member, Arts Council of Great Britain Literature Panel, 1966–69; since 1973, Member, Society of Authors. Committee of Management. Recipient: *Transatlantic Review* prize, for fiction, 1966.

PUBLICATIONS

Verse

Landscape Any Date.   Edinburgh, M. Macdonald, 1963.
Two and Two Make One: Poems.   Preston, Lancashire, Akros, 1966.
Two Elegies.   London, Turret Books, 1968.
Eight Poems for Gareth.   Frensham, Surrey, Sceptre Press, 1970.
Between Appointments.   Frensham, Surrey, Sceptre Press, 1971.
Twelve Poems for Callum.   Preston, Lancashire, Akros, 1972.
One Man Two Women.   London, Sheep Press, 1974.
Egyptian Room, Metropolitan Museum of Art.   Rushden, Northamptonshire,
   Sceptre Press, 1974.

Novels

The Umbrella Man.   London, Allison and Busby, 1971.
About a Marriage.   London, Allison and Busby, and New York, Stein and
   Day, 1972.
Girl with Red Hair.   London, Hutchinson, 1974.

Short Stories

Pictures from an Exhibition.   London, Allison and Busby, and New York, Dial
   Press, 1970.
Penguin Modern Stories 3, with others.   London, Penguin, 1970.
Farewell, Fond Dreams.   London, Hutchinson, 1975.

Other

Book 2000: Some Likely Trends in Publishing.   London, Association of Assistant
   Librarians, 1969.
Walter and the Balloon (juvenile).   London, Heinemann, 1973.
Beyond the Words: Eleven Writers in Search of a New Fiction.   London, Hut-
   chinson, 1975.

Editor, with Alex Hamilton, Factions: Eleven Original Stories.   London,
   Joseph, 1974.
Editor, with Dulan Barber, Members of the Jury: The Jury Experience.   London,
   Wildwood House, 1975.
Editor, with Michael Bakewell and B. S. Johnson, You Always Remember the
   First Time.   London, Quartet, 1975.
Editor, with Martin Seymour-Smith, Horrible People.   London, Joseph, 1975.
Editor, A New English Writing.   London, Hutchinson, 1975.

Manuscript Collection: National Library of Scotland, Edinburgh.

Giles Gordon comments:

I fear my poetry becomes less important to me as my prose fiction becomes more important to me. I seem to be able to use prose in a more flexible way than I am able to use poetry. I think it is important (for one's self respect, if nothing else) to recognise one's limitations as a writer by the time one is, say, thirty. My limiatations as a poet are considerable, and I doubt whether I shall publish in future more than the occasional new poem. If it isn't impossibly arrogant (which it is), I like to think that my real poetry is in my prose. Which is not to say that I write "poetic prose": quite the contrary.

*   *   *

As a novelist and short-story writer Giles Gordon is courageously experimental, being obsessed both by the feeling that "the world is not for us" (i.e., he is interested in giving non-anthropomorphic accounts of events) and by questions of identity that can best be described as Pirandellian. Yet, though his attempts to work out these themes in prose are valuable and intelligent, and will in due course play their part in his work, his most memorable prose has been written when he was directly moved (an article on the loss of a child; an account of his friend and fellow-writer B. S. Johnson's suicide and funeral), and is itself direct and moving. The foregoing remarks are relevant to his poetry: while he fully understands the different role of the poem – by virtue of the rhythm and, in particular, its line – we find a similar dichotomy between the intellectual and the directly emotional (though by no means uncontrolled), and a similar promise of a future reconciliation between the two attitudes.

But the poems in *Two and Two Make One* nonetheless go beyond his prose in finding, in landscape (of Provence), mysterious although significant parallels to human experience. Unlike the bulk of his fiction, these poems sometimes seem to be trying to ask the question, "How is the world for us?" rather than making the statement that it *is* not; at other times he sees (interestingly) people *as* landscapes:

> All things are in two, have sides or halves,
> one always complementary to the other.
> In the sky, sun and moon; man and woman
> on earth. . . .

In *Twelve Poems for Callum* he becomes more direct. These celebrate the birth of a son against the hideous background of world events, and in them the author is simply asking the question of how he can reconcile his delight with the horrors perpetrated by the world which he – and now his son – are a part. As the doomed Dubcek returns from Moscow to Prague the child

> cries in his sleep
> mutters in his growing
> convinces my dreams
> that something
> is real.

– Martin Seymour-Smith

GOTLIEB, Phyllis. Canadian. Born in Toronto, Ontario, 25 May 1926. Educated at public schools in Toronto; University of Toronto, B.A. in English language and literature 1948; M.A. 1950. Married Calvin Gotlieb in 1949; has three children. Address: 29 Ridgevale Drive, Toronto, Ontario M6A 1K9, Canada.

PUBLICATIONS

Verse

> *Who Knows One?* Toronto, Hawkshead Press, 1962.
> *Within the Zodiac.* Toronto, McClelland and Stewart, 1964.
> *Ordinary, Moving.* Toronto, Oxford University Press, 1969.
> *Doctor Umlaut's Earthly Kingdom.* Toronto, Calliope Press, 1974.

Novels

> *Sunburst.* Greenwich, Connecticut, Fawcett, 1964; London, Coronet, 1966.
> *Why Should I Have All the Grief?* Toronto, Macmillan, 1969.

Plays

> *Doctor Umlaut's Earthly Kingdom* (broadcast, 1970; produced Ontario, 1972). Published in *Poems for Voices,* Toronto, CBC Publications, 1970.
> *Garden Varieties* (broadcast, 1973; produced Ontario, 1973).

> Radio Plays: *Doctor Umlaut's Earthly Kingdom,* 1970; *Garden Varieties,* 1973.

Critical Studies: Reviews by Fred Cogswell, in *Canadian Literature* (Vancouver), by Mary Keyes, in *Canadian Forum* (Toronto), January 1970; by Michael Hornyansky, in *University of Toronto Quarterly,* July 1970; by Louis Martz, in *Yale Review* (New Haven, Connecticut), Summer 1970; by Daisy Alden, in *Poetry* (Chicago), April 1971.

Phyllis Gotlieb comments:

My work, poetry or prose, makes use of any aspect of human culture and experience I can manage to find out about: family, childhood, growing up in Toronto; Jewish background, either learned or experienced, Talmud or Kabbala, rational or mystic; early interests in Greek and Roman cultures; folklore all over the world; enthusiasms for as much science as I can understand: biology, medicine, astronomy, anthropology; painting, sculpture. I'd like to call myself a universalist except that the abstract leaves me floundering. Humanity is my department.

*   *   *

Phyllis Gotlieb has written in two, seemingly disparate sub-genres: science fiction stories and a novel, and poems of a more esoteric focus. Yet the common theme which binds the two strains and which is most easily seen in *Within the Zodiac*, is also appropriate to each. In all her work there is a preoccupation with the unity of all things in the universe and an exploration of the energy which binds them. Such a concern pertains naturally enough to the science fiction stories and these need not be considered as more than largely well-written examples of the school. It is not, however, a theory which is so easily situated in literary forms which look away from the explicatory for their narrative or stylistic emphasis. And in dealing with her theory in such contexts, Gotlieb meets with varied success.

In *Within the Zodiac*, for example, the early poems are marred by a dry style and the essentially cerebral and yet curiously over-clear statements in which they attempt to objectify the myriad, incongruous aspects of the universe. These early poems lack any poetic rhythm and any personal response to the universe they so dispassionately detail. In the poem "Day Falcon," however, Gotlieb seeks in memory for congruity within this apparent incongruity, developing her personal myth in brilliant, naturalistic description. And, as a result, the poem rises above the others. Like "Day Falcon," the later poems in the collection open the more personal avenues of memory ("A Bestiary of the Garden for Children Who Should Know Better") and the Jewish tradition ("Who Knows One"). The point-of-view to which these final *Zodiac* poems lean is more fully assumed in *Ordinary, Moving*, a vastly more successful collection of poems.

In *Ordinary, Moving*, Gotlieb becomes more intimate with her creation, while maintaining an intellectual reserve and without becoming sentimental. She still considers ideas that are metaphysical and catholic but now views then as weighted equally with skeletal parts, bricks and old telephone numbers. Indeed, by grounding her musings in homely objects, she simultaneously strengthens her myth of unity and avoids the aridity of the *Zodiac* poems. Here, the rhythms are actively present and if the musical patterns (as well as the sense of family memory) is Jewish in sensibility, it is nevertheless accessible to gentile readers. This is not to suggest that Gotlieb's characteristic economy of words, sparsity of figures and avoidance of allusions have been altered. Rather, her personal myth has been expanded and made sufficiently comprehensible that it supersedes the need for more traditional links. At last in *Ordinary, Moving*, the reader not only understands what Gotlieb is saying, but feels he has himself experienced it before.

The novel *Why Should I Have All the Grief?*, however, lies outside the experience of most readers. It cannot be denied that the suffering of the Jews fits into Gotlieb's spectrum of universality, but its expression in this novel is too strongly dependent on a response to Jewish sentiment to appeal to those who lack it. Moreover, Gotlieb worries over her plot with an attention bordering on hysteria and the denouement is very early given away. Unable to do his own thinking and stranger in an alien, Talmudic culture, the reader cannot identify as he does with the *souvenirs* of the *Ordinary, Moving* poems, cannot asssociate himself with the joys and sufferings of the fictional world presented or the larger universe assumed, and quickly loses interest.

That he is not disinterested in the *Ordinary, Moving* poems is a significant statement of the appeal of anchoring the suggested in the familiar. The collage of *Ordinary, Moving* demonstrates that Gotlieb did, indeed, "like all writers [spend her youth] listening in buses, cars & cafes / trams & subways / streets & alleyways . . . ." And furthermore, it celebrates the concentric concatenation of energies in which all that she overheard is joined and in which the reader by the last line also becomes part of the unity and then "begin[s] again."

– S. R. Gilbert

GRAHAM, Henry. British. Born in Liverpool, Lancashire, 1 December 1930. Educated at Liverpool College of Art. Painter: exhibitions in London and Northern England; gave up painting for poetry at the age of 30. Since 1969, Lecturer in Art History, Liverpool Polytechnic. Poetry Editor, *Ambit* magazine, London. Recipient: *Ambit* prize, 1968; Arts Council award, 1969, 1971. Address: Flat 2, Bath House, Parkgate Parade, Parkgate, Wirral, Cheshire, England.

PUBLICATIONS

Verse

Soup City Zoo: Poems, with Jim Mangnall. London, Anima Press, 1968.
Good Luck to You Kafka/ You'll Need It Boss. London, Rapp and Whiting, 1969.
Passport to Earth. London, Rapp and Whiting-Deutsch, 1971.

Henry Graham comments:

My early influences in writing were the modern American poets, Pound, Olson, Duncan, etc. But now the Englishness of all the English arts interests me more; Auden, for instance, is one of the poets I admire most. The arts, and especially poetry, are not an attempt on my part to communicate, but are a way of looking into myself and the universe. If, as sometimes seems to happen, others are interested in and find in me what lies outside themselves, good; if not, good.

*   *   *

Henry Graham is a poet who never formed part of the so-called "Liverpool Scene," though he is sometimes included in anthologies of Pop Poetry. His background, however, is much like that of the other Liverpool poets who emerged in the late 1960's. He is a painter, and has worked as a jazz-musician. Experience of the other arts seems to have turned him, not towards popular materials, but towards an attempt at hermetic synthesis, of the sort one finds in poetry by Frenchmen such as Blaise Cendrars and Pierre Reverdy. Graham is by no means an even writer, nor is he a particularly prolific one. But he has produced a handful of poems with real control and authority. Perhaps the following lines will give an idea of what he can do on top form:

> A soprano sings. The poem
> limps on. The cat yawns. It feels
> the air with the fine
> wires on its nose. It yearns
> to wear away the white
> marble of milk it commands
> morning and evening. . . .

– Edward Lucie-Smith

GRAHAM, W(illiam) S(ydney). British. Born in Greenock, Renfrewshire, Scotland, 19 November 1918. Educated at Greenock High School; Workers Educational Association College, Newbattle Abbey, Edinburgh, 1 year. Married. Lecturer, New York University, 1947–48. Recipient: Atlantic Award, 1947. Address: 4 Mountview Cottages, Madron, Penzance, Cornwall, England.

PUBLICATIONS

Verse

    Cage Without Grievance. London, Parton Press-David Archer, 1942.
    The Seven Journeys. Glasgow, Maclellan, 1944.
    2nd Poems. London, Editions Poetry, 1945.
    The Voyages of Alfred Wallis. London, Anthony Froshang, 1948.
    The White Threshold. London, Faber, 1949.
    The Nightfishing. London, Faber, and New York, Grove Press, 1955.
    Malcolm Mooney's Land. London, Faber, 1970.
    Penguin Modern Poets 17, with David Gascoyne and Kathleen Raine. London, Penguin, 1970.

Manuscript Collection: National Library of Scotland, Edinburgh.

Critical Studies: "Notes on a Poetry of Release" by the author, in *Sewanee Review* (Tennessee), 1947; "W. S. Graham's Threshold" by Edwin Morgan, in *Nine 3* (London), Spring 1950; *Babel to Byzantium* by James Dickey, New York, Farrar Straus, 1968.

W. S. Graham comments:

I do recognise a Scots timbre in my "voice" although I can't see myself, in any way, as characteristic of Scots poetry.

Major themes: The difficulty of communication; the difficulty of speaking from a fluid identity; the lessons in physical phenomena; the mystery and adequacy of the aesthetic experience; the elation of being alive in the language.

Although I love the ever-present metronome in verse, I am greedy for my rhythmic say. The gesture of speech often exists, moving seemingly counter to the abstract structure it is in. The three-accent line, not specially common in the body of English poetry, even a kind of strait-jacket, interested me enough for me to keep to it for a bit and try to ring the changes within.

As far as I can discern, my verse is influenced by the prose of Joyce and Beckett and by the verse of Marianne Moore, Pound and Eliot. And the texture of my verse shows, I think, a fondness for Anglo-Saxon and Scandinavian roots, also for translations of early Irish and Scottish Gaelic verse.

*   *   *

Probably because he was one of the most verbally gifted poets of his generation in Scotland, W. S. Graham had a struggle to clarify a personal style that first carried large acknowledgements of other wordsmiths like Dylan Thomas, Gerard Manley Hopkins, and James Joyce. His early volumes – *Cage Without Grievance, The Seven Journeys,* and *2nd Poems* – have a tendency to thrash around with adjectives and to produce obscurely exciting effects, yet his devotion to the *word,* and his sense of the poem as a voyage of discovery, were not perverse. In exploring the self, and the poet's relation to his living audience and the audience of all the dead, Graham was working within a network of image and reference that was anchored to his Clydeside upbringing – indeed all his poetry is haunted by sea and shipyards, and by place-names from the countryside around Glasgow. The best of the early poems show a distinctive lyricism ("O Gentle Queen of the After-noon") and a deepening sense of mortality ("Many Without Elegy").

In *The White Threshold* and *The Nightfishing* Graham produced a very remarkable poetry, strong, musical, and intense, where the central sea imagery feeds a range of subtly related themes: his autobiography, wartime shipwrecks and drownings, fish-ing, and the metaphorical "white threshold" of all life and death which Herman Melville had tried to plumb before him. Apart from the two long title-pieces in these volumes, there are several shorter poems of great beauty and force: "Listen. Put on Morning," "Gigha," "Men Sign the Sea," "Night's Fall Unlocks the Dirge of the Sea," and "Letter VI." A growing lucidity humanizes the verse, but without removing its obsessional preoccupation with the endless dyings and metamorphoses of the self:

> I bent to the lamp. I cupped
> My hand to the glass chimney.
> Yet it was a stranger's breath
> From out of my mouth that
> Shed the light.

Was the preoccupation too obsessional? Graham has published little since 1955, and is now a rather isolated figure. But this best poetry stands firm still, and is not likely to be forgotten.

– Edwin Morgan

GRAVES, Robert (Ranke).   British.   Born in London in 1895. Educated at Char-terhouse School, Surrey; St. John's College, Oxford, B.Litt. 1926. Served with the Royal Welsh Fusiliers in World War I; was refused admittance into the armed forces in World War II. Married to Nancy Nicholson; to Beryl Pritchard; has seven children. Professor of English, Egyptian University, Cairo, 1926. Settled in Deyá, Mallorca, in 1929; with the poet Laura Riding established the Seizin Press and *Epilogue* magazine. Left Mallorca during the Spanish Civil War; settled in Glampton-Brixton, Devon during World War II; returned to Mallorca after the war. Clark Lecturer, Trinity College, Cambridge, 1954; Professor of Poetry, Oxford University, 1961–66; Arthur Dehon Little Memorial Lecturer, Massachusetts Insti-tute of Technology, Cambridge, 1963. Recipient: Bronze Medal for Poetry, Olympic Games, Paris, 1924; Hawthornden Prize, for fiction, 1935; Black Memorial Prize, for fiction, 1935; Femina Vie Heureuse-Stock Prize, 1939; Russell Loines Poetry Award, 1958; National Poetry Society of America Gold Medal, 1960; Foyle Poetry

Prize, 1960; Arts Council Poetry Award, 1962; Italia Prize, for radio play, 1965; Queen's Gold Medal for Poetry, 1968; Gold Medal for Poetry, Cultural Olympics, Mexico City, 1968. M.A.: Oxford University, 1961. Honorary Member, American Academy of Arts and Sciences, 1970. Address: c/o A. P. Watt and Son, 26–28 Bedford Row, London W.C.1, England.

PUBLICATIONS

Verse

Over the Brazier.   London, Poetry Bookshop, 1916.
Goliath and David.   London, Chiswick Press, 1916.
Fairies and Fusiliers.   London, Heinemann, 1917; New York, Knopf, 1918.
Treasure Box.   London, Chiswick Press, 1919.
Country Sentiment.   London, Secker, and New York, Knopf, 1920.
The Pier-Glass.   London, Secker, and New York, Knopf, 1921.
Whipperginny.   London, Heinemann, and New York, Knopf, 1923.
The Feather Bed.   Richmond, Surrey, Hogarth Press, 1923.
Mockbeggar Hall.   London, Hogarth Press, 1924.
Welchman's Hose.   London, The Fleuron, 1925.
(Poems).   London, Benn, 1925.
The Marmosite's Miscellany (as Paul Boyle).   London, Hogarth Press, 1925.
Poems (1914–1926).   London, Heinemann, 1927; New York, Doubleday, 1929.
Poems (1914–1927).   London, Heinemann, 1927.
Poems 1929.   London, Seizin Press, 1929.
Ten Poems More.   Paris, Hours Press, 1930.
Poems 1926–1930.   London, Heinemann, 1931.
To Whom Else?   Deyá, Mallorca, Seizin Press, 1931.
Poems 1930–1933.   London, Barker, 1933.
Collected Poems.   London, Cassell, and New York, Random House, 1938.
No More Ghosts: Selected Poems.   London, Faber, 1940.
(Poems).   London, Eyre and Spottiswoode, 1943.
Poems 1938–1945.   London, Cassell, 1945; New York, Creative Age Press, 1946.
Collected Poems (1914–1947).   London, Cassell, 1948.
Poems and Satires 1951.   London, Cassell, 1951.
Poems 1953.   London, Cassell, 1953.
Collected Poems 1955.   New York, Doubleday, 1955.
Poems Selected by Himself.   London, Penguin, 1957.
The Poems of Robert Graves.   New York, Doubleday, 1958.
Collected Poems 1959.   London, Cassell, 1959.
More Poems 1961.   London, Cassell, 1961.
Collected Poems.   New York, Doubleday, 1961.
New Poems 1962.   London, Cassell, 1962; as *New Poems,* New York, Doubleday, 1963.
The More Deserving Cases: Eighteen Old Poems for Reconsideration.   N.p., Marlborough College Press, 1962.
Man Does, Woman Is 1964.   London, Cassell, and New York, Doubleday, 1964.
Love Respelt.   London, Cassell, 1965.
Collected Poems 1965.   London, Cassell, 1965.
Seventeen Poems Missing from "Love Respelt".   Privately printed, 1966.

Colophon to "Love Respelt". Privately printed, 1967.
(Poems), with D. H. Lawrence, edited by Leonard Clark. London, Longman, 1967.
Poems 1965–1968. London, Cassell, 1968; New York, Doubleday, 1969.
Poems about Love. London, Cassell, and New York, Doubleday, 1969.
Love Respelt Again. New York, Doubleday, 1969.
Beyond Giving: Poems. Privately printed, 1969.
Poems 1968–1970. London, Cassell, 1970.
Advice from a Mother. London, Poem-of-the-Month Club, 1970.
The Green-Sailed Vessel. Privately printed, 1971.
Poems 1970–1972. London, Cassell, 1972; New York, Doubleday, 1973.
Corgi Modern Poets in Focus 3, with others, edited by Dannie Abse. London, Corgi, 1971.
Deya. London, Motif Editions, 1973.
Timeless Meeting: Poems. London, Bertram Rota, 1973.

Recordings: *Robert Graves Reading His Own Poems,* Argo and Listen, 1960; *Robert Graves Reading His Own Poetry and The White Goddess,* Caedmon; *The Rubaiyat of Omar Khayyam,* Spoken Arts.

Plays

John Kemp's Wager: A Ballad Opera. Oxford, Blackwell, and New York, T. B. Edwards, 1925.

Radio Play: *The Anger of Achilles,* 1964.

Novels

No Decency Left, with Laura Riding (as Barbara Rich). London, Cape, 1932.
The Real David Copperfield. London, Barker, 1933; as *David Copperfield by Charles Dickens, Condensed by Robert Graves,* edited by Merrill P. Paine, New York, Harcourt Brace, 1934.
I, Claudius: From the Autobiography of Tiberius Claudius, Emperor of the Romans, Born B.C. 10, Murdered and Deified A.D. 54. London, Barker, and New York, Smith and Haas, 1934.
Claudius the God and His Wife Messalina: The Troublesome Reign of Tiberius Claudius Caesar, Emperor of the Romans (Born B.C. 10, Died A.D. 54), As Described by Himself; Also His Murder at the Hands of the Notorius Agrippina (Mother of the Emperor Nero) and His Subsequent Deification, As Described by Others. London, Barker, 1934; New York, Smith and Haas, 1935.
"Antigua, Penny, Puce." Deya, Mallorca, Seizin Press, and London, Constable, 1936; as *The Antigua Sramp,* New York, Random House, 1937.
Count Belisarius. London, Cassell, and New York, Random House, 1938.
Sergeant Lamb of the Ninth. London, Methuen, 1940; as *Sergeant Lamb's America,* New York, Random House, 1940.
Proceed, Sergeant Lamb. London, Methuen, and New York, Random House, 1941.
The Story of Marie Powell: Wife to Mr. Milton. London, Cassell, 1943; as *Wife to Mr. Milton: The Story of Marie Powell,* New York, Creative Age Press, 1944.
The Golden Fleece. London, Cassell, 1944; as *Hercules, My Shipmate,* New York, Creative Age Press, 1945.

King Jesus. New York, Creative Age Press, and London, Cassell, 1946.

Watch the North Wind Rise. New York, Creative Age Press, 1949; as *Seven Days in Crete,* London, Cassell, 1949.

The Islands of Unwisdom. New York, Doubleday, 1949; as *The Isles of Unwisdom,* London, Cassell, 1950.

Homer's Daughter. London, Cassell, and New York, Doubleday, 1955.

Short Stories

The Shout. London, Elkin Mathews and Marrot, 1929.

¡Catacrok! Mostly Stories, Mostly Funny. London, Cassell, 1956.

Collected Short Stories. New York, Doubleday, 1964; London, Cassell, 1965.

Other

On English Poetry. New York, Knopf, and London, Heinemann, 1922.

The Meaning of Dreams. London, Cecil Palmer, 1924; New York, Greenberg, 1925.

Poetic Unreason and Other Studies. London, Cecil Palmer, 1925.

My Head! My Head! Being the History of Elisha and the Shumanite Woman; With the History of Moses as Elisha Related It, and Her Questions to Him. London, Secker, and New York, Knopf, 1925.

Contemporary Techniques of Poetry: A Political Analogy. London, Hogarth Press, 1925.

Another Future of Poetry. London, Hogarth Press, 1926.

Impenetrability; or, The Proper Habit of English. London, Hogarth Press, 1926.

The English Ballad: A Short Critical Survey. London, Benn, 1927.

Lars Porsena; or, The Future of Swearing and Improper Language. London, Kegan Paul Trench Trubner, and New York, Dutton, 1927; revised edition, as *The Future of Swearing and Improper Language,* Kegan Paul Trench Trubner, 1936.

A Survey of Modernist Poetry, with Laura Riding. London, Heinemann, 1927; New York, Doubleday, 1928.

Lawrence and the Arabs. London, Cape, 1927; as *Lawrence and the Arabian Adventure,* New York, Doubleday, 1928.

A Pamphlet Against Anthologies, with Laura Riding. London, Cape, 1928; as *Against Anthologies,* New York, Doubleday, 1928.

Mrs. Fisher; or, The Future of Humour. London, Kegan Paul Trench Trubner, 1928.

Goodbye to All That: An Autobiography. London, Cape, 1929; New York, Cape and Smith, 1930; revised edition, New York, Doubleday, and London, Cassell, 1957, London, Penguin, 1960.

T. E. Lawrence to His Biographer Robert Graves. New York, Doubleday, 1938; London, Faber, 1939.

The Long Week-end: A Social History of Great Britain 1918–1939, with Alan Hodge. London, Faber, 1940; New York, Macmillan, 1941.

Work in Hand, with others. London, Hogarth Press, 1942.

The Reader over Your Shoulder: A Handbook for Writers of English Prose, with Alan Hodge. London, Cape, 1943; New York, Macmillan, 1944.

The White Goddess: A Historical Grammar of Poetic Myth. London, Faber, and New York, Creative Age Press, 1948; revised edition, Faber, 1952, 1966; New York, Knopf, 1958.

The Common Asphodel: Collected Essays on Poetry 1922–1949.   London, Hamish Hamilton, 1949.

Occupation: Writer.   New York, Creative Age Press, 1950; London, Cassell, 1951.

The Nazarene Gospel Restored, with Joshua Podro.   London, Cassell, 1953; New York, Doubleday, 1954.

The Crowning Privilege: The Clark Lectures 1954–1955; Also Various Essays on Poetry and Sixteen New Poems.   London, Cassell, 1955; as *The Crowning Privilege: Collected Essays on Poetry,* New York, Doubleday, 1956.

Adam's Rib and Other Anomalous Elements in the Hebrew Creation Myth: A New View.   N.p. Trianon Press, 1955; New York, Yoseloff, 1958.

The Greek Myths.   London and Baltimore, Penguin, 2 vols., 1955.

Jesus in Rome: A Historical Conjecture, with Joshua Podro.   London, Cassell, 1957.

They Hanged My Saintly Billy.   London, Cassell, 1957; as *They Hanged My Saintly Billy: The Life and Death of Dr. William Palmer,* New York, Doubleday, 1957.

Steps: Stories, Talks, Essays, Poems, Studies in History.   London, Cassell, 1958.

5 Pens in Hand.   New York, Doubleday, 1958.

Food for Centaurs: Stories, Talks, Critical Studies, Poems.   New York, Doubleday, 1960.

The Penny Fiddle: Poems for Children.   London, Cassell, 1960; New York, Doubleday, 1961.

Greek Gods and Heroes.   New York, Doubleday, 1960; as *Myths of Ancient Greece,* London, Cassell, 1961.

Selected Poetry and Prose, edited by James Reeves.   London, Hutchinson, 1961.

The Siege and Fall of Troy (juvenile).   London, Cassell, 1962; New York, Doubleday, 1963.

The Big Green Book.   New York, Crowell Collier, 1962.

Oxford Addresses on Poetry.   London, Cassell, and New York, Doubleday, 1962.

Nine Hundred Iron Chariots: The Twelfth Arthur Dehon Little Memorial Lecture.   Cambridge, Massachusetts Institute of Technology, 1963.

Hebrew Myths: The Book of Genesis, with Raphael Patai.   New York, Doubleday, and London, Cassell, 1964.

Ann at Highwood Hall: Poems for Children.   London, Cassell, 1964.

Majorca Observed.   London, Cassell, and New York, Doubleday, 1965.

Mammon and the Black Goddess.   London, Cassell, and New York, Doubleday, 1965.

Two Wise Children (juvenile).   New York, Harlin Quist, 1966; London, W. H. Allen, 1967.

Poetic Craft and Principle.   London, Cassell, 1967.

Spiritual Quixote.   London, Oxford University Press, 1967.

The Poor Boy Who Followed His Star (juvenile).   London, Cassell, 1968; New York, Doubleday, 1969.

The Crane Bag and Other Disputed Subjects.   London, Cassell, 1969.

On Poetry: Collected Talks and Essays.   New York, Doubleday, 1969.

Poems: Abridged for Dolls and Princes (juvenile).   London, Cassell, 1971.

Difficult Questions, Easy Answers.   London, Cassell, 1972; New York, Doubleday, 1973.

Editor, with Alan Porter and Richard Hughes, *Oxford Poetry, 1921.*   Oxford, Blackwell, 1921.

Editor, *John Skelton (Laureate), 1460(?)–1529.*   London, Benn, 1927.

Editor, *The Less Familiar Nursery Rhymes.* London, Benn, 1927.

Editor, *English and Scottish Ballads.* London, Heinemann, and New York, Macmillan, 1957.

Editor, *The Comedies of Terence.* New York, Doubleday, 1962; London, Cassell, 1963.

Translator, with Laura Riding, *Almost Forgotten Germany*, by Georg Schwarz. Deyá, Mallorca, Seizin Press, London, Constable, and New York, Random House, 1936.

Translator, *The Transformations of Lucius, Otherwise Known as The Golden Ass*, by Apuleius. London, Penguin, 1950; New York, Farrar Straus, 1951.

Translator, *The Cross and the Sword*, by Manuel de Jésus Galván. Bloomington, Indiana University Press, 1955; London, Gollancz, 1956.

Translator, *The Infant with the Globe*, by Pedro Antonio de Alarcon. London, Trianon Press, 1955; New York, Yoseloff, 1958.

Translator, *Winter in Majorca*, by George Sand. London, Cassell, 1956.

Translator, *Pharsalia: Dramatic Episodes of the Civil Wars*, by Lucan. London, Penguin, 1956.

Translator, *The Twelve Caesars*, by Suetonius. London, Penguin, 1957.

Translator, *The Anger of Achilles: Homer's Iliad.* New York, Doubleday, 1959; London, Cassell, 1960.

Translator, with Omar Ali-Shah, *Rubaiyat of Omar Khayyam.* London, Cassell, 1967; Tucson, Arizona, Omen Press, 1972.

Translator, *The Song of Songs.* New York, Clarkson Potter, and London, Collins, 1973.

Bibliography: *A Bibliography of the Works of Robert Graves* by Fred H. Higginson, London, Nicholas Vane, 1966.

Manuscript Collections: Lockwood Memorial Library, State University of New York at Buffalo; New York City Public Library; University of Texas Library, Austin.

*   *   *

The poetry of Robert Graves may, allowing for anticipations and regressions, be divided into four main phases: from his schoolboy beginnings in 1906 until his discovery of the poetry of the American poet Laura Riding (now Laura Jackson) in 1925; the duration of his literary and personal association with Miss Riding (1926–39); the period of his war-time sojourn in a South Devon farmhouse and of the first years of his return to Mallorca (1939–56); and what may be called the years in which he emerged into world fame. The two main events in his poetic life have been the impact upon him of four years' trench warfare in World War I, and his response to the poetry and personality of Laura Riding. While the effect of Graves's war experiences has been adequately appreciated by his critics, the influence of Miss Riding has been very seriously underestimated, owing, one feels, to failure to understand her poetry. Whether the general verdict on this poetry will be reversed or not (one suspects that it may be, from the private interest that has been shown in it), it is certainly true to say that no one who will not make the effort to understand Miss Riding's poetry (she stopped writing it in 1939) can hope to understand Graves's. (That this is a statement he himself fully endorses does not prove it to be correct, but it is a fact not irrelevant for students of his poetry.)

As Graves has written in a note to the most recent English edition of his *Collected Poems* (1965), ". . . I always aimed at writing more or less as I still do."

This is only another way of saying that his development has been less a matter of a series of fresh inventions, or successions of changed attitudes, than of a continuously expanding awareness of his purposes as a poet. His faith in the poem he has to write – although not attended by any careless arrogance about his capacities to write it – has been as great as that of any English poet, perhaps greater. In this sense the poem, for Graves, is a thing outside himself, a task of truth-telling – and not a thing to be invented or "composed." Poem-writing is a matter of absolute truthfulness to the emotional mood of self-revelation. Graves is not a craftsman who invents shapes in stone, to his own desires; but one who seeks, by means of intuition, to discover the exact shape in the middle of the stone, in which he has absolute faith.

If one of the signs of a major as distinct from a minor poet is development, then Graves is certainly a major poet. Yet his experiments have always been within the limits of tradition. As a schoolboy he worked on hosts of complicated rhyme-schemes and verse-forms, including the Welsh *englyn,* as well as with assonance and dissonance. For his subject-matter he drew on the worlds of chivalry, romance and nursery rhyme. Much of his technical facility and his capacity to use folk-themes without parodying them he owed to his father, Alfred Perceval Graves, who was a graceful minor Irish poet.

Graves was one of a group of war-poets which included Sassoon and Owen; but unlike theirs his poetry did not mature during the war, and he has rejected nearly all his war poetry. Much of his immediately post-war poetry, written under the twin (and opposing) influences of war-trauma and pastoral marriage, he has also rejected. It is technically accomplished, charming, and with an underlying complexity that is not as typically Georgian as is its surface. Graves was at this time working – under the influence of W. H. R. Rivers, the anthropologist – on the Freudian theory that poetry was therapeutic, a view he largely abandoned in the later Twenties.

Little of the poetry of Graves's first period has been preserved in his *Collected Poems*; but its main positive features – delight in nonsense, preoccupation with terror, the nature of his love for women – have survived into his later poetry. What was purged was softness and cloying over-sweetness. A poem (preserved) such as *The Pier Glass* (1921) perfectly illustrates the qualities of the early poems and at the same time delineates the area that the later poems were to explore so meticulously and movingly. Written in the person of a lonely female ghost doomed to wander a lonely mansion, it conjures up a picture of utter lifelessness, so that the ghost cries to her "sullen pierglass, cracked from side to side" for "one token" this life exists, "So be it only this side Hope"; anything but "this phantasma." Graves was to explore the life "this side Hope," only to find it dangerous and phantasmagoric; but his poetry gained immensely in vitality and depth.

Laura Riding was on the fringes of the American Fugitive Group (which included John Crowe Ransom, Allen Tate and Robert Penn Warren) and it was in *The Fugitive* that Graves first encountered her work. What influenced him was not her procedures – which were, rhythmically, totally unlike his – but the content of her poems and the personality that went with this. The poems of his maturity are in no sense at all imitations of hers; but her remarkably complicated view of life (and therefore the work in which she expressed this) are relevant to them: he shared, or rather, attempted devotedly to learn, this view, and the material of the poems is his struggle to accommodate himself lovingly to it and to her. The process proved impossible in the end, as he foresaw in "Sick Love," written in the late Twenties: "O Love, be fed with apples while you may," this begins; and it ends:

> Take your delight in momentariness,
> Walk between dark and dark – a shining space
> With the grave's narrowness, though not its peace.

The poems Graves wrote in his second period record, with great directness and in a diction of deliberate hardness and strength, the nerve-strains of impossible love ("To the galleys, thief, and sweat your soul out" one begins) and his attempt to achieve an existence that accorded with the goodness that Graves and (at that time) Laura Riding saw as residing in poetry above every other human activity. These are therefore extremely "existential" poems, and to be understood they must be read in this way: they are at once an account of a condition of romanticized devoted-ness, of a search for perfection (always tempered with ironic realism and earthly masculine robustness) and of human failures. Poems such as "The Legs" describe the distractions that Graves saw as tempting him from the concentration his single-minded quest for poetic wisdom required. His "historical grammar of poetic myth," *The White Goddess*, is essentially a generalization from his experiences of these years of devoted struggle to serve a savagely demanding muse, whom in "On Portents" he has seen as a vast propeller, a "bladed mind" strongly pulling through the "ever-reluctant element" of Time. These poems, by which – together with those of the succeeding phase – Graves will probably be chiefly remembered, provide what will almost certainly become the classic latter-day record of romantic love; this is so not least because of their unsentimentality, their tough and unidealistic acceptance of the author's strong masculine recalcitrance. Thus, his mood changes from confidence –

> We tell no lies now, at last cannot be
> The rogues we were – so evilly linked in sense
> With what we scrutinized that lion or tiger
> Could leap from every copse, strike and devour us.
>   – "End of Play"

– to zestful gloom –

> Yet why does she
> Come never as longed-for beauty
> Slender and cool, with limbs lovely to see. . .?
>   – "The Succubus"

As he wrote in 1965, "My theme was always the practical impossibility, tran-scended only by miracle, of absolute love continuing between man and woman." It is the tension between "practical impossibility" and "miracle," a tension reflected in universal experience, that gives Graves's poetry its unique power.

    The poems of Graves's third phase, written when he had abandoned his prodi-gious enterprise of creating – with Laura Riding – an existence in which poetry and what it represents would be a natural way of life (for more details of this, see Laura Riding's Introduction to her *Collected Poems*, 1938), reflect upon the meaning of his experience:

>   her image
> Warped in the weather, turned beldamish.
> Then back came winter on me at a bound,
> The pallid sky heaved with a moon-quake.
>
> Dangerous had it been with love-notes
> To serenade Queen Famine. . . .
>   – "A Love Story"

They also discover new love, in some of the most beautiful love lyrics in English:

> Have you not read
> The words in my head,
> And I made part
> Of your own heart?
>   – "Despite and Still"

Finally they humorously state his position and accept that fame has caught up with him, as in "From the Embassy," where he refers to himself as "ambassador of Otherwhere / To the unfederated States of Here and There."

The poetry of Graves's most recent phase has continued to develop. More technically impeccable than ever, more consciously cunning in its artistry than anything that has gone before it, it lacks the tension of the earlier work – but never the convincing tone of a man in love. It owes a good deal to the Sufist ideas by which Graves has been influenced in recent years, and it discovers the peaceful figure of the Black Goddess who lies behind the crueller one of the White Goddess. Love, to Graves in these new poems, walks "on a knife-edge between two different fates": one fate is to consort with the White Goddess, and is physical; the other, more difficult yet more rewarding, to find peace in the domains of the Black Goddess. Frequently the poems are so lapidary as to remind the reader of Landor; but they reach a greater power than ever Landor achieved when they envisage the hell of a world made dead by a too great reliance upon physical passion. Of one who is trapped in this hell, who in departing too casually has said, "I will write," he says in a poem of the same title:

> Long letters written and mailed in her own head –
> There are no mails in a city of the dead.

Graves's latest poems provide, in their explorations of the possibilities of a world purged of what he calls "the blood sports of desire," and of the agonies of alienation from such a world, a fitting sequel to those of his earlier years. He will be, perhaps, the last romantic poet to operate within wholly traditional limits – and his mastery of these is not in question.

– Martin Seymour-Smith

GREENE, Jonathan (Edward). American. Born in New York City, 19 April 1943. Educated at Bard College, Annandale-on-Hudson, New York, B.A. Married; has two daughters. Since 1965, Founding Editor, Gnomon Press, Lexington, Kentucky. Since 1966, Apprentice Printer, then Assistant Production Manager, and currently Production Manager and Designer, University Press of Kentucky. Recipient: National Endowment for the Arts grant, 1969. Address: 450 West Sixth Street, Lexington, Kentucky 40508, U.S.A.

Publications

Verse

The Reckoning. Annandale-on-Hudson, New York, Matter Books, 1966.
Instance. Lexington, Kentucky, Buttonwood Press, 1968.
The Lapidary. Los Angeles, Black Sparrow Press, 1969.
A 17th Century Garner. Lexington, Kentucky, Buttonwood Press, 1969.
An Unspoken Complaint. Santa Barbara, California, Unicorn Press, 1970.
Scaling the Walls. Lexington, Kentucky, Gnomon Press, 1974.
Glossary of the Everyday. Toronto, Coach House Press, 1974.
Quiet Goods. Monterey, Kentucky, Larkspur Press, 1975.
Once a Kingdom Again. Berkeley, California, Sand Dollar, 1975.

Other

Translator, *The Poor in Church*, by Arthur Rimbaud. Lexington, Kentucky, Polyglot Press, 1973.

Jonathan Greene comments:

Friendships early on with "deep image" poets important; close ties with Robert Kelly, Robert Duncan and Robin Blaser.

No school, but a tradition involving individual poets felt strongly: Blake, Yeats and more recent incarnations.

*   *   *

Jonathan Greene may be placed among the group of writers affiliated (through shared concerns rather than "influence") with Robert Kelly. (Others include Charles Stein and Harvey Bialy and the prose writer Richard Grossinger.) Kelly published and wrote the introduction for Greene's first book and was his teacher and friend at Bard College. The hermetic tradition as mediated through such writers as Blake, H. D., and Robert Duncan is a major informing presence in Greene's work. One consequence is a frequently baffling abstractness and allusiveness, but even in the obscurest poems there is evident a care for the weight and sound of each syllable. Greene speaks of "the work, / which is / love / persistent" and of how "the *care- / takers* / portion out / their harvests, / the bounty." The bounty for us, in the most successful poems, is a delicate but tough lyricism – see, for example, "The Definition" from *The Lapidary*. Much influenced by Jung, Greene writes out of a sense of poetry as "given" from a source "beyond" and thus inevitably dealing in archetypal material. "A Palimpsest" opens:

> The old story keeps writing itself.
> Dark woods & the turn of the road
> again. I do not write it. *A turn*
> *of the road,* writes itself. *A*
> *changed life,* interpolates from
> an unknown source. Underneath,
> the writing still goes on.
> The true writing.

And a haiku-like poem from *Instance* puts it more imagistically:

> the old tales are told,
> migratory birds
> come home to
> the heart

It should be added that Greene's uncollected recent work shows a welcome inclusion of more directly personal subject matter, while retaining the qualities of ear and of access to depth evidenced in his earlier books.

– Seamus Cooney

GREGOR, Arthur. American. Born in Vienna, Austria, 18 November 1923; emigrated to the United States, 1939, naturalized, 1945. Educated at Newark College of Engineering, New Jersey, B.S. in electrical engineering 1945. Engineer, Electronic Transformer Corporation, New York, 1945–54; Editor, Whitney Publications, New York, 1955–61; Senior Editor, Macmillan Company, publishers, New York, 1972–73. Since 1973, Associate Professor and Director of the Creative Writing Center, Hofstra University, Hempstead, New York. Recipient: First Appearance Prize (*Poetry*, Chicago), 1948; Palmer Award, 1962. Address: 49 Greenwich Avenue, New York, New York 10014, U.S.A.

PUBLICATIONS

Verse

Octavian Shooting Targets: Poems. New York, Dodd Mead, 1954.
Declensions for a Refrain: Poems. New York, Poetry London-New York Books, 1957.
Basic Movements: Poems. New York, Gyre Press, 1966.
Figure in the Door. New York, Doubleday, 1968.
A Bed by the Sea: Poems. New York, Doubleday, 1970.
Selected Poems. New York, Doubleday, 1971.
The Past Now. New York, Doubleday, 1975.

Plays

Continued Departure (produced New York, 1968). Published in *Accent* (Urbana, Illinois), 1951.
Fire (produced Urbana, Illinois, 1952).
The Door Is Open (produced New York, 1970).

Other

1 2 3 4 5 (juvenile).   Philadelphia, Lippincott, 1956.
The Little Elephant (juvenile).   New York, Harper, 1956.
Animal Babies (juvenile).   New York, Harper, 1959.

Critical Studies: Reviews by Laurence Lieberman, in *Yale Review* (New Haven, Connecticut), Spring 1968; by Hayden Carruth, in *Hudson Review* (New York), Spring 1968; by Robert A. Carter, in *Modern Poetry Studies* (Buffalo, New York), Autumn 1971; by Thomas Lask, in *The New York Times*, 9 December 1971; by Christopher Collins, in *The Nation* (New York), 15 February 1972; by F. D. Reeve, in *Poetry* (Chicago), January 1973.

Arthur Gregor comments:

I have tried to explore and to articulate what I consider the poetic reality in myself – a reality which lies in all. My influences have been art, nature, and those in whom throb powerfully the magic, the mystery of life.

*   *   *

During a time when the evolution of American poetry has been defined by large movements with clearly directed aims, Arthur Gregor has followed a decidedly independent, sometimes contrary course. In part it is a question of his European origin. He was born and raised in Vienna, and has traveled extensively in the Old World; his poetry relies upon images and allusions drawn from European history and culture. But the distinction is more basic than this. If we agree that the great movement of American poetry in the past 25 years has been away from the symbolist tradition and the dominance of such poets as Eliot and Yeats, and toward a poetry based not only on native themes and idioms but on an objectivist view of reality (which does not preclude mythic values), then Gregor has clearly stood against the main stream with his insistence upon the continuing human validity of symbolist modes of perception. It has not been an argued insistence. Though Gregor has been a journalist and editor, as well as an engineer, he has rarely resorted to theoretical statements about his own work. But in his poetry his philosophical affinities are clear: they are with the great symbolists of the European tradition, and particularly with such poets of the richly colored, central European imagination as Rilke and Hofmannsthal.

It is easy to overemphasize the programmatic importance of these distinctions, however. Gregor fits comfortably enough in the present American literary scene. In tone and verbal texture his verse resembles the contemporary free-form writing of most American poets. In fact from his first poems in the 1940's Gregor used a freer, more flexible line than the formalist conventions of that period sanctioned. He could never have been classed with the academics. On the other hand his early work did show an ornateness of diction and figure which seemed very baroque at the time, as if this European poet had taken the manner of Wallace Stevens and converted it to foreign ends, though the actual influence of Stevens, if it existed at all, was superficial. From these beginnings Gregor moved toward quieter, gentler poems that reached ever farther into his mystical view of experience. An evocation of unseen presences, a realization of history or of the minds of ancestors, a glimpse of the "elsewhere" that lies somehow within the defined particulars of each new place: these and similar themes occupied him more and more. It is difficult to say precisely what his religious orientation may be; his poems are written always obliquely, as if alongside the standard forms of spiritual evolution, not within them. Allusions can be detected to Hebrew, Christian, Gnostic, and Vedantic motifs, but they are allusions of feeling, not form, of spirit, not substance. His vision is clearly his own. And in his poems about people, though they are often richly erotic, it is the essential mystery of the person toward which the vision aspires.

The danger of Gregor's vision is that words will fail its mysteriousness and turn into mere talk – talking about what cannot be sufficiently embodied, the failure of symbolism. It is a danger that Gregor has not always surmounted. But in his best poems – some of those about his parents and his travels – his vision is conveyed intact. It is a private vision, hence in some sense exclusive or even elitist, at odds with the prevailing temper of the age. Yet Gregor's work has a gentleness and seriousness which have won it considerable popularity in recent years, especially among young people, and his somewhat alien voice has become a distinct and useful element in the American literary sensibility of the time.

– Hayden Carruth

GREGORY, Horace (Victor).   American.   Born in Milwaukee, Wisconsin, 10 April 1898. Educated at the Milwaukee School of Fine Arts, Summers 1913–16; German-English Academy, Milwaukee, 1914–19; University of Wisconsin, Madison, B.A. 1923. Married Marya Zaturenska, *q.v.*, in 1925; has two children. Free-lance Writer, New York and London, 1923–34. Member of the English Department, 1934–60, and since 1960, Professor Emeritus, Sarah Lawrence College, Bronxville, New York. Associate Editor, *Tiger's Eye* magazine, New York. Recipient: Lyric Prize, 1928, Levinson Prize, 1934, and Union League Civic and Arts Foundation Prize, 1951 (*Poetry*, Chicago); Levinson Award, 1936; Loines Award, 1942; Guggenheim Fellowship, 1951; Academy of American Poets Fellowship, 1961; Bollingen Prize, 1965. Member, National Institute of Arts and Letters. Address: Palisades, Rockland County, New York 10964, U.S.A.

PUBLICATIONS

Verse

> *Chelsea Rooming House: Poems.*   New York, Covici Friede, 1930; as *Rooming House*, London, Faber, 1932.
> *No Retreat: Poems.*   New York, Harcourt Brace, 1933.
> *Wreath for Margery.*   New York, Modern Editions Press, 1933.
> *Chorus for Survival.*   New York, Covici Friede, 1935.
> *Poems 1930–1940.*   New York, Harcourt Brace, 1941.
> *Selected Poems.*   New York, Viking Press, 1951.
> *Medusa in Gramercy Park.*   New York, Macmillan, 1961.

Alphabet for Joanna: A Poem (juvenile). New York, Holt Rinehart, 1963.
Collected Poems New York, Holt Rinehart, 1964.

Other

Pilgrim of the Apocalypse: A Critical Study of D. H. Lawrence. New York, Viking Press, 1933; London, Secker, 1934; revised edition, as *D. H. Lawrence: Pilgrim of the Apocalypse*, New York, Grove Press, 1957.
The Shield of Achilles: Essays on Beliefs in Poetry. New York, Harcourt Brace, 1944.
A History of American Poetry 1900–1940, with Marya Zaturenska. New York, Harcourt Brace, 1946.
Poet of the People: An Evaluation of James Whitcombe Riley, with James T. Farrell and Jeanette Covert Nolan. Bloomington, Indiana University Press, 1951.
Amy Lowell: Portrait of the Poet in Her Time. New York, Nelson, 1958.
The World of James McNeill Whistler. New York, Nelson, 1959; London, Hutchinson, 1961.
The Dying Gladiators and Other Essays. New York, Grove Press, 1961.
Dorothy Richardson: An Adventure in Self-Discovery. New York, Holt Rinehart, 1967.
The House on Jefferson Street: A Cycle of Memories. New York, Holt Rinehart, 1971.
Spirit of Time and Place: The Collected Essays of Horace Gregory. New York, Norton, 1973.

Editor, with Eleanor Clark, *New Letters in America.* New York, Norton, 1937.
Editor, *Critical Remarks on the Metaphysical Poets.* Mount Vernon, New York, Golden Eagle Press, 1943.
Editor, *The Triumph of Life: Poems of Consolation for the English-Speaking World.* New York, Viking Press, 1943.
Editor, *The Portable Sherwood Anderson.* New York, Viking Press, 1949.
Editor, *Snake Lady*, by Violet Paget. New York, Grove Press, 1954.
Editor, *Selected Poetry*, by Robert Browning. New York, Rinehart, 1956.
Editor, with Marya Zaturenska, *The Mentor Book of Religious Verse.* New York, New American Library, 1957.
Editor, with Marya Zaturenska, *The Crystal Cabinet: An Invitation to Poetry.* New York, Holt Rinehart, 1962.
Editor, with others, *Riverside Poetry 4: An Anthology of Student Verse.* New York, Twayne, 1962.
Editor, *Evangeline and Selected Tales and Poems of Longfellow.* New York, New American Library, 1964.
Editor, *Selected Poems*, by E. E. Cummings. New York, Harcourt Brace, 1965.
Editor, with Marya Zaturenska, *The Silver Swan: Poems of Romance and Mystery.* New York, Holt Rinehart, 1966.
Editor, *Selected Poems of George Gordon, Lord Byron.* New York, Crowell, 1969.

Translator, *Poems*, by Catullus. New York, Covici Friede, 1931.
Translator, *Poems*, by Catullus. New York, Grove Press, and London, Thames and Hudson, 1956.
Translator, *The Metamorphoses*, by Ovid. New York, Viking Press, 1958.
Translator, *Love Poems of Ovid.* New York, New American Library, 1964.

Critical Studies: "Horace Gregory Issue" of *Modern Poetry Studies* (Buffalo, New York), May 1973.

*   *   *

Horace Gregory is perhaps best known as the translator of Catullus and Ovid. But he has also published critical studies on Amy Lowell, D. H. Lawrence, James McNeill Whistler and others, as well as collaborating with his wife, the poet Marya Zaturenska, on *A History of American Poetry 1900–1940*, and on the editing of an anthology for young readers, *The Crystal Cabinet: An Invitation to Poetry*.

Elizabeth Drew has written that his "emotional range is perhaps the most comprehensive among modern poets," and Louis Untermeyer wrote that Gregory "does not share Eliot's disillusions or Crane's disorganization," a statement that is unfair to all three poets. However, poems like "Valediction to My Contemporaries" compare interestingly with Hart Crane's "The Bridge" in their language, their idealism, their purposes; and many of Gregory's efforts to recapture in monologues the pathos and cacophony of life in the modern city remind one of Eliot. In the final analysis, however, authenticity and integrity may not be enough; subtleties of syntax, powers of condensation, originality of imagery, distinguish Eliot and Crane from those who wrote with comparable verve.

Gregory is academic, ordered, descriptive, even-paced; he might be quite properly compared with MacLeish for his intellectual ambition, rhetorical power, and sense of American history. Most of his poems are based on classical subjects in one way or another, though he often juxtaposes classical imagery with modernistic impressions; he also has many poems about paintings, European scenes, and – like MacLeish – his country's cultural history. His well-known poem on Emerson recapitulates Emerson's life in an investigation of the intellectual's role ("To know too well, to think too long") in a land where action and immortality are even more akin than rhetoric and relevance. Gregory, like MacLeish, bears a heavy weight of idealism at all times, perhaps more than his country's history can support. Because the idealism is more muted in his Chelsea rooming house poems, they are perhaps more appealing than his poems with more epic ambitions. In poems like "McAlpin Garfinkel, Poet" and "Time and Isidore Lefkowitz," Gregory seems to have absorbed the influence of Edwin Arlington Robinson and to have looked forward to the work of poets like Kenneth Fearing:

> Look at Isidore Lefkowitz,
> biting his nails, telling how
> he seduces Beautiful French Canadian
> Five and Ten Cent Store Girls,
> beautiful, by God, and how they cry
> and moan, wrapping their arms
> and legs around him
> when he leaves them . . . .

In an age when we have come to think of poems as the swiftly captured sound of madness, Gregory's work stands as a celebration of order, with the glimpsed backstreet life crying out to have a part of that order and the consideration due to it:

How can I unlearn
the arts of love within a single hour;
how can I close my eyes before a mirror,
believe I am not wanted, that hands, lips, breast
are merely deeper shadows behind the door
where all is dark?

– David Ray

GRIEVE, Christopher Murray.   See MacDIARMID, Hugh.

GRIFFITHS, Bryn (lyn David). Welsh.   Born in Swansea, Glamorganshire. Left
school at age 14; attended Coleg Harlech, Merioneth, 1961–62. Served in the
Merchant Navy for 7 years. Address: c/o J. M. Dent and Sons Ltd., Aldine House,
26 Albermarle Street, London W1X 4QY, England.

PUBLICATIONS

Verse

The Mask of Pity.   Llandybie, Carmarthenshire, Christopher Davies, 1966.
The Stones Remember.   London, Dent, 1967.
Scars.   London, Dent, 1969.
At the Airport.   Frensham, Surrey, Sceptre Press, 1971.
The Survivors.   London, Dent, 1971.
Beasthoods: Poems.   London, Turret Books, 1972.
Starboard Green.   Blackwood, Monmouthshire, Imble Publications, 1973.
Dark Convoy: Sea Poems.   Solihull, Warwickshire, Aquila, 1974.

Recording: *Poems*, with Bryan Walters, Argo, 1974.

Plays

Radio Plays: *The Sailor*, 1967; *The Dream of Arthur*, 1968.

Other

Editor, *Welsh Voices: An Anthology of New Poetry from Wales.*   London, Dent,
1967.

591

Bryn Griffiths comments:

I am primarily concerned with the present of man and his future, and particularly the symbiotic relationship of mankind with other life on this planet. I also draw on my Welsh background for themes – sources from Celtic myth and history – and am trying, slowly, to hammer out, through syllabic structures of words, a personal poetic vision of our world.

*   *   *

After a somewhat mixed experience as a welder, painter, labourer, seaman and car-tester, Bryn Griffiths started his writing career at a time when, partially as a result of the activities of the "pop" poets, the general public was being persuaded to take an increasing interest in poetry readings – an interest which Griffiths has subsequently done a good deal to encourage and sustain. As his poetry is pithy, down-to-earth, and direct in impact, it is hardly surprising that, from the beginning, it has had a great appeal for listeners, as well as readers. In fact, his earliest work seems to reflect both the strength and weakness of the poet whose platform performance is almost equal to his technical skill – the ability to communicate a rich variety of thought and feelings to a wide audience, combined with an occasional tendency to content himself with superficial impressions.

With the publication of his second volume, *The Stones Remember*, it became apparent that Griffiths was undergoing a period of rapid development and exploring his own experience at great depth. He has always been preoccupied with the landscape, people and traditions of his native Wales, but with this volume, and *Scars*, which followed two years later, he produced clear evidence of having found an individual voice. *The Survivors* is largely concerned with his experiences on two trips to Australia, but even in that vast continent, impressed as he is by the strange grandeur of his new environment, he looks back to his native country: "I take you with me, Wales, wherever I go."

– Howard Sergeant

GRIGSON, Geoffrey (Edward Harvey). English. Born in Pelynt, Cornwall, 2 March 1905. Educated at St. Edmund Hall, Oxford. Married; has several children. Formerly, Staff Member, *Yorkshire Post*, Leeds, and Literary Editor, *Morning Post*, and BBC, London. Founding Editor, *New Verse*, London, 1933–39. Recipient: Duff Cooper Memorial Prize, 1971; Oscar Blumenthal Prize (*Poetry*, Chicago), 1971. Address: Broad Town Farm, Broad Town, Swindon, Wiltshire, England.

PUBLICATIONS

Verse

Several Observations: Thirty Five Poems. London, Cresset Press, 1939.
Under the Cliff and Other Poems. London, Routledge, 1943.
The Isles of Scilly and Other Poems. London, Routledge, 1946.

Legenda Suecana: Twenty-Odd Poems. London, privately printed, 1953.
The Collected Poems of Geoffrey Grigson, 1924–1962. London, Phoenix House, 1963.
A Skull in Salop and Other Poems. London, Macmillan, and Chester Springs, Pennsylvania, Dufour, 1967.
Ingestion of Ice-Cream and Other Poems. London, Macmillan, 1969.
Discoveries of Bones and Stones. London, Macmillan, 1971.
Penguin Modern Poets 23, with Edwin Muir and Adrian Stokes. London, Penguin, 1973.
Sad Grave of an Imperial Mongoose. London, Macmillan, 1973.
The First Folio. London, Poem-of-the-Month Club, 1973.
Angles and Circles. London, Gollancz, 1974.

Other

Henry Moore. London, Penguin, 1943.
Wild Flowers in Britain. London, Collins, and New York, Hastings House, 1944.
Samuel Palmer: The Visionary Years. London, Kegan Paul, 1947.
The Harp of Aeolus and Other Essays on Art, Literature, and Nature. London, Routledge, 1947.
An English Farmhouse and Its Neighbourhood. London, Parrish, 1948.
The Scilly Isles. London, Elek, 1948.
Places of the Mind. London, Routledge, 1949.
The Crest on the Silver: An Autobiography. London, Cresset Press, 1950.
Flowers of the Meadow. London, Penguin, 1950.
Wessex. London, Collins, 1951.
A Master of Our Time: A Study of Wyndham Lewis. London, Methuen, 1951.
Essays from the Air (broadcasts). London, Routledge, 1951.
West Country. London, Collins, 1951.
Gardenage; or, The Plants of Ninhursaga. London, Routledge, 1952.
The Female Form in Painting, with Jean Cassou. London, Thames and Hudson, and New York, Harcourt Brace, 1953.
Freedom of the Parish. London, Phoenix House, 1954.
Gerard Manley Hopkins. London, Longman, 1955; revised edition, 1962.
The Englishman's Flora. London, Phoenix House, 1955.
English Drawing from Samuel Cooper to Gwen John. London, Thames and Hudson, 1955.
Corot. New York, Metropolitan Museum, 1956.
Painted Caves. London, Phoenix House, 1957.
England. London, Thames and Hudson, 1957; New York, Studio Publications, 1958.
Fossils, Insects, and Reptiles. London, Phoenix House, 1957; in *The Shell Nature Book*, 1964.
Art Treasures of the British Museum. London, Thames and Hudson, and New York, Abrams, 1957.
The Three Kings. Bedford, Gordon Fraser, 1958.
The Wiltshire Book. London, Thames and Hudson, 1957.
English Villages in Colour. London, Batsford, 1958.
Looking and Finding and Collecting and Reading and Investigating and Much Else (juvenile). London, Phoenix House, 1958; revised edition, London, Baker, 1970.
The Shell Guide to Trees and Shrubs. London, Phoenix House, 1958; in *The Shell Nature Book*, 1964.

A Herbal of All Sorts. London, Phoenix House, and New York, Macmillan, 1959.

The Shell Guide to Wild Life. London, Phoenix House, 1959; in *The Shell Nature Book*, 1964.

English Excursions. London, Country Life, 1960.

Samuel Palmer's Valley of Vision. London, Phoenix House, 1960.

Christopher Smart. London, Longman, 1961.

Poets in Their Pride (juvenile). London, Phoenix House, 1962; New York, Basic Books, 1964.

The Shell Country Book. London, Phoenix House, 1962.

The Shell Book of Roads. London, Ebury Press, 1964.

Shapes and Stories: A Book about Pictures (juvenile), with Jane Grigson. London, Baker, 1964; New York, Vanguard Press, 1965.

The Shell Nature Book (includes *The Shell Guide to Wild Life, The Shell Guide to Trees and Shrubs, The Shell Guide to Flowers of the Countryside,* and *Fossils, Insects, and Reptiles,* by Geoffrey Grigson, and *Birds and Beasts* by James Fisher). London, Phoenix House, and New York, Basic Books, 1964.

The Shell Country Alphabet. London, Joseph, 1966.

Shapes and Adventures (juvenile), with Jane Grigson. London, Marshbank, 1967; as *More Shapes and Stories: A Book about Pictures,* New York, Vanguard Press, 1967.

Shapes and People: A Book about Pictures (juvenile). London, Baker, and New York, Vanguard Press, 1969.

Poems and Poets. London, Macmillan, and Chester Springs, Pennsylvania, Dufour, 1969.

Notes from an Odd Country. London, Macmillan, 1970.

Shapes and Creatures (juvenile). London, Black, 1973.

The Contrary View: Glimpses of Fudge and Gold. London, Macmillan, 1974; Totowa, New Jersey, Rowman and Littlefield, 1974.

A Dictionary of English Plant Names. London, Allen Lane, 1974.

Britain Observed: From Rubens to Ben Nicholson. London, Phaidon, 1975.

Editor, with others, *The Year's Poetry.* London, Lane, 1934.

Editor, *The Arts Today.* London, Lane, 1935.

Editor, with Denys Kilham Roberts, *The Year's Poetry, 1937–38.* London, Lane, 1938.

Editor, *New Verse: An Anthology.* London, Faber, 1939.

Editor, *The Journals of George Sturt.* London, Cresset Press, 1941.

Editor, *The Romantics: An Anthology.* London, Routledge, 1942; Cleveland, World, 1962.

Editor, *Visionary Poems and Passages; or, The Poet's Eye.* London, Muller, 1944.

Editor, *The Mint: A Miscellany of Literature, Art, and Criticism.* London, Routledge, 2 vols., 1946, 1948.

Editor, *Before the Romantics: An Anthology of the Enlightenment.* London, Routledge, 1946.

Editor, *Poems of John Clare's Madness.* London, Routledge, 1949.

Editor, *Poetry of the Present: An Anthology of the Thirties and After.* London, Phoenix House, 1949.

Editor, *Selected Poems of William Barnes, 1800–1866.* London, Routledge, and Cambridge, Massachusetts, Harvard University Press, 1950.

Editor, *Selected Poems,* by John Clare. London, Routledge, 1950.

Editor, *Selected Poems,* by John Dryden. London, Grey Walls Press, 1950.

Editor, *Poems,* by George Crabbe. London, Grey Walls Press, 1950.

Editor, *The Victorians: An Anthology.* London, Routledge, 1950.

Editor, *Thornton's Temple of Flora*, by Robert John Thornton. London, Collins, 1951.

Editor, *Poems*, by Samuel Taylor Coleridge. London, Grey Walls Press, 1951.

Editor, *About Britain* series. London, Collins, 13 vols., 1951.

Editor, with Charles Harvard Gibbs-Smith, *People, Places and Things*. London, Grosvenor Press, and New York, Hawthorn Press, 4 vols., 1954.

Editor, *The Three Kings: A Christmas Book of Carols, Poems, and Pieces*. Bedford, Gordon Fraser, 1958.

Editor, *Country Poems*. London, Hulton, 1959.

Editor, *The Cherry Tree: A Collection of Poems* (juvenile). London, Phoenix House, and New York, Vanguard Press, 1959.

Editor, *The Concise Encyclopaedia of Modern World Literature*. London, Hutchinson, and New York, Hawthorn Books, 1963; revised edition, Hutchinson, 1970; Hawthorn Books, 1971.

Editor, *O Rare Mankind! A Short Collection of Great Prose* (juvenile). London, Phoenix House, 1963.

Editor, *Poems*, by Walter Savage Landor. London, Centaur Press, 1964; Carbondale, Southern Illinois University Press, 1965.

Editor, *The English Year: From Diaries and Letters*. London, Oxford University Press, 1967.

Editor, *A Choice of William Morris's Verse*. London, Faber, 1969.

Editor, *A Choice of Thomas Hardy's Poems*. London, Macmillan, 1969.

Editor, *A Choice of Robert Southey's Verse*. London, Faber, 1970.

Editor, *Thirty-Eight Poems*, by Pennethorne Hughes. London, Baker, 1970.

Editor, *Rainbows, Fleas, and Flowers* (juvenile). London, Baker, 1971; New York, Vanguard Press, 1974.

Editor, *Unrespectable Verse*. London, Allen Lane, 1971.

Editor, *The Faber Book of Popular Verse*. London, Faber, 1971; as *Gambit Book of Popular Verse*, Boston, Gambit, 1971.

Editor, *The Faber Book of Love Poems*. London, Faber, 1973.

Editor, *Cotton*. London, Penguin, 1974.

Manuscript Collections: British Museum, London; Birmingham University Library.

Critical Study: in *Times Literary Supplement* (London), 31 July 1969.

Geoffrey Grigson comments:

I deduce from my poems that I write by this conviction: graces enter and exist in living; they start up, vanish, and are seen again in glimpses. It is sentimental treason to suppose that we can be anaesthetized or satisfied by these graces, but the grand treason, realizing the constancy of the bad and the worst, is not as well to admit and celebrate and be thankful for these consolatory graces, or viaticum.

*   *   *

Geoffrey Grigson is one of the most interesting of the so-called "Auden generation" of English poets who began writing in the 1930's; but his merits as a poet have always been overshadowed by his activities as an entrepreneur of letters. For several years in the thirties Grigson was editor of the influential magazine *New*

Verse, and throughout his life he has been an active and polemical critic. His early poetry was marked by its precise, imagistic observations of the contemporary scene; Grigson was a believer in the brief snapshot of reality, presented without elaboration or comment, though the political preoccupations so evident in the poetry of Auden or Spender were often implicitly present in his verse. These early poems were redeemed from flatness by Grigson's delicate and very personal sense of rhythm. They can still be read with pleasure, although at the same time they are very much of their period, when poets were following up Eliot's fascination with urban landscape, and were actively interested in sociological enquiry: the 1930's movement called Mass Observation echoes the title of Grigson's book of poems *Several Observations.*

His later poetry, though still anchored to the discipline of exact description, is less austere and more overtly emotional. In addition to his original discipleship of Auden and the Imagists, Grigson developed a great admiration for John Clare, and much of his description of natural objects recalls the precise botanical observations of Ruskin or Hopkins. Although Grigson remains what he has always been, a writer of short poems, there are pieces in his *Collected Poems* that show he has occasionally been more ambitious, like the short verse play "The Islanders," and a rather impressive sequence of love poems called "Legenda." Yet a brief poem like "Elms under Cloud" remains most typical of Grigson's art:

> Elms, old-men with thinned-out hair,
> And mouths down-turned, express
> The oldness of the English scene:
>
> And up the hill a pale road reaches
> To a huge paleness browned with scattered,
> Irritated cloud . . . .

– Bernard Bergonzi

GRUBB, Frederick (Crichton-Stuart). British. Born near Salisbury, Wiltshire, 18 June 1930. Educated at Trinity College, Cambridge, M.A. 1960; London University, Ph.D. Recipient: Arts Council bursary, 1966. Address: 243 Haverstock Hill, London N.W.3, England.

PUBLICATIONS

Verse

Title Deeds and Other Poems. London, Longman, 1961.
September Sun. Frensham, Surrey, Sceptre Press, 1969.
Frog. Rushden, Northamptonshire, Sceptre Press, 1972.

Other

A Vision of Reality: A Study of Liberalism in Twentieth Century Verse. London, Chatto and Windus, and New York, Barnes and Noble, 1965.

Frederick Grubb comments:

Descendant of Lord Bute who was satirised by Charles Churchill and whose inept policies did Britain the service of losing the American colonies. Never "educated" but played pub darts at a "public" school, attended Trinity College, Cambridge (M.A.), has Ph.D., London, for research on "Relation Between Feeling and Values in T. S. Eliot," and lives by work and the dole.

Socialist (i.e. fights capitalism), enjoys (red) wine if cheap, travels (frugally) in remote areas of Latin countries, prefers a pub to a club and a workers caff to a restaurant and a bedsitter to a flat. Unlikely to be invited to a Foyles Literary Lunch: he expropriated the expropriators.

Agrees with T. S. Eliot that "art is not a career, it's a mug's game." Is not a member of any organization or committee, neither owns, attends, hears nor sees telly, radio, discs, cinema, theatre, concerts, galleries, newspapers, junkets, house, or car, dislikes all ornaments, and believes that art is an individual activity with (one hopes) social meaning and culture is individuals communicating to (one hopes) individuals. A revival of satire of the Augustan type is needful.

Prefers Russian literature, British poetry to Byron, the best 1930's work to current writing. Loathes Hardy, but likes Larkin, Nicholson, Hughes, Middleton, Hamburger, Martin Bell, and thirty others, often Scots or Welsh. His poems were fussy and elaborate, but does not agree with W. H. Auden that poems can be rewritten – or withdrawn. Now aims at clarity, austerity, moments of vividness and force in resolutely structured or free designs with unity of thought-form and feeling-pattern.

*   *   *

The poetry of Frederick Grubb is made up of maddening starts and stops. In his output there is scarcely one complete poem. Dr. Grubb's erudition has been proverbial for some years now, and he was advocating Yeats, Rilke, Valéry and Péguy as long ago as 1953 when he was still an undergraduate. Yet all his study of literature has not served to show him how to shape a line or frame an image as adeptly as the newcomer who went down last year.

Perhaps the answer to this puzzle is that Frederick Grubb is grappling with concerns more difficult than the deftness of lines or the immediate appeal of imagery. There is a dichotomy in the author of *A Vision of Reality*, and it is a curiously post-Romantic one. As an artist and critic of literature Dr. Grubb seems to attach himself to works which are self-substantive and finely wrought; the poems of Valéry, Rilke and Yeats, in fact. But as a socialist and social critic he seeks to subjoin such grecian urns to the soiled crockery of humanity as a means of making it whole. In other words, he has trouble in relating his aesthetic and political concerns.

This dilemma is not new. It accounts for the vagueness of Shelley, the triviality of Wilde, the evasiveness of Auden. Other practitioners have compounded their honour with their safety and set politics at a considerable remove from art. Yet *A Vision of Reality* is a critical book that only a poet could have written, and the same is true of Frederick Grubb's poetry.

If we read it, we read it as fragments. Thus:

> Landscape already tinged with regret
> How shall we keep you, externally passing away
> Clouds drift into clouds, trees to another forest
> Caves into cathedrals, rivers into seas . . .
> – from "The Imperfect Day"

> Anyone could walk in. The gates creaking.
> The parterre mature if not overblown.
> The orangery reeks . . . .
> – from "The Hall of Mirrors in the Evening"

> The ice that froze his uncle's ambition
> Thawed, burned in him: his Moscow was the throne . . .
> – from "Napoleon III"

> Uncommon people? Yes, but commonness
> Is not so rare you cannot breed from it . . .
> – from "Talented Families"

> Lascaux was closed, the taint of breath
> – First since the last, that dried the paint –
> Mildewed the pigments . . .
> – from "Cave"

> Under drizzle,
> Among traffic, dominated by constructions
> The spirit
> Is at a solemn music but not for long . . .
> – from "A Short View of Music"

> Two moving dots, slow, sure, dutiful, go
> Along the row of elms, to pealing bells.
> An ageing couple
> My parents worship in the church below . . .
> – from "Elegy"

The poetry does not last as long as the prose sense of these pieces, the prose sense seldom as long as the external form. But among much that is tortuous, certain lines, like the ones quoted, stand out clear. They survive, wrenched out of context, because the context does little to help them.

It would appear that this student of mythopoeic poetry is in search of a myth for himself. He may disturb the conventional reader by his refusal to take an easy way out of his intellectual labyrinth. But it must be said that the tortuosities of Frederick Grubb carry more conviction than the dexterity of many rivals who on the surface seem more accomplished.

– Philip Hobsbaum

GRUFFYDD, Peter. British. Born in Liverpool, Lancashire, 12 April 1935. Educated at University College of North Wales, Bangor, 1957–60, B.A. (honours) in English 1960. Served in the Royal Army, 1955–57. Lecturer in Liberal Studies, Rochdale College of Art, Lancashire, 1965–67; taught English, Volkhochschule, Munich, 1970–72. Free-lance writer, translator, and actor. Recipient: Gregory Award, 1963; Welsh Arts Council award, 1968; Arts Council of Great Britain award, 1972. Address: Grosvenor Hotel, Llanberis, Carnarvonshire, North Wales.

PUBLICATIONS

Verse

> *Triad: Thirty-Three Poems,* with Harri Webb and Meic Stephens. Merthyr Tydfil, Glamorganshire, Triskel Press, 1963.
> *The Shivering Seed.* London, Chatto and Windus, and Middletown, Connecticut, Wesleyan University Press, 1972.

Play

Radio Play: *The Cuckoo,* 1968.

Peter Gruffydd comments:

I am, and have always felt myself to be, a lone wolf – with no labels, manifestos, or luggage other than words.

My poems involve cyclic themes of life, birth, death, love, individuals in everyday or esoteric "environments."

It seems to me that any modern poet has the whole scope of techniques and stylistic devices, the poet's tool bag, in English, from Chaucer to now, at his fingertips – should he either need or care to use them. The field is completely open.

What I try to achieve in poetry is truth to the object and the image in "true" words.

No modern poet expects to live by selling his work, but the standard of payment (in the few that do pay) is unspeakably low in British periodicals. *C'est la vie!*

*   *   *

Many of Peter Gruffydd's poems are about Wales, particularly in his last collection, *The Shivering Seed.* Some are evocations of place, the accumulation of sharp details of a scene where he employs vivid images: "the dog which, deaf, / Maps out again its world of odours"; "this fire-flicked / Brasswink and elbow-kept room"; "the sour steel sky." Other Welsh poems are "exposures" of the more corrupt, confused and unintelligent of his compatriots, and these rather bitter indictments have been criticised as stale and pompous – best left to other writers with a closer, wittier knowledge of the much-battered targets flayed by Gruffydd. But he is not without a sense of irony (unusual in Celtic practitioners), and is occasionally very funny at the expense of the narrower specimen of Welshman.

His main talent consists in describing objects and landscape, rather than in forming significant conclusions about them. Often he stretches his material too thinly over too many lines, being consciously "poetic" while evading the necessity of asking himself what a particular experience may signify.

Gruffydd is effective as a sensitive observer of childhood, recording a sense of awe in the face of nature and capturing a child's first shock of wonder or apprehension. Though at his best the language has a tautness, richness and density, it is possible to detect influences – such as, inevitably, Dylan Thomas's – on Gruffydd's work which have not yet been completely assimilated into his own, original voice. There is much, however, in his work that is impressive, promising a distinctive accomplishment in the future.

– John Tripp

GUEST, Barbara. American. Born in Wilmington, North Carolina, 6 September 1920. Educated at the University of California, Berkeley, A.B. 1941. Married Lord Haden-Guest in 1948 (divorced, 1954); Trumbull Higgins, 1954; has two children. Editorial Associate, *Art News*, New York, 1951–54. Recipient: Yaddo Fellowship, 1958; Longview Foundation Award, 1960. Address: 1148 Fifth Avenue, New York, New York 10028, U.S.A.

PUBLICATIONS

Verse

The Location of Things. New York, Tibor de Nagy Press, 1960.
Poems: The Location of Things, Archaics, The Open Skies. New York, Doubleday, 1962.
The Blue Stairs. New York, Corinth Books, 1968.
I Ching: Poems and Lithographs, with Sheila Isham. New York, Mourlot, 1969.
Moscow Mansions. New York, Viking Press, 1973.

Plays

The Ladies Choice (produced New York, 1953).
The Office (produced New York, 1963).
Port (produced New York, 1965).

Other

Robert Goodnough, with B. H. Friedman. Paris, G. Fall, 1962.

Manuscript Collection: University of Kentucky, Lexington.

Barbara Guest comments:

Frequent traveller – usually Europe once a year with several longer periods in Paris and London – with subsequent effect on poetry.

Involved with painters, beginning with Abstract-Expressionists of the 1950's to present time. Their influence on my work is very strong.

*   *   *

The poems of Barbara Guest ignore almost every convention in metrics in English and American poetry – past and present; this fact can create difficulties for the reader and leaves one searching for analogies in painting, the art which she has been closely identified with as editor and commentator, in order to describe her work. Paintings are her subject in several poems, their effect reminiscent of the full bright canvasses of Matisse, without frames. In "Passage," for John Coltrane, she compares the two arts directly:

> Words
>   after all
> are syllables *just*
> and you put them
>   in their place
>   notes
>   sounds
> a painter using his stroke . . .
> slashed as it was with color
>   called "being"
>   or even "it"

A typical poem by Barbara Guest is a pastiche of colors, shapes, natural setting in which the objects create the mood. She constantly explores problems in aesthetics, how beauty makes itself felt, enjoying "the transformed colors and shapes that the imagination makes possible," as William Van O'Connor once said of Wallace Stevens' work. Her poems are a search for a definable form, as if she were discovering the shape of things for the first time. She tells the painter Robert Motherwell, for example, in "All Elegies Are Black and White":

> (How wise you are to understand
> the use of orange with blue.
> "Never without the other.")

For all their distinctive charm, however, a reader may wonder how concretely the poems relate to this world, this time, and how as reader, viewer, audience, one can participate in the poet's original discovery, in the poetic excitement and awe and wonder that prompted her highly imaginative and impressionistic response. Many of the poems lack moral weight, a social or ethical grounding.

Guest writes as if the Imagist movement began yesterday, saying "no ideas but in things," moving persistently toward some revelation no one else has discovered. At its best, her poetry brings together the Imagist delight in objects, landscapes, and seascapes, and the uneasiness of a person attuned to suffering, anxiety, pain. At one point, she wonders "if this new reality is going to destroy me." But the dominant note, as in "Now," is one of joy and confidence in the lyrical beauty that surrounds her:

It's Autumn
It's Fall. A red cloth with
Yellow leaves is chosen. And the
Sophisticated color of mauve
Burnt orange for the touch. To affect
A change. Where the ripe dawn
Hurries a red is.
                    – "Dieu soit en cette maison"

                                                        – Michael True

---

GUEST, Harry (Henry Bayly Guest). British. Born in Penarth, Glamorganshire, Wales, 6 October 1932. Educated at Malvern College, Worcestershire, 1946–50; Trinity Hall, Cambridge, 1951–54, B.A. in modern languages 1954; the Sorbonne, Paris, 1954–55, D.E.S. 1955 (thesis on Mallarmé). Married Lynn Guest in 1963; has one daughter and one son. Assistant Master, Felsted School, Essex, 1955–61; Head of Modern Languages Department, Lancing College, Sussex, 1961–66; Assistant Lecturer, Yokohama National University, Japan, 1966–72. Agent: Michael Bakewell, 118 Tottenham Court Road, London W.1. Address: 1 Alexandra Terrace, Exeter, Devon EX4 6SY, England.

PUBLICATIONS

Verse

Private View. London, Outposts Publications, 1962.
A Different Darkness. London, Outposts Publications, 1964.
Arrangements. London, Anvil Press Poetry, 1968.
The Cutting-Room. London, Anvil Press Poetry, 1970.
Penguin Modern Poets 16, with Jack Beeching and Matthew Mead. London, Penguin, 1970.
The Place. Rushden, Northamptonshire, Sceptre Press, 1971.
Text and Fragment, The Inheritance, Miniatures. Southampton, Hampshire, Earth Ship 13, 1972.
The Achievement of Poetry. Rushden, Northamptonshire, Sceptre Press, 1974.

Plays

The Inheritance (broadcast, 1973). Included in *Text and Fragment, The Inheritance, Miniatures,* 1972.

Radio Plays: *Beware of Pity,* translation of a play by Stefan Zweig, 1962; *Trial of Strength,* translation of a play by G. A. Golfar, 1964; *The Inheritance,* 1973.

Other

Another Island Country (essays).   Tokyo, Eikôsha, 1970.

Translator, with Lynn Guest and Kajima Shozo, *Post-War Japanese Poetry*.   London, Penguin, 1972.

Harry Guest comments:

(1970) Lyrical analysis of personal relationships, bisexual love, landscapes, etc. Certain amount of intellectual demand: European rather than transatlantic: syllabics or stress-length lines: high premium on musicality.

I admire Klee, the early Godard, Debussy's piano music.

(1974) *Private View* is a poem in XIV sections dealing with the relationships between art and reality, imagination and love. "Matsushima" (1967) examines the shadow-line crossed when death is felt in the marrow as inevitable. "Metamorphoses" (1968) uses a highly condensed, elliptical language for its "Six Poems on Related Themes." *The Place* is 15 connected meditations about a holiday on the west coast of Japan, and *Miniatures* is 36 brief poems recording a visit with the poet's daughter to a volcanic island.

The short poems in various structural forms are primarily lyrical or narrative – love-poems like "The Summers of Nowhere" or "At Shoreham"; problems of perception like "Allegories," "Autumns," or "Nocturnes for the Dead of Winter"; or of art – "The Painter . . .," "Cinema."

The kind of poetry that most appeals to me has music and density, appeals to the senses as much as to the mind and spirit.

*   *   *

Harry Guest's poems have appeared in numerous magazines, ranging from *The Poetry Review* and *Outposts* to the *Yokohama Journal of Post-Graduate English Studies*, but his first individual publication was *Private View*, a long poem in 14 sections, published by Outposts Publications, who also published a selection of his poems under the title of *A Different Darkness*. The former, and five poems from the latter, were reprinted in the Anvil Press volume, *Arrangements*, together with other poems written between 1957 and 1967. *Private View* is a series of reflective poems arising out of a visit to an art exhibition, largely concerned with the relationship between the artist and his subject, as well as the part played by the artist. Like most of Guest's poetry, it makes its impact by means of skilfully manipulated images and association of ideas. In *Arrangements* Harry Guest divides his work under such headings as "Problems," "Relationships," "Criticisms," "Narratives," "Techniques," but this does not give a clear idea of his real virtues as a poet. One might remark upon his skill and note his interest in the techniques of other writers, reflected in such poems as "Statement," "About Baudelaire," and "Elegy for Jean Cocteau." Some critics have praised his "travel" poems; but Guest has a line all his own and rarely writes a simple descriptive poem. "A Bar in Lerici" or "Matsushima" shows how he uses the new environment to effect new insights into the human situation. Perhaps best of all are his poems on the man-woman relationship, the marital relationship in particular, on which he can be lyrical and tender without losing control over his material.

In *The Cutting Room*, written in Japan, Harry Guest has extended his range of subject and treatment, and produced his most ambitious work to date.

– Howard Sergeant

GULLANS, Charles (Bennett). American. Born in Minneapolis, Minnesota, 5 May 1929. Educated at the University of Minnesota, Minneapolis, B.A. 1948, M.A. 1951; King's College, Durham (Fulbright Fellow, 1953–55); Stanford University, California (Fellow in Creative Writing, 1952), Ph.D. 1956. Taught at the University of Washington, Seattle, 1955–61. Since 1961, Member of the English Department, Associate Professor, 1965–72, and since 1972, Professor of English, University of California, Los Angeles. Recipient: University of California Institute of Creative Arts Fellowship, 1965. Address: 405 Hilgard, Los Angeles, California 90024, U.S.A.

PUBLICATIONS

Verse

Moral Poems.   Palo Alto, California, John Hunter Thomas, 1957.
Arrivals and Departures.   Minneapolis, University of Minnesota Press, 1962.

Other

The Decorative Designers, 1895–1931: An Essay.   Los Angeles, University of California Library, 1970.
A Bibliography of the Published Writings of J. V. Cunningham.   Los Angeles, University of California Library, 1973.

Editor, *The English and Latin Poems of Sir Robert Ayton.*   Edinburgh, Blackwood, 1963.
Editor, with John Espey, *A Checklist of Trade Bindings Designed by Margaret Armstrong.*   Los Angeles, University of California Library, 1968.

Translator, with Franz Schneider, *Last Letters from Stalingrad.*   New York, Morrow, 1962.

Manuscript Collection: University of California, Los Angeles.

Critical Study: "A Study of the Poetry of Charles Gullans" by Mary Cecile Caestecker, in *The Barat Faculty Review* (Lake Forest, Illinois), January 1966.

Charles Gullans comments:

"After these successful operations we reached a fortress called Thilutha, situated in the middle of the river, a place rising in a lofty peak and fortified by nature's power as if by the hand of man. Since the difficulty and the height of the place made it impregnable, an attempt was made with friendly words (as was fitting) to induce the inhabitants to surrender; but they insisted that such defection would be untimely. But they went so far as to reply, that as soon as the Romans had got possession of the interior, they also would go over to the victors, as appendages of the kingdom. After this, as our ships went by under their very walls, they looked on in respectful silence without making any move." Ammianus Marcellinus, XXIV, 2, 1–2.

*   *   *

Published in 1962, Charles Gullans' *Arrivals and Departures* remains one of the best books of poems of our period. Volumes by other poets contain individual poems as good or better than any of Gullans'; yet few can equal *Arrivals and Departures* as a book, whole and unified in its diversity and variety. The book is divided into three sections: "Love and Landscapes," "Friends and Relations," and "Metaphysicians and Marvels." The progression is not an arbitrary grouping of poems with similar themes, as in most books of verse. One needs to read the poems in the order printed; not because they form a sequence, but because of the deliberate arrangement, each poem and each section informing the rest. The book is a sort of record or impression of a wholly civilized man: almost fragile love poems can stand with bitter satire; poems of great originality can bear the comparison one inevitably makes with his translations from Rilke, Petrarch, Jose-Maria de Heredia, and Nietzsche. It takes a man of courage and equal talent to put his own poems beside those of masters; but the poems of Gullans can bear such comparison; and the translations show another dimension of his mind, his understanding, his gift. They are part of the contents of an urbane, educated, aware mind; and that is one thing the book is about.

I cannot do justice to Gullans in this short notice. Only a close examination of his stylistic virtues, his intellectual and emotional integrity, and his poetic virtuosity could do such justice. His translation of Rilke's "The Panther" is the finest I know in English; and he boldly follows it with one of his own best poems, "First Love," a beautifully rendered piece. Other good poems include "After Analysis" and the two poems titled "Midsummer Day" and "Autumn: An Ode." His "Autumn Burial: A Meditation" is a great poem.

– James Korges

GUNN, Thom (son William). British. Born in Gravesend, Kent, 29 August 1929. Educated at University College School, London; Trinity College, Cambridge, B.A. 1953, M.A. 1958; Stanford University, California, 1954–55, 1956–58. Served in the British Army, 1948–50. Member of the English Department, University of California, Berkeley, 1958–66. Poetry Reviewer, *Yale Review*, New Haven, Connecticut,

1958–64. Since 1966, Free-lance Writer. Recipient: Levinson Prize (*Poetry*, Chicago), 1955; Maugham Award, 1959; Arts Council of Great Britain award, 1959; National Institute of Arts and Letters grant, 1964; Rockefeller award, 1966; Guggenheim Fellowship, 1971. Address; 1216 Cole Street, San Francisco, California 94117, U.S.A.

PUBLICATIONS

Verse

(*Poems*).   Oxford, Fantasy Press, 1953.
Fighting Terms.   Oxford, Fantasy Press, 1954; revised edition, New York, Hawk's Well Press, 1958; London, Faber, 1962.
The Sense of Movement.   London, Faber, 1957; Chicago, University of Chicago Press, 1959.
My Sad Captains and Other Poems.   London, Faber, and Chicago, University of Chicago Press, 1961.
Selected Poems, with Ted Hughes.   London, Faber, 1962.
A Geography.   Iowa City, Stone Wall Press, 1966.
Positives, with Ander Gunn.   London, Faber, 1966; Chicago, University of Chicago Press, 1967.
Touch.   London, Faber, 1967; Chicago, University of Chicago Press, 1968.
The Garden of the Gods.   Cambridge, Massachusetts, Pym Randall Press, 1968.
The Explorers: Poems.   Crediton, Devon, Gilbertson, 1969.
The Fair in the Woods.   Oxford, Sycamore Press, 1969.
Poems 1950–1966: A Selection.   London, Faber, 1969.
Sunlight.   New York, Albondocani Press, 1969.
Last Days at Teddington.   London, Poem-of-the-Month Club, 1971.
Moly.   London, Faber, 1971.
Corgi Modern Poets in Focus 5, with others, edited by Dannie Abse.   London, Corgi, 1971.
Moly and My Sad Captains.   New York, Farrar Straus, 1973.
Mandrakes.   London, Rainbow Press, 1974.
Song Book.   New York, Albondocani Press, 1974.
To the Air.   Boston, Godine Press, 1974.

Recording: *Thom Gunn Reading "On the Move"*, Listen, 1963.

Other

Editor, *Poetry from Cambridge 1951–52: A Selection of Verse by Members of the University.*   London, Fortune Press, 1952.
Editor, with Ted Hughes, *Five American Poets.*   London, Faber, 1963.
Editor, *Selected Poems of Fulke Greville.*   London, Faber, and Chicago, University of Chicago Press, 1968.
Editor, *Ben Jonson.*   London, Penguin, 1974.

Critical Studies: by Martin Dodsworth, in *The Survival of Poetry*, London, Faber, 1970; essay by the author in *Corgi Modern Poets in Focus 5*, 1971; "The Stipulative Imagination of Thom Gunn" by John Miller, and "A Critical Performance of Thom

Gunn's *Misanthropos*'' by Merle E. Brown, in *Iowa Review* (Iowa City), Winter 1973; ''My Suburban Muse'' by the author, in *Seven Modern Poets*, edited by Geoffrey Summerfield, London, Penguin, 1974.

*   *   *

The British poets who came to prominence in the 'fifties, Philip Larkin, Kingsley Amis, John Wain and lesser figures who shared their outlook, were alert and intelligent, but distrust of the high-flown romanticism which had so recently been in fashion led them towards a cautious use of imagery and a preference for a poetically neutral tone as well as a socially neutral attitude. Thom Gunn was an odd man out among these contemporaries in the sense that he favoured dramatic flourishes rather than poetic caution, and that from the first he experimented with poetic forms that in their harsh and rigid rhetoric tended to stress the power of the will:

> Over the map a moment, face to face:
> Across from Hitler, whose grey eyes have filled
> A nation with the illogic of their gaze,
> The rational man is poised, to break, to build.

The ''rational man'' here is Claus von Stauffenberg and the subject of a fine poem is the bomb plot against Hitler. It is typical of Gunn that he should implicitly regard the violence as not only rational and necessary but almost desirable: breaking comes before building. Some critics have seen in this attitude nothing more than a liking for sado-masochism as represented by his poems about black-jacketed motor cyclists, and a worship of action as opposed to sensibility:

> I praise the overdogs from Alexander
> To those who would not play with Stephen Spender

he has written in a poem giving a blessing to ''all the toughs through history.'' Yet these excesses of style and subject are perhaps a price that must be paid for the scope and magnificence of Gunn's best poetry. He is capable of tenderness untouched by sentimentality as in ''Lerici,'' a poem about death by drowning, and intellectual subtlety and complexity mark all his writing. The powerful images and rhythms he habitually uses seem both to modify and enhance what has been called his Jacobean language.

The sequence of poems called ''Misanthropos,'' which takes up a third of his volume *Touch,* deals with the situation of the last man left alive after atomic war and shows his tough humanism at full stretch. Vivid verses, most intelligently varied, reveal the last man setting traps, making skins from moles and rabbits, and learning to forget the past with its ''relentless memory of monstrous battle'' until he becomes purely a vehicle for action and ''nothing moves at the edges of the mind.'' At the end of the sequence, which is highly dramatic (and was performed originally on radio), he is seen as the first man, bent, small and furred, sifting mounds of dirt:

> He is a nose.
> He picks through the turned earth, and eats. A mouth.

He meets and helps creatures as inadequate as himself, beginning a new human cycle.

In other hands ''Misanthropos'' would have been merely grandiose, as bad as most of the poems written about Hiroshima and the concentration camps. Gunn's poem succeeds because of the masterly assurance of his tone and the sobriety and plainness of the language. It is an imaginative achievement beyond the reach of any other poet of his generation.

– Julian Symons

GUSTAFSON, Ralph (Barker). Canadian. Born in Lime Ridge, Quebec, 16 August 1909. Educated at Bishop's University, Lennoxville, Quebec, B.A. 1929, M.A. 1930; Oxford University, B.A. 1933. Married Elisabeth Renninger in 1958. Taught at Bishop's College School, 1930, and St. Alban's School, Brockville, Ontario, 1934. Worked for the British Information Services, 1942–46. Since 1960, Music Critic, Canadian Broadcasting Corporation. Since 1963, Professor of English and Poet-in-Residence, Bishop's University. Recipient: Prix David, 1935; Canada Council Senior Fellowship, 1959, award, 1968, 1971. M.A.: Oxford University, 1963; D.Litt.: Mount Allison University, Sackville, New Brunswick, 1973. Address: P.O. Box 172, North Hatley, Quebec, Canada.

PUBLICATIONS

Verse

    The Golden Chalice.   London, Nicholson and Watson, 1935.
    Alfred the Great (verse play).   London, Joseph, 1937.
    Epithalamium in Time of War.   New York, privately printed, 1941.
    Lyrics Unromantic.   New York, privately printed, 1942.
    Flight into Darkness: Poems.   New York, Pantheon Books, 1944.
    Rivers among Rocks.   Toronto, McClelland and Stewart, 1960.
    Rocky Mountain Poems.   Vancouver, Klanak Press, 1960.
    Sift in an Hourglass.   Toronto, McClelland and Stewart, 1966.
    Ixion's Wheel: Poems.   Toronto, McClelland and Stewart, 1969.
    Themes and Variations for Sounding Brass.   Sherbrooke, Quebec, Progressive Publications, 1972.
    Selected Poems.   Toronto, McClelland and Stewart, 1972.
    Fire on Stone.   Toronto, McClelland and Stewart, 1974.

Short Stories

    The Brazen Tower.   Tillsonburg, Ontario, Roger Ascham Press, 1974.

Other

    Poetry and Canada.   Ottawa, Canadian Legion Educational Service, 1945.

    Editor, *Anthology of Canadian Poetry (English).*   London, Penguin, 1942.
    Editor, *A Little Anthology of Canadian Poets.*   New York, New Directions, 1943.

Editor, "Canadian Poetry Issue" of *Voices* (New York), 1943.
Editor, *Canadian Accent: A Collection of Stories and Poems by Contemporary Writers from Canada.* London, Penguin, 1944.
Editor, *The Penguin Book of Canadian Verse.* London, Penguin, 1958; revised edition, 1967, 1975.

Bibliography: "Ralph Gustafson: A Bibliography in Progress" by L. M. Allison and W. Keitner, in *West Coast Review* (Burnaby, British Columbia), June 1974.

Manuscript Collections: State University of New York, Buffalo; Queen's University, Kingston, Ontario; University of Saskatchewan, Saskatoon.

Critical Studies: *Literary History of Canada,* Toronto, University of Toronto Press, 1966; *Oxford Companion to Canadian History and Literature,* Toronto, Oxford University Press, 1968; "Ralph Gustafson: A Review and Retrospect" by Robin Skelton, in *Mosaic* (Winnipeg, Manitoba), 1974.

Ralph Gustafson comments:

Living is prerequisite to the making of poems. Sensitivity and the intelligence to shape experience are the next essentials. The engagement with life must achieve more than facts. The stance must transcend domesticity and egotism. Humility accompanies the exaltation of facts; a compassion transforms the malevolence. The whole man is a moral man.

Having lived and become, the whole man being a poet is as it is. Disposition is by a concatenation of genes and God. By gift or by acquisition, the committed man can't get by without verbal passion. The manipulation of words is as important as clarification of experience. The meaning equally resides in its physical existence. Pace and music become cognition. Delight goes with the precise world.

Poetry is almost impossible.

*   *   *

Ralph Gustafson is one of the most prolific, various and technically accomplished of contemporary Canadian poets. After a somewhat unpromising start with a volume of romantic lyrics and sonnets and a poetic play on the subject of King Alfred in the mid-thirties, Ralph Gustafson found an original style and an individual voice in the sardonic and tender poetry produced during and after World War II. *Flight into Darkness* assimilated, rather than shook off, influences of Hopkins and Donne and demonstrated the relevance of the metaphysical dialectic to the problem of preserving an individual integrity in the kaleidoscopic new world of the post-war breakdown.

The poet's elliptical and intensely allusive style took on a new subtlety and his work a wider field of interest in three volumes published since 1960, *Rivers among Rocks, Rocky Mountain Poems* and *Sift in an Hourglass.* In these, travel across Canada, especially to the Rockies and the mountains of the north-west coast, and to Italy, Greece and the Scandinavian countries, has provided the stimulus for a prolific outburst of poetry in which the themes of nature, art, history, love and sex are given a highly individual treatment. As Professor Earle Birney has written:

"Ralph Gustafson has a way all his own of fusing music and passion with sophisticated feeling and graceful craft. . . . A stylist given to paradox and poetic wit, he is
nonetheless serious, and his sensitive judgments rise from a warm heart."

Mr. Gustafson has written also a number of prize-winning short stories and has
edited three influential anthologies for Penguin Books.

– A. J. M. Smith

GUTHRIE, Ramon. American. Born in New York City, 14 January 1896. Edu-
cated at Mt. Hermon, 1912–14; University of Toulouse, Docteur en Droit 1922; the
Sorbonne, Paris, 1919, 1922–23. Served in the American Field Service, 1916–17;
United States Army Air Corps, 1917–19; Office of Strategic Services during World
War II. Married Margarite Maurey in 1922. Assistant Professor of Romance Lan-
guages, University of Arizona, Tucson, 1924–26. Professor of French, 1930–63, and
since 1963, Professor Emeritus, Dartmouth College, Hanover, New Hampshire.
Recipient: National Endowment for the Arts grant, 1969, 1971; Marjorie Peabody
Waite Award, 1970. M.A., 1939, and D.Litt., 1971, Dartmouth College. Address:
Norwich, Vermont 05055, U.S.A. *Died 22 November 1973.*

PUBLICATIONS

Verse

Trobar Clus. Northampton, Massachusetts, S4N, 1923.
A World Too Old. New York, Doran, 1927.
Scherzo, From a Poem to be Entitled "The Proud City." Hanover, New Hamp-
shire, Arts Press, 1933.
Graffiti. New York, Macmillan, 1959.
Asbestos Phoenix. New York, Funk and Wagnalls, 1968.
Maximum Security Ward, 1964–1970. New York, Farrar Straus, 1970; London,
Sidgwick and Jackson, 1971.

Novels

Marcabrun: The Chronicle of a Foundling Who Spoke Evil of Women and of Love
and Who Followed Unawed the Paths of Arrogance Until They Led to Madness,
and of His Dealings with Women and of Ribald Words, the Which Brought Him
Repute as a Great Rascal and as a Great Singer. New York, Doran, 1926.
Parachute. New York, Harcourt Brace, 1928; London, Howe, 1929.

Other

Editor, with George E. Diller, French Literature and Thought since the
Revolution. New York, Harcourt Brace, 1942.

Editor, with George E. Diller, *Prose and Poetry of Modern France.* New York, Scribner, 1964.

Translator, *The Revolutionary Spirit in France and America.* London, Allen and Unwin, 1928.

Bibliography: by Alan Cooke, in *Ramon Guthrie Kaleidoscope,* Lunenburg, Vermont, Stinehour Press, 1963.

Critical Studies: *Ramon Guthrie Kaleidoscope,* Lunenburg, Vermont, Stinehour Press, 1963; *The New Poets* by M. L. Rosenthal, New York, Macmillan, 1967; "La Poésie de Ramon Guthrie" by L. Véza, in *Etudes Anglaises* (Paris), January-March 1967; review in *Dartmouth Alumni Magazine* (Hanover, New Hampshire), December 1968.

Ramon Guthrie comments:

One critic (L. Véza) characterizes my work as "un auto-portrait constamment retouché." While agreeing with this appraisal, I also see my poetry as an act of self-exploration aimed at discovering what I am and how I see and re-act to the universe within and about me.

As for style, I am eclectic. I tend to use rhyme less than I formerly did.

In my formative years I am conscious of having been influenced by Arnaut Daniel, Bertran de Born, Rimbaud, Mallarmé and some of Pound's early work.

*   *   *

The voice that speaks in Ramon Guthrie's poems often belongs to a buffoon, but what it says is no laughing matter. The point of view is basically that of the satirist, conservative, out of key with the time, a kind of J. Alfred Prufrock fully aware of his own hesitancy and ineffectuality in the face of disaster. It is the voice of one willing to face the full implications of his debased humanity, but still insisting on his own terms, even in his dilapidated condition. He is that half-clown waiting for Godot or that partly self-conscious metaphysician in Stevens' "The Comedian as the Letter C."

I mention these other characters by way of comparison, not in any sense suggesting that Guthrie can be defined in anyone else's terms, for one of the principal marks of his poetry is the singular and unique style. Nonetheless, the tradition within which he works is obvious enough, as he himself has acknowledged: the tradition of Baudelaire and Pound, with at times striking resemblances to Laforgue, the early T. S. Eliot, e.e.cummings, and other experimentalists who lived in Paris, as Guthrie did, during the period immediately after World War I. In various stages of his career, the voice, the persona changes, making, as the speaker in "Coda" says,

> "a constantly retouched
> self-portrait" to be hung upon the wall
> of some quaint village bordel tucked
> in a lane between the church's apse
> and the charnel house perhaps –

Many of the poems, particularly those published up to about 1965, reflect Guthrie's attraction to the Dadaist movement, to painters and other artists sympathetic to the "erstwhile infant Pope of Unreason." Specific examples include "Wunday the Worst of Weptober," "Masque for Luis Buñuel," and "Variations on a Threne for Tristan Tzara (1896–1963)," a fitting elegy for the founder of Dada, which concludes with the following lament:

> *Tzara, I don't like your being dead.*
> *Somehow you seem less cut out for it*
> *than almost anyone I ever knew.*

In the last section of *Asbestos Phoenix*, however, Guthrie returns to a preoccupation, political in content and tragic in tone, that had appeared earlier in his career, particularly in "Postlude: For Goya," written in 1938. In a group of poems, including a translation of a lyric of Louis Aragon written and circulated clandestinely during the Nazi occupation of France, Guthrie enumerates the principal horrors of modern war – Guernica, Lidice, Quang Ngai. And "Scherzo for a Dirge," prompted by a letter from one of his former students, a draft resister, ends with the following prayer:

> Listen, Lord God of Hosts
> whatever it is that you are up to, please
> lay off it, for Jesus' sake. Amen.

Particularly in his latest volume, *Maximum Security Ward*, "a single poem composed of a number of movements," Guthrie masters his own material, in a sustained, authoritative, and comprehensive rendering of one man's experience. All the elements of the earlier poems are there: the First World War, in "Side by Side"; the Lost Generation in Paris, in "Montparnasse" and "For Approximately the Same Reason Why a Man Can't Marry His Widow's Sister"; and the sense of loss and near despair as a member of "the race of napalm Santa Clauses / Sheep herded by glib lies that greed concocts." In the midst of a series of scenes of people caught in riots, of soldiers about to die in wars around the world, he hopes for the opportunity of one last say, from the coffin:

> I'd like to give one last galvanic jerk
> and flip up straight and look all living beings
> in the eye – all human ones, that is
> (because, less lucky than are cats and cows
> and bumblebees, they know that they are living)
> and speak out clear: "I hate life. I who am
> no longer living can speak this truth . . ."
> then flop back flat into the casket with a happy
> or, at least, contented or vacuous, smirk upon my face –
> soundly dead for keeps this time.
> *That, mes amis, would be worth living long enough to see!*

"And yet, and yet . . . ," as several of the poems caution, he stops short of total despair. For every Himmler, Johnson, Quisling, Calvin, there are also Beethoven, Blake, Chardin, Giotto, Villon, Rembrandt, William Carlos Williams, Ravel. There are the artist and his subject. And in "The Making of the Bear," one of the concluding poems in *Maximum Security Ward* and surely one of the most beautiful long lyrics in recent American poetry, the poet affirms life. He is, as one might have suspected, still something of a Romantic. Working alone, in isolation – somewhat in the matter of Guthrie as a poet – the artist paints, in a cave, a subject of his own choosing, in his own style:

> There
> in that total lack of light
> is where my bear is.
> No one will ever see him
> but he still
> is there.

– Michael True

GUTTERIDGE, Don(ald George). Canadian. Born in Point Edward, Ontario, 30 September 1937. Educated at the University of Western Ontario, London, 1956–60, 1962–63, B.A. (honours) 1960. Married Anne Barnett in 1961; has one daughter and one son. English Teacher, Elmira School Board, Ontario, 1960–62; Teaching Fellow, University of Western Ontario, 1962–63; Head of the Department of English, Ingersoll School Board, Ontario, 1963–64, and London Board of Education, Ontario, 1964–68. Since 1968, Assistant Professor of Education, University of Western Ontario. Recipient: President's Medal, University of Western Ontario, 1971; Canada Council Travel Grant, 1973. Address: 114 Victoria Street, London, Ontario N6A 2B5, Canada.

PUBLICATIONS

Verse

Riel: A Poem for Voices. Fredericton, New Brunswick, Fiddlehead, 1968; revised edition, Toronto, Van Nostrand Reinhold, 1972.
The Village Within: Poems Toward a Biography. Fredericton, New Brunswick, Fiddlehead, 1970.
Death at Quebec and Other Poems. Fredericton, New Brunswick, Fiddlehead, 1971.
Perspectives. London, Ontario, Pennywise Press, 1971.
Saying Grace: An Elegy. Fredericton, New Brunswick, Fiddlehead, 1972.
Coppermine: The Quest for North. Ottawa, Oberon Press, 1973.

Novel

Bus-Ride. Nairn, Ontario, Nairn Publications, 1973.

Other

Language and Expression: A Modern Approach (textbook). Toronto, McClelland and Stewart, 1971.

Critical Studies: "Poetry Chronicle" by Edward A. Lacey, in *Edge 9* (Edmonton, Alberta), Summer 1969; *Survival: Themes in Canadian Literature* by Margaret Atwood, Toronto, House of Anansi, 1971.

Don Gutteridge comments:

One of our poets has called Canada a "country without a mythology"; little wonder, then, that my work – like that of many Canadian writers – is concerned with the sense of place and the perspective of time, with roots into the past and what myths can be made in the face of such vast geography and empty stretches of history. My work takes two forms: personal poems about my childhood village and narrative poems on Canadian historical figures (real and imagined). Though quite different in content and form, these two types are related in that they share my concern for making something of my own past as well as that of my country, and my belief, however naive, that the two are somehow connected.

*   *   *

"History is the biography of great men," Carlyle once said, and Don Gutteridge would probably agree with him, for to the teacher (who was born in an historic section of Ontario and teaches in the old city of London, Ontario) history and biography are very much a unity. So far he has published poems of two types: historical and autobiographical.

The historical poems are the more familiar, although to date these have not won him too many readers. His widest read work, *Riel: A Poem for Voices*, might at first glance seem an ideal script for a radio documentary about the leader of the two Métis uprisings on the Canadian prairies, for the long poem is constructed, as a mason would construct a wall, of bits and pieces – editorials, letters, lyrical interludes.

Gutteridge promises to tell "what Riel really was in Canadian terms," and the short lyric poems are always on the verge of revealing some psychological or universal truth:

> When my body
> swings like a
> dead tongue
> from the white-man's
> scaffolding,
> will there be
> an eloquence
> to tell. . . .

Riel remains an enigma wrapped up in a mystery swinging from the white man's scaffolding. *Riel* is a labour of love, but essentially a pastiche, and as such unrevealing and undramatic.

The same might be said of *Death at Quebec and Other Poems* and *Coppermine: The Quest for North* which attempt to build dramatic monologues on the personalities of early missionaries and explorers as revealed through their writings. Gutteridge deserves credit for spotting the poetic possibilities in these figures from the past, but the language he uses is neither of the period nor particular to the person, and so seems inappropriate.

Although the historical poems are so far more adventurous than the autobiographical poems, it is perhaps in this latter area that Gutteridge may develop in the future. *Saying Grace: An Elegy* is a short, impressionistic poem written on the death of his mother. It includes these moving lines, somewhat quirky, yet moody and effective:

> Death does not
> "take us," it
> moves into the
> waiting spaces
>
> is welcome.

> – John Robert Colombo

HAINES, John (Meade). American. Born in Norfolk, Virginia, 29 June 1924. Educated at art schools in Washington, D.C., and New York. Served in the United States Navy, 1943–46. Married Jo Ella Husey in 1960; Jane Everett, 1970; has four step-children. Homesteaded in Alaska, 1947–69. Free-lance Writer. Poet-in-Residence, University of Alaska, Anchorage, 1972–73; University of Washington, Seattle, 1974. Currently, Visiting Lecturer, University of Montana, Missoula. Recipient: Corcoran Gallery Sculpture Prize, 1948; Jennie Tane Award (*Massachusetts Review*), 1964; Guggenheim Fellowship, 1965; National Endowment for the Arts grant, 1967. Address: 517 12th Street, Pacific Grove, California 93950, U.S.A.

PUBLICATIONS

Verse

Winter News: Poems.   Middletown, Connecticut, Wesleyan University Press, 1966.
Suite for the Pied Piper.   Menomonie, Wisconsin, Ox Head Press, 1967.
The Mirror.   Santa Barbara, California, Unicorn Press, 1971.
The Stone Harp.   Middletown, Connecticut, Wesleyan University Press, and London, Rapp and Whiting-Deutsch, 1971.
The Legend of Paper Plates.   Santa Barbara, California, Unicorn Press, 1970.
Twenty Poems.   Santa Barbara, California, Unicorn Press, 1971.
Leaves and Ashes: Poems.   Santa Cruz, California, Kayak Books, 1974.

Other

Translator, *El Amor Ascendia*, by Miguel Hernández.   Menomonie, Wisconsin, Ox Head Press, 1967.

615

Manuscript Collection: University of Alaska Library, Fairbanks.

Critical Studies: Review by Paul Zweig, in *The Nation* (New York), 27 March 1967; Ira Sadoff, in *Seneca Review* (Geneva, New York), April 1971; William Witherup, in *Kayak* (Santa Cruz, California), 1972; Paul Zweig, in *Parnassus* (New York), Winter 1972–73; "John Haines Issue" of *Stinktree* (Memphis, Tennessee), November 1972.

John Haines comments:

Most of the poems for which I am known (*Winter News*) grew out of my experience in the Alaskan wilderness. It is a poetry of solitude, of the solitary man, and even the isolated man. The subject matter is drawn mainly from nature and its citizens – animals, birds, trees, ice and the weather, and the occasional human traveler. The poems are subjective, being parts of a continuing interior monologue; but it seems to me they contain plenty of actual sticks and stones to stumble on and be bruised by.

For a time in the late 1960's I became preoccupied with events in the outside world – politics, social conflict, all that absorbed so many of us during that time. I tried to deal with this in my poetry (*The Stone Harp*). In a few poems I think I was successful, but on the whole I was too remote from the events for them to dominate my poetry as convincingly as the natural world had up until that time.

For a number of reasons I became dissatisfied with the isolation I had been living in, and made a decisive break with it in 1969. The poems I've written since then reflect a certain restlessness and searching. They are increasingly concerned with people, even though they still look to the world of nature for many of their metaphors.

I am interested in the teaching of poetry, as much for the opportunity it affords for a personal discovery of poets and poetry as for any other reason. Teaching has given me a chance to develop some ideas about poetry, ideas that have been half-formed for years.

I am interested in the longer poem, and have become disenchanted with the narrow, imagistic "self" poem so abundant today. I feel the poetry dominant in the United States today is of a low order, lacking in strong ideas and often devoid of emotion. It might be unwise to try and predict the course of one's own work, but I expect my own to become more open to ideas, and to risk a greater involvement in the human community. I would like to find a larger place in my poetry for the experience of the American west and northwest, especially the movement of its early people from Asia and Alaska into the southwest.

*   *   *

John Haines homesteaded in Alaska in 1947 at a place over sixty miles from Fairbanks. All through the 1950's and into the 1960's he and his wife lived there in a house they built. In some seasons they lived off the country, but as time went on and recognition came – a Guggenheim grant and steady publication – the Haineses ranged farther and lived more easily.

John Haines's work recurrently links to the animals and the land: moose, caribou, owls; snow, wind, cold. In the literature of our time, he evokes a totem feeling.

His presence in the American scene slowly became known through the 1950's and then more rapidly in the 1960's, through work in little magazines of small circulation but special reputation: *The Sixties, Kayak, Chicago Choice, The San Francisco Review.* Where these magazines do circulate, they count; and in them the poems of John Haines, trenchant but quiet, appear. And now and then the Haines criticism drops into place, a voice distanced, serious, uncompromising – different, but carefully not part of any coterie.

From a few poetry readings, down country, "in the lower 48," his reputation grew; by 1969 with a conference of Alaska writers at Alaska Methodist University in which his accomplishment was celebrated, he began to go national in reputation. In recent years he has resided prevalently in California, from whence he currently operates, with readings all over the nation and with occasional guest professorships at colleges and universities.

– William Stafford

HALL, Donald (Andrew, Jr.). American. Born in New Haven, Connecticut, 20 September 1928. Educated at Phillips Exeter Academy, New Hampshire; Harvard University, Cambridge, Massachusetts (Garrison and Sergeant prizes, 1951), B.A. 1951; Oxford University (Henry Fellow; Newdigate Prize, 1952), B.Litt. 1953; Stanford University (Creative Writing Fellow), 1953–54. Married Jane Kenyon in 1972; has two children. Junior Fellow, Society of Fellows, Harvard University, 1954–57. Assistant Professor, 1957–61, Associate Professor, 1961–66, and since 1966, Professor of English, University of Michigan, Ann Arbor. Poetry Editor, *Paris Review,* Paris and New York, 1953–62; Member of the Editorial Board for Poetry, Wesleyan University Press, 1958–64. Literary Consultant, Harper and Row, publishers, New York. Lived in England, 1959–60, 1963–64. Recipient: Lamont Poetry Selection Award, 1955; Edna St. Vincent Millay Memorial Prize, 1956; Longview Foundation Award, 1960; Guggenheim Fellowship, 1963, 1972. Address: 1715 South University, Ann Arbor, Michigan 48104, U.S.A.

PUBLICATIONS

Verse

(*Poems*).   Oxford, Fantasy Press, 1952.
Exile.   Privately printed, 1952.
To the Loud Wind and Other Poems.   Cambridge, Massachusetts, Harvard Advocate, 1955.
Exiles and Marriages.   New York, Viking Press, 1955.
The Dark Houses.   New York, Viking Press, 1958.
A Roof of Tiger Lilies: Poems.   New York, Viking Press, and London, Deutsch, 1964.
The Alligator Bride.   Menomonie, Wisconsin, Ox Head Press, 1968.
The Alligator Bride: Poems New and Selected.   New York, Harper, 1969.
The Yellow Room Love Poems.   New York, Harper, 1971.
A Blue Wing Tilts at the Edge of the Sea.   London, Secker and Warburg, 1975.

Recording: *Today's Poets 1,* with others, Folkways, 1967.

Play

An Evening's Frost (produced New York, 1965).

Other

Andrew the Lion Farmer (juvenile). New York, Watts, 1959; London, Methuen, 1961.
String Too Short to Be Saved: Childhood Reminiscences. New York, Viking Press, 1961; London, Deutsch, 1962.
Henry Moore: The Life and Work of a Great Sculptor. New York, Harper, and London, Gollancz, 1966.
Marianne Moore: The Cage and the Animal. New York, Pegasus, 1970.
As the Eye Moves: A Sculpture by Henry Moore. New York, Abrams, 1970.
The Gentleman's Alphabet Book. New York, Dutton, 1972.
Writing Well. Boston, Little Brown, 1973.
Playing Around. Boston, Little Brown, 1974.

Editor, *The Harvard Advocate Anthology.* New York, Twayne, 1950.
Editor, with Robert Pack and Louis Simpson, *New Poets of England and America.* Cleveland, Meridian, 1957.
Editor, *Whittier.* New York, Dell, 1961.
Editor, with Robert Pack, *New Poets of England and America: Second Selection.* Cleveland, Meridian, 1962.
Editor, *Contemporary American Poetry.* London, Penguin, 1962; revised edition, 1971.
Editor, *A Poetry Sampler.* New York, Watts, 1962.
Editor, with Stephen Spender, *The Concise Encyclopedia of English and American Poets and Poetry.* London, Hutchinson, and New York, Hawthorn Books, 1963; revised edition, 1970.
Editor, with Warren Taylor, *Poetry in English.* New York, Macmillan, 1963; revised edition, 1970.
Editor, *The Faber Book of Modern Verse,* revised edition. London, Faber, 1965.
Editor, *A Choice of Whitman's Verse.* London, Faber, 1968.
Editor, *The Modern Stylists: Writers on the Art of Writing.* New York, Free Press, 1968.
Editor, *Man and Boy: An Anthology.* New York, Watts, 1968.
Editor, *American Poetry: An Introductory Anthology.* London, Faber, 1969.
Editor, *The Pleasures of Poetry.* New York, Harper, 1971.

Critical Studies: by Ralph J. Mills, Jr., in *Iowa Review* (Iowa City), Winter 1971; "Donald Hall Issue" of *Tennessee Poetry Journal* (Martin), Winter 1971.

                                    *   *   *

   In an early and still brilliant poem, "Elegy for Wesley Wells," Donald Hall hits a characteristic note: a grief for the older person who has died, and somehow taken some of his nobility with him. Mr. Hall's moving poem in memory of Edwin Muir casts Muir also as one of the noble old grandfathers. This noble mourning for the old we see in his lament for the death of the old World War I pilot, his sense of the greatness of Henry Moore, his care for old men like Ezra Pound. His grief for what goes when fine old men go seems now – in a time of hatred of the old – dissident, but that grief in his work is something that readers coming after us will find precious, and honor.

A second complex of experiences that surfaces in Mr. Hall's work, and surfaces unmistakably, like a buried tree rising in the Missouri, is a complex centering around animal and vegetable processes, instinctual changes. This second knot of awarenesses does not have to do with moral nobility at all, but with certain instinctual processes which move like glaciers slowly and almost invisibly, but are just as unstoppable. Many persons living in this century have the illusion these processes are under their control, but Mr. Hall has a deep sense of their uncontrollability. His major poem on this theme is the opening poem in *A Roof of Tiger Lilies*, called "The Snow." He uses the metaphor of snow descending for instinctual processes. The snow falls whether it wants to or no. He mentions that a baby really does not want to fall out of the mother's body, he wants to remain in his "airy tent," but, like snow, he has to fall. Through the baby's birth then, the baby understands death. And anyone who studies falling snow will sense the glacial slide of the instincts, anyone watching snow then "sleeps himself" back to his babyhood; the whole world becomes once more particles of his infant body.

Toward the end of the poem, Mr. Hall notices that the snow, as it melts, goes through "the cycles of water" – another process. And yet Mr. Hall admits he cannot enter joyfully into these Processes: "I cannot open the door to the cycles of water."

Perhaps because he clings so to the nobility he saw embodied in some old men, he cannot give himself to death, confident that he will be reborn, that "all things die and are born again." His poetry often then gives us the experience of a being held unwillingly inside one room of time, a life reluctantly lived out inside one body. The sense of being trapped in a room of time is like the sensation that your birth was somehow unhappily fated, that your unhappy mother and father conceived you while playing in some ritual they could not escape ("In the Kitchen of the Old House"), or like the sensation of clay being trapped to form a massive human body, clay which gracefully agrees to be both massive and human (see his many poems on Henry Moore sculptures).

These two experiences – of grief for permanent loss of civilization, and of wonder at the processes inside animals and plants, their unstoppable slide toward death and resurrection – are both *human* experiences, independent of art. A third experience to which his work returns often is a more specifically artistic experience – the experience of pleasure.

Just as politics is the art of gaining power over others, art is an investigation of pleasure. Poetry investigates spiritual joy, imaginative delights, the joy of sound by itself, or, as in concrete poetry, even the delight of type. We recall that the Puritans, who were suspicious of pleasures, removed art objects from their churches, preferring the pure white boards. Mr. Hall's investigation of pleasure then is also relevant to New England history, but this time goes against the grain of the New England past.

"The Long River" is a poem about pleasure. His speculations and tentative probings have been given body in wonderfully vivid and blocky pictures, images heavy like sculptures. He describes first the danger a New Englander (or an American in general) feels as he approaches pleasure:

> The musk-ox smells
> in his long head
> my boat coming. When
> I fell him there,
> intent, heavy,

> the oars make wings
> in the white night,
> and deep woods are close
> on either side
> where trees darken.
>
> I rowed past towns
> in their black sleep
> to come here. I passed
> the northern grass
> and cold mountains.
>
> The musk-ox moves
> when the boat stops,
> in hard thickets. Now
> the wood is dark
> with old pleasures.

The words carry the strong self-sufficient force of pleasure itself, and music carries an instinctive archaic resonance, that means the music is coming from deep, inward, and archaic parts of the consciousness, from a very ancient brain. I think this poem is one of the best poems written since the Second World War.

  Mr. Hall is not prolific, he does not have an immense number of good poems, but when a poem is good, it is solid all the way through, and absolutely genuine. Some of his new poems, such as the love poem "Gold," continue to embody, not superficial intellectual speculations, but "old pleasures."

– Robert Bly

HALL, J(ohn) C(live).   British.   Born in London, 12 September 1920. Educated at Leighton Park, Reading, Berkshire; Oriel College, Oxford. Married; has two children. Formerly, a book publisher. Since 1955, Member of the Staff, *Encounter* magazine, London. Address: 198 Blythe Road, London W14 0HH, England.

PUBLICATIONS

Verse

  Selected Poems, with Keith Douglas and Norman Nicholson.   London, John
    Bale and Staples, 1943.
  The Summer Dance and Other Poems.   London, Lehmann, 1951.
  The Burning Hare.   London, Chatto and Windus-Hogarth Press, 1966.
  A House of Voices.   London, Chatto and Windus, 1973.

Other

Edwin Muir. London, Longman, 1956.

Editor, *New Poems 1955,* with Patric Dickinson and Erica Marx. London, Joseph, 1955.
Editor, with Willa Muir, *Collected Poems of Edwin Muir, 1921–1958.* London, Faber, 1960.
Editor, with G. S. Fraser and J. Waller, *The Collected Poems of Keith Douglas,* revised edition. London, Faber, 1966.

*   *   *

J. C. Hall's early poems, collected in *The Summer Dance,* though reflective and carefully formed, lack any strongly individual quality. As he himself acknowledged:

> All these long years I've pondered how to make
> A poetry I could truly call my own.

In the next volume, *The Burning Hare,* the influence of Edwin Muir is all-pervasive. "Before This Journeying Began" and "The Double Span" are dedicated to him, and "The Island" reads like a pastiche of Muir. Hall is a conservative poet, conscious of his debt to literary tradition, and "The Playground by the Church," with its allusions to Valéry, is typical of his meditative poetry, which questions and explores the world of ideas and of philosophical apprehensions.

His latest book, *A House of Voices,* relies less than the previous collections on myth and symbol, although Hall remains aware of their potency. The tone of the verse is more relaxed, and the poems are more firmly rooted in the world of everyday experience. In "The Double" Hall ends on a note of metaphysical speculation, but the first three stanzas are more humorous and colloquial than anything in his earlier work:

> I often wonder what he was really like,
> That identical boy – whether he knew of me
> Taking the rap, riding round on my bike
> Secretly proud of the devil I dared not be.

Hall's patient search for a poetry truly his own appears finally to have been successful.

– John Press

HALL, Rodney. Australian. Born in Solihull, Warwickshire, England, 18 November 1935; emigrated to Australia during his childhood. Educated at City of Bath Boys' School; Brisbane Boys' College; University of Queensland, Brisbane, B.A. 1971. Married to Maureen Elizabeth MacPhail; has three daughters, Imogen, Delia, Cressida. Free-lance Scriptwriter and Actor, 1957–67, and Film Critic, 1966–67, Australian Broadcasting Commission, Brisbane. Tutor, New England University

School of Music, Armidale, New South Wales, Summers 1967–71; Youth Officer, Australian Council for the Arts, 1971–73. Since 1962, Advisory Editor, *Overland* magazine, Melbourne; since 1967, Poetry Editor, *The Australian* daily newspaper, Sydney. Travelled in Europe, 1958–60, 1963–64, 1965, and in the United States, 1974. Australian Department of Foreign Affairs Lecturer in India, 1970, and Malaysia, 1972. Recipient: Australian National University Creative Arts Fellowship, Canberra, 1968; Commonwealth Literary Fund Fellowship, 1970; Literature Board Fellowship, 1973. Address: P.O. Box 118, North Quay, Queensland, Australia.

PUBLICATIONS

Verse

Penniless till Doomsday.   London, Outposts Publications, 1962.
Four Poets, with others.   Melbourne, Cheshire, 1962.
Forty Beads on a Hangman's Rope: Fragments of Memory.   Newnham, Tasmania, Wattle Grove Press, 1963.
Eyewitness: Poems.   Sydney, South Head Press, 1967.
The Autobiography of a Gorgon.   Melbourne, Cheshire, 1968.
The Law of Karma: A Progression of Poems.   Canberra, Australian National University Press, 1968.
Heaven, In a Way.   Brisbane, University of Queensland Press, 1970.
The Soapbox Omnibus.   Brisbane, University of Queensland Press, 1973.

Recording: *Romulus and Remus*, University of Queensland Press, 1971.

Novel

The Ship on the Coin.   Brisbane, University of Queensland Press, 1971.

Other

Social Services and the Aborigines, with Shirley Andrews.   Canberra, Federal Council for Aboriginal Advancement, 1963.
Focus on Andrew Sibley.   Brisbane, University of Queensland Press, 1968.

Editor, with Thomas Shapcott, *New Impulses in Australian Poetry.*   Brisbane, University of Queensland Press, 1968.
Editor, *Australian Poetry 1970.*   Sydney, Angus and Robertson, 1970.
Editor, *Poems from Prison.*   Brisbane, University of Queensland Press, 1973.

Rodney Hall comments:

I suppose the only way I'd be prepared to describe my own work is to say that it is basically non-confessional. It is my hope that each poem may take on an independent life of its own. If this is possible the emotional experience, it would seem to me, becomes available to the reader in a far more pure and direct form than is generally possible with confessional poetry, where the poet as a person perpetually obtrudes and everything is limited to his vision of himself. My experiences are nearly always projected into imaginary situations – often in an attempt to relate them back to that skeleton of our world-view, legends and myths.

I have also concentrated on a special form, which I call a Progression. This consists of many short poems, each capable of standing alone, tightly inter-related so that they become something akin to a single long poem with all the peaks left in and the discursive passages cut. I have published five of these progressions so far. The average length is forty poems, the largest is sixty-six.

                              *   *   *

Though Rodney Hall has lived in Australia since he was thirteen, there is about his poetry – its pace and alertness – a quality of suavite and intellectual precision that is quite different from any Australian-born poet, even Peter Porter, who has become the most cosmopolitan of Australian expatriate writers. Although widely published over the past decade, Rodney Hall has in many ways remained elusive as a poet. This is partly because his early collections (most notably *Forty Beads on a Hangman's Rope*) were not widely available, though they establish many of the concerns and attitudes explored in Hall's later volumes. Many Australian readers find themselves unable to accept easily the idea of a poetry which draws its vigour and nourishment, not from regional landscape or current urban dilemmas, but from a deeply felt social awareness, a concern with large issues (through the medium of specifically located personae) rather than with small evidences. Rodney Hall has consistently worked out and developed his poetic preoccupations through what he calls "progressions": cycles of small, often glittering and elegant, pieces which are part of a largely conceived mosaic delineating some overall social or aesthetic vision: *Forty Beads on a Hangman's Rope* was the first of these, followed by *The Autobiography of a Gorgon, The Law of Karma* and, more recently, shorter cycles ("Social Studies," "Folk Songs," etc.). In these works, not only are the overriding preoccupation and poetic conceptualising relatively unfamiliar in Australian verse, but also the essentially cool and reedy nature of Hall's language contrasts with the more readily identifiable cadence of many of his contemporaries. It is notable that Rodney Hall is one of the few poets of his generation who has influenced the work of younger contemporaries, particularly those who do not seek salvation in the derivations of "open form" practised by the imitators of current American verse.

                                                  – Thomas W. Shapcott

---

HAMBURGER, Michael (Peter Leopold). British. Born in Berlin, 22 March 1924; emigrated to England in 1933. Educated at schools in Germany; George Watson's School, Edinburgh; The Hall, Hampstead, London; Christ College, Oxford, B.A. in modern languages, M.A. 1948. Served as an infantryman, non-commissioned officer, and lieutenant, Royal Army Educational Corps, 1943–47. Married Anne Beresford, *q.v.*, in 1951 (marriage dissolved, 1970); remarried Anne Beresford, 1974; has three children. Assistant Lecturer in German, University College, London, 1952–55; Lecturer, then Reader in German, University of Reading, Berkshire, 1955–64; Florence Purington Lecturer, Mount Holyoke College, South Hadley, Massachusetts, 1966–67; Visiting Professor, State University of New York at Buffalo, 1969, and at Stony Brook, 1970; Visiting Fellow, Wesleyan University, Middletown, Connecticut, 1971; Visiting Professor, University of Connecticut, Storrs,

1972; Regents Lecturer, University of California, San Diego, 1973; Visiting Professor, University of South Carolina, Columbia, 1973. Recipient: Bollingen Fellowship, 1959, 1965; Deutsche Akademie für Sprache und Dichtung Translator's Prize, 1964; Tieck-Schlegel Prize, 1967; Arts Council Translation Prize, 1969; Levinson Prize (*Poetry*, Chicago), 1972. Fellow, Royal Society of Literature, 1972. Address: 34a Half Moon Lane, London S.E.24, England.

PUBLICATIONS

Verse

Later Hogarth.   London, Cope and Fenwick, 1945.
Flowering Cactus: Poems 1942–49.   Aldington, Kent, Hand and Flower Press, 1950.
Poems 1950–1951.   Aldington, Kent, Hand and Flower Press, 1952.
The Dual Site: Poems.   New York, Poetry London–New York Editions, 1957; London, Routledge, 1958.
Weather and Season: New Poems.   London, Longman, and New York, Atheneum, 1963.
In Flashlight: Poems.   Leeds, Northern House, 1965.
In Massachusetts.   Menomonie, Wisconsin, Ox Head Press, 1967.
Feeding the Chickadees.   London, Turret Books, 1968.
Travelling: Poems 1963–68.   London, Fulcrum Press, 1969.
Penguin Modern Poets 14, with Alan Brownjohn and Charles Tomlinson.   London, Penguin, 1969.
Home.   Frensham, Surrey, Sceptre Press, 1969.
Travelling I–V.   London, Agenda Editions, 1972.
Ownerless Earth: New and Selected Poems 1950–1972.   Cheadle, Cheshire, Carcanet Press, and New York, Dutton, 1973.
Conversations with Charwomen.   Rushden, Northamptonshire, Sceptre Press, 1973.

Plays

The Tower, adaptation of a play by Peter Weiss (produced New York, 1974).

Radio Play: *Struck by Apollo,* with Anne Beresford, 1965.

Other

Reason and Energy: Studies in German Literature.   London, Routledge, and New York, Grove Press, 1957; revised edition, London, Weidenfeld and Nicolson, 1971; as *Contraries: Studies in German Literature*, New York, Dutton, 1971.
Hugo von Hofmannsthal: Zwei Studien.   Göttingen, Sachse and Pohl, 1964; translated as *Hofmannsthal: Three Essays*, Princeton, New Jersey, Princeton University Press, 1970; Cheadle, Cheshire, Carcanet Press, 1974.
From Prophecy to Exorcism: The Premisses of Modern German Literature.   London, Longman, 1965.
Zwischen den Sprachen: Essays und Gedichte.   Frankfurt, Fischer, 1966.

The Truth of Poetry: Tensions in Modern Poetry from Baudelaire to the 1960's. London, Weidenfeld and Nicolson, 1969; New York, Harcourt Brace, 1970.

A Mug's Game: Intermittent Memoirs. Cheadle, Cheshire, Carcanet Press, 1973.

Editor and Translator, *Beethoven: Letters, Journals, and Conversations.* London, Thames and Hudson, and New York, Pantheon Books, 1951; revised edition, London, Cape, 1966.

Editor, and Translator with others, *Poems and Verse Plays,* by Hugo von Hofmannsthal. New York, Pantheon Books, and London, Routledge, 1961.

Editor and Translator, with Christopher Middleton, *Modern German Poetry, 1910–1960: An Anthology with Verse Translations.* London, MacGibbon and Kee, and New York, Grove Press, 1962.

Editor, and Translator with others, *Selected Plays and Libretti,* by Hugo von Hofmannsthal. New York, Pantheon Books, and London, Routledge, 1963.

Editor, *Das Werk: Sonette, Lieder, Erzählungen,* by Jesse Thoor. Frankfurt, Europäische Verlagsanslalt, 1965.

Editor and Translator, *East German Poetry: An Anthology in German and English.* Oxford, Carcanet Press, and New York, Dutton, 1972.

Editor, *Selected Poems,* by Thomas Good. London, St. George's Press, 1974.

Translator, *Poems,* by Hölderlin. London, Nicholson and Watson, 1943: revised edition, as *Hölderlin: His Poems,* London, Harvill Press, 1952; New York, Pantheon Books, 1953; revised edition, as *Selected Verse,* London, Penguin, 1961; revised edition, as *Poems and Fragments,* London, Routledge, 1966; Ann Arbor, University of Michigan Press, 1967.

Translator, *Twenty Prose Poems of Baudelaire.* London, Editions Poetry, 1946; revised edition, London, Cape, 1968.

Translator, *Decline: 12 Poems,* by Georg Trakl. St. Ives, Cornwall, Latin Press, 1952.

Translator, *The Burnt Offering,* by Albrecht Goes. New York, Pantheon Books, and London, Gollancz, 1956.

Translator, *Egmont,* by Goethe, in *Classic Theatre 2,* edited by Eric Bentley. New York, Doubleday, 1959.

Translator, with Yvonne Kapp, *Tales from the Calendar,* by Bertoit Brecht. London, Methuen, 1961.

Translator, with Christopher Middleton, *Selected Poems,* by Günter Grass. London, Secker and Warburg, and New York, Harcourt Brace, 1966.

Translator, *Poems,* by Hans Magnus Enzensberger. Newcastle upon Tyne, Northern House, 1966.

Translator, *Lenz,* by Georg Büchner, with *Immensee* by Theodor Storm and *A Village Romeo and Juliet* by Gottfried Keller. London, Calder and Boyars, 1966; in *Leonce and Lena, Lenz, Woyzeck,* 1972.

Translator, with others, *O the Chimneys,* by Nelly Sachs. New York, Farrar Straus, 1967; as *Selected Poems, Including the Verse Play "Eli,"* London, Cape, 1968.

Translator, with Jerome Rothenberg and the author, *Poems for People Who Don't Read Poems,* by Hans Magnus Enzensberger. New York, Atheneum, and London, Secker and Warburg, 1968; as *Poems,* London, Penguin, 1968.

Translator, *And Really Frau Blum Would Very Much Like to Meet the Milkman: 21 Short Stories,* by Peter Bichsel. London, Calder and Boyars, 1968.

Translator, *Journeys: Two Radio Plays: The Rolling Sea at Setúbal, The Year Lacertia,* by Günter Eich. London, Cape, 1968.

Translator, with Christopher Middleton, *Poems,* by Günter Grass. London, Penguin, 1969.

Translator, with Matthew Mead, *The Seeker and Other Poems,* by Nelly Sachs. New York, Farrar Straus, 1970.

Translator, *Stories for Children,* by Peter Bichsel. London, Calder and Boyars, 1971.

Translator, with Christopher Middleton, *Selected Poems,* by Paul Celan. London, Penguin, 1972.

Translator, *Leonce and Lena, Lenz, Woyzeck,* by Georg Büchner. Chicago, University of Chicago Press, 1972.

Manuscript Collections: University of Texas, Austin; Lockwood Memorial Library, State University of New York, Buffalo; University of Reading, Berkshire.

Critical Studies: "The Subject Beneath the Subject" by the author, in *Christian Science Monitor* (Boston), 31 January 1967; "Across Frontiers: Michael Hamburger as Poet and Critic" by Jon Glover, in *Stand* (Newcastle upon Tyne), 1970; "Rhythm" by the author, in *Agenda* (London), x, 4, and xi, 1, 1972, 1973; "More New Poetry" by Terry Eagleton, in *Stand* (Newcastle upon Tyne), 1973; "Forward, Ay, and Backward" by Martin Dodsworth, in *The Guardian* (London), 5 April 1973; "Ownerless Earth" by Donald Davie," in *New York Times Book Review,* 28 April 1974; "Travellers" by John Matthias, in *Poetry* (Chicago), April 1974.

*   *   *

Michael Hambuger's is a poetry of ideas made as sensuous as possible by being passed through images of nature, tinged very frequently with a decent uncloying melancholy. The turning point in his poetry is made in *Weather and Season* in which all the traditionally metrical, iambic and rhyming forms have almost entirely been disbanded because, as he stated in the reading he gave at the University of Iowa in 1969 (and I paraphrase) "in my previous books I used the traditional forms to protect myself from the pressure and intensity of my feelings; whereas I subsequently came to feel that, in writing the later poems, I no longer wished to evade or mask these feelings." This frank, direct criticism of an earlier stance, together with his decision to shuck off the encrustments of such forms, has brought rewards. In few Poems, "In a Cold Season" for instance, and then with particular reason, has he since consistently used iambic; and the form of his work now more closely integrates with both his ideas and their emotioned, originating pressures, making it impossible to consider the form and content as separable adjuncts of each other.

The poetry has two contexts. One is that of men socialized into a dilemma which may be resolved only by the using of the charged, moral conscience ("In a Cold Season"); the other context is nature, although as one critic has recently, and justly, pointed to some affinity with Edward Thomas, so I suggest that he is no more a nature poet than Thomas is. Leavis in *New Bearings* has indicated that for Thomas nature was used as the arena of delicate and scrupulous psychological re-enactment, and for Hamburger this is also valid. In "Brixton" (from *In Flashlight*), which is a suburb of south east London, more recently a black ghetto, children of black, and of white parents "Kick dead leaves for conkers." But this is a slight example. Many of the poems cohere in his pamphlet *In Flashlight,* to form an exploration of the use and stamina of memory. In the poem of that name, for instance, Hamburger expresses, firstly, his sense of the "Unchanged, unchanging regions," which ambiguously refers to nature; but they are regions in which his wives walk, so that the unchanging relationships between them and him are reflected in that of unchanging nature. Then follows his apprehension of death, disease, or ageing, the experience of each figured in the horrifying stranger, against whom, significantly, the church is no protection. Hamburger again discovers the memory of the "Sweet wives, sweet virgins"; and this succouring, uncloyed memory witnesses the treasurable but active power of remembered experience which, if valuable, does not die. His memory is not used to directly console, or to combat the fear, also experienced; yet intrinsically, although this is not even its first value, it does precisely this. Although when the memory of the wives re-emerges, after the experience of fear, it has been tested, qualified, validated and changed by the fear of death, as has the fear been. The two are mutually qualifying strata of experience, and through the persistence of both in the poem, we are able to evaluate our two central experiences and emphasize accordingly. Nothing is rejected.

A similar capacity for valuation, issuing directly from responsive memory, which absorbs the two nodes of experience seen here as change through exploration and settled recurrence, is examined in "Tides" and "The Road" (*Weather and Season*). In the latter, memory is the recognising faculty by which the conscious mind penetrates its unconscious, to find natural images built there into an ideal country – an absolute, alluring and unattainable – and which the teller does "not look for . . . when awake."

The question of identity, subsumed in the role of poet in "Man of the World" (*Weather and Season*), is more inclusively embodied in "The Search" (*Weather and Season*). In that search, "as commanded," the familiar country of the man's origins is discovered as alien, and when, through tracts of nature, he reaches the village, the symbolic ideal is released to him, to be discovered as actual, in its alien quality as

Why, Mors, need we tell you, mors, MORS.

Expectedly enough this is the last poem of *Weather and Season*.

The extrapolation from biography into criticism is dubious, and the question of the text and its alogical relationship to biographical (historical) data is ground already struggled over, and the issue has largely, one hopes, been decided against historicism. Nevertheless I think it's relevant here to indicate that Hamburger is a Jew, of German birth, and that he with most of his family emigrated to England in the year of Hitler's rise to power, and averted for themselves the Nazi holocaust. Hamburger is acutely fitted to write such a poem as "The Search," with all its narrower, more defined implications. It is the Jewish component of this poet that hiddenly but with integrated power explores the landscape of nature and village and finds that the search discovers his origins and death to be identical.

The same qualification permits him to write of the issues of conscience in relation to Eichmann. Eichmann's is a "test case." For if the Jews should by virtue of their insistent history care to extend mercy to Eichmann on trial at Jerusalem "for crimes against humanity," "the evil that men do" will not, to paraphrase, in this instance live as indelibly after them. There is evident irony in such paraphrase, but it is clear that if the Jews could extend mercy, they would be working against the example impressed without mercy on them. One other concern in the poem (which is also one in Hannah Arendt's *Eichmann at Jerusalem*) is with the (moral) deterioration of language through society's use of euphemism. The code, for instance, used by the Nazis to refer to their destruction of European Jewry was *The Final Solution* (cf. Gerald Reitlinger). Clearly such euphemisms weaken the conscience not merely of the individual user, but also that social conscience embodied in the direct, perceptive use of language, that valid currency which a healthful society must share and constantly re-invigorate. Eliot has declared in another context that "Humankind cannot bear very much reality," but it is Hamburger's alert and intelligent contenton that it is the burden of humanity as well as its necessary precondition for survival that it use language as searchingly as possible and with as faithful a rendering of the referents in experience, and interpretation of them, as can be. Mercy, honesty and perception are in this context integral:

Dare break one word and words may yet be whole.

This (final) line from "In a Cold Season" conveniently joins to my last statement of how Hamburger is concerned with language. His language is quiet and naturally spoken, even when speaking of violence. The intensity of the poetry is in the *un*extraordinary and seemingly non-manipulative but exact use of ordinary language – "the sea, that basher of dumb rock" – and its unassumingly painful exploration of painful experience ("For a Family Album"). Its intensity is also in the scrupulous testing of experience impossible of logical accounting for ("The Road"), and in the questioning of the problem all artifact poses as the creative impulsion abstracts from the "raw" but, because raw, valuable experience ("Man of the World"). So that metaphoric imagery is used rarely. The images are visually referential; or else the metaphors live in consideration of the metaphysical data as if the data was actual, or physically tangible. And these are fed through hovering, tentative but persistent rhythms fitted to their unrhymed, speech-moulded cadences.

– Jon Silkin

HAMILTON, (Robert) Ian. British. Born in King's Lynn, Norfolk, 24 March 1938. Educated at Darlington Grammar School; Keble College, Oxford, B.A. Married; has one son. Editor, *Tomorrow*, Oxford, 1959–60. Since 1962, Editor, *The Review*, London. Since 1965, Assistant Editor, *Times Literary Supplement*, London, and Poetry Reviewer, *The Observer*, London. Since 1974, Founding Editor, *The New Review*, London. Recipient: Gregory Award, 1963. Address: Flat 6, 72 Westbourne Grove, London W.2, England.

PUBLICATIONS

Verse

Pretending Not to Sleep: Poems. London, The Review, 1964.
The Visit: Poems. London, Faber, 1970.
Anniversary and Vigil. London, Poem-of-the-Month Club, 1971.

Other

A Poetry Chronicle: Essays and Reviews. London, Faber, 1963; New York, Barnes and Noble, 1973.

Editor, *The Poetry of War, 1939–45.* London, Alan Ross, 1965.
Editor, *Selected Poetry and Prose*, by Alun Lewis. London, Allen and Unwin, 1966.

Editor, *The Modern Poet: Essays from "The Review."* London, Macdonald, 1968; New York, Horizon Press, 1969.
Editor, *Eight Poets.* London, Poetry Book Society, 1968.
Editor, *Selected Poems,* by Robert Frost. London, Penguin, 1973.
Editor, with Colin Falck, *Poems since 1900.* London, Macdonald, 1974.

*   *   *

Response in our time to the problem of how to render intimate and profound emotion in poetry has been extremely varied; often confused. Some poets have preferred to keep off the terrain almost altogether, sublimating pure feeling while employing it as the driving-force for a poetry which makes general, impersonal statements of another kind. Some have taken masks to disguise it, expressing it obliquely or with ironic detachment. Others have adopted the very direct, confessional manner, holding nothing back, hoping that the raw, detailed truth of their utterances will validate the poetry which contains them. Ian Hamilton's achievement has been to establish an alternative different from any of these: an area where personal feeling can be expressed not only with vividness and fidelity to experience but also with a subtlety and a reticence which do not diminish its force. It is a very private, very individual mode of writing; but the emotions are recognizable and universal.

Hamilton's output has been small. His one volume, *The Visit,* contained some thirty poems only, written during seven years; and beyond it, there are so far only a few uncollected new poems printed in magazines, or as yet unpublished. All the poems are short, none exceeding twenty lines. They are most of them direct and simple; or simple once the situation – between father and son, poet and wife, poet and child – has been grasped. Dwelling on significant human moments has been a very deliberate choice. In a note in the *Bulletin* of the Poetry Book Society (Summer 1970), Hamilton defines his poems as "dramatic lyrics . . . the intense climactic moment of a drama." The reader must supply "the prose part . . . the background data" from clues inside the brief statements the poems make. Yet reading Hamilton is never a matter of puzzling out a wilfully cryptic technique. The authenticity and strength – and the interest and relevance for the reader – of the emotions, are immediately apparent. Re-reading gradually uncovers the full situation, the exact intention, affording an increasing sense of the scrupulousness and delicacy with which he handles images and verbal effects.

Sorrow, alarm, tragedy are never far away in Hamilton's verse, but they are contained (in both senses) in small human gestures or minute, careful observations of objects: the movements of hands, or hair, or breath, the play of light in a room, a sudden scent. In "Trucks," the light from the vehicles at night

> Slops in and spreads across the ceiling,
> Gleams, and goes.

The sick, or dreaming, loved one speaks suddently:

> You're taking off, you say,
> And won't be back.
> Your shadows soar.

But her remoteness from him will turn again into a kind of closeness, if he can only wait:

> Very soon
> The trucks will be gone. Bitter, you will turn
> Back again. We will join our cold hands together.

An entire situation is caught in thirteen very simple lines in which images of light and shadow, the gestures of hands, enact its "climactic moment"; sensitive judgment of punctuation and line-endings captures a speaking tone which movingly renders both the intimacy and the alarm. In "Father, Dying," petals from a rose suggest the dying flower, but act also, in words of quiet yet intense physical immediacy, as images for the dying man:

> Trapped on your hand
> They darken, cling in sweat, then curl
> Dry out and drop away.

The end of the poem, as the man's hand bleeds from the thorns on the bare stem, suggests effects in the poetry of Sylvia Plath:

> "My hand's
> In flower," you say, "My blood excites
> This petal dross. I'll live."

There is a certain debt here to a more florid confessional poetry; but the economy and precision, the avoidance of overt drama, are something only Hamilton achieves.

The poems towards the end of *The Visit* are no less moving and arresting, but tend even more towards the laconic; as if the poet feels he can suggest all the more by saying even less. Hamilton's immense skill (very much a personal technical skill) in writing short poems of great tenderness and resonance has tempted many imitators who lack his resource and judgment. As a poet who has helped to keep certain areas of personal sensitivity open at a time when crudity and rhetoric have invaded so much personal verse, his place is assured. But the difficulty of emulating him should be clearly demonstrated by the fine complexity and irony of "Friends," an uncollected poem in which even the plain-looking title contributes a dimension of bitter meaning:

> "At one time we wanted nothing more
> Than to wake up in each other's arms."
> Old enemy,
> You want to live forever
> And I don't
> Was the last pact we made
> On our last afternoon together.

– Alan Brownjohn

HAMPTON, Christopher. British. Born in London, 3 May 1929. Educated at Ardingly College, Sussex, 1944–46; Guildhall School of Music, London (Piano Prize, 1953, Principal's Prize, 1954), 1948–53, A.G.S.M. (Associate, Guildhall School of Music) 1953. Married Kathleen Hampton in 1956; has one daughter. Pianist, accompanist, proof-reader, 1954–61; Director of Studies, Shenker Institute, Rome, 1962–66; Teacher, Davies School of English, London, 1966–67. Since 1968, Lecturer, Polytechnic of Central London. Recipient: Cobbold Prize, 1972. Address: 161 Southwood Lane, London N6 5TA, England.

PUBLICATIONS

Verse

An Exile's Italy.   Leiston, Suffolk, Stuart Thonnesen, 1972.

Other

Island of the Southern Sun (juvenile).   London, Chatto and Windus, 1962.
The Etruscans and the Survival of Etruria.   London, Gollancz, 1969; as *The Etruscan Survival,* New York, Doubleday, 1970.

Editor, *Poems for Shakespeare.*   London, Globe Playhouse Trust, 1972.

Translator, *The Fantastic Brother* (juvenile), by Réné Guillot.   London, Methuen, 1961; Chicago, Rand McNally, 1963.

Christopher Hampton comments:

Since each of us carries within himself, at least potentially, those obscure intangibles and myths that determine the underlying rhythms of identity and being, we have to find ways of getting at them and making something of them. They have to be transposed, caught and held within the forms of another and less fugitive reality, symbolic and imaginative, or let go. And for me poetry is a reality of this order. Poems are mediators, carriers, transmitters of the essences of feeling. In a world in which time and change put each of us continually at risk and in doubt, a poem is one way to reflect on and to embody the discoveries and rewards of the struggle. What one is after is an exact correspondence, a verbal equivalent that will mirror the rhythms of the life within and around one. A poem is a way of recording and of celebrating the impact of momentary vision; of getting at roots and sources; of attempting some kind of affirmation. As I see it:

> The attempt's what matters – against time's slow attritions
> To pit memory and feeling and to hold intact
> Snatched fragments, building from them what we can.

An Exile's Italy, the collection from which this fragment comes, is a sequence of 34 poems embodying at different levels both the metaphor implicit in the title and the experience of the place itself. In its metaphorical sense, the idea of exile involves the recognition that dispossession, loss, captivity, exclusion are terms of existence that one has to live with and accept. But the awareness of this underlying condition also inevitably involves one in the search for place, equilibrium and identity. In face of the alienating facts of time, of change, of familiarity, of strangeness, one is in pursuit. *"Cosi l'animo preso entra in desire . . . e mai non posa / fin che la cosa amata il fa gioire,"* as Dante had it in the lines from *Purgatorio* that I have used as an epigraph. "The committed spirit, possessed by desire . . . can know no rest till the loved object be enjoyed entire" – this is the feeling that governs all the poems. In the search for possession one has to register the fact that all that is most worth having must always remain in the deepest sense beyond possession, or that it can be possessed only in terms of the moment, unless in the poem itself. For what else can one do with the marvellous quivering presences around one except to try and live them through "as constancies between death's stopped notes, held / High up and uncorrupted as life sheds its moment"; and then let them go? Yet, having known them, having been marked by them, broken into, made to see, we may (perhaps) absorb then as potentiality, as sources of the energy and vividness we are after. And maybe then a little of the intangible vitality of the external world will have got into us – which we have to find the voice, the sensuous equivalent for, somehow, if we can. All that is lost is there, waiting for us. We have an inheritance, if we can free ourselves from the blunting routines, the rule of "the weak and the tame." Waking the dead, we become lovers and are changed by what we've stirred, referred back to the vitality and vividness in things, and so potentially at least to ourselves. Though dispossession and defeat are there for many, perhaps even for all (whether as victims of puritan oppression or of the intolerance of the system, as in a number of the monologues in my book, or in the act of life itself), beyond this there is also the hurt of the search for possession. These are conditions we have to face and meet, if possible, since they define the terms of the struggle for survival and for solvency, for continuity and replenishment. Death is always coming at us, to deny and to haunt; but also as part of the pattern of life, which is there to be celebrated through the intangible gifts of Being. Alive, we

> bear the hurt of contact
> Like a voice between us who know –
> Though caught in the glare of sun and stone – this keeps us
> Close to love, and will not let us go.

*   *   *

Christopher Hampton was trained as a musician at the Guildhall School of Music and Drama but after working for a time as pianist and conductor, he abandoned music in order to concentrate upon a writing career, though he has published a number of musicological articles. Before he went to Italy in 1962 he was an active and enthusiastic member of the Group, the gathering of poets who met regularly to discuss and analyse each other's poems, and he was represented in *A Group Anthology,* edited by Edward Lucie-Smith and Philip Hobsbaum.

Hampton's poems have been published in a large number of British and American periodicals and for his first collection, *An Exile's Italy,* he was awarded first prize at the East Anglian Festival of poetry and the arts. He has also published two children's books as well as a book on the art and culture of the Etruscans, *The Etruscans and the Survival of Etruria.*

As might be expected, the poems which make up the sequence *An Exile's Italy* were inspired by his experience as a teacher in Italy. In a way this is unfortunate since many of Hampton's best poems, such as "The Grandmother," "Home for Incurables," and "The Man with the Club Foot," are not (at the time of writing) yet available in volume form, and to appreciate Hampton's stature as a poet his work must be seen as a whole. Be that as it may, *An Exile's Italy* is an interesting sequence which admirably sets the modern Italy in sharp juxtaposition with the ancient world of Cato and Cicero. "A Non-Roman Asserts His Independence" is a satirical piece on the ancient scene; "Cato Castigates the Fish-Breeders" ridicules the effeminacy and extravagances evident in the years between the Punic Wars; and in "The Veteran Takes a Disaffected View of Britain" the Roman soldier stationed in Britain complains about life in 44 A.D. "Forgotten on the fringe of things."

– Howard Sergeant

HANSON, Kenneth O. American. Born in Shelley, Idaho, 24 February 1922. Educated at schools in Shelley; University of Idaho, Pocatello and Moscow, B.A. 1942; University of Washington, Seattle. Since 1956, Professor of Literature and Humanities, Reed College, Portland, Oregon. Delegate to the first Institute in Chinese Civilization, Formosa (Fulbright Fellowship), 1962. Recipient: Bollingen commission award, 1962; Rockefeller Award, 1966; Lamont Poetry Selection Award, 1966; Asia Society translation commission award, 1971; Amy Lowell Traveling Scholarship, 1973. Address: Reed College, Portland, Oregon 97202, U.S.A.

PUBLICATIONS

Verse

8 *Poems 1958.* Portland, Oregon, privately printed, 1958.
Poems. Portland, Oregon, Portland Art Museum, 1959.
Five Poets of the Pacific Northwest, with others, edited by Robin Skelton. Seattle, University of Washington Press, 1964.
The Distance Anywhere. Seattle, University of Washington Press, 1967.
Saronikos and Other Poems. Portland, Oregon, Press-22, 1970.
The Uncorrected World. Middletown, Connecticut, Wesleyan University Press, 1973.

Other

Editor, *Clear Days: Poems by Palamás and Elytis, in Versions by Nikos Tselepides.* Portland, Oregon, Press-22, 1972.

Critical Study: "On Translation," interview with William Stafford, in *Madrona* (Seattle), Summer 1973.

Kenneth O. Hanson comments:

Chief influences on my work have been Pound, Williams, the Chinese language, the Greek landscape, Prévert, Cavafy, and my third-grade teacher Miss Warwas, who taught me how to pay attention.

*   *   *

The first poem in Kenneth O. Hanson's *The Distance Anywhere* describes a skin-diver who hangs "hours on the surface of one world / and stares into another." A frequent visitor to Greece and a serious student of classical Chinese culture, Hanson might in those lines be describing a central situation in his poems. As an observer he likes to be inconspicuous ("Beginning the day with ouzo / you're one jump ahead. / I stick to beer''), and reticent (''Sometimes / a thing can be made / too clear'').

His rhetoric is colloquial, understated. His more formal tone, usually elegiac, is closer to Waley's and Rexroth's translations from Chinese poetry than to British or American models:

> What is empty? What is full? Only
> the four corners of the past stand pat.

Most of *The Uncorrected World* is set in Greece; a few poems at the book's end long for Greece and meditate on what it means to be a traveller, and to be back in America. Throughout the book age-old Greece and its current political situation collide:

> This rocky
> landscape Hesiod how could he
> plow a straight furrow?
> Three thousand years.
> Sun. Moon. Stone. Sky.
> Against the whitewashed wall.
> Official pronouncements.

But the world is uncorrected, and Greek political life is a manifestation, rather than a cause, of that fact. Hanson in Greece is a shrewd version of the American innocent abroad, but Hanson even at home is a traveller, because we all are:

> We like to seem importunate
>
> before this world of change.
> O plains o vasty deep o marge and void
> etc. We move but not through distance
>
> into time, as if the fatal toad
> in time's thin stone still faintly ticked
> somewhere beyond. Aficionados of the moon!
>
> O distances we gaze into!

– William Matthews

HANSON, Pauline.   American.   Born in Massachusetts. Since 1950, Assistant to the Director, Yaddo, Saratoga Springs, New York. Recipient: Eunice Tietjens Memorial Prize (*Poetry*, Chicago), 1965; National Endowment for the Arts grant, 1972; National Institute of Arts and Letters award, 1972. Address: Yaddo, Saratoga Springs, New York 12866, U.S.A.

PUBLICATIONS

Verse

The Forever Young.   Denver, Swallow, 1948.
The Forever Young and Other Poems.   Denver, Swallow, 1957.
Across Countries of Anywhere.   New York, Knopf, 1971.

Critical Studies: Comments, by May Swenson, George P. Elliott, and Malcolm Cowley on the dust jacket of *Across Countries of Anywhere*, 1972.

*   *   *

The landscape of Pauline Hanson's poetry is stark, vast, and abstract; seasons slip into seasons, years into centuries, one dead into many, the flesh into spirit – and all are unspecified. Frequently, the nameless persona stands before the altars of the night ("Like Anyone Who Waits Here" from *Across Countries of Anywhere* or "Poems for the Night" from *The Forever Young and Other Poems*) and struggles to think her way out of the silence and into a knowledge of death, love, and her place in the scheme of things. The roads she travels are time and space; the people she meets are spectres and shadows:

> And once, beyond the words of it,
> slowly then all suddenly,
> imagined in the longest night
> the way, the only way, was time. . .
>
> When you touched me, when I touched you,
> when your shadows, when my shadows,
> shimmered into the sensuous flesh
> of my body, of your body:
> lust into lust we moved and then –
> then dreamed from every secret self
> of our remembering, it was
> like lost . . . like found . . . like always love.
>
> – "The Ways"

Whether Hanson practices a mental athleticism as she speculates on atomic theory, astrophysics and Hindu mysticism in "The Questions of the One Question," or whether in her less pretentious long poem, "The Forever Young and Never Free" (originally titled "The Forever Young"), she fashions her story in the form of arduous questionings, she characteristically leads her reader through tight parad-oxes and tortured syntax unrelieved by conventional imagery to an understanding of life's mysteries.

In "The Forever Young" and many other of her poems, it is a particular death, the death of her lover, that lies behind all the deaths she probes and gives her verse its poignancy and power. This lover also figures in poems where the living and dead are fused in love and love transcends the bonds of time:

> Love is to the farthest place –
> love is to so far a place
> from always its greater distances,
> to see where death was, I look back.
> — "And I Am Old To Know"

Hanson's refusal to employ figurative language and her insistence on a limited vocabulary of familiar but haunting words used repetitively contribute to the ritual-istic, hypnotic quality of her poetry:

> Where the constant winter was,
> where stricken from myself I went
> into the cold and colder sweep
> of snow on snow already deep.
> — "The Ways"

At times her heavy dependence upon repetition coupled with her habit of leaving her pronouns without referents renders her verse unintelligible rather than ambigu-ous; but generally, her craft does not falter and the austere language is poetically effective. That she can evoke concrete images is illustrated in several of her poems. Eager to celebrate the living and contrast it to the unknown, she recalls a "small bird's crimson flight" ("The Forever Young"). In "So Beautiful Is the Tree of Night" the arched branches of the great tree are etched against the sky. In the grotesque lines of "We Meet," she appalls us with her piteous image of the hanging jew child:

> . . . . Of God who for these hours is to let him hang here –
> with his hands tied, with his feet tied – put here for others to look at –
> put up here as high as he has seen at home branches hang and
> he reached up his hand but could not touch the flowers on them,
> could not touch the shining apples on them.

But these images are rare. Generally, her poetry is one of questioning, examining life's paradoxes. Like Gerontion, she keeps reminding her reader and herself to "think now." Her setting is astral; the ways she travels take her beyond time; and her place is nowhere and anywhere as she tries to answer "Who I am?"

— Carol Simpson Stern

HARPER, Michael S(teven). American. Born in Brooklyn, New York, 18 March 1938. Educated at City College of Los Angeles, A.A. 1959; California State Univer-sity, Los Angeles, B.A. 1961, M.A. in English 1963; University of Iowa, Iowa City, M.A. 1963; University of Illinois, Urbana, 1970–71. Married Shirley Ann Buffing-ton in 1965; has one daughter and two sons. Taught at Contra Costa College, San Pablo, California, 1964–68; Reed College and Lewis and Clark College, Portland, Oregon, 1968–69; California State University, Hayward, 1970. Since 1971, Director of the Writing Program, and Professor of English, Brown University, Providence, Rhode Island. Recipient: National Institute of Arts and Letters Award, 1972; Black

Academy of Arts and Letters Award, 1972. Address: 26 First Street, Barrington, Rhode Island 02806, U.S.A.

PUBLICATIONS

Verse

> *Dear John, Dear Coltrane.* Pittsburgh, University of Pittsburgh Press, 1970.
> *History Is Your Own Heartbeat.* Urbana, University of Illinois Press, 1971.
> *Photographs: Negatives: History as Apple Tree.* San Francisco, Scarab Press, 1972.
> *Song: I Want a Witness.* Pittsburgh, University of Pittsburgh Press, 1972.
> *Debridement.* New York, Doubleday, 1973.
> *Nightmare Begins Responsibility.* Urbana, University of Illinois Press, 1974.

Other

> Editor, *Heartblow: Black Veils* (anthology). Urbana, University of Illinois Press, 1974.

*   *   *

Michael S. Harper's collections reveal a broad diversity of themes and his disparate interests, ranging from music (jazz and blues), to nature (birth and death), to history and myth. But it is soon apparent that they are manifestations of a highly sensitized Black within whom all these themes coalesce and are translated into emotional and spiritual expressions. Harper states that "relationships between speech and body, between men, between men and cosmology are central to my poetry."

In some respects his poetry defies characterization for it is free of form, and yet it is controlled by personal rhythms emanating from his deeply rooted jazz and blues impulses. (He tells us for example that "Billie Holiday played piano in my family's house when I was 12.") At the same time his writing manifests a historical sense affording him what T. S. Eliot called a perception "not only of the pastness of the past, but of its presence." Harper believes that man must not allow himself to be dislocated from his historical continuum: "When there is no history there is no metaphor." His poetry is at once a synthesis and an articulation of this sensibility.

In another respect, Africa is viewed as the "potent ancestor" providing "a strong ancestral base that reflects the African spirit wherever it is located":

> And we go back to the well: Africa,
> the first mode, and man, modally,
> touched the land of the continent,
> modality: we are one; a man is another
> man's face, modality, in continuum,
> from man, to man, contact-high, to man. . . .

It is out of this spiritual and historical consciousness as well that Michael Harper defines relationships between people and the cosmos, and generates metaphor:

This suture is race
as it is blood,
long as the frozen
lake building messages
on typewritten paper,
faces of my ancestors,
warm in winter only
as their long scars touch ours.

His poetry is challenging, but for the most part it is rewarding.

– Charles L. James

———————

HARRIS, (Theodore) Wilson. British. Born in New Amsterdam, British Guiana, now Guyana, 24 March 1921. Educated at Queen's College, Georgetown. Married to Margaret Whitaker. Government Surveyor, in the 1940's, and Senior Surveyor, 1955–58, Government of British Guiana. Visiting Lecturer, State University of New York at Buffalo, 1970; Writer-in-Residence, Scarborough College, University of Toronto, 1970; Commonwealth Fellow in Caribbean Literature, Leeds University, Yorkshire, 1971; Visiting Professor, University of Texas, Austin, 1972. Delegate to the National Identity Conference, Brisbane, 1968; to UNESCO Symposium on Caribbean Literature, Cuba, 1968. Recipient: Arts Council grant, 1968, 1970; Guggenheim Fellowship, 1973. Address: c/o Faber and Faber Ltd., 3 Queen Square, London WC1N 3AU, England.

PUBLICATIONS

Verse

Fetish. Georgetown, British Guiana, privately printed, 1951.
Eternity to Season. Georgetown, British Guiana, privately printed, 1954.

Novels

The Guiana Quartet:
  Palace of the Peacock. London, Faber, 1960.
  The Far Journey of Oudin. London, Faber, 1961.
  The Whole Armour. London, Faber, 1962.
  The Secret Ladder. London, Faber, 1963.
Heartland. London, Faber, 1964.
The Eye of the Scarecrow. London, Faber, 1965.
The Waiting Room. London, Faber, 1967.
Tumatumari. London, Faber, 1968.
Ascent to Omai. London, Faber, 1970.
Black Marsden. London, Faber, 1972.

Short Stories

> *The Sleepers of Roraima.* London, Faber, 1970.
> *The Age of the Rainmakers.* London, Faber, 1971.

Other

> *Tradition and the West Indian Novel.* London and Port of Spain, Trinidad, New Beacon Books, 1965.
> *Tradition, The Writer and Society: Critical Essays.* London and Port of Spain, Trinidad, New Beacon Books, 1967.

Manuscript Collections: University of the West Indies, Mona, Kingston, Jamaica; University of Texas, Austin; University of Indiana, Bloomington.

Critical Studies: "The Necessity of Poetry" by Louis James, and "Kyk-over-Al and the Radicals" by Edward Brathwaite, in *New World* (Georgetown, Guyana), 1966.

Wilson Harris comments:

Fetish and *Eternity to Season,* along with other miscellaneous poems of the early 1950's, stand at the beginning of an exploration which extends deeper and further at a later stage in my work in the novel over the 1960's. The development of the novels is foreshadowed, to some extent, in the earlier poems. Constant to that exploration within poem and novel is the use I continue to make of the brooding continental landscape of Guiana as a gateway of memory between races and cultures, Amerindian, European, African, Asian.

*   *   *

The poetry of Wilson Harris, like his contribution to the art of the novel since 1960 (he has published no poetry since this date), is outside the present mainstream of Caribbean writing in English. Like Martin Carter, also of Guyana, his metaphorical perception and expression are more akin to that of the Martiniquan poet Aimé Césaire and the Cuban writer Alejo Carpentier. One does not find in Harris' work the clear air of the anglophone islands' poets. His sensibility has been formed by the world of the Guyanese forest and its rivers, its complexities and contradictions:

> The world-creating jungle
> travels eternity to season. Not an individual artifice
> this living movement
> this tide
> this paradoxical stream and stillness rousing reflection.
>
> The living jungle is too full of voices
> not to be aware of collectivity,
> and too swift with unseen wings
> to capture certainty.

– "Amazon"

639

Harris' poetry is to be found in *Kyk-over-Al* and in the privately published *Eternity to Season*, which contain his most important poems. He does not concern himself with social conditions, individual problems, the "historical" colonial past, or a possible or impossible future. His themes are time (into which he subsumes history), creation, separation and unity. His burden is not the Faustian ego but the environmental collective. There is some evidence of the operation of a Hegelian/ Marxist dialectic in his poems. When individuals appear in his poetry, they are gigantic mythologized figures like Hector "hero of time," Agamemnon, Achilles (the great runner) and Teiresias. Harris uses these figures, and simple material existences like rice, water and charcoal to initiate journeys both (and often simultaneously) into cosmic space and human time:

> The tall trees lean
> and darken the world beside bright and glowing honey:
> sunshine meets each shadowy bloom, flower or leaf:
> blue sky is far aloft like the dot of a bird's
> black speck, the blackness melts in heaven.
> > – from "Teiresias"

> In this dark village the noble dead speed like the wind.
> The wind in its pride, ruler of its domain, full of feats of dust
> and honours conferred by time, strides on the meadows of eternity.
> The bright blossoms' grime, the blue
> steadfast premonitions of space remain free to this whirling brain.
> > – from "Achilles"

Because of the nature of Harris' perception, some of his poetry is obscure (although most of it deposits its meaning after repeated reading) and sometimes (perhaps through the need to make meaning clear) Harris eschews metaphor for "prose" statement:

> But earth cannot simply be
> a cosmic and arbitrary discovery! what of its changing roots
> and purposive vitality? External and internal
> forces are separate illusions that move
> beyond the glitter and the gloom with a knife to cut inner and outer times
> > from each other
> as they weave and interweave in the tapestry of life. . . .

Earlier in this same poem, "Amazon," this *statement* had been already almost magically expressed as:

> Branches against the sky smuggle to heaven the extreme beauty
> of the world: the store-house of that very heaven
> breaks walls to drop tall streams like falls.

> The green islands of the world
> and the bright leaves lift their tender blossom of sunrise
> to offset arenas of sunset
> and wear a wild rosette like blood.

> This self same blossom burns the clouds. . . .

Nor is Harris alone in this paradoxical riverain and arboreal continuum. Two hundred years before his time, George Pinckard, an English army doctor, travelling

on Guyanese water, received and recorded the same kind of environmental breakdown and unification that Harris has transmuted into poetry:

> The watery medium made no impression upon the eye, but the open azure
> expanse was seen the same, whether we looked upwards or downwards.
> We seemed suspended in the centre of a hollow globe, having the same
> concave arch above and below, with an inverted and an upright forest on
> either hand. At one spot we met a huge mass of earth resembling a small
> island, floating down the silent river, with a variety of plants and shrubs
> growing upon it; and from the water being invisible, the perfect reflection
> of this little plantation gave it the appearance of a clump of young trees
> calmly moving in a wide vacuum, with each plant growing perpendicularly
> upward and downward, in precise resemblance. If we held out a hand or
> an oar . . . the same was seen below, without discovering the limpid
> medium between them. In short we seemed to move, like our globe itself,
> in ethereal space.
> — *Notes on the West Indies*, London, 1806, vol. 2, pages 470–71

From this world, Harris has derived his sensibility. His achievement has been the
creation of it into poetry. And at its best, this poetry moves even beyond recreation into enactment; so that often we are able to participate in the creation (out
of elements of space, time and material) of the poet's vision:

> Touched by vision
> the light fingertips of rain pass softly
> to change the stone and burden of her perfection
> into rapt walls that house joy and pain and living imperfection.
> Her cheeks are the dark glow of blood
> beneath the frail temper of space and eternity, the history
> of her flesh and blood is strange and new.
> — from "The Vision at the Well"

— Edward Brathwaite

HARRISON, Jim (James Thomas Harrison). American. Born in Grayling, Michigan, 11 December 1937. Educated at Michigan State University, East Lansing, B.A.
1960; M.A. in comparative literature. Married Linda King in 1960; has two children. Formerly, Assistant Professor of English, State University of New York,
Stony Brook. Now lives on a farm in Michigan. Recipient: National Endowment
for the Arts grant, 1967, 1968, 1969; Guggenheim Fellowship, 1969. Agent: Robert
Datilla, 225 East 49th Street, New York, New York. Address: Box 120a, Lake
Leelanau, Michigan 49653, U.S.A.

PUBLICATIONS

Verse

Plain Song. New York, Norton, 1965.
Locations. New York, Norton, 1968.

Walking.   Cambridge, Massachusetts, Pym Randall Press, 1969.
Outlyers and Ghazals.   New York, Simon and Schuster, 1971.
Letters to Yesenin.   Fremont, Michigan, Sumac Press, 1973.

Novels

Wolf.   New York, Simon and Schuster, 1971.
A Good Day to Die.   New York, Simon and Schuster, 1973.

Jim Harrison comments:

I write "free verse" which is absurdly indefinite as a name for what any poet
writes. I consider myself an "internationalist" and my main influences to be
Neruda, Rilke, Yeats, Bunting, Lorca, and, in my own country, Whitman, Hart
Crane, Robert Duncan and Ezra Pound. Not that this helps much other than to
name those I esteem, and, perhaps vacantly, wish to emulate. Most of my poems
seem rural, vaguely surrealistic though after the Spanish rather than the French.
My sympathies run hotly to the impure, the inclusive, as the realm of poetry. A
poet, at best, speaks in the "out loud speech of his tribe," deals in essences
whether political, social or personal. All of world literature is his province though
he sees it as a "guild" only to be learned from, as he must speak in his own voice.

                                     *   *   *

Jim Harrison seems most at home in his poems when he is alone in the woods of
Northern Michigan, where he lives. He is a poet of the physical world and the
natural world. His work is immersed in sensations – the taste of blackberry brandy,
the smell of manure and kerosene – and many of his most forceful poems show a
close observation of animals and a great sympathy for them, for starving swans, for
wolves turned mad or murderous by the imprisonment men impose upon them.
    Harrison's is a grainy, tactile kind of writing. An increased adeptness and rich-
ness of description are the primary gains that resulted from his work with longer
forms in *Locations.* That talent for description serves him well in his professed
intention to write about "audible things, things moving/at noon in full raw light";
still, one could wish that Harrison were more concerned with spiritual matters, that
he had more of the religious tenderness possessed by a poet like Roethke. Largely
in the ghazals which comprise the most of *Outlyers* an adolescent and cruel side of
Harrison surfaces. The ghazals are pervaded by a kind of sneering humor, an
American tough-guy stance that can be ugly, especially when he deals with women.
In countless couplets Harrison either insults, ogles, or accuses women, and continuously pictures or imagines females suffering a myriad of indignities and cruelties.
    In a series of poems, *Letters to Yesenin,* that has appeared since *Outlyers,*
Harrison confesses to having reached an emotional dead-end, unable to love,
exhausted and inured. The poems, however, are encouraging not only because they
have a feel of genuine honesty in contrast to the locker-room honesty of the
ghazals, but because in them Harrison seems to have found a form that suits his
considerable talent, especially his facility for creating a sense of natural speech.

                                                              – Lawrence Russ

HARRISON, Keith (Edward). Australian. Born in Melbourne, Victoria, 29 January 1932. Educated at Trinity Grammar School, Melbourne; Melbourne Teachers' College, 1951; University of Melbourne (Masefield Prize, 1954), 1952–54, B.A. in English and French 1954; University of Iowa, Iowa City, 1966–67, M.A. 1967. Married Inger Christina Götesdotter Haglund in 1965; has two daughters. Tutor, University of London Extra-Mural Department, 1963–65; Visiting Poet, University of Iowa, 1966; Lecturer in English, York University, Toronto, 1966–68. Since 1968, Assistant Professor of English, and since 1970, Director of the Arts Program, Carleton College, Northfield, Minnesota. Recipient: Canada Council grant, 1968; Department of Health, Education, and Welfare Seminar on South Asian Studies Fellowship, 1969, 1970; Arts Council of Great Britain award, 1972. Address: 200 College Street, Northfield, Minnesota 55057, U.S.A.

PUBLICATIONS

Verse

> *Points in a Journey and Other Poems.* London, Macmillan, 1967; Chester Springs, Pennsylvania, Dufour, 1968.
> *Two Variations on a Ground.* London, Turret Books, 1968.
> *Songs from the Drifting House.* London, Macmillan, 1972.

Manuscript Collection: Carleton College Library, Northfield, Minnesota.

Keith Harrison comments:

Teaching still seems to me the best and worst job for a poet. Young people are so starved at their high schools for good literature – good art of any kind – that introducing them to poetry both at an interpretive and a creative level is an urgent necessity, as well as an exciting challenge. The trick is to find enough time for your own work – and no university poet whom I know has solved that one, except by becoming a public institution, an "instant personality."

To get to more substantial matters: I think there are stable mythic patterns. Chiefly: to grow, it would seem that artists, as well as everybody else, have to go through hell. Modern man is a neurotic mess and that is the ground we have to stand on. The evasive strategies of madness, suicide or incoherence simply won't do. The difficult thing, the damnably difficult thing, is to take one's private predicament and by imaginative heat to forge something hard and emblematic out of it. One hopes that on the other side of all that one will be able to write a poetry that is full of sunlight and broad humour (there is too little *pleasure* in contemporary poetry) – but there is no easy way out of hell. I have just finished a book of very dark poems and I hope the darkness is made acceptable by the validity and accuracy of the language. (I also hope it's the last dark thing that I ever do.)

Poetry readings are currently the dullest and most ill-organized form of entertainment we have. I would like, both as a writer and a reader, to improve them to the level of, say, a concert given by a group of bright young musicians. The whole art of poetry – writing, understanding, reading aloud – is still in its infancy in this country, and in most others.

*   *   *

An Australian, Keith Harrison has lived and studied in both England and America for a considerable number of years. Like so many poets, he has found it necessary to work through the experiences of childhood before being able to experiment with new styles and ideas. His first book, *Points in a Journey*, records in an eight-part autobiographical poem, the discoveries he has made about himself, his family and his background. The second part of this book consists of a series of dramatic monologues of which the most outstanding is "Leichardt in the Desert" (Leichardt was a nineteenth-century German explorer who died while attempting to cross the Australian desert):

> I did not choose to make this westward journey
> Into the dry rock country of the dead
> Where in the torpid light the lizards
> Flick from our tracks into the mean rock shadows;
> To slash that tunnel through the mountain forest,
> Cross the grasslands, wade the inland rivers –
> I did not choose; say rather I was called. . . .

Other pieces of interest are "The Island Weather of the Newly Betrothed," "Wife Waiting" and "Dentist at Work." The third section contains more formal experiments, set in Spain and London, and these poems are not quite so successful as the rest.

In *Songs from a Drifting House*, Keith Harrison still persists in the role of ironic observer, commenting upon life as he sees it on his travels. "Swedish Vignettes" and "Midwestern Blues" make their point with due economy. The title of the book is taken from a series of lyrics which are pleasant enough but in no way outstanding. There are some competent translations from Ronsard, Baudelaire and Rimbaud, but overall one gains the impression of a poet lacking a real sense of direction. Harrison undoubtedly has talent, but so far his promise is greater than his achievement.

– Howard Sergeant

HARRISON, Tony. British. Born in Leeds, Yorkshire, 30 April 1937. Educated at Cross Flats County Primary, Leeds, 1942–48; Leeds Grammar School, 1948–55; University of Leeds, 1955–60, B.A. in classics, Postgraduate Diploma in linguistics. Married Rosemary Dietzsch in 1962; has one daughter and one son. Lecturer in English, Ahmadu Bello University, Zaria, Northern Nigeria, 1962–66, and Charles University, Prague, 1966–67; Editor, with Jon Silkin and Ken Smith, *Stand*, Newcastle upon Tyne, 1968–69. Delegate, Conference on Colonialism and the Arts, Dar-es-Salaam, Tanzania, July 1971. Recipient: Northern Arts Fellowship, University of Newcastle upon Tyne and University of Durham, 1967–68; Cholmondeley Award, 1969; UNESCO Fellowship, 1969; Faber Memorial Award, 1972. Address: 9 The Grove, Gosforth, Newcastle upon Tyne NE3 1NE, Northumberland, England.

PUBLICATIONS

Verse

Earthworks. Leeds, Northern House, 1964.
Newcastle Is Peru. Newcastle upon Tyne, Eagle Press, 1969.
The Loiners. London, London Magazine Editions, 1970.
Corgi Modern Poets in Focus 4, with others, edited by Jeremy Robson. London, Corgi, 1971.
Voortrekker. Ashington, Northumberland, MidNAG, 1972.

Plays

Aikin Mata, with James Simmons, adaptation of *Lysistrata* by Aristophanes (produced Zaria, Northern Nigeria, 1965). Ibadan, Oxford University Press, 1966.
The Misanthrope, adaptation of a play by Molière (produced London, 1973). London, Rex Collings, and New York, Third Press, 1973.
Phaedra Brittanica, adaptation of the play by Racine (produced London, 1975). London, Rex Collings, 1975.

Other

Editor, "New Writing from Czechoslovakia" issue of *Stand* (Newcastle upon Tyne), x, 2, 1969.
Editor and Translator, *Poems of Pallades of Alexandria.* London, Anvil Press Poetry, 1973.

Critical Studies: by James Simmons, in *The Honest Ulsterman* (Belfast), September-October 1970; Jeremy Robson, in *Corgi Modern Poets in Focus 4,* 1971; "The Prosodies of Free Verse" by Donald Wesling, in *Twentieth Century Literature in Retrospect,* edited by Reuben A. Brower, Cambridge, Massachusetts, Harvard University Press, 1971; Irving Wardle, in *The Times* (London), 23 February 1973; "Molière Remodelled" by Benedict Nightingale, in *New Statesman* (London), 2 March 1973.

*   *   *

Tony Harrison, who has been described by the poet, critic and discriminating editor David Wright as "the white hope of English poetry," is certainly one of the most accomplished technicians of his generation. His brilliant translation of Molière, a deserved success on the stage, aptly demonstrates that form, intelligently and experimentally employed, is still viable. His use of "the floating s" (the transfer of an apostrophe s to the following line), his vigour and nerve and faith to the spirit of the original: all these contribute to one of the greatest successes in translation of recent years. It is as readable as it is performable. His skill as a translator is also to be seen in *The Poems of Pallades of Alexandria* and in his contributions to Peter Jay's *Greek Anthology.*
Harrison is not a poet who works from the excitement words create in him; he begins, rather, with an idea or a theme and then clothes it with his verbal imagination. One may (so far) miss in him the kind of richness that is to be found in some

of the best Latin-American poetry (from some of the *Modernistas* onward); but that one should think of missing it at all is tribute to his very evident potentialities. His caution, at a time when complete carelessness and the tendency to splurge on without thought is perfectly acceptable, is in any case, admirable; his well-judged daring in translation shows that he has the capacity to do justice to his linguistic resources, which are considerable.

As it is, Harrison's elegant and originally angled poems work primarily by means of wit (in the Empsonian sense), and their emotional substance is conveyed by means of carefully chosen modes of tone and the force of particular lines. He is an intellectual, though never a cold, poet – one would suspect that the influence of Empson, though never disastrous as in the case of the early John Wain, has been a strong one. He shows something of Empson's ability to clothe a complex idea in a form of words that is passionate and yet not over-emotional; he has Empsonian restraint, and one suspects that his political position is somewhat near to Empson's at least in the sense that his powerful feelings are as powerfully restrained by intelligence – an intelligence so acute that it is sometimes felt as despair. Harrison is refreshing because he turns his energies, which are considerable, not to the fashionable literary world or what it may vaguely feel it wants at any given time, but to the exploration of what can be done with the colloquial and the unfamiliar. This suggests that he may soon feel ready to plunge more directly into his own imagination, which may have positively startling results on a poetic scene that is still dominated – in terms of gifts – by Philip Larkin. "On Not Being Milton," aside from its subtle puns, its characteristic wit and its strong sense of history, contains hints of the latent power that I have suggested Harrison possesses:

> Read and committed to the flames, I call
> these sixteen lines that go back to my roots,
> my *Cahier d'un retour au pays natal*,
> my growing black enough to fit my boots.
>
> The stutter of the scold out of the branks
> Of condescension, class and counter-class
> thickens with glottals to a lumpen mass
> of Ludding morphemes closing up their ranks.
> Each swung cast-iron Enoch of Leeds stress
> clangs a forged music on the frames of Art,
> the looms of owned language smashed apart!
>
> Three cheers for mute ingloriousness!
>
> Articulation is the tongue-tied's fighting.
> In the silence round all poetry we quote
> Tidd the Cato Street conspirator who wrote:
>
> *Sir, I Ham a very Bad Hand at Righting.*

Not all that Harrison writes is as effectively compressed and moving and sardonic as this fine poem; but much is. In him, for the first time for many years, we have an intellect combined with what was once called a heart. It is cheering that even at his weakest he has no trace of sentimentality; that almost all he writes is worthy of discussion at a high critical level.

– Martin Seymour-Smith

HARSENT, David. English. Born in Devonshire, 9 December 1942. Married; has two children. Worked in bookselling. Recipient: Gregory Award, 1967; Arts Council bursary, 1969. Lives in Buckinghamshire.

PUBLICATIONS

Verse

Tonight's Lover. London, The Review, 1968.
A Violent Country. London, Oxford University Press, 1969.
Ashridge. Oxford, Sycamore Press, 1970.
After Dark. London, Oxford University Press, 1973.

*   *   *

David Harsent's first collection of poetry, *A Violent Country*, contains poems about madness and death, a series of love poems deeply veined with sadness and terror, and a sequence in which a woman probes her anguished existence.

There is, obviously, little easy terrain in this country, and Harsent does not flinch from penetrating the deepest undergrowth. Occasionally he revels in the gore and desolation, and then the poems seem contrived and over-sentimental. But for the most part, Harsent writes with harsh accuracy, richly conveying the violence:

> . . . the crushed
> head, the raw
> excresence at
>
> the gaping jaw –
> rubbery bleb
> of its own
>
> congealing guts.
> > – "The Woman and the Cat"

But Harsent's major talent lies in the exactness and authority with which he communicates the deep crises raging within – a dreamlike, obsessive world of impotence, hopelessness, and madness. In "The Woman and the Cat," the real horror is not the eyes of the cat cracking "like a trodden grape," but the woman's eyes, like a camera, recording every detail, visualising the moment of impact, picturing precisely the process of death.

The series of poems about the woman are among the most powerful and disturbing that Harsent has written. Moving slowly through her house and garden – reminiscent of an Ingmar Bergman movie – the woman's mind is full of blood imagery, guilt, and doom. Through meticulous examination of objects, soft words and stillness, she exorcises both pain and passion; but waking in the morning, her words – real or dreamed – return to haunt her through the day, until:

> That evening, tired of speech
> she tests
> the astringency of song.
> > – "The Woman's Soliloquies"

Pain and anguish are less blatant in *After Dark*, but uncertainties linger and the poignancy remains intense. The poems are generally softer, more reflective and more obviously personal. The poet lives quietly in the country:

> I have bogged down in this odd village;
> my children belong to the place.
> At night I can hear the cows
> coughing in a field behind the house.
>
> I close my eyes
> and invent arrivals.
>   – "After Dark"

Harsent is constantly reminded of his childhood – strange, passionate, less ordered than the present, it underlines the inadequacies of his adult life. Perhaps the strongest "presence" is the austere landscape – a wildness surrounding his neat interior, reflecting his love and his solitude in its bleak depths:

> Too tired for sleep and knowing of no way
> to quieten you, I've walked to this cold bench.
>
> Above the fields
> mountains of purple cloud lumber through drizzle.
>
> Between your open window and this place
> the land is dark and wringing wet.
>   – "Figures in a Landscape"

Later in the volume the uncertainties harden; there is less looking back. He begins to anticipate death, lured by signs of withering skin, "insights of fatigue," a switchblade drawn across the palm. The volume ends with a poem about a suicide. Hurtling toward the street, the man's last glimpse is of the sky:

> a fractured blue, and clouds
> like dark pools where his other lives submerged.
>   – "Leap Off the City Skyline"

There are no half measures for Harsent. Death is the totality, and suffering the way toward it. How vital then, to remember passion, to always hope for love:

> . . . how lovers might
> suffer the fierce light flensing their lives
>
> of all but one bald fact;
> how they might lie awake by those blunt hills
> breathing each other's breath
> and feeling the island slipping with the tides.
>   – "Acid Landscapes"

There is an extraordinary power in Harsent's poetry. If he can withstand a slight tendency to sentimentalize, he will undoubtedly emerge as a major poet of his generation.

– Roland Turner

HARTNETT, Michael. Irish. Born in Ireland, 18 September 1941. Married; has one daughter. Worked as a civil servant, security guard, dishwasher, postman, tea-boy, and housepainter, 1961–68. Since 1969, Telephonist, General Post Office, Dublin. Contributor to *The Irish Times*, Dublin, and Radio Eireann. Editor, with James Liddy and Liam O'Connor, *Arena* magazine, Dublin, 1963–65. Address: 19 St. Aidan's Park Avenue, Narino, Dublin 3, Ireland.

PUBLICATIONS

Verse

> *Anatomy of a Cliché.* Dublin, Dolmen Press, 1968.
> *Tao: A Version of the Chinese Classic of the Sixth Century B.C.* Dublin, New Writers Press, 1969.
> *The Hag of Beare: A Rendition of the Old Irish.* Dublin, New Writers Press, 1969.

Other

> Editor, with Desmond Egan, *Choice.* Dublin, Goldsmith Press, 1973.

Critical Study: Interview in *The Poet Speaks*, edited by Peter Orr, London, Routledge, and New York, Barnes and Noble, 1966.

Michael Hartnett comments:

> *Major themes:* The woman as human being; deaths (not *Death*); "nature" in human terms.
> *Characteristic Subjects:* Love Poems; the hunting of animals; wake poems.
> *Usual Verse Forms:* Lyric, syllabic, assonantal, rhyme (sparingly), metric (rarely in the classical sense); developing more complex forms.
> *General Sources and Influences:* Mainstream English poetry; Gaelic poetry.
> *Characteristic Stylistic Devices:* Compound words; anglosaxon (*not* in the D. H. Lawrence sense) vocabulary; the animal as symbol.

*   *   *

Michael Hartnett's achievement as a poet so far has been distinguished by its emotional intensity, its scrupulous attention to the subtleties of craftsmanship, its thematic variety, and its essentially experimental and adventurous character. In his work, intelligence and music play equally important parts. There is no arid intellectualizing, no meaningless melody. Reading through his output so far, one has the sense of a dedicated artist who refuses to admit anything shabby or shoddy into his work. Some critics in fact say that Hartnett is fastidious to the point of being finicky, that his obsession with technique conceals very serious emotional limitations. This, to my mind, is a complete misreading of Hartnett's purpose and achievement. Hartnett, as far as I can see, has the full equipment for a poet of stature. He is well on his way to becoming a master of language, his *own* language; he has a keen ear for the subtlest rhythms; almost everything he writes haunts the reader for its cutting insight expressed in appropriate verbal music; and, above all, his poems at their best have that quiet authority which is the surest mark of confidence.

Take, for example, the last of "Four Sonnets," from *Selected Poems*:

> I saw magic on a green country road –
> That old woman, a bag of sticks her load,
>
> Blackly down to her thin feet a fringed shawl,
> A rosary of bone on her horned hand,
> A flight of curlews scribing by her head,
> And ashtrees combing with their frills her hair.
>
> Her eyes, wet sunken holes pierced by an awl,
> Must have deciphered her adoring land:
> And curlews, no longer lean birds, instead
> Become ten scarlet comets in the air.
>
> Some incantation from her canyoned mouth,
> Irish, English, blew frost along the ground,
> And even though the wind was from the South
> The ashleaves froze without an ashleaf sound.

The picture of that old woman is completely, yet concisely, imagined. The form is old enough for anyone's taste; but the diction is novel and energetic. This blend of the old and the new is reflected in the imagery of the poem:

> curlews, no longer lean birds, instead
> Become ten scarlet comets in the air.

In his vision of the past as a source of vitality and inspiration, Michael Hartnett has produced a moving, elegant version of the Chinese classic, the *Tao*, and a magnificent translation of the greatest of Old Irish poems, *The Hag of Beare*. This latter poem shows Hartnett's technical dexterity at its most brilliant. He makes a fine, sustained attempt to convey something of the rhythms of the original by interlocking assonance and by alliteration. Many Irish poets have tried to translate this marvellous lament for lost youth, this outcry against the ravages of time. I think that Michael Hartnett's is the best.

Very fine, too, are his translations of the *Gipsy Ballads* of Garcia Lorca. It is obvious that no translator can fully capture Lorca's magic; all he can hope to do, at best, is to suggest something of its nature and effects. In his versions of Lorca's "The Flight," "San Miguel," "Gabriel" and "Ballad of the Black Sorrow," Michael Hartnett succeeds in making precisely that suggestion.

What have we then? We have a gifted and dedicated poet, as intensely interested in the cultures of other lands as in that of his own. In his mid-thirties, Hartnett is already one of the most accomplished and enterprising poets now writing in Ireland. I believe that he will soon have a growing international reputation.

– Brendan Kennelly

HART-SMITH, William. Australian. Born in Tunbridge Wells, Kent, England, 23 November 1911. Educated in Scotland; St. Clair, Walmer, Kent; Gunnersbury Preparatory School, London; Belmont Primary School, Auckland, New Zealand; Seddon Memorial Technical College, Auckland. Served in the Australian military forces, 1941–43. Married P. A. McBearn in 1949 (marriage dissolved, 1964); Dorothy O'Donnell, 1964; has four children. Clerk, New Zealand Shipping Company, Auckland, 1926–27; Radio Salesman and Mechanic, Wisemans Ltd., Auckland, 1927–30; Radio Serviceman, Auckland, 1930–36, and Baden-Cameron Company, Hobart, Tasmania, 1936–37; Radio Copywriter and Announcer, Station 2CH, Sydney, 1937–44; Free-lance Writer, Sydney, 1944–47; Tutor Organizer, Adult Education Department, Canterbury, New Zealand, 1948–55; Advertising Copywriter, Jack Penny Ltd., Christchurch, 1956–60; Manager, Christchurch Office, 1960–62, and Advertising Manager, Sydney, 1962–66, Charles Kidd and Company; Radio Technician, Amalgamated Wireless of Australasia, Sydney, 1966–70. Since 1970, Part-time Lecturer in English, Western Australian Institute of Technology, Perth. President, Poetry Society of Australia, 1963–64. Recipient: Crouch Memorial Medal, 1959; Grace Leven Prize, 1966. Agent: Angus and Robertson Ltd., 102 Glover Street, Cremorne, New South Wales 2090. Address: c/o Western Australian Institute of Technology, Hayman Road, Bentley, Perth, Western Australia 6102, Australia.

Publications

Verse

Columbus Goes West. Adelaide, Economy Press, 1943.
Harvest. Melbourne, Georgian House, 1945.
The Unceasing Ground: Poems. Sydney, Angus and Robertson, 1946.
Christopher Columbus: A Sequence of Poems. Christchurch, Caxton Press, 1948.
On the Level: Mostly Canterbury poems. Timaru, New Zealand, Timaru Herald, 1950.
Poems in Doggerel. Wellington, Handcraft Press, 1955.
Poems of Discovery. Sydney, Angus and Robertson, 1959.
The Talking Clothes: Poems. Sydney, Angus and Robertson, 1966.
Poetry from Australia: Pergamon Poets 6, with Judith Wright and Randolph Stow, edited by Howard Sergeant. Oxford, Pergamon Press, 1969.

Critical Study: Australian Literature by E. Morris Miller and F. T. Macartney, revised edition, Sydney, Angus and Robertson, 1956.

William Hart-Smith comments:

Except on very rare occasions, I was never forced to learn poetry at school which, in those days, usually meant memorising poems and afterwards pulling them to pieces in order to "understand" them. I think I owe my love of poetry to one man. His name was Mr. Waller. That's all I know about him. He taught us for a short while – arithmetic and algebra – at Gunnersbury Prep. School. Always, a few minutes before end of period, he would take a book out from under the lid of his desk and read poetry to us. Tears used to trickle down his face. I shall never forget how utterly spellbound I was when he read us Poe's "The Raven," and Coleridge's

"Ancient Mariner." He never commented on the poems, or on poetry. Just read it. We were eleven- and twelve-year olds: uncouth on principle and grubby because it was the thing. Mr. Waller had difficulty maintaining discipline. His gown was torn and faded. His mortar-board was threadbare. He spoke in a curious "wet" sort of way which we used to make fun of. In public, I did the same. In private, I couldn't wait for him to read poetry to me. I owe Mr. Waller a debt I can only repay by writing poetry myself.

I didn't begin to write poetry, though, until much later. In the Auckland Public Library one evening when I was twenty, looking for my usual reading on radio theory and practice, I came upon a book put back in the wrong place. It was *Birds, Beasts and Flowers* by D. H. Lawrence. There and then I read it right through and, from then on, just about everything Lawrence wrote. Lawrence's poems, and, oddly enough, *First and Last Things* by H. G. Wells (I read his entire opus also) started me writing poetry too. But it was eight years before anyone accepted anything. One can talk of influences, themes and so forth; but I don't think it really matters, in a note such as this, what they were and are. Sufficient to say I have loved poetry ever since Mr. Waller made a twelve-year old respond to it, without coercion. Except perhaps to say that American poets have influenced me more than British, Eastern ideas more than Western; and Aboriginal Mythology a great deal.

*   *   *

Over the years since 1936, William Hart-Smith, who left England at the age of twelve, has consistently written of his adopted country, Australia, and sometimes of New Zealand where he has also lived some years. His spare economy of language, the simple, usually free, shapes of his poems and the lucidity and apparent casualness of their statements have kept his work from becoming fashionable, but also lent it strength. He seems to have found his way easily into both his new countries as providers of symbol and background, and his pithy conversational rhythms have much in common with their speech.

Few of his poems take much space to make their point. His one long poem, *Christopher Columbus*, consists of forty-three short poems, few of more than page-length, each devoted to some aspect of Columbus' story and each complete in itself. Comment is kept at a minimum; with Hart-Smith, it is selection that does the commenting; and he chooses his momentary glimpses of the voyages, or his quotations from the documents, much as a good documentary film-maker does, for their visual or human illuminations.

There is, indeed, something of document in many of his poems, directed as they are towards objects, events or persons. To write this kind of verse, into which the poet as person intrudes so minimally, is not easy, if the poet is to avoid a cool pedestrianism of vision. This danger for Hart-Smith's poetry is increased by the fact that though his vision is individual, ironic and continually interesting, it does not seem to be directed through any deep interior conviction or world-view. This apparent lack of thematic connection between separate poems is reinforced by the lack of much change or apparent poetic development over the years, though there has been a perceptible increase in tautness of manner, a sharpening of his use of language, and a lessening in his earlier more lyrical attack.

An important influence in his work was the "Jindyworobak" movement, through which a group of Australian poets attempted to work their way into a "native" attitude to Australian themes. Hart-Smith was one of the most distinguished of the poets in the movement, and his verse still displays some of their characteristic tenets. In a comment on the movement's achievement, he once wrote: "It is more than a few rather fanatical individuals trying to be exclusively and most Aboriginally Australian in the English language; it's a case of a number of creative writers pointing the way back to . . . the childhood of the human race, 'to a land that is common to us all.' '' His poems, he says, are "poems of discovery," "attempts to record moments of understanding." Their concentration on objects and events of the outer world is motivated by this attempt to re-see them in a fresh light.

At his best, he does this with memorable individuality. Such poem-titles as "Boomerang," "Bathymeter," "A Snail," "Number," "Candles" indicate the directions in which he turns the searchlight of his verse.

Though he has published a number of books of verse, no complete collection has yet appeared. When this happens, it will be possible to see that, instead of a succession of descriptive and commentary verses, he has produced a gallery of portraits and still-lifes that illuminate the world from the viewpoint of an original and ironic mind.

– Judith Wright

HARWOOD, Gwen(doline Nessie). Australian. Born in Taringa, Queensland, 8 June 1920. Educated at Brisbane Girls' Grammar School. Married Frank William Harwood in 1945; has four children. Formerly, Organist at All Saints' Church, Brisbane. Currently, Secretary to a Consultant Physician, Hobart. Recipient: *Meanjin* prize, 1958, 1959; Commonwealth Literary Fund grant, 1973. Address: 89 Augusta Road, Hobart, Tasmania 7008, Australia.

PUBLICATIONS

Verse

Poems. Sydney, Angus and Robertson, 1963.
Poems: Volume Two. Sydney, Angus and Robertson, 1968.
New and Selected Poems. Sydney, Angus and Robertson, 1974.

Plays

The Fall of the House of Usher, music by Larry Sitsky (produced Hobart, 1965).
Commentaries on Living, music by James Penberthy (produced Perth, 1972).
Lenz, music by Larry Sitsky, adaptation of the story by Georg Büchner (produced Sydney, 1973).

Manuscript Collection: Australian National Library, Canberra.

Critical Studies: by David Moody, in *Meanjin* (Melbourne), no. 4, 1963; "The Poet as Döppelganger" by Dennis Douglas, in *Quadrant* (Sydney), April 1969; "Gwen Harwood and the Professors" by A. D. Hope, in *Australian Literary Studies*

(Hobart), 1972, and a reply to Professor Hope by Dennis Douglas, in *Australian Literary Studies* (Hobart), May 1973; "Artists and Academics in the Poetry of Gwen Harwood" by John B. Beston, in *Quadrant* (Sydney), 1974.

Gwen Harwood comments:

My major themes are music and musicians; the celebration of love and friendship. I write in a number of styles but the qualities I value most in poetry are power and clarity. I want my poems "to shape joy from the flux of sense."

*   *   *

For over a decade Gwen Harwood has been delighting Australian readers with a steady flow of excellent poems written under her own and at least two pen names. Though not stylistically adventurous she is a virtuoso of the character study, choosing her subjects and sometimes victims from a milieu of outwardly polite, inwardly primitive middleclass Australians, often with academic backgrounds.

Her two chief poetic protagonists through whose reactions she sifts and analyses both blatant and subtle aspects of a predominantly bourgeois morality are Professor Eisenbart, a middle-aged academic, and Kröte, an aging declassé music teacher. Though in her satirical manner and expert use of the iambic line she may be said to resemble superficially A. D. Hope, the true affinity of her poetry is with the scarifying humour and intricate characterisation of the fiction of Patrick White.

In her first book, simply entitled *Poems*, surrounded by a body of perfectly wrought individual pieces of the calibre of the philosophical "Hesperian," the scathingly witty "Critic's Nightwatch" and the beautiful, compassionate "At the Sea's Edge," is the central sequence "Professor Eisenbart." Here in eight self-contained yet thematically linked poems she depicts the arrogant yet vulnerable professor seduced at a prize-giving concert – "a sage fool trapped / by music in a copper net of hair" – caught napping at a visit to the zoo, lecturing his mistress on elementary physics at the seaside and so on, "Too old to love, too young to die."

Kröte the musician is the central character of her second book *Poems: Volume Two*. He, like Eisenbart, brings a cultured European consciousness to bear on the not-quite-barbarous wilderness of Australian society in the Sixties. In his isolated crises of suffering and near despair he becomes a persona of the poet in a largely unsympathetic environment.

Gwen Harwood's innate love of music sounds throughout her books. Whether she is examining the spectacle of domesticity versus art, as in "Burning Sappho," or poking sophisticated fun at pedantic get-togethers, "Academic Evening" and "Cocktails at Seven," music is invariably invoked as a saving grace and guardian angel of the embattled, non-conforming poet-witness of the contemporary scene.

– Bruce Beaver

HARWOOD, Lee. British. Born in Leicester, 6 June 1939. Educated at state schools; Queen Mary College, London, B.A. (honours) in English 1961. Married to Jud Walker; has one son, Blake. Monumental mason's mate, 1961; library and museum assistant, 1962–64, 1965–66; packer, 1964; assistant, 1966–67, and manager of the poetry department, 1971, Better Books, London; bus conductor, Brighton, 1969; lived in the United States, 1970, 1972–73; Writer-in-Residence, Aegean School of Fine Arts, Paros, Greece, Summer 1971, 1972. Editor, *Night Scene* magazine,

London, 1963; Co-Editor, *Night Train* magazine, London, 1963; Co-Editor, *Horde* magazine, London, 1964; Editor, with Claude Royet-Journoud, *Soho* magazine, London and Paris, 1964; Editor, *Tzarad* magazine, London and Brighton, 1965–69. Since 1973, Co-Editor, *Boston Eagle*. Recipient: Poets Foundation Award (USA), 1966. Address: c/o 9 Highfield Road, Chertsey, Surrey, England.

PUBLICATIONS

Verse

Title Illegible. London, Writers Forum, 1965.
The Man with Blue Eyes. New York, Angel Hair Books, 1966.
The White Room. London, Fulcrum Press, 1968.
The Beautiful Atlas. Brighton, Sussex, Kavanagh, 1969.
Landscapes. London, Fulcrum Press, 1969.
The Sinking Colony. London, Fulcrum Press, 1970.
Penguin Modern Poets 19, with John Ashbery and Tom Raworth. London, Penguin, 1971.
The First Poem. Brighton, Sussex, Unicorn Bookshop, 1971.
New Year. London, Wallrich, 1971.
Captain Harwood's Log of Stern Statements and Stout Sayings. London, Writers Forum, 1973.
H.M.S. Little Fox. London, Oasis Books, 1975.

Recording: *Landscapes,* Stream, 1968.

Other

Translator, *A Poem Sequence,* by Tristan Tzara. Gillingham, Kent, ARC Publications, 1969; revised edition, 1973.
Translator, *Destroyed Days,* by Tristan Tzara. Colchester, Essex, Voiceprint Editions, 1971.
Translator, *Selected Poems,* by Tristan Tzara. London, Trigram Press, 1975.

Critical Studies: Comments by John Ashbery and Ed Dorn on the dust jacket of *The White Room,* 1968; review in *Records and Recording* (London), April 1969; by Raymond Gardiner, in *The Guardian* (London), 8 July 1970; interview with Victor Bockris, in *Pennsylvania Review* (Philadelphia), no. 1, 1970; in *Southern Review* (Baton Rouge, Louisiana), 1971.

Lee Harwood comments:

Schools of poetry seem totally irrelevant today when "new writing" is becoming more and more international, both in its aspirations and its audiences. My explaining my own work would be ridiculous – if one can explain art, why bother to create it? Long live the object – which is common property.

*   *   *

Lee Harwood's work represents an interesting new development in the English poetic tradition. He seems open to both American and French influences. The American influences come not from the Beats or the Black Mountain poets, but from those who are best defined as "School of New York" – the writers who were associated with the Abstract Expressionist painters, the late Frank O'Hara, John Ashbery, and Kenneth Koch. The French ones seem to come from Dada and from Surrealism – Tristan Tzara and Paul Eluard. To this is added what Ashbery has described as "a soft-focus quality" which seems entirely English. Harwood's poems are often constructed to allow the reader several choices of meaning – he enters into the poem, and collaborates with the poet in completing it. The deliberate, rather coat-trailing aestheticism of much of the work is spiced with a sly humour.

– Edward Lucie-Smith

HAYDEN, Robert (Earl). American. Born in Detroit, Michigan, 4 August 1913. Educated at Wayne State University, Detroit, A.B.; University of Michigan, Ann Arbor (Hopwood Award, 1938, 1942), M.A. 1944. Married; has one daughter. Teaching Fellow, University of Michigan, 1944–46; Member of the English Department, Fisk University, Nashville, Tennessee, 1946–68. Visiting Professor, 1968, and since 1969, Professor of English, University of Michigan. Bingham Professor, University of Louisville, Kentucky, Spring 1969; Visiting Poet, University of Washington, Seattle, Summer 1969, University of Connecticut, Storrs, 1971, and Denison University, Granville, Ohio, 1971; Staff Member, Breadloaf Writers Conference, Middlebury, Vermont, 1972. Member, and Poetry Editor, *World Order*, Baha'i Faith. Recipient: Rosenwald Fellowship, 1947; Ford Grant, 1954; World Festival of the Arts Prize, Dakar, Sengal, 1966; Russell Loines Award, 1970. Address: 1201 Gardner Avenue, Ann Arbor, Michigan 48104, U.S.A.

PUBLICATIONS

Verse

Heart-Shape in the Dust.   Detroit, Falcon Press, 1940.
The Lion and the Archer, with Myron O'Higgins.   Nashville, Tennessee, Counterpoise Press, 1948.
Figures of Time: Poems.   Nashville, Tennessee, Hemphill Press, 1955.
A Ballad of Remembrance.   London, Paul Breman, 1962.
Selected Poems.   New York, October House, 1966.
Words in the Mourning Time: Poems.   New York, October House, 1970.
The Night-Blooming Cereus.   London, Paul Breman, 1972.

Recording: *Today's Poets*, with others, Folkways, 1967.

Other

How I Write 1, with Judson Philips and Lawson Carter.   New York, Harcourt Brace, 1972.

Editor, *Kaleidoscope: Poems by American Negro Poets.* New York, Harcourt Brace, 1967.

Editor, with David J. Burrows and Frederick R. Lapides, *Afro-American Literature: An Introduction.* New York, Harcourt Brace, 1971.

Editor, "Modern American Poetry," in *The United States in Literature.* Chicago, Scott Foresman, 1972.

Critical Study: Review by Julius Lester, in *The New York Times Book Review,* 24 January 1971.

Robert Hayden quotes a conversation in *How I Write 1,* 1972:

I write poetry because I prefer it to prose, for one thing. Because, for another, I'm driven, impelled to make patterns of words in the special ways that poetry demands. Maybe whatever it is I'm trying to communicate I can most truthfully express in poems. I think I have other reasons, too. At best, though, I can make only very tentative statements, and they're subject to change without notice. I suppose I could say, with fear of contradicting myself later, that writing poetry is one way I have of coming to grips with both inner and external realities. I also think of my writing as a form of prayer – a prayer for illumination, perfection. No, I'm not satisfied with any of this. It's all beginning to sound pompous, high-falutin, but it's about as close as I can come to an answer. Most poets don't consciously analyze their reasons for being poets anyway. One doesn't choose to be a poet any more than he chooses to be born. If one could answer the question, "Why do you go on living?" then perhaps one could come up with a convincing answer to "Why do you write poetry?"

*   *   *

In his first book, *Heart-Shape in the Dust,* Robert Hayden foreshadowed his later themes. There were poems in the racy language of urban Blacks, like "Bacchanal," poems of personal emotion like "Obituary," written for his father, poems of social imports like "Speech." This book established Hayden's reputation as one of the most promising of the younger poets. His language was simple, colorful, and direct. His fluid verse encompassed the ballad, blank verse, the sonnet, and free verse. His themes covered the personal, the social, local color, and world events. This wide range showed that from the beginning he was "opposed to the doctrinaire and the chauvinistic."

In *The Lion and the Archer* (with Myron O'Higgins) Hayden writes in a denser, more baroque style, abandoning the dialect and colloquialism of his first book. "A Ballad of Remembrance" has a surreal effect, with glittering, whirling, nightmare images. "Homage to the Blues" adds to his pictures of Black life, and like Sterling Brown's "Ma Rainey" was one of the earliest tributes to a specific Black singer. "Magnolias in Snow" is one of his simpler, more direct lyrics, but is moving in its personal emotion.

Hayden's movement toward a more complex poetry was confirmed in *A Ballad of Remembrance,* which won him the grand prize for poetry in English at the first World Festival of Negro Arts at Dakar, Senegal in 1966. The book contained two long poems which are among his finest achievements. "Middle Passage" depicts the horrors of the slave ships and the seizure of the *Amistad* by Cinquez and other captives. "Runagate Runagate" is a narrative of escape from slavery celebrating

Harriet Tubman who led more than three hundred slaves to freedom. In these poems Hayden speaks with varied voices, using compelling rhythms, irony, and allusions.

Selected Poems, Words in the Mourning Time, and *The Night-Blooming Cereus* are his three latest books. All along Hayden has written poems hinting of nightmare and evil, such as "The Wheel," but in *Cereus* the tone of the whole book has this disquieting quality. It is most evident in "Ballad of the True Beast," where the suspicion of the villagers toward two men who had seen a fabled monster and reported it as harmless caused the villagers to persecute the two, and the two men themselves to become bosom enemies.

Hayden's poetry is characterized by flexibility and control of rhythms, sensuous images, a Negro folk quality, and allusiveness. He has written of Negro history and folk lore and also of world events and personal feelings. At times he writes with directness and simplicity as in "Those Winter Mornings," "The Web," and "The Wheel." At other times he writes in a baroque, richly ornamented manner. He has created his own stanza forms with patterns of lines of varying length, in flexible rhythms, unrimed or with imperfect rimes. His best poems are an enduring contribution to American poetry.

– Dudley Randall

HAYS, H(offman) R(eynolds). American. Born in New York City, in 1904. Educated at Cornell University, Ithaca, New York, B.A.; Columbia University, New York, M.A.; University of Liège, Belgium. Married to Juliette Levine; has two children. Acting Head of Drama Department, Fairleigh Dickinson University, Rutherford, New Jersey, 1960–63; Coordinator of the Drama Program, Southampton College, Long Island University, New York, 1965–69. Recipient: Putnam Award, 1964. Address: Box 22, Baiting Hollow Road, East Hampton, New York 11937, U.S.A.

Publications

Verse

Strange City. Boston, Four Seas, 1929.
Selected Poems 1933–1967. San Francisco, Kayak Books, 1968.

Play

Medicine Show, with Oscar Saul, music by Hanns Eisler (produced New York, 1940).

Novels

Stranger on the Highway. Boston, Little Brown, 1943; London, Hale, 1947.
Lie Down in Darkness. New York, Reynal, 1944; London, Hale, 1948.

The Takers of the City. New York, Reynal, 1946; London, Sampson Low Marston, 1947.
The Envoys. New York, Crown, 1953.

Other

From Ape to Angel: An Informal History of Social Anthropology. New York, Knopf, 1958; London, Methuen, 1959.
In the Beginnings: Early Man and His Gods. New York, Putnam, 1963.
The Kingdom of Hawaii. Greenwich, Connecticut, New York Graphic Society, 1964.
The Dangerous Sex: The Myth of Feminine Evil. New York, Putnam, 1964; London, Methuen, 1966.
Charley Sang a Song, with Daniel Hays. New York, Harper, 1964.
Explorers of Man: Five Pioneers in Anthropology. New York, Crowell Collier, 1971.
Birds, Beasts, and Men: A Humanistic History of Zoology. New York, Putnam, 1972; London, Dent, 1973.

Editor and Translator, *12 Spanish American Poets: An Anthology.* New Haven, Connecticut, Yale University Press, 1943.

Translator, *The Trial of Lucullus: A Play for Radio,* by Bertolt Brecht. New York, New Directions, 1943; in *Plays of Brecht,* London, Methuen, 1960.
Translator, *Selected Poems of Bertolt Brecht.* New York, Reynal, 1947.
Translator, *The Selected Writings of Juan Ramón Jiménez.* New York, Farrar Straus, 1957.
Translator, *The Selected Poems of Jorge Carrera Andrade.* New York, New York University Press, 1972.

Critical Studies: by Millen Brand and Allen Planz, in "H. R. Hays Issue" of *Voyages* (Washington, D.C.), Winter 1969.

H. R. Hays comments:

I don't use "verse forms," don't have characteristic subjects, belong on the whole to the generation which developed out of imagism after William Carlos Williams, Pound, Eliot, etc. I suppose W. C. Williams, Latin-American and French surrealism are the chief influences. My poetry adds up to an autobiography of my reactions to the world in which I have found myself.

                    *   *   *

H. R. Hays is one of the hidden poets of America. I say hidden because, beyond his reputation as the author of some books on anthropology for the general reader, his most widely known appearance as a poet occurs in his role as translator, a role in which he must *seem* to be invisible or transparent, subordinating himself to the effort of transmittimg another man's poetry. His endeavors in this area have been exemplary and influential. The recently reissued *12 Spanish American Poets,* originally published in 1943 and difficult to obtain, has been acknowledged by such poets as James Wright, David Ignatow, and Robert Bly as an important discovery for them in terms of their own art. Hays' volumes of Brecht and Jiménez translations are likewise highly regarded.

Accomplished translating of this sort is, of course, a poetic achievement, a genuine literary contribution to the language; but Hays is a fine poet in his own right as well. His selected work of thirty-four years, gathered in a small, handsome book, reveals a poetry that is subtle, meditative, often calm, full of the closest observation of objects, the life of nature, and seasonal change: ". . . the iris blades / Emerge / Sharp, green, / From old trash, / Warm with / Secret life." Throughout his work there is evident a deep sense of history and its ironies, of social and political injustice, of the failures and delusions of modern life. Like the Latin American poets he admires, Hays speaks out on these matters, sometimes in direct fashion, at other times in an exaggerated irrational mode appropriate to the realities he must cope with. Recurrently one encounters – particularly, though not exclusively, in later poems – an infusion of elements of the mysterious, the dreamlike, the surreal:

> Oh there are marvels in the souls of children –
> Prophetic insects, stones that grow. They see
> Life in a drowned hair
> And know that death flies into rooms
> On a bird's wings.

Writing in a manner both precise and perceptive, Hays has produced a number of handsome and moving poems which deserve the attention of more readers.

– Ralph J. Mills, Jr.

HAZO, Samuel (John). American. Born in Pittsburgh, Pennsylvania, 19 July 1928. Educated at Notre Dame University, Indiana, (Mitchell Award, 1948), B.A. (magna cum laude) 1948; Duquesne University, Pittsburgh, M.A. 1955; University of Pittsburgh, Ph.D. 1957. Served in the United States Marine Corps, 1950–53. Married to Mary Anne Sarkis; has one son. Instructor, Shady Side Academy, 1953–55. Since 1955, Member of the English Department, Dean of the College of Arts and Sciences, 1961–66, and since 1965, Professor of English, Duquesne University. Visiting Professor, University of Detroit, 1968. Since 1966, Director, International Poetry Forum, Pittsburgh. Contributing Editor, *Mundus Artium* magazine, Athens, Ohio; Poetry Editor, *America*, Washington, D.C. United States State Department Lecturer in the Middle East and Greece, 1965, in Jamaica, 1966. Recipient: Pro Helvetia Foundation grant (Switzerland), 1971. D.Litt.: Seton Hill College, Greensburg, Pennsylvania, 1965. Address: 785 Somerville Drive, Pittsburgh, Pennsylvania 15243, U.S.A.

PUBLICATIONS

Verse

Discovery and Other Poems. New York, Sheed and Ward, 1959.
The Quiet Wars. New York, Sheed and Ward, 1962.

Listen with the Eye, photographs by James P. Blair.   Pittsburgh, University of
   Pittsburgh Press, 1964.
My Sons in God: Selected and New Poems.   Pittsburgh, University of Pittsburgh
   Press, 1965.
Blood Rights.   Pittsburgh, University of Pittsburgh Press, 1968.
The Blood of Adonis, with Adonis (Ali Ahmed Said).   Pittsburgh, University of
   Pittsburgh Press, 1971.
Twelve Poems, with George Nama.   Pittsburgh, Byblos Press, 1972.
Seascript: A Mediterranean Logbook.   Pittsburgh, Byblos Press, 1972.
Once for the Last Bandit: New and Previous Poems.   Pittsburgh, University of
   Pittsburgh Press, 1972.
Quartered.   Pittsburgh, University of Pittsburgh Press, 1974.
Inscripts.   Pittsburgh, Byblos Press, 1975.

Other

Hart Crane: An Introduction and Interpretation.   New York, Barnes and Noble,
   1963.

Editor, *The Christian Intellectual: Studies in the Relation of Catholicism to the
   Human Sciences.*   Pittsburgh, Duquesne University Press, 1963.
Editor, *A Selection of Contemporary Religious Poetry.*   Glen Rock, New Jersey,
   Paulist Press, 1963.

Critical Study: "Swimming in Sharkwater: The Poetry of Samuel Hazo" by R. H.
W. Dillard, in *Hollins Critic* (Hollins College, Virginia), February 1969.

Samuel Hazo comments:

Suffice it to say that I regard poetry as the best form of conversation with largely
unknown readers or hearers whose answer is hopefully their attention and assent.
The rest is for critics to discover and evaluate.

*   *   *

Samuel Hazo's first two collections, *Discovery* and *The Quiet Wars,* introduced a
meditative Christian poet concerned with the tough and enduring realities of death
and suffering. He displayed the technical mastery necessary to avoid portentousness and unearned statement; his style is at once traditional and colloquial – that of
a thinking modern man's believable metrical utterance.
Listen with the Eye, a small collection of poems with accompanying photographs
by James Blair, involves a technical departure of some importance; many of the
poems are cast in a strongly iambic free verse. The result is not so much rhythmic
freedom as it is a stronger sense of the weight of each line. This quality distinguishes the new poems of *My Sons in God,* a collection of new and selected earlier
poems in which the union of style and theme marks the arrival of an important
American poet. Among the new poems is a group of "transpositions" from the
Arabic of Ahmed Ali Said, the contemporary Lebanese poet; here again this fresh
technical influence brings to Hazo's own poems an additional firmness of line. A
larger selection of Said's poems, *The Blood of Adonis,* appeared in 1971.

Once for the Last Bandit: New and Previous Poems hones down the selection of early poems which appeared in *My Sons in God;* it includes generous selections from that book and from *Blood Rights.* Nearly half of the book is given over to the title sequence, a group of poems having some qualities of a journal, or as Hazo calls it, "an almanac of a penman in transit." The sinuous, heavily iambic free verse is a genuine new direction for Hazo; while his themes of loss, God, and persistence are still central, a larger variety of starting points and tones has become available to this very resourceful, still vitally developing poet.

– Henry Taylor

HEANEY, Seamus. Irish. Born in County Derry, 13 April 1939. Educated at St. Columb's College, Derry; Queen's University, Belfast, B.A. (honours) in English. Married; has two sons. Secondary School Teacher, 1962–63; Lecturer, St. Joseph's College of Education, Belfast, 1963–66. Since 1966, Lecturer in English, Queen's University. Recipient: Eric Gregory Award, 1966; Cholmondeley Award, 1967; Geoffrey Faber Memorial Prize, 1968; Maugham Award, 1968; Denis Devlin Memorial Award, 1973. Address: 16 Ashley Avenue, Belfast 9, Northern Ireland.

PUBLICATIONS

Verse

> *Eleven Poems.* Belfast, Festival Publications, 1965.
> *Death of a Naturalist.* London, Faber, and New York, Oxford University Press, 1966.
> *Room to Rhyme,* with Dairo Hammond and Michael Longley. Belfast, Arts Council of Northern Ireland, 1968.
> *A Lough Neagh Sequence.* Manchester, Phoenix Pamphlet Poets Press, 1969.
> *Door into the Dark.* London, Faber, and New York, Oxford University Press, 1969.
> *Night Drive: Poems.* Crediton, Devon, Gilbertson, 1970.
> *Boy Driving His Father to Confession.* Frensham, Surrey, Sceptre Press, 1970.
> *Land.* London, Poem-of-the-Month Club, 1971.
> *Wintering Out.* London, Faber, 1972; New York, Oxford University Press, 1973.

Other

> Editor, with Alan Brownjohn and Jon Stallworthy, *New Poems 1970–1971.* London, Hutchinson, 1971.
> Editor, *Soundings 2.* Belfast, Blackstaff Press, 1974.

*　　*　　*

Seamus Heaney has attracted considerable attention with his volume entitled *Death of a Naturalist*, in which he writes of his boyhood spent on a farm in Northern Ireland. His poems are strong, accurate in observation, and concentrated:

> Between my finger and my thumb
> The squat pen rests.
> I'll dig with it.

The poems express boyish wonder, curiosity and affright. The curious title of the book comes from a poem about the invasion of a flax-dam by a hoard of frogs:

> The great slime kings
> Were gathered there for vengeance and I knew
> That if I dipped my hand the spawn would clutch it.

Imaginative terror is expressed as effectively in "Personal Helicon," which describes a youngster staring into a deep well, and the poem ends in subtle symbolism:

> Now, to pry into roots, to finger slime,
> To stare big-eyed Narcissus, into some spring
> Is beneath all adult dignity. I rhyme
> To see myself, to set the darkness echoing.

In "Follower" we see the child following his father as he guides the horse-plough:

> I stumbled in his hob-nailed wake,
> Fell sometimes on the polished sod;
> Sometimes he rode me on his back
> Dipping and rising to his plod.

In contrast we have "At a Potato Digging," in which labourers swarm after a mechanical digger as it "Spins up a dark shower of roots and mould." Typical of Mr. Heaney's felicity of phrase is this couplet from a poem about turkeys:

> He lorded it on the claw-flecked mud
> With a grey flick of his Confucian eye.

In recent poems Mr. Heaney has turned for his themes to the south-west coast. In poems about Gallarus Oratory and the abandonded Blasket Islands he evokes folk traditions and ancient piety.

– Austin Clarke

HEATH-STUBBS, John (Francis Alexander). British. Born in London, 9 July 1918. Educated at Queen's College, Oxford, B.A. (honours) in English 1942, M.A. 1972. English teacher, Hall School, Hampstead, London, 1944–45; Editorial Assistant, Hutchinson and Company, publishers, London, 1945–46. Gregory Fellow in Poetry, Leeds University, 1952–55; Visiting Professor of English, University of Alexandria, Egypt, 1955–58, and the University of Michigan, Ann Arbor, 1960–61. Lecturer in English, College of St. Mark and St. John, London, 1963–72. Recipient:

Arts Council bursary, 1965; Queen's Gold Medal for Poetry, 1974. Fellow, Royal Society of Literature, 1953. Address: 35 Sutherland Place, London W.2, England.

PUBLICATIONS

Verse

Wounded Thammuz. London, Routledge, 1942.
Beauty and the Beast. London, Routledge, 1943.
The Divided Ways. London, Routledge, 1947.
The Charity of the Stars. New York, Sloane, 1949.
The Swarming of the Bees. London, Eyre and Spottiswoode, 1950.
A Charm Against the Toothache. London, Methuen, 1954.
The Triumph of the Muse and Other Poems. London, Oxford University Press, 1958.
The Blue-Fly in His Head: Poems. London, Oxford University Press, 1962.
Selected Poems. London, Oxford University Press, 1965.
Satires and Epigrams. London, Turret Books, 1968.
Artorius. Providence, Rhode Island, Burning Deck, 1970; London, Enitharmon Press, 1973.
Penguin Modern Poets 20, with F. T. Prince and Stephen Spender. London, Penguin, 1971.
Indifferent Weather: Occasional Poems. London, Ian McKelvie, 1975.

Plays

The Talking Ass (produced London, 1953). Included in *Helen in Egypt and Other Plays,* 1958.
Helen in Egypt and Other Plays (includes *The Talking Ass, The Harrowing of Hell*). London, Oxford University Press, 1958.

Other

The Darkling Plain: A Study of the Later Fortunes of Romanticism in English Poetry from George Darley to W. B. Yeats. London, Eyre and Spottiswoode, 1950.
Charles Williams. London, Longman, 1955.
The Verse Satire. London, Oxford University Press, 1969.
The Ode. London, Oxford University Press, 1969.
The Pastoral. London, Oxford University Press, 1969.

Editor, *Selected Poems of Shelley.* London, Falcon Press, 1947.
Editor, *Selected Poems of Tennyson.* London, Falcon Press, 1947.
Editor, *Selected Poems of Swift.* London, Falcon Press, 1947.
Editor, with David Wright, *The Forsaken Garden: An Anthology of Poetry 1824–1909.* London, Lehmann, 1950.
Editor, *Images of Tomorrow: An Anthology of Recent Poetry.* London, SCM Press, 1953.
Editor, with David Wright, *The Faber Book of Twentieth Century Verse: An Anthology of Verse in Britain 1900–1950.* London, Faber, 1953; revised edition, 1965, 1975.

Editor, *Selected Poems of Alexander Pope.* London, Heinemann, 1964; New York, Barnes and Noble, 1966.
Editor, with Martin Green, *Homage to George Barker on His 60th Birthday.* London, Martin Brian and O'Keeffe, 1973.

Translator, *Poems from Giocomo Leopardi.* London, Lehmann, 1946.
Translator, *Aphrodite's Garland.* London, Crescendo Press, 1952.
Translator, with Peter Avery, *Thirty Poems of Hafiz of Shiraz.* London, Murray, 1955.
Translator, with Iris Origo, *Selected Poetry and Prose,* by Giacomo Leopardi. London, Oxford University Press, 1966; New York, New American Library, 1967.
Translator, *The Horn/Le Cor,* by Alfred de Vigny. Richmond, Surrey, Keepsake Press, 1969.

Critical Studies: *Poetry and Personal Responsibility* by George Every, London, SCM Press, 1948; "John Heath-Stubbs: A Poet in Alexandria" by Shafik Megally, in *Cairo Bulletin of English Studies,* 1959; *The Price of an Eye* by Thomas Blackburn, London, Longman, and New York, Morrow, 1961; *Rule and Energy* by John Press, London, Oxford University Press, 1963.

John Heath-Stubbs comments:

Influenced at Oxford by teaching of C. S. Lewis and Charles Williams; also by friendship with fellow undergraduate poets Sidney Keyes, Drummond Allison, and William Bell.

*   *   *

There is a certain Byzantine quality in much of John Heath-Stubbs' poetry. An encyclopaedic knowledge of past cultures and a continual application of this knowledge is reminiscent of Byzantium. It is significant that Heath-Stubbs wrote a poem about Alexandria, that other great centre of Hellenistic and early Christian culture. "Alexandria" is, significantly, the longest poem in *The Swarming of the Bees.* The poem summarizes much of Heath-Stubbs' early poetry. It displays his use of a rather recondite knowledge of myth and legend and his blending of the humanistic and Christian traditions, and it demonstrates his highly sophisticated, stylized technique. His preference for the past is also revealed: the poet carries his account of Alexandria down only to early Christian times.

Heath-Stubbs is a poet of the modern city as well. In *A Charm Against the Toothache,* the megalopolis is modern London. In the same volume the poet begins to speak in his own voice. "Poem after Solstice" is a reaction to the termination of an unfortunate and unsatisfactory love; and in "Address Not Known," more direct and conversational, a failure of earthly love is revealed. In Heath-Stubbs' poetry there is a continual contrast between the *civitas dei* and the *civitas mundi,* divine love and earthly love.

Yet it would be erroneous to assume that his early poems were mere exercises in virtuosity, while the later poetry alone reveals the artist's private experience. Heath-Stubbs has been labelled a neo-Romantic on the basis of early poems, such as some of those included in *The Divided Ways.* One of the poems in *The Divided Ways,* "The Hill," is an account of a profoundly personal religious experience. The hill of the title is a spiritual vantage point, perhaps associated with Golgotha, where the protagonist is dissolved by the heat of the sun. This heat, at first suggestive of the justice of God, eventually proves to be his Love, but not before the speaker has undergone a profound change accompanied by fear and suffering.

John Heath-Stubbs' poetry is conspicuous for its erudition; its technical virtuosity, partly dependent upon the poet's sensitive musical ear; and a strong critical sense that is especially evident in his satire. He is at his best when he is using his sense of history and his moral sensitivity to reveal the shoddiness of modernity.

– John Van Domelen

HECHT, Anthony (Evan). American. Born in New York City, 16 January 1923. Educated at Bard College, Annandale-on-Hudson, New York, B.A. 1944; Columbia University, New York, M.A. 1950. Served in the United States Army during World War II. Married Patricia Harris in 1954 (divorced, 1961); Helen D'Alessandro, 1971; has two sons, Jason and Adam. Taught at Kenyon College, Gambier, Ohio, 1947; University of Iowa, Iowa City, 1948; New York University, 1959; Smith College, Northampton, Massachusetts, 1956–59; Bard College, 1962–67. Since 1967, Member of the English Department, State University of New York, Rochester. Hurst Professor, Washington University, St. Louis, 1971. Recipient: American Academy in Rome Fellowship, 1951; Guggenheim Fellowship, 1954, 1959; *Hudson Review* Fellowship, 1958; Ford Fellowship, for drama, 1960, for verse, 1968; Brandeis University Creative Arts Award, 1964; Rockefeller Fellowship, 1967; Loines Award, 1968; Pulitzer Prize, 1968; Academy of American Poets Fellowship, 1969. Chancellor, Academy of American Poets, 1971. Member, National Institute of Arts and Letters. Address: 19 East Boulevard, Rochester, New York 14610, U.S.A.

PUBLICATIONS

Verse

A Summoning of Stones. New York, Macmillan, 1954.
The Seven Deadly Sins: Poems. Northampton, Massachusetts, Gehenna Press, 1958.
Struwwelpeter. Northampton, Massachusetts, Gehenna Press, 1958.
The Hard Hours: Poems. New York, Atheneum, and London, Oxford University Press, 1967.
Aesopic: Twenty Four Couplets. . . . Northampton, Massachusetts, Gehenna Press, 1967.

Other

Editor, with John Hollander, *Jiggery-Pokery: A Compendium of Double Dactyls.* New York, Atheneum, 1967.

Translator, with Helen Bacon, *Seven Against Thebes*, by Aeschylus. New York, Oxford University Press, 1973.

*   *   *

It is strange to confront a contemporary who actually admits God. Anthony Hecht believes not only in Jehovah, but in Satan. His poems question not the existence of Evil and Death, but their perpetuation before an allegedly Just and hopefully Merciful God. Hecht has a powerful sense of death, and as poet he renders Death more immediate, nearer than Life; with his old Jew, "He is saying a prayer for all whom this room shall kill."

There are a classic intensity and expansiveness in his poems. At best the distant voice also achieves a profound personal, but never incredible, honesty. His is the kind of poem many have tried to "make," usually through some "revolutionary" technique which affects one more as a mistake than a mode. Hecht's poetry is not "revolutionary"; he works squarely within tradition.

It would be as impossible as undesirable to escape the consciousness of antiquity. Poems are titled to Jason and Adam (who, while they *are* the poet's sons, rely on their mythic namesakes for poetic existence); *Seven Deadly Sins* focused on nearly-medieval, sometimes epigrammatic, descriptions of the archetype sins, with accompanying woodcuts.

Hecht's technique is traditional. He is fond of the narrative element, the decasyllabic line, and in general works unabashedly, audibly with accentual-syllabic verse. He even writes sonnets, and without the euphemisms of elaborate typography or convoluted structure.

What is noteworthy is not Hecht's control of the conventions – many have shown their ability at "exercises" – or even his probable refusal to let the conventions control *him*. Rather, one notices the form, the craft or ingenuity not at all and senses the mode of the poem is not only transparent, but inevitable.

Hecht's poems especially achieve impact through unexpected juxtapositions of imagery, clashes which spark new imaginings for the reader. In the poem "Jason" the untouchable myth in golden rooms of the reader's imagination is suddenly destroyed:

> Dream how a little boy alone
> With a wooden sword and the top of a garbage can
> Triumphs in gardens full of marigold.

At times, especially in *The Hard Hours*, Hecht can bespeak the entire horror of the Jewish experience; or again, the vision is the personal, and at its poetic best, timeless experience of dying. The mode of the poems arises, finally and appropriately, with the energy and voice of Old Testament prophecy, the product of a vision which is at once confessional and cultural.

– Joseph Wilson

HELWIG, David (Gordon). Canadian. Born in Toronto, Ontario, 5 April 1938. Educated at the University of Toronto, B.A. 1960; University of Liverpool, M.A.

1962. Married Nancy Keeling in 1959; has two children. Assistant Professor of English, Queen's University, Kingston, Ontario. Address: 73 Baiden Street, Kingston, Ontario, Canada.

PUBLICATIONS

Verse

    Figures in a Landscape.   Ottawa, Oberon Press, 1967.
    The Sign of the Gunman.   Ottawa, Oberon Press, 1969.
    The Best Name of Silence.   Ottawa, Oberon Press, 1972.

Play

    A Time in Winter (produced Kingston, Ontario, 1967).   Included in *Figures in a Landscape*, 1967.

Novel

    The Day Before Tomorrow.   Ottawa, Oberon Press, 1971.

Short Stories

    The Streets of Summer.   Ottawa, Oberon Press, 1969.

Other

    A Book about Billie (documentary).   Ottawa, Oberon Press, 1972.

    Editor, with Tom Marshall, *Fourteen Stories High: Best Canadian Stories of 71.*   Ottawa, Oberon Press, 1971.
    Editor, with Joan Harcourt, *72, 73, and 74: New Canadian Stories.*   Ottawa, Oberon Press, 3 vols., 1972–74.

Critical Study: "Spells Against Chaos" by Tom Marshall, in *Quarry* (Kingston, Ontario), Spring 1968.

*   *   *

    David Helwig's recent muse is more violent, blacker, and more political than that of his early poetry. It is not a development that seems congenial to his strengths. In the poetry of *The Sign of the Gunman* there are a curious stridency and rhetorical pose that seem artificial and laboured:

        They are burning our cities
        They are shooting at us with bullets.

This is not great poetry. It is not even good, and it goes hand in hand with occasional distasteful revelling in sutures and seared flesh that reminds one of nothing so much as Tom Lehrer:

> Somewhere is a photograph
> of a man in two pieces
> burned until he is only
> two pieces of a cooked man.

When the violence is necessary to greatness, as it is in "Apollo and Daphne," it is right and felt as a right conclusion to the poem. Helwig, however, does not escape the fasionable Canadian taste for Frye-esque mythology where Harlequin and the acrobat, like the Zeus of his "Metamorphosis," appear to stand for more than they are, gesturing for significance.

Fortunately the strength of his early poetry is present even in his more recent work – a strength that owes much to a fine-edged description that is like the Wyeth he admires. There is something of the Pacific North-West School (William Stafford for instance) in Helwig's "Still Life" or "Sunday Breakfast":

> Orange, one egg, tea in a cup
> of blue and white, composing silences
> against the hurt nerves fluttering.

This affection for the familial and the domestic is never sentimental though, never McKuenized. A classic of toughness is his poem "A Shaker Chair":

> I see in the Shaker rocking chair
> stillness turning, stillness moving,
> contemplation and silent standing,
> even the denial of the body.

Occasionally too one senses Helwig's debt to the impressionist transformation of simple painterly objects into a larger life, a debt that gives us echoes of Stevens:

> We swim before we walk. The tropic sea
> within the caul is home.

Certainly the inflexions are Stevens's and they are congenial to an attractive toughness in the verse that saves Helwig's taste for darkness, secrecy, night and their magic from being mere fantasy.

Like many Canadian artists Helwig seemed to find his voice abroad. Liverpool nurtured him and in his best poems one hears not the Mersey sound or poets but the voices of "the old women / climbing Brownlow Hill / in the killing fog" that he celebrates in "Liverpool."

In the best of his poetry there is a fine sense of detachment. That is why his poems on Diefenbaker, the Orange Lodge, and American political issues are so weak. His spontaneous emotion is too close to their creation. The picture one retains of him is of a distant walker, a figure in his own landscape, above the world he deplores and celebrates – the world he describes in "Christmas, 1965" in which "Silence / had overwhelmed the noise of men" leaving only the poet's voice.

– D. D. C. Chambers

HENDERSON, Hamish. British. Born in Blairgowrie, Perthshire, Scotland, 11 November 1919. Educated at Blairgowrie High School; Dulwich College, London; Downing College, Cambridge, M.A. Served with the Highland Division during World War II. Married; has two daughters. Since 1951, Lecturer and Research Fellow, School of Scottish Studies, Edinburgh University. Recipient: Maugham Award, 1949. Lives in Edinburgh.

PUBLICATIONS

Verse

Elegies for the Dead in Cyrenaica. London, Lehmann, 1948.
Freedom Come-All-Ye, in Chapbook special issue (Aberdeen), iii, 6, 1967.

Other

Editor, and Contributor, Ballads of World War II Collected by Seumas Mor Maceanruig. Glasgow, Caledonian Press, 1947.

Critical Study: The Poet Speaks, edited by Peter Orr, London, Routledge, and New York, Barnes and Noble, 1966.

*   *   *

Hamish Henderson's one book of verse, Elegies for the Dead in Cyrenaica, was published as long ago as 1948; and was the product of the desert war which inspired so much of the best English poetry of World War II, including that of Keith Douglas. Appearing when it did, it tended to miss the tide of interest in "war poetry" which had been nourished by the conflict itself. The fact that the author has never produced another collection has also not aided his reputation. Yet Henderson has always had a small band of admirers, and re-reading his elegies it is easy to see why.

The book has two advantages – it can be read complete, as a whole, not just as a collection of poems written in different moods and on different occasions; and it has a comfortable relationship to the modernist tradition (something more likely to happen with Scottish poets than with English ones). Henderson was obviously much influenced by the Eliot of Four Quartets – it was difficult not to be, at that period; that is, if one hadn't succumbed to the influences of Dylan Thomas or Edith Sitwell. But one also hears within his work the voices of Europe – Goethe and Hölderlin, who supply him with epigraphs; and the Alexandrian Greek, Cavafy, whom he quotes. The poems are that comparatively rare thing in 20th century English poetry – successful philosophical verse.

He combines this philosophical bent with a delicate naturalism, and a skilful control of tone, which means that these comparatively long poems can rise up into the "high" style and leave it again without difficulty, just as the author requires. Here is an example, from the beginning of the Second Elegy:

At dawn, under the concise razor-edge
of the escarpment, the laager sleeps. No petrol fires yet
blow flame for brew-up. Up on the pass a sentry
inhales his Nazionale. Horse-shoe-curve of the bay
grows visible beneath him. He smokes and yawns.
Ooo-augh,
                  and the limitless
shabby lion-pelt of the desert completes and rounds
his limitless ennui.

One suspects, at a distance of more than a quarter of a century, that this is the
kind of war-time verse most likely to last and be read by posterity.

– Edward Lucie-Smith

HENDRIKS, A(rthur) L(emière). Jamaican. Born in Kingston, 17 April 1922
Educated at Jamaica College; Ottershaw College, Surrey, England. Married Gisela
Schiffers in 1969; has four children. Clerk, Arthur Hendricks Furniture Company,
Jamaica, 1940–50; Sales Manager, Radio Jamaica Ltd., 1950–60; General Manager,
Jamaica Broadcasting Corporation, 1961–64; Caribbean Director, Thomas Televi-
sion Ltd., London, 1964–71. Since 1971, Free-lance Writer. Address: Box 1360,
Hamilton, Bermuda; or, c/o 85 Caledonian Road, London N.1, England.

PUBLICATIONS

Verse

On This Mountain and Other Poems.   London, Deutsch, 1965.
These Green Islands.   Kingston, Jamaica, Bolivar Press, 1971.
Muet.   London, Outposts Publications, 1971.
Madonna of the Unknown Nation.   London, Workshop Press, 1974.

Other

Editor, with Cedric Lindo, The Independence Anthology of Jamaican
Literature.   Kingston, Jamaica, Arts Celebration Committee of the Ministry
of Development, 1962.

*   *   *

A. L. Hendriks is one of perhaps a half dozen impressive contemporary West
Indian poets. His poetry is less agitated by themes of race, alienation and identity
than is much West Indian writing, and the impression his poems make on the
reader is that they are the private meditations of a delicate soul. There is a certain

671

sobriety in his idiom, a coolness in approach, and a feeling of control and tranquility. His tone is subdued, his voice without stridency or affectation; the rhythms are
quiet and they engage the person or subject in a private way. Some of his best
poems join sympathy for a particular place, a sense of its quality and particularity,
with a capacity for attentive listening. The poetry seems to me to be a mode of
intimate access to some truth of experience not yet articulated, not yet quite held:

> This thin and oval stone, cold upon the brown earth,
> is not dumb, nor is the grass, nor the curved stick
> lying smooth by the brook's edge; you may listen
> and through the unapparent sense learn from them
> a new music, secret, and played on no instrument.

In some of his poems, for example "Song for My Brothers and Cousins" and
"On This Mountain," Hendriks is troubled out of his secluded world and contemplative posture:

> We no longer belong to a private
> society and cannot hide
> private misdemeanours, we are
> one people in one house and cannot leave it.

The idea trembling on the edge in this stanza is never brought to the passionate
explicitness that it would have in the verse of Edward Brathwaite, for example.
Indeed, the feeling, even in his more public poems, is less torn and troubled. It has,
on the other hand, an unaffected inward dignity, of the kind that is to be seen in
his restrained but sensitive relish for the old in "An Old Jamaican Woman Thinks
about the Hereafter":

> What would I do forever in a big place, who
> have lived all my life in a small island?
> The same parish holds the cottage I was born in, all
> my family, and the cool churchyard.

In all of Hendriks's poetry we find a sensibility which thrives on smallness,
coolness, and a fine human simplicity.

– William Walsh

HENRI, Adrian (Maurice). British. Born in Birkenhead, Cheshire, 10 April 1932.
Educated at St. Asaph Grammar School, North Wales, 1945–51; King's College,
Newcastle, B.A. (honours) in fine arts 1955. Married Joyce Wilson in 1958 (sepa-
rated). Lecturer, Manchester College of Art and Design, 1961–64, and Liverpool
College of Art, 1964–68. Member of the Liverpool Scene, poetry-rock group,
1968–70, American tour, 1969. Painter: Exhibitions in Liverpool, 1962, 1965, 1968;
Biennale della Giovane Pintura, Milan, 1968; One-Man Show, Institute of Contem-
porary Arts, London, 1968. Since 1970, full-time writer, singer, and painter, with
occasional work with Grimms, and Henri and Friends groups. Recipient: Arts
Council of Northern Ireland prize, for painting, 1964; John Moore Exhibition Prize,

1972. Agents: (literary) Deborah Rogers, 29 Goodge Street, London W.1; (performance) Alan Cottam Entertainments, 65 Renshaw Street, Liverpool 1, Lancashire. Address: 21 Mount Street, Liverpool L1 9HD, Lancashire, England.

PUBLICATIONS

Verse

The Mersey Sound: Penguin Modern Poets 10, with Roger McGough and Brian Patten. London, Penguin, 1967.
Tonight at Noon. London, Rapp and Whiting, 1968; New York, McKay, 1969.
City. London, Rapp and Whiting, 1969.
Talking after Christmas Blues, music by Wallace Southam. London, Turret Books, 1969.
Poems for Wales and Six Landscapes for Susan. Gillingham, Kent, ARC Publications, 1970.
Autobiography. London, Cape, 1971.
America. London, Turret Books, 1972.

Recordings: (with Liverpool Scene) *St. Adrian Co., Broadway and 3rd*, RCA, 1970; *Heirloon*, RCA, 1970; *Recollections*, Charisma, 1972; (solo) *Adrian Henri*, Canon, 1974; *Autobiography*, Canon, 2 records, 1974.

Plays

I Wonder: A Guillaume Apollinaire Show, with Michael Kustow (produced London, 1968).

Television Play: *Yesterday's Girl*, 1973.

Novel

I Want, with Nell Dunn. London, Cape, 1972.

Other

Environments and Happenings. London, Thames and Hudson, 1974; as *Total Art: Environments, Happenings, and Performances*, New York, Praeger, 1974.

Guest Editor, *The Poetry Review* (London), Spring 1971.

Critical Study: "Notes on Painting and Poetry" by the author, in *Tonight at Noon*, 1968.

Adrian Henri comments:

(1970) I was trained as a painter and still paint and exhibit paintings. I make a living primarily by performing the works that I write, mostly with music. I think of myself as a maker, and presenter, of images in various media. "Pop Poet" is, I think, the most common label.

My major influences are T. S. Eliot, Apollinaire, Mallarmé, Ginsberg, Olson and recently Tennyson, Creeley and Hugh MacDiarmid; also the prose of Joyce and William Burroughs. I am an autobiographical poet: my poems are extensions of my own life, some fact, some fantasy. For this reason I write perhaps more love-poems than anything else. I am excited by new uses of language in the mass-media, like TV commercials or pop songs, and am only interested in "older" verse-forms (i.e. rhyme, etc.) as they survive in modern society, e.g. ballad and particularly Blues. I would like my poems to be read by as many people as possible, since I can't see any point either personally or politically in writing for an elite minority. I think by doing readings and by working with the "Liverpool Scene" I am beginning to reach a bigger and largely "non-literary" audience.

(1974) Since a serious heart illness in 1970 my way of life, and to some extent my way of working, has changed somewhat. At the moment my poetry is perhaps quieter and more "traditional" in character. Since spending some time in Somerset and Shropshire I have become interested in the English landscape tradition, notably Wordsworth and Housman, and the Pre-Raphaelite painters. My work as a painter is similarly involved in an investigation into the possibilities of landscape.

*   *   *

Adrian Henri is perhaps the most "typical" of the Liverpool pop-poets because of the way in which he mixes topical references, material drawn from pop-songs and from jazz, and a wide range of references to modern painting and the Modern Movement in general. These are made to relate to personal experience and the poet's own immediate context and the result appeals by its directness, gentleness and honesty. From the technical point of view Henri's poetry is interesting because it tries to make use of techniques derived both from jazz and from the procedures of contemporary painting – there is a lot of "verbal collage," for example. Particularly characteristic are the lists of objects and images which ultimately derive from Whitman, but which the poet seems to feel are representative of the fragmentary nature of contemporary experience.

– Edward Lucie-Smith

HEPPENSTALL, Rayner.   British.   Born in Huddersfield, Yorkshire, 27 July 1911. Educated locally and at the Collège Sophie-Berthelot, Calais, France, 1928; University of Leeds, Yorkshire, 1929–33, B.A. 1932; University of Strasbourg, France, 1931. Served in the Royal Artillery and the Royal Army Pay Corps, 1940–45. Married Margaret Edwards in 1937; has two children and five grandchildren. Schoolmaster, Eastbrook Senior Boys' School, Dagenham, Essex, 1934; Free-lance Writer, 1935–39. Producer, Features and Drama Department, BBC Radio, London, 1945–67. Recipient: Arts Council Novel Prize, 1966. Address: 31 Churton Street, London, S.W.1, England.

Publications

Verse

First Poems. London, Heinemann, 1935.
Sebastian. London, Dent, 1937.
Proems: An Anthology of Poems, with others. London, Fortune Press, 1938.
Blind Men's Flowers Are Green. London, Secker and Warburg, 1940.
Poems 1933–1945. London, Secker and Warburg, 1947.

Plays

The Fool's Saga, in Three Tales of Hamlet, with Michael Innes. London,
  Gollancz, 1950.
A Clean Break, and Daily Bread, adaptations of plays by Jules Renard (pro-
  duced Mull, Scotland, 1969).

Radio Plays and Dramatized Documentaries: The Death of a Prophet, The Rising
in the North, and The Battle for St. David's, in the early 1950's; The Green Bay
Tree, adaptation of novel by Paul Desjardins, 1960; The Generations, 1961;
Renard, 1961; The Literate Killer, 1968; Vautrin (four parts), based on works by
Balzac, 1969; The General's Daughter, 1969; A Pretty Liar, 1971; Dr. Satan,
1971; A Tidy Little Man, 1972; The Case of Eugene Weidmann, 1972; The Murder
of Jean Jaures, 1972; The Trial of Eugene Aram, 1974; Axel, with James Laver,
adaptation of the work by Villiers de l'Isle Adam; and others.

Television Plays: The Seventh Juror, 1972; The Bells, 1974.

Novels

The Blaze of Noon. London, Secker and Warburg, and Chicago, Alliance
  Book Company, 1939.
Saturnine. London, Secker and Warburg, 1943; revised and extended version,
  as The Greater Infortune, London, Peter Owen, 1960.
The Lesser Infortune. London, Cape, 1953.
The Connecting Door. London, Barrie and Rockliff, 1962.
The Woodshed. London, Barrie and Rockliff, 1962.
The Shearers. London, Hamish Hamilton, 1969.

Other

Apology for Dancing (ballet criticism). London, Faber, 1936.
Léon Bloy. Cambridge, Bowes, and New Haven, Connecticut, Yale Univer-
  sity Press, 1954.
Four Absentees (memoirs). London, Barrie and Rockliff, 1960.
The Fourfold Tradition (criticism). London, Barrie and Rockliff, and New
  York, New Directions, 1961.
The Intellectual Part (memoirs). London, Barrie and Rockliff, 1963.
Raymond Roussel. London, Calder and Boyars, and Berkeley, University of
  California Press, 1966.

Portrait of the Artist as a Professional Man (memoirs).   London, Peter Owen, 1969.

A Little Pattern of French Crime.   London, Hamish Hamilton, 1969.

French Crime in the Romantic Age.   London, Hamish Hamilton, 1970.

Bluebeard and After: Three Decades of Murder in France.   London, Peter Owen, 1972.

The Sex War and Others.   London, Peter Owen, 1973.

Reflections on the Newgate Calender.   London, W. H. Allen, 1975.

Editor, *Existentialism*, by Guido de Ruggiero.   London, Secker and Warburg, 1947; New York, Social Science Publishers, 1948.

Editor, *Imaginary Conversations* (radio scripts).   London, Secker and Warburg, 1948.

Editor, *Architecture of Truth.*   London, Thames and Hudson, 1957.

Translator, *Atala and René*, by F. R. de Chateaubriand.   London, Oxford University Press, 1963.

Translator, with Lindy Foord, *Impressions of Africa*, by Raymond Roussel.   London, Calder and Boyars, and Berkeley, University of California Press, 1966.

Translator, *A Harlot High and Low,* by Honoré de Balzac.   London, Penguin, 1970.

Translator, *When Justice Falters,* by René Floriot.   London, Harrap, 1972.

Rayner Heppenstall comments:

(1970) The usual subjects. A variety of forms and devices. Much affected by Yeats, Blake and minor French symbolists, perhaps also Gerard Manley Hopkins.

(1974) I have written no original verse for almost a quarter of a century. I do not disown what I once did, but view it with no more than autobiographical interest. I take no interest in the verse of my younger contemporaries.

*   *   *

Rayner Heppenstall's literary career has followed a familiar pattern. As a young man he regarded himself primarily as a poet, but after the age of thirty he turned exclusively to prose. In his autobiography, *The Intellectual Part,* he speaks dismissively of poetry as a literary mode, and regards his last collection *Poems 1933–1945* as marking a distinctive farewell to verse. Indeed, this book contained very little written after 1940. In 1933 Heppenstall contributed to an early number of *New Verse,* the important English poetry magazine of the thirties, but he never subscribed to its programme of socially concerned verse and precise observation; indeed, in a later number Heppenstall was repudiated and abused by its combative editor, Geoffrey Grigson. Heppenstall's principal influence was Gerard Manley Hopkins, who was then beginning to be seriously read and imitated by English poets. Heppenstall's poetry shows Hopkins's influence in its verbal contortions and its emphatic grappling with spiritual crises. (Though not a Christian, Heppenstall teetered for a while on the brink of conversion to Catholicism.) Formally, it is skillfully controlled and at times, as in the sequence called "Sebastian," it rises to an impressive if frigid rhetoric. But its frequent obscurity looks like the product of affection rather than genuine complexity of thought and imagination. However, one of his last poems, "Instead of a Carol," dated 1940, deserves to be remembered as a crisp presentation of a wartime moment.

– Bernard Bergonzi

HERNTON, Calvin C. American. Born in Chattanooga, Tennessee, 28 April 1933. Educated at Howard High School, 1946–50; Talladega College, Alabama, 1950–54, B.A. 1954; Fisk University, Nashville, Tennessee, 1954–56, M.A. in sociology 1956; Columbia University, New York, 1961. Has one child. Social Worker, Youth House, New York, 1956; Instructor in Sociology, Benedict College, Columbus, South Carolina, 1956–57, Alabama Agricultural and Mechanical College, Huntsville, 1957–58, Edward Waters College, Jacksonville, Florida, 1958–59, and Southern University, Baton Rouge, Louisiana, 1959–60; Social Investigator, Department of Welfare, New York, 1961–62; Writer-in-Residence, Central State University, Wilberforce, Ohio, 1969. Writer-in-Residence, 1970, and since 1971, Associate Professor of Afro-American Literature, Oberlin College, Ohio. Co-Founder, *Umbra* magazine, New York, 1963. Address: c/o Wendy Weil, Julian Bach Literary Agency, 3 East 48th Street, New York, New York 10017, U.S.A.

PUBLICATIONS

Verse

The Coming of Chronos to the House of Nightsong: An Epical Narrative of the South. New York, Interim Books, 1964.

Plays

Glad to Be Dead (produced Jacksonville, Florida, 1958).
Flame (produced Jacksonville, Florida, 1958).
The Place (produced Oberlin, Ohio, 1972).

Novel

Scarecrow. New York, Doubleday, 1974.

Other

Sex and Racism in America. New York, Doubleday, 1965; as *Sex and Racism,* London, Deutsch, 1969.
White Papers for White Americans. New York, Doubleday, 1966.
Coming Together: Black Power, White Hatred, and Sexual Hangups. New York, Random House, 1971.

Calvin C. Hernton comments:

I used to make statements about what I wrote, how I wrote it, my method, my process, my poetics, and that stuff. But I don't do that anymore. My poetry is my statement. However, I will say this much. I write about anything, and from as many possible standpoints. I've written poems about war, hatred, racism, racial violence, social and personal suffering and joy as well; poems about trees, making love, loss of love, the blues, being scared in an airplane, persons I've known such as musicians, painters, friends, lovers, enemies and people rushing along the streets with umbrellas open with it no longer raining; poems about whatever I happen to feel necessary at the time; poems for children, women, and poems for nobody but myself! I have noticed that one thing runs through all of my poems no matter what the subject, style or poetic level: and this is an almost too human concern for humanity.

*   *   *

Calvin C. Hernton's poetry is concerned with the plight of the black masses, the coming of age of the existential Negro, and the misconceptualization of race relations in the United States:

> Laughter and scorn on the lips of Edsel automobiles
> instructing the populace to love God, be kind to puppies
> and the Chase Manhattan National Bank
> Because of this there is no Fourth of July this year
> No shouting, no popping of firecrackers, no celebrating,
>   no parade
> But the rage of a hopeless people
> Jitterbugging
>   in the streets.

He speaks of creative impersonalization:

> I am not a metaphor or symbol.
> This you hear is not the wind in the trees,
> Nor a cat being maimed in the street.
> I am being maimed in the street.
> It is I who weep, laugh, feel pain or joy.

And finally he symbolizes America spiritually replenished through organic changes in her total civilization:

> to see ALL Americans in freedom and passion for one another, lift ourselves above that lifeless thing (materialism). What America needs most now is room, a kind of transcendent humanity, whereby all men and women can work, love and acquire self-esteem without having to maim one another in the struggle.

— Corrine E. Bostic

HEWITT, Geof. American. Born in Glen Ridge, New Jersey, 1 September 1943. Educated at Cornell University, Ithaca, New York (Academy of American Poets Prize, 1966), 1962–66, B.A. 1966; Johns Hopkins University, Baltimore, 1966–67, M.A. 1967; University of Iowa, Iowa City, 1967–69, M.F.A. 1969. Married Janet Lind Hewitt in 1971; has one son, Benjamin Starr. Assistant Editor, *Epoch Magazine*, Ithaca, New York, 1964–66; Editor-in-Chief, *The Trojan Horse* magazine, Ithaca, New York, 1965–66; Gilman Teaching Fellow, Johns Hopkins University, 1966–67; Teaching Assistant, University of Iowa, 1967–69; Instructor, Coe College, Cedar Rapids, Iowa, 1969, and University of Hawaii, Honolulu, 1969–70. Since 1966, Founding Editor, The Kumquat Press, Montclair, New Jersey, later Enosburg, Vermont; since 1970, Contributing Editor, *Cornell Alumni News*, Ithaca, New York; since 1971, Contributing Editor, *New Letters*, Kansas City, Missouri. Recipient: Coordinating Council of Literary Magazines grant, 1967, 1969; Vermont Council on the Arts grant, 1974. Address: R.D.4, Enosburg, Vermont 05450, U.S.A.

PUBLICATIONS

Verse

Poem and Other Poems.   Montclair, New Jersey, Kumquat Press, 1966.
Waking Up Still Pickled.   Aurora, New York, Lillabulero Press, 1967.
Stone Soup.   Ithaca, New York, Ithaca House, 1974.

Other

Editor, *Quickly Aging Here: Some Poets of the 1970's.*   New York, Doubleday, 1969.
Editor, *Selected Poems of Alfred Starr Hamilton.*   Highlands, North Carolina, Jargon, 1969.
Editor, *Living in Whales: Stories and Poems from Vermont Public Schools.*   Montpelier, Vermont Council on the Arts, 1972.

Critical Studies: Reviews by Michael Benedikt, in *Poetry* (Chicago), December 1968, and by Thomas Lask, in *The New York Times,* 20 February 1970.

Geof Hewitt comments:

I write poetry when I can. There is a tension between the public and the private person, between ambition and sloth, between the joy of language and the sincerity of silence.

Poetry is not a "career" for me, nor am I presumptious enough to claim it as a way of life.

I write what I can whenever I can, sometimes call it "poetry," and am always grateful when it comes.

*   *   *

Geof Hewitt's poetry, even from such early poems as "The Gift" and "Laramie, 1851," both written about 1965, relies heavily on humor and word-play. These two poems, the former relatively serious, the latter more farcically playful, both announce and anticipate technique and tone to come; the former turns on two connotations of the word "fail," while the latter juggles word permutations like a slap-happy acrobat ("mugs," "smug," and "gums," all within four lines), while both exhibit a sense of humor, whether about himself or others. While many of Hewitt's poems stick close to his own experience and describe convincingly real, if occasionally bizarre events ("The Couple Parking on the Motorcycle," for example, which could be subtitled, "love in gear"), Hewitt sometimes makes a leap into science fiction – related poetry, and some of his s.f. poetry is among the more interesting poetry of this sort. "The Frozen Man" is about a man, quick frozen, who wakes up in the future to find himself merely another t.v. dinner; "My Martian Girl Friend" describes the attributes of a extraterrestrial dream girl, and "At One with the Blue Night" manages to be at once both a metaphysical journey in the vein of *2001* and a highly lyrical love poem.

Hewitt's poetry displays the exuberance of someone excited, rather than intimidated, by the possibilities of language, a poet not afraid to use its full resources: connotation, anagrams, punning, or outrageous internal rhymes we're more accustomed to encountering in nonsense poetry: "men too cool to coo through glass" (from "November 23, 1971"). It takes daring, an admirable penchant for risk-taking which Hewitt has in abundance, to attempt being funny about a serious subject in as slapstick a way as Hewitt is in these lines from "Shudder":

> For months there were hints she was disenchanted:
> the banana peel in the bathtub, a roller
> skate balanced on the ladder rung
> while you repaired the roof of your now-empty

– Duane Ackerson

HEWITT, John (Harold). British. Born in Belfast, Northern Ireland, 28 October 1907. Educated at Methodist College, Belfast; Queen's University, Belfast, B.A. 1930, M.A. 1951. Married Roberta Black in 1934. Art Assistant, then Deputy Director, Belfast Museum and Art Gallery, 1930–57; Art Director, Herbert Art Gallery and Museum, Coventry, 1957–72, now retired. Associate Editor, *Lagan* magazine, 1945–46; Poetry Editor, *Threshold* magazine, Belfast, 1957–61. Fellow, Museums Association, D.Litt.: New University of Ulster, Coleraine, 1974. Member, Irish Academy of Letters, 1960. Address: 11 Stockman's Lane, Belfast BT9 7JA, Northern Ireland.

PUBLICATIONS

Verse

Conacre. Belfast, privately printed, 1943.
No Rebel Word: Poems. London, Muller, 1948.

Tesserae. Belfast, Festival Publications, 1967.

Collected Poems 1932–1967. London, MacGibbon and Kee, 1968.

The Day of the Corncrake: Poems of the Nine Glens. Belfast, Glens of Antrim Historical Society, 1969.

The Planter and the Gael, with John Montague. Belfast, Arts Council of Northern Ireland, 1970.

An Ulster Reckoning. Coventry, privately printed, 1971.

Out of My Time. Belfast, Blackstaff Press, 1974.

Play

The Bloody Brae (produced Belfast, 1957). Published in *Threshold* (Belfast), Autumn 1957.

Other

Coventry: The Tradition of Change and Continuity. Coventry, Coventry Corporation, 1966.

Editor, with Sam H. Bell and Nesca A. Robb, *The Arts in Ulster: A Symposium.* London, Harrap, 1951.

Editor, *Poems of William Allingham.* Dublin, Dolmen Press, 1967.

Editor, *Rhyming Weavers and Other Country Poets of Antrim and Down.* Belfast, Blackstaff Press, 1974.

Critical Studies: "Regionalism into Reconciliation: The Poetry of John Hewitt" by John Montague, in *Poetry Ireland* (Dublin), Spring 1964: "The Poetry of John Hewitt" by Seamus Heaney, in *Threshold* (Belfast), Summer 1969; "John Hewitt: Ulster Poet" by Terence Brown, in *Topic 24* (Washington, Pennsylvania), 1972.

John Hewitt comments:

My poetry is a quest for identity as an individual, as an Irishman of settler stock, as a twentieth-century man.

In imagery, for evocation of mood, I seek accuracy of sensory experience. My verse is low-charged, conversational in tone. I normally use regular forms, largely iambic; now free verse tends to replace blank verse, but with renewed interest in sonnet.

Influences: Wordsworth, Frost, Yeats, Pound, Edward Thomas.

                              *   *   *

John Hewitt, Ulster's senior poet, presents the paradox of largely rural inspiration, and an urban (Belfast) background. As he says in "The Lonely Heart":

> My father was a city schoolmaster
> for forty years acclimatised to air
> stale with hot breath, wet jerseys, chalk and crumbs,
> in a tall building islanded in slums.

He first began to publish in the socialist thirties, both nature lyrics like "The Leaf" or "The Little Lough," and others in which he asserted his identity as an Irishman of Planter stock:

> Once alien here my fathers built their house,
> claimed, drained, and gave the land the shape of use. . . .
> – from "Once Alien Here"

In the 1940's these two themes came together in a series of long poems, the best known being *Conacre* which was privately published in 1943 and later appeared in Geoffrey's Grigson's anthology, *Poetry of the Present* (1949). Several others appeared in *Lagan,* the leading Ulster magazine of the period, grouped under the title of "Freehold"; as well as the private world of "The Lonely Heart" there was the more public:

> To Ulster then, my region, now I turn,
> new to sworn service, with so much to learn. . . .
> – from "The Glittering Sod"

The poems of this period were part of a conscious attempt to foster Ulster Regionalism, as a companion to the Lallans movement in Scotland. In his extended essay, "Ulster Poets, 1800–1850," first read to the Belfast Literary Society (January, 1950) Hewitt sketched what he calls the "true Ulster tradition," ignoring the Gaelic writers of the province in favour of rural bards and rhyming weavers. But in his first English collection, *No Rebel Word,* he allowed himself to be presented (in the preface by Geoffrey Taylor) as part of the tradition of English nature poetry; a few poems apart, the only hint of defiance is in the title.

Something similar occurs in his *Collected Poems* where, with a kind of retrospective modesty, Hewitt has tended to skimp the more controversial aspects of his career. But a careful reading will discover a development in his thinking about Ulster, especially in the parable poem, "The Colony," which compares the Protestant position to that of a Roman settlement in the declining Empire. There is a more detached note in the later poems, due to his leaving Belfast for an English gallery (cf. "An Irishman in Coventry"). But his affection for the landscape of Antrim remains a constant factor, as Donegal was for the nineteenth century fore-runner whose poems he edited for the Irish Arts Council, William Allingham.

– John Montague

HIDDEN, (Frederick) Norman. British. Born in Portsmouth, Hampshire, 24 October 1913. Educated at St. Johns, Porthcawl, Glamorganshire; Hereford Cathedral School; Brasenose College, Oxford, M.A., Dip.Ed.; University of Michigan, Ann Arbor. British Liaison Officer with United States Army Headquarters in Europe during World War II. Taught at Kings School, Macclesfield, Cheshire; Goole Grammar School, Yorkshire; Hornchurch Grammar School, Essex. Since 1964, Senior Lecturer in English, College of All Saints, London. Since 1967, Founding Editor, *Workshop New Poetry,* London. Formerly, Parliamentary Candidate and Borough Councillor. Member, General Council and Executive Committee, 1967–73, Chairman, 1968–71, and since 1974, Vice-President, The Poetry Society,

London. Since 1967, Member, Executive Committee, The English Association. Awarded Civil List pension, 1974. Address: 2 Culham Court, Granville Road, London N4 4JB, England.

PUBLICATIONS

Verse

These Images Claw.   London, Outposts Publications, 1966.

Other

Dr. Kink and His Old Style Boarding School: Fragments of Autobiography.   London, Workshop Press, 1973.
A Study Guide to "Under Milk Wood."   London, Study Tapes, 1973.

Editor, *A National Anthology of Student Poetry.*   London, University of London Institute of Education Students Association, 1968.
Editor, *Say It Aloud.*   London, Hutchinson, 1972.

Critical Studies: "A Declaration of Intent" by the author, in *Labour Monthly* (London), February 1968; by Dick Russell, in *The Teacher* (London), 22 September 1972; by Raymond Gardiner, in *The Guardian* (London), 9 January 1973.

*   *   *

Norman Hidden's verse exploits Georgian concerns in free verse, and without the gentility that was popular fifty years ago. "Brown Girl" begins:

> Around your thigh
> you smooth the cocoa stocking-top
> with firm and self-caressing hands.
> The nipple of your skin snakes lazily
> as waves on far-off sands.

"Transition: London to Nice" again shows a typically Georgian preoccupation with new types of traffic, ("Poof! poof! go the rockets of the jet plane / as it geometrically pierces / the shapeless wet clouds / thick over Northolt") but is written, perhaps, less regularly than it would have been by J. D. C. Pellow or Herbert Asquith, the poets with whom Hidden has most in common. "These Images Claw" is more ambitiously modernist; presented, in short lines that sometimes look (on the page) a little like those of Pound's *Cantos*, it mixes disparate images in an attempt to reflect Hidden's mental chaos and sense of artistic modesty, in which it totally succeeds. Some of the "clawing images" are memories, such as "a little rouge" on "the beldame's cheek" (a film, perhaps?), some are invention, such as "the hornets' smashed nest"; but in the end, "only the

683

quiver grass / shakes in the fields": this is an uncannily accurate metaphor for the reader's feeling as he slips Hidden's *oeuvre* back onto the shelf.

– Martin Seymour-Smith

HIGHAM, Charles. British. Born in London, 18 February 1931. Educated at Cranleigh, Clayesmore. Film Critic, *Nation*, Sydney, 1961–63; Literary Editor, *The Bulletin*, Sydney, 1963–68. Film Critic, Sydney *Morning Herald*, 1955–63; Australian Correspondent, *Sight and Sound*, London, and *Hudson Review*, New York. Currently, Hollywood correspondent, *New York Times*. Visiting Regents Professor, University of California, Santa Cruz, 1969. Recipient: Poetry Society Prize, London, 1949; Sydney *Morning Herald* prize, 1956. Agent: John Cushman Associates, 25 West 43rd Street, New York, New York 10036, U.S.A.

PUBLICATIONS

Verse

> *A Distant Star.* Aldington, Kent, Hand and Flower Press, 1951.
> *Spring and Death.* Aldington, Kent, Hand and Flower Press, 1953.
> *The Earthbound and Other Poems.* Sydney, Angus and Robertson, 1959.
> *Noonday Country: Poems 1954–1965.* Sydney, Angus and Robertson, 1966.
> *The Voyage to Brindisi and Other Poems, 1966–1969.* Sydney, Angus and Robertson, 1970.

Other

> *Hollywood in the Forties*, with Joel Greenberg. London, Zwemmer, and Cranbury, New Jersey, A. S. Barnes, 1969.
> *The Films of Orson Welles.* Berkeley, University of California Press, 1970.
> *Hollywood Cameramen: Sources of Light*, Bloomington, Indiana University Press, and London, Thames and Hudson, 1970.
> *Ziegfeld.* Chicago, Regnery, 1972; London, W. H. Allen, 1973.
> *Hollywood at Sunset.* New York, Saturday Review Press, 1972.
> *Cecil B. DeMille.* New York, Scribner, 1973; London, W. H. Allen, 1974.
> *The Art of the American Film, 1900–1971.* New York, Doubleday, 1973.
> *Ava.* New York, Delacorte Press, and London, W. H. Allen, 1974.

> Editor, with Alan Brissenden, *They Came to Australia: An Anthology.* Melbourne, Cheshire, 1961; London, Angus and Robertson, 1962.
> Editor, with Michael Wilding, *Australians Abroad: An Anthology.* Melbourne, Cheshire, 1967.
> Editor, *Australian Writing Today.* London, Penguin, 1968.
> Editor, with Joel Greenberg, *The Celluloid Muse: Hollywood Directors Speak.* London, Angus and Robertson, 1969; Chicago, Regnery, 1971.

Critical Study: in *Times Literary Supplement* (London), 23 September 1960.

Charles Higham comments:

My poems are written in a large variety of largely invented forms, and sometimes words; and their subject matter is equally various. The ocean – a dominating prescence in the world I live in – swamps, jungles, strange towns, animals and birds all form the basis of what I believe is essentially a poetry of the senses, and of primitive nature. I try to strike through to the places that are still untouched by man's ruinings; hence my deep passion for Australia, the West Indies, above all Luzon in the Philippines and parts of Japan. If I were asked to set a landscape which my poems live in, I would say: a green sky, with a mid-day moon; palms slanting from a swamp from which rise strange wading and flying birds; a lonely figure digging for clams on a fringing beach beyond which lies the enormous, flat, metallic Pacific.

In the early part of 1974, after a long hiatus, I began writing a new series of poems based on Rilkean exotic themes.

                              *   *   *

Although he is an Englishman, Charles Higham has adapted to his Australian identity with remarkable intelligence. His best poems, most of which deal with Australian experience or history, present an interesting and revealing point of view that is, so to say, both involved and yet detached. This newer, Australian poetry is considerably superior to his earliest, English poetry, which was feebly derivative (even neo-Georgian), debilitated and lacking in self-confidence or purpose. He can still write too patly, without tension, relying too much on technical convention, as in these lines from "Rushcutter's Bay":

> In winter, trapped by gloom, we long for this:
> The body stripped, sex in blue trunks, the leap
> Of water to be carved by pressing shoulders. . . .

But in his powerful "The Kelly Show" – surely an extraordinary poem to have come from one who is not a native of Australia – the tight rhyming form (in which he usually chooses to write) is vitalized by a personal rhythm and a tragic urgency. His weaknesses – a tendency to cliché, a fondness for making trite or commonplace points, as well as others already mentioned – have vanished. The last stanza reads:

> The curtain falls; she waves a final hand.
> He quotes his jot of evidence; he treads
> Into the proper place; his smile is bland.
> Applause demands her curtsey into beds,
> And so she lewdly nods her short assent.
> He drops and twists: the watchers nod their heads
> And write his name upon the continent.

> – Martin Seymour-Smith

HILL, Geoffrey. British. Born in Bromsgrove, Worcestershire, 18 June 1932. Educated at Fairfield Junior School; County High School, Blomsgrove; Keble College, Oxford. Senior Lecturer in English, University of Leeds. Recipient: Gregory Award, 1961; Hawthornden Prize, 1969; Geoffrey Faber Memorial Prize, 1970; Whitbread Award, 1971; Alice Hunt Bartlett Award, 1971; Heinemann Award, 1972. Fellow, Royal Society of Literature, 1972. Lives in Leeds, Yorkshire, England.

PUBLICATIONS

Verse

(Poems). Oxford, Fantasy Press, 1952.
For the Unfallen: Poems 1952–1958. London, Deutsch, 1959; Chester Springs, Pennsylvania, Dufour, 1960.
Preghiere. Leeds, Northern House, 1964.
Penguin Modern Poets 8, with Edwin Brock and Stevie Smith. London, Penguin, 1966.
King Log. London, Deutsch, and Chester Springs, Pennsylvania, Dufour, 1968.
Mercian Hymns. London, Deutsch, 1971.

Critical Studies: by Christopher Ricks, in *London Magazine,* November 1964; Jeffrey Wainwright, in *Stand* (Newcastle upon Tyne), x,1, 1968; Martin Dodsworth, in *Stand* (Newcastle upon Tyne), xiii, 1, 1971–72; Michael Launchbury, in *Delta* (Sheffield), Spring 1972; "The Poetry of Geoffrey Hill" by Jon Silkin, in *British Poetry since 1960,* edited by Michael Schmidt and Grevel Lindop, Oxford, Carcanet Press, 1972; "Beyond Modernism: Christopher Middleton and Geoffrey Hill" by Wallace D. Martin, in *Contemporary Literature* (Madison, Wisconsin), xii, 4, 1972; Michael Wilding in *New Poetry* (Sydney), xx, 1–2, 1973.

*   *   *

Geoffrey Hill's powerful, peremptory talent has made the sharpest impact on the current poetic scene, although he has, as yet, published only three collections of verse. He is a poet of pain and economy. His attention is preoccupied with absolutes, with death, God, war, love, time. He has the courage of his subjects, which are not conceived of as the abstractions of reason – they are too thronged and dense for that – but as the stark observations of a collected and suffering soul:

> Let mind be more precious than soul; it will not
> Endure. Soul grasps its price, begs its own peace,
> Settles with tears and sweat, is possibly
> Indestructible.

Unterrified of grandeur, quite without fashionable glibness or cleverness, almost suspicious of fluency, he sees life as agonisingly under the jurisdiction of tragedy. The movement of his lines, which is both organic and severely controlled, and the use of language crammed with meaning, are strong enough to support and supple enough to project such an individual vision:

> Tragedy has all under regard.
> It will not touch us but it is there –
> Flawless, insatiate – hard summer sky
> Feasting on this, reaching its own end.

The complex syntax, a function of the genuinely intellectual grapple of a distinguished mind, recalls Donne:

> . . . not yielding their abused
> Bodies and bonds to those whom war's chance saves
> Without the law. . . .

The blend of common and splendid language, which at critical points becomes one and the same – "cliché rinsed and restored . . . as responsible speech," is the way Hill puts it – calls up the name of Ben Jonson. And Hill is a traditional poet, in a secret, personal and ancient way.

The double and paradoxical impression made on the reader by Hill's finest poems, which seem as much born as constructed, is on the one hand an excess of consciousness and on the other a resolute objectivity. Light must be poured in on every corner of the poet's experience. The ambiguities and the temptations (to facility or indulgence) of the poet's position are as much part of the theme as the explicit subject. At the same time the reader is aware of a solid, external universe which exists in its own – maimed – right and in which the poet himself is an object, not just a manipulator. Hill addresses a universe which is brutally – and it must be added – beautifully, *there*.

In some remarks on the splendid "Funeral Music," a sequence developed out of a bloody episode in the Wars of the Roses, Hill speaks of his attempt at "a florid grim music broken by grunts and shrieks." This characteristic comment suggests something of the curiously potent combination of ceremonial richness and animal realism in these extraordinary poems. They spring from and realise a most individual force and they compose an original, compelling body of verse, which wants only volume to qualify as very considerable work indeed. Marks of that quality are evident in the power of the feeling, in the intellectual complexity and the total vision, in the scrupulous (occasionally almost obsessive) fidelity to the subject and to the poet's own nature, in the rhythmic vitality and in the exploratory skill which can discover and recover so many resources in the language.

– William Walsh

HINE, Daryl. Canadian. Born in Burnaby, British Columbia, 24 February 1936. Educated at McGill University, Montreal, 1954–58, B.A. in classics 1958; University of Chicago, M.A. 1965, Ph.D. in comparative literature 1967. Lived in Europe 1958–62. Assistant Professor of English, University of Chicago, 1967–69. Since 1968, Editor, *Poetry*, Chicago. Recipient: Canada Foundation-Rockefeller Fellowship, 1958; Canada Council grant, 1959; Ingram Merrill grant, 1962, 1963; National Endowment for the Arts grant, 1969. Address: Poetry Magazine, 1228 North State Street, Chicago, Illinois 60610, U.S.A.

PUBLICATIONS

Verse

>*Five Poems.* Toronto, Emblem Books, 1955.
>*The Carnal and the Crane.* Montreal, Contact Press, 1957.
>*The Devil's Picture Book: Poems.* London and New York, Abelard Schuman, 1960.
>*Heroics: Five Poems.* Fontainebleau, France, Gosswiller, 1961.
>*The Wooden Horse: Poems.* New York, Atheneum, 1965.
>*Minutes: Poems.* New York, Atheneum, 1968.
>*The Homeric Hymns and The Battle of the Frogs and the Mice.* New York, Atheneum, 1972.

Plays

>*The Death of Seneca* (produced Chicago, 1968).

Radio Play: *Alcestis,* 1972 (UK).

Novel

>*The Prince of Darkness & Co.* London and New York, Abelard Schuman, 1961.

Other

>*Polish Subtitles: Impressions from a Journey.* London and New York, Abelard Schuman, 1962.

Critical Study: *Alone with America* by Richard Howard, New York, Atheneum, 1969.

*   *   *

When *The Carnal and the Crane* appeared in 1957, Northrop Frye described Daryl Hine's first book of poems as "a brilliant series of phrases" moving "across a mysteriously dark background." Now, four books of poetry, a novel and a travel book later, the phrases retain their brilliance and the background its mystery. Elegance is characteristic of all of Hine's writing which may be appreciated for its formal qualities if not for its expressiveness. His work resembles nothing more than an excellent, clear, but very dry wine.

The poet has called his first book "rhapsodic" and surreal in imagery and structure, *The Carnal and the Crane* was followed by *The Devil's Picture Book*, a more crafted work. *The Wooden Horse*, which explored the possibilities of dramatic monologues, led Hine to his most intimate book to date, *Minutes*. This gave way to a technical *tour de force*, *The Homeric Hymns*, translations from once-oral Greek poems written anonymously in the Homeric manner. With these noble-sounding praises, the worlds of poetry and classical scholarship merge for Hine, as in the dactylic hexameters of the first line of "To Apollo": "How should I hymn you, Apollo, so handsomely sung of already?"

Hine's classical learning, far from being confined to *The Homeric Hymns*, reverberates rather than echoes with Greek, Roman, Christian and even Celtic references throughout all his poetry. It is an attractive characteristic of his work that he can capture an image with crystal clarity in a Symbolist fashion, as in "Les Yeux de la Tête" from *Minutes:*

> A tiny palace and a formal garden
> In miniature, lawns, flowers, jewelled trees
> By Fabergé, and in the midst a fountain
> Whose precious drops like tear drops fill the eyes.

Hine's poems proceed from image to image, building on the principle of polarity, finding in the irreconcilability of opposites proof of the inability of people to merge, the impossibility of history, in a world in which "all our wisdom is unwillingness."

— John Robert Colombo

HIRSCHMAN, Jack. American. Born in New York City, 13 December 1933. Educated at City College of New York, 1951–55, B.A. 1955; Indiana University, Bloomington, A.M. 1957, Ph.D. 1961. Married Ruth Hirschman in 1954; has one son, David, and one daughter, Celia. Instructor, Dartmouth College, Hanover, New Hampshire, 1959–61; Assistant Professor, University of California, Los Angeles, 1961–66. Painter and Collage-maker: Exhibitions in Venice, California, 1972, and Los Angeles, 1972. Associated with *Tree* magazine, Bolinas, California. Address: 19688 Grandview, Topanga, California, U.S.A.

PUBLICATIONS

Verse

Fragments. New York, privately printed, 1952.
A Correspondence of Americans. Bloomington, Indiana University Press, 1960.
Two, with lithographs by Arnold Belkin. Los Angeles, Zora Gallery, 1963.
Interchange. Los Angeles, Zora Gallery, 1964.
Kline Sky. Northridge, California, privately printed, 1965.
Yod. London, Trigram Press, 1966.
London Seen Directly. London, Goliard Press, 1967.
Wasn't It Like This in the Woodcut. London, Cape Goliard Press, 1967.
William Blake. Topanga, California, Love Press, 1967.
A Word in Your Season, with Asa Benveniste. London, Trigram Press, 1967.

Ltd. Interchangeable in Eternity: Poems of Jackruthdavidcelia Hirschman. London, privately printed, 1967.
Jerusalem: A Three Part Poem. Topanga, California, Love Press, 1968.
Aleph, Benoni and Zaddik. Los Angeles, Tenfingers Press, 1968.
Jerusalem, Ltd. London, Trigram Press, 1968.
Shekinah. Mill Valley, California, Maya, 1969.
Broadside Golem. Venice, California, Box Zero, 1969.
Black Alephs: Poems 1960–1968. New York, Phoenix Bookshop, and London, Trigram Press, 1969.
NHR. Goleta, California, Christopher's Press, 1970.
Scintilla. Bolinas, California, Tree Books, 1970.
Soledeth. Venice, California, Q Press, 1971.
DT. Santa Barbara, California, Yes Press, 1971.
The Burning of Los Angeles. Venice, California, J'Ose Press, 1971.
HNYC. Topanga, California, Skyline Press, 1971.
Les Vidanges. Venice, California, Beyond Baroque Press, 1972.
The R of the Ari's Raziel. Los Angeles, Press of the Pegacycle Lady, 1972.
Adamnan. Santa Barbara, California, Christopher's Press, 1972.
Aur Sea. Bolinas, California, Tree Books, 1973.
Cantillations. Santa Barbara, California, Yes/Capra Press, 1973.
Djackson. Salt Lake City, Rainbow Resin Press, 1974.

Other

Editor, *Artaud Anthology.* San Francisco, City Lights Books, 1965.

Translator, with Victor Erlich, *Electric Iron,* by Vladimir Mayakovsky. Mill Valley, California, Maya, 1970.
Translator, *Love Is a Tree,* by Antonin Artaud. Fairfax, California, Red Hill Press, 1972.
Translator, *A Rainbow for the Christian West,* by René Depestre. Fairfax, California, Red Hill Press, 1972.
Translator, *The Exiled Angel,* by Luisa Pasamanik. Fairfax, California, Red Hill Press, 1973.
Translator, *Igitur,* by Stéphane Mallarmé. Los Angeles, Press of the Pegacycle Lady, 1973.
Translator, *Wail for the Arat Beggars of the Casbah,* by Ait Djafer. Los Angeles, Papa Bach Books, 1973.

Jack Hirschman comments:

(1970) Poetry is man at his most complete state of consciousness. As I write this, in March of 1969, I am conscious of whirling bodies of Vietnamese women and children in the long process of death; and aware that "poetry does nothing" is a truth; I reject that truth for the poem I am now going to plunge into. Long live the creative act! May the overlords of the world learn the real meaning of death.

(1974) Putting my poems, my visual works, and my kabbalist interests together, my poetry may be seen more and more to reflect – through the amuletic/hieroglyphic tradition – a politically Left position which sees Hanoi as the extension of the idea of Blake's *Jerusalem.* Free to translate from many languages, and moreover to broadcast such works, as well as my own, on Pacifica Radio in Los Angeles, my works reveal all that is beautifully decayed in western capitalistic societies in the hope that the interchange between the present West and the future Asia and Africa takes place, so to speak, across the arc of rainbows rather than the broken backs of those who still have not forfeited the earth to machinery.

*   *   *

Introducing his first book, Karl Shapiro hailed Jack Hirschman exuberantly as "an inventor" who had "evolved his own particular version of the language" and who was "a kind of Hart Crane, without Crane's fatal humorlessness." Such praise is hard to live down, or up to. For years Hirschman's subsequent work appeared mainly in fugitive small editions – many of them experiments in format, such as *Interchange*, with its loose cards to be shuffled, or *LTD.*, hand-calligraphed on paper strips – and until the 1969 London collection, *Black Alephs*, he seemed an isolated figure. Recently, however, he has worked in collaboration with David Meltzer and appears regularly in the latter's bi-annual of cabbalistic lore and poetry, *Tree*. In his writing, while the content has grown more esoteric, the emphasis on linguistic originality has continued. The early work owed much to a Dylan Thomas-like *Hwyl* and to the comic gusto of the Joyce of *Finnegans Wake*. But what is disarming in a first book can grow tiresome, and those who find the associated names of Crane, Thomas, and Joyce portentous in a depressing way will not read Hirschman's later work with much reward. Both in verse and in the "breath-style" prose-poems of recent years, the writing communicates more a generalized energy and afflatus than any very strictly definable meaning or emotion. The effect aimed at seems usually to be a hectic visionary intoxication and exaltation, as in these opening lines of "Drive":

> What a whine of a mouth in the engine of robot tit
> what an eye of blue chrome thorax my sweet
> necrophiliac my yackity rattling spit hiss my
> lilith leather slashwhip desire my voluptuous
> lynch

Still, when he cares to, Hirschman can write more quietly and convincingly, as in this poem, also from *Black Alephs:*

> I've had enough of love
> to know
> death a little
> way away is
> sleeping,
>
> her hand where she left it,
> on me, her hair
> tumbled over her mouth half
> open for
> more.

– Seamus Cooney

HITCHCOCK, George. American. Born in Hood River, Oregon, 2 June 1914. Educated at the University of Oregon, Eugene, B.A. Worked as laborer, shipfitter, smelter-man, mason, carpenter, and gardener. Formerly, Lecturer in English, San

Francisco State College. Currently, Lecturer in Literature, University of California, Santa Cruz. Since 1964, Editor and Publisher, *Kayak* magazine and Kayak Books, San Francisco, later Santa Cruz. Recipient: National Endowment for the Arts grant, 1968, 1969. Address: 325 Ocean View, Santa Cruz, California 95062, U.S.A.

PUBLICATIONS

Verse

> *Poems and Prints,* with Mel Fowler.   San Francisco, San Francisco Review, 1962.
> *Tactics of Survival and Other Poems.*   San Francisco, Bindweed Press, 1964.
> *The Dolphin with the Revolver in Its Teeth.*   Santa Barbara, California, Unicorn Press, 1967.
> *The One Whose Approach I Cannot Evade.*   Santa Barbara, California, Unicorn Press, 1967.
> *Two Poems.*   Santa Barbara, California, Unicorn Press, 1967.
> *A Ship of Bells: Poems.*   San Francisco, Kayak Books, 1968.
> *Twelve Stanzas in Praise of the Holy Chariot.*   San Francisco, Kayak Books, 1969.
> *The Rococo Eye.*   LaCrosse, Wisconsin, Juniper Books, 1970.

Play

> *The Busy Martyr* (produced Medford, Massachusetts, 1963).   Published in *First Stage* (Lafayette, Indiana), Winter 1962–63.

Novel

> *Another Shore.*   Santa Cruz, California, Kayak Books, 1972.

Other

> Editor, with Robert Peters, *Pioneers of Modern Poetry.*   San Francisco, Kayak Books, 1967.
> Editor, *Losers Weepers: Poems Found Practically Anywhere.*   San Francisco, Kayak Books, 1969.

George Hitchcock comments:

I'm not very good at this. My verse is largely subconscious in its origins and rational tampering with these well-springs – in my case at least – is likely to pollute the water.

*   *   *

George Hitchcock has mastered the technique of blending the surreal with the actual: his poems float, believably, from what appears to be subconscious impulse to the surface world that has demanded the poem. Unlike most of America's "surreal" poets, Hitchcock does not strain for his images; they emerge in spite of themselves, almost as if they've existed for all time, waiting to be discovered by a poet who would not elaborate them to death. Hitchcock observes without intellectual frippery; the observation, if fresh, is enough. Children, whose senses have not yet grown callouses, see this way:

> Flotillas of leaves set sail in the birch trees.
> They are answering the call of birds, their brothers;
> they too would like to ascend like sonatas of glass
> from pianos, but the twigs, the limbs, the roots
> hold them back.
>
>   In such an April
> we would all fly upward like sparks, but some emblem
> in our shoes detains us.
>   – "The Ascension"

The vocabularly is adult, but the vision is new.

Hitchcock's vision, however unstrained, goes *into* things, and it is here that the surreal blends with the actual. If we believe the statement, it is not surreal, whatever the nature of its texture. Hitchcock describes a sinking ship:

> I watch her
> dissolve into the arms of her
> false twin caught in their watery hair
> the plumes of terns
> over their unknown name the keels
> and sails of magic schooners
>   – from "Portrait While Sinking"

and, in "A Voyage":

> Summer passes.
> The melon,
> split
> to the heart,
> reveals
> its secret
> cargo
> of mosquitoes.

Notice that Hitchcock avoids the fashionable trap of bolstering his images with surprising adjectives: he is sure enough of his vision that the mosquitoes need not assume an unlikely color, or somehow become more human than they already are.

His work includes some of the best poetry that has been written about the war in Vietnam. After a while, most war poems sound the same, inspired as they are by the tragedy of hatred and the innocence of hatred's victims. But Hitchcock avoids revelling in useless rhetoric and his war poetry retains the best qualities of surrealism:

> Freedom, a dancing girl,
> lifts her petticoats of gasoline,
> and on the hot sands of a deserted beach
> a wild horse struggles, choking
> in the noose of diplomacy.
> – from "Scattering Flowers"

Through his Kayak Press, Hitchcock has become an important force in the new American poetry: his magazine, *Kayak*, sometimes the most exciting of all the little magazines, has made available a variety of new forms, many of which Hitchcock has explored in his own work. These include found poetry, "cut-ups," and collaborations.

– Geof Hewitt

HOBSBAUM, Philip (Dennis). British. Born in London, 29 June 1932. Educated at Belle Vue Grammar School, Bradford, Yorkshire; Downing College, Cambridge, 1952–55, B.A. 1955, M.A. 1961; Royal Academy of Music, London, licentiate 1956; University of Sheffield, 1959–62, Ph.D. 1968. Married Hannah Kelly in 1957 (marriage dissolved, 1968). Lecturer in English, Queen's University, Belfast, 1962–66. Lecturer, 1966–72, and since 1972, Senior Lecturer in English, University of Glasgow. Co-Editor, *Poetry from Sheffield*, 1959–61; Editor, *Delta*, Cambridge, 1954–55. Address: Department of English, The University, Glasgow, Scotland.

PUBLICATIONS

Verse

> *The Place's Fault and Other Poems.* London, Macmillan, and New York, St. Martin's Press, 1964.
> *Snapshots.* Belfast, Festival Publications, 1965.
> *In Retreat and Other Poems.* London, Macmillan, and Chester Springs, Pennsylvania, Dufour, 1966.
> *Coming Out Fighting.* London, Macmillan, and Chester Springs, Pennsylvania, Dufour, 1969.
> *Some Lovely Glorious Nothing.* Frensham, Surrey, Sceptre Press, 1969.
> *Women and Animals.* London, Macmillan, 1972.

Other

> *A Theory of Communication: A Study of Value in Literature.* London, Macmillan, 1970; as *Theory of Criticism*, Bloomington, Indiana University Press, 1970. '
> *A Reader's Guide to Charles Dickens.* London, Thames and Hudson, and New York, Farrar Straus, 1973.

Editor, with Edward Lucie-Smith, *A Group Anthology.* London, Oxford
   University Press, 1963.
Editor, *Ten Elizabethan Poets. . . .* London, Longman, 1969.

Manuscript Collection: University of Texas, Austin.

Critical Studies: Reviews by P. N. Furbank, in *The Listener* (London), May 1964,
and by G. S. Fraser, in *The New York Review of Books,* 1964; *The Modern Writer and
His World* by G. S. Fraser, London, Penguin, 1964.

Philip Hobsbaum comments:

I have been associated, as founder of "The Group," with Lucie-Smith, MacBeth,
Porter, Bell and Redgrove.

*   *   *

Trained under both Leavis and Empson, the leading figure in a set of poets who
used to meet for regular stringent self-criticism, the Group, yet in his roots very
much a man of the left, of working-class and Jewish origins, in prose a forceful and
aggressive critic of what seem to him fashionable shams, Philip Hobsbaum does not
work out, in practice, as the sort of poet such a background would suggest. One of
his earliest admirers was a poet whose background and attitudes seem entirely
opposite, John Betjeman, and he resembles Betjeman at least in his gift for creating
a memorable and dense local atmosphere: the atmosphere of a life, in a school
class-room, in a provincial university, in a pub, which is shabby, alive, sensitive
and vulnerable.
   The persona of the poems figures as a kind of almost Tony Hancock character,
bewailing his own fatness, his decaying teeth, his short sight and astigmatism (in
one poem, mistaking the steps down to a pub lavatory for a flat grille he falls
smash on his face). Awkward and slightly shocking incidents recur in his poems:
the tutor at a provincial university making love clumsily under the desk on the
floor, with a great thrashing of legs, to a not particularly glamorous girl student.
His latest volume has a certain resemblance to Meredith's *Modern Love,* the story
of the simultaneous break up of a lecturer's marriage and his affair with a student,
and of his subsequent loneliness. He is a poet of the painful and awkward concrete
detail of life, writing verse which has a plodding exactness but disdains any lyrical
grace or attempt at memorable condensation of phrase. The honesty of what Hardy
called "unadjusted impressions," reinforced first by resentment and then by pity,
is at the heart of his achievement. There are humour and satire, too, but of a burly,
straightforward sort. He is in the line, perhaps, of poets like Crabbe and of the
Hardy of *Satires of Circumstances.* Readers who are at first put off by a drab texture
and a flat deliberation of verse movement find themselves in the end caught up in
the authenticity of Hobsbaum's social observation and, even more, his ruthless
observation of himself.

– G. S. Fraser

HOCHMAN, Sandra. American. Born in New York City, 11 September 1936. Educated at Bennington College, Vermont, B.A. 1957. Married Harvey Leve in 1965; has one child, Ariel. Actress. Poet-in-Residence, Fordham University, New York, 1965. Recipient: Yale Series of Younger Poets Award, 1963. Address: 180 East 79th Street, New York, New York 10021, U.S.A.

PUBLICATIONS

Verse

Voyage Home: Poems. Paris, Two Cities, 1960.
Manhattan Pastures. New Haven, Connecticut, Yale University Press, 1963.
The Vaudeville Marriage: Poems. New York, Viking Press, 1966.
Love Poems. Hong Kong, privately printed, 1966.
Love Letters from Asia: Poems. New York, Viking Press, 1968.
Earthworks: Poems 1960–1970. New York, Viking Press, 1971; London, Secker and Warburg, 1972.
Futures: New Poems. New York, Viking Press, 1974.

Plays

The World of Günter Grass (produced New York, 1966).

Screenplay: *Year of the Woman* (also director), 1973.

Novel

Walking Papers. New York, Viking Press, 1971.

Other

The Magic Convention (juvenile). New York, Doubleday, 1971.

Sandra Hochman comments:

> my written voice, my gift, is an instrument for memory,
> love, praise & revelation; in my poems i swallow my pride and turn
> to the authentic teachers of the dreaming mind.
> My work springs out of an inability to forget the loneliness of
> childhood and feeds upon all the metaphors of Nature & Revelation.

*   *   *

The flat, sometimes throwaway, delivery of Sandra Hochman's lines surprises the reader with unexpected, often ominous, echoes: "I scrape death from the black spots of a radish" ("I Live with Solomon"). This richness makes a carriage ride through Central Park subsume the great voyages of legend and history ("Hansoms") and supports the shock when "Old spring umbrellas / Bloom in the looking glass / As if in preparation for thunder" ("I Walk into the Pharmacy of Sleep"). "Poem for Alexandra," which might serve as Hochman's testament, traces this genesis of the miraculous: ". . . ridiculous stops / Are always turned to advantage – in improbable times / We discover whatever mystery we can." Though "The Love Singer" reduces a street bard to a "miracle-monger," art is the ultimate miracle, directing its force against both external and internal enemies: "David . . . / Turned all songs to a stone / And overthrew the flesh" ("The Problem of David"). The poems about clowns and magic in *The Vaudeville Marriage* root art in the commonplace it must ultimately transcend: ". . . I am / Aware of the tricks. They must be / What ugly feet are to the swan" ("The Magic Convention").

This immanence of wonder in the ordinary creates an appropriate landscape for Hochman's many poems about dreams that recreate the adult's vanished past, childhood dreams that persist, and dreams indistinguishable from the waking state. However frightening, however false, dreams shape the world: "She tries to construct / A small tower out of ivory and horn. / Dreams are nails . . ." ("Constructions: Upper East Side"). The travel poems of *Love Letters from Asia* celebrate a parallel world of waking miracles: ". . . How / Can this be all / And be so true? I / Breathe my whole life / In one morning . . . / I tremble / All day / In a glass / Of water" ("Written at Vivian Court").

Poems in this volume and new poems in *Earthworks* dramatize this vulnerable but renascent selfhood through a fusion with the spirit of vegetation and, ultimately, in works like "The New Life," with the blossoming foetus within: ". . . Tonight / My marrow flowers into coral." Only lovers, whether in foreign landscapes or even beneath the sea in "The Couple," lack this regenerative power.

Hochman hymns her daughter's birth as compensation for the violently disrupted past, accessible only in dreams, of the earlier volumes: ". . . Then, in a white room, / A doctor behind a mask – perhaps a woman, / Perhaps a man – took out our childhood" ("How We Get Rid of Our Childhood"). Hochman's witty novel, *Walking Papers*, defines the ambiguous central incident of this poem as an abortion, but the literal treatment dissipates the force of the episode. Though the novel provides a scenario for many of the poems and often echoes their language, it tends to diminish their evocative power. That the poems generate as much force as they do is a tribute to Hochman's short, spare lines and often flat language, sometimes merely lists of objects. The poems make no attempt to seduce with sound effects, and generally only the early poems use rhyme, usually in a final couplet. The casual tone, often self-deprecating, curbs excesses in paeans to vegetative and female fecundity. And Hochman can be directly, hilariously funny: "When a wheel broke, it was not the wheel of life, / Buddha's great wheel of birth and endless death, / It was the pierced flat tire of the car / Dying beneath the windows" ("About My Life at That Time"). But ultimately Hochman succeeds with a rhythm that creates the shape of an image, the contours and the stuff of a mood, as in "The Spy":

> If only there were a perfect word
> I could give it to you – a word like some artichoke
> That could sit on the table, dry, and become itself.

– Burton Kendle

HOFFMAN, Daniel (Gerard). American. Born in New York City, 3 April 1923. Educated at Columbia University, New York, A.B. 1947 (Phi Beta Kappa), M.A. 1949, Ph.D. 1956. Served in the United States Army Air Force, 1943–46; Legion of

Merit. Married Elizabeth McFarland in 1948; has two children. Instructor in English, Columbia University, 1952–56; Visiting Professor, University of Dijon, 1956–57; Assistant Professor, 1957–60, Associate Professor, 1960–65, and Professor of English, 1965–66, Swarthmore College, Pennsylvania. Since 1966, Professor of English, University of Pennsylvania, Philadelphia. Fellow of the School of Letters, Indiana University, 1959; Elliston Lecturer, University of Cincinnati, 1964; Lecturer, International School of Yeats Study, Sligo, Ireland, 1965; Consultant in Poetry, Library of Congress, Washington, D.C., 1973–74. Recipient: New York Y.M.H.A. Poetry Center Introductions Award, 1951; Yale Series of Younger Poets Award, 1954; Ainsley Prize, 1957; American Council of Learned Societies Fellowship, 1962, 1966; National Institute of Arts and Letters grant, 1967; Ingram Merrill Foundation grant, 1971. Since 1972, Chancellor, Academy of American Poets. Address: Department of English, University of Pennsylvania, Philadelphia, Pennsylvania 19174, U.S.A.

PUBLICATIONS

Verse

> *An Armada of Thirty Whales.* New Haven, Connecticut, Yale University Press, 1954.
> *A Little Geste and Other Poems.* New York and London, Oxford University Press, 1960.
> *The City of Satisfactions.* New York and London, Oxford University Press, 1963.
> *Striking the Stones: Poems.* New York and London, Oxford University Press, 1968.
> *Broken Laws.* New York and London, Oxford University Press, 1970.
> *Corgi Modern Poets in Focus 4,* with others, edited by Jeremy Robson. London, Corgi, 1971.
> *The Center of Attention.* New York, Random House, 1974.

Other

> *Paul Bunyan: Last of the Frontier Demigods.* Philadelphia, University of Pennsylvania Press-Temple University, 1952.
> *The Poetry of Stephen Crane.* New York, Columbia University Press, 1957.
> *Form and Fable in American Fiction.* New York and London, Oxford University Press, 1961.
> *Barbarous Knowledge: Myth in the Poetry of Yeats, Graves, and Muir.* New York and London, Oxford University Press, 1967.
> *Poe Poe Poe Poe Poe Poe Poe.* New York, Doubleday, 1972; London, Robson Books, 1973.
> "Poetry since 1945," in *Literary History of the United States,* revised edition, edited by R. E. Spiller and others. New York, Macmillan, 1974.

> Editor, *The Red Badge of Courage and Other Stories,* by Stephen Crane. New York, Harper, 1957.
> Editor, *American Poetry and Poetics: Poems and Critical Documents from the Puritans to Robert Frost.* New York, Doubleday, 1962.

Editor, with Samuel Hynes, *English Literary Criticism: Romantic and Victorian.* New York, Appleton Century Crofts, 1963; London, Peter Owen, 1966.

Editor, *Discovery: Prize-Winning Campus Poems 1967–1972.* New York, Academy of American Poets, 1974.

Bibliography: *Daniel Hoffman: A Comprehensive Bibliography* by Michael Lowe, Norwood, Pennsylvania, Norwood Editions, 1973.

Critical Studies: *Alone with America* by Richard Howard, New York, Atheneum, 1969; "Daniel Hoffman's Poetry of Affection" by William Sylvester, in *Voyages* (Washington, D.C.) Winter 1970; "Daniel Hoffman" by Jeremy Robson, in *Corgi Modern Poets in Focus 4,* 1971; Interview with W. B. Patrick, in *Daniel Hoffman: A Comprehensive Bibliography,* 1973.

Daniel Hoffman comments:

The titles of my books, I now see, mark out an unpremeditated design in my work thus far. The character of my early verse is fairly suggested by the title poem in *An Armada of Thirty Whales*, a sportive fable which both celebrates the natural order and suggests that man is limited by his place in it. The theme is elaborated and mythologized in *A Little Geste*, a sequence of eight poems which recreates a 14th century legend (of Robin Hood) as a fertility ritual and dramatizes the conflicts between natural freedom and the harsh restraints of social order. The title poem of my third book, *The City of Satisfactions*, is a free-verse obsessional nightmare enactment of The Great American Dream – a frantic derailed train trip westward in search of treasure, in endlessly receding images evoked by the perpetual recession of the land, the treasure, the satisfactions.

"Striking the stones to make them sing" is the line in my fourth book from which I take its title: an image of the poet's task. The stones may be the pavements that surround us, for my work has come to range between the sea and the city, to include the natural order and its instinctual joys and also the chaos and anguish exacted from us by the intricate disorder of our mechanistic and unmemoried society.

I make no manifestos, save: Keep imagination free to speak its revelations of the true.

*   *   *

A French plane crashed because the pilot did not know enough English, according to a report which is, metaphorically, impeccable. The triumph of radio English has a levelling effect which makes television sound, at times, almost regional. Stephen Spender may be the last author to hold American and British affiliations in a kinetic equilibrium. Even Robert Bly, who has the most profound range of both theory and practice among contemporary American poets, does not have a normative influence on both sides of the ocean. Quite possibly, the days of literary giants, of a Rilke, Valéry, or Neruda, are over in any language, but the international sweep of English imposes upon all anglophonic poets the necessity of stipulating the boundaries or the assumptions of their provinces, so that the technical stance of a poet, today, has an emotional resonance.

Daniel Hoffman's scansion is modern insofar as he frequently resorts to a shifting visual pattern of spacing, a line of varying length for rhetorical purposes of either reinforcement or of counterpoint. He both demonstrates and denotes his practise in the conclusion of *The Center of Attention:*

The Poem

Arriving at last,

It has stumbled across the harsh
Stones, the black marshes.

The appearance on the page is modern, but actually evokes traditional rhythms. The first line has two unmistakably strong beats, and the isolation of the first line invites a pause, so that the first word of the next line cannot be slighted. The distinction between stressed and unstressed is sharp and consistent. Later on in the poem –

Carved on memory's staff
The legend is nearly decipherable

– one finds a line that echoes a trochaic and choriambic, followed by a line with three primary stresses and a secondary. His lines are like a steady shifting of traditional meters, but never move into the cadences of unmistakable prose. His diction is consistently generic; he prefers to evoke a sense of swerving rather than the precisely classificatory hyperbole. The "stones" and "marshes" do not indicate a world out there, to be photographed, but are emblematic of an inner struggle, the "harsh, black" struggle of writing. The legend, what is read, what is available to all, like a scroll or a saint's life, is "nearly decipherable,"

Casting its message
In a sort of singing.

"A sort of," in the sense of "approximate" but the phrase has also the decipherably older meaning of "a particular kind" as when Swift writes about "a sort of jabber." Hoffman's use of rhyme, however sparing and occasional, however attenuated semantically or prosodically, brings him close to a tradition which bypasses Whitman and which assumes a correlation between literary and social decorum. In "The Sonnet," he contrasts his memory of Louise Bogan's faith in the sacredness of form to the formlessness of bearded youths and rumpled girls.

His province is conservative, a poetry that indirectly evokes, without imitating them, the worlds of Yeats and Muir, a "sort of singing" to make older ways of feeling accessible today. He is less interested in discovering new perceptions than in finding new ways of expressing feelings common to people now and in the past. He is chary of assuming a common knowledge and is sparing in specific literary references. When he quotes Mallarmé, "donner un sens plus pur aux mots de la tribu," the allusion to his own interest in Poe is decipherable, but the central meaning of the quotation expresses his own aim. (Actually his poetry should be seen as one aspect of his total literary production.)

With his concern for *bon sens*, his development has been a shift of emphasis rather than an experimentation with new assumptions. He has put successively rigorous restraints upon his lines. The title "City of Satisfactions" has ironic overtones; whereas the multiple meanings of "Broken Laws" – legal, or natural identity papers or

> The broken laws
> Almost deciphered on
> This air we breathe

– occurred in a collection that was considerably less ironic than the predecessors. Irony implies a commonly held set of social assumptions, and has, perhaps, inevitably hierarchical implications of shared values. In the increasing pluralism of assumptions, Hoffman has brought the center of his attention to what can be shared. Each line has a sharply delimited focus, so that overtones emerge from the sequence of lines, and from the sequence of poems.

His most recent book, *The Center of Attention,* is almost a single book length poem, as if he were moving toward a latter-day Lucretian disquisition, in a sort of singing, "On the Nature of Feelings." The title poem – to sum it up – sets forth the basic conflicts between peace and violence, between the impulses to save and to destroy a would-be suicide who is the "center of attention." The conflict is never totally absent in the "elementals": Wind, Wave, Trees, Raven, Boar, the poems of places, directions and death. The trend in the collection is toward an increasingly abstract interiorization, and sense of death, so that the final poem – about poetry – affirms what has been his central concern all along, that the poem, by evoking a lost sense of order, should provide an immediate experience of order.

– William Sylvester

HOLBROOK, David (Kenneth). British. Born in Norwich, Norfolk, 9 January 1923. Educated at Colman Road Primary School; City of Norwich School; Downing College, Cambridge (Exhibitioner), 1941–42, 1945–47, M.A. 1946. Served as a Tank Troop Officer, and Explosives and Intelligence Officer, in the East Riding of Yorkshire Yeomanry, 1942–45. Married Margot Holbrook in 1949; has four children. Assistant Editor, *Our Time* magazine, London, 1947–48; Assistant Editor, Bureau of Current Affairs, London, 1948–51; Tutor in Adult Education and School Teacher, 1951–61: Tutor at Bassingbourn Village College, Cambridgeshire, 1954–61; Fellow, King's College, Cambridge, 1961–65; Part-time Lecturer in English, Jesus College, Cambridge, 1968–70; Writer-in-Residence, Dartington Hall, Devon (Elmgrant Trust grant), 1970–72; Assistant Director of Studies, Downing College, Cambridge, 1973–74. Attended Dartmouth Seminar on English Syllabus Reform, Hanover, New Hampshire, 1966; British Council Lecturer in Germany, 1969; appointed Compton Lecturer in Poetry, University of Hull, Yorkshire, 1970 (resigned); visited Australia on British Council grant to work with English teachers, 1970. Recipient: Writing Fellowship, King's College, Cambridge, and Cambridge University Press, 1961; Leverhulme Senior Research Fellowship, 1964; Arts Council grant, 1970. Agent: Christine Bernard, 7 Well Road, London N.W.3. Address: New Farm House, Madingley, Cambridge, England.

PUBLICATIONS

Verse

Imaginings. London, Putnam, 1961.
Against the Cruel Frost. London, Putnam, 1963.

701

Penguin Modern Poets 4, with Christopher Middleton and David Wevill.   London, Penguin, 1963.
Object Relations. London, Methuen, 1967.
Old World, New World. London, Rapp and Whiting, 1969.

Plays

The Borderline, music by Wilfred Mellers (opera for children; produced London, 1959).
The Quarry, music by John Joubert (opera for children). London, Novello, 1967.

Novel

Flesh Wounds. London, Methuen, 1966.

Short Stories

Lights in the Sky Country. London, Putnam, 1962.

Other

Children's Games. Bedford, Gordon Fraser, 1957.
English for Maturity. London, Cambridge University Press, 1961.
Llareggub Revisited (on Dylan Thomas). London, Bowes and Bowes, 1962.
The Secret Places: Essays on Imaginative Work in English Teaching and on the Culture of the Child. London, Methuen, 1964.
English for the Rejected. London, Cambridge University Press, 1964.
The Quest for Love. London, Methuen, 1964.
I've Got to Use Words. London, Cambridge University Press, 1966.
The Flowers Shake Themselves Free (songs set by Wilfred Mellers). London, Novello, 1966.
The Exploring Word. London, Cambridge University Press, 1967.
Children's Writing. London, Cambridge University Press, 1967.
Human Hope and the Death Instinct. Oxford, Pergamon Press, 1971.
The Masks of Hate in Art, Thought and Life in Our Time. Oxford, Pergamon Press, 1971.
Sex and Dehumanisation: The Problem of False Solutions in the Culture of an Acquisitive Society. London, Pitman, 1972.
Dylan Thomas and the Code of Night. London, Athlone Press, 1972.
The Pseudo-Revolution: A Critical Study of Extremist "Liberation" in Sex. London, Stacey, 1972.
English in Australia Now. London, Cambridge University Press, 1973.
T. F. Powys: Love under Control. London, Covent Garden Press, 1974.
Gustav Mahler and the Courage to Be. London, Vision Press, 1974.
Sylvia Plath and the Problem of Existence. London, Athlone Press, 1975.

Editor, *Iron Honey Gold* (anthology of verse). London, Cambridge University Press, 1961.
Editor, *People and Diamonds* (anthology of stories). London, Cambridge University Press, 1962.

Editor, *Thieves and Angels* (anthology of drama).   London, Cambridge University Press, 1963.

Editor, *Visions of Life* (anthology of prose).   London, Cambridge University Press, 1964.

Editor, with Elizabeth Poston, *The Cambridge Hymnal.*   London, Cambridge University Press, 1967.

Editor, *Plucking the Rushes* (anthology of Chinese poetry).   London, Heinemann, 1968.

Editor, *I've Got to Use Words* (course for less-abled children).   London, Cambridge University Press, 1969.

Editor, *The Case Against Pornography.*   London, Stacey, 1972.

Editor, *The Honey of Man.*   Melbourne, Nelson, 1973.

Critical Studies: in *Time* (New York), 14 August 1964; *Times Literary Supplement* (London), 21 January 1965; in school edition of *Flesh Wounds*, London, Longman, 1967; in *Sunday Times Colour Supplement* (London), 19 May 1968; essay by the author, in *Poetry Book Society Bulletin* (London), Christmas 1969; *Towards a Moral Approach to English Studies* (on David Holbrook and F. R. Leavis) by Gordon Pradl, Harvard University, unpublished dissertation, 1971; "David Holbrook's Humanities" by Roger Poole, in *Books and Bookmen* (London), September 1973.

David Holbrook comments:

A few people have seen that all my work is of a piece – Dr. Gordon Pradl, for instance, in his dissertation at Harvard. In my poetry and prose fiction I am trying to find what meaning there might be in normal, everyday existence – assuming that it should be possible, *there*, to find a sense of having existed to some point. I have kept deliberately to domestic, quotidian living, searching for transcendence in that, since I believe we are doomed if we cannot. In my books for teachers and my anthologies I have tried to encourage those in education to cherish creativity in children, in the sense of helping to explore their normal existence, through symbolism, to find meaning in it.

To this exploration of authenticity, searching for what Maslow calls "peak-moments" in ordinary life, the hollow postures of hate are the greatest enemy. I have therefore tried to diagnose the schizoid trends in contemporary culture to show that they are false, and a bluff, from "James Bond" myths, to the sex novel, and pornography. At the same time I have tried to show how genuine artists may be engaged with schizoid problems of identity, and of not knowing where to find a sense of the meaning in life – namely Dylan Thomas, Sylvia Plath, and Gustav Mahler. In doing so I have come to find the prevalent "model" of man unsatisfactory – the belief of those from Freud to Lorenz, who seem to think instincts of aggression and sex are primary. I believe that culture and symbolism are man's primary needs – and I am trying to apply this view in educational books, in criticism, and in my own writing. This revolution in thought about man I believe to be part of a widespread change – encompassing psychoanalysis, phenomenology, post-Kantian philosophy, and philosophical anthropology. I find more interest in this revolution in Europe and America – while at home in England the thinking minority have betrayed "the people" into a new barbarism which is destroying values and making a more creative future impossible. Intellectuals slavishly follow the Sunday papers, or the trendy fashions, or the trivialities of television – and proclaim their right to indulge in pornography and other vices. The onslaught of this new Barbarism will make all our efforts towards a more creative education,

towards new and more visionary works of the imagination, and even towards good
community life useless – unless there is a change of heart. And meanwhile, all one
can do is to go on as best one can, with creative writing, and trying to warn of the
dangers to survival in cultural nihilism.

*   * ˙   *

The subject matter of David Holbrook's poetry is, for the most part, domestic,
personal and everyday: it is of the "real world" of which he is an advocate in so
much of his critical and educational writing. It is a world that is explored with
feeling and compassion and from which morals are drawn or implied. If not directly
didactic, there is usually an undertow of didacticism to be detected in his poetry. It
can be personal to the point of being candid. Thus in the poem "To His Wife
Going to Bed" (the title itself is point enough) it is gooseflesh which is exposed
"drawing your petticoat off – showing your husband what he after clings to in
bed." Mind you, it is gooseflesh transfigured by being "like wind-
touched-on-water." Sometimes the poems are personal to the point of embarrassment when in "Fingers in the Door" his emotion on seeing the pain caused by
closing his child's fingers in a door jamb makes him wish "myself dispersed in
hundred thousand pieces" when it was "For her I cast seed into her mother's
womb."

But it is this sympathy for the pain and distress of others, and the ability to
express it, that informs his best poems. In "Unholy Marriage," a poem about the
death of a young girl pillion passenger on a motor-cycle who lies "anointed only by
the punctured oil" while her parents wait worrying because "she's late tonight,"
the simple unemphasised ending –

> Some news? They hear the gate
> A man comes: not the best.

– gives strength to the direct emotion of what has gone before.

The language employed in most of his poems is straightforward and unadorned:

> This is the sort of evening on which to write a poem

– a reaction, one imagines, against the verbosity of the forties which he castigates
in his crtical works. Though sometimes, when combined with the long freely
written lines he employs, it tends towards a looseness of form which can compromise the strength of the feelings expressed. If there is a weakness in Holbrook's
verse it is this, and the influence of a romanticism deriving from what would seem
an idiosyncratic interpretation of the work of D. H. Lawrence and other literary
heroes. The strength of his verse is its obvious and direct honesty, despite the
pitfalls of naivety into which it sometimes leads him.

– John Cotton

HOLDEN, Molly. British. Born in London, 7 September 1927. Educated at Commonweal Grammar School, Swindon, Wiltshire; King's College, London, B.A.
(honours) in English 1948, M.A. 1951. Married Alan Holden in 1949; has one son
and one daughter. Disabled by multiple sclerosis in 1964. Recipient: Arts Council
award, 1970; Cholmondeley Award, 1972. Address: 58 Willow Road, Bromsgrove,
Worcestershire, England.

PUBLICATIONS

Verse

> *The Bright Cloud.* London, Outposts Publications, 1964.
> *To Make Me Grieve.* London, Chatto and Windus-Hogarth Press, 1968.
> *Air and Chill Earth.* London, Chatto and Windus, 1971.
> *A Speckled Bush.* London, Poem-of-the-Month Club, 1974.
> *The Country Over.* London, Chatto and Windus, 1975.

Novels

> *The Unfinished Feud* (juvenile). Leicester, Brockhampton Press, 1970; New
>   York, Hawthorn Books, 1971.
> *A Tenancy of Flint.* London, Chatto and Windus, 1971.
> *White Rose and Wanderer.* London, Chatto and Windus, 1972.
> *Reivers' Weather.* London, Chatto and Windus, 1973.

Critical Study: by Martha Byers, in *British Poetry since 1960*, edited by Michael
Schmidt and Grevel Lindop, Oxford, Carcanet Press, 1972; "The Poetry of Molly
Holden" by Roger Alma, in *Poetry Nation 2* (Manchester), 1974.

Molly Holden comments:

My major theme is the English countryside, although town-born and bred, but
always near enough to open land to feel that that was where I belonged and which I
wanted to preserve, even if only in words. My verse-forms are usually free,
although I have used rhyme a little more lately. Any influences on my work are
those of English literature. Reviewers have mentioned Clare, Thomas Hardy,
Edward Thomas, Housman. These I proudly accept while wishing and feeling my
tone to be my own.

*   *   *

There is a sense in which any poet, on publication, is offering hostages to
fortune. This would seem especially so in the case of Molly Holden whose subject
matter is external nature, her tone quietly contemplative and her language and
forms basically traditional. It is as if Hardy, Frost and Edward Thomas are
constantly hovering in the wings and the dangers of invidious comparisons or just
becoming lost in the legions of "nature poets" are acute and obvious. What is it
then which sees her succeeding in a field where the competition is so strong and
failure so frequent, which sees her making something freshly individual from a
poetic vein which some might feel to be exhausted? First, of course, is the need for
a keenly accurate eye and that it should be directed by a critical faculty which
allows of a judicious selection from what is observed, the choice and juxtaposition
of just the right details to make the observation illuminating and to the point. This
Molly Holden has and exercises: a winter frost is "sharp and white as acid" or the
bark of a crack willow "plateaux of outer rind rooted in pith." In "Sanctuary" she
describes a derelict railway station –

> The unpatched road
> leads only to a farm. Building and gates
> have been destroyed – Wire boundaries the track
> which now is grass, rails gone and signals down

– where it is the reverberating ambiguity of "signals down" that clinches it; and in "Piper's Hill" we encounter what is basically a painter's eye:

> Now colour separates and age
> makes individuals of them all, edges
> the tags of forest with resisting oaks
> that stain towards the darker heart
> of evergreen on higher contour lines.

But there is more than this. Not vision so much, though in poems such as "Revelation" Molly Holden does capture most skilfully those fleeting moments of realization:

> Only the shrinking snow
> revealed all this and, likely,
> such a state of thaw and I
> would not coincide again.

No, it is more a matter of a deeply personal involvement and concern which gives an edge of intense feeling to poems which could, otherwise, so easily lapse into the commonplace. As in "The Dying Publican" when:

> Upstairs there ebbed away
> the life of more than a man.

Molly Holden conveys in her poems that sense of life which reaches out beyond the individual to where one is part of the very environment in which one finds oneself. It is this which enables her to write so sympathetically in "Winter Quarters" of a gipsy family taking shelter in a deserted house –

> This was for hibernation only, no need
> to make for comfort; a roof to keep out the snow
> was all they wanted

– where human beings share with external nature the primeval instinct to survive. It adds up to an intense awareness of an order in which we all share, and without which

> the fields would jumble, the hedges stray
> and the fork in the road lead nowhere of importance.
> – from "Hill In Winter"

Then there is her technical skill. The ability to tell a story directly and simply as in "Seaman, 1941," or to handle lines with a deftness which pushes the meaning forward while knitting the poem neatly together:

> The theory works. After an edge-flowered spinny
> the red soil greens, in thin and tenuous lines
> that strengthen, heighten, grow in bulk and gold,
> until the corn, in summer fullness, shines.
> – from "Severn Harvests"

Indeed, Molly Holden's felicitous pursuit of a line of argument through a poem can give, as in "The Gap" for example, a unity and completeness which result in a pleasingly aesthetic whole.

That Molly Holden is an invalid can add a poignancy to some of her poems. Certain poems allude to this and an anguished note is heard from time to time, but it is so controlled that it enriches rather than intrudes:

> Poetic justice is imperfectly exemplified in me
> who, as a child, as a girl, was persuaded that
> I felt as earth feels, the furrows in my flesh.
> — from "Illness"

In this, as in all else, Molly Holden's unsentimental and tight hold on her use of language produces quietly forceful poems that steadily grow on you.

— John Cotton

HOLLANDER, John. American. Born in New York City, 10 October 1929. Educated at Columbia University, New York, A.B. 1950 (Phi Beta Kappa), M.A. 1952; Indiana University, Bloomington, Ph.D. 1959. Married Anne Loesser in 1953; has two daughters. Junior Fellow, Society of Fellows, Harvard University, Cambridge, Massachusetts, 1954–57; Lecturer, Connecticut College, New London, 1957–59; Instructor, 1959–61, Assistant Professor, 1961–63, and Associate Professor of English, 1963–66, Yale University, New Haven, Connecticut. Since 1966, Professor of English, Hunter College, City University of New York. Gauss Lecturer, Princeton University, New Jersey, 1962; Visiting Professor, Indiana University, 1964; Lecturer, Salzburg Seminar in American Studies, 1965; Overseas Fellow, Churchill College, Cambridge, 1967–68. Member of the Poetry Board, Wesleyan University Press, 1959–62; Editorial Assistant for Poetry, *Partisan Review*, New Brunswick, New Jersey, 1959–66; Contributing Editor, *Harper's* magazine, New York, 1969–71. Recipient: Yale Series of Younger Poets Award, 1962; National Institute of Arts and Letters grant, 1963; National Endowment for the Arts grant, 1973. Fellow, American Academy of Arts and Sciences. Address: 88 Central Park West, New York, New York 10023, U.S.A.

PUBLICATIONS

Verse

A Crackling of Thorns. New Haven, Connecticut, Yale University Press, 1958.
Movie-Going and Other Poems. New York, Atheneum, 1962.
A Beach Vision. Privately printed, 1962.
A Book of Various Owls (for children). New York, Norton, 1963.
Visions from the Ramble. New York, Atheneum, 1965.
The Quest of the Gole (for children). New York, Atheneum, 1966.
Philomel. London, Turret Books, 1968.
Types of Shape: Poems. New York, Atheneum, 1969.
The Night Mirror: Poems. New York, Atheneum, 1971.
Town and Country Matters: Erotica and Satirica. Boston, David R. Godine, 1972.
Selected Poems. London, Secker and Warburg, 1973.

The Head of the Bed.   Boston, Godine Press, 1974.
Tales Told of the Father.   New York, Atheneum, 1975.

Play

An Entertainment for Elizabeth, Being a Masque of the Seven Motions; or, Terpsichore Unchained (produced New York, 1969). Published in *English Renaissance Monographs 1* (Amherst, Massachusetts), 1972.

Other

The Untuning of the Sky: Ideas of Music in English Poetry, 1500–1700.   Princeton, New Jersey, Princeton University Press, 1961.
Images of Voice.   Cambridge, Heffer, and New York, Chelsea House, 1969.
The Immense Parade on Supererogation Day (juvenile).   New York, Atheneum, 1972.

Editor, *Selected Poems,* by Ben Jonson.   New York, Dell, 1961.
Editor, with Harold Bloom, *The Wind and the Rain: An Anthology of Poems for Young People.*   New York, Doubleday, 1961.
Editor, with Anthony Hecht, *Jiggery-Pokery: A Compendium of Double Dactyls.*   New York, Atheneum, 1967.
Editor, *Poems of Our Moment.*   New York, Pegasus, 1968.
Editor, *Modern Poetry: Essays in Criticism.*   London, Oxford University Press, 1968.
Editor, *American Short Stories since 1945.*   New York, Harper, 1968.
Editor, with others, *The Oxford Anthology of English Literature.*   New York and London, Oxford University Press, 2 vols., 1973.
Editor, with Reuben Brower and Helen Vendler, *I. A. Richards: Essays in His Honor.*   New York, Oxford University Press, 1973.

Manuscript Collection: Beinecke Library, Yale University, New Haven, Connecticut.

Critical Studies: *Alone with America* by Richard Howard, New York, Atheneum, 1969; "The Poem as Silhouette: A Conversation with John Hollander" by Philip L. Gerber and Robert J. Gemmett, in *Michigan Quarterly Review* (Ann Arbor), ix, 1970; "The Sorrows of American Jewish Poetry" by Harold Bloom, in *Commentary* (New York), March 1972; " 'I Carmina Figurata' di John Hollander" by Cristina Giorcelli, in *Scritti in Ricordo di Gabriele Baldini*, Rome, Edizione di Storia e Letteratura, 1972; "Some American Masks" by David Bromwich, in *Dissent* (New York), Winter 1973.

*   *   *

John Hollander has been compared to Ben Jonson by Richard Howard, and the exuberant classicism of Jonson, the sense that art was *hard work*, does inform the whole of Hollander's poetic career. Yet Hollander is one of several American poets of his generation (I think of Ashbery, Merwin, Merrill as analogues) who started out in the Fifties largely under an alien guise, as though they were going to be wit-poets of the age of Eliot and Auden. There is in early Hollander (*A Crackling of Thorns*) a technical debt to Auden as to Jonson and Marvell, but deep poetic influence has nothing to do with overt structures, and Hollander's true precursors, creators of his stance and sensibility, provokers of his authentic poetic anxieties, came out of a very different Anglo-American tradition: the Romantic skepticism of Shelley; the Epicurean nihilism of Rossetti, Pater and Wilde; the American elegiac intensities of Stickney, aspects of Stevens, and of Hart Crane; and the equally American tormented pathos of the Yiddish poet Moshe Leib Halpern.

Movie-Going evidenced Hollander's rapid darkening into his own tradition of visionary skepticism and self-conscious yet essentially wild phantasmagoria. The climax of Hollander's first phase is in the long poem, *Visions from the Ramble*, an American Expressionist brief epic in the mode of Crane's *The Bridge*. The poem is stunningly ambitious, but possibly written too soon in the poet's life, and several of its parts are clearly much more successful than the poem as a whole, which, though coherent, is self-divided and even uneasy in its tone, despite the continuous exuberance of invention and the sustained technical mastery.

A middle phase of Hollander's poetry truly begins not with *Types of Shape*, an almost brilliantly despairing collection, but with *The Night Mirror*, a book of introspective lyrics of the poet's first full maturity, and one of the genuinely distinguished volumes of its generation. Themes of mortality, of the sense that no spring can follow past meridian, are expressed here with a directness of emotional power previously untouched by Hollander. The satirical and erotic verse of *Town and Country Matters* gives ebullient release to Hollander's other side, the now energized and grotesque wit of an inharmonious skeptic whose scholarly obsession always has been harmony. With the long poem or quasi-Stevenian sequence, "The Head of the Bed," Hollander opens himself fully to American nostalgias and American nightmares, and achieves his masterpiece, at least to date, giving us a work comparable to the best we have had since the death of Stevens in 1955.

– Harold Bloom

HOLLO, Anselm (Paul Alexis). United States Resident. Born in Helsinki, Finland, 12 April 1934; son of the professor and translator J. A. Hollo. Educated at schools in Helsinki and Cedar Rapids, Iowa; Helsinki University; University of Tübingen, Germany, B.A. (equivalent). Married Josephine Wirkus in 1957. Translator and Book Reviewer for German and Finnish periodicals, and secretary to his grandfather, Professor Paul Walden, 1955–58; Program Assistant and Co-Ordinator, BBC, London, 1958–66. Visiting Lecturer, State University of New York, Buffalo, Summers 1967, 1969; Visiting Lecturer, 1968–69, Lecturer in English and Music, 1970–71, and Head of the Translation Workshop, 1971–72, University of Iowa, Iowa City; Associate and Visiting Professor, Bowling Green University, Ohio, 1972–73; Poet-in-Residence, Hobart and William Smith College, Geneva, New York, 1973–74, and Michigan State University, East Lansing, 1975. Contributing Editor, *Modern Poetry in Translation*, London, and *New Letters*, Kansas City, Missouri; Poetry Editor, *Iowa Review*, Iowa City, 1971–72. Address: 112 Washington Street, Geneva, New York 14456, U.S.A.

PUBLICATIONS

Verse

Sateiden Valilla (Rainpause). Helsinki, Otava, 1956.
St. Texts and Finnpoems. Birmingham, Migrant Press, 1961.

Loverman.   New York, Dead Language Press, 1961.
We Just Wanted to Tell You.   London, Writers Forum, 1963.
And What Else Is New.   Chatham, Kent, New Voice, 1963.
History.   London, Matrix Press, 1964.
Trobar: Loytaa (Trobar: To Find).   Helsinki, Otava, 1964.
Here We Go.   Newcastle upon Tyne, Strangers Press, 1965.
The Claim.   London, Goliard Press, 1966.
For the Sea: Sons and Daughters We All Are.   Ryde, Isle of Wight, privately
   printed, 1966.
The Going-On Poem.   London, Writers Forum, 1966.
Poems/Runoja (bilingual edition).   Helsinki, Otava, 1967.
Isadora and Other Poems.   London, Writers Forum, 1967.
Leaf Times.   Exeter, Exeter Books, 1967.
The Man in the Tree-Top Hat.   London, Turret Books, 1968.
The Coherences.   London, Trigram Press, 1968.
Tumbleweed: Poems.   Toronto, Weed/Flower Press, 1968.
Haiku, with John Esam and Tom Raworth.   London, Trigram Press, 1968.
Waiting for a Beautiful Bather: Ten Poems.   Milwaukee, Morgan Press, 1969.
Maya: Works, 1959–1969.   London, Cape Goliard Press, and New York,
   Grossman, 1970.
America del Norte and Other Peace Herb Poems.   Toronto, Weed/Flower Press,
   1970.
Message.   Santa Barbara, California, Unicorn Press, 1970.
Sensation 27.   Canton, New York, Institute of Further Studies, 1972.
Some Worlds.   New Rochelle, New York, Elizabeth Press, 1974.

Other

The Minicab War, with Gregory Corso and Tom Raworth.   London, Matrix
   Press, 1961.
Surviving in America, with Jack Marshall and Sam Hamod.   Iowa City, Cedar
   Creek Press, 1972.

Editor, and Translator, *Kaddisch,* by Allen Ginsberg.   Wiesbaden, Limes,
   1962.
Editor, and Translator, *Red Cats: Selections from the Russian Poets.*   San Fran-
   cisco, City Lights Books, 1962.
Editor, *Jazz Poems.*   London, Vista Books, 1963.
Editor, and Translator, *In der Flüchigen Hand der Zeit,* by Gregory Corso.
   Wiesbaden, Limes, 1963.
Editor, and Translator, *Huuto ja Muita Runoja,* by Allen Ginsberg.   Turku,
   Finland, Tajo, 1963.
Editor, and Translator, *Kuolema van Gogh Korvalle,* by Allen Ginsberg.
   Turku, Finland, Tajo, 1963.
Editor, and Translator, with Markku Lahtela, *Idan ja Lannen Runot.*   Helsinki,
   Weilin and Goos, 1963.
Editor, *Negro Verse.*   London, Vista Books, 1964.
Editor, and Translator, *Selected Poems,* by Andrei Voznesensky.   New York,
   Grove Press, 1964.
Editor, and Translator, *Nain Ihminen Vastaa.*   Turku, Finland, Tajo, 1964.
Editor, and Translator, *Five Feet Two,* by Rolf-Gunter Dienst.   Nottingham,
   Tarasque Press, 1965.
Editor, and Translator, *Word from the North: New Poetry from Finland.*   Black-
   burn, Lancashire, Screeches Press, 1965.

Editor, and Translator, *Helsinki: Selected Poems*, by Pentti Saarikoski. London, Rapp and Whitling, 1967.

Editor, and Translator, *Selected Poems*, by Paavo Haavikko. London, Cape Goliard Press, and New York, Grossman, 1968.

Editor, and Translator, *The Twelve and Other Poems*, by Aleksandr Blok. Lexington, Kentucky, Gnomon Press, 1971.

Translator, *Some Poems*, by Paul Klee. Lowestoft, Suffolk, Scorpion Press, 1962.

Translator, *A Man Survives*, by Vladimir Maximov. New York, Grove Press, 1963.

Translator, *John Lennon Panee Omiaan*. Helsinki, Otava, 1964.

Translator, *Das Manilaseil*, by Veijo Meri. Munich, Carl Hanser Verlag, 1964.

Translator, *491*, by Lars Gorling. New York, Grove Press, 1966.

Translator, *The Trees of Vietnam*, by Matti Rossi. Mexico City, El Corno Emplumado, 1966.

Translator, *The Erotic Minorities*, by Lars Ullerstam. New York, Grove Press, 1966; London, Calder and Boyars, 1967.

Translator, *In the Jungle of Cities*, by Bertold Brecht. New York, Grove Press, 1966.

Translator, *Hispanjalainen Jakovainaa*, by John Lennon. Helsinki, Otava, 1966.

Translator, *In the Dark, Move Slowly: Poems*, by Tuomas Anhava. London, Cape Goliard Press, and New York, Grossman, 1969.

Translator, with Sidney Berger, *Thrymskvitha* (Icelandic Skald). Iowa City, Windhover Press, 1970.

Translator, with Robin Fulton, *Paavo Haavikko and Tomas Transtromer*. London, Penguin, 1974.

Translator, *Querelle*, by Jean Genet. New York, Grove Press, 1974.

Translator, *Emmanuelle, The Anti-Virgin*, by Emmanuelle Arsan. New York, Grove Press, 1974.

Anselm Hollo comments:

(1970) Poems are *given*: they are also "graphs of a mind moving" (Philip Whalen). Each poem, if and when it works, is a singular, at times even "unique" formal, emotional, intellectual entity, posing no problems to the poet beyond those contained in itself. The sources are in the poet's life – and that includes his reading, his given "place" at any given "time," his awareness of all animate and inanimate objects (and subjects) around him. When he is in love, he writes, "for love"; and writing, he is, stands, falls, gets up and walks again, *in love.* That is the "House of Light," the "portable state of grace," described in one of the world's greatest poems, the Cherokee Indian "Spell for the Attraction of Affections."

(1974) One way or another, most of us poets tend to aim for the "direct hit," that deeply satisfying *ouch!* of the inner gunfighter toppling over on the dusty little main street of the Reader's Heart. ... The Temper of that "hit" is various; inflated reputations are proposed on what in another medium, say painting or sculpture, would be instantly recognized and rejected as miserable tear-jerkers. However, no poet ever was, is, or will ever be in total control of his or her radar installation. The Built-In Shit Detector (invented by the late Mr. Hemingway) is always liable to freak out and start regurgitating into the system the very substance it was supposed to eliminate. It may take a long time, perhaps years, perhaps forever, to discover such malfunction and its causes. However, one keeps on trying, and when the poem is there, one knows it, and you know it too.

*   *   *

The poetry of Anselm Hollo is fun. In his later verse, furthermore, we come to expect the unexpected with every turn of the page, almost with every new line; and we are seldom disappointed. Of late years, too, his diction has become less "English" (meaning decorous) and more "American" (meaning slangy and colloquial). But his poetry always has been unadorned and keyed to the rhythms of common speech. He speaks, that is, as "one of us" not from a platform, and this is surprising in view of the years he spent as a program director on the BBC. Or perhaps in his diction he is compensating for the fact that his father was an eminent professor of philosophy and theory of education at the University of Helsinki.

Mr. Hollo's career as a translator began at the University of Helsinki also, where he translated many European classics into Finnish including Cervantes, Dostoievski, and Henry James. I mention this because Mr. Hollo is still better known as a translator (especially for his magnificent translations into English of Alexander Blok and Andrei Voznesensky) than he is as a poet. In view of the fact that his own verse has now appeared in more than 18 anthologies and that he has published four substantial books of poems, a much wider recognition of his poetic achievement seems long overdue. Another fact delaying such recognition may be that Mr. Hollo is primarily a *comic* poet. (What is he laughing at? people ask themselves uneasily, Himself? Me? The world? The nature of things? T. S. Eliot never behaved like that.) Can it be that people have been conditioned into expecting poets to be *serious* and are at a loss with one who has an overmastering sense of the ridiculous, the absurd?

One of the recurrent themes in his most recent book, *Sensation*, is the science fiction dream, which, it turns out, is only the old romantic pursuit of the blue flower in disguise:

> Let me tell you, the captain knew
> exactly what he would do
> soon as he reached the destination
> he would fuse with her
> plumulous essence
> & they would become a fine furry plant
> later travelers would run their sensors over
> to hear it hum
> "call me up in dreamland"
> by the old minstrel known as "the van"
> ultimate consummation of long ethereal affair
> he knew he would miss
> certain small addictions
> acquired in the colonies
> visual images baloney sandwiches
> but those would be minor deprivations
> hardly bothersome in the vita nuova
> he was flying high
> he was almost there
> & that is where
> we leave him to go hurtling through the great warp
> & at our own ineffable goals

A second recurrent theme is the goddess Maya, who is, he explains,

> the energy
> put forth in producing
> the performance of the world.

It follows, of course, that Mr. Hollo himself is an aspect of this goddess:

> through two layers of glass
> the far end of this restaurant
> a man
> whose head is
> a glob
> of light
> like anybody's
> any body
> he is formless form
> by means of maya
> & all her daughters, assumes
> innumerable forms
> of which I am one
> eating out alone.

It bucks a man up when he is eating out alone to think of himself as part of the cosmic force which makes possible "the performance of the world." Like the science fiction theme, the maya theme is comic, cheerful, with romantic overtones.

On occasion Mr. Hollo pokes fun at a sombre romantic classic, here Verlaine's "Il Pleur dans Mon Coeur":

> after Verlaine
> right now
> it is raining in Iowa City
> but it ain't rainin in my heart
> nor on my head
> because my head
> it wears a big floppy heart, ha ha
> it wears a big floppy heart.

The tragic note enters his poetry rarely and usually in his translations, and even here, as in this brief poem from the Finnish, with an element of comic surprise:

> go to the lakeshore go
> throw in a feather and a stone
>
> the stone   floats
> it is the day your son comes home
> – from "Tumbleweeds"

A quieter more intimate tone prevails in some of his earlier lyrics, as in "Webern":

> switch off the light
> the trees stand together
>
> easier then
> to be in our bodies

growing quietly
"dem tode entgegen"

slow it is
a slow business

to grow a few words
to say love.

Mad as the world is, Mr. Hollo suggests, we'll all get home sometime; and this irrepressible hunch, the root of his cheerfulness, balances his laughter at the mad stock race of experience in "About Her":

outside
some human beings were roaring
to one another

inside and no doubt
contrapuntally he was whispering
to the typewriter's erratic pulse

the words on the paper
and the words in his head
never quite the same

the stock cars were tearing round the track
they seemed to be going a great deal faster
than they were "in fact"

it was a poem in fact
about writing a poem while waiting
for the whole world to come home.

A traveler through many countries and languages, Mr. Hollo has a slightly off-planet slant on human affairs. Like Puck, he is convinced of our absurdity, but like Oberon, beneficient. Of his diction, Peter Schjedahl has commented, "His slight verbal hesitance succeeds in communicating the sense of a man anxious lest his words misrepresent his feelings." And it is very important to this poet that such misunderstandings never occur. Verbal finery and decoration might get in the way of the laughter, the cheerfulness, the outgoing spirit.

– E. L. Mayo

HOLLOWAY, John. British. Born in London, 1 August 1920. Educated at County School, Beckenham, Kent; New College, Oxford (Open History Scholar), M.A. 1945, D.Phil. 1947. Served in the British Army, 1941–45. Married Audrey Gooding in 1946; has two children. Temporary Lecturer in Philosophy, New College, 1945, Fellow, All Souls College, 1946–60, and John Locke Scholar, 1947,

Oxford; Lecturer in English, Aberdeen University, 1949–54. University Lecturer in English, 1954–66, Fellow of Queens' College, 1955, Reader in Modern English, 1966–72, and since 1972, Professor of Modern English, Cambridge. Byron Professor, University of Athens, 1961–63; Alexander White Professor, University of Chicago, 1965; Hinkley Professor, Johns Hopkins University, Baltimore, 1972. Litt.D.: Aberdeen University, 1954; Cambridge University, 1969. Fellow, Royal Society of Literature, 1956. Address: Queens' College, Cambridge, England.

PUBLICATIONS

Verse

The Minute and Longer Poems.   Hessle, Yorkshire, Marvell Press, 1956.
The Fugue and Shorter Pieces.   London, Routledge, 1960.
The Landfallers: A Poem in Twelve Parts.   London, Routledge, 1962.
Wood and Windfall.   London, Routledge, 1965.
New Poems.   New York, Scribner, 1970.

Other

Language and Intelligence.   London, Macmillan, 1951; Hamden, Connecticut, Archon Books, 1971.
The Victorian Sage: Studies in Argument.   London, Macmillan, and New York, St. Martin's Press, 1953.
The Chartered Mirror: Literary and Critical Essays.   London, Routledge, 1960; New York, Horizon Press, 1962.
The Story of the Night: Studies in Shakespeare's Major Tragedies.   London, Routledge, 1961; Lincoln, University of Nebraska Press, 1963.
The Colours of Clarity: Essays on Contemporary Literature and Education.   London, Routledge, and Hamden, Connecticut, Archon Books, 1964.
The Lion Hunt: A Pursuit of Poetry and Reality.   London, Routledge, and Hamden, Connecticut, Archon Books, 1964.
Widening Horizons in English Verse.   London, Routledge, 1966; Evanston, Illinois, Northwestern University Press, 1967.
A London Childhood (autobiography).   London, Routledge, 1966; New York, Scribner, 1968.
Blake: The Lyric Poetry.   London, Arnold, 1968.

Editor, *Poems of the Mid-Century.*   London, Harrap, 1957.
Editor, *Selected Poems,* by Percy Bysshe Shelley.   London, Heinemann, 1959; New York, Macmillan, 1960.
Editor, *Little Dorrit,* by Charles Dickens.   London, Penguin, 1967.
Editor, with Joan Black, *Later English Broadside Ballads.*   London, Routledge, 1974.

John Holloway comments:

A few guiding ideas would be: indifference to all modishness; constant study and innovation; concentration and density; refusal to compromise over difficulty; an interest in folk, street ballad, and popular poetry; and, more recently, interest in a "classic" style, strictly in Eliot's sense.

*   *   *

Although John Holloway has never been thought of primarily as a poet, he has published several volumes of verse during the course of an active career as critic, scholar and teacher. During the 1950's he was sometimes regarded as a Movement poet, and it is true that he contributed to the Movement anthology, *New Lines*, in 1956. But apart from his attachment to fairly strict and traditional verse forms, Holloway had little in common with the other contributors. His characteristic tone was grave, even solemn, rather than ironic, and his poetry was directed to myth rather than social comment. Holloway did, however, resemble some of his contemporaries in being influenced by the terse, formal lyrics of Robert Graves, though in his case the reflective, mythopoeic poetry of Edwin Muir was equally influential. In Holloway's first collection, *The Minute*, there were a number of memorable, well-realized poems, such as "Journey to the Capital," "Poem for Deep Winter" and "Warning to a Guest." But there was, equally, a pervasive sense that the will was too much involved in the production of Holloway's poetry; many of his poems were well-written and carefully structured, but somehow lacking in content or point. And this tendency has become more pronounced in his subsequent poetry, much of which is frankly dull. The dedication to the ideal of writing poetry remains strong and commands respect but the spirit seems lacking. A book-length poem like *The Landfallers* is serious and ambitious rather than convincing or enjoyable; Holloway's gifts are more apparent in his evocations of Greek landscape in *Wood and Windfall*.

– Bernard Bergonzi

HONIG, Edwin. American. Born in New York City, 3 September 1919. Educated in public schools, New York; University of Wisconsin, Madison, B.A. 1941, M.A. 1947. Served in the United States Army, 1943–46. Married Charlotte Gilchrist in 1940 (died, 1963); Margot S. Dennes, 1963; has two children, Daniel and Jeremy. Library Assistant, Library of Congress, Washington, D.C., 1941–42; Instructor in English, Purdue University, Lafayette, Indiana, 1942–43, New York University and Illinois Institute of Technology, Chicago, 1946–47, University of New Mexico, Albuquerque, 1947–49, and Claremont College, California, Summer 1949; Instructor, 1949–52, and Briggs Copeland Assistant Professor, 1952–57, Harvard University, Cambridge, Massachusetts. Associate Professor, 1957–60, since 1960, Professor of English, and since 1962, Professor of Comparative Literature, Brown University, Providence, Rhode Island. Visiting Professor, University of California, Davis, 1964–65. Poetry Editor, *New Mexico Quarterly*, Albuquerque, 1948–52. Director, Rhode Island Poetry in the Schools Program, 1968–72. Phi Beta Kappa Poet, Brown University, 1962. Recipient: Guggenheim Fellowship, 1948, 1962; *Saturday Review* prize, 1957; New England Poetry Club Golden Rose, 1961; Bollingen grant, for translation, 1962; National Institute of Arts and Letters grant, 1966; Amy Lowell Traveling Fellowship, 1968. M.A.: Brown University, 1958. Address: 32 Fort Avenue, Cranston, Rhode Island 02905, U.S.A.

PUBLICATIONS

Verse

The Moral Circus: Poems. Baltimore, Contemporary Poetry, 1955.
The Gazabos: Forty-One Poems. New York, Clarke and Way, 1959; augmented
   edition, as *The Gazabos: Forty-One Poems, and The Widow,* 1961.
Poems for Charlotte. New York, privately printed, 1963.
Survivals: Poems. New York, October House, 1965.
Spring Journal. Providence, Rhode Island, Hellcoal Press, 1968.
Spring Journal: Poems. Middletown, Connecticut, Wesleyan University Press,
   1968.
Four Springs. Chicago, Swallow Press, 1972.
Shake a Spear with Me, John Berryman: New Poems (includes the play Orpheus
   Below).   Providence, Rhode Island, Copper Beech Press, 1974.
At Sixes. Providence, Rhode Island, Bruning Deck Press, 1974.

Plays

The Widow (produced Chicago, 1953).   Included in *The Gazabos: Forty-One
   Poems, and The Widow,* 1961.
The Phantom Lady, adaptation of a play by Calderón (produced Washington,
   D.C., 1965).   Included in *Calderón: Four Plays,* 1961.
Calderón: Four Plays, adaptations by Edwin Honig.   New York, Hill and
   Wang, 1961.
Cervantes: Eight Interludes, adaptations by Edwin Honig.   New York, New
   American Library, 1964.
Calisto and Melibea (produced Stanford, California, 1966).   Providence, Rhode
   Island, Hellcoal Press, 1972.
Life Is a Dream, adaptation of a play by Calderón (broadcast, 1970; produced
   Providence, Rhode Island, 1971).   New York, Hill and Wang, 1970.

Radio Play: *Life Is a Dream,* 1970 (UK).

Other

García Lorca. New York, New Directions, 1944; London, Editions Poetry,
   1945; revised edition, New Directions, 1962; London, Cape, 1968.
Dark Conceit: The Making of Allegory. Evanston, Illinois, Northwestern
   University Press, 1959; London, Faber, 1960; revised edition, New York,
   Oxford University Press, 1966; Providence, Rhode Island, Brown University
   Press, 1973.
Calderón and the Seizures of Honor. Cambridge, Massachusetts, Harvard
   University Press, 1972.

Editor, with Oscar Williams, *The Mentor Book of Major American Poets.* New
   York, New American Library, 1961.
Editor, with Oscar Williams, *The Major Metaphysical Poets.* New York, Wash-
   ington Square Press, 1968.
Editor, *Spenser.* New York, Dell, 1968.

Translator, *The Cave of Salamanca,* by Miguel de Cervantes.   Boston, Crysalis,
   1960.

Translator, *Selected Poems of Fernando Pessoa*. Chicago, Swallow Press, 1971.
Translator, *Divan and Other Writings*, by García Lorca. Providence, Rhode
Island, Bonewhistle Press, 1974.

Bibliography: in *Books and Articles by Members of the Department: A Bibliography* by
George K. Anderson, Providence, Rhode Island, Brown University Department of
English, 1967.

Manuscript Collection: John Hay Library, Brown University, Providence, Rhode
Island.

Critical Studies: "The Voice of Edwin Honig" by John Hawkes, in *Voices* (Vinal-
haven, Maine), January–April 1961; "To Seize Truth Assault Dogmas" by Robert
Taylor, in *The Providence Sunday Journal* (Rhode Island), 4 March 1962; " 'Spring'
Breakthrough in the New Poetry" by James Schevill, in *San Francisco Examiner-
Chronicle*, 5 January 1969; "Double Exposure" by L. Alan Goldstein, in *The Nation*
(New York), 19 May 1969.

Edwin Honig comments:

Matters that may have influenced my becoming a writer (though perhaps this is
only a nice rationalization) were an early sense of exclusion owing to my being
blamed for my younger brother's accidental death when I was five, and a severe,
nearly fatal bout with nephritis when I was nine. A positive influence was my
illiterate grandmother, who spoke Spanish, Arabic, and Yiddish (but no English); I
lived with her and my grandfather for a few years after my parents were divorced
when I was twelve. Experiences of this sort urged certain necessities upon me: one
was to write instead of choking; another, to make sense of the world around me –
but sense that would not exclude my own fantasy. Both my poetry and my
criticism seem to rise out of such a mixed need: the criticism that creates – Spain
(Calderón and García Lorca) as well as allegory – and the poetry that criticizes
persons and places I have loved and distrusted – the "moral circuses" where the
"gazabos" live.

My best poems are either unfinished or still merely notes in a notebook. Some
poems got away (were printed) but have since been excluded from my books
because they did not seem substantial enough or true. In the same way I quarrel
constantly with the poems written by contemporaries old and young. No poet
writing in English in the last sixty years has mastered his art or has resisted the
nervous need to keep changing his style; and so none has been able to write as a
complete human being. Perhaps Rilke and Lorca succeeded in a few poems. (I find,
now that I have written the penultimate sentence, that I am echoing an opinion of
Gottfried Benn.) I have taken to translating and to writing plays out of impatience
with poetry and criticism; but I go on writing poetry – to stop would be a
self-betrayal.

(This was written in 1966, and might just as well stand for what I feel today,
though I think the statement bleaker than need be. There are probably more than
two poets, for instance, who have done a service to the language or their language
in the last sixty years, and I am almost willing to admit that Pound is one.)

*   *   *

Not in the last dilettantish, Edwin Honig's poetry shows careful craftsmanship, breadth of learning, sharp perceptions, and deep authentic feeling. In the earlier volumes, obviously influenced by Eliot and the prevailing standards of modernism, the feeling is often, though not always, insulated by technical virtuosity and layers of erudition. Recently, however, Honig has moved away from the poem as carefully constructed artifact to a looser, though by no means formless, open-ended continuing poem (*Four Springs*). The new form does not diminish any of his technique or learning, nor does it suddenly transform him into a poet easily accessible to the casual reader, but it does more readily release depths of personal emotion. A headnote to *Four Springs* observing that "in 1966 or so I began writing a poem that very soon went beyond my conception of when or where it would end" and that the book's three concluding sections "continue the story to the present date, my fiftieth birthday" gives some evidence of an intention to explore further potential in this new form.

Honig's critical study of García Lorca calls attention to "his problematical forcing of the door of the constant enemy, death." The comment sheds as much light on Honig himself as it does on Lorca. His book titles (viz., *Survivals*, *Spring Journal*, *Four Springs*) – and indeed the poet's work as a whole – affirm life, but the affirmation is wrested, often fiercely and explicitly, from the omnipresent threat of death. "Death with its cup of hopefulness / needs nourishment / but won't be fed by leftovers – / tired grief, / bewilderment of life's exhaust."

– Rudolph L. Nelson

HOOKER, Jeremy. British. Born in Warsash, Hampshire, 23 March 1941. Educated at St. Peter's, Southbourne, 1954–59; University of Southampton, 1959–65, B.A. 1963, M.A. 1965. Married Susan Hope Gill in 1968; has one son. Since 1965, Lecturer in English, University College of Wales, Aberystwyth. Recipient: Eric Gregory Award, 1969. Address: Brynbeidog, Llangwyryfon, Aberystwyth, Cardiganshire, Wales.

PUBLICATIONS

Verse

The Elements. Llandybie, Carmarthenshire, Christopher Davies, 1972.

Other

John Cowper Powys. Cardiff, University of Wales Press, 1973.

Critical Studies: by Philip Pacey, in *Poetry Wales* (Cardiff), Autumn, 1972; John Tripp, in *Planet* (Llangeilo Tregaron, Cardiganshire), February–March 1973; Randall Jenkins, in *Anglo-Welsh Review* (Pembroke Dock, Wales), Spring 1973.

Jeremy Hooker comments:

So far I have written from a sense of strong personal attachment to southern localities familiar to me since childhood, but where the presence of history and prehistory and also of other writers, such as Hardy, the Powys brothers, Richard Jefferies and Edward Thomas, is palpable. Thus I have attempted to establish my own way of experiencing, and also that of my forebears who were predominately agricultural labourers, the life of places that have strong literary and historical associations – associations that work both with and against the individual experience I try to express. There is, in the south, an opposition between continuity and discontinuity, and often a sense that all the air has been breathed, so that the relationship, and sometimes the struggle, between the living and the dead, the present and the past is one of my principal themes. Above all, I am moved to write by the physical nature of the landscape itself, by the coexistence of such phenomena as Stonehenge and Porton, the Cerne giant and the jets from Boscombe Down, and by a sense of family history that is inseparable from this landscape. Living in Wales has helped to bring these themes into focus by distancing me from their place of origin, but also by making me aware of the Welsh poet's relationship to his material, which is quite different from that of the majority of his English counterparts.

I suppose everything that is implied by "belonging" and "not belonging" can be said to be at the root of my work. My inclination is to write extended sequences and sequences of related lyrics rather than occasional poems.

*   *   *

With a thin collection called *The Elements,* Jeremy Hooker provided only 11 poems, although the fine sequence "Elegy for the Labouring Poor" is a long one. Most of the poems are correspondingly austere, a few almost crumbling at the touch. But Hooker's work is quite excellent, and much praised, especially in Wales. He went there to work as a lecturer, and his attitude is one of curiosity expressed in eloquent terms combined with the utmost respect for Welsh history and traditions, realising that the Welsh have a mind of their own, and doing his best to comprehend their foibles and whims.

The stark countryside of mid-Wales with its own associations finds a place in his most recent work, and he seems to have gained from this experience a desire to establish connections with the past. The clear sense of history in his poems, and his intense pre-occupation with a search for personal roots, elicit considerable sympathy from some Anglo-Welsh practitioners. He understands, completely, a poet's love of his land and his desperate need to relate to his own people. Thus, his own integrity has been a quiet, steady example to others, and those poets he particularly admires – Edward Thomas, David Jones, R. S. Thomas, Roland Mathias and John Ormond – all contain lessons of restraint that heated Celts could usefully absorb.

It is Hooker's dignified reticence that appeals, each word and line fully scrutinised for its allotment of truth and accuracy before being committed to the page; his refusal to embroider, to gloss, or to shout noisily. He reminds one of some patient, skilful sculptor working very slowly to chip away the best pieces from a slab of recalcitrant granite. Such work has the cleanliness of a skelton, picked clean of flesh:

> He moves like timber on a swell,
> In mud gaiters and clay-coloured cord,
> Bent to it, sculpting a furrow.
> Mould's his name: James Mould
> With shoots in Hants and Wiltshire.
> His blunt boot-prints, fugitive
> As the cloud at his rear,
> Are unseen by the camera that exhumes
> Celtic patterns from suave downland.
> But the tread's purposeful.
> – "Elegy for the Labouring Poor"

And here is a love poem, called "There":

> As sent to badger dark in the warm soil;
> As moist places to the secret mole;
> As essential darkness to earth itself:
> Love, the night surrounds us.
> We are the confluence of underground streams.
> We grow together and in daylight
> Flow out apart, now each in each, remade.

Hooker's grave and impressive "Elegy" is a brave, imaginative and moving sequence which wrestles with the heartbreaking problem of trying to pierce the darkness of the botched lives of his rural ancestors in Hampshire and Dorset, in the days of harsh poverty, cottage slums, dawn-to-dusk grafting in the fields, burning thatch, redcoats, and "Captain Swing." The melancholy tread of his verse ("Nothing lasts / But the mortal nature of all that's unique"), the grapple to make some sense of the shaping landscape and the earth's continuity, fuse to make his undertaking a serious, conherent and ambitious one. A small complaint laid at his door is that there is too much landscape in his work and not enough human figures. But Jeremy Hooker is already a fine poet on the evidence of only two slender offerings, having pushed forward from his first selection in the anthology *Introduction 1*. Whether he chooses, in the future, to be published in Wales or England, it will be interesting to watch his development.

– John Tripp

HOPE, A(lec) D(erwent). Australian. Born in Cooma, New South Wales, 21 July 1907. Educated at Sydney University, B.A. 1928; Oxford University, B.A. 1931. Married Penelope Robinson in 1938; has three children. English Teacher, New South Wales Department of Education, 1933–36; Lecturer in English and Education, Sydney Teachers College, 1937–45; Senior Lecturer in English, Melbourne University, 1945–50. Professor of English, 1950–69, and Library Fellow, 1969–72, Canberra University College, later Australian National University; now retired. President, Australian Society of Authors, 1966. Recipient: Britannica-Atlantic Award, 1965; Levinson Prize (*Poetry*, Chicago), 1969; Ingram Merrill Foundation Award, 1969. Litt.D.: Australian National University, 1972. O.B.E. (Officer, Order of the British Empire), 1972. Agent: Tim Curnow, Curtis Brown (Australia) Pty.

Ltd., P.O. Box 19, Paddington, New South Wales 2021. Address: 66 Arthur Circle, Forrest, A.C.T. 2063, Australia.

PUBLICATIONS

Verse

> *The Wandering Islands.* Sydney, Edwards and Shaw, 1955.
> *Poems.* Sydney, Angus and Robertson, and London, Hamish Hamilton, 1960; New York, Viking Press, 1962.
> (*Poems*), edited by Douglas Stewart. Sydney, Angus and Robertson, 1963.
> *Collected Poems 1930–1965.* Sydney, Angus and Robertson, London, Hamish Hamilton, and New York, Viking Press, 1966.
> *New Poems 1965–1969.* Sydney, Angus and Robertson, 1969; New York, Viking Press, 1970.
> *Dunciad Minor: An Heroick Poem.* Melbourne, Melbourne University Press, 1970.
> *Collected Poems 1930–1970.* Sydney and London, Angus and Robertson, 1972.
> *Selected Poems.* London, Angus and Robertson, 1973.

Other

> *Australian Literature 1950–1962.* Melbourne, Melbourne University Press, 1963.
> *The Cave and the Spring: Essays on Poetry.* Adelaide, Rigby, 1965; Chicago, University of Chicago Press, 1970.
> *A Midsummer Eve's Dream: Variations on a Theme by William Dunbar.* Canberra, Australian National University, and New York, Viking Press, 1970; Edinburgh, Oliver and Biyd, 1971.

> Editor, *Australian Poetry 1960.* Sydney, Angus and Robertson, 1960.

Bibliography: *A. D. Hope: A Bibliography,* Adelaide, Libraries Board of South Australia, 1968.

*   *   *

A. D. Hope's poetry is of two main kinds, elegies and satires: the nobility of vision and decorum of such poems as "The Death of The Bird" and "X-ray Photograph," and lengthy mock heroic satires like *Dunciad Minor* and "Conversation with Calliope" (744 lines assiduously reconciling erudition with jokiness).

These two extremes, however, are bound by Hope's narrow prosodic range and the constant assertion of sources in European culture. There is an uncomfortably insistent sense of "Literature" in his verseforms and in the echo of celebrated lines; this is emphasised by a very particular avoidance of specifically Australian themes and speech rhythms. It is as if Hope's work belongs to the English-writing tradition but not to the present English-speaking world. It is inclined to be mandarin and to make a point of standing against modernism, as Australia itself has remained (till very recent years) largely outside the social and intellectual environment of modernism and most of what has followed. Possibly it is the poetry of a man isolated from his sources.

As with other twentieth century classicists, A. D. Hope's traditional forms too often have the effect of obstructing any affinity with the living concerns of our own time; however his finest poems tower above such strictures:

> See how she strips her lily for the sun:
> The silk shrieks upward from her wading feet;
> Down through the pool her wavering echoes run;
> Candour with candour, shade and substance meet.

These are the opening lines of a magnificent poem about Susannah and the elders, combining sensuousness with high seriousness. As for the satires, they are often heavy-handed against trivial faults; but in "The Martyrdom of St Teresa" the regular rhythms and rhymes are turned to savage effect again and again:

> She was so small a saint, a holy
> Titbit upon the butcher's block –
> Death chose the cuts with care and slowly
> Put on his apron, eyed the clock
>
> And sitting down serenely waited
> Beside the plump brown carcass there,
> Which kings had feared and the popes hated,
> Which had known neither hate nor fear;
>
> While through all Spain mysterious thunder
> Woke cannibal longings in the blood,
> Inviting man to put asunder
> The flesh that had been joined with God.
>
> The little nuns of her foundation
> Arrived on foot, by mule or cart,
> Each filled with meek determination
> To have an elbow, or the heart.

The slyness of his wit is in every stanza: "Inviting man to put asunder / The flesh that had been joined with God."

How lumpish, by comparison, is his use of the same verseform in a declamatory poem about the ploughshare and the sword (!) which opens with this stanza:

> Home the farmer carts his sheaves,
> Homeward rides a laurelled brow:
> Living bread and barren leaves,
> Yet the sword puts down the plough.

In the context of Australian poetry in the 1940's and 1950's, still dominated by the Norman Lindsay Sydney Charm School (led by Kenneth Slessor and Douglas Stewart) A. D. Hope brought a fresh savagery, a ruthless iconoclasm – as with the closing lines of "Imperial Adam":

> . . . Adam watching too
> Saw how her dumb breasts at their ripening wept,
> The great pod of her belly swelled and grew,
>
> And saw its water break, and saw, in fear,
> Its quaking muscles in the act of birth,
> Between her legs a pigmy face appear,
> And the first murderer lay upon the earth.

– Rodney Hall

HOROVITZ, Michael. British. Born in Frankfurt, Germany, 4 April 1935; emigrated to England at the age of 2. Educated at William Ellis School, London; Brasenose College, Oxford, B.A. in English. Married to the poet Frances Horovitz; has one son, Adam Albion. Since 1959, Editor and Publisher, *New Departures* magazine, London, later Bisley, Gloucestershire. Painter and singer; director of the Live New Departures road show. Address: Piedmont, Bisley, Stroud, Gloucestershire GL6 7BU, England.

PUBLICATIONS

Verse

Declaration. London, New Departures, 1963.
Strangers. London, New Departures, 1965.
Nude Lines for Barking (in Present Night Soho). London, Goliard Press, 1965.
High Notes from When I Was Rolling in Moss. London, New Departures, 1966.
Poetry for the People: A Verse Essay in "Bop" Prosody. London, Latimer Press, 1966.
Bank Holiday: A New Testament for the Love Generation. London, Latimer Press, 1967.
The Wolverhampton Wanderer: An Epic of Football. London, Latimer Press, 1969.
Love Poems. London, New Departures, 1971.

Other

Alan Davie. London, Methuen, 1963.

Editor, *Children of Albion: Poetry of the "Underground" in Britain.* London, Penguin, 1969.

Translator, with Stefan Themerson, *Europa,* by Anatol Stern. London, Gabberbocchus, 1962.

Critical Studies: "Of Relative Importance" by Barry Cole, in *Ambit 26* (London), 1966; Afterword to *Children of Albion* by the author, 1969; "Poetry Explodes" by

Adrian Mitchell, in *The Listener* (London), 14 May 1970; "Vanessa's Hangups" by Jeff Nuttall, in *Ambit 48* (London), 1971; "Blake and the Voice of the Bard in Our Time" by the author, in *Books* (London), Winter 1972; "The Need for the Non-Literary" by the author, in *Times Literary Supplement* (London), 29 December 1972.

*   *   *

It is difficult to separate Michael Horovitz's poetry from his public image. This isn't said in a derogatory sense, but more in acceptance of the fact that his alive, good-humoured, and enthusiastic appearances at readings, and his total commitment to a less-hackneyed approach to the writing and presentation of poetry, are always reflected in his work. It too is full of surprises, and it jabs at the reader with light, fast punches which are full of a deceptive power.

Just as Horovitz's promotional activities have been maintained over the years, so has his work sustained a constant tone, one which, in its colour and vigour, overcomes certain limitations of depth and precision. As with many enthusiastic people, Horovitz's use of words is sometimes noted more for its liveliness than its accuracy. He sprays language at the reader, and if a little of it falls by the wayside then one has to learn to ignore this and instead allow oneself to be swept along on the crest of the wave of words which carries the narrative.

There are, it's only fair to say, certain Horovitz poems which do aim at a greater degree of control than is evident in much of his writing, and these often contain an appealing lyricism. But his reputation rests primarily on the longer poems, in particular his magnum opus, *The Wolverhampton Wanderer*, in which the role of the football star as a working-class hero – and a symbol of the true energy of our society – is tied in with the role of the poet as a kind of wandering bard. If any one work of Horovitz's is to be recommended it is this, and its racy, humorous style is remarkably effective.

Whether Horovitz can develop as a poet is something which only time will tell. Not that his achievements to date should be under-estimated. But so far he has tended to function essentially on the surface-level, philosophically speaking, and one would like to see him attempting a deeper work, a work which would still project his involvement with contemporary life and at the same time extend it to take in larger social and political issues.

– Jim Burns

HOSKINS, Katherine (de Montalant).   American.   Born in Indian Head, Maryland, 25 May 1909. Educated at Smith College, Northampton, Massachusetts, A.B. 1931. Married Albert Learnard Hoskins in 1935; has one child. Recipient: Brandeis University Creative Arts Award, 1957; Guggenheim Fellowship, 1958; Longview Award, 1958. Lives in Weston, Massachusetts, U.S.A.

PUBLICATIONS

Verse

A Penitential Primer: Poems.   Cummington, Massachusetts, Cummington Press, 1945.

Villa Narcisse: The Garden, The Statues, and the Pool. New York, Noonday
   Press, 1956.
The Partridge Tree. San Francisco, Poems in Folio, 1957.
Out in the Open: Poems. New York, Macmillan, 1959.
Excursions: New and Selected Poems. New York, Atheneum, 1967.

Manuscript Collection: Library of Congress, Washington, D.C.

Katherine Hoskins comments:

My themes appear to consist of Nature and People wherever I happen to be –
often, in thought at least, south of the Mason-Dixon Line. My influences are
probably my admirations – George Herbert, Andrew Marvell, Wallace Stevens, J.
C. Ransom, Yeats and Spenser. I have been considerably blamed for complication
of verse forms, use of inversions and archaic words. Still and all, to quote Apollinaire, "each of these poems commemorates an event in my life."

                         *   *   *

In Katherine Hoskins' poems, common occasions acquire uncommon value. A
pine overhanging a pond, a child skating on the pond form a harmony "too
delicate, too lone to hold / . . . a second more / against the continents at arms."
But in a certain miraculous way, they do hold: the peace they signify fills the
watcher's consciousness, "swells . . . / to the world's rim, shoves off / the clawing
continents and down, down, down."
   During a country wedding a sudden flurry of leaf-patterned shadows on a white
church wall distracts the congregation. And we are reminded, ever so lightly, that
human occasions exist within larger patterns. Friend and kin glance outward "To
where these little twisters blow, / To where the prime, the five-point / Stag sleeps
under the hill." But nature quiets, and the congregation resumes its business:
"faced forward to the old pattern."
   The lover of beauty and order, the "debased artistocrat," is offended by grace-
less ski boots, skis, leaning against a wall "Like careless planking" – "Her
unclassed child's appliances for pleasure." But it is the child, she understands, who
saves her values: "Self-multiplying quartz refracts all things"; so does the child
assimilate a diverse world, find order and meaning in unlikely possibilities.
   Mrs. Hoskins' tone, in these and in her poems generally, is reflective, quiet. Her
ironies are lightly underlined, almost always countered by larger affirmations.
There are, of course, instances of sustained acerbity – "Success," for example,
which is entirely concerned with images "straw or carved." Some few poems give
us a sense of terror: the mutilated body in "After the Late Lynching," "All down
one side no ribs / But broken things that moved"; the wild spirit in "The Municipal
Swimming Pool," "Who rests a bloody head against the drain / and clings with
battered nails, be-dazed from scrabbling / fifty feet of naked concrete box."
   Yet these poems, based firmly on daily life and common human recognitions,
rich in formal resources, are often curiously remote. Partly, this is a consequence
of language that moves too easily toward the general and emotionally dead. At the
climactic moment of "Pity as Power," when Louie Guevin comes back after death
to visit his daughter, "She wasn't she says, afraid / But apprehensive." Is
"apprehensive" really the word the daughter would have used? And if it is, why
should we understand what she felt? Even so fine a poem as "The Byfield Rabbit"

is marred by what may be called poetic diction. The "wheel-whir, bee-hum, bird song / In single sound arose" is soft and quiet like the summer work day it describes, but it does not evoke fresh responses.

There is also an unresisted tendency to make sure we understand the poet's meaning, to give us a nudge, usually at the end of the poem. The effect is to make the major event of the poem merely an illustration of homely wisdom. We need not be told at the end of "Luxury," for instance, that the rowboat, which is lust, "perseveres against the waking hours." Mrs. Hoskins is an accomplished poet, certainly. What she sometimes lacks is not technical skill, but courage. Courage to follow through the implications of her thought, and to let them stand for themselves.

– Jacqueline Hoefer

HOUÉDARD, dom(Pierre-)Sylvester. British. Born in Guernsey, 16 February 1924. Educated at Elizabeth College, Guernsey; Jesus College, Oxford; Collegio Santanselmo, Rome, Ph.L. Served in the Far East during World War II. Benedictine monk: Prinknash Abbey, Gloucester, since 1949. Librarian, Farnborough Abbey, 1959–61. Literary Editor for the New Testament, Jerusalem Bible, 1961. Since 1965, Founding Member and Vice-President, Association of Little Presses. Visual Poetry exhibited: St. Catherine's College, Oxford, 1964; Gallerie Riquelme, Paris, 1964; Gallerie Bressy, Lyons, 1965; Gallerie Denise-Davy, Paris, 1965; Kornblee Gallery, New York, 1965; ICA, London, 1965; Signals Gallery, London, 1965; Tyler School of Art, Philadelphia, 1966; Peacetower, Los Angeles, 1966; Midland Gallery, Nottingham, 1966; Galeria Universitaria Aristos, Mexico City, 1966; Galeria Juana Mordo, Madrid, 1966; Gallery 10, London, 1966; Kunstcentrum 'tvenster, Rotterdam, 1966; Arnolfini, Bristol, 1966; Galeria Barandiaran, San Sebastian, Spain, 1966; Castello del Valentino, Turin, 1966; Subscription Rooms, Stroud, Gloucestershire, 1966; Brighton Festival, 1967; Lisson Gallery, London, 1967; New Metropole Arts Centre, Folkestone, Kent, 1967; French Institute, London, 1967; Festival de Fort Boyard, Rochefort-sur-Mer, France, 1967; Studio 2-B, Bergamo, Italy, 1967; Festival of Spain, 1967; Absalom, Bath, 1968; Gallerie nächst St. Stephan, Vienna, 1968; Totem-1 Gallery, Salford, Lancashire, 1968; Westfälische Kunstverein, Münster, 1969; Fine Arts Gallery, Vancouver, 1969; Axis, Bristol, 1969; Ceolfrith Gallery, Sunderland, 1970; Stedelik Museum, Amsterdam, 1970; Victoria and Albert Museum, London (and tour), 1970–72; Bear Lane Gallery, Oxford, 1970, 1971; Avelles Gallery, Vancouver, 1971; Art Centre, Bristol, 1971; Laing Gallery, Newcastle upon Tyne, 1971, 1972; Oval House, London, 1974; LYC Museum, Brampton, Cumberland, 1974. Vice-President, The Poetry Society, 1974. Address: Prinknash Abbey, Gloucester GL4 8EX, England.

PUBLICATIONS

Verse

Yes-No. Daneway, Gloucestershire, Daneway Press, 1963.
Thalamus-Sol. Maidstone, Kent, St. Albert's Press, 1964.

Rock Sand Tide. Woodchester, Gloucestershire, Daneway Press–Openings Press, 1964.
Frog-Pond-Plop. Woodchester, Gloucestershire, Openings Press, 1965.
Atom. Woodchester, Gloucestershire, Openings Press, 1965.
Kinkon. London, Writers Forum, 1965; revised edition, as *Op and Kinkon Poems and Some Non-Kinkon,* 1965.
Worm-Wood/Womb-Word. Daneway, Gloucestershire, Daneway Press, 1966.
A Book of Chakras (8 Yantrics): Studies Towards Mechanical Fingers by dsh for Inner Moon Pointing. Watford, Hertfordshire, Watford School of Art, 1966.
To Catch a Whiteman by His Manifesto. Corsham, Wiltshire, Openings Press, 1967.
Tantric Poems, Perhaps. London, Writers Forum, 1967.
Book of 12 Mudras. Corsham, Wiltshire, Openings Press, 1967.
Book of Mazes and Troytowns. Corsham, Wiltshire, Openings Press, 1967.
Easter Frog Toy for Pesach-Skipover. Corsham, Wiltshire, Openings Press, 1967.
Eros A-Gape. London, Lisson Delta Publications, 1967.
Semaine Euclidienne. Sherborne, Dorset, South Street Publications, 1968.
Poster for the Breakdown of Nations 4th-World Conference. London, Resurgence Publications, 1968.
Deus-Snap. Corsham, Wiltshire, Openings Press, 1968.
Miniposters. Sherborne, Dorset, South Street Publications, 1968.
The Sun-Cheese Wheel-Ode: A Double-Rolling-Gloster Memorial for Ken Cox. Sherborne, Dorset, South Street Publications, 1969.
A Snow Mouse. Bristol, Axis Multiple, 1969.
En Trance. Bristol, Axis Multiple, 1969.
12 Nahuatl Dancepoems from the Cosmic Typewriter. Sherborne, Dorset, South Street Publications, 1969.
Texts, edited by John Sharkey. London, Lorrimer Books, 1969.
Streets Go Both Crazy Ways at Once. Sherborne, Dorset, South Street Publications, 1969.
Book of Battledores. Sherborne, Dorset, South Street Publications, 1969.
Book of Onomastikons. Sherborne, Dorset, South Street Publications, 1969.
Splendid Weeping. Corsham, Wiltshire, Openings Press, 1969.
Successful Cube Tranceplant in Honor of Chairman Mao. Openings Press, 1970.
Ode to the Colonels. Corsham, Wiltshire, Openings Press, 1970.
Grove Sings: Reflecting Poem for ihf. Sunderland, Ceolfrith Bookshop and Gallery, 1970.
Auto-de-Chakra-Struction. Oxford, Bear Lane Gallery, 1971.
Main Calm Line. London, National Poetry Centre, 1972.
Like Contemplation. London, Writers Forum, 1972.

Other

Translator, *Office of Our Lady* (the Encalcat Office). London, Darton Longman Todd, 1962.

Bibliography: in *Dom Sylvester Houédard,* edited by Charles Verey, Sunderland, Ceolfrith Arts Centre, 1972.

Critical Studies: In *Dom Sylvester Houédard,* edited by Charles Verey, Sunderland, Ceolfrith Arts Centre, 1972.

dom Sylvester Houédard comments:

inevitably i feel my own work as the continuation of the unbroken traditions of benedictine poets & artists – beginning with the monastic literati of the ancient west who *created* civilization & the european cultural revolution until the mimetic embourgeoisification of art as revivalism – with the neo-isms of *re*naissance thru *neo*gothic – even for part of this period tho not right up till napoleon III's salon des refusés there is a wu-wei quality of playing the stringless lute in benedictine baroque as contrasted with the jesuit – & poetmonks in the west have always cultivated what newman calls "the alliance of benedict & virgil." eg:

s-abbo s-adelhard agobard b-alcuin s-aldhelm (the concretist) s-angilbert s-bede s-bertharius (caedmon) s-dunstan (another concretist) florus fridoard gerbert (sylvester II) heiric hepidamn-the-newsallust herimann v-hildebert hincmar b-hrabanus-maurus (concrete) abbess hroswitha the ladycatullus playwright hucbald itier-de-vassy lawrence of durham lupus modoin notkerbalbulus s-odo otfrid s-pascasiusradbert peter-the-venerable sigebert-the-newovid theodulf & walafridstrabo-the-newvirgil – not to mention the preservers & copiers of not only the pagan latin poets including the erotica but also of pagan icelandic sagas & (tho the danes later destroyed these mss) the earlier british poets (& celtic monkpoets were as honoured as their nonmonk-poets) – for similar reasons sahagun & other friars preserved the nahuatl poetry of aztec & earlier mexico.

to the modern contemplative & poet it is hard not to see the sweep of so called avantgarde creativeness from eg the impressionists & thru dada cage concrete antimimesis autodestructive streetguerilla & authentic je-je communication-dialog structures as so many searches for innerpath social liberation & the creative poetic monastic transcendental experience & vision of seeing things change into what they are – but i feel too this equally strong empathy with the monk-prophet poets of other cultures – tho particularly with the siberian shamans & the feathery flowerdrum heart-&-face-making nahuatl singers & the welsh englynion makers & the zen haiga/haiku makers – yinyang acceptance of yinyang tension is the unifying field of west scriptorium & east zenga – onepointed poetry as spiritual askesis.

*   *   *

"There are certain fundamental types of questioning abt language that shld have occurred in English poetry before it got withered by the festival of britain." So dom Sylvester Houédard wrote in 1964, and his output in the last decade has tried to supply this lack of questioning, sometimes within previously accepted parameters of how poetry works, but more often through a radical denudation of subjective and expressionist language elements, producing a cool flicker of mathematical permutations and/or of sound-effects and/or of visual patterns. The works by which he is best-known are his "typestracts" – typed designs of exraordinary ingenuity which increasingly came to be ikons for contemplation, topological tantric forms linked to language or "poetry" only by the lingering literary hookup anything typewritten still tends to retain, or by a title like "slipping sideways into god" which slips the typestract into both poetry and religion, however nonverbal the design in itself.

Western and oriental meditation join their influences in his work, whether in the "sun/bridesroom" (sol/thalamus) Christmas poem or in his version of Basho's Zen-directed haiku "frog / pond / plop," both using the spatialist techniques of concrete poetry. His ecumenical inclusiveness has been held against him, and his "borderblurs" (to use his own term for the dissolving of art-categories) have been regarded with some suspicion as well as admiration. But in the history of the avant-garde in Britain he has a distinctive place.

– Edwin Morgan

HOWARD, Richard. American. Born in Cleveland, Ohio, in 1929. Educated at Columbia University, New York (Editor, *Columbia Review*); the Sorbonne, Paris. Poetry Editor, *American Review*, New York; Director, Braziller Poetry Series. Fellow of Morse College, Yale University, New Haven, Connecticut. Free-lance literary and art critic and translator. Recipient: Guggenheim Fellowship, 1966; Harriet Monroe Memorial Prize, 1969, and Levinson Prize, 1973 (*Poetry*, Chicago); American Institute of Arts and Letters grant, 1970; Pulitzer Prize, 1970. Address: 37 West 12th Street, New York, New York 10011, U.S.A.

PUBLICATIONS

Verse

Quantities: Poems. Middletown, Connecticut, Wesleyan University Press, 1962.
The Damages: Poems. Middletown, Connecticut, Wesleyan University Press, 1967.
Untitled Subjects: Poems. New York, Atheneum, 1969.
Findings: Poems. New York, Atheneum, 1971.
Two-Part Inventions: Poems. New York, Atheneum, 1974.

Other

Alone with America: Essays on the Art of Poetry in the United States since 1950. New York, Atheneum, 1969; London, Thames and Hudson, 1970.

Editor, *Preferences: 51 American Poets Choose Poems from Their Own Work and from the Past.* New York, Viking Press, 1974.

Translator, *The Voyeur,* by Alain Robbe-Grillet. New York, Grove Press, 1958.
Translator, *The Wind,* by Claude Simon. New York, Braziller, 1959.
Translator, *The Grass,* by Claude Simon. New York, Braziller, 1960.
Translator, *Two Novels* (*Jealousy* and *In the Labyrinth*), by Alain Robbe-Grillet. New York, Grove Press, 1960.
Translator, *Najda,* by André Bréton. New York, Grove Press, 1961.
Translator, *The Automobile Graveyard,* by Fernando Arrabal (produced New York, 1961).
Translator, *Last Year at Marienbad,* by Alain Robbe-Grillet. New York, Grove Press, and London, Calder and Boyars, 1962.

Translator, *Mobile,* by Michel Butor.   New York, Simon and Schuster, 1963.

Translator, *Manhood,* by Michel Leiris.   New York, Grossman, 1963; London, Cape, 1968.

Translator, *Force of Circumstance,* by Simone de Beauvoir.   New York, Simon and Schuster, 1963; London, Deutsch-Weidenfeld and Nicolson, 1965.

Translator, *Erasers,* by Alain Robbe-Grillet.   New York, Grove Press, 1964; London, Calder and Boyars, 1966.

Translator, *For a New Novel: Essays on Fiction,* by Alain Robbe-Grillet.   New York, Grove Press, 1966.

Translator, *The Poetics of Paul Valéry,* by Jean Hytier.   New York, Doubleday, 1966.

Translator, *Natural Histories,* by Jules Renard.   New York, Horizon Press, 1966.

Translator, *History of Surrealism,* by Maurice Nadeau.   New York, Macmillan, 1967; London, Cape, 1968.

Translator, *Histoire,* by Claude Simon.   New York, Braziller, 1968; London, Cape, 1969.

Translator, *The Immoralist,* by André Gide.   New York, Knopf, 1970.

Translator, *May Day Speech,* by Jean Genet.   San Francisco, City Lights Books, 1970.

Translator, *Professional Secrets: An Autobiography,* by Jean Cocteau.   New York, Farrar Straus, 1970; London, Vision Press, 1972.

Translator, *Fall into Time,* by E. M. Cioran.   New York, Quadrangle Books, 1970.

Translator, *The Battle of Pharsalus,* by Claude Simon.   New York, Braziller, and London, Cape, 1971.

Translator, *A Happy Death,* by Albert Camus.   New York, Knopf, and London, Hamish Hamilton, 1972.

Translator, *Critical Essays,* by Roland Barthes.   Evanston, Illinois, Northwestern University Press, 1972.

Translator, *Rosa,* by Maurice Pons.   New York, Dial Press, 1972.

Translator, *Project for a Revolution in New York,* by Alain Robbe-Grillet.   New York, Grove Press, 1972; London, Calder and Boyars, 1973.

Translator, *The Fantastic,* by Tzvetan Todorov.   Cleveland, Case Western Reserve University Press, 1973.

More than 100 other translations of French works published.

*   *   *

In the slightly more than ten years since the appearance of his first book, *Quantities,* Richard Howard, who is now 44, has established himself firmly in a distinguished career as one of our brightest young poets, critics, editors, and translators. And the course of his poetic development seems to me to represent the difficult and treacherous job of surmounting and transforming his learning, sophistication, brilliance, and knowingness, instead of simply displaying it. As with Auden, for example, an acknowledged model for Howard, he is so good at writing interesting and skilful poems that he tends to be taken in by his own cleverness, writing poems that are merely skilful and interesting rather than compelling or passionate – poetry that arises inevitably out of the self's confrontation with itself and the world.

In *Quantities,* with variety of subject, flexibility and power of language and structure, and penetration of insight, Howard has much to say coupled with a virtuoso ability to say it. ''The Return from Montauk,'' for example, presents a beautifully balanced moment in terms of a natural yet complex and ambiguous symbol. The speaker is riding a train at nightfall, and, looking to the east, he sees an image of the setting sun reflected in a window:

> A red suicide
> Descending where, before, the hopes
> Of every day mounted to their
> Customary wreck.

This double perspective is completed when he turns toward the west, and sees through the train window the actual setting sun – imagining, however, in line with the logic of his previously-established conception, that it is the rising sun:

> With another eye
> I see, in the brilliant glass,
> Love, like another sun, rising
> In the western sky.

Thus, at the moment of sunset, he can envision, out of the literal structure of the perception itself, the sunrise, and at the moment of despair, the rebirth of hope.

It is a clear and delicate poem, intricately wrought, suggesting implications that go far below its pellucid surface – a thematically central poem in the book as a whole, for Howard characteristically deals with the knife-edge upon which opposites are balanced, but his vision of the abyss which falls between them is neither deep nor powerful, and hence the tension in his poems is often not strong. There is too much of the dandified manner and not enough of the presence of a man. Order is best when it comes out of energy, not out of literature.

With *The Damages* we find an increased assurance and depth, coupled with an increasing prolixity and confirmation of his bright knowingness. In "For Hephaistos," we find the inevitable and moving confrontation with Auden, who "taught me, taught us all a way / To speak our minds," and the speaker's grateful sense of being free from his master:

> only now, at last
> Free of you, my old ventriloquist,
> Have I suspected what I have to say
> Without hearing you say it for me first.

In "The Encounter," we find a marvelously erotic and mysterious confrontation between a nameless Hero and The Female, which rises convincingly to the level of myth. And there are, on the other hand, Jamesian and Proustian vignettes of childhood ("Seeing Cousin Phyllis Off," "Intimation of Mortality," "Private Drive"); poems of friends, literature, and travel ("Seferiades," "Even the Most Beautiful Sunset"); and the clever poems, such as "To Aegidius Cantor," "Eusebius to Florestan," and "Bonnard: A Novel," which continue his own line of literary ventriloquism and which anticipate the extended fascination Howard is to develop for the "dramatic monologue" in his next volume.

Thus, *Untitled Subjects*, awarded the Pulitzer Prize in poetry for 1970, consists entirely of fifteen such monologues (mostly in the form of letters), spoken by such nineteenth-century Worthies as Sir Walter Scott, Ruskin, Thackeray, and Mrs. William Morris, and arranged chronologically from 1801 to 1915. Howard alludes to Browning in his dedication, "the great poet of otherness," and quotes that poet's saying, "I'll tell my state as though 'twere none of mine." This clearly implies that Browning was writing about himself while pretending to be speaking in the voices of others, and I think this is true. But I do not think either that this makes him simply a poet of otherness or that Howard's dramatic monologues are very similar to his master's. Browning's great poems in this manner characteristically present a vivid person in a moment of crisis or intense self-awareness and self-revelation, and thus do not normally allow for the ease and reflectiveness of letter-writing. On the deepest level, these poems tell us more about Browning than about their ostensible subjects, and they are the better for that.

But Howard's do not, nor do they, with their epistolary manner, typically present a character under duress. When Keats spoke of the chameleon poet, surely he had more in mind than this. What they do, in fact, is "to bring history alive," as the jacket blurb for a historical novel or costume drama might say: they bring the past closer to us, first, by treating it as if it were present, and second, by making it personal and intimate – putting back in, as it were, what the histories leave out. Thus, for example, "1864" is spoken by Thackeray the year after his death, and is a sort of bitter retrospective of his life, career, and particularly his unfortunate marriage: "I had not found what I wanted, nor wanted / What I found." This is good, but it is neither a crisis-situation nor as much Howard as Fra Lippo Lippi is Browning. It is, rather, skilful and interesting, an intelligent piece of literary legerdemain.

Similar poems make up the first part of *Findings*, and this time Howard does not hesitate to write a 14-page poem, "November, 1889," spoken by Browning himself as he nears the moment of death. Revealingly, Howard puts these words into his master's mouth:

> what is dead or dying
> is more readily apprehended by us
> than what is part of life.
> Nothing in writing is
> easier than to raise the dead.

Perhaps this *is* more Howard than Browning, and so he moves on in the second part to more personal poems of love and friendship. But he is still so over-civilized, so full of grace, learning, polish, and elegance, as to seem the victim of his own gifts, keeping himself and his life – even when he does write about these things – at such a distance from the poems that they emerge as snowflakes under glass rather than the prowling animals they have every right to be. The bravura technique becomes, in short, a technique of evasion; no poet need trifle, especially a poet such as Howard who has potentially much to say.

– Norman Friedman

HOWELL, Anthony. British. Born in London, 20 April 1945. Educated at Leighton Park School, Berkshire; Royal Ballet School, London; Centre de la Danse Classique, Cannes. Married Signe Lie in 1972. Dancer with the Royal Ballet, London, 1966. Lecturer in Creative Writing, Grenoble University, 1969–70. Editor of Softly Loudly Books, London. Address: 11 Ascham Street, London N.W.5, England.

PUBLICATIONS

Verse

Sergei de Diaghileff (1929).   London, Turret Books, 1968.
Inside the Castle: Poems.   London, Barrie and Rockliff-Cresset Press, 1969.
Imruil: A Naturalized Version of His First Ode-Book (pre-Islamic Arabic).   London, Barrie and Rockliff-Cresset Press, 1970.
Femina Deserta.   London, Softly Loudly Books, 1971.
Anchovy.   London, Tetrad, 1973.

Other

Editor, *Erotic Lyrics.*   London, Studio Vista, 1970.

Anthony Howell comments:

I write poetry because I was brought up in Reading. You write poetry do you? He writes poetry because he was brought up in Slough. She writes poetry. It doesn't write poetry. We write poetry because we were brought up. They write poetry because they were brought up in blazers.

*   *   *

Anthony Howell's *Inside the Castle,* his first collection, was a crowded book, comparable with Keat's *Poems* of 1817 in that it marked the emergence of a young man of much talent unable or unwilling to refine a capacity for confusion when he saw that he could employ it to keep a poem going when inspiration failed. The book also contained three very good poems ("The Growing Family," "The Head," and "A Reason for Fidelity") where in each case one clear poetic impulse worked the whole way through, nothing sounded forced, and the only obvious debt was to John Crowe Ransom and the Fugitives generally.

Imruil: A Naturalized Version of His First Ode-Book takes a handful of footnotes in an academic crib to the Mu'Allaqat or "Seven Suspended Odes" of pre-Islamic Arabia, and uses them as "a metaphor-cluster" in the making of an original sequence.. A comparison of these verses and the texts of the scholar R. S. Rattray, from whence they are derived, would make a useful exercise for students of literary mechanics. More importantly, this Borgesian game provides Howell with a mask in the shape of a well-fitting *persona* in front of his own feelings, the opacities of *Inside the Castle* are refined, and a number of individual poems reach a high level of lyrical excellence:

> Inhaling the wind out of the East
> One can tell it has satisfied
> The camphor leaves. "Bring
> Me a gift with nothing in your hands . . ."

Later work in magazines and pamphlets has shown the influence of John Ashbery.

– Robert Nye

HOWES, Barbara. American. Born in New York City, 1 May 1914. Educated at Beaver Country Day School, Boston; Bennington College, Vermont, B.A. 1937. Married William Jay Smith, *q.v.*, in 1947 (divorced, 1965); has two sons, David and Gregory. Editor, *Chimera* magazine, New York, 1943–47. Lived in Florence for four years, and in Oxford, France, and Haiti. Recipient: Bess Hopkin Prize, 1949, and Eunice Tietjens Prize, 1959 (*Poetry*, Chicago); Guggenheim Fellowship, 1955; Brandeis University Creative Arts Award, 1958; National Institute of Arts and Letters award, 1971; New England Poetry Club Golden Rose, 1973; Christopher Book Award, 1974. Agent: John Schaffner, 425 East 51st Street, New York, New York 10022. Address: Brook House, North Pownal, Vermont 05260, U.S.A.

PUBLICATIONS

Verse

The Undersea Farmer. Pawlet, Vermont, Banyan Press, 1948.
In the Cold Country: Poems. New York, Bonacio and Saul-Grove Press, 1954.
Light and Dark: Poems. Middletown, Connecticut, Wesleyan University Press, 1959.
Looking Up at Leaves. New York, Knopf, 1966.
The Blue Garden. Middletown, Connecticut, Wesleyan University Press, 1972.

Christmas Card Poems: *Lachrymae Christi and In the Old Country*, with William Jay Smith, 1948; *Poems: The Homecoming and The Piazza*, with Smith, 1949; *Two French Poems: The Roses of Saadi and Five Minute Watercolor*, with Smith, 1950; *The Triumph of Love*, 1953; *Turtle*, 1955; *Early Supper*, 1956; *Lignum Vitae*, 1958; *The Snow Vole*, 1960; *Two Poems: Landscape, Deer Season; Dream of a Good Day*, 1962; *Looking Up at Leaves*, 1963; *Gulls*, 1964; *Leaning into Light*, 1965; *Wild Geese Flying*, 1966; *Elm-Burning*, 1967; *Otis*, 1968; *Talking to Animals*, 1969; *Returning to Store Bay*, 1970; *Evening: Crown Point*, 1971; *Reginae Coeli*, 1972; *Entrance, Casuarinas*, with Gregory Jay Smith, 1972 – all privately printed. Other Occasional Poems: *To W. H. Auden on His Fiftieth Birthday*, 1957; *An Epithalamium: For Petie and Frank Palmer*, 1964; *Hubert Walking: A Profile; For Mother: A Log: On Her Eightieth Birthday*, 1968; *A Liking for People and Animals*, 1968; *Millefleurs: For the Presentation of a Tapestry*, 1969; *For Helen and Bob Allen*, 1970; *Gold Beyond Gold*, 1970; *The Sixth Color of the Afternoon*, 1974 – all privately printed.

Other

Editor, *23 Modern Stories.* New York, Knopf, 1963.
Editor, *From the Green Antilles: Writings of the Caribbean.* New York, Macmillan, 1966; London, Souvenir Press, 1967.

Editor, with Gregory Jay Smith, *The Sea-Green Horse: A Collection of Short Stories* (juvenile).   New York, Macmillan, 1970.

Editor, *The Eye of the Heart: Short Stories from Latin America.*   Indianapolis, Bobbs Merrill, 1973.

Manuscript Collection: Yale University Library, New Haven, Connecticut.

Critical Studies: *Selected Criticism* by Louise Bogan, New York, Noonday Press, 1955; *Modern American Poetry,* edited by Louis Untermeyer, New York Harcourt Brace, 1962.

Barbara Howes comments:

(1970) [I am] a poet, a woman, a wife, a mother: all these things go to make up one's outline.

I am interested in form, and also in what I call "creative form," the working out of a unique form for that one poem. Also interested in the possibilities of free verse. Basically, in what will happen to me and my work next.

I am not very good at discussing my own work. In the essay in *Poets on Poetry* (edited by Howard Nemerov, New York, Basic Books, 1966), I probably stated things as well as I could. As I suggested above, one never knows what one will do next, or, as W. H. Auden said much more eloquently, one never knows if one will write another poem till one has done it. I have been especially influenced perhaps by Emily Dickinson, Yeats, Frost, Hopkins; really, in some way, by about everyone I read. I am much interested in trying to adapt Old French and other forms to modern or contemporary subjects and emotions. Am also interested in the fascinations and complexities of translation.

Basically, I am trying to deal with my experience through my writing; this is how to a degree one can order what one sees and what happens.

(1974) I guess I'll stand by what I said before. All one can do is do the best you can, and keep at it; all the dress-ups of worrying about reviews and getting to know the "right" people are disaster for the serious poet. You just have to keep on at dealing with your experience, whatever it is.

As it turns out, I seem to write about things I see, my children, my friends, my house, my attachments, our animals, the view from any window, in no special order or arrangement. *Place* (physical, not social), which so affects one, comes into it. If you can be attached to people, to a place or places, to ideas, to trees, you will be less likely to fall into the trap of the snarling little ego, which so ranges abroad. Too many writers give in to violence and spite. It is more interesting, though, to be alive, to find what stimulates the imagination, to meet what is beyond one's powers: then a poem may be hatching.

*   *   *

Barbara Howes's last three volumes – *Light and Dark, Looking Up at Leaves,* and *The Blue Garden* – represent a gradual smoothing out and cooling off. In the first, we find that she is an explorer of the abyss, the inner self, and the forbidden. In "City Afternoon," for example, after sensing the vibrations of an unseen subway, an escalator, a disposal unit, and the cooped-up people in a large apartment building, she concludes by hearing, in a lull, the Iron Maiden closing on its spikes.

Or again, in "The Undersea Farmer," the poem comes to its end by taking us back up out of the water and toward the land, as Arnold's Forsaken Merman's wife did, but still urges that we keep hold of our "subaqueous lifeline," as Margaret did not. And, in "The Nuns Assist at Childbirth," she wonders what the nun can make of this "Rude life" pouring "From the volcano," "Tragic, regenerate, wild."

She is especially good about women, treating them in terms of genuine passion and sexuality. "Danae," for example, compassionately and frankly sees bed as their destiny, whether it supports agony or joy. And she does not avoid the personal, as in "Indian Summer," where she ponders the man asleep in her arms. Nor is she afraid of love, as in "The Balcony," which portrays a true interchange between human beings. And "The New Leda" is one of her best. Leda awaits the god's arrival; a nun awaits Christ: what will be their various destinies? – lust, new life, or emptiness? The poem ends with a powerful appeal to the speaker's "Sisters, wastrels," to give over "sacrifice and harm/ And deprivation."

The next two books, however, reveal a somewhat more complacent pattern. Each is divided similarly into two parts, entitled variously "A Short Way by Air" and "Vermont Poems," and "Away" and "At Home," which seems generally to refer to her habit of dividing her time between the West Indies and New England. Thus the one section contains poems of warmth and lushness, while the other embodies a more wintry climate, with human relations cutting across the categories.

Thus, for example, the first section of *Leaves* deals with seascapes, seabirds, fish, swimming, and boating, but it also has a remarkable poem called "Flight," in which a Russian spaceman, a Goya picture, a boy murdered on a subway, and the speaker's reflections on "the outer spaces of the mind" revealed by such brutality, are effectively made into symbols of one another. In "My Dear, Listen," she says:

> An artist should keep
> The pathway open
> To his inward life. . . .

The intensity of the cold is felt in the second section, especially in "The Snow Hole," which tells of a trip to a cleft in the mountains in which can be seen never-melting snow, and which concludes: "Chilled through/ By now, we touch the world." And in the title poem, as well as in "A Few Days Ago," the speaker experiences an almost mythic identification with trees.

And yet the overall impression left by this book is more placid and low-keyed than that of *Light and Dark*. Miss Howes is still a very good poet, bright and resourceful, but less turbulent and anguished. She is rather the keen observer and compassionate commentator than the involved participant, and she has settled on a calm concision of style which tends to flatten the emotional power of her insights – even in such a painful poem as "Flight," which concludes:

> Realizing of him
> That nothing is the same as one young man, one son,
> One good bet, gone.

This is well said, and there is a poignant urgency in the last three repetitive phrases and final verb, but it is still a bit too level in tone.

This impression is confirmed and strengthened by a reading of the latest book. Again, a few poems deal with nightmare ("Sweet Sleep") and the deeps of the mind ("Focus"), but many are given over to jewel-like creature poems reminiscent of, but not as taut as, some of Marianne Moore's work in this line ("Luke, Captive," "The Ostrich Tree"), or to bric-a-brac and *objets d'art* ("Millefleurs," "Gold *Beyond* Gold") whose presence I was less than enthusiastic about in *Light and Dark*. And as the language continues almost imperceptibly to slacken, the

typography of the stanzas seems to grow more intricate, as if Miss Howes unwit-
tingly feels the need to compensate for her loss of intensity:

> From that old cow in the field
> A calf was born;
> He struggles now to rise –
> No, he cannot
> Yet, on his tapestry legs. . . .
> – from "Still-life: New England"

   She wrote, in *Light and Dark,* that "the wild cannot rest with the tame," and
"the strange/Wild frantic clear-eyed ones are gone" ("Lament"), and if her recent
work is any sign, she is right. For if the influence of the wild ones persists in her
poems, she is nevertheless demonstrating that she is not entirely one of them
herself.

– Norman Friedman

HOWITH, Harry. Pseudonym for journalism: **Marc Wyman.** Canadian. Born in
Ottawa, Ontario, 11 August 1934. Educated at Carleton University, Ottawa
(University Medal in Journalism, 1957), B.A. 1956, B.J. 1957. Ottawa Correspon-
dent, Co-operative Press, Ottawa, 1957–59; Editor, *Flight Comment,* Royal Canadian
Air Force, 1960–62; Research Assistant, Royal Commission on Publications,
Ottawa, 1960–61; Editor and Publications Officer, Department of Northern Affairs
and National Resources, Ottawa, 1962–64; Publications Officer, North York Board
of Education, Toronto, 1964–65. Assistant Master in English, 1966–67, Chairman of
the English Department, 1967–69, Assistant to the Academic Dean, 1970–71, and
English Master, 1972–73, Centeanial College, Toronto. Recipient: Canada Council
scholarship, 1959, and grant, 1969, 1970. Address: c/o 335 Crichton Street, Ottawa,
Ontario, Canada.

PUBLICATIONS

Verse

   Street Encounter. Ottawa, Blue "R" Press, 1962.
   Burglar Tools. Ottawa, Bytown Books, 1962.
   *Two Longer Poems: The Seasons of Miss Nicky by Harry Howith and Louis Riel by
     William Hawkins.* Toronto, Patrician Press, 1965.
   Total War. Toronto, Contact Press, 1967.
   Fragments of the Dance. Toronto, Village Book Store Press, 1969.
   The Stately Homes of Westmount. Montreal, DC Books, 1973.

Play

   You Bet Your Love (produced Ottawa, 1957).

Other

   Report of the Royal Commission on Publications, with others.   Ottawa, Queen's
   Printers, 1961.

Manuscript Collection: University of New Brunswick Library, Fredericton.

Harry Howith comments:

   His poetry is about love, loss, time, death, and the excrescences of contemporary urban society. It used both sentiment and heavy-handed irony; it is characterized by wit, and by precision of diction.
   The poets whose work he most admires are: Eliot, Mayakovsky, and Rilke.
   He thinks of himself as a teacher, journalist, editor, poet, and administrator,
more or less in that order.

                                    *   *   *

   "He has a fondness for the romantic," Raymond Souster wrote of Harry Howith
after reading the latter's *Fragments of the Dance*. The collection does have more
than its share of lines that run "Here, little darling, is my warm hand: / give me
your shivering fingers" and poems about loving that end wryly: "And it's supposed
to be a crime. . . . / Be my accomplice." But a more touchy tone can be detected
in *Fragments of the Dance*, a more public and political tone and subject, that may be
summarized, perhaps, in a single line from the title poem which talks about "the
dooms of empires written with a feather."
   This new concern is fully explored in *The Stately Homes of Westmount*, Howith's
latest collection, which includes poems about the "stately homes" in the fashionable districts of three cities: Westmount (the exclusive area of Montreal), Rosedale
(of Toronto), and Rockcliffe (of Ottawa). In the Rosedale poem, Howith notes the
passing of "Wit into humour: Style into fashion: Scorn into hatred," and condemns
the decline of civilized values by pushing the observation to its nth degree in
"MYSTERY, BABYLON THE GREAT, THE MOTHER OF HARLOTS AND
ABOMINATIONS OF THE EARTH." The Westmount and Rockliffe poems are
written more formally but retain a colloquial tone. Here is a verse taken from the
latter poem:

>   sloganeering and invective,
>   hubristic ignorance elevated
>   to dogma; it's not so much
>   the boring arrogance of nonstop

One can detect a manic intensity, and a Canadian can discern the "Ottawa Valley"
accent, with its over-enunciation of every word. The tone corresponds to the
treatment of the subject in poems like "In Memory of Ezra Pound," the last two
verses of which run:

>   You leave for us, cant-cranky
>   but monumental, the Cantos,
>   and your veritable invention
>
>   of made-new verse: if we
>   could sing or even hear correctly,
>   we too might praise Benito Mussolini.

One wonders what links, in the poet's mind, poetic modernism and Italian fascism, for the poem does not say.

This is not meant to suggest *The Stately Homes of Westmount* is lacking in wit, irony, insight or a wide range of reference, for these may be found in profusion in many of the poems. There is, too, the note of self-examination in "The New Nationalism," which in its conclusion finds the poet wondering whether

> . . . there's much difference after all
> between nationalism and rheumatism.
> (P.S.: This makes me, according to my niece,
> a male chauvinist pig.)

Howith is plainly irritated with the world around him, with its ambiguities, certainties and pretentions. As Swift preferred horses, Howith admires penguins – in an effective poem with a clever and characteristic title: "If the World Were My Poem, I'd Revise It."

– John Robert Colombo

HOYEM, Andrew. American. Born in Sioux Falls, South Dakota, 1 December 1935. Educated at Pomona College, Claremont, California, B.A. 1957. Served as a lieutenant in the United States Navy, 1957–60. Married Sally Cameron Heimann in 1961 (divorced, 1964); Judith B. Laws, 1971. Partner, with Dave Haselwood, Auerhahn Press, San Francisco, 1961–64; Owner, Andrew Hoyem, printer, San Francisco, 1965–66; Partner, Grabhorn-Hoyem, publishers, San Francisco, 1966–73. Since 1973, Owner, Andrew Hoyem, printer. Address: 4040 17th Street, San Francisco, California 94114, U.S.A.

PUBLICATIONS

Verse

> *The Wake.* San Francisco, Auerhahn Press, 1963.
> *Lafayette Park Place.* San Francisco, Auerhahn Press, 1964.
> *The Music Room.* San Francisco, Dave Haselwood, 1965.
> *Stranger.* San Francisco, San Francisco Arts Festival, 1965.
> *Happy Birthday.* San Francisco, Andrew Hoyem, 1965.
> *Chimeras: Transformations of "Les Chimères" by Gerard de Nerval.* San Francisco, Dave Haselwood, 1966.
> *A Romance.* San Francisco, Andrew Hoyem, 1966.
> *The Pearl,* with John Crawford, translation of the Middle English poem. San Francisco, Grabhorn Hoyem, 1967.
> *Vengeance.* San Francisco, Grabhorn Hoyem, 1967.

Articles: Poems 1960–1967. London, Cape Goliard Press, and New York, Grossman, 1969.
Try. San Francisco, Grabhorn Hoyem, 1971.
Aim. San Francisco, Grabhorn Hoyem, 1972.
Still Life. New York, Valenti Angelo, 1973.
Petit Mal. San Francisco, Grabhorn Hoyem, 1973.

Critical Studies: Reviews by Gilbert Sorrentino, in *Kulchur 12* (New York), Winter 1963; by Robert B. Shaw, in *Poetry* (Chicago), March 1972.

Andrew Hoyem comments:

I am associated with the San Francisco "renaissance" of poetry of the late Fifties and Sixties which is hardly a school, for one of its advantages is variety.

*   *   *

Andrew Hoyem is a poet so highly eclectic and derivative in style that one is forced to suspect that he has, as yet, failed to discover his own inner voice – or that, if he has, he does not yet know how to speak in it. When he is direct, as in the prose-poem "The Korean Conflict," he is simply ineffective; but his more recondite work, while it demonstrates an excellent grasp of its sources, does not have enough individual quality to make it memorable. "Birds. Moss. Pebbles. Frog. / Fade. / The five finger fern" is good enough for a diary entry, but as pastiche of Japanese or Imagist verse it only reminds us of failures. "Spook Sheep," his "transformation" of de Nerval's most famous sonnet, only manages to be either literal or to change the French into an English de-fused of poetry. He can glide easily enough from satirical observation –

> This bachelor deluding himself
> whose children play in the streets

– to an archaic "Old High Poesy" manner for which it is hard to see the point:

> Fain should I barren Beauty's breast
>   suck shameless to secrete
> faint praise, fame, and fortunes of war,
>   at issue from her teat.

It is all very well to point to irony, Pound, the Provençal; but this lacks attack, appears debilitated by any strong sense of direction besides simply wanting to write poetry. One can at present, regretfully, point only to an evident intelligence and a certain charm and delicacy as Hoyem's positive virtues. But if a poet lacks energy and a personal rhythm then he needs very special qualities indeed to spark him into life; the pleasant and pacific impression that Hoyem's poetry gives, when read as a whole, is not enough.

– Martin Seymour-Smith

HUFANA, Alejandrino G. Filipino. Born in San Fernando, La Union, Philippines, 22 October 1926. Educated at the University of the Philippines, Quezon City, A.B. in English 1952, M.A. in comparative literature 1961; University of California, Berkeley (Rockefeller Fellowship, 1961–62), 1957–58, 1961–62; Columbia University, New York (John D. Rockefeller III Fund Fellowship, 1968–70), M.S. in library science 1969. Served with the North Luzon guerillas, 1944. Married Julita Quiming in 1957; has four daughters. Secretary and English teacher, Cebu Chinese High School, 1952–54. Research Assistant in Social Science, 1954–56, Member of the English Department, 1956–71, since 1971, Associate Professor of English and Comparative Literature, and since 1972, Principal Researcher in Iloko Literature, University of the Philippines. Since 1970, Director of the Library, and since 1971, Editor, *Pamana* magazine, Cultural Center of the Philippines, Manila. Co-Founding Editor, *Signatures* magazine, 1955, *Comment* magazine, 1956–67, *Heritage* magazine, 1967–68, and *University College Journal*, later *General Education Journal*, 1961–72; Editor, *Panorama* magazine, 1959–61. Managing Editor, University of the Philippines Press, 1965–66. Artist: Exhibition in Elmira, New York, 1957, and Manila, to 1972. Recipient: Republic Cultural Heritage Award, 1965. Address: 54 Mabini Street, Area I, University of the Philippines, Diliman, Quezon City, Philippines.

PUBLICATIONS

Verse

> *13 Kalisud.* Quezon City, Collegian New Review, 1955.
> *Sickle Season: Poems of a First Decade, 1948–1958.* Quezon City, Kuwan, 1959.
> *Poro Point: An Anthology of Lives: Poems 1955–1960.* Quezon City, University of the Philippines, 1961.
> *The Wife of Lot and Other New Poems.* Quezon City, Diliman Review, 1971.

Plays

> *Man in the Moon* (produced La Union, 1956, Manila, 1970; revised version, produced Quezon City, 1972). Published in *Panorama* (Quezon City), December 1960.
> *Curtain-Raisers: First Five Plays* (includes *Gull in the Wind, Honeymoon, Ivory Tower, Terra Firma, View from Origin*). Quezon City, University of the Philippines Social Science Research Council, 1964.
> *The Unicorn,* in *Pamana 1* (Manila), June 1971.
> *Salidom-ay,* in *Pamana 2* (Manila), September 1971.

Other

> *Mena Pecson Crisologo and Iloko Drama.* Quezon City, Diliman Review, 1963.
> *Notes on Poetry.* Quezon City, Diliman Review, 1973.

> Editor, *Aspects of Philippine Literature.* Quezon City, University of the Philippines, 1967.
> Editor, *A Philippine Cultural Miscellany, Parts I and II.* Quezon City, University of the Philippines, 1968, 1970.

Editor, with others, *Introduction to Literature*.   Quezon City, Alemar Phoenix, 1974.

Reviews and articles published in periodicals.

Manuscript Collections: University of the Philippines Library, Quezon City; State University of New York, Syracuse.

Critical Studies: "The Poetry So Far of A.G. Hufana" by Jean Edwardson, in *Collegian New Review* (Quezon City), January 1954; "Mutineer, Sight Ascending" by Leonard Casper, in *The Wayward Horizon: Essays on Modern Philippine Literature*, Manila, Community Publishers, 1961; "Poet's Portrait Gallery" by Andres Cristo-bal Cruz, in *Sunday Times* (Manila), 26 November 1961; "Dive in a Hypnosis: The Poetry of Alejandrino G. Hufana" by Albert Casuga, in *Philippine Writing 2* (Man-ila), 1963; *New Writing from the Philippines: A Critique and Anthology* by Leonard Casper, Syracuse, New York, Syracuse University Press, 1966; "Hufana: Rebel-lious Poet" by Florentino S. Dauz, in *Graphic* (Manila), 8 September 1966; "A Poet's Romance with Art" by Jolico Cuadra, in *Chronicle Magazine* (Manila), 1 July 1967; *Poetry in the Plays of A. G. Hufana* by Bernardita Castillo, University of Bohol, unpublished thesis, 1973.

Alejandrino G. Hufana comments:

The pre-publication discipline of any poet should be like the pre-performance training of the athlete or prize-fighter. All flaws considered in public must as such turn the performer back to the privacy of the grind for a repeat. Only birds, or such creatures, are born to the grace of what they do, which also happens to excuse their plunder to live.

*   *   *

Alejandrino G. Hufana is a fascinating and highly original poet. Some of his plans sound somewhat formidably grandiose, but such schemes often result in curtailed versions of the original intention – which must, almost certainly, in the case of mere sections of a work extending to more than 1,000 typescript pages each, be a good thing. Hufana studied in America, and has absorbed much from American poetry – in particular from that neglected master of epigram, Edwin Arlington Robinson. Deeply rooted in the complex culture of his native country, Hufana employs an ambitiously idiosyncratic diction that some non-Filipino readers have taken as evincing a lack of mastery of the English language –

> Unclothing so the Zambul Bali Dag
> May for her dead infanta deep be soft
> The black she-parent grieving on the crag
> A lullaby invokes: "Arrow aloft
> Time for your sleep, piece-of-my-thigh,
> The fletcher is not false, time for your dream,
> Meat will be yours. . . ."

– but this is a serious error. One of Hufana's main aims is to discover and to express what is authentically Filipino, and this, given so complicated and foreign-influenced a culture (there are Filipinos writing in the national language, which is an artifact, and Spanish, as well as in English) is bound to yield results that have an odd appearance to the outside world. Hufana has been called the most successful "anthropological" poet writing in the English language, and the lines quoted above may confidently be employed as evidence in support of such a view. It is high time that both a British and an American publisher put out a comprehensive selection of his poetry.

– Martin Seymour-Smith

HUFF, Robert. American. Born in Evanston, Illinois, 3 April 1924. Educated at Wayne State University, Detroit, A.B. in English 1949, A.M. in humanities 1952. Served as an aerial gunner and bombardier in the Eighth Air Force, 1943–46. Married Sally Ann Sener in 1959; has three children. Instructor, Wayne State University, 1950–52, 1957–58, University of Oregon, Eugene, 1952–53, Fresno State College, California, 1953–55, and Oregon State University, Corvallis, 1955–57, 1958–60; Poet-in-Residence and Assistant Professor, University of Delaware, Newark, 1960–64. Since 1964, Member of the English Department, and currently, Professor of English, Western Washington State College, Bellingham. Writer-in-Residence, University of Arkansas, Fayetteville, 1967. Poetry Editor, *Concerning Poetry,* Bellingham, Washington. Recipient: Indiana University School of Letters Fellowship, 1957; Bread Loaf Writers' Conference Scholarship, 1961; MacDowell Colony Fellowship, 1963. Address: 2820 Eldridge Street, Bellingham, Washington 98225, U.S.A.

PUBLICATIONS

Verse

Colonel Johnson's Ride and Other Poems. Detroit, Wayne State University Press, 1959.
Poems. Portland, Oregon, Portland Art Museum, 1959.
The Course: One, Two, Three, Now! Detroit, Wayne State University Press, 1966.
The Ventriloquists. Chicago, Swallow Press, 1975.

Recordings: *The Sound of Pacific Northwest Poetry,* with others, Washington State Poetry Foundation, 1968; *Robert Huff Reading at the Poetry Center of New York,* McGraw Hill, 1970.

Manuscript Collections: University of Kentucky, Lexington; Wayne State University, Detroit; Carnegie Library, State University of New York, Syracuse.

Critical Studies: Reviews by John Haislip, in *Northwest Review* (Eugene, Oregon), Summer 1967; by William Heyen, in *Poetry* (Chicago), February, 1968.

* * *

Robert Huff is a poet who generally writes in traditional forms; his mentors, as he himself makes clear in *The Course*, are Roethke, Frost, and Yeats. His poetry in *The Course* is an autobiographical unfolding of his life from childhood through recent years; topics include finding his vocation as a poet, memories of relatives, enduring the personal and historical shocks life has to deal him. The book might be regarded, like Delmore Schwartz's great short story ("In Dreams Begin Responsibilities") from which it gets its subtitle ("One, Two, Three, Now!"), as a sort of autobiographical fiction in which the author, like the photographer of that story, tries to get a good fix, the proper artistic slant, on the fluid stuff of life. Like all of us, Huff is both involved and a spectator, human being and artist. Like the confessional poets, he is working close to the nerve ends:

> These days I'm really sure I'm tranquilized
> When any little signal says I'm ready,
> Like this sweet thing teasing my inner ear
> Into a dream of hearing rubber whisper
> Along the humped blacktop back to that boy
> Spoiled sick to death between one smart fool's ad
> And this mean pen at a dead end hanging tight
> Until the good pill works its trick of bells.
>
>   – from "Fixed"

This is powerful poetry, as are other poems in *The Course*, including the title poem, "If It's an Owl," "How Not to Make a Model in a Bottle in a Bar in Ithaca," and especially, "Getting Drunk with Daughter"; the last is surely one of the finest poems ever written by an American poet, as is "Rainbow" in Huff's earlier collection, *Colonel Johnson's Ride*. Huff's language is dense and heavily allusive; occasionally, as in "Previews," the allusions seem to come too fast and to be too personal to really work for the reader. On the whole, this isn't true.

Many of Huff's poems deal with loss, and the things, like drink and death, that accelerate our sense of loss. There is, however, a moving affirmation underlying this work, a suggestion of the spiritual gains that move in to fill the gaps. This is evident in "Rainbow" ("And I am glad/That I have wounded her, winged her heart,/And that she goes beyond my fathering"), and again in "Although I Remember the Sound":

> Although I remember the sound
> The young snag made when I felled it,
> It was not noise or music mattered then.
> Briefly, the tree was silent on the ground.
>
> Of what it was that mattered I recall
> Simply, among the chips and dust
> And keener near the center of the cut,
> The sweet, new smell which rose after the fall.

            – Duane Ackerson

HUGHES, Glyn. British. Born in Middlewich, Cheshire, 25 May 1935. Educated at Altrincham Grammar School, Cheshire, 1946–52; Regional College of Art, Manchester, 1952–56, 1958–59, National Diploma in Design, 1956, Art Teacher's Diploma, 1959. Married Wendy Slater in 1959 (marriage dissolved), has one son; married Roya Liakopoulos, 1974. Art teacher in secondary schools in Lancashire and Yorkshire, 1956–65, and in H.M. Prison, Manchester, 1969–71; Extra-Mural Lecturer in Art, University of Manchester, 1971–73. Member of the Manchester Institute of Contemporary Arts Committee, 1966–69. Recipient: Welsh Arts Council Prize, 1969; Arts Council bursary, 1970, 1973. Agent: David Higham Associates Ltd., 5–8 Lower John Street, Golden Square, London W1R 4HA. Address: 28 Lower Millbank, Sowerby Bridge, Yorkshire HX6 3ED, England.

PUBLICATIONS

Verse

The Stanedge Bull. Manchester, Manchester Institute of Contemporary Arts, 1966.
Almost-Love Poems. Oxford, Sycamore Press, 1968.
Love on the Moor: Poems 1965–1968. Manchester, Phoenix Pamphlet Poets Press, 1968.
Neighbours: Poems 1965–1969. London, Macmillan, and Chester Springs, Pennsylvania, Dufour, 1970.
Presence. London, Poem-of-the-Month Club, 1971.
Towards the Sun: Poems and Photographs. Manchester, Phoenix Pamphlet Poets Press, 1971.
Rest the Poor Struggler: Poems 1969–1971. London, Macmillan, 1972.

Other

Letters from John Cowper Powys to Glyn Hughes, edited by Bernard Jones. Stevenage, Hertfordshire, Ore Publications, 1971.
Millstone Grit (on Yorkshire and Lancashire). London, Gollancz, 1975.

Glyn Hughes comments:

I spent my childhood in North Cheshire, and my passion was for long, solitary cycle-rides and walks when I trespassed through that pastoral, rather eighteenth-century countryside, the secrets of which were guarded by gamekeepers and farmers behind the walls of parks and thick agricultural hedges. (There is a description of my discovery of "nature" in my book *Millstone Grit.*) Therefore, the first poetry to appeal to me belonged to that particularly English tradition of "nature poetry" – Wordsworth, John Clare, William Barnes, Edward Thomas, D. H. Lawrence. I went to the College of Art in Manchester; for better and for worse the long experience of *looking* at things during that impressionable period brought a character to my verse – as my reviewers usually point out. After art school, I shunned the almost obligatory fate of becoming a school teacher, and lived in a dilapidated cottage where I tried to keep my wife, my child, and myself from a quarter-acre of land and a minute income from gardening for other people. My garden was a little paradise amongst the Lancashire and Yorkshire industrial towns; and the conflict between my cottage and garden (the embodiments of the ideals of my youth) and the towns (which represented a vile history of which I knew little) produced the realisations that made my first relatively clear poems – the ones collected in *Neighbours*. In various ways, I tried to set the vivid realisations of life in circumstances that denied that vividness – for example, in the story of a farmer's wife who sees the possibility of romantic love but who draws back into the familiar drudgery of farm life ("Love on the Moor"); or in the small excitement of playing with a child on a snowy moor, which ends in a cold room (metaphorically and actually cold). Because of my own troubled marriage, I also wrote many fictions of the bed and hearth.

Just as I was beginning to write clearly, I found Alvarez's *The New Poetry* anthology, and the two poets who appealed to me – R. S. Thomas and Ted Hughes – had a regrettable influence. My reviewers made me pay for that influence. Having paid that debt, I would direct readers to "The Letter," "The Voyage," and "The Flower," which were ignored by the reviewers, but now, after several years, still seem justified; to "Cold" and to "Love on the Moor"; and to scatterings of lines in "Curlews" and "Woodside Cottage" and one or two other poems. My second collection, *Rest the Poor Struggler*, continues in very much the same territory as *Neighbours*, but with, I think, more lucid poems (though the book is technically marred by my restlessness during the period in which I wrote it). Since then I have written only a few poems. My main work has been a prose assessment of my experience of Lancashire and Yorkshire (*Millstone Grit*).

I came to Greece in early 1974, and in the future will be spending perhaps half of each year here, where politics (particularly during this alarming summer of 1974) are of more importance than it ever seemed to be in England. I have begun, tentatively, a novel, and am working on several poems.

*   *   *

One of the purposes of art is to bring order to the complexity of our experiences so that the truth behind them can be explored and revealed, and one aspect of this truth is to be discovered in the observation of man both against and as part of the terrain he inhabits. In the visual arts the Chinese can do this superbly; and so does Hardy, for example, in his novels where a sense of values and proportion is revealed which is a truth in itself. It is such an exploration of how the nature and quality of life are shaped and influenced by the environment (a sort of poetic ecology) which marks out Glyn Hughes' poems in his Phoenix Pamphlet *Love on the Moor* and in his first full collection *Neighbours*. As Hughes said in his introduction to *Love on the Moor*: "My idealism about how people ought to live is implicit in every poem." This has been maintained in his later collections.

The terrain of Glyn Hughes' poems is one of those harsh, unrelenting inbred bits of country-side that still endure in Twentieth Century England,

> the last place of rickets and bow legs
> aching from their grip of iced roads.
> Where the stranger's stared-at smile is unreturned,
> the stranger's house is shunned.
>   – from "Rock Bottom"

Even the joys of Spring sunshine are hard won:

> The fractured land bursts into grass.
> A farmer, woken by the sun and us,
> yaps like a terrier at the field's edge
> to defend his growth. We laugh,
> point, joke. Old walls glow
> like unripe apples as we cross his field
> to see the coltsfoot flowers.
> — "Towards the Sun"

Hughes' approach is as equally uncompromising and well suited to his subject matter. Unsentimental, it is not without compassion, as illustrated in "Love on the Moor" where the farmer's wife, stirred for a moment by the smile of a visiting salesman —

> What might
> have been that trickle of light
> to the cinders of her heart
> stopped at a scowling grate

— calls her man who shambles out

> From his kitchen doze
> fly open, feet in oven —
> not that he'd ever lied
> he would be different.

Hughes' ability to touch on just the right nuance of feeling, in situations where the slightness of its manifestation belies its depth, is quite remarkable.

The life described is harsh; but hashness is not indulged for the sake of it, rather it is allied to the quality of life portrayed:

> We communicate
> in other ways: we poke the grate,
> and whether we rise early or rise late
> is boasted from the roof. Each broods alone
> with a false air of no-one at home.
> — from "Neighbours"

It is a life withdrawn, pulled into itself — like a snail into its shell — in order to render it bearable. It is Glyn Hughes' achievement not only to have described his terrain with economy and accuracy, but to have expressed the spirit of it with a sensitivity which is masterly.

— John Cotton

HUGHES, Ted. British. Born in Mytholmroyd, Yorkshire, in 1930. Educated at Mexborough Grammar School, Yorkshire; Pembroke College, Cambridge, B.A. 1954, M.A. 1959. Served in the Royal Air Force, 2 years. Married the poet Sylvia Plath in 1956 (died, 1963); Carol Orchard, 1970; has one son and one daughter. Worked as rose gardener and night watchman; Reader for Rank Organization. Since 1965, Editor, with Daniel Weissbort, *Modern Poetry in Translation* magazine, London. Recipient: New York Poetry Center First Publication Award, 1957; Guinness Award, 1958; Guggenheim Fellowship, 1959; Maugham Award, 1960; Hawthornden Prize, 1961; City of Florence International Poetry Prize, 1969; Queen's Gold Medal for Poetry, 1974. Address: c/o Faber and Faber Ltd., 3 Queen Square, London WC1N 3AU, England.

PUBLICATIONS

Verse

The Hawk in the Rain. London, Faber, and New York, Harper, 1957.
Lupercal. London, Faber, and New York, Harper, 1960.
Selected Poems, with Thom Gunn. London, Faber, 1962.
The Burning of the Brothel. London, Turret Books, 1966.
Recklings. London, Turret Books, 1966.
Scapegoats and Rabies: A Poem in Five Parts. London, Poet and Printer, 1967.
Animal Poems. Crediton, Devon, Gilbertson, 1967.
Fuve Autumn Songs for Children's Voices. Crediton, Devon, Gilbertson, 1968.
The Martyrdom of Bishop Farrer. Crediton, Devon, Gilbertson, 1970.
A Crow Hymn. Frensham, Surrey, Sceptre Press, 1970.
A Few Crows. Exeter, Rougemont Press, 1970.
Crow: From the Life and Songs of the Crow. London, Faber, 1970; New York, Harper, 1971; revised edition, Faber, 1972.
Corgi Modern Poets in Focus 1, with others, edited by Dannie Abse. London, Corgi, 1971.
Crow Wakes: Poems. London, Poet and Printer, 1971.
Poems, with Ruth Fainlight and Alan Sillitoe. London, Rainbow Press, 1971.
Eat Crow. London, Rainbow Press, 1972.
Selected Poems 1957–1967. London, Faber, 1972; New York, Harper, 1973.
In the Little Girl's Angel Gaze. London, Steam Press, 1972.

Plays

The Calm (produced Boston, 1961).
The Wound (broadcast, 1962). Included in *Wodwo,* 1967.
Seneca's Oedipus (produced London, 1968). London, Faber, 1969; New York, Doubleday, 1972.
Beauty and the Beast (televised, 1968; produced London, 1971). Included in *The Coming of the King and Other Plays,* 1970.
The Coming of the King and Other Plays (includes *The Tiger's Bones; Beauty and the Beast; Sean, The Fool, The Devil and the Cats*). London, Faber, 1970;

augmented edition, as *The Tiger's Bones and Other Plays for Children* (includes *Orpheus)*, New York, Viking Press, 1973.

Sean, The Fool, The Devil and the Cats (produced London, 1971).   Included in *The Coming of the King and Other Plays*, 1970.

The Coming of the King (televised, 1972).   Included in *The Coming of the King and Other Plays*, 1970.

Orghast (produced Persepolis, 1971).

The Iron Man (televised, 1972).   London, Penguin, 1973.

The Story of Vasco, music by Gordon Crosse (produced London, 1974).

Radio Plays: *The House of Aries*, 1960; *A Houseful of Women*, 1961; *The Wound*, 1962; *Difficulties of a Bridegroom*, 1963; *Dogs*, 1964.

Television Plays: *Beauty and the Beast*, 1968; *The Coming of the King*, 1972; *The Iron Man*, 1972.

Other

Meet My Folks! (juvenile).   London, Faber, 1961; Indianapolis, Bobbs Merrill, 1973.

The Earth-Owl and Other Moon-People (juvenile).   London, Faber, 1963; New York, Atheneum, 1964.

How the Whale Became (juvenile).   London, Faber, 1963; New York, Atheneum, 1964.

Nessie the Mannerless Monster (juvenile).   London, Faber, and New York, Chilmark Press, 1964; as *Nessie the Monster*, Indianapolis, Bobbs Merrill, 1974.

Wodwo (miscellany).   London, Faber, and New York, Harper, 1967.

The Iron Man: A Story in Five Parts (juvenile).   London, Faber, 1968; as *The Iron Giant: A Story in Five Parts*, New York, Harper, 1968.

Poetry Is (juvenile).   New York, Doubleday, 1970.

Seasons Songs (juvenile).   New York, Viking Press, 1975.

Editor, with Patricia Beer and Vernon Scannell, *New Poems 1962*.   London, Hutchinson, 1962.

Editor, with Thom Gunn, *Five American Poets*.   London, Faber, 1963.

Editor, *Here Today*.   London, Hutchinson, 1963.

Editor, *Selected Poems*, by Keith Douglas.   London, Faber, and New York, Chilmark Press, 1964.

Editor, *Poetry in the Making: An Anthology of Poems and Programmes from "Listening and Writing."*   London, Faber, 1967.

Editor, *A Choice of Emily Dickinson's Verse*.   London, Faber, 1971.

Editor, *A Choice of Shakespeare's Verse*.   London, Faber, 1971; as *Poems: With Fairest Flowers While Summer Lasts: Poems from Shakespeare*, New York, Doubleday, 1971.

Editor, *Selected Poems*, by Yehuda Amichai.   London, Penguin, 1971.

Editor, *Crossing the Water*, by Sylvia Plath.   London, Faber, 1971; as *Crossing the Water: Transitional Poems*, New York, Harper, 1971.

*   *   *

That Ted Hughes should be presented as a "nature poet" (through the kind of grouping in which he is found in school anthologies and the like) is not surprising; his poems teem with wild life, sometimes noble (horses, for example), more often predatory (pike, hawks, jaguars, foxes, wolves, crows, rats). "His images have an admirable violence," wrote Edwin Muir of Hughes's first book, *The Hawk in the Rain*, and the violence is that of "Nature red in tooth and claw." Human life is seen in terms of brute physical activity, and there is a particular obsession with the animal-like trench-fighting of the First World War.

"The Thought-Fox" (from *The Hawk in the Rain)* gives a good picture of the physical origin, and the physical impact, of Hughes's poems: the fox seen as a presence gradually approaching,

> Brilliantly, concentratedly,
> Coming about its own business

> Till, with a sudden sharp hot stink of fox
> It enters the dark hole of the head.

This physical vividness is more apparent in the earlier poems, but sometimes at the expense of clarity and coherence. In *Lupercal*, his second book, Hughes manages something altogether sparer, in "Hawk Roosting" and "View of a Pig": here he avoids his habitual temptations of verbal grotesqueness (e.g. "how loud and above what/Furious spaces of fire do the distracting devils/Orgy and hosannah . . .") and turbulent diction ("The cradled guns, damascus, blued, flared").

Many of the poems can be seen as parables of human life, but generally expressed in such spurts of energy that the tamed and untamed worlds blur. Certainly the world revealed is one that has little to do with 20th-century urban England, and indeed part of Hughes's appeal is no doubt due to the stress on primitivism. The features of this landscape are those of his childhood in that odd enclave of the West Riding of Yorkshire where the mills and factories have encroached on something rural and remote but have not managed to dominate it – a half industrial world which shares something with D. H. Lawrence's Erewash Valley. In both Hughes and Lawrence, this childhood background is constantly drawn on and evoked, as somehow a "realer" place than anywhere else. This is borne out in Hughes's prose short stories, too, in such pieces as "Sunday," with its vivid and sickening memory of rat-baiting.

There is also much of the sea, as the first fierce chaos and the destructive eater of the land. In "Pibroch" (from Hughes's book, *Wodwo*) the sea, a stone, the wind, a tree, are all seen caught up in a vortex of change and destruction:

> Minute after minute, aeon after aeon,
> Nothing lets up or develops.
> And this is neither a bad variant nor a tryout.
> This is where the staring angels go through.
> This is where all the stars bow down.

The manner of many of these later poems has become more disjointed and runic, and often less concentrated, as if to accommodate a wider range of subject-matter. Hughes's interest in folk-tales and primitive oral poetry is also more apparent, particularly in his continuing sequence of "Crow" poems. Yet here and there are vivid examples still of the odd visual angle which Hughes can command, as in the opening of "Thistles":

Against the rubber tongues of cows and the hoeing hands of men
Thistles spike the summer air
Or crackle open under a blue-black pressure.

Hughes's influence has been marked on a number of his contemporaries and immediate juniors, such as Peter Redgrove, David Wevill, Harold Massingham and Ted Walker. He was a particularly potent force in the late 1950's, when reviewers inevitably contrasted his arrival with the "Movement" poems represented in *New Lines* (though in fact when Robert Conquest came to edit *New Lines 2* he included four poems by Hughes). Very large claims have been made for him: A. Alvarez has called him "a poet of the first importance." Certainly he is one of the two best-known post-Dylan Thomas poets in Britain today (the other being Philip Larkin) – or was until recently, with the advent of the mass-audience platform poets from Liverpool and Newcastle. He is himself a most impressive reader of his own work, his voice and manner being entirely consonant with the craggy, hewn quality of his poems.

– Anthony Thwaite

HUGO, Richard (Franklin).   American.   Born in Seattle, Washington, 12 December 1923. Educated at the University of Washington, Seattle, B.A. 1948, M.A. 1952. Served as a bombardier in the United States Army Air Corps during World War II. Worked for the Boeing Company, Seattle, 1951–63. Since 1964, Member of the English Department, and currently, Professor of English, University of Montana, Missoula. Recipient: Theodore Roethke Prize and Helen Bullis Award *(Poetry Northwest);* Northwest Writers Award, 1966; Rockefeller Fellowship, 1967. Address: 2407 Wylie, Missoula, Montana 59801, U.S.A.

PUBLICATIONS

Verse

A Run of Jacks.   Minneapolis, University of Minnesota Press, 1961.
Five Poets of the Pacific, with others, edited by Robin Skelton.   Seattle, University of Washington Press, 1964.
Death of the Kapowsin Tavern.   New York, Harcourt Brace, 1965.
Good Luck in Cracked Italian.   Cleveland, World, 1969.
The Lady in Kicking Horse Reservoir.   New York, Norton, 1973.

Manuscript Collection: University of Montana, Missoula.

Richard Hugo comments:

Usually I find a poem is triggered by something, a small town or an abandoned house, that I feel others would ignore.

*   *   *

Central to Richard Hugo's poems is his concern for place and a rhythmic facility that repeatedly compresses the language.

> Word's gone back to the commercial world:
> if you sail that region, stop there.
> You will see our work and you can worship
> when the sun is flat and shafts of cream
> spray between our pillars from the sea.
> Odd dark birds weave through black and pink
> we planned. As for natives there,
> they farm, die often from some fever
> we have never seen, make love
> more frequently than we, and when we sweat
> erecting pillars, they laugh above their hoes.
> – final stanza of "Paestum"

Such linguistic intensity is risky: Hugo surely is not appealing to a "general audience," but to that reader who is willing to stay with the tight rhythms, demanding cadences, long enough that their dominance becomes incidental, at which point the content begins to assert itself.

In an introduction to the work of four American Indian Poets, Hugo wrote (in the *American Poetry Review*) "Indians come from a recently destroyed civilization . . . the Indian sensibility is something like those of the 20th Century giants, especially Yeats and Eliot, who felt we inherited ruined worlds that, before they were ruined, gave man a sense of self-esteem, social unity, spiritual certainty and being at home on earth."

Hugo's awareness of ruined civilizations is especially evident in *Good Luck in Cracked Italian*, a depressing travelogue, poems written upon his first visit to Italy since the war, when he was a flyer. Hugo's poems in this book express guilt and the sense that since the war many cities have become ugly through both physical and spiritual ruination. Neon and greed have absorbed a finer culture. Each poem finds new human metaphors to express this theme.

> I'll never think of virgin angels here.
> Did I walk this street before,
> protesting: I am kind. You switch the menu,
> gyp me on the bill. Remember me? My wings?
> The silver target and the silver bomb?
> Take the extra coin. I only came
> to see you living and the fountains run.
> – final stanza of "Napoli Again"

In his most recent book, *The Lady in Kicking Horse Reservoir*, Hugo's language is typically dense and rhythmic, and his fascination with place remains strong, but the tone of the poems is lightened by the mirror he turns upon himself, and the growing variety of subjects for his poems. With them, Hugo totters and crashes from bar to bar in Scotland, Italy, Spain, and Montana, his home.

> Home. Home. I knew it entering.
> Green cheap plaster and the stores
> across the street toward the river
> failed. One Indian depressed
> on Thunderbird. Another buying
> Thunderbird to go. This air
> is fat with gangsters I imagine
> on the run. If they ran here
> they would be running from
> imaginary cars. No one cares
> about the wanted posters
> in the brand new concrete block P.O.
>
>   – first stanza of "The Only Bar in Dixon"

In this book, Hugo portrays himself as a highly intemperate person: this apparent lack of control, which adds such an important dimension to his poems of place and occasion, nevertheless works at sharp odds with the rigid control he exercises over the language.

The Lady in Kicking Horse Reservoir includes two short poems which, by their appearance on the page with so much white space beneath them, announce themselves as a departure from the rest of his work. Here they are, complete:

> Mercy Jesus Mercy
> cries a stone
> b 1586
> d 1591
> and Tennyson's brook
> drones on
>
>   – "Somersby"

> I don't come here after June when rattlesnakes
> come out of caves and snore on stones
> along the stream, though trout and trout remain
> and I am keen to harm. Yellow bells have fangs
> and jack pines rattle in the slightest wind.
>
>   – "Taneum Creek"

Some of Hugo's finest poems, not yet available in a collection, appeared recently as a special supplement to *American Poetry Review*. In these poems, Hugo's sense of humor, somewhat muted in earlier work, provides another dimension to his bauchy bar-hopping disgust. He seems more open in these poems, too, and the language, though still compressed, slackens just a bit. He writes that he has stopped drinking:

> I'm in Milltown. You remember that bar, that beautiful bar
> run by Harold Herndon where I pissed five years away
> but pleasantly. And now I can't go in for fear
> I'll fall sobbing to the floor. God, the ghosts in there.
> The poems. Those honest people from the woods and mill.
> What a relief that was from school, from that smelly
> student-teacher crap and those dreary committees
> where people actually say 'considering the lateness
> of the hour.' Bad times too. That depressing summer
> of '66 and that woman going – I've talked too often
> about that. Now no bourbon to dissolve the tension,
> to find self love in blurred fantasies, to find the charm
> to ask a woman home. What happens to us, John?
>
>   – from "Letter to Logan from Milltown"

Humor introduces optimism, the work brightens, and the reader hungers for more.

– Geof Hewitt

HUNT, Sam. New Zealander. Born in New Zealand, 4 July 1946. Recipient: Young Poets Award, 1971. Agent: Alister Taylor, Box 87, Martinborough, New Zealand. Address: Bottle Creek, Paremata, Wellington, New Zealand.

PUBLICATIONS

Verse

Between Islands. Privately printed, 1964.
A Fat Flat Blues (When Morning Comes). Wellington, Bottle Press, 1969.
Selected Poems 1965–1969. Wellington, Wellington Training College, 1970.
A Song about Her. Wellington, Bottle Press, 1970.
Postcard of a Cabbage Tree. Wellington, Bottle Press, 1970.
Bracken Country. Wellington, Alister Taylor, 1971.
Letter to Jerusalem. Wellington, Bottle Press, 1971.
Bottle Creek Blues. Wellington, Bottle Press, 1971.
Bottle Creek. Wellington, Alister Taylor, 1972.
Beware the Man. Wellington, Triple P Press, 1972.
Birth on Bottle Creek. Wellington, Triple P Press, 1972.
South into Winter. Wellington, Alister Taylor, 1973.
Roadsong Paekakariki. Wellington, Triple P Press, 1973.

Recording: *Beware the Man,* with Mammal.

Other

Bow-Wow (juvenile). Wellington, Alister Taylor, 1974.

Sam Hunt comments:

If in any, I'd see myself in the lyric tradition.

*   *   *

Sam Hunt's poems – love-lyrics, celebrations of people and places and of memories of childhood – seem to spring from a sort of grateful astonishment at the world. It is a young man's poetry, Romantic, limited in its scope and achievement, but lit with flashes of insight, as in these lines from "A School Report":

Working with these young kids in the pastel
clay frontier, we live near bulldozer blades.
The school I came to yesterday had loads
of children waiting: that was all:
the road up the valley still a shingle path.
The town planners never predicted such birth.

"We live near bulldozer blades" catches accurately much of New Zealand's town-
scapes that are *peopled* but still not *settled,* the unpredicted "birth" of a growing
country.

On the printed page many of Hunt's poems look flat and prosaic, and his syllabic
lines lack the stressed delivery of the spoken voice. In fact, of course, they are
written for performance, as Hunt's own readings on the record *Beware the Man*
demonstrate. At his best, he can achieve an unaffectedly simple, singing line, as in
these closing stanzas of "Song about Her":

Two years out of practice
writing cool Platonic songs about
a girl too innocent to seize
the hot rod of a V8 lout,

I'm singing now because the shellbanks
shine and in the sun here, sober,
smoking her last night's butts,
I know I love her.

– Alan Roddick

HUTCHINSON, (William Patrick Henry) Pearse. Irish. Born in Glasgow, Scotland, 16 February 1927. Educated at Christian Brothers School, Dublin; University
College, Dublin; Salzburg Seminar in American Studies, 1952. Translator, International Labor Organization, Geneva, Switzerland, 1951–53; Drama Critic, Radio
Eireann, 1957–61, and Telefis Eireann, 1968. Gregory Fellow in Poetry, University
of Leeds, 1971–73. Lived in Barcelona, 1954–57, 1961–67. Recipient: Butler Award,
for Gaelic writing, 1969. Address: School of English, University of Leeds, Leeds
LS2 9JT, England.

PUBLICATIONS

Verse

Tongue Without Hands. Dublin, Dolmen Press, 1963.
Faoistin Bhacach (Imperfect Confession). Dublin, Clóchomhar, 1968.
Expansions. Dublin, Dolmen Press, 1969.
Watching the Morning Grow. Dublin, Gallery Books, 1973.

Other

Translator, *Poems*, by Josep Carner. Oxford, Dolphin Book Company, 1962.
Translator, *Friend Songs: Medieval Love-Songs from Galaico-Portuguese*.
Dublin, New Writers Press, 1970.

Pearse Hutchinson comments:

Themes: Growing-up. Near-madness. Near-despair. The colour bar. The horrors
of puritannical Irish Catholicity. Xenophobia and xenophilia. Travel (especially
Spain). The built-in dangers (to truth) of all revolt. The difficulty, tenuous possibility, and utter necessity, of love. Friendship. Social injustice. God. Pity.
Forms: Free verse and strictly rhyming metres.
Influences: Hard to say – but I suppose Auden, Cavafy, the 17th century Gaelic
poet Pierce Ferriter, and the contemporary Catalans Salvador Espriu (especially as
to cadence) and Pere Quart.

                              *   *   *

Mr. Pearse Hutchinson has lived for seven years in Spain and his first volume
consisted of verse translations from the work of a Catalan poet, Josep Carner. The
effect of his experiences abroad can be plainly seen in his two collections of
poems, *Tongue Without Hands*, and *Expensions*. His delight in Mediterranean colour
is shown in "Málaga":

> The scent of unseen jasmine on the warm night beach.
>
> The tram along the sea road all the way from town
> through its wide open sides drank unseen jasmine down.
> Living was nothing all those nights but that strong flower.

Equally gay is the lyrical "Fireworks in Córdoba":

> Cocks and coins and golden lupins,
> parachutes and parasols and shawls,
> pamplinas, maltrantos, and glass lawyers,
> giant spermatozoa, dwarf giants,
> greengage palms, and flying goldfish. . . .

Mr. Hutchinson is one of the few Irish poets of to-day who writes of political
oppression and bad social conditions. In "Questions" he describes attempts to
suppress the use of the Catalan language by imprisonment and violence in a
province:

> Where one fine day, the gun smiles, and everyone rumours a thaw,
> but next night, the gun kills, and all remember the law.

Mr. Hutchinson writes in various measures, including free verse. The poems
which he has written on Irish life, both in city and country, are brisk, satiric and
ironic, as in "Men's Mission":

> Some Lenten evening sharp, at five to eight,
> pick a suburban road both long and straight
> and leading – which do not? – to a Catholic church:
> you'll see, whisked out through every creaking gate,
> men only, walking all at the same brisk rate.

"Fleadh Cheoil" (a popular musical festival) is a lively account of a country town *en fête:*

> each other door in a mean twisting main street,
> flute-player, fiddler and penny-whistler
> concentrating on one sense only
> such a wild elegance of energy gay and sad
> few clouds of lust or vanity could form:
> the mind kept cool, the heart kept warm;
> therein the miracle, three days and nights
> so many dances played and so much drinking done,
> so many voices raised in singing but none
> in anger nor any fist in harm.

From the manufacturing centres of England and Scotland, exiles "in flashy ties and frumpish hats" return for a few days to hear "an ancient music." "Friday in a Branch Post-Office" tells of the weekly queue of septuagenarians waiting patiently for their meagre old age pension and ends with an ironic comment:

> We don't need a statue of Cú Chulainn
> in our Branch Post-Office.

The reference reminds us of Yeats' tribute to the statue of the ancient Irish hero in the General Post Office in Dublin.

– Austin Clarke

HUWS, Daniel. Welsh. Born in London, 28 June 1932. Educated at Llangefui County School; Bryanston School; Peterhouse, Cambridge. Agent: Miss Olwyn Hughes, 100 Chetwynd Road, London N.W.5, England. Address: Penrhyncoch, Cardiganshire, Wales.

PUBLICATIONS

Verse

Noth. London, Secker and Warburg, 1972.
Buzzards. Rushden, Northamptonshire, Sceptre Press, 1974.
From an Old Book of Riddles. Rushden, Northamptonshire, Sceptre Press, 1974.

Other

Editor, with Maldwyn Mills, *Fragments of an Early Fourteenth Century "Guy of Warwick."* Oxford, Blackwell, 1974.

*   *   *

As we may gather from lines like these –

> We know our crags, our climbs, our controlled terrors,
> As we know our own hearthsides. We manage nicely.

– the manners of Daniel Huws' verse are staunch, a little downright, self-confident within known limits but respectful of what may lie beyond those limits. On the negative side, we have a propensity for a verse whose well-shaped laboriousness tends to leave flat unfelt material just where it is ("A Mountain Land," "The Knot," "For Better or Worse," "In the Cafe"), despite occasional jabs at over-resonant metaphor: "The world's womb has closed to the seed / Of vitality boxed in our dark hold."

On the other hand his very firmness of touch can serve him well in poems which try to encompass modes of awareness that are not so easily circumscribed. Through a crisp definition of what *can* be defined ("So much was certain . . .") a space is cleared for the strangeness beyond immediate notice – see "Escape," "Waking in the Small Hours," "A Dawn." And there is a similar efficacy in some of his miniatures, achieved through the adroit placing of a single image, as in "The Oranges Won't Grow," "The Burden," or "The Piercing Wind." The latter is worth quoting, though it is a happy find somewhat to the side of the main line of his conscious endeavour:

> Was there not wood to hew
> And stone to quarry?
> Had you not eyes?
> Had you not hands?
>
> The piercing wind questions.
>
> Answerless,
> I huddle behind children.

– Robin Fulton

IGNATOW, David. American. Born in Brooklyn, New York 7 February 1914. Educated in Brooklyn public schools. Married Rose Graubart in 1938; has one son, David, and one daughter, Yaedi. Worked as salesman, public relations writer, editor, shipyard handyman, newspaperman, and treasurer and president of a bindery firm. Instructor, New School for Social Research, New York, 1964–65; Visiting Lecturer, University of Kentucky, Lexington, 1965–66; Lecturer, University of Kansas, Lawrence, 1966–67, and Vassar College, Poughkeepsie, New York.

1967–69. Since 1969, Poet-in-Residence, York College, City University of New York, Jamaica, and Adjunct Professor, Columbia University, New York. Associate Editor, *American Scene* magazine, 1935–37; Literary Arts Editor, *New York Analytic* magazine, 1937; Co-Editor, *Beloit Poetry Journal*, Wisconsin, 1950–59; Poetry Editor, *The Nation*, New York, 1962–63. Since 1969, Consulting Editor, *Chelsea* magazine, New York, and since 1972, Associate Editor, *American Poetry Review*, Philadelphia. Recipient: National Institute of Arts and Letters Award, 1964; Guggenheim Fellowship, 1965, 1973; Shelley Memorial Award, 1966; Rockefeller Fellowship, 1968; National Endowment for the Arts grant, 1969. Address: 155–01 90th Avenue, Jamaica, New York 11432, U.S.A.

PUBLICATIONS

Verse

> *Poems.*   Prairie City, Illinois, Decker Press, 1948.
> *The Gentle Weight Lifter.*   New York, Morris Gallery, 1955.
> *Say Pardon.*   Middletown, Connecticut, Wesleyan University Press, 1961.
> *Figures of the Human: Poems.*   Middletown, Connecticut, Wesleyan University Press, 1964.
> *Rescue the Dead.*   Middletown, Connecticut, Wesleyan University Press, 1968.
> *Earth Hard: Selected Poems.*   London, Rapp and Whiting, 1968.
> *Poems 1934–69.*   Middletown, Connecticut, Wesleyan Univuersity Press, 1970.
> *Facing the Tree.*   Chicago, Swallow Press, 1973.
> *The Notebooks of David Ignatow,* edited by Ralph J. Mills, Jr.   Chicago, Swallow Press, 1973.
> *Facing the Tree.*   Boston, Little Brown, 1975.
> *Selected Poems,* edited by Robert Bly.   Middletown, Connecticut, Wesleyan University Press, 1975.

> Recording: *Today's Poets 3,* with others, Folkways.

Other

> Editor, *Political Poetry.*   New York, Chelsea, 1960.
> Editor, *Walt Whitman: A Centennial Celebration.*   Beloit, Wisconsin, Beloit College, 1963.
> Editor, *William Carlos Williams: A Memorial Chapbook.*   Beloit, Wisconsin, Beloit College, 1963.

Bibliographies: *A Checklist of Writings* by Robert A. Smith, Storrs, University of Connecticut Library, 1966; in *Tennessee Poetry Journal* (Martin), Winter 1970.

Manuscript Collections: Lockwood Memorial Library, State University of New York, Buffalo; Olin Library, Wesleyan University, Middletown, Connecticut.

Critical Studies: by Edwin Honig, in *New Mexico Quarterly* (Albuquerque), Spring 1951; by James Wright, in *Chelsea 12* (New York), September 1962; by Victor

Contoski, in *University Review* (Kansas City, Missouri), Spring 1968; by Robert Bly in *New Leader* (New York), 22 May 1968; by Paul Zweig, in *The Sixties* (Madison, Minnesota), Summer 1968; *The Suspect in Poetry* by James Dickey, New York, Doubleday, 1971; "Earth Hard: The Poetry of David Ignatow" by Ralph J. Mills, Jr., in *North Shore Review* (Chicago), Winter, 1973; "Circumscriptions: The Poetry of David Ignatow" by Jerome Mazzaro, in *Salamagundi* (New York), Spring 1973; "American Poetry in and out of the Cave" by James Moore, in *The Lamp in the Spine* (St. Paul, Minnesota), Spring 1973.

David Ignatow comments:

(1970) I suppose it may be said that my early poems originated in the William Carlos Williams' school of hard core realism literally presented, free of the conventional rhyme and/or rhythm patterns. After my second book I found myself deeply interested in the school of surrealism.

I am constantly aware of the absolute and imminent tragedy of men in and among themselves through every level of their existence, socially, politically, privately, in love, family, business affairs. I deal with the entire range of experience given to each man in his life, as I seek through this apprehension of tragedy the saving grace, the cause for living in the act of serving tragedy itself. I dance with Yeats and Williams on the graves of the dead, as I would wish it done to me, in pleasure and homage to the dead.

My form is usually very free, content and/or idea determining it, while I use every conceivable device traditional and new for the proper realization of the poem. My private life, lives of my friends, lives of important men and women, historical events, scientific developments, the works of mythologies, philosophical treatises, the poems and novels of friends and interesting writers, all feed me with materials for poems. But most particularly, it is often history as it is being enacted today from which I draw a sense of the life of the times, with frequent reference to my life in that context. I search for *now*, using the method of introspection and dream in tandem with objective events or things.

In my poetry I have tried especially to make my life a metaphor for existence in these times, to the extent that I experience it. Each poem ultimately is designed with that purpose in mind, no matter the subject. It is for this reason that more than several critics have noticed the metaphysical basis to my work, Randall Jarrell for example, in a brief review many years ago. While I seek for the meaning to the experience, at the same time I am allowing the poem as it takes shape also to contribute its understanding of the experience. Language plays a decisive role in my projection of the experience though never losing sight of the objective event itself.

However, frequently in recent years I have presented completely fictitious events, given them an objective reality so to speak, as I explore the possibilities of the surrealist poem through this device. I have been led to surrealism by internal as well as external events, in a search for absolute understanding of the nature of relationships among us. These have suggested the need for a surrealistic approach. I don't know though whether I wish to continue in that phase, as I discover in myself a delight in projecting a sort of dream quality in the poem, as if it were from here that we take our final shape.

After having written some of the most bitter, terrifying dead end poems, with no place else to go from there, I conceive of the necessity for re-establishing relationships with myself and with the world on still another level, while life goes on. To quote in full from a recent paragraph I submitted for a recording of my poems by Scholastic Records, Inc.: "To me, the act of writing is a gesture of independence. I write with the thought of gaining control over my materials and over myself. With this achieved, I feel free once more to return to the balance and poise I prefer in my life, providing the poem of that moment has released me from the pressure, to my satisfaction. That does not happen often or long enough, as I am continually examining and re-examining my relations with the world and with myself. The poems that get written are what they are, poems; but I suppose, put all together, serve as an index to my way of life. I am very glad that this life within and without is so restless and disturbing to me since I get so much pleasure in writing about it.''

(1974) I would only add that much of my early and perhaps later poetry was in response to the pessimism and withdrawal in the poetry of T. S. Eliot. I took my cue in the manner with which to respond from William Carlos Williams, but this is to acknowledge that Eliot played a deeply important role in shaping much of my thinking on my life and the world around me. In other words, I found myself as a kind of mediator between Eliot and Williams, giving respect to the qualities of both and, out of the necessities in my life, shaping my own poems out of an identity with Eliot's own problems while seeking for a resolution in the energy and freedom manifest in Williams' work.

*   *   *

The poems of David Ignatow are often poems about the city for he has lived all of his life in the area of metropolitan New York. Yet such poems do not involve themselves with the particulars of place, the names of streets, restaurants, bookstores, as do Frank O'Hara's *Lunch Poems,* which revel in those details. Ignatow seeks a more fundamental reality and proceeds to reveal it through an imaginative activity that strips away inessentials until it arrives at the bare, frequently terrifying, truth. One is tempted to say that Ignatow provides us with the dreams of the city-dwellers, dreams disclosing the real nature of their lives. Thus his poems, with their deceptive simplicity of language and style, take the forms of parable or nightmare or monologue in which the speaker, perhaps intent on talking to himself, comes to a revelation of his deepest agonies and desires. But however concerned he is with the life around him, Ignatow also envisages the patterns, moments, and crises of his own existence in his work. So he writes in "I Am Well," a poem dedicated to William Carlos Williams, whose concentration in poetry on the immediate environment and use of everyday speech have influenced Ignatow:

> Say, what is it . . .
> I have put a knife in the sun:
> gleam of my self in transport –
> knife of my dream: sacrificial
> edge to see me through. I am
> exposed to you, offered
> by desires from the sea.
> Fish me from the flood,
> bring me shiny to shore,
> my unsteady dream. Knife
> that can bring solace, cut me
> where I am not free. Rose
> of my dying fill me,
> I breathe for you,
> I am awake,
> I am well.

Running through all of his work is what might be called a spiritual, even religious quest, a search for qualities which will redeem the violence, suffering and guilt in life. A parable version of this continuing pursuit of Ignatow's is evident in a poem such as "The Dream" from *Say Pardon:*

> Someone approaches to say his life is ruined
> and to fall down at your feet
> and pound his head upon the sidewalk.
> Blood spreads in a puddle.
> And you, in a weak voice, plead
> with those nearby for help;
> your life takes on his desperation.
> He keeps pounding his head.
> It is you who are fated;
> and you fall down beside him.
> It is then you are awakened,
> the body gone, the blood washed from the ground,
> the stores lit up with their goods.

In *Rescue the Dead,* Ignatow enters even more complicated centers of experience, confronting in his series of "Ritual" poems various aspects of evil, disorder and irrationality, taking up, in some highly personal pieces, the problems of marriage. This is an ambitious collection and shows how remarkably this poet has grown and extended himself. Beyond the malice, both individual and military, and the trials of married intimacy he countenances in his recent poetry, Ignatow achieves something of that redemptive vision he has been looking for. There is a feeling of a certain blessedness, of a love for and profound bond with others and with the physical world in "The Hope," "Night at an Airport," "Anew," and "Walk There" which liberates the spirit and renews it:

> Walk.
> See the sky splattered with leaves.
> Ahead, is that too the sky
> or a clearing?
> Walk there.

Never a participant in the momentary fads and fancies of the literary life, David Ignatow has quietly and persistently developed his art over the past two decades and now emerges as one of the very best poets of his generation.

– Ralph J. Mills, Jr.

IRBY, Kenneth. American. Born in Bowie, Texas, 18 November 1936. Educated at the University of Kansas, Lawrence, B.A. 1958; Harvard University, Cambridge, Massachusetts, M.A. 1960; University of California, Berkeley, M.L.S. 1968. Served in the United States Army, 1960–62. Formerly, reviewer of books and records for *Kulchur* magazine, New York. Address: 1614 Russell, Berkeley, California 94703, U.S.A.

PUBLICATIONS

Verse

The Roadrunner.   Placitas, New Mexico, Duende Press, 1964.
Kansas-New Mexico.   Lawrence, Kansas, Dialogue Press, 1965.
Movements/Sequences.   Placitas, New Mexico, Duende Press, 1965.
The Flower of Having Passed Through Paradise in a Dream: Poems 1967.   Annandale-on-Hudson, New York, Matter Books, 1968.
Relation: Poems 1965–1966.   Los Angeles, Black Sparrow Press, 1970.
To Max Douglas.   Privately printed, 1971.
The Snow Queen.   San Francisco, Turtle Island Foundation, 1973.

Kenneth Irby comments:

My closest associates (if that makes a "school") are Robert Kelly, Larry Goodell, Clayton Eshleman.

My concern *seems* to have been muchly with *pastoral* verse – that is, poetry that *feeds* us – drawing on a common Great Plains mysticism in the face of the landscape, that the landscape, *especially*, demands of us. But the concern of *poetry* is not finally at all limited.

*   *   *

The uniqueness of Kenneth Irby's vision is a product of the confrontation between the regionalist tradition and modern poetics. Like Robert Kelly and Clayton Eshleman, who are almost precisely his contemporaries, he has learned much from Charles Olson and Robert Duncan, but his themes and, in a sense, even his technique derive more significantly from his reading of James C. Malin, the historian of the Great Plains. For Malin, as for Charles Olson, the experience of space is the controlling fact of American history. In *Relation*, his first major publication, Irby arrives at a re-definition of pastoralism which is rooted in this understanding that "the landscape demands us and reveals us." That is, the pastoral world is neither distant nor a simple-minded idealization. It is the *literal* world which must be recovered from the false dichotomy of abstract Nature and urban artifice: "salvation is only to pass into the space all people live in." Irby conceives of his work as a gathering of evidence which reveals that participation in the actual is the only source of spiritual revelation.

Irby's most significant book to date is *To Max Douglas*, a sequence of poems addressed to a young poet who died of an overdose of heroin. It is not strictly speaking an elegy; it is rather an investigation of spiritual possibilities and dangers inherent in a spatio-temporal landscape, the Missouri-Kansas border region, which Irby and Douglas shared: "Kansas and Missouri is a zone / as violent of movement / as the San Andreas Fault." These controlled, densely-articulated poems clearly demonstrate that Irby is possessed of a precise ear and a voice which is capable of achieving, at once, pastoral calm and genuine poetic energy.

– Don Byrd

IRELAND, Kevin (Mark).   New Zealander.   Born in Auckland, 18 July 1933. Married. Founding Editor, *Mate* magazine, Auckland. Address: 2 Earnoch Avenue, Takapuna, Auckland, New Zealand.

PUBLICATIONS

Verse

Face to Face: Poems.   Christchurch, Pegasus Press, 1963.
Educating the Body: Poems.   Christchurch, Caxton Press, 1968.
A Letter from Amsterdam: Poems.   London, Amphadesma Press, 1972.
A Grammar of Dreams: Poems.   Wellington, Te Wiata Press, 1974.
Orchids Hummingbirds: Poems.   Auckland, Auckland University Press–Oxford University Press, 1974.

*   *   *

> Thin men
> write gaunt poems
> and each word
> sticks out
> like a rib

writes Kevin Ireland in "Deposition" – except that, regardless of the shape of the poet, his poems have not always been as "gaunt"; indeed, his latest poems are often quite "plump."

Whatever their shape, the problem is the old one of *form* and *content*. Seeking a congenial form, Ireland adopted, early on, a strict discipline of brief stanzas with short lines of one to three feet, and with complex rhyme-schemes and patterns of words or phrases recurring from stanza to stanza.

His poems are mostly witty, whimsical conceits and explorations of metaphors; one such is "Running a Risk":

> I laid both hands
> upon her heart:
> I staked my life
> against that part
>
> by risking all
> shy lovers thrive:
> my hands are full
> I'm still alive.

After some ten years' writing in such a strict mode, however, there are signs that Ireland is feeling its limitations irksome. The more open and relaxed love-poems of *A Letter from Amsterdam* suggest a return to a freer style – or perhaps an advance towards a new, and different, manner altogether.

– Alan Roddick

IREMONGER, Valentin. Irish. Born in Dublin, 14 February 1918. Educated at Christian Brothers School, Dublin; Colaiste Mhuire; Abbey Theatre School of Acting, Dublin. Married Sheila Manning in 1948; has one son and four daughters. Associated with the Abbey Theatre Company, Dublin, 1939–40, and the Gate Theatre, Dublin, 1942–44. Entered the Irish Foreign Service in 1946: Third Secretary, 1946–48; Private Secretary to the Foreign Minister, 1948–50; First Secretary, successively in the Political, Consular, and Economic Divisions, 1950–55; First Secretary, 1956–59, and Counsellor, 1959–64; Ambassador to Sweden, Norway, and Finland, 1964–68; Ambassador to India, 1968–73. Since 1973, Irish Ambassador to Luxembourg. Poetry Editor, *Envoy* magazine, Dublin, 1949–51. Recipient: AE Memorial Award, 1945. Address: Department of Foreign Affairs, Iveagh House, Dublin 2, Ireland.

PUBLICATIONS

Verse

On the Barricades, with Robert Greacen and Bruce Williamson. Dublin, New Frontiers Press, 1944.
Reservations. Dublin, Envoy, and London, Macmillan, 1950.
Horan's Field and Other Reservations. Dublin, Dolmen Press, 1972.

Play

Wrap Up My Green Jacket (broadcast, 1947; produced Belfast, 1952). Published in *The Bell* (Dublin), 1949.

Other

Editor, with Robert Greacen, *Contemporary Irish Poetry.* London, Faber, 1949.
Editor, *Irish Short Stories.* London, Faber, 1960.

Translator, *The Hard Road to Klondike,* by Donall MacAmlaigh. London, Routledge, 1962.
Translator, *An Irish Navvy: The Diary of an Exile,* by Donall MacAmlaigh. London, Routledge, 1966.

*   *   *

Valentin Iremonger was one of the most interesting and original of Irish poets to emerge during the 1940's. In Ireland this was not an especially stimulating period for literature. The death of W. B. Yeats in 1939 had left the field more open to the younger generation, but censorship was still rigorous and continued to make Irish writers feel outsiders in their own society. It was appropriate that the title of Iremonger's first publication in book form, *On the Barricades,* should suggest a determination to challenge both tradition and the establishment. His early poems, though not revolutionary in the broader context of English and American writing of the period, brought a contemporary urban note into Irish poetry for the first time. A deep concern with the alien position of the poet in society was also apparent.

Several of the earlier poems develop this theme. Others explore a sense of disorientation within the individual himself. At times each situation is seen to reflect the other and the two themes interconnect.

Iremonger was quick to achieve an authoritative and individual style. There are occasional suggestions of Patrick Kavanagh, F. R. Higgins and Auden in the earlier work, but right from the start the writing was forthright and incisive; the imagery and diction, though concrete, were vital and vivid. Later Iremonger began to cultivate a greater richness and wrote poems carried forward by a rhapsodic sweep which rarely faltered. A change in subject-matter accompanied this stylistic development. Iremonger's interest in the position of the poet vis-à-vis society was replaced by a concern for the position of man in relation to time. Poems like "Clear View in Summer," "Elegy for the Commencement of Winter," "Lackendarragh," and "Poem in the Depths of Summer" are passionate celebrations of living in which the passion derives from an awareness of impermanence and impending loss. They are filled with the kind of tragic joy which brims over in some of Dylan Thomas's poems, notably "Poem on His Birthday." Iremonger's elegies do not reach quite such a high level but they are splendid achievements.

Two other important poems among Iremonger's later work are "Hector" and "Icarus." In "Hector" he describes the situation of the Trojan hero before his final battle with Achilles, and uses it to evoke a fatalistic attitude towards death. "Icarus" relates the predicament of the legendary flier to the situation of the modern aviator. It is one of his most imaginative and skilful poems, and has appeared widely in anthologies.

Iremonger's output has apparently dwindled since the publication of *Reservations* in 1950. The greater part of *Horan's Field and Other Reservations* consists of poems from the earlier collection. Several of the most recent poems look back with acute regret to the past out of a context of present frustration. The long poem "Horan's Field" provides a vehement expression of this feeling:

> We were famous people in our day
> And to all and to the boy
> I feel now holding this pen
> I send my reminiscent love.
> Marise, Marise, the world is at us all.
> It falls upon us like a Himalayan peak
> And we are trapped, no hope at all . . .

More and more for Iremonger the writing of a poem has become an act which places a portion of the poet's imaginative life within a "reservation" fencing it safely away from the destructive pressures of everyday living.

Though primarily a lyric poet, Iremonger has also written some plays. The most highly regarded of these is *Wrap Up My Green Jacket*, a verse play based on the tragedy of Robert Emmet. The most romantic of Ireland's revolutionaries, Emmet was executed after leading an abortive rising against the British in 1803. The powerful rhetoric of the play both faithfully reflects and implicitly criticises the histrionic but courageous character of a patriot who was to be followed by the men of 1916 in making the sacrificial, heroic gesture of a foredoomed revolt.

– Rivers Carew

JACKSON, Alan. Scottish. Born in Liverpool, Lancashire, 6 September 1938. Educated in Edinburgh schools; Royal High School; Edinburgh University,

1956–59, 1964–65, left without degree. Married Margaret Dickson in 1963; has two sons, Kevin and Yorick. Laborer; trainee psychiatric nurse, 1959–60; Secretary, Scottish Committee of 100, 1961–62. Since 1965, Founding Director, Kevin Press, Edinburgh; since 1967, Director, Live Readings, Scotland. Recipient: Scottish Arts Council bursary, 1967. Address: 17 Cathcart Place, Edinburgh 11, Scotland.

PUBLICATIONS

Verse

Under Water Wedding: Poems. Edinburgh, privately printed, 1961.
Sixpenny Poems. Bristol, privately printed, 1962.
Well Ye Ken Noo. Bristol, privately printed, 1963.
All Fall Down: Poems. Edinburgh, Kevin Press, 1965.
The Worstest Beast. Edinburgh, Kevin Press, 1967.
Penguin Modern Poets 12, with Jeff Nuttall and William Wantling. London, Penguin, 1968.
The Grim Wayfarer. London, Fulcrum Press, 1969.
Idiots Are Freelance. Dyce, Aberdeenshire, Rainbow Books, 1973.

Alan Jackson comments:

I regard the poet as the Blakean "bard" who turns the eye in, tries to bring the dark to light.

Themes: family (particularly the mother), sex (particularly as against Christian morality and also searching my own perversities), death of religion and the absence of myth, man as a pernicious life-form.

Verse forms: many, longer ones often rhyming, always close to speech, but interest in longer unrhymed rhythms and eluding grammar increasing; dozens of very short unrhymed highly compressed poems. Poems often kept for over a year, then to be worked and re-worked. Clarity desired but not immediate understanding.

Main influence, Jung; can see few limits to his importance. Main admiration: Norman Mailer. Nietzsche somewhere between the two. I try not to be influenced by poets, though I try to absorb lessons about writing. Finally, a man should not know what is characteristic of him.

*   *   *

Alan Jackson's best work has subtle sympathy, ironic wit, technical dexterity and satirical verve, although other pieces express a raucous violence shrieking in concert with the fashionable taste for what Robert Lowell has called "raw, huge, blood-dripping gobbets of unreasoned experience" – as in "Fraulein," where a "shocking" tale of rape followed by syphilis appears merely sensational because presented in complete isolation from the rest of the environment. When he resists the temptation to drop his literary pants in public, however, his verse shows that although he is still young he has already attained individual achievement as a symbolist-cum-satirist, with such bitter brevities as "Loss" where, using a thin Scots close to urban speech, he turns conventional flower imagery to most unconventional ends in revealing the all too frequent fate of beauty in the Scottish climate. Most often, however, he writes in English, and in at least one poem, "Was a Shame," the influence of Blake is as evident in style as in content, theme, and feeling. But elsewhere his work reveals an original stylist with a highly personal voice, capable of a stimulating variety of themes and forms, from the epigrammatic wit of "Young Politician" ("What a lovely lovely moon. / And it's in the constituency too") to the controlled passion of rage and sorrow in the couplets picturing man as "the worstest beast" and to the sensuous richness and strangeness of the poem called "3 1/g 4" (three little green quarters) which explores the mysteries of time and fate in terms of the superstitions of science and science-fiction.

– Alexander Scott

JACKSON, Laura (Riding).   See **RIDING, Laura.**

JACOB, Paul.   Indian.   Born in Kerala, 27 April 1940. Educated at St. Columba's School, New Delhi; Madras Christian College; St. Stephen's College, Delhi. Member of the Staff, *The Century* magazine, New Delhi, 1963–65. Since 1966, Member of the Editorial Staff, *Enact* magazine, Delhi. Lives in New Delhi, India.

PUBLICATIONS

Verse

Sonnets.   Calcutta, Writers Workshop, 1968.
Alter Sonnets.   Calcutta, Writers Workshop, 1969.
Swedish Exercises.   Calcutta, Writers Workshop, 1973.

*   *   *

Paul Jacob's poetry seems to be a continuous search for the perfect poetic form. His first two volumes consisted of exercises in the sonnet form, written in a taut, controlled style. In his recent volume, *Swedish Exercises*, he experiments with the Italian sestina consisting of six six-line stanzas. He has tried his hand at limericks and at present is writing English poems in the Urdu *ghazal* form.

This concern with form is a challenge Paul Jacob sets for himself and it suits his obliquely suggestive style. Though he never writes poetry of plain statement, his

poems, rather than appearing obscure, give the impression of almost a total communicability at a non-logical level:

> Anywhere there are children is no flaw, but youth
> Must come out of darkness, newspaperish tar,
> Forever celluloid, soundtrack, should warm up
> As you review gulmohar, amaltaz, summerspring to truth.

(Gulmohar and amaltaz are orange and yellow flowering trees that blossom in India
in late spring and summer.)

Paul Jacob uses words skilfully and sensitively, but sometimes also a little
self-consciously as in his favourite antithetical devices like "A lifelong sleep, a
deathshort sleeplessness," or "My bed shall not make others, others shall make my
bed." The central theme of all his poems is self-exploration, but the frame of
reference ranges from love to religion:

> May every true prayer be repetition
> Vain like a baby. May prayer itself be whole
> Over this weekend the earth shall burn for you.

Like most Indian writers who are bilingual (Paul Jacob happens to be trilingual)
he is interested in translation. He has translated plays from Hindi and Malayalam
into English.

– Meenakshi Mukherjee

JACOBSEN, Josephine. Canadian. Born in Coburg, Ontario, 19 August 1908.
Educated privately, and at Roland Park Country School, Baltimore, 1915–18. Mar-
ried Eric Jacobsen in 1932; has one son. Poetry Consultant, 1971–73, and since
1973, Honorary Consultant in American Letters, Library of Congress, Washington,
D.C. Agent: McIntosh and Otis, 18 East 41st Street, New York, New York 10017.
Address: 220 Stony Ford Road, Baltimore, Maryland 21210, U.S.A.

PUBLICATIONS

Verse

> *Let Each Man Remember.*   Dallas, Kaleidograph Press, 1940.
> *For the Unlost.*   Baltimore, Contemporary Poetry, 1946.
> *The Human Climate: New Poems.*   Baltimore, Contemporary Poetry, 1953.
> *The Animal Inside: Poems.*   Athens, Ohio University Press, 1966.
> *The Shade-Seller: New and Selected Poems.*   New York, Doubleday, 1974.

Other

> *The Testament of Samuel Beckett*, with William Randolph Mueller. New York,
> Hill and Wang, 1964; as *The Testament of Samuel Beckett: A Study*, London,
> Faber, 1966.
> *Ionesco and Genet: Playwrights of Silence*, with William Randolph Mueller. New
> York, Hill and Wang, 1968.
> *From Anne to Marianne: Some American Women Poets* (lecture). Washington,
> D.C., Library of Congress, 1973.
> *The Instant of Knowing* (lecture). Washington, D.C., Library of Congress,
> 1974.

Manuscript Collection: Mugar Memorial Library, Boston University.

Critical Studies: "Poetry and Preaching" by Hugh Kerr, in *Theology Today* (Princeton, New Jersey), October 1964; Richard Ohmann, in *Wisconsin Studies in Contemporary Literature* (Madison), Autumn 1965; "The Matter and Manner of Beckett" by David Helsa, in *Christian Scholar* (New York), Winter 1965; "Enduring Saturday" by Anthony Burgess, in *Spectator* (London), 29 April 1966; "The Human Condition," in *Irish Press* (Dublin), 11 June 1966; "The Essential Q," in *Times Literary Supplement* (London), 30 June 1966; John Logan, in *Epoch* (Ithaca, New York), Autumn 1966; "Art in Transition" by Laurence Lieberman, in *Poetry* (Chicago), March 1967; Rosemary Dee, in *Commonweal* (New York), 20 December 1968.

Josephine Jacobsen comments:

I don't really value very highly "statements" from a poet in regard to her own work. I can perhaps best introduce my own poetry by saying what I have not done, rather than by defining what I have done. I have not involved my work with any clique, school, or other group; I have tried not to force any poem into an overall concept of "how I write poetry" when it should be left to create organically its own individual style; I have not been content to repeat what I have already accomplished or to establish any stance which would limit the flexibility of discovery. I have not confused technical innovation, however desirable, with poeic originality or intensity. I have not utilized poetry as a social or political lever. I have not conceded that any subject matter, any vocabulary, any approach or any form is in itself necessarily unsuitable to the uses of poetry. I have not tried to establish a reputation as poet on any grounds but those of my poetry.

*   *   *

"Terrestrial, we learned the accurate measure / Of sharpness is the brevity of touch," wrote Josephine Jacobsen in her early volume, *For the Unlost*. Capturing the brief but significant moment which reveals the essence of a subject has remained her forte. "Precise in its every act," the dance is an apt and frequent metaphor in poems celebrating our fleeting, earthly pleasures; its ephemeral beauty, a figure for the "art of our mortality." She sizes up existence by striking to the core. There she finds the shining boy that preceded the greedy, frightened man and the integral marble which shadows the hypocritical monument. In "The Big Hotel Closed Yesterday for the Winter" short scenes depicting rich snobs and selfish, superannuated virgins veer toward the sentimental, only to be cut dead by a savage wit, worthy of Dorothy Parker, which strips away the veneer. In poems written in time of war, she speaks directly; ever clear-eyed, she has strength to view the horrors of the "ugly feast," though her voice catches at the poignancy of suffering and loss. "*At dreadful high noon,*" she writes in "Lines to a Poet," "*You may speak only to our heart, / Our honor and our need.*"

Continuing her explorations in *The Human Climate*, she discovers more darkness at the center, and here her lines give up their meaning less easily. Hunger for experience and "utter freedom" leads to momentary confusion: "The blinded eye will have all color." Urgency, even wildness, marks poems in which personae strive for release from "deadly limit." Lost souls are caught in psychological binds, playing games lovers play. The young man travels to the brink of suicide; the old man treads the customary path of penury and loneliness. Here, despite the vivid pointillism, the poet's design can be obscure: details are precise, but the outline remains blurred. In "Variations on Variety." the object is clearer, as the vaudeville show becomes a paradigm of our transitory nature. In "April Asylum" old ladies like "docile sentient dead" watch Technicolor films, sacraments which bring them "lonely and together" a blessing in the empty morning hours. Probing ever more inward, Jacobsen seeks in *The Animal Inside* the mysterious soul which cannot be caught or tamed, but which, "Seen, can be loved." Brilliant flashes of color, flickering images of shadows, water, and fire entice the reader into the marvelous poetic world but often leave him in a cul-de-sac. She examines the dying revolutionary, the deaf-mutes isolated in a ballpark, the ancient lady exhumed with her curious case, but maintains dramatic distance from them; despite analysis they remain inscrutable. The persona views religious spectacles, a ritual Indian sacrifice, a haunting All Soul's Day litany, from an original perspective; the Son of Man is seen in the tropical swamp, and Peter is called "crucifixion's clown." The poet seems, however, more in sympathy with wildlife. She reads chaos in a dessicated starfish and finds identity in the awkwardness and hurt of a fiddler crab. "Almost nothing concerns me but communication," she writes, and if here she sometimes meets with failure, the adventure of these poems is worth the risk.

– Joseph Parisi

JAFFIN, David. American. Born in New York City, 14 September 1937. Educated at the University of Michigan, Ann Arbor (Hopwood Award, 1956; Oreon E. Scott Award), 1955–56; New York University (Penfield Fellow), 1956–66, B.A. 1959 (Phi Beta Kappa), M.A. 1961, Ph.D. in history 1966. Married Rosemarie Jaffin in 1961; has two sons. Graduate Assistant, New York University, 1961–62; Lecturer in European History, University of Maryland European Division, Germany, 1966–69. Currently, Theological Student, University of Tübingen, Germany. Address: 7406 Moessingen, Baestenhardt, Laerchenstrasse 1, Germany.

PUBLICATIONS

Verse

Conformed to Stone. New York, Abelard Schuman, 1968; London, Abelard Schuman, 1970.
Emptied Spaces. London, Abelard Schuman, 1972.
Objects. Sheffield, Yorkshire, Headlands Publications, 1973.
Late March. Rushden, Northamptonshire, Sceptre Press, 1973.

Of. Rushden, Northamptonshire, Sceptre Press, 1974.
As One. New Rochelle, New York, Elizabeth Press, 1974.
In the Glass of Winter. London, Abelard Schuman, 1974.

Critical Studies: in *Library Journal* (New York), 15 September 1968; *Yorkshire Post* (Leeds), 9 September 1972; *Bristol Evening Post*, 9 November 1972; by Edward Lucie-Smith, in *Emptied Spaces*, 1972, and *In the Glass of Winter*, 1974; *Workshop New Poetry 18* (London), 1973; *Poet Lore* (Boston), Summer 1974.

David Jaffin comments:

My art is one of intense compression, both of form and meaning. I seek to create a world at once visually alive, tangible/explicit and yet abstract, inward and res- trained. I feel the poetic process as an intensification of consciousness. I break through/break down those words inspired in my mind (revising over and over again while I'm writing), to derive their intrinsic form and relation. Jacques Lipschitz told me that my poems were sculpted as from stone. There must never be a word too many, no decoration, ornament, rhetoric. The craft involves the unity of image, sound, sense, tone and idea. The poem itself is a state of being, not a theme to be developed with the "poetic trimmings." The poem simply is, is not about. But craftsmanship itself is only the prerequisite for the spiritual process. A "state of being" means for me a personal and new definition of reality. All meaningful art must be this. I often describe this via tangible objects, thereby actualizing the senses. My aesthetic moves on two levels, the one being physically alive, so vivid as to be almost touched, and yet when these poems succeed they create an absolute stillness and control. I am told my poems gain by constant re-reading. I always present them at least twice at public readings.

*   *   *

Both *Conformed To Stone* and *Emptied Spaces*, David Jaffin's first and second books in The Abelard Poets series, have a sculptural quality; the poems are spare, chiselled down to the essentials. The title of each is appropriate; the first collection contains more people among its statuary: "Creatures of Stone," "The Idiot," "Woodcarver," "Self Portrait"; the second collection moves away from human models to still lifes more remote from human life, though the artistic (and particul- arly, the sculptural) motif remains. In the latter book, Jaffin seems to be hollowing out his previous forms, trying for a sort of negative space to complement the positive space the previous book occupied; things defined by their absence, as in "Door Partly Opened":

> You let the light
>   in,
> Angled-off,
>
> Your hands closed as a
> Shadow hanging there
>
> You let the light
>   in
> As far as your face
>   could allow.

Poems like this remind one of French poets like Valéry, with their sense of moments of time mysteriously arrested; the poet seems to be inviting us to study some scene closely and at the same time denying total entrance. The poems are restrained, dignified, pictorial, superficially simple, but turning frequently on the ambiguities inherent in language; reading them is bracing, like stepping through ice that was not as thick as we thought. The poem above, like a number of others, turns on such ambiguities, and on the suggestion, beneath the ice of the poem, of deeper, philosophical ambiguities. The observed person in this poem is the one who has opened the door and shed light on the speaker, and yet, the light becomes merely a mask for the observed, himself no more than a shadow silhouette. The last two lines suggest a deliberate act of will as well as physical obstruction of the light, and remind us of the different disguises we wear; that openness and shedding light on things, illuminating others, can be a mask too. Such subtleties make David Jaffin's poetry rewarding.

– Duane Ackerson

JAY, Peter (Anthony Charles).   British.   Born in Chester, Cheshire, 24 May 1945. Educated at Lancing College, Sussex; Lincoln College, Oxford (Exhibitioner; Newdigate Prize, 1965). Editor, with John Aczel, *New Measure* magazine, Oxford, 1965–69. Currently, Free-lance writer, and Publisher, Anvil Press Poetry, London. Assistant Director of Poetry International, London, 1969. Recipient: Rockefeller grant, 1968. Address: c/o Anvil Press Poetry, 69 King George Street, London SE10 8PX, England.

PUBLICATIONS

Verse

Adonis and Venus.   Santa Barbara, California, Peter Whigham, 1968.

Other

Editor, *The Greek Anthology.*   London, Allen Lane, and New York, Oxford University Press, 1973.

Translator, *The Song of Songs.*   London, Anvil Press Poetry, 1974.
Translator, with Petru Popescu, *The Still Unborn about the Dead*, by Nichita Stanescu.   London, Anvil Press Poetry, and Iowa City, Iowa, International Writing Program, 1974.
Translator, with Peter Whigham, *The Poems of Meleager.*   London, Anvil Press Poetry, 1974.

*   *   *

Unnecessarily shy about publishing his own poetry, Peter Jay is the outstanding translator of his generation, and certainly the finest to emerge since Michael

Hamburger. His versions of the Rumanian poet George Bacovia are the most brilliant of all renderings into English since Hamburger's Hölderlin. Jay is also a brilliant parodist, exposing the weaknesses of his victims with deadly geniality (and very funnily indeed). He is an extremely serious, fastidious poet, and none of his original poetry is less than presentable, which is unusual in an age of low standards. His difficulty lies in discovering his own style, and some of the poems reflect too keenly his awareness of and sensitivity to many differing manners (Italian, ancient Greek, German, Rumanian). Pound, much admired by him, may not have been a useful influence: like that of so many poets who have been dazzled by Pound, Jay's natural manner in no way resembles his; this seems, as in other cases, to have worked as an inhibitory influence. Jay is very stylish, only occasionally lapsing (in earlier poems) into a kind of hermeticism that does not work in English poetry. So far he has said less than he has expressed; yet one feels that he wishes for greater explicitness. But his descriptions of his moods already have a distinction that marks him out as one of the few truly serious original poets of his generation – as in "The Gallery":

> There are days when the mind grazes,
> circling itself like an answer
> lazily guessing its question.
> Slowly they assemble, one
> by one: some whose faces
> shine with the smile of certain
> gestures long recalled. . . .

– Martin Seymour-Smith

JENNINGS, Elizabeth (Joan). British. Born in Boston, Lincolnshire, 18 July 1926. Educated at Oxford High School; St. Anne's College, Oxford, M.A. in English language and literature. Assistant, Oxford City Library, 1950–58; Reader, Chatto and Windus Ltd., publishers, London, 1958–60. Since 1961, Free-lance Writer. Recipient: Arts Council award, 1953, bursary, 1965, 1968, grant, 1972; Maugham Award, 1956; Richard Hillary Memorial Prize, 1966. Agent: David Higham Associates Ltd., 5–8 Lower John Street, Golden Square, London W1R 4HA. Address: 11 Winchester Road, Oxford OX2 6NA, England.

PUBLICATIONS

Verse

(*Poems*). Oxford, Fantasy Press, 1953.
A Way of Looking: Poems. London, Deutsch, 1955; New York, Rinehart, 1956.
The Child and the Seashell. San Francisco, Poems in Folio, 1957.
A Sense of the World: Poems. London, Deutsch, 1958; New York, Rinehart, 1959.
Song for a Birth or a Death and Other Poems. London, Deutsch, 1961; Chester Springs, Pennsylvania, Dufour, 1962.
Penguin Modern Poets 1, with Lawrence Durrell and R. S. Thomas. London, Penguin, 1962.

Recoveries: Poems. London, Deutsch, and Chester Springs, Pennsylvania, Dufour, 1964.

The Mind Has Mountains. London, Macmillan, and New York, St. Martin's Press, 1966.

The Secret Brother and Other Poems for Children. London, Macmillan, and New York, St. Martin's Press, 1966.

Collected Poems 1967. London, Macmillan, and Chester Springs, Pennsylvania, Dufour, 1967.

The Animals' Arrival. London, Macmillan, and Chester Springs, Pennsylvania, Dufour, 1969.

Lucidities. London, Macmillan, 1970.

Hurt. London, Poem-of-the-Month Club, 1970.

Folio, with others. Frensham, Surrey, Sceptre Press, 1971.

Relationships. London, Macmillan, 1972.

Other

Let's Have Some Poetry. London, Museum Press, 1960.

Every Changing Shape (religion and poetry). London, Deutsch, 1961.

Poetry Today, 1957–60. London, Longman, 1961.

Frost. Edinburgh, Oliver and Boyd, 1964; New York, Barnes and Noble, 1965.

Christianity and Poetry. London, Burns and Oates, 1965; as *Christian Poetry*, New York, Hawthorn Books, 1965.

Editor, with Dannie Abse and Stephen Spender, *New Poems 1956: A P.E.N. Anthology.* London, Joseph, 1956.

Editor, *The Batsford Book of Children's Verse.* London, Batsford, 1958.

Editor, *An Anthology of Modern Verse 1940–1960.* London, Methuen, 1961.

Editor, *A Choice of Christina Rossetti's Verse.* London, Faber, 1970.

Translator, *The Sonnets of Michaelangelo.* London, Folio Society, 1961; revised edition, London, Allison and Busby, 1969; New York, Doubleday, 1970.

Manuscript Collections: Oxford City Library; University of Washington, Seattle.

Critical Study: by Margaret Byers, in *British Poetry since 1960*, edited by Michael Schmidt and Grevel Lindop, Oxford, Carcanet Press, 1972.

Elizabeth Jennings comments:

I do not much care for writing about my own poems. The main reason for this is, I believe, that it makes one too self-conscious. However, I would like to say that I am always interested in what I am writing at present and hope to write in the future. I like to experiment with different poetic forms, and, at this time, I am constantly seeking for more and more clarity. I am working on a series of prose poems about paintings (painting is my second favourite art), and a series of poems, in various forms and from several viewpoints, on religious themes. I have also been writing poems about craftsmen and various aspects of nature, particularly sky-scapes. For me, poetry is always a search for order. I started writing at the age of thirteen and wrote only one 4-line poem I now wish to preserve from childhood. My Roman Catholic religion and my poems are the most important things in my life.

*   *   *

Elizabeth Jennings's *Collected Poems*, drawing on seven books of poems over a period of fourteen years, shows a remarkable unity of tone and theme, repetitive and yet gaining strength from that very fact. The most notable development has been one of giving greater prominence to the immediate and the circumstantial, and yet clearly the later poems of mental agony and illness come from the same person who wrote such pure and clear lyrics and meditations as the early "Delay," "Reminiscence," and "The Island."

Apart from purity and clarity, the epithets most often attached to Elizabeth Jennings's work have been (apart, again, from the obvious and meaningless "femi-nine") "reserved" and "abstract." Yet the tone and matter of many of the poems are frequently as confessional as almost anything one finds in Robert Lowell, Sylvia Plath and Anne Sexton; and the concreteness of experience, particularly in some of the later poems, is plainly there – even, in the weaker pieces, to the point of mere literalness and banality.

More significant is the contemplative formality, the cool and deliberate effort to give shape and order to experience. This is particularly sharpened in the later poems of sickness and breakdown, in which this formality preserves a composure which, running counter to what the poems are *about*, adds to, rather than dimi-nishes, the tension felt like an unheard note behind the level cadences and the calm words. It seems a thoroughly earned, worked-for art. The composure is schooled by self-discipline, and the confessional nakedness demands a kind of reverence rather than the prurience which some more heart-baring contemporaries invite.

Many of the earlier poems were concerned with identity, and with the working out of the significance of people in their relationships to places and situations. Very often these took a "type" ("The Planners," "The Stranger," "The Idler," "Bell-Ringer," "The Climbers," "Fishermen," and so on) and, rather in the manner of Edwin Muir, drew illuminations and conclusions from the careful elaboration of the chosen central image. Later, places themselves seem to become an obsession, and there are many poems which draw for their nourishment on Elizabeth Jennings's frequent and protracted visits to Italy: "Letter from Assisi," "Santa Maria Mag-giore, Rome," "The Roman Forum," "A Roman Window," "Men Fishing in the Arno." It would be a misapprehension to take these as postcard poems: certainly they set the scene and preserve it, but the search is always for the true significance of balance, juxtaposition, and the figures in the landscape. Such a piece of observa-tion as "Fountain" is – as Miss Jennings herself has commented – as much about power and authority as the examined thing itself. It ends:

> It is the elegance here, it is the taming,
> The keeping fast in a thousand flowering sprays,
> That builds this energy up but lets the watchers
> See in that stress an image of utter calm,
> A stillness there. It is how we must have felt
> Once at the edge of some perpetual stream,
> Fearful of touching, bringing no thirst at all,
> Panicked by no perception of ourselves
> But drawing the water down to the deepest wonder.

There follow poems which are more specifically religious meditations (Elizabeth Jennings is a devout Roman Catholic), and then the desperate but still tenuously calm poems of sickness in *Recoveries*. At this period there is also a handful of extremely good poems about family life, with its tensions and misunderstandings, most finely and wonderingly expressed in "One Flesh" (chronologically out of order, incidentally, both in *The Mind Has Mountains* and the *Collected Poems*). This ends:

> Strangely apart, yet strangely close together,
> Silence between them like a thread to hold
> And not wind in. And time itself's a feather
> Touching them gently. Do they know they're old,
> These two who are my father and my mother
> Whose fire, from which I came, has now grown cold?

The mental-hospital poems are, as suggested earlier, not the ravings or illuminations of someone whose barriers have been broken down. There is no trace, either, of self-pity. Instead, the daily routine of doctors, nurses and fellow-patients is observed with an uncanny blend of compassion, detachment, and a poise which is on the edge of despair but somehow never topples over. Only in the nine free-association poems – attempts at automatic writing in a kind of jumpy, self-conscious *vers libre* – is there a disappointing sense of something tried and failed. Several of the poems in the recent book *The Animals' Arrival* seem to show a temporary dilution of her habitual themes into something almost banal; but they are still piercingly honest, sensitively faithful to the experiences they record.

– Anthony Thwaite

JEROME, Judson. American. Born in Tulsa, Oklahoma, 8 February 1927. Educated at the University of Oklahoma, Norman, 1943–45; University of Chicago, M.A. 1950; Ohio State University, Columbus, Ph.D. 1955. Married Martha-Jane Pierce in 1948; has one son and four daughters. Professor of Literature, Antioch College, Yellow Springs, Ohio, 1953–72; Chairman of the Humanities Division, College of the Virgin Islands, St. Thomas, 1963–65; Director of the Center for Documentary Arts, Antioch Columbia, Columbia, Maryland, 1969–70. Since 1961, Columnist ("Poetry: How and Why"), *Writer's Digest*, Cincinnati. Since 1972, Free-lance Writer. Recipient: Huntington Hartford Fellowship, 1959; Amy Lowell Traveling Fellowship, 1960. Agent: Ann Elmo, 54 Vanderbilt Avenue, New York, New York 10017. Address: Downhill Farm, Hancock, Maryland 21750, U.S.A.

PUBLICATIONS

Verse

> *Light in the West.* Francestown, New Hampshire, Golden Quill Press, 1962.
> *The Ocean's Warning to the Skin Diver and Other Love Poems.* Point Richmond, California, Crown Point Press, 1964.

Serenade.   Point Richmond, California, Crown Point Press, 1968.
I Never Saw. . . .   Chicago, Whitman Press, 1974.

Plays

Winter in Eden (produced Yellow Springs, Ohio, 1955).   Included in *Plays for
an Imaginary Theatre*, 1970.
The Wandering Jew (produced Yellow Springs, Ohio, 1963).
Candle in the Straw (produced St. Paul, Minnesota, 1963).   Included in *Plays for
an Imaginary Theatre*, 1970.
The Glass Mountain (produced St. Thomas, Virgin Islands, 1964).   Included in
Plays for an Imaginary Theatre, 1970.
Plays for an Imaginary Theatre (includes *Winter in Eden, Candle in the Straw, The
Glass Mountain, Drums*).   Urbana, University of Illinois Press, 1970.

Novel

The Fell of Dark.   Boston, Houghton Mifflin, 1966.

Other

The Poet and the Poem.   Cincinnati, Writer's Digest, 1963; revised edition,
1974.
Poetry: Premeditated Art.   Boston, Houghton Mifflin, 1968.
Culture Out of Anarchy: The Reconstruction of American Higher Learning.   New
York, Herder, 1970.
Families of Eden: Communes and the New Anarchism.   New York, Seabury
Press, 1974.

Manuscript Collection: Boston University Library.

Judson Jerome comments:

I believe that a new culture is transforming Western Civilization, and that poets
have supplied and are supplying its vision, which essentially is a shift from a
mechanistic to an organic world view. By leaving institutions behind and retiring
with my family to a rural commune, I am hoping to become a more active
participant in this ongoing revolution of consciousness.
My monthly column in *Writer's Digest* continues to be my letter to the world.

*   *   *

In his poetry, fiction and essays, Judson Jerome has been examining contemporary American life in a way intended to define possibilities of cultural order. Poetry
he has described as a vital, liberating illusion: "It is less ecstasy or rebellion or
confession than a steady voice that tells a lie so completely that hearts are moved
and people live by it." This conception of poetry has moral and aesthetic roots. It
involves acknowledgement of radical human fault: "Acting/is honest, the courage

to accept / our false condition." And it emphasizes the powers of traditional poetic techniques. Jerome has located tradition in American poetry in the writings of Emily Dickinson, E. A. Robinson and Robert Frost; and his own attention to technique is part of his attempt to clarify experience. In "Cages," for example, he works against meter to convey the limits of human freedom: "dear child with touching hands, / night, day, age, youth, our veins, / our very ribs, are cage."

This interest in technique and in the magical aspect of poetry is behind his *Plays for an Imaginary Theatre*, a collection of related plays, essays and lyrics. The mixed format is peculiarly appropriate to Jerome's talents as poet and critic; and the plays themselves are lyric extravaganzas, less plays of character than plays of ideas, of the possibilities of reconciling a radical individualism and the competing claims of communal order.

At times in the plays, as in the poetry, the verbal facility, the deliberate sense of artifice, approaches a kind of self-indulgence. At its best, however, Jerome's writings, with their enthusiasm and discipline, provide humane, clarifying insight.

– Jerry Paris

JOHNSON, B(ryan) S(tanley). British. Born in London, 5 February 1933. Educated at King's College, London, B.A. (honours) in English. Married Virginia Ann Kimpton in 1964; has two children. Since 1964, Poetry Editor, *Transatlantic Review*, London and New York. Founder, with Alan Burns, "Writers Reading" program to encourage and organize prose readings at colleges and universities, 1969. Gregynog Arts Fellow, University of Wales, Aberystwyth, 1970. Recipient: Gregory Award, 1963; Maugham Award, 1967; Grand Prix, Tours and Melbourne Short Film festivals, 1968; Grandara Prize, 1971. Agent: Michael Bakewell Associates, 118 Tottenham Court Road, London W.1. Address: 9 Dagmar Terrace, London N.1, England. *Died 13 November 1973.*

PUBLICATIONS

Verse

Poems. London, Constable, and New York, Chilmark Press, 1964.
Poems Two. London, Trigram Press, 1972.
Dublin Unicorn. Nottingham, Byron Press, 1973.
Penguin Modern Poets 25, with Zulfikar Ghose and Gavin Ewart. London, Penguin, 1974.

Plays

You're Human Like the Rest of Them (also director: televised, 1967). Published in New English Dramatists 14, London, Penguin, 1970.
B. S. Johnson Versus God (Whose Dog Are You? and You're Human Like the Rest of Them) (produced London, 1971).

Television plays and documentaries: *The Evacuees*; *The Smithsons on Housing*; *On Reflection: Alexander Herzen*; *Samuel Johnson*; *The Unfortunates*; *Architecture of Bath*; *Charlie Whildon Talking, Singing and Playing*; *You're Human Like the Rest of Them*, 1967; *Up Yours Too, Guillaume Apollinaire*, 1968; *Paradigm*, 1969; *Not Counting the Savages*, 1971; *Fat Man on a Beach*, 1974.

Novels

Travelling People. London, Constable, 1963.
Albert Angelo. London, Constable, 1964.
Trawl. London, Secker and Warburg, 1966.
The Unfortunates. London, Secker and Warburg, 1969.
House Mother Normal. London, Collins, 1971.
Christie Malry's Own Double-Entry. London, Collins, 1972; New York, Viking Press, 1973.
See the Old Lady Decently. London, Hutchinson, and New York, Viking Press, 1975.

Short Stories

Statement Against Corpses, with Zulfikar Ghose. London, Constable, 1964.
Penguin Modern Stories 7, with others. London, Penguin, 1971.

Other

Street Children, photographs by Julia Trevelyan Oman. London, Hodder and Stoughton, 1964.
Aren't You Rather Young to Be Writing Your Memoirs? (essays). London, Hutchinson, 1973.

Editor, *The Evacuees.* London, Gollancz, 1968.
Editor, with Margaret Drabble, *London Consequences* (a group novel). London, Greater London Arts Association, 1972.
Editor, *All Bull: The National Servicemen.* London, Allison and Busby, 1973.

Theatrical Activities:

Director: **Plays** – *Backwards*, and *The Ramp*, by Johnnie Quarrell, London, 1970. **Television** – *You're Human Like the Rest of Them*, 1967; *Up Yours Too, Guillaume Apollinaire*, 1968; *Paradigm*, 1969.

B. S. Johnson comments:

I do not believe poetry is limited to verse.
One of the first to be interested in syllabic metres in recent years (say since the war), and have carried out various experiments with syllabic metres. For fuller account, see note to my volume *Poems*, 1964.

Major themes: corroding effect of time, decay in general, unrequited love, unfor-
giveness, solipsism.

*   *   *

Because B. S. Johnson is so widely known as a novelist of distinction it is
important to remind ourselves that not only is he a poet, but that he is primarily a
poet. Here it is interesting to compare one of his most successful poems, "Evening: Barents Sea," with his novel *Trawl*, for both of them are derived from the
same experience. The poem is descriptive and evocative:

> the thin coast
> (of grey Norway is it, or of Russia?)
> distinguished only as a formal change
> in the pattern of clouds on our port side
>
> on deck the strung lights illuminate no
> movement but the sullen swill of water
> in the washer.

In one line only is there an oblique reference to that other trawl –

> the trawl of unquiet mind drops astern

– which is to be directly explored and developed in the novel. "Why do I trawl the
delicate mesh of my mind over the snagged and broken floor of my past?" asks the
hero of *Trawl*. Indeed, the novel, with its counterpointing of present and past
emotions and experiences, is, in fact, an extended prose-poem and a most successful one at that. I suspect that it is this poetic quality of his novels and the
frequently sparse nature of his actual poems which find critics regarding B. S.
Johnson's poetry as marginal to his novels and even to his life.

In some senses this is not altogether untrue. It is difficult, for example, to view
parts of the poem "Nine Stages Towards Knowing," say "Theatregoer," in any
other light. But the best of Johnson's poems do stand in their own right. "Knowing," itself, and "Laying-out" are poems that seek their own depth of meaning –

> Knowledge of her was
> earned like miners' pay.

– where, in contrast to his novels, the poet seeks to pare the experience down to its
essentials. On occasions, as in "The Bonepit Testes Series," Johnson strives too
directly to make his point and the poem tends to collapse under the strain. But
when he allows his point to emerge obliquely and of itself from the matter of the
poem his success is marked. The experimental "Three Gregynog Englynion" are a
case in point; take "Fern":

> Hook headed hairy young fern, springy, curled,
> coy greeny thruster set on
> its own spread revelation.

– John Cotton

JOHNSON, Louis. New Zealander. Born in Wellington, 27 September 1924. Educated at Wellington Teachers' Training College. Has three children. School teacher, 1951–54; Editor, *New Zealand Parent and Child* magazine, 1955–59; Assistant Editor, Department of Education School Publications Branch, Wellington, 1963–68; Officer in Charge, Department of Information Bureau of Literature, Port Moresby, Papua New Guinea, 1968–69. Founding Editor, *Numbers* magazine, Wellington, 1954–60. Editor, New Zealand Broadcasting Corporation Poetry programme, 1964, and "Column Comment" television programme, 1968. Since 1970, Free-lance Writer. Secretary, New Zealand P.E.N., 1954–59. Recipient: New Zealand Literary Fund grants. Address: 6/11A Redan Street, St. Kilda, Melbourne, Victoria 3182, Australia.

PUBLICATIONS

Verse

> *Stanza and Scene: Poems.* Wellington, Handcraft Press, 1945.
> *The Sun among the Ruins.* Christchurch, Pegasus Press, 1951.
> *Roughshod among the Lilies.* Christchurch, Pegasus Press, 1952.
> *Poems Unpleasant,* with Anton Vogt and James K. Baxter. Christchurch, Pegasus Press, 1952.
> *Two Poems: News of Molly Bloom, The Passionate Man and the Casual Man.* Christchurch, Pegasus Press, 1955.
> *The Dark Glass.* Wellington, Handcraft Press, 1955.
> *New Worlds for Old: Poems.* Wellington, Capricorn Press, 1957.
> *The Night Shift: Poems on Aspects of Love,* with others. Wellington, Capricorn Press, 1957.
> *Bread and a Pension: Selected Poems.* Christchurch, Pegasus Press, 1964.
> *Land Like a Lizard: New Guinea Poems.* Brisbane, Jacaranda Press, 1970.

Other

> Editor, *New Zealand Poetry Yearbook 1–11.* Wellington, Reed, 3 vols., 1951–54; Christchurch, Pegasus Press, 8 vols., 1955–64.

Critical Studies: *A Way of Saying* by Kendrick Smithyman, Auckland, Collins, 1965; *Aspects of Poetry in New Zealand* by James K. Baxter, Christchurch, Caxton Press, 1967.

Louis Johnson comments:

I'm a sort of personal-liberal-existentialist of an atheistic inclination.

When I was beginning to write verse, in the early 1940's, New Zealand was just "coming of age" in the art through the works of Mason, Curnow, Glover, Fairburn, etc., and it seemed to me that their "nationalism" was rather overdone, limited, and parochial, especially since my own earlier poetic interests were people like Auden, Yeats, Pound, men whose vision appeared unlimited by the back fence. But from the "broad view" I turned to personal experience, the "known and felt" thing rather than the "New Zealand thing" as prescribed by Curnow, probing the field of human relationships – especially those between men and women, the way we live here and now – and became known as "the poet of subtopia."

I have been concerned, in my work, with the way in which people have grown up in, and been shaped by, our small, restricted community; a great deal of the work has been written on themes of childhood and growth, the nature of reality and the manner of our illusions; there is also a strong social strain, almost political at times, in some of it.

My work has gone through several different stages of method – from an over-dressed abstractionism to, recently, a direct, colloquial "language as she is spoke" approach. Suddenly, in middle-age, I have found my feet as a poet in the mysteries of love; of a new volume in the process of being put together, my friend and colleague James K. Baxter has said: "I didn't think any Kiwi would write love poetry like it. It's the best we've got."

*   *   *

"At the centre of it there is always a mystery," Louis Johnson wrote of the act which is a poem. "Poetry is an act of faith," he insisted at another time. "To the poet, nothing is unbelievable." The central mystery to which he refers is the imagination much as Coleridge conceived of it; the faith is faith in the potential power of imagination, as it may be for a child to whom "possibility is actual." The nominally real must be illusion; conversely, a lot of living may be disillusioning. Life is often an offence to the man able to imagine. To be adult is to be deprived, given over to a reality which endorses the probable at the expense of the possible.

Although sometimes Johnson would seem to want to appear a social realist, opinions of the kind above are at the heart of his view. He rejected a popular doctrine of the poet's obligation to respect "the reality prior to the poem" because the reality foreseen was thought to be too narrowly understood. The common impression of Johnson's vigorous, copious, ostensibly worldly poems is of writing at odds with his announced principles. His most evident engagement is with the external (or even extrinsic) show of life in a cultural province, whether urban, suburban or rural, which implies an accentuating of what is contemporary and thus peculiar because particular. He has been freely and loudly criticized because his sense of the contemporary and of what he has referred to as formalism persuades him into practices which strike readers as wilful or gratuitously *farouche*. At his best, he is a formalist. Disillusioned, he is a disenchanted romantic. At his most effectively contemporary – in which role he came near to founding a School – he is highly persuasive. At such times he is closest to the tradition, whether he is being a propagandist, a persuader, or a polemicist.

– Kendrick Smithyman

JOHNSON, Ronald. American. Born in Ashland, Kansas, 25 November 1935. Educated at Columbia University, New York, B.A. 1960. Served in the United States Army, 1954–56. Poet-in-Residence, University of Kentucky, Lexington, 1971, and University of Washington, Seattle, 1972. Recipient: Inez Boulton Award (*Poetry*, Chicago), 1964; National Endowment for the Arts grant, 1969, 1974; Anderson Fellowship, 1972. Address: 2509 Sacramento, San Francisco, California 94115, U.S.A.

Publications

Verse

A Line of Poetry, A Row of Trees. Highlands, North Carolina, Jargon, 1964.
Assorted Jungles: Rousseau. San Francisco, Auerhahn Press, 1966.
Gorse/Goose/Rose and Other Poems. Bloomington, Indiana University Fine Arts Department, 1966.
Sunflowers. Woodchester, Gloucestershire, John Furnival, 1966.
Io and the Ox-Eye Daisy. Dunsyre, Lanarkshire, Wild Hawthorn Press, 1966.
The Book of the Green Man. New York, Norton, and London, Longman, 1967.
The Round Earth on Flat Paper. Urbana, Illinois, Finial Press, 1968.
Reading 1 and *2.* Urbana, Illinois, Finial Press, 2 vols., 1968.
Valley of the Many-Colored Grasses. New York, Norton, 1969.
Balloons for Moonless Nights. Urbana, Illinois, Finial Press, 1969.
The Spirit Walks, The Rocks Will Talk. Highlands, North Carolina, Jargon, 1969.
Songs of the Earth. San Francisco, Grabhorn Hoyem, 1970.
Maze/Mane/Wane. Cambridge, Massachusetts, Pomegranate Press, 1973.

Other

The Aficionado's Southwestern Cooking (cookbook). Albuquerque, University of New Mexico Press, 1968.

Translator, *Sports and Divertissments*, by Erik Satie. Edinburgh, Wild Hawthorn Press, 1965; Urbana, Illinois, Finial Press, 1969.

Manuscript Collection: University of Kansas, Lawrence.

Ronald Johnson comments:

(1970) I have been primarily influenced by the Black Mountain "school" of poetry – i.e., Charles Olson out of Ezra Pound, Louis Zukofsky and Williams.

To see the world in a grain of sand, to see the *word* in a grain of sand, this is where the poem begins. Thoreau questioned: "Who placed us with eyes between a microscopic and a telescopic world?" All is built from this position – a solid construct in the apparently invisible, exact words illuminating the ineffable. A grain of sand if looked at long enough waxes first as glowing, then as large as a moon. The architects tell us that large and small are a matter of placement, and that galactic and atomic are simply humming-birds within humming-birds, etc. To write a poem is to begin with words, and is it not where word becomes wor(l)d the primal poem exists? And it is only an arc from there to *whirled* and "the push of numerous humming-birds from a superior bush."

(1974) After ten years of writing and walking out there in the trees, I have found, as William Blake knew all along, that the trees are in the head. I am at present at work on two projects – one, a re-writing of Milton's *Paradise Lost* in terms of 20th century cosmology, and two, a book entitled *Wor(l)ds*. This is a long work in the tradition of Pound's *Cantos* and Olson's *Maximus*, about the structure of the Universe.

*   *   *

Ronald Johnson's poems are filled with the energy of discovery: he observes, hypothesizes, and moves on to new discovery. There is no form that he regularly employs; rather, his poems create their own form, the length and placement of the line dictated by no tradition. Occasionally, as in "Sunflowers," which balances on a center axis, suggesting concrete poetry, the visual appeal of the poem detracts from the text. As always, Johnson surrounds his words with air:

> The sky is apple-green.
> > A sower casts his seed
> > in a dark field,
> > > while the sun, become pale as silver,
> > > encircles
> > > > his head.

Johnson's work frequently incorporates the poetry of earlier writers, to the extent that only the most sophisticated reader will know the source: perhaps this does not matter. Surely Johnson considers these borrowings and their sources important, and the long poem *The Book of the Green Man* has five pages of notes which credit a wide range of authors. Johnson's recent book, *Valley of the Many-Colored Grasses*, devotes two pages to "Emerson, On Goethe." There is the paragraph as Emerson wrote it, followed by Johnson's version, which adheres faithfully to the text of the original. Where Emerson begins: "Nature will be reported. All things are engaged in writing their history . . .," Johnson has it:

> NATURE WILL BE
>
> > reported.
> > > All things
> > are engaged in writing their history.

This is either a beautiful compliment or an insult of sorts.

One could debate endlessly the pros and cons of this poetry, which is not academic, but surely research-oriented. I prefer the rare poems in which Johnson lets himself do all the talking, even though he might feel that talk is merely paraphrase. For when he is willing to put us into direct contact with himself, all the energy of discovery mentioned earlier opens heavy doors:

> What is myth, but the power to tell
> the truth of it? In words
> not even the *real* planted here –
> with its rootlets reaching from the base
> arrested in a movement down,
> or its bright green
> of leaves, caught in transpiration –
> could tell. For truth
> includes not only the even row
> of kernels, but grey-black
> growths, that I have seen split
> the greenest husk.

> – & *Kan*:
> in which scholars
> cannot see the simplicity of a kernel . . .
> — "Indian Corn"
>
> – Geof Hewitt

JOHNSTON, George (Benson). Canadian. Born in Hamilton, Ontario, 7 October 1913. Educated at the University of Toronto, B.A. 1936, M.A. 1945. Served in the Royal Canadian Air Force, four years. Married to Jeanne McRae; has three sons and three daughters. Assistant Professor of English, Mount Allison University, Sackville, New Brunswick, 1946–48. Since 1950, Member of the English Department, and currently, Professor of English, Carleton University, Ottawa. LL.D.: Queen's University, Kingston, Ontario, 1971. Address: 22 Third Avenue, Ottawa K1S 2J6, Ontario, Canada.

PUBLICATIONS

Verse

> *The Cruising Auk.* Toronto, Oxford University Press, 1959.
> *Home Free.* Toronto, Oxford University Press, 1966.
> *Happy Enough.* Toronto, Oxford University Press, 1972.

Other

> Translator, *The Saga of Gisli.* Toronto, University of Toronto Press, and London, Dent, 1963.
> Translator, *The Faroe Islanders' Saga.* Ottawa, Oberon Press, 1975.

Critical Studies: by George Whalley, in *Canadian Literature 35* (Vancouver), Winter 1968; by Lawrence W. Jones, in *Canadian Literature 48* (Vancouver), Spring 1971.

George Johnston comments:

(1970) First volume, *The Cruising Auk*, was considered light verse in mainly conventional forms.

Second volume, *Home Free*, is part light verse, part serious, also largely conventional in form.

(1974) My work has been progressively less ironic and the light verse tone has pretty much faded out, for better or worse I don't know.

*   *   *

The poetry of George Johnston, that most engaging Canadian poet, written between 1959 and 1972, shows itself as distinctively individual and very much of a piece, the characteristic tone and idiom having been established almost from the beginning. Not that it isn't difficult to define the tone of verse which on the one side hesitates on the edge of pathos, and on the other leans back from the brink of farce. Perhaps we could say of it that it blends in an inimitably individual way sentiment and daftness, or flippancy and a strong and central orthodoxy. Perhaps this is no more than to say, human experience being as enigmatically complex as it is, that the poet's eye registers nuances which the ordinary person, or just the rest of us, loses in a blur of emotional cliché and commonsense expectation. The technique by which Johnston establishes some shade of feeling or being varies from point to point: sometimes it may be a grave disparity between the solemn treatment and the ridiculous subject, as in "Noctambule":

> Mr. Murple's got a dog that's long
> And underslung and sort of pointed wrong;
> When daylight fades and evening lights come out
> He takes him round the neighbour lawns about
> To ease himself and leak against the trees
> The which he does in drops and by degrees
> Leaving his hoarded fluid only where
> Three-legged ceremonious hairy care
> Has been before and made a solemn sign.

Or it may be, as in "Fields," by the use of a bent parallel, two stanzas laid out side by side, with a small, distorting explosive in the second; or it may be by the adoption of a certain simplicity or even simple-mindedness of attitude as in many of the poems of *The Cruising Auk*; or it may be by a neatly modulating use of repetition, a device he uses very frequently to achieve a strikingly disconcerting effect, as in the last stanza of "Eating Fish."

Johnston's versification is skillful in a traditional way, and indeed the normality of his rhythms and figuration makes even more impressive the individuality of the approach. The central characteristic of that approach is the sort of wit which sees at once what is discrepant in the situation or the character. The wit in Johnston is not merely clever or sharp but issues from some fundamental sagacity and repose. It is conveyed in diction of an almost Chinese precision and clarity and with a tone of calm and moderate good sense which adds to its point and sharpness.

What makes him so fine a comic poet is that his wit operates within a certain context of desperation, the humour is played out against a background suggestive of anxiety and distress. Like his own Mr. Goom,

> . . . he finds he needs a drink
> Or else a Turkish bath to chase
> His apperception from the brink
> Of darkness to a brighter place.

Not only Mr. Goom but all his characters have this sense of treading on the brink of darkness: Mr. Murple, Mrs. Beleek, Mrs. Belaney, Mrs. McGonigle, Miss Knit, Poor Edward and Miss Decharmes. In the same way the fantastic, which is so strong an element in his vision, works itself out against an ordinary suburban life, in a tar-warm city where people put ingenious stuff around their gardens "to baffle bugs and coax the ground":

The call of the dufuflu bird
For which I have an ear
Falls like the uncreating word,
But only some can hear.

And often at the droop of day
When evening grumbles in
The great dufuflu has his say
Above the braffic's din . . .

Graceful, pointed, odd, George Johnston's is a poetry modest in its pretension, effective in its individuality, successfully conveying a valid human vision. His universe is wry and peculiar but wholly recognisable, crazy but within everybody's competence and recognition. His poetry, in its wit, urbanity and fantasy, adds a genuinely different note to the canon of modern Canadian work.

– William Walsh

JONAS, George. Canadian. Born in Budapest, Hungary, 15 June 1935; left Hungary in 1956, and lived briefly in Austria and England before settling in Canada. Educated at the Lutheran Gymnazium, Budapest; studied Theatre and Film Arts with F. Hont, Budapest. Married Barbara Amiel in 1974; has one child by a previous marriage. Editor, Light Entertainment, Hungarian Broadcasting Corporation, 1956. Script Editor, 1962–67, Chief Story Editor, 1968–70, and since 1970, Television Drama Producer, Canadian Broadcasting Corporation, Toronto. Recipient: Canada Council grant, 1968, 1971. Address: c/o Canadian Broadcasting Corporation, Box 500, Terminal A, Toronto, Ontario, Canada.

PUBLICATIONS

Verse

The Absolute Smile. Toronto, House of Anansi, 1967.
The Happy Hungry Man. Toronto, House of Anansi, 1970.
Cities. Toronto, House of Anansi, 1973.

Plays

The European Lover, music by Tibor Polgar (Canada tour, 1966).
The Glove, music by Tibor Polgar (produced Toronto, 1974).

Radio Plays: *Of Mice and Men*, 1963; *To Cross a Bridge*, 1964; *The Redl Affair*, 1966; *The Agent Provocateur*, 1966; *Fasting Friar*, 1967, *Master and Man*, 1967; *Mr. Pym Passes By*, 1967; *First and Vital Candle*, 1967; *Catullus*, 1967; *Tell His*

Majesty, 1968; *Ave Luna, Morituri Te Salutant*, 1970; *The Sinking of the Mary Palmer*, 1972.

Television Plays: *The Major*, 1964; *The Family Man*, 1972; *Ave Luna, Morituri Te Salutant*, 1973.

Critical Studies: *Robert Fulford in Conversation with George Jonas*, televised, 1968; in *University of Toronto Quarterly*, January 1968; *Poetry* (Chicago), June 1969; *Canadian Literature* (Vancouver), Summer 1969; *Dennis Lee in Conversation with George Jonas*, televised, 1970.

*   *   *

George Jonas is, in the world of which he writes, an outsider, almost an exile. The authorities of his post-Kafka Hungarian childhood haunt him in a new land-scape. And indeed there is much in the brittle descriptive quality of his verse that is un-Canadian (with the exception of Quebec) and reminiscent of poets like Zbigniew Herbert and Miroslav Holub. The world he inhabits is one of dream and waking, just this side of nightmare – full of ordinary conversations about dinner or the cleaning lady and yet somehow torn out of life like collage pictures from a magazine.

The format of *The Happy Hungry Man* – interspersed as it is with photographs of Kent State troopers, Iris the scrotum-stroker, or a rampaging river – adds to this sense of disconnection. There is a narrative life to the poems in this collection, held together thinly by the marginal glosses on each poem, but one's sense of the poems overall is of disorder and disarray – a world where all coherence is long gone.

In many ways Jonas's world is like Auden's, but without the toughness of rhyme that gives to Auden's ballads their edge. Largely the connexion is a Horatian tone: the sense of the domestic as paradigmatic of a world gone ruinous. And added to it is the terror that lurks without, the more terrifying in its apparently motiveless malignity:

> For someone who has bravely tried
> To keep his head and distance
> And live as sharks or apples do
> Without mercy or assistance,
> It is astonishing to see
> That it is still not over
> And lately at night the stars
> Threaten to move closer.

Jonas's answer is to "have elected to live / In legal separation from the world," but this separation is never wholly satisfactory and his lovers return to haunt him – "your breasts' shape, the full length of your limbs" – as he searches the past for analogies of himself – "I am only trying to show / How fully we resembled you / As young men." In the end it is death, resolution, desire, old age that remain with him – "wondering how I'll feel / In 1985."

– D. D. C. Chambers

JONES, Brian. British. Born in 1938. Married; has two children. Recipient: Cholmondeley Award, 1967; Gregory Award, 1968.

PUBLICATIONS

Verse

Poems. London, Alan Ross, 1966.
A Family Album. London, Alan Ross, 1968.
Interior. London, Alan Ross, 1969.
The Mantis Hand and Other Poems. Gillingham, Kent, ARC Publications, 1970.
For Mad Mary. London, London Magazine Editions, 1974.

Play

Radio Play: *The Lady with a Little Dog*, 1962.

*   *   *

The poems in Brian Jones's books of verse cover a narrow area of subject-matter. Repeatedly he returns to the same material – family life, the married state, parents and children. When he strays outside this, as he sometimes does, he tends to write poems which, though extremely competent, read like the work of a score of other poets – the naturalistic norm of post-war poetry in Britain. The other poems, though they have the same kind of surface and use the same kind of diction, seem to me a different matter. *A Family Album,* which contains Jones's best work, is a series of monologues – each monologue a portrait of the person who speaks, and offering glimpses of those who surround him.

The idea of loss seems to dominate these monologues. The most forcefully created character is Aunt Emily – some of the poems concerning her are in fact transferred from an earlier collection, and it is clear that this deprived, eccentric spinster haunts Jones's imagination, and provides a kind of antonym for himself. Yet Emily's hovering shadow of madness is perhaps the poet's, too.

The verse itself, examined it detail, has many felicities, without ever being pioneering. The civilized ease of the writing comes out in a concluding stanza like the following:

> And when she came from hospital
> thin in the cold air, thin like a slip of a girl,
> with our boy like a doll bundled against
> her girl's breast, and from a taxi
> stepped into the neighbour's gaze,
> she and my child were the frail and total
> grounds for my praise.

– Edward Lucie-Smith

JONES, D(ouglas) G(ordon). Canadian. Born in Bancroft, Ontario, 1 January 1929. Educated at McGill University, Montreal, B.A.; Queen's University, Kingston, Ontario, M.A. Married; has four children. Currently, Professeur Titulaire, English Department, University of Sherbrooke, Quebec. Address: P.O. Box 356, North Hatley, Quebec, Canada.

PUBLICATIONS

Verse

Frost on the Sun. Toronto, Contact Press, 1957.
The Sun Is Axeman. Toronto, University of Toronto Press, 1961.
Phrases from Orpheus. Toronto, Oxford University Press, 1967.

Other

Butterfly on Rock: A Study of Themes and Images in Canadian Literature. Toronto, University of Toronto Press, 1970.

Critical Studies: "D. G. Jones: Etre chez soi dans le monde" by George Bowering, in Ellipse 13 (Sherbrooke, Quebec), 1973; "The Masks of D. G. Jones" by E. D. Blodgett, in Canadian Literature 60 (Vancouver), Spring 1974.

D. G. Jones comments:

A lyric poetry, relying heavily on a visual imagination ("rhyme of images") and on phrasing (or relationship in rhythm and sound of words to each other and to overall curve of statement) to create a line or sequence with a sense of inevitability or authority. Finally metaphysical (rather than descriptive, social, etc.) in intention. Attempts to digest for own use major influences of 20th century poetry (imagist – symbolist – metaphysical) and to connect with native Canadian tradition of two generations.

Aim: to create or recreate my life – to make sense of my life. Themes: sense, sustaining sense, of the infinite potentiality of life; poignance of supremely precious, supremely ephemeral character of each actual life; vast reservoirs of energy in nature; inability of contemporary society or culture to make that energy or vitality available in human affairs, in inner space, to make our life profound.

> It is the route out, where
> oil sludge mixes with the sea,
>
> A loneliness.

*   *   *

Verbal clarity, economy, precision, and a purity of imagery characterize the poetry of D. G. Jones. These aesthetic qualities are related to a philosophical state of mind and a quality of emotion which give the poetry an unusual consistency of tone and meaning. The relation between an ''emptiness'' or ''barrenness'' perceived in nature, on the philosophical plane (recurrent images in Jones), and an aesthetic of purity in poetry is familiar, especially in Mallarmé, and Jones can be usefully compared to the French master. Jones derives more directly from the Imagists, however, from H. D., and from Ezra Pound as critical mentor; later affinities are with Wallace Stevens and Marianne Moore. He is authentic in himself, also, and does not resemble so much as parallel these poets in general ways.

His first book, *Frost on the Sun*, already showed the taint of philosophic disenchantment and affected the shine of purity. His second, *The Sun Is Axeman*, revealed a marked advance in control and assurance and a full development of these features. Themes of silence, alienation, and emptiness recur – ''a string of notes / limned on the stillness of a void'' . . . ''skeletons of trees'' . . . ''And silence like a snow is everywhere.'' A number of poems, with their patina of perfection, dealing with lighter subject matter – ''Clotheslines,'' ''Schoolgirls'' – remind one of Gautier, the father of the aesthetes. A cosmic pessimism – ''the universe bleeds into darkness'' – underlies these poems.

The most recent book, *Phrases from Orpheus*, is marked by personal suffering not unlike that of W. D. Snodgrass in *Heart's Needle*, but there is no further resemblance. Jones is not confessional; his book gives expression to pain and passion through the indirections of poetry, through the myth of Orpheus, through images and the incantations of symbolism, and through irony. Here ''stars are not polite, and / even plants are / violent''; there is comfort in ''that relatively immortal blue gas / the sky. . . .'' The poetry transcends the personal, and at its best achieves a noble indifference or stoicism that touches on the heroic without rhetoric or mannerism.

Phrases from Orpheus is a deeply moving book and one of the most important to appear in Canada in recent years. It has, unfortunately, been neglected in the hubbub created by numerous young poets appearing on the scene and by the phenomenon of popularity affecting poetry; but the book will no doubt take its place as one of the finest to appear in the fifties and sixties.

– Louis Dudek

JONES, David (Michael). British. Born in Brockley, Kent, 1 November 1895. Educated at the Camberwell School of Art, London, 1910–14; Westminster School of Art, London, 1919–21. Served with the Royal Welsh Fusiliers, 1915–18. Worked with Eric Gill in Wales, 1924–27. Engraver, book illustrator, painter and water colourist: Exhibitions – National Gallery, 1940, 1941, 1942; Paris, 1945; Brooklyn, New York, 1952–53; One-Man Show in Edinburgh and the Tate Gallery, 1954–55; National Book League, London, 1972. Works acquired by Tate Gallery, Victoria and Albert Museum, National Museum of Wales, Sydney Art Gallery, Toronto Art Gallery, Arts Council of Great Britain, British Council. Recipient: Hawthornden Prize, 1938; Loines Award, 1954; Harriet Monroe Memorial Prize, 1956, and Levinson Prize, 1961 (*Poetry*, Chicago); Welsh Arts Council Award, 1960, 1969; Royal National Eisteddfod of Wales Gold Medal for Fine Arts, 1964; Corporation of London Midsummer Prize, 1968. D.Litt.: University of Wales, 1960. Honorary Member, Royal Society of Painters in Water Colours. Fellow, Royal Society of Literature. C.B.E. (Commander, Order of the British Empire), 1955. Companion of

Honour, 1974. Address: Monksdene, 2 Northwick Park Road, Harrow, Middlesex, England. *Died 28 October 1974.*

PUBLICATIONS

Verse

> *The Anathemata: Fragments of an Attempted Writing.* London, Faber, 1952; New York, Chilmark Press, 1963.
> *The Tribune's Visitation.* London, Fulcrum Press, 1969.
> *The Sleeping Lord and Other Fragments.* London, Faber, 1974.

> Recording: *David Jones Reads His Own Poems*, Argo, 1967.

Other

> *In Parenthesis: Seinnyessit e gledyf ym penn mameu.* London, Faber, 1937; New York, Viking Press, 1961.
> *David Jones* (paintings). London, Penguin, 1949.
> *Epoch and Artist: Selected Writings*, edited by Harman Grisewood. London, Faber, and New York, Chilmark Press, 1959.
> *An Introduction to "The Rime of the Ancient Mariner."* Cambridge, Rampant Lions Press, 1972.

Critical Study: "David Jones Issue" of *Agenda* (London), June 1967.

*   *   *

Perhaps one of the most important facts about David Jones is his mixed parentage, which combined the traditions of England and Wales. His father's family was Welsh-speaking on both sides. His mother was English, the daughter of a Thamesside mast-and-block maker. Through his father he derived an intense interest in Wales and its traditions; his father being a printer, D. J. acquired a heightened regard for the printed page. His mother was a competent artist, whose delicately and sensitively drawn pictures adorned the walls of his home as a boy. Early visits to Wales fed his imagination with concrete images which later would be linked with the ancient literary and historical traditions, which were to be woven into his writing.

His reputation as a writer rests on two works – *In Parenthesis* and *The Anathemata*. *In Parenthesis* is not a realistic war novel; it only "happens to be concerned with war"; it is, in the words of the author, a "shape in words." It is in fact a poem – an epic poem. Nowhere in modern literature can there be seen so clearly traced, in all its profound intricacy, the two strands of the tradition of this Island. We see the Welshman and the Englishman yoked to the machines of war, showing forth from the depths of their being the traditions that bind them into separate peoples. It was the experience of war which fired his imagination and made him conscious of the presence of these two traditions in his own person. Arthur and Alfred sit together on the throne of his heart.

The Anathemata is a meditation on the Christian sacrifice, its preparation in pre-history, its enacting in history and its continued re-enacting and re-calling, the *anamnesis*, in time, in the Christian Mass. The conditioning act in D. J.'s life came with his submission to the Roman Catholic Church. It is clear that this was not a purely spiritual experience, but the conversion of the whole man. There was a willing acceptance of the profound implications of the Incarnation. There is a glorious materialism in his work, a materialism which matches, or perhaps derives from, the materialism of the Incarnation. His work is sacramental. This may account for the slow recognition of his greatness. But the international awards won by his two works, and his subsequent poems, are an indication of his gradual acceptance, and his name is now being closely linked with those of Joyce, Pound, and Eliot.

– Aneirin Talfan Davies

JONES, Evan (Lloyd). Australian. Born in Melbourne, Victoria, 20 November 1931. Educated at Melbourne High School; University of Melbourne (Services' Canteen Fund Scholar, 1954–55), B.A. 1953, M.A. in history 1957; Stanford University (Writing Fellow, 1958–60), California, M.A. in English 1959. Married Judith Ann Jones in 1954; Margot Jones, 1966; has four children. Tutor, then Senior Tutor in History, University of Melbourne, 1955–58; Lecturer in English, Australian National University, Canberra, 1960–63. Lecturer, 1964, and since 1965, Senior Lecturer in English, University of Melbourne. Address: Department of English, University of Melbourne, Parkville, Victoria 3052, Australia.

PUBLICATIONS

Verse

   Inside the Whale: Poems. Melbourne, Cheshire, 1960.
   Understandings: Poems. Melbourne, Melbourne University Press, 1967.

Other

   Kenneth Mackenzie. Melbourne, Oxford University Press, 1969.

   Editor, "Australian Poetry since 1920," in *The Literature of Australia*, edited by
      Geoffrey Dutton. London, Penguin, 1964.
   Editor, with Geoffrey Little, *The Poems of Kenneth Mackenzie.* Sydney, Angus
      and Robertson, 1972.

Evan Jones comments:

   My poetry is characteristically highly formal in structure, diverse in diction. Forms range from the sestina to unrhymed trimeter. Early influences were a multitude of English, American and Australian poets, but especially W. H. Auden. Most poems are concerned in one way or another with the problem of maintaining or achieving coherence and equanimity in the face (as the anonymous blurb of my second book put it, rather heavy-handedly) of loneliness, separation and death: in the face of being a thinking and sentient being here and now.

*   *   *

Although Evan Jones has, to date, published only two collections of verse, he must be considered one of the influential poets of his period and place: Melbourne in the late 1950's and early 1960's. The first book, *Inside the Whale*, is full of student work in the once fashionable vein of what A. D. Hope calls "the discursive mode." At times, in this volume, Evan Jones almost appears to be self-parodying, as he practices older English stanzaic forms and apostrophizes the Melbourne University. Other poems, however, such as the much anthologised "Noah's Song," became key demonstrations of "the habit of irony" that pervaded University literary circles in the 1950's.

The second collection abandons this youthful donnish guise and concerns itself with a closer approach to the characteristic early adult experiences: love, marriage, estrangement. In these later poems, Evan Jones, though no longer a determinedly donnish poet, demonstrates a considerable erudition and an even more considerable command of language and cadence in a way that is always unspectacular, but often brilliantly sharp and precise. Although he has published in various journals in recent years, Evan Jones has not yet released a further collection. On the basis of a sampling of fugitive publications, he seems to have settled into a line of quiet, reflective verse. He is, however, the sort of poet one would not be surprised to find emerge suddenly with some long and large-ranging epic after a gestation period of several years. Should he produce nothing more, Jones is assured of a place in the re-animation and re-direction of Australian poetry that occurred, in Melbourne, at the end of the 1950's.

– Thomas W. Shapcott

JONES, Glyn. Welsh. Born in Merthyr Tydfil, 28 February 1905. Educated at Castle Grammar School, Merthyr Tydfil; St. Paul's College, Cheltenham. Married Phyllis Doreen Jones in 1935. Formerly a schoolmaster in Glamorgan; now retired. Chairman, Yr Academi Gymreig (English Section). Recipient: Welsh Arts Council Prize, for non-fiction, 1969; Christian Gauss Award, 1973. D.Litt.: University of Wales, 1974. Address: 158 Manor Way, Whitchurch, Cardiff, Wales.

PUBLICATIONS

Verse

Poems. London, Fortune Press, 1939.
The Dream of Jake Hopkins. London, Fortune Press, 1954.

Play

> *The Beach of Falesa*, music by Alun Hoddinott (produced Cardiff, 1974). London, Oxford University Press, 1973.

Novels

> *The Valley, The City, The Village.* London, Dent, 1956.
> *The Learning Lark.* London, Dent, 1960.
> *The Island of Apples.* London, Dent, and New York, Day, 1965.

Short Stories

> *The Blue Bed.* London, Cape, and New York, Dutton, 1937.
> *The Water Music.* London, Routledge, 1944.
> *Selected Short Stories.* London, Dent, 1971.

Other

> *The Dragon Has Two Tongues* (essays on Anglo-Welsh writers). London, Dent, 1968.

> Translator, with T. J. Morgan, *The Saga of Llywarch the Old.* London, Golden Cockerel Press, 1955.

Manuscript Collection: National Library of Wales, Aberystwyth.

Critical Study: *Glyn Jones* by Leslie Norris, Cardiff, University of Wales Press, 1973.

Glyn Jones comments:

I began my literary career as a poet and I hope to end it in the same way.

I believe I am usually thought of as belonging to the Anglo-Welsh group of poets (Dylan Thomas, Vernon Watkins, R. S. Thomas, David Jones, etc.), poets who are Welsh but who write in English.

The poets who have meant most to me are G. M. Hopkins, D. H. Lawrence, Walt Whitman, Dylan Thomas, plus some of the poets of my own country – I mean writers of poems in the Welsh language. I admire poets who are word- and language-conscious; but that does not mean I am indifferent to what the poet says. Hopkins appeals to me so much because I am in sympathy with his agonising over language, and I also find acceptable his subject matter and what he has to say about it.

*   *   *

Better known as a short story writer and novelist, Glyn Jones began as a poet, his first poems appearing in *The Dublin Magazine* in 1931. His recent critical work,

The Dragon Has Two Tongues, reveals that not till later did he become well acquainted with the intricate rhyme-schemes and density of texture of much of the poetry in the Welsh language: the concern for *words* rather than ideas which he showed from the beginning was therefore a Welsh instinct, a natural eloquence which decorated and "blew up" the narrative line, sounding off a country of echoes on either side. Admiration for the rich and sensuous imagery of D. H. Lawrence is reflected in his earliest poems, but, this impetus exhausted, he turned to a kind of proletarian poetry, inspired by the *hen benillion* of the peasant past. Although far from the "public school communism" of the contemporary English mode, the effect of this was not very different on occasion from the neo-romanticisms of Auden. Out of this windy alley grew other poems, realist rather than proletarian, "poems built up solid out of concrete nouns," strongly consonantal (a painter's poems, perhaps, for Glyn applied sounds to his poem much as he would apply blocks of colour to his canvas):

> The sky tilts suddenly, its sleety herringbone
> Of pouring rain spills thick across the dock,
> Shags up the furry liner's side, its blurred
> Black iron cliff immense above the dock-wall,
> Pelts the sheety concrete, sprawls its gusty growth
> Its hiss of cold grey grass across the tingling streets.
> – "Dock"

His reading of G. M. Hopkins reinforced this development, and meetings with Dylan Thomas from 1934 onwards strengthened his view that the craft was more important than the audience, that social implications were secondary. At its least successful, his new mode of writing had a glutinous quality that could slough the reader; at its best, a distinctive glory of words and images that illuminated the greys of the natural scene:

> Blush-feathered, frocked, above the grey-bled sea
> He bears my beating heart with rosy webs,
> The fire-bird, the flame-silked through the grieving sea-rain, swift
> On hot flushed petal-flesh his flashing wings.
> – "Gull"

After 1940 he wrote much less poetry, through his smaller output included the radio ode, "The Dream of Jake Hopkins" and the well-known "Merthyr," both of which made use of a humour and irony which had so far appeared only in his short stories. Novels and translations from the Welsh absorbed him, and it was 1967 before he broke poetic silence again with "Images of Light and Darkness." Unmoved by fashion, he was writing still out of that *cwm-taf* of images, that echo-making mountain of words before which his house had long stood, and the lyrical impulse was now uppermost. In "Profile of Rose" with which he opened 1969, despite its narrative line and tragic symbolism, the lyrical note is still strong:

> Hair-bowed Rose, deep in lush grass of the river
> Bank, watched through the crystal unflawed block of
> Afternoon, broad waters of her tenth birthday
> Under sunglare, bottomless ebony
> Sheeted with green and shine, and elms black
> Along the far brink, and the gold field
> Beyond, a shallow dishful of buttercup
> Liquor.

There are many who look at this "shallow dishful" wistfully and ask only that Glyn Jones shall honour his declared intention to end, as he began, by writing poetry.

– Roland Mathias

JONES, (Everett) LeRoi. Pseudonym: **Imamu Amiri Baraka.** American. Born in Newark, New Jersey, 7 October 1934. Educated at Central Avenue School and Barringer High School, Newark; Rutgers University, Newark; Howard University, Washington, D.C., B.A. 1954; New School for Social Research, New York; Columbia University, New York. Served in the United States Air Force, 1954–56. Married Hettie Cohen in 1958 (divorced, 1965); Sylvia Robinson (Bibi Amina Baraka), 1966; has five children. Taught at the New School for Social Research, 1961–64; State University of New York, Buffalo, Summer 1964; Columbia University, 1964, 1966–67; Visiting Professor, San Francisco State College. Founder, *Yugen* magazine and Totem Press, New York, 1958; Co-Editor, with Diane DiPrima, *Floating Bear* magazine, New York, 1961–63. Founding Director, Black Arts Repertory Theatre, Harlem, New York, 1964–66. Since 1966, Founding Director, Spirit House, Newark. Involved in Newark politics: Member of the United Brothers, 1967; Committee for Unified Newark, 1968. Member of the International Coordinating Committee, Congress of African Peoples; Chairman, Congress of Afrikan People; Secretary-General, National Black Political Assembly. Recipient: Whitney Fellowship, 1961; Obie Award, for drama, 1964; Guggenheim Fellowship, 1965; Dakar Festival Prize, 1966; National Endowment for the Arts grant, 1966. Address: C.A.P., 502 High Street, Newark, New Jersey 07102, U.S.A.

PUBLICATIONS

Verse

Preface to a Twenty Volume Suicide Note. New York, Totem Press, 1961.
The Dead Lecturer. New York, Grove Press, 1964.
Black Art. Newark, Jihad Publications, 1966.
A Poem for Black Hearts. Detroit, Broadside Press, 1967.
Black Magic: Poetry 1961–1967. Indianapolis, Bobbs Merrill, and London, MacGibbon and Kee, 1969.
It's Nation Time. Chicago, Third World Press, 1970.
Spirit Reach. Newark, Jihad Publications, 1972.

Plays

A Good Girl Is Hard to Find (produced Montclair, New Jersey, 1958).
Dante (produced New York, 1961; as *The 8th Ditch*, produced New York, 1964). Included in *The System of Dante's Hell*, 1965.
Dutchman (produced New York, 1964; London, 1967). Included in *Dutchman and The Slave*, 1964.

The Slave (produced New York, 1964; London, 1972). Included in *Dutchman and The Slave*, 1964.

Dutchman and The Slave. New York, Morrow, 1964; London, Faber, 1965.

The Baptism (produced New York, 1964; London, 1971). Included in *The Baptism and The Toilet*, 1967.

The Toilet (produced New York, 1964). Included in *The Baptism and The Toilet*, 1967.

Jello (produced New York, 1965). Chicago, Third World Press, 1970.

Experimental Death Unit #1 (produced New York, 1965). Included in *Four Black Revolutionary Plays*, 1969.

A Black Mass (produced Newark, 1966). Included in *Four Black Revolutionary Plays*, 1969.

The Baptism and The Toilet. New York, Grove Press, 1967.

Arm Yrself and Harm Yrself (produced Newark, 1967). Newark, Jihad Publications, 1967.

Slave Ship: A Historical Pageant (produced Newark, 1967; New York, 1969). Newark, Jihad Publications, 1969.

Madheart (produced San Francisco, 1967). Included in *Four Black Revolutionary Plays*, 1969.

Home on the Range (produced Newark and New York, 1968). Published in *Drama Review* (New York), Summer 1968.

Police, in *Drama Review* (New York), Summer 1968.

The Death of Malcolm X, in *New Plays from the Black Theatre*, edited by Ed Bullins. New York, Bantam, 1969.

Great Goodness of Life (A Coon Show) (produced New York, 1969). Included in *Four Black Revolutionary Plays*, 1969.

Four Black Revolutionary Plays (includes *Experimental Death Unit #1, A Black Mass, Great Goodness of Life (A Coon Show), Madheart*). Indianapolis, Bobbs Merrill, 1969; London, Calder and Boyars, 1971.

Junkies Are Full of (SHHH . . .), and Bloodrites (produced Newark, 1970). Published in *Black Drama Anthology*, edited by Woodie King and Ron Milner, New York, New American Library, 1971.

BA-RA-KA, in *Spontaneous Combustion: Eight New American Plays*, edited by Rochelle Owens. New York, Winter House, 1972.

Screenplays: *Dutchman*, 1967; *A Fable*, 1971.

Novel

The System of Dante's Hell. New York, Grove Press, 1965; London, MacGibbon and Kee, 1966.

Short Stories

Tales. New York, Grove Press, 1967; London, MacGibbon and Kee, 1969.

Other

Blues People: Negro Music in White America. New York, Morrow, 1963; London, MacGibbon and Kee, 1965.

Home: Social Essays. New York, Morrow, 1966; London, MacGibbon and Kee, 1968.

Cuba Libre. New York, Fair Play for Cuba Committee, 1966.
Black Music. New York, Morrow, 1967.
In Our Terribleness: Some Elements and Meaning in Black Style, with Fundi (Billy Abernathy). Indianapolis, Bobbs Merrill, 1970.
A Black Value System. Newark, Jihad Publications, 1970.
Raise Race Rays Raze: Essays since 1965 (as Imamu Amiri Baraka). New York, Random House, 1971.
The Creation of the New Ark. Washington, D.C., Howard University Press, 1974.

Editor, *Four Young Lady Poets.* New York, Corinth Books, 1962.
Editor, *The Moderns: New Fiction in America.* New York, Corinth Books, 1964; London, MacGibbon and Kee, 1965.
Editor, with Larry Neal, *Black Fire: An Anthology of Afro-American Writing.* New York, Morrow, 1968.
Editor, *African Congress: A Documentary of the First Modern Pan-African Congress.* New York, Morrow, 1972.
Editor, with Diane DiPrima, *The Floating Bear: A Newsletter, Numbers 1–37.* La Jolla, California, Laurence McGilvery, 1974.

Bibliography: "LeRoi Jones: A Checklist to Primary and Secondary Sources" by Stanley Schatt, in *Bulletin of Bibliography* (Westwood, Massachusetts), April–June 1971.

LeRoi Jones comments:

(1970) I identify with the "Black" school.
My major theme? The evolution of man.
(1974) The first step is Socialist Revolution.

* * *

LeRoi Jones, a black, man, writer of stories, poems, plays, jazz books, a cut-open type who is not noticeable on a bus, mid-thirties, medium height, handsome, wiry body in motion & at ease, can move anywhere and moves anyone who reads him, comes to where he is or where his work has appeared. Eyes open to the world straight on and busy with it. Who used to play softball with other poets, black & white, mix it up to relax, began to raise two half-white daughters with his first wife, moved with ease then, found he had to lose the ease and jump into conscience with acts and words. . . . Arrested in Newark, his own city, "for possession of firearms" (and the words like guns) and jailed, for his part in the black ghetto uprising: a leader. Winding up on the committee to re-structure: a builder, not a destroyer. . . . Memories of Newark; all the deaths . . .

There are the easy-way folks who play safe, and men like Che, or Roi, or Lumumba. In the work, Roi mocks those whose roads even *look* easier. A man who can be wrong, but before you take it in, he has done something else terribly right, some dynamic to set the world's eyes into a new stance. Roi, divided into three parts: memories, nostalgia of when we were young; the present, with the skill taut and extended like maleness, writing or speaking truth as if it were the sex act; and the next cycle of time, toward which he is reaching, leaping. An impatient man, of course. A gentle man. Voice breaking onstage as he reads about the death of the lovely black girl he loved: a slim man weeping for all deaths.

All his work is drawn, and quartered, from life. I refer to no bibliographies; Roi, too, can and doesn't. His work: the stories talk about the smell of terror, the man as a black with an army or a whore, the kid growing up kicked in a ghetto, playing hard and tough in nightspots, screwing, running, a thickness & pungency of kinds of pursuit. Or what moves a man, to the sort of rage that is "The Toilet" or the scathing, scathed torture of "Dutchman"? In our history, has there been anyone unmoved by those tragedies he assaults? He loves some people. And he hates vividly and aloud: the fake & phony, halfwit barbaric rituals sold as a civilized life in middleclass America, the garb & trappings of people who buy retirement as a goal and die without having lived. He is *concerned*, a serious man with a dry sense of humor, an intellectual man, literate as you please, who has influenced many of the writers near him: and does not choose to use this obviously, does not need to point to the computer mythology back of the fine writing. It works. Like Cleaver's, like Lenny Bruce's. Years ago his plays produced shockwaves, the establishment giving an angry groan when confronted with his mirrors, all the assumed bases for sanity threatened or criticized. Supermarkets and stockmarkets okay, and white Sun Cities, but to hell with a good look at a faggotty bishop, for instance, or the army, or the voices of the body and other honest juices . . . a man whose eyes turned on before that became a slogan for magazine ads.

He will change us, and he will use force as necessary. With all his language stern and odd enough to crisp through the smug intentions of the oversecure. The density of his language is twice that of most prose men, excepting perhaps Burroughs'. He has to speak for a million men and reach a million others who are too different. The writing is not separable from the life; the forces forged from the same matter & with the same intent. The life-figures in his works are grotesques, large enough to be archetypes, but none is larger than the trait represented. No one is comfortable in Roi's writings, *because* no one is comfortable. He can isolate and then illustrate. Roi is related by blood to The Living Theatre, to Rochelle Owens, Ed Sanders, Jacov Lind . . . he is American, and from the same country as Jose Cuevas, Heinrich Kley, Gerald Scarfe. He makes a stark line move out hard enough to break the sound barrier. With the entire body raw to the world, to receive and to transmute and give it all back to us in essence.

– Carol Bergé

JONG, Erica. American. Born in New York City, 26 March 1942. Educated at Barnard College, New York (George Weldwood Murray Fellow, 1963), 1959–63, B.A. 1963 (Phi Beta Kappa); Columbia University, New York (Woodrow Wilson Fellow, 1964), M.A. 1965; Columbia School of Fine Arts, 1969–70. Married Allan Jong in 1966. Lecturer in English, City College of New York, 1964–66, and University of Maryland European Division, Heidelberg, Germany, 1967–68; Instructor in English, Manhattan Community College, New York, 1969–70. Since 1971, Instructor in Poetry, YM–YWHA Poetry Center, New York. Recipient: Bess Hokin Prize (*Poetry*, Chicago), 1971; New York State Council on the Arts grant, 1971; Madeline Sadin Award (*New York Quarterly*), 1972; Alice Fay di Castagnola Award, 1972; National Endowment for the Arts grant, 1973. Agents: Deborah Rogers Ltd., 29 Goodge Street, London W.1, England; Betty Anne Clark, International Famous Agency, 1301 Avenue of the Americas, New York, New York 10019. Address: 20 West 77th Street, New York, New York 10024, U.S.A.

PUBLICATIONS

Verse

> *Fruits and Vegetables.* New York, Holt Rinehart, 1971; London, Secker and
> Warburg, 1973.
> *Half-Lives.* New York, Holt Rinehart, 1973; London, Secker and Warburg,
> 1974.

Novel

> *Fear of Flying.* New York, Holt Rinehart, 1973; London, Secker and War-
> burg, 1974.

Critical Studies: in *St. Louis Post-Dispatch*, 16 May 1971; "The Comestible Muse,"
in *The Nation* (New York), 28 June 1971; "Eat, Darling, Eat!," in *Village Voice*
(New York), 2 September 1971; *Saturday Review* (New York), 18 December 1971;
Library Journal (New York) 15 April 1973; *Publishers Weekly* (New York), 7 May
1973; *Hartford Courant* (Connecticut), 1 July 1973; Grace Shulman, in *Ms.* (New
York), August 1973.

Erica Jong comments:

Though I have been writing since childhood, my first formal training in poetry
came at Barnard College, where I studied from 1959–63. At that time I loved the
poetry of Auden, Yeats, Keats, Byron and Alexander Pope, cultivated the command of formal verse, and developed an abiding interest in satire. My early
university poems were mostly expert, satirical and somewhat academic. I went on
to do a thesis on Alexander Pope in Columbia's graduate English department. In
my early and mid-twenties, however, I became much more interested in French
surrealist poetry and its South American derivatives. I came to love the poetry of
Neruda and Alberti, and I learned the value of poetry which delved deep into the
unconscious and relied on the association of images. It seems to me that these two
influences – crisp satire and an abiding belief in the importance of unconscious
material – have shaped my voice as a poet. I believe that poetry can be serious and
comic at the same time, formal yet free. I think I was also liberated to write out of
a frankly female persona by reading the work of such poets as Anne Sexton, Sylvia
Plath, Muriel Rukeyser, Carolyn Kizer, Adrienne Rich. It has been very important
to me – both in poetry and fiction – to write freely about women and women's
sexuality. Throughout much of history, women writers have capitulated to male
standards, and have paid too much heed to what Virginia Woolf calls "the angel in
the house." She is that little ghost who sits on one's shoulder while one writes and
whispers, "Be nice, don't say anything that will embarrass the family, don't say
anything your man would disapprove of. . . ." The "angel in the house" castrates
one's creativity because it deprives one of essential honesty, and many women
writers have yet to win the freedom to be honest with themselves. But once the
right to honesty has been established, we can go on to write about anything that
interests us. We need not *only* write about childbirth, menstruation and other
supposedly feminist topics. I resist the subject matter fallacy in any of its forms.
Writing should not be judged on the basis of its subject, but on the artistry with

which that subject is treated. It seems to me that all three of my published books (*Fruits and Vegetables*, *Half-Lives* and *Fear of Flying*) have certain themes in common: the search for honesty within oneself, the difficulty of resolving the conflicting needs for security and adventure, the necessity of seeing the world both sensuously and intelligently at the same time. Having said all that, I should add that my views about my writing will probably be entirely different by the time this is printed.

*   *   *

Erica Jong is one of a new generation of American women poets, marked by a frank acceptance of the fact of femaleness, but also by a kind of anguish at being able to be so candid. Sylvia Plath is the patron saint of this generation of poets, yet one senses in them a toughness, an earthiness, a rejection of the impulse towards self-destruction. Mrs. Jong, in particular, has also been influenced by the cheerful, rather ribald surrealism which invaded the work of New York School poets through the example of Frank O'Hara. Her work is highly pictorial – one is constantly reminded that New York is an art city even more than it is a literary city.

This kind of poetry demands, and usually gets, a personal reaction. Either one reels back in shock from the candour, the gaudiness and the energy; or one begins to relish the swagger with which it is done. The passive male muse, so graphically described in a poem called "Arse Poetica," seems a better joke than many a male poet has managed to produce recently.

But Mrs. Jong's work is not all joking:

> The corruption begins with the mouth,
> the tongue, the wanting.
> The first poem in the world
> is *I want to eat.*

Impossible not to respect the direct candour about mortal appetites which informs the best of her work.

– Edward Lucie-Smith

JOSEPH, M(ichael) K(ennedy). New Zealander. Born in Chingford, Essex, England, 9 July 1914. Educated at Auckland University College, B.A. 1933, M.A. 1934; Merton College, Oxford, B.A. 1938, B.Litt. 1939, M.A. 1945. Served in the British Army in the Royal Artillery, 1940–46. Married Mary Julia Antonovich in 1947; has five children. Lecturer in English, 1945–49, and Senior Lecturer, 1950–59, Auckland University College. Associate Professor of English, 1960–69, and since 1970, Professor of English, University of Auckland. Recipient: Hubert Church Prose Award, 1958; Jessie Mackay Poetry Award, 1959. Address: Department of English, University of Auckland, Private Bag, Auckland, New Zealand.

Publications

Verse

Imaginary Islands. Auckland, privately printed, 1950.
The Living Countries. Auckland, Paul's Book Arcade, 1959.
Inscription on a Paper Dart. Auckland, Auckland University Press–Oxford University Press, 1974.

Novels

I'll Soldier No More. Auckland, Paul's Book Arcade, and London, Gollancz, 1958.
A Pound of Saffron. Auckland, Paul's Book Arcade, and London, Gollancz, 1962.
The Hole in the Zero. Auckland, Paul's Book Arcade, and London, Gollancz, 1967; New York, Dutton, 1968.

Other

Byron the Poet. London, Gollancz, 1964.

Editor, *Frankenstein*, by Mary Shelley. London, Oxford University Press, 1969.

M. K. Joseph comments:

From about 1944–54, I was writing poetry; now novels and research. I admire the poets I teach – especially Pope, Byron, Yeats, Auden.

When I was writing verse, I was trying for something with a definite, fairly traditional shape, and a comprehensible meaning, not esoteric, not personal. I suppose I am interested in consciousness and self-consciousness, expressed in poems about New Zealand, about religion and about literature. These interests probably come out now in my novels.

*   *   *

In a note written at the request of an anthologist, M. K. Joseph said, "If poetry as dialogue seems in danger of extinction, we should take all the more seriously the idea of poetry as making. The poem is an object which we make and set down, like an antique torso in an abandoned city, good, self-sufficient, durable, waiting for the people to come back." In many ways, this could be a description of his own verse, which, even in its lighter form, is always well made, with firm artistry. Yet the sense of dialogue is there as well, for Professor Joseph's poems are also always about something.

He brings to poetry a mind nourished on classical and modern literatures, a quirky imagination, compassion and a concern with religion, art and history. Although he writes of the great truths, of time, love, dissolution, the arrogance of intellect, the guises of sophistry, and what is and what could be, a spirit of luminous joy keeps him from solemnity. This is the case, for instance, in "Mercury Bay Eclogue" in which he moves from a response to a New Zealand landscape through a meditation on New Zealand and European history and on the truth of poetry to an epiphanic enfolding of them all in the transcendence of peace and love.

Some of his poems recall war experiences, others define the New Zealand thing in places and history, others take their point of departure from concepts of modern science or medieval philosophy. All are sustained by a sympathetic awareness of Western culture, including Catholic tradition, which gives his poetry an amplitude rare in New Zealand writing. More than once, as in his satirical "Secular Litany," he contrasts the variety and richness of Mediterranean culture with the plodding materialism of New Zealanders. His other witty parodies and satires proceed from a positive and balanced Christian humanism.

It may sometimes be thought that the virtues of his poetry lie in its intellectual resourcefulness and its richness of allusion, and that it is emotionally rather reticent or low-powered. Some of his poetry supports such a view. The bulk of it does not. Even in such a sequence as "The Lovers and the City," based upon the characters of *Romeo and Juliet*, there is a sensitivity to broad human needs and a compassion that give the poems a glow of benignity which subsumes a recognition of the agonies of physical and spiritual love. His poetry is, in its way, academic poetry, scholarly poetry, urbane, gracious, allusive, and strengthened by a closer understanding of and affinity to the great Western traditions that most of his contemporaries possess. Yet it has tenderness and pity which its formal grace accentuates rather than muffles. And an eye for the freakish, the grotesque and the marvellous enables him to illuminate the ordinary with a sudden radiant perception of the inexhaustible wonders of man and the universe.

– J. C. Reid

JUSTICE, Donald (Rodney). American. Born in Miami, Florida, 12 August 1925. Educated at the University of Miami, B.A. 1945; University of North Carolina, Chapel Hill, M.A. 1947; Stanford University, California, 1947–48; University of Iowa, Iowa City (Rockefeller grant, 1954), Ph.D. 1954. Married Jean Ross in 1947; has one son, Nathaniel. Visiting Assistant Professor, University of Iowa, Columbia, 1955–56; Assistant Professor, Hamline University, St. Paul, Minnesota, 1956–57; Lecturer, 1957–59, Assistant Professor, 1959–63, and Associate Professor, 1963–66, University of Iowa; Associate Professor, State University of New York, Syracuse, 1966–70; Visiting Professor, University of California, Irvine, 1970–71. Since 1971, Professor of English, University of Iowa. Poet-in-Residence, Reed College, Portland, Oregon, 1962. Recipient: Lamont Poetry Selection Award, 1959; Inez Boulton Prize, 1960, and Harriet Monroe Memorial Prize, 1965 (*Poetry*, Chicago); Ford Fellowship, in theatre, 1964; National Endowment for the Arts grant, 1967; National Institute of Arts and Letters award, 1974. Address: Department of English, University of Iowa, Iowa City, Iowa 52240, U.S.A.

Publications

Verse

> *The Summer Anniversaries.* Middletown, Connecticut, Wesleyan University
> Press, 1960.
> *A Local Storm.* Iowa City, Stone Wall Press, 1963.
> *Night Light.* Middletown, Connecticut, Wesleyan University Press, 1967.
> *Four Poets,* with others. Pella, Iowa, C.U.I. Press, 1967.
> *Sixteen Poems.* Iowa City, Stone Wall Press, 1970.
> *From a Notebook.* Iowa City, Seamark Press, 1972.
> *Departures.* New York, Atheneum, 1974.

Other

> Editor, *The Collected Poems of Weldon Kees.* Iowa City, Stone Wall Press,
> 1960.
> Editor, with Paul Engle and Henri Coulette, *Midland.* New York, Randon
> House, 1961.
> Editor, with Alexander Aspel, *Contemporary French Poetry.* Ann Arbor,
> University of Michigan Press, 1965.
> Editor, *Syracuse Poems 1968.* Syracuse, New York, Syracuse University
> Department of English, 1968.

Critical Study: *Alone with America* by Richard Howard, New York, Athenuem,
1969.

Donald Justice comments:

Major themes: none. Characteristic subjects: childhood, death, madness, love.
Usual verse forms: I began with standard meters, including some accentuals, and
the usual forms associated with these, moved on toward syllabics and a general
relaxation of meters and "forms," and now write mostly free, or relatively free.
Sources and influences: memory and language itself chief sources; influences
many, both in English and other languages. Stylistic devices: none I know of. I
cannot make a personal statement about my poetry, other than this.

*   *   *

The idea of loss is a continuous one in Donald Justice's first book, *The Summer
Anniversaries,* and one that deepens and becomes more complex as his career
advances. In his second full-length book, *Night Light,* the idea is extended to
include the loss of love, the decline of self and, ultimately, the loss of self. Just as
the past exercises its peculiar strength by having become past, so the self can be
more compelling, paradoxically present when lost:

He has come to report himself
A missing person

The authorities
Hand him the forms . . .

They reassure him
That he can be nowhere

But wherever he finds himself
From moment to moment,

Which, for the moment, is here.
And he might like to believe them.

But in the mirror
He sees what is missing.

It is himself. . . .

In another poem Justice is speaking as much about the body of his work as he is the formal embodiment of his vision:

I indulge myself
In rich refusals.
Nothing suffices.

I hone myself to
This edge. Asleep, I
Am a horizon.
                              – "The Thin Man"

From the very beginning Justice has fashioned his poems, honed them down, freed them of rhetorical excess and the weight, however gracefully sustained, of an elaborate diction. His self-indulgence, then, has been with the possibilities of plain statement. His refusal to adopt any other mode but that which his subject demands – minimal, narcissist, negating – has nourished him.

Often the subjects in Justice's poems remind one of the paintings of Edward Hopper. Attention is paid to the passing and ephemeral conditions of the present. There is a painful sense that life as it is lived escapes us even in its most ordinary aspects and most durable guises. It is that need in Justice's poems to recover banal views and average moments, to rescue what otherwise would be lost forever, which gives them their sadness, and their success.

If absence and loss are inescapable conditions of life, the poem for Justice is an act of recovery. It synthesizes, for all its meagreness, what is with what is no longer; it conjures up a life that persists by denial, gathering strength from its own hopelessness, and exists, finally and positively, as an emblem of survival.

– Mark Strand

KALLMAN, Chester (Simon). American. Born in Brooklyn, New York, 7 January 1921. Educated at Brooklyn College, B.A.; University of Michigan, Ann Arbor. Lived for long periods in Italy, Greece, and Austria. Recipient: National Institute of Arts and Letters grant, 1955; Ingram Merrill Foundation grant, 1964; Morton Dauwen Zabel Prize (*Poetry*, Chicago), 1970. Address: Democharous 23, Marasleiou, Athens 601, Greece. *Died 17 January 1975.*

PUBLICATIONS

Verse

> *Storm at Castelfranco.* New York, Grove Press, 1956.
> *Absent and Present.* Middletown, Connecticut, Wesleyan University Press, 1963.
> *The Sense of Occasion.* New York, Braziller, 1971.

Plays

> *The Rake's Progress*, with W. H. Auden, music by Igor Stravinsky (produced Venice, 1951; New York, 1953; London, 1962). London, and New York, Boosey and Hawkes, 1951.
> *Bluebeard's Castle*, adaptation of the libretto by Bela Balazs, music by Bartok. London and New York, Boosey and Hawkes, 1952.
> *Delia; or, A Masque of Night*, with W. H. Auden, in *Botteghe Oscure 12* (Rome), 1953.
> *Falstaff*, adaptation of the libretto by Arrigo Boito, music by Boito. New York, G. Ricordi, 1954.
> *The Magic Flute*, with W. H. Auden, adaptation of the libretto by Schikaneder and Giesecke, music by Mozart. New York, Random House, 1956; London, Faber, 1957.
> *The Abduction from the Seraglio*, adaptation of the libretto by C. F. Bretzner, music by Mozart (produced Stratford, Connecticut, 1956).
> *Panfilo and Loretta*, music by Cesar Chavez (produced New York, 1957).
> *Anne Boleyn*, adaptation of the libretto by Felice Romani, music by Donizetti. New York, G. Ricordi, 1959.
> *Elegy for Young Lovers*, with W. H. Auden, music by Hans Werner Henze (produced Glyndebourne, Sussex, 1961). Mainz, B. Schotts Söhne, 1961.
> *The Seven Deadly Sins of the Lower Middle Class*, with W. H. Auden, adaptation of the work by Brecht, music by Kurt Weill (produced Edinburgh and London, 1961). Published in *Tulane Drama Review* (New Orleans), September 1961.
> *Don Giovanni*, with W. H. Auden, adaptation of the libretto by Lorenzo da Ponte, music by Mozart. New York and London, G. Schirmer, 1961.
> *Die Bassariden (The Bassarids)*, with W. H. Auden, music by Hans Werner Henze (produced Salzburg, 1966; London, 1974). Mainz, B. Schotts Söhne, 1966.
> *The Entertainment of the Senses*, with W. H. Auden, music by John Gardner (produced London, 1974). Published in *Thank You Fog*, by Auden, London, Faber, and New York, Random House, 1974.

Chester Kallman comments:

[On schools of poetry] I know I am not "Beat." I like to think I am neither "academic" nor "Confessional." If there is a "school" that believes in the integrity of the verse line, I hope I may qualify to join it.

*   *   *

Chester Kallman's poetry is the outgrowth of an urbane, witty sensibility; "civilized" is a description that immediately comes to mind no matter where one opens his collection *Absent and Present.* The book opens with a dedication to Kallman's collaborator on Stravinsky's opera, *The Rake's Progress,* the late W. H. Auden, certainly the great modern celebrant, in poetry, of the civilized virtues. Sometimes the poems (particularly in the section titled "City and Country Beasts") read somewhat like modern fables out of Aesop or La Fontaine as in "Patronage":

> The grasshopper approached the ant
> To ask for a Creative Grant:
>
> "My singing made your labors light."
> The puzzled ant refused outright:
>
> "Was *that* noise you? I never know
> What's on my pocket radio."

As this poem suggests (and the other work generally bears this out), Kallman's poems reflect a classical bent not unlike Auden's; these poem are frequently in rhyme and deal with the age-old topics: country and city life, social life and gossip, the artist's lot, love and loss. The poems' angle of attack varies considerably: there are poems that verge on epigram or aphorism ("Notes for an Ars Poetica" is a good example of the latter, or a series of the latter), others, as mentioned earlier, are fables, and there is an impressive, and moving, longer poem, a dramatic poem interweaving his mother's remarks and his reflections on her, entitled "*The Only Child:* Theme and Variations" and there is even a shaped poem (not too successful), "Persistence." Occasionally the cleverness wears thin, or the aphorisms ring a bit wooden, but none-the-less, Kallman has assembled a collection that displays versatility and reminds us that work still remains to be done within traditional forms.

– Duane Ackerson

KANDEL, Lenore. American. Born in New York City. Recipient: Borestone Poetry Award, 1962. Address: 925 Sanchez Street, San Francisco, California 94114, U.S.A.

PUBLICATIONS

Verse

A Passing Dragon.   Studio City, California, Three Penny Press, 1959.
A Passing Dragon Seen Again.   Studio City, California, Three Penny Press,
    1959.
The Exquisite Navel.   Studio City, California, Three Penny Press, 1959.
The Love Book.   San Francisco, Stolen Paper Review Editions, 1966.
Word Alchemy.   New York, Grove Press, 1967.

Lenore Kandel comments:

Major theme – awareness of it all. Awareness of same as characteristic subjects
– the creature and the planet, the angel and the star. Forms – as the subject
demands. Sources – as above. Influences – as above. Devices – clarity that flies.

*   *   *

Lenore Kandel is an amazing lady who seems to have vanished from the public
world of literature at the height of her success. Her most noted work is *The Love
Book* – a passionate and explicit work which in turn became a *cause célèbre*. Its
strong erotic content was perhaps even more provocative to the prurient and
blue-nose alike because it was written by a woman celebrating love-making in an
active voice, the voice usually relegated to the male poet:

> . . . [*The Love Book*] deals with physical love and the invocation, recogni-
> tion, and acceptance of the divinity in man through the medium of phy-
> sical love. In other words, it feels good. It feels so good that you can step
> outside your private ego and share the grace of the universe. This simple
> and rather self-evident statement, enlarged and exampled poetically, raised
> a furor difficult to believe . . .
>
> – from *Word Alchemy*

The Love Book is a marvelously balanced hymn of praise and ascension and
remains, to date, her most fully-realized accomplishment. Like *Dark Brown* by
Michael McClure, *The Love Book* attempts to create an erotic and positive physical
love poetry unique in American literature.

Her only other collection, *Word Alchemy*, is a selection of shorter poems written
from 1960 to 1967. It is uneven in its voice and strength. The most satisfying poems
are those which combine precision, wit and sensitivity. For instance, "Melody for
Married Men":

> I like to watch the young girls walk
> swinging their hips and hair
> swinging their hopes and dreams in magic circles
> they never walk alone, but move in twos and threes
> confiding audacities to each other
> twitching their tails and giggling
> while thirty year old men watch from their windows
> drinking coffee with their wives and making fantasies
> of Moslem heaven

or this exerpt from "Spring 61":

> yesterday we went to the ocean and prised mussels
> from low-tide rocks
> cooked them with onion   carrots   celery seed
>   (delicious)
> cut fingers healed in sea water . . .

reflect her ability to translate material into forthright and clear language. Many other poems in the collection have the tendency to become strident and break into areas of prose and polemic and lose power because of a lessening of attention to transformative language.

> Those who read modern poetry do so for pleasure, for insight, sometimes for counsel. The least they can expect is that the poet who shares his visions and experiences with them do so without hypocrisy. To compromise poetry through fear is to atrophy the psyche. To compromise poetry through expedience is the soft, small murder of the soul."
>
> – from the preface to *Word Alchemy*

– David Meltzer

KAVANAGH, P(atrick) J(oseph). British. Born in Worthing, Sussex, in 1931. Educated at the Douai School; Merton College, Oxford, M.A. Formerly, Lecturer, University of Indonesia, Djarkarta. Recipient: Richard Hillary Memorial Prize, 1966; Arts Council bursary, 1967; *The Guardian* Fiction Prize, 1969. Lives in Gloucestershire, England.

PUBLICATIONS

Verse

One and One: Poems.   London, Heinemann, 1959.
On the Way to the Depot.   London, Chatto and Windus-Hogarth Press, 1967.
About Time.   London, Chatto and Windus-Hogarth Press, 1970.
Edward Thomas in Heaven.   London, Chatto and Windus–Hogarth Press, 1974.

Plays

Television Plays: *William Cowper Lived Here* (documentary), 1971; *Journey Through Summer* (documentary), 1973.

Novels

A Song and Dance.   London, Chatto and Windus, 1968.
A Happy Man.   London, Chatto and Windus, 1972.

Other

The Perfect Stranger (autobiography).   London, Chatto and Windus, 1966.

*   *   *

As a poet P. J. Kavanagh is a difficult case – which means that he is interesting. Although skilled in the use of free rhythms and thoroughly professional in his procedures, he has nothing like the robustness to be considered as a major poet, and the content of his work shows no development – but to be a good minor poet has always been an achievement. How good is he? His main fault, and it is a serious one, has been well stated by a critic: ". . . the final impression, despite [his] neat descriptiveness, is of someone being a little too breezy in his acceptance, with a slightly maddening optimism." Kavanagh is a television entertainer, a failed comedian and a whimsy-sentimental purveyor of middlebrow travelogues: this presumably pot-boiling aspect shows up, which it should not, in his verse. And yet he loves nature and is exceedingly accurate in his descriptions of it. What he has learned from Edward Thomas, Andrew Young, Edmund Blunden and others has been well assimilated. But something happened between his admittedly immature early poetry and his later (if not, perhaps, his latest) work: incompetently equipped to deal with suffering as a young poet, he was none the less prepared to confront it; now that he is competently equipped his poetry might actually be described as a series of exercises in how to avoid it. If no other way will do, he is prepared to be deliberately banal or sentimental.

Yet when all this has been said – and it has to be said – Kavanagh is imaginative, intelligent and has a fine sense of delicacy. Occasionally, too, he can be angry – and when he is, he is very effective. An example is his sharp satire on the simple-minded Bardic posturings of Ted Hughes in "The Famous Poet," who, while snarling "right in the teeth of Life's snarl" does not really manifest quite the same attitude towards

> Two charabancs
> Of Poetry Students in summery clothes necking and laughing.
> In dove-light he watches them straighten their clothes and faces,
> Thrilled, soon, to frown in the presence of Truth.

Furthermore, Kavanagh's poetry, though it shows no intellectual advance, has consistently improved: observation increasingly takes the place of sentimentality (the habit of giggling banality has not yet been shed), and the rhythms are stronger and more confident. "Commuter" (this, like "The Famous Poet," is from *Edward Thomas in Heaven*) may even be seen as an oblique attempt to avoid the fault of "maddening optimism": what it observes is by no means "breezy" in that manner which has become too notoriously associated with this poet. Broad description of "an open station platform in the Dordogne" narrows to the sinister precision of:

> the rest of us waited, standing beside our cases.
> When it arrived she left him and climbed on the train
> Her face like dawn because of their conversation.
> She suddenly turned, grabbed his neck in the crook of her arm,
> Gave him the bones of her head, the bones of her body, violently,
> Then climbed on again alone. Her face hardened
> In seconds as the train moved away from her island.
> Tight lipped she looked around for a seat on the sea.

This clearly demonstrates that Kavanagh is not a person who does not understand or has not seen suffering; his problem is rather to "place" it in his poetry. It should not be implied that it is his duty to indulge it – rather that he should not pretend it away. His poetry shows some signs that he is concerned to purge away its false elements.

– Martin Seymour-Smith

KEARNS, Lionel (John). Canadian. Born in Nelson, British Columbia, 16 February 1937. Educated at the University of British Columbia, Vancouver, B.A. in English 1961, M.A. 1964; School of Oriental and African Studies, London, 1964–65. Married Dolly Revati Maharaj in 1960 (separated); has four children. Lived in Mexico and Trinidad. Since 1966, Assistant Professor of English, Simon Fraser University, Burnaby, British Columbia. Recipient: Canada Council fellowship, 1964, 1965, and grant, 1968, 1973. Address: Department of English, Simon Fraser University, Burnaby, British Columbia, Canada.

PUBLICATIONS

Verse

Songs of Circumstance. Vancouver, Tish Press, 1963.
Listen George. Montreal, Imago Press, 1965.
4 Poeter, with others. Stockholm, Bok Ock Bild, 1966.
Pointing. Toronto, Ryerson Press, 1967.
By the Light of the Silvery McLune: Media Parables, Poems, Signs, Gestures, and Other Assaults on the Interface. Vancouver, Daylight Press-Talon Books, 1969.
About Time. Prince George, British Columbia, Caladonia, 1974.

Film-Poems, with Gordon Payne: The Birth of God, 1973; Negotiating a New Canadian Constitution, 1974.

Critical Studies: in Tish 1–30 (Vancouver), 1961–64; Canadian Literature 20 and 37 (Vancouver), Spring 1964 and Summer 1968; Rhymes and Reasons, edited by John Robert Colombo, Toronto, Holt Rinehart, 1971.

Lionel Kearns comments:

I am currently experimenting with and investigating the poetic possibilities of film and the filmic possibilities of poetry.

*   *   *

"Poems represent a spontaneous projection of my own concern at any particular moment," Lionel Kearns wrote about the verse in his first large-scale book *Pointing*. The poems are clever and sometimes private. "Recall," for instance, ends:

> They will perceive only
> an insignificant
> hiss of words
> in the wind.

In "Poet as Salesman" he seems at odds with inner life. "Anguish," he writes, "want some?"

Kearns' other major book is *By the Light of the Silvery McLune*, and the pun on the name of the Toronto media pundit Marshall McLuhan is a clue to the kind of poems that are in the book. From a poet concerned with semantics and semiology, Kearns has become a poet concerned with performance and effect. In the new book are shaggy-dog poems, essentially stand-up comic routines, like "Telephone," which begins:

> After completing his call
> Roderick discovered
> the phone-booth had no door.

It ends, many pages later, on this note:

> so that today
> no one knows whether Roderick
> is living or dead.

Perhaps it is possible to see in Kearns' work – which has so far only touched the surface of an imaginative world of its own making – an intelligence at work that will radically alter the relationship of the reader and the writer. One direction he might move in is into a West Coast Surrealism. At present he remains what George Bowering has dubbed him: "Lionel Kearns, the linguistic poet."

– John Robert Colombo

KELL, Richard (Alexander). British. Born in Youghal, County Cork, Ireland, 1 November 1927. Educated at Methodist College, Belfast; Wesley College, Dublin, 1944–46; Trinity College, Dublin, B.A. (honours) in English and French literature 1952. Married Muriel Adelaide Nairn in 1953; has four children. Assistant Teacher, Kilkenny College, Ireland, and Whinney Bank School, Middlesborough, Lancashire; Assistant Librarian, Luton Public Library, Bedfordshire, 1954–56, and Brunel College of Technology, Uxbridge, Middlesex, 1956–59; Assistant Lecturer, 1960–65, and Lecturer in English, 1966–70, Isleworth Polytechnic, London. Since 1970, Senior Lecturer in English, Newcastle upon Tyne Polytechnic. Address: 18 Rectory Grove, Gosforth, Newcastle upon Tyne NE3 1AL, England.

PUBLICATIONS

Verse

(Poems).   Oxford, Fantasy Press, 1957.
Control Tower.   London, Chatto and Windus-Hogarth Press, 1962.
Six Irish Poets, with others, edited by Robin Skelton.   London, Oxford University Press, 1962.
Differences.   London, Chatto and Windus-Hogarth Press, 1969.

Richard Kell comments:

   The poems in my first collection, largely reflective and descriptive, were written without any awareness of a predominant theme; in retrospect, however, it appears that one of my main concerns was the opposition between negative and positive states (restraint and freedom, deprivation and fulfillment, apathy and love, scepticism and faith, inner blindness and vision), often with a note of regret for the elusiveness of the second. Though some aspect of the theme itself was implied fairly frequently, the experiences that represented it were varied – ranging from the sight of some empty coal carts to a meditation focused on the image of a Buddhist goddess. In my second collection the same kind of dichotomy emerges, but with an emphasis on harmony and conflict as concomitants of diversity. As for technique, I like to combine fairly well-defined verse forms – of many types, and not necessarily traditional – with rhythmic flexibility. In the choice and syntactic ordering of words I aim at intelligibility as well as imaginative precision (which does not preclude double meanings when these are useful). In general my poetry tends to be quiet and controlled rather than effusive: I love freedom but am distrustful of excess.

                              *   *   *

   Richard Kell was a slow developer, for his first collection, *Control Tower,* did not appear until he was thirty-five. It suggested that Kell was a Movement poet with a slight Irish accent. The hint of Yeat's tower in the title might be fortuitous, but there is a stronger echo in "The Swan" (one of Kell's best poems) which recalls another favourite Yeatsian emblem: "Cumbrous wings whacking the startled air / And terror swirls the surface of the lake." But Kell avoids an emphatic Yeatsian rhetoric, and a more immediate model is a quieter poet, Robert Graves, whose influence is apparent in "Citadels." Kell's qualities, as revealed in *Control Tower,* were those of several other British poets of the fifties: formal skill and a satisfying precision of statement, plus a tendency to comment on experience rather than to explore it from within, and a comparatively narrow emotional range. There was also a tendency, ultimately derived from Auden, to lean heavily on a highly charged abstraction such as "love": "Down the long approach / Of love, to love's darkness." But Kell's most positive quality was his capacity to render experience in clear visual images and a firm draughtsmanlike line. As a first collection *Control Tower* is both accomplished and promising. Unfortunately the promise has not so far been fulfilled, for his second book, *Differences,* is a disappointment. Trying for more immediate treatment of emotional themes, in less formal verse, Kell has become pedestrian and even slack, though there is still a pervasive intelligence about his writing.

– Bernard Bergonzi

KELLY, Robert. American. Born in Brooklyn, New York, 24 September 1935. Educated at the City College of New York, A.B. 1955; Columbia University, New York, 1955–58. Married Helen Kelly in 1969. Translator, New York, 1956–58. Lecturer in English, Wagner College, New York, 1960–61. Instructor in German, 1961–62, Instructor in English, 1962–64, Assistant Professor, 1964–69, Associate Professor, 1969–74, and since 1974, Professor of English, Bard College, Annandale-on-Hudson, New York. Assistant Professor of English, State University of New York, Buffalo, Summer 1964; Visiting Lecturer, Tufts University, Medford, Massachusetts, 1966–67; Poet-in-Residence, California Institute of Technology, Pasadena, 1971–72. Editor, *Chelsea Review*, New York, 1958–60; Founding Editor, with George Economou, *Trobar* magazine, 1960–64, and Trobar Books, 1962–64, New York; Contributing Editor, *Caterpillar*, New York, 1969–73. Since 1963, Editor, *Matter* magazine and Matter publishing company, New York, later Annandale-on-Hudson, New York. Fellow in Fiction, New York City Writers Conference, 1967. Agent: Black Sparrow Press, P.O. Box 25603, Los Angeles, California 90025. Address: Department of English, Bard College, Annandale-on-Hudson, New York 12504, U.S.A.

PUBLICATIONS

Verse

    Armed Descent. New York, Hawks Well Press, 1961.
    Her Body Against Time (bilingual edition). Mexico City, El Corno Emplumado, 1963.
    Round Dances. New York, Trobar Books, 1964.
    Tabula. Lawrence, Kansas, Dialogue Press, 1964.
    Enstasy. Annandale-on-Hudson, New York, Matter, 1964.
    Matter/Fact/Sheet/1. Buffalo, New York, Matter, 1964.
    Matter/Fact/Sheet/2. Annandale-on-Hudson, New York, Matter, 1964.
    Lunes, with *Sightings* by Jerome Rothenberg. New York, Hawks Well Press, 1964.
    Lectiones. Placitas, New Mexico, Duende Press, 1965.
    Words in Service. New Haven, Connecticut, Robert Lamberton, 1966.
    Weeks. Mexico City, El Corno Emplumado, 1966.
    Songs XXIV. Cambridge, Massachusetts, Pym Randall Press, 1967.
    Twenty Poems. Annandale-on-Hudson, New York, Matter, 1967.
    Devotions. Annandale-on-Hudson, New York, Salitter Books, 1967.
    Axon Dendron Tree. Annandale-on-Hudson, New York, Matter, 1967.
    Crooked Bridge Love Society. Annandale-on-Hudson, New York, Salitter Books, 1967.

A Joining: A Sequence for H.D.   Los Angeles, Black Sparrow Press, 1967.
Alpha.   Gambier, Ohio, Pothanger Press, 1968.
Finding the Measure.   Los Angeles, Black Sparrow Press, 1968.
Songs I–XXX.   Cambridge, Massachusetts, Pym Randall Press, 1968.
Sonnets.   Los Angeles, Black Sparrow Press, 1968.
From the Common Shore, Book 5.   Great Neck, New York, George Robert
   Minkoff, 1968.
We Are the Arbiters of Beast Desire.   Berkeley, California, MBVL Editions,
   1969.
A California Journal.   London, Big Venus, 1969.
The Common Shore, Books I–V: A Long Poem about America in Time.   Los
   Angeles, Black Sparrow Press, 1969.
Kali Yuga.   London, Cape Goliard Press, 1970; New York, Grossman, 1971.
Flesh: Dream: Book.   Los Angeles, Black Sparrow Press, 1971.
Ralegh.   Los Angeles, Black Sparrow Press, 1972.
The Pastorals.   Los Angeles, Black Sparrow Press, 1972.
Reading Her Notes.   Uniondale, New York, privately printed, 1972.
The Tears of Edmund Burke.   Annandale-on-Hudson, New York, Printed by
   Helen, 1973.
Whaler Frigate Clippership.   Lawrence, Kansas, Tansy Publications, 1973.
The Mill of Particulars.   Los Angeles, Black Sparrow Press, 1973.
The Loom.   Los Angeles, Black Sparrow Press, 1975.

Recording: *Finding the Measure,* Black Sparrow Press, 1968.

Plays

The Well Wherein a Deer's Head Bleeds (produced New York, 1964).   Published in *A Play and Two Poems,* with Diane Wakoski and Ron Loewinsohn,
   Los Angeles, Black Sparrow Press, 1968.
Eros and Psyche, music by Elie Yarden (produced New Paltz, New York,
   1971).   New Paltz, New York, privately printed, 1971.

Novels

The Scorpions.   New York, Doubleday, 1967; London, Calder and Boyars,
   1969.
Cities.   West Newbury, Massachusetts, Frontier Press, 1971.

Other

Statement.   Los Angeles, Black Sparrow Press, 1968.
In Time (essays).   West Newbury, Massachusetts, Frontier Press, 1971.
Sulphur.   Altadena, California, privately printed, 1972.
A Line of Sight.   Los Angeles, Black Sparrow Press, 1974.

Editor, with Paris Leary, *A Controversy of Poets: An Anthology of Contemporary
   American Poetry.*   New York, Doubleday, 1965.

Critical Studies: by Paul Blackburn, in *Kulchur* (New York), 1962; by Hyatt Waggoner, in *American Poetry from the Puritans to the Present,* Boston, Houghton Mifflin,

1968; review by Diane Wakoski, in *Poetry* (Chicago), 1972; "Robert Kelly Issue" of *Vort* (Bloomington, Indiana), 1974.

Robert Kelly comments:

What help can I give the reader who would come to my work? First, tell him it is not *my* work, only Work, itself, somehow arisen through (or in spite of) my instrumentality. My personality is its enemy, only distracts. But what is there for the reader who reads to find the man? He'll find the man. The man is always there, the stink of him, the hope and fear he confuses with himself, the beauty of him, struggle, dim intuitions of a glory that is not personal, but that only persons can inhabit and share. That we are human in the world, and share our thoughts.

And this sharing of thought, perception, is what becomes the world. The world is our shared thought.

But in language the unperceived or newly perceived can arise, to break the fabric of the ordinary consensus of our lives. News from nowhere, a new handle for an old day.

Invited to introduce my work to the general reader, never!, the *specific* reader, I rehearse for our mutual benefit two answers my work has given, and I here transcribe.

1967.   Prefix to *Finding the Measure:*

> Finding the measure is finding the mantram,
> is finding the moon, as index of measure,
> is finding the moon's source;
> > > if that source
> is Sun, finding the measure is finding
> the natural articulation of ideas.
> > > > The organism
> of the macrocosm, the organism of language,
> the organism of I combine in ceaseless naturing
> to propagate a fourth,
> > > the poem,
> > > > from their trinity.
>
> Style is death. Finding the measure is finding
> a freedom from that death, a way out, a movement
> forward.
> > > Finding the measure is finding the
> specific music of the hour,
> > > > the synchronous
> consequence of the motion of the whole world.

(Measure as distinct from meter, from any precompositional grid or matrix super-imposed upon the fact of the poem's own growth "under hand.")

1973.   Prefix to *The Mill of Particulars:*

> Language is the only genetics.
> > Field
> "in which a man is understood & understands"
> > & becomes
> > what he thinks,
> becomes what he says
> > > following the argument.

When it is written that Hermes or Thoth invented language, it is meant that language is itself the psychopomp, who leads the Individuality out of Eternity into the conditioned world of Time, a world that language makes by discussing it.

> So the hasty road
> & path of arrow
> must lead up
> from language again
> > & in language the work be done,
> work of light,
> > beyond.

Through manipulation and derangement of ordinary language (*parole*), the conditioned world is changed, weakened in its associative links, its power to hold an unconscious world-view (consensus) together. Eternity, which is always there, looms beyond the grid of speech.

I have spoken a little about my motives and my intentions. I have not presumed to speak about the work itself, which must, true to its name, do its own work, and try to lure the reader to dance with it.

One word of abandon-caution: I am not concerned with sources. The poem is "sensuous in its intention to impress," says W. C. Williams. Many lights flicker in the water, many images are reflected. But the point is to jump in. Or at least to lift the cup and drink.

*   *   *

The density of Robert Kelly's poems is balanced by their liveliness. He has, for the time, found "the measure," as expressed in the "prefix" to *Finding the Measure* [quoted above]. Precisely what Kelly means by "style" is a puzzle: I accept the above credo as Kelly's way of saying that the individual poem must create its own form. One would be tempted to say that his style is *not* death, but nevertheless a style. Kelly shares with many of America's best poets an unpredictability: his use of the language is sure but never without surprises. Our most lauded poets, the dandies, either work the language beautifully or play with it cleverly. Kelly plays language and is not afraid to mix various approaches within one poem:

> blacks menaced by rising boredom, whites
> > stung by neuter anopheles
> lie at the foot of Uranus' throne
> > – for the retail is deadlier
> > > than the hail,
> wipeth stockes oute
> > > & buggeth corne
> > > > – "Of Earth"

Kelly's "freedom" is, perhaps, his willingness to experiment with a variety of forms. In one long, rambling poem, "The Alchemist," Kelly's voice shifts frequently but always seems his own:

> the origin, far side of a lake
> is always shadow
> the voice goes around
> it easily in one hour . . .

The poem deals with change, and achieves tonal changes of its own: "& if we do not get up and destroy all the congressmen / turn them into naked men and let the sun shine on them / set them down in a desert & let them find their way out. . . ." Kelly's rhetoric is dense but not tiring. The language always pivots on an image; the energy of this turning produces sparks:

> The alchemist
>
> weeping in the Spanish field
> in a cloak chewed into rags by its symbols
>
> a body,
> under it,
> whose name is love & which only of all light love can eat

Kelly may not like it, but he does have a style; the style of a poet whose work cannot be characterized except by his attitude. It is this attitude that marks him as one of America's most promising young poets.

In *Flesh: Dream: Book*, Kelly is again at an energetic peak, exploring formal as well as free verse. The book contains a lovely sequence of eighteen sonnets, as well as numerous other poems (of such gentle, natural rhythms!) that make lasting tactile impressions, and harken the priorities suggested by the book's title:

> Fish you caught
> delight me
> five years ago
> getting you wet
>
> nourished on
> delight
>   sat on the bank
> waiting for that life
> to come up
> that was food
> how
>
> cool your body is

> dream a world
> have
> enough for me
>
> darkness a crag, shy
> fingers at your throat
> feeling
> down the breasts' way
>
> a stroke or
> trait
> from which a line

from a hydrant
along the street
water

seeks its home
– the final two of "Nine Songs for Helen"

– Geof Hewitt

KENNEDY, X. J. Pseudonym for Joseph Charles Kennedy. American. Born in
Dover, New Jersey, 21 August 1929. Educated at Seton Hall College, South
Orange, New Jersey, B.Sc. 1950 (Phi Beta Kappa); Columbia University, New
York, M.A. 1951; the Sorbonne, Paris, Cert. Litt. 1956. Served in the United States
Navy, 1951–55. Married Dorothy Mintzlaff in 1962; has five children. Teaching
Fellow, 1956–60, and Instructor, 1960–62, University of Michigan, Ann Arbor;
taught at the University of North Carolina, Greensboro, 1962–63. Assistant Profes-
sor, 1963–67, Associate Professor, 1967–73, and since 1973, Professor of English,
Tufts University, Medford Massachusetts. Visiting Lecturer, Wellesley College,
Massachusetts, 1964, and the University of California, Irvine, 1966–67; Bruern
Fellow in American Literature, University of Leeds, 1974–75. Poetry Editor, *Paris
Review*, Paris and New York, 1962–64. Editor, with Dorothy M. Kennedy,
Counter/Measures magazine, 1972–74. Recipient: Hopwood Award, 1959; Bread
Loaf Writers Conference Fellowship, 1960; Lamont Poetry Selection Award, 1961;
Bess Hokin Prize (*Poetry*, Chicago), 1961; National Endowment for the Arts grant,
1967; Shelley Memorial Award, 1970. Agent: Curtis Brown Ltd., 60 East 56th
Street, New York, New York 10022. Address: Department of English, Tufts
University, Medford, Massachusetts 02155, U.S.A.

PUBLICATIONS

Verse

Nude Descending a Staircase: Poems, Song, A Ballad. New York, Doubleday,
   1961.
Growing into Love. New York, Doubleday, 1969.
Bulsh. Providence, Rhode Island, Burning Deck, 1970.
Breaking and Entering. London, Oxford University Press, 1972.
Emily Dickinson in Southern California. Boston, Godine Press, 1974.

Other

Editor, with James E. Camp, *Mark Twain's Frontier.* New York, Holt Rinehart, 1963.
Editor, *An Introduction to Poetry* (textbook). Boston, Little Brown, 1966;
   revised edition, 1971, 1974.

Editor, with Keith Waldrop and James E. Camp, *Pegasus Descending: A Book of the Best Bad Verse.* New York, Macmillan, and London, Collier Macmillan, 1971.

Editor, *Messages: A Thematic Anthology of Poetry.* Boston, Little Brown, 1973.

Critical Studies: "Squibs" by Bernard Waldrop, in *Burning Deck 2* (Providence, Rhode Island), Spring 1963; "Recent Poetry: The End of an Era" by Louis L. Martz, in *Yale Review* (New Haven, Connecticut), Winter 1970; review by Stephen Tudor, in *Spirit* (South Orange, New Jersey), Spring 1970; by Henry Taylor, in *Masterplots Annual,* New York, Salem Press, 1970; in *Times Literary Supplement* (London), 24 December 1971.

X. J. Kennedy comments:

[I belong to] the Wolgamot School (group of young poets including Donald Hall, W. D. Snodgrass, and Keith Waldrop, centering around the literary historian John Barton Wolmagot, begun at the University of Michigan in the 1950's).

Nearly always write in rime and metre. Favor narratives, lyrics to be sung.

*   *   *

X. J. Kennedy belongs to the "academic" wing of contemporary American poetry despite the avowal he once made to an anthologist: "I do not believe in conventional theories of English prosody but in the ear's ability to chop off a line when it has run out of time." Essentially, he is an extremely witty lightweight, a poet with a cunning ear and a deft hand with rhyme and off-rhyme. A good many of his poems are written to be sung to popular tunes, and they contrast this "folk" basis with a cool sophistication of content.

The kind of tradition to which Kennedy belongs goes back to John Crowe Ransom, and it also owes something to the ballads which Auden was writing in the thirties. It is impossible to read his work without delight at its neatness, swiftness and, above all, its sense of fun. It is equally impossible not to notice its restriction of emotional range.

– Edward Lucie-Smith

KENNELLY, (Timothy) Brendan. Irish. Born in Ballylongford, County Kerry, 17 April 1936. Educated at St. Ita's College, Tarbert, County Kerry; Trinity College, Dublin, Ph.D. 1967; Leeds University. Married Margaret O'Brien in 1969; has one daughter. Junior Lecturer, 1963–66, Lecturer, 1966–69, Associate Professor, 1969–73, and since 1973, Professor of Modern Literature, Trinity College, Dublin. Cornell Professor of English Literature, Swarthmore College, Pennsylvania, 1971–72. Recipient: A. E. Memorial Award, 1967. Address: 19 St. Alban's Park, Sandymount, Dublin, Ireland.

PUBLICATIONS

Verse

Cast a Cold Eye, with Rudi Holzapfel.   Dublin, Dolmen Press, 1959.
The Rain, The Moon, with Rudi Holzapfel.   Dublin, Dolmen Press, 1961.
The Dark about Our Loves, with Rudi Holzapfel.   Dublin, John Augustine,
  1962.
Green Townlands: Poems, with Rudi Holzapfel.   Leeds, Bibliographical Press,
  1963.
Let Fall No Burning Leaf.   Dublin, New Square Publications, 1963.
My Dark Fathers.   Dublin, New Square Publications, 1964.
Up and At It.   Dublin, New Square Publications, 1965.
Collection One: Getting Up Early.   Dublin, Allen Figgis, 1966.
Good Souls to Survive: Poems.   Dublin, Allen Figgis, 1967.
Dream of a Black Fox.   Dublin, Allen Figgis, 1968.
Selected Poems.   Dublin, Allen Figgis, 1969; New York, Dutton, 1971.
A Drinking Cup: Poems from the Irish.   Dublin, Allen Figgis, 1970.
Bread.   Dublin, Tara Telephone Publications, 1971.
Love-Cry.   Dublin, Allen Figgis, 1972.
Salvation, The Stranger.   Dublin, Tara Telephone Publications, 1972.
The Voices.   Dublin, Gallery Press, 1973.

Novels

The Crooked Cross.   Dublin, Allen Figgis, 1963; Boston, Little Brown, 1964.
The Florentines.   Dublin, Allen Figgis, 1967.

Other

Editor, *The Penguin Book of Irish Verse.*   London, Penguin, 1970; revised
  edition, 1972.

Critical Studies: B.A. Thesis by Antonella Ceoletta, University of Venice, 1973;
M.Litt. Thesis by Frances Gwynn, Trinity College, Dublin, 1974.

Brendan Kennelly comments:

  I used to divide my poetry into rather facile categories, such as poems written
about the countryside, poems written about the city, and poems that tried to
express some sort of personal philosophy. I think now that such categories are
false and I believe instead that I select appropriate images from aspects of my
experience and try to use them in such a way that they express what goes on
within. This involves a continued struggle to discover and develop a proper language, my *own* language, carefully selected from the words of the world in which I
live. I believe there is poetry in ordinary everyday life and that the poet is one who
tries to stay awake to that. There is this continual battle between civilized sluggish-
ness and sharp seeing, seeing-into. The poem is born the moment one sees into and

through one's world, and when one expresses that seeing-into in a totally appropriate language. By totally appropriate I mean a language of complete alertness, a vital and buoyant idiom. As I try to write I know that I am involved in an activity which is a deliberate assertion of energy over indifference, of vitality over deadness, of escitement and ecstasy over dullness and cynicism. Yet the poem must take account of all these negatives. In fact, it must often use them as its raw material, but, by a .sort of dynamic, inner alchemy of language, rhythm and image, transform those negatives into living, singing forms. Poetry is for me a challenge, a mystery, a consolation, a source of bewilderment, a joy.

*   *   *

In a recent volume entitled *Collection One: Getting Up Early,* Brendan Kennelly has given us a selection from a number of slender books published during the last ten years. The poet, who comes from Kerry, draws frequently on vigorous local stories, as in "Moloney at the Wake" and "Moloney Remembers the Resurrection of Kate Finucane." In these and other poems he evokes the "Kingdon of Kerry":

> Between the Banner County and the Kingdom
> The burly Shannon strides into the sea.
> In rocky desolation, the unploughed parishes end;
> The outnumbering waves insist
> That the river is nobody's friend.

Mr. Kennelly is now Professor of Modern Literature at Trinity College, Dublin, and, in contrast to his local poems, his poems are now filled with the sights and sounds of city life, such as "Ambulance":

> Braying on its mercy mission,
> The white hysterical bully
> Blows all things out of its way,
> Cutting through the slack city
> Like a knife through flesh.
> People respect potential saviours
> And immediately step aside,
> Watching it pitch and scream ahead,
> Ignoring the lights, breaking the rules,
> Lurching on the crazy line
> Between the living and the dead.

Notable among these poems is an elegy on the late Frank O'Connor, which begins:

> Climbing the last step to your house, I knew
> That I would find you in your chair,
> Watching the light die along the canal. . . .

The themes range from emigration, children's hospital, old men sharing "the sun's enormous charity" to a sonnet about a negro:

> My mother fine. But
> Man, she think the whole world made of coconut.

The Crooked Cross is the poet's first novel and it describes the effects of a drought on a remote village. A handsome gypsy girl, a publican, an old sailor and a water diviner are among the lively characters. This is a poet's novel with an allegorical context. In lighter mood is *The Florentines,* which tells of the adventures of a young student who takes up a post-graduate course of mythology in England.

– Austin Clarke

KESSLER, Milton. American. Born in Brooklyn, New York, 9 May 1930. Educated at DeWitt Clinton High School, New York; Harvard University, Cambridge, Massachusetts; University of Buffalo, New York, B.A. (magna cum laude) 1957 (Phi Beta Kappa); University of Washington, Seattle, M.A. 1962; Ohio State University, Columbus, 1959–63. Married Sonia Berer in 1952; has three children. Teaching Assistant, University of Washington, 1957–58; Instructor, Boston University, 1957–58, and Ohio State University, 1958–63; Lecturer in English, Queens College, City University of New York, 1963–65. Since 1965, Poet-in-Residence and Associate Professor of English, Harpur College, State University of New York, Binghamton. Visiting Professor, University of the Negev, Beersheba, Israel, 1971–72. Co-Editor. *Choice* magazine, Buffalo, New York. Recipient: Bread Loaf Writers Conference Robert Frost Fellowship, 1961; Yaddo Fellowship, 1965, 1966, 1969, 1973; MacDowell Foundation Fellowship, 1966; New York State Research Foundation Fellowship, 1966, and Distinguished Fellowship, 1969; National Endowment for the Arts grant, 1967. Address: 25 Lincoln Avenue, Binghamton, New York 13905, U.S.A.

PUBLICATIONS

Verse

A Road Came Once. Columbus, Ohio State University Press, 1963.
Called Home. Vestal, New York, Black Bird Press, 1967.
Woodlawn North: A Book of Poems. Boston, Impressions Workshop, 1970.
Sailing Too Far. New York, Harper, 1973.

Play

Pale Is This Good Prince (oratorio), based on adaptations of Egyptian songs, with Gerald E. Kadish, music by Karl Korte (produced Washington, D.C., 1973). "Love Songs and Tomb Songs of Ancient Egypt" published in *Alcheringa* (New York), Spring 1973.

Milton Kessler comments:

(1970) Poetry is my private, almost my secret life. My poetry is the home I return to or the home to which I turn.

In my poems each word is another room, sky, another voice, gesture, spiritual configuration, atmosphere, like the change in a face that experiences invisible changes in its spirit, or the changes in his body felt by an asthmatic like myself. The poem is written, is reaching, into spatial planes or densities: within my arms, across the alley, beyond the far mountain, memory or sound, into my side, on the other side of this table. All in one line. It neither follows the natural breath nor the metrical music. I dream of it as very slow, to be held forever like that revery of St. Joan's weeping face in Carl Dreyer's silent masterpiece. In the line "Grandmother / Celia / save / my / David" each word is another place, each word illuminates another surface of a globe from within, each word addresses another phase of life, even though the whole sentence seems to be a clear linear development. Of course, what I say here is a kind of fiction, the fiction I need to remember myself. I surrender myself to the poems: my impurity, my wrath, my tenderness, my confusion. Regardless of the specific situation, I want each-poem to embody my whole life. The universe must and does remind me of itself as God reminded Job. I am overheard and seen through by those who are wiser. It is not a poetry of wisdom or defenses. I do not possess a returning hero's wisdom. I can't imagine telling anyone how to live his life or what poetry should be. I think of my poems as prayer. I write for a miracle; the hurt, stalled people of my poems pray for a miracle, and sometimes, in the poems, it comes to pass. I write often, perhaps too often, of my Jewish family as it moves so vulnerably through its ordinary days. I am often frightened. My poems reach for solace, for miracles, sometimes even for the comfort of acknowledged delusions.

> Now, somewhere, as if I were really holy,
> I know that my savior is lonely.

(1974) Now three or four years later there is a difference, of course. An operation on my thyroid, a year in Israel, many readings in the United States, England, and Israel, and the coming of age of my children, a change in energy and desire has formed through which I hope to be able to express the rest of my experience of life in poems. And I do now feel that I am old enough to tell people what I think, what I have learned. I want to take some action in this world that will help. I've been in correspondence with poets in prison. For my sake, for the sake of poetry, I want their work to be known. I have a title for my next book, an idea and just the first few poems so far, *American Experiments*, poems of the daily life of Americans, which is much of the life I live. I will be reflecting as well on my own past life, representative past life, especially the period of World War II. That does seem now a very long time ago, long enough to turn back to, and I do feel the pressure of the end of the century. Since 1969 four more years of war and news of war. The end of the century in sight but no end to the wars. Yet I think I am less frightened than I was then and more in touch with the flow of life.

*   *   *

Milton Kessler is the kind of writer whose earnestness, whose sympathy for the people and things he writes about, wins the sympathy of his readers. If we take Jung's notion that each man orients himself primarily by one of four basic means – intellect, feeling, sensation, or intuition – it is clear that Kessler's primary mode is feeling. Most of the best poems in *A Road Came Once* are poems of strong feeling for family and for the sorrows and troubles of other people – poems like "The El-Painter's Daughter" and "The Clerk Retires." His tone is often reminiscent of a Jewish cantor's, an energetic wailing tone which conveys the feeling that any life, no matter how small it may seem, is a thing worthy of high drama.

One of the faults of Kessler's past work, however, is that sometimes his language is so lofty and dramatic that it becomes melodramatic or removed from the simple subject of the poem; it makes it seem as if he were so anxious to bring the subject to a ''higher'' level that the kernel, the basic incident, gets left behind on the ground. For instance, in ''The Game'' Kessler tries to build a father watching his football-playing son's injury into a kind of Homeric lament, but the language grows too self-consciously grand, melodramatic and obtrusive. In addition, Kessler's poems are sometimes simply obscure.

Since his first volume, at readings and in poems that have come out in magazines, Kessler has shown that he has done a great deal to overcome his difficulties with obscurity and grandiose diction. (A particularly fine poem of his to appear recently is ''Songs for Paul Blackburn,'' in *Choice 7–8,* Buffalo.) His poetry also has become more fanciful on occasion, and more joyous.

– Lawrence Russ

KGOSITSILE, Keorapetse (William). South African. Born in Johannesburg, 19 September 1938. Educated at Madibane High School, Johannesburg, 1958; Lincoln University, Pennsylvania; University of New Hampshire, Durham; Columbia University, New York; New School for Social Research, New York (African-American Institute Fellow). Married to Melba Kgositsile. Since 1971, Poet-in-Residence, North Carolina Agricultural and Technical State University, Greensboro. African Editor-at-Large, *Black Dialogue,* San Francisco. Recipient: Conrad Kent Rivers Award, 1969; National Endowment for the Arts grant, 1969. Address: c/o Shakong, 610 West 115th Street, New York, New York 10025, U.S.A.

PUBLICATIONS

Verse

Spirits Unchained. Detroit, Broadside Press, 1969.
For Melba. Chicago, Third World Press, 1970.
My Name Is Afrika. New York, Doubleday, 1971.

Other

Editor, *The Word Is Here: Poetry from Modern Africa.* New York, Doubleday, 1973.

*   *   *

''Because finally things have come to this,'' writes Keorapetse Kgositsile, ''White world gray grim cold turning me into a killer / Because I love love.'' The lines are ironic and paradoxical. Yet, their underlying truth argues a radical and profound humanism – the key to understanding the revolutionary poetic vision of this young South African-in-exile.

In Kgositsile's cosmology, love transcends Western definitions: it is not simply felt, or sung about, or sought after; nor is it an essentially individual experience. Rather, love finds its true definition in the commitment of the individual to both self and nation. For Blacks, nation is all Black people, wherever they may live; they are united by a bond forged outside of time: "Searching past the pretensions of knowledge / We move to the meeting place / The pulse of the beginning the end and the beginning." Thus, the subjects of his first volume of poetry, *Spirits Unchained*, are the Africans and African Americans who dedicated themselves to Black liberation. Among the most moving of the poems are the lyrical "Elegy to David Diop," and the strident "When Brown Is Black," whose hero, H. Rap Brown, becomes the metaphor for the long awaited insurrection of the oppressed: ". . . Go on, brother, say it. Talk / the talk slaves are afraid to live."

Militancy softens in *For Melba*, the volume dedicated to his wife; but Kgositsile never loses sight of the larger vision. The intense anguish and joy of interpersonal love – beautiful in itself – are but stepping stones to a union whose strength and commitment will spawn the future Black nation. When, finally, in *My Name Is Afrika*, songs of celebration and love give way to exhortation, it is, again, in the interest of the long view: "Gut it is will move us from the gutter . . . to the rebirth of real men."

– Saundra Towns

KINNELL, Galway. American. Born in Providence, Rhode Island, 1 February 1927. Educated at Princeton University, New Jersey, A.B. 1948; University of Rochester, New York, M.A. 1949. Served in the United States Navy, 1945–46. Married to Inés Delgado de Torres; has one daughter and one son. Formerly, Member of the Faculty, University of Grenoble, France; Poet-in-Residence, Juniata College, Huntingdon, Pennsylvania, and University of California, Irvine, 1968–69. Field Worker, Congress of Racial Equality, 1963. Recipient: Fulbright Scholarship, 1955; Longview Foundation Award, 1962; National Institute of Arts and Letters grant, 1962; Bess Hokin Prize, 1965, and Eunice Tietjens Memorial Prize, 1966 (*Poetry*, Chicago); Rockefeller grant, 1967; Cecil Hemley Prize, 1968; Brandeis University Creative Arts Award, 1968; National Endowment for the Arts grant, 1969; Amy Lowell Traveling Fellowship, 1969; Shelley Memorial Award, 1972; Guggenheim Fellowship, 1974. Address: Sheffield, Vermont 05866, U.S.A.

PUBLICATIONS

Verse

What a Kingdom It Was. Boston, Houghton Mifflin, 1960.
Flower Herding on Mount Monadnock. Boston, Houghton Mifflin, 1964.
Poems of Night. London, Rapp and Carroll, 1968.

Body Rags. Boston, Houghton Mifflin, 1968; London, Rapp and Whiting, 1969.
The Hen Flower. Frensham, Surrey, Sceptre Press, 1970.
First Poems 1947–1952. Mount Horeb, Wisconsin, Perishable Press, 1970.
The Book of Nightmares. Boston, Houghton Mifflin, 1971.
The Shoes of Wandering. Mount Horeb, Wisconsin, Perishable Press, 1971.
The Avenue Bearing the Initial of Christ into the New World: Poems 1946–1964. Boston, Houghton Mifflin, 1974.

Recording: *Today's Poets 5,* with others, Folkways.

Novel

Black Light. Boston, Houghton Mifflin, 1966; London, Hart Davis, 1967.

Other

3 Self-Evaluations, with Anthony Ostroff and Winfield Townley Scott. Beloit, Wisconsin, Beloit Poetry Journal, 1953.
The Poetics of the Physical World. Fort Collins, Colorado State University, 1969.

Translator, *Bitter Victory,* by Rene Hardy. New York, Doubleday, and London, Hamish Hamilton, 1956.
Translator, *Pre-Columbian Ceramics,* by Henri Lehmann. London, Elek, 1962.
Translator, *The Poems of François Villon.* New York, New American Library, 1965.
Translator, *On the Motion and Immobility of Douve,* by Yves Bonnefoy. Athens, Ohio University Press, 1968.
Translator, *The Lackawanna Elegy,* by Yvan Goll. Fremont, Michigan, Sumac Press, 1970.

Bibliography: *Galway Kinnell: A Bibliography and Index of His Published Works and Criticism of Them,* Potsdam, New York, State University College Frederick W. Crumb Memorial Library, 1968.

*　　　*　　　*

In the winter of 1946–47, when I was teaching at Princeton University, a dark-shocked student, looking more like a prize fighter than a literary man, showed me a poem, maybe his first. I remember it as a Wordsworthian sonnet, not what the avant-garde of Princeton, Blackmur or Berryman, would have taken to – old diction, no modern flair. But the last couplet had a romantic fierceness that amazed me. The man who had done that could go beyond any poetic limits to be assigned. I was reckless enough to tell him so.

I was to lecture at Black Mountain that summer. He took a bit of his G.I. money and came along. Apart from some works of mine which seemed to move him, it was to Yeats that he gave himself with the totality that has always characterized him. By the fall he had written the first form of a four-page poem, "A Morning Wake among the Dead" (later called "Among the Tombs"), which foreshadowed in volcanic latency all his later long poems. The death-haunted, tragic Kinnell had already spoken, though it would take years for the fact to be recognized.

When I left Princeton in 1948 to go abroad, Galway Kinnell, who was graduating with highest honours (though that had taken a fight with the usual pedantic guardians), had applied for a Woodrow Wilson grant and for entrance to the Princeton graduate school. I heard in Florence that he had been denied both. It may be to a poet's advantage to get flung out of the academic rat-race; but it seemed an outrage at the time. He beat around for a year or so at odd teaching jobs, graduate work, endlessly rewriting "Meditations among the Tombs." I had gone to Chicago, then in the last boldness of the Hutchins' upheaval. Kinnell came out, saw some administrators of that persuasion, and on the basis of dynamism alone was made director of the Great Books Program at the Downtown College. So we were together again for a few fruitful years. We had entered so far into each other's style by then that each could suggest lines for the other's poems, as Johnson is said to have done for Goldsmith.

In form, Kinnell was still using a romantic and Miltonic pentameter almost totally remade under impacts from Donne and the moderns – meter purposely broken up, rhymes concealed – a demonic wrestling with traditional measures. His matter was the reaffirmation of the Promethean and pioneer daring of America, to which I also, after the neo-Augustinian resignations of the war, was committed. He wrote a whole volume of Western poems which did not find a publisher, though some of them, revised, appear in the first sections of *What a Kingdom It Was*.

About 1956 Kinnell was able to get abroad. It was not too late for his "Prairie" style to be infused with French modernism, though without losing its passionate immediacy. The most remarkable fruit of this is "The Supper after the Last," in *What a Kingdom*, a symbolist vision and statement, at one time Promethean-romantic and mysteriously avant-garde.

Kinnell's break with traditional form has continued, leading to his espousal of free verse as the only possible medium for an American poet. It is significantly to Whitman that he has returned, with some inspiration from William Carlos Williams. But anyone who will take the twisted rhymes of the earlier Kinnell and set them beside the free verse of recent works – that staggering diptych of animal poems, "The Porcupine" and "The Bear" in *Body Rags* – will sense how far everything that has occurred, both in content and form, was within the province of the original Apocalyptic vision of "A Morning Wake among the Dead."

What distinguishes that vision from anything else on the contemporary scene is its continuation of the titanism of the last century – whatever flamed from Goethe's *Faust* through Melville, Nietzsche, Rimbaud, to Rilke, Yeats, Jeffers. There is a sense in which Galway Kinnell has remained faithful to this heritage, though for a long time it handicapped him among those of a more oblique and verbal trend, poets who grew up as it were after Pound. Thus a review of *Body Rags* (in the *New York Review of Books*) spent most of its time complaining that Kinnell didn't write like Berryman – as if he hadn't had his chance at that and decided early against it.

Within Kinnell's passionate and personal vein, two drifts have revealed themselves, that of the longer poem prefigured in "A Morning Wake," "The Avenue Bearing the Initial of Christ," and "The Last River," and that of clarified small lyrics aimed at an ultimate transparency. The lyrical tendency reaches its earliest perfection in "First Song" ("Then it was dusk in Illinois") as in the other tender pieces ("Island of Night," "A Walk in the Country") published in Rolfe Humphries' *New Poems* though not included by Kinnell in any of his volumes. So too with "Spring Oak," a poem that illustrates Kinnell's critical pronouncement in his Beloit "Self-Study": "Only meaning is truly interesting." Even in the most recent book there are such distillates, "The Falls" and "How Many Nights." Reading them, as the "Self-Study" had also said, is "like opening a window on the thing the poem is talking about":

831

> How many nights
> have I lain in terror,
> O Creator Spirit,
> Maker of night and day,
>
> only to walk out
> the next morning over the frozen world
> hearing under the creaking of snow
> faint, peaceful breaths . . .
> . . . snake,
> bear, earthworm, ant . . .
>
> and above me
> a wild crow crying "*yaw yaw yaw*"
> from a branch nothing cried from ever in my life.

Against such poems, the underworld involvement of "The Last River" goes another road, groping through caves and antres of "the flinty, night-smelling depths," "waiting by the grief-tree of the last river."

Kinnell's second book, *Flower Herding on Mount Monadnock*, as the title suggests (strange the Indian name for that solitary mountain on a peneplane should hold the Greek root of the One), is largely in the lyrical mode. Even the Wagnerian love-death has wonderfully refined itself in "Poems of Night":

> A cheekbone,
> A curved piece of brow,
> A pale eyelid
> Float in the dark,
> And now I make out
> An eye, dark,
> wormed with the far-off, unaccountable lights.

While the title poem and "Spindrift" – "Sit down / By the clanking shore / Of this bitter, beloved sea" – stand at the pinnacle of the poignantly pure and deeply transparent.

At the moment I have before me various sketches of a new long poem, *The Book of Nightmares*. For oceanic participation, the section on childbirth ("Maud Moon") goes beyond anything Kinnell has done before:

> It is all over, little one,
> the flipping
> and overleaping,
> the watery
> somersaulting alone in the oneness
> under the hill, under
> the old, lonely bellybutton pushing forth again
> in remembrance, all over,
> the drifting there furled like a flower, pressing
> a knee down the slippery
> walls, sculpting the whole world, hearing
> a few cries from without not even as promises, the stream
> of omphalos blood humming all over you.

What distinguishes this from the work of any other poet (though parallels can be found: Roethke, Rilke, even Whitman) is the intuitive immediacy of its entrance into pre-birth and subhuman organic nature.

Of all the poets born in the twenties and thirties, Galway Kinnell is the only one who has taken up the passionate symbolic search of the great American tradition.

– Charles G. Bell

KINSELLA, Thomas. Irish. Born in Dublin, 4 May 1928. Educated at University College, Dublin. Married Eleanor Walsh in 1955; has two daughters and one son. Worked in the Irish Civil Service, 1948–65, retired from the Department of Finance. Writer-in-Residence, 1965–67, and Professor of English, 1967–70, Southern Illinois University, Carbondale. Since 1970, Professor of English, Temple University, Philadelphia. Director, Dolmen Press, Dublin, and Cuala Press, Dublin; Founder, Peppercanister publishers, Dublin, 1972. Artistic Director, Lyric Players Theatre, Belfast. Recipient: Guinness Award, 1958, Irish Arts Council Triennial Book Award, 1961; Denis Devlin Memorial Award, 1967, 1970; Guggenheim Fellowship, 1968, 1971. Member, Irish Academy of Letters, 1965. Address: Department of English, Temple University, Philadelphia, Pennsylvania, 19122, U.S.A.

PUBLICATIONS

Verse

The Starlit Eye. Dublin, Dolmen Press, 1952.
Three Legendary Sonnets. Dublin, Dolmen Press, 1952.
The Death of a Queen. Dublin, Dolmen Press, 1956.
Poems. Dublin, Dolmen Press, 1956.
Another September. Dublin, Dolmen Press, and Philadelphia, Dufour, 1958; revised edition, Dolmen Press, and London, Oxford University Press, 1962.
Moralities. Dublin, Dolmen Press, 1960.
Poems and Translations. New York, Atheneum, 1961.
Downstream. Dublin, Dolmen Press, 1962.
Six Irish Poets, with others, edited by Robin Skelton. London and New York, Oxford University Press, 1962.
Wormwood. Dublin, Dolmen Press, 1966.
Nightwalker. Dublin, Dolmen Press, 1967.
Nightwalker and Other Poems. Dublin, Dolmen Press, London, Oxford University Press, and New York, Knopf, 1968.
Poems, with David Livingstone and Anne Sexton. London and New York, Oxford University Press, 1968.
Tear. Cambridge, Massachusetts, Pym Randall Press, 1969.
Butcher's Dozen. Dublin, Peppercanister, 1972.
A Selected Life. Dublin, Peppercanister, 1972.
Finistere. Dublin, Dolmen Press, 1972.
Notes from the Land of the Dead and Other Poems. Dublin, Cuala Press, 1972; New York, Knopf, 1973.
New Poems, 1973. Dublin, Dolmen Press, 1973.
Selected Poems 1956–1968. Dublin, Dolmen Press, and London, Oxford University Press, 1973.

Vertical Man.   Dublin, Peppercanister, 1973.
The Good Fight.   Dublin, Peppercanister, 1973.
One.   Dublin, Peppercanister, 1974.

Other

Davis, Mangan, Ferguson? Tradition and the Irish Writer, with W. B. Yeats.
Dublin, Dolmen Press, 1970.

Translator, *The Breastplate of St. Patrick.* Dublin, Dolmen Press, 1954; as
Faeth Fiadha: The Breastplate of St. Patrick, 1957.
Translator, *The Exile and Death of the Sons of Usnech,* by Longes Mac n-
Usnig.   Dublin, Dolmen Press, 1954.
Translator, *Thirty Three Triads, Translated from the XII Century Irish.*   Dublin,
Dolmen Press, 1955.
Translator, *The Tain.*   Dublin, Dolmen Press, 1969; London and New York,
Oxford University Press, 1970.

Bibliography: by Hensley Woodbridge, in *Eire-Ireland* (St. Paul, Minnesota), 1966.

Critical Studies: *The New Poets: American and British Poetry since World War II* by
M. L. Rosenthal, New York and London, Oxford University Press, 1967; "Thomas
Kinsella Issue" of *The Hollins Critic* (Hollins College, Virginia), iv, 4, 1968; "The
Poetry of Thomas Kinsella" by Robin Skelton, in *Eire-Ireland* (St. Paul, Minne-
sota), iv, 1, 1968; *Eight Contemporary Poets* by Calvin Bedient, London, Oxford
University Press, 1974.

Thomas Kinsella comments:

It is my aim to elicit order from significant experience, with a view to acceptance
on the basis of some kind of understanding. Major themes are love, death and the
artistic act. Methods various and developing.

                              *   *   *

Thomas Kinsella might be described as an intellectual troubador, his desire to
sing increasingly crossed by a need to explain. In his first book, *Poems,* traditional
love lyrics, like "Soft to Your Places" and "Midsummer", were balanced by
others like "Ulysses", where a dense vocabulary was pressed into the service of a
still emerging vision. It was the elegant world of Richard Wilbur, with a metaphysical twist and an Irish music.
Another September represented a more thorough cultivation of the same private
garden. The romantic dandy is still in evidence ("Fifth Sunday after Easter") but
his presence does not unduly impede Kinsella's clarification of his main theme: an
obsession with time. Its expression varies from the conventional ballad stanzas of
"In the Ringwood", based on the Irish *aisling* or vision poem,

> Dread, a grey devourer,
> Stalks in the shade of love.
> The dark that dogs our feet
> Eats what is sickened of.
> The End that stalks Beginning
> Hurries home its drove,

to the more analytic pose of "Baggot Street Deserta", with the poet, against his favourite backdrop of nocturnal Dublin, declaring that we must "endure and let the present punish."

The principal reproach that might be levelled against *Another September* is that the poems were not sufficiently anchored in time and place. But a less remote quality was evident towards the end of the collection, especially in the sombre "Thinking of Mr. D". And in his second major collection, Kinsella emerges clearly as a *persona* with the "pious clerkly" hand of "Priest and Emperor" now leading to the dejected face which gazes into "A Mirror in February":

> Now plainly in the mirror of my soul
> I read that I have looked my last on youth
> And little more; for they are not made whole
> That reach the age of Christ.

Downstream can be said to mark Kinsella's change of gear from lyric to meditative; as he says in "Time's Mischief":

> He must progress
> Who fabricates a path, though all about
> Death, Woman, Spring, repeat their first success.

The most noticeable change is his determination to grapple with public themes, from the local history and politics of "A Country Walk" to the problem of Hiroshima in "Old Harry". Perhaps too deliberately, for in the latter poem Truman is dignified with a moral complexity alien to his character, while the most striking effects are lavished on the atom bomb's destruction of "the notorious cities of the plain"!

The same determination flows over into *Nightwalker*, the title poem of which exposes the moral vacuum of modern Ireland. But the monologue technique and diction are still close to early Eliot, and like "Chrysalides" and "Dick King" in *Downstream*, one has to turn to the more private poems to catch Kinsella's distinctive quality. The sequence on marital love, "Wormwood", is heavy with portentousness, but contains at least one poem, "First Light", where despair is crystallised, drop by terrible drop. And there are some moving attempts to face the problem of physical suffering:

> The girl whimpers in bed, remote
> Under the anaesthetic still.
> She sleeps on her new knowledge, a bride
> With bowels burning and disarrayed.
> > – "Our Mother"

This vision of life as ordeal is more fully enunciated in the magnificently romantic intimacies of the long poem, "Phoenix Park". As well as a celebration of married love, it is also a farewell to his native Dublin, and one waits to see how America will affect Kinsella's work. For with his seriousness of purpose, and strength of intellect, went a Parnassian quality which can only benefit from a more experimental poetic climate. His translation of the early Irish epic, *The Tain*, does not wholly succeed in "making it new", but "A Hand of Solo" and "Hen Woman", parts of a new poetic sequence, show a relaxing of technique which augurs well.

"Notes from the Land of the Dead" is incorporated in *New Poems, 1973* which, with *Selected Poems 1956–1968*, amounts to a new definition of his career. But he has also established a private press, for broadsides like *Butcher's Dozen* and his

835

meditation on John F. Kennedy, *The Good Fight*. So in his late forties his career presents the paradox of definitive achievement and increasing adventurousness, a strong combination. The private and public life, love and waste, these are the antimonies that engage Kinsella's intensely serious gaze.

– John Montague

KIRKUP, James (Falconer). British. Born in South Shields, Durham, 23 April 1923. Educated at South Shields High School; Durham University, B.A. 1941. Gregory Fellow in Poetry, Leeds University, 1950–52; Visiting Poet and Head of the Department of English, Bath Academy of Art, Corsham, Wiltshire, 1953–56; Travelling Lecturer, Swedish Ministry of Education, Stockholm, 1956–57; Professor of English, University of Salamanca, Spain, 1957–58, and Tohoku University, Sendai, Japan, 1959–61; Lecturer in English Literature, University of Malaya, Kuala Lumpur, 1961–62; Professor of English Literature, Nagoya University, Japan, 1969–72. Since 1963, Professor of English Literature, Japan's Woman's University, Tokyo; since 1968, Professor of English Literature and Poet-in-Residence, Amherst College, Massachusetts. Literary Editor, *Orient/West Magazine*, Tokyo, 1963–64; Founder, *Poetry Nippon*, Nagoya, 1966. Recipient: Atlantic-Rockefeller Award, 1950; Japan P.E.N. Club International Literary prize, 1965. Fellow, Royal Society of Literature, 1962. Address: BM-Box 2870, London WC1V 6XX, England.

PUBLICATIONS

Verse

Indications, with John Ormond and John Bayliss. London, Grey Walls Press, 1942.
The Cosmic Shape: An Interpretation of Myth and Legend with Three Poems and Lyrics, with Ross Nichols. London, Forge Press, 1946.
The Drowned Sailor and Other Poems. London, Grey Walls Press, 1947.
The Submerged Village and Other Poems. London, Oxford University Press, 1951.
The Creation. Hull, Lotus Press, 1951.
A Correct Compassion and Other Poems. London, Oxford University Press, 1952.
The Spring Journey and Other Poems of 1952–1953. London, Oxford University Press, 1954.
The Descent into the Cave and Other Poems. London, Oxford University Press, 1957.
The Prodigal Son: Poems 1956–1959. London, Oxford University Press, 1959.
The Refusal to Conform: Last and First Poems. London, Oxford University Press, 1963.
Japan Marine. Tokyo, Japan P.E.N. Club, 1965.
Paper Windows: Poems from Japan. London, Dent, 1968.
Japan Physical: A Selection, with Japanese Translations by Fumiko Miura. Tokyo, Kenkyusha, 1969.
White Shadows, Black Shadows: Poems of Peace and War. London, Dent, 1970.

The Body Servant: Poems of Exile.   London, Dent, 1971.
Broad Daylight.   Frensham, Surrey, Sceptre Press, 1971.
A Bewick Bestiary.   Ashington, Northumberland, MidNAG, 1971.
Transmental Vibrations.   London, Covent Garden Press, 1971.

Plays

Upon This Rock: A Dramatic Chronicle of Peterborough Cathedral (produced
   Peterborough, 1955).   London, Oxford University Press, 1955.
Masque: The Triumph of Harmony (produced London, 1955).
The True Mistery of the Nativity (televised, 1960).   London and New York,
   Oxford University Press, 1956.
The Meteor, adaptation of a play by Friedrich Dürrenmatt (produced London,
   1956).   London, Cape, 1973; New York, Grove Press, 1974.
*The True Mistery of the Passion: Adapted and Translated from the French Medieval
   Mystery Cycle of Arnoul and Simon Grélan* (televised, 1960; produced Bristol,
   1960).   London and New York, Oxford University Press, 1962.
The Physicists, adaptation of a play by Friedrich Dürrenmatt (produced London,
   1963; New York, 1964).   London, French, and New York, Grove Press,
   1964.
The Magic Drum (produced Newcastle upon Tyne, 1972).   New York, Knopf,
   1972.
Brand, adaptation of the play by Ibsen, in *The Oxford Ibsen*, volume 3, edited
   by James Walter MacFarlane.   London, Oxford University Press, 1972.

Television Plays: *The Peach Garden*, 1954; *Two Pigeons Flying High*, 1955; *The
True Mistery of the Passion*, 1960; *The True Mistery of the Nativity*, 1960.

Novel

The Love of Others.   London, Collins, 1962.

Other

The Only Child: An Autobiography of Infancy.   London, Collins, 1957.
Sorrows, Passions, and Alarms: An Autobiography of Childhood.   London, Col-
   lins, 1959.
These Horned Islands: A Journal of Japan.   London, Collins, and New York,
   Macmillan, 1962.
Tropic Temper: A Memoir of Malaya.   London, Collins, 1962.
England, Now.   Tokyo, Seibido, 1964.
Japan Industrial: Some Impressions of Japanese Industries.   Osaka, PEP Publica-
   tions, 2 vols, 1964, 1965.
Japan Now.   Tokyo, Seibido, 1966.
Frankly Speaking.   Tokyo, Eichosha, 1966.
Tokyo.   London, Phoenix House, and South Brunswick, New Jersey, A. S.
   Barnes, 1966.
Filipinescas: Travels Through the Philippine Islands.   London, Phoenix House,
   1968.
Bangkok.   London, Phoenix House, and South Brunswick, New Jersey, A. S.
   Barnes, 1968.
One Man's Russia.   London, Phoenix House, 1968.

Aspects of the Short Story: Six Modern Short Stories with Commentary. Tokyo, Kaibunsha, 1969.
Streets of Asia London, Dent, 1969.
Hong Kong and Macao. London, Dent, and South Brunswick, New Jersey, A. S. Barnes, 1970.
Japan Behind the Fan. London, Dent, 1970.
Insect Summer (juvenile). New York, Knopf, 1971.
Heaven, Hell, and Hari-Kari. London, Angus and Robertson, 1974.

Editor, *Shepherding Winds: An Anthology of Poetry from East and West.* London, Blackie, 1969.
Editor, *Songs and Dreams: An Anthology of Poetry from East and West.* London, Blackie, 1970.

Translator, with Julian Shaw, *The History and Practice of Magic,* by Paul Christian. London, Forge Press, 1952.
Translator, with Leopold Sirombo, *The Vision and Other Poems,* by Todja Tartschoff. London, Newman and Harris, 1953.
Translator, *The Dark Child,* by Camara Laye. New York, Noonday Press, 1954; London, Collins, 1955; as *The African Child,* Collins, 1959.
Translator, *Ancestral Voices,* by Doan-Vinh-Thal. London, Collins, 1956.
Translator, *The Radiance of the King,* by Camara Laye. London, Collins, 1956.
Translator, *The Girl from Nowhere,* by H. T. von Gebhardt. London, University of London Press, 1958, New York, Criterion Books, 1959.
Translator, *The Evil Eye,* by P. Boileau and T. Narcejac. London, Hutchinson, 1959.
Translator, *Memoirs of a Dutiful Daughter,* by Simone de Beauvoir. Cleveland, World, and London, Weidenfeld and Nicolson-Deutsch, 1959.
Translator, *Don Carlo,* by Schiller, and *The Prince of Homburg* by Heinrich von Kleist, in *Classic Theatre,* volume 2, edited by Eric Bentley. New York, Doubleday, 1959.
Translator, *Don Tirburcio's Secret,* by Jeanne Loisy. London, University of London Press, 1959; New York, Pantheon, 1960.
Translator, *A Summer Gone,* by Heinrich E. Klier. London, Bles, 1959.
Translator, *The Captive,* by Ernst von Salomon. London, Weidenfeld and Nicolson, 1961.
Translator, *It Began in Babel: The Story of the Birth and Development of Races and Peoples,* by Herbert Wendt. London, Weidenfeld and Nicolson, 1961; Boston, Houghton Mifflin, 1962.
Translator, *Dangerous Spring,* by Margaret Benary-Isbert. London, Macmillan, 1961.
Translator, *The Other One,* by Simone Martin-Chauffier. London, University of London Press, 1961.
Translator, *The Gates of Paradise,* by Jerzy Andrzejewski. London, Weidenfeld and Nicolson, 1962.
Translator, *Trouble in Brusada,* by Fritz Brunner. London, University of London Press, 1962.
Translator, *Fast as the Wind,* by Gine V. Leclercq. London, University of London Press, 1962.
Translator, *Nuno,* by L. N. LaVolle. London, University of London Press, 1962.
Translator, *The Sins of the Father,* by Christian Geissler. London, Weidenfeld and Nicolson, 1962.
Translator, *My Friend Carlo,* by Gine V. Leclercq. London, University of London, Press, 1963.

Translator, with Oliver Rice and Abdullah Majid, *Modern Malay Verse.* London, Oxford University Press, 1963.

Translator, *Daily Life of the Etruscans,* by Jacques Heurgon. New York, Macmillan, 1964.

Translator, *The Heavenly Mandate,* by Erwin Wickert. London, Collins, 1964.

Translator, *My Great-Grandfather and I,* by James Kruess. London, University of London Press, 1964.

Translator, *Daily Life in the French Revolution,* by Jean Robiquet. London, Weidenfeld and Nicolson, 1964; New York, Macmillan, 1965.

Translator, *Immensee,* by Theodor Storm. London, Blackie, 1965.

Translator, *Tales of Hoffman.* London, Blackie, 1966.

Translator, *The Little Man,* by Erich Kastner. London, Cape, 1966.

Translator, *Michael Kohlhaas: From an Old Chronicle.* London, Blackie, 1967.

Translator, *A Dream of Africa,* by Camara Laye. London, Collins, 1968.

Translator, *The Eternal Virgin,* by Paul Valéry. Orient Editions, 1970.

James Kirkup comments:

Characterized by a very wide variety of themes and verse forms, including many oriental subjects and techniques. Most deeply influenced by Japanese and Chinese poetry, as well as by French. No English or American influences. Major themes: the sea, loneliness, music, painting, photography, sport, travel, the Orient, peace and war, science and space exploration, UFO's, legend, people, psychical research, medicine, satire, social criticism.

In my poetry I have attempted always to express an essence both of myself and of experience, a crystallization of my personal awareness of this world and worlds beyond. I feel I am slowly developing, after nearly thirty years of writing poetry, a voice that is only my own, and illuminating areas of experience and technique untouched by other poets. I am original, so I do not strive for originality for its own sake, or experiment with form unless the subject demands it. My aim is to be perfectly lucid yet to provide my candour with serious and mysterious undertones of sound and meaning.

*   *   *

The blurb on the dust wrapper of James Kirkup's collection *The Body Servant* includes this statement by the American poet and novelist, James Dickey: "With Kirkup's work I don't feel that facility is the problem, as it is with many writers." The long list of published work both in collections and numerous periodicals underlines this, though it could be that facility itself presents its own problems. Certainly Kirkup sometimes gives the impression of being able to knock off a passable poem at the drop of a hat. Subject matter is never lacking: his dustbin, photographs in a railway compartment, the New Year, a pet cat, have all suggested poems as Royal occasions have prompted such bits of unofficial laureateship as a Chant Royal on the Queen's Coronation or a Ceremonial Ode on her birthday. The very lists of acknowledgements in his earlier collections read like a roll call of past magazines: *Poetry London, Mandrake, The Wind and the Rain,* and *Nine,* among others.

Kirkup's first collection, *The Drowned Sailor,* was published in 1947 and was very much a collection of its time in its style and language. A determined poeticism may be the best way of describing it with its peppering of enormous abstractions such as "memory's mountain" or "the candelabra of the soul." The other poets of the time (vide Wrey Gardiner's *Poetry Quarterly*) were full of such stuff as if there was an urgency to plump out otherwise flat poems, a sort of poetic padded bra'; but Kirkup was too adept at this for his own good. It was in Kirkup's second collection, *The Submerged Village,* that something distinctive was to be observed. There were still oddly old-fashioned pieces ("The Ship," "Music at Night" and "Poem for a New Year") which read like those poems the leisured gentlemen of previous centuries were so adept at "turning" as they would put it – competent, agreeable but strangely impersonal. But amongst these were poems such as the title poem itself, "The Submerged Village," where it was as if the poet had taken a cool hard look at his subject and determined to deny himself the indulgence of his particular facility:

> Calm, the surrounding mountains look upon
> the steeple's golden cross, that still
> emerges from the centre of the rising lake.
> Like a sinking raft's bare mast and spar
> anchored to earth by chains of stone.

The facility is still there, of course; but used to the purpose of the poem and not as a merely decorative addition.

This progress towards an individual voice and style was to flower in the next collection, *A Correct Compassion,* in which the title poem can stand with the finest poems written since the war. Here, in a poem written after watching the performance of an operation at the General Infirmary, Leeds, Kirkup combines keenly observed detail –

> The glistening theatre swarms with eyes, and hands, and eyes.
> On green-clothed tables, ranks of instruments transmit
>   a sterile gleam.
> The masks are on, and no unnecessary smile betrays
> A certain tension, true concomitant of calm.

– while using the whole as a prolonged and deftly handled metaphor:

> – For this is imagination's other place,
> Where only necessary things are done, with the supreme the grave
> Dexterity that ignores technique; with proper grace
> Informing a correct compassion, that performs its love,
>   and makes it live.

It is as if from the controlled skill of the surgeon Kirkup has, as the poem makes clear, not only learnt something concerning the nature of art, but has found a parallel for his own technique. Anthoer poem in this collection, "Matthew Smith," begins:

> Yours, brother, is a masculine art,
> The business of doing what you see.

And in a sense with *A Correct Compassion* Kirkup's, too, becomes a masculine art to be followed up in the collection *A Spring Journey.*

It is true that the old temptations remain and "Rhapsody on a Bead Curtain" sees the facility at work wringing out to the last drop the metaphor of a bead curtain as a shower. But firmness prevails almost to the point of harshness in "Medusa":

> those frog-like legs
> Seem barely able to support
> That sad, amorphous bum

where Kirkup is in danger of overbalancing the other way. Poems such as "The Ventriloquist," "A Visit to Brontë Land," "Photographs in a Railway Compartment" and "Summertime in Leeds" reassure us, however, that Kirkup has found his true voice:

> No idle toy would have tempted Branwell
> From the "Bull," and brandy; or kept that sister
> From her tragic poems. They knew they had nothing but the moor
> And themselves. It is we, who want all, who are poor.

and that he will stick to it, though tempted, like Branwell, by the "bull" as he sometimes is.

Since *A Spring Journey* James Kirkup has published numerous collections. Some have been serious volumes, some rather more playful like *The Body Servant* with its journey over the body's parts and old chestnuts such as the part without a bone. But if, as it should be, a poet is to be remembered by his best work then a "selected poems" for Kirkup is long overdue, if only as a show case for some of the more pleasing poems to have been written in the past decades.

– John Cotton

KIZER, Carolyn. American. Born in Spokane, Washington, in 1925. Educated at Sarah Lawrence College, Bronxville, New York. Formerly, teacher, translator, and State Department Poet-in-Residence, Pakistan. Currently, Director of the National Endowment for the Arts Literary Program. Since 1959, Founding Editor, with David Wagoner, *Poetry Northwest,* Seattle. Address: 510 East Franklin Street, Chapel Hill, North Carolina 27514, U.S.A.

PUBLICATIONS

Verse

The Ungrateful Garden. Bloomington, Indiana University Press, 1961.
Five Poets of the Pacific Northwest, with others, edited by Robin Skelton. Seattle, University of Washington Press, 1964.
Knock upon Silence. New York, Doubleday, 1965.
Midnight Was My Cry: New and Selected Poems. New York, Doubleday, 1971.

*   *   *

Carolyn Kizer works in terms of the twinned tensions of life, those central paradoxes so directly felt by women. She poses the problem of the woman poet boldly in her remarkable "A Muse of Water":

> We who must act as handmaidens
> To our own goddess, turn too fast,
> Trip on our hems, to glimpse the muse
> Gliding below her lake or sea,
> Are left, long-staring after her
> Narcissists by necessity . . .

Mother and Muse, she can write tenderly of her own mother, who taught her to love nature even at its most loathsome, "a whole, wild, lost, betrayed and secret life / Among its dens and burrows." And though she has a poem on "Not Writing Poetry about Children" they are everywhere in her work. So are cats, symbols of the female condition, as in "A Widow in Wintertime,"

> trying
> To live well enough alone, and not to dream
> Of grappling in the snow, claws plunged in fur,
>
> Or waken in a caterwaul of dying.

The daring and diffidence of womanhood are celebrated in poems of companionship, like "For Jan, In Bar Maria." But her most constant, resonant theme is love and loss, analysed in detail in the sequence "A Month in Summer." This ends with a quotation from Basho and it is in the fatalism of that ancient civilisation that Carolyn Kizer finds a refuge and an artistic remedy for her womanly woes:

> "O love long gone, it is raining in our room."
> So I memorize these lines,
>   without salutation, without close.

She must be one of the best woman poets around, profoundly committed to the process of life, however painful.

– John Montague

KNIGHT, Etheridge. American. Born in Corinth, Mississippi, 19 April 1931. Educated in public schools. Served in the Korean War. Married Sonia Sanchez, *q.v.* (divorced); Mary McAnally in 1970; has two children. Poet-in-Residence, University of Pittsburgh, 1968, Hartford University, West Hartford, Connecticut, 1970, and Lincoln University, Jefferson City, Missouri, 1970–71. Poetry Editor, *Motive*, Nashville, Tennessee, 1970–71; Co-Editor, *Black Box*, Washington, D.C., 1971–72. Recipient: National Endowment for the Arts grant, 1972; Guggenheim Fellowship, 1974. Address: c/o Broadside Press, 12651 Old Mill Place, Detroit, Michigan 48238, U.S.A.

PUBLICATIONS

Verse

Poems from Prison.   Detroit, Broadside Press, 1968.
The Idea of Ancestry.   Rome, 1968.
2 Poems for Black Relocation Centers.   Detroit, Broadside Press, 1968.
For Black Poets Who Think of Suicide.   Detroit, Broadside Press, 1972.
A Poem for Brother Man.   Detroit, Broadside Press, 1972.
Belly Song and Other Poems.   Detroit, Broadside Press, 1973.

Recordings: *Poems from Prison* (tape), Broadside; *Tough Poems for Tough People*, Caedmon.

Other

Editor, *Voce negre dal carcere.*   Rome, Laterza, 1968; as *Black Voices from Prison*, New York, Pathfinder Press, 1970.

*   *   *

In 1960, Etheridge Knight was sentenced to serve twenty years in Indiana State Prison. He was to say later: "I died in 1960 from a prison sentence and poetry brought me back to life." His collection *Poems from Prison* was published during this time and shortly thereafter he was released from prison on parole. Even though he has not been as prolific as some other Black poets, Knight has proven to be an especially significant voice of the sixties and seventies. His poetry is an explication in verse of a Malcolm X theme defining a new frame of reference to the prison experience for poor Blacks and Whites.

Knight spells out a direct relationship between "men behind prison walls and men behind the myriad walls that permeate [the American] society." His philosophy captures the themes of Malcolm X when he states that "crime, criminality, and alienation can be understood as being the by-product of a society/culture whose technology has far outstripped its humanism." In this respect, prison is viewed as "the ultimate oppression" of Black people in the larger prison outside. That philosophy is summed up simply and effectively in his "The Warden Said to Me the Other Day":

> The warden said to me the other day
> (innocently, I think), "Say, etheridge,
> why come the black boys don't run off
> like the white boys do?"
> I lowered my jaw and scratched my head
> and said (innocently, I think), "Well, suh,
> I ain't for sure, but I reckon its cause
> we ain't got no wheres to run to."

Knight's style is particularly suited to his ends. His poems are almost rigidly patterned (among his offerings is a brief series of Haiku poems), meticulously structured, tough in terminology, yet they never seem forced or restrained or without eloquence. He is sometimes as disarmingly simple as Langston Hughes; he is capable of shifting with piston smoothness from the concrete to the abstract:

This year there is a gray stone wall damming my stream,
   and when
the falling leaves stir my genes, I pace my cell or flop
   on my bunk
and stare at 47 black faces across the space. I am all of them,
they are all of me, I am me, they are thee, and I have no sons
to float in the space between.

– Charles L. James

KNOEPFLE, John. American. Born in Cincinnati, Ohio, 4 February 1923. Educated at Xavier University, Cincinnati, Ph.B. 1949, M.A. 1951; St. Louis University, Ph.D. 1967. Served in the United States Navy, 1942–46: Purple Heart. Married Margaret Sower in 1956; has one daughter and three sons. Producer-Director, WCET Educational Television, Cincinnati, 1953–55; Assistant Instructor, Ohio State University, Columbus, 1956–57; Instructor, Southern Illinois University, East St. Louis, 1957–61, St. Louis University High School, 1961–62, and Mark Twain Institute, Clayton, Missouri, Summers 1962–64; Assistant Professor, Maryville College, St. Louis, 1962–66, and Washington University College, St. Louis, 1963–66; Associate Professor, St. Louis University, 1966–72; Consultant, Project Upward Bound, Washington, D.C., 1967–70. Since 1972, Professor of Literature, Sangamon State University, Springfield, Illinois. Recipient: Rockefeller Fellowship, 1967. Address: 1008 West Adams, Auburn, Illinois 62615, U.S.A.

PUBLICATIONS

Verse

Poets at the Gate, with others. St. Louis, Arts Festival of Washington University, 1965.
Rivers into Islands: A Book of Poems. Chicago, University of Chicago Press, 1965.
Songs for Gail Guidry's Guitar. New York, New Rivers Press, 1969.
An Affair of Culture and Other Poems. La Crosse, Wisconsin, Northeast-Juniper Books, 1969.
After Gray Days and Other Poems. Prairie Village, Kansas, Crabgrass Press, 1970.
The Intricate Land: A Book of Poems. New York, New Rivers Press, 1970.
The Ten-Fifteen Community Poems. Poquoson, Virginia, Back Door Press, 1971.
Whetstone: A Book of Poems. Shawnee Mission, Kansas, BkMk Press, 1972.
Deep Winter Poems. Lincoln, Nebraska, Three Sheets, 1972.

Other

> *Voyages to the Inland Sea: Essays and Poems*, with Lisel Mueller and David
> Etter.   La Crosse, Wisconsin Center for Contemporary Poetry, 1971.
> *Dogs and Cats and Things Like That: A Book of Poems for Children.*   New York,
> McGraw Hill, 1971.
> *Our Street Feels Good: A Book of Poems for Children.*   New York, McGraw
> Hill, 1972.
> *Regional Perspectives: An Examination of America's Literary Heritage*, with oth-
> ers, edited by John Gordon Burke.   Chicago, American Library Association,
> 1973.

> Translator, with Robert Bly and James Wright, *Twenty Poems of César
> Vallejo.*   Madison, Minnesota, Sixties Press, 1962.
> Translator, with Robert Bly and James Wright, *Neruda and Vallejo: Selected
> Poems.*   Boston, Beacon Press, 1971.

Critical Studies: "Masks of Self-Deception" by Lloyd Goldman, and "The Reflective Art of John Knoepfle" by Raymond Benoit, in *Minnesota Review 8* (St. Paul),
1968.

John Knoepfle comments:

(1970) I consider myself a poet of the American Middle West, but aware of the
same cosmic problems that beset everyone anywhere.
Poems written since the publication of *Rivers into Islands* are less nostalgic. They
show bias toward events – often surrealistic ones – that occur in such moments
when public and private experience overlaps. The poetry does not attempt to
analyze the content of these two kinds of experience so much as it tries to
reproduce the dynamics of their encounter. This has not been particularly intentional on my part; it is simply the way the poems have been moving, perhaps in an
effort to get away from a propagandist/fatalist dilemma which seems at the moment
largely irrelevant. The past in these poems and the midcontinent as place are there,
then, not so much as subject matter outside of the poet as they are a part of a
community of experience which I feel deeply involved in.
(1974) I am more and more concerned with the nature of a voice that is adequate
that can articulate the overlapping of public and private experience, some voice
that is neither totally egocentric nor totally masked speech: how to capture such a
voice.

                    *   *   *

John Knoepfle's poetry moves between farcical humor and a serious search for
spiritual illumination. A desire for communion with God informs much of the work
in *Deep Winter Poems* and *The Ten-Fifteen Community Poems*, two recent pamphlets,
but this is also underscored, especially in the latter pamphlet, by desire for communion between people. In numerous poems, religious ritual, particularly that of
Catholicism, plays its part, and sometimes, as in an hilarious poem in *An Affair of*

Culture ("Tunnel Blaster on Bear and Brotherhood"), the farcical and religious strains blend into a ludicrous parody of the mass:

> he thought hed hunt bear with his brother
> but the bear ate his brother
> and he shot the bear
> he came back in here on the monday
> with a bearmeat sandwich
> wanted me to eat half of it
> see how a bearmeat sandwich tasted
> I told him Im damned the day
> I ate any mans brother
> but he said there wasnt nothing to it
> the bear didnt have time to digest his brother

This sort of outrageous humor takes risks, and Knoepfle, as in this poem, frequently succeeds; he has a good feeling for colloquial speech, and a good sense of his Midwestern locales. He is less successful when he tries for the spareness and starkness of Creeley, in poems like "At Forty," and flatly expresses his spiritual needs:

> god look down
> on me look
> down on me
> look at my
> face and tell
> me something

Many of Knoepfle's poem are concerned with death, whether actual, as in the first poem quoted, or impending, as in the second poem. In his major collection, *Rivers into Islands,* "Evening Departure" pictures the deceased as leaving on a train waving goodbye; another, "Night of Stars and Flowers," apparently again pictures death, but merely as an electing to be somewhere else. "The White Mule" is about a ghostly mule abandoned down in the mines who feeds on lost men. Poems like these, and many of the others about trains and rivers and other Midwestern scenes, are very evocative. Knoepfle has a real talent for the short poem, a talent that is particularly apparent where the rivers of verse in the first two parts of *Rivers into Islands* break up into the islands of short poems in the last part. His short poems seem even shorter in the collections since this one, terser, more compressed, with a greater sense of pressure pushing at their seams. His humor and colloquial grace remain strong assets.

– Duane Ackerson

KNOTT, Bill (William Kilborn Knott).   American.   Born in Gratiot County, Michigan, 17 February 1940. Educated at Carson City High School, Michigan. Served as a Private in the United States Army. Recipient: National Endowment for the Arts grant, 1968. Address: c/o Big Table Books, Follett Publishing Company, 1010 West Washington Boulevard, Chicago, Illinois 60607, U.S.A.

PUBLICATIONS

Verse

The Naomi Poems, Book One: Corpse and Beans. Chicago, Follett, 1968.
Aurealism: A Study: A Poem. Syracuse, New York, Salt Mound Press, 1970.
Are You Ready Mary Baker Eddy?, with James Tate. San Francisco, Cloud
    Marauder Press, 1970.
Auto-Necrophilia: The Bill Knott Poems, Book 2. Chicago, Follett, 1971.
Nights of Naomi. Somerville, Massachusetts, Barn Dream Press, 1971.

Bill Knott comments:

I identify with the "Aurealist" School, or the group known as "Posthumous
Poets."
Influences: Yvette Mimieux movies. John Logan's ideas and personal example of
dedication.
Major theme is avoidance of major themes. Characteristic subjects are my death
in 1966 and subsequent posthumous existence, and my virginity.
My usual verse form is iambic prose poems.

                                *   *   *

The poems of Bill Knott, who is St. Geraud (1940–1966), are often very brief,
deeply psychological lyrics, and he is a master of this form. "Hair Poem," two
lines long, is characteristic:

> Hair is heaven's water flowing eerily over us
> Often a woman drifts off down her long hair and is lost

The sensuality of Knott's work imbues it with value beyond that of the Freudian
level where most "Confessional" poets take their steambaths. Knott shares with
his reader the possibility of an organic unity, a world where hair and heaven's
water are the same elusive obtainables: his "death" may well suggest the view that
life and death, equally permeated by identical organic elements, are also the same.
   Knott's enormous success with the "deep image" arises from his stance. He
seems to live in a world where heaven's water is commonplace, and hair is not. His
surrealism arises from what seems to be a surreal existence where the tables and
perceptions are turned completely; metaphor, therefore, is reversed, and the world
is seen through a crystal lens:

> If bombing children is preserving peace, then
> my fucking you is a war-crime.
>   – from "Nuremburg, USA"

At times the image is tied to nothing but itself and its effect relies simply on the
suggested idea, as in "Cueballs have invented insomnia in an attempt to forget
eyelids," from *Nights of Naomi,* a 32-page sequence where the surrealist jars the
reader over and over: accept the metaphorical condition or don't bother to read any
further. The poem begins, "Prefontal lightningbolt too lazy to chew the sphinx's
loudest eyelash. . . . Only a maze can remember your hair of buttered blowguns."

847

It makes for thick reading, and the reader must indeed accomodate Knott's unusual stance in a world where "They squeezed your blood back into grapes." The reward is a trip through unvisited rooms of experience, with one of the finest poetic imaginations in print, "Years spent wandering in front of a stab."

– Geof Hewitt

KOCH, Kenneth. American. Born in Cincinnati, Ohio, 27 February 1925. Educated at Harvard University, Cambridge, Massachusetts, A.B. 1948; Columbia University, New York, M.A. 1953, Ph.D. 1959. Served in the United States Army, 1943–46. Married Mary Janice Elwood in 1955; has one daughter. Lecturer in English, Rutgers University, New Brunswick, New Jersey, 1953–54, 1955–56, 1957–58, and Brooklyn College, 1957–59; Director of the Poetry Workshop, New School for Social Research, New York, 1958–66. Since 1959, Member of the English Department, and since 1970, Professor of English, Columbia University. Associated with the magazine *Locus Solus*, 1960–62. Recipient: Fulbright Fellowship, 1950; Guggenheim Fellowship, 1961; National Endowment for the Arts grant, 1966; Ingram Merrill Foundation Fellowship, 1969; Harbison Award, for teaching, 1970; Frank O'Hara Prize (*Poetry*, Chicago), 1973. Address: Department of English, Columbia University, New York, New York 10027, U.S.A.

PUBLICATIONS

Verse

> *Poems.* New York, Tibor de Nagy Gallery, 1953.
> *Ko; or, A Season on Earth.* New York, Grove Press, 1960.
> *Permanently.* New York, Tiber Press, 1960.
> *Thank You and Other Poems.* New York, Grove Press, 1962.
> *Poems from 1952 and 1953.* Los Angeles, Black Sparrow Press, 1968.
> *When the Sun Tries to Go On.* Los Angeles, Black Sparrow Press, 1969.
> *Sleeping with Women.* Los Angeles, Black Sparrow Press, 1969.
> *The Pleasures of Peace and Other Poems.* New York, Grove Press, 1969.
> *Penguin Modern Poets 24*, with Kenward Elmslie and James Schuyler. London, Penguin, 1973.

Plays

> *Bertha* (produced New York, 1959). Included in *Bertha and Other Plays*, 1966.
> *The Election* (also director: produced New York, 1960). Included in *A Change of Hearts*, 1973.
> *Pericles* (produced New York, 1960). Included in *Bertha and Other Plays*, 1966.
> *George Washington Crossing the Delaware* (produced New York, 1962). Included in *Bertha and Other Plays*, 1966.

The Construction of Boston (produced New York, 1962).   Included in *Bertha and Other Plays*, 1966.

Guinevere; or, The Death of the Kangaroo (produced New York, 1964).   Included in *Bertha and Other Plays*, 1966.

The Tinguely Machine Mystery; or, The Love Suicides at Kaluka (also co-director: produced New York, 1965).   Included in *A Change of Hearts*, 1973.

Bertha and Other Plays (includes *Pericles, George Washington Crossing the Delaware, The Construction of Boston, Guinevere; or, The Death of the Kangaroo, The Gold Standard, The Return of Yellowmay, The Revolt of the Giant Animals, The Building of Florence, Angelica, The Merry Stones, The Academic Murders, Easter, The Lost Feed, Mexico, Coil Supreme*).   New York, Grove Press, 1966.

The Scotty Dog (produced New York, 1967).   Included in *A Change of Hearts*, 1973.

The Apple (produced Philadelphia, 1968).   Included in *A Change of Hearts*, 1973.

The Moon Balloon (produced New York, 1969).   Included in *A Change of Hearts*, 1973.

The Artist, music by Paul Reif, adaptation of the poem "The Artist" by Kenneth Koch (produced New York, 1972).   Poem included in *Thank You and Other Poems*, 1962.

A Little Light (produced Amagansett, New York, 1972).

A Change of Hearts: Plays, Films, and Other Dramatic Works 1951–1971 (includes the contents of *Bertha and Other Plays*, and *E. Kology; The Moon Balloon; Without Kinship; Ten Films: Because, The Color Game, Mountains and Electricity, Sheep Harbor, Oval Gold, Moby Dick, L'Ecole Normale, The Cemetery, The Scotty Dog*, and *The Apple; Youth*; and *The Enchantment*).   New York, Random House, 1973.

Other

Wishes, Lies and Dreams: Teaching Children to Write Poetry.   New York, Random House, 1970.

Rose, Where Did You Get That Red? Teaching Great Poetry to Children.   New York, Random House, 1973.

Editor, with David Shapiro, *Learn Something America.*   Bedford, Massachusetts, Bedford Museum, 1968.

Theatrical Activities:

Director: **Plays** – *The Election*, New York, 1960; *The Tinguely Machine Mystery* (co-director, with Remy Charlip), New York, 1965.

*   *   *

Kenneth Koch was one of the three principal poets of the "New York school" in the middle and late 1950's, a somewhat amorphous and short-lived group which also included John Ashbery and Frank O'Hara. The three had joined forces while students at Harvard before transferring their activities to New York, where they became associated with the painters who were then ascendant in the American art world, a group known as "abstract expressionists." To a certain extent the poets seemed to be bringing to verbal constructs the principles of abstract expressionism, i.e., they used words totally abstractly and evocatively. At the same time their prosodic practice was in revolt against the academic austerity of mid-century American poetry, and their use of syntax and measure resembled that of the contemporaneous Beat movement. What distinguished the two groups, if anything, was the New York poets' retention of an earlier idea of art as in some sense a puristic activity, not socially amenable, and of the art object as distinct from and perhaps superior to the objects of "ordinary reality." In addition Koch was, during a period of residence abroad, deeply influenced by current French poetry with its emphasis on psychological particularism.

These groupings and distinctions have long since broken down, of course. Koch's association with New York poetry was, in effect, his apprenticeship. Much of his early work was very far out indeed; some was frankly incomprehensible, even to the poet. Since then Koch has elevated his lyric view to another level, not in the least "realistic" but better organized and more simplified than his earlier view, with the result that some of his recent work has been extremely effective. The freedom of his earlier verbal technique has given him a felicity which occasionally still descends to surrealistic glibness but which at its best is remarkably inventive and accurate. At the same time, substantially fixed in his poems is a depth of metaphysical concern that gives them the drive and intensity of genuinely serious experiments.

One distinction of the New York poets was their devotion to the lyric theater. Their connection with "off-Broadway" and "off-off-Broadway" gave them opportunities for experiments with dramatic writing that were open to few poets elsewhere in the country, and some of Koch's best writing occurs in the several books of plays he has published, books which have been generally neglected, however, by American poetry-readers and critics.

– Hayden Carruth

KOLLER, James. American. Born in Oak Park, Illinois, in 1936. Has two daughters and one son. Since 1964, Editor, *Coyote Journal* and Coyote Books, San Francisco, then New Mexico and Maine. Recipient: National Endowment for the Arts grant, 1968, 1973. Address: P.O. Box 629, Brunswick, Maine 04011, U.S.A.

PUBLICATIONS

Verse

Two Hands: Poems 1959–1961. Seattle, James B. Smith, 1965.
Brainard and Washington Street Poems. Eugene, Oregon, Toad Press, 1965.
Some Cows: Poems of Civilization and Domestic Life. San Francisco, Coyote Books, 1966.

The Dogs and Other Dark Woods. San Francisco, Four Seasons Foundation, 1966.
I Went to See My True Love. Buffalo, Audit East/West, 1967.
California Poems. Los Angeles, Black Sparrow Press, 1971.
Messages. Canton, New York, Institute of Further Studies, 1972.
Dark Woman, Who Lay with the Sun. San Francisco, Tenth Muse, 1972.
The Tracks Run Together. Santa Fe, New Mexico, Fourwing Press, 1974.

Manuscript Collections: University of Connecticut, Storrs; Simon Fraser University, Burnaby, British Columbia.

Critical Studies: "Eyes and 'I' " by Richard Duerden, in *Poetry* (Chicago), May 1966; "James Koller Issue" of *Savage 2* (Chicago), 1972.

*   *   *

James Koller is an earthy poet; perhaps even "raunchy" would not be the wrong adjective to put to his work, which seeks out communion with nature and sex at a visceral level. Though his work calls to mind, with its spontaneous, collage-like technique, the Beat or Black Mountain poets, he is less cerebral, or mystical, in approach than a poet like Olson or Ginsberg; his poetry is direct, sensual, wrenched still steaming from the innards of the other life he encounters – when he speaks of stepping inside a bear's body, the intentions are by no means as metaphysical as in the poems of identification with animal life of, for instance, Kinnell or Dickey.

He is interested in the retreat to a more primitive relationship with nature, with ecstasy and the dangerous, slippery terrain around madness. He takes the sort of risks that can result in bad taste, but also in sudden gains, as in "I Get Crazy in the Full Moon" from *California Poems*:

> I crawled over the dark ground
> planting squash, an owl
> over my shoulder, the moon
>
> she throws back her head, stretches
> her arms hands, ripple of muscle
> skin, the moon
>
> clouds, shadows
> between us
> the ground mostly lighted
>
> the flower first, fruit
> full & rounded
> the softest curve, ripple, moon
>
> the laughter very soft

– Duane Ackerson

KOPS, Bernard. British. Born in London, 28 November 1926. Educated in London elementary schools to age 13. Married Erica Gordon in 1956; has four children. Has worked as a docker, chef, salesman, waiter, lift man, and barrow boy. Recipient: Arts Council bursary, 1957. Agent: David Higham Associates, 5–8 Lower John Street, London W.1. Address: Flat 1, 35 Canfield Gardens, London N.W.6, England.

PUBLICATIONS

Verse

> *Poems.* London, Bell and Baker Press, 1955.
> *Poems and Songs.* Lowestoft, Suffolk, Scorpion Press, 1958.
> *An Anemone for Antigone.* Lowestoft, Suffolk, Scorpion Press, 1959.
> *Erica, I Want to Read You Something.* Lowestoft, Suffolk, Scorpion Press, and New York, Walker, 1967.
> *For the Record.* London, Secker and Warburg, 1971.

Plays

> *The Hamlet of Stepney Green* (produced Oxford, 1957; London and New York, 1958). London, Evans, 1959.
> *Goodbye World* (produced Guildford, Surrey, 1959).
> *Change for the Angel* (produced London, 1960).
> *The Dream of Peter Mann* (produced Edinburgh, 1960). London, Penguin, 1960.
> *Enter Solly Gold*, music by Stanley Myers (produced Wellingborough, Northamptonshire, and Los Angeles, 1962; London, 1970). Published in *Satan, Socialites, and Solly Gold: Three New Plays from England*, New York, Coward McCann, 1961; in *Four Plays*, 1964.
> *Home Sweet Honeycomb* (broadcast, 1962). Included in *Four Plays*, 1964.
> *The Lemmings* (broadcast, 1963). Included in *Four Plays*, 1964.
> *Stray Cats and Empty Bottles* (televised, 1964; produced London, 1967).
> *Four Plays* (includes *The Hamlet of Stepney Green, Enter Solly Gold, Home Sweet Honeycomb, The Lemmings*). London, MacGibbon and Kee, 1964.
> *The Boy Who Wouldn't Play Jesus* (juvenile; produced London, 1965). Published in *Eight Plays: Book 1*, edited by Malcolm Stuart Fellows, London, Cassell, 1965.
> *David, It Is Getting Dark* (produced Rennes, France, 1970). Paris, Gallimard, 1970.

> Radio Plays: *Home Sweet Honeycomb*, 1963; *The Lemmings*, 1963; *Born in Israel*, 1963; *The Dark Ages*, 1964; *Israel: The Immigrant*, 1964.

> Television Plays: *I Want to Go Home*, 1963; *Stray Cats and Empty Bottles*, 1964; *The Lost Years of Brian Hooper*, 1967; *Alexander the Greatest*, 1971; *Just One Kid*, 1974.

Novels

> *Awake for Mourning.* London, MacGibbon and Kee, 1958.
> *Motorbike.* London, New English Library, 1962.

Yes from No-Man's Land. London, MacGibbon and Kee, 1965; New York, Coward McCann, 1966.

The Dissent of Dominick Shapiro. London, MacGibbon and Kee, 1966; New York, Coward McCann, 1967.

By the Waters of Whitechapel. London, Bodley Head, 1969; New York, Norton, 1970.

The Passionate Past of Gloria Gaye. London, Secker and Warburg, 1971; New York, Norton, 1972.

Settle Down Simon Katz. London, Secker and Warburg, 1973.

Partners. London, Secker and Warburg, 1975.

Other

The World Is a Wedding (autobiography). London, MacGibbon and Kee, 1963; New York, Coward McCann, 1964.

Critical Studies: "Bernard Kops" by Colin MacInnes, in *Encounter* (London), May 1960; "The Kitchen Sink" by G. Wilson Knight, in *Encounter* (London), December 1963; Deep Waters of Whitechapel" by Nina Sutton, in *The Guardian* (London), 6 September 1969.

Bernard Kops comments:

Kops creates specific relationships in order that they might relate universally. He writes compulsively, for himself, and even if his work is acceptable to others, this is a secondary process. Nevertheless, he is pleased that he can sell his work and be able to live by writing. Kops is obsessed by family themes; this runs throughout his work. The relationships are of people bound up together in an intense emotional and intellectual involvement. He believes that the great themes of Shakespeare, Racine, Sophocles, O'Neill have lasted and will last because they deal with themes common to every human being. *King Lear* and its dream and despair lives for us because it lives through us – it is US. We give it life and constantly renew it. Kops is also obsessed with death but only because he is obsessed with life. He believes motives are impossible to ultimately define, but actions are not subjective and one must judge a man by his actions. He likes ambiguity. But he also believes in strict discipline, and thinks that the writer must know exactly what he is doing even if he has shown the subjectivity and complexity of human relationships. He writes constantly about the backgrounds and the people and things he knows, or thinks he knows. The only things that he is really certain about are: the existence of love, the need for it and that "they" no longer exist. There are only US left on this earth. Kops writes about this.

*   *   *

Bernard Kops's reputation stands on his plays and novels, yet these very substantial writings can be said to arise from the wellsprings of a talent and an approach to literature which is entirely that of a poet.

And, further, it is that of a special sort of poet – the sort contained in the familiar quotation about "the poet's eye in a fine frenzy rolling." Kops's poems usually exhibit a tendency to the frenetic – a free-wheeling fantasy, an extravagence of language and gesture, an explosive celebration of the things that he loves or that excite him, and an apocalyptic rejection of things that he hates or that appall him. He draws a great deal of his poetry from his fervent Jewishness – but not merely in the form of his sense of racial difference, or his horror at the Nazi holocaust. Many of his most successful poems grow out of his family's presence in the foreground of his experience, from which he can create universalised images for what he sees as the sad, proud, lonely, laughable continuity of human life. "Somewhere upon these impossible stairs," he wrote in a poem entitled "Prayer at Forty," "we are attempting love."

Though his poetic output has never been large, his assertion in it of the need to go on "attempting love" has been unflagging – and has figured equally large throughout his considerable oeuvre of plays, novels and that splendid poet's autobiography, *The World Is a Wedding*. That determined assertion has been his poetry's source of power, and its most lasting quality.

– Douglas Hill

KÖRTE, Mary Norbert. American. Recipient: National Endowment for the Arts grant, 1969. Address: 7034 Mesa Drive, Aptos, California 95003, U.S.A.

PUBLICATIONS

Verse

Hymn to the Gentle Sun. Berkeley, California, Oyez, 1967.
Beginning of Lines: Response to "Albion Moonlight." Berkeley, California, Oyez, 1968.
The Generation of Love. New York, Bruce Publications, 1969.
My Day Was Beautiful, How Was Yours? The Going (two poems). Berkeley, California, Oyez-White Rabbit, 1969.
A Breviary in Time of War. San Francisco, Cranium Press, 1970.
The Midnight Bridge. Berkeley, California, Oyez, 1970.

*   *   *

"Is she a mother or a sister?" asked Jenny, our oldest daughter, then six years old.

Sister Mary Norbert Körte had just left our San Francisco flat with three of her teenage students from Saint Rose Academy, a private girls' college-preparatory school where she taught English, Latin, music and religion, and conducted a poetry workshop. All of us had talked animatedly about poetry, music, politics, and drank Chinese tea and ate marvelous chocolatechip cookies Sister and the girls had baked for the occasion. The Sister wore a snow-white habit whose cowl framed her well-scrubbed bright face. An open face radiating humor, vitality and intelligence.

If we'd been drinking sherry and had it been late at night I might have converted right then and there.

My three daughters had never seen a nun in their livingroom before and would peer in until they were spotted and run back to their rooms where God only knows what odd information was passed around.

"Does she fly?" asked Maggie, four years old, already familiar with TV lore.

"Who's her husband?" asked Amanda, two years old, clear about the order of things, the structure of families.

"She's a poet," I told them because that's a word and presence all of us were familiar with in our household.

Before she left the Dominican Order in 1968 it would have been easy enough to relegate her poems to that convenient category, Devotional Poetry, and allow her work to remain un-read alongside works of other so-called "devotional poets" of that period: Brother Antoninus, Thomas Merton, Father Daniel Berrigan – poets deeply committed to poetry as an extension of the spiritual life and who, like Sister Mary Norbert Körte, were active in presence and voice to the anti-war movement.

"Devotional Poetry" is a term too often used to exile readers from the poem. Discerning poetry readers know that a poem and the act of writing a poem are devotions. The inward process of bringing a poem to the page is in many ways no different than a meditation or prayer. The emptying of shells, the self opening itself into its most vulnerable points, all come into play during moments of creation. A poem is testimony to the poet's devotions. Its existence on the page or in the air affirms the proposition in *Deuteronomy* [30:19]: "I call heaven and earth to witness against you this day, that I have set before thee life and death, the blessing and the curse; therefore choose life, that thou mayest live, thou and thy seed. . . ."

A poet in his work transcends the institutions of the soul. A poem is always one to One. Mary's work from the beginning (*Hymn to the Gentle Sun*) has eluded movements or categories, yet speaks directly to paradoxes that surround the human condition. Almost bereft of self-consciousness, the poems are always about self-process, a continuous event and not static as icons. Sacred or secular, the most useful poetry speaks clearly and is able to translate top-heavy directives and metaphors into lucid realities. Mary Norbert Körte's work is aware of this value and is open and deeply honest.

– David Meltzer

KOSTELANETZ, Richard. American. Born in New York City, 14 May 1940. Educated at Brown University, Providence, Rhode Island, A.B. 1962; Columbia University, New York, M.A. 1966; King's College, London (Fulbright Fellowship, 1964–65). Married Anne Louise Tidaback in 1962 (divorced, 1965). Since 1965, Free-lance Writer. Visual Poetry exhibited at the Stedelijk Museum, Amsterdam, and tour, 1970–71; New York University, 1970; Bear Lane Gallery, Oxford, 1970; Bookshop Gallery, Sunderland, 1970; Indiana University, Bloomington, 1970; Galerie Im Hof, Giessen, Germany, 1971; Galleria U., Montevideo, 1972; El Centro de Arte y Communicacion, Buenos Aires, 1972; Virginia Commonwealth University, Richmond, 1973. Contributing Editor, *Arts in Society*, *The Humanist*, and *Lotta Poetica*. Recipient: Pulitzer Fellowship, 1965; Guggenheim Fellowship, 1967. Address: 38th Floor, 80 Pine Street, New York, New York 10005, U.S.A.

PUBLICATIONS

Verse

Visual Language.   New York, Assembling Press, 1970.
I Articulations, bound with *Short Fictions.*   New York, Kulchur Foundation, 1974.

Novel

In the Beginning.   Somerville, Massachusetts, Abyss, 1971.

Short Stories

Accounting.   Brescia, Italy, Amodulo, 1972; Sacramento, California, Poetry Newsletter, 1973.
Ad Infinitum.   Freidrichsfehn, Germany, International Artists' Cooperation, 1973.
Short Fictions, bound with *I Articulations.*   New York, Kulchur Foundation, 1974.

Other

The Theatre of Mixed-Means: An Introduction to Happenings, Kinetic Environments, and Other Mixed-Means Performances.   New York, Dial Press, 1968.
Master Minds: Portraits of Contemporary American Artists and Intellectuals.   New York, Macmillan, 1969.
The End of Intelligent Writing: Literary Politics in America.   New York, Sheed and Ward, 1974.
Recyclings: Volume One, 1959–67 (autobiography).   New York, Assembling Press, 1974.

Editor, *On Contemporary Literature: An Anthology of Critical Essays on Major Movements and Writers of Contemporary Literature.*   New York, Avon, 1964; revised edition, 1969.
Editor, *The New American Arts.*   New York, Horizon Press, 1965.
Editor, *Twelve from the Sixties.*   New York, Dell, 1967.
Editor, *The Young American Writers: Fiction, Poetry, Drama, and Criticism.*   New York, Funk and Wagnalls, 1967.
Editor, *Beyond Left and Right: Radical Thought for Our Time.*   New York, Morrow, 1968.
Editor, *Imaged Words and Worded Images.*   New York, Outerbridge and Dienstfrey, 1970.
Editor, *Possibilities of Poetry: An Anthology of American Contemporaries.*   New York, Dell, 1970.
Editor, *John Cage.*   New York, Praeger, 1970; London, Allen Lane, 1971.
Editor, *Moholy-Nagy.*   New York, Praeger, 1970; London, Allen Lane, 1974.
Editor, *Assembling, Second Assembling, Third Assembling,* and *Fourth Assembling.*   New York, Assembling Press, 4 vols., 1970–73.
Editor, *Future's Fictions.*   New York, Panache, 1971.
Editor, *Human Alternatives: Visions for Us Now.*   New York, Morrow, 1971.

Editor, *Social Speculations: Visions for Us Now.* New York, Morrow, 1971.
Editor, *In Youth.* New York, Ballantine, 1972.
Editor, *Seeing Through Shuck.* New York, Ballantine, 1972.
Editor, *Breakthrough Fictioneers: An Anthology.* New York, Something Else Press, 1973.
Editor, *The Edge of Adaptation: Man and the Emerging Society.* New York, Prentice Hall, 1973.
Editor, *Essaying Essays.* New York, Oolp, 1974.

Critical Studies: *Once Again,* edited by Jean-François Bory, New York, New Directions, 1968; "Poetry and Space" by Carolo Alberto Sitta, in *The Gazette* (Modena, Italy), 4 November 1970; "Figured Verse and Calligrams" by Massin, in *Letter and Image,* Paris, Gallimard, and New York, Van Nostrand, 1970; *Text-Bilder/Visuelle Poesie International,* edited by Klaus Peter Dencker, Cologne, DuMont Schauberg, 1972.

Richard Kostelanetz quotes from "After Sentences" to *I Articulations,* 1974:

In visual poetry, unlike other kinds, the way that words are placed on the page is the primary means of enhancing language; pictorial shaping makes words poetic by generating semantic and symbolic connotations that would not otherwise be present. Conversely, language in visual poetry would have considerably different meanings if presented in uniform, horizontal type; for one thing, it would lack the poetic dimensions that the pictorial increment provides. Visual poetry is not synonymous with "concrete," although all anthologies with "concrete" in the title included some visual work. The principal characteristic of "concrete" appears to be the counter-syntactical use of language; and although most pictorial poetry likewise eschews conventional linguistic syntax, that is not its primary particularity. "Visual poetry" is a genre, or a species of *poetic* literature, as distinct from fictional literature or expository writing. The epithet is useful as a critical-historical classification that, like a genus-term in biology, tells us not only what the work at hand is, but also what it isn't.

Visual poetry is an intermedium between poetry and design. One man's visual poetry is another man's "design" and a third man's "Art." The form of word-image art provided me, as a professional essayist, with a sure means of avoiding the conventions of expository writing, for I assumed from the beginning that a writer's poetry should evolve from processes different from, if not contrary to, prose. Certain things can be articulated in visual poetry that cannot be said in prose, and vice versa.

Visual poetry depends not only upon design but upon language, revealing, intrinsically, why one word was chosen, rather than another; it exploits the advantages of non-verbal communication without relinquishing language. A pictorial poem creates a field of visual-verbal communication; and though both the visual and the verbal dimensions are perceived simultaneously, their relationship is usually comprehended progressively. Some pictorial poets try, often with the help of professional collaborators, to realize the precision of commercial design; but since my own works belong to poetry, rather than design, some of them reveal, perhaps too conspicuously, the presence of the poet's own hand. My aims include not only the communication of information but the making of a visual-verbal field that makes an impression comparable to the "after-image" of painting. The designer Jan Tschichold once said that "typography is the arranging of words to be read," implying that words were servants of an ulterior message; in pictorial poetry, words stand mostly as an end in themselves. What distinguishes my own pictorial poems from those of others has been, I think, the complete avoidance so far of any visual materials other than letters.

*   *   *

The appropriate descriptive term for Richard Kostelanetz's creative work is "visual poetry," indicating a specialized genre within poetry, or an intermedium between poetry and painting. His visual poems are non-linear and non-syntactic, in contrast to those "shape poems" whose ancestry is traceable back through Apollinaire and George Herbert to the illuminated manuscript and Chinese ideogram. They are consciously counter-conventional poems, reflecting a comprehensive knowledge of contemporary literary practice and deliberate avoidance of it, although they employ such specifically literary devices as punning, wit, allusion, alliteration, parallelism and contrast. Constructivism and minimalism in the visual art tradition have also influenced Kostelanetz. His early poems in *Visual Language*, written around 1967, are usually mimetic, often employing only one letter or word, and often erotic in content. In his second collection, *I Articulations*, he creates more complex structures involving synonyms, multiple repetitions and more philosophical concerns, frequently about the nature of language itself.

His style is immediately recognizable, not only because he has published more visual poetry than any other American practitioner, but because of his distinctive technical means – a common letter-stencil and shamelessly amateur calligraphy which represent calculated avoidance of the polished finish of commercial design. Another recognizable aspect of his style is the strict limitation he places on himself. In these volumes he uses no visual material other than letters in non-syntactic formations. This methodology mirrors his aesthetic conviction that a radical formal constraint is essential to true creativity.

DISINTEGRATION
DISINTEGRATION
DISINTEGRATION
DISINTEGRATION

© 1968, 1970 by Richard Kostelanetz

From this style and its ramifications, he has moved into fiction – "sequential forms that still eschew the prosaic form of expository sentences" – and his most recent poems and fictions consist entirely of numbers, thus emphasizing that formal pattern and relationship, rather than semantic content or extrinsic reference, is at the center of his art.

Although traditionalists may object to such expansion of the genre, Kostelanetz's work continually challenges more moderate notions of "new directions" in poetry. It incorporates the values which have governed his work as a critic, anthologist and proponent of the avant-garde movement in America. Visual enhancement of language, he says, is not an exclusive successor to the past, but "one propitious future for literature."

– Jane Augustine

KUMIN, Maxine. American. Born in Philadelphia, Pennsylvania, 6 June 1925. Educated at Radcliffe College, Cambridge, Massachusetts, A.B. 1946, M.A. 1948. Married Victor M. Kumin in 1946; has three children. Instructor, 1958–61, and Lecturer in English, 1965–68, Tufts University, Medford, Massachusetts; Consultant, Central Atlantic Regional Educational Laboratory, 1967–69, and Board of Coordinated Educational Services, Nassau County, New York, 1967–72. Since 1971, Lecturer in English, Newton College of the Sacred Heart, Massachusetts; since 1972, Visiting Lecturer in English, University of Massachusetts, Amherst. Scholar, 1961–63, and since 1972, Officer, The Society of Fellows, Radcliffe Institute, Cambridge, Massachusetts. Recipient: Lowell Mason Palmer Award, 1960; National Endowment for the Arts grant, 1966; William Marion Reedy Award, 1968; Eunice Tietjens Memorial Prize, (*Poetry*, Chicago), 1972; Pulitzer Prize, 1973. Address: 40 Bradford Road, Newton Highlands, Massachusetts 02161, U.S.A.

PUBLICATIONS

Verse

Halfway. New York, Holt Rinehart, 1961.
The Privilege. New York, Harper, 1965.
The Nightmare Factory. New York, Harper, 1970.
Up Country. New York, Harper, 1972.

Novels

Through Dooms of Love. New York, Harper, 1965; as *A Daughter and Her Loves*, London, Gollancz, 1965.
The Passions of Uxport. New York, Harper, 1968.
The Abduction. New York, Harper, 1971.
The Designated Heir. New York, Viking Press, 1974.

Other

Sebastian and the Dragon (juvenile). New York, Putnam, 1960.
Spring Things (juvenile). New York, Putnam,1961.
Summer Story (juvenile). New York, Putnam, 1961.
Follow the Fall (juvenile). New York, Putnam, 1961.
A Winter Friend (juvenile). New York, Putnam, 1961.
Mittens in May (juvenile). New York, Putnam, 1962.
No One Writes a Letter to the Snail (juvenile). New York, Putnam, 1962.
Archibald the Traveling Poodle (juvenile). New York, Putnam, 1963.
Eggs of Things (juvenile), with Anne Sexton. New York, Putnam, 1963.
More Eggs of Things (juvenile), with Anne Sexton. New York, Putnam, 1964.
Speedy Digs Downside Up (juvenile). New York, Putnam, 1964.
The Beach Before Breakfast (juvenile). New York, Putnam, 1964.
Paul Bunyan (juvenile). New York, Putnam, 1966.
Faraway Farm (juvenile). New York, Norton, 1967.
The Wonderful Babies of 1809 and Other Years (juvenile). New York, Putnam, 1968.
When Grandmother Was Young (juvenile). New York, Putnam, 1969.
When Mother Was Young (juvenile). New York, Putnam, 1970.
When Great Grandmother Was Young (juvenile). New York, Putnam, 1971.
Joey and the Birthday Present (juvenile), with Anne Sexton. New York, McGraw Hill, 1971.

*   *   *

One hears echoes in the poems of Maxine Kumin of poets slightly older and better known than herself – poets as diverse as John Logan and Robert Lowell (in "Pasture Poems" and "Country House"), or Anne Sexton and Adrienne Rich (in "The Masochist" and "For My Great Grandfather: A Message Long Overdue"). One can say this without implying that Kumin is in any way inferior to these writers or even imitative of their work. She is a master, in her own way, of several diverse styles, competent always in conveying the special nature of an event and skillful in her manner of saying it.

In "For My Son on the Highways of His Mind," for example, a mother expresses concern for her son, as he hitchhikes across the country, in a language and rhythm made popular by folk singers of the 1970's. Between verses of narrative, in which she describes his adventures – some real, some imagined – the speaker repeats the following refrain:

> Dreaming you travel light
> Guitar pick and guitar
> Your bedroll sausage-tight
> They take you as you are

For all its diversity, however, the poetry of Maxine Kumin is often the poetry of a special world, unmistakably upper middle-class, comfortable, urbane, safe in its place at the center of things and fully alive to the pleasures of Boston city life and New Hampshire farm country. Perhaps for this reason, "The Nightmare Factory" the title for her third book of poems, appears almost pretentious, as if affluence made self-pity a full-time occupation. To an admiring reader, her talent appears to lend itself more naturally to less sensational topics: as in "to a blind friend teaching me braille," or in "halfway" and "on being asked to write a poem for the centenary of the civil war" – both of which draw upon her Jewish background and her early life in Germantown, Pennsylvania. Though that too is a special world few people share, she gives it authority and dominance by an unusual combination of sophisticated thought and a simple style.

Maxine Kumin once said that Marianne Moore's statement, "We must be as clear as our natural reticence allows us to be," marked her for life. "I have tried always to do this, both in diction and in intent to the point of pain." Such precision of language and strength of purpose give Kumin's poetry a place among the best American writing in recent years. As winner of the Pulitzer Prize, for *Up Country* (1972), she will undoubtedly find that larger, more appreciative audience that, as a master craftsman, she deserves.

– Michael True

KUNITZ, Stanley (Jasspon). American. Born in Worcester, Massachusetts, 29 July 1905. Educated at Harvard University, Cambridge, Massachusetts (Garrison Medal, 1926), A.B. (summa cum laude) 1926 (Phi Beta Kappa), A.M. 1927. Served in the United States Army, 1943–45. Married Helen Pearce in 1930 (divorced, 1937), has one daughter; Eleanor Evans in 1939 (divorced, 1958); Elise Asher in 1958. Editor, *Wilson Library Bulletin*, New York, 1928–43. Member of the Faculty, Bennington College, Vermont, 1946–49; Professor of English, State University of New York, Potsdam, 1949–50, and Summers, 1949–53; Lecturer, New School for Social Research, New York, 1950–57; Visiting Professor, University of Washington, Seattle, 1955–56, Queens College, Flushing, New York, 1956–57, Brandeis University, Waltham, Massachusetts, 1958–59, and Yale University, New Haven, Connecticut, 1970. Director, YM–YWHA Poetry Workshop, New York, 1958–62. Danforth Visiting Lecturer, United States, 1961–63. Lecturer, 1963–67, and since 1967, Adjunct Professor of Writing, Columbia University, New York. Since 1968, Chairman, Writing Department, Fine Arts Work Center, Provincetown, Massachusetts. Since 1969, Editor, Yale Series of Younger Poets, Yale University Press, New Haven, Connecticut. Since 1974, Consultant in Poetry, Library of Congress, Washington, D.C. Formerly, Cultural Exchange Lecturer, U.S.S.R. and Poland. Fellow, Yale University, 1969. Recipient: Oscar Blumenthal Prize, 1941, and Levinson Prize, 1956 (*Poetry*, Chicago); Guggenheim Fellowship, 1945; Amy Lowell Traveling Fellowship, 1953; Harriet Monroe Award, 1958; Pulitzer Prize, 1959; Ford grant, 1959; National Institute of Arts and Letters grant, 1959; Brandeis University Creative Arts Award, 1964; Academy of American Poets Fellowship, 1968. Litt.D.; Clark University, Worcester, Massachusetts, 1961. Member, National Institute of Arts and Letters. Chancellor, Academy of American Poets, 1970. Address: 157 West 12th Street, New York, New York 10011, U.S.A.

PUBLICATIONS

Verse

Intellectual Things. New York, Doubleday, 1930.
Passport to the War: A Selection of Poems. New York, Holt Rinehart, 1944.
Selected Poems 1928–1958. Boston, Little Brown, 1958; London, Dent, 1959.

The Testing-Tree: Poems.   Boston, Little Brown, 1971.
The Terrible Threshold: Selected Poems, 1940–1970.   London, Secker and Warburg, 1974.

Other

Editor (as Dilly Tante), *Living Authors: A Book of Biographies.*   New York,
   Wilson, 1931.
Editor, with Howard Haycraft and Wilbur C. Hadden, *Authors Today and
   Yesterday: A Companion Volume to "Living Authors."*   New York, Wilson, 1933.
Editor, with others, *The Junior Book of Authors.*   New York, Wilson, 1934;
   revised edition, 1961.
Editor, with Howard Haycraft, *British Authors of the Nineteenth Century.*   New
   York, Wilson, 1936.
Editor, with Howard Haycraft, *American Authors, 1600–1900: A Biographical
   Dictionary of American Literature.*   New York, Wilson, 1938.
Editor, with Howard Haycraft, *Twentieth Century Authors: A Biographical
   Dictionary of Modern Literature.*   New York, Wilson, 1942; *First Supplement,*
   with Vineta Colby, 1955.
Editor, with Howard Haycraft, *British Authors Before 1800: A Biographical
   Dictionary.*   New York, Wilson, 1952.
Editor, *Poems,* by John Keats.   New York, Crowell, 1964.
Editor, with Vineta Colby, *European Authors, 1000–1900: A Biographical
   Dictionary of European Literature.*   New York, Wilson, 1967.
Editor and Translator, with Max Hayward, *Poems of Akhmatova.*   Boston,
   Little Brown, 1973; London, Harvill Press, 1974.

Translator, with others, *Antiworlds,* by Andrei Voznesensky.   New York,
   Basic Books, 1966; London, Oxford University Press, 1967.
Translator, with others, *Antiworlds and the Fifth Ace,* by Andrei Voznesen-
   sky.   New York, Doubleday, 1967.
Translator, with others, *Stolen Apples,* by Yevgeny Yevtushenko.   New York,
   Doubleday, 1972.
Translator, with others, *Story under Full Sail,* by Andrei Voznesensky.   New
   York, Doubleday, 1974.

Critical Studies: *The Contemporary Poet as Artist and Critic,* edited by Anthony
Ostroff, Boston, Little Brown, 1964; "The Poetry of Stanley Kunitz" by James
Hagstrum, in *Poets in Progress,* edited by Edward Hungerford, Evanston, Illinois,
Northwestern University Press, 1967; "Man with a Leaf in His Head" by Stanley
Moss, in *The Nation* (New York), 20 September 1971; "Voznesensky and Kunitz on
Poetry," in *The New York Times Book Review,* 16 April 1972.

Stanley Kunitz comments:

   Since my *Selected Poems* I have been moving toward a more open style, based on
natural speech rhythms. *The Testing-Tree* (1971) embodied my search for a transparency of language and vision. Maybe age itself compels me to embrace the great
simplicities, as I struggle to free myself from the knots and complications, the
hang-ups, of my youth. I keep trying to improve my controls over language, so that
I won't have to tell lies. And I keep reading the masters, because they infect me

with human possibility. I am no more reconciled than I ever was to the world's wrongs and the injustice of time. The poetry I admire most is innocent, luminous, and true.

*   *   *

One of the truly powerful and skilled poets of our time, Stanley Kunitz has been writing for four decades and has still – in spite of a Pulitzer Prize in 1959 which brought some public acclaim – to receive the wide recognition among readers he so obviously deserves. Some of this neglect may perhaps be accounted for by Kunitz's slow and careful production, which has resulted in only four collections of his work, and by the severe, exacting standards he applies to himself. This poet has, moreover, avoided all the changes of literary fad and fashion, preferring to labor in the main tradition of the lyric poem that includes Yeats and the Metaphysicals.

Many of Kunitz's earlier poems explore the vast, uncharted reaches of the inner world, the territories of the self. In such poems as "Geometry of Moods" and "Science of the Night," the inward self assumes the mysterious proportions of a cosmos of infinite spaces; other pieces, "Approach of Autumn," "Postscript," "End of Summer," and "Green Ways," for example, use imagery of earth, season, vegetation, to reflect the speaker's condition. The concluding stanza of "Green Ways" discloses Kunitz's forceful manner which always presses against imposed formal restraints and also reveals the constant struggle in his writing to preserve and identify the human element in life:

> Let me proclaim it – human be my lot! –
> How from the pit of green horse-bones
> I turn, in a wilderness of sweat,
> To the moon-breasted sybilline,
> And lift this garland, Danger, from her throat
> To blaze it in the foundries of the night.

The self is everywhere threatened in Kunitz's poetry, finding no solace in theological convictions and little to cling to in the turmoil of the present age: "I suffer the twentieth century," he writes in "Night Letter"; "the nerves of commerce wither in my arm." But the self, under attack, never collapses, refuses to be annihilated; instead, its integrity and toughness increase; it takes for weapons of resistance love between individuals and the act of writing which impose "form and value," to borrow R. P. Blackmur's terms, on the disorder and chaos of experience. So it is that intelligence and emotion contend for the upper hand in his poems, thus creating a stunning, terrible dramatic tension. This tension remains as well in the magnificent poems of parable and nightmare such as "Father and Son," "The Surgeons," and "Open the Gates," where apocalyptic terror, enigma, and nihilistic forces are endured to come at last into profound human realizations. To whatever theme Kunitz turns his masterful imagination and superior craftsmanship, the emergent poem is of the highest quality. His newest poems in *The Testing-Tree* carry even further the strength and excellence of his previous work, and the recent volume of his translations of the Russian poet Anna Akhmatova demonstrate a new, compelling virtuosity in his writing.

– Ralph J. Mills, Jr.

KYGER, Joanne. American. Born 19 November 1934. Educated at Santa Barbara College, California. Married to John Boyce. Lived in Japan, 1960–64. Performer and Poet in experimental television project, 1967–68. Recipient: National
Endowment for the Arts grant, 1968. Lives in California.

PUBLICATIONS

Verse

The Tapestry and the Web. San Francisco, Four Seasons Foundation, 1965.
The Fool in April: A Poem. San Francisco, Coyote Books, 1966.
Places To Go. Los Angeles, Black Sparrow Press, 1970.
Joanne. New York, Angel Hair Books, 1970.
Desecheo Notebook. Berkeley, California, Arif Press, 1971.
Trip Out and Fall Back. Berkeley, California, Arif Press, 1974.

Joanne Kyger comments:

I myself am a West Coast poet, but I also feel an affinity for much of the work
of the younger New York poets.

My vision of the poet changes so I can stay alive and the muse can stay alive. I
report on my states of consciousness and the story I am telling.

*   *   *

In a sequence entitled "Imaginary Apparitions," Joanne Kyger writes, "But this
is clearly an enactment / Cut through / I can see all this / and part of an idea." This
troublesome space in which sight is in the process of forming itself into thought is
the location of her vision. She seems well aware, in fact, that the Greek root of
"idea" is "*idein*" (to see), and her work is an investigation of a consciousness in
which the modern distinction does not apply. In "Descartes and the Splendor Of,"
she turns to at least the most visible source of this distinction, accepts his methodology and in part his language in order to re-discover what Charles Olson calls
"the *primitive* abstract." "As I move thru language," she writes, "and transfer the
delicacy of vision into the moving and written word, so all thought not transferred
on that level is lost and degenerated." To Kyger, this consciousness which produces private dreams and public mythologies is a matter of fact, even a domestic
place: "I wish to allow great unimpeded / Grandeur like a rising storm / to take
over / and do the dishwashing." The vision is never allowed to float away into
obscurity or mystery.

The voice in Kyger's poems is at times almost frantic, at times ironic, at times
simply and beautifully lyrical. In the control of a fine intelligence and an ear
precisely attuned to the rhythms of speech, it is also a voice which is capable of
drawing a sense of brutal reality ("like a dark red bruise, the house") and zany
fantasy ("the Great Pigs waddle off in the sky") into a seamless poetic world.

– Don Byrd

LAL, P. Indian. Born in Kapurthala, Punjab, 28 August 1929. Educated at St. Xavier's School, Calcutta, B.A. 1950; Calcutta University, M.A. in English literature 1952. Married Shyamasree Devi in 1955; has one son and one daughter. Professor of English, St. Xavier's College, Calcutta, 1952–67; now Honorary Professor. Since 1967, Professor of English, University of Calcutta. Visiting Professor, Hofstra University, Hempstead, New York, 1962–63, and University of Illinois, Urbana, 1968; Prentiss M. Brown Visiting Professor, Albion College, Michigan, Spring 1973; Robert L. Morton Visiting Professor, Ohio University, Athens, 1973–74. Founder and Secretary, Writers Workshop, publishers, and Editor, *Writers Workshop Miscellany*, Calcutta; Editor, with Alfred Schenkman, *Orient Review and Literary Digest*, 1954–58. Delegate, P.E.N. Conference, New York, 1966. Recipient: Jawaharlal Nehru Fellowship, 1969. Awarded the Padmashri title by the Goverment of India, 1970. Address: 162/92 Lake Gardens, Calcutta 45, India.

PUBLICATIONS

Verse

The Parrot's Death and Other Poems. Calcutta, Writers Workshop, 1960.
Love's the First: Poems. Calcutta, Writers Workshop, 1962.
"Change!" They Said: New Poems. Calcutta, Writers Workshop, 1966.
Draupadi and Jayadratha and Other Poems. Calcutta, Writers Workshop, 1967.
Yakshi from Didarganj: Poems. Calcutta, Writers Workshop, 1969.
Creations and Transcreations: Three Poems, Selections from the Subhasita-Ratna-Kosa, and The First 92 Slokas from the Mahabharata. Calcutta, Dialogue Publications, 1968.
The Man of Dharma and the Rasa of Silence. Calcutta, Writers Workshop, 1974.

Other

The Art of the Essay. Delhi, Atma Ram, 1951.
An Annotated Mahabharata Bibliography. Calcutta, Writers Workshop, 1967.
The Concept of an Indian Literature: Six Essays. Calcutta, Writers Workshop, 1968.
Transcreation: Two Essays. Calcutta, Writers Workshop, 1971.
The Lemon Tree of Modern Sex and Other Essays. Calcutta, Writers Workshop, 1973.

Editor, *The Merchant of Venice*, by William Shakespeare. Delhi, Atma Ram, 1952.
Editor, with K. R. Rao, *Modern Indo-Anglian Poetry.* New Delhi, Kavita, 1959.
Editor, *T. S. Eliot: Homage from India: A Commemoration Volume of 55 Essays and Elegies.* Calcutta, Writers Workshop, 1967.
Editor, *The First Workshop Story Anthology.* Calcutta, Writers Workshop, 1967.
Editor, *Modern Indian Poetry in English: The Writers Workshop Selection: An Anthology and a Credo.* Calcutta, Writers Workshop, 1969.
Editor, *Selected Poems: A Selection of Lyrics,* by Manmohan Ghose. Calcutta, Writers Workshop, 1969.
Editor, *The First Writers Workshop Literary Reader.* Calcutta, Writers Workshop, 1970.

Editor, *The Second Writers Workshop Literary Reader.* Calcutta, Writers Workshop, 1973.

Translator, *Premchand: His Life and Work,* by Hans Raj Rahbar. Delhi, Atma Ram, 1957.
Translator, with Jai Ratan, *Godan,* by Premchand. Bombay, Jaico Books, 1957.
Translator, *Great Sanskrit Plays in New English Transcreations.* New York, New Directions, 1964.
Transcreator, *Sanskrit Love Lyrics.* Calcutta, Writers Workshop, 1965.
Transcreator, *The Bhagavad-Gita.* Calcutta, Writers Workshop, 1965.
Translator, *The Golden Womb of the Sun.* Calcutta, Writers Workshop, 1965.
Transcreator, *The Dhammapada.* New York, Farrar Strauss, 1967.
Translator, *The Jap-Ji: Fourteen Religious Songs.* Calcutta, Writers Workshop, 1967.
Translator, *The Isa-Upanisad.* Calcutta, Writers Workshop, 1967.
Transcreator, *Some Sanskrit Poems.* Calcutta, Writers Workshop, 1967.
Transcreator, *The Farce of the Drunk Monk.* Calcutta, Writers Workshop, 1962.
Transcreator, *The Avyakta-Upanisad.* Calcutta, Writers Workshop, 1969.
Translator, *The Mahabharata.* Calcutta, Writers Workshop, 72 monthly vols., 1969–74.
Translator, *More Songs from the Jap-Ji.* Calcutta, Writers Workshop, 1969.
Transcreator, *Ghalib's Love Poems.* Calcutta, Dialogue Publications, 1970.
Translator, *The Mahanarayana Upanisad.* Calcutta, Writers Workshop, 1971.
Transcreator, with Shyamasree Devi, *Tagore's Last Poems.* Calcutta, Writers Workshop, 1972.
Transcreator, *The Brhadaranyaka Upanisad.* Calcutta, Writers Workshop, 1974.

Critical Studies: "P. Lal's Poetry" by Nita Pillai, in *Poetry India* (Bombay), i,3, 1965; *P. Lal: An Appreciation* by S. Mokashi-Punekar, Calcutta, Writers Workshop, 1968; "P. Lal: A Major Indo-English Poet" by Subhas C. Saha, in *The Banasthali Patrika* (Banasthali), January 1969; "The Poetry of P. Lal" by Suresh Kohli, in *Thought* (Delhi), xx,30, 1969.

*   *   *

P. Lal is a key figure in the landscape of Indo-English creative writing. He has played a multiple role with remarkable success. Poet, ideologist for Indo-English creativity, avant-garde publisher for markedly new writing, translator of classics, responsible orientalist, he has filled a varied bill, which, in return, has conditioned his own growth through sudden transitions and empirical intuitions. The movement he seemed to lead in the early post-Independence years rallied a good many competent rebels around him under the simple banner: Indians can create in English; but they must break with the past genre of the pompous and the amorphous! To that slogan no contenders are left, and the movement should have reached the more painful state of self-examination with the question: Is that enough? But Lal's pluralist approach has skilfully doctored the movement into a painless transition. In the process, not only Lal's organising ability but his poetic practice has played a role, not exactly by trend-setting but by ice-breaking. Lal's poetry cannot be isolated from the multiple role he has played; it forms a setting for his growth.

Lal's first four collections mark a development, in themes, in technique, even in objectives, though the corpus is too thin to reveal it fron book to later book. Since 1960, he has been bringing out collections at regular intervals; but before that is a fifteen-year stretch of apprenticeship. An early poem like "Beside the Pipal," recording a delicately veined Indian pastorale, is an index of some early ambition to poetise on national themes, abandoned under the compulsion of international norms, but restored to a later collection (*"Change!" They Said*) under a renewed sense of national commitment. An oddly rhetorical piece like "On Transience" in an early collection (*The Parrot's Death*) is the token of competent kitten play, too good to be thrown away but too out of character to fit into a stabler manner cultivated later:

> and when the winds howl, their raucous breath
> convulses the green continence of earth.

To make these rhetorical convulsions click is a sign of healthy apprenticeship and can prove a second string to the bow when social commitments demand a raucous breath, as in *"Change!" They Said*: Lal's most stable manner, however, was the green continence of earth.

A studied and taut delicacy which seldom lapses into aestheticism may well be the most fascinating undertone of Lal's verse. A painfully keen love of beauty in nature, in flowers, birds and trees, is ever rendered sturdy by a vigorous man-centredness. Lal's perceptions are delicate and firm; he sketches them in clean strokes:

> A mustard of butterflies
> Hovers round a lovely eye.

Not just a poetic image that, but a perception. Lal shows the same delicacy in love, a theme that dominates his second collection *Love's the First*. Fortunately for us, Lal is not ashamed of his cleverness and we get fine cavalier swashbuckling:

> Love, twin-fuselaged
> Sweeps serenely thus
> (Weather Report: Unfair)
> To passion's terminus.

Lal constantly returns to the manner of spare expression and self-control. And while he belongs to the avant-garde, he must have his roses, petals, leaves and bees to stand by him. Why? We get a clue in poems of another kind, what may be described as lyrics of human behaviour. Lal constantly returns to an adoration of civilized behaviour, a fine instance of which is "The Letter" – a poem written in a mood of agonized gratitude to a brother whose letter opens up old wounds again by its painful but civil talk. Lal's love for language is the greater for its being the index of a rooted civility which is its distinctive feature. The same quality illuminates his effort at self-control and often at self-accusation; and that returns us to Lal the organizer. The finest expression of this "culture" is seen in a really ripe poem like "The Leaf" (in *"Change!" They Said*) in which he accurately sums up the stages of his life:

> Cupped in decrepit easy chair
> Mellow gum in eyes.

Lal's care for words is not a part of his technique but a part of his vision of life – its beauty and tautness. Words, for Lal, are the indices of summations inherent in humanity's past experience, and Lal constantly tries to connect:

Here meaning is in fragrances
And life is the careful delivery of leaf.

Such attitudes cannot but compel Lal to seek roots in an Indian tradition; two trends are already significant – Lal's growing impatience with the rootless highbrow, and with the monstrous outgrowths of India's hurried social transformation which has inspired some raucous social satire of late; and a growing orientalism, primarily for translation, but inspiring poems like *Draupadi and Jayadratha,* which are revealing an altogether different Lal.

– Shankar Mokashi-Punekar

LAMANTIA, Philip. American. Born in San Francisco, California, 23 October 1927. Educated in San Francisco public schools. Assistant Editor, *View* magazine, New York, 1944. Address: c/o City Lights Books, 261 Columbus Avenue, San Francisco, California 94133, U.S.A.

PUBLICATIONS

Verse

Erotic Poems. Berkeley, California, Bern Porter, 1946.
Tower, with *Manifesto* by Max Finstein. San Francisco, Golden Mountain Press, 1958.
Ekstasis. San Francisco, Auerhahn Press, 1959.
Destroyed Works: Hypodermic Light, Mantic Notebook, Still Poems, Spansule. San Francisco, Auerhahn Press, 1962.
Touch of the Marvelous. Berkeley, California, Oyez, 1966.
Selected Poems, 1943–1966. San Francisco, City Lights Books, 1967.
Penguin Modern Poets 13, with Charles Bukowski and Harold Norse. London, Penguin, 1969.
The Blood of the Air. San Francisco, Four Seasons Foundation, 1970.

Other

I Demand Extinction of Laws Prohibiting Narcotic Drugs. San Francisco, Auerhahn Press, 1959.
Narcotica, with Antonin Artaud. San Francisco, Auerhahn Press, 1959.

Critical Study: Prefatory Note by Parker Tyler to *Touch of the Marvelous,* 1966.

Philip Lamantia comments:

I consider myself essentially a surrealist, but as Breton qualified this, it is *not* a "school," but a way of life.

868

I understand the act of poetry as the maximum volatile expression of Imagination, a *central power*, relating all levels of conscious and unconscious thought and being. I believe in poetry as a means of unqualified individual liberation. I believe in the poetry of primal melody and the revelation of the mysteries of cosmic being.

*   *   *

Although Philip Lamantia's life has been one of change and travel the poetry has continued its function as a tightly controlled inner ritual, and the poem has been continually characterized by a highly burnished surface that seems to gleam with such stillness that if the poem was turned from side to side light would glance off it. It was as a Surrealist that he was published, at the age of fifteen, by Charles Henri Ford and Parker Tyler in their magazine *View*. André Breton, then living in the United States, called him "a voice that rises once in a hundred years." The shifting of image, the layering of association that is characteristic of surrealism has continued in his work, and his language has the hardness of a glimpse through a prism:

> The mermaids have come to the desert
> They are setting up a boudoir next to the camel
> who lies at their feet of roses.

But with his first book, *Erotic Poems*, he felt that he had broken with the surrealists, and it was a lyric physicality that gave the book its dominant mood. Though there was still a complex surface imagery in the poems it was, as he had titled it, a collection of erotic poems. The language often had a closeness of physical contact that was almost like a breath:

> The crash of your heart
> beating its way through a fever of fish
> is heard in every crowd of that thirsty tomorrow
> and your trip ends in the mask of my candle-lit hair.

A consciousness of brutality has continued in his poetry, even though he is sometimes able to shake it off long enough to see it at a distance from himself. The poem sometimes becomes obsessive in its awareness of cruelty:

> Come my ritual wax and circles
> my rose spitting blood
> When the day is lit up by our magic candles
> and the hours yell their sadistic songs and suck hard
> into the night when the cats invade our skulls

A similar cruelty is apparent in this example of early work finally published in *Touch of the Marvelous*:

> The hanged girl in my mirror watches with horror
> as I exchange my eyes for yours
> But, too late
> I pull the gun's trigger
> and the mirror shatters

But his work shifted away from this obsessiveness, and he began to find another imagery in his experience, and he was able to write "From a window I see the world / As I would see love." It was after this affirmation that his wanderings began. Of the younger group of San Francisco poets, Lamantia was the first to begin experimenting with altered states of consciousness. He was initiated into the Washo Indian peyote rites in Nevada in 1953, and then spent three years in Mexico, living for some time with the Cora Indians of Nayarit. It was at the close of this period that he destroyed all of his earlier work, and it was not until the late 1950's that he began publishing again. The poems he had destroyed were eventually published in 1962. He spent much of the 1960's in Europe, continuing his search into the forces and the planes of the poem.

Lamantia's work, coming out of a forties dominated in the United States by Eliot and Frost, Stevens and Cummings, seemed to be an entirely new element, an entirely new structuring of the emotions of the poem. Despite the efforts of Ford and others there had not been any wide attention paid to the surrealists, and the first American writing in the idiom forced a belated recognition of the power of surrealist technique. This is not to say that Lamantia became a poet with any kind of popular following, but he was widely read by other poets. In any outline of the main currents of American poetry of the 1940's his name must be considered as one of the forces that led to the burst of surrealist poetry in the United States in the 1950's and 1960's.

– Samuel Charters

LANGLAND, Joseph (Thomas). American. Born in Spring Grove, Minnesota, 16 February 1917. Educated at Spring Grove High School; Santa Ana Junior College, California, A.A. 1936; University of Iowa, Iowa City, B.A. 1940, M.A. 1941, 1946–48. Served in the United States Army, 1942–46. Married the artist, Judith Gail Wood in 1943; has one daughter and two sons. School Teacher, Winneshiek County, Iowa, 1936–38; Instructor, Dana College, Blair, Nebraska, 1941–42; Assistant Professor, then Associate Professor, 1948–59, University of Wyoming, Laramie. Since 1959, Professor of English, University of Massachusetts, Amherst. Visiting Professor of Poetry, University of British Columbia, Vancouver, 1960, San Francisco State College, 1961, University of Washington, Seattle, 1964, and the University of Oregon, Eugene, 1968, 1969. Poetry Editor, *Massachusetts Review*, Amherst, 1960–66. Recipient: Ford Fellowship, 1953; Fund for the Advancement of Education in the Humanities grant, 1953; Amy Lowell Traveling Fellowship, 1955; Melville Cane Award, 1964; National Endowment for the Arts grant, 1966. D.Litt.: Luther College, Decorah, Iowa, 1974. Address: 16 Morgan Circle, Amherst, Massachusetts 01002, U.S.A.

PUBLICATIONS

Verse

For Harold. Augsburg, Germany, 1945.
The Green Town. New York, Scribner, 1956.
A Little Homily. Northampton, Massachusetts, Apiary Press, 1960.

The Wheel of Summer. New York, Dial Press, 1963.
Songs and Half-Songs. Boston, David R. Godine, 1975.
Adlai Stevenson. Iowa City, Iowa, Stone Wall Press, 1975.

Recording: *Today's Poets 1*, with others, Folkways, 1967.

Other

Editor, with James B. Hall, *The Short Story.* New York, Macmillan, 1956.
Editor, with Paul Engle, *Poet's Choice.* New York, Dial Press, 1962.

Translator, with Tamas Aczel and Lazlo Tikos, *Russian Underground Poems 1958–1970.* New York, Harper, 1973.

Critical Studies: in *Southern Review* (Baton Rouge, Louisiana) i, 4, 1965; in *Tri-Quarterly 5* (Evanston, Illinois), 1966.

Joseph Langland comments:

I began writing in relative isolation. While I know many of the living poets and have corresponded with many, I have never espoused a special group or followed any central creed or statement in poetry.

I join colloquial American speech to the traditions. While much of my immediate subject material has come from the landscape and life of rural America, its true subject is usually the relationship of the individual to the world. Forms are various, sources numerous. I think I am my own man. Presently, I am deeply interested in exploring the chaotic condition of American (and likely world) culture. My orientation is oral rather than visual; in all I write I wish never to neglect the singing voice, even in the harshest poem. All subjects pursue some kind of form, either out of themselves or their situations.

                  *   *   *

Joseph Langland's best poems occur when a personal vision of history unites with a song-like immediacy, when his particular emotional intensity and subtlety meet with craft and intellect unnoticed – as in the long poem ("An Open Letter") to Ralph Ellison, and in many of the "Sacrifice" poems of *The Wheel of Summer.*

There is no discordance in such poems, and an authority rings in the voice and diction of "A Hiroshima Lullaby." The same power and quality are in early poems ("War"); and in "Norwegian Rivers" or "Dandelion" a quiet appropriateness fills both vision and voice:

> You are both a small sun
> and a pale moon.
> When you come
> flowering through the daylight
> my blood smiles in its skin.

But Langland finds horror, too ("Buchenwald"), or an expansive and "moving" sadness, as in "Libertyville," one of the Stevenson sequence.

The sequence of "Sacrifice" poems in Langland's award-winning volume relates the different deaths a boy experiences on a Minnesota farm as he comes of age. These are the sacrifices the world makes, it seems, to the spiritual education and filling of a man, and lest this seem presumptuous, the wheel becomes a cycle of dyings – from all various causes and sources – which the maturing youth comes to participate in and even, finally, perpetrate. All nature is caught in this cycle of dying, and in the poems a consciousness remembers joining, becoming aware of the deaths surrounding it and whirling mysteriously away into the past; the consciousness forms and wakens so that finally the "wheel of summer" is natural, a cause and celebration as well as death. Not surprisingly, then, the poems often function as loving equations, metaphors, although much of the surprise inherent in the structure of individual poems dissipates when the poems are placed in sequence or when Langland's concern for "first principles" strikes against his contemporary feeling for the intrinsic holiness of separate things.

– Joseph Wilson

LARKIN, Philip (Arthur). British. Born in Coventry, Warwickshire, 9 August 1922. Educated at King Henry VIII School, Coventry; St. John's College, Oxford, B.A. 1943, M.A. 1947. Since 1955, Librarian, Brynmor Jones Library, University of Hull, Yorkshire. Jazz feature writer, *Daily Telegraph,* London, 1961–71; Visiting Fellow, All Souls College, Oxford, 1970–71. Recipient: Arts Council Prize, 1965; Queen's Gold Medal, 1965; Cholmondeley Award, 1973; Loines Award, 1974. D.Litt: University of Belfast, 1969; University of Leicester, 1970; University of Warwick, 1973; University of St. Andrews, 1974; University of Sussex, Brighton, 1974. Fellow, Royal Society of Literature. Address: Brynmor Jones Library, The University, Hull, Yorkshire, England.

PUBLICATIONS

Verse

The North Ship: Poems. London, Fortune Press, 1945; revised edition, London, Faber, 1966.
XX Poems. Belfast, privately printed, 1951.
(Poems). Oxford, Fantasy Press, 1954.
The Less Deceived. Hessle, Yorkshire, Marvell Press, 1955; New York, St. Martin's Press, 1960.
The Whitsun Weddings. London, Faber, and New York, Random House, 1964.
The Explosion. London, Poem-of-the-Month Club, 1970.
Corgi Modern Poets in Focus 5, with others, edited by Jeremy Robson. London, Corgi, 1971.
High Windows. London, Faber, and New York, Farrar Straus, 1974.

Recordings: *The Less Deceived,* Listen, 1960; *Philip Larkin Reads and Comments on "The Whitsun Weddings,"* Listen.

872

Novels

> *Jill.* London, Fortune Press, 1946; revised edition, London, Faber, and New York, St. Martin's Press, 1964.
> *A Girl in Winter.* London, Faber, 1947; New York, St. Martin's Press, 1957.

Other

> *All What Jazz: A Record Diary 1961–68.* London, Faber, and New York, St. Martin's Press, 1970.

> Editor, *The Oxford Book of Twentieth Century Verse.* Oxford, Clarendon Press, 1973.

Manuscript Collection: British Library, London.

Critical Studies: *Philip Larkin* by David Timms, Edinburgh, Oliver and Boyd, 1973; New York, Barnes and Noble, 1974; "Philip Larkin Issue" of *Phoenix 11–12* (Manchester), Autumn–Winter 1973–74.

*   *   *

It would be difficult to guess from Philip Larkin's first volume, *The North Ship*, that here were the beginnings of a considerable poet. Certainly it attracted little attention on its first appearance in 1945. Looking back now, one can see what seem to be hints, in a few lines and cadences, of what was to come; but this may be hindsight. A wan Yeatsianism, a steely touch of Auden here and there – these are the book's characteristics, and remarkable only in that they show none of the influences one would expect from an Oxford poet in the 1940's: there is no studied literariness, and no flushed and verbose New Apocalypse rhetoric. These poems are careful, yearning and a little dim.

It was in 1946 that Larkin wrote the first poems of his maturity: "Waiting for Breakfast" (which is attached as a "coda" to the 1966 Faber reissue of *The North Ship*) and "Wedding-wind," chronologically the first piece in *The Less Deceived.* Without showing any overt influence of Hardy, they mark the liberation and sense of direction which reading Hardy's poems had given Larkin. In Larkin's own words, spoken in a radio programme:

> When I came to Hardy it was with the sense of relief that I didn't have to try and jack myself up to a concept of poetry that lay outside my own life. . . . One could simply relapse back into one's own life and write from it.

This did not mean that in some way he became anything like what more recently have been called "confessional" poets: the emotional content of Larkin's poems is strong, but the tone is reserved, wry, often resigned, and never self-indulgently revelatory. The "human shows" of Hardy's verse fitted congenially into Larkin's temperament, as did Hardy's unselfpitying pessimism.

After *The North Ship,* Larkin did not publish another book of poems (with the exception of two slim pamphlets) until *The Less Deceived* appeared from the Marvell Press in 1955. (His two novels, *Jill* and *A Girl in Winter*, came in the interim, but – though above average pieces of work – they have no place in this entry.) *The*

Less Deceived, though coming from an obscure press and without any barrage of publicity such as a richer publisher might have laid down, was quite quickly received with enthusiasm. The appearance of Robert Conquest's anthology *New Lines* in 1956, and the journalistic conscription of Larkin into the so-called "Movement" because of his inclusion in that book, probably hindered the acceptance of Larkin's true merits as much as they helped, though it did not take keen critical eyes to see that he was more like, say, Kingsley Amis than Dylan Thomas or W. S. Graham. Yet neither does he share very much, in outlook or style, with such companions in *New Lines* as Elizabeth Jennings, D. J. Enright or Thom Gunn. As for the supposed "neutral tone" of what have been called the Faceless Fifties, Larkin's voice is far too individual to be docketed with that label.

It is a voice that commands a range from the light mockery of "I Remember, I Remember" to the wincing brutality of "Sunny Prestatyn," from the tenderness (joyously rapt in the first, gravely compassionate in the second) of "Wedding-wind" and "Love Songs in Age" to the spiritual bleakness of "Mr. Bleaney." Some of Larkin's poems have that lightness of tone without levity that Auden used to command so well: "Toads," "Toads Revisited," "Naturally the Foundation Will Bear Your Expenses." His two longest, most sustained poems – "Church Going" from *The Less Deceived* and "The Whitsun Weddings" from the 1964 book of that title – use combinations or progressions of several of these tones. "Church Going" moves, through seven carefully-patterned 9-line stanzas, from easy, colloquial, mockingly casual beginnings, through reflection and half-serious questioning, to a rhetorical solidity at the close which is of such weight and deliberation that some readers have mistakenly supposed that Christianity is thereby being endorsed, which in fact is what the poem sets out with great pains *not* to do. Rather, what is being acknowledged – as in several of Larkin's poems, such as "An Arundel Tomb" – is the strange power of inherited order and habit. Like so many leading poets of the century (Eliot and Yeats are examples), Larkin's attitudes are often conservative, even "reactionary": see, for instance, two more recent and uncollected poems – "Posterity" (*New Statesman,* London, 28 June 1968) and "Homage to a Government" (*Sunday Times,* London, 19 January 1969). But he is not really a "public" poet at all, though he reflects common experiences and common concerns. He has no easy answers, but he does not wallow in fashionable *angst* either. There is an agnostic stoicism in his work, which confronts change, diminution, death with sardonic resignation. Though he would not relish the description, there is nobility in this.

"The Whitsun Weddings," which proceeds through its eight 10-line stanzas with none of the subdued gear-crashing of "Church Going," is the finest example of Larkin's temper, tone and technique. Its level descriptive sweep, its amused human observation, its intelligent sense of the inexplicable, all move with complete inevitability to the mysterious closing lines as the train with its load of newly-married couples slows as it reaches its destination:

> And as the tightened brakes took hold, there swelled
> A sense of falling, like an arrow-shower
> Sent out of sight, somewhere becoming rain.

The force of this is partly cumulative, but it has a lot to do with an unerring ear for individual cadences too: that "sense of falling" which one hears in:

> So
> To pile them back, to cry,
> Was hard, without lamely admitting how
> It had not done so then, and could not now.
> – "Love Songs in Age"

> They show us what we have as it once was,
> Blindingly undiminished, just as though
> By acting differently we could have kept it so.
>
> — "Reference Back"

> Life is first boredom, then fear.
> Whether or not we use it, it goes,
> And leaves what something hidden from us chose,
> And age, and then the only end of age.
>
> — "Dockery and Son"

Unlike any other important modern British poet (with the exception of the otherwise utterly different Dylan Thomas), Larkin has constructed no system into which his poems can fit: like Parolles in *All's Well*, he seems to say "simply the thing I am shall make me live." It is an individual achievement, and a memorable one.

— Anthony Thwaite

LATTIMORE, Richmond (Alexander). American. Born in Paotingfu, China, 6 May 1906. Educated at Dartmouth College, Hanover, New Hampshire, A.B. 1926 (Phi Beta Kappa); Christ Church, Oxford (Rhodes Scholar), B.A. 1932, M.A. 1964; University of Illinois, Urbana, A.M. 1927, Ph.D. 1934. Served in the United States Naval Reserve, 1943–46: became lieutenant. Married Alice Bockstahler in 1935; has two sons. Assistant in Classics and English, 1926–28, and in Philosophy, 1933–35, University of Illinois; Assistant Professor of Classics, Wabash College, Crawfordsville, Indiana, 1928–29; Assistant Professor, 1935–41, Associate Professor, 1945–48, and Professor of Greek, 1948–71, Bryn Mawr College, Pennsylvania. Visiting Lecturer, University of Chicago, 1947, and Columbia University, New York, 1948, 1950; Taft Lecturer, University of Cincinnati, Ohio, 1952; Turnbull Lecturer, Johns Hopkins University, Baltimore, 1956; Lord Northcliffe Lecturer, University College, London, 1961; Fulbright Lecturer, Oxford University, 1963–64; Centennial Professor, University of Toronto, 1966. Senior Fellow, Center for Hellenic Studies, Washington, D.C., 1960–65. Honorary Student, Christ Church, Oxford, 1971. Recipient: American Academy in Rome Fellowship, 1934; Rockefeller Fellowship, 1946; Fulbright Scholar, 1951; National Institute of Arts and Letters grant, 1954; American Council of Learned Societies award, 1959; Bollingen translation award, 1962. Litt.D.: Dartmouth College, 1958. Member, National Institute of Arts and Letters; American Academy of Arts and Sciences. Address: 123 Locust Grove Road, Rosemont, Pennsylvania, 19010, U.S.A.

PUBLICATIONS

Verse

Hanover Poems, with A. K. Laing. New York, H. Vinal, 1927.
Poems. Ann Arbor, University of Michigan Press, 1957.

Sestina for a Far-Off Summer: Poems 1957–1962.   Ann Arbor, University of
  Michigan Press, 1962.
Selected Poems.   Oxford, Harlequin Poets, 1965.
The Stride of Time: New Poems and Translations.   Ann Arbor, University of
  Michigan Press, 1966.
Poems from Three Decades.   New York, Scribner, 1972.

Other

Themes in Greek and Latin Epitaphs.   Urbana, University of Illinois Press, 1942.
The Poetry of Greek Tragedy.   Baltimore, Johns Hopkins University Press,
  1958.
Story Patterns in Greek Tragedy.   Ann Arbor, University of Michigan Press, and
  London, Athlone Press, 1964.

Editor, with David Green, *Complete Greek Tragedies* (and translator of *Oresteia*
  by Aeschylus and *Alcestis, Helen, The Trojan Women,* and *Rhesus* by Euripides).   Chicago, University of Chicago Press, 4 vols., 1959.

Translator, *Early Philosophies of Greece,* by M. McClure.   New York, Apple-
  ton, 1935.
Translator, *Some Odes of Pindar.*   New York, New Directions, 1942.
Translator, *The Odes of Pindar.*   Chicago, University of Chicago Press, 1947.
Translator, *The Iliad of Homer.*   Chicago, University of Chicago Press, 1951.
Translator, *The Oresteia of Aeschylus.*   Chicago, University of Chicago Press,
  1953.
Translator, *Greek Lyrics: Translated into Close Approximation of the Original
  Meter.*   Chicago, University of Chicago Press, 1955; revised edition, 1960.
Translator, *Works and Days, Theogony, The Shield of Herakles.*   Ann Arbor,
  University of Michigan Press, 1959.
Translator, *The Frogs of Aristophanes.*   Ann Arbor, University of Michigan
  Press, 1962.
Translator, *The Revelation of John.*   New York, Harcourt Brace, 1962.
Translator, *The Odyssey of Homer.*   New York, Harper, 1967.
Translator, *Iphigenia at Tauris,* by Euripides.   New York, Oxford University
  Press, 1973.

Bibliography: *Richmond Lattimore: A Bibliography*, Chicago, University of Chicago
Press, 1971.

*   *   *

  Richmond Lattimore's poetry, as it appears in his last volume, *Poems from Three
Decades,* which brings together his three formerly published books of verse plus
thirty four new poems, is an impressive achievement. Lattimore is a thorough
student and admirer of the classics, which he taught for many years at Bryn Mawr
College, as well as a translator and critic of ancient Greek poetry; it is, therefore,
not surprising that he draws a considerable part of his inspiration from classical
themes, without, however, becoming their mere imitator or their slave. He is
equally moved and inspired by the contemporary scene, the more recent European
and American past and even by the Far East, where he was born in 1906. Thus, the
most heterogeneous events, places and writers have excited him to compose arresting verse, his subjects ranging from Mycenean linear B tablets to the hulk of the

Lusitania or a tourist poster about Mount Athos. In this wide world of roughly three thousand years in which he moves, his vision is always deeply humane and the tone he adopts calm – he is never "confessional" or "didactic" in the strict sense of the word – but always beneath the surface of his verse you can sense the *lacrimae rerum*. Occasionally you also come across a good-natured humorous outburst.

The technique Lattimore employs varies. He can be traditional in the forms he chooses – the sonnet, the sestina, the terza rima, etc. – or he can branch out into blank and free verse, where a variety of conversational and regular rhythms are blended. Enjambment is frequently employed as well as rhymes and half-rhymes, in which he excells. His language is on the whole simple, and if occasionally rarer words are used, they are always combined with common words that can carry them. He clearly believes in the "intimacy and appeal of common speech." His imagery is fresh and well developed and his lyricism pleasingly subdued; there is no rhetoric and the use of similes and of extended mataphors is sparse. The one weakness in his style is the use of usual and outworn adjectives: yellow willows, small island, pale cinders, old beards, black wrongs, green trees, white plaster, sweet weather.

But Lattimore is not only a distinguished original poet. He is also a most able translator and adaptator of great poetry in other languages, classical Greek, Latin, Anglo-Saxon, Italian, French and modern Greek. The most important of his translations are those of Homer, Pindar and Aeschylus' *Oresteia*. As so rightly and so often said, every generation must make its own translations of the classics, and Lattimore's rendering of the *Iliad* into contemporary English verse is by far the best we have today, a great and lasting achievement.

– Constantine Trypanis

LAUGHLIN, James. American. Born in Pittsburgh, Pennsylvania, 30 October 1914. Educated at Le Rosey, Switzerland; Choate School, Connecticut, 1930–32; Harvard University, Cambridge, Massachusetts, A.B. 1939. Married Margaret Keyser in 1942 (divorced, 1952); Ann Clark Resor in 1956; has four children. Since 1936, Founding Editor and President, New Directions Publishing Corporation, New York. Director, Goethe Bicentennial Foundation, 1949, and the Aspen Institute of the Humanities, 1950; Member, United States National Commission for UNESCO, 1960–63. President, Intercultural Publications; Chairman, Creative Writing Panel, Institute for International Education Conference on Arts Exchange; Trustee, Allen-Chase Foundation; Co-Trustee, Thomas Merton Legacy Trust, D.Litt.: Hamilton College, Clinton, New York, 1969. Member, American Academy of Arts and Sciences; Chevalier, Legion of Honor, France. Address: 333 Avenue of the Americas, New York, New York 10013, U.S.A.

PUBLICATIONS

Verse

Some Natural Things. New York, New Directions, 1945.
Report on a Visit to Germany. Lausanne, Switzerland, Held, 1948.

877

A Small Book of Poems. Milan, Schweiwiller, and New York, New Directions, 1948.

The Wild Anemone and Other Poems. Verona, Valdonega, and New York, New Directions, 1957.

Confidential Report and Other Poems. London, Gaberbocchus, 1959; as *Selected Poems,* New York, New Directions, 1960.

Pulsatilla (bilingual edition), translated by Mary de Rachewiltz. Milan, All' insigna del presce d'oro, 1961.

Die Haare auf Grossvaters Kopf (bilingual edition), translated by Eva Hesse. Zurich, Verlag der Arche, 1966.

Quel che la Matita Scrive (bilingual edition), translated by Mary de Rachewiltz. Rome, Guanda, 1970.

The Pig: Poems. Mount Horeb, Wisconsin, Perishable Press, 1970.

The Woodpecker. Santa Barbara, California, Yes Press, 1971.

Other

Skiing: East and West, with Helene Fischer. New York, Hastings House, 1947.

Editor, *New Directions in Prose and Poetry.* New York, New Directions, 28 vols., 1937–74.

Editor, *Poems from the Greenberg Manuscripts: A Selection from the Works of Samuel B. Greenberg.* New York, New Directions, 1939.

Editor, with Albert Hayes, *A Wreath of Christmas Poems.* New York, New Directions, 1942.

Editor, *Spearhead: Ten Years' Experimental Writing in America.* New York, New Directions, and London, Falcon Press, 1947.

Editor, with Hayden Carruth, *A New Directions Reader.* New York, New Directions, 1964.

Editor, with Naomi Burton and Patrick Hart, *The Asian Journal of Thomas Merton.* London, Sheldon Press, 1974.

*   *   *

James Laughlin is known to many as the publisher who has been a particular friend to avant-garde writers in America. His firm, New Directions, which he founded in 1936 to print works then seriously neglected – especially by Ezra Pound and William Carlos Williams – has expanded over the years and now is one of the foremost publishing houses in the world devoted to serious imaginative writing. But until recently Laughlin's own poetry was little known, partly because he wrote little but chiefly because it has been published reticently and distributed among friends and associates. In the past few years, however, his poems have begun to appear in many anthologies and have been translated into several other languages.

The poems are in colloquial diction, arranged according to what Laughlin calls "prosody of the eye": when typed on a typewriter each line of the poem must be no more than one space (occasionally two) longer or shorter than the opening line. The verbal tension arises from a contrast between this intentional artificiality of design and the freedom of the colloquial, sometimes singsongy aural cadence. Beyond this, the poems rely for effect on the directness and acuteness of the poet's insight, as in "A Modest Proposal":

> I think I can offer this
> simple remedy for a part
>
> at least of the world's
> ills and evil I suggest
>
> that everyone should be
> required to change his
>
> name every ten years I
> think this would put a
>
> stop to a whole lot of
> ambition compulsion ego
>
> and like breeders of dis-
> cord and wasted motion.

A stop, too, to biographical directories; and that, one feels, would probably be o.k. with Laughlin.

– Hayden Carruth

———————————

LAYTON, Irving (Peter). Canadian. Born in Neamtz, Romania, 12 March 1912; emigrated to Canada in 1913. Educated at MacDonald College, Sainte Anne de Bellevue, Quebec, B.Sc. in agriculture 1939; McGill University, Montreal, M.A. 1946. Served in the Canadian Army, 1942–43. Married Betty Frances Sutherland in 1946; the writer Aviva Cantor, 1961; has two sons and one daughter. Lecturer, Jewish Public Library, Montreal, 1943–58; High School teacher in Montreal, 1954–60; Part-time Lecturer, 1949–65, and Poet-in-Residence, 1965–66, Sir George Williams University, Montreal; Writer-in-Residence, University of Guelph, Ontario, 1968–69. Since 1969, Professor of English Literature, York University, Toronto. Co-Founding Editor, *First Statement*, later *Northern Review*, Montreal, 1941–43; Associate Editor, *Contact* magazine, Toronto, and *Black Mountain Review*, North Carolina. Recipient: Canadian Foundation Fellowship, 1957; Canada Council Award, 1959, 1967, Senior Arts grant and travel grant, 1973; Governor-General's Award, 1960; President's Medal, University of Western Ontario, 1961. D.C.L.: Bishop's University, Lennoxville, Quebec, 1970. Address: 122 St. Clement's Avenue, Toronto, Ontario, Canada.

PUBLICATIONS

Verse

Here and Now. Montreal, First Statement Press, 1945.
Now is the Place: Stories and Poems. Montreal, First Statement Press, 1948.
The Black Huntsman. Privately printed, 1951.

Cerberus, with Raymond Souster and Louis Dudek.   Montreal, Contact Press, 1952.
Love the Conqueror Worm.   Montreal, Contact Press, 1953.
In the Midst of My Fever.   Palma, Mallorca, Divers Press, 1954.
The Cold Green Element.   Toronto, Contact Press, 1955.
The Blue Propeller.   Toronto, Contact Press, 1955.
The Blue Calf and Other Poems.   Toronto, Contact Press, 1956.
Music on a Kazoo.   Toronto, Contact Press, 1956.
Improved Binoculars: Selected Poems.   Highlands, North Carolina, Jargon, 1956.
A Laughter in the Mind.   Highlands, North Carolina, Jargon, 1958; augmented edition, Montreal, Editions d'Orphée, 1959.
A Red Carpet for the Sun: Collected Poems.   Toronto, McClelland and Stewart, and Highlands, North Carolina, Jargon, 1959.
The Swinging Flesh (poems and stories).   Toronto, McClelland and Stewart, 1961.
Balls for a One-Armed Juggler.   Toronto, McClelland and Stewart, 1963.
The Laughing Rooster.   Toronto, McClelland and Stewart, 1964.
Collected Poems.   Toronto, McClelland and Stewart, 1965.
Periods of the Moon: Poems.   Toronto, McClelland and Stewart, 1967.
The Shattered Plinths.   Toronto, McClelland and Stewart, 1968.
The Whole Bloody Bird (obs, aphs, and pomes).   Toronto, McClelland and Stewart, 1969.
Selected Poems, edited by Wynne Francis.   Toronto, McClelland and Stewart, 1969.
Five Modern Canadian Poets, with others, edited by Eli Mandel.   Toronto, Holt Rinehart, 1970.
Collected Poems.   Toronto, McClelland and Stewart, 1971.
Nail Polish.   Toronto, McClelland and Stewart, 1971.
Lovers and Lesser Men.   Toronto, McClelland and Stewart, 1973.
Selected Poems.   London, Charisma Books, 1974.
The Pole-Vaulter.   Toronto, McClelland and Stewart, 1974.
Seventy-Five Grub Poems.   Athens, Hermes, 1974.

Other

Engagements: The Prose of Irving Layton, edited by Seymour Mayne.   Toronto, McClelland and Stewart, 1972.

Editor, with Louis Dudek, *Canadian Poems 1850–1952.*   Toronto, Contact Press, 1952.
Editor, *Pan-ic: A Selection of Contemporary Canadian Poems.*   New York, Alan Brilliant, 1958.
Editor, *Poems for 27 Cents.*   Montreal, privately printed, 1961.
Editor, *Love Where the Nights Are Long: Canadian Love Poems.*   Toronto, McClelland and Stewart, 1962.
Editor, *Anvil: A Selection of Workshop Poems.*   Montreal, Kuritzky Frohlinger, 1966.
Editor, *Poems to Colour: A Selection of Workshop Poems.*   Toronto, privately printed, 1970.
Editor, *Anvil Blood: A Selection of Workshop Poems.*   Toronto, privately printed, 1973.

Bibliography: "Irving Layton: A Bibliography in Progress 1931–1971" by Seymour Mayne, in *West Coat Review* (Burnaby, British Columbia), January 1973.

Manuscript Collections: Sir George Williams University, Montreal; University of Saskatchewan, Saskatoon; University of Toronto.

Critical Studies: "Layton on the Carpet" by Louis Dudek, in *Delta 9* (Montreal), October-December 1959; "The Man Who Copyrighted Passion" by A. Ross, in *Macleans Magazine* (Toronto), 15 November 1965; "Personal Heresy" by Robin Skelton, in *Canadian Literature* (Vancouver), Winter 1965; "A Grab at Proteus: Notes on Irving Layton" by George Woodcock, in *Canadian Literature* (Vancouver), Spring 1966; "That Heaven-Sent Lively Ropewalker, Irving Layton" by Hayden Carruth, in *Tamarack Review* (Toronto), Spring 1966; "Satyric Layton" by K. A. Lund, in *Canadian Author and Bookman* (Toronto), Spring 1967; "A Poet of Occasions" by Mike Doyle, in *Canadian Literature* (Vancouver), Autumn 1972.

*   *   *

The most prolific of Canadian poets and certainly the most fluent since Bliss Carman, Irving Layton has published 15 volumes of verse between *Here and Now* (1945) and the *Collected Poems* of 1965, and since then new collections have appeared regularly. A various and indeed an uneven poet, Layton has shown a steady advance in technical accomplishment and in emotional and intellectual maturity. The shrill and strident verses of the earliest volumes had some success in shocking the bourgeoisie with sexual frankness and an uninhibited vocabulary, but they seem rather old-fashioned today and in any case were overshadowed by the later poetry that began with the two volumes of 1954 and 1955, *In the Midst of My Fever* and *The Cold Green Element*. Reviewing the first of these, the critic Northrop Frye wrote: "The question of whether Mr. Layton is a real poet is settled. . . . An imaginative revolution is proclaimed all through this book: when he says that 'something has taught me severity, exactness of speech' or 'has given me a turn for sculptured stone,' we see a new excitement and intensity in the process of writing. At last it is possible to see what kind of poet Mr. Layton is, and he proves to be not a satirist at all but an erudite elegiac poet, whose technique turns on an aligning of the romantic and the ironic."

In spite of an unmistakably romantic conception of the poet as the voice of the earth and the sun iterating a gospel of the natural and the instinctive that is personal and emotional – and straight out of Blake, Whitman and Lawrence – Layton is in his handling of language, metre, and poetic technique a thoroughly classical poet, the best of whose love poems are quite genuinely in the tradition of Ovid and Catullus. The quality of his sensibility can be seen in the vividness and accuracy of his perceptions and can be illustrated in a line or two:

> The maples glisten with the season's rain;
> The day's porous, as October days are,
> And objects have more space about them.
>
> All field things seem weightless, abstract,
> As if they'd taken one step back
> To see themselves as they literally are
> After the dementia of summer.

The *Collected Poems* contains 385 titles, of which perhaps fifty or sixty must rank with the best lyrical and reflective poems of the mid-century in English. The rest consists of squibs, satires, casual jottings, mordant light verse and some often rather childish curses and polemics, but these (along with the strange glorification of military violence found in *The Shattered Plinths*) should not be allowed to obscure the significance of Layton's contribution to North American poetry.

– A. J. M. Smith

LEE, Dennis (Beynon). Canadian. Born in Toronto, Ontario, 31 August 1939. Educated at the University of Toronto, B.A. 1962. M.A. in English literature 1964. Married Donna Youngblut in 1962 (separated); has two daughters. Instructor in English, University of Toronto, Rochdale College, Toronto, and York University, Toronto. Editor, House of Anansi Press, Toronto, 1967–73. Recipient: Governor-General's Award, 1973. Address: 35 Britain Street, Toronto M5A 1R7, Ontario, Canada.

PUBLICATIONS

Verse

Kingdom of Absence. Toronto, House of Anansi, 1967.
Civil Elegies. Toronto, House of Anansi, 1968.
Wiggle to the Laundromat (juvenile). Toronto, New Press, 1970.
Civil Elegies and Other Poems. Toronto, House of Anansi, 1972.
Alligator Pie (juvenile). Toronto, Macmillan, 1974.
Nicholas Knock and Other People (juvenile). Toronto, Macmillan, 1974.

Other

Editor, with R. A. Charlesworth, *An Anthology of Verse.* Toronto, Oxford University Press, 1964.
Editor, with R. A. Charlesworth, *The Second Century Anthologies of Verse, Book 2.* Toronto, Oxford University Press, 1967.
Editor, with Howard Adelman, *The University Game.* Toronto, House of Anansi, 1968.
Editor, *T. O. Now: The Young Toronto Poets.* Toronto, House of Anansi, 1968.

Dennis Lee comments:

In *Civil Elegies*, the book of mine which I consider important, I was working from the cadences and the fusion of passion and intellect that I find in Pindar, Hölderlin and Purdy. The heavily revised version of 1972 grows out of my concern for a more supple voice than in the first edition.

*   *   *

"They are poets who write for real . . . they're accessible to people with a wide range of consciousness . . . reading them in one sitting is a self-contained pleasure." This is Dennis Lee discussing a group of contemporary poets in *Read Canadian: A Book about Canadian Books* (1972); needless to say, these are essential qualities of Lee's own work. His range of consciousness is wide enough to encompass the academy (he teaches at York University), the market place (he was the first editor of House of Anansi Press), and the anti-establishment (he helped found Rochdale College, a free university that flourished in Toronto in the 1960's).

Lee's poetic reputation rests on a single volume, *Civil Elegies and Other Poems*, which establishes the poet as a concerned citizen of liberal-leftist persuasion, worried by world trends. "Sibelius Park," a ruminating poem about Toronto life, ends ominously: "There is nothing to be afraid of." Other poems celebrate the "excellent pleasures," which are ultimately found wanting, of bourgeois life.

It is not in the short poems but in the longish elegies that Lee makes his mark. The nine elegies are basically free verse (one is tempted to say "free prose"), meditations on "the quality of Canadian civilization." The ruminations were inspired by George Grant, the moral philosopher and author of the influential book *Lament for a Nation* (1965), who saw Canada as a conservative country on a liberal continent engulfed by modern technology. In "Elegy 6," Lee peers into the future: "Though I do not deny technopolis I can see only the bread and circuses to come." By turns ponderous and profound, the elegies are as much concerned with the past as they are with the future, and references to historical and literary figures abound. It is in "Elegy 2" that Lee presents the reader with his measure of the past and standard for the future:

> Master and Lord, there was a
> measure once.
> There was a time when men could say
> my life, my job, my home
> and still feel clean.
> The poets spoke of earth and heaven. There were no symbols.

– John Robert Colombo

LEE, Don L. American. Born in Little Rock, Arkansas, 23 February 1942. Educated at Dunbar Vocational High School, Chicago; Chicago City College, A.A. 1966; Roosevelt University, Chicago, 1966–67. Served in the United States Army, 1960–63. Apprentice Curator, DuSable Museum of African American History, Chicago, 1963–67; Stock Department Clerk, Montgomery Ward, Chicago, 1963–64; Post Office Clerk, Chicago, 1964–65; Junior Executive, Spiegels, Chicago, 1965–66. Taught at Columbia College, Chicago, 1968; Writer-in-Residence, Cornell University, Ithaca, New York, 1968–69; Poet-in-Residence, Northeastern Illinois State College, Chicago, 1969–70; Lecturer, University of Illinois, Chicago, 1969–71; Writer-in-Residence, Morgan State College, Baltimore, 1972–73. Since 1971, Writer-in-Residence, Howard University, Washington, D.C. Editor, *Black Books Bulletin*, Chicago; *Black Pages Series*; Third World Press, Chicago. Recipient: National Endowment for the Arts grant, 1969; Kuumba Workshop Black Liberation Award, 1973. Address: Institute of Positive Education, 7848 South Ellis Avenue, Chicago, Illinois 60619, U.S.A.

PUBLICATIONS

Verse

Think Black. Detroit, Broadside Press, 1967.
Black Pride. Detroit, Broadside Press, 1968.
Back Again, Home. Detroit, Broadside Press, 1968.
One Sided Shoot-Out. Detroit, Broadside Press, 1968.
For Black People (And Negroes Too). Chicago, Third World Press, 1968.
Don't Cry, Scream. Detroit, Broadside Press, 1969.
We Walk the Way of the New World. Detroit, Broadside Press, 1970.
Directionscore: Selected and New Poems. Detroit, Broadside Press, 1971.
Book of Life. Detroit, Broadside Press, 1973.

Recording: *Rappin' and Readin'*, Broadside Press, 1971.

Other

Dynamite Voices: Black Poets of the 1960's. Detroit, Broadside Press, 1971.
From Plan to Planet: Life Studies: The Need for Afrikan Minds and Institutions. Detroit, Broadside Press, 1973.
Enemies: The Clash of Races. Chicago, Third World Press, 1974.

Editor, with Patricia L. Brown and Francis Ward, *To Gwen with Love.* Chicago, Johnson Publishing Company, 1971.
Editor, "Pan African Issue" of *The Journal of Black Poetry* (San Francisco), 1971.

Critical Studies: "Black Poetry's Welcome Critic" by Hollie I. West, in *The Washington Post* (Washington, D.C.), 6 June 1971; "A Black Poet Faces Reality" by Vernon Jarrett, in *Chicago Tribune*, 23 July 1971; "The Relevancy of Don L. Lee as a Contemporary Black Poet" by Annette Sands, in *Black World* (Chicago), June 1972; "Some Black Thoughts on Don L. Lee's *Think Black:* Thanks by a Frustrated White Academic Thinker" by Eugene E. Miller, in *College English* (Champaign, Illinois), May 1973.

*   *   *

Of the strong young Black poets of the "Black arts movement" that began in the United States in the late 1960's, Don L. Lee is one of the most powerful and persuasive in content, one of the most creative and influential in technique.

His poetry, consciously utilitarian, is directed to a Black audience, with themes centering around self-identity and self-definition, self-determination, the human-ness of Black people and the depravity of white people ("unpeople"), and self-help through collective and institutional efforts. Examples are "In the Interest of Black Salvation," which shows disillusionment with orthodox Euro-American religion; "Move Un-Noticed to Be Noticed," an exhortation for sincerity in Blacks; "The Wall," a celebration of Black pride; "Back Home Again," which depicts an excursion into an alien (white) "establishment" world and a subsequent return to Blackness; "But He Was Cool," a satire on vapid and showy life styles affected by some Blacks; and "Re-Act for Action," a cry for aggression against racial injus-tices.

Lee's poems convey spontaneity and emotional compulsion as well as ideological commitment. He prefers the speech of the Black urban masses. Much of his poetry seems intended for oral delivery. (He is in demand for readings of his poetry.) He frequently achieves desired aural effects through extra vowels or consonants, phonetic spellings, elisions. He is fond of playing with words, particularly syntactic reversals and the breaking of words into components – for irony, purposeful double meaning, emphasis of components of meaning, aural effects, and other reasons. He is partial to scattered spatial arrangements, broken words, unconventional syntax, and unconventional punctuation, favoring the ampersand and diagonal. His imagery is strong, concrete, and specific. Frequently he builds up a poem's tension incrementally, withholding its point or resolution until the end at which time the poem's logic or impact is made manifest.

– Theodore R. Hudson

LEE, Laurie. British. Born in Stroud, Gloucestershire, 26 June 1914. Educated at Slad Village School, Gloucestershire, and Stroud Central School. During World War II made documentary films for the General Post Office film unit, 1939–40, and the Crown Film Unit, 1941–43, and travelled as a scriptwriter to Cyprus and India; Publications Editor, Ministry of Information, 1944–46; member of the Green Park Film Unit, 1946–47. Married Catherine Francesca Polge in 1950; has one daughter. Caption Writer-in-Chief, Festival of Britain, 1950–51. Recipient: Atlantic Award, 1944; Society of Authors Traveling Award, 1951; Foyle Award, 1956; Smith Literary Award, 1960. Fellow, Royal Society of Literature. M.B.E. (Member, Order of the British Empire), 1952. Lives in Slad, Stroud, Gloucestershire, and London, England.

PUBLICATIONS

Verse

The Sun My Monument. London, Hogarth Press, 1944; New York, Doubleday, 1947.
The Bloom of Candles: Verse from a Poet's Year. London, Lehmann, 1947.
My Many-Coated Man. London, Deutsch, 1955; New York, Coward McCann, 1957.
(Poems). London, Vista Books, 1960.
Pergamon Poets 10, with Charles Causley, edited by Evan Owen. Oxford, Pergamon Press, 1970.

Recording: *Laurie Lee Reading His Own Poems,* with Christopher Logue, Jupiter, 1960.

Plays

The Voyage of Magellan: A Dramatic Chronicle for Radio (broadcast, 1946). London, Lehmann, 1948.
Peasants' Priest: A Play. Canterbury, H. J. Goulden, 1947.

Radio Play: *The Voyage of Magellan,* 1946.

885

Other

Land at War. London, His Majesty's Stationery Office, 1945.
We Made a Film in Cyprus, with Ralph Keene. London, Longman, 1947.
A Rose for Winter: Travels in Andalusia. London, Hogarth Press, 1955; New York, Morrow, 1956.
Cider with Rosie (autobiography). London, Hogarth Press, 1959; as *The Edge of Day: A Boyhood in the West of England,* New York, Morrow, 1960.
Man Must Move: The Story of Transport (juvenile), with David Lambert. London, Rathbone Books, 1960; as *The Wonderful World of Transportation,* New York, Doubleday, 1961; revised edition, 1969; as *The Wonderful World of Transport,* London, Macdonald, 1969.
The Firstborn (essay on childhood). London, Hogarth Press, and New York, Morrow, 1964.
As I Walked Out One Midsummer Morning (autobiography). London, Deutsch, and New York, Atheneum, 1969.

Editor, with Christopher Hassall and Rex Warner, *New Poems 1954.* London, Joseph, 1954.

Translator, *The Dead Village,* by Avigdor Dagan. London, Young Czechoslovakia, 1943.

*   *   *

A first encounter with Laurie Lee's poems immediately reveals that they are loaded with charm, and almost always in the best sense of that tricky word. Their furniture is traditionally "poetic" – seas, moons, flowers, stars, girls, animals – and their mode romantic, but a fine tact protects the poems from the dangerous slide into sentimentality. Laurie Lee is a fluent creator of images and odd correspondences: sometimes one fancies one hears, though not too loudly, the echoing voice of Lorca:

> You were adventure's web,
> the flag of fear I flew
> riding black stallions
> through the rocky streets.

And sometimes, in his exact observations of physical details, he reminds one of Andrew Young – "holes suck in their bees," and "The birdlike stars droop down and die, / The starlike birds catch fire." Indeed, the outside world fills him, as it does Andrew Young, with a sort of devout pleasure.

But these influences, if they are influences and not coincidences, only occasionally intrude. Overall a Laurie Lee poem is very much his and no one else's. His rhythms, verbal textures, visual aperçus are all his own.

It stops there, though. If there are some melancholy poems, they are always of a personal and introspective sort. He does not take account of the miseries, not to say atrocities, that are happening all around us. When he looks outward it is at the physical world, but not the suffering people in it, and when he cerebrates he never pushes his thinking very far. A result of this is that, in spite of the numerous felicities, his final effect is one of slightness. You will find in his poems no exclamation marks – but no questions either. One wishes that a man with his sensibility and his technical adroitness might range farther afield, might explore more deeply the larger experiences whose absence makes, in the end, these poems miniatures. However, he has not done that.

This may account for the smallness of his output. And it says something for his critical judgment that he has not made that slightness seem more slight by printing too much.

– Norman MacCaig

LEEMING, Owen (Alfred). New Zealander. Born in Christchurch, 1 August 1930. Educated at the University of Canterbury, Christchurch, 1949–52, M.A. in French 1952; studied musical composition in Paris, 1954–55. Radio Announcer, New Zealand Broadcasting Corporation, Christchurch, 1953–54; Talks Producer, Pacific Service, 1956–59, Home Service, 1959–62, BBC, London; Television Producer, New Zealand Broadcasting Corporation, Wellington, 1962–64; UNESCO Consultant, Dakar, Senegal, 1965–66, and Kuala Lumpur, Malaysia, 1971–72. Recipient: New Zealand Government Bursary, 1954; Katherine Mansfield Menton Fellowship, 1970. Address: 21 rue de la Liberté, 13980 Alleins, France.

PUBLICATIONS

Verse

Venus Is Setting. Christchurch, Caxton Press, 1972.

Plays

The Quarry Game (produced Wellington, 1970).

Radio Plays: *Order,* 1969 (UK); *Yellow,* 1970; *Reefer's Boys,* 1971 (UK).

Television Play: *White Gardenia* (on Katherine Mansfield), 1969.

Critical Study: *A Way of Saying* by Kendrick Smithyman, Auckland, Collins, 1965.

Owen Leeming comments:

"A mental camera, finely polished," is what a reviewer of *Venus Is Setting* called me, adding, "Owen Leeming's creative imagination is more intricately geared to world history than that of any other New Zealand poet." It is true that when I use sense-images in poems I try to focus them as sharply as possible. I am also conscious of the reach of time, although I think people and places have stimulated me more. My poetry is not frightened of long lines or difficult forms. What I should like a reader to feel in my work is the excitement of mind exploring the

887

world of the body, and of the body of the world flowing back into the mind, with it all holding together.

*   *   *

Brought up a Catholic and neo-Thomist, Owen Leeming first made a considerable impact as a poet with "The Priests of Serrabonne," a massive elaborately-structured palinode of renunciation:

> I think of priests who cowed me, tall soutaned
> Caners who vaunted their humility, their wall
>   Of pride hung with a small
> Black cross. They are singing now, controlled
>   In me . . .

This poem, a sort of post-Hopkins "Stanzas from the Grande Chartreuse," is impressive for its muted rhetoric and bleak honesty of personal statement. It is hardly typical of Leeming's more customary style of writing, which is sophisticated, detached, and highly cerebral, reflecting close familiarity with modern French poetry, and the montage effects of one who has worked professionally in theatre and television.

Venus Is Setting, a rigorous selection from perhaps a dozen years' output, has a few poems – "Instance of Death," "At Home with Cold," "My Cousin James" – which record simply and directly moments of experience and recollection, in what might be called the English manner. But Leeming seems more often driven, from intuitions which may be triggered off by a place or an incongruous occasion, into free-ranging intellectual reverie: the result, pared down with verbal economy, becomes a sequence often stimulating but sometimes bizarrw. His interest in musical composition may account for the contrasting forms and movement of elaborate set-pieces like "Masks" and "Visions, Limited." It is in a tone-poem like "Verdun," and a few Cavafy-style lyrics of real intensity, that he has come nearest to achieving his declared aim of "exploring the idea of a secular metaphysic."

– James Bertram

LEHMANN, Geoffrey (John). Australian. Born in Sydney, New South Wales, 28 June 1940. Educated at Shore School, Sydney, and Sydney University, Degree in arts, 1960, and in law, 1963. Qualified as a solicitor in 1963. Since 1969, Principal, C. R. Wilcox and Lehmann, Sydney. Address: 8 Highfield Road, Lindfield, New South Wales, Australia.

PUBLICATIONS

Verse

The Ilex Tree, with Les A. Murray. Canberra, Australian National University Press, 1965.
A Voyage of Lions and Other Poems. Sydney, Angus and Robertson, 1968.
Conversation with a Rider. Sydney, Angus and Robertson, 1972.
From an Australian Country Sequence. London, Poem-of-the-Month Club, 1973.

Novel

   A Spring Day in Autumn.   Melbourne, Nelson, 1974.

Other

   Editor, *Comic Australian Verse.*   Sydney, Angus and Robertson, 1972.

Critical Study: Review by Roy Fuller, in *London Magazine*, January 1967.

Geoffrey Lehmann comments:

   I regard myself as somewhat old-fashioned because I think that poetry should be
enjoyable. I have written a number of poems about members of my family, but
started writing on these themes just before Robert Lowell made this mode popular.
   There are a number of Graeco-Roman poems influenced by Pound and Cavafy in
which Rome is used as the symbol for modern civilization, city life and overpopulation. These poems deal with the love-hate relationship that an individual has
with his city and contrast private longings with official duties. They use lions and
dolphins as symbols of imagination, the natural order and purity.
   There are a group of poems about members of my family including a grandfather
who died of morphia, self-administered, and another grandfather who built the first
Anglican church in New Guinea and died shortly afterwards of tropical diseases.
These two deaths blighted the lives of my parents early in their childhood and
indirectly affected me very considerably. The poems about my family were motivated by the wish to relive the experiences which made my family what they are,
rather than mere nostalgia, although this is an important emotion for me. Amongst
Australian poets probably Kenneth Slessor has influenced me most. Recent poems
are more spare in their language and free in their form, and attempt to follow
thought patterns.

                              *   *   *

   Among the younger generation of Australian poets Geoffrey Lehmann is possibly
the most prolific as well as the most immediately approachable. His verse relies
largely on conventional techniques, being for the most part unrhymed iambic
pentameters or simple stanzaic patterns of alternative rhymes and half-rhymes.
   A penchant for sequences of homely, familial anecdotes and episodes in the lives
of his father and grandfather has lent a deceptively simple aura to his reputation. In
reality he is a poet of genuine subtleties and complex affiliations with standards of
moderation and saneness that seem out of place, even anachronistic, in the present
age. This appears to have led him to identify his thought and poetic persona with
the immediate and the distant past rather than to take an existential stance in the
present.
   To date his most effective work is to be found in the excellent sequence entitled
"Monologues for Marcus Furius Camillus, Governor of Africa" that opens his
second book. Adopting the guise of a provincial administrator during ancient Rom's
decadence he narrates a series of episodes in the Roman's career that have caused
him to review his life and allegiances. Meditating upon the carefree life of dolphins

or the degradation of lions in the Roman arenas, the governor lives and moves
through these poems, one of the eternal contemporaries of literature.

– Bruce Beaver

LEHMANN, John. British. Born in Bourne End, Buckinghamshire, 2 June 1907;
brother of the actress Beatrix Lehmann, and the novelist Rosamond Lehmann.
Educated at Eton (King's Scholar); Trinity College, Cambridge, B.A. Journalist in
Vienna for several years prior to 1938. General Manager, 1931–32, 1938–46, and
Partner, 1940–46, Hogarth Press, London; Founder and Managing Director, John
Lehmann Ltd., publishers, London, 1946–52. Founding Editor, *New Writing,
Daylight, New Writing and Daylight*, and *Penguin New Writing*, London, 1936–50, and
The London Magazine, 1954–61; Advisory Editor, *The Geographical Magazine*, Lon-
don, 1940–45; Editor, New Soundings, BBC Third Programme, 1952. Visiting
Professor, University of Texas, Austin, 1970–71, State University of California,
San Diego, 1970–71, and University of California, Berkeley, 1974. Chairman, Brit-
ish Council Editorial Advisory Panel, 1952–58; President, Alliance Française in
Great Britain, 1955–64; Member, Angko-Greek Mixed Commision, 1962–68. Since
1967, President, Royal Literary Fund. Recipient: Prix du Rayonnement Française,
1961; Foyle Prize, 1964. Officer, 1954, and Commander, 1961, Order of King
George of the Hellenes; Officer, Legion of Honor, France, 1958; Grand Officer,
Etoile Noir, 1960; Officer, Order of Arts and Letters, France, 1965. Fellow, Royal
Society of Literature, C.B.E. (Commander, Order of the British Empire), 1964.
Address: 85 Cornwall Gardens, LOndon S.W.7, England.

PUBLICATIONS

Verse

> *The Bud, Burial, Dawn, Grey Days, The Lover, The Mountain, Ruin, The
> Gargoyles, Turn Not, Hesperides.* Privately printed, 10 broadsheets, 1928.
> *A Garden Revisited and Other Poems.* London, Hogarth Press, 1931.
> *The Noise of History.* London, Hogarth Press, 1934.
> *Forty Poems.* London, Hogarth Press, 1942.
> *The Sphere of Glass and Other Poems.* London, Hogarth Press, 1944.
> *The Age of the Dragon: Poems, 1930–1951.* London, Longman, 1951; New
> York, Harcourt Brace, 1952.
> *The Secret Messages.* Stamford, Connecticut, Overbrook Press, 1958.
> *Collected Poems, 1930–1963.* London, Eyre and Spottiswoode, 1963.
> *Christ the Hunter.* London, Eyre and Spottiswoode, 1965.
> *Photograph.* London, Poem-of-the-Month Club, 1971.
> *The Reader at Night and Other Poems.* Toronto, Basilike, 1974.

Other

> *Prometheus and the Bolsheviks.* London, Cresset Press, 1937; New York,
> Knopf, 1938.

Evil Was Abroad. London, Cresset Press, 1938.

New Writing in England. New York, Critics Group Press, 1939.

Down River: A Danubian Study. London, Cresset Press, 1939.

New Writing in Europe. London, Penguin, 1940.

The Open Night (essays). London, Longman, and New York, Harcourt Brace, 1952.

Edith Sitwell. London, Longman, 1952.

In My Own Time: Memoirs of a Literary Life. Boston, Little Brown, 1969.

    I. The Whispering Gallery: Autobiography. London, Longman, and New York, Harcourt Brace, 1955.

    II. I Am My Brother: Autobiography. London, Longman, and New York, Reynal, 1960.

    III. The Ample Proposition: Autobiography. London, Eyre and Spottiswoode, 1966.

Ancestors and Friends. London, Eyre and Spottiswoode, 1962.

A Nest of Tigers: Edith, Osbert, and Sacheverell Sitwell in Their Times. London, Macmillan, and Boston, Little Brown, 1968.

Holborn: An Historical Portrait of a London Borough. London, Macmillan, 1970.

Editor, with Denys Kilham Roberts and Gerald Gould, *The Year's Poetry: A Representative Selection.* London, Lane, 1934.

Editor, with Denys Kilham Roberts and Gerald Gould, *The Year's Poetry: 1935: A Representative Selection.* London, Lane, 1935.

Editor, with Denys Kilham Roberts, *The Year's Poetry: 1936: A Representative Selection.* London, Lane, 1936.

Editor, *New Writing.* London, Bodley Head, 2 vols., Lawrence and Wishart, 3 vols., 1936–38; with Christopher Isherwood and Stephen Spender, London, Hogarth Press, 2 vols., 1938–39; Hogarth Press, 1 vol., 1939.

Editor, *Writer in Arms,* by Ralph Fox. London, International Publishing, 1937.

Editor, with Stephen Spender, *Poems for Spain.* London, Hogarth Press, 1939.

Editor, *Penguin New Writing 1–40.* London, Penguin, 1940–50.

Editor, *Folios of New Writing.* London, Hogarth Press, 4 vols., 1940–41.

Editor, *"New Writing" and "Daylight."* London, Hogarth Press, 5 vols., 1942–47; London, Lehmann, 1 vol., 1946.

Editor, *Poems from "New Writing," 1936–1946.* London, Lehmann, 1946.

Editor, *French Stories from "New Writing."* London, Lehmann, 1947; as *Modern French Stories,* New York, New Directions, 1948.

Editor, *Demetrios Capetanakis: A Greek Poet in England.* London, Lehmann, 1947; as *Shores of Darkness: Poems and Essays,* New York, Devin Adair, 1949.

Editor, *Shelley in Italy: An Anthology.* London, Lehmann, 1947.

Editor, *Orpheus: A Symposium of the Arts.* London, Lehmann, and New York, New Directions, 1948.

Editor, *English Stories from "New Writing."* London, Lehmann, 1951.

Editor, *Best Stories from "New Writing."* New York, Harcourt Brace, 1951.

Editor, *Pleasures of "New Writing": An Anthology of Poems, Stories, and Other Prose Pieces from the Pages of "New Writing."* London, Lehmann, 1952.

Editor, *Modern French Stories.* London, Faber, 1956.

Editor, with Cecil Day Lewis, *The Chatto Book of Modern Poetry, 1915–1955.* London, Chatto and Windus, 1956.

Editor, *The Craft of Letters in England: A Symposium.* London, Cresset Press, 1956; Boston, Houghton Mifflin, 1957.

Editor, *Coming to London.* London, Phoenix House, 1957.

Editor, *Italian Stories of Today.* London, Faber, 1959.

Editor, *Selected Poems,* by Edith Sitwell. London, Macmillan, 1965.

Editor, with Derek Parker, *Selected Letters of Edith Sitwell.* London, Macmillan, 1970.

Manuscript Collection: Humanities Research Center, University of Texas, Austin.

* * *

During the 1940's John Lehmann published a number of prose poems which came as near as has yet proved possible to making a success of that difficult form in the English language. Many of them ("Spring Light," for instance, and "After the Fire") remain a tribute to Mr. Lehmann's command of the language. But a continual preoccupation with form and language, while it led to an enviable ease, in some respects inhibited his development as a poet. "The Sphere of Glass," one of his best poems, demonstrates a wholeness and intactness of form which make it much more than a conventional autobiographical anecdote; elsewhere, however, his poems are marked by a certain predictability of "poetic" language which can weaken them. One or two of the poems of the 1940's reflect as well as any other war poems not only the "style" but the emotion of the time, and deserve a place in any anthology of the period. His more recent poems are more organic than the earlier ones; their sum is greater than their parts, and quotation does them less than justice. If a slackening of impetus is hinted at by the rarer appearances of his poems in print, the poems that have appeared within the past ten years have also shown a more sober apprehension of the relative places of technique and "inspiration" in the making of a poem. It is much to be hoped that this always interesting poet will turn a little from accomplished literary journalism, and from the writing of interesting autobiography, and publish more poetry.

– Derek Parker

LEONARD, Tom. British. Born in Glasgow, Lanarkshire, 22 August 1944. Educated at Lourdes Secondary School, Glasgow; since 1973, M.A. candidate, Glasgow University. Married in 1971. Recipient: Scottish Arts Council bursary, 1971. Address: 56 Eldon Street, Glasgow G3 6NJ, Scotland.

PUBLICATIONS

Verse

Six Glasgow Poems. Glasgow, Midnight Press, 1969.
A Priest Came On at Merkland Street. Glasgow, Midnight Press, 1970.
Poems. Dublin, E. and T. O'Brien, 1973.

Critical Studies: "A Scots Quartette" by Edwin Morgan, in *Eboracum* (York), Winter 1973; "Tom Leonard: Man with Two Heads" by Tom McGrath, in *Akros* (Preston, Lancashire), April 1974.

*   *   *

Tom Leonard is one of the most interesting of the younger Scottish poets who emerged during the 1960's. His reputation in Scotland has tended to centre on his poems in Glasgow dialect, but in fact, as the publication of his first general collection, *Poems,* made clear, he is a man of many styles, a restless formal experimenter whose language is laid with surprises, traps, and ironies. There is a considerable element of humour, sometimes fantastic and sometimes moderately black, to attract the reader, and a recurring deadpan strangeness is characteristic. Some of the ironical effects are slight, joky, throwaway. But in the best poems, like "simile please / say cheese," the interlock of images and ideas forces the humour to work in unusual and meaningful ways. The Glasgow poems make use of local idiom and pronunciation for a range of effects, from the bold outspoken backchat of schoolgirls skipping their bus-fares ("A Scream") to the more sophisticated meshing of religion and football in "The Good Thief." These poems take the risk of being obscure to English readers (though the book provides a translation) for the sake of offering a tribute to the much-attacked Glasgow environment – not that the tribute is anything but unsentimental.

– Edwin Morgan

LePAN, Douglas (Valentine). Canadian. Born in Toronto, Ontario, 25 May 1914. Educated at University of Toronto Schools; University College, University of Toronto, B.A.; Merton College, Oxford, M.A. Served in the Canadian Army, 1942–45. Married to Sarah Katharine Chambers; has two sons. Lecturer, University of Toronto, 1937–38; Instructor and Tutor in English Literature, Harvard University, Cambridge, Massachusetts, 1938–41. Joined Canadian Department of External Affairs, 1945: First Secretary on the Staff of the Canadian High Commissioner in London, 1945–48; various appointments in the Department of External Affairs, including that of Special Assistant to the Secretary of State, Ottawa, 1949–51; Counsellor and later Minister Counsellor at the Canadian Embassy, Washington, D.C., 1951–55; Secretary and Director of Research, Royal Commission on Canada's Economic Prospects (Gordon Commission), 1955–58; Assistant Under-Secretary of State for External Affairs, 1958–59. Professor of English Literature, Queen's University, Kingston, Ontario, 1959–64. Principal, University College, 1964–70, and since 1970, University Professor, University of Toronto. Since 1964, Member, Canada Council. Recipient: Guggenheim Fellowship, 1948; Governor-General's Award, for poetry, 1954, for fiction, 1965; Oscar Blumenthal Prize (*Poetry*, Chicago), 1972. D.Litt.: University of Manchester, 1964. Fellow, Royal Society of Canada, 1968. Address: Massey College, 4 Devonshire Place, Toronto 5, Canada.

PUBLICATIONS

Verse

The Wounded Prince and Other Poems. Toronto, Clarke Irwin, and London,
    Chatto and Windus, 1948.
The Net and the Sword: Poems. Toronto, Clarke Irwin, and London, Chatto
    and Windus, 1953.

Novel

The Deserter. Toronto, McClelland and Stewart, 1964.

*   *   *

When a man of letters is also a man of affairs, his public life cannot but
influence his writing. Douglas LePan, who holds degrees from the University of
Toronto and Oxford, saw action in the Italian Campaign of World War II. He
joined the Department of External Affairs and rose to become Assistant Under-
Secretary of State. Then he left to become a professor of English and finally
principal of University College, University of Toronto. His careers have influenced
his poetry in interesting ways.

His two books of poems are largely concerned with his war experiences. The
Wounded Prince views the grim events ironically and paradoxically. The Net and the
Sword, which received the Governor-General's Award, recreates the Italian Campaign and views man mercilessly pitted against the forces of destruction. Along
with paintings by the War Artists in the National Gallery in Ottawa, these war
poems are a valuable record of the achievements of Canadian soldiers overseas.
Both books are mature works full of rich, intellectualized imagery.

Like a public man, LePan is very much concerned with the responsibility of man.
He admires the muscular man, whether gladiator, soldier, or coureur de bois. In The
Net and the Sword, he has a poem on the latter:

> Thinking of you, I think of the coureur de bois,
> Swarthy men grown almost to savage size
> Who put their brown wrists through the arras of the woods
> And were lost – sometimes for months.

But he is also concerned with the repercussions of action, not with those "whose
care is how they fall, not why." This has led him to theorize about the Canadian
experience. The title of a poem in The Wounded Prince has beome a catch-phrase of
the period: "A Country Without a Mythology."

His only novel, The Deserter, concerns social responsibility and was awarded a
Governor-General's Award. It probes the meaning of war to a soldier who deserts –
not before or during a campaign, but after the armistice. LePan has recently
published a number of essays on social philosophy – further evidence of his
concern for the roots of the Canadian community.

– John Robert Colombo

LERNER, Laurence (David). British. Born in Cape Town, South Africa, 12 December 1925. Educated at the University of Cape Town, B.A. 1944, M.A. 1945; Pembroke College, Cambridge, B.A. 1949. Married Natalie Winch in 1948; has four children. Schoolmaster, St. George's Grammar School, Cape Town, 1946–47; Assistant Lecturer, then Lecturer in English, University College of the Gold Coast, Legon, Ghana, 1949–53; Extra-Mural Tutor, then Lecturer in English, Queen's University of Belfast, 1953–62. Lecturer, then Reader, 1962–70, and since 1970, Professor of English, University of Sussex, Brighton. Visiting Professor, Earlham College, Richmond, Indiana, and University of Connecticut, Storrs, 1960–61; University of Illinois, Urbana, 1964; University of Munich, 1968–69. Address: 232 New Church Road, Hove, Sussex BN3 4EB, England.

Publications

Verse

(Poems). Oxford, Fantasy Press, 1955.
Domestic Interior and Other Poems. London, Hutchinson, 1959.
The Directions of Memory: Poems 1958–1962. London, Chatto and Windus, 1963.
Selves. London, Routledge, 1969.
Folio, with others. Frensham, Surrey, Sceptre Press, 1971.
A.R.T.H.U.R.: The Life and Opinions of a Digital Computer. Hassocks, Sussex, Harvester, 1974.

Novels

The Englishmen. London, Hamish Hamilton, 1959.
A Free Man. London, Chatto and Windus, 1968.

Other

The Truest Poetry. London, Hamish Hamilton, 1960.
The Truthtellers: Jane Austen, George Eliot, and D. H. Lawrence. London, Chatto and Windus, 1967.
The Uses of Nostalgia: Studies in Pastoral Poetry. London, Chatto and Windus, 1972.
Hardy's "The Mayor of Casterbridge": Tragedy or Social History? Brighton, Sussex University Press, 1974.

Editor, *Shakespeare's Tragedies: A Selection of Modern Criticism.* London, Penguin, 1963.
Editor, with John Holmstrom, *George Eliot and Her Readers: A Selection of Contemporary Reviews.* London, Bodley Head, 1966.
Editor, *Shakespeare's Comedies: A Selection of Modern Criticism.* London, Penguin, 1967.
Editor, with John Holmstrom, *Thomas Hardy and His Readers: A Selection of Contemporary Reviews.* London, Bodley Head, 1968.

Translator, *Spleen,* by Charles Baudelaire. Belfast, Festival Publications, 1966.

Laurence Lerner comments:

My poems are comprehensible, sad, modern in subject-matter more than in form,
written infrequently and with intense concentration. The recent ones are dramatic
to the extent of being Protean. I wish I could write more poems than I do.

*   *   *

Like the best of his criticism, Laurence Lerner's poetry is sensible, direct and
aware of the complexities of human behaviour. Many of the poems in his first
collection, *Domestic Interior*, are reactions to different environments; their strength
lies not so much in description as in the way they establish a mental *rapport* with
the external world, in which closely-observed incidentals find their place in a wider
pattern of experience:

> While shaping eyes stare from the moving train:
> Or else a water-colour landscape glows
> Grey-green and tawny under a wash of rain,
> Or blue with blobs of cabbages in rows.

Most of these poems are "efficient" and well-argued, in a sense which reminds one
of the best Thirties' poetry, though occasionally the argument only partly conceals
a certain diffuseness of detail. In the more successful ones, however, like the
title-poem and "Meditation on the Toothache" (in actual fact, a meditation on the
imagination), a powerful social concern is firmly rooted in the trivia of the individual life, and in the means by which these may be absorbed into artistic creation.
The dramatic sense which is evident in "Domestic Interior" and "Mimesis" – both
poems in which the subject is approached through a number of protagonists – also
appears in a very different form in the long poem "The Desert Travellers" (*Critical
Quarterly*, Manchester, Winter 1962), a finely sustained dramatic monologue based
on the journeys of the 14th-century Arab geographer, Ibn Battuta.

Lerner's second collection, *The Directions of Memory*, is more adventurous in
technique, and shows a willingness to handle more difficult kinds of experience.
Though one still occasionally feels that a poem has not found its ideal form, there
is a more subtle sense of construction and a growing skill in the use of imagery.
Several of the most striking poems deal with sexual relationships, sometimes from
the woman's point of view. These range from the aggression-dream ("Housewife as
Judith") to the qualified celebration of "The Anatomy of Love" and the fine
"Midnight Swim," a poem in which a profoundly disturbing situation is conveyed
through a brilliantly-controlled central metaphor. The same could be said of the
most moving poem in the volume, "Years Later," the monologue of an unborn
Jewish child, the victim (with its mother) of a Nazi atrocity. This and other poems
("The Little Girl in Rags Fills in Her Application" and, in its way, "Macbeth")
show an admirable lack of insularity in their attempt to understand the pressure of
socially-destructive forces on the individual. Like the more personal poems, they
show a determination to face up to the more disturbing aspects of life with honesty,
intelligence and, at times, with wit.

The same combination of qualities persists, with increasing verbal power, in
Lerner's most recent collection, *Selves*, as well as in his vigorous and resourceful
versions of Baudelaire. The central section of *Selves* includes a group of monologues in which various victims of human cruelty – a laboratory rat, a monkey
involved in a feeding experiment, a battery-reared cockerel – comment on their
situations with grimly humorous logic. Though in one sense such poems are a
natural extension of Lerner's interest in current psychological theory, their real

originality comes from the skill with which they render essentially inarticulate suffering in terms of a recognizable human idiom. In other poems ("The Merman," "Adam Names the Creatures," "Information Theory"), the concern with communication extends to the nature of language itself. Here, the deliberate assumption of inarticulateness becomes a powerful device for exploring the gap between words and reality:

> When humans talk they split their say in bits
> And bit by bit they step on what they feel.
> They talk in bits, they never talk in all.
> So live in wetness swimming they call "sea";
> And stand on dry and watch the wet waves call
> They still call "sea".
> > Only their waves don't call.
> > > – "The Merman"

In addition to the long poem "The Desert Travellers," the volume also contains a number of more personal poems, notably "My Naked Room," "The Dreamwork," "Address to the Tooth of a Whale and to an Unborn Child" and "A Wish." Despite occasional faults of structure and a tendency to stay within established forms, such poems movingly record both the profits and losses of human love, often with striking sympathy for the woman's point of view.

– Arthur Terry

LESLIE, Kenneth. Canadian. Born in Pictou, Nova Scotia, 1 November 1892. Educated at Dalhousie University, Halifax, Nova Scotia, B.A. 1912; University of Nebraska, Lincoln, M.A. 1914; Harvard University, Cambridge, Massachusetts. Married Nora S. Totten in 1960; has four children by first marriage. Formerly, Editor of the *Protestant*. Currently, Editor of *New Man*. Recipient: Tweedsmuir Prize, 1938; Governor-General's Award, 1939. Address: Pine Haven Estates, Armdale, Nova Scotia, Canada. *Died 7 October 1974.*

PUBLICATIONS

Verse

Windward Rock: Poems. New York, Macmillan, 1934.
Such a Din. Halifax, Nova Scotia, John McCurdy, 1935.
Lowlands Low. Halifax, Nova Scotia, John McCurdy, 1936.
By Stubborn Stars and Other Poems. Toronto, Ryerson Press, and Boston, Humphries, 1938.
Songs of Nova Scotia. Privately printed, 1964.
The Poems of Kenneth Leslie. Ladysmith, Quebec, Ladysmith Press, 1970.
O'Malley to the Reds and Other Poems. Armdale, Nova Scotia, privately printed, 1972.

Other

The Red Judge and Other Anecdotes: Reminiscences of Two Great Law Courts of Bengal. Rangoon, Rangoon Times Press, 1934.
Hungary: Christian or Pagan? An Eye-Witness Report. New York, New Christian Books, 1950.
Christ, Church and Communism. Gravenhurst, Ontario, Northern Book House, 1962.

*   *   *

There have been, of course, a number of poets and writers in this century who have been able to sustain their literary excellence while indulging a career in business or a profession: Wallace Stevens, William Carlos Williams, C. P. Snow come immediately to mind. But Kenneth Leslie has tried to juggle too much, to keep too many clubs simultaneously in the air to remember to be a first-rate poet. Had he not spread himself quite so thinly through politics (*Life* proclaimed the danger it thought he represented by including his name in 1949 in a list of important fellow travelers), *and* preaching, *and* editing, *and* teaching, *and* farming, *and* singing, *and* driving a cab, he may or may not have been less of a man, but he would unquestionably have been able to focus more of himself on his poetry.

Not that Kenneth Leslie did not begin well and get better. Almost undoubtedly he merits more than the neglect he has largely endured since 1939, when he was presented with the Governor General's Award in Canada. Perhaps the recent publication of a collection of his work by a commercial press and his own private publication of an edition that includes pieces that *The Poems of Kenneth Leslie* omits will signal a revival that will elevate him to the Canadian pantheon along with E. J. Pratt, W. W. E. Ross, Roy Daniells, and others. Beginning with *Windward Rock* in 1934, in which he shared some of the technique and motives of his friend Robert Frost, Leslie went on to develop his own strong humanitarian voice by the time of the publication of *By Stubborn Stars* in 1938. It was in that volume that he succeeded more consistently than ever before – or since – in harnessing form to put it in fine equilibrium with sense and in controlling his tendency to deal with abstractions through abstractions. There was dross even in that collection, but there is calm power in Leslie that makes one tend to overlook the lapses; it is the effect of standing alondside a powerful and often lyrical human being.

– Alan R. Shucard

LEVENSON, Christopher. British. Born in London, 13 February 1934. Educated at Downing College, Cambridge, 1954–57, B.A. 1957; University of Iowa, Iowa City, M.A. 1970. Conscientious Objector: worked with the Friends Ambulance Unit International Service, 1952–54. Married Ursula Frieda Lina Fischer in 1958; has three sons. Taught at the International Quaker School, Eerde, Holland, 1957–58; English Lektor, University of Munster, West Germany, 1958–61; taught at Rodway Technical High School, Margotsfield, Gloucestershire, 1962–64. Since 1968, Member of the English Department, Carleton University, Ottawa, Ontario. Editor, *Delta* magazine for two years. Recipient: Eric Gregory Award, 1960. Address: Department of English, Carleton University, Ottawa 1, Ontario, Canada.

PUBLICATIONS

Verse

New Poets 1959, with Iain Crichton Smith and Karen Gershon. London, Eyre and Spottiswoode, 1959.
Cairns. London, Chatto and Windus-Hogarth Press, 1969.
Stills. London, Chatto and Windus-Hogarth Press, 1972.

Other

Editor, Poetry from Cambridge. London, Fortune Press, 1958.

Translator, Van Gogh, by Abraham M. W. J. Hammacher. London, Spring Books, 1961.
Translator, The Golden Casket: Chinese Novellas of Two Millenia (translation from the German version). London, Allen and Unwin, 1965.
Translator, The Leavetaking, and Vanishing Point (two novels), by Peter Weiss. London, Calder and Boyars, 1966.

*   *   *

A considerable body of verse by Christopher Levenson was published in volume form as long ago as 1959. It may be found in Edwin Muir's compilation for Eyre and Spottiswoode, New Poets. Nobody took sufficient notice at the time. Yet a discerning reader should have felt that here was a distinctive voice:

> Exiled ambassadors of their heart's country, refugees
> Carry their futures in one attache case. . . .
>
> In the distorting mirrors of my travels,
> Where is tomorrow, now that yesterday
> Is bartered for snapshots? . . .
>
> Past the last city, on to the great plain,
> The fevered air grows still, the lights behind us,
> Thrown from a thousand scattered windows, blur:
> We are alone. . . .

It was no accident that the author called this early collection "In Transit." The word "transit" occurs throughout his work which is that of an exile observing the scenes he passes through:

> They came here in transit, would not learn the language
> Their children gabble, had not meant to stay,
> But gradually drained of will, subsided into
> The institutional gray. . . .

This is a later poem – "Transit Camp" – and the rhymes, though obtrusive, seem an attempt to variegate the obsessively post-Auden verse. But, outside his theme of displaced people, Levenson has little to say. His most famous poem, "Cairns," an elegy on Sylvia Plath, seems to me a rhetorical failure. His attempts to understand situations in personal lives such as divorce or drug-addiction are, though compassionate, clumsy. But, from his earliest verse to his latest, the plight of the wanderer evokes a characteristic Levenson cadence, at once memorable and haunting. This may well be his real contribution to poetry today:

> I stand, tenebral, gazing down on a city
> lost under smoke but luminous, to overhear
> its many baffled night sounds, catch its drift
>
> of hasty farewells, and sift through memory
> a half-heard language I no longer know
> in a remote country. . . .

– Philip Hobsbaum

LEVERTOV, Denise. American. Born in Ilford, Essex, England, 24 October 1923. Educated privately. Served as a Nurse in World War II. Married the writer Mitchell Goodman in 1947; has one son. Emigrated to the United States in 1948; naturalized in 1955. Taught at the YM–YWHA Poetry Center, New York, 1964, City College of New York, 1965, and Vassar College, Poughkeepsie, New York, 1966–67; Visiting Lecturer, Drew University, Madison, New Jersey, 1965, and University of California, Berkeley, 1969; Visiting Professor, Massachusetts Institute of Technology, Cambridge, 1969–70, University of Cincinnati, Ohio, Spring 1973, and Tufts University, Medford, Massachusetts, 1973–74, 1974–75. Poetry Editor, *The Nation*, New York, 1961. Honorary Scholar, Radcliffe Institute for Independent Study, Cambridge, Massachusetts, 1964–66. Recipient: Bess Hokin Prize, 1960, Harriet Monroe Memorial Prize, 1964, Inez Boulton Prize, 1964, and Morton Dauwen Zabel Prize, 1965 (*Poetry*, Chicago); Longview Award, 1961; Guggenheim Fellowship, 1962; National Institute of Arts and Letters grant, 1966, 1968. D.Litt.: Colby College, Waterville, Maine, 1970; University of Cincinnati, 1973. Address, c/o New Directions, 333 Avenue of the Americas, New York, New York 10013, U.S.A.

PUBLICATIONS

Verse

The Double Image. London, Cresset Press, 1946.
Here and Now. San Francisco, City Lights Books, 1957.
Overland to the Islands. Highlands, North Carolina, Jargon, 1958.
5 Poems. San Francisco, White Rabbit Press, 1958.
With Eyes at the Back of Our Heads. New York, New Directions, 1959.
The Jacob's Ladder. New York, New Directions, 1961; London, Cape, 1965.

O Taste and See: New Poems. New York, New Directions, 1964.
City Psalm. Berkeley, California, Oyez, 1964.
Psalm Concerning the Castle. Madison, Wisconsin, Perishable Press, 1966.
The Sorrow Dance. New York, New Directions, 1967; London, Cape, 1968.
Penguin Modern Poets 9, with Kenneth Rexroth and William Carlos Williams.
    London, Penguin, 1967.
Three Poems. Mount Horeb, Wisconsin, Perishable Press, 1968.
A Tree Telling of Orpheus. Los Angeles, Black Sparrow Press, 1968.
The Cold Spring and Other Poems. New York, New Directions, 1968.
A Marigold from North Vietnam. New York, Albondocani Press-Ampersand
    Books, 1968.
Embroideries. Los Angeles, Black Sparrow Press, 1969.
Relearning the Alphabet. New York, New Directions, and London, Cape,
    1970.
Summer Poems 1969. Berkeley, California, Oyez, 1970.
A New Year's Garland for My Students, MIT 1969–70. Mount Horeb, Wiscon-
    sin, Perishable Press, 1970.
To Stay Alive. New York, New Directions, 1971.
Footprints. New York, New Directions, 1972.

Recording: *Today's Poets 3*, with others, Folkways.

Short Story

In the Night: A Story. New York, Albondocani Press, 1968.

Other

The Poet in the World (essays). New York, New Directions, 1973.

Editor, *Out of the War Shadow: An Anthology of Current Poetry.* New York,
    War Resisters League, 1967.
Editor and Translator, with Edward C. Dimock, Jr., *In Praise of Krishna: Songs
    from the Bengali.* New York, Doubleday, 1967; London, Cape, 1968.

Translator, *Selected Poems of Guillevic.* New York, New Directions, 1969.

Bibliography: *A Bibliography of Denise Levertov* by Robert A. Wilson, New York,
Phoenix Bookshop, 1972.

Critical Studies: *Denise Levertov* by Linda Wagner, New York, Twayne, 1967; *Out
of the Vietnam Vortex* by James Mersmann, Lawrence, University Press of Kansas,
1974; Colman McCarthy, in *Washington Post* (Washington, D.C.), 1974; Hayden
Carruth, in *Hudson Review* (New York), 1974.

*   *   *

Although she is frequently associated with the Projectivist or Black Mountain
poets (the names derive from Charles Olson's influential essay on poetic composition, "Projectivist Verse," and from Black Mountain College, where a number of

901

these poets were once students or teachers), including Robert Duncan, Charles
Olson and Robert Creeley, Denise Levertov's career as a writer really has its
origins in England. It was in London that she was born, of a Welsh mother and a
father who was a Russian-Jew and also an Anglican clergyman. In an age of mass
education, she was educated at home and read in her father's library. Her first
book of poems, displaying talent but very much influenced by the somewhat vague,
imprecise tendencies of a romanticism current in much British poetry of the World
War II period, appeared in 1946; the following year she married the young American novelist Mitchell Goodman and later came to the United States to live, a move
obviously decisive for her art.

   It was not until a decade later that Miss Levertov produced another collection –
Here and Now – with the then new series of Pocket Poets launched by Lawrence
Ferlinghetti. The change in her writing during the intervening years is complete; she
had come under the commanding but liberating spell of William Carlos Williams,
Ezra Pound, H.D., and doubtless others, the effect of which was to bring about an
accurate concentration upon (to apply some words of Robert Creeley's) "the
particulars of [her] own experience, the literal *things* of an immediate environment." Freer in form, her new poems are concrete, precise, intense, and shaped,
the result of what must have been the most difficult kind of transformation since it
meant a total alteration of sensibility and imagination. As she says in "Art," a
version after Gautier, included in her next book – a book that firmly established her
as one of the finest young poets in America:

> The best work is made
> from hard, strong materials,
>   obstinately precise –
> the line of the poem, onyx, steel.

   If these lines are accepted as an artistic credo – though she has written several
different ones equally demanding – it is clear that Miss Levertov has never swerved
from them as an ideal, and has, moreover, seldom failed to come up to their
measure in her actual practice. The material she now draws on for her poems is
what presents itself within the context of living, the circle of her personal
experience: "the authentic," as she says in a later poem, is the end of her aesthetic
search. So she may write of a conversation overheard on a street in New York, an
old man walking his dogs, the profound aspects of her marriage. In "A Window"
the observation that among the multitude of city windows one continues to blaze
brightly brings Miss Levertov's imagination to the point of vision:

> Among a hundred windows shining
>   dully in the vast side
> of greater-than-palace number such-and-such
>   one burns
> these several years, each night
>   as if the room within were aflame.

But it would be a mistake to view her work as limited to the external world of
objects, things, and other persons. Though she is concerned to rejoice in the reality
that surrounds her, there is evident a very strong element of inwardness, even
mysticism, in the poetry, so that the particulars of outward experience are met by
responses from within; and quite a few poems focus solely on an inner space of
consciousness where the images and revelations of dream or vision manifest themselves. While Miss Levertov discloses no orthodox commitment of any sort in her
work, it is hard not to see a strong religious impulse making itself felt there. Yet
this impulse refuses to be separated from the poet's deep *human* compassion, an

unbreakable attachment to earthly reality, veneration for and wonder at man's physical body, the endless variety of life, and a feeling that poetry, rising from mysterious, unfathomable sources in the poet's being, is inextricably bound up with all these aspects of existence. The last stanzas of "The Jacob's Ladder," from the volume of that title, illustrate in part this important side of her writing; here man and angels come together, and poetry struggles upward with its author as the spiritual creatures descend into the world:

> A stairway of sharp
> angles, solidly built.
> One sees that the angels must spring
> down from one step to the next, giving a little
> lift of the wings:
>
> and a man climbing
> must scrape his knees, and bring
> the grip of his hands into play. The cut stone
> consoles his groping feet. Wings brush past him.
> The poem ascends.

Miss Levertov's recent work shows no lessening of her accomplishment, and her collection, *The Sorrow Dance,* is remarkable for the elegiac sequence for her sister Olga and for the series of poems about the Viet Nam war. Two subsequent books are intensely preoccupied with questions of war, politics, and social change, though her newest volume, *Footprints,* while not abandoning such considerations, returns to aspects of the meditative and lyric manner evident before. Few poets of her generation can claim the depth and relevance, imaginative strength and careful craftsmanship so plain to see in Denise Levertov's writing.

– Ralph J. Mills, Jr.

LEVI, Peter (Chad Tiger), S. J. British. Born in Ruislip, Middlesex, 16 May 1931. Educated at Beaumont College, Berkshire, 1946–48; Campion Hall, Oxford, M.A. 1961. Since 1948, Member, The Society of Jesus. Currently, Tutor in Classics, Campion Hall, Oxford. Address: c/o Campion Hall, Oxford, England.

PUBLICATIONS

Verse

Earthly Paradise. Privately printed, 1958.
The Gravel Ponds: Poems. London, Deutsch, and New York, Macmillan, 1960.
Orpheus Head. Privately printed, 1962.
Water, Rock and Sand. London, Deutsch, and Chester Springs, Pennsylvania, Dufour, 1962.

903

The Shearwaters.   Oxford, Allison, 1965.
Fresh Water, Sea Water: Poems.   Llandeilo, Carmarthen, and London, Black Raven Press-Deutsch, 1965.
Pancakes for the Queen of Babylon: Ten Poems for Nikos Gatsos.   London, Anvil Press Poetry, 1968.
Ruined Abbeys.   London, Anvil Press Poetry, 1968.
Life Is a Platform.   London, Anvil Press Poetry, 1971.
Death Is a Pulpit.   London, Anvil Press Poetry, 1971.
Penguin Modern Poets 22, with Adrian Mitchell and John Fuller.   London, Penguin, 1973.

Other

Beaumont: 1861–1961.   London, Deutsch, 1961.
The Light Garden of the Angel King: Journeys in Afghanistan.   New York, Collins, 1972.

Editor, *The English Bible from Wycliff to William Barnes.*   London, Constable, 1974.
Editor, *Pope.*   London, Penguin, 1974.

Translator, with Robin Milner-Gulland, *Selected Poems of Yevtushenko.*   London, Penguin, 1962.
Translator, *Guide to Greece,* by Pausanias.   London, Penguin, 2 vols., 1971.

*   *   *

There is a quietude, and beauty, at the centre of Peter Levi's best poems which will make them endure. They also possess that strangeness and solidity which are integral to most fine poetry. He is never fashionable and he uses no rhetoric, but his unobtrusive control of language and imagery creates a world which is distinct from that of any other poet. As Eliot has written, "To be original with the *minimum* of alteration, is sometimes more distinguished than to be original with the *maximum* of alteration."

In connection with his own work Peter Levi once wrote: "One might expect a Catholic poet to imitate more than I do the immense ghost of Hopkins, but his negative virtues are what one most envies; his not being subject to Catholic delusions of grandeur, or the ecstatic violence of phrase and shabby poverty of conception, or the mere linguistic vices that hang like an aura around so many Catholic reputations. A Catholic poet needs to begin as Hopkins did and as Baudelaire did from the truth of his own mind, a truth not easily attained to. It seems important that the only poet from whom I have consistently tried to learn . . . is Horace." This "truth of his own mind" is complex and valuable; it cannot be expressed in any way other than by the poems themselves – certainly not by a few lines of expository prose. But certain themes which run through his poetry from the beginning can, I suppose, be pointed out. I quote from "Over the Roof, High in among the Gloom . . ." from his book, *The Gravel Ponds*:

> and here my mind returns, day and night,
> accepting with an instinctive ease
> this nest where the mind hangs at peace,
> this intellectual liberty and light.

Some of what Peter Levi seeks to achieve in his poetry is put clearly in these lines from the poem which opens his volume *Water, Rock and Sand*:

> yet I can strain and hope
> for words and for a shape
> which unregarded might
> praise reason and be bare or clear as light.

John Bayley defined the quality of these poems well when he wrote: "All poetry of the *Water, Rock and Sand* kind surely represents not a network of agile syntax but a real and sensuous world, a place, a landscape of both actuality and association." He then goes on to say that Peter Levi brings with him "a garden . . . where his friends and his moods are found, and also his infinitely quiet and courteous sadness . . . which never obtrudes on us but sharpens our sense of this personal and fascinating place."

This sadness is perhaps best expressed in one of Fr. Levi's most moving poems, "For Peter Hacker." I quote the last two stanzas:

> All those philosophies have gone,
> since pleasure, doubt, the sense of death
> teach schoolmasters their own lesson
> in voices tangible as breath,
> and adolescents, studying what I write,
> note the dead foliage and the dying light.
>
> Now an intense reflective rage
> by seasonal rebirth and loss
> rips away words, page after page,
> ringing eros on thanatos;
> I study bare landscape, question the dead,
> listen to cold rain falling in my head.

Peter Levi has also written two longer poems, *Pancakes for the Queen of Babylon* and *Canticum*. The former is, like his earlier books, permeated by imagery of land and sea, but here, while remaining real places, they have become part of visionary experience. This poetry is sometimes deep and clear, like the magic and light of landscapes seen in waking dreams:

> I am always thinking about early morning
> these woods have been much ruined and confused.

Occasionally there seems to me too much abstraction and fancy in these poems – a vice of the surrealist tradition – but the finest have been made, to use Louis Zukofsky's phrase, "out of deep need." Single lines and images shine out with disturbing power, and after several rereadings a larger pattern begins to shape. I quote *Pancakes for the Queen of Babylon*:

> Poetry is burnt out.
> It is in the necessity to speak.

Peter Levi has since published two important books, *Life Is a Platform*, a new collection of lyric poems, and *Death Is a Pulpit*, containing poems written for public performance. The latter are long and their quality cannot be conveyed adequately by brief quotation. Most impressive is "Christmas Sermon." *Life Is a Platform* includes some of the most moving and rhythmically powerful poems Peter Levi has written. I shall close by quoting the first stanza of "For Miranda and Iain":

> Drowsy tree. In the end it revives
> and the sky suddenly begins to flash
> scattering masses of the mist and leaves;
> abundant pure smells, then the thundercrash.
> Apollo barks, the god's in his machine,
> the light is mine and the darkness is mine.

– William Cookson

LEVINE, Philip. American. Born in Detroit, Michigan, 10 January 1928. Educated at Wayne State University, Detroit, B.A. 1950, M.A. 1955; University of Iowa, Iowa City, M.F.A. 1957; Stanford University, California (Fellowship in Poetry, 1957). Married Frances Artley in 1954; has three sons. Since 1958, Member of the Department of English, California State University, Fresno. Recipient: San Francisco Foundation Joseph Henry Jackson Award, 1961; Chaplebrook Award, 1968; National Endowment for the Arts grant, 1969, 1970 (refused); Frank O'Hara Prize (*Poetry*, Chicago), 1972; National Institute of Arts and Letters grant, 1973. Address: 4549 North Van Ness Avenue, Fresno, California 93704, U.S.A.

PUBLICATIONS

Verse

> *On the Edge.* Iowa City, Stone Wall Press, 1963.
> *Silent in America: Vivas for Those Who Failed.* Iowa City, Shaw Avenue Press, 1965.
> *Not This Pig: Poems.* Middletown, Connecticut, Wesleyan University Press, 1968.
> *Five Detroits.* Santa Barbara, California, Unicorn Press, 1970.
> *Thistles: A Poem Sequence.* London, Turret Books, 1970.
> *Pili's Wall.* Santa Barbara, California, Unicorn Press, 1971.
> *Red Dust.* Santa Cruz, California, Kayak Books, 1971.
> *They Feed They Lion.* New York, Atheneum, 1972.
> *1933: Poems.* New York, Atheneum, 1974.

Other

> Editor, with Henri Coulette, *Character and Crisis: A Contemporary Reader.* New York, McGraw Hill, 1966.

Critical Studies: by X. J. Kennedy, in *Poetry* (Chicago), 1964; Robert Dana, in *North American Review* (Mt. Vernon, Iowa), 1964; Hayden Carruth, in *Hudson*

Review (New York), 1968; "Personally, I'd Rather Be in Fresno" by Stuart Peter-freund, in *New: American and Canadian Poetry 15* (Trumansburg, New York), May 1971; "They Feed They Lion" by Robert D. Spector, in *Saturday Review* (New York), 11 March 1972; "A Gathering of Poets" by Richard Schramm, in *Western Humanities Review* (Salt Lake City), Autumn 1972; "Recent Poetry" by Marie Borroff, in *The Yale Review* (New Haven, Connecticut), Autumn 1972; "Borges and Strand, Weak Henry, Philip Levine" by James McMichael, in *Southern Review* (Baton Rouge, Louisiana), Winter 1972; "Interview with Philip Levine," in *American Poetry Review* (Philadelphia), i, 1, 1972; " 'The True and Earthly Prayer': Philip Levine's Poetry" by Ralph J. Mills, Jr., in *American Poetry Review* (Philadelphia), iii, 2, 1974.

Philip Levine comments:

It's difficult for me to talk about my poetry because I'm mainly aware of how much it's changed over the years. I began writing when I was about 19; I was outraged by America, and I thought poetry would help me communicate that outrage. I thought I'd write these poems, publish them, and people would shape up or change or love me. Well, it didn't happen that way, and by the time I tried to publish anything I'd written I was 26 years old and had fallen in love with the beast itself, the poem. My first great love was Stephen Crane; that lasted a week; then Eliot, another few weeks; Dylan Thomas, Auden, Yeats, and many others until I came across Williams, and he stuck. I've written in a variety of styles and ways: traditional meters, which dominate my first book, then syllabics, and the rest, and for the past several years in free verse mainly. Some themes have remained through the 25 years: I try to pay homage to the people who taught me my life was a holy thing, who convinced me that my formal education was a lie: these were the men and women I met as an industrial worker and bum in America; they were mainly Southerners – so many of whom had come to Detroit in my boyhood to find work – and they were closer, I believe, to some great truths about people, to the truth that we are the children of God, and that we were meant to come into this world and live as best we could with the beasts and the trees and plants and to leave the place with our love and respect for it intact, and to leave it our selfs. These people, both Black and white, were mainly rural people, and the horror of the modern world was clearer to them than to me, and the beauty and value of the world was something they knew in a way I did not, first hand. So, I learned from them, and I owe them my hope and maybe more. They're in my poems from the start, and so are the animals and plants they loved and showed me. The magic and mystery of that city, Detroit, its immense energy and its carnival atmosphere during WWII and other cities I came to know later, especially Barcelona. My childhood appears only in the work of the last few years, but it now dominates my work, and the book I'm now finishing will deal mainly with those years. Of course the landscapes of California and Spain – where I lived for two years recently – are much in the work.

My favorite poem is "Spring and All" by Williams. My favorite living poet, Zbigniew Herbert. My favorite book? Waley's *170 Poems from the Chinese* or Rexroth's *100?* I can have them both.

*   *   *

Though Philip Levine's work has appeared widely since the mid-fifties, it was not till the publication of *Not This Pig* (1968) that he reached the large generally appreciative audience he most certainly deserves. Unremittingly grim, yet as hard on himself as on all that troubles him, he creates a virtual rogue's gallery caught compassionately at dramatic moments of decline: peopling his poems are drunks, draft-dodgers, boxers, Hell's Angels, midgets, poor neighbors. The following passage from the important sequence "Silent in America" will give some idea of his degree of involvement as well as his method:

> For a black man whose
> name I have forgotten who danced
> all night at Chevy
> Gear & Axle,
> for that great stunned Pole
> who laughed when he called me Jew
> Boy, for the ugly
> who had no chance,
> the beautiful in
> body, the used and the unused,
> those who had courage
> and those who quit –
>
>   .   .   .
>
> all my energy,
> all my care for
> those I cannot touch
> runs on my breath like a sigh. . . .

The poet writes often of his family, as the guilty father/husband whose vulnerability threatens the lot of them. Such poems, invariably tender, may be his most moving, and there is at least one which has significance for the way it relates the poet and his family to their world, "The Morning after the Storm," the third section of which goes:

> The winds and the dogs
> brought down the garbage.
> Ostrichlike, my wife picks
> at the tidbits on the lawn.
>
> The wet winds gust,
> and her night clothes flap around her –
> in her 40th year
> she stoops and pecks and clears
>
> our little yard;
> she turns away from nothing,
> grounds, bottles, bones,
> egg shells, animal fat,
>
> the splintered plastic guns,
> the burned-out bulbs
> and swollen batteries,
> all the refuse of this house.
>
> The sky clenches again.
> Our three sons grow toward war.
> Child of the land, Indian,
> you cannot live here any more.

In recent years Philip Levine has travelled, particularly in Spain, and what is most striking about the poems that have come of that experience is that they display the same toughness with self and, when called for, an equal degree of compassion for others. Whether in Fresno or Barcelona the poet is never less than fully human, and one finds oneself admiring the man as much as the poet. On the evidence of work done in the last few years he is a poet who is not likely to stop growing.

– Lucien Stryk

L'HEUREUX, John (Clarke). American. Born in South Hadley, Massachusetts, 26 October 1934. Educated at the National Academy of Theatre Arts, 1952; College of the Holy Cross, Worcester, Massachusetts, 1952–54; Boston College, A.B. 1959, M.A. in philosophy 1960, M.A. in English 1963; Harvard University, Cambridge, Massachusetts. Married Joan Polston in 1971. Entered the Society of Jesus, 1954; ordained a priest, 1966; requested laicization, 1970; married with Vatican approval, 1971. Writer-in-Residence, Georgetown University, Washington, D.C., 1965; and Regis College, Weston, Massachusetts, 1970; Visiting Lecturer, Tufts University, Boston, 1971; Visiting Professor, Harvard University, 1973. Since 1973, Assistant Professor of English, Stanford University, California. Staff Editor, 1968–70, and since 1970, Contributing Editor, *The Atlantic*, Boston. Agent: Lynn Nesbit, International Famous Agency, 1301 Avenue of the Americas, New York, New York 10019. Address: Department of English, Stanford University, Stanford, California 94305, U.S.A.

PUBLICATIONS

Verse

    Quick as Dandelions: Poems. New York, Doubleday, 1964.
    Rubrics for a Revolution. New York, Macmillan, 1967.
    One Eye and a Measuring Rod: Poems. New York, Macmillan, 1968.
    No Place for Hiding: New Poems. New York, Doubleday, 1971.

Novels

    Tight White Collar. New York, Doubleday, 1972.
    The Clang Birds. New York, Macmillan, 1972.

Short Stories

    Family Affairs. New York, Doubleday, 1974.

Other

    Picnic in Babylon: A Jesuit Priest's Journal, 1963–1967. New York, Macmillan, 1967.

Manuscript Collection: Boston University.

*   *   *

A remark that John L'Heureux made in *Picnic in Babylon: A Jesuit Priest's Journal, 1963–1967* gives some insight into what he wishes to do in poetry. Stressing the harm done to American poetry by Poe's jingles and Whitman's "over developed ego," he said that "with the singular exception of Emily Dickinson there is no American poetry until 1900."

What one finds in L'Heureux's poetry, in other words, is a sensibility compatible with the interior religious struggles described in Dickinson and in her admirers among twentieth century poets. In a sequence called "The Problem of God," he expresses something of the impatience Dickinson felt toward divinity: "The trouble with Christ is / he always comes at the wrong time." Yet, as one might suspect, the quarrel between L'Heureux and God is merely temporary. In fact, in the early poems their relationship (in "Death of a Man" and "The Unlikely Prophet") and his familiarity with God's chosen (in "The Journey" and "Joseph") appear too comfortable to be believed.

He is essentially a poet of celebration and of reconciliation, as James Dickey has said, who goes "eagerly toward events and people, open-handed and open-hearted." The final section of L'Heureux's poem, "The Death of Kings," an epitaph for John F. Kennedy, conveys his essential faith in the nature of things:

> The end is vision:
> stones roll back and wonder cracks
> like morning on a disbelieving world.
> No Lazarus standing gray and stupid
> in his linen bands, but we – harlequins
> and fools – stride the fired air
> with feet of bronze. Laughter
> is our music. Let the earth tremble.

L'Heureux's strength of feeling and wit as a lyric poet exhibit themselves most fully in his recent poems, as in "The Command" and "Narcissus," whose passion and self-knowledge indicate a much wider range of feeling than the earlier conventionally religious poems. And in "A Pleasing Fragrance," the best of the old and the new directions come together:

> He was crowing
> on the rooftop
> of his sanctity
> when the house burned
> down. Crazy old cock
> larger than death
>
> he thought
> before the conflagration.
> . . .
> And so he's gone,
> poor roasted soul,
>
> in blazing glory.
> He made, despite himself,
> a good holocaust.

In his latest books, both poetry and fiction, L'Heureux recounts his struggle with and ultimate decision to leave the Jesuits. But the religious pilgrimmage continues, and in poems such as "Incarnation" and "Foolsgold" it remains as much of a preoccupation as ever.

– Michael True

LIEBERMAN, Laurence (James). Born in Detroit, Michigan, 16 February 1935. Educated at the University of Michigan, Ann Arbor (Hopwood Award, 1958), B.A. 1956, M.A. in English, 1958; University of California, Berkeley. Married Bernice Braun in 1956; has one son and two daughters. Former Poetry Editor, *Orange County Illustrated* and *Orange County Sun,* California. Taught at Orange Coast College, Costa Mesa, California, 1960–64; College of the Virgin Islands, St. Thomas, 1964–68. Associate Professor of English, 1968–70, and since 1970, Professor of English, University of Illinois, Urbana. Recipient: Yaddo Fellowship, 1963, 1967; Huntingdon Hartford Foundation Fellowship, 1964; National Endowment for the Arts grant, 1966; University of Illinois Center for Advanced Study grant, 1971. Address: Department of English, University of Illinois, Urbana, Illinois 61801, U.S.A.

PUBLICATIONS

Verse

The Unblinding: Poems. New York, Macmillan, 1968.
The Osprey Suicides. New York, Macmillan, and London, Collier Macmillan, 1973.

Other

The Blind Dancers: Ten Years of American Poetry 1964–74. Urbana, University of Illinois Press, 1975.

Editor, *The Achievement of James Dickey: A Comprehensive Selection of His Poems with a Critical Introduction.* Chicago, Scott Foresman, 1968.

Critical Study: "Fool, Thou Poet" by Vernon Young, in *Hudson Review* (New York) Winter 1973–74.

Laurence Lieberman comments:

The subject which I have found most arresting in the last few years is underwater swimming and diving and spearfishing. My aim is to continue to cultivate a medium for a richly descriptive poetry of nature, which is at the same time visionary, capable of registering and evoking a wide range of spiritual states.

The poet who has had the strongest influence on my recent work is Theodore Roethke.

*   *   *

While many of the younger American poets who made their literary debuts in the latter part of the 1960's – that is, in the generation following that of Ginsberg, Bly, Wright, and Kinnell – have developed in directions which enable us to place them in one or another of the large categories of recent poetic tendencies in America, Laurence Lieberman has preferred to proceed on his own. His earlier work, gathered in *The Unblinding,* offers ample evidence of the gifts he possesses, a good ear, a sensitivity to the rich potentialities of diction, and an acute awareness of the extraordinary complexity of the most commonplace event or act of observation. There is a deep impulse in his writing to unfold by means of a subtle and intricate proliferation of language the covert aspects and angles of experience as he envisages it. Words, then, become the keys for unlocking the structure and the details of what the poet sees or undergoes; but in this process words are themselves an integral element of the perception. Hence a density of language in Lieberman's poems which seems at times elaborate, even ornamental, though the latter is true only in weaker pieces.

With the appearance of his second collection, *The Osprey Suicides,* Lieberman makes decisive strides into maturity and accomplishment. Sometimes the early poems failed for lack of a considerable enough subject or theme, one commensurate with the author's talents; but the new poems reveal a forceful grip on substantial materials and a marvelous working out of their possibilities. Like Roethke and James Dickey, who are perhaps closest to him in influence, Lieberman is frequently concerned with nature, though very much in his own way, creating through a full, beautifully textured line a feeling of the intimate relation between man and environment, the poet and the immediate context of the mysterious, fluctuating, complicated existence in which he finds himself. Whether concentrated on nature or other kinds of experience, Lieberman's poems are written with great skill and strong imagination, the result of careful attention to craft and to a fascinated vision of the world.

– Ralph J. Mills, Jr.

LIFSHIN, Lyn (Diane). American. Born in Burlington, Vermont, 12 July 1942. Educated at Syracuse University, New York, B.A. 1961; University of Vermont, Burlington, M.A. 1963; Brandeis University, Waltham, Massachusetts; State University of New York, Albany; Bread Loaf School of English, Vermont. Married Eric Lifshin in 1963. Teaching Fellow, State University of New York, Albany, 1964–66; Educational Television Writer, Schenectady, New York, 1966; Writing Consultant, Mental Health Department, Albany, New York, 1967; Instructor, State University of New York, Cobleskill, 1968, 1970. Recipient: Yaddo Fellowship, 1970, 1971; MacDowell Fellowship, 1973. Address: 2142 Apple Tree Lane, Niskayuna, New York 12309, U.S.A.

PUBLICATIONS

Verse

Why Is The House Dissolving. San Francisco, Open Skull Press, 1968.
Femina 2. Oshkosh, Wisconsin, Abraxas Press, 1970.
Leaves and Night Things. West Lafayette, Indiana, Baby John Press, 1970.
Black Apples. Trumansburg, New York, Crossing Press, 1971; revised edition, 1973.
Tentacles, Leaves. Belmont, Massachusetts, Helleric Press, 1972.
Moving by Touch. Traverse City, Michigan, Cotyledon Press, 1972.
Lady Lyn. Milwaukee, Morgan Press, 1972.
Mercurochrome Sun Poems. Tacoma, Washington, Charis Press, 1972.
I'd Be Jeanne Moreau. Milwaukee, Morgan Press, 1972.
Love Poems. Durham, New Hampshire, Zahir Press, 1972.
Forty Days, Apple Nights. Milwaukee, Morgan Press, 1973.
Audley End Poems. Long Beach, California, Mag Press, 1973.
The First Week Poems. Plum Island, Massachusetts, Zahir Press, 1973.
Museum. Albany, New York, Conspiracy Press, 1973.
All the Women Poets I Ever Liked Didn't Hate Their Fathers. St. Petersburg, Florida, Konglomerati, 1973.
The Old House on the Croton. San Lorenzo, California, Shameless Hussy Press, 1973.
Poems. Minneapolis, Northstone, 1974.
Selected Poems. Trumansburg, New York, Crossing Press, 1974.
Upstate Madonna. Trumansburg, New York, Crossing Press, 1974.
The Old House. Oakland, California, Capra, 1974.
Shaker Poems. Chatham, New York, Omphalos Press, 1974.
Thru Blue Post, New Mexico. Fredonia, New York, Basilik, 1974.
Blue Fingers. Milwaukee, Wisconsin, Shelter Press, 1974.
Plymouth Women. Milwaukee, Wisconsin, Morgan Press, 1974.

Bibliography: by Marvin Malone, in *The Wormwood Review* (Stockton, California), xii, 3, 1971.

Critical Studies: by Bill Katz, in *Library Journal* (New York), June 1971, and December 1972; Carol Rainey, in *Road Apple Review* (Albuquerque, New Mexico), Summer-Fall 1971; Victor Contoski, in *Northeast* (La Crosse, Wisconsin), Fall-Winter 1971–72; James Naiden, in the *Minneapolis Star*, 18 April 1972; Dave Etter, in *December* (West Springs, Illinois), 1972; "Lyn Lifshin" by Jim Evans, in *The Windless Orchard* (Fort Wayne, Indiana), Summer 1972; Eric Mottram, in *The Little Magazine* (New York), Summer-Fall 1972.

Lyn Lifshin comments:

I'm usually better at doing something than talking about how and why I do it. One time I spent days trying to say how I wanted the words to be connected to touch the reader's body. Somehow. Except that sounded strange and so I tore it up. . . . It seems to me that the poem has to be sensual (not necessarily sexual, tho that's ok too) before it can be anything else. So rhythm matters a lot to me, most, or at least first. Before images even. I want whoever looks at, whoever eats the poem to feel the way old ebony feels at 4 o'clock in a cold Van Cortlandt mansion, or the smell of lemons in a strange place, or skin.

Words that I like to hear other people say the poems are are: strong, tight, real, startling, tough, tender, sexy, physical, controlled – that they celebrate (Carol Rainey), reflect joy in every aspect of being a woman (James Naiden).

I always steal things I like from people: other poets, especially from blues, old black and country blues rhythms (after most readings, people come and ask how, where I started reading the way I do; another mystery, really). So I was glad to have Dave Etter say that *Black Apples* "comes on like a stack of Cannonball Adderley records, blowing cool, blowing hot, sometimes lyrical and sweet, sometimes hard bop, terse and tough."

*   *   *

In the relatively short time that she has been writing, Lyn Lifshin has developed her talent in ways that extend the significance of her work. Her poems are, characteristically, brief lyrics, often imagistic, that move towards sudden, revelatory metamorphoses. Her earlier poems focus on personal experience. She writes with a hard, disarming candor about sexual love, its familiarities and the powerful transforming element in which it occurs. Sometimes there are visions of fulfillment: "how far away / are the mountains / he kept / saying / could we touch them." More often, there are images of absence and vacancy: "every / time I came / close to you / the place that / was you / changed to air." She uses phantasmagoric imagery to evoke the horror of everyday domestic life in which people have no contact with one another. Her style is deceptively casual: sometimes subversively prosaic, sometimes cool and flamboyant.

Her more recent poems involve a shift from contemporary ghosts and ruins to the American colonial past, in the "Old House on the Croton" poems, and to pre-Columbian Indian culture, in *Museum*. These new poems are even more spare than her personal poems, and their effect is to suggest that those personal poems are ultimately less about contemporary life than about a horror that intrudes, as she writes of the Old House on the Croton, upon the most domestic life: "this must have been the last / room to think of war in." And here, as in the personal poems, there issues from within that horror and vulnerability something tough and sustaining. Her enumeration of the sacrifices of the Indian poor, for example, quietly evokes the ferocity of the human will to survive: "the poor / cocoa corn / flour wool or / a plucked eyelash."

– Jerry Paris

LINDSAY, (John) Maurice. Scottish. Born in Glasgow, 21 July 1918. Educated at Glasgow Academy, 1928–36; Scottish National Academy of Music, now the Royal Scottish Academy of Music, Glasgow, 1936–39. Served in the Cameronians (Scottish Rifles) at the Staff College, Camberley, and in the War Office during World War II. Married Aileen Joyce Gordon in 1946; has one son and three daughters. Drama Critic, *Scottish Daily Mail*, Edinburgh, 1946–47; Music Critic, *The Bulletin*, Glasgow, 1946–60; Editor, *Scots Review*, 1949–50. Programme Controller, 1961–62,

Production Controller, 1962–64, and Features Executive and Chief Interviewer, 1964–67 Border Television, Carlisle. Since 1964, Editor, with Douglas Young, Saltire Modern Poets series, Edinburgh. Since 1967, Director, Scottish Civic Trust, Glasgow. Recipient: Atlantic-Rockefeller Award, 1946. Address: 11 Great Western Terrace, Glasgow G12 0UP, Scotland.

PUBLICATIONS

Verse

The Advancing Day. Privately printed, 1940.
Perhaps To-morrow. Oxford, Blackwell, 1941.
Predicament. Oxford, Alden Press, 1942.
No Crown for Laughter: Poems. London, Fortune Press, 1943.
The Enemies of Love: Poems 1941–1945. Glasgow, Maclellan, 1946.
Selected Poems. Edinburgh, Oliver and Boyd, 1947.
Hurlygush: Poems in Scots. Edinburgh, Serif Books, 1948.
At the Wood's Edge. Edinburgh, Serif Books, 1950.
Ode for St. Andrews Night and Other Poems. Edinburgh, New Alliance Publications, 1951.
The Exiled Heart: Poems 1941–1956, edited by George Bruce. London, Hale, 1957.
Snow Warning and Other Poems. Arundel, Sussex, Linden Press, 1962.
One Later Day and Other Poems. London, Brookside Press, 1964.
This Business of Living. Preston, Lancashire, Akros, 1971.
Comings and Goings: Poems. Preston, Lancashire, Akros, 1971.
Selected Poems, 1942–1972. London, Hale, 1973.

Plays

Fingal and Comala (produced Braemar, 1953; London, 1958).
The Abbott of Drimmock, music by Thea Musgrave (produced London, 1957).
The Decision, music by Thea Musgrave (produced London, 1967). London, Chester, 1967.

Other

A Pocket Guide to Scottish Culture. Glasgow, Maclellan, 1947.
The Scottish Renaissance. Edinburgh, Serif Books, 1949.
The Lowlands of Scotland: Glasgow and the North. London, Hale, 1953; revised edition, 1973.
Robert Burns: The Man, His Work, The Legend. London, MacGibbon and Kee, 1954; revised edition, 1968.
Dunoon: The Gem of the Clyde Coast. Dunoon, Town Council of Dunoon, 1954.
The Lowlands of Scotland: Edinburgh and the South. London, Hale, 1956.
Clyde Waters: Variations and Diversions on a Theme of Pleasure. London, Hale, 1958.
The Burns Encyclopaedia. London, Hutchinson, 1959; revised edition, 1970.
Killochan Castle, with David Somervell. Derby, Pilgrim Press, 1960.
By Yon Bonnie Banks: A Gallimaufry. London, Hutchinson, 1961.

The Discovery of Scotland: Based on Accounts of Foreign Travellers from the Thirteenth to the Eighteenth Centuries. London, Hale, and New York, Roy, 1964.

Environment: A Basic Human Right. Glasgow, The Scottish Civic Trust, 1968.

The Eye Is Delighted: Some Romantic Travellers in Scotland. London, Muller, 1970.

Portrait of Glasgow. London, Hale, 1972.

Editor, *Poetry Scotland One, Two, Three.* Glasgow, Maclellan, 1943, 1945, 1946.

Editor, *Sailing To-morrow's Seas: An Anthology of New Poems.* London, Fortune Press, 1944.

Editor, *Modern Scottish Poetry: An Anthology of the Scottish Renaissance, 1920–1945.* London, Faber, 1946; revised edition, 1966.

Editor, with Fred Urquhart, *No Scottish Twilight: New Scottish Stories.* Glasgow, Maclellan, 1947.

Editor, *Selected Poems of Sir Alexander Gray.* Glasgow, Maclellan, 1948.

Editor, *Poems,* by Sir David Lyndsay. Edinburgh, Oliver and Boyd, 1948.

Editor, with Hugh MacDiarmid, *Poetry Scotland Four.* Edinburgh, Serif Books, 1949.

Editor, with Helen Cruickshank, *Selected Poems of Marion Angus.* Edinburgh, Serif Books, 1950.

Editor, *John Davidson: A Selection of His Poems.* London, Hutchinson, 1961.

Editor, with Edwin Morgan and George Bruce, *Scottish Poetry One* to *Six.* Edinburgh, Edinburgh University Press, 1966–72; with Alexander Scott and Roderick Watson, *Scottish Poetry Seven,* Glasgow, University of Glasgow Press, 1974.

Editor, *A Book of Scottish Verse,* revised edition. London, Oxford University Press, 1967.

Editor, *Scotland: An Anthology.* London, Hale, 1974.

Short stories and television and music criticism published in periodicals and anthologies.

Manuscript Collection: National Library of Scotland, Edinburgh.

Critical Studies: Preface by George Bruce to *The Exiled Heart: Poems 1941–1956,* 1957; Alexander Scott, in *Whither Scotland?,* edited by Duncan Glen, London, Gollancz, 1971; *Studies in Scottish Literature, 1971,* Columbia, University of South Carolina Press, 1973; "A Different Way of Being Right: The Poetry of Maurice Lindsay" by Donald Campbell, in *Akros* (Preston, Lancashire), April 1974.

Maurice Lindsay comments:

I began writing because, from an early age, I wanted to try to retrieve some tangible aspects from my own experience of living: in other words, to probe the nature of satisfaction, whatever is "reality." Most theories of poetry seem to me pompous, egotistical, and more or less irrelevant. I have therefore never worked to any "programme."

Born a Scot and brought up in Scotland, in spite of being subjected to an anglified public school education, I became fascinated with that part of my literary heritage written in Scots, and for a number of years wrote enthusiastically in Lallans (as Lowland Scots was called by the poets of the "second wind" phase – the expression was Eric Linklater's – of the "Scottish Renaissance" movement, instituted by Hugh MacDiarmid in the 1920's and so dubbed by Denis Saurat). By the early 1950's this concentration on language for its own sake, particularly a language in decline spoken more thinly and by fewer people every year, seemed to me to be forcing a wedge behind that modern Scotland of which I was a part, and the language in which I, and some others, were writing. I therefore turned my attention to writing in the tongue I, and the majority of Scots, actually speak: a kind of Scotticised English. I have been attacked for "betraying" Lallans. This is nonsense. A Scots writer may have a choice of three languages in which to write. That choice depends upon circumstances all valid in the contemporary context. There can therefore be no "right" language and no "wrong." I am entirely in favour of teaching Scots literature and language in Scottish schools so that what exists already may continue to be enjoyed and understood. But the pressures of the modern world cannot be resisted. Compulsion is not saving Ireland's Erse. Not even an independent Scottish Government could successfully decree the survival of the Scots tongue as a fully spoken medium.

Life is for people to live. My interest in people, which led me to become a radio and television interviewer at one point, has provided a constant theme for my later poetry. Early training as a musician perhaps accounts for the fascination that rhyme and half-rhyme have always exercised upon me. I have seen poetry as one way, perhaps the best, of making sense out of life, and I have therefore been less interested in free verse than in verse in more closely ordered forms.

I deplore the present British academic practice of collecting young poets into groups – "The Beats," "The Movement," "The Confessionals" – each of which reflects, at most, the fashion of half a decade, and their underlying implication that only the newest group's work is of interest or value. Poets can't and shouldn't try to change their styles to keep up with every latest teenage fashion. While a poet and his work must be of, and reflect, the age in which he lives, a poet at fifty may take a different, though no less valid, view of that age than a poet at twenty. The notions that poets are expendable at twenty-five and that each new fashion is an "advance" on the one before, are to me as absurd as would be an evolutionary interpretation of the Arts.

From all of this it may have become apparent that I believe the poet's job is to develop his talents and get on with his art, ignoring the cat-calls of the cliques and the compartmentalising of the more fashion-conscious critics. What is, or is not, of permanent value will be assessed by calmer standards long after the outcome is of personal concern to the poet.

*   *   *

Maurice Lindsay began publishing verse during the Second World War, and much of his early work is in a high Romantic style that has not worn well, yet from the beginning he showed himself capable of smaller and more personal poems, concentrated upon individuals rather than issues, in which his grasp of traditional form met subject matter drawn from the contemporary world and resulted in something satisfying. *The Enemies of Love: Poems 1941–1945* is his most representative collection of this period, while the volume *Hurlygush*, with its introduction by Hugh MacDiarmid, stands as testament to an upflare of enthusiasm for what was then called Lallans. The Scots tongue proved useful to Lindsay in that it permitted him to bring comic elements into his poems exploring the vagaries of human character, but by the time his mature work began to appear it was plain that he could be true to his origins without recourse to dialect.

917

Four collections – *The Snow Warning, One Later Day, This Business of Living,* and *Comings and Goings* – show Lindsay at his best, and the proportion of work from these books which has found its way into his *Selected Poems* is correctly large. A sense of measure, an approval of order and continuity and grace, characterises Lindsay's attitude to experience, but there is usually at least an implication of intenser feeling held in reserve. This makes for a grown-up tone which dwells upon certain favourite subjects – music, children, animals – but does not vary much from poem to poem. There are an obvious honesty and sincerity to lines such as these, which observe the end of innocence in a four-year-old child:

> Alone beside himself, head-in-air
> he wanders gently through a fading season,
> almost for the last time aware
> of how a moment feels, before the lesion
> of growing into thought begins to hurt;
> the falling burn turn into a complaint
> it can't communicate . . .

The half-rhymes within the lines (thought / hurt, complaint / communicate) testify to the care with which Lindsay nowadays examines his experience. There is a sense of patiently teasing out the meaning. Large gestures of all kinds, verbal and intellectual, are eschewed, although a well-defined awareness of his own identity does not prevent the poet from attaching value to what he considers – in a somewhat sentimentally pantheistic way – to be the "healing last word" of Nature. If Lindsay looks at a river he is apt to celebrate "torn water endlessly mended." Humankind in his reckoning is "the rhythm, not the range," a typical modesty, but one which has not protected him from a critical charge of week-ending with his own talents, of a sort of Scottish neo-Georgianism.

There is some bite to this criticism, but if it leads to neglect of what is persistently decent and well-achieved in Lindsay's verse then its perpetrators do no service to a genuine poet. It is not unlikely that his quiet voice will be heard when a number of louder and shriller ones have been forgotten.

— Robert Nye

LIPSITZ, Lou. American. Born in Brooklyn, New York, 29 October 1938. Educated at the University of Chicago, B.A. 1957; Yale University, New Haven, Connecticut, M.A. 1959, and Ph.D. in political science 1964. Married; has two children. Reporter, *Daily Standard,* Celina, Ohio, 1957–58. Instructor, University of Connecticut, Storrs, 1961–64. Since 1964, Associate Professor of Political Science, University of North Carolina, Chapel Hill. Recipient: National Endowment for the Arts grant, 1967. Address: 416 Westwood Drive, Chapel Hill, North Carolina, U.S.A.

PUBLICATIONS

Verse

Cold Water. Middletown, Connecticut, Wesleyan University Press, 1967.

Other

Editor, *American Politics: Behavior and Controversy.*   Boston, Allyn and Bacon, 1967.

*   *   *

Lou Lipsitz, like so many other American poets in the last decade, has been influenced by the great modern European and Latin American poets such as Neruda, Vallejo, and Voznesensky. But whereas many other young poets have merely taken the grand style of surrealism and passion and turned it either flippant or blandly mechanical, Lipsitz shares the spirit that informs the originals.

He has written a genuine urban poetry which deals with the callousness and despair of the city but maintains its own concern and gentleness. His range of emotions is wide, and he has written marvelous poems of personal joy and tenderness ("Cold Water," "A Note"), of humor which is not strident but rather pervaded by an affection for the human spirit ("Pancho Villa," "Why I Left My Job"), and of the spiritual imagination ("Night Train," "The Pipes"); but the poems which are perhaps the most impressive are the ones in which he demonstrates the rare and important capacity to feel, to comprehend, the difficult life of another being.

He explores the desperation of prize fighters from the slums, the awkward strangeness of young boys entering manhood, the suffering of emotionally disturbed children, with a fully engaged perceptiveness, portraying them in lines whose accuracy and force are at least as much a proof of his empathy and love as they are of his talent or skill.

– Lawrence Russ

LIVESAY, Dorothy.   Canadian.   Born in Winnipeg, Manitoba, 12 October 1909. Educated at Trinity College, University of Toronto, 1927–31, B.A. 1931; the Sorbonne, Paris, Diploma, 1932; London Institute of Education, 1959; University of British Columbia, Vancouver, M.Ed. 1966. Married Duncan Macnair in 1937 (died); has one son and one daughter. Social Worker, Englewood, New Jersey, 1935–36, and Vancouver, 1936–39, 1953–55; Correspondent, *Toronto Daily Star,* 1946–49; Documentary Scriptwriter, Canadian Broadcasting Corporation, 1950–55; Lecturer in Creative Writing, University of British Columbia, 1955–56, 1965–66; High School Teacher, Vancouver, 1956–58; UNESCO English Specialist, Paris, 1958–60, and Zambia, 1960–63; Writer-in-Residence, University of New Brunswick, Fredericton, 1966–68; Associate Professor of English, University of Alberta, Edmonton, 1968–71. Currently, Visiting Lecturer, University of Victoria, British Columbia. Recipient: Governor-General's Award, 1945, 1948; Lorne Pierce Medal, 1947; President's Medal, University of Western Ontario, 1954; Canada Council grant, 1958, 1964, 1971. D.Litt.: University of Waterloo, Ontario, 1973. Address: Department of English, University of Victoria, P.O. Box 1700, Victoria, British Columbia, Canada.

PUBLICATIONS

Verse

Green Pitcher. Toronto, Macmillan, 1928.
Signpost. Toronto, Macmillan, 1931.
Day and Night: Poems. Toronto, Ryerson Press, 1944.
Poems for People. Toronto, Ryerson Press, 1947.
Call My People Home. Toronto, Ryerson Press, 1950.
New Poems. Toronto, Emblem Press, 1955.
Selected Poems, 1926–1956. Toronto, Ryerson Press, 1957.
The Colour of God's Face. Vancouver, Unitarian Service Committee, 1965.
The Unquiet Bed. Toronto, Ryerson Press, 1967.
Poets Between the Wars, with others, edited by Milton T. Wilson. Toronto, McClelland and Stewart, 1967.
The Documentaries: Selected Longer Poems. Toronto, Ryerson Press, 1968.
Plainsongs. Fredericton, New Brunswick, Fiddlehead, 1971.
Collected Poems: The Two Seasons. Toronto, Ryerson Press, 1972.

Short Stories

A Winnipeg Childhood. Winnipeg, Peguis Press, 1973.

Other

Editor, *The Collected Poems of Raymond Knister.* Toronto, Ryerson Press, 1949.
Editor, with Seymour Mayne, *Forty Women Poets of Canada.* Montreal, Ingluvin, 1971.

Manuscript Collection: University of Alberta, Edmonton.

Critical Studies: "My New Found Land" by W. E. Collin, in *The White Savannahs,* Toronto, Macmillan, 1936; "Out of Silence and Across the Distance: The Poetry of Dorothy Livesay" by P. Stevens, in *Queen's Quarterly 4* (Kingston, Ontario), Winter 1969; "Dorothy Livesay: The Love Poetry" by P. Stevens, in *Canadian Literature* (Vancouver), Winter 1971; "Livesay's Two Seasons" by Robin Skelton, in *Canadian Literature* (Vancouver), Autumn 1973.

Dorothy Livesay comments:

(1970) Early lyrical and imagist poetry became social and documentary (30's and 40's) and reverted to personal statement (50's and 60's). Influenced recently by West Coast movement (projective verse).
  Themes and subjects: love and personal psychological relationships between lovers, parents, children. Problems of individual relationships to the question of our

age: achieving the just society, how to stop war, how to understand other races and peoples. Recently in *The Unquiet Bed* my theme has been the importance of oneness with another person. If this harmony is achieved, many other harmonies spring from it.

I like to experiment with new forms, to find the subtleties for music in English words and word-arrangements. Poetry is speech and communication and should be said aloud.

(1974) In the past three years I have been giving readings of my poetry to universities across Canada and to women's organizations. The great and encouraging response of women to my poetry is due, perhaps, to the fact that for forty years I have been writing of matters that concern women: love, marriage and its bonds, childbirth, childhood: the need for peace in the world to give children a growing place. But perhaps the greatest response has been to my love poetry, as in *The Unquiet Bed* and *Plainsongs* – now incorporated in *Collected Poems: The Two Seasons.*

*   *   *

Dorothy Livesay is one of the pioneers of modernism in Canadian poetry. Her early work in *Green Pitcher,* published when she was nineteen, while showing the influence of Imagism current at that time, was also distinguished by its simple lyricism and a rare maturity of spirit.

A start in newspaper writing was followed by university studies in Toronto and in France, and led eventually to a career in social work. Coincident with Livesay's studies at the Sorbonne, 1931–32, was the publication of *Signpost* which is a personal document and consists, in the main, of poems conceived before the politicizing process which befell Western intellectuals in the early 1930's. The suggestion exists, though, in this second chapbook, that Livesay's concerns are going to become progressive, political and committed. The private and the lyrical give way to social awareness which is informed not only by personal involvement in the lives of the under-privileged, but also by the world struggle against fascism. Out of this ambience comes *Day and Night,* a volume of socially relevant and committed writing. The institutional quality of social zeal, and that sense of *movimento* typical of the time were muted and improved upon by new well-springs of humanist affirmation in *Poems for People. Call My People Home* and *New Poems* are two chapbooks with an interim note about them, but with indications of a return to a more private verse concerned with the experiences of love and the joyful and evocative liberation of art. Following the publication of Livesay's *Selected Poems, 1926–1956,* the poet's work seemed to mark time briefly until the emergence of a re-enforced sense of the musical phrase and new rhythms. In *The Colour of God's Face,* a chapbook inspired by work and residence in Zambia, the strength of Livesay's rhythms is noteworthy, as is her success in balancing the imagistic with the interpretative. Influences of the Canadian West Coast *TISH*-movement are also at work in her later poems as evidenced in *The Unquiet Bed,* a collection which, with its private intensities, relies on established spareness and discipline, but which is also rich in the rhythm and musicality of its statement.

The process of shifting literary and political orientation did not affect profoundly Livesay's basic style. She continued to write in simple and direct verse forms with variations in tone from the lyrical and subdued, through the emotional and political to the genuinely humane and passionate.

Livesay's 1968 collection, *The Documentaries,* is a selection of key poems like

"The Outrider" and "Call My People Home" which have a particular value not only as significant statement, but as milestones in the career of Dorothy Livesay.

– Michael Gnarowski

———————

LIVINGSTONE, Douglas (James). South African. Born in Kuala Lumpur, Malaya, 5 January 1932. Educated at Kearney College, Natal, South Africa; qualified in Pathogenic Bacteriology, Pasteur Institute, Salisbury, Rhodesia. Officer in Charge, Pathological Laboratory, Broken Hill (Kabwe) General Hospital, Zambia, 1959–63. Since 1964, Bacteriologist in charge of marine work, Natal. Recipient: Guinness Prize, 1965; Cholmondeley Award, 1970. Address: c/o C.S.I.R., P.O. Box 17001, Congella, Natal, South Africa.

PUBLICATIONS

Verse

The Skull in the Mud.   London, Outposts Publications, 1960.
Sjambok and Other Poems from Africa.   London and New York, Oxford University Press, 1964.
Poems, with Thomas Kinsella and Anne Sexton.   London and New York, Oxford University Press, 1968.
Eyes Closed Against the Sun.   London and New York, Oxford University Press, 1970.
A Rosary of Bone.   Cape Town, David Philip, 1974.

Play

The Sea My Winding Sheet (broadcast, 1964).   Durban, The Theatre Workshop Company, 1971.

Radio Play: *The Sea My Winding Sheet,* 1964 (Rhodesia).

Douglas Livingstone comments:

Some African themes, especially animals: to reflect the nature of man. Happier with "form." Attempts to "shape" poem to subject. Influences unknown, but favorite poets: Chaucer, John Clare, Catullus, Shelley, Marvell, Donne, Cavafy, E. A. Robinson, Wilfred Owen and Sylvia Plath among the dead.

*   *   *

Douglas Livingstone might be described as a poet without roots in any particular country or environment, which makes him rather difficult to place for the reader who automatically thinks in terms of nationalities. Born in Kuala Lumpur of middle-class Scottish parents, Livingstone spent his early years in Malaya, Australia, Ceylon, Scotland, South Africa, Rhodesia and Zambia. In Rhodesia he studied and qualified in pathological bacteriology. As he himself observes somewhat ruefully: "I have been to more schools than I care to remember, in several continents, but which to call a capillary, let alone a tap-root, had me foxed."

His earliest work appeared in *Outposts* and his first small collection of poems, *The Skull in the Mud*, was published by Outposts Publications in 1960. Although uneven in quality, this collection already exhibited the characteristics which the critics welcomed on the appearance of his second volume, and had an extraordinary vitality which, surprisingly enough for any Rhodesian or South African poet, owed nothing at all to Roy Campbell. Indeed, though it was obvious that Livingstone had read widely, no strong literary influences were anywhere apparent. In *The Skull in the Mud* Livingstone refers to himself as a "muscoid Jonah" and takes up his position as "sentry in the shade," recording what he sees with scrupulous attention to detail, yet never quite maintaining the stance of detached observer. He is, in fact, deeply committed to what he sees and apprehends, without knowing why he is so affected by the scene. There are both movement and compassion in these poems, the best of which reflect local colour and conditions; but it is the title poem which most fittingly expresses his individuality and allows him scope for the satirical streak which he has since developed with success.

Livingstone had moved to South Africa by the time his second collection, *Sjambok*, appeared, though the poems were all written in Zambia. *Sjambok* commanded immediate attention for its energy and power, its vigorous employment of language, and its originality in describing animals and landscape. It is curious that no one seems to have noticed the connection between his choice of title (*sjambok*=whip of plaited leather) and that of the magazine founded by Roy Campbell and William Plomer in 1926 (*voorslag*=whiplash) in order to "sting with satire the mental hindquarters . . . of the bovine citizenry of the Union." Certainly Livingstone is concentrating more and more upon the satirical element, though the satire is directed at social evils in general rather than those of South Africa in particular. Despite the superficial qualities so highly praised by the critics – the descriptive skill, the evocative phraseology and precision of imagery – *Sjambok* shows that Livingstone is preoccupied with the disrupting effects of Western civilisation upon primitive peoples and traditions. The ambivalence to be detected in his attitudes owes something to the unsettled nature of his own life as well as that of the African continent; and when he extends his range and raises his sights, as in "Suicide Note" and "Johnny Twenty-Three," he can be exceptionally shrewd and perceptive.

– Howard Sergeant

LIYONG, Taban lo. Ugandan. Born in Uganda, in 1938. Educated at Gulu High School; Sir Samuel Baker School; Government Teacher Training College, Kyambogo; Knoxville College, Tennessee; University of North Carolina, Chapel Hill; Georgetown University, Washington, D.C.; Howard University, Washington, D.C., B.A. in literature and journalism 1966; University of Iowa, Iowa City, M.F.A.

Since 1968, Member of the Institute for Development Studies Cultural Division, and currently Lecturer in English, University of Nairobi. Address: Department of English, University of Nairobi, P.O. Box 30197, Nairobi, Kenya.

PUBLICATIONS

Verse

> *Eating Chiefs: Lwo Culture from Lolwe to Malkal.* London, Heinemann, 1970; New York, Humanities Press, 1971.
> *Franz Fanon's Uneven Ribs: With Poems More and More.* London, Heinemann, 1971.
> *Another Nigger Dead: Poems.* London, Heinemann, 1972.
> *Ballads of Underdevelopment.* Nairobi, East African Literature Bureau, 1974.

Novel

> *Meditations in Limbo.* Nairobi, Equatorial Publishers, 1970.

Short Stories

> *Fixions and Other Stories.* London, Heinemann, 1969.
> *The Uniformed Man.* Nairobi, East African Publishing House, 1971.

Other

> *The Last Word: Cultural Synthesism.* Nairobi, East African Publishing House, 1969.
> *Popular Culture of East Africa: Oral Literature.* Nairobi, Longman, 1972.
> *Thirteen Offensives Against Our Enemies.* Nairobi, East African Literature Bureau, 1973.

> Editor, *Sir Apolo Kagwa Discovers England.* London, Heinemann, 1974.

Taban lo Liyong comments:

We have a saying, roughly translated it reads: Chicken lost their teeth through too much talking. I am therefore retiring from writing at the end of 1974 to devote myself to the long postponed scholarly study of Nietzsche. By then the following books will have been completed: *A Calendar of Wisdom* (proverbs in verse); *The African Tourist* (culture criticism); *To Still a Passion* (last poems); *The American Education of Taban lo Liyong*; *The Lubumbashi Lectures*; *Meditations* (last version of *Meditation in Limbo*); and *East African Anthology* (comprehensive anthology of literature from Zinjanthropus to Extelcom).

*   *   *

A wry and acerbic wit, a ready sense of humor, an equally ready sense of tragedy, and a staggeringly wide range of reference points are the most obvious qualities of the poetry of Taban lo Liyong. His two books of poems, *Franz Fanon's Uneven Ribs* and *Another Nigger Dead,* indicate these dimensions by their titles alone, to say nothing of the cornucopia (Taban is certainly copious and also, at times, corny) of work the reader finds himself confronted with (or assaulted by) when he begins to read them. "Language / is a figure / of speech," begins the first poem in his first book. "Bless the african coups / tragedy now means a thing to us," begins the initial poem in his second volume.

More than almost any other African poet, Taban lo Liyong's poems reflect the odyssey of his life as African and poet ranging from facetiousness to seriousness and from pathos to intentional bathos. His subject matter one minute is the break up of a "modern" African marriage (in the poem which begins "i walked among men in america for a year . . .") and the next minute the development of modern poetry (in "The Best Poets," a marvellous ramble through the history of poetic theory).

Call Taban lo Liyong a prodigy, a genius, a freak or an apostate; he might well be pleased with any or all of those titles. If there is any one fault in his work, in fact, it is that there is so much in his two volumes that a reader may be overwhelmed. His is not a poetry which one reads to while away an evening or calm one's nerves after a harrowing day. It is a poetry that demands as much from its reader as it gives in return – a high price for quality merchandise.

– Joseph Bruchac

LOCHHEAD, Liz. Scottish. Born in Motherwell, Lanarkshire, 26 December 1947. Educated at Dalziel High School, Motherwell, 1960–65; Glasgow School of Art, 1965–70, Diploma in Art. Currently, Art Teacher at Bishopbriggs High School, Glasgow, and other schools in Glasgow and Bristol. Recipient: BBC Scotland Prize, 1971; Scottish Arts Council Award, 1973. Address: c/o 13 Tillanburn Road, Newarthill, Motherwell, Lanarkshire, Scotland.

PUBLICATIONS

Verse

Memo for Spring.   Edinburgh, Reprographia, 1972.

Play

Screenplay: *Now and Then,* 1972.

Liz Lochhead comments:

I want my poems to be clear. They should make sense to my landlady and the man in the corner shop. But be capable of being pondered over by the academics round at the University if they like to. Probably I'd hope they'd find a lot of controlled ambiguities, puns – a lot of puns – and word play and double-meanings. I hope they'd find them funny, with a lot of irony, but I'm growing as I get older to distrust irony, despise the way an ironic stance can allow one both to say something and deny responsibility for it, hate the way this kind of cowardice has to hide behind its mask. I like to set up what are, I suppose, essentially dramatic situations within a poem. The poems are almost invariably about people and they tell stories. Above all, I want everything to become so visually alive that it's real, physical, palpable. This I'm always trying for, and I suppose it is exactly what almost every other writer tries to do too.

*   *   *

There is a directness about Liz Lochhead's work that makes it extremely communicative, and she herself has said of her poetry (in an interview with Julie Davidson in *The Scotsman*, 10 June 1972): "I want people to understand it immediately, and I want it to entertain them." However, she distinguishes it from pop-poetry, and indeed its effects often involve more verbal devices and subtleties than might appear at a glance or on a first hearing. Its main characteristics are freshness and truth to experience. An ability to talk about very ordinary things – her young sister trying on her shoes, a trip from Glasgow to Edinburgh, her grandmother knitting, the clang of steelworks, a child carrying a jug of milk, the end of a love-affair – is in a few poems flattened out towards triviality or the prosaic, but for the most part the warmly observing eye and ear are convincingly on target. The experience has a Glasgow and Lanarkshire background, but it is encouraging too that one of her best poems is a "Letter from New England," where elements of ironical comment on small-town life are entertainingly presented through patterned speech-structures and the persona of a surprised visitor.

– Edwin Morgan

LOEWINSOHN, Ron(ald William). American. Born in Iloilo, Philippines, 15 December 1937. Educated at San Francisco State College; University of California, Berkeley, A.B. 1967 (Phi Beta Kappa); Harvard University, Cambridge, Massachusetts (Woodrow Wilson Fellow, 1967–68; Danforth Fellow, 1967–70; Harvard University Graduate Prize Fellow, 1967–70), M.A. 1969, Ph.D. 1971. Taught poetry workshops at San Francisco State College, 1960–61, and the Center for Adult Education, Cambridge, Massachusetts, 1968; Teaching Fellow, Harvard University, 1968–70. Since 1970, Member of the English Department, University of California, Berkeley. Editor, *Change*, 1963, *Sum*, 1964, and *R.C. Lion*, 1966–67, all in Berkeley. Recipient: Poets Foundation Award, 1963; Academy of American Poets Irving Stone Award, 1966. Lives in California, U.S.A.

PUBLICATIONS

Verse

Watermelons. New York, Totem Press, 1959.
The World of the Lie. San Francisco, Change Press, 1963.
Against the Silences to Come. San Francisco, Four Seasons Foundation, 1965.
L'Autre. Los Angeles, Black Sparrow Press, 1967.
Lying Together, Turning the Head and Shifting the Weight, The Produce District and Other Places, Moving – A Spring Poem. Los Angeles, Black Sparrow Press, 1967.
Three Backyard Dramas with Mamas. Santa Barbara, California, Unicorn Press, 1967.
The Sea, Around Us. Los Angeles, Black Sparrow Press, 1968.
The Step. Los Angeles, Black Sparrow Press, 1968.
These Worlds Have Always Moved in Harmony, in *A Play and Two Poems*, with Diane Wakoski and Robert Kelly. Los Angeles, Black Sparrow Press, 1968.
Meat Air: Poems 1957–1969. New York, Harcourt Brace, 1970.
The Leaves. Los Angeles, Black Sparrow Press, 1973.

Other

Editor, *Embodiment of Knowledge*, by William Carlos Williams. New York, New Directions, 1974.

*   *   *

So many young American poets owe allegiance and inspiration to the work of William Carlos Williams that we might well, remembering the 17th century Jonsonians known as the Tribe of Ben, speak now of the Tribe of Bill. Ron Loewinsohn's first book was one of the many bearing a prefatory commendation by Williams; it bore too an introduction by that senior Tribesman, Allen Ginsberg, acclaiming the younger man expansively as part of the "great wave of Poetry . . . breaking over America now." In the years since 1959, Loewinsohn has gone on unobtrusively working in the Williams mode, acknowledging his source with almost insistent modesty (he is currently writing a critical book on Williams and his selected poems, *Meat Air*, is dedicated to him as "informing spirit"), but adding too a note we might connect with Ginsberg – that of a greater sexual explicitness than Williams ever permitted himself (e.g., the poem title "The Romaunt of the Rose Fuck"), still however in the service of a poetry of love. If Loewinsohn's work shows perhaps less sophisticated agility of mind than that of the deceptively mild-seeming doctor of Rutherford, it brings no less gusto to the celebration of the local and the demotic, and to the inventing of beauty in the literal particulars of the common world. *Three Backyard Dramas with Mamas* gives a touching Californian incarnation to the Persephone myth. "The Distractions; The Music" moves effectively between the social world of work and glimpsed violence and the private world of love and beauty. Noteworthy in Loewinsohn is a genuinely sweet lyricism; it's relevant that a recurring motif in his work is the figure of Mozart, exemplar of a lucid, unforced, unegoistic beauty. Here is the end of a short poem called "K. 282":

> The door
> is open & he is playing at his ease.
> He is maybe 18, the beloved of
> God, & is in love himself. Beauty
> falls from him as easily as the sun
> falls thru the windows. His fingers
> follow the play of his mind, dancing
> over the keys as he waits. He is 18,
> it is late summer, he can wait easily
> all day. the door is open. forever.

– Seamus Cooney

LOGAN, John (Burton). American. Born in Red Oak, Iowa, 23 January 1923. Educated at Coe College, Cedar Rapids, Iowa, B.A. in zoology 1943; University of Iowa, Iowa City, M.A. in English 1949; Georgetown University, Washington, D.C. Married; has nine children. Tutor, St. John's College, Annapolis, Maryland, 1947–51; Associate Professor, The General Program, University of Notre Dame, Indiana, 1951–63; Visiting Professor, Department of English, University of Washington, Seattle, 1965, and San Francisco State College; Fellow, Indiana School of Letters, Summers 1965, 1969. Since 1966, Professor of English, State University of New York, Buffalo. Editor, *Choice*, Chicago. Recipient: National Endowment for the Arts grant, 1966, 1968; Miles Modern Poetry Award, 1967; Rockefeller grant, 1968; Morton Dauwen Zabel Award (*Poetry*, Chicago), 1974. Address: Department of English, State University of New York, Buffalo, New York 14214, U.S.A.

PUBLICATIONS

Verse

Cycle for Mother Cabrini. New York, Grove Press, 1955.
Ghosts of the Heart: New Poems. Chicago, University of Chicago Press, 1960.
Spring of the Thief: Poems 1960–1962. New York, Knopf, 1963.
The Zig-Zag Walk: Poems 1963–1968. New York, Dutton, 1969.
The Anonymous Lover: New Poems. New York, Liveright, 1973.

Recording: *Today's Poets 5*, with others, Folkways.

Play

Of Poems, Youth and Spring. New York, French, 1962.

Other

Tom Savage: A Boy of Early Virginia (juvenile). Chicago, Encyclopedia Britannica Press, 1962.

Critical Studies: by Robert Bly, in *The Sixties 5* (Madison, Minnesota), 1961; James Dickey, in *Babel and Byzantium*, New York, Farrar Straus, 1967; Jerome Mazzaro, in *Salmagundi 8* (Flushing, New York), 1968; Paul Carroll, in *The Poem in Its Skin*, Chicago, Follett, 1968.

John Logan comments:

I think of poetry as a reaching, an anonymous loving, which occasionally becomes personal when there are those present who care to listen. I began using stresses, in my first book. Moved to syllabic writing in my second and third books, invented the thirteen syllable line for my "Monologues of the Son of Saul" in my third book and then moved toward a form which adapts slant rhyme to free verse couplets and triplets, which I used for my fourth book. I think of Ogden Nash as an influence in this "delayed rhyme" technique. I don't know who my other influences are, except for Rilke. Stories of the Old Testament and the lives of poets (Southwell, Heine, Rimbaud, Keats, Cummings, Crane) are important sources.

*   *   *

Despite the admiring remarks of distinguished poets and critics, John Logan has not been a popular poet in his native country, and the reasons are not hard to discover. Chiefly, of course, he early became known as a writer of religious verse of a particularly orthodox cast, replete with the conventional symbology of church ritual, and though he has more and more tended to break free both of the overt religious concerns and the metaphorical staples, it is only very recently that he has developed a style to which many of us can respond.

A more important factor in explaining Logan's relation to prospective readers of his verse has been the unfortunate misreading of the poetry by those who might have been expected to do better. Where even sensitive observers have seen nothing but orthodoxy in Logan's early poetry, a few have seen the radical ambiguity which so distinguishes Logan's approach to his materials. Too often the rather prosaic voice and straightforward presentation of sequential observations have been mistaken for ideological certitude and dully competent versification: Unnoticed have been the subtle exorcisms, the parody, the intuitive rejection of resolutions legitimized by a Catholicism that continues, whatever its failings, to hold Logan in its embrace. In fact, only in a recent study by Jerome Mazzaro has the relation between Logan's poetic artifacts and his thematic concerns been successfully explored, to the extent that Logan's witty rhymes and absurd puns, for example, may be understood as essential to his verse, rather than as somehow frivolous posturings.

Logan's poetry evinces a remarkable quality of tenderness, of genuine love of creation, and the use of devices to undercut his sombre and touching evocations is a necessary element in his achievement of a modern voice. Occasionally, even in the most recent work, a quality of ingenuous exclamation and breathless wonderment intrudes, and one senses a wilful generation of excitement that is only half-felt. The language, which has been called prosaic, is often richly ornamented, though he relies on metaphor only sparingly, and there is a distinct playfulness which regularly vies with the more reverential tones that dominate the verse. Similarly, the poems in Logan's third volume, *Spring of the Thief,* as well as the pieces that have lately appeared in various magazines, have been marked by a kind of erotic sensuality that has qualified and deepened the piety which rings in his utterance. This is no doubt related to Logan's quest for self-knowledge and the basically religious transcendence of self-love, so that the masturbatory reveries toward which so many of the better poems tend may be seen as part of a larger struggle, not as a manifestation of purely sexual despair.

Many of Logan's poems explore the spiritual and artistic lives of others, such as Rimbaud, Heine, and Keats, not to mention a host of religious figures, but the explorations are carried on in such a way that they implicate Logan's own problems at every turn. What fascinates Logan is the identity in certain men, especially artists, between scapegoat and priest, and it is this identity that he continually probes, searching out the sacramental qualities of a life in which too often the lovely and tender are obscured by the ugly.

– Robert Boyers

LOGUE, Christopher. British. Born in Portsmouth, Hampshire, 23 November 1926. Educated at Pryor Park College, Bath; Portsmouth Grammar School. Served in the British Army, 1944–48 (including two years in army prison). Lived in France, 1951–56. Contributor, *Private Eye*, London. Lives in London.

Publications

Verse

Wand and Quadrant. Paris, Olympia Press, 1953.
The Weekdream Sonnets. Paris, Jack Straw, 1955.
Devil, Maggot, and Son. Amsterdam, Stols, 1954; Tunbridge Wells, Kent, Peter Russell, 1955.
She Sings, He Sings. Rome, Estratto da Botteghe Oscure, 1957.
A Song for Kathleen. London, Villiers Publications, 1958.
The Song of the Dead Soldier, To the Tune of McCafferty: One Killed in the Interests of Certain Tory Senators in Cyprus. London, Villiers Publications, 1959.
Count Palmiro Vicarion's Book of Limericks. Paris, Olympia Press, 1959.
Memoranda for Marchers. Privately printed, 1959.
Songs. London, Hutchinson, 1959; New York, McDowell Obolensky, 1960.
Songs from "The Lily-White Boys." London, Scorpion Press, 1960.
Count Palmiro Vicarion's Book of Bawdy Ballads. Paris, Olympia Press, 1962.
Logue's A. B. C. London, Scorpion Press, 1966.
I Shall Vote Labour. London, Turret Books, 1966.
The Words of Christopher Logue's Establishment Sings, Etcetera. London, Poet and Printer, 1966.
Selections from a Correspondence Between an Irishman and a Rat. London, Goliard Press, 1966.
Gone Ladies, music by Wallace Southam. London, Turret Books, 1968.
Rat, Oh Rat. London, privately printed, 1968.
SL. Privately printed, 1969.
The Girls. London, Turret Books, 1969.

New Numbers. London, Cape, 1969; New York, Knopf, 1970.
Twelve Cards. London, Lorrimer, 1972.

Recordings: *Christopher Logue Reading His Own Poetry*, with Laurie Lee, Jupiter, 1960; *The Death of Patroclus*, adapted from Book XII of Homer's *Iliad*, Spoken Arts.

Plays

The Trial of Cob and Leach: A News Play (produced London, 1959).
The Lily-White Boys (lyrics only), with Henry Cookson, music by Tony Kinsey and Bill LeSage (produced London, 1960).
Trials by Logue (Antigone and *Cob and Leach)* (produced London, 1960).
Creon (produced London, 1961).
Friday, adaptation of a work by Hugo Klaus. London, Davis Poynter, 1972.

Screenplay: *Savage Messiah,* 1972.

Television Play: *The End of Arthur's Marriage,* with Stanley Myers, 1965.

Novel

Lust (as Count Palmiro Vicarion). Paris, Olympia Press, 1959.

Other

The Arrival of the Poet in the City: A Treatment for a Film. Amsterdam, Yellow Press, and London, Mandarin Books, 1963.

Editor, *True Stories.* London, New English Library, 1966.
Editor, *True Stories from "Private Eye."* London, Deutsch, 1973.

Translator, *The Man Who Told His Love: Twenty Poems Based on Pablo Neruda's "Los Cantos d'Amores."* London, Scorpion Press, 1958.
Translator, *Patrocleia* (from Book XVI of Homer's *Iliad*). London, Scorpion Press, 1962; as *Patrocleia of Homer,* Ann Arbor, University of Michigan Press, 1963.
Translator, *Pax* (from Book XIX of Homer's *Iliad*). London, Turret Books, Rapp and Carroll, 1967.

Theatrical Activities

Actor: **Films** – *Dante's Inferno,* 1966; *The Peasant's Revolt,* 1966; *The Devils,* 1970.

*   *   *

Christopher Logue was one of the few really cosmopolitan figures in the British poetry of the nineteen-fifties. His first collection of poems was published in Paris, and he was one of the earliest English writers to show an interest in Pablo Neruda, with his set of translations or, rather, adaptations, *Red Bird Dancing on Ivory*. These texts later became the material for one of the earliest experiments with poetry-and-jazz, experiemtns which led directly to the now flourishing poetry-and-pop scene. In fact, Logue throughout his career has shown a restless impatience with conventional boundaries for poetry. He has experimented with the night-club or cabaret song, as Auden did; one of his poems has been used as the theme-song for a film (the film version of Nell Dunn's novel, *Poor Cow*); and a good number have appeared on posters. Often, those which appeared on posters were written especially for the medium, which enabled Logue to explore two themes at once – his interest in visual design, and his feeling that poetry should be a "popular" art-form, the vehicle for a political or social message. Part, at least, of his reputation is based on his protest-poems, which he reads to brilliant effect at recitals and concerts.

Few living British poets have such a paradoxical *oeuvre*, however. Side by side with his political poems, which frequently owe a good deal to the example of Brecht, Logue has been making an adaptation of the *Iliad*. Two sections of this have so far been published, under the titles *Patrocleia* and *Pax*. Clearly, these are influenced by Ezra Pound: some passages are in a high rhetorical style, others slangy and almost colloquial. Homer speaks to us as a modern author, and the *Iliad* often lives as freshly as the day when it was first composed.

– Edward Lucie-Smith

LONGLEY, Michael. Irish. Born in Belfast, Northern Ireland, 27 July 1939. Educated at the Royal Belfast Academical Institution, 1951–58; Trinity College, Dublin, B.A. (honours) in classics 1963. Married to Edna Broderick; has one daughter and one son. Assistant Master, Avoca School, Blackrock, 1962–63, Belfast High School and Erith Secondary School, 1963–64, and Royal Belfast Academical Institution, 1964–69. Since 1970, Assistant Director, Arts Council of Northern Ireland, Belfast. Recipient: Eric Gregory Award, 1965. Address: 18 Hillside Park, Stranmillis, Belfast 9, Northern Ireland.

PUBLICATIONS

Verse

Ten Poems. Belfast, Festival Publications, 1965.
Room to Rhyme, with Seamus Heaney and David Hammond. Belfast, Arts Council of Northern Ireland, 1968.
Secret Marriages: Nine Short Poems. Manchester, Phoenix Pamphlet Poets Press, 1968.
Three Regional Voices, with Barry Tebb and Iain Crichton Smith. London, Poet and Printer, 1968.
No Continuing City: Poems 1963–1968. London, Macmillan, and Chester Springs, Pennsylvania, Dufour, 1969.
Lares. London, Poet and Printer, 1972.
An Exploded View: Poems 1968–1972. London, Gollancz, 1973.

Other

Editor, *Causeway: The Arts in Ulster.* Belfast, Arts Council of Northern Ireland, and Dublin, Gill and Macmillan, 1971.

Editor, *Under the Moon, Over the Stars: Young People's Writing from Ulster.* Belfast, Arts Council of Northern Ireland, 1971.

*   *   *

Michael Longely is one of several interesting young Irish poets who made their debut during the 1960's. He was part winner of the Eric Gregory Award in 1965 and his first collection *No Continuing City* appeared four years later. The work as a whole was already mature although a number of the poems dated from Longley's undergraduate years. His second volume, *An Exploded View,* showed he had acquired greater technical assurance and had further humanized and extended his thematic range.

Longley's work includes a considerable amount of free verse but it also provides a convincing demonstration of the continuing validity of rhyme and metre. He has accommodated contemporary idiom within a wide variety of traditional forms ranging from *terza rima* and sonnet to octo-syllabic eight-line stanzas. Some of the earlier poems, both in tone and structure, indicated a profound and profitable study of the "metaphysical" poets. Without the example of John Donne, Longley could hardly have written as he does of moths:

> Who hazard all to be
> Where we, the only two it seems,
> Inhabit so delightfully
> A room it bursts its seams
> And spills on to the lawn in beams . . .
> — from "Epithalamion"

Longley's gift for finding symbols in a given environment to express interior meaning is already apparent in "Epithalamion." Later he carried the process much further. The most elaborate example is "The Hebrides," a lengthy monologue on the achievement and extension of self-knowledge. The poem is remarkable for the imaginative energy of its imagery and for the accomplished handling of a stanza composed of six lines of varying lengths:

> Along my arteries
> Sluice those homewaters petroleum hurts.
> Dry docks, gantries,
>
> Dykes of apparatus educate my bones
> To track the buoys
> Up sea lanes love emblazons
> To streets where shall conclude
> My journey back from flux to poise, from poise
> To attitude.

A prominent place in Longley's work is occupied by heroes who belong to what Frank O'Connor called the submerged population group. They range from John Clare and Emily Dickinson to Walter Mitty and jazz musicians like Bix Beiderbecke. Longley's pantheon is also generously peopled with mythological figures

taken, interestingly, from Greek myths rather than those of his own land. Sometimes the mythologizing process is extended to real people. One of 'these is Dr.
Johnson and another is the poet's baby nephew who inspired "Christopher at
Birth." This ends with a series of heraldic images which could have been taken
from some mediaeval tapestry and which turn the poem away from a consideration
of the personal implications of the child's birth to place it against the backdrop of
history.

A mythologizing process also takes place in some of Longley's poems about the
animal world. "Swans Mating" describes the pairing in terms which load the
physical act with overtones of numinous significance:

> This was a marriage and a baptism,
> A holding of breath, nearly a drowning,
> Wings spread wide for balance where he trod,
> Her feathers full of water and her neck
> Under the water like a bar of light.

Longley's deep sympathy with the animal world is self-evident. The variety of
creatures in his poems is so large that there is a feeling at times of having wandered
into a nature reserve. Longley undoubtedly looks on animals with a kindly eye.
Sometimes they suggest the working of elemental forces; thus the badger "manages
the earth with his paws." But the red tooth and claw find no place in Longley's
vision of nature and his animals are never put to use as images of cruelty or
menace.

In the earlier poems Longley made effective use of certain resonant words, such
as "brainstorm," "histories" and "anthem," but tended to over-exploit them. His
technique is now more finely honed and he no longer finds it necessary to resort to
such props. At the same time he has retained his ability to suggest the mysteries
which underlie the appearances of life. "Casualty," a poem about a decaying
sheep, has this kind of awareness in spite of the absence of the earlier poeticisms:

> For the ribs began to scatter
> The wool to move outward
> As though hunger still worked there
>
> As though something that had followed
> Fox and crow was desperate for
> A last morsel and was
> Other than the wind or rain.

Reaction to the Northern Ireland troubles has given rise to some of Longley's
most compassionate poems. One of these links the delayed effects on his father of
wounds incurred in the Great War with the murders in Belfast of three British
soldiers and a bus conductor. In the present circumstances particularly it is not
surprising that Longley should sometimes give an impression of *déracinement* but so
far there is no sign that he may reject the fractured and psychically scarred society
to which he is heir as so many Irish writers before him have done. On the contrary
he makes a point of claiming Ireland as his country "though today / *Timor mortis
conturbat me.*"

Longley's attitude towards his craft, conservative in the best sense as it is, seems
likely to be as well defended as his Irish identity. In an early poem called "The
Ornithological Section" he drew a humorous parallel between taxidermy and the
creative process, implying that the latter also was a species of embalmment. It was
an amusing articulation of a traditional point of view. Recently he has declared an
ambition to be the last poet in Europe to find a rhyme. Again it is clear that

Longley's tongue is partly in his cheek but there is an underlying seriousness to the remark.

– Rivers Carew

———————

LORDE, Audre (Geraldin). American. Born in New York City, 18 February 1934. Educated at Hunter College, New York, B.A. 1959; Columbia University, New York, M.L.S. 1961. Married Edwin A. Rollins in 1962; has one daughter and one son. Staff Member, Mount Vernon Public Library, New York, 1961–63; Instructor, Town School, New York, 1966–68; Poet-in-Residence, Tougaloo College, Mississippi, 1968; Instructor, City College of New York, 1968–70, and Lehman College, New York, 1969–70. Since 1970, Lecturer, John Jay College of Criminal Justice, New York. Recipient: National Endowment for the Arts grant, 1968; New York State Council on the Arts Public Service Award, 1972. Address: 207 St. Paul's Avenue, Staten Island, New York 10304, U.S.A.

PUBLICATIONS

Verse

The First Cities. New York, Poets Press, 1968.
Cables to Rage. Detroit, Broadside Press, and London, Paul Breman, 1970.
From a Land Where Other People Live. Detroit, Broadside Press, 1973.
New York Head Shop and Museum. Detroit, Broadside Press, 1974.

*   *   *

Audre Lorde is a poet of the physical. Whether the subject is poetry, "I am black because I come from the earth's inside / Take my word for jewel in your open light," or the destruction of innocence, "My sister has my tongue / . . . And I presume her trustless as a stone," the language is bold, immediate, almost visceral in nature. Whatever the time of action, the poems themselves invariably devolve upon concrete scenes and objects, whose larger meanings are carried by the leanness and precision of imagery, the compactness and passion of line.

Yet, the beauty and power of words clothe a profound and bitter anguish, born of loss, disillusion, and the painful recognition of the transience of all things human – particularly human love. The poet is not easily – if ever – reconciled; however, an indomitable spirit continually seeks a more favorable accommodation. The struggle begins with the harsh recognition of human betrayal: "We have no passions left to love the spring / Who had suffered autumn as we did, alone." Because self will not be silenced, passion returns – as rage: "We were brown free girls / Love singing beneath their skin / . . . we purchased bridges with our mothers' bloody gold." The scathing denunciation is never fully retracted. It will mellow, however, with the gradual apprehension that the enemy cannot be particularized; that human betrayal,

935

if it exists, is the result of a much larger movement: human mutability. This is the insight that informs the virtuoso pieces "Martha," and "Bridge Through My Windows." Perhaps the final accommodation is the recognition that a universe whose only constant is change is inherently antagonistic to the human spirit. In such a world, the poet seems to suggest, one must create beauty, truth and love: "Thus I hold you / frank in my heart's eye." In this, her vision is both timeless and existential.

– Saundra Towns

———————————

LOWBURY, Edward (Joseph Lister).   British.   Born in London, 6 December 1913. Educated at St. Paul's School, London, 1927–33; University College, Oxford (Newdigate Prize, 1934, Matthew Arnold Memorial Prize, 1937), 1933–37, B.A. (honours) 1936, B.M., B.Ch. 1939; London Hospital, University of London, M.A. 1940, D.M. 1957. Specialist in Pathology, Royal Army Medical Corps, 1943–47. Married Alison Young, daughter of the poet Andrew Young, in 1954; has three daughters. Bacteriologist, 1946–49, and currently, Member, Medical Research Council Scientific Staff, Birmingham Accident Hospital; since 1960, Consultant Adviser in Bacteriology, Birmingham Regional Hospital Board; since 1960, Honorary Director, Hospital Infection Research Laboratory, Birmingham. Editor, *Equator* magazine, Nairobi, Kenya, 1945–46. Visited the United States as a World Health Organization Consultant in 1965. Fellow, Royal College of Pathologists; John Keats Memorial Lecturer, Guy's Hospital, London, 1973. Recipient: Honorary Research Fellowship, University of Birmingham, 1957. Member, Royal College of Physicians, 1972; Fellow, Royal Society of Literature, 1974. Address: 79 Vernon Road, Birmingham B18 9SQ, England.

PUBLICATIONS

Verse

>   *Fire: A Symphonic Ode.*   Oxford, Blackwell, 1934.
>   *Crossing the Line.*   London, Hutchinson, 1946.
>   *Metamorphoses.*   Privately printed, 1955.
>   *Time for Sale.*   London, Chatto and Windus-Hogarth Press, 1961.
>   *New Poems.*   Richmond, Surrey, Keepsake Press, 1965.
>   *Daylight Astronomy.*   London, Chatto and Windus-Hogarth Press, and Middletown, Connecticut, Wesleyan University Press, 1968.
>   *Figures of Eight.*   Richmond, Surrey, Keepsake Press, 1969.
>   *Green Magic* (for children).   London, Chatto and Windus, 1972.
>   *Two Confessions.*   Richmond, Surrey, Keepsake Press, 1973.
>   *The Night Watchman.*   London, Chatto and Windus-Hogarth Press, 1974.

Other

>   *Facing North* (miscellany).   London, Mitre Press, 1960.
>   *Thomas Campion: Poet, Composer, Physician,* with Timothy Salter and Alison Young.   London, Chatto and Windus, and New York, Barnes and Noble, 1970.

936

Manuscript Collection: Birmingham University Library.

Critical Study: "Edward Lowbury" by John Press, in *Southern Review* (Baton Rouge, Louisiana), Spring 1970.

Edward Lowbury comments:

Poetry is an obsessional activity through which, at intervals in my medical life, I have been able to work off accumulated tension; it is, for me, an exploration, through words, of various experiences, and in particular of painfully exciting or disturbing or conflicting experiences – love: hardship and loss; the attritions of time; childhood and age; nature and the unknown; experiences in my medical work. In the poem I discover verbal, visual and metrical equivalents to represent the conflicts and ambiguities of the world about which I write. When the components shape themselves into structures (i.e. poems) with an inner tension, with what I judge to be the correct balance of thought and feeling, of harmony and discord, and when the structures give me – and others – a simultaneous feeling of surprise and inevitability, I feel I have found whatever it was I was looking for in my "exploration." I usually take many wrong turnings before I find (if I ever do find) the right one; I think I can recognise when I have struck the right path and the place where I should stop but I realize that neither the writer nor any individual critic can make categorical judgements.

*   *   *

The poetry of Edward Lowbury demonstrates that there is still a place for the competent neo-Georgian who has understood and purged himself of the vices of the original Georgian school. He had a fine master in his late and great father-in-law, Andrew Young. He has shown no development, but has worked hard to record his observations sensitively and in a well-handled verse – his work on Thomas Campion has served him in good stead here. Such a poem as "The Collector" shows him at his best: too over-dependent on Young, certainly, to achieve a really individual voice – but there is the minimum of irrelevant chatter, and the poet means what he says. He collects bluebells, then other kinds of flowers – but discovers that he can never get enough, so that he ends:

> A lifetime brought this new collector's itch:
> In a world of flowers, names, necessities –
> To see how many I could do without:
> And at last the distant shout
> "Come home" finds me exulting in a wealth
> Of unpossessions – all of it, perhaps,
> A practice-run for doing without myself.

This is his most successful manner. In love poetry, or less precisely observed nature poetry, he is more awkward; nor do his attempts at the colloquial come off, as the opening of "Astrology" aptly demonstrates: "So it's true, all that nonsense / About the stars controlling destiny: / True, anyway, for migrant birds! . . ." But he is at all times a modest and unstrident poet, whose quiet achievement outstrips that of many of his better known contemporaries.

– Martin Seymour-Smith

LOWELL, Robert (Traill Spence, Jr.). American. Born in Boston, Massachusetts, 1 March 1917.· Educated at St. Mark's School; Harvard University, Cambridge, Massachusetts, 1935–37; Kenyon College, Gambier, Ohio, A.B. (summa cum laude) 1940 (Phi Beta Kappa). Conscientious objector during World War II: served prison sentence, 1943–44. Married the writer Jean Stafford in 1940 (divorced, 1948); the writer Elizabeth Hardwick, 1949, has one daughter; third marriage, has one daughter. Worked for Sheed and Ward, publishers, New York, 1941–42. Taught at the University of Iowa, Iowa City, 1949–50, 1952–53; Salzburg Seminar on American Studies, 1952; Boston University; New School for Social Research, New York; Harvard University. Consultant in Poetry, Library of Congress, Washington, D.C., 1947–48; Visiting Fellow, All Souls College, Oxford, 1970. Since 1970, has taught at Kent University, Canterbury. Recipient: Pulitzer Prize, 1947; National Institute of Arts and Letters grant, 1947; Guggenheim Fellowship, 1947, 1974; Harriet Monroe Poetry Award, 1952; Guinness Prize, 1959; National Book Award, 1960; Harriet Monroe Memorial Prize, 1961, and Levinson Prize, 1963 (*Poetry*, Chicago); Bollingen Poetry Translation Award, 1962; New England Poetry Club Golden Rose, 1964; Ford grant, for drama, 1964; Obie Award, for drama, 1965; Sarah Josepha Hale Award, 1966; Copernicus Award, 1974. Member, American Academy of Arts and Letters. Address: 15 West 67th Street, New York, New York 10023, U.S.A.

PUBLICATIONS

Verse

The Land of Unlikeness. Cummington, Massachusetts, Cummington Press, 1944.
Lord Weary's Castle. New York, Harcourt Brace, 1946.
Poems 1938–1949. London, Faber, 1950.
The Mills of the Kavanaughs. New York, Harcourt Brace, 1951.
Life Studies. London, Faber, 1959; augmented edition, New York, Farrar Straus, 1959; Faber, 1968.
Imitations. New York, Farrar Straus, 1961; London, Faber, 1962.
For the Union Dead. New York, Farrar Straus, 1964; London, Faber, 1965.
Selected Poems. London, Faber, 1965.
Near the Ocean. New York, Farrar Straus, and London, Faber, 1967.
The Voyage and Other Versions of Poems by Baudelaire. New York, Farrar Straus, and London, Faber, 1968.
Notebook 1967–1968. New York, Farrar Straus, 1969; augmented edition, as Notebook, London, Faber, and Farrar Straus, 1970.
For Lizzie and Harriet. London, Faber, and New York, Farrar Straus, 1973.
History. London, Faber, and New York, Farrar Straus, 1973.
The Dolphin. London, Faber, and New York, Farrar Straus, 1973.
Poems: A Selection, edited by Jonathan Raban. London, Faber, 1974.

Plays

Phaedra, adaptation of the play by Racine (produced London, 1961). Included in Phaedra and Figaro, New York, Farrar Straus, 1961; as Phaedra, London, Faber, 1963.
The Old Glory (Benito Cereno and My Kinsman, Major Molineux) (produced New York, 1964; Benito Cereno produced London, 1967). New York, Farrar

Straus, 1964; expanded version, including *Endecott and the Red Cross* (produced New York, 1968), London, Faber, 1966; Farrar Straus, 1968.

Prometheus Bound, adaptation of a play by Aeschylus (produced New Haven, Connecticut, 1967; London, 1971). New York, Farrar Straus, 1969; London, Faber, 1970.

Other

Editor, with Peter Taylor and Robert Penn Warren, *Randall Jarrell 1914–1965*. New York, Farrar Straus, 1967.

Robert Lowell comments:

I belong to no "school" of poetry, but various living or once-living poets have fascinated me – W. C. Williams, Pound, Tate Ransom, Eliot, and Yeats. And many, many others, though perhaps I've tried to be a chameleon in vain.

A critical statement on my own verse? I know about my verse, I have been looking at it for a long time since I first started to write and revise. But this question must not be answered. One must only analyse oneself with great seriousness, or casually and intuitively. All these things you inquire about are subjects for the professors, their subjects, their inventions. I suppose these things have value, but go against the intellect. I don't like to read such pieces, see a writer I understand laid on the surgeon's table, see what was comprehensible made dull.

*   *   *

Some modern artists, like Piet Mondrian or Franz Kline, have exploited a personal calligraphy throughout their artistic lives. But the greatest modern artists, typically, have innovated ceaselessly, moving from style to style and continually destroying their old solutions in search of new matter and manner. The latter sort of artist, as inventive as Edison, includes Picasso and Stravinsky; in literature, Yeats, Joyce, Pound and Roethke.

While the degree of Robert Lowell's achievement is difficult to assess at this time, he clearly belongs among the changing innovators of modern art. In his thirty years of publishing, he has confounded his admirers by renouncing an achieved style and exploring new territory. Because of his dissatisfaction with his achievement and because that achievement has already been considerable, he has the potential to become the major poet in English of the last half of this century, as Yeats – who recurrently judged himself a failure, and set out to improve his art – was the major poet of the first half.

Lowell has had to resist the temptation to become a monument; it is a temptation actively offered: the literary entrepreneurs of the academy and the press would like to cast him in bronze as The Genius of Contemporary Poetry, so that they could stop thinking about poetry. Lowell's strength has been his obdurate commitment to artistic excellence. Monuments do not wrote poems. It is up to him, whether in fifty years he looks as Yeats looks to us now, or whether he more closely resembles another intelligent innovator, but a man of less achievement, the laureate Robert Bridges.

Lowell's first collection was a small edition of *The Land of Unlikeness* in 1944. The best of these poems were revised and reprinted in *Lord Weary's Castle* in 1946; the years at the end of the war were astonishingly productive. The petulance and melodrama of much of *The Land of Unlikeness* disappeared; *Lord Weary's Castle* was simply the most powerful book of poems written in our language since *The Tower*. The poems were formal, a tight decasyllable always rhymed; yet the violent energy of the diction – especially embodied in a series of monosyllabic verbs which were frequently tactile – hammered against the decasyllabic cage. Enjambment was violent, caesura eccentric, and the din deafening. Subject matter was painful conflict, particularly within the confines of a rigorous Catholicism to which Lowell brought a strong element of New England Calvinism. Pain, tight form, energetic diction and syntax all combine in this passage from "New Year's Day":

> In the snow
> The kitten heaved its hindlegs, as if fouled,
> And died. We bent it in a Christmas box
> And scattered blazing weeds to scare the crow
> Until the snake-tailed sea-winds coughed and howled
> For alms outside the church whose double locks
> Wait for St. Peter. . . .

This poem is medial in its violence, for *Lord Weary's Castle* varies from an extreme which is close to the spitting jerkiness of the poems left behind in *Land of Unlikeness*, nearly too angry or painful for coherent speech, to the relatively smooth narrative couplet of later poems like "After the Surprising Conversions" and "Between the Porch and the Altar." The celebrated "Quaker Graveyard at Nantucket" is medial also, but leans toward the earlier, more violent style. The later narrative poems include character and start Lowell toward the inclusiveness which he has always envied in the novel. The prosody and diction diminish in violence, and resemble the model that Lowell himself has named, the Robert Browning of "My Last Duchess" and of "Sordello." Perhaps the best of the dramatic monologues belongs to Lowell's second major book, *The Mills of the Kavanaughs*, the magnificent "Mother Marie Therese":

> The bell-buoy, whom she called the Cardinal,
> Dances upon her. If she hears at all,
> She only hears it tolling to the shore,
> Where our frost-bitten sisters know the roar
> Of water, inching, always on the move
> For virgins, when they wish the times were love,
> And their hysterical hosannas rouse
> The loveless harems of the buck ruffed grouse,
> Who drums, untroubled now, beside the sea –
> As if he found our stern virginity
> *Contra naturam*. . . .

The style and manner are perfectly achieved; one could imagine the poet spending the rest of his life comfortably in this decasyllabic rocking chair. But the modern artist is typically unable or unwilling to work within the limits of his known abilities. In the title poem of this volume, Lowell failed. Lyric obscurity and ellipsis prevented his narrative. For several years, Lowell printed virtually nothing; eight years elapsed before the next volume, *Life Studies*.

The new book was a thorough departure. It was autobiographical, it was largely free verse, and the American edition included prose. Instead of noble thunder out of Virgil and Calvin, one read, "Tamed by Miltown, we lie on mother's bed." In the decade of the fifties, Lowell had gone through enormous changes in his personal life; he was divorced, he left the Catholic church, he experienced the first of the attacks of madness which have committed him to mental hospitals on several occasions, he was remarried, and he became a father. His attitude toward his old poetry shifted; in conversation he told friends that his old poetry seemed melodramatic, posturing. And modern poetry, in general, he felt, was inferior to the modern novel because it excluded so much of reality. Psychotherapists turned him more directly to examining his own experience, in particular his childhood; one started him on a prose autobiography, which became the excellent "91 Revere Street," which was included in the American *Life Studies*. The poet W. D. Snodgrass was a student of Lowell's at Iowa, and began to write poems out of his own life, in a manner which has been called confessional; Lowell observed the possibility, and has acknowledged his indebtedness. Yet another source of his change (and there are doubtless more to be found) was the vogue of poetry reading; in America the enormous popularity of the poetry reading has conditioned American poets to the sound of their own poems in their own mouths. The vogue did not begin until after *Lord Weary's Castle*. Reading his old poems aloud to audiences, Lowell found himself wanting to relax them, to make them more like speech. In this source of change he resembled Yeats, whose poems became more speech-like when he found himself writing for the stage; contact between voice and audience showed up poetic diction of early work, for both men.

Whatever the sources, *Life Studies* was a superb book. There are echoes of earlier Lowell, even to intact iambic pentameters, but the voice is usually quieter and more intimate, as in this passage from "Skunk Hour":

> One dark night,
> my Tudor Ford climbed the hill's skull;
> I watched for love-cars. Lights turned down,
> they lay together, hull to hull,
> where the graveyard shelves on the town . . . .
> My mind's not right.

Lowell's readers tended to argue the merits of the disparate styles, without seeming able to encompass the whole man. But Lowell was to confound them further, In 1961 he brought out *Imitations,* a collection of translations which are largely inaccurate on purpose, adaptations which either attempt obliquely to express the feeling of the original or frankly to use the translated images to make new Lowell poems. As with Ezra Pound's translations, many of which could be called imitations, Lowell's readers are allowed in this volume to observe a part of the education of a major poet: his assimilation – which sometimes includes distortion – of his sources.

In 1964–65 Lowell published two books. *For the Union Dead* carried on the styles of *Life Studies*, with especial success in the title poem, but with energy that frequently reminds us of *Lord Weary's Castle*. In *The Old Glory*, Lowell collected his first attempts at theatre (he has also been translating – or imitating – plays; his *Phaedra* has been produced on several occasions). The plays ran successfully in New York, and *Benito Cereno* had good notices in particular. In 1967 Lowell published a brief collection of poems and imitations called *Near the Ocean*. Along with *The Mills of the Kavanaughs*, it is among his lesser work. The imitations are of quality, but the seven original poems, largely written in an elliptical neo-classic tetrameter couplet, fail to make a new resting place for the poet. They seem to thresh and founder within received or achieved moods of diction, not necessarily Lowell's. They seem dissatisfied with their own definition. They remind one of the earlier failures. After *The Land of Unlikeness* came *Lord Weary's Castle*, after *The Mills of the Kavanaughs, Life Studies*.

Yet after *Near the Ocean* came *Notebook 1967–1968*, in 1969. It is another failure, grander in its scope and more abysmal in its sinking. The line is generally iambic, and at first glance seems a return to the high bravado of *Lord Weary*; but really the rhythm is slack, and the meter metronomic. The series of unrhymed fourteen-liners imitates John Berryman's *Dream Songs* in ellipses and in subject matter. Lowell writes topical poems – on assassinations and political campaigns – as if he were striving to become known as the conscience of his times; these verses read like prayers to Stockholm. One looks back to *Lord Weary's Castle* and *Life Studies* for confirmation; yes, he made great poems. Perhaps he will make them again.

Or perhaps he will simply rewrite *Notebook* over and over again, for the rest of his life, like an old actor constantly making farewell appearances. In 1970 he published *Notebook,* in which, as he wrote, "about a hundred of the old poems have been changed, some noticeably. More than 90 new poems have been added." In 1973, *Notebook* divided into two, and spawned a third collection. *History* included most of the *Notebook* poems, revised, and added 80 new poems. *For Lizzie and Herriet* reprinted from *Notebook* the 60-odd poems about Lowell's former wife and his daughter, "In another order, in other versions. . . ." The third 1973 book was *The Dolphin,* more than 100 further exercises in the form – 14 lines, still mostly unrhymed, frequently iambic – which has dogged the poet for 6 years. One of the new *History* poems talks about opening "an old closet door," to find "myself / covered with quick-lime, my face deliquescent . . . / by oversight still recognizeable . . .":

> Ah the swift vanishing of my older
> generation – the deaths, suicide, madness
> of Roethke, Berryman, Jarrell and Lowell,
> "the last the most discouraging of all
> surviving to dissipate *Lord Weary's Castle*
> and nine subsequent useful poems
> in the seedy grandiloquence of *Notebook.*"

Lowell quotes (and rewrites; the critic said "good" not "useful") an unnamed critic, who spoke not only of "the seedy grandiloquence" of *Notebook,* but of its "self-serving journalism." Reading these latest versions, a reader might find the poems more "self-exploiting" than "self-serving." One senses the life lived in order to provide material for poems; one sees the cannibal-poet who dines off portions of his own body. And the bodies of his family. The verse remains strangely lacking in sensuality, monotonously heavy, sensational, and dishonest.

– Donald Hall

LOWENFELS, Walter. American. Born in New York City, 10 May 1897. Served in the Army Air Force in World War I. Married Lillian Apotheker in 1926; has four children. Worked as a journalist in Philadelphia. Recipient: Richard Aldington Award, 1929; *Mainstream* Award, 1957; Longview Foundation Award, 1963. Address: Boulder Drive, Peekskill, New York 10566, U.S.A.

PUBLICATIONS

Verse

Episodes and Epistles. New York, Thomas Seltzer, 1925.
Finale of Seem: A Lyrical Narrative. London, Heinemann, 1929.
Apollinaire: An Elegy. Paris, Hours Press, 1930.
U.S.A. with Music: An Operatic Tragedy. Paris, Carrefour, 1930.
Elegy for D. H. Lawrence. Paris, Carrefour, 1932.
The Suicide. Paris, Carrefour, 1934.
Sonnets of Love and Liberty. New York, Blue Heron Press, 1955.
American Voices. New York, Roving Eye Press, 1959.
Some Deaths: Selected Poems 1929–1962. Highlands, North Carolina, Jargon, 1964.
Translations from Scorpius. Monmouth, Maine, Poetry Dimension Press, 1966.
We Are All Poets, Really, edited by Allen De Loach. Buffalo, New York, Intrepid Press, 1967.
Thou Shalt Not Overkill: Walter Lowenfels' Peace Poems, edited by Lillian Lowenfels. Belmont, Massachusetts, Hellric Publications, 1968.
Found Poems and Others. New York, Barlenmir House, 1972.

Other

Anonymous, The Need for Anonymity. Paris, Carrefour Editions, 1930.
To an Imaginary Daughter. New York, Horizon Press, 1964.
Land of Roseberries. Mexico City, El Corno Emplumado, 1965.
The Portable Walter: From the Prose and Poetry of Walter Lowenfels, edited by Robert Gover. New York, Grove Press, 1968.
My Many Lives: The Autobiography of Walter Lowenfels: II. The Poetry of My Politics. Homestead, Florida, Olivant Press, 1969.
The Life of Fraenkel's Death: A Biographical Inquest, with Howard McCord. Pullman, Washington State University Press, 1970.
The Revolution Is to Be Human. New York, International Publishers, 1973.
Reality Prime: Pages from a Journal. New York, Cycle Press, 1974.

Editor and Translator, *Song of Peace: Based on Poems by Paul Eluard, Nicolas Guillén, Horace, M. Lukenin, Gabriela Mistral, Vitêslave Nezval, Tu Fu.* New York, Roving Eye Press, 1959.
Editor, *Walt Whitman's Civil War.* New York, Knopf, 1960.
Editor, *Poets of Today: A New American Anthology.* New York, International Publishers, 1964.
Editor, *Where is Vietnam? American Poets Respond: An Anthology Of Contemporary Poems.* New York, Doubleday, 1967.
Editor, *New Jazz Poets* (recording and text). New York, Folkways, 1967.
Editor, *The Writing on the Wall: 108 American Poems of Protest.* New York, Doubleday, 1969.
Editor, *In a Time of Revolution: Poems from Our Third World.* New York, Random House, 1969.
Editor, *From the Belly of the Shark: A New Anthology of Native Americans: Poems by Chicanos, Eskimos, Hawaiians, Puerto Ricans in the U.S.A., With Related Poems by Others.* New York, Vintage Books, 1973.

Manuscript Collection: Yale University, New Haven, Connecticut.

Walter Lowenfels comments:

   Writing begins with a mechanical mastery over inanimate objects: paper, carbon, typewriter, dictionary, postage stamps, cluttered desk, etc. Considering that typewriter keys are made of steel, the process can be considered partly metallurgical – the technology of pouring the language into a mold precisely the shape of what the writer wants to get the O.K. of the inspector he never sees – the audience.
   "Anyone," said Willard Gibbs of his scientific discoveries, "having these desires, will make these discoveries."

                                    *   *   *

   "The main point is to survive," Walter Lowenfels wrote in 1959, at age 62. His verse from the twenties, long poems on love and death, influenced Kenneth Rexroth. In the thirties, the almost "geological" cataclysym of the Great Depression generated "Steel 1937." Feeling that that poem was inadequate, Lowenfels abandoned poetry to fight for civil and labor rights until his imprisonment in the McCarthy period. That led him to "socialist surrealism," a looser poetry with a wacky texture:

> I saw the Impossibilists looking at the measurement
> of a billionth of a second,
> tying molecules in knots,
> announcing: "Today is obsolete."

Lowenfels quotes Rimbaud: "it is absolutely necessary to be modern." Then he finds a use for these perceptions, quoting Leonardo: "the artist is the first politician." Tomorrow is today, he says in "The Autobiography of My Poems," and the political goals of the thirties – equality of the Negro before the law and the rights of labor – have been met because people like him worked and suffered. He opens his elegy for a soldier killed in the Korean War:

> Spring raided our street,
> broke through the thin glass of daybreak,
> found houses asleep,
> neighbor's cyclamen bush
> redder than it was yesterday.

Spring, no doubt, arrested the cyclamen bush. It is interesting to flip back and forth between Lowenfel's poetry and his prose. "Speech to the Court," a logical, noble defense at his own trial, is in careful prose which would convince any careful listener. The later poem, "Speech to the Court," brings the universe into it:

> Pity the poor
> dinosaur
> he doesn't live here
> anymore.

Atomic war is a possibility which disturbs a poet whose theme, in 1927, was "humanity is killing itself and doesn't even know it." In the twenties, as now, he

tried to write "not poems as literature but as a bridge over the desert of our age."
He is a personal poet and a political poet. Henry Miller called him "probably *the*
poet of the age."

– Michael André

LUCIE-SMITH, (John) Edward (McKenzie). British. Born in Kingston, Jamaica,
27 February 1933. Educated at King's School, Canterbury; Merton College,
Oxford, B.A. 1954. Education Officer, Royal Air Force, 1954–56. Free-lance Journalist. Co-Founder, Turret Books, London, 1965. Recipient: Rhys Memorial Prize,
1962; Arts Council Triennial Poetry Prize, 1962. Fellow, Royal Society of Literature. Address: 24 Sydney Street, London S.W.3, England.

PUBLICATIONS

Verse

(Poems). Oxford, Fantasy Press, 1954.
A Tropical Childhood and Other Poems. London and New York, Oxford
　University Press, 1961.
Penguin Modern Poets 6, with Jack Clemo and George MacBeth. London,
　Penguin, 1964.
Confessions and Histories. London and New York, Oxford University Press,
　1964.
Fir-Tree Song. London, Turret Books, 1965.
Jazz for the N.U.F. London, Turret Books, 1965.
A Game of French and English. London, Turret Books, 1965.
Three Experiments. London, Turret Books, 1965.
Gallipoli – Fifty Years After. London, Turret Books, 1966.
Cloud Sun Fountain Statue. Cologne, Hansjörg Mayer, 1966.
Silence, music by Wallace Southam. London, Turret Books, 1967.
"Heureux Qui, Comme Ulysse . . ." London, Turret Books, 1967.
Borrowed Emblems. London, Turret Books, 1967.
Towards Silence. London, Oxford University Press, 1968.
Teeth and Bones. London, Pebble Press, 1968.
Six Kinds of Creature. London, Turret Books, 1968.
Snow Poem. London, Turret Books, 1969.
Egyptian Ode. Stoke Ferry, Norfolk, Daedalus Press, 1969.
Six More Beasts. London, Turret Books, 1970.
Lovers. Frensham, Surrey, Sceptre Press, 1970.
The Rhino. London, Steam Press, 1971.
A Girl Surveyed. London, Hanover Gallery, 1971.
The Yak, The Polar Bear, The Dodo, The Goldfish, The Dinosaur, The Parrot
　(posters). London, Turret Books, 1971.
The Well-Wishers. London and New York, Oxford University Press, 1974.

Other

Mystery in the Universe: Notes on an Interview with Allen Ginsberg. London, Turret Books, 1965.
Op Art, edited by Duncan Taylor. London, BBC Publications, 1966.
What Is a Painting? London, Macdonald, 1966.
Thinking about Art: Critical Essays. London, Calder and Boyars, 1968.
A Beginner's Guide to Auctions (as Peter Kershaw). London, Rapp and Whiting, 1968.
Movements in Art since 1945. London, Thames and Hudson, 1969; as *Late Modern: The Visual Arts since 1945,* New York, Praeger, 1969.
A Concise History of French Painting. London, Thames and Hudson, and New York, Praeger, 1971.
Eroticism in Western Art. London, Thames and Hudson, 1972.
Symbolist Art. London, Thames and Hudson, 1972.
The First London Catalogue: All the Appurtenances of a Civilized, Amusing, and Comfortable Life. London, Paddington Press, and New York, Two Continents, 1974.

Editor, *Rubens.* London, Spring Books, 1961.
Editor, *Raphael.* London, Batchworth Press, 1961.
Editor, with Philip Hobsbaum, *A Group Anthology.* London, Oxford University Press, 1963.
Editor, *The Penguin Book of Elizabethan Verse.* London, Penguin, 1965.
Editor, *The Liverpool Scene.* London, Rapp and Carroll, and New York, Doubleday, 1967.
Editor, *A Choice of Browning's Verse.* London, Faber, 1967.
Editor, *The Penguin Book of Satirical Verse.* London, Penguin, 1967.
Editor, *Holding Your Eight Hands: A Book of Science Fiction Verse.* New York, Doubleday, 1969; London, Rapp and Whiting, 1970.
Editor, with Patricia White, *Art in Britain, 1969–70.* London, Dent, 1970.
Editor, *British Poetry since 1945.* London, Penguin, 1970.
Editor, with Simon Watson-Taylor, *French Poetry Today: A Bi-Lingual Anthology.* London, Rapp and Whiting-Deutsch, 1971.
Editor, *Primer of Experimental Poetry, 1870–1922.* London, Rapp and Whiting, 1971.

Translator, *Manet,* by Robert Rey. Milan, Uffici Press, 1962.
Translator, *Jonah: Selected Poems of Jean-Paul de Dadelsen.* London, Rapp and Carroll, 1967.
Translator, *Five Great Odes,* by Paul Claudel. London, Rapp and Whiting, 1967; Chester Springs, Pennsylvania, Dufour, 1970.
Translator, *The Muses,* by Paul Claudel. London, Turret Books, 1967.

Edward Lucie-Smith comments:

My activities, though various, seem to revolve about poetry and the modern arts in general. I hate the term "poet." I'm simply a man who tries to react honestly to the world.

Since I was one of the founder-members of "The Group," and for some years chairman of its discussions, I'm in that sense a "Group" poet. Nowadays I can't think of anyone who writes much like me.

I think my development as a poet could be described roughly as follows: I began in the wake of the Movement, among a group of undergraduate poets at Oxford which included Anthony Thwaite, George MacBeth, Adrian Mitchell and Geoffrey Hill. I was then a poet of tight conventional forms and my chief subject was childhood experience. Under the influence of the sessions of "The Group," I began to write longer poems, often dramatic monologues, which were greatly influenced by Browning. Poems of this sort appear in my second volume, *Confessions and Histories.* At this period I gradually became dissatisfied with conventional verse forms and especially with their lack of real flexibility. I began to look for forms which would give: (*a*) greater colloquialism, (*b*) greater simplicity, and (*c*) greater concision. The results of these experiments can be seen in my third book, *Towards Silence,* and I have continued them in my more recent work. The metrical principle in most of my recent poetry is twofold – a strict syllabic "ground," and a melody of strong and light stresses. I use the syllabic pattern to syncopate the metre I have chosen which is usually mismatched to it, e.g. dactyls and a seven- or eleven-syllable line. The effect is, I think, very like that of Greek or Latin poetry, without strictly copying Greek or Latin forms. The influences are various: Catullus, the Elizabethan experiments with classical metre and especially Campion, Rochester (for his colloquial directness), French medieval poetry, and Pound. I am very concerned to preserve strict prose-order of words. A common criticism of my recent work is that it is too "thin" – not complex enough. My translators, on the other hand, tend to complain of simplicity which conceals difficulty.

I am interested in extending the scope of poetry – in writing poster-poems and poems to be set to music, for example.

My themes are, I think, commonly erotic (poems about love), historical and aesthetic (poems about artists and works of art, etc.), and occasionally religious.

I consider publishing and promoting other poets an important part of my activity and I am one of three partners in a private press (Turret Books) which has published many leading British and American poets, and also new ones.

*   *   *

The immediate impression on surveying Edward Lucie-Smith's poetry is that of progress and variety, from the neatly turned and rhymed "Movement" verses of his Fantasy Press pamphlet of 1954 to the experimentation and freedom of syllabics in his latest collection, *Towards Silence,* 1968.

The second impression is that of a conscious artistry – not only in individual poems, but in the compilation of the collections themselves. The poems in *Towards Silence,* for example, gain from being read as a collection, though clearly each poem will stand in its own right. The danger with such poetry can be that the artistry too finely applied tends to exclude feeling; but in the best of Lucie-Smith's poetry this certainly is not so. In the early personal poems about his boyhood – such as "A Tropical Childhood" and "The Lesson" – the feeling is clearly expressed:

> I cried for knowledge which was bitterer
> Than any grief. For there and then I knew
> That grief has uses.

In the later poems, as in the group about artists in the collection *Confessions and Histories* – e.g. the popular "Caravaggio Dying" and the, to my mind, much better "Soliloquy in the Dark" – he succeeds in expressing an empathy not only with the situations he takes as his subject-matter but with the feelings of the characters in those situations. The same is true of the later group of poems based on the Tristan legend:

> His vows broken, he sleeps renewed.
> Love's salt dries on him.

The poems in *Towards Silence* signal a progress into a more markedly direct simplicity of statement and form, though the implications and overtones may be far from being so, as in that near perfect poem "Silence," which rounds off the collection:

> Hear
> Your own noisy machine, which
> Is moving towards silence.

From the same period comes the remarkable translation of Paul Claudel's *Five Great Odes* in which he captures the quality and feeling of this high, near-baroque poetry. To set this translation beside the simple directness of the work in *Towards Silence* is to illustrate the versatility of Edward Lucie-Smith and the range of his achievement.

– John Cotton

———————————

MacADAMS, Lewis (Perry, Jr.) American. Born in San Angelo, Texas, 12 October 1944. Educated at Princeton University, New Jersey, B.A. 1966; State University of New York, Buffalo, M.A. 1968. Married Phoebe Russell in 1967; has two sons. Formerly, Switchman on the Southern Pacific Railroad. Currently, Director, Bolinas Community Public Utility District, California. Recipient: Poets Foundation Award, 1967. Address: Box 40, Overlook Road, Bolinas, California 94924, U.S.A.

PUBLICATIONS

Verse

> *City Money: Poems.* Oxford, Burning Water Press, 1966.
> *Water Charms.* San Francisco, Dariel Press, 1968.
> *The Poetry Room.* New York, Harper, 1970.
> *Dance.* Canton, New York, Institute of Further Studies, 1972.
> *Now Let Us Eat of This Pollen and Place Some on Our Heads, For We Are to Eat
> of It.* New York, Harper, 1973.

Other

> *A Bolinas Report: Reportage and Exhortation.* San Francisco, Zone Press, 1971.
> *Tilth: Interviews.* Bolinas, California, Bolinas Future Studies Center, 1972.

Editor, with others, *Where the Girls Are: A Guide to Eastern Women's Colleges.* New York, Dial Press, 1966.

Critical Study: review by John Koethe, in *Poetry* (Chicago), April 1972.

Lewis MacAdams comments:

I would like to introduce myself to you as the work of a poet that derides masks. It's that the wind sings through me, and there is no personality there – anywhere. "Speech" is the state of human things, and the words of the poet telescope elemental space and fire into geometry, which is the dance of sexual joy. It is incredible to be listed in the middle of a huge book linked with thousands of humans only because we all write in the various forms of English, so I would like to say Hello to Bob Marley in Jamaica, to Haile Selassie, to Chinua Achebe, and to Kwesi Brew. I am the words of an average man trained to composition and honed by consciousness and gravity to song. And alot of meat's gone down the pike before. And now, here is a poem by me and Tom Clark:

100 Poets in "The Rolling Stone"

such a smile, like having you near
and so many other poets I
yet never shall my song omit
to sigh and moan, more fit for Ovid
than Shakespeare, for David Bowie
than the Troggs, or Mike "Eggs" Benedict.

We shall not be mooed at gracefully
this afternoon, nor shall we either feel
a hard-on. One inch deeper in shit.
Well, at least it's my shit,
you think. It's
Ocean Lee's shit,
justly entitled Cupid's Hill.

I'd embrace those struggling rocks
with John and Ed and so many a
happy face. Wal kick my ass.
The neck, in which strange graces lurk
has eyes, and looks up into my face.
And I realized I was in a body
that would not die.

*   *   *

Lewis MacAdams of West Texas and now of Bolinas who looks sometimes like Jerry Lee Lewis writes poems as easy as walking. They amble and dance and are filled with high-energy good nature and accuracy. They demonstrate a poet's acrobatic love of language and lingo and display the joy of putting the right words together to resonate a unique music.

He is a serious writer who never takes the serious stance too seriously. He keeps everything in focus, even romance. Lessons you learn in the clear-eyed school of poetry.

MacAdams is also a graceful and informative prose writer. A privately printed journal detailing events during the Bolinas oil-spill disater and *Tilth* are prime examples of his abilities.

The poems and prose hold his voice whether read aloud or in the silence of paper. Song tones and overtones move constantly through his work. Quite an accomplishment. Not even 30 years old and he already knows what to keep in and what to leave out of a poem. A knowledge often absent in poets twice his age. He knows what to leave in and what to take out and how to keep the music in tact. Amen.

– David Meltzer

MacBETH, George (Mann). Scottish. Born in Shotts, Lanarkshire, 19 January 1932. Educated at King Edward VII School, Sheffield, Yorkshire; New College, Oxford, B.A. (honours) in classical greats 1955. Married Elizabeth Browell Robson in 1955. Editor, *Poet's Voice* programme, 1958–65, *New Comment* programme, 1959–64, and since 1965, *Poetry Now* programme, BBC, London. Since 1952, Editor, Fantasy Poets series, Fantasy Press, Oxford. Recipient: Geoffrey Faber Memorial Award, 1964. Lives in Richmond, Surrey. Address: c/o British Broadcasting Corporation, Broadcasting House, London W.1, England.

PUBLICATIONS

Verse

A Form of Words: Poems.   Oxford, Fantasy Press, 1954.
Lecture to the Trainees.   Oxford, Fantasy Press, 1962.
The Broken Places: Poems.   Lowestoft, Suffolk, Scorpion Press, 1963; New York, Walker, 1968.
Penguin Modern Poets 6, with Jack Clemo and Edward Lucie-Smith.   London, Penguin, 1964.
A Doomsday Book: Poems and Poem-Games.   Lowestoft, Suffolk, Scorpion Press, 1965.
The Twelve Hotels.   London, Turret Books, 1965.
Missile Commander.   London, Turret Books, 1965.
The Calf.   London, Turret Books, 1965.
The Humming Bird: A Monodrama.   London, Turret Books, 1966.
The Castle.   Privately printed, 1966.
The Screens.   London, Turret Books, 1967.
The Colour of Blood: Poems.   London, Macmillan, and New York, Atheneum, 1967.

The Night of Stones: Poems. London, Macmillan, 1968; New York, Atheneum, 1969.
A War Quartet. London, Macmillan, 1969.
A Death. Frensham, Surrey, Sceptre Press, 1969.
Zoo's Who. Privately printed, 1969.
The Burning Cone. London, Macmillan, 1970.
The Bamboo Nightingale. Frensham, Surrey, Sceptre Press, 1970.
Poems. Frensham, Surrey, Sceptre Press, 1970.
The Hiroshima Dream. London, Academy Editions, 1970.
Two Poems. Frensham, Surrey, Sceptre Press, 1970.
A Prayer, Against Revenge. Rushden, Northamptonshire, Sceptre Press, 1971.
The Orlando Poems. London, Macmillan, 1971.
Collected Poems, 1958–1970. London, Macmillan, 1971.
A Farewell. Rushden, Northamptonshire, Sceptre Press, 1972.
Lusus: A Verse Lecture. London, Fuller d'Arch Smith, 1972.
A Litany. Rushden, Northamptonshire, Sceptre Press, 1972.
Shrapnel. London, Macmillan, 1973.
Prayers. Solihull, Warwickshire, Aquila, 1973.
The Vision. Rushden, Northamptonshire, Sceptre Press, 1973.
A Poet's Year. London, Gollancz, 1973.
Elegy for the Gas Dowsers. Rushden, Northamptonshire, Sceptre Press, 1974.
Shrapnel, and A Poet's Year. New York, Atheneum, 1974.

Plays

The Doomsday Show (produced London, 1964). Published in *New English Dramatists 14*, London, Penguin, 1970.
The Scene-Machine, music by Anthony Gilbert (produced Kassel, Germany, 1971; London, 1972). Mainz, Germany, B. Schott's Söhne, 1971.

Other

Noah's Journey (juvenile). London, Macmillan, and New York, Viking Press, 1966.
Jonah and the Lord (juvenile). London, Macmillan, 1969; New York, Holt Rinehart, 1970.
My Scotland: Fragments of a State of Mind. London, Macmillan, 1973.

Editor, *The Penguin Book of Sick Verse.* London, Penguin, 1963.
Editor, *The Penguin Book of Animal Verse.* London, Penguin, 1965.
Editor, *Poetry 1900–1965: An Anthology.* London, Longman-Faber, 1967.
Editor, *The Penguin Book of Victorian Verse: A Critical Anthology.* London, Penguin, 1969.
Editor, *The Falling Splendour: Poems of Alfred, Lord Tennyson.* London, Macmillan, 1970.

Manuscript Collections: University of California, Los Angeles; State University of New York, Buffalo.

Critical Studies. *The New Poets: American and British Poetry since World War II* by M. L. Rosenthal, London and New York, Oxford University Press, 1967; ''The

Poetry of George MacBeth'' by D. M. Black, in *Scottish International* (Edinburgh), August 1968; Roger Garfitt, in *British Poetry since 1960*, edited by Michael Schmidt and Grevel Lindop, Oxford, Carcanet Press, 1972.

*   *   *

George MacBeth is the most inventive poet of his generation in Britain. His fluency with ideas is accompanied by an equally pronounced skill in versification. He has been very influential, and although he is eclectic in style it is already possible to point to passages in other poets' work which show his influence. He disclaims the title of an intellectual, but he has a seminal intelligence which is perhaps the strongest in British poetry since Auden. Like Auden, he is a popular poet: even his most recondite pieces are written for the general public. Often he overestimates the public's willingness to work at a poem and consequently he can be obscure. But every poem is well planned – he is not hermetic and does not subscribe to a closed aesthetic order or a professional poets club in the manner of Robert Graves. He is a very prolific writer and publishes a lot in pamphlets and limited editions and his poems are often seen in magazines. He tends to operate a poetic canon when collecting his poems into books, but some of his most interesting achievements (such as "The Crab-Apple Crisis" and "Amelia's Will") are uncollected.

MacBeth's first book, *A Form of Words*, is now a collector's piece. These intellectual shavings from the later Caroline poets and from Empson were almost parodies, but revealed for the first time his playfulness with words. His second book, *The Broken Places*, is still, in many ways, his strongest. His preoccupation with violence and cruelty, which has been much remarked on, is present in this book in poems such as "Report to the Director," "The Disciple," "Drop," and "The Son," but so in other poems is a classically sustained note of elegy and a sympathetic talent for autobiography. It should be stressed that the caricature of him as a poet obsessed with the gamiest forms of nastiness is a simplification amounting to a calumny. *The Broken Places* also contains some of the first of MacBeth's dandified interpretations of the past. He has celebrated authors who are men of action like Hemingway and D'Annunzio and he has a natural sympathy for the larger-than-life artists of the late nineteenth century. One of the most original poems in *The Broken Places* is "The Spider's Nest," an ingenious monologue spoken by Eugene Lee-Hamilton, the crippled English poet who lived in Florence. Fin-de-siècle enthusiasms have grown on him until the diction and rhythms of some of his recent poems have acquired a drugged and purple solemnity which is not his best style.

A Doomsday Book is a collection of poems in honour of Homo Ludens, a figure MacBeth, like Auden, places very high in the Pantheon of fallen man. The tone of MacBeth's macabre jokes, such as "Fin-du-Globe" (an apocalyptic card-game poem) and "The Ski Murders," is equivocal. He has a love of picture-stories and games with rules and has used them in poems to take the portentousness out of death and violence. He is not frivolous but appears frequently as a player: his finest work is as detailed and energetic as a medieval Triumph of Death. Both *The Colour of Blood* and *The Night of Stones* show him continuing to explore his major themes but also experimenting with techniques of the avant-garde. MacBeth's originality as a poet lies in the use he makes of the hundreds of styles available to the modern poet. He is not a dedicated innovator and after producing a suitably outrageous experimental poem, he will often write another in a traditional mode. His realisations of Chinese poems in *The Colour of Blood* are hilarious bits of chinoiserie and show him ready to use concrete poetry and sound poetry for his own purposes. In his copious output there are many remarkable poems about animals and a number of successful ones for children, of which "Noah's Journey" is the most considerable. "At Crufts" and "Fourteen Ways of Touching the Peter" from *The Night of Stones* are vignettes in syllabics of pedigree dogs and his own cat. Here is part of his description of the Chow:

> . . . your
> tail
>
> over-curled
> as if attempting
> to open
>
> yourself
> like a tin
> of pilchards. . . .

No poet writing today has put so much of the touchable surface of life into his poetry. Yet MacBeth's concerns are ultimately with the major options of poetry – the unswervable matters of death and life, war and love. It is not possible to forecast what so volatile a poet will do next, but he has written enough good poems already to earn him a high place in the history of post-war English verse.

– Peter Porter

MacCAIG, Norman (Alexander). Scottish. Born in Edinburgh, 14 November 1910. Educated at Royal High School, Edinburgh; Edinburgh University, M.A. (honours) in classics 1932. Married Isabel Munro in 1940; has two children. Schoolteacher, 1934–67, and Headmaster, 1969–70, Edinburgh; Fellow in Creative Writing, Edinburgh University, 1967–69. Lecturer in English Studies, 1970–72, and since 1972, Reader in Poetry, University of Stirling. Recipient: Scottish Arts Council Award, 1957, 1966; Society of Authors grant, 1964, prize, 1967; Heinemann Award, 1967. Fellow, Royal Society of Literature, 1965. Address: 7 Leamington Terrace, Edinburgh 10, Scotland.

PUBLICATIONS

Verse

Far Cry: Poems.   London, Routledge, 1943.
The Inward Eye.   London, Routledge, 1946.
Riding Lights: Poems.   London, Hogarth Press, 1955; New York, Macmillan, 1956.
The Sinai Sort: Poems.   London, Hogarth Press, 1957.
A Common Grace.   London, Chatto and Windus-Hogarth Press, 1960.
A Round of Applause.   London, Chatto and Windus-Hogarth Press, 1962.
Measures.   London, Chatto and Windus, 1965.

Surroundings. London, Chatto and Windus-Hogarth Press, 1966.
Rings on a Tree. London, Chatto and Windus-Hogarth Press, 1968.
A Man in My Position. London, Chatto and Windus-Hogarth Press, 1969.
Midnights. London, Poem-of-the-Month Club, 1970.
Three Manuscript Poems. Exeter, Devon, Rougemont Press, 1970.
Selected Poems. London, Hogarth Press, 1971.
Penguin Modern Poets 21, with George Mackay Brown and Iain Crichton Smith.
   London, Penguin, 1972.
The White Bird. London, Chatto and Windus, 1973.
The World's Room. London, Chatto and Windus, 1974.

Other

Editor, *Honour'd Shade: An Anthology of New Scottish Poetry to Mark the
   Bicentenary of the Birth of Robert Burns.* Edinburgh, Chambers, 1959.
Editor, with Alexander Scott, *Contemporary Scottish Verse 1959–1969.* London,
   Calder and Boyars 1970.

Critical Studies: in *Akros 7* (Preston, Lancashire), 1968.

*   *   *

Norman MacCaig's earliest poetry, published in the nineteen-forties, was in the
energetically obscure romantic manner of the period and followed the example of
Dylan Thomas. Then, after some years of silence, his volume *Riding Lights*, published in 1955, showed the emergence of a tougher and more intellectually disciplined manner. MacCaig had evidently been reading Donne with great attention,
and Donne's influence dominates this volume, almost to the extent of pastiche in
some poems:

> I who had nowhere else to go now do
> Such journeys (here) as lie from me to you,
> And think them nothing; which Time thinks them too.

In MacCaig's poetry of the late fifties this influence was better assimilated; it left
on his work the largely beneficial result of intellectual rigour and tight formal
control. He is a prolific but somewhat repetitive poet, with a number of themes or
preoccupations which he constantly returns to.
   MacCaig might be called a Scots metaphysician by temperament: he has more
overtly philosophical interests than most British poets, and he is deeply concerned
with questions of perception, of how we know and understand the world. Many of
his poems are dominated by speculations about the relations between the observer
and that which he observes; and in his love-poems MacCaig tends to use these
questions as a suggestive though sometimes obscure source of metaphor. MacCaig
is very much a Scotsman, although he has never attempted to write in Scots. He
frequently turns to aspects of Highland landscape as the starting point for poems;
in his less successful pieces the subject tends to disappear in abstract speculation;
in the better poems the landscape or natural object the poet is contemplating
preserves its identity and is presented to the reader in a sharply rendered way.
MacCaig is a talented and intelligent poet, yet one whose substantial *oeuvre* remains

disappointingly limited, though one may applaud the honesty of the poet in not attempting to move beyond what he clearly realises are his limitations.

– Bernard Bergonzi

MacDIARMID, Hugh. Pseudonym for Christopher Murray Grieve. British (Scottish). Born in Langholm, Dumfriesshire, 11 August 1892. Educated at Langholm Academy; Broughton Student Centre, Edinburgh; Edinburgh University. Married Margaret Skinner in 1918 (divorced, 1932), has one son and one daughter; Valda Trevlyn in 1934, has one son. Journalist, 1912–15, 1920–30; Editor, *The Scottish Chapbook*, Montrose, Angus, 1922–23; *The Scottish Nation*, Montrose, Angus, 1923; *The Northern Review*, Edinburgh, 1924; *The Voice of Scotland*, Dunfermline, Fife, 1938–39, Glasgow, 1945–49, and Edinburgh, 1955–58. Co-Founder, Scottish Nationalist Party. Recipient: Foyle Poetry Prize, 1963; Scottish Arts Council Award, 1969. LL.D.: Edinburgh University, 1957. Granted civil list pension, 1951. Professor of Literature, Royal Scottish Academy, 1974. Address: Brownsbank, Biggar, Lanarkshire, Scotland.

PUBLICATIONS

Verse

Annals of the Five Senses. Montrose, Angus, C. M. Grieve, 1923.
Sangschaw. Edinburgh, Blackwood, 1925.
Penny Wheep. Edinburgh, Blackwood, 1926; edited by John C. Weston, Amherst, University of Massachusetts Press, 1971.
A Drunk Man Looks at the Thistle. Edinburgh, Blackwood, 1926.
The Lucky Bag. Edinburgh, Porpoise Press, 1927.
To Circumjack Cencrastus; or, The Curly Snake. Edinburgh, Blackwood, 1930.
First Hymn to Lenin and Other Poems. London, Unicorn Press, 1931.
Second Hymn to Lenin. Thakeham, Sussex, Valda Trevlyn, 1932; London, Stanley Nott, 1935.
Tarras. Edinburgh, The Free Man, 1932.
Scots Unbound and Other Poems. Stirling, Eneas Mackay, 1932.
Stony Limits and Other Poems. London, Gollancz, 1934.
Selected Poems. London, Macmillan, 1934.
Direadh. Dunfermline, Fife, The Voice of Scotland, 1938.
Speaking for Scotland. London, The Lumpen Press, 1939.
Cornish Heroic Song for Valda Trevlyn. Glasgow, Caledonian Press, 1943.
Selected Poems, edited by R. Crombie Saunders. Glasgow, Maclellan, 1944.
Speaking for Scotland: Selected Poems of Hugh MacDiarmid. Baltimore, Contemporary Poetry, 1946.
Poems of the East-West Synthesis. Glasgow, Caledonian Press, 1946.
A Kist of Whistles: New Poems. Glasgow, Maclellan, 1947.

Selected Poems of Hugh MacDiarmid, edited by Oliver Brown. Glasgow, Maclellan, 1954; as *Poems of Hugh MacDiarmid*, Glasgow, Scottish Secretariat, 1955.

In Memoriam James Joyce: from A Vision of World Language. Glasgow, Maclellan, 1955.

Stony Limits and Scots Unbound and Other Poems. Edinburgh, Castle Wynd Printers, 1956.

Three Hymns to Lenin. Edinburgh, Castle Wynd Printers, 1957.

The Battle Continues. Edinburgh, Castle Wynd Printers, 1957.

The Kind of Poetry I Want. Edinburgh, K. D. Duval, 1961.

Collected Poems of Hugh MacDiarmid. New York, Macmillan, and Edinburgh, Oliver and Boyd, 1962; revised edition, edited by John C. Weston, Macmillan, 1967.

Bracken Hills in Autumn. Edinburgh, Colin H. Hamilton, 1962.

The Blaward and the Skelly. Hemel Hempstead, Hertfordshire, privately printed, 1962.

Poems to Paintings by William Johnstone 1933. Edinburgh, K. D. Duval, 1963.

Two Poems: The Terrible Crystal: A Vision of Scotland. Skelmorlie, Ayrshire, Duncan Glen, 1964.

The Ministry of Water: Two Poems. Glasgow, Duncan Glen, 1964.

Six Vituperative Verses. Privately printed, 1964.

Poet at Play and Other Poems, Being a Selection of Mainly Vituperative Verses. Privately printed, 1965.

The Fire of the Spirit: Two Poems. Glasgow, Duncan Glen, 1965.

Whuchulls: A Poem. Preston, Lancashire, Akros, 1966.

A Lap of Honour. London, MacGibbon and Kee, 1967; Chicago, Swallow Press, 1969.

Early Lyrics: Recently Discovered among Letters to his Schoolmaster and Friend George Ogilvie, edited by J. K. Annand. Preston, Lancashire, Akros, 1968.

The Clyack-Sheaf. London, MacGibbon and Kee, 1969.

More Collected Poems. London, MacGibbon and Kee, and Chicago, Swallow Press, 1970.

Selected Poems, edited by David Craig and John Manson. London, Penguin, 1970.

The Hugh MacDiarmid Anthology: Poems in Scots and English, edited by Michael Grieve and Alexander Scott. London, Routledge, 1972.

Song of the Seraphim. London, Covent Garden Press, 1973.

Complete Poems. London, Martin Brian and O'Keeffe, 1974.

Other

Contemporary Scottish Studies: First Series. London, Parsons, 1926.

The Present Position of Scottish Music. Montrose, Angus, C. M. Grieve, 1927.

Albyn; or, Scotland and the Future. London, Paul Trencher Trubner, and New York, Dutton, 1927.

The Present Position of Scottish Arts and Affairs (published anonymously). Dalbeattie, Kirkcudbright, The Stewartry Observer, 1928.

The Scottish National Association of April Fools (as Gillechriosd Mac A'Ghreidhir). Aberdeen, University Press, 1928.

Scotland in 1980. Montrose, Angus, C. M. Grieve, 1929.

Warning Democracy (as C. H. Douglas). London, C. M. Grieve, 1931.

Five Bits of Miller. London, privately printed, 1934.

At the Sign of the Thistle: A Collection of Essays. London, Stanley Nott, 1934.

Scottish Scene; or, The Intelligent Man's Guide to Albyn, with Lewis Grassic Gibbon. London, Jarrolds, 1934.

Charles Doughty and the Need for Heroic Poetry. St. Andrews, The Modern Scot, 1936.

Scottish Eccentrics. London, Routledge, 1936.

Scotland and the Question of a Popular Front Against Fascism and War. Whalsay, Zetland, The Hugh MacDiarmid Book Club, 1938.

The Islands of Scotland: Hebrides, Orkneys and Shetlands. London, Batsford, and New York, Scribner, 1939.

Lucky Poet: A Self-Study in Literary and Political Ideas, Being the Autobiography of Hugh MacDiarmid. London, Methuen, 1943.

Cunningham Graham: A Centenary Study. Glasgow, Caledonian Press, 1952.

The Politics and Poetry of Hugh MacDiarmid (as Arthur Leslie). Glasgow, Caledonian Press, 1952.

Francis George Scott: An Essay on the Occasion of His Seventy-Fifth Birthday, 25th January 1955. Edinburgh, Macdonald, 1955.

Burns Today and Tomorrow. Edinburgh, Castle Wynd Printers, 1959.

David Hume: Scotland's Greatest Son. Edinburgh, Paperback Booksellers, 1962.

The Man of (Almost) Independent Mind (on Hume). Edinburgh, Giles Gordon, 1962.

When the Rat Race Is Over: An Essay in Honour of the Fiftieth Birthday of John Gawsworth. London, Twyn Barlwm Press, 1962.

Hugh MacDiarmid on Hume. Edinburgh, Giles Gordon, 1962.

The Ugly Birds Without Wings. Edinburgh, Allan Donaldson, 1962.

Sydney Goodsir Smith. Edinburgh, Colin H. Hamilton, 1963.

The Company I've Kept (autobiography). London, Hutchinson, 1966; Berkeley, University of California Press, 1967.

The Uncanny Scot: A Selection of Prose, edited by Kenneth Buthlay. London, MacGibbon and Kee, 1968.

Selected Essays, edited by Duncan Glen. London, Cape 1969; Berkeley University of California Press, 1970.

An Afternoon with Hugh MacDiarmid: Interview at Brownsbank on 25th October 1968, with Duncan Glen. Privately printed, 1969.

A Political Speech. Edinburgh, Reprographia, 1972.

Editor, *Northern Numbers, Being Representative Selections from Certain Living Scottish Poets.* Edinburgh, T. N. Foulis, 2 vols., 1920, 1921; Montrose, Angus, C. M. Grieve, 1922.

Editor, *Robert Burns, 1759–1796.* London, Benn, 1926.

Editor, *Living Scottish Poets.* London, Benn, 1931.

Editor, *The Golden Treasury of Scottish Poetry.* London, Macmillan, 1940.

Editor, *William Soutar: Collected Poems.* London, Dakers, 1948.

Editor, *Poems*, by Robert Burns. London, Grey Walls Press, 1949.

Editor, with Maurice Lindsay, *Poetry Scotland Four.* Edinburgh, Serif Books, 1949.

Editor, *Scottish Arts and Letters: Fifth Miscellany.* Glasgow, Maclellan, 1950.

Editor, *Selections from the Poems of William Dunbar.* Edinburgh, Oliver and Boyd, 1952.

Editor, *Selected Poems of William Dunbar.* Glasgow, Maclellan, 1955.

Editor, *Love Songs*, by Robert Burns. London, Vista Books, 1962.

Editor, *Henryson.* London, Penguin, 1970.

Translator, *The Handmaid of the Lord*, by Ramon Maria de Tenreiro. London, Secker, 1930.

Translator, *The Birlinn of Clanranald* (as Alexander Macdonald of Ardnamurchan). St. Andrews, Abbey Book Shop, 1935.

Translator, with Elspeth Harley Schubert, *Harry Martinson: Aniara: A Review of Man in Time and Space*. London, Hutchinson, and New York, Knopf, 1963.

Translator, *The Threepenny Opera*, by Bertolt Brecht. London, Eyre-Methuen, 1973.

Bibliography: "A Hugh MacDiarmid Bibliography" by W. R. Aitkin, in *Hugh MacDiarmid: A Critical Survey*, edited by Duncan Glen, Edinburgh and London, Scottish Academic Press, 1972.

Manuscript Collections: National Library of Scotland, Edinburgh; Edinburgh University; Yale University, New Haven, Connecticut; State University of New York, Buffalo.

Critical Studies: *Hugh MacDiarmid: A Festschrift*, edited by K. D. Duval and others, Edinburgh, K. D. Duval, 1962; "*Hugh MacDiarmid*" (*C. M. Grieve*), by Kenneth Buthlay, Edinburgh, Oliver and Boyd, 1964.

Hugh MacDiarmid comments:

My purpose as a poet has been to revive the independent Scottish tradition of poetry, and to that end to restore the literary use of Scots for all the purposes of modern literary expression. In the past 30 years I have moved from the short lyrics which constituted my first two volumes, to very long discursive poems embracing scientific and political subject matter, and a world-wide concern with linguistics (especially in my very long poem, *In Memoriam James Joyce*, 1955). The opinion has been widely expressed that I am the first poet to employ Scots as a medium for high poetry. I believe this to be correct, and other aspects of my more recent poetry have been hailed as bracketing me as a Communist poet with Neruda, Yevtushenko, and Brecht.

*   *   *

The three great ages of Scottish poetry – the sixteenth century, the eighteenth and the twentieth – have each produced its dominating figure. The sixteenth century had that dour master of technique and melancholy passion, with a begging-bowl never far from his hand, William Dunbar; the eighteenth century had Robert Burns, who summed up the technical experimentation in colloquial verse forms of his predecessors since the Union of 1707, and whose tree spread such luxuriant branches that very few successors of merit could find sustenance under its all-pervading shade; and the twentieth century has "Hugh MacDiarmid," who combines both Dunbar's technical dexterity and Burns's idealism (though not his acceptance of the common man, with all his faults), but who differs from both Dunbar and Burns in at least one respect – that he has proved a fruitful influence, albeit not producing exactly the kind of crop he perhaps envisaged.

MacDiarmid's early experimentings included Georgian work of extraordinary badness, some of it under various pseudonyms, as if he were casting around systematically for an authentic voice. Under the pseudonym "Hugh MacDiarmid" he found it about 1922, when he began publishing in magazines those pieces which were to make up *Sangschaw*, published in 1925, a collection of Scots lyrics which put Scottish poetry back on the European map from which it had been absent for at least a century, a process continued through *Penny Wheep* and the long sequence *A Drunk Man Looks at the Thistle*.

"Back to Dunbar!" was the young MacDiarmid's battle cry. He was thinking, perhaps, not so much of Dunbar's not particularly wide range of subject matter as of the fact that Dunbar was part of a European chorus of voices in a way that none of the post-Burnsians, with their concern for purely local and often trivial matter, remotely were.

The Scots which MacDiarmid used in these early poems was "synthetic," in the sense that he retrieved words out of Jamieson's *Dictionary of the Middle Scots Tongue* and paid scant attention to the geographical limitations of those Scottish dialects into which the Scots tongue fragmented after Knox sanctioned the issuing of *The Bible* in English rather than waiting for the Scots versions being prepared, thus making English the language for matters of life and death. But "synthetic" is a misleading word, infinitely inferior to Burns's word, "Lallans," the language of the Lowlands. For MacDiarmid breathed life into these dead parts, and never used an old word without miraculously making it suddenly vibrant, an image fully relevant to our time:

I' the how -dumb*-deid o' the cauld hairst* nicht	(*) depth; harvest
The warl' like an eemis* stane	(*) insecure
Wags i the lift*:	(*) sky
An' my eerie memories fa'	
Like a yowdendrift*.	(*) gale driving down
Like a yowdendrift so's I couldna read	
The words cut oot i the stane	
Had the fug* o fame	(*) moss
An' history's hazelraw*	(*) lichen
No' yirdit* thaim.	(*) buried

Lyrics like this one, "The Eemis Stane," are concentrated into their very essence.

Like Pound and Eliot, MacDiarmid's allusions to the past – sometimes a past commemorated in simple folk-songs, sometimes in the literature of Europe – were digested and re-issued to illuminate his modern purpose. His imagery in these days was cosmic, his highest concerns, the fundamental human *what* and *why*. His was a highly subjective vision of metaphysical reality:

Lay haud o' my hert and feel	
Fountains outloupin* the starns*	(*) outjumping; stars
Or see the Universe reel	
Set gaen my eident harns.	

Together with this search after an answer to the fundamental questions which have occupied all major poets – What am I? What is my place or purpose in the Universe? – MacDiarmid also sought out and analysed the basic issues of nationality as manifested in Scotland. The two often came together:

> He canna Scotland see wha yet
> Canna see the Infinite,
> And Scotland in true scale to it.

There was scarcely any aspect of Scotland's traditional values which MacDiarmid did not question, contemptuously rejecting the traditional answers, from Harry Lauderism to the concept of a Scotland politically subjected to England and forced since 1707 to accept her European contacts second-hand through English sensibilities.

To Circumjack Cencrastus, based on the Celtic symbol of the Snake of Wisdom with its tail in its mouth, betrayed the first signs of the preacher (latent in every Scot), a deterioration which marred some of the poems in *First Hymn to Lenin* and *Scots Unbound*, in spite of its masterly revelation of MacDiarmid's genius in making music out of Scots vocables, and *Second Hymn to Lenin*.

For MacDiarmid, Lenin had become a kind of Gothicised Christ-substitute. The poet's preoccupation with Communism, albeit of a kind which did not endear him to the Communist Party during the thirties, and his abandonment both of the Scots tongue and of fixed verse forms for a freer, wider-ranging verse in English (with generous snippets from other languages) seeking, Goethe-like, to produce a poetry of total experience, may be seen in *Stony Limits*, *A Kist of Whistles*, and *In Memoriam, James Joyce*, as well as in his *Collected Poems*, which contains part of his epic, *The Kind of Poetry I Want*. Indeed, an epic imaginative scale, and an epic structural looseness now became the characteristics of a poet whose first impact had been made through the utmost economy of concentration. The attempt totally to synthesise life, in the end, leads inevitably to a kind of heroic failure. There are vast prosy tracts, chopped-up "borrowings" from the works of other authors, and a good deal of linguistic demonstration by the way. Indeed, MacDiarmid's way of looking at Science as a kind of material "thingness" is already as old-fashioned as his historicist belief in the inevitable coming of an ultimate Marxist society, in which the processes of change would somehow miraculously cease. Yet, however barren these mountainous journeyings, MacDiarmid is never intellectually uninteresting, and the reader is now and then allowed to relax by lush meadows of poetry in the richest later-MacDiarmid vein between the stern ascents.

MacDiarmid's Communism rather than his Scottish Nationalism estranged the support of many Scots during the nineteen thirties and forties. The Scotland he envisages is a radical Scotland sufficiently courageous to take back control of her own destiny and occupy her place by the rights of intellectual and artistic achievement in the European concert of nations.

Despite MacDiarmid's being received back into the arms of the Communist Party, and despite his affirmation of policies condemned even by radicals outside the Soviet Union (for instance, the invasion of Czechoslovakia), I see his Communism as essentially a vision of the spirit, a state of organisation where every man would have the right and the opportunity to develop his potential to the full. For MacDiarmid is a psychological rebel firmly on the side of humanity (even if once he did remark that he would be prepared to sacrifice a sizeable number of human beings for the sake of one good lyric), an individual confidently rooted in his own idealism:

> I stand to my position, do what I can,
> And will never be turned into "a strong silenced man,"
> For I am corn and not chaff, and will neither
> Be blown away by the wind, nor burst with the flail,
>
> But will abide them both
> And in the end prevail.

For I am like Zamyatin. I must be a Bolshevik
Before the Revolution, but I'll cease to be one quick
When Communism comes to rule the roost.
For real literature can exist only where it's produced
By madmen, hermits, heretics,
Dreamers, rebels, sceptics. . . .

When one has absorbed MacDiarmid's poetry and prose (uneven, ranging from
rock-like and masterly writing to slovenly journalism marred by cheap and unfair
invective) – the best of his prose is anthologised in *The Uncanny Scot* – it is still
difficult to "place him."

"I am a volcano," he once declared, and to some the sheer volume of the
volcano's output seems daunting. Of one thing, however, I am certain. MacDiarmid's remarkable achievement within that enormous range guarantees him a place
alongside Yeats, Pound, Eliot and Wallace Stevens as one of the greatest writers of
the twentieth century.

– Maurice Lindsay

MacEWEN, Gwendolyn (Margaret). Canadian. Born in Toronto, Ontario, 1 Sep-
tember 1941. Educated in public schools. Married Nikos Tsingos in 1972. Since
1960, Part-time Librarian, Children's Public Library, Toronto. Recipient: Canadian
Broadcasting Corporation prize, 1965; Canada Council Scholarship, 1965, 1969,
Senior Arts grant, 1973; Governor-General's Award, 1970. Lives in Toronto. Agent:
Anne McDermid, David Higham Associates, 5–8 Lower John Street, London
W1R 3PE, England.

PUBLICATIONS

Verse

Selah. Privately printed, 1961.
The Drunken Clock. Privately printed, 1961.
The Rising Sun. Toronto, Contact Press, 1963; as *The Rising Fire*, 1964.
A Breakfast for Barbarians. Toronto, Ryerson Press, 1966.
The Shadow-Maker. Toronto, Macmillan, 1969.
Armies of the Moon. Toronto, Macmillan, 1972.

Recording: *Open Secrets*, CBC Toronto, 1971.

Plays

Radio Plays: *Terror and Erebus*; *Tesla*; *The World of Neshiah*; *The Death of the
Loch Ness Monster*; *The Sweet Breath of the Pard*; *A Celebration of Evil.*

Novels

> *Julian the Magician.* Toronto, Macmillan, and New York, Corinth Books, 1963.
> *King of Egypt, King of Dreams.* Toronto, Macmillan, 1972.

Short Stories

> *Noman.* Ottawa, Oberon Press, 1972.

Manuscript Collection: University of Toronto.

Critical Studies: "To Improvise an Eden" by Ian Sowton, in *Edge 2* (Montreal), 1964; by George Whalley, in *Quarry* (Kingston, Ontario), 1967; "They Shall Have Arcana" by George Whalley, in *Queen's Quarterly* (Kingston, Ontario), 1967; "MacEwen's Muse" by Margaret Atwood, in *Canadian Literature* (Vancouver), Summer 1970; *Butterfly on Rock*, by D. G. Jones, Toronto, University of Toronto Press, 1970; *15 Canadian Poets* by Gary Geddes, Toronto, Oxford University Press, 1971.

Gwendolyn MacEwen comments:

Major themes include the discovery of mythological patterns and archetypal forces which are present in modern life – the exploration of the meaning of time – human time, cosmic time – frequent use of irony, paradox, dualism to express ambiguous human state – pre-occupation with the bi-polarity of life. Also the discovery of the transcendental realities of human love and all human relationships – the search for a reality which resolves all contradictions.

*   *   *

"Gwendolyn MacEwen is preoccupied with time and its multiple meanings, with the ambivalences of existence, with the archetypal patterns that emerge and re-emerge from ancient times to now," as George Woodcock wrote in his entry devoted to the poet in the *Supplement to the Oxford Companion to Canadian History and Literature* (1973). This may be so, yet the explanation seems heavy beside the achievement, which is light, graceful, imaginative, and refreshingly free of pretension.

The quest for a leader, or saviour, or cultural hero, has taken Ms. MacEwen through two novels and a collection of short stories, all essentially poetic. *Julian the Magician* creates an imaginary alchemist out of wholecloth. With *King of Egypt, King of Dreams*, she finds her mythic man in the person of Ikhnaton, the heretic-pharaoh of Ancient Egypt, and this permits her to present the vision in the form of historical fiction. Perhaps the most successful of the prose works is *Noman*, in which the poet's fancy is free to make wide connections without the need to create a credible personality for her mysterious "Noman." The elusive figure, a kind of Jean Sans Terre, "became whatever he encountered."

If *Noman* is poetry written in the form of prose, Ms. MacEwen's books of verse are very much poetry. From *The Rising Fire* (1963) to *The Armies of the Moon* (1972), her poems have grown more self-contained and her vision of the magical properties of everyday things has grown clearer. Like a mediaeval alchemist, she turns base experiences into rare epiphanies. Coupled with the imaginative insights there is a *fey* quality to her writing which, playful and elusive, may be found in her description, say, of a cat hiding behind its own shadow, or her lines "there are so many places for places to hide," or her view that the moon is sending Morse Code messages to the earth. And in "The Vacuum Cleaner Dream" she imagines herself an angelic char "vacuuming the universe." It is only slightly upsetting when she finds among the debris "the sleeping body of my love."

A sense of the magic and wonderful movement of Ms. MacEwen's work can be felt in the final stanza of "The Discovery," from *The Shadow-Maker*, the volume for which she received the Governor-General's Award for Poetry:

> When you see the land naked, look again
> (burn your maps, that is not what I mean),
> I mean the moment when it seems most plain
> is the moment when you must begin again.

– John Robert Colombo

MACKAY, Florence Ruth.   See GILBERT, Ruth.

MACKIE, Alastair (Webster).   Scottish.   Born in Aberdeen, 10 August 1925. Educated at Skene Square School, 1930–37; Robert Gordon's College, Aberdeen, 1937–43; University of Aberdeen, 1946–50, M.A. (honours) in English 1950. Served in the Royal Air Force, 1943, and the Royal Navy, 1944–46. Married Elizabeth Law in 1951; has two children. English Teacher, Stromness Academy, Orkney, 1951–59. Since 1959, English Teacher, Waid Academy, Anstruther, Fife. Recipient: Saltire Prize, 1963; Scottish Arts Council bursary, 1973. Address: 13 St. Adrian's Place, Anstruther, Fife, Scotland.

PUBLICATIONS

Verse

Soundings.   Preston, Lancashire, Akros, 1966.
Clytach.   Preston, Lancashire, Akros, 1972.

Critical Studies: Introduction to *Contemporary Scottish Verse 1959–1969*, edited by Norman MacCaig and Alexander Scott, London, Calder and Boyars, 1970; *Whither*

Scotland?, edited by Duncan Glen, London, Gollancz, 1971; Robert Garioch, in *Lines Review 42–43* (Edinburgh), 1972; Alexander Scott, in *Glasgow Review 1,* Summer 1972; *The MacDiarmid Makars 1923–1972*, by Alexander Scott, Preston, Lancashire, Akros, 1972; "The Progress of Scots" by J. Herdman, in *Akros 20* (Preston, Lancashire), 1972; J. A. K. Annand, and Donald Campbell, in *Akros 21* (Preston, Lancashire), 1973.

Alastair Mackie comments:

My work is directed towards developing the limits of Scots as a vehicle for poetry in the contemporary setting as I am placed in regard to it. I continue the work of MacDiarmid and attempt to annex areas where his influence has not extended. For example, I have written a space sequence in Scots called "Captus Cupidine Coeli." I work for a more extended canon of Scots in order to give Scots poetry bulk and variety. I am more attracted to English translations of European poets – Amichai, Holub, Herbert – than to any contemporary English poetry.

*   *   *

The publication of Alastair Mackie's collection of poems, *Clytach* (barbarous words) in 1972 was a matter of consequence to the continuing tradition of poetry in Scots. The book is yet another vindication of the claim Hugh MacDiarmid made fifty years previously to the effect that poetry in the Scots tongue could still contribute apprehensions and perceptions relevant to contemporary life which could not be conveyed in English. In his previous collection, *Soundings*, Mackie's poems in English showed terseness and temper. In his "Notes on 'The Truce' by Primo Levi" he writes:

> Auschwitz in due time
> exported its surplus
>
> Afterwards, the truce
> when the soiled ex-objects
>
> took to trains and began
> their picaresque novels.

This tight-lipped speech has a secure base in the Aberdeenshire dialect which was Alastair Mackie's birthright, though the style witnesses to other influences. His poems in Scots, however, have a rich texture and an intimate responsiveness to his subjects, as well as an ironic turn of phrase that is art and part of his Scots idiom. The wide range of the poet's interest is evident from the titles of the poems in *Clytach*. These include: "The Cosmonaut Hero," "Binary Sets," "Orpheus and Eurydice," "Lines from Mallarmé," "Leopardi on the Hill," "Scots Pegasus," and "Still-Life: Cézanne." Just how appropriate his Scots is to this last subject is clear even from a few phrases. He describes the table on which the apples are set:

> The white claith wid aye jist
> cowp doun like a lynn aneth the aipples' wecht.
>
> (the white cloth would always just
> tumble down like a waterfall beneath the apples' weight.)

He again refers to the apples in the phrase "Yon was mason's work." To re-enact in words the sense of durability and solidity – as if it were the weight of the world that was being presented – requires a language that has retained physical characteristics. One of the best poems that Mackie has written, "Mongol Quine" (Mongol Girl), presents the child with a blunt directness that draws one up sharply. Mackie writes –

> Her blond baa-heid wags   (Her blond ball-head wags)
> frae side to side

– yet the poem ends gently and mysteriously with the words:

> Ayont the hert-brak her een
> are set for ever on an unkent airt.
>
> (Beyond the heartbreak her eyes
> are set forever on an unknown place.)

Though the Scots may initially daunt readers unacquainted with it, the centrality of Mackie's interests and comments makes a study of the work of this writer very desirable for all interested in the developments in contemporary poetry.

– George Bruce

MACLEAN, Alasdair. Scottish. Born in Glasgow, Lanarkshire, 16 March 1926. Recipient: Cholmondeley Award, 1974; Heinemann Award, 1974. Address: Sanna, Kilchoan, Ardnamurchan, Argyllshire, Scotland.

PUBLICATIONS

Verse

From the Wilderness. London, Gollancz, 1973.

*   *   *

The attempt to come to grips with the fundamental questions about life with which serious literature ought to concern itself need not of itself relate to the physical location of the writer. Alasdair Maclean left university to work a croft near Ardnamurchan, in Argyll. His first volume, *From the Wilderness*, did not appear before the public until he was into his forties, although something of his quality could be seen from anthologised poems in the annual *Scottish Poetry* and others. He is therefore a late starter, at any rate so far as publication is concerned. All to the good, since it means that for the most part he wants to say things, not merely to gyrate like some youthful virtuoso for the sake of attracting fashionable attention. He also has an assured and personal voice.

He tells his reader bluntly what to expect from him:

> I leave the foothills of the images
> and climb. What I pursue's not means but ends.
> You may come, if you've a mind to travelling.
> Meet me at the point where the language bends.

At his best, Maclean writes with a hard, direct economy, drawing his imagery and the strength of his thought from the way of life he loves and with which he is familiar. For instance, there is the countryman's unsentimental approach to matters of life and death, focussed into "Hen Dying":

> The other hens have cast her out.
> They batter her with their beaks
> Whenever they come across her.
> Most of them are her daughters.
> Hens are inhuman.

His poem "Rams," using the same terse short-sentence style, builds up a powerful apprehension of nature's sexual prodigality, and mindless directorial force, a fact which the ingenuity of *homo sapiens* often contrives for comfort to fudge:

> I found a ram dead once.
> It was trapped by the forefeet
> in the dark waters of a peatbog,
> drowned before help could arrive
> by the sheer weight of its skull.
> Maiden ewes were grazing near it,
> immune to its clangerous lust.
> It knelt on the bank, hunched over its own image
> its great head buried in the great head facing it.
> Its horns, going forward in the old way,
> had battered through at last to the other side.

Not a word, not a rhythm is false there; and Maclean has many poems with this quality in his first collection. There is also some harsh satire apparently arising, though not always admitting such origin, out of the unconfessed awareness of the Gael that his way of life and his culture are now peripheral, and that, rant as he may against the urban-dwelling Lowlander, the Gael himself has been his own worst enemy. Not all of these outbursts are entirely plausible, as in "Eagles":

> An eagle of that breed once, for a joke,
> picked up a stunted Highlander
> and flew him south, witless from the journey
> but fertile still,
> Hence your race of Lowland Scots.

Inevitably, as in every collection, there are some bookfiller pieces in which there is evident the metaphysical influence of the later, and poetically drier, Norman MacCaig; such a poem is "Sea and Sky," its feyly sentimental conclusion so out of keeping with the firmness of this poet's best texture and direct-sounding voice:

I'd choose the sky for burial
though, if such were possible.
I'd have mountains at my head and feet.
When Gabriel blew his trumpet I'd arrive
before God's kindness became strained.
The clouds would ease my bones
more than the hard rocks of Ardnamurchan.
Not worms would feed on me but larks.

Fanciful trifling of that sort is far below the level of a poet who can ring fierce, rough honesty out of the stoney fields of Ardnamurchan, and the hard life their isolation demands. To me, Maclean is certainly the most interesting Scottish poet to make his appearance for at least a couple of decades.

– Maurice Lindsay

MacLEISH, Archibald. American. Born in Glencoe, Illinois, 7 May 1892. Educated at the Hotchkiss School, Lakeville, Connecticut; Yale University, New Haven, Connecticut, A.B. 1915; Harvard University, Cambridge, Massachusetts, LL.D. 1919. Served in the United States Army, 1917–19: Captain. Married Ada Hitchcock in 1916; has three children. Lecturer in Government, Harvard University, 1919–21; Attorney, Choate Hall, and Stewart, Boston, 1920–23; Editor, *Fortune* magazine, New York, 1929–38; Curator of the Niemann Foundation, Harvard University, 1938; Librarian of Congress, Washington, D.C., 1939–44; Director, United States Office of Facts and Figures, 1941–42, Assistant Director of the Office of War Information, 1942–43, and Assistant Secretary of State, 1944–45, Washington, D.C. Delegate to the UNESCO drafting conference, London, 1945, and United States Member of the Executive Board, UNESCO, 1946. Rede Lecturer, Cambridge University, 1942; Boylston Professor of Rhetoric and Oratory, Harvard University, 1949–62; Simpson Lecturer, Amherst College, Massachusetts, 1964–67. Recipient: Shelley Memorial Award, 1932; Pulitzer Prize, for verse, 1933, 1953, for drama, 1959; New England Poetry Club Golden Rose, 1934; Levinson Prize (*Poetry*, Chicago), 1941; Bollingen Prize, 1952; National Book Award, 1953; Sarah Josepha Hale Award, 1958; Tony Award, for drama, 1959; Academy of American Poets Fellowship, 1965; Academy Award, 1966. M.A.: Tufts University, Medford, Massachusetts, 1932; Litt.D.: Wesleyan University, Middletown, Connecticut, 1938; Colby College, Waterville, Maine, 1938; Yale University, 1939; University of Pennsylvania, Philadelphia, 1941; University of Illinois, Urbana, 1947; Rockford College, Illinois, 1952; Columbia University, New York, 1954; Harvard University, 1955; Carleton College, Northfield, Minnesota, 1956; Princeton University, New Jersey, 1965; University of Massachusetts, Amherst, 1969; York University, Toronto, 1971; LL.D.: Dartmouth College, Hanover, New Hampshire, 1940; Johns Hopkins University, Baltimore, 1941; University of California, Berkeley, 1943; Queen's University, Kingston, Ontario, 1948; University of Puerto Rico, Rio Piedras, 1953; Amherst College, 1963; D.C.L.: Union College, Schenectady, New York, 1941; L.H.D.: Williams College, Williamstown, Massachusetts, 1942; University of Washington, Seattle, 1948. Commander, Legion of Honor, France; Commander, El Sol del Peru. President, American Academy of Arts and Letters, 1953–56. Address: Conway, Massachusetts 01341, U.S.A.

PUBLICATIONS

Verse

Songs for a Summer's Day (A Sonnet-Cycle). New Haven, Connecticut, Yale
   University Press, 1915.
Tower of Ivory. New Haven, Connecticut, Yale University Press, and London,
   Oxford University Press, 1917.
The Happy Marriage and Other Poems. Boston, Houghton Mifflin, 1924.
The Pot of Earth. Boston, Houghton Mifflin, 1925.
Streets in the Moon. Boston, Houghton Mifflin, 1926.
The Hamlet of A. MacLeish. Boston, Houghton Mifflin, 1928.
Einstein. Paris, Black Sun Press, 1929.
New Found Land: Fourteen Poems. Boston, Houghton Mifflin, and Paris, Black
   Sun Press, 1930.
Before March. New York, Knopf, 1932.
Conquistador. Boston, Houghton Mifflin, 1932; London, Gollancz, 1933.
Frescoes for Mr. Rockefeller's City. New York, Day, 1933.
Poems, 1924–1933. Boston, Houghton Mifflin, 1933; as *Poems*, London, Boris-
   wood, 1935.
Public Speech: Poems. New York, Farrar and Rinehart, and London, Boris-
   wood, 1936.
Land of the Free – U.S.A. New York, Harcourt Brace, and London, Boris-
   wood, 1938.
America Was Promises. New York, Duell, 1939; London, Lane, 1940.
Actfive and Other Poems. New York, Random House, 1948; London, Lane,
   1950.
Collected Poems, 1917–1952. Boston, Houghton Mifflin, 1952.
Songs for Eve. Boston, Houghton Mifflin, 1954.
Collected Poems. Boston, Houghton Mifflin, 1963.
"The Wild Old Wicked Man" and Other Poems. Boston, Houghton Mifflin,
   1968; London, W. H. Allen, 1969.
The Human Season: Selected Poems 1962–1972. Boston, Houghton Mifflin,
   1972.

Recording: *Archibald MacLeish Reads His Own Poetry*, Caedmon.

Plays

Nobodaddy. Cambridge, Dunster House, 1926.
Union Pacific (ballet scenario; produced New York, 1934). Published in *The
   Book of Ballets*, New York, Crown, 1939.
Panic: A Play in Verse (produced New York, 1935). Boston, Houghton Mif-
   flin, 1935; London, Boriswood, 1936.
The Fall of the City: A Verse Play for Radio (broadcast, 1937). New York,
   Farrar and Rinehart, and London, Boriswood, 1937.
Air Raid: A Verse Play for Radio (broadcast, 1938). New York, Harcourt
   Brace, 1938; London, Lane, 1939.
The States Talking (broadcast, 1941). Published in *The Free Company Presents*,
   edited by James Boyd, New York, Dodd Mead, 1941.
The American Story: Ten Radio Scripts (includes the plays *The Admiral,
   American Gods, The American Name, Between the Silence and the Surf,*

Discovered, Many Dead, Names for Rivers, Ripe Strawberries, Socorro, When Your Sons Forget) (broadcast, 1944).   New York, Duell, 1944.

The Trojan Horse (broadcast, 1952).   Boston, Houghton Mifflin, 1952.

This Music Crept by Me upon the Waters (broadcast, 1953).   Cambridge, Massachusetts, Harvard University Press, 1953.

J.B.: A Play in Verse (produced New Haven, Connecticut, and New York, 1958; London, 1961).   Boston, Houghton Mifflin, 1958; London, Secker and Warburg, 1959.

The Secret of Freedom (televised, 1959).   Included in *Three Short Plays*, 1961.

Three Short Plays: The Secret of Freedom, Air Raid, The Fall of the City.   New York, Dramatists Play Service, 1961.

Our Lives, Our Fortunes, and Our Sacred Honor (as *The American Bell*, music by David Amram, produced Philadelphia, 1962).   Published in *Think* (Armonk, New York), July–August, 1961.

Herakles: A Play in Verse (produced Ann Arbor, Michigan, 1965).   Boston, Houghton Mifflin, 1967.

Evening's Journey to Conway, Massachusetts: An Outdoor Play.   New York, Grossman, 1967.

Scratch, suggested by *The Devil and Daniel Webster* by Stephen Vincent Benet (produced New York, 1971).   Boston, Houghton Mifflin, 1971.

Screenplays: *Grandma Moses*, 1950; *The Eleanor Roosevelt Story*, 1965.

Radio Plays: *The Fall of the City*, 1937; *Air Raid*, 1938; *The States Talking*, 1941; *The American Story* series, 1944; *The Son of Man*, 1947; *The Trojan Horse*, 1952; *This Music Crept by Me upon the Waters*, 1953.

Television Play: *The Secret of Freedom*, 1959.

Other

Housing America, by the Editors of Fortune.   New York, Harcourt Brace, 1932.

Jews in America, by the Editors of Fortune.   New York, Random House, 1936.

Background of War, by the Editors of Fortune.   New York, Knopf, 1937.

The Irresponsibilities: A Declaration.   New York, Duell, 1940.

The Next Harvard, As Seen by Archibald MacLeish.   Cambridge, Massachusetts, Harvard University Press, 1941.

A Time to Speak: The Selected Prose of Archibald MacLeish.   Boston, Houghton Mifflin, 1941.

The American Cause.   New York, Duell, 1941.

A Free Man's Books: An Address.   Mt. Vernon, New York, Peter Pauper Press, 1942.

American Opinion and the War: The Rede Lecture.   Cambridge, University Press, and New York, Macmillan, 1942.

A Time to Act: Selected Addresses.   Boston, Houghton Mifflin, 1943.

Poetry and Opinion: The Pisan Cantos of Ezra Pound: A Dialogue on the Role of Poetry.   Urbana, University of Illinois Press, 1950.

Freedom Is the Right to Choose: An Inquiry into the Battle for the American Future.   Boston, Beacon Press, 1951; London, Lane, 1952.

Poetry and Journalism.   Minneapolis, University of Minnesota Press, 1958.

Emily Dickinson: Papers Delivered at Amherst College, with others.   Amherst, Massachusetts, Amherst College Press, 1960.

Poetry and Experience. Boston, Houghton Mifflin, and London, Bodley Head, 1961.

The Dialogues of Archibald MacLeish and Mark Van Doren, edited by Warren V. Busch. New York, Dutton, 1964.

The Eleanor Roosevelt Story. Boston, Houghton Mifflin, 1965.

A Continuing Journey. Boston, Houghton Mifflin, 1968.

The Great American Frustration. Stamford, Connecticut, Overbrook Press, 1968.

Editor, *Law and Politics*, by Felix Frankfurter. New York, Capricorn Books, 1962.

Bibliography: *A Catalogue of the First Editions of Archibald MacLeish* by Arthur Mizener, New Haven, Connecticut, Yale University Library, 1938; *Archibald MacLeish: A Checklist* by Edward J. Mullahy, Kent, Ohio, Kent State University Press, 1973.

Manuscript Collections: Library of Congress, Washington, D.C.; Yale University, New Haven, Connecticut; Harvard University, Cambridge, Massachusetts.

* /   *   *

Archibald MacLeish's lines, "And what became of him? Fame became of him" apply very well to himself – for fame is certainly what became of Archibald MacLeish: few poets have known more honor in their own time, and he has been accorded a respect rare in American cultural life. As Librarian of Congress for some years, as an active and influential government adviser· under Franklin Roosevelt, as Assistant Secretary of State, as Harvard professor, as winner of the Bollingen Prize, the National Book Award, the Pulitzer prize, and as an active figure in the world of virtually every art and half-art in America, MacLeish has either moved toward public taste or made it move toward him. His work reveals a highly sensitive awareness of what appeals to the public – there is in it the high-sounding authority of really great art – and because he has been such an eminent man of letters, his ultimate reputation will depend as much on the assessment of his use of office as on his lyrics; he will be subject to the researches of those who want to set straight the social record of American poetry. People will want to know if he really should have advised E. E. Cummings against reading his poem on the Hungarian Revolution at the Boston arts festival, and whether he shouldn't have tried harder to find funds for those poets – Maxwell Bodenheim and others – who dunned him for help while he was Librarian of Congress.

In fact, MacLeish's responsibilities have been so heavy that it is a wonder he has had the time for such an immense outpouring of poems, radio dramas, and plays – all informed by his sense of history, of America's past. This vision is generic, often even jingoistic ("There was a time, Tom Jefferson, / When freedom made free men. The new found earth and the new freed mind"). MacLeish has always worked for a sense of the sublime, and he was never so infected with Pound's notions as to turn away from abstraction and rhetoric when he needed it. Nor has he been afraid, in courting a public audience, to run into charges, perhaps jealously inspired, that he is the poet of the middle-brow, the playwright of the mass man. His warning of the impending doom of mankind, in *J.B.*, is at once an obvious and topical parallel, but it is also a convincing attempt to meet a sense of historical responsibility which MacLeish obviously feels with great depth and sincerity. In short, MacLeish ranks with Robinson Jeffers and Carl Sandburg in the penetration of popular taste.

But it is also an age when poets are judged by their technical innovations, and in this sense MacLeish cannot stand beside Cummings, Pound, or Williams. Like many poets MacLeish may find his most ambitious works absorbed, utterly consumed, by their audience: perhaps it is enough that men left a performance of *J.B.* inspired and went out to lead better lives – while his quieter work lives on in shorter, more private lyrics, scattered through a dozen volumes. In MacLeish's canon such shorter poems are those like "The Snow Fall" and "The Linden Trees" and "Poem in Prose" ("Wherever she is there is sun / And time and a sweet air / Peace is there / Work done"). And his sense of the magic of places, of the sweetness of energy spent, may survive: "This poem is made for my wife / I have made it plainly and honestly / The Mark is on it / Like the burl of the knife." Long after the speeches ("They say: We were young. We have died. Remember us") one goes on admiring the simple and straightforward ("There are always curtains and flowers / And candles and baked bread / And a cloth spread / And a clean house"). It is perhaps the high dignity of his verse that everyone will acknowledge and remember.

– David Ray

MACLEOD, Joseph (Todd Gordon). Pseudonym. **Adam Drinan.** British (Scottish). Born in Ealing, Middlesex, 24 April 1903. Educated at Rugby School, 1917–22; Balliol College, Oxford, 1922–25, B.A. 1925, M.A. 1945; Inner Temple, London, called to the Bar 1928. Married Kathleen Macgregor Davis in 1928 (died, 1953); Maria Teresa Foschini; has one son and one daughter. Director and Lessee, Festival Theatre, Cambridge, 1933–36; Newsreader and Commentator, BBC, London, 1938–45; Managing Director, Scottish National Film Studios, 1946–47. Secretary, Huntingdonshire Divisional Labour Party, 1937–38, and Parliamentary Candidate. Toured Holland as a guest of the Dutch Government, 1946, and the U.S.S.R. as a guest of the Soviet Government, 1947. Honorary Life Member, British Actors' Equity, 1970. Recipient: Royal Society of Arts Silver Medal, 1944; Scottish Arts Council prize, for drama, 1952, for verse, 1973. Address: Via delle Ballodole 9/7, Trespiano, Florence, Italy.

PUBLICATIONS

Verse (as Adam Drinan)

> *The Cove: A Sequence of Poems.* London, privately printed, 1940.
> *The Men of the Rocks.* London, Fortune Press, 1942.
> *Women of the Happy Island.* Glasgow, Maclellan, 1944.

Verse (as Joseph Macleod)

The Ecliptic.   London, Faber, 1930.
Foray of Centaurs.   Paris, This Quarter, 1931.
The Passage of the Torch.   Edinburgh, Oliver and Boyd, 1951.
Script from Norway (under both names).   Glasgow, Maclellan, 1953.
An Old Olive Tree,   Edinburgh, Macdonald, 1971.

Novel

Overture to Cambridge.   London, Allen and Unwin, 1934.

Plays

The Suppliants of Aeschylus with a Verse Sequel (produced Cambridge, 1933).
A Woman Turned to Stone (produced Cambridge, 1934).
Overture to Cambridge (produced Cambridge, 1934).
Miracle for St. George (produced Cambridge, 1935).
The Ghosts of the Strath.   London, Fortune Press, 1943.
Leap in September (produced Perth, 1952).

Screenplay: *Someone Wasn't Thinking,* 1947.

Other

Beauty and the Beast.   London, Chatto and Windus, 1927.
The New Soviet Theatre.   London, Allen and Unwin, 1943.
Actors Cross the Volga.   London, Allen and Unwin, 1946.
A Job at the BBC (autobiography).   Glasgow, Maclellan, 1947.
A Soviet Theatre Sketch-Book.   London, Allen and Unwin, 1951.
Piccola Storia del Teatro Britannico (A Short History of the British Theatre).   Florence, Sansoni, 1958.
People of Florence.   London, Allen and Unwin, 1968.
The Sisters d'Aranyi (biography).   London, Allen and Unwin, 1969.

Manuscript Collection: National Library of Scotland, Edinburgh.

Joseph Macleod comments:

Though Auden and I were greeted in the U.S.A. as a "Dawn in Britain," I never belonged to his school, nor any other I'm aware of. Like most of my poetic generation I was liberated from the word-joys of classical verse (greek melic) by the actuality – accuracies of Ezra Pound. Seeking accuracy has avoided some of the dangers of having a responsive technique and a wide vocabulary. It results in words sometimes outré or obsolete, or can break through the inadequacies of formal grammar.

On the other hand, most of my adult life has been spent in the performing arts (theatre, politics, broadcasting): and the habit of thinking into other people's ears has probably given my verse spoken rhythms and reactions, scottish (Highland father, Perthshire mother) or english (circumstances).

Each word makes up its poem, each poem its book, each book a new part of the same long voyage of discovery. Locality and people: each makes up the other. Without them one would have no personal awareness: so they make up me too. In these circumstances I can't know my direction unless I know the way the world is going. The world is confused by men of action, of commerce and of cruelty. But poetic thought is not confined to these: it can refuse people. For this reason I find my work getting more and more metaphysical. For that reason I feel as much out of sympathy now with the often thoughtless sensationalism of the 70's as I did with the often thoughtless sentimentalism of the 30's.

Poetry = fact + thought = experience. I would like to see myself as a poet who crystallizes (and possibly illuminates?) his and others' experience by discovering it in words.

But readers may not see my work so; and I have no idea of its public effect. Does this matter?

*   *   *

Joseph Macleod divides his long poem *The Ecliptic*, published in 1930, into twelve sections, each under a sign of the zodiac. "Each," he writes in his introduction, "thus contributes to a single consciousness." Preoccupation with the idea of a "single consciousness" occurs when it is under threat. Those poets who mattered most in the twenties were much concerned with the fragmentation of cultures and consciousness. In his note on this section, "Cancer," Macleod writes: "There is a phase in the twenties when this disintegration becomes complete." He was referring to age only but the comment has, by chance, the other application. It is not surprising that this section carries more conviction than the others, forty years after the poem was written. Influenced by Pound in method and style, it has a robust directness that is Macleod's own:

> But the Crab is nobody
> Nobody
> Nobody

The poem ends on the word "Nothing."

And there was nothing more from Macleod until some twelve years later, when he began to write poetry dealing with life in the Hebrides under the pseudonym of Adam Drinan. Some of his forebears came from Drinan in Skye. He discovered he had roots in an ancient way of life which he could admire. His poetic problem was how to relate his modern sense of rhythm to the movement of island speech. The temptation of a poet with an exquisite ear was to imitate the cadences of the Gaelic tongue. The desire to identify aurally might become a substitute for genuine identification with the mores and social concerns of the people and indeed those verses which witness to Macleod's social conscience resolve his poetic problem completely. When his lyrical lament is stiffened by references to the "rusty English trawler" that threatens the livelihood of the natives, he writes fine poems such as "Our Pastures Are Bitten and Bare." A delicate balance, however, was involved. How frequently he sustained it may be gathered from his books *The Men of the Rocks* and *Women of the Happy Island.*

The simplification to Adam Drinan was a temporary, but successful, solution to the dilemma of poetic identity. *Script from Norway*, published in 1953 under both names, capitalised on both sides of the personality, by presenting this poem in dramatic form, though the breach was not healed. Yet later Joseph Macleod was to

write some of his finest poems, those particularly where he spoke out of suffering.
When he writes

> Now that the sun is stopping
> now that the paralysed moon
> is gnawn away

we know we are in the presence of a man who is

> too wise to include or exclude terror.

This has the penetration of maturity but it may still relate to the lively observation
of the young man who wrote in *The Ecliptic:*

> Butcherboys, square basketed, run to make warm their errands.

– George Bruce

MAC LOW, Jackson. American. Born in Chicago, Illinois, 12 September 1922.
Educated at the University of Chicago, 1939–43, A.A. 1941; Brooklyn College,
New York, 1955–58, A.B. (cum Laude) in philosophy 1958. Married to the painter
Iris Lezak; has two children. Free-lance music teacher, English teacher, translator
and editor, 1950–66; reference book editor, Funk and Wagnalls, 1957–58, 1961–62,
and Unicorn Books, 1958–59; copy editor, Alfred A. Knopf, 1965–66, all in New
York. Member of the editorial staff, and Poetry Editor, 1950–54, *Why?*, later
Resistance, a pacifist-anarchist magazine. Since 1966, Instructor, American Lan-
guage Institute, New York and Poetry Editor of *WIN* magazine, New York.
Address: 1764 Popham Avenue, Bronx, New York 10453, U.S.A.

PUBLICATIONS

Verse

The Pronouns: A Collection of 40 Dances – for the Dancers – 6 February–22 March
    1964. New York, Jackson Mac Low, 1964; London, Tetrad Press, 1970.
Manifestos. New York, Something Else Press, 1966.
August Light Poems. New York, C. Eshleman, 1967.
22 Light Poems. Los Angeles, Black Sparrow Press, 1968.
23rd Light Poem: For Larry Eigner. London, Tetrad Press, 1969.
Stanzas for Iris Lezak. New York, Something Else Press, 1970.

Recordings: A Reading of Primitive and Archaic Poems, with others, Broadside;
    From a Shaman's Notebook, with others, Broadside.

974

Plays

Biblical Play (produced New York, 1955).
The Marrying Maiden: A Play of Changes, music by John Cage (produced New York, 1960).
Verdurous Sanguinaria (produced New York, 1961). Act I published in *Tulane Drama Review* (New Orleans), Winter 1965.
Thanks: A Simultaneity for People (produced Wiesbaden, 1962).
Letters for Iris, Numbers for Silence (produced Wiesbaden, 1962).
A Piece for Sari Dienes (produced Wiesbaden, 1962).
Thanks II (produced Paris, 1962).
The Twin Plays: Port-au-Prince and Adams County Illinois (produced New York, 1963). New York, Something Else Press, 1966.
Questions and Answers: A Topical Play (produced New York, 1963).
Play (produced New York, 1965).
Asymmetries No. 408, 410, 485 (produced New York, 1965).
Asymmetries, Gathas and Sounds from Everywhere (produced New York, 1966).

Composer: incidental music for *The Age of Anxiety* by W. H. Auden, produced New York, 1954; for *The Heroes* by John Ashberry, produced New York, 1955.

Theatrical Activities:

Actor: **Plays** – in *Tonight We Improvise* by Pirandello, New York, 1959, and other plays.

Jackson Mac Low comments:

I consider myself a composer: of poetry, music, and theatre works.

I do not think that I belong to any particular school of poetry, but my work is closely related to that of such composers as John Cage, Morton Feldman, Earle Brown, Christian Wolff, and La Monte Young, and it has close affinities with the work of such "concrete" poets as Emmett Williams.

While my earliest work (1937–40) uses mostly free verse and experimental forms, the poems between 1940 and 1954 tend to alternate between traditional metrical forms (and variations on them) and experimental forms, most of which are varieties of free verse. However, from 1954, the poems, plays, and simultaneities incorporate methods, processes, and devices from modern music, including the use of chance operations in composition and/or performance, silences ranging in duration from breath pauses to several minutes, and various degrees of improvisation by performers. Many of the works are "simultaneities" – works performed by several speakers and/or producers of musical sounds and noises at once. These range from completely instrumental pieces (e.g., "Chamber Music for Barney Childs," 1963), thru works combining speech and other sounds (e.g., *Stanzas for Iris Lezak* as simultaneity, 1960), to ones involving only speech (e.g., "Peaks and Lamas," 1959). Other features include indeterminacy (the quality of a work which is in many ways different at every performance) and various degrees of "syntacticalness," ranging from structures that are essentially strings of unrelated words to ones that are partially or fully syntactical in the ordinary sense of the word. Works after 1960 use various proportions of chance and choice in composition and performance. The most recent performance poems (e.g., "Velikovsky Dice-Song," 1968) incorporate multiple slide projections or movies.

*   *   *

Jackson Mac Low's multifarious activities as an artist are all directed toward the exploration of limits and boundaries: the boundary between poetry and music, poetry and drama, even poetry and dance; or, taken differently, the limits of ego, of will, of meaning, of significant order. Although he has written in traditional metrical forms and continues to write in an uninhibited variety of free verse which he calls "spontaneous expression," his most characteristic work, and the mode in which he has made his most interesting discoveries, has its most direct analogues in the music of John Cage, La Monte Young, and Lukas Foss. That is, the poem is a product of the "collaboration" between the poet and the indeterminant, synchronous world. Elements of randomness are admitted in the composition of the poem, or in works which are scored for performance, areas of freedom are allowed to the performers.

In *22 Light Poems*, which is perhaps Mac Low's most beautifully conceived book, the central device is a more or less randomly prepared chart which is keyed to playing cards. "1st Light Poem" is purely a result of random selection from the chart. Others admit "coincidental" input from the environment in which the poem is written, allow concrete events to stand in place of poems, or freely mix his own spontaneous expression with random material. Despite the indeterminacy, however, *22 Light Poems* as well as imaginative realizations of the dances in *The Pronouns* and the "simultaneities" like *Stanzas for Iris Lezak* withstand remarkably rigorous formal analysis. Order, given an opportunity, thrives.

Mac Low's work adduces cogent evidence that the classic western attitudes toward meaning derive from categorical distinctions which result alternatively in radical isolation of consciousness and ruthless exploitation of the external world. The act of the poem as Mac Low conceives it, rather than isolating the poet in his vision, opens free and useful intercourse between the poet and the external world.

– Don Byrd

MACNAB, Roy (Martin). South African. Born in Durban, 17 September 1923. Educated at Hilton College, Natal; Jesus College, Oxford, M.A. Naval Officer, 1942–45. Married to Rachel Mary Heron-Maxwell; has one son and one daughter. Cultural Attaché, South African High Commission, London, 1955–59; Counsellor for Cultural and Press Affairs, South African Embassy, Paris, 1959–67. Since 1968, Director, South African Foundation, London. Fellow, Royal Society of Arts. Address: 7 Lincoln Street, London SW3, England.

Publications

Verse

Testament of a South African. London, Fortune Press, 1947.
The Man of Grass and Other Poems. London, St. Catherine Press, 1960.

Other

> *South and Central Africa.* New York, McGraw Hill, 1954.
> *Journey into Yesterday: South African Milestones in Europe.* Cape Town, H. Timmins, and London, Bailey Brothers and Swinfen, 1962.
> *The French Colonel* (biography). Cape Town and London, Oxford University Press, 1975.

> Editor, with Martin Starkie, *Oxford Poetry 1947.* Oxford, Blackwell, 1947.
> Editor, with Charles Gulston, *South African Poetry: A New Anthology.* London, Collins, 1948.
> Editor, *Towards the Sun: A Miscellany.* London, Collins, 1950.
> Editor, *Poets in South Africa: An Anthology.* Cape Town, Maskew Miller, 1958.

Manuscript Collection: Thomas Pringle Collection, Rhodes University, Grahamstown.

Critical Studies: by Anthony Delius, in *Books Abroad* (Norman, Oklahoma), Summer 1955; Guy Butler, in *Listener* (London), 24 May 1956; William Plomer, in *London Magazine,* February 1957; *A Critical Survey of South African Poetry in English,* by G. M. Miller and Howard Sergeant, Cape Town, Balkema, 1957; *South African Poetry*, Pretoria, University of South Africa, 1966.

*   *   *

Roy Macnab's first book of poetry strikes the reader as a very sincere attempt to convey the poet's thoughts and feelings, but unfortunately the result is somewhat obscured by his struggle with words, a struggle which he seems to have been aware of himself in "The Word":

> Said he, the word is a faithless flirt,
> Not a lover to your art,
> Deceiving with a warm coquetry
> Your dreamfilled youth
> A spidery dilettante, fondling
> Your silver web of thought.

Half-hidden behind this veil of words one senses a very genuine feeling for nature, a deep compassion for the less fortunate among his fellow men and a natural tenderness which finds its best expression in the poem "To a Child." In the poem "The Sick Room" this compassion rises to an impotent fury which unfortunately spoils the poetry and thus proves the truism that genuine involvement does not guarantee genuine poetry.

Although the poems cover a variety of subjects, one experience seems to overshadow all other events in the author's life – his active participation in the Second World War. This experience left him with a feeling of restless discontent and, like the soldiers of Erich Remarque's books he is constantly searching for a meaning or a purpose in his present life that is noble enough to merit the sacrifices of the war that made it possible, and he is inevitably disappointed. His heroes come back from the War "Battered but unbroken in the time of test," and this is what they find:

Reluctantly turning tomorrow's pages
Where no new sensation is stored,
Only the inevitable dullness of Friday's wages
And further occasion for being bored.
      – from "Turning To-Morrow's Pages"

Even those soldiers who died on the battlefield are not allowed to rest in peace, and Macnab is haunted by the knowledge that consequent ages may change their attitude to his heroes. This feeling he expresses in one of his most successful poems, "El-Alamein Revisited":

Six feet is no depth for tragic men
Said the wind and the wind never ceases
To pile up high the soft grey tombs,
And move them where it pleases. . . .

In his disgust with urban life and its tedium Macnab turns to the pioneers, the settlers, the seekers of gold, for it is in these people that he finds the spirit of exploration that so obviously appeals to him.

– Kirsten Holst Petersen

MACPHERSON, (Jean) Jay. Canadian. Born in London, England, 13 June 1931; emigrated to Canada in 1940. Educated at Carleton University, Ottawa, B.A. 1951; University College, London, 1951–52; University of Toronto, M.A. 1955, Ph.D. 1964. Since 1954, Member of the English Department, Victoria College, University of Toronto. Recipient: *Contemporary Verse* prize, 1949; Levinson Prize (*Poetry,* Chicago), 1957; President's Medal, University of Western Ontario, 1957; Governor-General's Award, 1958. Address: Department of English, Victoria College, University of Toronto, Toronto 181, Ontario, Canada.

PUBLICATIONS

Verse

Nineteen Poems. Deyá, Mallorca, Seizin Press, 1952.
O Earth Return. Toronto, Emblem Books, 1954.
The Boatman. Toronto, Oxford University Press, 1957.

Other

The Fovr Ages of Man: The Classical Myths (textbook). New York, St. Martin's Press, and Toronto, Macmillan, 1962.

978

Critical Studies: by Kildare Dobbs, in *Canadian Forum* (Toronto), xxxvii, 438; "Poetry" by Northrop Frye, in "Letters in Canada: 1957," in *University of Toronto Quarterly*, xxvii; "The Third Eye" by James Reaney, in *Canadian Literature 3* (Vancouver); Milton Wilson, in *Fiddlehead 34* (Fredericton, New Brunswick); Munro Beattie, in *Literary History of Canada*, Toronto, University of Toronto Press, 1965.

*   *   *

Jay Macpherson's *The Boatman* has been reprinted five times since its first publication in 1957, and has been accepted with enthusiasm by academic critics as well as the general public. The book is a subtly organised suite of lyrics, elegiac, pastoral, epigrammatic, and symbolist, which utilises the traditional forms of quatrain and couplet with great metrical virtuosity and a remarkable flair for the presentation of serious philosophical and, indeed, religious themes in verse that is sometimes beautifully lyrical and sometimes comic in the tradition of Lear or Gilbert or the nursery rhymes – and sometimes both at once.

The book has as its unifying theme the transmutation of time-bound physical reality into the eternal and the spiritual through the magical intermediary of man's imagination. Symbol and myth are the instruments, and the drama of man's fall and redemption is worked out in terms derived from the Bible, Milton, Blake, and such modern poets and scholars as Robert Graves and Northrop Frye. Among the protagonists whose fables supply the seeds of the mystical drama unifying the book are Noah, Leviathan, Sheba, Mary of Egypt, Eurynome, Merlin, Helen, and such symbolic figures as The Plowman, The Fisherman, The Shepherd, and the Angels. One of the reasons for the success of these poems is that they take the reader into the world of childhood's faith in the unquestionable truth of fairy tale and legend. The elegance and grace of the writing and the authority with which wit and a sense of comedy are conveyed in verse that is both timeless and contemporary give the book an appeal also to the most sophisticated of readers.

– A. J. M. Smith

MacSWEENEY, Barry. British. Born in Newcastle upon Tyne, Northumberland, 17 July 1948. Educated at Rutherford Grammar School; Harlow Technical College, 1966–67. Married Elaine Randell in 1972. Formerly, Free-lance Journalist. Currently, Director, Blacksuede Boot Press; Editor, with Elaine Randell, *Harvest* and *The Blacksuede Boot*, Barnet, Hertfordshire. Recipient: *Stand* Prize, 1967; Arts Council grant, 1971. Address: 6 Sherard Mansions, 46 Well Hall Road, London S.E.9, England.

PUBLICATIONS

Verse

Poems 1965–1968: The Boy from the Green Cabaret Tells of His Mother. Hastings, Sussex, The English Intelligencer, 1967; New York, McKay, 1969.
The Last Bud. Newcastle upon Tyne, Blacksuede Boot Press, 1969.

Joint Effort, with Peter Bland.   Barnet, Hertfordshire, Blacksuede Boot Press,
    1970.
Flames on the Beach at Viareggio: Poems.   Barnet, Hertfordshire, Blacksuede
    Boot Press, 1970.
Our Mutual Scarlet Boulevard.   London, Fulcrum Press, 1970.
The Official Biography of Jim Morrison, Rock Idol, with *12 Poems and a Letter*, by
    Elaine Randell.   London, Curiously Strong, 1971.
Brother Wolf.   London, Turret Books, 1972.
5 Odes.   London, Transgravity Advertiser, 1972.
Dance Steps.   London, Joe DiMaggio Press, 1972.
Fog Eye.   London, Ted Cavanagh, 1973.
6 Odes.   London, Ted Cavanagh, 1973.
Pelt Feather Log.   London, Grosseteste Press, 1975.

Other

*Elegy for January: An Essay Commemorating the Bi-Centenary of Chatterton's
    Death.*   London, Menard Press, 1970.

Barry MacSweeney comments:

   Influenced by Shelley, Pound, Blake, Rimbaud; try to reach into the gap between
the "real" and the Vita Nuova of the Ideal; the air between the poet and his "dark
ideals," some political poetry; lyrical, romantic; Newcastle and Northumberland
are a great influence, the hard and sometimes vaporous geography of the fells and
valleys. Music is also an influence: Berlioz, Bartok, Vivaldi, Debussy. Also helped
revive the poem as the spoken medium; doing many readings. Hard, industrial
landscapes of childhood and youth, reflected in the poems, lucid and tensile words
like steel or coal; then, softer words reflecting the hills and streams where I go
fishing and shooting.

                              *   *   *

   The diversification of English poetry in the 1960's meant that attention was
frequently focused on poets operating from, or at least with their roots in, the
provinces. Some areas, of course, received more publicity than others. Liverpool
was a breeding-ground for the so-called "pop" poets, but an equally lively – and in
many ways more fertile – scene developed in and around Newcastle. Barry Mac-
Sweeney was an important member of the Newcastle poetry community, and time
has proved that he is one of the most talented of the various poets who survived
the initial wave of group enthusiasm and went on to establish themselves as
individuals.
   MacSweeney's early work, as represented in *The Boy from the Green Cabaret Tells
of His Mother*, has a strong sense of the geography of his locality, and there are
frequent references to its physical appearance. But more important, the rhythm of
the poems, and their structure, seems to be shaped by the twin influences of the
city and the country. It would be wrong to call MacSweeney an urban poet
because, like many provincials, he's obviously keenly aware of often being on the
edge of the moors, or close to the coast. The land, and the sea, spill into his

poems, balancing them, and keeping them from becoming merely bright exercises in urban playfulness.

In some later poems MacSweeney changed his area of operation to produce work which had, in his own words, "to do with dreams: either sleep, fantasy, or the luxurious influence of various hallucinogens." Although a worthwhile experiment, and displaying a sure skill in construction, the poems lacked the directness and concern of the earlier work, and one wondered if MacSweeney had lost his way in a fashionable maze. But more recent writings have shown that this was not so. The excellent poem-sequence, *Brother Wolf*, demonstrated that his talents were strong enough to survive a futile journey. Indeed, they possibly benefited from it by learning how to discard the unnecessary. *Brother Wolf* is rich in form and content, and is an essential part of the MacSweeney canon.

MacSweeney has long since lost any limitations imposed by being classified as a regional poet, although it's true to say that the grittiness and colour of the North-East still touches his writing. He has now become one of the most confident and skilled of the younger English poets, and is amongst the handful likely to produce a sustained and vigorous body of work.

– Jim Burns

MADGE, Charles (Henry). British. Born in Johannesburg, South Africa, 10 October 1912. Educated at Winchester College; Magdalene College, Cambridge. Married to Kathleen Raine, *q.v.* (marriage dissolved), has one son and one daughter; Inez Pearn, has one son and one daughter. Reporter, *Daily Mirror*, London, 1935–36; founded Mass Observation, 1937; Staff Member, National Institute of Social and Economic Research, 1940–42; Research Staff, Policy and Economic Planning, 1943; Director, Pilot Press, London, 1944; Social Development Officer, Stevenage, 1947–50; Professor of Sociology, University of Birmingham, 1950–70. Member, United Nations Technical Assistance Mission, Thailand, 1953–54, India, 1957–58, Southeast Asia, 1959–60; Leader, Mission to Ghana, United Nations Economic Commission for Africa, 1963. Address: La Rivière, 81-Mirandol, France.

PUBLICATIONS

Verse

The Disappearing Castle. London, Faber, 1937.
The Father Found. London, Faber, 1941.

Other

Mass Observation, with T. Harrisson. London, Muller, 1937.
War-Time Pattern of Saving and Spending. Cambridge, University Press, and New York, Macmillan, 1943.
Industry after the War: Who Is Going to Run It?, with Donald Tyerman. London, Pilot Press, 1943.

Survey Before Development in Thai Villages. New York, U.N. Secretariat, 1957.
Evaluation and the Technical Assistance Expert: An Operational Analysis. Paris, UNESCO, 1961.
Society in the Mind: Elements of Social Eidos. London, Faber, and New York, Free Press of Glencoe, 1964.
Art Students Observed, with Barbara Weinberger. London, Faber, 1973.

Editor, with Humphrey Jennings, *May the Twelfth: Mass Observation Day-Surveys 1937, by over 200 Observers.* London, Faber, 1937.
Editor, with T. Harrisson, *First Year's Work, 1937–38, by Mass Observation.* London, Lindsay Drummond, 1938.
Editor, with T. Harrisson, *Britain, by Mass Observation.* London, Penguin, and New York, Famous Books, 1938.
Editor, with T. Harrisson, *War Begins at Home, by Mass Observation.* London, Chatto and Windus, 1940.
Editor, *Target for Tomorrow* series. London, Pilot Press, 1943–45.
Editor, *Pilot Guide to the General Elections.* London, Pilot Press, 1945.
Editor, *Pilot Papers: Social Essays and Documents, 1945–47.* London, Pilot Press, 1947.

*   *   *

Charles Madge, who was born in Johannesburg in 1912 and educated at Winchester and Cambridge (where he came under the influence of William Empson), is an intellectual poet, which may to some extent explain why his poetry has never received the attention it deserves. His earliest poems, collected in *The Disappearing Castle,* demonstrate his readiness to try out new ideas and techniques in his search for an effective medium of communication. If they display many of the weaknesses of the experimentalist, such as ambiguous statements, imprecise images, occasional striving after effects, and surrealistic word-play almost for its own sake, they also hint at his potentialities and reveal an original turn of mind. "Solar Creation," "In Conjunction," "Fortune," and the sequence entitled "Delusions" are among the best of these poems. Like many other poets of the thirties, Madge was concerned with social conditions and "the strain of being man upright in the flat world," but even in these early pieces there is little evidence of the over-simplified analysis of the situation such as those proffered by the Auden-Spender group with whom he has been identified. He had closer affinities with the *Twentieth Century Verse* group of poets, led by Julian Symons, whose theory that the poet ought to be "the perfect mass-observer" was probably derived from Madge's contribution to the development of Mass Observation as a valid instrument of social research.

Madge's second volume, *The Father Found,* marks a distinct advance in technical proficiency. The romantic landscapes, the verbal tricks and ambiguities, have all been discarded, and the poems are written in a controlled and compact language, of which psychological concepts and accurate scientific references form an integral part, against a localised background of filling-stations, factories, traffic, theodolites, airwaves and television. Such poems as "Binocular Vision," "Drinking in Bolton," and "Through the Periscope" indicate the change that had taken place and show a new objectivity in Madge's approach to his chosen themes. If the language presents any difficulties, they arise from the intractable nature of the material he is working upon and his highly individual way of looking at things. As he observes in "Philosophical Poem":

> This window by a curious trick can see
> Workaday things and a white rising planet.

Charles Madge has succeeded in translating his philosophical beliefs into action in the sociological sphere, so that his theories have been tested by experience; direct activity in the sociological field in its turn has assisted his creative work by keeping him in close touch with reality; while the dual nature of his vision has enabled him to perform "the curious trick" by which he establishes the connection between "workaday things" and the "white rising planet." It can, therefore, be argued that his best poetry has social value.

This is confirmed by the later and, as yet, uncollected pieces such as "Visions of Camden Town," "In the Lens of Observation," "For an Altar," the sequence "Poem by Stages," and the long poem entitled "The Storming of the Brain," which can best be described as a poetic treatment, in allegorical form acceptable at several levels, of the conflict between detached intellectualism and the unruly and unpredictable forces of life. With "The Storming of the Brain" before us it is possible not only to ascertain the progress Madge has made, but also to trace the direction in which he seems to be moving. First it was necessary to effect a reconciliation between his romantic impulses and his trained scientific methods, and then his intellectual beliefs had to be related to his idealistic concern for humanity in such a way as to maintain his artistic integrity and yet provide a basis for positive action.

In "The Storming of the Brain" Madge lays emphasis upon the need for the integration of society as distinct from the prevailing tendency towards division into armed ideological camps, and indicates what seems to him to be the only practical way in which unity of purpose can be achieved.

– Howard Sergeant

MAHON, Derek. British. Born in Belfast, Northern Ireland, 23 November 1941. Educated at Belfast Institute; Trinity College, Dublin, B.A. 1965. English Teacher, Belfast High School, Newtownabbey, County Antrim, 1967–68. Since 1969, Lecturer in English, The Language Centre of Ireland, Dublin. Founding Editor, *Ariel*; since 1970 Co-Editor, *Atlantis*, Dublin. Recipient: Eric Gregory Award, 1965. Lives in London.

PUBLICATIONS

Verse

> *Twelve Poems.* Belfast, Festival Publications, 1965.
> *Night-Crossing.* London, Oxford University Press, 1968.
> *Ecclesiastes.* Manchester, Phoenix Pamphlet Poets Press, 1970.
> *Beyond Howth Head.* Dublin, Dolmen Press, 1970.
> *Lives.* London, Oxford University Press, 1972.
> *The Man Who Built His City in Snow.* London, Poem-of-the-Month Club, 1972.

Other

> Editor, *Modern Irish Poetry.* London, Sphere, 1972.

*   *   *

Derek Mahon is one of a number of young poets to have emerged from Northern Ireland in the last dozen years. Having said that, one has to add that the difference in his work from that of his contemporaries is as marked as their geographical distinction. For one thing, he is eclectic in his metres and his influences; almost defiantly so. When he is at his most local topographically, as in "Day Trip to Donegal," he is most metropolitan in his technique:

> How could we hope to make them understand?
> Theirs is a sea-mind, mindless upon land
> And dead. Their systematic genocide
> (Nothing remarkable that millions died)
> To us is a necessity
> For ours are land-minds, mindless in the sea.

This refers to the herring and whiting brought home to a fishing-village, probably Killybegs. Notice the dexterous handling of what could have been a tricky stanza-form, the reference to the Holocaust in that nonchalant parenthesis. Derek Mahon's feet only seem to falter; for him, hesitancy is a special effect.

This is true not of the poem in question but of other witty, tricky poems in Mahon's output. Consider, for example, "My Wicked Uncle," "An Unborn Child," "April on Toronto Island," "De Quincey in Later Life" from his first collection; "Job's Comforter," "I Am Raftery," "Consolations of Philosophy," and "Edvard Munch" from his second.

But, as the titles indicate, this shows a poet eclectic not only in his techniques but in his themes. By and large, there is an absence of pressure behind the deftly executed transitions. We shall not find in the De Quincey poem the aching nostalgia that the Opium Eater achieved in a page or so of his *Confessions* when he wrote of Anne of Oxford Street. Mr. Mahon speaks of the occasional cries of despair in the paintings of Munch, but the despair is spoken of, not confronted. These poems are triumphs of prosody rather than empathy.

The exceptions to this general remark are striking. The end of a relationship is characterized by the death of the speaker's potential descendants as well as himself:

> They will have buried
> My great-grandchildren, and theirs,
> Beside me by now
>
> With a subliminal
> Batsqueak of reflex lamentation.
> Our hair and excrement
>
> Litter the rich earth
> Changing, second by second,
> To civilizations. . . .
>   – "An Image from Beckett"

This reveals Mahon as essentially an elegist. Indeed, his interest in the charnel house provides him with his richest imagery:

> They buried him slowly above the sea,
> The young Presbyterian minister
> Rumpled and windy in the sea air . . .
>
> When we start breaking up in the wet darkness
> And the rotten boards fall from us, and the ribs
> Crack under the constriction of tree roots. . . .

Derek Mahon can make being born seem like an escape to the grave, the coming of spring to Toronto Island resemble a visitation of winter. It is in this area that the aesthete shows, behind his ironic mask, a sombre countenance. And this is never more so in what is, perhaps, Mahon's finest poem to date, "At Carrowdore Churchyard." It is an elegy on Louis MacNeice which takes on, characteristically enough, a measure of MacNeice's manner to invoke an attitude towards life which is as much that of Derek Mahon as of the fine Irish poet whom he commemorates:

> . . . Maguire, I believe, suggested a blackbird
> And over your grave a phrase from Euripides.
>
> Which suits you down to the ground, like this churchyard
> With its play of shadow, its humane perspective.
> Locked in the winter's fist, these hills are hard
> As nails, yet soft and feminine in their turn
> When fingers open and the hedges burn.
> This, you implied, is how we ought to live –
>
> The ironical, loving crush of roses against snow,
> Each fragile, solving ambiguity. So
> From the pneumonia of the ditch, from the ague
> Of the blind poet and the bombed-out town you bring
> The all-clear to the empty holes of spring.
> Rinsing the choked mud, keeping the colours new.

– Philip Hobsbaum

MAJOR, Clarence. American. Born in Atlanta, Georgia, 31 December 1936. Educated at the Art Institute, Chicago, 1952–54; Armed Forces Institute, 1955–56; New School for Social Research, New York, 1972. Served in the United States Air Force, 1955–57. Taught in the Harlem Education Program Writers Workshop, New York, 1967, and the Teachers and Writers Collaborative, New York, 1967–72. Since 1972, Member of the Faculty, Sarah Lawrence College, Bronxville, New York. Associate Editor, *Proof Magazine*, Chicago, 1959–60; Editor, *Coercion Review*, Chicago, 1958–65; Associate Editor, *Caw!* magazine, 1967–68, and *Journal of Black Poetry*, 1967–70. Recipient: National Endowment for the Arts grant, 1970; New York Cultural Foundation grant, 1971. Agent: Marcia Higgins, William Morris Agency, 1350 Avenue of the Americas, New York, New York 10019, U.S.A.

PUBLICATIONS

Verse

The Fires That Burn in Heaven. Privately printed, 1954.
Love Poems of a Black Man. Omaha, Nebraska, Coercion Press, 1964.
Human Juices. Omaha, Nebraska, Coercion Press, 1965.
Swallow the Lake. Middletown, Connecticut, Wesleyan University Press, 1970.
Symptoms and Madness. New York, Corinth Books, 1971.

Private Line. London, Paul Breman, 1971.
The Cotton Club: New Poems. Detroit, Broadside Press, 1972.
The Syncopated Cakewalk. New York, Barlenmir House, 1974.

Novels

All-Night Visitors. New York, Olympia Press, 1969.
NO. New York, Emerson Hall, 1973.

Other

Dictionary of Afro-American Slang. New York, International Publishers, 1970;
   as *Black Slang: A Dictionary of Afro-American Talk*, London, Routledge, 1971.
The Dark and Feeling: Black American Writers and Their Work. New York,
   Third Press, 1974.

Editor, *The New Black Poetry.* New York, International Publishers, 1969.

Critical Studies: in *New York Times*, 7 April 1969; *Quarterly Journal of Speech* (New York), April 1971; *Saturday Review* (New York), 3 April 1971; *Chicago Sun-Times*, 28 April 1971; *Poetry* (Chicago), August 1971; *Virginia Quarterly Review* (Charlottesville), Winter 1971; *New York Times Book Review*, 1 July 1973; *Interviews with Black Writers*, edited by John O'Brien, New York, Liveright, 1973.

Clarence Major comments:

I am trying to break through the artificial effects of language. I'm also trying to break down the artificial distinctions between poetry and fiction.

*   *   *

With others of the loose association known variously as the new, young, or revolutionary black poets, Clarence Major is concerned to use the black reality in ways that will indicate a departure from the Euro-American cultural sensibility and provide the artistic equivalent of nationalist revolutionary politics. For Major, more so than for others in the group, achievement of that public program must come through exploration of interior experiences, and for that reason he notably carries the implications of the emerging black esthetic furthest toward renewal of technical practice.
In some of his works, particularly verse in the recent *Cotton Club*, titles provide reference to the familiar social realm and thus orient the reader to historical reality. Other times the concrete experiential reference emerges gradually as in musical lyrics. Whether the externally referential detail is personal as in the verses about intimate relationships in *Symptoms and Madness* or alluding to events in lives of friends and acquaintances as in several of the poems included in *Private Line*, the poems are cast subjectively as dramas of feelings, sometimes in conflict, other times their complexities resolved by time, and occasionally verging on direct assertion because of the author's sense of detachment. Always, however, the dynamic of Major's poems derives from the logic of emotional knowledge.

The premise of such verse holds that the structures of feeling, in art as in life, have been shaped by experience uniquely black and personal, and it follows that the patterns of expression, therefore, must be intrinsic to poetic execution. Obvious evidence appears in such a poem as "Breakup" where Major runs phrases together, omits utility words, and punctuates in ways to suggest that gesture, intonation, and nuance supply part of the meaning:

> really. dumb young, back
> then you know i knew your
> husband. knew you guess you
> got into levels. of me, too
> remember you so smart too
> much for college. too much
> for your ol man, too.

As the internal play with sounds suggests, this verse partakes of popular speech but does not reflect it. The stylized usage shows Major's interest lies in the sound clusters providing the beat he believes is unique to black art – distinguishing it from the sight-based and melodic poetry of Euro-American tradition.

Fundamental as it is to communication, the devotion to sound often produces verse that not only defies conceptualizing but also results in such attention to the sensations of words that the poem becomes intensely private. At its best, however, Major's technique of raising feeling above the original stimulation in external experience suspends it within the consciousness of the poet to become available to bold symbolist treatment. "Surprising Love," for example, verges on failure but the risk is well taken:

> O supreme sledgehammer of reposing verbal stacks of
> nouns verbs adjectives charming, not
> with witches of middleages full of pale death, but
> the soft, waiting form of myself as male, not
> metallic elements, defined by ghost cities nor crises
> nor color or courts nor the vulgar solitude of
> my "birthday," but by the gushing tar, the
> agitation of surprising love, or more precisely
> She.

Major's poetic energy – he has published in more than one hundred magazines and journals – and experimental nerve promise us much. With the other poets of his generation he may be making another black renaissance in America, this one to survive.

– John M. Reilly

MANDEL, Eli(as Wolf). Canadian. Born in Estevan, Saskatchewan, in 1922. Educated at the University of Saskatchewan, Saskatoon; University of Toronto. Served in Europe with the Army Medical Corps during World War II. Since 1946, Member, Department of English, currently Professor of English, University of Alberta. Recipient: President's Medal, University of Western Ontario, 1963;

Governor-General's Award, 1968; Canada Council Award, 1971. Address: Department of English, University of Alberta, Edmonton, Alberta, Canada.

PUBLICATIONS

Verse

> *Trio,* with Gael Turnbull and Phyllis Webb.   Toronto, Contact Press, 1954.
> *Fuseli Poems.*   Toronto, Contact Press, 1960.
> *Black and Secret Man.*   Toronto, Ryerson Press, 1964.
> *An Idiot Joy.*   Edmonton, Alberta, Hurtig, 1967.

Other

> *Criticism: The Silent Speaking Words.*   Toronto, C.B.C. Publications, 1966.
> *Irving Layton.*   Toronto, Forum House, 1969.

> Editor, with Jean-Guy Pilon, *Poetry 62.*   Toronto, Ryerson Press, 1961.
> Editor, *Five Modern Canadian Poets.*   Toronto, Holt Rinehart, 1970.
> Editor, with Desmond Maxwell, *English Poems of the Twentieth Century.*   Toronto, Macmillan, 1971.
> Editor, *Contexts of Canadian Criticism.*   Chicago, University of Chicago Press, 1971.
> Editor, *Poets of Contemporary Canada 1960–1970.*   Toronto, McClelland and Stewart, 1972.

*   *   *

"I am a fable looking for a plot," Eli Mandel wrote in "Aesop" in *Black and Secret Man.* "Actually, I am an unwritten tale." The search for the tale to tell has taken Eli Mandel from Greek mythology and Old Testament fable to modern Freudian and Jungian theories of human motivation. What has remained constant – from his "Minotaur Poems" in *Trio,* where his work appeared with that of Phyllis Webb and Gael Turnbull, to his latest book, *An Idiot Joy* – is his feeling for tortured imagery, his sense of the grotesque, his urbane tone of irony, and his language which is by turns dramatic and melodramatic.

It might be argued that Eli Mandel is an academic poet in the best sense of that term. He is interested in the mythopoeic theories of Northrop Frye, and sees in the act of criticism itself (especially in his radio talks published as *The Silent Speaking Words*) an inevitable counterpoint to the practice of poetry. When he edited *Poetry 62* with Jean-Guy Pilon, he isolated the imaginative and dramatic strains in Canadian poetry. To all his writing, he brings a heightened sense of the immediacy of the imaginative act, which owes something to the writing of William Blake.

His first book, *Fuseli Poems,* is full of fragmentation and a concern for anthropology and myth. Writing about "The Anarchist-Poets" in *Black and Secret Man,* he advises the reader to "step carefully through this rubble of words. / Can you really say which wrecks were once poems, / which weapons?" In "The Burning Man" from *An Idiot Joy,* he stresses the anarchic quality of the poetic imagination: "I'm a walking crime wave." His poem "In the 57th Century of Our Lord" begins, "Semitic and secret I plan new evasions, / survival, the tribal rite."

Eli Mandel's imagery, often full of literary allusions, is usually bold and arresting. The hermatic and the heroic battle it out within his poems – Orpheus and Hercules united in one man. He ends "Pictures in an Institution" with the following lines:

> Notice: there will be no further communication
> lectures are cancelled
> all students are expelled
> the reading of poetry is declared a public crime.

– John Robert Colombo

MANHIRE, Bill. New Zealander. Born in Invercargill, 27 December 1946. Educated at Otago Boys High School; University of Otago, Dunedin, M.A. (honours) 1968, M.Litt. 1970; University College, London, 1970–73, M.Phil. 1973. Married Barbara McLeod in 1970: has one daughter. Since 1973, Lecturer in English, Victoria University, Wellington. Editor, Amphedesma Press, Dunedin. Agent: Toby Eady Associates, 313 Fulham Road, London, England. Address: Department of English, Victoria University of Wellington, Private Bag, Wellington, New Zealand.

PUBLICATIONS

Verse

Malady. Dunedin, Amphedesma Press, 1970.
The Elaboration. Wellington, Square and Circle, 1972.

Other

Editor, *New Zealand Universities Arts Festival Yearbook 1969.* Dunedin, Arts Festival Committee, 1969.

*   *   *

Bill Mahire's published work so far is notable for its elegant economy of language and the subtlety of its aural effects. The poems in *The Elaboration,* which date back some years, tend to imagism, with all that the label implies: most are uncluttered, pared-down, concentrating intently on single events without comment or explanation. Their rhythms arise naturally our of their content; each line finds its own length. There are a few exceptions; and influences (Pound, and in one case John Crowe Ransom) are still apparent. But this is to be expected in a young poet trying out various voices. His own voice does, in the end, emerge strongly: a rather quiet, sane, but faintly mysterious accent, a tone blending humour, sadness and patience, usually unrhetorical but capable of surprises. He has poignantly memorable lines:

> And you kneeling among sand
> Pardoning the fishes
>
> Morag Morag
>
> Who will tend your ridiculous garden?
> How will the crops fatten?

This is effective partly because of its delicate handling of rhythm. Elsewhere the impact is made by touches of surrealism, a mode which is used increasingly in Bill Manhire's later work. For example:

> . . . in the garden we discover
> the skating-rink, women ticking
> with white frost as if they
> mean to go off. A farmer from
> Balclutha sends a platoon of sheep
>
> out on to the ice. In their little
> boots they are quite graceful.

The few longer, more descriptive poems he has published recently suggest an expansion in his range; it will be awaited with interest.

– Fleur Adcock

MANIFOLD, John (Streeter). Australian. Born in Melbourne, Victoria, 21 April 1915. Educated at Geelong Grammar School, Victoria; Jesus College, Cambridge, 1934–37, B.A. (honours) in modern languages 1937. Served with the Intelligence Corps, 1940–46. Married the singer Katharine Hopwood in 1940 (died, 1969); has one son and one daughter. President, Brisbane Realist Writers Group, 1956–66; President, Fellowship of Australian Writers, Queensland Branch, 1959; Commonwealth Literary Fund Lecturer at the universities of New England, Queensland, and South Australia. Currently, Vice-President, National Council of Realist Writers' Groups, and Poetry Editor, *The Realist*. Since 1971, President, the Bach Society of Queensland. Toured China in 1963 as a guest of the Association for Cultural Relation with Foreign Countries; toured the U.S.S.R. in 1963 as a guest of the Union of Soviet Writers; Delegate, International Writers' Meeting, Berlin, 1965. Agent: David Higham Associates Ltd., 5–8 Lower John Street, Golden Square, London W1R 4HA, England. Address: 361 Wynnum North Road, Wynnum, Queensland 4178, Australia.

PUBLICATIONS

Verse

The Death of Ned Kelly and Other Ballads. London, Favil Press, 1941.
Trident, with Hubert Nicholson and David Martin. London, Fore Publications, 1944.
Selected Verse. New York, Day, 1946; London, Dobson, 1948.
Nightmares and Sunhorses. Melbourne, Overland, 1961.
Op. 8: Poems 1961–69. Queensland, Queensland University Press, 1970.
Broadsheets. Brisbane, privately printed, 1973.

Other

The Amorous Flute: An Unprofessional Handbook for Recorder Players and All Amateurs of Music. London, Workers Music Association, 1948.
The Music in English Drama from Shakespeare to Purcell. London, Barrie and Rockliff, 1956.
The Violin, The Banjo and the Bones: An Essay on the Instruments of Bush Music. Ferntree Gully, Victoria, Ram's Skull Press, 1957.
Who Wrote the Ballads? Notes on Australian Folksong. Sydney, Australasian Book Society, 1964.

Editor, *Bandicoot Ballads.* Ferntree Gully, Victoria, Ram's Skull Press, 1950–.
Editor, *The Queensland Centenary Pocket Songbook.* Sydney, Edwards and Shaw, 1959.
Editor, *The Penguin Australian Songbook.* Melbourne, Penguin, 1964.

John Manifold comments:

My verse is old-fashioned. It is about women, horses, soldiers, revolutionists, landscapes, myths, and history. A lot of it is narrative. I enjoy wrestling with the strict forms – the apparently artless ballad being just as strict a form in its way as the apparently artful sonnet or limerick. I learnt from "Banjo" Paterson, Heredia, Heine, Aragon, and more recently Brecht, to strive for clarity, brevity, balance and impersonality.

Melius est quod reprehendent nos grammatici quam non intelligant populi (Saint Augustine).

*   *   *

John Manifold's *Selected Verse* was well received upon publication both in England and the United States. It centred around a brilliantly cool yet ardent sonnet series that was directly derived from the work of Auden. Manifold was able to bring his own heritage – wealthy pioneer ancestry, brilliant Cambridge career, conversion to Communism – unobtrusively but ingratiatingly into these poems, giving them a lightness and cultivatedness that was disarming and unexpected in Australian poetry of the late 1940's. Returning to Australia, Manifold retired to a small village outside Brisbane and, with his wife, taught local children how to make, and perform upon, antique musical instruments – recorders, lutes, citterns. His poetry became influenced by his own attempts to revive and reanimate early Australian bush-ballad traditions, the results of which were not very convincingly shown in his next collection, *Nightmares and Sunhorses*. Manifold has published a number of volumes on Elizabethan and Jacobean music, as well as Australian folksong. His most important recent work, however, is the verse collection *Op. 8*, which includes a number of recent sonnets that recapture the wit and poise of his earlier work, as well as other work that remains admirably and unashamedly elegant. (Elegant in sensibility, not affectation.) John Manifold has been a personal influence on a number of Australian poets, from David Campbell to Rodney Hall. His writing perhaps captures only part of the man's complex and individual personality. But in itself that remains something of a nectar to be savoured and remembered.

– Thomas W. Shapcott

MARSHALL, Jack. American. Born in Brooklyn, New York, 25 February 1937. Educated at Lafayette High School, Brooklyn. Has one son. Shipping clerk, salesman, farmhand, steel mill hand, deck hand; Copywriter, J. C. Penney, New York; longshoreman, San Francisco. Taught in poetry workshops at the University of Iowa, Iowa City, California Western College, San Diego, and San Francisco State College. Address: 554 Jersey Street, San Francisco, California 94114, U.S.A.

PUBLICATIONS

Verse

The Darkest Continent. New York, For Now Press, 1967.
Bearings: Poems. New York, Harper, 1969.
Surviving in America, with Anselm Hollo and Sam Hamod. Iowa City, Cedar Creek Press, 1972.
Floats. Iowa City, Cedar Creek Press, 1972.
Bits of Thirst. Iowa City, Cedar Creek Press, 1973.
Arriving on the Playing Fields of Paradise. Iowa City, Cedar Creek Press, 1974.

Jack Marshall comments:

My poems are playful investigations and perceptions of alternate realities. I write them because no one else does. I write them as ecstatically as I can; music and metaphor being the compression-chamber of the senses.

*   *   *

In his book, *Bearings*, Jack Marshall impresses one as a poet with considerable energy and talent who cannot always harness them successfully; often the poem gets the upper hand, its forceful rhetoric becoming mannered, unclear, or somewhat rambling. Marshall has a talent for stately speech and a rich vocabulary, packing his lines with strong sounds and closely-bunched movements of imagery and thought. The problem is that often his lines are *too* dense; they become crabbed, straining the reader's attention, or else they get caught up in following associations of emotion and image that draw away from the poem's main thrust.

When his poems succeed, some of the same qualities apparent in the poorer poems make the successes impressive ones – density of sound and sense, dramatic tone, specificity, variety of vocabulary and image. A great number of his best poems (like "Setting Out" and "On the President's State Visit to Mexico") make an extensive use of syntactical parallelism, a device which at once accomodates his forceful rhetoric, producing a kind of persistent thrust, and also provides a simple structure which tends to prevent excessive convolution or rambling courses of association.

It isn't apparent whether or not the poems are arranged chronologically, but there seems to be a considerable improvement in the poems of the third and fourth sections over those in the first and second, and a more personal and relaxed tone enters the book in poems like "Walking Across Brooklyn Bridge" and "For Kathleen, Gone on a Brief Journey." It should be added that in poems which have appeared in various places since his first book Marshall has assumed a new, freer style which allows him to make series of non-rational associations without cramping the poem or seeming to get lost in it.

– Lawrence Russ

MASSINGHAM, Harold (William). British. Born in Mexborough, Yorkshire, 25 October 1932. Educated at Mexborough Grammar School, 1943–51; Manchester University, 1951–54, BA. in English 1954. Married Patricia Audrey Moran in 1958; has three sons and one daughter. School teacher, Manchester Education Committee, 1955–70. Since 1971, Tutor, Extra-mural Department, University of Manchester. Co-Founder, *Manchester University Poetry*, 1953. Recipient: Cheltenham Festival Guinness Prize, 1962; Arts Council award, 1965; Cholmondeley award, 1968. Address: 29 Moorland Road, Manchester M20 OBB, Lancashire, England.

PUBLICATIONS

Verse

Black Bull Guarding Apples. London, Longman, 1965.
Creation. Oxford, Sycamore Press, 1968.
The Magician: A Poem Sequence. Manchester, Phoenix Pamphlet Poets Press, 1969.
Storm. Frensham, Surrey, Sceptre Press, 1970.
Snow-Dream. Frensham, Surrey, Sceptre Press, 1971.
The Pennine Way. London, BBC Publications, 1971.

Frost-Gods. London, Macmillan, 1971.
Doomsday. London, Poem-of-the-Month Club, 1972.

Harold Massingham comments:

As a poet, and apart from certain lyrics and fanciful poems for children, my main concern is to re-live, explore and re-present native experience in concrete terms. Some poems embody natural forces, birth-dreams and animal-nightmares; some relate to the North of England, especially a Yorkshire childhood; others celebrate persons and occasionally treat of domestic issues. The tendency is to create sensuous, physical, elemental impressions in a thick texture of tight phrasing and concrete imagery: most of which imagery has its genesis in my early life. I am indebted to Keats for the earliest impulse to use my own verbal resources (see also *London Magazine* ix, 1); Laurie Lee and Dylan Thomas were later fugitive influences; and for many years my main stylistic influence has been Anglo-Saxon verse, in its ruggedness, deliberate alliterations and seemingly irregular (pre-iambic) rhythms. I have translated a great deal of it, usually as "free versions." Non-literary inspirations have been Van Gogh and Beethoven. I have no orthodox political or religious affiliations, but certain pantheistic sympathies and a preoccupation with self-expression and with the genesis and individuality of things.

*   *   *

Harold Massingham was born in 1932 in Mexborough, Yorkshire, the son of a collier, and spent the first twenty years of his life there. The poems of his first book of verse, *Black Bull Gardening Apples,* are very much those of a Northerner ("The air nips, blonds, it is eye-living light. / North-born, I could do worse than house in it"). It is concerned with the history and climate of Northern England and the "separateness" of animals (bull, rat, lizard, spider, frog, jackdaw). The language is terse, the description compact and imaginative (of the rat: "He was filthy silk"). People are represented by a snuff addict, a war veteran, his children, his mining father. Half-rhymes are usual. Significantly, there are versions of the Anglo-Saxon "The Seafarer" and "The Wanderer."

Frost-Gods also celebrate "Northness." Most of these poems are unrhymed; the writing is both more sophisticated and more fanciful ("tree-rain / Fell like isaac-newton apples"). Animals are still represented: a swan, an Alsatian, a cow ("this suede Empress"). There are translations of thirteen Anglo-Saxon riddles and three longer Anglo-Saxon poems. One poem describes the old and the poor in a cafeteria, another ("Winter in Wensleydale") is a very typical poem of landscape and season. These are two of the most successful, and illustrate the two main manifestations of Massingham's talent. There are also two nightmare poems: one childish ("Flitter-Rats"), one adult ("Nightmare of Blazing Vultures"). These are not so successful; nor is his children's verse, some of which appeared in *The Magician.* He is a poet who writes best about animals, natural objects, ordinary people. When he has his eye on these, his poems benefit. Humour, satire, political intention, are entirely absent. This is an art of straightforward projection, making the reader see what the poet sees, with very little variation of theme or tone.

– Gavin Ewart

MATCHETT, William H(enry). American. Born in Chicago, Illinois, 5 March 1923. Educated at Westtown School, Philadelphia; Swarthmore College, Pennsylvania, B.A. (highest honors) 1949; Harvard University, Cambridge, Massachusetts, M.A. 1950, Ph.D. 1957. Conscientious Objector; Civilian Public Service, 1943–46. Married Judith Wright in 1949; has two sons and one daughter. Teaching Fellow, Harvard University, 1953–54. Instructor, 1954–56, Assistant Professor, 1956–60, Associate Professor, 1960–66, and since 1966, Professor of English, University of Washington, Seattle. Member of the Editorial Board, *Poetry Northwest*, Seattle, 1961–66; since 1963, Editor, *Modern Language Quarterly*. Recipient: *Furioso* Prize, 1952. Address: Department of English, GN-30, University of Washington, Seattle, Washington 98195, U.S.A.

PUBLICATIONS

Verse

Water Ouzel and Other Poems. Boston, Houghton Mifflin, 1955.

Other

Poetry: From Statement to Meaning, with Jerome Beaty. New York, Oxford University Press, 1965.
The Phoenix and the Turtle: Shakespeare's Poem and Chester's "Loues Martyr." The Hague, Mouton, 1965.

Editor, *The Life and Death of King John,* by William Shakespeare. New York, New American Library, 1966.

William H. Matchett comments:

Minor poetry in a minor key, moving from the natural image to the, hopefully not forced, small affirmation. The early influence was the heavy hand of Eliot. If there is any increased freedom in my recent poetry, it is the direct influence of the poetry and criticism of Paul Hunter.

*   *   *

Subdued, civil, and marked by an easy grace, William H. Matchett's poems have found favor in several reprintings. Long before Ecology became the fashionable cry, he praised the fragile lives of wild birds, now become extinct, or nearly so, by the wanton hand of predatory man. His sensitive descriptions of nature are based on acute observation and conveyed through personification and perky humor, but they often close in pessimism. "Hang on to the end!" he urges the Ivory Bill, "You still may thrive / The Fates of us all are linked." He places little trust, however, in "the human pest," concluding there may be room for delicate wildfowl when man is extinct. Viewing man against man in war, he despairs, "lacking the strength to put the world in order." In other topographical poems, casual, conversational sketches preface philosophical meditations on nature as a source of grace and "second sight." Dry reflection follows the vivid portraiture of "Old Inn on the

995

Eastern Shore,'' but finally gives way to mockery. The impression of nature is short-lived, ''insight will fade''; the student soon considers himself ''no sinne,'' and ''Will go in to bathe before dinner.''

This penchant for the didactic is more pronounced in compact rimed lyrics on a simple wedding, a Quaker funeral, Spring, and September, where aphorisms and moral tags render the scenes curiously bloodless. More spirited are the several internal monologues by personages caught in dramatic moments. Blood-thirsty and self-righteous, Mather, scourge of witches, rants to his angry God. Surrounded by dust and dry earth, Kruger waits placidly for death. The selfish patriarch remembers the powers of youth; imperious still in strengthless old age, he is aware of the symbolism of a flower but oblivious to the granddaughter who brings it. The visiting poet slyly avoids, then confronts, his imperceptive admirers – and the vision of his younger, better self. In ''Packing a Photograph from Firenze'' Matchett's several themes and methods join. Leaving an old house soon to be replaced by a modern jungle of structural steel, a home for statisticians who ''doodle death with indelible ink,'' he marks the end of a life cycle and reaffirms the values of crooked lines, dirty fingers, fertile minds, living things.

– Joseph Parisi

MATHIAS, Roland (Glyn). British (Welsh). Born in Talybont-on-Usk, Breconshire, 4 September 1915. Educated at Caterham School; Jesus College, Oxford (Meyricke Exhibitioner, 1934; Honorary Scholar, 1936), B.A. (honours) in modern history 1936, B.Litt. 1939, M.A. 1944. Married Mary (Molly) Hawes in 1944; has three children. Headmaster, Pembroke Dock Grammar School, Wales, 1948–58, The Herbert Strutt School, Belper, Derbyshire, 1958–64, and King Edward's Five Ways School, Birmingham, 1964–69; Schoolmaster-Fellow, Balliol College, Oxford, 1961, and University College, Swansea, 1967; Visiting Lecturer, University of Rennes, France, 1970, University of Brest, France, 1970, and University of Alabama, Birmingham, 1971. Since 1961, Editor, *The Anglo-Welsh Review*, Brecon. Recipient: Welsh Arts Council bursary, 1968, award, 1969, and prize, 1972. Address: Deffrobani, Maescelyn, Brecon, Wales.

PUBLICATIONS

Verse

Days Enduring and Other Poems. Ilfracombe, Devon, Stockwell, 1943.
Break in Harvest and Other Poems. London, Routledge, 1946.
The Roses of Tretower. Pembroke Dock, Pembrokeshire, Dock Leaves Press, 1952.
The Flooded Valley. London, Putnam, 1960.
Absalom in the Tree. Llandybie, Carmarthenshire, Gomer, 1971.

Short Stories

> *The Eleven Men of Eppynt and Other Stories.*   Pembroke Dock, Pembrokeshire,
> Dock Leaves Press, 1956.

Other

> *Whitsun Riot: An Account of a Commotion Amongst Catholics in Herefordshire and
> Monmouthshire in 1605.*   London, Bowes, 1963.
> *Vernon Watkins.*   Cardiff, University of Wales Press, 1974.
>
> Editor, with Sam Adams, *The Shining Pyramid.*   London, Bowes, 1963.
> Editor, with Sam Adams, *The Shining Pyramid and Other Stories by Welsh
> Authors.*   Llandybie, Carmarthenshire, Gomer, 1970.

Critical Study: "The Poetry of Roland Mathias" by Jeremy Hooker, in *Poetry
Wales* (Llandybie), Summer 1971.

Roland Mathias comments:

In my earlier poetry the sense of "place" was very strong. . . . Even love poems
used the "place" or "history" symbol.

Of recent years the process has changed. The secret "place" is always Wales,
but since my return to it physically there has been a blurring of the remembered
image by the present reality. In consequence I have become slightly more personal
in my poetry, in an overt sense, but there are more people about, more predicaments than mine. I think of history still, of my stock, my parents, family love, and
my own insufficiency in the line of descent. For me the old Nonconformist sense
of guilt is not inhibiting and useless: it gives me a particular vision of the present
through the past, a measurement. Out of it I can write.

*   *   *

Roland Mathias was born in 1915 at Talybont-on-Usk in Breconshire, a border
county which is still largely rural in character. Although he has spent much of his
adult life in Pembrokeshire and England, this borderland of his birth, where "Nigh-
tingales struggle with thorn-trees for the gate of Wales" and where Welsh and
English have rubbed shoulders for hundreds of years, remains an important part of
his personal landscape. He has written that in his earlier poetry "the sense of
'place' was very strong . . . it was always of tremendous importance to me to know
exactly *where* I was and what mood the place engendered in me. People might help
to form that mood but the moment of ignition was always (or almost always)
produced by solitude, the particular place and the history of men in that place."

In all his writing his appreciation of landscape is profoundly enriched by his
sense of history and his concern for truth. He has no time for loose rhetoric or the
easy attitude. His poetry presents a consistent view of the world expressed in a
tough and concentrated verse of considerable individuality.

Alliteration is a powerful unifying device and with its help he often creates a
rhythmic undertow which tugs against the surface flow. His images are concrete,

hardly ever merely pictorial, but suggestive of layers of meaning beneath the obvious. His poetry is not always easy, but it is always rewarding.

– John Stuart Williams

MATTHEWS, William. American. Born in Cincinnati, Ohio, 11 November 1942. Educated at Yale University, New Haven, Connecticut, B.A. 1965; University of North Carolina, Chapel Hill, M.A. 1966. Married Marie Harris in 1963 (divorced, 1974); has two sons. Instructor in English, Wells College, Aurora, New York, 1968–69. Since 1969, Assistant Professor of English, Cornell University, Ithaca, New York. Since 1966, Co-Founding Editor, Lillabulero Press, and *Lillabulero,* Aurora, New York; since 1969, Member, Wesleyan University Press Editorial Board. Address: Department of English, Cornell University, Ithaca, New York 14850, U.S.A.

PUBLICATIONS

Verse

Broken Syllables.   Aurora, New York, Lillabulero Press, 1969.
Ruining the New Road.   New York, Random House, 1970.
The Cloud.   Boston, Barn Dream Press, 1971.
The Moon.   Baltimore, Penyeach Press, 1971.
Poems for Tennessee, with Robert Bly and William Stafford.   Martin, Tennessee Poetry Press, 1971.
Sleek for the Long Flight: New Poems.   New York, Random House, 1972.
Without a Mouth.   Norfolk, Virginia, Penyeach Press, 1972.
The Secret Life.   Rochester, New York, Valley Press, 1972.

Critical Studies: in *Tennessee Poetry Journal* (Martin), Spring 1970; interview in *Ohio Review* (Athens), Spring 1972.

William Matthews comments:

My poems hope to speak for themselves. Much of their speech would be silence. Just as an architect uses walls to organize space, I use the words of a poem to organize silences. In those silences, the echoes, reverberations, assents, denials and secrets of my poems occur. These mute events are closely linked to the silences and strange landscapes in the natural world. That natural world, to an American, is large, often melodramatic, and strange – even in the most settled regions, where I have spent most of my life. My poems aren't self-consciously or programmatically American, but it matters – for all my travels – that I have lived here so long, in certain places, with certain people.

The language in my poems is the language one would love if he had grown up loving much British poetry and much American speech. I have grown to love American poetry and what I have heard of British (and Canadian) speech, but the memories of childhood are intense ones, indelible it seems. Of course it is all mixed, in moil, when I write. But I know from listening to what I have written that I love in language those moments which blur the distinctions between "formal" and "street" language. I distrust such categories, so I blur them often. I love best those poems which seem just to have emerged from a thicket of silence and intense emotion. Burrs still cling to them. Such poems I want most to read, and to write.

*   *   *

Although he belongs to no particular "school," William Matthews is among a handful of young American poets who first published in early *Kayak* during the mid-Sixties and who still seem to share each other's influences and enthusiasms. With Russell Banks and a few other student writers at the University of North Carolina at Chapel Hill, Matthews founded *Lillabulero* in 1966 – a magazine of considerable standing that published many young poets during significant stages of their early development. Matthews' abilities as an editor, and his considerable intelligence as a critic, have helped make him an important figure in contemporary American poetry.

Many of his poems are of the "deep image" tradition that is associated with *Kayak*, and expressive of a common poetic voice, shared at times by such fine poets as Bly, Wright, Merwin, Simic, Knott, and many others. For Matthews, this concern with the image manifests itself in careful and extensive use of metaphor and simile. He is capable of terrific compression – good, tight language – and his penchant for comparisons can become obvious and tiring, especially because there's no verbal fat to hide those metaphoric bones. Here is the first third of "Driving All Night":

> My complicated past is an anthology,
> a long line painted on the plains.
> I feel like literary history
> about to startle the professors.
>
> But it's not true.
>
> Days ahead, snow heaps up
> in the mountains
> like undelivered mail.

Taken to its extreme, this tendency obscures the poem by calling to question the poet's credibility who seems so preoccupied with being original that he fails to establish reason. Here is all of "Why We Are Truly a Nation":

> Because we rage inside
> the old boundaries,
> like a young girl leaving the Church,
> scared of her parents.
>
> Because we all dream of saving
> the shaggy, dung-caked buffalo,
> shielding the herd with our bodies.
>
> Because grief unites us,
> like the locked antlers of moose
> who die on their knees in pairs.

Aside from this basic reservation, I find Matthews to be an inventive and fascinating poet. His best work deals with experience and goes past metaphoric examination. In "Another Beer," the meditational absorption of each beer, with the metaphoric toast preceding each glassful, takes the poem beyond definition, to sharing, of experience:

> The last beer is always for the road.
> The road is what the car drinks
> traveling on its tongue of light
> all the way home.

Matthews is barely thirty, and his many poems to date have experimented in almost all poetic forms; also, he has given considerable attention to translation. His still-unwritten books may well reflect experience and consequent narrative as highly as his work in print reflects an active, intelligent word-smith of unusual imaginative power.

– Geof Hewitt

MAYNE, Seymour. Canadian. Born in Montreal, Quebec, 18 May 1944. Educated at McGill University, Montreal (Chester Macnaghten Prize, 1962), B.A. (honours) 1965; University of British Columbia, Vancouver, M.A. 1966, Ph.D. 1972. Lecturer, The Jewish Institute, Montreal, 1964, and University of British Columbia, 1972. Since 1973, Assistant Professor of English, University of Ottawa. Co-Editor, *Cataract* magazine, Montreal, 1961–62; Editor, *Catapult* magazine, Montreal, 1964; Managing Editor, Very Stone House, Vancouver, 1966–69. Poetry Editor, Ingluvin Publications Ltd., Montreal, 1970–73. Recipient: Canada Council bursary, 1969, and grant, 1973. Address: Department of English, University of Ottawa, Ottawa K1N 6N5, Ontario, Canada.

PUBLICATIONS

Verse

> *That Monocycle the Moon.* Montreal, Jewish Public Library, 1964.
> *Tiptoeing on the Mount.* Montreal, McGill University Press, 1965; revised edition, Montreal, Catapult, 1965.
> *From the Portals of Mouseholes.* Vancouver, Very Stone House, 1966.
> *Touches.* Vancouver, University of British Columbia, 1966.
> *I Am Still the Boy.* Vancouver, Western Press, 1967.
> *Ticklish Ticlicorice.* Vancouver, Very Stone House, 1969.
> *The Gigolo Teaspoon.* Vancouver, Very Stone House, 1969.
> *Earseed.* Vancouver, Very Stone House, 1969.
> *Anewd.* Vancouver, Very Stone House, 1969.
> *Mutetations.* Vancouver, Very Stone House, 1969.
> *Manimals* (poems and prose). Vancouver, Very Stone House, 1969.

Mouth. Kingston, Ontario, Quarry Press, 1970.
For Stems of Light. Vernon, British Columbia, Very Stone House, 1971;
     revised edition, Ottawa, Valley Editions, 1974.
Face. Burnaby, British Columbia, Blackfish, 1971.

Other

Editor, with P. Lane, *Collected Poems of Red Lane.* Vancouver, Very Stone
     House, 1968.
Editor, with Dorothy Livesay, *Forty Women Poets of Canada.* Montreal, Inglu-
     vin, 1971.
Editor, *Engagements: The Prose of Irving Layton.* Toronto, McClelland and
     Stewart, 1972.

Translator, with Catherine Leach, *The Genealogy of Instruments,* by Jerzy
     Harasymowicz. Ottawa, Valley Editions, 1974.

Bibliography: *Jews in Canadian Literature: A Bibliography,* revised edition, edited by
David Rome, Montreal, Canadian Jewish Congress and Jewish Public Library,
1964.

Critical Studies: by Peter Stevens, in *Canadian Forum* (Toronto), March 1968;
"Other Vancouverites" by A. W. Purdy, in *Canadian Literature 35* (Vancouver),
Winter 1968; "New Poetry of the East" by Tom Marshall, in *New: American and
Canadian Poetry 15* (Trumansburg, New York), April-May 1971.

Seymour Mayne comments:

What I have to say about poetry is written into the poems and titles of my books.
I have learned from the early study of Biblic poetry and Hebraic liturgy and prayer.
More immediately I wish to acknowledge the Montreal poets whose work and
example taught me much: A. M. Klein, Irving Layton, Louis Dudek, John Sutherland, Leonard Cohen, F. R. Scott, A. J. M. Smith, and other less known men and
women.

*   *   *

As an editor of two little magazines called *Cataract* and *Catapult*; as a founder of
two private presses named Very Stone House and Ingluvin Press; as a broadcaster
of radio documentaries on literary subjects; as the compiler of the prose writings of
Irving Layton; and as many other things as well, Seymour Mayne has made a name
for himself in the world of Canadian poetry.
    But reputations of this sort are ephemeral and double-edged. Perhaps what he
will be known for in the future is his own poetry which has been appearing for the
last decade and attracting increased interest of late. He has not been an experimental poet (his concrete work has the sense of *déjà vu*) but he has been persistent. His
central publication to date is *Mouth*, a full-length collection of miscellaneous poems,
some of which chart the relationship of the various bodily orifices and, in a

Freudian fashion, find a link between or among them. As he writes in "Fang of Light":

> and make the mouth
> one vibrating hoop
> of his whole
> orificial self.

The mood and image are there, but the language, especially the diction, is mixed and not always specific or emotional.

There are various contradictory themes in embryo – or in suspension – in Mayne's poetry, and these include: human desire as against bodily guilt; human transcendence as against whimsical reasonableness or ironic insight. Perhaps it is through a Jewish reconciliation of these opposites that Mayne's poetry will pass. The necessary drive is there, for the poet writes in "You Don't Scream":

> Tear yourself away.
> Bleed, if you must.
> A fever will rise in your eyes
> and burn like a need.

– John Robert Colombo

MAYO, E(dward) L(eslie). American. Born in Dorchester, Massachusetts, 26 July 1904. Educated at the University of Minnesota, Minneapolis (Payne Prize, 1932), B.A. (magna cum laude) 1932, M.A. Married Myra Margaret Buchanan Morton in 1936; has three children. Since 1947, Professor of English, Drake University, Des Moines, Iowa. Recipient: Oscar Blumenthal Prize (*Poetry*, Chicago), 1942; Amy Lowell Traveling Fellowship, 1953, 1954. D.Litt.: Iowa Wesleyan College, Mount Pleasant, 1960. Address: 1532 Twenty-fourth Street, Des Moines, Iowa 50311, U.S.A.

PUBLICATIONS

Verse

The Diver: Poems. Minneapolis, University of Minnesota Press, 1947.
The Center Is Everywhere. New York, Twayne, 1954.
Summer Unbound and Other Poems. Minneapolis, University of Minnesota Press, 1958.
Selected Poems. Iowa City, Prairie Press, 1973.

Critical Study: "E. L. Mayo: A Modern Metaphysical" by John Ciardi, in *University of Kansas City Review* (Missouri), 1947.

E. L. Mayo comments:

I owe a dual homage to the Metaphysicals, especially Donne, and to the French Symbolists. The Symbolist influence first reached me indirectly through Yeats, Eliot, etc. If to these you add a penchant for the plainness of diction which I found in both Hardy and E. A. Robinson, you should be able to place my school pretty accurately.

When I began writing, Eliot and Frost were the main luminaries on the horizon. Hardy and Housman were almost as important. All these poets used traditional forms, meter, rhyme, stanza form – but with a difference. Such, in general, have been my own procedures. I have no objection to good free verse but I feel that poets haven't yet begun to discover the full potentialities of rhythm and sound. Contemporary experiemts with free verse force the poet back on imagery, everything else being secondary. That is, he isn't using all the resources at his disposal. My effort in poetry is to avail myself of all these resources.

*   *   *

According to John Ciardi, some of the poems of E. L. Mayo are "happy evidence of how far poetry has come in a hundred years toward acquiring a wholly natural mastery of the commonest details of ordinary living." Ciardi goes on to praise Mayo's "intellectual fire," "verbal felicity," and capacity to create symbols and images that conspire toward a "sudden burgeoning of second meanings." "Mayo has long ago achieved his technical majority," Ciardi wrote in 1947, and "the personality that emerges from his poems is invariably attractive." James Wright, in *Poetry*, in 1958, commented that Mayo's poems "smolder with a kind of subdued bitterness," praised his work as "unpretentious," and found the poet "daring and successful precisely because he does not overburden his language." From Mayo's volume, *Summer Unbound*, Wright singled out "Handbag" and "Three Ladies" for special praise, but found the entire volume "severe, tough," with a natural modernity. An earlier review of "The Diver" (printed in *Poetry*, 1948) also spoke of Mayo's modernity, relating it to "his rejection of surface meaning": "And there is that most typical contemporary phenomenon: the poem drawing skilfully upon all levels of experience – including, even, the conventionally poetic ... the poet has assimilated many modern voices to his own voice." Freshness was what this critic found in Mayo's "Iron Gate":

> To pass the thirtieth year is but to be
> Other than one expected, barer here
> The heart is than it was in many a year,
> No longer cluttered with bright privacies.
>
> Here Solomon perceives he is not wise
> And with an eye upon the second prize
> Divides desire with possibility . . .
> The sea gull in his proper breast
> Beats louder now against a thinner door. . . .

He "snatches the shining runners as they fly –" yet "even the awkward song is excellent." The poem is surpassed perhaps only by "On Growing Invisible," in which Mayo later speaks "From the bland, snow-crusted eminence / Of sixty," comparing himself to "a mild smiling Cheshire gentleman / Cat of sixty fading softly away," and concluding: "My vision will continue to expand / Brobdingnagian / Until I comprehend all humankind / Without being there." Poems like this latter one, found in *The Center Is Everywhere*, are good examples of the metaphysical style many critics have noted in Mayo. Indeed, what gives his poems their unique appeal may be the heavy, out-in-the-open tension that exists in his poems between the metaphysical and the idiomatic, for the poems also "pretend to be simple prose-like utterances, whereas in fact the best of them contain an echoing poetic meaning which begins to release itself a split second after we have read the words. There is an assumed lightness of touch here, a note not quite of irony but almost of timidity, behind which the richer meanings can be heard . . . He understands what form does to an idea, and is not afraid to write something which is in itself trivial but in its poetic context is not" (David Daiches). Milton Crane has defined Mayo's "obvious principle" of unity as "an admirable clarity and lucidity of expression and a determination to shun the clichés which make much modern poetry seem a kaleidoscope in which the same unevocative images and abstractions are constantly reshuffled into new patterns." One could write at length of Mayo's success in knowing "the true, secret name of the river," of opening up in his poems "the mystery of better and of worse," of dealing with that angel whose "name was Loneliness," of speaking of the ghost to whom flesh is only a door, of hearing the "Wind – I said – Breaker of ties, breaker of promises." In "The Diver" Mayo dealt with the poet's trip down into the sea of experience, where "in his brain / The jungles of the sea must flower still"; in another poem he said poetry is a mirror, "showing / Clearer than to our shadowy sense, the glowing / And waning of a more than mortal creature." Just as "moles are very little / And worlds are very big," the poet and his world are unfairly matched. But perhaps the best introduction to Mayo's work is to cite his simple, yet powerful poem on El Greco:

> See how the sun has somewhat not of light
> Falling upon these men who stand so tall;
> See how their eyes observe some inward sight
> And how their living takes no room at all –
> Their passing stirs no air, so thin they are –
> Behind them see small houses with small doors;
> The light from an unfamiliar star
> That lights their walls and falls across their floors.
> What shall we say when one of these men goes
> Into his house and we no longer see
> His eyes observing something that he knows?
> And if their houses brim with radiancy
> Why does no light come through as those doors close?

– David Ray

McAULEY, James (Phillip). Australian. Born in Lakemba, New South Wales, 12 October 1917. Educated at Fort Street High School; Sydney University, M.A., Dip.Ed. Married Norma Abernethy in 1942; has five children. Lecturer in Government, Australian School of Pacific Administration, 1946–60. Since 1961, Professor of English, University of Tasmania, Hobart. Since 1956, Editor, *Quadrant*, Sydney. Recipient: Carnegie grant, 1967. Address: 11 Marsh Street, New Town, Tasmania 7008, Australia.

PUBLICATIONS

Verse

The Darkening Ecliptic (as Ern Malley), with Harold Stewart. Melbourne,
   Reed and Harris, 1944; as *Poems*, Melbourne, Lansdowne Press, 1961.
Under Aldebaran. Melbourne, Melbourne University Press, 1946.
A Vision of Ceremony: Poems. Sydney, Angus and Robertson, 1956.
The Six Days of Creation: Poems. Adelaide, Australian Letters, 1963.
(Poems), selected and introduced by the author. Sydney, Angus and Robert-
   son, 1963.
Captain Quiros: A Poem. Sydney, Angus and Robertson, 1964.
Surprises of the Sun: Poems. Sydney, Angus and Robertson, 1969.
Collected Poems 1936–1970. Sydney, Angus and Robertson, 1971.

Other

Poetry and Australian Culture, with *Felons and Folksongs* by Russell B. Ward.
   Canberra, Canberra University College, 1955.
The End of Modernity: Essays on Literature, Art and Culture. Sydney, Angus
   and Robertson, 1959.
C. J. Brennan. Melbourne, Lansdowne Press, 1963.
Edmund Spenser and George Eliot: A Critical Excursion. Hobart, University of
   Tasmania, 1963.
A Primer of English Versification. Sydney, Sydney University Press, and Lon-
   don, Methuen, 1966; as *Versification: A Short Introduction*, East Lansing,
   Michigan State University Press, 1966.
The Personal Element in Australian Poetry. Sydney, Angus and Robertson,
   1970.

Editor, *Generations: Poetry from Chaucer to the Present Day.* Melbourne, Nelson, 1969.

Critical Studies: *James McAuley* by Vivian Smith, Melbourne, Lansdowne Press,
1956; "James McAuley: The Landscape of the Heart" by David Bradley, in *The
Literature of Australia*, edited by Geoffrey Dutton, London, Penguin, 1964.

*   *   *

   Many poets, confronted with the deliquescence of order and the material confusions and spiritual emptiness of today, feel they must either attempt to forge a
symbolic order of their own, or discover in one or other of the orders already
available from the past a picture within which their art can still function as a
meaningful interpretation of their time. This dilemma confronted James McAuley
especially, since his need for spiritual dedication and moral direction has always
been acute. As an adolescent he was deeply affected by the ethical relativism
which has emerged from modern studies of human moral and religious behaviour,
and the history of his poetic development has closely followed his attempts to
satisfy this need.
   As an undergraduate at the University of Sydney, it was already clear that his
verse was of high aspiration and achievement. During World War II his work lay in

New Guinea, and for some time after he remained involved in problems of administration there. The question of social change and the impact of European culture on
primitive peoples set off a further meditation on the emptiness of the new world-
view being imposed on these races.

His first book, *Under Aldebaran*, contained some undergraduate poems as well as
work emerging from the war years. The most ambitious of these, "The Blue
Horses," meditates on the function of imagination and art in social change and
revolution. The remarkable "Incarnation of Sirius" pursues this further, presenting
an apocalyptic vision of cyclical revolution alternating with periods of calm. This
vision seems to have faced him with the need for some over-riding principle of
order for art and life. Other poems explore the implications of human love,
culminating in the poem "The Celebration of Love." The period of tension and
exploration (symbolised in such poems as "Henry the Navigator") led to his
conversion to Catholicism soon after.

His second book, *A Vision of Ceremony*, contains many lyrics of great beauty,
emerging from his conversion, in some of which, such as "An Art of Poetry," he
applies his new faith to his meditations on the function of art. A certain loss of
tension in the book as a whole, and a somewhat doctrinaire manner, detract from
the undoubted gains in serenity and the new celebrative spirit of the book as a
whole. For a number of years he worked on a long epic poem, *Captain Quiros*,
which was finally published eight years after *A Vision of Ceremony*. In this he
merges the hero-figure who had appeared in earlier poems such as "Henry the
Navigator" and the "Prometheus" sequence in the figure of the explorer Quiros,
who set out to discover the Great South Land (Australia) and to establish there a
new religious settlement, but failed in the task.

The poem, moving and often beautiful, contains some splendid descriptive passages but fails in narrative and dramatic power. Certain inner contradictions are
visible, which perhaps parallel the failure of the real Quiros. The main figure
emerges only hazily, and the bridge-passages of narrative often seem flat. The
seven-line rhymed stanza used throughout seems more suited to the contemplative
than the dramatic use; but the poem is marked by grace, lucidity and sincerity, and
as one of the few attempts at religious apologia today has an interest of its own.

McAuley is now a Professor of English, and has published several books of
criticism. As a young man he was one of those concerned in the famous "Ern
Malley" hoax poems. His work has had much influence, especially on the younger
Catholic poets. Though he has written satirical and occasional verse, his most
successful work has been in the lyric mode, to which he seems to have returned
since the publication of *Captain Quiros*.

– Judith Wright

McAULEY, James J(ohn). Irish. Born in Dublin, 8 January 1936. Educated at
Clongowes Wood College, 1948–53; University College, Dublin, 1960–62, B.A.
1962; University of Arkansas, Fayetteville, 1966–68, M.F.A. 1971. Married Joan
McNally in 1958 (divorced, 1968), has three children; Almut R. Nierentz, 1968, has
two children. Journalist, Electricity Supply Board, Dublin, 1954–66; Lecturer, Municipal Gallery of Modern Art, Dublin, 1965–66; Graduate Assistant, University of

Arkansas, 1966–68; Assistant Professor and Director of the Creative Writing Program, Lycoming College, Williamsport, Pennsylvania, 1968–70. Assistant Professor, 1970–73, and since 1973, Associate Professor of English, Eastern Washington State College, Cheney. Art Critic, *Kilkenny Magazine*, Dublin, 1960–66; Associate Editor, *Poetry Ireland*, Dublin, 1962–66; Arts Consultant, *Hibernia National Review*, Dublin, 1964–66; Book Reviewer, *Irish Times*, Dublin, 1964–66; Reporter, *North West Arkansas Times*, Fayetteville, 1967. Recipient: National Endowment for the Arts grant, 1972. Agent: Lordly and Dame Inc., 51 Church Street, Boston, Massachusetts 02116. Address: 624 Lincoln, Cheney, Washington 99004, U.S.A.

PUBLICATIONS

Verse

Observations. Blackrock, Ireland, Mount Salus Press, 1960.
A New Address. Dublin, Dolmen Press, London, Oxford University Press, and Chester Springs, Pennsylvania, Dufour, 1965.
Draft Balance Sheet: Poems 1963–1969. Dublin, Dolmen Press, London, Oxford University Press, and Chester Springs, Pennsylvania, Dufour, 1970.

Play

The Revolution (produced Dublin, 1966).

Critical Studies: review of *Draft Balance Sheet*, in *Hibernia* (Dublin), 1970; *Choice*, edited by Michael Hartnett and Desmond Egan, Dublin, Goldsmith Press, 1973.

James J. McAuley comments:

My first book, *Observations*, consists of sixteen confessional lyrics; very young poems, imitative, private. *A New Address* is the offspring of my two-year love affair with *Roget's Thesaurus*: poems resulting from my preoccupation with words, their sounds and associations. *Draft Balance Sheet* resulted from my two-year study of Poetry and Poetics under James Whitehead at Arkansas. *The Revolution*, a satire on Easter, 1916, and its end result, the modern Irish state, is currently under revision in "silence, exile, and cunning" (as it has been since 1960 or thereabouts).

I've given up the search for my own "voice"; prefer the freedom to invent voices, masks, personae. I try to "sing whatever is well-made."

*   *   *

James J. McAuley's poetry has changed very considerably, perhaps not altogether convincingly, since his move from Ireland to America. His newer, distinctly American tone, hardly seems natural to him – although the themes of his poems are clearly ones of his natural choice. Unlike such a poet as John Montague, who has also been closely associated with America, McAuley seems half-inclined to drop his "Irishry," which may in his case be a mistake. (Denise Levertov did turn from an English neo-Georgian into a modernist American – but she married an American and became an American citizen.) Easily the best of McAuley's poetry is his sharp and telling satire on things Irish; this is of course a special prerogative of Irish writers from (to give the remark a characteristically paradoxical Irish air) the Englishman Swift onwards; but McAuley does it well, and lends a dimension of his own to his criticism of Ireland, which is not genial. Other poetry, though composed with great care, tends to be over-literary, falsely fastidious, a shade over-graceful. But the good taste and the intelligence are certainly present: this stanza from "Stella" (dating from the early 1960's) demonstrates both his defects and his virtues:

> The swan pierced by an arrow lies
> Immortal on sharp stars
> Above the bowed head ringing with the tones,
> Vibrations, plangent chords of love.
> About him, night sounds:
> A leaf touching his shoulder
> Whispered, descended, dying
> At his feet.

– Martin Seymour-Smith

McCLURE, Michael. American. Born in Maryville, Kansas, 20 October 1932. Married to Joanna McClure; has one daughter. Recipient: National Endowment for the Arts grant, 1967, 1974; Guggenheim Fellowship, 1973; Magic Theatre Alfred Jarry Award, for drama, 1973; Rockefeller Fellowship, for drama, 1975. Agent: Sterling Lord Agency, 660 Madison Avenue, New York, New York 10021. Address: 264 Downey Street, San Francisco, California 94117, U.S.A.

PUBLICATIONS

Verse

Passage. Big Sur, California, Jonathan Williams, 1956.
Peyote Poem. San Francisco, Semina, 1958.
For Artaud. New York, Totem Press, 1959.
Hymns to St. Geryon and Other Poems. San Francisco, Auerhahn Press, 1959.
The New Book: A Book of Torture. New York, Grove Press, 1961.
Dark Brown. San Francisco, Auerhahn Press, 1961.
Two for Bruce Conner. San Francisco, Oyez, 1964.
Ghost Tantras. San Francisco, privately printed, 1964.
Double Murder! Vahroooooooohr! Los Angeles, Semina, 1964.
Love Lion, Lioness. San Francisco, privately printed, 1964.
13 Mad Sonnets. Milan, East 128, 1964.
Poisoned Wheat. San Francisco, privately printed, 1965.
Dream Table. San Francisco, Dave Haselwood, 1965.
Unto Caesar. San Francisco, Dave Haselwood, 1965.
Mandalas. San Francisco, Dave Haselwood, 1965.
Hail Thee Who Play: A Poem. Los Angeles, Black Sparrow Press, 1968.

Love Lion Book. San Francisco, Four Seasons Foundation, 1968.
The Sermons of Jean Harlow and the Curses of Billy the Kid. San Francisco,
Four Seasons Foundation, 1969.
The Surge: A Poem. Columbus, Ohio, Frontier Press, 1969.
Hymns to St. Geryon and Dark Brown. London, Cape Goliard Press, 1969.
Lion Fight. New York, Pierrepont Press, 1969.
Star. New York, Grove Press, 1971.
99 Theses. Lawrence, Kansas, Tansy Press, 1972.
The Book of Joanna. Berkeley, California, Sand Dollar Press, 1973.
Rare Angel (writ with ravens blood). Los Angeles, Black Sparrow Press,
1974.
September Blackberries. New York, New Directions, 1974.
Solstice Blossom. Berkeley, California, Arif Press, 1974.

Plays

The Feast (produced San Francisco, 1960). Included in *The Mammals*, 1972.
Pillow (produced New York, 1961). Included in *The Mammals*, 1972.
The Growl, in *Four in Hand* (produced Berkeley, California, 1970). Published
in *Evergreen Review* (New York), April–May 1964.
The Blossom; or, Billy the Kid (produced New York, 1964). Milwaukee, Great
Lakes Books, 1967.
The Beard (produced San Francisco, 1965; New York, 1967; London,
1968). San Francisco, privately printed, 1965; revised version, New York,
Grove Press, 1967.
The Shell (produced San Francisco, 1970). London, Cape Goliard Press, 1968.
The Cherub (produced Berkeley, California, 1969). Los Angeles, Black Spar-
row Press, 1970.
The Charbroiled Chinchilla: The Pansy, The Meatball, Spider Rabbit (produced
Berkeley, California, 1969). Included in *Gargoyle Cartoons*, 1971.
Little Odes, Poems, and a Play, The Raptors. Los Angeles, Black Sparrow
Press, 1969.
*The Brutal Brontosaurus: Spider Rabbit, The Meatball, The Shell, Apple Glove,
The Authentic Radio Life of Bruce Conner and Snoutburbler* (produced San
Francisco, 1970). Included in *Gargoyle Cartoons*, 1971.
The Meatball (produced London, 1971). Included in *Gargoyle Cartoons*, 1971.
Spider Rabbit (produced London, 1971). Included in *Gargoyle Cartoons*, 1971.
The Pansy (produced London, 1972). Included in *Gargoyle Cartoons*, 1971.
Gargoyle Cartoons (includes *The Shell, The Pansy, The Meatball, The Bow, Spider
Rabbit, Apple Glove, The Sail, The Dear, The Authentic Radio Life of Bruce
Conner and Snoutburbler, The Feather, The Cherub*). New York, Delacorte
Press, 1971.
Polymorphous Pirates: The Pussy, The Button, The Feather (produced Berkeley,
California, 1972). *The Feather* included in *Gargoyle Cartoons*, 1971.
The Mammals (includes *The Blossom, The Feast, Pillow*). San Francisco,
Cranium Press, 1972.
The Pussy, The Button, and Chekov's Grandmother; or, The Sugar Wolves (pro-
duced New York, 1973).
Gorf (produced San Francisco, 1974).
The Derby (produced Los Angeles, 1974).

Radio Play: *Music Peace*, 1974.

Television Play: *The Maze* (documentary), 1967.

Novels

The Mad Cub. New York, Bantam, 1970.
The Adept. New York, Delacorte Press, 1971.

Other

Meat Science Essays. San Francisco, City Lights Books, 1963; revised edition,
San Francisco, Dave Haselwood, 1967.
*Freewheelin' Frank, Secretary of the Angels, as Told to Michael McClure by Frank
Reynolds.* New York, Grove Press, 1967.

Editor, with James Harmon, *Ark II/Moby I.* San Francisco, Editorial Offices,
1957.
Editor, with David Meltzer and Lawrence Ferlinghetti, *Journal for the Protection
of All Beings.* San Francisco, City Lights Books, 1961.

Bibliography: *A Catalogue of Works by Michael McClure, 1956–1965* by Marshall
Clements, New York, Phoenix Book Shop, 1965.

Manuscript Collection: Simon Fraser University, Burnaby, British Columbia.

Critical Studies: "This Is Geryon," in *Times Literary Supplement* (London), 25
March 1965; interview in *San Francisco Poets,* edited by David Meltzer, New York,
Bantam, 1971.

                              *   *   *

Michael McClure is aware of the choices. Moving into the language (if not the
life) like a candidate for a doctoral degree in hedonism, he evinces his zeal with
grunts, howls, and meaty whines. He seeks the revelations; is opposite to another
poet's "telephone-pole men," each of whom is content to resemble his neighbor.
This man, within a play written and directed by others, prepares the program notes,
in which his role is illustrated. So that that which may appear as iconoclasm or
affectation becomes an effective style in confirmation of the new reverence for
body-freedom.
   The Libran, refiner of art, works from others' initial strengths (McClure follows
work Blake and Artaud began; his language has added no new words to common
parlance as has Sanders' or Ginsberg's today; his explorations into sound are more
timid than Cage's) but the Libran adds inimitability of his touch. One recognizes his
form and idioma, sans signature. It is sensual above sexual; despite apparently
radical moves in *Dark Brown* and *The Beard,* the language is more classical than
innovatory, more musical than bestial. When he was young he risked more. Disguised as a lion-maned nude, but never naked, this celebrant chants the body with
the elegance of the average caryatid. In his better experiments he resists balancing
sensuality with intellect (his weak point, as with most Librans). And he looks
typically Libra, moderate in all respects. Air-sign and verbal, he's in love with
sound; as a romantic, he shuns the experiences offered by dissonance.
   Conscious of status quo, both as observer and participant, he is eager to lend his
energy to the fashionable changes. The mutability produces interesting variations

on his theme. His ambition exceeds his abilities, with great results: the challenges are in the wisdom of the poem just around the next page or year. An exciting, difficult role, at the edge of the true hand-to-hand revolution of language. The life and work come through of a piece: both vivid, and memorable, neither modest nor monumental.

– Carol Bergé

McCUAIG, Ronald. Australian. Born in Newcastle, New South Wales, in 1908. Educated in Newcastle and Sydney. Married; has two sons. Formerly, Radio Journalist. Member of the Editorial Staff, *The Bulletin*, Sydney.

PUBLICATIONS

Verse

Vaudeville. Sydney, privately printed, 1938.
The Wanton Goldfish. Sydney, privately printed, 1941.
Quod Ronald McCuaig. Sydney, Angus and Robertson, 1946.
The Ballad of Bloodthirsty Bessie and Other Poems. Sydney, Angus and Robertson, 1961.

Other

Tales Out of Bed (essays and short stories). Sydney, Allied Authors and Artists, 1944.
Literature. Canberra, Australian News and Information Bureau, 1962.
Gangles (juvenile). London, Angus and Robertson, 1972.
Tobolino (juvenile). London, Angus and Robertson, 1975.

*   *   *

Ronald McCuaig is still remembered with affection by readers of the *Sydney Bulletin* in its last burst of glory as the leading Australian weekly journal of literature and comment up to the late 1950's. McCuaig's early poetry was self-confessedly influenced by the more strident abrasiveness of early Eliot and Pound. However, his "Vaudeville" sequence seems today more heavily indebted to C. J. Dennis' famous comic masterpiece, "The Sentimental Bloke."

McCuaig worked on the *Bulletin* staff for many years and regularly contributed topical light verse to the "Aboriginalities" and "Society" pages, often under a *nom-de-plume*. His work was gathered together in *The Ballad of Bloodthirsty Bessie and Other Poems*. Much of the topicality has faded, but a number of poems, particularly those influenced by McCuaig's interest in music, retain their original charm and zest. His most ambitious work is contained in a sequence "Scenes from Childhood" whose ten elegies display formal ingenuity with a pervasively nostalgic lyricism. Of these Douglas Stewart has written: "In these elegies his eclecticism turns the verse of *Piers Plowman* into a sestina, combines a hint from Mallarmé with a rhythm of Campion's, paraphrases a Chopin Study, draws a ballad out of 'Auld Lang Syne,' and begins an anecdote of his childhood with an homage to Debussy that turns into a song in pràise of Renoir." Ronald McCuaig has published almost nothing since that volume.

– Thomas W. Shapcott

McDONALD, Nan(cy May). Australian. Born in Eastwood, New South Wales, 25 December 1921. Educated at Hornsby Girls' High School; University of Sydney, B.A. Editor, Angus and Robertson Ltd., publishers, Sydney, 1943–73. Address: 24 Yates Avenue, Mount Keira, New South Wales, Australia.

PUBLICATIONS

Verse

Pacific Sea. Sydney and London, Angus and Robertson, 1947.
The Lonely Fire. Sydney and London, Angus and Robertson, 1954.
The Lighthouse and Other Poems. Sydney, Angus and Robertson, 1959.
Selected Poems. Sydney, Angus and Robertson, 1969.

Other

Editor, *Australian Poetry 1953.* Sydney, Angus and Robertson, 1953.

Nan McDonald comments:

Much of my work could be called pastoral or nature poetry. I have tried to capture the characteristic quality of landscape in those parts of Australia most familiar to me. Other poems deal more directly with human beings, some taking historical characters and incidents for their subjects. My Christian belief has had a strong general influence on my work.

My poems are varied in form, but are usually rhymed (though the rhyme scheme is often irregular), and more often have long lines than short. The most common length would be 40–60 lines. My longest poem, "The Lighthouse," is about 1000 lines and is in semi-dramatic form. It has been broadcast by the Australian Broadcasting Commission.

*   *   *

Many of Nan McDonald's poems deal with the isolation and loneliness of man. This is a condition not only of her madmen, the eccentrics, the hatters, but of us all. Often man is seen as victim of the elements, of both land and sea. To the Australian bush Nan McDonald gives a weird, melancholic Lawrentian air, a "strange darkness is in the sunlight." There is a sense of stillness, of quiet brooding, of timelessness about her Australia. The sea which features in a number of her poems often plays a sinister, pitiless role with man once more as victim: "Lord God, how lonely is man on this dark sea." In her poetry, Australia's early settlers remind us of Cowper's castaway and Australia becomes what so many of her artists have made her, an outer symbol of an inner reality.

Not all is foreboding about the land; some of her poems are celebrations of nature and its ability to withstand the onslaughts of man, but even then there is an underlying tension, "under it all a voice of foreboding is calling."

When she describes events such as an earthquake or a mining disaster she gives to these events a deeper meaning so that we quickly realise that they are symbolic of the human condition in which we are all buried alive.

It is interesting that in her last book of verse Australia has taken on a somewhat different aspect and has moved from a purgatory to a place of refuge for the victims of a war-torn Europe, a place of renewal. The mention of renewal reminds us that in spite of the fact that Nan McDonald believes that "all our houses [are] condemned" her poems also celebrate the "miracle of being." Over all the darkness there is a ray of light, a deep religious faith in a merciful God. Unfortunately this expression of faith is often too impersonal and cliché-ridden to move us.

– Anna Rutherford

McDONALD, Roger. Australian. Born in Young, New South Wales, 23 June 1941. Educated at the University of Sydney, 1959–62, B.A. 1962. Married Rhyll McMaster in 1967; has two children. School Teacher, Murrumburrah and Wellington, New South Wales, 1963–64; Producer, Educational Radio and Television, Brisbane, Queensland, and Hobart, Tasmania, 1964–69; Copy Editor, Open University Publishing Division, Bletchley, Buckinghamshire, 1972. Since 1969, Editor, University of Queensland Press, Brisbane. Delegate, Hari Sastra National Literature Conference, Sabah, Malaysia, 1973. Address: c/o University of Queensland Press, P.O. Box 42, St. Lucia, Queensland 4067, Australia.

PUBLICATIONS

Verse

Citizens of Mist.   Brisbane, University of Queensland Press, 1968.
Airship.   Brisbane, University of Queensland Press, 1975.

Other

Editor, *The First Paperback Poets Anthology.*   Brisbane, University of Queensland Press, 1974.

1013

Roger McDonald comments:

I would like to think that an introspective strain in my poetry is made acceptable, even interesting, by firmly physical writing. I find abstractions impossible to approach without the armour of careful description. I like to find things said in precise and evocative ways in the work of other writers, and hope that the qualities I prefer can be found in my own work.

*   *   *

Reading Roger McDonald's poetry one is struck by his fascination with the past, with extracting details from past happenings and making them unique to the present. This is in fact a poetry of moments. Almost cinematically the action is seen to stop – and the frozen frame examined. But seldom does he conclude the poem by, as it were, setting the film in motion again; more often he slightly recasts the details and leaves it at that. It is as if he is saying: Now, at this unrepeatable point of time, I'm going to declare all I have shown you to be a mere collage of appearances whose independent and contemporary meanings already assert themselves, a leap ahead of any attempt I might make at interpretation.

The poem "Two Summers in Moravia" is a clear example of this. In the first summer (looking back to wartime),

> This was a day
> when little happened
> though inch by inch everything changed.
> A load of hay narrowly crossed the bridge,
> the boy caught a fish underneath in shade,
> and ducks quarrelled in the reeds

and in the second summer, the present-time of the poem, he records an almost unchanged scene but, like positive to negative, simple details seem unaccountably reversed; there is a brooding feeling, a threat, the suggestion that some other dimension moves within them.

In another recent poem, "The Hollow Thesaurus," a similar process is applied to language itself, so that here McDonald is writing about his medium as a means of demonstrating his use of it:

> Names for everything I touch
> were hatched in bibles, in poems cupped by madmen
> on rocky hills, by marks on sheets of stone,
> by humped and sticky lines in printed books.
>
> Lexicographers burned their stringy eyeballs black
> for the sake of my knowing. Instinctive generations
> hammered their victories, threaded a chain,
> and lowered their strung-up wisdom in a twist
> of molecules. But with me in mind
> their time was wasted.
>
> When the bloodred, pewter, sickle, sick or meloned moon
> swells from nowhere,
> the chatter of vast informative print
> spills varied as milk. Nothing prepares me
> even for common arrivals like this.

Look. The moon comes up. Behind certain trees are bats
that wrench skyward like black sticks.
Light falls thinly on grass, from moon and open door.
This has not happened before.

These recent poems are markedly more original in concept than those in his first book, *Citizens of Mist,* where, although he sustained his interest in gradual decay (whether the doomed politeness of Victorian gentility or flies buzzing about a carcass) by setting it within a context of collapse on a massive scale, the implications remained narrow. There was a tendency for the universal to be cramped by the particular, where now the particular is its point of release.

He is a careful, thoughtful writer. His output is not large but his position in Australian literature is assured. Compact and intelligent, this is a poetry that is never quirky or flashy. Its limitation is that it might be thought too even, too neat, too safe.

Roger McDonald is also a book editor of distinction and is having an important influence on the directions being taken in poetry and prose in Australia today.

– Rodney Hall

McFADDEN, David. Canadian. Born in Hamilton, Ontario, 11 October 1940. Attended public schools. Married to Joan Pearce; has two children. Teller, Canadian Imperial Bank of Commerce, 1960; Junior Gardener, Royal Botanical Gardens, Hamilton, 1961; Traffic Clerk, International Harvester, Burlington, Ontario, 1962. Since 1962, Proofreader, *Spectator,* Hamilton. Recipient: Canada Council bursary, 1968. Address: 86 Garside Avenue North, Hamilton 27, Ontario, Canada.

PUBLICATIONS

Verse

The Poem Poem.   Toronto, Weed/Flower Press, 1967.
The Saladmaker: A Humility Cycle.   Montreal, Imago Books, 1968.
Letters from the Earth to the Earth.   Toronto, Coach House Press, 1968.
The Great Canadian Sonnet.   Toronto, Coach House Press, 1970.
Intense Pleasure.   Toronto, McClelland and Stewart, 1972.
Poems Worth Knowing.   Toronto, Coach House Press, 1973.

David McFadden comments:

Writing poems is one aspect of my function as a cosmic lover.

My major theme is my self which includes my daily experiences and feeble attempts to understand them. I find that everything is beautiful, so I have no characteristic subjects. I try to keep my poems open for anything, indisciminately, and have no idea what I'll be writing about tomorrow, or what form it will require. As for my "usual verse forms" and "characteristic stylistic devices," I find I do not like to analyse them; the best way to keep them natural and self-appropriate is to let them percolate below conscious level where everything happens faster than the speed of light.

*   *   *

"I'm particularly pleased to inhabit the same world as McFadden," wrote Alfred Purdy when he read the manuscript of *Intense Pleasure*, "even if he's crazy as a bedbug." Although David McFadden – a poet and newspaperman who lives and writes in Hamilton, Ontario, a community not celebrated for its artists – has been publishing short collections of his poems and Richard Brautigan-like prose for the last decade, it was not until 1972, with the appearance of *Intense Pleasure*, that McFadden's work reached a wide public and the nature of his singular talent became clear.

McFadden is not as "crazy as a bedbug," for he is as "crazy as a fox" – and as witty and often as irrelevant as Dick Gregory and any number of stand-up comedians who specialize in witty one-liners and put-downs and one-upmanships. Many of his poems are nightclub routines with fast lines like: "He knew he was pregnant," "I'm addicted to toothpicks," "Now I'm middle-aged I want to be an alligator." The poems are amusing, lively and light, and often exhausted on a single reading.

In the poem "Ova Yoga," McFadden writes, "Inside every chicken is a human being trying to get out," and inside McFadden there is another poet beginning to be heard. This is the observer of modern society beset – but not swallowed up by – the incongruities and irrationalities of the contemporary world. This is the poet who in one poem presents a midget's-eye view of the world, who in another discovers Adolf Hitler living in Hamilton and arranges an interview. This is the poet who is attracted to the pop and kitsch characteristics of Canadian advertising: "This is Bruce Marsh speaking / for Kraft Foods in Canada."

On first reading one might mistake this McFadden for the stand-up comedian. But the emerging poet is one who like Apollinaire seeks to celebrate "the heroic of the everyday," who tries to grant a modicum of immortality to such things as "three Motorcycles parked diagonally at the curb / in front of 111 Brucedale Avenue." One looks to the Liverpudlian poets for something approximating McFadden's tone; but to long-dead but always-resurrectible Dadaists and Surrealists for McFadden's sense of the nostalgia of the evanescent. Thus David McFadden is the prophet of the ephemeral present.

– John Robert Colombo

McFADDEN, Roy. British. Born in Belfast, Northern Ireland, 14 November 1921. Educated at Regent House School, Newtownards, County Down; Queen's University, Belfast. Co-Editor, *Ulster Voices*, 1941–42, *Rann: An Ulster Quarterly of Poetry*, 1948–53, and *Irish Voices*, 1953, all in Belfast. Lives in Belfast.

PUBLICATIONS

Verse

A Poem: Russian Summer.   Dublin, Gayfield Press, 1942.
Three New Poets, with Alex Comfort and Ian Seraillier.   London, Grey Walls
   Press, 1942.
Swords and Ploughshares.   London, Routledge, 1943.
Flowers for a Lady.   London, Routledge, 1945.
The Heart's Townland.   London, Routledge, 1947.
Elegy for the Dead of the "Princess Victoria."   Lisburn, Northern Ireland, Lis-
   nagarvey Press, 1952.
The Garryowen.   London, Chatto and Windus, 1972.

Critical Studies: in *Rann 20* (Belfast); by Michael Longley, in *Causeway: The Arts in
Ulster,* Belfast, Arts Council of Northern Ireland, 1971.

Roy McFadden comments:

> – I am of Northern Ireland, born
> To exile in a local street –

Post-Yeats. He was blind and tone-deaf. I see and hear. I was born Irish of a
Geordie mother.

*   *   *

Roy McFadden produced his striking first collection during the war when
presumably people were too busy to take notice of it. It was called *Swords and
Ploughshares* – an appropriate title for what is in fact a war-book. Its vision is
minatory, its verse is prophetic. Roy McFadden is an Irishman and sees his native
mountain, "Slieve Donard," amid the waste of sky and flame of wings in terms of
another Ararat. His "Train at Midnight" strides through fields whose very green
flaunts the insurgent flag of the Irish Republic. War prevails in his inventive
rehandling of ballad form, particularly "An Irish Peasant Woman Summons Her
Absent Children":

> Call them home from foreign lands,
> Send my love imperative;
> Holding hope between my hands
> Theirs the hope I have to give,
> Hands of hope imperative.
>
> Stars still walk on secret hills
> Hope is still a peasant's child;
> The cities hoard their seven ills,
> But I hold wisdom undefiled,
> Willing to history this child . . .

> Call them home where there is light
> And still a candle and a prayer;
> Call them through the twisted night,
> Yesterday is dying there,
> Past the hope of priest or prayer . . .
>
> Call them home. Send undefiled
> This my love imperative.
> Hope is still a peasant's child
> Theirs the hope I have to give,
> Child of hope imperative.

But, in McFadden's subsequent two books, the ghost of Yeats beats too insistently upon the door. The diction, too, becomes lush and over-romantic. After these he published no collection for twenty-five years.

However, in his recent book *The Garryowen,* Mr. McFadden matched his early skill with a wisdom conferred by experience. Here we have an authority all the better for being unforced. It is a craftsmanlike book all through, but "Glenarm," "Roger Casement's Rising," "Premonition," and various poems in the sequence "Family Album" are especially poignant. Like his distinguished contemporary John Hewitt, Roy McFadden has not only learned from the Anglo-Irish tradition but carried it forward. And, like John Hewitt, his reputation should be consolidated before long by the issue of a Collected Poems.

– Philip Hobsbaum

McGINLEY, Phyllis. American. Born in Ontario, Oregon, 21 March 1905. Educated at Ogden High School, Utah; Sacred Heart Academy, Ogden; University of Utah, Salt Lake City; University of California, Berkeley. Married Charles L. Hayden in 1937; has two children. Formerly, Schoolteacher, Utah and New York; worked for an advertising agency, New York City; Staff Writer, *Town and Country,* New York. Member, Advisory Board, *The American Scholar,* Washington, D.C. Recipient: Christopher Book Award, 1955; Poetry Society Award, 1955; Catholic Writers Guild Award, 1955; Edna St. Vincent Millay Award, 1955; St. Catherine de Siena Medal, 1956; Catholic Institute of the Press Award, 1960; Pulitzer Prize, 1961; Catholic Poetry Society Spirit Gold Medal, 1962; Laetare Medal, Notre Dame University, 1964; Campion Award, 1967. D.Litt.: Wheaton College, Illinois, 1956; St. Mary's College, Notre Dame, Indiana, 1958; Marquette University, Milwaukee, 1960; Dartmouth College, Hanover, New Hampshire, 1961; Boston College, 1962; Wilson College, Chambersburg, Pennsylvania, 1964; Smith College, Northampton, Massachusetts, 1964; St. John's University, Jamaica, New York, 1964. Member, National Institute of Arts and Letters. Address: 60 Beach Avenue, Larchmont, New York 10538, U.S.A.

PUBLICATIONS

Verse

On the Contrary. New York, Doubleday, 1934.
One More Manhattan. New York, Harcourt Brace, 1937.
A Pocketful of Wry. New York, Duell, 1940.
Husbands Are Difficult; or, The Book of Oliver Ames. New York, Duell, 1941.
Stones from a Glass House: New Poems. New York, Viking Press, 1946.
A Short Walk from the Station. New York, Viking Press, 1951.
The Love Letters of Phyllis McGinley. New York, Viking Press, 1954; London, Dent, 1955.
Merry Christmas, Happy New Year. New York, Viking Press, 1958; London, Secker and Warburg, 1959.
Times Three: Selected Verse from Three Decades. New York, Viking Press, 1960; as Times Three: Selected Verse from Three Decades with Seventy New Poems, London, Secker and Warburg, 1961.
A Wreath of Christmas Legends. New York, Macmillan, 1967.
Christmas con and pro. Berkeley, California, Hart Press, 1971.
Confessions of a Reluctant Optimist, edited by Barbara Wells Price. Kansas City, Missouri, Hallmark Editions, 1973.

Plays

Small Wonder (lyrics only; revue; produced New York, 1948).

Screenplay: The Emperor's Nightingale, 1951.

Other

The Horse Who Lived Upstairs (juvenile). Philadelphia, Lippincott, 1944.
The Plain Princess (juvenile). Philadelphia, Lippincott, 1945.
All Around the Town (juvenile). Philadelphia, Lippincott, 1948.
A Name for Kitty (juvenile). New York, Simon and Schuster, 1948; London, Muller, 1950.
The Most Wonderful Doll in the World (juvenile). Philadelphia, Lippincott, 1950.
The Horse Who Had His Picture in the Paper (juvenile). Philadelphia, Lippincott, 1951.
Blunderbus (juvenile). Philadelphia, Lippincott, 1951.
The Make-Believe Twins (juvenile). Philadelphia, Lippincott, 1953.
The Year Without Santa Claus (juvenile). Philadelphia, Lippincott, 1957.
The Province of the Heart (essays). New York, Viking Press, 1959; London, Catholic Book Club, 1963.
Lucy McLockett (juvenile). Philadelphia, Lippincott, 1959; Leicester, Brockhampton Press, 1961.
Sugar and Spice: The ABC of Being a Girl (juvenile). New York, Watts, 1960.
Mince Pie and Mistletoe (juvenile). Philadelphia, Lippincott, 1961.
The B Book (juvenile). New York, Crowell Collier, 1962.
Boys Are Awful (juvenile). New York, Watts, 1962.
How Mrs. Santa Claus Saved Christmas (juvenile). Philadelphia, Lippincott, 1963.

A Girl and Her Room (juvenile).   New York, Watts, 1963.
Sixpence in Her Shoe (autobiographical).   New York, Macmillan, 1964.
Wonderful Time (juvenile).   Philadelphia, Lippincott, 1966.
Saint-Watching.   New York, Viking Press, 1969; London, Collins, 1970.

Editor, *Wonders and Surprises: A Collection of Poems.*   Philadelphia, Lippincott,
1968.

*   *   *

A complacent *ubi sunt* mood dominates the best verse of Phyllis McGinley.
"Epithalamion (If Spenser Had Been on the Staff of *The Bride's Magazine*)," a
strong early poem, parodies both the romantic and spiritual bases of modern
marriage: "So tall, so slim, visaged so like a garden / (Coiffure by Antoine; skin by
Elizabeth Arden), . . . (Prayer by the pastor; marriage – we trust – by Heaven)."
However, the final invocation to ". . . scatter pleasure o'er the marriage bed! /
(Mattress by Simmons; bed by W. and J. Sloane)" confirms the earlier hints that
material things not only threaten but also reinforce civilized values, in this case the
values of an educated suburbanite with a love for New York, an outlook that both
enriches and seriously limits McGinley's verse. Only occasionally does she dramat-
ize the ultimate antithesis of the worldly and spiritual: the portrait of the Reverend
Dr. Harcourt simultaneously acknowledges and undercuts his eloquence on "Art,
Education, God, the Early Greeks, / Psychiatry, Saint Paul, true Christian charity, /
. . . All things but Sin. He seldom mentions Sin" ("Community Church").
  In her "occasional" poems, the same wry regret laments the imminent closing of
a gourmet importer ("Dirge over a Pot of Pâté de Foie Gras") or the reversal of
values during the Depression ("Trinity Place"). This dual focus continues through
the forties with a graceful sonnet to the "Good Humor Man," or the ambitious
World War II poem, "On Every Front," in which the speaker flees the frightening
radio news for the comfort of her garden, only to discover an increasingly horrifying Book of the Creatures: "The mole, / Devious, secret, like a virus, / Bored from
within upon the iris." The poem shrewdly avoids a positive ending but, perhaps
reluctant to rest with a bleak perception, concludes with facile irony: "I took up
arms and, stoutly met, / Slew twenty slugs with no regret."
  This unwillingness to explore the full implications of ambitious poems flaws even
The Love Letters of Phyllis McGinley, her best volume. She stays brilliantly within
her range in "Mrs. Sweeney among the Allegories," a delicate parody of Eliot's
poetry, *The Confidential Clerk*, and a puzzled middle-brow sensibility: "Gnomic, the
jests of Ina Claire / Scampered on super-cadenced feet. / Eggerson spoke of
Brussel Sprouts. / Entered at left the Paraclete." Often, her tight tetrameters
perfectly reflect the movement of her wit: "And even white is partly black / In
books by François Mauriac" ("From Any Angle It's a Viper's Tale"). And she can
skillfully vary strict meters to create a mood in which moralizing wit achieves
authentic emotion: "Coquettes with doctors; hoards her breath / For blandish-
ments; fluffs out her hair; / And keeps her stubborn suitor, Death, / Moping upon
the stair" ("The Old Beauty"). Unfortunately, such tight forms rarely succeed with
serious themes, but seem more suited to comic, or bemused speculations, such as
the series "Saints Without Tears." For her celebrations of family life and female
self-assessment, McGinley wisely attempts more expansive forms, such as the
ballade and, in poems like "The Doll House," syllabic or free verse.
  The difficulty of "placing" McGinley is most evident in her famous "In Praise of
Diversity," a hymn to human variety that often disconcertingly shifts to a comic
tone: "Praise *con amor'* or *furioso* / The large, the little, and the soso." The mood
of the poem never sufficiently recovers to accommodate the final prayer. Though

their elements do not completely fuse, such poems suggest McGinley's continual enlargement of the boundaries of her craft. Her comic poems, which rarely depend on the obsessive sound magic of a poet like Updike, or on explosive wit or word play, project a sensibility that wears its impressive erudition gracefully and muses without bitterness on the passing of values simultaneously attractive and absurd, as in "A Threnody: 'The New Rolls-Royce Is Designed to Be Owner Driven. No Chauffeur Required' "·

> Splendor decays, despite the walnut table
> Sliding from under the dash. Who now will stow
> The wicker hampers away? For ladies in sable,
> Who'll spread the cloth, uncork the Veuve Cliquot?

– Burton Kendle

McGOUGH, Roger. British. Born in Liverpool, Lancashire, 9 November 1937. Educated at St. Mary's College, Crosby, Lancashire; Hull University, Yorkshire, B.A. in French and geography, Cert.Ed. Formerly, Lecturer, Liverpool College of Art. Poetry Fellow, University of Loughborough, Leicestershire, 1973–75. Currently, a member of "The Scaffold" (humor, poetry and music group). Agent: Hope, Leresche and Steele, 11 Jubilee Place, London S.W.3, England.

PUBLICATIONS

Verse

The Mersey Sound: Penguin Modern Poets 10, with Adrian Henri and Brian Patten. London, Penguin, 1967.
Frinck, A Life in the Day of, and Summer with Monika: Poems (novel and verse). London, Joseph, and New York, Ballantine, 1967.
Watchwords. London, Cape, 1969.
After the Merrymaking. London, Cape, 1971.
Out of Sequence. London, Turret Books, 1973.
Gig. London, Cape, 1973.
Sporting Relations. London, Eyre Methuen, 1974.

Recordings: The Incredible New Liverpool Scene, CBS, 1967; McGough McGear, Parlophone; "Scaffold" Live at Queen Elizabeth Hall, Parlophone; "Scaffold" L. the P., Parlophone; Grimms, Island; Fresh Liver, Island.

Plays

Birds, Marriages and Deaths, with others (produced London, 1964).
The Chauffeur-Driven Rolls (produced Liverpool, 1966).
The Commission (produced Liverpool, 1967).

The Puny Little Life Show (produced London, 1969).   London, Penguin, 1973.
Stuff (produced London, 1970).

*   *   *

English critics have shown a surprising inability to cope with the "Pop Poetry" boom. Regularly, since the first appearance of the Liverpool poets on the national scene, they have predicted that the whole thing must soon come to an end, must be recognized as no more than an aberration, a flash in the pan. As I write, in 1974, the three principal Liverpool poets – Henri, McGough and Patten – are still very much with us, still publishing volumes of verse which seem to find eager readers.

When my anthology, *The Liverpool Scene*, was first published in 1967, Roger McGough was the poet whom the critics felt most inclined to forgive. They detected in him a lyricism, a simplicity and a lack of American influence which made him more acceptable than the others. Surprisingly, it is McGough, in the ensuing years, who has remained closest to the Pop milieu. He makes his living as a performer, rather than as a writer, and the group with whom he works, The Scaffold, have achieved a celebrity which stretches a long way beyond the poetry circuit, and have even managed, on one occasion, to top the English hit parade.

The result has been, perhaps, that he has not developed as interestingly as his colleagues. The virtues of his poetry remain very much what they always were – charm, high-spirits, and an astonishing capacity for inventing puns. Surely no English writer since W. S. Gilbert has had a cleverer touch with these:

> Or when I'm 91
> with silver hair
> & sitting in a barber's chair
> may rival gangsters
> with hamfisted tommyguns burst in
> & give me a short back & insides.

It seems to me that when McGough adds these qualities to a rarer, but extremely attractive, lyric melancholy about the ups-and-downs of love, then he is producing work which, for all its feather-lightness, is quite likely to survive.

– Edward Lucie-Smith

McGRATH, Thomas M. American. Born near Sheldon, North Dakota, 20 November 1916. Educated at Sheldon public schools; University of North Dakota, Grand Forks, B.A. in English 1939 (Phi Beta Kappa); Louisiana State University, Baton Rouge, M.A. in English 1940; New College, Oxford (Rhodes Scholar), 1947–48. Served in the United States Army Air Force, 1943–46. Married Eugenia Juanopoulos in 1960; has one son. English Instructor, Colby College, Waterville, Maine, 1940–41; Assistant Professor, Los Angeles State College, 1950–54, and C. W. Post College, Long Island, New York, 1960–61; Associate Professor, North Dakota State University, Fargo, 1962–67. Since 1969, Associate Professor of English, Moorhead State College, Minnesota. Formerly, Film Writer; Editor, *California Quarterly*. Since 1960, Founding Editor, with Eugenia McGrath, *Crazy Horse*, Fargo. Recipient: Swallow Book Award, 1955; Amy Lowell traveling scholarship, 1965; Guggenheim Fellowship, 1967; National Endowment for the Arts grant, 1974. Address: 615 South 11th Street, Moorhead, Minnesota 56560, U.S.A.

PUBLICATIONS

Verse

First Manifesto.   Baton Rouge, Louisiana, Swallow, 1940.

Three Young Poets, with William Peterson and James Franklin Lewis, edited by Alan Swallow.   Prairie City, Illinois, Decker Press, 1942.

The Dialectics of Love.   Prairie City, Illinois, Decker Press, 1944.

To Walk a Crooked Mile.   New York, Swallow-Morrow, 1947.

Longshot O'Leary's Garland of Practical Poesie.   New York, International Publishers, 1949.

Witness to the Times.   Los Angeles, privately printed, 1954.

Figures from a Double World.   Denver, Swallow, 1955.

Letters to an Imaginary Friend.   Denver, Swallow, 1962.

New and Selected Poems.   Denver, Swallow, 1962.

Letter to an Imaginary Friend, Parts I and II.   Chicago, Swallow Press, 1970.

The Movie at the End of the World: Collected Poems.   Chicago, Swallow Press, 1973.

Voyages to the Inland Sea III, with others, edited by John Judson.   La Crosse, University of Wisconsin Center for Contemporary Poetry, 1973.

A Sound of One Hand.   Minneapolis, Minnesota Writers Publishing House, 1975.

Novel

The Gates of Ivory, The Gates of Horn.   New York, Mainstream Publishers, 1957.

Other

About Clouds (juvenile).   Los Angeles, Melmont Publishers, 1959.

Beautiful Things (juvenile).   New York, Vanguard Press, 1960.

Manuscript Collection: North Dakota State University, Fargo.

Critical Studies: by Tom Bond, in *Measure 2* (Boston), 1958; Charles Potts, in *Small Press Review* (Paradise, California), 1974.

Thomas McGrath comments:

Some of the work is a restructuring of traditional forms; some of it is open and "free." I have written a lot of short haiku-like poems and I'm now working on what may turn out to be the longest poem in America. I think the poems are quite personal in idiom, often "autobiographical" and politically revolutionary.

*   *   *

Thomas McGrath, who was born on a farm in North Dakota and studied at the University of North Dakota and Oxford, served for three years in the army, largely in the Aleutian Islands. He has worked as a teacher, a writer of children's books, and a film scenarist; for his political sympathies he has found himself blacklisted. He calls his long poem *Letter to an Imaginary Friend* a "pseudo-autobiography"; the work is comparable, perhaps, to that of Malcolm Lowry in fiction – it is highly imagistic, centered in a sense of the stars, and it shuttles confidently back and forth between memory and current impression. McGrath excels in the expansive integration of diverse materials and the welding together of voices and tones of language:

> So, that winter, we got wood up from the river
> While the migrant bourgeois of Morehead slalomed south on their chins
> And my auld acquaintance broke like a covey of quail
> And rode the rods to Detroit or soonered westerly.

His strong sense for the American countryside and the past reminds one of MacLeish, but there is more emphatic sounding of strong and gutteral personal idiom and emotion. McGrath's work – stylistically at a polar remove from that of Robert Bly – does much to contribute to a feeling that American poetry enjoys a healthy and salubrious range. There is also, in McGrath's long poem, a sharp sense of nature, derived perhaps partly from Frost:

> So, worked together. Fed the wood to the saw
> That had more gaps than teeth. Sweated, and froze
> In the dead-still days, as clear as glass, with the biting
> Acetylene of the cold cutting in through the daylight,
> And the badman trees snapping out of the dusk
> Their icy pistols. So, worked, the peddlers pack of us.

He has real enthusiasm for "the vagrant farms of the north: Montana, Saskatchewan, / With the farmers still on them, merrily plowing away," and he expresses with some power the history of political conscience: "A mile east, in the dark, / The hunger marchers slept in the court house lobby . . . hoped they were building / The new society, inside the shell of the old –." But the police arrive and "we fought down the stairs." In such lines McGrath lives in the idealism of the Thirties:

> But *then* was a different country . . . To talk of the People
> Is to be a fool. But they were the *sign* of the People,
> Those talkers
> Went underground about 1941
> Nor hide nor hair of 'em since; not now, in the Year
> Of the Dog . . .
> Their voices got lost in the rattle of voting machines
> In the Las Vegas of the national politic.

McGrath's long six-beat lines build chantingly, from epiphany to epiphany, from "vagrant farms of the north" to "the little lost towns . . . towns of the dark people: a depot, a beer joint, a small / Fistful of lights flung east as the red-ball train goes past." His *New and Selected Poems* contains, in fact, so many beautiful lyrics that one can say only the most hopeful things about his work and its direction.

– David Ray

McKEOWN, Tom (Thomas Shanks McKeown). American. Born in Evanston, Illinois, 29 September 1937. Educated at the University of Michigan, Ann Arbor, 1957–62, B.A. 1961, M.A. 1962. Instructor, Alpena College, Michigan, 1962–64, and Wisconsin State University, Oshkosh, 1964–68. Instructor, Stephens College, Columbia, Missouri, 1968–74. Recipient: Hopwood Award, University of Michigan, 1968; Wurlitzer Foundation grant, 1972; Yaddo grant, 1973. Address: General Delivery, Pentwater, Michigan 49449; or, English Department, Stephens College, Columbia, Missouri 65201, U.S.A.

PUBLICATIONS

Verse

Alewife Summer. Albuquerque, New Mexico, Road Runner Press, 1967.
Last Thoughts: Poems. Madison, Wisconsin, Abraxas Press, 1969.
The Winds of the Calender. Albuquerque, New Mexico, Road Runner Press, 1969.
Drunk All Afternoon. Madison, Wisconsin, Abraxas Press, 1969.
The Milk of the Wolf. Columbia, Missouri, Assari Press, 1970.
The Cloud Keeper. Dublin, Seafront Press, 1972.
The House of Water. Fredonia, New York, Basilisk Press, 1974.
The Luminous Revolver. Fremont, Michigan, Sumac Press, 1974.
Driving to New Mexico. Santa Fe, New Mexico, Sunstone Press, 1974.

Critical Studies: "Contemporary Poetic Statements," in *Road Apple Review* (Oshkosh, Wisconsin), 1971; in *December Magazine* (Western Springs, Illinois), December 1971; in *Back Door* (Poquon, Virginia), 1971; in *New Voices in American Poetry: An Anthology*, Cambridge, Massachusetts, Winthrop, 1973.

Tom McKeown comments:

Have several unfinished novels but I have little interest in them now. Poetry is my full-time obsession.

I lean toward the surreal in poetry. Like experimentation rather than the tired, heavy academic stuff.

Write in free verse almost entirely. No major themes really other than the usual ones: love, death, separation, alienation, war, etc. I am mainly concerned with the *dream* and the poetic possibilities that arise out of the *dream*. This is the area of the surreal where a non-sequitur progression of images or image clusters are drawn from the unconscious mind. The surreal deals with the landscapes of dreams and thus there are infinite possibilities for new and startling creations. Always there is a possibility for a *satori* or sudden illumination. Have been influenced perhaps by Neruda, Bréton and Trakl.

Recently, my poems have been reaching more toward the mystical and supernatural.

*   *   *

Tom McKeown is a poet who is able to be both concrete and surreal in his poetry. He admits the influence on his verse of such Spanish and Latin American poets and Lorca and Neruda; like Neruda, his surrealism has a strong grip on the natural landscape in which McKeown lives. Like other young American poets such as Greg Kuzma, McKeown manages a synthesis of the concrete and the surreal, the traditions of English nature poetry and Spanish and French surrealism. McKeown is one of the most promising exponents of this approach. He also sees the poet as a shaman in a poem from *Drunk All Afternoon* called "The Buffalo, Our Sacred Beast":

> I am running with them
> through the streets, drunk
> on buffalo milk and nourished
> by dung.
> I carry a flag with a buffalo on it
> and on my staff I spin a human skull.

In an essay he contributed to *Their Place in the Heat*, McKeown notes that he is attracted to both the nature/mythic/archetypal approach and the surreal approach as well in his writing. The former approach is evident in the poem quoted above, in which McKeown sees himself as a medicine man leading the buffalo back to trample the civilization that crushed them. Another poem (in a three poet issue of the *Road Apple Review*), "Aztec Dream," also evokes ancient rites, again involving human sacrifice:

> a thin dagger parts the softness of air
> of youth of flesh giving over all happy
> silence to the carved gods of stone . . .

McKeown is, however, basically a compassionate poet; even in the first poem, he half apologizes to the human victims for the well-merited revenge of the buffalo, and one of his strongest groups of poems is a small collection of four elegies, *Last Thoughts*, which contains one of the strongest denunciations of the Viet Nam War, all the stronger for bringing it home in "Body En Route":

> A twenty year old boy
> is en route home. Killed
> in Viet Nam. En route home
> to the funeral parlor.
> Home. En route to Oshkosh.
> Twenty below zero. Heavy snow.
> He is riding home to be lifted
> from the baggage car
> of the Chicago-Northwestern.
> Quietly and smoothly
> he will be driven home
> through the frozen luminous streets.
> Nothing stirs in the gray houses.
> Silence from his metal box.
> The park is without voices.
> The wind blows a terrible darkness.

– Duane Ackerson

McNEILL, Anthony. Jamaican. Born in Kingston, 17 December 1941. Educated at Excelsior College, 1952; St. George's College, 1953–59; Nassau Community College, 1964–65; Johns Hopkins University, Baltimore, 1970–71, M.A. 1971; University of Massachusetts, Amherst, since 1971. Married Olive Samuel in 1970; has one child. Civil service clerk, Port Maria and Kingston, 1960–64; journalist, The Gleaner Company, Kingston, 1965–66; scriptwriter, JIS radio, Kingston, 1966–68; trainee manager, Jamaica Playboy Club-Hotel, Ocho Rios, 1968–69; Editorial Assistant, *Jamaica Journal*, Kingston, 1970. Since 1971, Teaching Assistant, University of Massachusetts. Recipient: Jamaica Festival Literary Competition prize, 1966, 1971; Silver Musgrave Medal, 1973.

PUBLICATIONS

Verse

Hello Ungod. Baltimore, Peacewood Press, 1971.
Reel from "The Life-Movie." Mona, Jamaica, Savacou Publications, 1972.

Critical Studies: "An Extreme Vision" by Mervyn Morris, in *Sunday Gleaner* (Kingston), 28 January 1973; Wayne Brown, in *Jamaica Journal* (Kingston), March-June 1973.

*   *   *

Anthony McNeill is the first and most accomplished poet to appear out of the "now" generation of the anglophone Caribbean. McNeill is "new" in the sense that coming to maturity in the late sixties, he is past the rhetorical colonial assertions and dramatic nationalist self-doubts of the *entre des guerres* writing which gave us Carter, Roach and the early Derek Walcott. He is very much into his own "thing." That thing is "now" in that it deals with clairol and speed, and is very much concerned with splitting, suicide and animal/identity. But there is nothing gratuitously "today" about these energies and work. Here is a poet of patient, scrupulous craftsmanship, concerned with rhythm, cadence, form and the fission-able, rather than fashionable qualities of his word:

> Aunt Angel is three She swallows
> the virus and sickens No one
> can assist A terrible
> needle shies up her body and sticks
>
> at a hundred and plus . . .
> – from "Elegy Plus"

His most definitive collection to date is *Reel from "The Life-Movie."* It contains 30 poems, eighteen of which appear in his earlier 20-poem *Hello Ungod*. The two together give a fair idea of McNeill's thematic interests and poetic development. He begins (setting/style) as a "lyrical" "Nature" poet:

and this cliff
where swallows confirm
the sooncome of rain
of long evenings adrift
from your meaning again and again.
                    – from "Cliff-Walking"

But this is no traditional "Nature" where metaphors come to rest in contemplation
of superordinate glories. Note the "*adrift / from your meaning*" in that last line of
the poem which just before said "and my eyes ride / upward, oaring me back / to
loneliness" (my italics). It is this modern/urban problem and paradox, the concern
of anglophone poetry from Auden through Lowell to Plath, that quickly comes to
dominate his page. The sense of interior loneliness so pervades McNeill's poetry,
in fact, that even physical love ("Mummy+," "Dermis") is vitiated by it, until the
persona/victim loses his hold of self and becomes "other": as in the zoo-poem
"Rimbaud Jingle," for example:

When you trip
on my skin of sickness, bruised blue,

I'll slip from my cage and into
the pure life of lions. I'm death-
sick of being two . . .

which leads to a frighteningly clear and "cool" contemplation of the anti-solutions:
suicide ("Who'll see me dive?") and/or the use of hallucinogens:

The lady freaks
out to her loveliness
lost irrevocably lost The Lady cries out
for ships The Lady cries out for Paris . . .

The Lady gets sexy & rings
a towering eunuch into her hell
            – from "The Lady Accepts the Needle Again"

But what makes McNeill an important new voice is his comprehensive perception
of this agony: the result of interior loneliness is not just personal freak, but social
impasse ("Reel," "American Leader") and cultural, perhaps even cosmic catastrophe ("Hello Ungod," "Black Space"). All the post-Dostoevsky archetypes
gather in his poetry, suffering from the death of God: the mad clown, the schizophrenic, the ape, Aunt Angel, The Lady, Godot, Dracula, and the dread ikons from
McNeill's own formative experience of the Kingston ghetto: Brother Joe, Saint
Ras, and Don Drummond, the sacred trombone-man. All these walk through a
broken, shadowed wordscape "whose irradiant stop is light"; whose "true country" is "Both doubt and light."
    It is from this double (paradoxical, sometimes schizoid) vision that McNeill's
remarkable sensibility expresses itself. But his development contains its own perils.
More and more the light of his poetry seems to radiate not from the sun, no matter
how distant, but from an agnostic space lit only by the flicker of a (life)-*movie*, so
that the poet finds himself locked into the "ponderous ingot / that weights down
the base of / his / box," until only a dark solar doubt (unseen ungod) is left:

At twenty-nine guru
I'm still unprepared;
one day I will shatter

yank loose in the wind
as a man stuck together with pins.
When the god comes, I'll tell him *the perfect flamingo he gifted is gone.*

– "Flamingo"; my italics

But this, surely, with one so seriously embattled with his own talent, can only be a temporary or apparent illumination. McNeill's "solutions" over the next few years will be one of the major achievements in our literature.

– Edward Brathwaite

McWHIRTER, George. Canadian. Born in Belfast, Northern Ireland, 26 September 1939. Educated at Grosvenor High School, Belfast, 1951–57; Queen's University, Belfast, 1957–62, B.A. 1961; University of British Columbia, Vancouver (Macmillan Prize), 1968–70, B.A. 1970. Married to Angela Coid; has one daughter and one son. Assistant Master, Kilkeel Secondary School, Northern Ireland, 1962–64, and Bangor Grammar School, Northern Ireland, 1964–65; English Teacher, University of Barcelona, Spain, 1965–66, and Alberni Secondary School, Port Alberni, British Columbia, 1966–68. Since 1970, Assistant Professor of Creative Writing, University of British Columbia. Associate Editor, *Prism International*, Vancouver, 1970–73; Editor, *Words from the Inside*, Kingston, Ontario, 1973. Recipient: Canada Council grant, 1969; Commonwealth Poetry Prize, 1972. Address: 4637 West 13th Avenue, Vancouver 8, British Columbia, Canada.

PUBLICATIONS

Verse

Catalan Poems. Ottawa, Oberon Press, 1971.
Columbuscade. Vancouver, Hoffer Publications, 1974.

Short Stories

Bodyworks. Ottawa, Oberon Press, 1974.

George McWhirter comments:

My work to date has been preoccupied with people and substance: people as consumers of substance and at the same time as those consumed by substance. He who eats will in turn be eaten. Such was the base of *Catalan Poems.* The family, man, woman, and child, one flesh, one substance was the central dramatic vehicle for this. *Columbuscade* uses the idea of Columbus to deal with the impossibility of escape from the flesh in terms of space: we can jump no farther than ourselves. Even if there was a new world, few would embark; the superscription of the book runs, "All are chosen for the crew, but few embark fearing a new world." This is the fundamental dilemma in my most recent book of poems, as yet unpublished, *Reina del Nar Poems*, which is set in the Belfast shipyards. Recently, I've come to regard things and substance as part of the infinite imagination of light. The unknown is the point of disembarkation, the intellect provides place names as we pass, the real rudder in the rear of the head is the intuition. The main thing that poetry does for me is turn ideas or intimations into the properties of the five senses; this is what life itself does for us. Poetry, in short, is life.

*   *   *

George McWhirter has been accused of producing "deftly crafted anachronisms – still, cold and timeless to the point of utter irrelevance." But the same critic, a Canadian, acknowledged the poet's skill, describing *Catalan Poems* as "a collection of exquisitely sculptured impersonal lyrics." The barrier between poet and reader in this case appears to have derived from the fact that McWhirter's poems were not set in Canada and did not present a Canadian point of view.

To an outsider the virtues of the book are more apparent. The skill is certainly present: there are vividly memorable images such as these lines about a man plucking and eating grapes from a bunch:

> Seconds drop *pip* into a dish.
> Time plants a sprig of green bone
> In the empty glass."

The style is impressionistic, highly visual, and admittedly somewhat detached. It would be unfair, though, to dismiss this collection as impersonal or irrelevant. It is not confessional, first-person poetry; but there are sharply-observed portraits of people – market-women, a prostitute, a soldier, and in particular the aging, anxious but undauntedly swaggering Eduardo with his long-suffering wife; and insights into the uneasy commitments and compromises of the Catholic faith (far from irrelevant when one remembers that the poet comes from Belfast). Here and elsewhere we are free to draw our own parallels. George McWhirter's world is not a comfortable one, but we cannot ignore his picture of it.

– Fleur Adcock

MEAD, Matthew. British. Born in Buckinghamshire, 12 September 1924. Served in the British Army, 1942–47, including three years in India, Ceylon and Singapore. Married to Ruth Adrian. Formerly, Editor, *Satis* magazine, Edinburgh. Has lived in Germany since 1962, currently in Bad Godesberg.

Publications

Verse

A Poem in Nine Parts. Worcester, Migrant Press, 1960.
Identities. Worcester, Migrant Press, 1964.
Kleinigkeiten. Newcastle upon Tyne, Malcolm Rutherford, 1966.
Identities and Other Poems. London, Rapp and Carroll, 1967.
The Administration of Things. London, Anvil Press Poetry, 1970.
Penguin Modern Poets 16, with Harry Guest and Jack Beeching. London, Penguin, 1970.
In the Eyes of the People. Edinburgh, Satis Press, 1973.

Other

Translator, with Ruth Mead, *Shadow Land: Selected Poems of Johannes Bobrowski.* London, Donald Carroll, 1966; revised edition, London, Rapp and Whiting, 1967.
Translator, with Ruth Mead, *Generation,* by Heinz Winfried Sabais. Edinburgh, Malcolm Rutherford, 1967.
Translator, with Ruth Mead and others, *O the Chimneys,* by Nelly Sachs. New York, Farrar Straus, 1967; as *Selected Poems of Nelly Sachs,* London, Cape, 1968.
Translator, with Ruth Mead, *Generation and Other Poems,* by Heinz Winfried Sabais. London, Anvil Press Poetry, 1968.
Translator, with Ruth Meade, *Amfortiade and Other Poems,* by Max Höltzer. Edinburgh, Malcolm Rutherford, 1968.
Translator, with Ruth Mead, *Horst Bienek.* Santa Barbara, California, Unicorn Press, 1969.
Translator, with Ruth Mead, *Elisabeth Borchers.* Santa Barbara, California, Unicorn Press, 1969.
Translator, with Ruth Mead and Michael Hamburger, *The Seeker and Other Poems,* by Nelly Sachs. New York, Farrar Straus, 1970.
Translator, with Ruth Mead, *Selected Poems,* by Johannes Bobrowski and Horst Bienek. London, Penguin, 1971.
Translator, with Ruth Mead, *Mitteilungen / Communications,* by Heinz Winfried Sabais. Darmstadt, Eduard Roether Verlag, 1971.

Critical Studies: by Christopher Middleton, in *London Magazine,* 1964; in *Neue Deutsche Literatur* (Berlin), February 1965.

Matthew Mead comments:

I have tried not to avoid what has happened in poetry and psycho-politics during this century. In plain politics the failure of socialism has been important to my verse. Eliot and Pound are obvious influences on style but a good deal of basic Housman is lurking in the background. I admire the poetry and prose of Michael Roberts. Of the Germans, Gottfried Benn has said many things to their end, but the important poem by a contemporary is, for me, Sabais's *Generation*. I use any form I can.

"And all's to do again."

*   *   *

Matthew Mead has been spoken of as a modernist, a social critic, a poet who is proletarian and unacademic. On the contrary, his qualities are those of literary accomplishment. He can turn an epigram or a ballade as well as anyone writing today. The reader may feel his way through deliberately fragmented *hommages* to Ezra Pound or Robert Creeley to light upon such finely tooled verses as

> Bodies are rolled from bed to scuffed slippers
> and day stiff-jointed; in sense repetition;
> in spring one more spring; the figure
> in a worn carpet traced with a dull eye.
>
> And the house old, the wind's sound, each ache
> lent art and length, given due weight
> the dragging footfall. For this are we bent
> and gnarled and wrinkled – to cross the room. . . .

It is not that Mr. Mead is an escapist; his translations of Bobrowski, done in collaboration with his wife, would assure us of that. Rather he is a Poundian in a sense deeper than that of technical allegiance: an aesthete distressed by the blood and chaos of totalitarian Europe. The poem quoted, "To Redistort a Weltanschauung," comes from his retrospective collection, *Identities*. Here is an extract from his more recent *The Administration of Things*:

> What she herself believes
> No man alive conceives
>
> We tell the lawful tale
> (All fictions else must fail)
>
> And loyal beyond the lie
> Nor daring to deny
>
> That what we have she gave
> We make of what we have
>
> Lending it length and art
> Embellishing each part
>
> A faith to ravage noon
> With phases of the moon. . . .

It is clear that writing such as this resembles nothing so much as the more Elizabethan lyrics of Donne –

> But come bad chance
> And we join to it our strength
> And we teach it art and length
> Itself o'er us to advance. . . .

– or the more lapidary verse of Marvell –

> . . . Caesar's head at last
> Did through his laurels blast
> . . . And if we must speak true
> Much to the man is due. . .

At present, in Mr. Mead's original work, there is a gap between subject and presentation. Those who have followed his work with interest all these years must hope that he will turn this characteristic hiatus to dramatic use. Or, if not that, then they must wish him to find a range of subject matter suited to the cool detachment of his technique.

– Philip Hobsbaum

MELTZER, David. American. Born in Rochester, New York, 17 February 1937. Educated in public schools in Brooklyn and Los Angeles; Los Angeles City College; University of California, Los Angeles. Married Christina Meyer in 1958; has three daughters. Editor, *Maya*, Mill Valley, California, 1966–71. Currently, Editor, *Tree*, Bolinas, California. Recipient: Council of Literary Magazines grant, 1972; National Endowment for the Arts grant, 1974. Address: Box 9005, Berkeley, California 94709, U.S.A.

PUBLICATIONS

Verse

Poems, with Donald Schenker. San Francisco, privately printed, 1957.
Ragas. San Francisco, Discovery Books, 1959.
The Clown: A Poem. Larkspur, California, Semina, 1960.
The Process. Berkeley, California, Oyez, 1965.
In Hope I Offer a Fire Wheel. Berkeley, California, Oyez, 1965.
The Dark Continent. Berkeley, California, Oyez, 1967.
Nature Poem. Santa Barbara, California, Unicorn Press, 1967.
Round the Lunch Box: Rustic and Domestic Home Movies for Stan and Jane Brakhage. Los Angeles, Black Sparrow Press, 1969.
Yesod. London, Trigram Press, 1969.
From Eden Book. Mill Valley, California, Maya, 1969.
Abulafia Song. Santa Barbara, California, Unicorn Press, 1969.
Greenspeech. Santa Barbara, California, Christopher Books, 1970.
Luna. Los Angeles, Black Sparrow Press, 1970.
Letters and Numbers. Berkeley, California, Oyez, 1970.
Bronx Lil / Head of Lillin S.A.C. Santa Barbara, California, Capra Press, 1970.
32 Beams of Light. Santa Barbara, California, Capra Press, 1970.
Knots. Bolinas, California, Tree Books, 1971.
Bark: A Polemic. Santa Barbara, California, Capra Press, 1973.

Hero/Lil.   Los Angeles, Black Sparrow Press, 1973.
Tens: Selected Poems 1961–1971, edited by Kenneth Rexroth. New York, McGraw Hill Herder, 1973.
The Eyes, The Blood.   San Francisco, Mudra, 1973.
Bark.   Santa Barbara, California, Capra Press, 1973.
French Broom.   Berkeley, California, Oyez, 1974.
Blue Rags.   Berkeley, California, Oyez, 1974.

Recordings: *The Serpent Power*, Vanguard, 1968; *Poet Song*, Vanguard, 1969.

Novels

The Agency Trilogy.   North Hollywood, California, Essex House, 1968.
Orf.   North Hollywood, California, Essex House, 1969.
The Martyr.   North Hollywood, California, Essex House, 1969.
The Brain-Plant Tetralogy: Lovely, Healer, Out, and Glue Factory.   North Hollywood, California, Essex House, 1970.
Star.   North Hollywood, California, Brandon House, 1970.

Other

We All Have Something to Say to Each Other: Being an Essay Entitled "Patchen" and Four Poems.   San Francisco, Auerhahn Press, 1962.
Introduction to the Outsiders (essay on Beat Poetry).   Fort Lauderdale, Florida, Rodale Books, 1962.
Bazascope Mother (essay on Robert Alexander).   Los Angeles, Drekfesser Press, 1964.
Journal of the Birth.   Berkeley, California, Oyez, 1967.
Isla Vista Notes: Fragmentary, Apocalyptic, Didactic Contradictions.   Santa Barbara, California, Christopher Books, 1970.
Birth.   New York, Ballantine, 1973.
The Secret Garden: An Anthology of Texts from the Jewish Mystical Tradition.   New York, McGraw Hill-Herder, 1974.

Editor, with Michael McClure and Lawrence Ferlinghetti, *Journal for the Protection of All Beings.*   San Francisco, City Lights Books, 1961.
Editor, *The San Francisco Poets.*   New York, Ballantine, 1971.
Editor, *Birth: An Anthology.*   New York, Ballantine, 1973.

Manuscript Collections: Washington University, St. Louis; University of Indiana, Bloomington; University of California, Los Angeles.

Critical Studies: *David Meltzer: A Sketch from Memory and Descriptive Checklist* by David Kherdian, Berkeley, California, Oyez, 1965; *6 Poets of the San Francisco Renaissance* by David Kherdian, Fresno, California, Giligia Press, 1967.

*   *   *

A Californian since he was fourteen and a San Franciscan since 1959, David Meltzer has affinities with the other West Coast poets grouped in the *New American*

Poetry anthology of 1959, and more specifically with fellow-workers in cabalistic lore like Jack Hirschman and the painter Wallace Berman. Rock musician, editor of a journal of the Jewish mystical tradition, and pornographer, he writes poems that are lyrical, esoteric, and erotic. A recent sequence, "Lil," blends the Lilith myth with tangy particulars of contemporary urban California. For example:

> Lil in the teenage blond,
> Tight purple pants
> Legs spread apart.
> Looks thru orange shades
> Right thru my seams
> & seems to smile.

Meltzer has written, "Poetry is the special use of language which welds invisible & visible worlds into words generating great power," and while his power isn't often intense, this blending of the magical and mythic with the local and contemporary is his most distinctive note (see, for instance, his poem "For Raymond Chandler"). Also effective is his work commemorating ancestral racial presences, such as "From a Midrash": "The stories retell themselves. They are memory & they invent my songs. In my head, I swear, Eden flourishes."

– Seamus Cooney

MEREDITH, Willliam (Morris, Jr.). American. Born in New York City, 9 January, 1919. Educated at Lenox School, Massachusetts; Princeton University, New Jersey (Woodrow Wilson Fellow, 1946–47), B.A. (magna cum laude) 1940. Served in the United States Army Air Force, 1941–42, and in the United States Navy, 1942–46, 1952–54. Copy-boy and Reporter, *The New York Times*, 1940–41; Resident Fellow in Creative Writing, Princeton University, 1947–48, 1949–50, 1965–66; Associate Professor of English, University of Hawaii, Honolulu, 1950–51. Since 1955, Member of the Department, and since 1965, Professor of English, Connecticut College, New London. Taught at Bread Loaf Writers Conference, Vermont, Summers 1958–62. Opera Critic, *Hudson Review*, New York, 1955–56. Member, Connecticut Commission on the Arts, 1963–65; Director of the Humanities, Upward Bound Program, 1964–68. Recipient: Yale Series of Younger Poets Award, 1943; Harriet Monroe Memorial Prize, 1944, and Oscar Blumenthal Prize, 1953 (*Poetry*, Chicago); Rockefeller grant, for criticism, 1948, for poetry, 1968; *Hudson Review* fellowship, 1956; National Institute of Arts and Letters grant, 1958; Ford Fellowship, for drama, 1960; Loines Award, 1966; Van Wyck Brooks Award, 1971; National Endowment for the Arts grant, 1972. Member, National Institute of Arts and Letters; since 1964, Chancellor, Academy of American Poets. Address: Department of English, Connecticut College, New London, Connecticut 06320, U.S.A.

PUBLICATIONS

Verse

> *Love Letter from an Impossible Land.*   New Haven, Connecticut, Yale University Press, 1944.
> *Ships and Other Figures.*   Princeton, New Jersey, Princeton University Press, 1948.
> *The Open Sea and Other Poems.*   New York, Knopf, 1958.
> *The Wreck of the Thresher and Other Poems.*   New York, Knopf, 1964.
> *Earth Walk: New and Selected Poems.*   New York, Knopf, 1970.

Play

> *The Bottle Imp* (libretto), music by Peter Whiton (produced Wilton, Connecticut, 1958).

Other

> Editor, *Shelley.*   New York, Dell, 1962.
> Editor, *University and College Poetry Prizes, 1960–66, in Memory of Mrs. Fanny Fay Wood.*   New York, Academy of American Poets, 1966.
> Editor, with Mackie L. Jarrell, *Eighteenth Century Minor Poets.*   New York, Dell, 1968.

> Translator, *Alcools: Poems 1878–1913,* by Guillaume Apollinaire.   New York, Doubleday 1964.

Manuscript Collection: Middlebury College, Vermont.

*   *   *

Introducing William Meredith's *Love Letter from an Impossible Land,* Archibald MacLeish observed that this poet's "instincts are sound" ("He seems to know, without poisoning himself in the process, which fruits are healthful and which fruits are not"). The consistencies in his three subsequent volumes have proved MacLeish's prediction true. Although his meters have loosened in recent books, Meredith remains a formal poet who achieves imaginative participation in his subjects by creating them at an aesthetic distance. Poise and understanding are sought and revealed in the subjection of the facts of experience to an imaginative yet rational order. If the experience in a Meredith poem begins as a brute fact or raw emotion, it is transmuted into a shapelier, more civil and more intelligible image of itself. His work renders emotional force into forms. In a period when many poets sacrifice convention and form for force and immediacy, the risks in this aesthetic are evident. Yet the reader responsive to the legitimate demands such poetry makes will find among the resulting poems those which acknowledge the forces which engendered them. In his elegy to the sailors lost in a sunken submarine (the title poem from *The Wreck of the Thresher*) Meredith writes:

Why can't our dreams be content with the terrible facts?
The only animal cursed with responsible sleep,
We trace disaster always to our own acts.
I met a monstrous self trapped in the black deep:
All these years, he smiled, *I've drilled at sea
For this crush of water*. Then he saved only me.

Confronting the inexplicable tragedy of meaningless death, Meredith characteristically concludes, "Whether we give assent to this or rage / Is a question of temperament and does not matter."

This poem reflects two of his abiding concerns, the threat of death and the
loneliness of the sea, already enunciated in the last ten poems of his first book.
Service as a naval aviator in two Pacific wars has marked out for Meredith a part
of his *donnée*: images of oceanic space, the lonely sky, distant islands seen from
vast heights, the unknown destinies of men in wartime, and the responses of an
American to Oriental cultures (Japan, Korea, Hawaii) recur in his poems. Characteristically, he deals with such themes pictorially, fixing his images as though in a
painting, imposing upon them the designs imagination discovers and the forms and
meters appropriated by a scrupulously sensitive ear. His instinct is to render such
design; in "Rus in Urbe" (from *The Open Sea)* he chooses "In a city garden an
espalliered tree," not nature unadorned but nature shaped by human skill and
imagination. Yet in a later poem, "Roots" (from *The Wreck of the Thresher)*, a
dialogue narrative in the mode of Frost, he discovers in nature itself the pattern
which in "Rus in Urbe" imagination had to wrest by altering the shapes of trees.

The new poems in Meredith's latest book, *Earth Walk: New and Selected Poems*,
use a conversational, coloquial style, as in "Walter Jenks' Bath": "These are my
legs. I don't have to tell them, legs, / Move up or down or which leg." With like
informality of diction Meredith explores dreams, probes memory, creates characters, and, as in the title poem, makes his wry statement about being himself at a
time when almost everyone else is preoccupied by somebody else's moon walk.
The formality of this recent work is less a matter of surface and detail (such as
regular stanza, rhythm, rhyme) than formerly, but the design of the experience is
quietly interiorized in each poem. His tone is modest rather than boisterous, his
range deceptively larger than the voice whose speech provides the style.

Meredith has published also a complete translation of *Alcools* by Apollinaire, a
poet whose intuitive mode of apprehending experience would seem quite different
from his own. In his poem "For Guillaume Apollinaire," Meredith writes, "But
these poems –/ How quickly the strangeness would pass from things if it were not
for them." The same may be said of his own best work.

– Daniel Hoffman

MERRILL, James (Ingram). American. Born in New York City, 3 March 1926.
Educated at Lawrenceville School; Amherst College, Massachusetts, B.A. 1947.
Served in the United States Army, 1944–45. Recipient: Oscar Blumenthal Prize,
1947, Levinson Prize, 1949, Harriet Monroe Prize, 1951, Eunice Tietjens Memorial
Prize, 1958, and Morton Dauwen Zabel Prize, 1966 (*Poetry*, Chicago); National
Book Award, 1967; Bollingen Prize, 1973. Member, National Institute of Arts and
Letters, 1971. Address: 107 Water Street, Stonington, Connecticut 06378, U.S.A.

PUBLICATIONS

Verse

Jim's Book: A Collection of Poems and Short Stories. New York, privately
   printed, 1942.
The Black Swan. Athens, Icaros, 1946.
First Poems. New York, Knopf, 1951.
Short Stories. Pawlet, Vermont, Banyan Press, 1954.
The Country of a Thousand Years of Peace and Other Poems. New York, Knopf,
   1959; revised edition, New York, Atheneum, 1970.
Selected Poems. London, Chatto and Windus-Hogarth Press, 1961.
Water Street: Poems. New York, Atheneum, 1962.
The Thousand and Second Night. Athens, Christos Christian Press, 1963.
Violent Pastoral. Cambridge, Massachusetts, privately printed, 1965.
Nights and Days: Poems. New York, Atheneum, and London, Chatto and
   Windus-Hogarth Press, 1966.
The Fire Screen: Poems. New York, Atheneum, 1969; London, Chatto and
   Windus, 1970.
Two Poems. London, Chatto and Windus, 1972.
Braving the Elements. New York, Atheneum, 1972; London, Chatto and Win-
   dus, 1973.
The Yellow Pages. Cambridge, Massachusetts, Temple Bar Bookshop, 1974.

Plays

The Bait (produced New York, 1953). Published in Artists' Theatre: Four
   Plays, edited by Herbert Machiz, New York, Grove Press, 1960.
The Immortal Husband (produced New York, 1955). Published in Playbook:
   Plays for a New Theatre, New York, New Directions, 1956.

Novels

The Seraglio. New York, Knopf, 1957; London, Chatto and Windus, 1958.
The (Diblos) Notebook. New York, Atheneum, and London, Chatto and Windus, 1965.

Manuscript Collection: Washington University, St. Louis.

Critical Studies: Interview, in Contemporary Literature (Madison, Wisconsin), ix,1,
1968; Alone with America by Richard Howard, New York, Atheneum, 1969; interview, in Saturday Review of the Arts (New York), December 1972; "Feux d'Artifice" by Stephen Yenser, in Poetry (Chicago), June 1973; Richard Saez, in Parnassus
(New York), 1974.

*   *   *

James Merrill was one of a group of particularly gifted young men who, beginning to write after World War II, extended the dominant neo-metaphysical mode of

mid-century American poetry into a final, popular phase during the 1950's. Others with whom he was loosely associated, although there was no formal school nor even, in the usual sense, a "movement," were such poets as Howard Nemerov, Richard Wilbur, William Meredith, and W. S. Merwin. In part their work represented a revulsion against the excessive sociality of the war, a retreat into private and immutable themes; and in part it was an attempt to carry on the successes of the previous poetic generation, and to exploit the esthetic principles of the reigning critics, especially John Crowe Ransom, Allen Tate, and R. P. Blackmur.

Merrill's poetry is characterized by a modest formality of utterance. Whether in fixed forms or free verse, he writes with a dry yet unpedantic diction which gives the effect of seriousness and intelligence on one hand, and of a certain detachment on the other. But in spite of this Eliotean impersonalism, his poetry relies far less on a rhetoric of heavy, self-conscious irony than that of most of his contemporaries; instead it is simply, gently understated. In retrospect his work of the fifties and early sixties seems better than some of the more "brilliant" work that was popular at the time. Generally, Merrill's themes are those of his, or probably any, age: death and birth and rebirth, the passage of time, appearance and reality, the role of imagination, etc. His poems, meditative and semi-dramatic, arise from private and domestic experience, from travel, from reading, from life in the academic and business worlds.

To say that this phase of American poetry has ended, however, is premature. It has changed, to a degree it has frayed out, and it has been superseded in popularity by the very different poetry of the Beat and Black Mountain poets. But those among the later neo-metaphysical poets who have retained their imaginative vigor and who have courageously stuck to their esthetic principles will certainly respond, as poets universally respond, to the changing life around them, and they will do so in terms of the kind of poetry they know best. Radical though these changes are, and will be, in contemporary America, to judge by his past-performance Merrill will be among the most successful in adapting to them.

– Hayden Carruth

MERWIN, W(illiam) S(tanley). American. Born in New York City, 30 September 1927. Educated at Princeton University, New Jersey, A.B. in English 1947. Married Diana Whalley in 1954. Tutor to Robert Graves' son, Mallorca, 1950; Playwright-in-Residence, Poet's Theatre, Cambridge, Massachusetts, 1956–57; Poetry Editor, *The Nation*, New York, 1962; Associate, Théâtre de la Cité, Lyons, France, 1964–65. Recipient: Yale Series of Younger Poets Award, 1952; *Kenyon Review* fellowship, 1954; National Institute of Arts and Letters grant, 1957; Arts Council of Great Britain bursary, 1957; Rabinowitz Research Fellowship, 1961; Bess Hokin Prize, 1962, and Harriet Monroe Memorial Prize, 1967 (*Poetry*, Chicago); Ford grant, 1964; Chapelbrook Award, 1966; National Endowment for the Arts grant, 1968; P.E.N. Translation Prize, 1969; Rockefeller grant, 1969; Pulitzer Prize, 1971; Academy of American Poets Fellowship, 1973; Shelley Memorial Award, 1974. Address: c/o Ford, Atheneum Publishers, 122 East 42nd Street, New York, New York 10017, U.S.A.

PUBLICATIONS

Verse

A Mask for Janus.   New Haven, Connecticut, Yale University Press, 1952.
The Dancing Bears.   New Haven, Connecticut, Yale University Press, 1954.
Green with Beasts.   London, Hart Davis, and New York, Knopf, 1956.
The Drunk in the Furnace.   New York, Macmillan, and London, Hart Davis, 1960.
The Moving Target: Poems.   New York, Atheneum, 1963; London, Hart Davis, 1967.
The Lice: Poems.   New York, Atheneum, 1967; London, Hart Davis, 1969.
Three Poems.   New York, Phoenix Book Shop, 1968.
Animae: Poems.   San Francisco, Kayak Books, 1969.
The Carrier of Ladders.   New York, Atheneum, 1970.
Signs: A Poem.   Iowa City, Stone Wall Press, 1971.
Chinese Figures: Second Series.   Mount Horeb, Wisconsin, Perishable Press, 1971.
Japanese Figures.   Santa Barbara, California, Unicorn Press, 1971.
Asian Figures.   New York, Atheneum, 1972.
Writings to an Unfinished Accompaniment.   New York, Atheneum, 1974.

Plays

Darkling Child, with Dido Milroy (produced 1956).
Favor Island (produced Cambridge, Massachusetts, 1957).
Eufemia, adaptation of the play by Lope de Rueda, in *Tulane Drama Review* (New Orleans), December !958.
The Cid, adaptation of the play by Corneille (produced Coventry, England, 1960). Published in *Classic Theatre,* edited by Eric Bentley, New York, Doubleday, 1961.
The Gilded West (produced Coventry, England, 1961).
Turcaret, adaptation of the play by Alain Lesage, in *Classic Theater,* edited by Eric Bentley, New York, Doubleday, 1961.
The False Confession, adaptation of the play by Marivaux (produced New York, 1963). Published in *Classic Theatre,* edited by Eric Bentley, New York, Doubleday, 1961.
Yerma, adaptation of the play by Garcia Lorca (produced New York, 1966).

Other

A New Right Arm (essay).   Oshkosh, Wisconsin, Road Runner Press,
Selected Translations, 1948–1968.   New York, Atheneum, 1968.
The Miner's Pale Children.   New York, Atheneum, 1970.

Editor, *West Wind: Supplement of American Poetry.*   London, Poetry Book Society, 1961.

Translator, *The Poem of the Cid.*   New York, New American Library, and London, Dent, 1959.
Translator, *The Satires of Perseus.*   Bloomington, Indiana University Press, 1961.

Translator, *Some Spanish Ballads.* London, Abelard Schuman, 1961; as
Spanish Ballads, New York, Doubleday, 1961.
Translator, *The Life of Lazarillo de Tormes: His Fortunes and Adversities.* New
ʸorḳ, Doubleday, 1962.
Translator, *The Song of Roland,* in *Medieval Epics.* New York, Modern Lib-
rary, 1963.
Translator, *Transparence of the World: Poems of Jean Follain.* New York,
Atheneum, 1969.
Translator, *Products of the Perfected Civilization: Selected Writings,* by Sebastian
Chamfort. New York, Macmillan, 1969.
Translator, *Voices: Selected Writings of Antonio Porchia.* Chicago, Follett,
1969.
Translator, *Twenty Love Poems and a Song of Despair,* by Pablo Neruda. Lon-
don, Cape, 1969.
Translator, with others, *Selected Poems: A Bilingual Edition,* by Pablo Neruda,
edited by Nathaniel Tarn. London, Cape, 1969; New York, Delacorte
Press, 1972.
Translator, with Clarence Brown, *Selected Poems of Osip Mandelstam.* London,
Oxford University Press, 1973; New York, Atheneum, 1974.

Bibliography: "Seven Princeton Poets," in *Princeton Library Chronicle* (New Jersey), Autumn 1963.

Critical Studies: "W. S. Merwin Issue" of *Hollins Critic* (Hollins College, Virginia)
June 1968; *Alone with America* by Richard Howard, New York, Atheneum, 1969.

*   *   *

W. S. Merwin has been, during the past two decades, one of the most prolific of
American poets. He has published several books of his own poetry, and numerous
books of translations, including such major works as *The Song of Roland* and *The
Poem of the Cid.* He has a thorough knowledge of several European languages, a
broad acquaintance with all European literature – ancient, medieval, and modern –
and he has lived in Europe, chiefly in England and France, for many years. Hence
his development as a poet has been somewhat divergent from the main course of
American poetry at home. Where American poetry of recent years may be broadly
characterized by its movement away from the Yeatsian symbolism of mid-century
and toward the objectivism of Williams and Zukofsky, Merwin's recent poetry has
shown an affinity with the linguistic experiments of modern French verse, moving
toward ultra-symbolism and ultra-surrealism.

He began, however, like most poets of his age, squarely in the symbolist tradition. His first two books are roughly divided between long meditations, lyrico-
dramatic in form, on esthetic and epistemological themes, somewhat in the manner
of Wallace Stevens, and short lyrics with a seventeenth-century flavor. Some of
these latter, like "When I Came from Colchis" and "Song of Three Smiles," are
deservedly famous; no poet has excelled Merwin in his ability to combine syntax,
rhyme, and simple metaphor into musical structures of gentle irony. But clearly he
became dissatisfied with the artifice of these poems, and in his next books he
turned toward a plainer style, sometimes verging on the narrative techniques of
Robert Frost, in which he explored themes from his personal and family history,
relationships to nature, etc. Again, however, he became dissatisfied with what he
was doing, and after a few years moved to escape, not this time from artifice, but

from triviality. He wanted poems which would reach to the center of his immediate psychic experience.

If we can trace a more or less consistent progression of linguistic experiment from Mallarmé through Apollinaire to Breton and Eluard, a progression with analogies in music and psychology, then Merwin's recent poetry appears to be a further step. He now writes poems which comprise discrete statement of metaphor, often superficially unrelated, which meet and combine at their remotest connotative extensions, where they produce an unexpected illumination of a fundamental emotional complex. He is like a modern composer; not an atonalist, far from it, but a row composer or, better, a jazz improviser working at the outer limits of the chordal series. Merwin has been hailed as the "new American surrealist," but this is a misleading simplification. His poems bear unmistakable evidence of conscious artistry and hard creative endeavor that are inimical to the motifs of spontaneity in doctrinaire surrealism. Though syntactically very different, Merwin's verse perhaps bears a closer resemblance to the work of Jean Follain.

On its surface, however, Merwin's recent poetry does conform to the contemporary American mode: unrhymed, freely metered, contained in a studiously simple but exact diction. In spite of their strangeness his best poems convey a sense of striking fitness and inevitability. To a certain extent the lyricism of his first poems has been revived, but now with a more certain and necessary connection to the poem's inner substance. Some of his new poems are attempts to define the personal experience of social break-up, and perhaps it is significant that in 1968 Merwin returned to the United States, after many years abroad, on a visit which has been prolonged into an apparently permanent stay. Contemporary American criticism, in its methodological poverty, is scarcely fitted to deal with Merwin's poetry, with the result that many published statements about his work are sheer critical folly; but among fellow poets and serious readers his new work is awaited with an eagerness of attention that is accorded to few other writers in America.

– Hayden Carruth

MEYERS, Bert. Member of the English Department, Pitzer College, Claremont, California. Lives in Claremont, California.

Publications

Verse

Early Rain. Denver, Swallow, 1960.
The Dark Birds. New York, Doubleday, 1968.

Other

Translator, with Odette Meyers, *Lord of the Village*, by François Dodat. Reno, Nevada, West Coast Poetry Review, 1973.

*   *   *

Bert Meyers' language is lucid and unambiguous. His imagery is the most striking aspect of his work, particularly the presence in it of two distinct kinds. The first is a familiar kind of metaphor which at its best can be witty, as with the pigeons who "fly by / applauding themselves" ("Pigeons"), or elegiac, as in "People were flowers that grew by the shore;/ twilight takes them home,/ they fade together at their tables" ("Gulls Have Come Again"), or sensuously evocative, as in "October smokes a long cigar / and hangs its leather in the sun" ("October Poem"). But such images can also seem ostentatious or appliquéd: "airplanes punch the town with invisible fists of sound" ("Icon"), or "A needle's eye / in his tattered head / is losing his life's thread" ("The Accident"). These neither stimulate the mind nor challenge the emotions.

But Meyers also offers images which invite meditation rather than explication and have obvious affinities with the "deep image" of such diverse voices as Robert Bly and Jerome Rothenberg. Not that the *kind* guarantees success. "Surely a dead moth's / the skull of a tiny horse,/ and the moon's a saint / who pities the sea" ("Funeral") – only the first half of this pair wins assent, the emotionalism of the second seeming factitious. An image can look like the first kind but get its power from being the second, as in "The huge root lies like a head / on a vacant field" where what matters is not the visual analogy but the ominous and mysterious feeling. This kind of imagery sustains Meyers' best poems, such as "Cigarette" ("You sigh as you tap / your way to the end. / The hand is a blind child / called to the blackboard") or his best single piece, "Windy Night":

> The sound of the wind
> is the sound of a man
> alone with himself
> in the forest of sleep.
>
> A tree, a mind holding on.
>
> So many dry leaves fall,
> then at last the rain.

– Seamus Cooney

MEZEY, Robert. American. Born in Philadelphia, Pennsylvania, 28 February 1935. Educated at Kenyon College, Gambier, Ohio, 1951–53; University of Iowa, Iowa City, 1956–60, B.A. 1959; Stanford University, California (Poetry Fellow, 1961), 1960–61. Served in the United States Army, 1953–55: discharged as subversive. Married Ollie Simpson in 1963; has two daughters and one son. Instructor, Western Reserve University, Cleveland, 1963–64, and Franklin and Marshall College, Lancaster, Pennsylvania, 1965–66; Assistant Professor, Fresno State University, California, 1967–68. Currently, Associate Professor of English, University of Utah, Salt Lake City. Currently, Poetry Editor, *TransPacific*, Yellow Springs, Ohio. Recipient: Lamont Poetry Selection Award, 1960; Ingram Merrill Foundation Fellowship, 1973. Address: 116 Q Street, Salt Lake City, Utah 84103, U.S.A.

PUBLICATIONS

Verse

Berg Goodman Mezey: Poems. Philadelphia, New Ventures Press, 1957.
The Wandering Jew. Mount Vernon, Iowa, Hillside Press, 1960.
The Lovemaker: Poems. Iowa City, Cummington Press, 1961.
White Blossoms: Poems. Iowa City, Cummington Press, 1965.
Favors. Fresno, California, privately printed, 1968.
The Book of Dying: Poems. Santa Cruz, California, Kayak Books, 1970.
The Door Standing Open: New and Selected Poems 1954–1969. Boston, Houghton Mifflin, and London, Oxford University Press, 1970.

Other

Last Words: for John Lawrence Simpson, 1896–1969. Iowa City, Cummington Press, 1970.

Editor, with Stephen Berg, *Naked Poetry: Recent American Poetry in Open Forms.* Indianapolis, Bobbs Merrill, 1969.
Editor and Translator, *Poems from the Hebrew.* New York, Crowell, 1973.

Translator, *The Mercy of Sorrow*, by Uri Zri Greenberg. Philadelphia, Three People Press, 1965.

Critical Study: by Ralph J. Mills, Jr., in *American Poetry Review* (Philadelphia), Fall 1974.

Robert Mezey comments:

There are many schools of poetry; I don't feel allegiance to any. Of my contemporaries, I especially admire Galway Kinnell, Bob Dylan, Philip Levine, Charles Simic, Luis Salinas.

My poems are largely mysterious to me – I don't want to analyze them. I have written love poems, poems of outrage at daily universal fraud and cruelty, expressions of gratitude to mountains and trees, jokes, messages, enigmas, obscenities. My theme is mortality and life everlasting. Influences: Catullus, Po Chu-i, Herbert (both George and Zbigniew), Ecclesiastes, Blake, Clare, Loren Eiseley, Cabeza de Vaca, Sam Cooke, Kenneth Rexroth, Issa Archilocus, John Fowles, and a dog named Nina.

*   *   *

Robert Mezey is a metaphysical poet not because like Donne he ransacks scholastic philosophy for images, but because like Hamlet and all true metaphysicians he is given to asking unanswerable questions about himself and the world. He is not, however, a "philosophical poet." A great weight of passion accumulates behind his studied reserve and what finally emerges over the dam is intensely felt, tightly controlled poetry.

Early in his career, Robert Mezey came under the influence of the formalist critic and poet Yvor Winters, and *The Lovemaker*, Mr. Mezey's early book, betrays this influence clearly. Of Winters and his own subsequent development he writes wryly in a note appended to a group of his poems in *Naked Poetry*, an anthology of American poems in open forms edited by himself and Stephen Berg:

> When I was quite young I came under unhealthy influences – Yvor Winters, for example, and America, and my mother, though not in that order. Yvor Winters was easy to exorcise; all I had to do was meet him. My mother and America are another story and why tell it in prose?
>
> Once in Iowa City a friend said, "Why do you write in rhyme and meter? Your poetry is nothing like your life." "What do we know of another's life," I thought, but I had nothing to say. I no longer write in rhyme and meter, and still my life is not much like my poetry. At least, I don't think so. It is possible I'm not a poet at all. But I am a man, a Piscean, and unhappy, and therefore I make up poems.

Robert Mezey is a poet all right and an important one, but there is no doubt that a kind of passionate melancholy underlies most of his poetry. Yeats said "Out of our quarrel with the world we make rhetoric; out of the quarrel with ourselves, poetry"; Mr. Mezey is never rhetorical, but his quarrel really seems to be with the nature of things. He avoids the Hardian rhetoric against the universe through the adroit use of images which supply objective correlatives for his own moods. In "There," for example, microcosm (the poet) and macrocosm (the world) seem to fuse together:

> It is deep summer. Far out
> at sea the young squalls darken
> and roll, plunging northward,
> threatening everything. I see
> the Atlantic moving in slow
> contemplative fury
> against the rocks, the frozen
> headlands, and the towns sunk deep
> in a blind northern light. Here,
> far inland, in the mountains
> of Mexico, it is raining
> hard, battering the soft mouths
> of flowers. I am sullen, dumb,
> ungovernable. I taste myself
> and I taste those winds, uprisings
> of salt and ice, of great trees
> brought down, of houses and cries
> lost in the storm; and what breaks
> on that black shore breaks in me.

The tone here is perhaps more Byronic than usual in his poems, where urban images have their place along with natural ones. But the poem does show quite clearly his strategy for making turbid and passionate feelings objective through the use of corresponding images from the natural world.

Mr. Mezey thinks of himself as having abandoned traditional meter and rhyme. His and Berg's anthology is exclusively concerned with poems in what he calls "open form." Yet as one reads over the poem just quoted one becomes aware that a great measure of the force of the poem is owing to the tightly controlled rhythms employed. No line in the poem contains more than four stresses or less than three, a close approach to "regular" meter; yet these fluctuations in line length do much to suggest the fluctuating pressures of the storm and the sea. One senses too that such powerful rhythmic control had to be exerted to keep the poem from exploding all over the page. And the control over raw emotion manifests itself mainly through the poet's handling of rhythm.

Mr. Mezey obviously values clarity in a writer. Three things, I think, account for the unfailing clarity of these passionate poems. Two have already been mentioned, sharp clear images, many of which turn out to be objective correlatives, rhythmic control, and frequent, unobtrusive, but effective employment of articulatory symbolism: the forced miming by the organs of speech of the very action or object being described. To illustrate, I quote from another of his poems about autumn, "Touch It." This is the second stanza:

> Past the thinning orchard the fields
> are on fire. A mountain of smoke
> climbs the desolate wind, and at its roots
> fire is eating dead grass with many small teeth.

The very shaping of the words in the final line here enforces upon the reader a sort of *chewing* action. Or again, in "There,"

> it is raining
> hard, battering the soft mouths
> of flowers

simply shaping the words pantomimes the effect the words describe.

These three factors, and perhaps many more that have escaped me, but at least these three, make possible shaping the raw emotion of these poems toward the extraordinary clarity they achieve.

– E. L. Mayo

MICHIE, James. British. Born in London in 1927. Educated at Trinity College, Oxford. Worked as an Editor, and as a Lecturer at London University. Currently, Director, The Bodley Head, publishers, London.

PUBLICATIONS

Verse

Possible Laughter. London, Hart Davis, 1959.

Other

Editor, with Kingsley Amis, *Oxford Poetry 1949.* Oxford, Blackwell, 1949.
Editor, *The Bodley Head Book of Longer Short Stories.* London, Bodley Head, 1974.

Translator, *The Odes of Horace.* New York, Orion, 1963; London, Hart Davis, 1964.

Translator, *The Poems of Catullus: A Bilingual Edition.* London, Hart Davis, and New York, Random House, 1969.

Translator, *The Epigrams of Martial.* London, Hart Davis, MacGibbon and New York, Random House, 1973.

*   *   *

James Michie is better known as a translator, probably, than as an original poet, which is hardly surprising considering the wit and energy of his versions of Horace, Catullus and Martial. These translations are not "modern" in the usual sense – they have nothing in common, for example, with the free renderings and "homages" of Pound or Lowell – but are cast in the neo-classical tradition of Pope and Dryden in which the order of English rhyme and meter offers a kind of substitute satisfaction for the unrenderable richnesses of Latin. Thus Catullus' celebrated

> Odi et amo. Quare id faciam, fortasse requiris?
> Nescio, sed fieri sentio et excrucior

becomes, in Michie's version,

> I hate and love. If you ask me to explain
>   The contradiction,
> I can't, but I can feel it, and the pain
>   Is crucifixion.

Michie's own poetry thus far is collected in one slender volume – very slender indeed, with thirty-two poems, few of which are longer than a page. They reflect some of the qualities of the Latin verse which Michie has translated, the economy, the sophistication and particularly the good natured cynicism about human nature. The chief English influence seems to have been the light (but serious) black doggerel of Auden during the 'thirties, with its popular ballad forms and quick, surprising imagery. In "Quiet, Child," for example, Michie observes

> Glumly we chew on with murder
>   Long past the appetite of hate.
> Nothing but their shadows' outlines
>   Left, like grease-stains on a plate,
> People leaning over bridges
>   Quietly evaporate.
>
> And big as a telephone directory
>   His bomber's casualty list,
> Gloved, the pilot leaves behind him,
>   Represented by a mist,
> Individuals who were furious,
>   But no longer now exist.

The poems vary considerably in theme and metrical form, from the Betjeman-like "Park Concert" to the more troubled, individual voice of "Nightmare" and "At Any Rate," with their darker observations about human cruelty and helplessness. Time is the enemy, with its subtle erosions:

The hours, pretending they do not know how to combine,
Walk up as charming freebooters, unarmed, disclaiming
Allegiance to that remote and iron-grey battle-line.

Fidelity is weak. The lovers may

>   hold like amulets
>   Precious hands, or go linking
>   Arms, but no one gets
>   Cleanly through without slinking.
>   Quite innocent,
>   Moving to kiss, although they hadn't meant
>   It, they'll find themselves archly winking.

The prevailing tone of Michie's verse, however, is neither brutal nor tragic but much more in the spirit of the wise man in "The End of the Sage" who dies

>   "Much wiser and much dafter,
>   Now that I quite agree
>   To become dead,
>   I achieve a witticism,
>   And I see at last," he said,
>   "Hazy like foothills possible laughter."

– Elmer Borklund

MIDDLETON, (John) Christopher. British. Born in Truro, Cornwall, 10 June 1926. Educated at Felsted School, Essex; Merton College, Oxford, B.A. 1951, D.Phil. 1954. Served in the Royal Air Force, 1944–48. Married Mary Freer in 1953; has three children. Lecturer in English, Zurich University, 1952–55; Senior Lecturer in German, King's College, University of London. Since 1965, Professor of Germanic Languages and Literature, University of Texas, Austin. Recipient: Geoffrey Faber Memorial Prize, 1964; Guggenheim Fellowship, 1974. Address: Department of German, University of Texas, Austin, Texas 78712, U.S.A.

PUBLICATIONS

Verse

Poems. London, Fortune Press, 1944.
Nocturne in Eden: Poems. London, Fortune Press, 1945.
Torse 3: Poems 1949–1961. London, Longman, and New York, Harcourt Brace, 1962.
Penguin Modern Poets 4, with David Holbrook and David Wevill. London, Penguin, 1963.
Nonsequences: Selfpoems. London, Longman, 1965; New York, Norton, 1966.
Our Flowers and Nice Bones. London, Fulcrum Press, 1969.

Die Taschenelefant: Satire. Berlin, Verlag Neue Rabenpresse, 1969.
The Fossil Fish: 15 Micropoems. Providence, Rhode Island, Burning Deck, 1970.
Briefcase History: 9 Poems. Providence, Rhode Island, Burning Deck, 1972.
Fractions for Another Telemachus. Rushden, Northamptonshire, Sceptre Press, 1974.

Play

The Metropolitans (libretto), music by Hans Vogt. Kassel, Alkor Editions, 1964.

Other

Editor and Translator, with Michael Hamburger, *Modern German Poetry 1910–1960: An Anthology with Verse Translations.* London, MacGibbon and Kee, and New York, Grove Press, 1962.
Editor and Translator, with William Burford, *The Poet's Vocation: Selections from the Letters of Hölderlin, Rimbaud, and Hart Crane.* Austin, University of Texas Press, 1967.
Editor, *German Writing Today.* London, Penguin, 1967.
Editor, *Selected Poems*, by Georg Trakl, translated by Robert Grenier and others. London, Cape, 1968.

Translator, *The Walk and Other Stories*, by Robert Walser. London, John Calder, 1957.
Translator, with others, *Primal Vision*, by Gottfried Benn. New York, New Directions, 1960.
Translator, with others, *Poems and Verse Plays*, by Hugo von Hoffmansthal. New York, Pantheon, 1961.
Translator, with Michael Hamburger, *Selected Poems*, by Günter Grass. London, Secker and Warburg, and New York, Harcourt Brace, 1966.
Translator, *Jakob von Gunter*, by Robert Walser. Austin, University of Texas Press, 1969.
Translator, *Selected Letters*, by Friedrich Nietzsche. Chicago, University of Chicago Press, 1969.
Translator, with Michael Hamburger, *Poems*, by Günter Grass. London, Penguin, 1969.
Translator, *The Quest for Christa T.*, by Christa Wolf. New York, Farrar Straus, 1970.
Translator, with Michael Hamburger, *Selected Poems*, by Paul Celan. London, Penguin, 1972.
Translator, *Selected Poems*, by Friedrich Hölderlin and Eduard Mörike. Chicago, University of Chicago Press, 1972.
Translator, *Inmarypraise* by Gunter Grass. New York, Harcourt Brace, 1974.
Translator, *Kafka's Other Trial: The Letters to Felice*, by Elias Canetti. New York, Schocken Books, 1974.

*   *   *

Christopher Middleton's work claims attention both for its extraordinary technical skill and because it is the meeting point of many influences. Middleton is well-known for his translations of German poetry, and, naturally enough, one detects in his own poetry affinities with that which has been written in post-war Germany, notably by the members of the "group of 47" who are his contemporaries. Middleton, however, lacks the close engagement with contemporary politics which has been the hallmark of much German poetry. What he possesses instead is an engagement with the notion of literature, with the *ways* of saying something, as well as with the subject-matter itself. The two earliest books of verse he now acknowledges, *Torse 3* and *Nonsequences*, are very various, but nearly every poem is marked by a characteristic obliqueness. The poet deliberately reminds the reader of this in the epigraph to the first of these volumes, which is one of the definitions of the word "torse," taken from the *Shorter Oxford English Dictionary:* "A developable surface; a surface generated by a moving straight line which at every instant is turning, in some plane or other through it, about some point or other in its length."

Middleton has also been one of the leading figures in the recent revival of "modernism" which has taken place in English verse – a revival which, paradoxically, has rather an antiquarian tinge about it. A poem such as "Southern Electric Teddygirl," in *Torse 3*, is based on material which could quite easily have attracted Philip Larkin, who is superficially a very different sort of writer. But the manner is that of early Eliot:

> Recrossing the ankles
> Her winkle-pickers bruise, to resume
> Into Orpington
> Her airy trail.

– Edward Lucie-Smith

MILES, Josephine (Louise). American. Born in Chicago, Illinois, 11 June 1911. Educated at the University of California, Los Angeles, A.B. 1932 (Phi Beta Kappa); University of California, Berkeley, M.A. 1934, Ph.D. 1938. Since 1940, Member of the English Department, and since 1973, University Professor, University of California, Berkeley. Recipient: Shelley Memorial Award, 1936; Phelan Award, 1937; American Association of University Women fellowship, 1939; Guggenheim Fellowship, 1948; National Institute of Arts and Letters grant, 1956; Oscar Blumenthal Prize (*Poetry,* Chicago), 1959; American Council of Learned Societies Fellowship, 1965; Linguistic Society of America Fellowship, 1967; National Endowment for the Arts grant, 1967. D.Litt.: Mills College, Oakland, California, 1965. Fellow, American Academy of Arts and Sciences. Address: 2275 Virginia Street, Berkeley, California 94709, U.S.A.

PUBLICATIONS

Verse

Lines at Intersection. New York, Macmillan, 1939.
Poems on Several Occasions. New York, New Directions, 1941.
Local Measures. New York, Reynal, 1946.

After This Sea. San Francisco, Book Club of California, 1947.
Prefabrications. Bloomington, Indiana University Press, 1955.
Poems, 1930–1960. Bloomington, Indiana University Press, 1960.
Civil Poems. Berkeley, California, Oyez, 1966.
Bent. Santa Barbara, California, Unicorn Press, 1967.
Kinds of Affection. Middletown, Connecticut, Wesleyan University Press, 1967.
Saving the Bay. San Francisco, Open Space, 1967.
Fields of Learning. Berkeley, California, Oyez, 1968.
American Poems. Berkeley, California, Cloud Marauder Press, 1970.
To All Appearances: New and Selected Poems. Urbana, University of Illinois Press, 1974.

Recording: *Today's Poets 2*, with others, Folkway, 1968.

Play

House and Home (produced Berkeley, California, 1960). Published in *First Stage* (Lafayette, Indiana), Fall 1965.

Other

Wordsworth and the Vocabulary of Emotion. Berkeley and Los Angeles, University of California Press, 1942.
Pathetic Fallacy in the 19th Century: A Study of the Changing Relation Between Object and Emotion. Berkeley and Los Angeles, University of California Press, 1942.
The Vocabulary of Poetry: Three Studies. Berkeley and Los Angeles, University of California Press, 1946.
The Continuity of Poetic Language: Studies in English Poetry from the 1540's to the 1940's. Berkeley, University of California Press, 1951.
  I. *The Primary Language of Poetry in the 1640's.* Berkeley, University of California Press, 1948.
  II. *The Primary Language of Poetry in the 1740's and 1840's.* Berkeley, University of California Press, 1950.
  III. *The Primary Language of Poetry in the 1940's.* Berkeley, University of California Press, 1951.
Eras and Modes in English Poetry. Berkeley, University of California Press, 1957; revised edition, 1964.
Renaissance, Eighteenth-Century and Modern Language in English Poetry: A Tabular View. Berkeley, University of California Press, 1960.
Ralph Waldo Emerson. Minneapolis, University of Minnesota Press, 1964.
Style and Proportion: The Language of Prose and Poetry. Boston, Little Brown, 1967.
Poetry and Change: Donne, Milton, Wordsworth, and the Equilibrium of the Present. Berkeley, University of California Press, 1974.

Editor, with Mark Schorer and Gordon McKenzie, *Criticism: The Foundations of Modern Literary Judgment.* New York, Harcourt Brace, 1948; revised edition, 1958.
Editor, with others, *Idea and Experiment.* Berkeley, University of California Press, 1950.

Editor, *The Poem: A Critical Anthology.* New York, Prentice Hall, 1959; revised edition as *The Ways of the Poem*, 1973.
Editor, *Classic Essays in English.* Boston, Little Brown, 1961; revised edition, 1965.

Translator, with others, *Modern Hindi Poetry.* Bloomington, Indiana University Press, 1965.

Manuscript Collections: State University of New York, Buffalo; Washington University, St. Louis; University of California, Berkeley.

Critical Studies: "Distance and Surfaces" by Robert Beloof, in *Prarie Schooner* (Lincoln, Nebraska), Winter 1958–59; in *Voyages* (Washington, D.C.), Fall 1968.

Josephine Miles comments:

Interest in poetry of spoken thought, of meditation, of literally making sense of ideas. Main themes, human doubt and amazement. A strong beat of meaning playing against the beat of pattern. Some critics say "western," but I am not aware of this.

*   *   *

Josephine Miles shares, with William Carlos Williams and his followers, credit for exalting "the American idiom" into the standard language of poetry – a feat surrounded by risk, by the danger of being charged with flatness and being forsaken by all but the most sensitive of critics. Her achievement is that she has successfully laid aside her academic powers (she is one of the land's best scholars) in order to paint with a great gentleness – and sense of their fragility and evanescence – the landscapes of the American scene – its speech, jazz, billboards, comics and assasinations, and those dark streets of towns where three creeks meet. She has raised these materials into a high form of poetry; and her insights in poems provide an enlightening commentary on American life. In clearing her vision of scholarship, in renouncing sophistication and working exclusively with native materials, Miss Miles offers, essentially, the *persona* of a Willa Cather schoolmarm discoursing gently on the wisdom she has acquired from the prairies and a few rides in tin cars. Even when confessing her scholarship ("Bad quartos were my first love") she remains matter of fact. Her skill is in rendering the quotidian stillness of an American street; and she avoids exoticism, even in her treatment of "Bombay" and "Tehachapi South." She is most at home rendering the sadness, the matter-of-factness, the every-evening miracle, of the moon rising over the lumber yard, and perhaps a whiskey bottle; the rendering is pure, strikes life's tonic note of recognition. Her work is at once primitive and sophisticated, like that of Chekhov and Dr. Williams. It must be said too that an undercurrent of sharp physical pain runs through her poems. The fact that she must *be* helped, physically, as well as offer her help to the world, must partly account for the strikingly developed theme of the acknowledgement of others – a sense of the connectedness of people, of obligation, of gratitude reciprocal and eternal. And her elegy on the death of John Kennedy is not only rhythmically enchanting and original, but is a major statement on violence in America, on the resentment of real *qualitas* in

American life, on the assertion of mediocrity and the insistence of enshrining it or turning power over to it: with the metaphor of Daniel Boone's shooting of the bear, Miss Miles transforms history and myth in such a way that many readers feel that she alone has offered an adequate explanation for the Kennedy assassination. Her work imparts the riches of a rare and compassionate sensibility.

– David Ray

MILLER, Vassar (Morrison). American. Born in Houston, Texas, 19 July 1924. Educated at the University of Houston, B.S. 1947, M.A. 1952. Formerly, Instructor in Creative Writing, St. John's School, Houston. Address: 1615 Vassar Street, Houston, Texas 77006, U.S.A.

PUBLICATIONS

Verse

Adam's Footprint. New Orleans, New Orleans Poetry Journal, 1956.
Wage War on Silence: A Book of Poems. Middletown, Connecticut, Wesleyan University Press, 1960.
My Bones Being Wiser: Poems. Middletown, Connecticut, Wesleyan University Press, 1963.
Onions and Roses. Middletown, Connecticut, Wesleyan University Press, 1968.
If I Could Sleep Deeply Enough. New York, Liveright, 1974.

Vassar Miller comments:

Traditional lyrics, but also free verse and syllabic. Religious themes, though also more humanistic of late.

*   *   *

To say that Vassar Miller was once Poet Laureate of Texas (1963) may raise some eyebrows and evoke glib remarks about the sweet singer of the purple sage. Any such response is at once stopped by even a cursory reading of her deeply felt, spare poems. In the midst of an expanding society (she is a native of Houston, Texas) she is an interior poet, modest in diction without being trivial in theme. Rather than sing the vastness of the Western Spirit, she examines in carefully wrought poems the individual soul in the individual body; and her poems body forth the implications for us all of her experience. Many of her best poems are what we call "religious" – but they are religious in the quiet mode of Herbert, rather than in the more convoluted and even shrill manner of Crashaw and Berryman. She does not wish to believe; she believes. Nor does she deny the hard realities and difficulties of writing about the religious experience, though she writes from the assurance of faith (perhaps even grace) and the stability of a fully civilized sensibility. Some of her poems are damaged by easy rhetorical victories (as when Pontius Pilate says "The gods will play some joke – / And then get angry every time it works"), trite phrasing ("the afternoons so beautiful"), cliché of emotional response (as in the set responses to religious holidays and E. B. Browning's grave), and even rigid metrical handling ("It would be best to travel light / Between the darkness and the light"). Her best poems avoid these faults. She is most successful in traditional forms, as in the villanelle "Hot Air" ("Soft my pleasure came") and in the sonnet, as in "Reverent Impiety," "Judas," and many others. And although many of her secular poems are moving ("So that I felt relief / to see your existence wrapped up / in death's lying precision, / pomp prayed and sung / then given discreetly to / the lithe ruin of worms"), and some explore the meanings of love in animal imagery to powerful effect ("the dog whines, rattling her chain, / not comprehending her crime / when her occupation is love"), Miller's best work remains in her religious poems, as in the sonnet "The Wisdom of Insecurity" which contains the lines: "God will not play our games nor join our fun, / Does not give tit for tat, parade His glories. / And chance is chance, not providence dressed neat, / Credentials hidden in its wooden leg." Miller's books (*My Bones Being Wiser* is the best of her published volumes) are all informed by hard intelligence, insight, and a gift for language.

– James Korges

MILLWARD, Eric. British. Born in Longnor, Staffordshire, 12 March 1935. Educated at Longnor Church of England School, 1941–46; Buxton College, 1946–54. Married Anne Craig in 1961; has two sons. Currently, Chief Steward, British Airtours Ltd., Gatwick Airport, Surrey. Since 1971, Secretary, Conservation Society, Sussex Branch. Since 1973, Poetry Editor, *Towards Survival*, Coventry. Address: Hope Cottage, 67 Hillside, Horsham, Sussex, England.

PUBLICATIONS

Verse

A Child in the Park.   Walton-on-Thames, Surrey, Outposts Publications, 1969.

Eric Millward comments:

My work has been mainly poetry, but contains occasional short stories, mostly of a futuristic nature.

Of late, poems have dealt increasingly with care for, and proper treatment of, the earth and *all* its inhabitants, resulting in the recently completed collection, *Earthwords.*

*   *   *

The work of Eric Millward has appeared in magazines and anthologies for more than a decade now. Yet it has never achieved permanence between the covers of a hard-back volume. However, of many uncollected poets, he is one whose poems deserve collection.

Eric Millward's verse at first sight seems to relate to a tradition deriving from Clare, Hardy, Edward Thomas and Edmund Bluden. But he is not, any more than these earlier poets, simply pastoral. His themes are various, as instanced by the titles of his better poems: "Children with Hands," "Spastic," "Cows," "The Girl's Confession," "The Widow's Bird," "Mrs. Monk," "When His Wife Died," "Sudden Rain," "A Short Life," "The Cat Returns," "A Winter Wedding" and (perhaps the two best) "Freeing a Bird" and "A Child in the Park." These last two are essentially religious poems. The plot of "Freeing a Bird" unfolds itself with a decision of narrative that builds up the sense that the sparrow will eventually fall into our hands as we, in our turn, fall into the hands of God. The point is not insisted upon, but, when caught at length, the sparrow is "a sheeted bundle" and it is thrown out into the night "like crumbs." What comes out clearly is the alienation between one species and another and the sense that there is a similar lack of contact between man and his maker:

> And we, who might perhaps presume to teach,
> Should count the missions we initiate
> That end in failure to communicate.

"A Child in the Park" is a poem of the same kind. It is a meditative lyric on a large scale, couched in metres which are traditional but highly expressive. Like the previous poem, it recounts a story with a strongly allegorical bent:

> It may be some perverse desire
> For pain that lets me watch my child
> Wander away in the terrible park
> Towards a distant target, called
> By a half-heard, compelling bark
> To cuddle some ungainly cur . . .

The child, of course, loses his perspective and finds himself alone. Naturally, the father obeys his instinct to run after the child and soothe his fears. But the allegory becomes marked if we mentally capitalize the protagonists, for the final stanzas are a reproach by the mortal Child of the heavenly Father:

> Thus, it is said, we are allowed
> To wander in our wider park,
> The staying word withheld, until,
> Straying toward the half-heard bark,
> We totter, lose our balance, fall,
> Are then set up and reassured.
>
> Yet hardly can this claim be proof
> Of ultimate love while some still fall
> Who go unaided to their fate.
> Could fathers find acceptable
> A love which can discriminate,
> To one child's cry remain aloof?
>
> Meanwhile we wandering children move
> Within our park, unheld by hands,
> Some finding peace which grows from trust
> In power that loves and understands;
> Some, loving children, doubting, must
> Concede the power, question the love.

To call Eric Millward a religious poet seems true enough, but the statement must be qualified. This poetry is, for all its formal certainty, allied to the reproaches, the questionings, the cries like dead letters sent by a line of poets, from Donne to Andrew Young, which constitute a major English tradition. The poems of Eric Millward, collected and made available to the public, would show him to be one of the most distinguished representatives of that tradition today.

– Philip Hobsbaum

MILNE, (Charles) Ewart. Irish. Born in Dublin, 29 May 1903. Educated at Nuns Cross National School, Wicklow; Christ Church Cathedral Grammar School, Dublin. Married Kathleen Ida Bradner in 1927 (marriage dissolved), has one son; Thelma Dobson in 1948, has two sons. Formerly, teacher; seaman, 1920–30; Book Reviewer, *Irish Times*, Dublin; Staff Member, *Ireland Today*, Dublin, 1937–40; Estate Farm Manager, 1947–61. Since 1968, Book Reviewer, *The Irish Press*, Dublin. Throughout his career, an "inveterate letter-writer." Address: 46 De Parys Avenue, Bedford, England.

Publications

Verse

Forty North, Fifty West.   Dublin, Gayfield Press, 1938.
Letter from Ireland.   Dublin, Gayfield Press, 1940.
Listen Mangan: Poems.   Dublin, At the Sign of the Three Candles Press, 1941.
Jubilo: Poems.   London, Muller, 1944.
Boding Day: Poems.   London, Muller, 1947.
Diamond Cut Diamond: Selected Poems.   London, Bodley Head, 1950.
Elegy for a Lost Submarine.   Burnham on Crouch, Essex, Plow Poems, 1951.
Galion: A Poem.   Dublin, Dolmen Press, 1953.
Life Arboreal.   Tunbridge Wells, Kent, Pound Press, 1953.
Once More to Tourney: A Book of Ballads and Light Verse, Serious, Gay, and Grisly.   London, Linden Press, 1958.
A Garland for the Green.   London, Hutchinson, 1962.
Time Stopped: A Poem Sequence with Prose Intermissions.   London, Plow Poems, 1967.

Manuscript Collection: State University of New York, Buffalo.

Cricitical Studies: "Self Portrait" by the author, in *Poetry Ireland* (Dublin), April 1949; "The Poetry of Ewart Milne" by Peter Russell, in *Chantecleer* (London) i,3, 1953; "The Poetry of Ewart Milne" by Lawrence Lipton, in *Poetry* (Chicago), September 1955; *A Poet's War: British Poets in the Spanish Civil War,* by Hugh Ford,

Philadelphia, University of Pennsylvania Press, 1965; "Recent Poetry" by Terry Eagleton, in *Stand* (Newcastle upon Tyne), 1967; Penelope Palmer, in *Agenda* (London), 1968.

Ewart Milne comments:

I am not very interested in writing about my work in poetry, "talking shop" as it seems to me, and I think the best way a poet can introduce his work to the public is through the verse itself. After all, to ask a hen how (and why) it lays an egg would surely seem pretty pointless, if not downright ridiculous, to her, though no doubt if pressed, and being a patient fowl, she might reply that no egg was ever laid without toil, and sometimes painful toil, at that! So with me, for although some of my poems have been well-nigh spontaneous creations, taken down in longhand and then typed out with scarcely any alterations, in the main they begin as bits and pieces, or semi-finished pieces, which have to be worked over and polished again and again. Sometimes I write them as prose pieces, as Yeats said he did, and then work them up until they satisfy me, either in their rhythmic sound, or roughly speaking in classical metre and shape. It is all protracted and heavy toil – the idea being that the end-product should show no signs of the blood, sweat, and tears that went into its making. Afterwards there is usually some sense of exaltation, of triumph and pride – but this is often short-lived, and followed by a depression which insists the piece is not yet up to scratch, and one must start over again.

In a previous biographical sketch, I wrote of my Anglo-Irish Dublin background (in a Protestant household), and mentioned the Elizabethan and Romantic periods as among the chief formative influences of my early days. But circumstances also played a part, indeed a chief part: since as well as "the troubles," there was not really enough family money for me to go to Trinity College, so I went to sea instead; and so on. Quite early, too, I read Hardy's novels, and some of his poetry, and it was his "philosophy" (of scientific humanism) that seemed nearest my own outlook, when Church of Ireland teachings were slipping away. But given that one was subject to circumstance and chance, and the "Immament Will" of Him I thought of as the great "Stone Father," one could still plot out one's own graph, although caged one could still sing, one could express one's ideas, in a chosen medium (once one had found that medium), about it all. Had not Matthew Arnold said that the real function of poetry was the application of ideas to life? In the Thirties – and I wrote little poetry though a lot of prose before 1930 – this "application of ideas" to include social attitudes and political ideologies was acceptable and fashionable, following the breaking by Eliot and Pound of the strait-jacket into which the Georgians had tightlaced English poetry, or so it was held. But though I included politics, or rather a half-baked philosophy about politics, in my poet's repertoire, I was just as interested in the cat on the mat – and the rat on the mat, for that matter. And not simply because of any ideas I might have had about them, but because of what they looked like to me, objectively. And subjectively, since although I don't at all *want* to be "part of all that I have met," willy-nilly, ruefully, I am.

Now because some of my then work was rhetorical to a degree – and has been so since – and although it doesn't seem to me important whether a poet writes in accentual hexameters or blank verse, or that most unfree of poetic dictions, rhythmic free verse, provided that *what* he says fits like a glove with *how* he says it, perhaps I had better put in a word on my attitude to rhetoric. Beside, the word itself is presently one of the literary dirty words, to be flung by poets and poetry critics at poets whose work displeases in outlook. Sometimes it's difficult to know what they mean by rhetoric, since they all mean different things. Rhetoric is not poetry in itself, but some good poetry, at any rate in the past, has been rhetorical in tone and framework. I would say most "committed" poetry is *bound* to be rhetorical, to some degree. On the other hand, W. H. Auden recently condemned some of his early work, that of his "pink" Thirties period, on the grounds that it was too rhetorical, and that it had not saved one Jew from the Gas-chambers. It would be difficult to argue the point on this, and I won't try. But to keep Mr. Auden company, I would say that I abjure and renounce quite a number of my own poems over even a longer period, that between the Thirties and the Sixties, indeed: but it is precisely for their *content* – for their Leftish outlook, above all where any pro-Soviet views were expressed – that I do so. Bad politics, or woefully mistaken politics, must lead to bad rhetoric, I've no doubt, and to even worse poetry. However, while seeking to extenuate nothing, I may perhaps point out that there was then a rising gale blowing across the sociological-political arenas of the world, when I (speaking here only for myself) was trying to get my head out from under the huge wings of Eliot, Pound, and Yeats, and what with taking some of the gale in the teeth, and coping with such towering literary fathers, it *was* a struggle. Perhaps those of us who survived with voices recognisably our own were lucky, however much we owed (or thought we owed) to our protogenetic parents.

Oddly, perhaps, my own early period, that of the late Twenties, was not "pink" at all, but straightforward literary, and influenced mainly by Hardy and Lawrence. But it was mostly prose, short stories, I was trying to write, and little of it survived. And in the Thirties, it was not one's poetry that was noticed, so much as one's *politics.* Even so, my colour then was not so much pink as orange, white, and green (in that order). Pink came later, or rather red. Don't ask me to colour myself or my work *now*, since the answer is obvious: deep blue! Just the same, I believe poets will never really be at home in politics, no matter of what shade, right across the spectrum. "Pick up a stone, look at it, handle it, and then hammer out some words to express stone as a universal truth, and in relation to yourself," said an artist friend of my early days to me. It was an old truth, but he meant that what mattered was the language the poets used, or I should say, created, in the re-statement of old truths in new terms. Any true poet must create a new language, *his* language, recognisable as his and only his. That is really what he is required to do, his vital task, and nothing less. But he need not drag the actual tongue in which he creates out by the roots to make his own speech-song – though, like the later Joyce, he may feel obliged to. Moreover, do what he may to mask and disguise it, the poet's own character, or lack of character, *will* show up in his poetry. There are exceptions, yes. What sort of character had Shakespeare, what sort of a character was he? Does anyone know, does Dr. Rowse really know? Certainly *I* don't! Neither do I know if "there is a Divinity which shapes our ends," but some poems, and some poets, seem to me trail *something* Divine as they go: and they are not necessarily those who subscribe either to the forms of religion or of atheism – or of humanistic politics.

All that concerns me is to sketch and paint and present, like a moving panoramic graph, poems of circumstance and allegory and ballad and true story, as affecting my own life, and of my past in relation to my present, as objectively and effec-tively as I can, with pieces also of inconsequential irrelevance that is part of my make-up, and thus of my poetry, which *is* my way of life. I am strict only to make sure the voice is my own, with as few echoes of other voices as possible, except where I may catch an echo of some dead poet, like a star from the air. And to sift and retain the more significant among my notes in my workshop, and work on them, as a diamond-cutter might work on a rough stone. I am an experimenter in everything I do in life, I teach myself how as I go along, and in poetry this means that I compose a poem as the lines occur to me, and leave them and come back to them, and chisel away at them, or paint them up or down, depending whether they seem like a bit of sculpture or a portrait or landscape. But I repeat once more, poetry is my way of life (and one can become savagely rejectful of one's way of life, as is known), as surely as sculpture and painting are the ways of life of sculptors and artists. It is still necessary to say this, here in the Western world on the edge of Europe. Praise or blame about my work, though I value criticism and have had far too little of it of any value, make not the slightest difference to me now, and really, they never did. I may be uplifted by praise: cast down by blame, but both conditions are superficial and indeed extraneous to me as, busily spinning words like silken threads from myself, I weave about me a coloured cloak that will cocoon me when I sleep. Indifference, not praise or blame, is the real killer for poets as for any artists. But I doubt if indifference is overcome by the kind of ego-incest about themselves and their work which is all too prevalent in national and regional poetry circles today. Which brings me back to where I began by saying I am not greatly interested in writing about myself and/or my work. The personality is whom I am least interested in the world is my own.

*   *   *

Ewart Milne began to write in the late thirties when the new poets were concerned with political and social problems. He has published a dozen volumes, widely ranging in their themes and varied in their moods. He spent some years in the British Merchant Navy, became a teacher, was for some time an ambulance driver in the Spanish Civil War. Of his experiences at sea he has written little except for the moving "Elegy for a Lost Submarine," and an effective allegory, "The Waterside Poem":

> Shanghaied aboard
> We signed on later because we must.
> In a smelly cabin among charts and paraffin
> We signed on for the round trip:
> Where we were bound for had been left blank.
>
> And a hard going we had of it.
> You were below then, in the stokehold, while I
> Swung overside in a bosun's chair
> Was repainting the ship's name on the rusty bow.
> Her name was, as I remember, the steamship Earth.

He has written a number of moving poems, however, about the tragic events which he witnessed in Spain. He has experimented in diverse metrical forms but usually writes in free verse. His opinions are Leftist, but he avoids purely political themes and concentrates on social conditions in Ireland and elsewhere.

A Garland for the Green was inspired by his return to his native country and is romantic in its mood. In contrast, two successive volumes, *Letter from Ireland* and *Listen Mangan*, are satiric in modd. His style is direct and, by disciplined selection, can, at its best, be evocative, as in "Tinker's Moon":

> A potato patch to thin on the way, a hen to kill,
> And hunger again: and sleep again:
> And a moonlight flit while the salmon leaps
> From a smouldering spot by the riverside;
> The tinker's children take their chance, and bide.

Once More to Tourney is, as the subtitle indicates, a book of light verse, gay and grisly by turn. In an introduction to this volume, Mr. J. M. Cohen notes that the poet has a voice of his own and belongs to no school: "His poems are as easy to read as nursery-rhymes, and as tough as a saloon-bar argument."

Mr. Milne's most recent volume, *Time Stopped*, is a long dramatic poem in a variety of measures, mostly rhymed, deeply tragic in its mood. Written in the first person, it describes how a poet discovers from the letters after her death that his wife had been unfaithful to him with a friend of his. By the use of deliberate plain statement, the tragic mood is set:

> In nineteen sixty-four the United States Medical Council
> Decreed that cigarette smoking constituted a health hazard
> And could cause death from lung cancer; in that year
> In that summer in that September when you died

The bitterness and disillusion expressed in the poem will remind readers of *Modern Love*, that cycle of irregular sonnets by George Meredith. Even in its despairing mood, the poem is guarded by its own discipline:

> I sat by her bedside and watched her die
> And the hopeless and defeated one   that was I
> The helpless one the condemned one   that was I
> Left over   left to live on   mercilessly
> Left with the fallen bricks of my house of poetry.

– Austin Clarke

MITCHELL, Adrian. British. Born in London, 24 October 1932. Educated at Dauntsey's School, Wiltshire; Christ Church, Oxford (Editor, *Isis* magazine, 1954–55), 1952–55. Served in the British Army, 1951–52. Reporter, *Oxford Mail*, 1955–57, and *Evening Standard*, London, 1957–59; Columnist and Reviewer, *Daily Mail, Woman's Mirror, The Sun, The Sunday Times, Peace News, The Black Dwarf,* and *The Guardian*, all in London. Instructor, University of Iowa, Iowa City, 1963–64; Granada Fellow in the Arts, University of Lancaster, 1967–69; Fellow, Wesleyan University Center for the Humanities, Middletown, Connecticut, 1971. Recipient: Eric Gregory Award, 1961; P.E.N. Translation Prize, 1966; Tokyo Festival Television Film Award 1971. Agent: Miss Irene Josephy, 35 Craven Street, Strand, London W.C.2; or, Karen Kitzig, Wender and Associates, 1545 Broadway, New York, New York 10036, U.S.A. Address: c/o Jonathan Cape Ltd., 30 Bedford Square, London W.C.1, England.

PUBLICATIONS

Verse

(*Poems*).   Oxford, Fantasy Press, 1955.
Poems.   London, Cape, 1964.
Peace Is Milk.   London, Peace News, 1966.

Out Loud.   London, Cape Goliard Press, and New York, Grossman, 1968.
Ride the Nightmare: Verse and Prose.   London, Cape, 1971.
Cease-Fire.   London, Medical Aid Committee for Vietnam, 1973.
Penguin Modern Poets 22, with John Fuller and Peter Levi.   London, Penguin, 1973.

Recording: *Poems*, with Stevie Smith, Argo, 1974.

Plays

The Ledge (libretto), music by Richard Rodney Bennett (produced London, 1961).
The Persecution and Assassination of Jean-Paul Marat as Performed by the Inmates of the Asylum of Charenton under the Direction of the Marquis de Sade, adaptation of the play by Peter Weiss (produced London, 1964; New York, 1965).   London, John Calder, 1965; New York, Atheneum, 1966.
The Magic Flute, adaptation of the libretto by Schikaneder and Giesecke, music by Mozart (produced London, 1966).
US, with others (produced London, 1966).   Published as *US: The Book of the Royal Shakespeare Production US/Vietnam/US/Experiment/Politics . . .*, London, Calder and Boyars, 1968; as *Tell Me Lies: The Book of the Royal Shakespeare Production US/Vietnam/US/Experiment/Politics . . .*, Indianapolis, Bobbs Merrill, 1968.
The Criminals, adaptation of a play by José Triana (produced London, 1967; New York, 1970).
Tyger: A Celebration of the Life and Work of William Blake (produced London, 1971).   London, Cape, 1971.
Tamburlane the Mad Hen (for children; produced Devon, 1971).
Man Friday (televised, 1972; produced London, 1973).   Included in *Man Friday*, and *Mind Your Head*, 1974.
Mind Your Head (produced Liverpool, 1973; London, 1974).   Included in *Man Friday, and Mind Your Head*, 1974.
The Inspector General, adaptation of a play by Gogol (produced Nottingham, 1974).
Man Friday, and *Mind Your Head*.   London, Eyre Methuen, 1974.

Screenplays: *Tell Me Lies* (lyrics only), 1968; *The Body* (commentary), 1969.

Radio Play: *The Island* (libretto), music by William Russo, 1963.

Television Plays: *Animals Can't Laugh*, 1961; *Alive and Kicking*, 1971; *William Blake* (documentary), 1971; *Man Friday*, 1972.

Initiated and helped write several student shows: *Bradford Walk*, Bradford College of Art; *The Hotpot Saga*, *The Neurovision Song Contest*, and *Lash Me to the Mast*, University of Lancaster; *Move Over Jehovah*, National Association of Mental Health; *Poetry Circus*, Wesleyan University.

Novels

If You See Me Comin'.   London, Cape, 1962; New York, Macmillan, 1963.
The Bodyguard.   London, Cape, 1970; New York, Doubleday, 1971.
Wartime.   London, Cape, 1973.

Other

Editor, with Richard Selig, *Oxford Poetry 1955*. Oxford, Fantasy Press, 1955.
Editor, *Jump, My Brothers, Jump: Poems from Prison*, by Tim Daly. London,
    Freedom Press, 1970.
Editor, with Brian Elliott, *Bards in the Wilderness*. Melbourne, Nelson, 1971.

Adrian Mitchell comments:

My mind and imagination and my life have been altered by many things and many
people. Other people's poetry has been among my most important experiences and
I don't just mean great poetry. Politically speaking, it was poetry as much as
anything else which pushed me first in the direction of left-wing political action (in
which I include committee work, demonstrating, envelope-addressing as well as
poetry). To cite some of the poets who have educated and influenced me: Wilfred
Owen, Walt Whitman, Kenneth Patchen, Alex Comfort, Brecht, Beckett, John
Arden, Allen Ginsberg and most of all, William Blake. (But I've been influenced by
hundreds of others, most of all by my close friends and my family and a teacher
called Michael Bell.) I'm sometimes called a committed poet. So's your old man.
There are many poets who because they turn their back on politics, believe they
are somehow not engaged. But their indifference or their silence contributes
towards the status quo. And the status quo demands, at different periods, exploitation, starvation, poverty, mass-murder, torture, vile prisons, the stunting of children's imaginations and – in some part of the world during every day of my lifetime
– war. When the revolution comes, I expect some poetry to make some contribution toward it – every revolution so far has had its own songs and poems. That
contribution towards changing the world may be very small, but the smallest
contribution helps when it's a matter of changing the world. (I don't think that
poets should sit down and say: I've got to write a political poem.) But I think a
poet, like any other human being, should recognise that the world is mostly
controlled by political forces and should become politically active. And if a poet
attempts to live his politics, his poems will become politically active too.

                              *   *   *

Adrian Mitchell is currently the leading "committed" poet in Britain. His work
directs itself to political and social issues (the H-bomb, the war in Vietnam), and,
as he himself declares: "Direct contact is very important. There is more satisfaction from reading to an audience than from seeing one's work in print." Perhaps
more than any other poet, Mitchell is responsible for the growth of the fashion for
large-scale poetry readings in Britain, and he has played a large part in getting
poetry accepted as part of the "protest culture" of the young, and has considerably
refurbished the image of the poet as a natural rebel. These things naturally make it
very difficult to assess what he writes simply as literature. It is clear, for instance,
that Mitchell does not expect some of his poems to outlast the occasions for which
they were written. So far as the more topical ones are concerned, posterity will
require a good deal of scholarly elucidation if it is to understand all the references.
Yet it is equally plain that the poet hopes that at least some of his work will have
staying power. Despite the comparisons which are often made between Mitchell
and the American Beats, he is really very European, with a European concern for a
fairly tightly structured way of writing (it is worth remembering, for example, that
he began his career in the wake of the Movement, and was first published in

establishment journals, such as the *London Magazine*). Mitchell's immediate ancestor is clearly not Allen Ginsberg but W. H. Auden, and one often catches echoes in his work of the political verses of the poets of the 30's. There is also a direct influence from Brecht, and on the whole the poets whom Mitchell most closely resembles are some of his own German contemporaries, such as Hans Magnus Ensenzberger and Erich Fried, though his language seldom has their degree of concentration and pithiness. The weakness of Mitchell's work is its pop sentimentality; its virtues are a passionate anger and a colloquial directness.

– Edward Lucie-Smith

MITCHELL, David (John). New Zealander. Born in Wellington, 10 January 1940. Educated at Wellington Boys College, 1953–57, School Certificate, 1955; Victoria University, Wellington, 1958–59. Married Elsebeth Nielsen in 1963; has one daughter. Address: 99 Jervois Road, Herne Bay, Auckland, New Zealand.

PUBLICATIONS

Verse

Orange Grove. Auckland, Poets Cooperative, 1969.
Pipe Dreams in Ponsonby. Auckland, Associations of Oriental Syndics-New Zealand Arts Council, 1972.

Critical Study: "He Sing fr You" by C. K. Stead, in *Islands* (Christchurch), Spring 1972.

*   *   *

The physical appearance of David Mitchell's poetry – spacing, setting, punctuation, part-phonetic spelling, etc. – places it at once in the general current that flows out of the work of the Americans Pound, W. C. Williams and Charles Olson. A Mitchell poem is not sequential in any obvious sense except that some things follow others. There is neither logic nor narrative. Each poem is a succession of images, juxtaposition, associations, dissociations, around a central subject or idea. The writing picks out and heightens each phrase, even each word, which is a note of music before it is a sign pointing to anything beyond itself. At their best (and Mitchell is a talented poet whose public readings are expecially effective in bringing out the best in his work) the poems are lyrical, nostalgic, wry, generous in feeling and confident in tone. Where they fail it is a failure of denotation. Words used too exclusively for their musical qualities and secondary resonances begin to look under-employed, suggesting the transient brightness of a pop culture rather than the basic stuff which alone endures changes of taste. But Mitchell has also a fine ear for the music latent in the roughest vernacular speech, and this, together with his sense of humour, is likely to keep his poetry concrete and to strengthen its fibre as he goes on writing. Mitchell is a genuine stylist on a literary scene that has been most remarkable for hacking fence posts out of kauri logs, and as such he is surely welcome.

– C. K. Stead

MOAT, John. British. Born in Mussoorie, India, 11 September 1936. Educated at Exeter College, Oxford. Married; has two children. Co-Founder, The Arvon Foundation. Currently, Free-lance Writer. Lives in North Devon. Agent: A.D. Peters and Co., 10 Buckingham Street, London W.C. 2, England.

PUBLICATIONS

Verse

Sixpence per Annum: 12 Poems. Newbury, Berkshire, Phoenix Press, 1966.
Thunder of Grass: Poems. London, Barrie and Rockliff-Cresset Press, 1970.
The Ballad of the Leat. Gillingham, Kent, ARC Publications, 1973.

Novels

Heorot. London, Barrie and Rockliff-Cresset Press, 1968.
The Tugen and the Toot. London, Barrie and Jenkins, 1973.

Other

A Standard of Verse. Newbury, Berkshire, Phoenix Press, 1969.

*   *   *

John Moat has published one collection of verse, *Thunder of Grass.* The work in it exhibits a Yeatsian smoothness, which, while moving more interestingly towards the rhythms of speech, still stays close to Yeats's special brand of rhetoric for its effects:

> I inherited the garden towards dawn
> And keep it with a very moderate art;
> Though this may prosper now a child is born
> To simplify complexities of heart:
> The toil is simple while the love is one;
> Two kids would tear a toiling soul apart.
> For charity I work a routine spell
> As premium to save my brat from hell.

Moat does better than "routine spells" in some of the sequence entitled "The Overtures" – notably Overture 37, a love poem where the strong sense of his wife's identity prevents him from drifting off into self-enchantment with what he has to say about it, and words are used for other than musical purposes. He is, on the evidence of this single book, a Romantic who needs plenty of room to transcend his own rather limited idea of what a poem can be. Some longer poems – "Winter Passage," "Stages of Solar Eclipse" – show a possible way forward.

– Robert Nye

MOKASHI-PUNEKAR, Shankar. Indian. Born in Dharwar, Mysore State, 8 May 1928. Educated at K.E.B.'s High School, Dharwar; K.E.B.'s Arts College; Karnatak College, Dharwar, M.A. 1953, Ph.D. 1965. Married; has five children. Assistant Lecturer in English, Lingaraj College, Belgaum, 1954–56, and Kishinchand Chellaram College, Bombay, 1956–61; Principal, Sri Poornaprajna College, Udipi, 1967–68. Lecturer, 1961–69, and since 1969, Assistant Professor of English, Indian Institute of Technology, Bombay. Editor, *Jayakarnatak*, 1950–51; Music Critic, *The Times of India*, Bombay, 1965–67. Address: Department of Humanities, Indian Institute of Technology, Powai, Bombay 76, India.

PUBLICATIONS

Verse

> *The Captive: Poems.* Bombay, Popular Prakashan, 1965.
> *The Pretender.* Calcutta, Writers Workshop, 1967.
> *An Epistle to Professor David McCutchion.* Calcutta, Writers Workshop, 1970.

Other

> *The Later Phase in the Development of W. B. Yeats: A Study in the Stream of Yeats's Later Thought and Creativity.* Dharwar, Karnatak University, 1966.
> *P. Lal: An Appreciation.* Calcutta, Writers Workshop, 1968.
> *Indo-Anglian Creed and Other Essays.* Calcutta, Writers Workshop, 1972.
> *Interpretations of the Later Poems of W. B. Yeats.* Dharwar, Karnatak University Press, 1973.

> Translator, *The Cycle of the Seasons*, by Kalidasa. Bombay, Sigma, 1966.

Shankar Mokashi-Punekar comments:

I am a poet cursed with a wide diversification of ability and consequent sapping of single-minded energy. I stand for proto-classical values; these involve me in controversies wherein I sometimes use verse for illustration, sometimes for mounting an attack; by and large, I am a lyricist with a high content of ratiocinative passion.

I wish to be a cosmopolitan Hindu in both theme and style, but I love to use – and wherever possible fuse – the terminology and imagery of Christian theology to express my Hindu inspiration. I am confident of selling my ideas in a decade or so.

As a lyricist, I wish not to repeat or practise any single form as a demonstration of having evolved a manner. I want each poem to be faithful to its kind. Within its kind, I try to achieve the fullest possible expression and rhythm. Unfortunately, I find that English does not have certain kinds of inspiration, and if it had them once, it has now evolved social manners which make them sound false or repellent or outmoded – ethical inspiration, bardic self-confidence, clear-cut distinction between friend and enemy (blurred by the Liberal credo), for instance. Nazism made nationalism odious to the English ear, but I cannot help being a nationalist; am I to pare myself to fit into contemprary English stereotypes? Certainly not. I prefer to remain halted, outlandish, even incommunicative; as a compensation, I try to pack my poems with thought and imagery valuable in themselves and hope for the best. I am confident of my prosody and brook no criticism on that score. The turn of my idiom has raised some controversy, but my non-British thought is bound to militate against the culture-created idiom of English. In my opinion, poetry pre-exists single poems, and no single poem can have finality. It is an index, and a good reader alone can drown the shortcomings of a poem in the poetry he can perceive. Our love makes things complete, said Yeats.

*   *   *

In India most of the successful poets in English come from a certain socio-economic background in the urban areas where the exposure to the English language is the most intense. In such company Shankar Mokashi-Punekar stands out as a unique and solitary voice. He is different from the others both in his attitude to the English language and in his response to life. He is a critic as well as a poet, and his two activities are not unconnected. In his criticism he puts forward entirely original and thought-provoking ideas, often taking unfashionable stands. For example, in 1967 he wrote a serious and cogent critical article on the poetry of Sarojini Naidu, when no one who read or wrote English poetry in India regarded her to be anything more than a facile versifier. He even justified her archaisms and poetic inversions on the ground that the mere existence of these devices cannot disqualify a poem from critical consideration. He does not hesitate to use such devices in his own poetry.

Mokashi-Punekar's poetry reflects what in his monograph on the poetry of P. Lal he calls "a new philosophy of English." This apparently consists of an attempt to be free from the associations that English words have for people in English speaking countries, and a refusal to be blindly guided by the poetic standards set by someone else in another country. In his poetry this results in an occasional oddity of syntax and diction which is sometimes his strength and occasionally his weakness. His poems vary from witty epigrams, whimsical ballads and sonnets to dramatic monologues, sketches combining prose and poetry, and long poems of philosophic reflections. The general impression is that of a poet whose imagination is verbal and cerebral rather than visual. His poems are often interspersed with literary and academic references, but his most memorable poem, "The Pioneers-II," is remarkably free of these.

Apart from being a critic and a poet in English Mokashi-punekar is also a translator. His translation from Sanskrit poetry has a deliberate quaintness achieved through the use of rhyme, inversions and outmoded words such as "lass" and "affrighted." One may question the validity of such usage in a modern translation, but Mokashi-Punekar translates, as he does everything else, with such total conviction in matters of principle that no one can take his work casually.

– Meenakshi Mukherjee

————————

MOLE, John. British. Born in Taunton, Somerset, 12 October 1941. Educated at King's School, Bruton, Somerset; Magdalene College, Cambridge, 1961–64, B.A. (honours) in English 1964, M.A. Married Mary Norman in 1968; has two sons. English Teacher, Haberdashers' Aske's School, Elstree, Hertfordshire, 1964–73; Exchange Teacher, Riverdale Country School, New York 1969–70. Since 1973, Chairman of the English Department, St. Albans Grammar School, Hertfordshire. Editor, with Peter Scupham, Cellar Press, Hitchin, Hertfordshire. Recipient: Eric Gregory Award, 1970. Address: 142c St. Albans Road, Sandridge, St. Albans, Hertfordshire, England.

PUBLICATIONS

Verse

A Feather for Memory. London, Outposts Publications, 1961.
The Instruments. Manchester, Phoenix Pamphlet Poets Press, 1970.
Something about Love. Oxford, Sycamore Press, 1972.
The Love Horse. Manchester, E. J. Morton, 1974.
Scenarios. Berkhamsted, Hertfordshire, Priapus Press, 1975.
A Partial Light. London, Dent, 1975.

Other

Understanding Children Writing, with others. London, Penguin, 1973.

John Mole comments:

Apart from the routine essays, I didn't write much at school except for deeply purple prose in our true-blue magazine. I preferred novels, and, as for poetry, I was more concerned to know about it than to read it; I was, at least, aware that there was something intellectually distinguished about claiming an interest in *modern* poetry – anyone could read novels, but I went on reading them. Then, one Sunday in 1960, I picked up the "Review" section of the *Observer* and noticed a front page spread of poems by Robert Graves called "Symptoms of Love." I began reading, casually, became disconcertingly excited, and by the time I had finished the sequence I knew that I wanted to write poetry. Robert Graves wasn't an unfamiliar name to me; after all, he wrote novels – but what was this? So off I went and fashioned lapidary love poems with titles like "Prodigal Daughter," "Bard in Exile" etc. (see my first pamphlet in the Outposts series). I sent them to Graves who was, at that time, Professor of Poetry at Oxford and he said kind things; he even rewrote the closing lines of one of them in order to tighten up the syntax. It was important to get the shape right; mere feeling, as a later Oxford professor remarked, was too easy. I was hooked. Swinburne had kissed the baby Graves while he was still in his pram, and now Graves had corrected my syntax. The line was clear. I belonged.

Since then, I have gone on writing and come, increasingly (I hope), to belong to myself. I find poetry very difficult to talk about except in terms of my shifting enthusiasm for different poets and my permanent concern for patterning and craftmanship. I enjoy what W. H. Auden calls "hanging around language" and there's usually some verbal sport going on in my most overtly "serious" poems whether it be called syllables or manipulating couplets. I don's believe that counting and manipulating, mathematical or geometric though they may sound, squeeze out feeling; I think they squeeze it *in*. In general, I hope that the best of my work may be memorable and capable of moving my readers. Anything else to be said about it must be said by others if they will.

*   *   *

Wit is not a word that figures much in recent critical writing, perhaps because it expresses a quality of penetrating sharpness of intellect that does not itself figure much in recent poetry. Yet it is the word which first comes to mind when discussing the work of John Mole. This is not just because Mole has written humorous poetry, *vide* his longish jazz poem published in the magazine *Encounter* and the delightful adaptions of "Chantefables" from the French of Robert Desnos where the pleasure they give is derived from the display of technical high jinks, as in "The Owls":

> Mother owls make beau –
> tiful mothers, a few
> might brew more nourishing mouse stew
> than they do,
> but most of them muddle through.

The mind behind and the intellectual pressure driving all John Mole's work is what distinguishes it from the mindless, attention-seeking stuff which is constantly attempting to force itself upon us. Mole's poems force themselves upon us through the impetus of their logical progression. "The Instruments" and "Frogman" both get to grips with their own specific terrors because of the precision with which they are presented:

> Polish the blades
> But hold them away from the light.
> Sharpen the edges
> But do not demonstrate how keen they are,
> Show him his photograph
> But let it be a bad likeness.
>
> – from "The Instruments"

Parodoxically it is the precise description of a nightmarish imprecision which is so effective, for as "Frogman" tells us "I had always been afraid of what I could not feel."

In his domestic poems, "Not Flouring Pastry" and "Wife," for example, the same technical astuteness allows the expression of a compassionate understanding of everyday marital scenes under which tick the time-bombs of passion:

> Strange I feel it
> Grow unhomely.

"Depths" would seem to be a key poem in John Mole's work to date. It is a poem which deals directly with what is basic to the theme of all his serious poetry, and a poem which states prophetically:

> Such a depth
> Is fearful, nothing moves
> But thoughts of what may start there
> Even at this moment
> Coming up.

– John Cotton

MONTAGUE, John (Patrick).   Irish.   Born in Brooklyn, New York, 28 February 1929. Educated at St. Patrick's College, Armagh; University College, Dublin, B.A. in English and history 1949, M.A. 1952; Yale University, New Haven, Connecticut (Fulbright Scholar), 1953–54; University of Iowa, Iowa City, M.F.A. 1955. Worked for State Tourist Board, Dublin, 1956–61. Taught at the Poetry Workshop, University of California, Berkeley, Spring 1964 and 1965, University College, Dublin, Spring and Summer 1967, and Spring 1968, and the Experimental University of Vincennes. Currently, Lecturer in Poetry, University College, Cork. Member, Irish Academy of Letters. Address: Department of English, University College, Cork, Ireland.

PUBLICATIONS

Verse

Forms of Exile. Dublin, Dolmen Press, 1958.
The Old People. Dublin, Dolmen Press, 1960.
Poisoned Lands and Other Poems. London, MacGibbon and Kee, 1961; Chester Springs, Pennsylvania, Dufour, 1963.
Six Irish Poets, with others, edited by Robin Skelton. London, Oxford University Press, 1962.
All Legendary Obstacles. Dublin, Dolmen Press, 1966.
Patriotic Suite. Dublin, Dolmen Press, 1966.
Home Again. Belfast, Festival Publications, 1967.
A Chosen Light. London, MacGibbon and Kee, 1967; Chicago, Swallow Press, 1969.
The Rough Field. Dublin, Dolmen Press, and London, Oxford University Press, 1972.
Hymn to the New Omagh Road. Dublin, Dolmen Press, 1968.

The Bread God: A Lecture, with Illustrations in Verse. Dublin, Dolmen Press, 1968.
A New Siege. Dublin, Dolmen Press, 1969.
The Planter and the Gael, with John Hewitt. Balfast, Arts Council of Northern Ireland, 1970.
Tides. Dublin, Dolmen Press, 1970; Chicago, Swallow Press, 1971.
Small Secrets. London, Poem-of-the-Month Club, 1972.
A Fair House (translations from Irish). Dublin, Cuala Press, 1973.
The Cave of Night. Cork, Golden Stone, 1974.
O'Riada's Farewell. Cork, Golden Stone, 1974.

Recording: *The Northern Muse*, with Seamus Heaney, Claddagh, 1968.

Play

The Rough Field (produced London, 1973).

Short Stories

Death of a Chieftain and Other Stories. London, MacGibbon and Kee, 1964; Chester Springs, Pennsylvania, Dufour, 1967.

Other

Editor, *The Dolmen Miscellany of Irish Writing.* Dublin, Dolmen Press, 1962.
Editor, with Liam Miller, *A Tribute to Austin Clarke on His Seventieth Birthday, 9 May 1966.* Dublin, Dolmen Press, and Chester Springs, Pennsylvania, Dufour, 1966.
Editor, *The Faber Book of Irish Verse.* London, Faber, 1974.

Critical Studies: *The New Poetry* by M. L. Rosenthal, New York and London, Oxford University Press, 1967; by John MacInerney, in *Hibernia* (Dublin), 15 December 1972; D. S. Maxwell, in *The Critical Quarterly* (London), Summer 1973; Derek Mahon, in *Malahat Review* (Victoria, British Columbia), July 1973; Thomas Dillon Redshaw, in *Studies* (Dublin), Spring 1974; *John Montague* by Frank Kersnowski, Lewisburg, Pennsylvania, Bucknell University Press, 1975.

John Montague comments:

I am usually classed as an Irish poet and that is true insofar as I am deeply involved with the landscape and people of Ireland, particularly Ulster. In Gaelic poetry, Ireland appears both as a maiden and a hag, a sort of national muse, and her hold is still strong, especially now that her distinctive culture is being submerged. But underneath these tribal preoccupations beats a more personal struggle, the effort to affirm lovingly, to salvage some order, in the face of death and change. The technique is a blend of post-modern (Williams and Pound) and old Gaelic poetry, which could also be regarded as an aspect of nationality, for an Irish poet (following Joyce, Yeats, Beckett) has a better chance of being international than an English writer. But my effort to understand as much of the modern world as possible serves only to illuminate the destruction of that small area from which I initially came, and that theme in turn is only part of the larger one of continually threatened love. We must warn and warm ourselves against a new ice age.

*   *   *

John Montague's poetry has displayed, from the very start, a blend of lyrical grace and ironic grotesquerie, and a fusion of sensuality and wit, which, in combination with his ability to handle both personal and public themes, make him an outstanding figure among his contemporaries. Concerned with the state of his native country, and particularly of Ulster, he has made a typically Irish use of wry nostalgia, but has also developed a strong historical sense which is decisive enough to prevent that romantic excess which mars the political and nationalist poetry of many other and earlier writers. Moreover, having learned much from Pound and W. C. Williams, his work is always concrete and precise in imagery and deft in its handling of speech rhythms. Eschewing the pulsating rhetoric of the followers of Yeats, he may sometimes seem to prefer elegance to ecstasy, but the clarity and accuracy of his language reveal to the percipient reader an intellectual passion and a direct sensuality which are much more disturbing than the blurred sublimities of the camp-followers of nineteenth century romanticism. He does not equate obscurity with profundity, but rather strives to present a numinous clarity. In "The Answer" he describes a cottage on the Dingle peninsula as a place

> where even something
> tinny like a two-legged horned alarm-clock
> was isolated into meaning . . . .

Montague has an astonishing capacity to "isolate" a perception "into meaning" without losing physical immediacy. "Petrel" opens with an image of dazzling clarity:

> High
> A curl of light
> Under the sun

"Omagh Hospital" opens with an equally immediate image, and continues with a statement of almost unbearable simplicity:

> Your white hair
> on the thin rack
> of your shoulders
>
> it is hard to
> look into the eyes
> of the dying.

The directness and muscularity of Montague's language frequently produce lines and phrases which startle with their aphoristic strength or their compact clarity. "Everything dies into birth" he tells us in "Lame de Fond," and in other poems provides us with "the spike / Of each small nipple / A wild strawberry," "the steel/Sheathed stream," "rigorous as trees / Reduced by winter," "the fernlike talon uncurls," all images in which delicate and precise observation is matched to economy of utterance.

It would be a disservice to Montague to so emphasize this almost ascetic economy of language as to imply a lack of broad human sympathy or a pervasive narrow reticence. In many poems he indulges in exuberant humour and in others he uses the reverberant language of intense passion. No-one could ever, surely, forget the magnificiently parodic refrain of "The Siege of Mullingar,"

> *Puritan Ireland's dead and gone,*
> *A myth of O'Connor and O'Faolain*

or the superb sensuality and dexterity of "Life Class," the symbolic power and obsessiveness of "The Pale Light," in which an archetypal vision is given physical immediacy to a degree almost beyond the bearable.

Montague is not, however, only a maker of lyrics. He is one of the most adventurous of all Irish poets, and his long poem, *The Rough Field*, a cool survey and passionate lament about Ulster, is the closest thing to a poem of real political substance that has come out of Anglo-Irish poetry for forty years. Using cut-up and collage techniques together with verse forms modelled both upon Gaelic and Anglo-American patterns, he contemplates Ulster with wit, compassion, and cold rage. It is a personal poem and a public poem at once; the perceptions of the observant exile and the troubled participant are fused into one comprehensive vision by the skilled and committed intelligence of a master craftsman.

John Montague is now clearly one of the most skilled and interesting poets alive, and one of the most original and disturbing.

– Robin Skelton

MOORE, Nicholas. British. Born in Cambridge, 16 November 1918; son of the philosopher G. E. Moore. Educated at Dragon School, Oxford; Leighton Park School, Reading; Trinity College, Cambridge, B.A. Married Priscilla Patience Craig (marriage dissolved), has one daughter; Shirley Putnam, 1953, has one son and one daughter (died). Editor, *New Poetry*, 1944–45, and *Seven*; Editorial Assistant, Editions Poetry London. Has held jobs in horticulture, and written horticultural journalism. Recipient: Patrons Prize (*Contemporary Poetry*, Baltimore), 1945; Harriet Monroe Memorial Prize (*Poetry*, Chicago), 1947. Address: 89 Oakdene Road, St. Mary Cray, Kent BR5 2AL, England.

PUBLICATIONS

Verse

> *A Wish in Season: Poems.* London, Fortune Press, 1941.
> *The Island and the Cattle.* London, Fortune Press, 1941.
> *A Book for Priscilla: Poems.* Cambridge, Epsilon Pamphlets, 1941.
> *Buzzing Around with a Bee and Other Poems.* London, Editions Poetry, 1942.
> *The Cabaret, The Dancer, The Gentleman: Poems.* London, Fortune Press, 1942.
> *The Glass Tower: Poems 1936–43.* London, Editions Poetry, 1944.
> *Three Poems,* with Fred Marnau and Wrey Gardiner. London, Grey Walls Press, 1944.

Thirty-five Anonymous Odes. London, Fortune Press, 1944.
The War of the Little Jersey Cows: Poems by Guy Kelly. London, Fortune Press, 1945.
Recollections of the Gala: Selected Poems, 1943–1948. London, Editions Poetry, 1950.
Identity: Poems. London, Cadenza Press, 1969.
Resolution and Identity. London, Covent Garden Press, 1970.
Spleen (31 versions of Baudelaire's poem). London, Black Suede Boot Press-Menard Press, 1973.

Plays

Lock and Key (produced Oxford, 1956).

Other

Henry Miller. Wigginton, Hertfordshire, The Opus Press, 1943; Folcroft, Pennsylvania, Folcroft Editions, 1969.
The Tall Bearded Iris. London, Collingridge, and New York, Transatlantic Arts, 1956.

Editor, with John Bayliss and Douglas Newton, *The Fortune Anthology.* London, Fortune Press, 1942.
Editor, *The P L Book of Modern American Short Stories.* London, Editions Poetry, 1945.
Editor, with Douglas Newton, *Atlantic Anthology.* London, Fortune Press, 1945.

Critical Studies: "The Glass Tower" by Kenneth Gee, in *The New English Weekly* (London), 10 May 1945; G. W. Stonier, in *The New Statesman* (London), 1945; "The Poetry of Nicholas Moore" by G. S. Fraser, in *Poetry Quarterly* (London), 1945; Preface by Kenneth Rexroth to *New British Poets*, New York, New Directions, 1949; "Nicholas Moore: A Problem Poet" by Margaret Crosland, in *Poetry Quarterly* (London), Spring 1952.

Nicholas Moore comments:

Writing in *The Spectator* on January 8th 1943, Sheila Shannon wrote, in a review of "Some New Poets" as follows: "But too many of the poets under review here write poems as the result of their education; too few of them use any but a single sense at a time in conjunction with the mind. It was with delight and relief that, after much reading, I came across Nicholas Moore's poem in *Poetry Folios*. It is poetry written by a man functioning in all his senses and having a mind and an imagination equal to the tasks of conception and construction. Moore has sensibility; he has great sense of enjoyment; he can be witty and gentle; he can also be silly and trivial, which is the result of an unusual and refreshing exuberance."
    Whether I deserve this or not, of course, I don't know, but it does represent, in part at least, what I would like to be true.
    So, too, with "In much of Moore's writing there is a sense of justice, a morality that refuses to have anything to do with any morality bespoken by rulers or

bewildered crowds,'' or, ''but Mr. Moore is really a reflective poet, his best poems take their shape and movement from his thought, and grow with it; in the later poems in this book, his consciousness has a greater range, and the words of the poems bring to life other words and ideas that are not on the page but are discovered in reading. He is a civilized poet who has much to say, and to say well, against the evils of his civilization. . . . He can also write with some faith and hope which one feels to be real,'' from Kenneth Gee; and G. W. Stonier's ''the intricacy of workmanship makes one want to reject one meaning for another more intricate; or we turn the poem over feelingly like a scarab,'' and ''I should like to emphasize Mr. Moore's accomplishment in these various phases. Nevertheless, the poems which appeal most are those in which vividness of phrase is matched by vividness of idea. . . . It comes naturally to him to see sharply and form patterns, and an epigrammatic gaiety is one of the surprises of his talent.''

Some of these comments might seem to be mutually exclusive; but that, really, is the point. Victoria Sackville-West in another review (of *Three Poems*) described me as ''slightly surrealist.'' At that time, I thought this a silly comment, but now on reflection I'm not sure that most of the poems of mine I like best myself are not ''slightly surrealist.''

I do not consider myself a romantic – though I have written some romantic poems – ''Ode to Sexual Beauty'' and ''The Aquatic Stag'' for instance – because that seemed appropriate to the particular theme, or particular time and place. In its early days I was associated with The New Apocalypse movement, and contributed to *The White Horseman*. But once it started calling itself – or was it Herbert Read who called it? – The New Romanticism, I was out of sympathy. My own personal tastes – in poetry – were more for the Southern group of writers in America, particularly Ransom and John Peale Bishop, and for the Metaphysicals (Donne, Herbert, Vaughan), and the Elizabethans: Shakespeare, of course; Marlowe; Webster; and especially Ralegh and Fulke Greville.

In other words, I believed – and do believe – in a poetry of greater universality and width of range than any narrow categorising can encompass.

*   *   *

In the nineteen-forties Nicholas Moore was well known as a talented and prolific poet, whose work appeared frequently in little magazines and anthologies. He published several collections, of which the most substantial were *The Glass Tower* and *Recollections of the Gala*. But after the appearance of the latter volume Moore appeared to stop writing completely, and this silence was broken only in the late sixties, when he once more began to contribute verse to literary reviews.

Nicholas Moore's origins in the late nineteen-thirties are evident in the prevalent influence of Auden, and particularly of Auden's songs and light verse. Moore picked up and carried on Auden's talent for the mellifluous but slightly cerebral lyric. Other influences were Blake, notably the ''Songs of Innocence and Experience,'' and, most interestingly, Wallace Stevens. Moore read and admired Stevens many years before he became a prominent and even fashionable poet; indeed, Stevens was almost wholly unknown in England in the nineteen-forties, when Moore was paying him the tribute of deliberate imitation in a poem such as ''Ideas of Disorder at Torquay.'' From Stevens Moore acquired a flowing music and a deliberate rhetoric that stiffened the colloquial thirties manner and the throwaway wit. Moore's poems of the early forties were sometimes excessively fluent, with a suggestion of more manner than matter. But *Recollections of the Gala* is a very accomplished collection which represents Moore's poetry at its best, variously fantastic, sardonic and lyrical. His most recent work is as adroit and witty as ever; particularly in *Spleen*, a set of thirty-one versions of a famous Baudelaire poem, which provides a series of dazzling variations on a theme.

– Bernard Bergonzi

MORAES, Dom(inic Frank). British. Born in Bombay, India, 19 July 1938, son of Frank Moraes, editor of the *India Express*. Educated at Jesus College, Oxford, B.A. 1959. Married Judith St. John in 1963 (marriage dissolved), has one son; Leslie Naidu, 1970. Formerly, Scriptwriter, Granada Television; Documentary Film-maker. Since 1972, Editor, *The Asian Magazine*, Hong Kong. Recipient: Hawthornden Prize, 1958. Address: *The Asian Magazine*, 31 Queen's Road Central, Hong Kong.

PUBLICATIONS

Verse

A Beginning. London, Parton Press, 1957.
Poems. London, Eyre and Spottiswoode, 1960.
Penguin Modern Poets 2, with Kingsley Amis and Peter Porter. London, Penguin, 1962.
15 Poems for William Shakespeare. Stratford-upon-Avon, 1964.
John Nobody. London, Eyre and Spottiswoode, 1965.
Poems 1955–1965. New York, Macmillan, 1966.
Bedlam Etcetera. London, Turret Books, 1966.

Other

Green Is the Grass (on cricket). Bombay, Asia Publishing House, 1951.
Gone Away: An Indian Journal. London, Heinemann, and Boston, Little Brown, 1960.
My Son's Father: An Autobiography. London, Secker and Warburg, 1968; as *My Son's Father: A Poet's Autobiography,* New York, Macmillan, 1969.
The Tempest Within: An Account of East Pakistan. New York, Barnes and Noble, 1971.
From East and West: A Collection of Essays. New Delhi and London, Vikas, 1971.
A Matter of People. London, Deutsch, 1974; as *This Burdened Planet,* New York, Praeger, 1974.

Editor, *Voices for Life: Reflections on the Human Condition.* New York, Praeger, 1975.

Translator, *The Brass Serpent,* by T. Carmi. London, Deutsch, 1964.

*   *   *

Amongst Indian poets writing in English today perhaps the best-known is Dom Moraes. It is true that neither in his themes nor in his imagery, neither in the landscape of his poetry nor in his references and allusions is there anything distinctively Indian; but this does not matter much since "Indianness," whatever it may be, is not a poetic virtue *per se*. Moraes's first book of poems, *A Beginning*, published when he was only 19, won the Hawthornden Prize and brought him immediate fame; he was the first non-English poet to win it.

What distinguishes Moraes among Indian poets is his powerful organic sensibility, a very skilful use of words in metrical and verse-patterns, a striking imagery and an authentic personal experience. His difficulty at the moment seems to be that he has not as yet found any convincingly felt solution of his personal problems. This is a difficulty which is almost inevitable in the early poetry of a young poet who is honest, sincere and individual. As a result of this difficulty, however, the style of some of his poems tends to overweigh "the idea." For example, in "Vivisection" (*John Nobody*) the "virgin" (modern version) betrays her own deepest instincts and kills the "unicorn" (original version). The sustained imagery of the poem does not breathe any new life into the commonplace conclusion. Similarly in "The General" (*John Nobody*) the poet speaks of the dilemma of living in a world of horror and violence in which the attitude of neither "the anchorite" nor "the clown" is appropriate – both of them are killed – and there seems to be no permanent escape from contingent becoming into pure being; the elaborate set-up of the story of these poems is hardly justified by the fairly simple conclusions and emotional dilemmas of the poet's situation. The machinery (myths, references, allusions, etc.) is quite often excessive for the jobs that the poet plans. The poet does not always achieve creative mastery of his personal experience. We get to know that he is deeply "troubled" and is searching for solutions. There is an intimation that he accepts life and love and the necessity of struggle against the evil in oneself. Considering the gifts of the poet, it is reasonable to expect that this intimation will obtain convincing poetic realization in due course of time.

Not all the poems, however, suffer from this incompleteness. There are many poems in which the aim and scope of the poet are "impersonal" and these succeed very well. Such for instance are "Figures in the Landscape" (*A Beginning*), "Kanheri Caves" (*A Beginning*) and "Melancholy Prince" (*John Nobody*). In "Figures in the Landscape" the poet re-interprets the story of the Pied Piper to suggest the trustfulness and innocence of the children and the Piper's betrayal – of which he is aware – of that trust. The poem on the Kanheri Caves re-creates in clear sharp detail the poetic impression of the caves and makes skilful use of the scientific hypothesis of evolution and Keats's reference to "stout Cortez" to intimate the cyclic nature of life and civilization; the poem is also an excellent illustration of Moraes's command of word-music. "Melancholy Prince" may not say anything fresh or original about *Hamlet* – hard task to do so – but it conveys admirably the tragedy of Ophelia and the peculiar atmosphere of the play. It is in these comparatively "public" poems that Moraes has greater variety of interest and success to offer than in his purely "personal" poems. He has been deeply concerned of late with public issues such as racial segregation in England, and we may expect him to modulate what he has himself recognized as "a small whimper" and attempt a larger mode without losing his individuality of response and style.

– S. Nagarajan

MORGAN, Edwin (George).   Scottish.   Born in Glasgow, 27 April 1920. Educated at Rutherglen Academy; Glasgow High School; Glasgow University, 1937–40, 1946–47, M.A. 1947. Served in the Royal Army Medical Corps, 1940–46. Assistant Lecturer, 1947–50, Lecturer, 1950–65, Senior Lecturer, 1965–71, and since 1971, Reader in English, Glasgow University. Recipient: Cholmondeley Award, 1968; Scottish Arts Council award, 1969, 1973; P.E.N. Memorial Medal, 1972. Address: 19 Whittingehame Court, Glasgow G12 0BG, Scotland.

PUBLICATIONS

Verse

   The Vision of Cathkin Braes. Glasgow, Maclellan, 1952.
   The Cape of Good Hope. Tunbridge Wells, Kent, Peter Russell, 1955.
   Starryveldt. Frauenfeld, Switzerland, Gomringer Press, 1965.
   Scotch Mist. Cleveland, Renegade Press, 1965.
   Sealwear. Glasgow, Gold Seal Press, 1966.
   Emergent Poems. Stuttgart, Hansjörg Mayer, 1967.
   The Second Life. Edinburgh, Edinburgh University Press, 1968.
   Gnomes. Preston, Lancashire, Akros, 1968.
   Proverbfolder. Corsham, Wiltshire, Openings Press, 1969.
   Penguin Modern Poets 15, with Alan Bold and Edward Brathwaite. London, Penguin, 1969.
   The Horseman's Word: A Sequence of Concrete Poems. Preston, Lancashire, Akros, 1970.
   Twelve Songs. West Linton, Peeblesshire, Castlelaw Press, 1970.
   The Dolphin's Song. Leeds, School of English Press, 1971.
   Glasgow Sonnets. West Linton, Peeblesshire, Castlelaw Press, 1972.
   Instamatic Poems. London, Ian McKelvie, 1972.
   The Whittrick: A Poem in Eight Dialogues. Preston, Lancashire, Akros, 1973.
   From Glasgow to Saturn. Cheadle, Cheshire, Carcanet Press, and Chester Springs, Pennsylvania, Dufour, 1973.

Other

   Essays. Cheadle, Cheshire, Carcanet Press, 1974.

   Editor, *Collins Albatross Book of Longer Poems: English and American Poetry from the Fourteenth Century to the Present Day.* London, Collins, 1963.
   Editor, with George Bruce and Maurice Lindsay, *Scottish Poetry One to Six.* Edinburgh, Edinburgh University Press, 1966–72.
   Editor, *New English Dramatists 14.* London, Penguin, 1970.

   Translator, *Beowulf.* Aldington, Kent, Hand and Flower Press, 1952; Berkeley, University of California Press, 1962.
   Translator, *Poems from Eugenio Montale.* Reading, Berkshire, University of Reading School of Art, 1959.
   Translator, *Sovpoems: Brecht, Neruda, Pasternak, Tsvetayeva, Mayakowsky, Martynov, Yevtushenko.* Worcester, Migrant Press, 1961.
   Translator, with David Wevill, *Sándor Wëores and Ferenc Juhász: Selected Poems.* London, Penguin, 1970.

Translator, *Wi the Haill Voice: Poems by Mayakovsky.*   Oxford, Carcanet Press,
   1972.

Manuscript Collection: National Library of Scotland, Edinburgh

Critical Studies: by Tom Buchan, in *Scottish International* (Edinburgh), August 1968;
"Scottish Poets: Edwin Morgan and Iain Crichton Smith" by Robin Fulton, in
Stand (Newcastle upon Tyne), x, 4, 1969; *Worlds: Seven Modern Poets*, London,
Penguin, 1974; *Contemporary Scottish Poetry* by Robin Fulton, Edinburgh, M. Mac-
donald, 1974.

                              *   *   *

   One obvious aspect of Edwin Morgan's inherent Scottishness is the extent and
penetration of his versatility. Another is his ability to reach the universal through
the particular.
   Morgan's first paper-back collection, *The Vision of Cathkin Braes,* was brought
out in 1952, when its author was thirty-two. There is thus no published Morgan
juvenilia. *The Vision of Cathkin Braes* confidently sets out staking-pegs round all, or
almost all, the poetic territory Morgan has since developed, even though it was
meant to show only one side of Morgan's work, *Dies Irae and Other Poems,* which
never appeared, being designed to show another.
   The title poem, in which the poet and his love "strayed in the red rays / Of the
lingering sun" to Cathkin Braes, near Glasgow, there to encounter a company
which included "Gaunt Jenny Geddes, the Minister's delight," "McGonagal . . . a
figure somewhat comical," "Knox, Lauren Bacall, Wordsworth and St. Mungo
Park," already balances irony and wit on an exact and precise choice of vocabulary. His skill as a creative translator is also thus early apparent. "Verses for a
Christmas Card" combines Morgan's interest in the experimental use of language
with Dunbar-like Scots overtones:

> O angellighthoused harbourmoon,
> Glazegulfgalaxeval governoon,
> Jovegal allcapellor jupiterror
> And you brighdsun of venusacre,
> Respour this leidyear Phoenixmas
> With starphire and restorying dazz
> Bejeweleavening cinderill
> To liftlike pace and goodquadrille.
> All men reguard, from grace our fere,
> And sun on us to kind and chere.

   Morgan's verse translation into modern English of *Beowulf* is not only without
doubt the only living re-creation of this poem so far to be achieved, but a narration
which holds the contemporary reader's interest partly because Morgan has satisfac-
torily solved the problem of handling the unrhymed stressed line, and partly
because the lines themselves fulfil Morgan's own requirement of them that they
should be "able to contract to terseness, and to expand to splendour" with sufficient flexibility and variety to carry us through just under three thousand two
hundred of them.
   Something of the Anglo-Saxon practice of alliteration rubbed off on Morgan's

next poem, *The Cape of Good Hope.* It is an exploration through four lyrical movements, in the first of which the poet cries to the

> Great Lucretian deep,
> Wean my libertinism
> Pillow my nescience
> Cradle my revolt.
> I chose the emptiness
> When fullness appalled me,
> I ran to the barrens
> When the warrens choked me . . . .

In the company of his "brothers in the throat of desolation," Leonardo, Michelangelo, Newton, Beethoven, Melville and Mayakovsky, the poet finds that "The throat of desolation is silent as I turn / Through the great world of matter to my heart," to learn that "out of casting off," the poet

> wins
> Arrival, and where he left his hope
> Trussed in the common human chains
> He journeys into the whole of verity
> Beyond the reach of vanity
> And hears in verity the evangel of joy
> According to hope and according to the world.

Three further distinctive collections of translations or re-creations followed. To have been able, on the one hand, to bring vividly to life in English the sophisticated glancing half-lights of Eugenio Montale's poetry, and on the other, in *Sovpoems,* to provide direct and effective versions of poems by Brecht, Pasternak, Tsvetayeva, Martynov and others into English, and Mayakovsky into Scots (*Wi the Haill Voice*) is achievement of sustained and remarkable breadth.

In his excellent introduction to *Sovpoems,* Morgan makes clear the challenges of social responsibility and intelligibility that the best of the poets of the East throw out to us. He himself has developed for his own purposes their directness of expression and their concern for humankind rather than for artificial literary style, combining these qualities with a warm compassion and a highly personal cynicism. His finest book, despite a tendency in some of the poems to break out into a Whitmanesque rhetoric ("The Death of Marilyn Monroe"), is *The Second Life,* which reflects not only his belief that poetry should acknowledge its environment, but also his interest in a poetry of time-and-space-exploration. He himself has said of his own "brand of free verse" that his effects are "built up over paragraphs rather than within single lines." For that reason, it is difficult to quote effectively from such poems as "King Billy," "Glasgow Green," "The Death of Marilyn Monroe" or the title poem, in which Morgan's feelings for Glasgow carry a more than local significance:

> Many things are unspoken
> in the life of a man, and with a place
> there is an unspoken love also
> in the undercurrents, drifting, waiting its time.

From Glasgow to Saturn also contains some fine poems, like "Kirkegaard's Song," and repeats many of the kind of successes achieved in the earlier volume. However, it also betrays a growing preoccupation with experimentation for its own sake – Morgan would probably call the less tensioned examples "disposable verse," as indeed it is! – and an irritating fondness for visual linguistic jokiness.

In both of the more recent collections, Morgan includes examples of concrete poetry. One may feel that this particular *genre* is no more than a passing fashion, with its limited possibilities for reverberation and satisfaction, yet still be aware that Morgan's best examples, particularly the humorous ones, stand comparison with anything of their kind to be found in international collections of concrete work.

– Maurice Lindsay

MORGAN, (George) Frederick. American. Born in New York City, 25 April 1922. Educated at St. Bernard's School, New York, 1927–35; St. Paul's School, Concord, New Hampshire, 1935–39; Princeton University, New Jersey, 1939–43, A.B. 1943. Served as a Staff Sergeant in the United States Army Tank Destroyer Corps, 1943–45. Married Constance Canfield in 1942 (divorced), has six children (one deceased); Rose Fillmore in 1957 (divorced); Paula Deitz in 1969. Founder, with Joseph Bennett and William Arrowsmith, and since 1947, Editor, *The Hudson Review,* New York. Since 1974, Chairman of the Advisory Council, Department of Romance Languages and Literatures, Princeton University. Recipient: National Endowment for the Arts grant, 1966, 1968, 1969. Address: c/o The Hudson Review, 65 East 55th Street, New York, New York 10022, U.S.A.

PUBLICATIONS

Verse

A Book of Change. New York, Scribner, 1972.

Other

Editor, *The Hudson Review Anthology.* New York, Random House, 1961.
Editor, *The Modern Image: Outstanding Stories from "The Hudson Review."* New York, Norton, 1965.

Critical Studies: by John Fandel, in *Commonweal* (New York), 27 October 1972; James Finn Cotter, in *America* (New York), 13 January 1973; "Poetry Not Written To Be Poetry" by Guy Davenport, in *The New York Times Book Review,* 1 April 1973.

Frederick Morgan comments:

My poems attempt to express my sense of the nature of things and of the meaning of my own life and destiny. They deal with the full range of human emotion and the perennial lyric themes: time, death, love, pain and joy. Some are immediately personal, others more general and philosophical; some are poems of direct recollection, others trace the development of different stages of awareness. All my poems are interrelated, forming sequences whose impact is cumulative. Thus they all, in an important sense, form part of a single, continually developing work.

*   *   *

The title of Frederick Morgan's single collection of verse thus far, *A Book of Change*, clearly indicates his indebtedness to Eastern thought, though less to the *I Ching* itself – the "Book of Changes" – than to the quietism of Tao and, especially, the *Chuang Tzu*. The specific changes Morgan describes are the stages of his own life – his childhood, his first marriage, World War II, the death of a son and, at much greater length, an extremely happy third marriage; the lesson of the changes is the rejection of intellectualism as a means of understanding, much less controlling the course of life:

> But we,
> race of sad apes grown sensitive and smart,
> think that by thinking we shall know the world.
> Sad error, since the world as object known
> ever recedes beyond our nervous grasp:
> the very thinking pushes it away.

Wisdom means cheerful submission, the "letting go" of the ego:

> Letting go into God is almost physical;
> .   .   .   .   .   .
> But we forget, because we're caught up in the network
> of hopes, desires, fears – and because we try
> to live in an illusion of permanence.
> .   .   .   .   .   .
> the self is cunning and will play its pleasant games
> as long as we allow. . . .

The final poem of the collection asserts

> After twenty-five years
>   to be in touch with myself
> To bring it all together and, what's more, to love –
>
> this is ripeness, the golden fruit
> of the great world-tree that dies, and lives.

Taoism, while much less mysterious to Westerners these days than it once was, is so hostile to the intellect that even to pose questions is a species of error, as the parables of the *Chuang Tzu* are designed to show. But the final issue is not so much the strangeness of the doctrine – the "true spirit" of Dante is, after all, hardly less foreign to us now – as it is Morgan's failure to embody rather than merely state his discoveries. Yeats once observed that rhetoric is the will doing the work of the imagination, and in this sense Morgan's poetry is often rhetorical, embarrassingly flat and prosaic. Only in a few isolated instances (in the poem describing his response to a Joseph Cornell collage, for example, or in the quirky, Whitmanesque

"Barbershop Poem") is Morgan able to fuse image and statement in a way which makes it possible for his readers to feel, at least for the moment, what it must be like to share his attractive point of view and eminently un-Western contentment.

– Elmer Borkland

MORGAN, (Colin) Pete(r).   British.   Born in Leigh, Lancashire, 7 June 1939. Educated at Normanton School, Buxton, Derbyshire, 1950–57. Served in the Royal Army Infantry, 1958–63. Married Kate Smith in 1965; has one daughter and one son. Recipient: Scottish Arts Council bursary, 1969; Arts Council of Great Britain award, 1973. Agent: David Higham Associates, 5–8 Lower John Street, Golden Square, London W.1. Address: Moorsams House, Tommy Baxter Street, Robin Hood's Bay, North Yorkshire, England.

PUBLICATIONS

Verse

A Big Hat or What? Edinburgh, Kevin Press, 1968.
Loss of Two Anchors. Edinburgh, Kevin Press, 1970.
Poems for Shortie. Solihull, Warwickshire, Aquila, 1973.
The Grey Mare Being the Better Steed. London, Secker and Warburg, 1973.

Plays

Still the Same Old Harry (produced Edinburgh, 1972).

Screenplay (documentary): *Gardens by the Sea*, 1973.

Other

Editor, *C'mon Everybody: Poetry of the Dance.* London, Corgi, 1963.

*   *   *

The first words in Pete Morgan's Introduction to his anthology, *Poetry of the Dance,* are: "Plato said it – 'The dance is god-like in itself. It is a gift from heaven.'" These words also describe Pete Morgan's poetry at its best. As his poems bound along, or dance, with effortless ease, and as they present their innocent pictures of knights, stallions, "the bull with the rumpus horn," my Moll and partner Joe, the impression is of something given, not made. His poems seem to be immediately original without any special seeking after difference, yet their origins are evident. They begin in the world of nursery rhymes. Nursery rhymes have a known audience which they captivate. Equally Pete Morgan poems have an audience or rather many audiences which respond to his excellent readings. Some of the poems are well suited for ballad-style music settings. Yet despite the immediacy of communication and surface simplicity of the poems, beneath is a psychological curiosity and a sharpness of perception which reveal the poet has not sold out his intelligence.

"The White Stallion" begins:

> There was that horse
>   that I found then
>   my white one
> big tall and lean as
>   and mean as hell

The supple movement, the momentary halt in the penultimate line, and the unexpected drive of the last line, is the work of a craftsman who has learned from, amongst others, Auden, though the last poems of Yeats have also been caught in Morgan's ear to his advantage. More significant perhaps is the use he makes of the commonplace "mean as hell." He rejoices in the lively vernacular phrase. There is so much delight in his first book, *A Big Hat or What?*, in such poems as "My Moll and Partner Joe," "Whoops! I nearly smiled again," "Elegy for Arthur Prance," and "My enemies have sweet voices," that the subtle tones and undertones may not be regarded.

In Pete Morgan's second book, *Loss of Two Anchors*, the stock imagery is used more personally. In "The Rainbow Knight's Confession" the dance measure is less jaunty, and the characteristic question of today, identity – who is the knight, what does the armour conceal? – emerges as the poem progresses. The deliberate ambiguity of the opening line followed by the conscious placing of the romantic imagery, suggests a mature mind using the pieces on the board as a means of self-discovery. The poem begins:

> My armour *becomes* me.
> I have it to the letter now –
> even the colour of my steed,
> a much deliberated
> white.

Pete Morgan at thirty four is one of the most interesting talents of his generation.

– George Bruce

MORGAN, Robert. British. Born in Glamorgan, Wales, 17 April 1921. Educated at Fircroft College, Birmingham, 1949–51; College of Education, Bognor Regis, Sussex, 1951–53, Dip.Ed. 1953; Southampton University, 1969–70, Advanced Diploma in Special Education. Married Jean Elizabeth Morgan in 1953; has two daughters. Coal miner in South Wales, 1936–48. Currently, school teacher in Portsmouth. Painter for many years: gallery exhibitions in London, South Wales, Southampton, and Portsmouth, and one-man shows at the Plestor Gallery, Selborne, Wiltshire, 1966, the Mermaid Theatre, London, 1967, and the Winchester Art Gallery, Wiltshire, 1972. Formerly, Art Organizer for Welsh Artists Workshop,

Cardiff. Address: 44 Martin Avenue, Denmead, Portsmouth, Hampshire PO7 6NS, England.

PUBLICATIONS

Verse

The Night's Prison: Poems, and Rainbow Valley: A Play for Broadcasting. London, Hart Davis 1967.
Poems and Extracts. Exeter, Exeter University Press, 1968.
On the Banks of the Cynon. Gillingham, Kent, ARC Publications, 1973.
The Storm. Llandybie, Carmarthenshire, Christopher Davies, 1974.

Plays

Rainbow Valley (broadcast, 1967). Included in *The Night's Prison: Poems, and Rainbow Valley: A Play for Broadcasting,* 1967.
Voices in the Dark, in *Anglo-Welsh Review 40* (Pembroke Dock, Wales), 1969.
The Master Miners (produced Cardiff, 1971). Published in *Anglo-Welsh Review 47* (Pembroke Dock, Wales), 1971.
Fragments of a Dream (produced Cardiff, 1971). Published in *Anglo-Welsh Review 54* (Pembroke Dock, Wales), 1972.

Radio Plays: *Rainbow Valley,* 1967; *The Master Miners,* 1972.

Bibliography: exhibition catalogue, Winchester, Southern Arts Association, 1972.

Critical Studies: by M.H.G. Norman, in *Anglo-Welsh Review 40* (Pembroke Dock, Wales), 1969; Preface to exhibition catalogue, Winchester, Southern Arts Association, 1972.

Robert Morgan comments:

As a poet, the main body of my work is connected with coal mines and the mining valleys of South Wales. Some of the poems cover my life as a boy in the mines, and they show the humanity, the cruelty, the ironies and the sudden brief beauties of the Welsh valleys – above ground and in the Deeps and Levels below.

In my verse-plays, which were written many years after leaving the mines, I explore my mining experiences in more poetic detail, often using ghost characters as a literary vehicle to explore and strengthen the mining underground atmosphere. A small section of my poems is devoted to handicapped children, those whom I am connected with in my professional job as head of a remedial department in a secondary school.

Another section of my work covers pastoral poems. These are connected with the rural landscape around my village home in Hampshire, England.

*   *   *

With his collection *The Night's Prison*, Robert Morgan produced a fine document about the South Wales coalfields. He was a miner for 12 years and wrote out of real experience, unlike some other Anglo-Welsh poets who lived in the mining areas but never went down a pit. No other poet since the late Idris Davies has written quite so vivid and bitter a tract about life in the depressed valleys. Morgan sums up much of the essence of his work in these lines:

> I know there are bright places
> Under the brow of the hill slag
> But it was in the shadows I
> Wandered where the truth was thickest.

He has been criticised for returning endlessly to the "oblique, remembered streets" and the "stale shadows / of burning hills," but perhaps such repetition is inevitable, given the limitations of the subject-matter. Also, being very much *inside* the experience, he tends to rush to emotional climaxes, anxious to *move* the reader, to make him share his own harsh memories. The fatal shadow of Dylan Thomas falls on these lines, too:

> He lies in his city room in the bandage
> of dark clinging to runaway years
> of green time in the mist of memories.

But, despite the occasional uneven, untidy lapses, the clichéd symbols and repetitive vocabulary ("buckled hands," "musical silence," and "silica" often recur), Morgan's poems are usually forceful and, indeed, informative in the best sense when he concentrates on tight description (reminding us that he is also a talented painter and sculptor):

> We are charmed by thin mice
> Eating crumbs and blind
> Flies dancing in the lamp's
> Cold light and we are always
> Curious of the black, squeezed
> Roads behind cross-sticks where
> Our grandfathers worked as boys.

Among his fully effective poems are "Gomer," "Farewell on a Wet Day," and "Blood Donor," which are chiselled and steely, far superior to some of his looser, hastier constructions. One of his most anthologised pieces is "The Carpenter," which is not about Wales at all and so escapes from the pull of inheritance and Morgan's customary burning necessity to remain faithful to his past and to his dead comrades. This is a fine poem, and so, too, is his long broadcast play *Rainbow Valley*, where he has room to spread himself, as it were, capturing all the simple emotion and the stark tragedy through individual voices naming their own fears and memories.

One still cannot say whether his mining past, which he has already looted and ransacked, will continue to sustain Robert Morgan's work, though he has written an excellent poem, "Maladjusted Boys," and others stemming from his experience as a compassionate teacher of backward children. The mining seam could be worked out, and he may have to look elsewhere for nourishment to avoid becoming trapped and sealed within a monotonous theme. Even the bleak but dignified history of the Welsh pits cannot bear too much repeating, and Morgan has already achieved much by leaving a small monument to them in his poetry. His vitality, faith, honesty and sincerity are unquestioned, and the possible extension of his range may be hinted at in these, his own words:

> The background is overgrown with dreams
> And the horizon fades into smooth tips
> Sprinkled with the blood of coal.
> But the weight of time strengthens
> The corner stones of my heritage.

– John Tripp

MOSS, Howard. American. Born in New York City, 22 January 1922. Educated at the University of Michigan, Ann Arbor, 1939–40; University of Wisconsin, Madison, 1940–43, B.A. 1943; Harvard University, Cambridge, Massachusetts, Summer 1942; Columbia University, New York, 1946. Book Reviewer, *Time*, New York, 1944; Instructor in English, Vassar College, Poughkeepsie, New York, 1944–46. Since 1948, Poetry Editor, *The New Yorker*. Recipient: Janet Sewall Davis Award (*Poetry*, Chicago), 1944; National Institute of Arts and Letters Award, 1968; Ingram Merrill Foundation grant, 1972; National Book Award, 1972. Member, National Institute of Arts and Letters. Address: 27 West 10th Street, New York, New York 10011, U.S.A.

PUBLICATIONS

Verse

The Wound and the Weather: Poems. New York, Reynal, 1946.
The Toy Fair: Poems. New York, Scribner, 1954.
A Swimmer in the Air: Poems. New York, Scribner, 1957.
A Winter Come, A Summer Gone: Poems 1946–1960. New York, Scribner, 1960.
Finding Them Lost and Other Poems. New York, Scribner, and London, Macmillan, 1965.
Second Nature: Poems. New York, Atheneum, 1968.
Selected Poems. New York, Atheneum, 1971.
Chekhov. New York, Albondocani Press, 1972.
Buried City: Poems. New York, Atheneum, 1975.

Plays

The Folding Green (produced Cambridge, Massachusetts, 1954; New York, 1964).
The Oedipus Mah-Jongg Scandal (produced New York, 1968).
The Palace at 4 A.M. (produced East Hampton, New York, 1972). Published in Quarterly Review of Literature (Princeton, New Jersey), Spring 1973.

Other

The Magic Lantern of Marcel Proust. New York, Macmillan, 1962; London, Faber, 1963.
Writing Against Time: Critical Essays and Reviews. New York, Morrow, 1969.
Instant Lives (satire). New York, Saturday Review Press, 1973.

Editor, *Keats.* New York, Dell, 1952.
Editor, *The Nonsense Books of Edward Lear.* New York, New American Library, 1964.
Editor, *The Poet's Story.* New York, Macmillan, 1973.

Manuscript Collection: Syracuse University Library, New York.

Critical Studies: *Alone with America* by Richard Howard, New York, Atheneum, 1969; "Recent Poetry: Exiles and Disinterments" by Laurence Lieberman, in *Yale Review* (New Haven, Connecticut), Autumn 1971; "A Gathering of Poets" by Richard Shramm, in *Western Humanities Review* (Salt Lake City), Autumn 1972.

                              *   *   *

Imagine a set of fraternal twins, brothers at once terribly alike and needfully disparate. Who choose different facets of the same life to lead. Each achieving in different facets of the same craft; whose wishes and careers cast into patterns geographically separate and with startlingly similar results . . . supposing that each "brother" becomes deeply involved in the course of a major magazine, as an editor and as a creative writer; that each excels over a devoted period of long years' work; and that the two men, not having met or discussed, choose strong foreign interests to correspond to the intimately American identity of each . . .

The two men might be Howard Moss, poetry editor for the *New Yorker* for over twenty years, poet and playwright, native of New York City and admirer of England and Ireland; and Cid Corman, editor of *Origin* (Series 1–3), native of Boston, experiencer of Italy and Japan. Their physical resemblance is astonishing. Moss being a compact version of Corman's bigger corpus. Where Corman is heavy and flowing, a big man, Moss is formed into compact energy, fastidiousness, and order. They look as alike as brothers. And the magazines: Corman's is, of course, since the Black Mountain days, one of the most influential of the avant garde in the past twenty years. And Moss's section of the *New Yorker* has presented poetry in mass media in an impact undeniable on the American scene.

Howard Moss is, like Corman, the proven and respected possessor of a lucid, compressed poetic style that expresses a dynamic sensitivity to his world. Moss revels in the soft speech-pattern of Ireland's common folk; Corman, for years a visitor to Japan, now lives there. Both men are brown-eyed, affable, gregarious, kindly men, with that distance between upper lip and nose that betokens a generosity of spirit. Both are at once intimately a part of and separate from the realm of the massive creativity of our age. Each has the courage of the editor and the individuality of the creative, and it is to the credit of each that such risk and responsibility are accepted for the greater good.

Howard Moss is deeply engrossed in his interests in. the theatre. An accomplished playwright whose "experiments" with dialogue extend into his poetic techniques, he is an avid theatre-goer and commentator on avant garde theatre. He is the recipient of kudos for his criticism and has gathered such pieces into two stimulating collections. An admirer of Chekov, and of such Americans as Elizabeth Bishop and W.S. Merwin, he involves himself with the shaping of his magazine by himself reading and selecting from 150 poems a week (of the thousand or so that are submitted, from all over the world). His own work bears the imprint of the width, breadth, romanticism, and toughness of his Russian heritage, winning him a distinguished place in American letters.

– Carol Bergé

MOSS, Stanley. American. Born in New York City, 21 June 1935. Educated at Trinity College, Hartford, Connecticut; Yale University, New Haven, Connecticut. Married to Dr. Jane Z. Moss. Currently, Poetry Editor, *New American Review*, New York. Recipient: Rockefeller grant, 1967. Address: 241 Central Park West, New York, New York 10024, U.S.A.

PUBLICATIONS

Verse

The Wrong Angel.   New York, Macmillan, 1966.
The Wrong Angel (augmented edition).   London, Anvil Press Poetry, 1969.

*   *   *

If it is true that a first-rate poet is one whose poetic powers demonstrably grow over a period of time, it is difficult to determine the rank in which Stanley Moss stands. Since he has published but a single volume and an expanded version of that volume in the two-and-a-half decades of his poetic life, there is no real means to measure the range of his work.

Yet *The Wrong Angel* is not an infirm base on which to rest what is essentially a one-book reputation. It is gathered from a number of pieces that appeared in good periodicals and is divided into five sections, the most obviously cohesive of which is the fourth, "Poems on a Theme of Antony and Cleopatra." The last of the poems in this group, "Another Reply for Pompey," is a powerful statement tinged with Moss's characteristic tough humor, of man's becalmed ambition whipped up by a rising gale. It perverts the traditional tale of Pompey's respect for hospitality and refusal to gain the world by permitting his captain to cut loose the ship from its mooring to send the sleeping Caesar, Antony, and Lepidus to oblivion; in Moss's version, Pompey begins by ordering the cutting of the cable, and, as his sense of decency is further diminished by ambition rationalized, he ends by commanding the cutting of his guests' throats.

Moss has a way of soaring like Pompey's ambition – of slipping the anchor of the pedestrian and cutting the throat of the anticipated. But for a few poems, best forgotten, about a wide-eyed young man seeking himself abroad, he fills a moment

– biblical, present, any moment – with an exquisite sense of immediacy, often of ironic ominousness, of "the wrong angel." He watches his father: "Death hooks over the corner of his lips. / The wrong angel takes over the lesson." Moss is precisely the right poet to finger the wrong angel.

– Alan R. Shucard

MTSHALI, Oswald (Joseph).   South African.   Born in Vryheid, Natal, 17 January 1940. Educated at Inkamana High School, Natal. Married to Margaret Mtshali. Driver for a local engineering firm, 1963–65. Since 1965, messenger and general delivery man for a Johannesburg investment company. Address: P.O. Box 8266, Johannesburg, South Africa.

PUBLICATIONS

Verse

> *Sounds of a Cowhide Drum.*   Johannesburg, Renoster Books, 1971; London, Oxford University Press, and New York, Third Press, 1972.

Oswald Mtshali comments:

I am neither a Romantic nor a Traditionalist. Maybe I am a socially involved poet of South Africa as Charles Dickens was a socially involved novelist of England.

I consider Lorca, Allen Ginsberg and Yevtushenko as some of the poets I admire. I draw my themes from my life as I live and experience it. I write in the free verse form because it allows me more freedom in expression without the restriction of metre and rhyme. I depict the life of humanity as a whole as reflected in my environment, Mofolo Village; my community, Soweto; my society, Johannesburg; my country, South Africa. As an aspirant black poet in South Africa, I have no model poet on whom to base my style.

*   *   *

Oswald Mtshali's *Sounds of a Cowhide Drum* sold over 10,000 copies in South Africa in less than a year. Most of his poems deal with racial tensions. Some, as he says, punch "wildly at the immense powers," but many more successfully control narrative, imagery and the details of linguistic connotation in witty, anecdotal sketches of individuals under pressure or of bitterly ludicrous social injustices. More interestingly still, some longer poems, such as "Snowfall on Mount Frere," achieve a mode of emblematic narration (not unlike the Irish *aisling*) in which political pressure is recast in terms of the natural landscape of the oppressed country. Mtshali's ability to control larger structures, together with his acute visual memory, exploited in vivid analogies –

> A newly-born calf
> is like oven-baked bread
> steaming under a cellophane cover

or

> The skin was pale and taut
> like a glove on a doctor's hand

– could lead to developments in his work that will make him not only a man with an urgent and well-spoken message, but a poet with a unique voice of international validity.

– Anne Cluysenaar

MUDIE, Ian (Mayelston). Australian. Born in Hawthorn, South Australia, 1 March 1911. Educated at Scotch College, Adelaide. Served in the Australian Army, 1941–45. Married Renée Dunford Doble in 1935; has two sons. Lecturer in Creative Writing, Adult Education Department, University of Adelaide, 1959–66; Editor-in-Chief, Rigby Ltd. publishers, Adelaide, 1960–66. President, Fellowship of Australian Writers, 1959–60; Member, Literature Committee, Adelaide Festival of Arts, 1960–72; Member, South Australian Advisory Committee to the Australian Broadcasting Commission, 1963–70. Currently, Regional Vice-President, Australian Society of Authors. Recipient: W. J. Miles Memorial Prize, 1943; Commonwealth Literary Fund Fellowship, 1946; Grace Leven Prize, 1963. Address: 8 Bristol Street, Glenelg South, South Australia 5045, Australia.

PUBLICATIONS

Verse

Corroborēe to the Sun.   Melbourne, Hawthorn Press, 1940.
This Is Australia.   Adelaide, Frank E. Cork, 1941.
Their Seven Stars Unseen.   Adelaide, Jindyworobak Publications, 1943.
The Australian Dream.   Adelaide, Jindyworobak Publications, 1943.
Poems: 1934–1944.   Melbourne, Georgian House, 1945.
The Blue Crane: Poems.   Sydney, Angus and Robertson, 1959.
The North-Bound Rider.   Adelaide, Rigby, 1963.
Look, The Kingfisher!   Melbourne, Hawthorn Press, 1970.

Other

The Christmas Kangaroo (juvenile).   Adelaide, Frank E. Cork, 1946.
Riverboats. Adelaide, Rigby, 1962.
Wreck of the Admella (history).   Adelaide, Rigby, 1966; London, Angus and Robertson, 1967.
Rivers of Australia (juvenile).   Adelaide, Rigby, and San Francisco, Tri-Ocean Books, 1966; London, Angus and Robertson, 1968.
Pageant Stone: The First Hundred Years of John Martin's. Privately printed, 1968.
The Heroic Journey of John McDouall Stuart (biography).   Sydney, Angus and Robertson, 1968.
River Murray Sketchbook, with Jeanette McLeod.   Adelaide, Rigby, and San Francisco, Tri-Ocean Books, 1969.
Australia Today (juvenile).   Sydney, Hicks and Smith, and London, Kaye and Ward, 1970.
New Zealand Today (juvenile).   Sydney, Hicks and Smith, and London, Kaye and Ward, 1973.
Glenelg Sketchbook.   Adelaide, Rigby, 1974.

Editor, *Poets at War: An Anthology of Verse by Australian Servicemen.*   Melbourne, Georgian House, 1944.
Editor, *Jindyworobak Anthology 1946.*   Adelaide, Jindyworobak Publications, 1946.
Editor, with others, *Verse in Australia.*   Adelaide, Australian Letters, 4 vols., 1958–61.
Editor, with Colin Thiele, *Australian Poets Speak.*   Adelaide, Rigby, 1961.
Editor, *Favourite Australian Poems.*   Adelaide, Rigby, 1963.

Bibliography: *Ian Mudie: A Bibliography*, Adelaide, South Australia Libraries Board, 1970.

Ian Mudie comments:

Ian Mudie came into prominence as one of the Australian nationalist poets of the nineteen-thirties. He became associated with Rex Ingamells's Jindyworobak Movement and, as well as doing much to widen the use of Australian terms and turns of speech in serious Australian poetry, introduced the use of ideas from Aboriginal religion and mythology to apply symbolically to modern national problems. He has also found much of his symbolism in the scenery of the Australian Outback. Possibly his best-known poem is "They'll Tell You about Me," which is largely a catalogue of figures and incidents from Australian literature, history, and folklore. During recent years his poetry has tended to be quieter in tone and more personal, varying in mood from tender to bitter.

He has been called "a Wordsworth in blucher boots," a "serpent of mediocrity," and the founder of a truly Australian poetry. He is completely a compulsive poet, and has said "between one attack of poem-producing and the next I find it difficult to believe I am capable of writing poetry. His work varies from loose free verse expressed in speech-rhythms to strictly formal poetry. One critic has remarked that much of Mudie's work is not easy to accept as verse until it is read aloud, when the fact that it is poetry becomes inescapable.

He is not aware of having consciously attempted to achieve anything in poetry except to get the poem of the moment out of his system and fails to see that he has accomplished anything more with his poetry than that.

*   *   *

Ian Mudie has been publishing verse since 1934 and in this forty year span there have been many modifications and realignments of poetic orthodoxy. Although Mudie has practised in a number of forms and adopted various stances, ranging from the loud voiced jackeroo to the meditative nature lover to, more recently, the bemused urban victim of the generation gap, yet he will be remembered, probably, for a handful of poems of simple nationalistic assertiveness, written for, and in, a voice calculated to hold its own with any public bar stridency. These well known, and successfully extrovert larrikin-poems are, within the corpus of Ian Mudie's work, gestures. Mudie, the poet, is obviously more complex than this. Through all his collections one is aware of a simple but genuine preoccupation with Man In A Landscape. When the landscape and the man converge, as in the broad-brimmed slang poems, Mudie achieves his best poetic expression. The quieter poems, particularly in the earlier work, have to struggle with a much more intractable tyranny of form. Mudie, though prolific, has never expressed the exhiliration of conquering merely formal problems and obstacles. The lyric poems, therefore, tend to work doggedly towards their ends. Perhaps the most totally successful collection of poems by Ian Mudie is *The Blue Crane.* In this book the poet comes closest to relaxing his guard in the lyrical pieces, and certainly reaches his most convincing peak in the broad-accented poems. But more important, there is no sense of dichotomy between the two genres. Mudie has continued to write and to publish. His most recent work accepts naturally and without presumption certain lessons of the folk-rock culture. It also is pervaded with the forced reflectiveness of the once-active participant: the preoccupations are direct and physical, the recognitions point otherwise.

– Thomas W. Shapcott

MULDOON, Paul. Irish. Born in County Armagh, Northern Ireland, 20 June 1951. Educated at St. Patrick's College, Armagh; Queen's University, Belfast. Recipient: Eric Gregory Award, 1972. Address: Keenaghan, Duncannon, County Tyrone, Northern Ireland.

PUBLICATIONS

Verse

Knowing My Place.   Belfast, Ulsterman Publications, 1971.
New Weather.   London, Faber, 1973.

*   *   *

Paul Muldoon is an excellent technician who has achieved individuality very yoing. He has been compared with other young Irish poets, but in fact his distinction is marked out by a sense of apartness, in style as in subject-matter. He writes of love, for instance, as though it were a dispersion of one's sole self. Proximity is defined in terms of pain:

> Often when the wind has gathered
> The trees together and together
>
> One tree will take
> Another in her arms and hold . . .
>
> It is no real fire.
> They are breaking each other.
>
> Often I think I should be like
> The single tree, going nowhere . . .

If Muldoon identifies with anything at all, it is with such creatures as the hedgehog:

> The hedgehog gives nothing
> Away, keeping itself to itself.
> We wonder what a hedgehog
> Has to hide, why it so distrusts . . .

For Muldoon, ships are in bottles, the sea is in shells, the illusion of depth is created by carefully appointed mirrors. There is a paradox in using such careful artistry to communicate distance, remoteness, departure. It is seen at its most remarkable in "Good Friday, 1971. Driving Westward." Characteristically enough, the allusion to Donne signifies unlikeness. This is a poem about people remote from each other. The growing hiatus between intending lovers is symbolized in terms of driving a car:

> Errigal stepped out suddenly in our
> Path and the thin arm tightened round the waist
> Of the mountain and for a time I lost
> Control and she thought we hit something big
> But I had seen nothing, perhaps a stick
> Lying across the road. I glanced back once
> And there was nothing but a heap of stones . . .

A cairn or funeral mound for their love? One has to read this precise and enigmatic poem carefully. The words are never simply what they stand for and the poet's skilled play with them does more than his explicit statement to countenance a wary distrust of life. Paul Muldoon is certainly an original. His next collection of poems should dispel any illusions that some of his readers retain about contact or contiguity.

– Philip Hobsbaum

MURPHY, Richard. Irish. Born in County Mayo, 6 August 1927. Educated at
Canterbury Cathedral Choir School (Cathedral Chorister, 1940); King's School,
Canterbury (Milner Scholar), 1941–42; Wellington College, Berkshire, 1943–44;
Magdelen College, Oxford, 1945–48, M.A. 1948; the Sorbonne, Paris, 1954–55.
Married Patricia Davis in 1955 (divorced); has one daughter. Director, English
School, Canea, Crete, 1953–54; Writer-in-Residence, University of Virginia, Char-
lottesville, 1965; Visiting Fellow, Reading University, Berkshire, 1968; Compton
Lecturer in Poetry, University of Hull, Yorkshire, 1969; O'Connor Professor of
Literature, Colgate University, Hamilton, New York, 1971; Visiting Professor of
Poetry, Bard College, Annandale-on-Hudson, New York, 1972. Recipient: AE
Memorial Award, 1951; Guinness Award, 1962; Arts Council bursary, 1967. Fellow,
Royal Society of Literature, 1968. Address: Cleggan, County Galway, Ireland.

PUBLICATIONS

Verse

> *The Archaeology of Love.* Dublin, Dolmen Press, 1955.
> *The Woman of the House: An Elegy.* Dublin, Dolmen Press, 1959.
> *The Last Galway Hooker.* Dublin, Dolmen Press, 1961.
> *Six Irish Poets,* with others, edited by Robin Skelton. London and New York,
>   Oxford University Press, 1962.
> *Sailing to an Island.* London, Faber, 1963; New York, Chilmark Press, 1964.
> *Penguin Modern Poets 7,* with Jon Silkin and Nathaniel Tarn. London, Pen-
>   guin, 1965.
> *The Battle of Aughrim and The God Who Eats Corn.* London, Faber, and New
>   York, Knopf, 1968.

Recording: *The Battle of Aughrim,* Claddagh, 1969.

*   *   *

Richard Murphy's output is small, his central achievement so far a group of four
or five long poems, of very slow growth, in which his family and his chosen place
in the west of Ireland are commemorated. These poems are deeply meditated and
solid. They are not all equally successful, and there are unevennesses within the
poems themselves. And perhaps because of their low key, and perhaps because a
part of their subject matter belongs to an Irish Ascendancy tradition that has
withered away, these poems – and even Murphy's shorter poems, which have not
quite the same characteristics – have not yet established themselves as firmly as
they deserve to. They are there nevertheless, strenuously simple, the evidence of
Murphy's dedication and determination.
    The earliest, "The Last Galway Hooker," is typical of the strengths and limita-
tions of Murphy's method. The poem concerns the history of an old sailing boat
bought from a Connemara fisherman: the image of the boat itself, sailing temporarily in the poet's possession, is the structural strength of the poem. The image is
adequate by its nature, without further manipulation, for the poem's purpose –
which has to do with the past, as it is embodied in the artefact, passing though the
poet's hands into the future. Upon this sturdy structure the relevant facts accumulate, in verse of the lowest possible intensity. At its best the diction, gently
mannered, incandesces faintly against the general level of statement:

> Fastest in the race to the gull-marked banks
> What harbour she hived in, there she was queen. . . .

At its worst it sinks well below the danger level:

> We met here last summer, nineteen fifty-nine,
> Far from the missiles, the moon-shots, the money. . . .

But lapses of this kind, though they might seem ruinous, remain merely local and diminish the poem scarcely at all.

They are rare in Murphy's more recent poems, though these do not always have the same structural strength as "The Last Galway Hooker" – or "The Woman of the House" or "The God Who Eats Corn." "The Cleggan Disaster," for example, though it is more vigorous than these, squanders a great deal of its energy in a fine storm description that remains mere description, a distortion of the poem's form.

The Battle of Aughrim is a long radio script, in four sequences of lyrics, that sets out to investigate the reality of one great historic event. To speak only of technique, the work covers a far wider range of modes than Murphy has managed elsewhere, introducing, most notably, a harsh voice that promises new strength – especially when, as seems inevitable, Murphy opens himself to his intensest feelings.

– Thomas Kinsella

MURRAY, Les(lie) A(llan). Australian. Born in Nabaic, New South Wales, 17 October 1938. Educated at Taree High School; University of Sydney (Co-Editor, *Arna and Hermes*; Literary Editor, *Honi Soit*), 1957–60, 1962. Served in the Royal Australian Naval Reserve, 1960–61. Married Valerie Gina Maria Morelli in 1962; has one son and one daughter. Translator, Australian National University, Canberra, 1963–67. Recipient: Grace Leven Prize, 1965; Australian Commonwealth Literary Fund Fellowship, 1968; Australian Council for the Arts grant, 1970. Address: 7 Giles Street, Kingston, Canberra, A.C.T. 2604, Australia.

PUBLICATIONS

Verse

The Ilex Tree, with Geoffrey Lehmann.   Canberra, Australian National University Press, 1965.
The Weatherboard Cathedral: Poems.   Sydney, Angus and Robertson, 1969.
Poems Against Economics.   Sydney and London, Angus and Robertson, 1973.

Other

Translator, *An Introduction to the Principles of Phonological Description*, by Trubetzkoy.   The Hague, Nijhoff, 1968.

Les A. Murray comments:

Themes, subjects: legion, but principally the country, its people, landscapes, folklore, humour and so on. War in various aspects (the aircraft of the Pacific war flew over my childhood and I grew up with the ghosts of Gallipoli and, because we were of Scots descent, the '45). Human religious impulses and experiences too: natural religion mainly; though a Catholic by conversion, I can't handle specifically Christian poetry yet. Ancestors, relatives, neighbours, friends. A Welsh friend said once my characteristic figure was a horseman in a forest with a violin, and I said, yes, he was killed at Culloden and Bapaume and plays for dances at our local hall.

I try to write with clarity, lucidity and resonance, to reach as many people as possible, not just university readers. Heavy Australian bias in my work both natural and deliberate – try to write for all people in our commonwealth and keep us one community. Try to be universal through or at least while being Australian. Tend to preach doctrine that poets have no rights, only duties, especially that of service.

One of my most deeply held standards is that of a mistrustful love of people, and a resolve always to write about them with compassion and respect, avoiding the ultimately contemptuous, aren't-they-quaint-animals tone deeply infused in the very structure of modern, especially educated, English. Also distrust sophistication that shows and intellect that works as the clothes rather than the bones of a work.

I usually prefer to use fairly fixed measures, more often rhymed than not. My stanzas are most often quatrains, though tercets, quintains and sextains occur. Used refrains and repetitions a lot once, but less now. Pretty close attention to sound effects and placement of effects within lines and larger units. Use names of places and people a fair bit. Narrative forms common. Write as much for reading aloud as for the page, so pay close attention to pace. Have risky affection for effects derived from interplay of disparate emotions – stark terror and humour, for instance. Some use of primitive modes, particularly Australian Aboriginal and American Indian.

At my best I've achieved and maintained a certain lucid, kindly ringing tone I was aiming at, and a style capable of making real some things which are important to me and to a *few* others, anyway.

*   *   *

Les A. Murray's share of *The Ilex Tree*, published in collaboration with his friend Geoffrey Lehmann, consolidated a poetic reputation won and maintained throughout his college years. Though he is a student of modern languages, his poetry reflects no linguistic eclecticism or syntactic experimentation, as in the followers of Ezra Pound and T. S. Eliot, but is in the main written with an energetic and straightforward grasp of the strengths and latent possibilities of the English language. The breadth of his work has expanded over the past few years and he hardly ever writes in the shorter lyrical forms but uses a fairly free form of rarely less than fifty lines.

He was born and grew up on his father's dairy farm on the northern coast of New South Wales and in his own words "learned to read from an encyclopaedia." His celebration of country childhood is beautifully portrayed in "Spring Hail," a poem full of the fire and ice of the springing season. In the long meditation on his widowed father and farming antecedents, "An Evening Alone at Bunyah," and the more personal "Noontide Axeman," he captures the sense of loneliness verging on alienation ever-present in the Australian bushland and partially tamed countryside.

This innate sense of belonging to the land and yet isolated from it and other inhabitants is explored further in "The Away Bound Train" and "The Insolent

Familiar." The latter is especially remarkable for the paradoxical feeling of detached engagement which it generates while externally describing a stroll through a seaside holiday resort and witnessing a brawl outside a pub. In such poems as these Les A. Murray exerts a strong, exciting talent in modern Australian letters.

– Bruce Beaver

MUSGRAVE, Susan. Canadian. Born in Gort, Galway, Ireland, 3 December 1951. Recipient: Canada Council travel grant, 1970, bursary, 1972. Agent: McIntyre and Stanton, 1851 Welch Street, North Vancouver, British Columbia. Address: Box 10, Port Clements, Queen Charlotte Islands, British Columbia, Canada.

PUBLICATIONS

Verse

Songs of the Sea-Witch.   Vancouver, Sono Nis Press, 1970.
Skuld.   Frensham, Surrey, Sceptre Press, 1971.
Mindscapes.   Toronto, House of Anansi, 1971.
Birthstone.   Frensham, Surrey, Sceptre Press, 1972.
Entrance of the Celebrant.   Toronto, Macmillan, and London, Fuller d'Arch Smith, 1972.
Equinox.   Rushden, Northamptonshire, Sceptre Press, 1973.
Kung.   Rushden, Northamptonshire, Sceptre Press, 1973.
Grave-Dirt and Selected Strawberries.   Toronto, Macmillan, 1973.

Other

Gullband Thought Measles Was a Happy Ending (juvenile).   Vancouver, J. J. Douglas, 1974.

*   *   *

A reading of Susan Musgrave's poetry leaves me with the same disquieting feeling I had upon completing Sylvia Plath's *Ariel*, knowing that the death she tried to exorcise in her poetry had to be attempted again, and with success. It is not just that Musgrave imitates Plath, writing, in "Exposure":

> . . . .I have lived too long in a thick
> black shoe like a foot, I have stepped
> through too many days and uncovered my
> face on too many coins. . . .
>
> I have given up three times unsuccessfully
> and been shifted
> in and out of dreams like the
> opium alleys in the downtown night.
> I demand a sanity trial, I want you
> all there to witness my one
> symbolic disguise.
> Yes I am resting briefly in catatonia,
> campaigning the Creativity of Nothing –
> it may be the simplest resolution
> I've ever decided to make.

Nor is it only that their feminine stances are alike, and that their treatment of men, fascination with lesbianism, and intoxication with blood unite them. Rather, the resemblance is deeper and more disturbing. It lies in Musgrave's obsessive preoccupation with death which runs through all her poetry, making her the celebrant of death, the "spilled child" she writes so poignantly about, and making her transform the nights, the dreams, the sea, the womb, and life itself into death. My sense of unease is increased by the frequency with which Musgrave places herself at the "edge of things" in her poetry. In "Night and Fog" she ends, pleading:

> Stay with me. Out on the
> trailing edges of darkness
> I scatter their last bones before me
> to my will.

Or in "The Opened Grave" she writes:

> I remember the beginning
> like the first day of the world.
> I floated like a scar along some river
> listening for an answer
> Whenever I called. This dream,
> on the edge of things, troubled me –
> the dream I was lost and halfway there.

Normally, I would reject this kind of critical observation, arguing that poems are autonomous and ought not to be read as portents of things to come or as indices of a writer's psychological state. My only excuse in this instance is that the precariousness of the mood, the obsessive, poignant treatment of death, nightmares, and fears, the preoccupation with the question of sanity, and the frequently expressed desire for vacancy, for the sound that is no sound, all draw against the self-control the poetry seems to display, making it suspect and recalling the sinister bell heard behind Plath's poetry.

Many of Musgrave's poems read like unfamiliar myths in which witches and ghosts enact their spells, exposing man and love to ruin. In the poem "Gathering in the Host's Wood," cold Skuld, the Elf-Queen, rules over the dead, turning fire and passion into ash as she in the guise of a toad embraces the persona who is inhabiting the form of a squirrel. Musgrave writes with skill when she depicts her weird, magical, witch-like kingdom. Her eye for detail when she selects waterbugs, beetles, white moths, and gray insects to participate in the black rites is true, but rarely is she able to capture the rhythms that could lend her details the aura of bewitchment. She is more skilful when she takes a sound in Canada, or a river, and imbues it with terror. "Mackenzie River, North" illustrates this when she writes:

> . . . . The river is not our only hunter.
> White against the road
> the slow rain drives us back
> against the ground.
> Wolves smell us out of our bones,
> fish grow bored and swim away.
> There is nothing about us
> but fear

> And moving,
> always moving,
> out of the night
> it comes.

Finally, she is at her best when she unexpectedly numbs us with her image of death in the midst of love, in "Finding Love":

> From my bed I could hear
> the ripe wound open, the thick sea
> pouring in. I told you, then,
> the first lie I had in my heart;
> the carcass of a dull animal
> slipped between our sights.

Musgrave's range is limited, her theme obsessive and disquieting, but her images are stark and vivid, her magical presences haunting, and her sense of the whimsical and bizarre is unerring.

– Carol Simpson Stern

NABOKOV, Vladimir. Pseudonym: V. Sirin (for Russian works). American. Born in St. Petersburg, now Leningrad, Russia, 23 April 1899; left Russia in 1919, and lived in Berlin, 1922–37, and France, 1937–40; since 1940 has lived in the United States; naturalized citizen, 1945. Educated at Prince Tenishev School, St. Petersburg, 1910–17; Trinity College, Cambridge, B.A. 1922. Married Véra Slonim in 1925; has one son. Instructor in Russian Literature and Creative Writing, Stanford University, California, Summer 1941; Lecturer in Russian, Wellesley College, Massachusetts, 1941–48; Professor of Russian Literature, Cornell University, Ithaca, New York, 1948–59. Research Fellow, Museum of Comparative Zoology, Harvard University, Cambridge, Massachusetts, 1942–48; Visiting Lecturer, Harvard University, Spring 1955. Recipient: Guggenheim Fellowship, 1943, 1953; National Institute of Arts and Letters grant, 1951; Brandeis University Creative Arts Award, 1963; American Academy of Arts and Letters Award of Merit Medal, 1969; National Medal for Literature, 1973. Address: c/o McGraw-Hill Book Company, Trade Division, 1221 Avenue of the Americas, New York, New York 10020, U.S.A.; or, c/o Weidenfeld and Nicolson, 5 Winsley Street, London W.1, England.

Publications

Verse

(*Poems*).   St. Petersburg, privately printed, 1916.
(*Two Paths*).   Petrograd, privately printed, 1918.
Gorniy Put' (The Empyrean Path).   Berlin, Grani, 1923.
Grozd' (The Cluster).   Berlin, Gamayun, 1923.
Stikhotvoreniya, 1920–1951 (Poems).   Paris, Rifma, 1952.
Poems.   New York, Doubleday, 1959; London, Weidenfeld and Nicolson, 1961.
Poems and Problems.   New York, McGraw Hill, 1971; London, Weidenfeld and Nicolson, 1972.

Plays

Smertj (Death), *Deduschka* (Grandfather), *Poljus* (The Pole), *Trajedija gospodina Morna* (The Tragedy of Mr. Morn), and *Tschelowek in SSSR* (The Man from the USSR), published in *Rul* (Berlin), 1923–27.
Izobreteniye Val'sa, in *Russkiya Zapiski* (Paris), 1938; translated as *The Waltz Invention* (produced St. Paul, Minnesota, 1968).   New York, Phaedra, 1966.
Sobytiye (The Event) (produced Paris, 1938; New York, 1941).   Published in *Russkiya Zapiski* (Paris), 1938.

Screenplay: *Lolita*, 1962.

Novels

Mashen'ka.   Berlin, Slovo, 1926; translated by the author and Michael Glenny as *Mary*, New York, McGraw Hill, 1970; London, Weidenfeld and Nicolson, 1971.
Korol', Dama, Valet.   Berlin, Slovo, 1928; translated by the author and Dmitri Nabokov as *King, Queen, Knave*, New York, McGraw Hill, and London, Weidenfeld and Nicolson, 1968.
Zashchita Luzhina (The Luzhin Defense).   Berlin, Slovo, 1930; translated by the author and Michael Scammell as *The Defense*, New York, Putnam, and London, Weidenfeld and Nicolson, 1964.
Podvig' (The Exploit).   Paris, Sovremennïya Zapiski, 1932; translated by the author and Dmitri Nabokov as *Glory*, New York, McGraw Hill, 1971; London, Weidenfeld and Nicolson, 1972.
Kamera Obskura.   Paris, Sovremennïya Zapiski, and Berlin, Parabola, 1933; translated by W. Roy as *Camera Obscura*, London, Long, 1937; revised and translated by the author as *Laughter in the Dark*, Indianapolis, Bobbs Merrill, 1938; London, Weidenfeld and Nicolson, 1961.
Otchayanie.   Berlin, Petropolis, 1936; translated by the author as *Despair*, London, Long, 1937; revised edition, New York, Putnam, and London, Weidenfeld and Nicolson, 1966.
Priglashenie na Kazn'.   Paris, Dom Knigi, 1938; translated by the author and Dmitri Nabokov as *Invitation to a Beheading*, New York, Putnam, 1959; London, Weidenfeld and Nicolson, 1960.
The Real Life of Sebastian Knight.   New York, New Directions, 1941; London, Editions Poetry, 1945.

Bend Sinister. New York, Holt, 1947; London, Weidenfeld and Nicolson, 1960.

Dar. New York, Izdatel'stvo Imeni Chekhova, 1952; translated by the author and Michael Scammell as *The Gift,* New York, Putnam, and London, Weidenfeld and Nicolson, 1963.

Lolita. Paris, Olympia Press, 2 vols., 1955; New York, Putnam, 1958; London, Weidenfeld and Nicolson, 1959.

Pnin. New York, Doubleday, and London, Heinemann, 1957.

Pale Fire. New York, Putnam, and London, Weidenfeld and Nicolson, 1962.

Ada; or, Ardor: A Family Chronicle. New York, McGraw Hill, and London, Weidenfeld and Nicolson, 1969.

Transparent Things. New York, McGraw Hill, 1973.

Look at the Harlequins. New York, McGraw Hill, 1974.

Short Stories

Vozvrashchenie Chorba (The Return of Chorb). Berlin, Slovo, 1930.

Soglyadatay (The Spy). Paris, Russkiya Zapiski, 1938; translated by the author and Dmitri Nabokov as *The Eye,* New York, Phaedra, 1965; London, Weidenfeld and Nicolson, 1966.

Nine Stories. New York, New Directions, 1947.

Vesna v Fial'te i Drugie Rasskazi (Spring in Fialta and Other Stories. New York, Izdatel'stvo Imeni Chekhova, 1956.

Nabokov's Dozen: A Collection of 13 Stories. New York, Doubleday, 1958; London, Heinemann, 1959.

Nabokov's Quartet. New York, Phaedra, 1966; London, Weidenfeld and Nicolson, 1967.

A Russian Beauty and Other Stories, translated by Dmitri Nabokov. New York, McGraw Hill, and London, Weidenfeld and Nicolson, 1973.

Other

Nikolai Gogol. New York, New Directions, 1944; London, Editions Poetry, 1947.

Conclusive Evidence: A Memoir. New York, Harper, 1951; as *Speak, Memory: A Memoir,* London, Gollancz, 1952; revised edition, as *Speak, Memory: An Autobiography Revisted,* New York, Putnam, 1966; London, Weidenfeld and Nicolson, 1967.

Nabokov's Congeries: An Anthology. New York, Viking Press, 1968.

Strong Opinions (essays). New York, McGraw Hill, 1973.

Editor and Translator, *Eugene Onegin,* by Aleksandr Pushkin. New York, Pantheon Books, and London, Routledge, 4 vols., 1964.

Translator, *Nikolka Persik* (Colas Breugnon), by Romain Rolland. Berlin, Slovo, 1922.

Translator, *Anya v Strane Chudes* (Alice in Wonderland), by Lewis Carroll. Berlin, Gamayun, 1923.

Translator, *Three Russian Poets: Verse Translations from Pushkin, Lermontov and Tyutchev.* New York, New Directions, 1945; as *Poems by Pushkin, Lermontov and Tyutchev,* London, Drummond, 1948.

Translator, with Dmitri Nabokov, *A Hero of Our Times,* by Mikhail Lermontov. New York, Doubleday, and London, Mayflower, 1958.

Translator, *The Song of Igor's Campaign: An Epic of the Twelfth Century.* New York, Knopf, 1960; London, Weidenfeld and Nicolson, 1961.

Numerous papers on lepidoptera published in scientific journals, since 1920.

Bibliographies: *Vladimir Nabokov: Bibliographie des Gesamtwerks* by Dieter E. Zimmer, Hamburg, Rowohlt, 1963, revised edition, 1964; *Nabokov: A Bibliography* by Andrew Field, New York, McGraw Hill, 1974.

Critical Studies: *The Art of Vladimir Nabokov: Escape into Aesthetics* by Page Stegner, New York, Dial Press, 1966; *Nabokov: His Life in Art* by Andrew Field, Boston, Little Brown, 1967; *Nabokov: The Man and His Work,* edited by L. S. Dembo, Madison, University of Wisconsin Press, 1967; *For Vladimir Nabokov on His Seventieth Birthday,* edited by Charles Newman and Alfred Appel, Jr., Evanston, Illinois, Northwestern University Press, 1970, and London, Weidenfeld and Nicolson, 1971; *Vladimir Nabokov* by Julian Moynahan, Minneapolis, University of Minnesota Press, 1971; *Nabokov's Deceptive World* by W. Woodlin Rowe, New York, New York University Press, 1971.

*   *   *

Leaving aside the 999 lines of doggerel in his novel *Pale Fire,* Vladimir Nabokov's verse in English has been collected in two volumes, *Poems* and *Poems and Problems.* The first group in the latter book are of the most interest – 39 poems in Russian, dating from 1917 to 1967, with facing English translations by Nabokov himself. They compare interestingly with his autobiographical prose volume *Speak, Memory,* being pervaded as is that text by themes of sadness and images of loss. Without the existence of Nabokov's prose, however, it is doubtful that these verses would have attracted attention. As it is, they genuinely illuminate a certain section of his imagination – that which celebrates a Russia now gone forever, if indeed it ever existed. A Russia of the mind. A Russia necessary to Nabokov.

Fourteen other poems in *Poems and Problems* were originally written in English, and are observably less elegant in rhythm and diction. The volume has curiosity value in being perhaps the first publication ever to contain poems and chess-problems in one book. Those who find the problems poetic may well find the poems problematical.

– Robert Nye

NANDY, Pritish. Indian. Born in Bhagalpur, Bihar, 15 January 1947. Educated at La Martiniere, Calcutta; Presidency College, Calcutta. Married. Since 1968, Editor, *Dialogue Calcutta,* later *Dialogue India.* Address: 5 Pearl Road, Calcutta 17, India.

PUBLICATIONS

Verse

Of Gods and Olives: 21 Poems. Calcutta, Writers Workshop, 1967.
I Hand You in Turn My Nebbuk Wreath: Early Poems. Calcutta, Dialogue, 1968.
On Either Side of Arrogance. Calcutta, Writers Workshop, 1968.
Rites for a Plebeian Statue: An Experiment in Verse Drama. Calcutta, Writers Workshop, 1969.
From the Outer Bank of the Brahmaputra. New York, New Rivers Press, 1969.
Masks to Be Interpreted as Messages. Calcutta, Dialogue, 1970.
Collected Poems. London, Oxford University Press, 1973.

Other

Editor, *Getting Rid of Blue Plastic: Poems Old and New*, by Margaret Randall. Calcutta, Dialogue, 1968.
Editor, *Some Modern Cuban Poems.* Calcutta, Dialogue, 1968.
Editor, *Selected Poems of Subhas Mukhopadhyay.* Calcutta, Dialogue, 1969.
Editor, *Selected Poems of Parvez Shahedi.* Calcutta, Dialogue, 1969.
Editor, *Selected Poems of G. Sankara Kurup.* Calcutta, Dialogue, 1969.
Editor, *Selected Poems of Agyeya.* Calcutta, Dialogue, 1969.
Editor and Translator, *The Complete Poems of Samar Sen.* Calcutta, Dialogue, 1970.
Editor, *Selected Poems of Amrita Pritam.* Calcutta, Dialogue, 1970.
Editor, *Indian Poetry in English Today.* New Delhi, Sterling, 1973.

Translator, *Ravana's Lament: A Selection from the Abhiseka Swarga of the Meghnad-Badh Kavya of Michael Madhusudhan Datta.* Calcutta, Dialogue, 1969.

Critical Studies: *The Poetry of Pritish Nandy*, by Satyabrata Pal, Calcutta, Writers Workshop, 1969; "Workpoints for a Study of Pritish Nandy's 'In Transit, Mind Seeks' " by Satyabrata Pal, in *Banasthali Vidyapith Magazine*, 1969.

Pritish Nandy comments:

Trying to achieve an entirely new breakthrough in form and evolve a new language to characterise Indian writing in English. Feel that creative writing in English by Indians is generally imitative in both form and approach. What is required is a new language that will be characteristic and structurally powerful, with a logic of its own. It is this Indian English that must be worked out and that is what I am trying to do. Also trying to discover/build a tradition for Indo-Anglian poetry: the fusion of a modern language with the myths and symbols we have. Indian writers in English till now have ignored this quest for a tradition, which I consider vital for a living poetry. Finally: a personal quest – a secular, politically-involved poet has his own peculiar problems.

*   *   *

Pritish Nandy's early poems are often in short-line free verse; others form typographical pictures, or use Cummings-style spacing. He sceptically mingles Indian, classic, and Christian imagery, with gentle irony towards gods who "have aged and are not aware," or Christ who "came third in the contest / with death / and wrote a poem on the cross." Nandy indeed pities those who have to live with him – he "shreds their magic faith into a million assumptions." He is equally skeptical about such rationalists as the recluse found.dead: "having read too much of / Salinger / he had checkmated himself in one/man chess." Indeed, "To understand by cataloguing is like / splitting hairs on a bald head."

Perhaps this is why he thinks English poetry stopped at Auden (American "never began"); he most frequently alludes to Spanish-language poets, notably Lorca. His own effort is to combine, and symbolize: "What you cannot explain in terms of symbols is lost forever like blind totems and ruins in an old man's face." For words are only "masks to be interpreted in terms of messages."

He was long preoccupied with the frustrations of penetrating to realities, or saying anything meaningful if one did; he praised a friend for seeking "a new level of communication" and so compacted his own images as to make very sur-real sense: "your eyes bled like a violet tiger / as I watched the winds strangle / whispers of the apocalypse." But certain themes are clear: death, loneliness, suffering – and the mitigations of love, sex, friendship.

In *Masks to Be Interpreted as Messages* he changed to short statements in rhythmic prose, and in his best-known poem, "Calcutta, If You Must Exile Me," states in brutally direct style the cruelties which revolt him. Next year, the Bangla Desh horrors jolted him into plain, moving statements of sympathy with all victims of hate: in India, Vietnam, or Colombia "the marauders changed their name but the sufferers each time were the same." At times he despairs – "blood is a country you and I have loved in vain" – but he no longer thinks of leaving: "Dark city I shall not disown you again." And though he writes for those who cannot read the language he uses, "my voice is the voice of my people, for I speak of their loves and ambitions and secret shames."

Later, he found consolation in translating Tagore's last poems, a "devastating confrontation with death"; the message, of "haunting simplicity," is that "death is but a new birth of the spirit into the great unknown." Modern Indian poetry, he says, draws "strength from the bedrock of our tradition," yet is "violent, anguished, brutally contemporary." His own certainly is.

– George McElroy

NATHAN, Leonard (Edward). American. Born in Los Angeles, California, 8 November 1924. Educated at Georgia Institute of Technology, Atlanta, 1943; University of California, Los Angeles, 1946–47; University of California, Berkeley, B.A. (summa cum laude) 1950, M.A. 1952, Ph.D. in English 1961. Served in the United States Army during World War II. Married Carol Nash in 1949; has three children. Instructor, Modesto Junior College, California, 1954–60. Since 1960, Member of the Department of Rhetoric, Chairman of the Department, 1969–72, currently Professor of Rhetoric, University of California, Berkeley. Recipient: Phelan Award, 1959; Longview Award, 1961; University of California Creative Awards Fellowship, 1967; National Institute of Arts and Letters grant, 1971. Agent: Margaret Rebhan, 69 Northgate, Berkeley, California 94708. Address: 1135 Fresno Avenue, Berkeley, California 94707, U.S.A.

PUBLICATIONS

Verse

Western Reaches: A Collection of Poems.   San Jose, California, Talisman Press,
   1958.
The Glad and Sorry Seasons.   New York, Random House, 1963.
The Matchmaker's Lament and Other Astonishments.   Northampton, Massa-
   chusetts, Gehenna Press, 1967.
The Day the Perfect Speakers Left.   Middletown, Connecticut, Wesleyan
   University Press, 1969.
Flight Plan.   Berkeley, California, Cedar Hill Press, 1971.

Recording: *Confessions of a Matchmaker*, Fantasy-Galaxy, 1972.

Other

The Tragic Drama of William Butler Yeats: Figures in a Dance.   New York,
   Columbia University Press, 1965.

Editor, *Talisman Anthology.*   Georgetown, California, Talisman Press, 1963.

Translator, with others, *Modern Hindi Poetry.*   Bloomington, Indiana Univer-
   sity Press, 1965.
Translator, *First Person, Second Person*, by Ageyeya.   Berkeley, California,
   Center for South and Southeast Asia Studies, 1971.

Leonard Nathan comments:

I have always tried a wide variety of topics and styles. I guess I am aiming at
some sort of middle style that can move up or down at need and is inclusive
enough to encompass a good range of experience. I think that overly personal
poetry suffers from the same limits as so-called objective poetry: it reduces important poetic and human possibilities. I find that I have tended, as many others of my
generation, to "open" my verse up over the years, and to simplify and avoid the
literary. This often results in a loose iambic line in poems that have a lot of
forward momentum and aim at a strong climax, or a shorter less conventionally
metrical line in poems that move slowly toward a *diminuendo* ending. Poets who
have meant a lot to me as a poet are Wallace Stevens, Josephine Miles, William
Stafford and Richard Wilbur. If I have an obsessive theme it is how things (people
and others) do or don't relate: or, to use a more portentous word, communion or its
lack. ("Real meeting" is always something like religious experience, even when the
subject is a bad marriage, an alcoholic, or guilt.) I write poem by poem – have no
program, no grand design, but hope only to make what I do at the moment as good
as it can be.

*   *   *

In his review of *The Glad and Sorry Seasons* for *Poetry*, John Woods quite rightly observed that Leonard Nathan has a "preference for statements of revelation" and that his demands on metaphor are relatively minor. Nathan convinces by conclusive statement, seldom by narrative or emotional persuasion. Although he inclines toward declarative and reductionist poetry, his lines are not so concentrated as, say, W. S. Merwin's, nor has he Merwin's power to startle and amaze through revelation. Leonard Nathan employs a steady iambic meter, with frequent variation in end rhymes. His lines seldom fail; they are refined, restrained, and well polished.

The dominant tonality of *The Glad and Sorry Seasons* is autumnal. The poet is middle-aged and wise, detached and reflective:

> I sweeten by the minute, bodying
> The spirit of my seed; hear how I sing
> Inside my skin – that's blood, that growing sound,
> The psalm of mellowing . . . .

The following lines from "First Girl," while perhaps uncharacteristic of Nathan's lyrics, reveal the intensity he is capable of:

> As she bent, I woke, and felt a pull like water
> And saw above her head a foreign blue,
> And nothing was homely, even my heavy body,
> And what I had never learned I always knew.

This snow queen, resplendent in frosted radiance, has transformed the poet and "crystalized the wildest flux of nature." But the time of ecstasy is past and "too long ago for second thoughts."

The Day the Perfect Speakers Left seems to bemoan the disintegration of high culture and humanistic values. Several poems strike a pose reminiscent of Ezra Pound's "Hugh Selwyn Mauberley," in its condemnation of our "botched civilization," our "old bitch gone in the teeth." In Nathan's "The Crisis" a shadowy figure, a Greek or Jew, has come "To see his children's children, how they escaped / His law, his love, his unpronounceable name." The title poem of this volume confirms the notion and may remind one of Arnold's "Dover Beach." The birds have assembled for what the poet fears is final migration:

> And leave-taking was another,
> Sadder version of dusk we were attending,
> And as though a whole age were going out,
> Its head covered, and going out with it
> A purpose including stars and stones.

Poems detailing the splendor of small acts, and little gestures, also find their way into the volume, as in "An Answer of Sorts":

> A neighbor sings in her small backyard,
> As if she were in a procession
> To a temple. She has simply forgotten herself
> In the roses. Let her be. Let her be.

For Nathan there is an endless fascination with the mechanics of verse writing. The consistently polished flow of his lines is both remarkable and lamentable; one soon craves roughness in line and subject. Perhaps it is Leonard Nathan's very control of his materials and of the energy contained in them that keeps his poems, while always of craft, from becoming poems of authority.

– John R. Cooley

NAUDÉ, Adèle. South African. Born in Pretoria, 14 August 1910. Educated at Rustenburg Girls' High School, Rondebosch; University of Cape Town, B.A. 1930. Widow of D. F. Hugo Naudé; has one daughter. Formerly, Editor of various women's journals. Currently, Free-lance Journalist and Radio Scriptwriter. Address: Apartment C, 2 Scott Road, Claremont, Cape Province, South Africa.

PUBLICATIONS

Verse

Pity the Spring. Cape Town, Balkema, 1953.
No Longer at Ease: Poems. Cape Town, Balkema, 1956.
Only a Setting Forth: Poems. Cape Town, Human and Rousseau, 1965.
Time and Memory. Cape Town, Maskew Miller, 1973.

Other

Verhale vit die Griekse Legendes. Cape Town, Oxford University Press, 1949.
Konig Arthur en sy Ridders. Cape Town, Oxford University Press, 1950.
Gentlemen's Relish: Dishes with a Difference. Cape Town, privately printed, 1956.
Strooihoed en Sonbril (travel). Cape Town, Human and Rousseau, 1965.
Tousandale aan my Voete (travel). Cape Town, Human and Rousseau, 1968.
Gregory Kaapse Pikkewyn: The Jackass Penguins of the Cape and Present-Day Pollution. Cape Town, David Philip, 1971.
Rondebosch and Round About. Cape Town, David Philip, 1973.

Critical Studies: by E. Pereira, in *South African Poetry: A Critical Anthology*, Pretoria, Communications of the University of South Africa, 1966; D. R. Beeton, in *UNISA English Studies* (Pretoria), June 1968.

Adèle Naudé comments:

Verse forms mainly traditional. Subject matter: nature, human relationships, European art and cultures.

*   *   *

Adèle Naudé's first volume, *Pity the Spring*, strikes the note of seasonal decay and painful regeneration which recurs throughout her work:

> Pity the spring that yet unknowing bears
> The seeds of autumn's rotting fruit within
> Her youthful self. . . .

Traditional in form (she describes herself as "mainly a stanza poet, with little runs of free verse in between"), her poems are intensely personal explorations of thought, feeling, and human relationships, through images drawn from art and nature. The need for poetic expression, for truths intuitively perceived and sensitively rendered, informs the firm lines of "Stone Man":

> It was but stone
> And yet it had a force
> That dragged the sculptor's hand
> Along an unfamiliar course
> And led him to an alien land. . . .

Taking its cue from Eliot's "Journey of the Magi," her second volume, *No Longer at Ease*, is full of self-questioning, but there is greater assurance of tone and technique in the empathic exploration of everyday things. She is fascinated by shifts of focus, by the insights gained through changing perspectives. Equally important is her probing of classical myth, and awed experiencing of Mediterranean culture, in the evocative "Oracle of Delphi" and "In the Old Orchard" (reminiscent of Roy Campbell in its structural control and starkly physical portrayal of seasonal process):

> How cold the old arthritic trees
> Knotted in their strings of pain!
> The lupins push their pliant bodies
> Close to take the winter's strain. . . .

> Now red the sod and warm the soil
> And friable with youth interred.
> The trees receive Persephone,
> Fair ransom for the massacred.

Her third volume, *Only a Setting Forth*, is notable for the "inner vision" she attains to through the commonplaces of chance encounters and shifting perspectives. There is wry acceptance, tautly phrased, in "The Unpossessed": "I fear no loss / Though never at rest; / None has yet lost / The unpossessed," and a recurrence of the ironic note and epigrammatic style first encountered in *No Longer at Ease*. Again, however, it is the Mediterranean- (and Cape-) inspired poetry which is most finely felt and wrought, and which places her in the front rank of contemporary South African poets.

Of her latest volume, *Time and Memory*, Adèle Naudé remarks: ". . . although it is the same voice, the eye is different. I am looking at life from a different point of view." It remains to be seen whether this latest change of focus results merely in variations on a theme, or does in fact signal a new direction.

– E. Pereira

NEAL, Larry (Lawrence P. Neal). American. Born in Atlanta, Georgia, 5 September 1937. Educated at a Roman Catholic high school, Philadelphia; Lincoln University, Pennsylvania, B.A. 1961; University of Pennsylvania, Philadelphia. Married. Former Art Editor, *Liberator* magazine, and education director of the Panther party. Co-Editor, *The Cricket* magazine; Contributing Editor, *Journal of Black Poetry*. Recipient: Guggenheim Fellowship, 1971. Address: 12 Jumel Terrace, New York, New York 10032, U.S.A.

PUBLICATIONS

Verse

    Black Boogaloo: Notes on Black Liberation. San Francisco, Journal of Black Poetry Press, 1968.

Other

    Editor, with LeRoi Jones, *Black Fire: An Anthology of Afro-American Writing.* New York, Morrow, 1968.

*   *   *

Larry Neal is a foremost and influential theorist, interpreter, and spokesman of the current "Black arts movement." He has declared that "Black Art . . . speaks directly to the needs and aspirations of Black America. . . . It proposes a separate symbolism, mythology, critique, and iconology."

His poems are informed by events and situations in, or touching upon, the lives of the masses of Black people. They often celebrate an elitism, a flair, an élan often associated with Black life styles. For example, he says about a jazzman's identifying hat, ". . . the pork-pie hat reigns supreme, / the elegance of style / gleaned from the city's underbelly / . . . defying the sanctity of white / America." His poetic Black icons are not often those from traditional history books but rather the likes of Charlie Parker, the folk-hero "Shine," Malcolm X, the Signifying Monkey from Black oral lore, and Langston Hughes. There is in his work an element of spiritualism, frequently Islamic, sometimes approaching the mystical and mythological.

Sensitive to the poetic inherent in Black oral culture, Neal usually employs common language, current as well as older folk idioms, a conversational or "rapping" tone (e.g., ". . . instant time, my man, history is one quick / fuck; you no sooner in then you come, a quick fuck"). The flow of his lines frequently connotes non-verbal sounds, as in "Kuntu" with its suggestion of talking drums. He often makes allusions to jazz music and musicians, and his technical effects are suggestive of jazz music. His imagery is deft and clear, although at times somewhat ethnocentric. He is an adroit cataloguer. Most of his poetry, in the free verse style, is irregularly structured, or it is complex in such a way that the overall schema, like intricately structured jazz, is not immediately apparent.

– Theodore R. Hudson

NEMEROV, Howard. American. Born in New York City, 1 March 1920. Educated at Fieldston School, New York; Harvard University, Cambridge, Massachusetts, A.B. 1941. Served in the Royal Canadian Air Force and the United States Air Force, rising to the rank of First Lieutenant, 1941–45. Married Margaret Russell in 1944; has three children. Instructor in English, Hamilton College, Clinton, New York, 1946–48; Member of the Literature Faculty, Bennington College, Vermont, 1948–66; Professor of English, Brandeis University, Waltham, Massachusetts, 1966–69. Since 1969, Professor of English, Washington University, St. Louis. Visiting Lecturer, University of Minnesota, Minneapolis, 1958–59; Writer-in-Residence, Hollins College, Virginia, 1962–64; Consultant in Poetry, Library of Congress, Washington, D.C., 1963–64. Associate Editor, *Furioso*, Madison, Connecticut, later Northfield, Minnesota, 1946–51. Recipient: *Kenyon Review* Fellowship in Fiction, 1955; Oscar Blumenthal Prize, 1958, Harriet Monroe Memorial Prize, 1959, and Frank O'Hara Prize, 1971 (*Poetry*, Chicago); *Virginia Quarterly Review* Short Story Award, 1958; National Institute of Arts and Letters grant, 1961; New England Poetry Club Golden Rose, 1962; Brandeis University Creative Arts Award, 1962; National Endowment for the Arts grant, 1966; Theodore Roethke Award, 1968; Guggenheim Fellowship, 1968; St. Botolph's Club Prize, 1968; Academy of American Poets Fellowship, 1970. D.L.: Lawrence University, Appleton, Wisconsin, 1964; Tufts University, Medford, Massachusetts, 1969. Fellow, American Academy of Arts and Sciences, 1966. Member, National Institute of Arts and Letters, 1965. Address: Department of English, Washington University, St. Louis, Missouri 63130, U.S.A.

PUBLICATIONS

Verse

The Image and the Law. New York, Holt, 1947.
Guide to the Ruins. New York, Random House, 1950.
The Salt Garden. Boston, Little Brown, 1955.
Mirrors and Windows. Chicago, University of Chicago Press, 1958.
New and Selected Poems. Chicago, University of Chicago Press, 1960.
The Next Room of the Dream: Poems and Two Plays. Chicago, University of Chicago Press, 1962.
Five American Poets, with others, edited by Ted Hughes and Thom Gunn. London, Faber, 1963.
The Blue Swallows. Chicago, University of Chicago Press, 1967.
The Winter Lightning: Selected Poems. London, Rapp and Whiting, 1968.
The Painter Dreaming in the Scholar's House. New York, Phœnix Book Shop, 1968.
Gnomes and Occasions: Poems. Chicago, University of Chicago Press, 1972.

Novels

The Melodramatists. New York, Random House, 1949.
Federigo; or, The Power of Love. Boston, Little Brown, 1954.
The Homecoming Game. New York, Simon and Schuster, 1957.

Short Stories

> *A Commodity of Dreams and Other Stories.* New York, Simon and Schuster, 1959; London, Secker and Warburg, 1960.
> *Stories, Fables and Other Diversions.* Boston, Godine Press, 1971.

Other

> *Poetry and Fiction: Essays.* New Brunswick, New Jersey, Rutgers University Press, 1963.
> *Journal of the Fictive Life.* New Brunswick, New Jersey, Rutgers University Press, 1965.
> *Reflexions on Poetry and Poetics.* New Brunswick, New Jersey, Rutgers University Press, 1972.

> Editor, *Poets on Poetry.* New York, Basic Books, 1965.

Critical Studies: *Howard Nemerov* by Peter Meinke, Minneapolis, University of Minnesota Press, 1968; *The Critical Reception of Howard Nemerov: A Selection of Essays and a Bibliography*, edited by Bowie Duncan, Metuchen, New Jersey, Scarecrow Press, 1971; *The Shield of Perseus*, by Julia Bartholomay, Gainesville, University of Florida Press, 1972.

*   *   *

Howard Nemerov's poems are, on the one hand, often about bugs, birds, trees, and running water. On the other, they are about the Great American Society and its works, e.g. the loyalty oath, the committee, the Indian-head nickel, and the packaged meat in the super-market. And they are about Lot's wife, and Lu Chi, and Vermeer. They are about history and nature, and about everyman, who participates in and speaks for both.

Nemerov does not seek to impose a vision upon the world so much as to listen to what it says. He works in closer relationship with literal meaning than is at present fashionable; consequently, his worst fault is sententiousness, but his corresponding virtue is a clarity whose object is not to diminish the mystery of the world but to allow it to appear without the interposition of a peculiar individuality, or of fancy-work or arabesque. He is, as much as any modern can be, a romantic poet, a religious poet who has no religion:

> . . . and history is no more than
> The shadows thrown by clouds on mountainsides,
> A distant chill when all is brought to pass
> By rain and birth and rising of the dead.
> – from "Runes," X

He is a prophet, especially in the polemical and ironic mode, without portfolio. When he writes about history, as Stanley Hyman has said, his theme is "history from the point of view of the losers." Thus when he wants to write about Moses, he does so from the point of view of Pharaoh after the Red Sea debacle; and instead of writing about Perseus, he presents the nitwitted predecessors of that hero, who approached Medusa without a mirror and were turned to stone. To judge by his later poems, being turned to stone is the least agreeable and most probable fate for human beings and their institutions together.

Nemerov is an intellectual but in no obtrusive way a "literary" poet, except insofar as he uses a variety of traditional verse forms. There are rhymed quatrains, songs, sonnets, sestinas, most notably a loose blank-verse line well exemplified in his two short plays, *Endor* and *Cain*. Nemerov's voice is spare and flexible. He allows himself no flourishes, except in irony, e.g. at the expense of Santa Claus, the "annual saviour of the economy," who "speaks in the parables of the dollar sign: / Suffer the little children to come to Him." The over-all effect is of great intellectual and lyric power held in firm control. The poems are like the seeds Nemerov so often speaks of: small, but greatly generative. What they generate in us is painstaking and sometimes painful attention to the insides and outsides of things, and to the subtle relationships between them.

The world, for Nemerov, is a great writing in which we are characters attempting to read our own sentence. We are to see (not solve) our secret in seeds and seasons, in trout pools and in paintings and in poems:

> . . . knowing the secret,
> Keeping the secret – herringbones of light
> Ebbing on beaches, the huge artillery
> Of tides – it is not knowing, it is not keeping,
> But being the secret hidden from yourself.
> – from "Runes," XV

Being is extraordinarily painful: "from nose-picking to the Crucifixion / One terrible continuum extends / Binding disaster to discovery." The point of faith is that you sweat your *being* out. But there is more than sweat. Happiness is "helpless" before the fall of white water which purges away "all this filth" of history and mortality. Nemerov accepts again and again the river-runs of time and language in which the reflections of our stony monuments break and disappear.

– Julia Randall

NEWLOVE, John (Herbert). Canadian. Born in Regina, Saskatchewan, 13 June 1938. Married Susan Mary Phillips in 1966; has two step-children. Senior Editor, McClelland and Stewart Ltd., publishers, Toronto. Recipient: Koerner Foundation grant, 1964; Canada Council grant, 1965, 1967; Governor-General's Award, 1973. Address: c/o McClelland and Stewart Ltd., 25 Hollinger Road, Toronto 16, Ontario, Canada.

PUBLICATIONS

Verse

Grave Sirs: Poems. Vancouver, Robert Reid, 1962.
Elephants, Mothers and Others. Vancouver, Periwinkle Press, 1963.

Moving In Alone.   Toronto, Contact Press, 1965.
Notebook Pages.   Toronto, Charles Pachter, 1966.
Four Poems.   Platterville, Wisconsin, It, 1967.
What They Say.   Toronto, Weed/Flower Press, 1967.
Black Night Window.   Toronto, McClelland and Stewart, 1968.
The Cave.   Toronto, McClelland and Stewart, 1970.
Lies.   Toronto, McClelland and Stewart, 1972.

*   *   *

John Newlove has moved from an initial stage of matter-of-fact, personal recollection through a middle phase of essentially negative vision and a conscious edging towards marginal projectivism, to a latter condition in which there has been a noticeable darkening of his horizons coupled with a new intellectual toughness, and a more studied method in his technique.

In the early poems the most consistent locus is that of a series of private observations, and the tone – understandably personal and not infrequently nostalgic – is honest and outspoken. The correlatives are of youthful experiences; the remembered journey; the sense and sensation of simply being alive. A sombre shift takes place with *Moving In Alone* and with *What They Say* where death, isolation and the pointlessness and ugliness of existence become the hallmarks of much of what Newlove has to say. There is also a sense of a kind of desperate activity; movement; travel in the tumbleweed moods of the hitch-hiker which suggests rootlessness and a worrisome escape.

Disengagement and the poet's alienation continue to dominate *Black Night Window*, Newlove's most ambitious collection, and stamp him with the mark of small "e" existentialism. He continues to be autobiographical although his perspective transcends the purely subjective, and his imagination grapples effectively with abstraction and succeeds in striking a balance between his own vision, the ideas of poetry, and the larger consciousness of collective man.

Newlove's marginal projectivism stems from the technical bias of the Canadian West Coast *TISH*-movement with which the poet has links. His early style has a laconic, forthright quality with later development into the relative complexities of jigsaw structuring of concrete, immediate and precise images.

– Michael Gnarowski

NICHOL, Barrie Phillip (bpNichol). Canadian. Born in Vancouver, British Columbia, 30 September 1944. Attended the University of British Columbia, Vancouver. Formerly, taught grade school. Co-Editor, *GrOnk* magazine, Toronto. Recipient: two Canada Council grants; Governor-General's Award, 1971. Address: c/o The Village Bookstore, 29 Gerrard Street West, Toronto, Ontario, Canada.

PUBLICATIONS

Verse

Cycles Etc.   Cleveland, 7 Flowers Press, 1965.
Scraptures: 2nd Sequence.   Toronto, Ganglia Press, 1965.
Strange Grey Town, with David Aylward.   Toronto, Ganglia Press, 1966.
Tonto or.   Toronto, Ganglia Press, 1966.
Calendar.   Woodchester, Gloucestershire, Openings Press, 1966.
Scraptures: 3rd Sequence.   Toronto, Ganglia Press, 1966.
Scraptures: 4th Sequence.   Niagara Falls, New York, Press Today Niagara, 1966.
Fodder Folder.   Toronto, Ganglia Press, 1966.
Portrait of David.   Toronto, Ganglia Press, 1966.
A Vision in the U of T Stacks.   Toronto, Ganglia Press, 1966.
A Little Pome for Yur Fingertips.   Toronto, Ganglia Press, 1966.
Langwedge.   Toronto, Ganglia Press, 1966.
Alaphbit.   Toronto, Ganglia Press, 1966.
Stan's Ikon.   Toronto, Ganglia Press, 1966.
The Birth of O.   Toronto, Ganglia Press, 1966.
Chocolate Poem.   Toronto, privately printed, 1966.
Last Poem with You in Mind.   Toronto, Ganglia Press, 1967.
Konfessions of an Elizabethan Fan Dancer.   London, Writers Forum, 1967.
bp (including *Journeying and The Returns, Letters Home,* and a recording, *Borders*).   Toronto, Coach House Press, 1967.
Scraptures: 10th Sequence.   Toronto, Ganglia Press, 1967.
Scraptures: 11th Sequence.   Toronto, Fleye Press, 1967.
Ruth.   Toronto, Fleye Press, 1967.
The Year of the Frog: A Study of the Frog from the Scraptures: Ninth Sequence.   Toronto, Ganglia Press, 1967.
Ballads of the Restless Are.   Sacramento, California, Runcible Spoon Press, 1968.
Dada Lama: A Sound Sequence in Six Parts.   London, Cavan McCarthy, 1968.
The True Eventual Story of Billy the Kid.   Toronto, Weed/Flower Press, 1970.
Still Water.   Vancouver, Talonbooks, 1970.
Beach Head.   Sacramento, California, Runcible Spoon Press, 1970.
MONO tones.   Vancouver, Talonbooks, 1971.
Love: A Book of Remembrances.   Vancouver, Talonbooks, 1971.
ABC: The Aleph Beth Book.   Ottawa, Oberon Press, 1971.
The Martyrology.   Toronto, Coach House Press, 1972.

Recording: *Motherlove,* Allied Records, 1968.

Novels

Andy and For Jesus Lunatic: Two Novels.   Toronto, Coach House Press, 1969.

bpNichol comments:

primarily i consider myself to be serving an apprenticeship in language, hopefully to find ways out of the self-imposed trap it has evolved into.

i suppose if i have a general theme it's the language trap and that runs thru the centre of everything i do. in this regard Bill Bissett first pointed the direction with a poem called "They Found th Wagon Cat in Human Body." hence style is disregarded in favor of reproduction of actual states of mind in order to follow these states thru the particular traps they become in search of possible exits. hence for me there is no discrepancy to pass back and forth between trad poetry, concrete poetry, sound poetry, film, comic strips, the novel or what have you in order to reproduce the muse that musses up my own brain.

as large influences i would like to note Chester Gould's *Dick Tracy*, Walt Kelly's *Pogo*, & Winsor McKay's *Dreams of a Rarebit Fiend & Little Nemo in Slumberland.* In addition the poetry of Olson and Creeley, e. e. cummings, gertrude stein & james joyce, rube goldberg, & the children's books by Dr. Seuss.

*   *   *

bpNichol is internationally known as the Canadian concrete poet, a role bestowed on him by that self-conscious international movement.

Konfessions of an Elizabethan Fan Dancer consists of typewriter poems, visual poetry dependent on the identical size of typewriter letters. "The Return of the Repressed," reminiscent of a genetic chart, evolves in time:

```
                          Q
            OOOOOOOOOOⓍOOOOOQOOOO
            OOOOOOOOOOⓍOOOOOQOOOOO
            OOOOOOOOOOⓍOOOOOQOOOO
            QQQQQQQQQQQQQQQQQQQQQQ
            QQQQQQQQQQQQQQQQQQQQQQ
            QQQQQQQQQQQQQQQQQQQQQQ
            QQQQQQQQQQQQQQQQQQQQQQ
```

The progenitor is replaced by his sons. Nichol uses the more extravagant Press-On Type for "tight imagistic" effects, not meant as pictures, he says, but as "syllabic and sub-syllabic messages to who care to listen." In "Window," Nichol paints with letters the aural and emotional complex suggested by a window; "imagism" seems to be an appropriate analogue. *Still Water* is a box of poems on cards, cleanly printed in sans-serif type. Many are funny, like this rap at high coo:

> 2 leaves touch
> bad poems are written

Others are one-liners using onomatopoetic permutations: "beyond a bee yawned abbey on debby honda beyond." Although one-line poems are in vogue, their creators seem defensive, probably because scale in poetry and in painting has grown larger through this century, more heroic, more inclusive.

In any case, there is nothing new or unusual about Nichol's concrete poetry. In his book on Canadian literature, Northrop Frye concluded that the country's literary energy had been absorbed in meeting a standard, a self-defeating enterprise because real standards can only be established, not met. Canadian writing, according to Frye, is academic in the pejorative sense, an imitation of a prescribed model, second rate in conception, not merely execution.

The poetry which is loosely called concrete, however, is self-investigative. Richard Kostelanetz, a theoretician of the movement, compares it to minimalism.

Like minimal artists, concrete poets will restrict themselves to the means of making statements. Nichol writes a poem on mortality which consists of a rhyme:

FLOWERS
(hours)

The Toronto Research Group, in which Nichol is prominent, investigates translation and narrative in an imaginative rather than critical context. The very process of imitation seems to have freed Nichol from that malaise.

The Martyrology, a recent two-volume large-scale work, is certainly readable. It's about a bunch of saints he made up. Saint Ranglehold, for instance, is the patron of the sea, and he gives lovers a hard time on their Petrarchan voyages; were there such things as ''the good'' and ''the bad'' saints, Nichol asks, where would we place him?

> a ship in perilous storm
> the lover doth compare his state to
>
> often he loses
>   (sinking out of view)
>
> dedications change as frequently as the moon
>
> riding the white waves
> patterns seem strangely familiar
>
> ruler of the ships & sea
> saint ranglehold guides lovers with a flaccid hand
>
> snickers knowingly
> as they flounder on dry land

Saint Reat, like Charles Olson, had difficulty breathing and, as a wanderer in search of breath, he is the patron saint of poetry. Saint Orm, a loser, gets kicked Kafka-style around a circus. Nichol has a special devotion to Saint Orm. These saints are neither Eastern nor Christian but very tough. It takes a Dick Tracy or Emma Peel to handle them.

> random brain stranded in the station
>
> sam & dick & emma peel
> oh how the real world gets lost in you
>
> the loose ends shrivel
>   & are gone
>
> faces denote the places growing song

The Martyrology is a creation myth. The saints once lived in the clouds. Saint And was the first to leave. Orm followed, expecting rain. Saint Iff had a terrible time, landing in the desert and dying near water. Only Saint Rike and the lady of past nights stayed behind, and their tale is curious indeed. But so are the other tales.

—Michael André

_____

NICHOLL, Louise Townsend. American. Born in Scotch Plains, New Jersey. Educated at Smith College, Northampton, Massachusetts, B.A. Formerly, Reporter, *Evening Post,* New York; Associate Editor, E. P. Dutton and Company, publishers, New York. Since 1956, Free-lance Writer and Editor. Founding Editor, *The Measure: A Journal of Poetry,* New York. Member, Poetry Society of America Executive Board. Recipient: Academy of American Poets Fellowship, 1954; Catholic Poetry Society Spirit Gold Medal, 1965; Lowell Mason Palmer Award, 1965; Shelley Memorial Award, 1971. Address (business): 3 West 46th Street, New York, New York 10036, U.S.A.

PUBLICATIONS

Verse

> *Water and Light.* New York, Dutton, 1939.
> *Dawn in Snow.* New York, Dutton, 1941.
> *Life Is the Flesh.* New York, Dutton, 1947.
> *The Explicit Flower.* New York, Dutton, 1952.
> *The Collected Poems.* New York, Dutton, 1953.
> *The Curious Quotient.* New York, Dutton, 1956.
> *The World's One Clock.* New York, St. Martin's Press, 1959.
> *The Blood That Is Language.* New York, Day, 1967.

Other

> *The Blossom Print.* New York, Dutton, 1938.

*   *   *

Louise Townsend Nicholl is one of those lady writers who give authors with three names a bad reputation. Old-fashioned and predictable, she prefers nature-studies, particularly from the religious angle, which, despite accumulated detail, remain lifeless and remote. Her relentless rimes depict trees, flowers, houses, birds with postcard simplicity, yet less vividly. Striving for painterly effect, she gathers several surface aspects into metrical catalogues or stretches obvious metaphors into intolerable conceits. Facile associations, strained into semblance, pile up into anticlimaxes, while labored lines result in strange illogic. Acute pain, tense struggle, serious philosophical questioning find no place in this genteel world where even death is gentle. Her easy ramblings reveal the cozy landscape of a comfortable mind. Yet so often she tells of her longing to escape. Thus, her "antique nature" finds respite in sweet nostalgia, occasionally mixed with patriotic pap. Her attempts at the poetry of "uplift" and inspiration are usually just cloying. She enjoys, to use her phrase, "looking back obscurely," and old grammar school prescriptions for poetic form seem to have been taken to heart. Rather than showing us, however, she merely tells of her selective domain in general terms – *splendor, beauty, magnificence, ecstasy* – grand in sound though vague in meaning. If she does not jar us with novelty, intrigue us with an original viewpoint, or startle us into a new awareness, that may be because these are not her intentions. It is easy and it may be unfair to accuse her of failing to achieve that for which she does not strive. Throughout a prolific career she has remained faithful to her earliest formula, which she has continued to express in decorative lines that are not without the charm of the pleasant and familiar.

—Joseph Parisi

NICHOLSON, Norman (Cornthwaite). British. Born in Millom, Cumberland, 8 January 1914. Educated at local schools. Married Yvonne Gardner in 1956. Frequent public lecturer. Recipient: Heinemann Award, 1945; Cholmondeley Award, 1967; Northern Arts Association Grant, 1969; Society of Authors bursary, 1973. M.A.: Manchester University, 1959. Fellow, Royal Society of Literature, 1945. Agent: David Higham Associates, 5-8 Lower John Street, Golden Square, London W1R 4HA. Address: 14 St. George's Terrace, Millom, Cumberland LA18 4DB, England.

PUBLICATIONS

Verse

Selected Poems, with John Hall and Keith Douglas. London, John Bale and Staples, 1943.
Five Rivers. London, Faber, 1944; New York, Dutton, 1945.
Rock Face. London, Faber, 1948.
The Pot Geranium. London, Faber, 1954.
Selected Poems. London, Faber, 1966.
No Star on the Way Back: Ballads and Carols. Manchester, Manchester Institute of Contemporary Arts, 1967.
A Local Habitation. London, Faber, 1972.
Hard of Hearing. London, Poem-of-the-Month Club, 1974.

Recording: *Poems*, with Tony Connor, Argo, 1974.

Plays

The Old Man of the Mountains (produced London, 1945). London, Faber, 1946.
Prophesy to the Wind: A Play in Four Scenes and a Prologue (produced London, 1949). London, Faber, 1950.
A Match for the Devil (produced Edinburgh, 1953). London, Faber, 1955.
Birth by Drowning (produced Mirfield, Yorkshire, 1959). London, Faber, 1960.

Television Play: *No Star on the Way Back*, 1963.

Novels

> *The Fire of the Lord.* London, Nicholson and Watson, 1944; New York,
>   Dutton, 1946.
> *The Green Shore.* London, Nicholson and Watson, 1947.

Other

> *Man and Literature.* London, S.C.M. Press, 1943.
> *Cumberland and Westmoreland.* London, Hale, 1949.
> *H. G. Wells.* London, Barker, and Denver, Swallow, 1950.
> *William Cowper.* London, Lehmann, 1951.
> *The Lakers: The Adventures of the First Tourists.* London, Hale, 1955.
> *Provincial Pleasures.* London, Hale, 1959.
> *Portrait of the Lakes.* London, Hale, 1963.
> *Greater Lakeland.* London, Hale, 1969.

> Editor, *An Anthology of Religious Verse Designed for the Times.* London,
>   Penguin, 1942.
> Editor, *Wordsworth: An Introduction and Selection.* London, Phoenix, and
>   New York, Dent, 1949.
> Editor, *Poems,* by William Cowper. London, Grey Walls Press, 1951.

Manuscript Collection: National Collection of Poetry Manuscripts, London.

Critical Studies: *Christian Themes in Contemporary Poets* by Kathleen Morgan, London, S.C.M. Press, 1965; "The Provincial Poetry of Norman Nicholson" by Philip Gardner, in *Toronto Review.*

Norman Nicholson comments:

(1970) The most obvious characteristic of my poetry is the fact that I draw by far the greater amount of my imagery from my own immediate environment – i.e., from the fells, dales, farms, sea-shore and estuaries of the English Lake District, and from the houses, streets, blast furnaces, mines, etc. of the small industrial town of Millom where I still live in the house where I was born. But, though the topographical element is prominent in my earlier verse, I do not think of myself primarily as a local poet. On the contrary, I feel that, through drawing on my knowledge of the place and the people where and among whom I have spent all my life, I am able to say what I want to say about man in relation to his physical environment and about human society, man in relation to man. In particular, I believe that in a small, somewhat isolated town like Millom, the problems of society, the dwelling-together of people of different types, ages and class, and the pattern of the repetition and variation shown from generation to generation, can be seen on a scale small enough for the mind to grasp it whole.

(1974) After the publication of *The Pot Geranium,* I wrote very little poetry for about ten years, but then began writing again and produced the poems collected together under the title of *A Local Habitation,* which was The Poetry Book Society's Autumn Choice for 1972. This work is, on the whole, more direct, more colloquial in tone, and, though I am as concerned as ever with the problem of environment, the new poems deal more with people than with places, and in particular with the people of Millom, with my family and other memories of childhood and youth. I have also written a number of lighter poems which have not yet been published but have been included in a number of anthologies and in my public readings of my own verse.

*   *   *

Norman Nicholson is very much a poet of the Cumberland area, and very much a poet of the Christian faith; these twin themes run through most of his published work from *Five Rivers* onward. He writes very often of the landscape around Millom, the little town where he was born – only fifteen miles from the Lakeland of Wordsworth, Coleridge, Southey, with whom he evidently feels a deep sympathy; and he frequently speaks through the mouths of the often wryly humorous characters who live in the roughly beautiful Cumberland landscape, "Where the rocks stride about like legs in armour/And the steel birches buckle and bounce in the wind. . . ."

His talent is for somewhat laconic observation of the natural scene, of landscape and wild and human life; the fact that he has made a selection from Wordsworth is significant. His unintellectualized faith often sees Christianity epitomized in acts of nature. He has written on modern European literature from a religious standpoint, and has edited an anthology of religious verse; his own verse-play *The Old Man of the Mountains* is a reworking of the story of Elijah and the raven, set in the contemporary Cumberland landscape.

Nicholson's choice of words is straightforward and unambiguous, and if there is a certain ambiguity at the heart of his verse, it is the ambiguity which as a Christian poet he has set out to reconcile with inner certainty. Most of his poems, however assured, seem to end with a question. Unfashionably direct in language and philosophy, he is perhaps one of the finest landscape poets writing at the present time.

—Derek Parker

NIMS, John Frederick. American. Born in Muskegon, Michigan, 20 November 1913. Educated at De Paul University, Chicago; University of Notre Dame, Indiana, A.B. 1937, M.A. 1939; University of Chicago, Ph.D. in comparative literature 1945. Married Bonnie Larkin in 1947; has four children. Taught at the University of Notre Dame, 1939–45, 1946–58; University of Toronto, 1945–46; Visiting Fulbright Professor of American Literature, Bocconi University, Milan, 1952–53, and University of Florence, 1953–54; Visiting Professor of American Studies, University of Madrid, 1958–60 (Smith-Mundt grant); Professor of English, University of Illinois, Urbana, 1961–65, Chicago Circle, 1965–73; Visiting Professor of English and Comparative Literature, Harvard University, Cambridge, Massachusetts, 1964, 1968–69, and Breadloaf School of English, Vermont, 1965–69. Since 1973, Professor of English, University of Florida, Gainesville. Associate Editor, 1945–48, Guest Editor, 1960–61, *Poetry*, Chicago. Recipient: Harriet Monroe Memorial Prize, 1942, Guarantors Prize, 1943, and Levinson Prize, 1944 (*Poetry*, Chicago); National Endowment for the Arts grant, 1967; National Institute of Arts and Letters grant, 1968. Address: Department of English, University of Florida, Gainesville, Florida 32601, U.S.A.

PUBLICATIONS

Verse

Five Young American Poets: Third Series, with others. New York, New Directions, 1944.
The Iron Pastoral. New York, Sloane, 1947.
A Fountain in Kentucky and Other Poems. New York, Sloane, 1950.
Knowledge of the Evening: Poems 1950–1960. New Brunswick, New Jersey, Rutgers University Press, 1960.
Of Flesh and Bone. New Brunswick, New Jersey, Rutgers University Press, 1967.

Other

Western Wind: An Introduction to Poetry. New York, Random House, 1974.

Editor, with others, *The Poem Itself.* New York, Holt, 1960.
Editor, *Ovid's Metamorphoses: The Arthur Golding Translation.* New York, Macmillan, 1965.

Translator, *The Poems of St. John of the Cross.* New York, Grove Press, 1959; revised edition, 1968.
Translator, *Andromache,* in *Euripides III* of *The Complete Greek Tragedies.* Chicago, University of Chicago Press, 1959.
Translator, *The Graveyard by the Sea and Other Poems.* New Brunswick, New Jersey, Rutgers University Press, 1970.
Translator, *Sappho to Valéry: Poems.* New Brunswick, New Jersey, Rutgers University Press, 1971.

*   *   *

There has always been a tradition of elegance in American poetry, and it is to this tradition that John Frederick Nims belongs. He has an ease of tone which is very civilized, and an admirable virtuosity when it comes to the handling of verse. He is able to convince his readers that poetry can reject the "barbaric yawp" of Whitman without surrendering the power to communicate. Immediately after the war, Nims was one of the pioneers of a new style in American verse, a style which, for a time, carried all before it with its urbanity. His first full collection, *The Iron Pastoral,* appeared in 1947, the same year as Richard Wilbur's *The Beautiful Changes,* and Nims, as much as Wilbur, was one of the leaders of the reaction against modernism which swept through American poetry in the forties. The manner which was then established has since been challenged by a very different sort of poetry. But Nims, no less than Wilbur, was highly original in the context of the time, and his work seems likely to be remembered not only for its unfailing grace, but as marking an important turning-point in the development of the literary tradition. Meanwhile, it has continued to give pleasure to all those poetry-readers whose taste is not entirely at the mercy of the dictates of fashion.

—Edward Lucie-Smith

NORRIS, Leslie. Welsh. Born in Merthyr Tydfil, Glamorgan, 21 May 1921. Educated at Cyfthfa Castle School, 1931–38; City of Coventry College, 1947–48; University of Southampton (Ralph Morley Prize, 1958), 1955–58, Dip.Ed., M.Phil., 1958. Served in the Royal Air Force, 1940–42. Married Catherine Mary Morgan in 1948. Teacher, Grass Royal School, Yeovil, Somerset, 1948–52; Deputy Head, Southdown School, Bath, 1952–55; Head Teacher, Aldingbourne School, Chichester, 1956–58; Principal Lecturer in Degree Studies, College of Education, Bognor Regis, Sussex, 1958–73. Since 1973, Visiting Professor of English, University of Washington, Seattle. Recipient: Welsh Arts Council Award, 1967, 1968; Alice Hunt Bartlett Prize, 1970. Agent: Charles Schlessiger, Brandt and Brandt, 101 Park Avenue, New York, New York 10017. Address: Plas Nant, Northfields Lane, Aldingbourne, Chichester, Sussex, England.

PUBLICATIONS

Verse

Tongue of Beauty. London, Favil Press, 1941.
Poems. London, Falcon Press, 1946.
The Ballad of Billy Rose. Leeds, Northern House, 1964.
The Loud Winter. Cardiff, Triskell Press, 1967.
Finding Gold. London, Chatto and Windus-Hogarth Press, 1967.
Curlew. St. Brelade, Jersey, Armstrong, 1969.
Ransoms. London, Chatto and Windus, 1970.
His Last Autumn. Rushden, Northamptonshire, Sceptre Press, 1972.
Mountains, Polecats, Pheasants and Other Elegies. London, Chatto and Windus, 1973.
Stone and Fern. Winchester, Southern Arts Association, 1973.
Wthan Moonfields. Llandysul, Cardiganshire, Gomer, 1973.
The Dove and the Tree. Llandysul, Cardiganshire, Gomer, 1973.

Recording: *Poems,* with Dannie Abse, Argo, 1974.

Other

Glyn Jones. Cardiff, University of Wales Press, 1973.

Editor, *Vernon Watkins, 1906–1967.* London, Faber, 1970.

Manuscript Collection: National Library of Wales, Aberystwyth, Cardiganshire.

Critical Studies: by Sam Adams, in *Poetry Wales* (Cardiff), 1972; R. Jenkins, in *The Anglo-Welsh Review* (Pembroke Dock), 1972; Ted Walker, in *Priapus* (London), 1972.

Leslie Norris comments:

My poetry is an attempt to recreate, not to describe. The birds or animals or people or buildings or trees existing in my poems, must exist root branch claw skin and stone. The texture of my words must be made of feathers or bones bark or whatever, the lines must move with real muscle. I think I am a Jungian poet, bringing up the images from some unknown source. The poems come unbidden, and my task is to recognise them; often I am well towards the end of a poem before I know what it is "about." But afterwards I work with unremitting labor to make sure of the poem's clarity, to make its surface perfect. I think my poems ought to be like onions; the golden outer skin flawless, the weight surprisingly heavy, solid, much more than you'd expect; then when the outer skin is peeled, there is the moist, pearly inner layer of meaning, then another and another.

Somewhere in the process you might begin to weep.

                          *   *   *

To say that Leslie Norris was born in an industrial town in South Wales, and that this fact has had an enormous effect on his poetry, could give an entirely wrong impression of his work. The particular industrial town, Merthyr, stands where the South Wales coalfield abruptly ends and where the lovely National Park of the Brecon Beacons begins. There is in fact far more about nature in Leslie Norris's work than there is about the "charred hills" of industry and he is as different from the truly mining-valley poets like Idris Davies and Robert Morgan as it is possible to be. Merthyr itself has a strong literary tradition and the poet was encouraged to write in school from a quite early age. This Wordsworthian "seed-time," his childhood and youth in Merthyr, has been a wonderfully fruitful source of material and inspiration for his poetry and some of his best and most moving poems ("Dead Boys," "A Blunt Invasion") deal with his memories of his Merthyr schooldays or become reflections arising from incidents which took place during this period. The boxing tradition was almost as powerful in Merthyr as the literary one and Leslie Norris has written movingly about this too; what is probably his most popular poem, "The Ballad of Billy Rose," anthologized about eighty times, concerns this at first sight rather unpromising subject. His nature poetry, fresh, unsentimental, drenched in the atmosphere of high moorland or autumnal splendour, can be largely descriptive like the admirable "Buzzard," or, like "Looking at Snowdrops" and "Ransomes," be fine syntheses of natural observation and compassionate memory of dead poets like Hart Crane and Edward Thomas. There is about the current work of Leslie Norris a restlessness, an intelligence, a compassion which make him a poet whose new works one awaits with excitement.

—Glyn Jones

NORSE, Harold. American. Born in New York City. Educated at New York University, M.A. Lived in Europe and North Africa, 1953–68. Currently, part-time teacher, University of California, San Jose. Editor, *Bastard Angel* magazine, San Francisco. Recipient: Swallow Press New Poetry Series Award, 1953; National Endowment for the Arts grant, 1974. Address: 29B Guy Place, San Francisco, California 94105, U.S.A.

PUBLICATIONS

Verse

The Undersea Mountain: Poems. Denver, Swallow, 1953.
The Dancing Beasts. New York, Macmillan, 1962.
Karma Circuit: 20 Poems and a Preface. London, Nothing Doing in London, 1967.
Penguin Modern Poets 13, with Charles Bukowski and Philip Lamantia. London, Penguin, 1969.
Hotel Nirvana. San Francisco, City Lights Books, 1974.

Other

The Roman Sonnets of G. C. Belli. New York, Grove Press, 1960.

*   *   *

Harold Norse has suffered from a number of disadvantages, as far as making a poetic reputation is concerned. An expatriate and a slow starter, he does not seem to have sought, and certainly has not managed to find, a regular market for his work. A protegé, like Ginsberg, of William Carlos Williams, his mature poems are related to the Beats, yet retain a sufficient stylistic distance to prevent him from being swept up into the Beat movement as a whole, and borne along on its current of energy.

It must also be admitted that he is an uneven writer. His first book, which he now seems to have rejected almost totally, is *The Undersea Mountain*, published in 1953. The prevailing influence is that of Hart Crane. These lines, from a poem called "The Tankers," are exactly in the manner of Crane's *The Bridge*:

> The gunmount flashes, flashing metal grey
> also the opaque aft, as down the harbor
> estuary under steam towards turquoise streams
> she plies.
>> And dagger-eyed the gull veers overhead.

Norse next surfaced, seven years later, with a remarkable book of translations – from the sonnets in Roman dialect of G. C. Belli. What these seem to have enabled him to do was to relate his feeling for American vernacular to his feeling for Europe. Belli, with his baroque use of an exuberantly popular diction, was the liberating influence Norse needed.

His more recent poems, couched in the ranging free-verse which is now an accepted American idiom, tend to vary in quality according to the amount of information, and the kind of information, he manages to pack in to them. Quite a few people do the drug poem, and the tantric poem, rather better than Norse. His speciality, if only he would realise it, is of a more traditional kind – he charts the meetings of the Old World and the New with a kind of exuberant delicacy. His best essay in this manner is the appropriately titled "Classic Frieze in a Garage," which takes an idiom which is basically the one Pound forged for *The Cantos* and uses it in a personal, and, to me, extremely seductive way:

> perfect! & how strange! garage
>   swallows sarcophagus!
> mechanic calmly spraying
>   paint on a
>   fender
> observed in turn by lapith & centaur!

—Edward Lucie-Smith

NOTT, Kathleen (Cecilia). British. Born in London. Educated at Mary Datchelor School, London; King's College, London; Somerville College, Oxford, B.A. (honours) in philosophy, politics and economics. Worked in Army Education and with Air Raid Precautions in World War II. President, Progressive League, London, 1958–60. Since 1960, Editor of International P.E.N.'s Bulletin of Selected Books, London. Since 1966, Vice-President, International P.E.N., British Centre. Recipient: Arts Council Bursary, 1968. Agent: Hope Leresche and Steele, 11 Jubilee Place, London SW3 3TE. Address: 5 Limpsfield Avenue, Thornton Heath, Surrey CR4 6BG, England.

PUBLICATIONS

Verse

Landscapes and Departures. London, Editions Poetry, 1947.
Poems from the North. Ashford, Kent, Hand and Flower Press, 1956.
Creatures and Emblems. London, Routledge, 1960.

Novels

Mile End. London, Hogarth Press, 1938.
The Dry Deluge. London, Hogarth Press, 1947.
Private Fires. London, Heinemann, 1961.
An Elderly Retired Man. London, Faber, 1963.

Other

The Emperor's Clothes: An Attack on the Dogmatic Orthodoxy of T. S. Eliot, Graham Greene, Dorothy Sayers, C. S. Lewis and Others. London, Heinemann, 1954.
A Clean Well-Lighted Place. London, Heinemann, 1960.
Objections to Humanism, with others. London, Hodder and Stoughton, 1963.
A Soul in the Quad. London, Routledge, 1969.
Philosophy and Human Nature. London, Hodder and Stoughton, 1970.

Editor, with C. Day Lewis and Thomas Blackburn, New Poems 1957: A P.E.N. Anthology. London, Joseph, 1957.

Translator, Northwesterly Gale, by Lucien Chauvet. London, Hutchinson, 1947.
Translator, Son of Stalin, by Riccardo Bacchelli. London, Secker and Warburg, 1956.
Translator, The Fire of Milan, by Riccardo Bacchelli. London, Secker and Warburg, 1958.

Critical Study: in Times Literary Supplement (London), 1963.

Kathleen Nott comments:

I am primarily a poet, but I had a philosophical training and I am very much concerned with ethics and aesthetics. A Soul in the Quad took over five years to write and is a largish book describing in an autobiographical and intellectual-social setting what I conceive the relations of poetry and philosophy to be.

I regard poetry as a special language and an existential one. It is the language of beings of rather peculiar physiological and psychological organization. It works out as the most favourable selection and balance of the colours, implications, weights, stresses and relations of words – most favourable, that is, to project a highly authentic personal vision (which may be of a momentary kind). Hence rhythmical and musical sense strikes me as paramount.

*   *   *

As a philosopher Kathleen Nott is a humanist but also a respectful opponent of logical positivism and the "scientism" of Karl Popper. Her position is in fact a remarkably original and interesting one, and it is in her poetry that we find it most subtly and yet explicitly stated. For, like Valéry, she believes in the formulative power of music (in the Valérian sense of that preconceived rhythm that "visits" a poet before he is consciously aware of its content or significance). Thus rhythm is an important aspect of her work: she seldom works within strictly conventional forms, but her line is elegantly formed and controlled. This is also the strongest feature of her work – its weaknesses are unconfident or blurred diction, and an apparent inability to do justice to her initial impulse. Thus "Absolute Zero" begins promisingly:

> There are no tall engines standing in the polar North
> or none that is ready for use. They are all
> sheeted and hooded with the snow: who could discern them
> among faceless pines
> and blinded firs?

But this vision gradually peters out into a confusion of metaphors, only to recover itself at the end of the poem: the result is unintentionally elliptical. There seems little explanation for the wrenched diction ("and at last to be seen of eyes . . .") that characterizes the middle section of the poem. Fortunately this does not always happen: "Nature's Betrayal," about Wordsworth and nature, is in a tighter form, and there is more control of meaning and metaphor as well as of rhythm. At her best Kathleen Nott is an interesting philosophical poet whose thinking, in this form, deserves more attention than it has been given.

—Martin Seymour-Smith

NOWLAN, Alden A. Canadian. Born in Windsor, Nova Scotia, 25 January 1933. Married to Claudine Orser; has one son. Formerly, News Editor, *The Observer*, Hartland, New Brunswick, and *The Telegraph Journal*, St. John, New Brunswick. Since 1968, Writer-in-Residence, University of New Brunswick, Fredericton. Recipient: Canada Council Fellowship, 1961, Special Award, 1967; Governor-General's Award, 1968; Guggenheim Fellowship, 1968; President's Medal, The University of Western Ontario, for short story, 1969, 1971. D.Litt.: University of New Brunswick, 1971. Address: 676 Windsor Street, Fredericton, New Brunswick, Canada.

PUBLICATIONS

Verse

The Rose and the Puritan. Fredericton, University of New Brunswick, 1958.
A Darkness in the Earth. Eureka, California, Hearse Press, 1959.
Wind in a Rocky Country. Toronto, Emblem Books, 1960.
Under the Ice. Toronto, Ryerson Press, 1961.
Five New Brunswick Poets, with others, edited by Fred Cogswell. Fredericton, New Brunswick, Fiddlehead, 1962.
The Things Which Are. Toronto, Contact Press, 1962.
Bread, Wine and Salt. Toronto and Vancouver, Clarke Irwin, 1967.
A Black Plastic Button and a Yellow Yoyo. Toronto, Charles Pachter, 1968.
The Mysterious Naked Man: Poems. Toronto, Clarke Irwin, 1969.
Playing the Jesus Game: Selected Poems. Trumansburg, New York, New Books, 1970.
Between Tears and Laughter. Toronto, Clarke Irwin, 1971.

Novel

Cautious Persons Named Kevin O'Brien. Toronto, Clarke Irwin, 1973.

Short Stories

Miracle at Indian River. Toronto, Clarke Irwin, 1968.

Alden Nowlan comments:

I write about what it is like to be Alden Nowlan because that is the only thing I know anything about.

*   *   *

Something of the spirit of Edwin Arlington Robinson's Tilbury Town or Edgar Lee Masters' Spoon River informs the concise, realistic, and often bitterly ironic studies of rural and still primitive central New Brunswick which make up some of the most striking pages of the Canadian poet Alden Nowlan's volumes of verse. Both *The Things Which Are* and *Bread, Wine and Salt* attain a power and maturity that transcend the merely local.

A perception of beauty at the heart of violence and a sharpness and intensity of vision that give a breathing body to thought and idea make Nowlan's poetry relevant both as expression and meditation. One poem, for example, reveals a compassionate understanding of the half savage "incestuous kings" of the logging camps who drink and brawl on Saturday nights on Stoney Ridge; another depicts the agony of a young boy tormented by sexual desire in a joyless puritan community; and a third offers love and understanding to the body of a young woman imagined murdered, stripped and hidden in "the grove beyond the barley." In an epigram entitled "The Genealogy of Morals" the poet equates the childhood dreams and fears of St. Francis and Gilles de Raisse: "The same nightmares instruct the evil, as inform the good."

In an interesting autobiographical document, which must have helped him win his Guggenheim Fellowship, Nowlan spoke of his ancestor Padraig O'Nolin, who crossed the Atlantic in 1787 and cleared a plot of ground in Nova Scotia. "He is said to have come to his new homestead carrying only a musket and a salt shaker. From old Patrick's loins have come politicians, prostitutes, rum runners, farmhands, village idiots, Baptist ministers, Catholic priests, cavalrymen, draft dodgers, fortune tellers, burglars and me."

—A. J. M. Smith

NUTTALL, Jeff. British. Born in Clitheroe, Lancashire, 8 July 1933. Educated at Hereford School of Art, graduated in 1951; Bath Academy of Art, graduated in 1953. Served in the Royal Army Education Corps. Married Jane Louch in 1954.

Has taught in the Art Departments of several secondary schools; Lecturer, Fundamental Studies Department, Bradford College of Art, Yorkshire, 1968–70. Since
1970, Lecturer in Fine Art, Leeds College of Art. Has exhibited paintings and
constructions. Formerly, Editor, *My Own Mag*. Address: 461 Huddersfield Road,
Wyke, Bradford, Yorkshire, England.

PUBLICATIONS

Verse

> *The Limbless Virtuoso*, with Keith Musgrove.   London, Writers Forum, 1963.
> *Songs Sacred and Secular*.   London, privately printed, 1964.
> *Poems I Want to Forget*.   London, Turret Books, 1965.
> *Pieces of Poetry*.   London, Writers Forum, 1965.
> *Isabel*.   London, Turret Books, 1967.
> *Journals*.   Brighton, Sussex, Unicorn Bookshop, 1968.
> *Penguin Modern Poets 12*, with Alan Jackson and William Wantling.   London,
>   Penguin, 1968.
> *Love Poems*.   Brighton, Sussex, Unicorn Bookshop, 1969.
> *Selected Poems*.   London, Horizon, 1970.
> *Poems 1962–69*.   London, Fulcrum Press, 1970.

Play

> *Barrow Bags* (produced Bradford, Yorkshire, 1972).

Novels

> *Come Back Sweet Prince: A Novelette*.   London, Writers Forum, 1966.
> *The Case of Isabel and the Bleeding Foetus*.   London, Turret Books, 1967.
> *Mr. Watkins Got Drunk and Had to Be Carried Home*.   London, Writers
>   Forum, 1968.
> *Oscar Christ and the Immaculate Conception*.   London, Writers Forum, 1968.
> *Pig*.   London, Fulcrum Press, 1969.
> *Snipe's Spinster*.   London, Calder and Boyars, 1974.

Other

> *Bomb Culture* (social criticism).   London, MacGibbon and Kee, 1968; New
>   York, Delacorte Press, 1969.

Jeff Nuttall comments:

I make a line out of a rhythmic figure. The previous figure suggests the
subsequent one. The rhythmic figures owe much to Parker's saxophone phrasing.
I look to my obsessions to provide me with syllables to fill out the necessary
figure.

I am hardly at all concerned with direct verbal/syntactical "meaning." Silly to call my verse "obscure" unless you're short sighted.

*   *   *

Jeff Nuttall goes a little crazy. He mentions it in *Bomb Culture*, his book of social criticism:

> The phone goes. Criton. I don't want to see or speak to anybody. I've recently had a nervous crack-up and managed to pass it off to the family as flu – three wincing days bound in the sheets, trying to dull my screaming nerves. I want to hibernate. And now Criton rings.

Think of that passage while reading "Insomnia":

> Shall I do it, get up?
> Curl like a hurt furred animal?
> Shall I curl like an early embryo
> All hairy, simian, gone wrong?
> Curl up out there, out of the bed,
> Red, raw bitten under my itch of pelt,
> All huddled up, all curled on my side?

The man suffers from more than insomnia. "Insomnia" appeared in *Poems I Want to Forget*. Again the title misleads, for Nuttall does not want to forget his poems out of temperamental disdain or wispy diffidence; underground poets do not cotton to the wispy. Rather he wants to forget the pain. In *Bomb Culture* he remarks on a similar subterfuge in Ginsberg:

> Ginsberg read, and it registered that what had seemed over-messianic, grotesquely self-exposing and self-lacerating in print, was, in fact, a gay thing, the violent images delivered with a mischievous twinkle, and incredible milky gentleness flowing out from this one man into the minds and bodies of the audience.

Oscar Christ and the Immaculate Conception epitomizes the discrepancy between a gay manner and a horrific subject. It is a cheaply-printed, woolly and daffy underground collage-novel-poem about a Russian girl murdered in World War II by her S.S. lover:

> That night I woke and said
> "What's your name, Oscar?"
> "Christ," he said.

But the grotesquerie underlines the significance, as the woman by admirable sleight of hand comes to typify all contemporary women; they offer themselves to men who oblige by murdering them. "I Hadn't Meant Murder," in *Poems I Want to Forget*, is about a similar impulsive murder of a lover. Nuttall is a little crazy, and he thinks society, in *Bomb Culture*, is completely crazy. Nuclear war, to his underground mind, is inevitable. The goal of life is death, said Freud, and Nuttall sees it in himself and in society.

—Michael André

NYE, Robert. British. Born in London, 15 March 1939. Educated at Dormans Land, Sussex; Hamlet Court, Westfield, Essex; Southend High School. Married Judith Pratt in 1959 (divorced); Aileen Campbell, 1966; has four sons and two daughters. Free-lance Writer. Contributes critical articles and reviews to British periodicals, notably *The Scotsman*, Edinburgh, and *The Times* and *The Guardian*, London. Since 1967, Poetry Editor, *The Scotsman*; since 1971, Poetry Critic, *The Times*. Recipient: Eric Gregory Award, 1963; Scottish Arts Council bursary, 1970, and publication award, 1970; James Kennaway Memorial Award, 1970. Lives in Edinburgh. Address: c/o Calder and Boyars Ltd., 18 Brewer Street, London W.1, England.

PUBLICATIONS

Verse

Juvenilia 1. Lowestoft, Suffolk, Scorpion Press, 1961.
Juvenilia 2. Lowestoft, Suffolk, Scorpion Press, 1963.
Darker Ends. London, Calder and Boyars, and New York, Hill and Wang, 1969.
Agnus Dei. Rushden, Northamptonshire, Sceptre Press, 1973.
Two Prayers. Richmond, Surrey, Keepsake Press, 1974.
Five Dreams. Rushden, Northamptonshire, Sceptre Press, 1974.

Plays

Sawney Bean, with William Watson (produced Edinburgh, 1969; London, 1972). London, Calder and Boyars, 1970.
Sisters (broadcast, 1969; produced Edinburgh, 1973). Included in *Three Plays*, 1974.
Fugue (screenplay), in *Lines Review 38* (Edinburgh), 1971.
The Seven Deadly Sins: A Mask, music by James Douglas (produced Stirling, 1973). Rushden, Northamptonshire, Omphalos Press, 1974.
Three Plays (includes *Fugue*, *Sisters*, and *Penthesilea*, adaptation of the play by Heinrich von Kleist). London, Calder and Boyars, 1974.

Radio Play: *Sisters*, 1969.

Novel

Doubtfire. London, Calder and Boyars, 1967; New York, Hill and Wang, 1968.

Short Stories

Tales I Told My Mother. London, Calder and Boyars, and New York, Hill and Wang, 1969.
Penguin Modern Stories 6, with others. London, Penguin, 1970.

Other

Taliesin (juvenile).   London, Faber, 1966; New York, Hill and Wang, 1967.
March Has Horse's Ears (juvenile).   London, Faber, 1966; New York, Hill and Wang, 1967.
Wishing Gold (juvenile).   London, Macmillan, and New York, Hill and Wang, 1970.
Poor Pumpkin (juvenile).   London, Macmillan, and New York, Hill and Wang, 1971.
Cricket (juvenile).   Indianapolis, Bobbs Merrill, 1973.

Editor, *A Choice of Sir Walter Ralegh's Verse.*   London, Faber, 1972.
Editor, *William Barnes of Dorset: A Selection of His Poems.*   Cheadle, Cheshire, Carcanet Press, 1973.
Editor, *A Choice of Swinburne's Verse.*   London, Faber, 1973.

Translator, *Beowulf* (juvenile).   London, Faber, and New York, Hill and Wang, 1968.
Translator, *Aucassin and Nicolette* (juvenile).   Indianapolis, Bobbs Merrill, 1973.

Manuscript Collections: University of Texas, Austin; Colgate University, Hamilton, New York.

Critical Studies: by George MacBeth, in *London Magazine,* 1961; "Recent Developments in British Poetry" by Michael Nott, in *Poetry* (Chicago), May 1961; "Secretary of Hidden Powers," in *Times Literary Supplement* (London), 1963.

*   *   *

The career of Robert Nye has been a peculiar one. He began with some éclat, publishing poems in *The London Magazine* and *Delta* when he was only sixteen years of age. One of these lyrics, "Other Times," is almost his best. It appears, somewhat revised, in what looks like his definitive collection so far, *Darker Ends*:

> Midsummer's liquid evenings linger even
> And melt the wind in autumn, when bonfires
> Burn books and bones, and lend us foreign faces.
> At such a heart's November I might wish
> For summer's heir to come, with his cruel kiss
> Sealing the promises we could not keep. . . .

One may feel that there are a few too many possessives here – "midsummer's," "heart's," "summer's." And yet the poem is purged in diction from its earlier version in *Juvenilia 1* (1961):

> Midsummer's liquid evenings linger even
> And leave four hours of autumn bonfires –
> Terre Gaste of your sleevelessness; imp and scraps,
> The oily rags, old bike spokes, bones and cans
> And executed dolls forstitched and lax
> Folding pink little arms precipitant to ash. . . .

This, in its turn, was altered from the first published version, in *Delta*, Autumn 1956, where we have "a tragedy of autumn bonfires / Raw with a gardener's rubbish, flesh and scraps. . . ." The older, more austere Nye appears to have spent the intervening years weeding through several of his teenage pastures. There is no doubt that some fine Gravesian lyrics are the result. What he has done with "Other Times," he has also done with "Kingfisher," "I've Got Sixpence" and "At Last." In this final draft, Mr. Nye appears to have found his poetic feet in a rhythm not all that way after Andrew Young:

> Dear, if one day my empty heart,
> Under your cheek, forgets to start
> Its life-long argument with my head –
> Do not rejoice that I am dead
> And need a colder, harder bed,
> But say: "At last he's found the art
> To hold his tongue and lose his heart."

Clearly, Mr. Nye is rising on the stepping-stones of his former romantic selves to finer things. After the baroque ambitions of his earlier years, he looks about to emerge as a poet of distinction, wit and epigram.

—Philip Hobsbaum

OAKES, Philip. British. Born in Burslem, Staffordshire, 31 January 1928. Educated at Royal School, Wolverhampton; Wolverhampton and Darwen Grammar School. Married to Stella Fleming; has one son and one daughter. Scriptwriter for Granada Television and BBC, London, 1958–62; Film Critic, *Sunday Telegraph*, London, 1963–65; Assistant Editor, *Sunday Times Magazine*, London, 1965–67. Currently, Arts Columnist, *Sunday Times*, London. Agent: Curtis Brown Ltd., 13 King Street, London W.C.2. Address: Pinnock Farm House, Pluckley, Kent, England.

PUBLICATIONS

Verse

Unlucky Jonah: Twenty Poems. Reading, Berkshire, Reading University School of Art, 1954.
In the Affirmative. London, Deutsch, 1968.
Notes by the Provincial Governor. London, Poem-of-the-Month Club, 1972.
Married/Singular. London, Deutsch, 1973.

Play

Screenplay: *The Punch and Judy Man*, with Tony Hancock, 1962.

Novels

Exactly What We Want. London, Joseph, 1962.
The God Botherers. London, Deutsch, 1969; as *Miracles: Genuine Cases
Contact Box 340*, New York, Day, 1971.
Experiment at Proto. New York, Coward McCann, and London, Rapp and
Whiting-Deutsch, 1973.

Philip Oakes comments:

I consider myself an all-round writer, subject at any time to the demands of
poetry. Poetry flavors much of my work – as a script writer, and as a film critic –
it couldn't be kept out.

I was labelled a "Movement" poet in the 1950's, but this is literary-political
journalism, which has nothing to do with me. I still subscribe to "Movement"
virtues – form, discipline, etc. – but school's out.

I suppose I write from a finely balanced schizophrenia: a need for domestic
order on one hand, an occasional lunge for freedom on the other. I invent my own
forms. As far as influences go, the most important poets in my life have been (and
still are) John Donne, W. H. Auden, Philip Larkin, Robert Graves, and Rudyard
Kipling. I write a lot about duty, love (ironically, I'm afraid), and eccentrics that I
rather admire. These are the heroes of my ballads – a man who hunted unicorns, a
sea-captain who sails to meet mermaids, a football referee known as Spring-Heeled
Jack. Like Larkin I'm stuck on the eternal verities. The rest is probably journalism.

*   *   *

Despite a comparatively slender output, and the competing pressures of journalism and novel-writing, Philip Oakes remains one of the best of the generation of
English poets who emerged in the 1950's, and were loosely grouped under the label
of the "Movement." His early poems provided social and moral comments in tight,
clipped forms in the characteristic manner of the Movement; but Oakes was less
severely formal and intellectual than some of his contemporaries. A mild but
authentic vein of lyricism lies not far below the cool, conversational surface.
Indeed, there is a basic human warmth, recalling Thomas Hardy, at the heart of
Oakes' practice as a poet. In his work of the sixties and seventies, collected in *In
the Affirmative* and *Married/Singular*, he has written of personal and domestic
themes, in direct language and unfussily formal verse. At times, admittedly, the
low-key descriptions are merely flat, and the metre occasionally falters. But Oakes'
successes are more frequent – notably in his admirable evocations of the pieties
and crises of modern family life.

—Bernard Bergonzi

O'GORMAN, Ned (Edward Charles O'Gorman). American. Born in New York City, 26 September 1929. Educated at St. Michael's College, Vermont, A.B.; Columbia University, New York, M.A. Taught at Brooklyn College, New York; New School of Social Research, New York; Manhattan College, New York; Editor, *Jubilee* magazine, New York, 1962–65; State Department American Studies Specialist in Chile, Argentina and Brazil, 1965. Since 1966, Director, Addie Mac-Collins library and Storefront School, New York. Recipient: Guggenheim Fellowship, 1956, 1962; Lamont Poetry Selection Award, 1958. Agent: Harold Matson Company, 22 East 40th Street, New York, New York 10016. Address: 56 West 11th Street, New York, New York 10011, U.S.A.

PUBLICATIONS

Verse

> *The Night of the Hammer: Poems.* New York, Harcourt Brace, 1959.
> *Adam Before His Mirror.* New York, Harcourt Brace, 1961.
> *The Buzzard and the Peacock.* New York, Harcourt Brace, 1964.
> *The Harvesters' Vase.* New York, Harcourt Brace, 1968.
> *The Flag the Hawk Flies.* New York, Knopf, 1972.

Other

> *The Storefront: A Community of Children on Madison Avenue and 129th Street.* New York, Harper, 1970.
> *The Blue Butterfly* (juvenile). New York, Harper, 1971.
> *The Wilderness and the Laurel Tree: A Guide to Parents and Teachers on the Observation of Children.* New York, Harper, 1972.

> Editor, *Prophetic Voices: Essays and Words in Revolution.* New York, Random House, 1969.

Manuscript Collection: Immaculata College, Malvern, Pennsylvania.

*　　*　　*

Ned O'Gorman's poems hope that, in the collision of metaphysical and metaphorical opposites, theme and meaning will arise. Compressed and "lush," there is a mystery and lyric extravagance to the poems which, when most successful, provoke a lasting dreamlike quality.

Images repeat exotic light, birds, water, colors, honey, holy oils, vegetables, seeds, centers and sun, in a luxuriant usage of – oftentimes – a pentameter. There are many examples. The result can be overwhelming. At other times O'Gorman's poems have the impact of an abstract painting of planes and trajectories ("What Three?" and "Written on the Occasion in Cairo . . .").

The conflicts underlying the poems are intelligent, abstract, controlled, metaphysical. The reader is attracted by the beauty of composition in many poems; real chaos is only mentioned here, but it is of a different world. O'Gorman's best poems address themselves seriously to *things*, making a concrete frame of reference available in direct statement:

> The Donkey who is in the field
> in this increasing fall is
> tall as a hedge of wild rose.

Imagery when solely the representative of concept at least must not seem so, unless it is allegory. The poet must have a personal stake in the poem and must risk it as O'Gorman does in his finest efforts, such as "The Graveyard," "In Honor of the Mother of God," "The Aunt," and "To the Memory of Lydia Hoffman." When this expenditure is not made we sense, with a reviewer of *The Flag the Hawk Flies*, that the "imagery touches on nothing real," that the poet merely "names." Or perhaps it is true that in the contemporary world a vision of horror – as in "War" – strikes us as natural and credible while O'Gorman's visions of beauty seem extravagant. This is tragic, yet the poet must take account of the fact or risk a failure – no matter of great beauty.

—Joseph Wilson

O'GRADY. Desmond (James Bernard). Irish. Born in Limerick, 27 August 1935. Educated at St. Michael's Primary School, Limerick; Sacred heart College, Limerick; Cistercian College, Roscrea, Co. Tipperary; Harvard University, Cambridge, Massachusetts, M.A. in Celtic studies 1964. Married; has four children. Taught at Berlitz School, Paris; Cambridge Institute and British Institute, Rome; St. George's English School, Rome; English Language School, Rome; Roxbury Latin School, West Roxbury, Massachusetts; Harvard University. Since 1965, Senior English Master, Overseas School of Rome. Irish Representative, European Community of Writers Congresses, Florence, Belgrade, Premio Taormina, Rome. Address: 1/A Via Catalena, Rome, Italy.

PUBLICATIONS

Verse

Chords and Orchestrations. Limerick, Echo Press, 1956.
Reilly. London, Phoenix Press, 1961.
Professor Kelleher and the Charles River. Cambridge, Massachusetts, Carthage Press, 1964.
Separazione. Rome, Edizioni Rapporti Europei, 1965.
The Dark Edge of Europe: Poems. London, MacGibbon and Kee, 1967.
The Dying Gaul. London, MacGibbon and Kee, 1968.
Hellas. Dublin, New Writers Press, 1971.
Separations. Dublin, Goldsmith Press, 1973.
Pen and Ink. Dublin, Goldsmith Press, 1973.
Sing Me Creation. Dublin, Dolmen Press, 1974.

Other

Translator, *Off Licence: Translations from Irish, Italian and Armenian Poetry.* Dublin, Dolmen Press, 1968.

Desmond O'Grady comments:

My early work dealt with the experience of growing up on the west coast of Ireland, with the leaving of that place for the cities of the Continent and America and the need to connect my life there with the one I had left. My later work deals with the theme of "the journey" and the theme that emerges from that, "separation"; separation from people, places, things.

My middle work, the long poem *The Dying Gaul,* was an attempt at making a self portrait of what it is to be a Celt. It is this "persona" that journeys and is "separated" in my later work. He is a "wandering Celt" who records his wanderings and experiences and attempts to connect what was left with what is found.

The Prologue of my volume *Sing Me Creation* gives an attempt at condensing my purpose:

> Who saw everything to the ends
> of the land began
> at the end of a primary road.
> Who saw the mysteries, knew
> secret things, went a long
> journey and found the whole story
> cut in stone.
> His purpose: praise, search,
> his appointed pain, and the countries
> of the world that housed
> his image. Weary,
> worn out with his labours,
> he returned and told
> what he's seen and learned
> to help kill the winter.

There is also a great deal of translation from the languages of others under the general title *The Unauthorised Version.* These were done principally to learn the methods of those poets, classical and modern, whose work I admire, the better to extend my own range and at the same time to make their work available to young Irish poets who may not have heard of them or cannot read them in the original in the hope that I might make some contribution to the revitalisation of verse being written in Ireland by the young.

                         *   *   *

Desmond O'Grady spent some years in Paris but has been teaching in Rome since 1965. In his second collection, *Reilly,* he uses as a satirical *persona* a bohemian young man and describes amusingly his reckless adventures in Dublin:

table and shelves cleared of books and belongings,
the firegrate stuffed with stale fish-and-chips
and a dry whiskey bottle.
Finger-rubbed into the windowpane dust:
Reilly Rotted Here.

The Dark Edge of Europe is a selection from O'Grady's previous work. Many of his poems evoke Paris and Italy, and the imagery in them is contemporary in its unexpectedness, as in "Girl and Widow on a Sea Park Bench":

In this park by the sea, marvellous
As marble, under the fronded green of the palms,
The sun strafing
The stones with flat tracers of light, water like mercury
Tinnular out of the fountain.
You come to me out of the gold stained day like a word.

Mr. O'Grady spent his early years in Limerick and many of his poems are inspired by his return visits, as in "Homecoming":

The familiar pull of the slow train
trundling after a sinking sun on shadowed fields.
White light splicing the broad span of the sky.
Evening deepens grass, the breeze,
like purple smoke, ruffles its surface.
Straight into herring-dark skies the great cathedral spire
is sheer Gothic.

Like Joyce and other Irish writers, Mr. O'Grady expresses in compressed lines the effect of Puritanic education:

Unwinking eyes of saints and hushed confession queue –
For one loud nervous boot
Of frightened heart,
I felt the Churcheyed, fidget fear of schooltied youth.

Sometimes he objectifies his early experiences as in his depiction of an old man, who turns

for the safest healer
To a clean and bandaged silence of the heart.

—Austin Clarke

OKAI, John. Ghanaian. Born in Ghana. Educated at the Gorky Literary Institute, Moscow, M.A.(Litt.) 1967; University of Ghana, Accra; University of London. Recipient: Royal Society of Arts Fellowship, 1968. Lived in the U.S.S.R., 1961–67. Lives in London.

PUBLICATIONS

Verse

Fiowerfall. London, Writers Forum, 1969.
The Oath of Fontomirom and Other Poems. New York, Simon and Schuster,
  1971.

*   *   *

The use of musical rhythms in poetry is nothing unusual, but few contemporary
writers make so great a use of the musical heritage of their culture as does John
Okai. The sounds of the talking drums of Ghana figure strongly in his poems and
the titles of most of them, such as "Fugue for Fireflies" and "Okponglo Concerto" bear witness of the musical bent of his work. The repetition and alliterative
forms which are a part of traditional verse are brought by Okai into the English
language, producing effects which are often close to hypnotic, as in "Modzawe"
where the line "Let human beings be human beings again" is repeated six times
and Okai refers to traditional drums, allowing the musicality of their names to
shape his lines:

> Descend O God! descend O God!
> To the echo-wail-boom and music of
> The Dodonpo and the Odono
> And the festive Bintim Obonu . . .

His Ghanaian background is not the only source Okai draws from, however.
Having studied in England, America and Russia, Okai can refer as familiarly to
apple trees as to palms and his poems often contain catalogues of people and
places reflecting this catholic experience:

> the swallow
>   and the bougainvillea . . .
> modigliani's woman with a necklace . . .
> leonardo da vinci's mona lisa
> the parrot
>   and the bougainvillea . . .
> shostakovich's leningrad symphony . . .
> dvorak's new world symphony (part two) . . .
> the sparrow
>   and the bougainvillea
> frank lloyd wright's falling water . . .
> ya-na's palace at wa in ghana . . .

If there is a fault in Okai's work, it may be that some of his lines take on a
singsong quality, seeming to sacrifice sense in favor of sound, for Okai can be
more alliterative in his writing than was Old English verse. His "Sunset Sonata" is
filled with such lines as:

Still stand stubborn
    To stones that strangle the dawn,
Still stand stubborn
    To stones that maim the morn,
Still stand stubborn
    To stones that assail the sun . . .

and because of this some critics attempt to easily dismiss Okai, not seeing that even in his most highly alliterative passages there is still meaning.

It cannot be denied that Okai's work is assertive and, especially when read aloud, charged with vitality. His recent work has been a great influence in enlivening the poetry scene in Ghana and the directions in which his poems move take advantage of a rich and, in English, relatively unexplored patrimony.

—Joseph Bruchac

OKARA, Gabriel (Immomotime Obainbaing).   Nigerian.   Born in the Ijaw country, near the Niger Delta, in 1921. Educated at Government College, Umuahia; trained as a book-binder. Principal Information Officer, Eastern Regional Government, Enugu.

PUBLICATIONS

Verse

Poetry from Africa, with others, edited by Howard Sergeant.   Oxford, Pergamon Press, 1968.

Novel

The Voice.   London, Deutsch, 1964; New York, Africana, 1970.

*   *   *

One of the most gifted, and certainly the least literary, of the African poets is Gabriel Okara. Okara has proved to be what can only be described as a "natural," in that he is highly original in both outlook and expression, and appears to have learned his craft without being influenced unduly by the stylistic mannerisms of any other poet. This, however, has not been without considerable effort on his part. "In order to capture the vivid images of African speech," he observed in an article (printed in *Transition*), "I had to eschew the habit of expressing my thoughts first in English. It was difficult at first, but I had to learn." That he has been successful in capturing the African scene, the African colour and excitement, and the changing African moods, is evidenced by such poems as "The Mystic Drum," "Were I to Choose," "Adhiambo," and "Piano and Drums."

There is, in fact, almost a mystical quality about his work which seems to spring from his racial inheritance, his instincts and sensitivity rather than from his intellect, and he exhibits a curious power when he draws upon the great oral traditions to release this nervous energy, as in "The Mystic Drum." In "Adhiambo" he tries to define his feelings on the subject: "Maybe I'm a medicine man/hearing talking saps/seeing behind trees," and in "Piano and Drums," he writes of the jungle drums "telegraphing the mystic rhythm, urgent, raw like bleeding flesh." In other poems which will probably make more impact upon non-African readers he is practical and down to earth, extremely perceptive in his judgements, and almost analytical in his approach, as in "Once Upon a Time" – "There was a time indeed/they used to shake hands with their hearts" – and "You Laughed and Laughed and Laughed" where the ancient world of Africa merges with the modern world.

—Howard Sergeant

OLSON, Elder (James). American. Born in Chicago, Illinois, 9 March 1909. Educated at the University of Chicago, B.A. 1934 (Phi Beta Kappa), M.A. 1935, Ph.D. 1938. Married Ann Elizabeth Jones in 1937 (divorced, 1948); Geraldine Louise Hays in 1948; has four children. Instructor, Armour Institute of Technology, Chicago, 1938–42. Assistant Professor, 1942–48, Associate Professor, 1948–53, and since 1954, Professor of English, University of Chicago. Visiting Professor, University of Puerto Rico, Rio Piedras, 1952–53; University of Frankfurt; Powell Professor of Philosophy, 1955, Visiting Professor of Literary Criticism, 1958–59, and Patten Lecturer, 1964, University of Indiana, Bloomington; Rockefeller Visiting Professor, University of the Philippines, Quezon City, 1966–67. Recipient: Witter Bynner Award, 1927; Guarantors Prize, 1931, and Eunice Tietjens Memorial Prize, 1953 (*Poetry*, Chicago); Poetry Society of America Chap-Book Award, 1955; Academy of American Poets Award, 1956; Longview Foundation Award, 1958; Balch Award (*Virginia Quarterly Review*, Charlottesville), 1965; Quantrell Award, University of Chicago, 1966. Address: Department of English, University of Chicago, Chicago, Illinois 60637, U.S.A.

PUBLICATIONS

Verse

    Thing of Sorrow: Poems.   New York, Macmillan, 1934.
    The Cock of Heaven.   New York, Macmillan, 1940.
    The Scarecrow Christ and Other Poems.   New York, Noonday Press, 1954.
    Poems and Plays 1948–58.   Chicago, University of Chicago Press, 1958.
    Collected Poems.   Chicago, University of Chicago Press, 1963.

Plays

A Crack in the Universe, in First Stage (Lafayette, Indiana), Spring 1962.
The Abstract Universe: A Comedy of Masks, in First Stage (Lafayette, Indiana), Summer 1963.

Other

General Prosody, Rhythmic, Metric, Harmonics. Chicago, University of Chicago Press, 1938.
Critics and Criticism, with others. Chicago, University of Chicago Press, 1952.
The Poetry of Dylan Thomas. Chicago, University of Chicago Press, 1954.
Tragedy and the Theory of Drama. Detroit, Wayne State University Press, 1961.
The Theory of Comedy. Bloomington, Indiana University Press, 1968.

Editor, American Lyric Poems: From Colonial Days to the Present. New York, Appleton Century Crofts, 1963.
Editor, Aristotle's "Poetics" and English Literature: A Collection of Critical Essays. Chicago, University of Chicago Press, 1965.

*   *   *

The early poems from Thing of Sorrow which now make up Part I of Elder Olson's Collected Poems are elegiac, deliberately understated and restrained in their expression of some lasting preoccupations: the beauties of this earth, despite our disappointments ("The Tale"); the relationship between the artist's personal sorrows and his work ("Wishes for His Poem"); and, most important by far, the compensations available to a mind able at least to contemplate its losses and vulnerability. Thus Olson writes (in "To Man") that, whatever our limitations:

> – Bird, beast, flower, and star
> Are of no thing but thought,
> Since if mind wills, they are,
> Or if mind wills, are not.
>
> The Rose surviving Time
> Is patterned in your brain;
> Without such paradigm
> No rose had ever been. . . .
>
> Be comforted at length,
> Be brave; till you are free,
> Accept this frailty
> That tenders you this strength.

Nevertheless any possible acceptance is more than overshadowed by the awareness of loss, particularly the passing of love:

It is that love goes in the end.
It is that of all this amazement and pain,
The bright harm, the royal woe,
The brilliant wound and the stain,
Naught shall remain
To emblazon one rose-leaf,
To illumine a prism of snow
Or a rainbow's crystal, to
Incline the course of wind
A gull's-wing's width, to bend
The worn sea to a grave:

. . . And the mind knows this well;
But the heart breaks if it believes.

The tones remain muted throughout, nearly feminine in Olson's preference for short lines and delicate, internal sound patterns. The influences attractive to a young poet starting out in the 1930's are not what one might expect – Eliot, Yeats and Pound – but rather, it seems, Léonie Adams and Louise Bogan.

The poems which stand as Part II of the *Collected Poems* suffer by being torn from the context of *The Cock of Heaven*, a long philosophical sequence which Olson has described as "an epitome of human history . . . the destruction of the world, and the causes of both destruction and creation . . . [and] the universal catastrophe." Devised in terms of expert imitations of the whole range of voices at work in English poetry (and not only English poetry at that), from the Anglo Saxon through T. S. Eliot, these eighty-seven pieces, now radically diminished to twenty-five, create an uncertain focus and effect. The despairing tones of *Thing of Sorrow* are still present, rendered more forcefully (man is a poor talking animal "possessed by angels and impelled by fiends"), but Olson now seems haunted by the possible revelations behind Christian symbols. The opening "text" asserts: "it is manifest that Man is eternally damned . . . And I consider that to save this world God Himself must needs be born into it; and even then even He can but make it worthy to be destroyed." The relationship between Christian doctrine and Olson's apparently naturalistic view of life is not easy to define, but perhaps the poet's own statement, in the tender "Nocturnal for His Children," comes close. After surveying various theories of divinity and the divine plan he concludes:

My children, I cannot tell
Which of these is right.
I never heard God's voice,
To me no angels descend.
All I know is my soul
Which is, like this night sky,
Far more dark then bright,
Yet in that dark waste
While I watch out its night
All strives from dark to light:

Not knowing false from true,
I yet know good from bad;
I cannot think my God
Worse than myself: I
Demand a nobler faith.

Many of the poems which follow *The Cock of Heaven* come close to ultimate despair:

> I mourn, not grieving, no, at grievous death,
> But at the resurgence after death,
> And the death again, and senseless resurgence still.
>
> Cycle on cycle, wheeling Infinity,
> Boundless Abyss, where all things rise and fall,
> You are my sickness . . .

but once more the power of mind to grasp its position offers some measure of consolation, even dignity:

> I thought once that I should have at a man's age
> Some wisdom hard and pure as diamond
> To make the center of a new steadfast world,
>
> Or some bauble, at least, for a toy – accurate enough
> To catch the universe in its gay reflex,
> Like Paris reflected in a jewel,
>
> And perhaps after all I have it: at last recognizing
> The treadmill as a treadmill: asking of my empty journeys
> Nothing, in the end, but to spare my private nobility.

The finest later poems are varied in the best sense of the term. There are the familiar elegiac strains ("For the Demolition of a Theater"), the same concern for the Christian symbols of death and mortality ("Crucifix") and, increasingly, a new display of informal humor and relaxed good nature ("Exhibition of Modern Art," "Directions to the Armourer," "Able, Baker, Charlie, Et Al." and the superb "Childe Roland, Etc." and "Entertainment for a Traveller"). When Olson treats his most serious themes with quick, metaphorical wit the results are memorable (as in "The Last Entries in the Journal," which may well be his best poem to date). The good will of generous acceptance now dominates almost entirely:

> I praise the weaknesses
> That make us fellows;
> Fine faults, that keep us kin. . . .
>
> To that implacable Angel, the stern Scribe
> Of heaven or of our consciences, I wish
> Short memory, bad ink, a sputtering pen:
>
> Our faults, our common faults, have kept us kin.

In recent years, with *Tragedy and the Theory of Drama* and *The Theory of Comedy*, Elder Olson has established himself as an indispensible critic. The poetry is much less widely known, which is a great pity, considering its seriousness and technical brilliance. But then one of Olson's virtues as a critic and a poet is that he has never been in a hurry. What he has done is likely to last.

—Elmer Borklund

ONDAATJE, (Philip) Michael. Canadian. Born in Colombo, Ceylon, 12 September 1943. Educated at St. Thomas' College, Colombo; Dulwich College, London; Bishop's University, Lennoxville, Quebec; University of Toronto, B.A.; Queen's University, Kingston, Ontario, M.A. Married to Betty Kimbark; has one daughter and one son. Taught at the University of Western Ontario, London, 1967–71. Since 1971, Member of the Department of English, Glendon College, York University, Toronto. Editor, *Mongrel Broadsides.* Recipient: Ralph Gustafson Award, 1965; Epstein Award, 1966; E. J. Pratt Medal, 1966; President's Medal, University of Western Ontario, 1967; Canada Council grant, 1968; Governor-General's Award, 1971. Address: Department of English, Glendon College, York University, Toronto, Ontario, Canada.

PUBLICATIONS

Verse

The Dainty Monsters. Toronto, Coach House Press, 1967.
The Man with Seven Toes. Toronto, Coach House Press, 1969.
The Left-Handed Poems: Collected Works of Billy the Kid. Toronto, House of Anansi, 1970; New York, Norton, 1974.
Rat Jelly. Toronto, Coach House Press, 1973.

Play

The Collected Works of Billy the Kid (produced Stratford, Ontario, 1973; New York, 1974). New York, Norton, 1974.

Other

Leonard Cohen. Toronto, McClelland and Stewart, 1970.

Editor, *The Broken Ark* (animal verse). Toronto, Oberon Press, 1971.

Theatrical Activities

Director: **Films** – *Sons of Captain Poetry,* 1971; *Carry on Crime and Punishment,* 1972; *Royal Canadian Hounds,* 1973; *Farm,* 1974.

*   *   *

Michael Ondaatje's first book of poems, *The Dainty Monsters,* elicits prophecy. Its poems forecast the possibility that their successors will be poems of the first intensity. Ondaatje was included among the group that a year previously was heralded as the "New Wave" poets. There was nothing much new about this group. The poetry largely derived from the William Carlos Williams/Black Mountain school; eventually from that great re-animator Ezra Pound. The method has been persistent elsewhere for years. What was inadvertently refreshing was the presence of three or four Canadian poets whose practice indicated a choice counter to the standard derivation. Ondaatje was one of these.

His shaping of language was formal and musical; his content was balanced. Departing from the prevailing lack of metrical challenge to dispersed rhythm, aware of verbal sound inherent in the meaning, unaffianced to the egocentric confessional, Ondaatje engages attention. His shapings of a poem do not leak either salt tears or sawdust or inarticulations or empty spaces. The first essential is here: sheer love of language. Otherwise he can be what he wants to be: metaphysician, sociologist, domestic or saint.

His area is dainty monsters. That is satisfyingly contemporary enough. His universal monsters live in Toronto:

> When snows have melted
> how dull to find just grass and dog shit.
> Why not polemic bones of centaurs
> – remnants of a Toronto bullet,
> punishment for eating gladioli.

Why not? It is good to have his centaurs back, his sows like chinless duchesses on spread thighs watching

> the sun
> fingersnapping out the dying summer.

He doesn't want hippopotami barred from public swimming pools. He is equally aware that

> Deep in the fields
> behind stiff dirt fern
> nature breeds the unnatural.

You can look but you better not touch, a title of one of his poems tells us:

> We must build new myths
> to wind up the world,
> provoke new christs
> with our beautiful women.

He is on a mythopoeic voyage from Lilith in Eden,

> pivoting on the horn
> of corrupted unicorns,

to modern man on his cold mountain, moving "with fast passion from necessity," and, mutilated, drowning "in the beautiful dark orgasm of his mouth."

He shows evidence of having that rarest of all elements, presently almost destroyed by the tearings of metal and the dark idiocy of its manufacturers: comic perspective and rescuing wit high on poetry and hospitals:

> Three floors down
> my appendix
> swims in a jar
> O world, I shall be buried all over Ontario.

—Ralph Gustafson

OPPEN, George. American. Born in New Rochelle, New York, 24 April 1908. Educated in California public schools. Served in the United States Army, 1943–45. Married Mary Colby in 1928; has one daughter. Publisher, To Company, Toulon, France, 1930–33; Member, Objectivist Press Co-op, New York, 1934–36. Formerly, tool and die maker, cabinet-maker, mechanic, and building contractor; shopowner and furniture builder in Mexico City. Recipient: Pulitzer Prize, 1969. Address: 2811 Polk Street, San Francisco, California 94109, U.S.A.

PUBLICATIONS

Verse

Discrete Series. New York, Objectivist Press, 1934.
The Materials. New York New Directions, 1962.
This in Which. New York, New Directions, 1965.
Of Being Numerous. New York, New Directions, 1968.
Alpine: Poems. Mount Horeb, Wisconsin, Perishable Press, 1969.
Collected Poems. London, Fulcrum Press, 1973.
Seascape: Needle's Eye. Fremont, Michigan, Sumac Press, 1973.

*   *   *

George Oppen strikes me as being one of the best and one of the worst of poets. The vantage from which he writes is high: the poetry of George Oppen declaims, defines, and finally establishes for us a series of dicta by George Oppen. This is the poet's task, amply stated by Oppen:

> It is the business of the poet
> "To suffer the things of the world
> And to speak them and himself out."
>   – from "The Building of the Skyscraper"

In Section 9 of the long poem, *Of Being Numerous,* he writes:

> Yet I am one of those who from nothing but man's way of
> thought and one of his dialects and what has happened
> to me
> Have made poetry. . . .

And, in "Route":

> I have not and never did have any motive of poetry
> But to achieve clarity.

So Oppen's goal has been clarity, and perhaps this, achieved, is enough. But one suspects that the poet whose aim is clarity must tackle seemingly insoluble problems if his work is to distinguish itself. Oppen's out is to attempt clarification of everything; but no indication of humility and a great many self-assured statements can strain the wary reader's belief. This is not to deny that when Oppen hits, he hits hard, and many of his poems provide compelling testimony to the success of his mission. But in Oppen's books, these same poems, side by side, often seem echoes of one another: the clarity that one has defined is slightly changed by the next. What remains constant is Oppen's refusal to put down his pen and to wrestle bodily with the facts as he sees them. In short, there is a bothersome detachment here, as if Oppen has discounted himself from the viewpoint of his poem. This results in uneven poetry, often too engaged with games instead of play:

> Because the known and the unknown
> Touch,
>
> One witnesses –
> It is ennobling
> If one thinks so.
>
> If to know is noble
>
> It is ennobling.
>   – *Of Being Numerous*, section 31

One of my principal difficulties with Oppen is his frequent use of abstraction and the equally disturbing double negative. I find myself distrusting these devices, not for themselves, but because they occur so often. He writes of women "In the streets, weakened by too much need/Of too little" (*Of Being Numerous*, section 34), and seeks "Not to reduce the thing to nothing" ("Route"). The double negative often becomes more ponderous than it deserves: "Like hawks we are at least not/Nowhere . . ." ("Technologies"); and, again from *Of Being Numerous*: "That which one cannot/Not see."

In spite of this, it would be unfair to deny that Oppen is attempting a poetry far more difficult than most poets will dare, and the finest moments of his work raise questions (rather than answers) that will haunt every reader:

> Wars that are just? A simpler question: In the event,
> will you or will you not want to kill a German. Because,
> in the event, if you do not want to, you won't.
>   – from "Route"

And, when he is willing to settle for just the moment of poetry, Oppen is without equal, as in "A Boy's Room":

> A friend saw the rooms
> of Keats and Shelley
> At the lake, and saw "they were just
> Boys' rooms" and was moved
>
> By that. And indeed a poet's room
> Is a boy's room
> And I suppose that women know it.
>
> Perhaps the unbeautiful banker
> Is exciting to a woman, a man
> Not a boy gasping
> For breath over a girl's body.

In his most recent book, *Seascape: Needle's Eye*, Oppen works with an even finer edge of clarity, turned towards the ocean. This may be Oppen's most accessible poetry to date, and his openness results in the achievement he hopes for in "Route":

> We have begun to say good bye
> To each other
> And cannot say it
>   – final stanza of "Anniversary Poem"

> One writes in the presence of something
> Moving close to fear
> I dare pity no one
> Let the rafters pity
> The air in the room
> Under the rafters
> Pity
> In the continual sound
> Are chords
> Not yet struck
> Which will be struck
> Nevertheless yes
>   – from "Silver as . . ."

—Geof Hewitt

OPPENHEIMER, Joel (Lester). American. Born in Yonkers, New York, 18 February 1930. Educated in Yonkers public schools; Cornell University, Ithaca, New York, 1947–48; University of Chicago, 1948–49; Black Mountain College, North Carolina, 1950–53. Married Rena Furlong in 1952 (divorced, 1960); has four children. Production Manager, Arrow Typographic Service, New York, 1964; Project Director, Poetry Project at St. Mark's Church in-the-Bowery, New York, 1966–68; Director, Teachers and Writers Collaborative, New York, 1968. Since 1969, Poetry Consultant, Bobbs Merrill, Inc., publishers, Indianapolis and New York, and Poet-in-Residence, City College of New York. Editor, *Kulchur*, New York; regular contributor, *The Village Voice*, New York. Recipient: National Endowment for the Arts grant, 1968. Address: Westbeth, 463 West Street, New York, New York 10019, U.S.A.

PUBLICATIONS

Verse

The Dancer. Highlands, North Carolina, Jargon, 1952.
The Dutiful Son. Highlands, North Carolina, Jargon, 1957.
The Love Bit and Other Poems. New York, Totem Press, 1962.
A Treatise. New York, Brownstone Press, 1966.
Sirventes on a Sad Occurrence. Mount Horeb, Wisconsin, Perishable Press, 1967.

In Time: Poems, 1962–1968. Indianapolis, Bobbs Merrill, 1969.
On Occasion. Indianapolis, Bobbs Merrill, 1973.

Plays

The Great American Desert (produced New York, 1961). New York, Grove
  Press, 1965.
Miss Right (produced New York, 1962).
Like a Hill (produced New York, 1963).

Other

The Wrong Season (on baseball). Indianapolis, Bobbs Merrill, 1973.

*   *   *

Joel Oppenheimer was actually a student at that mythical institution, Black
Mountain College, and he calls Olson, Creeley, and Ginsberg his "teachers and
makers" ("The Excuse" from *In Time*), but in fact his real teacher and maker-
mentor has been William Carlos Williams, and he shares an interest in what might
be called the occasional poem with his contemporaries, Paul Blackburn and Frank
O'Hara. His poems are constructed of talk, the most effective being poems like
"Sirventes on a Sad Occurrence" which describes an old lady in a tenement in
New York who could not control her bowels and shamed herself and her daughter
on the stairs to their apartment. Oppenheimer is best when he is, as in this poem,
describing the occasions of everyday occurrences, and uttering his compassion and
sympathy with the life of humble people.
   Oppenheimer's writing style is typified by hip jargon used by New York artists,
Olson-style punctuation, and a continuous line which is punctuated with line-breaks
that give the voice pauses where the syntax affords none. His long monologues are
personal meditations on everyday occasions such as his wife's breasts or a ball
game in the park or going to work, but use those occasions or subjects to spin off
into a meditation on how good the world is in spite of everything. The banal style
of writing/talking of the poems actually serves as a foil to disarm the reader and
suddenly allow him to see that perhaps one kind of poem *is* the simple occasion of
being human and appreciating that fact.
   The poems are quiet and patient, like an old teacher, waiting for the reader to
stop and look at his own life with as much tenderness as Oppenheimer looks at his.
At times, the poems have an insidious internal rhyming structure which will pun on
old poems or songs or sayings. Poems like "The Cop Out" illustrate this sense of a
poem's music which he shares with Blackburn and Creeley. Oppenheimer is a
master of the everyday; one feels that the poems ask us all to live intelligently and
above all with some mercy for others. They are proper poems for a time in which
every educated man writes poems and uses the act of writing and the poem itself to
help with his own enlightenment. The actual modesty of the poems underneath the
seeming self-agrandizement of whole poems about the trivia of existence is touching and compelling for its humane reminder of how important each of us thinks his

life is and yet how each of us knows, underneath, how little any of us count for in the larger view.

—Diane Wakoski

ORLOVITZ, Gil. American. Born in Philadelphia, Pennsylvania, 7 June 1918. Married Maralyn Orlovitz in 1954; has three children. Screenplay Writer, Columbia Pictures, Hollywood, and free-lance television screenplay writer, in the 1950's; Softcover Book Editor, Universal Publishing and Distributing Corporation, New York, 1960–69. Address: 235 West 107th Street, New York, New York 10025, U.S.A. *Died 10 July 1973.*

PUBLICATIONS

Verse

Concerning Man. Pawlet, Vermont, Banyan Press, 1947.
Keep to Your Belly. New York, Louis Brigants-Intro, 1952.
The Diary of Dr. Eric Zeno. San Francisco, Inferno Press, 1953.
The Diary of Alexander Patience. San Francisco, Inferno Press, 1958.
The Papers of Professor Bold. Eureka, California, Hearse Press, 1958.
Selected Poems. San Francisco, Inferno Press, 1960.
The Art of the Sonnet. Nashville, Tennessee, Hillsboro Publications, 1961.
Couldn't Say, Might Be Love. London, Barrie and Rockliff, 1969.
More Poems. Fredericton, New Brunswick, Fiddlehead, 1972.

Plays

Stevie Guy, in *Quarterly Review of Literature* (Princeton, New Jersey), vi, 1 and 3, 1951.
Case of the Neglected Calling Card (produced New York, 1952).
Noone (produced New York, 1953).
Stefanie (produced New York, 1954).
Gray, in *Literary Review* (Rutherford, New Jersey), Winter 1959–60.

Novels

Milkbottle H. London, Calder and Boyars, 1967; New York, Dell, 1968.
Ice Never F. London, Calder and Boyars, 1970.

Short Stories

The Story of Erica Keith and other Stories, Poems and a Play. Berkeley, California, Miscellaneous Man, 1957.

Other

Editor, *Award Avant-Garde Reader*.   New York, Award House, 1965.

Critical Studies: "Paradox Made Manifest" by Robert Nye, in *The Scotsman* (Edinburgh), 8 April 1967; "Literary Exile in Residence" by Hale Chatfield, in *Kenyon Review* (Gambier, Ohio), 1969.

*   *   *

Gil Orlovitz lays words on the page as the painter lays colors on the canvas, or the composer sets out notes on the score. Like the symphonic composer, he achieves his end through the interplay of sounds; like the painter, he uses his medium to create the effect of light and shadow. But unlike both the painter and the composer, his medium is words – the substance of daily communication among men. The majority of poets concern themselves with the material of saying and doing – neither of which concerns the painter or composer. Orlovitz, like the composer and painter, devotes himself entirely to the expression of being, to the vision of existence – along with several contemporary philosophers. "Too much verse is written *about* phenomena . . .," he says. "My intent is . . . to transmit thru image the paradoxes of experienced phenomena. My intent is to make the phenomenon itself one of symbols."

With Orlovitz, words point to the experience, words *are* the experience. The communication of an Orlovitz poem, then, does not occur – as he puts it – "on the rational-intellectual level, but on the *feeling* level." As one may communicate through a wink, a smile, a shrug – or more violently, through a knife thrust in the belly – Orlovitz communicates on an experiential/existential level. Like the smile of Buddha which, according to Zen tradition, was transmitted from one master to another for centuries, the poetry of Orlovitz transmits anger, grief, awe, the act of lovemaking and love itself – the stuff of which life is made.

His "Lyrics" and "Flamencos" express an essential *joie de vivre*; his "Elegies" are of a more somber side. The "Numbers," "Medians," "Inscriptions," "Conjugates," "Relationships," "Indexes" (in four series), and "Masterindexes" are concerned with more complex – sometimes more tenuous, diffuse, delicate – aspects of the human condition. The "Gnomics," like haiku, encapsulate. It is with *The Art of the Sonnet* that Orlovitz joins the discipline of tradition with his unique talent of communication. This series (existing in nearly 300 individual parts) is the heart itself measuring out the acts of existence – each beat separate, distinct, but all joined in the continuum of the universal whole.

In the "Biographical Masques," Orlovitz creates a character to express the varied facets of the individual in and out of contact with the social environment. The essence of each of these series is best described in his own words. *The Diary of Dr. Eric Zeno* concerns "the errant ganglia of a Western Christian psychoanalyst." *The Diary of Alexander Patience* concerns "a self-confessed but unreliable stoic," *The Papers of Professor Bold* "a somewhat rococo academician." "The personality of an ordained American minister ruminating upon religious attitudes not confined to any one sect" is the subject of "The Diary of Matthew Parson." In "The Letters of Great Ape," "the effort is made to crack the substance of the self-made image and to expose the ruthless comedy of the living parallax." And finally "M'sieu Mishiga" is "a psychiatrically nonclassifiable lunacy . . . the major principles of sanity, as our *zeitgeist* has them, are put to test and protest."

The vast remainder of his poetic work exists as individual poems of varying length. Some have caused controversy; for instance, after the radio broadcast of "The Rooster" by the *Beliot Poetry Journal*, Beliot College dropped its sponsorship of the magazine. This poem was later broadcast throughout the world and is available on record.

Orlovitz is still growing, still writing poetry (as well as novels, short stories and plays), still using words to build a view of the universe of outstanding value.

—Milton Van Sickle

ORMOND, John. Welsh. Born in Dunvant, near Swansea, Glamorgan, 3 April 1923. Educated at Swansea Grammar School, 1935–41; University College of Swansea, 1941–45, B.A. 1945. Married Glenys Roderick in 1946; has three children. Staff Writer, *Picture Post*, London, 1945–49; Sub-Editor, *South Wales Evening Post*, Swansea, 1949–55; BBC Television News Assistant, Cardiff, 1955–57. Since 1957, BBC Documentary Film-maker, Cardiff. Recipient: Welsh Arts Council prize, 1970, bursary, 1973. Agent: Oxford University Press, Ely House, 37 Dover Street, London W. 1. Address: 15 Conway Road, Cardiff, Wales.

PUBLICATIONS

Verse

> *Indications*, with James Kirkup and John Bayliss. London, Grey Walls Press, 1942.
> *Requiem and Celebration.* Llandybie, Carmarthenshire, Christopher Davies, 1969.
> *Corgi Modern Poets in Focus 5*, with others, edited by Dannie Abse. London, Corgi, 1971.
> *Definition of a Waterfall.* London, Oxford University Press, 1973.

> Recording: *Poets of Wales*, with Raymond Garlick, Argo.

Other

> Documentary Films include: *Under a Bright Heaven* (on Vernon Watkins), 1966; *A Bronze Mask* (on Dylan Thomas), 1968; *The Fragile Universe* (on Alun Lewis), 1969; *R. S. Thomas: Priest and Poet*, 1971.

Critical Studies: by Leslie Norris, in *Poetry Wales* (Cardiff), Winter 1969; Robert Shaw, in *Poetry* (Chicago), November 1970; introduction by Dannie Abse to *Corgi Modern Poets in Focus 5*, 1971; "The Poetry of John Ormond" by Randal Jenkins, in *Poetry Wales* (Cardiff), Summer 1972.

John Ormond quotes from his comment in *Corgi Modern Poets in Focus 5*, London, Corgi, 1971:

A number of my poems are elegiac in tone and I suppose this to be an indication of something in my nature, perhaps part of a Celtic characteristic. The ancient Welsh poetic tradition of lament cannot be dismissed as mere literary convention. Some of the reasons for it can be found in history but the factor of temperament, too, is strong. I do not work consciously in the minor key; but I am aware that I am continually concerned with "life's miraculous poise between light and dark."

In some ways my poems are forms in which I work out and test my relationship with the past. They sometimes start in celebrations of kinships and loyalties. Sometimes they are interim accounts of feelings and attitudes arrived at as the result of asking questions, mainly about beginnings and ends, which I cannot answer. They are also about coming to terms with the fact that, for me, there may never be answers. But I would add that this situation, together with my commitment to my roots, does not invalidate loving laughter, and even something approaching a mischievousness with words, as elements which can be present in the making of a poem.

In some ways a poet is a strange mixture of humility and of a self-confidence which borders on self-esteem. Without the latter how could he dare produce work in the face of what all the great poets have written? Excitement, a sureness about his talent, will sustain a young practitioner. What reason had I, seven or eight years ago, to start again? As a young man I wrote and published many pieces I then called poems; and later destroyed many more before falling into near-silence. I can give no reasons except that one is finally stuck with being the person one is. I think I learned the truth of what Valéry meant when he said that to expect perfection is, in itself, a kind of arrogance. I remember that a poet, with whom I had been discussing the general contemporary crisis of faith and the difficulty of being a lyric poet at all in the present age, remarked, "You cannot play a tune upon a slack string." And I recall that Wallace Stevens wrote, "One reads poetry with one's nerves."

*   *   *

John Ormond was born in 1923 at Dunvant, a small mining village near Swansea, the son of a master-shoemaker. After university, he became a staff-writer on *Picture Post* in London, and then a documentary film producer for BBC Wales. His two most recent volumes, *Requiem and Celebration*, and *Definition of a Waterfall*, marked a welcome late development after years spent in a creative cul-de-sac.

His poetry is mainly concerned with three themes: a continuing journey into the past to recapture his early roots, and the once-simple certainties of a small, warm community (his affectionate portraits of family and the more eccentric villagers are full of wryness, wit, and compassion); the task of "freezing" his ancestry and inheritance in a series of panels which, if these were paintings, would combine to give the impression of a splendid chronicle in oils; and the more ambitious effort to probe the riddle of existence, in which he finds no easy, cushioned consolations, but tenaciously drills away with his imagination and intellect to pierce a fragment of the mystery. Those parts of his work which are concerned with a quest for revelation and the painfully-hard lesson of acceptance of the human condition are deep, complex and moving elegies of considerable power – lifting the reader, in their brave crippled vision and sculpted eloquence, above mundane everyday affairs, and offering a brief, tormenting glimpse of eternity behind a corner of the curtain. His own doubt never sinks into self-pity or negative despair. Somehow, within his own longing and bafflement, and the struggle to communicate his thought, he succeeds in celebrating life and persuades us to maintain a veneration for it. Stark, meaningless pessimism, without a shred of hope or comfort, is not to be countenanced.

Among contemporary Anglo-Welsh poets, Ormond's singular technical contribution, after his long creative silence, has been to forge a distinctive style at once sinewy and lyrical, carpentered to a detailed millimetre (he has been praised for the richness and textural density of his verse), and increasingly adequate to cope with the philosophical complexity of much of his subject-matter. Thus, knots of supreme intellectual difficulty are gradually unravelled by his discovery of an appropriate, and long-sought-for, method of expression.

As a craftsman, Ormond's dedication is total, his poems often travelling through countless revisions before they are considered fit for publication. He releases nothing, not even a lighter-hearted "portrait," until it is as near-perfect as he can make it, as well-made as any example of his father's craft. In the present period of so much poetic drab and wild, loose forms, such meticulous refinement and high polish of language and structure are things for which we should be grateful.

Here is the last stanza from his fine poem, "My Dusty Kinsfolk":

> Early and lately dead, each one
> Of you haunts me. Continue
> To tenant the air where I walk in the sun
> Beyond the shadow of yew.
> I speak these words to you, my kin
> And friends, in requiem and celebration.

—John Tripp

O'SULLIVAN, Vincent (Gerard). New Zealander. Born in Auckland, 28 September 1937. Educated at the University of Auckland, M.A. 1959; Lincoln College, Oxford, B.Litt. 1962. Married. Formerly, Lecturer, Victoria University, Wellington. Currently, Senior Lecturer, Waikato University, Hamilton. Editor, *Comment*, Wellington, 1963–66. Recipient: Commonwealth Scholarship, 1960; Macmillan Brown Prize, 1961; Jessie Mackay Award, 1965; Farmers Poetry Prize, Sydney, 1967. Address: Pukeroro, R.D. 3, Hamilton, New Zealand.

PUBLICATIONS

Verse

Our Burning Time. Wellington, Prometheus, 1965.
Revenants. Wellington, Prometheus, 1969.
Bearings. Wellington and London, Oxford University Press, 1973.

Other

Opinions: Chapters on Gissing, Rolfe, Wilde. London, Unicorn Press, 1959.
Apollinaire: A Letter to the Editor of the Dublin Magazine. Edinburgh,
   Tragara Press, 1970.

Editor, *An Anthology of Twentieth-Century New Zealand Poetry.* London,
   Oxford University Press, 1970.

*   *   *

The most striking feature of Vincent O'Sullivan's first book of poems, *Our Burning Time*, is the nervous intensity with which themes are picked up, and the taut elegance of the phrasing. Effects are often superimposed, so that an "Elegy for a Schoolmate" can begin flatly:

> On the other side of the world I heard
> That she died in a Newton kitchen,
> Her head in someone else's oven.
>
> I'd never thumped her nor called her names
> With the others, and so I had nothing
> To sorrow or anger about. . . .

and end:

> But she takes her place among immortal things.
> With the potter's wheel at the bottom of a dry pit,
> With the hands of Egyptian ladies held like thin,
>   brown leaves,
> Their collars of beaten gold, and a basalt dog.

These two manners – colloquial and eloquent – come together most successfully in the early "poems of place" (most notably in Greece and Ireland), but marry uneasily in personal lyric.

Revenants, a longer second collection, shows less nervousness, greater fluency, and a strong flavour of *fin-de-siècle*. A sonnet sequence on Charles Meryon called "Long Harbour" (the New Zealand port of Akaroa, where the young Frenchman early came) spans the globe in the same way that Meryon included the Southern Alps in a late etching of Paris. There are lyrics vivid as a sketch by Guys:

> Where have they gone, those tall girls
> who pass us, hands in pockets,
> their white coats fading between the branches,
> mist in their hair? . . .

All this promise, with some undoubted successes, reaches a fully achieved style of great compression and variety in *Bearings*, and the still uncollected work that has followed it in many periodicals. O'Sullivan is certainly one of the most cultivated and accomplished poets now writing in New Zealand: his style, like his subject-matter, is international; in verse or prose, he should now command a wide hearing.

—James Bertram

OWENS, Rochelle. American. Born in Brooklyn, New York, 2 April 1936. Educated at Lafayette High School, Brooklyn, graduated 1953; Herbert Berghof Studio; New School for Social Research, New York. Married George Economou, *q.v.*, in 1962. Worked as clerk, typist, telephone operator. Member, Playwrights Unit, Actors Studio; Member, The New Dramatists Committee; Founding Member, New York Theatre Strategy. Recipient (for drama): Rockefeller-Office for Advanced Drama Research grant, 1965; Ford Grant, 1965; Creative Artists Public Service grant, 1966; Yale University Drama School Fellowship, 1968; Obie Award, for best play, 1968, for distinguished writing, 1971; Guggenheim Fellowship, 1971. Agents: Elizabeth Marton, 96 Fifth Avenue, New York, New York 10011; or, Michael Imison, Dr. Jan Van Loewen Ltd., 81-83 Shaftesbury Avenue, London, England. Address: 606 West 116th Street, No. 34, New York, New York 10027, U.S.A.

PUBLICATIONS

Verse

Not Be Essence That Cannot Be. New York, Trobar Press, 1961.
Four Young Lady Poets, with others, edited by LeRoi Jones. New York, Corinth Books, 1962.
Salt and Core. Los Angeles, Black Sparrow Press, 1968.
I Am the Babe of Joseph Stalin's Daughter. New York, Kulchur Press, 1972.
Poems from Joe's Garage. Providence, Rhode Island, Burning Deck, 1973.
The Joe 82 Creation Poems. Los Angeles, Black Sparrow Press, 1974.
Selected Poems. New York, Seabury Press, 1974.

Recordings: *A Reading of Primitive and Archaic Poetry,* with others, Broadside; *From a Shaman's Notebook,* with others, Broadside.

Plays

Futz (produced Minneapolis, 1965; New York, Edinburgh and London, 1967). New York, Hawk's Well Press, 1961; revised version in *Futz and What Came After,* 1968; in *New Short Plays 2,* London, Methuen, 1969.
The String Game (produced New York, 1965). Included in *Futz and What Came After,* 1968.
Istanbul (produced New York, 1965). Included in *Futz and What Came After,* 1968.

1157

Homo (produced Stockholm and New York, 1966; London, 1969). Included in *Futz and What Came After*, 1968.

Beclch (produced Philadelphia and New York, 1968). Included in *Futz and What Came After*, 1968.

Futz and What Came After (includes *Beclch, Homo, The String Game, Istanboul*). New York, Random House, 1968.

The Karl Marx Play (produced New York, 1973). Included in *The Karl Marx Play and Others*, 1974.

The Karl Marx Play and Others (includes *Kontraption, He Wants Shih, Farmer's Almanac, Coconut Folksinger, O.K. Certaldo*). New York, Dutton, 1974.

Screenplay: *Futz* (additional dialogue), 1969.

Short Stories

The Girl on the Garage Wall. Mexico City, El Corno Emplumado, 1962.
The Obscenities of Reva Cigarnik. Mexico City, El Corno Emplumado, 1963.

Other

Editor, *Spontaneous Combustion: Eight New American Plays.* New York, Winter House, 1972.

Bibliography: in *The Off-Broadway Book*, Indianapolis, Bobbs Merrill, 1973.

Manuscript Collection: Mugar Library, Boston University.

Critical Studies: by Jack Kroll, in *Newsweek* (New York), 1967, 1973; Harold Clurman and Jerome Rothenberg, in *Futz and What Came After*, 1968; Ross Wetzsteon, 1969, Michael Feingold, 1970, and Michael Smith, 1973, in *The Village Voice* (New York).

Rochelle Owens comments:

(1970) I use language at times with a visceral, painter's tongue/eye. I will alter and extend language, transform and nobilize, bless and judge like Isaiah or Roberta? Or Job, for the helluv it! My sources are my skin! And secret scrolls left to me by the prophets of the Old World who still like me! Those who prepare anthologies must smile!

(1974) The process of poetry is growth, authentic, inevitable, the direction of urgency and exploration, the range of language possibilities extensive and sublime, the discovery of the panoramic range of the mind, the eternal curiosity of the aesthetic sensibility. If I write, I am aware of the breath generalized to include all that lives and is, the existence of the thing that is conscious because I am aware of it in the manifold ways of human experience.

*   *   *

Rochelle Owens is better known as a playwright than as a poet, but perusal of her poems shows them to be close to her theatrical imagination and an essential stimulus to it. In poetry (as distinct from poetic drama) she can concentrate her energies exclusively on verbal invention, coining words, splitting them, splashing them disjunctively on the page, disrupting grammar and free-associating with maximum tonal contrast:

> O IF I FORGET THEE O ZION
> LET AMERICA'S BALLS RUST

In her recent collection, *I Am the Babe of Joseph Stalin's Daughter*, both her verbal incandescence and dramatic proclivities emerge. As in her play *Futz*, she fearlessly explores the psychic realities of deviant personae. The Deebler Woman poems and "Bernard Fruchtman in Town & Country" create voices speaking fragments of plays. "The Voluminous Agony of Karl Marx" plainly grew into *The Karl Marx Play*, in which Marx, a modern Hebrew prophet cries out to Yahweh, as Job did, to relieve his boils so he can sit down and "write the book."

Owens, herself Jewish and married to a Greek, relishes Old Testament themes and the Mediterranean arena of contrast between Jew and Christian, Turk and Greek, which metaphorically extends to other conflicts – black *vs.* white, male *vs.* female, always juxtaposing ancient and traditional faith and language with contemporary slang and secular thought. Her most recent work, *The Joe 82 Creation Poems*, is a sequence of over a hundred poems titled for the gut-creative act which inspires graffiti on the New York subways. Although its subtitle is "a theater piece," this sequence nevertheless has strongly biblical and epic qualities. In the voices of a primal couple, Wild-Man and Wild-Woman, Owens redesigns the myths of creation in terms of the immediate creativity of every mind confronting its own experience. It is an ambitious task, with impressive results. Still an innovator and still young, this poet is enlarging her originality of thought and exuberance of language to create a new vision of the world which rests on the old virtues of praise and joy:

> O World (Yes)
>
> Thy feet   are graced with everything!

—Jane Augustine

OXLEY, William. British. Born in Manchester, Lancashire, 29 April 1939. Educated at College of Commerce, Manchester; qualified as Chartered Accountant. Married Patricia Holmes in 1963; has two daughters. Office Boy, Salford, Lancashire, 1955–57; Articled Clerk, Manchester, 1957–64. Chartered Accountant, Deloitte and Company, London, 1964–68. Since 1968, Chartered Accountant for a merchant bank, London. Since 1971, Editor, Ember Press, Esher, Surrey and *Littack, New Headland,* and *Laissez Faire,* Epping, Essex, and Associate Editor, *The Village Review,* Newport, Essex; since 1972, Associate Editor, *Orbis,* Bakewell, Derbyshire. Address: 27 Brook Road, Epping, Essex, England.

PUBLICATIONS

Verse

The Dark Structures. London, Mitre Press, 1967.
New Workings. Epping, Essex, privately printed, 1969.
Passages from Time: Poems from a Life. Epping, Essex, Ember Press, 1971.
The Icon Poems. Epping, Essex, Ember Press, 1972.
Opera Vetera. Epping, Essex, privately printed, 1973.
Mirrors of the Sea. London, Quarto Press, 1973.

Other

Sixteen Days in Autumn (travel). Privately printed, 1972.

William Oxley comments:

At this time, I have one basic aim, and that is to change the present climate of
poetry in the United Kingdom, away from the dry academic poetry of the
Establishment, and away from the formless morass of undisciplined hysteria
offered as the alternative to Establishment poetry by those I would choose to call
the poets of the Alternative Establishment. Towards this end the magazine *Littack*
was founded in 1971, and a systematic programme of poetics is being worked out
in open forum by a number of poets, of whom the original cadre are becoming
known as the Vitalist Poets.

*   *   *

William Oxley's poetry lacks a crisp voice, and often runs the danger of being
swamped by its feeling or thinned out in the service of its notions: "What measure,
father, you asked of poetry./I rather ask it of man." The need for moral clarity,
not the same thing as depth, can turn his language into mere attempted persuasion;
this combines with an archness in the presentation of the speaker (that "rather" in
the lines quoted) which can turn the verses irrevocably toward the prosaic. In his
polemical manifesto, he argues, "*Littack 1* laid new attitude of mind. A new circuit
was established – it is now necessary to run a current through" (from "The Vitalist
Memorandum," from *Littack*, October 1972). Ironically most of Oxley's poems are
like circuits without currents:

> Through dust-occluded glass, half-broken
> and most light precluding, I watch
> first mechanical assaults against old
> foundations. A familiar pattern witnessed.

Here the play with "occluded" and "precluded" prevents him from seeing that
he's told us the same thing twice, and the enervating effect of the summarizing
clause at the end of the quatrain is characteristic. All too often the description is
flaccid and the anagogic leap is faulty. Not until his latest book, *Mirrors of the Sea*

do his lyrics begin to sing, caught up in more daring, less calculated imaginative excursions. In this book he begins to compose in "the sequence of the musical phrase" as Pound urged, though he may also rely too much on typography to enhance the undertaking. What's missing is still some sense of rectifying or enchanting metaphor, a caressing urge of the language past its domain of the egocentered cuddling of one's reaction to experience, and into a newly rapt ordering of vision. Oxley seldom lets us see anything but his own attitudes: "I am forced to apprehend about all things/There hangs the silent asking of dead faces." *The Dark Structures* and *Opera Vetera* contain early verse filled with poeticized abstractions, and as Oxley continues to struggle against his tendency to reaffirm platitudes, his advance has been real, though he has yet to demand of himself a set of risks beyond the safe discursive designs of prose.

—Charles Molesworth

PACK, Robert. American. Born in New York City, 19 May 1929. Educated at Dartmouth College, Hanover, New Hampshire, B.A. 1951; Columbia University, New York, M.A. 1953. Married Patricia Powell in 1961; has one son. Taught at Barnard College, New York, 1957–64; Middlebury College, Vermont; Poetry Workshop of the New School for Social Research, New York; Bread Loaf Writers Conference, Vermont. Editor, *Discovery*, New York. Recipient: Fulbright Fellowship, 1956; National Institute of Arts and Letters grant, 1957; Borestone Mountain Poetry Award, 1964; National Endowment for Arts grant, 1968. Lives in Georgetown, Connecticut.

PUBLICATIONS

Verse

The Irony of Joy. New York, Scribner, 1955.
A Stranger's Privilege. Hessle, Yorkshire, Asphodel Books, and New York, Macmillan, 1959.
Guarded by Women. New York, Random House, 1963.
Selected Poems. London, Chatto and Windus, 1964.
Home from the Cemetery. New Brunswick, New Jersey, Rutgers University Press, 1969.
Nothing But Light. New Brunswick, New Jersey, Rutgers University Press, 1972.

Other

Wallace Stevens: An Approach to His Poetry and Thought. New Brunswick, New Jersey, Rutgers University Press, 1958.
The Forgotten Secret (juvenile). New York, Macmillan, 1959.
What Did You Do? (juvenile). New York, Macmillan, 1961.
How to Catch a Crocodile (juvenile). New York, Knopf, 1964.

Editor, with Donald Hall and Louis Simpson, *New Poets of England and America.* Cleveland, Meridian, 1957.

Editor and Translator, with Marjorie Lelach, *Mozart's Librettos.* Cleveland, World, 1961.

Editor, with Donald Hall, *New Poets of England and America: Second Selection.* Cleveland, Meridian, 1962.

Editor, with Tom Driver, *Poems of Doubt and Belief: An Anthology of Modern Religious Poetry.* New York, Macmillan, 1964.

Editor, with Marcus Klein, *Literature for Composition on the Theme of Innocence and Experience.* Boston, Little Brown, 1966.

Editor, with Marcus Klein, *Short Stories: Classic, Modern, Contemporary.* Boston, Little Brown, 1967.

*   *   *

Robert Pack's poetry asserts man's connection to all levels of creation. "Grieving on a Grand Scale," a representative work, ranges from the imagined death of a lover, through speculations on the inevitable demise of the entire scale of nature, to the impending fate of the narrator himself. Though the poem resolves ". . . to mourn softly, without hope of resurrection," the final lines comfort with the image of an unknowing, yet elegiac universe: ". . . young deer/Do not move – their loose watery lips/Slide over their gums with a sound like weeping." Pack avoids sentimentality by acknowledging both human involvement in "the crooked weasel's crooked chase" ("Canoe Ride"), and the horror, however stylized, of the cycle of existence: ". . . lace/Of mouse bones in owl feces" ("The Black Ant"). That carnage defines and fuses with human beauty implies frightening questions. Poems like "Descending" interpret the terror implicit in the universe as the real cost of exclusion from paradise, but generally Pack, while negating traditional answers, substitutes only an openness to the wonders of creation, whatever its origin: ". . . above, no missing God/I miss; high satisfying sky though, and below,/Chrysanthemums in garb of gaiety" ("Raking Leaves"). The key image of delight is the family; "Breakfast Cherries" celebrates the richness of ephemeral family moments. In "Everything Is Possible," the expectant father achieves the illusion of godhead, while the husband in "Were It Not" sees daily life as a recapitulation of paradise. Though children "redeem all sorrow," such redemption never completely calms latent anxiety; even the exultant "Welcoming Poem for the Birth of My Son" acknowledges ". . . that far city where my fears hide." "The Mountain Ash Tree" with its equivocally symbolic berries is Pack's most complex version of man's precarious optimism; despite the ominous appearance and bitter taste of the fruit, its unraveled meanings force the reader to share the final affirmation: "I am still alive."

Because of the relatedness of all elements in the universe, man can revert to the "hermit crab" comfort of "shell" and "tentacles" ("My House"), while the stone reciprocally thrusts forward to ". . . leaves,/A leaf, my tongue . . ." ("To the Muse"). This diversity parallels man's ability to play several family roles simultaneously in a perpetual series of frightening but reassuring traps. A son, struggling to distinguish mother from wife and himself from his dead father, invokes his father's return in a way that ironically suggests a renewal of the whole process: "Dreaming, I seek your skeleton below;/I dig the worms and find your embryo" ("Father"). Most powerful of such poems is "The Boat," in which the speaker, with deadpan earnestness, accepts both the fusion and separateness of roles: "I dressed my father in his little clothes,/Blue sailor suit, brass buttons on his coat./He asked me where the running water goes./. . . He told me where all the running water goes,/And dressed me gently in my little clothes." If the family generates order, however unstable, sexual love generates the family.

Because Pack sees this love as a variant of complex natural phenomena, his love poems fuse tenderness with fierce eroticism: "The snow now hurtles from my eyes./I can do nothing. Nothing now can stop./The hemlock trees are hair and thighs/And in I drop" ("Let There Be Snow!"). Though long poems like "Home from the Cemetery" and "The Last Will and Testament of Art Evergreen" understandably lack the sustained intensity of the shorter lyrics, these ambitious works reveal Pack's characteristic command of symbolic image and his tact in suiting varying mood and tone to the demands of the overall pattern, in both cases Pack's obsessive equation of acceptance of death with acceptance of life.

While Pack often creates bitterly comic passages or infuses an entire poem with sly irony, his attempts at social satire, as in "Routine," disappoint. However, "The Children" roots Vietnam protest into the perpetual cycle of human guilt and avoids both polemic and easy answers. Pack's stylistic signature is the repetition, sometimes varied, of verb forms: "I grow by choosing what I choose to know" ("Song to Myself"), or the Cummingesque double infinitive, playful yet capable of supporting intricacies of thought: ". . . beyond/what the stars/shall have time ever to learn to forsake" ("He Dies Alive"). Pack's special contribution, among a variety of traditional and free metrical forms that never seem arbitrary or defy careful reading, is a moral nursery rhyme in which a convincingly guileless speaker agonizes toward a solution that both repels and involves the reader, a solution that is ultimately no solution: "I shot an otter because I had a gun" leads through six tortured stanzas only to "He shot an otter because he had a gun" ("The Shooting").

—Burton Kendle

PADGETT, Ron. American. Born in Tulsa, Oklahoma, 17 June 1942. Educated at Columbia University, New York (Boar's Head Poetry Prize and George E. Woodberry Award, 1964), A.B. 1964; Fulbright Fellow, Paris, 1965–66. Married; has one son. Since 1968, has taught poetry workshops at St. Mark's-in-the-Bowery, New York, and poetry writing in New York public schools. Since 1973, Founding Editor, with Joan Simon and Anne Waldman, Full Court Press, New York. Recipient: Gotham Book Mart prize, 1964; Poets Foundation grant, 1965, 1968. Address: 342 East 13th Street, New York, New York 10003, U.S.A.

PUBLICATIONS

Verse

In Advance of the Broken Arm: Poems. New York, "C" Press, 1964.
Sky: An Opener. London, Goliard Press, 1966.
Bean Spasms: Poems and Prose, with Ted Berrigan. New York, Kulchur Press, 1967.

Tone Arm.   Brightlingsea, Essex, Once Press, 1967.
100,000 Fleeing Hilda, with Joe Brainard.   New York, Boke Press, 1967.
Bun, with Tom Clark.   New York, Angel Hair Books, 1968.
Some Thing, with Ted Berrigan and Joe Brainard.   Privately printed, n.d.
Great Balls of Fire.   New York, Holt Rinehart, 1969.
Sweet Pea.   New York, Aloe Editions, 1971.
Poetry Collection.   London, Strange Faeces Press, 1971.
Back in Boston Again, with Ted Berrigan and Tom Clark.   Philadelphia, Telegraph Books, 1972.

Plays

Seventeen: Collected Plays, with Ted Berrigan.   New York, "C" Press, 1965.

Novel

Antlers in the Treetops.   Toronto, Coach House Press, 1973.

Short Stories

2/2 Stories for Andy Warhol.   New York, "C" Press, 1965.

Other

The Adventures of Mr. and Mrs. Jim and Ron, with Jim Dine.   London, Cape Goliard Press, 1970.

Editor, with David Shapiro, *An Anthology of New York Poets*.   New York, Random House, 1970.

Translator, *The Poet Assassinated*, by Guillaume Apollinaire.   New York, Holt Rinehart, 1968.
Translator, *Entretiens avec Marcel Duchamp/Dialogues with Marcel Duchamp* (bilingual edition).   New York, Viking Press, 1970; London, Thames and Hudson, 1971.
Translator, with Bill Zavatsky, *The Poems of A. O. Barnabooth*, by Valéry Larbaud.   Tokyo, Mushinsha Books, 1974.

Critical Study: "The New American Poetry" by Jonathan Cott, in *The New American Arts*, New York, Horizon Press, 1966.

Ron Padgett comments:

I have been recognized by others as belonging to the so-called New York "school" of poetry, but I have trouble recognizing myself in that disguise.

*   *   *

Deeply influenced by modern painting and its techniques, Ron Padgett modulates poems beyond traditional limits. In "Wonderful Things," for example, his diction varies from the language of formal elegy ("Anne, who are dead . . .") to that of insanity ("Seriously, I have this mental (smuh!) illness . . ."). Then, taking a new direction, he wraps the whole poem, retroactively, in the disarmingly ingenuous diction of a master storyteller ("and that's what I want to do / tell you wonderful things").

A naive world surfaces in this poetry: mysterious appearances, holes in the sky, falling clouds, ghosts, secret notes, funny animals, elves:

DECEMBER

I will sleep
in my little cup.

At its purest, its effect is wonder:

A child draws a man and the earth
is covered with snow.

Padgett's power comes from this voice. When it speaks directly, it is the clearest voice of a child in modern poetry. When it speaks indirectly, the irony is clear.

Behind his irony, Padgett grows full of Dada ("What modern poetry needs / is a good beating"), ready to parody anything established ("When I see birches / I think of nothing . . . One could do worse than see birches"). Like the Dadaists, he can pit Art against Life with ease:

Let's take a string quartet
Playing one of Beethoven's compositions
We may explain it as the scratching
Of a horse's hair against a cat's gut
Or we may explain it as the mind
Of a genius soaring up to an infinite
Horse's hair scratching against an infinite cat's gut.

The dilemma Padgett especially enjoys is that of the man who climbs after a ball of gold in the sky, actually gets it, but then doesn't know what to do with it:

And . . . the way Madison Avenue really
Does go to Heaven
And then turns around and comes back, disappointed.

In his own search for values, Padgett is deeply affected by Surrealism's black humor, unmistakeable imagery, and its antipathy towards the merely rational. Intellectual history, Padgett writes,

Is now only an imitation of itself
Like a car
Driving towards itself in the rain
Only to be photographed from behind
As we all eventually are . . .
Breaking the visible chains of logic.

1165

Whether he is, like a wise fool, proclaiming

> Socrates was a mute, this is generally not known
> But understood at some hilarious fork
> For a few years! oh

or, like a child full of belief, stretching his hand into a painting to pick up one chocolate from a box, "Breaking the visible chains of logic" is what Padgett is about.

– Edward B. Germain

PAGE, P(atricia) K(athleen). Canadian. Born in Swanage, Dorset, England, 23 November 1916; emigrated to Canada in 1919. Educated at St. Hilda's School for Girls, Calgary, Alberta; Art Students League, and Pratt Institute, New York. Married William Arthur Irwin in 1950; has three step-children. Formerly, sales clerk and radio actress, St. John, New Brunswick; filing clerk and historical researcher, Montreal; Script Writer, National Film Board, Ottawa, 1946–50. Recipient: Bertram Warr Award (*Contemporary Verse*, Vancouver), 1940; Oscar Blumenthal Award (*Poetry*, Chicago), 1944; Governor-General's Award, 1955. Address: 3260 Exeter Road, Victoria, British Columbia, Canada.

PUBLICATIONS

Verse

> *Unit of Five*, with others. Toronto, Ryerson Press, 1944.
> *As Ten as Twenty.* Toronto, Ryerson Press, 1946.
> *The Metal and the Flower.* Toronto, McClelland and Stewart, 1954.
> *Cry Ararat! Poems New and Selected.* Toronto, McClelland and Stewart, 1967.
> *Leviathan in a Pool.* Vancouver, Blackfish, 1973.

Critical Studies: by Daryl Hine, in *Poetry* (Chicago), 1968; "Traveller, Conjuror, Journeyman" by the author, in *Canadian Literature* (Vancouver), Autumn 1970; *The Bush Garden* by Northrop Frye, Toronto, House of Anansi, 1971; "The Poetry of P. K. Page" by A. J. M. Smith, in *Canadian Literature* (Vancouver), Autumn 1971.

*   *   *

P. K. Page is an artist of many aspects; she has written a romance and short stories; under her married name of P. K. Irwin she is a painter of deserved repute. But it is a poet that she has worked longest, producing a small but interesting body of verse over the past quarter of a century.

P. K. Page began to publish in the early 1940's and in her own early twenties. Montreal was still – as it had been in the years before World War II – the most active literary centre for English as well as French Canada, and it was here that P. K. Page first emerged as a member of the group which produced *Preview*, a literary journal whose cosmopolitan aspirations somewhat belatedly aimed at the social realist ideals of the English thirties. One of the leading figures of the *Preview* group was in fact a British poet, Patrick Anderson, temporarily resident in Montreal, and another was F. R. Scott, an instigator of the Montreal movement of the 1930's. P. K. Page's earliest poems were published in *Preview*, and immediately she appeared – with Anderson and Scott – as one of the most accomplished poets of the group. In 1944, with four other poets, she contributed a group of poems to *Unit of Five*, and two years later published her first independent book, *As Ten as Twenty*. Since then her production has been slight, governed by a rigorously selective self-criticism; in 1954 she published *The Metal and the Flower*, and her next volume – *Cry Ararat!* in 1967 – was a selection from the best of her early work, with a small group of seventeen recently written poems added.

P. K. Page's early verse was largely dominated by social protest, but by the end of the forties her preoccupations had changed and so, inevitably, had the content of her work. She became more concerned with isolated human situations, the plight of the solitary or of those whom circumstances have condemned to seem contempt-ible, and some of her poems of this period are really highly condensed novels or minute imaginary biographies, like "The Stenographer" and "The Landlady"; they come as close as any writer can to the meeting of satire and compassion.

From the inner landscapes of such poems P. K. Page has moved towards a mystical concern with the view out of the self towards images – Cook's Glasshouse Mountains in Australia, an aboriginal bark drawing, Mount Ararat itself – that suggest in Blakeian or Asian vision the way of liberation from the alienated, prisoned self:

> The bird in the thicket with his whistle
> the crystal lizard in the grass
> the star and shell
> tassel and bell
> of wild flowers blowing where we pass,
> this flora-fauna flotsam, pick and touch,
> requires the focus of the total I.
>
> A single leaf can block a mountainside;
> all Ararat be conjured by a leaf.

P. K. Page's philosophic development is paralleled in form; both developments are hinted in the last verse of her poem, "After Rain":

> And choir me too to keep my heart a size
> larger than seeing, unseduced by each
> bright glimpse of beauty striking like a bell,
> so that the whole may toll,
> its meaning shine
> clear of the myriad images that still –
> do what I will – encumber its pure line.

The progressive purification of the line is clearly evident in P. K. Page's work. In the earlier poems the line is long and flowing, with the kind of full eloquence that belonged alike to the English and the Canadian forties. In the more recent poems there is still a fluidity, but it is more controlled, sparser, yet totally moving, like the crystal jet that flows from a Japanese bamboo pipe into its rock basin.

In sum, P. K. Page's is poetry to be read on and off the page. It has the accuracy of rhythm, period and internal echo that make it eminently speakable; it is also dense with intent, and needs dwelling on to extract the quality and meaning that lie deeper than its considerable immediate attractiveness.

– George Woodcock

PARKINSON, Thomas (Francis).   American.   Born in San Francisco, California, 24 February 1920. Educated at the University of California, Berkeley, A.B., M.A., Ph.D. Married to the painter Ariel Parkinson; has two daughters. Since 1948, Member, Department of English, currently, Professor of English, University of California, Berkeley. Recipient: Guggenheim Fellowship, 1957; Institute of Creative Art Fellowship, 1963. Address: 1001 Cragmont, Berkeley, California 94708, U.S.A.

PUBLICATIONS

Verse

Men, Women, Vines.   Berkeley, California, Ark Press, 1959.
Thanatos: Earth Poems.   Berkeley, California, Oyez, 1965.
Protect the Earth (includes essays).   San Francisco, City Lights Books, 1970.
Homage to Jack Spicer and Other Poems: Poems 1965–1969.   Berkeley, California, Ark Press, 1970.

Play

Twenty-Five Years of the Endless War.   Berkeley, California, Thorp Springs Press, 1973.

Other

W. B. Yeats, Self-Critic: A Study of His Early Verse.   Berkeley, University of California Press, and London, Cambridge University Press, 1951.
W. B. Yeats: The Later Poetry.   Berkeley, University of California Press, and London, Cambridge University Press, 1964.

Editor, A Casebook on the Beat.   New York, Crowell, 1961.
Editor, Masterworks of Prose.   Indianapolis, Bobbs Merrill, 1962.
Editor, Robert Lowell: A Collection of Critical Essays.   New York, Prentice Hall, 1968.

Thomas Parkinson comments:

My poetry is primarily meditative poetry written in various forms but moving increasingly toward a formal free verse that makes use of all the devices of historical poetry in English, not excluding rhyme. My main concerns are the relation of man to nature, of history to wilderness, and of death to love.

*   *   *

From his position on the Berkeley campus Thomas Parkinson has witnessed first-hand the free speech movement, war resistance and protest, and the student strikes which have been so prominently focused there. His poetry and essays traverse an astonishingly wide range from public, often political, topics to events personal and confessional. Parkinson has himself escaped death by inches, has seen death close at hand, and shows painful awareness of the infinite varieties of dying. His poetry reveals a continual amazement over the very process and flux of life, the cruel ecology of organisms, the fragility, and the mystery of it all. It is like being at the beach at low tide, watching the squirting, crawling, opening abundance of life until you can absorb no more, "And the entire planet screams in the mind, an interminable / feeding, and swelling and expiring."

Parkinson's *Protect the Earth* contains short environmental and political essays and a long poem, "Litany for the American People," which records his outrage over inhuman governmental actions. The book is based on Parkinson's conviction that "so long as human beings go on building up levels of tolerance against the abominable, the abominable will grow." It records his deep concern for the quality of human life and his rages against human arrogance and environmental insensitivity. Parkinson sees himself as a Franciscan; he is also a poet ecologist in sympathy if not in league with Barry Commoner and Paul Ehrlich.

The poetry of *Homage to Jack Spicer* and *Thanatos: Earth Poems* is considerably more personal. The eight "Spicer" poems span eighteen years of close friendship with Spicer, between 1947 and 1965. There is also the pain of watching Spicer, also a writer, tear and drink himself dead. "He was a battered radio / in the city dump, connections busted, batteries shot . . . ," dead at forty. Parkinson also refers to his "Dry Season" during this period. He is shot in his office by a "poor lunatic" who believes he is a Communist. His student assistant is killed and sixty pieces of bird shot hit Parkinson in the face and jaw. "My wound / throbs and my wired jaw / Aches." It is a time when "clocks fail, hearts / stumble," poison and violence surround him yet he can affirm "violence only creates more violence." Still, for Parkinson "surviving's not enough," he seeks not merely law and order but inner order, and the "expression of an inner psychological harmony." *Thanatos* presents both a series of "Soliloquies for the Dead," the dying, and a further search, through solitude, for the inner order he craves. He recognizes in life:

> A spark ongoing, and in the ever-branching
> heavens of the night
> A life-tree bearing on and on.

With the *Thanatos* poems Parkinson's lines are less tightly imagistic, more expansive and more memorable, as seen in "Death as Solitude":

> Moon passes and sun sets, whatever is holy rests
> In the rising susurrah. From their quiet, ecstasy.
> And the sanctified earth turns and turns.

– John R. Cooley

PARVIN, Betty.   British.   Born in Cardiff, Glamorgan, 10 October 1916. Educated at Heathfield House Convent School; extramural classes at the University of Nottingham and the University of Leicester. Married D. F. McKenzie Parvin in 1941; has one son. During World War II, worked as a secretary in the Civil Service. Secretary, 1966–71, and since 1973, Vice-Chairman, Nottingham Poetry Society. Member, Advisory Panel, East Midlands Arts Association; Reviewer, *Outposts*, London. Recipient: Lake Aske Memorial Award, 1968, 1971; Manifold Century Scholarship, 1968. Address: "Bamboo," Bunny Hill Top, Costock, near Loughborough, Leicestershire LE12 6UX, England.

PUBLICATIONS

Verse

A *Stone My Star*.   London, Outposts Publications, 1961.
The Bird with the Luck: Twelve Poems.   Nottingham, Byron Press, 1968.
Sketchbook from Mercia.   London, Manifold Publications, 1968.
Sarnia's Gift.   Loughborough, Leicestershire, Griffin Press, 1972.
A Birchtree with Finches.   Nottingham, N.P.S. Publications, 1974.

Other

Editor, *Poetry Nottingham*.   Nottingham, N.P.S. Publications, 1970.

Manuscript Collection: Nottingham Central Library.

Critical Study: Introduction by G. S. Fraser to *The Bird with the Luck*, 1968.

Betty Parvin comments:

When G. S. Fraser read some of my first poems in the early sixties he remarked: "You have a Parnassian gift. Don't let it go!" From that time I ceased to denigrate its Palgravian roots or to attempt consciously to change my style. Poets I have learned to revere since force-fed schooldays have contemporized my work without my conscious manipulation, but still when the rhyme would chime, I permit it. Not unnaturally, many of these poets have similar roots: Hardy, Edward and R. S. Thomas, Larkin, Day Lewis, Wilbur, Fraser and the lesser known but to my mind considerable woman poet Madge Hales. But among the younger moderns who have surely influenced me are: Plath, Heaney, Patten . . . I watch for Martin Booth's new work.

My theme is whatever warms me emotionally; I am past the time of powerful bias, unless it be for the beautiful – that which, some would persuade us, has never existed.

For a brief time I became involved in groups and group poetry readings; have returned with some relief to working alone, though inclusion in textbooks and anthologies has resulted in calls upon me to read and talk about my poems in schools, etc. – a valuable contact with my "public," and one which I enjoy.

*   *   *

Betty Parvin is more widely known and respected among readers of poetry than her four small booklets would appear to indicate, for her work has been published in a number of magazines and anthologies and has been translated into Portuguese and Byelorussian. There is nothing that might be regarded as pretentious in her poetry and no attempt is made at intellectual hair-splitting, though her poems are informed by a cool intelligence and control of language that do not give way to sentimentality or egotism. She concentrates largely upon her own everyday experiences – memories of youth and childhood, encounters with people, family connections, places she has visited or lived in, or moods "caught on the wing at play in timeless Wales." An ivy-wreathed gateway or a gothic window is enough to stimulate her creative imagination. Yet it would be a mistake to regard her as a domestic poet. She has such an individual way of looking at things, whether it is the absurd gait of a magpie or gulls searching for food in the "green harbour muck," and of placing them in some kind of perspective, that the reader is subtly brought into contact with fundamentals, the paradox and underlying reality of life itself. In such poems as "Gulls Aground," "Welsh Cottagers," and "Mothering," Betty Parvin is to be seen at her best.

– Howard Sergeant

PATTEN, Brian. British. Born in Liverpool, Lancashire, 7 February 1946. Educated at Sefton Park Secondary School, Liverpool. Formerly, Editor, *Underdog*, Liverpool. Recipient: Eric Gregory Award, 1967; Arts Council grant, 1969. Address: c/o Allen and Unwin, Museum Street, London W.C.1, England.

PUBLICATIONS

Verse

Portraits. Liverpool, privately printed, 1962.
The Mersey Sound: Penguin Modern Poets 10, with Adrian Henri and Roger McGough. London, Penguin, 1967.
Little Johnny's Confession. London, Allen and Unwin, 1967; New York, Hill and Wang, 1968.
Atomic Adam. London, Fulham Gallery, 1967.
Notes to the Hurrying Man: Poems, Winter '66–Summer '68. London, Allen and Unwin, and New York, Hill and Wang, 1969.
The Home Coming. London, Turret Books, 1969.
The Irrelevant Song. Frensham, Surrey, Sceptre Press, 1970.
Little Johnny's Foolish Invention: A Poem (bilingual edition), translated by Robert Sanesi. Milan, Tipographia Bertieri, 1970.

At Four O'Clock in the Morning.   Frensham, Surrey, Sceptre Press, 1971.
The Irrelevant Song and Other Poems.   London, Allen and Unwin, 1971.
When You Wake Tomorrow.   London, Turret Books, 1972.
*The Eminent Professors and the Nature of Poetry as Enacted Out by Members of the
    Poetry Seminar One Rainy Evening.*   London, Poem-of-the-Month Club, 1972.
The Unreliable Nightingale.   London, Rota, 1973.

Recordings: *Selections from Little Johnny's Confession and Notes to the Hurrying
Man and New Poems,* Caedmon, 1969; *Vanishing Trick,* 1972.

Short Stories

Two Stories.   London, Covent Garden Press, 1973.

Other

The Elephant and the Flower: Almost-Fables (juvenile).   London, Allen and
    Unwin, 1970.
Manchild (juvenile).   London, Covent Garden Press, 1973.
Jumping Mouse (adaptation of an American Indian folk tale).   London, Allen
    and Unwin, 1973.

Editor, with Pat Krett, *The House That Jack Built: Poems for Shelter.*   London,
    Allen and Unwin, 1973.

Brian Patten comments:

(1970) Outside poetry I feel there are too many ways of saying things for me to
be able to speak clearly. So the poems are their own statements. A translation into
words of a world beyond words is the best I can say about them.

*   *   *

The young Liverpool poet Brian Patten made a big reputation for himself on the
strength of his first two volumes of verse – and, of course, his own youth. When
he first appeared on the scene Patten was commonly identified as a pop-poet – a
label apparently justified not only by his working-class background, but by poems
such as "Little Johnny's Confession," which in fact was the title poem of his first
volume. Yet the pop-references seemed to fall naturally into place, to be part of
what the poet was trying to say, and not just fashionable decoration. At the same
time, Patten declared his wish to write "the hard lyric." His book *Notes to the
Hurrying Man* showed what he meant by this. The poetry has a song-like quality,
plaintive and nostalgic, yet is sufficiently dense and sufficiently abrupt in its
transitions to avoid looking like words in search of a tune. Patten's touch is not
infallible – he can be both clumsy and sentimental – but reviewers have rightly
recognised a potentially important talent.

– Edward Lucie-Smith

PATTERSON, Raymond R(ichard). American. Born in New York City, 14 December 1929. Educated at Lincoln University, Pennsylvania, 1947–51, A.B. 1951; New York University, 1954–56, M.A. 1956. Served in the United States Army, 1951–53. Married Boydie Alice Cooke in 1957; has one child, Ama. Children's Supervisor, Youth House for Boys, New York, 1956–58; Instructor in English, Benedict College, Columbia, South Carolina, 1958–59; English Teacher in New York City Public Schools, 1959–68. Since 1968, Lecturer in English, City College of the City University of New York. Recipient: Borestone Mountain award, 1950; National Endowment for the Arts grant, 1969. Address: 2 Lee Court, Merrick, New York 11566, U.S.A.

PUBLICATIONS

Verse

  Twenty-Six Ways of Looking at a Black Man and Other Poems. New York, Award Books, and London, Tandem, 1969.

Critical Study: by Aaron Kramer, in *Freedomways* (New York), 1970.

Raymond R. Patterson comments:

For me writing poetry is an exploration of the possibilities of experience; a poem written is a poem dis-covered, providing useful knowledge about the territory we travel through.

*   *   *

Contemporary Black poetry is rooted in the social upheaval that gripped the United States during the 1950's and 1960's, when, in a last ditch push for full integration, Black people – North and South – took to the streets. The result of their effort was the recognition, by some, that the country would cede nothing through protest. From that political truth grew the Black Power Movement. Its cultural arm, the Black Arts Movement, views all art as a weapon in the struggle for Black liberation. In this context, the aim of Black literature is the total revaluation of the ideas and images by which Blacks have traditionally defined themselves.

  Poet Raymond R. Patterson reflects the influence of all these forces. The result has been a body of poetry that is seminal in its explorations of black life. Concerned more with the psychological that the physical, Patterson is the poet-chronicler, capturing in verse the revolution in Black thought that created the 1960's. "Come into my black hands. / Touch me. Feel the grip / And cramp of angry circumstance. . . ." From the crucial admission of individual rage – a rage given force and articulation in real life by Malcolm X – the poet moves on to attack the various ploys used by Blacks to navigate the American holocaust: "Black boys push carts in alligator shoes," while aspiring integrationists ". . . carry the word in Brooks Brothers suits," and the tiny elite, while fully convinced of its infallibility, are "Thinking, sometimes . . . / Someone lied. Sometimes thinking suicide." But all is illusion and self-deception, insists the poet; beneath the carefully controlled masks, "There is enough / Grief- / Energy in / The Blackness / Of the whitest Negro / To incinerate / America."

Incineration is the key to "Riot Rimes U.S.A.," the eighty-five poem sequence that is Patterson's most popular work. The poems are humorous and ironic by turn, in their first person depictions of the Harlem riot of 1965. From the poet's perspective, that event was the high point of the African experience in America: "My mama hadn't said one word / To my daddy for two whole years. / But after the riots, she was so happy / She was crying tears . . . / Nothing suits a family like a big strong male."

– Saundra Towns

PAYNE, Basil. Irish. Born in Dublin, 22 June 1928. Educated at Christian Brothers School, Dublin; University College, Dublin. Married; has six sons and one daughter. Formerly, Drama Critic, the *Irish Times* and the *Irish Press*, Dublin; Scriptwriter, Editor and Critic, Radio Telefis Eireann, Dublin, 1963–73. Since 1974, Poet-in-Residence, Glassboro State College, New Jersey. Recipient: Guinness Prize, 1964, 1966. Address: Cortona, 137 Rathfarnham Road, Dublin 14, Ireland.

PUBLICATIONS

Verse

> *Sunlight on a Square: Poems.* Dublin, John Augustine, 1962.
> *Love in the Afternoon.* Dublin and London, Gill and Macmillan, 1971.
> *Another Kind of Optimism.* Dublin and London, Gill and Macmillan, 1974.

Plays

> *In Dublin's Quare City* (produced Dublin, 1973).

> Radio Plays: *The Onlooker*, 1969; *Don't Call Me Honey.*

> Television Plays: *Missing Believed Dead; A Boy and a Ball.*

Other

> Editor and Translator, *Elegy for the Western World*, by Hans Carossa. Dublin, University of Dublin Press, 1964.

> Translator, *Collected Poems*, by Karl Gustav Gerold. Dublin, Dolmen Press, 1972.

Basil Payne comments:

Major Themes: (1) Hidden recesses of selfhood. (2) Confessional – Family Album poems (man and wife; father and son; etc.). (3) Dublin as subject matter and/or objective correlative of personal experience. (4) Childhood. (5) Poems of social protest.

General Influences: Environmental mainly. But also Eliot, Brecht, Rilke, and Lowell (I have translated Carossa, Brecht, and Rilke).

I use most verse forms but value irony and tenderness as invaluable in reaching a singular poetic statement.

*   *   *

The forty poems in Basil Payne's *Love in the Afternoon* are divided into three sections: "Pilgrimage," "From a Family Album," and "Public and Private Eye." The divisions give an idea of his territory and the way he walks it. He writes about his memories of growing up in the South Circular Road district of Dublin; of watching his father shaving with a cut-throat razor, his mother doing the wash in a zinc bathtub; of journeys, neighbours, accidents, pruning the roses; of other Irish poets; and of love between man and wife and parent and child. This last is Payne's most ambitious theme. His tone is relaxed, pleasant, chatty to a fault:

> Watching my father shaving in the kitchen
> Before a cracked mirror: this was my four-years-old high-light
> In our otherwise humdrum daily domestic ritual . . .
>
> Father died having breakfast (*from natural causes*
> The Coroner's verdict recorded). My electric razor purrs.
> My young son complains it causes T.V. interference.

Contact with the accent of common speech is never quite foregone, and the poet asks our pardon for his one obvious vice of being "so dissolutely *nice*."

– Robert Nye

---

p'BITEK, Okot. Ugandan. Born in Gulu, Northern Uganda, in 1930. Educated at Gulu High School; King's College, Budo; University of Bristol; Oxford University, B. Litt. 1963; studied Law at Aberystwyth University, Wales. Formerly, taught school near Gulu. Director, Uganda National Theatre and Cultural Center.

PUBLICATIONS

Verse

Lak tar miyo kinyero wi lobo? (in Acoli: Are your teeth white, then laugh!). Kampala, Uganda, Eagle Press, 1953.

1175

The Song of Lawino (translated from Acoli by the author). Nairobi, Kenya,
   East African Publishing House, 1966.
Song of Ocol. Nairobi, Kenya, East African Publishing House, 1970.
Song of a Prisoner. New York, Third Press, 1971.
Horn of My Love. London, Heinemann, 1973.

*   • *   *

Okot p'Bitek is undoubtedly among the most original of African poets. In using
traditional African themes and rhythms to incorporate European ideas and
experiences he has fashioned a new and personal use of the English language,
which finds its most characteristic expression in *Song of Lawino*.

Song of Lawino is a lyrical cycle of poems reflecting the poet's roving eye. Its
biting satire is aimed at once at traditional African society, as well as the European
sophistication which impinges on it, yet does not spare those elements which bridge
these separate cultures. But the exploration is not without compassion and huge
gusts of humour. p'Bitek thus represents for East African poetry that increasingly
evident phenomenon of the writer so far emancipated from the wrath of Colonialism that he can afford to laugh at his own circumstance and that of the society
around him.

His themes range from attitudes on polygamy through the phases of social
evolution to religion in Africa. Within this panorama individuals, as symbols of a
class group or point of view in the community, rush around with T.V. cameras
taking close-ups of each other. If the result is not beautiful or profound, it is clear
and disturbing.

The poet's technique is light-weight narrative and recalls the story-telling delivery
which is so familiar a feature of African culture. The images are stark and irides-
cent, embodying worlds of wisdom in their sharp thrusts, yet not overburdened or
obscured by an excess of local myth.

Song of Lawino though lyrical in style is a dramatic situation worked out through
many Acts. In it we see compounded the very fundamentals of African Art, an
all-embracing expression of *persona*. The music, poetry, dance and dramatic art are
interlaced and indivisible. The poet achieves all this by the impressive naturalness
of his device of juggling the rhythms from, say, the prose narrative patterns to
sudden three-line stanzas of personal affirmation. One can hear the cadences of
Arabic influences floating over the plains of his African expression in the high-
pitched and taut melodies of desert horns.

But though p'Bitek at first acquaintance seems an extrovert poet, closer contact
reveals a depth of feeling and use of ideas. He does however leave the matter open
and draws few conclusions for his readers.

– Lenrie Peters

PERRY, Grace. Australian. Born in Melbourne, Victoria. Educated at Sydney
University, M.B., B.S., qualified as physician. Married to Harry Kronenberg; has

three children. Has held several pediatric appointments. Currently in general practice. Editor, *Poetry Magazine*, Sydney, 1962-64. Since 1963, Writing School and Festival Director. Since 1964, Proprietor, South Head Press, Sydney, and Editor, *Poetry Australia*, Sydney. Address: c/o South Head Press, 350 Lyons Road, Five Dock, New South Wales 2046, Australia.

PUBLICATIONS

Verse

I Am the Songs You Sing and Other Poems.   Sydney, Consolidated Press, 1944.
Red Scarf.   Sydney, Edwards and Shaw, 1964.
Frozen Section.   Sydney, Edwards and Shaw, 1967.
Two Houses: Poems 66–69.   Sydney, South Head Press, 1969.
Berrima Winter.   Sydney, South Head Press, 1974.
Journal of a Surgeon's Wife.   Sydney, South Head Press, 1975.

Manuscript Collection: Mitchell Library, Sydney.

Critical Studies: by James Libdroth, in *Spirit* (South Orange, New Jersey), Spring 1970; J. G. Tulip, in *Southerly* (Sydney), no. 2, 1973; J. E. Chamberlin, in *Hudson Review* (New York), Summer 1973; Fred Holzknect, in *Makar* (Brisbane), 1973.

Grace Perry comments:

My poetry? You may as well ask what does the crocodile have for dinner. Many times, I have been down to the grey-green greasy Limpopo River all set about with fever trees, but I am still sitting in the wait-a-bit thorn bush rubbing my sore nose and pondering the answer.

I do not consider poetry a religion. It does not matter with which holy trinity the century began – Allen Tate's conversational or the imagist trio of 1911. I am where I am now, my own bible, my own horizon. The view is not the same from my small window. I have passed through the painful structures of rejection systems that afflict the young, who walk the old road as if houses and trees were not there. The novoice of the determined inner city inhabitant, upon the page, may be difficult to differentiate from the unpoems of other cities.

Yet I am greedy for many lives, and do my best to live them, moving from surgery to sea coast to countryside – more than "two houses." The important thing is to know who I am, where and when. Within the sensitive shell deficient receptive body, I need to cut off excessive stimuli. It would be impossible for me to survive in an office now for more than a few days – the traffic noise, the telephones, the pressure of people erode my substance.

I believe all of us build around ourselves that elaborate and delicate structure (after our death to be known as "The Work") out of the rummage rooms of the mind and physical elements detached from the immediate environment, erecting each day ·the more or less complex delusional systems by which we survive. The eidolons which are mine may have little significance to anyone else; for each man his own language. I speak out of myself words I do not fully understand but somewhere, out there, I know someone is listening.

*   *   *

Grace Perry was a poet long before she was a doctor. Her first work was published before her 18th year. Yet the apparently unlike careers of medico and poet have overlapped in recent years and her books have appeared regularly. Much of her verse is heavily textured with powerful verbs and there is always an awareness of the distinction of poetry as imaginatively heightened speech, in some instances as an almost ceremonial chant.

Two engrossing themes occur and sometimes interact throughout her poetry: the never-ending search for the inner self, the anima, shown as an allegory of the separated lover hymning or bewailing the elusive ideal, and the omnipresent aware-ness of mortality, death and decay, interpreted and personified as a patient suffer-ing from a virulent disease, often terminal.

In *Red Scarf* she separated these themes, concentrating on the search for love in the long sequence "Where the Wind Moves," while the latter part of the book brought together a number of pieces descriptive and interpretative of lives changing and intensifying under the stress of serious illness. Her recent book *Frozen Section* offers a wider scope of subject matter but the two major themes – the perennial poetic juxtaposition of love and death – are developed and expanded in a number of poems and sequences.

– Bruce Beaver

PETERS, Lenrie (Leopold). Gambian. Born in Bathurst, 1 September 1932. Edu-cated at Trinity College, Cambridge; University College Hospital, London, M.B., B.Chir. Since 1966, Surgical Registrar, Northampton General Hospital. Fellow, Royal College of Surgeons. Address: 34 Howitt Close, Howitt Road, London N.W.3, England.

PUBLICATIONS

Verse

Poems. Ibadan, Nigeria, Mbari, 1964.
Satellites. London, Heinemann, 1967.
Katchikali. London, Heinemann, 1971.

Novel

The Second Round. London, Heinemann, 1965.

         *   *   *

Two biographical influences stand out in the poetry of Lenrie Peters. The first is that he is a surgeon and the second is that he has been considerably influenced by an adulthood spent outside Africa. Surgery is the source of many of his most effective images and themes. No poem demonstrates this more effectively than "Sounds of the Ocean" which frequently resorts to the image of a surgeon groping in the body of a patient to represent the precarious search and exploration for limited objectives through which man eventually achieves self realisation and the peace that this brings:

> Hand fumbling with bowel
> Or wringing out the brain
> Reaches no further than
> The moment allows.

The end of the poem holds out the hope that this fumbling search will produce results:

> But there will be for each
> Who seeks with dedication
> A solitary triumph of peace.

The guarded optimism of "Sounds of the Ocean" is a recurrent note in Peters' poetry which never seeks, however, to conceal the agony, the uncertainty, and the loneliness of the search that leads to self realisation.

The second biographical fact – Peters' African birth and his subsequent physical alienation from Africa – comes out in many ways. He is continually remembering Africa and realises in poetry the physical return to it which so far has not occurred. It is significant that his only novel so far, *The Second Round*, is based on the experiences of a doctor returning to his home after many years of study abroad. The impression one gets is of the poet continually balancing the alternatives in his mind – a felt duty to Africa and a duty to himself which dictates continued residence in Europe. These poetic returns abound in his poetry:

> I shall return
> When daylight saunters on
> When evening shadows the berry
> And fiery night the sun.

Like others of Peters' poems, however, this is not just a simple return to a country; there is the implication of a return to a basic state of nature which requires an elimination of outward trappings; the return is in fact a spiritual rather than a physical return. Other "Homecoming" poems show a similar meaningful ambiguity. Peters' vicarious returns are thus symbolically significant.

In spite of his sojourn abroad, the poet is concerned with the fate of Africa. The consequences of independence, the broken promises, the petty tyrannies are all reflected in the long poem "In the Beginning," where Peters exploits his talent for broken pieces of suggestive dialogue to picture the relationship between the ordinary voter and his new rulers:

"But excuse me, Sir;
We're free.
Why do we have to beg?"
Industrial development
Dams, factories, the lot –
change the face of the Continent.
"I see
But my children –
beg pardon Sir,
will they go to school?"
Later!
"Will they have food to eat
and clothes to wear?"
Later I tell you!
"Beg pardon Sir;
a house like yours?"
Put this man in jail.

The concern for the common man in the hands of authority is treated in contexts
other than the African:

Every time they shut the gates
And hang up notices
On steel plates
That love-making is forbidden
After eight

This has more of the background of Hyde Park than of Freetown's Victoria Park as
has his "Song" which pictures prostitutes "selling old boot / On wet pavements."
Peters has succeeded in making a harmony of his two backgrounds and he uses
each without self-consciousness. The range of his interests is very wide. Very few
African poets would write a eulogy of Winston Churchill, whom Peters seems
genuinely to have admired. The explosion of the Chinese bomb is similarly the
unlikely subject of another poem. The result of all this is that Peters is an
unlocalised poet, whose concern is ultimately for the general human predicament.

– Eldred D. Jones

PETERSEN, Donald. American. Born in Minneapolis, Minnesota, 11 November
1928. Educated at the Sorbonne, Paris, 1948–49; Carleton College, Northfield,
Minnesota, B.A. 1950; Indiana University, Bloomington; University of Iowa, Iowa
City, M.F.A. 1952. Married Jeanine Ahrens in 1952; has four children. Taught at
the University of Iowa, 1954–56. Since 1956, Member of the English Department,
and currently, Professor of English, State University of New York, Oneonta.
Assistant Editor, *Western Review*, Iowa City, 1950–55. Address: Department of
English, State University of New York, Oneonta, New York 13820, U.S.A.

PUBLICATIONS

Verse

The Spectral Boy.   Middletown, Connecticut, Wesleyan University Press, 1964.

*   *   *

Donald Petersen is a formalist, an elegist, and a pastoral poet whose works are rooted in his small town (rural America) and big city (Paris) experiences. Despite the fact that he studied under such poets as Robert Lowell, Karl Shapiro, Paul Engle, and John Berryman, he regards himself as neither a literary nor an academic poet.

His work is pervaded by a haunting nostalgia for things of value which lend genuine feeling to his lines without becoming mournful:

> Home is a place of resurrections. Fears
> I ran away from, sorrows that I fled,
> Come back to haunt me now from other years.
> Two neighbors I remember best are dead.

Petersen states, "My memory plays a large role in making a poem. A poem of mine is often an amalgam of old and new verse, and its subject matter is often concerned with memory. It is also likely to be, in unlikely terms, a religious poem." Central to his poetry are attempts to experience renewal or to effect regeneration through relationships to time, to nature, to religion, and between individuals. The range of these relationships is frequently evinced through "the terrifying extremes" of hot and cold and their possible harmony:

> Then summer slid beneath her cold inversion
> With sunny slopes and crowded canopies,
>   But we were happy.
>
> Fell winter without tears that when they freeze
> Can pierce the summer-keeping heart and be
>   Forever dripping.
>
> Desire these days, my dear, that we may be
> Two ever-shifting dunes of fine white snow,
>   Made one completely.

Mr. Petersen further describes himself as one of the few remaining poets who writes in complete sentences. But his poetry is rigidly formed, a characteristic which he accounts for because he is dealing with very "slippery" content.

– Charles L. James

PETRIE, Paul (James).   American.   Born in Detroit, Michigan, 1 July 1928. Educated at Wayne State University, Detroit, 1946–51, B.A., M.A.; University of

Iowa, Iowa City, Ph.D. 1957. Married to Sylvia Spencer; has two daughters and one son. Since 1959, Member of the English Department, and currently, Professor of English, University of Rhode Island, Kingston. Address: 66 Dendron Road, Peace Dale, Rhode Island 02879, U.S.A.

PUBLICATIONS

Verse

Confessions of a Non-Conformist.   Mount Vernon, Iowa, Hillside Press, 1963.
The Race with Time and the Devil.   Francestown, New Hampshire, Golden Quill
    Press, 1965.
The Leader: For Martin Luther King, Jr.   Providence, Rhode Island, Hellcoal
    Press, 1968.
From under the Hill of Night: Poems.   Nashville, Tennessee, Vanderbilt Univer-
    sity Press, 1969.
The Idol.   Kingston, Rhode Island, Biscuit City Press, 1973.
The Academy of Goodbye.   Hanover, New Hampshire, University Press of New
    England, 1974.

Paul Petrie comments:

My whole approach to poetry, both thematic and technical, is governed by a hatred of dogmatic theorizing, and since the twentieth century represents the very apotheosis of theorizing, a paradise for half-baked creeds and counter-creeds, I find myself in a "school" of one. If there is any critical notion which I find appealing, it is Keats' idea of Negative Capability, but even that has its limitations. In short I believe that there is nothing that cannot be said in poetry and that there is no limitation on the way it can or should be said. A poem need not be "new" or "old," in "free verse" or "meter," "understated" or "overstated" – all that it must be is a good poem.

As for my own work, I would describe it as lyrical, relatively emotional, dramatic in its inclusion of opposites with a stronger current of movement than is common in verse today, and perhaps an over-indulgence in the doctrine of statement through images. My major strengths are rhythm and organization; my major weaknesses are a lack of exact detail and firm diction. I have a personal notion of the poem as an act of praise (be it positive or negative in theme and tone), and I tend to regard poetry as a semi-religious vocation, but I do not demand that others share these attitudes and I can think of excellent poems which would stretch these terms to the breaking point. The poems will remain; the theory will go.

*   *   *

Dr. Paul Petrie is well known to students of contemporary American poetry. For two decades his poems have appeared in a wide variety of literary journals, magazines, and in three volumes, Confessions of a Non-Conformist, The Race With Time and the Devil, and From under the Hill of Night. A sense of death-in-life and our fragile mortality seems to be the exclusive concern of the three volumes. Haunted by death in his dreams and plagued by it in his waking life, Dr. Petrie, in an intense and passionate creative act, transforms his fear and dread into art. As *The Race with Time and the Devil* suggests, such an act is not an easy or an unambiguous triumph. His best poems are alive with the sense of a real person's struggle to achieve an elemental relationship with and understanding of the natural cycles of life and death.

From the first volume to the third, there is a clear movement toward concentration, sharpness and mastery of medium. *Confessions of a Non-Conformist* is an adequate work, though not particularly original. *The Race with Time and the Devil* is a marked improvement and contains a number of fine poems, especially the five poem sequence "Pictures of Departure," "The Last Words of Frederick II," "Chain," "The Church of San Antonio De La Florida," "Morning Psalm," and "In Defense of Colds." The most recent collection, *From under the Hill of Night,* deserves the most praise. Poems such as "Under the Hill of Night," "The Party," "Mark Twain," "Kindertoten," and "Notes of a Would-Be Traveler," are excellent. In them, Dr. Petrie has achieved fully his desire to articulate his organic sense of his world.

– Richard Damashek

PETTY, W(illiam) H(enry). British. Born in Bradford, Yorkshire, 7 September 1921. Educated at Bradford Grammar School, 1931–40; Peterhouse, Cambridge, B.A. 1946, M.A. 1950; University of London, B.Sc. 1953. Served in the Royal Artillery, 1941–45. Married Margaret Bastow in 1948; has two daughters and one son. Senior Assistant, London County Council Library Services, 1946–47; Administrative Assistant, Borough of Doncaster, later, English Teacher, Central Technical High School, 1947–51; Assistant Education Officer, North Riding County Council, 1951–57, and West Riding County Council, 1957–64. Deputy Education Officer, 1964–73, and since 1973, County Education Officer, Kent County Council. National Executive, Society of Education Officers, 1971. Recipient: Cheltenham Festival Prize, 1968; Camden Festival Prize, 1970. Address: Godfrey House, Hollingbourne, near Maidstone, Kent, England.

PUBLICATIONS

Verse

No Bold Comfort. London, Outposts Publications, 1957.
Conquest. London, Outposts Publications, 1967.

Critical Studies: in the *Times Literary Supplement* (London), July 1957; by Vernon Scannell, in *Outposts* (London), Summer 1957; in *Poetry Review* (London), Winter 1958; in the *Times Educational Supplement* (London), July 1967.

W. H. Petty comments:

An experience – intellectual, emotional, visual – itself informs me when I should write a poem. The process of writing always reveals connections, often subtle connections, with other experiences of which I had not been conscious before beginning to write the poem. The process of writing also indicates the techniques, such as rhythm, rhyme and word and line patterns – or, at times, the deliberate avoidance of these – which appear to be the most effective means of expression. I never "force" a poem: I never pre-determine a technique. This means that the poems I write are comparatively few in number – which seems to me advantageous in the circumstances of today.

*   *   *

Although only two booklets of W. H. Petty's work have been published, his poems have appeared in a wide range of magazines and anthologies, and he has been awarded prizes in the Cheltenham Festival of Literature and the Camden Festival of Music and the Arts. *No Bold Comfort* is a collection of 20 lyrics, mostly descriptive of scenes or events which seem to have been thrust upon the poet's attention – "Futility in Cagnes," "Nightmare in Bruges," "Skinningrove Steel-Works," etc. – rather than having been selected as subjects to illustrate a central theme, though there are also a few reflective poems about life in general or personal experience in particular which reveal the poet's philosophy.

Even in his earliest poems, W. H. Petty exhibited a fastidious concern for language and form, but undoubtedly the most noticeable feature of his modest style was the capacity to evoke a scene or recreate an atmosphere by means of striking visual imagery. In poem after poem one comes across such phrases as "the town's white angularities and the morning tables bright as tight fruit," "the village fat with snow," and "the rough kidney cobbles of the Pennine streets"; and occasionally a masterly use of monosyllables to achieve the desired effect, as in "Market":

> So the high sun brings all things here to pattern
> Even the fat cattle amiably
> Ambling between the buxom-windowed shops
> To curt death.

Conquest is a long poem in which the poet reviews his past from childhood to the present, touching upon life in Bradford and Cambridge, and holidays at home and abroad, in the belief that "to contemplate our past is to savour / Mastery, for the past only exists / when the spool of memory is turned / By one's self." W. H. Petty turns the spool to considerable purpose here.

– Howard Sergeant

PICKARD, Tom. British. Born in Newcastle upon Tyne, Northumberland, in 1946. Educated in Newcastle secondary schools. Married to Constance Pickard; has one son and one daughter. Worked for a seed merchant, 1962–63, for a construction company, 1963, and for a wine merchant, 1964, all in Newcastle. Co-Founder

and Manager of the Mordern Tower Book Room, 1963–72, and the Ultima Thule
Bookshop, 1969–73, Newcastle. Recipient: Northern Arts Minor Award, 1965; Arts
Council grant, 1969, 1973. Address: 2 Hubert Terrace, Gateshead, County Durham
NE8 2HE, England.

PUBLICATIONS

Verse

High on the Walls. London, Fulcrum Press, 1967; New York, Horizon Press,
    1968.
New Human Unisphere. Newcastle-upon-Tyne, Ultima Thule Books, 1969.
An Armpit of Lice. London, Fulcrum Press, 1970.
The Order of Chance. London, Fulcrum Press, 1971.
Dancing under Fire. Philadelphia, Middle Earth, 1973.

Play

Television Play: Squire, 1974.

Novel

Guttersnipe. San Francisco, City Lights Books, 1972.

Critical Studies: "Tom Pickard" by Eric Mottram, in Lip 1 (Philadelphia), 1972;
interview in Contact 6 (Philadelphia), 1973.

*   *   *

Tom Pickard's first book had a rightly enthusiastic and characteristically truthful
Foreword by Basil Bunting. Here was someone, he said, who had "escaped education," and over whom "tradition and fashion" had no power. For Pickard, victim
of an educational system that still has little interest in catering for the socially
underprivileged but gifted personality, left school at fourteen. He had not heard of
the Greek Anthology, and yet his "unbookish" lyrics had some resemblance (as
Bunting pointed out) to the earliest writers in that collection. So here we had the
fresh poetry of a young man who had little to inspire him beyond his own impulse,
and who could not look at his art with formalized or official or academic eyes. The
title poem, "High on the Walls," may be slight; but its vision is pure and it parallels
mental events – as such miniaturistic descriptive poems must:

> Strange to be higher
> than a bird, to watch
> them eat
>
> when startled (the only
> defence to be above)
> take flight, and land
> at my feet.

"To My Unborn Child" would doubtless be classed as "obscene" by some ("our heads met / when both of them / bent to kiss / your mother's womb"), and is biologically incorrect (his head "met," at that stage, his unborn child's feet); but it has perfect simplicity, and its directness is not at all directed towards the fashionably obscene. "Rape," too, in Newcastle dialect (and excellently done), taps real experience. Pickard was at this stage simply not aware of gentility, or even of the nature of the savage hostility of the Northern English establishment to the arts in general (to which Bunting refers in his Foreword). These were minor poems, but tough and innocent: true responses.

The Order of Chance was a grave disappointment. Bunting had written: "Mr. Pickard has yet to read most of the English classics, which must change his writing more or less, perhaps not always for the better. He is poor, and must feel the temptation to dilute his spirit till it is acceptable to the flock of inferior poets who pick up all the gleanings society leaves for literature." This happened; but the gleanings he picked up were not those of academic or over-literary poets who haunt the pages of the modish weeklies, but instead those of pseudo-"drop-outs" or ignorant English imitators of American styles. Once he had sung; now, for the most part, he swore – he repeated what he had already said well enough, on the subject of human nastiness and establishment complacency, and he imitated himself. The language of the newer poems has lost its purity, its freshness: Pickard has discovered gentility, and wants to offend it. But he is not sharp enough to be a good satirical poet; his intellect is not fully formed; the reader no longer gains the impression of independence; the candour has vanished, to be replaced (for the most part) by an almost monotonous aggressiveness – and one that lacks poetic edge. Once again the Arts Council Writer's Award has struck. There is no poem about the committee that gave him this: instead he gives them the mindless and routine blasphemy that is the sure sign of neutralization: they may easily lean back with educated indulgence.

> Fuck the virgin mary
>   bless Eve for her fruit
> let's eat her apple and fuck our fill
>   god gave us cocks and cunts
> for joys and thrills
>   bite deep the juice is sweet
> bless Eve for her fruit.

This is abject, and one can certainly not point to any intellectual compensation for its tiredness of diction or its sleek, ingratiating sexism: it merely reiterates, without distinction, a somewhat old-fashioned and over-simplified view. But Pickard is not yet thirty, and there is some chance that he will move from being a spoiled poet to a once again independent one – who can, as Bunting (again) said, learn to "sing with a longer breath." One hopes for this, for he possesses a distinctive lyrical gift.

– Martin Seymour-Smith

PIERCY, Marge. American. Born in Detroit, Michigan, 31 March 1936. Educated at the University of Michigan, Ann Arbor (Hopwood Award), B.A. 1957; Northwestern University, Evanston, Illinois, M.A. 1958. Married Robert Shapiro in

1962. Agent: Peter Matson, The Matson Agency, 22 East 40th Street, New York, New York 10016. Address: Box 943, Wellfleet, Massachusetts 02667, U.S.A.

PUBLICATIONS

Verse

Breaking Camp: Poems.   Middletown, Connecticut, Wesleyan University Press, 1968.
Hard Loving: Poems.   Middletown, Connecticut, Wesleyan University Press, 1969.
A Work of Artifice.   Detroit, Red Hanrahan Press, 1970.
4-Telling, with others.   Trumansburg, New York, The Crossing Press, 1971.
When the Drought Broke.   Santa Barbara, California, Unicorn Press, 1971.
To Be of Use.   New York, Doubleday, 1973.

Recording: *Laying Down the Tower,* The Black Box.

Novels

Going Down Fast.   New York, Simon and Schuster, 1969.
Dance the Eagle to Sleep.   New York, Doubleday, 1970; London, W. H. Allen, 1971.
Small Changes.   New York, Doubleday, 1973.

Marge Piercy comments:

I don't write in the traditional forms of English verse but in measures derived from spoken American. I use both the short line we learned from William Carlos Williams and the long prophetic line from Whitman through Allen Ginsberg, but basically I use my ears. I make poems that are spoken primarily and read with the eyes secondarily. I am always trying to learn how to say what I mean, and how to mean more truthfully. For the last four years, I have published in the alternate press (what we used to call underground papers) and women's papers and journals about as often as in poetry or literary magazines.

I am a committed radical and feminist. I don't understand distinctions between private and social poetry: love, after all, is supposed to be between people. On the other hand, I consider the attempt to build new kinds of relationships as political as a picket line. Half the human race (my half) has been sat on under every form of economic organization. I want my poems to be useful – in the broadest and not necessarily conscious sense – to the people I speak them to or who read them. I am also concerned with the remaking of the symbols we use according to our own values and what we would be.

*   *   *

Marge Piercy's activism in the revolutionary movement among young Americans in the 1960's is reflected in her tough-minded poems, as is her disillusionment with the antifeminism within the organizations she worked with. She says: "My first, my strongest identification now is with women's liberation, but I still feel a larger connection to the Movement in general." Her poetry is seldom overtly political; she writes chiefly about complex human relationships in which little comes easily to her. But if *Hard Loving* – the title of her second collection – is a persistent theme, she is able to face her emotions and dilemmas with intelligence and a gift for apt metaphor. "Letter to Be Disguised as a Gas Bill" is a vituperative poem, rescued from the dangers of that genre by a sustained series of fresh comparisons:

> Your face scrapes my sleep tonight
> sharp as a broken girder.
> My hands are empty shopping bags.

"Song of the Fucked Duck" also rises above anger, relentlessly analyzing the manipulative mentality of the revolutionary organizer, yet full of the personal pain of a particular failed relationship. (Piercy has also written a much-anthologized essay on this theme, "The Grand Coolie Dam," describing and protesting the Movement men's relegation of women to subservient roles.)

Not all of her poems are angry. Tenderness and warm feeling for both men and women inform such poems as "Gracious Goodness," "Unclench Yourself," and "For Jeriann's Hands":

> you move like a bow drawn taut and released.
> sometimes your wrists are transparent.
> .   .   .   .
> you are warm as a baker's oven.
> you are stubborn and hardy as a rubber mat.

Piercy, who has also written novels dealing with activism and personal relationships in dynamic interconnection, belongs to a group of young poets associated with the magazine *Hanging Loose*. Like them, she writes a poetry of direct statement, characterized by a refusal to avoid or compromise with the difficulties of everyday life, especially (in her case) the difficulties of being a woman. She is among the growing number of women writers committed to bringing neglected female experience into literature. She is still young and growing as a poet; her honesty and intensity may be expected to carry her into even deeper and more searching studies of human feeling in collision with collective forces.

– Jane Augustine

PILLIN, William. American. Born in Alexandrowsk, Russia, 3 December 1910. Educated at Lewis Institute, Chicago; Northwestern University, Evanston, Illinois; University of Chicago. Married Polia Pillin in 1934; has one son. Since 1948, self-employed Artist-Potter. Recipient: Jeanette Sewell Davis Award (*Poetry*, Chicago), 1937. Address: 4913 Melrose Avenue, Los Angeles, California 90029, U.S.A.

PUBLICATIONS

Verse

Poems.   Prairie City, Illinois, Decker Press, 1939.
Theory of Silence.   Los Angeles, George Yamada, 1949.
Dance Without Shoes.   Francestown, New Hampshire, Golden Quill Press,
    1956.
Passage after Midnight.   San Francisco, Inferno Press, 1958.
Pavanne for a Fading Memory.   Denver, Swallow, 1963.
Everything Falling.   Santa Cruz, California, Kayak Books, 1971.

Critical Studies: by James Dickey, in *Poetry* (Chicago), May 1959; Felix Anselm, in
Prairie Schooner (Lincoln, Nebraska), Winter 1959–60; introduction by Robert Bly
to *Everything Falling*, 1971; Stewart Granger, in *Northwest Review* (Eugene, Oregon),
Spring 1972.

William Pillin comments:

Earlier poems in strict classical forms, later poems depending largely on cadence
and free of rhyme. Characteristic subjects: I identify myself with the great mass of
ordinary people, not necessarily in an ideological sense, but in terms of needs,
aspirations, attitudes. My moonlight shines in a backyard, not on a formal garden,
and I observe the stars from a kitchen window. General influences are poets who
emphasize imagery and the surreal: Neruda, Vallejo, Lorca, etc., and poets whose
emphasis is social, like Brecht.
    Felix Anselm in his *Prairie Schooner* review wrote the following: "His world is
characterized by a hopeless nostalgia . . . a gentle and affectionate appreciation of
the small things of daily living that issue touches of warmth and beauty." If his
estimate is correct, I have been successful in my literary intentions.

                              *   *   *

William Pillin's poetry shows evidence of more resources than results. He often
draws his subject matter from his immigrant background: the Eastern European
culture, pulverized by the urban pressures of twentieth-century Los Angeles, is
alternately celebrated for its other-worldliness and lamented in its imminent evapo-
ration. But the rhetoric we hear most óften resounds with self-conscious nostalgia:
"To you I say a farewell daily." The poet, too haunted by memories to speak with
unchecked force, leaves behind a language of enervated regret, a prosaic numbering
that ends by numbing the senses still further:

> My nights are haunted by footsteps
> on the wind. The sky, the trees
> are kisses of memory on my forehead.

The lack of incisive presentation of sensory images, and the blurring of metaphors
by abstraction, prevent Pillin's joy its fullest rendering. He presents his description
of the poem as "at best / a black bordered / post-card of grief," but the border is
drawn without sufficient care, and it threatens to take over the entire space of the

poem. His irony might be tenser, his wit more agile, but too often the syntax of exposition turns stanzas into what Edmund Wilson called "shredded prose."

Besides this nostalgic poetry of the Jewish immigrant, Pillin attempts several love poems, and poems on aesthetic subjects, the latter usually in praise of some artist. This sort of subject matter is rendered more successfully, and emotions are clearer and more forceful. He wishes his daughter's piano playing will "continue somewhat green / and ignorantly sweet." His kiln grins "like a pot-bellied devil / licking with a glowing tongue / opaline on stone jars." But when he strives for a larger scope, the inflated language goes limp, exemplified by the poem on Isadora Duncan, which begins: "Hallucinatory, like theatrical twilight, is her passage." The weak passive construction and the alliterating, but over-obvious, adjective are unfortunately his characteristic weaknesses. When we are told that the city contains "nudities on streetcorners / instigating youths to bacchanalian cakewalks," we are told too much and allowed to see too little. Pillin's poetry displays more emotion than skill, and while that limits it, it marks it as unusual, for he never descends to the merely glib, though he seldom sings his distress into rapture.

– Charles Molesworth

PILLING, Christopher (Robert). British. Born in Birmingham, Warwickshire, 20 April 1936. Educated at King Edward's School, Birmingham, 1947–54; University of Leeds, Yorkshire, 1954–57, B.A. (honours) 1957; Institute of French Studies, La Rochelle, France, 1955; Loughborough College, University of Nottingham, 1958–59, Cert.Ed. 1959. Married Sylvia Pilling in 1960; has one son and two daughters. Assistant in English, Ecole Normale, Moulins, France, 1957–58; French Teacher, Wirral Grammar School, Cheshire, 1959–61, King Edward's Grammar School, Birmingham, 1961–62, and Ackworth School, Pontefract, Yorkshire, 1962–71, 1972–73. Since 1973, Chairman of the Department of Modern Languages, Knottingley High School, Yorkshire. Committee Member, Whitwood and District Arts Association, Yorkshire, 1970–71. Recipient: Arts Council New Poets Award, 1970, grant, 1971. Address: The Headlands, 18 Barnsley Road, Ackworth, near Pontefract, Yorkshire WF7 7NB, England.

PUBLICATIONS

Verse

Snakes and Girls. Leeds, University of Leeds School of English Press, 1970.
Fifteen Poems. Leeds, University of Leeds School of English Press, 1970.
In All the Spaces on All the Lines. Manchester, Phoenix Pamphlet Poets Press, 1971.
Wren and Owl. Leeds, University of Leeds School of English Press, 1971.
Andrée's Bloom and the Anemones. Rushden, Northamptonshire, Sceptre Press, 1973.

Critical Study: by Julian MacKenney, in *Poetry and Audience* (Leeds), 1 May 1970.

*   *   *

In All the Spaces on All the Lines and *Snakes and Girls* show Christopher Pilling bringing out, at his best, the subjective depths of everyday domestic moments by forming around them multiple concrete and abstract analogies, as in "Sunscape," "Old Celtic Cocoon," and "Partial Ellipse" (all in *Snakes and Girls*). The opening of the third of these illustrates how concretely observant this poetic evocation can be:

> My wife's wedding ring is no longer
> Circular:
>
> A gold curve
> Is all I see on a hand-coloured
>
> Background.
> One does not think the world is
>
> Round.

More discursive poems tend to be less fully achieved, but do suggest Pilling's developing intellectual grasp of his life-loving orientation:

> The world is not so sinister, suck dark.
> The left-handed is another turn of truth.
> The poet needs an ambidextrous strain.
> The words must not go to the ends of the earth.
> Hammer them to the gallows of a poem
> And let them cry of a spirit they have denied.

Though not poetically successful, "Crow Answers by Flight" takes on Ted Hughes' poem intelligently, and one senses that the younger poet has a more than lyrical basis for future work.

– Anne Cluysenaar

———————

PITCHFORD, Kenneth S(amuel). American. Born in Moorhead, Minnesota, 24 January 1931. Educated at the University of Minnesota, Minneapolis, B.A. (summa cum laude) 1952; Oxford University (Fulbright Fellow); New York University (Penfield Fellowship, 1957), M.A. 1959. Served in the United States Army,

1953–55. Married to the poet Robin Morgan; has one child. Member, Department of English, New York University, 1958–62; Writer-in-Residence, Yaddo, Saratoga Springs, New York, Summer 1958; taught at the Poetry Workshop, New School for Social Research, New York, 1960; Associate Editor, *The New International Yearbook*, New York, 1960–66. Currently, Free-lance Editor, New York. Recipient: Borestone Mountain Award, 1964. Address: 109 Third Avenue, New York, New York 10003, U.S.A.

PUBLICATIONS

Verse

The Blizzard Ape: Poems. New York, Scribner, 1958.
A Suite of Angels and Other Poems. Chapel Hill, University of North Carolina Press, 1967.
Color Photos of the Atrocities: Poems. Boston, Little Brown, 1973.

Kenneth Pitchford comments:

I consider myself a writer. My medium, then, is language. Any form that can be composed of words is of interest to me. Alongside the poems I write, I have also written plays, stories, a novel, essays, etc.

I began writing poetry to express the inexpressible sensation of being alive – before I knew that a formal discipline called poetry existed. In college, I achieved the mastery of traditional forms of poetry under superb taskmasters, but while my first book of poems reflects these acquired skills, I feel that my own poetic bent has always lain elsewhere. My second book of poems shows the attempt to put "schooling" behind me and seize my own sense of poetry more directly. My third book begins to show me a configuration that is uniquely my own.

This "growing into myself" is also reflected in the progression of subject matter that has preoccupied me. Previous to the first book, my work was an uncontrolled outcry about the despair and ignorance that was the lot of a working-class young-ster – and the sources of beauty open to such a one. In the first book, written during the McCarthyist Fifties, I had not become so domesticated that this subject matter was totally obscured. But with the second book, several strands come together: the exploration and laying to rest of a tortuous psychological journey from suicide and sexual conflict toward intimations of personal liberation; and a growing refusal to accept the amount of general suffering required to maintain the present shape of society. In the new poems, the commitment is totally to political revolution and a struggle to imagine what social liberation would be like. I find myself embittered now about the years of "training" I underwent in the 1950's – training designed to transform intransigence into passivity and to drive wedges between thought and action, literary values and human needs, taste and utility. I see the whole literary endeavor as presently pursued to be the stutterings of a dying culture. The attempt to tell some part of the truth will be considered propaganda; the urgent outcry will be considered vulgar; the abandonment of outworn forms and assumptions will be seen as inartistic. Yet the revolutionary poet, in trying to re-create himself, will take all these risks, will attempt to fuse thought and action, value and need, and in so doing, perhaps, build a new language strong enough to be of help in the growing worldwide struggle for human liberation from want, greed and domination. Whether the new world that emerges will want to remember such writing is really unimportant. Venceremos!

*   *   *

. . . I might have made some greater difference than I did
(though never enough, never mind total)
but all my poems were trying to curry favor
with the *Kenyon Review* and other extinct areas of sensibility
when there was this rage in me that only now has exploded into the
realization that my right to be sensitive, to love the art of any suffering
people, was taken from me by their calling me
faggot faggot faggot – and that all I have to do to reclaim that right
is the realize how faggot is my salvation, whatever they called Chopin.

– "I've Never Been To Majorca"

Kenneth Pitchford's festering rage is well concealed in *The Blizzard Ape*. The poems are chiselled and carefully wrought: many are written as lyrics to be set to music and use the ballad form and colloquial idiom to sing jauntily of the barmaid propositioned by a customer in Tony's Hashhouse, or to sing the "Young Buck's Sunday Blues" when he discovers that his hell raisin' woman has left him to seek comfort with a preacher "full a' brimstone, cash, and hell." Others evoke fleeting moods and meditate upon the difficulty of making a poem speak and the loss experienced when the poem is perfected; finally, a very few, "A Bride's Song," "Still-Life from a Packing Plant," and "The Solipsist at Midnight," strike the macabre note later sustained in many of the poems on conjury and others in *A Suite of Angels*. The spectre of death that chills the lovers' kiss in "A Bride's Song," and the still-life image of the cow slaughtered in the kill room where ". . . red-aproned men have come, / affixed the cable to bruise the senseless neck, replaced the hooks through the achilles tendons, hoisted the body upwards, set casters / in the grooves of the shiny rail above them, to send it wheeling down rows of skinners and cutters" brutally hint at the rage mounting in the poet as he confronts the butchery and violence in, society and in himself which have done their best to slay his gentler, more delicate instincts.

In *A Suite of Angels* a number of the poems continue to rework Greek myths and write in an objective voice designed to win favor from the *Kenyon Review*, but most begin to speak in the first person confessional voice, and begin to dredge up the painful memories from the past and recreate the nightmares of his present marriage. Many express the ambivalence Pitchford feels towards himself as a man and towards women as they have been defined in their traditional roles. The scene of the bull slaughtered repeats itself; the male is transformed into a Wer-Man, turned into this creature by his lust for men but held prisoner by women who demand to feed his blood hunger. The poems speak of moments in childhood when he heard the muffled, scuffling sounds of his father wringing the necks of mallards which his sister later cleaned; when he heard his sister talking of wanting to take her mother's place in her father's bed; when he decried his father's crime of denying him love. Finally, in "Nightmares," his nightmares and those of his wife war upon the two of them: he haunted by his role as Wer-Man, male supremacist, sucking his wife's blood because long ago he was denied his other love; she struggling with spectres of nazi doctors with their scalpels, come to sterilize, rape, or otherwise mutilate her. He becomes the nazi doctors; she the Wer-man's mistress: both trace their nightmares to the wrongs done them by their parents and by an evolutionary history that made the male the dominant species; both briefly overcome the fiendish tortures of sleep when their love finally unites them.

1193

But *Color Photos of the Atrocities* allows no such easy solution to the anti-gender struggle. Pitchford's rage has burst; he has found his cause. Although the reader may find the poems too wordy, the cant of revolution, egalitarianism, racism, sexism, gay liberationism, and militant feminism too much a part of the nostalgia of the 1960's, Pitchford believes he must abandon his old controls and struggle painfully to make explicit the plight of the effeminist married to Robin Morgan (authoress of *The Monster* and a radical feminist herself) who wants to come to terms with his feelings·for her, their son, Blake, his lover, Michael, and the future movement which now consumes him. In this volume, all atrocities, Auschwitz, the holocaust, the Attica prison riots, and the mass killings of Brazil's Indians, are one to Pitchford: all bespeak the brutality and violence which has defined The Man, the white straight male, whom Pitchford now identifies with the Establishment, the Kennedys, Rockefellers, and all the moguls. The faggot is their prisoner who awaits a revolution in which, as Pitchford declares, "he will risk his whole self or die." But the enemy is also the faggot himself who cannot entirely get rid of the violence in him that has always made him oppressor, and who cannot survive if the force he believes in, the liberated woman, is to have her way. For she, in Pitchford's poems, must become the real heroine of the revolution and pull the trigger that kills him. Pitchford dreams of a time:

> . . . when there is no more religion or family or
>   male domination
>   or money or property or mine or yours or
>   forced obedience
> . . . when women are free
>   not only to shape their own lives
>   but to realize a vision of liberation
>   that will shape the lives of all of us
> . . . when men are able
>   to hug and kiss babies not for show,
>   but able to care for them in every sense
>   and for each other
> . . . when I'm no longer called queer
>   for wishing my father had held me
>   with a love like that,
>   for loving still any rare stray
>   glimmer of tenderness in a man. . . .

– "The Flaming Faggots"

But the poetry sees this as a dream; and the reality he wrestles with is one in which suicide or murder seem the more necessary outcomes. At their best, these poems candidly capture the joy of fatherhood, the delight derived from simple domestic moments, and the dizzying pleasure found in music. At their worst, they are too insistent, propagandistic, repetitive, and voguish.

– Carol Simpson Stern

PITTER, Ruth. British. Born in Ilford, Essex, 7 November 1897. Educated at Coburn School for Girls, East London. War Office Clerk during World War I.

Painter for Walberswick Peasant Pottery Company, Suffolk, 1918–30, and from 1930, Partner, Deane and Forester, London. Now retired. Recipient: Hawthornden Prize, 1937; Heinemann Award, 1954; Queen's Gold Medal for Poetry, 1955. Companion of Literature, 1974. Address: The Hawthorns, Chilton Road, Long Crendon, Aylesbury, Buckinghamshire, England.

PUBLICATIONS

Verse

First Poems. London, Cecil Palmer, 1920.
First and Second Poems 1912–1925. London, Sheed and Ward, 1927; New York, Doubleday, 1930.
Persephone in Hades. Privately printed, 1931.
A Mad Lady's Garland. London, Cresset Press, 1934; New York, Macmillan, 1935.
A Trophy of Arms: Poems 1926–1935. London, Cresset Press, and New York, Macmillan, 1936.
The Spirit Watches. London, Cresset Press, 1939; New York, Macmillan, 1940.
The Rude Potato. London, Cresset Press, 1941.
Poem. Shirley, Suffolk, Shirley Press, 1943.
The Bridge: Poems 1939–1944. London, Cresset Press, 1945; New York, Macmillan, 1946.
Pitter on Cats. London, Cresset Press, 1947.
Urania (selections from A Trophy of Arms, The Spirit Watches and The Bridge). London, Cresset Press, 1950.
The Ermine: Poems 1942–1952. London, Cresset Press, 1953.
Still by Choice. London, Cresset Press, 1966.
Poems 1926–1966. London, Barrie and Rockliff-Cresset Press, 1968; as Collected Poems, New York, Macmillan, 1969.
End of Drought. London, Barrie and Jenkins, 1975.

Critical Study: Preface by the author to Poems 1926–1966, 1968.

Ruth Pitter comments:

I am not even a professional writer, just a poet; the occupations of my life other than this have been simply to gain a subsistence, and I have mostly worked with my hands.
I look at life, and listen inside myself, and try to express what I feel mostly in the well-worn forms of our tradition. From infancy I have intently observed nature (including people), fascinated chiefly by the mysteries of things.

*   *   *

In a literary period of revolution, reflecting that of Western society, the poetry of Ruth Pitter stands as an isolated monument, untouched by the changes, both technical and moral, around it. She says in the Foreword to her *Collected Poems* that "I have been trying to write poetry since 1903, when I was about five; but I produced little that I now think worth keeping until about the age of thirty." That is a long, and humble apprenticeship. The humility comes from an ever closer dedication to Christian Faith, of an almost Traherne-like individuality and isolation. The persistence comes from a character obstinate, assured and humorous. As she also says, "I have had strange thoughts at times about comedy." They not only emerge in much of her verse. They also play a part in securing her in her assurance of her own idiom as a craftsman in that verse, by making her self-critical without at the same time freezing her muse into sterility. Seriousness, a necessary ingredient of poetry, can be damaged, even crippled, by self-laughter.

For sixty years Miss Pitter has practised her art, obstinately personal, rather as a goldsmith at his bench. She uses words as that precious metal, manipulating it into verbal shapes of recognised modes: the sonnet, the *terza rima*, the couplet and blank verse. In all those shapes it is lucid, simple. Its vowels echo round the halls of the English Pantheon, where Milton has entoned and Spenser sung. But it is a music on its own, self-taught, self-tuned. It is poetry, not merely verse.

That must be why, some thirty years ago, Hilaire Belloc spoke to me about her one day at lunch, saying that he had written an introduction to a book of poems by a young woman of remarkable skill and intellectual and spiritual force. She has persisted since then, singing her own song. It is mainly a *Magnificat*, in praise of life as she has encountered it, close up and through the sharp eye of an intense curiosity. She has not dissipated her literary vitality on professional writing, such as literary journalism, nor, as far as I know, on prose work of any kind. She has been solely a poet, and has made her living at work wholly apart from this major activity which, to be secure in its achievement, demands as much fidelity and patience as marriage. Hers has been a monophilic art, sustained, as I have said, by bouts of extraneous humour, as when she writes verse about cats and gardening, amusing relaxations from the demands of her more devout work.

That work is based upon religious faith, not dogmatic but metaphysical and exalted. It is astonishingly beautiful, and clothed in sensuous phrases and images. Like the swallows (she calls them "freemasons of the air"), in a poem which is a masterpiece, she is one of those "Spirits who can sleep on high / And hold their marriage in the sky." That is an example of close observation of the goings-on of nature, and of the imaginative power to translate such earthy traffic into terms of spiritual symbolism.

This process occupies most of her work. Again and again, she sets out demurely, almost cataloguing something she has noticed in her daily round and common task; then suddenly it is turned round, irradiated, and made to reveal a divine significance. Thus, in a poem called "The Apple Tree," she says:

> A dear and blessed thing to see,
> The lovely laden apple-tree.
> I sit me down his boughs below,
> The cold and tortuous musings go;
> I from the lowest branches take
> Four apples for my childhood's sake.

Somehow, that takes us back to Genesis and the Garden of Eden, and the springtime of the mind. Note, too, how the obsolete device of inversion, so much frowned on today, adds to the effect of total return to the garden of prime innocence.

Much more could be said about her work: its simplicity, its quiet self-assurance; but its source and strength can be summed up in her short lyric "For Sleep or Death":

Cure me with quietness,
Bless me with peace;
Comfort my heaviness,
Stay me with ease.
Stillness in solitude
Send down like dew;
Mine armour of fortitude
Piece and make new:
That when I rise again
I may shine bright
As the sky after rain,
Day after night.

– Richard Church

PLANZ, Allen. American. Born in New York City, 2 January 1937. Educated at New York University, M.A. 1961. Married to Doris Sommers; has one child. Formerly taught at Hunter College, New York, University of North Carolina, Chapel Hill, and Queens College, New York. Poetry Editor, *The Nation*, New York, 1969–70. Currently, "independent fisherman." Delegate, International Poetry Conference, Stony Brook, New York, 1968. Recipient: Midsouth Literary Competition prize; New York Poetry Center Younger Poets prize, 1963; Swallow Press New Poetry Series Award, 1969. Address: Westbeth, 463 West Street, New York, New York 10014, U.S.A.

PUBLICATIONS

Verse

Poor White and Other Poems. Lanham, Maryland, Goosetree Press, 1964.
Studsong. New York, Lower East Press, 1968.
A Night for Rioting. Chicago, Swallow Press, 1969.

Other

American Wilderness. San Francisco, Sierra Club Books, 1970.

Allen Planz comments:

Recently, I've come to think of my best work as discovery – discovering again the ancient relations between man and earth, man and man, man and woman, the excess of joy and terror and splendor which in rediscovery becomes celebration, toward which each poem strives, praising earth and the people on it.

*   *   *

In *A Night for Rioting*, Allen Planz combines visions of urban and rural deterioration. The process of decay, due to technology and industry, occurs wherever modern man locates himself. The disintegration caused by an increasingly object-oriented culture ("gentlemen delivered to chrome by a caress") has radiated outward from the cities to poison the land as well.

In Planz's poetry, speed is both subject and essence of style. Automobiles signify the quest for masculinity and the rapidly accelerating pace of life. However exhilarating though it may be, velocity without positive direction is meaningless and destructive ("sons wild / on curves who met their manhood on a wall"). Similarly, the growing speed and friction of the urban machine and its component parts inevitably lead to violence.

A country that worships power, speed and violence is more than a bit frightening, and Planz concedes this ("if ever I get the courage / to have a son") while capturing the culture:

> I put on a uniform & laid down my life
>
> & thereafter lived in dread of it,
> thru fear & violence
> becoming quite American.

As a resistance poet, he speaks out against the threatening array of anti-life forces – the dollar, the dictator, and the diplomat ("admen felt for their sex in watchpockets"). The land that remains unoccupied (place and state of mind) is where the revolutionary takes hold ("now as a man, dizzy still with gravity / and hard loving, I name my upland rapture"). The land is real:

> . . . nothing but the land survives,
> for only the land lasts, outlasting
> citizen, city, empire.

The revolt starts with one man ("having found a rifle / a good thing to lie by") in the natural world, a guerilla who recognizes the need to reverse ongoing destructive processes and the cost of the effort ("My heart, my land, it is the courage to starve to death / I work to give or to get").

– Carl Lindner

PLOMER, William (Charles Franklyn).   British.   Born in Transvaal, South Africa, 10 December 1903. Educated at Spondon House School; Beechmont, Sevenoaks,

Kent; Rugby School, Warwickshire; St. John's College, Johannesburg. Served in the Naval Intelligence Division, 1940–45. Lived in Japan in the 1920's. Editor, with Roy Campbell, *Voorslag*, 1928; Fiction Reviewer, *Spectator*, London, 1933–38; succeeded Edward Garnett as Literary Adviser to Jonathan Cape, publishers, London, 1937. President, Poetry Society, London, 1968–71. Since 1968, President Kilvert Society, Hereford. Recipient: Queen's Gold Medal for Poetry, 1963; Whitbread Award, 1973. D.Litt.: Durham University, 1958. Fellow, Royal Society of Literature, 1951. C.B.E. (Commander, Order of the British Empire), 1968. Address: c/o Jonathan Cape Ltd., 30 Bedford Square, London W.C.1, England. *Died 21 September 1973.*

PUBLICATIONS

Verse

    Notes for Poems.   London, Hogarth Press, 1927.
    The Family Tree.   London, Hogarth Press, 1929.
    The Fivefold Screen.   London, Hogarth Press, 1931; New York, Coward McCann, 1932.
    Visiting the Caves.   London, Cape, 1936.
    Selected Poems.   London, Hogarth Press, 1940.
    The Dorking Thigh and Other Satires.   London, Cape, 1945.
    A Shot in the Park.   London, Cape, 1955.
    Borderline Ballads.   New York, Noonday Press, 1955.
    Collected Poems.   London, Cape, 1960; revised edition, 1973.
    A Choice of Ballads.   London, privately printed, 1960.
    Taste and Remember.   London, Cape, 1966.
    Celebrations.   London, Cape, 1972.

Plays

    Gloriana, music by Benjamin Britten (produced London, 1953).   London, Boosey and Hawkes, 1953.
    Curlew River, music by Benjamin Britten (produced London, 1964).   London, Faber, 1964.
    The Burning Fiery Furnace, music by Benjamin Britten (produced London, 1966).   London, Faber, 1966.
    The Prodigal Son, music by Benjamin Britten (produced Aldeburgh, Suffolk, 1968).   London, Faber, 1968.

Novels

    Turbott Wolfe.   London, Hogarth Press, and New York, Harcourt Brace, 1926.
    Sado.   London, Hogarth Press, 1931; as *They Never Came Back*, New York, Coward McCann, 1932.
    The Case Is Altered.   London, Hogarth Press, and New York, Farrar and Rinehart, 1932.
    The Invaders.   London, Cape, 1934.
    Museum Pieces.   London, Cape, 1952; New York, Noonday Press, 1954.

Short Stories

I Speak of Africa.   London, Hogarth Press, 1927.
Paper Houses.   London, Hogarth Press, and New York, Coward McCann, 1929.
The Child of Queen Victoria.   London, Cape, 1933.
Curious Relations, with Anthony Butts (as William D'Arfey).   London, Cape, 1945; New York, Sloane, 1947.
Four Countries.   London, Cape, 1949.

Other

Cecil Rhodes.   London, Davies, and New York, Appleton, 1933.
Ali the Lion: Ali of Tebeleni, Pasha of Janina, 1741–1822.   London, Cape, 1936; as *The Diamond of Janina: Ali Pasha 1741–1822*, Cape, and New York, Taplinger, 1970.
Double Lives: An Autobiography.   London, Cape, 1943; New York, Noonday Press, 1956.
At Home: Memoirs.   London, Cape, and New York, Noonday Press, 1958.
Conversation with My Younger Self.   Ewelme, Oxfordshire, privately printed, 1963.
Address Given at the Memorial Service for Ian Fleming.   Privately printed, 1964.
Remarks When Opening the George Gissing Exhibition at the National Book League, London . . . 23 July 1971.   London, privately printed, 1971.
The Butterfly Ball and the Grasshopper Feast (juvenile).   London, Cape-Times Newspapers Ltd., 1973.
Autobiography of William Plomer.   London, Cape, 1975.

Editor, *Japanese Lady in Europe*, by Haruko Ichikawa.   London, Cape, and New York, Dutton, 1937.
Editor, *Kilvert's Diary 1870–1879.*   London, Cape, 3 vols., 1938–40; abridged edition, Cape, 1944; New York, Macmillan, 1947; revised edition, Cape, and Macmillan, 3 vols., 1960.
Editor, *Selected Poems of Herman Melville.*   London, Hogarth Press, 1943.
Editor, *Curious Relations*, by William D'Arfey.   London, Cape, 1945.
Editor, with Anthony Thwaite and Hilary Corke, *New Poems 1961: A P.E.N. Anthology.*   London, Hutchinson, 1961.
Editor, *A Message in Code: The Diary of Richard Rumbold, 1932–1960.*   London, Weidenfeld and Nicolson, 1964.
Editor, *Burn These Letters: Alice Lemon to Winifred Nicol, 1959–62.*   London, Cape, 1973.

Translator, with Jack Cope, *Selected Poems of Ingrid Jonker.*   London, Cape, 1968.

Bibliography: in *William Plomer* by John R. Doyle, New York, Twayne, 1969.

William Plomer comments:

In my book *At Home* I alluded to the poet's consciousness both of his alienation from the rest of mankind and of his membership of mankind. "Poetry," I wrote,

"is an attempt to fuse together the sense of difference and the sense of sameness."
In this it resembles love: and love has not been a rare impulse or theme in my
work.

A concern with persons, in their times and places, has always been a main
motive force in my poetry. Because of that, my poems have narrative and dramatic
tendencies, and a good many have taken ballad-like forms, sometimes being concerned with the blending or juxtaposition of the monstrous with the commonplace,
or the pathetic and absurd with the tragic or ominous.

I am inclined to hold, with Coleridge, that "works of imagination should be
written in very plain language"; with Nicanor Parra that "En poésia se permite
todo," provided (as he wisely added) you improve on the blank page; and with Wei
T'ai, a Chinese poet of the 11th century, that poetry presents the thing in order to
convey the feeling, and should be exact about the thing and reticent about the
feeling.

*   *   *

The life-work, so far as William Plomer's poetry is concerned, falls into three
groups conditioned by his environment: his childhood and early manhood in South
Africa, two later years spent in Japan, and the rest of his life in the hurly-burly of
the English literary scene. But the most outstanding characteristic of this work is
its precise unity of mood and detachment. He was eighteen when he wrote his first
book, a novel called *Turbott Wolfe*. It is really a poem in prose, but the observation
in it, and the recoil of a mind governed almost entirely by a critical fastidiousness
of taste and sensation, was already present, and already mature. This book was
recently reprinted, so the reader who wants to estimate the growth and sustenance
of Mr. Plomer's writing, both in verse and prose, may start at the beginning. An
almost Mozartean precocity both of technique and perceptiveness will be found.

Such a consciousness of one's own capabilities, such self-criticism, might have
reduced Mr. Plomer's work to aridity, but for the presence in his nature, so far as
one can judge from his writing, of a passionate sense of ethical responsibility,
something he shares with another precise writer, E. M. Forster. Each watches his
own writing syllable by syllable, and pronounces it as it were aloud, upon his lips,
to engrave the words upon the air. The result in effect is a startling clarity of
expression, comparable to looking out at life through over-strong lenses. This has
an exhilarating effect. All is so vivid, things both near and far take on an indelibil-
ity. We call this quality irony.

It is, therefore, as an ironist that William Plomer is likely to be classified by
time. Irony was apparent in his early novel. It continues throughout his work
wherever he has been placed. It makes him withdraw, sometimes even with a recoil
of disgust, from the goings-on of human society, and even from nature, when
Mother Earth is in one of her extravagant or horrific moods. This habit of irony
has imposed a discipline on his idiom that reduces its statement to frequent
under-statement. In his early poems it was startling because young writers are
usually inclined to exuberance. He was never so, except in an occasional savagery
of critical punch, or whip-crack.

The detachment to which I have referred is another remarkable quality consistent
throughout his life-work. It has given him the habit of microscopic observation,
such as one finds in the verse of Gerard Hopkins. As he says of a character in one
of his poems, "Let me, he thought, attain the bird's eye view." He has fulfilled that
intention himself, and this has given a richness of detail to his poetry that commands the reader to close attention, so that the precision shall not be overlooked.
"It was no longer the fashion to be gentle," he says, and that conveys much of the

intellectual austerity which gives the texture to his work. Especially in his "ballads" he allows this characteristic full rein. They are all social satires, fierce and derisive, and since the present fashion in both life and art is for hard hitting, these ballads have made Mr. Plomer famous. They combine folk-rhythms (the naïve statement of the broadsheet) with hard intellectual analysis and criticism, as in the poem about the murder of President Kennedy. But he carries the form further, in such ballads as "The Philhellene," and remarkably in the subtle and deeply philosophic "Reading in the Garden," in which he confesses:

> Mine is a more than midway,
> An afternoon moment, where
> Life is not snatched or guzzled,
> Nor clung to, but all in view.

That is a good summing up of his whole conscious career. The lack of greed, of fear, we find to be the commandant of that clarity of form which has enabled him to keep "all in view."

It is inevitable that such detachment should induce an elegiac tinge into his work. Who can look on at the human drama dispassionately without sensing the tragic element underlying our gestures? It causes this poet to coin such phrases as "laughter dying of wounds." His somewhat grim humanism, stoic in origin, is softened by this admission of personal emotion. Otherwise he would have remained only a satirist. His capacity for enjoyment, which is another name for love, adds. flesh and blood to that skeletal structure of mind. As he says

> I also soon shall hear the sunset gun –
> But in between times life has been such *fun*!

So the fun, as well as the anger, adds to the dimension of this man's poetry, and, I suspect, to its durability. I see him as one

> Who is at home with death
> More than he guesses;
> The rose will die, and a skull
> Gives back no caresses.

To be at home with death is to be a seer who can frame life concisely. That is what Mr. Plomer has done in his body of poetry.

– Richard Church

PORTER, Hal. Australian. Born in Albert Park, Melbourne, Victoria, 16 February 1911. Educated at Kensington State School, 1917; Bairnsdale State School, Victoria, 1918–21; Bairnsdale High School, 1922–26. Married Olivia Parnham in 1939 (divorced, 1943). Cadet Reporter, *Bairnsdale Advertiser*, 1927. Schoolmaster, Victorian Education Department, 1927–37, 1940; Queen's College, Adelaide, 1941–42; Prince Alfred College, Kent Town, South Australia, 1943–46; Hutchins School, Hobart, Tasmania, 1946–47; Knox Grammar School, Sydney, 1947; Ballarat College, Victoria, 1948–49; Nijimura School, Kure, Japan (Australian Army Education), 1949–50. Director, National Theatre, Hobart, 1951–53. Chief Librarian of

Bairnsdale and Shepparton, 1953–61. Full-time Writer since 1961. Australian Writers Representative, Edinburgh Festival, 1962. Lecturer for the Australian Department of External Affairs, in Japan, 1967. Recipient: Sydney Sesquicentenary Prize, 1938; Commonwealth Literary Fund Fellowship, 1956, 1960, 1964, 1968, 1972, and Subsidy, 1957, 1962, 1967; *Sydney Morning Herald* Prize, 1958; Sydney Journalists' Club Prize, for fiction, 1959, for drama, 1961; *Adelaide Advertiser* Prize, for fiction, 1964, 1970, for non-fiction, 1968; *Encyclopedia Britannica* Award, 1967; Captain Cook Bi-Centenary Prize, 1970. Address: Glen Avon, Garvoc, Victoria 3275, Australia.

PUBLICATIONS

Verse

The Hexagon. Sydney, Angus and Robertson, 1956.
Elijah's Ravens. Sydney, Angus and Robertson, 1968.
In an Australian Country Graveyard. Sydney, Angus and Robertson, 1973.

Plays

The Tower (produced London, 1964). Melbourne, Penguin, 1963.
The Professor (as *Toda-San*, produced Adelaide, 1965; as *The Professor*, produced London, 1965). London, Faber, 1966.
Eden House (produced Melbourne, 1969; as *Home on a Pig's Back*, produced Richmond, Surrey, 1972). Sydney, Angus and Robertson, 1969.
Parker (produced Ballarat, Victoria, 1972).

Novels

A Handful of Pennies. Sydney, Angus and Robertson, 1958; London, Angus and Robertson, 1959.
The Tilted Cross. London, Faber, 1961.
The Right Thing. Adelaide, Rigby, and London, Hale, 1971.

Short Stories

Short Stories. Adelaide, Advertiser Press, 1942.
A Bachelor's Children. Sydney and London, Angus and Robertson, 1962.
The Cats of Venice. Sydney, Angus and Robertson, 1965.
Mr. Butterfry and Other Tales of New Japan. Sydney, Angus and Robertson, 1970.
Selected Stories. Sydney and London, Angus and Robertson, 1971.
Fredo Fuss' Love Life. Sydney, Angus and Robertson, 1973.

Other

The Watcher on the Cast-Iron Balcony (autobiography). London, Faber, 1963.
Australian Stars of Stage and Screen. Adelaide, Rigby, 1965.

The Paper Chase (autobiography).   Sydney, Angus and Robertson, 1966.
The Actors: An Image of the New Japan.   Sydney, Angus and Robertson, 1968.
Criss-Cross (autobiography).   Sydney, Angus and Robertson, 1973.

Editor, *Australian Poetry 1957.*   Sydney, Angus and Robertson, 1957.
Editor, *Coast to Coast 1961–1962.*   Sydney, Angus and Robertson, 1963.
Editor, *It Could Be You.*   Adelaide, Rigby, 1972; London, Hale, 1973.

Bibliography: *A Bibliography of Hal Porter* by Janette Finch, Adelaide, Libraries Board of South Australia, 1966.

Manuscript Collection: Mitchell Library, Sydney.

Critical Studies: "The Craft of Hal Porter" by Peter Ward, in *Australian Letters* (Adelaide), October 1962; in *Profile of Australia* by Craig McGregor, Melbourne, Penguin, 1968; essay by Robert Burns, in *Meanjin 1* (Melbourne), 1969.

Hal Porter comments:

A great deal of my writing that could be actual poems overflows into the short stories, novels, autobiographies, and plays. I belong to no school unless there is a school of poets who prefer rigid verse forms, rigid schemes, "old-fashioned" disciplines.

Major themes: Australian landscape, the anguishes of living and loving, disenchantment. Usual verse forms: always rigid ones, but of many varieties, including the sonnet. Never *vers libre*, and not even blank verse. I need to work within a steel frame of rhyme and metre – in this cage I can wrestle with words until they obey me; outside it, I suspect (although I've never even thought of trying this freedom), I should be tricked, cheated, tripped up by words.

I'm not conscious of *direct* influences but the fact that I've strong preferences for disciplined poets suggests that I might be influenced by their intentions, their discipline, their machinery, though not by their topics or their attitudes. I find that, as I get older, I can handle the machinery better – why not? – and that what I intend saying with clarity is less smudged and decorated than formerly. A slow maturer, I look forward to writing "good" poetry very soon.

*   *   *

Hal Porter is perhaps better known as novelist, short story writer and dramatist than as a poet. Yet such a listing of literary attainments gives some idea of this versatile writer's talents. He is also a much praised autobiographer and as a black and white artist his drawings illustrating the article "South Gippsland and Its Towns" are a graphic *tour de force*.

His first book of poems, *The Hexagon*, disclosed an essentially fastidious poetic talent almost hidden beneath a tumultuous surge of images and stylish word-play. It was not until his second book, *Elijah's Ravens*, was released that his poetic development could be gauged.

Many poems originally appearing in *The Hexagon* are included in the later collection in altered versions that display general improvements in technique and an overall clarification of content. The new poems, though no less rich in imagery than the earlier pieces, have clearer statements to make and a number are devoted to exploring and gauging aspects of love, its finding and loss.

The best poems are "Soldier Farmer," an essentially sympathetic portrait seen against the harsh background of the country's capricious moods, "The Sheep," a brilliantly witty evocation of the economically important yet naturally stupid animals seen as unwitting judges of their own lot ("the visors carved with grieving mourn beneath judicial wigs"), and "Hobart Town, Van Dieman's Land (11th June, 1837)," a historical character sketch in the vividly evocative setting of Sir John Franklin who perished "in attempting the North West Passage."

– Bruce Beaver

PORTER, Peter (Neville Frederick). Australian. Born in Brisbane, Queensland, 16 February 1929. Educated at the Church of England Grammar School, Brisbane; Toowoomba Grammar School. Married Jannice Henry in 1961; has two daughters. Formerly, journalist, bookseller, clerk; worked in advertising for ten years. Compton Lecturer in Poetry, University of Hull, 1970–71; Visiting Lecturer in English, University of Reading, Autumn 1972. Currently, Free-lance Writer. Address: 42 Cleveland Square, London W.2, England.

PUBLICATIONS

Verse

Once Bitten, Twice Bitten: Poems. London, Scorpion Press, 1961.
Penguin Modern Poets 2, with Kingsley Amis and Dom Moraes. London, Penguin, 1962.
Poems Ancient and Modern. Lowestoft, Suffolk, Scorpion Press, and New York, Walker, 1964.
Words Without Music. Oxford, Sycamore Press, 1968.
A Porter Folio: New Poems. Lowestoft, Suffolk, Scorpion Press, 1969.
The Last of England. London and New York, Oxford University Press, 1970.
Epigrams by Martial. London, Poem-of-the-Month Club, 1971.
After Martial. London, Oxford University Press, 1972.
Preaching to the Converted. London, Oxford University Press, 1972.

Plays

Radio Plays: *The Siege of Munster*, 1971; *The Children's Crusade*, 1973.

Other

Solemn Adultery at Breakfast Creek: An Australian Ballad, music by Michael Jessett. Richmond, Surrey, Keepsake Press, 1968.

Jonah. London, Secker and Warburg, 1973.
In Italy, with Anthony Thwaite, photographs by Roloff Beny. London, Thames and Hudson, and New York, Harper, 1974.

Editor, *New Poems, 1971–72: A P.E.N. Anthology of Contemporary Poetry.* London, Hutchinson, 1972.
Editor, *A Choice of Pope's Verse.* London, Faber, 1972.
Editor, with Anthony Thwaite, *The English Poets: From Chaucer to Edward Thomas.* London, Secker and Warburg, 1974.

Manuscript Collections: Lockwood Memorial Library, State University of New York, Buffalo; University of Indiana, Bloomington; British Museum, London.

Critical Studies: by Clive James, in *The Review 24* (Oxford); Roger Garfitt, in *British Poetry since 1960: A Critical Anthology*, edited by Michael Schmidt and Grevel Lindop, Oxford, Carcanet Press, 1972.

*   *   *

Peter Porter has steadily built up a reputation as one of the most substantial and various talents among the English poets of the middle generation. An expatriate Australian who does not intend to return to the country of his birth (see "Sidney Cove, 1788" in *Poems Ancient and Modern* and "Recipe" in *A Porter Folio* for examples of his ironic and mistrusting attitude towards it), he casts a scathing and rueful eye on contemporary English civilisation; and yet is inescapably held by it. The loyalty is not only an aversion to an Australia where, he felt, writing in the *TLS* in 1971, "nobody has any natural talent and the Great Supervisor fails me over a whole range of Anglo-Saxon virtues." It is a positive adoption of England, and indeed Europe (in the wider cultural sense, not the constricted one of the Market "Europeans"). It is a respect for, and a comfort in the sense of, "the continuity of the living and the dead which I find in England":

> Sailing away from ourselves, we feel
> The gentle tug of water at the quay –
> Language of the liberal dead speaks
> From the soil at Highgate, tears
> Show a great water table is intact.
> You cannot leave England, it turns
> A planet majestically in the mind.

To this point of affirmation, which is nevertheless much qualified by a brooding, increasing sense of the presence of death in his more recent poetry, he has moved through a series of volumes which have been unerring in their recording of the follies of mankind in general with a satire that is grave, sometimes brutal and always acutely observant. He has a considerable flair for a kind of bitter, epigrammatic wit and for elaborately entertaining fantasy (for example, "Fair Go for Anglo-Saxons" in *A Porter Folio*). If there is scarcely any lyric ease or relaxation in his writing, it is not all impassioned seriousness: he can often be extremely funny, sometimes in a sad self-deprecating vein but more often in a way which exorcises the facts of ageing and death with mordant, pertinacious satire (in *Preaching to the Converted*, "Sex and the Over Forties" and "Affair of the Heart" show this side of his talent).

The strong positive element in Porter's poetry is there in his celebration of the high points of European culture (particularly in the field of music). The great artist survives death, remains a living presence in the sonatas of a Scarlatti or the portraits of a Giotto. But the lines on Giotto's portrait of Dante display the ambivalence out of which springs much of Porter's most arresting and absorbing verse:

> I've eaten in a restaurant named for you
> and seen your posthumous life-mask. You tell us
> we never get home but are buried in eternal exile.

Art is enduring, but death is even more enduring than art; and life is, at best, a kind of exile from any imaginable happiness or reassurance.

The poems on personal themes, frequently deriving from dreams (he describes his dreams as a kind of private cinema) or centred on his own personal life-patterns against a garish urban background, are, as a result, largely wry, angry, and self-reproaching; though the emotions are never simple. His love poetry presents that emotion as a tarnished thing, pitiable and unsuccessful, unsuited for treatment in a sensuous or delicate style:

> What I want is a particular body,
> The further particulars being obscene
> By definition. The obscenity is really me,
> Mad, wanting mad possession: what else can mad mean?

His entire style is formal and compressed, with moments of measured solemnity and some successful excursions into the grand manner. There is an air of highly intelligent, witty, intensely committed yet immensely zestful conversation about it; though he is rarely colloquial. This distinguishes him very clearly from contemporaries whose quest for a mode of self-revealing frankness leads them into mawkish self-indulgence or grandiose diffuseness. But Porter has achieved an impressive expansion of range, through the medium of his "versions" of the great Roman satirist, in his volume *After Martial*. Porter both updates Martial, making his satires pointful in a modern age of high, permissive living and egotistic pretentiousness, and preserves the spirit of the original. Otherwise, great formal artists of the past and present – Bach, Shakespeare, Laclos, Hardy, Stravinsky – remain his principal admirations; though a ranging, lively and formidable intellect draws him equally to Marston, Christopher Smart, Schopenhauer, Rilke, Mahler, Auden. There is considerable brilliance, and obvious relish, in his employment of the great as mentors, and in a sense, companions, in a life-situation out of which it is difficult to make final sense or derive any ultimate hope. But the governing emotion in Porter's poetry is a fierce moral emphasis, suggesting that at least something may be wrested from the human predicament if we confront and understand the inadequacy and impermanence of life itself. At his best, Porter has made some of the most powerful and moving statements in the poetry of the last decade in England: his treatment of the traditional major themes – love, war, death – becomes steadily more convincing and original as his work develops.

– Alan Brownjohn

POWELL, Craig. Australian. Born in Wollongong, New South Wales, 16 November 1940. Educated at Sydney Boys' High School; Sydney University, M.B., B.S. 1964; New South Wales Institute of Psychiatry. Married Janet Eileen Dawson in 1965; has one daughter and one son. Resident Medical Officer, Royal Prince Alfred Hospital, 1965, and Western Suburbs Hospital, Sydney, 1966; Medical Officer, later Junior Psychiatrist, Parramatta Psychiatric Centre, Sydney, 1968–72. Since 1972, Psychiatrist, Brandon Mental Health Centre, Manitoba, Canada. Member, Australian and New Zealand College of Psychiatrists (M.A.N.Z.C.P.), 1971. Recipient: *Poetry Magazine* Award, 1964; Commonwealth Literary Fund grant, 1966, 1968, 1972; Henry Lawson Festival Award, 1969. Agent: South Head Press, 350 Lyons Road, Five Dock, New South Wales 2046, Australia. Address: Box 420, Brandon, Manitoba R7A 5Z5, Canada.

PUBLICATIONS

Verse

A Different Kind of Breathing: Poems.   Sydney, South Head Press, 1966.
I Learn by Going: Poems.   Sydney, South Head Press, 1968.
A Country Without Exiles.   Sydney, South Head Press, 1972.

Manuscript Collection: Mitchell Library, Sydney.

Critical Study: "Gauging Honesty, Engaging Voice" by William H. New, in *Poetry Australia 49* (Sydney), 1973.

Craig Powell comments:

A number of aims: (i) to write honestly – I don't find that easy; (ii) to write with absolute clarity – this is also difficult, and unfashionable besides.

I am less preoccupied with traditional forms than I used to be, though I will still write, say, villanelles and sestinas out of sheer delight in their intricacy. Technique is still only a means to an end, a way of getting it said. It has been said of my work, "One feels one is looking through the poetry at something else. The poetry is rooted in experience."

In sum, I am a puzzled middle-class family man, using poems and the practice of psychiatry to validate my existence. So far, surviving.

*   *   *

Just as Melbourne University, in the late 1950's, produced a group of lively poets who forced readers to reconsider available currency, so Sydney University in the early 1960's produced three poets who were to epitomise the counter-claim of a revived Vitalist tradition. These were Geoffrey Lehmann, Les A. Murray, and Craig Powell. Of the three, Powell has been least concerned with expounding large scale Life Views. Indeed, his most characteristic verse has been confined within the limitations of the sonnet and the triolet forms.

As a medical practitioner, Craig Powell has openly expressed an admiration of the American poet-medico Merrill Moore, who was reputed to have filing cabinets of sonnets stored away. Powell has never achieved, however, the relaxed assurance of Merrill Moore. His work is essentially dramatic, a performance. For this reason, he is most successful in poems that deal with themes of violence or conflict. Undoubtedly his best work is in the group of hospital and psychiatric poems in his third volume, or in the openly rhetorical "In Memory of Hans Mueller," possibly one of the most effective poems written in Australia on the Vietnam theme. In poems of a personal or lyric tone, one senses an underlying discomfort, with the result that the gestures often fail to convince. Craig Powell is still a young and developing writer. His best work has an admirable vigour and punch – and a formal control – that promise considerable scope for growth and development.

– Thomas W. Shapcott

PRINCE, F(rank) T(empleton). South African. Born in Kimberley, Cape Province, 13 September 1912. Educated at Christian Brothers' College, Kimberley; Balliol College, Oxford; Princeton University, New Jersey, 1935–36; Study Groups Department, Chatham House, 1937–40. Served in the Intelligence Corps, 1940–46. Married Pauline Elizabeth Bush in 1943; has two children. Member of the English Department, 1946–56, and since 1957, Professor of English, University of Southampton. Visiting Fellow, All Souls College, Oxford, 1968–69; Clark Lecturer, Cambridge University, 1973. Address: Department of English, University of Southampton, Hampshire, England.

PUBLICATIONS

Verse

Poems. London, Faber, 1938.
Soldiers Bathing and Other Poems. London, Fortune Press, 1954.
The Stolen Heart. San Francisco, The Press of the Morning Sun, 1957.
The Doors of Stone: Poems 1938–1962. London, Hart Davis, 1963.
Memoirs in Oxford. London, Fulcrum Press, 1970.
Penguin Modern Poets 20, with John Heath-Stubbs and Stephen Spender. London, Penguin, 1971.

Other

The Italian Element in Milton's Verse. Oxford, Clarendon Press, 1954.
In Defense of English: An Inaugural Lecture. Southampton, University of Southampton Press, 1959.
William Shakespeare: The Poems. London, Longman, 1963.

Editor, *Samson Agonistes*, by Milton.   London, Oxford University Press, 1957.

Editor, *The Poems*, by Shakespeare.   London, Methuen, and Cambridge, Massachusetts, Harvard University Press, 1960.

Editor, *Paradise Lost, Books I and II*, by Milton.   London, Oxford University Press, 1962.

Editor, *Comus and Other Poems*, by Milton.   London, Oxford University Press, 1968.

Translator, *Sir Thomas Wyatt*, by Sergio Baldi.   London, Longman, 1961.

*   *   *

F. T. Prince, in introducing his collected poems, *The Doors of Stone*, said these were all he wished to preserve of his published work. They amounted to fewer than 50 poems. From this one may judge the poet's acute fastidiousness, his inability to accept anything from himself that is not of the best. Hence the extraordinary quality of these poems: "Soldiers Bathing," perhaps the finest individual poem of the war, and "The Old Age of Michelangelo," exquisite like the sculptor's cartoon that links it with the previous poem.

Whereas his native South Africa, in its physical beauty of flower and fauna and the heroic quality of its legends, provided Prince with the themes of his early poems, leaving us with gems such as "Moonflower" and "The Babiaantje," the broad tradition of European civilisation and in particular Renaissance Italy exerted a later and more profound influence on his writing, not only as poet but as critic and university teacher. The poems issuing from this influence reveal the gravity and clearness of his thought and imagery, a concern for language that is masterly in its accuracy and its elegance. In fact, when so much of the verse of our time, though powerful, lacks polish, Prince is outstanding for his artistry, chiselling at his images and at his construction so that his poems are always finished, carrying no ballast, nothing in the rough. They demand reading and re-reading that nothing be lost of them.

Handling the English language as a master craftsman is one thing but what really makes Prince's work memorable is his own humanity and compassion, a sombre note amounting almost to melancholy, marking much of what he writes. In "Soldiers Bathing," for instance, as he watches his "band / Of soldiers who belong to me," he sees them transformed by his compassion:

> All pathos now. The body that was gross
> Rank, ravenous, disgusting in the act or in repose,
> All fever, filth and sweat, its bestial strength
> And bestial decay, by pain and labour grows at length
> Fragile and luminous.

The same quality of compassionate feeling also distinguishes his most beautiful cycle of love poems, the final sequence, "The Question," surely one of the finest love poems of our time, where the language twists the heart through the maze that all lovers know:

> For we know nothing but that, long ago,
> We learnt to love God whom we cannot know.
> I touch your eyelids that one day must close,
> Your lips as perishable as a rose:
> And say that all must fade, before we know
> *The thing we know of but we do not know.*

Although a streak of melancholy runs through much of Prince's poetry, there is a measure of comfort there, too. In relating a particular experience, whether at war or in love, to man's broader experience as revealed by artists and writers of the distant past, and in the final resort, to the Son of Man himself, as revealed by God, something of the loneliness of the moment departs:

> . . . as I drink the dusky air,
> I feel a strange delight that fills me full,
> Strange gratitude, as if evil itself were beautiful,
> And kiss the wound in thought, while in the west
> I watch a streak of red that might have issued from Christ's breast.

Regret at the thinness of Prince's poetic production is surely tempered by gratitude for what we have.

– Roy Macnab

PROKOSCH, Frederic. American. Born in Madison, Wisconsin, 17 May 1908. Educated at Haverford College, Pennsylvania, 1922–25, M.A. 1926; Yale University, New Haven, Connecticut, 1930–31, Ph.D. 1933; King's College, Cambridge, 1935–37, M.A. 1937. Instructor in English, Yale University, 1932–34; Printer, of modern poetry, in Bryn Mawr, Pennsylvania, Cambridge, Florence, Venice and Lisbon, 1933–40; Cultural Attaché, American Legation, Stockholm, 1943–45; Visiting Lecturer, University of Rome, 1950–51. Squash-Racquets Champion of France, 1933–39, and of Sweden, 1944. Recipient: Guggenheim Fellowship, 1937; Harper Prize, 1937; Harriet Monroe Memorial Prize (*Poetry*, Chicago), 1941; Fulbright Fellowship, 1951. Address: "Ma Trouvaille," Plan de Grasse, Alpes Maritimes, France.

PUBLICATIONS

Verse

Three Mysteries. New Haven, Connecticut, privately printed, 1932.
Three Sorrows. New Haven, Connecticut, privately printed, 1932.
Three Deaths. New Haven, Connecticut, privately printed, 1932.
Three Images. New Haven, Connecticut, privately printed, 1932.
The Voyage. Bryn Mawr, Pennsylvania, privately printed, 1933.
The Dolls. Bryn Mawr, Pennsylvania, privately printed, 1933.
The Grotto. Bryn Mawr, Pennsylvania, privately printed, 1933.
The Enemies. Bryn Mawr, Pennsylvania, privately printed, 1934.
The Survivors. Bryn Mawr, Pennsylvania, privately printed, 1934.
Going Southward. Bryn Mawr, Pennsylvania, privately printed, 1935.
The Red Sea. Cambridge, privately printed, 1935.
Andromeda. Cambridge, privately printed, 1935.

The Assassins. Cambridge, privately printed, 1936.

The Assassins (collection). New York, Harper, and London, Chatto and Windus, 1936.

The Sacred Wood. Cambridge, privately printed, 1936.

The Carnival: Poems. New York, Harper, and London, Chatto and Windus, 1938.

Death at Sea: Poems. New York, Harper, and London, Chatto and Windus, 1940.

Sunburned Ulysses. Lisbon, privately printed, 1941.

Among the Caves. Lisbon, privately printed, 1941.

Song. New York, privately printed, 1941.

Song. Stockholm, privately printed, 1943.

Fable. New York, privately printed, 1944.

Chosen Poems. London, Chatto and Windus, 1944; New York, Doubleday, 1947.

The Flamingoes. Rome, privately printed, 1948.

Snow Song. Paris, privately printed, 1949.

Boat Song. Venice, privately printed, 1950.

Wood Song. Florence, privately printed, 1951.

Phantom Song. Naples, privately printed, 1952.

Banquet Song. Barcelona, privately printed, 1953.

Temple Song. Stuttgart, privately printed, 1954.

Fire Song. Zurich, privately printed, 1955.

Island Song. Hong Kong, privately printed, 1956.

Jungle Song. Bangkok, privately printed, 1957.

The Death Ship. Singapore, privately printed, 1958.

The Ghost City. Antwerp, privately printed, 1959.

The Mirror. Vienna, privately printed, 1960.

Novels

The Asiatics. New York, Harper, and London, Chatto and Windus, 1935.

The Seven Who Fled. New York, Harper, and London, Chatto and Windus, 1937.

Night of the Poor. New York, Harper, and London, Chatto and Windus, 1939.

The Skies of Europe. New York, Harper, 1941; London, Chatto and Windus, 1942.

The Conspirators. New York, Harper, and London, Chatto and Windus, 1943.

Age of Thunder. New York, Harper, and London, Chatto and Windus, 1945.

The Idols of the Cave. New York, Doubleday, 1946; London, Chatto and Windus, 1948.

Storm and Echo. New York, Doubleday, 1948; London, Faber, 1949.

Nine Days to Mukalla. New York, Viking Press, and London, Secker and Warburg, 1953.

A Tale for Midnight. Boston, Little Brown, 1955; London, Secker and Warburg, 1956.

A Ballad of Love. New York, Farrar Straus, 1960; London, Secker and Warburg, 1961.

The Seven Sisters. New York, Farrar Straus, 1962; London, Secker and Warburg, 1963.

The Dark Dancer. New York, Farrar Straus, 1964; London, W. H. Allen, 1965.

The Wreck of the Cassandra. New York, Farrar Straus, and London, W. H. Allen, 1966.

The Missolonghi Manuscript. New York, Farrar Straus, and London, W. H. Allen, 1968.
America, My Wilderness. New York, Farrar Straus, and London, W. H. Allen, 1971.

Other

Translator, *Some Poems of Friedrich Hölderlin.* New York, New Directions, 1943; London, Grey Walls Press, 1947.
Translator, *Love Sonnets of Louise Labé.* New York, New Directions, 1947; London, Grey Walls Press, 1948.

Manuscript Collection: University of Texas, Austin.

Critical Study: *Frederic Prokosch* by Radcliffe Squires, New York, Twayne, 1964.

Frederic Prokosch comments:

A poet is ill-advised to make a "personal statement," i.e., a *credo*. He cannot possibly do justice to himself in this manner. It will sound stilted, coy, pompous, irrelevant, even false. As I meditate on the question of why my poetry is totally unlike all other contemporary poetry, I feel puzzled; but I conclude that my conception of a poem is not the current one. To use a poem as a "confessional," a "protest," or a manifesto, a self-analysis or in any way as a self-indulgence, seems to me to abuse and degrade the true function of poetry. A poem should aim for the perfection, the timeless and impersonal "stillness" of a Chinese vase. I think of Yeats and Rilke; I think of Catullus, Goethe and Hölderlin. The present is not an age for poetry, needless to say. The timeless, impersonal stillness is drowned in an orgy of howls and moans, not to mention vituperations, indignations, and masturbations.

*　　　*　　　*

Frederic Prokosch made his reputation with three volumes, *The Assassins, The Carnival,* and *Death at Sea,* published just before or at the beginning of the second World War. His poetry impressed T. S. Eliot and Edwin Muir, and it shows the evidence of influences, particularly those of Eliot himself and Yeats, which it was impossible for any ripening talent to avoid at that period. His work has, however, an undoubted poetic individuality. In the first place it is elaborate, sumptuous, formal, musical, characteristically checking the usual long gliding line with a shorter, sharper turn. In the second, there is something of an older, a more traditional and European, manner in the poet's calm assumption of a public pose, in his treatment of the grand, impressive theme, in the formal clarity of his diction and his intricately rhyming patterns. Not that he isn't, clearly, highly sensitive to the strains of his own violent times. He is intensely moved by the combination in reality of style and disaster, by the blend, for example, in "The Country House" of platonic, shadowed lawns, cool airs, instinctive poise, and howling conflagration, or in "Molière" of the suppressed presence in an intricately spun civilisation, with its lucid laws of reason, its learning and perception, of Othello's howl and Dido's unforgettable cave. He is much preoccupied with Yeats's rough beast, and he is conscious beneath the mask of civilisation of the hooked, retaliating nightmare and the horrible disorderly whirlpool. The particular attractiveness of the poetry comes from its joining a cool and cultivated surface to a nightmare vision of inward and inevitable fatality. In Frederic Prokosch's reading of life, the clipped and ordered park, the salon, the formal avenue he so much appreciates and so finely evokes, are "rosy with the approaching glow and spectacle of Hell."

– William Walsh

PRYNNE, J(eremy) H(alward).   British.   Born in the United Kingdom, 24 June 1936.

PUBLICATIONS

Verse

Force of Circumstance and Other Poems. London, Routledge, 1962.
Kitchen Poems. London, Cape Goliard Press, and New York, Grossman, 1968.
Day Light Songs. Pampisford, Cambridgeshire, R. Books, 1968.
Aristeas. London, Ferry Press, 1968.
The White Stones. Lincoln, Grosseteste Press, 1969.
Fire Lizard. Barnet, Hertfordshire, Blacksuede Boot Press, 1970.
Brass. London, Ferry Press, 1971.
Into the Day. Cambridge, Street Editions, 1972.
A Night Square. London, Albion Village Press, 1973.
Wound Response. Cambridge, Street Editions, 1974.

*   *   *

J. H. Prynne's poetry is at the least a worthy attempt at a totally interior monologue, but it raises the questions of whether the English language can accommodate an absolutely alyrical style – and of whether a strategy of evasion, based on statements that have a resolutely inner reference can yield apprehensible truths. Is Prynne's work in effect simply hideously and disingenuously mannered, or do its oddities convey a sense of human existence hitherto unaccessible?

> . . . The
> moraine runs axial to the Finchley Road
> including hippopotamus, which isn't a
> joke any more than the present fringe
> of intellectual habit. They did live as
> the evidence is ready, for the successive
> drift. . . .

This poem, "The Glacial Question, Unsolved," does contain several references; and its method is much the same commendably, no doubt, as Alexander Cozens' was in his Blot Drawings. The lack of any discernible rhythm, the bleak "jokes" – these are disturbing; but are they potent ironies, or do they belong to a private notebook? How hard is it to write this kind of poetry if you set your mind to it? Is it original or merely eccentric? The reader has to thank Prynne for raising such questions in the mind by the courageous use of a procedure involving the ju-jitsu-like use of dehumanized boredom which, like any movement in the human mind, may be viewed as a partial achievement. One may add that this poetry ingeniously calls forth its own brand of criticism.

– Martin Seymour-Smith

PRYS-JONES, A(rthur) G(lyn). British (Welsh). Born in Denbigh, North Wales, 7 March 1888. Educated at Llandovery College, Carmarthenshire; Jesus College, Oxford (History Scholar), B.A. (honours) 1912, M.A. 1912. Formerly, Assistant Master, Dulwich College, London; Inspector of Schools, Wales; Staff Inspector, Secondary Education, Wales, 1919–49; now retired. Secretary, Welsh Committee, Festival of Britain, 1950–52; Co-Founder and former Chairman, Cardiff Little Theatre; former Chairman, Cardiff Literary Society. Currently, Vice-President, Cardiff Writers Circle; President, English Section, Welsh Academy. O.B.E. (Officer, Order of the British Empire), 1949. Address: 50 Coombe Lane West, Kingston-upon-Thames, Surrey KT2 7BY, England.

PUBLICATIONS

Verse

Poems of Wales. Oxford, Blackwell, 1923.
Green Places: Poems of Wales. Aberystwyth, Cardiganshire, Gwasg Aberystwyth, 1948.
A Little Nonsense. Cowbridge, Glamorgan, Eastgate Press, 1954.
High Heritage: Poems of Wales. Llandybie, Carmarthenshire, Christopher Davies, 1969.

Other

Gerald of Wales: His "Itinerary" Through Wales and His "Description" of the Country and Its People. London, Harrap, 1955.
The Story of Carmarthenshire. Llandybie, Carmarthenshire, Christopher Davies, 2 vols., 1959, 1972.

Editor, *Welsh Poets: A Representative English Selection from Contemporary Writers.* London, Erskine Macdonald, 1917.
Editor, *The Fountain of Life: Prose and Verse from the Authorized Version of the Bible.* London, Pan Books, 1949; Boston, Beacon Press, 1950.
Literary Editor, *The National Songs of Wales.* London, Boosey and Hawkes, 1959.

A. G. Prys-Jones comments:

My themes are almost entirely concerned with the past history, traditions, personalities and scenery of Wales: and my approach is essentially simple, lyrical and
romantic. I aim at making my poems pass the test of being read or declaimed
aloud, and thus suitable for individual or choral speech. A number have been set
to music and published as songs. If I have succeeded at all, it is in this direction,
and also in having interpreted the past of Wales, more especially for its young
people. In my writing I often use some of the simpler metrical and alliterative
devices of Welsh poetry.

*   *   *

Most of the veteran A. G. Prys-Jones's poems in his volume *High Heritage* (1969)
appeared in *Poems of Wales* (1923) and *Green Places* (1948). He himself has modestly
suggested that *High Heritage* is intended as an anthology for verse-speaking in
schools, and certainly it is a book eminently suitable for this purpose. He has
brought into modern English verse something of the visual imagery shaped by his
native Welsh tongue. Technically adept, he has a very delicate sense of rhythm, as
shown in "Spring Comes to Glamorgan," and a refined gift for the original image:

> And how the ragged medicants of mist
> In shifty garb rise up from stealthy lairs
> Thrusting their shapeless hands about your face.

Prys-Jones's style is unfashionable nowadays, but he manages to project the
Georgian manner into the turbulent present or past, maintaining a regular rhyme-
scheme and a firm stanza-structure. Thus, his well-known, rollicking "Henry Morgan's March on Panama":

> Twelve hundred famished buccaneers,
> Bitten, blistered and bled,
> A sweltering mob, accursed and flayed
> By the fierce sun overhead:
> Twelve hundred starving scarecrows
> With hardly a crust to eat,
> And only sips from festering pools
> In that grim, monstrous heat.

This has been called "Chestertonian heroic verse in the style of the twenties," and
such a strict structure does tend to limit the intention that certain poems are
supposed to fulfil. Soaked in history, most of his work involves celebration or
nostalgia, reflecting the formal Georgian mode, which could be so exquisite and yet
so fustian, He has no time for jagged irregularity, being interested only in building
and holding a consistent form. In this he has long reached a mastery, and it is a
pity that the stock phrases of "modern" criticism are not equipped to cope with
skilled structures like Prys-Jones's, even if his content now appears to be somewhat obsolete. He has a high command of language, splendidly shaped, and many
moments of rare beauty which could make a welcome return in our own gloomy
time – such as this musical glimpse of a historic Wales:

The tides of evening pass, deep-drenched with rose
And all the perfumes of the summer night.

– John Tripp

PUDNEY, John (Sleigh). British. Born in Langley, Buckinghamshire, 19 January 1909. Educated at Gresham's School, Holt, Norfolk. Served in the Royal Air Force, 1940–45. Married Crystal Herbert in 1934 (divorced, 1955); Monica Forbes Curtis, 1955; has three children. Producer and Writer for the BBC, London, 1934–37; Correspondent of the *News Chronicle*, London, 1937–41; Book Critic, *Daily Express*, London, 1947–48; Literary Editor, *News Review*, London, 1948–50. Director of Putnam and Company, publishers, London, 1953–63. Recipient: C. P. Robertson Memorial Trophy, 1965. Address: 4 Macartney House, Chesterfield Walk, Greenwich Park, London SE10 8HJ, England.

PUBLICATIONS

Verse

Spring Encounter. London, Methuen, 1933.
Open the Sky: Poems. London, Boriswood, 1934; New York, Doubleday, 1935.
Dispersal Point and Other Air Poems. London, Lane, 1942.
Beyond This Disregard: Poems. London, Lane, 1943.
South of Forty: Poems. London, Lane, 1943.
Almanack of Hope: Poems. London, Lane, 1944.
Ten Summers: Poems [1933–1943]. London, Lane, 1944.
Flight above Cloud. New York, Harper, 1944.
Selected Poems. London, Lane, 1946.
Selected Poems. London, British Publishers Guild, 1947.
Low Life: Verses. London, Lane, 1947.
Commemorations: Poems. London, Lane, 1948.
Sixpenny Songs. London, Lane, 1953.
Collected Poems. London, Putnam, 1957.
The Trampoline. London, Joseph, 1959.
Spill Out: Poems and Ballads. London, Dent, 1967.
Spandrels: Poems and Ballads. London, Dent, 1969.
Take This Orange. London, Dent, 1971.
Selected Poems 1967–1973. London, Dent, 1973.

Plays

The Little Giant (produced London, 1972).
Ted (televised, 1972; produced Leatherhead, Surrey, 1974).

Television Play: *Ted*, 1972.

1217

Novels

Jacobson's Ladder. London, Longman, 1938.
Estuary: A Romance. London, Lane, 1948.
Shuffley Wanderers: An Entertainment. London, Lane, 1948.
The Accomplice. London, Lane, 1950.
Hero of a Summer's Day. London, Lane, 1951.
The Net. London, Joseph, 1952.
A Ring for Luck. London, Joseph, 1953.
Trespass in the Sun. London, Joseph, 1957.
Thin Air. London, Joseph, 1961.
The Long Time Growing Up. London, Dent, 1971.

Short Stories

And Lastly the Fireworks: Stories. London, Boriswood, 1935.
Uncle Arthur and Other Stories. London, Longman, 1939.
It Breathed Down My Neck: A Selection of Stories. London, Lane, 1946; as
    Edna's Fruit Hat and Other Stories, New York, Harper, 1946.
The Europeans: Fourteen Tales of the Continent. London, Lane, 1948.

Other

The Green Grass Grew All Round. London, Lane, 1942.
*Who Only England Knows: Log of a Wartime Journey of Unintentional Discovery of
    Fellow-Countrymen.* London, Lane, 1943.
World Still There: Impressions of Various Parts of the World in Wartime. Lon-
    don, Hollis and Carter, 1945.
Saturday Adventure (juvenile). London, Lane, 1950.
Sunday Adventure (juvenile). London, Lane, 1951.
Music on the South Bank: An Appreciation of the Royal Festival Hall. London,
    Max Pavash, 1951.
Monday Adventure (juvenile). London, Evans, 1952.
His Majesty King George VI: A Study. London, Hutchinson, 1952.
The Queen's People. London, Harvill Press, 1953.
The Thomas Cook Story. London, Joseph, 1953.
Tuesday Adventure (juvenile). London, Evans, 1953.
Wednesday Adventure (juvenile). London, Evans, 1954.
The Smallest Room: A History of Lavatories. London, Joseph, 1954; New York,
    Hastings House, 1955; revised edition, as *The Smallest Room: With an
    Annexe*, Joseph, 1959.
Six Great Aviators (juvenile). London, Hamish Hamilton, 1955.
Thursday Adventure (juvenile). London, Evans, 1955.
Friday Adventure (juvenile). London, Evans, 1956.
The Grandfather Clock (juvenile). London, Hamish Hamilton, 1957.
Crossing the Road (juvenile). London, Hamish Hamilton, 1958.
*The Seven Skies: A Study of the British Overseas Airways Corporation and Its
    Forerunners.* London, Putnam, 1959.
Home and Away: An Autobiographical Gambit. London, Joseph, 1960.
A Pride of Unicorns: Richard and David Atcherley of the R.A.F. London, Old-
    bourne, 1960.
Bristol Fashion: Some Accounts of the Earlier Days of British Aviation. London,
    Putnam, 1960.

Spring Adventure (juvenile).   London, Evans, 1961.
Summer Adventure (juvenile).   London, Evans, 1962.
The Hartwarp Light Railway (juvenile).   London, Hamish Hamilton, 1962.
The Hartwarp Dump (juvenile).   London, Hamish Hamilton, 1962.
The Hartwarp Balloon (juvenile).   London, Hamish Hamilton, 1963.
The Hartwarp Circus (juvenile).   London, Hamish Hamilton, 1963.
Autumn Adventure (juvenile).   London, Evans, 1964.
The Camel Fighter.   London, Hamish Hamilton, 1964.
The Hartwarp Bakehouse (juvenile).   London, Hamish Hamilton, 1964.
The Hartwarp Explosion (juvenile).   London, Hamish Hamilton, 1965.
Winter Adventure (juvenile).   London, Evans, 1965.
Tunnel to the Sky (juvenile).   London, Hamish Hamilton, 1965.
The Hartwarp Jets (juvenile).   London, Hamish Hamilton, 1967.
The Golden Age of Steam.   London, Hamish Hamilton, 1967.
Suez: De Lesseps' Canal.   London, Dent, 1968.
A Draught of Contentment.   London, New English Library, 1971.
Crossing London's River.   London, Dent, 1972.
Brunel and His World.   London, Thames and Hudson, 1973.
London's Docks.   London, Thames and Hudson, 1975.

Editor, with Henry Treece, *Air Force Poetry.*   London, Lane, 1944.
Editor, *Laboratory of the Air: An Account of the Royal Aircraft Establishment of the Ministry of Supply, Farnborough.*   London, Central Office of Information, 1948.
Editor, *Pick of Today's Short Stories.*   London, Odhams, Putnam, and Eyre and Spottiswoode, 13 vols., 1949–1963.
Editor, *Popular Poetry.*   London, News of the World, 1953.
Editor, *The Book of Leisure.*   London, Odhams, 1957.
Editor, *The Harp Book of Toasts.*   London, Harp Lager, 1963.
Editor, *The Batsford Colour Book of London.*   London, Batsford, 1965; New Rochelle, New York, Soccer Associates, 1966.
Editor, *Flight and Flying.*   London, Hamish Hamilton, and New York, David White, 1968.

Manuscript Collection: University of Texas, Austin.

John Pudney comments:

I have been writing poetry on and off since I was seventeen and a good deal of it has been published.

I don't feel competent to make any critical analysis of my own work. I would only suggest that the publication of *Selected Poems 1967–1973* marks something of a departure from my previous work which is associated in many people's minds with World War II and the post-war years.

*   *   *

The poetry of John Pudney seems to fall into two distinct periods: the poems written prior to 1957, the best of which can be found in his *Collected Poems*; and the poems he produced after a silence of several years, published in *Spill Out, Spandrels,* and *Take This Orange,* volumes which form the basis of his latest *Selected*

Poems. As Pudney himself remarks, "I am a bit like a football match – divided into two halves."

Although Pudney had previously produced two collections of pleasant, if innocuous, verse, he was little known as a poet until the war years, when within a very short time he almost became a best-seller. His three slim volumes, *Dispersal Point, Beyond This Disregard* and *South of Forty,* all inspired by the war, seemed fittingly to express the moods, thoughts, and feelings of the inarticulate young men and women caught up in the turmoils of war. Pudney himself served with the R.A.F. and he was able to communicate not only his own personal experience, but that of countless others, in such poems as "Crew Room," "Happy-Go-Lucky," "Air Gunner," "Night Fighter Patrol," and "The New Story":

> Limply the broadcast words balloon on air,
> Stale as the comic jokes: now gunfire only
> Is real: and the brief handclasps which must tear
> The lonely from the lonely.

The prevalent moods reflected in these poems were those of personal loss and loneliness, frustration and compassion. It was as if Pudney had needed the stimulus of war to find his voice and develop an individual style. Most popular of these poems were those featuring Jones, Johnny, or Smith, no doubt representing in their different ways the common man faced with the immensities of war:

> Less said the better.
> The bill unpaid, the dead letter,
> No roses at the end
> Of Smith, the ghost.

"For Johnny," written on the back of an envelope during an air-raid, became quite famous after it was used in the film *The Way to the Stars,* and subsequently was almost an embarrassment to the poet, since he had written better poems which tended to be obscured by the attention paid to this one poem.

For some years after the publication of his *Collected Poems* John Pudney wrote little or no poetry, then in the mid-sixties he seemed to acquire a fresh burst of creative energy and a new sense of urgency. Within a period of six years he has produced three volumes of poetry, followed by *Selected Poems,* which also contains poems written between 1971 and 1973. Not that this break with the past was immediately successful, for it took some time for Pudney to regain his confidence and get into his stride. There was, initially, a too-deliberate effort to be "with it," to introduce the modern scene with all its paraphernalia of supermarkets, television, and motorways, etc. at a rather superficial level ("O what can ail thee, knight at arms / My moral cathode ray"), and to deal with fashionable themes such as Vietnam ("The burned children / Climb the ladders of newsprint again"). It is not a little significant that in deciding the contents of *Selected Poems* practically everything in *Spill Out* has been discarded, though it is reassuring to note that the mordant "Hymn to a Practical Carpenter" has been retained, if under another title:

> Bless if you can, O Lord, the inventive man.
> Having been crucified on that hill, I'm sure you will.
> When the sharp – or were they sharp? – nails went in,
> The job was part of a process, not a sin
> The planning of the cruciform device
> No doubt needed, and had, expert advice.

What is most striking about the later poems is the freedom in language, style and treatment, and the wider range of material. John Pudney, having gained his second breath, is now writing with greater assurance and skill than ever before. He is able to use autobiographical material to much greater effect, whether he goes back to childhood, as in "Growing," or attempts to analyse his feelings and apprehensions at the time of the motor accident in which he was involved ("Casualty"). His social commentaries have more bite and are more pointedly on target, if less predictable in ideas:

> The manufacturer
> Would not have made your rifle
> If there were only cardboard targets.
> If there were not real stuff
> A cardboard rifle would have been enough.

and his references to the establishment or the predicament of mankind make far more impression upon the reader. Above all, when he writes of personal relationships there is in evidence a lyrical awareness of nuances and an extraordinary development of tensions, in which language is heightened without becoming precious or uncolloquial, as in "Lute for Love," "Celebration," "Afterthoughts," "Mortality," "There Is This Mystery," "Could Be Simple," and other poems that might reasonably be described as the result of coming to terms with life and forging a personal philosophy.

– Howard Sergeant

PURCELL, Sally (Anne Jane). British. Born 1 December 1944. Educated at Lady Margaret Hall, Oxford (Countess of Warwick prize, 1965), B.A. 1966, M.A. 1970. Since 1969, Honorary Secretary, Foundation for Islamic Culture, Oxford; since 1969, Joint General Editor, Fyfield Books, Oxford and Cheadle, Cheshire. Recipient: Arts Council award, 1971. Address: 19 Crown Street, Oxford, England.

PUBLICATIONS

Verse

The Devil's Dancing Hour. London, Anvil Press Poetry, 1968.
The Holly Queen. London, Anvil Press Poetry, 1972.

Other

Editor, with Libby Purves, *The Happy Unicorns: The Poetry of the Under-25's.* London, Sidgwick and Jackson, 1971.
Editor, *George Peele.* Oxford, Carcanet Press, 1972.
Editor and Translator, *Monarchs and the Muse: Poems by Monarchs and Princes of England, Scotland, and Wales.* Oxford, Carcanet Press, 1972.
Editor, *Charles d'Orleans.* Cheadle, Cheshire, Carcanet Press, 1973.

Translator, *Provençal Poems*.   Oxford, Carcanet Press, 1969.
Translator, *The Exile of James Joyce*, by Hélène Cixous.   New York, David
   Lewis, 1972.

Sally Purcell comments:

I was brought up as a classicist, and I believe in courtesy, craftsmanship and
honesty.

*   *   *

Sally Purcell read Medieval French at Lady Margaret Hall, Oxford, and she has
published a volume of translations from the troubadour poetry of Provence. Her
researches and studies have clearly coloured her own poetry both in its context and
texture. Many of her poems, in the form of dramatic lyrics, explore the mysteries
and characters of classical and medieval legends, and their very titles are indicative
of their nature: "Bale-Fires on the Dark Moor," "Loquitur Arthurus," or "Tarot
XII." The settings, too, are in keeping: misty shires, a drowned winter world, a
petrified chalcedony forest or a ring of standing stones. What gives the poems their
special quality is Sally Purcell's imaginative insight into that twilight world of
superstition, replete with "prodigies and signs of doom," and especially her ability
to pinpoint the accompanying physical sensations of such a world:

> Queen Proserpina walks
>   through late autumn;
> the glowing fruit of ice
>   that she holds
> covers the dying sun, & chills
>   all ripeness to the bone

A smouldering sensuality is ever present where, as an "Imráma," it waits to
entrap the unwary and the pretentious:

> the muse medusa caresses her body,
> glories in her flesh firmness,
> smiles at the promises they assume
> who believe in her advances.

The best way to describe the texture of her verse is as an intellectual sensuality
where the precise syntax both knits the poems together and leads the reader into
them, while the involvement of the physical senses creates the necessary suspension of disbelief. Thus in "Baroque Episode" Sally Purcell is able to engage the
reader in an imagined world where

> Mingling blood for love's token
> He hopes to symbolise affection's depth
> Achieve the untenable equation
> That added selves make one,
> And seal in a small bottle changefulness.

It is a world where self-delusion is rife, and in "Oxford, Early Michaelmas Term"
she draws a modern parallel where "hypnotised by hearsay, by skilful propaganda

– the aesthetes flower gently." It is in the few poems where Sally Purcell relates her themes to the contemporary world that one senses promise for the future development of her work. Meanwhile, those in which she has created the strangely brooding world of legendary figures are an achievement in themselves.

– John Cotton

PURDY, A(lfred) W(ellington). Canadian. Born in Wooller, Ontario, 30 December 1918. Educated at Dufferin Public School, Trenton, Ontario; Albert College, Belleville, Ontario; Trenton Collegiate Institute, Ontario. Married Eurithe Parkhurst in 1941; has one son. Has held numerous jobs; taught at Simon Fraser University, Burnaby, British Columbia, Spring 1970; Poet-in-Residence, Loyola College, Montreal, 1973. Recipient: Canada Council Fellowship, 1960, 1965, Senior Literary Fellowship, 1968, 1971, and award, 1973; President's Medal, University of Western Ontario, 1964; Governor-General's Award, 1966. Address: Rural Route 1, Ameliasburgh, Ontario, Canada.

PUBLICATIONS

Verse

The Enchanted Echo. Vancouver, privately printed, 1944.
Pressed on Sand. Toronto, Ryerson Press, 1955.
Emu, Remember! Fredericton, University of New Brunswick, 1956.
The Crafte So Longe to Lerne. Toronto, Ryerson Press, 1959.
Poems for All the Annettes. Toronto, Contact Press, 1962.
The Blur in Between: Poems 1960–61. Toronto, Emblem Books, 1962.
The Cariboo Horses. Toronto, McClelland and Stewart, 1965.
North of Summer: Poems from Baffin Island. Toronto, McClelland and Stewart, 1967.
Poems for All the Annettes (selected poems). Toronto, House of Anansi, 1968.
Wild Grape Wine. Toronto, McClelland and Stewart, 1968.
Spring Song. Frederiction, New Brunswick, Fiddlehead, 1968.
Love in a Burning Building. Toronto, McClelland and Stewart, 1970.
Five Modern Canadian Poets, with others, edited by Eli Mandel. Toronto, Holt Rinehart, 1970.
The Quest for Ouzo. Trenton, Ontario, M. Kerrigan Almey, 1970.
Selected Poems. Toronto, McClelland and Stewart, 1972.
Hiroshima Poems. Trumansburg, New York, Crossing Press, 1972.
On the Bearpaw Sea. Vancouver, privately printed, 1973.
Sex and Death. Toronto, McClelland and Stewart, 1973.

Other

Editor, *The New Romans: Candid Canadian Opinions of the United States.* Edmonton, Alberta, Hurtig, and New York, St. Martin's Press, 1968.

Editor, *Fifteen Winds: A Selection of Modern Canadian Poems*. Toronto, Ryerson Press, 1969.

Editor, *I've Tasted My Blood: Poems 1956–1968*, by Milton Acorn. Toronto, Ryerson Press, 1969.

Editor, *Storm Warning: The New Canadian Poets*. Toronto, McClelland and Stewart, 1971.

Critical Studies: "In the Raw: The Poetry of A. W. Purdy" by Peter Stevens, in *Canadian Literature* (Vancouver), Spring 1966; interview by Gary Geddes, in *Canadian Literature* (Vancouver), 1969.

A. W. Purdy comments:

Themes? Sex and death (which last naturally includes life). Subjects? Anything that appeals to me. Form? Pretty irregular, but generally with rhythm running somewhere, sometimes off rhymes and assonance. Influences? Very many, including the usual big names (Pound, Eliot, Yeats); also César Vallejo, Neruda, Superveille, Charles Bukowski, Robinson Jeffers, etc., etc. Style? I have some strong prejudices against schools of any kind, including most particularly the Creeley-Olson Black Mountain bunch and their imitators. I do not dismiss these people and believe it is possible to learn much from them, but only IF one remains oneself, something most of them apparently find difficult. I believe that when a poet fixes on one style or method he severely limits his present and future development. By the same token I dislike the traditional methods of rhyme and metre when used without variation, ditto traditional forms. But I use rhyme, metre and (occasionally) standard forms when a poem seems to call for it. Rules tend to be exclusive of anything outside their own strictures: I think most traditional poets would agree with this, but go right on using traditional metre and rhymes – poets like prime ministers are all against war and on the side of truth and justice.

Perhaps I should say that: I began to write nearly forty years ago, influenced at that time by people whom I don't appreciate very much now. For instance, I like some of G. K. Chesterton's poems, and his influence no doubt remains with me but is, I think, difficult to discern in what I write today. At one time iambic metrics were so deeply implanted in my mind that it took me years of not-trying to break out of iambics to finally break out of iambics. I suppose other people's styles were apparent in my stuff until publication of *Poems for All the Annettes* in '62, and this book (and also *Blur in Between*, published '62 but earlier poems than *Annettes*) is the transitional period between what I was and am and change into. I have a fixation about change, which can also be regarded as a self-conscious weakness as well as a strength. And yet I wrote a poem in Athens, Greece, in January, 1969 ("The Time of Your Life"), which is probably the best I've ever written; at least I think so now.

*   *   *

A. W. Purdy has been publishing poetry for a generation and writing it for longer. His first collection, *The Enchanted Echo*, appeared in 1944; since then he has published many books and brochures of verse. Nevertheless, it was only during the middle sixties, already well into middle age, that he came into prominence as one of Canada's leading poets, prolific in print, vigorous in statement, energetic in travelling the land to read his verse publicly and in travelling the world to gather material for poems whose external form of travelogue or journalism was the vehicle for deeper poetic-philosophic statement.

Purdy is unusual in the strongly academic world of Canadian poetry in his lack of a university background, which has probably been an advantage, since it has led him to wander far and freely, to work at many callings, and to bring a wide, down-to-earth experience to his writing. On the technical side, it has liberated him from ordered disciplines and from the literary fashions that sweep North American campuses, so that he has been able to spend many years working out his own poetic goals, taking from Williams on the one hand, from Auden and Thomas on the other, from Pratt and Birney in between, what he wanted and no more; by this means he has progressed from the traditional lyricism of *The Enchanted Echo* to the open forms and personal voice of later books like *The Cariboo Horses* and *Hiroshima Poems*.

What has struck one about Purdy's verse since the early sixties is its essentially oral impact. It is free verse in the truest form: fluent, untrammeled by conventions, and yet possessing rhythmic and grammatical forms that distinguish it from statement in prose.

Purdy's poems are always near to experience; the concept emerges from the poem, not the poem from the concept. Many of them rise out of actual episodes in the poet's life. A high proportion of the pieces in *Cariboo Horses* and *Wild Grape Wine* were based on his wanderings over Canada; *North of Summer* (set in the Arctic) and *Hiroshima Poems* are collections that emerge from specific journeys; in fact their constituent poems were often written during the journeys in question. The interval between conception and creation is surprisingly short, and the poems often seem to serve Purdy as a journal, so immediate is the response. This leads to unevenness in tone and quality, though Purdy controls this to an extent by weeding out much of a voluminous production. At his least successful, the result is a harsh flatness; the poem remains a mere observation or even a mere joke. At his best, the result can be a controlled lyrical freedom.

Memory is for Purdy a form of intense experience, and thus, while he often writes the poetry of travel, geographical poetry, he also writes the poetry of tradition, historical poetry, intimately linked with his own Loyalist ancestry, and with the long-settled regions of Ontario in which he grew up. In recent years the strain of continuity has become very marked in his verse; he goes back to the history of the village of Ameliasburgh where he lives; he goes back to land where his forefathers farmed after they fled from the United States, as in "My Grandfather's Country" from *Wild Grape Wine* – a volume much concerned with Ontario memories:

> But the hill-red has no such violence of endings
> the woods are alive
> and gentle as well as cruel
> unlike sand and sea
> and if I must give my heart to anything
> it will be here in the red glow
> where failed farms sink back into earth
> the clearings join and fences no longer divide
> where the running animals gather their bodies together
> and pour themselves upward
> into the tips of falling leaves
> with mindless faith that presumes a future . . .

A special characteristic of Purdy's poetry is its intellectual directness. It is often densely allusive, but never obscure. He draws freely on the funds of knowledge which a generalizing and self-educated mind accumulates, and some of his poems show a remarkable ability to bring images drawn from great sweeps of time and place into a meaningful relationship with what he sees before him in the everyday contemporary world, so that, watching cowboys' horses in a British Columbian village, he can end a poem:

> Only horses
> > no stopwatch memories or palace ancestors
> not Kiangs hauling undressed stone in the Nile Valley
> and having stubborn Egyptian tantrums or
> Onagers racing through Hither Asia and
> the last Quagga screaming in African highlands
> > lost relatives of these
> > whose hooves are thunder
> the ghosts of horses battering thru the wind
> whose names were the wind's common usage
> whose life was the sun's
> > arriving here at chilly noon
> > in the gasoline smell of the
> > dust and waiting 15 minutes
> > at the grocer's.

Rarely has poetry of such apparent spontaneity so accurately trapped the fresh reactions and roving speculations of a highly original mind. With vigour and humour, Purdy has moved from an early dependence on Canadian romantic models to a personal and highly independent style.

– George Woodcock

RAINE, Kathleen (Jessie). British. Born in London, 14 June 1908. Educated at County High School, Ilford; Girton College, Cambridge, M.A. in natural sciences 1929. Married to Charles Madge, *q.v.* (marriage dissolved); has one daughter and one son. Research Fellow, Girton College, Cambridge, 1955–61; Andrew Mellon Lecturer, National Gallery of Art, Washington, D.C., 1962. Recipient: Harriet Monroe Memorial Prize, 1952, and Oscar Blumenthal Prize, 1961 (*Poetry*, Chicago); Arts Council award, 1953; Chapelbrook Award; Cholmondeley Award, 1970; Smith Literary Award, 1972. D.Litt.: Leicester University, 1974. Address: 47 Paultons Square, London S.W.3, England.

PUBLICATIONS

Verse

> *Stone and Flower: Poems 1935–43.* London, Nicholson and Watson, 1943.
> *Living in Time: Poems.* London, Editions Poetry, 1946.
> *The Pythoness and Other Poems.* London, Hamish Hamilton, 1949; New York, Farrar Straus, 1952.

Selected Poems. New York, Weekend Press, 1952.

The Year One: Poems. London, Hamish Hamilton, 1952; New York, Farrar Straus, 1953.

The Collected Poems of Kathleen Raine. London, Hamish Hamilton, 1956; New York, Random House, 1957.

Christmas 1960: An Acrostic. London, privately printed, 1960.

The Hollow Hill and Other Poems, 1960–1964. London, Hamish Hamilton, 1965.

Six Dreams and Other Poems. London, Enitharmon Press, 1968.

Ninfa Revisited. London, Enitharmon Press, 1968.

Pergamon Poets 4: Kathleen Raine and Vernon Watkins, edited by Evan Owen. Oxford, Pergamon Press, 1968.

A Question of Poetry. Crediton, Devon, Gilbertson, 1969.

Penguin Modern Poets 17, with David Gascoigne and W. S. Graham. London, Penguin, 1970.

The Lost Country. Dublin, Dolmen Press, and London, Hamish Hamilton, 1971.

Three Poems Written in Ireland. London, Poem-of-the-Month Club, 1973.

On a Deserted Shore. Dublin, Dolmen Press, and London, Hamish Hamilton, 1973.

Other

William Blake. London, Longman, 1951; revised edition, 1965, 1969.

Coleridge. London, Longman, 1953.

Poetry in Relation to Traditional Wisdom. London, Guild of Pastoral Psychology, 1958.

Blake and England (Founders Memorial Lecture, Girton College). Cambridge, W. Heffer, 1960; Folcroft, Pennsylvania, Folcroft Editions, 1974.

Defending Ancient Springs (essays). London and New York, Oxford University Press, 1967.

The Written Word. London, Enitharmon Press, 1967.

Blake and Tradition. Princeton, New Jersey, Princeton University Press, 1968; London, Routledge, 1969.

William Blake. London, Thames and Hudson, 1971.

Faces of Day and Night (autobiography). London, Enitharmon Press, 1972.

Yeats, The Tarot and the Golden Dawn. Dublin, Dolmen Press, 1972; New York, Humanities Press, 1973.

Farewell Happy Fields (autobiography). London, Hamish Hamilton, 1973.

Death in Life, Life in Death (on Yeats). Dublin, Dolmen Press, 1974.

Blake and Antiquity. Princeton, New Jersey, and London, Princeton University Press, 1974.

David Jones: Solitary Perfectionist. Ipswich, Suffolk, Golgonooza Press, 1974.

Editor, with Max-Pol Fouchet, *Aspects de Littérature Anglaise, 1918–1945.* Paris, Fontaine, 1947.

Editor, *Letters of Samuel Taylor Coleridge.* London, Grey Walls Press, 1950.

Editor, *Selected Poems and Prose of Coleridge.* London, Penguin, 1957.

Editor, with George Mills Harper, *Thomas Taylor the Platonist: Selected Writings.* Princeton, New Jersey, Princeton University Press, and London, Routledge, 1969.

Editor, *A Choice of Blake's Verse.* London, Faber, 1974.

Editor, *Shelley.* London, Penguin, 1974.

Translator, *Talk of the Devil*, by Dénis de Rougemont. London, Eyre and Spottiswoode, 1945.

Translator, *Existentialism*, by Paul Foulquié. London, Dobson, 1948.

Translator, *Cousin Bette*, by Honoré de Balzac. London, Hamish Hamilton, 1948.

Translator, *Lost Illusions*, by Honoré de Balzac. London, Lehmann, 1951.

Translator, with R. M. Nadal, *Life's a Dream*, by Calderon de la Barca. London, Hamish Hamilton, 1968; New York, Theatre Arts Books, 1969.

Manuscript Collections: British Museum, London; University of Texas, Austin; University of California, Irvine.

Kathleen Raine comments:

I began as a poet of spontaneous inspirations, drawing greatly on nature and fortified by my more precise biological studies. Though I was born in London, my poetic roots were in wild Northumberland where I lived as a child. Most of my poems have been written in Cumberland or Scotland, some in Italy, Greece or France, but very few in London, where I at present live.

I have studied the symbolic language of Blake, Shelley, Yeats, Coleridge, and other poets of the "Romantic" tradition; who employ that language of analogy inseparable from the Perennial Philosophy (of which Christianity is our own cultural branch) which regards man as a spiritual and immortal being. Increasingly, in an atheist society, the meaning of words, and the symbolic implications, of traditional poetry become changed or lost. And this makes it difficult, if not impossible, for a poet of my kind to be anthologized with writers committed to another view of the nature of things. I have much sympathy for the young generation now reacting against materialist culture; but I am too firmly rooted in the civilization of the past to speak their language.

*   *   *

The young poets who caught the widest public attention in the 1930's were a group of Oxford poets, W. H. Auden, C. Day-Lewis, Stephen Spender, and Louis MacNeice. A group of Cambridge poets of the same generation, Kathleen Raine, William Empson, Ronald Bottrall, and Miss Raine's second husband Charles Madge, attracted on the whole less public attention. It was not that they were less politically engaged – two good Cambridge poets, John Cornford and Julian Bell, died in the Spanish Civil War; it was, perhaps, that there was a greater austerity in the Cambridge tradition. Miss Raine studied the natural sciences, not literature, at Cambridge, and an exactness of natural observation (very notable in her first volume, *Stone and Flower*, beautifully illustrated by Barbara Hepworth) is one of the main qualities of her poetry. Another is a beautifully natural and graceful lyrical movement, and a third is what might be called a transparency of diction. She has never attempted wit poetry, or the poetry of personal self-analysis, "confessional" poetry: in gathering together her *Collected Poems* she said in her preface that she had at first excluded all poems of "mere human emotion" but, persuaded by a friend that this was a too grandly austere statement – might not Chaucer and Shakespeare be described as poets of "mere human emotion"? – she substituted for that phrase the phrase "the transient." Miss Raine thinks of herself as a poet in a Platonic or neo-Platonic tradition that has included Spenser, Milton, Blake,

Shelley and Yeats in its members among the poets of the greater English tradition. The combination of the approach of a trained botanist and geologist with neo-Platonic mysticism may seem strange, but a link could be found in Miss Raine's interest in abstract art, in the sculptures of Barbara Hepworth and the drawings of Ben Nicolson. Both these artists might be thought of as seeking in outward nature archetypal forms, or Platonic ideas, as might another English artist whom Miss Raine greatly admires, Henry Moore. Such artists and the older poets whom she has praised in her book of essays *Defending Ancient Springs* might be thought of as Miss Raine's deepest sources. She has little sympathy with most contemporary poetry, feeling that even her old Cambridge friend, William Empson, is in his poetry and prose her spiritual antagonist. Poetry is only true poetry for her if it utters in traditional language the truths of the perennial philosophy, of ancient wisdom, of ancient revelation. Working on Blake over many years of patient scholarship, she has been concerned with the Blake who created a mythology and a cosmology, not with the Blake who spoke of "the lineaments of gratified desire." It follows that, though her poetry has always been admired by sound judges, some have found it thin and unearthly, speaking too much for what Yeats called soul, not enough for what Yeats called self, not enough for "the fury and the mire of human veins." Her lyrical sweetness, the beauty of the voice that is heard in the poems, is praised, but the vision itself found abstract or schematic. Carefully reading and listening with the inner ear will tell another story. Only a very proud and passionate woman would wage such a stern war, through all her work, against human pride and passion. These are the poems of a sybil, perhaps, of a rapt visionary, but not of a saint.

– G. S. Fraser

RAKOSI, Carl. American. Born in Berlin, Germany, 6 November 1903. Educated at the University of Wisconsin, Madison, B.A. 1924, M.A. 1926; University of Pennsylvania, Philadelphia, M.A. in social work, 1940; University of Chicago; University of Texas, Austin. Married Leah Jaffe in 1939; has one daughter and one son. Instructor, University of Texas, 1928–29; Social Worker, Chicago, New Orleans, Brooklyn, St. Louis, and Cleveland, 1932–45; Executive Director, Jewish Family and Children's Service, Minneapolis, Minnesota, 1945–68; Writer-in-Residence, University of Wisconsin, 1969–70. Since 1955, engaged in private practice of psychotherapy, Minneapolis. Recipient: National Endowment for the Arts award, 1969, fellowship, 1972. Address: 4451 Colfax Avenue South, Minneapolis, Minnesota 55409, U.S.A.

PUBLICATIONS

Verse

Selected Poems. New York, New Directions, 1941.
Two Poems. New York, Modern Editions Press, 1942.
Amulet. New York, New Directions, 1967.
Ere-VOICE. New York, New Directions, 1971.

Critical Studies: "The Objectivist Poet: Interviews with Oppen, Rakosi, Reznikoff, and Zukofsky" by L. S. Dembo, in *Contemporary Literature* (Madison, Wisconsin) x, 2; "The Poetry of Carl Rakosi" by L. S. Dembo, in *The Iowa Review* (Iowa City), ii, 1.

Carl Rakosi comments:

I am identified with the Objectivists but it is questionable whether the term has meaning any more.

*   *   *

Carl Rakosi was a member of a group of poets in the thirties who called themselves "The Objectivists." Louis Zukofsky, Charles Reznikoff, and George Oppen were other poets identified with this group. Rakosi and Oppen both went unpublished for many years between the thirties and the present time, either writing secretly or not writing at all, as they were both involved with active social protest against the oppression of the laboring classes and, as is usually the case, when active politics reign in a man's life, he has no place for the more meditative art of poetry.

Now as older men, they have both begun to write and publish prolifically. Rakosi, who led his life as a social worker in the Midwest still concerns his poems with pithy practical comments of life and its injustices. Ironically, however, his best poems are pastoral observations of the natural world, often with tiny comments such as those you might find in early Japanese or Chinese poetry.

Rakosi's poetry is short and spritely and not at all meditative, though seemingly made up of conclusions about the meaning of the world. It feels like the language of a man who has been active all of his life and now has comments about everything he has experienced, slightly wry and not at all uncritical, though delivered with friendliness. As a poet, he is a sort of gadfly, not taking on any epic subjects (perhaps even having wry words about such subjects), but stinging and buzzing about everything, a reminder that to live intelligently is never to relax or to leave unnoticed any slightly foolish thing – the poet as commentator on all of life.

– Diane Wakoski

RAMANUJAN, A(ttipat) K(rishnaswami). Indian. Born in Mysore, 16 March 1929. Educated at the University of Mysore, B.A. 1949, M.A. in English 1950; Indiana University, Bloomington (Fulbright and Smith-Mundt fellowships, 1959), Ph.D. in linguistics 1963. Married Molly Daniels in 1962; has two children. Taught in India, 1950–58. Member of the Faculty since 1962, and since 1968, Professor of Dravidian Studies and Linguistics, departments of Linguistics and South Asian Languages, University of Chicago. Visiting Assistant Professor of Indian Studies, University of Wisconsin, Madison, Summer 1965; Visiting Associate Professor, University of California, Berkeley, 1967. Consultant, Peace Corps Malayalam

Project, Milwaukee, 1965. Recipient: American Institute of Indian Studies Fellowship, 1963; Indiana School of Letters Fellowship, 1963; Tamil Writers' Association Award, 1969. Address: 5629 South Dorchester Avenue, Chicago, Illinois 60637, U.S.A.

PUBLICATIONS

Verse

The Striders.   London and New York, Oxford University Press, 1966.
No Lotus in the Navel (in Kannada).   Dharwar, Manohar Granthmala, 1969.
Relations.   London, Oxford University Press, 1972.

Other

Proverbs (in Kannada).   Dharwar, Karnatak University, 1955.
The Literature of India, with others.   Chicago, University of Chicago Press, 1974.

Translator, *Fifteen Poems from a Classical Tamil Anthology.*   Calcutta, Writers Workshop, 1965.
Translator, *The Yellow Fish* (into Kannada), by Molly Ramanujan.   Dharwar, Manohar Granthmala, 1966.
Translator, *The Interior Landscape: Love Poems from a Classical Tamil Anthology.*   Bloomington, Indiana University Press, 1967; London, Peter Owen, 1970.
Translator, *Speaking of Siva.*   London, Penguin, 1973.

Critical Study: in *Poetry Book Society Bulletin* (London), April 1966.

*   *   *

A. K. Ramanujan achieved recognition when his first book of poems, *The Striders*, was recommended by the Poetry Society of London. He is, as his name reveals, a South Indian, and from the notice on the jacket of his book we learn that he is now living in Chicago, teaching Linguistics at the University there. This biographical information is relevant in reading his poems which are mostly poems of memory. They have their origin in an emotion arising from the Indian experience of the poet which is now recollected in an American environment – not always in a mood of tranquillity. Many of them are based on the predicament of a person who has been brought up in a traditional culture – such as that of South India – living now in a culture very different from it. One of the best poems in the collection which exemplifies these remarks is "Conventions of Despair." The poem opens quietly with the description of a modern hell whose representative figure is the Marginal Man nursing martinis in his hand. But the hell to which the poet feels he is consigned is the Hindu hell in which he must

> translate and turn
> till I blister and roast
> for certain lives to come, "eye-deep"
> in those Boiling crates of Oil.

This is the punishment to which he is condemned for loving a prohibited person. In this Hindu hell he will be compelled to

> weep
> iron tears for winning what I should have lost;
> see Them with lidless eyes
> saw precisely in two equal parts
> (one of the sixty-four arts
> they learn in That Place)
> a once-beloved head
> at the naked parting of her hair.

The worst of his punishments, however, is to catch a glimpse of a grandchild

> bare
> her teen-age flesh to the pimps
> of ideal Tomorrow's crowfoot eyes
> and the theory of a peacock-feathered future.

The poet rejects both versions of hell – "conventions of despair" – and prefers simply to live in the present without any kind of "future," content with continuous existence as it is now. He prefers an "archaic despair." In the system of Hindu thought known as the Advaita Vedanta it is held that the chain of birth, death, and rebirth began with existence itself:

> It is not obsolete yet to live
> in this many-lived lair
> of fears, this flesh.

The poet does not however say anything about the hopefulness of the complementary Vedantic belief that the chain can be ended if we so will.

Ramanujan's rhythms are generally very close to the relaxed rhythms of speech; his images are carefully chosen to fit the content in all their details; the ordinary diction is used in a surprising, original and acceptable way; the poems are well balanced and usually contain in themselves the principle of their growth and development. At the moment Ramanujan's poems may not have much to say, but there is a habit of thought in them that, combined with his already strong craftsmanship, promises to make him perhaps the most considerable Indian poet in English.

– S. Nagarajan

RAMSEY, Paul. American. Born in Atlanta, Georgia, 26 November 1924. Educated at the University of Chattanooga, Tennessee; University of North Carolina, Chapel Hill, B.A., M.A.; University of Minnesota, Minneapolis, Ph.D. 1956. Served in the United States Navy during World War II. Married to Bets Ramsey; has four children. Taught at the University of Alabama, Tuscaloosa, 1948–50, 1953–57; Elmira College, New York, 1957–62; Raymond College, Stockton, California, 1962–64; University of the South, Sewanee, Tennessee, 1964–66. Professor of

English, 1966–70, since 1966, Poet-in-Residence, and since 1970, Alumni Distinguished Service Professor, University of Tennessee, Chattanooga. Recipient: Folger Library Senior Fellowship, 1967; Roberts Memorial Prize (*Lyric*, Bremo Bluff, Virginia), 1972. Address: Department of English, University of Tennessee, Chattanooga, Tennessee 37401, U.S.A.

PUBLICATIONS

Verse

>*Triptych*, with Sy Kahn and Jane Taylor.   Stockton, California, Raymond College Press, 1964.
>*In an Ordinary Place.*   Raleigh, North Carolina, Southern Poetry Review Press, 1965.
>*A Window for New York.*   San Francisco, Two Windows Press, 1968.
>*The Doors: Poems of 1968.*   Martin, Tennessee Poetry Press, 1968.
>*The Answerers.*   San Francisco, Two Windows Press, 1970.
>*The Running on the Boardwalk.*   Athens, University of Georgia Press, 1975.

Other

>*The Lively and the Just: An Argument for Propriety.*   University, Alabama, University of Alabama Press, 1962.
>*The Art of John Dryden.*   Lexington, University of Kentucky Press, 1969.

Critical Study: review in *Virginia Quarterly Review* (Charlottesville), 1968.

Paul Ramsey comments:

My poetry deals with varied themes: some important ones are returnings, the real price of things, doors, explorations, kinds of knowledge. For years I wrote only traditional forms, mostly accentual-syllabics. In the last few years I have written much free verse as well as iambics, syllabics, and other forms, including some poems in prose. My longest poem is in blank verse mixed with some free verse. My free verse includes short-line, long-line, and other kinds. My work has been influenced by Allen Tate, Robert Lowell, and Dryden, nursery rhymes, Robert Creeley, Donald Justice, Theodore Roethke and the epigrams of J. V. Cunningham and David Zimmerman. The landscapes of Tennessee, Maine, New York State, California, and more recently Ireland work in my poems. As do cities. As does the sea. And the Book of Jude and other biblical sources. And rocks and ghosts.

*   *   *

Paul Ramsey in his best work often combines the virtues of men whose work he has studied carefully: John Dryden, Allen Tate, and Yvor Winters. The combination may at first seem strange. Yet Dryden is godfather to our critical wars and poetical age; and Tate and Winters were not so far apart as poets as their critical squabbles suggested. Aiming for compression, some of Ramsey's early poems were so tightly packed that they seemed more cryptic than epigramatic. The quatrain "Art" is an often cited example ("Art is act / Betrayed by passion and by artifact / Till images encounter their repose"). Aiming at a general loosening of the poetic line and at a more conversational vocabulary in the fashionable manner, some of his later poems (and the whole book *The Doors: Poems of 1968*) have become diffuse, sketchy, even lacking in content. Yet superb lines appear in both the tight early poems ("Art" ends: "The mind must learn to suffer what it knows") and the diffuse later experiments ("The Doors" sequence ends with the line "Blood loosens the rust of the keys"); and in all the poems, one finds subtle metrical skill as well as intellectual integrity and grace. Ramsey's profoundly Christian humanitarian outlook gives moving substance to many of his poems, and informs others with moral strength and character. This habit of mind evidences itself in such poems as the apology to Wordsworth, an apology for having taught that man's poems badly; and to the assertion in the challenging and important critical work *The Lively and the Just*, that of the English Odes examined in the book Wordsworth's Intimations Ode is the greatest. Such a remark, coming from a Dryden scholar and a student of the so-called "New Criticism" is a measure of rigorous intellectual integrity.

No poet writes great poems all the time; nor even good poems. One must, I think, pass over such experiments as *The Doors* and most of Ramsey's "occasional" poems, as one would any other poet's. Then one finds a solid body of work. He has written at least one major poem, "Address to Satan," 14 iambic pentameter lines in two stanzas riming a-a-b-b-c-c-c, and beginning "Now curl about your wisdom and be still, / Old serpent-tooth." In addition he had written some very fine poems, "Forest" and "Even Umpires Wager with Pascal" among them. The poems of a man of such skill and integrity will survive, past fads and fashions. The man who wrote such poems as "Address to Satan" and "Forest" is still composing. His lively verbal imagination will, knock wood, give us more good poems.

– James Korges

RANDALL, Dudley (Felker). American. Born in Washington, D.C., 14 January 1914. Educated at Wayne State University, Detroit, A.B. 1949; University of Michigan, Ann Arbor, M.A.L.S. 1951. Served in the United States Army Signal Corps, 1943–46. Married Ruby Hands in 1935 (marriage dissolved); Mildred Pinckney in 1942 (marriage dissolved); Vivian Spencer in 1957; has one daughter. Librarian, Lincoln University, Jefferson City, Missouri, 1951–54, Morgan State College, Baltimore, 1954–56, and Wayne County Federated Library System, Detroit, 1956–69. Since 1969, Librarian and Poet-in-Residence, University of Detroit. Since 1965, Founding Publisher, Broadside Press, Detroit. Visited Paris, Prague and the U.S.S.R. with a delegation of black artists, 1966. Recipient: Wayne State University Tompkins Award, for fiction and poetry, 1962, for poetry, 1966; Kuumba Black Liberation Award, 1973. Agent: Contemporary Forum, 2528a West Jerome Street, Chicago, Illinois 60645. Address: 12651 Old Mill Place, Detroit, Michigan 48238, U.S.A.

PUBLICATIONS

Verse

Ballad of Birmingham. Detroit, Broadside Press, 1965.
Dressed All in Pink. Detroit, Broadside Press, 1965.
Booker T. and W. E. B. Detroit, Broadside Press, 1966.
Poem, Counterpoem, with Margaret Danner. Detroit, Broadside Press, 1966.
Cities Burning. Detroit, Broadside Press, 1968.
On Getting a Natural. Detroit, Broadside Press, 1969.
Love You. London, Paul Breman, 1970.
More to Remember: Poems of Four Decades. Chicago, Third World Press, 1971.
Green Apples. Detroit, Broadside Press, 1972.
After the Killing. Chicago, Third World Press, 1973.

Other

Editor, with Margaret Burroughs, *For Malcolm: Poems on the Life and the Death of Malcolm X.* Detroit, Broadside Press, 1967.
Editor, *Black Poetry: A Supplement to Anthologies Which Exclude Black Poets.* Detroit, Broadside Press, 1969.
Editor, *The Black Poets: A New Anthology.* New York, Bantam, 1971.

Dudley Randall comments:

Writes poetry of the Negro. Formal, reflective, with occasional humor.

*   *   *

Dudley Randall's verse eases its audience into a pleased approval of the poet's viewpoint. Take, for example, what must be his most famous piece, "Booker T. and W.E.B." References to the doctrines of the famous black leaders in this imagined dialogue seem even-handed, each speaker uses in-group language in a manner appropriate to his personality, and the dispute quite appropriately has no logical resolution within the poem. On the other hand, Randall's heavy end-rhymes develop qualitative contrasts as Washington admonishes ". . . do not grouse, / But work, and save, and buy a house" and DuBois responds that Washington should "try his little plan, / But as for me, I'll be a man." Upon second thought auditors may feel there is less than justice in this mock dialogue in which just one participant gets mocked, but it has been a delight.

Randall generates such verse between the poles of a wit modulated by the rhythms of popular idiom and a strong ethical concern. Frequently he works as a satirist invoking the integrity of discipline and good sense to censure those who sanctify getting high ("Hail, Dionysos"), indulge themselves in fashionable introspection ("Analysands"), or parade as "stone" revolutionaries ("Abu"). The satiric structure, as often as not, builds upon enumeration as in "F.B.I. Memo" where the perfect spy is equipped with beard, Afro, tiki, dashiki, Swahili, and the cry "Kill the Honkies"; and deceptive simplicity is the background for wit, as in "Black Poet, White Critic" where Randall blandly records the critic's advice to write on universal themes symbolized by a white unicorn: "A *white* unicorn?"

Wit, the popular idiom, and an ethical concern are good for more than satire, however. The metaphoric identification of black speech with the Southern land in "Laughter in the Slums" lyrically images a soul world as vividly as Jean Toomer ever did, while "Roses and Revolutions" conveys a prophecy in a striking metaphysical image.

We owe much to Dudley Randall, for his devotion to art that delights and instructs led him to found the very important Broadside Press, first publisher of a number of the new black American poets. Appropriately, though, the epitome of his entire project, as poet and publisher of poets, is to be found in his own verse. Try his beautiful elegy "Langston Blues." It's all there: wit, popular form, and feeling that defies objective description. It's perfect.

– John M. Reilly

———————————

RANDALL, Julia. American. Born in Baltimore, Maryland, 15 June 1923. Educated at Bryn Mawr School, Baltimore; Bennington College, Vermont, A.B. 1945; Johns Hopkins University, Baltimore, M.A. 1950. Lived in Paris, 1952–54. Assistant Professor, 1962–66, and since 1966, Associate Professor of English, Hollins College, Virginia. Recipient: *Sewanee Review* Fellowship, 1957; National Endowment for the Arts grant, 1966; National Institute of Arts and Letters grant, 1968. Address: Department of English, Hollins College, Virginia 24020, U.S.A.

PUBLICATIONS

Verse

The Solstice Tree: Poems.   Baltimore, Contemporary Poetry, 1952.
Mimic August: Poems.   Baltimore, Contemporary Poetry, 1960.
4 Poems.   Hollins College, Virginia, Tinker Press, 1964.
The Puritan Carpenter.   Chapel Hill, University of North Carolina Press, 1965.
Adam's Dream.   Hollins College, Virginia, Tinker Press, 1966.
Adam's Dream: Poems.   New York, Knopf, 1969.

Julia Randall comments:

It seems to me quite beyond the call of duty, modesty, or even common sense to answer questions about one's own verse. Influences? The usual ones for our time: Eliot, Yeats, Rilke, Stevens, Thomas; behind them Hopkins, Wordsworth, Dickinson, the great ambiguous ghost of Milton, and the lesser ghosts of hymn- and ballad-makers. Also, very importantly, musicians, painters, naturalists, novelists, philosophers, and prophets. My subjects are drawn about equally from nature (especially the Maryland-Virginia countryside) and from the arts, which is to say about half my poems are literal and half imaginary. They are personal or local, rather than dramatic or topical. My forms are frequently traditional quatrains, but tend now toward something larger or looser with either sustained or irregular use of slant rhyme. I belong to no school that I know of. I try to achieve at least an articulation of the questions that particular experience seems to pose: how do we attach ourselves to or separate ourselves from each other, or from time? how do we know? where or to whom do we most belong? how do we mean? I try to write complete poems, sensible to the eye and ear as well as to the mind.

*   *   *

The poems of Julia Randall are tough and compressed, with a complexity that demands much of the reader, hard lines in the traditional sense, taut and metaphysical; but they are also lyrical and musically beautiful, written in a language that sings even as it tightens into knots of fused word and idea. The poems are highly allusive and are often witty in the fullest sense; language leaps to imagination and words contort themselves for the mind's delight. They are highly charged entities in which the arcane and archaic are alloyed with metaphysical passion into an active communion with the colloquial and the immediate. The days of her poems are precise and detailed, often carefully dated, but they open out, forward and back, into thought, memory and belief, into what can best be termed imaginative meditation – the mind fully at work in the harmonies (and disharmonies) of the present, not analyzing and organizing it but rather experiencing it down to the very bone.

Her earlier poems were more self-consciously aesthetic, almost hermetic at times, but even in them, she wrote from a commitment to the immediacy of experience, to learning from the inside out. For example, in the poem "Inscape I" from her first book, *The Solstice Tree:*

You

that curl the blind hand over the breast,
sing for a sign, sign for a feast,

fasten the blade, explore the vein,
learn the familiar blood.

Her later poems have become more openly personal, less artificially wrought, while losing none of the compressed intensity of the early poems. She addresses the world and her "masters" (Stevens and Rilke, Wordsworth, Lawrence, Woolf and Yeats); she invokes them, plant and poet, stone and artist, demanding of them and of herself "what we see clear, but clumsily half-tell." What she sees is the world of bone and blood and words, but also the power of being itself, beyond and through them all:

I walked by the stream. The hay was loud
with bugs escaping; they know
what danger is. I too
feared once the many-bladed mower.
Once, but not now.

– R. H. W. Dillard

RANDALL, Margaret. Mexican. Born in New York City, 6 December 1936. Educated at the University of New Mexico, Albuquerque. Married Sam Jacobs in 1955 (divorced, 1958); Sergio Mondragón in 1962 (marriage dissolved, 1968); has lived with Robert Cohen since 1969; has four children. Has lived in Mexico since 1961. Editor, the English-Spanish quarterly, *El Corno Emplumado*, Mexico City, 1962–69. Since 1969, Writer for the Cuban Book Institute, Havana. Delegate, Congress for Intellectuals from the Third World, Havana, 1968, and Seminar on Latin American Women, Santiago, Chile, 1972. Recipient: National Institute of Arts and Letters grant, Carnegie Fund grant, and Gutman Foundation grant, 1960. Address: Apartado Postal 13–546, Mexico City 13, Mexico.

PUBLICATIONS

Verse

    Giant of Tears and Other Poems. New York, Tejon Press, 1959.
    Ecstasy Is a Number: Poem. New York, Gutman Foundation, 1961.
    Poems of the Glass. Cleveland, Renegade Press, 1964.
    Small Sounds of the Bass Fiddle. Albuquerque, New Mexico, Duende, 1964.
    October. Mexico City, El Corno Emplumado, 1965.
    25 Stages of My Spine. New Rochelle, New York, Elizabeth Press, 1967.
    Water I Slip Into at Night. Mexico City, privately printed, 1967.
    So Many Rooms Has a House, But One Roof. Nyack, New York, New Rivers Press, 1968.
    Getting Rid of Blue Plastic: Poems Old and New, edited by Pritish Nandy. Calcutta, Dialogue, 1968.
    With Our Hands. Vancouver, New Star Books, 1974.

Other

    La Gloria de Crazy Horse. Santiago, Chile, Quimantú, 1973.
    Part of the Solution: Portrait of a Revolutionary (miscellany). New York, New Directions, 1973.

    Editor, *Los Hippies: Expressión de Una Crisis.* Mexico City, Siglo XXI, 1968.
    Editor, *Las Mujeres.* Mexico City, Siglo XXI, 1970.
    Editor, *La Mujer Cubana Ahora.* Havana, Cuban Book Institute, 1972.
    Editor, *Mujeres en la Revolución.* Mexico City, Siglo XXI, 1973.
    Editor, *Poems from Latin America.* San Francisco, Peoples' Press, 1973.
    Editor, *Women in Latin America.* San Francisco, Peoples' Press, 1974.

    Translator, with Sergio Mondragón, *Her Body Against Time,* by Robert Kelly. Mexico City, El Corno Emplumado, 1963.

Manuscript Collection: New York University Library.

Critical Study: "The Sense of the Risk of the Coming Together" by Alvin Greenberg, in *Minnesota Review* (St. Paul), vi, 2, 1966.

Margaret Randall comments:

There are no longer any separations between the poem (or writing of any kind) and life, the revolution, the changing balance of powers in the world and the change within the human being as she/he struggles to become the "new man" (or woman) Che spoke of and was. The poem is no longer valuable to me except as a documentary of the life experience and the experience of struggle, and as a vehicle for growth, struggle, revolution. I want to put my writing at the service of a true history and the people's liberation struggles.

*   *   *

The strength of Margaret Randall's poetry comes from its position on the immediate edges of experience: experience fresh and untempered whatever its quality (loving or violent), and brought forth directly as an offering of the poet's own self. She has been consistently a poet whose major concern is to confront whatever happens – however new and however great the risks – prepared to grow, as artist and person, from that encounter, always seeking to "create a new language for this, a new place." The dangers of such an approach are great – that the experience will be too raw, too unformulated, to become meaningful, or that, particularly in areas of political or social concern, failure to find the new words may cause one to fall back on sloganizing – but the values, as she shows, are well worth the risk: giving a sense of the immediacy of the poet living through a significant encounter (with self, dreams, other people, events, new places), discovering herself in the midst of that encounter, and opening up to the reader the potential for a similar discovery.

Thus her poems deal, for the most part, with, as she says in "Everyone Comes to a Lighted House," "people moving together" and with her own emergence, as detailed in "Eyes," through such encounters to new vision:

> The dream went on but I woke up.
> The bus is full my stop's coming up everyone has new eyes.

The brief prose pieces she has been writing lately, a number of which are included in her recent book, *Part of the Solution*, present in greater detail encounters comparable to those which take place in the poems; they are not actually stories but meetings, generally bizarre and traumatic, in which the poet confronts, or has forced upon her, experiences which call her entire sense of self, society, or relationships into question. Again, as in all her work – and in the movement of her life as well – what is pre-eminent is the sense of risk, and of risk as potential for the new, for learning and growth, as in "So Many Rooms Has a House, But One Roof":

> One side a surface where the hole forms, opens,
> to persist means look through
> or change
> as water runs over the found object.

One changes, she indicates, not by becoming something different but by self-discovery, even in the act of writing; the encounters around which her writing centers become the potential for creativity in both her life and her poetry, and the odds which she describes Fidel risking in the mountains become as well her own sense of challenge and possibility, as she concludes in "Both Dreams": "in forests we'll conquer because we have to."

– Alvin Greenberg

RANSOM, John Crowe. American. Born in Pulaski, Tennessee, 30 April 1888. Educated at Vanderbilt University, Nashville, Tennessee, A.B. 1909 (Phi Beta Kappa); Christ Church, Oxford (Rhodes Scholar), B.A. 1913. Served in the United States Army, 1917–19. Married Robb Reavill in 1920; has three children. Assistant in English, Harvard University, Cambridge, Massachusetts, 1914. Member of the Faculty, 1914–27, and Professor of English, 1927–37, Vanderbilt University. Carnegie Professor of Poetry, 1937–58, and since 1958, Professor Emeritus, Kenyon College, Gambier, Ohio. Visiting Lecturer in English, Chattanooga University, Tennessee, 1938; Visiting Lecturer in Language and Criticism, University of Texas, Austin, 1956. Member of the Fugitive Group of Poets: Founding Editor, with Allen Tate, *The Fugitive*, Nashville, 1922–25; Editor, *Kenyon Review*, Gambier, Ohio, 1937–59. Formerly, Honorary Consultant in American Letters, Library of Congress, Washington, D.C. Recipient: Guggenheim Fellowship, 1931; Bollingen Prize, 1951; Loines Award, 1951; Brandeis University Creative Arts Award, 1958; Academy of American Poets Fellowship, 1962; National Book Award, 1964; National Endowment for the Arts award, 1966; Emerson-Thoreau Medal, 1968; National Institute of Arts and Letters Gold Medal, 1973. Member, American Academy of Arts and Letters, and American Academy of Arts and Sciences. Address: Kenyon College, Gambier, Ohio 43022, U.S.A. *Died 3 July 1974.*

PUBLICATIONS

Verse

Poems about God.   New York, Holt, 1919.
Armageddon, with A Fragment, by William Alexander Percy, and Avalon, by
    Donald Davidson.   Charleston, Poetry Society of South Carolina, 1923.
Chills and Fever: Poems.   New York, Knopf, 1924.
Grace after Meat.   London, Leonard and Virginia Woolf, 1924.
Two Gentlemen in Bonds.   New York, Knopf, 1927.
Selected Poems.   New York, Knopf, 1945; London, Eyre and Spottiswoode,
    1947; revised edition, 1963, 1969.
Poems and Essays.   New York, Knopf, 1955.

Recording: Poems, Decca, 1966.

Other

God Without Thunder: An Unorthodox Defense of Orthodoxy.   New York, Har-
    court Brace, 1930; London, Gerald Howe, 1931.

The World's Body. New York, Scribner, 1938.

The New Criticism. New York, New Directions, 1941.

Poetics. New York, New Directions, 1942.

A College Primer of Writing. New York, Holt, 1943.

American Poetry at Mid-Century . . ., with Delmore Schwartz and John Hall Wheelock. Washington, D.C., Library of Congress, 1958.

Exercises on the Occasion of the Dedication of the New Phi Beta Kappa Hall . . . . Williamsburg, Virginia, College of William and Mary, 1958.

Beating the Bushes: Selected Essays 1941–1970. New York, New Directions, 1972.

Editor, *Topics for Freshman Writing: Twenty Topics for Writing, with Appropriate Material for Study.* New York, Holt, 1935.

Editor, *The Kenyon Critics: Studies in Modern Literature from the "Kenyon Review."* Cleveland, World, 1951.

Editor, *Selected Poems,* by Thomas Hardy. New York, Macmillan, 1961.

*   *   *

The body of John Crowe Ransom's verse is small. Its implications are large. He has devoted as much time and thought to criticism as to poetry, and each naturally illumines the other. In one of the essays collected under the title *The New Criticism* (new nearly thirty years ago) he makes a nice distinction between scientific discourse and poetry. The first reduces, emasculates, renders docile the several worlds it deals with. Poetry "intends to recover the denser and more refractory original world which we know loosely through our perceptions and memories." And also, he might have added, were he considering his own poems, through the wisdom of the heart. The world that these recover for us is notably "refractory," since its inhabitants, men and women, girls and boys, creatures of fantasy, all carry the burden of duality. Robert Penn Warren has noted that Ransom once spoke to him of man as "a kind of 'oscillating mechanism.' " It is the tensions, the ambiguities, the paradoxes, in which we are involved that his work implacably, if quietly, reveals.

The scene is often a domestic one in a provincial context (he has confessed that probably most of his poems "are about familiar and familial situations; domestic and homely things"). These preoccupations, like his characteristic technical graces, set his work apart from that of his juniors. The argument of a poem may hark back to what his fellow-Southerners call "the war between the States," or even to a war recorded in the Apocrypha, rather than to any less remote conflict. In any case, civil war, without or within, is repeatedly made present to us. Thus, when Ransom writes an "Eclogue" about Jane Sneed and John Black, he reminds us, however tacitly, that this pair is not alone in being

> one part love
> and nine parts bitter thought.

Although he was to reject it, the sonnet sequence called "Two Gentlemen in Bonds" remains of interest because it deals with the fraternal quarrel between body and mind. A later poem, "Painted Head," which takes an anonymous portrait for its subject, has a like theme. For all his devotion to the discriminations of the intellect, Ransom does not slight the claims of the body that houses it. Even his wittiest pieces, like that about the doughty "Captain Carpenter" and his more accessible "Survey of Literature," show him wryly conscious of the duality governing our lives. The latter opens:

In all the good Greek of Plato
I miss my roastbeef and potato.

It ends by crying God's mercy on the sinner (=the poet)

With no belly and no bowels,
Only consonants and vowels.

His own work is attentive to both necessities.

Another chief feature of it is that it mingles wit with a tenderness usually absent from that of his fellow self-styled "Fugitives," who were less concerned to define what they fled to than what they fled from: our industrialized, mechanized, divisive civilization.

Among Ransom's most moving lyrics are those on the deaths of children, in one instance an unlikeable little boy ("A pig with a pasty face, so I had said"), in another a mischievous small girl. What occupies the poet is the way that their entrance into the kingdom of death their elders' feeling about them. A superficially simple poem is apt to be rich with subtleties, as is "Janet Waking." This treats of a child's first confrontation with death – that of her pet hen. As often as one rereads these lines, one is struck by the delicacy that governs Ransom's diction, happily marrying Latinate words with curt prose, by his careful twisting of syntax for the sake of emphasis, by the way in which he pleasures us with slight variations in his handling of metre. The tone, as usual, is gently ironic. The irony carries the weight of the meaning, which is not light. These felicities are the hallmark of Ransom's poems.

– Babette Deutsch

RAWORTH, Tom (Thomas Moore Raworth).   British.   Born in Bexleyheath, Kent, 19 July 1938. Educated at St. Joseph's Academy, London, 1949–54; University of Essex, Colchester 1967–71, M.A. 1971. Married Valarie Murphy in 1959; has five children. Owner and Publisher, Matrix Press, and Editor, *Outburst*, London, 1959–64; Founding Editor, with Barry Hall, Goliard Press, London, 1965–67; Poet-in-Residence, Department of Literature, University of Essex, 1969–70; Fiction Instructor, Bowling Green State University, Ohio, 1972–73. Poet-in-Residence, North-eastern Illinois University, Chicago, 1973–74. Visiting Lecturer, University of Texas, Austin, 1974. Recipient: Alice Hunt Bartlett Prize, 1969; Arts Council grant, 1970, 1972; Cholmondeley Award, 1972; New York Committee on Poetry Award, 1972, 1973. Address: c/o T. A. Raworth, Esq., 8 Avondale Road, Welling, Kent, England.

PUBLICATIONS

Verse

Weapon Man.   London, Goliard Press, 1965.
Continuation.   London, Goliard Press, 1966.

The Relation Ship: Poems. London, Goliard Press, 1967; New York, Grossman, 1969.
Haiku, with John Esam and Anselm Hollo. London, Trigram Press, 1968.
The Big Green Day. London, Trigram Press, 1968.
Lion, Lion. London, Trigram Press, 1970.
Moving. London, Cape Goliard Press, and New York, Grossman, 1971.
Penguin Modern Poets 19, with John Ashbery and Lee Harwood. London, Penguin, 1971.
Pleasant Butter. Northampton, Massachusetts, Sand Project Press, 1972.
Tracking. Bowling Green, Ohio, Doones Press, 1972.
Time Being, with Asa Benveniste and Ray DiPalma. London, Blue Chair, 1972.
Here. Bowling Green, Ohio, privately printed, 1973.
An Interesting Picture of Ohio. Bowling Green, Ohio, privately printed, 1973.
Back to Nature. London, Joe DiMaggio Press, 1973.
Act. London, Trigram Press, 1973.
Ace. London, Cape Goliard Press, 1974.
Bolivia. London, Secret Books, 1974.
Nicht Wahr, Rosie? London, Fulcrum Press, 1975.

Recording: *Little Trace Remains of Emmett Miller,* Stream Records, 1969.

Play

Screenplay: *A Plague on Both Your Houses,* 1966.

Novels

Betrayal. London, Trigram Press, 1967.
A Serial Biography. London, Fulcrum Press, 1969.
Cancer. West Newbury, Massachusetts, Frontier Press, 1974.
Sic Him Oltorf! San Francisco, Zephyrus Image, 1974.

Other

The Minicab War (parodies), with Anselm Hollo and Gregory Corso. London, Matrix Press, 1961.

Editor, "Rainer M. Gerhardt Issue" of *Work 4* (Detroit), 1968.

Translator, with David Ball, *Provence – Point Omega,* by René Char. New York, Frontier Press, 1969.
Translator, with Valarie Raworth, *From the Hungarian.* Bowling Green, Ohio, privately printed, 1973.

Manuscript Collection: Wilbur Cross Library, University of Connecticut, Storrs.

Critical Study: by Jeff Nuttall, in *Poetry Information 9–10* (London), 1974.

*   *   *

Tom Raworth has been slow in making a reputation because his poems are among the densest and most difficult of those published by the English "new generation." Raworth's style is both abrupt and elliptical. The reader must make sudden jumps and sidesteps to keep pace with the poet. At the same time, there is an unmistakable feeling of tension and energy in the language, of "something going on." Raworth's resemblance to the French surrealists is marked, and his work, like Lee Harwood's, seems the sign of a possible change of direction in British poetry.

– Edward Lucie-Smith

RAY, David. American. Born in Sapulpa, Oklahoma, 20 May 1932. Educated at the University of Chicago, B.A. 1952, M.A. 1957. Married Judy Ray in 1970; has three daughters and one son. Member of the Faculty, Wright Junior College, Chicago, 1957–58, Northern Illinois University, DeKalb, 1958–60, and Cornell University, Ithaca, New York, 1960–64; Assistant Professor of Literature and Humanities, Reed College, Portland, Oregon, 1964–66; Lecturer in English, University of Iowa, Iowa City, 1969–71. Since 1971, Professor of English, University of Missouri, Kansas City. Editor, *Chicago Review*, 1956–57; Associate Editor, *Epoch*, Ithaca, New York, 1960–64. Since 1971, Editor, *New Letters*, Kansas City, Missouri. Recipient: *New Republic* Young Writers Award, 1958; Breadloaf Writers Conference Robert Frost Fellowship, 1964. Address: Department of English, University of Missouri, Kansas City, Missouri 64110, U.S.A.

PUBLICATIONS

Verse

X-Rays: A Book of Poems. Ithaca, New York, Cornell University Press, 1965.
Dragging the Main and Other Poems. Ithaca, New York, Cornell University Press, 1968.
A Hill in Oklahoma. Shawnee Mission, Kansas, Bkmk Press, 1973.
Gathering Firewood: New Poems and Selected. Middletown, Connecticut, Wesleyan University Press, 1974.

Other

Editor, *The Chicago Review Anthology.* Chicago, University of Chicago Press, and London, Cambridge University Press, 1959.
Editor, *From the Hungarian Revolution: A Collection of Poems.* Ithaca, New York, Cornell University Press, 1966.
Editor, with Robert Bly, *A Poetry Reading Against the Vietnam War.* Madison, Minnesota, American Writers Against the Vietnam War, 1966.
Editor, with Robert M. Farnsworth, *Richard Wright: Impressions and Perspectives.* Ann Arbor, University of Michigan Press, 1973.

David Ray comments:

I like the comparisons that have been made of my poems to X-rays or to found objects, as my poems are attempts to render verbal equivalents of what happens inside me or in persons or things I have found in the world and which have given me and sometimes them a different context through my finding them.

*   *   *

Like other disciples of W. C. Williams, but none, perhaps so faithfully and persistently, David Ray continues to turn out strong, sharp, direct poem after poem without the help of most of the prosodic conventions. Avoiding regular meter, Ray prefers the casual (hence surprising) turn of thought, the plainest of colloquial diction, until, as when we round the bend of a perfectly ordinary road and see a great holm oak, his poem reveals itself.

It's no use saying of one of his poems: "An accident; it just happened." The miracle happens too frequently. Let us scrutinize "Love Letter" (from *X-Rays*), a poem which (after that title) begins paradoxically among bills and loneliness:

> For months now you've hated me
>   and sent on angry letters
> From creditors without comment
>   though you've had to address
> New envelopes; your anger
>   is joined to theirs
> And I take it broadside

Then, through an instant landscape as symbolic as real, comes the shift of tone:

>   here in an empty apartment
> Where I watch the cars plunge
>   past all night, where I own
> A morning moon above distant farms
>   and my cough annoys no one.

Perhaps the little landscape owes something to the Chinese poets? In any case the vowel melody of the concluding lines (own-moon-no one) along with *m*'s and *n*'s provides an unobtrusive and delightful music that seems inseparable from the images there.

Rhythmic elements are also operative. By stress-count the poem goes 3, 3, 3, 2, 3, 2, 3, 3, 3, 3, 4, 3, and since the next-to-last line has four it looms vastly. Rhythm is often working for Ray when the reader least suspects it.

The technique of David Ray's poetry is sophisticated; its total effect, as in the prose of the late George Orwell, is one of unalloyed sincerity. Every line seems washed in the astringencies of simplicity and surprise.

– E. L. Mayo

REANEY, James (Crerar). Canadian. Born near Stratford, Ontario, 1 September 1926. Educated at Elmhurst Public School, Easthope Township, Perth County; Stratford High School; University College, Toronto (Epstein Award, 1948), M.A. in English, Ph.D. 1956. Married Colleen Thibaudeau in 1951; has two living children. Member of the English Department, University of Manitoba, Winnipeg, 1949–56. Since 1960, Member of the English Department, Middlesex College, University of Western Ontario, London. Founding Editor, *Alphabet* magazine, London, 1960–71. Active in little theatre groups in Winnipeg and London. Recipient: Governor General's Award, for verse, 1950, 1959, for drama, 1963; President's Medal University of Western Ontario, 1955, 1958. Agent: Sybil Hutchinson, Apt. 409, Ramsden Place, 50 Hillsboro Avenue, Toronto, Ontario M5R 1S8, Canada.

PUBLICATIONS

Verse

The Red Heart. Toronto, McClelland and Stewart, 1949.
A Suit of Nettles. Toronto, Macmillan, 1958.
Twelve Letters to a Small Town. Toronto, Ryerson Press, 1962.
The Dance of Death at London, Ontario. London, Ontario, Alphabet, 1963.
Poems. Toronto, New Press, 1972.
Sticks and Stones: The Donnellys, Part One. Erin, Ontario, Porcépic Press, 1975.

Plays

Night-Blooming Cereus (broadcast, 1959; produced Toronto, 1960). Included in *The Killdeer and Other Plays*, 1962.
The Killdeer (produced Toronto, 1960; Glasgow, 1965). Included in *The Killdeer and Other Plays*, 1962; revised version (produced Vancouver, 1970), in *Masks of Childhood*, 1972.
One-Man Masque (produced Toronto, 1960). Included in *The Killdeer and Other Plays*, 1962.
The Easter Egg (produced Hamilton, Ontario, 1962). Included in *Masks of Childhood*, 1972.
The Killdeer and Other Plays (includes *Sun and Moon, One-Man Masque, Night-Blooming Cereus*). Toronto, Macmillan, 1962.
Sun and Moon (produced Winnipeg, Manitoba, 1971). Included in *The Killdeer and Other Plays*, 1962.
Names and Nicknames (produced Winnipeg, Manitoba, 1963). Included in *School Plays*, 1973.
Apple Butter (puppet play; also director: produced London, Ontario, 1965). Included in *School Plays*, 1973.
Let's Make a Carol: A Play with Music for Children, music by John Beckwith. Waterloo, Ontario, Waterloo Music Company, 1965.
Listen to the Wind (produced London, Ontario, 1965; Woodstock, New York, 1967). Vancouver, Talonbooks, 1972.
Colours in the Dark (produced Stratford, Ontario, 1967). Vancouver and Toronto, Talonbooks-Macmillan, 1970.
Three Desks (produced Calgary, 1967). Included in *Masks of Childhood*, 1972.
Masks of Childhood (includes *The Killdeer, Three Desks, Easter Egg*). Toronto, New Press, 1972.

Apple Butter and Other Plays for Children (includes *Names and Nicknames, Ignoramus, Geography Match*).   Vancouver, Talonbooks, 1973.

Radio Play: *Night-Blooming Cereus*, 1959.

Other

The Boy with an "R" in His Hand (juvenile).   Toronto, Macmillan, 1965.

Bibliographies: in *James Reaney* by Alvin A. Lee, New York, Twayne, 1968; in *James Reaney* by Ross G. Woodman, Toronto, McClelland and Stewart, 1971.

Theatrical Activities:

Director: **Plays** – *One-Man Masque and Night-Blooming Cereus*, Toronto, 1960; *Apple Butter*, London, Ontario, 1965.

Actor: **Plays** – in *One-Man Masque and Night-Blooming Cereus*, Toronto, 1960.

James Reaney comments:

My poetry can probably best be summed up in three words: What I've tried to do and what I keep trying to do is Listen to the Wind, see Colours in the Dark.

*   *   *

One of the most original and imaginative poets in Canada, James Reaney has published only a small body of work in the past two decades, but it is poetry with a powerful consistency and concentration of mind. His plays have added to the body of his work, and so has his critical writing and editorial direction of the magazine *Alphabet*, which he founded and edited for ten years.

Alphabet, following the critical theories of Northrop Frye, under whom Reaney once studied, is concerned with "the iconography of the imagination," and successive issues have developed specific mythopoeic themes in poetry, prose, and the fine arts. Reaney as editor sometimes took up characteristic positions critical of science and of rationalism, but his own poetry is both wider and deeper (more personally focused) than these ideas would suggest. It is as a poet that he makes his strongest impact, and his imagination seems to be ordered by deep inner necessity rather than by any special theory or criticism.

His first book, *The Red Heart*, already contains the essential elements of his view of life. It offers dazzling and provocative leaps of fantasy, free-wheeling satire, and wild surrealist wit. But there are also deeply serious poems which set the tone for the book and for Reaney's later work.

These poems deal with death, with the universal stage of nature marked by change and destined for ultimate extinction, and with the mystery of the perishable individual heart and mind. Against this backdrop, the world of human concerns withers into insignificance, and thus provides the subject for Reaney's brilliant secular satires.

Further, in the context of death and human folly, the poetry reveals a powerful attachment to childhood memories and emotions. Against the world of childhood, the adult world becomes polarized as its opposite, the scene of triviality and horror.

Reaney's second book, *A Suit of Nettles*, is a complex satire, purportedly directed at Canadian life in Ontario Province, but really concerned with life generally, under the guise of an animal allegory. The poem is a metrical *tour-de-force* in imitation of Spenser's *Shepheardes Calender*. Language is used with a good deal of archaizing arbitrariness and artificial word-placing, but the whole effect is one of great skill and virtuosity in satirical handling. The themes of the earlier book are formalized into what is now clearly a unifying vision, and in technical skill the whole is a professional execution of a full and unified work.

The nature of this vision is thoroughly traditional and recognizably Christian. The *contemptus mundi* is fully explored in the farm and goose allegory; and the complementary theme of eternal order is only touched on here and there. In all his work so far, the Christian resolution appears in only two crucial passages, one at the close of *The Dance of Death*, and the other toward the end of *A Suit of Nettles*, in the November section.

A Suit of Nettles is Reaney's most ambitious and satisfying book. The collections published since are minor developments of his central themes. *Twelve Letters to a Small Town* is written in the style of mock infantilism; it explores the world of childhood in the satirical secular dimension. *The Dance of Death at London, Ontario* is an imitation of the late medieval genre, continuing the same satire on a more general social canvas.

– Louis Dudek

REDGROVE, Peter (William).   British.   Born in Kingston, Surrey, 2 January 1932. Educated at Queen's College, Cambridge. Married to Barbara Redgrove (separated); has three children. Formerly scientific journalist and editor; Visiting Poet, University of Buffalo, New York, 1961–62; Gregory Fellow in Poetry, Leeds University, 1963–65. Since 1966, Poet-in-Residence, Falmouth School of Art, Cornwall. Visiting Professor, Colgate University, Hamilton, New York, 1974–75. Recipient: Fulbright Fellowship, 1961; Arts Council grant, 1969, 1970; *Guardian* Prize, for fiction, 1973. Address: c/o Routledge and Kegan Paul, Publishers, 68–74 Carter Lane, London EC4U 5EL, England.

PUBLICATIONS

Verse

The Collector and Other Poems.   London, Routledge, 1960.
The Nature of Cold Weather and Other Poems.   London, Routledge, 1961.
At the White Monument and Other Poems.   London, Routledge, 1963.
The Force and Other Poems.   London, Routledge, 1966.
The God-Trap.   London, Turret Books, 1966.
The Old White Man.   London, Poet and Printer, 1968.

Penguin Modern Poets 11, with D. M. Black and D. M. Thomas. London, Penguin, 1968.

Work in Progress MDMLXVIII. London, Poet and Printer, 1968.

The Mother, The Daughter and the Sighing Bridge. Oxford, Sycamore Press, 1970.

The Shirt, The Skull and the Grape. Frensham, Surrey, Sceptre Press, 1970.

Love's Journeys. Cardiff, Second Aeon, 1971.

The Bedside Clock. Oxford, Sycamore Press, 1971.

Folio, with others. Frensham, Surrey, Sceptre Press, 1971.

Love's Journeys: A Selection. Crediton, Devon, Gilbertson, 1971.

Dr. Faust's Sea-Spiral Spirit and Other Poems. London, Routledge, 1972.

Two Poems. Rushden, Northamptonshire, Sceptre Press, 1972.

The Hermaphrodite Album, with Penelope Shuttle. London, Fuller D'Arch Smith, 1973.

Sons of My Skin: Poems 1954–74. London, Routledge, 1975.

Plays

The Sermon: A Prose Poem (broadcast, 1964). London, Poet and Printer, 1966.

Three Pieces for Voices. London, Poet and Printer, 1972.

In the Country of the Skin (broadcast, 1973). Privately printed, 1973.

Radio Plays: *The White Monument,* 1963; *The Sermon,* 1964; *The Anniversary,* 1964; *In the Country of the Skin: A Radio Dramatization,* 1973.

Novels

In the Country of the Skin. Rushden, Northamptonshire, Sceptre Press, 1972; London, Routledge, 1973.

The Terrors of Dr. Treviles, with Penelope Shuttle. London, Routledge, 1974.

Other

Editor, *Poet's Playground 1963.* Leeds, Schools Sports Association, 1963.

Editor, *Universities Poetry 7.* Keele, Universities Poetry Management Committee, 1965.

Editor, with John Fuller and Harold Pinter, *New Poems 1967: A P.E.N. Anthology.* London, Hutchinson, 1967.

Manuscript Collection: Humanities Research Center, Austin, Texas.

*   *   *

Peter Redgrove has been one of the most prolific poets of his generation, and the richness and the density of the material have alike tended to ward off any kind of critical judgement. Basically, Redgrove seems to resemble Ted Hughes who was his friend and contemporary at Cambridge. Both are essentially expressionist writers, both are more interested in imagery than in formal structure, and this imagery rises from the natural world. Redgrove differs from Hughes in pushing these characteristics much further than Hughes is prepared to. Reviewers have often noticed the violence of imagery and language – a violence which tends to seem mannered when applied to situations which do not seem to call for it. Less often commented upon has been the poet's tendency to transfer a favourite image or trope, or even a whole set of images, from one poem to another, so that the work becomes all one fabric, and the thing which occasioned a particular poem something of almost no importance. At its worst, Redgrove's work can seem a compulsive outpouring of words, which overwhelms subject and emotion alike, which rolls along in a flurry of rhetoric and poetic self-satisfaction. At its best it shows extraordinary insights – few poets have more subtly explored the link between the individual creativity of the writer and the blind will to breed and continue which one discovers in the natural world. One finds things in Redgrove which remind one of the insights of certain 20th-century British artists, most particularly Henry Moore. Just as Moore has an astonishing command of evolving sculptural metaphor, so Redgrove does the same thing with words. A poem such as "The House in the Acorn" does not describe something, but simply *is* the situation which it presents. The real question of course is the proportion of misses to the proportion of hits – and also, perhaps, Redgrove's failure to show any very consistent development.

– Edward Lucie-Smith

REED, Henry. British. Born in Birmingham, Warwickshire, 22 February 1914. Educated at the King Edward VI School, Birmingham; University of Birmingham, M.A. Served in the Royal Army, 1941–42. Teacher and free-lance journalist, 1937–41; Staff Member, Foreign Office, London, 1942–45. Since 1945, broadcaster, journalist, and radio writer. Address: c/o Jonathan Cape Ltd., 30 Bedford Square, London WC1B 3EL, England.

PUBLICATIONS

Verse

A Map of Verona: Poems.   London, Cape, 1946; New York, Reynal, 1947.
Lessons of the War.   New York, Chilmark Press, 1970.

Plays

Moby Dick: A Play for Radio from Herman Melville's Novel (broadcast, 1947).   London, Cape, 1947.
Leopardi: The Unblest, The Monument (broadcast, 1949, 1950).   Included in The Streets of Pompeii and Other Plays for Radio, 1971.
The Streets of Pompeii (broadcast, 1952).   Included in The Streets of Pompeii and Other Plays for Radio, 1971).
The Great Desire I Had (broadcast, 1952).   Included in The Streets of Pompeii and Other Plays for Radio, 1971.
Return to Naples (broadcast, 1953).   Included in The Streets of Pompeii and Other Plays for Radio, 1971.
A Very Great Man Indeed (broadcast, 1953).   Included in Hilda Tablet and Others: Four Pieces for Radio, 1971.

The Private Life of Hilda Tablet (broadcast, 1954). Included in *Hilda Tablet and Others: Four Pieces for Radio*, 1971.

The Queen and the Rebels, adaptation of a play by Ugo Betti (broadcast, 1954; produced London, 1955). Included in *Three Plays*, 1956.

The Burnt Flower-Bed, adaptation of a play by Ugo Betti (produced London, 1955). Included in *Three Plays*, 1956.

Summertime, adaptation of a play by Ugo Betti (produced London, 1955). Included in *Three Plays*, 1956.

Island of Goats, adaptation of a play by Ugo Betti (produced New York, 1955). Published as *Crime on Goat Island*, London, French, 1960.

Vincenzo (broadcast, 1955). Included in *The Streets of Pompeii and Other Plays for Radio*, 1971.

Three Plays (includes *The Queen and the Rebels*, *The Burnt Flower-Bed*, and *Summertime*, adaptations of plays by Ugo Betti). London, Gollancz, 1956.

A Hedge, Backwards (broadcast, 1956). Included in *Hilda Tablet and Others: Four Pieces for Radio*, 1971.

The Primal Scene, As It Were . . . (broadcast, 1958). Included in *Hilda Tablet and Others: Four Plays for Radio*, 1971.

Corruption in the Palace of Justice, adaptation of a play by Ugo Betti (broadcast, 1958; produced New York, 1963).

The Advertisement, adaptation of a play by Natalia Ginzburg (produced London, 1968; New York, 1974). London, Faber, 1969.

The Streets of Pompeii and Other Plays for Radio (includes *Leopardi: The Unblest*, *The Monument*; *The Great Desire I Had*; *Return to Naples*; *Vincenzo*). London, BBC, 1971.

Hilda Tablet and Others: Four Pieces for Radio (includes *A Very Great Man Indeed*; *The Private Life of Hilda Tablet*; *A Hedge, Backwards*; *The Primal Scene, As It Were . . .*). London, BBC, 1971.

Radio Plays: *Noises On*, 1947; *Noises – Nasty and Nice*, 1947; *Moby Dick*, 1947; *Pytheas*, 1947; *Leopardi* (includes *The Unblest*, 1949, and *The Monument*, 1950); *A By-Election of the Nineties*, 1951: *The Dynasts*, 1951; *Malatesta*, 1952; *The Streets of Pompeii*, 1952; *The Great Desire I Had*, 1952; *Return to Naples*, 1953; *All for the Best*, 1953; *A Very Great Man Indeed*, 1953; *The Private Life of Hilda Tablet*, 1954; *Hamlet; or, The Consequences of Filial Piety*, 1954; *The Battle of the Masks*, 1954; *The Queen and the Rebels*, 1954; *Emily Butler*, 1954; *The Burnt Flower-Bed*, 1955; *Vincenzo*, 1955; *Crime on Goat Island*, 1956; *A Hedge, Backwards*, 1956; *Don Juan in Love*, 1956; *Alarica*, 1956; *Irene*, 1957; *Corruption in the Palace of Justice*, 1958; *The Primal Scene, As It Were . . .*, 1958; *The Auction Sale*, 1958; *The Island Where the King Is a Child*, 1959; *One Flesh*, 1959; *Not a Drum Was Heard*, 1959; *Musique Discrète*, with Donald Swann, 1959; *The House on the Water*, 1961; *A Hospital Case*, 1961; *The America Prize*, 1964; *Zone 36*, 1965; *Summertime*, 1969; *The Two Mrs. Morlis*, 1971.

Other

The Novel since 1939. London, Longman, 1946.

Translator, *Perdu and His Father*, by Paride Rombi. London, Hart Davis, and Toronto, Clarke Irwin, 1954.

Translator, *Larger Than Life*, by Dino Buzzati. London, Secker and Warburg, 1962.

*   *   *

Henry Reed, although he has published only one collection of poems, *A Map of Verona*, is a much underrated writer. He is better known for the highly amusing dramatic pieces he has written for radio than for his poems.

A Map of Verona divides itself fairly simply into four sections – poems written about the last World War, personal poems, dramatic monologues, and a sequence entitled "Tintagel." Reed is also a comic poet, and he is certainly the only writer of importance who has (in "Chard Whitlow") parodied T. S. Eliot with complete success. This too must be taken into account.

Henry Reed is a poet with a fine ear, a strongly disciplined sense of form, and passionate feelings. The personal poems, which will be considered first, are all the more effective because emotion is never allowed to get out of hand; Reed always eschews chaos. The title poem of his book is a good example of all his finest qualities. Here are its first two stanzas:

> The flutes are warm: in to-morrow's cave the music
> Trembles and forms inside the musician's mind,
> The lights begin, and the shifting lights in the causeways
> Are discerned through the dusk, and the rolling river behind
>
> And in what hour of beauty, in what good arms,
> Shall I those regions and that city attain
> From whence my dreams and slightest movements rise?
> And what good Arms shall take them away again?

Here is nostalgia without a trace of sentimentality. Every word is carefully chosen and placed. All this can be found in other personal poems where, by sheer artistry, the poet can communicate and, at the same time, keep the distance which all very good poems of human feeling must have if they are not to fall into bathos or formlessness.

"Morning," "The Return," "Outside and In," and "The Door and the Window" all fall into this group of personal poems. The last named has the beautiful opening stanza:

> My love, you are timely come, let me lie by your heart,
> For waking in the dark this morning, I woke to that mystery,
> Which we can all wake to, at some dark time or another:
> Waking to find the room not as I thought it was,
> But the window further away, and the door in another direction.

The sensibility which informs such poems as these is evident in a rather different way in the poems about the Army written during the 1939 war. *Here*, Reed displays irony as well as observation. There is a section entitled "Lessons of the War" which is composed of three parts, "Naming of Parts," "Judging Distances," and "Unarmed Combat." In the first of these poems, the training of soldiers and the arrival of Spring are most dexterously and tellingly blended. The second stanza runs:

> This is the lower sling swivel. And this
> Is the upper sling swivel, whose use you will see
> When you are given your slings. And this is the piling swivel,
> Which in your case you have not got. The branches
> Hold in the gardens their silent eloquent gestures,
> Which in our case we have not got.

All the futility of war is rendered in these lines. Nature goes on while men train in order to kill their enemy across the English Channel. The last lines of "Naming of Parts" complete what is, in its own very individual way, a most remarkable poem about war:

> . . . and the almond-blossom
> Silent in all of the gardens and the bees going backwards and forwards,
> For to-day we have naming of parts.

Henry Reed always writes with a skill which conceals itself. This becomes more and more clear in the sequence called "The Desert" (also much concerned with war) and "Tintagel." In the latter, this poet's descriptive gifts are shown at their most intense. Part One, "Tristram" contains these lines:

> The ruin leads your thoughts
> Past the moment of darkness when silence fell over the hall,
> And the only sound rising was the sound of frightened breathing . . .
> To the perpetually recurring story,
> The doorway open, either in the soft green weather,
> The gulls seen over the purple-threaded sea, the cliffs,
> Or open in mist . . . .

"Tintagel" also demonstrates Reed's ability to enter into the characters of others, which we find in the two monologues, "Chrysothemis" and "Philoctetes." In these poems, his highly-developed dramatic gift is clearly evident, especially in the matter of dialogue. Reed really brings Philoctetes to life in lines such as the following:

> To my companions become unbearable,
> I was put on this island. But the story
> As you have heard it is with time distorted,
> And passion and pity have done their best for it . . .
> . . . They seized me and forced me ashore,
> And wept.

The poet is completely identified with Philoctetes and his plight.

Finally we must glance at "Chard Whitlow (Mr. Eliot's Sunday Evening Post-script)," Henry Reed's brilliant parody of the T. S. Eliot of *Four Quartets*. Here we have just two passages from what is not a long piece:

> Seasons return, and to-day I am fifty-five
> And this time last year I was fifty-four,
> And this time next year I shall be sixty-two.

> I think you will find this put,
> Far better than I could ever hope to express it,
> In the words of Kharma: "It is, we believe,
> Idle to hope that the simple stirrup-pump
> Can extinguish hell."

This is true parody, both uproariously funny and shrewdly ironic. Eliot's tone is perfectly caught, and Reed's mockery is not unkind but illustrates the ownership of a fine ear and a mastery of language.

Why such a good poet has written so little poetry is strange. The BBC has a way of inadvertently making its poet-employees either "dry-up" altogether or else produce a poem only now and then (Terence Tiller is another case in point). But Henry Reed has written a handful of poems that may well last; these are probably the war poems. His command over verse-forms and language is flawless. Perhaps, in old age, he will return to poetry again. It would be a loss to English literature if he did not.

– Elizabeth Jennings

REED, Ishmael. Afro-American. Born in Chattanooga, Tennessee, 22 February 1938. Attended the University of Buffalo, New York, for three years. Married to Carla Blank-Reed; has one child by a previous marriage. Guest Lecturer in American Literature, University of California, Berkeley, 1968, 1969; Lecturer, University of Washington, Seattle, 1969. Since 1971, Vice-President (Editorial), Yardbird Publishing Corporation, and Editor, *Yardbird Reader*, Berkeley, California. Recipient: National Endowment for the Arts grant, 1974. Address: 6 Bret Harte Way, Berkeley, California 94708, U.S.A.

PUBLICATIONS

Verse

Catechism of D Neoamerican HooDoo Church. London, Paul Breman, 1970.
Conjure: Selected Poems 1963–1970. Amherst, University of Massachusetts Press, 1972.
Chattanooga: Poems. New York, Random House, 1973.

Novels

The Free-Lance Pallbearers. New York, Doubleday, 1967; London, MacGibbon and Kee, 1968.
Yellow Back Radio Broke-Down. New York, Doubleday, 1969; London, Allison and Busby, 1971.
Mumbo-Jumbo. New York, Doubleday, 1972.
The Last Days of Louisiana Red. New York, Random House, 1974.

Other

The Rise, Fall, and . . .? of Adam Clayton Powell (as Emmett Coleman). New York, Bee-Line Books, 1967.

Editor, *19 Necromancers from Now.* New York, Doubleday, 1970.

Ishmael Reed comments:

Themes – personal, magic, race, politics; no particular verse form.

*　　　*　　　*

Ishmael Reed is a satirist who today is primarily a novelist, but like many other Black American writers he started his literary career writing poetry. *Conjure* is his first collection of poetry and although it was not published until 1972 it is made up of renderings dating back to 1963 – four years before his first novel.

Many of these poems foreshadow the subjects of his novels and point up the fact that his more recent preoccupations are the result of thinking over an extended period of time. For example, in his introduction to *19 Necromancers from Now*, Reed writes that because "Black writers have in the past written sonnets, iambic pentameter, ballads, [and] every possible Western gentleman's form," they have sacrificed their own originality. He further says that "Sometimes I feel that the condition of the Afro-American writer in this country is so strange that one has to go to the supernatural for an analogy." It is from this feeling that Reed has developed the view that the Black artist should function as a "conjuror" who employs "Neo-HooDoo" as a means of freeing his fellow victims from the psychic attack of his oppressors.

Ishmael Reed's poems are not unique either in their intent or their responsibility but they are poignant earlier examples of the dynamic wit and unabashed approach which he demonstrates in his novels. It is scathing, uncompromising satire, but he is always in full control. A typical example of his thematic focus on the incompatibility of Western civilization and the cultures of Africa and Asia is illustrated in this excerpt from "Badman of the Guest Professor":

> its not my fault dat yr tradition
> was knocked off wop style & left in
> d alley w/pricks in its mouth. i
> read abt it in d papers but it was no
> skin off my nose
> wasnt me who opened d gates & allowed
> d rustlers to slip thru unnoticed. u
> ought to do something about yr security or
> mend yr fences partner

and again in his prosey dictum from "The Ghost of Birmingham," a poem for which he feels impelled to apologize because it "shows the influence of people I studied in college":

> There has never been in history another culture as the
> Western civilization – a culture which has practiced the belief
> that the physical and social environment of man is subject to
> rational manipulation and that history is subject to the will and
> action of man; whereas central to the traditional cultures of
> the rivals of Western civilization, those of Africa and Asia, is a
> belief that it is environment that dominates man.

Reed's works are certainly controversial among both Black and White critics, but he wouldn't have it any other way.

– Charles L. James

1255

REEVE, F(ranklin) D(olier). American. Born in Philadelphia, Pennsylvania, 18 September 1928. Educated at Princeton University, New Jersey, A.B. 1950; Columbia University, New York, A.M. 1952, Ph.D. 1958. Married Helen Schmidinger in 1956; has three children. Taught at Columbia University, 1952–61; American Council of Learned Societies – U.S.S.R. Academy of Sciences Exchange Professor, University of Moscow, 1961, Associate Professor and Chairman of the Russian Department, 1962–64, Professor of Russian, 1964–66, and since 1967, Adjunct Professor of Letters, Wesleyan University, Middletown, Connecticut. Visiting Professor, Oxford University, 1964. Since 1973, Visiting Professor, Yale University, New Haven, Connecticut. Formerly, Member of the International Longshoreman's Association and the American Labor Party. Currently, a Justice of the Peace. Fellow, Saybrook College, Yale University. Recipient: Ford Fellowship, 1955; American Council of Learned Societies Fellowship, 1961; Ingram-Merrill Foundation award, 1961; National Institute of Arts and Letters grant, 1970. Lives in Higganum, Connecticut, U.S.A.

PUBLICATIONS

Verse

The Stone Island. Middletown, Connecticut, Salamander Press, 1964.
Six Poems. Middletown, Connecticut, Salamander Press, 1964.
In the Silent Stones: Poems. New York, Morrow, 1968.
The Blue Cat. New York, Farrar Straus, 1972.

Play

The Three-Sided Cube (produced New London, Connecticut, 1972).

Novels

The Red Machines. New York, Morrow, 1968.
Just over the Border. New York, Morrow, 1969.
The Brother. New York, Farrar Straus, 1971.
White Colors. New York, Farrar Straus, 1973.

Other

Aleksandr Blok: Between Image and Idea. New York, Columbia University Press, 1962.
Robert Frost in Russia. Boston, Little Brown, 1964.
On Some Scientific Concepts in Russian Poetry at the Turn of the Century. Middletown, Connecticut, Wesleyan University Center for Advanced Studies, 1966.
The Russian Novel. New York, McGraw Hill, 1966; London, Muller, 1967.

Editor and Translator, *Five Short Novels of Turgenev.* New York, Bantam, 1961.
Editor and Translator, *An Anthology of Russian Plays.* New York, Random House, 2 vols., 1961, 1963.

Editor and Translator, *Great Soviet Short Stories.* New York, Dell, 1963.

Editor and Translator, *Dostoevsky's Short Stories.* New York, Bantam, 1966.

Editor and Translator, *Contemporary Russian Drama.* New York, Pegasus, 1968.

Editor and Translator, *Nobel Lecture by Alexander Solzhenitsyn.* New York, Farrar Straus, 1972.

F. D. Reeve comments:

The play between the surface – things as seen – and the depths – the naturalistic and moral interpretations of things – is the life of poetry. Traditions supply the concepts, the forms, which we train oursleves to use to catch the experience of change. Reality's landscape is bleak, but a poem's landscape delights the eye and the mind by moving forward and back out of the present, transfixing change in the tensions among words, ferrying between what really is and the fictions of the imagination. The substance of poetry is metaphor, at times given in colloquial language and images from casual life, at times given in strict verse patterns and difficult images of implication. The mask of the poet – philosopher, songster, clown, apostle – conceals his face but not his personality, dances before the reader until the reader picks up his own and puts on a new consciousness.

*   *   *

F. D. Reeve's first collection, *In the Silent Stones,* is mostly rhymed and metrical – jingling anapests or more flexible iambics. A sign of uncertainty is the frequency with which elaborate stanza forms are undertaken only to be modified. Devices often seem tricks of the trade rather than expressive means: "I head for the heart of a girl / on the soft white breast of the world." But the wit can be amusing, even when it merely decorates a banal observation: "The conversation seesaws on the rim of a teacup. / Highwire ladies drop to save a faux pas. . ." ("Summer Circus"). One is aware of echoes – of the "Movement" ("Chinese Poem"), of Lowell ("The Plaque . . . for My Classmates Killed in Korea"), of Stevens ("A Tangram").

The Blue Cat shows more rhythmic subtlety and less ostentation (though a line like "That shallop symmetry burst from the hawse of her father" is hardly unforced). The imagery continues to be uneven, varying from the witty-elusive – "Like ribs around my body this armillary sphere / cages the fancy with old bars new Marco Polos must unbend" ("Hands") – to the merely flashy – "her hair / swinging like ten pendulums in love" ("The Blue Cat's Daughter"). Outstanding in the book, however, is a sequence of fourteen poems on the life of Thoreau which often achieves a moving intensity in evoking the New England moral climate. As Reeve gives himself to Thoreau we hear the voice of man with more on his mind than self-display:

> Immoral slave who pleads a moral cause,
> bankrupt in Heaven and on earth a stone,
> man sets his course against the natural laws,
> plotting the steps to seize the beautiful
>
> but coming, after all, to his own wet bones.

– Seamus Cooney

REEVES, James. British. Born in London, 1 July 1909. Educated at Stowe School, Buckinghamshire; Cambridge University, M.A. (honours) in English 1931. Has one son and two daughters. Taught in schools and colleges of education, 1933–52. Since 1951, General Editor, The Poetry Bookshelf series, William Heinemann Ltd., publishers, London; since 1960, General Editor, Unicorn Books, London. Address: Flints, Rotten Row, Lewes, Sussex, England.

PUBLICATIONS

Verse

The Natural Need. Deyá, Mallorca, Seizin Press, and London, Constable, 1936.
The Imprisoned Sea. London, Editions Poetry, 1949.
XIII Poems. Privately printed, 1950.
The Password and Other Poems. London, Heinemann, 1952.
The Talking Skull. London, Heinemann, 1958.
Collected Poems 1929–1959. London, Heinemann, 1960.
The Questioning Tiger. London, Heinemann, 1964.
Selected Poems. London, Allison and Busby, 1967.
Subsong. London, Heinemann, 1969.
Poems and Paraphrases. London, Heinemann, 1972.
Collected Poems 1929–1974. London, Heinemann, 1974.

Plays

Mulcaster Market: Three Plays for Young People. London, Heinemann, 1951.
The King Who Took Sunshine: A Comedy for Children in Two Acts. London, Heinemann, 1954.
A Health to John Patch: A Ballad Operatta. London, Boosey and Hawkes, 1957.

Other

The Wandering Moon (juvenile). London, Heinemann, 1950; New York, Dutton, 1960.
The Blackbird in the Lilac: Verses for Children. London, Oxford University Press, and New York, Dutton, 1952.
English Fables and Fairy Stories, Retold (juvenile). London, Oxford University Press, 1954; New York, H. Z. Walck, 1960.
The Critical Sense: Practical Criticism of Prose and Poetry. London, Heinemann, 1956.
Pigeons and Princesses (juvenile). London, Heinemann, 1956.
Prefabulous Animiles (juvenile). London, Heinemann, 1957; New York, Dutton, 1961.
Mulbridge Manor (juvenile). London, Heinemann, 1958.
Teaching Poetry: Poetry in Class Five to Fifteen. London, Heinemann, 1958.
The Exploits of Don Quixote, Retold. London and Glasgow, Blackie, 1959.
Titus in Trouble (juvenile). London, Bodley Head, 1959.
Ragged Robin (juvenile). London, Heinemann, and New York, Dutton, 1961.
Hurdy-Gurdy: Selected Poems for Children. London, Heinemann, 1961.

Fables from Aesop, Retold. London and Glasgow, Blackie, 1961.
A Short History of English Poetry 1340–1940. London, Heinemann, 1961; New York, Dutton, 1962.
Sailor Rumbelow and Britannia (juvenile). London, Heinemann, 1962.
The Story of Jackie Thimble (juvenile). London, Chatto and Windus, 1964.
The Strange Light (juvenile). London, Heinemann, 1964.
Three Tall Tales: Chosen from Traditional Sources. London, Abelard Schuman, 1964.
Understanding Poetry. London, Heinemann, 1965; New York, Barnes and Noble, 1968.
Rhyming Will (juvenile). London, Hamish Hamilton, 1967; New York, McGraw Hill, 1968.
The Cold Flame: Based on a Tale from the Collection of the Brothers Grimm. London, Hamish Hamilton, 1967; New York, Meredith, 1969.
The Trojan Horse (juvenile). London, Hamish Hamilton, 1968; New York, Watts, 1969.
Heroes and Monsters: Legends of Ancient Greece Retold. London, Blackie, 1969.
Essays: Commitment to Poetry. London, Heinemann, 1969; as *Commitment to Poetry,* New York, Barnes and Noble, 1969.
Mr. Horrox and the Grath (juvenile). London, Abelard Schuman, 1969.
The Angel and the Donkey (juvenile). London, Hamish Hamilton, 1969; New York, McGraw Hill, 1970.
Inside Poetry, with Martin Seymour-Smith. London, Heinemann, and New York, Barnes and Noble, 1970.
Maildun the Voyager (juvenile). London, Hamish Hamilton, 1971.
How to Write Poems for Children. London, Heinemann, 1971.
The Path of Gold (juvenile). London, Hamish Hamilton, 1972.
The Forbidden Frost (juvenile). London, Heinemann, 1973.
How the Moon Began (juvenile). London, Abelard Schuman, 1973.
Complete Poems for Children. London, Heinemann, 1973.
The Lion That Flew (juvenile). London, Chatto and Windus, 1974.
Two Greedy Bears (juvenile). London, Hamish Hamilton, 1974.

Editor, *The Modern Poet's World.* London, Heinemann, 1935; revised edition, as *Poet's World,* 1948, 1957.
Editor, with Denys Thomson, *The Quality of Education: Methods and Purposes in the Secondary Curriculum.* London, Muller, 1947.
Editor, *The Writer's Way: An Anthology of English Prose.* London, Christophers, 1948.
Editor, *Orpheus: A Junior Anthology of English Poetry.* London, Heinemann, 1949.
Editor, with Norman Culpan, *Dialogue and Drama.* London, Heinemann, 1950.
Editor, *Selected Poems,* by D. H. Lawrence. London, Heinemann, 1951.
Editor, *The Speaking Oak: English Poetry and Prose: A Selection.* London, Heinemann, 1951.
Editor, *Selected Poems,* by John Donne. London, Heinemann, 1952; New York, Macmillan, 1958.
Editor, *The Bible in Brief: Selections from the Text of the Authorized Version of 1611.* London, Wingate, 1954.
Editor, *Heinemann Junior Poetry Books.* London, Heinemann, 4 vols, 1954.
Editor, *Selected Poems,* by John Clare. London, Heinemann, 1954; New York, Macmillan, 1957.
Editor, *The Merry-Go-Round: A Collection of Rhymes and Poems for Children.* London, Heinemann, 1955.

Editor, *Gullivers Travels: The First Three Parts.* London, Heinemann, 1955.
Editor, *Selected Poems,* by Gerard Manley Hopkins. London, Heinemann, 1956; New York, Macmillan, 1957.
Editor, *Selected Poems,* by Robert Browning. London, Heinemann, 1956; New York, Macmillan, 1957.
Editor, *A Golden Land: Stories, Poems, Songs New and Old.* London, Constable, and New York, Hastings House, 1958.
Editor, *The Idiom of the People: English Traditional Verse from the Manuscripts of Cecil Sharp.* London, Heinemann, and New York, Macmillan, 1958.
Editor, *Selected Poems,* by Emily Dickinson. London, Heinemann, 1959; New York, Barnes and Noble, 1966.
Editor, *Selected Poems,* by Samuel Taylor Coleridge. London, Heinemann, 1959.
Editor, *The Personal Vision. . . .* London, Poetry Book Supplement, 1959.
Editor, *The Rhyming River: An Anthology of Verse.* London, Heinemann, 4 vols, 1959.
Editor, with William Vincent Aughterson, *Over the Ranges.* Melbourne, Heinemann, 1959.
Editor, *The Everlasting Circle: English Traditional Verse.* London, Heinemann, and New York, Macmillan, 1960.
Editor, with Desmond Flower, *The War 1939–45.* London, Cassell, 1960.
Editor, *Great English Essays.* London, Cassell, 1961.
Editor, *Selected Poems and Prose,* by Robert Graves. London, Hutchinson, 1961.
Editor, *A First Bible: An Abridgement for Young Readers.* London, Heinemann, 1962.
Editor, *Georgian Poetry.* London, Penguin, 1962.
Editor, *Gulliver's Travels: Parts I-IV.* London, Heinemann, 1964.
Editor, *The Cassell Book of English Poetry.* London, Cassell, and New York, Harper, 1965.
Editor, *Selected Poems,* by Jonathan Swift. London, Heinemann, and New York, Barnes and Noble, 1967.
Editor, with Martin Seymour-Smith, *A New Canon of English Poetry.* London, Heinemann, and New York, Barnes and Noble, 1967.
Editor, *An Anthology of Free Verse.* Oxford, Blackwell, 1968.
Editor, *The Christmas Book.* London, Heinemann, and New York, Dutton, 1968.
Editor, *The Reader's Bible.* London, Tandem, 1968.
Editor, *The Sayings of Dr. Johnson.* London, Baker, 1968.
Editor, *Poets and Their Critics,* vol. 3. London, Hutchinson, 1969.
Editor, *One's None: New Rhymes for Old Tongues.* London, Heinemann, 1968; New York, Watts, 1969.
Editor, *Homage to Trumbull Stickney.* London, Heinemann, 1968.
Editor, with Martin Seymour-Smith, *The Poems of Andrew Marvell.* London, Heinemann, and New York, Barnes and Noble, 1969.
Editor, *A Vein of Mockery* (anthology). London, Heinemann, 1973.
Editor, *Selected Poems,* by Thomas Gray. London, Heinemann, 1973; as *The Complete English Poems of Thomas Gray,* New York, Barnes and Noble, 1973.
Editor, *Five Late Romantic Poets.* London, Heinemann, 1974.

Translator, *Primrose and the Winter Witch,* by František Hrubín. London, Hamlyn, 1964.
Translator, *The Golden Cockerel,* by Alexander Pushkin. New York, Watts, 1969.

James Reeves comments:

The subject matter of my poems is the life of the individual, his relations with other people, the situation of the individual in an increasingly collectivist society. On the one hand I write poems, romantic or anti-romantic, about my own emotional problems, and on the other hand satires about the difficulty of remaining a poet. I acknowledge as influences all good English poets from Langland onwards, and bad poets as examples of how not to write. My style and technique are in what I conceive to be the English tradition, and that I believe is based on the nature and genius of the language. I believe in poetry as poetry, not poetry as propaganda, journalistic word games and other forms of exhibitionism including conscious experimentalism. All satisfactory poems are experiments: only the failures look like experiments. I have never climbed on any fashionable bandwagon. My poetic world is the world of the private man.

*   *   *

For long it was commonplace to hear James Reeves referred to as a member of the "school of Graves," on the strength of his friendship with the older poet – and of the fact that Graves' and Laura Riding's Seizin Press had published his first collection, *The Natural Need*, in 1936. In fact the early poems included in this volume, which contained a prefatory poem by Laura Riding, owe at least as much to Eliot, Pound, Richard Aldington and the imagists as they do to Graves or Laura Riding. On the other hand, Reeves' later poems, most particularly those collected in the two volumes published since the *Collected Poems*, owe more to Edmund Blunden, Andrew Young and John Crowe Ransom than to Graves – whose consistency of energy and attack his poetry has never pretended to have. This myth of Reeves' debt to Graves is worth scotching, although the most acute criticism of his poetry has never assumed it.

Reeves' poetry requires rigorous selection. There are some metrical wastes, where energy and linguistic inventiveness have been low, and where consequently the effect is commonplace and even "Georgian" in the worst sense. *Selected Poems*, which might have been a revelation, is a valuable pointer towards what Reeves can achieve at his best, but does not stringently enough exclude the slack and sentimental, nor yet quite skilfully enough select the sharp and the strongly impelled.

Reeves at his best writes in three distinct manners; but, as the late Edwin Muir wrote in reviewing one of his volumes, "Perfection does not call attention to itself": the surface of the poems is not striking. Most approachable of Reeves' manners is his quiet pastoralism, which in its way is as authentic as that of Blunden, although less observant of natural detail and frequently with a wryly satiric look at human obtrusions. In "Ghosts and Persons" he writes of "slow heads drowsing over sums" and the "mower's distant sound" whining through high windows, but also of "The forward smile and stupid eyes/Of a youthful village charmer." Human "progress" in its urbanizing forms amuses Reeves, but finally, especially in pastoral settings, arouses his resentment.

Reeves' angry, Kafkaesque manner, as beautifully exemplified in "Greenhallows" – ostensibly an account of a journey to an interview for an important position – is less familiar, more original and harder to interpret. In this vein, Reeves appears violently to reject his normally calm acceptance of his bourgeois background and to express attitudes quite alien to his usual self as expressed in poetry. The same kind of uncharacteristic energy is to be found in the sequence "Letter Before a Journey" and in some of the satirical poems included in *The Questioning Tiger*.

Finally, Reeves is the author of a handful of deeply felt, and powerfully expressed lyrics, such as "All Days But One," which begins:

> All days but one shall see us wake to make
> Our last confession:
> Bird notes at dawn revive the night's obsession.

Guilt, regret, anger, desire for stability – these are among the staple elements in Reeves' best poetry. Few have more memorably portrayed the pains, pleasures and sinister or unhappy nature of the conventional life than Reeves; few are more startling beneath a tranquil surface.

– Martin Seymour-Smith

REID, Alastair. British. Born in Whithorn, Wigtonshire, Scotland, 22 March 1926. Educated at the University of St. Andrews, Scotland, M.A. (honours) 1949. Served in the Royal Navy, 1943–46. Has one son. Taught at Sarah Lawrence College, Bronxville, New York, 1950–55; Fellow in Writing, Columbia University, New York, 1966; Visiting Professor of Latin American Studies, Antioch College, Yellow Springs, Ohio, 1969–70; Seminar Instructor in Latin American Literature, Oxford University and St. Andrews University, 1972–73. Since 1959, Staff Writer and Correspondent, *The New Yorker*. Gave lecture tours for the Association of American Colleges, 1966, 1969. Recipient: Guggenheim Fellowship, 1957, 1958. Lives in London and Spain. Agent: C. & J. Wolfers Ltd., 3 Regent Square, London W.C.1, England.

PUBLICATIONS

Verse

To Lighten My House: Poems. Scarsdale, New York, Morgan and Morgan, 1953.
Oddments Inklings Omens Moments: Poems. Boston, Little Brown, 1959; London, Dent, 1961.
Corgi Modern Poets in Focus 3, with others, edited by Dannie Abse. London, Corgi, 1971.

Other

I Will Tell You of a Town (juvenile). Boston, Houghton Mifflin, 1955; London, Hutchinson, 1957.
Fairwater (juvenile). Boston, Houghton Mifflin, 1956.
A Balloon for a Blunderbuss (juvenile). New York, Harper, 1957.
Allth (juvenile). Boston, Houghton Mifflin, 1958.
Ounce Dice Trice. Boston, Little Brown, 1958; London, Dent, 1961.

Millionaires, with Bob Gill.   New York, Simon and Schuster, 1959.
Supposing (juvenile).   Boston, Little Brown, 1960; London, Sidgwick and Jackson, 1973.
Passwords: Places, Poems, Preoccupations.   Boston, Little Brown, 1963; London, Weidenfeld and Nicolson, 1965.
To Be Alive (juvenile).   New York, Macmillan, 1966.
Mother Goose in Spanish, with Anthony Kerrigan.   New York, Crowell, 1967.
Uncle Timothy's Traviata.   New York, Delacorte Press, 1967.
La Isla Azul (juvenile).   Barcelona, Editorial Lumen, 1973.

Translator, with others, *Ficciones*, by Jorge Luis Borges.   New York, Grove Press, and London, Weidenfeld and Nicolson, 1965.
Translator, *We Are Many*, by Pablo Neruda.   London, Cape Goliard Press, 1967; New York, Grossman, 1968.
Translator, with Anthony Kerrigan, *Jorge Luis Borges: A Personal Anthology*.   New York, Grove Press, 1967; London, Cape, 1968.
Translator, with Ben Belitt, *A New Decade: Poems 1958–67*, by Pablo Neruda.   New York, Grove Press, 1968.
Translator, with others, *Selected Poems: A Bilingual Edition*, by Pablo Neruda, edited by Nathaniel Tarn.   London, Cape, 1970; New York, Delacorte Press, 1972.
Translator, *Extravagaria*, by Pablo Neruda.   London, Cape, 1972; New York, Farrar Straus, 1974.
Translator, with others, *Selected Poems*, by Jorge Luis Borges.   New York, Delacorte Press, and London, Penguin, 1972.
Translator, *Sunday Sunday*, by Mario Vargas Llasa.   Indianapolis, Bobbs Merrill, 1973.

Manuscript Collections: State University of New York, Buffalo; National Library of Scotland, Edinburgh.

Critical Study: in *Corgi Modern Poets 3*, edited by Dannie Abse, 1971.

*   *   *

Mirrors, magic, ghosts, cats, frogs, children – the subjects give hints as to the kind of poet Alastair Reid might be, but the list may mislead unless the context is given. The name of his poem "Cat-Faith" may also mislead, until one sees that this is his device for approaching his own concern about the hazard of life; so he depicts, with astonishment and gratitude, the creature, which, secure in its individuality, is beautifully adapted for survival. He applies his observation to himself:

> Yet to endure that unknown night by night
> must we not be sure, with cat-insight,
> we can afford its terrors, and that full day
> will find us at the desk, sane, unafraid –
> cheeks shaven, letters written, bills paid?

Perhaps the last line, despite the question mark, moves too securely; yet the delicacy of the human poise, the threat to it and the blessing are of concern to Alastair Reid. In "A Game of Glass" he writes:

> How can I trust my luck?
> Whatever way I look,
> I cannot tell which is the door,
> And I do not know who is who.

He uses the talisman of childhood to present *his* sense of adult life, which despite the query about identity, he accepts as a blessing:

> The point is seeing – the grace
> beyond recognition.

Again in the same poem, "Growing Flying Happening," he writes:

> Amazement is the thing.
> Not love, but the astonishment of loving.

This condition of perception is to be in Eden and he knows

> No angel drives us out,
> but time,
>   . . .
> The garden is not ours.

Despite these references there is not the concentration in his writing of the true visionary poet. He is rather an investigator, who looks sometimes with amused curiosity at Oddments Inklings Omens Moments, as the title of one of his books implies, but frequently registering and perceiving more than the avowed modest intention and more than the easy, smooth flow of the line might, at first, suggest. "Let your ear be gentle," Alastair Reid writes, and the hope is that it will hear what others ears do not, for

> The tune at first is odd, though still familiar.

– George Bruce

REXROTH, Kenneth. American. Born in South Bend, Indiana, 22 December 1905. Educated at the Art Institute, Chicago; New School for Social Research, New York; New York Art Students League. Married Andree Dutcher in 1927 (died 1940); Marie Kass, 1940 (divorced, 1948); Marthe Larsen, 1949 (divorced, 1961); has two children. Conscientious objector during World War II. Past occupations include farm worker, factory hand, insane asylum attendant. Painter: one-man shows held in Los Angeles, New York, Chicago, San Francisco, Paris. Columnist, *San Francisco Examiner*, 1958–68. Since 1953, San Francisco correspondent for *The Nation*, New York; since 1968, Columnist for *San Francisco Magazine*, and the *San Francisco Bay Guardian*. Since 1968, Lecturer, University of California, Santa Barbara. Recipient: Guggenheim Fellowship, 1948; Eunice Tietjens Award (*Poetry*, Chicago), 1957; Shelley Memorial Award, 1958; Amy Lowell Fellowship, 1958; National Institute of Arts and Letters grant, 1964. Member, National Institute of Arts and Letters. Address: 1401 East Pepper Lane, Santa Barbara, California 93108, U.S.A.

Publications

Verse

In What Hour. New York, Macmillan, 1941.
The Phoenix and the Tortoise. New York, New Directions, 1944.
The Art of Wordly Wisdom. Prairie City, Illinois, Decker Press, 1949.
The Signature of All Things: Poems, Songs, Elegies, Translations, and Epigrams. New York, New Directions, 1950.
The Dragon and the Unicorn. New York, New Directions, 1952.
In Defense of the Earth. New York, New Directions, 1956; London, Hutchinson, 1959.
The Homestead Called Damascus. New York, New Directions, 1963.
Natural Numbers: New and Selected Poems. New York, New Directions, 1963.
The Complete Collected Shorter Poems of Kenneth Rexroth. New York, New Directions, 1967.
Penguin Modern Poets 9, with Denise Levertov and William Carlos Williams. London, Penguin, 1967.
The Collected Longer Poems of Kenneth Rexroth. New York, New Directions, 1968.
The Heart's Garden, The Garden's Heart. Cambridge, Massachusetts, Pym Randall Press, 1967.
The Spark in the Tinder of Knowing. Cambridge, Massachusetts, Pym Randall Press, 1968.
Sky Sea Birds Trees Earth House Beasts Flowers. Santa Barbara, California, Unicorn Press, 1970.
New Poems. New York, New Directions, 1974.

Recording: *In the Cellar*, with Lawrence Ferlinghetti, Fantasy.

Plays

Beyond the Mountains (includes *Phaedra, Iphigenia, Hermaios, Berenike*) (produced New York, 1951). New York, New Directions, and London, Routledge, 1951.

Other

Bird in the Bush: Obvious Essays. New York, New Directions, 1959.
Assays (essays). New York, New Directions, 1961.
An Autobiographical Novel. New York, Doubleday, 1966.
Classics Revisited. Chicago, Quadrangle Books, 1968.
The Alternative Society: Essays from the Other World. New York, Herder, 1970.
With Eye and Ear (literary criticism). New York, Herder, 1970.
American Poetry: In the Twentieth Century. New York, Herder, 1971.
The Rexroth Reader, edited by Eric Mottram. London, Cape, 1972.
The Elastic Retort: Essays in Literature and Ideas. New York, Seabury Press, 1973.
Communalism: From Its Origins to the 20th Century. New York, Seabury Press, 1974.

Editor, *Selected Poems*, by D. H. Lawrence. New York, New Directions, 1948.

Editor, *The New British Poets: An Anthology.* New York, New Directions, 1949.

Editor, *Four Young Women: Poems.* New York, McGraw Hill, 1973.

Editor, *Tens: Selected Poems 1961–1971*, by David Meltzer. New York, McGraw Hill Herder, 1973.

Editor, *The Selected Poems of Czeslav Milosz.* New York, Seabury Press, 1973.

Translator, *Fourteen Poems*, by O. V. de L.-Milosz. San Francisco, Peregrine Press, 1952.

Translator, *100 Poems from the Japanese.* New York, New Directions, 1955.

Translator, *100 Poems from the Chinese.* New York, New Directions, 1956.

Translator, *30 Spanish Poems of Love and Exile.* San Francisco, City Lights Books, 1956.

Translator, *100 Poems from the Greek and Latin.* Ann Arbor, University of Michigan Press, 1962.

Translator, *Poems from the Greek Anthology.* Ann Arbor, University of Michigan Press, 1962.

Translator, *Selected Poems*, by Pierre Reverdy. New York, New Directions, 1969; London, Cape, 1973.

Translator, *Love and the Turning Earth: 100 More Classical Poems.* New York, New Directions, 1970.

Translator, *Love and the Turning Year: 100 More Chinese Poems.* New York, New Directions, 1970.

Translator, *100 Poems from the French.* Cambridge, Massachusetts, Pym Randall Press, 1970.

Translator, with Ling O. Chung, *The Orchid Boat: Women Poets of China.* New York, Herder, 1972.

*   *   *

In America the relationship between poetry and simplicity is a fixed and almost natural necessity; poets working with what William Carlos Williams called "the American idiom" try to capture the intimacy and appeal of straightforward speech, and because Kenneth Rexroth has succeeded in making even his most intellectual poems seem as natural as campfire talk, he is one of America's great poets. He has mastered the art of talking, in his poems, to anyone: his dead mother or father, the master W.C.W., or to the classic philosophers; he is willing, for the sake of this intimacy and naturalness – in pursuit of his goal of a classical severity – to take fantastic risks with sentiment, with grief. His elegy for Dylan Thomas, "Thous Shalt Not Kill," made famous by a recording of Rexroth reading it with a jazz background, when he was one of the leading figures in the San Francisco Renaissance (a movement, in fact, very much sparked by the admiration of the young for Rexroth and his work), was condemned by many critics as maudlin; but it is a lasting and powerful work in which the *ubi sunt* of those who have been destroyed by materialism rings as if through a hollow corridor in hell. Rexroth's poetry is *factual*; he can report in a poem ("The summer of nineteen eighteen / I read *The Jungle* and *The* / *Research Magnificent.* That fall / My father died and my aunt / Took me to Chicago to live"); he can make quiet wit erupt in a bestiary poem or an epigram; or he can achieve what Richard Eberhart called "calmness and grandeur, as if something eternal in the natural world has been mastered," but in whatever he writes Rexroth's sense of nature dominates; the love of nature is rich in his work, and his early books like *The Dragon and the Unicorn* are hymns to nature – memorable in their celebration of fishing, reading the classics, lovemaking, meditating; and his voice is noted for its *naturalness.* He writes without pretence, and perhaps this is the true meaning of a classic poet: he can speak to anyone, deeply, directly, and if there is pain and work behind the seeming ease with which he speaks, it is part of his art to hide that effort. Many of his long poems perhaps aim at giving "expression to certain general ideas of more or less social importance for our time"; Rexroth is all on the side of content and message. But to me his most powerful poems are those, like "For a Masseuse and Prostitute" in which he is most a wisecracking natural, even though he has hidden "electric life" in his poem. There is a precision in his short lyrics, and in his translations, that is by force ruled out in his longer, more rhetorical poems in which he comes to terms with this or that body of theory. His own views are available in his criticism. His judgement is that "from the death of Longfellow to the day Allen Ginsberg took off his clothes, the American poet was not an important factor in American life. He was not a factor at all." And yet his own career has argued forcefully and by example for the importance of the poet in all his concerns, public and private.

– David Ray

REZNIKOFF, Charles. American. Born in Brooklyn, New York, 31 August 1894. Educated at the School of Journalism, University of Missouri, Columbia, 1910–11; New York University Law School, LL.B. 1915; called to the bar, 1916. Married Marie Syrkin in 1930. Recipient: Jewish Book Council of America Kovner Award, 1963; Morton Dauwen Zabel Award, 1971. Address: 180 West End Avenue, Apartment 22F, New York, New York 10023, U.S.A.

PUBLICATIONS

Verse

Rhythms.   Brooklyn, New York, privately printed, 1918.
Poems.   New York, Samuel Roth, 1920.
Uriel Acosta: A Play and a Fourth Group of Verse.   New York, Cooper Press, 1921.
Chatterton, The Black Death, and Meriwether Lewis: Three Plays.   New York, Sunwise Turn, 1922.
Coral, and Captive Israel: Two Plays.   New York, Sunwise Turn, 1923.
Nine Plays.   New York, privately printed, 1927.
Five Groups of Verse.   New York, privately printed, 1927.
Jerusalem the Golden.   New York, Objectivist Press, 1934.
In Memoriam: 1933.   New York, Objectivist Press, 1934.
Separate Way.   New York, Objectivist Press, 1936.
Going To and Fro and Walking Up and Down.   New York, Future Press, 1941.

Inscriptions: 1944–1956. New York, privately printed, 1959.
By the Waters of Manhattan: Selected Verse. New York, New Directions, 1962.
Testimony: The United States (1885–1890), Recitative. New York, New Directions, 1965.
Testimony: The United States (1891–1900), Recitative. New York, privately printed, 1968.
By the Well of Living and Seeing. New York, privately printed, 1969.
By the Well of Living and Seeing: Selected Poems, edited by Seamus Cooney. Los Angeles, Black Sparrow Press, 1974.

Novels

By the Waters of Manhattan. New York, Charles Boni, 1930.
The Lionhearted: A Story about the Jews in Medieval England. Philadelphia, Jewish Publication Society of America, 1944.

Other

Testimony. New York, Objectivist Press, 1934.
Early History of a Sewing-Machine Operator, with Nathan Reznikoff. New York, privately printed, 1936.
The Jews of Charleston: A History of an American Jewish Community, with Uriah Z. Engelman. Philadelphia, Jewish Publication Society of America, 1950.
Family Chronicle: "Early History of a Seamstress," by Sarah Reznikoff, "Early History of a Sewing-Machine Operator," by Nathan Reznikoff, "Needle Trade," by Charles Reznikoff. New York, privately printed, 1963; London, Norton Bailey, 1969.

Translator, *Stories and Fantasies from the Jewish Past*, by Emil Cohn. Philadelphia, Jewish Publication Society of America, 1961.

Charles Reznikoff comments:

"Objectivist," images clear, the meaning not stated but suggested by the objective details and the music of the verse; words pithy and plain; without the artifice of regular meters; themes, chiefly Jewish, American, urban.

*   *   *

Charles Reznikoff's poems have an honored place in the history of the American poet's search for simplicity. The spirit of his work was stated in *Five Groups of Verse*:

> How difficult for me is Hebrew:
> even the Hebrew for *mother*, for *bread*, for *sun*
> is foreign. How far have I been exiled, Zion.

He chose to express the exile's loneliness as he wandered through Manhattan, his Judaism providing resonances, echoes, parallels to what he sees – the ghetto funeral: "two girls of twelve or so at a table / in the Automat, smiling at each other

/ and the world," "men and women with open books before them," in the Cooper Union Library, "come merely for warmth not light." Reznikoff's controlled sympathy goes out to the city's derelicts and scrubwomen; it is to be remembered that he was very much the contemporary of the proletarian and Jewish novelists such as Henry Roth, who were doing much the same thing in prose fiction. And yet Reznikoff was passionately involved in the imagist's (and more narrowly, the Objectivist's) search for terseness, for the objecthood of ideas. Poems like "A Sunny Day" show a heavy Pound influence, and some of his poems read like illustrations of the classic imagist ideal:

> I like this secret walking
> in the fog;
> unseen, unheard,
> among the bushes
> thick with drops;
> the solid path invisible
> a rod away –
> and only the narrow present is alive.

Always, he has suppressed the elegant, excised the elaborate, kept his focus on simple objects, relying on pure statement to attest to his passion. One often sees in his work the Objectivist's deliberate and almost amused or stunned confusion of people and objects: "There is no furniture for a room / like a beautiful woman." Or,

> What are you doing in our street among the automobiles,
> horse?
> How are your cousins, the centaur and the unicorn?

Often it is only through the spatial disposition of such simple statements that Reznikoff can hope to impart his vision:

> The shopgirls leave their work
> quietly.
>
> Machines are still, tables and chairs
> darken.
>
> The silent rounds of mice and roaches begin.

One is reminded of painters like Edward Hopper, and of cubist notions of highlighting certain effects to the entire exclusion of others. One feels that Reznikoff must have sacrificed a vast array of powers in order to risk all with the objectivist treatment of the experience of urban alienation. Often one feels a straining toward a savage mysticism:

> To the savage, perhaps, each bird has a message;
> I know that they shriek only to themselves.
> The stars in their courses did not fight for us.

Reznikoff obviously approached at times some terrible cliff of Being, where – if poets step off – they fly or become metamorphized unrecognizably. He clung to his code; and his work will be more easily defined by consequence – it will live because it is centered in objects that seem eternal, and because the clarity is actualized, the feeling beyond challenge. In his books Reznikoff chose to deal well with just a few themes, and he succeeded admirably in doing so. Had he chosen to step off that cliff he would very likely be one of our major poets.

– David Ray

———————

RICH, Adrienne (Cecile).   American.   Born in Baltimore, Maryland, 16 May 1929. Educated at Roland Park Country School, Baltimore, 1938–47; Radcliffe College, Cambridge, Massachusetts, A.B. (cum laude) 1951 (Phi Beta Kappa). Widow; has three sons. Lived in the Netherlands, 1961–62. Taught at the YM-YWHA Poetry Center Workshop, New York, 1966–67; Visiting Poet, Swarthmore College, Pennsylvania, 1966–68; Adjunct Professor, Graduate Writing Division, Columbia University, New York, 1967–69; Lecturer, 1968–70, Instructor, 1970–71, and Assistant Professor of English, 1971–72, City College of New York; Fannie Hurst Visiting Professor of Creative Writing, Brandeis University, Waltham, Massachusetts, 1972–73. Phi Beta Kappa Poet, College of William and Mary, Williamsburg, Virginia, 1960, Swarthmore College, 1965, and Harvard University, Cambridge, Massachusetts, 1966. Recipient: Yale Series of Younger Poets award, 1951; Guggenheim Fellowship, 1952, 1961; Ridgely Torrence Memorial Award, 1955; National Institute of Arts and Letters award, 1960; Amy Lowell Traveling Scholarship, 1962; Bess Hokin Prize, 1963, and Eunice Tietjens Memorial Prize, 1968 (*Poetry*, Chicago); National Translation Center grant, 1968; National Endowment for the Arts grant, 1969; Shelley Memorial Award, 1971; National Book Award, 1974. D.Litt.: Wheaton College, Norton, Massachusetts, 1967. Lives in New York City. Address: c/o W. W. Norton Company, 55 Fifth Avenue, New York, New York 10003, U.S.A.

PUBLICATIONS

Verse

A *Change of World.*   New Haven, Connecticut, Yale University Press, 1951.
(*Poems*).   Oxford, Fantasy Press, 1952.
The Diamond Cutters and Other Poems.   New York, Harper, 1955.
Snapshots of a Daughter-in-Law: Poems 1954–1962.   New York, Harper, 1963; London, Chatto and Windus, 1970.
Necessities of Life: Poems 1962–1965.   New York, Norton, 1966.
Selected Poems.   London, Chatto and Windus, 1967.
Leaflets: Poems 1965–1968.   New York, Norton, 1969; London, Chatto and Windus, 1972.
The Will to Change: Poems 1968–1970.   New York, Norton, 1971; Chatto and Windus, 1973.
Diving into the Wreck: Poems 1971–1972.   New York, Norton, 1973.

Recording: *Today's Poets 4*, with others, Folkways; *Adrienne Rich*, Stanford, 1973.

*   *   *

Adrienne Rich began to write poetry at a very early age. Her first book, which was published when she was twenty-two years old, won the annual competition conducted by Yale University Press for books by beginning poets. It was a remarkable performance. She showed herself to be a young woman of emotional and intellectual maturity, possessing an easy command of verbal technique, and from that time on she appeared to be launched on a brilliant, if somewhat conventional, literary career. Her writing unmistakably fell within the "neo-metaphysical" convention of mid-century American poetry, characterized by its use of fixed forms and its metrical and dictional concision. Her themes were personal and ethical, her aesthetic roughly Kantian, her view of human reality more or less Existential. She began to publish in many prominent magazines, she travelled abroad, she translated from several foreign literatures, especially the Dutch. In short, although she was younger than most of them, she soon took her place among the leading eastern poets of the time, Robert Lowell, Elizabeth Bishop, John Berryman, etc.

The first traces of dissatisfaction with what she was doing appeared in her third book, *Snapshots of a Daughter-in-Law* (1963). The later poems in the book show a relaxation of form that has continued and intensified since then; but a relaxation of surface only. Rhyme and conventional meter have been abandoned; but her diction is, if anything, tighter than ever, and her poems give an effect of inner formalism that is the opposite of lyrical. She writes now with explosive force, with short lines, hard images, in poems of restless energy. She does not hesitate to write apothegmatically when symbols or dramatic actions fail. These stylistic changes have been accentuated by her involvement in radical politics during recent years, and many of her poems explore the theme of revulsion from traditional cultural and social values. The apex of this work so far is probably a sequence called "Homage to Galib" in which she has loosely adapted the form of the Urdu poet's ghazals, writing with intense concentration on themes of personal transformation, rebirth amidst chaos, erotic need, and social revolution. These are interfused to make a conceptual unity that is both autonomous and socially connected. As Miss Rich has written elsewhere, "Love is political."

Many poets, probably most poets, in America today are writing *about* revolution. The poetry of Adrienne Rich *is* revolution. In its actual methodological progress it denies the older humanist concept of the world of imagination as separate from or contrary to ordinary reality; it shows the poem at work not only as a part of reality but as a creating and transforming part. Thus her poetry makes and at the same tine exemplifies a new aesthetic. It has nothing to do with discredited social realism, but a good deal to do with the existential notion of the artist as self-creator, extended to a social plane. It is poetry that is functional, connected, and in the completest sense programmatic, while at the same time it disclaims none of the purely instrumental developments of any other poetry. It undoubtedly relates to certain aspects of the work of Pound and Williams in an earlier generation, but at least in its direction and emphasis, and very likely in its philosophical grounding, it is new. It is one of the most important continuing experiments in American literature.

– Hayden Carruth

RICHARDS, I(vor) A(rmstrong). British. Born in Sandbach, Cheshire, 26 February 1893. Educated at Clifton College; Magdalene College, Cambridge, B.A. 1914, M.A. 1918, D.Litt. 1932. Married Dorothy Eleanor Pilley in 1926. Lecturer in

English, Cambridge University, 1919; Fellow, Magdalene College, 1926; Visiting Professor, Tsing Hua University, Peking, 1929–30. Visiting Lecturer, 1931, University Lecturer, 1939, University Professor, 1943–63, and since 1963, Professor Emeritus, Harvard University, Cambridge, Massachusetts. Director, the Orthological Institute of China, 1936–38. Corresponding Fellow, British Academy, 1959; Honorary Fellow, Magdalene College, 1964. Recipient: Loines Award, 1962; Companion of Honour, 1964; Emerson-Thoreau Medal, 1970; Brandeis University Creative Activity Medal, 1972. Litt.D.: Harvard University, 1944. Honorary Member, American Academy of Arts and Letters. Address: Magdalene College, Cambridge, England.

PUBLICATIONS

Verse

> Goodbye Earth and Other Poems. New York, Harcourt Brace, 1958; London, Routledge, 1959.
> The Screens and Other Poems. New York, Harcourt Brace, 1960; London, Routledge, 1961.
> Internal Colloquies: Poems and Plays. London, Routledge, 1972.

Plays

> A Leak in the Universe (produced Cambridge, Massachusetts, 1954). Published in Playbook: Five Plays for a New Theatre, New York, New Directions, 1956.
> Tomorrow Morning, Faustus! An Infernal Comedy. New York, Harcourt Brace, and London, Routledge, 1962.
> Why So, Socrates? A Dramatic Version of Plato's Dialogues: Euthyphro, Apology, Crito, Phaedo. New York, Harcourt Brace, and London, Cambridge University Press, 1964.

Other

> The Meaning of Meaning, with C. K. Ogden. London, Routledge, 1923; New York, Harcourt Brace, 1956.
> Principles of Literary Criticism. London, Paul Trench Trubner, 1924; New York, Harcourt Brace, 1925.
> The Foundations of Aesthetics, with C. K. Ogden. New York, Lear, 1925.
> Science and Poetry. London, Paul Trench Trubner, 1926; revised edition, 1935; as Poetries and Sciences, New York, Norton, 1970.
> Practical Criticism: A Study of Literary Judgment. London, Paul Trench Trubner, 1929; New York, Harcourt Brace, 1950.
> Mencius on the Mind: Experiments in Multiple Definitions. London, Paul Trench Trubner, and New York, Harcourt Brace, 1932.
> Basic Rules of Reason. London, Paul Trench Trubner, 1933.
> Coleridge on Imagination. London, Paul Trench Trubner, 1934; New York, Norton, 1950.
> Basic in Teaching: East and West. London, Paul Trench Trubner, 1935.
> The Philosophy of Rhetoric. New York and London, Oxford University Press, 1936.

Interpretation in Teaching. New York, Harcourt Brace, and London, Paul Trench Trubner, 1938.

How to Read a Page: A Course in Effective Reading, with an Introduction to a Hundred Great Words. New York, Norton, 1942; London, Paul Trench Trubner, 1943.

Basic English and Its Uses. New York, Norton, and London, Paul Trench Trubner, 1943.

A World Language: An Address. New York, New York Herald Tribune, 1944.

The Pocket Book of Basic English: A Self-Teaching Way into English with Directions in Spanish, French, Italian, Portuguese, German. New York, Pocket Books, 1945; revised edition, 1946; as *English Through Pictures,* 1957.

Learning Basic English: A Practical Handbook for English-Speaking People, with Christine Gibson. New York, Norton, 1945.

Nations and Peace. New York, Simon and Schuster, 1947.

The Republic of Plato: A Version in Simplified English. London, Paul Trench Trubner, 1948.

French Self-Taught with Pictures, with M. H. Ilsley and Christine Gibson. New York, Pocket Books, 1950.

Spanish Self-Taught Through Pictures, with Ruth C. Metcalf and Christine Gibson. New York, Pocket Books, 1950.

The Wrath of Achilles: The Iliad of Homer, Shortened. New York, Norton, 1950.

German Through Pictures, with others. New York, Pocket Books, 1953.

Hebrew Through Pictures, with David Weinstein and Christine Gibson. New York, Pocket Books, 1954.

Italian Through Pictures, with Italo Evàngelista and Christine Gibson. New York, Pocket Books, 1955.

Speculative Instruments. London, Routledge, 1955.

First Steps in Reading English, with Christine Gibson. New York, Washington Square Press, 1957.

French Through Pictures, with M. H. Ilsley and Christine Gibson. New York, Pocket Books, 1959.

A First Workbook of French, with M. H. Ilsley and Christine Gibson. New York, Washington Square Press, 1960.

Coleridge's Minor Poems: A Lecture. Missoula, Montana State University, 1960.

Russian Through Pictures, with Evelyn Jasiulko and Christine Gibson. New York, Washington Square Press, 1961.

Design for Escape: World Education Through Modern Media. New York, Harcourt Brace, 1968.

So Much Nearer: Essays Towards a World English. New York, Harcourt Brace, 1968.

Poetries: Their Media and Aims, edited by Trevor Eaton. The Hague, Mouton, 1973.

Beyond: Springs of the Human Endeavor: Studies in the Iliad, the Republic, Job, the Divine Comedy, and Prometheus Unbound. New York, Harcourt Brace, 1974.

Editor, with C. K. Ogden, *The Times of India Guide to Basic English.* Bombay, Times of India Press, 1938.

Editor, *The Portable Coleridge.* New York, Viking Press, 1950.

Editor and Translator, *Republic,* by Plato. Cambridge, University Press, 1966.

Critical Studies: *I. A. Richards: Essays in His Honor* (includes bibliography), edited by Reuben Brower, Helen Vendler, and John Hollander, London and New York, Oxford University Press, 1973.

I. A. Richards comments:

Since *A Leak in the Universe* I have felt that other work ought for me to give place, and priority of importance, to any poems that were going forward. This doesn't mean that other jobs have, as a rule, been willing to do so. They have been able to plead contracts and date lines.

In a 1948 article (reprinted in my *Speculative Instruments*, p. 41) I implied a need for "a poetic account of prose" to transmute "a prose account of poetry." Both phrases ask for wary interpretations. I did not then foresee how they might look to me when, five years later, I first took to writing verse. My poems proved to be colloquies between selves professing to be me or between components of these selves. Moreover, what these beings or voices spoke *about* was commonly that *for* and *to* which they spoke. This led them unavoidably to require high intricacy in metre and rhyme scheme. Possession is a tricky matter. Internal voices need all the controls they can contrive. Make it hard enough for the speakers and there is a better chance that something may be said.

They taught me so to be at most a moderator. I had been deliberately and with explicit intent beating up heavyweight prose about poetry through three full decades. It was refreshing to spread some sail. The more so since I found myself being taken now close up along the other side of the great veil. What prose had tried to analyse let verse learn to put together. They were concerned in their different ways with the same enigma: "What's it about but doubt?"

My type specimen, both for aims and for intricacy of means, is "Waking Thoughts" (*Times Literary Supplement*, 13th December, 1965). And it was comfortingly like the closure of a circle when Conrad Aiken, the first and best reviewer *Principles* (1924) had (see *A Reviewer's ABC*, p. 75), sent me a postcard saying: "What a magnificent thing. Total satisfaction, that's what! It says it all. Thanks." The voices in the poem, however, keep on telling me that they still have something to say.

*   *   *

It was only at the age of sixty that I. A. Richards, after having established a position as the most ranging and supple (and subtle) theorist and practical critic of poetry of his day began to write verse. Those whose lives and thoughts had been greatly influenced by such great books as *Principles of Literary Criticism*, *Practical Criticism*, and *Mencius on the Mind* found in the poems not a different personality, or different preoccupations, but the same man: after a life so long (to adapt Chaucer) he had learned the hard craft. The central mystery of life for Richards has always been the mystery of language – the way in which the words we use "tease us out of thought," hint at or whisper of meanings we had not intended to put into them. "The question is," said Humpty-Dumpty to Alice, "who is to be master?" Can we make words mean just what we want them to mean, as Humpty-Dumpty thought: or should we take their orders about what they mean, as Alice thought? For Richards, the answer is a compromise: we can push words around a little, but they can push us around too though in directions we do not expect. In a cosmos in which there is not any obvious order or direction, they can help us to create order and direction: or perhaps they nudge us into doing so, and there may be some order and direction – but benign or ominous? – after all. In his handling of rhythms, a certain ghostliness and wistfulness, combined with a gift for making disconcerting jokes, Richards resembles poets like Hardy or de la Mare, poets of the suggestion and the half-tone, poets who leave it to the reader to work a riddle out, rather than a poet about whom he has written brilliantly, T. S. Eliot. One catches echoes sometimes also of his own most brilliant pupil, Empson, and through it all, as Mrs. Joan Bennett has noted, there runs the serious wit of Donne. Some critics have been put off Richards's poems by the thought that this is merely a sage versifying thoughts that his prose has made familiar to us. But there is a mage as well as a sage here; and the poems are thoughts versified – they are what Pound called *logopoeia*, the riddling, teasing, and delighting dance of words and thoughts.

– G. S. Fraser

RICKWORD, (John) Edgell. Born in Colchester, Essex, 22 October 1898. Educated at Colchester Grammar School; Pembroke College, Oxford. Served in the Royal Army during World War I. Editor, *Calendar of Modern Letters*, 1925–27; Associate Editor, *Left Review*, 1934–38; Editor, *Our Time*, 1944–47. Recipient: Arts Council Prize, 1966. Address: c/o E. and J. Stevens, 2 Prospect Road, London N.W.2, England.

PUBLICATIONS

Verse

Behind the Eyes. London, Sidgwick and Jackson, 1921.
Invocations to Angels, and The Happy New Year. London, Wishart, 1928.
Twittingpan and Some Others. London, Wishart, 1931.
Collected Poems. London, Bodley Head, 1947.
Fifty Poems. London, Enitharmon Press, 1970.
Collected Poems and Translations. Cheadle, Cheshire, Carcanet Press, 1974.

Short Stories

Love One Another: Seven Tales. London, Mandrake Press, 1929.

Other

Rimbaud: The Boy and the Poet. London, Heinemann, and New York, Knopf, 1924; revised edition, Castle Hedingham, Essex, Daimon Press, 1963.
William Wordsworth 1770–1850. London, Bureau of Current Affairs, 1950.
Essays and Opinions 1921–1931, edited by Alan Young. Cheadle, Cheshire, Carcanet Press, 1974.

Editor, *Scrutinies by Various Writers.* London, Wishart, 1928.
Editor, *Scrutinies Volume II.* London, Wishart, 1931.
Editor, with Jack Lindsay, *A Handbook for Freedom: A Record of English Democracy Through Twelve Centuries.* London, Lawrence and Wishart, 1939.

RICKWORDCONTEMPORARY POETS

Editor, *Soviet Writers Reply to English Writers' Questions.* London, Society for Cultural Relations with the U.S.S.R., 1948.
Editor, *Further Studies in a Dying Culture,* by Christopher Caudwell. London, Bodley Head, 1949.
Editor, *Radical Squibs and Loyal Ripostes: Satirical Pamphlets of the Regency Period, 1819–1821.* Bath, Adams and Dart, 1971.

Translator (as John Mavin), with Douglas Mavin Garman, *Charles Baudelaire: A Biography,* by François Porché. London, Wishart, 1928.
Translator, *La Princesse aux Soleils, and Harmonie* (bilingual edition), by Ronald Firbank. London, Enitharmon Press, 1973.

Critical Studies: "The Poetic Mind of Edgell Rickword" by David Holbrook, in *Essays in Criticism* (Aylesbury, Buckinghamshire), July 1962; in *English Poetry 1900–1950: An Assessment,* by C. H. Sisson, London, Hart Davis, 1971.

Edgell Rickword comments:

Traditional idiosyncratic.

*   *   *

Edgell Rickword is old enough to have served in the First World War, and his memories of that experience are preserved in a few distinguished poems that deserve to be better known. Here, for instance, is the opening of "The Soldier Addresses His Body":

> I shall be mad if you get smashed about;
> we've had good times together, you and I;
> although you groused a bit when luck was out,
> and a girl turned us down, or we went dry.

Here and in the poems that Rickword went on to write in the 1920's one sees a remarkable poise; an openness to disparate elements of experience, together with an ability to relate them in a poetic fashion that may have been ironical but was also deeply felt. Rickword came to poetic maturity in the period when T. S. Eliot was extolling the Metaphysical virtues, and above all the capacity to fuse thought and feeling in a single response. Eliot found this quality in such poets as Donne and Marvell, who were greatly talked about and admired in the twenties, but Rickword was one of the few English poets who were able to make creative use of their example. Some of his verse is undoubtedly open to the charge of being over-intellectual and hence obscure, but the obscurity, where it exists, arises from the poet's determination to pursue a particular argument to its conclusion, rather than from mere mystification for its own sake. There are times, admittedly, when Rickword's diction seems a little too consciously mannered and arch; lines such as "as though your spirit, overweighed, / tired of the saxophone's pert nonchalance" may seem a slightly faded example of the bright twenties' manner, though the poem from which they are taken, "Strange Party," is impressive as a whole. In addition to his poems of serious wit, Rickword was a sharp but urbane satirist of the cultural scene of the twenties. After 1930 he wrote no more poetry, except for "To the Wife of a Non-interventionist Statesman," a brilliant piece of harsh political satire arising from the Spanish Civil War. It was a real loss for English poetry that such an admirable writer produced so little, and equally unfortunate that what he has written is not better known.

– Bernard Bergonzi

RIDDELL, Alan. Australian. Born in Townsville, Queensland, 16 April 1927. Educated at Merchiston Castle School, Edinburgh; Edinburgh University, M.A. Served in the Royal Navy. Founding Editor, *Lines Review*, Edinburgh, 1952–55, 1962–67. Since 1963, Sub-Editor, *Daily Telegraph*, London. Educational Supplement Editor, *Sydney Morning Herald*, 1969–70. Concrete and Visual Poetry Exhibitions – One Man Show: New 57 Gallery, Edinburgh, 1971; Group Shows: Homage to Apollinaire, ICA, London, 1968; Gallery A, Sydney, 1969; Expo/Internacional de Novisima Poesia, Buenos Aires, 1969; International Concrete Poetry, Zagreb, 1969; Stedelijk Museum, Amsterdam, 1970; Elvaston Gallery, London, 1972; New 57 Gallery, Edinburgh, 1973; Europlia 73, Brussels, 1973. Recipient: Heinemann Award, 1956; Scottish Arts Council Prize, 1968. Address: 23 Chapel Side, Bayswater, London W.2, England.

PUBLICATIONS

Verse

> *Beneath the Summer.* Edinburgh, Macdonald, 1953.
> *Majorcan Interlude.* Edinburgh, Macdonald, 1960.
> *The Stopped Landscape and Other Poems.* London, Hutchinson, 1968.
> *Eclipse.* London, Calder and Boyars, 1972.

Other

> Editor, with others, *Young Commonwealth Poets '65.* London, Heinemann, 1965.
> Editor, *Typewriter Art.* London, London Magazine Editions, 1975.

Manuscript Collection: National Library of Scotland, Edinburgh.

*   *   *

As editor of *Lines Review* at two periods, first from 1952 to 1955 and again from 1962 to 1967, Alan Riddell made a valuable contribution to Scottish literary life at a time when, unlike now, the opportunities for publishing poetry in Scotland were meagre. His own poetry, not prolific, shows little interaction with the varieties of language and mode in the range of work he edited: it is withdrawn, rather, to a relatively confined and private area. Its slightness cannot be denied but need not be insisted upon, since it does not itself make any strong claim upon the reader's involvement. Undoubtedly *felt* personal experience tends to be dissipated through recourse to blatant clichés ("the muddy lies of time," "time's ever spinning wheel"), and even in a poem which sharply records memories of his Australian boyhood he is content to relate his subsequent life to these terms: "So the voyage / began, and ever the distance grew outward / from the centre that was and ever / the reefs became thicker, the storms more frequent and fierce." Thus both his joys and his wounds slip in and out of his often chatty verse too smoothly for the reader to grasp much.

On the other hand, short clear poems describing moments of unusual perception ("Dream," "Goldfish at an Angle," "Boulders Underwater") point in another direction and, following this, his sensibility has found a more satisfactory medium in his concrete poems. Granted, he works here well within the frontiers charted by others, and indulges in "impure" elements such as verbal and pictorial puns: yet this frankly literary content of his graphic poems does allow him to comment on human predicaments with a more fully realised impact than in his ealier work.

– Robin Fulton

RIDING, Laura (Mrs. Schuyler B. Jackson).   American.   Born in New York City, 16 January 1901. Address: Box 35, Wabasso, Florida 32970, U.S.A.

PUBLICATIONS

Verse

> *The Close Chaplet* (as Laura Riding Gottschalk).   New York, Adelphi, and London, Hogarth Press, 1926.
> *Voltaire: A Biographical Fantasy* (as Laura Riding Gottschalk).   London, Hogarth Press, 1927.
> *Love As Love, Death As Death.*   London, Seizin Press, 1928.
> *Poems: A Joking Word.*   London, Cape, 1930.
> *Twenty Poems Less.*   Paris, Hours Press, 1930.
> *Though Gently.*   Deyá, Mallorca, Seizin Press, 1930.
> *Laura and Francisca: A Poem.*   Deyá, Mallorca, Seizin Press, 1931.
> *The Life of the Dead.*   London, Barker, 1933.
> *The First Leaf.*   Deyá, Mallorca, Seizin Press, 1933.
> *Poet: A Lying Word.*   London, Barker, 1933.
> *Americans.*   Los Angeles, Primavera, 1934.
> *The Second Leaf.*   Deyá, Mallorca, Seizin Press, 1935.
> *Collected Poems.*   New York, Random House, and London, Cassell, 1938.
> *Selected Poems: In Five Sets.*   London, Faber, 1970; New York, Norton, 1973.

Novels

> *No Decency Left,* with Robert Graves (as Barbara Rich).   London, Cape, 1932.
> *14A,* with George Ellidge.   London, Barker, 1934.
> *A Trojan Ending.*   Deyá, Mallorca, Seizin Press, London, Constable, and New York, Random House, 1937.

Short Stories

> *Experts Are Puzzled.* London, Cape, 1930.
> *Progress of Stories.* Deyá, Mallorca, Seizin Press, and London, Constable, 1935.
> *Lives of Wives.* London, Cassell, and New York, Random House, 1939.

Other

> *A Survey of Modernist Poetry*, with Robert Graves. London, Heinemann, 1927; New York, Doubleday, 1928.
> *A Pamphlet Against Anthologies*, with Robert Graves. London, Cape, 1928; as *Against Anthologies*, New York, Doubleday, 1928.
> *Contemporaries and Snobs.* London, Cape, 1928.
> *Anarchism Is Not Enough.* London, Cape, and New York, Doubleday, 1928.
> *Four Unposted Letters to Catherine.* Paris, Hours Press, 1930.
> *The World and Ourselves: Letters about the World Situation from 65 People of Different Professions and Pursuits.* London, Chatto and Windus, 1938.
> *The Telling.* London, Athlone Press, 1972; New York, Harper, 1973.

> Editor, *Everybody's Letters.* London, Barker, 1933.
> Contributing Editor, *Epilogue I, II,* and *III.* Deyá, Mallorca, Seizin Press, and London, Constable, 1935, 1936, 1937.

> Translator, with Robert Graves, *Almost Forgotten Germany*, by Georg Schwarz. Deyá, Mallorca, Seizin Press, London, Constable, and New York, Random House, 1936.

Laura (Riding) Jackson comments:

My first book of poems was published as by Laura Riding Gottschalk, this surname being mine by an early marriage which terminated in divorce. Thereafter my name, authorial and personal, was Laura Riding, until 1941, when I married Schuyler B. Jackson, American poet and critical writer; my authorial name became then Laura (Riding) Jackson, with "Laura Riding" used for re-publication of work so signed. After the publication of my *Collected Poems* (1938), and my return to the U.S.A. in 1939 – I had been long abroad – I renounced poetry, for reasons of principle. I now permit the republication of my poems if a statement on this renunciation accompanies them.

In my high-school years I received extraordinarily good language-education. At Cornell University I was also very fortunate in teachers (in languages, literature, history). I left before completing my undergraduate career, living then, as a young professor's wife, in the sphere of two other universities, doing some studying, and continuing the writing of poems, become important to me at Cornell – and publishing some in magazines. At the close of 1925, after a period of uncertainty, I went abroad to live. I had found my American fellow-poets more concerned with making individualistic play upon the composition-habitudes of poetic tradition than with what concerned me: how to strike a personal accent in poetry that would be at once an authentic truth-impulsion, of universal force; I saw them as combining something less than complete poetic seriousness with something less than complete personal seriousness. In the English and cross-Atlantic literary atmosphere, there was, instead of crowding individualism, a loose assemblage of unsure positions, occupied with a varying show of modernistic daring; I had there solitariness in which to probe the reality of poetry as a spiritual, not merely literary, inheritance.

In my pursuits abroad, which, besides poetry, included criticism, story-writing, activity in printing and publishing ventures, the editing of a literary-critical miscellany, I became increasingly aware of the prime dependence of worth, in everything formed of words, on observance of the linguistic integrities. I conceived of a work that would help to dissipate the confusion existing in the knowledge of word-meanings – where, I believed, all probity of word must start. This project did not take deep root until after I returned to America. My husband joined me in it, bringing to it poetic experience and linguistic learning and a moral sense of language of his own, and strong-heartedness for facing difficulties, of which there were many, within and outside the task. The resultant book was far advanced when he died, in 1968. I am trying to complete it.

[Asked if she considers herself primarily a poet, Laura (Riding) Jackson says:] Up to 1940 I considered myself centrally a poet, with every other writing activity coming under a government of values (a unity of values prerequisite for truth) that I conceived of as centrally poetic. This moral and spiritual emphasis on poetry I took to be practically justified by the linguistic urgency in poetry towards rightness of word; poetry seemed where the verbal maximum could be one with and the same as the truth-maximum. When, after long-sustained faith in this seeming poetic potential, and pressing of the linguistic possibilities of poetic utterance towards further and further limits, I comprehended that poetry had no provision in it for ultimate practical attainment of that rightness of word that *is* truth, but led on ever only to a temporizing less-than-truth (the lack eked out with illusions of truth produced by physical word-effects), *I stopped.* I stopped – but I went on to search for the way to that rightness of word that is truth, and as the natural yield of words cultivated for truth's sake, not as the product of an *art* of words. . . . And in so doing I did not, renouncing poetry, transfer allegiance to some other form of literary procedure. I intensified my application to the problem of the knowledge of the meanings of words, and, for the rest, dedicated myself to the saying of what I might be able to say with a more far-reaching trueness of word than I had attained in any special literary climate, poetic or otherwise.

[Asked if she identifies herself with a particular school of poetry, she explains:] I have never belonged to any "school" of poetry – though the values I defined for the poetic use of words, which were nothing other than the values of language treated not only as a verbal discipline but one on which the intellectual integrity and total spiritual worth of poems depended, became associated in people's minds as a school of my instituting. (Thus W. B. Yeats, in a letter: "I wrote today to Laura Riding . . . that her school was too thoughtful, reasonable, truthful, that poets were good liars. . . .") All I did was to endeavor to make poetic goodness – the goodness of the "good" poem – comprehensive enough for the good poem to be no mere performance on the stage of a tradition, but something *literally* good, having so much reality as language that it fulfilled the function of language of authenticating the reality of the experiences of human consciousness (this function still only very imperfectly fulfilled in human speaking and writing, on the whole). This amounted to making the linguistic conscience the monitor of poetic goodness.

I had no models, in my particular approach to the question of what "good" is in poetry, no collaborators: the approach was, simply, a unique kind of seriousness directed upon poetry. I lessoned poets with whom I had association, in this work of literal poetic goodness. Though all took away something, and in one case at least the something was massive, none gave much thought to the depths of general principle from which this "higher" literalism, this new poetic gospel of linguistic probity, came – their interest, and therefore their gains, did not exceed the literary. Many poets outside personal range, known and unknown to me, have taken away something variedly, from the linguistic atmosphere of my poems, with superficial results – appearances of new linguistic distinction, and verbal sophistication, not backed by internal events of new experience in terms of principle, the travel within to new places in thought. In the case of one poet never more than a stranger to me, every abstractable manner of tone, diction, rhythmic movement, of mine was worked into the technique of this other – with not mere period-consequences. An application of my method of textual testing of poetic substance to a certain poem, in a book in which I was a collaborator, became the starting point from which a particular poet drew out the line of a critical career; and the resultant diffusion of the idea of such a method caused it to have further part in poetry-criticism developments, in further separation from its background-thought, as the mark of the "new" (for a time). Thus was it with me as to influences, being of a "school," or generating a "school": I have no influences on myself to record, or membership in any school. (In the early twenties I was made an honorary member of the group of Southern poets that called itself "The Fugitives." But I had no programmatic association with them. The membership was a tribute to my work.) My influence on others, directly and remotely, has been extensive and wasted. I think the reason of this is in the moral condition of poets; they have taken on the morals of their time which are not good enough for a thorough concern with goodness, poetic or otherwise.

*   *   *

In an early poem, Laura Riding asks:

> But for familiar sense what need can be
> Of my most singular device or me . . .
> "As Well As Any Other"

The "singular device" became more and more recognizable as a virtue of dedication in the development of the whole of her work: criticism, stories, editorial and collaborative writings, as well as the poems, and then the later post-poetic rebeginning in a new closeness to words themselves as "secreting in their meanings a natural eloquence of truth" (a recent comment of hers). Her purposes were and are supra-individual: she is bent upon locating the yet unfound in thought, saying the yet unsaid "For All Our Sakes" (the title of another early poem). Her work implies necessary reorientations of values and positions: it tends to test the minds of its readers and critics.

To turn to Laura Riding's poetry is to turn to her thought also. She warns:

> The nicest thought is only gossip
> If merchandized into plain language and sold
> For so much understanding to the minute . . .
> "The Talking World"

Some of the poems will be found immediately lucid. Others, the kind to which the long-celebrated difficulty is attributed, will make one stop – not just "stop and think" but stop and read. If this necessity is "difficulty," it is associated with the virtues of the poems, and contributory to a happy consequence in the immediate freshness they have on each return to them. The language has precision, but also litheness of expression-movement; it is language alive and at work. Because there is a right way in, and no other way, one may feel puzzled or dazzled until it is found. A poem of hers is a process; one must travel with it, and, if one does, one "understands" because the process develops and defines itself. This approach is outlined as a reading-method in *A Survey of Modernist Poetry* (pp. 138–49), with reference to "The Rugged Black of Anger."

The strong quality of personal voice and presence permeating Laura Riding's poems can induce the idea that they are full of private references, while her never-absent governing sense of the universal context of all particular contexts can suggest the label "abstract." These two tendences are interlocked, function as a unity, and so demand integration in the readers' minds: no poem-subject of hers is so general that there is not an immediate personal bearing, but its large force will be lost if realistic private identifications are sought for. When she writes, for instance, of "the tragedy of selfhood / And self-haunting," the case is (she avers) not a narrative of personal tragedy but of the approach to knowledge of the human necessity of graduation from the self as tragic. Thus her sensibility of personal crisis as an aspect of a total human event of crisis makes itself felt, as it pulsates through the *Collected Poems*, within an ever-widening emphasis upon the universal context:

> The lone defiance blossoms failure,
> But risk of all by all beguiles
> Fate's wreckage into similar smiles.
>   "Doom in Bloom"

Much of her thought has a quality of inexorability: "The mercy of truth – it is to be truth." Her poetic standard was for the perfect: the rightness stipulated was "for always"; she meant real survival, minds on the side of permanence:

> Whole is by breaking and by mending.
> The body is a day of ruin,
> The mind, a moment of repair.
> A day is not a day of mind
> Until all lifetime is repaired despair . . .
>   "Autobiography of the Present"

Death, in her poetic – and general – sense of the nature of things, is, as she has recently put it, "the reality of the necessity of an end, for that which has a limit. But the coming to a term of the limited is not mere predestined nullification: the mark of the end is a mark of rightness, and so death has, thus, aspects of significance and character which spell the perfect and the true, not mortality and loss." The mental perspective in which she views death can be found in depiction both stern and touched with happy wit:

> Exchange the multiplied bewilderment
> For a single presentation of fact by fairness;
> And the revelation will be instantaneous.
> We shall all die quickly.
>   "There Is Much at Work"

Her controls of the solemn and the large themes, the report of their reality as belonging intimately to the human experience, are everywhere firm. But not only is severity of definition and vision tempered with tenderness: the culminating words are often of a profoundly tender cheer, as in the transcendent "The Flowering Urn," where the fond supersedes the grim:

> . . . Will rise the same peace that held
> Before fertility's lie awoke
> The virgin sleep of Mother All:
> The same but for the way in flowering
> It speaks of fruits that could not be.

("Mother All" comes with characteristic cleanness. She uses such figures with serious ontological intent, not for purposes of mythological rhetoric.)

There is an essence of simplicity in these poems. Their many questions are approaches to answers. "What knows in me? / Is it only something inside / That I can't see?" comes from the beginning, and "What were we, then, / Before the being of ourselves began?" from the end, of the *Collected Poems* progression, while almost at its centre "As Many Questions As Answers" reveals the implicit unity of the process. This spirit of simplicity brings the problem of knowledge within the intelligence's intimate range; it informs not only Laura Riding's poems but also such propositions of hers as "we experience reality to the degree to which we are at once a question about reality and its answer" (*Epilogue III*, 1937). She has not been afraid to let her intelligence press its points with the insistence of a child-like refusal to settle for no-answer. She pictures the alternative to this mental mode in rather passionate assault:

> Too orthodox maturity
> For such heresy of child-remaining –
> On these the dusty blight of books descends,
> Weird, pundit babyhoods
> Whose blinking vision stammers out the past
> Like a big-lettered foetus-future.
>
> "Unread Pages"

The internal simplicity of her poetic offering, the unity of its motivations and attitudes – so much missed when readers do not read *into* it, but content (or discontent) themselves with surface impressions of "difficulty" or "obscurity" – can provide a key to her ultimate renouncing of poetry. One might say that she moved from an initial belief that the answers we must find with our right questions could be found in poetry by its implicit invitation to (its demand of) truthfulness of word – never, for her, an obscure intellectualized or sentimentally spiritualized ideal, but a literal objective – to an ultimate feeling that poetry itself limits achievement in the unclosable gap between the verbal realms of question and answer. Her preface to the *Collected Poems* of 1938 is a soaring and persuasive defence of poetry; that to her *Selected Poems* of 1970 tells how she has "devoutly renounced allegiance to poetry as a profession and faith in it as an institution." To turn from one preface to the other is to feel one's loose world of poetry and prose, ordinary and literary language, tightening into tensions that suggest the labour of opening up that "other language-path" that has been Mrs. Jackson's commitment since 1940. The appearance of *The Telling* in its book form has afforded sight of the transformed context, a newly simple view of the objective of truth of word as more than a categorically literary one.

The primary effect of Laura Riding's work as a whole is that it is "there." It stands firm as a monument in the shifting literary scene, a contribution of grave substance. Acknowledgement of her work's right to candid regard is avoided, in much comment on it, by concentrating on her and her poems as the source of "influence" on a handful of other poets. Such fractioning approaches tend to reduce her poetry, her thought, her language, to the status of a repository of complicated ideas, and her personal nature to that of one pressing programmes of ideals. One finds the persons influenced represented as having purged and simplified the one, in profiting from it, and having survived the moral overtaxing of the other. Thus is blocked appreciation both of the specific internal potency of her work, and, in general, of the true power of influence which resides in what a work means self-definingly and what it excites itself of fresh resolve of mind to distinct expression, kindred in sincerity. (This power is also, as in Laura Riding's work itself, "there.")

To the effect of Laura Riding's working self, there is testimony from two statements by Robert Graves (*Epilogue III*, 1937, and the preface to his own *Collected Poems*, 1938): ". . . my personal experience satisfied me that you have no motive outside that of saying what you say, that there is no discrepancy between what you say and what you do, and that what you say in general you apply to every major and minor particular of daily existence. . ."; "I have to thank Laura Riding for her constructive and detailed criticism of my poems in various stages of composition – a generosity from which so many contemporary poets besides myself have benefited."

– Alan Clark

RIDLER, Anne (Barbara). British. Born in Rugby, Warwickshire, 30 July 1912. Educated at Downe House School; King's College, London, diploma in journalism 1932. Married Vivian Ridler in 1938; has four children. Member of the editorial department, Faber and Faber, publishers, London, 1935–40. Recipient: Oscar Blumenthal Prize, 1954, and Union League Civic and Arts Foundation Prize, 1955 (*Poetry*, Chicago). Address: 14 Stanley Road, Oxford, England.

PUBLICATIONS

Verse

Poems. London, Oxford University Press, 1939.
A Dream Observed and Other Poems. London, Editions Poetry, 1941.
The Nine Bright Shiners. London, Faber, 1943.
The Golden Bird and Other Poems. London, Faber, 1951.
A Matter of Life and Death. London, Faber, 1959.
Selected Poems. New York, Macmillan, 1961.
Some Time After and Other Poems. London, Faber, 1972.

Plays

Cain (produced Letchworth, Hertfordshire, 1943; London, 1944). London, Editions Poetry, 1943.
The Shadow Factory (produced London, 1945). London, Faber, 1946.
Henry Bly (produced London, 1947). Included in *Henry Bly and Other Plays*, 1950.
Henry Bly and Other Plays (includes *The Mask* and *The Missing Bridegroom*). London, Faber, 1950.
The Mask and The Missing Bridegroom (produced London, 1951). Included in *Henry Bly and Other Plays*, 1950.
The Trial of Thomas Cranmer, music by Bryan Kelly (produced Oxford, 1956). London, Faber, 1956.
The Departure, music by Elizabeth Maconchy (produced London, 1961). Included in *Some Time After and Other Poems*, 1972.

Who Is My Neighbour? (produced Leeds, 1961). Included in *Who Is My Neighbour? and How Bitter the Bread*, 1963.
Who is My Neighbour? and How Bitter the Bread. London, Faber, 1963.
The Jesse Tree: A Masque in Verse, music by Elizabeth Maconchy (produced Dorchester, Oxfordshire, 1970). London, Lyrebird Press, 1972.

Other

Olive Willis and Downe House: An Adventure in Education. London, Murray, 1967.

Editor, *Shakespeare Criticism, 1919–1935.* London and New York, Oxford University Press, 1936.
Editor, *The Little Book of Modern Verse.* London, Faber, 1941.
Editor, *Best Ghost Stories.* London, Faber, 1945.
Editor, *The Faber Book of Modern Verse*, revised edition. London, Faber, 1951.
Editor, *The Image of the City and Other Essays*, by Charles Williams. London, Oxford University Press, 1958.
Editor, *Shakespeare Criticism, 1935–1960.* London and New York, Oxford University Press, 1963.
Editor, *Poems and Some Letters of James Thomson.* London, Centaur Press, 1963.
Editor, *Thomas Traherne.* London, Oxford University Press, 1966.

*   *   *

Anne Ridler's poems demonstrate a triumph (minor, but still perfectly valid) of intelligence and skill in dealing with quiet, domestic themes and "occasional" subjects: meditations on married love, observations and celebrations of children, recordings of places and pictures. They are characteristically low-toned, but a distinct and not at all tepid personality comes through, with a strong sense of loyalty, the need for roots, and an awareness of the divine transfiguring the commonplace.

The quality of the best earlier poems (such as "At Parting" and "For a Child Expected" in *The Nine Bright Shiners*) lies partly in their assured rhythmical sense, traditional and yet not slavishly so, and partly in the transparent sweetness of their diction:

> Since we through war a while must part
> Sweetheart, and learn to lose
> Daily use
> Of all that satisfied our heart:
> Lay up those secrets and those powers
> Wherewith you pleased and cherished me these two years.

It is a note not often heard in contemporary English poetry; the saccharine flavour of women's magazine verse is quite different. Anne Ridler has herself said that she has learned from Wyatt, and Eliot seems to have been a liberating and beneficial modern influence; but Mrs. Ridler's proper poetic ancestry seems to lie in the 17th century, in Herbert. In "Deus Absconditus" (from *The Golden Bird*), Eliot and Herbert both seem somewhere in the background, but not obtrusively so:

Here he is endured, here he is adored.
And anywhere. Yet it is a long pursuit,
Carrying the junk and treasure of an ancient creed,
To a love who keeps his faith by seeming mute
And deaf, and dead indeed.

Mrs. Ridler's most ambitious work has been in partly or wholly dramatic form
(e.g., *Cain, The Shadow Factory, The Trial of Thomas Cranmer*, the Christmas broadcasts and the title-poem from *The Golden Bird*), but none of these is wholly
satisfactory. Much the best of the longer poems is "A Matter of Life and Death,"
which gave its title to her 1959 volume. This is a two-voiced meditation, of mother
and child, on a birth:

I did not see the iris move,
I did not feel the unfurling of my love . . .

I have seen the light of day,
Was it sight or taste or smell?
What I have been, who can tell?
What I shall be, who can say?

Anne Ridler is not at all a prolific poet, and her slimness of output, together with
her lack of any self-assertiveness, seems unjustly to have made her work much less
noticed than it should be.

– Anthony Thwaite

ROBINSON, Roland (Edward). British. Born in Balbriggan, Ireland, 14 June
1912. Educated in secondary schools. Member, Kirsova Ballet, 1944–47. Ballet
Critic, 1956–66, and currently, Book Reviewer, *Sydney Morning Herald*. Editor,
Poetry Magazine, Sydney. President, Poetry Society of Australia. Recipient: Grace
Leven Award, 1952; Commonwealth Literary Fellowship, 1954; Australian Council
for the Arts grant, 1973; Australian Book Council Award, for non-fiction, 1974.
Address: Woollahra Golf Club, O'Sullivan Road, Rose Bay, New South Wales
2029, Australia.

PUBLICATIONS

Verse

Beyond the Grass-Tree Spears: Verse. Adelaide, Jindyworobak Publications-
    Georgian House, 1944.
Language of the Sand: Poems. Sydney, Lyre Bird, 1948.
Tumult of the Swans. Sydney, Edwards and Shaw, 1953.
Deep Well. Sydney, Edwards and Shaw, 1962.

Grendel. Brisbane, Jacaranda Press, 1967.
Selected Poems. Sydney, Angus and Robertson, 1971.

Play

Television Play: *The Ballad of the Aborigines,* 1972.

Short Stories

Black-Feller, White-Feller. Sydney, Angus and Robertson, 1958.

Other

Legend and Dreaming: Legends of the Dream-Time of the Australian Aborigines. Sydney, Edwards and Shaw, 1952.
The Feathered Serpent: The Mythological Genesis and Recreative Ritual of the Aboriginal Tribes of the Northern Territory of Australia. Sydney, Edwards and Shaw, 1956.
The Man Who Sold His Dreaming. Sydney, Currawong Publications, 1965.
Aborigine Myths and Legends. Melbourne, Sun Books, 1966.
The Australian Aborigine in Colour. Sydney, Reed, 1968.
The Drift of Things, 1914–1952 (autobiography). Melbourne, Macmillan, 1973.

Editor, *Wandjina: Children of the Dreamtime: Aboriginal Myths and Legends.* Brisbane, Jacaranda Press, 1968.

Critical Study: by Evan Jones, in *The Literature of Australia,* Melbourne, Penguin, 1964.

Roland Robinson comments:

[I belong to the] Jindyworobak school – devoted to poetry with distinctive Australian environment.

Themes are Australia, its fauna and flora, its human inhabitants, Aboriginal and European. Latest theme is involvement in Mankind in its modern environment of cities, industry, etc.

A poem should have the texture and character of its subject. I detest abstract cerebral verse. A poem's sound should argue for its sense. A poem's form should be sculptural. A poet should bring all his senses alive on the page: sight, hearing, taste, smell. A poem's rhythm should express its emotion. A poem should agonize to find its own unique form whether it be a Shakespearean sonnet or the Twenty-third Psalm. Prescribed form is meaningless.

Influences are Edward Thomas, Anglo-Saxon Poetry, Ted Hughes, R. S. Thomas.

*   *   *

Something of a legend in his own lifetime, Roland Robinson has become a familiar figure reading (brilliantly) his own poems in lecture halls and schools across Australia, his shock of white hair flowing and, latterly, a white wolfhound in attendance. His own career has been colourful enough, ranging from jackeroo to ballet critic for the *Sydney Morning Herald* to greenkeeper of a municipal golf links. He was largely instrumental in organising a writer's cooperative publishing venture (the Lyre Bird Writers series) around 1950 and has, in the early 1970's, revived this series in order to publish the work of younger poets. With this background of activity and variety, it is perhaps surprising that Roland Robinson's own poetry remained for so long centrally concerned with a very private search through the desert and bird-and-animal landscape of outback Australia, a lyrical and often delicate Wanderer's voyage of discovery and communion. The many short lyrics published in magazines and even books over some twenty years were collected and arranged in the volume *Deep Well* in a way that showed them to be, not merely occasional campfire nature pieces, but components of a definite search and expression of a centrally understood vision. *Deep Well* remains the centre of Roland Robinson's achievement, and must be regarded as expressing something close to the very core of that poetic reawakening that began in Australia during the Second World War years, a reawakening that for the first time directed Australians unself-consciously to their own landscape, and with a language at last equipped to approach it. It is interesting that of the two poets most occupied with this task one, Douglas Stewart, was a New Zealander; the other, Roland Robinson, was born in Ireland. Roland Robinson will be remembered for naming, for us, points of a journey both private and universal.

– Thomas W. Shapcott

ROBSON, Jeremy. British.   Born in Llandudno, Carnarvonshire, Wales, 5 September 1939. Educated at Haberdashers' Aske's School; Regent Street Polytechnic, London, diploma in journalism, 1960. Married Carole de Botton in 1964. Editor, Aldus Books, London, 1963–69. Poetry Critic, *Tribune*, London, 1962–72; Chief Editor, Vallentine, Mitchell, publishers, London, 1969–72; Editor, Woburn Press, London, 1972–73. Since 1974, Managing Director, Robson Books, London. Poetry and Jazz Concert organizer. Address: 37 Briardale Gardens, London NW3 7PN, England.

PUBLICATIONS

Verse

Penny Pamphlet.   London, Writers Club, 1961.
Poems for Jazz.   Leicester, L. Weston, 1963.
Thirty-Three Poems.   London, Sidgwick and Jackson, 1964.
In Focus.   London, Allison and Busby, 1970.
Poems Out of Israel.   London, Turret Books, 1970.

Recordings: *Blues for the Lonely*, Columbia; *Before Night*, Argo; *Poetry and Jazz in Concert*, Argo; *Poetry and Jazz in Concert 250*, Argo.

Other

> Editor, *Letters to Israel: Summer 1967.*   London, Vallentine Mitchell, 1968.
> Editor, *Poems from Poetry and Jazz in Concert: An Anthology.*   London, Souvenir Press, 1969.
> Editor, *The Young British Poets.*   London, Chatto and Windus, 1971.
> Editor, *Corgi Modern Poets in Focus 2* and *4.*   London, Corgi, 2 vols, 1971.
> Editor, *Poetry Dimension I: A Living Record of the Poetry Year.*   London, Robson Books, 1973.

*   *   *

Jeremy Robson's poetry reveals a man assuming the position of an ordinary person in an ordinary world – then turning aside, now and then, into a poem that expresses and comments on the unease, the distaste, the pain, even the horror which that world bears in upon his perceptions. Clearly his everyman persona is at the mercy of outer forces:

> Call my name, sing your psalms, make your war,
> speak your speech, Save my Soul. . .
> Break down my door: I wait.

His poems are replete with the oppressions and diminutions we suffer in the city: underground rush hours, domination by all officialdom and authority, the importunings of the media and of the consumer society, the heaped-up grinding annoyances "of the season's / fickle mood, of today's speech, tomorrow's / march, of the drizzle in the amber lights." But among his experience of these workaday miseries he does not overlook the larger fears and oppressions that afflict us: political upheaval and military threat, social and racial conflict, cruelty and murder, "Rivers to the ocean / lovers to the war. . . ."

He communicates these concerns in a restrained free verse, often partially disciplined by semi-stanzaic forms of irregular rhyme. His use of language is determinedly colloquial, reflecting the "ordinariness" of his chosen persona, but leaving options for frequent ironic asides and moments of humour on the one hand and a heightening into emotional intensity on the other. Recently his output of poetry has slackened somewhat – as have his public appearances (he was one of the prime movers of the poetry-reading boom in Britain during the sixties). But his most recent work shows a steady strengthening and maturing of his poetic intentions, and an ever more sure touch in their expression.

– Douglas Hill

ROCHE, Paul. British.   Born in India, 25 September 1928. Educated at Gregorian University, Rome, Ph.B., Ph.L. 1949. Married to Clarissa Tanner; has five children. Instructor, Smith College, Northampton, Massachusetts, 1957–59. Since 1972, Poet-in-Residence, California Institute of the Arts, Valencia. Recipient: Bollingen Foundation Fellowship, 1958; Alice Fay di Castagnola Award, 1965; Alice Hunt

Bartlett Prize, 1966. Agents: International Famous Agency, 1301 Avenue of the Americas, New York, New York, 10019, U.S.A.; Miss Christina Bernard, 7 Well Road, London N.W.3. Address: The Stables, The Street, Aldermaston, Berkshire, England.

PUBLICATIONS

Verse

> *The Rank Obstinacy of Things: A Selection of Poems.* New York, Sheed and Ward, 1962.
> *22 November 1963 (The Catharsis of Anguish).* London, Adam Books, 1965.
> *Ode to the Dissolution of Mortality.* New York, Madison Avenue Church Press, 1966.
> *All Things Considered: Poems.* London, Duckworth, 1966; as *All Things Considered and Other Poems,* New York, Weybright and Talley, 1968.
> *To Tell the Truth: Poems.* London, Duckworth, 1967.
> *Te Deum for J. Alfred Prufrock.* New York, Madison Avenue Church Press, 1967.
> *Lament for Erica: A Poem.* Bembridge, Isle of Wight, Yellowsands Press, 1971.

> Recording: *Ad Nauseam; or, Death at Fun City,* Mercury Records, 1972, Phonogram, 1973.

Play

> Screenplay: *Oedipus the King,* 1967.

Novels

> *O Pale Galilean.* London, Harvill Press, 1954.
> *Vessel of Dishonour.* London, Sheed and Ward, 1962; New York, New American Library, 1963.

Other

> *The Rat and the Convent Dove and Other Tales and Fables.* Aldington, Kent, Hand and Flower Press, 1952.

> Translator, *The Oedipus Plays of Sophocles.* New York, New American Library, 1958.
> Translator, *The Orestes Plays of Aeschylus.* New York, New American Library, 1963.
> Translator, *Prometheus Bound,* by Aeschylus. New York, New American Library, 1964.
> Translator, *The Love-Songs of Sappho.* New York, New American Library, 1966.
> Translator, *3 Plays of Plautus.* New York, New American Library, 1968.

1290

Translator, *Philoctetes, lines 676–729,* by Sophocles.   Bembridge, Isle of Wight, Yellowsands Press, 1971.

Translator, *Three Plays of Euripides: Alcestis, Medea, The Bacchae.*   New York, Norton, 1974.

Critical Studies: by John Engels, in *Minnesota Review* (St. Paul), 1963; Patricia deJoux, in *The Times* (London), 5 January 1968; John Moffitt, in *America* (New York), May 1968.

Paul Roche comments:

(1970) There is always a "sufficient reason" even for the worst of happenings, and it is always sufficiently human. I say in my work: "Father forgive them for they know not what they do: and forgive *me.*" Poetry is awareness heightened to the point of love. It is a way of apprehending the intensity of being. I try to re-create experience more intensely, reduce it to a luminous whole, render intuitive the meaning and metaphysics of the universe – and so feed myself and others the kernel of being. My greatest influences have been the Bible (Authorised or Douay), Shakespeare, Hopkins, Eliot, Aeschylus, Sophocles, Euripides and Sappho.

(1974) For me poetry is an incantation of exact experience that seizes the mind and the heart; it is the orchestration of language towards maximum perception; it is condensed verbal impact. . . . Poetry and art are the unique channels through which knowledge is humanised: enters the blood-stream, is made part of ourselves. Although I write my poems to please myself (to purge myself), I am fully aware of using myself as the exemplar for all human beings, and so ultimately I write for humanity. However embedded in the particular consciousness (even confessional) of a poet his poem is, for me it is only successful if it reaches universality. Which is to say, if anyone (or almost anyone . . . some people are just too bovine to bother with) picking up that poem is wounded, is hit, is illuminated, and can say: "This is about *me.* Or it may not exactly be about me, but I now know what it is like to be that person."

*   *   *

An Englishman, born in India and educated at Rome, Paul Roche has lived in the United States, the West Indies and Mexico in addition to his own country. Perhaps as a result of an outlook that has never been constricted by national boundaries, he has never been unduly influenced by localised coteries – though profiting from them all in his application of poetic technique – and his poetry is equally enjoyed in Britain and America.

For the poems in *All Things Considered,* he received the Alice Fay di Castagnola Award of the Poetry Society of America and the Alice Hunt Bartlett Award of the British Poetry Society. His skill as a translator has certainly had an impact upon his own creative writing so that even what he calls his "mere verse" has a liveliness and an interest often lacking in the work of other poets. In his more serious poetry, whether he writes about events or personal relationships, or draws upon mythology or religion, or makes use of his own personal experience as a starting-point, he has a happy knack of spotlighting major issues in a somewhat playfully ironic and often humorous manner, whilst getting to grips with realities. One might well describe one of his methods (and he has many) as approaching the metaphysical through the physical; he has written a whole series of poems about inanimate objects ("The Brick," "The Spent Matchstick," "The Hairbrush," "The Nail-Scissors," etc.).

His "Act of Love" still remains the finest poem ever written on this difficult subject, and his "Paradigm of Love" is a remarkable example of wordplay used in a valid and effective way. In *To Tell the Truth* he continues his exploration of the significance of experience in a variety of styles, encompassing the satirical "Spring Song of the Petroleum Board Meeting," the re-writing of Eliot's "Prufrock," and the lyrical "Her Love Longs for Tears." His *As Far as I Can See* (a collection not yet published) shows that Roche is working towards greater freedom in his choice of form, and at the same time becoming more concerned with what man is making of his environment, a preoccupation reflected in such intricate pieces as "The American Dream" and "Ad Nauseam; or, Death at Fun City."

– Howard Sergeant

RODDICK, Alan. New Zealander. Born in Belfast, Northern Ireland, 22 July 1937. Educated at Auckland Grammar Achool; University of Auckland; University of Otago, Dunedin, B.D.S. 1960. Married Patricia Woods in 1959; has three daughters and one son. Currently a Dentist, in private practice. Editor, Radio Poetry Programme, New Zealand Broadcasting Corporation, 1968–69, 1973–74. Address: 42 Albert Street, Invercargill, New Zealand.

PUBLICATIONS

Verse

The Eye Corrects: Poems 1955–1965. Auckland, Blackwood and Janet Paul, 1967.

*   *   *

No critic or anthologist has yet done justice to Alan Roddick's poetry, perhaps because it has only its merits as poetry to recommend it. The subject matter is not in itself arresting, the manner is not in any obvious sense innovatory, and Roddick has lacked the advantage (in terms of publicity) gained by poets who start their careers belonging to a movement. He has had to make his way on his own.

Precision, particularity, hardness of outline, descriptive exactness, flexibility of form, wit – these are some of the qualities of Roddick's poetry. The run of the lines commonly matches the action of the subject; the poem is beautifully shaped to the event it describes. He is fond of paradoxes – particularly the paradoxes of mirrors, which (like poems) reflect and yet are not the world. Time, memory, love, the responsibilities and discoveries of parenthood – if his subjects are commonplaces they are also eternal. They are seen in the suburban and domestic setting in which they have been experienced, seen good-humouredly, without Larkinish distaste, but with no room for decorative sentiment either.

The other side of Roddick's poetic merits may be a caution that will not chance its arm. In one poem ("A Patient") he has ventured into unusual territory, making poetry of his day-to-day experience as a dentist. In a recent verse-letter he has experimented technically with a form borrowed from the Russian of Pushkin. Otherwise he has remained within narrow bounds. But Roddick has the kind of literary intelligence and tact that knows you cannot extend yourself stylistically by acts of will. It must be something that happens to the whole man. In the meantime he remains a rare example among New Zealand poets of a perfect miniaturist.

– C. K. Stead

RODGERS, Carolyn M. Afro-American. Born in Chicago, Illinois, in the 1940's. Educated at the University of Illinois, Urbana, 1960–61; Roosevelt University, Chicago, 1961–65. Y.M.C.A. Social Worker, Chicago, 1965; Lecturer in Afro-American Literature, Columbia University, New York, 1968, University of Washington, Seattle, 1970, and Indiana University, Bloomington, Summer 1973; Writer-in-Residence, Albany State College, Georgia, 1971, and Malcolm X College, Chicago, 1972. Formerly, Mid-West Editor, *Black Dialogue*, New York. Recipient: Conrad Kent Rivers Award, 1968; National Endowment for the Arts grant, 1969; Society of Midland Authors Award, 1970. Address: 5954 South Bishop, Chicago, Illinois 60636, U.S.A.

PUBLICATIONS

Verse

Paper Soul. Chicago, Third World Press, 1968.
Two Love Raps. Chicago, Third World Press, 1969.
Songs of a Blackbird. Chicago, Third World Press, 1969.
Now Ain't That Love. Detroit, Broadside Press, 1969.
For H. W. Fuller. Detroit, Broadside Press, 1970.
Long Rap/Commonly Known as a Poetic Essay. Detroit, Broadside Press, 1971.

Carolyn M. Rodgers comments:

I seek to tell the truth. To explore the human condition, the world's condition. To illuminate the ordinary, the forgotten, the overlooked, to show that the specific me is often the general you and us. To exemplify God working in man and the consequences of man defying and denying God, not only in himself but in the universe. I seek to write simply, so that a child might understand; and to write simply profoundly, so that the educated, the intellectual may enjoy and find mental food, find delight. The Light. Truth. My gift is not my own. What is written by me is written through me. I am an instrument. An inkpen of God's.

*　　*　　*

Carolyn M. Rodgers's allegiances are broad and general. The old generation must yield to a revolutionary age, but one cannot "forget the bridge that you crossed over on." The flames of Detroit, Watts, Newark produced Black martyrs, but there is still an ambivalence when the speaker of "Eulogy" asks how tears shed for a single, materialistic, Black soul can be ignored. The song of the Black poet is as universal as eating, sleeping, copulating, and a baby's face ("To the White Critics" and "You Name It"), but the creator often longs for a bus ride to see the sun set or to sing a *sui generis* lyric ("Breakthrough"). The fact is we must "see, the changes are so many / there are several of me and / all of us fight to show up at the same time."

One critic has said that Carolyn Rodgers moves between two worlds, the Bourgeoisie and the Black masses. Another has called her a masterful storyteller giving Black people back to themselves. Both, I think, have set forth partial truths. They have refused to see the poet's canon for what it really is. The poems in *Paper Soul* and *Songs of a Blackbird* are, more than anything else, personal. A hundred and fifty years ago this word would have caused no furor, but in an age of *littérature engagé* it sounds like an indictment. That is not its intent.

Miss Rodgers is personal because there are so many selves that compose her makeup, and poetical honesty demands their expression. Thus, she can be the ironical humorist in "Portrait of a White Nigger" and demand that her audience stop laughing in "Unfunny Situation." She can champion armed revolution at one point ("U Name This One") and praise the singular efforts of a Black magazine editor at another ("For H. W. Fuller"). And some of her finest efforts are poems that deal unapologetically with the lives and loves of Carolyn Rodgers. She speaks self-deprecatingly and honestly about those things that have hurt, embarassed, appeased, or thrilled her in the past ("Now Ain't That Love," "6:30," and "I Remember"). She moves easily from the self of mixed sexual, astronomical, and technical metaphors ("Written for Love of an Ascension-Coltrane") to the poet who employs dialectal spellings to record a telephone conversation with her prose-lytizing mother. When she is deeply in love with a revolutionary speaker (not his sentiments) she says so ("Plagiarism for a Trite Love Pome"). Of course, there are all the stock situations of the new Black poetry: Black men vis-a-vis white women, the permanent wave vs. the natural, the establishment's mocking response to horrors it has created, etc. But finally Carolyn Rodgers is a woman speaking to a wide audience about occasions (whether overheard conversations or passionate love affairs) in her own multifaceted life.

– Houston A. Baker, Jr.

RODITI, Edouard (Herbert). American. Born in Paris, 6 June 1910. Educated at Elstree School, Hertfordshire; Charterhouse, Godalming, Surrey; Balliol College, Oxford; University of Chicago, B.A. 1939; University of California, Berkeley. Art Critic, *L'Arche;* Contributing Editor, *Antaeus,* New York, *European Judaism,* Amsterdam, *The Expatriate Review,* and *Shantih.* Recipient: Gulbenkian Foundation

grant, 1969. Agent: Hope Leresche and Steele, 11 Jubilee Place, London S.W.3.
Address: 8 Gregoire de Tours, Paris 6, France.

PUBLICATIONS

Verse

Poems for F.   Paris, privately printed, 1935.
Prison Within Prison: Three Elegies on Hebrew Themes.   Prairie City, Illinois,
    Press of J. A. Decker, 1941.
Pieces of Three, with Paul Goodman and Meyer Liben.   Harrington, New
    Jersey, 5×8 Press, 1942.
Poems 1928–1948.   New York, New Direction, 1949.
New Hieroglyphic Tales: Prose Poems.   San Francisco, Kayak Books, 1968.
Surrealist Poetry and Prose.   Los Angeles, Black Sparrow Press, 1973.
Thrice Chosen: Poems on Jewish Themes.   Bolinas, California, Tree Books, 1974.
Emperor of Midnight.   Los Angeles, Black Sparrow Press, 1974.

Short Stories

The Delights of Turkey.   New York, New Directions, 1974.

Other

Oscar Wilde.   New York, New Directions, 1947.
Dialogues on Art.   London, Secker and Warburg, 1960; New York, Horizon
    Press, 1961.
Joachim Karsch.   Berlin, Verlag Gebr. Mann, 1960.
De l'Homosexualité.   Paris, Editions Sedimo, 1962.
Magellan of the Pacific.   London, Faber, 1972; New York, McGraw Hill, 1973.

Translator, *Young Cherry Trees Secured Against Hares,* by André Breton.   New
    York, View Editions, and London, A. Zwemmer, 1946.
Translator, *The Pillar of Salt,* by Albert Memmi.   London, Elek, 1956.
Translator, *The Essense of Jewish Art,* by Ernest Namenyi.   New York and
    London, Thomas Yoseloff, 1960.
Translator, *Memed, My Hawk,* by Yashar Kemal.   London, Harvill Press,
    1961.
Translator, *Toros y Toreros,* by Pablo Picasso.   London, Thames and Hudson,
    1961.
Translator, *Art Nouveau,* by Robert Schmutzler.   London, Thames and Hud-
    son, 1964.

Manuscript Collection: Special Collections, University of California at Los Angeles
Library.

Critical Studies: by Alvin Rosenfeld, in *Judaism* (New York), Spring 1969; Sidney
Rosenfeld, in *Books Abroad* (Norman, Oklahoma), Summer 1972.

Edouard Roditi comments:

Originally a Surrealist, I have sought to broaden the scope of Surrealist poetry so that it can include elegiac, didactic or metaphysical poetry in addition to more strictly lyrical poetry.

My major themes are those that have inspired a great number of poets of the past, ranging from Horace to Baudelaire and T. S. Eliot; in my devotional poetry, however, I have always remained within a strictly Jewish tradition. The American poet and philosopher Paul Goodman has compared me, as an elegiac poet, to Rilke and also to Eliot. I suppose I remain too philosophical a poet to have an important following, as my very critical approach to the philosophical themes that I handle excludes any surprising innovations of style or of thought that would not, in my opinion, withstand the tests of time.

I feel that my work now illustrates a very clear and positive evolution in the course of which I have achieved, as a poet, almost all that I had proposed to achieve. I do not feel the need to add much more to what I have already written, though much of my poetry of recent years remains unpublished, partly because I still may wish to correct it before publication.

*   *   *

Edouard Roditi is two poets, both evolved from that exhausted European romanticism he grew up with that appears in his earliest, adolescent poems:

> The sky oppresses me, its vault
> Of stone-grey clouds has kept my mind
> Imprisoned in sepulchral gloom . . .

The conventional Roditi, encouraged and goaded by Eliot, began and remains elegiac, in cadence typically iambic, often end-rimed, becoming over the years slightly more lyrical, more rhythmically varied, enjambing more: a poetry of loss, loneliness, moral outrage, nearly always with en echo of literature in the lines:

> Lady, there being nothing more to say
> About your beauty that has not been said
> By other men about their other loves . . .

The other mature Roditi is surrealist. In 1927 he began drawing upon correspondences between the world of surrealism and the world of his anterior temporal lobe seizures, seizures characterized by deeply rhythmic intense hallucinations of unusually vivid colors and symbolic forms, rather than by convulsions and unconsciousness. Encouraged by Desnos, and the Paris surrealists, Roditi recorded and organized a mythic, metamorphic land beyond nightmare – for its images do not invade consciousness, rather the other way around: consciousness seems to invade the dream, opening its shifting symbols to daylight exploration. These are the "vision mantras," as Roditi labeled them in 1928, finally collected in *New Hieroglyphic Tales* (1968), 40 years after the first were written. A remarkable poetry, especially in the light of many more recent, often less ambitious or successful surrealist experiments. As in his conventional poetry, the tone is elegiac, but the images come as startingly clear as dreams:

And she gazed into the green eyes, her own eyes, and
lay down on the black slab of the sea. And as the
last woman's steel body stiffened, brittle relic
exposed upon the black marble altar of a dead planet,
out of her mouth rose a star: the last star.

At Oxford University that same year, Roditi wrote the first manifesto of surrealism in English, "The New Reality," which was generally ignored. So were his 1930's experiments in black humor and the surrealist absurd. (Some of these are included in his more recent Black Sparrow volume.) In spite of this initial neglect, the surrealist Roditi has obscured the accomplishments of the conventional poet. As reality has come to seem more and more surreal itself, Roditi's conception has become more meaningful. "I accept reality as if it were a found object of an ambiguous nature," Roditi has written. "Those [interpretations of it] that I choose remain, of course, the ones which reveal most clearly my sense of being personally threatened by . . . an alien and hostile force."

– Edward B. Germain

ROOK, (William) Alan. British. Born in Ruddington, Nottinghamshire, 31 October 1909. Educated at Uppingham School, Rutland; Oxford University, 1936–39, B.A. (honours) in English 1939. Served as a Major in the Royal Artillery. Since 1947, Managing Director, Skinner, Rook and Chambers, Ltd. Fellow, Royal Society of Literature. Address: Stragglethorpe Hall, Lincoln, England.

PUBLICATIONS

Verse

Songs from a Cherry Tree. Oxford, Halls, 1938.
Soldiers, This Solitude. London, Routledge, 1942.
These Are My Comrades: Poems. London, Routledge, 1943.
We Who Are Fortunate. London, Routledge, 1945.

Other

Not as a Refuge (literary criticism). London, Lindsey Drummond, 1948.
Diary of an English Vineyard. London, Wine and Spirit Publications, 1972.

Editor, with A. W. Sandford, Oxford Poetry 1936. Oxford, Blackwell, 1936.

*   *   *

Alan Rook was one of the most prolific poets of World War II, but he fell silent immediately the war ended. The coincidence is surely a little too pat? Reading Rook's poems now, thirty years after they were written, one sees that they were precisely adapted to the taste of their time, and in many ways antagonistic to that of ours. The diction has a lush fullness which appealed to the war-time taste for the romantic; and in his first volume – the bulk of it, incidentally, written before war broke out – there are, in uneasy juxtaposition to this romanticism, distinct echoes of the work Auden was doing in the late thirties.

Yet this volume also contains at least one poem of real interest – Robin Skelton rightly chose it for his representative anthology, *Poetry of the Forties*. This poem is "Dunkirk Pier," and it is one of the few English attempts to sum up the experience of defeat – a muted, but still genuine echo of the kind of poetry Aragon wrote in *Les Yeux d'Elsa*:

> Deeply across the waves of our darkness fear,
> like the silent octopus, feeling, groping, clear
> as a star's reflection, nervous and cold as a bird,
> tells us that pain, tells us that death is near.

What is still valid about Rook's poems is that they encapsulate a mood, a way of feeling otherwise out of reach. The poetic means are often imperfect, but the interest lies in the meeting of the individual and the time – just as it does with much of the poetry of the First World War.

– Edward Lucie-Smith

―――――――――

ROOT, William Pitt. American. Born in Austin, Minnesota, 28 December 1941. Educated at the University of Washington, Seattle, B.A. 1964; University of North Carolina, Greensboro, M.F.A. 1967. Married Judy Bechtold in 1965; has one daughter. Instructor, Slippery Rock State College, Pennsylvania, 1967; Assistant Professor of English, Michigan State University, East Lansing, 1967–68; Stegner Creative Writing Fellow, Stanford University, California, 1968–69; Lecturer in Writing, Mid-Peninsula Free University, 1969–70; Visiting Writer-in-Residence, Amherst College, Massachusetts, 1971. Recipient: American Academy of Poets university prize, 1966; Rockefeller grant, 1969; Guggenheim grant, 1970; National Endowment for the Arts grant, 1973. Address: c/o Atheneum Publishers, 122 East 42nd Street, New York, New York 10017, U.S.A.

PUBLICATIONS

Verse

The Storm and Other Poems. New York, Atheneum, 1969.
Striking the Dark Air for Music. New York, Atheneum, 1973.

William Pitt Root comments:

I write both poetry and fiction and in my mind they so utterly overlap in origin and in the feelings I experience as I write, that I find no distinction useful. So far I've been most active and successful with poems.

Sources: my experiences, real/imagined. I consider ideas to be secondary, emotions primary. My "devices" for relaying emotion are dramatic rather than rational. I try to show, not explain. The juxtapositions of tone, music, rhythm (silences and accelerations) over the grid of subject matter, these things create substance. I cannot make use of allusions, literary or topical, so I don't; when I need them I'll try them. I've most admired and envied Roethke's "Greenhouse" and "North American" poems, Williams' lyrics, Frost's monologues, Lorca's tragedies and ballads, Faulkner, Whitman, Neruda, Blake, men who give most from their experience, their opening to experience, who extend us. In poems we need air and light, room and time for the weather to change and to change us.

*   *   *

William Pitt Root's first book impresses one with its solidity: dense physical detail; evenly-paced, full sounds; and a strong emotional weightiness. He succeeds, not with leaps of imagination (he uses few similes and little of the dream-world), but by careful description of emotionally significant scenes or situations and occasional, direct statements of feeling. He says:

> . . . I am a bear
> as clumsy off the ground
> as I am strong among trees.

The heart of *The Storm* is death. There are poems about dead or dying men, raccoons, fish, girls, flowers, turtles, crows, and starlings. But the primary death, the one to which Root returns again and again in his books, is the death of his father, which occurred while Root was a child. One senses in so many of his poems a subterranean aggression which seems strongly connected to the frustrations and angers, the Oedipal force, of the relationship to his dying father. One feels "a pale brutal ferocity spreading its strength" throughout the poems. He also makes us feel the sorrow, though, and the intense love and admiration he had for his father.

Root's second book, *Striking the Dark Air for Music*, shows a change in both style and intent. The poems are more introspective; there is more abstraction and direct statement, less physical detail. He continues to be concerned with death and dying, but he is more involved in self-examination, in recognizing his faults and fixations, in attempting to change. Not only does he show uncommon openness in his self-scrutiny, but there seems to be genuine growth, the poems at the end of the book having a lighter spirit, joyous and mystical.

– Lawrence Russ

ROSELIEP, Raymond (Francis). American. Born in Farley, Iowa, 11 August 1917. Educated at Loras College, Dubuque, Iowa, B.A. 1939; Catholic University of America, Washington, D.C., M.A. 1948; University of Notre Dame, Indiana, Ph.D. 1954. Ordained a Roman Catholic secular priest, 1943; Assistant Pastor in Gilbertville, Iowa, 1943–45. Instructor, 1946–48, Assistant Professor, 1948–60, and Associate Professor, 1960–66, Loras College; Poet-in-Residence, Georgetown University, Washington, D.C., Summer, 1964. Since 1966, Resident Chaplain, Holy Family Hall, Dubuque, Iowa. Managing Editor, *Witness*, Dubuque, Iowa, 1945–46. Poetry Editor, *Sponsa Regis*, published by the Benedictine Order, 1959–66. Member, Gallery of Living Catholic Authors, 1957. Recipient: Society of Midland Authors Award, 1968. Address: Holy Family Hall, 3340 Windsor Extension, Dubuque, Iowa 52001, U.S.A.

PUBLICATIONS

Verse

> *The Linen Bands.* Westminster, Maryland, Newman Press, 1961.
> *The Small Rain.* Westminster, Maryland, Newman Press, 1963.
> *Love Makes the Air Light.* New York, Norton, 1965.
> *Voyages to the Inland Sea IV*, with others. La Crosse, University of Wisconsin Center for Contemporary Poetry, 1974.
> *Flute over Walden.* West Lafayette, Indiana, Vagrom Chap Books, 1975.

Critical Studies: "Priest and Poet: A Note on the Art of Raymomd Roseliep" by John Logan, in *Mutiny* (Northport, New York), Spring 1961; "The Poetry of Raymond Roseliep" by Thomas P. McDonnell, in *Four Quarters* (Philadelphia), May 1961; "Magic and the Magician" an interview with Dennis Hayes, in *Today* (Notre Dame, Indiana), October 1963; "Four Poets Take Note of *The Linen Bands* of Raymond Roseliep" by Sam Bradley, Charles Philbrick, Gil Orlovitz, and James L. Weil, in *Mutiny* (Northport, New York), iv, 1; "Priesthood and Poetry" by Gerald Meath, in *The Tablet* (London), 1 January 1966.

Raymond Roseliep comments:

Sometimes people ask me, Why do you write a poem? and I remember once asking that question of Stephen Spender. I'd say I write a poem because I can't write a musical score, paint a picture, sculpt, or design a building, and I gave up dancing when I became a priest. A poem seems to be the right form for what I want to express. Sometimes I feel many of my poems should be short stories, and probably they would if I had the patience to work in that medium. If I had other talents in the fine arts, I'm certain I would shape my vision in one or another of their molds. I recall Stephen Spender telling me *he* could work fairly well in some of these areas, but he said practically the same thing I'm saying now about the "rightness" of poetry for a particular vision.

I write to find out what I'm thinking. And because I'm moving in an art structure, naturally I want to *make* something beautiful. Something with the order and harmony and radiance which Thomas Aquinas asked of a piece of beauty – I still believe his *id quod visum placet*, "that which delights the beholder," is our best definition of what's beautiful. I delight myself as first beholder (every writer is his own first and often most appreciative audience); then I hope to give this experience of delight to others. Personally I feel a pressing need to share these ordered thoughts and feelings; not all writers do. I always say beauty is beauty twice when shared. Like Hopkins' "azurous hung hills." They were made by the Master Artificer and just stood there beautiful, "the beholder wanting." They needed the necessary eye of a witness other than the artist.

Of course there's another step beyond "delighting" an audience – and I keep it pretty much in mind too: this business of being "useful" to readers. Maurois stated it poignantly one time when he said, "If [a writer's] own conflict resembles that of many of his fellow men, it may, through his efforts, become less obsessive and troublesome to them – in which case he will have the additional pleasure of having been helpful." This twofold function of "delighting" and "instructing" (being useful) I know is pure Horace.

The inspiration or subject of my poems may evolve from almost anything or anyone – a tire, a violet, a football, tomato juice, a young lover, a toothache, air, fire, water, earth, stuff from books or history or dreams or the world of ideas, religion, blue jeans, bandannas, frogs, children, Indians, cats, drugs, war, popcorn – or from anywhere. A poem's experience may be my own, or it may be vicarious or fictional. Inspirations arrive any time. The worst time is at night after I'm well established in bed. If I don't get up and write down the rough idea for a poem, or some delicious phrase that visits me at this unseasonable moment, I lose it.

A poem takes time. I spend more time revising than in first-drafting a poem. I remember what Housman said once, that his effort as poet was not so much to find the right word as to reject the wrong one. Yeats defended the practice early in his career: "A line will take us hours maybe; / Yet if it does not seem a moment's thought, / Our stitching and unstitching has been naught." It's hard to say how long it takes to write a single poem. Sometimes an hour – for a first draft of a fairly short poem like a sonnet. Maybe five to umpteen hours. And I don't always write "in one sitting." Sometimes I assemble the skeleton on a bus or plane or while listening to a bad lecture, or just almost any time I have a ball point and something to scratch on. I write on the backs of old envelopes, whatever's handy – once I scribbled some verses on my shirt cuff (the left one).

Felix Stefanile wrote me in one of his letters: "I hope you always try to write poetry that is both un-easy and not easy; it is the only kind of art worth the allegiance." I know my poetry is sometimes "un-easy and not easy" because there's pain in it; and there's something ambiguous about pain, something you don't want to clearly define about pain. *Should* a poem be clearly defined anyway? And so, people sometimes consider me "obscure." In reply I can only say that I want my reader to do some of the work, for one thing; and I don't want to overstate my case, for another; I don't want to explain the emotion, or I'm likely to have not a poem but a psychiatric profile. Understatement, then, is any poet's desideratum, maybe even a weapon for self-protection. A poem is distilled significance.

Knowing that I have made something and have given something is the reward of a poem. Occasionally there's a bonus when I write a poem about a certain someone and offer it to my subject as a gift. The most delightful response to a gift-poem was the one I received from Marianne Moore. I had sent her my lines about her reading in Chicago, a poem that started with the cadence, "Peacock elegant the lady wore a necklace microphone," and went on to picture her as that rare bird with "dark jewels" and "a particular flight." She sent me a peacock feather.

"Love is the word of all work," George Eliot said, and love is at the core of my poems. I try to incarnate spiritual reality and spiritualize or humanize material reality. To help in this transfiguration of matter keeps me aware that a poet is, after all, an animal with the sun in his belly. The one thing his poetry must do, as Auden said, is to praise all it can for being and happening. My students took another view: they used to cite Augustine's *vinum daemonum* as descriptive of my poems – they translated it "devilish wine." I like that too.

*   *   *

Raymond Roseliep is a teacher and a Catholic priest who writes a catholic, well-crafted, and direct love poetry. As the poet John Logan enthusiastically explains in the preface to Roseliep's first volume: "These three, the priest, the poet, the teacher, are held together either by mere love, which is the thinnest of threads if it's not the strongest, or by art, or by both. I think that in Father Roseliep they are held together by both."

Some poems express the love of the divine representative, the priest, for the worshipper and penitent, but, more often, Roseliep's poems deal with the love of the teacher and scholar for the student ("Room 210: Shakespeare"). "Love," we will see, "makes the air light" and it joins all things. After the "small rain" of the real, through love – and these poems –

> light
> will wheel to a
> point
> sharper than rain.

The expression of a "supernatural" love depends on imagery more than intensity or emotion, and Roseliep's poems succeed because, in transcending the "small rain," a human love for the physical is evident. The priestly vows to keep at bay the world where love is "materialized" only intensify – as they did for Hopkins – everything; his vow to keep to a love which will not "touch" only makes his perceptions as man and poet the more impassioned and poignant: this is effective and obvious in "For Denise, Distracting," or "Your Hair Falls Blackbird," and again

> on our terrace, robin lithe
> and robin bloused, skirted, blown
> was a girl brilliant as pain.

Roseliep's love extends to language and its rhythms. In such poems as "Alan" and "GI" he attempts a return to the energy of Anglo-Saxon; he is able to use the immediate image with facility, and although obviously capable in accentual syllabics, Roseliep most often achieves effect with vivid language and syllabics ("Convent Infirmary," or "Rembrandt's 'Young Girl at an Open Half-Door'" are examples). His poems are direct in their love and repeatedly risk the reader with strong emotion. It is to Roseliep's credit that only occasionally can he be charged with sentimentalism.

– Joseph Wilson

<hr />

ROSENBLATT, Joseph. Canadian. Born in Toronto, Ontario, 26 December 1933. Educated at Central Technical School, and George Brown College, Toronto. Married to Faye Smith; has one son. Fornerly, a laborer, factory worker, plumber's mate, grave digger, civil servant; worked for the Canadian Pacific Railway for seven years. Currently, Editor, *Jewish Dialog* magazine, Toronto. Recipient: Canada Council grant, 1966, 1968, 1973. Address: 136A Walmer Road, Toronto, Ontario, Canada.

PUBLICATIONS

Verse

> *Voyage of the Mood.*   Don Mills, Ontario, Heinrich Heine Press, 1963.
> *The LSD Leacock: Poems.*   Toronto, Coach House Press, 1966.
> *Winter of the Luna Moth.*   Toronto, House of Anansi, 1968.
> *Greenbaum.*   Toronto, Coach House Press, 1971.
> *The Bumblebee Dithyramb.*   Erin, Ontatio, Press Porcépic, 1972.
> *The Blind Photographer*, with drawings.   Erin, Ontario, Press Porcépic, 1973.
> *Dream Craters.*   Erin, Ontario, Press Porcépic, 1974.
> *Vampires and Virgins.*   Toronto, McClelland and Stewart, 1975.

Joseph Rosenblatt comments:

My own verse and prose-poems basically attack the human condition and society with its crass materialism and phony value-structure.

My poetry is traditional and influenced by American poets such as Hart Crane and Robert Frost. My poems are concerned with the Moloch or Mammon monster of society and the insatiable appetite of the creature. The monster finds its expression in my animal poems.

For example, in my bat poems the psyche of man is found in this terrestrial animal of darkness. Therefore my kinship is with Swift and misanthropes. My super hero is Ambrose Bierce. In nearly all my poems the quest of man is spiritual cannibalism – soul theft and the protein of money – I use the traditional devices of poetry in my work such as rhyme, assonance and metric extension.

*   *   *

Joseph Rosenblatt "is a poet of the small presses," but he is, nevertheless, well-known in Canada. At times he has seemed, superficially, more interested in the world of plants, insects and animals than that of human beings; but this is more an aspect of his fascination with the unusual, the rare, and the minute than a lack of sympathy with the race of men. He has said, "I only deal with the bizarre," but adds that his newer poems are "more directly confessional poems, written without the intervention of imagery or my old animal disguises." Lately, he has been drawing as well as writing poems, and in the drawings images of grotesque, and curiously human, though debased, animals and reptiles abound. He has had exhibitions of his drawings in several Toronto galleries and his last book (*The Blind Photographer*) might more properly be called a book of drawings illustrated by poems than the opposite. He has said that "drawings are the lazy man's way to writing anti-poems, poems without intellectualizing and verbalizing." It is typical of Rosenblatt to hint that he is not much interested in thoughtful technique; in fact, in both poems and drawings, he is always meticulously careful of detail. His interest in "insect and plant sexuality" is extraordinary and Norman Snider has said rightly that "Rosenblatt is a miniaturist in his sensibility, his poems are minute and exquisite observations of the tiny phenomena of nature." It only remains to add that, in the real meaning of the word, wit is the prime mark of his work.

– John Newlove

ROSENTHAL, M(acha) L(ouis).   American.   Born in Washington, D.C., 14 March 1917. Educated at the University of Chicago, B.A. 1937, M.A. 1938; New York University, Ph.D. 1949. Married Victoria Himmelstein in 1939; has two sons and one daughter. Instructor, Michigan State University, East Lansing, 1939–45. Since 1945, Member of the English Department, and since 1961, Professor of English, New York University. Poetry Editor, *The Nation*, New York, 1956–61. United States Cultural Exchange Program Visiting Specialist in Germany, 1961, Pakistan, 1965, and Poland, Romania, and Hungary, 1966. Since 1970, Poetry Editor, *The Humanist* and *Present Tense*, both in New York. Recipient: American Council of Learned Societies Fellowship, 1942, 1950; Guggenheim Fellowship, 1960, 1964. Agent: Fox Chase Agency, Lincoln Building, 60 East 42nd Street, New York, New York 10017. Address: Department of English, New York University, 19 University Place, New York, New York 10003, U.S.A.

PUBLICATIONS

Verse

> *Blue Boy on Skates: Poems.*   New York and London, Oxford University Press, 1964.
> *Beyond Power: New Poems.*   New York and London, Oxford University Press, 1969.
> *The View from the Peacock's Tail: Poems.*   New York and London, Oxford University Press, 1972.

Other

> *Effective Reading: Methods and Models*, with W. C. Hummel and E. V. Leichty. Boston, Houghton Mifflin, 1944.
> *Exploring Poetry*, with A. J. M. Smith.   New York, Macmillan, 1955; revised edition, 1973.
> *A Primer of Ezra Pound.*   New York, Macmillan, 1960.
> *The Modern Poets: A Critical Introduction.*   New York and London, Oxford University Press, 1960.
> *The New Poets: American and British Poetry since World War II.*   New York and London, Oxford University Press, 1967.
> *Randall Jarrell.*   Minneapolis, University of Minnesota Press, 1972.
> *Poetry and the Common Life.*   New York and London, Oxford University Press, 1974.

Editor, with T. Jameson, *A Selection of Verse*. Totowa, New Jersey, Littlefield, 1952.

Editor, with Gerald D. Sanders and John Herbert Nelson, *Chief Modern Poets of
Britain and America*. New York, Macmillan, 1962; revised edition, 1970.

Editor, *Selected Poems and Two Plays of W. B. Yeats*. New York, Macmillan,
1962; revised edition, 1973.

Editor, *The William Carlos Williams Reader*. New York, New Directions,
1966; London, MacGibbon and Kee, 1967.

Editor, *The New Modern Poetry: An Anthology of British and American Poetry
since World War II*. New York, Macmillan, 1967; revised edition, New
York, Oxford University Press, 1969.

Editor, *100 Postwar Poems: British and American*. New York, Macmillan, 1968.

Critical Studies: "In Spite of Solitude" by Stuart Holroyd, in *John O'London's*, 2
March 1961; "Judgements and Interpretations" by Thomas Lask, in *The New York
Times*, 25 April 1967; "The Lyre in the Larger Pattern" by Robert D. Spector, in
Saturday Review (New York), 10 June 1967; "Voices of Victims" by Robie
Macauley, in *The New York Times Book Review*, 10 September 1967; Thomas Lask,
in *The New York Times*, 29 August 1969; "Sensibilities" by William Heyen, in
Poetry (Chicago), March 1970; Frederick Feirstein, in *Library Journal* (New York), 8
November 1972.

M. L. Rosenthal comments:

I *want* each poem to be and say at least as much as the insight behind it – its
dynamics to betray more than I realized.

*   *   *

With the publication of three volumes of poetry since 1964, the distinguished
critic and teacher M. L. Rosenthal has emerged as a genuinely important poet in his
own right. Rosenthal is capable of considerable variety in tone and form, and this
flexibility provides suitable expressive parallels to the breadth of his subject matter.
The tone of individual poems varies, for example, from the playfulness of "Jim
Dandy," and the sardonic and transforming wit of "Love in the Luncheonette,"
to the controlled grief of "I Strike a Match . . . ," and the poems range in form
from the disciplined lyricism of "Visiting Yeats's Tower" to more open forms with
deceptively relaxed conversational rhythms. In addition, certain poems explore
within the framework of a single work the relationships between prose and verse
themselves.

Rosenthal's subject matter is drawn from deeply felt personal experience; from
Biblical allusions; from literary references to such diverse figures as, among others,
Keats, Pasternak, Rilke, Hart Crane, and Mayakovsky; and occasionally from
political and historical events. But the triumph of individual poems lies in Rosenthal's ability to place in new and contemporary perspective some of the great and
traditional themes: love and death; youth and age; innocence and experience; the
identity of man.

The key perhaps to this diversity of style and content is Rosenthal's inclusive
and paradoxical concept of the poet himself: in his own case a combination of "a
'tragic view of life' *and* an optimistic 'nature.'" Throughout his work one is aware

of the pained intensity of a deeply compassionate man who observes the contradictory behavior of those "Sentimental scorpions," human beings, and who yearns
nevertheless – as "Seniority, or It Stands to Reason" indicates – for ultimate
metaphors of reconciliation:

> These autumn leaves, with their gold or crimson sheen,
> could hardly recommend the fresh young green
> spring leaves for mature responsibilities.
> You need *experience* to capture sun for trees.

– Gaynor F. Bradish

ROSS, Alan. British. Born in Calcutta, India, 6 May 1922. Educated at Hailey-
bury; St. John's College, Oxford. Served in the Royal Naval Voluntary Reserve,
1942–47. Married Jennifer Fry in 1949; has one son. Staff Member, British Council,
1947–50; Staff Member, *The Observer*, London, 1950–71. Since 1961, Editor, *London
Magazine*. Currently, Managing Director, London Magazine Editions, formerly Alan
Ross Publishers, London. Recipient: Atlantic-Rockefeller Award, 1946. Fellow,
Royal Society of Literature, 1971. Address: Clayton Manor, near Hassocks,
Sussex, England.

PUBLICATIONS

Verse

> *Summer Thunder.* Oxford, Blackwell, 1941.
> *The Derelict Day: Poems in Germany.* London, Lehmann, 1947.
> *Something of the Sea: Poems, 1942–1952.* London, Verschoyle, 1954; Boston,
> Houghton Mifflin, 1955.
> *To Whom It May Concern: Poems, 1952–57.* London, Hamish Hamilton, 1958.
> *African Negatives.* London, Eyre and Spottiswoode, 1962.
> *North from Sicily: Poems in Italy, 1961–64.* London, Eyre and Spottiswoode,
> 1965.
> *Poems 1942–67.* London, Eyre and Spottiswoode, 1967.
> *A Calcutta Grandmother.* London, Poem-of-the-Month Club, 1971.
> *Tropical Ice.* London, Covent Garden Press, 1972.
> *The Taj Express: Poems 1967–1973.* London, London Magazine Editions, 1973.
> *Open Sea.* London, London Magazine Editions, 1975.

Other

> *Time Was Away: A Notebook in Corsica.* London, Lehmann, 1948.
> *The Forties: A Period Piece.* London, Weidenfeld and Nicolson, 1950.
> *The Gulf of Pleasure* (travel). London, Weidenfeld and Nicolson, 1951.

Poetry 1945–50. London, Longman, 1951; Folcroft, Pennsylvania, Folcroft Editions, 1974.

The Bandit on the Billiard Table: A Journey Through Sardinia. London, Verschoyle, 1954; revised edition, as *South to Sardinia.* London, Hamish Hamilton, 1960.

Australia 55: A Journal of the M.C.C. Tour (cricket). London, Joseph, 1955.

Cape Summer, and The Australians in England. London, Hamish Hamilton, 1957.

The Onion Man (children's book). London, Hamish Hamilton, 1959.

Danger on Glass Island (children's book). London, Hamish Hamilton, 1960.

Through the Caribbean: The M.C.C. Tour of the West Indies 1959–1960 (cricket). London, Hamish Hamilton, 1960.

Australia 63 (cricket). London, Eyre and Spottiswoode, 1963.

The West Indies at Lord's (cricket). London, Eyre and Spottiswoode, 1963.

The Wreck of the Moni (juvenile). London, Alan Ross, 1965.

A Castle in Sicily (juvenile). London, Alan Ross, 1966.

Editor, *Selected Poems of John Gay.* London, Grey Walls Press, 1950.

Editor, with Jennifer Ross, *Borrowed Time,* by F. Scott Fitzgerald. London, Grey Walls Press, 1951.

Editor, *Abroad: Travel Stories.* London, Faber, 1957.

Editor, *The Cricketers Companion.* London, Eyre and Spottiswoode, 1960.

Editor, *Poetry Supplement.* London, Poetry Book Society, 1963.

Editor, *London Magazine Stories 1–9.* London, London Magazine Editions, 1964–74.

Editor, *Leaving School.* London, London Magazine Editions, 1966.

Editor, *Living in London.* London, London Magazine Editions, 1974.

Translator, *Undersea Adventure,* by Philippe Diolé. New York, Messner, 1953.

Translator, *Sacred Forest,* by Pierre Gaisseau. London, Weidenfeld and Nicolson, 1954.

Translator, *Death Is My Trade,* by Robert Merle. London, Verschoyle, 1954.

Translator, *Seas of Sicily,* by Philippe Diolé. London, Sidgwick and Jackson, 1955; as *Gates of the Sea,* New York, Messner, 1955.

Manuscript Collection: Arts Council of Great Britain, London.

*   *   *

Alan Ross began as what is vaguely called a war poet. He was in Germany during the early part of the Occupation, and his subjects were German gun sites and military hospitals, day and night in Hamburg, Lüneburg Heath, the dark night of the soul that as he saw it was closing on Germany. The subjects were grim, but the poet's spirit did not fully reflect them; his awareness of the sensuous world was too strong. "Lüneburg," for instance, has a refrain: "The courtroom holds the afternoon in chains." The idea is to convey that Germany too is in chains, but the verse that follows might reflect a peaceful life in Oxford:

> October settles on water and weeping willows.
> Under stone bridges, leaves like boats
> Drift golden. . . .

Many years later, when preparing his collected poems, Ross changed many of these early pieces in a remarkable way, stiffening and sharpening them, making

exact what had been vague. "Sengwarden" originally began and ended: "At Sengwarden the silence is the space in the heart." (As a young poet Ross had a
weakness for this kind of romantic and not very meaningful statement.) This line
has been dropped, and the revised poem begins:

> Something (but what) could be made of this.
> Two U-boat officers turning to piss
> In swastika shapes against a wall.

These revised early poems which bear only the relationship of mood to their
originals are certainly among his best work. In general he shows a love of colour
and gaiety that sometimes declines to mere prettiness. He has written about cricket
at Brighton and the World Cup, the Grand Canal and mine dances in Johannesburg,
the Autostrada del Sole and the Finchley Road. He records the scene very vividly,
but too often seems content just to do that without looking beneath or outside it.
"Beyond the window the tyre-coloured road deflates / Like a tube at night" his
poem about the Finchley Road begins. One appreciates the ingenious aptness of the
image, but it is expressive only upon a superficial level. Sometimes a general moral
is drawn in the last verse, in an attempt to add meaningfulness to a poem which is
really no more than a record of observations.

Perhaps Ross was unlucky in the period at which he began writing. His natural
tendency to romantic excess was encouraged by the War and by the poets most in
favour at the time. In the Thirties or the Fifties his tendency to see everything in
terms of brightly coloured pictures would have been controlled, and this in fact he
has tried to do himself. The poems he wrote in Africa between 1958 and 1960 offer
pictures just as clear as those in his earlier work but some of them, like "Rock
Paintings," "Sometime Never" and "Such Matters as Rape" go a good deal
further by expressing some involvement with the scenes described. These, and the
rewritten early poems, suggest a possible new line of development in the next
decade.

– Julian Symons

ROTHENBERG, Jerome. American. Born in New York City, 11 December 1931.
Educated in New York public schools, 1937–48; City College of New York, B.A.
1952; University of Michigan, Ann Arbor, M.A. 1953. Served in the United States
Army, Germany, 1953–55. Married Diane Brodatz in 1952; has one son. Instructor,
City College of New York, 1959–60; Lecturer in English, Mannes College of Music,
New York, 1961–70; Regents Professor, University of California, San Diego, 1971;
Visiting Lecturer in Anthropology, New School for Social Research, New York,
1971–72. Since 1960, Founding Publisher, Hawk's Well Press, New York. Editor,
with David Antin, *Some/Thing*, New York; Editor, *Floating World*, New York;
Ethnopoetics Editor, *Stony Brook*, New York; Editor, with Dennis Tedlock,
Alcheringa: A First Magazine of Ethnopoetics, New York. Recipient: Longview Foun-
dation Award, 1961; National Endowment for the Arts grant, 1969; Wenner-Gren
Foundation grant, 1969; Guggenheim grant, 1974. Address: c/o New Directions
Inc., 333 Sixth Avenue, New York, New York 10014, U.S.A.

PUBLICATIONS

Verse

White Sun, Black Sun.   New York, Hawk's Well Press, 1960.
The Seven Hells of the Jigoku Zoshi.   New York, Trobar Books, 1962.
Sightings I-IX, with *Lunes* by Robert Kelly.   New York, Hawk's Well Press, 1964.
The Gorky Poems (bilingual edition).   Mexico City, El Corno Emplumado, 1966.
Between 1960–1963.   London, Fulcrum Press, 1967.
Conversations.   Los Angeles, Black Sparrow Press, 1968.
Poems 1964–1967.   Los Angeles, Black Sparrow Press, 1968.
Offering Flowers, with Ian Tyson.   London, Circle Press, 1968.
Sightings I-IX & Red Easy a Color.   London, Circle Press, 1968.
Poland/1931.   Santa Barbara, California, Unicorn Press, 1969.
The Directions, with Tom Phillips.   London, Tetrad Press, 1969.
Poems for the Game of Silence 1960–1970.   New York, Dial Press, 1971.
A Book of Testimony.   Bolinas, California, Tree Books, 1971.
Net of Moon, Net of Sun.   Santa Barbara, California, Unicorn Press, 1971.
A Valentine No a Valedictory for Gertrude Stein.   London, Judith Walker, 1972.
Esther K. Comes to America.   Greensboro, North Carolina, Unicorn Press, 1973.
Seneca Journal I: A Poem of Beavers.   Madison, Wisconsin, Perishable Press, 1973.
The Cards.   Los Angeles, Black Sparrow Press, 1974.
The Pirke and the Pearl.   San Francisco, Tree Books, 1974.
Poland/1931 (complete edition).   New York, New Directions, 1974.

Play

The Deputy, adaptation of a play by Rolf Hochhuth (produced New York, 1964).   New York, French, 1965.

Other

Editor and Translator, *New Young German Poets.*   San Francisco, City Lights Books, 1959.
Editor, *Ritual: A Book of Primitive Rites and Events* (anthology).   New York, Something Else Press, 1966.
Editor, *Technicians of the Sacred: A Range of Poetries from Africa, America, Asia, and Oceania.*   New York, Doubleday, 1968.
Editor, *Shaking the Pumpkin: Traditional Poetry of the Indian North Americas.*   New York, Doubleday, 1972.
Editor, with George Quasha, *America a Prophecy: A New Reading of American Poetry from Pre-Columbian Times to the Present.*   New York, Random House, 1973.
Editor, *Revolution of the Word: A New Gathering of American Avant-Garde Poetry.*   New York, Seabury Press, 1974.

Translator, *The Flight of Quetzalcoatl*, from a Spanish prose version of the original Aztec by Angel Maria Garibay.   Brighton, Sussex, Unicorn Bookshop, 1967.

Translator, with Michael Hamburger and the author, *Poems for People Who Don't Read Poems*, by Hans Magnus Enzensberger. New York, Atheneum, and London, Secker and Warburg, 1968; as *Poems*, London, Penguin, 1968.

Translator, *The Book of Hours and Constellations*, by Eugen Gomringer. New York, Something Else Press, 1968.

Translator, *The 17 Horse Songs of Frank Mitchell, Nos. X-XIII*. London, Tetrad Press, 1969.

Critical Studies: in *The Sullen Art*, edited by David Ossman, New York, Corinth Books, 1963; "Interview with Jerome Rothenberg," in *The Craft of Poetry*, edited by William Packard, New York, Doubleday, 1974; *Vort 6* (Bloomington, Indiana), 1974; *Boundary 2* (Binghamton, New York), 1975.

Jerome Rothenberg comments:

I think of myself as making poems that other poets haven't provided for me & for the existence of which I feel a deep need.

I look for new forms & possibilities, but also for ways of presenting in my own language the oldest possibilities of poetry going back to the primitive & archaic cultures that have been opening up to us over the last hundred years.

I believe that everything is now possible in poetry, & that our earlier "western" attempts at closed definitions represent a failure of perception we no longer have to endure.

I have recently been translating American Indian poetry (including the "meaningless" syllables, word distortions & music) & have been exploring ancestral sources of my own in the world of Jewish mystics, thieves & madmen.

My personal manifesto reads: 1) I will change your mind; 2) any means (=methods) to that end; 3) to oppose the "devourers"=bureaucrats, system-makers, priests, etc. (W. Blake); 4) "& if thou wdst understand that wch is me, know this: all that I have sd I have uttered playfully – & I was by no means ashamed of it" (J. C. to his disciples, The Acts of St. John).

*   *   *

In a poetry world today where each member makes his place by being unique, and each new body of work creates its own definitions, it should be tautological to say that Jerome Rothenberg writes a different poetry from anyone else. However, Rothenberg's poetry is special because it combines so many elements that haven't been combined before. His poetry is remarkable because it is a beautiful combination of lyric and commentary. Its technique is often surrealistic without having the purposes of surrealism at heart. It is ethnic without making one aware of the fact. It is religious and secular at the same time. It is intimate without being autobiographical. And it is experimental without being hard to understand or tedious to listen to. His poetry has influenced many American poets who have been struggling with the mode of "personal poetry," looking for a way to write it without being self-absorbed.

Jerome Rothenberg is one of those interesting poets who started his career by forming his own magazines, his own contemporary colleagues, his own press, and while not ignoring other schools of poetry or poets in the more "established" world of poetry, felt no need to gain recognition in the traditional ways. Consequently, he published more than a dozen books with small presses before publishing his selected poems, *Poems for the Game of Silence 1960–1970.*

He has proved that if you do your own work with integrity and energy, the world will come to you and appreciate your skills, for he is one of the most highly respected and loved poets in New York, and one hears nothing but praise for his poetry in places where Rothenberg has given poetry programs.

One of the most imposing works by Jerome Rothenberg is his long on-going series of poems, called *Poland/1931.* This is a magnificent set of poems which use as their source materials Rothenberg's background as an American Jew born of European parents. Most of the poems in this series are written in the incantatory style we have now come to associate with Rothenberg, using lists of images, often surrealistic, to intone a mood, to create a landscape of feelings and ideas merged together with ecstatic language. The first poem in the series, "The Wedding," is typical of the action of all the poems. Archetypal subjects give a picture of life that everyone can understand, even though they come from special sources:

> poland poland poland poland poland
> how thy bells wrapped in their flowers toll
> how they do offer up their tongues to kiss the moon
> old moon old mother stuck in the sky thyself
> an old bell with no tongue a lost udder
> poland thy beer is ever made of rotting bread
> thy silks are linens merely thy tradesmen
> dance at weddings where fanatic grooms
> still dream of bridesmaids still are screaming
> past their red mustaches poland
> we have lain awake in thy soft arms forever

The triumph of all the poems in this series is that they are autobiographical without being about Rothenberg's personal life or himself. They give us an intimate feeling of closeness to the mind and the voice without details of the life.

Another very impressive group of poems is Rothenberg's *The Seven Hells of Jigoku Zoshi,* imagistic poems about the punishments for breaking archetypal taboos. These poems sing off the page and remind the reader how possible the lyric still is in English. But even more satisfying, they also comment compassionately on all of our lives, on how much we need from others, and how much pain and punishment all of us suffer. This is from "The Second Hell," where thieves are ground in mortars:

> The thieves the thieves the lovely thieves are no more
> The shore is washed by the sea
> The sea is combed by the wind
> The wind sleeps all day in the chimney
> It moves through the house in the evening
> It wakes us, it opens a door for the sea
> It walks where the thieves walked
> It leads us into a night without windows
> Comfort me, stay with me light of my eyes
> The lovely thieves are no more

Rothenberg has also done a considerable amount of translation, especially of contemporary German poetry, and one of his primary concerns is primitive poetry. Many of the surrealistic techniques of his own poetry are directly related to his study of primitive poetry all over the world. He has compiled two anthologies with those interests in mind: *Technicians of the Sacred,* an anthology of primitive poetry

with an appendix of contemporary poems which he sees as bearing some resem-
blence to ancient poetry, and *Shaking the Pumpkin,* an anthology of American Indian
poetry. *America a Prophecy,* edited with George Quasha, attempts to review American poetry from the standpoint of the oral and experimental tradition. Many of
Rothenberg's innovations in poetry, including a multi-media version of *Poland/1931*
in collaboration with the composer, Charles Morrow, and photographer, Lawrence
Fink, demonstrate a continuation of the most ancient religious and oral traditions in
poetry. He is a powerful poet whose work demonstrates what he has been preaching for many years: that there is some "deep image" or magical spirit in all good
poetry, from all ages, which rests in back of a poem and communicates beyond
language through the voice. He has created the possibility for all of us to hear the
poetry of image through his own magnificent images.

– Diane Wakoski

ROWBOTHAM, David (Harold).   Australian.   Born in Toowoomba, Queensland,
27 August 1924. Educated at Toowoomba Grammar School; University of Sydney
(Lawson Prize, 1949); University of Queensland, Brisbane (Ford Medal, 1948),
B.A. Served in the Royal Australian Air Force, Southwest Pacific, 1942–45. Mar-
ried Ethel Jessie Matthews in 1952; has two daughters. Editorial Staff Member, *The
Australian Encyclopedia,* 1950–51; Columnist, *Toowoomba Chronicle,* 1952–55; Broad-
caster, Australian Broadcasting Commission National Book Review Panel, 1957–63.
Literary and Theatre Critic, 1955–64, Chief Book Reviewer, 1964–69, and since
1969, Arts Editor, *The Courier-Mail,* Brisbane. Commonwealth Literary Fund
Lecturer, University of Queensland, 1956, 1964, and University of New England,
Armidale, New South Wales, 1961; Senior Tutor in English, University of Queen-
sland, 1965–69. Advisory Editor, *Poetry Magazine,* Sydney. Since 1964, Council
Member, Australian Society of Authors. Recipient: *Sydney Morning Herald* Compe-
tition prize, 1949; Grace Leven Prize, 1964; Xavier Society Award, 1966; Australian
Commonwealth Literary Fund travel grant, 1972. Address: 28 Percival Terrace,
Holland Park, Brisbane, Queensland, Australia.

PUBLICATIONS

Verse

   Ploughman and Poet.   Sydney, Lyre Bird Writers, 1954.
   Inland: Poems.   Sydney, Angus and Robertson, 1958.
   All the Room.   Brisbane, Jacaranda Press, 1964.
   Bungalow and Hurricane: New Poems.   Sydney, Angus and Robertson, 1967.
   The Makers of the Ark.   Sydney, Angus and Robertson, 1970.
   The Pen of Feathers.   Sydney, Angus and Robertson, 1971.
   Selected Poems.   Brisbane, University of Queensland Press, 1975.

Novel

The Man in the Jungle.   London and Sydney, Angus and Robertson, 1964.

Short Stories

Town and City: Tales and Sketches.   Sydney, Angus and Robertson, 1956.

Other

Brisbane.   Sydney, University of Sydney, 1964.

Editor, *Queensland Writing.*   Brisbane, Fellowship of Australian Writers, 1957.

Critical Studies: in *Australian Literature,* by Cecil Hadcraft, London, Heinemann, 1960; *Creative Writing in Australia,* by John K. Ewers, Melbourne, Georgian House, 1966; *Focus on David Rowbotham,* by John Strugnell, Brisbane, University of Queensland Press, 1969; "Some Recent Australian Poetry" by Ronald Dunlop, in *Poetry Australia* (Sydney), 1972.

David Rowbotham comments:

In reading my work backwards (for the purposes of making a selection), I find my beginnings true to subsequent ends. I have been concerned with being and words. I have not been engaged with furnishing values and fighting causes, only with seeing and speaking as myself in the issue called life, and wherever time has taken me. All that a poet has to do is: merely to be. This can still be a task when so many of us have made the most natural things the hardest of all. A common review observation about my early work (in the 1950's) – "landscape is not enough" – has never been enough, for me, in terms of a really human view. No element of one's self – in my case it was landscape – should be disowned by the self though others depreciate or dismiss it. I would only regret, not disown, poems unworthy as poems of their (my) origins. Neither should a writer working in the element of nature disown what has not been admitted or discerned: his element of man. I acknowledge – as a guidance to my earlier work done among my Australian home-countryside, and to my later work done (say) within the sense of surrounding larger worlds – that man and landscape (outer? inner?) can not be separated, and that it never occurred to me whether or not they could be. I also acknowledge that poetry is a passion before it is anything else; I have been concerned with a language for living. We are farmers of ourselves, said Donne; and I would not mind if the whole of my work, from poems about ploughmen to poems about men in space, were seen and summed up in light of that remark.

*   *   *

David Rowbotham began writing and publishing after World War II as a young follower of the *Bulletin* school of nature poets in Australia, a school that encouraged Australian writers to look closely at and reaffirm their own regional identity and meaning. Such a coming to terms with Australian landscape was important at that time, but it threatened our poetry with an ever expanding wash of minor bird and billabong versification. David Rowbotham wrote a number of very delicate lyrics in his first book, *Ploughman and Poet,* but his second collection, *Inland,* though it contained probably his most anthologised – and one of his best – poems, "Mullabinda," did not really prepare his readers for the change in direction, to a more introverted and personal poetry, that was first displayed in the volume *All the Room.*

From this point on, Rowbotham's poetry has struggled its way doggedly, and with considerable effort, into areas of response and experience far removed from the gentle sunny Darling Downs countryside of the earlier books. It is a measure of Rowbotham's integrity that he has not paid easy court to current fashionable styles and mannerisms, even when they have been shown to be amendable to the sort of personal self-exploration he has been struggling to realize. At its worst, then, his later work, in *Makers of the Ark* and *The Pen of Feathers,* is marred by a residue of quatrain-making habits not fully explored or justified. At its best, the recent poetry counterpoints a conservative vocabulary and rhythm with an intensely felt response to the poet's own discoveries and concerns, which have been thought through with an almost painful honesty to their own relevance in Rowbotham's poetic search. David Rowbotham is becoming one of the significant loners in Australian poetry.

– Thomas W. Shapcott

———————

ROWLAND, J(ohn) R(ussell). Australian. Born in Armidale, New South Wales, 10 February 1925. Educated at Cranbrook School; University of Sydney, B.A. Married Moira Armstrong in 1956; has one son and two daughters. Member of the Department of Foreign Affairs: Canberra, 1944, 1949–52, 1959–65; Moscow, 1946–48; London, 1948–49, 1957–59; Saigon, 1952–55; Washington, D.C., 1955–57. Ambassador to the U.S.S.R., 1965–68; High Commissioner to Malaysia, 1969–72. Since 1973, Ambassador to Austria, Czechoslovakia, and Hungary. Address: Australian Embassy, Vienna, Austria.

PUBLICATIONS

Verse

The Feast of Ancestors: Poems. Sydney, Angus and Robertson, 1965.
Snow. Sydney, Angus and Robertson, 1971.

Other

Translator, *A Poem on Various Points of View and Other Poems,* by Robert Ivanovich Rozhdestvenskii. Melbourne, Sun Books, 1968.

J. R. Rowland comments:

Very much a spare-time poet; primarily a diplomat – unfortunately. Lyric verse; poems usually not longer than thirty lines; strongly visual; mostly personal in theme rather than social or philosophical.

*   *   *

The settings of J. R. Rowland's poems reflect the fact that he has lived in many varied and various parts of the world. Yet whether it be the Australian desert, winter in Moscow, a hotel room in Cairo or Southeast Asia, it is always possible for him in just a few lines to create a landscape and an atmosphere. What helps him so much to achieve this effect is his eye for the tiny but important detail and his gift for the unusual, apt, and fresh image, simile or metaphor.

We are always aware that this is a man with a quiet, dry sense of humour, a man able to laugh at human foibles and pretensions but at the same time questioning his right to do so, realising how easy it is to be "the slick observer." There is a cavalier touch to his verse, the touch of a man who is concerned but who knows that there is nothing worse than taking oneself too seriously.

Much of his verse is personal, concerned with what he himself has described as domesticities. These deal with his wife, children, and ordinary everyday events of family life. To all of these incidents he gives a depth and singularity and if his family holiday by the sea seems a little dull to us he reminds us that

> Lara and Zhivago
> Had no children, nor is laundry mentioned
> By Lawrence in a similar situation
>   With Frieda in the cottage at Thirroul:
> It makes a certain difference to the tone.
> Exaltation needs to be alone

> – from "At Noosa"

His special plea is for originality, for men of vision. Against the dull, monotonous routine of suburbia where "admirals pick tomatoes / In their back garden," he sets the Australian continent. This for him is a "half-unearthly country," a land of mystery, a visionary landscape, "a cure for habit." For Rowland the East has the same ability to stir the imagination, both have a "promise / Of strangeness and discovery." There is a celebration not only of the Australian landscape but of the people enveloped by it, of "the natural human pulse / Of Country living." With horror the poet looks at the trends of urban Australia and suggests that

> To find some essence ours, that is the land's,
> True to its nature, fitted to its ends,
> Direct, attuned and native, we return

> To men and buildings of the primary age.

> – from "The Hotel Namatjira"

> – Anna Rutherford

ROWSE, A(fred) L(eslie). British. Born in St. Austell, Cornwall, 4 December 1903. Educated at Christ Church, Oxford (Douglas Jerrold Scholar), M.A. in English Literature 1929. Since 1925, Fellow, All Souls College, Oxford. President of the English Association, 1952–53; Millar Visiting Professor, University of Illinois, Urbana, 1952–53; Raleigh Lecturer, the British Academy, 1957; Visiting Professor, University of Wisconsin, Madison, 1959–60; Trevelyan Lecturer, Cambridge University, 1958; Research Associate, Huntington Library, San Marino, California, 1962–69; Beatty Memorial Lecturer, McGill University, Montreal, 1963. D.Litt.: Oxford University, 1953; University of Exeter, 1960; D.C.L.: University of New Brunswick, Fredericton, 1960. Fellow, British Academy, 1958; Fellow, Royal Society of Literature. Address: All Souls College, Oxford, England.

PUBLICATIONS

Verse

> *Poems of a Decade, 1931–1941.* London, Faber, 1942.
> *Poems Chiefly Cornish.* London, Faber, 1944.
> *Poems of Deliverance.* London, Faber, 1946.
> *Poems Partly American.* London, Faber, 1959.
> *Poems of Cornwall and America.* London, Faber, 1967.
> *Strange Encounter.* London, Cape, 1972.

Short Stories

> *West Country Stories.* London, Macmillan, 1945.
> *Cornish Stories.* London, Macmillan, 1967.

Other

> *On History: A Study of Present Tendencies.* London, Paul Trench Trubner, 1927; as *Science and History: A New View of History,* New York, Norton, 1928.
> *Politics and the Younger Generation.* London, Faber, 1931.
> *The Question of the House of Lords.* London, Hogarth Press, 1934.
> *Queen Elizabeth and Her Subjects,* with G. B. Harrison. London, Allen and Unwin, 1935.
> *Mr. Keynes and the Labour Movement.* London, Macmillan, 1935.
> *Sir Richard Grenville of the Revenge: An Elizabethan Hero.* London, Cape, and Boston, Houghton Mifflin, 1937.
> *Tudor Cornwall: Portrait of a Society.* London, Cape, 1941; revised edition, London, Macmillan, and New York, Scribner, 1969.
> *A Cornish Childhood: Autobiography of a Cornishman.* London, Cape, 1942; New York, Macmillan, 1947.
> *The Spirit of English History.* London, Longman, 1943; New York, Oxford University Press, 1945.
> *The English Spirit: Essays in History and Literature.* London, Macmillan, 1944; revised edition, 1966; New York, Funk and Wagnalls, 1967.
> *The Use of History.* London, English Universities Press, 1946; New York, Macmillan, 1948; revised edition, English Universities Press, and New York, Collier, 1963.

The End of an Epoch: Reflections on Contemporary History. London, Macmillan, 1947.

The England of Elizabeth: The Structure of Society. London, Macmillan, 1950; New York, Macmillan, 1951.

The English Past: Evocations of Places and Persons. London, Macmillan, 1951; New York, Macmillan, 1952; revised edition, as *Times, Persons, Places: Essays in Literature,* New York, Macmillan, 1965.

History of France, by Lucien Romier (translated and completed). London, Macmillan, and New York, St. Martin's Press, 1953.

A New Elizabethan Age? London, Oxford University Press, 1952.

An Elizabethan Garland. London, Macmillan, and New York, St. Martin's Press, 1953.

The Expansion of Elizabethan England. London, Macmillan, and New York, St. Martin's Press, 1955.

The Churchills: The Story of a Family. London, Macmillan, and New York, Harper, 1966.
  I. *The Early Churchills: An English Family.* London, Macmillan, and New York, Harper, 1956.
  II. *The Later Churchills.* London, Macmillan, 1958; as *The Churchills: From the Death of Marlborough to the Present,* New York, Harper, 1958.

The Elizabethans and America. London, Macmillan, and New York, Harper, 1959.

St. Austell: Church, Town, Parish. St. Austell, Cornwall, Warne, 1960.

All Souls and Appeasement: A Contribution to Contemporary History. London, Macmillan, 1961; as *Appeasement: A Study in Political Decline 1933–1939,* New York, Norton, 1961.

Ralegh and the Throckmortons. London, Macmillan, 1962; as *Sir Walter Ralegh, His Family and Private Life,* New York, Harper, 1962.

William Shakespeare: A Biography. London, Macmillan, 1962; New York, Harper, 1963.

Christopher Marlowe: A Biography. London, Macmillan, 1964; as *Christopher Marlowe: His Life and Works,* New York, Harper, 1965.

A Cornishman at Oxford: The Education of a Cornishman. London, Cape, 1965.

Shakespeare's Southampton: Patron of Virginia. London, Macmillan, and New York, Harper, 1965.

Bosworth Field and the Wars of the Roses. London, Macmillan, 1966; as *Bosworth Field: From Medieval to Tudor England,* New York, Doubleday, 1966.

The Contribution of Cornwall and Cornishmen to Britain. Newton Abbot, Devon, Seale-Hayne Agricultural College, 1969.

The Cornish in America. London, Macmillan, 1969; as *The Cousin Jacks: The Cornish in America,* New York, Scribner, 1969.

The Elizabethan Renaissance:
  I. *The Life of the Society.* London, Macmillan, 1971; New York, Scribner, 1972.
  II. *The Cultural Achievement.* London, Macmillan, 1972.

The Tower of London in the History of the Nation. London, Weidenfeld and Nicolson, and New York, Putnam, 1972.

The Abbey in the History of the Nation, in *Westminster Abbey.* London, Weidenfeld and Nicolson, 1972.

Shakespeare the Man. London, Macmillan, 1973.

Windsor Castle in the History of the Nation. London, Weidenfeld and Nicolson, 1974.

Simon Forman: Sex and Society in Shakespeare's Age. London, Weidenfeld and Nicolson, 1974; New York, Scribner, 1975.

Peter, The White Cat of Trenarren.   London, Joseph, 1974.

Editor, with M. I. Henderson, *Studies in Cornish History*, by Charles Hender-
son.   London, Oxford University Press, 1935.
Editor, *The West in English History.*   London, Hodder and Stoughton, 1949.
Editor, *Shakespeare's Sonnets.*   London, Macmillan, and New York, Harper,
1964; revised edition, as *Shakespeare's Sonnets: The Problems Solved*, Macmil-
lan and Harper, 1973.
Editor, *A Cornish Anthology.*   London, Macmillan, 1968.
Editor, *The Two Chiefs of Dunboy: A Story of 18th Century Ireland*, by J. A.
Froude.   London, Chatto and Windus, 1969.
Editor, with John Betjeman, *Victorian and Edwardian Cornwall from Old
Photographs.*   London, Batsford, 1974.

A. L. Rowse comments:

A Celt, growing up in Cornwall, I was early influenced by the Irish poets,
especially Yeats. At Oxford I discovered the poetry of T. S. Eliot, whose work,
help, and friendship became the most fruitful and enduring affiliation in my career
of writing. He first published my work in prose as well as verse, and recognizably
wrote the blurbs for the first three volumes of my poems. In my early verse I was
particularly interested in exploring the emotion of fear, and – naturally, owing to
long years of illness – in expressing the heightened sensitivity, the extra-sensory
experiences, that went with it. Wartime brought renewed health, a more varied and
outgoing response, some reconciliation with life, which I always found difficult.
Hence the strain of bitterness, an iron element, that runs all through my work,
disgust with human foolery, *contemptus mundi*, though not in a religious sense, any
more than with Yeats. (Swift much influenced my outlook from youth on.)

As a Celt I have an extra-sensitivity to atmosphere and have given it expression
all along, chiefly in relation to Cornwall, but also in Oxford and America. (Very
few British poets have been inspired to write about America.) Places speak to me
rather than people and are apt to mean more to me. My inner life, from which the
poetry springs, has been withdrawn – my outer life has gone into history and
politics. But the inner life has always meant more, and by keeping it apart I have
kept a flow of inspiration going, where some of my more publicized contemporaries
have dried up. One should never be too self-conscious about the springs of art. I
don't mind paying the price of not having my poetry noticed – rather a joke really –
since it enables me to continue to write. (The joke is on the critics: the combined
work in prose and verse, history and literature, is evidently too much for them at
present, though they should see that there is a rare literary phenomenon to be
investigated.)

A self-contained life, withdrawn from the public eye, a solipsistic outlook, is best
for an artist in the hideous contemporary world, so discouraging to real poetry
(other than journalistic) – what Yeats described as "this filthy modern tide." He
held fast to "his ghostly solitude" as I do. So, I have held by Yeats, early and late,
with no more compassion for fools than he or Swift had.

I find traditional verse forms sufficient for what I have to say. Earlier I was
attracted by disjoined couplets in rhyme and half-rhyme, like Wilfred Owen,
another Celt. Neither blank verse nor free verse has been altogether blank or free
with me: each has always had a good deal of unobtrusive decoration, internal as
well as end-rhymes, and much alliteration (instinctive, the unconscious mark of the
poet). Eliot liked (as well as published) my poetry and used to say that I should
give myself more to it; but I was afraid of losing inspiration if I forced myself and

worked at it: I prefer to trust to the creative urges of the unconscious. However, before I die I should like to write one long narrative poem on a Cornish theme.

Perhaps I have given to history – and wasted on politics – something of what should have gone to poetry.

*   *   *

Readers and admirers of A. L. Rowse's autobiographical books have on the whole failed to follow the history of his personality into the field of his poetry, which continues to reveal one of the most complex, sometimes irritating, always sensitive and interesting personalities of our time. His earlier collections (*Poems Chiefly Cornish* or *Poems of a Decade*) chronicle his love-hate relationship with Cornwall, and through the four subsequent volumes his landscape poems continue to be remarkably vivid. But the personal note continues, too, and grows stronger. Sometimes it is recognisably the tone in which Dr. Rowse conducts his public altercations: "The Cornish crowd / Into the compartment, chattering / As ever with platitudinous vacuity"; but, more rewardingly, it is dark, melancholy, inward-turned: "A public man, scarred with injuries, / Seared by sad experience, without illusion / Or any hope, dedicated to despair," But then there is the note of simple pleasure, in such traditionally pure verses as "How Many Miles to Mylor" and "Child's Verses for Winter." Dr. Rowse's poetry shows almost as many faces as his prose (he is historian, literary critic, editor, biographer, short-story writer). Sturdily in traditional forms, it opens out his personality – as it should – more fully than his critics have understood, and it is much undervalued.

– Derek Parker

RUBIN, Larry (Jerome). American. Born in Bayonne, New Jersey, 14 February 1930. Educated at Columbia University, New York, 1949–50; Emory University, Atlanta, Georgia, B.A. 1951 (Phi Beta Kappa), M.A. 1952, Ph.D. 1956. Instructor, 1956–58, Assistant Professor, 1958–65, Associate Professor, 1965–73, and since 1973, Professor of English, Georgia Institute of Technology, Atlanta. Visiting Professor of American Literature (Smith-Mundt Award), University of Krakow, Poland, 1961–62; Fulbright Lecturer in American Literature, University of Bergen, Norway, 1966–67, Free University of Berlin, 1969–70, and University of Innsbruck, Austria, 1971–72. Recipient: Poetry Society of America Reynolds Lyric Award, 1961, Prize 1973; Sidney Lanier Award, Oglethorpe University, 1964. Address: Box 15014, Druid Hills Branch, Atlanta, Georgia, 30333, U.S.A.

PUBLICATIONS

Verse

The World's Old Way. Lincoln, University of Nebraska Press, 1962.
Lanced in Light. New York, Harcourt Brace, 1967.
All My Mirrors Lie. Boston, Godine Press, 1975.

Manuscript Collection: Special Collections, Woodruff Memorial Library, Emory University, Atlanta.

Critical Studies: by Charles Beaumont, in *Georgia Review* (Athens), Winter 1963; "A Catalogue of Nine" by Felix Stefanile, in *Poetry* (Chicago), February 1964; John R. Willingham, in *Library Journal* (New York), August 1967; Louis Ginsberg, in *The Poetry Society of America Bulletin* (New York), February 1968; "A Point in Time, A Place in Space" by F. H. Griffin Taylor, in *The Sewanee Review* (Tennessee), Spring 1969.

Larry Rubin comments:

My themes are the familiar ones of time, love, death, friendship, isolation, childhood; when I write about family life, I find myself dealing, on the whole, with familial guilt, rather than familial devotion. I have also been emphasizing, of late, the vulnerability of the lover, and of the friend. I am concerned with betrayals, but also with reconciliations. I try to get quickly to the core of feeling, without relying on extraneous and obscure allusions or on cumbersome mythologies. It is in Emily Dickinson's poetry that I find most clearly the compactness and incisiveness that I aim for. In my poetry I try to fulfil my own critical test of a poem, and that is that it should make an immediate emotional impact upon the reader. My usual verse forms include a sort of modified blank verse, a free verse form which I try to control carefully, and a four-line iambic tetrameter stanza with slant rhymes, often in varying positions in each stanza.

*   *   *

Larry Rubin's poems take the reader into a subtle and private world, their subject-matter apparently determined by circumstance rather than consciously chosen by the author. His experience, after the death of his parents, as a Jew, a bachelor, a teacher, an expatriate momentarily in love, is recounted and dutifully catalogued.

In the early poems, the voice is appropriate to the subject, but later it falters, particularly in *Lanced in Light*, where the speaker's involvement with various subjects seems distant, casual, almost disinterested. As a poet, Rubin is always competent – rather like a veteran reporter whose articles show extensive know-ledge, an acute ear, a facility in language, but sometimes a mere academic interest in the topic under discussion, as in "Souvenir," "After Italy," "in lower case," and "The Uninvolved."

The poems in *The World's Old Way*, on the other hand, are consistently witty, lively, precise, inviting, and repay repeated readings. Several of them belong in any collection of the best short lyrics published in America since 1960, particularly "A Note on Library Policy" and that perfect stylistic parody of its subject "Emily Dickinson on Etiquette":

If God came calling at my house,
I'd ask him in for tea
And comment on the lovely day
That brought such Deity.

I'd ask him were his angels well,
And if his saints had dined;
Somehow I'd steer the table talk
On well-accepted lines.

But should he fail to take the hint
And probe my soul in two,
I'd rise a little formally
And end the interview.

Almost as successful, in metrical skill and total effect, are "The Anarchist," "God Opens His Mail," "For a Poet's Wife, Who Has Conceived" (which begins, "You bear creation's double burden"), and several of the poems from the sequence entitled "Greek Family Life."

One looks for a similar authority in all his work. In searching for a new direction or in deepening his own very personal style, Rubin will undoubtedly regain that sophistication in manner and method that he exhibited so frequently in the early poems. Indeed, in "The Discard" and "Annual Checkup," published after his second volume, it appears that that has already begun to happen.

– Michael True

RUKEYSER, Muriel. American. Born in New York City, 15 December 1913. Educated at Fieldston Schools, 1919–30; Vassar College, Poughkeepsie, New York; Columbia University, New York, 1930–32. Has one son. Vice-President, House of Photography, New York, 1946–60. Taught at Sarah Lawrence College, Bronxville, New York, 1946, 1956–57. Since 1967, Member, Board of Directors, Teachers-Writers Collaborative, New York. Recipient: Yale Series of Younger Poets Award, 1935; Oscar Blumenthal Prize, 1940, Levinson Prize, 1947, and Eunice Tietjens Memorial Prize, 1962 (*Poetry,* Chicago); Harriet Monroe Award, 1941; National Institute of Arts and Letters Award, 1942; Guggenheim Fellowship, 1943; American Council of Learned Societies Fellowship, 1963; Swedish Academy translation award, 1967. D.Litt.: Rutgers University, New Brunswick, New Jersey, 1961. Member, National Institute of Arts and Letters. Agent: Monica McCall, International Famous Agency, 1301 Avenue of the Americas, New York, New York 10019. Address: Westbeth, 463 West Street, New York, New York 10014, U.S.A.

PUBLICATIONS

Verse

Theory of Flight. New Haven, Connecticut, Yale University Press, 1935.
U.S. 1. New York, Covici Friede, 1938.

Mediterranean. Privately printed, 1938.
A Turning Wind: Poems. New York, Viking Press, 1939.
The Soul and Body of John Brown. New York, privately printed, 1940.
Wake Island. New York, Doubleday, 1942.
Beast in View. New York, Doubleday, 1944.
The Children's Orchard. San Francisco, Book Club of California, 1947.
The Green Wave. New York, Doubleday, 1948.
Orpheus. San Francisco, Centaur Press, 1949.
Elegies. New York, New Directions, 1949.
Selected Poems. New York, New Directions, 1951.
Body of Waking. New York, Harper, 1958.
Waterlily Fire: Poems 1932–1962. New York, Macmillan, 1962.
The Outer Banks. Santa Barbara, California, Unicorn Press, 1967.
The Speed of Darkness. New York, Random House, 1968.
29 Poems. London, Rapp and Whiting, 1970.
Breaking Open. New York, Random House, 1973.

Play

The Color of the Day (produced Poughkeepsie, New York, 1961).

Novel

The Orgy. New York, Coward McCann, 1965; London, Deutsch, 1966.

Other

Willard Gibbs (biography). New York, Doubleday, 1942.
The Life of Poetry. New York, Current Books, 1949.
Come Back Paul (juvenile). New York, Harper, 1955.
One Life (biography of Wendell Willkie). New York, Simon and Schuster, 1957.
I Go Out (juvenile). New York, Harper, 1961.
Bubbles (juvenile). New York, Harcourt Brace, 1967.
Poetry, and Unverifiable Fact: The Clark Lectures. Claremont, California, Scripps College, 1968.
The Traces of Thomas Hariot. New York, Random House, 1971.

Translator, with others, *Selected Poems of Octavio Paz.* Bloomington, Indiana University Press, 1963; revised edition, New York, New Directions, 1973.
Translator, *Sun Stone,* by Octavio Paz. New York, New Directions, 1963.
Translator, with Leif Sjöberg, *Selected Poems of Gunnar Ekelöf.* New York, Twayne, 1967.
Translator, *Three Poems by Gunnar Ekelöf.* Lawrence, Kansas, T. Williams, 1967.

*   *   *

Much has been said about the feminine voice in poetry, usually by male critics. No one seems to know exactly what the "true" feminine voice is, except that somewhere between the despair and the joy of woman's second-class existence, a kind of experience is finally being written. Sylvia Plath wrote from this sensibility and a number of new lady poets have missed the joy expressed between the lines, where Plath had made words that work together. The assumption that despair should somehow outweigh joy in serious feminine poetry results from the Dickinson (and now, Plath) tradition.

Reading the work of Muriel Rukeyser, one quickly learns that feminism is not so easily defined. Once again, the near-answer is revealed for what it is, and we are thrown back to the poem itself. Rukeyser's work can be despairing, but her responses have larger potential. Even in moments of sad recollection, Rukeyser's voice is not entirely despondent:

> When I was three, a little child read a story about a rabbit
> who died, in the story, and I crawled under a chair   :
> a pink rabbit   :   it was my birthday, and a candle
> burnt a sore spot on my finger, and I was told to be happy.
>   – from "Effort at Speech Between Two People"

Here, Rukeyser has successfully combined the elements of mature narrative with a verbal sense of what it was like to live through that third birthday. The poem is not cute, in any of its aspects, and in spite of succeeding lines ("I am unhappy. I am lonely. Speak to me.") never indulges in outright despondency. It is the hope for communication that has initially caused the poem which survives, echoed by lively images, and imbuing the poem ultimately with a sense of optimism:

> I stood in a crowded street that was live with people,
> and no one spoke a word, and the morning shone.
> Everyone silent, moving. . . . Take my hand. Speak to me.

Rukeyser's work is always tough, however, and never assumes the false authority that is so often mistaken for wisdom. She investigates nearly every aspect of life, from the desparate haircutting of a boy who needs work to "The Power of Suicide," one of her tight, excellent four-line poems:

> The potflower on the windowsill says to me
> In words that are green-edged red leaves:
> Flower   flower   flower   flower
> Today for the sake of all the dead   Burst into flower.

The simplicity of such a poem makes explication impossible: what gimmicks of "style" has the poet employed? One knows only that the poem is bound by a natural rhythm, and seems to relate a part of the poet's experience.

Some of Rukeyser's long poems, in particular "The Speed of Darkness," title poem of the book in which it appears, are among the finest we'll have to carry with us into the next century. Her vocabulary is truly of our generation, but she's writing poems of a longer endurance:

> Whoever despises the clitoris despises the penis
> Whoever despises the penis despises the cunt
> Whoever despises the cunt despises the life of the child.
>
> Resurrection music,   silence,   and surf.

In "Waterlily Fire," she curiously mixes hard consonant sounds with a softer, feminine voice:

> We pray : we dive into each other's eyes.
> Whatever can come to a woman can come to me.
> This is the long body : into life from the beginning. . . .

The toughness of these poems suggests that "feminine," with all its present connotations, is not the correct adjective for Miss Rukeyser's work. The frankness of her love poems (read "What I See") combined with her muted optimism also makes for memorable poetry.

For the moment, such "optimism" seems the only valid voice that any poet, regardless of sex, can bring to his work. Anything else is a lie, or why would the poet trouble to write at all?

Muriel Rukeyser's poetry *is* feminine, but only because the poet is a lady. It is enduring because the poet has retained all of her "seventeen senses," and utilizes every one of them in her work:

> : After I am dead, darling,
>   my seventeen senses gone,
> I shall love you as you wish,
>   no sex, no mouth, but bone –
>   in the way you long for now,
> with my soul alone.

> : When we are neither woman nor man
>   but bleached to skeleton –
> when you have changed, my darling,
>   and all your senses gone,
>   it is not me that you will love:
> you will love everyone.
>
> – "What They Said"

– Geof Hewitt

RUSSELL, (Irwin) Peter. British. Born in 1921. Served in the British Army, 1939–46. Owner of bookshop and poetry press, 1950–63. Has lived in Venice since 1964. Address: Castello 3611, Venice 30122, Italy.

PUBLICATIONS

Verse

Picnic to the Moon. Privately printed, 1944.
Descent: A Poem Sequence. Tunbridge Wells, Kent, privately printed, 1952.
The Spirit and the Body: An Orphic Poem. Fairwarp, Sussex, privately printed, 1956.
Images of Desire: Discreete Sonets. London, Gallery Bookshop, 1962.
Dreamland and Drunkenness. London, Gallery Bookshop, 1963.
Complaints to Circe. London, privately printed, 1963.

Visions and Ruins: An Existentialist Poem. Aylesford, Kent, Saint Albert's
  Press, 1964.
Agamemnon in Hades. Aylesford, Kent, Saint Albert's Press, 1965.
The Golden Chain: Lyrical Poems 1964–1969. Venice, privately printed, 1970.
Paysages Légendaires. London, Enitharmon Press, 1971.

Other

  Editor, *Ezra Pound: A Collection of Essays . . . to Be Presented to Ezra Pound on
    His Sixty-Fifth Birthday.* London, Peter Nevill, and New York, New Direc-
    tions, 1950.
  Editor, *Money Pamphlets by £.* London, Peter Russell, 6 vols., 1950–51.
  Editor, with Khushwant Singh, *A Note . . . on G. V. Desani's "All about H.
    Hatterr" and "Hali."* London and Amsterdam, Szeben, 1952.
  Editor, *ABC of Economics,* by Ezra Pound. Tunbridge Wells, Kent, Pound
    Press, 1953.

  Translator, *Three Elegies of Quintilius.* Tunbridge Wells, Kent, Pound Press,
    1954.
  Translator, *Landscapes,* by Camillo Pennati (bilingual edition). Richmond, Sur-
    rey, Keepsake Press, 1964.
  Translator, *The Elegies of Quintilius.* London, Anvil Press Poetry, 1973.

                              *   *   *

For me, Peter Russell is the major neglected talent of our time – the author of
the finest book of purely "English" lyrics (*The Golden Chain*) of the last twenty
years; the author of a gigantic, mostly unpublished epic poem, *Ephemoron*, running
to some two thousand pages; the author of *Paysages Légendaires*, a book impreg-
nated with great wisdom and that music the Celts call the "cael moer" or the
"great music." In Peter Russell, we are dealing with not just the Poundian theory
of the multilingual poet of the future (and Russell was Pound's greatest disciple),
but with the realization of such a poet as fact. The sheer magnitude of the job of
investigating the innumerable works produced by Russell since *Picnic to the Moon* in
1944 is not a sufficient excuse for not trying. Still less is it an excuse for the
wanton neglect of a poet of whom such a figure as Hugh MacDiarmid has written:
"Peter Russell is, in my opinion, a writer who has so far received nothing like due
recognition . . . no one in Great Britain today has rendered anything like the
disinterested, many-sided and sustained service to Poetry" – the latter comment
referring to Russell's work as editor of *Nine* and as publisher of so many of today's
established figures long before they were known.
  Of *Paysages Légendaires*, Hugh McKinley's phrase "tribute open-eyed, yet illuminate, of life entire" is remarkably apposite. This is how the poem opens:

            Palladian villas and the changing seasons

            An old man digging in the shade

            The gold sun varnishes
            The small viridian of the elms
            And gilds the hidden cadmium of the glades.

In fact, its way of expression throughout is best described as an open-eyed style.
  So, too, it is a rare book of unimpeachable seriousness and poetic wisdom.

Perhaps the most interesting feature of *Paysages Légendaires* (and the explanation of its style) is the absence of a close or particularly tense (or over-tense) verbal and syntactical density, which induces an unusual clarity in the verse. And this goes a long way towards compensating for the major disadvantage of a modern sequential but non-narrative long poem, namely, the breaks in continuity which so trouble the average reader. It is a poem that reads well.

The sheer intelligence of the poem commands respect; but what matters is that one feels it is an extraordinarily "aware" poem – a poem aware of, and in touch with the main-stream of human thought. This awareness of the "now" is undoubtedly achieved by a profound knowledge of the "then" and exemplifies what is, perhaps, the poem's central pre-occupation:

> It will take time to build again,
> To build the soul's tall house,
> The tower of the wandering self
> Foursquare beneath the moon.

Many people, myself among them, think that poetry – the "real" of the thing, the heart's meat of the matter – is the line, or lines of words that are necklace-perfect. Something that glitters with ineffable quality, wisdom, beauty, LIFE – a kind of instant of revelation in words, the discovery, as Russell puts it, that

> Every natural effect has a spiritual cause
> (That which is above, is below).

Indeed, if poetry is the unshakable line, memorable phrase – then Peter Russell is probably the greatest English poet now writing.

Myth is the stuff of thought one might say and *Paysages Légendaires* is a "thoughtful poem." There is little concrete description, and, where there is, the object tends towards the emblematic and metaphorical. There is, however, one short passage where the descriptive element is uppermost:

> Sweet bones are growing in the earthly night
>
> Slow maturations in the endless dark
> Of subterranean galleries, telluric force
> That broods whole centuries upon a single grain
> That crumbles or coagulates.

One gets a sense of the tremendousness of life, its continual working; the key word is "broods" – it reveals brilliantly the meaning behind the description, the life within.

Apart from the practical problem of the range of this poet's work, there is one other problem, which is only a "problem" in the framework of present day poetry's dusty picture. This derives from the fact that the more one reads Russell's poetry, the more one realises that it demands imagination. In poem after poem, one finds the feeling transcending the flat detail of experience. So, too, there is a copious knowledge displayed of life both past and present, and there is that true linguistic metamorphosis at times, which provides a permanent frame – be it only a single good line – in which the present is held up before our eyes to be seen in infinite terms. Therefore, parodying Pound, these poems must "go to the imaginative" if they are to be understood, and to the serious if they are to be loved.

– William Oxley

RUTSALA, Vern. American. Born in McCall, Idaho, 5 February 1934. Educated at Reed College, Portland, Oregon, B.A. 1956; University of Iowa, Iowa City, M.F.A. 1960. Served in the United States Army, 1956–58. Married Joan Colby in 1957; has three children. Since 1961, Associate Professor, Lewis and Clark College, Portland, Oregon. Visiting Professor, University of Minnesota, Minneapolis, 1968–69; Bowling Green State University, Ohio, 1970. Editor, *December* magazine, Western Springs, Illinois, 1959–62. Recipient: National Endowment for the Arts grant, 1974. Address: Department of English, Lewis and Clark College, Portland, Oregon 97219, U.S.A.

PUBLICATIONS

Verse

The Window: Poems. Middletown, Connecticut, Wesleyan University Press, 1964.
Small Songs: A Sequence of Poems. Iowa City, Stone Wall Press, 1969.
The Harmful State. Lincoln, Nebraska, Best Cellar Press, 1971.
Laments. New York, New Rivers Press, 1975.

Other

Editor, *British Poetry 1972*. Phoenix, Arizona, The Baleen Press, 1972.

Critical Study: by Norman Friedman, in *Chicago Review*, June 1967.

Vern Rutsala comments:

Many of the poems in *The Window* are centered in and around houses – often houses in some worn suburb – and are concerned with what might be seen in such an area. The central image of the window is appropriate, then, and the poems reflect both what can be observed and what happens within. More recent work follows this pattern though its focus is usually much more inward. Though the rhythms I use are relatively free, I often like to make use of regular stanza forms. My themes are not unusual – the common obsessions of poets: how does one live? why is the world as it is? Recently I have become interested in the possibilities of the prose poem and have completed a manuscript, called *Paragraphs*, which explores directions that differ a good deal from my earlier work.

Assessing my own "progress" is difficult. I keep working.

*   *   *

Vern Rutsala seems to me to have one of the keenest poetic responses to contemporary middle class society that I can remember since Cummings, Auden, the earlier Karl Shapiro, and some of Louis Simpson. His special achievement in *The Window* is to have made the furniture of everyday bourgeois life in America available to the uses of serious poetry. He is thus somewhat like one of the better

1327

Pop artists, such as Edward Kienholz, who makes assemblages out of found objects – the chassis of an old car, for example – and, with a few skilfully-constructed wire figures, can confront us with ourselves as we fumble erotically in the back seat with our dates in a doomed search for pleasure and joy ("Lovers in Summer").

But there is here not merely a familiar world of skate keys, wagons, bicycles ("Sunday"); there is also a commanding vision which governs the shaping of that world. He hears the glacier knocking in the cupboard and the rumble of violence and despair hidden within our domestic walls. Rutsala deals card after card, building up unbearably to a remorseless climax, until not a corner is left for us to hide in, nothing is spared – not a toothbrush, family album, mantlepiece clock, visit from relatives, souvenir ashtray, flushing of the toilet, garden hose – nothing escapes his illumination of things so ordinary that we have forgotten them, so close we haven't seen them, revealing what we thought we already knew but never quite understood.

Each aspect of our lives, each object of our mundane environment, is a badge of the numb but terrible disparity between life's possibilities and the horror of diminishment we are all suffering from. A bathroom mirror is a symbol of the abyss, which is not simply the inevitable loss of childhood in growing up; more, it is the crushing emptiness of spirit characteristic of living in an imperialistic, commercial, and technological civilization ("Gilbert and Market"). In such a society, even childhood is no Eden, and children are not spared ("Playground"). "Nightfall" is one of the most moving poems in the book:

> Night settles like a damp cloth
> over the houses. The houses that are shut,
> that show no wear. Lawns
> are patrolled by plywood flamingoes
> or shrubbery clipped from magazines.

The poem continues on to reveal our compulsive housecleaning, sports pages, basement workshops, repairing skills, dinner, dishes in the kitchen sink, bills, two cars, committee meetings, unused telephone appointment pads – and our desperate and suicidal children. Then, as the time for sleep comes, some of us lie awake in the glow of a cigarette, fascinated by disappointment and heartbreak. And the poem concludes, perfectly:

> Dawn lies coiled in clocks.
> There are no conclusions here. The dark is there.
> Cigarettes burn down and are ground out
> in souvenir ashtrays from vacations by the sea.

The Window does, however, suffer from two rather serious flaws: its language is overly even in tone, and its persona is not sufficiently a part of the world he sees so clearly. For all its brilliance of imagery and metaphor, Rutsala's style rarely varies from a characteristic levelness of diction, and the net effect is somewhat monotonous. And although an "I" or a "we" does appear here and there, the speaker seems more a witness and an observer than a participant, making the impact of his world more remote than it should be. The first fault awaits Rutsala's future development (*Small Songs*, his only other work I have seen, is a rather minor effort), but the second is on its way to being redeemed by the end of this volume.

"The Adventurer" is the last poem in the book, and in a situation somewhat reminiscent of Auden's "Who's Who," the speaker works out a series of contrasts between his own sedentary and domesticated existence and that of his adventurous friend, concluding:

Your actions comment on my life,
but you smudge your face
for maneuvers behind the wrong lines.
Here the war is endless, the enemy obscure.

He is not saying that our sterile suburbs are really romantic, after all. Ordinary life *is* dull, and a life of action *is* exciting. But that very dulness is the enemy, and must be conquered – the most difficult adventure of all, and the most dangerous. Surely the communiqués Rutsala has been sending back to the home front should help in mobilizing the rest of us for this enigmatic campaign, for they are aiding us in making the enemy less obscure.

– Norman Friedman

SANCHEZ, Sonia. American. Born in Birmingham, Alabama, 9 September 1934. Educated at New York University; Hunter College, New York, B.A. 1955. Has three children. Staff Member, Downtown Community School, 1965–67, and Mission Rebels in Action, 1968–69, San Francisco; Instructor, San Francisco State College, 1967–69; Lecturer in Black Literature, University of Pittsburgh, 1969–70, Rutgers University, New Brunswick, New Jersey, 1970–71, Manhattan Community College, New York, 1971–73, and Amherst College, Massachusetts, 1972–73. Recipient: P.E.N. Writing Award, 1969; National Institute of Arts and Letters grant, 1970. Ph.D. (Honorary) in Fine Arts: Wilberforce University, Ohio. Address: 86 College Street, Amherst, Massachusetts 01002, U.S.A.

PUBLICATIONS

Verse

Homecoming. Detroit, Broadside Press, 1969.
WE a BaddDDD People. Detroit, Broadside Press, 1970.
Broadside No. 34. Detroit, Broadside Press, 1970.
It's a New Day: Poems for Young Brothas and Sistuhs. Detroit, Broadside Press, 1971.
Love Poems. New York, Third Press, 1973.
A Blues Book for Blue Black Magical Women. Detroit, Broadside Press, 1973.

Recordings: *Homecoming,* Broadside Voices; *We a BaddDDD People,* Broadside Voices.

Plays

The Bronx Is Next (produced New York, 1970).
Sister Son/ji (produced Evanston, Illinois, 1971).
Dirty Hearts, '72, in *Scripts 1* (New York), November 1971.

Other

The Adventures of Fat Head and Square Head (juvenile). New York, Third
Press, 1973.
The Afternoon of Smallhead, Fathead and Squarehead (juvenile). New York,
Third Press, 1974.

Editor, *Three Hundred Sixty Degrees of Blackness Comin' at You*. N.p., 5X
Publications, 1972.
Editor, *Three Hundred Sixty Degrees of Blackness Comin' at You*. 5X Publica-
tions, 1972.
Editor, *We Be Word Sorcerers: 25 Stories by Black Americans*. New York,
Bantam, 1973.

*   *   *

Sonia Sanchez is a strong and popular poetic voice of the so-called "Black arts
movement." She directs her poetry to Black people, concentrating on such themes
as Black identity and pride, identification of the source of the Black man's difficulties (the white man and his values and actions), e.g., the "right on: wite america"
poems; guidance, instructions, and exhortations for Black directed self-
improvement, e.g., the "TCB-en Poems" in *We a BaddDDD People*; love, e.g.,
"black magic"; exposure and chastisement of white-minded, apathetic, predatory,
or faddishly revolutionary Blacks, e.g., "blk/rhetoric." Her relatively recent conversion to the Nation of Islam (Black Muslims) is reflected in the content of (and
by the absence of profanity in) her more recent poetry, e.g., "let us begin the real
work."

As her recordings and public readings would indicate, Miss Sanchez seems to
write for her own speaking voice – a sort of sing-song monotone that, curiously,
has a lilting quality. One is struck by the contrast of her strong statements with her
feminine inflection, intonation, pacing, and timbre. Frequently she punctuates her
lines with a gentle "yeh," elongates sounds, sustains parts of words, particularly
word endings, sustains or raises the pitch slightly at line or poem endings. Her
language is vigorous, direct, conversational, unabashed, by some standards coarse,
and it is not often infused with poetic indirection or metaphor. Her diction is that
of the Black urban masses. She employs "Black grammar," e.g., "we bees real /
bad"; "Black speech" sounds, e.g., "white motha / fucka"; elisions, e.g., "blk"
for black; extra vowels and consonants to approximate elongated sounds, e.g.,
"soooooo"; nonstandard spellings, e.g., "amurica"; non-words, e.g., the approximation of musical sounds in "a / coltrane / poem"; word components, e.g., "sun
day"; diagonals; and ampersands. In the free verse style, she frequently uses open
and irregular spatial arrangements, practically never uses symmetrical or formulaic
structures.

– Theodore R. Hudson

SANDERS, Ed. American. Born in Kansas City, Missouri, 17 August 1939. Educated at New York University, B.A. in classics 1963. Married Miriam Kittell in

1961; has three children. Since 1962, Editor and Publisher, *Fuck You: A Magazine of the Arts*, and *Dick*, New York. Since 1964, Organizer and Lead Singer of The Fugs, a literary-political rock group. Since 1965, Professor, Free University of New York; Owner, Peace Eye Bookstore, New York. Recipient: National Endowment for the Arts grant, 1966, 1969. Address: Westbeth, 463 West Street, New York, New York 10014, U.S.A.

PUBLICATIONS

Verse

> *Poem from Jail.*   San Francisco, City Lights Books, 1963.
> *King Lord – Queen Freak.*   Cleveland, Renegade Press, 1964.
> *The Toe-Queen: Poems.*   New York, Fuck You Press, 1964.
> *Banana: An Anthology of Banana-Erotic Poems.*   New York, Fuck You Press, 1965.
> *The Complete Sex Poems of Ed Sanders.*   New York, Fug-Press, 1965.
> *Peace Eye.*   Buffalo, New York, Frontier Press, 1965; revised edition, Cleveland, Frontier Press, 1967.
> *Shards of God.*   New York, Grove Press, 1971.
> *Egyptian Hieroglyphics.*   Canton, New York, Institute of Further Studies, 1973.

Other

> *The Family: The Story of Charles Manson's Dune Buggy Attack Battalion.*   New York, Dutton, 1971; London, Hart Davis, 1972.
> *Votel* (on Abbie Hoffman).   New York, Warner, 1972.

> Editor, *Bugger: An Anthology.*   New York, Fuck You Press, 1964.
> Editor, *Despair: Poems to Come Down By* (anthology).   New York, privately printed, 1964.

*   *   *

Ed Sanders' poems burn up incredible amounts of energy, with the nervous excitement of his poetry flashing into the reality of the person at work, consciously creating, and extremely together. As has been noted by Ted Berrigan in his review of Sanders' book *Peace Eye* in *Kulcher 20*: "The language is abrupt, it is rude and burning cold, as ancient as it is current, as literary as it is (and it is) of the streets." Sanders is interested in assault (action) leading to change. The combination of energy and change becomes revolutionary when there is a result that is recognizable, when the scope of an ideology embraces the highest possible denominator or the greatest number of people. Sanders has set his sights high and with extraordinary power and range has written a number of poems whose subjects and mood pinpoint the position of the individual in relationship to American society. Within this framework you find the man: Ed Sanders. Poetry is probably the only means of expressing the non-visual aspects of that part of your personality which drifts up through consciousness to be transformed into clear vision. Sanders' sense of himself breaks down into the idea of language as a weapon with clarity hinging on the performance so that the poet often seems inside his words, not around them, invisible while remaining on the surface, breaking even further to the point where his intelligence cuts off the vision, knowing where to stop, with perfect understanding and timing. The poems, and the language he uses, are almost "noble," their strength based on the theory that there is nothing and nowhere to hide. The fact that behind the physical and mental energy there is a tremendous warmth shining at a somewhat lower volume shadows and makes almost secondary the fact that Sanders is one of the most original poets writing today.

– Lewis Warsh

SANDY, Stephen. American. Born in Minneapolis, Minnesota, 2 August 1934. Educated at Yale University, New Haven, Connecticut, A.B.; Harvard University, Cambridge, Massachusetts, Ph.D. Instructor in English, Harvard University, 1963–67; Fulbright Lecturer, University of Tokyo, 1967–68; Visiting Assistant Professor, Brown University, Providence, Rhode Island, 1968–69; Currently, Professor of English, Bennington College, Vermont. Currently, Vice-President, Banyan Press. Address: White Creek, Eagle Bridge, New York 12057, U.S.A.

PUBLICATIONS

Verse

Caroms. Groton, Massachusetts, Groton Press, 1960.
Mary Baldwin. Dublin, Dolmen Press, 1962.
The Destruction of Bulfinch's House. Cambridge, Massachusetts, Identity, 1964.
Stresses in the Peaceable Kingdom. Boston, Houghton Mifflin, 1967.
Home Again, Looking Around. Cambridge, Massachusetts, Halty Ferguson, 1968.
Catullus LVIII: To Caelius. Tokyo, The Voyagers Press, 1969.
Japanese Room. Providence, Rhode Island, Hellcoal Press, 1969.
Jerome. Bennington, Vermont, Grel Press, 1970.
A Dissolve, music by Richard Wilson. New York, G. Schirmer, 1970.
Light in the Spring Poplars, music by Richard Wilson. New York, G. Schirmer, 1970.
Roofs. Boston, Houghton Mifflin, 1971.
Home from the Range, music by Richard Wilson. New York, G. Schirmer, 1971.
Soaking, music by Richard Wilson. New York, G. Schirmer, 1971.
Elegy, music by Richard Wilson. New York, G. Schirmer, 1972.
Can, music by Richard Wilson. New York, J. Fischer, 1973.

Play

Hieronymo: An Antiphonai Cantata, music by Henry Brant. New York, MCA Music, 1973.

Manuscript Collection: Houghton Library, Harvard University, Cambridge, Massachusetts.

Critical Studies: "Like the Bones of Dreams" by Heather Ross Miller, in *The American Scholar* (Washington, D.C.), Autumn 1967; by Vernon Young, in *Hudson Review* (New York), Winter 1971–72; Richard Howard, in *American Poetry Review* (Philadelphia), May-June 1973.

*   *   *

In *Stresses in the Peaceable Kingdom*, Stephen Sandy captures the incongruities inherent in modern life and writes of his loss of innocence and struggle to find a place in a world where modern technology has destroyed the old idols, dirtied the landscape, and sullied man's soul. Employing a style which combines conversational ease with clarity and precision of diction, and drawing on his keen sensitivity and penetrating powers of observation, Sandy's poems are a series of epiphanies which compel the reader to see vividly the objects or moments he renders. The theme of loss runs through most of his poems, be it loss of innocence, or past traditions, or of old landmarks like the Grand Union, or of myths, or of the rural landscapes that are now streaked with tollways. Too often the poems are tinged with nostalgia although Sandy occasionally escapes this mood and treats loss with good humor, wit, or painful irony. In some poems it is the ravishes of technology that Sandy depicts, as in "The Destruction of Bulfinch's House" where he renders the old mansion-turned-tenement in a mood reminiscent of Eliot's "Preludes"; in others he writes whimsically of technology's products. In "Can," he transforms a can into "a bent tin soldier," jobless, knocking about, grinning through jagged teeth. In "The Woolworth Philodendron," he rescues the "proto gewgaw" from its sullen state in the "greenhouse of simulex and excelsior" and brings it home to grow again in complicity with the sun. In "Soaking" it is the delights of the bath that he evokes, making us feel the microbubble of air that tickles his spine and the warm water that creeps above his earlobes, and making us hear the squeak of his soles on the enamel tub and the gurglings of his stomach magnified by the water. In "The Hunter's Moon," amused by a cocky dragonfly buzzing him, his eye becomes a magnifying glass reflecting the insect's wing: ". . . floating / like seaweed or a / mote down the eye's film, / he stained the sky with / four mica-seamed wings, / just able to hold / onto his outrigged / eyes, spying——." In "Hiawatha" and "Home from the Range," Sandy protests against man's indifference to humanity and decries his loss of innocence. These poems practice a painful irony. In the former, he movingly describes his boyhood haunt:

>   . . . . Behind our fall
> in the hollow we hid laughing,
> quaffing the yellow mist; once,
> dizzily bracing, gave streams of urine to the torrent.
> Our selves. In that shade, shreds of sunlight and water
> spattered us, held us. In that place we
> were of it: outside was make-believe. Then
> sun alone webbed our eyes; the misty
> light walked on our legs

and goes on to parallel the destruction of the fall which was part of his boyhood trust in the myth of the Indian's wildness and nobility with the Indians' relinquishment of their sacred relics to the white man who had conquered them and the attendant destruction of their civilization. In "Home from the Range" the refrain from the folksong is used ironically to describe the poet's return, not from the range where deer and antelope play, but from the firing range where he has lost part of his hearing.

In *Roofs*, Sandy's most recent collection, he presents a series of poems that traces his journey from New England to Japan and back again and reflects upon the paradoxes in the modern Japanese experience and in his own reaction to it. Again in this volume as in the first, his strength lies in his ability to see deeply and create word pictures as delicate and enduring as those painted on a Japanese screen. Again he pits past against present in his poems and explores the conflicts which arise when different cultures confront each other and when two cultures who share a common heritage make war upon each other. In this volume, his poems of protest against the war are more intense and personal than before. His elegy "Charley" on the death of a friend killed in the demilitarized zone and "Moving Out" bewilder and pain the reader. Finally, this volume develops a technique to satisfy a problem posed in the earlier collection. In "Breaks" from *Stresses in the Peaceable Kingdom*, Sandy cannot remember the outlines of his lover's face nor the timbre of her voice. "It is time, the space between us, wins" he writes and goes on to liken the difficulty of keeping her in perspective to the difficulty of moving a cobweb without altering the spaces that separate its filaments. In *Roofs*, Sandy continues to want to preserve the spaces, to make them felt, but here, in "Intersections," he finds a technique which allows him to depict disparate elements while forcing us to feel the distance that separates them and know the impossibility of synthesizing them. He preserves tension and the sense of space by actually employing large spaces between the print on the page. Sandy's skill as an artist is more certain in this volume: he captures the stylized figures of Japan's past, his verbal plays are less ostentatious and self-conscious than they were in the earlier volume, and the world he draws is more complex.

– Carol Simpson Stern

SAROYAN, Aram. American. Born in New York City, 25 September 1943; son of the writer William Saroyan. Educated at Trinity High School, New York; University of Chicago; New York University; Columbia University, New York. Married Gailyn McClanahan in 1968; has two daughters. Founding Editor, *Lines*, 1964–65, and Publisher, Lines Books, New York. Recipient: National Endowment for the Arts grant, 1966, 1968. Address: 11 Alder, Bolinas, California 94924, U.S.A.

PUBLICATIONS

Verse

 Poems, with Jenni Caldwell and Richard Kolmar. New York, Acadia Press, 1963.
 In. Eugene, Oregon, The Bear Press, 1964.
 Top. New York, Lines Books, 1965.

Works.   New York, Lines Books, 1966.
Sled Hill Voices.   London, Goliard Press, 1966.
(Poems).   New York, Lines Books, 1967.
Poems.   Cambridge, Massachusetts, Lines Books, 1967.
Coffee Coffee.   New York, 0 to 9 Books, 1967.
© *1968 by Aram Saroyan.*   New York, Kulchur Press, 1968.
(Poems).   New York, Random House, 1968.
Pages.   New York, Random House, 1969.
Words and Photographs.   Chicago, Big Table Books, 1970.
The Beatles.   Cambridge, Massachusetts, Barn Dream Press, 1970.
5 Mini-Books.   Palisades, California, privately printed, 1971.
Cloth: An Electric Novel.   Chicago, Big Table Books, 1971.
The Rest.   Philadelphia, Telegraph Books, 1971.
Poems.   Philadelphia, Telegraph Books, 1972.
By Air Mail, with Victor Bockris.   London, Strange Faeces Press, 1972.

Manuscript Collection: Special Collections, University of California, Los Angeles.

Aram Saroyan comments:

I write on a typewriter, almost never in hand (I can hardly handwrite, I tend to draw words), and my machine – an obsolete red-top Royal Portable – is the biggest influence on my work. This red hood holds the mood, keeps my eye happy. The typeface is a standard pica; if it were another style I'd write (subtly) different poems. And when a ribbon gets dull my poems I'm sure change.

– 1966.

ELECTRIC POETRY

By electric I mean instantaneous – without any reading process at all; and therefore continuous – as the Present is – without beginning, middle, or end.

– 1968.

(1974) Having spent the past five years largely organizing my previous work and seeing most of it into print, I now find myself writing again, but with a new orientation.

Although I regard my work as a concrete poet, and my later work with the book form itself (*Words and Photographs, Cloth, 5 Mini-Books,* and *The Beatles*) as valid, I feel I have explored this direction as thoroughly as I am able, and hence I am no longer personally interested in it. My new writing, which began with my settling in Bolinas, California, in August 1972, is primarily a return to and an extension of my earlier work as a poet *(Poems)* in which I wrote about my life as honestly as I could, employing conventional syntax. I feel I made a breakthrough in this mode with a poem.called "Lines for My Autobiography," written over a period of three days in Bolinas; and seemingly on the momentum of this work have followed three books (the third currently in the writing) – *Lines for My Autobiography, Friendly Persuasion,* and *Poetry in Motion.* With the second of these books, I began composing poems in hand.

*   *   *

Aram Saroyan's first-published poetry, written during the 1960's, established him as an experimental poet whose chief interest was concrete and "minimal" poetry.

These poems, skillful as they are, do not often extend beyond a kind of poster-like play with words and the letters of the alphabet. They become objects instantly perceived, and thus fuel for lengthy contemplation for readers so inclined. Such a poem is the untitled one-word "crickets" repeated for 37 or 42 lines, depending on which anthology you find it in. I suppose the length of this poem depends on size of the page, and perhaps Saroyan would accept the notion that a two-line version is likewise complete if printed on a shallow page:

> crickets
> crickets

The concept may well be an isolation of the components of conscious thought, and in a poem like the one just quoted, repetition and the word itself mimes its subject, and the ubiquitous nature of the crickets' song. A favorite of mine is his "My arms are warm" printed directly over his name; many of the letters used for the statement are those in "Aram Saroyan." Saroyan writes that his "concrete / minimal work now seems to have a lot to do with the strange 'time' the Sixties was for most of us. The one-word poem has *no* time in it, it can be read instantly – and this seemed to me 'perfect' for a while. Now I'm interested less in perfection and more in 'time' – I like lines, sentences, stanzas. . . ."

Saroyan's latest book, *Poems*, which he says contains his earliest poems, exemplifies his current interest in the more "traditional" forms, heavily influenced, as ever, by the "New York School," where nothing is too mundane for a place in the poem. Even Saroyan's "traditional" poems are uncommonly spare: here is all of "Almost Midnight":

> I type & think & look at the painting of Poe & out
> the window there's the top of my head, to the left
> and behind me, is the bookcase.

At times this perfected attention captures completely the glimmer of city life, and it is in poems like these that Saroyan's work most distinctly justifies the glorification of the ordinary:

> This morning I ate (bacon
> & eggs) and
> tied my tie
> in a hurry
> when I went outside
> gilt was flashing
> in the sidewalk
> and the street
> sounded like a movie

– Geof Hewitt

SARTON, May. American. Born in Wondelgem, Belgium, 3 May 1912, daughter of the historian of science George Sarton; emigrated to the United States in 1916; naturalized, 1924. Educated at the Shady Hill School and The High and Latin School, both in Cambridge, Massachusetts. Apprentice, then Member, and Director of the Apprentice Group, Eva Le Gallienne's Civic Repertory Theatre, New York,

1930–33; Founder and Director, Apprentice Theatre, New York, and Associated Actors Inc., Hartford, Connecticut, 1933–36. Taught Creative Writing and Choral Speech, Stuart School, Boston, 1937–40. Documentary Scriptwriter, Office of War Information, 1944–45. Poet-in-Residence, Southern Illinois University, Carbondale, Summer 1945; Briggs-Copeland Instructor in English Composition, Harvard University, Cambridge, Massachusetts, 1950–53; Lecturer, Breadloaf Writers' Conference, Middlebury, Vermont, 1951–52, and Boulder Writers Conference, Colorado, 1953–54; Phi Beta Kappa Visiting Scholar, 1959–60; Danforth Lecturer, 1960–61; Lecturer in Creative Writing, Wellesley College, Massachusetts, 1960–63; Poet-in-Residence, Lindenwood College, St. Charles, Missouri, 1964, 1965; Visiting Lecturer, Agnes Scott College, Decatur, Georgia, Spring 1972. Recipient: New England Poetry Club Golden Rose, 1945; Bland Memorial Prize, 1945 (*Poetry*, Chicago); American Poetry Society Reynolds Prize, 1953; Bryn Mawr College Donnelly Fellowship, 1953; Guggenheim Fellowship, 1954; Johns Hopkins University Poetry Festival Award, 1961; National Endowment for the Arts grant, 1966; Sarah Josepha Hale Award, 1972. Litt.D.: Russell Sage College, Troy, New York, 1958; New England College, Henniker, New Hampshire, 1971. Fellow, American Academy of Arts and Sciences. Address: Box C, York, Maine 03909, U.S.A.

PUBLICATIONS

Verse

Encounter in April. Boston, Houghton Mifflin, 1937.
Inner Landscape. Boston, Houghton Mifflin, 1939; with a selection from *Encounter in April,* London, Cresset Press, 1939.
The Lion and the Rose. New York, Rinehart, 1948.
The Leaves of the Tree. Ithaca, New York, Cornell College Chapbook, 1950.
The Land of Silence and Other Poems. New York, Rinehart, 1953.
In Time like Air. New York, Rinehart, 1957.
Cloud, Stone, Sun, Vine: Poems, Selected and New. New York, Norton, 1961.
A Private Mythology: New Poems. New York, Norton, 1966.
As Does New Hampshire and Other Poems. Peterborough, New Hampshire, Richard R. Smith, 1967.
A Grain of Mustard Seed: New Poems. New York, Norton, 1971.
A Durable Fire: New Poems. New York, Norton, 1972.
Collected Poems, 1930–1973. New York, Norton, 1974.

Plays

Underground River. New York, Play Club, 1947.

Screenplays: *Toscanini: The Hymn of Nations,* 1944; *Valley of the Tennessee,* 1944.

Novels

The Single Hound. Boston, Houghton Mifflin, and London, Cresset Press, 1938.
The Bridge of Years. New York, Doubleday, 1946.

Shadow of a Man.   New York, Rinehart, 1950; London, Cresset Press, 1952.
A Shower of Summer Days.   New York, Rinehart, 1952; London, Hutchinson, 1954.
Faithful Are the Wounds.   New York, Rinehart, and London, Gollancz, 1955.
The Birth of a Grandfather.   New York, Rinehart, 1957; London, Gollancz, 1958.
The Small Room.   New York, Norton, 1961; London, Gollancz, 1962.
Joanna and Ulysses.   New York, Norton, 1963; London, Murray, 1964.
Mrs. Stevens Hears the Mermaids Singing.   New York, Norton, 1965; London, Peter Owen, 1966.
Miss Pickthorn and Mr. Hare: A Fable.   New York, Norton, 1966; London, Dent, 1968.
The Poet and the Donkey.   New York, Norton, 1969.
Kinds of Love.   New York, Norton, 1970.
As We Are Now.   New York, Norton, 1973; London, Gollancz, 1974.

Other

The Fur Person: The Story of a Cat.   New York, Rinehart, 1957; London, Muller, 1958.
I Knew a Phoenix: Sketches for an Autobiography.   New York, Holt Rinehart, 1959; London, Peter Owen, 1963.
Plant Dreaming Deep (autobiography).   New York, Norton, 1968.
Journal of a Solitude.   New York, Norton, 1973.
Punch's Secret (juvenile).   New York, Harper, 1974.

Critical Studies: *May Sarton* by Agnes Sibley, New York, Twayne, 1972; "Home to a Place of Exile: The *Collected Poems* of May Sarton" by Henry Taylor, in *Hollins Critic* (Hollins College, Virginia), June 1974.

                              *   *   *

Bare of nuance and ambiguity, May Sarton's verse is often indistinguishable from ordinary prose. Within her limits, her earnest and bookish sensibility has for forty years reassured readers about the joys and even the anguishes of love, and the dedication necessary to generate art from everyday life, often at the expense of love and other relationships; beginning with *The Lion and the Rose*, many poems have soothingly transcribed the response of an aroused conscience to the horrors of war, and the deep, but curable, guilt of our racism. Her first volume articulates a view of the universe that supports many later poems on the relation between art and nature, between the artist and his work: "Objects and people / exist within this world / only if they can find their places / in a pattern" ("Portrait of One Person – As by Chirico"). Sometimes Sarton more concisely and effectively stylizes nature: ". . . the Japanese look of sleet / When it slants back the way the wind blows" ("To the Weary"), a perception that still charms many years later in *A Private Mythology*: "How Japanese the rain looked / In Cambridge" ("A Child's Japan"). As early as *The Land of Silence*, Sarton reveals an occasional skill at capturing natural detail: "As shadows made a river of the road" ("Evening Journey"). Unfortunately, she failed to develop this strength until her later volumes. Many poems celebrate specific works of art, from the early "Portrait of the Artist," which praises both the evocative and organizational power of van Cleve's self-portrait, to "Dutch Interior," which 35 years later analyzes de Hooch's skill at suggesting both the psychology and formal function of the woman in the painting. Avoiding undue modesty, Sarton places an equally high value on her own efforts: "A Letter to James Stephens" prays to transform the "Quick-burning fire of youth" to ". . . that bush of flame / That . . . contained the angel who could speak God's name. . . ." Sometimes this intense dedication collides with a familiar metaphor: "Imagine a moment when student and teacher / (Long after the day and the lesson are over) / Will soar together to the pure immortal air / And find Yeats, Hopkins, Eliot waiting there" ("Poet in Residence").

Nor are Sarton's perpetual love poems convincing, whether the youthful ecstasies of *Encounter in April* or the paeans to love at 60 of *A Durable Fire*. The lover/antagonist achieves neither credible humanity nor symbolic force as an ultra-human principle in an allegory. Since Sarton consistently uses the Shakespearean sonnet, but has difficulties with the final couplet, the poems never reach the resolution implicit in the form. Infrequently in the first volume, the final lines embody a sensuousness that suggests a real relationship and the metrical skill to dramatize it: "Now let us rest. Now let me lay my hand / In yours – like a smooth stone on the smooth sand" ("Sonnet 15"). Too often, however, the couplets strive for Millay's flippancy or Drayton's wit, but stumble: "I am come home to you, for at the end, / I find I cannot live without you, friend" ("Sonnet 14"). Even the competent "Autumn Sonnets" in *A Durable Fire* suffer from Sarton's predilection for familiar abstraction and rhetoric: "Truth is, her daily battle is with death, / Back to the wall and fighting for her breath" ("Sonnet 6").

For all her insistence on strict form and her occasional success with slant rhymes, Sarton is best with free verse. *A Private Mythology*, her strongest volume, succeeds with short poems on Japan, perhaps suggested by haiku, which concentrate on image and eliminate the superfluous moral addenda flawing much of her work: "We regretted the rain / Until we saw the mists / Floating the mountains / On their dragon-tails" ("On the Way to Lake Chuzen-ji"). Other poems in the collection display a previously concealed humor and some assurance with conventional forms, especially in "A Late Mowing," in which vivid images vivify the traditional comfort of the eternality of the natural cycle; "A sky flung down to earth as daises" returns reassuringly in the final stanza: "While overhead your dazzling daisy skies / Flower in the cold, bright mowing that will keep." The success of *A Private Mythology* suggested that Sarton's eclecticism and moral earnestness had found an authentic voice, but other recent volumes are less encouraging. *A Durable Fire* keeps her signature vocative command to a minimum; but "Elegy (for Louise Bogan)" embarasses not only with Sarton's familiar rhetorical question, but also with a general failure of taste and technique: "Louise, Louise, why did you have to go / In this hard time of wind and shrouding snow[?]" And *A Grain of Mustard Seed* makes a series of awkward pronouncements on American outrages of the 1960's. Despite these flaws and a continuing fondness for stereotyped treatment of abstract themes in abstract language, Sarton's verse has at least transcended the Henleyesque bravado of *Inner Landscape* and has apparently won an audience in a dozen published volumes. Sarton's great problem has always been a tendency toward excessive length and repetition in individual works and a willingness to publish everything. Even the new *Collected Poems* stops short of the ruthlessness necessary to eliminate the inferior. However, Sarton has produced enough competent, low-keyed verse to support her credo (expressed in "Second Thoughts on the Abstract Gardens of Japan"):

> Unbuttoned ego. I have staked
> My life on controlled native powers;
> My garden, so untamed, still has not lacked
> Its hard-won flowers.

– Burton Kendle

SAVORY, Teo. American. Born in Hong Kong. Educated privately in Hong Kong; Royal College of Music, London, and Conservatoire in Paris; studied with Harry Plunket Greene. Married Alan Brilliant, *q.v.*, in 1958. Scriptwriter and Producer, American National Theatre and Academy, New York. Since 1966, Editor-in-Chief, Unicorn Press and *Unicorn Journal*, Santa Barbara, California, later Greensboro, North Carolina. Recipient: National Endowment for the Arts grant, 1969. Address: R.F.D. 1, Housatonic, Massachusetts; or, Unicorn Press Inc., P.O. Box 3307, Greensboro, North Carolina 27402, U.S.A.

PUBLICATIONS

Verse

Traveler's Palm: A Poetry Sequence. Santa Barbara, California, Unicorn Press, 1967.
The House Wrecker. Santa Barbara, California, Unicorn Press, 1967.
A Christmas Message Received During a Car Ride. Aptos, California, Grace Hoper Press, 1967.
Snow Vole: A Poetry Sequence. Santa Barbara, California, Unicorn Press, 1968.
Transitions. Greensboro, North Carolina, Unicorn Press, 1973.
Dragons of Mist and Torrent. Greensboro, North Carolina, Unicorn Press, 1974.

Novels

The Landscape of Dreams. New York, Braziller, 1960.
The Single Secret. New York, Braziller, and London, Gollancz, 1961.
A Penny for the Guy. London, Gollancz, 1963; as *A Penny for His Pocket*, Philadelphia, Lippincott, 1964.
To a High Place. Santa Barbara, California, Unicorn Press, 1971.

Short Stories

17 Fables. Greensboro, North Carolina, Unicorn Press, 1975.

Other

Translator, *Corbière, Supervielle, Prévert, Jammes, Michaux, Guillevic, Queneau, Eich.* Santa Barbara, California, Unicorn Press, 8 vols., 1967–71.
Translator, *Guillevic.* London, Penguin, 1974.
Translator, *Zen Poems*, by Nhat Hanh. Greensboro, North Carolina, Unicorn Press, 1974.
Translator, *Euclidians*, by Guillevic. Greensboro, North Carolina, Unicorn Press, 1975.

*   *   *

Teo Savory could be a contemporary version of Colette. She has starred on the stage, and produced books of a high quality – verse, verse translation, and novels.

In her fiction, strong plot line and an engaging dialogue are her trademarks. Her poetry seems less economical. The vividness of such a novel as *To a High Place* could effectively be transferred to the poetry. Similarly, her translations seem close to the mark, but I would like to see her make the same imaginative leaps she uses in her prose.

The Unicorn Press and *Unicorn Journal*, both of which she founded in 1966, have produced a striking number of original books and translations.

– Glenna Luschei

SCANNELL, Vernon. British. Born in Spilsby, Lincolnshire, 23 January 1922. Educated at Queen's Park School, Aylesbury, Buckinghamshire; University of Leeds, Yorkshire, 1946–47. Served in the Gordon Highlanders, 1941–45. Married Josephine Higson in 1954; has five children. Formerly, amateur and professional boxer. Teacher of English, Hazlewood School, Limpsfield, Surrey, 1955–62. Free-lance Writer and Broadcaster since 1962. Recipient: Heinemann Award, 1961; Arts Council grant, 1967, 1970; Cholmondeley Award, 1974. Fellow, Royal Society of Literature, 1960. Address: Folly Cottage, Nether Compton, Sherborne, Dorset, England.

PUBLICATIONS

Verse

> *Graves and Resurrections: Poems.* London, Fortune Press, 1948.
> *A Mortal Pitch.* London, Villiers, 1957.
> *The Masks of Love.* London, Putnam, 1960.
> *A Sense of Danger.* London, Putnam, 1962.
> *Walking Wounded.* London, Eyre and Spottiswoode, 1965.
> *Epithets of War: Poems 1965–1969.* London, Eyre and Spottiswoode, 1969.
> *Mastering the Craft.* Oxford, Pergamon Press, 1970.
> *Selected Poems.* London, Allison and Busby, 1971.
> *Company of Women.* Frensham, Surrey, Sceptre Press, 1971.
> *Corgi Modern Poets in Focus 4,* with others, edited by Jeremy Robson. London, Corgi, 1971.
> *The Winter Man.* London, Allison and Busby, 1973.
> *The Apple-Raid and Other Poems* (for children). London, Chatto and Windus, 1974.

Plays

> Radio Plays: *A Man's Game,* 1962; *A Door with One Eye,* 1963; *The Cancelling Dark,* music by Christopher Whelen, 1965.

Novels

The Fight.   London, Peter Nevill, 1953.
The Wound and the Scar.   London, Peter Nevill, 1953.
The Big Chance.   London, Longman, 1960.
The Shadowed Place.   London, Longman, 1961.
The Face of the Enemy.   London, Putnam, 1961.
The Dividing Night.   London, Putnam, 1962.
The Big Time.   London, Longman, 1965.

Other

Edward Thomas.   London, Longman, 1962.
The Dangerous Ones (juvenile).   Oxford, Pergamon Press, 1970.
The Tiger and the Rose: An Autobiography.   London, Hamish Hamilton, 1971.

Editor, with Patricia Beer and Ted Hughes, *New Poems 1962.*   London, Hutchinson, 1962.

Manuscript Collection: British Museum, London.

Vernon Scannell comments:

Major themes: violence, the experience of war, the "sense of danger" which is part of the climate of our times; these are contrasted with poems of a more private nature which affirm the continuity and indestructibility of the creative spirit. Some verse satire; the work is traditional, very direct and firmly rooted in recognizable human experience.

*   *   *

Vernon Scannell's poems began to appear in the magazines in the late 1940's but (despite the 1961 Heinemann Award for Literature, which was given to his book *The Masks of Love*) it was not until the publication of *A Sense of Danger* in 1962 that he showed his real talent as a skilful memorialist of the aspirations, daydreams, lusts, disillusionments and ironies of a bruised, wry and incorrigible romantic. One supposes that it was for this romanticism that he was enlisted as a contributor to *Mavericks*, the anthology intended to be a counterblast to the suggested calm severities of *New Lines*; but in fact Scannell's poems in his later books (*A Sense of Danger* and *Walking Wounded*) have more in common with Philip Larkin than with anyone represented in *Mavericks*. The world of Scannell's incendiaries, suicides, psychopaths, adulterers – as well as telephone calls, pubs, insurance agents and radio interviews – is thoroughly mid-20th century urban, acutely and mordantly observed.

Scannell's technical organisation of a poem is generally sound (he works easily and fluently within received forms), but his language is less sure – for example, in "The Fair":

> The night sniffs rich at pungent spice,
> Brandy snap and diesel oil:
> The stars like scattered beads of rice
> Sparsely fleck the sky's deep soil . . .

But this overheated metaphorical glow does not appear at all in the real successes of *A Sense of Danger*, such as "Dead Dog," "My Father's Face," "The Telephone Number," and "Hearthquake." Scannell's elegiac mood, well seen in the first two of these poems, is even better handled in *Walking Wounded*, best of all in "The Old Books" and the title-poem, which recreates a wartime memory of soldiers

> Straggling the road like convicts loosely chained,
> Dragging at ankles exhaustion and despair.

But the common concern of most of Scannell's poems is with something more immediate, the ordinary hurts of the ordinary world, the dark places and betrayals of everyday experience. Colloquial, easy, even winsome, the tone of voice is generally poised above a pessimism which is lightened with wit and even, sometimes, with coarseness. It has a brutal and unequivocal honesty:

> What captivates and sells, and always will,
> Is what we are: vain, snarled up, and sleazy.
> No one is really interesting until
> To love him has become no longer easy.

– Anthony Thwaite

SCHEVILL, James (Erwin). American. Born in Berkeley, California, 10 June 1920. Educated at Harvard University, Cambridge, Massachusetts, B.S. 1942. Served in the United States Army, 1942–46. Married Margot Helmuth Blum in 1967; has two children by an earlier marriage. Member of the Faculty, California College of Arts and Crafts, Oakland, 1950–59; Member of the Faculty, 1959–68, and Director of the Poetry Center, 1961–68, San Francisco State College. Since 1969, Professor of English, Brown University, Providence, Rhode Island. Recipient: National Theatre Competition prize, 1945; Dramatists Alliance Contest prize, 1948; Fund for the Advancement of Education Fellowship, 1953; Phelan Biography Competition prize, 1954; Phelan Playwriting Competition prize, 1958; Ford grant, for work with Joan Littlewood's Theatre Workshop, 1960; Rockefeller grant, 1964; William Carlos Williams Award (*Contact* magazine), 1965; Roadstead Foundation award, 1966. Agent: Bertha Case, 42 West 53rd Street, New York, New York 10019; or, Dr. Suzanne Czech, International Copyright Bureau Ltd., 53a Shaftesbury Avenue, London W.1, England. Address: Department of English, Brown University, Providence, Rhode Island 02912, U.S.A.

PUBLICATIONS

Verse

Tensions. San Francisco, Bern Porter, 1947.
The American Fantasies. San Francisco, Bern Porter, 1951.
The Right to Greet. San Francisco, Bern Porter, 1956.
Selected Poems 1945–1959. San Francisco, Bern Porter, 1959.

Private Dooms and Public Destinations: Poems 1945–1962. Denver, Swallow, 1962.
The Stalingrad Elegies. Denver, Swallow, 1964.
Release. Providence, Rhode Island, Hellcoal Press, 1968.
Violence and Glory: Poems 1962–1968. Chicago, Swallow Press, 1969.
The Buddhist Car and Other Characters. Chicago, Swallow Press, 1973.
Pursuing Elegy. Providence, Rhode Island, Copperbeech Press, 1974.

Plays

High Sinners, Low Angels, music by James Schevill, arranged by Robert Commanday (produced San Francisco, 1953). San Francisco, Bern Porter, 1953.
The Bloody Tenet (produced Providence, Rhode Island, 1956; Shrewsbury, Shropshire, 1962). Included in *The Black President and Other Plays,* 1965.
The Cid, adaptation of the play by Corneille (broadcast, 1963). Published in *Classic Theatre Anthology,* edited by Eric Bentley, New York, Doubleday, 1961.
Voices of Mass and Capital A, music by Andrew Imbrie (produced San Francisco, 1962). New York, Friendship Press, 1962.
The Master (produced San Francisco, 1963). Included in *The Black President and Other Plays,* 1965.
American Power: The Space Fan and The Master (produced Minneapolis, 1964). Included in *The Black President and Other Plays,* 1965.
The Black President and Other Plays (includes *The Bloody Tenet* and *American Power: The Space Fan and The Master*). Denver, Swallow, 1965.
The Death of Anton Webern (produced Fish Creek, Wisconsin, 1966). Included in *Violence and Glory: Poems 1962–1968,* 1969.
This Is Not True, music by Paul McIntyre (produced Minneapolis, 1967).
The Pilots (produced Providence, Rhode Island, 1970).
Oppenheimer's Chair (produced Providence, Rhode Island, 1970).
Lovecraft's Follies (produced Providence, Rhode Island, 1970). Chicago, Swallow Press, 1971.
The Ushers (produced Providence, Rhode Island, 1971).
The American Fantasies (produced New York, 1972).
Emperor Norton Lives!, music by James Schevill (produced Salt Lake City, Utah, 1972).
Fay Wray Meets King Kong (produced Providence, Rhode Island, 1974).
Sunset and Evening Stance; or, Mr. Krapp's New Tapes (produced Providence, Rhode Island, 1974).

Radio Plays: *The Sound of a Soldier,* 1945; *The Death of a President,* 1945; *The Cid,* 1963 (Canada).

Other

Sherwood Anderson: His Life and Work. Denver, University of Denver Press, 1951.
The Roaring Market and the Silent Tomb (biographical study of the scientist and artist Bern Porter). Oakland, California, Abbey Press, 1956.
Breakout! In Search of New Theatrical Environments. Chicago, Swallow Press, 1973.

Editor, *Six Historians*, by Ferdinand Schevill. Chicago, University of Chicago Press, and London, Cambridge University Press, 1956.

James Schevill quotes from *The Prairie Schooner* (Lincoln, Nebraska), 1970:

With the increasing restrictions of poetry to filler material in magazines, to short books of less than a hundred pages for "economy," to exclusive anthology status – the short poem has become a tormented form. Often it is too complex for its own flow. It tries to compress everything into nothing. Or, in self-defense, its simplicity is so extreme that it is merely sentimental instead of musical. If the approach is fashionably confessional, it may attempt to compress an autobiography into a page, losing the most significant details in a few pulverizing images. If the approach is narrative or dramatic, the story and the drama are often condensed into an oblique obscurity that loses the strength of both narrative and drama. If the approach is prophetic, metaphysical, the poem may seem overweighted, filled with puffed-up profundity that reflects personality rather than vision. It is not, of course, that short poems have lost their value; it is rather that the apparatus of poetry – books, magazines, readings, and criticism no matter what the viewpoints – tends to limit and deny the life-giving range of poetry that is essential. If we permit short, pseudo-lyrical forms to dominate not only do they become corrupted, but the longer narrative and dramatic forms are forsaken for the novel, the play, and the work of non-fiction. The sad result is the loss of a wide variety of subject matter that was once the domain of poetry and is now the essence of prose.

The only answer to the dominance of pseudo-lyrical forms is a greater exploration of dramatic forms and increased experimentation with the possibility of performance poems. While the poem must be personal and use the forms, the climate, of our "confessional" and psychological age, the danger is self-indulgence, self-pity. Somehow, while remaining personal, a balance must be struck by means of characterization, dramatic portrayal of situations and actions, a recovery of important social subject matter so that the poem does not remain a mere splinter of isolation.

Performance poems can always help in this respect, particularly since poetry readings are so fashionable nowadays. Everyone has sat through too many poetry readings where the poet, no matter how good his work may be on the page, has simply read his work perfunctorily and at the lowest level of audibility. Boredom is the result.

Consequently, the performance poem offers a wide range of exciting possibilities to be explored. The aim is to bring the arts together again, to make poetry the central unifier of the arts that it once was. As far as subject matter, imagery, and rhythm are concerned, performance poems provide formal opportunities of infinite variations. In a time of specialization, the poet can achieve a new unity of the arts in performance that has been too rarely attempted in poetry readings.

*   *   *

James Schevill, dramatist as well as poet, can make almost anything interesting: side by side in his large selected collection *Private Dooms and Public Destinations: Poems 1945–1962* there are pieces on the painter Seurat, the death of a cat, a meditation on trees, an Irish castle, a man working a hydraulic drill, and gambling in Las Vegas. It is perhaps inevitable that some of these subjects, and they are typical, move him more than others, and that his greatest thrust be reserved for the things that most matter to him (his wartime experiences as a coastguardsman, a scientist like Fabre), yet he is never trivial and poem after poem offers sharp

responses and insights. He is, in short, a poet all the way, a somewhat rare species
in our time, and has the vitality and the natural equipment to make so strenuous a
poetic life possible: curiosity, sensitivity, wide learning and a truly impressive gift
with language, reminding one at times of Dylan Thomas'. Here is the first stanza of
"The Blue Jay" from the above mentioned collection:

> Blue jay in the garden,
> Cocky bastard!
> Boor on stilts in your Cyrano plume
> Where the purple wistaria hangs like grapes.
> Go flirt in the boggy woods;
> In the gardens of spring,
> When the grosbeak sings from the song-struck tree,
> What are you but a duenna to beauty,
> The claptrap chaperon?

If it is true that reading the poet on such a variety of subjects, however unified
the vision from piece to piece, can be a dizzying experience, his volume *The
Stalingrad Elegies* offers something altogether different: it is a daring, deeply imaginative and altogether successful experiment, surely one of the most interesting
books to come out of the mid-60's. Here the poet has found a theme – a licked
German army trapped in the snows of Stalingrad and their attempts, for the most
part puny, occasionally noble, to get their feelings into letters home – that taxes his
talent to the full, and the talent shows itself to be formidable. One can read the
book as one reads an exciting story, so carefully is the volume structured and
variety assured – through the selection of sufficiently dissimilar types, through the
choice of stanza patterns and meters. Here in one of the shortest poems a soldier
writes his wife:

> Bury your face in your hands
> in order to forget;
> *You said that*
> *in your last letter . . .*
> Two months of happiness
> We had as man and wife,
> Then I marched into
> The dark nights of the east,
> My hands slipping
> from your body
> As if it were only a dream of sex,
> Not a marriage . . . I live
> In a sense of space
> And time so huge
> that they devour
> Every human face.
> I can't even imagine your flesh
> Any more; too cold . . .
> You are the wife of death.

James Schevill, a poet of strong gifts and generous impulses, has created a
durable body of work, some of it, as in *The Stalingrad Elegies*, of major order.

– Lucien Stryk

SCHMIDT, Michael (Norton). Mexican. Born in Mexico City, 2 March 1947. Educated at Christ's Hospital, Horsham, Sussex; Harvard University, Cambridge, Massachusetts; Wadham College, Oxford, B.A. in English 1970. Since 1969, Managing Director, Carcanet Press Ltd., publishers, Oxford, later Cheadle, Cheshire; since 1972, Fellow, Manchester Poetry Centre; since 1973, Editor, with C. B. Cox, *Poetry Nation*, Manchester. Agent: Andrew Mylett, Hughes Massie Ltd., 69 Great Russell Street, London W.C.1. Address: c/o Carcanet Press, 266 Councillor Lane, Cheadle Hulme, Cheadle, Cheshire, England.

PUBLICATIONS

Verse

Black Buildings. Oxford, Carcanet Press, 1969.
One Eye Mirror Cold. Oxford, Sycamore Press, 1970.
Bedlam and the Oakwood: Essays on Various Fictions. Oxford, Carcanet Press, 1970.
Desert of Lions. Oxford, Carcanet Press, 1972.
It Was My Tree. London, Anvil Press Poetry, 1972.

Other

Editor, with Grevel Lindop, *British Poetry since 1960: A Critical Survey.* Oxford, Carcanet Press, 1972.

Translator, with Ed Kissam, *Flower and Song: Aztec Poetry.* London, Anvil Press Poetry, 1975.

*   *   *

For a poet still early in his career, Michael Schmidt displays a formidable precocity. It is formidable because it is not showing off, not posturing, but has a confidence which seems to arise from the whole personality of the poet. Schmidt almost never writes poems of direct individual feeling, but he is not, on this account, ever devious or obscure; he never assaults us either with joy or grief, but he is never cold. He has read much and travelled much. From his travels much of the basic material of his work is drawn. It supplies him with imagery and description. Even in the early work of 1968 in *It Was My Tree*, sympathy for others is generalised and distanced by the utmost care in the use of language. Here, for example, are some lines from a poem called "Cancer":

> . . . Find out
> who is this discoloured
> body always half-awake
> to itself. A music
>
> from the unrusting
> instruments. How deep
> the body drinks, customary
> thirst, the frightened moon.

There is no lack either of compassion or powerful feeling here, but it is checked by the immediacy of imagery. The same thing happens in the last stanza of "For Pasternak":

> Flowers have fallen on us
> yellow like wings, fragrant
> with the powder of the air; small petals
> delicate as the sky. We have been
> unable to hold them.

That last line is close to sadness, but grief is not allowed to overflow.

In his booklet of 1969, Michael Schmidt continued in much the same vein. Since then he has brought out two full-scale volumes, *Bedlam and the Oakwood* and *Desert of the Lions*. There are no violent developments to be discerned in either of these volumes but rather a surer grasp of Schmidt's early manner, a keener awareness of language and its potentialities for imagery and description. If he is to be faulted, then one can only do so by pointing out the lack of any lyrical element in his poems and often an unconscious unwillingness to confront the reader directly. The appearance of concealment is at present only a minor blemish, though there are moments when one longs for the poet to appear fully himself, for the curtain to be raised. The following is an example of what I mean, taken from "Nailed like Stoats":

> Around you the suppliant
> generosity to gifted invalids –
> a lifetime of it. Critics were kept at bay.
> Your correspondence was meticulously edited.

Echoes of other poets are hard to find in Schmidt's work but, certainly in this poem, one can detect a small debt to early and middle period Auden. *Bedlam and the Oakwood* is divided into sections, and Part I is called "Biographies." Schmidt gives us most vivid portraits of famous writers, as in "Jonathan Swift's Body," "Samuel Johnson's Marriage" and "Hatching." In these pieces the poet identifies himself completely with his chosen characters and makes them truly alive. In another section, places are also powerfully summoned up; one thinks particularly of "Luncheon" and "Venice: A Letter to Robert Browning."

"Some Fictions," yet another section of *Bedlam and the Oakwood*, does show an inclination on the poet's part to reveal himself in the round, but he is more willing to display his thoughts than his feelings, and he is usually quick to move on to other people or to characters from literature. This tendency is evident in a poem called "Appendix":

> This reading leaves me seated,
> in the gateway to some unlosable wisdom,
> and here at least I am no cynic.

In these lines, and the following ones from "Flown Eagle," Schmidt comes closest to setting aside his finely chosen language and careful rhythms and telling us about himself:

> I have had to dispose of eagles, and the
> things they seemed to touch: sky,
> liner, and the deserted sea
> which leaves me smaller territory.

Starting with such an accomplished though somewhat limited technique together with so much external material to work upon, Schmidt could hardly advance, in *Desert of the Lions*, except by way of more personal revelation or a real lyric impulse. The latter does not appear but, even if only unobtrusively, the former fitfully does. Amid the scintillating and accurately conveyed settings we come upon such passages as the following:

> I follow you hunting with jar and trowel,
> with gloves, this poison tail.
> > – from "Scorpion"

> Speak cautiously before morning
> of fishermen – the men
> with nets, with hooks, with knives.

> I eavesdrop on them
> from our balcony . . .
> > – from "Before Morning"

> We can move near.
> We cannot touch this bird, stiff,
> almost a sawdust dummy, but on fire.
> > – from "Reconciliation"

In such poems as these and "Funerals," "Hypothesis," the title poem itself, and "Tourist Waking," this poet can be sensed. Wherever he goes, he enters a new country, city, landscape, and transforms them by the power of his sharp visual gift and his control over form. For so young a man, all this, together with his understanding of many different people, is quite exceptional. Yet this very achievement makes it extremely hard to predict where he can move next. A more varied feeling for movement and sound would certainly be a definite advance, together with a more intimate revelation of such an interesting personality. We have the intellect; now we want more of the heart.

– Elizabeth Jennings

SCHMITZ, Dennis. American. Born in Dubuque, Iowa, 11 August 1937. Educated at Loras College, Dubuque, B.A. 1959; University of Chicago, M.A. 1961. Married Loretta D'Agostino in 1960; has five children. Instructor in English Literature, Illinois Institute of Technology, Chicago, 1961–62, and University of Wisconsin, Milwaukee, 1962–66. Since 1966, Member of the Faculty, and currently, Associate Professor of English, California State University, Sacramento. Recipient: New York Poetry Center Discovery Award, 1968; Big Table Series of Younger Poets Award, 1969. Address: 1348 57th Street, Sacramento, California 95819, U.S.A.

PUBLICATIONS

Verse

We Weep for Our Strangeness.   Chicago, Follett, 1969.
Double Exposures.   Oberlin, Ohio, Triskelion Press, 1971.

Dennis Schmitz comments:

Subjects: Death & birth in nature & human rituals. Personal experiences in farm
and wild areas. Influences: Jung, Bible, Chuang Tzu, Herman Melville, Jean Giono.

*   *   *

In the death-haunted poems in Dennis Schmitz's *We Weep for Our Strangeness* a
dying rabbit's intestines wind "like roads / between the bones," a remembered
farm "fed / on the blue hillsides," ants slide "their hills / wave on lipless wave /
down the long bay of grass."
Landscape endures, though in ceaseless modification by glacier, flood, burial,
river, ants. Man seems "lost" here, in the religious sense of the word. And indeed
God is named often in these poems, and appears still more frequently. In the
book's last poem, "The Rescue," three men are lost on a canoe trip. One of them
– Peter! – is sick. Finally a small plane flies over:

> we signal
>
> we are here, to those above
> that we have suffered
> the lonely ocean of green
> life.

Has the plane spotted them? They can't be sure, but one of them says hopefully
that help will come, someone will rescue them:

> yes,
> I said to Jack, yes he will.

Neither the religious echoes nor the emotional urgency of Schmitz's poems
assumes a loud voice. His style is colloquial, his diction Midwestern. The conversational tone and sparse punctuation would make for swift, fluid poems, were not his
lines consistently slowed – sometimes nearly broken down – by enjambment.
Sometimes the result is needlessly knotty:

> %s are the signs. I remember
>   the birds broke up
> on the table. top. scratches
> like soft entrails we read sad
>   tidings if we are to believe
>   examine the corners

and so on.

1350

Such lapses are few. The three relaxed and fully achieved eclogues beginning the book are beyond the capabilities of most of his contemporaries. Among them he stands out for the authenticity of his vision, its thick obsession with death and its convincing religiousity:

> because you have loved your body closes its doors
> because you have eaten now the poor came.
> & your plate is clean as the skull of God.

– William Matthews

SCHROEDER, Andreas (Peter). Canadian. Born in Hoheneggelsen, Germany, 26 November 1946. Educated at the University of British Columbia, Vancouver, 1966–71, B.A. 1969, M.A. in creative writing and comparative literature 1971; University of Toronto, 1968. Editorial Assistant, *Prism International*, Vancouver, 1968–69; Member, Board of Directors, British Columbia Film Cooperative, 1970–71; Editor, *Poetry Canada*, Toronto, 1970–71. Since 1969, Founding Editor, with J. Michael Yates, *Contemporary Literature in Translation*, Vancouver; since 1970, Literary Critic, *Vancouver Province-Pacific Press*; since 1971, Editorial Board Member, *The Canadian Fiction Magazine*, Prince George, British Columbia. Recipient: Canada Council grant, 1968, bursary, 1969, 1971; Gordon Woodward Memorial award, for prose, 1969; National Film Board grant, 1970; Canadian Film Development grant, 1971. Address: Box 2058, Mission, British Columbia, Canada.

PUBLICATIONS

Verse

   The Ozone Minotaur. Vancouver, Sono Nis Press, 1969.
   File of Uncertainties. Vancouver, Sono Nis Press, 1971.
   uniVerse, with David Frith. Vancouver, MASSage Press, 1971.

Plays

   Screenplays: *The Plastic Mile,* 1969; *Immobile,* 1969; *The Pub,* 1970; *The Late Man,* 1972.

Short Stories

   The Late Man. Vancouver, Sono Nis Press, 1971.

Other

   Editor, with J. Michael Yates, *Contemporary Poetry of British Columbia.* Vancouver, Sono Nis Press, 2 vols., 1970, 1972.
   Editor, with Rudy Wiebe, *Stories of the Pacific Northwest.* Toronto, Macmillan, 1974.

Translator, with Michael Bullock, *The Stage and Creative Arts*. Greenwich, Connecticut, New York Graphic Society, 1969.

Translator, *Collected Stories of Ilse Aichinger*. Vancouver, Sono Nis Press, 1974.

Critical Studies: "The Relevance of Surrealism with Some Canadian Perspectives" by Paul Green, in *Mosaic* (Winnipeg, Manitoba), Summer 1969; "The O-Zone and Other Places" by Alan Shucard, in *Canadian Literature 48* (Vancouver), Spring 1971; "Swarming of Poets" by George Woodcock, in *Canadian Literature 50* (Vancouver), Winter 1971; "A Certain Degree of Madness" by Patricia Morley, in *Ottawa Journal*, 13 May 1972.

Andreas Schroeder comments:

While I have always made considerable use of the surreal mode in both my poetry and prose, my more recent work varies greatly with respect to its surreality. The first book of verse which I published (*The Ozone Minotaur*) was a fairly orthodox example of the genre; the second (*File of Uncertainties*) was only occasionally characteristic of it. I find myself moving more and more toward that thin line where reality and surreality mesh, where a couple making love and a couple killing each other appear involved in identical acts. The result tends often to be cinematic, for which reason many of the stories have proven themselves easily adaptable to film scripts. My poetry, too, makes increasing use of a more linear logic.

*   *   *

Andreas Schroeder, German-born though he emigrated in childhood, is unusually international among Canadian poets in his literary affiliations. It is impossible to consider him as a poet apart from his activities as editor of *Contemporary Literature in Translation*. His imaginative world is related to Kafka's and, equally, to that of Borges, and his poems have an intellectual complexity rare among young North American poets but relating him directly to the Modernist tradition. He has published two books of verse, *The Ozone Minotaur* and *File of Uncertainties*; the development between them is considerable. The earlier poems are largely neo-surrealist in character, seeking to give verisimilitude to implausible but potent myths, such as "Introduction" in which "three men in tails" cross a cornfield to a creek:

> . . . The man in the middle
> of the stream is stepping on the fish;
> he is intent. The fish swim through
> him and he walks through the fish.
> Notice that he is not surprised. The
> man on the other bank is sifting debris
> into a notebook; notice him. The man on
> the bank is now measuring the size of
> the sand grains.
> The man in the middle of the creek is
> walking on.
> He is stepping on the fish.

Schroeder's later poems, in *File of Uncertainties*, explore ambiguities of condition and consciousness like those exemplified in the man through whom the fish swim as he walks through them. The recognition of multiple consciousness, and the sense of being trapped in many selves, are in these later poems more explicit, more apprehensive, more convincing:

> Now, my constant fear:
> To stumble across my own remains
> when this snow melts.

– George Woodcock

SCHUYLER, James (Marcus). American. Born in Chicago, Illinois, 9 November 1923. Educated at Bethany College, West Virginia. Lived in Italy for several years. Currently, Staff Member, Museum of Modern Art, New York. Recipient: Frank O'Hara Prize (*Poetry*, Chicago), 1969; National Endowment for the Arts grant, 1969, 1972. Address: 49 South Main Street, Southampton, New York 11968, U.S.A.

PUBLICATIONS

Verse

Salute. New York, Tiber Press, 1960.
May 24th or So. New York, Tibor de Nagy Editions, 1966.
Freely Espousing: Poems. New York, Doubleday, 1969.
The Crystal Lithium. New York, Random House, 1972.
Penguin Modern Poets 24, with Kenneth Koch and Kenward Elmslie. London, Penguin, 1973.
Hymn to Life: Poems. New York, Random House, 1974.

Recording: *A Picnic Cantata*, music by Paul Bowles, Columbia, 1955.

Play

Unpacking the Black Trunk, with Kenward Elmslie (produced New York, 1965).

Novels

Alfred and Guinevere.   New York, Harcourt Brace, 1958.
A Nest of Ninnies, with John Ashbery.   New York, Dutton, 1969.

                              *   *   *

   James Schuyler is a poet of the New York School who doesn't particularly care
for New York City, preferring those neighboring artistic retreats, Vermont and
Long Island. He espouses:

     the sinuous beauty of words like allergy
     the tonic resonance of
     pill when used as in
     "she is a pill"
     on the other hand I am not going to espouse any short stories in
                              which lawn mowers clack.
     No, it is absolutely forbidden
     for words to echo the act described; or try to. Except very directly
     as in
     bong. And tickle.

His friends Robert Dash and Fairfield Porter are landscape painters and so, in a
sense, is Schuyler. He describes what he sees, which is what he loves, and cheers.
He sees time, for instance, in its subcategory, the seasons:

                         It's
               not – "the fly buzzed"
               finding moods, reflectives:
               fall
               equals melancholy, spring,
               get laid: but to turn it all
               one way: in repetition, change:
               a continuity, the what
               of which you are a part.

He sees. But he doesn't like people who can't see, who claim what they are seeing
is an example of something they've read. Schuyler talked to the fog about this very
matter:

                         Fog
               you are like the tedium you recall: "Walking
               across Central Park it was beautiful this
               morning." "I know I know"
               she glassily grimaced, "just like
               a Chinese painting." Thanks, fog:
               it's handy, getting to know someone
               so instantly you don't want to
               know them any better or further.

Schuyler also writes letters to the days of June. Like nature and like Fairfield
Porter, he is prolific. Lately he's broken his collections into sequences, autumn at
Kenward's place in Vermont, a really great and ongoing love affair, spring in
(Saratoga) Springs.

He talks casually about ecstasy, and he's not nearly as theoretical and acerbic as these three quotes indicate. "Salute" is more representative:

> Past is past, and if one
> remembers what one meant
> to do and never did, is
> not to have thought to do
> enough? Like that gather-
> ing of one of each I
> planned, to gather one
> of each kind of clover,
> daisy, paintbrush that
> grew in that field
> the cabin stood in and
> study them one afternoon
> before they wilted. Past
> is past. I salute
> that various field.

– Michael André

SCHWERNER, Armand. American. Born in Antwerp, Belgium, 11 May 1927. Educated at Cornell University, Ithaca, New York, 1945–47; University of Geneva, Switzerland, 1947–48; Columbia University, New York, B.S. 1950, M.A. 1964. Served in the United States Navy, 1945–46. Married Doloris Holmes in 1961; has two children. Formerly, Instructor in English and French, Barnard School for Boys, Riverdale, New York; Instructor in English, Long Island University, New York, 1963–64. Instructor, 1964–66, Assistant Professor, 1966–69, Associate Professor, 1969–73, and since 1973, Professor of English, Staten Island Community College, City University of New York. Recipient: New York State Arts Council grant, 1973; National Endowment for the Arts grant, 1973. Address: 30 Catlin Avenue, Staten Island, New York 10304, U.S.A.

PUBLICATIONS

Verse

The Lightfall.   New York, Hawk's Well Press, 1963.
The Tablets I-VIII Transmitted Through Armand Schwerner.   West Branch, Iowa, Cummington Press, 1968.
(if personal).   Los Angeles, Black Sparrow Press, 1968.
Seaweed.   Los Angeles, Black Sparrow Press, 1969.
The Tablets I-XV Presented by the Scholar-Translator, Transmitted Through Armand Schwerner.   New York, Grossman, 1971.
The Bacchae Sonnets.   Omaha, Nebraska, Cummington Press, 1974.

Other

> Stendhal's "The Red and the Black": Notes and Criticism. New York, Study
> Master Publications, 1963.
> The Domesday Dictionary, with Donald M. Kaplan. New York, Simon and
> Schuster, 1963; with Louise J. Kaplan, London, Cape, 1964.
> A Farewell to Arms: A Critical Commentary. New York, Study Master
> Publications, 1963.
> The Sound and the Fury: A Critical Commentary, with Jerome Neibrief. New
> York, American R.D.M. Corporation, 1964.
> John Steinbeck's "Of Mice and Men." New York, Monarch Press, 1965.
> John Steinbeck's "The Red Pony" and "The Pearl." New York, Monarch
> Press, 1965.
> Andre Gide's "The Immoralist," "Strait Is the Gate" and Other Works: A Critical
> Commentary. New York, Monarch Press, 1966.
> Dos Passos' "U.S.A." and Other Works. New York, Monarch Press, 1966.
> Albert Camus' "The Stranger": A Critical Commentary. New York, Monarch
> Press, 1970.

> Translator, Redspell: Poems from the American Indian. Mount Horeb, Wiscon-
> sin, Perishable Press, 1975.

Critical Studies: "Son of the Cantos?" by Stanley Sultan, in *Chelsea* (New York),
1971; by Allen Planz, in *The Nation* (New York), 19 June 1972; John Shawcross, in
American Poetry Review (Philadelphia), March 1973; Diane Wakoski, in *Parnassus*
(New York), Spring 1973.

                              *   *   *

Armand Schwerner is a multi-talented man and that can be seen plainly in the
gigantic scope of his most important collection of poems, *The Tablets*. These
amazing poems have a number of qualities that make them praiseworthy and one
which makes them stand apart from other poems. *The Tablets* is the closest thing I
have seen to a theatrical or oral poetry produced today. They are not merely sound
poems, by the way, and I do not mean to imply that. They are poems which the
reader/listener must hear before he can understand their whole reality.

The Tablets are poems which satirize the fashionable inclination for poets to be
anthropologists, and translators and purveyors of pre-historic knowledge. They
purport to be a series of Icelandic tablets dug up by some archaeologist and
translated by a theologian-scholar who himself actually makes up half the poetry
out of the missing sections. The character of the author-translator is a brilliant act
of self-satire by Schwerner himself, who like classical comedians has taken the
absurd and ridiculous world he lives in and embodied the ridiculous, satirized it at
times, while also creating a beautiful religious and love poetry, as well as a witty
game, out of the whole business. The author-translator is so important in this piece
that he must be performed, and Schwerner lives in the right age of poetry, for he is
a magnificent performer of his own drama.

The Tablets are a topical poetry, for they satirize the poetry world of the 60's and
70's, and they also take advantage of a convention of our times, that poets read
their own poems aloud. Yet, this satiric undercurrent is not such a limitation, for
the poems themselves are filled with pathos and humor and beautiful images.
Schwerner, who began as an academic poet, was opened up to the wider possibilities of poetry by the avant garde poet, Jackson Mac Low in the early 1960's. But

that he was ready to put this influence to good use is evident from the success of *The Tablets.*

– Diane Wakoski

SCOTT, Alexander. British (Scottish). Born in Aberdeen, 28 November 1920. Educated at Aberdeen Academy, 1933–39; Aberdeen University, 1939–41, 1945–47, M.A. (honours) in English 1947. Served in the Royal Army, 1941–45: Military Cross, 1945. Married Catherine Goodall in 1944; has two sons. Assistant Lecturer, Edinburgh University, 1947–48. Lecturer, 1948–63, Senior Lecturer, 1963–71, and since 1971, Head of the Department of Scottish Literature, Glasgow University. Editor, *Northeast Review,* 1945–46; *Scots Review,* 1950–51; *Saltire Review,* Edinburgh, 1954–57; General Editor, The Scottish Library, Calder and Boyars, publishers, London, 1968–71. Since 1972, General Editor, The Scottish Series, Routledge and Kegan Paul, publishers, London. Since 1968, Secretary, Universities Committee on Scottish Literature. Recipient: Festival of Britain Award, for poetry, 1951, for verse drama, 1951; Arts Council Award, for drama, 1952; Scottish Community Drama Association Award, 1954; Scottish Arts Council Publication Award, 1969. Agent: S.C.O., 2 Clifton Street, Glasgow G.3. Address: 5 Doune Gardens, Glasgow G20 6DJ, Scotland.

PUBLICATIONS

Verse

> *The Latest in Elegies.* Glasgow, Caledonian Press, 1949.
> *Selected Poems.* Edinburgh, Oliver and Boyd, 1950.
> *Mouth Music: Poems and Diversions.* Edinburgh, M. Macdonald, 1954.
> *Cantrips.* Preston, Lancashire, Akros, 1968.
> *Greek Fire.* Preston, Lancashire, Akros, 1971.
> *Double Agent.* Preston, Lancashire, Akros, 1972.
> *Selected Poems 1943–1974.* Preston, Lancashire, Akros, 1975.

Plays

> *Prometheus 48* (produced Aberdeen, 1948). Aberdeen, S.R.C., 1948.
> *Untrue Thomas.* Glasgow, Caledonian Press, 1952.
> *Right Royal* (produced Glasgow, 1954).
> *Shetland Yarn.* London, Evans, 1954.
> *Tam O'Shanter's Tryst* (produced Glasgow, 1955).
> *The Last Time I Saw Paris.* Edinburgh, Saltire Review, 1957.
> *Truth To Tell* (produced Glasgow, 1958).

Other

> *Still Life: William Souter 1898–1943* (biography).   London, Chambers, 1958.
> *The MacDiarmid Makars, 1923–1972* (criticism).   Preston, Lancashire, Akros, 1972.

> Editor, *Selected Poems of William Jeffrey.*   Edinburgh, Serif Books, 1951.
> Editor, *The Poems of Alexander Scott, 1530–1584.*   Edinburgh, Oliver and Boyd, 1952.
> Editor, *Diaries of a Dying Man,* by William Soutar.   Edinburgh, Chambers, 1955.
> Editor, with Norman MacCaig, *Contemporary Scottish Verse.*   London, Calder and Boyars, 1970.
> Editor, with Michael Grieve, *The Hugh MacDiarmid Anthology: Poems in Scots and English.*   London, Routledge, 1972.
> Editor, with Douglas Gifford, *Neil M. Gunn: The Man and the Writer.*   Edinburgh, Blackwood, 1973.

Manuscript Collection: National Library of Scotland, Edinburgh.

Critical Studies: by Norman MacCaig, in *Akros 9* (Preston, Lancashire), 1969; George Bruce, in *Akros 19* (Preston, Lancashire), 1972; Lorn Macintyre, in *Akros 25* (Preston, Lancashire), 1974.

Alexander Scott comments:

I write in both English and Scots, the latter being my first speech. With me a poem begins itself, as it were, from a phrase which flashes into the mind unbidden and which may present itself in either English or Scots. Since the inception of any poem of mine is to that extent voluntary, I am not bothered, in any one case, by having to make a choice between the two languages. The choice is already made for me, by the initial words themselves, as they rise into the consciousness. Any other procedure, in my view, would be a falsehood so fundamental as to make a mockery of the poetic act.

*   *   *

Hugh MacDiarmid has said, with a typically Scottish finality, "We have no use for emotions, let alone sentiments, but are solely concerned with passions." If this is not true, regrettably, of all Scots, it is true of Alexander Scott, except that emotions do occasionally creep in – but not subversively, since a stiffening pith in the centre prevents them from deliquescing into sentimentality. He represents, in fact, more than any living Scots poet other than MacDiarmid, those characteristic elements that define the Scots tradition and which are centred on a stubborn, passionate and sardonic realism that eschews the egotistical sublime, that deals with a remarkably high hand with what makes the substance of so much poetry – love, death, God, the Devil, etc. – and that robustly refuses to ignore the grit that forms the pearl, or even the grit. He also provides in himself a flat contradiction of the comical assumption that the Scots are dour, inarticulate and humourless and informs his work with the spirited gusto that makes, for example, Burns so heart-warming a writer.

Because these are his characteristic qualities, unsubtle sensibilities have been known to accuse him of a lack of sympathy, of brashness, of a brutal and unfeeling response to the tears of things. He can be shocking. But the hard directness of his statements (he is an Aberdonian and writes in granite) is infused with a real sympathy, a real tenderness, made triumphantly explicit in his love poems.

The bulk and the best of his poems are in Scots. Since this was his natural speech when he was young and since he has studied it in a scholarly, and respon-sive, way ever since, it is not surprising that he handles it with a lively naturalness that craftily exploits the wide range of expressive sounds that this almost too onomatopoeic language offers for use, or abuse. This Scots is muscular, athletic, with no fat on its bones, and is quite free from the pedantic antiquarianism that flaws the work of some other Scottish writers. And if his language is contempor-ary, so are his themes. He takes account of, but is not obsessed by, the past, either his own or his country's.

As for his poems in English, they could not have been written by anyone else. All the same, more of the author gets into the Scots poems – though in *Cantrips* there are some which offer evidence of a new thing in Scott's work, an exploration of looser forms which point forward to what may well be a new sort of achieve-ment.

The plays not surprisingly share most of the characteristics of the poems, except that they mainly concern themselves with situations originally reasonable enough but roisterously developed according to the curious logic of farce. The life they have, and it is plenty, derives from Scott's comic invention, in plot and dialogue, and that healthy gusto which is so prominent a feature in all his work.

– Norman MacCaig

SCOTT, F(rancis) R(eginald). Canadian. Born in Quebec City, 1 August 1899. Educated at Quebec High School; Bishop's College, Lennoxville, Quebec, B.A. 1919; Magdelen College, Oxford (Rhodes Scholar), B.A. 1922, B.Litt. 1923; McGill University, Montreal, B.C.L. 1927, called to the Quebec Bar, 1927. Married Marian Mildred Dale in 1928; has one son. Teacher, Quebec High School, 1919; Bishop's College School, Lennoxville, 1920; Lower Canada College, Montreal, 1923. Assis-tant Professor of Federal and Constitutional Law, 1928–34, Professor of Civil Law, 1934–1954, Macdonald Professor of Law, 1955–67, Dean of the Faculty of Law, 1961–64, and Visiting Professor, French Canada Studies Programme, 1967–69, McGill University. Visiting Lecturer, University of Toronto Law School, 1953–54, and Michigan State University, East Lansing, 1957. National Chairman, C.C.F. Party, 1942–50. U.N. Technical Assistant, Burma, 1952. Chairman, Canadian Writ-ers Conference, 1955. Civil Liberties Counsel before the Supreme Court of Canada, 1956–64. Formerly, Co-Founding Editor, with A. J. M. Smith, *McGill Fortnightly Review*, Montreal, 1925; Editor, *Canadian Journal of Economic and Political Science*, Toronto; *Canada Forum*, Toronto; *Canada Mercury*; *Preview*, Montreal; *Northern Review*, Montreal; *Tamarack Review*, Toronto. Recipient: Guggenheim Fellowship, 1940; Guarantor's Prize (*Poetry*, Chicago), 1945; Royal Society of Canada Fellow-ship, 1947, and Lorne Pierce Medal, 1962; *Northern Review* Award, 1951; Banff

Springs Festival Gold Medal, 1958; Quebec Government Prize, 1964; Canada Council Molson Award, 1965. LL.D.: Dalhousie University, Halifax, Nova Scotia, 1958: University of Manitoba, Winnipeg, 1961; Queen's University, Kingston, Ontario, 1964; University of British Columbia, Vancouver, 1965; Université de Montréal, 1966; Osgoode Hall Law School, Downsview, Ontario, 1966; McGill University, 1967; LL.B.: University of Saskatchewan, Saskatoon, 1965. Honorary Member, American Academy of Arts and Sciences, 1967. Companion, Order of Canada, 1967. Address: 451 Clark Avenue, Westmont, Montreal 217, Quebec, Canada.

PUBLICATIONS

Verse

Overture: Poems.   Toronto, Ryerson Press, 1945.
Events and Signals.   Toronto, Ryerson Press, 1954.
The Eye of the Needle: Satires, Sorties, Sundries.   Montreal, Contact Press, 1957.
Signature.   Vancouver, Klanak Press, 1964.
Selected Poems.   Toronto, Oxford University Press, 1966.
Trouvailles: Poems from Prose.   Montreal, Delta Canada, 1967.
Poets Between the Wars, with others, edited by Milton T. Wilson.   Toronto, McClelland and Stewart, 1967.
The Dance Is One.   Toronto, McClelland and Stewart, 1973.

Other

Canada Today: A Study of Her National Interests and National Policy.   London and Toronto, Oxford University Press, 1938.
Make This Your Canada: A Review of C.C.F. History and Policy, with David Lewis.   Toronto, Central Canada Publishing, 1943.
Canada after the War: Attitudes of Political, Social, and Economic Policies in Post-War Canada, with Alexander Brady.   Toronto, Canadian Institute of Internal Affairs, 1944.
Cooperation for What? United States and Britain's Commonwealth.   New York, Institute of Pacific Relations, 1944.
The World's Civil Service.   New York, Carnegie Endowment for International Peace, 1954.
Evolving Canadian Federalism.   Durham, North Carolina, Duke University Press, 1958.
The Canadian Constitution and Human Rights (radio talks).   Toronto, Canadian Broadcasting Corporation, 1959.
Civil Liberties and Canadian Federalism.   Toronto, University of Toronto Press, 1959.
Dialogue sur la Traduction, with Anne Hébert.   Montreal, Editions HMH, 1970.

Editor, with A. J. M. Smith, New Provinces: Poems of Several Authors.   Toronto, Macmillan, 1936.
Editor, with A. J. M. Smith, The Blasted Pine: An Anthology of Satire, Invective and Disrespectful Verse, Chiefly by Canadian Writers.   Toronto, Macmillan, 1957; revised edition, 1967.

Editor, with Michael Oliver, *Quebec States Her Case: Speeches and Articles from Quebec in the Years of Unrest.*   Toronto, Macmillan, 1964.

Translator, *St. Denys Garneau and Anne Hébert.*   Vancouver, Klanak Press, 1961.

Critical Studies: *Ten Canadian Poets,* edited by Desmond Pacey, Toronto, Ryerson Press, 1958; *The Literary History of Canada,* edited by Carl F. Klinck, Toronto, University of Toronto Press, 1965; "The Road Back to Eden: The Poetry of F. R. Scott," in *Queen's Quarterly* (Kingston, Ontario), Autumn 1972.

F. R. Scott comments:

I see Life as "making," and therefore primarily poetic. Only part of my making has taken the form of poetry.

*   *   *

F. R. Scott has been a kind of "double agent" who has succeeded in combining an active public life in politics and university teaching with the contemplative and yet very active and practical life of a poet. While still an undergraduate at McGill he helped to introduce the new poetry of the Eliot-Pound tradition into Canada, and for more than thirty years he has been a leader of groups of younger poets and a stimulating force in the poetry scene. His own verse is divided into satirical poetry, a pungent form of social and political criticism, love poems ranging from the simple to the metaphysically or psychologically complex, and nature poems, which begin with simple examples of a northern imagism and develop into an elegance of style and a richness of allusion that suggest at times a Canadian Marvell.

"Lakeshore," the fine poem that stands at the beginning of *Selected Poems,* may be cited as an example. Written in a series of irregularly rhymed stanzas, it begins with the immediate and the personal – the poet standing by the "bevelled edge" of a lake in the air and the sunshine, then plunging into the breathless dark of the subaqueous world below. The senses stimulate the mind, and the theme of the poem becomes Man's history, which extends back into pre-history, before man developed lungs and ceased to be fish. With its unifying symbol of water as the source of life, the poem establishes a contact in awareness with biological history, stretching back to the primordial beginnings of life, and also (as we emerge again to the surface of the lake) with the earthbound now of "a crowded street." This poem is characteristic of Scott's mature non-satirical poetry. The themes and motives of much of his most completely articulated work are seen in it at their clearest and most direct. The fascination with water, as an element and as a symbol; the identification of the poet's self with Man and of the sensuous perceptive physical being with Mind; and the inescapable tendency to interchange the language and imagery of science (especially biology, geology, and psychology) with the language and imagery of religion are all seen in this poem as well as in a dozen other of Scott's more recent metaphysical lyrics and in the remarkable series of poems resulting from his travels in India, Burma, and the Far East.

Scott has managed, more successfully than most, to unify his public life of social responsibility with the private, perceptive and contemplative life of the poet. All his poems, from the gayest and lightest expressions of delight in life through his witty and sometimes savage satires to the metaphysical lyrics, are informed and qualified by a sense of responsibility and an inescapable sincerity, serious but never solemn.

– A. J. M. Smith

SCOTT, Tom. Scottish. Born in Glasgow, Lanarkshire, 6 June 1918. Educated at Hyndland Secondary School, Glasgow; Madras College, St. Andrews, Scotland; Edinburgh University, M.A., Ph.D. Served in the Royal Army Pay Corps, 1939–44. Married Heather Fretwell in 1963; has one son and twin daughters. Formerly, Editor, Scottish Literature Series, Pergamon Press, Oxford. Recipient: Atlantic-Rockefeller Award, 1950; Carnegie Senior Fellowship and Scholarship; Arts Council Award, 1972. Address: Duddingston Park, Edinburgh 15, Scotland.

PUBLICATIONS

Verse

Seeven Poems o Maister Francis Villon. Tunbridge Wells, Kent, Peter Russell, 1953.
An Ode til New Jerusalem. Edinburgh, M. Macdonald, 1956.
The Ship and Ither Poems. London and New York, Oxford University Press, 1963.
At the Shrine o the Unkent Sodger: A Poem for Recitation. Preston, Lancashire, Akros, 1968.
Musins and Murgeonins. Thurso, Caithness Books, 1975.

Other

A Possible Solution to the Scotch Question. Edinburgh, M. Macdonald, 1963.
Dunbar: A Critical Exposition of the Poems. Edinburgh, Oliver and Boyd, and New York, Barnes and Noble, 1966.
Tales of King Robert the Bruce (juvenile). Oxford, Pergamon Press, 1969.

Editor, with John MacQueen, *The Oxford Book of Scottish Verse.* Oxford, Clarendon Press, 1966.
Editor, *Late Medieval Scots Poetry: A Selection from the Makars and Their Heirs down to 1610.* London, Heinemann, and New York, Barnes and Noble, 1967.
Editor, *The Penguin Book of Scottish Verse.* London, Penguin, 1970.

Critical Study: "Tom Scott" by John Herdman, in *Akros 16* (Preston, Lancashire), April 1971.

Tom Scott comments:

After some years writing in English, to my own dissatisfaction, I found myself beginning to write in my native Scots, suppressed by my English education, in Sicily. Since that conversion I have written mostly in that language, my own reworking of it, for verse, and in English for prose.

At the centre of my work is a vision of the Good Society. My poems mainly take two modes: visions of that society, and satires of existing society and its evils. Technically I have been much influenced by Villon, Dunbar, and Lewis Grassic Gibbon, and stick close to traditional forms, in the main. I have recently revived the verse epistle for social criticism, owing perhaps something to Fergusson and Burns, but very much brought up to date. I am a Scottish nationalist and more concerned with the salvation of my nation than that of my own soul, believing that "he who saveth his soul shall lose it." I have a personal vision of Yeshua of Nazareth, but it accords little and quarrels much with orthodox religion. I am a writer, with no capacity for religion as such, being an observer rather than a man of action. My social vision is moral-aesthetic rather than scientific – old fashioned utopian socialism, I suppose.

*   *   *

Tom Scott began publishing poems in English about 1941, but it was another ten years before he found his own voice in his native Scottish tradition. He has since become probably the most talented poet to keep alive the great renaissance of Scots as a language for poetry which began with the poems Hugh MacDiarmid wrote in the nineteen-twenties and thirties. Like MacDiarmid, Tom Scott stems directly from three great poets (often misleadingly labelled the Scottish Chaucerians): Henryson, Dunbar, and Gavin Douglas.

Scott is a modernist whose work is rooted in the Pound/Eliot tradition which he has grafted onto a number of mediaeval Scottish and European sources. His first important book was *Seeven Poems o Maister Francis Villon*. This met with the approval of Ezra Pound and belongs to that small group of great translations which read like original poems and help to revitalise the poetry of a nation – the finest previous example in Scots, apart from MacDiarmid's version of Alexander Blok's *The Stranger* contained in *A Drunk Man Looks at the Thistle*, is Gavin Douglas's *Aeneid*. I quote the first stanza of Tom Scott's "Ballat o the Leddies o Langsyne" to give some indication of the quality of his Villon:

> Tell me whaur, in whit countrie
> Bides Flora nou, yon Roman belle?
> Whaur Thais, Alcibiades be,
> Thon sibbit cuisins; can ye tell
> Whaur clettaran Echo draws pell-mell
> Abuin some burn owrehung wi bine
> Her beauties's mair nor human spell –
> Ay, whaur are the snaws o langsyne?

But Scott is by no means only a translator. His original work contains a number of moving lyrics. "The Annunciation" is a good example:

Ye'll lig your bridal nicht yourlane
    Your legs aspar til nocht but air,
And it sall get in you a Son
    Yet nevir pairt your maiden hair.

Ye'll gie your Bairn the name I say.
    And let nae lover stier ye, will ye,
Till He has seen the licht o day
    And broached your virgin nipples til ye.

Tak tent nou – I maun gang my road –
    Ilka word I've said is true:
And aa I've ever envied God
    Is the bairnin o a lass like you!

Scott has also written a number of long poems including "The Ship" and *At the Shrine o the Unkent Sodger*. The latter is a passionate meditation on the horror of war from the beginning of history until the recent crimes of the concentration camps, civilian bombing, Hiroshima, Nagasaki, and Vietnam. There are many flashes of insight, particularly into the economic causes of war. Like Ezra Pound, Tom Scott is committed to a radical reform of our financial system as the most practical way of preventing wars. The metre is a five stress blank verse line, at times making use of a silent stress indicated by a full-stop or a dash. This is probably closer to the natural speech rhythms of Scots than iambics are to present day English. But the poem might have gained if more variety of metre had been used. Tom Scott has elsewhere shown his ability to use complicated rhyme schemes with great skill, both in his Villon and in his fine translation of the Anglo-Saxon poem *A Dream o the Rude*. His blank verse is diffuse by comparison, and, in places, seems to make rhetoric inevitable. Apostrophes, for example, are now probably just as unusable in Scots as they are in English.

But Scott's long poems have an honesty and rough-hewn strength which only things deeply felt could have produced. At a time when so much verse writing is concerned with trivia, it is good to see a poet with the courage to tackle major subjects. *At the Shrine o the Unkent Sodger* ends with a powerful vision of a world order built out of an internationalism that is organically part of nationalism, a "Federal Union o Nations," without loss of distinctions and individuality:

The starns maintain their hard integritie
In universal peace ayont aa comprehension,
Their true separateness the guarantee
That atween them sall be harmonie.

. . . .
Sae fowk, in this coman warld,
Sall aa be entities like starns in space,
Never mair thegither nor when maist apairt,
Never mair apairt nor when maist thegither,
Like tones in chords in some gret symphonie –
And life be love, as it is meant to be.

                     – William Cookson

SCOVELL, E(dith) J(oy). British. Born in Sheffield, Yorkshire, in 1907. Educated at Casterton School, Westmorland; Somerville College, Oxford, B.A. 1930. Married Charles Sutherland Elton in 1937; has two children. Lives in Oxford, England.

PUBLICATIONS

Verse

Shadows of Chrysanthemums and Other Poems. London, Routledge, 1944.
The Midsummer Meadow and Other Poems. London, Routledge, 1946.
The River Steamer and Other Poems. London, Cresset Press, 1956.

*   *   *

The gentle talent of E. J. Scovell has been drowned out by the tumult of competing voices. Her range may be limited, but her poems are distinguished by an attention to detail and an almost mystical sense of the process of life. Of a baby's head, she writes:

> Now even the captive light still in a sheltered room,
> Claiming you as its kind, pours round your head in bloom,
> So melting where it flows that the strong, armour-browed
> Skull seems as precious as cloud;
>
> Or seems a field of corn by the wind liquefied
> Streaming over the arches of a round hill-side.
> Contours and skin make tender the planes of light and shadow,
> The pale and darker gold of an upland meadow . . .

Delicately touched, this is, and quietly spoken. So much so, indeed, that the ear deadened by the apocalyptic beat of the drop-out poets and their British admirers may well not descern the patterning of rhymes and half-rhymes, the oddly displaced stress that is part of the charm of Miss Scovell's poetry:

> Under the pent-house branches the eight swans have come
> Into the black-green water round the roots of the yew;
> Like a beam descending the lake, the stairway to their room . . .
>   – "A Dark World"

Miss Scovell's original books were published in the 1940's, and there was a retrospective collection in 1956. This seems to be her last word on the matter; she has published nothing since. Yet *The River Steamer*, as her collected poems are called, has some good work apparently dating up to its period of publication, and nothing finer than the title poem, a meditation on the passing years and one remarkable for its sustained allegory:

1365

> Waiting for a spirit to trouble the water,
>
> Waiting for a spirit from beneath or over
> To trouble the surface of the river
> From which the hours like clouds reflected gaze
> White, and the daylight shine of all earth's days
>
> Waiting for a spirit to dissolve the glass . . .

How could this poem have passed, as it has, virtually unnoticed? An essentially religious poet in the same ambience, for all the individual differences, as Anne Ridler, Joan Barton, Stevie Smith – E. J. Scovell herself, one feels, would expect no higher praise than that.

– Philip Hobsbaum

SCULLY, James (Joseph).   American.   Born in New Haven, Connecticut, 23 February 1937. Educated at Southern Connecticut State College, New Haven, 1955–57; University of Connecticut, Storrs, B.A. 1959 (Phi Beta Kappa), Ph.D. 1964. Married Arlene Steeves in 1960; has two children. Instructor, Rutgers University, New Brunswick, New Jersey, 1963–64; taught at Hartford Street Academy, Connecticut, 1968–69. Since 1964, Associate Professor of English, University of Connecticut. Visiting Associate Professor, University of Massachusetts, 1973. Recipient: Ingram Merrill Foundation Fellowship, 1962; Lamont Poetry Selection Award, 1967; Contributors' Prize (*The Far Point*, Winnipeg, Manitoba), 1969; Jennie Tane Award (*Massachusetts Review*, Amherst), 1971; Guggenheim Fellowship, 1973. Address: Warrensville Road, Mansfield Center, Connecticut 06250, U.S.A.

PUBLICATIONS

Verse

The Marches: A Book of Poems.   New York, Holt Rinehart, 1967.
Communications, with Grandin Conover.   Amherst, The Massachusetts Review, 1970.
Avenue of the Americas.   Amherst, University of Massachusetts Press, 1971.
Santiago Poems.   Willimantic, Connecticut, Curbstone Press, 1975.

Other

Editor, *Modern Poetics.*   New York, McGraw Hill, 1965; as *Modern Poets on Modern Poetry*, London, Collins, 1966.

Translator, with C. J. Herington, *Prometheus Bound*, by Aeschylus.   New York, Oxford University Press, 1975.

James Scully comments:

Some premises and intentions:

*A body of poetry is put together as a life is.

*To write inside out, experientially. Not deform the felt perception by hedging it with arbitrary thematic caution.

*To be *in* the poetry, not a spectator/manipulator of it.

*To avoid the striking of poses because these are little more than personalized prisons.

*Poetry is for real, no fiction. Though it may be fictive, and it must be coherent – which is how it differs from most other modes of reality.

*To dramatize only that reality which has a felt significance.

*Unconsciousness (mystery) is what poetry dispels, realization (revelation) being the end in view.

*Realization as revelation is a process. It is arrived at step by step with no end to the arriving.

*Realization being evolutionary, nothing gets lost: as brackishness in blood, Latin in English – past informs present.

*Revelation broods on complexity, the questions too basic to be answered (too basic to be easily formulated even), whereas mystery generates mere surface complication.

*To admit anything and everything, including arguments, theories, opinions, etc. The point is not to take these at face value, as ends in themselves, but as clues. For instance, a political theory functions much as a word does – more elaborate in some ways, less so in others, but essentially similar. Its power is the power of allusion: it's an instrument for pointing toward realities that are too complex ever to be fully and definitively grasped.

*Not to explain, explanations violate reality, but to burn off the mist that obscures it.

*To write as transparently as possible. Because poetry isn't the most important thing in the world, though it may be the only means we have of approaching and apprehending what is.

*If everything that lives is holy, then there is nothing to hide or banish. What's damnable, or morally warped, is the categorical declaration that certain aspects of our reality (e.g. political, sexual, metaphysical, whatever) are off-limits to poetry. Nothing is taboo. Except, of course, in the psychic provinces.

*Poetic truth is whole truth, at once personal and common. At best that is. Poems are (a) people speaking.

*Any poetry must be able to accomodate people, people who speak in their own voices.

*What makes sense: to work the language that is ours, not one like private property that is merely one's own. To take seriously the shopworn language we take for granted, and allow it consciousness.

*Not to mythicize oneself or others, but to realize that everyone has mythic dimensions.

*Poetry, like the Duomo of Siena, is a common enterprise: communal coherence too accomodating to be egocentric.

*   *   *

The poems in James Scully's *The Marches* are meditative, dense as the persistence ot the past in the present,

<blockquote>
as if,
rockbound, this were the kingdom come,

and the hunched fields were crystal-clear
Jerusalem, and life was judged
vibration in the summer air.
</blockquote>

Connecticut, northern France, Lake Bled in Yugoslavia, Venice, Gibralter, Lake Sunapee in New Hampshire – wherever, "you could almost hear / lost gods breathing in the earth." Another noise is time passing:

<blockquote>
. . . pink-pale clouds march
as far as the mind can reach, wilting,
central Jersey spread under like spilt milk.
</blockquote>

Avenue of the Americas is a far less scattered book, focused by loss. A child is dead at six months, a brilliant and extravagant friend is dead, rapacious grief runs through the poems. Scully's language is less measured than before, more various – discursive, argumentative and lyrical all in the same few lines. Organizing themes are Edenic America, friendship and family, the failure of art to console and its power to instruct, the spiritual collapse of American political life in the 1960's. The rock-like past of *The Marches* is transmogrified by history, by evolution, and seems to be spending itself as fast as the present:

<blockquote>
Even the beautiful are too
    heartsick for beauty,
astronauts will never make it to the stars
but burn up.
</blockquote>

The book includes translations from Joseph Brodsky, whose political themes underscore Scully's own.

Occasionally so ambitious they fail of their own philosophical weight. Scully's newer poems have the urgency and personal risk of letters to a beloved friend (and one group of poems in *Avenue of the Americas* was evidently written as such a series of letters). But the poems are not "confessional," nor does the poet set himself up in them as representative man. They move toward the wider life which is their persistent obsession by a manifest sense that language, perhaps more than history or evolution, is our shared life:

<blockquote>
Maybe that's what poetry is, one of the species
claiming grandeur.
It's that helpless.
</blockquote>

– William Matthews

SCUPHAM, (John) Peter. British. Born in Liverpool, Lancashire, 24 February 1933. Educated at The Perse, Cambridge, 1942–47; St. George's, Harpenden,

1947–51; Emmanuel College, Cambridge, 1954–57. Served in the Royal Army Ordnance Corps, National Service. Married Carola Braunholtz in 1957; has one daughter and three sons. English Teacher, Skegness Grammar School, Lincolnshire,
1957–61. Since 1961, Chairman of the English Department, St. Christopher School,
Letchworth, Hertfordshire. Editor, with John Mole, Cellar Press, and Owner,
Mandeville Press, both in Hitchin, Hertfordshire. Address: 2 Taylor's Hill, Hitchin,
Hertfordshire SG4 9AD, England.

PUBLICATIONS

Verse

The Small Containers. Stockport, Cheshire, Phoenix Pamphlet Poets Press,
1972.
The Snowing Globe. Manchester, E. J. Morten, 1972.
Children Dancing. Oxford, Sycamore Press, 1972.
The Nondescript. Stockport, Cheshire, Phoenix Pamphlet Poets Press, 1973.
The Gift. Richmond, Surrey, Keepsake Press, 1973.
Prehistories. London, Oxford University Press, 1975.

Critical Studies: in New Statesman (London), 29 September 1972; by Michael Lon-
gley, in Phoenix 9 (Stockport, Cheshire), Winter 1972; in Irish Times (Dublin), 6
January 1973; in The Teacher (London), 2 March 1973; in Encounter (London), 18
May 1973.

Peter Scupham comments:

I feel with Auden that poetry is a game of knowledge, and I enjoy the complexity
of rules that make the game worth playing. I enjoy, and hope my work demonstrates, formalities, ironies, technical complexities, patterns, elegance. But since
the game is a game of knowledge, I also hope my poems are about something, that
they possess a strong sense of the reality of people and objects. The game should
be played for someone or something else's sake; not for the poet's. I enjoy
tightrope-walking, cadence, clarity, celebrations; I dislike the raw, the self-
absorbed, the cosmic. The poets for whom I feel particular elective affinities would
include James Reeves, Norman Cameron, Louis MacNeice, Richard Wilbur, John
Crowe Ransom. I would like my best poems to unite the dance of beauty with the
dance of death.

*   *   *

The subject matter of Peter Scupham's poetry reflects the wide ranging interests
of a lively mind: archaeology in "Un Peu d'Histoire: Dordogne"; jazz in "Fats
Waller"; children and family life in "Small Pets," "Four Fish," and "Family
Ties"; and so we could go on. The poetry itself is marked by a scrupulous care in
the use of language and form which results in a precision of expression and depth
of feeling. Scupham is keenly aware of our vulnerability, of that incidence of
tragedy that lies close to the surface of even everyday domestic life:

> All this dark humus
> A soft compound of shared sufferings.
> The earth is knit together with absences.

– from "At Home"

and that is not without menace where in the nursery:

> The small child tosses. It is not easy
> To have wolves wished upon you.
> They wait patiently beside the bed.

– from "Wolves"

This awareness can be intensely personal too, and when it is it gives an added edge to his poetry. A poem such as "Unpicked" is a dramatic illustration of this:

> I know the drowning fly, the shorn dark hair,
> The soldier weeping on his iron bed
> In some old hutment by a windy square.
> I know the unhealing sutures in my head.
> I am unpicked; I cannot face alone
> The vigorous, careless damage I have done.

Scupham's poetry is that of a committed conscience, where the sense of a common bond between all humanity, past and present, is never far off, and responsibility is shared. This is to be seen most clearly in a remarkably strong poem "The Nondescript" which Scupham wrote for Friends of the Earth, where the use of the first person in the poem manages to be strongly impersonal and yet all embracing:

> I am plural. My interests are manifold
> I see through many eyes. I am fabulous

so that the poem manages to address the reader while involving him as a participant in its tragic consequences:

> I have prepared a stone inheritance
> It flourishes beneath my fertile tears.

"I have a conviction that a poem should be about something," Scupham wrote in an introduction to his Phoenix Pamphlet *The Small Containers*, and I suspect that the subject of poems such as "The Nondescript" and "Unpicked" are what he likes them to be about.

– John Cotton

SEIDEL, Frederick (Lewis). American. Born in St. Louis, Missouri, 19 February 1936. Educated at Harvard University, Cambridge, Massachusetts, A.B. 1957. Married Phyllis Munro Ferguson in 1960; has one daughter. Writer-in-Residence,

Rutgers University, New Brunswick, New Jersey, 1964. Recipient: National Endowment for the Arts grant, 1968. Address: 164 East 93rd Street, New York, New York 10028, U.S.A.

PUBLICATIONS

Verse

Final Solutions: Poems. New York, Random House, 1963.

*   *   *

Past is ever present in Frederick Seidel's *Final Solutions*, as juxtaposed and overlapping time-frames trace the psychic travels of memorable souls. Uneasy, frightened, struggling, and tormented, personae reveal through internal monologues histories whose significance is both individual and universal. But, whether in painful resignation or in fitful turmoil, speakers' voices are modulated into meticulously wrought lines. The frequent contrast between the noisome details of suffering and the controlled tone of its expression results in powerful tension, agony heightened by an ominous placidity. "The Heart Attack," a remarkable evocation of ancient times, conveys eternal themes of lust, hurt, and regret in polished rimes; a long-departed mistress fills an old man's dreams with coy and spiteful recollections and gets a sort of revenge by her "presence" at the poem's dramatic close. The widower finds himself still held in the power of a wife who "killed / Him in her dreams every day," a masochistic thrall perpetuated by his scolding granddaughter. The retired Jewish analyst in "Daley Island" holds on, locked like the land in a sea of memory. Surrounded by the squalid artefacts of a Parisian spring, the soldier is drawn back by a half-remembered vision of idealism at Harvard and a desire for a girl with "Unmarriageable Minoan eyes, / All intuition, delicately lidded."

Occasionally, the subtle, inferential handling of material gives way to an unfortunate bluntness. "Americans in Rome" proceeds by means of extended reveries and short dramatic scenes to show tenderness confronted by social realities, but leads to self-righteous pity for poor souls who "can give to piety / Their ego, for amnesia," and ends in a crude critique of religious hypocrisy. In "The Beast Is in Chains," time-shifts operate once more, but in facile comparisons of wars (Napoleon's and the Allies') and in obvious commentary upon a fragile peace maintained by American flags in the City of Light. More successful is "A Year Abroad," in which the persona travels to and through modern Germany, with flashes of "Jew-baiting mothers" in Cologne, and further back still to the city of the Roman Varus, a journey made a parable of civilization versus freedom. In the final poem, "The Sickness," the poet gives a virtuoso display of his powers. Graphic scenes in Bellevue are pitted in ironic counterpoint against the world outside, where "others try life, try dope . . . join the Reserves, / Or take the wife their life deserves." Following this unsettling prelude, the final mad fantasies of escape build to terrifying hallucinatory scenarios driven by crazy, relentless logic climaxing in breathless release. In lines such as these, Seidel answers his own question: "What / Else is there but – to live – to care . . .?"

– Joseph Parisi

SERGEANT (Herbert) Howard. British. Born in Hull, Yorkshire, 6 May 1914. Educated at the College of Commerce, Hull; Metropolitan College, St. Albans, 1935–39; School of Accounting, London, 1939–42. Married Jean Crabtree in 1944; has four children. Accountant, 1935–39, District Chief Accountant, 1939–41, Broadcast Relay Services, Northern England; Travelling Accountant, British Air Ministry and Ministry of Aircraft Production, 1941–49; Company Secretary and Chief Accountant, Jordan and Sons, publishers, London, 1949–54, and E. Austin and Sons, London, 1954–63; Lecturer in Accountancy, Economics and English Literature, Norwood Technical College, London, 1963–65; Senior Lecturer in Accountancy, Wandsworth Technical College, London, 1965–68. Senior Lecturer in Management Studies, 1969–72, and since 1972, Joint Head, Brooklands School of Management, Surrey. Since 1943, Founding Editor, *Outposts*, London. Reader and Judge for the E. C. Gregory Trust Awards; British Commonwealth Editor, for the Borestone Mountain Poetry Awards (U.S.A.). Address: 72 Burwood Road, Walton-on-Thames, Surrey, England.

PUBLICATIONS

Verse

The Leavening Air. London, Fortune Press, 1946.
The Headlands. London, Putnam, 1953.

Other

The Cumberland Wordsworth. London, Williams and Norgate, 1950.
Traditions in the Making of Modern Poetry. London, Britannicus Liber, 1951.
A Critical Survey of South African Poetry in English, with G. M. Miller. Cape Town, Balkema, 1957.

Editor, *For Those Who Are Alive: An Anthology of New Verse.* London, Fortune Press, 1946.
Editor, *An Anthology of Contemporary Northern Poetry.* London, Harrap, 1947.
Editor, *These Years: An Anthology of Contemporary Poetry.* Leeds, Arnold, 1950.
Editor, with Robert Conquest and Michael Hamburger, *New Poems 1953: A P.E.N. Anthology.* London, Joseph, 1953.
Editor, *Selected Poems of John Milton.* London, Grey Walls Press, 1953.
Editor, with Dannie Abse, *Mavericks.* London, Editions Poetry and Poverty, 1957.
Editor, *Selected Poems*, by A. J. Bull. London, Outposts Publications, 1966.
Editor, *Commonwealth Poems of Today.* London, Murray, 1967.
Editor, *New Voices of the Commonwealth.* London, Evans, 1968.
Editor, with Jean Sergeant, *Poems from Hospital.* London, Allen and Unwin, 1968.
Editor, *Poetry from Africa.* Oxford, Pergamon Press, 1968.
Editor, *Universities' Poetry 8.* Keele, Staffordshire, Universities Poetry Management Committee, 1968.
Editor, *Poetry from Australia.* Oxford, Pergamon Press, 1969.
Editor, *The Swinging Rainbow: Poems for the Young.* London, Evans 1969.
Editor, *Poetry from India.* Oxford, Pergamon Press, 1969.

Editor, *Poetry of the 1940's*.   London, Longman, 1970.
Editor, *Happy Landings*.   London, Evans, 1971.
Editor, *Evans Book of Children's Verse*.   London, Evans, 1972.
Editor, *African Voices*.   London, Evans, and New York, Lawrence Hill, 1973.
Editor, *For Today and Tommorow*.   London, Evans, 1974.

Critical Study: "The Poetry of Howard Sergeant" by Lionel Monteith, in *Poetry Quarterly* (London), Spring 1951.

*   *   *

Howard Sergeant is a teacher, an editor of distinction, and, perhaps chiefly, a poet. In 1943 he founded *Outposts*, publishing poetry by unestablished poets of Britain and the Commonwealth. This courageous, discriminating Little Magazine, a "model of its kind" (*Sunday Times*) is the longest lived of Little Magazines in England. Sergeant edits the Outposts Modern Poets Series established in order "to help poets who have reached a certain stage of development and who might not otherwise have the opportunity of placing their work before the public." Many of the poets whose work first appeared in this series have since placed their work with established publishers; amongst these are Alan Sillitoe, Ruth Fainlight, Molly Holden, and Kevin Crossley-Holland.

Devotion to publishing other poets with his discriminating breadth of perception, has unjustly obscured the fact that Howard Sergeant is himself a poet of note. The *Leavening Air* is early work. *The Headlands* sequence, intended, he writes, "to be autobiographical," is "an exploration into mental development in which 'the sea' is the unconscious or subconscious mind . . . and all the sea imagery is intended to be symbolic of mental experience – the tricks the mind plays." The poem widely anthologized from *The Headlands* is "The Inland Sea." The whole volume, its original use of ballad quatrain, its half-rhymes, para-rhymes within sustained, deeply rooted, universal metaphor are, set beside Philip Larkin's *The Less Deceived* (1955), indicative. Time will give this very English poet his place.

– Anne Tibble

SEXTON, Anne.   American.   Born in Newton, Massachusetts, 9 November 1928. Educated at Garland Junior College, Boston; Radcliffe Institute, Cambridge, Massachusetts (Scholar), 1961–63. Married Alfred M. Sexton in 1948 (divorced, 1974); has two daughters. Fashion Model, Boston, 1950–51. Taught at Wayland High School, Massachusetts, 1967–68. Lecturer in Creative Writing, 1970–71, and since 1972, Professor of Creative Writing, Boston University. Crawshaw Professor of Literature, Colgate University, Hamilton, New York, 1972. Honorary Member, Phi Beta Kappa, 1968. Recipient: Bread Loaf Writers Conference Robert Frost Fellowship, 1959; Levinson Prize (*Poetry*, Chicago), 1962; American Academy of Arts and Letters Traveling Fellowship, 1963; Ford grant, 1964; Shelley Memorial Award, 1967; Pulitzer Prize, 1967; Guggenheim Fellowship, 1969. Litt.D.: Tufts University, Medford, Massachusetts, 1970; Regis College, Weston, Massachusetts, 1971; Fairfield University, Connecticut, 1971. Fellow, Royal Society of Literature. Agent:

Claire Degener, Sterling Lord Agency, 75 East 55th Street, New York, New York
10022. Address: 14 Black Oak Road, Weston, Massachusetts 02193, U.S.A. *Died 4
October 1974.*

PUBLICATIONS

Verse

To Bedlam and Part Way Back.   Boston, Houghton Mifflin, 1960.
All My Pretty Ones.   Boston, Houghton Mifflin, 1962.
Selected Poems.   London, Oxford University Press, 1964.
Live or Die.   Boston, Houghton Mifflin, 1966; London, Oxford University
   Press, 1967.
Poems, with David Livingstone and Thomas Kinsella.   London and New York,
   Oxford University Press, 1968.
Love Poems.   Boston, Houghton Mifflin, and London, Oxford University
   Press, 1969.
Transformations.   Boston, Houghton Mifflin, 1971; London, Oxford University
   Press, 1972.
The Book of Folly.   Boston, Houghton Mifflin, 1972; London, Chatto and
   Windus, 1974.
O Ye Tongues.   London, Rainbow Press, 1973.
The Death Notebooks.   Boston, Houghton Mifflin, 1974.
The Awful Rowing Towards God.   Boston, Houghton Mifflin, 1975.

Play

Mercy Street (produced New York, 1969).

Other

Eggs of Things (juvenile), with Maxine Kumin.   New York, Putnam, 1963.
More Eggs of Things (juvenile), with Maxine Kumin.   New York, Putnam,
   1964.
Joey and the Birthday Present (juvenile), with Maxine Kumin.   New York,
   McGraw Hill, 1971.

Critical Studies: "Les Belles Dames sans Merci" by Geoffrey H. Hartman, in
Kenyon Review (Gambier, Ohio), Autumn 1960; "The Hungry Sheep Looks Up" by
Neil Meyers, in *Minnesota Review* (Minneapolis), Fall 1960; "A Return to Reality"
by Cecil Hemley, in *Hudson Review* (New York), Winter 1962–63; "Seven Voices"
by M. L. Rosenthal, in *Reporter* (New York), 3 January 1963; "Interview with
Anne Sexton" by Patricia Marx, in *Hudson Review* (New York), Winter 1965;
Contemporary American Poetry by Ralph J. Mills, Jr., New York, Random House,
1965; "In Spite of Artifice" by Hayden Carruth, in *Hudson Review* (New York),
Winter 1966–67; "O Jellow Eye" by Philip Legler, in *Poetry* (Chicago), May 1967;
"Achievement of Anne Sexton" by Robert Boyers, in *Salmagundi* (New York),
Spring 1967; interview with Barbara Kevles, in *Paris Review* (Paris and New York),
Spring 1971.

Anne Sexton comments:

It is said that I am part of the so-called "confessional school." I prefer to think of myself as an imagist who deals with reality and its hard facts.

I write stories about life as I see it. As one critic put it I am "metaphor-mad." I work happily within strict forms that differ poem by poem or in what I call loose poems. Each time I look for the voice of the poem and each time it is a different one. I have been influenced by Rilke, Rimbaud, Kafka, Neruda. My themes deal with life and death, insanity, daughterhood, motherhood and love. My poems are intensely physical.

*   *   *

The poetry of Anne Sexton has been classified, and with some justification, by many of her critics, as "confessional" verse, a form of poetic self-revelation and autobiography that does not hesitate to disclose the most intimate or terrible aspects of the writer's existence, including love or family relationships and even the suffering and humiliation of mental breakdown. The term "confessional" seems first to have been applied to Robert Lowell's *Life Studies* (1959), a volume bringing startling changes into his work, particularly through a focus on himself, his friends and family. Mrs. Sexton's initial collection, *To Bedlam and Part Way Back*, with its equally disturbing forays into the most private areas of experience, its exposure of mental illness and hospitalization, ties of love and hate between child and parents, and attempted suicide, followed a year later. Within a short period, new work by John Berryman, the late Sylvia Plath, and others, gave rise to the notion of a confessional school, though this idea is oversimplified and evades the considerable differences between poets.

In the books succeeding her first, Mrs. Sexton has continued unhesitantingly to test the raw edges of her personal feelings, to confront the darkest and most threatening forces within herself, to undergo the excruciating agonies caused by religious disbelief in conflict with a deep-seated desire for faith. *Live or Die*, perhaps the finest of her collections so far, lays down in a series of poems dated like a private journal in verse from January 1962 to February 1966 the thematic pattern of her writing, also neatly summarized in the title borrowed from Saul Bellow. The wish to let go of life struggles desperately against the will to live, and to find existence in some way worthy of the effort. Significantly, the final poem in the volume is called "Live," and in it Mrs. Sexton discovers reasons for her affirmation, though she is first struck by an awareness of rebirth within: "Today life opened inside me like an egg." The sun nourishing life, the presence of lovers "sprouting in the yard," her husband and daughters, and a litter of Dalmatian puppies – all bring her, in spite of evil and guilt, to affection and celebration at the poem's conclusion.

Sexton's *Love Poems* examines amatory relationships with her usual force and frankness, but here the pleasures and joys of love outweigh its complexities, loneliness, and recurrent pain. In her work to date, including the recent *Transformations* (nightmare rewritings of fairy tales) and *The Book of Folly*, she has created and expanded her own poetic style, one which is close to speech, capable of handling sudden shifts of thought and emotion or sharp flights into the hallucinatory and irrational; this style carries the conviction of an authentic voice and personality addressing us directly, passionately from an open encounter with existence.

– Ralph J. Mills, Jr.

SEYMOUR A(rthur) J(ames). Guyanese. Born in Georgetown, British Guiana, now Guyana, 12 January 1914. Educated at Queen's College, Georgetown. Married Elma Bryce in 1937; has three daughters and three sons. Chief Information Officer, Government Information Service, British Guiana, 1954–62; Development Officer, Caribbean Organization, Puerto Rico, 1962–64; Public Relations Officer, Demerara Bauxite Company, Ltd./Guyana Bauxite Company, Ltd., Guyana, 1965–73. Since 1973, Cultural Relations Adviser, Ministry of Information, Culture and Youth, Guyana. Editor, *Kyk-over-Al* literary magazine, Georgetown, 1945–61; Editor, Miniature Poets Series; Poetry Editor, *Kaie* magazine of the National History and Arts Council, Guyana, 1965. Recipient: Golden Arrow of Achievement, from the President of the Republic of Guyana, 1970. Address: 23 North Road, Bourda, Georgetown, Guyana.

PUBLICATIONS

Verse

Verse. Georgetown, Guyana, Daily Chronicle, 1937.
More Poems. Georgetown, Guyana, Daily Chronicle, 1940.
Over Guiana, Clouds. Georgetown, Guyana, Demerara Standard, 1945.
Sun's in My Blood. Georgetown, Guyana, Demerara Standard, 1945.
The Guiana Book. Georgetown, Guyana, Argosy, 1948.
Leaves from the Tree. Georgetown, Guyana, Miniature Poets, 1951.
Water and Blood: A Quincunx. Georgetown, Guyana, Miniature Poets, 1952.
Selected Poems. Georgetown, Guyana, privately printed, 1965.
Monologue. Georgetown, Guyana, privately printed, 1968.
Patterns. Georgetown, Guyana, privately printed, 1970.
I, Anancy. Georgetown, Guyana, privately printed, 1971.
Black Song. Georgetown, Guyana, privately printed, 1972.
Passport. Georgetown, Guyana, privately printed, 1972.
Song to Man. Georgetown, Guyana, privately printed, 1973.
Italic. Georgetown, Guyana, privately printed, 1974.

Other

A Survey of West Indian Literature. Georgetown, Guyana, Kyk-over-Al, 1950.
Caribbean Literature (radio talks). Georgetown, Guyana, privately printed, 1951.
Window on the Caribbean (sociological comment). Georgetown, Guyana, privately printed, 1952.
Edgar Mittelholzer: The Man and His Work. Georgetown, Guyana, National History and Arts Council, 1968.
Introduction to Guyanese Writing. Georgetown, Guyana, National History and Arts Council, 1971.
Looking at Poetry. Georgetown, Guyana, privately printed, 1974.
I Live in Georgetown. Georgetown, Guyana, privately printed, 1974.

Editor, *Anthology of West Indian Poetry.* Georgetown, Guyana, Kyk-over-Al, 1952; revised edition, 1957.
Editor, *Anthology of Guyanese Poetry.* Georgetown, Guyana, Kyk-over-Al, 1954.
Editor, *Themes of Song.* Georgetown, Guyana, privately printed, 1959.

Editor, with Elma Seymour, *My Lovely Native Land* (anthology of Guyana). London, Longman, 1971.

Editor, *New Writing in the Caribbean.* Georgetown, Guyana, Government of Guyana, 1972.

Bibliography: *A. J. Seymour: A Bibliography,* by Joan Christiani, Georgetown, Guyana, National Library, 1974.

Manuscript Collection: National Library, Georgetown, Guyana.

Critical Study: "A Study of the Poetry of A. J. Seymour" by Celeste Dolphin, in *New World Fortnightly* (Georgetown, Guyana), 1965.

A. J. Seymour comments:

I would feel that primarily I am a Love poet. I am strongly aware of political shifts in the Community climate in my own country and in the region. Historical personalities stimulate me, and myths and legends of the continent and archipelago also interest me.

I am very conscious of form in poetry – sonnets, terza rima, quatrains and rhyme generally. But everything is grist to the poetic mill and my present influences are W. B. Yeats, Borges, Neruda, and T. S. Eliot.

*   *   *

Like Frank Collymore, A. J. Seymour has not, over the years, only written poetry. He has also been concerned to encourage its writing in others. He edited the now defunct literary magazine, *Kyk-over-Al,* between 1945 and 1961, which, apart from a fair proportion of poems in its individual numbers, devoted three entire issues to anthologies. He produced a series "The Miniature Poets," featuring the work of writers like Martin Carter, Cecil Herbert and Phillip Sherlock; he conducted (and still conducts) writers workshops; and his weekly broadcast literary programmes did much to encourage an interest in the emerging Caribbean literature of the 1950's. He is also a critic, lecturer, and reader of considerable calibre. But above all, A. J. Seymour is a poet.

Three main themes emerge from this work: a feeling for heroes of history or literature, usually accompanied by a sense of violence and doom:

> In killing, there must be a fierce, dark joy.
> – To stab a pulsing throat and see the blood
> Spurt angry purple from the quivering gash.
> Or choke life out with muscles tense and hard,
> And hammering temples, gloating at the sight
> Of thick veins swelling snake-like from the skin. . . .
> – from "Caligula," Selected Poems

> The engine failing,
> The shattered peace,
> The athlete lost within his stride,
> The look over the edge of the abyss. . . .
> – from "Othello," Monologue

a feeling for the continuity of Caribbean and Guyanese history, centred through the persona of an epic hero:

> He dreamed not that the ocean would bear ships
> Heavy with slaves in the holds, to spill their seed
> And fertilise new islands under whips

> . . . dreamt not indeed
> Massive steel eagles would keep an anxious watch
> For strange and glittering fish where now was weed.
> – "For Christopher Columbus," *The Guiana Book*

Seymour has also been concerned to weave a local past using Amerindian mythology – "Amalivaca," for instance, and "The Legend of Kaieteur." But these, with their over-emphatic singing pentametres are not as successful as the poems of the first group (the "literary" poems) where, as will be seen from the earlier quotations, he achieves real eloquence, or, as with "Diocletian," a certain sharpness of focus:

> I dream of Diocletian in his age   '
> Walking alone within his cabbage garden.

> A gaunt old man with power upon his face
> Straighter than furrows, and images of power
> Still moving in those deepest eagle eyes.

With these poems, in fact, we reach the paradox of Caribbean "colonial" poetry which tends, like the verse of Frank Collymore, to avoid "social reality"; or, as with Seymour's, to be most technically at home with the "literary." But Seymour is also a "transitional" poet, preparing the way, in "Tomorrow Belongs to the People," for writers like Martin Carter:

> Ignorant
> Illegitimate
> Hungry sometimes,
> Living in tenement yards
> Dying in burial societies
> The people is a lumbering giant
> That holds history in his hand.

But it is in the third group of poems, those that disclose Seymour's personal perception of the living world and living love, that we find, perhaps, the most certain successes:

> Time spirals upright this unflowing river
> This waterrise through the earth safely miracled
> This phallus from the deeps unbound and liquid,

> Reversal of the dying desert . . .
> – from "The Well," *Selected Poems*

and

Nearly all women sleep when they are loved

Maybe the body has to coil again
From its full stretch, maybe the drowned brain
Emerges from its Springtide into rest
Maybe they bank their ectasy in dreams
Against a future anguish and devaluation

But as the unhurried stars wheel overhead
Above a thousand million nests of love
One or two women lie and think and glow.
                    – "Springtide," *Monologue*

                                    – Edward Brathwaite

SEYMOUR-SMITH, Martin. British. Born in London, 24 April 1928. Educated at Highgate School, 1939–46; St. Edmund Hall, Oxford (Poetry Editor, *Isis*, 1950–51), 1948–51, B.A. (honours) 1951, M.A. Served as a Sergeant in the British Army in the Near East, 1947–48. Married Janet de Glanville in 1952; has two daughters. Tutor to Robert Graves' son, Mallorca, 1951–54; school master, 1954–60. Since 1960, Free-lance Writer. Visiting Professor of English and Poet-in-Residence, University of Wisconsin, Parkside, 1971–72. Editorial Assistant, *The London Magazine*, 1955–56; Poetry Editor, *Truth* magazine, London, 1955–57, and *The Scotsman*, Edinburgh, 1964–67; Literary Adviser, Hodder and Stoughton, publishers, London, 1963–65; General Editor, Gollancz Classics series, Victor Gollancz Ltd., publishers, London, 1967–69. Agents: Anthony Sheil Associates Ltd., 52 Floral Street, London WC2 9DA; Wallace Aitken and Sheil, 118 East 61st Street, New York, New York 10021, U.S.A. Address: 36 Holliers Hill, Bexhill-on-Sea, Sussex TN40 2DD, England.

PUBLICATIONS

Verse

Poems, with Rex Taylor and Terence Hards. Dorchester, Dorset, Longman, 1952.
(*Poems*). Oxford, Fantasy Press, 1953.
All Devils Fading. Palma, Mallorca, Divers Press, 1954.
Tea with Miss Stockport: 24 Poems. London and New York, Abelard Schuman, 1963.
Reminiscences of Norma: Poems 1963–1970. London, Constable, 1971.

Other

Robert Graves.   London, Longman, 1956; revised edition, 1965, 1970.
Bluff Your Way in Literature.   London, Wolfe, 1966; New York, Cowles, 1968.
*Fallen Women: A Sceptical Inquiry into the Treatment of Prostitutes, Their Clients,
    and Their Pimps in Literature.*   London, Nelson, 1969.
Poets Through Their Letters.   London, Constable, and New York, Holt Rine-
    hart, 1969.
Inside Poetry, with James Reeves.   London, Heinemann, and New York,
    Barnes and Noble, 1970.
Guide to Modern World Literature.   London, Wolfe, 1973; as *Funk and
    Wagnalls' Guide to World Literature,* New York, Funk and Wagnalls, 1973.
Sex and Society.   London, Hodder and Stoughton, 1975.

Editor, *Poetry from Oxford.*   London, Fortune Press, 1953.
Editor, *Shakespeare's Sonnets.*   London, Heinemann, 1963; New York, Barnes
    and Noble, 1966.
Editor, *A Cupful of Tears: Sixteen Victorian Novelettes.*   London, Wolfe, 1965.
Editor, *Every Man in His Humour,* by Ben Jonson.   London, Benn, 1966; New
    York, Hill and Wang, 1968.
Editor, with James Reeves, *A New Canon of English Poetry.*   London, Heine-
    mann, and New York, Barnes and Noble, 1967.
Editor, with James Reeves, *The Poems of Andrew Marvell.*   London, Heine-
    mann, and New York, Barnes and Noble, 1969.
Editor, *Longer Elizabethan Poems.*   London, Heinemann, and New York,
    Barnes and Noble, 1970.

Manuscript Collection: University of Texas, Austin.

Critical Study: "Poetry of Exactness" by Robert Nye, in *The Scotsman* (Edinburgh), September 1963.

Martin Seymour-Smith comments:

(1970) My earlier poems tended to be "traditional" in form, while the later ones
are much freer – although they make full but irregular use of rhyme. Browning
seems to be a much more persistent influence than until recently I would have liked
to acknowledge. I seem to write many poems about people: they could be described, I suppose, as biographical poems. If I had to sum up the kind of poem I
should like to write (a hypothetical question), I should probably say "something
like Jacques Audiberti, but wholly anglicized and laced with plenty of native
humour." But I find answering questions like this damaging as I write few poems
and tend to conserve my energies for them. I like a compact sort of poetry, and
rely heavily on the non-manufacturing side of myself in order to produce first
drafts.
(1974) An introduction to my work as a poet for the general reader would, I
suppose, say that I am essentially a "phenomenological" poet but that I value
coherence; that many people don't seem to understand what I am about except
when I am "being funny"; that I never "submit" poems to anyone (except God),
but only send them when requested; that I find the general atmosphere of unread-
poeticule-sucking-up-to-unread-poeticule irrelevant to what I am trying to do, since

for any poet poetry is a lonely business; that I would rather have, say, six (no, *ten*) readers than a thousand carrion-fed unminds; that there are contemporary poets whose poems I admire and to which I can respond; that there is nothing left for me but to do exactly what I have to do, in poetry, when I have to do it and in whatever way it should be done; that I would rather be a poet than any kind of dogmatist; that good grocerdom is undoubtedly more difficult than good poetdom, but then in poetry the standards are considerably higher, too high.

*   *   *

Hart Crane once said: "Poetry, in so far as the metaphysics of absolute knowledge extends, is simply the concrete evidence of the experience of knowledge. It can give you a ratio of fact and experience, and in this sense it is both perception and thing perceived according as it approaches a significant articulation or not."

Apart from a Fantasy Press pamphlet and an early book, *Poems*, Martin Seymour-Smith has published only two collections, *Tea With Miss Stockport* and *Reminiscences of Norma*, but the poems in these books which do not approach a significant articulation are few, for Seymour-Smith is nothing if not fastidious – of language, and of the occasions when language may permissibly aspire to poetry. Whether he is writing simply about subtle thoughts and feelings, or with succinct irony at the expense of his own sensitivity, his concern is the same: to "test" the moment of self-knowledge by applying to it the resources of an intelligent imagination. He is not a poet who finds questions in his experience – in data "given" before the poem happens – and then sets about providing himself, and us, with easy, knowing answers. Each poem is itself a questioning; when an answer is offered it is usually tentative, an understatement of what has been understood, and then that answer is often further qualified by self-satire, as though the poet were mistrustful of where the poem might take him, the satire being there to clarify his perception of his meaning. This makes for an intense and caustic poetry of much exactness. See especially "The Northern Monster" in the 1963 collection, and the thirteen poems which comprise Section III of *Reminiscences of Norma*, and give that book its title.

– Robert Nye

SHAPCOTT, Thomas W(illiam). Australian. Born in Ipswich, Queensland, 21 March 1935. Educated at Ipswich Grammar School, 1949–50; University of Queensland, Brisbane, B.A. in arts 1968. Served in the National Service, 1953. Married Margaret Hodge in 1960; has three daughters and one son. Clerk, H. S. Shapcott, Public Accountant, Ipswich, 1951–63; Partner, Shapcott and Shapcott, Accountants, Ipswich, 1963–72. Since 1972, Public Accountant, Sole Trader, Ipswich. Fellow, Australian Society of Accountants, 1970. Churchill Fellow (U.S.A. and England), 1972. Member, Australian Arts Council Australian Literature Board, 1973. Recipient: Grace Leven Prize, 1961; Sir Thomas White Memorial Prize, 1967; Sydney Myer Charity Trust Award, 1968, 1970. Address: P.O. Box 91, Ipswich Quay, Queensland 4305, Australia.

PUBLICATIONS

Verse

Time on Fire: Poems. Brisbane, Jacaranda Press, 1961.
Twelve Bagatelles. Adelaide, Australian Letters, 1962.
The Mankind Thing. Brisbane, Jacaranda Press, 1964.
Sonnets 1960–1963. Brisbane, privately printed, 1964.
A Taste of Salt Water: Poems. Sydney, Angus and Robertson, 1967.
Inwards to the Sun: Poems. Brisbane, University of Queensland Press, 1969.
Fingers at Air: Experimental Poems 1969. Ipswich, Queensland, privately printed, 1969.
Begin with Walking. Brisbane, University of Queensland Press, 1972.
Interim Report. Ipswich, Queensland, privately printed, 1972.

Play

The Seven Deadly Sins, music by Colin Brumby (produced Brisbane, 1970). Brisbane, privately printed, 1970.

Other

Focus on Charles Blackman (art monograph). Brisbane, University of Queensland Press, 1967.

Editor, with Rodney Hall, *New Impulses in Australian Poetry.* Brisbane, University of Queensland Press, 1968.
Editor, *Australian Poetry Now.* Melbourne, Sun Books, 1969.
Editor, *Poets on Record.* Brisbane, University of Queensland Press, 1970–73.

Manuscript Collections: Australian National Library, Canberra; Fryer Library, University of Queensland, Brisbane.

Critical Studies: by L. Clancy, in *Meanjin Quarterly* (Melbourne), 1967; Carl Harrison-Ford, in *Meanjin Quarterly* (Melbourne), 1972.

Thomas W. Shapcott comments:

My apprenticeship was a self-directed soakage of key poets of the early 1950's (Dylan Thomas, e. e. cummings, T. S. Eliot) followed by an increasing awareness of Australian poets and poetry (Slessor and Judith Wright initially, later A. D. Hope and Vincent Buckley). Experimental writing was unfashionable in Australia in the 1950's so my early published work, including the first volume, *Time on Fire,* practised a strain of lyricism I was later to grow out of. In this period I discovered the sonnet form, a lasting influence in directing me to the tensions and interplay between form and content. Subjectively, I think I am an intensely regional poet, though my concern has always been with issues of personality and belief.

*   *   *

1968 saw the publication of an anthology entitled *New Impulses in Australian Poetry*. One of the poets behind these new impulses was the co-editor of the volume, Thomas W. Shapcott, who with several volumes of poetry to his credit is firmly established as one of the leading poets of his generation.

Shapcott's first volume, *Time on Fire* doesn't prepare one at all for the experimentation that one finds increasingly in his poetry. It is very much a young man's work, partly autobiographical it would seem, telling of young love, courtship, marriage, the birth of the first child. These are conventional lyrics, many in the sonnet form, a form which, along with all his experimentation, he has returned to again and again, constantly exploring its possibilities and exploiting the tensions it can provide between form and content. One never feels that Shapcott is indulging in experiment for experiment's sake. On the contrary one feels the constant struggle to express thoughts in words:

> It is my tongue, only, falters. Language remains
> monstrous.

Moreover, recent publication of some of his poems written over fifteen years ago shows that his interest in innovation in form is not a recent one. The lack of innovation in his early published work points not to the poet but rather to the conservatism of the poetry editors of that period.

There is an infinite variety in his subject matter: personal experiences, mythological, religious, historical themes, urban life, social problems, all are there. Yet with this variety one is still able to pinpoint basic concerns. Perhaps the one that he returns to most of all is the question of time. Time, like fire, is all-consuming; struggle as we may against it, we are doomed to defeat. Linked to this question and possibly an answer to it is the poet's attempt to define himself. "Self is beyond grasp" is a line from his first volume. In the minotaur sequence in *Inwards to the Sun* he uses the myth to explore the nature of man, the duality, that we, like the minotaur, partake of. Like the minotaur, we are trapped in our own labyrinths, living in "inconsolable privacy," "in a crowd that hurls again and again the noisy cry / of loneliness."

In his latest volume, *Begin with Walking*, "anonymity" continues to haunt him; there is a cry to God for definition, "God, O God define us." Shapcott attempts this definition through his verse:

> This   is where I begin to exist.
> Blank
> Page
>
>   – "This Blank Page"

Perhaps we could say that his verse is not only his attempt to define himself, but also his challenge to time:

> I make
> a self into this page to placate
> my time-veined fears
>   – "Time on Fire"

>   – Anna Rutherford

SHAPIRO, David (Joel). American. Born in Newark, New Jersey, 2 January
1947. Educated at Columbia University, New York, B.A. (magna cum laude) 1968;
Clare College, Cambridge (Kellett Fellow, 1968–70), B.A. (honours) 1970. Married
Lindsay Stamm in 1970. Since 1970, Editorial Associate, *Art News*, New York.
Since 1972, Instructor, Columbia University. Since 1963, a violinist with various
orchestras including the New Jersey Symphony and the American Symphony.
Recipient: Gotham Book Mart Avant-Garde Poetry Award, 1962; Bread Loaf Writers Conference Robert Frost Fellowship, 1965; Ingram Merrill Foundation Fellow-
ship, 1967; Book-of-the-Month Club Fellowship, 1968; Creative Artists Public Service Fellowship, 1974. Address: 560 Riverside Drive, Apartment 16K, New York,
New York 10027, U.S.A.

PUBLICATIONS

Verse

Poems.   Privately printed, 1960.
A Second Winter.   Privately printed, 1961.
When Will the Bluebird.   Privately printed, 1962.
January: A Book of Poems.   New York, Holt Rinehart, 1965.
Poems from Deal.   New York, Dutton, 1969.
A Man Holding an Acoustic Panel.   New York, Dutton, 1971.
The Dance of Things.   New York, Lincoln Center, 1971.
The Page-Turner.   New York, Liveright, 1973.

Other

Editor, with Kenneth Koch, *Learn Something, America.*   Bedford, Massachusetts, Bedford Museum, 1968.
Editor, with Ron Padgett, *An Anthology of New York Poets.*   New York, Random House, 1970.

Translator, *Writings of Sonia Delauney.*   New York, Viking Press, 1974.

Composer: incidental music for *The Scotty Dog* by Kenneth Koch, produced
New York, 1967.

Critical Study: in the *New York Review of Books*, Christmas 1971.

David Shapiro comments:

Simone Weil said, "The Fool, taken literally, is speaking the truth." Often, in
my favorite poets, paradoxia and "nonsense" achieve not so much the ambiguity
analysed denotatively and connotatively by Mr. Empson, but a pointing to logos by
its extreme absence. As early tribes were obsessed by shadows, convinced that an
animal's shadow was part of the animal, so Stein, Carroll, Borges employ the
techniques of "nonsense" because they are convinced, like me, that the poet's task
is to subdue – in Rimbaud's terms – the formless. If the task of positivism was to

expunge nonsense, the work of poetry is to use it. That is "the meaning of meaninglessness," to use nonsense and uncertainty and discontinuity as the central tone and abiding metaphor of our peculiar predicament.

*   *   *

David Shapiro is one of the most gifted members of what has come to be called the "New York School" of poetry, a loose confederation of talents inspirited by the work of the late Frank O'Hara, John Ashbery, and Kenneth Koch.

Shapiro's poetry, although profoundly influenced by John Ashbery, whose sinuous intelligence and command of French poetic sources has stamped Shapiro's imagination, is nonetheless thoroughly original in the production of his imagery. The Shapiro image, nervous, agitated, associative in the psychoanalytic sense of eliciting connections from puns, sense confusions (both mystical and Rimbaudian), and fabulous and incredible synecdoches often leaves the reader gasping for meaning. However, there is throughout his work a hard rock of intelligence and arbitrariness and it is these which give assurance that his work will continue to explore and colonize the *terra incognita* between private worlds – childhood, music, love, suffering, madness – and the concerns of the reader. A very large talent, David Shapiro will surely, as his new book *The Page-Turner* demonstrates, emerge as one of the major American poets of this decade.

– Arthur A. Cohen

SHAPIRO, Harvey. American. Born in Chicago, Illinois, 27 January 1924. Educated at Yale University, New Haven, Connecticut, B.A. 1947; Columbia University, New York, M.A. 1948. Served in the United States Army Air Force during World War II: Distinguished Flying Cross. Married Edna Lewis Kaufman in 1953; has two sons. Instructor in English, Cornell University, Ithaca, New York, 1949–50, 1951–52; Creative Writing Fellow, Bard College, Annandale-on-Hudson, New York, 1950–51. Staff Member, *Commentary*, New York, 1955–56, and *The New Yorker*, 1956–57. Since 1957, Staff Member, and since 1964, Assistant Editor, *The New York Times Magazine*. Recipient: YMHA Poetry Center Award, 1952; Swallow Press New Poetry Series Award, 1954; Rockefeller grant, 1967. Address: 264 Hicks Street, Brooklyn, New York 11201, U.S.A.

PUBLICATIONS

Verse

The Eye: Poems. Denver, Swallow, 1953.
The Book and Other Poems. Cummington, Massachusetts, Cummington Press, 1955.
Mountain, Fire, Thornbush. Denver, Swallow, 1961.

> *Battle Report: Selected Poems.*   Middletown, Connecticut, Wesleyan University
>   Press, 1966.
> *This World.*   Middletown, Connecticut, Wesleyan University Press, 1971.

Critical Studies: by David Ignatow, in *The Nation* (New York), 24 April 1967;
"Rebels in the Kingdom" by Jascha Kessler, in *Midstream* (New York), April 1972.

Harvey Shapiro comments:

My earlier work is marked by a preoccupation with Jewish (Hebraic) themes. In
my later work I have followed mainly chassidic teachings. My later poems are free
verse (earlier poems were more formal), anecdotal (based on autobiographical
anecdotes), attempts to discover "The Way" (a way of right living). They have
urban settings. They are concerned with marriage and the tensions of city life. But
many have mystical (kabbalistic or chassidic or zen) underpinnings. Martin Buber
has been an influence throughout.

*   *   *

From the first, Harvey Shapiro's poems have been concerned with the poignancy
and gentleness of Jewish religion, and it may be that only readers raised in the
same tradition, with rhythms of Yiddish argument and the sonorities of the synagogue running in their ears, can respond to them completely. Yet in his best work
Shapiro speaks to, and for, everyone. He himself is a Jew from New York City,
one of a number who have contributed important work to modern American poetry:
Charles Reznikoff, Louis Zukofsky, Delmore Schwartz, etc. But Shapiro is
younger than any of these, and though he may have been influenced in his early
years by Schwartz, he has followed the route of most poets who began writing
after World War II; that is, his early formalist manner changed to something more
free and direct as he took part in the withdrawal from academic modes which
characterized American poetry during the late 1950's and 1960's. With this came a
heightening of the poignancy of his themes – poignancy driven to the brink of
terror – as he responded to the cultural and social crises of his own generation.
    In the 1950's Shapiro could still rely on the power of the traditional Jewish
vision, as in these lines from "Feast of the Ram's Horn":

> Feast of the ram's horn. Let the player rise.
> And may the sound of that bent instrument,
> In the seventh month, before the seventh gate,
> Speak for all the living and the dead,
> And tell creation it is memorized.
>
> Let Isaac be remembered in the ram
> That when the great horn sounds, and all are come,
> These who now are gathered as one man
> Shall be gathered again. Set the bright
> Scales in the sky until that judgment's done.

But now such assurance is rarely with him. Many of his most effective poems are
short, like this one, which he in savage irony entitled "Ditty":

> Where did the Jewish god go?
> Up the chimney flues.
> Who saw him go?
> Six million souls.
> How did he go?
> All so still
> As dew from the grass.

Another ironically titled poem, "The Kingdom," which is quoted here in entirety, is no more than part of a sentence:

> Battering at the door
> Of a pretend house
> With pretend cries
> Of rage and loss
> As I sit remembering
> Quiet
> And dead white.

Uncertainty, nostalgia and love of ancestors, fear of what is coming, a faith that seems useless – these are the coordinates of Shapiro's poetry today. Often it is very moving. He has written:

> There is no reason for survival.
> As we drift outward
> The tribal gods wave farewell.

In effect, Shapiro's poems are the gestures of one who waves back.

– Hayden Carruth

SHAPIRO, Karl (Jay). American. Born in Baltimore, Maryland, 10 November 1913. Educated at the University of Virginia, Charlottesville, 1932–33; Johns Hopkins University, Baltimore, 1937–39; Pratt Library School, Baltimore, 1940. Served in the United States Army, 1941–45. Married Evelyn Katz in 1945 (divorced, 1967); Teri Kovach, 1969; has three children. Associate Professor, Johns Hopkins University, 1947–50; Visiting Professor, University of Wisconsin, Madison, 1948, and Loyola University, Chicago, 1951–52; Lecturer, Salzburg Seminar in American Studies, 1952; State Department Lecturer, India, 1955; Visiting Professor, University of California, Berkeley and Davis, 1955–56, and University of Indiana, Bloomington, 1956–57; Professor of English, University of Nebraska, Lincoln, 1956–66, and University of Illinois, Chicago Circle, 1966–68. Since 1968, Professor of English, University of California, Davis. Editor, *Poetry*, Chicago, 1950–56, *Newberry Library Bulletin*, Chicago, 1953–55, and *Prairie Schooner*, Lincoln, Nebraska, 1956–66. Consultant in Poetry, Library of Congress, Washington, D.C., 1946–47. Recipient: Jeannette Davis Prize, 1942, Levinson Prize, 1942, Eunice Tietjens Memorial Prize, 1961, and Oscar Blumenthal Prize, 1963 (*Poetry*, Chicago); *Contemporary Poetry* prize, 1943; National Institute of Arts and Letters grant, 1944;

Guggenheim Fellowship, 1944, 1953; Pulitzer Prize, 1945; Shelley Memorial Award, 1946; Kenyon School of Letters Fellowship, 1956, 1957; Bollingen ·Prize, 1969. Fellow in American Letters, Library of Congress. Member, American Academy of Arts and Sciences, and National Institute of Arts and Letters. Address: 1119 Bucknell Drive, Davis, California 95616, U.S.A.

PUBLICATIONS

Verse

Poems. Baltimore, Waverly Press, 1935.
Five Young American Poets, with others. New York, New Directions, 1941.
Person, Place and Thing. New York, Reynal, 1942; London, Secker and War-
burg, 1944.
The Place of Love. Melbourne, Comment Press, 1942.
V-Letter and Other Poems. New York, Reynal, 1944; London, Secker and
Warburg, 1945.
Essay on Rime. New York, Reynal, 1945; London, Secker and Warburg, 1947.
Trial of a Poet and Other Poems. New York, Reynal, 1947.
Poems, 1940–1953. New York, Random House, 1953.
The House. San Francisco, privately printed, 1957.
Poems of a Jew. New York, Random House, 1958.
The Bourgeois Poet. New York, Random House, 1964.
Selected Poems. New York, Random House, 1968.
White-Haired Lover. New York, Random House, 1968.

Play

The Tenor, music by Hugo Weisgall. New York, Merion Music Company,
1956.

Novel

Edsel. New York, Geis, 1971.

Other

English Prosody and Modern Poetry. Baltimore, Johns Hopkins University
Press, 1947.
A Bibliography of Modern Prosody. Baltimore, Johns Hopkins University
Press, 1948.
Beyond Criticism. Lincoln, University of Nebraska Press, 1953; as A Primer
for Poets, 1965.
In Defense of Ignorance (essays). New York, Random House, 1960.
Start with the Sun: Studies in Cosmic Poetry, with James E. Miller, Jr., and
Bernice Slote. Lincoln, University of Nebraska Press, 1960.
The Writer's Experience, with Ralph Ellison. Washington, D.C., Library of
Congress, 1964.
A Prosody Handbook, with Robert Beum. New York, Harper, 1965.

Randall Jarrell. Washington, D.C., Library of Congress, 1967.
To Abolish Children and Other Essays. Chicago, Quadrangle Books, 1968.
The Poetry Wreck. New York, Random House, 1975.

Editor, with Louis Untermeyer and Richard Wilbur, *Modern American and Modern British Poetry,* revised shorter edition. New York, Harcourt Brace, 1955.
Editor, *American Poetry.* New York, Crowell, 1960.
Editor, *Prose Keys to Modern Poetry.* New York, Harper, 1962.

Bibliography: *Karl Shapiro: A Bibliography* by William White, Detroit, Wayne State University Press, 1960.

Manuscript Collection: Library of Congress, Washington, D.C.

*   *   *

The poetic career of Karl Shapiro is remarkable for its high accomplishment in various styles – all of them his own creations – and for its abrupt, unpredictable departures into new and fruitful artistic territories. From *Person, Place and Thing,* published while he was still in the army, to the bold cycle of love poems, *White-Haired Lover,* his writing shows considerable range as well as changing interests and attitudes. His criticism, of which we can say little here, is perceptive, vigorous, and frequently outspoken; the opinions and judgments it expresses usually reflect the stylistic or other preoccupations of his poetry.

Much of Shapiro's earlier work, and that of his American contemporaries John Berryman, Delmore Schwartz, Muriel Rukeyser, Weldon Kees, and others, demonstrates a concern with the life and institutions of modern society. Like Auden, MacNeice, and Spender in England, whose influence they doubtless felt, these poets struggled towards individual styles that would embrace both personal intuition and public experience. No one is more successful in this achievement than Shapiro: the poetry of his first three books is polished, elegant, witty, conversational, but also marked by deep compassion and humanity quite evident in such poems as "Auto Wreck," "The Leg," and "Elegy for a Dead Soldier." A large number of pieces from the 1940's explore with surgical skill the ironies, hypocrisies, prejudices, and illusions of America and its institutions. "University" begins: "To hurt the Negro and avoid the Jew / Is the curriculum." In his poem about Hollywood he concentrates on its falsities, its manufactured dreams, but also wonders if it doesn't express something inherent in the nation:

> O can we understand it? Is it ours,
> A crude whim of a beginning people,
> A private orgy in a secluded spot?

And the poem "Necropolis" confronts the inequalities which persist between rich and poor even beyond the boundaries of death, reputedly the great equalizer.

In all of these poems Shapiro's voice and conscience are representative of humanity, take man's part before the spectacle and trials of modern existence; yet we find some poems – the sequence "Recapitulations" is an example – that reveal more closely his own life and private feelings. With *Trial of a Poet,* the first of several indications of change and experiment appears – in this instance, two prose poems which look forward to Shapiro's radical adoption of that form later for an entire book, *The Bourgeois Poet.* In addition, the new "Adam and Eve" sequence

with which he opens his selected *Poems, 1940–1953* announces a growing fascination
with Jewish themes that leads directly on to his initial, unexpected departure from
previous work in *Poems of a Jew*, a collection that includes both earlier and recent
pieces and whose introduction is provocative; in it he attempts to identify a
"Jewish consciousness" that is man "absolutely committed to the world" but also
"essentially himself, beyond nationality, defenseless against the crushing impersonality of history." He cites Joyce's Leopold Bloom, "neither hero nor victim," as
the best example of this "free modern Jew." Together with the controversial but
enormously stimulating volume of critical essays, *In Defense of Ignorance* (the title
and contents of which attack intellectualism and the New Criticism), published two
years later, *Poems of a Jew* starts Shapiro off on a poetically rewarding quest for
identity. If his criticism occasionally overstates matters, that is probably necessary
in order to overthrow his allegiance to the literary prescriptions handed down by
Eliot and the New Critics and to take up the support of such strong but too often
neglected writers as Whitman, Lawrence, Henry Miller, and W. C. Williams.

   The Bourgeois Poet, which follows after these first repudiations of artistic and
intellectual convention, provides a complete breakthrough into novel, difficult areas
of literary form. The prose poem, utilizing the prose paragraph, has a fine tradition
in French literature but has seldon proved manageable in English. However, Shapiro's success is remarkable; the poems have a marvelous flexibility in mood, tone,
and temper; they shift from the satirical to the lyric to the dreamlike or irrational
with rhythmic facility and strength. This book belongs in a line of descent from
Rimbaud, Joyce's *Ulysses*, Henry Miller, Céline, and Isaac Singer.

   Shapiro's newest work does not simply try to repeat *The Bourgeois Poet*; he
undertakes a certain artistic retrenchment in the love poems, though they profit
immensely from his prose experiments and are themselves frank, intimate, tender,
and moving – the latest instance of powerful exploratory imaginative gifts.

                                                                – Ralph J. Mills, Jr

---

SHELTON, Richard. American. Born in Boise, Idaho, 24 June 1933. Educated at
Harding College, Searcy, Arkansas, 1951–53; Abilene Christian College, Texas,
B.A. in English 1958; University of Arizona, Tucson, M.A. 1960. Served in the
United States Army, 1956–58. Married Lois Bruce in 1956; has one son. Teacher,
Lowell School, Bisbee, Arizona, 1958–60; Director, Ruth Stephan Poetry Center,
Tucson, 1964–65. Instructor, 1960–64, Assistant Professor, 1969–73, and since 1973,
Associate Professor of English, University of Arizona, Tucson. Recipient: Interna-
tional Poetry Forum United States Award, 1970; Borestone Mountain Award,
1972. Address: 1548 West Plaza De Lirios, Tucson, Arizona 85705, U.S.A.

PUBLICATIONS

Verse

   Journal of Return. San Francisco, Kayak Books, 1969.
   The Tattooed Desert. Pittsburgh, University of Pittsburgh Press, 1971.
   The Heroes of Our Time. Lincoln, Nebraska, Best Cellar Press, 1972.
   Of All the Dirty Words. Pittsburgh, University of Pittsburgh Press, 1972.
   Calendar: A Cycle of Poems. Phoenix, Arizona, Baleen Press, 1972.
   Among the Stones. Pittsburgh, Monuments Press, 1973.

Critical Studies: in the *Chicago Tribune Magazine*, 22 January 1970; in *Prairie Schooner* (Lincoln, Nebraska), Summer 1972; in *Poetry* (Chicago), July 1972 and July 1973; in the *San Francisco Chronicle*, 27 May 1973.

Richard Shelton comments:

I hope my work reflects something of the Sonora Desert, in which I have lived for fifteen years.

*   *   *

Richard Shelton, one of the finest poets now writing in the United States, has shown through two remarkable books the new possibilities of surrealism for the American writer. Shelton's poems are frequently as regional as those of Stafford or Haines or Berry, but he also brings to this poetry the surrealist poet's awareness of the subconscious. The result is a poetry that manages a highly successful and original fusion of the inner and outer worlds. As even the title of his first major collection, *The Tattooed Desert*, suggests, this is a writer interested in probing both the wilderness outside himself in his adopted Southwest and the equally vast wilderness within. This is a lot of territory to cover, but Shelton traverses it all; there are powerful poems about the Southwest, and equally powerful poems about the spiritual desolation surrounding his father's death. In fact, the latter poems from *The Tattooed Desert* are among Shelton's finest, and illustrate the strong emotional charge his best work carries. Here is "Reunion" entire (Shelton's work virtually demands total quotation; as Martin Grossman has pointed out, there is a strong emotional thread to the best poems, and it would be wrong to sever the thread):

> once a year at midnight
> the ghost of my father walks
> in wearing his scars
> on the outside of his bandages
> asking directions *which*
> *way are we going*
> *how far to silence*
>
> maps flapping on the walls
> the walls falling in and me
> waiting as usual while the future
> limps from door to door
> on its broken toes
>
> sliding into a chair
> and tucking one leg under him
> his bloated head begins
> to fall toward his right
> shoulder as he gives me a long
>
> wink and says *I'm going*
> *to get drunk again tonight*
> *god how I dread it*

1391

Shelton is a careful, though by no means timid, artist; even a short collection like
the fine *The Heroes of Our Time* (from Greg Kuzma's Best Cellar Press) contains
scarcely a weak poem, and he brings this sort of care to his second major
collection, *Of All the Dirty Words*, a book that shows Shelton's continued growth
from the work in his excellent first book; almost all the poems in the title section
are successful, as are any number of others: "The Heroes of Our Time," "A Small
Voice," "The Other World," "Why I Never Went into Politics," and "Her," to
name just a few. The desert of Richard Shelton, the world of his poems, is not the
sterile wasteland too many poets inherited from Eliot, but a painted desert alive
with images that redeem the barrenness. His imagination reminds us that the mind
may be a desert, but its mirages are real.

– Duane Ackerson

SHERWIN, Judith Johnson. American. Born in New York City, 3 October 1936.
Educated at the Dalton Schools, New York, graduated 1954; Radcliffe College,
Cambridge, Massachusetts, 1954–55; Barnard College, New York, B.A. (cum laude)
1958; Columbia University, New York (Woodrow Wilson Fellow, 1958), 1958–59.
Married James T. Sherwin in 1955; has three children. Promotion Manager, Arrow
Press, New York, 1961. Recipient: Academy of American Poets prize, 1958; Yaddo
Fellowship, 1964; Poetry Society of America Fellowship, 1964; Aspen Writers
Workshop Rose Fellowship, 1967; Yale Series of Younger Poets Award, 1968.
Agent: Carl Brandt, Brandt and Brandt, 101 Park Avenue, New York, New York
10017. Address: 27 West 86th Street, New York, New York 10024, U.S.A.

PUBLICATIONS

Verse

Uranium Poems. New Haven, Connecticut, Yale University Press, 1969.
Impossible Buildings. New York, Doubleday, 1973.

Plays

Belisa's Love (produced New York, 1959).
En Avant, Coco (produced New York, 1961).
two untitled multimedia works (produced Brussels, 1971, 1972).
Waste (multimedia; produced London, 1972).

Short Stories

The Life of Riot. New York, Atheneum, 1970.

Judith Johnson Sherwin comments:

My poetry comes across in readings as drama or music more than as text. I enjoy reading with cool jazz or with quiet electronic music which provides spaces in the sound and between the sounds. Much of my poetry is meant to be sung or chanted or belted out in the shower.

All my life I have refused to let myself be limited to any theory of what poetry should be, either in form or in content. I write traditional sonnet sequences and I write surreal poems and sound poems. Every form, every technique is of equal interest; I should feel dissatisfied with my mind if there were any approach to poetry that did not excite me to see if I could go out and do likewise.

My writing, poetry, fiction and drama, is both feminist and political, but it is neither didactic nor hortatory. I write about my life as a woman and as a political animal because that's where my life is, those are the questions I have to face. However, I don't know the answers; any answer I examine is hypothesis, not conclusion.

I try to make a rough music, a dance of the mind, a calculus of the emotions, a driving beat of praise out of the pain and mystery that surround me and become me. My poems are meant to make your mind get up and shout.

*   *   *

Judith Johnson Sherwin's *Uranium Poems* are characterized by a diction in which words pile up and hammer on each other without breath-break, like endless German adjectives before the noun. The style suits her theme: uranium mining destroys the earth to procure ores to make bombs that destroy the world. She is dealing metaphorically with the various deaths that permeate and undermine our lives, especially the death that haunts love, and inscrutable bitter deaths – Eichmann's murders, Marilyn Monroe's suicide. The names of mines – Happy Jack, Mary Kathleen – become persons; the names of ores – coffinite, stillwellite – indicate emotions. Her lines embody high contrasts, shaped with great rhetorical selfconsciousness, avoiding syntactical cliché, while her vocabulary is tough and slangy, borrowed from life on garbage-strewn streets. It is hard to be human in this destructive atmosphere but the poet is struggling:

> THAT SILENCE WAS THE LOVESONG
> I WROTE YOU LAST NIGHT WHEN
> SHAKING ITS HONKY-TONK TAMBOURINE HAIR
>   THE NIGHT
> SAID TO ME do you need
> anybody?
>   no sweetheart I SAID what
> i need if i could find
> it maybe a surgically clean mind . . .

In her more recent collection, *Impossible Buildings*, Sherwin is still hard-headed but her language and forms are less rough-hewn, are often almost old-fashioned in their rhymes and metres. In "Materials," a sequence of ten sonnets, each poem focusses on a natural substance – ice, wood, water – and makes each an elegant metaphor for an aspect of love, weaving these into a philosophical commentary reminiscent of the metaphysical poets. Other poems reveal other intricate moods of love, but the prevailing theme of the book is larger than love, as the title poem makes clear. "Impossible buildings" are built by the artist's mind at work:

>   the construction is
>   the information. like Escher's it has less
>   to do with conservation than with
>   recirculation: to pass the same new
>   world through me again . . .

This poetry also reflects a woman's concerns, but not in any stereotyped way. Sherwin is always intelligent and unflinchingly perceptive, contributing to high quality art by women and insight into women's experience which this period in history needs. Her full humanity is what is finally impressive.

– Jane Augustine

SIEBRASSE, Glen. Canadian. Born in Edmonton, Alberta, 5 November 1939. Educated at Loyola College, Montreal. Co-Editor, *Yes* magazine, Montreal, 1956–60, 1964–67. Managing Editor, 1965–71, and since 1972, Editor, *Delta Canada*, Montreal. Recipient: Junior Canada Council Grant, 1966; Junior Quebec grant, 1968; President's Medal, University of Western Ontario, 1969; Canada Council travel grant, 1971. Address: 351 Geráld Street, Lasalle 690, Quebec, Canada.

PUBLICATIONS

Verse

    The Regeneration of an Athlete.   Montreal, Delta Canada, 1965.
    Man: Unman.   Montreal, Delta Canada, 1969.
    Jerusalem.   Montreal, Delta Canada, 1971.

Other

    Editor, "Canadian Issue" of *Vanderbilt Poetry Review 2* (Nashville, Tennessee), 1973.

Glen Siebrasse comments:

These books contain all the poetry I never wished to write.

                    *   *   *

"My poetry has often been interpreted as a study in death," Glen Siebrasse has explained. "Death is the only thing we have time to fear," he added in a poem. If by death is meant decline as well as decomposition, then this characterization of his theme is as good as any. Like the monk with the skull labelled "Memento Mori" at his elbow as he works, Siebrasse is ever-conscious of the presence of what has been affectionately called "the great leveller."

Perhaps the central book to this theme or obsession is *The Regeneration of an Athlete* which charts decline and laments the impossibility of ascent. Even birth is depicted in terms of caricature, as in "Woman Gives Birth to a Frog":

> we mock life:
> grow each day
> weaker.
>
> The bones swell in our skull heads.

Ever aging, even lovers are advised to leave evidence of their mortality. In "Harrison," he writes:

> build for a thousand years that others
> coming after
> will note men stopped here
> embracing, even under the bombs.

This is a difficult poetry, sometimes rewarding, sometimes merely puzzling. Siebrasse's poems are, as Peter Stevens noted in the *Supplement to the Oxford Companion to Canadian History and Literature* (1973), "carefully organized; some sometimes thickly, even opaquely, textured." The writing is technically unexceptional, except when the poet is moved to create, *sui generis*, a new tone and technique, as in "The Field":

> The field contains the hunter and the hare:
> the hunter kills the hare,
> kills the field,
> kills himself;
> the field begins itself again,
> begins the hare,
> begins the hunter:
> the field contains the hunter and the hare.

– John Robert Colombo

SIEGEL, Eli. American. Born in Dvinsk, Latvia, 16 August 1902; emigrated to the United States in 1905; naturalized, 1912. Educated at Baltimore City College, 1916–19. Married the writer Martha Baird in 1944. Associated with V. F. Calverton in founding *Modern Quarterly*, Baltimore, 1923. Columnist, *Baltimore American*, 1925; Book Reviewer, *New York Evening Post*, and *Scribner's*, New York, 1926–35. Conducted poetry readings in New York, 1926–40. Founder and Teacher since 1940 of Aesthetic Realism (defined as "the seeing that the world, art, and self explain each other: each is the aesthetic oneness of opposites"). Recipient: *The Nation* Prize, 1925. Address: c/o Definition Press, 141 Greene Street, New York, New York 10012, U.S.A.

PUBLICATIONS

Verse

Hot Afternoons Have Been in Montana: Poems. New York, Definition Press, 1957.
Hail, American Development. New York, Definition Press, 1968.

Plays

The Appraisal of a Ghost; Haste Me to Know It; The Imperfect Soliloquy; Who Is Ophelia?; The Great Dumb Show; A Mother Commands and Is Rebuked; Gertrude's Wrong Choice; Hamlet Is an Army; Ophelia Enclosed No Longer; Hamlet's Enemies Contrive; Infinite Jest, or, The Mortuary Songster; Family Versus the Universe; The Rites of Actuality (13 plays produced New York, 1962–63); revised version, as Hamlet Revisited: Hamlet and His Father, Hamlet and Ophelia, Hamlet and the World (produced New York, 1963).
The Ordinary Doom (produced New York, 1967).
Double Viewpoint (produced New York, 1967).

Other

The Aesthetic Method in Self-Conflict. New York, Definition Press, 1946.
Psychiatry, Economics, Aesthetics. New York, Definition Press, 1946.
Is Beauty the Making One of Opposites? New York, Terrain Gallery, 1955.
Art as Life. New York, Terrain Gallery, 1957.
Personal and Impersonal: Six Aesthetic Realists. New York, Terrain Gallery, 1959.
Aesthetic Realism: Three Instances. New York, Terrain Gallery, 1961.
A Rosary of Evil. New York, Terrain Gallery, 1964.
Williams' Poetry Talked About, and William Carlos Williams Present and Talking: 1952. New York, Terrain Gallery, 1964; revised edition, as The Williams-Siegel Documentary, Including: Williams' Poetry Talked About, and William Carlos Williams Present and Talking: 1952, edited by Martha Baird and Ellen Reiss, New York, Definition Press, 1970.
Damned Welcome: Aesthetic Realism Maxims. New York, Terrain Gallery, 1964.
What's There? Lou Bernstein's Photographs: An Aesthetic Realism Art Inquiry. New York, Terrain Gallery, 1965.
Aesthetic Realism Is Contemporary; or, A Hundred Merry Tales of This World: Being Bulletins Read by the Hamlet Revisited Company, 1963, 1964, 1965. New York, Terrain Gallery, 1965.
James and the Children: A Consideration of Henry James's "The Turn of the Screw," edited by Martha Baird. New York, Definition Press, 1968.
The "Modern Quarterly" Beginnings of Aesthetic Realism, 1922–1923. New York, Definition Press, 1969.
Goodbye Profit System. New York, Definition Press, 1970.
Children's Guide to Parents and Other Matters. New York, Definition Press, 1971.
The Francis Sanders Lesson and Two Related Works. New York, Defintion Press, 1974.

Manuscript Collection: State University of New York, Buffalo.

Critical Studies: Selden Rodman, in *Saturday Review* (New York), August 1957; "Whole in Brightness" by Walter Leuba, in *New Mexico Quarterly* (Albuquerque), Autumn 1957; autobiographical article by the author, in *Literary Review* (Rutherford, New Jersey), Winter 1957–58; "Ghosts and Benedictions" by Hugh Kenner, in *Poetry* (Chicago), November 1968; Kenneth Rexroth, in *The New York Times Book Review*, 23 March 1969; *Aesthetic Realism: We Have Been There: Six Artists on the Siegel Theory of Opposites*, by Ted van Griethuysen and others, New York, Definition Press, 1969; Selden Rodman, in *100 American Poems*, New York, New American Library, 1972.

Eli Siegel comments:

If the sameness and difference of America were to become musical, it would be poetry. Every fact has music in it. The poet looks for it. (From the preface to *Hail, American Development*).

Poetry, like life, states that the very self of a thing is its relations, its having-to-do with other things. Whatever is in the world, whatever person, has meaning because it or he has to do with the whole universe: immeasurable and crowded reality. . . . Humor and poetry I see as utterly amiable; the relation of the light and heavy, the humorous and grave, I regard as a mighty and pressing critical problem. The jocose moments in "Hot Afternoons Have Been in Montana" were missed by early commentators: fish can move fast in dark pools and so on. (From the preface to *Hot Afternoons Have Been in Montana: Poems*).

*   *   *

Eli Siegel is known mainly on the basis of William Carlos Williams' enthusiasm for his work – a long and interesting letter from Williams appears in lieu of a preface in Siegel's collection *Hot Afternoons Have Been in Montana*. In this letter, Williams speaks of the unexpectedness – some might say the quirkiness – of Siegel's style. In fact, the poet's Aesthetic Realism, as he names it, is clearly a personal variation on the Objectivism of Louis Zukofsky and his colleagues. Siegel's poems seem to me extremely variable in quality, despite the enthusiasm of Williams' recommendation. His worst faults are slightness, and a slightly sugary whimsicality. His best work, however, has a romantic purity which harks back to Wordsworth – one even catches the Wordsworthian accent in this statement about the merits of free verse:

> Free verse is when
> You're at ease with something
> You mean with your whole heart.

– Edward Lucie-Smith

SILKIN, Jon. British. Born in London, 2 December 1930. Educated at Wycliffe and Dulwich colleges; University of Leeds (Gregory Fellow, 1958–60), B.A.

(honours) 1962. Served in the Army Education Corps, 1948–50. Formerly, Extramural Lecturer, University of Leeds, and University of Newcastle; Beck Visiting Lecturer of Writing, Denison University, Granville, Ohio; Visiting Lecturer, Writers Workshop, University of Iowa, Iowa City, 1968–69; Visiting Writer, Australian Arts Council and University of Sydney, 1974. Since 1952, Founding Co-Editor, and since 1968, Editor with Lorna Tracy and David Heal, *Stand*, Newcastle upon Tyne; since 1964, Co-founding Editor, Northern House, publishers, Newcastle upon Tyne. Recipient: Northern Arts Minor Award, 1965; Faber Memorial Prize, 1966. Agent: Anthony Shiel, 52 Floral Street, Covent Garden, London W.C.2. Address: 58 Queen's Road, Newcastle upon Tyne NE2 2PR, England.

PUBLICATIONS

Verse

> *The Portrait and Other Poems.* Ilfracombe, Devon, Stockwell, 1950.
> *The Peaceable Kingdom.* London, Chatto and Windus, 1954; New York, Yorick Books, 1969.
> *The Two Freedoms.* London, Chatto and Windus, and New York, Macmillan, 1958.
> *The Re-ordering of the Stones.* London, Chatto and Windus-Hogarth Press, 1961.
> *Flower Poems.* Leeds, Northern House, 1964.
> *Penguin Modern Poets 7*, with Richard Murphy and Nathaniel Tarn. London, Penguin, 1965.
> *Nature with Man.* London, Chatto and Windus-Hogarth Press, 1965.
> *Poems New and Selected.* London, Chatto and Windus, and Middletown, Connecticut, Wesleyan University Press, 1966.
> *Three Poems.* Cambridge, Massachusetts, Pym Randall Press, 1969.
> *Killhope Wheel.* Ashington, Northumberland, MidNAG, 1971.
> *Amana Grass.* London, Chatto and Windus-Hogarth Press, and Middletown, Connecticut, Wesleyan University Press, 1971.
> *Air That Pricks Earth.* Rushden, Northamptonshire, Sceptre Press, 1973.
> *The Principle of Water.* Cheadle, Cheshire, Carcanet Press, 1974.

Other

> *Isaac Rosenberg, 1890–1918: A Catalogue of the Exhibition Held at Leeds University, May-June 1959, Together with the Text of Unpublished Material*, with Maurice de Sausmarez. Leeds, University of Leeds, 1959.
> *Out of the Battle: Poetry of the Great War* (criticism). London and New York, Oxford University Press, 1972.

> Editor, *Living Voices: An Anthology of Contemporary Verse.* London, Vista Books, 1960.
> Editor, *Poetry of the Committed Individual: A "Stand" Anthology of Poetry.* London, Gollancz-Penguin, 1973.

> Translator, *Against Parting*, by Nathan Zach. Newcastle upon Tyne, Northern House, 1968.

Critical Studies: by John Fuller, in *London Magazine*, October 1966; Merle E. Brown, in *Iowa Review* (Iowa City), i, 1, 1969; "Alone in a Mine of Reality: A Matrix in the Poetry of Jon Silkin" by Anne Cluysenaar, in *British Poetry since 1960: A Critical Survey*, edited by Michael Schmidt and Grevel Lindop, Oxford, Carcanet Press, 1972; in *Times Literary Supplement* (London), 19 July 1974; in *The Tablet* (London), 10 August 1974.

*   *   *

After his two early volumes, *The Peaceable Kingdom* and *The Two Freedoms*, in which the seeds of later developments are still overlaid with an occasional uncertainty of style and tone, Jon Silkin achieved an impressive maturity with *The Re-ordering of the Stones*. His later volume, *Nature with Man*, represents both an extension and a specialisation of the earlier book.

In both of these later volumes, Silkin writes a poised, slow-moving, reflective poetry which manages to be at once meditative and dramatic. He probes the human and political meanings of growth, suffering, destruction and creativity, but through a strikingly focused and sensuous range of imagery. This combination, of a tone which is essentially that of a maturely reflective speaking-voice, with a pungent and concrete mode of simile and metaphor, is the distinctive hall-mark of Silkin's poetry. The poems show an acute attention to the detail of rhythm and movement, alternating complex and comulative patterns of thought and feeling with curt, elliptical statements; and it is through this interchange of reflection and immediacy, the abstract and the directly sensuous, that they achieve at their best the sense of a public, rhetorical tone which is at the same time flexibly expressive and dramatic. In several of Silkin's poems, this originality of style hardens into mannerism and artifice, so that the need to maintain a certain quality of tone and stance seems to be dictating the developments of image and feeling; but at its best, Silkin's poetry has widened the possibilities of tone and feeling for its generation.

In *Nature with Man*, Silkin examines the delicate contrasts and continuities between human and natural life-forms. The central sequence of the volume is a series of "Flower-poems," each of which tries to render the intricately inward life of a particular flower in a way which is both faithful to the flower's autonomy as a living thing, and yet simultaneously resonant of human concerns. The sequence has uneven success; but it interestingly embodies, in its preoccupation with both general human issues and minutely specific detail, that concern with the achievement of a "moral sensuousness" – a re-fruiting of human sensibilities through the sensuous discriminations of language – which has been the continuing theme of Silkin's work.

– Terry Eagleton

SILLITOE, Alan. British. Born in Nottingham, 4 March 1928. Educated in various Nottingham schools up to the age of 14. Served as a radio operator in the Royal Air Force, 1946–49. Married Ruth Fainlight, *q.v.*, in 1959; has two children. Travelled in France, Italy and Spain, 1952–58. Since 1970, Literary Adviser to W. H. Allen and Company, publishers, London. Recipient: Authors Club prize, 1958;

Hawthornden Prize, for fiction, 1960. Address: c/o W. H. Allen and Company, 43 Essex Street, London W.C.2, England.

PUBLICATIONS

Verse

Without Beer or Bread.   London, Outposts Publications, 1957.
The Rats and Other Poems.   London, W. H. Allen, 1960.
A Falling Out of Love and Other Poems.   London, W. H. Allen, 1964.
Love in the Environs of Voronezh.   London, Macmillan, 1968; New York, Doubleday, 1970.
Shaman and Other Poems.   London, Turret Books, 1968.
Poems, with Ted Hughes and Ruth Fainlight.   London, Rainbow Press, 1971.
Barbarians and Other Poems.   London, Turret Books, 1974.
Storm: New Poems.   London, W. H. Allen, 1974.

Plays

The Ragman's Daughter (produced Felixstowe, Suffolk, 1966).
All Citizens Are Soldiers, with Ruth Fainlight, adaptation of a play by Lope de Vega (produced Stratford upon Avon and London, 1967).   London, Macmillan, and Chester Springs, Pennsylvania, Dufour, 1969.
This Foreign Field (produced London, 1970).

Screenplays: *Saturday Night and Sunday Morning*, 1960; *The Loneliness of the Long Distance Runner*, 1961; *The Ragman's Daughter*, 1974.

Novels

Saturday Night and Sunday Morning.   London, W. H. Allen, and New York, Knopf, 1958.
The General.   London, W. H. Allen, and New York, Knopf, 1960.
Key to the Door.   London, Macmillan, and New York, Knopf, 1961.
The Death of William Posters.   London, Macmillan, and New York, Knopf, 1965.
A Tree on Fire.   London, Macmillan, and New York, Knopf, 1967.
A Start in Life.   London, W. H. Allen, 1970; New York, Scribner, 1971.
Travels in Nihilon.   London, W. H. Allen, 1971; New York, Scribner, 1972.
Raw Material.   London, W. H. Allen, 1972; New York, Scribner, 1973.
Flame of Life.   London, W. H. Allen, 1974.

Short Stories

The Loneliness of the Long Distance Runner.   London, W. H. Allen, and New York, Knopf, 1959.
The Ragman's Daughter.   London, W. H. Allen, and New York, Knopf, 1963.
Guzman Go Home.   London, Macmillan, and New York, Doubleday, 1968.
Men, Women, and Children.   London, W. H. Allen, 1973; New York, Scribner, 1974.

Other

> *The Road to Volgograd* (travel).   London, W. H. Allen, and New York, Knopf, 1964.
> *The City Adventures of Marmalade Jim* (juvenile).   London, Macmillan, 1967.

Critical Studies: *Alan Sillitoe*, London, Times Authors Series, 1970; *Alan Sillitoe* by Allen Richard Penner, New York, Twayne, 1972.

Alan Sillitoe comments:

I use poetry to express emotions that can't be expressed in any other medium.

I am incapable of analysing my own poetry. When I first began to write I considered myself more a poet than a writer. However, novels and stories seem to have overtaken me – though I still am, and still consider myself to be, primarily a poet. A great deal of my "poetry" gets into my prose work, and it is often difficult to find a dividing line. If I have any aim in poetry it is to use images and language as a means of breaking through to new experience – that is to say, old experiences that have not been described before.

*   *   *

Alan Sillitoe is much better known as a novelist than he is as a poet, and one cannot help feeling that, in essence, this is the correct verdict. Yet it is also true to say that Sillitoe has not received credit for his poems. His first and most substantial collection, *The Rats*, was mostly written in the 1950's; and the poems in it reflect the boredom and impatience which many radical writers felt with the English society of that epoch. The "rats" of the title are the forces of conformity:

> They are the government, these marsh-brained rats
> Who give protection from outsider cats . . .

But, in addition to satires, the book also contains a number of tender love poems.

This impatience with society and the way it is going is just one of the characteristics which suggest a comparison with D. H. Lawrence. Lawrence, like Sillitoe, came from the working-class, from Nottingham, made his reputation as a novelist, and spent much time as an expatriate. Like Lawrence's, Sillitoe's poems have been consistently undervalued. More recent work, such as the poems in *Love in the Environs of Voronezh*, shows a marked increase in technical control, but also a continuing impatience with poetic convention – radical conventions as well as conservative ones. Sillitoe seems to write a poem because there is something which, as he sees it, needs to be said. The quality of the "saying" tends to vary a good deal from poem to poem, but one is always aware of the direct thrust of a powerful literary personality.

– Edward Lucie-Smith

SIMIC, Charles. American. Born in Yugoslavia, 9 May 1938; emigrated to the United States in 1949. Educated at Oak Park High School, Illinois; University of Chicago, 1956–59; New York University, 1959–61, 1963–64, 1964–65, B.A. 1964. Served in the United States Army, 1961–63. Married Helene Dubin in 1965; has one daughter. Formerly, Proofreader, *Chicago Sun-Times*. Taught English at California State College, Hayward. Since 1966, Editorial Assistant, *Aperture* magazine, New York. Recipient: Guggenheim Fellowship, 1972; National Endowment for the Arts grant, 1974. Address: Old Mountain Road, Northwood, New Hampshire 03261, U.S.A.

PUBLICATIONS

Verse

> *What the Grass Says.* San Francisco, Kayak Books, 1967.
> *Somewhere among Us a Stone Is Taking Notes.* San Francisco, Kayak Books, 1969.
> *Dismantling the Silence.* New York, Braziller, and London, Cape, 1971.
> *White.* New York, New Rivers Press, 1972.
> *Return to a Place Lit by a Glass of Milk.* New York, Braziller, 1974.

Other

> Editor and Translator, *Five Gardens*, by Luan Lauc. New York, New Rivers Press, 1970.
> Editor and Translator, *Selected Poems of Ivan V. Lalic.* New York, New Rivers Press, 1970.
> Editor and Translator, *Four Yugoslav Poets: Ivan V. Lalic, Brank Miljkovic, Milorad Pavic, Ljubomir Simovic.* Aurora, New York, Lillabulero Press, 1970.
> Editor and Translator, *The Little Box: Poems*, by Vasco Popa. Washington, D.C., Charioteer Press, 1970.

*   *   *

Part nursery-rhyme for the psychologically distressed, part surrealistic copy-book for the disenchanted, Charles Simic's poetry aggressively adopts the contemporary mode. The speaker of the poems is laconic, almost aphasic, and his characteristic utterances are parables, fables, intimations, and myths-in-the-making. Always concerned with interiority, the verse presents a barren exterior, and its *disjecta membra* float between the vortex of an engulfing portentousness and a cascading froth of agonized subjectivity. "I'm like a cold glass of milk / the stars will drink before going to bed." Is this gigantism, or slippery bathos? The very tonelessness of this poetry makes it difficult to answer readily. Often the poems seem translated from primitive texts, figments of some codex, the central legend of which remains indecipherable. There are unnamed crimes in the past, some allusive blood-curse so ancient that retribution and relinquishment are alike impossible: "the stone coughs up its secret pit / which will prove to be just another stone."

Simic's poetry resembles Mark Strand's and W. S. Merwin's; he incorporates the pained sensitivity of the former while juggling the mythic conundrums of the latter.

The typical Simic poem uses a very limited vocabulary, draws plain images from un-adorned objects (which include bones as well as stars), and generates tension from surreal lacunae and juxtapositions, while hinting darkly at the ineffable. The poems are spare, but whether from an almost silent awe or concise defeat depends in part on the reader's sensibility: "A voice that wanted / To equal the silence / That surrounds it." He seems to owe as much to Jakov Lind or Kafka as to any older American writer. Indeed, his poems sometimes sound like Sylvia Plath's, but stripped of her pyrotechnic vocabulary and whipsaw syntax:

> Thumb, loose tooth of a horse.
> Rooster to his hens.
> Horn of a devil. Fat worm
> They have attached to my flesh
> At the time of my birth.
> It takes four to hold him down,
> Bend him in half, until the bone
> Begins to whimper.

We move from disjunct images to a colloquial, almost nonchalant terror. This passage goes slack when compared to Plath's "Cut," but the worm, the whimper, and the devil's horn are characteristic of Simic's almost-Transylvanian imagination. These poems often seek to establish a morality, at least a psychology, firmly grounded in the human body, but often that body sustains (at least imagined) mutilations in order to render the interior agony ("Hang the meat on the hook / So that I may see what I am").

   Such mutilations occur not in the heat of the battle, nor in daily struggle, but rather like after-thoughts of the apocalypse, an ending that sends us all back to primitive origins, for in the daemonized land of Simic's imagination, everything is circular:

> Whoever swings an ax
> Knows the body of man
> Will again be covered with fur.
> . . . He who cannot
> Grow teeth will not survive.

In such an utterly reduced psychological landscape, Simic turns easily to anthropo-morphizing material objects and small domestic creatures: he has poems called "Spoon," "Knife," and "Fork," as well as "Spiders," and "The Animals." The last has these post-diluvean lines:

> Alone, without a model –
> It will be up to me
> To imagine, out of the stone and debris
> That are left, a new species.

Reading Simic is sometimes like listening to a student of Jung discussing the survivor-complex, while illustrating his lecture with mediaeval wood-cuts:

> Let us kneel pinch of nothing
> And pray sliver of pain. . . .
> My voice now the mad captain
> Thrown in chains by his suffering crew.

The poetry of the exacerbated, deracinated neurotic can scarcely be carried any further, yet we're told "The worst is still to come." There is in Simic's poetry at its best a numbed disorientation that never surrenders at least the memory, or the fading hope, of what it is to be fully human. But such hope is far from blithe. If anything, his poetry rebukes its own humanistic echoes. Such injured flesh as supports these fevered, dessicated messages casts the shadows of its distrust everywhere. A condemned man's face is "dark and twisted / As if death meant straining to empty one's bowels." Always beneath the horror lurks the possibility that agony is as mundane as mere subsistence, and equally pervasive, equally unremarkable.

Occasionally, Simic's poetry exhibits considerable flaws: "Concerning My Neighbours, the Hittites," for example, overflows with a surrealistic tide of unredeemed cliches. The marvellous and the shopworn cancel each other out. Like much neo-surrealistic poetry written by his contemporaries such as Michael Benedikt and James Tate, Simic's poetry might be seen as comic excess, a saturnalian indulgence in the madness of language, but surrounded as his is by broken bones and spilt blood, it's difficult to appreciate the humor. Gallows humor might constitute part of it, but the poems lack the verbal gloss to fit that category comfortably. Simic's strength resides in his insistence, not his release. Of the stone he says, "I answered your questions / until your hardness entered my voice." The unrelenting sameness of the diction in these poems forms their beauty and much of their weakness; while exceedingly egocentric they often sound anonymous. Perhaps the mode developed by Robert Bly and James Wright, a kind of second-wave post-Hiroshima imagism, has become too homogenized, too replete with facile practitioners.

The last poem of Simic's major volume is called "*errata*," and contains these two directives:

> Each time a hat appears
> think of Isaac Newton
> reading the Old Testament
> Remove all periods
> They are scars left by words
> I couldn't bring myself to say

A mundane object putatively represents the paradox of a scientist obsessed by ancient thunderings: a fitting exemplum of the typical Simic poem. Then we are asked to imagine that the *un-spoken* words leave the scars; this, too, typifies Simic's poetic, for his poems are often the residue, the smoke, of some more searing utterance that he has not yet mouthed. Though he's put a period down for the moment, he reminds us there is more he must say, still more to bring back, to bring forth.

– Charles Molesworth

SIMMONS, James (Stewart Alexander). British. Born in Londonderry, Northern Ireland, 14 February 1933. Educated at Foyle College, Londonderry; Campbell College, Belfast; University of Leeds, Yorkshire, B.A. (honours) in English 1958. Married to Laura Stinson; has four daughters and one son. Has taught at Friends School, Lisburn, Northern Ireland; Ahmadu Bello University, Zaria, Nigeria. Since 1968, Member of the English Department, New University of Ulster, Coleraine.

Editor, *Poetry and Audience*, Leeds, 1957–58. Founder, *The Honest Ulsterman*, Portrush, Northern Ireland. Recipient: Eric Gregory Award, 1962. Address: 15 Kerr Street, Portrush, Northern Ireland.

PUBLICATIONS

Verse

Ballad of a Marriage.   Belfast, Festival Publications, 1966.
Late But in Earnest: Poems.   London, Bodley Head, 1967.
Ten Poems.   Belfast, Festival Publications, 1968.
In the Wilderness and Other Poems.   London, Bodley Head, 1969.
Songs for Derry, music by the author.   Belfast, Ulsterman Publications, 1969.
No Ties.   Belfast, Ulsterman Publications, 1970.
Energy to Burn: Poems.   London, Bodley Head, 1971.
No Land Is Waste, Dr. Eliot.   Richmond, Surrey, Keepsake Press, 1972.
The Long Summer Still to Come.   Belfast, Blackstaff Press, 1973.
West Strand Visions.   Belfast, Blackstaff Press, 1974.

Recordings: *City and Western*, Outlets Records; *Pubs*, BBC.

Play

Aikin Mata: The Lysistrata of Aristophanes, with T. W. Harrison.   Ibadan, Oxford University Press, 1966.

Other

Editor, *Out on the Edge.*   Leeds, Leeds University, 1958.
Editor, *Ten Irish Poets: An Anthology.*   Cheadle, Cheshire, Carcanet Press, 1974.

Manuscript Collections: University of Texas, Austin; New University of Ulster, Coleraine.

Critical Study: Interview with Robert Chapman, in *Confrontations* (Brooklyn, New York), Spring 1975.

James Simmons comments:

Love poet and moralist. Very sympathetic to aspects of the folk revival; the songs and singing of Ewan MacColl; poetry as entertainment (Roger McGough, etc.) and as a way of life (Beatnik poets); the writing of pop music with range and depth of feeling; and ideas (Bob Dylan, Christopher Logue, etc.)

Started in the manner of D. H. Lawrence but knew more about popular songs than poetry. Very badly educated. Innumerable shallow influences. Imitator and singer of ballads, admirer of Hopkins' last sonnets and *The Loss of the Eurydice*, e. e. cummings' "I Sing of Olaf," *The Rubaiyat of Omar Khayyam*. Antipathy to T. S. Eliot; love much of Auden, some of Geoffrey Hill, Jeffers, Masters. Now write mostly in more or less traditional forms with no ordinary intelligence. Formality under duress. Influenced more by single poems, even verses, than by poets.

*   *   *

James Simmons is a curiously vulnerable poet, despite his rumbustious style and the projected, even cultivated, persona of the good-humouredly lecherous boozer:

> Our youth was gay but rough,
> much drink and copulation.
> If that seems not enough
> blame our miseducation.

His rhymes thump steadily home giving the careless reader an impression of verbal insensitivity, and the humour is sometimes so robust that a superficial reading can leave one unaware of the quality of Simmons' sensibiltiy, which may well account for the unfortunate reception given to his collections by certain reviewers. The poem "One of the Boys," from which the four lines quoted above are taken, can be seen as a joyfully iconoclastic romp:

> the great careers all tricks,
> the fine arts all my arse,
> business and politics
> a cruel farce.

But the final lines get under the surface of this defensive philistinism, to point its emptiness and the subconscious awareness of its emptiness in its practitioners:

> Though fear of getting fired
> may ease, and work is hated
> less, we are tired, tired
> and incapacitated.
> On golf courses, in bars,
> crutched by the cash we earn,
> we think of nights in cars
> with energy to burn.

There is a sympathetic understanding here of a tragic sense of loss, which reminds me, obliquely, of the purport of that line in Philip Larkin's poem "Mr. Bleaney":

> That how we live measures our own nature.

And though "One of the Boys" is heavily rhymed, the rhymes can be seen to underpin the poem and as by no means intrusive. But while this poem succeeds, Simmons' style and stance are replete with the dangers of the sentimental "good-natured tart" variety, and it can involve a deal of casuistry as when in "The

Wife-swappers'' the poet attempts to equate (and therefore justify) a taste for lechery with an honest harmlessness:

> It's people who believe absurdities
> who must, to feel secure, lock up their lives,
> that in the end commit atrocities.
> I play strip-poker with my neighbours' wives.

As if atrocities were the monopoly of prudes and puritans!

It could be said, of course, that Donne, too, indulged in such sophistry; but he employed considerably more wit and subtlety, if that can be considered a defence. It all comes down to the fact, I suppose, that Simmons sees the poet as an entertainer and moralist, and while he never fails to entertain (no mean achievement) the entertainer sometimes elbows out the moralist. Yet, for the most part, not very far from the clowning and posturing surface of his more swashbuckling poems there is always a hint of *carpe diem* or an awareness of values missed:

> Your dumbness on a walk
> was better than my clown's talk.
> You showed me what you meant . . .
> > – from "Goodbye Sally"

and at its best Simmons' poetry can express an understanding of and empathy with certain aspects of the human tragedy which are only considered minor because they occur with such frequency and are common to so many. Notice here, in "Antigone's Hour," how he moderates the often heavy beat of his poetry to a minor key as it were, so that the tragic element is, in fact, in the very ordinariness of what is often seen as an extraordinary situation:

> All risks are a tribute
> to the adventurous dead.
> Gathering fine small flowers
> was all they wanted said . . .

the poem ending:

> No guards observed them
> acting the clown.
> Their own doubts what to do
> next let them down.

The very real strength of Simmons' poetry resides in his basic humanity, and his sympathy and preference for the human condition however fallible and whatever its faults, as in "Stephano Remembers":

> We were distracted by too many things . . .
> the wine, the jokes, the music, fancy gowns
> We were no good as murderers, we were clowns.

The constant use of the "clown" as an archetype is a clue here.

– John Cotton

SIMPSON, Louis (Aston Marantz). American. Born in Jamaica, West Indies, 27 March 1923. Educated at Murro College, Jamaica, 1933–40, Cambridge Higher Schools Certificate, 1940; Columbia University, New York, B.S. 1948, A.M. 1950; Ph.D. 1959. Served in the United States Army 1943–45: Purple Heart and Bronze Star. Married Jeanne Claire Rogers in 1949 (divorced, 1954), has one son; Dorothy Roochvarg, 1955, has one son and one daughter. Editor, Bobbs-Merrill Publishing Company, New York, 1950–55; Instructor, Columbia University, 1955–59; Professor of English, University of California, Berkeley, 1959-67. Since 1967, Professor of English, State University of New York, Stony Brook. Recipient: American Academy in Rome Fellowship, 1957; *Hudson Review* Fellowship, 1957; Edna St. Vincent Millay Award, 1960; Guggenheim Fellowship, 1962, 1970; American Council for Learned Societies Grant, 1963; Pulitzer Prize, 1964; Columbia University Medal for Excellence, 1965. Address: P.O. Box 91, Port Jefferson, New York 11777, U.S.A.

PUBLICATIONS.

Verse

> *The Arrivistes: Poems 1940–1949.* Paris, privately printed, 1949; New York, Fine Editions Press, n.d.
> *Good News of Death and Other Poems.* New York, Scribner, 1955.
> *The Dream of Governors: Poems.* Middletown, Connecticut, Wesleyan University Press, 1959.
> *At the End of the Open Road: Poems.* Middletown, Connecticut, Wesleyan University Press, 1963.
> *Five American Poets,* with others, edited by Thom Gunn and Ted Hughes. London, Faber, 1963.
> *Selected Poems.* New York, Harcourt Brace, 1965; London, Oxford University Press, 1966.
> *Adventures of the Letter I.* London, Oxford University Press, 1971; New York, Harper, 1972.

> Recording: *Today's Poets 1,* with others, Folkways, 1967.

Plays

> *The Father Out of the Machine: A Masque,* in *Chicago Review,* Winter 1951.
> *Andromeda,* in *Hudson Review* (New York), Winter 1956.

Novel

> *Riverside Drive.* New York, Atheneum, 1962.

Other

> *James Hogg: A Critical Study.* Edinburgh, Oliver and Boyd, 1962; New York, St. Martin's Press, 1963.
> *Air with Armed Men* (autobiography). London, London Magazine Editions, 1972; as *North of Jamaica,* New York, Harper, 1972.

Editor, with Donald Hall and Robert Pack, *New Poets of England and America.* Cleveland, Meridian, 1957.

Editor, *An Introduction to Poetry.* New York, St. Martin's Press, 1967; London, Macmillan, 1968.

Bibliography: in *Louis Simpson* by Ronald Moran, New York, Twayne, 1972.

Manuscript Collection: Library of Congress, Washington, D.C.

Critical Studies: "The Poetry of Louis Simpson" by C. B. Cox, in *Critical Quarterly 8* (Manchester), Spring 1966; "The Wesleyan Poets – II" by Norman Friedman, in *Chicago Review 19*, 1966; *Louis Simpson*, by Ronald Moran, New York, Twayne, 1972.

Louis Simpson comments:

(1970) I have written about many subjects: war, love, American landscape and history. For several years I have been writing in free form. Influences: many poets, English and American – particularly Eliot and Whitman. I believe that poetry rises from the inner life of the poet and is expressed in original images and rhythms. Also, the language of poetry should be closely related to the language in which men actually think and speak.

(1974) My earliest published work was in traditional forms. I was much taken with the lyricism of the Tudor poets. At the end of the 1950's I began writing in irregular, unrhymed lines – I was attempting to write verse that would sound like speech. My subjects, from first to last, have been taken from life – that is, I do not write metaphysical or argumentative verse, I try to create, or recreate, an experience. I like to write narrative – I find it perhaps the most satisfying kind of poetry, when it works. In most of my poems there is a narrative or dramatic element. I believe that in poetry ideas are most effective when they are transformed into images. The movement of the poem as a whole, and the rhythm of the lines, are of first importance.

*   *   *

Louis Simpson's *Selected Poems* contains portions from his four previous volumes – *The Arrivistes, Good News of Death, A Dream of Governors,* and *At the End of the Open Road* – as well as a dozen "New Poems." The last two volumes alone, published only four years apart, reveal his remarkable growth. Dealing with war, love, history, the emptiness of modern American life, and the American in Europe, *A Dream* is knowing and intelligent but somewhat too formal, avoiding simultaneously the pressure of passion and the perspective of vision.

The Open Road, which received the Pulitzer Prize in Poetry for 1964, is a very different matter entirely. Simpson has found the key to the meaning and power of his themes. The development of a poem from the routine to the timeless, from the external to the internal, and from situation to response, is no longer a matter of mere machinery but rather of vital shock. It is not simply that his style is getting more experimental, but more that this flexibility is a sign of growth in the character and thought of the speaker, an openness to life whereby the poet risks being changed by what he experiences, and Simpson is on his way to becoming a major poet.

Here we have another group of poems about America, but they are much more penetrating than those in *A Dream.* "In California," for example, begins: "Here I am, troubling the dream coast / With my New York face." And this is "In the Suburbs" entire:

> There's no way out.
> You were born to waste your life.
> You were born to this middleclass life
> As others before you
> Were born to walk in procession
> To the temple, singing.

There are also the three poems at the end inspired by Whitman, who was also hailed in "In California": Simpson knows that "The Open Road goes [now] to the used-car lot," and that, since the past keeps repeating itself, it cannot be cancelled out. And then, finally, that "At the end of the open road we come to ourselves." He has come a long way from the somewhat easy Sherwood-Andersonianism of "Hot Night on Water Street" and "The Boarder" from *A Dream.* America's emptiness is now seen in its historical context, and thus the poet's satire has cause and direction.

Then there is a group of four wonderful love poems – "Summer Morning," "The Silent Lover," "Birch," and "The Sea and the Forest" – which are by far more meaningful and passionate than his earlier erotic lyrics. In "Summer Morning," for example, the speaker remembers having been with a girl in a hotel room in an abandoned section of New York fifteen years ago, and he feels the weight of the intervening time, concluding:

> So I have spoiled my chances.
> For what? Sheer laziness,
>
> The thrill of an assignation,
> My life that I hold in secret.

And finally, there is a remarkable piece called "American Poetry," a marvel of concise meaning, which I quote in full:

> Whatever it is, it must have
> A stomach that can digest
> Rubber, coal, uranium, moons, poems.
>
> Like the shark, it contains a shoe.
> It must swim for miles through the desert
> Uttering cries that are almost human.

Simpson has digested the indigestible, and has now embarked on his long swim through the desert.

Thus we find him realizing, two years later, in "The Laurel Tree":

> I must be patient with shapes
> Of automobile fenders and ketchup bottles.
> These things are the beginning
> Of things not visible to the naked eye.

And, in a confrontation between the speaker and an unearthly visitor, in "Things," the latter tells him: "Things which to us in the pure state are mysteries, / Are your simplest articles of household use." To which the speaker replies:

> I have suspected
> The Mixmaster knows more than I do,
> The air conditioner is the better poet.

The spirituality of the mundane is surely a Whitmanesque theme, and Simpson returns in his next book, *Adventures of the Letter I,* to his obsession with America:

> I myself am the union of these states,
> offering liberty and equality to all.
> I share the land equally, I support the arts,
>
> I am developing backward areas.
> I look on the negro as myself, I accuse myself
> of sociopathic tendencies, I accuse my accusers.

I think he has wittily captured the authentic Whitman mood and cadence here – and then the feeling falls and he becomes depressed. But once more he must learn to be patient, he says, and to "breathe in, breathe out, / and to sit by the bed and watch."

Adventures is a marvelous and varied book, fulfilling all of his earlier promise and carrying it a stage further. It begins, for example, with a strange and fable-like section on Volhynia Province, where the poet creates an imaginary version of the part of old Russia his mother came from. And there is a section called "Individuals," which contains a very effective and affecting narrative portrait, "Vandergast and the Girl," reminiscent in subject and tone of E. A. Robinson. "When I go for a walk with Tippy," says the narrator, an anonymous townsman, "I pass the unweeded tennis court, / the empty garage, windows heavily shuttered." This is the lugubrious and clichéd tale of an insurance man who left his wife and children for a redhead, and whom the girl then left in turn. But the conclusion, clear-eyed and compassionate, is anything but clichéd:

> Was it worth it? Ask Vandergast.
> You'd have to be Vandergast, looking through his eyes
> at the house across the street, in Orange, New Jersey.

Here he lives alone now, and perhaps he remembers his days of passion:

> Maybe
> he talks to his pillow, and it whispers,
> moving red hair.
>
> In any case, he will soon be forty.

In order to digest the trash of ordinary life like this, to see the light of meaning in the trivial, Simpson has had to go into himself and to learn to be patient indeed – to learn what Keats spoke of as "negative capability." "I have always lived," says the speaker in "An American Peasant," "as though I knew the reason":

> Like a peasant I trust in silence.
> And I don't believe in ideas
> unless they are unavoidable.

Perhaps the shadow of a garden is becoming visible as the desert swim nears the shore at last.

– Norman Friedman

SIMPSON, R(onald) A(lbert). Australian. Born in Melbourne, Victoria, 1 February 1929. Educated at Royal Melbourne Institute of Technology, Associateship Diploma of Art; Melbourne Teachers' College, Primary Teachers' Certificate, 1951. Married to Shirley Simpson; has two children. Lecturer in Art, 1968–71, and since 1972, Senior Lecturer, Caulfield Institute of Technology, Melbourne. Poetry Editor, *The Bulletin*, Sydney, 1963–65. Since 1969, Poetry Editor, *The Age*, Melbourne, and Advisory Editor, *Poetry Magazine*, Sydney. Address: 29 Omama Road, Murrumbeena, Melbourne, Victoria 3163, Australia.

PUBLICATIONS

Verse

The Walk along the Beach: Poems. Sydney, Edwards and Shaw, 1960.
This Real Pompeii. Brisbane, Jacaranda Press, 1964.
After the Assassination and Other Poems. Brisbane, Jacaranda Press, 1968.
Diver. Brisbane, University of Queensland Press, 1972.

Other

Editor, "Australian Poetry" in *International Literary Annual*. London, Calder, 1959.

R. A. Simpson comments:

As a poet I use words in an effort to understand and clarify experiences. I get my main joy from poetry in the use of words; the struggle for clarification is the painful region. My early poetry was stiff and formal: I believe, and hope, that my recent work shows greater ease and freedom. My background as an art teacher has partly contributed to my recent experiments in "concrete poetry."

I do not see myself merely as an Australian poet, though there are obvious Australian attitudes in my poetry – and I have used Australian themes. Most present-day Australian poets would seriously believe that the best poetry being written today here and overseas reflects some kind of international style – a sense of the poet's responsibility to human beings in general. Australian poets feel part of the larger flow of ideas, even if they are not main contributors to the birth of ideas.

*   *   *

One of a group of Melbourne poets who came to prominence in the 1950's and to influence in the 1960's, R. A. Simpson has carefully maintained certain essential characteristics more consistently than have his fellow poets Vincent Buckley, Chris Wallace-Crabbe and Evan Jones, all of whom have modified their original formal regularity and slightly academic (or, at least, cloistered) affectations of irony and equipoise. Ron Simpson, in his first collection, *The Walk along the Beach*, quite firmly demonstrated a mind concerned with paring language down, with understatement, and with letting the image work with a minimum of encumbrances. The early poems were overtly concerned, however, often with the aftermath of guilt, heritage of a Catholic boyhood and subsequent loss of faith. Indeed, even through Simpson's most recent poetry, *Diver*, the innate direction of mind is through channels of justification or expiation. Though there may be no God, for Simpson, there is still an implied Judgement.

The verse style that worries its way through these concerns is, still, strangely tight-lipped and reticent. At its weakest it seems hesitant, hardly daring to indulge even in connectives. At its best it is a strikingly taut and resonant instrument capable of playing upon (and preying upon) those central nervous gropings and ambivalences that our own speech can enmesh us in. The poetry of R. A. Simpson is not graceful or elegant. It is self-guarded, and keeps catching itself off guard. It has remained outside current fashions, both in the 1960's and 1970's. Its essential honesty sustains it. It is a poetry one can return to many times, and always with gain.

– Thomas W. Shapcott

SINCLAIR, Keith. New Zealander. Born in Auckland, 5 December 1922. Educated at Mount Albert Grammar School, Auckland; University of Auckland, B.A. 1945, M.A. 1946, Ph.D. 1954. Served in the New Zealand Army, 1941–44, and Navy, 1944–46. Married Mary Land in 1947; has four sons. Lecturer, 1947–59, Associate Professor, 1959–62, and since 1962, Professor of History, University of Auckland. Carnegie Visiting Fellow, Institute of Commonwealth Studies, London, 1954; Visiting Fellow, Australian National University, Canberra, 1967, and Cambridge University, 1968–69. Since 1967, Editor, *New Zealand Journal of History*, Auckland. Labour Party Parliamentary Candidate, 1969. Recipient: Walter Frewen Lord Prize for History, London, 1951; Ernest Scott Prize, for history, Melbourne, 1958, 1961; F. P. Wilson Prize for History, Wellington, 1966; Hubert Church Prize, for prose, 1966; Jessie Mackay Prize, 1974. Litt.D.: University of Auckland. Address: 13 Mariqosa Crescent, Birkenhead, Auckland, New Zealand.

PUBLICATIONS

Verse

Songs for a Summer and Other Poems. Christchurch, Pegasus Press, 1952.
Strangers or Beasts: Poems. Christchurch, Caxton Press, 1954.
A Time to Embrace. Auckland, Paul's Book Arcade, 1963.
The Firewheel Tree. Auckland, Auckland University Press and Oxford University Press, 1973.

Other

The Maori Land League: An Examination into the Source of a New Zealand Myth. Auckland, University of Auckland, 1950.

Imperial Federation: A Study of New Zealand Policy and Opinion 1880–1914. London, Athlone Press, 1955.

The Origins of the Maori Wars. Wellington, New Zealand University Press, 1957; revised edition, 1961.

A History of New Zealand. London, Penguin, 1959; revised edition, Wellington and London, Oxford University Press, 1961; Penguin, 1969.

Open Account: A History of the Bank of New South Wales in New Zealand, 1861–1961, with William F. Mandle. Marrickville, New South Wales, Whitcombe and Tombs, 1961.

William Pember Reeves: New Zealand Fabian. Oxford, Clarendon Press, 1965.

The Liberal Government, 1891–1912: First Steps Towards a Welfare State. Auckland, Heinemann, 1967.

Editor, *The Maori King,* by John Eldon Gorst. Auckland, Oxford University Press, 1959.

Editor, *Distance Looks Our Way: The Effects of Remoteness on New Zealand.* Auckland, University of Auckland, 1961.

Editor, with Robert Chapman, *Studies in a Small Democracy: Essays in Honour of Willis Airey.* Auckland, Paul's Book Arcade, and Sydney, Angus and Robertson, 1963.

Critical Study: *A Way of Saying: A Study of New Zealand Poetry* by Kendrick Smithyman, Auckland and London, Collins, 1965.

Keith Sinclair comments:

The main influence on my early verse of which I was conscious was John Donne; more recently, perhaps Yeats and Robert Graves. In general I have been influenced by contemporary New Zealand poets, especially James K. Baxter, in the early 1950's. My main subjects have been love of various sorts – of country, especially the coast, of children and family and women. I have thought that the intellect and feeling are inseparable in life and in poetry.

*   *   *

Three pointers toward changing sensibility: John Donne, Dylan Thomas, and Theodore Roethke. But pointers only of a way: to name names is not to describe, still less to define. From Donne's example Keith Sinclair learned, as he has said, to admire "a witty clarity, a clarity within which wits may find obscurity," although Sinclair is rarely obscure. From Thomas, an artifice, a rhetoric, which shows, say, in "The Sleeping Beauty" sequence, but he has not been alive to metric – his own is idiosyncratic – as Thomas was, or as interested in the artifice of regulated patterns. For many years he respected, and still respects, Roethke whose practical bearing, whose homeliness, but most (probably) his evident sense of pitch rather than tone may be thought at least partly to have persuaded Sinclair to that increased directness, that lowered pitch which has served his poems well in recent years.

If these men helped shape a talent they did not do so totally. At his earliest, Sinclair's poems were his and no one else's; of those of recent years the same is to be said. Poems like "Goat Island Valley" and "Explaining Rain" (published in *Landfall* in 1967) clearly are mature expressions of what was present in a younger man's writing. The intelligence, the wit, the ebullience (not the exuberance) of his poems remain constant, producing a particular decorum which subsumes on the one hand what was once referred to as a fantastic element and, on the other, a sensuous if not sensual directness. The sensibility is not dissociated. The traditionalist and the contemporary man are one, with the family man, the Professor of History, the biographer, and the Labour Party candidate. If the latter emphasise the man of public conscience, of public obligation, the poems emphasise the man responsive to private conscience, of less advertised but not necessarily smaller or less significant pieties.

– Kendrick Smithyman

SISSMAN, L(ouis) E(dward). American. Born in Detroit, Michigan, 1 January 1928. Educated at Detroit Country Day School, 1937–44; Harvard University, Cambridge, Massachusetts (Garrison Prize, 1949), 1944–49, B.A. (honors) 1949. Married Anne Bierman in 1958. Copy Editor, 1950–51, and Production Manager, 1951–52, Prentice-Hall Incorporated, publishers, New York; Aide, John F. Kennedy Senatorial Campaign, Boston, 1952; Copywriter, John C. Dowd Advertising, Boston, 1953–56; Senior Writer, 1956–62, Supervisor, 1962–66, and Creative Vice-President, 1966–72, Kenyon and Eckhardt Advertising, Boston. Since 1972, Creative Vice-President, Quinn and Johnson Advertising, Boston. Book Reviewer, *The New Yorker*; Contributing Editor, *Atlantic Monthly*, Boston. Phi Beta Kappa Poet, Harvard University, 1971. Recipient: National Spelling Bee Prize, 1941; Guggenheim Fellowship, 1968; National Institute of Arts and Letters Award, 1969. Address: Box 107, Still River, Massachusetts 01467, U.S.A.

PUBLICATIONS

Verse

Dying: An Introduction.   Boston, Little Brown, 1968.
Scattered Returns.   Boston, Little Brown, 1969.
Pursuit of Honor.   Boston, Little Brown, 1971.

L. E. Sissman comments:

Since I reject the notion that the English verse tradition is defunct and must be replaced with tuneless effusions and verbal *objets trouvés*, I write traditional, scanning, stanzaic verse, with special emphasis on iambic pentameter and the couplet. My poems tend to be long, segmented, exceedingly specific evocations of my time and place; I hope to achieve some sort of universality by wedding colloquial, allusive contemporary language to traditional form. I experiment both with language and with time sequences and often invent words based on existing roots. I am preoccupied with character and action; though there is a fictional cast to my work, it is not "narrative" in the old-fashioned sense. The tone of most of my verse is dry and ironic, though I don't hesitate to use the organ-like capabilities of the line of Shakespeare and Milton for large effects. I was early influenced by them and by Donne, Herbert, Pope, Yeats, Eliot, and Auden, though I doubt that any of these influences are superficially apparent in my recent work.

*   *   *

In a literary age dominated by free verse, one comes upon the work of L. E. Sissman with a feeling akin to shock. What is one to make of a writer who insists upon reclaiming traditional poetic forms that have practically disappeared from American poetry: couplets, quatrains, and even an occasional sonnet? As narrator and raconteur, Sissman resembles the public poets of the Augustan age more than he does the confessional poets of his own time.

In "The West Forties: Morning, Noon, and Night" and in "Scattered Returns," the title poem of his second volume, he adopts the attitude of an eighteenth century coffee house wit, of John Gay in "Trivia; On Walking the Streets of London," taking as his subject the occupations, sights, sounds, and diversions of people caught in a lively, chaotic, and occasionally melancholy urban environment.

With a few variations, including a general unconcern for matters political, Sissman might be James Russell Lowell, casting a sardonic eye on the contemporary Brahmin scene: Central Park South, Riverside Drive, Harvard Square, the Boston Common, with an occasional Journey to Provincetown and Bar Harbor, off season. Like his nineteenth century predecessor, Sissman serves as an editor of *Atlantic*; in his monthly column, "Innocent Bystander" and in several early poems, he indicates a concern for the contemporary world, as seen through the eyes of a very worldly and dispassionate observer. Occasionally, the poet's object of satire is himself, as in "Upon Finding *Dying: An Introduction* by L. E. Sissman Remaindered at 1 s":

> novels all the Reage
> Short weeks ago, now smutched with rusts and rots
> Upon their colored calyces; memoirs
> Of august personages laid to rest
> As early as October; ghosts of Mod
> Nonce-figures, once in, now as dead as God;
> And there, a snip under a blackleg sign,
> "These books reduced to 1 s.," there is mine,
> *Dying: An Introduction.* Well, if you
> Preach about dying, you must practice, too.

Sissman is fond of echoing other poets, risking an old joke here, an outrageous pun there. His city eclogues borrow something from the atmosphere of the pub scene and the episode involving the carbuncular young man in Eliot's *Wasteland*. A parody entitled "Just a Whack at Epsom," rhyming aba, begins with this line: "We rot and rot and rot and rot." Appropriating the sounds of Yeats, he describes his undergraduate room (R-34, Lowell House, Harvard, 1945), as "A pleasure dome of Klees and Watteaus made."

In his first three books, Sissman has extended the range of American poetry, giving new life to a tradition that can only enrich it further. And in poems such as

"The Big Rock-Candy Mountain," an elegy for an itinerate farm worker, one hears another voice that has become increasingly significant and powerful in his later work.

– Michael True

SISSON, C(harles) H(ubert). British. Born in Bristol, 22 April 1914. Educated at the University of Bristol, 1931–34, B.A. (honours) in philosophy and English literature 1934; University of Berlin and University of Freiburg, 1934–35; the Sorbonne, Paris, 1935–36. Served in the British Army Intelligence Corps, India, 1942–45. Married Nora Gilbertson in 1937; has two children. Assistant Principal, 1936–42, Principal, 1945–53, Assistant Secretary, 1953–62, and Under Secretary, 1962–68, Ministry of Labour, London; Assistant Under Secretary of State, 1968–71, and Director of Occupational Safety and Health, 1971–73, Department of Employment, London. Recipient: Senior Simon Research Fellowship, University of Manchester, 1956. Agent: A. D. Peters and Company, 10 Buckingham Street, London WC2N 6BU. Address: Moorfield Cottage, The Hill, Langport, Somerset, England.

PUBLICATIONS

Verse

> *Versions and Perversions of Heine.*   London, Gaberbocchus, 1955.
> *Poems.*   Fairwarp, Sussex, Peter Russell, 1959.
> *Twenty-One Poems.*   Sevenoaks, Kent, privately printed, 1960.
> *The London Zoo: Poems.*   London, Abelard Schuman, 1961.
> *Numbers.*   London, Methuen, 1965.
> *Catullus.*   London, MacGibbon and Kee, 1966; New York, Orion Press, 1967.
> *The Discarnation; or, How the Flesh Became Word and Dwelt among Us.*   Sevenoaks, Kent, privately printed, 1967.
> *Metamorphoses: Poems.*   London, Methuen, 1968.
> *Roman Poems.*   Sevenoaks, Kent privately printed, 1968.
> *In the Trojan Ditch: Collected Poems and Selected Translations.*   Cheadle, Cheshire, Carcanet Press, 1974.

Novels

> *An Asiatic Romance.*   London, Gabberbocchus, 1953.
> *Christopher Homm.*   London, Methuen, 1965.

Other

> *The Spirit of British Administration and Some European Comparisons.*   London, Faber, and New York, Praeger, 1959.
> *Art and Action* (essays).   London, Methuen, 1965.
> *Essays.*   Sevenoaks, Kent, privately printed, 1967.

English Poetry 1900–1950: An Assessment.   London, Hart Davis, 1971.
The Case of Walter Bagehot.   London, Faber, 1972.

Critical Studies: by Martin Seymour-Smith, in *X* (London), ii, 3, 1961, in *Agenda* (London), Summer-Autumn 1970, and in *Guide to Modern World Literature*, London, Wolfe, 1973; Donald Davie, in *Listener* (London), 9 May 1974; Robert Nye, in *Times Literary Supplement* (London), 29 November 1974.

C. H. Sisson comments:

My verse is about things that I am, at the moment of writing, just beginning to understand. When I have understood them, or have that impression, the subject has gone, and I have to find another. Or stop. Generally, my resolution is to stop, but another subject is found in time, and I begin again. I began by stopping, so to speak, for having written some verse as an adolescent, I gave up at twenty because I had a great respect for poetry and did not think I could write it. The war and exile produced a few hesitant verses, wrung from me, but I stopped again without really having begun. A more productive start was about 1950, when I was already on the declining side *del cammin di nostra vita*; no wonder therefore that my themes have often been age, decline and death, with the occasional desperate hopes of the receding man. Naturally some facility has come with practice, and the risk now is less from stopping than from going on. One comes to understand too much, or to think one does.

As to verse forms, whether they are what is called regular, or not, it is a small matter: I have written in both kinds. What matters is the rhythm, which is the identifying mark of the poem. If one fails there is no need for a poem; better shut up.

Influences: all one's interests bear, in unexpected ways, on what one writes; still more, one's poetry may be prophetic of interests one is about to have. The influence of other poets – generally in youth – is deadly while it lasts. There is, however, a deliberate, mature learning which is beneficial. For this purpose I have found translations of the greatest value, with the Latins as the great, though not the only, masters. What I aim at is to make plain statements, and not more of them than I need. "It is the nature of man that puzzles me"; I should like to leave a few recognizable – not novel – indications. The man that was the same in Neolithic and in Roman times, as now, is of more interest than the freak of circumstances. This truth lies at the bottom of a well of rhythm.

*   *   *

Two years before the publication of his collection *The London Zoo* in 1961, C. H. Sisson had made a name with his *The Spirit of British Administration*, the result of a comparative study of public administration in several European countries. This book was notable for its wit and for the sharpness of the mind involved. The same qualities are to be found in his poetry and in many cases their terrains overlap. Thus the long title poem of *The London Zoo* gains point and edge from the author's own involvement in the world of the City and administration that he satirizes:

> And who am I, you ask, thus to belly-ache
> At my betters? I'll tell you, I am one of the same lot
> – Without lobsters and limousine, but, like the rest,
> Expending my best energies on the second best.

Not so in his poems, however, where his attitude to that particular world can be seen summarized in his brief epitaph "On a Civil Servant":

> Here lies a civil servant. He was civil
> To everyone, servant to the devil.

Much of Sisson's poetry is uncomfortable in that it looks at our pretensions and society with a critical and unflinching eye. When it looks at our beliefs it can be even more disquieting, as in "Knole" where the unthinking nature of the deer in winter is compared with that of those who pass them on their way home from church, or in "The Aeroplane" where below there are those who are "gathered round the Easter cup," yet "up here it is empty."

His poetry, though written from an uncompromisingly intellectual standpoint, is informed by a depth of feeling which is unusual in such; an idea is not something to consider dispassionately but to feel strongly even emotionally. Thus a somewhat conventional satire on the cash-nexus will explode violently into:

> Suddenly you are in bed with a screeching tear-sheet
> This is money at last without her nightdress
> Clutching you against her fallen udders and sharp bones
> In an unscrupulous and deserved embrace.

It is this depth of feeling allied to an astringency of intellect that makes C. H. Sisson's poems and style peculiarly and remarkably his own.

– John Cotton

SITWELL, Sacheverell. British. Born in Scarborough, Yorkshire, 15 November 1897; younger brother of the poets Dame Edith and Sir Osbert Sitwell. Educated at Eton; Balliol College, Oxford. Married Georgia Doble in 1925; has two sons. High Sheriff of Northamptonshire, 1948–49. Succeeded to the baronetcy, 1969. Address: Weston Hall, Towcester, Northamptonshire, England.

PUBLICATIONS

Verse

The People's Palace. Oxford, Blackwell, 1918.
Doctor Donne and Gargantua: First Canto. London, Favil Press, 1921; Boston, Houghton Mifflin, 1930.
The Hundred and One Harlequins. London, Grant Richards, and New York, Boni and Liveright, 1922.
Doctor Donne and Gargantua: Canto the Second. London, Favil Press, 1923.
The Thirteenth Caesar and Other Poems. London, Grant Richards, 1924; New York, Doran, 1925.
Poor Young People, with Edith and Osbert Sitwell. London, The Fleuron, 1925.

Doctor Donne and Gargantua: Canto the Third. Stratford-upon-Avon, privately printed, 1926.
Exalt the Eglantine and Other Poems. London, The Fleuron, 1926.
The Cyder Feast and Other Poems. London, Duckworth, and New York, Doran, 1927.
(Poems). London, Benn, 1928.
Two Poems, Ten Songs. London, Duckworth, 1929.
Doctor Donne and Gargantua: The First Six Cantos. London, Duckworth, and Boston, Houghton Mifflin, 1930.
Canons of Giant Art: Twenty Torsos in Heroic Landscapes. London, Faber, 1933.
Collected Poems. London, Duckworth, 1936.
Selected Poems. London, Duckworth, 1948.
"Forty-Eight Poems," in *Poetry Review* (London), Summer 1967.
Tropicalia. Edinburgh, Ramsay Head Press, 1972.
To Henry Woodward. London, Covent Garden Press, 1972.
Agamemnon's Tomb. Edinburgh, Tragara Press, 1972.
Rosario d'Arabeschi, Basalla ("as the Moors call it") and Dionysia, A Triptych of Poems, The Strawberry Feast, Ruralia, To E.S., Variations upon Old Names of Hyacinths, Lily Poems, The Archipelago of Daffodils, A Charivari of Parrots, Flowering Cactus, A Look at Sowerby's English Mushrooms and Fungi, Auricula Theatre, Lyra Varia, The House of the Presbyter, Nigritian, Twelve Summer Poems of 1962, Doctor Donne and Gargantua (Cantos Seven and Eight), Badinerie, An Indian Summer, Temple of Segesta, l'Amour au theatre italien, and *A Notebook upon My New Poems.* Badby, Northamptonshire, Brackley Smart, 23 vols., 1972–74.

Play

All at Sea: A Social Tragedy in Three Acts for First-Class Passengers Only, with Osbert Sitwell. London, Duckworth, 1927; New York, Doubleday, 1928.

Other

Southern Baroque Art: A Study of Painting, Architecture and Music in Italy and Spain of the 17th and 18th Centuries. London, Grant Richards, and New York, Knopf, 1924.
All Summer in a Day: An Autobiographical Fantasia. London, Duckworth, and New York, Doran, 1926.
German Baroque Art. London, Duckworth, 1927; New York, Doran, 1928.
A Book of Towers and Other Buildings of Southern Europe. London, Frederick Etchells and Hugh Macdonald, 1928.
The Gothick North: A Study of Medieval Life, Art, and Thought. Boston, Houghton Mifflin, 1929.
I. *The Visit of the Gypsies.* London, Duckworth, 1929.
II. *These Sad Ruins.* London, Duckworth, 1929.
III. *The Fair-Haired Victory.* London, Duckworth, 1930.
Beckford and Beckfordism: An Essay. London, Duckworth, 1930.
Far From My Home: Stories: Long and Short. London, Duckworth, 1931.
Spanish Baroque Art: With Buildings in Portugal, Mexico, and Other Colonies. London, Duckworth, 1931.
Mozart. New York, Appleton, and London, Davies, 1932.

Liszt.   London, Faber, and Boston, Houghton Mifflin, 1934; revised edition, London, Cassell, and New York, Philosophical Library, 1955.

Touching the Orient: Six Sketches.   London, Duckworth, 1934.

A Background for Domenico Scarlatti, 1685–1757; Written for His Two Hundred and Fiftieth Anniversary.   London, Faber, 1935.

Dance of the Quick and the Dead: An Entertainment of the Imagination.   London, Faber, 1936; Boston, Houghton Mifflin, 1937.

Conversation Pieces: A Survey of English Domestic Portraits and Their Painters.   London, Batsford, 1936; New York, Scribner, 1937.

Narrative Pictures: A Survey of English Genre and Its Painters.   London, Batsford, 1937; New York, Scribner, 1938.

La Vie Parisienne: A Tribute to Offenbach.   London, Faber, 1937; Boston, Houghton Mifflin, 1938.

Roumanian Journey.   London, Batsford, and New York, Scribner, 1938.

Edinburgh, with Francis Bamford.   London, Faber, and Boston, Houghton Mifflin, 1938.

German Baroque Sculpture.   London, Duckworth, 1938.

Trio: Dissertations on Some Aspects of English Genius, with Edith and Osbert Sitwell.   London, Macmillan, 1938.

The Romantic Ballet in Lithographs of the Time, with Cyril W. Beaumont.   London, Faber, 1938.

Old Fashioned Flowers.   London, Country Life, 1939.

Mauretania: Warrior, Man, and Woman.   London, Duckworth, 1940.

Poltergeists: An Introduction and Examination Followed by Chosen Instances.   London, Faber, 1940.

Sacred and Profane Love.   London, Faber, 1940.

Valse des Fleurs: A Day in St. Petersburg and a Ball at the Winter Place.   London, Faber, 1941.

Primitive Scenes and Festivals.   London, Faber, 1942.

The Homing of the Winds and Other Passages in Prose.   London, Faber, 1942.

Splendours and Miseries.   London, Faber, 1943.

British Architects and Craftsmen: A Survey of Taste, Design, and Style During Three Centuries 1600 to 1830.   London, Batsford, 1945; revised edition, 1946, New York, Scribner, 1946.

The Hunters and the Hunted.   London, Macmillan, 1947; New York, Macmillan, 1948.

The Netherlands: A Study of Some Aspects of Art, Costume and Social Life.   London, Batsford, 1948; revised edition, 1974; New York, Hastings House, 1974.

Morning, Noon and Night in London.   London, Macmillan, 1948.

Theatrical Figures in Porcelain: German 18th Century.   London, Curtain Press, 1949.

Spain.   London, Batsford, 1950; revised edition, 1951.

Cupid and the Jacaranda.   London, Macmillan, 1952.

Truffle Hunt with Sacheverell Sitwell.   London, Hale, 1953.

Fine Bird Books 1700–1900, with Hanasyde Buchanan and James Fisher.   London, Collins, and New York, Van Nostrand, 1953.

Selected Works of Sacheverell Sitwell.   Indianapolis, Bobbs Merrill, 1953.

Portugal and Madeira.   London, Batsford, 1954.

Old Garden Roses: Part One, with James Russell.   London, Collins, 1955.

Selected Works of Sacheverell Sitwell.   London, Hale, 1955.

Denmark.   London, Batsford, 1956.

Great Flower Books 1700–1900: A Bibliographical Record of Two Centuries of Finely-Illustrated Flower Books, with Wilfrid Blunt and Patrick M. Synge.   London, Collins, 1956.

Arabesque and Honeycomb.   London, Hale, 1957.

Malta. London, Batsford, 1958.

Journey to the Ends of Time:
  I. *Lost in the Dark Wood.* London, Cassell, and New York, Random House, 1959.

Bridge of the Brocade Sash: Travels and Observations in Japan. London, Weidenfeld and Nicolson, 1959; Cleveland, World, 1960.

Golden Wall and Mirador: From England to Peru. London, Weidenfeld and Nicolson, and Cleveland, World, 1961.

The Red Chapels of Banteai Srei, and Temples in Cambodia, India, Siam and Nepal. London, Weidenfeld and Nicolson, 1962.

Monks, Nuns, and Monasteries. London, Weidenfeld and Nicolson, 1965.

Southern Baroque Revisited. London, Weidenfeld and Nicolson, 1967.

Baroque and Rococo. New York, Putnam, 1967.

Gothic Europe. London, Weidenfeld and Nicolson, and New York, Holt Rinehart, 1969.

For Want of a Golden City (autobiography). London, Thames and Hudson, and New York, Day, 1973.

The Netherlands. London, Batsford, 1974.

Bibliography: *A Bibliography of Edith, Osbert and Sacheverell Sitwell* by Richard Fifoot, London, Hart Davis, 1963; New York, Oxford University Press, 1964.

*   *   *

Born in 1897, Sir Sacheverell Sitwell was the youngest member of a brilliant family who, rejecting an assured status as members of the highest country gentry, flung themselves from early youth with dashing enthusiasm into the practice of the arts of prose and poetry and the appreciation of all the arts. They were, for a time, during the 1920's, brilliantly in fashion, and then suddenly out of it. Edith Sitwell attained her highest reputation during the Second World War with her bold, sweeping, and direct poems about the horrors of war and the strange mercies of God. Sir Osbert Sitwell, from whom Sir Sacheverell inherited the baronetcy, attained his highest reputation with his series of autobiographical writings, after the Second World War, in which he made his father, Sir George Reresay Sitwell, one of the greatest comic figures in European fiction. Sir Sacheverell, who has visited almost every country, and seen almost every important art-work in the world, never quite attained the fame of his elder brother and sister, though his almost Trollopeian or Jamesian output of books is larger than theirs, and his early autobiographical fantasia, *All Summer in a Day* (1926), is a masterpiece of poetic prose which neither of his siblings equalled. Between 1948 (when he published his *Selected Poems,* chosen from fifteen previous volumes) and 1972, he found no one willing to risk publishing more poems, though publishers rightly leap for his prose (his book about Japan made me resee, with fresh eyes, many things I thought I had already seen). Yet what I have seen of his poems since 1948 – a large selection was printed some years ago in the Poetry Society's *Poetry Review,* then edited by John Smith – seemed to me, retrospectively, to prove Sir Sacheverell's contention in a letter that he had been writing *better* poems, on the whole, since 1948. It was simply that Sitwells, first under Grigson and Leavis; and then under Robert Conquest and the "Movement," were out. The "movement," as such, is dead, and there is a growing tendency among young and serious poetic aestheticians, like Dr. Veronica Forrest-Thomson, to recognise that a poem is not a "slice of life," prose chunked up into clumsy verse, but a rational artifice, whose importance is much less in its outward reference to an "external world" which we know only through verbal conventions than in its inner play of interstresses of sound and sense. Poetry, in other words, is less a criticism of life than a criticism of *language*. When this new aesthetics prevails, as I think it will, Sir Sacheverell will have his due, and his siblings be restored to favour. People will no longer worry about the "meaning" but taste the crispness of

> The parrot's voice snaps out –
> No good to contradict –
> What he says he'll say again:
> Dry facts, dry biscuits

and the colour and lushness of

> Let light like honey shine upon your skin:
> When you're hot and like a comb of fire
> Glide back into this shade,
> Bend that heavy branch down with your hand upon its fruit,
> Ripe cherries and a honeycomb must make my bread and wine.

> – G. S. Fraser

SKELTON, Robin. Canadian. Born in Easington, East Yorkshire, England, 12 October 1925. Educated at Pocklington Grammar School, near York; Christ's College, Cambridge, 1943–44; University of Leeds, Yorkshire, B.A. 1950, M.A. in English 1951. Served in the Royal Air Force, 1944–47. Married Sylvia Mary Jarrett in 1957; has three children. Assistant Lecturer, 1951–54, and Lecturer in English, 1954–63, Manchester University. Associate Professor, 1963–66, since 1966, Professor of English, Director of the Creative Writing Program, 1967–73, and since 1973, Chairman of the Department of Creative Writing, University of Victoria, British Columbia. Manager, Lotus Press, Hull, 1950–52. Poetry Reviewer, 1956–57, and Drama Reviewer, 1958–60 *Manchester Guardian*; Art Reviewer, *Victoria Daily Times*, British Columbia, 1964–66. Founder Member, Peterloo Group (poets and painters), Manchester, 1957–60; Founding Secretary, Manchester Institute of Contemporary Arts, 1959–62. Centennial Lecturer, University of Massachusetts, Amherst, 1962–63; Visiting Professor, University of Michigan, Ann Arbor, 1967. Editor, with John Peter, 1967–71, and since 1972, Editor, *Malahat Review*, Victoria; since 1972, Director, Pharos Press, Victoria. Broadcaster, BBC, Canadian Broadcasting Corporation, and All India Radio. Collage Maker: one man shows, Victoria, 1966, 1968. Fellow, Royal Society of Literature, 1966. Address: Department of Creative Writing, University of Victoria, Victoria, British Columbia, Canada.

PUBLICATIONS

Verse

Patmos and Other Poems. London, Routledge, 1955.
Third Day Lucky: Poems. London and New York, Oxford University Press, 1958.

Begging the Dialect: Poems and Ballads. London and New York, Oxford University Press, 1960.

Two Ballads of the Muse. Cambridge, Rampant Lions Press, 1960.

The Dark Window: Verses. London and New York, Oxford University Press, 1962.

A Valedictory Poem. Victoria, British Columbia, privately printed, 1963.

An Irish Gathering. Dublin, Dolmen Press, 1964.

A Ballad of Billy Barker. Victoria, British Columbia, privately printed, 1965.

Inscriptions: Verses. Victoria, British Columbia, Morriss Printing Company, 1967.

Because of This. Manchester, Manchester Institute of Contemporary Arts, 1968.

The Hold of Our Hands. Victoria, British Columbia, privately printed, 1968.

Selected Poems 1947–1967. Toronto, McClelland and Stewart, and London, Oxford University Press, 1968.

Answers. London, Enitharmon Press, 1969.

An Irish Album. Dublin, Dolmen Press, 1969.

The Hunting Dark. London, Deutsch, 1971.

Remembering Synge: A Poem in Homage for the Centenary of His Birth, 16 April 1871. Dublin, Dolmen Press, 1971.

A Different Mountain. San Francisco, Kayak Books, 1971.

Private Speech: Messages, 1962–1970: Poems. Vancouver, Sono Nis Press, 1971.

Three for Herself. Rushden, Northamptonshire, Sceptre Press, 1972.

Musebook. Victoria, British Columbia, Pharos Press, 1972.

A Christmas Poem. Victoria, British Columbia, privately printed, 1972.

Country Songs. Rushden, Northamptonshire, Sceptre Press, 1973.

Timelight. London, Heinemann, 1974.

Fools Wisdom. London, Enitharmon Press, 1975.

Other

John Ruskin: The Final Years. Manchester, John Rylands Library and Manchester University Press, 1955.

The Poetic Pattern. London, Routledge, 1956; Berkeley, University of California Press, 1958.

Painters Talking: Michael Snow and Tony Connor Interviewed. Manchester, Peterloo Group, 1957.

Cavalier Poets. London, Longman, 1960.

Poetry. London, English Universities Press, 1963; New York, Dover, 1965.

The Writings of J. M. Synge. London, Thames and Hudson, 1971.

The Practice of Poetry. London, Heinemann, and New York, Barnes and Noble, 1971.

J. M. Synge and His World. London, Thames and Hudson, 1971.

J. M. Synge. Lewisburg, Pennsylvania, Bucknell University Press, 1972.

The Poet's Calling. London, Heinemann, 1975.

Editor, *Leeds University Poetry.* Leeds, Lotus Press, 1949.

Editor, with D. Metcalfe, *The Acadine Poets, Series I–III.* Hull, Yorkshire, Lotus Press, 1950.

Editor, *J. M. Synge: Translations.* Dublin, Dolmen Press, 1961.

Editor, *Four Plays and The Aran Islands,* by J. M. Synge. London and New York, Oxford University Press, 1962.

Editor, *Edward Thomas' Selected Poems.* London, Hutchinson, 1962.

Editor, *J. M. Synge: Collected Poems.* London, Oxford University Press, 1962.

Editor, *Six Irish Poets: Austin Clarke, Richard Kell, Thomas Kinsella, John Montague, Richard Murphy, Richard Weber.* London, Oxford University Press, 1962.

Editor, *Viewpoint: An Anthology of Poetry.* London, Hutchinson, 1962.

Editor, *Five Poets of the Pacific Northwest.* Seattle, University of Washington Press, 1964.

Editor, *Poetry of the Thirties.* London, Penguin, 1964.

Editor, *Selected Poems of Byron.* London, Heinemann, 1964; New York, Barnes and Noble, 1966.

Editor, *Collected Poems,* by David Gascoyne. London, Oxford University Press-Deutsch, 1965.

Editor, *The Irish Renaissance: A Gathering of Essays, Letters and Memoirs from the Massachusetts Review.* Dublin, Dolmen Press, and London, Oxford University Press, 1965.

Editor, with Ann Saddlemyer, *The World of W. B. Yeats: Essays in Perspective.* Seattle, University of Washington Press, 1965; revised edition, 1967.

Editor, *Poetry of the Forties.* London, Penguin, 1968.

Editor, *Georges Zuk: Selected Verse.* San Francisco, Kayak Books, 1969.

Editor, *Riders to the Sea,* by J. M. Synge. Dublin, Dolmen Press, 1969.

Editor, *Introductions from an Island: A Selection of Student Writing.* Victoria, British Columbia, University of Victoria, 5 vols., 1969–74.

Editor, with Alan Clodd, *Collected Verse Translations,* by David Gascoyne. London, Oxford University Press-Deutsch, 1970.

Editor, *The Cavalier Poets.* London, Faber, and New York, Oxford University Press, 1970.

Editor, *Herbert Read: A Memorial Symposium.* London, Methuen, 1970.

Editor, *The Collected Plays of Jack B. Yeats.* London, Secker and Warburg, and Indianapolis, Bobbs Merrill, 1971.

Editor and Translator, *Two Hundred Poems from the Greek Anthology.* London, Methuen, and Seattle, University of Washington Press, 1971.

Editor, *Some Sonnets from "Laura in Death" after the Italian of Francesco Petrarch,* by J. M. Synge (bilingual edition). Dublin Dolmen Press, 1971.

Manuscript Collections: MacPherson Library, University of Victoria, British Columbia; University of Texas, Austin.

Robin Skelton comments:

I have been called a Muse Poet, a Lyrical Poet, a Confessional Poet, a Traditional Poet, an Innovative Poet, a Romantic Poet, a British Poet, an Irish Poet, and a Canadian Poet. I hope I am all these things and more. I relish most the compliment paid me by a very old lady, the mother of an eminent British poet, who said (to somebody else) of my work, "All human life is there!" I would like to think that this is the case. All my life I have tried to work in terms of Rabelais' dictum, "Everything that God allows to happen I allow to be written about". This has resulted in my finding myself using, and being used by, many different attitudes and emotions to an extent which makes it impossible for me to sum up a poetry which is, after all, my life and the life of those forces which have spoken through me. There is no point in listing my "masters" or the major "influences" upon my work, for I have learned something from almost every poet I have read from

Homer to the present. I could perhaps suggest that the writings of Jung, to which I was introduced by Herbert Read, have been important to me for a quarter of a century, as also has been the Neo-Platonist Tradition from which he drew. I cannot stand back from my poetry and see it clearly, for, thank God, it is still in the writing; and therefore still changing its shape. Perhaps some critic other than I may detect connections between the poetry I have made and the authors I have edited or written about. Perhaps another critic may uncover a central theme or themes and disclose my "philosophy". I myself am in doubt. I can only respond to an editor's request for auctorial comment by parodying Archibald MacLeish's rightly famous line and saying "A poet should not mean, but be", and pray that I may continue to "be" a poet, by which I mean merely a man through whom poems continue to arrive.

*   *   *

In his crucial middle years Robin Skelton moved from England to Canada, where he has lived since 1962. He remains, more than any other poet now writing in Canada, a man of two worlds, European and North American. This condition has been reflected in his work as an editor; he has followed up his two excellent anthologies of recent English verse by editing from Victoria in British Columbia an international literary journal, *The Malahat Review*, perhaps the only magazine in which Canadian poetry competes on an egalitarian basis with poetry of other traditions. The effect of emigration on his own poetry has been to create a feeling of distance – rather than detachment – from significant experience: an inverted telescope view of situations and states of mind which one senses are in reality nearer to the poet than their magic realist aloofness at first suggests. Skelton's poetry from the beginning reflected the analytical and strongly patterned frame of mind that dominates his excellent critical work on Ruskin and on the Irish poets. He began in the Movement manner of the British fifties, writing in a flat and almost audibly north country tone the deliberately unexciting verse which was favoured at that time in contrast to the emotional manner of the forties. Since then, however, his poetry had developed an individual style – reflective and, in the later poems especially, marked often by a stoic melancholy. Narrative, and especially the narrative of the feelings – feelings prompted by memory and the sense of exile – is a mode which Skelton has particularly developed, though, with a fine and continually experimental craftsmanship, he has written in a variety of lyric and satiric moods. Recently, in *Private Speech*, his verse has turned towards the gnomic, and in his *Poems from the Greek Anthology* he has explored the ambiguous borderland between translation and parody.

– George Woodcock

SKINNER, Knute (Rumsey). American. Born in St. Louis, Missouri, 25 April 1929. Educated at Culver-Stockton College, Canton, Missouri, 1947–49; Colorado State College, Greeley, A. B. in speech and drama 1951; Middlebury College, Vermont, M.A. in English 1954; University of Iowa, Iowa City, Ph.D. in English 1958. Married Linda Kuhn in 1961; has two sons. English Teacher, Boise High School, Idaho, 1951-54; Instructor in English, University of Iowa, 1960–61; Assistant Professor of English, Oklahoma College for Women, Chickasha, 1961–62.

Part-time Lecturer, 1962–70, and since 1971, Associate Professor of English, Western Washington State College, Bellingham. Recipient: Huntington Hartford Foundation Fellowship, 1961; National Endowment for the Arts grant, 1974. Address: 2600 Hampton Place, Bellingham, Washington 98225, U.S.A.; or, Killaspuglonane, Kilshanny, County Clare, Ireland (summer).

PUBLICATIONS

Verse

   Stranger with a Watch.   Francestown, New Hampshire, Golden Quill Press, 1965.
   A Close Sky over Killaspuglonane.   Dublin, Dolmen Press, 1968.
   In Dinosaur Country.   Greeley, Colorado, Pierian Press, 1969.
   The Sorcerers: A Laotian Tale.   Bellingham, Washington, Goliards Press, 1972.
   Hearing of the Hard Times.   Dublin, Dolmen Press, 1973.

Manuscript Collection: Humanities Research Center, University of Texas, Austin.

Critical Studies: "From Ireland the American" by Gregory FitzGerald, in *Ann Arbor Review* (Michigan), Summer 1968; by Thomas Churchill, in *Concerning Poetry* (Bellingham, Washington), Fall 1968; "Killaspuglonane" by Harry Chambers, in *Phoenix* (Manchester), Summer 1969; X. J. Kennedy, in *Concerning Poetry* (Bellingham, Washington), Fall 1969.

Knute Skinner comments:

I have attempted to embody (emphasis on body) love and death. In other poems I have analyzed character. In a few I have attempted to enter nature and have gone so far as to find spirit in a cow. I am no longer as interested in the distant and abstract as I am in my immediate surroundings, and some of my recent poems are set in Killaspuglonane, my adopted townland. My influences are varied and usual. I began by writing rhymed stanzas and now write mostly free verse – though I still use rhyme, meter, syllabic or accentual if the poem asks for it.

                              *   *   *

Knute Skinner creates from remarkably disparate sources. His poems of love, death and isolation in *Stranger with a Watch* are powerfully underscored by a wry and acid humor which etches at the surface of experience to reveal inner situations and private struggles. He writes elegies for the living as well as the dead – mourns the mourners. In his constant interplay of mind and senses and in his perception of physical decay and time he recalls Hardy, Housman, and Yeats. Here is ironic laughter at twisted circumstance; here is understatement, word-play and a combination of metaphysical and sensual imagery; here is concern with madness, prophecy, and the stripping of poetic language to its bones and marrow. In form Skinner ranges widely and easily from lyric to epigram, from sonnet to ballad to free-style;

but his vision is peculiarly his own. By his criticism he reveals how things are and thereby implies how they ought to be – how love should not be a commodity, how men should not journey alone, how formality and self-consciousness should not divert people from genuine feeling. Through his poems the reader catches glimpses of lost connections – of time, places, and people that are not what they were – and a sense of love's fragility and ineffability. In *A Close Sky over Killaspuglonane*, Skinner allies himself with his Irish heritage, reflecting the land, the people, and the traditions of Clare county. Here he writes most strongly out of a sense of place. *In Dinosaur Country* displays an exuberant sense of life through humor which can be gentle, whimsical and uproarious. Unflinchingly, Skinner reintroduces "gross" material into the life experience via poetry. He makes poems of "Blackheads," "Phlegm," "Urine," and presents "A Poem for the Class of 69" (in the concrete poetic style). His laughter is compelling and human, reminding the reader that nothing is ugly or alien unless he makes it so.

– Carl Lindner

SLAVITT, David (Rytman). Pseudonym. **Henry Sutton.** American. Born in White Plains, New York, 23 March 1935. Educated at Phillips Academy, Andover, Massachusetts, graduated 1952; Yale University, New Haven, Connecticut, 1952–56, B.A. (magna cum laude) 1956; Columbia University, New York, M.A. 1957. Married Lynn Meyer in 1956; has three children. Instructor, Georgia Institute of Technology, Atlanta, 1957–58; Associate Editor, *Newsweek* magazine, New York, 1958–65. Address: 44 Coolidge Avenue, Cambridge, Massachusetts 02138, U.S.A.

PUBLICATIONS

Verse

Suits for the Dead. New York, Scribner, 1961.
The Carnivore. Chapel Hill, University of North Carolina Press, 1965.
Day Sailing and Other Poems. Chapel Hill, University of North Carolina Press, 1969.
Child's Play. Baton Rouge, Louisiana State University Press, 1972.
Vital Signs. New York, Doubleday, 1975.

Novels

Rochelle; or, Virtue Rewarded. London, Chapman and Hall, 1966; New York, Delacorte Press, 1967.
The Exhibitionist (as Henry Sutton). New York, Geis, 1967; London, Geis, 1968.
Feel Free. New York, Delacorte Press, 1968; London, Hodder and Stoughton, 1969.
The Voyeur (as Henry Sutton). New York, Geis, and London, Hodder and Stoughton, 1969.

Vector (as Henry Sutton). New York, Geis, 1970; London, Hodder and
   Stoughton, 1971.
Anagrams. London, Hodder and Stoughton, 1970; New York, Doubleday,
   1971.
ABCD. New York, Doubleday, 1972; London, Hamish Hamilton, 1974.
The Liberated (as Henry Sutton). New York, Doubleday, 1973; London, W.
   H. Allen, 1974.
The Outer Mongolian. New York, Doubleday, 1973.
The Killing of the King. New York, Doubleday, and London, W. H. Allen,
   1974.

Other

Translator, *The Eclogues of Virgil.* New York, Doubleday, 1971.
Translator, *The Eclogues and the Georgics of Virgil.* New York, Doubleday,
   1972.

Manuscript Collection: Beinecke Rare Book Library, Yale University, New Haven,
Connecticut.

Critical Study: interview in *The Writer's Voice*, edited by George Garrett, New
York, Morrow, 1973.

*   *   *

In 1961, in the introduction to David Slavitt's first book of poems, John Hall
Wheelock said that "one of the distinguishing characteristics of Mr. Slavitt's poetry
is a severe restraint in the use of figurative language. It is the brilliance and clarity
of his work, its brisk pace and taut resonance of line, its ironic and sardonic
counterpoint, and, above all, its dramatic tensions, rather than any striking use of
imagery or metaphor, that make it memorable." Slavitt's later books have borne
out that description of his poetry, for he is a classicist – not one of the Eliot
generation's neo-classicists who still depended so heavily on the "romantic image,"
but a genuine classicist, using reason and wit to order his experience, to explain it,
to describe it rather than (like a romantic) to embody it or transcend it.
   The voice of Slavitt's poetry is literally that of a man talking, an intelligent and
urbane man, a man of wit and no little wisdom, speaking of life and more increasingly of death, often playfully, more often very seriously. His version of Virgil's
Eclogues and *Georgics*, not strictly a translation of Virgil's poetic musings, but an
application of Slavitt's own very striking voice and vision to those musings, is (not
surprisingly) his finest book of poems, audacious, even arrogant, and brilliant
throughout, a genuine translation of Virgil's approach to things into Slavitt's own
well-honed modern classical idiom and a commentary on that approach as well.
   As aware as any classical poet was of poetry as a self-conscious confidence
trick, Slavitt is also aware of its real and necessary values. In his version of the
eighth eclogue, he says:

Madness –
schizoid, of course – but it works, and you and I
can read, hear, give ourselves up to the poem,
and all our hurts too are healed, at least for a time.
We're all like dogs. A bone, a sop, distracts,
or the howl of another dog. We take it up,
one or two at a time, and then whole packs,
pouring out a grief we never felt
or sharing a real grief with all the others,
which becomes a public occasion, a communion,
a kind of celebration, a kind of prayer.

   David Slavitt masters the madness of that con game in his poems, and he speaks
in a voice that is distinctive and immediately recongizable as his. In a romantic
time, he has gone his own way, and it has proven to have been a way well worth
the going.

– R. H. W. Dillard

SMITH, A(rthur) J(ames) M(arshall). American. Born in Montreal, Quebec,
Canada, 8 November 1902. Educated at McGill University, Montreal (Editor,
McGill Literary Supplement), B.Sc. in arts 1925, M.A. 1926; University of Edin-
burgh, Ph.D. 1931. Married Jeannie Dougal Robins in 1927; has one son. Assistant
Professor, Ball State Teachers College, Muncie, Indiana, 1930–31; Instructor,
Doane College, Crete, Nebraska, 1934–35; Assistant Professor, University of South
Dakota, Vermillion, 1935–36. Instructor, 1931–33, since 1936, Member of the
English Department, and since 1960, Professor of English and Poet-in-Residence,
Michigan State University, East Lansing; now retired. Visiting Professor, Univer-
sity of Toronto, 1944, 1945, University of Washington, Seattle, 1949, Queen's
University, Kingston, Ontario, 1952, 1960, University of British Columbia, Van-
couver, 1956, Dalhousie University, Halifax, Nova Scotia, 1966–67, Sir George
Williams University, Montreal, Summers 1967, 1969, and McGill University,
1969–70. Co-Founding Editor, with F. R. Scott, *McGill Fortnightly Review*, Montreal, 1925. Recipient: Guggenheim Fellowship, 1941, 1942; Harriet Monroe
Memorial Prize (*Poetry*, Chicago), 1943; Governor-General's Award, 1944; Rockefeller Fellowship, 1944; Lorne Pierce Medal, 1966; Canada Centennial Medal,
1967; Canada Council Medal, 1968. D.Litt.: McGill University, 1958; LL.D.:
Queen's University, 1966; D.C.L.: Bishop's University, Lennoxville, Quebec, 1967.
Address: 640 Bailey Street, East Lansing, Michigan 48823, U.S.A.

PUBLICATIONS

Verse

   News of the Phoenix and Other Poems. Toronto, Ryerson Press, and New York,
     Coward McCann, 1943.

A Sort of Ecstasy: Poems New and Selected.   Toronto, Ryerson Press, and East
  Lansing, Michigan State College Press, 1954.
Collected Poems.   Toronto, Oxford University Press, 1962.
Poems: New and Collected,   Toronto, Oxford University Press, 1967.
Poets Between the Wars, with others, edited by Milton T. Wilson.   Toronto,
  McClelland and Stewart, 1967.

Other

Some Poems of E. J. Pratt: Aspects of Imagery and Theme.   St. John's, New-
  foundland, Memorial University, 1969.
Towards a View of Canadian Letters: Selected Essays 1928–1972.   Vancouver,
  University of British Columbia Press, 1973.

Editor, with F. R. Scott, *New Provinces: Poems of Several Authors.*   Toronto,
  Macmillan, 1936.
Editor, *The Book of Canadian Poetry.*   Toronto, Gage, and Chicago, University
  of Chicago Press, 1943, 1948, 1957.
Editor, *Seven Centuries of Verse: English and American, from the Early English
  Lyrics to the Present Day.*   New York, Scribner, 1947, 1957, 1967.
Editor, *The Worldly Muse: An Anthology of Serious Light Verse.*   New York,
  Abelard Schuman, 1951.
Editor, with M. L. Rosenthal, *Exploring Poetry.*   New York, Macmillan, 1955;
  revised edition, 1973.
Editor, with F. R. Scott, *The Blasted Pine: An Anthology of Satire, Invective and
  Disrespectful Verse, Chiefly by Canadian Writers.*   Toronto, Macmillan, 1957;
  revised edition, 1967.
Editor, *The Oxford Book of Canadian Verse: In English and French.*   Toronto
  and New York, Oxford University Press, 1960; revised edition, 1965.
Editor, *Masks of Fiction: Canadian Critics on Canadian Prose.*   Toronto, McClel-
  land and Stewart, 1961.
Editor, *Masks of Poetry: Canadian Critics on Canadian Verse.*   Toronto, McClel-
  land and Stewart, 1962.
Editor, *Essays for College Writing.*   New York, St. Martin's Press, 1965.
Editor, *The Book of Canadian Prose.*   Toronto, Gage, 2 vols, 1965, 1973.
Editor, *100 Poems: Chaucer to Dylan Thomas.*   New York, Scribner, 1965.
Editor, *Modern Canadian Verse: In English and French.*   Toronto, Oxford
  University Press, 1967.
Editor, *The Collected Poems of Anne Wilkinson and a Prose Memoir.*   Toronto,
  Macmillan, 1968.

Critical Studies: *Ten Canadian Poets,* by Desmond Pacey, Toronto, Ryerson Press,
1958; "A Salute to A. J. M. Smith" by various authors, in *Canadian Literature*
(Vancouver), Winter 1963; *Literary History of Canada,* edited by Carl F. Klinck,
Toronto, University of Toronto Press, 1965; *The McGill Movement,* edited by Peter
Stevens, Toronto, Ryerson Press, 1969; *Odysseus Ever Returning* by George Wood-
cock, Toronto, McClelland and Stewart, 1970.

*   *   *

A. J. M. Smith holds an important place in Canadian poetry, not merely for his own verse, but also for his part in creating and sustaining the modern movement and in giving Canadian poets a sense of distinctiveness as writers interpreting a unique culture in appropriate language.

It was in the Thirties that Smith began to gain an international reputation, but his Canadian career began in the Twenties. His earliest poems appeared when he was a student at McGill University in Montreal, where he edited the *McGill Literary Supplement*, and later, in 1925, founded with his fellow poet F. R. Scott the *McGill Fortnightly Review*, the first Canadian avant garde literary journal, dedicated to liberating Canada poetically and politically from colonialist attitudes. As important, in 1936, was the appearance of *New Provinces: Poems of Several Authors*, the Canadian equivalent of *New Signatures*, in which the writers who are since recognized as the pioneers in a distinctive Canadian voice in poetry, Smith, Scott, A. M. Klein, and E. J. Pratt, appeared together. The book's importance – like that of Smith's own poetry – lay in the fact that it showed how a poetry sensitive to a special environment and a local tradition could take on a cosmopolitan character, drawing from and contributing to a wider tradition in a way merely colonial poets have never been able to do.

Later, Smith balanced this achievement by demonstrating a continuity in Canadian poetry between the colonial and national eras through publishing the definitive series of Canadian poetry anthologies, beginning with *The Book of Canadian Poetry* in 1943 and ending with *Modern Canadian Verse* in 1967.

In his own work, Smith is a poet, given to metaphysical speculation, who sustains at the same time a high emotional intensity and a lapidary craftsmanship by which he has sought to make his poems

> as hard
> And as smooth and as white
> As a brook pebble cold and unmarred. . . .

Smith, in fact, is a poet little bound by time or place. Even the poems he wrote during the Thirties are much less tied to the period than those of most younger poets then writing in English. Indeed, if there is anything that Smith retains to place him in the period through which he has worked and lived, it is a slight rococo tang that reminds one of the Twenties rather than of the later decades in which almost all his verse was written. Yeats and the Sitwells are much more his natural mentors than Auden and his circle.

If the world Smith creates in his poems is autonomous in time, it seems equally free in place. Only a very few of his satirical poems are parochial enough for non-Canadians to follow them with difficulty. It is true that Smith declared his intent

> To hold in a verse as austere
> As the spirit of prairie and river,
> Lonely, unbuyable, dear,
> The North, as a deed, and for ever.

But even in his rather imagistic poems on Canadian landscapes the result is usually a glimpse into the same detached and personal world as that where (in Smith's only apparently less literal poems) the Phoenix does not die and "The bellow of good Master Bull / Astoundeth gentil Cow. . . ." The familiar cedars and firs and wild-duck calls in a poem like "The Lonely Land" lead us into a landscape in its feeling as mythological as any painted by Poussin for the encounters of Gods and mortals:

This is a beauty
of dissonance,
this resonance
of stony strand,
this smoky cry
curled over a black pine
and wind-battered branch
when the wind
bends the tops of the pines
and curdles the sky
from the north.

Besides such landscape poems, and poems devoted to the metaphysical contemplation of death, Smith often resorts in his verse to those sublime forms of literary criticism – the only really creative ones: parody, translation (he has rendered Gautier and Mallarmé excellently), deliberate pastiche, and the tribute, in the manner of his finely rendered "To Henry Vaughan." All these are more than feats of imitative virtuosity; they are the emphatic approaches of a poet who can, when he desires, be resoundingly himself.

Smith's aims are spareness, clarity, balance, the austerity of a latter-day classicism enriched by the discoveries of the Symbolists and the Imagists. One is aware of the unending search for words that are "crisp and sharp and small," for a form as "skin-tight" as the stallions of his poem "Far West." Occasionally the visions clarified through Smith's bright glass are too sharp for comfort, the detachment too remote for feeling to survive. More often they are saved by the dense impact of the darker shapes that lie within the crystal, the

shadows I have seen, of me deemed deeper
That backed on nothing in the horrid air.

It is this enduring sense of the shapeless beyond shape that gives Smith's best poems their peculiar rightness of tension, and makes his austerities so rich in implication.

– George Woodcock

SMITH, Iain Crichton. British. Born on the Isle of Lewis, Outer Hebrides, Scotland, 1 January 1928. Educated at the University of Aberdeen, M.A. (honours) in English 1950. Served as a Sergeant in the British Army Education Corps, 1950–52. Secondary School Teacher, Clydebank, 1952–55. Since 1955, Teacher of English, Oban High School. Recipient: Scottish Arts Council Award, 1966, Prize, 1968, and Publication Award, 1968; BBC Award, for television play, 1970; Book Council Award, 1970; Silver Pen Award, 1971. Address: 42 Combie Street, Oban, Argyll, Scotland.

PUBLICATIONS

Verse

The Long River.   Edinburgh, M. Macdonald, 1955.
New Poets 1959, with others.   London, Eyre and Spottiswoode, 1959.
Deer on the High Hills: A Poem.   Edinburgh, Giles Gordon, 1960.
Thistles and Roses.   London, Eyre and Spottiswoode, 1961.
The Law and the Grace.   London, Eyre and Spottiswoode, 1965.
Biobuill is Sanasan Reice (in Gaelic).   Glasgow, Gairm Publications, 1965.
Three Regional Voices, with Michael Longley and Barry Tebb.   London, Poet
    and Printer, 1968.
At Helensburgh.   Belfast, Festival Publications, 1968.
From Bourgeois Land.   London, Gollancz, 1970.
Selected Poems.   London, Gollancz, 1970.
Penguin Modern Poets 21, with George Mackay Brown and Norman MacCaig.
    London, Penguin, 1972.
Love Poems and Elegies.   London, Gollancz, 1972.
Hamlet in Autumn.   Edinburgh, M. Macdonald, 1972.
Eadar Fealla-dhà is Glaschu (in Gaelic).   Glasgow, University of Glasgow Cel-
    tic Department, 1974.
Notebooks of Robinson Crusoe.   London, Gollancz, 1974.

Novels

Consider the Lilies.   London, Gollancz, 1968; as *The Alien Light*, Boston,
    Houghton Mifflin, 1969.
The Last Summer.   London, Gollancz, 1969.
My Last Duchess.   London, Gollancz, 1971.
Goodbye, Mr. Dixon.   London, Gollancz, 1974.

Short Stories

Burn is Aran (includes verse; in Gaelic).   Glasgow, Gairm Publications, 1960.
An Dubh is an Gorm (in Gaelic).   Aberdeen, Aberdeen University, 1963.
Maighsirean is Ministearan (in Gaelic).   Inverness, Club Leabhar, 1970.
Survival Without Errors and Other Stories.   London, Gollancz, 1970.
The Black and the Red.   London, Gollancz, 1973.
An t-Adhar Amaireaganach (in Gaelic).   Inverness, Club Leabhar, 1973.

Plays

An Coileach (in Gaelic; produced Glasgow, 1966).   Glasgow, An Comunn Gaid-
    healach, 1966.
A' Chuirt (in Gaelic; produced Glasgow, 1966).   Glasgow, An Comunn Gaid-
    healach, 1966.

Other

The Golden Lyric: An Essay on the Poetry of Hugh MacDiarmid.   Preston, Lan-
    cashire, Akros, 1967.

Iain Am Measg nan Reultan (in Gaelic; juvenile).   Glasgow, Gairm Publications,
1970.

Translator, *Ben Dorain,* by Duncan Ban Macintyre.   Preston, Lancashire,
Akros, 1969.
Translator, *Poems to Eimhir,* by Sorley Maclean.   London, Gollancz, and New-
castle upon Tyne, Northern House, 1971.

Bibliography: in *Lines Review* (Edinburgh), no. 29, 1969.

Critical Study: interview in *Scottish International* (Edinburgh), 1971.

Iain Crichton Smith comments:

Interested in the conflict between discipline and freedom, as shown in the title
The Law and the Grace. No particular sources, except that I admire Lowell's work.

*   *   *

Iain Crichton Smith's poetry is complexly textured, with its frequent passages of
colloquial movement interwoven with, or juxtaposed to a decorative wit or a highly
styled imagery; its themes by turn personal and bookish, descriptive and philosophical; its emotional and intellectual background sometimes Gaelic and sometimes
English. He is capable of failure and of felicity in all these modes, and his work is
full of fine lines and images, and of his own particular clichés, such as an indefinite
use of the word "air," of an adjective like "incurious," and of the image of
distorted faces seen in spoons. These are mannerisms, which should not distract
the reader unduly.
    Smith's work, especially in poetry, is a long, sustained attempt to understand
experience and communicate it in artistic expression. Religion, power, evil, loneliness, hopelessness, love, death: these are perhaps his main preoccupations. Sometimes didacticism and dogmatism take over, as in a good number of poems in *From
Bourgeois Land,* and occasionally books are used as a substitute for thought or
experience instead of an addition, but his serious, intelligent, perceptive quest
continues after these intervals, and has by now produced an impressive body of
work, impressive in its commitment and concern, and also in its original and
sensitive use of language and technique.
    In "The White Noon" (his contribution to *New Poets 1959)* there are examples of
poetry being prised out of a theme: the concentration here goes into the line or
stanza but "Grace Notes," a short sequence of sonnets, foreshadows the overall
poem-control which becomes more characteristic in his later work. *Thistles and
Roses* (1961) shows a further movement towards integrated, unified statement
within the poem, as in "Love Songs of a Puritan (B)," or "Old Woman," where
compassion rather than wit is the driving force. There is also a fine love-poem "By
Ferry to the Island," where the images make powerful linkages: old iron, white
diamonds, plough, raw naked twilight, rusty ring. *Deer on the High Hills* does a
stylish, philosophical dance, full of remote, unpredictable symbols, creating delicately a mood suggestive of the deer-world (at least as seen through human eyes).
The Law and the Grace is the most varied of the earlier collections, within the
psychological ruthlessness of poems like those on the old (Highland) woman –

> two eyes like lochs staring up
> from heather gnarled by a bare wind
> beyond the art and dance of Europe

– with description which shows delicate perception (the "mineral laughter" and "almost aloof delightedness of water" in the poem "At Tiumpan Head, Lewis"); with poems on death; and with love poems of a bleak, sardonic but haunting melody ("At the Reservoir" and "At the Firth of Lorne"). *From Bourgeois Land* is more uneven, and the poems not closely connected with the central theme are probably the best. The second poem in this collection (on the Free Church minister's house, seen after his death) has a fine structure, with excellent play of detail, strong juxtapositions and a well-judged dénouement. The *Selected Poems* includes work published in periodicals, such as the vivid, journalistic "World War One" sequence, "She Teaches Lear," a good piece of meditative poetic argument, and "Shall Gaelic Die?," a reflection on language and death. In *Hamlet in Autumn* many of the poems seem to have relapsed into a cold intellectuality, losing the human warmth that had been slowly won in preceding collections; there is an interesting criss-crossing of images in "On a Summer's Day" and a strange *gravitas* in "For John Maclean." *Love Poems and Elegies* has fresh examples of his restrained, conversational style, without the intrusion of verbal wit, hard clear detail (as in "The Burial"), a further deepening of his preoccupation with death, and in the "Poems for S" section of the book a bare and direct poetry which seems to be a transcript of experience rather than an imagined experience. These are perhaps the sketches for finer poems.

Imagery is central to Smith's concept of poetry. Robin Fulton, in an interesting essay on Smith's poetry (in *Lines Review*, 42–43, 1972) comments: "– what surprises us is the ellipsis in the thought, the unexpected associations, often heightened indeed by the very orderliness of the syntax," and he goes on to remark that Smith moves to this style, from a more colloquial, discursive one, towards the end of a poem, after the context has been prepared. Where the imagery and style are in controlled harmony, bonded into the structure of the poem, the writing is of a high order.

– Derick S. Thomson

SMITH, John. British. Born in High Wycombe, Buckinghamshire, 5 April 1924. Educated at St. James's Elementary School, Gerrards Cross. Director, 1946–58, Managing Director, 1959–71, and since 1972, Advisory Director, Christy and Moore Ltd., literary agents, London. Editor, *Poetry Review*, London, 1962–65. Recipient: *Adam International* Prize, 1953. Address: Flat 2, Chartwell Court, Brighton, Sussex, England.

PUBLICATIONS

Verse

Gates of Beauty and Death: Poems (as C. Busby Smith). London, Fortune Press, 1948.

The Dark Side of Love.   London, Hogarth Press, 1952.
The Birth of Venus: Poems.   London, Hutchinson, 1954.
Excursus in Autumn.   London, Hutchinson, 1958.
A Letter to Lao Tze.   London, Hart Davis, 1961.
A Discreet Immortality.   London, Hart Davis, 1965.
Five Songs of Resurrection.   Privately printed, 1967.
Four Ritual Dances.   Privately printed, 1968.
Entering Rooms.   London, Chatto and Windus-Hogarth Press, 1973.

Plays

The Mask of Glory (produced, 1956).
Mr. Smith's Apocalypse: A Jazz Cantata, music by Michael Garrick.   London,
   Robbins Music, n.d.

Other

Jan le Witt: An Appreciation of His Work, with Herbert Read and Jean Casson.
   London, Routledge, 1971.
The Broken Fiddlestick (juvenile).   London, Longman, 1971.
The Early Bird and the Worm (juvenile).   London, Burke, 1972.

Editor, with William Kean Seymour, *The Pattern of Poetry.*   London, Burke,
   1963.
Editor, *My Kind of Verse.*   London, Burke, 1965; New York, Macmillan, 1968.
Editor, *Modern Love Poems.*   London, Studio Vista, 1966.
Editor, with William Kean Seymour, *Happy Christmas.*   Philadelphia, Westmin-
   ster Press, and London, Burke, 1968.
Editor, *My Kind of Rhymes.*   London, Burke, 1973.

John Smith comments:

I suppose, as briefly as possible, I would describe my poetry as lyrical, metaphysical, formal, sardonic.

                              *   *   *

A certain civilised coolness at first seemed the main characteristic of John
Smith's poetry. Admirers of *The Dark Side of Love* – and there were a considerable
number – seemed to be looking, like the poet, back to the elegant verse-makers of
the seventeenth century: "As any man / With any woman lies / Let him in sleep
her lovely limbs discover. . . ." Fortunately, the slightly overblown felicity of the
early poems was controlled, in later collections, by a developing intelligence which
in that early volume had informed the long "Conversations with the Moon." In
subsequent books, while the language remains highly literate and elegant, unsophis-
ticated in everything except its dexterity, the tone has become increasingly and
more subtly esoteric; the allusions less romantically projected. Yet Smith has
remained largely unnoticed by critics, unanthologised despite some eminently suitable pieces. This may be because he has declined to interest himself in various
schools of poetry, has remained unassociated with any movement (except in his

interesting experiments in writing verse for recital with jazz, which has resulted in some of the most successful pieces in that *genre* – again largely unnoticed, presumably because more serious than the Liverpool words-and-pop simplicities). Smith has steadfastly refused to be self-indulgent, preferring a private, though not difficult, wit to public clowning. His most recent verse has shown him as a valuable guide to contemporary social life, sometimes terrifying in its vision into psychiatric darkness, sometimes funny. He is perhaps the least recognised good poet writing in England at the moment.

– Derek Parker

SMITH, Ken(neth John).   British.   Born in Rudston, East Yorkshire, 4 December 1938. Educated at Hull and Knaresborough grammar schools; University of Leeds, Yorkshire, B.A. in English literature, 1963. Served in the Royal Air Force, 1958–60. Married Ann Minnis in 1960; has two daughters and one son. Taught in an elementary school, Dewsbury, Yorkshire, 1963–64, and in a technical college, Batley, Yorkshire, 1964–65; Tutor, Exeter College of Art, Devon, 1965–69; Instructor in Creative Writing, Slippery Rock State College, Pennsylvania, 1969–72. Since 1972, Visiting Poet, Clark University, and College of the Holy Cross, both in Worcester, Massachusetts. Since 1963, Editor, with Jon Silkin, *Stand*, Newcastle upon Tyne. Recipient: Gregory Award, 1967. Address: c/o 2 Lamplugh Square, Bridlington, East Yorkshire, England.

PUBLICATIONS

Verse

  Eleven Poems.   Leeds, Northern House, 1964.
  The Pity.   London, Cape, 1967.
  Academic Board Poems.   Harpford, Devon, Peeks Press, 1968.
  A Selection of Poems.   Gillingham, Kent, ARC Publications, 1969.
  Work, Distances: Poems.   Chicago, Swallow Press, 1972.

Ken Smith comments:

  After nearly four years in the U.S. I seem to be neither British nor American – my work seems to me most influenced by America now – though reaching back into its roots in childhood and the North of England – to which I intend to return soon. But the categorisations "Northern" or even "British" or "American" seem to me mere critical tags: I'm a poet even if I write prose, by the act of turning my experience through the imagination, and by the act of writing – for me the act of surviving.
  Themes: environment (hence nature), domestic, human relations and human attitudes, our subjective world implanted in an indifferent objectivity. Usual verse forms – free, intuitively worked, organic. General sources: any – many accidental

and incidental, but environment and history, the sense of being alive, etc. Literary sources – many and scattered, too many to mention but mostly twentieth century.

Amongst other things, I want to express the way we live, and comment on it: the way we live in society, the way our environment is and we with it, how we form community – the minute ways in which the shapes of our lives are expressed in habits, gestures, buildings, our conscious and unconscious reactions to weather, landscape, each other – how we bind our lives down to the smallest detail distinguishing individual or community. So in this sense I am interested in custom, and in speech, and so in language, and so in process. The poem itself is a process more than a product of this interest. I want a language that enacts and makes living, that is living rather than merely representative: a language metaphoric in itself.

*   *   *

Ken Smith's poetry is characterised, at its best, by a coincidence of formal syntax with austere passion. When either of these goes awry, or is diminished, the poetry reads thinly. Thus in his first book, *The Pity*, his two best known poems move with a richness of feeling and insight, both of these released through formal, spoken syntax. Released is the proper word; the reader receives a building tension which eventually finds its expressive release without a loosening of the syntactic structure. In "The Pity" (the title poem) the images of bat and fish –

> The horned and hanging bat sees a bat's world.
> Fish quiver in the shallows, cold as their element,
> thinking water. I wore contempt, grew hatred

– are used to open out sensually the perception of submission to their environment. Smith implies that the human creature may behave like a fish or bat as he or she submits without struggle to his context; but the deepest part of the insight is reserved for the implication that men, equipped with intelligence, need not always submit, or merge indecipherably with their surroundings.

This nexus of resistance and change is also examined in "Family Group," but here the change, one supposes intimately experienced by the poet, is equivocally appraised. The alteration of the family's circumstances, from those of a farm labourer's to a small-shop owner's, is weighed carefully. For each gain substantiated by independence and physical well-being, there is a corresponding loss (not apparently recognised by the mother and father) which, ironically, is a loss of response inevitably entailed by their town life, a life which aims at reducing the hardships of exposure but which at the same time reduces the responses. On the face of it, my account attributes to Smith a reactionary conservatism, but because the gains and losses can be and are weighed by the son (the poet) the heuristic comparison between the two experiences points not to an either/or choice but to the richer consciousness that is able, through both experiences, to weigh, compare, and qualify both, without blindly committing himself to either. Here the value is in response.

What is Smith's poetry committed to? The propriety of the question is indicated in the strengths – the dogged, at times dourly formed love for the resisting, struggling individual who, through no apparently remediable flaw other than individuality, is condemned to suffer, without society being able, or willing, to help. Where help implies a change of heart. What has developed here, of course, is the deepening realisation of society's intractable nature, an apprehension that has not so much hardened Smith against it, as opened out his tenderness for those individuals who seem society's inevitable victims. This emerges clearly, the tenderness, I mean, in "Eli's Poem" from Smith's second book, *Work, Distances: Poems*:

> Now I am with a crazy woman
> who hurts herself with ashes and briars
> running in the scrub. She takes blankets
> and stuffs them under her skirt for a child . . .
> Now she is out on the hill wailing
> cutting her flesh on the stiff grass
> where I go to her lamenting.

What is to be done? Here the unornamented language, the starkness of the sensuous apprehension and enactment, which is one of Smith's strengths, expresses the aloneness of the creature, loved for her almost intolerable strangeness, which the poet would not abandon. The almost monotonous drone of the rhythms, both alert and repetitive, builds one's sense of the woman, without the poet having to spell out his feelings for her. The commitment to her is realised through narrative, rhythm, and tone, that is, through characteristically central literary means. And by making clear his allegiance to her, he qualifies his attitude to society, which in this instance is tolerant but uncomprehending.

More recently, in so-far-uncollected poems, such as "Lake" and "Fly," the more formal syntax of the earlier poems takes over, the loss of which threatened to disperse those very feelings which, one supposes, the disjointing of the syntax was meant to release. The casual *movement* but not casual tone of these poems implements a lucid intensity which disencumbers itself of everything but those physically cited details which serve to interconnect feelings. That is, the physical details act as nodes of feelings:

> A month back the lake
> I stood by spreading its bulk
>
> cracked whipped and cried
>
> and fought its bed: animals
> stirring, seeds pressing out
>
> from milkweed's grip
>
> and
>
>
> come back to the world brought me
> out of long sleep. Love,
> as you stir from your dream's
> untrembling be still for me. . . .
>   – from "Lake"

– Jon Silkin

SMITH, Michael. Irish. Born in Dublin, 1 September 1942. Educated at O'Connell's School, Dublin; University College, Dublin, B.A. and H.Dip. in Education. Married; has one daughter. Since 1966, teacher of Latin and English, St. Paul's

College, Raheny, Dublin. Editor, New Irish Poets series of the New Writers Press, Dublin, and *The Lace Curtain*, Dublin. Address: 19 Warrenmount Place, SCR, Dublin 8, Ireland.

PUBLICATIONS

Verse

With the Woodnymphs.   Dublin, New Writers Press, 1968.
Dedications.   Dublin, New Writers Press, 1968.
Homage to James Thompson (B.V.) at Portobello.   Dublin, New Writers Press, 1969.
Poems.   London, Advent Press, 1971.
Times and Locations.   Dublin, Dolmen Press, 1972.

Michael Smith comments:

I belong to a school of poetry which probably originated in Ireland with Patrick Kavanagh; might be called cosmopolitan parochialism as its underlying belief is that poets achieve universality by working in the context of their home environment.

The psychological condition out of which most of my poetry comes is not unlike that of Manzoni when he wrote, "An immense multitude, one generation after the other, passing on the face of the earth, passing on its own native piece of earth, without leaving a trace in history, is a sad phenomenon the importance of which cannot be overlooked."

I am living in a small house in Dublin's old quarter, an area of ancient ruin and obsolescence, where the troubled ghosts of Swift and Mangan are omnipresent and where the people still have traditions so that the past is alive. My poetry is a fusion of this environment and that condition which I have used Manzoni's words to suggest. As regards form, I believe it cannot be discussed apart from the poem. As a purely lyric poet, I can only say that I do not think the resources of language or, to use Pound's terms, logopeia, phanopeia, and melopeia, can be considered in isolation from the actual writing of a poem. They are simply things that happen, I hope necessarily, when the poem is being written: the impulse, the moment, the insight dictate all terms. Resulting from this view of poetic methodology I see my poems as short, intense inquiries and revelations which, at present, work against the background of a primeval Dublin so far without expression in literature, notwithstanding Joyce and O'Casey.

*   *   *

Times and Locations shows Michael Smith to be a maker of short poems which increase their effect as they are re-read. Some are so delicate that the basis of their imagery in genuine observation emerges only slowly; in others, a blunt first impact is later seen to encompass a range of more subtle feeling. He catches very well the atmosphere of localities, of moments of intensity due to imagined or actual events:

> Something ordered, yet desperate and violent –
> A rose, say, or an old man's humiliation.

Already an able and attractive writer, he will gain in depth, perhaps, by the gradual loosening of what is still a very "literary" style, and by a more direct, elaborated approach to the seriousness of his Irish (and universal) subject-matter.

– Anne Cluysenaar

SMITH, Sydney Goodsir.   Scottish.   Born in Wellington, New Zealand, 26 October 1915. Educated at Edinburgh University; Oxford University, M.A. Taught English to the Polish Army in Scotland for the War Office. Married; has two children. Joined the British Council, Edinburgh, 1945. Currently free-lance writer, journalist, and broadcaster. Recipient: Atlantic-Rockefeller Award, 1946; Festival of Britain Scots Poetry Prize, 1951; Oscar Blumenthal Prize (*Poetry*, Chicago), 1956; Thomas Urquhart Award, 1962. Address: 25 Drummond Place, Edinburgh 3, Scotland. *Died January 1975.*

PUBLICATIONS

Verse

   Skail Wind: Poems.   Edinburgh, Chalmers Press, 1941.
   The Wanderer and Other Poems.   Edinburgh, Oliver and Boyd, 1943.
   The Deevil's Waltz.   Glasgow, Maclellan, 1946.
   Selected Poems.   Edinburgh, Oliver and Boyd, 1947.
   Under the Eildon Tree: A Poem in xxiv Elegies.   Edinburgh, Serif Books, 1948.
   The Aipple and the Hazel.   Edinburgh, Caledonian Press, 1951.
   So Late in the Night: Fifty Lyrics 1944–1948.   London, Peter Russell, 1952.
   Cokkils.   Edinburgh, M. Macdonald, 1953.
   Omens: Nine Poems.   Edinburgh, M. Macdonald, 1955.
   Orpheus and Euridice: A Dramatic Poem.   Edinburgh, M. Macdonald, 1955.
   Figs and Thistles.   Edinburgh, Oliver and Boyd, 1959.
   The Vision of the Prodigal Son.   Edinburgh, M. Macdonald, 1960.
   Kynd Kittock's Land.   Edinburgh, M. Macdonald, 1965.
   Girl with Violin.   Dublin, Dolmen Press, and London, Oxford University Press, 1968.
   Fifteen Poems and a Play.   Edinburgh, Southside, 1969.
   Collected Poems.   London, Calder and Boyars, 1975.

Play

   The Wallace: A Triumph (produced Edinburgh, 1960).

Novel

   Carotid Cornucopius: Caird o the Cannon Gait and Voyeur o the Outluik Touer: A Drammatick, Backside, Bogbide, Bedride or Badside Buik, by Gude Schir Skedderie Smithereens.   Glasgow, Caledonian Press, 1947.

Other

A Short Introduction to Scottish Literature.   Edinburgh, Serif Books, 1951.

Editor, *Robert Fergusson 1750–1774: Essays by Various Hands to Commemorate the Bicentenary of His Birth.*   Edinburgh, Nelson, 1952.

Editor, *Gavin Douglas: A Selection of His Poetry.*   Edinburgh, Oliver and Boyd, 1959.

Editor, with J. Delancey Ferguson and James Barke, *The Merry Muses of Caledonia,* by Robert Burns.   Edinburgh, M. Macdonald, 1959; New York, Putnam, 1964.

Editor, with K. D. Duval and others, *Hugh MacDiarmid: A Festschrift.*   Edinburgh, K. D. Duval, 1962.

Editor, *Bannockburn: The Story of the Battle and Its Place in Scottish History.*   Stirling, Scots Independent, 1965.

Editor, *A Choice of Burns's Poems and Songs.*   London, Faber, 1966.

Critical Studies: by Norman MacCaig, in *Saltire Review* (Edinburgh), April 1954; Alexander Scott, in *Lines Review* (Edinburgh), Summer 1956; Kurt Wittig, in *The Scottish Tradition in Literature,* Edinburgh, Oliver and Boyd, 1958; Thomas Crawford, in *Studies in Scottish Literature,* edited by G. Ross Roy, Columbia, University of South Carolina, 1969.

*   *   *

In *Skail Wind,* the talent of Sydney Goodsir Smith *(il miglia fabbro,* alias "the Great Auk") was still in the process of settling itself down from that linguistic ferment stirred up by the highly individual brew of Scots which the poet had made for himself, deciding this was the only language in which he wished to write. Much of his early verse indulges in the thick sound-play of Scots for its own sake. His third collection, *The Deevil's Waltz,* however, contains one or two lyrics which have remained among Smith's best: "Largo," for instance, in which that feeling of impotence against impersonal forces so commonly experienced in our society is powerfully expressed through the symbolism of the last fishing-boat fishing from this Fife Coast harbour:

And never the clock rins back,	
The free days are owre;	
The warld shrinks, we luik	
Mair t'our maisters ilka hour –	
Whan yon lane* boat I see	(*)lonely
Daith and rebellion blinn* ma ee.*	(*)blind; eye

Smith's absorption of the Scots tradition produced in the title poem of *The Deevil's Waltz* a stirring of that renaissance note of unbridled merriment practised by Dunbar in "The Dance of the Sevin Deidly Synnis," and to some extent by Burns in "The Jolly Beggars" and "Tam O'Shanter":

We kenna hairt, we kenna heid,	
The Deevil's thirled* baith quick and deid.	(*)enslaved
Jehovah snores, and Christ his sel	
Lowps in the airms of Jezebel.	

But it was as a love-poet that Smith was most fully to develop: a love-poet steeped not only in the literature of his own country and in world literature, but in the red blood of passion itself:

Hairt, ma hairt, forgae*	(*)forgo
This dirlin* o' ma saul	(*)piercing
Ye steer* ma deeps til* a reel of flame	(*)stir; to
Like a smashed coal.	

For Smith, love and thought, sex and emotion, illumine and complete a single total experience, as they also did for Burns.

Smith's love-poems are set firmly in a modern urban setting:

I loe* ma luve in a lamplit bar	(*)love
Braw on a wuiden stool,	
Her knees cocked up and her neb* doun	(*)nose
Slorpan* a pint o' yill*	(*)swilling; ale

His supreme achievement is *Under the Eildon Tree.* Using the myth of Thomas the Rhymer, the poet laments the loves of some of the world's, and classical mythology's, great lovers – Orpheus and Eurydice, Dido and Aeneas, Burns and Highland Mary – in a series of elegies each of which is a variation on the single theme: love as experienced by the poet. The allusions to world literature fall thick and fast, but are woven into the texture of the verse so naturally and with such musical skill that they contribute much towards the depth of the poem which surely makes it the finest sustained love-poem of the twentieth century. The opening lines of "Elegy xiii" illustrate the extraordinary quality of the poem:

Ah, she was a bonnie cou!	
Saxteen, maybe sevinteen, nae mair,	
Her mither in attendance, *comme il faut*	
Pour les jeunes filles bien élevées,	
Drinkan like a bluidie whaul* tae!	(*)a whale
Wee breists, round and ticht* and fou*	(*)tight; full
Like sweet Pomona in the orange grove;	
Her shanks were lang, but no owre lang, and plump,	
A lassie's shanks,	
Wi the meisurance o' Venus –	
Achteen inch the hoch* frae heuchle-bane* til knap*	(*)thigh; hip-bone
Achteen inch the cauf* frae knap til cuit*	(*)knee-cap
As is the true perfection calculate	(*)calf;ankle
By the Auntients efter due regaird	
For this and that,	
The true meisurance	
O' the Venus dei Medici,	
The Aphrodite Anadyomene	
And all the goddesses o' hie antiquitie –	
Siclike were the shanks and hochs	
O' Sandra the cou o' the auld Black Bull.	

Smith's patriotism has found expression in his play *The Wallace*, performed at the Edinburgh International Festival of Music and Drama. This love of language for its own sake has resulted in his Joycean prose fantasy in Scots, *Carotid Cornucopius*, although the evident artificiality of the language strain prevents it touching the depths of associative meaning achieved in Joyce's *Ulysses*. Smith's mastery of the Scots colloquial style of the Eighteenth Century Revival has enabled him to adapt it to contemporary satirical use (though his satire is always warmed by good humour). and even to address a long verse-letter "To Robert Fergusson" in the earlier poet's own favourite stanza-form.

In an age when most major poets have developed the image to carry full technical weight, Smith's style is almost bare of imagery, and the few that he uses are often commonplace. Consequently, like the little girl in the nursery rhyme, when he is bad he is horrid! Happily, however, he is often very, very good; especially so when the force of his passion and the power of his imagination transmute whichever aspect of love he is writing about into a stuff more durable than the experiences which inspired him. He is thus, after MacDiarmid, the most powerful Scots-writing poet of the Scottish Renaissance movement.

– Maurice Lindsay

SMITH, Vivian (Brian). Australian. Born in Hobart, Tasmania, 3 June 1933. Educated at the University of Tasmania, Hobart, M.A.; University of Sydney, Ph.D. Married Sybille Gottwald in 1960; has two daughters and one son. Formerly, Lecturer in French, University of Tasmania. Currently, Senior Lecturer in English, University of Sydney. Address: 19 McLeod Street, Mosman, New South Wales 2088, Australia.

Publications

Verse

The Other Meaning: Poems.   Sydney, Edwards and Shaw, 1956.
An Island South.   Sydney, Angus and Robertson, 1967

Other

James McAuley.   Melbourne, Lansdowne Press, 1965; revised edition, 1970.
Les Vigé en Australie (juvenile).   Melbourne, Longman, 1967.
Vance Palmer.   Melbourne, Oxford University Press, 1971.
Robert Lowell.   Sydney, Sydney University Press, 1974.

Editor, *Australian Poetry 1969.*   Sydney, Angus and Robertson, 1969.

Vivian Smith comments:

Within the context of Australian poetry I am, I suppose, something of a regionalist since most of my poems are about Hobart and Tasmania, though Sydney too has been one of the poles of my inspiration. I usually write in traditional forms, and my lyrics try to affirm both the sense of a personal inner world and the inescapable presence of the actual.

*   *   *

In the 1950's there appeared to be a blossoming of fresh young poetic talent, predominantly regional in origin, in Australia: David Rowbotham in Queensland, Randolph Stow in West Australia, and, in Tasmania, Christopher Koch and Vivian Smith. In his first volume, *The Other Meaning*, Smith showed a sensitive response to his environment. The "other meaning" which he sought was some aspect of the transient that gave it either definition or awareness.

In *An Island South*, the influence of the then-predominantly academic poets of dry wit in England and America is more apparent. Vivian Smith has published only occasional poems since that volume. His work has a reticence that sometimes underplays the deftness of observation and precision of control that give his best work a true luminosity. Though his themes have tended to remain persistently close to immediate response, Smith has appreciably hardened the texture of his poems to a gemlike precision. If he does not appear to have justified the early anticipations of his admirers, his work has grown in its own terms and with honesty and quiet dignity.

– Thomas W. Shapcott

SMITH, William Jay. American. Born in Winnfield, Louisiana, 22 April 1918. Educated at Blow School, St. Louis, 1924–31; Cleveland High School, 1931–35; Washington University, St. Louis, 1935–41, B.A. 1939, M.A. in French, 1941; Institut de Touraine, Tours, France, 1938; Columbia University, New York, 1946–47; Wadham College, Oxford (Rhodes Scholar), 1947–48; University of Florence, 1948–50. Served as a Lieutenant in the United States Naval Reserve, 1941–45. Married Barbara Howes, *q.v.*, in 1947 (divorced, 1965), has two sons; Sonja Haussmann in 1966, has one step-son. Assistant in French, Washington University, 1939–41; Instructor in English and French, 1946–47, and Visiting Professor of Writing and Acting Chairman, Writing Division, 1973, 1974–75 Columbia University; Instructor in English, 1951, and Poet-in-Residence and Lecturer in English, 1959–64, 1966–67, Williams College, Williamstown, Massachusetts. Writer-in-Residence, 1965–66, Professor of English, 1967–68 and since 1970, Hollins College, Virginia. Consultant in Poetry, 1968–70, and Honorary Consultant, 1970–74, Library of Congress, Washington, D.C. Poetry Reviewer, *Harper's*, New York, 1961–64; Editorial Consultant, Grove Press, New York, 1968–70. Democratic Member, Vermont House of Representatives, 1960–62. Recipient: Young Poets Prize, 1945, and Union League Civic and Arts Foundation Prize, 1964 (*Poetry*, Chicago); Alumni Citation, Washington University, 1963; Ford Fellowship, for drama, 1964; Henry Bellamann Major Award, 1970; Loines Award, 1972; National Endowment for the Arts grant, 1972. D.Litt.: New England College, Henniker, New Hampshire, 1973. Agent: Martha Winston, Curtis Brown Ltd., 60 East 56th Street, New York, New York 10022. Address: Upper Bryant Road, West Cummington, Massachusetts 01265, U.S.A.

PUBLICATIONS

Verse

Poems.   Pawlet, Vermont, Banyan Press, 1947.
Celebration at Dark: Poems.   London, Hamish Hamilton, and New York, Farrar
    Straus, 1950.
Typewriter Birds.   New York, Caliban Press, 1954.
The Bead Curtain: Calligrams.   Florence, privately printed, 1957.
Poems 1947–1957.   Boston, Little Brown, 1957.
*Prince Souvanna Phouma: An Exchange Between Richard Wilbur and William Jay
    Smith.*   Williamstown, Massachusetts, Chapel Press, 1963.
The Tin Can and Other Poems.   New York, Delacorte Press, 1966.
New and Selected Poems.   New York, Delacorte Press, 1970.
A Rose for Katherine Anne Porter.   New York, Albondocani Press, 1970.
At Delphi: For Allen Tate on His Seventy-Fifth Birthday, 19 November 1974.   Wil-
    liamstown, Massachusetts, Chapel Press, 1974.

Play

The Straw Market, music by the author (produced Washington, D.C., 1965;
    New York, 1969).

Other

Laughing Time (juvenile).   Boston, Little Brown, 1955; London, Faber, 1956.
Boy Blue's Book of Beasts (juvenile).   Boston, Little Brown, 1957.
Puptents and Pebbles: A Nonsense ABC (juvenile).   Boston, Little Brown, 1959;
    London, Faber, 1960.
Typewriter Town (juvenile).   New York, Dutton, 1960.
The Spectra Hoax (criticism).   Middletown, Connecticut, Wesleyan University
    Press, 1961.
What Did I See? (juvenile).   New York, Crowell Collier, 1962.
My Little Book of Big and Little: Little Dimity, Big Gumbo, Big and Little
    (juvenile).   New York, Macmillan, 3 vols., 1963.
Ho for a Hat! (juvenile).   Boston, Little Brown, 1964.
If I Had a Boat (juvenile).   New York, Macmillan, 1966.
Mr. Smith and Other Nonsense (juvenile).   New York, Delacorte Press, 1968.
Around My Room and Other Poems (juvenile).   New York, Lancelot Press,
    1969.
Grandmother Ostrich and Other Poems (juvenile).   New York, Lancelot Press,
    1969.
Children and Poetry: A Selective Annotated Bibliography, with Virginia Haviland.
    Washington, D.C., Library of Congress, 1969.
Louise Bogan: A Woman's Words.   Washington, D.C., Library of Congress,
    1971.
The Streaks of the Tulip: Selected Criticism.   New York, Delacorte Press, 1972.

Editor and Translator, *Selected Writings of Jules Laforgue.*   New York, Grove
    Press, 1956.
Editor, *Herrick.*   New York, Dell, 1962.

Editor, with Louise Bogan, *The Golden Journey: Poems for Young People.*
Chicago, Reilly and Lee, 1965; London, Evans, 1967.
Editor, *Poems from France* (juvenile).   New York, Crowell, 1967.
Editor, *Poems from Italy* (juvenile).   New York, Crowell, 1972.

Translator, *Scirroco,* by Romualdo Romano.   New York, Farrar Straus, 1951.
Translator, *Poems of a Multimillionaire,* by Valéry Larbaud.   New York,
Bonaccio and Saul, 1955.
Translator, *Two Plays by Charles Bertin: Christopher Columbus and Don
Juan.*   Minneapolis, University of Minnesota Press, 1970.
Translator, *Children of the Forest* (juvenile), by Elsa Beskow.   New York,
Delacorte Press, 1970.
Translator, *The Pirate Book* (juvenile), by Lennart Hellsing.   New York,
Delacorte Press, 1970.

Manuscript Collection: Washington University, St. Louis.

Critical Studies: "William Jay Smith," in *Modern Verse in English, 1900–1950,*
edited by Lord David Cecil and Allen Tate, New York, Macmillan, 1958; "William
Jay Smith," in *The Hollins Poets,* edited by Louis D. Rubin, Charlottesville, Univer-
sity Press of Virginia, 1967; *Authors of Books for Young People,* by Martha E. Ward
and Dorothy A. Marquardt, Metuchen, New Jersey, Scarecrow Press, 1967; "The
Lightness of William Jay Smith" by Dorothy Judd Hall, in *Southern Humanities
Review* (Auburn, Alabama), Summer 1968; "A Poet Named Smith" by Jean G.
Lawlor, in *Washington Post* (Washington, D.C.), 9 March 1969; "An Interview with
William Jay Smith" by Alizavietta Ritchie, in *Voyages* (Washington, D.C.), Winter
1970.

William Jay Smith comments:

I am a lyric poet, alert, I hope, as one of my fellow poets, Stanley Kunitz, has
put it, "to the changing weathers of a landscape, to the motions of the mind, to the
complications and surprises of the human comedy." I believe that poetry should
communicate: it is, by its very nature, complex, but its complexity should not
prevent its making an immediate impact on the reader. Great poetry must have
resonance: it must resound with the mystery of the human psyche, and possess
always its own distinct, identifiable, and haunting, music. My recent poems have
been written in long unrhymed lines because the material with which I am dealing
seems to lend itself to this form, which is often close to, but always different from,
prose. I have always used a great variety of verse forms, especially in my poetry
for children. I believe that poetry begins in childhood and that a poet who can
remember his own childhood exactly can, and should, communicate to children.

*   *   *

William Jay Smith's first book, *Poems,* announced a poet of exotic subjects, high
patina, and exquisite music, a combination suggestive of early Wallace Stevens.
Such poems as "The Peacock of Java," "On the Islands Which Are Solomon's,"

and "Of Islands" transform a seascape of atolls which "brings, even/To the tree of heaven, heaven." Other poems, like "The Barber" and "The Closing of the Rodeo," initiate Smith's satirical rendering of the American commonplace, while "Cupidon" reflects his interest in incremental ballad form and fantasy. This early work seemed a very deft performance in the then-dominant metaphysical style, but Smith has always sounded a note of his own – his lightness, dexterity, elegance, and wit reflect not only the prevailing influence of Eliot, Tate, and Ransom, but also earlier poets who had influenced them.

During World War II, Smith served as a liaison officer aboard a Free French naval vessel, and he began his civilian career as a teacher of French literature at Columbia. He published a distinguished translation of Valéry Larbaud in 1955 and of Jules Laforgue in 1956. The qualities of formal versification, precarious poise, and wit in his early verse seem akin to those of Laforgue, the dreamwork suggestive of Larbaud. Further clues to his own verse are offered in Smith's two critical studies. *The Spectra Hoax* is an entertaining reconstruction of the successful leg-pull by Witter Bynner and Arthur Davidson Ficke, who not only concocted a fictitious school of poets in 1916–18, but, writing pseudonymously as its members, begat better poems than when using their own names and more conventional styles. The following year Smith's introduction to a selection of the poems of Robert Herrick described that poet as "a master of understatement [who] knows what to omit," "a perfect miniaturist; nothing is too small for him to notice or too great to reduce in size." These and other occasional essays are collected in *Streaks of the Tulip: Selected Criticism.*

His translations and studies of English, French, and American poets suggest the range and sources of Smith's fascination with satire, fantasy, and word-play, his comprehension of the true seriousness of successful light verse, and his devotion, until his most recent work, to brief lyrics, conventional forms, aesthetic distance from his subjects, and a burnished surface – as in his little poem "Tulip" which offers "Magnificence within a frame." Similar qualities animate his several books of verse for children; he has written, "I believe that poetry begins in childhood and that a poet who can remember his own childhood exactly can, and should, communicate to children." (One such communication, *Typewriter Town* [1960], anticipates by several years the vogue for concrete poetry among writers for adults.)

These qualities and Smith's characteristic lightness of touch are blended into an unmistakably American idiom in *Poems 1947–1957,* especially in "Letter," "Death of a Jazz Musician," and "American Primitive":

> Look at him there in his stovepipe hat,
> His high-top shoes, and his handsome collar;
> Only my Daddy could look like that,
> And I love my Daddy like he loves his Dollar.
> The screen door bangs, and it sounds so funny –
> There he is in a shower of gold;
> His pockets are stuffed with folding money,
> His lips are blue, and his hands feel cold.
>
> He hangs in the hall by his black cravat,
> The ladies faint, and the children holler:
> Only my Daddy could look like that,
> And I love my Daddy like he loves his dollar.

With *The Tin Can and Other Poems* and since, Smith, like most of the poets of his generation, moved on from the style he had mastered to a new, freer prosody, in which the dark side of experience is presented in a more unmediated way than in poems like "American Primitive" which had enclosed it in a play of wit and form:

O dreadful night! . . . What train will come? . . . What tree is that?
  . . . a sycamore – the mottled bark stripped bare,

Desolate in winter light against the track, and I continue on to
  the mudflats

By the roaring river where garbage, chicken coops, and houses rush
  by me on mud-crested waves,

And at my feet are dead fish – catfish, gars – and there in a little
  inlet

Come on a deserted camp, the tin can in which the hoboes brewed their
  coffee stained bitter black

As the cinders sweeping ahead under a milkweed-colored sky along a
  darkening track

    And gaze into a slough's green stagnant foam,
      and know that the way out is never back,
                                    but down,
                              down . . .

          What train will come
            to bear me back
          across so wide a town?

At least one reviewer of *The Tin Can* suggested that the hitherto elegant Mr. Smith had succumbed to the prosier incantations of Allen Ginsberg. As with Ginsberg, this loose, rolling line makes possible the inclusion in Smith's work of many grubby realities which, like Herrick, he had earlier tended to omit or to transfigure. Smith's sensibility, however, has little in common with the Beat bard's; a likelier *point d'origine* for these recent poems is in the free verse and surreal observations of the contemporary by Valéry Larbaud. His long unrhymed line makes possible an amplitude of feeling as well as inclusiveness of subject, and in it Smith continues to explore both his descent into the inarticulate and the terrifying ("My voice goes out like a funicular over an abyss, and my hands hang at my sides, clenching the void; / My dreams are filled with bitter oranges and carrots, signifying calumny and sorrow") and his intimations of the unity of all things, as in "The Tin Can," a poem of withdrawal from the world and the resultant gift of vision to the spirit.

                                                            – Daniel Hoffman

---

SMITHYMAN, (William) Kendrick. New Zealander. Born in Te Kopuru, Auckland, 9 October 1922. Educated at Seddon Memorial Technical College; Auckland Teachers College; Auckland University College. Served in the New Zealand Artillery and the Royal New Zealand Air Force, 1941–45. Married Mary Stanley in 1946;

has three sons. Primary School Teacher, 1946–63. Since 1963, Senior Tutor, Department of English, University of Auckland. Visiting Fellow in Commonwealth Literature, University of Leeds, Yorkshire, 1969. Recipient: British Council grant, 1969; New Zealand Literary Fund grant, 1969; Jessie Mackay prize, 1970. Address: Department of English, University of Auckland, Auckland, New Zealand.

PUBLICATIONS

Verse

Seven Sonnets. Auckland, Pelorus Press, 1946.
The Blind Mountain and Other Poems. Christchurch, Caxton Press, 1950.
The Gay Trapeze. Wellington, Arena Press, 1955.
The Night Shift: Poems on Aspects of Love, with others. Wellington, Capricorn Press, 1957.
Inheritance: Poems. Auckland, Blackwood and Janet Paul, 1962.
Flying to Palmerston: Poems. Wellington, Oxford University Press, 1968.
Earthquake Weather. Auckland, Auckland University Press, and London, Oxford University Press, 1972.
The Seal in the Dolphin Pool. Auckland, Auckland University Press, and London, Oxford University Press, 1974.

Other

A Way of Saying: A Study of New Zealand Poetry. Auckland and London, Collins, 1965.

Editor, The Land of the Lost (novel), by William Satchell. Auckland, Auckland University Press, and London, Oxford University Press, 1971.

*   *   *

If the precise observation of detail is one requirement of a poet, Kendrick Smithyman begins with a genuine advantage. Many of his poems enshrine curious and unexpected details of New Zealand life and landscape, as well as strange material from often esoteric reading. His vocabulary, too, is extremely varied, and this, combined with a packed elliptical style, a habit of exploiting the less-used secondary meanings of words and a kind of syntactical juggling makes his poems, especially of his earlier period, frequently hard to understand. But few of them do not repay extra effort, for Mr. Smithyman's restless, leaping mind confronts a wide variety of ontological concepts, problems of being and of personal relations, questions of human identity, as well as aspects of married love and parenthood.

Not a great number of his poems relate directly to the New Zealand scene. When he does begin with such a setting, as in "Gathering the Toheroa" or "Just an Evening in the Ranges," it is only to move at once beyond it to meditate on mortality or the puzzle of meaning. Irony, sometimes gentle, sometimes cutting, sustains many of them. At times his poems suggest a strenuous wrestling with words and forms as if the raid on the inarticulate were indeed a bloody and an exhausting business. But his skilful craftsmanship, as well as his exuberant intellectual curiosity produce, in the main, pieces of a dense, rich substance, wry in flavour. The mind they disclose is akin to that of a 17th century Metaphysical.

During his poetic career, Mr. Smithyman has assimilated elements from several contemporary poets, perhaps most noticeably American ones, Robert Lowell among them. Yet his work always sounds an individual note, in part because, despite the complicated verbal structure, a colloquial character is frequently maintained. His poetry gains greatly in effect and in intelligibility by being read aloud.

From *The Blind Mountain* to *Flying to Palmerston*, he shows a gradual increase of directness, with fewer ellipses, more stylistic control and greater urbanity. He has always possessed wit, in its several 18th century senses, and increasingly in his poetry there have appeared a verbal wit and a kind of ironical gaiety which intensify, rather than negate, his essential seriousness and strength of feeling. What may sometimes teeter on the edge of cynicism or flippancy becomes an ironic or wryly sad comment on time, change, emotional sterility or cultural dryness. His awareness of the social scene in New Zealand, if most often expressed indirectly, goes deeper than that of more overtly socially critical poets. One of the most sophisticated craftsmen New Zealand has so far produced, Kendrick Smithyman brings a quite distinctive, highly selective imagination and a masterly command of technique to bear on subjects which are never trivial.

– J. C. Reid

SNODGRASS, W(illiam) D(eWitt). American. Born in Wilkinsburg, Pennsylvania, 5 January 1926. Educated at Geneva College, Beaver Falls, Pennsylvania, 1943–44, 1946; State University of Iowa, Iowa City, 1949–55, B.A. 1949, M.A. 1951, M.F.A. 1953. Served in the United States Navy, 1944–46. Married Lila Jean Hank in 1946 (divorced, 1953); Janice Wilson in 1954 (divorced, 1966); Camille Rykowski in 1967; has one daughter, one son and one step-daughter. Instructor in English, Cornell University, Ithaca, New York, 1955–57, University of Rochester, New York, 1957–58, and Wayne State University, Detroit, 1959–67. Since 1968, Professor of English and Speech, Syracuse University, New York. Visiting Teacher, Morehead Writers Conference, Kentucky, Summer 1955, and Antioch Writers Conference, Yellow Springs, Ohio, Summers 1958–59. Recipient: Ingram Merrill Foundation Award, 1958; *Hudson Review* Fellowship, 1958; Longview Award, 1959; Poetry Society of America Special Citation, 1960; Yaddo Resident Award, 1960, 1961, 1965; National Institute of Arts and Letters grant, 1960; Pulitzer Prize, 1960; Guinness Award (UK), 1961; Ford Fellowship, for drama, 1963; Miles Award, 1966; National Endowment for the Arts grant, 1966; Academy of American Poets Fellowship, 1972; Guggenheim Fellowship, 1972. Member, National Institute of Arts and Letters, 1972; Fellow, Academy of American Poets, 1973. Address: R.D. 1, Erieville, New York 13061, U.S.A.

PUBLICATIONS

Verse

Heart's Needle. New York, Knopf, 1959; Hessle, Yorkshire, Marvell Press, 1960.

After Experience: Poems and Translations. New York, Harper, and London, Oxford University Press, 1968.
Remains: Poems (as S. S. Gardons). Mount Horeb, Wisconsin, Perishable Press, 1970.

Other

In Radical Pursuit: Critical Essays and Lectures. New York, Harper, 1975.

Editor, *Syracuse Poems 1969.* Syracuse, Syracuse University Department of English, 1969.

Translator, with Lore Segal, *Gallows Songs,* by Christian Morgenstern. Ann Arbor, University of Michigan Press, 1967.

Bibliography: *W. D. Snodgrass: A Bibliography* by William White, Detroit, Wayne State University Press, 1960.

Manuscript Collection: Lockwood Library, State University of New York, Buffalo.

W. D. Snodgrass comments:

I am usually called a "confessional" poet or else an "academic" poet. Such terms seem to me not very helpful.

I first became known for poems of a very personal nature, especially those about losing a daughter in a divorce. Many of those early poems were in formal metres and had an "open" surface. All through my career, however, I have written both free verse and formal metres. At first, I published more of the formal work because it seemed more successful to me. Recently, my free (or apparently free) verse seems more successful, so I publish more of it. My poems now are much less directly personal and often experiment with multiple voices or with musical devices. My work almost always goes very slowly and involves long periods of gestation and revision. This is not because I am particularly perfectionistic, but because it takes me so long to get through the conscious areas of beliefs and half-truths into the subrational areas where it may be possible to make a real discovery.

*   *   *

The considerable reputation of W. D. Snodgrass rests on two volumes of verse in which the main element is the confessional: the poet appears as a sad, self-revealing figure whose main concern in poetry (see the paper on "Finding a Poem" at the end of *Heart's Needle*) is to write "what he really thinks." If this entails a markedly autobiographical approach, that is justified in the interests of sincerity, innocence and truthful writing about "the self he cannot help being." This kind of emphasis sets Snodgrass among other, probably more notable, confessional poets of the sixties – John Berryman, Sylvia Plath, Anthony Hecht, the later Robert Lowell, some of whom gave enthusiastic welcomes to his first book. If he lacks the ability of most of those poets to generalise, movingly, from personal experience and make public statements, Snodgrass, at his best, works this personal territory with integrity and resource.

These very personal poems are set in an American landscape which the poet evokes with nostalgic inventiveness, working natural details into his plots with a patient, meditated skill:

> After the sharp windstorm
> of July Fourth, all that summer
>   through the gentle, warm
> afternoons, we heard great chain saws chirr
>   like iron locusts. Crews
> of roughneck boys swarmed to cut loose
> branches wrenched in the shattering wind, to hack free
> all the torn limbs that could sap the tree.
>
> In the debris lay
> starlings dead.

The careful syllabic metre adopted here (the poem is from his title-sequence in *Heart's Needle*, about the daughter from whom he was separated by divorce) testifies to a zealous craftsmanship for which he has also been much admired, although it seems often to mute his themes and produce an awkwardness of technique, especially in rhyming. Sometimes this care (more noticeable in his less successful second book, *After Experience*) and the consistent attempt to be completely serious give his poems an air of solemnity: certainly the best are those where the self-scrutiny involves humour without a sacrifice of gravity: "These Trees Stand . . ." and the much-praised "April Inventory" (*Heart's Needle*).

Sceptical critics of Snodgrass's verse detect the lack of a basic extrovert energy in his writing, a lurking sentimentality, a kind of complacent accomplishment in his handling of distressful material, and a readiness to assume that his readers can accept without quibbling the personal attitudes which his poetry embodies. What they miss is his abundant skill in the ordering of external detail in those poems where he feels he can develop the theme fully without resort to veiled implication or allegory. Poems like "The Operation," and "The Campus on the Hill" (*Heart's Needle*) and (though less strikingly) "Planting a Magnolia" (*After Experience*) show this faculty at its best, and have none of the self-pity or mawkish violence of his more indulgent writing.

– Alan Brownjohn

SNYDER, Gary (Sherman). American. Born in San Francisco, California, 8 May 1930. Educated at Reed College, Portland, Oregon, B.A. in anthropology 1951; Indiana University, Bloomington, 1951–52; University of California, Berkeley, 1953–56; studied Buddhism in Japan, 1956–64, 1965–68. Married Masa Uehara in 1967; has two children. Lecturer in English, University of California, Berkeley, 1964–65. Recipient: Bess Hokin Prize, 1964, and Levinson Prize, 1968 (*Poetry*, Chicago); Bollingen Foundation Research Grant for Buddhist Studies, 1965; National Institute of Arts and Letters prize, 1966; Guggenheim Fellowship, 1968. Lives in California. Address: c/o New Directions Publishing Corporation, 333 Avenue of the Americas, New York, New York 10014, U.S.A.

PUBLICATIONS

Verse

Riprap.   Kyoto, Japan, Origin Press, 1959.
Myths and Texts.   New York, Totem Press, 1960.
Hop, Skip, and Jump.   Berkeley, California, Oyez, 1964.
Nanoa Knows.   San Francisco, Four Seasons Foundation, 1964.
Riprap and Cold Mountain Poems.   San Francisco, Four Seasons Foundation, 1965.
Six Sections from Mountains and Rivers Without End.   San Francisco, Four Seasons Foundation, 1965; London, Fulcrum Press, 1968.
Three Worlds, Three Realms, Six Roads.   Marlboro, Vermont, Griffin Press, 1966.
A Range of Poems.   London, Fulcrum Press, 1966.
The Back Country.   London, Fulcrum Press, 1967; New York, New Directions, 1968.
The Blue Sky.   New York, Phoenix Book Shop, 1969.
Four Changes.   Privately printed, 1969.
Sours of the Hills.   Brooklyn, New York, Portents, 1969.
Regarding Wave.   New York, New Directions, 1970; London, Fulcrum Press, 1971.
Anasazi.   Santa Barbara, California, Yes Press, 1971.
Turtle Island.   New York, New Directions, 1974.

Recording: *Today's Poets 4,* with others, Folkways.

Other

Earth House Hold: Technical Notes and Queries to Fellow Dharma Revolutionaries.   New York, New Directions, and London, Cape, 1969.

Bibliography: in *Schist 2* (Willimantic, Connecticut), Summer 1974.

Critical Studies: "Gary Snyder Issue" of *In Transit* (Eugene, Oregon), 1969.

*   *   *

Gary Snyder was born in San Francisco in 1930, was brought up in the states of Washington and Oregon, and since 1952 has lived part of the time in San Francisco and part in Japan. He has worked at many different jobs, and has studied under the Zen master, Oda Sessō Rōshi.

Thomas Parkinson speaks of "the peculiar blending of Zen Buddhism with IWW political attitudes, Amerindian lore, and the mystique of the wilderness" in Snyder's poetry, and later observes that his aim is "not to achieve harmony with nature but to create an inner human harmony that equals to the natural external harmony" ("The Poetry of Gary Snyder," in *Southern Review*, July 1968). Indeed though Snyder writes about nature, he is far from the Romantic's idea of the Nature Poet. His valuing of the primitive tribe and its relation to the earth is not a sentiment but a call for action, and his beliefs are practically and explicitly worked out in both his poetry and his prose.

His literary antecedents are Ezra Pound and Kenneth Rexroth, but their influences were quickly absorbed. There is an echo of Pound's "River Merchant's Wife" in the first poem of Snyder's first book, "Mid August at Sourdough Mountain Lookout," but it is already fully Snyder's poem. It conveys an intense clarity of sensation and does so by statement, not by metaphor or symbol. We are invited to test the statement against only the most available of human experiences, the knowledge of what it feels like to be up a mountain, for instance, or of what water tastes like. Snyder is not, indeed, interested in the unique experience but in the shared or sharable experience, and this is why his poetry is so different from that of the "confessional" poets, even though he writes (like them) largely in the first person.

The shared experience is implicitly compared to an awakening – to wonder, to awareness, and to sympathy. In another poem he recalls how, on a walking tour fifteen years before, he and his first wife met at a mountain lookout. It ends:

> I don't know where she is now;
> I never asked your name.
> In this burning, muddy, lying,
> blood-drenched world
> that quiet meeting in the mountains
> cool and gentle as the muzzles of
> three elk, helps keep me sane.
> – from *A Range of Poems*

The image at the end is characteristic of Snyder: precise, unrhetorical, and definitive. It resolves and cancels out the large generalities of the third and fourth lines quoted. In a sense the image is the whole poem. And this too is characteristic, for Snyder perceives and communicates largely through images.

They are not static images, however. There are few still lifes in Snyder's poetry. His writing is full of things caught in motion: on the coast "mussels clamp to sea-boulders / Sucking the spring tides"; or a deer runs with

> stiff springy jumps down the snowfields
> Head held back, forefeet out,
> Balls tight in a tough hair sack.
> – from *A Range of Poems*

The structure of his poems varies anywhere from the traditionally shaped poem ending with a summation, like "Hop, Skip, and Jump," to the poem of thematic juxtaposition, like "Bubbs Creek Haircut." The second method is the more common, and is used with variety and inventiveness in most of his poems.

Not only is his poetry carefully and sensitively structured, it is kept alive at every point by the rhythms and the language. The stressed and unstressed syllables are quite sharply distinguishable and group easily into tight clear rhythmic units. The language is consistently powerful: it is cool, firm, and exact, with no ambitions toward a grand style to intrude between him and his perceptions. Snyder records the world attentively, as an act of love, with all his senses opened to it.

– Thom Gunn

SOLT, Mary Ellen. American. Born in Gilmore City, Iowa, 8 July 1920. Educated at Iowa State Teachers College, now State College of Iowa, B.A. 1941; University of Iowa, Iowa City, M.A. 1948; Indiana University, Bloomington, Summers 1957, 1958. Married Leo Frank Solt in 1946; has two children. English Teacher, Dinsdale High School, Iowa, 1941–42; Hubbard High School, Iowa, 1942–44; Estherville High School, Iowa, 1944–46; University High School, Iowa City, 1946–48; Bentley School, New York, 1949–52. Since 1970, Member of the Comparative Literature Department, Indiana University. Recipient: *Folio* award, 1960. Address: 836 Sheridan Road, Bloomington, Indiana 47401, U.S.A.

PUBLICATIONS

Verse

> *Flowers in Concrete.* Bloomington, Indiana University Department of Fine Arts, 1960.
> *A Trilogy of Rain.* Privately printed, 1970.
> *Eyewords.* New York, White Rose Press, 1972.

Other

> Editor, with Willis Barnstone, *Concrete Poetry: A World View.* Bloomington, Indiana University Press, 1968.

*   *   *

Mary Ellen Solt is not only a concrete poet herself but also a well-known aesthetician of the "concrete poetry" movement. She stipulates that the definition of concrete poetry must be broad, covering visual, phonetic, kinetic, constructivist, and expressionist poems. She says, "The concrete poet seeks to relieve the poem of its century-old burden of ideas, symbolic reference, allusion and repetitious emotional content. ... the concrete poem communicates first and foremost its structure." Her own practice is rather classically mimetic and centrally located in the spectrum of what is labelled "concrete." In her collection *Flowers in Concrete*, she arranges the letters of flower-names in differing typefaces to suggest the natural shape of that flower – zinnia, geranium, forsythia. (She had the assistance of a typographer, John Dearstyne, after drawing the originals by hand.) Despite the disclaimer quoted above, her poem "Dogwood: Three Movements" has clear symbolic reference to the tree out of which Christ's cross was hewn, although the poem is primarily an evocation of the blossom's delicacy.

As with almost all concrete and visual poets, wit is a principal literary device with Solt. Her "Moonshot Sonnet" is a fine example. Her comment on it, in *Concrete Poetry: A World View*, reads:

> Made by copying the scientists' symbols on the first photos of the moon in the *New York Times*: there were exactly fourteen "lines" with five "accents" ... so the poem is both a spoof of old forms and a statement about the necessity for new.

Solt's 1968 poem (or poem-sequence) is very different from *Flowers in Concrete* both in form and theme. It could be called a "happening" or guerilla theater, consisting of a set of ten posters reflecting the terrible events of that year: civil riots, the assassinations of King and Kennedy, Resurrection City, and the presidential elections. They employ such concrete imagistic devices as the A in USA turned upside down to resemble a falling bomb, and punning on the "nix" in Nixon. This poem has been performed four times, most recently in 1970 with readers and slides of historical texts during the exhibition Expose Concrete Poetry at Indiana University.

Solt's extensive comments as editor of *Concrete Poetry: A World View* have served to explain and clarify this international movement to American readers, as well as to introduce multitudinous examples of this intermedial genre. Her own work indicates the range – from the pastoral lyric of flower-names to the poem-as-public-demonstration – which she herself has called for. It is to be expected that her present interest in semiotics will carry her in a new direction.

– Jane Augustine

SORRENTINO, Gilbert. American. Born in Brooklyn, New York, 27 April 1929. Educated in New York public schools, and at Brooklyn College. Served in the United States Army Medical Corps, 1951–53. Married; has three children. Editor and Publisher, *Neon* magazine, New York, 1966–60. Editor, Grove Press, New York, 1965–70. Recipient: Guggenheim Fellowship, for fiction, 1973; National Endowment for the Arts grant, 1974. Address: 463 West Street, New York, New York 10014, U.S.A.

PUBLICATIONS

Verse

    The Darkness Surrounds Us. Highlands, North Carolina, Jargon, 1960.
    Black and White. New York, Totem Press, 1964.
    The Perfect Fiction. New York, Norton, 1968.
    Corrosive Sublimate. Los Angeles, Black Sparrow Press, 1971.

Play

    Flawless Play Restored: The Masque of Fungo. Los Angeles, Black Sparrow Press, 1974.

Novels

    The Sky Changes. New York, Hill and Wang, 1966.
    Steelwork. New York, Pantheon Books, 1970.
    Imaginative Qualities of Actual Things. New York, Pantheon Books, 1971.

Short Story

Splendide-Hôtel.   New York, New Directions, 1973.

Manuscript Collection: University of Delaware, Newark.

Critical Studies: in *Grosseteste Review* (Pensnett, Staffordshire), vi, 1–4, 1973; *Vort 6* (Silver Spring, Maryland), Fall 1974.

Gilbert Sorrentino comments:

I do not champion a "poetry of statement" and I despise narrative in verse. What I look for in my work is a verse dense in its particulars, but flexible in its total structure.

*   *   *

In some of his early poems, Gilbert Sorrentino spent himself on subjects that neither deserved nor demanded anything more than superficial treatment. Thus, Sorrentino's poetic response was facile: in "A Classic Case," no love was wasted on Major Hoople, but the poem never reaches beyond itself to demonstrate Hoople's foibles. The reader's appreciation of Hoople is wholly dependent on the poem's rhetoric: "lovely" is sarcastic and the carefully chosen nouns are proof of Hoople's hatefulness:

> Tomorrow he'll get up, put on
> his fez, and stand behind
> his gut. The sagging furniture
> his friends,
> lovely Major Hoople.

In *The Perfect Fiction*, Sorrentino rises above this presumed response of readers to rhetoric and selected objects. Strong emotion is no longer merely implied, and our idea of the poet is significantly enlarged:

> It is one man alone, what
> other way
> to say it. I am sick of myself.

And,

> A stinking city full of stinking
> people. What things they do
> are not flowers, but are sometimes
> flowery.

One may disagree with the vision but at least its expression is direct. Sorrentino seems so at odds with his world that an objective response to his work *as poetry* becomes difficult. Where the statement was once too weak, it is now dangerously strong.

But there is much delight, too, in Sorrentino's recent work, and here we find nice counterpoint to his bitter moments:

> There is no instance that was not love:
> at one time
> or another. The seasons move
>
> into the past. The seasons shove
> one another away, sunshine or rime.

Even when he lapses into the earlier type of comment, Sorrentino has new teeth, and his wit, though primitive, pushes the poem's focus beneath the surface:

> She has a kind of adoration
> for her crotch, as if it had
>
> a brain, almost as if piss
> did not pour forth from it,
> several times a day. Likewise
>
> her anus is revered.

Sorrentino's insistence on using the almost archaic "pour forth" garnishes the poem with another level of language, suggesting a new toughness and richness.

Corrosive Sublimate bears out the promise of *The Perfect Fiction* – in this recent book, Sorrentino's attention brings significance to whatever subject he writes about. The poems do not look for easy targets but start, instead, within the poet and seem to move with him out onto the streets. Sorrentino's aloneness, his sense of a time passed, is a continual refrain throughout the book, which fulfills the message of "Anatomy":

> Certain portions of the heart
> die, and are dead. They are
> dead.
>
> Cannot be exorcised or brought
> to life.
>
> Do not disturb yourself
> to become whole.
>
> They are dead, go down
> in the dark and sit with them
> once in a while.

These poems rise like words Sorrentino sends up during such visits. Here is "The Morning Roundup" with which the collection begins:

> I don't want to hear any news on the radio
> about the weather on the weekend. Talk about that.
>
> Once upon a time
> a couple of people were alive
> who were friends of mine.
>
> The weathers, the weathers they lived in!
> Christ, the sun on those Saturdays.

– Geof Hewitt

SOUSTER, (Holmes) Raymond. Canadian. Born in Toronto, Ontario, 15 January 1921. Educated at University of Toronto schools; Humberside Collegiate Institute, Toronto. Served in the Royal Canadian Air Force, 1941–45. Married Rosalie Lena Geralde in 1947. Since 1939, Staff Member, and currently, Securities Custodian, Canadian Imperial Bank of Commerce, Toronto. Editor, *Direction*, Sydney, Nova Scotia, 1943–46; Co-Editor, *Contact*, Toronto, 1952–54; Editor, *Combustion*, Toronto, 1957–60. Chairman, League of Canadian Poets, 1968–72. Recipient: Governor-General's Award, 1965; President's Medal, University of Western Ontario, 1967; Centennial Medal, 1967. Address: 39 Baby Point Road, Toronto, Ontario M6S 2G2, Canada.

PUBLICATIONS

Verse

Unit of Five, with others. Toronto, Ryerson Press, 1944.
When We Are Young. Montreal, First Statement Press, 1946.
Go To Sleep, World: Poems. Toronto, Ryerson Press, 1947.
City Hall Street. Toronto, Ryerson Press, 1951.
Cerberus, with Louis Dudek and Irving Layton. Montreal, Contact Press, 1952.
Shake Hands with the Hangman. Toronto, Contact Press, 1953.
A Dream That Is Dying. Toronto, Contact Press, 1954.
For What Time Slays. Toronto, Contact Press, 1955.
Walking Death. Toronto, Contact Press, 1955.
Selected Poems, edited by Louis Dudek. Toronto, Contact Press, 1956.
Crêpe-Hanger's Carnival: Selected Poems 1955–58. Toronto, Contact Press, 1958.
Place of Meeting: Poems 1958–60. Toronto, Isaac's Gallery, 1962.
A Local Pride: Poems. Toronto, Contact Press, 1962.
12 New Poems. Lanham, Maryland, Goosetree Press, 1964.
The Colour of the Times: The Collected Poems of Raymond Souster. Toronto, Ryerson Press, 1964.
Ten Elephants on Yonge Street: Poems. Toronto, Ryerson Press, 1965.
As Is. Toronto, Oxford University Press, 1967.
Lost and Found: Uncollected Poems. Toronto, Clarke Irwin, 1968.
So Far So Good: Poems 1938–1968. Ottawa, Oberon Press, 1969.
The Years. Ottawa, Oberon Press, 1971.
Selected Poems. Ottawa, Oberon Press, 1972.
Change-Up. Ottawa, Oberon Press, 1974.

Novels

The Winter of the Time (as Raymond Holmes). Toronto, Export Publishing, 1949.
On Target (as John Holmes). Toronto, Village Book Store Press, 1973.

Other

Editor, Poets 56: Ten Younger English-Canadians. Toronto, Contact Press, 1956.

Editor, *Experiment: Poems 1923–1929*, by W. W. E. Ross. Toronto, Contact Press, 1958.

Editor, *New Wave Canada: The New Explosion in Canadian Poetry*. Toronto, Contact Press, 1966.

Editor, with John Robert Colombo, *Shapes and Sounds: Poems of W. W. E. Ross*. Toronto, Longman, 1968.

Editor, with Douglas Lochhead, *Made in Canada: New Poems of the Seventies*. Ottawa, Oberon Press, 1970.

Editor, with Richard Woollatt, *Generation Now* (textbook). Toronto, Longman, 1970.

Editor, with Douglas Lochhead, *100 Poems of Nineteenth Century Canada* (textbook). Toronto, Macmillan, 1973.

Editor, with Richard Woollatt, *Sights and Sounds* (textbook). Toronto, Macmillan, 1973.

Editor, with Richard Woollatt, *These Loved, These Hated Lands* (textbook). Toronto, Macmillan, 1974.

Manuscript Collection: Rare Book Room, University of Toronto Library.

Critical Studies: "Groundhog among the Stars" by Louis Dudek, in *Canadian Literature* (Vancouver), Autumn 1964; "To Souster with Vermont" by Hayden Carruth, in *Tamarack Review* (Toronto), Winter 1965; introduction by Michael Macklem to *Selected Poems*, 1972.

Raymond Souster comments:

Whoever I write to, I want to make the substance of the poem so immediate, so real, so clear, that the reader feels the same exhilaration – be it fear or joy – that I derived from the experience, object or mood that triggered the poem in the first place. . . . I like to think I'm "talking out" my poems rather than consciously dressing them up in the trappings of the academic school. For many years I held to the theory that all poetry must be written out of a sudden spontaneous impulse in which the poet is unbearably moved to write down the words of that vision. Now I am more inclined to echo the view of Giuseppi Ungaretti when he says: "Between one flower gathered and the other given, the inexpressible Null."

*   *   *

The title of a book of poems by Raymond Souster is *As Is*. That is exactly the way the world is to be found in the work of Souster, as is, without idealistic impositions, without ideological distortion. The area of his approach and the locality it is centred upon can be pursued through any of his titles. He is after "The Colour of the Times" without sentimental illusions. "Shake Hands with the Hangman," he tells us, realistically but without sombre destitution; life is "A Dream That Is Dying." Mortal but with comic integrity, we are engaged in a "Crêpe-Hanger's Carnival." His "Place of Meeting" is Toronto. No Canadian poet has exploited a Canadian city for more truth than Souster has Toronto. It is "A Local Pride" for him. But be careful. You may not have as much pride in your city as you think you have:

> The finger of Christ
> points straight from his pedestal
> on the Church of the Sailors
> down history-crawling streets
> to Joe Beef's, the oldest
> loudest tavern in town.

On its streets you are likely to meet a drunk on crutches,

> Like this one now: this corpse,
> This living death coming toward you.

Our urban world is not likely to turn out pretty – not if you have Souster's perspicacious eye and his peripatetic shoes. Harbouring all the compassion in the world, you are likely to be arrested for loitering. Move on and take refuge in computerization. Get cardboarded. It is the only safe way to escape the penalties of being human. Even so, you are likely to get punched:

> Wrap yourself well in that cheap coat that holds back
>   the wind like a sieve,
> you have a long way to go, the streets are dark, you
>   may have to walk all night before you can find
> another heart as lonely.

In this disillusioned stance, there is always the danger of becoming an inverted romantic. The bum is the hero. There is always the cynic's disease of blaming man for the cold glitter of the inimical stars. The city of Toronto is responsible for the acne on a girl's face. This is the shuffle dealt out by the freaked-out poets.

Souster does not whine. He knows we are all a little mad, that after our last beer the door opens on nothing, on darkness

> into which we walk
> dead drunk or chanting poetry
>
> but upright, still with the living
> my friend.

He can apostrophize a drunken clock, a hollyhock, and birds

> which any moment
> may begin to sing!
>
> Who knows, my heart
> may beat again
> quick as the slap
> of the first skipping rope
> of spring.

Yonge Street is the ugliest main street of Toronto. Souster has ten grey elephants going up it, literally and metaphorically:

> Ten grey eminences moving
> with the daintiest of steps
> and the greatest unconcern
> up the canyon.

His circus roller coaster takes off into the Empyrean.

Souster says: "I want to make the substance of the poem so immediate, so real, so clear, that the reader feels the same exhilaration – be it fear or joy – that I derived from the experience, object or mood that triggered the poem in the first place." He does.

– Ralph Gustafson

SOYINKA, Wole (Akinwande Oluwole Soyinka).   Nigerian.   Born in Abeokuta, 13 July 1934. Educated at Government College, Ibadan; University of Leeds, York-shire, 1954–57, B.A. (honours) in English. Married; has children. Play Reader, Royal Court Theatre, London, 1958–59; Research Fellow in Drama, University of Ibadan, 1960–61; Lecturer in English, University of Ife, 1962–63; Senior Lecturer in English, University of Lagos, 1964–67; Director of the School of Drama, University of Ibadan, 1969–72. Since 1972, Research Professor in Drama, University of Ife. Founding Director of the Orisun Theatre and the 1960 Masks theatre, Lagos and Ibadan. Political Prisoner, Lagos and Kaduna, 1967–69. Recipient: Dakar Negro Arts Festival award, for drama, 1966; John Whiting award, for drama, 1966; Jock Campbell Award (*New Statesman*), for fiction, 1968. D.Litt: University of Leeds, 1973. Agent: Morton Leavy, Weissberger and Frosch, 120 East 56th Street, New York, New York 10022, U.S.A. Address: c/o University of Ife, London Office, 56 Hallam Street, London W.1, England.

PUBLICATIONS

Verse

  Idanre and Other Poems.   London, Methuen, 1967; New York, Hill and Wang, 1968.
  A Shuttle in the Crypt.   London, Eyre Methuen-Rex Collings, and New York, Hill and Wang, 1972.

Plays

  The Swamp Dwellers (produced Ibadan and London, 1958; New York, 1968).   Included in *Three Plays*, 1963; *Five Plays*, 1964.
  The Lion and the Jewel (produced Ibadan, 1959; London, 1966).   London, Ibadan, and New York, Oxford University Press, 1963.
  The Invention (produced London, 1959).
  A Dance of the Forests (produced Ibadan, 1960).   London, Ibadan, and New York, Oxford University Press, 1963.
  The Trials of Brother Jero (produced Ibadan, 1960; Cambridge, 1965; London, 1966; New York, 1967).   Included in *Three Plays*, 1963; *Five Plays*, 1964.
  Camwood on the Leaves (broadcast, 1960).   London, Eyre Methuen, 1972; in *Camwood on the Leaves, and Before the Blackout*, 1974.

Three Plays: The Trials of Brother Jero, The Swamp Dwellers, The Strong Breed. Ibadan, Mbari, 1963.

The Strong Breed (produced Ibadan, 1964; London, 1966; New York, 1967). Included in *Three Plays,* 1963; *Five Plays,* 1964.

Kongi's Harvest (produced Ibadan, 1964; New York, 1968). London, Ibadan, and New York, Oxford University Press, 1967.

Five Plays: A Dance of the Forests, The Lion and the Jewel, The Swamp Dwellers, The Trials of Brother Jero, The Strong Breed. London, Ibadan, and New York, Oxford University Press, 1964.

Before the Blackout (produced Ibadan, 1964). Lagos, Orisun Editions, 1971; in *Camwood on the Leaves, and Before the Blackout,* 1974.

The Road (produced London, 1965). London, Ibadan, and New York, Oxford University Press, 1965.

Madmen and Specialists (produced Waterford, Connecticut, and New York, 1970; revised version, produced Ibadan, 1971). London, Methuen, 1971; New York, Hill and Wang, 1972.

The Jero Plays: The Trials of Brother Jero and Jero's Metamorphosis. London, Eyre Methuen, 1972.

The Bacchae: A Communion Rite, adaptation of the play by Euripides (produced London, 1973). London, Eyre Methuen, 1973; New York, Norton, 1974.

Collected Plays:
   I. *A Dance of the Forest, The Swamp Dweller, The Strong Breed, The Road, The Bacchae.* London and New York, Oxford University Press, 1974.
   II. *The Lion and the Jewel, Kongi's Harvest, The Trials of Brother Jero, Metamorphosis, Madmen and Specialists.* London and New York, Oxford University Press, 1974.

Camwood on the Leaves, and Before the Blackout: Two Short Plays. New York, Third Press, 1974.

Radio Play: *Camwood on the Leaves,* 1960 (U.K.).

Television Plays: *Joshua: A Nigerian Portrait,* 1962 (Canada); *Culture in Transition,* 1963 (U.S.A.).

Novels

The Interpreters. London, Deutsch, 1965; New York, Macmillan, 1970.
Season of Anomy. London, Rex Collings, 1973; New York, Third Press, 1974.

Other

The Man Died: Prison Memoirs. London, Eyre Methuen-Rex Collings, and New York, Harper, 1972.

Editor, *Poems of Black Africa.* London, Secker and Warburg, 1974; New York, Hill and Wang, 1975.

Translator, *The Forest of a Thousand Daemons: A Hunter's Saga,* by D. A. Fagunwa. London, Nelson, 1968; New York, Humanities Press, 1969.

Critical Study: *The Writing of Wole Soyinka* by Eldred Jones, London, Heinemann, 1972.

Theatrical Activities:

  Director: **Plays** – by Brecht, Chekhov, Clark, Easmon, Eseoghene, Ogunyemi, Shakespeare, Synge, and his own works; *L'Espace et la Magie*, Paris, 1972.

                          *   *   *

  Wole Soyinka's first volume of collected poems, *Idanre and Other Poems*, is a significant guide to the direction of the author's work. Soyinka first made his name as a writer of light satirical verse in poems like "Telephone Conversation," "The Immigrant," and "The Other Immigrant," all of which he has excluded from this collection. A pre-occupation with more sombre themes is represented by "Requiem" (also, and more surprisingly, excluded from the collected poems) where he explores the continuing but tenuous relationship between the dead and the living. He expresses this elusive relationship in a series of delicate images suggestive of barely perceptible contact:

> You leave your faint depressions
> Skim-flying still, on the still pond's surface.
> Where darkness crouches, egret wings
> Your love is gossamer.

  Soyinka's pre-occupation with death and beyond is one of the features of his later poetry and drama. It is one of the central themes of his play *The Road*. Soyinka seems, for example, to have become increasingly fascinated by the instant transformation from life to death which is caused by death at speed. His poem "Death in the Dawn" ends with the startled recognition by a victim of a car crash of this transformation:

> Brother,
> Silenced in the startled hug of
> Your invention – is this mocked grimace
> This closed contortion – I?

Several pictures of this kind occur in Soyinka's prose, poetry, and drama. Indeed one of his impressive features is his consistency between genres and over the whole period of his writing. Similar passages can be quoted from his drama and his novel *The Interpreters*. This one from *The Road* illustrates the vivid poetic qualities even of his prose:

> . . . a madness where a motor-car throws itself
> against a tree – Gbram! And showers of crystal
> flying on broken souls.

  In a magazine interview Soyinka spoke about his "personal intimacy which I have developed with a certain aspect of the road . . . it concerns the reality of death. . . ." Death on the road has burned itself into Soyinka's consciousness through a series of personal encounters.
  Death on the road is a kind of sacrifice to "progress," a notion which Soyinka treats with extreme scepticism. But sacrifice – self-sacrifice – martyrdom is another

theme with which Soyinka has become increasingly concerned. Society often destroys its greatest benefactors; indeed it is ironically through the willingness of
sensitive souls to suffer martyrdom if necessary that society advances. This is the
central theme both of his play *The Strong Breed* and "The Dreamer," a poem
based on the idea of the Crucifixion. The dreamer (like Eman in *The Strong Breed*)
is martyred in his prime, but in the final stanza of the poem there is the suggestion
that out of his bitter suffering arises a new and powerful growth:

> The burden bowed the boughs to earth
> A girdle for the see
> And bitter pods gave voices birth
> A ring of stones
> And throes and thrones
> And incense on the sea.

This theme, that society needs these victims for its own salvation, is a very
important one in Soyinka's writing. The captain in his play *A Dance of the Forests* is
emasculated and sold into slavery for sticking to his principles – in this case a
refusal to fight in a causeless war. There is evidence of Soyinka's growing concern
with man's incorrigible urge for self-destruction through war. Nowhere is this
better portrayed than in the long poem "Idanre" in which, using what he has now
become the dominant figure in his writing, Ogun, he pictures the god who, having
been invited by men to fight on their behalf, is unable to distinguish friend from
foe:

> He strides sweat encrusted
> Bristles on risen tendons
> Porcupine and barbed. Again he turns
> Into his men, butcher's axe
> Rises and sinks
>
> Behind it, a guest no one
> Can recall.

The poem "Idanre" neatly exhibits Soyinka's poetic. In his essay "And after the
Narcissist" (*African Forum*, Spring 1968) he had put forward Ogun as the perfect
symbol of the unity of the creative and destructive principle:

> Primogenitor of the artist as the creative human, Ogun is the antithesis of
> cowardice and Philistinism, yet within him is contained also the comple-
> ment of the creative essence, a blood thirsty destructiveness.

In "Idanre" the contradictory union of death and growth is frequently pictured:

> growth is greener where
> Rich blood has spilt; brain and marrow make
> Fat manure with sheep's excrement.

Soyinka's work is an attempt to formulate a meaning out of the contradictory
forces that goven human life and actions. This is why Ogun who unites these two
qualities without separating them is now so important in Soyinka's symbolism.
  Soyinka himself effects a similar indissoluble fusion in his work between African
and European influences. European dramatic and poetic conventions are fused with
African conventions and ways of thought to produce an original type of poetry. He
invokes the pantheon of Yoruba gods to forge a new ethic whose validity is not

confined to Africa. He imbues English with a verve and an expansiveness which spring from the imagic nature of Yoruba speech. This is what makes Soyinka, both as an African and as a world writer.

– Eldred D. Jones

SPARK, Muriel (Sarah).   British.   Born in Edinburgh. Educated at James Gillespie's School for Girls, Edinburgh. Married S. O. Spark in 1937 (divorced); has one child. Worked in the Political Intelligence Department of the British Foreign Office during World War II. General Secretary of the Poetry Society, and Editor of the *Poetry Review*, London, 1947–49. Recipient: *The Observer* Story Prize, 1951; Italia Prize, for radio drama, 1962; Black Memorial Prize, 1966. LL.D.: University of Strathclyde, Glasgow, 1971. O.B.E. (Officer, Order of the British Empire), 1967. Lives in Rome. Address: c/o Macmillan and Company, 4 Little Essex Street, London W.C.2, England.

PUBLICATIONS

Verse

> *The Fanfarlo and Other Verse.*   Aldington, Kent, Hand and Flowers Press, 1952.
> *Collected Poems I.*   London, Macmillan, 1967.

Plays

> *The Party Through the Wall* (broadcast, 1957).   Included in *Voices at Play*, 1961.
> *The Interview* (broadcast, 1958).   Included in *Voices at Play*, 1961.
> *The Dry River Bed* (broadcast, 1959).   Included in *Voices at Play*, 1961.
> *Danger Zone* (broadcast, 1961).   Included in *Voices at Play*, 1961.
> *Doctors of Philosophy* (produced London, 1962).   London, Macmillan, 1963.

> Radio Plays: *The Party Through the Wall*, 1957; *The Interview*, 1958; *The Dry River Bed*, 1959; *The Ballad of Peckham Rye*, 1960; *Danger Zone*, 1961.

Novels

> *The Comforters.*   London, Macmillan, and Philadelphia, Lippincott, 1957.
> *Robinson.*   London, Macmillan, and Philadelphia, Lippincott, 1958.
> *Memento Mori.*   London, Macmillan, and Philadelphia, Lippincott, 1959.
> *The Ballad of Peckham Rye.*   London, Macmillan, and Philadelphia, Lippincott, 1960.
> *The Bachelors.*   London, Macmillan, 1960; Philadelphia, Lippincott, 1961.

The Prime of Miss Jean Brodie. London, Macmillan, 1961; Philadelphia, Lippincott, 1962.
The Girls of Slender Means. London, Macmillan, and New York, Knopf, 1963.
The Mandelbaum Gate. London, Macmillan, and New York, Knopf, 1965.
The Public Image. London, Macmillan, and New York, Knopf, 1968.
The Driver's Seat. London, Macmillan, and New York, Knopf, 1970.
Not to Disturb. London, Macmillan, 1971; New York, Viking Press, 1972.
The Hothouse by the East River. London, Macmillan, and New York, Viking Press, 1972.
The Abbess of Crewe: A Modern Morality Tale. London, Macmillan, and New York, Viking Press, 1974.

Short Stories

The Go-Away Bird and Other Stories. London, Macmillan, 1958; Philadelphia, Lippincott, 1960.
Voices at Play (includes radio plays). London, Macmillan, 1961.
Collected Stories I. London, Macmillan, 1967; New York, Knopf, 1968.

Other

Child of Light: A Reassessment of Mary Shelley. London, Tower Bridge Publications, 1951.
Emily Brontë: Her Life and Work, with Derek Stanford. London, Peter Owen, 1953.
John Masefield. London, Peter Nevill, 1953.
The Very Fine Clock (juvenile). New York, Knopf, 1958; London, Macmillan, 1969.

Editor, with Derek Stanford, *Tribute to Wordsworth.* London, Wingate, 1950.
Editor, *A Selection of Poems,* by Emily Brontë. London, Grey Walls Press, 1952.
Editor, with Derek Stanford, *My Best Mary: The Letters of Mary Shelley.* London, Wingate, 1953; Folcroft, Pennsylvania, Folcroft Editions, 1972.
Editor, *The Brontë Letters.* London, Peter Nevill, 1954.
Editor, with Derek Stanford, *Letters of John Henry Newman.* London, Peter Owen, 1957.

Critical Studies: *Muriel Spark* by Karl Malkoff, New York, Columbia University Press, 1968; *Muriel Spark* by Peter Kemp, London, Elek, 1974.

*   *   *

"What's good enough for Archimedes / Ought to be good enough for me" ("Elementary"): Muriel Spark's verse mocks the inadequacy of scientific definition and rejoices in "An odd capacity for vision." Though "Against the Transcendentalists" elevates "poets" over "visionaries" and hopes ". . . that if Byzantium / Should appear in Kensington / The city will fit the size / Of the perimeter of my eyes / And of the span of my hand," the poem paradoxically celebrates the miracle these limits create: "The flesh made word." And the Kensington that obsesses a number of other poems is "Kensington of dreadful night" ("The Pearl-Miners"), where the persona invokes "latent Christ" ("Elegy in a Kensington Churchyard"). Sometimes the miraculous becomes merely the talking steel chairs of familiar satire on human interchangeability with artifacts ("A Visit"). Conversely, the elegant colloquialism of "Fruitless Fable," a chronicle of Mr. Chiddicott's sudden enslavement by his "perfected tea-machine," raises the poem from mock-heroic moral fable ("Alas, the transience of bliss –") to genuine fantasy. Occasionally fantasy dramatizes obsession with ". . . my other / who sounds my superstition like a bagpipe" ("Intermittence"), or with ". . . the momentary name I gave / To a slight stir in a fictitious grave" ("Evelyn Cavallo").

Spark's most ambitious fusion of obsession with fantasy creates the "tremorous metropolis" of "The Ballad of the Fanfarlo," a hallucinatory "settlement of fever," in which vocal traffic lights and ether bowls seem as ordinary or extraordinary as everything else. This nightmare continuation of Baudelaire's prose satire traces the quest of the Romantic poet Samuel Cramer for his alter ego Manuela de Monteverde and the dancer Fanfarlo, but significantly changes the tone of the original. Baudelaire's Cramer ultimately edits a socialist journal and presumably no longer signs Manuela's name to "quelques folies romantiques," while Spark's hero, either true to his early vision or atoning for his defection, is willing to endure the horrors of "No-Man's Sanitorium" in his quest. Despite a generous epigraph from Baudelaire, the poem's atmosphere and stanza form suggest "The Ancient Mariner" and, at times, "Sir Patrick Spens" as filtered through Coleridge's "Dejection: An Ode": "The new moon like a pair of surgical forceps / With the old moon in her jaws." Only in such passages, when Spark defines Romantic art through parody, does the poem achieve the simultaneous recreation and mockery of Baudelaire toward which it aims.

Cramer is funnier in a brief appearance as a visiting journalist in "The Nativity," when he replies to rumors of mysterious happenings at the inn: "No good to me if it's local." "The Nativity," Spark's longest religious poem, precariously blends faith and fantasy in a portrait of bizarre wise men: "You with the nose on top of your head, smell out / The principalities of heaven for all of us." Riddling wit defines the limits of religious mystery in shorter works, "Conundrum," "Holy Water Rondel," and "Faith and Works" ("We are the truest saint alive / As near as two and two make five"). Even an apparently secular exercise like "The Rout," which fuses, in the manner of Marianne Moore, a news article about a battle between bees and wasps in a village church with a dispatch from Cromwell, reinforced by quotations from Lawrence and The Pocket Book of British Insects: The Honey Bee, produces not only the eloquent parody of "The murder of innumerable bees," but also an elegant questioning of man's relation to the rest of creation. Like Spark's seemingly casual treatment of religion, the moralizing is always implicit, offhand. However complex her tone, Spark's forms are generally traditional. The more controlled the verse, the more the strictness of the pattern causes a concentration in theme that becomes incantatory:

> These eyes that saw the saturnine
>
> Waters no provident whim made wine
> Fail to infuriate the dull
> Heart of Midlothian, never mine.

> – "Edinburgh Villanelle"

> – Burton Kendle

SPEAR, Charles.   New Zealander.   Born in Owaka, in 1910. Formerly a journalist and teacher. Currently, Lecturer in English, University of Canterbury, Christchurch. Address: Department of English, University of Canterbury, Christchurch, New Zealand.

PUBLICATIONS

Verse

Twopence Coloured: Poems.   Christchurch, Caxton Press, 1951.

*   *   *

With one volume of poems, *Twopence Coloured,* which has had no successor, Charles Spear has made a special place for himself in New Zealand poetry. Unlike most of the poets of his time, except R. A. K. Mason, his work pays little attention to the people, the landscape or the specific national concerns of New Zealand. His subject-matter derives in great part from his own experiences in European countries, their history, literature, and scenery, and from his own generous reading. His poems are not, however, descriptive, but subtle, at times enigmatic, pieces, conveying a mood or a sensation and delicately using symbolism to express a mature acceptance of the inevitability of pain, change, sacrifice and loss, while yet remaining curious about life and what it brings.

A number of poems in *Twopence Coloured,* too, show a response to the accidentals of social life, places and things which, in their elusiveness and occasional preciosity, recall the poems of Wilde, Dowson and others of the Nineties. The technical assurance, breadth of allusion and cultivated sensibility which mark the poems make the poetic persona they present a very intriguing one indeed. Mr. Spear does not embark upon subjects beyond his range, but within it achieves an exquisite finish and completeness, so that his best pieces are admirable artefacts.

– J. C. Reid

SPENDER, Stephen (Harold).   British.   Born in London, 28 September 1909; son of the writer Harold Spender. Educated at University College School, London; University College, Oxford. Served as a fireman in the National Fire Service, 1941–44. Married Agnes Marie Pearn in 1936; Natasha Litvin, 1941; has one son and one daughter. Editor, with Cyril Connolly, *Horizon* magazine, London, 1939–41; Co-Editor, 1953–66, and Corresponding Editor, 1966–67, *Encounter* magazine, London. Counsellor, UNESCO Section of Letters, 1947. Elliston Lecturer, University of Cincinnati, 1953; Beckman Professor, University of California, Berkeley, 1959; Visiting Professor, Northwestern University, Evanston, Illinois, 1963; Clark Lecturer, Cambridge University, 1966; Visiting Professor, University of Connecticut, Storrs, 1968–70; Mellon Lecturer, Washington, D.C., 1968; Northcliffe Lecturer, London University, 1969. Since 1970, Professor of English Literature, University College, London. Consultant in Poetry in English, Library of Congress, Washington, D.C., 1965–66. Honorary Member, Phi Beta Kappa, Harvard University, Cambridge, Massachusetts; Fellow of the Institute of Advanced Studies,

Wesleyan University, Middletown, Connecticut, 1967. Recipient: Queen's Gold Medal for Poetry, 1971. D.Litt.: University of Montpelier; Loyola University, Chicago. Honorary Member, American Academy of Arts and Letters, 1969. C.B.E. (Companion, Order of the British Empire), 1962. Address: 15 Loudoun Road, London N.W.8, England.

PUBLICATIONS

Verse

Nine Experiments by S. H. S.: Being Poems Written at the Age of Eighteen.   London, privately printed, 1928.
20 Poems.   Oxford, Blackwell, 1930.
Poems.   London, Faber, 1933; New York, Random House, 1934; revised edition, Faber, 1934.
Vienna.   London, Faber, 1934; New York, Random House, 1935.
At Night.   Cambridge, privately printed, 1935.
The Still Centre.   London, Faber, 1939.
Selected Poems.   London, Faber, 1940.
I Sit by the Window.   N.p., Linden Press, n.d.
Ruins and Visions.   London, Faber, and New York, Random House, 1942.
Spiritual Exercises (To Cecil Day Lewis).   London, privately printed, 1943.
Poems of Dedication.   London, Faber, 1946; New York, Random House, 1947.
Returning to Vienna 1947: Nine Sketches.   Pawlet, Vermont, Banyan Press, 1947.
The Edge of Being.   London, Faber, and New York, Random House, 1949.
Sirmione Peninsula.   London, Faber, 1954.
Collected Poems 1928–1953.   London, Faber, and New York, Random House, 1955.
Inscriptions.   London, Poetry Book Society, 1958.
Selected Poems.   New York, Random House, 1964; London, Faber, 1965.
The Generous Days: Ten Poems.   Boston, D. R. Godine, 1969; augmented edition, as The Generous Days, London, Faber, and New York, Random House, 1971.
Descartes.   London, Steam Press, 1970.
Art Student.   London, Poem-of-the-Month Club, 1970.
Penguin Modern Poets 20, with John Heath-Stubbs and F. T. Prince.   London, Penguin, 1971.

Recordings: Stephen Spender Reading His Own Poems, Argo, 1958; Stephen Spender Reading His Own Poems, Caedmon.

Plays

Trial of a Judge (produced London, 1938).   London, Faber, and New York, Random House, 1938.
Danton's Death, with Goronwy Rees, adaptation of a play by Georg Büchner (produced London, 1939).   London, Faber, 1939; in From the Modern Repertory, edited by Eric Bentley, Bloomington, Indiana University Press, 1958.
To the Island (produced Oxford, 1951).

Mary Stuart, adaptation of the play by Schiller (produced New York, 1957; Edinburgh and London, 1958). London, Faber, 1959.

Lulu, adaptation of the play by Frank Wedekind (produced New York, 1958).

Rasputin's End, music by Nicholas Nabokov. Milan, Ricordi, 1963.

Novel

The Backward Son. London, Hogarth Press, 1940.

Short Stories

The Burning Cactus. London, Faber, and New York, Random House, 1936.

Engaged in Writing, and The Fool and the Princess. London, Hamish Hamilton, and New York, Farrar Straus, 1958.

Other

The Destructive Element: A Study of Modern Writers and Beliefs. London, Cape, 1935; Philadelphia, Saifer, 1953.

Forward from Liberalism. London, Gollancz, and New York, Random House, 1937.

The New Realism: A Discussion. London, Hogarth Press, 1939.

Life and the Poet. London, Secker and Warburg, 1942; Folcroft, Pennsylvania, Folcroft Editions, 1974.

Jim Braidy: The Story of Britain's Firemen, with William Sansom and James Gordon. London, Drummond, 1943.

Citizens in War – and After. London, Harrap, 1945.

Botticelli. London, Faber, 1945; New York, Pitman, 1948.

European Witness (on Germany). London, Hamish Hamilton, and New York, Reynal, 1946.

Poetry since 1939. London and New York, Longman, 1946.

Crossman. London, Hamish Hamilton, and New York, Harper, 1950.

World Within World: The Autobiography of Stephen Spender. London, Hamish Hamilton, and New York, Harcourt Brace, 1951.

Europe in Photographs. London, Thames and Hudson, 1951.

Shelley. London, Longman, 1952.

Learning Laughter (on Israel). London, Weidenfeld and Nicolson, 1952; New York, Harcourt Brace, 1953.

The Creative Element: A Study of Vision, Despair, and Orthodoxy among Some Modern Writers. London, Hamish Hamilton, 1953.

The Making of a Poem (essays). London, Hamish Hamilton, 1955; New York, Norton, 1962.

The Imagination in the Modern World: Three Lectures. Washington, D. C., Library of Congress, 1962.

The Struggle of the Modern. London, Hamish Hamilton, and Berkeley, University of California Press, 1963.

Ghika: Paintings, Drawings, Sculpture, with Patrick Leigh Fermor. London, Lund Humphries, 1964; Boston, Boston Book and Art Shop, 1965.

The Magic Flute: Retold. New York, Putnam, 1966.

Chaos and Control in Poetry. Washington, D.C., Library of Congress, 1966.

The Year of the Young Rebels. London, Weidenfeld and Nicolson, and New York, Random House, 1969.

Love-Hate Relations: A Study of Anglo-American Sensibilities. London, Hamish
  Hamilton, and New York, Random House, 1974.
W. H. Auden: A Tribute. New York, Macmillan, 1975.

Editor, with Louis MacNeice, *Oxford Poetry 1929.* Oxford, Blackwell, 1929.
Editor, with Bernard Spencer, *Oxford Poetry 1930.* Oxford, Blackwell, 1930.
Editor, with John Lehmann and Christopher Isherwood, *New Writing, New
  Series I* and *II.* London, Hogarth Press, 1938, 1939.
Editor, with John Lehmann, *Poems for Spain.* London, Hogarth Press, 1939.
Editor, *A Choice of English Romantic Poetry.* New York, Dial Press, 1947.
Editor, *Selected Poems,* by Walt Whitman. London, Grey Walls Press, 1950.
Editor, with Elizabeth Jennings and Dannie Abse, *New Poems 1956: A P.E.N.
  Anthology.* London, Joseph, 1956.
Editor, *Great Writings of Goethe.* New York, New American Library, 1958.
Editor, *Great German Short Stories.* New York, Dell, 1960.
Editor, *The Writer's Dilemma.* London, Oxford University Press, 1961.
Editor, with Donald Hall, *The Concise Encyclopedia of English and American
  Poets and Poetry.* London, Hutchinson, and New York, Hawthorn Books,
  1963; revised edition, 1970.
Editor, with Irving Kristol and Melvin J. Lasky, *Encounters: An Anthology from
  Its First Ten Years.* London, Weidenfeld and Nicolson, and New York,
  Basic Books, 1963.
Editor, *Selected Poems,* by Abba Kovner and Nelly Sachs. London, Penguin,
  1971.
Editor, *A Choice of Shelley's Verse.* London, Faber, 1971.
Editor, *D. H. Lawrence: Novelist, Poet, Prophet.* London, Weidenfeld and
  Nicolson, and New York, Harper, 1973.
Editor, *The Poems of Percy Bysshe Shelley.* New York, Heritage Press, 1974.

Translator, *Pastor Hall,* by Ernst Toller. London, Lane, 1939.
Translator, with J. L. Gili, *Poems,* by García Lorca. London, Dolphin, and
  New York, Oxford University Press, 1939.
Translator, with J. B. Leishman, *Duino Elegies,* by Rainer Maria Rilke. Lon-
  don, Hogarth Press, and New York, Norton, 1939; revised edition, Hogarth
  Press, 1948, Norton, 1963.
Translator, with J. L. Gili, *Selected Poems,* by García Lorca. London, Hogarth
  Press, 1943.
Translator, with Frances Cornford, *Le dur Désir de Durer,* by Paul Eluard.
  London, Faber, and New York, New Directions, 1950.
Translator, *The Life of the Virgin Mary (Das Marien-Leben)* (bilingual edition),
  by Rainer Maria Rilke. London, Vision Press, and New York, Philosoph-
  ical Library, 1951.
Translator, with Frances Fawcett, *Five Tragedies of Sex* (includes *Spring's
  Awakening, Earth-Spirit, Pandora's Box, Death and Devil, Castle Wetterstein),*
  by Frank Wedekind. London, Vision Press, 1952.

Bibliography: *The Early Published Poems of Stephen Spender: A Chronology* by A. T.
Tolley, Ottawa, Carleton University, 1967.

*   *   *

In *The Destructive Element* Stephen Spender described the difficulties of writing
about contemporaries: "One is dealing in a literature of few accepted values. At

best one can offer opinions . . . at worst, bookmaking, or stockbroking." He goes on to consider a question vital to understanding his own work; he is interested in writers "faced by the destructive element, i.e., by the experience of an all-pervading Present, which is a world without belief." It is easily possible to regard Spender's poetry sympathetically as a near-traumatic reaction to "a void in the present," and much of his personal experience, e.g., his commitment and later disengagement involving communism, can be interpreted as a search for belief. Even the intensity of his well-known personal and literary loyalties (e.g., with Auden and Isherwood) and the value he has given to them in his autobiographies assume a new dimension in this light. Even in his journalism, his book on the Youth Aliyah effort to make homes for Jewish children in the Kibbutzim of Israel (*Learning Laughter*), his book based on journals kept on a trip through Germany in 1945 (*European Witness*), his book on student unrest, a reader can discern a kind of seeking for belief; there is an element of wander-literature, even of Quixote – for Spender's faults are those of idealistic generalizing, of a frequent, often irritating naïvety.

His search for a metaphor in Berlin is perhaps illustrative: "At first Berlin seemed less damaged than I had expected, but as we approached the centre of the town it produced the same impression of desolation as all the other large German towns. . . ." A picture emerges, of a haunted palace – something out of Poe: "Charwomen responsible for the upkeep of the Chancellory, and still performing their tasks, concealed on their persons hammers with which they broke off fragments of the yellow marble top of this [Hitler's] desk as souvenirs in exchange for a few cigarettes." He concludes that "the Nazi and the Fascist leaders were often disappointed artists," somehow linking up the Nazi fate with "the gloom of Tennyson, the ennui of Baudelaire and the pessimism of Thomas Hardy." Spender carries away a piece of Hitler's desk. Commenting on its significance as an "unholy relic," he concludes that the Nazis taught us the necessity of choosing between good and evil.

Earlier, a friend had remarked on Spender's poems: "When you write in this way you are filled with social despair, and you have no religious or political beliefs whatever. Directly, out of a sense of conscience, you try to introduce a constructive idea into your writing, you fail." "All the same," Spender replies, "one must look for a constructive idea. If one has the sense of despair and of evil, then one must look for the sense of hope and of good with which to confront despair and evil."

It is perhaps this idealism, and the linking of abstraction with imagery (a Spender play concerns "the belief that man / can overthrow systems of injustice / and build systems of justice") that determine the final tone of a Spender poem.

> The secret of these hills was stone, and cottages
> Of that stone made,
> And crumbling roads
> That turned on sudden hidden villages

he writes in "The Pylons." But soon comes the intervention of politics, of the dark awareness:

> Now over these small hills they have built the concrete
> That trails black wire:
> Pylons, those pillars
> Bare like nude, giant girls that have no secret.

On thinks sometimes that Spender wanted to be the kind of poet George Orwell might have been; and appropriately, his best poems are perhaps those about the

Spanish Civil War, in *The Still Centre* (especially "A Stop Watch and an Ordnance Map" and "Fall of a City"), though poems like "I Think Continually of Those Who Were Truly Great," "The Express," and "The Landscape near an Aerodrome" are justly famous. Certain lines of Spender's echo through the minds of anyone familiar with a modern anthology:

> Eye, gazelle, delicate wanderer,
> Drinker of horizon's fluid line;
> Ear that suspends on a chord
> The spirit drinking timelessness. . . .

And who can forget the opening lines of "The Express"?

> After the first powerful plain manifesto
> The black statement of pistons, without more fuss
> But gliding like a queen, she leaves the station

passing

> gasworks and at last the heavy page
> Of death, printed by gravestones in the cemetery.

With the "jazzy madness" of the train we feel a growing confidence in the poet's power, his own confidence in his own as the train arrives at "Edinburgh or Rome."

Perhaps it is difficult to recapture a sense of relevance when it comes to remembering why Spender thought C. Day Lewis shouldn't be afraid of communists, or how Spender himself changed toward "the god that failed" but we can easily recall from some distance the way Spender has developed certain obsessive ideas about death and fame:

> For how shall we prove that we really exist
> Unless we hear, over and over,
> Our ego through the world persist
> With all the guns of the self-lover?

Through everything Spender has written has run the same idealism. And a reader can hear it as he speaks in *European Witness* of "a desire to see an International Review for Europe, on the very highest level, in which the best German writers were published side by side with English and French, and perhaps with Russian ones too." There everything was going to be "discussed very seriously and with equal frankness by thinkers of all nations, since they would be on a level which was human and not immediately controversial." Spender's final appeal to many readers is probably to an idealism they have themselves failed to keep alive.

– David Ray

SQUIRES, (James) Radcliffe. American. Born in Salt Lake City, Utah, 23 May 1917. Educated at the University of Utah, Salt Lake City, B.A. 1940; University of

Chicago (John Billings Fiske Prize, 1946), A.M. 1945; Harvard University, Cambridge, Massachusetts, Ph.D. 1952. Served in the United States Navy, 1941–45. Married Eileen Mulholland in 1945. Instructor, Dartmouth College, Hanover, New Hampshire, 1946–48. Since 1952, Professor of English, University of Michigan, Ann Arbor. Fulbright Professor of American Culture, Salonika, Greece, 1959–60. Editor, *Chicago Review*, 1945–46, and since 1970, *Michigan Quarterly Review*, Ann Arbor. Recipient: *Voices* magazine Young Poets Prize, 1947. Address: 7270 Warren Road, Ann Arbor, Michigan 48105, U.S.A.

PUBLICATIONS

Verse

Cornar. Philadelphia, Dorrance, 1940.
Where the Compass Spins. New York, Twayne, 1951.
Fingers of Hermes: Poems. Ann Arbor, University of Michigan Press, and London, Cresset Press, 1965.
The Light under Islands: Poems. Ann Arbor, University of Michigan Press, and London, Cresset Press, 1967.
Daedalus. Ann Arbor, Michigan, Generation Press, 1968.
Waiting in the Bone. Omaha, Nebraska, Cummington Press, 1973.

Other

The Loyalties of Robinson Jeffers. Ann Arbor, University of Michigan Press, and London, Oxford University Press, 1956.
The Major Themes of Robert Frost. Ann Arbor, University of Michigan Press, and London, Cresset Press, 1963.
Frederic Prokosch. New York, Twayne, 1964.
Allen Tate: A Literary Biography. Indianapolis, Bobbs Merrill, 1971.

Editor, *Allen Tate and His Work: Critical Evaluations.* Minneapolis, University of Minnesota Press, and London, Oxford University Press, 1972.

Radcliffe Squires comments:

I suppose that my major themes involve a belief I have that we have gotten too far out of Nature, we humans, ever to be able to think of it as home again. This has shaken our beliefs far more than the loss of religion has, so that it often seems to me that the only faith man is capable of today is one in which he tells himself that he cannot be good, but that at least he can be wicked, which is better than being nothing. Though this gloomy view haunts much of what I do, my poems owe more to a sense of place, mountains, the Mediterranean, than they do to any dogma.

Technically my verse tends to fall into blank verse with occasional or accidental rhyme. I am not a formalist, but I should feel sheepish to turn out a poem with less metrical discipline than iambics provide. Even so, if I should have to choose between meter and metaphor, I should take metaphor, for metaphor seems to me the essence of poetry, the poem within a poem. Luckily, poetry never insists on taking one thing or the other. I believe there are colorings in my verse that come from Thomas Hardy, Robinson Jeffers, T. S. Eliot, Wallace Stevens, W. H. Auden, and C. P. Cavafy. At any rate, I have admired these poets very deeply.

*   *   *

The quiet voice of Radcliffe Squires speaks through an extraordinary imagination. His poems are romantic in theme, yet metaphysical, heroic in scope, and yet delicate. It is as if the visionary élan of a Robinson Jeffers were grafted on to lyrical, narrative gifts of a Robert Frost.

Although all Squires's poems share common properties – wit, thought, and a philosophy of nature in which Man is a sacred, yet ruinous intrusion – they tend to fall into four distinct groups. His longer poems are parables drawn from mythology: Beowulf, Hercules, Daedalus. Squires uses these heroes as emblems of human creativity and self-discovery, often blurring the edge of his narrative with hermetic allusions. In his last three books, these long mythical poems are offset by shorter ones describing places, principally in Western America and Greece, by elegies and love poems, and by poems that might best be described as speculative.

It is in his speculative moods that Squires writes his most finished poems. In "Sunday in the Laboratory," the poet turns from an aquarium of newts "hardly less transparent than glass" to "The after-image of that human embryo / The size of a hand" whose "body is all the stupor of time."

Waiting in the Bone, anticipated by the earlier "Bone House," suggests that behind a prevailing sense of loss lies hope. Bones are the source of life, of blood. "We shall come up from the bone now. / We shall learn to weep again." Or, to quote the last line of "Self as an Eye," "A squint of tears can hold the sun."

Radcliffe Squires is an evocative poet, so good at his best that no one interested in poetry today should be ignorant of his work.

– Anne Stevenson

STAFFORD, William (Edgar). American. Born in Hutchinson, Kansas, 17 January 1914. Educated at the University of Kansas, Lawrence, B.A. 1936, M.A. 1947; University of Iowa, Iowa City, Ph.D. 1954. Conscientious Objector during World War II; active in Pacifist organizations, and since 1959, Member, Oregon Board, Fellowship of Reconciliation. Married Dorothy Hope Frantz in 1944; has two daughters and two sons. Member of the English Department, 1948–54, 1957–60, and since 1960, Professor of English, Lewis and Clark College, Portland, Oregon. Assistant Professor of English, Manchester College, Indiana, 1955–56; Professor of English, San Jose State College, California, 1956–57. Consultant in Poetry, Library of Congress, Washington, D.C., 1970–71. United States Information Agency Lecturer in Egypt, Iran, Pakistan, India, Nepal, and Bangladesh, 1972. Recipient: Yaddo Foundation Fellowship, 1955; Oregon Centennial Prize, for poetry, for short story, 1959; Union League Civic and Arts Foundation Prize (*Poetry*, Chicago), 1959; National Book Award, 1963; Shelley Memorial Award, 1964; National Endowment for the Arts grant, 1966; Guggenheim Fellowship, 1966; Melville Cane Award, 1974. D.Litt.: Ripon College, Wisconsin, 1965; Linfield College, McMinnville, Oregon, 1970. Address: Department of English, Lewis and Clark College, Portland, Oregon 97219, U.S.A.

PUBLICATIONS

Verse

West of Your City: Poems.   Los Gatos, California, Talisman Press, 1960.
Traveling Through the Dark.   New York, Harper, 1962.
Five American Poets, with others, edited by Thom Gunn and Ted Hughes.
    London, Faber, 1963.
Five Poets of the Pacific Northwest, with others, edited by Robin Skelton.   Seat-
    tle, University of Washington Press, 1964.
The Rescued Year.   New York, Harper, 1966.
Eleven Untitled Poems.   Mount Horeb, Wisconsin, Perishable Press, 1968.
Weather: Poems.   Mount Horeb, Wisconsin, Perishable Press, 1969.
Allegiances.   New York, Harper, 1970.
Temporary Facts.   Athens, Ohio, Duane Schneider Press, 1970.
Poems for Tennessee, with Robert Bly and William Matthews.   Martin, Tennes-
    see Poetry Press, 1971.
Someday, Maybe.   New York, Harper, 1973.
That Other Alone: Poems.   Mount Horeb, Wisconsin, Perishable Press, 1973.

Recording: Today's Poets 2, with others, Folkways, 1968.

Other

Down in My Heart (experience as a conscientious objector during World War
    II).   Elgin, Illinois, Brethren Publishing House, 1947.
Friends to This Ground: A Statement for Readers, Teachers, and Writers of
    Literature.   Champaign, Illinois, National Council of Teachers of English,
    1967.
Leftovers, A Care Package: Two Lectures.   Washington, D.C., Library of Con-
    gress, 1973.

Editor, with Frederick Candelaria, The Voices of Prose.   New York, McGraw
    Hill, 1966.
Editor, The Achievement of Brother Antoninus: A Comprehensive Selection of His
    Poems with a Critical Introduction.   Chicago, Scott Foresman, 1967.
Editor, with Robert H. Ross, Poems and Perspectives.   Chicago, Scott Pores-
    man, 1971.

Critical Studies: "William Stafford Issue" of Northwest Review (Eugene, Oregon),
Spring 1974, and of Modern Poetry Studies (Buffalo, New York), Spring 1975.

William Stafford comments:

My poetry seems to me direct and communicative, with some oddity and variety.
It is usually not formal. It is much like talk, with some enhancement.
Often my poetry is discursive and reminiscent, or at least is that way at one
level: it delivers a sense of place and event; it has narrative impulses. Forms are
not usually much evident, though tendencies and patterns are occasionally flirted

with. Thomas Hardy is my most congenial poetry landmark, but actually the voice I most consistently hear in my poetry is my mother's voice.

*   *   *

The *Lares* and *Penates* are presences to be reckoned with in William Stafford's poetry. At the centre is his strong sense of the domestic in its best sense. And beyond the hearth world that informs his moral vision is the landscape, present, like Roethke's, in a way that is total. More than that, it is a moral landscape – one whose storms are to be wrestled with, not easy, and rarely sentimental. His nature has its moral intimations which are both sustaining and reinforming, and the wilderness ("before the Indians pulled the West over the edge of the sky") informs his sense of opposition to a meaningless mechanical world. The wildcat cornered ("all there is left of the wilderness") manifests the lunacy of a world in which rockets are the only protection. Indeed, it is Stafford's sense of the "natural" as norm that enables him to use the lizard as judge of the folly of weaponry – the feeling of imminent transformation where the terror of the lizard's prehistoric ancestors is correlative to the horror of the bomb's doom.

But if, as he says, "we live in a terrible season," it is not just the bomb but the *taedium* of modern life with its faceless bland acceptances that alarms him. It is these predatory jelly-fish that he fears in "At the Chairman's Housewarming": "Go back wishy-washy to your sheltered bay, / but let me live definite, shock by shock." And more, as with Stevens, Stafford's desire to escape from illusory ideologies leads him to revel in the anguish and the intensity of the everyday:

> Better to stand in the dark of things and crash,
> hark yourself, blink in the day, eat bitter bush
> and look out over the world.

Those whom Stafford admires and celebrates are the heirs of the radical ideal. Among these are the Indians who withstand the inroads of the sociologists – most poignantly in "The Concealment: Ishi, the Last Indian" in the cycle to Dag Hammarskjöld. For there the Indian, who is the spirit of Hammarskjöld as well, is also the spirit of his father – the independent mind worrying the surface of things and forcing it to yield:

> Your life was a miracle
> and could build out of shadows
> anything: your restless thought has made the world haunted.

Stafford's heroes are ferociously non-average. Like Joe Champion, the first white settler in "The Museum at Tillamook," they have about them the garments of a past whose morality informs the poet.

Occasionally the nostalgia or the homespun becomes sentimental, but this is rarely the case. The intensity of the experience – its almost Proustian detail of smell and sound – and the honesty of the response prevent that. The question keeps being asked: "Is there a way to walk that living has obscured?" And this question enlivens Stafford's search for roots – the home that is the homestead, and a homestead, as in "The Farm on the Great Plains," that refers him back to life as it is now:

> My self will be the plain,
> wise as winter is gray,
> pure as cold posts go
> pacing toward what I know.

His reverence is for the sense of mystery at the heart of an ostensibly simple nature:

> So the world happens twice –
> once what we see it as;
> second as it legends itself
> deep, the way it is.

It is in this way that the sensuous apprehension of the immediate grain of sand on the knife blade gives a strength to his larger almost apocalyptic abstractions – "Summer will rise till the houses fear."

Stafford's sense of himself as pilgrim and spokesman is an abiding one. His best poetry is informed with the desire to feel and affirm the mysterious and unknowable moral force that his landscape provides: "I am the one / to live by the hum that shivers till the world can sing." It takes him beyond the strength to endure that he speaks of in "A Dedication" to the affirmation of an ongoing creation that is his "Vocation": "Your job is to find what the world is trying to be."

– D. D. C. Chambers

STALLWORTHY, Jon (Howie).   British.   Born in London, 18 January 1935. Educated at Dragon School, 1940–48; Rugby School, Warwickshire, 1948–53; Magdalen College, Oxford (Newdigate Prize, 1958), 1955–59, B.A. 1958, B.Litt. 1961. Served in the Oxfordshire and Buckinghamshire Light Infantry, Royal West African Frontier Force, 1953–55. Married Gillian Waldcock in 1960; has one daughter and two sons. Editor, Oxford University Press, London, 1959–71, and since 1972, Clarendon Press, Oxford. Visiting Fellow, All Souls College, Oxford, 1971–72. Recipient: Duff Cooper Memorial Award, 1974. Address: The Mill House, Wolvercote, Oxford, England.

PUBLICATIONS

Verse

The Earthly Paradise.   Oxford, privately printed, 1958.
The Astronomy of Love.   London, Oxford University Press, 1961.
Out of Bounds.   London, Oxford University Press, 1963.
The Almond Tree.   London, Turret Books, 1967.
A Day in the City.   Exeter, Exeter Books, 1967.
Root and Branch.   London, Chatto and Windus-Hogarth Press, and New York, Oxford University Press, 1969.
Positives.   Dublin, Dolmen Press, 1969.
A Dinner of Herbs.   Exeter, Rougemont Press, 1970.
Hand in Hand.   London, Chatto and Windus-Hogarth Press, 1974.
The Apple Barrel: Selected Poems 1956–1963.   London, Oxford University Press, 1974.

Other

Between the Lines: Yeats's Poetry in the Making. Oxford, Clarendon Press, 1963.
Vision and Revision in Yeats's "Last Poems." Oxford, Clarendon Press, 1969.
Wilfred Owen. London, Chatto and Windus-Oxford University Press, 1974.

Editor, *Yeats: Last Poems: A Casebook.* London, Macmillan, 1968; Nashville, Tennessee, Aurora, 1970.
Editor, with Seamus Heaney and Alan Brownjohn, *New Poems 1970-1971.* London, Hutchinson, 1971.
Editor, *The Penguin Book of Love Poetry,* London, Penguin, 1973; as *A Book of Love Poetry,* New York, Oxford University Press, 1974.

Translator, with Jerzy Peterkiewicz, *Five Centuries of Polish Poetry,* revised edition. London, Oxford University Press, 1970.
Translator, with Peter France, *The Twelve and Other Poems,* by Alexander Blok. London, Eyre and Spottiswoode, and New York, Oxford University Press, 1970; as *Alexander Blok,* London, Penguin, 1974.

                            *   *   *

Jon Stallworthy is a quiet poet, a fastidious craftsman, whose talent did not reveal itself fully until the publication of his collection, *Root and Branch.* His earlier poems were carefully wrought, but lacked the individuality and style that are apparent in the looser but still controlled forms of *Root and Branch.*

The central poem in this collection is "The Almond Tree," which seeks to discover meaning in the agonizing event of the birth of a mongol son. Such poems are notoriously hard to write, and at the beginning this one achieves a rather high degree of success as it laconically describes the poet, unaware of disaster, driving to the hospital hoping for a son. Then it collapses into more contrived modes, ending with the bathetic

> I have learnt that to live is to suffer,
> to suffer is to live.

Such a failure is, however, understandable: other more successful poems in the volume show that Stallworthy is capable of a more original brand of compassion when he writes less painfully near to the event. "A Poem about Poems about Vietnam" memorably attacks the glib ease of the "protest" poets: those killed in the conflict

> whisper in their sleep
> louder from underground than all
> the mikes that were hung upon your lips
> when you were at the Albert Hall.

But one of Stallworthy's themes is compassion, concern for suffering, and in "Bread" he illustrates how concern can be meaningful: as he eats the bread for his breakfast he remembers

> stick limbs and hunger-blown
> bellies; the aftermath
> of drought, flood flotsam, cyclone
>
> fodder. And sawdust crams my mouth.

That is an admirable and convincing record of how anguish at that suffering from which one is removed by circumstance can be more than a mere emotion. Now that he has eschewed traditional formal strictness, Stallworthy seems to write better and more imaginatively. Sometimes the exquisiteness for which he strives seems to be dwarfed by the largeness of his subject – as in "War Song of the Embattled Finns 1939"; increasingly, however, the care of his writing and his almost imagistic talent for description match up to his subjects.

– Martin Seymour-Smith

STANFORD, Ann. American. Born in La Habra, California, 25 November 1916. Educated at Stanford University, California (Phelan Fellowship, 1938), B.A. 1938 (Phi Beta Kappa); University of California, Los Angeles, M.A. in journalism 1958, M.A. in English 1961, Ph.D. in English and American literature 1962. Married Roland Arthur White in 1942; has three daughters and one son. Executive Secretary, 1957–58, Instructor in Journalism, 1958–59, and Poetry Workshop Instructor, 1960–61, University of California, Los Angeles. Assistant Professor, 1962–66, Associate Professor, 1966–68, and since 1968, Professor of English, San Fernando Valley State College, later California State University, Northridge. Editor, *Uclan Review*, Los Angeles, 1961–64; since 1969, Co-Founding Editor, San Fernando Valley State College Renaissance Editions; since 1971, Member, Editorial Board, *Early American Literature*, Geneseo, New York. Formerly, Poetry Reviewer, *Los Angeles Times*. Recipient: Yaddo Fellowship, 1957, 1967; Borestone Mountain Award, 1960; San Fernando Valley State College fellowship, 1966; National Endowment for the Arts grant, 1967, 1974; Shelley Memorial Award, 1969; National Institute of Arts and Letters Award, 1972. Address: 9550 Oak Pass Road, Beverly Hills, California 90210, U.S.A.

PUBLICATIONS

Verse

In Narrow Bound. Gunnison, Colorado, Swallow, 1943.
The White Bird. Denver, Swallow, 1949.
The Weathercock. San Jose, California, Talisman Press, 1956.
Magellan: A Poem to Be Read by Several Voices. San Jose, California, Talisman Press, 1958.
The Weathercock. New York, Viking Press, 1966.
The Descent: Poems. New York, Viking Press, 1970.

Other

Editor, *The Women Poets in English: An Anthology.* New York, McGraw Hill, 1972.

Translator, *The Bhagavad Gita: A New Verse Translation.* New York, Herder, 1970.

1483

Ann Stanford comments:

I try to set down the inner experiences of human beings, especially their relationships to time and the world. The expression is by means of imagery drawn from the
visible, especially the natural, scene. The verse forms vary from traditional metrical
verse to free verse in long or short cadences.

                              *   *   *

Ann Stanford's poetry thrives in the realm of reverie, bordered by nightmare,
"beset by spirits," whose voices reveal the world as a "sifting down of shadows."
Objects, often classified, are seldom sharply defined; human actions, attended by
larger forces, turn either febrile or hollow. Whatever comforts are presented bob
along in a welter of surrender: though "sleepy and warm," in "Night Rain," she
falls back to sleep where she can say, "I dream of the great horned owl / Snatching
birds like plums out of trees." Inside the "black ball of [her] mind," she protects
the "one white thought," but it's unclear whether this is a node of joy or concentrated pain. Imagine the extreme situations of Sylvia Plath done over into the
sensibility of H.D. and you have some of this poetry's texture: she invokes the
"blessed dark that runs across the day" as an opening force.

Her method reveals through abstration, and though she wants to "descend from
ideal to actual touch," her motions are often upward. Upon descent, however, she
discovers the "earth with all its destinies," and promise and threat take the shape
of an unknown future buried in an immutable plan:

> The noun
> Is what is feared: to name the sly
> Commotion of the blood which runs
> Unplanned as leaves to their own ways.

Filled with earth and sky, kernel and shell, this poetry presents assured and limited
returns – its horrors are all in the coming and going – but it lacks instantaneous
images where accuracy might break open into ecstasy. A poetry of general nouns
and basic verbs, its lyricism rides along on stores of emotion: "From the center of
our body / Come the bright flowers." The main accomplishment here derives from
a quiet honesty; it offers the sureness of craft and the surprises of self-possession.
Her victories originate in her willingness to ignore the odds and keep watch at
night. She shuns, to advantage, the ordinary and domestic subjects, but hasn't
perhaps the complete frenzy to fathom the Blakean excesses; her language is her
own, but she is too satisfied with it to complete her experiments. "Caught between
never and now," she makes all she can of her patience and her predicament, and
her ways are sufficiently beautiful.

– Charles Molesworth

STANLEY, George. American. Born in San Francisco, California, in 1934. Edu-
cated at San Francisco State College, B.A. 1969, M.A. 1971. Served in the United
States Army, 1953–56. Recipient: National Endowment for the Arts grant, 1968.
Address: 2504 York Street, Vancouver 9, British Columbia, Canada.

PUBLICATIONS

Verse

The Love Root.   San Francisco, White Rabbit Press, 1958.
Tete Rouge/Pony Express Riders.   San Francisco, White Rabbit Press, 1963.
Flowers.   San Francisco, White Rabbit Press, 1965.
Beyond Love.   San Francisco, Open Space-Dariel Press, 1968.
You.   Vancouver, New Star Books, 1974.

George Stanley comments:

(1970) I feel like I can't imagine ever writing another poem and this is the way I usually feel when I feel anything about poetry – I want to distinguish feeling about poetry from compulsively thinking about it. I used to do a lot more of that than I do now. I used to hang on to being a "poet," as an identity. I don't do that now. I have written a few poems that I think are exciting and even beautiful; and I don't think that about much poetry of anyone's. These poems have usually come when I was least expecting them, and I got caught up in the excitement of bringing them into being.

Major influences on my work have been Virgil, Milton, Hopkins, Whitman, Crane, Ginsberg, Spicer and Duncan. A strong recent influence on my life and writing is Whitehead's *Process and Reality.*

(1974) I write a line or two of poetry in my journal from time to time (when I get caught off guard). I'm a poet – *force majeure* by now; if this is identity it's not easily extricable from anything I'd call being. It goes back a long way. But I don't identify with the identity as it has been historically conditioned – bourgeois poet – I don't shit on it either, only on poetasters, some evidence of how many of these there are is the size of your book. I am at present working with the *Western Organizer* newspaper in Vancouver and preparing to write a book on homosexuality and society.

*   *   *

George Stanley's poetry emerges significantly out of his relationship with Jack Spicer, whose poetics and poetry were a vital force in San Francisco's North Beach in the saloon-schoolrooms of the mid-1950's. Spicer's considerable impact as poet and teacher has not yet been properly evaluated. It is hoped a much clearer idea of his powers will be revealed in the long-awaited long-delayed collected and uncollected works (edited by Robin Blaser).

Stanley maintains a particular, tenacious, and individual voice in all his work. He has published only four small books, and at this writing only two of the titles remain in print. Each book is complete, self-contained, exemplary. Each book reveals a clear development and advancement of his abilities.

Though Stanley's work has "opened" in the past few years via extending control over the poem by expanding vocabulary and line, his work remains tightly-reined against excess. Like a juggler he knows the balances. The elegiac tone pervading much of the work is kept in check with a tough no-nonsense stance. It is George Stankey's intelligence and devotion to grace accomplished in the act of creation that sustain his work and make it of constant interest to the reader.

It is hoped that his selected poems, *You* (poems 1957–1968) will make George Stanley's work more accessible to a larger audience.

– David Meltzer

––––––––––

STARBUCK, George (Edwin). American. Born in Columbus, Ohio, 15 June 1931. Educated at the California Institute of Technology, Pasadena, 1947–49; University of California, Berkeley, 1950–51; University of Chicago, 1954–57; Harvard University, Cambridge, Massachusetts, 1957–58. Served in the United States Army, 1952–54. Married Janice King in 1955 (divorced, 1961); Judith Luraschi, 1962 (divorced, 1968); Kathryn Salyer, 1968; has five children. Fiction Editor, Houghton Mifflin Company, Boston, 1958–61. Member of the English Department, State University of New York, Buffalo, 1963–64; Associate Professor, 1964–67, and Director, Writers Workshop, 1967–70, University of Iowa, Iowa City. Since 1971, Professor of English, Boston University. Recipient: Yale Series of Younger Poets Award, 1960; American Academy in Rome Fellowship, 1961, 1962; Guggenheim Fellowship, 1961. Address: Department of English, Boston University, Boston, Massachusetts 02215, U.S.A.

PUBLICATIONS

Verse

Bone Thoughts. New Haven, Connecticut, Yale University Press, 1960.
White Paper: Poems. Boston, Little Brown, 1966.
Three Sonnets. Iowa City, Windhover Press, n.d.

Recording: *George Starbuck*, Carillon Records, 1960.

George Starbuck comments:

I am the illegitimate son of Auden by a pregnancy he carefully concealed and would shudder to acknowledge. I have the American academic's common interest in common speech. Do I exchange gossip and advice with a set of peers? No. Am I proud of that? No.

Characterize my poems? In subject, obsessed by wars, religions, beautiful weird Americans, beautiful weird American talk. In impulse, utterly frivolous and formal. Put it this way: One of my poems is a 156-line acrostic in dactylic monometer, heavily alliterated. No poet in his right mind would attempt such a thing. Audiences tell me it's one of my most fluent and forceful and serious poems. What am I to do? For me, the long way round, through formalisms, word-games, outrageous conceits (the worst of what we mean by "wit") is the only road to truth. No other road *takes* me. Put it another way: Rather than chisel away at the rock of language, hoping to leave the world an Easter present of great stone Truths, I dump the rock, a piece at a time, into acid. The acid is brute, arbitrary, simple: this it eats, this it rejects. But find the right acid, and suddenly the rock will, of itself, yield up a whole shaped world – a world I *could not have known* was there. Lovely complexity of fact, of the pre-existent. Fossils, yes. How do you bring them to light? Not by regarding the language as bland *medium* for your own exquisite machinations. Not by chiseling at it. By genuine *experiment* on it – the putterer's destructive prank. Some writers' lives are a search for the philosopher's stone. My search is for *aqua regia*. Not *aqua fortis*.

None of your lesser "acid." Against marble, rhyme. Shakespeare had the idea. Rhyme, pun, palindrome – whatever may do violence *enough* to the shapes we think we have already given Truth. Put it yet another: *Conscious* slavery to the language. The only alternatives are unconscious slavery, or the sainthood of the wholly silent. And if the slave still merely grumbles and wisecracks under his breath, if he shies from the full fervor of insurrection, at least he will know whose fault and choice it is.

Affinities? My great admirations are for Frost, Auden, Hopkins, Dylan Thomas, Merwin, Plath – all lovers of the spoken English sentence, all but the first two fascinated with both the syntax and the metaphysics of metaphor. But who to *lump* me with? Wilbur? Dugan? Hecht? Hollander? A lesser, drearier catalog of names? How does a poet know? James Wright never glommed onto an ounce of Frost's tone or sense or way with American speech, until after he thought he had broken with Frost as a model.

Important experience? Majoring in mathematics at CalTech. Studying the standard textbooks of 1950: Brooks and Warren, O. Williams' anthologies. More recently, winning a long legal battle for free speech in the State University of New York, and in the process realizing that maybe I had never, myself, hazarded in public a truly difficult, unpopular, or dangerous truth. (See "truth" again. I love to bandy bad words.)

*   *   *

George Starbuck has been for more than a decade a consistently enjoyable poet. His first volume *Bone Thoughts* reached, for poetry, a very large audience, which is not hard to understand when one takes into account his technical prowess alone, little short of spectacular, with rhyme, meter, alliteration, etc., deployed as practically nowhere else. If the poet gives the impression that he has done all the homework, his craft sits lightly, and as in the following lines from the second of "Three Dreams on a Warm Sabbath," metrically so dexterous, one finds something of his by now well-known wryness:

> Here is the peak of pressure, here of heat,
> here the descending tension in the feet,
> and here we have the computed muscle-tone.
> The moment, you notice, passes and is gone,
> and if the observer's eye should blink, is lost. . . .

Wit, even when forced by a poet like George Starbuck to do its own serious work, is today more derogated than ever before, partly as the result of the high value placed on directness and depth of involvement, and his type is often perfunctorily labeled academic, even when writing, as the poet does in "Communication to the City Fathers of Boston," on a subject to tax the gifts of the most direct of involved responders:

> When New York mushrooms into view, when Boston's
> townspeople, gathered solemnly in basements,
> feel on their necks the spiderwebs of bombsights,
> when subway stations clot and fill like beesnests
> making a honey-heavy moan, whose business
> will it be then to mourn, to take a busman's
> holiday from his death, to weep for Boston's?

Yet *Bone Thoughts* did have its share of the kind of skilful set pieces common to American verse in the 1950's, and those interested enough in the poet – and there were many – to await his second volume with anticipation, must have had doubts about his ability to adjust to a very different poetic mood in the mid-1960's. *White Paper*, the poet's second volume, did not disappoint, for if in *Bone Thoughts* he could write on the subject of war so jazzy a piece as "War Story," whose first stanza goes:

> The 4th of July he stormed a nest.
> He won a ribbon but lost his chest.
> We threw his arms across the rest
>   And kneed him in the chin.
>   (You knee them in the chin
>   To drive the dog-tag in.)

in *White Paper* the response to the threats of the time, not to speak of a new war, larger and more ominous than many thought possible, was sombre and very moving. The book contains at least two such poems, "Poem Issued by Me to Congressmen . . ." and "Of Late," among the strongest of their type ever done by an American. Here is the first stanza of the latter:

> "Stephen Smith, University of Iowa sophomore, burned what
>   he said was his draft card."
> And Norman Morrison, Quaker, of Baltimore, Maryland,
>   burned what he said was himself.
> You Robert McNamara, burned what you said was a
>   concentration
> of the enemy aggressor.
> No news medium troubled to put it in quotes.

The poet's craftsmanship rose, in *White Paper*, to the occasion offered by a conscience directly involved in a burning world, and the achievement was and continues to be of a very high order.

—Lucien Stryk

STEAD, C(hristian) K(arlson). New Zealander. Born in Auckland, 17 October 1932. Educated at Mount Albert Grammar School; Auckland University, B.A. 1954, M.A. (honours) 1955; Bristol University (Michael Hiatt Baker Scholar), Ph.D.

1961. Married Kathleen Elizabeth Roberts in 1955; has two daughters and one son. Lecturer in English, University of New England, New South Wales, 1956–57. Member of the English Department, 1960–69, and since 1969, Professor of English, Auckland University. Recipient: Poetry Awards Incorporated prize (U.S.A.), 1955; Readers Award (*Landfall*, Christchurch), 1959; Winn-Manson Katherine Mansfield Award, for fiction and for essay, 1960, and Fellowship, 1972; Nuffield Travelling Fellowship, 1965. Address: 37 Tohunga Crescent, Parnell, Auckland 1, New Zealand.

PUBLICATIONS

Verse

Whether the Will Is Free: Poems 1954–62. Auckland, Paul's Book Arcade, 1964.
Crossing the Bar. Auckland, Auckland University Press – Oxford University Press, 1972.

Novel

Smith's Dream. Auckland, Longman Paul, 1971.

Other

The New Poetic: Yeats to Eliot. London, Hutchinson, 1964; New York, Harper, 1966.

Editor, New Zealand Short Stories: Second Series. London and Wellington, Oxford University Press, 1966.
Editor, Measure for Measure: A Casebook. London, Macmillan, 1971.
Editor, Selected Letters and Journals of Katherine Mansfield. London, Penguin, 1973.

Critical Studies: by Roy Fuller, in *London Magazine*, July 1964; *New Zealand*, by W. J. Cameron, New York, Prentice Hall, 1965; James Bertram, in *Islands 2* (Christchurch), 1972.

C. K. Stead comments:

I am always troubled that I can't write more poems than I do, that although I am a fairly conscientious and hard-working person, the Muse will not warm to these virtues, in fact, seems bored by them. I don't take the view that poets who wrote more than I do are less demanding of themselves; that "more means worse." I envy their fluency and still hope one day to learn the trick.

Reviewers tell me (with an emphasis that varies, of course, from approval to disapproval) that my poems are disciplined. This seems to suggest labour, conscious effort, self-control – all the qualities that go (for example) into my critical prose. But for me the discipline by which poems are achieved is quite different and still something I don't properly understand. I have to step out of the world in which I fill various roles (critic, professor, committee member, family man, etc.) and in which the clock rules. I have to sink back into myself to a point where all the trappings, all the things that are accidental, are lost. Then what is dredged up will sometimes seem worth polishing and putting on display.

Although I have on one occasion worked a poem into being through literally hundreds of drafts (an experience which was itself a kind of "possession," and not at all pleasant) it is usually true for me that hard labour doesn't help, and that Keats's dictum holds: "If poetry comes not as naturally as the leaves to the tree it might as well not come at all." To be in that rare state where poetry comes naturally is for me the greatest felicity. I am always afraid that it will never happen again.

I am a self-regarding younger son. My natural tone is secure but not definitive. I am a liberal, fitted neither for moralising nor for command. But when I am able to burrow deep enough I discover another self who (though not very likable) is perhaps the best of the poet in me. I conceive of this person as German, romantic, authoritarian, detached yet full of passion, above all a musician. To learn that a poet I admire (Yeats, for instance, or the New Zealander James K. Baxter) could not sing in tune shocks me almost to disbelief.

When I write poetry I very often have in mind the image of a place; and whatever the subject or "approach" of the poem, that image will carry through into the final form. But I also have the feeling that if a poem is merely personal it may be trivial; and I often catch myself, in the process of writing, nudging the personal vision towards some kind of general or public utterance.

In my earlier poems influences are clearly apparent but I don't think I am much influenced any longer by other poets. For better or worse, I seem to have found my own form. Though I still write occasionally in formal stanzas, more often I find myself writing a cluster of short pieces, all springing out of one mood, one experience, one preoccupation, which together make up the poem. I like to write with as little punctuation as possible, accommodating line-length and syntax to one another in a free-flowing verse-sentence in which words echo one another and the pauses and runs of sound parallel the sense.

To be invited to write about oneself is, of course, a trap. What can a poet say about his own work except that he does the best he can and that he hopes someone else will enjoy it?

*   *   *

In 1965 C. K. Stead named Truth, Generosity and Delight as the qualities which he would like his poems to manifest, although in such a way that the three would not readily be separable. His idea of Truth, of "responses to occasions" and of fidelity to experience which cannot presume to think itself total but may justly be selective, wants to be more than simply honest. His poems should be true as long as they recognise that poetry serves "Art before Principle, because Art serves the world which Principle admonishes."

He has never been a prolific poet, a fluent writer. Yet throughout, perhaps because of that conception of the true as the selective which connotes definition as discrimination, he has been a versatile writer. What he does, he does well, whether poetry, fiction, or criticism. These functions imply distant roles, misleadingly. "Pictures in a Gallery Undersea" is a tacit fiction presented as a sequence of pieces, a poet of manner and poise which is itself an act of criticism, and a tribute to his scholarship. Broadly speaking, the poems of Stead's first book are personal in a usual sense or literary, in some fairly evident sense, whether as subject or as exploration of a different aspect of technique.

"Only what lies behind," Stead says in a poem written before leaving Australia, "falls into shape." His immediate occasion then was the appreciation of the sense of loss as a state of value able to enhance and to be enhanced; the line has a peculiar resonance. One may take it that Stead was quite aware that this is a dogmatic statement which is simultaneously open and direct, and pregnant and cryptic. Cryptic, as a comment on life which comments too on an art. Pregnant, in that it becomes virtually a statement of principle, of the necessary reduction of formalist writing or the reduction of a rhetoric in pursuit of that passionate declaration which used to be contemplated as "essential form," an organisation which does not permit any distinction of "form" and "structure" still less of "form and content"; the upshot in Stead's case is a poetry more "natural," in terms of aesthetic, and as a correlative, a poetry of a "natural order" or "natural morality."

Earlier poems may, for instance, indeed they did, comment on the wilful man stationed in a largely determinist situation. Stead's later poems do not offer us comment, but rather experience, very near direct experience.

—Kendrick Smithyman

STEPANCHEV, Stephen. American. Born in Mokrin, Yugoslavia, 30 January 1915. Educated at the University of Chicago, A.B. 1937 (Phi Beta Kappa), M.A. 1938; New York University, Ph.D. 1950. Served as a Lieutenant in the United States Army, 1941–45: Bronze Star. Instructor in English, Purdue University, Layfayette, Indiana, 1938–41; New York University, 1946–47, 1948–49. Member of the English Department, 1949–64, and since 1964, Professor of English, Queens College, Flushing, New York. Fulbright Professor of American Literature, University of Copenhagen, Spring 1957. Recipient: Society of Midland Authors Prize (*Poetry*, Chicago), 1937; National Endowment for the Arts grant, 1968. Address: Department of English, Queens College, Flushing, New York 11367, U.S.A.

PUBLICATIONS

Verse

Three Priests in April. Baltimore, Contemporary Poetry, 1956.
Spring in the Harbor. Flushing, New York, Amity Press, 1967.
Vietnam. Los Angeles, Black Sparrow Press, 1968.
A Man Running in the Rain. Los Angeles, Black Sparrow Press, 1969.
The Mind. Los Angeles, Black Sparrow Press, 1972.
The Mad Bomber. Los Angeles, Black Sparrow Press, 1972.
Mining the Darkness. Los Angeles, Black Sparrow Press, 1974.

Other

American Poetry since 1945: A Critical Survey.   New York, Harper, 1965.

                            *   *   *

A New York poet-professor, Stephen Stepanchev writes lucid, urbane poems which depict dream- or city-scapes, remember parents or childhood, recount quarrels with a lover, or observe a fellow-victim of life with sympathy. Mostly they're first-person poems and usually the speaker is a wry detached observer: "The telephone squatted all day/In the equilibrium of indifference./No one called that wrong number,/Me, poking among dead men's words" ("A Visit"). The poems rely for their energy on a rapid montage of images, rendered in a succession of simple declarative sentences without much rhythmic intensity (like much current image-centered poetry, they might well be translations). The images are usually clever, seldom memorable. "November withdraws like a junkie," he writes, or "I was of two minds, like traffic," or "I live in the rice paddies of my desperation": one registers the effect, admires the invention, and passes on unmoved. Sometimes one cannot even admire: "Yesterday I poured gasoline all over myself/And flamed like a monk/To move you" seems both lurid and unpleasantly exploitative. Still, the general effect in an agreeable one, well represented by the following complete poem from *The Mad Bomber*, called "In the Gallery":

> Repetition makes a garden,
> But these roses are, clearly, unemployed.
> Nature does so much better than this painter
> I am expected to admire. My attention
> Wanders to a gallery guest whose hair
> Is a lair of lights, whose face dreams
> Like a wheat field, and whose eyes glisten
> With tears induced by her contact lenses.
> I mix her in my martini and drink
> Her down at the window overlooking the East
> River, where the moon is breaking up in shivers.

—Seamus Cooney

STEPHENS, Alan (Arthur).   American.   Born in Greeley, Colorado, 19 December 1925. Educated at the University of Colorado, Boulder, 1946–48; University of Denver, Colorado, A.B., M.A. 1950; Stanford University, California; University of Missouri, Columbia, Ph.D. 1954. Served in the United Stated Army Air Force, 1943–45. Married Frances Jones in 1948; has three sons. Assistant Professor of English, Arizona State University, Tempe, 1954–58. Since 1959, Member of the English Department, University of California, Santa Barbara. Recipient: Swallow Press New Poetry Series Award, 1957. Address: 326 Canon Drive, Santa Barbara, California 93105, U.S.A.

Publications

Verse

The Sum: Poems. Denver, Swallow, 1958.
Between Matter and Principle. Denver, Swallow, 1963.
The Heat Lightning. Brunswick, Maine, Bowdoin College Museum of Art, 1967.
Tree Meditation and Others. Chicago, Swallow Press, 1970.

Other

Editor, *Selected Poems,* by Barnaby Googe. Denver, Swallow, 1961.

Alan Stephens comments:

I caught my share of the academic influenzas of the late '40's and early '50's. As for style, themes, and all that: I used to write like this:

> Heavily from the shadeless plain to the river
> The Bull slants down and bends his head to draw
> Bright water in, that goes unbroken ever.

But now I write like this –

> – suppose that the words came in
> the way a flight of blackbirds
> I once watched entered a tree
> in the winter twilight:
> finding places for themselves
> quickly along the bare branches
> they settled into their singing
> for the time.

> *   *   *

Alan Stephens is a nature poet. Up to this time, his main interest has been to render nature faithfully, but as a realization of a meditative response which answers to the sensibility in natural objects. He seeks an effect similar to that of Wordsworth's early "Influence of Natural Objects." Stephens has remarked about his own poems that they are "descriptive meditations rather than meditative descriptions. . . ." To this end he wishes his poetry naked, the form invariably open, the expression spare. His utterances are, however, either clipped directions, like a dramatist's for the setting of scenes, or discursive meanderings, too often simple only for being denuded of figurative speech. Hence, from "A Breath," a stanza of this sort:

> A quiet, cool, spring morning –
> the sun up, and its light
> crossing things without emphasis,
> merely bringing out the pale colors.

Of course, the limitations of this manner are sometimes quite successfully accommodated to a larger context, as in "Home Rock."

While society and socially conscious or sophisticated speech are almost entirely absent from Stephens' quiet poetry, his work is effective in those instances where domestic man is projected against a natural backdrop. In such cases, he usually works with a motif of black and white, of darkness and tenuously comforting light. Meditating on the omnivorous incursion of dark space even into his own beard, the speaker of "To Fran" achieves this minimal consolation:

> it must be we belong in it – at once remotely
> and intimately; the way a sheepherder's fire at night belongs
> in the distance on a desert upland.

And returning from the moonlit night and "the black shadow of the house," the speaker of "Sounds" reports that:

> I go back in, and hunch over
> The familiar hiss of my pencil tip
> Racing across the lighted page.

—David M. Heaton

STEPHENS, Meic. Welsh. Born in Pontypridd, Glamorgan, 23 July 1938. Educated at University College of Wales, Aberystwyth and Bangor, A.B. (honours) in French; University of Rennes, France, Diplome de Langue et de Littérature Française. Married Ruth Wynn Meredith in 1965; has three daughters. French Master, Ebbw Vale Grammar School, 1962–66. Director, Triskel Press, Merthyr Tydfil, Glamorgan, 1962–67. Founding Editor, 1965, and since 1969, Editor, with Gwilym Rees Hughes and Sam Adams, *Poetry Wales*, Llandybie. Staff Journalist, *Western Mail*, Cardiff. Founding Member, English Language Section, Academy of Letters in Wales (Yr Academi Gymreig). Welsh Nationalist Party (Plaid Cymru) Candidate for Merthyr Tydfil, 1966. Since 1967, Assistant Director, Welsh Arts Council. Address: 9 Museum Place, Cardiff, Wales.

PUBLICATIONS

Verse

> *Triad: Thirty-Three Poems*, with Peter Gruffydd and Harri Webb. Merthyr Tydfil, Glamorgan, Triskel Press, 1963.
> *Exiles All.* Llandybie, Carmarthenshire, Christopher Davies, 1973.

Other

> *A Reader's Guide to Wales: A Selective Bibliography.* London, National Book League, 1973.

> Editor, with John Stuart Williams, *The Lilting House: An Anthology of Anglo-Welsh Poetry, 1917–1967.* London, Dent, and Llandybie, Carmarthenshire, Christopher Davies, 1969.
> Editor, with R. Brinley Jones, *Writers of Wales* series. Cardiff, University of Wales Press, 1969–74.
> Editor, *Artists in Wales.* Llandysul, Cardiganshire, Gomer, 2 vols., 1971, 1973.
> Editor, *The Welsh Language Today.* Llandysul, Cardiganshire, Gomer, 1973.

Meic Stephens comments:

I write little and think my most substantial contribution has been as Editor of *Poetry Wales,* and now as Assistant Director (Literature) of the Welsh Arts Council I am associated with most literary activities in Wales.

Most of my poems are about the industrial valleys of Glamorgan. They are all Welsh in reference. It is in my ballads and topical songs that I have celebrated the nationalist cause and these are my most popular works in that they are often sung in public. I have also translated poems from French, Welsh and Breton into English and it is the literature of those languages which have most influenced my own poetry. I believe that Wales and her literature should be restored to their former place as part of the European heritage by political means, namely the establishment of a Welsh government. I admire English literature but deplore the anglicanisation of Wales. I am especially interested in the culture of small European nations like the Irish, Scots, Basques, Flemings, Catalans and Bretons.

I am the first poet in Wales to publish visual and concrete poems and the pioneer of this form among young poets in our country. The poets I most admire are Hugh MacDiarmid, Emile Verhaeren, David Jones and Gwenallt Jones.

*   *   *

Meic Stephens has been primarily concerned in recent years with the problem of explaining, through his poetry, the predicament of many of his compatriots in Wales who feel themselves to be "exiled," emotionally and intellectually, from their proper Welsh heritage. Brought up English-speaking and learning Welsh as an adult, he is well aware of this condition — not only in his own country but elsewhere in Europe. His deep-rooted social commitment is made vivid by the convincing detail embedded in his "nationalist" poems and those to do with memories of a dwindling valley community. He has also done much as an editor of commendable severity, and as a small publisher, for writers of talent and promise.

His own poems are extremely well-made; he writes sparingly and produces perhaps three or four a year. He is a meticulous craftsman, even if some of his images tend to be a trifle threadbare, tired, and banal, coming perilously near cliché. One of his best, in my view, is a sonnet about Christmas 1968 when the major Welsh-language poet, Gwenallt Jones, died, with this fragment of prayer for his daughters:

> may they belong
> to Wales as he did, cherishing most of all
> his faith, his language and his living song.

Predictions are dangerous, but one feels that Stephens's mark in the future, providing he develops at the pace he has been keeping, could well be made as a continuous explorer of this "spiritual homelessness" among a large segment of his people. A stoic, not easily given to rose-tinted illusion, he possesses the necessary credentials and could bring the right unsentimental and unromantic approach to the task.

—John Tripp

STEVENS, Peter. Canadian. Born in Manchester, Lancashire, England, 17 November 1927. Educated at Nottingham University, B.A. (honours) in English, Cert. Ed., 1951; McMaster University, Hamilton, Ontario, M.A., 1964; University of Saskatchewan, Saskatoon, Ph.D. in English, 1969. Married; has three children. Chairman of the English Department, Hillfield College, Hamilton, Ontario, 1957–64; Lecturer, Extension Division, McMaster University, 1961–64; Assistant Professor of English, University of Saskatchewan, 1964–69. Since 1969, Associate Professor of English, University of Windsor, Ontario. Recipient: Canada Council Award, 1969. Address: 2055 Richmond Street, Windsor 15, Ontario, Canada.

PUBLICATIONS

Verse

    Plain Geometry.   Toronto, Ganglia Press, 1968.
    Nothing But Spoons.   Montreal, Delta Canada, 1969.
    Leaves from Falling Trees.   London, Writers Forum, 1969.
    Breadcrusts and Glass.   Fredericton, New Brunswick, Fiddlehead, 1972.

Other

    Editor, *The McGill Movement: A. J. M. Smith, F. R. Scott, and Leo Kennedy.*   Toronto, Ryerson Press, 1969.
    Editor, *Forum: Canadian Life and Letters 1920–1970: Selections from "The Canadian Forum."*   Toronto, University of Toronto Press, 1972.

Peter Stevens comments:

I deal with the local landscape and places: the prairie, its place in my own personal and family life, its past, its geologic history, its "mythology." I write usually in free verse paragraphs and have experimented with some concrete forms: a method of using anagrams I call Anagrammatics. General influences are simply Canada and being Canadian – Canadian writers I admire and whose work has probably made an impression on mine are Al Purdy and Earle Birney. I admire the technical facility of Auden and early Ezra Pound. I have paid attention to the North American-ness of W. C. Williams, particularly as it emerges in a Canadian manner in the poetry of W. W. E. Ross and Raymond Souster.

*   *   *

Peter Stevens is a poet who reflects the immigrant experience. Coming to Canada from Britain, he brought a poetic sensibility influenced by the low-toned writing of the English 1950's. That sensibility has since been modified by Canadian experience, and the result is a manner that is undramatic, deliberately uncolourful, but – rather like an early spring landscape in the Prairies where Stevens spent much of his time in Canada – slowly revealing subtleties of perception and tone, pleasing gradations in the range of grey and brown. Generally speaking, there is little metaphorical or adjectival colour in Stevens' poems; the images are meant to speak dryly for themselves, as in the opening lines of "Fuschia":

> blood drops belled
> hanging in hedges
> above the bay curved
> under cliffs I remember
> an island in my past . . .

or in "Seeing Is Seeing Is Believing in Poetry":

> A stalker lurches across the snow.
> His shadow stretches inhuman long
> across snow's glistening crust of ice.
>
> A rabbit sits stark still, then spurts away
> to black trees, dark lines blacker on the white,
> as this dense shadow slides into his eye.
>
> All I see is rabbit flashing into shadows
> away from stealthy shadow: no comment.
> The eye does not speak, it does not think. . . .

The poems I have quoted come from *Breadcrusts and Glass*, most recent and best of Stevens' several small books. They show his sharp, thoughtful perception of the natural world; other poems show him equally sharply aware of the anomalies and frustrations of the plastic life, and here emerges an ironic, almost acerbic view of the self, and, at times, a curious questioning consciousness of literature as pretension.

—George Woodcock

STEVENSON, Anne. American. Born in Cambridge, England, 3 January 1933. Educated at University High School, Ann Arbor, Michigan, 1947–50; University of Michigan, Ann Arbor (Hopwood Award, 1951, 1952, 1954), B.A. 1954 (Phi Beta Kappa), M.A. 1962; Radcliffe Institute, Cambridge, Massachusetts, 1970–71. Married R. L. Hitchcock in 1955 (divorced), has one daughter; Mark Elvin in 1962 (divorced), has two sons. School Teacher, The Lillesden School, Kent, 1955–56, Westminster School, Georgia, 1959–60, and The Cambridge School, Massachusetts, 1961–62; Advertising Manager, A. and C. Black, publishers, London, 1956–57; Tutor, Department of Extra-Mural Studies, University of Glasgow, 1970–73; Counsellor, Open University, Paisley, Renfrew, 1972–73. Recipient: University of Dundee Creative Writing Fellowship, 1973. Agent: A. D. Peters, 10 Buckingham Street, London W.C.2., England. Address: 156 Wilton Street, Glasgow G20 6BS, Scotland.

PUBLICATIONS

Verse

Living in America. Ann Arbor, Michigan, Generation Press, 1965.
Reversals. Middletown, Connecticut, Wesleyan University Press, 1969.
Correspondences: A Family History in Letters. Middletown, Connecticut, Wesleyan University Press, and London, Oxford University Press, 1974.
Travelling Behind Glass: Selected Poems 1963–1973. London, Oxford University Press, 1974.

Other

Elizabeth Bishop. New York, Twayne, 1966.

Critical Studies: by Dorothy Donnelly, in *Michigan Quarterly Review* (Ann Arbor), Fall 1966, and April 1971.

Anne Stevenson comments:

The poets I most admire, and have been "influenced by" are the Elizabethans (Wyatt, Raleigh, Greville), the Metaphysicals (Donne and Marvell), the less mad Blake, and lately, Yeats, Frost, Wallace Stevens and Elizabeth Bishop. I admire what is controlled, finely wrought and yet passionate. Lately I have turned with interest to Robert Browning whose dramatic monologues suggested the dramatic form of my latest book, *Correspondences.* I have perhaps too little patience with sprawling "mysticism," but I like Haiku in Blyth's translations.

I think my own work quiet, somewhat cynical, more than usually domestic. I'm always conscious of having something to say in every poem.

*   *   *

Anne Stevenson's two books of verse, *Reversals* and *Correspondences*, are the work of an exceptionally disciplined, as well as of a highly gifted poet. *Correspondences*, the later and more developed of the two, forms a remarkable unity. It is, as the sub-title informs us, "A Family History in Letters" – a genealogical tree traces the relationships. The family is a New England one, and I suspect the poet's sense of what New England is has been sharpened by long residence on the other side of the Atlantic. Indeed, she tells us as much, in the last poem in the collection, where "Kay Boyd," who is the author's surrogate, writes to her widowed father. Speaking of herself, she tells us: "She lives a long way from Eden. The tug back/is allegiance to innocence which is not there."

One of the most fascinating things about Anne Stevenson's work, taken as a whole, to the English reader, is the relationship between her kind of naturalism and the kind of naturalistic writing usually encountered in England. The difference lies in a much greater spareness. One notices, in both her books, how every unnecessary word is pared away.

—Edward Lucie-Smith

STEWART, Douglas (Alexander). Australian. Born in Eltham, New Zealand, 6 May 1913. Educated at New Plymouth Boys High School; Victoria University College, New Zealand. Married Margaret Coen in 1946; has one daughter. Literary Editor, *The Bulletin*, Sydney, 1940–61. Since 1961, Literary Adviser, Angus and Robertson Ltd., publishers, Sydney. Recipient: Encyclopedia Britannica Award, 1968. Agent: Angus and Robertson Ltd., 221 George Street, Sydney, New South Wales. Address: 2 Banool Avenue, St. Ives, New South Wales 2075, Australia.

PUBLICATIONS

Verse

Green Lions: Poems.   Auckland, Whitcombe and Tombs, 1937.
The White Cry: Poems.   London, Dent, 1939.
Elegy for an Airman.   Sydney, Frank C. Johnson, 1940.
Sonnets to the Unknown Soldier.   Sydney and London, Angus and Robertson, 1941.
The Dosser in Springtime.   Sydney and London, Angus and Robertson, 1946.
Glencoe.   Sydney and London, Angus and Robertson, 1947.
Sun Orchids.   Sydney and London, Angus and Robertson, 1952.

The Birdsville Track and Other Poems. Sydney and London, Angus and
  Robertson, 1955.
Rutherford and Other Poems. Sydney and London, Angus and Robertson,
  1962.
The Garden of Ships: A Poem. Sydney, Wentworth Press, 1962.
(*Poems*), selected and introduced by the author. Sydney, Angus and Robert-
  son, 1963; as *Selected Poems*, 1969.
Collected Poems, 1936–1967. Sydney and London, Angus and Robertson,
  1967.
Poems: A Selection. Sydney, Angus and Robertson, 1972.

Plays

The Fire on the Snow (broadcast, 1941). Included in *The Fire on the Snow
  and The Golden Lover*, 1944.
The Golden Lover (broadcast, 1943). Included in *The Fire on the Snow and
  The Golden Lover*, 1944.
Ned Kelly (produced Sydney, 1944). Sydney and London, Angus and Robert-
  son, 1943.
The Fire on the Snow and The Golden Lover: Two Plays for Radio. Sydney
  and London, Angus and Robertson, 1944.
Shipwreck (produced Sydney, 1948). Sydney, Shepherd Press, 1947.
Four Plays (includes *The Fire on the Snow, The Golden Lover, Ned Kelly,
  Shipwreck*). Sydney and London, Angus and Robertson, 1958.
Fisher's Ghost: An Historical Comedy (produced Sydney, 1961). Sydney,
  Wentworth Press, 1960.

Radio Plays: *The Fire on the Snow*, 1941; *The Golden Lover*, 1943; *An
Earthquake Shakes the Land*, 1944.

Short Stories

A Girl with Red Hair and Other Stories. Sydney and London, Angus and
  Robertson, 1944.

Other

The Flesh and the Spirit: An Outlook on Literature. Sydney and London,
  Angus and Robertson, 1948.
The Seven Rivers (on angling). Sydney, Angus and Robertson, 1966.

Editor, *Coast to Coast: Australian Stories.* Sydney, Angus and Robertson,
  1945.
Editor, with Nancy Keesing, *Australian Bush Ballads.* Sydney, Angus and
  Robertson, 1955.
Editor, with Nancy Keesing, *Old Bush Songs and Rhymes of Colonial Times,
  Enlarged and Revised from the Collection of A. B. Paterson.* Sydney,
  Angus and Robertson, 1957.
Editor, *Voyager Poems.* Brisbane, Jacaranda Press, 1960.
Editor, *The Book of Bellerive,* by Joseph Tischler. Brisbane, Jacaranda Press,
  1961.

Editor, *Modern Australian Verse: Poetry in Australia II.* Sydney, Angus and Robertson, 1964; Berkeley, University of California Press, 1965.

Editor, *Selected Poems,* by Hugh McCrae. Sydney, Angus and Robertson, 1966.

Editor, *Short Stories of Australia: The Lawson Tradition.* Sydney, Angus and Robertson, 1967.

Editor, with Nancy Keesing, *The Pacific Book of Bush Ballads.* Sydney, Angus and Robertson, 1967.

Editor, with Nancy Keesing, *Bush Songs, Ballads, and Other Verse.* Penrith, New South Wales, Discovery Press, 1968.

Critical Study: *Douglas Stewart* by Nancy Keesing, Sydney, Oxford University Press, 1967.

*   *   *

Douglas Stewart is the most versatile writer in Australia today. He has published books of poetry, poetic drama, fiction, essays and criticism and is an editor of perception and influence. In poetry, no Australian has been more prolific than Stewart and few as experimental although his experiments have more to do with enlarging the range of existing forms than with the invention of new types of poetry. "Stewart understands rhyme today probably better than anyone else living," R. D. Fitzgerald has said.

In all its forms Stewart's poetry displays a distinctively original view of life and a lyrical, witty but highly disciplined style. He often makes a poetic comment on huge events by pin-pointing some little-known region, nearly forgotten tragedy or happening or old traveller's tale to which his readers may supply wider or universal meanings. A ballad sequence, *Glencoe,* although it described a seventeenth-century Scottish highlands massacre, was Stewart's commentary on World War II; his verse plays *The Fire on the Snow* (Scott's last Antarctic expedition) and *Ned Kelly* (a notorious bush-ranger) dramatized Stewart's preoccupation with man as hero; a recent series of "explorer" poems arise from his belief that "the scientist is the modern equivalent of the explorer who, in his quest for truth and his enlargement of the human mind, is the colleague, not the enemy, of the artist."

Stewart avoids abstract images when he ponders abstractions but selects aspects of life or landscape to typify abstract ideas. Man himself is always central to Stewart's work and to express the heroism and endurance of man he often uses images of snow and ice:

> Till mind is dulled to stone
> And body is creaking wood
> With a sap of ice in the veins.

—from *The Fire on the Snow*

At all stages of his writing Stewart has returned to short, closely observed lyrics about the small plant forms and animals of the Australian landscape. These lyrics, he says "are essentially an exploration of the mysteries of creation and evolution, especially the duality of the universe (or God); good and evil, or apparent good and evil, like the flower and the centipede, both coming from the same Hand":

The rock swallows the snake,
Chilly and black as it vanishes;
In rain and moss the year
Moves in the sandstone crevices
Where like the snake itself
Earth's darkest impulses brood.
Long stems, sharp leaves awake –
O look where the wet moss flourishes
Tall crimson orchids appear,
Snake-headed, with darting tongue,
Now this way striking, now that,
As if indeed they had sprung
From the black snake's rotting side
Under the sandstone shelf
To spill on the green air
Their dewdrops of dark thought
Like venom and like blood.

—"Kindred"

Stewart's most recent work ("Elegy," "Memories of a Veteran") indicates a possible change to more open autobiographical statement. In it he abandons the use of mouthpieces and speaks directly in the ballad-like poetry which he has gradually forged into flexible and adaptable forms peculiarly his own.

—Nancy Keesing

STEWART, Harold (Frederick).   Australian.   Born in Sydney, New South Wales, 14 December 1916. Address: Higashisenouchicho 29, Kitashirakawa, Sakyo-ku, Kyoto, Japan.

PUBLICATIONS

Verse

> *The Darkening Ecliptic*, with James McAuley (as Ern Malley).   Melbourne, Reed and Harris, 1944; as *Poems*, Melbourne, Lansdowne Press, 1961.
> *Phoenix Wings: Poems 1940–6.*   Sydney and London, Angus and Robertson, 1948.
> *Orpheus and Other Poems.*   Sydney, Angus and Robertson, 1956.

Other

> *A Net of Fireflies: Japanese Haiku and Haiku Paintings with Verse Translations and an Essay.*   Tokyo and Rutland, Vermont, Charles E. Tuttle, 1960.

> Translator, *A Chime of Windbells: A Year of Japanese Haiku in English Verse.*   Tokyo and Rutland, Vermont, Charles E. Tuttle, 1969.

Harold Stewart comments:

Poetry founded on Tradition is to me not only a way of life but a spiritual method, a kind of Yoga, both mantric and bhaktic, yoking the poet by means of words with the Word. The poet, in turn, has a ministerial function, mediating between the Muse and the reader, and it is his duty to praise and express his gratitude for the inspiration which he receives from above. As a follower of Tradition, I am opposed to "modernism" of every kind in art and thought. My aim is not to be contemporary, but timeless.

Although some of my earlier work treated European themes, since about 1950 I have concentrated entirely on giving poetic expression to certain of the Traditional Doctrines of the Far East, especially those of Buddhism, Taoism and Hinduism. During the past century, Oriental scholarship has opened up the vast treasure houses of the metaphysical, religious and artistic traditions of Asia; yet these have remained largely unexplored by Western poets.

I have devoted the past thirty years to their study, drawing poetic inspiration from these rich resources and endeavouring to acclimatize English poetry to these old but newly rediscovered regions of the spirit, both by direct translation and by original composition. At first I drank from the fountainheads, India and China; but since coming to live in Japan, I have turned to a more personal expression of religious devotion, to the Pure Land School of Buddhism, Jodo Shinshu, as well as attempting to capture some of the natural and cultural atmosphere of Kyoto and its environs.

My poetic methods have always been strictly Traditional, using the regular metres of English verse, often with rhyme, and a modern English diction of a slightly heightened tone, but striving always for greater clarity and simplicity in expressing sometimes difficult and unfamiliar subjects.

I think that I can fairly claim the discovery of two new principles of stanza formation: the inverted stanza, in which the order of rhymes is inverted from the previous one, the two stanzas alternating in various patterns; and the variation stanza, in which each new stanza is formed by a different permutation of a fixed number of rhymes.

*   *   *

In his sensitive study of James McAuley's Poem "Prometheus" in *Workshop* ii, 1, Harold Stewart praises McAuley for using a method which is obviously his own. Stewart writes, "It is only through the myth that reality can be presented in the round: the superficially realist work can give only a one-sided and distorted projection." McAuley's method consists in the presentation of a myth, and at the same time of incorporating into that presentation what the poet himself has called "interpretative words and phrases." In his poem "The Myths" Stewart expresses the same idea in a more poetic form:

> Myths are a never-empty urn
> Of meaning: poets thence in turn
> Pour out the symbols that presage
> The rise or ruin of their age.

Stewart draws his material not only from European myth but also from the myths of Buddhism and Taoism, and thus endeavours to give his poetry a universal timeless appeal: "My aim is not to be contemporary, but timeless."

Mr. Stewart seems to be struggling along with Plato, the Christian Saints and

Eastern gurus to overcome his earthly desires, his burden of flesh, in order to be liberated into pure spirit and a feeling of oneness with nature. When he achieves this, in "The Annunciation," for example, the poet savours the rare moment of illumination and insight:

> Rarely is flesh from purpose thus untied
> It is as though my aching blood were still.

The struggle to obtain this spiritual freedom is the subject of the main body of the poetry, including a very personal interpretation of the myth of Orpheus and Eurydice. Through this personal use of the myths the poet casts new light on his subjects and in turn enriches our understanding of the myths.

—Kirsten Holst Petersen

STOUTENBURG, Adrien. Pseudonym: **Lace Kendall.**   American.   Born in Darfur, Minnesota, 1 December 1916. High School education. Librarian, Hennepin County Library, Richfield, Minnesota, 1949–50; Reporter, *Richfield News*, 1950–52; Editor, Parnassus Press, Berkeley, California, 1956–58. Recipient: Edwin Markham Award and Michael Stone Fellowship, Poetry Society of America, 1961; Lamont Poetry Selection Award, 1964; Borestone Mountain Award, 1970, 1972. Agent: Curtis Brown Ltd., 60 East 56th Street, New York, New York 10022. Address: 9340 East Center Avenue, Denver, Colorado 80231, U.S.A.

PUBLICATIONS

Verse

Heroes, Advise Us: Poems.   New York, Scribner, 1964.
Short History of the Fur Trade.   Boston, Houghton Mifflin, 1969; London, Deutsch, 1970.
Out There.   New York, Viking Press, 1971; London, Bodley Head, 1972.

Other

The Model Airplane Mystery (juvenile).   New York, Doubleday, 1943.
Timberline Treasure (juvenile).   Philadelphia, Westminster, 1951.
The Silver Trap (juvenile).   Philadelphia, Westminster, 1954.
Stranger on the Bay (juvenile).   Philadelphia, Westminster, 1955.
Remembered Island (juvenile), with Barbara Ritchie (as Barbi Arden).   New York, Holt Rinehart, 1956.
River Duel (juvenile).   Philadelphia, Westminster, 1956.

Snowshoe Thompson (juvenile), with Laura Nelson Baker. New York, Scribner, 1957.

In This Corner (juvenile). Philadelphia, Westminster, 1957.

Wild Treasure: The Story of David Douglas (juvenile), with Laura Nelson Baker. New York, Scribner, 1958.

Wild Animals of the Far West. Berkeley, California, Parnassus Press, 1958.

Honeymoon (juvenile). Philadelphia, Westminster, 1958.

Four on the Road (juvenile). Philadelphia, Westminster, 1958.

Scannon: Dog with Lewis and Clark (juvenile), with Laura Nelson Baker. New York, Scribner, 1959.

Houdini: Master of Escape (juvenile; as Lace Kendall). Philadelphia, Macrae Smith, 1960.

Good-by Cinderella (juvenile). Philadelphia, Westminster, 1960.

The Blue-Eyed Convertible (juvenile). Philadelphia, Westminster, 1961.

Beloved Botanist: The Story of Carl Linnaeus (juvenile), with Laura Nelson Baker. New York, Scribner, 1961.

Little Smoke (juvenile; as Lace Kendall). New York, Coward McCann, 1961.

Lady in the Jungle (juvenile), with Laura Nelson Baker (as Nelson Minier). Philadelphia, Macrae Smith, 1961.

Window on the Sea (juvenile). Philadelphia, Westminster, 1962.

Elisha Kent Kane: Arctic Challenger (juvenile; as Lace Kendall). Philadelphia, Macrae Smith, 1963.

The Secret Lions (juvenile; as Lace Kendall). New York, Coward McCann, 1963.

The Mud Ponies (juvenile; as Lace Kendall). New York, Coward McCann, 1963.

Dear, Dear Livy: The Story of Mark Twain's Wife (juvenile), with Laura Nelson Baker. New York, Scribner, 1963.

A Time for Dreaming (juvenile). Philadelphia, Westminster, 1963.

The Things That Are (verse for children). Chicago, Reilly and Lee, 1964.

Walk into the Wind (juvenile). Philadelphia, Westminster, 1964.

Rain Boat (juvenile; as Lace Kendall). New York, Coward McCann, 1965.

Explorer of the Unconscious: Sigmund Freud (juvenile), with Laura Nelson Baker. New York, Scribner, 1965; as *Freud: Explorer of the Unconscious*, London, Whiting and Wheaton, 1967.

The Crocodile's Mouth: Folk-Song Stories (juvenile). New York, Viking Press, 1966.

Masters of Magic (juvenile; as Lace Kendall). Philadelphia, Macrae Smith, 1966.

American Tall Tales (juvenile). New York, Viking Press, 1966.

A Vanishing Thunder: Extinct and Threatened Birds (juvenile). New York, Doubleday, 1967.

Tigers Training, Dancing Whales: Wild Animals of the Circus, Zoo, and Screen (juvenile; as Lace Kendall). Philadelphia, Macrae Smith, 1968.

Listen America: A Life of Walt Whitman (juvenile), with Laura Nelson Baker. New York, Scribner, 1968.

American Tall-Tale Animals (juvenile). New York, Viking Press, 1968.

Animals at Bay: Rare and Rescued American Wildlife (juvenile). New York, Doubleday, 1968.

Fee, Fi, Fo, Fum: Friendly and Funny Giants (juvenile). New York, Viking Press, 1969; as *The Giant Who Sucked His Thumb and Other Stories*, London, Deutsch, 1972.

People in Twilight: Vanishing and Changing Cultures. New York, Doubleday, 1971.

Haran's Journey (juvenile; as Lace Kendall). New York, Dial Press, 1971.

Adrien Stoutenburg comments:

Nature and history have a predominant place in my work. Two long, narrative poems of mine have historical backgrounds – "This Journey," written about Capt. Robert F. Scott's fatal journey to the South Pole; and the age-old exploitation of animals in the title poem of *Short History of the Fur Trade.* I write chiefly so-called free verse, though in a long poem I sometimes introduce rhymed lines for variation. Wild animals are often subjects in my work. Death, the mechanical destruction of the natural environment, the threat of nuclear holocaust are frequent themes. Although I admire many poets, I am not aware of any strong outside influence on my work. I do not seek for descriptive language but language that is connotative, and strung with fresh imagery or statement. Though I sometimes use surreal images, I am concerned for clarity and accuracy. There is no room in poetry for untruth, whether of the imagination or of fact.

*   *   *

Adrien Stoutenburg's poetry is richly sensual, well attuned to the plant and animal life of our planet in a way that, at its best, is strongly reminiscent of D. H. Lawrence and Theodore Roethke:

> There is such a buzz here;
> my ears whirl with it,
> and the wind spinning it
> into legs, arms, squeaking trees,
> motes, mites, and the precise blue tick
> inside my wrist, my temple. . . .

—from "Who Love to Lie with Me"

She has a unique power for bringing such disparate parts of creation together, for showing the essential oneness of life, as she does with great success is her fine long poem "This Journey," in which she discovers the victory underlying Scott's defeat in his attempt to reach the South Pole first. The long title poem from *Short History of the Fur Trade* manages to also suggest, and draw on, two opposed emotions: anger and disgust at human destruction of wild life (as particularly exemplified in the career of John Jacob Astor) motivated by nothing better than greed and the frivolous desire for rare furs, and, on the other hand, an acute awareness of the beauty and vitality of this wild life that was crushed to benefit the callous and the rich. She recreates the beauty of these vanished breeds of animals before our eyes at the same time she chronicles their destruction. In some of the shorter poems in this second volume, she suggests (again, the lyrical and the satirical are often mixed, counterbalancing one another and giving the poems greater complexity as a result) the possibility that we can, as Gary Snyder has also said, re-establish some communion with nature on at least an individual basis, whatever others may be doing to destroy the ecological balance:

> I am thinking of doing over my room,
> of plastering wings on it,
> of letting clouds in through the attic,
> of collecting moles
> and training them to assemble in an oval
> for a rug as bright as black water.

—from "Interior Decoration"

Though she senses that the excitement she feels in the presence of wild life is perhaps becoming extinct, she is also willing to implicate herself in what is going wrong with our world; she would invite lions into her home, as in "Open House" (one of several titles in her second collection that conjures up Roethke), but knows how far removed hers is from the life of lions:

> For this I might sacrifice
> the chicken in the freezer,
> or the lunch reserved
> for our spoiled kittens
> who yearn to be lions
> but cannot conquer
> their lust for cans
> packed with tuna
> and the long, green bones of mermaids.

Obviously, the satire here is self-satire. The nature poetry that abounds in both *Heroes, Advise Us* and *Short history of the Fur Trade* goes beyond eulogy and lyrical appreciation to teach us, too: Ms. Stoutenburg reminds us, particularly in the latter book, of how easily the love of nature can be corrupted into a destructive lust for it, of the culpability of us all in what is happening to our planet. This is the sort of teaching that can help, since it is informed by passion; these poems abound in "the long green bones of mermaids," the magical image that darts for the heart and swims inside to stay.

—Duane Ackerson

STOW, (Julian) Randolph. Australian. Born in Geraldton, Western Australia, 28 November 1935. Educated at Guildford Grammar School, Western Australia; University of Western Australia, Nedlands, B.A. 1956. Formerly, Anthropological Assistant, working in Northwest Australia and Papua New Guinea. Taught at the University of Adelaide, 1957; Lecturer in English Literature, University of Leeds, Yorkshire, 1962, and University of Western Australia, 1963; Lecturer in English and Commonwealth Literature, University of Leeds, 1968–69. Recipient: Australian Literature Society Gold Medal, 1957, 1958; Miles Franklin Award, 1958; Commonwealth Fund Harkness Travelling Fellowship, 1964–66; Britannica-Australia Award, 1966. Address: c/o Richard Scott Simon Ltd., 36 Wellington Street, London WC2E 7BD, England.

PUBLICATIONS

Verse

Act One: Poems. London, Macdonald, 1957.
Outrider: Poems 1956–1962. London, Macdonald, 1962.

A Counterfeit Silence: Selected Poems. Sydney and London, Angus and Robertson, 1969.
Poetry from Australia: Pergamon Poets 6, with Judith Wright and William Hart-Smith, edited by Howard Sergeant. Oxford, Pergamon Press, 1969.

Novels

A Haunted Land. London, Macdonald, 1956; New York, Macmillan, 1957.
The Bystander. London, Macdonald, 1957.
To the Islands. London, Macdonald, 1958; Boston, Little Brown, 1959.
Tourmaline. London, Macdonald, 1963.
The Merry-Go-Round in the Sea. London, Macdonald, 1965; New York, Morrow, 1966.

Other

Midnite: The Story of a Wild Colonial Boy (juvenile). Melbourne, Cheshire, and London, Macdonald, 1967; New York, Prentice Hall, 1968.

Editor, *Australian Poetry 1964.* Sydney, Angus and Robertson, 1964.

Bibliography: *Randolph Stow: A Bibliography,* Adelaide, Libraries Board of South Australia, 1968.

Critical Studies: by the author on his own work: "Raw material," in *Westerly* (Nedlands, Western Australia), 1961; "The Quest for Permanence" by Geoffrey Dutton, in *Journal of Commonwealth Literature* (Leeds, Yorkshire), September 1965; "Outsider Looking In" by W. H. New, in *Critique* (Minneapolis), ix, 1, 1967; "Waste Places, Dry Souls" by Jennifer Wightman, in *Meanjin* (Melbourne), June 1969; "Voyager from Eden" by Brandon Conron, in *Ariel (Canada)* (Calgary, Alberta), October 1970; *The Merry-Go-Round in the Sea* by Edriss Noall, Sydney, Scoutline Publications, 1971.

*   *   *

Randolph Stow's already considerable poetic reputation both overseas and in Australia rests on a comparatively small amount of published poetry. However, he is also a novelist who has written in both genres concurrently and the worlds and visions of his novels and of his poetry are interwoven. A discussion of his poetry should not forget these links and it is relevant to note the title of his selected poetry – *A Counterfeit Silence* on whose title page he quotes Thornton Wilder (*The Bridge of San Luis Rey*): "Even speech was for them a debased form of silence; how much more futile is poetry, which is a debased form of speech."

Stow's youthful poetry displayed technical mastery. He often contained great passion in graceful and ingenious traditional forms and frequently wrote a ballad-like verse which he has continued to use and to develop from time to time. Many of his early poems were autobiographical and displayed a sometimes almost oppressive awareness of the physical features of his Western Australian childhood and of its people expressed in lively and telling images: ". . . living where the sun/rolled on the land like a horse in a cloud of dust."

A series of Sydney Nolan's paintings decorate Stow's second book, *Outrider*. After this publication the term "surrealist" was heard of his work, wrongly I think. He has not, in that volume or later, abandoned effects and forms of great simplicity. Poems like "Ruins of the City of Hay" are many-sided, intricately stratified and dreamlike, but actual experience is their base. One may need a key to perceive the reality and logic but nothing in them is over or beyond reality, or beyond wit and irony:

> But the wind of the world descended on lovely Petra
> and the spires of the towers and the statues and belfries fell.
> The bones of my brothers broke in the breaking columns.
> The bones of my sisters, clasping their broken children,
> cracked on the hearthstones, under the rooftrees of hay.
> I alone mourn in the temples, by broken altars
> bowered in black nightshade and mauve salvation-jane.

> —from "Ruins of the City of Hay"

Stow has an acute, and acutely Australian, sense of dynasty. He is close in time and in imagination to his forebears who explored, possessed, named and tamed territories: "I am the country's station; all else is fever./Did we ride knee to knee down canyons, or did I dream it!" ("Strange Fruit"). This dynastic vision is clearest and most open in "Stations," a suite for three voices and three generations. A man, woman and youth speak for each generation, brilliantly evoking the history of a place and family; the whole concludes with this affirmative couplet spoken by the woman:

> Across the uncleared hills of the nameless country
> I write in blood my blood's abiding name.

In "Thailand Railway" a dying Australian prisoner of war thinks of "children on horseback, hordes of my own country," rejects the utterance of "some warning or some charge, some testament" to enjoin: "think of the childless dead and be our sons."

Stow's poetry is international by virtue of his wide reading, his allusiveness in sound, rhythm and sense but unmistakably national as to its imagery, viewpoint and frequent use of Australian idiom.

> —Nancy Keesing

STRAND, Mark. American. Born in Summerside, Prince Edward Island, Canada, 11 April 1934. Educated at Antioch College, Yellow Springs, Ohio, B.A. 1957; Yale University, New Haven, Connecticut (Cook Prize and Bergin Prize, 1959), B.F.A. 1959; University of Florence (Fulbright Fellow), 1960–61; University of Iowa, Iowa City, M.A. 1962. Married Antonia Ratensky in 1961 (divorced, 1973); has one daughter. Instructor, University of Iowa, 1962–65; Fulbright Lecturer, University of Brazil, Rio de Janeiro, 1965–66; Assistant Professor, Mount

Holyoke College, South Hadley, Massachusetts, 1967; Visiting Professor, University of Washington, Seattle, 1968, 1970; Adjunct Associate Professor, Columbia University, New York, 1969; Visiting Professor, Yale University, 1969; Associate Professor, Brooklyn College, New York, 1970–72. Since 1973, Bain-Swiggett Lecturer, Princeton University, New Jersey. Recipient: Ingram Merrill Foundation Fellowship, 1966; National Endowment for the Arts grant, 1967; Rockefeller Award, 1968. Address: 3 East 10th Street, New York, New York 10003, U.S.A.

PUBLICATIONS

Verse

Sleeping with One Eye Open.   Iowa City, Stone Wall Press, 1964.
Reasons for Moving: Poems.   New York, Atheneum, 1968.
Darker: Poems.   New York, Atheneum, 1970.
The Story of Our Lives.   New York, Atheneum, 1973.
The Sergeantville Notebook.   Providence, Rhode Island, Burning Deck, 1973.
Elegy for My Father.   Iowa City, Windhover Press, 1973.

Other

Editor, *The Contemporary American Poets: American Poetry since 1940.* Cleveland, World, 1969.
Editor, *New Poetry of Mexico.*   New York, Dutton, 1970; London, Secker and Warburg, 1973.
Editor and Translator, *The Owl's Insomnia: Selected Poems of Rafael Alberti.*   New York, Atheneum, 1973.

Translator, *18 Poems from the Quechua.*   Cambridge, Massachusetts, Halty Ferguson, 1971.

Critical Studies: "Mark Strand: Darker" by James Crenner, in *Seneca Review* (Geneva, New York), April 1971; "A Conversation with Mark Strand," in *Ohio Review* (Athens), Winter 1972; "Dark and Radiant Peripheries: Mark Strand and A. R. Ammons" by Harold Bloom, in *Southern Review* (Baton Rouge, Louisiana), Winter 1972.

*   *   *

Not allied with any of the various "schools" of poetry, Mark Strand writes in a readable, deceptively simple, almost traditional style that enhances the strange power with which he expresses disquieting thoughts. He strikes deeply into the heart of modern man; he awakens anxiety, guilt, and desperation; he arouses responses that most readers would prefer to leave dormant. He does it with ease, skill, and wit. There is an eeriness in his lyrics that is transferred to his reader; and with each rereading of a poem one is pulled deeper into "the encircling dark":

> Something is happening
> that you can't figure out.
> Things have been put in motion.
> Something is in the air.
>
> —"Something Is in the Air"

By frequent restatement of his themes, he develops a tonal consistency that is a great part of his growing strength and persuasion. Here is an imagination vitally concerned with man in the world today; or is there a world today, and is man in it?

> All places that have been
> With me will wear away.
> I do not lift my voice
> Or raise a hand. I am
> Not capable of force,
> Feeling myself at stake.
>
> —"Standing Still"

But the question concerns not only "All places that have been/With me." Who is the "me"? And why is he "Not capable of force"? What is at stake here? Do we find it in the following?

> I look at you
> and see myself
> under the surface. . . .
>
> It will always be this way.
> I stand here scared
> that you will disappear,
> scared that you will stay.
>
> —"The Man in the Mirror"

The man in the mirror pulls the reader in too, and we cannot take our eyes from it – or put it down. It is existence that is at stake, an existence that is not quite real, however: a reflected existence that is not quite life itself. We are afraid of life.

We are afraid because of the illness of our world. Some of the symptoms are developed in "From a Litany," first published in April 1969 in *The New Republic:*

> Let those in office search under their clothes for the private life.
> They will find nothing.
> Let them gather together and hold hands.
> They shall have nothing to hold.
> Let the black suited priests stand for the good life.
> Let them tell us to be more like them.
> For that is the nature of the sickness.

And what remains? There seems to be no hope. Where can we go?

> My parents rise out of their thrones
> Into the milky rooms of clouds. How can I sing?
> Time tells me what I am. I change and am the same.
> I empty myself of my life and my life remains.

These lines from "The Remains" (originally the title poem of *Darker*) leave us trying to escape from the vacuum which Strand has presented to us, but in which we have been all the time. But can it be a vacuum if we fill it? We are in a dream that Strand has made very, very real; so real that we suddenly awaken from it – not quite the same. He has made us face the questions. And still we want to go on, as he does: "One foot in front of the other,/that is the way I do it." We reach the point where

> We are reading the story of our lives
> as though we were in it,
> as though we had written it.

There can be no doubt that this is a major voice speaking, and we are eager for it to go on.

—Holly Stevens

STRYK, Lucien. American. Born in Chicago, Illinois, 7 April 1924. Educated at Indiana University, Bloomington, B.A. 1948; University of Maryland, College Park, M.F.S. 1950; University of London; the Sorbonne, Paris, M.F.S.; University of Iowa, Iowa City, M.F.A. 1956. Served in the United State Army, 1943–45. Married; has two children. Since 1958, Member of the English Department, and currently Professor of English, Northern Illinois University, DeKalb. Visiting Lecturer, Niigeta University, Japan, 1956–58, and Yamaguchi University, Japan, 1962–63; Fulbright Lecturer, Iran, 1961–62. Recipient: Grove Press Fellowship, 1960; Yale University Asia Society grant, 1961; Ford Foundation Faculty Fellowship, University of Chicago, 1963; Isaac Rosenbaum Award (*Voices*, Detroit), 1964; Swallow Press New Poetry Series Award, 1965; National Translation Grant, 1969. Agent: Doubleday Author Lecture Service, 277 Park Avenue, New York, New York 10017. Address: Department of English, Northern Illinois University, DeKalb, Illinois 60115, U.S.A.

PUBLICATIONS

Verse

Taproot: A Selection of Poems. Oxford, Fantasy Press, 1953.
The Trespasser: Poems. Oxford, Fantasy Press, 1956.
Notes for a Guidebook. Denver, Swallow, 1965.
The Pit and Other Poems. Chicago, Swallow Press, 1969.
Awakening. Chicago, Swallow Press, 1973.

Other

> Editor and Translator, with Takashi Ikemoto, *Zen: Poems, Prayers, Sermons, Anecdotes, Interviews.* New York, Doubleday, 1965.
> Editor, *Heartland: Poets of the Midwest.* DeKalb, Northern Illinois University Press, 1967.
> Editor, *World of the Buddha: A Reader.* New York, Doubleday, 1968.
> Editor and Translator, with Takashi Ikemoto, *Afterimages: Zen Poems of Shinkichi Takahashi.* Chicago, Swallow Press, and London, Alan Ross, 1970.
>
> Translator, with Takashi Ikemoto, *Zen Poems of China and Japan: The Crane's Bill.* New York, Doubleday, 1973.
> Translator, with Takashi Ikemoto, *Twelve Death Poems of the Chinese Zen Masters.* Providence, Rhode Island, Hellcoal Press, 1973.

Manuscript Collection: Mugar Memorial Library, Boston University.

Critical Studies: *On Writing, By Writers,* Boston, Ginn, 1966; Peter Michelson, in *Chicago Review,* June 1967; Interviews in *Chicago Review,* xxv, 3, 1973, and *American Poetry Review* (Philadelphia), 1974.

Lucien Stryk comments:

I consider myself primarily a poet, though I am seriously interested in Oriental philosophy. Some critics, particularly Peter Michelson, have associated me with other poets and "schools" but, frankly, I like to think of myself as an "independent."

I don't think a grown-up poet can do much about the content of his verse: he either has or hasn't worthy concerns, he is either small or large-minded, and such things as his politics and social attitudes generally get into his verse, one way or another. My chief concern as a poet is to *make* something, something firmly enough crafted to assure its life for longer than one hurried reading. How to get this done is the main study of my life, and I have developed certain methods of using the line within a patterned (by no means conventionally patterned) stanza or unit which, hopefully, help me in the task. I suppose that what some critics have called my economy of statement has to a certain degree been influenced by my work as a translator of Zen poetry, but I'm far from certain about that.

Anyhow, I try for a firm line and, most important of all, image and/or metaphor without which, so far as I'm concerned, there cannot be poetry. Whatever else he is – and he had better be much more – the poet is an active finely-tuned sensorium, his eye working perfectly with his ear, and his fingers touching delicately. When the poet *is* that, and when his theme is worthy, he *may* produce a good poem. Yet the making of a good poem is never less than a mystery, and no poet would really want to be anything less, however much he despairs.

*   *   *

For two decades, from *Taproot* (1953) to *Awakening* (1973), war has haunted Lucien Stryk's poetry. War has been the bone beneath the smile, the human constant against which love, loyalty, reverence, and all other qualities or notions of higher being must survive as best they can. This is a deep and complex awareness in Stryk, and is grounded in the poet's own memories: "memories [that] converge to form a shaft of pain" ("The Stack among the Ruins"). Generated by "the gibbet and the gas chamber," by the bombing of a Red Cross ship, by "the screaming victims thrown/From out the burning hospital/Into the burning town," the early poem "Song" from *The Trespasser* indicates just how pervasive these memories are. "Song" ends:

> The withered trees are in bloom again,
>   The earth is ripe and warm,
> But now we watch the lecher worm
>   That stains the vestal bud
> And like a fighter in the sun
>   The acrobatic bird.

We can see here the extent to which his song and vision have been colored. The mind that contemplates even the spring carries with it and always will the horrors of the past. From here on, Stryk, metaphorically speaking, will project into the body of every bird the propensities of the warplane. In "Summer," from *Awakening*, the poet's neighbor

>   scowls up at my maple, rake
> clogged and trembling,
> as its seeds spin down –
>
>   not angels, moths, but paratroopers
> carried by the wind,
> planting barricades along his eaves.

However this is read, whatever irony is directed against the sensibility that obsessively reads nature in martial terms, what is clear is that the poet understands this predilection and its origins only too well. Poem after poem will tell us that he had his fill of that life at war, that repulsive anti-life. At the same time, I think, Stryk would agree that the whole of life somehow has to be gotten into each poem.

Stryk's poems are the embodiment of an evolution that carries him along from the despair of the early work to the more balanced and hopeful strains of the later. *Taproot* and *The Trespasser* name the experiences that will temper the life's work. War becomes known, in part, through the occasional realization of love, its divine opposite. In "For Helen" from the former volume Stryk declares

>   I know that all
> True lovers and their words but serve
> A love more tender than their own. Our
> Child, the pollened wind, the swirl of
> Homing birds proclaim its power.

In *Notes for a Guidebook*, the poet's selves become students, wanderers, tourists, beachcombers. The presences of the poems visit for a first time or return to familiar places and wonder how best to live in such a world of flux and seeming contradiction. This volume seems occasionally to labor for ultimate truth and morality, for something to hold to once and for all. *Notes*, I believe, represents a tense and crucial period in the poet's life. In *The Pit and Other Poems*, Stryk comes to grips with the function and worth of his life's work, "this house/of paper" as he terms it. The recognition of this book is that the poem must change, that life is motion, that systems are at once fluid and rooted in a divine One, that if there is no final way to resolve pain and loss and death forever, a man can still come to an ease, can become, as Whitman said, a "cosmos." In "Memo to the Builder" of his house, Stryk directs: "Build me a home/The living day can enter, not a tomb." The title poem, filled with horrifying images of a pit of bodies, ends: "Ask anyone who/Saw it: nobody won that war." This represents a resolution for the poet, an insistence that, although war is a human fact and constant, its acceptance is wrong and a man could and should publish it for what it is and also, at the same time, properly distance himself from it. As he says in "Zen: The Rocks of Sesshu,"

> The weed also has the desire
>   To make clean,
> Make pure, there against the rock.

As it is in *Notes*, in *The Pit* the same desire for a spiritual calm is apparent. What is new with this book, and what deepens and matures in *Awakening*, is a dimension of peace in the face of what were previously almost debilitating conflicts and fears. "Ask anyone who/Saw it: nobody won that war" – in its straightforwardness, in its staunchness, this is a note of celebration that prefigures the grace and wisdom of Stryk's most recent work.

—William Heyen

STUART, Dabney. American. Born in Richmond, Virginia, 4 November 1937. Educated at Davidson College, North Carolina, 1956–60, A.B. 1960; Harvard University, Cambridge, Massachusetts (Summer Poetry Prize, 1962), A.M. 1962. Instructor in English, College of William and Mary, Williamsburg, Virginia, 1961–65. Since 1965, Member of the English Department, currently Associate Professor of English, Washington and Lee University, Lexington, Virginia. Visiting Professor, Middlebury College, Vermont, 1968–69. Currently, Poetry Editor, *Shenandoah*, Lexington. Recipient: Howard Willett Research Prize, College of William and Mary, 1962; Poetry Society of America Dylan Thomas Prize, 1965; John M. Glenn grant, Washington and Lee University, 1967, 1969, 1971. Address: Department of English, Washington and Lee University, Lexington, Virginia 24450, U.S.A.

PUBLICATIONS

Verse

The Diving Bell. New York, Knopf, 1966.
A Particular Place: Poems. New York, Knopf, 1969.
Corgi Modern Poets in Focus 3, with others, edited by Dannie Abse. London, Corgi, 1971.

Manuscript Collection: James Branch Cabell Library, Virginia Commonwealth University, Richmond, Virginia.

Critical Studies: by X. J. Kennedy, in *Shenandoah* (Lexington, Virginia), Autumn 1966; John Unterecker, in *Shenandoah* (Lexington, Virginia), Autumn 1969; Dannie Abse, in *Corgi Modern Poets in Focus 3*, 1971; a biographical statement by the author, in *Contemporary Poetry in America*, edited by Miller Williams, New York, Random House, 1973.

Dabney Stuart comments:

I feel I have done as much as I am capable of doing in the traditional verse forms of lyric poetry, and that now the essential task is to find, or more properly invent, forms of my own. Which is to say that in terms of my life as a poet I am just the other side of apprenticeship.

*   *   *

Dabney Stuart has received impressive tributes for his skill, his intelligence, and his veracity to experience. In his first book, *The Diving Bell*, he revealed himself as a master of the well-made poem. His command of language and his confident handling of relatively traditional forms are combined there with a gentle candour which enables many of the poems to transcend the category of Lowellesque confessional verse into which they run the risk of falling. There is nothing trite about his contribution to this genre. For example, in a poem for the small daughter whom he seldom sees he speaks of her as a conjuror: "Your voice a wand, you called the olives grapes," but adds later:

> Yet, deserting your role,
> You called me by my name –
> I'd rather
> Have been that metaphor, your father.

Here language is both image and instrument.

His second book makes a necessary advance into more adventurous territory. It includes, in fact, a number of poems about places, contemplative in tone, dwelling on stone and water, air and stillness. But it explores also deeper regions of symbol and myth, psychic landscapes, in forms which owe little to tradition.

There is always a danger that this kind of poem may not come off. A few here, even in Stuart's accomplished hands, fail. About those which do not it is, in a sense, impossible to make final judgments: their success depends very much on the range of experience and the type of attention which the reader brings to them, and on the reverberations they cause in his mind. Many of the poems in this book have a haunting resonance which gives more with every reading.

—Fleur Adcock

SUMMERS, Hollis (Spurgeon, Jr.). American. Born in Eminence, Kentucky, 21 June 1916. Educated at Georgetown College, Kentucky, A.B. 1937; Bread Loaf School of English, Middlebury College, Vermont, M.A. 1943; University of Iowa, Iowa City, Ph.D. 1949. Married Laura Vimont Clarke in 1943; has two children. Taught at Holmes High School, Covington, Kentucky, 1937–44; Professor of English, Georgetown College, 1945–49, and the University of Kentucky, Lexington, 1949–59. Since 1959, Distinguished Professor of English, Ohio University, Athens. Adviser, Ford Foundation Conference on Writers in America, 1958; Lecturer, Arts Program, Association of American Colleges, 1958–63; Danforth Lecturer, 1963–66. Recipient: Fund for the Advancement of Education grant, 1951; *Saturday Review* Poetry Award, 1957; Colleges of Arts and Sciences Award, 1958. LL.D.: Georgetown College, 1965. Address: 181 North Congress Street, Athens, Ohio 45701, U.S.A.

PUBLICATIONS

Verse

The Walks near Athens. New York, Harper, 1959.
Someone Else: Sixteen Poems about Other Children. Philadelphia, Lippincott, 1962.
Seven Occasions. New Brunswick, New Jersey, Rutgers University Press, 1965.
The Peddler and Other Domestic Matters. New Brunswick, New Jersey, Rutgers University Press, 1967.
Sit Opposite Each Other. New Brunswick, New Jersey, Rutgers University Press, 1970.
Start from Home. New Brunswick, New Jersey, Rutgers University Press, 1972.

Novels

City Limit. Boston, Houghton Mifflin, 1948.
Brighten the Corner. New York, Doubleday, 1952.
Teach You a Lesson, with James Rourke (as Jim Hollis). New York, Harper, 1955; London, Foulsham, 1956.
The Weather of February. New York, Harper, 1957.
The Day after Sunday. New York, Harper, 1968.
The Garden. New York, Harper, 1972.

Short Stories

How They Chose the Dead. Baton Rouge, Louisiana State University Press, 1973.

Other

Editor, *Kentucky Story: A Collection of Short Stories.* Lexington, University of Kentucky Press, 1954.

Editor, with Edgar Whan, *Literature: An Introduction.* New York, McGraw
  Hill, 1960.
Editor, *Discussions of the Short Story.* Boston, Heath, 1963.

Hollis Summers comments:

  Could these words serve, some of them, as a statement of faith?

> A poem is moving down a summer street,
> Darkly, unsure, yet pretending
> That assumption is a name for fact;
>
> Pretending even street and season,
> It walks with carefully balanced faith to meet
> A space for turning, to bring
> The eyes, even if blinded for the act,
> To look back,
>   To ask the reason
> For the movement:
>   Darkness again, perhaps, or
> Darkness barred with slanted light from an opened door.

—from "A Poem Is Moving Down a Summer Street"
  in *The Walks near Athens*

> You can tell almost all in a poem.
> Tears, semen, and bowel movements
> Come precisely with fairly simple aids:
> Color and consistency charts
> Stapled to the wish to show and shout.
>
> I also wish to show and shout,
> Look at me, look here, look out
> From where you read, considering the poems I need.
> I'm sorry I have been reared
> Believing poems that said, "Look there."
>
> A poem is room enough to skin a cat in;
> A poem is shaking a stick at a cat;
> A poem is skinning a cat more ways than one.

—from "For Three Specific Friends"
  in *The Peddler and Other Domestic Matters*

*   *   *

  Since *The Walks near Athens,* Hollis Summers' poetry has been characterized by
an ease of expression, an effortlessness that balances his classical elegance with
rhythms so casual that they seem spontaneous. The beginning lines of "On
Looking at Television's Late Movies," for example, move so surely that they seem
almost offhand:

> John Keats sank into nothingness
> Over a star or the song of a bird
> Or a vase or marbles, or even the sea
> In which he assumed his name was writ.

The lines turn their corners perfectly, as the poem begins to turn on its ironies. Summers' labor has always been to understand the assumptions that we consider facts, and to write clearly about them. This poem ends: "In the water where Keats wrote I have read/Permanence. I am glad he is dead."

Here and throughout Summers' poetry, romantic notions of beauty (perhaps the most important word in his work) are turned mercilessly on the spit of experience. Faiths built on notions of meaning or permanence are held in the light for what they are. We sing, Summers concludes in the title poem of *Seven Occasions*, "for no final reason." "Song to Be Attached" from *The Peddler and Other Domestic Matters* might serve as a metaphor for his unrelenting vision. Three stanzas tell us to "Decorate the carcass/Thread with amethyst," to "Deck the bowels with ruby." But the poem concludes:

> Braise in precious ointment
> Drench it if you will
> Decorate the carcass
> It is a carcass still.

It is not easy to say these things. In "Song for a Dead Lady" from *Sit Opposite Each Other*, Summers tells us that "it is good she is dead . . ./But I had to live a long time/To say this song." Summers is one of America's finest, most underrated poets. Volume after volume has clarified a voice and a vision that will come to engage us as among the most memorable of our time.

—William Heyen

SUTTON, Henry.   See **SLAVITT, David.**

SWARD, Robert S.   American; Canadian Landed Immigrant.   Born in Chicago, Illinois, 23 June 1933. Educated at Von Steuben High School, Chicago; San Diego Junior College, California, 1951; University of Illinois, Urbana, 1953–56, B.A. (honors) 1956 (Phi Beta Kappa); Bread Loaf School of English, Middlebury, Vermont, Summers 1965–58; University of Iowa, Iowa City, M.A. 1958; University of Bristol (Fulbright Fellow), 1960–61. Served in the United States Navy in Korea, 1951–53. Married Diane Kaldes in 1960 (divorced); has four daughters and one son. Research Fellow, 1956–58, and Poet-in-Residence, Spring 1967, University of Iowa; Lecturer in English, Connecticut College, New London, 1958–59; Visiting Writer-in-Residence, Cornell University, Ithaca, New York, 1962–64; Poet-in-Residence,

Aspen Writers' Conference, Colorado, Summer 1967. Since 1969, Poet-in-Residence, University of Victoria, British Columbia. Since 1970, Founding Editor and Publisher, Soft Press, Victoria. Recipient: Dylan Thomas Award, 1958; Yaddo Fellowship, Summers 1959–69; MacDowell Colony Fellowship, Summers 1959–72; Guggenheim Fellowship, 1964; University of New Mexico D. H. Lawrence Fellowship, 1966. Agent: Ms. Helen Brann, Sterling Lord Agency Inc., 660 Madison Avenue, New York, New York 10021. Address: 1050 Saint David Street, Victoria, British Columbia, Canada.

PUBLICATIONS

Verse

Advertisements: Poems.   Chicago, Odyssey Chapbook Publications, 1958.
Uncle Dog and Other Poems.   London, Putnam, 1962.
Kissing the Dancer and Other Poems.   Ithaca, New York, Cornell University Press, 1964.
Thousand-Year-Old Fiancée and Other Poems.   Ithaca, New York, Cornell University Press, 1965.
In Mexico and Other Poems.   London, Ambit, 1966.
Horgbortum Stringbottom, I Am Yours, You Are History.   Chicago, Swallow Press, 1970.
Quorum/Noah.   Victoria, Soft Press, 1970.
Songs from the Jurassac Shales.   Victoria, Soft Press, 1970.
Hannah's Cartoon.   Victoria, Soft Press, 1970.
Gift.   Victoria, privately printed, 1970.
Raspberry (as Dr. Soft).   Victoria, privately printed, 1971.
Risk.   Victoria, privately printed, 1971.
Poems: New and Selected 1957–1973.   Chicago, Swallow Press, 1973.

Play

Events Surrounding the Supposed Progress of Four Homosexual Karate Experts Through the Streets of Chicago to the Palace of Hugh Hefner, with Lawrence Russell (produced Bellingham, Washington, 1971).

Other

Editor, *Cloud Nine: Vancouver Island Poems.*   Victoria, Soft Press, 1973.

Bibliography: by John Gill, in *New: American and Canadian Poetry* (Trumansburg, New York), 1973.

Manuscript Collection: Rare Books and Special Collections, Washington University Library, St. Louis.

Critical Studies: Introduction by William Meredith to *Kissing the Dancer and Other Poems,* 1964; *A Controversy of Poets,* New York, Doubleday, 1965; "A Poetry Chronicle" by Constance Urdang, in *Poetry* (Chicago), 17 February 1972.

Robert Sward comments:

Person, place and thing. Things of this world, things of that world. Measures based upon speech phrases, syllable-count and syllable no-count. Collage, free-verse, song, speech, protest. Rock. Acid-Rock. Architecture. Stand-up burlesque comedians. Flashing lights. Lights that are not flashing. Silence. Silence. Space. New Mexico. New Hampshire. Mt. Monadnock. Love. Judith. Barbara, Michael, Alexis. White houses and yellow houses. The thousand-year-old fiancée. Robert David Cohen. Wayne Boohers. The thinker, Increase Mather. Ether. Fire. Aquarian ascendant. The mystic Baba RamDass. The man Richard Alpert. Michael Dennis Browne, the poet. "Who am I?" "Whence have I come?" "Where am I going?" Tantra says: *I am all this.*

*   *   *

A striking feature of Robert Sward's poetry is its range: he is a master of unique observation, gifted with emotional recall, capable of goofy humor as well as experiments in disdain, and properly turned off by war and the diplomatic posture of his native America. Sward's recently published "Statement of Poetics" – a poem that appeared in *New: American & Canadian Poetry 20* – may indicate Sward's attitudes accurately enough, though it may also indicate his disdain for unanswerable poetic questions. He is outrageous as often as not, seeming capable of walking on words halfway between double exposures of put-on and truth:

> Talk
> people talking, getting that
> into one's poetry that
> is my poetics. Love
> hate lies laughing stealings
> self-confession self-destruction
> get them all get
> them all into writing.
> No one has to
> read them. No one
> has to publish them.
> I am more and
> more for unpublished poetry.

Sward's delight with language is evident in all his poetry, and the reader senses a healthy dose of play at work in every poem. He revels in the power of the final word, which he uses with delight against the innocent as well as those who have crossed him. He writes in "Mothers-In-Law" (both of whom he lost through divorce) that the first of them:

> required, upon departure,
> The services of three gentlemen
>   with shoehorns
> To get her back into her large black
> Studebaker.

The reader experiences vicarious pleasure imagining the lady in question thumbing through Robert's book. It may be play of an adolescent nature, but how grand to have a poet awaken the childishness within us.

Indeed, if we accept spontaneity as a primary quality of childhood, Sward's childishness is virtually unequalled. The poetry that results is sometimes half-baked, but so direct of statement that we feel, unquestionably, the poet's complete, warty presence: I'll take this kind of unguarded, risky stuff anyday in preference to the urbane, sophisticated verse of poets (half his age!) who write within only a limited range of highly selected posturings. Sward is willing to let his reader hate him; yet he, himself, escapes the pit of self-hatred. At times, his spontaneity works against him, as in the polemic "In Mexico," where after describing his opposition to American war policies, he concludes: "What a country!/For even/Your stupidity,/The Charm/Of Your/Tastelessness,/Vitality,/Greed// *America, get out/Of Vietnam,/The Dominican Republic,/Africa, Europe/Southeast Asia//* Has begun to smell/Has begun to smell/I would say/Like the Pentagon,/Like senility/Like death." I believe poems written without deference to academic standards should rise above such standards, not be vulnerable to the kind of bitchy complaint that says the subjects "stupidity" and "charm" are not capable of their verbs, and the abstract image is not even linguistically interesting, unless Sward intends a different subject. In any case, spontaneity in this instance results in dull rhetoric.

For each of his few failed risks, Sward has many poems that win against the odds; his only form, the integrity of his voice. The language is tight, the words comprehensible, and he can move up off the page, out of the words, like a man coming into sunlight. I admire his fullness, and will end with excerpts from two distinctly different poems:

> Pine cones, aspen,
> Starlight, the light
> World one way, then another
> The light rising,
> The light drawn up into stars
>
> Voice is light,
> The world is light
> The stars, their hands
> Striking through

—from "San Cristobal"

> It's a calculated risk, whatever you do.
> A man has cancer of the rectum. You
> take out his rectum and
> maybe he dies of heart failure.
> Or he's fine and goes on for 20 years.

—from "Risk"

—Geof Hewitt

SWENSON, May. American. Born in Logan, Utah, 28 May 1919. Educated at Utah State University, Logan, B.A. 1939. Editor, New Directions Press, New

York, 1959–66. Poet-in-Residence, Purdue University, Layfayette, Indiana, 1966–67; Poetry Seminar Instructor, University of North Carolina, Greensboro, 1968–69, and Lothbridge University, Alberta, 1970. Recipient: Rockefeller Fellowship, 1955, 1967; Breadloaf Writers' Conference Robert Frost Fellowship, 1957; Guggenheim Fellowship, 1959; William Rose Benet Prize, 1959; Longview Foundation Award, 1959; Amy Lowell Traveling Fellowship, 1960; National Institute of Arts and Letters Award, 1960; Ford Fellowship, for drama, 1964; Brandeis University Creative Arts Award, 1966; Utah State University Distinguished Service Gold Medal, 1967; Lucy Martin Donnelly Fellowship, Bryn Mawr College, 1968; Shelley Memorial Award, 1968. Member, National Institute of Arts and Letters. Address: 73 The Boulevard, Sea Cliff, New York 11579, U.S.A.

PUBLICATIONS

Verse

Another Animal.   New York, Scribner, 1954.
A Cage of Spines.   New York, Holt Rinehart, 1958.
To Mix with Time: New and Selected Poems.   New York, Scribner, 1963.
Poems to Solve.   New York, Scribner, 1966.
Half Sun, Half Sleep: New Poems.   New York, Scribner, 1967.
Iconographs: Poems.   New York, Scribner, 1970.
More Poems to Solve.   New York, Scribner, 1971.

Recording: Today's Poets 2, with others, Folkways, 1968.

Play

The Floor (produced New York, 1966). Published in First Stage (West Layfayette, Indiana), vi, 2, 1967.

Other

The Contemporary Poet as Artist and Critic.   Boston, Little Brown, 1964.

Translator, Windows and Stones: Selected Poems, by Tomas Transtromer.   Pittsburgh, University of Pittsburgh Press, 1972.

Manuscript Collection: Rare Book Room, Washington University Library, St. Louis.

Critical Studies: "The Poetry of May Swenson" by Betty Miller Davis, in Prairie Schooner (Lincoln, Nebraska), Winter 1960; "About May Swenson" by John Hall Wheelock, in Wilson Library Bulletin (New York), January 1962; "One Knows by Seeing" by Richard Moore, in The Nation (New York), 10 August 1963; "Turned Back to the Wild by Love" by Richard Howard, in Tri-Quarterly (Evanston, Illinois), 1966; "A Ball with Language" by Karl Shapiro, in The New York Times Book Review, 7 May 1967; "The Art of Perceiving" by Ann Stanford, in Southern Review (Baton Rouge, Louisiana), January 1969.

May Swenson comments:

I devise my own forms. My themes are from the organic, the inorganic, and the psychological world. I tend to create a typographical or iconographic frame for my poems *after* the text is complete.

*   *   *

May Swenson is extremely deft and inventive with sounds and shapes in language. And with that, she is reckless, an attempter of oddities. A juggler and acrobat, she has performed so consistently that her poems find their way into many well known magazines, such as *Harper's, The Atlantic,* and *The New Yorker.*

Her agile language has brought fame. Another quality has saved her from the hovering envy of competing writers: she forces her talent into metaphysical attempts and into the service of causes that have solid appeal.

To hear her read to an audience is to become aware of what she has yoked together. Her voice is intense, not at ease – at work. And her surprising, fountaining lines go steadily into their blend of brilliance and integrity. It is the combination that distinguishes her.

She is from the West – Utah. But she has made New York City into her place. An example, an emblem for the foregoing characterizations, is her poem "On Seeing Rocks Cropping Out of a Hill in Central Park":

> Boisterous water arrested, these rocks
> are water's body in death. Transparent
>
> water falling without stop makes a wall,
> the frenzied soul of rock its white breath.
>
> Dark water's inflated wave, harsh spray
> is ghost of a boulder and cave's
>
> marble, agitated drapery. Stillness
> water screams for, flying forth,
>
> the body of death. Rock dreams
> soul's motion, its hard birth.

—from Half Sun Half Sleep

—William Stafford

TAGLIABUE, John. American. Born in Cantu, Como, Italy, 1 July 1923. Educated at Columbia University, New York, B.A. 1944 (Phi Beta Kappa), M.A. in art and literature 1945, 1947–48; University of Florence, Italy (Fulbright Scholar), 1950–52. Married Grace Ten Eyck in 1946; has two daughters. Lecturer in American Poetry, American University of Beirut, Lebanon, 1945–46, and Washington

State College, Pullman, 1946–47; Assistant Professor of American Literature, Alfred University, New York, 1948–50; Fulbright Lecturer in American Poetry, University of Pisa, Italy, 1950–52, and Tokyo University, Japan, 1958–60. Member of the English Department, 1953–58, Associate Professor, 1960–71, and since 1971, Professor of English, Bates College, Lewiston, Maine. Formerly, Poet-in-Residence, Bennett College, Greensboro, North Carolina, International Institute of Madrid, Spain, and the University of Rio Grande do Norte, Natal, Brazil. Recipient: Bates College grant, 1969. Agent: Russell and Volkening, 551 Fifth Avenue, New York, New York 10017. Address: 59 Webster Street, Lewiston, Maine, U.S.A.

PUBLICATIONS

Verse

Poems.   New York, Harper, 1959.
A Japanese Journal.   San Francisco, Kayak Books, 1966.
The Buddha Uproar: Poems.   San Francisco, Kayak Books, 1967.
The Doorless Door.   Tokyo, Mushinsha Press, 1970.

Plays

A Journal Concerning Noh, in First Stage (Layfayette, Indiana), Spring 1963.
Mario in the Land of the Unicorns: A Puppet Play, in Carolina Review 16, Spring 1964.

Manuscript Collection: George Arents Research Library, Syracuse University, New York.

John Tagliabue comments:

(1970) Poetry is all a matter of design, play, ritual, decorations, symbolism, and like our life it is always changing. I have been writing poems for many years and my moods and styles have changed – sometimes as I see new places, new people, get new suggestions – and yet something which at the moment I can't say in prose doesn't seem to change. I like poems and dances to help make us realize many festivals, all kinds of holidays.

(1974) Often and there are thousands of them, written in many moods, in many countries, in many religions and love affairs, the poems speak, sing, dance, celebrate for themselves-and-others. I must let it go at that now. The many Travel Journals that I've been keeping might help; they are related to the USA and Italy, Spain, France, England, Greece, Lebanon, Syria, Mexico, Guatemala, Brazil, Peru, Japan, and some other places.

*   *   *

John Tagliabue is an unashamedly happy poet, content – too – to be an inexorably minor one. In an age of what Robert Graves once called "posterity-conscious heavyweights" this is no bad thing; but one has to add that many of Tagliabue's poems, charming though they are, are almost too insubstantial to make their presence felt at all. They tend to blow away before one has finished reading them:

> Mountain
> of Chinese noodles,
> heaven for a poor man.

This is too obvious, too matter-of-fact, to achieve the true quality of the kind of miniaturist Japanese poetry that has so entranced and influenced this author. Many attempts, of course, have been made to carry over this quality into English verse, and very few of them have succeeded. It is perhaps unfortunate that Tagliabue has confined so much of his poetic intention to the effort. When he becomes more thoughtful he is not only enchanted by life (which is the chief, and attractive, feature of his verse as a whole) but also enchanting, as in "Friendship":

> Sleep sat next to me
> Like a man on the subway.
> Sleep said, Write a poem.
> I said, You are a poem.
> Sleep was my friend.
> Always between places
> we are closing our eyes
> and growing. We are
> always going towards
> each other or poetry.
> Sleep said, Have I written you?
> You said, I am sleepy.

—Martin Seymour-Smith

TARN, Nathaniel. British. Born in Paris, France, 30 June 1928. Educated at Cambridge University, B.A. (honours) 1948, M.A. 1952; the Sorbonne and Ecole des Hautes Etudes, Paris, Cert. C.F.R.E.; University of Chicago, M.A. 1952, Ph.D. 1957; London School of Economics; School of Oriental and African Studies, University of London. Married; has two children. Has worked as an anthropologist in Guatemala and Burma. Formerly, Member of the Faculty, University of Chicago, and University of London; Visiting Professor, State University of New York, Buffalo, and Princeton University, New Jersey, 1969–70. Since 1970, Professor of Comparative Literature, Rutgers University, New Brunswick, New Jersey. General Editor, Cape Editions, and Director, Cape Goliard Limited, publishers, London, 1967–69. Recipient: Guinness Prize, 1963. Address: c/o Talese, Random House, 210 East 50th Street, New York, New York 10022, U.S.A.

PUBLICATIONS

Verse

> Old Savage/Young City. London, Cape, 1964; New York, Random House,
> 1965.
> Penguin Modern Poets 7, with Richard Murphy and Jon Silkin. London,
> Penguin, 1965.
> Where Babylon Ends. London, Cape Goliard Press, and New York, Gross-
> man, 1968.
> The Beautiful Contradictions. London, Cape Goliard Press, 1969; New York,
> Random House, 1970.
> October: A Sequence of Ten Poems Followed by Requiem Pro Duabus Filiis
> Israel. London, Trigram Press, 1969.
> The Silence. Milan, M'Arte, 1970.
> A Nowhere for Vallejo: Choices, October. New York, Random House, 1971;
> London, Cape, 1972.
> Lyrics for the Bride of God: Section: The Artemision. Bolinas, California,
> Tree Books, 1973.
> The Persephones. Santa Barbara, California, Christopher's Books, 1974.

Other

> Editor, and Translator with others, Con Cuba: An Anthology of Cuban Poetry
> of the Last Sixty Years. London, Cape Goliard Press, and New York,
> Grossman, 1969.
> Editor, and Translator with others, Selected Poems: A Bilingual Edition, by
> Pablo Neruda. London, Cape, 1970; New York, Delacorte Press, 1972.
>
> Translator, The Heights of Macchu Picchu, by Pablo Neruda. London, Cape,
> 1966; New York, Farrar Straus, 1967.
> Translator, Stelae, by Victor Segalen. Santa Barbara, California, Unicorn
> Press, 1969.

Nathaniel Tarn comments:

Poetry for me is the discovery of a sound which arises out of unimpeded
listening. The sound, once recognized, can assume a number of voices; my
life-history happens to have given me no convincing English of my own. I have
always been fascinated by the interplay between restricted and elaborated codes,
between common parlances and formal rhetorics. Form is usually allowed to grow
out of content, though I am aware of moving towards more and more open form as
I discover that there is less and less that *cannot* be discussed in poetry. In the
early work, my anthropological experience prompted me to speak out of various
personae associated with *Old Savage*; an old, wise Amerindian or Melanesian,
aware of what our culture has done to his, forgiving, sad at his own destruction
principally because it mirrors the destruction of the whole natural earth. Dropping
anthropology as a profession has enabled me to speak as an anthropologist and add
the dialectic of observer and observed to the previous one-dimensional picture. As
a result, politics have become a major factor in recent work such as *The Beautiful
Contradictions*. This complex material is offset by simple lyrical-erotic sequences

such as occur in *October.* The aim is to work towards more and more satisfactory resolutions of the tension between simplicity and complexity.

We may be living at a time when only the exasperation of contradictions is possible for the artist; synthesis is closed to him because of the intolerable weight of new information he must shoulder each day. In this situation, poetry is more than ever a discipline, the means whereby a poet not only discovers, but literally creates, himself out of the total flux. Silence is more than poetry's complement: it is that which poetry must sink back into the moment it ceases to perform this function. It follows that poetry for poetry's sake – decoration *et al.* – is intolerable.

Translation is (i) a duty within the Republic of Letters; (ii) a way of allowing various voices to speak; (iii) a means of letting air into the stale bed of English letters. Editorial activity is an extension of translation, not only from languages but from disciplines. *Transformation* is a key concept, linking early allegiances to Surrealism with present interests in Structuralism.

*   *   *

That Nathaniel Tarn is a professional anthropologist and that he is a learned and highly informed exponent (as his editorship of Cape Editions demonstrates) of cosmopolitan art and thought are facts of importance in the consideration of his poetry. In an era when the impact of European and South American poetry is being more universally felt among younger poets than ever before, Tarn's poetry is nevertheless the most non-traditional and foreign-influenced of any British poet now writing. It seems appropriate that he was born in the cosmopolitan city of Paris. The chief single influence upon him has undoubtedly been the Chilean poet, Pablo Neruda, whose long poem *The Heights of Macchu Picchu* he has translated with conspicuous success.

Tarn is a "difficult" poet in the sense that his poems yield up little of their meaning when a traditional type of interpretation is applied to them. He eschews what he would call the false neatness of the traditional English-language poem (as well exemplified in Graves, Andrew Young, or Roy Fuller) and embraces a procedure in which the only brake (but an important one) to unconscious, wholly intuitive writing is rhetoric. The sprawlingness of his verse, its relentless search for space, particularly recalls the veteran surrealist Pablo Neruda. An individual line such as "Streets like flexed muscles cannot knock me out" clinches the matter.

Tarn's use of language is only semi-surrealist, however; his many descriptions of landscape, evocative of both its appearance and its atmosphere, make use of a remarkably consistent range of metaphor and imagery. His quest – one that is felt to be desperate if we are to judge from his language – is to rediscover the primitive in the midst of the civilized – hence the title of his first volume, *Old Savage/Young City.* In this he has almost certainly been influenced, though not at any superficial level, by the French anthropologist Claude Lévi-Strauss. Characteristic of the thought underlying his poems are these lines from "Old Savage/Young City,"

> On the day the earth achieved enlightment –
> as it is said: each blade of grass shall know itself
> knowing the wind it bends to its own purpose . . .,

which clearly reflect the influences of Oriental thought and folk-poetry. If Tarn is religious, he is religious only in the most primitive – that is to say, pre-civilized – sense. "For the Death of Anton Webern Particularly," one of his simpler poems, is not always successful in the avoidance of cliché; but it aptly illustrates both his concerns and his faith:

I need to ask what Sunday God first churned
his cauldron world in such a manner that we all deal death. . . .
And how, at last, the notes
composed by fragile Webern survive the boil and music in the bubbles.

His most recent long poem, *The Beautiful Contradictions*, describing "the quest for reality" continuing from innocence through "every shade of complexity to the exhaustion of human capacities," again, perhaps more emphatically, demonstrates his debt to Lévi-Strauss and his extremely radical interpretation of historical and anthropological data. Its weakness lies, again, in its sprawlingness and rhythmical innocuousness – Tarn's energy has become dispersed in his dialectic rather than in his technique or his language – but it is nonetheless a notably serious poem in theme.

—Martin Seymour-Smith

TATE, Allen. American. Born in Winchester, Kentucky, 19 November 1899. Educated at Georgetown Preparatory School, Washington, D.C.; Vanderbilt University, Nashville, Tennessee, B.A. 1922. Married Caroline Gordon, in 1924; Isabella Stewart Gardner, *q.v.*, 1959; Helen Heinz, 1967; has three children. Member of the Fugitive Group of Poets: Founding Editor, with John Crowe Ransom, *The Fugitive*, Nashville, 1922–25. Editor, *Sewanee Review*, Tennessee, 1944–46; Editor, Belles Lettres series, Henry Holt and Company, New York, 1946–48. Lecturer in English, Southwestern College, Memphis, Tennessee, 1934–36; Professor of English, The Woman's College, Greensboro, North Carolina, 1938–39; Poet-in-Residence, Princeton University, New Jersey, 1939–42; Lecturer in the Humanities, New York University, 1947–51. Since 1951, Professor of English, University of Minnesota, Minneapolis: Regents' Professor, 1966; Professor Emeritus, 1968. Visiting Professor in the Humanities, University of Chicago, 1949; Fulbright Lecturer, Oxford University, 1953, University of Rome, 1953–54, and Oxford and Leeds universities, 1958–59; Department of State Lecturer at the universities of Liège and Louvain, 1954, Delhi and Bombay, 1956, the Sorbonne, Paris, 1956, Nottingham, 1956, and Urbino and Florence, 1961; Visiting Professor of English, University of North Carolina, Greensboro, 1966, and Vanderbilt University, 1967. Phi Beta Kappa Orator, University of Virginia, Charlottesville, 1936, and University of Minnesota, 1952; Phi Beta Kappa Poet, College of William and Mary, Williamsburg, Virginia, 1948, and Columbia University, New York, 1950; Member, Phi Beta Kappa Senate, 1951–53. Since 1948, Fellow, and since 1956, Senior Fellow, Kenyon School of English (now School of Letters, Indiana University, Bloomington). Consultant in Poetry, Library of Congress, Washington, D.C., 1943–44. Recipient: Guggenheim Fellowship, 1928, 1929; National Institute of Arts and Letters grant, 1948; Bollingen Prize, 1957; Brandeis University Creative Arts Award, 1960; Gold Medal of the Dante Society, Florence, 1962; Academy of American Poets Fellowship, 1963. Litt.D.: University of Louisville, Kentucky, 1948; Coe College, Cedar Rapids, Iowa, 1955; Colgate University, Hamilton, New York, 1956; University of Kentucky, Lexington, 1960; Carleton College, Northfield, Minnesota, 1963; University of the South, Sewanee, Tennessee, 1970; M.A.: Oxford University, 1958. Member, American Academy of Arts and Letters. President, National Institute of Arts and Letters, 1968. Since 1964, Member, Board of Chancellors, Academy of American Poets. Address: Running Knob Hollow Road, Sewanee, Tennessee 37375, U.S.A.

PUBLICATIONS

Verse

The Golden Mean and Other Poems, with Ridley Wills. Privately printed, 1923.
Mr. Pope and Other Poems. New York, Minton Balch, 1928.
Ode to the Confederate Dead: Being the Revised and Final Version of a Poem Previously Published on Several Occasions: To Which Are Added Message from Abroad and The Cross. New York, Minton Balch, 1930.
Poems: 1928–1931. New York, Scribner, 1932.
The Mediterranean and Other Poems. New York, Alcestis Press, 1936.
Selected Poems. New York and London, Scribner, 1937.
Sonnets at Christmas. Cummington, Massachusetts, Cummington Press, 1941.
The Winter Sea: A Book of Poems. Cummington, Massachusetts, Cummington Press, 1944.
Poems, 1920–1945: A Selection. London, Eyre and Spottiswoode, 1947.
Poems, 1922–1947. New York, Scribner, 1948.
Two Conceits for the Eye to Sing, If Possible. Cummington, Massachusetts, Cummington Press, 1950.
Poems. New York, Scribner, 1960.
The Swimmers and Other Selected Poems. London, Oxford University Press, 1970; New York, Scribner, 1971.

Play

The Governess, with Anne Goodwin Winslow (produced Minneapolis, 1962).

Novel

The Fathers. New York, Putnam, 1938; London, Eyre and Spottiswoode, 1939; revised edition, Denver, Swallow, and Eyre and Spottiswoode, 1960.

Other

Stonewall Jackson: The Good Soldier: A Narrative. New York, Minton Balch, 1928; London, Cassell, 1930.
Jefferson Davis: His Rise and Fall: A Biographical Narrative. New York, Minton Balch, 1929.
Reactionary Essays on Poetry and Ideas. New York and London, Scribner, 1936.
Reason in Madness: Critical Essays. New York, Putnam, 1941.
Invitation to Learning, with Huntington Cairns and Mark Van Doren. New York, Random House, 1941.
Sixty American Poets, 1896–1944: A Preliminary Checklist. Washington, D.C., Library of Congress, 1945.
On the Limits of Poetry: Selected Essays, 1928–1948. New York, Swallow Press-Morrow, 1948.
The Hovering Fly and Other Essays. Cummington, Massachusetts, Cummington Press, 1949.

The Forlorn Demon: Didactic and Critical Essays. Chicago, Regnery, 1953.
The Man of Letters in the Modern World: Selected Essays, 1928–1955. Cleveland, Meridian, and London, Thames and Hudson, 1955.
Collected Essays. Denver, Swallow, 1959.
Christ and the Unicorn: An Address. . . . Iowa City, Cummington Press, 1966.
Essays of Four Decades. Chicago, Swallow Press, 1969; London, Oxford University Press, 1970.
Modern Literature and the Lost Traveller. Nashville, Tennessee, George Peabody College for Teachers, 1969.
The Translation of Poetry. Washington, D.C., Library of Congress, 1972.

Editor, with others, *Fugitives: An Anthology of Verse.* New York, Harcourt Brace, 1928.
Editor, with Herbert Agar, *Who Owns America? A New Declaration of Independence.* Boston, Houghton Mifflin, 1936.
Editor, with A. Theodore Johnson, *America Through the Essay: An Anthology for English Courses.* New York, Oxford University Press, 1938.
Editor, *The Language of Poetry.* Princeton, New Jersey, Princeton University Press, and London, Oxford University Press, 1942.
Editor, *Princeton Verse Between Two Wars: An Anthology.* Princeton, New Jersey, Princeton University Press, and London, Oxford University Press, 1942.
Editor, with John Peale Bishop, *American Harvest: Twenty Years of Creative Writing in the United States.* New York, Fischer, 1942.
Editor, *Recent American Poetry and Poetic Criticism: A Selected List of References.* Washington, D.C., Library of Congress, 1943.
Editor, *A Southern Vanguard* (the John Peale Bishop memorial anthology). New York, Prentice Hall, 1947.
Editor, *The Collected Poems of John Peale Bishop.* New York, Scribner, 1948.
Editor, with Caroline Gordon, *The House of Fiction: An Anthology of the Short Story.* New York, Scribner, 1950; revised edition, 1960.
Editor, with Lord David Cecil, *Modern Verse in English, 1900–1950.* London, Eyre and Spottiswoode, and New York, Macmillan, 1958.
Editor, with John Berryman and Ralph Ross, *The Arts of Reading.* New York, Crowell, 1960.
Editor, *Selected Poems of John Peale Bishop.* London, Chatto and Windus, 1960.
Editor, with Robert Penn Warren, *Selected Poems,* by Denis Devlin. New York, Holt Rinehart, 1963.
Editor, *T. S. Eliot: The Man and His Work.* New York, Delacorte Press, 1966; London, Chatto and Windus, 1967.
Editor, *The Complete Poems and Selected Criticism of Edgar Allan Poe.* New York, New American Library, 1968.
Editor, *Six American Poets: From Emily Dickinson to the Present: An Introduction.* London, Oxford University Press, 1972.

Translator, *The Vigil of Venus.* Cummington, Massachusetts, Cummington Press, 1943.

Bibliographies: "Allen Tate: A Checklist" by Willard Thorp, in *Princeton University Library Bulletin* (New Jersey), April 1942; reprinted, with "Allen Tate: A Checklist Continued" by James Korges, in *Critique* (Minneapolis), x, 2, 1968.

Critical Studies: *The Last Alternatives* by R. K. Meiners, Denver, Swallow, 1962; *Tradition and Dream* by Walter Allen, London, Phoenix House, 1964; *Allen Tate: A Literary Biography* by Radcliffe Squires, Indianapolis, Bobbs Merrill, 1971.

*   *   *

Before he attained his twenty-fifth birthday, Allen Tate had become one of the masters of the "modernist" idiom of his century. He had learned how to employ a classical wit as an antidote against bathos. He had learned to center his poems in images, most of which, like a warning buoy in shoal water, radiated signals of alarm. Like Mallarmé he conceived of poetry as emerging from "language in a state of crisis." Like Mallarmé he felt it was better to suggest than to state. Like T. S. Eliot he tended to underline the theme of "dissociation" by turning nervously from image to image, wryly fragmenting his perceptions. At the same time, however, like Eliot once again, he also wished for a poetry as fluid, confident and innocent as music. As a result of this discrepancy between practice and desire, Tate's poetic career became a search for some way of broadening modern poetry, of making it live in an expanded cultural configuration, a vision which could exceed the confines of mere feeling while still containing and supporting feeling.

At first three possible courses seemed open to him. He could apply intellect to feeling, hardening and extending sensibility in the manner of the 17th-century metaphysical poets. Or possibly intellect could extend feeling toward a religious emotion. Or perhaps he could relate his feelings to an ancestral past, to some personal, familial tradition. None of these methods quite succeeded, and many of Mr. Tate's poems written in his late twenties and early thirties take as their theme some failure of cognition. Many of these poems are successful poems technically but they are written about "failure," a word which became a favorite revenant in his criticism. He documented in the poem "The Wolves" (1931) the failure of intellect alone to save the individual sensibility from the terror of life. Similarly, a merely intellectual approach to religion, as in the poem "The Cross" (1928), succeeded only in converting feeling into coldly impersonal ontogeny. And the ancestral poems, such as "Emblems" (1930), seemed to most readers to bite the bullet too hard, to narrow down too much on some experience vaguely bloodshot and guilty. It is not at all surprising that Mr. Tate's most successful poem written before the age of thirty is his "Ode to the Confederate Dead," wherein he makes no effort to break from a purely personal view of the subject matter; indeed, in a gloomy way, the poem celebrates that view.

The celebrations of failure, however, were preparations for success, for Mr. Tate has succeeded in his search for a broader, more triumphant poetry. In this respect "The Mediterranean" (1932) is a crucial and transitional poem wherein for the first time in his career Mr. Tate was able to make personal experience into public experience, and he was able to do this by paralleling a subjective experience with a mythic-historical occurrence in the *Aeneid*. The method is predictive of Mr. Tate's great poem "Seasons of the Soul" (1943) as well as of his superb late poems in terza rima, "The Swimmers," "The Buried Lake," and "The Maimed Man," which are parts of a longer work still in progress. In these poems the most personal experiences – dreams, early loves, and so forth – stand as in a montage with spiritual equivalences in profound Christian history or epic, St. Augustine's *Confessions* or Dante's *Divine Comedy*. In these poems – wherein the religious vision pacifies those parts of the soul which in the younger poet quarrelled all too bitterly – intellect finds its proper place as does the rage of pure sensibility. Personal tradition becomes mankind's tradition in the basic rhythms of doubt and faith, sin and salvation. Because these poems possess certain things in common with T. S. Eliot's later poetry, their remarkable originality has gone unnoticed. Yet they are not like Eliot's poetry. Indeed, they bid farewell to one of the exquisite tortures which Eliot made a cliché of the 20th century. Instead of contrasting modern man with his past so as to show him ignoble, these poems solemnly compare man with his past so as to show him his place in man's continuing capacity for spiritual nobility. They belong with the finest and most magisterial examples of the meditative lyric written in this century.

—Radcliffe Squires

TATE, James (Vincent). American. Born in Kansas City, Missouri, 8 December 1943. Educated at the University of Missouri, Kansas City, 1963–64; Kansas State College, Pittsburg, B.A. 1965; University of Iowa, Iowa City, M.F.A. 1967. Visiting Lecturer, University of Iowa, 1965–67, and University of California, Berkeley, 1967–68; Assistant Professor, Columbia University, New York, 1969–71, Emerson College, Boston, 1970–71, and University of Massachusetts, Amherst, 1971–72. Since 1967, Poetry Editor, *The Dickinson Review*, North Dakota. Currently, Associate Editor, Pym Randall Press, Cambridge, Massachusetts, and Barn Dream Press; Consultant, Coordinating Council of Literary Magazines. Phi Beta Kappa Poet, Brown University, Providence, Rhode Island, 1972. Recipient: Yale Series of Younger Poets Award, 1966; National Endowment for the Arts grant, 1968, 1969. Address: 863 Massachusetts Avenue, Cambridge, Massachusetts 02139, U.S.A.

PUBLICATIONS

Verse

Cages. Iowa City, The Shepherds Press, 1966.
The Destination. Cambridge, Massachusetts, Pym Randall Press, 1967.
The Lost Pilot. New Haven, Connecticut, Yale University Press, 1967.
The Torches. Santa Barbara, California, Unicorn Press, 1968; revised edition, 1971.
Notes of Woe: Poems. Iowa City, Stone Wall Press, 1968.
Mystics in Chicago. Santa Barbara, California, Unicorn Press, 1968.
Camping in the Valley. Chicago, Madison Park Press, 1968.
Row with Your Hair. San Francisco, Kayak Books, 1969.
Is There Anything. Fremont, Michigan, Sumac Press, 1969.
Shepherds of the Mist. Los Angeles, Black Sparrow Press, 1969.
The Oblivion Ha-Ha. Boston, Little Brown, 1970.
Amnesia People. Pittsburg, Kansas, Little Balkans Publishing Company, 1970.
Deaf Girl Playing. Cambridge, Massachusetts, Pym Randall Press, 1970.
Are You Ready Mary Baker Eddy?, with Bill Knott. San Francisco, Cloud Marauder Press, 1970.

Wrong Songs.   Cambridge, Massachusetts, Halty Ferguson, 1970.
Hints to Pilgrims.   Cambridge, Massachusetts, Halty Ferguson, 1971.
Apology for Eating Geoffrey Movius' Hyacinth.   Santa Barbara, California, Unicorn Press, 1971.
Nobody Goes to Visit the Insane Anymore.   Santa Barbara, California, Unicorn Press, 1971.
Absences: New Poems.   Boston, Little Brown, 1972.

James Tate comments:

I am in the tradition of the Impurists: Whitman, Williams, Neruda. . . . I am trying to combine words in such a way as to lend a new life, a new hope, to that which is lifeless and hopeless. If the vision in the poems is occasionally black, it is so in order to see more clearly the fabric of which that blackness is made, and thereby understand the source. If the source is understood, there is the possibility of correcting it.

In my poems it seems one of the recurring themes must be the agony of communication itself: despair and hatred are borne out of this failure to communicate. The poem is man's noblest effort because it is utterly useless.

I use the image as a kind of drill to penetrate the veils of illusion we complacently call the Real World, the world of shadows through which we move so confidently. I want to split that world and release the energy of a higher reality. There is nothing I won't do because I see a new possibility each day.

*   *   *

In 1967, then 23 years old, James Tate won the Yale Series of Younger Poets award for his first book, *The Lost Pilot.* The bored world of contemporary American poetry was jolted: one so young doesn't often gain such recognition, and the foreward by Dudley Fitts said Tate "sounds . . . like no one I have ever read – utterly confident, with an effortless elegance of control, both in diction and in composition, that would be rare in a poet of any age and that is particularly impressive in a first book."

More than most of his peers, Tate understands the magic of language itself as distinguished from language that seeks to share the magic of ideas. *The Lost Pilot* bore out the claims of the foreward, but in spite of all the fine use of language, only a few of the poems take on enough substance to stick. Those which most closely reveal Tate retain the elegance, and substance shadows charm. The poet's imagination, like a circus, offers both a fun house and the house of horrors. The title poem, an elegy to his father (1922–1944), addresses conceptions of "father" and stereotypes of astronauts, as well as a cosmological question involving worlds. It is a poem that stretches for, and attains, true importance.

Within two years of *The Lost Pilot,* Tate had another dozen collections in print or accepted for publication (surely a record of sorts), and the critics began to make their claims and demands. Maybe if he could write good poems younger than anyone else, he could also get wisdom sooner. At an age when many writers benefit from neglect, Tate was busy with public readings and what must have been a gratifying if insatiable demand for his new poems.

Most amazing of all this is how gracefully Tate rode it out. He seemed to enjoy himself, and to be aware of the position he was in. At the same time, there were poems like "The Hermit" whose final, second quatrain casts a shadow on what we consider to be required sociability:

> From the mountainside,
> I watch their fallen faces
> rise, and scarcely believe
> the luck I have had.

A question surfaces: how much of grace is just plain tact? What wear is done to the soul in the name of manners?

Enough of claims and demands. At thirty, Tate has already written some extraordinary poems; he has an energy of language that may well demand over-production, imagination flooding and sometimes drowning sensibility. The resulting poems can be heavily imagistic, flashy, and confusing, like the two-line "Flushing & Swarming":

> She dreamed of excreting white plankton
> then woke with a hiccup of white hatchets.

The poem seems to center on the idea of white excrement; the difference between dream and reality, however, is not this impossible color, but the substance. Who "she" is, why she would have such a strange experience, and of what importance it all is, Tate characteristically neglects to mention.

Tate's more recent work has taken a fascinating turn towards the depth suggested by "The Lost Pilot," where the imagination is trained on credible events, however zany. Here are the opening lines of "Apology for Eating Geoffrey Movius' Hyacinth":

> It has come to this,
> a life of uncalculated passion
> for the barely wriggling throb
> of the invisible tube of force
> that manufactures a laugh
> for smothering pentagons,
> fructifying useless poems,
> and salvaging broken-hearted penguins.

It may be Tate's concept that the laugh can smother a pentagon, his idea of "useless poems" that fortify an attitude of unchecked absurdity.

When he abandons this stance, to write openly of himself and those poeple he loves, he demonstrates the self-awareness that balances him between redemption and the curse of prodigal attention:

> To be something different like a brussels sprout
> it's as if we were ants so far away
> made of charcoal made of dust,
> good enough to erase and coming down
>
> if I had not grown up dissolving into
> the swan the way they think of me.

> —from "The Blue Canyon"

To retain this balance requires the abundance of grace which he alone so naturally has.

> —Geof Hewitt

THIELE, Colin (Milton). Australian. Born in Eudunda, South Australia, 16 November 1920. Educated at Adelaide Teachers College, South Australia, 1937–38; University of Adelaide, B.A. 1941, Dip.Ed. 1947, Dip.T. Served in the Royal Australian Air Force, 1942–45. Married Rhonda Gill in 1945; has two daughters. Taught at Port Lincoln High School, South Australia 1946–55, and Brighton High School, 1956. Lecturer, 1957–62, Senior Lecturer in English, 1962–63, Vice-Principal, 1964, and since 1965, Principal, Wattle Park Teachers College, Adelaide. Formerly, National Book Reviewer, Australian Broadcasting Commission; Commonwealth Literary Fund Lecturer in Australian Literature. Member, 1964–68, and since 1969, Fellow, Australian College of Education; since 1967, Council Member, Australian Society of Authors. Recipient: W. J. Miles Memorial Prize, 1944; Commonwealth Jubilee Radio Play Prize, 1951; Fulbright Scholarship, 1959; Grace Leven Prize, 1961; Commonwealth Literary Fund Fellowship, 1967. Address: 24 Woodhouse Crescent, Wattle Park, South Australia, Australia.

PUBLICATIONS

Verse

    Progress to Denial. Adelaide, Jindyworobak Publications, 1945.
    Splinters and Shards. Adelaide, Jindyworobak Publications, 1945.
    The Golden Lightning: Poems. Adelaide, Jindyworobak Publications, 1951.
    Man in a Landscape. Adelaide, Rigby, 1960.
    In Charcoal and Conté. Adelaide, Rigby, 1966.
    Selected Verse (1940–1970). Adelaide, Rigby, 1970.

Plays

    Burke and Wills (broadcast, 1949). Included in *Selected Verse (1940–1970),* 1970.

    Radio Plays: *Burke and Wills,* 1949; *Edge of ice,* 1951; *The Shark Fishers,* 1953; *Edward John Eyre,* 1962.

Novel

    Labourers in the Vineyard. Adelaide, Rigby, 1970.

Short Stories

    The Rim of the Morning. Adelaide, Rigby, 1966.

Other

    The State of Our State. Adelaide, Rigby, 1952.
    The Sun on the Stubble (juvenile). Adelaide, Rigby, 1962.
    Gloop, The Gloomy Bunyip (juvenile). Brisbane, Jacaranda Press, 1962; as *Gloop the Bunyip,* Adelaide, Rigby, 1970.

Storm Boy (juvenile).   London, Angus and Robertson, 1963; Chicago, Rand
   McNally, 1966.
February Dragon (juvenile).   London, Angus and Robertson, Adelaide, Rigby,
   and San Francisco, Tri-Ocean, 1965.
Mrs. Munch and Puffing Billy (juvenile).   Adelaide, Rigby, 1967; San Fran-
   cisco, Tri-Ocean, 1968.
Barossa Valley Sketchbook.   San Francisco, Tri-Ocean, 1968.
Heysen of Hahndorf (biography).   Adelaide, Rigby, and San Francisco, Tri-
   Ocean, 1968.
Blue Fin (juvenile).   Adelaide, Rigby, 1969; New York, Harper, 1974.
Yellow Jacket Jock (juvenile).   Melbourne, Cheshire, 1969.
Flash Flood (juvenile).   Adelaide, Rigby, 1970.
Flip Flop and Tiger Snake (juvenile).   Adelaide, Rigby, 1970.

Editor, *Jindyworobak Anthology.*   Adelaide, Jindyworobak Publications, 1953.
Editor, *Looking at Poetry.*   London, Longman, 1960.
Editor, with Ian Mudie, *Australian Poets Speak.*   Adelaide, Rigby, 1961.
Editor, with Greg Branson, *One-Act Plays for Secondary Schools.*   Adelaide,
   Rigby, 3 vols, 1962, 1964; revised version as *Setting the Stage,* and *The
   Living Stage,* 1969, 1970.
Editor, *Favourite Australian Stories.*   Adelaide, Rigby, 1963.
Editor, *Handbook to Favourite Australian Stories.*   Adelaide, Rigby, 1964.
Editor, with Greg Branson, *Beginners, Please.*   Adelaide, Rigby, 1964.
Editor, with Greg Branson, *Plays for Young Players.*   Adelaide, Rigby, 1970.

Critical Studies: *Reading Time 36* (New South Wales), July 1970; *Children's
Libraries Newsletter,* May 1972.

Colin Thiele comments:

Main themes are man and his environment on the one hand (note title of fourth
book – *Man in a Landscape*) and the discovery of the universal in the particular,
on the other. Therefore interested in regional and local people going about their
work (*In Charcoal and Conté* is largely a portrait gallery in verse), yet nevertheless
concerned with great human issues – happiness, humour, tragedy, death.
   Verse ranges in style from free verse to sonnets. Prefer metaphor as a device,
and sharp Australian images.
   Love of country scenes and people of German descent reflects own early
background. Verse often sardonic and ironic in flavour.

*   *   *

   Colin Thiele's poetry ranges over a wide variety of subjects; from pastoral life
and country personalities to city dwellers and destroyers, from secret love to oval
barrackers, from Magellan to car salesmen. Throughout many of his poems there is
a note of regret and anger at what is happening to the world today, a sharp
criticism of modern civilization with its efficiency experts and bulldozers, the joint
destroyers of humanity and nature.
   There is a strong note of human compassion in his poetry and it is soon obvious
that his concern and fondness is for the common man, indeed many of his best

poems are those which are portraits of the bush personalities. Colin Thiele would have us believe that he is opposed to the "world of the hypocritical hush," to pretentions of any description and no doubt he is. It is a pity that this dislike for pretentiousness does not carry over into his verse. If it did we would be saved the "Nature's guerdons," the "pantheistic altars," and the "rumpy ecstasies." Heinrich Heidenreich, the hero of one of his poems doesn't dismount from his horse, instead he "unloads the vast/And pendent pudding of his loins." Nor does he look upon his children but "Upon his blood's renascent brood." At times his ventures into rhyme are almost as unfortunate as his sorties into poetic diction. A stanza from "Bill Crawford" should serve to illustrate both weaknesses. In this poem a group of railway fettlers have eaten half a ton of fruit and the result is predictable. Being railway fettlers we would have a good idea of how they would describe their complaint. And how about Colin Thiele?

> But untried stomachs rued the raid
> That generated with a rush
> Such gastric yeastiness that made
> The whole camp scatter to the bush.

Not all descends to this level, and it is unfortunate that such faults mar what could otherwise, in some cases, have been enjoyable poems.

—Anna Rutherford

THOMAS, D(onald) M(ichael). British. Born in Redruth, Cornwall, 27 January 1935. Educated at Redruth Grammar School; University High School, Melbourne; New College, Oxford, B.A. (honours) in English, 1958, M.A. Since 1963, Senior Lecturer in English, Hereford College of Education. Visiting Lecturer in English, Hamline University, St. Paul, Minnesota, 1967. Recipient: Richard Hillary Memorial Prize, 1960; Eric Gregory Award, 1962. Address: 10 Greyfriars Avenue, Hereford, England.

PUBLICATIONS

Verse

Personal and Possessive. London, Outposts Publications, 1964.
Penguin Modern Poets 11, with D. M. Black and Peter Redgrove. London, Penguin, 1968.
Two Voices. London, Cape Goliard Press, and New York, Grossman, 1968.
Logan Stone. London, Cape Goliard Press, and New York, Grossman, 1971.
The Shaft. Gillingham, Kent, ARC Publications, 1973.
Love and Other Deaths. London, Elek, 1975.

Other

> Editor, *The Granite Kingdom: Poems of Cornwall.* Truro, Cornwall, Barton, 1970.
> Editor, *Selected Poems of John Harris.* Padstow, Cornwall, Lodenek Press, 1973.

D. M. Thomas comments:

My poetry does not move far from the great twin cities of love and death. Early poems (see *Penguin Modern Poets 11*) use science fiction themes as images of desire and separation. More recently, my most obsessive themes have been sexuality, family deaths and a search for lost roots in the brimming landscape of West Cornwall.

*   *   *

D. M. Thomas established his poetic reputation through his connection with Science Fiction. His science fiction poems are not at all experimental in technique – rather, they are closely linked to Victorian poetry, and especially to the monologues of Browning (who has had a pervasive influence on many contemporary British poets – George MacBeth is another example). What is new and fresh about Thomas's work is its interest in narrative – an aspect of their work which most contemporary poets neglect. He is an extremely able craftsman, and his poems are very effective when read aloud. The deliberate, considered style, instead of seeming dull and unspontaneous, helps to carry the listener along with the story the poet is telling. One's interest is seized by the content itself, rather than by the manner. Because the style is so closely linked to the necessities of narrative, it is hard to give any impression of Thomas's work through brief quotation – each poem, indeed, tends to develop a vocabulary as well as a rhythm of its own.

—Edward Lucie-Smith

THOMAS, R(onald) S(tuart). British (Welsh). Born in Cardiff, Glamorgan, in 1913. Educated at University College, Bangor; St. Michael's College, Llandaff; University of Wales, Degree in Classics, 1935. Ordained Deacon, 1936, Priest, 1937. Curate of Chirk, 1936–40; Curate of Hanmer, 1940–42; Rector of Manafon, 1942–54; Vicar of St. Michael's, Eglwysfach, 1954–67. Since 1967, Vicar of St. Hywyn, Aberdaron, with St. Mary, Bodferin. Recipient: Heinemann Award, 1955; Queen's Gold Medal for Poetry, 1964; Welsh Arts Council Award, 1968. Address: Aberdaron, Pwllheli, Caernarvon, Wales.

PUBLICATIONS

Verse

The Stones of the Field. Carmarthen, Druid Press, 1946.
An Acre of Land. Newtown, Montgomeryshire Printing Company, 1952.
The Minister. Newtown, Montgomeryshire Printing Company, 1953.
Song at the Year's Turning: Poems 1942–1954. London, Hart Davis, 1955.
Poetry for Supper. London, Hart Davis, 1958; Chester Springs, Pennsylvania, Dufour, 1961.
Judgment Day. London, Poetry Book Society, 1960.
Tares. London, Hart Davis, and Chester Springs, Pennsylvania, Dufour, 1961.
Penguin Modern Poets 1, with Lawrence Durrell and Elizabeth Jennings. London, Penguin, 1962.
The Bread of Truth. London, Hart Davis, and Chester Springs, Pennsylvania, Dufour, 1963.
Pietá. London, Hart Davis, 1966.
Not that He Brought Flowers. London, Hart Davis, 1968.
Pergamon Poets 1, with Roy Fuller, edited by Evan Owen. Oxford, Pergamon Press, 1968.
Postcard: Song. N.p., Fishpaste Postcard Series, 1968.
The Mountains. New York, Chilmark Press, 1968.
H'm: Poems. London, Macmillan, and New York, St. Martin's Press, 1972.
Selected Poems 1946–1968. · London, Hart Davis MacGibbon, 1973; New York, St. Martin's Press, 1974.
What Is a Welshman? Llandybie, Carmarthenshire, Christopher Davies, 1974.

Other

Words and the Poet. Cardiff, University of Wales Press, 1964.
Young and Old (juvenile). London, Chatto and Windus, 1972.

Editor, *The Batsford Book of Country Verse.* London, Batsford, 1961.
Editor, *The Penguin Book of Religious Verse.* London, Penguin, 1963.
Editor, *Selected Poems,* by Edward Thomas. London, Faber, 1964.
Editor, *A Choice of George Herbert's Verse.* London, Faber, 1967.
Editor, *A Choice of Wordsworth's Verse.* London, Faber, 1971.

Critical Studies: in *Welsh Anvil* (Llandybie), 1949, 1952; in *Critical Quarterly* (Manchester), ii, 4, 1960; in *A Review of English Literature* (Leeds), iii, 4, 1960; in *Anglo-Welsh Review* (Pembroke Dock, Wales), xiii, 31, 1963; "R. S. Thomas Issue" of *Poetry Wales* (Llandybie), Winter 1972.

*   *   *

In a Welsh-language play, "Buchedd Garmon," by Saunders Lewis, an influential Welsh writer and one of the founders of the Welsh Nationalist Party, a significant passage occurs in which Wales is seen by one of the characters as a "vineyard placed in my care . . . to deliver unto my children . . . an eternal heritage. . . . And behold, the swine rush on her to rend her." To understand much of the work of R. S. Thomas one must think of him not as just another rural poet writing in English but rather in relation to these words of Saunders Lewis. He is the antithesis of the rootless, cosmopolitan poet, or even the urban poet; there is nothing about him of the dilettante, the gimmickist or the art-for-art's-saker.

Although he is probably the most famous Anglo-Welsh poet after Dylan Thomas he has nothing in common, except his surname and his nationality, with his one-year-younger fellow-countryman. Where Dylan Thomas was self-regarding, R. S. Thomas is deeply concerned with his own people and his own community; where the one was obscure, prodigal of imagery and a technical masochist, the other, although the master of a style every bit as individual in its own way, is lucid, sparing, austere; where the one was precocious and spasmodic in his development, the talent of the other was slow to unfold and has followed a line of steadily increasing mastery and authority.

Dylan Thomas was inclined to think of the poet as a man apart, a "genius," without concern for politics, religion, or ordinary involvement or commitment.

R. S. Thomas is much nearer a tradition in Wales which sees the poet as part of, and concerned with, the community in which he lives; in fact some of the themes of R. S. Thomas's poetry have much in common with those of certain modern Welsh-language poet-patriots, grave and committed writers like Saunders Lewis, Gwenallt and Waldo Williams, than with many of those of his English contemporaries. Like the Welsh writers, he sees with bitterness, sometimes perhaps with despair, the rural decay, the cultural erosion and the depopulation which afflict the Welsh countryside. Another important theme has been his attitude to his parishioners, men of the Welsh farming uplands and their families. Towards them his attitude has been steadily unromantic but also ambivalent and increasingly tolerant. He was repelled at first by their stolidity, their oafish unresponsiveness; and their sweat-sour clothes and their phlegm – in both senses of the word – appalled him. But in spite of his almost Caradoc Evans-like vision of these people he acknowledges, even as early as *The Stones of the Field*, that they have their virtues and that they are, in fact, "winners of wars." The isolation of the parson from his people has occupied him too ("Country Cures," "The Country Clergy") and his own problems as a poet ("To a Young Poet"). And some of his best poems spring from his pastoral calling and its ministrations ("Evans," "The Mill," "On the Farm"). Alun Lewis has a fine phrase in one of his poems – "within the parish of my care." The parish of R. S. Thomas's care is the Wales of the small farms, and his achievement has been to give his themes and his characters, limited and remote, by his passionate concern, universal significance.

—Glyn Jones

THOMSON, Derick S(mith). Scottish. Born in Stornoway, Outer Hebrides, 5 August 1921. Educated at Bayble Public School; Nicolson Institute, Stornoway, 1926–39; University of Aberdeen, 1939–41, 1945–47; Cambridge University, 1947–48; University College of North Wales, Bangor, 1950. Served in the Royal Air Force. Married Carol Galbraith in 1952; has five children. Assistant in Celtic,

University of Edinburgh, 1948–49; Reader in Celtic, University of Aberdeen, 1956–63. Lecturer in Welsh, 1949–56, and since 1963, Professor of Celtic, University of Glasgow. Since 1952, Editor, *Gairm*, Glasgow; since 1961, Editor, *Scottish Gaelic Studies*, Aberdeen. Chief, Gaelic Society of Inverness, 1969–70. Since 1964, President, Scottish Gaelic Texts Society; since 1968, Chairman, Gaelic Books Council. Recipient: Festival of Britain prize, 1951; Scottish Arts Council Publication Award, 1971. Address: 41 Aytoun Road, Glasgow S.1, Scotland.

PUBLICATIONS

Verse

An Dealbh Briste (The Broken Picture). Edinburgh, Serif Books, 1951.
Eadar Samhradh is Foghar (Between Summer and Autumn). Glasgow, Gairm Publications, 1967.
An Rathad Cian (The Far Road). Glasgow, Gairm Publications, 1970.
The Far Road and Other Poems. Edinburgh, M. Macdonald, 1971.
The Far Road. New York, New Rivers Press, 1971.

Other

The Gaelic Sources of Macpherson's "Ossian." Edinburgh, Oliver and Boyd, 1952.
Edward Lhuyd in the Scottish Highlands, 1699–1700, with John Lorne Campbell. Oxford, Clarendon Press, 1963.
An Introduction to Gaelic Poetry. London, Gollancz, and New York, St. Martin's Press, 1974.

Editor, *Branwen Uerch Lyr: The Second of the Four Branches of the Mabinogi Edited from the White Book of Rhydderch with Variants from the Red Book of Hergest and from Peniarth.* Dublin, Institute for Advanced Studies, 1961; revised edition, 1968.
Editor, with Ian Grimble, *The Future of the Highlands.* London, Routledge, 1968.

Critical Studies: by Iain Crichton Smith, in *Lines Review 36* (Edinburgh); Donald MacAuley, in *Lines Review 39* (Edinburgh); John Macinnes, in *Scottish International* (Edinburgh), January 1972.

Derick S. Thomson comments:

I regard myself, of course, primarily as a Gaelic poet, but have been in the habit of making line-for-line translations of many of my own poems, preserving to a large extent the rhythms of the originals. Perhaps because I live daily in the Gaelic and English-speaking worlds, it might be said that my sensibility is a bilingual one, and I am aware of drawing on the traditions of both Gaelic and English literature, though the words themselves must derive most of their resonance from their Gaelic associations.

English was my lisping language, both in speech and verse. I had begun to repair this monoglot image by the age of five, but was in my late teens before becoming powerfully attracted to Gaelic as a writing language. There were political overtones in this attraction, but it has long hardened into a habit, and I have not attempted original English verse for the last twenty-five years.

The main preoccupations of my verse have been: personal themes (especially in *An Dealbh Briste*); the building up of a fairly detailed impression of my experience of life in the island of Lewis (culminating in *An Rathad Cian*), and allied to that theme, the experience of alienation; the Scottish nation. For many years I think the mainspring of my verse was a sensuousness which often has associations with Lewis and my upbringing there. In recent years there has been more acerbity and anger, and more fun and ridicule, in my verse.

I became attracted to free verse in my teens, and have worked off and on in that medium since then. I now find it difficult to say what I want to say in another form. I hope that I have contributed significantly to the development of style in Gaelic.

*   *   *

The fact that Derick S. Thomson grew up on the island of Lewis and has perforce spent his adult life in very different surroundings gives a distinct context to his memories of earlier life. But as well as this richly detailed personal history we also find a sharp focus on social, economic and linguistic circumstances, for those very years, the twenties and early thirties, coincided with the last years of a fully indigenous communal life in the area, so that his memories of boyhood are inextricably linked with his feelings about the erosion of Gaelic society.

Thus while Lewis is a geographical anchor, with its place-names further indicating a deep historical context, the island also has a parallel, non-geographical existence in the poet's mind and feelings. It has been subjected to the alchemy of memory and appears in many transformations (monster, sweet-heart, standing-stone, emigrant ship). Similarly, the nostalgia exists on several different levels. It is relatively straightforward in references to, say, "a coffinful of songs" being laid in the earth. It can be blended with a polemical sharpness, the latter being directed not only towards attempts to improve the purely material aspects of highland life, but also towards that indifference within the beleaguered community which in effect becomes an ally of intrusion from without. And at the level where the poet recognises the apparent insolubility of his dilemma yet refuses to abandon it, the nostalgia is clearly only one element in a complex response:

> The heart tied to a tethering post, round upon round of rope
> till it grows short,
> and the mind free.
> I bought its freedom dearly.

It is worth adding that Thomson's role as a Gaelic writer is not confined to his poetry, for while in that poetry he explores the shifting connections between past and present, as they affect both himself as an individual and the society to which he belongs, he is also actively engaged as a scholar, entrepreneur and propagandist in a wide range of practical activities aimed at preserving and reviving the culture of that society.

—Robin Fulton

THWAITE, Anthony (Simon). British. Born in Chester, Cheshire, 23 June 1930. Educated in Leeds; Sheffield; the United States, 1940–44; at Kingswood School, Bath; Christ Church, Oxford, B.A. (honours) 1955, M.A. 1959. Military Service, 1949–51. Married Ann Harrop in 1955; has four daughters. Visiting Lecturer in English Literature, Tokyo University, Japan, 1955–57; Radio Producer, BBC London, 1957–62; Literary Editor, *The Listener*, London, 1962–65; Assistant Professor of English, University of Libya, Benghazi, 1965–67; Literary Editor, *New Statesman*, London, 1968–72. Since 1973, Co-Editor, *Encounter*, London. Recipient: Richard Hillary Memorial Prize, 1967; Henfield Writing Fellowship, University of East Anglia, Norwich, Summer 1972. Address: The Mill House, Tharston, Norfolk NOR 7OW, England.

PUBLICATIONS

Verse

(*Poems*). Oxford, Fantasy Press, 1953.
Home Truths. Hessle, Yorkshire, Marvell Press, 1957.
The Owl in the Tree: Poems. London, Oxford University Press, 1963.
The Stones of Emptiness: Poems 1963–66. London, Oxford University Press, 1967.
Penguin Modern Poets 18, with A. Alvarez and Roy Fuller. London, Penguin, 1970.
Points. London, Turret Books, 1972.
Inscriptions. London, Oxford University Press, 1973.
New Confessions. London, Oxford University Press, 1974.

Other

Essays on Contemporary English Poetry: Hopkins to the Present Day. Tokyo, Kenkyusha, 1957; revised edition, as *Contemporary English Poetry: An Introduction*, London, Heinemann, 1959; Chester Springs, Pennsylvania, Dufour, 1961.
Japan in Colour, with Roloff Beny. London, Thames and Hudson, and New York, McGraw Hill, 1967.
The Deserts of Hesperides: An Experience of Libya. London, Secker and Warburg, and New York, Roy, 1969.
Poetry Today 1960–1973. London, Longman, 1973.
In Italy, with Peter Porter. London, Thames and Hudson, 1974.

Editor, with Hilary Corke and William Plomer, *New Poems 1961*. London, Hutchinson, 1961.
Editor, and Translator with Geoffrey Bownas, *The Penguin Book of Japanese Verse.* London, Penguin, 1964.
Editor, with Peter Porter, *The English Poets: From Chaucer to Edward Thomas.* London, Secker and Warburg, 1974.

Manuscript Collection: Brynmor Jones Library, University of Hull, Yorkshire.

*   *   *

The continuing thread in Anthony Thwaite's poetry is his concern for technical accuracy. In his first book, *Home Truths*, he appeared in the uniform of The Movement, but this was an accident of timing rather than a conviction of style. These early poems are as abstract and didactic as Thom Gunn's and perhaps lack Gunn's interesting subject matter, but they are amazingly self-sufficient in form and accomplishment. Read now, they can be seen as the honing of a fine technique, a process which has borne fruit in the more relaxed mode of his later work. The sealed definitive line, once it is matched by experience, provides an excellent base for poetry. "To My Unborn Child," from this early collection, is a key poem, being written in his first style but pointing to the special concerns of his second book, *The Owl in the Tree*. One stanza, bearing a fine conceit, shows Thwaite's two styles in forceful union:

> Collision of erratic spores
> Moved eyes to bud, fingers to swell
> Out of the light, and now he walks
> On water, and is miracle.

For a time, Thwaite turned to the day-to-day sights of suburban life and the domestic round for his inspiration. His poems were deliberately lightened of their intellectual matter, but his eye grew sharper and his technical skill more self-effacing. He kept his love of the weighty and didactic, however, and the best two poems in *The Owl in the Tree*, "Mr. Cooper" and "Manhood's End," dealt with that traditional subject, death. Thwaite's next collection, *The Stones of Emptiness*, shows his talent in its maturity. Many of the poems in it derive from his experience of Libya and especially of the contrast between the present-day decrepitude and the traditional severity of Islam. In "Arabic Script," he finds a symbol for the Mohammedan world in the characters of its written language:

> you see the stern
> Edge of the language, Kufic, like a scimitar
> Curved in a lash, a flash of consonants
> Such as swung out of Medina that day
> On the long flog west, across ruins and flaccid colonials,
> A swirl of black flags, white crescents, a language of swords.

The long sequence, "The Letters of Synesius," written in a finely controlled free verse, and uniting the sensibilities of the ancient and modern worlds, is his finest achievement to date.

—Peter Porter

TIEMPO, Edith (Lopez). Filipino. Born in Nueva Vizcaya, 22 April 1919. Educated at Silliman University, Dumaguete City, B.S.E. 1947; University of Iowa, Iowa City, M.A. 1949; University of Denver, Colorado, Ph.D. 1958. Married to E. K. Tiempo; has two children. Since 1961, Professor of English, currently Chairman of the English Department, Silliman University. Visiting Professor of English, Western Michigan University, Kalamazoo, 1963–64, 1965–66, and Wartburg College, Waverly, Iowa, 1964–65. Recipient: Rockefeller Grant, 1949, 1971; Palanca

Award, for poetry, 1967, for short story, 1969; Asia Foundation Grant, 1971. Address: Department of English, Silliman University, Dumaguete City, Philippines.

PUBLICATIONS

Verse

   The Tracks of Babylon and Other Poems.   Denver, Swallow, 1966.

Novel

   A Blade of Fern.   Manila, A. S. Florentino, 1974.

Short Stories

   Abide, Joshua and Other Stories.   Manila, A. S. Florentino, 1964.

Other

   Poetry in Image and Statement.   Manila, New Day, 1974.

Critical Study: by A. O. Constantino, in *Solidarity* (Manila), August 1968.

Edith Tiempo comments:

   I am more a fictionist and critic of poetry than a poet. Perhaps my poetry might not fit under any one "school" because, although I write in English, I often work with myths and folk metaphors not easily recognizable outside my geographical milieu. Possible influences are Robert Frost; Nashville group; W. H. Auden's British Socialist group.

   The main problem from the beginning has been the projection of the universal through particulars that are (even psychically sometimes) alien to the language medium. But art and communication are miraculous; I feel that this polarity can actually give a valid kind of mystery to the utterance; I feel this has been the case in some of my poems (e.g. "The Tracks of Babylon" and "The Pestle," both published in *Poetry*, Chicago). This kind of "incongruity" is the reason that the poetry has come so slowly – I hope to be able to work more and more meaningfully within this tension between the language and the material.

   One American critic criticized my poetry for its use of "archaisms" (the nearest equivalents to transliterating a certain indigenous tone), and praised the poems that are toughened in tone by the abstract, "intellectual" vocabulary. Understandably, I feel easier working with images of the natural world, and like Yeats and Frost I would let these images reveal their final tough meaningfulness through the peepholes that the poet quite often directs himself to "stumble" upon.

*   *   *

Edith Tiempo's poetry is reminiscent of W. B. Yeats and T. S. Eliot by whom she was deeply influenced, but her finely chiselled images are put to different purposes from theirs. Mrs. Tiempo's symbols develop a theme common to all her work – one's failure to establish meaningful relationships with others. Her poetry is both cerebral and sensuous. She overwhelms the reader with images which reflect the urgency of the efforts to comprehend formless experience. Her telescoping of past and present lend to these attempts the timelessness and terror of universalised experience. Her poem "The Tracks of Babylon" shows that the search can end only in paradox. The quest for an ordering principle in life becomes futile by one's very obsessiveness. In old age, "Not death, but Memory is the beast" to be feared ("Green Hearts") as man awakes to "bruise [his] hands on the living cage" of his own self ("Lament for the Littlest Fellow"). Yet there is no bitterness because self-knowledge suffuses the old man's disorientation and enables him to live harmoniously with others ("The Return").

Most Asian writers are similarly engaged in the quest for an identity but Mrs. Tiempo's treatment of the issue is different from that, say, of her compatriots R. Demetillo and A. G. Hufana, and Malaysia's Wong Phui Nam: they trace the quest historically while she is interested only in its impact on the quality of personal life; theirs is a poetry of self-concern, hers one of communication. It is the manner in which she effects this communication that enables her to hold her own against English poets not only in the Philippines but also elsewhere in Asia.

—Abdul Majid bin Nabi Baksh

TILLER, Terence (Rogers). British. Born in Truro, Cornwall, 19 September 1916. Educated at Latymer Upper School, Hammersmith, London; Jesus College, Cambridge (Chancellor's Medal, 1936), B.A. (honours) in history 1937, M.A. 1940. Married; has two daughters. Research Scholar and Director of Studies, 1937–39, and University Lecturer in Medieval History, 1939, Cambridge University; Lecturer in English History and Literature, Fuad I University, Cairo, Egypt, 1939–46. Radio Writer and Producer, Features Department, 1946–65, and since 1965, Drama Department, BBC London. Lives in Roehampton, London.

PUBLICATIONS

Verse

Poems. London, Hogarth Press, 1941.
The Inward Animal. London, Hogarth Press, 1943.
Unarm, Eros. London, Hogarth Press, 1947.
Reading a Medal and other Poems. London, Hogarth Press, 1957.
Notes for a Myth and Other Poems. London, Hogarth Press – Chatto and Windus, 1968.

Plays

The Death of Adam (produced Edinburgh, 1950).

Radio Plays: *The Death of a Friend,* 1949; *Lilith,* 1950; *The Tower of Hunger,* 1952; *The Death of Adam, The Passion of Our Lord, The Harrowing of Hell, The Ascension, The Death of Pilate,* 1962; *Philider and England,* 1965; *Final Meeting,* 1966; *The Elizabethan Underworld,* 1966; *Richard Parson,* 1967; *The Story of Kasper Hauser,* 1968; *Euphorion,* 1969; *Aphrodite the Luxuriant Pig,* 1970; *Road to Astolat,* 1972.

Other

Editor, with others, *Personal Landscape: An Anthology of Exile.* London, Editions Poetry, 1945.
Editor, with Anthony Cronin, *New Poems 1960: A P.E.N. Anthology.* London, Hutchinson, 1960.
Editor and Co-Translator, *The Inferno,* by Dante. London, BBC Publications, 1966; New York, Schocken Books, 1967.
Editor, *Chess Treasury of the Air.* London, Penguin, 1966.

Terence Tiller comments:

I am a poet only insofar as my other interests and occupations are *coloured* by my being a poet. Of course I look at history, novels, music, radio, etc., etc., *differently* because of that. But I don't, and can't, and would never have been able to, earn my living as a poet.

I have been called, and am willing to call myself, "a modern metaphysical." Certainly, I have been more influenced by the "metaphysicals" than by any other poets except Dante and Rilke. Minor, sometimes transient, influences, include obvious names like Hopkins, Eliot, early-to-middle Auden. Most of *them* would/would have disown/disowned me! As far as verse-form is concerned, I tend almost exclusively towards the "traditional," while allowing myself such "license" as I need for specific purposes. I feel strongly that regular prosody is a "springboard" that a poet abandons at his own risk. (Always provided that he can cope with it! Whatever else I am or am not, I am a *technician* in verse.)

Themes? Almost entirely a-political as far as poetry is concerned – except that poetry and politics involve morality, and I am fairly committed *there* (though not with any "party" or "sectarian" affiliation). I would claim to be a polymath, and to attempt poems as a kind of syncretism of the emotions, speculations, and symbolic coincidences, that arise out of my physical and mental experience.

*   *   *

Terence Tiller's first volume, *Poems,* is immature, but foreshadows certain positive qualities of his later work: the ability, for example, to control complex verse patterns, accomplished rhetoric and an impressive, if cold, heraldic use of imagery. *The Inward Animal* reflects Tiller's experiences as a civilian in the Middle East of the war years, where he was associated with the "Personal Landscape" group: Lawrence Durrell, Bernard Spencer, and Robin Fedden. Flanked by two poems, "Eclogue for a Dying House" and "The Birth of Christ," which attempt in social and religious modes respectively to generalise the pattern of war, exile and single strangeness, the volume's theme in Tiller's own words is to explore the impact of that strangeness which "must have shaken, and perhaps destroyed, many a customary self. There will have been a shocked and defensive rebellion; reconciliation must follow; the birth of some mutual thing in which the old and the new, the self and the alien, are combined after war. . . . The birth of something at once myself, the new self and 'Egypt' is the 'inward animal.'" Such a dialectic makes the volume sound somewhat more schematised than it actually is, but underlines the fact that Tiller has always applied stratagems in his work and has never minimised the importance of pure craft. Rilke and the Metaphysicals are presences in *The Inward Animal.* Tiller preferred (until his most recent work) assonance to rhyme, using rhyming only when he wished to enact finality. The poems are strongest where they rise from some observed scene or persons, least sensuous when "Egypt" is missing from the record, even if one allows some dramatic cogency in the ordering of individual poems. Once or twice it becomes difficult to distinguish the "metaphysical" idiom from highly accomplished *New Statesman* competition verse:

> The silence that I break was more profound,
> and purer sound
> – as being absent is a kind
> of closer bridal in the mind.

It is difficult to see what purpose this allusiveness achieves. The impact of such poems as "Bathers," "Sphinx," "The Convalescent Party," and "Egyptian Dancer" (interesting to compare with Bernard Spencer's "Egyptian Dancer at Subra": these gifted poets seem on occasion to have tackled topics in collusion) is immediate – and lasting. Another feature of *Inward Animal* is a happy sensuousness that counterpoints the heraldic coldness, arrived at by dense and witty use of figure, perhaps more *concettist* than metaphysical, though Tiller rarely suppresses the tenor of his metaphors. *Inward Animal* abounds with felicities:

> the flags that slap his plunging knee,
> and the cold stocking of the stream.

> —from "Bathers"

or:

> and the soft lath of woman bears
> a heaven's agonising weight.

> —from "The Incubus"

"Europa," the second of four folk songs, wittily reads a locomotive and its shed as a modern version of a fertility myth and demonstrates Tiller's virtuosity.

Unarm, Eros is perhaps Tiller's finest collection. The bold sensuousness, the wit and enigma of the surface work together. It is difficult to isolate particular triumphs, but perhaps "Perfumes," "Roman Portraits," "Hospital" (compare Spencer's "In a Foreign Hospital"), "Beggar," an example of strict, compassionate observation, and "Image in a Lilac Tree" incise themselves most sharply. *Reading a Medal* contains individual poems as striking as any Tiller has written, but a general impression persists of pressure diffused, lyricism of less intensity, puzzles not altogether worth solving and the impression is more strongly marked in the most recent collection, *Notes for a Myth*. Tiller is reported to have remarked that "mere experience is a distraction" (doubtless he meant something more subtle) but one can barely avoid applying this somewhat ironically to his later work, where the tensions, the concrete situations that underlay *The Inward Animal* and *Unarm, Eros* have been gravely attenuated. The poems have tended to become longer, to retreat further into pattern and myth. The social commentator who kept such good company with the introvert has disappeared. But Tiller's poetry has already asserted its own lingering resonances. He remains something of a poet's poet and must always appeal to those who respond to the mystery of the vocation.

—Ian Fletcher

TILLINGHAST, Richard. American. Born in Memphis, Tennessee, 25 November 1940. Educated at the University of the South, Sewanee, Tennessee (Assistant Editor, *Sewanee Review*), A.B. 1962; Harvard University, Cambridge, Massachusetts (Woodrow Wilson Fellow), A.M. 1968, Ph.D. 1970. Has taught at Harvard University. Since 1968, Assistant Professor of English, University of California, Berkeley. Recipient: University of California Creative Arts Institute Award, 1970. Address: 1300 Arch Street, Berkeley, California 94708, U.S.A.

PUBLICATIONS

Verse

The Keeper. Cambridge, Massachusetts, Pym Randall Press, 1968.
Sleep Watch. Middletown, Connecticut, Wesleyan University Press, 1969.

*   *   *

Richard Tillinghast's *Sleep Watch* amazed its readers with a startling, ingenious way of seeing things. Here is an animal describing God's bungling of Creation: "Later on when he saw that things had gone wrong/ . . . it rested him to look at us/And I found I could love him in his weakness/as I never could before/the beauty left his face. . . ." Here is "Waking on the Train": "after the commuters/cigars windows being jerked open/your body begins to know it hasn't slept/It thinks of all the parts of itself/that would touch a bed. . . ."

Many of Tillinghast's poems touch on that dream-like area of consciousness between waking and sleeping. Everything real is in doubt, and that may be desirable. "Is everything sliding?" he asks in a poem called "Everything Is Going to Be All Right" and answers himself, "Nothing/to worry about –/Getting lost means sliding in all directions."

The present American fashions in poetry – Eastern mysticism, Nature worship, confession – hover dangerously about Tillinghast's work, but they are kept at bay by his delicate obliqueness plus a hawk's eye for metaphor. "I put the cap back onto the pen/the way a court reunites a/mother and child." "I am alert at once/and think of the cat/coasting on its muscles. . . ."

One of the best poems in *Sleep Watch* is about rising from a childhood illness and confronting the world of health. The poet senses an undefined disappointment in his parents; he has not given them cause to mourn: "For them I am closing the door to the place/where the dead children are stored,/where the pets have gone to heaven."

A certain self-consciousness has led Tillinghast to develop his own style. He uses spaces where one would normally expect punctuation, allowing his poem to lie on the page between breathing intervals, like directions for speech. Self-consciousness and sensitivity: there is an abundance of this. It will be interesting to see where Tillinghast goes after having given us this brilliant tour of his complex psyche.

—Anne Stevenson

TODD, Ruthven. American. Born in Edinburgh, Scotland, 14 June 1914. Educated at Fettes College; Edinburgh College of Art. Has one son, the writer Christopher Todd. Farm laborer on the Isle of Mull for two years; Assistant Editor, *Scottish Bookman,* Edinburgh. Moved to London, 1935, and to New York, 1947. Operated The Weekend Press, New York, 1950–54. Visiting Professor, State University of New York, Buffalo, Summer 1972. Recipient: National Institute of Arts and Letters grant, 1954; Guggenheim Fellowship, 1960, 1967; Chapelbrook Fellowship, 1968; Ingram Merrill Foundation Fellowship, 1970. Agent: David Higham Associates Ltd., 5-8 Lower John Street, Golden Square, London W.1, England; or, Harold Ober Associates, 40 East 49th Street, New York, New York 10017, U.S.A. Address: Ca'n Bieló, Mallorca, Spain.

PUBLICATIONS

Verse

Proems: An Anthology of Poems, with others. London, Fortune Press, 1938.
Poets of Tomorrow: First Selection, with others. London, Hogarth Press, 1939.
Ten Poems. Edinburgh, privately printed, 1940.
Until Now. London, Fortune Press, 1942.
Poems for a Penny. Edinburgh, privately printed, 1942.
The Acreage of the Heart. Glasgow, Maclellan, 1943.
The Planet in My Hand: Twelve Poems. London, privately printed, 1944.
The Planet in My Hand. London, Grey Walls Press, 1946.
In Other Worlds: Twelve Poems. New York, Piper's Press, 1951.
Love Poem for the New Year, 1952. New York, Weekend Press, 1951.
A Masterpiece of Shells. New York, Bonacio and Saul-Grove Press, 1954.
A Poem: Indian Spring. Martha's Vineyard, Massachusetts, privately printed, 1954.
Indian Pipe. Martha's Vineyard, Massachusetts, privately printed, 1955.
Funeral of a Child (bilingual edition), translated by Elaine Kerrigan and Camilo

Jose Cela. Madrid and Palma, Papeles de Son Armadans, 1962.
Garland for the Winter Solstice: Selected Poems. London, Dent, and Boston, Little Brown, 1962.
The Geography of Faces (bilingual edition), translated by Antonio Molina. Madrid and Palma, Papeles de Son Armadans, 1964.
John Berryman 1914–1972. London, Poem-of-the-Month Club, 1972.
Lament of the Cats of Rapallo. London, John Roberts Press, 1973.
McGonagall Remembers Fitzrovia in the 1930s. London, Michael Parkin Fine Arts, 1973.

Novels

Over the Mountain. London, Harrap, and New York, Knopf, 1939.
The Lost Traveller. London, Grey Walls Press, 1942; augmented edition, New York, Dover, 1968.
Unholy Dying (as R. T. Campbell). London, John Westhouse, 1945.
Take Thee a Sharp Knife (as R. T. Campbell). London, John Westhouse, 1946.
Adventure with a Goat: Two Stories (includes *Adventures with a Goat* and *Apollo Wore a Wig*; as R. T. Campbell). London, John Westhouse, 1946.
Bodies in a Bookshop (as R. T. Campbell). London, John Westhouse, 1946.
Death for Madame (as R. T. Campbell). London, John Westhouse, 1946.
The Death Cap (as R. T. Campbell). London, John Westhouse, 1946.
Swing Low, Swing Death (as R. T. Campbell). London, John Westhouse, 1946.
Loser's Choice. New York, Hermitage House, 1953.

Other

The Laughing Mulatto: The Story of Alexander Dumas. London, Rich and Cowan, 1939.
First Animal Book (juvenile). London, Peter Lunn, 1946.
Tracks in the Snow (essays). London, Grey Walls Press, and New York, Scribner, 1947.
Space Cat (juvenile). New York, Scribner, 1952; London, Chatto and Windus, 1955.
The Tropical Fish Book. New York, Fawcett, 1953; revised edition, 1956.
Space Cat Visits Venus (juvenile). New York, Scribner, 1955; London, Chatto and Windus, 1956.
Space Cat Meets Mars (juvenile). New York, Scribner, 1957.
Space Cat and the Kittens (juvenile). New York, Scribner, 1958.
Tan's Fish (juvenile). Boston, Little Brown, 1958; London, Dent, 1960.
William Blake the Artist. London, Studio Vista, and New York, Dutton, 1971.

Editor, *Life of William Blake,* by Alexander Gilchrist. London, Dent, and New York, Dutton, 1942; revised edition, Dent, 1945.
Editor, *A Song to David and Other Poems,* by Christopher Smart. London, Grey Walls Press, 1947.
Editor, *Songs of Innocence and of Experience,* by William Blake. New York, United Book Guild, and London, Falcon Press, 1947.
Editor, *America: A Prophesy,* by William Blake. New York, United Book Guild, 1947.

Editor, *A Century of British Painters*, by Richard and Samuel Redgrave. London, Phaidon Press, 1947.

Editor, *Poems, Selected and Introduced*, by William Blake. London, Grey Walls Press, 1949.

Editor, *Selected Poetry*, by William Blake. New York, Dell, 1960.

Editor, *Blake's Dante Plates*. London, Book Collecting and Library Monthly, 1968.

Manuscript Collections: Lockwood Memorial Library, State University of New York, Buffalo; Humanities Research Center, University of Texas, Austin; National Library of Scotland, Edinburgh; Boston University.

Ruthven Todd comments:

In the fifty or so years during which I've been trying to write poems I guess that I must have written, and, unfortunately, printed rather more than I should have done in the way of weak, derivative and just simply bad poems. There have been periods during which the poems seemed to come so easily that I didn't have time to look at them properly. Still, I think that I can dismiss most of the bad stuff as slips made in climbing toward what I hope is a personal point of view and a personal voice. Today each poem that I manage to finish takes much more work than some of these earlier verses, and, though I regret the decline in production, I trust that the poems which I do produce are better than my earlier efforts.

When I look through my earlier poems I realize that, although I may not be happy with them, I cannot change them, beyond the correction of a grammatical error or of punctuation to make the sense more obvious. I know that many of my closest friends have adjusted the poems of their youth to fit their maturity. However, warts and all, I'd rather let them stay as errors from which I hope I learned to do better. Also, in a way, poems are a kind of autobiography and belated revision can only be a Stalinist rewriting of history. Of course, this doesn't mean that I don't keep a poem around me for several years, sometimes, before I print it (I'm speaking of my development in the last dozen or more years). However, once I've printed it in a book (for a magazine is only a trial run to see how it feels when printed), I wouldn't know what to do with it if I was to start tinkering with it.

So far as I know, none of my poems can be called obscure. Many of them have been written in what are the basically conventional forms, so adequately described by Babette Deutsch. However, call it what you will, I have played with scansion and rhythm as I thought fit. In my better poems I hope I have achieved a speaking voice making a balanced statement rather than indulged in the metronomic hypnosis of the regular beat. One of the hardest things, in writing English prose, is to avoid writing in hexameters. I do it myself, but see no reason why I should indulge in that ease in writing poems.

Finally, I have to admit that I have no reason to complain but I really have never had enough time to spend on my poetry. A part of this can be laid to financial considerations, but I fear that the major cause is an imbedded sense of curiosity about the world in which I live. As a child I thought that I could learn to know everything about everything. I have trimmed my ambitions throughout the years but, as any reader of my poems will recognize, I have done a great deal of research into matters which have taken up much time. As a person I do not regret the spread of my interests. And, anyhow, what could have been expected from a Gemini whose given name, although spelled Ruthven, is pronounced "Riven"? The

Shorter Oxford English Dictionary defines that as "Split, cloven, rent, torn asunder."

*   *   *

Most of Ruthven Todd's successful poems were produced before he was thirty, and are concerned either with horrified anticipation of the Second World War ("It Was Easier"), or with fascinated investigation of his Scottish ancestry and environment ("Personal History"), or with an effective combination of both these themes ("In September 1937"). In such pieces he achieves a style which is at once simple and atmospheric, where wit and feeling run in double harness. But in many of the early poems the wit is too consciously Audenesque, the passion inflated to Dylan Thomas grandiloquence, while some show more critical than creative energy in their concern with painters and other poets. The outbreak of the war deprived Todd of one main theme, and removal to the United States cut him off from his Scottish roots. Apart from a fine love poem ("A Narrow Sanctuary") and an effective contrast between past and present ("Broken Arrowheads at Chilmark, Martha's Vineyard"), his later work is more concerned with the surfaces of things than with their depths. Where the best of the earlier poems attempt to express major themes, and are sometimes most movingly successful, the later are so minor in quality that their emotional impact is slight.

—Alexander Scott

TOMLINSON, (Alfred) Charles. British. Born in Stoke-on-Trent, Staffordshire, 8 January 1927. Educated at Queens' College, Cambridge, B.A. 1948; London University, M.A. 1955. Married Brenda Raybould in 1948; has two daughters. Since 1956, Member of the Faculty, currently, Reader in English Poetry, University of Bristol. Visiting Professor, University of New Mexico, Albuquerque, 1962–63; O'Connor Professor of Literature, Colgate University, Hamilton, New York, 1967. Artist: One Man Show – Institute for Contemporary Arts, London, 1972. Recipient: Bess Hokin Prize, 1956, Levinson Prize, 1960, Oscar Blumenthal Prize, 1960, Union League Civic and Arts Foundation Prize, 1961, Inez Boulton Prize, 1964, and Frank O'Hara Prize, 1968 (*Poetry*, Chicago); University of New Mexico D. H. Lawrence Fellowship, 1963; University of Texas National Translation Center grant, 1968; Institute of International Education Fellowship, 1968. Lives in Ozleworth Bottom, Gloucestershire, England.

PUBLICATIONS

Verse

> *Relations and Contraries.* Aldington, Kent, Hand and Flower Press, 1951.
> *The Necklace.* Oxford, Fantasy Press, 1955; revised edition, London, Oxford University Press, 1966.
> *Seeing Is Believing: Poems.* New York, McDowell Obolensky, 1958; London, Oxford University Press, 1960.
> *A Peopled Landscape: Poems.* London, Oxford University Press, 1963.
> *Poems: A Selection,* with Tony Connor and Austin Clarke. London, Oxford University Press, 1964.
> *American Scenes and Other Poems.* London, Oxford University Press, 1966.
> *The Mattachines.* Cerillos, New Mexico, San Marcos Press, 1968.

To Be Engraved on the Skull of a Cormorant. London, The Unaccompanied
  Serpent, 1968.
Penguin Modern Poets 14, with Alan Brownjohn and Michael Ham-
  burger. London, Penguin, 1969.
The Way of a World. London, Oxford University Press, 1969.
America West Southwest. Cerillos, New Mexico, San Marcos Press, 1969.
Renga, with others. Paris, Gallimard, 1970; translated by the author, London,
  Penguin, 1972.
Worlds and Images. London, Covent Garden Press, 1972.
Written on Water. London, Oxford University Press, 1972.
The Way In and Other Poems. London, Oxford University Press, 1974.

Other

The Poem as Initiation. Hamilton, New York, Colgate University Press,
  1967.

Editor, *Marianne Moore: A Collection of Critical Essays.* New York, Pren-
  tice Hall, 1970.
Editor, *William Carlos Williams: A Collection of Critical Essays.* London,
  Penguin, 1972.

Translator, *Versions from Fyodor Tyutchev, 1803–1873.* London, Oxford Uni-
  versity Press, 1960.
Translator, with Henry Gifford, *Castilian Ilexes: Versions from Antonio
  Machado.* London, Oxford University Press, 1963.
Translator, *Ten Versions from Trilce,* by César Vallejo. Cerillos, New
  Mexico, San Marcos Press, 1970.

Critical Studies: "Negotiations: American Scenes and Other Poems" by Michael
Kirkham, in *Essays in Criticism* (Oxford), July 1967; "Charles Tomlinson" by
Calvin Bedient, in *Iowa Review* (Iowa City), Spring 1970; "The Poetry of Charles
Tomlinson" by Michael Edwards, in *Agenda 9* (London), 1970.

Charles Tomlinson comments:

My theme is relationship. The hardness of crystals, the facets of cut glass; but
also the shifting of light, the energizing weather which is the result of the
combination of sun and frost – these are the images for a certain mental climate,
components for the moral landscape of my poetry in general. One critic has
described that climate as Augustan. But it is an Augustanism that has felt the
impact of French poetry – Baudelaire to Valéry – and of modern American poetry.
A phenomenological poetry, with roots in Wordsworth and in Ruskin, is what I
take myself to be writing. Translation has been an accompanying discipline and so
have drawing and painting.

*   *   *

A rootedness in things, an intelligence of eye and ear, has informed Charles
Tomlinson's poetry from the beginning. What Donald Davie wrote in his introduction to *The Necklace,* Tomlinson's collection of poems published in 1955, applies

with probably greater force to his most recent poetry: "The world of these poems is a public one, open to any man who has kept clean and in order his nervous sensitivity to the impact of shape and mass and colour, odour, texture, and timbre. The poems appeal outside of themselves only to the world perpetually bodied against our senses. They improve that world. Once we have read them, it appears to us renovated and refreshed, its colours more delicate and clear, its masses more momentous, its sounds and odours sharper, more distinct."

Mr. Tomlinson is also a visual artist and there is a quality of *seeing*, a beauty derived from a minute observation of particular things, in his finest work. His words exactly fit his objects, whereas bad poetry erects a barrier between our perceptions and external reality. Allied to this is a lack of rhetoric, and a stillness, which can perhaps be exemplified best by quoting the first stanza of "Farewell to Van Gogh," from his second book:

> The quiet deepens. You will not persuade
>   One leaf of the accomplished, steady, darkening
> Chestnut-tower to displace itself
>   With more of violence than the air supplies
> When, gathering dusk, the pond brims evenly
>   And we must be content with stillness.

But Charles Tomlinson's work has not remained static. In *American Scenes*, there is a quality of *sound* which reinforces and vitalizes what was at times in the early work mere precision of visual description. These poems exemplify Louis Zukofsky's statement: "To see is to inform all speech." The more clearly Mr. Tomlinson sees and hears the greater definition he gets into his rhythms:

> Your quiet ministers
> to windless air, but the ear
> pricks at an under-stir
> as the leaves clench tighter
> in their shrivellings.

The best of these poems grow out of "solitary, sharpened perception" (to quote one of them) in desert places, or the heart of Winter:

> Between the graves, you find
> a beheaded pigeon, the blood and grain
> trailed from its bitten.crop, as alien to all
> the day's pallor as the raw
> wounds of the earth, turned above
> a fresh solitary burial.

In the "American Scenes" section of this book, it is the desolation of ghost towns ("Speak of the life that uselessness has unconstrained"), and of the desert that has produced some of the most solid and lucid poetry to be published in England in the sixties. In many of these poems also there is a concern for people. This is particularly present in "Death in the Desert," in memory of an old Hopi doll-maker.

Good poets often discover poets that they are particularly suited to translate and Tomlinson is no exception. His collaboration with Henry Gifford in versions of the Spanish poet Antonio Machado, *Castilian Ilexes*, has enriched English poetry, added a new dimension, and this is the one justification for the translation of poetry. A love of people also permeates these poems. One of the most moving, "Lament of the Virtues and Verses on Account of the Death of Don Guido," is an elegy which has, at the same time, a lightness, hilaritas, that could not have come out of England. It is a creative achievement to have brought this across so that the poem has become part of the English tradition:

> The here
> and the there,
> cavalier,
> show in your withered face,
> confess the infinite:
> the nothingness.
> Oh the thin cheeks
> yellow
> and the eyelids, wax,
> and the delicate skull
> on the bed's pillow!

In his most recent books, *The Way of a World* and *Written on Water*, Tomlinson continues to define his perceptions of people, landscape, air and water. In "Clouds," from the former collection, he has almost overcome the immense difficulties involved in finding adequate words for such intangibles, though here, of course, Shakspere has excelled him. At times, in Tomlinson's later poetry, there is an over-complexity of language – the vocabulary and sentence structure have the effect of distancing the reader from the subject matter of the poems. But there are several powerful poems in both *The Way of a World* and *Written on Water*. I quote "The Apparition" in full:

> I dreamed, Justine, we chanced on one another
>   As though it were twenty years ago. Your dark
> Too vulnerable beauty shone
>   As then, translucent with its youth,
> Unreal, as dreams so often are,
>   With too much life. 'Tomorrow,'
> You said, 'we plough up the pastureland.'
>   The clear and threatening sky
> New England has in autumn – its heightened blue,
>   The promise of early snow – were proofs enough
> Of the necessity, though of what pastureland
>   You spoke, I'd no idea. Then
> Reading the meaning in your face, I found
>   Your pastureland had been your hallowed ground which now
> Must yield to use. And all of my refusals,
>   All I feared, stood countered
> By the resolve I saw in you and heard:
>   While death itself, its certain thread
> Twisted through the skein of consequence
>   Seemed threatened by the strength
> Of those dead years. It was a dream –
>   No more; and you whom death
> And solitude have tried, must know
>   The treachery of dreams. And yet I do not think it lied,
> Because it came, without insistence,
>   Stood for a moment, spoke and then
> Was gone, that apparition,
>   Beyond the irresolute confines of the night,
> Leaving me to weigh its words alone.

Charles Tomlinson's finest poems are rhythmic units of beauty. They fix moments of heightened perception, of sound and sight, in permanent words. I think particularly here of "The Well," in the Mexican section of *American Scenes*. It is a complete, perfectly balanced statement (consequently it is impossible to substantiate what I am saying by a quotation) while being a complex pattern of things felt with roots extending at the same instant into many areas of experience both past and present.

—William Cookson

TONKS, Rosemary (D. Boswell). British. Born in London. Married. Has lived in West Africa and Pakistan. Poetry Reviewer, BBC European Service. Address: 46 Downshire Hill, London N.W.3, England.

PUBLICATIONS

Verse

Notes on Cafés and Bedrooms. London, Putman, 1963.
Iliad of Broken Sentences. London, Bodley Head, 1967.

Novels

Opium Fogs. London, Putnam, 1963.
Emir. London, Adam Books, 1963.
The Bloater. London, Bodley Head, 1968.
Businessmen as Lovers. London, Bodley Head, 1969; as *Love among the Operators*, Boston, Gambit, 1970.
The Way Out of Berkeley Square. London, Bodley Head, 1970; Boston, Gambit, 1971.
The Halt During the Chase. London, Bodley Head, 1972; New York, Harper, 1973.

Other

On Wooden Wings: The Adventures of Webster (juvenile). London, Murray, 1948.
The Wild Sea Goose (juvenile). London, Murray, 1951.

Rosemary Tonks comments:

I have developed a visionary modern lyric, and, for it, an idiom in which I can write lyrically, colloquially, and dramatically. My subject is city life – with its sofas, hotel corridors, cinemas, underworlds, cardboard suitcases, self-willed buses, banknotes, soapy bathrooms, newspaper-filled parks; and its anguish, its enraged excitement, its great lonely joys.

*   *   *

Rosemary Tonks's strength as a poet is an unusual adventurousness of style. Her weakness is self-consciousness. Her work has developed, so to speak, "against the tide." Gaudy and exclamatory, it deliberately flouts the rules laid down for contemporary English poets by English critics. At a time when French poetry in general has been out of favour with English-speaking readers, Rosemary Tonks seems to have read a vast range of French poets, and shows signs of being especially attracted to those least in tune with the tradition of her fellow-countrymen. Eluard seems to attract her in particular. The result is work that occasionally reads like a good translation:

> What a night! My past is very close.
> Dark rag-and-satin April in the city
> Moves its water lily breezes, one by one. My fading letters!
> My café-au-lait sentences that groaned for love and money!

Nevertheless one grows to respect her defiance of "good taste" and accepted rules. She deserves the phrase A. Alvarez once applied to her: "an original sensibility in motion."

—Edward Lucie-Smith

TORRES, Emmanuel. Filipino. Born in Manila, 29 April 1932. Educated at Ateneo de Manila University, Quezon City, B.A. in education 1954; University of Iowa, Iowa City (Smith-Mundt Scholar), M.A. in English 1957. Member of the Faculty, 1958–64, and since 1965, Associate Professor of English, Ateneo de Manila University. Since 1960, Curator, Ateneo Art Gallery, Quezon City. Since 1965, Art Critic, *Manila Times.* First Vice-President, Art Association of the Philippines, 1964–65. Recipient: United States State Department Specialist Grant, 1962; British Council Grant, 1964; Rockefeller Research Grant, 1965; Palanca Award, 1966. Lives in Quezon City.

PUBLICATIONS

Verse

Angels and Fugitives: Poems.   Manila, Bookmark, 1966.

Emmanuel Torres comments:

My poems deal thematically (the better ones at any rate) with the doubtful comforts of individual solitude and complacency and the importance of humane communication and communion; the need to acknowledge and come to terms with the irrational, the unpredictable, the mysterious in the human condition; the difficulty of sustaining courage and love in a world of unspectacular, banal, unheroic urban dailiness. Stylistically the poems owe a great deal to the Symbolists, also something to Zen. Generally they tend to create a tension between the precise image and the elusive feeling, between the heroic stance and the banal circumstance, between the naked cry and the cool suggestion, between having to make explicit meaning and leaving gaps in the meaning.

*   *   *

Writing about Emmanuel Torres should be easy, as we edited the same college magazine together, started to paint after college and exhibit our paintings together with other poets, moved into art criticism, and are now entangled in projects involving the more basic problems of aesthetics.

When Torres was preparing his first volume of poems, the prize-winning *Angels and Fugitives*, I wrote an introduction which later appeared as an epilogue. But this did not and does not matter. With or without introduction, Torres' poetry is one of the best performances of word and symbol among the works of Philippine poets writing in the English language today.

Although Torres can be exotic and deliberately philosophical in his use of language (e.g., his Mu Ch'i poem), he prefers to employ commonplace, almost banal images and situations for his poems. But this is merely his method. Torres' vision is anything but trite: it is that of a seer seeking out the angelic and fugitive Pattern or Configuration even in the most ordinary things or acts, like a wash basin by a window, a girl dozing off in an armchair, a pair of old shoes, and so on.

This seeking after the extraordinary in the ordinary – the tension between the spiritual and the humdrum – is characteristic of his poetry.

—Leonidas V. Benesa

TOULSON, Shirley. British. Born in Henley-on-Thames, Oxfordshire, 20 May 1924. Educated at Birkbeck College, University of London. Formerly, free-lance journalist. Since 1967, Features Editor, *The Teacher* (journal of the National Union of Teachers), London. Address: 63 Denmark Road, Wimbledon, London S.W.19, England.

PUBLICATIONS

Verse

Shadows in an Orchard. London, Scorpion Press, 1960.
Circumcision's Not Such a Bad Thing after All and Other Poems. Richmond, Surrey, Keepsake Press, 1970.

All Right Auden, I Know You're There: A Quick Thought. Leicester, Offcut
Press, 1970.
For a Double Time. Frensham, Surrey, Sceptre Press, 1970.
The Fault, Dear Brutus: A Zodiac of Sonnets. Richmond, Surrey, Keepsake
Press, 1972.

Other

Education in Britain. London, Evans, 1974.

Editor, *The Remind-Me Hat and Other Stories* (juvenile). London, Evans,
1973.

Shirley Toulson comments:

I consider I have a very minor talent which occasionally gets triggered off into
expression by some personal, highly charged event. My conscious effort in writing
is to give a disciplined more impersonal pattern to the original emotion; for this
reason I work usually in fairly rigorous verse forms. The poets I read a lot of are
Yeats and Auden, but I do not think they have any discernible influence on my
work.

*   *   *

Shirley Toulson is the sort of poet whose work appears in magazines, and then in
small collections under the imprint of such houses as Scorpion Press (*Shadows in
an Orchard*) and The Keepsake Press (*Circumcision's Not Such a Bad Thing after
All* and *The Fault, Dear Brutus*).
Hardly the sort of publishing history to help win éclat or reputation, it nevertheless indicates a certain degree of humility, a self-recognition of minority. What it
does not indicate is that her poems exemplify a quiet mastery of a less than limited
range, even if her writing might, to some, be too easily characterised as that
familiar contemporary mode – the domestic, balanced uneasily over hinted turbul-
ences, as in "Watching" or "Dustbins," both of them poems in which ordinary
fascinations are contemplated to a point in which they are made to elicit her
perceptions of an individual predicament.
Her collection of 1970, from which these two poems come, is probably her best.
Earlier, in *Shadows in an Orchard*, her poems showed an attractive concentration
on real settings, real incidents. But even in the reluctantly poetic area of the city
("Fulham in Winter" and "Tube Train," for instance) the result of her interest in
what, in the late Fifties, was not well-covered terrain, produced what appears a
too-easily achieved melancholy, even if her strictness could not permit digressions
from the realities before her.
By the time of *Circumcision's Not Such a Bad Thing after All*, technical
assurance had grown considerably, although her attempt at a villanelle ("Learning
to Read") simply sounds like most other attempts at the cumulative vowel-tune.
The preciosity of form here devalues the compassion behind the impulse to write.
In earlier poems, "Cripples" or "Films for Defectives," that compassion was
obvious, and controlled enough.

However, *The Fault, Dear Brutus* was to show Miss Toulson engaging with the frivolous, if difficult, technical problems involved in "a Zodiac of Sonnets." The overall effect of this girlish, sweetly illustrated volume is one of an almost regrettable neatness and charm, thankfully toughened at odd moments by failures of what Alvarez would call "gentility." Each poem, writes Miss Toulson, "is centred round the birthday of a particular individual." Zodiacal play was common in medieval literature (in Chaucer, for example); so Miss Toulson's personal but moral concern can be seem as updating an old technique. There may even be a certain amount of mischievousness in her purpose. Yet for all that it appears little more than a pleasant digression from the compassionate concerns which are the strengths of her earlier work.

—Douglas Dunn

TOYNBEE, (Theodore) Philip. British. Born in Oxford, 25 June 1916; son of the historian Arnold Toynbee. Educated at Rugby School, Warwickshire, 1930–34; Christ Church, Oxford, 1935–38. Served in the Intelligence Corps, 1940–42, the Ministry of Economic Warfare, 1942–45, and at S.H.A.E.F. in France and Belgium, 1944–45. Married Anne Barbara Denise Powell in 1939 (divorced, 1950); Frances Genevieve Smith, 1950; has five children. Editor, *Birmingham Town Crier*, 1938–39; Literary Editor, Contact Publications, London, 1945–46. Since 1950, Member of the Editorial Staff, *The Observer*, London. Address: The Barn House, Brockweir, near Chepstow, Monmouthshire, England.

PUBLICATIONS

Verse

The Pantaloon series (novels in verse):
    Pantaloon; or, The Valediction. London, Chatto and Windus, and New York, Harper, 1961.
    Two Brothers: The Fifth Day of the Valediction of Pantaloon. London, Chatto and Windus, 1964; New York, Harper, 1965.
    A Learned City: The Sixth Day of the Valediction of Pantaloon. London, Chatto and Windus, 1966.
    Views from a Lake: The Seventh Day of the Valediction of Pantaloon. London, Chatto and Windus, 1968.

Novels

The Savage Days. London, Hamish Hamilton, 1937.
A School in Private. London, Putnam, 1941.
The Barricades. London, Putnam, 1943; New York, Doubleday, 1944.
Tea with Mrs. Goodman. London, Horizon, 1947; as *Prothalamium: A Cycle of the Holy Grail*, New York, Doubleday, 1947.

The Garden to the Sea. London, MacGibbon and Kee, 1953; New York, Doubleday, 1954.
Thanatos: A Modern Symposium, with Maurice Richardson. London Gollancz, 1963.

Other

Friends Apart: A Memoir of Esmond Romilly and Jasper Ridley in the Thirties. London, MacGibbon and Kee, 1954.
Comparing Notes: A Dialogue Across a Generation, with Arnold Toynbee. London, Weidenfeld and Nicolson, 1963.
Towards the Holy Spirit. London, SCM Press, 1973.
The Age of the Spirit: Religion as Experience. New York, Harper, 1974.

Editor, *Fearful Choice: A Debate on Nuclear Policy.* London, Gollancz, 1958; Detroit, Wayne State University Press, 1959.
Editor, *Underdogs: 18 Victims of Society.* London, Weidenfeld and Nicolson, 1961; as *Underdogs: Anguish and Anxiety: 18 Men and Women Write Their Own Case-Histories,* New York, Horizon Press, 1962.

Translator, *Kérillis on the Causes of the War,* by Henri de Kérillis and Raymond Cartier. London, Putnam, 1939.

Critical Study: introduction by the author to *Two Brothers,* 1964.

Philip Toynbee comments:

What I am trying to do in *Pantaloon* – no doubt over-ambitiously – is to write something like a modern equivalent of *Don Quixote, The Prelude, Faust,* and *A la Récherche du Temps Perdu,* all in one. That's to say a tragi-comic epic whose hero is representative, but not in the least typical, of the years 1914–1950. Above all I want to stand at a distance from my own hero, and by means of this device give a fair hearing and showing to all the important ideas and human types of the age, without explicitly endorsing any of them. It is part of the old struggle, in fact, to escape from romanticism and return to a classical outlook and method. My chosen medium is verse – in a great many different forms.

I hope the wide variety of verse styles in the *Pantaloon* will speak for themselves. There is a reason, or several reasons, for every one of them.

*   *   *

Although Philip Toynbee has been known for most of his life as a critic and an experimental novelist, his long poem or verse novel, *The Valediction of Pantaloon,* which has been appearing in successive volumes since 1961, indicates that he is also a gifted poet, even if he did not turn to writing poetry until middle age. The poem has an ingenious pattern. It is supposedly set in the closing years of the twentieth century, when the elderly narrator, Dick Abberville, aristocrat and sometime rebel, considers his early life. Within this elaborate and distancing structure Toynbee looks back to the 1930's, the period when he himself developed

1563

as a writer; the recollections may not be strictly autobiographical, but they seem to have some relation to Toynbee's own experience.

The verse is adroit and well-written; if there are occasional echoes of Eliot and Auden or MacNeice, one is also reminded of Victorian narrative poetry, with pleasant suggestions of Clough or Tennyson. But it is hard to see that Toynbee has effectively solved the problems of writing a long narrative poem in our age; if anything, he underlines the difficulties. In particular, his determination to vary the verse form for expressive purposes from one volume to the next, and within different sections of the same volume, indicates a certain formal restlessness, which is conspicuously unlike the assurance with which the major Romantic and Victorian poets handled the extended verse narrative.

—Bernard Bergonzi

TREMAYNE, Sydney (Durward). Scottish. Born in Ayr, 15 March 1912. Educated at Ayr Academy, 1917–27. Served as a fireman in London during World War II. Married Lily Hanson in 1931 (marriage dissolved), has two sons; Constance Lipop in 1946. Journalist, *Yorkshire Evening News*, Leeds, 1929, and for newspapers in Harrowgate, Selby, Northampton, Sunderland, and Newcastle-upon-Tyne, 1929–38. Staff Member, 1938, Chief Sub-Editor, 1939–48, Leader Writer, 1948–54, and since 1969, Special Writer, the *Daily Mirror*, London. Leader Writer, the *Daily Herald*, later *The Sun*, London, 1954–69. Recipient: Scottish Arts Council Award, 1970. Agent: Anthony Shiel Associates Ltd., 52 Floral Street, London WC2E 9DA. Address: Blawan Orchard, Westerham Hill, Kent, England.

PUBLICATIONS

Verse

For Whom There Is No Spring. London, Pendulum Press, 1946.
Time and the Wind. London, Collins, 1948.
The Hardest Freedom. London, Collins, 1951.
The Rock and the Bird. London, Allen and Unwin, 1955.
The Swans of Berwick. London, Chatto and Windus – Hogarth Press, 1962.
The Turning Sky. London, Hart Davis, 1968.
Selected and New Poems. London, Chatto and Windus, 1973.

Critical Study: by Austin Clarke, in the *Irish Times* (Dublin), 10 December 1955.

Sydney Tremayne comments:

I have written verse since the age of eleven but did not publish until the Second World War. My poems have arisen out of the need to clarify experience and from pleasure in language. All are written to be heard. I hope, simply, that they speak for themselves.

*   *   *

Sydney Tremayne at the beginning of his practice as a poet used largely the language of romantic poetry. He never rejected it, nor did he develop an interest in new verse techniques, yet thanks to his genuineness, his literary discrimination, and an ability to recognize those subjects that have a special meaning for him, his poems have a winning freshness and frequently authority. He has a robust and immediate response to the animals that he sees – as it were – at his door, as in "Earth Spirits":

> The world of the young hare
> Is hairy as his milky mother's teat
> Who suckles him and rolls him off his feet,
> Licks him with rapid care,
> Then leaves him with a leap to his own care
> Among forget-me-nots to sit and stare.

He has the genuineness to take this poem no further, but in his poem, "The Fox," he begins with a glimpse of the animal:

> Out of the corner of his yellow eye
> Glanced round his shoulder. Seeing nothing there
> Skirted the tall dry biscuit coloured grass. . . .

He then associates the image with a person,

> One who was brave and frightened, fugitive,
> Fox coloured hair.

The poem ends:

> Swiftly comes
> The verbal thought how many years she's dead.
> The fox has slipped away in the dark wood.

He has achieved a poise whereby he can use natural imagery (without ever falling for the discredited pathetic fallacy) as a means of disclosing the delicately balanced, sometimes threatened, always isolated life of man in a natural environment. The disclosure is tactfully and tenderly made in "Outposts in Winter":

> We two adrift in winter share with birds
> Confinement in the dark, that comes,
> Silence banked upon silence, stranding words.

This poem from Tremayne's collection, *The Turning Sky*, shows an increasing freedom of movement between fact and idea, a recognition that even the conditioning natural world becomes words in poetry. This flexibility, when applied to the details of the environment, which has been the material of his better poems, has given a new depth to some of the most recent poems, as in "Wanting News":

Waiting for words to fall into the box
And ice to drop from hedges, wanting news,
Missing your voice, cold stillness, builds unease:
The eye looks round for movement, like a fox.

Some of Sydney Tremayne's poems have been referred to as water colour painting. It is true that some have the merit and limitation of that art. The better poems rebut the allegation. It would seem that after sixty he is in a position to take further the developments of his later poems.

—George Bruce

TRIPP, John. Welsh. Born in Bargoed, Glamorgan, 22 July 1927. Educated at Whitchurch Senior School, Cardiff; Morley College, London, Diploma in Moral Philosophy. Served as a Sergeant in the Royal Army Pay Corps, 1945–48. BBC News Researcher and Sub-Editor, London, 1951–58; Press Officer, Indonesian Embassy, London, 1958–67; Information Officer, Central Office of Information, London, 1967–69. Since 1969, Free-lance Writer, Cardiff. Member, English Language Section, Welsh Academy of Letters. Recipient: Welsh Arts Council Bursary, 1969, 1972. Address: 2 Heol Penyfai, Whitchurch, Cardiff, Wales.

PUBLICATIONS

Verse

Diesel to Yesterday. Cardiff, Triskel Press, 1966.
The Loss of Ancestry. Llandybie, Carmarthenshire, Christopher Davies, 1969.
The Province of Belief. Llandybie, Carmarthenshire, Christopher Davies, 1971.
Bute Park and Other Poems. Cardiff, Second Aeon, 1972.
The Inheritance File. Cardiff, Second Aeon, 1974.

Play

Radio Play: The Seed of Dismemberment, 1972.

Manuscript Collection: National Library of Wales, Aberystwyth.

Critical Studies: by Sam Adams, in Poetry Wales (Cardiff), 1969; Roland Mathias, in Anglo-Welsh Review (Pembroke Dock, Wales), 1970; Charles Elliott, in Anglo-Welsh Review (Pembroke Dock, Wales), 1972; "Poetry in Wales" by Glyn Jones, in *British Poetry since 1960: A Critical Survey*, edited by Michael Schmidt and Grevel Lindop, Oxford, Carcanet Press, 1972.

John Tripp comments:

The major themes in my work have to do with Wales, its history and people, from the viewpoint of one who is extremely conscious of his roots. I have tried to create a small document about my country, its harsh past, its difficult present, and its chances for the future – including the preservation of the Welsh language. This subject-matter has often been framed within a tight, terse verse-form which has been described as "tough and steely." (There have also been many references to my wryness, dryness, irony and "gallows humor.") But one has tried to keep a cold eye and a warm heart on the raw material – which is often recalcitrant – to find a union of reason and emotion in pulling away from the sentimental nostalgia and discursive rhetoric of much of the poetry common to the overstating Celt. Our problem has always been one of economy.

I suppose I am still a modern who reeks of the museum, caught between two cultures, and well aware of a vacuum of disinheritance.

                    *   *   *

Most of John Tripp's writing is set in Wales. Like many poets, he is thin in generalization, better in sharp particulars:

> Snow mucks to slush, the yellow
> streaks of dog piss on the lovewalk,
> thin layered frost on their crud
> at the trees' base . . .

Too much of his work consists of praise of the Welsh and denunciation of the English. The insight missing in his simply nationalistic poems comes out when he speaks, not of the Welsh, but of individual Welshmen – Lloyd George, Aneurin Bevan, Jack Jones, and, best of all, R. Williams Parry, whom, in a sustained analogy, he represents as "The Bard of Winter":

> He was a careful little man
> who looked more like a bank manager
> than a bard: chalk-striped
> suit, waistcoat, hornrimmed spectacles,
> and horror behind the eyes.
> In the woods and fields of Gwynedd
> he was frightened when he saw the fear
> of wood-pigeon, wild fowl, hare and fox . . .
>
> He was buried on a January day
> too cold to lift its head –
> a day of honest weather he might have liked
> and fitting for a true poet . . .
> On the hillside at Bethesda
> under the snow his wild companions
> nestle for shelter.

1567

The language never catches fire, but, equally, Mr. Tripp seems never at a loss for a subject. He gets a good deal of humour and observation, too, into these wry professions of a middle-aged Welshman. It may well be, however, that for all his toughness and irony, Mr. Tripp is insufficiently interested in the craft of verse to make the best of his talent. On the other hand, a novel or a collection of stories from his pen would be interesting to read.

—Philip Hobsbaum

TRYPANIS, Constantine (Athanasius). Greek. Born in Chios, 22 January 1909. Educated at Chios Classical Gymnasium, 1920–26; University of Athens M.A. 1931, D.Phil. 1939; University of Berlin, 1932–34; University of Munich, 1935–37; Oxford University, M.A. 1946. Served as a Sub-Lieutenant in the Greek Army, 1940–41. Married Alice Macris in 1942; has one daughter. Lecturer in Classics, University of Athens, 1939–47. Bywater and Sotheby Professor of Byzantine and Modern Greek Language and Literature, and Fellow, Exeter College, Oxford, 1947–69. Since 1969, Emeritus Fellow. Since 1969, University Professor of Classics, University of Chicago. Visiting Professor, Hunter College, New York, 1963, Harvard University, Cambridge, Massachusetts, 1963–64, and University of Vienna, 1971. Member, Medieval Academy of America; Corresponding Member, Academy of Athens. Recipient: Academy of Athens Koraes Prize, 1933; Heinemann Award, 1960. D.Litt: Oxford, 1970. Fellow, Royal Society of Literature. Archon Hieromnemon, Oecumenical Patriarchate. Address: 5825 South Dorchester Avenue, Chicago, Illinois 60637, U.S.A.

PUBLICATIONS

Verse

Pedasus: Twenty-Four Poems. Reading, Berkshire, University of Reading School of Art, 1955.
The Stones of Troy. London, Faber, 1957.
The Cocks of Hades. London, Faber, 1958.
Grooves in the Wind (The Stones of Troy and The Cocks of Hades). New York, Chilmark Press, 1964.
Pompeian Dog. London, Faber, 1964; New York, Chilmark Press, 1965.
The Elegies of a Glass Adonis. New York, Chilmark Press, 1967.
The Glass Adonis. London, Faber, and New York, Chilmark Press, 1973.

Plays

Radio Plays: *Oedipus King,* 1955 (U.K.); *Oedipus at Colonus,* 1958 (U.K.); *Antigony,* 1958 (U.K.); *Persians,* 1958 (U.K.)

Other

Eric Arthur Barber. 1888–1965.   London, Oxford University Press, 1967.

Editor, *Alexandrian Poetry.*   Athens, Garouphalias, 1943.
Editor, *Medieval and Modern Greek Poetry: An Anthology.*   Oxford, Claren-
don Press, 1951.
Editor and Translator, *Callimachus: Aetia, Iambi, Lyric Poems, Hecale, Minor
Epic and Elegiac Poems, Fragments of Epigrams, Fragments of Uncertain
Location.*   London, Heinemann, and Cambridge, Massachusetts, Harvard
University Press, 1958.
Editor, with P. Maas, *Sancti Romani Melodi Cantica.*   Oxford, Clarendon
Press, 2 vols., 1963, 1970.
Editor, *Fourteen Early Byzantine Cantica.*   Vienna, Academy of Austria,
1968.
Editor, *The Penguin Book of Greek Verse.*   London, Penguin, 1970.

Manuscript Collection: Library of the State University of New York, Buffalo.

Critical Study: by W. H. Auden, in *Encounter* (London), 1956.

Constantine Trypanis comments:

Themes come from the Greek world – ancient, medieval, and modern. Both
traditional forms and free verse have been used. Classical Greek poetry and the
poetry of Yeats have influenced me.

*   *   *

Born in the island of Chios, Constantine Trypanis had an English nanny and
spoke fluent and correct English from his childhood. For many years he was
Professor of Byzantine and Medieval Greek at Oxford, and, in the 1950's particularly, was noted for his kindness and sympathy to young poets – it was a flowering
period for poets in Oxford – and began, in middle age, to write poems himself,
modestly asking for advice from poets much younger than himself. He uses in
poetry his marvellous knowledge of Greek history and literature and his special
sense of the pathos of the periods of Greece in the Hellenistic, Rome-dominated
period and after the conquest of Constantinople by the Ottoman Turks. In his
sense of the fragility and irony of a great tradition in decline he resembles the great
modern Alexandrian poet, Kavafis or Cavafy and Auden, who adored Cavafy,
greeted one of Trypanis's earlier volumes with delight (and Auden, like Eliot,
tended rather studiously to avoid reviewing his contemporaries). Trypanis's longest
and most distinguished poem, *The Glass Adonis*, is a study of a great culture in the
stage of vitrification. He writes a formal but not in the least stiff English, rather
like the English of the other Greek who chose English for his medium, the late
Demetrios Capetanakis. His poems are learned and allusive but full of profound
and simple pathos in the emotions they express.

—G. S. Fraser

TURCO, Lewis (Putnam). American. Born in Buffalo, New York, 2 May 1934. Educated at Suffield Academy, Connecticut, 1947–49; Meriden High School, Connecticut, 1949–52; University of Connecticut, Storrs, 1956–59, B.A. 1959; University of Iowa, Iowa City, 1959–60, 1962, M.A. 1962. Served in the United States Navy, 1952–56. Married Jean Cate Houdlette in 1956; has one son and one daughter. Instructor, University of Connecticut, Spring 1959; Editorial Assistant, University of Iowa Writers Workshop, 1959–60; Instructor, 1960–64, and Poetry Center Founding Director, 1961–64, Cleveland State University; Assistant Professor, Hillsdale College, Michigan, 1964–65. Assistant Professor, 1965–68, Associate Professor, 1968–70, since 1969, Director of the Writing Arts Program, and since 1970, Professor of English, State University of New York, Oswego. Visiting Professor of English, State University of New York, Potsdam, 1968–69. Since 1968, Honorary Trustee, Theodore Roethke Memorial Foundation, Saginaw, Michigan. Recipient: Yaddo Fellowship, 1959; Academy of American Poets Prize, 1960; Bread Loaf Writers Fellowship, 1961; Helen Bullis Prize (*Poetry Northwest*, Seattle), 1972. Agent: Del Walker, 475 Fifth Avenue, New York, New York 10017. Address: 54 West 8th Street, Oswego, New York 13126, U.S.A.

PUBLICATIONS

Verse

Day after History: A Selection of Poems. Arlington, Virginia, Samisdat, 1956.
Fixing This World. Cleveland, privately printed, 1960.
First Poems. Francestown, New Hampshire, Golden Quill Press, 1960.
The Sketches of Lewis Turco and Livevil: A Mask. Cleveland, American Weave Press, 1962.
Image Tinged with No Color. Oswego, New York, privately printed, 1966.
School Drawing. Oswego, New York, privately printed, 1966.
My Country Wife. Oswego, New York, privately printed, 1966.
Awaken, Bells Falling: Poems 1959–1967. Columbia, University of Missouri Press, 1968.
The Inhabitant. Northampton, Massachusetts, Despa Press, 1970.
Pocoangelini: A Fantography. Northampton, Massachusetts, Despa Press, 1971.
The Weed Garden. Orangeburg, South Carolina, Peaceweed Press, 1973.

Plays

Dreams of Stone and Sun (produced Storrs, Connecticut, 1959). Published in *Theatre Journal* (Oswego, New York), Fall 1971.
The Elections Last Fall (produced Oswego, New York, 1969). Published in *Polemic 6* (Cleveland), 1961.

Other

The Book of Forms: A Handbook of Poetics. New York, Dutton, 1968.
The Literature of New York: A Bibliography. Oneonta, New York State English Council, 1970.
Creative Writing in Poetry. Albany, State University of New York, 1970.

Poetry: An Introduction Through Writing. Reston, Virginia, Reston Publishing Company, 1973.

Freshman Composition and Literature. Saratoga Springs, New York, Empire State College, 1973.

Editor, *The Spiritual Autobiography of Luigi Turco.* Ann Arbor, Michigan, University Microfilms Books, 1969.

Bibliography: "Lewis Turco: A Bibliography of His Works and of Criticism of Them," in *F. W. Crumb Memorial Library Bibliographies,* Potsdam, State University of New York, 1972.

Manuscript Collection: Harriet Monroe Modern Poetry Library, University of Chicago.

Critical Studies: "The Formalism of Lewis Turco" by Hyatt H. Waggoner, in *Concerning Poetry* (Bellingham, Washington), Fall 1969; "Craft and Vision: An Interview with Lewis Turco" edited by David McLean, in *Dekalb Literary Arts Journal* (Clarkston, Georgia), 1970; "The Progress of Lewis Turco" by William Heyen, in *Modern Poetry Studies,* v, 2, 1971; "A Certain Slant of Light" by Herbert Coursen, Jr., in *Bartleby's Review* (Machias, Maine), 1972; "The Poetry of Lewis Turco: An Interview" by Gregory Fitz Gerald and William Heyen, in *Costerus* (Amsterdam, Holland), ix, 1973.

Lewis Turco comments:

I regard myself as a formalist in the broadest sense of the word, not in the traditional sense, meaning perhaps an accentual-syllabic metrist; rather, in the experimental sense, meaning that the poem is the product of the whole poet, including his mind, bent on giving coherent language form to the human experience. I can only quote and echo Benjamin Britten, who said, "I try to write as Stravinsky has written and Picasso has painted. They were the men who freed music and painting from the tyranny of the purely personal. They passed from manner to manner as a bee passes from flower to flower. I try to do the same. Why should I lock myself inside a narrow personal idiom?"

*   *   *

Most of the work in Lewis Turco's *First Poems* is too stiff metrically, or too pretty, or too ingenious, or too heavily moral and wise. Turco was not willing to allow his poems to well up from their own subtle senses of themselves, was not willing to allow them to do what they wanted to do. In *The Sketches,* a collection of twenty-five character sketches and a mask, Turco moves toward the natural style that will come to fruition in *Awaken, Bells Falling: Poems 1959–1967,* and especially in *The Inhabitant,* about which Conrad Aiken has said: "*The Inhabitant* is the best new poem I've read in something like thirty years – profoundly satisfying to me, speaks my language, such a relief to have WHOLE meaning again, instead of this pitiable dot-and-dash splinter-poetry, or sawdust cornflakes which we usually get."

In *The Inhabitant* Turco is willing to allow his subject to surface when and how it must. As he says in "School Drawing," "There is a road: no one is walking there." Even the furniture of the inhabitant's house is allowed to sing its own songs. Turco's later work is skillful to such an extent that even the effects of accentual-syllabics are conversational, unstrained. "The Portrait of a Clown" describes that portrait in the room of the inhabitant's daughter as she sleeps, and concludes:

> how will the clown
>   maintain his equipoise as a
>   world as a
> room tips the frame tilts shades
>
>   of aquamarine the bold lines
>   of a face
> ride over the sleeping child.

– William Heyen

TURNBULL, Gael (Lundin). British. Born in Edinburgh, 7 April 1928. Married; has three children. Medical Practitioner; currently in general practice. Recipient: Union League Civic and Arts Foundation Prize (*Poetry*, Chicago), 1965; Alice Hunt Bartlett Prize, 1968. Address: 61 Belmont Road, Malvern, Worcestershire WR14 1PN, England.

PUBLICATIONS

Verse

Trio, with Eli Mandel and Phyllis Webb. Toronto, Contact Press, 1954.
The Knot in the Wood and Fifteen Other Poems. London, Revision Press, 1955.
Bjarni Spike-Helgi's Son and Other Poems. Ashland, Massachusetts, Origin Press, 1956.
A Libation. Glasgow, The Poet, 1957.
With Hey, Ho. . . . Birmingham, Migrant Press, 1961.
To You, I Write. Birmingham, Migrant Press, 1963.
A Very Particular Hill. Edinburgh, Wild Hawthorn Press, 1963.
Twenty Words, Twenty Days: A Sketchbook and a Morula. Birmingham, Migrant Press, 1966.
Briefly. Nottingham, Tarasque Press, 1967.
A Trampoline: Poems 1952–1964. London, Cape Goliard Press, 1968.
I, Maksoud. Exeter, University of Exeter, 1969.
Scantlings: Poems 1964–1969. London, Cape Goliard Press, 1970.
Finger Cymbals. Edinburgh, Satis, 1972.
A Random Sapling. Newcastle upon Tyne, Pig Press, 1974.

*   *   *

Gael Turnbull was born in Scotland and now lives in Worcester where he practices medicine. During his apprenticeship both as a physician and as a poet, however, he lived in North America where his early poems were published in, among other journals, *Black Mountain Review*. Until he returned to Britain in 1964, there was some confusion about whether he ought properly to be regarded as a Canadian, an American, or a British poet, and, evidently, at one point Donald Allen considered publishing a selection of Turnbull's poems (at Robert Duncan's suggestion) in his important anthology, *The New American Poetry*. Though Turnbull readily acknowledges his debt to poets like Duncan, Robert Creeley, Charles Olson, and Denise Levertov, he ought not to be looked upon as a kind of minor British Black Mountaineer. English poets like Basil Bunting, Roy Fisher, and Matthew Mead have also been important to his development and, in the end, the character of his best work turns out to be very personal and quite unique.

The danger for Turnbull is minimalism, and he is at his best when he is not attempting to refine and purify his writing down to the quintessential five or six four-syllable lines (or less) in the manner of Cid Corman, the early Creeley, or Ian Hamilton Finlay. For me, his strongest poem to date is a long piece in *A Trampoline* called "Twenty Words / Twenty Days" which ends: "and I remember an Edinburgh room and one saying, / when I asked what he'd done that day, how much – / I tore / it up . . . I wisnae pure enough when I wrote . . . I wisnae / pure enough. . . ." The poem, in fact, is marvellously *impure*. A word is chosen by a random method and each day's journal-like entry is constructed around it in a language as relaxed and supple as good prose but which has, in spite of its casual appearance on the page (it is broken up into units by dashes and ellipses), the concentration one expects from poetry. Rhythmically, it is very engaging: the rhythms of contemporary speech are handled as effectively as they are in William Carlos Williams. The poem is richly anecdotal. Turnbull responds to his responsibilities as a doctor and citizen, to his private experience as a husband and father, and to his memories and desires as a poet and as a man. The twenty days happened to be November 17th to December 6th, 1963, and while November 22nd was the date of John Kennedy's assassination, and while that event figures centrally enough, it is just as important for the final effect of the poem that on November 20th Turnbull prevented a child from choking during a tonsillectomy and "had pleasure in [his] skill" or that on December 2nd he woke up unexpectedly remembering a girl he had met years before "out walking in the Appalachians." The poem is a moving human document. One can say of it, as Turnbull writes elsewhere: "The phrases are apt / The scene is not unusual / The joy is in the attention."

Turnbull's work after *A Trampoline* is gathered in a second volume, *Scantlings*. The note on the title is important: "Of limited or prescribed dimension; a portion, an allotted quantity; a builder's or carpenter's measuring rod; in a building, the small beams or pieces of wood; in archery, the distance from a mark, within which a shot is not regarded as a miss." The most ambitious poem in the new book is "A Word," a piece in some ways related to "Twenty Words / Twenty Days" but which, I feel, suffers from its minimalist and concretist affinities. Any of one hundred and twelve phrases are meant to be interchangable in such a way that they may relate to any of twenty-eight nouns. The printed version, we are told in a note, "is no less final than any other." For example, the first four lines of the printed version, "a word / against silence / a love / impelled to be uttered," could also be "a love / against silence / a word / impelled to be uttered." And so on through all the permutations.

In the last several years Turnbull has been writing poems for oral performance in cooperation with a group of musicians and singers in Worcester, and he has had increasing contact with, and interest in, the theatre. He is also working on a long project, only fragments of which have been published, provisionally called "Residues." He seems to be in rapid development at the moment and it is difficult to anticipate at this writing either the final shape of "Residues" or what he will do next.

– John Matthias

TURNER, W(illiam) Price. British. Born in York, 14 August 1927. Educated at Whitehill Secondary School, Glasgow, 1941. Served in the Royal Engineers, 1945–47. Married Anne Hamilton Hill in 1950; has two children. Editor, *The Poet*, Glasgow, 1951–56; Television Captions Artist and Assistant Floor Manager, BBC, Glasgow, 1957–60; Sub-Editor, 1962–63, and Crime Fiction Reviewer, 1963–66, *Yorkshire Post*, Leeds. Tutor in Creative Writing, Swarthmore Adult Education Centre, Leeds, 1963–66; Creative Writing Fellow, Glasgow University, 1973–75. Recipient: Gregory Fellowship, Leeds University, 1960–62; Scottish Arts Council Publication Award, 1970. Address: 8 Methley Terrace, Chapel Alerton, Leeds LS7 3NL, England.

PUBLICATIONS

Verse

> *First Offence.* Bristol, Derek Maggs, 1954.
> *The Rudiment of an Eye: Poems.* London, Villiers Publications, 1955.
> *The Flying Corset: Poems.* London, Villiers Publications, 1962.
> *Fables from Life.* Newcastle-upon-Tyne, Northern House, 1966.
> *More Fables from Life.* Portrush, Northern Ireland, Ulsterman Publications, 1969.
> *The Moral Rocking-Horse: Poems.* London, Barrie and Jenkins, 1970.
> *Casting One's Bread.* Ashington, Northumberland, MidNAG, 1972.

Plays

> *Baldy Bane* (libretto). London, BBC Publications, 1967.

> Radio Plays: *The Lair of the Boneyard Clerk*, 1958; *The Symbol*, 1959; *The Refuge*, 1964; *Something to Remember You By*, 1969.

Novels

> *Bound to Die* (as Bill Turner). London, Constable, 1967; New York, Walker, 1967.
> *Sex Trap* (as Bill Turner). London, Constable, 1968.
> *Circle of Squares* (as Bill Turner). London, Constable, and New York, Walker, 1969.
> *Another Little Death.* London, Constable, 1970; New York, Walker, 1971.

Soldier's Woman. London, Constable, 1972.
Hot-Foot. London, Constable, 1973.

Critical Studies: by Michael Butler, in *Samphire 11* (Ipswich, Suffolk); Roy Fisher, in *The Birmingham Post*, 31 July 1971.

W. Price Turner comments:

A poet's devotion must be to his own truth; as soon as he starts worrying about the function of poetry, the social responsibility of the poet, or other ideological purgatives, he is lost. He becomes just another actor, conscious of his best profile.

Basically, I try to employ shifts of tone and perspective to liberate insights. I use humour and conversational rhythms to charge my ideas with the irrational dynamic which I believe essential to all poetry. I enjoy the challenge of exacting disciplines, aiming for a cross-weave of ideas against form. If I can entertain my readers, so much the better.

* * *

In one of the poems in his first collection *First Offence* W. Price Turner refers to "the lightning-white integrity/of all who stand alone," and independence of spirit and style are the marks of this witty and sharp-eyed (and sharp-tongued) poet. Both the wit and the observing eye have at times, but mainly in his early work, been overlaid by criss-crossing trains of metaphor that fail to explode or don't explode apropo: virtuoso leanings that remain clever rather than functional, and give a heaviness to otherwise promising poems like "The Back-Court Piper." But the back-court piper begging his stint in the streets of Govan (where Turner himself used to live, in the days of his "shoestring lyricism" and editorship of *The Poet*) is a true image of something that matters deeply to him; and poverty, honesty, and integrity are the subjects of a number of good poems, such as "The Angry Gambler," "Alien," "Song in Lean Times," and "The Moral Rocking-Horse."

From *The Rudiment of an Eye* to *The Flying Corset, Fables from Life* and later poems, increased skill in delineation goes with the emergence of a tone of voice that we recognize. The voice ranges between a mocking humour and a fairly swinging satire. It draws an alert bead on the contemporary world (colour supplements, landladies, "flying corsets," academics, trucks bullet-proofed with telephone directories), but seems more original and distinctive in allowing for an element of the grotesque, as in the rather macabre "Elegy for Seven Teeth," the surprising "Encounter" (with an onion), or the Gogolian incident of "Getting One's Bearings" – perhaps his best poem – where the poet carrying chairs on his back meets two men taking a table on a pram:

> They grinned at my strung trophies
> wielded like an animated nutcracker,
> and looked back laughing as I stopped
> to look after them, and we went down
> our different slopes, having
> exchanged perspectives.

– Edwin Morgan

TUWHARE, Hone. New Zealand Maori. Born in Kaikohe, 21 October 1922. Educated at Campbell's Kindergarten, Victoria Park; Kaikohe Primary School; Avondale Primary School; Mangere Central Primary School; Beresford Street School, Auckland; Seddon Memorial Technical College, Auckland, 1939–41; Otahuhu Technical College, 1941. Served in the Maori Battalion, 1945, and the New Zealand Second Divisional Cavalry, 1945–47. Married Jean Tuwhare in 1949; has three sons. Formerly, Member, Wellington Boilermakers Union; Amalgamated Society of Railway Servants; Wellington Public Service Association; Freezing Workers Union; Wellington Tramway Workers Union; and District Executive, Communist Party of New Zealand; President, Te Mahoe Local, New Zealand Workers Union, 1962–64. Since 1964, Member, Auckland Boilermakers Union. President, Birkdale Maori Cultural Committee, Auckland, 1966–68; Councillor, Borough of Birkenhead, Auckland, 1968–70; Organizer of the Maori Artists and Writers Conference, Te Kaha, 1973. Recipient: Internal Affairs Department travel grant, 1956; Robert Burns Centennial Fellowship, University of Otago, 1969. Agent: Longman Paul Ltd., Milford, Auckland. Address: P.O. Box 3417, C.P.O., Auckland, New Zealand.

PUBLICATIONS

Verse

No Ordinary Sun: Poems. Auckland, Blackwood and Janet Paul, 1964.
Come Rain Hail. Dunedin, University of Otago Bibliography Room, 1970.
Sapwood and Milk. Dunedin, Caveman Press, 1972.
Something Nothing. Dunedin, Caveman Press, 1973.

Critical Study: by M. P. Jackson, in *Landfall 74* (Christchurch), June 1965.

Hone Tuwhare comments:

Strongly influenced by translated works of Mayakovsky, Mao Tse-Tung, Garcia Lorca, Louis Aragon, Pablo Neruda and Shakespeare, and R. A. K. Mason of New Zealand, together with a close study of *Nga Moteatea me nga harikari o te Iwi Maori:* a collection of untranslated Maori songs. Also, the Old Testament.

*   *   *

Hone Tuwhare is the first Maori to achieve recognition as a poet in English. Politically aware and left-wing in outlook, he has been influenced by the poetry and personal encouragement of the Marxist writer R. A. K. Mason, whose effect is apparent less in subject-matter, however, than in such things as structure, economy in epithets and the urge to make poetry. Mr. Tuwhare's poems have their own individual character – a warmth of feeling, a touch of melancholy and an occasional dash of astringency. They are unique in New Zealand poetry in that they combine some elements of traditional Maori verse, the lament, for instance, with modern European forms. His imagery, too, as in "Not by Wind Ravaged," is often drawn from the special experience of the Maori, yet most of his work is thoroughly European in outlook and style.

His themes include the passing of the old Maori way of life, man's exploitation of Nature and of his fellow-man, and the consolations and joys of the New Zealand environment. One of his most impressive poems, "No Ordinary Sun," deals with the atom bomb. His language is fresh and uncluttered and his poetic forms are flexible and varied. At times perhaps somewhat deficient in the energy his subject seems to demand, his work has a clarity and freedom from wilful obscurity which have won him a wide audience. His single volume, *No Ordinary Sun*, has gone into several editions, making it the most-read book of New Zealand poetry of the 1960's.

– J. C. Reid

UNTERMEYER, Louis. American. Born in New York City, 1 October 1885. Educated at De Witt Clinton High School, New York. Editor of Publications, U.S. Office of War Information, and Associate Editor, Armed Services Editions, during World War II. Married Jean Starr in 1907 (marriage dissolved); Virginia Moore in 1926 (marriage dissolved); Esther Antin in 1933 (marriage dissolved); Bryna Ivens in 1948; has three sons. Designer and Factory Manager, Untermeyer-Robins, jewellers, New York, 1908–25. Poetry Editor, *American Mercury*, New York, 1934–37; Contributing Editor, *The Liberator*, New York; Editor of Publications, Decca Records, New York, 1945–58; Founder, with James Oppenheim, *Seven Arts* magazine, New York. Honnold Lecturer, Knox College, Galesburg, Illinois, 1937; Beecher Lecturer, Amherst University, Massachusetts, 1937; Poet-in-Residence, University of Michigan, Ann Arbor, 1939–40, University of Kansas, Lawrence, 1939, and University of Iowa, Iowa City, 1940. United States Delegate, International Cultural Conference, India, 1961, Japan, 1963. Consultant in Poetry, Library of Congress, Washington, D.C., 1961–63. Phi Beta Kappa Poet, Harvard University, Cambridge, Massachusetts, 1956; Honorary Member, Phi Beta Kappa. Recipient: Poetry Society of America Gold Medal, 1956; Sarah Josepha Hale Award, 1965; New England Poetry Club Golden Rose, 1966. D.H.L.: Union College, Schenectady, New York, 1967. Member, National Institute of Arts and Letters. Address: Great Hill Road, Newtown, Connecticut 06470, U.S.A.

PUBLICATIONS

Verse

First Love: A Lyric Sequence. Boston, Sherman French, 1911.
Challenge. New York, Century, 1914.
——————— and Other Poets. New York, Holt, 1916.
These Times. New York, Holt, 1917.
Including Horace. New York, Harcourt Brace, 1919.
The New Adam. New York, Harcourt Brace, 1920.
Heavens (parodies). New York, Harcourt Brace, 1922.

Roast Leviathan.   New York, Harcourt Brace, and London, Cape, 1923.
Collected Parodies.   New York, Harcourt Brace, 1926.
Poems, with Richard Untermeyer.   Privately printed, 1927.
Burning Bush.   New York, Harcourt Brace, and London, Cape, 1928.
Adirondack Cycle.   New York, Random House, 1929.
Food and Drink.   New York, Harcourt Brace, 1932.
First Words Before Spring.   New York, Knopf, 1933.
Selected Poems and Parodies.   New York, Harcourt Brace, 1935.
For You with Love: A Poem (juvenile).   New York, Golden Press, 1961; London, Collins, 1964.
Long Feud: Selected Poems.   New York, Harcourt Brace, and London, Longman, 1962.
One and One and One (juvenile).   New York, Crowell Collier, 1962.
Labyrinth of Love.   New York, Simon and Schuster, 1965.
This Is Your Day: A Poem (juvenile).   London, Collins, 1965.
Thanks: A Poem.   Indianapolis, Odyssey Press, 1965.
Thinking of You (juvenile).   New York, Golden Press, 1968.
You: A Poem (juvenile).   New York, Golden Press, 1969.

Novel

Moses.   New York, Harcourt Brace, 1928; London, Chapman and Hall, 1929.

Short Stories

The Donkey of God.   New York, Harcourt Brace, 1932; London, Gollancz, 1935.
Cat o' Nine Tales.   New York, American Heritage Press, 1975.

Play

Man and the Masses, adaptation of a play by Ernst Toller (produced New York, 1924).   New York, Doubleday, 1924.

Other

The New Era in American Poetry.   New York, Holt, 1919.
American Poetry since 1900.   New York, Holt, 1923; London, Grant Richards, 1924.
The Forms of Poetry: A Pocket Dictionary of Verse.   New York, Harcourt Brace, 1926; London, Cape, 1927; revised edition, Harcourt Brace, 1954.
Blue Rhine, Black Forest: A Hand- and Day-Book.   New York, Harcourt Brace, and London, Harrap, 1930.
Chip: My Life and Times: As Overheard by Louis Untermeyer (juvenile).   New York, Harcourt Brace, 1933.
The Last Pirate: Tales from the Gilbert and Sullivan Operas.   New York, Harcourt Brace, 1934.
Poetry: Its Appreciation and Enjoyment, with Carter Davidson.   New York, Harcourt Brace, 1934.
Songs to Sing to Children, with Clara Mannes.   New York, Harcourt Brace, 1935.

Heinrich Heine: Paradox and Poet. New York, Harcourt Brace, 1937; London, Cape, 1938.

Play in Poetry. New York, Harcourt Brace, 1938.

Doorways to Poetry. New York, Harcourt Brace, 1938.

From Another World: The Autobiography of Louis Untermeyer. New York, Harcourt Brace, 1939.

The Wonderful Adventures of Paul Bunyan: Now Retold. New York, Limited Editions Club, 1945.

French'Fairy Tales Retold. Paris, Didier, 1945.

All the French Fairy Tales. Paris, Didier, 1946.

More French Fairy Tales Retold. Paris, Didier, 1947.

A Century of Candymaking, 1847–1947. Privately printed, 1947.

Makers of the Modern World. New York, Simon and Schuster, 1955.

Lives of the Poets. New York, Simon and Schuster, 1959; London, W. H. Allen, 1960.

The Kitten Who Barked (juvenile). New York, Golden Press, 1962.

The Letters of Robert Frost to Louis Untermeyer. New York, Holt Rinehart, 1963.

Ezra Pound to Louis Untermeyer: Nine Letters Written to Louis Untermeyer by Ezra Pound, edited by J. A. Robins. Bloomington, Indiana University Press, 1963.

Robert Frost: A Backward Look. Washington, D.C., Library of Congress, 1964.

The Second Christmas. Kansas City, Missouri, Hallmark Editions, 1965.

Bygones: The Recollections of Louis Untermeyer. New York, Harcourt Brace, 1965.

The Paths of Poetry: 25 Poets and Their Poems. New York, Dial Press, 1966.

The Pursuit of Poetry: A Guide to Its Understanding and Appreciation. New York, Simon and Schuster, 1969.

Plants of the Bible (juvenile). New York, Golden Press, 1970.

Editor, *Modern American Poetry.* New York, Harcourt Brace, 1919; London, Cape, 1926; revised edition, Harcourt Brace, 1969.

Editor, *Modern British Poetry.* New York, Harcourt Brace, 1920; revised edition, 1969.

Editor, *Modern American and Modern British Poetry.* New York, Harcourt Brace, 1922; revised edition, 1969; revised shorter edition, with Richard Wilbur and Karl Shapiro, 1955.

Editor, *This Singing World: An Anthology of Modern Poetry for Young People.* New York, Harcourt Brace, 1923.

Editor, *Miscellany of American Poetry.* New York, Harcourt Brace, 1925.

Editor, *Walt Whitman.* New York, Simon and Schuster, 1926.

Editor, *This Singing World for Younger Children: Modern Poems.* New York, Harcourt Brace, 1926.

Editor, *Yesterday and Today: A Comparative Anthology of Poetry.* New York, Harcourt Brace, 1926.

Editor, *Emily Dickinson.* New York, Simon and Schuster, 1927.

Editor, *Conrad Aiken.* New York, Simon and Schuster, 1927.

Editor, *Yesterday and Today: A Collection of Verse (Mostly Modern) Designed for the Average Person of Nine to Nineteen and Possibly Older.* New York, Harcourt Brace, 1927.

Editor, with Clara and David Mannes, *New Songs for New Voices* (juvenile). New York, Harcourt Brace, 1928.

Editor, *American Poetry from the Beginning to Walt Whitman.* New York, Harcourt Brace, and London, Cape. 1932.

Editor, *The Book of Living Verse: English and American Poetry from the Thirteenth Century to the Present Day.* New York, Harcourt Brace, 1932; revised edition, 1939, 1945; as *The Albatross Book of Living Verse,* London, Collins, 1933; revised edition, 1960.

Editor, *The New Treasury of Verse.* London, Odhams Press, 1934.

Editor, *Rainbow in the Sky* (juvenile). New York, Harcourt Brace, 1935.

Editor, *Stars to Steer By* (juvenile). New York, Harcourt Brace, 1941.

Editor, *A Treasury of Great Poems, English and American.* New York, Simon and Schuster, 1942; revised edition, 1955.

Editor, *Complete Poems,* by Edgar Allan Poe. New York, Heritage Press, 1943.

Editor, *Poems,* by Henry Wadsworth Longfellow. New York, Heritage Press, 1943.

Editor, *Come In and Other Poems,* by Robert Frost. New York, Holt, 1943; enlarged edition, as *The Road Not Taken: An Introduction to Robert Frost,* 1951.

Editor, *The Pocket Book of Story Poems.* New York, Pocket Books, 1945; revised edition, as *Story Poems: An Anthology of Narrative Verse,* New York, Washington Square Press, 1957.

Editor, *Poems,* by John Greenleaf Whittier. New York, Heritage Press, 1945.

Editor, *Poems,* by Ralph Emerson. New York, Heritage Press, 1945.

Editor, *The Love Poems of Elizabeth Barrett Browning and Robert Browning.* New Brunswick, New Jersey, Rutgers University Press, 1946.

Editor, *The Book of Noble Thoughts.* New York, American Artists, 1946.

Editor, *A Treasury of Laughter.* New York, Simon and Schuster, 1946.

Editor, *The Rubaiyat,* by Omar Khayyam. New York, Random House, 1947.

Editor, with others, *The Pocket Treasury.* New York, Pocket Books, 1947.

Editor, *Poems,* by William Cullen Bryant. New York, Heritage Press, 1947.

Editor, *An Anthology of New England Poets from Colonial Times to the Present Day.* New York, Random House, 1948.

Editor, *The Pocket Book of American Poems.* New York, Pocket Books, 1948.

Editor, *The Love Poems of Robert Herrick and John Donne.* New Brunswick, New Jersey, Rutgers University Press, 1948.

Editor, *The Inner Sanctum Walt Whitman.* New York, Simon and Schuster, 1949.

Editor, with R. E. Shikes, *The Best Humor Annual: 1949–50* and *1951–52.* New York, Holt, 1951, 1952.

Editor, *Poems,* by Emily Dickinson. New York, Heritage Press, 1952.

Editor, *The Magic Circle: Stories and People in Poetry.* New York, Harcourt Brace, 1952.

Editor, *Early American Poets.* New York, Library Pubs, 1952.

Editor, *The Book of Wit and Humor.* Concord, New Hampshire, Mercury Books, 1953.

Editor, *A Treasury of Ribaldry.* New York, Doubleday, 1956; London, Elek, 1957.

Editor and Translator, *The Poems of Heinrich Heine.* New York, Heritage Press, 1957.

Editor, *The Golden Treasury of Poetry* (juvenile). New York, Golden Press, 1959; London, Collins, 1961.

Editor, *Britannica Book of Great American Writing.* Philadelphia, Lippincott, 2 vols, 1960.

Editor, *Lots of Limericks, Light, Lusty and Lasting.* New York, Doubleday, 1961; London, W. H. Allen, 1962; as *The Pan Book of Limericks,* London, Pan, 1963.

Editor, with Bryna Untermeyer, *Big and Little Creatures* (juvenile). New York, Golden Press, 1961.

Editor, with Bryna Untermeyer, *Old Friends and Lasting Favorites* (juvenile). New York, Golden Press, 1962.

Editor, with Bryna Untermeyer, *Fun and Fancy* (juvenile). New York, Golden Press, 1962.

Editor, with Bryna Untermeyer, *Wonder Tales* (juvenile). New York, Golden Press, 1962.

Editor, with Bryna Untermeyer, *Grimm's Fairy Tales* (juvenile). New York, Heritage Press, 1962.

Editor, with Bryna Untermeyer, *Creatures Wild and Tame* (juvenile). New York, Golden Press, 1963.

Editor, with Bryna Untermeyer, *Legendary Animals* (juvenile). New York, Golden Press, 1963.

Editor, with Bryna Untermeyer, *Creatures All* (juvenile). New York, Golden Press, 1963.

Editor, with Bryna Untermeyer, *Tall Tales* (juvenile). New York, Golden Press, 1963.

Editor, with Bryna Untermeyer, *Adventurers All* (juvenile). New York, Golden Press, 1963.

Editor, *An Uninhibited Treasury of Erotic Poetry.* New York, Dial Press, 1963.

Editor, *Love Sonnets.* Indianapolis, Odyssey Press, and London, Hamlyn, 1964.

Editor, *The World's Great Stories: Fifty-five Legends That Live Forever.* New York, M. Evans, 1964.

Editor, *Love Lyrics.* Indianapolis, Odyssey Press, and London, Hamlyn, 1965.

Editor, with Bryna Untermeyer, *The Golden Treasury of Children's Literature.* New York, Golden Press, 1966; as *The Children's Treasury of Literature in Colour,* London, Hamlyn, 1966.

Editor, *Merry Christmas: Legends and Traditions in Many Lands* (juvenile). New York, Golden Press, 1967.

Editor, *Songs of Joy from the Book of Psalms.* Cleveland, World, 1967.

Editor, *A Friend Indeed* (juvenile). New York, Golden Press, 1968.

Editor, *Lift Up Your Heart* (juvenile). New York, Golden Press, 1968.

Editor, *Your Lucky Stars* (juvenile). New York, Golden Press, 1968.

Editor, *Tales from the Ballet* (juvenile). New York, Golden Press, 1968.

Editor, with Bryna Untermeyer, *Adventure Stories* (juvenile). New York, Golden Press, 1968.

Editor, with Bryna Untermeyer, *Animal Stories* (juvenile). New York, Golden Press, 1968.

Editor, *Favorite Classics* (juvenile). New York, Golden Press, 1968.

Editor, *Tales and Legends* (juvenile). New York, Golden Press, 1968.

Editor, *The Firebringer and Other Great Stories: Fifty-five Legends that Live Forever.* New York, M. Evans, 1968.

Editor, *Words of Wisdom* (juvenile). New York, Golden Press, 1969.

Editor, *A Time for Peace: Verses from the Bible.* Cleveland, World, 1969.

Editor, *Men and Women: The Poetry of Love.* New York, Simon and Schuster, 1970.

Editor, *Roses: Selections.* New York, Golden Press, 1970.

Editor, *The Golden Book of Fun and Nonsense* (juvenile). New York, Golden Press, 1970.

Editor, *Treasury of Great Humor.* New York, McGraw Hill, 1972.

Editor, *50 Modern British and American Poets.* New York, McKay, 1973.

Editor, *Love Sonnets.* New York, Crown, 1974.

Translator, *Poems*, by Heinrich Heine. New York, Harcourt Brace, and London, Routledge, 1923.
Translator, *Fat of the Cat and Other Stories*, by Gottfried Keller. New York, Harcourt Brace, 1925.
Translator, *Heine: Poetry and Prose*. New York, Citadel Press, 1948.
Translator, *Cyrano de Bergerac*, by Edmond Rostand. New York, Heritage Press, 1954.

Bibliography: *Current Biography* (New York), January 1967.

Manuscript Collections: Lockwood Memorial Library, State University of New York, Buffalo; Library of Congress, Washington, D.C.

Louis Untermeyer comments:

I prefer to write of untraditional things in traditional forms. A critic in the *Boston Transport* wrote that "his is a social vision, his spirit a passionately energized command of the forces of justice." Edwin Muir wrote: "On every subject he treats, he gives opulent measure, an opulence within the reach of nobody in contemporary verse but himself." I have been called "a romantic ironist," but I prefer to think of myself as a somewhat ironic romanticist.

*   *   *

With an almost desperate optimism, Louis Untermeyer's personae move through the initiating lesson of the early *First Love* ("Love is not love that has not tasted sorrow") to the sentimental contentedness of the much later *For You with Love* ("Love is the memory time cannot kill"). Cities, with their "cheap music" and "evil alleys," and the "frantic drums" of war threaten the optimism throughout the volumes, but a "return to birds" whose "flight does not pollute the air," restores an energetic faith, a faith which admits both the curse of wisdom and its necessity in building "an earth made strong by disobedience." In his simple, traditional strophes, perhaps influenced by Heine, whose works he translated, Untermeyer is often artlessly familiar: Moses on Sinai, Eve in Eden, and God Himself in heaven speak with a common simplicity. Rhetoric, "man's noblest edifice," is less revered than the "mew and squawk" of nature's voice; the poet's art, neatly ridiculed in "The Purple Sonnet" ("What fulgid lure awoke the asphodels?") is "pale fireworks" mistaken for the "fierce and poignant flame" of life and love:

> His pain lives but in print; his tears are rolled
> And packed in small neat lyrics for the trade.

Ironically, the parodies, the most detached and intellectual of Untermeyer's works, are among the most successful, and admit a deep respect for poetry's art, disrespecting (fondly) only its excesses. Although the Mother Goose tales, retold by such poets as Yeats, Lindsay, and Masefield, offer good critical fun, the translations of Horace's ode "Integer Vitae" (Book I, 22) as might be done by Swinburne (who "alliteratively revolves all around it"), Poe (who "finds it full of lunar possibilities"), Sandburg (who "considers it on State Street, Chicago, Ill."), and

others display a dazzling virtuosity, parodying both the style and attitude characteristic of each poet. These lively early works pale later poems, and suggest the
potential, undeveloped in other works of his prolific and long career, of Untermeyer's nuance and wit.

– Carol A. Francis

UPDIKE, John (Hoyer). American. Born in Shillington, Pennsylvania, 18 March
1932. Educated in Shillington public schools; Harvard University, Cambridge,
Massachusetts, A.B. (summa cum laude) 1954; Ruskin School of Drawing and Fine
Arts, Oxford, 1954–55. Married Mary Pennington in 1953; has four children. Staff
Reporter, *The New Yorker*, 1955–57. Recipient: Guggenheim Fellowship, 1959;
Rosenthal Award, for fiction, 1960; National Book Award, for fiction, 1964; O.
Henry Award, for fiction, 1966. Member, National Institute of Arts and Letters.
Lives in Ipswich, Massachusetts.

PUBLICATIONS

Verse

> *The Carpentered Hen and Other Tame Creatures.* New York, Harper, 1958; as
> *Hoping for a Hoopoe*, London, Gollancz, 1959.
> *Telephone Poles.* New York, Knopf, and London, Deutsch, 1963.
> *Bath after Sailing.* West Haven, Connecticut, Pendulum Press, 1968.
> *Midpoint and Other Poems.* New York, Knopf, and London, Deutsch, 1969.
> *Seventy Poems.* London, Penguin, 1972.
> *Six Poems.* New York, Aloe Editions, 1973.
> *The Dance of the Solids.* New York, Scientific American, 1969.

Plays

> *Three Texts from Early Ipswich: A Pageant.* Ipswich, Massachusetts, 17th Cen-
> tury Day Committee, 1968.
> *Buchanan Dying.* New York, Knopf, and London, Deutsch, 1974.

Novels

> *The Poorhouse Fair.* New York, Knopf, and London, Gollancz, 1959.
> *Rabbit, Run.* New York, Knopf, 1960; London, Deutsch, 1961.
> *The Centaur.* New York, Knopf, and London, Deutsch, 1963.
> *Of the Farm.* New York, Knopf, 1965.
> *Couples.* New York, Knopf, and London, Deutsch, 1968.
> *Rabbit Redux.* New York, Knopf, 1971; London, Deutsch, 1972.
> *A Month of Sundays.* New York, Knopf, and London, Deutsch, 1975.

Short Stories

> *The Same Door.* New York, Knopf, 1959; London, Deutsch, 1962.
> *Pigeon Feathers and Other Stories.* New York, Knopf, and London, Deutsch, 1962.
> *Olinger Stories: A Selection.* New York, Knopf, 1964.
> *The Music School.* New York, Knopf, 1966.
> *Penguin Modern Stories 2*, with others. London, Penguin, 1969.
> *Bech: A Book.* New York, Knopf, and London, Deutsch, 1970.
> *Museums and Women and Other Stories.* New York, Knopf, 1972; London, Deutsch, 1973.
> *Warm Wine.* New York, Albondocani Press, 1973.

Other

> *The Magic Flute* (juvenile). New York, Knopf, 1962.
> *The Ring.* New York, Knopf, 1964.
> *Assorted Prose.* New York, Knopf, and London, Deutsch, 1965.
> *A Child's Calendar.* New York, Knopf, 1966.
> *Bottom's Dream: Adapted from William Shakespeare's "A Midsummer Night's Dream."* New York, Knopf, 1969.
> *A Good Place* (essay). New York, Aloe Editions, 1973.

> Editor, *Pens and Needles,* by David Levine. Boston, Gambit, 1970.

Bibliography: *John Updike: A Comprehensive Bibliography* by B. A. Sokoloff and Mark E. Posner, Norwood, Pennsylvania, Norwood Editions, 1973.

Critical Studies: interviews with the author in *Life* (New York), 4 November 1966, and in *Paris Review*, Winter 1968.

John Updike comments:

I began as a writer of light verse, and have tried to carry over into my serious or lyric verse something of the strictness and liveliness of the lesser form. My extensive prose writing has consumed much of the energy that might have gone into my development as a poet, though my long poem, "Midpoint," is an attempt to catch up.

*   *   *

The verse of John Updike is of little importance when set beside his own achievements in prose fiction. Specimens of it collected in *Hoping for a Hoopoe* and *Telephone Poles* do not require to be read, however, in that spirit of indulgence usually extended to novelists who have lost their way in poems. He is invariably neat, his wit is well-dressed, and he has a lively interest in form. The better of his verses look like superior exercises in the art of cheering oneself up by playing with words:

> Many-maned scud-thumper, tub
> of male whales, maker of worn wood, shrub-
> ruster, sky-mocker, rave!
> portly pusher of waves, wind-slave.

These four lines, which comprise a complete poem entitled "Winter Ocean," show the verse-making Updike's merits, and his strict limitations. Sophistication seizes upon a lyrical impulse and throttles it with style. It is as though G. M. Hopkins had settled for a job concocting elegant clues for crossword puzzles, or one of the Anglo-Saxon riddlers had been washed up on the staff of *The New Yorker*.

Updike is not always so slight – the title piece in the volume *Midpoint and Other Poems* shows him in a more serious or at any rate energetic mood.

– Robert Nye

URDANG, Constance (Henriette). American. Born in New York City, 26 December 1922. Educated at Fieldston School; Smith College, Northampton, Massachusetts, A.B. 1943; University of Iowa, Iowa City, M.F.A. 1956. Military Intelligence Analyst, United States Department of the Army, 1944–46. Married Donald Finkel, *q.v.*, in 1956; has two daughters and one son. Copy Editor, Bellas Hess Inc., publishers, New York, 1947–51; Editor, P. F. Collier and Son, publishers, New York, 1952–54. Recipient: *Carleton Centennial* Award, 1967. Lives in St. Louis, Missouri.

PUBLICATIONS

Verse

Charades and Celebrations: Poems.   New York, October House, 1965.
The Picnic in the Cemetery.   New York, Braziller, 1975.

Novel

Natural History.   New York, Harper, 1969.

Other

Editor, with Paul Engle, *Prize Stories '57.*   New York, Doubleday, 1957.
Editor, with Paul Engle and Curtis Harnack, *Prize Stories '59.*   New York, Doubleday, 1959.
Editor, *The Random House Vest Pocket Dictionary of Famous People.*   New York, Random House, 1962.

*   *   *

In *Charades and Celebrations*, Constance Urdang is preoccupied with three themes: the moon embodying the feminine principle; the equivocal nature of men labelled "heroes"; and experience viewed as a junkshop-collage of memories, relationships and reflections, a theme further developed in her unconventionally constructed novel-poem, *Natural History*.

Her "Moon Tree" poems are based on ancient associations of the moon with woman, evidently drawing on sources in Jung, in Harding's *Woman's Mysteries* and Briffault's *The Mothers*. Ishtar the moon-goddess as a fish, the moon as a cow, a panther, a she-bear, a hound, a hare – all symbolic phases of the female psyche are woven into assertions of the mystery, strength, beauty and cyclic nature of women's power:

> Moon-muse, mother, fountain that rises and falls
> Your daughters do not forget you.
> You make their weather. Their blood
> Ebbs and flows like the tide you make.

In the series of poems "The Idea of a Hero," Urdang is most at home with the bizarre history of the failed emperor of Mexico, Maximilian, who is seen through the eyes of people surrounding him. Epigraphs and the device of the persona enable her to present historical information as "eyewitness news" which passes naturally into commentary on the events, implicitly reflecting back on the publicity-created "heroes" of our own anti-heroic time:

> Being a hero
> Is a public job.

Urdang's third theme is loosely revealed in poems about her grandparents, children, a junkshop owner, and the "country of push-button patios." Her collage technique juxtaposes logically-unconnected scenes and events, mirroring the random flux of contemporary American life. Her novel-poem *Natural History* also follows this pattern:

> A long poem written not in, but by means of, prose. Its techniques that of
> the poem . . . Instead of using simple metaphors, use narrative sequences
> as metaphors. People, situations, as metaphors.

Following her own prescription, then, a St. Louis junkshop becomes a metaphor for brokenness and lives thrown away uselessly. The disheartening love affairs of her friends are metaphors for the general difficulty and superficiality of sexual and marital relationships. This collage method eliminates narrative padding and contributes to the continuing evolution of the novel form towards the terseness and density of poetry. Constance Urdang has produced a small but superior body of work. She belongs to a handful of women poets who have undertaken the major and long-neglected task of recording accurately the sensibilities of contemporary women.

– Jane Augustine

VALENTINE, Jean. American. Born in Chicago, Illinois, 27 April 1934. Educated at Milton Academy, 1949–52; Radcliffe College, Cambridge, Massachusetts, 1952–56, B.A. (cum laude) 1956. Married James Chace in 1957 (divorced, 1968); has two daughters. Poetry Workshop Teacher, Swarthmore College, Pennsylvania, 1968–70, Barnard College, New York, 1968, 1970, and Yale University, New Haven, Connecticut, 1970–74. Since 1970, Teacher of Remedial Composition and Writing Workshop, Hunter College, New York. Recipient: Yale Series of Younger Poets Award, 1965; National Endowment for the Arts grant, 1972. Address: 172 West 79th Street, New York, New York 10024, U.S.A.

PUBLICATIONS

Verse

Dream Barker and Other Poems. New Haven, Connecticut, Yale University Press, 1965.
Pilgrims. New York, Farrar Straus, 1969.
Ordinary Things. New York, Farrar Straus, 1974.

Manuscript Collection: Poetry Room, Lamont Library, Harvard University, Cambridge, Massachusetts.

*   *   *

In her first book, *Dream Barker,* Jean Valentine was obviously influenced by Robert Lowell. A touch of surrealism and a freshness of language hold in check any tendency to self-indulgence. Wit gives poignancy to evocations of Massachusetts ancestors:

> The New England landscape goes
> Like money: but here on Agassiz Walk we save
> Everything we have
> Under Great-Aunt Georgie's georgian bed . . .

The poems "Dream Barker," "First Love," and the elegant, punning verses "To My Soul" (after the Emperor Hadrian and Ronsard) stand out among others – wry, tender, disturbing. It is in her dramatic monologue, "The Little Flower," however, that Miss Valentine displays her most extraordinary talent, that of depicting character. A grandmother of eighty-three soliloquises to her granddaughter. Through the repetitiousness of a wandering, haunted memory the story emerges: the grandmother's husband had been an alcoholic; she blames herself as she excuses herself for having had him put away. The family, she feels, had turned against her:

> What could I do, it was such a shock, the money, and then
>   him never coming home and the drinking, I had the
>   children to think of, they never knew, Jack tried to
>   help him, first talking himself, then the doctors,
>   but nothing helped, he got worse, worse, he had had so
>   much, risen from nothing himself, and he became deluded
>   after the drop, losing more and more, he was on the
>   telephone talking business as if he were still what he
>   had been, then I had to call back, I was so ashamed,
>   and explain he wasn't well, everyone was very kind,
>   I couldn't go out of the house
> I had the children to think of
>   . . . They all blamed me . . .

In her second book, *Pilgrims*, Valentine has attempted to widen her area of concern to include more than her own experience of life and change in the 20th century. The poems are short and allusive. In "Torn Down Building," for instance, the images mean more than they seem to:

> Slowly, slowly our exploding time
> gives off its lives: a lens, an eyelash rub
> under the new ground broken
> under the new primary-color paint
> put up for someone to come to
> to start off from to cherish . . .

> – Anne Stevenson

VAN DUYN, Mona. American. Born in Waterloo, Iowa, 9 May 1921. Educated at the University of Northern Iowa, B.A. 1942; University of Iowa, Iowa City, M.A. 1943. Married Jarvis Thurston in 1943. Instructor in English, University of Iowa, 1944–46, and University of Louisville, Kentucky, 1946–50; Lecturer in English, Washington University, St. Louis, 1950–67; Lecturer, Salzburg Seminar in American Studies, 1973. Currently, Poetry Consultant, Olin Library Modern Literature Collection, Washington University. Since 1947, Editor, with Jarvis Thurston, *Perspective: A Quarterly of Literature*, St. Louis. Recipient: Eunice Tietjens Memorial Prize, 1956, and Harriet Monroe Memorial Prize, 1968 (*Poetry*, Chicago); Helen Bullis Prize (*Poetry Northwest*, Seattle), 1964; National Endowment for the Arts grant, 1966; Bollingen Prize, 1970; National Book Award, 1971; Guggenheim Fellowship, 1972. D.Litt.: Washington University, 1971; Cornell University, Ithaca, New York, 1972. Address: 7505 Teasdale Avenue, St. Louis, Missouri 63130, U.S.A.

PUBLICATIONS

Verse

Valentines to the Wide World: Poems. Iowa City, Cummington Press, 1959.
A Time of Bees. Chapel Hill, University of North Carolina Press, 1964.

To See, To Take: Poems. New York, Atheneum, 1970.
Bedtime Stories. Champaign, Illinois, Ceres Press, 1972.
Merciful Disguises: Poems Published and Unpublished. New York, Atheneum, 1973.

*   *   *

Mona Van Duyn's poems are homey and sophisticated, colloquial and formal, sincere and witty, charming and tough – all at the same time. Each of these characteristics provides joys for the reader. "Advice to a God," for instance, is based on the Greek legend of Zeus and Danae; "Death by Aesthetics" and "Paratrooper" recall Yeats' "Leda and the Swan" and Randall Jarrell's "Death of the Ball-Turret Gunner," respectively, employing similar imagery but with a momentum that expands the theme. Though a seemingly casual off-rhyme is used in most of the poems, the actual rhyme schemes are definite and often complex: abaaa, abaaa, baaaa ("A Kind of Music"); stanzas of aabbab ("The Gardener to His God"), abababa ("Open Letter, Personal"), and aaabbb ("Placet Experiri"); or even a sestina ("Sestina for Warm Seasons"). This kind of craft is pleasing; so too is the occasional use of a "strong line": "Curators mourn the perfect idea, for it crippled / outside of its case" ("Toward a Definition of Marriage"); or, "he breaks through the membrane of history and sees the trees" ("Paratrooper"); or, about dehydrated onions, "inoffensive to my notions of what an onion or a tear humanly means" ("An Essay on Criticism").

These are joys. But the prime joy of reading these poems lies in the mixture of the casual and the precise. The subtlety of the "attack" on the objects of the poems belies simplicity, and often the reader gasps in surprise at what the poem is doing. Here the basis of many of these poems is a complex image or analogy, often beautiful, sometimes ugly, reflecting the complexities of life which, once perceived, are obvious and unforgettable. So, "A Time of Bees," about a domestic problem of a beehive in a wall, is also about love and mystery. The bees are rooted out –

> such a mess of interrupted life dumped on newspapers
> – dirty clots of grubs, sawdust, stuck fliers, all smeared
> together with old honey

– dumped in the garbage can, and then later examined –

> the craze
> for life gets stronger in the squirming, whitish kind . . . .
> I feel it start, a terrible, lifelong heave
> taking direction. Unpleading, the men prod
> till all that grubby softness wants to give, *to give.*

And a section of a poem about truck-drivers' views of life from the highway:

> a statement so abstract
> that it's tiresome. Nothing in particular holds still in it

– is also about poetry –

> a discreetness of consumption
> . . . Its view is simultaneous
> discovery and reminiscence.

> – "Three Valentines to the Wide World

And in a poem addressed to her friends ("Open Letter, Personal"), we find the need to accept those things that bind us to each other:

> We know the quickest way to hurt each other, and we have
> used that knowledge. See, it is here, in the joined strands
> of our weaknesses, that we are netted together and heave
> together strongly like the great catch of mackerel that ends
> an Italian movie. I feel your bodies smell and shove
> and shine against me in the mess of the pitching boat. My friends,
> we do not like each other any more. We love.

– James Vinson

VARMA, Monika. Indian. Born in Allahabad, Uttar Pradish, 5 August 1916. Educated privately. Married Brigadier K. K. Varma in 1938; has two sons. Delegate, All India Poets Meet, June 1973. Recipient: *Caravan* magazine prize, 1956, 1958; *The Illustrated Weekly of India* prize, for short story, 1970; World Poetry Society Intercontinental Citation Honour Card, 1971. Address: Sokra Nala Farm, P.O. Krishak Nagar, Raipur, Madhya Pradish, India.

PUBLICATIONS

Verse

Dragonflies Draw Flame.   Calcutta, Writers Workshop, 1962.
Gita Govinda and Other Poems.   Calcutta, Writers Workshop, 1966.
Green Leaves and Gold.   Calcutta, Writers Workshop, 1970.
Quartered Questions and Queries.   Calcutta, Writers Workshop, 1971.
Past Imperative.   Calcutta, Writers Workshop, 1972.
Alakananda.   Calcutta, Writers Workshop, 1973.

Other

Translator, *A Bunch of Poems*, by Rabindranath Tagore.   Calcutta, Writers Workshop, 1966.

Transcreator, *The Gita Govinda of Jayadeva.*   Calcutta, Writers Workshop, 1968.
Transcreator, *Pather Panchali*, by Bibhuti Bhusan Banerjee.   Calcutta, Writers Workshop, 3 vols., 1973.

Manuscript Collection: Bangalore University Library, Mysore.

Critical Studies: "Some Poets of the Writers Workshop" by Amalendu Bose, in *Critical Essays on Indian Writings in English*, Dharwar, Karnatak University, 1968; "An Exchange Between Monika Varma and Amalendu Bose," in *Miscellany 30* (Calcutta), December 1968; S. C. Saha, in *Thought* (Delhi), June 1969; "Women Poets from Writers Workshop," in *Deccan Herald Magazine*, May 1972.

Monika Varma comments:

The two important points to remember in any understanding of my poetical works are that the metaphors are totally Indian, and the idioms are based on classical Indian philosophy.

Nobody writing English can be said to be devoid of influences of past poets. And Dylan Thomas is the Poet of all poets. But in my case, I think, I can say that a kind of transmutation has taken place in the crucible of Indian thinking.

The stress on "Indian" is obvious on reading all the references to birds, flowers, beasts, in the Nature poems. If the Lake Poets were influenced by their environment, my environment has also had a profound effect on me.

Besides being an Indian, I am a Bengali. The Bengali race is always sensitive to its surroundings. This fact shows up in all Bengali poetic writing and can be seen from my translations of the Tagore poems and finally, in the perfect prose statement of Bibhuti Bhusan Banerjee's *Pather Panchali*. The Bengali poets who have had a profound influence on me are Jibanananda Das and Ajit Dutta. Unfortunately the latter's works have never been translated and there isn't a really good translation of all Jibanananda Das's works.

My philosophical outlook and poetic statements are based on Indian philosophy but if any Western influence has to be sought it is Gerard Manley Hopkins. Though today my philosophical thinking is totally Indian, I have been greatly influenced by the New Testament and the Christ's Life as such, His parables, words, and the words of early Christian mystic saints.

Dr. S. Radhakrishnan's works, his comparative notes on the Western, Indian, and Islamic Sufi saints would also cover the metaphysical aspect of my poetry.

In fact, to understand and appreciate my works, the importance of the metaphysical aspect must be taken into consideration the whole time. Without this realization the subtleties are lost. The simplest statements have a depth of meaning.

It has not been a conscious effort, and it is only on analysis that I find that the metaphysical idiom is the most vital aspect in content. Even in style this is important.

I have, over and over again, in my poems talked about "Words." This love of words is a love of rhythm and music. At one time I was a dedicated student of Western classical music and it was the pure music of Bach that always appealed most to me. Therefore the rules of music, the idioms and phrases of the theory of music have walked into my verse.

The rhythm of words was originally learnt by a love of Swinburne's use of words and their toccata rhythm.

And, finally, a deep religious love for my land permeates my poetry.

*   *   *

There must be something in the exclusive use of the English language in the context of present-day India that eventually gives a number of poets a vague sense of limitation. There is no other explanation why so many of the more significant poets who started off by writing only in English have later taken up translation from an Indian language into English as a simultaneous activity. Outstanding examples are A. K. Ramanujam, P. Lal, Mokashi-Punekar, Gauri Deshpande, Suniti Namjoshi, and Paul Jacob.

Monika Varma is another such poet who finds a creative challenge in translation. She has five volumes of original poems (two more are about to be published), and her shorter lyrics have a remarkable capacity of vividly crystallizing a fleeting image or a passing thought, but to me her most impressive and sustained achievement so far is her English rendering of the work of a 12th century Sanskrit poet, Jayadeva. Jayadeva's *Gita Govinda* is on the surface a long love poem full of beautiful erotic images, but it has a symbolic and mystic undertone that gives the poem a universal significance. Monika Varma successfully conveys the mythic structure and the sensuous texture in contemporary English without doing violence to the spirit of the original. There is a sense of total devotion and enjoyment in this translation that recreates the *bhakti* quality of mediaval *vaishnavic* literature.

Monika Varma's own imaginative world is vivid with birds and trees and glow-worms that are not just objects in nature, but personally felt experiences. Grass is not just green but:

> Grass is in my mouth, my throat,
> grass is on my tongue, my taste,
> grass is my love, my touch.
> The scent of grass: green,.
> it is my life, my breath.

Here is a mature sensibility, sensitive to touch, to colour, to the seasons, and to the magic of the sound of words. On the whole her work has width of vision and a rootedness quite different in flavour form the academic sophistication of the "alienated" urban poets.

– Meenakshi Mukherjee

VAS DIAS, Robert. American. Born in London, England, 19 January 1931. Educated at Grinnell College, Iowa, B.A. 1953; Columbia University, New York, 1959–61. Served in the United States Army, 1953–55. Married Susan McClintock in 1961; has one son. Assistant Editor, Prentice Hall, publishers, New York, 1955–56; Staff Editor, Allyn and Bacon, publishers, Boston, 1956–57; Free-lance Editor, 1957–65; Instructor in English, Long Island University, Brooklyn, New York, 1964–66; Instructor, American Language Institute, New York University, 1966–71; Tutor and Poet-in-Residence, Thomas Jefferson College, Grand Valley State College, Allendale, Michigan, 1971–74. Director, Aspen Writers Workshop, Colorado, 1964–67, and National Poetry Festival, Thomas Jefferson College, 1971, 1973. Contributing Editor, *Mulch*, Amherst, Massachusetts, 1973–74. Address: 25 Cholmeley Park, London N.6, England.

PUBLICATIONS

Verse

Ribbed Vision: A Poem.   New York, privately printed, 1963.
The Counted.   New York, Caterpillar, 1967.
The Life of Parts; or, Thanking You for the Book on Building Birdfeeders.   Mount
   Horeb, Wisconsin, Perishable Press, 1972.
Speech Acts and Happenings.   Indianapolis, Bobbs Merrill, 1972.

Other

Editor, *Inside Outer Space: New Poems of the Space Age.*   New York, Doubleday, 1970.

Manuscript Collection: University of Virginia, Charlottesville.

Critical Study: by Linda W. Wagner, in *Red Cedar Review* (East Lansing, Michigan), 1973.

*   *   *

Blurbs on "slim" volumes of poetry usually announce that yet another "new
voice" has been found. From the contending multitude of small magazines, they
tell us, one more guardian of the great glottic heritage has emerged to celebrate
Language and Poetry. So Robert Vas Dias tells us in "Dump Poem" (*Speech Acts
and Happenings*) that this poem, *qua* poem, "is a genuine used poem / last-year's
model poem / shirt off someone's back poem / chair minus a leg poem / scrap husk
and rind poem / steakbone poem." It is a good poem because if you set fire to it
"you can hear its juices / sizzling and its light bulbs popping." But how do we test
the claim that the poem is palpable, therefore "genuine" and good? Poems like this
(for example, "Saturday Poem," "which is an idea I can taste") are mere reminders of the ingredients of a poem; like a successful dish, the real proof is not in the
recipe but in the product. In his brief foreword to the collection, Paul Blackburn
tells us that "This is a step for words. It surely is." Is it? Poems like "this" are
voyeuristic and self-contained, and agitatedly remind us, despite their slangy
"honesty," of the academic bromide: all art is ultimately about art.
    Vas Dias is best when managing small situations. His strength is in creating
unexpected visual and psychological complexities inherent in slight circumstances,
as in "Subway Sijo":

> In the rush hour she holds
>   several blue peacock feathers:
> I am trying to catch her eye
>   enticed by competitors.
> Soon I shall dance and fan
>   my many amazing eyes.

Yet, despite the several finely realized poems in *Speech Acts*, too many others are
crippled by manneristic tics which by now are not so much marks of individual
style as of generic idiosyncrasies: half-parentheses, caesura slashes, & for "and,"

cute punctuation ("deliberately . not . falling"). So, even when a poem is not directly about poetry, it struggles nervously toward a forced, minor epiphany by reliance on a tired inventory of typographical "techniques." We are never allowed to forget that the poet is practising his craft.

– Peter Desy

———————

VIERECK, Peter (Robert Edwin).   American.   Born in New York City, 5 August 1916. Educated at Horace Mann School for Boys, New York; Harvard University, Cambridge, Massachusetts, B.S. (summa cum Laude) 1937 (Phi Beta Kappa), M.A. 1939, Ph.D. 1942; Christ Church, Oxford, 1937–38. Served in the United States Army, 1943–45, and Instructor in History, United States Army University, Florence, Italy, 1945. Married Anya de Markov in 1945 (divorced, 1970), has two children; Betty Martin Falkenberg, 1972. Teaching Assistant, 1941–42, Instructor in German, and Tutor in History and Literature, 1946–47, Harvard University; Assistant Professor of History, 1947–48, and Visiting Professor of Russian History, 1948–49, Smith College, Northampton, Massachusetts. Associate Professor, 1948–55, Professor of History, 1955–65, and since 1965, holds Alumnae Foundation Chair of Interpretive Studies, Mount Holyoke College, South Hadley, Massachusetts. Visiting Lecturer in American Culture, Oxford University, 1953; Whittal Lecturer in Poetry, Library of Congress, Washington, D.C., 1954, 1963; Fulbright Lecturer, University of Florence, 1955; Elliston Lecturer, University of Cincinnati, Ohio, 1956; Visiting Professor, University of California, Berkeley, 1957, 1964, and City College of New York, 1964; State Department Cultural Exchange Lecturer in the U.S.S.R., 1961. Poetry Workshop Director, New York Writers Conference, 1965–67. Recipient: Eunice Tietjens Prize (*Poetry*, Chicago), 1948; Guggenheim Fellowship, 1948; Pulitzer Prize, 1949; Rockefeller grant, 1958; Horace Mann School Award, 1958; Twentieth Century Fund Scholarship, 1962. L.H.D.: Olivet College, Michigan, 1959. Address: 12 Silver Street, South Hadley, Massachusetts 01075, U.S.A.

PUBLICATIONS

Verse

> *Terror and Decorum: Poems 1940–1948.*   New York, Scribner, 1948.
> *Strike Through the Mask! New Lyrical Poems.*   New York, Scribner, 1950.
> *The First Morning: Lyrical Poems.*   New York, Scribner, 1952.
> *The Persimmon Tree: New Pastoral and Lyric Poems.*   New York, Scribner, 1956.
> *New and Selected Poems: 1932–1967.*   Indianapolis, Bobbs Merrill, 1967.

Play

> *The Tree Witch* (produced Boston, 1961). Published as *The Tree Witch: A Poem and a Play (First of All a Poem)*, New York, Scribner, 1961.

Other

> *Metapolitics: From the Romantics to Hitler.* New York, Knopf, 1941; revised
> edition, as *Metapolitics: The Roots of the Nazi Mind,* New York, Putnam,
> 1961.
> *Conservatism Revisited: The Revolt Against Revolt, 1815–1949.* New York,
> Scribner, 1949; London, Lehmann, 1950.
> *Shame and Glory of the Intellectuals: Babbitt Jr. vs. the Rediscovery of
> Values.* Boston, Beacon Press, 1953; revised edition, New York, Putnam,
> 1965.
> *Dream and Responsibility: Four Test Cases of the Tension Between Poetry and
> Society.* Washington, D.C., University Press of Washington, 1953.
> *The Unadjusted Man: A New Hero for Americans: Reflections on the Distinction
> Between Conforming and Conserving.* Boston, Beacon Press, 1956; revised
> edition, New York, Putnam, 1962.
> *Conservatism: From John Adams to Churchill.* Princeton, New Jersey, Von
> Nostrand, 1956.
> *Inner Liberty: The Stubborn Grit in the Machine* (lecture). Wallingford, Pennsyl-
> vania, Pendle Hill Pamphlets, 1957.
> *Conservatism Revisited, and the New Conservatism: What Went Wrong?* New
> York, Macmillan, 1962.

Critical Study: *Peter Viereck: Poet and Historian,* by Marie Henault, New York,
Twayne, 1969.

*   *   *

A nervous daring informs the characteristic verse of Peter Viereck. Occasionally,
the cleverness overreaches itself, when strained sound effects trivialize the image
of Nazi evil "Hiking in shorts through tyranny's Tyrols" ("Crass Times Redeemed
by Dignity of Souls"). But Viereck's gambles generally win; his sound patterns can
create the illusion of a new etymology: ". . . Aeneas on the boat from Troy /
Before harps cooled the arson into art" ("Lot's Wife"). This bravado works best
in his epic treatment of "Kilroy," and in "To a Sinister Potato," where echoes of
"Ode on a Grecian Urn" heighten the bizarre grandeur of the parody: "O vast
earth-apple, waiting to be fried, / Of all life's starers the most many-eyed, / What
furtive purpose hatched you long ago / In Indiana or in Idaho?" The zest animating
these poems from *Terror and Decorum* not only suits his frequent comic rhymes, or
his bastardized Spenserian language in "Ballad of the Jollie Gleeman," but also
supports the tender, frightening "Six Theological Cradle Songs," which use nursery
jingles and childhood games to dramatize the terror implicit in mortality. Sometimes, Viereck concentrates his frenzy to achieve the gnomic wit of the elegy for
Hart Crane, whose exotic polysyllables he elsewhere imitates: ". . . and he found /
New York was the clerks his daddy hired / Plus gin plus sea; then Hart felt tired, /
Drank both and drowned" ("Look, Hart, That Horse You Ride Is Wood").

Though the later volumes provide less outrageous fun than the first, they offer
greater control of ambitious themes. The straightforward comic verse falters, as in
"Full Cycle," a series of parodies of new critics and modern poets, including

Viereck himself. But Viereck develops an impressive group of poems with extraordinary personae; "To My Isis" wittily yet accurately summarizes Viereck's range from "Whatever shimmers . . . birch or trout" to ". . . Mud I also mimic: Let salivating wart-hogs gambol by, / Preening their bristles. All gross masks I'll try / But hairy spiders. These I still can't stomach." His most striking impersonations are of trees; an oak threatens a willow: "Your chance of passing next week's Woodlore Test / Is – bear it oakly – not the best. / You know the price! The beaver foreman claims / He needs just one more trunk to mend his dams" ("The Slacker Need Not Apologize"). Then an ironic "stage-direction" states: "beavers in overalls drag away storm-felled oak" (Viereck's frequent sub-title notes and epigraphs suggest a nervous, though charming editor, eager to help, but unwilling to compromise the integrity of his text). The willow survives: "Mere echo (-strummer?), mad (- or wild with truth?), / By contours of the winds lured far too far, / I'm left behind when even God flies south / (If 'God' means all the climate I ignore)." The dashes, questions, and parentheses heighten the struggling uncertainty already outlined by the dialectic format of the poem. Here, or in a Goethe/Crane debate in "Decorum and Terror," Viereck dramatizes viewpoints limited and belligerent that fuse for the reader into a compassionate accepting overview. Viereck's show-off rhymes: "Courtier's prance / Otto Kahn's," and play on "k" sounds ("barrack / Weimaric / Pyrrhic / wreck" are the rhymes in one quatrain) make both speakers less than Olympian and prepare for the triumphant final rhyme of "Viereck," which asserts the poet's fusion of decorous form and Romantic terror that are the antagonists of the poem.

Viereck's tree poems, while obviously allegories of particular human attitudes, are equally exciting as delicate versions of non-human psyche. After reading "The Slacker Apologizes," it is impossible to deny that a "crass young weed" would boast:

> Last night my stamen
> Could hear her pistil sigh . . .
> . . .
> My pollen's shy
> Deep nuzzling tells her: weeds must love or die.

Despite his skill in these poems and his flair for dialogue, both elegant and colloquial, Viereck disappoints with *The Tree Witch*, a morality play in verse which places man between the force of nature symbolized by a dryad and the force of technology and conformity symbolized by the Furies (disguised as maiden aunts). Viereck's fondness for dialectic and his familiar satiric targets produce episodes more repetitious than cumulative in their dramatic force, though there are some lovely lyrics, some amusing moments and, occasionally, an explosion of pithy magic: "Lively is not alive; a funeral pyre / Is snugger than a hearth a little while."

Viereck's exaltation of unromanticized nature is a constant in his work, finding strongest expression in "The Autumn Instant: Sky and Earth," which dramatizes the loving destructiveness of the cycle: "I am your sky; look up; my clouds are altars / To worship you with desecrating rain." Because of this frightening context in which nature and man exist, many Viereck poems praise the precarious splendor of the moment, often the moment of August ripeness, with Keatsian intensity, and "Sing the bewildered honor of the flesh" ("Some Lines in Three Parts"). Though his recent work has received insufficient acclaim, *New and Selected Poems* develops this obsessive theme with seemingly artless intensity – the fine sequence "Five Walks on the Edge" makes the Massachusetts coast an inevitable and powerful emblem fusing man's psychological, metaphysical and aesthetic limits; Viereck's characteristic formal control gives resonance and assurance to nervous uncertainties:

World, world, what wreath from soil so thin?
The roots replenish till the time
They don't replenish. Many times
The warmth is gaining. All the time
The loss is gaining anyhow.

– Burton Kendle

VILLA, José Garcia. Filipino. Born in Manila, 5 August 1908. Educated at the University of New Mexico, Albuquerque, B.A. 1933; Columbia University, New York. Has two sons. Has taught at the University of the Philippines, Quezon City, and Far Eastern University, Manila. Associate Editor, New Directions, publishers, New York, 1949–51; Poetry Workshop Director, City College of New York, 1952–63. Since 1964, Professor of Poetry, New School for Social Research, New York. Since 1968, Presidential Adviser on Cultural Affairs, Philippine Government. Recipient: National Institute of Arts and Letters grant, 1943; Guggenheim Fellowship, 1943; Bollingen Fellowship, 1951; Shelley Memorial Award, 1959; Philippines Cultural Heritage Award, 1962; Rockefeller Fellowship, 1963. D.Litt.: Far Eastern University, Manila, 1959; D.H.L.: University of the Philippines, 1973. Address: 780 Greenwich Street, New York, New York 10014, U.S.A.

PUBLICATIONS

Verse

Many Voices. Manila, Philippine Writers' League, 1939.
Poems by Doveglion. Manila, Philippine Writers' League, 1941.
Have Come, Am Here. New York, Viking Press, 1942.
Volume Two. New York, New Directions, 1949.
Selected Poems and New. New York, McDowell Obolensky, 1958.
Poems in Praise of Love. Manila, A. S. Florentino, 1962.
Poems 55: The Best Poems of José Garcia Villa as Chosen by Himself. Manila, A. S. Florentino, 1962.

Short Stories

Footnote to Youth: Tales of the Philippines and Others. New York, Scribner, 1933.
Selected Stories. Manila, A. S. Florentino, 1962.

Other

The Portable Villa. Manila, A. S. Florentino, 1962.
The Essential Villa. Manila, A. S. Florentino, 1965.

Editor, *Philippine Short Stories.* Manila, Philippines Free Press, 1929.
Editor, "E. E. Cummings Issue" of *Harvard Wake* (Cambridge, Massachusetts), 1945.

Editor, "Marianne Moore Issue" of *Quarterly Review* (New Haven, Connecticut), 1947.

Editor, *A Celebration for Edith Sitwell.* New York, New Directions, 1948.

Editor, *A Doveglion Book of Philippine Poetry.* Manila, Katha Editions, 1962.

*   *   *

José Garcia Villa is as yet the most distinguished contribution of the Philippines to world poetry in English, although a few younger poets are beginning to be recognized beyond Philippine frontiers. (Two minor poets – Carlos Bulosan and M. de Gracia Concepcion – who also had been published in America, are now dead.) A volume of his best poems as chosen by himself, *Poems 55,* is a little too thin and could be expanded to include 100 poems and still remain a distinguished volume of verse.

Villa started as a writer of short stories, then shifted to poetry and art, and for the last decade and a half he has been at work on a theory or philosophy of poetry, which he expects to publish in a multi-volume edition in the near future.

Now in his sixtieth year, he is still known in his country as an eccentric nonconformist. Early in college he was dismissed from the University of the Philippines for authoring a poem that was deemed obscene by college authorities. Thirty years later he received from his school an appointment as professorial lecturer in literature.

Villa's main achievement in poetry has been in experimentation; he has produced a number of poems considered original by critics native to the English language. Not having been born to English, he nevertheless has assiduously studied the language and has acquired a peculiar knowledge of it. This has enabled him to express himself in English with a high degree of originality which sometimes contains flashes of revelation. Some of his poems have been described as among the finest in the English language.

Mr. Villa has been concerned mainly with the individual human being, largely in his erotic and spiritual relations. He has been largely unconcerned, even in his prose fiction, with man as a social being, as a member of a larger community, with problems more complex and more difficult of solution. The possibility, therefore, is that the novelty of much of his poetry will wear off and his significance as a poet may decline. In fact, in the Philippines, although he is widely respected for the reputation which he has acquired among a number of foreign critics, Mr. Villa is not seriously regarded as a poet of significant achievement by the more thoughtful students of humane letters.

– Leopoldo Y. Yabes

VLIET, R(ussell) G. American. Born in Chicago, Illinois, in 1929. Educated at Southwest Texas State College, later, Southwest Texas State University, San Marcos, B.A. and M.A. 1952; Yale University, New Haven, Connecticut, 1955–56. Married Ann Rutherford in 1951; has one child. Recipient: Rockefeller grant, 1967. Agent: Lucy Kroll Agency, 119 West 57th Street, New York, New York 10019. Address: Route 1, Stanford, Vermont 01247, U.S.A.

PUBLICATIONS

Verse

Events and Celebrations. New York, Viking Press, 1966; London, Bodley
    Head, 1967.
The Man with the Black Mouth. Santa Cruz, California, Kayak Books, 1970.

Novel

Rockspring. New York, Viking Press, 1974.

                              *   *   *

The strongest of the pieces in R. G. Vliet's *Events and Celebrations* reveal an easy
command of a number of varying poetic modes. The two prose poems, "The
Journey" and the Kafka-like "The Ants," are not completely convincing (though
Vliet has a true narrative skill, as his later novella *Rockspring* demonstrates); but the
lyric sequence, "Clem Maverick," is immediately engaging. The twenty sections,
differing in style and point of view, sketch the career of a late, charismatic Country
Music star, the exploited and self-destructive victim of his own talent. The dark
side of Clem Maverick is barely suggested, however; Vliet is content here to
concentrate on the humor and pathos of the people who knew and loved and used
Maverick during his short life. The overall effect is a little indeterminate perhaps
but the virtuoso display of shifting dramatic voices is impressive.
  The most successful pieces in *Events and Celebrations* are the dramatic monologues (particularly "Robert it is eight months to the day") and the purely lyrical
poems which make up the first section of the book. The "events" which Vliet
celebrates are slight – a group of girls riding their horses down an icy street, a
group of boys fiercely at play – and sometimes not events at all, but merely bits of
nature carefully observed and lovingly described. "Love" is in fact the keynote of
the entire collection:

            Love's own form
                        is sufficient unto
            itself: never ask how or why:
            purpose puffs a grape, is its purple hue,
            packs apples; winged maples fly;
            horses dogs deer run wordlessly
            perfectly; the hand in love
            moves through its own country:
            love has no use for less than love:
            love made these poems. I don't know why.

These lines are slightly disingenuous, however, or at least a modest understatement
of Vliet's solid gifts. The closing invocation is in effect a prayer which answers its
own petition:

> I beg You mercy, mercy,
> You of the long black hair and the winter
> skin. I have served Thee. This
> I wear under my jacket now is no
> hunchback's hump, but a blotch of shriveled
> wings. Come down from the forthright
> northern country. Teach me the true,
> the harsh necessity. Strip me of error.
> Widen my eyes. Split my back open
> like a late dragonfly in summer thunder
> uncrinkling on the marshgrass of everyday
> surprise. I labor now, here.

– Elmer Borklund

WADDINGTON, Miriam. Canadian. Born in Winnipeg, Manitoba, 23 December 1917. Educated at Lisgar Collegiate Institute, Ottawa; University of Toronto, B.A. 1939, Diploma in Social Work, 1942, M.A. 1968; University of Pennsylvania, Philadelphia, M.S.W. 1945. Has two sons. Caseworker, Jewish Family Service, Toronto, 1942–44, 1957–60, and Philadelphia Child Guidance Clinic, 1944–45; Assistant Director, Jewish Child Service, Montreal, 1945–46; Lecturer and Supervisor, McGill School of Social Work, Montreal, 1946–49; Caseworker, Montreal Children's Hospital Speech Clinic, 1950–52, and John Howard Society, 1955–57; Supervisor, North York Family Service, 1960–62. Since 1964, Member of the English Department, and currently Associate Professor of Literature, York University, Toronto. Recipient: Canada Council Senior Fellowship, 1962, Academic Leave Fellowship, 1968. Address: 32 Yewfield Crescent, Don Mills, Ontario, Canada.

PUBLICATIONS

Verse

Green World. Montreal, First Statement Press, 1945.
The Second Silence. Toronto, Ryerson Press, 1955.
The Season's Lovers. Toronto, Ryerson Press, 1958.
The Glass Trumpet. Toronto, Oxford University Press, 1966.
Call Them Canadians. Ottawa, Queen's Printers and National Film Board, 1968.
Say Yes. Toronto, Oxford University Press, 1969.
Dream Telescope. London, Anvil Press Poetry, 1972.
Driving Home: Poems New and Selected. Toronto, Oxford University Press, 1972; London, Anvil Press Poetry, 1973.

Plays

Television Documentaries: *Chekov,* 1958; *Poe,* 1962.

Other

A. M. Klein.   Toronto, Copp Clark, 1970.

Editor, *The Collected Poems of A. M. Klein.*   New York, McGraw Hill, 1974.

Short stories, translations, and art criticism published in periodicals.

*   *   *

"Your poems fuse the flesh and the dream," wrote Anaïs Nin of the poetry of Miriam Waddington, who must be one of the finest lyric poets of the day. Of her books to date, the first three are full of images of changing seasons, green worlds, alfresco silences, lovers meeting and parting, flowers galore; the later ones branch out more from her native Manitoba to Canada as a country, and beyond, with evocative trips to Russia, Poland, Israel, and Germany. Common to both phases of her work are characteristic assertions of human worth and warmth, gentle imperatives, and a self-deprecating wit. Her imagery is intelligent without being intellectual, yet apt and derived from personal observation, as when she describes children playing hockey as being "stiff as flowers."

When *Driving Home: Poems New and Selected* appeared in 1972, it became apparent that hers was an essentially lyrical gift, for she sings of what is and finds in the world of desire the point of meeting of what was and what could have been. Hers is a poetry of acceptance rather than of search, for the important thing is to realize the values we have rather than those that we had or hope to have. While other poets were bemoaning the lack of a useable past or vainly engineering the future, she wrote in "Canadians":

> We look
> like a geography but
> just scratch us
> and we bleed
> history.

In other poems she describes bittersweet experiences with the directness of a folk tale and an awareness of modern psychology, for "in my mind / summer never ended." Her playfulness and relationship to the writers of Europe can be seen in the last lines of a characteristic poem, "Sad Winter":

> Dear Nelly Sachs,
> dear Nathalie Sarraute,
> isn't there anything
> you can teach me
> about how to write
> better in Canada?

– John Robert Colombo

WAGONER, David (Russell). American. Born in Massillon, Ohio, 5 June 1926. Educated at Pennsylvania State University, University Park, B.A. 1947; Indiana University, Bloomington, M.A. 1949. Served in the United States Navy, 1944–46. Married Patricia Parrott in 1961. Instructor, De Pauw University, Greencastle, Indiana, 1949–50, and Pennsylvania State University, 1950–54. Associate Professor, 1954–66, and since 1966, Professor of English, University of Washington, Seattle. Since 1966, Editor, *Poetry Northwest*, Seattle. Elliston Lecturer, University of Cincinnati, 1968. Recipient: Guggenheim Fellowship, 1956; Ford Fellowship, for drama, 1964; National Institute of Arts and Letters grant, 1967; Morton Dauwen Zabel Prize (*Poetry*, Chicago), 1967; National Endowment for the Arts grant, 1969. Address: 1075 Summit Avenue East, Seattle, Washington 98102, U.S.A.

PUBLICATIONS

Verse

Dry Sun, Dry Wind. Bloomington, Indiana University Press, 1953.
A Place to Stand. Bloomington, Indiana University Press, 1958.
The Nesting Ground. Bloomington, Indiana University Press, 1963.
Five Poets of the Pacific Northwest, with others, edited by Robin Skelton. Seattle, University of Washington Press, 1964.
Staying Alive. Bloomington, Indiana University Press, 1966.
New and Selected Poems. Bloomington, Indiana University Press, 1969.
Working Against Time. London, Rapp and Whiting, 1970.
Riverbed. Bloomington, Indiana University Press, 1972.
Sleeping in the Woods. Bloomington, Indiana University Press, 1974.

Play

An Eye for an Eye for an Eye (produced Seattle, 1973).

Novels

The Man in the Middle. New York, Harcourt Brace, 1954; London, Gollancz, 1955.
Money, Money, Money. New York, Harcourt Brace, 1955.
Rock. New York, Viking Press, 1958.
The Escape Artist. New York, Farrar Straus, and London, Gollancz, 1965.
Baby, Come On Inside. New York, Farrar Straus, 1968.
Where Is My Wandering Boy Tonight? New York, Farrar Straus, 1970.
The Road to Many a Wonder. New York, Farrar Straus, 1974.

Other

Editor, *Straw for the Fire: From the Notebooks of Theodore Roethke, 1943–1963.* New York, Doubleday, 1972.

Manuscript Collection: Rare Book Room, Washington University Library, St. Louis.

Critical Studies: "The Poetry of David Wagoner" by Robert Boyers, in *Kenyon Review* (Gambier, Ohio), 1970; "An Interview with David Wagoner," in *Crazy Horse 12* (Marshall, Minnesota), 1972; "On David Wagoner" by Sanford Pinsker, in *Salmagundi* (Saratoga Springs, New York), Spring-Summer 1973.

David Wagoner comments:

I have an affinity for the dramatic lyric, in tones ranging from the loud and satiric through the quiet and conversational.

*   *   *

There is an element of mystery, and of awe before the mystery, that plays about the edges of virtually every poem by David Wagoner, or at least those creations of his that one remembers, and it is this quality that has made him an elusive subject for observers of current poetry. While he has certainly been acknowledged as one of the prime poets of his generation, a certain reticence seems to afflict those who would represent him to the broader public relatively unfamiliar with his work. While there is no doubt that his writing has been distinguished by verbal dexterity, metaphorical ingenuity and by colloquial intensity, and that his imagination has been responsive to the serious problems that haunt Western culture and perplex the private individual, Wagoner has done something else that only his fellow poet James Dickey has articulated successfully: "It is when abandon, wild calculation and seriousness meet that his poetry really takes off, drawing the reader after him like the tail on a powerful, erratic kite."

That says it, and to fully understand what it means a good dose of Wagoner's potent medicine alone will do. For in Wagoner wildness and abandon have nothing whatever to do with the studied incoherence and randomness of much recent verse, nor is his seriousness related to the morbid melancholia and obsessional disgust that are staple features of the confessional tradition so many of us admire. In fact, even Wagoner's more depressing poems do not so much evoke a condition of nausea and breakdown as talk about it, try to overcome its influence by making it part of the convention which is the poem. He is less concerned with the intensity of madness and dislocation than he is with the intensity of creation, the resilience of the creative imagination. In the poem called "Going to Pieces," he speaks of terror, of dissociation, but he concocts an analogy for his condition that is, somehow, consoling. The analogy is at once richly relevant and a little preposterous, and the mystery is located precisely at that point in the poem where we know Wagoner is both pulling our leg and showing us the truth of the condition he describes. Often in Wagoner there is that irony which qualifies the sombre, and gives to the universal *angst* a meekly human dimension which is the enemy not of seriousness but of pretension.

Wagoner is not the poet to paint his significations large or to spell out the importance that abides in his concerns. He refuses to dissolve reality in meaning, and if his poems are sometimes gaudy, they are never merely clever – invention subserves serious intentions. If he sounds sometimes like other poets we identify with the emotive imagination, poets like Bly and Wright and Stafford, he is never content with the easy effects that characterize their verse, and the sudden metaphysical leaps many of their poems share are in Wagoner but one feature among many that dazzle, tease and give pleasure. Wagoner's poetry is, in fact, among the most moving and delightful things recent culture has given us.

– Robert Boyers

WAIN, John (Barrington). British. Born in Stoke-on-Trent, Staffordshire, 14 March 1925. Educated at The High School, Newcastle-under-Lyme, Staffordshire; St. John's College, Oxford, B.A. 1946, Fereday Fellow, 1946–49, M.A. 1950. Married Marianne Urmstrom in 1947 (marriage dissolved, 1956); Eirian James, 1960; has three children. Lecturer in English, University of Reading, Berkshire, 1947–55. Since 1973, Professor of Poetry, Oxford University. Director, Poetry Book Society Festival, "Poetry at the Mermaid," London, 1961. Churchill Visiting Professor, University of Bristol, 1967; Visiting Professor, Centre Universitaire Experimental, Vincennes, France, 1969; First Holder, Fellowship in Creative Arts, Brasenose College, Oxford, 1971–72. Recipient: Maugham Award, 1958. Fellow, Royal Society of Literature, 1960; resigned, 1961. Lives in Oxford. Address: c/o Macmillan and Company Ltd., 4 Little Essex Street, London W.C.2, England.

PUBLICATIONS

Verse

> *Mixed Feelings: Nineteen Poems.* Reading, Berkshire, Reading University School of Art, 1951.
> *A Word Carved on a Sill.* London, Routledge, and New York, St. Martin's Press, 1956.
> *Weep Before God: Poems.* London, Macmillan, and New York, St. Martin's Press, 1961.
> *Wildtrack: A Poem.* London, Macmillan, and New York, Viking Press, 1965.
> *Letters to Five Artists.* London, Macmillan, 1969; New York, Viking Press, 1970.
> *The Shape of Feng.* London, Covent Garden Press, 1972.

Play

Television Play: *The Young Visitors*, 1967.

Novels

> *Hurry on Down.* London, Secker and Warburg, 1953; as *Born in Captivity*, New York, Knopf, 1954.

Living in the Present.   London, Secker and Warburg, 1955; New York, Putnam, 1960.
The Contenders.   London, Macmillan, and New York, St. Martin's Press, 1958.
A Travelling Woman.   London, Macmillan, and New York, St. Martin's Press, 1959.
Strike the Father Dead.   London, Macmillan, and New York, St. Martin's Press, 1962.
The Young Visitors.   London, Macmillan, and New York, Viking Press, 1965.
The Smaller Sky.   London, Macmillan, 1967.
A Winter in the Hills.   London, Macmillan, 1970.

Short Stories

Nuncle and Other Stories.   London, Macmillan, 1960; New York, St. Martin's Press, 1961.
Death of the Hind Legs and Other Stories.   London, Macmillan, and New York, Viking Press, 1966.
The Life Guard.   London, Macmillan, 1971.

Other

Preliminary Essays.   London, Macmillan, and New York, St. Martin's Press, 1957.
Gerard Manley Hopkins: An Idiom of Desperation.   London, Oxford University Press, and Folcroft, Pennsylvania, Folcroft Editions, 1959.
Sprightly Running: Part of an Autobiography.   London, Macmillan, 1962; New York, St. Martin's Press, 1963.
Essays on Literature and Ideas.   London, Macmillan, and New York, St. Martin's Press, 1963.
The Living World of Shakespeare: A Playgoer's Guide.   London, Macmillan, and New York, St. Martin's Press, 1964.
Arnold Bennett.   New York, Columbia University Press, 1967.
A House for the Truth (critical essays).   London, Macmillan, 1972; New York, Viking Press, 1973.
Samuel Johnson.   London, Macmillan, 1974.

Editor, *Contemporary Reviews of Romantic Poetry.*   London, Harrap, and New York, Barnes and Noble, 1953.
Editor, *Interpretations: Essays on Twelve English Poems.*   London, Routledge, 1955; New York, Hillary House, 1957.
Editor, *International Literary Annual.*   London, John Calder, and New York, Criterion Books, 2 vols., 1959, 1960.
Editor, *Fanny Burney's Diary.*   London, Folio Society, 1960.
Editor, *Anthology of Modern Poetry.*   London, Hutchinson, 1963.
Editor, *Selected Shorter Poems of Thomas Hardy.*   London, Macmillan, and New York, St. Martin's Press, 1966.
Editor, *The Dynasts,* by Thomas Hardy.   London, Macmillan, and New York, St. Martin's Press, 1966.
Editor, *Selected Shorter Stories of Thomas Hardy.*   London, Macmillan, and New York, St. Martin's Press, 1966.
Editor, *Shakespeare: Macbeth: A Casebook.*   London, Macmillan, 1968.
Editor, *Shakespeare: Othello: A Casebook.*   London, Macmillan, 1971.
Editor, *Johnson as Critic.*   London and Boston, Routledge, 1973.

Critical Studies: "John Wain et le Magie de l'Individu" by Françoise Barriere, in *Le Monde* (Paris), 8 August 1970; "John Wain: Revolte et Neutralité" by Pierre Yvard, in *Etudes Anglaises* (Paris), October 1970; "The New Puritanism, The New Academism, The New . . ." by the author, in *A House for the Truth*, 1972.

*　　　*　　　*

John Wain's poetry, though intermittently anthologised, has been overshadowed by his versatility as novelist and critic. His earlier verse was associated by critics with "The Movement" or "The University Wits" as they were termed: Kingsley Amis, Robert Conquest, and others. Such poets reacted against the lax rhythms and indulgent rhetoric of much of the poetry of the 1940's. Influenced to some degree by William Empson, they preferred tight, if sometimes elaborate, forms such as terza rima and villanelle. This latter form indeed became virtually the Movement's "badge." It had entered the English tradition in the 1870's and 1880's through Austin Dobson, Andrew Lang and other "Parnassians," but was restricted to light verse. The aim of Wain and his associates was to use the form for seriously witty purposes and to ensure that the two lines that acted as refrains should at each repetition modify what preceded them so that though the actual form of words did not change, the tone and the significance did. Like the other "Movement" poets Wain, in his first collection, *Mixed Feelings*, preferred even-paced slow monosyllabic lines often carrying an aphoristic weight:

> When love as germ invades the purple stream
> It splashes round the veins and multiplies
> Till objects of desire are what they seem.

What separated Wain from his associates is of course more important. His diction tended to be somewhat generalised in an eighteenth-century manner (Dr. Johnson is one of Wain's heroes), but the moral dignity is crossed by faint touches of "metaphysical" wit.

Each succeeding volume has shown Wain advancing in range and technique. *A Word Carved on a Sill* is transitional in the sense that it clings still to the somewhat monotonous rhythms of *Mixed Feelings*, but "A Poem Feigned to Have Been Written by an Electronic Brain" reveals a journalistic immediacy and wit and a movement towards the public poem. In "The Bad Thing" he achieves a study of depressive states as distinguished as Keith Douglas's "Bête Noire."

Weep Before God contains Wain's most impressive work. "Time Was" returns to the metronomes of the first poems, but with delicate adjustments of caesura in the best Augustan way. The range of this volume widens; the rhythms become more adventurous, e.g. "Poem Without a Main Verb," "Anniversary," and "Brooklyn Heights": the first a riddling poem, the second a moving autobiographical reflection, the third a fine topographical meditation. "Anecdote of 2 a.m." is a direct, poignant and unsentimental lyric:

> I could not tell what dreams disturbed her heart.
> She spoke and never knew my tongue was tied.
> I longed to bless her but she lay apart.

With "A Song about Major Eatherly," which ponders the troubled later career of an American pilot involved in the nuclear assault on Japan in 1945, Wain successfully enters the difficult domain of public poetry. This poem is related by its principle of diversity in unity to *Wildtrack*, which consists of a single long poem on the theme of "human interdependence," passing freely from past to present and of considerable virtuosity of metre: terza rima, a free sestina, a sonnet, a mock dance-lyric, etc. Interesting, if uneven, the poem's most memorable sections are the passages of sentiment – "The Little Woman Addresses the Child in Her Womb" and the lyrical address to Samuel Johnson's mother presenting her son to Queen Anne to be touched for the King's Evil, "Gently, Sarah, Lift Your Son."

Wain's honest metronomes occasionally run flat and his diction is occasionally prosaic – "Survival was their magic and their art" – but these are defects of a poetry that is not ashamed, in touching what is centrally human, to risk sentimentality and banality.

– Ian Fletcher

WAKOSKI, Diane. American. Born in Whittier, California, 3 August 1937. Educated at the University of California, Berkeley, B.A. 1960. Married S. Shepard Sherbell in 1965 (divorced); Michael Watterlond, 1973. Clerk, British Book Centre, New York, 1960–63; English Teacher, Junior High School 22, New York, 1963–66; Lecturer, New School for Social Research, New York, 1969; Poet-in-Residence, California Institute of Technology, Pasadena, Spring 1972, University of Virginia, Charlottesville, Autumns 1972–73, and Wilamette University, Salem, Oregon, Spring 1974. Recipient: National Endowment for the Arts grant, 1966, 1968, 1973; Bread Loaf Writers Conference Robert Frost Fellowship, 1966; Cassandra Foundation Award, 1970; New York State Council on the Arts grant, 1971; Guggenheim grant, 1972. Address: P.O. Box 4786, Grand Central Station, New York, New York 10017, U.S.A.

PUBLICATIONS

Verse

Coins and Coffins. New York, Hawk's Well Press, 1962.
Four Young Lady Poets, with others. New York, Corinth Books, 1962.
Discrepancies and Apparitions: Poems. New York, Doubleday, 1966.
The George Washington Poems. New York, Riverrun Press, 1967.
Greed Parts One and Two. Los Angeles, Black Sparrow Press, 1968.
The Diamond Merchant. Cambridge, Massachusetts, Sans Souci Press, 1968.
Inside the Blood Factory. New York, Doubleday, 1968.
A Play and Two Poems, with Robert Kelly and Ron Loewinsohn. Los Angeles, Black Sparrow Press, 1968.
Thanking My Mother for Piano Lessons. Mount Horeb, Wisconsin, Perishable Press, 1969.
Greed Parts 3 and 4. Los Angeles, Black Sparrow Press, 1969.
The Moon Has a Complicated Geography. Palo Alto, California, Odda Tala Press, 1969.
The Magellanic Clouds. Los Angeles, Black Sparrow Press, 1970.
Greed Parts 5–7. Los Angeles, Black Sparrow Press, 1970.

The Lament of the Lady Bank Dick. Cambridge, Massachusetts, Sans Souci
   Press, 1970.
Love, You Big Fat Snail. San Francisco, Tenth Muse, 1970.
*Black Dream Ditty for Billy "The Kid" Seen in Dr. Generosity's Bar Recruiting for
   Hell's Angels and Black Mafia.* Los Angeles, Black Sparrow Press, 1970.
Exorcism. Boston, My Dukes, 1971.
On Barbara's Shore. Los Angeles, Black Sparrow Press, 1971.
The Motorcycle Betrayal Poems. New York, Simon and Schuster, 1971.
*The Pumpkin Pie, Or Reassurances Are Always False, Though We love Them. Only
   Physics Counts.* Los Angeles, Black Sparrow Press, 1972.
The Purple Finch Song. Mount Horeb, Wisconsin, Perishable Press, 1972.
Sometimes a Poet Will Hijack the Moon. Providence, Rhode Island, Burning
   Deck, 1972.
Smudging. Los Angeles, Black Sparrow Press, 1972.
The Owl and the Snake: A Fable. Mount Horeb, Wisconsin, Perishable Press,
   1973.
Greed Parts 8, 9, 11. Los Angeles, Black Sparrow Press, 1973.
Dancing on the Grave of a Son of a Bitch. Los Angeles, Black Sparrow Press,
   1973.
Winter Sequences. Los Angeles, Black Sparrow Press, 1973.
*Trilogy: Coins and Coffins, Discrepancies and Apperitions, The George
   Washington Poems.* New York, Doubleday, 1974.

Other

Form Is an Extension of Content. Los Angeles, Black Sparrow Press, 1972.

Critical Study: *A Terrible War: A Conversation with Diane Wakoski*, edited by Philip
Gerber and Robert Gemmett, Winnipeg, University of Manitoba, 1970.

*   *   *

  Some time in the early 1960's Diane Wakoski's poems began to appear on the
American scene. She did not make much of a splash at first; her language seemed
ordinary and prosy, meandering, talkative, rhythmless, a post-beat idiom incorporating technical jargon as well as street vocabulary but lacking the tension of poems
by Ginsberg or Corso. Yet to a few readers her poems signalled the arrival of a
remarkably inventive poetic imagination. She was associated with other writers in
New York who called themselves the "deep image" poets. It was nothing as grand
as a movement ot a school, and perhaps the reason for the association was no more
than the fun of associating; yet certain principles were observable. The chief was
that a poem should be organized, not verbally or formally, but in terms of the
consonance of imagery at an intuitive level. Not exactly an original idea; the
surrealists, among others, had been announcing it for years. But as it passed
through Wakoski's sensibility it issued in poems that were very unlike the difficult
preciosities of the surrealists, poems that were instead objective, lucid, readable,
and, in spite of their sprawling appearance, densely unified.
  Probably her most notable early work was the sequence called *The George
Washington Poems*, a series of conversations with a person who was called George
Washington but who was given a remarkably various identity. At times he was the
historical figure with the same name; at others he was a personal confidant, a
father substitute, a wayward lover or friend. Although much of the material of the

poems was personal, in parts the poet's consciousness expanded into the national consciousness, so that she addressed the "father of the country" in social-historical-sexual terms, her own body becoming a map of the states. It was a caprice, granted. The poet acknowledged as much in the flippant, easy manner of her writing. But it was a caprice capable of serious extensions, and in any case it was admirable preparation for her mature work.

Wakoski found her proper subject in the difficulty of being a woman in a world of changing values. To what extent her work was influenced by the movement for women's liberation is problematical. It seems clear that she would have come to her knowledge of her own sensibility without any suggestions from outside. She is extremely prolific; probably she is a compulsive writer. She has published at least seven major collections of poems since 1965. Her topics range widely over social and cultural experience, and her poems contain many sharply observed scenes of urban life from New York to Los Angeles. But again and again she returns to themes of sexual need, dread, jealousy, outrage, and anger, developed in images drawn spontaneously from contemporary reality. The titles of her books are some indication of the quality of her mind: *Inside the Blood Factory, The Motorcycle Betrayal Poems*, and, especially, *Greed*. This last is a long sequence still in progress, having appeared so far in several different volumes; its early parts may actually have been written before the George Washington sequence. It is in effect a series of poetic essays on the basic human condition, discursive and exploratory, often very acute.

But the impression should not be given that Wakoski's sensibility is only brittle or angry. The fathers and lovers in her poems may be actuated by greed, but so, often, is the poet herself, and all are held in the basic human bond of sympathy. This gives her work a moral and metaphysical resonance that the poetry of merely militant feminists seldom achieves. Indeed, though indignation and thwarted will are the springs which set many of her poems in motion, it is a rare poem that does not lead beyond these feelings into fundamental Aristotelean pity and woe, with the result that Wakoski reaches a great many readers who might otherwise be provoked by her aggressiveness. Her characteristic poems are too long to be quoted in full here, and too cohesive to be quoted in excerpts. But there is no doubt that she has become in a very few years one of the two or three most important poets of her generation in America.

– Hayden Carruth

WALCOTT, Derek (Alton). British. Born in Castries, St. Lucia, West Indies, 23 January 1930. Educated at St. Mary's College, St. Lucia; University of the West Indies, Kingston, Jamaica, B.A. 1953. Married; has three children. Taught at St. Mary's College and Jamaica College. Formerly, Feature Writer, *Public Opinion*, Kingston, and *Trinidad Guardian*, Port-of-Spain. Since 1959, Founding Director, Trinidad Theatre Workshop. Recipient: Rockefeller Fellowship, for drama, 1957; Guinness Award, 1961; Heinemann Award, 1966; Cholmondeley Award, 1969; Order of the Humming Bird, Trinidad and Tobago, 1969; Obie Award, for drama, 1971; Jock Campbell Award (*New Statesman*, London), 1974. Address: 165 Duke of Edinburgh Avenue, Diego Martin, Trinidad.

PUBLICATIONS

Verse

Twenty-Five Poems. Port-of-Spain, Trinidad, Guardian Commercial Printery,
    1948.
Epitaph for the Young. Bridgetown, Barbados Advocate, 1949.
Poems. Kingston, City Printery, 1953.
In a Green Night: Poems 1948–1960. London, Cape, 1962.
Selected Poems. New York, Farrar Straus, 1964.
The Castaway and Other Poems. London, Cape, 1965.
The Gulf and Other Poems. London, Cape, 1969; as The Gulf, New York,
    Farrar Straus, 1970.
Another Life. London, Cape, and New York, Farrar Sraus, 1973.

Plays

Henri Christophe: A Chronicle (produced St. Lucia, 1950; London,
    1951). Bridgetown, Barbados Advocate, 1950.
Henri Dernier: A Play for Radio Production. Bridgetown, Barbados Advocate,
    1951.
Sea at Dauphin (produced Trinidad, 1954; London, 1960). Mona, University
    College of the West Indies Extra-Mural Department, 1954; in The Dream on
    Monkey Mountain and Other Plays, 1971.
Ione: A Play with Music (produced Trinidad, 1957). Mona, University College
    of the West Indies Extra-Mural Department, 1954.
Drums and Colours (produced Trinidad, 1958). Published in Caribbean Quarterly
    (Kingston), vii, 1 and 2, 1961.
Ti-Jean and His Brothers (produced Port-of-Spain, Trinidad, 1958). Included in
    The Dream on Monkey Mountain and Other Plays, 1971.
Malcochon; or, Six in the Rain (produced St. Lucia, 1959; as Six in the Rain,
    produced London, 1960; as Malcochon, produced New York,
    1969). Included in The Dream on Monkey Mountain and Other Plays, 1971.
The Dream on Monkey Mountain (produced Toronto, 1967; Waterford, Connecti-
    cut, 1968; New York, 1971). Included in The Dream on Monkey Mountain
    and Other Plays, 1971.
In a Fine Castle (produced Jamaica, 1970; Trinidad, 1971; Los Angeles, 1972).
The Dream on Monkey Mountain and Other Plays (includes Ti-Jean and His
    Brothers, Malcochon, Sea at Dauphin, and the essay "What the Twilight
    Says"). New York, Farrar Straus, 1971; London, Cape, 1972.

*   *   *

The appearance of In a Green Night by Derek Walcott in 1962 was a landmark in
Caribbean literature in English. Although there had been poets of some quality
described elsewhere in this volume, the notable achievements of this literature had
been in prose. Walcott's volume marked a new level of poetic attainment. His
verse was distinguished by a combination of virtuosity with control; by a sure sense
of tone and nuance; and by delight in the sensuous and dramatic vitality of words.
In these strengths also lay potential weaknesses. His aural sensibility could trap
him into too extensive an echoing of other poets. His sheer pleasure in verbal

control could result in artificiality. Nevertheless, many of the poems remain sharply memorable today and need no allowances to be made either for Walcott's youth when writing them or for the formidable difficulties of a poet trying to find an authentic voice without the support of a vital tradition of Caribbean poetry in English behind him.

If Walcott's earlier verse too often echoes English poets, he aggressively rejects the Anglo-American clichés of Caribbean glamour, "Found only / In tourist booklets, behind ardent binoculars" ("Prelude"). He also rejects stereotypes within the Caribbean society; too easy acquiescence in emotional response: "Teach our philosophy the strength to reach / Above the navel" ("Tales of the Islands, I"); and the facile optimism of post-emancipation politics:

> This is a brief
> Ignored by our first parliaments, to chart
> The dangerous current of dividing grief. . . .
> > – "A Map of the Antilles"

Again, there are strengths and weaknesses. Walcott's attitudes were intelligent and necessary to a poet in the process of self-discovery, but there is a note of self-indulgent pessimism at times, too. The places he describes, such as La Guiara, Castiliane or D'Ennery, predominantly figure depression and futility, and his most precise and effective poem on human relationships in the volume ends

> Only the gulls, hunting the water's edge
> Wheel like our lives, seeking something worth pity.

On the other hand, his attempts to celebrate Caribbean beauty, such as "A Sea-Shantey," tend to be precious. There appears to be some emotional "blockage" here.

At this point it should be noted that, unlike another Caribbean poet, Edward Brathwaite, Walcott has made few excursions into poetry in the popular creole idiom of the West Indian masses. This by no means indicates that Walcott looks to Europe rather than to the Caribbean for inspiration. He has written a distinguished body of plays (outside our scope here) largely in dialect, and he has moved towards a flexible style that cannot be claimed as European rather than West Indian. He has used a comparatively "standard English" form in order to find the poetic medium that can most precisely express his complex, often ambiguous, attitudes to the Caribbean situation.

The personal isolation one sensed in his first poems has continued to be a theme through the later poems collected in *The Castaway*. This has not been negative, however; it has become increasingly the basis for a many-sided exploration of isolation – physically, culturally and in ways that Walcott sees as quintessential to the human being and the artist above all. The quest makes its own discoveries in the creation of the poem. His play-writing has widened the range of emotion and tone and the dramatic quality of his verse, always present, has been intensified. Now the Caribbean landscape, brilliant and sharply experienced, moves into the worlds of the poems. The struggle to find the perfect balance between depth of experience and control of expression, however, continues. At times they are not successfully resolved; at times the strains knot the syntax into lacunae of sense the reader has to struggle to decipher:

> The green wine bottle's gospel choked with sand,
> Labelled, a wrecked ship,
> Clenched seawood nailed and white as a man's hand.
> > – "The Castaway"

Nevertheless, in his fully successful poems, even an intimation of despair like that of the slum-dwellers in "Laventville," is transformed into a brilliantly orchestrated complex of anger and of compassion.

Walcott's sense of isolation as a poet is heightened by his Caribbean predicament in many ways. One of them is that in Europe the long tradition of the formal arts has given them an accepted validity. In the art of Chardin or Vermeer, for instance, though painted, a cracked coffee cup, a dented urn – everything – "IS" ("A Map of Europe"). What validity has art in a world that lacks the tradition of formally expressed culture ("an absence of ruins," as he describes it, in "The Royal Palms") and is dominated by the natural environment? Watching the peasant girls walking past the surf to vespers, Walcott reflects that nothing he can learn "from art or loneliness / Can bless them as the bell's / Transfiguring bell can bless" ("Crusoe's Island"). Yet not only has his tongue, like the bell's transfigured and blessed the scene; in the poem, his island setting has become a valid image of the modern artist facing the failure of traditional validities in art. Rejected by the young Walcott as a cliché, the vitality and colour of the Caribbean setting emerge in Walcott's mature verse to energise a vision at once intensely personal, Caribbean, and universal.

– Louis James

WALDMAN, Anne. American. Born in Millville, New Jersey, 2 April 1945. Educated at Bennington College, Vermont, B.A. in English literature 1966. Currently, Director of the Poetry Project, St. Mark's Church-in-the-Bowery, New York; Editor, *The World* magazine, New York; Editor with Lewis Warsh, *Angel Hair* and Angel Hair Books, New York; Founding Editor, with Ron Padgett and Joan Simon, Full Court Press, New York, 1973. Recipient: Dylan Thomas Award, 1967; National Endowment for the Arts grant, 1968. Address: St. Mark's Church-in-the-Bowery, New York, New York 10003, U.S.A.

PUBLICATIONS

Verse

On the Wing.   New York, Boke Press, 1967.
Giant Night.   New York, Angel Hair Books, 1968.
O My Life!   New York, Angel Hair Books, 1969.
Baby Breakdown.   Indianapolis, Bobbs Merrill, 1970.
Giant Night: Selected Poems.   New York, Corinth Books, 1970.
Icy Rose.   New York, Angel Hair Books, 1971.
No Hassles.   New York, Kulchur Foundation, 1971.
Memorial Day, with Ted Berrigan.   New York, Poetry Project, 1971.
Holy City.   Privately printed, 1971.
Goodies from Anne Waldman.   London, Strange Faeces Press, 1971.
Light and Shadow.   Privately printed, 1972.
The West Indies Poems.   New York, Boke Press, 1972.
Spin Off.   New York, Big Sky Books, 1972.
Self Portrait, with Joe Brainard.   New York, Siamese Banana Press, 1973.
Life Notes: Selected Poems.   Indianapolis, Bobbs Merrill, 1973.
Fast Speaking Woman.   San Francisco, City Lights Books, 1975.

Other

"The World" Anthology: Poems from the St. Mark's Poetry Project and *Another World*. Indianapolis, Bobbs Merrill, 1969, 1971.

Critical Studies: by Alicia Ostriker, in *Partisan Review* (New Brunswick, New Jersey), Spring-Summer 1971; "Queen Anne" by Susan Braudy, in *Newsweek* (New York), 22 November 1971; Gerard Malanga, in *Poetry* (Chicago), January 1974; Richard Morris, in *Margins* (Milwaukee, Wisconsin), October-November 1974.

Anne Waldman comments:

I am very interested in reading (performing) my work and am writing longer works to be vocalized, almost sung, though not always and absolutely. The short poems are snapshots. The range is open. I am sick of the label "New York School." It is misunderstood and stifling.

*   *   *

"The thing is don't worry. / You are doing what have to what you can . . ." Anne Waldman recommends in "How to Write," and her tone reveals an openness to experience, her subjects are reports on the experiences themselves. It is not an inward poetry – when Waldman does explore subjective areas the arrangement of words skipping about the page seems more imitative of a colloquy among friends than of a dark, confessional soliloquy. More often she is responding in a low-key, unpretentious manner to daily events: domestic life in a small apartment, an unrepentant touristic trip to Europe, and, most often, the streets and buildings of New York. For Waldman, urban life is all bits and pieces: the point is to look for the occasional jewel, or poem. General views, coherence, larger patterns are not only probably deceptive, but also cause one to miss the real things that are there, waiting. Anne Waldman's voice has much in it of the city-dweller: it is hard-edged, but finally sensitive; easily depressed, maybe, but always resilient – "All night on the phone talking to cold people / who remind you how cold you are . . . / But then freezing brings us all together."

– James Vinson

WALKER, Margaret (Abigail). American. Born in Birmingham, Alabama, 7 July 1915. Educated at Northwestern University, Evanston, Illinois, B.A. 1935; University of Iowa, Iowa City, M.A. 1940, Ph.D. 1965; Yale University, New Haven, Connecticut (Ford Fellow), 1954. Married Firnist James Alexander in 1943; has four children. Professor of English, West Virginia State College, Institute, 1942–43, and Livingston College, Salisbury, North Carolina, 1945–46. Since 1949, Professor of English, and since 1968, Director of the Institute for the Study of the History, Life and Culture of Black Peoples, Jackson State College, Mississippi. Recipient: Yale Series of Younger Poets Award, 1942; Rosenthal Fellowship, 1944; Houghton Mifflin Literary Fellowship, for fiction, 1966. Address: 2205 Guynes Street, Jackson, Mississippi 39213, U.S.A.

PUBLICATIONS

Verse

For My People.   New Haven, Connecticut, Yale University Press, 1942.
Ballad of the Free.   Detroit, Broadside Press, 1966.
Prophets for a New Day.   Detroit, Broadside Press, 1970.
October Journey.   Detroit, Broadside Press, 1973.

Novels

Come Down from Yonder Mountain.   Toronto, Longman, 1962.
Jubilee.   Boston, Houghton Mifflin, 1965.

Other

How I Wrote "Jubilee."   Chicago, Third World Press, 1972.
A Poetic Equation: Conversations Between Margaret Walker and Nikki Giovanni.   Washington, D.C., Howard University Press, 1974.

*   *   *

Margaret Walker's reputation as a poet rests mainly upon *For My People*, which in 1942 won the Yale Series of Younger Poets competition. These race-conscious poems, because of their prescient militancy, strength, and celebration of Black identity, purposes, and traditions, are admired by the current generation of young Afro-American poets and poetry readers.

This volume contains three groupings of poems, each demonstrating the author's creative resourcefulness and technical control. The first grouping is written in Miss Walker's rather distinctive experimental reverse-indented, paragraph-style stanzas. Some of the lines have sentence syntax, as in "Lineage"; some of the stanzas are clause structured, as in the title poem; some of the stanzas are paragraph structured, as in "Dark Blood." All show to advantage her skill in poetry-as-statement. Characteristically, each stanza in a poem is a catalog of images and evocative statements, and each stanza is an increment toward the poem's climax, point, or resolution. The second grouping is lively ballads and narratives informed or inspired by Negro folk characters, lore, and traditions. The language is infused with the idioms, cadences, and intonations of Negro oral traditions. The third grouping is sonnet variations, often informed too by what the author has seen, learned, and felt as a Negro American.

Margaret Walker's poetry since *For My People* mainly deals with current subjects, people, and events of significance to Afro-Americans. These later poems continue to be insightful, compassionate, and sincere; increasingly they have become utilitarian. Her imagery continues to be precise and graphic, perhaps more realistic and less romanticized than in her earlier work, and her language continues to be plain and direct. Her use of free verse techniques has increased.

– Theodore R. Hudson

WALKER, Ted (Edward Joseph Walker). British. Born in Lancing, Sussex, 28 November 1934. Educated at Steyning Grammar School; St. John's College, Cambridge, B.A. (honours) in modern languages 1956. Served in the Royal Naval Volunteer Reserve. Married Lorna Benfell in 1956; has two daughters and two sons. Head of the French Department, Southall Grammar School, Middlesex, 1958–61; Head of the Modern Languages Department, Bognor Regis School, Sussex, 1961–63; Assistant Spanish Master, Chichester High School, Sussex, 1963–64. Since 1971, Poet-in-Residence, New England College, Arundel, Sussex. Since 1962, Founding Editor, with John Cotton, *Priapus*, Berkhamsted, Hertfordshire. Recipient: Eric Gregory Award, 1964; Cholmondeley Award, 1966; Alice Hunt Bartlett Prize, 1968. Agent! Charles Schlessiger, Brandt and Brandt, 101 Park Avenue, New York, New York 10017. Address: Argyll House, The Square, Eastergate, Chichester, Sussex, England.

PUBLICATIONS

Verse

Those Other Growths. Leeds, Northern House, 1964.
Fox on a Barn Door: Poems 1963–4. London, Cape, 1965; New York, Braziller, 1966.
The Solitaries: Poems 1964–5. London, Cape, and New York, Braziller, 1967.
The Night Bathers: Poems 1966–8. London, Cape, 1970.
Poems for Cordelia. Rushden, Northamptonshire, Sceptre Press, 1972.
Gloves to the Hangman: Poems 1969–72. London, Cape, 1972.

Manuscript Collection: Lockwood Memorial Library, State University of New York, Buffalo.

Ted Walker comments:

My poetry seems to deal with loneliness and isolation. Since I live in the country, my imagery tends to be rural and even regional. My territory is Sussex and the Sussex coast.

*   *   *

Much of Ted Walker's poetry is in the great tradition of English Nature poetry. This has nothing to do with the versified nature or gardening notes which often pass for examples of this genre; but is a poetry which, while one of close and accurate observation, looks beyond external nature to where parallels are drawn and implications relating to the human condition are made:

> regret
the vacant seemliness
by which we live. For which we lost
that proper, vital gift of waste.
> – from "Crocuses"

It is a tradition of poetry which stretches in modern times from Wordsworth to Ted Hughes.

The territory of this poetry is the seashore with its inlets and breakwaters, and lonely parts of the English countryside, and the creatures that inhabit them. The vision expressed is that of the ultimate solitude of the individual soul when confronting the universe in which it finds itself; and the situation of man where he finds himself unsatisfied and incomplete in contrast to the aptness and completeness of the rest of the animal kingdom in relation to its environment. It is where man looks both within himself and out towards "that God I won't believe in" for something beyond his immediate environment to meet the spiritual loneliness which is reflected in the loneliness of the situations depicted in the poems. It is not without significance that the title of Walker's second collection was *The Solitaries*.

In Walker's third full length collection, *The Night Bathers*, there is a shift of emphasis. The same qualities of precise observation and craftsmanship are there; but the poet is growing older and the past begins to haunt the present to the point where it enriches it and gives it depth of meaning. The title poem reflects on the poet's relationship with his son as a parallel to that between himself and his own father:

> when he was young to understand
> why, momently out of the night
> and purposeful beyond the reach
> of all his worry, I had swum
> deep into banks of sea-fret
> too far to have to answer him.

There is, too, a clearly observable growth in Walker's technical mastery, which allows him to relax his earlier tight control and use a language closer to the colloquial. This development is continued in his latest collection, *Gloves to the Hangman*, where in poems such as "Letter to Barbados" there is an ease of expression which gives the poem an immediacy of reception without any diminution of strength:

> Dear far-off brother. Thank you for yours,
> And for the gift you send of little shells.

In fact in the longer narrative poem "Pig pig" there is, if anything, a resurgence of strength where the colloquial is allied to that ethological insight into brute nature that distinguished the best of Walker's earlier animal poems:

> Sunlight slammed on the dung
> between us. The men hung
> bare heads. Their cowardice
> fattened on my promise.

The result is a poetry of disturbing power.

> – John Cotton

WALLACE-CRABBE, Christopher (Keith). Australian. Born in Richmond, Victoria, 6 May 1934. Educated at Scotch College; University of Melbourne, Victoria,

B.A. 1956; M.A. (Lockie Fellow) 1964; Yale University, New Haven, Connecticut (Harkness Fellow), 1965–67. Married; has two children. Since 1968, Senior Lecturer in English, University of Melbourne. Visiting Fellow, University of Exeter, Devon, 1973. Address: 52 Glenard Drive, Heidelberg, Victoria 3084, Australia.

PUBLICATIONS

Verse

> *No Glass Houses.* Melbourne, Ravenswood Press, 1956.
> *The Music of Division.* Sydney, Angus and Robertson, 1959.
> *Eight Metropolitan Poems.* Adelaide, Australian Letters, 1962.
> *In Light and Darkness.* Sydney, Angus and Robertson, 1964.
> *The Rebel General.* Sydney, Angus and Robertson, 1967.
> *Where the Wind Came.* Sydney, Angus and Robertson, 1971.
> *Selected Poems: 1955–1972.* Sydney, Angus and Robertson, 1973.
> *Act in the Noon.* Melbourne, Cotswold Press, 1974.

Other

> *Melbourne or the Bush.* Sydney, Angus and Robertson, 1973.

> Editor, *Six Voices: Contemporary Australian Poets.* Sydney, Angus and Robert-
> son, 1963.
> Editor, *The Australian Nationalists.* Melbourne, Oxford University Press, 1971.
> Editor, *Australian Poetry '71.* Sydney, Angus and Robertson, 1971.

Critical Studies: "A Modest Radiance" by E. A. M. Colman, in *Westerly* (Ned-lands, Western Australia), 1969; "To Move in Light: The Poetry of Chris Wallace-Crabbe" by Peter Steele, in *Meanjin* (Melbourne), 1970.

Christopher Wallace-Crabbe comments:

My early poetry explored the nature of social order and of intellectual coherence in a world in which religious sanctions seemed irrelevant: my concern at this stage was to make poetic structures which testified to the strength which was inherent in human reason and (hopefully) to humorous resilience as a way of meeting the contradictions of experience. Later, finding my early poetry rather too stiff, rigo-rous and explicit, I came to seek more supple rhythms and more autonomous images – a poetry which was more fully charged with the physical world.

Over the past few years I have increasingly been trying to come to terms with violence: political, personal and intrapersonal. I am interested in the paradox that we tend most profoundly to worship vitality for its own sake, while we are bound at the same time to deplore such vitality as manifests itself in the form of violence. Poetry, like other constructive activities, issues from forces that are potentially destructive. The self, when it is most vital, is not reducible to a moral agent. These are the central concerns which I have been trying to dramatize in my recent poems. At the same time, inevitably, my poetry has been growing less formal, less architecturally shaped, and more sinuous, more shifting, more various in its effects and directions.

*   *   *

Christopher Wallace-Crabbe's volume of poems, *The Music of Division*, confirmed the promise indicated by the appearance of his work in Australian literary journals since the early 1950's. His first work was unusual in an Australian context in that it avoided the over-indulgence and exuberance normally associated with a young writer. *The Music of Division* exhibited a coolness and a quality of apparent detachment that looked forward to the early 1960's, rather than back to the more romantic 1950's of Australian poetry. In the first volume, the most notable poems are based upon observation of political forces, particularly as they implicate individual personalities in the tension between "public" and "private" responses. This preoccupation is developed and expanded in the later books, *In Light and Darkness* and *The Rebel General*, and is perhaps taken to its furthest stretch in the prize-winning long poem, "Blood Is the Water," included in the volume *Where the Wind Came*.

Such a continuous preoccupation with and development of the themes of power and political motivation has, interestingly enough, led Wallace-Crabbe away from the earlier detachment to an increasing relaxation and a sense of full humanness in his writing. He himself has written, "After stoical-formalist beginnings, I seek a poetry of Romantic fullness and humanity. I want to see how far lyrical, Dionysian impulses can be released and expressed without loss of intelligence." His *Selected Poems*, published in his fortieth year, would seem to mark a significant watershed in his work. It is worth noting that this volume commences with a series of "Meditations" which imply that he is reaching out in new directions, perhaps more fully exploring the vein of lyricism that has glittered tantalisingly throughout the volumes that preceded it and are abridged into it. The almost ruthless severity of the abridgement still indicates, however, that Christopher Wallace-Crabbe exercises a powerful and severe intelligence in the organisation of his compositions. At this point in his development he is certainly one of the leaders of his generation of Australian poets.

– Thomas W. Shapcott

WALSH, Chad. American. Born in South Boston, Virginia, 10 May 1914. Educated at Marion Junior College, Virginia, 1934–36; University of Virginia, Charlottesville, 1936–38, A.B. in French 1938 (Phi Beta Kappa); University of Michigan, Ann Arbor (Hopwood Award, for drama, 1939), 1938–43, A. M. in French 1939, Ph.D. in English 1943. Married Eva May Tuttle in 1938: has four daughters. Teching Fellow, University of Michigan 1942–43; Research Analyst, United States Army Signal Corps, Arlington, Virginia, 1943–45. Member of the English Department, 1945–52, since 1952, Professor of English, Department Chairman, 1959–69, and since 1969, Writer-in-Residence, Beloit College, Wisconsin. Fulbright Lecturer, Turku, Finland, 1957–58, and Rome, 1962; Visiting Professor of

English, Wellesley College, Massachusetts, 1958–59. Ordained Priest, Episcopal Church, 1949; since 1948, Assistant at St. Paul's Church, Beloit, Wisconsin. Founder, with Robert Glauber, *Beloit Poetry Journal*, 1950. Recipient: Catholic Poetry Society Spirit Gold Medal, 1964; Society of Midland Authors Award, 1965, 1970; Yaddo Fellowship, 1966. D.H.L.: Rockford College, Illinois, 1963; St. Norbert College, West De Pere, Wisconsin, 1972. Address: Department of English, Beloit College, Beloit, Wisconsin 53511, U.S.A.

PUBLICATIONS

Verse

The Factual Dark. Prairie City, Illinois, Decker Press, 1949.
Eden Two-Way. New York, Harper, 1954.
The Psalm of Christ: Forty Poems on the Twenty-Second Psalm. Philadelphia, Westminster Press, 1963.
The Unknowing Dance. New York and London, Abelard Schuman, 1964.
The End of Nature: Poems. Chicago, Swallow Press, 1969.
God at Large. New York, Seabury Press, 1971.

Novels

Knock and Enter. New York, Morehouse Barlow, 1953; London, Faith Press, 1959.
The Rough Years. New York, Morehouse Barlow, 1960.

Other

Stop Looking and Listen: An Invitation to the Christian Life. New York, Harper, 1947; London, SCM Press, 1948.
C. S. Lewis: Apostle to the Skeptics. New York, Macmillan, 1949.
Early Christians of the 21st Century. New York, Harper, 1950.
Campus Gods on Trial. New York, Macmillan, 1953; revised edition, 1962.
Faith and Behavior: Christian Answers to Moral Problems, with Eric Montizambert. New York, Morehouse Barlow, 1954.
Nellie and Her Flying Crocodile (juvenile). New York, Harper, 1956.
Behold the Glory (meditations). New York, Harper, 1956.
God at Large. New York, Seabury Press, 1960.
The Personality of Jesus. New York, Know Your Bible, 1961.
Why Go to Church?, with Eva Walsh. New York, Association Press, 1962.
Doors into Poetry (textbook). New York, Macmillan, 1962.
From Utopia to Nightmare. New York, Harper, and London, Geoffrey Bles, 1962.
The Story of Job. New York, Doubleday, 1963.

Editor, *Today's Poets: American and British Poetry since the 1930's.* New York, Scribner, 1965.
Editor, *Garlands for Christmas.* New York, Macmillan, 1965.
Editor, *The Honey and the Gall: Poems of Married Life.* New York, Macmillan, 1967.

Manuscript Collections: Lockwood Memorial Library, State University of New York, Buffalo; Beloit College Library, Wisconsin.

Critical Study: Introduction by Carl Bode, to *The Unknowing Dance*, 1964.

Chad Walsh comments:

As a boy, I had a strong quasi-pantheistic, quasi-scientific interest in nature. I roamed the fields and woods, did landscape paintings (as photographic as my ability would permit), daydreamed of being a forester or landscape architect. My interest in poetry began at about the age of ten. Two things triggered it. One was that my eldest brother, who had introduced me to the magic of language by reading Dickens aloud, became briefly interested in poetry. We memorized snatches of Shakespeare's sonnets and of Keats, and strode up and down the country lane near our home, reciting. About the same time my teacher, Miss Louise Johnston, told the students that each should write a poem about autumn. I recall only the ending of mine – "The leaves are falling fast, / Many of the birds are missing, / But cats will stay to the last." Anyway, she praised it, and from that time on I found myself writing poetry.

For a long time, playwriting vied with poetry. At the University of Virginia I had several one-act plays produced, and at the University of Michigan I won first place in the playwriting division of the Hopwood Awards. But what I most wanted to do was write verse dramas, and this appears not to be the right century. Had I lived in Elizabethan times, I suppose that would have been my specialty. Even many years later, after I went to teach at Beloit College, I wrote a full-length poetic tragedy, *King Saul*, which is still gathering dust.

I have published over twenty books in all, six of them poetry – and these are the books closest to my heart. I find it hard to "label" my poetry – I have experienced the influence, along the way, of diverse poets – Catullus, Villon, Dante, Shakespeare and minor Elizabethan poets, Donne, Keats, Baudelaire, Heine, Hopkins, Yeats, Frost, Eliot, Auden, etc., even Housman and Kipling. I suppose the two poets whose influence is most evident in my work are Frost and Auden.

I earn my living mainly as a college professor, with some moderate income from writing and from poetry readings and lectures that I give on campuses. I am also an Episcopal priest, but very definitely a part-time one, helping on weekends at the local church. Thos three-fold role sometimes suggests to people that I must lead a schizophrenic or polyphrenic life; if I do I am not aware of it.

Perhaps the most frequent theme in my verse is the dialogue between human and divine love. So far as subject-matter is concerned, many of my poems fall into categories: love, religion, nature, geographical impressions, social commentary, etc. I am always experimenting in various forms and tend to swing back and forth between relatively free verse and very complicated forms. I have invented a number of forms and used them extensively – such as the "quintina," the "circular sonnet," and the "rima quinta triplicata." In the last few years I have experimented a great deal with composing poetry directly on the tape recorder, so as to get as free and flowing a quality as possible. I want to experiment with devising a kind of poetic drama in which a number of voices (some perhaps taped) could be used; it would be a unified program of maybe 50 minutes duration. I think public poetry readings are evolving in this direction, and through them a thoroughly modern kind of verse drama may emerge.

I suppose I can best describe what I ideally want to be as a poet by saying that it seems to me the two best American poets of recent times are the late Theodore

Roethke and the living Robert Lowell. I'd like to have Roethke's heart and Lowell's head, to write poetry that somehow combines their strengths; in short, I'd like to be both Apollonian and Dionysian as Yeats was. Others must decide how close I come to this.

*   *   *

At the expense of inviting argument I maintain that Chad Walsh is the finest religious poet writing in America today. In evidence: he has taken a noble but gnarled tradition, reaffirmed its element of love, widened its technical range with unfailing ingenuity, and brought it home to an increased audience.

So far he has produced half a dozen volumes of verse. They all celebrate a God who is to be beloved more than venerated, and a mankind which is to be comprehended rather than condemned. They all benefit from the steady growth of his sensibility, a sensibility with at least two levels. One is a heightened, not dulled, response to the wildly assorted worlds around him. The other is a common-sense about the way his work will look to others. Reacting at one time against a preoccupation with form which led him to invent the circular sonnet and the quintina, he turned to the tape recorder and simply said his poetry as it came to him. Through these tapes he won a release. On the other hand, as he reported in *Hang Me Up My Begging Bowl*, he found two-thirds of that poetry "still uninteresting even after revision," and so discarded it. Of the remainder, printed in *Bowl*, most seems to me to be true poetry.

The scanner of sources will see especially in Chad Walsh's early lyrics the influence of Auden and Frost. Yet even at the outset he was his own man, whatever the influence in single lines or certain atmospheres. Though his continued concern for innovation has resulted in a diversity of manners, there is a firm, consistent core throughout his poetry.

Not surprisingly his best books are his later ones, *The Unknowing Dance* and *The End of Nature*. About his best poems there can always be disagreement among his readers. Among the many lyrics which move me are his stately ode "The Destruction by Fire of the Beloit College Chapel"; his urbanely metaphysical "Ode on a Plastic Stapes," where he meditates on man's replacement for a god-given bone in the poet's inner ear; his "Nuptial Hymn," addressing an uneasy young bridegroom on the bridal night; and the most recent of many invocations to his wife, "We were so busy being young." His most enduring poems relate man to God or man to woman; his least successful originate as reflections about his travels abroad.

He teaches literature at Beloit College. He is also an Anglican priest. He is also a compiler of poetry anthologies, the founder of a journal of poetry, and the poetry reviewer for one of the national newspaper weeklies. Above all, he is a poet who, after thirty years, composes with an obviously undiminished zest.

– Carl Bode

WANTLING, William. American. Born in Peoria, Illinois, 7 November 1933. Educated at Illinois State University, Normal (EPDA Fellow), B.S.Ed. 1969; currently studying for a graduate degree in education. Served in the United States

Marine Corps in Korea. Married; has two sons. Formerly, factory worker, surveyor, zoo-keeper, teacher, writer on electronics. Inmate, San Quentin State Penitentiary, California, 1958–63. Address: Route 1, Towanda, Illinois, U.S.A. *Died 4 May 1974.*

PUBLICATIONS

Verse

The Search, edited by Kirby Congdon.   Torrance, California, Hors Commerce Press, 1964.
Machine and Destiny: A Dirge for Three Artists.   Torrance, California, Hors Commerce Press, 1964.
Head First: Poems.   Staatsburg, New York, Erick Kiviat, 1964.
Heroin Haikus.   Chicago, Fenian Head Center Press, 1965.
Five Poem Songs.   Torrance, California, Hors Commerce Press, 1965.
Down, Off and Out.   Bensenville, Illinois, Mimeo Press, 1966.
The Source.   London, Dustbooks, 1966; El Cerrito, California, Dustbooks, 1967.
The Awakening.   London, Turret Books, 1967; revised edition, London, Rapp and Whiting, 1968.
Penguin Modern Poets 12, with Alan Jackson and Jeff Nuttall.   London, Penguin, 1968.
10,000 RPM and Diggin It, Yeah.   Cardiff, Second Aeon Publications, 1973.

Novels

Young and Tender.   New York, Bee Line Books, 1969.
Sick Fly.   Cardiff, Second Aeon Publications, 1970.

William Wantling comments:

I vacillate from (1) spare, realistic free verse to (2) mysticism, which employs rhyme and Welsh "Cynghanedd." Influenced by Dylan Thomas and Ernest Hemingway and still trying to synthesize these contrasting styles.

*   *   *

William Wantling has had a curious career, in that he is an "underground" American writer who has had an establishment success in England. Inclusion in the Penguin Modern Poets series, for instance, has probably brought him a wider spectrum of readers, and perhaps more readers absolutely, than he has ever had in America. Wantling's poetry is the direct product of personal experience. After serving as a Marine sergeant in the Korean War, he became a heroin addict in California in 1955. He served five-and-a-half years in San Quentin for forgery and narcotics convictions. In fact, he has been a denizen of the kind of America that frightens even Americans. No one would deny, least of all himself, that what he writes has a hit-or-miss quality. But his successes, when they come, are impressive.

For all the apparent casualness of his technique, Wantling works best in complete poems, and there is unfortunately only room to quote an untypical epigram here:

> Dreams
> are cages
> within which we
> observe the cages
> without

Yet the instinctive elegance and feeling for concision this displays are undoubtedly among his gifts.

– Edward Lucie-Smith

WARNER, Francis (Robert Le Plastrier). British. Born in Bishopthorpe, York-shire, 21 October 1937. Educated at Christ's Hospital, 1947–54; London College of Music, 1954–55; County Technical College, Guildford, Surrey, 1955–56; St. Catharine's College, Cambridge (Music Scholar), 1956–59. Married Mary Hall in 1958; has two daughters. Taught at St. Catharine's College, 1959–65. Since 1965, Fellow and Tutor in English Literature, and College Librarian, St. Peter's College, Oxford; currently University Lecturer in English. Founder, Pilgrim's Way Players, touring company, 1954, Cambridge University Elgar Centenary Choir and Orches-tra, 1957, and the Samuel Beckett Theatre, Oxford, 1967. Assistant Director, Yeats International Summer School, Sligo, Ireland, 1961–67; a Director, James Joyce Symposium, Dublin, 1967, and the James Joyce Foundation, Tulsa, Oklahoma. Recipient: Messing International Award, 1972. Agents: P. L. Representation, 33 Sloane Street, London S.W.1.; Margaret Kelley, 14 Pond View Road, Canton, Massachusetts, U.S.A. Address: St. Peter's College, Oxford, England.

PUBLICATIONS

Verse

Perennia. Cambridge, Golden Head Press, 1962.
Early Poems. London, Fortune Press, 1964.
Experimental Sonnets. London, Fortune Press, 1967.
Madrigals. London, Fortune Press, 1967.
The Poetry of Francis Warner. Philadelphia, Pilgrim Press, 1970.
Meeting Ends. Rushden, Northamptonshire, Sceptre Press, 1973.

Plays

Maquettes (produced Oxford, 1970; London, 1972). Oxford, Oxford Theatre Texts, 1972.
Lying Figures (produced Oxford, 1971; London, 1972). Oxford, Oxford Theatre Texts, 1972.

Meeting Ends (produced Edinburgh, 1973; London, 1974).   Cheadle, Cheshire,
Oxford Theatre Texts, 1974.

Other

Editor, *Garland: A Little Anthology of Poetry and Engravings.*   Cambridge, Gol-
den Head Press, 1968.
Editor, *Studies in the Arts: Proceedings of the St. Peter's College Literary
Society.*   Oxford, Blackwell, 1968; New York, Barnes and Noble, 1969.

Manuscript Collection: St. Louis University Library, Missouri; University Library,
Cambridge.

*   *   *

The Poetry of Francis Warner was compiled from several previous books and
"represents those poems written in the decade 1960–1969, with which the . . . poet
chooses to be associated, on which he stakes his reputation."
    The formal tradition of English poetry is very much alive in Mr. Warner's work.
There are ten "Experimental Sonnets" which, while they do not sustain the exact
form, do maintain the spirit of the Shakesperean sonnet. The elegy "Plainsong" is
written mostly in blank verse, and "A Legend's Carol" in eleven stanzas of
matched lines artfully arranged with both end and internal rhymes. Scarcely any of
the "Lyrical and Meditative Poems" fail to fall into a pattern of rhythm, rhyme, or
form. There are songs, lyrics, ballads, and even an aubade and a calypso ballad.
"Perennia" is composed in Spenserian stanzas except for Perennia's song which,
quite aptly, is written in the rhyme and meter of Swinburne's "Hymn to Proserpine."
    What of the wine that Mr. Warner pours into these familiar forms? The "Son-
nets" are deeply introspective; "The dark offstage preoccupies my mind," the poet
says, and, indeed, the thread of mutability stitches them together. "Plainsong"
seeks and finds a resolution for the final change of death in the constant renewal of
life, but "A Legend's Carol" undercuts this somewhat by seeing in the archetypal
birth of Mary's Son, the simultaneous death of Pan. "Lyrical and Meditative
Poems" are Mr. Warner at his best; they are too finely diverse to tarnish with a
generalization, but the poet seems to have accepted the urgings of "Venus and the
Poet": "Come, leave mutability, / Lie me down beneath this tree" – love does
provide both the ecstatic and only practical answer to the inevitability of change.
The long poem "Perennia" says this, too, in telling a lovely dream-myth.
    Hoping to introduce a poet to new followers often results in an earnest over-
simplifying of his work. Mr. Warner is a poet who should be read, not read about;
only then can one experience the incarnation he has achieved by mating word with
form.

– Norman T. Gates

WARNER, Rex (Ernest).   British.   Born in Birmingham, Warwickshire, 9 March
1905. Educated at St. George's School, Harpenden, Hertfordshire; Wadham College, Oxford, B.A. in classics and English literature 1928. Served in the Home
Guard, London, 1942–45. Married Frances Chamier Grove in 1929; Barbara Lady

Rothschild, 1949; remarried Frances Chamier Grove, 1966; has four children. Schoolmaster in Egypt and England, 1928–45; worked for the Control Commission in Berlin, 1945; Director, British Institute, Athens, 1945–47. Tallman Professor, Bowdoin College, Brunswick, Maine, 1962–63. Since 1963, Professor of English University of Connecticut, Storrs. Recipient: Black Memorial Prize, for fiction, 1961. Commander, Royal Order of the Phoenix, Greece, 1963. D.Litt.: Rider College, Trenton, New Jersey, 1968. Honorary Member, New England Classical Association. Address: Anchor House, St. Leonardi Lane, Wallingford, Berkshire, England.

<small>PUBLICATIONS</small>

Verse

> *Poems.* London, Boriswood, 1937; New York, Knopf, 1938; revised edition, as *Poems and Contradictions*, London, Lane, 1945.

Plays

> Screenplays: *World Without End* (documentary), 1953; *The Immortal Land* (documentary), 1958.

Novels

> *The Wild Goose Chase.* London, Boriswood, 1937; New York, Knopf, 1938.
> *The Professor.* London, Boriswood, 1938; New York, Knopf, 1939.
> *The Aerodrome.* London, Lane, 1941; Philadelphia, Lippincott, 1947.
> *Why Was I Killed? A Dramatic Dialogue.* London, Lane, 1943; Philadelphia, Lippincott, 1944.
> *Men of Stones: A Melodrama.* London, Lane, 1949; Philadelphia, Lippincott, 1950.
> *Escapade: A Tale of Average.* London, Lane, 1953.
> *The Young Caesar.* London, Collins, and Boston, Little Brown, 1958.
> *Imperial Caesar.* London, Collins, and Boston, Little Brown, 1960.
> *Pericles the Athenian.* London, Collins, and Boston, Little Brown, 1963.
> *The Converts.* London, Bodley Head, and Boston, Little Brown, 1967.

Other

> *The Kite.* Oxford, Blackwell, 1936; revised edition, London, Hamish Hamilton, 1963.
> *The English Public Schools.* London, Collins, 1945.
> *The Cult of Power: Essays.* London, Lane, 1946; Philadelphia, Lippincott, 1947.
> *John Milton.* London, Max Parrish, and New York, Chanticleer Press, 1950.
> *Views of Attica and Its Surroundings.* London, Lehmann, 1950.
> *E. M. Forster.* London, Longman, 1950.
> *Men and Gods.* London, MacGibbon and Kee, 1950; New York, Farrar Straus, 1951.

Ashes to Ashes: A Post-Mortem on the 1950–51 Tests, with Lyle Blair.   London, MacGibbon and Kee, 1951.

Greeks and Trojans.   London, MacGibbon and Kee, 1951.

Eternal Greece, with M. Hurlimann.   London, MacGibbon and Kee, 1951; New York, Viking Press, 1953.

Athens.   London, Thames and Hudson, 1956; New York, Studio Publications, 1957.

Athens at War: Retold from The History of the Peloponnesian War of Thucydides.   London, Bodley Head, 1970; New York, Dutton, 1971.

Men of Athens: The Story of Fifth Century Athens.   London, Bodley Head, and New York, Viking Press, 1972.

Editor, with Laurie Lee and Christopher Hassall, *New Poems 1954: A P.E.N. Anthology.*   London, Joseph, 1954.

Editor, *Look Up at the Skies! Poems and Prose,* by Gerard Manley Hopkins. London, Bodley Head, 1972.

Translator, *The Medea of Euripides.*   London, Lane, 1944; New York, Chanticleer Press, 1949.

Translator, *Prometheus Bound,* by Aeschylus.   London, Lane, 1947; New York, Chanticleer Press, 1949.

Translator, *The Persian Expedition,* by Xenophon.   London, Penguin, 1949.

Translator, *Hippolytus,* by Euripides.   London, Lane, and New York, Chanticleer Press, 1950.

Translator, *Helen,* by Euripides.   London, Lane, 1951.

Translator, *The Peloponnesian War,* by Thucydides.   London, Penguin, 1954.

Translator, *Fall of the Roman Empire: Marius, Sulla, Crassus, Pompey, Caesar, Cicero: Six Lives,* by Plutarch.   London, Penguin, 1958; revised edition, 1972.

Translator, *Poems of George Seferis.*   London, Bodley Head, 1960.

Translator, *War Commentaries of Caesar.*   New York, New American Library, 1960.

Translator, *Confessions of St. Augustine.*   New York, New American Library, 1963.

Translator, with Th. D. Frangopoulos, *On the Greek Style: Selected Essays in Poetry and Hellenism,* by George Seferis.   Boston, Little Brown, 1966.

Translator, *History of My Times,* by Xenophon.   London, Penguin, 1967.

Translator, *Moral Essays,* by Plutarch.   London, Penguin, 1971.

Bibliography: in *The Achievement of Rex Warner,* edited by A. L. McLeod, Sydney, Wentworth Press, 1965.

Manuscript Collection: University of Connecticut, Storrs.

*   *   *

Rex Warner's poetry celebrates the force of nature, symbolized usually by birds, either powerful, often ugly – "smothering an airpuff with heave of shoulder" ("Egyptian Kite") – or graceful – "easy on the flying twig's trapeze" ("Longtailed Tit"). In their plenitude and behavior, they reflect the immanent plan shaping the universe:

> designed so deftly that all air is advantage
> till, with few flaps, orderly as they left earth,
> alighting among curlew they pad on mud.
>
>   – "Mallard"

Frequently human beings submit their emotions to benevolent or tyrannical phenomena that manifest this same control: "to be awed by mountains, & feel the stars friendly" ("Sonnet"). Even in the political poems deleted from his revised edition, *Poems and Contradictions*, Warner plays on the agricultural implications of the Soviet emblem and attributes impending revolution to the working of this natural power: "For blight in the meadows, and for our master builders / let sickle be a staggerer and hammer heavy" ("Sonnet"). Thus, Warner dramatizes political change as the eruption of seasonal forces in the individual and society: "Come then, companions, this is the Spring of blood, / heart's heyday, movement of masses, beginning of blood" ("Sonnet").

Warner can create images startling yet ultimately appropriate: "These bottle-washer trees that give no shade" ("Palm Trees"). However, too often, even in the ambitious sonnet sequence "Contradictions," he depends on words like "love" and "lust" and "birth" and "seed" in contexts which fail to sustain the pulsating effect toward which this language aspires. This attempt, reinforced by elaborate sound and metrical patterns, to recreate the elemental surges of existence, ironically seems more literary than primeval: "All mud & mould shudders with life to-day; / birth bursts by flooding, bloodless without pain" ("Spring Song"). Sometimes, however, Warner masters complex effects of rhythm and alliteration: "Plover, with under the tail pine-red, dead leafwealth in down displayed" ("Lapwing"); but these long lines, whether derived from Hopkins or the fourteenth century alliterative revival, seem divorced from a living tradition and incapable of generating a new one.

Though Warner has published no verse for almost thirty years, except for his translations of George Seferis and classical dramatists, the promise of his best poetry has contributed to the distinguished style he has continuously polished in a stream of novels and translations of classical prose. His learning and eclecticism provide even minor verse with graceful echoes: the Virgilian "shores of leaning light" give resonance to "Spring Song," and the Audenesque "when kneecaps won't loose leg" enlivens the otherwise rhetorical promise of utopia in "Chorus." Besides this ability to evoke a whole range of other authors and traditions, Warner's real, though undeveloped, strengths lie in the compassionate wit of "Epithalamion and Hymn" – "Let moon and sun approve the fun / that Church and State allow" – and in the epigrammatic concentration of "Sonnet XV":

> sinking I see the certain fire and say:
> "There are the useful stars, & here am I!"

          – Burton Kendle

WARREN, Robert Penn. American. Born in Guthrie, Kentucky, 24 April 1905. Educated at Guthrie High School; Vanderbilt University, Nashville, Tennessee, B.A. (summa cum laude) 1925; University of California, Berkeley, M.A. 1927; Yale University, New Haven, Connecticut, 1927–28; Oxford University (Rhodes

Scholar), B.Litt. 1930. Married Emma Brescia in 1930 (divorced, 1950): Eleanor Clark, 1952; has two children. Assistant Professor, Southwestern College, Memphis, Tennessee, 1930–31, and Vanderbilt University, 1931–34; Assistant and Associate Professor, Louisiana State University, Baton Rouge, 1934–42; Professor of English, University of Minnesota, Minneapolis, 1942–50. Professor of Playwriting. 1950–56, Professor of English, 1962–73, and since 1973, Professor Emeritus, Yale University. Member of the Fugitive Group of poets: Co-Founding Editor, *The Fugitive*, Nashville, 1922–25. Founding Editor, *Southern Review*, Baton Rouge, Louisiana, 1935–42. Consultant in Poetry, Library of Congress, Washington, D.C., 1944–45. Recipient: Caroline Sinkler Award, 1936, 1937, 1938; Levinson Prize, 1936, and Union League Civic and Arts Foundation Prize, 1953 (*Poetry*, Chicago); Houghton Mifflin Literary Fellowship, 1939; Guggenheim Fellowship, 1939, 1947; Shelley Memorial Award, 1943; Pulitzer Prize, for fiction, 1947, for poetry, 1958; Robert Meltzer Award, Screen Writers Guild, 1949; Sidney Hillman Prize, 1957; Edna St. Vincent Millay Memorial Prize, 1958; National Book Award, 1958; *New York Herald-Tribune* Van Doren Award, 1965; Bollingen Prize, 1967; National Endowment for the Arts grant, 1968; Henry A. Bellaman Prize, 1970; Van Wyck Brooks Award, 1970; National Medal for Literature, 1970. D.Litt.; University of Louisville, Kentucky, 1949; Kenyon College, Gambier, Ohio, 1952; University of Kentucky, Lexington, 1955; Colby College, Waterville, Maine, 1956; Swarthmore College, Pennsylvania, 1958; Yale University, 1959; Fairfield University, Connecticut, 1969; Wesleyan University, Middletown, Connecticut, 1970; LL.D.: Bridgeport University, Connecticut, 1965. Member, American Academy of Arts and Letters. Address: 2495 Redding Road, Fairfield, Connecticut 06430, U.S.A.

PUBLICATIONS

Verse

Thirty-Six Poems. New York, Alcestis Press, 1935.
Eleven Poems on the Same Theme. New York, New Directions, 1942.
Selected Poems, 1923–1943. New York, Harcourt Brace, 1944; London, Fortune Press, 1951.
Brother to Dragons: A Tale in Verse and Voices. New York, Random House, 1953; London, Eyre and Spottiswoode, 1954.
Promises: Poems, 1954–1956. New York, Random House, 1957; London, Eyre and Spottiswoode, 1959.
You, Emperors and Others: Poems, 1957–1960. New York, Random House, 1960.
Selected Poems: New and Old, 1923–1966. New York, Random House, 1966.
Incarnations: Poems, 1966–1968. New York, Random House, 1968; London, W. H. Allen, 1970.
Audubon: A Vision. New York, Random House, 1969.
Or Else: Poem/Poems 1968–1973. New York, Random House, 1974.

Plays

Proud Flesh (in verse, produced Minneapolis, 1947; revised [prose] version, produced New York, 1947).
All the King's Men (produced New York, 1959). New York, Random House, 1960.

Novels

Night Rider. Boston, Houghton Mifflin, 1939; London, Eyre and Spottiswoode, 1940.

At Heaven's Gate. New York, Harcourt Brace, and London, Eyre and Spottiswoode, 1943.

All the King's Men. New York, Harcourt Brace, 1946; London, Eyre and Spottiswoode, 1948.

World Enough and Time: A Romantic Novel. New York, Random House, 1950; London, Eyre and Spottiswoode, 1951.

Band of Angels. New York, Random House, 1955; London Eyre and Spottiswoode, 1956.

The Cave. New York, Random House, and London, Eyre and Spottiswoode, 1959.

Wilderness: A Tale of the Civil War. New York, Random House, 1961; London, Eyre and Spottiswoode, 1962.

Flood: A Romance of Our Times. New York, Random House, and London, Collins, 1964.

Meet Me in the Green Glen. New York, Random House, 1971; London, Secker and Warburg, 1972.

Short Stories

Blackberry Winter. Cummington, Massachusetts, Cummington Press, 1946.

The Circus in the Attic and Other Stories. New York, Harcourt Brace, 1947; London, Eyre and Spottiswoode, 1952.

Other

John Brown: The Making of a Martyr. New York, Payson and Clark, 1929.

I'll Take My Stand: The South and the Agrarian Tradition, with others. New York, Harper, 1930.

Understanding Poetry: An Anthology for College Students, with Cleanth Brooks. New York, Holt, 1938; revised edition, 1950, 1960.

Understanding Fiction, with Cleanth Brooks. New York, Crofts, 1943; revised edition, Appleton Century Crofts, 1959.

A Poem of Pure Imagination: An Experiment in Reading, in *The Rime of the Ancient Mariner,* by Samuel Taylor Coleridge. New York, Reynal and Hitchcock, 1946.

Modern Rhetoric: With Readings, with Cleanth Brooks. New York, Harcourt Brace, 1949; revised edition, 1958, 1972.

Fundamentals of Good Writing: A Handbook of Modern Rhetoric, with Cleanth Brooks. New York, Harcourt Brace, 1950; London, Dobson, 1952; revised edition, Dobson, 1956.

Segregation: The Inner Conflict in the South. New York, Random House, 1956; London, Eyre and Spottiswoode, 1957.

Remember the Alamo! New York, Random House, 1958.

Selected Essays. New York, Random House, 1958; London, Eyre and Spottiswoode, 1964.

The Gods of Mount Olympus. New York, Random House, 1959; London, Muller, 1962.

The Legacy of the Civil War: Meditations on the Centennial. New York, Random House, 1961.

Who Speaks for the Negro? New York, Random House, 1965.
Homage to Theodore Dreiser. New York, Random House, 1971.
John Greenleaf Whittier's Poetry: An Appraisal and a Selection. Minneapolis, University of Minnesota Press, 1971.
A Conversation with Robert Penn Warren, edited by Frank Gado. Schenectady, New York, The Ido, 1972.

Editor, with Cleanth Brooks and J. T. Purser, *An Approach to Literature: A Collection of Prose and Verse with Analyses and Discussions.* Baton Rouge, Louisiana State University Press, 1936; revised edition, New York, Crofts, 1939, Appleton Century Crofts, 1952.
Editor, *A Southern Harvest: Short Stories by Southern Writers.* Boston, Houghton Mifflin, 1937.
Editor, with Cleanth Brooks, *Anthology of Stories from the Southern Review.* Baton Rouge, Louisiana State University Press, 1953.
Editor, with Albert Erskine, *Short Story Masterpieces.* New York, Dell, 1954.
Editor, with Albert Erskine, *Six Centuries of Great Poetry.* New York, Dell, 1955.
Editor, with Albert Erskine, *A New Southern Harvest.* New York, Bantam, 1957.
Editor, with Allen Tate, *Selected Poems,* by Denis Devlin. New York, Holt Rinehart, 1963.
Editor, with Robert Lowell and Peter Taylor, *Randall Jarrell 1914–1965.* New York, Farrar Straus, 1967.
Editor, *Faulkner: A Collection of Critical Essays.* New York, Prentice Hall, 1967.
Editor, *Selected Poems of Herman Melville.* New York, Random House, 1971.
Editor, *Selected Poems of John Greenleaf Whittier.* New York, Random House, 1971.
Editor, with Cleanth Brooks and R. W. B. Lewis, *American Literature: The Makers and the Making.* New York, St. Martin's Press, 2 vols., 1974.

Bibliography: *Robert Penn Warren* by M. N. Huff, New York, David Lewis, 1968.

Manuscript Collection: Beinecke Library, Yale University, New Haven, Connecticut.

Critical Studies: *Modern Poetry and the Tradition* by Cleanth Brooks, Chapel Hill, University of North Carolina Press, 1939; *Robert Penn Warren* by Klaus Poenicke, Heidelberg, 1959; *The Fugitive Group* by Louise Cowan, Baton Rouge, Louisiana State University Press, 1959; *Fugitives' Return,* edited by Rob Roy Purdy, Nashville, Tennessee, Vanderbilt University Press, 1959; *Robert Penn Warren: The Dark and Bloody Ground* by Leonard Casper, Seattle, University of Washington Press, 1960; *The Faraway Country* by Louis D. Rubin, Jr., Seattle, University of Washington Press, 1963; *The Hidden God* by Cleanth Brooks, New Haven, Connecticut, Yale University Press, 1963; *Robert Penn Warren,* edited by John Longley, New York, New York University Press, 1964; *Robert Penn Warren* by Charles H. Bohner, New York, Twayne, 1964; *The Burden of Time* by John L. Stewart, Princeton, New Jersey, Princeton University Press, 1965; *A Colder Fire* by Victor Strandberg, Lexington, University of Kentucky Press, 1965.

* * *

So much acclaim has been given his novels, critical studies and social comment, that it is well to emphasize that Robert Penn Warren is incontestably one of the most distinguished poets now writing. His poems are the meditations of a ghost-haunted philosopher, a man who can remember an agrarian way of life with families closely knit and rooted to the land, a man who has come as far from such pastoral simplicities as has his country and his region. A native of Kentucky, Warren grew up among a tale-telling, ballad-singing, proudly individualistic people. The American South has always had a distinctive regional culture and Warren had the fortune to begin writing as a member of its most influential literary party. Attending Vanderbilt University (1921–25), he studied with John Crowe Ransom and soon joined the Fugitive Movement along with Allen Tate, Donald Davidson, Stark Young, and others. These poets and critics wrote in the hope that the agrarian culture of the South could be preserved against the encroachments of industrial and mercantile values (see *I'll Take My Stand*, 1930). These social attitudes were reflected in their aesthetic, which embodied the values of a presumed stable and hieratic society; a devotion to classical literature; the influence of metaphysical poetry; and the conception of verse as public discourse, formal in diction, traditional in meter, impersonal in tone. These qualities appear, e.g. in the last stanza of Warren's early poem, "Problem of Knowledge":

> The rodent tooth has etched the bone,
> Beech bole is blackened by the fire:
> Was it a sandal smote the troughèd stone?
> We rest, lapped in the arrogant chastity of our desire.

The problem of knowledge has been Warren's continuing concern, but of all the Fugitives he was to move farthest from this conservative social and aesthetic position. After his *Selected Poems 1923–1943*, he published no lyrical verse until *Promises: Poems 1954–1956*, which embodied a style and an aesthetic markedly different from his Fugitive period. In the years since, he has remained true to this later style which he has put to increasingly adventurous uses.

A paradigm of Warren's lasting concerns is found in the poem "Original Sin: A Short Story," a short poem telling a long story indeed of the inescapability of man's knowledge of his fallen state. Its title suggests two permanent aspects of Warren's sensibility, his concern with the dark side of human nature and his commitment to narrative in a period when many poets have eschewed story for symbol, image, ideogram, or other non-discursive devices. These commitments are fully explored and dramatized in Warren's verse novel, *Brother to Dragons*. Here the narrative arises from the historical context most significant to a Southern man of letters. The story, based upon an actual set of events, involves the murderous Oedipal fixation of Lilburn Lewis, a nephew of Thomas Jefferson, whose motives are masked by self-righteousness and by his self-binding idealization of his mother's memory. The character of Lewis is dismaying to Jefferson, whose Augustan faith in human nature allowed no place for such irrationality and violence in one of his own blood, or in any man. Jefferson's idealism proves to be an abstraction which, like the nephew's insane self-righteousness, blinds its possessor to the truth of human nature. As the crime which Lewis commits is the wanton murder of his slave, the narrative poem thus involves also the special guilt of the old South, which Jefferson lamented but could neither assuage nor prevent. Warren's tale is in the Gothic vein (the same murder had been used by Poe as the plot of his verse drama *Politian*), but this is Gothicism deepened by moral responsibility and philosophical questing. The "dragon" of the title is the monster within man.

The brooding violence and terror that striate *Brother to Dragons* characterize Warren's later poetry also. With some poets one recalls lines or stanzas; with Warren it is often characters and actions which persist in the reader's memory: the folktale story of "The Ballad of Billy Potts," the terror and pity of "School Lesson Based on Word of the Tragic Death of Entire Gillum Family," the haunted sievings of time past in "Ballad of a Sweet Dream of Peace." In Warren's poems since *Promises* the narrative element is often subordinated to a brooding metaphysical contemplation of the event, the event itself sometimes not disclosed until the reader is well on into the long, looping sequences in which the poems are arranged. There is also a change in the metrical structure, the stressed meters and regular stanzas now replaced by broken rhythms; clusters of lines arranged in patterns the feelings compel, rather than in those a design proposes; and a beautifully controlled playing-off of speech against the silences of white space, of eye-breaks against the continuity of the brooding, solitary voice.

Selected Poems: New and Old 1923–1966 places the latest work first. The opening poem begins, "The stars are only a backdrop for / the human condition"; this line and a half introduce the two most frequent images in the recent verse: the vast impersonal grandeur of the stars, and the human condition, particularly the remembrance of that inexplicable affront, death. There are elegiac series of poems on the deaths of a boyhood companion ("Ballad: Between the Boxcars, 1923"), and of an old man ("Chain Saw at Dawn in Vermont," "Fall Comes in Back-Country Vermont"); a neighbor's remembered suicide ("The Day Dr. Knox Did It"); the death of the poet's father, his mother, his family's old Negro servant ("Mortmain," "Tale of Time"), as well as the imagined deaths of a Confederate and a Union soldier ("Two Studies in Idealism"). The brooding effort to re-experience, to understand, to explain, to endure these losses is counterpointed by images of stars, space, the diminution of the human scale when seen from an airplane – as in "Homage to Emerson, on Night Flight to New York," in which the poet tests but cannot accept the comforting transcendentalism of the philosopher who "had forgiven God everything," though he admits that "At 38,000 feet Emerson / Is dead right."

Later in the same poem he writes:

> Now let us cross that black cement which so resembles the arctic ice of
> Our recollections. There is the city, the sky
> Glows, glows above it, there must be
>
>
> A way by which the process of living can become Truth.
>
>
> Let us move toward the city. Do you think you could tell me
> What constitutes the human bond?

It is this "human bond," as well as how "the process of living can become Truth," which Warren is concerned to know, to experience, to celebrate. In *Audubon: A Vision*, a sequence of seven poems, Warren freely dramatizes an episode from an entry in the journal of the explorer-ornithologist. Audubon becomes a symbol of the artist in the New World, experiencing the grandeur and beauty of the natural environment and the meanness and violence of human life on the frontier. The tale is thematically similar to that in the earlier "The Ballad of Billy Potts," an encounter with greed, lust, and murder. The language of this long poem is so translucent that the reader is aware not of its diction but of the sensibility which records and responds to the action. "I did not know what was happening in my heart," writes the Audubon of the poem, but the reader knows that he has endured a confrontation with the darkest passions of human nature and has questioned the meaning of human existence; the poem concludes:

Tell me a story.

In this century, and moment, of mania,
Tell me a story.

Make it a story of great distances, and starlight.

The name of the story will be Time,
But you must not pronounce its name.

Tell me a story of deep delight.

Intrinsic with Warren's transfiguration of tragedy into "deep delight" are his celebrations of the senses and the human bonds of love. Warren's loyalties are deep and passionate, loyalties to a way of life he can define and pursue despite the difficulties of the divided soul and the contemporary "century, and moment, of mania." The accomplishment and range of his poetry, as well as the dramatic use of an agrarian sensibility to measure the imperfections of the human lot, suggest that Warren is one of the few living poets comparable to Robert Frost.

– Daniel Hoffman

WARSH, Lewis. American. Born in New York City, 9 November 1944. Educated at the City College of New York, B.A. 1966. Married. Since 1966, Editor, with Anne Waldman, *Angel Hair*, and Angel Hair Books, New York; since 1973, Co-Editor, *The Boston Eagle*. Recipient: National Endowment for the Arts grant, 1966; Poets Foundation Award, 1972. Address: 216 East 10th Street, New York, New York 10003, U.S.A.

PUBLICATIONS

Verse

The Suicide Rates. Eugene, Oregon, Toad Press, 1967.
Highjacking. New York, Boke Press, 1968.
Moving Through Air. New York, Angel Hair Books, 1968.
Chicago, with Tom Clark. New York, Angel Hair Books, 1969.
Two Poems. Windsor, Ontario, Orange Bear Reader, 1971.
Dreaming as One. New York, Corinth Books, 1971.
Long Distance. London, Ferry Press, 1972.
Part of My History. Toronto, Coach House Press, 1972.

Other

Translator, *Night of Loveless Nights*, by Robert Desnos. New York, The Ant's Forefoot, 1973.

Manuscript Collection: New York University Library.

*   *   *

Lewis Warsh is tall dark lean with long black rock & roll hair. He is soft spoken & smokes too many cigarettes.

He was born in the Bronx the year before the Atomic Bomb was dropped on Hiroshima & Nagasaki.

His poetry is clear, lyric, intelligent, romantic, matter-of-fact, exact & a constant pleasure to read.

His poetry moves easily on the page & it is an ease which sets him apart from other poets in his league who often work too hard at it & still can't pull it off. Or get it on.

Even in poems I find derivative I am always sure he will restate the source in his own voice. He usually does.

His poems retain a flexibility which keeps them moving on a page. His eyes are open to the value & weight of words & things.

His poems are (appear to be) the daily news.

They center almost exclusively within his living space. They remind me of those haiku-journals by Basho & Issa.

He rarely extends into cloud realms of abstract speculation. Whenever he gets too lofty he has the grace to balance (ballast) the poem by shooting the zeppelin down.

His poems are open, i.e., there are no secrets in them. Yet the real magic insists itself & remains in how they move & how easy they seem to read.

– David Meltzer

WATSON, Robert (Winthrop). American. Born in Passaic, New Jersey, 26 December 1925. Educated at Williams College, Williamstown, Massachusetts, B.A. 1946; University of Zurich, 1946–47; Johns Hopkins University, Baltimore, M.A. 1950, Ph.D. 1955. Served in the United States Naval Reserve, 1943–45. Married in 1952; has two children. Instructor, Johns Hopkins University, 1950–52, and Williams College, 1952–53. Member of the Faculty, 1953–65, and since 1965, Professor of English, University of North Carolina, Greensboro. Visiting Poet, San Fernando Valley State College, Los Angeles, 1968–69. Recipient: *American Scholar* Prize, 1961; National Endowment for the Arts grant, 1974. Address: 527 Highland Avenue, Greensboro, North Carolina 27403, U.S.A.

PUBLICATIONS

Verse

A Paper Horse. New York, Atheneum, 1962.
Advantages of Dark: Poems. New York, Atheneum, 1966.
Christmas in Las Vegas. New York, Atheneum, 1971.

>   *Watson on the Beach.*   Greensboro, North Carolina, SB Press, 1972.
>   *Selected Poems.*   New York, Atheneum, 1974.

Play

>   *A Plot in the Palace.*   Lafayette, Indiana, Purdue University Press, 1964.

Novel

>   *Three Sides of the Mirror.*   New York, Putnam, 1966.

Other

>   Editor, with Gibbons Ruark, *The Greensboro Reader.*   Chapel Hill, University
>   of North Carolina Press, 1964.

Critical Studies: by Thomas Lask, in *The New York Times,* 11 December 1971;
Grover Smith, in *Above Ground Review* (Arden, North Carolina), Winter 1971.

Robert Watson comments:

I am primarily a poet, but in my spare time I also enjoy writing fiction and
drama. Though I have written some criticisms and reviews, I write informative
prose only at the point of a gun.

With few exceptions the statements made by poets in our time about their work
seem pretentious, silly, boring or all three at once. Theories get much attention,
more than the poems from which they come; no theories for me. And if I try to
detail characteristics of my poetry, then I am writing my obituary. In vague terms I
try to make my work as musical (in the poetic sense), alive, and intimate as I can,
and try to get in the way people feel about their lives and their world. I do
dramatic, lyric and narrative poems in a wide variety of forms, most of my own
invention. What doesn't seem to fit poems I put in prose fiction.

*   *   *

Robert Watson's poetry is energetic and economical, splendidly suited to the
difficult art of creating characters in verse. Watson's first volume, *A Paper Horse,*
established these facts with far more authority and consistency than is usual in first
collections; the book demonstrates a mastery of staccato compression in a variety
of formal approaches ranging from free verse to strict rhyme and meter. Most of
the poems are soliloquies, spoken by a variety of characters particularly qualified
to speak of the loss of youth, freedom, or love. The surface bleakness of the
characters' lives is mitigated by Watson's compassion for them, and by his strong
and distinctive style.

Advantages of Dark does not reveal much stylistic development, but it extends the
range of starting points for Watson's poetry. In addition to a few soliloquies, there
are a number of satires of contemporary life, some of which portray with harrowing humor the willful recalcitrance of everyday inanimate objects. The book also

contains an ambitious long poem, "The City of Passaic," which evokes, through the lives of a few of its inhabitants, the life of the city where Watson was born. "Line for a President" also deserves mention as one of the very few convincing and genuine American poems on the assassination of President Kennedy.

Christmas in Las Vegas is something of a return to the bleakness of *A Paper Horse*. In his accustomed style, which suddenly appears to have been developed for just this purpose, Watson explores the brittle brilliance of modern urban life, in which people are almost indistinguishable from the machines they have become enslaved by. The somber tones of this collection, paradoxically deepened by the relentless presence of artificial light, are more profound than any Watson has struck before.

– Henry Taylor

WATSON, Roderick. Scottish. Born in Aberdeen, 12 May 1943. Educated at Aberdeen Grammar School, 1955–61; Aberdeen University, 1961–65, M.A. in English, 1965; Peterhouse, Cambridge (Lucy Jack Scholar), 1966–69, Ph.D. 1971. Married Celia Hall Mackie in 1966; has one son. Lecturer in English, University of Victoria, Vancouver, British Columbia, 1965–66. Since 1971, Lecturer in English, University of Stirling. Recipient: Scottish Arts Council bursary, 1970. Address: 19 Millar Place, Stirling FK8 1XD, Scotland.

PUBLICATIONS

Verse

28 Poems, with James Rankin. Aberdeen, Aberdeen University Poetry Society, 1964.
Poems. Preston, Lancashire, Akros, 1970.
Trio: New Poets from Edinburgh, with Valerie Simmons and Paul Mills, edited by Robin Fulton. New York, New Rivers Press, 1971.

Critical Studies: by Philip Hobsbaum, in *Lines Review 42–43* (Edinburgh), September 1972–February 1973; Donald Campbell, in *Akros 8* (Preston, Lancashire), March 1973; David Hewitt, in *Aberdeen University Review*, xliv, 3, 1973.

Roderick Watson comments:

The poem begins in the collision which happens when you say things by means of other things. But I am also concerned to preserve the integrity of these "other things." The images, experiences, and histories which one collects must be themselves too, and not merely the source material for striking metaphors. The long line

I use has been a great help in this. So I prefer an angular resistance in the language of poetry, a certain opacity, and a conclusion which retains some of the tension of the poem, rather than one which resolves it with a final epigrammatic flourish.

In the past I have identified this understanding with my origins in the Northeast of Scotland. I'm sure that this is true, but recently I have been thinking that it is not the whole story either. I don't know what the rest is yet.

*   *   *

Introducing the poems of Roderick Watson in *Trio: New Poets from Edinbugh*, Robin Fulton singled out three characteristic features of his work up to that date (1971): "a treatment of family history alongside the wider history of the century; an ability to localise and focus these wider movements; and the use of a long line and a full paragraph through which his verse can deliberate." The last word is well chosen. Punctuated by gaps which require the reader to stop and mark his words, Watson's twelve poems in that book have a slow, recollecting speech-rhythm that suits his preoccupation with stones, bones, cave paintings, the track of time. There is a kind of archaeology at the back of his imagination, typically active in "3 Stones," which contrasts a stone used as a weapon, a stone used for grinding corn, and a stone on which a message has been cut:

Leave wax and pigment   and ink the stone itself
– a beginner's exercise in lithography.
The printing shows old scars   lines   seams
a play of forces on matter   collected and recorded.
Time accumulates thus   and in quarries   mines
heart shafts   the deep places   it is true history
written on the walls.   This is a picture of it.
(And the track of ions too   in a cloud chamber).

Watson did post-graduate work on MacDiarmid, and the experience seems to have inspired him to try to write the kind of poetry MacDiarmid wants – "words coming from a mind / Which has experienced the sifted layers on layers / Of human lives." The result is occasionally clotted and repetitious, but full of possibilities for the future.

– Robert Nye

WATSON, Wilfred. Canadian. Born in Rochester, Kent, England, in 1911; emigrated to Canada in 1925. Educated at Malden Grammar School, England; University of British Columbia, Vancouver; University of Toronto, Ph.D. Served in the Royal Canadian Navy during World War II. Married to the writer Sheilah Watson. Since 1951, Member of the Faculty, currently, Professor of American Literature, University of Alberta, Edmonton. Recipient: Arts Council of Great Britain Award, 1953; Canadian Government Overseas Fellowship, 1955; Governor-General's Award, 1956; President's Medal, University of Western Ontario, 1962. Address: Department of English, University of Alberta, Edmonton, Alberta, Canada.

PUBLICATIONS

Verse

Friday's Child. London, Faber, 1955; New York, Farrar Straus, 1956.

Critical Studies: "Vision and Clarity: The Poetry of Wilfred Watson" by J. W. Bilsland, in *Canadian Literature* (Vancouver), Spring 1960; "First Night in Edmonton" by J. W. Bilsland, in *Canadian Literature* (Vancouver), Spring 1962; *Literary History of Canada*, edited by Carl F. Klinck, Toronto, University of Toronto Press, 1965.

*   *   *

Wilfred Watson's first book of poems, *Friday's Child*, received both the Governor-General's Award for Poetry in 1956 and the Award of the Arts Council of Great Britain for 1953–1955. Although no other books have followed, *Friday's Child* established him as an important, if unusual, Canadian poet. More than any other Canadian book it shows individual use being made of the influences of Hopkins, Yeats, Eliot, and especially Dylan Thomas.

These influences have been translated into largely traditional poems with an apocalyptic edge. He has written two poems on Dylan Thomas, "An Admiration for" and "A Contempt for." He frequently combines classical precision with an incantatory style. The opening of "Love Song for Friday's Child" shows his experimental vein:

> Then nor
> Any day nor
> Any movement neither
> But now – ever and ever. . . .

His poem on the painter Emily Carr ends: "And every bush an apocalypse of leaf."

As a playwright, particularly in his play "Cockrow and the Gulls," he shows a dramatic side to his work. "The Canticle of the H. in History," a long poem in *Poetry 62*, demonstrates an awareness of mixed modes, an almost beat utterance coupled with a concern for history and learning. He has studied with Marshall McLuhan and is married to the experimental novelist Sheila Watson, the author of *The Double Hook*.

– John Robert Colombo

WEBB, Francis (Charles). Australian. Born in Adelaide, South Australia, 8 February 1925. Educated at Christian Brothers schools, Chatswood and Lewisham; Sydney University. Served in the Royal Australian Air Force in Canada, during

World War II. Has worked for various Canadian publishers. Recipient: Commonwealth Literary Fund Fellowship, 1960. Address: c/o K. Snell, "Brewarrina,"
Thomas Road, Galston, New South Wales, Australia.

PUBLICATIONS

Verse

> A Drum for Ben Boyd. Sydney, Angus and Robertson, 1948.
> Leichhardt in Theatre. Sydney, Angus and Robertson, 1952.
> Birthday. Adelaide, Advertiser Printing Office, 1953.
> Socrates and Other Poems. Sydney, Angus and Robertson, 1961.
> The Ghost of the Cock: Poems. Sydney, Angus and Robertson, 1964.
> Collected Poems. Sydney, Angus and Robertson, 1969.

Critical Studies: "The World of Francis Webb" by Sylvia Lawson, in *Australian
Letters* (Adelaide), 1961; "Francis Webb and Robert Lowell" by Elizabrth Feltham,
in *Quadrant* (Sydney), 1962; "The Poetry of Francis Webb" by Vincent Buckley, in
Meanjin (Melbourne), 1963.

                                        *   *   *

   In some ways the most formidable poetic talent in Australia of the past twenty
years, Francis Webb developed and extended in his earlier work the Browning-type
dramatic monologue. Taking as his subject the legendary character of the early
19th-century Scottish business adventurer in New South Wales, his *A Drum for Ben
Boyd* won him immediate acclaim. This was followed by *Leichhardt in Theatre* in
which he attempted a poetic rather than drably realistic summation of the career of
the strange German explorer, half-charlatan, half-seer, who was later to achieve
something of an apotheosis in *Voss*, the brilliant novel by Patrick White.
   Already in his second book, an almost surreal element of clashing and káleido-
scopically merging imagery was in evidence. Even the most sympathetic readers
occasionally found it necessary to adopt a Coleridgian "willing suspension of
disbelief" to win through to an appreciation of his multi-faceted art.
   His next book, *Birthday*, was largely overlooked by the critics, though it contained the beautiful sequence of poems commemorating the life and works of St.
Francis of Assisi, "The Canticle." This sequence is one of his finest and most
lyrically sustained achievements, in which the technical prowess never impedes the
illumination of the content. With the appearance of *Socrates and Other Poems* it
became obvious that the poet was experiencing and interpreting the kind of existential endurance test that only saints and visionaries can come through in one piece.
Though there is a further brilliant attempt made at chronicling the trials and crises
of the explorer in "Eyre All Alone," the note appended to this sequence admits to
the poet's "seeing such a journey of discovery as suggestive of another which is
common to us all."
   In his 1964 collection, *The Ghost of the Cock*, the inward journey of discovery and
endurance is pressed to its farthest limits in the sequences "Around Costessey"
and "Ward Two." The vision of the poet has now become Promethean, that of the

sacrificial interpreter who, like Van Gogh, was all but consumed by the sun-bursts of poetic insight into nature and human existence.

– Bruce Beaver

WEBB, Harri. Welsh. Born in Swansea, Glamorgan, 7 September 1920. Educated at Glanmôr Grammar School, Swansea; Magdalen College, Oxford. Currently, Chief Librarian, Mountain Ash, Glamorgan. Active in the Welsh Republican Movement: since 1959, Member, Welsh Nationalist Party (Plaid Cymru). Recipient: Welsh Arts Council Prize, 1970. Address: Garth Newydd, Merthyr Tydfil, Glamorgan, Wales.

PUBLICATIONS

Verse

Triad: Thirty-Three Poems, with Peter Gruffydd and Meic Stephens. Merthyr Tydfil, Glamorgan, Triskel Press, 1963.
The Green Desert. Llandysul, Cardiganshire, Gomer, 1969.
A Crown for Branwen. Llandysul, Cardiganshire, Gomer, 1973.

Other

Dic Penderyn and the Merthyr Rising of 1831. Swansea, Gwasg Penderyn, 1956.
Our National Anthem: Some Observations on "Hen wlad fy nhadau." Merthyr Tydfil, Glamorgan, Triskel Press, 1964.

Harri Webb comments:

I am primarily, but not exclusively, a poet. As a Welsh poet, although not writing in the historic language of the country, one must be a leader.

I recognise that I am a poet with only one theme, one preoccupation, that implicit in being any sort of writer in Wales today. My work is unrepentently nationalistic and I seek no audience outside my own country.

*   *   *

Most of Harri Webb's poetry deals directly with some aspect of Wales: its landscape, culture, language, history, or national identity. In his collections The Green Desert and the recent A Crown for Branwen, his passionate concern for, and commitment to, the nationalist cause is total and remarkable. He possesses the well-known Welsh "lovely gift of the gab." His poems reveal his delight in language and his flowing facility, his wit and wide references (few Anglo-Welsh poets are as erudite about their country), his technical versatility ranging from simple folk verses to the most sophisticated forms, and a gift for the memorable phrase, as in the lyrical and delicate "Carmarthen Coast":

> In the steep hayfields, in the deep lanes
> Where the primroses linger till autumn
> And the white trefoils star the hedgerow grass,
> Where all the flowers bloom at once and forever,
> You are near, but may not cross, the frontier of time.
> Sweet heifers graze the saltings,
> The tide laps at the roots of elder and thorn,
> But the ferryman does not come to the ruined bellhouse.

Webb is also a popular balladist, pamphleteer, political journalist, and former Plaid Cymru candidate, and this background is shown in the considerable variety of approach and technique which characterises his work. There are many deeply-felt, nostalgic, sometimes bitter responses to what he sees as the tragedy of modern Wales, and odd political squibs like his famous "Ode to the Severn Bridge":

> Two lands at last connected
> Across the waters wide
> And all the tolls collected
> On the English side.

But the whiplash satire, clever parody, and biting mockery in his work are amply balanced by such powerful, profound and moving poems as "The Stone Face," a dramatic evocation of historical heroes in which he refers to "the special Welsh tone of voice / Half banter, half blind fervour" and which develops with urgency and authority. Nowhere is his love of Wales and the serious side of his talent seen more clearly than in this very fine poem.

Harri Webb's occasional rhetorical discursiveness, and the obligation he feels to preach his cause, have been viewed by sone cool critics as inhibiting his poetic intelligence. But his range of moods, forms, and styles, his sheer inventiveness and genial, high-spirited humour have placed him, through the last ten years, in the upper ranks of Anglo-Welsh bards. He is, in a real sense, a "poet of the people."

The simple sincerity, for example, of "Heat Wave," his address to an eminent long-dead Catholic Welshman exiled in Rome, commands the utmost respect:

> Will I,
> An Anglican atheist writing in the wrong language, exile,
> In the way of my century, here at home, earn something
> Of the understanding I feel for you, when future men,
> If there are any, read my dreams?

— John Tripp

WEBB, Phyllis. Canadian. Born in Victoria, British Columbia, 8 April 1927. Educated at the University of British Columbia, Vancouver, B.A. 1949; McGill

University, Montreal, 1953. Program Organizer, 1964–67, and Executive Producer, 1967–69, Canadian Broadcasting Corporation, Toronto. Currently, free-lance writer and broadcaster. Recipient: Canadian Government Overseas Award, 1957; Canada Council bursary, 1963, and Senior Fellowship, 1969. Address: c/o Bassek, R.R. 2, Ganges, British Columbia, Canada.

PUBLICATIONS

Verse

Trio, with Gael Turnbull and Eli Mandel.   Toronto, Contact Press, 1954.
Even Your Right Eye.   Toronto, McClelland and Stewart, 1956.
The Sea Is Also a Garden: Poems.   Toronto, Ryerson Press, 1962.
Naked Poems.   Vancouver, Periwinkle Press, 1965.
Selected Poems, 1954–1965, edited by John Hulcoop.   Vancouver, Talonbooks, 1971.

Manuscript Collection: University of Saskatchewan, Saskatoon.

Critical Studies: "The Structure of Loss" by Helen Sonthoff, in Canadian Literature (Vancouver), Summer 1961; "Phyllis Webb and the Priestess of Motion" by John Hulcoop, in Canadian Literature (Vancouver), Spring 1967; introduction by John Hulcoop to Selected Poems, 1954–1965, 1971.

*   *   *

Phyllis Webb's relatively few poems (those she decided to preserve for the 1971 Selected Poems – out of 20 years of work – amounted to only 116 sparsely printed pages) have slowly compelled the attention of a steadily growing group of readers.

Her first poems were published at the beginning of the 1950's in Contemporary Verse. Since then, her publication has always been sparse; there has seemed a reluctance in all her decisions to release a poem into print or speech, and her works when they appear are honed down to an extraordinary intellectual spareness. Publication has become even less copious with the years; she collaborated with Eli Mandel and Gael Turnbull in Trio in 1954, and published her own first volume, Even Your Right Eye, in 1956; it was six years before The Sea Is Also a Garden appeared, followed three years after by a collection of pieces ground to gem-like transparency and abstraction, appropriately entitled Naked Poems. Since 1965 she has published no new volume (even the Selected Poems contained nothing after 1965) and only a few poems in periodicals. Yet she continues to write in reclusion, to polish and, very often, to discard.

The careers of many Canadian poets – perhaps responding to an expansive movement within the culture – have been marked by a growing and unstemmed exuberance in production and in manner. In others, like Margaret Atwood, the self-conscious disciplining of the manner has not lessened the volume of production. For Phyllis Webb, growing maturity as a poet has meant growing withdrawal: a narrowing of the circle of the creative self in keeping with the somewhat solipsistic character of much of her verse. She has said – though she said it almost twenty years ago – that

> The public and the person are inevitably
> one and the same self.

But while this may have been true of the Phyllis Webb who in her early twenties campaigned as a socialist parliamentary candidate, it has not been true for many years of the poet who has been concerned with personal emotions, the loneliness of living, the knife-edge paths on which we painfully dance our way to death. Art she has seen as a "remedy" – not more; as "a patched, matched protection for Because."

The result was perhaps foreshadowed in the early poem, "Is Our Distress," which opens the *Selected Poems:*

> This our inheritance
> is our distress
> born of the weight of eons
> it skeletons our flesh,
> bearing us on
> we wear it
> though it bares us.

The philosophic pessimism – in unguarded moments breaking down into self-pity – which these lines suggest, tends to control the development of thought in Phyllis Webb's poems, the devolution away from the elaborate and the assured, which had led her towards the simplified view of the anarchists (so that the poems she has been working on for years are called "Kropotkin Poems"), the view that the less one demands of existence, the less one has to defend. One of "Some Final Questions," a section of *Naked Poems,* reads:

> *Now, you are sitting doubled up in pain.*
> *What's that for?*
>
> doubled up I feel
> small like these poems
> the area of attack
> is diminished

These lines say much of the poetic as well as the philosophic rule by which Phyllis Webb now lives. Her poems have become small, simple, as packed with meaning as stone artifacts. And, by a just paradox, her public presence had grown the farther she had personally retreated, into what often seems silence. Whatever she publishes in future will be the utterance of a poet who has learnt first the limitations and then the powers of her talent.

– George Woodcock

WEBER, Richard. Irish. Born in Dublin, 2 September 1932. Educated in Dublin public schools. Married; has one daughter. Formerly, Advisory Editor, *Icarus,* journal of Trinity College, Dublin; Poetry Editor, *Poetry Ireland,* Dublin; Assistant Warden in boys' clubs, Dublin, 1957–58; Lamplighter, London, 1959; Bookseller's

Assistant, London, 1959, Dublin, 1961; Secretary to Percy Lubbock, Lerici, Italy, 1960–61; Assistant Editor, *Bookseller*, London, 1961; Librarian, Chester Beatty Library, Dublin, 1961–65; Poet-in-Residence, University of Massachusetts, Amherst, 1967. Since 1967, Visiting Lecturer, Mount Holyoke College, South Hadley, Massachusetts. Honorary B.A.: University of Massachusetts, 1967. Address: Department of English, Mount Holyoke College, South Hadley, Massachusetts 01075, U.S.A.; or, Ballyknockan, Valleymount, County Wicklow, Ireland.

PUBLICATIONS

Verse

O'Reilly: Poems. Dublin, Dolmen Press, 1957.
The Time Being: A Poem in Three Parts: Autumn to Winter, Winter to Spring,
    Spring to Summer. Dublin, Dolmen Press, 1957.
Six Irish Poets, with others, edited by Robin Skelton. London and New York,
    Oxford University Press, 1962.
Lady and Gentleman. Dublin, Dolmen Press, 1963.
Stephen's Green Revisited: Poems. Dublin, Dolmen Press, 1968.

Richard Weber comments:

Being European I tend to use the traditional verse forms, but never, I hope, at the cost of losing the sound of spoken language. However, I began to write (at fifteen or so) in imitation of the American masters, Eliot and Pound, and in what I considered to be free verse. Major theme, subjects, are as with most poets: life, death, love, sex, poetry. Verse forms: whichever suit the poem wants to wear. Reviewers (some) suggest I am addicted to alliteration. I like listening to language; my poems must make sound-sense to me before I release them.

*   *   *

Richard Weber has written that verse "fills a place / in space / to help us smile / a while." This is a modest claim for a poet to make but it helps to explain Weber's predilection for expressing himself in terms of humour and wit. His main interest lies in the exploration of human relationships and of these, characteristically, he takes a gently ironical view. In some poems the poet's analysis is drily detached but generally this is counterbalanced by an intrinsic warmth of feeling. A basically good-humoured acceptance of experience is the norm in Weber's poetry in spite of an occasional wariness:

> The final success
> Before beauty
> Is not to possess
> But to let be.

Romantic and anti-romantic attitudes are both apparent in Weber but they complement, rather than oppose, each other. His verse reflects this in establishing a harmonious relationship between the tone of spoken language and a delicate, cool, water-colour kind of lyricism. A sequence of adaptations from Japanese poets represents Weber's lyrical style at its best. Some poems containing evocations of landscapes are notable for the same quality:

> Below a hillside in Italy
> The darkness filled the bay
> Like flood-water, pushing
> Down all opposition, submerging
> The ships, the olive trees, the town,
> The little gripping houses, the slipping rocks.

A vision of existence as a comedy tinged with sadness is central to Weber's outlook. His poetry is not the product of passionate involvement; it lacks drama, urgency, and daring, but it reflects a mature and well-balanced sensibility. A reassuringly sane and humorous celebration of "the miracle still continuing / Of ourselves and love surviving" is the essence of his achievement.

– Rivers Carew

WEDDE, Ian. New Zealander. Born in Blenheim, 17 October 1946. Educated at the University of Auckland, M.A. (honours) 1968. Married Rosemary Beauchamp in 1967; has one son. Formerly, forester, factory worker, gardener, and postman. British Council Teacher, Jordan, 1969–70; Poetry Reviewer, *London Magazine*, 1970–71; Broadcasting Editor, New Zealand Broadcasting Corporation, 1972. Recipient: Robert Burns Fellowship, University of Otago, 1972; Arts Council bursary, 1974. Address: 31 Currie Street, Port Chalmers, Dunedin, New Zealand.

PUBLICATIONS

Verse

Homage to Matisse. London, Amphedesma, 1971.
Made Over. Auckland, Stephen Chan, 1974.

Plays

Radio Plays: *Stations*, music by Jack Body, 1969; *Pukeko*, music by John Rimmer, 1972.

Other

Translator, with Fawwas Tuqan, *Selected Poems*, by Mahmud Darwish. Cheadle, Cheshire, Carcanet Press, 1974.

Ian Wedde comments:

Poems are ways out of solipsis, not necessarily the poet's. If the poems are any good, then he in writing & readers in reading are transported. Poems are not mirrors but creations, where "creations" is understood as a kind of present participle. I am myself sceptical about the "perfectibility" of men – I think they change to remain the same. For this reason, & because of what I've said above about poetry, & because poetry is not discrete but a function of men, I am not interested in poems as objects, potentially perfectible, but as processes which involve us. Naturally, the ways in which they do this are not unimportant. But the notion that poems "order" the world interests me only insofar as they may be said to do this by bringing us, through the intercourse in which they involve us, to cognition of varieties of the world's DISorder. This disorder, after all, can be every bit as shapely as the most exquisite *poème bien fait*, so called. My own impulse in writing poems is to inquire rather than describe. At the same time I am attracted by the idea of a *forma formans*, a shape or the ghost of a shape which, as Yves Bonnefoy has pointed out in his notes on translating Yeats, can determine the as yet uncertain "content" of which it becomes, reciprocally, an aspect. Mathematics can show us an exact principle of symmetry shared by one of the very oldest creatures, the nautilus, by a Greek temple, by innumerable supermarkets. With luck, poetry can offer us a similarly continuous and vital perspective.

*   *   *

Ian Wedde is among the most impressively gifted of the new generation of New Zealand writers. His talents are various: this is not the place to discuss his short stories or his perceptive criticism, but his translations of the Palestinian poet Mahmud Darwish belong properly in the field of his poetry and are an illuminating adjunct to certain fine poems of his own based on his experiences in Jordan.

As a poet Mr. Wedde is subtle, intelligent, and open to experience. He explores honestly and with sensitive attention subjects ranging over personal relations, love, suffering, politics, art. His observable influences, at least in the forms he uses, are American (Snyder, Creeley), but a wide background is apparent in his work, and although his tone is often colloquial, his use of language is skilful and far from casual.

Friendship is an important theme, and he frequently addresses friends in his poetry; the "Gulf Letters to Mark" are only one sample. Here as elsewhere he has touches of vigorous humour, but never forgets for long the sickening terrors which lie in wait for us all:

> What are we to do Mark before the violence
> in men's minds / dance ahead of the wide
> white sickle jaws & smack the heels
> of our palms together / *Yalla!* Let's
> go!
>   & play upon those taut spaces
> like Eric Clapton / brave words eh Mark?

In the powerful and effective "Losing the Straight Way," a painful loss is survived and transcended; the poem moves from delicate, allusive description through stages of hypnotic revelation and deep shock to close:

Their mouths crept together for comfort.
Their lips crept together for silence.
The mouths of their wounds
crept together for concealment.
Beneath white lips of scars
their blood ran on in silence.

– Fleur Adcock

WEISS, Theodore (Russell). American. Born in Reading, Pennsylvania, 16 December 1916. Educated at Muhlenberg College, Allentown, Pennsylvania, B.A. 1938; Columbia University, New York, M.A. 1940. Married Renée Karol in 1941. Instructor in English, University of Maryland, College Park, 1941, University of North Carolina, Chapel Hill, 1942–44, and Yale University, New Haven, Connecticut, 1944–47; Assistant Professor, 1947–52, Associate Professor, 1952–55, and Professor of English, 1955–66, Bard College, Annandale-on-Hudson, New York; Lecturer, New School for Social Research, New York, 1955–56; Visiting Professor of Poetry, Massachusetts Institute of Technology, Cambridge, 1961–62; Lecturer, New York City Young Men's Hebrew Association, 1965–67. Poet-in-Residence, 1966–67, and since 1968, Professor of English and Creative Writing, Princeton University, New Jersey. Since 1943, Editor and Owner, *Quarterly Review of Literature*, Annandale-on-Hudson, later, Princeton. Member, Wesleyan University Press Poetry Board, 1963–68. Since 1964, Honorary Fellow, Ezra Stiles College, Yale University. Recipient: Ford Fellowship, 1953; Wallace Stevens Award, 1956; National Endowment for the Arts grant, 1967, 1969; Ingram Merrill Foundation grant, 1974. D.Litt.: Muhlenberg College, 1968; Bard College, 1973. Address: 26 Haslet Avenue, Princeton, New Jersey 08540, U.S.A.

PUBLICATIONS

Verse

The Catch. New York, Twayne, 1951.
Outlanders. New York, Macmillan, 1960.
Gunsight. New York, New York University Press, 1962.
The Medium: Poems. New York, Macmillan, 1965.
The Last Day and the First: Poems. New York, Macmillan, 1968.
The World Before Us: Poems 1950–1970. New York, Macmillan, 1970.

Other

The Breath of Clowns and Kings: A Study of Shakespeare. New York, Atheneum, and London, Chatto and Windus, 1971.

Editor, *Selections from the Note-books of Gerard Manley Hopkins.* New York, New Directions, 1945.

Manuscript Collection: Princeton University Library, New Jersey.

Critical Studies: by Harry Berger, in *The Fat Abbot* (New Haven, Connecticut), Summer-Fall 1961; Richard Howard, in *Alone with America*, New York, Atheneum, 1969, and in *Perspective* (St. Louis), 1969.

Theodore Weiss comments:

"I am concerned in a proudly snippety time with the sustained poem, one that is more than merely personal and lyrical and happily fragmented. It is easy to go with the time or to cry out aginst it; but to do something with it, to take it by surprise, to make more of it (as poets usually have) than it can do itself – might that not still occupy poets? And let it be poetry, rather than the poor poet and his predicaments."

The above was printed in *A Controversy of Poets*, New York, Doubleday Anchor Books, 1965. I still more or less subscribe to this view.

                                    *   *   *

Theodore Weiss is not an easy poet to read. His poems are dense with their own music and as often as not two melodies or more are playing within one piece. The reader does not *adjust* to Weiss, but learns to read him, poem by poem. Weiss has accepted the challenge, and perhaps mastered the form, of extended verse. With *Gunsight*, a book-length, narrative poem, Weiss served notice that his earlier long poems were just a beginning. His principal interest, other than the language itself, seems to be stretching the sense of poetry beyond the physical (and mental) barrier imposed by the page.

Gunsight, which records the reactions of a wounded soldier to surgery, survives fifty-five pages as a poem because of Weiss's ability to keep the language moving. This is more than a single trick of rhythm; his skill at creating different levels of speech in contrapuntal rhythms and the simply believable imagery which he employs make the poem readily accessible:

>   Snowy masks
> bent over you,
>   voices flaking,
>   falling
> falling
>   through the seasick smell
>   *breathe in*
> LET ME GO, IT'S COLD.
>   Faces, walls
> fling up at you, cavernous waves, snow-kneading
> hands.
>   OH FIE, THAT SMELL
>   *breathe in.*

In his shorter work, Weiss's language is even richer. The poems have been meticulously constructed, and at times I wish that Weiss would loosen up a bit. The effect of so much careful writing can amount to bewilderment, or worse, some loss of credibility. Where is the "spontaneous overflow of emotion"? Oh, there is emotion here, plenty of it; but the craft, so keenly wrought, is a kind of barrier: Weiss describes carrots,

> coming up, tip-eyed,
> cocking
> this frizz of laughter cloddy earth
> must break loose in a tipsy
> wind to know.
> – from "Phenomenology of the Spirit"

Language as highly constructed as this needs breathing space, but Weiss is too good a poet to write slack lines.

In his 1968 book, *The Last Day and the First*, Weiss juxtaposes many typically brilliant longer poems ("Caliban Remembers" ought to be on the reading list of all college writing seminars) with some short lyrics. In this collection, the short poems seem to be a break with the sensibility that has created the difficult poems mentioned earlier. In "Fresh Paint," part of his suite for Boris Pasternak, Weiss allows himself a freer approach to poetic language:

> "Fresh paint?" I took that sign
> to be an invitation. Certainly,
> clumsy as I was looking more
> closely, it rubbed off on me,
>
> on hands and face and deeper
> still, as though my breath
> kept brushing it in and freshly. . . .

Weiss has demonstrated here, and with other poems in this collection, that he can write equally well, tight or loose. His forte remains the long narrative, but these shorter poems work wonderfully to provide the reader a moment of rest before studying still another example of how good poetry can be, regardless of length.

– Geof Hewitt

WEISSBORT, Daniel. British. Born in London, 1 May 1935. Educated at St. Paul's School, London, 1948–52; Queen's College, Cambridge, 1953–56, B.A. (honours) 1956. Married Jill Anderson in 1961; has two daughters and one son. Advisory Director, Poetry International, London, 1970–73. Since 1964, Co-Founding Editor, with Ted Hughes, *Modern Poetry in Translation*, London; since 1972, Director, Carcanet Press, Oxford, later Cheadle, Cheshire. Visiting Professor in Comparative Literature, University of Iowa, Iowa City, 1974–75. Since 1973, Member of the Poetry Society General Council, London. Recipient: Arts Council bursary, for translation, 1970, 1972; University of Iowa Writing Fellowship, 1973. Agent: John Johnson, 51–54 Goshen Buildings, 12–13 Henrietta Street, London WC2E 8LF. Address: 10 Compayne Gardens, London NW6 3DH, England.

PUBLICATIONS

Verse

The Leaseholder.   Oxford, Carcanet Press, 1971.
In an Emergency.   Oxford, Carcanet Press, 1972.

Other

Editor and Translator, *Natalya Gorbanevskaya: Poems, Trial, Prison.*   Oxford,
    Carcanet Press, 1972.
Editor and Translator, *Post-War Russian Poetry.*   London, Penguin, 1974.

Translator, *Scrolls: Selected Poems of Nikolai Zabolotsky.*   London, Cape, 1971.
Translator, *A History of the People's Democracies: Eastern Europe since Stalin,* by
    François Fetjö.   London, Pall Mall Press, 1971.
Translator, *The Rare and Extraordinary History of Holy Russia,* by Gustave
    Doré.   London, Alcove Press, 1972.
Translator, *Nose! Nose? No-se! and Other Plays,* by Andrei Amalriki.   New
    York, Harcourt Brace, 1973.

*   *   *

Daniel Weissbort is a poet with an uneasy conscience the causes of which are
hinted at rather than explored. The reader senses a temptation to guilt or sorrow
which – in poem after poem, lightly-handled though each may be – seeks to
undermine a personality bent on constructive, balanced living. The resulting tension
emerges most clearly in the less realistic scenarios: in "Distraction," for example,
where a knight's response to his own sorrow would seem to mean his abandonment
of the armour that makes a crusade possible. The "emergency" to which *In an
Emergency* refers remains, however, understated, with a curiously distinguished
reticence which will, one can't help hoping, give way to fuller if still partially veiled
expression.

– Anne Cluysenaar

WELCH, James.   American.   Born in Browning, Montana, in 1940. Educated at
the University of Montana, Missoula, B.A.; Northern Montana College, Harve.
Recipient: National Endowment for the Arts grant, 1969. Address: Roseacres Farm,
Route 6, Missoula, Montana 59801, U.S.A.

PUBLICATIONS

Verse

Riding the Earthboy 40. Cleveland, World, 1971.

Novel

Winter in the Blood. New York, Harper, 1974.

*   *   *

James Welch is a young poet whose Native American background helps shape his first volume of poetry, *Riding the Earthboy 40*, a book which is one of the strongest first volumes of poetry published in the United States in recent years. As is the case with such other fine young American Indian writers as Simon Ortiz, Leslie Silko, Duane Niatum, and Ray Youngbear, Welch brings to his writing a deep consciousness of the earth which makes his poems exciting and alive, full of depth and mystery. This consciousness, mingled with a sense of loss, makes for some of the most powerful moments in his poems, as in the last lines of "Thanksgiving at Snake Butte":

> On top, our horses broke, loped through
> a small stand of stunted pine, then jolted
> to a nervous walk. Before us lay
> the smooth stones of our ancestors, the fish,
> the lizard, snake and bent-kneed
>
> bowman – etched by something crude,
> by a wandering race, driven by their names
> for time: its winds, its rain, its snow
> and the cold moon tugging at the crude figures
> in this, the season of their loss.

Welch's poems frequently revolve around contemporary Indian experience, but without the sentimental overlay which too many bad non-Indian poets have brought to their writings about Native Americans. The images in Welch's poems are like the Northwest winds of a Montana winter, hard, crystal-cold and powerful as in "Christmas Comes to Moccasin Flat":

> Christmas comes like this: Wise men
> unhurried, candles bought on credit (poor price
> for calves), warriors face down in wine sleep.
> Winds cheat to pull heat from smoke . . .

or in "Going to Remake This World":

> From my window, I see bundled Doris Horseman,
> black in the blowing snow, her raving son,
> Horace, too busy counting flakes to hide his face.
> He doesn't know. He kicks my dog
> and glares at me, too dumb to thank the men
> who keep him on relief and his mama drunk . . .

His poem "The Man from Washington" is already a minor classic with its picture
of a Bureau of Indian Affairs bureaucrat – "a slouching dwarf with rainwater eyes
. . ." who promises

—

> that life would go on as usual,
> that treaties would be signed, and everyone –
> man, woman and child – would be innoculated
> against a world in which we had no part,
> a world of money, promise and disease.

With irony and honesty, James Welch has approached being an Indian and being a
poet in contemporary America and come out of it with poems which are always
memorable and, in some cases, close to great. It seems certain that he will continue
to be a vital force in American writing, not just as an Indian or a poet, but as both.

– Joseph Bruchac

WELSH, Anne. South African. Born in Johannesburg, 19 September 1922. Edu-
cated at Kingsmead School, Johannesburg; Roedean School, Brighton, Sussex,
England; University of Witwatersrand, Johannesburg; Somerville College, Oxford.
Married; has four children. Formerly, Lecturer in Economics, University of
Witwatersrand. Address: 10 Cecil Avenue, Melrose, Johannesburg, South Africa.

PUBLICATIONS

Verse

Set in Brightness. Cape Town, Purnell, 1968.

Other

Editor, *Africa South of the Sahara: An Assessment of Human and Material
Resources.* Cape Town and New York, Oxford University Press, 1951.

*   *   *

Imagery of light and darkness characterizes most of Anne Welsh's verse. The
underlying intuition is of a centre of light at the heart of darkness, and the
numerous brilliances of day are reminders of this perpetual mysterious spiritual
source, a "shining beyond shining." Nearly every poem is a viewing of material
items, touched by physical light and seen in terms of metaphorical radiance, and
each celebrates the re-discovery of this familiar mystery. A sense of awe unifies

the verse and literal reporting of externals is raised to a degree just short of explicit symbolism, since the chief concern is with essence and spirit. Anne Welsh is using traditional light-dark imagery, and she is not afraid of familiar truths; nevertheless, her vision is her own.

The observations are accurate. There is a painter's excitement, controlled by an almost clinical coolness of language, in colour, texture and the play of light, as the eye travels over tree, rock, wall, roof, sky and the wings of a flying bird. The poems are like watercolours, pleasing with their clear lines and pure tones. In them, through the intensity and steadiness of vision, the crude drabness of the city is transformed into something glowing and precious. The eye finds that it can graze on "an iron pasture" and the harsh concrete or tin surface becomes "jewel placed," "comforting." As the distressing defference between organic and inorganic dissolves, the ugly sterility of the South African town is absorbed into and made harmonious with its setting of a wild, spare, untarnished African landscape which the verse frequently suggests.

Clearly, this writer's concern is constantly to unify and relate, and a sense of community and of civilized compassion connects her with the inhabitants of her city-world. What especially touches her imagination are perimeter people – the clown, the deprived, the reject – as well as dancing children and circling birds. But these figures are always distanced: the tone is reserved, without being unfeeling, at times almost anonymous. Yet there is a distinct voice speaking in the poems. It is quiet and unemphatic; the language is clean, exact and taut. Anne Welsh is not a markedly experimental poet and her range is confined to a certain kind of contemplative lyric, written almost in the medium of heightened speech, but a speech with resonance.

Even a minor poet can be said to have attained a certain stature if her work contains an inner landscape of the mind. Here, the mind's country is unassertively individual and African, while yet having a universal, elemental quality. The themes and images which help create this world, sustained sometimes with a slight feeling of strain, are elaborated in the longer poems like "Cartage Possibilities," "Two Voices," "To-day." But more memorable and unified are the shorter, simpler "Time," "That Way," "Rejoicing," "View," "Feast Day," and "Speech." These are poised, and unanxious, in the right way. Each presents a single perception, illuminates the mystery apparent in the ordinary or looks out on a timeless world of dark radiance beyond the present.

– Ruth Harnett

WEVILL, David (Anthony). Canadian. Born in Yokohama, Japan, 15 March 1935. Educated at Trinity College School, Port Hope, Ontario; Fisher Park High School, Ottawa; Caius College, Cambridge, B.A. 1957. Married Assia Gutman in 1960. Lecturer in English, University of Mandalay, Burma, 1958–60. Since 1968, Fellow, National Translation Center, Austin, Texas. Recipient: Eric Gregory Award, 1963; Richard Hillary Memorial Prize, 1965; Arts Council Triennial Prize, 1965, and bursary, 1965, 1966; National Translation Center grant, 1966. Address, c/o National Translation Center, 2621 Speedway, Austin, Texas 78705, U.S.A.

Publications

Verse

> *Penguin Modern Poets 4*, with David Holbrook and Christopher Middleton.
>   London, Penguin, 1963.
> *Birth of a Shark: Poems.*   London, Macmillan, and New York, St. Martin's
>   Press, 1964.
> *A Christ of the Ice-Floes.*   London, Macmillan, and New York, St. Martin's
>   Press, 1966.
> *Firebreak: Poems.*   London, Macmillan, 1971.
> *Where the Arrow Falls.*   London, Macmillan, 1973; New York, St. Martin's
>   Press, 1974.

Other

> Translator, *Selected Poems of Terence Juhasz.*   London, Penguin, 1969.

Critical Study: "David Wevill's *A Christ of the Ice-Floes*: Vision of the Elemental
World" by Anthony Saroop, in *Pluck 1* (Edmonton, Alberta), 1967.

David Wevill comments:

I have tried to create complete poems, not just passing observations. So far I
think I have succeeded only in a few poems. I do not know what direction a poem
will take until it is finished: the theme therefore is unconscious. I have been much
taken with Spanish poetry: Lorca, Neruda, Machado, Paz. They have a terseness
which I admire and am only just, perhaps, starting to achieve. I do not use any
particular verse form: the poem takes its own form. I can't point to any particular
influences; these have been many – as much, say, from prose and painting as from
other poetry. Landscape is in my poetry not as "nature" but in the North American or Spanish sense, as something "out there."

*   *   *

David Wevill's poetry is one of intense personal responses intellectualized to a
high degree and of essentially religious stances conveyed in the language of organic
and frequently violent imagery. A Canadian poet in his origins – and in the
occasional reference – he is almost characteristically un-Canadian in his tone in that
sense of fatalistic ennui which distinguishes certain of his works. If there are
discernible affinities in his poems then these lie with contemporary British poetry
and it is as a British poet that one tends to see him.
    The common denominators of *Birth of a Shark* are visceral and metamorphic, with
a great deal of concentration on a concern which can be best described as that of
"life process." Wevill is most impressive in his ability to bring a sophisticated
method to the pulpy and primal matter which heaves convincingly and metabolic-
ally in his poems:

> The sun seeps into and through your bones.
> Flushing the clotted soil,
> Tapping bacteria, mites, and the locked
> Purses of beetles. And you, fiery and whole
>
> Are pure waste matter, aged to a diamond's strength;
> Your will and body, stone and root. . . .

A Christ of the Ice-Floes shows an extension of earlier interests and a firming of the intellectual posture which makes for the clipped and acerbic quality of Wevill's statement. A religious dimension associates itself with some of the poems as the poet engages in an elaborate and, at times, vicarious ritual of self-discovery which ranges through the metaphor of substitute lives; the experience of travel and geography; and an understanding fundamental to Wevill that life is cyclical and our knowledge of it regenerative:

> I hold my ancestry in my hand . . .
>
> The death of my limbs
> Must mean the nucleus is still alive.
>
> The afterlife at its roots searching for you. . . .

Technically, there is little departure from tried and true norms in Wevill's poems and his style is marked by a conventional sureness and an all-too-respectable limitation of experiment; yet he manages a discreet vividness and an authority and conviction in his statement which more than repay the reader.

– Michael Gnarowski

WHALEN, Philip (Glenn). American. Born in Portland, Oregon, 20 October 1923. Educated at Reed College, Portland, B.A. in literature and languages 1951. Served in the United States Army Air Force, 1943–46. Since 1955, part-time lecturer and teacher. Recipient: Poets Foundation Award, 1962; American Academy of Arts and Letters grant, 1965; Committee on Poetry grant, 1968. Address: 2427 Sutter Street, San Francisco, California 94115, U.S.A.

PUBLICATIONS

Verse

Three Satires. Portland, Oregon, privately printed, 1951.
Self-Portrait, from Another Direction. San Francisco, Auerhahn Press, 1959.
Like I Say. New York, Totem-Corinth, 1960.
Memoirs of an Interglacial Age, San Francisco, Auerhahn Press, 1960.
Monday in the Evening: 26 viii 61. Milan, 263 Milano, 1963.
Every Day: Poems. Eugene, Oregon, Coyote Books, 1965.

Highgrade: Doodles, Poems.   Eugene, Oregon, Coyote Books, 1966.
The Education Continues Along.   Eugene, Oregon, Toad Press, 1967.
On Bear's Head: Selected Poems.   New York, Harcourt Brace, 1969.
Severance Pay: Poems 1967–1969.   San Francisco, Four Seasons Foundation, 1970.
Scenes of Life at the Capital.   Bolinas, California, Grey Fox Press, 1971.

Novels

You Didn't Even Try.   San Francisco, Coyote Books, 1967.
Imaginary Speeches for a Brazen Head.   Los Angeles, Black Sparrow Press, 1972.

Other

The Invention of the Letter: A Beastly Morality (juvenile).   New York, Carp and Whitefish Press, 1967.

Philip Whalen comments:

I try to write in colloquial American speech, but I often fail because many of the subjects I'm interested in – Buddhism, Chinese and Japanese literature and painting and architecture, formal symphonic music, the history of science, historiography, archaeology – aren't much discussed by my fellow Americans. I try to do the best I can. I began studying English poetry at an early age and I continue to work at it. I like Chaucer and Skelton and the Elizabethans and Blake and W. B. Yeats and Dame Edith Sitwell, but I must read them with the help of the New English Dictionary, just as I read at Greek with the help of Liddell and Scott's *Lexicon,* French poetry with the *Nouvelle Petit Larousse Illustré*, Chinese poetry via Matthew's Chinese-English Dictionary, etc. Eliot, Pound, Robinson Jeffers, William Carlos Williams, E. E. Cummings, Kenneth Rexroth, Allen Ginsberg, Jack Kerouac, W. S. Burroughs, Gary Snyder, Lewis Welch, Gertrude Stein, Aeschylus, Su Tung-Po, Michael McLure, Ben Jonson, Walt Whitman, Emily Dickinson, Herman Melville, Nathaniel Hawthorne, Henry Thoreau, Wallace Stevens, Lady Murasaki, Mme. de Lafayette, Antonin Artaud, Aram Saroyan, Tom Clark, Gregory Corso, Samuel Johnson, Rilke, Joyce, Proust, George Chapman, Bernard Shaw, Tobias Smollett, Laurence Sterne, all influence me.

*   *   *

Philip Whalen's poems are often easy to read and endlessly fascinating when one stops to think about why the poems were written in the first place. I think most of Whalen's poems are written for the page – not necessarily to be read aloud – one of the reasons the voice behind most of the work seems, at times, almost impenetrable. I always think that whenever Whalen writes it's because he feels like writing – that if he's pushing himself in any way that that fact will enter the poem, will in fact become the topic of the poem itself as in "Trying Too Hard to Write a Poem Sitting on the Beach," which ends: "I'm not making it, I'm cold, I go into the house." Knowledge of things outside him is one way of making it, but he is also aware of the fact that using knowledge this way in his poems is almost too easy.

Instead, knowledge seems one way of getting through to himself; it's something to discuss or talk about with the final emphasis being the way in which we talk, with less emphasis on what is actually being said. A lot of Whalen's poems are filled with interesting and very detailed descriptions, as well as jottings and notes about what passes in front of his eyes, about where he is at the moment he is writing. Sometimes, when the mind is clear, that's all there is to write about, through the senses on to the page, the most valid and straightforward method of dealing directly with the present. Though all poetry reflects where the poet is while writing. Whalen gets on to the particular moment or mood, writes about it, then lets himself rise above it or slide off. What he teaches us is that poetry is very much in the air, as we are, and that attention, concentration and self-knowledge are the keys – with imagination necessary only as a means to wander from reality, the reality of the first person "I" talking and writing. Reading his poems I'm made aware of how possible it is to write – which is what I meant when I wrote that his poems are "easy" to read. His collected poems, *On Bear's Head*, seems the type of book one will never grow tired of turning to, picking up and reading from at leisure. Finally, his poems are emotional, with a delight in the emotion whether the feelings are pleasurable or sad, a delight in feeling and in the possibilities of feeling free and never questioning any alternative but the fact you're alive and doing it.

– Lewis Warsh

WHEELOCK, John Hall. American. Born in Far Rockway, Long Island, New York, in 1886. Educated at Harvard University, Cambridge, Massachusetts, A.B. 1908 (Phi Beta Kappa); University of Göttingen, Germany, 1909; University of Berlin, 1910. Married Phyllis E. deKay in 1940. Held various administrative positions including Editor and Senior Editor, 1911–54, and Editor, Poets of Today series, 1954–61, Charles Scribner's Sons, publishers, New York. Vice-President, Poetry Society of America, 1944–46; Honorary Consultant in American Letters, Library of Congress, Washington, D.C., 1967–73. Recipient: New England Poetry Club Golden Rose, 1937; Torrence Memorial Award, 1956; Borestone Mountain Award, 1957; Bollingen Prize, 1962; Harvard University Signet Society Medal, 1965; Poetry Society of America Gold Medal, 1972. D.H.L.: Otterbein College, Westerville, Ohio, 1942. Member, American Academy of Arts and Letters; Member, and formerly Vice-President, National Institute of Arts and Letters; Member, and Chancellor, 1947–71, Academy of American Poets. Address: 350 East 57th Street, New York, New York 10022, U.S.A.

PUBLICATIONS

Verse

Verses by Two Undergraduates, with Van Wyck Brooks. Privately printed, 1905.
The Human Fantasy. Boston, Sherman French, 1911.

1657

The Belovèd Adventure.   Boston, Sherman French, 1912.
Love and Liberation: The Songs of Adsched of Meru and Other Poems.   Boston,
    Sherman French, 1913.
Dust and Light.   New York, Scribner, 1921.
The Black Panther: A Book of Poems.   New York, Scribner, 1922.
The Bright Doom: A Book of Poems.   New York, Scribner, 1927.
Poems 1911–1936.   New York and London, Scribner, 1936.
Poems Old and New.   New York, Scribner, 1956.
The Gardener and Other Poems.   New York, Scribner, 1961.
Dear Men and Women: New Poems.   New York, Scribner, 1966.
By Daylight and in Dream: New and Collected Poems 1904–1970.   New York,
    Scribner, 1970.
In Love and Song: Poems.   New York, Scribner, 1971.

Other

Alan Seeger: Poet of the Foreign Legion.   New York, Scribner, 1918.
A Bibliography of Theodore Roosevelt.   New York, Scribner, 1920.
What Is Poetry?   New York, Scribner, 1963.

Editor, *The Face of a Nation: Poetical Passages from the Writings of Thomas
    Wolfe.*   New York, Scribner, 1939.
Editor, *Editor to Author: The Letters of Maxwell E. Perkins.*   New York,
    Scribner, 1950.

Translator, *Happily Ever After* (fairy tales).   New York, Scribner, 1939.

Manuscript Collection: Library of Congress, Washington, D.C.

*   *   *

For seventy years John Hall Wheelock's verses have reflected American poetry.
If there is a serious fault to his work, it is that he has followed, not led, other poets
– Whitman and Thoreau, Eliot and Roethke and Stevens; readers are reminded of
their worlds, beauties other than those Wheelock would confront.

One theme his imagery would treat is the silence he senses following a question
or a departing traveller. This "silence" invades his most pastoral scenes. Through
a dozen volumes of controlled verse we sense Wheelock plunging, for a new way,
any way to fill the silence. His exuberance/verbosity rises not from a need to
"pour out" himself, as with Whitman, but seems more a desperate effort to fill an
emptiness about him with words.

His simple directness softens with age, but he has not quit his joy for sympathy
with the absurd or truly recognized the ambivalent. His poems have acquired,
through years, a gentle sense of the ironic and the ambiguous, and time has gained
Wheelock objective distance from his subjects. Most important, there is an increasing reverence, a wonder which overwhelms his earlier emotion before the vacuum
which "could not be said / By the human voice. . . ."

– Joseph Wilson

WHIGHAM, Peter (George). British. Born in Oxford, 6 March 1925. Married Priscilla Minn in 1969; has two daughters and one son. Formerly, gardener, teacher, actor, reporter, BBC free-lance scriptwriter. Lecturer in Verse Composition, University of California, Santa Barbara, 1966. Since 1969, Member of the Department of Comparative Literature, University of California, Berkeley. Address: 1799 Spruce Street, Berkeley, California 94709, U.S.A.

PUBLICATIONS

Verse

> *Clear Lake Comes from Enjoyment,* with Denis Goacher. London, Spearman, 1959.
> *The Marriage Rite,* with Denis Goacher. Ditchling, Sussex, Ditchling Press, 1960.
> *The Ingathering of Love.* Santa Barbara, California, Unicorn Press, 1967.
> *The Blue Winged Bee: Love Poems of the VIth Dalai Lama and The Ingathering of Love.* London, Anvil Press Poetry, 1969.
> *Astapovo; or, What We Are to Do.* London, Anvil Press Poetry, 1970.
> *The Fletcher Song Book,* music by Preston Fletcher. London, Anvil Press Poetry, 1970.
> *The Crystal Mountain.* London, Anvil Press Poetry, 1970.

Other

> Translator, with Mary de Rachewiltz, *The Detail and the Design,* by Umberto Mastroianni. Bologna, Segnacolo, 1963.
> Translator, *Black Eros,* by Boris de Rachewiltz. London, Allen and Unwin, and New York, Lyle Stuart, 1964.
> Translator, *Introduction to African Art,* by Boris de Rachewiltz. New York, New American Library, 1965; London, John Murray, 1966.
> Translator, *The Poems of Catullus.* London, Penguin, 1966; revised edition, Penguin, and Berkeley, University of California Press, 1969.
> Translator, with Peter Jay, *The Poems of Meleager.* London, Anvil Press Poetry, 1974.

Peter Whigham comments:

[On "schools" of poetry] I recognise that the future literary historian, should he mention me at all, will have a category for me, but what that will be I am unable to say. Perhaps I can answer your question in a negative way, by saying I am against the influence of Yvor Winters (in America) and F. R. Leavis (in England).

I can say that my long maturing work on Catullus has been the principal means whereby I have been able to find my own voice. As regards "subject," I believe that this, rather than technique, is now the test of a poet's sincerity – a reversal of the situation Pound proclaimed earlier in the century. And as regards "influences," the single most influential contemporary figure has been Ezra Pound; historical figure, Catullus; country, Italy; notion, the world of fluid forces, or figuratively speaking, the age of the gods; circumstance, uncertainty of any continuing identity

other than that of being a poet. I simply do not find any "major" themes in my
work, or "ususal" verse forms or "characteristic" stylistic devices – though doubtless such are there to be discerned by others. As for "general sources and influences," to what I have already said could be added the English countryside and
Shakespeare's plays and poems, as pervasive throughout. Other indications of my
current attitude in literary matters can be found in the piece I wrote for the *Poetry
Book Society Bulletin* for Spring 1969, and in the blurb, written on my own behalf,
to the volume *Astapovo; or, What We Are to Do*. Finally, in the last few months, I
have found my interest turning to the Far East.

*   *   *

Peter Whigham's poetry deserves to be better known. He is one of the few
English poets of his generation to be firmly rooted in the modernist tradition and
has produced a considerable amount of interesting and varied writing as well as a
number of important translations. A few of his early poems are more likely to
survive than any produced by poets associated with "The Movement" or "The
Group." "The Orchard Is Not Cut Down" is short enough to quote in full:

> The orchard is gone. A space, con-
>   ventionally like Paaschendaele,
>   linearly framed by black rail-
> ings, rises to a wide field on
> which, inert, the milk-brown cows sun
>   themselves and where the busy mail-
>   van and the bus brightly curtail,
> on the road sudden as a gun
> the field, – the vanished grove.
>
>   No dream
>   of priest or king can empower mind
>   to seize the blossom on the wind;
> only, in passing, I have seen
>
>   swan leaning on confused swan
>   fall inwards like a folding fan.

Whigham is probably best known as the author of the Penguin Catullus, and to
have produced the liveliest English version of this poet is no mean achievement.
Cyril Connolly defined its quality when he wrote: "I feel that he has really lived
these poems; he brings back his translations as something that actually happened to
him, like Noah's dove with the olive, and this enables him to bring the longer
poems to life, in some cases for the first time."

The Blue Winged Bee is Whigham's finest collection of original poetry – most
impressive is a long poem, *The Ingathering of Love*. This is difficult to quote from
adequately as it creates its effect by the slow accumulation of images. Here are a
few lines to give a glimpse of its quality:

> All day the willow weeps by the summerhouse.
> Bits of grass, the detritus of summer, lie on the floor;
> the birds are muted
>   appeased by nest-building & egg laying:
> a plane fades like mild thunder and
> the sun, an atmosphere, pervades the grey sky.

Whigham's recent book, *Astapovo* is, I think, less successful. He seems here to have lost his own voice in a harsh stridency foreign to his earlier writing. This perhaps presents an example of the bad influence certain kinds of American poetry can exert on an English poet.

Whigham's most recent work is an interesting translation of Meleager.

– William Cookson

WHISTLER, (Alan Charles) Laurence. English. Born in Eltham, Kent, 21 January 1912; younger brother of the artist Rex Whistler. Educated at Stowe School; Balliol College, Oxford (Chancellor's Essay Prize, 1934), B.A. 1934. Served in the Rifle Brigade, 1939–45: Captain, 1942. Married Jill Furse in 1939 (died, 1944), one son and one daughter; Theresa Furse in 1950, one son and one daughter. Glass Engraver: goblets in point engraving, and church windows and panels at Sherborne Abbey; Moreton, Dorset; Checkendon, Oxfordshire; Ilton, Somerset; Eastbury, Berkshire; Guards Chapel, London. Recipient: King's Gold Medal for Poetry, 1934; Rockefeller-Atlantic Award, 1945. Honorary Fellow, Balliol College, Oxford, 1974. O.B.E. (Officer, Order of the British Empire), 1955; C.B.E. (Commander, Order of the British Empire), 1973. Fellow, Royal Society of Literature, 1960. Address: Little Place, Lyme Regis, Dorset, England.

PUBLICATIONS

Verse

Children of Hertha and Other Poems. Oxford, Holywell Press, 1929.
Proletaria, en avant! A Poem of Socialism. Oxford, Alden Press, 1932.
Armed October and Other Poems. London, Cobden Sanderson, 1932.
Four Walls: Poems. London, Heinemann, 1934; New York, Macmillan, 1935.
The Emperor Heart. London, Heinemann, 1936; New York, Macmillan, 1937.
In Time of Suspense. London, Heinemann, 1940.
Ode to the Sun and Other Poems. London, Heinemann, 1942.
Who Live in Unity. London, Heinemann, 1944.
¡OHO! Certain Two-Faced Individuals Now Exposed by the Bodley Head, with Rex Whistler. London, Lane, 1946.
The World's Room: The Collected Poems of Laurence Whistler. London, Heinemann, 1949.
The View from This Window: Poems. London, Hart Davis, 1956.
Audible Silence. London, Hart Davis, 1961.
Fingal's Cave: A Poem. Birmingham, F. E. Pardoe, 1963.
To Celebrate Her Living. London, Hart Davis, 1967.
On Llangynidr Bridge. Cambridge, Golden Head Press, 1968.
For Example: Ten Sonnets in Sequence to a New Pattern. Birmingham, F. E. Pardoe, 1969.
Way: Two Affirmations, in Glass and Verse. Cambridge, Golden Head Press, 1969.

Other

Sir John Vanbrugh, Architect and Dramatist 1664–1726.   London, Cobden San-
    derson, 1938.
Jill Furse: Her Nature and Her Poems, 1915–1944.   London, Chiswick Press,
    1945.
The Masque of Christmas: Dramatic Joys of the Festival Old and New.   London,
    Curtain Press, 1947.
The English Festivals.   London, Heinemann, 1947.
Rex Whistler 1905–1944: His Life and His Drawings.   London, Art and Tech-
    nics, 1948.
The Engraved Glass of Laurence Whistler.   Hitchin, Hertfordshire, Cupid Press,
    1952.
Rex Whistler: The Koenigsmark Drawings.   London, Richards Press, 1952.
The Kissing Bough: A Christmas Custom.   London, Heinemann, 1953.
The Imagination of Vanbrugh and His Fellow Artists.   London, Art and
    Technics-Batsford, 1954.
Stowe: A Guide to the Gardens.   London, Country Life, 1956; revised edition,
    London, Hillier, 1968.
Engraved Glass, 1952–58.   London, Hart Davis, 1959.
The Work of Rex Whistler, with Ronald Fuller.   London, Batsford, 1960.
The Initials in the Heart (autobiography).   London, Hart Davis, and Boston,
    Houghton Mifflin, 1964.
Pictures on Glass.   London, Cupid Press, 1972.

Editor, *Selected Poems of John Keats.*   London, Grey Walls Press, 1950.

*   *   *

Laurence Whistler has gained a double reputation, as a poet and as an engraver
on glass, whose work in both media is characterised by technical skill, elegance,
and lyrical sensibility. His notes on "Fore-Rhyme" and on "A Woven Sonnet"
reveal his preoccupation with poetic form and with the possibilities of extending
traditional formal patterns in the interests of greater exactness and imaginative
power.

Most of his early work, for all its easy grace, is little more than accomplished
verse-writing. The death of his beloved first wife, Jill Furse, gave him a powerful
poetic theme which preoccupied him over a long period. Indeed, many of his
poems, continually revised, may be regarded as parts of one long elegiac poem,
which appears to have assumed its final shape in *To Celebrate Her Living,* a volume
related to his prose work, *The Initials in the Heart.* The tone is varied, ranging from
lyrical tenderness to sombre reflection, and the movement of the verse sometimes
recalls the subtle yet direct mode of utterance perfected by the English Metaphysical poets:

> She whom I loved – she whom I love
> Years deep in abject death – who was,
> Who will be that to which I move
> In this or any world . . .

Apart from this sequence, Laurence Whistler's work includes a number of poems
which are likely to survive when the verse of flashier and inferior talents is
forgotten. The range and quality of his art are reflected in such poems as "The

Guest," "A Form of Epitaph," and "A Portrait in the Guards," an elegy on his brother Rex.

– John Press

WHITBREAD, Thomas (Bacon). American. Born in Bronxville, New York, 22 August 1931. Educated at St. James School, Maryland; Amherst College, Massachusetts, B.A. 1952 (Phi Beta Kappa); Harvard University, Cambridge, Massachusetts, M.A. 1953, Ph.D. 1959. Instructor, 1959–62, Assistant Professor, 1962–65, and since 1965, Associate Professor of English, University of Texas, Austin. Recipient: *Paris Review* Aga Khan Prize, for fiction, 1961; O. Henry Award, for fiction, 1962; National Endowment for the Arts grant, 1966. Address: Department of English, University of Texas, Austin, Texas 78712, U.S.A.

PUBLICATIONS

Verse

Four Infinitives. New York, Harper, 1964.

Other

Editor, *Seven Contemporary Authors: Essays on Cozzens, Miller, West, Golding, Heller, Albee and Powers.* Austin, University of Texas Press, 1966.

Thomas Whitbread comments:

Themes: time, change, love, the possibilities of human excellence. Subjects: my remembered past, my present, my anticipated future; public events, railroads, cemeteries, sports, other people, places and their auras, the mind and its creatures. Verse forms: sonnets, blank verse, various stanzaic patterns. Devices: irony, punning, use of verse forms for emphases, Tennysonian straightforwardness.

*   *   *

In a period that often admires mere surface complexity in poetry, Thomas Whitbread represents a refreshing return to poetry's main traditions. In his work, a surface directness and seeming simplicity deepen with a kind of surreptitious inevitability into new and striking insights. His method, a contemporary adaptation of Wordsworth's practise in the *Lyrical Ballads,* of finding the extraordinary in the common experiences of everyday life, is defined in the opening lines of "A Pool":

> This is a pool which bears deep looking into
> Beneath moon-shadow trees, beneath the mud
> I imagine at its bottom, and beneath
> All its appearances as just a pool.

Whitbread is traditional not only in this respect but in his handling of form as well. He is a highly disciplined technician with a sure ability to manipulate rhythmic and sound patterns. "Christmas Dinner" is a splendid example of the sureness of his ear, and he writes sonnets with genuine skill.

The poems collected in *Four Infinitives* are preoccupied with the conflict between permanence and impermanence, and this theme is suggested by the title with its reference to an active or verbal form capable of transformation or suspension to the substantive. The relative permanence of memory and art is postulated as answers to change, and the last two lines of "Christmas Dinner" crystallize this solution: "Always the juice lies locked in the grape-design/Cut-glassware while we take a walk in snow."

But the poems owe much of their strength to the fact that this formulation is deliberately an ambiguous one. The bicycle of childhood, and trains and railroad tracks, with their invitation to transience, retain their lure. The "National Limited" pauses "indefinitely" for revelation:

> I am all Ohio deep in night and snow.
> I am midway somewhere. Where, I do not know.
> $\qquad\qquad\qquad\qquad$ – from "A Pool"

And the poet's own art of printed words, no matter how disciplined, can dissolve into a dark motion:

> $\qquad\qquad$ . . . to think
> All of a sudden, that surely the river Styx
> Runs below this walk of bricks, and flows black ink . . .
> $\qquad\qquad\qquad\qquad$ – "Autumnal Meditation

> $\qquad\qquad\qquad\qquad\qquad$ – Gaynor F. Bradish

WHITE, Ivan. British. Born in Seven Kings, Essex, 23 May 1929. Married; has two children. Educated at the University of York; University of Manchester. Recipient: Guinness Prize, 1964. Address: 28 Pikes Lane, Glossop, Derbyshire, England.

PUBLICATIONS

Verse

Cry Wolf: A Poem of Urgency. London, Hephaestus Circle, 1962.
Crow's Fall. London, Cape Goliard Press, and New York, Grossman, 1969.

*   *   *

Ivan White is an intellectual – one may even say metaphysical – poet, of sensitivity, seriousness, modesty, sensibility and feeling. His poetry is only occasionally banal (". . . I thought of Keats and Dylan Thomas, / How suspect their respective loves became in death. / The one for a woman unmoved, / the other for humanity") and it is significant that when he is, he is also, usually, inaccurate (Fanny Brawne was not "unmoved"); but this comes from an uncharacteristically long, prosaic and rank bad "conversation" poem called "The Suspect Love." His best piece is the title piece from *Crow's Fall*, about a bird striking the stained-glass window of a buttress and killing itself:

> Falling into like black it scraped
> Mortar from arms that were flesh stripped.
>
> As earth broke over its slight head
> The beak point rasped against fluted
>
> Rock poised towards the impetus
> Of its feathered dive. . . .
>
> They replaced the glass. . . .
> . . . an act of half truth,
>
> Deep from which stress drove the dark bird
> Like a maxim that somehow strayed
>
> From its claw holes or grip on life
> That slipped, leaving no trace nor grief.

This may have been influenced or prompted by reading Ted Hughes; but it contains more thought, less hideously gratuitous violence, than anything by Hughes. Unfortunately White has written few other poems as effective: his chief fault seems to be an inability to discover a personal rhythm: too many of his poems are spoiled because they read like prose chopped arbitrarily into lines.

– Martin Seymour-Smith

WHITE, Kenneth. British. Born in Glasgow, Lanarkshire, 28 April 1936. Educated at the University of Glasgow, M.A. (honours) in French and German 1959; University of Munich; University of Paris. Married to Marie-Claude Charlut. Lecturer in English, the Sorbonne, Paris, 1962–63, and Faculty of Letters, Pau, France, 1967–68; Lecturer in French, University of Glasgow, 1963–67. Since 1969, Lecturer in English, University of Paris. Founder, *Jargon Papers*, Glasgow, *Feuillage*, Pau, and *The Feathered Egg*, Paris. Address: Residence d'Aspin III, 64000 Pau, France.

PUBLICATIONS

Verse

Wild Coal.   Paris, Club des Etudiants d'Anglais, 1963.
The Cold Wind of Dawn.   London, Cape, 1966.
The Most Difficult Area.   London, Cape Goliard Press, and New York, Grossman, 1968.

Other

En Toute Candeur (includes essays and verse), translated by Pierre Leyris.
Paris, Mercure de France, 1964.
Letters from Gourgounel (autobiography).   London, Cape, 1966.

Translator, *Selected Poems*, by André Breton.   London, Cape Goliard Press, 1969.
Translator, *Ode to Charles Fourier*, by André Breton.   London, Cape Goliard Press, 1969.

Manuscript Collection: National Library of Scotland, Edinburgh.

Critical Studies: by Hans ten Berge, in *Raster* (Amsterdam), Autumn 1970; *The Truth of Poetry* by Michael Hamburger, London, Weidenfeld and Nicolson, 1969; unpublished thesis by Lynn Taylor Novak, University of Southern California, Los Angeles, 1974.

Kenneth White comments:

I can call myself a poet providing the word be adequately defined. I like Elie Faure's description: "The poet is he who never ceases to have confidence precisely because he does not attach himself to any port . . . but pursues . . . a form that flies through the tempest and is lòst unceasingly in the eternal becoming."
The theme of my poetry (and prose) is the way to the complete and utter realisation of myself (which I see as the real and central content of art, without which it degenerates into a collection of more or less formally or psychologically interesting comments or objects). With a play on words and with the knowledge that "whiteness" is the synthesis of all colours, I tend, for the moment, to call this "complete realisation of myself" – "whiteness," and to translate moments of unity by terms indicative of whiteness. My aim, beyond the temporary realisations of "whiteness," is to ground this idea, this myth (as programme), to situate the ecstasy extensively, and find, discover, create a "white world."
In more philosophical terms, I see myself living in a world of separation and scission, and my aim, my desire is to move beyond this world of separation into unity. I find the theme in Hegel, who speaks of the early Greek world as "an immaculate world unadulterated by any scission." While the Heglian synthesis, however, is purely intellectual, ideal, my aim is concrete realisation.
In this direction, I have been influenced, or confirmed, by Whitman, and

Nietzsche (critique of present civilization, affirmation of life, will to self-realisation). Both of these, also, mean the end of a certain Western culture and, as I see it, an opening to the East (which can help us to discover a deeper West, create, in the West, a civilisation more existentially alive, more integrated, rather than merely mechanically active and essentially incoherent).

It's in the East that I find the terms and the vocabulary (and examples) more consonant with my search. In *L'Esprit Synthetique de la Chine*, Liou Kia-Hway speaks of the aim of Eastern life-thought (as contrasted with the radical dualism and abstraction of the West) as "a concrete totality which suffers no separation," penetrating beyond the dualisms into the "ground of being."

The way I see myself travelling towards this ground-realisation is the *sunyavada*, which Linnart Mäll, in his *Terminologia Indica*, translates as "The Zero Way" – "a quite original way of thought, so original it seems impossible to compare it with anything else."

My travelling on this way I express through poems (and prose), the poems, in general, expressing more intense moments of concentration, the prose recounting the travelling, attempting a synthesis of information, interspersed with moments of higher unity. The poems are characterised perhaps by intuitive rhythm, inner form, simplicity (i.e. a highly organised complexity, without elaboration) and a recurrent iconography (gulls and recent convergent image of the Rosy Gull), which makes for a characteristic "world." They are meant to satisfy demands, desires such as Bashō expresses: "There are many who write verse, but few who keep to the rules of the heart," understanding "heart" here not sentimentally, but as a psycho-sensual/intellectual synthesis, the poem itself being such a synthesis, uniting a content of ontological significance with an aesthetic of delight. "Before a poet can write haiku," writes Otsuji, and the same goes for poems in general as I understand them, "he must find a unity within his life which must come from the effort to discover his true self."

How far do I think I've travelled on my way? After passing through "the most difficult area," I'd say, with Paul Klee, "a little nearer to the heart of creation than is normal but still too far away."

*   *   *

If we except the more ecstatic passages, *Letters from Gourgounel* contains some of Kenneth White's most achieved writing to date in the sense that in the prose of that book we see his language engaging with substantial, particular experience more fully than has been the general rule in his poetry. It is not simply that much of his earlier poetry was too content with routine romantic gestures and unsubstantiated claims ("the deep-down poetry I trade my life for" . . . "I speak in knowledge to all men / the great things and the beautiful I bring"). It is rather that in his poetry he has set himself the difficult task of exploring those areas of experience where emptiness and silence may be sensed not in terms of negation but in terms of a more positive approach to a sense of immanence and revelation. Thus we have references to such phenomena as "this light that is / the limit of austerity / and makes words blind"; statements like "at the limits of saying / the soul flies to the mouth / and the poem is born"; and poems such as "In the Emptiness" which assert, in the emptiness, an experience of "reality right to the bone."

The general difficulty, then, is to reconcile the mystic's pull towards wordless-ness and the poet's ineradicable dependence on words. In particular, the poetry's frequent resort to assertion, to statements *about* experience, may be characterised both by abstractions and by a lack of clear focus upon such concrete details as are mentioned. To what extent White is going to solve such a problem, in a manner germane to his sensibility, remains to be seen. But there are several poems (e.g.

"Extraordinary Moment," "Sesshu") which do seem to indicate a possibility: these have clearly learned from oriental models, and their strength is that their focus on particulars *is* sharp and their implications are clear without being overspelt.

– Robin Fulton

WHITEHEAD, James. American. Born in St. Louis, Missouri, 15 March 1936. Educated at Central High School, Jackson, Mississippi; Vanderbilt University, Nashville, Tennessee, B.A. in philosophy 1959, M.A. in English 1960; University of Iowa, Iowa City, M.F.A. 1965. Married to Gen Graeber; has seven children. Member of the Faculty, Millsaps College, Jackson, Mississippi, 1960–63. Currently, Associate Professor of English, University of Arkansas, Fayetteville. Recipient: Bread Loaf Writers Conference Robert Frost Fellowship, 1967; Guggenheim grant, 1972. Address: Department of English, University of Arkansas, Fayetteville, Arkansas 72701, U.S.A.

PUBLICATIONS

Verse

Domains: Poems. Baton Rouge, Louisiana State University Press, 1966.

Novel

Joiner. New York, Knopf, 1971.

*   *   *

There is a strong sense of place and personality in James Whitehead's writing. In both his book of poems, *Domains*, and his more recent novel, *Joiner*, real people live in real houses. The novel contains flowerings of the earlier poems, suggesting the depth to which Mr. Whitehead's vision is rooted in the rich earth of the places and people he has known.

The concrete imagery of the poems in *Domains* often suggest Frost. Not a cold fire-under-ice Frost, but a passionate poet who sings the brakes and bayous of Mississippi as Frost sang the fields and west-running brooks of New Hampshire. Which is not to suggest that Mr. Whitehead is a nature poet; his river raises "floaters," drowned people, "Bringing a stern sight down to all of us / In the country where only the deaths of the aged were clear." His places are always peopled, and his poems suggest that there *was* a Dallas Tanksley, a Leroy Smith, and a dead baby brother.

Mr. Whitehead is a witty poet ("Walking Around," "Love Poem in Midwinter") with a fine feel for irony ("Desertions," "The Lawyer"), but his best poetry is imbued with a passionate sense of life and its evanescence. He is torn between the domains of the crusading spirit and of the lusting flesh, but in his loveliest lines they become one kingdom. At the end of his title poem, "Domains," he prays for the strength to see that he is ". . . not fit / To serve at once / Two dying bodies with equal wit." But in his best poems he does just that.

– Norman T. Gates

WHITMAN, Ruth. American. Born in New York City, 28 May 1922. Educated at Radcliffe College, Cambridge, Massachusetts, B.A. (magna cum laude) 1944. Married Morton Sacks in 1966; has two daughters and one son. Editorial Assistant, 1941–42, and Educational Editor, 1944–45, Houghton Mifflin Company, publishers, Boston; Editor, Harvard University Press, 1945–60; Poetry Editor, *Audience*, Cambridge, Massachusetts, 1958–63. Director, Cambridge Center for Adult Education Poetry Workshop, 1964–68. Since 1968, Scholar in Poetry, Radcliffe Institute, and since 1970, Instructor in Poetry, Radcliffe College. Since 1971, Director of the Massachusetts Schools Poetry Writing Program. Recipient: MacDowell Fellowship, 1962, 1964, 1972; Poetry Society of America Lyric Award, 1962, and Alice Fay di Castagnola Award, 1968; Tane Award (*Massachusetts Review*, Amherst), 1964; National Foundation for Jewish Culture grant, 1968, 1969; Radcliffe Institute grant, 1968, 1969; Jewish Book Council of America Kovner Award, 1969; Chanin Award, for translation, 1972; National Endowment for the Arts grant, 1974. Address: 70 Williston Road, Brookline, Massachusetts 02146, U.S.A.

PUBLICATIONS

Verse

    Blood and Milk Poems. New York, Clark and Way, 1963.
    The Marriage Wig and Other Poems. New York, Harcourt Brace, 1968.
    The Passion of Lizzie Borden: New and Selected Poems. New York, October House, 1973.

Other

    Editor and Translator, *An Anthology of Modern Yiddish Poetry.* New York, October House, 1966.

    Translator, with others, *Selected Poems*, by Alain Bosquet. New York, New Directions, 1962.
    Translator, with others, *Short Friday and Other Stories*, by Isaac Bashevis Singer. New York, Farrar Strauss, 1964; London, Secker and Warburg, 1967.
    Translator, with others, *The Séance and Other Stories*, by Isaac Bashevis Singer. New York, Farrar Straus, 1968; London, Cape, 1970.
    Translator, *Selected Poems*, by Jacob Glatstein. New York, October House, 1972.

Ruth Whitman comments:

(1970) The point of writing poetry is to celebrate all human experience and to communicate its value and intensity to other human beings. Technically, poetry must have a complete command of strict forms and then be free to abandon them and to use any device to make its rhetoric more direct and telling.

(1974) The best statement I have is this poem from *The Marriage Wig:*

A Spider on My Poem

Black one,
I was going to frighten you away,
but now I beg you,
stay!
You're what I need.
This poem needs real legs, faster than the eye.
And a belly with magic string in it
made from spit,
designed to catch and hold whatever flies by.
Also, the uninvited way
you came, boldly, fast as a spider,
till you paused all real in the middle of the page.
Everything I need.
Please stay.

*   *   *

Ruth Whitman's three volumes have established her as a significant American woman poet. From the beginning her poetry was personal, subjective, and strongly formal. Throughout Mrs. Whitman's poetry is the concern with the discovery of herself through her heritage. Jewish to the core, she explores that heritage in a variety of poems ("The Old Man's Mistress," "The Lost Steps," and "Touro Synagogue") about her family and homeland.

The Marriage Wig and Other Poems is a much fuller exploration of the experience of being Jewish and Ruth Whitman. The poems ring with an authenticity lacking in the first volume. Although a few of the poems strain after too much identification with the past, most are effective transformations of past and present.

Her third volume, *The Passion of Lizzie Borden: New and Selected Poems*, not only contains the best poems of the first volumes but some excellent new ones. In addition to the personal, autobiographical and heritage poems, Mrs. Whitman looks outward at the world larger than her family's, if not as definite. The poems still express Mrs. Whitman, but her feelings, emotions, ideas are embodied in recent experiences. Several important poems explore the Greek heritage which is finally and inevitably brought together in the last poems, "Passover 1970," with the Hebrew. The book may represent a closing out or exhaustion of these materials, though not of Mrs. Whitman. Her energy, vitality, and technical proficiency should enable her to continue her excellent work.

– Richard Damashek

WHITTEMORE, (Edward) Reed (Jr.). American. Born in New Haven, Connecticut, 11 September 1919. Educated at Yale University, New Haven, Connecticut, A.B. 1941; Princeton University, New Jersey, 1945–46. Served in the United States Army Air Force, 1941–45. Married Helen Lundeen in 1950; has four children. Member of the Faculty, 1947–62, Chairman of the English Department, 1962–64, and Professor of English, 1962–67, Carleton College, Northfield, Minnesota; Bain-Swiggett Lecturer, Princeton University, 1967–68. Since 1968, Professor of English, University of Maryland, College Park. Editor, *Furioso*, 1939–53, and *Carleton Miscellany*, 1960–64, both in Northfield, Minnesota. Since 1969, Literary Editor, *New Republic*, Washington, D.C. Consultant in Poetry, Library of Congress, Washington, D.C., 1964–65. Recipient: Emily Clark Balch Prize (*Virginia Quarterly Review*, Charlottesville), 1962; National Endowment for the Arts grant, 1968; National Institute of Arts and Letters Award of Merit, 1970. Litt.D.: Carleton College. 1971. Address: 3409 Woodley Road, N.W., Washington, D.C. 20016, U.S.A.

PUBLICATIONS

Verse

Heroes and Heroines: Poems. New York, Reynal, 1947.
An American Takes a Walk and Other Poems. Minneapolis, University of Minnesota Press, 1956.
The Self-Made Man and Other Poems. New York, Macmillan, 1959.
The Boy from Iowa: Poems and Essays. New York, Macmillan, 1962.
Return, Alpheus: A Poem for the Literary Elders of Phi Beta Kappa. Williamsburg, Virginia, King and Queen Press, 1965.
Poems, New and Selected. Minneapolis, University of Minnesota Press, 1967.
50 Poems 50. Minneapolis, University of Minnesota Press, 1970.
The Mother's Breast and the Father's House. Boston, Houghton Mifflin, 1974.

Other

Little Magazines. Minneapolis, University of Minnesota Press, 1963.
The Fascination of the Abomination: Poems, Stories and Essays. New York, Macmillan, 1963.
Ways of Misunderstanding Poetry. Washington, D.C., Library of Congress, 1965.
From Zero to the Absolute: Essays. New York, Crown, 1968.

Editor, *Browning.* New York, Dell, 1960.

*   *   *

In the essay "But Seriously," published in *The Fascination of the Abomination,* Reed Whittemore describes himself as a person with "the disposition, the temperament of a humorist," one of those who sides "pretty steadily" with those "mundane eccentrics who have stood on the sidelines with the game in progress, and made frosty remarks instead of cheering." His vision, like that of the man who craves balance in "A Porch Chair," is "urban,/Modern and secular" (*The Self-Made Man*). His approach frequently yields what he himself describes as the "ideal poem" of *The New Yorker:*

> a straightforward thing, in rhyme and stanzas, which displays the well-managed sensibility of an intelligent private individual at work on the world of his immediate neighbourhood.

Whittemore's materials are "his immediate neighbourhood" (paperboys, U.S. 1, Peck and Peck, popular magazines, a high school band, a radio, winter), "himself and his nearest and dearest." His hero is a self-made man, but one who, though he may *appear* god-like, the master of his destiny, to his audience, knows his own limitations: the void within him, the discontentment of trivial accomplishments and frustrated dreams. His hero can be Prufrockian:

> I have begun, been begun, more than most; I have even
> Started a book of beginnings (unfinished). . . .
> > – from "At the Beginning of My Sabbatical Year"

But, both as poet and modern man, Whittemore is not satisfied with this unheroic, "attendant lord" material; his heroes do not want to be "*so* middle class" (*The Boy from Iowa*). At times he is angry, as in "A Teacher":

> He hated them all one by one but wanted to show them
> What was Important and Vital and by God if
> They thought they'd never have use for it he was
> Sorry as hell for them, that's all, with their genteel
> Mercantile Main Street Babbitt
> Bourgeois-barbaric faces. . . .

At times he is bitter. He thinks of himself "As a Renaissance Man manqué, many parts, many interests / Yet to bear fruits" and asks:

> Why did the children shriek right under his window?
> Why were the days like a junk shop? – the hours in fragments,
> His desk still cluttered with coffee cups, Longfellow, stamps. . . .
> > – from "The Renaissance Man"

Frequently he is tired and sad, as in the conclusion of "The Renaissance Man" and in "Three Poems to Jackson":

> My third book will appear in the spring, a small book,
> A slight book,
> Containing no plays or long narrative poems,
> Borrowing hardly at all from the Middle Ages,
> Making few affirmations, avoiding inversions,
> Using iambics distrustfully, favoring lines
> Of odd lengths and irony.
> > I am forty.
> I seem to know the dimensions of what I can do
> And the season to do it in.

Or, looking out of his study window at the gray, cold winter and reflecting on Keats and Tennyson, poets who

have warn, sunny lands tucked away
In their serried works where galoshes, woodpiles, aspirin
And the like are never required,

he writes:

If I had talent to make such a place I would not,
I think, scribble about it but would just
Move in, settle down and endeavor to blot
From my memory all the aforesaid icicles,
Letting the future of literature go for heat
On earth, green trees for man, and the sweet
Ease of a life held in tropical trust.
                                    – "Out of My Study Window"

But most often Whittemore is quietly observing, committed to seeing and reassessing (deft, quick, though often strangely dispassionate), not far from his own description of "an ideal satirist who is happy in his work (taking it 'seriously') and who, though perhaps stuffed to the gills with subconscious aggressions, has also a sense of justice, truth, all that" (*The Fascination of the Abomination*). His is a genial satire "informed with pity" which proceeds from "a sense of all of us being in the same leaky boat." It may very well be a light satire, elusive and detached because it masks a deep involvement and concern:

I go digging for clams once every two or three years
Just to keep my hand in (I usually cut it),
And I'm sure that whenever I do so I tell the same story
Of how, at the age of four, I was trapped by the tide
As I clammed a sandbar. It's no story at all,
But I tell it and tell it. It serves my small lust
To be thought of as someone who's lived.

                                    – "Clamming"

Whittemore's gifts are many. Aside from his skilful satire, his concern with the peculiarly American problems of the non-heroic middle class aspirant, and his reflection of topical issues ("Lines Composed upon Reading an Announcement by Civil Defense Authorities Recommending That I Build a Bombshelter in My Backyard," "The Citizens Haven't Been Able"), his lyric voice is apparent in "On a Summer Sunday" and "Still Life" and he writes persuasively of the poetic process in "The Philadelphia Vireo." He is a poet so constantly aware of his "artistic heritage" (unlike the "zero-hunters" he describes in *From Zero to the Absolute*) that his poetry is saturated with literary allusions and echoes. At the same time its compression and direct simplicity, and its use of intensifiers, assure its immediacy.

                                    – Rosalie Murphy

WIENERS, John (Joseph).   American.   Born in Boston, Massachusetts, 6 January 1934. Educated at Boston College, A. B. in English 1954; Black Mountain College,

North Carolina, 1955–56; State University of New York, Buffalo (Teaching Fellow), 1965–67. Library Clerk, Lamont Library, Harvard University, Cambridge, Massachusetts, 1955–57; Actor and Stage Manager, Poets Theatre, Cambridge, 1956; Assistant Bookkeeper, 8th Street Bookshop, New York, 1962–63; Subscriptions Editor, Jordan Marsh Company, Boston, 1963–65; Class Leader, Beacon Hill Free School, Boston, 1973. Since 1957, Co-Founding Editor, *Measure*, Boston. Recipient: Poets Foundation grant, 1961; New Hope Foundation Award, 1963; National Endowment for the Arts grant, 1966, 1968; National Institute of Arts and Letters Award, 1968; Committe on Poetry grant, 1970, 1971, 1972. Address: 44 Joy Street, Boston, Massachusetts 02114, U.S.A.

PUBLICATIONS

Verse

The Hotel Wentley Poems. San Francisco, Auerhahn Press, 1958; revised edition, 1965.
Ace of Pentacles. New York, Carr and Wilson, 1964.
Chinoiserie. San Francisco, Dave Haselwood, 1965.
Hart Crane, Harry Crosby, I See You Going over the Edge. Detroit, Artists' Workshop Press, 1966.
King Solomon's Magnetic Quiz. Pleasant Valley, New York, Kriya Press, 1967.
Pressed Wafer. Buffalo, New York, Gallery Upstairs Press, 1967.
Selected Poems. London, Cape, 1968.
Unhired. Mount Horeb, Wisconsin, Perishable Press, 1968.
A Letter to Charles Olson. New York, Charters, 1968.
Asylum Poems. New York, Angel Hair Books, 1969.
Nerves. London, Cape Goliard Press, and New York, Grossman, 1970.
Youth. New York, Phoenix Book Shop, 1970.
Selected Poems. London, Cape, and New York, Grossman, 1972.

Plays

Still-Life (produced New York, 1961).
Asphodel in Hell's Despite (produced New York, 1963).
Anklesox and Five Shoelaces (produced New York, 1966).

Television Play: *The Spirit of Romance* (documentary), with Robert Danean, 1965.

Other

Untitled Essay on Frank O'Hara. New York, Doubleday, 1969.
A Memory of Black Mountain College. Cambridge, Massachusetts Institute of Technology Press, 1969.

Bibliography: "John Wieners: A Checklist" by George F. Butterick, in *Athanor 3* (Clarkson, New York), Summer-Fall 1973.

Critical Studies: by Denise Levertov, in *Poetry* (Chicago), February 1965; Robert Duncan, in *The Nation* (New York), 31 May 1965; Lewis Warsh, in *The Boston Phoenix*, January 1973; interview, in *Gay Sunshine* (San Francisco), March 1973.

John Wieners comments:

(1970) My themes are heartfelt ones of youth and manly desire. Their subjects are despair, frustration, ideal satisfaction, with Biblical and classical referential echoes. Their forms are declarative, orderly and true, without invention. General sources are Edna St. Vincent Millay, United States prose writers of the twentieth century, lyricists in the Greek anthology. Homer; Sappho; Horace; Virgilius; the songs of Geoffrey Chaucer, and subsequent strains of the English tradition. Characteristic stylistic devices are the direct address of German lieder, Near Eastern intimacy and Chinese abbreviation.

(1974) Poetry since 16 has been an obsession, every day, every minute, hearkening to the form of poetry, its practitioners and personables continues to remain fixed as divinities equal to those of the French novelists since 1945 or the Pléiades of court presentation. I have kept the sun and myself upon a balcony bent under its power to lead my attainment towards magnitudinous worldly success and ultimately the presentation towards one person of its worth. For what would it matter if I could not be of use or of importance to this possible derelict in the world's eyes, but to my heart, husband-god, king-emperor. And yet not that. Simply a poor person in need of myself.

Along its possession blossoms many rewards, leisure, conversation, books, friends, entertainment for the ultimate collected editions to merit his devotion.

*   *   *

I like John Wieners' poems and especially the casualness of the line which draws its lyric value out of the past into the moment and makes the world (not to say the life) it evokes alive, under a veil of sadness. That sadness appears to be one in which the highest and strongest emotions are written about almost langorously, the emotion slowing down the movement of words through the poet's head or the passage of the words from the lips to the page. At instances when the mind is alert, Wieners' tendency is an attempt to reconcile his life with the rest of the world and in doing this he addresses not his muse – directly – but through the muse or the medium through which his suffering flows, society, or the life that has forced him to separate himself from reality. I think it takes a lot of nerve to write about feeling sad if only because it means you are putting that feeling up front, are asking the reader to listen to your problems, what's bothering you.

A long time ago I realized that what I liked best about poetry, music, art, etc., were those works that brought me up – that either made me happy or were in some way inspiring. Listening to the Blues has always been difficult for this reason and listening to the Blues when down yourself is like drinking – a consolation, and a reminder of the pain and frustration that exist apart from your own troubles, whatever. Alone with himself, Wieners is faced not only with his memories but with the daemons that haunt it, making it all the more remarkable that the tone of his work is so soft, almost anonymous, clean and clear.

I'm writing now about his first large collection of poems, *Ace of Pentacles*, published in 1964, and less about the poet's earlier book, *The Hotel Wentley Poems*, published six years earlier. The latter mentioned work is much more direct as if Wieners' attention had surrounded various points of feeling which he could bounce off and rebounding rise, almost heroically, into the next line. In the work I've seen since 1964 there is less talk about unhappiness and more graphics, the emphasis on description with the commentary in the margin, suspended.

– Lewis Warsh

WILBUR, Richard (Purdy).   American.   Born in New York City, 1 March 1921. Educated at Amherst College, Massachusetts, B.A. 1942; Harvard University, Cambridge, Massachusetts, M.A. 1947. Served in the United States Army, 1943–45. Married Charlotte Ward in 1942; has one daughter and three sons. Member of the Society of Fellows, 1947–50, and Assistant Professor of English, 1950–54, Harvard University; Associate Professor of English, Wellesley College, Massachusetts, 1955–57. Since 1957, Professor of English, Wesleyan University, Middletown, Connecticut. General Editor, Laurel Poets series, Dell Publishing Company, New York. State Department Cultural Exchange Representative to the U.S.S.R., 1961. Recipient: Harriet Monroe Memorial Prize, 1948, and Oscar Blumenthal Prize, 1950 (*Poetry*, Chicago); Guggenheim Fellowship, 1952, 1963; American Academy in Rome Fellowship, 1954; Pulitzer Prize, 1957; National Book Award, 1957; Edna St. Vincent Millay Memorial Award, 1957; Ford Fellowship, for drama, 1960; Melville Cane Award, 1962; Bollingen Prize, for translation, 1963, and for verse, 1971; Sarah Josepha Hale Award, 1968; Brandeis University Creative Arts Award, 1970; Prix Henri Desfeuilles, 1971; Shelley Memorial Award, 1973. L.H.D.: Lawrence College, Appleton, Wisconsin, 1960; Washington University, St. Louis, 1964; D.Litt.: Amherst College, 1967. Member, American Academy of Arts and Sciences, and American Academy of Arts and Letters; Chancellor, Academy of American Poets. Agent: Gilbert Parker, Curtis Brown Ltd., 60 East 56th Street, New York, New York 10022. Address: Dodwells Road, Cummington, Massachusetts 01026, U.S.A.

PUBLICATIONS

Verse

The Beautiful Changes and Other Poems.   New York, Reynal, 1947.
Ceremony and Other Poems.   New York, Harcourt Brace, 1950.
Things of This World: Poems.   New York, Harcourt Brace, 1956; one section reprinted as *Digging to China*, New York, Doubleday, 1970.
Poems, 1943–1956.   London, Faber, 1957.
Advice to a Prophet and Other Poems.   New York, Harcourt Brace, 1961; London, Faber, 1962.
The Poems of Richard Wilbur.   New York, Harcourt Brace, 1963.
The Pelican from a Bestiary of 1120.   Stanbrook Abbey, Worcestershire, privately printed, 1963.
Prince Souvanna Phouma: An Exchange Between Richard Wilbur and William Jay Smith.   Williamstown, Massachusetts, Chapel Press, 1963.
Complaint.   New York, Phoenix Book Shop, 1968.
Walking to Sleep: New Poems and Translations.   New York, Harcourt Brace, 1969; London, Faber, 1971.
Seed Leaves.   Boston, Godine Press, 1974.

Recordings: *Poems*, Spoken Arts, 1959; *Richard Wilbur Reading His Own Poems*, Caedmon.

Plays

The Misanthrope, adaptation of the play by Molière (produced Cambridge, Massachusetts, 1955; New York, 1956). New York, Harcourt Brace, 1955; London, Faber, 1958.
Candide, with others, music by Leonard Bernstein, adaptation of the novel by Voltaire (produced New York, 1956; London, 1959). New York, Random House, 1957.
Tartuffe, adaptation of the play by Molière (produced Milwaukee, Wisconsin, 1964; New York, 1965). New York, Harcourt Brace, 1963; London, Faber, 1964.
School for Wives, adaptation of a play by Molière (produced New York 1971). New York, Harcourt Brace, 1971.

Other

Emily Dickinson: Three Views, with Louise Bogan and Archibald MacLeish. Amherst, Massachusetts, Amherst College Press, 1960.

Loudmouse (juvenile). London, Crowell Collier, and New York, Collier Macmillan, 1963.
Opposites (juvenile), with drawings by the author. New York, Harcourt Brace, 1973.

Editor, with Louis Untermeyer and Karl Shapiro, *Modern American and Modern British Poetry*, revised shorter edition. New York, Harcourt Brace, 1955.
Editor, *A Bestiary* (anthology). New York, Pantheon Books, 1955.
Editor, *Complete Poems of Poe*. New York, Dell, 1959.
Editor, *Selected Poems*, by John Keats. New York, Dell, 1959.
Editor, with Alfred Harbage, *Poems of Shakespeare*. London, Penguin, 1966; revised edition, as *The Narrative Poems, and Poems of Doubtful Authenticity*, 1974.

Translator, *The Funeral of Bobo*, by Joseph Brodsky. Ann Arbor, Michigan, Ardis, n.d.

Bibliography: *Richard Wilbur: A Bibliographical Checklist* by John P. Field, Kent, Ohio, Kent State University Press, 1971.

Manuscript Collection: Amherst College.

Critical Studies: *Richard Wilbur* by Donald L. Hill, New York, Twayne, 1967; *Richard Wilbur* by Paul F. Cummins, Grand Rapids, Michigan, Eerdmans, 1971.

*   *   *

Richard Wilbur's poetry has consistently provided us with so many pleasures that one must feel almost ungrateful to question the premises upon which he has founded his art. So serene and altogether orderly a style would hardly seem possible to us today were it not for his exemplary presence, and the epithet "classical" inevitably forms at the lips when one thinks of his characteristic virtues, so often remarked by others: poise, tact, formal and metrical regularity, musicality of diction, ingenuity of phrasing, and a basic human decency that permits him to deal with a wide range of subjects without every betraying a tendency towards unkindness or casual cynicism. Where he has been critical of people or views of one kind or another, of political expediency or middle-class timidity, he has been so in a way at once charitable and forgiving. Wilbur's is the sage, liberally earnest, slightly rhetorical voice of a fellow we should very much like to know, if we believed he really existed, an extremely intelligent, witty and entertaining fellow who neither beats his wife nor is likely to be found in the company of indecorous multitudes of whatever persuasion. In short, the voice that pulses ever so lightly in Wilbur's verse suggests a refinement of sensibility and a soundness of judgment so satisfying that one is hard put to discern in it the contours of a man as we have been accustomed to men in our experience. One is stirred by Wilbur's verse, stirred not feeling but to admiration and to a rather even-headed delight that falls quite short of ecstasy.

Clearly it is not Wilbur's concerns that have seriously affected his inability to prove terribly exciting or even interesting to most of his contemporaries. Stevens, after all, has proven a central figure in modern poetry, and there are sufficient Stevensian echoes in Wilbur to permit us to speak of his epistemological probings, without of course suggesting that they are either as obsessive, original, or philosophically elaborated as Stevens'. More important, probably, is the relationship to Williams, and Wilbur's insistence that we must find ideas in things; however, though Wilbur was aware of the older poet's example, as which American poet is not, he has proven all but incapable of learning from it. It is not only the rhetoric that obscures the things themselves, though the swelling orotunidites of Wilbur's lovely verse do often distract attention from what are his ostensible concerns. More significant is the fact that Wilbur does not really care for things. What his verse celebrates is not the hard things of this world, but the imagination that makes possible delight, its own and others', in appropriating things for a variety of spiritual and psychological purposes. He tells us in "The Beautiful Changes" that beauty exists in things whether or not it is perceived by beholders, and he is anxious to assure us in another poem that "Love Calls Us to the Things of This World" even as the poem itself suggests we are called not a little by constraint, that could we be other than what we are should hardly respond to things as ordinary reality dictates we must. For Wilbur, and there is no mistaking this, the call to things is equivalent to what he describes as "the punctual rape of every blessèd day." The hero is not the man who submits, but the audacious artist, the visionary, Wilbur's "Juggler": "For him we batter our hands / Who has won for once over the world's weight."

Clearly, then, there is a tension implicit in Wilbur's verse, just the sort of tension that might direct the poet's energies, leading him to the difficult resolutions we look for in a poem by Robert Lowell or, in a very different way, by Stevens. Instead, we get an elegant, contrapuntal playing off of effects, a few touches of airy whimsicality, and an almost total failure to establish relevant contexts for the observation of particulars. Thus a poem like "The Death of a Toad," which promises a limited pathos, despite the mock-heroic accents, dissolves in a kind of absurdity, Wilbur's essentially romantic imagination and purple diction conjuring for the dying frog "some deep monotone," "misted and ebullient seas and cooling shores," and "lost Amphibia's emperies." One can only wish it were all a put-on, but it is not: what utterly beautiful poetry is wasted by the proximity of these few silly lines. Wilbur is rarely to be caught in such unlikely, rather obvious errors of tact, but they point to a fundamental failing in his work which is the sense it evokes of ideas, people, things played with as counters in a not very important game. It is not that Wilbur doesn't care for the frog, but that he cares for it primarily to the degree that it releases particular imaginative faculties that make for poetry. Ultimately, it would seem, to care for the things of this world only as they may be transmuted into the materials of poetry is to make of poetry something less substantial, less fully human, less important than we should want it to be.

– Robert Boyers

WILD, Peter. American. Born in Northampton, Massachusetts, 25 April 1940. Educated at the University of Arizona, Tucson, 1958–62, 1965–67, B.A. 1962, M.A. 1967; University of California, Irvine, 1967–69, M.F.A. 1969. Married Sylvia Ortiz in 1966. Assistant Professor of English, Sul Ross State University, Alpine, Texas, 1969–71. Since 1971, Associate Professor of English, University of Arizona. Recipient: *Writer's Digest* Prize, 1964; Hart Crane and Alice Crane Williams Memorial Fund grant, 1969; *Art River Review* prize, 1972. Address: 1405 East Lester, Tucson, Arizona 85719, U.S.A.

PUBLICATIONS

Verse

The Good Fox. Glassboro, New Jersey, Goodly Company, 1967.
Sonnets. San Francisco, Cranium Press, 1967.
The Afternoon in Dismay. Cincinnati, Art Association of Cincinnati, 1968.
Mica Mountain Poems. Ithaca, New York, Lillabulero Press, 1968.
Joining Up and Other Poems. Sacramento, California, Runcible Spoon, 1968.
Mad Night with Sunflowers. Sacramento, California, Runcible Spoon, 1968.
Love Poems. Northwood Narrows, New Hampshire, Lillabulero Press, 1969.
Three Nights in the Chiricahuas. Madison, Wisconsin, Abraxas Press, 1969.
Poems. Portland, Oregon, Prensa de Lagar, 1969.
Fat Man Poems. Belmont, Massachusetts, Hellric Publications, 1970.
Terms and Renewals. San Francisco, Two Windows Press, 1970.
Grace. Pennington, New Jersey, Stone Press, 1971.
Wild's Magical Book of Cranial Effusions. New York, New Rivers Press, 1971.
Peligros. Ithaca, New York, Ithaca House, 1972.
New and Selected Poems. New York, New Rivers Press, 1973.
Cochise. New York, Doubleday, 1973.
The Cloning. New York, Doubleday, 1974.
Tumacacori. Berkeley, California, Two Windows Press, 1974.

Bibliography: in *Wild's Magical Book of Cranial Effusions*, 1971.

Critical Studies: "Eight Chapbooks," in *The Dragonfly* (Pocatello, Idaho), Fall and Winter 1970; Keeping Us Mad" by Brain Salchert, in *Wisconsin Review* (Oshkosh), Spring 1972; "Lillabulero's Pamphlets," in *Greenfield Review* (Greenfield Center, New York), June 1972; "Mud Men, Mud Women" by Robert Peters, in *Margins* (Milwaukee, Wisconsin), October-November 1974.

Peter Wild comments:

Both figuratively and in reality, I have always felt a necessity to spend a great deal of time in the open, in the outdoors. Hence, the deterioration of the natural environment, overpopulation and the erosion of man's cultural diversity are conditions of great concern to me. Furthermore, due to a strong sense of place, as a resident of the American Southwest, a region of the Anglo, Mexican and American Indian, I often hold conflicting sympathies and allegiances. This is not to imply that I consider myself either a "nature poet" or a regional poet – a poet must write for all men – but in general it may be of help for a reader to remember that the above concerns and circumstances of my life undoubtedly underlie and temper much of my writing.

*   *   *

Peter Wild's poetry demonstrates a brilliantly facile imagination and an ability to turn any world into a fantasy of magical tricks. His style of writing, properly referred to as surrealist, knits a surface poem with exotic and unreconcilible objects. You often feel that he is a magician pulling a rabbit out of his hat and letting doves fly out of his sleeves. His poems are most beautiful when they begin with some observation of natural phenomena and wander off into a speculation of its possibilities. The poem "Snakes" is a good example of this, as he begins the poem, "the rattlesnakes have begun to come out," and ends it when he fantasizes that he awakes in the night and hears a music outdoors and finds

> outside on the lawn, the road,
>   the housetops, our flowerbeds
>   were full of them, almost erect,
> their thin necks
>   swaying toward the moon
>   humming, smiling
>   sensuously
>   drinking in the light;
> while others sped
>   back and forth on great
>   rice paper wings,
> carrying messages
>   across the cloudness night . . .

Wild's poems are never overtly funny, yet they are filled with a kind of whimsy and a gentle sense of the "funniness" of the world. His poems are impersonal in that they are not autobiographical. Their personality comes from Wild's ability to imagine and describe any landscape he chooses and, again like a magician, fill it with bizarre and funny objects. William Matthews says of Wild's poems that "the effect is of a baroque telegram, or the wildest photo caption you'll ever read."

– Diane Wakoski

WILLARD, Nancy. American. Born in Ann Arbor, Michigan, 26 June 1936. Educated at the University of Michigan, Ann Arbor (Hopwood Award), B.A. 1958, Ph.D. 1963; Stanford University, California (Woodrow Wilson Fellow), M.A. 1960. Married to Eric Lindbloom; has one son. Currently, Lecturer in English, Vassar College, Poughkeepsie, New York. Recipient: Devins Memorial Award, 1967; O. Henry Award, for short story, 1970. Address: 133 College Avenue, Poughkeepsie, New York 12603, U.S.A.

PUBLICATIONS

Verse

In His Country: Poems. Ann Arbor, Michigan, Generation, 1966.
Skin of Grace. Columbia, University of Missouri Press, 1967.
A New Herball: Poems. Baltimore, Ferdinand-Roter Gallerias, 1968.
Nineteen Masks for the Naked Poet: Poems. Santa Cruz, California, Kayak Books, 1971.
The Carpenter of the Sun: Poems. New York, Liveright, 1974.

Short Stories

The Lively Anatomy of God: Stories. New York, Eakins Press, 1968.
Childhood of the Magician. New York, Liveright, 1973.

Other

Testimony of the Invisible Man: William Carlos Williams, Francis Ponge, Rainer Maria Rilke, Pablo Neruda. Columbia, University of Missouri Press, 1970.
The Merry History of a Christmas Pie: With a Delicious Description of a Christmas Soup (juvenile). New York, Putnam, 1974.
Sailing to Cythera and Other Anatole Stories (juvenile). New York, Harcourt Brace, 1974.

*   *   *

Of scholars and children, alike in the unpredictable movements of their attention, Nancy Willard writes in her first book:

> Their order belongs to eyes
> that the earth chooses
> to edit a work much vexed:
> > *de veritate rerum,*
> an occult, particular text.

Much of her poetry – like that of Williams, Ponge, Rilke, and Neruda, all of whom she has studied in her critical book, *Testimony of the Invisible Man* – aspires to be "a poetry of things," explicating that text and revivifying our awareness of the world. One way is the vivid image – "dragonflies / thin as barometer's blood," or (of a box of eggs) "the lid raised to show / a jury noncommital / as the bald heads of / a dozen uncles.'' Another requires a deeper attention, a probing below the surface of reality. In "The Water Diviner" the diviner speaks of her "gift":

> Less a gift for me than a burden
> of silence, this slow going blind
> to the green guests in my father's field,
> while the sun behind me scorches the men mowing.
> For the sake of that wind in the earth blowing
> I walk like a holy fool, past the barn and tree,
> with no ship but a broken rudder in my hand,
> calling the sea.

Her third book, *Nineteen Masks for the Naked Poet*, shows her leaving *Ding*-poetry to experiment with the loosely surrealist mode associated with Kayak press and magazine. Often merely whimsical, the playfulness can be evocative, as in "Putting His Finger in the Dyke, He Saves All Holland," where the mayor acclaims the poet-hero for saving them from the sea which "covers over the words of our fathers / and torments us with shipwrecks and bad dreams":

> This is the poet who took on himself
>
> our bad dreams and made them beautiful,
> our fathers' secrets and made them ours.

Uncollected recent poems seen in the anthology *Rising Tides*, such as "Marriage Amulet" and "For You, Who Didn't Know," show Nancy Willard dealing with more personal, even "confessional," subject-matter with no diminution of craft. If her next collection has many others of equal quality, it will have proven worth waiting for.

– Seamus Cooney

WILLIAMS, C(harles) K(enneth). American. Born in Newark, New Jersey, 4 November 1936. Educated at Bucknell University, Lewisburg, Pennsylvania; University of Pennsylvania, Philadelphia, 1955–59, B.A. 1959. Married Sarah Jones in 1965; has one daughter. Since 1972, Contributing Editor, *American Poetry Review*, Philadelphia. Recipient: Guggenheim Fellowship, 1974. Address: 506 Delancey Street, Philadelphia, Pennsylvania 19106, U.S.A.

PUBLICATIONS

Verse

A Day for Anne Frank. Philadelphia, Falcon Press, 1968.
Lies. Boston, Houghton Mifflin, 1969.
I Am the Bitter Name. Boston, Houghton Mifflin, 1972.

Critical Studies: by Richard Howard, in *Kenyon Review* (Gambier, Ohio), Summer 1970; L. E. Sissman, in the *Boston Sun-Globe*, 18 July 1972; "Politics and the Human Standard" by Morris Dickstein, in *Parnassus* (New York), Fall 1972; Richard Howard, in *American Poetry Review* (Philadelphia), November 1972.

C. K. Williams comments:

I don't think it would be pertinent for me to make a critical analysis of my own verse . . . if I could at all.

What I would really like would be to sing without meaning anything. There's a song: a man making a canoe, he's singing

> I am making a canoe
> I am making a canoe
>
> . . . yes, like that.

But we do suffer, hunger and love and war. And then find how much war there is within us . . . the apparently vicious, apparently irrational . . . and how much love, and how much hunger. And so song becomes charm, aversion, prayer, and we become all the painful, necessary abstractions that make us mean something. And more love, again, so that song is never quite lost, no matter how truthfully brutal the verse form. And again the intensity of the joy of life and song which, when it looks, has been riding oppression and shame toward death and cries out then with its double agony. And finally the desperate last hope in this age of bombs and perfect hatred that poetry does *something*, does *anything*, and to keep going.

*   *   *

"I am uncertain about just about everything – the use of poetry, the form of it," C. K. Williams has said, but judging from his poems, one would never guess that he was uncertain about anything. The tone is sure, swift, almost brittle in its certainty. Somewhat in the manner of Thomas Hardy or Stephen Crane, but with more despair, he shakes his fist in the face of God or god, saying:

> your lists of victims dear
> god like rows of sharp little teeth
> have made me crazy look
> I have crushed by poor balls
> for you I have kissed the blank
> pages drank the pissy chalice
> water and thrown up

The poems in *Lies* and *I Am the Bitter Name* are concerned principally with desperate, abandoned, but patient souls; and both books end with long poems about specific victims. "Come sit with me here / kiss me; my heart too is wounded / with forgiveness," the speaker says to the young girl, in "The Day for Anne Frank." And "In the Heart of the Beast – May 1970 –: Cambodia, Kent State, Jackson State," a person tired of forgiving, asks:

this is fresh meat right mr nixon
this is even sweeter than mickey schwerner or fred hampton
right?
even more tender than the cherokee nation or guatemala or
greece
having their asses straightened for them isn't it.

Such a heavy political message is uncharacteristic, however, of most of Williams'
poems, which belong more to the moral or even theological order. An exchange
between two Old Testament figures, for example, provided the title for his second
collection: "Abraham said to him, 'Art thou, indeed he that is called Death?' He
answered, and said, 'I am the Bitter Name!'"

But there is another aspect of Williams' work not so obvious as the ferocious
voice, the startling metaphor, the hard and bitter irony for which he is best known.
In "To Market," for example, a man manages to say "I love you," even as, in
metamorphosis, he becomes a machine; in "Wood," a young ruffian speaks to his
more conventional classmate from the grave; and in "Yours," the speaker promises
a poem to everyone in the world, as if each poem brought with it some hope, a
saving grace. Such poems suggest a range of feeling that may eventually take
Williams into new territory.

In an age of bestial death, as Williams calls it, telling "just what is" is achievement enough, "remembering iwo jima remembering the bulge seoul my lai."

In its precision, intensity, fury, his work gives full imaginative expression to a
kind of consciousness that many poets have only hinted at. It asks a great deal of
the reader, as all truly exceptional poetry must. One can only guess, at this time –
when Williams is still a young man – the possibilities in language and technique yet
available to him.

– Michael True

————————

WILLIAMS, Emmett. American. Born in Greenville, South Carolina, 4 April
1925. Educated at Kenyon College, Gambier, Ohio, B.A. 1949; University of Paris.
Served in the United States Army, 1943–46. Married Laura Powell MacCarteney in
1949, two daughters and one son; Ann Noël Stevenson in 1970, one son. Lived in
Europe, 1949–66: assistant to the ethnologist Paul Radin; associated with the Darm-
stadt group of concrete poets; Founding Member of the Domaine Poetique, Paris;
European Coordinator of the Fluxus group. Editor, Something Else Press, New
York, 1966–70. Artist-in-Residence, Fairleigh Dickinson University, Madison, New
Jersey, 1968, and University of Kentucky, Lexington, 1969; Professor of Critical
Studies, California Institute of the Arts, Valencia, 1970–72. Since 1972, Visiting
Professor of Art, Nova Scotia College of Art and Design, Halifax. Address: 5163
Duke Street, Halifax, Nova Scotia, Canada; or, West Glover, Vermont, 05875,
U.S.A.

PUBLICATIONS

Verse

Konkretionen. Darmstadt, Germany, Material, 1958.
13 Variations on 6 Words by Gertrude Stein (1958). Cologne, Galerie der
   Speigel, 1965.
Rotapoems. Stuttgart, Hansjörg Mayer, 1966.
The Last French-Fried Potato and Other Poems. New York, Something Else
   Press, 1967.
Sweethearts. Stuttgart, Hansjörg Mayer, 1967; New York, Something Else
   Press, 1968.
The Book of Thorn and Eth. Stuttgart, Hansjörg Mayer, 1968.
The Boy and the Bird. Stuttgart, Hansjörg Mayer, and New York, Wittenborn,
   1968.
A Valentine for Noël. Stuttgart, Hansjörg Mayer, 1973.
Selected Shorter Poems 1950–1970. Stuttgart, Hansjörg Mayer, 1974; New
   York, New Directions, 1975.

Plays

Ja, Es war noch da (produced Darmstadt, Germany, 1960). Published in *Nota 4*
   (Munich), 1960; as *Yes It Was Still There* (produced New York, 1965).
A Cellar Song for 5 Voices (produced New York, 1961).
4-Directional Song of Doubt for 5 Voices (produced Wiesbaden, Germany, 1962).
The Ultimate Poem (produced Arras, France, 1964).

Other

Variations Upon a Spoerri Landscape (lithographs). Halifax, Nova Scotia College of Art and Design Lithography Workshop, 1973.
Zodiac (lithographs). Tokyo, Gallery Birthday Star, 1974.

Editor, *Poésie et cetera américaine.* Paris, Biennale, 1963.
Editor, *An Anthology of Concrete Poetry.* New York, Something Else Press,
   1967.
Editor, *Store Days,* by Claes Oldenburg. New York, Something Else Press,
   1967.

Translator, *Anecdoted Topography of Chance . . .,* by Daniel Spoerri. New
   York, Something Else Press, 1966.
Translator, *The Mythological Travels of a Modern Sir John Mandeville, Being an
   Account of the Magic, Meatballs, and Other Monkey Business Peculiar to the
   Sojourn . . . upon the Isle of Symi, Together with Divers Speculations Thereon,*
   by Daniel Spoerri. New York, Something Else Press, 1970.

*   *   *

Emmett Williams' name is better known than his poetry, and one reason for this
discrepancy is that he edited *An Anthology of Concrete Poetry,* which has outsold its
competitors (including an anthology of mine), while most of his poetry remains

unpublished, particularly in his native country. Since *The Selected Shorter Poems* has only recently appeared, readers' understanding of his distinct achievement tends to be spotty. Unlike other American writers of his generation, Williams became closely involved, back in the fifties, with the European intermedia avant-garde, epitomized by the "Darmstadt Circle," in which he figured prominently. By the sixties, he was an initiator of Fluxus, an international post-Dada, mixed-means movement which won considerable attention at the time (but has so far escaped most historians of contemporary art and literature). Thus, his writing reflects, to an unusual degree, the experimental tradition in the non-literary arts. He echoed not Dylan Thomas but Kurt Schwitters, for instance, in his early "performance poems," to use the term that refers to poems whose most appropriate form is not the printed page but live performance.

It was Williams' good fortune to learn, back in the fifties, that English-language poetry could be composed in radically alternative ways – different not only from the academic poetry of that time but also from the declamatory expressionism of, say, Allen Ginsberg. Instead, Williams pioneered the art of "concrete poetry," in which the poet exchews conventional syntax (and related devices) to organize language in other ways. Rather than "free form" (whatever that might be), Williams favored such severe constraints as repetition, permutation, and linguistic minimalism. His masterpiece, the book-length *Sweethearts*, consists of one word (the title) whose eleven letters are visually distributed over 150 or so sequentially expressive pages, the work as a whole relating the evolution of a man-woman relationship. Like Williams' other work, *Sweethearts* is extremely witty; and like much else in experimental writing, it must be seen (and read) for its magic to be believed.

– Richard Kostelanetz

WILLIAMS, (David) Gwyn. British (Welsh). Born in Port Talbot, Glamorgan, 24 August 1904. Educated at Port Talbot Grammar School; University College of Wales, Aberystwyth, B.A.; Jesus College, Oxford, M.A. Married; has five children. Lecturer in English Literature, Cairo University, 1935–42; Assistant Professor of English, Alexandria University, Egypt, 1942–51; Professor of English, University of Libya, Benghazi, 1956–61; Professor of English Literature, Istanbul University, 1961–69. Address: Treweithan, Trefenter, Aberystwyth, Cardiganshire, Wales.

PUBLICATIONS

Verse

Existentialist Sonnets. Newton, Montgomeryshire Printing Company, 1953.
The Ascension of Man: Existential Verse. Ilfracombe, Devonshire, Arthur Stockwell, 1966.
Inns of Love: Selected Poems. Llandybie, Carmarthenshire, Christopher Davies, 1970.

Novel

This Way to Lethe.   London, Faber, 1962.

Other

An Introduction to Welsh Poetry From the Beginning to the Sixteenth Century.   London, Faber, and Philadelphia, Dufour and Saifer, 1953.
Green Mountain: An Informal Guide to Cyrenaica and Jebel Akhdar.   London, Faber, 1963.
Turkey: A Traveller's Guide and History.   London, Faber, 1967.

Editor, *Presenting Welsh Poetry: An Anthology of Welsh Verse in Translation and of English Verse by Welsh Poets.*   London, Faber, and Chester Springs, Pennsylvania, Dufour, 1959.

Translator, *The Rent That's Due to Love.*   London, Editions Poetry, 1950.
Translator, *The Burning Tree: Poems from the First Thousand Years of Welsh Verse.*   London, Faber, 1956; revised edition, as *Welsh Poems: Sixth Century to 1600,* 1973; Berkeley, University of California Press, 1974.
Translator, *In Defense of Wonder: A Welsh Poem,* by William Cynwal.   London, Golden Cockerel Press, 1960.

Gwyn Williams comments:

I write a poem when I experience something that requires a poem to be written, I suppose in an attempt to catch the experience, preserve it, give it an existence separate from my own. There are poems which are objects on my mental mantelshelf, some of them staying clean, others needing an occasional dusting, but most of them have gone further away from me than that. A long poem I am now writing with the idea of letting it carry off bees from my bonnet is already orbiting away from me. The experiences have occured mostly in Wales and round the eastern end of the Mediterranean. I use stanza forms as they come, half rhymes rather than full, some complex alliteration. Technically I have learnt most from translating Welsh poetry I like into English verse.

                    *   *   *

Gwyn Williams has won a high reputation as a translator of Welsh poetry. He has also written a fine travel book, *Turkey,* among many other volumes. He has travelled widely, and spent much of his working life teaching literature at universities in the Near East.

His selected poems, *Inns of Love,* shows how the better verse translators also happen to be good poets in their own right. Like Pound's, the output of Professor Williams may be seen at its best when working through other literatures, as if he needs a framework of translation to keep his intellect and imagination at full stretch. He uses the past, and masterpieces in other languages, as a sort of combined filter for his own peculiar vision.

The most ambitious poem in this splendidly entertaining collection is "Charlemagne in Constantinople," which occupies almost half the book. It is a long narrative work about Charlemagne's legendary encounter with Hu Gadarn in

Byzantium, based on the medieval Welsh version of the story in the 14th-century *Red Book of Hergest*. A highly individual treatment, one of its most intriguing features is the daring manner in which Williams employs an obtrusive 20th-century narrator – eloquent, flamboyant, witty, ironic – who marshals his characters, comments, draws parallels to their actions, juxtaposes past and present, legend and contemporary reality, and surveys the European and Eastern scenes of the story through the centuries. This produces a certain shock effect which might bring howls of protest from purists, but the method largely succeeds with the verve of its conversational style:

> Byzantium is the separate city, the ultimate Cokayne
> or the golden point of departure into decline;
> vision of a viable order or retreat into
> a fabricated region of potency; the landing
> on the Moon or the two-gun man doing
> his best with Eskimo Nell. As a ticket of entry you present
> bones, Mary's milk, the pill, the plunging neckline,
> the sports car, the space rocket or a glossy work on cooking.

This concluding passage, with a vigorous and almost vulgar tone, justifies itself by the way in which it clarifies Williams's interpretation of his sources, not treating it as a "museum piece gathering scholarly dust but as a living work of art." Looking deeply into the distant past becomes a way of understanding the present.

In another poem, "City under Snow," a fairly conventional subject evokes a fresh response:

> Mosques into snow-palaces; banks, bagnios,
> party headquarters and apartment blocks
> acquire an innocence; L. S. Lowry figures
> lean into flocked air;
>
> spittle, pigeon-dung, dogshit and broken
> glass, the layer of soot all iced over and
> a new fall powders the cleaned crotches
> of cobbled alleys.

Generally, *Inns of Love* and the later poems are the work of a writer for whom places remain important as nodal points where lines usually thought of as time, sensory impression, tradition, and a view of life intersect. And so the places in which he has lived and worked – Egypt, Libya, Turkey, and now Wales – are more than a background: they form an integral part of the experience which is the poem. Entry into the nature of a place eliminates the illusion of time and throws "hooks into the self," as Williams would put it.

The accomplishment of Gwyn Williams as a valuable verse-translator is considerable, and few more erudite and cultivated men have emerged from Wales – an academic who is yet very much involved in living and the future of his own country. He has recently made a separate, if less permanent, reputation on television as an articulate guide to the long history and archaeology of Wales.

– John Tripp

WILLIAMS, Herbert (Lloyd). British (Welsh). Born in Aberystwyth, Cardiganshire, 8 September 1932. Educated at Alexandra Road Boys School and Ardwyn Grammar School, Aberystwyth. Married Dorothy Edwards in 1954; has four sons and one daughter. Reporter, *Welsh Gazette*, Aberystwyth, 1951–53, and *Reading Standard*, Berkshire, 1953; Reporter and Sub-Editor, *Cambrian News*, Aberystwyth, 1953–56, and *South Wales Echo*, Cardiff, 1956–60; Sub-Editor, *Scottish Daily Mail*, Edinburgh, 1960–61, and *Birmingham Evening Mail*; Feature Writer, *South Wales Echo*, 1961–73. Since 1973, BBC Radio Producer, Cardiff. Address: 27 Fern Place, Fairwater, Cardiff, Wales.

PUBLICATIONS

Verse

Too Wet for the Devil and Other Poems. London, Outposts Publications, 1962.
The Dinosaurs. Cardiff, Triskel Press, 1966.
The Trophy. Llandybie, Carmarthenshire, Christopher Davies, 1967.
Corgi Modern Poets in Focus 1, with others, edited by Dannie Abse. London, Corgi, 1971.

Play

A Lethal Kind of Love (broadcast, 1968). Cardiff, John Jones, 1968.

Manuscript Collection: National Library of Wales, Aberystwyth.

Critical Study: by Dannie Abse, in *Corgi Modern Poets in Focus 1*, 1971.

*   *   *

Herbert Williams is an unambitious poet, avowedly diffident about his own talent; perhaps if he were more committed to the art his work would be tighter and more polished. As it is he succeeds best in low-key, sympathetic examinations of the society he lives in. He has a journalist's eye for detail and atmosphere, a warm social concern, and a healthy outward-looking attitude; his subjects tend to be drawn from everyday life in Wales – local characters, craftsmen and traders, sailors, a choir – individual or group portraits presented with natural, unemphatic realism. He can turn out a lively ballad ("A Man and a Half"), and is good with family occasions ("Morning in Aber"), although few of his poems are overtly personal.

At his best he is unsentimental, honest, and capable of the vivid, down-to-earth phrase which can bring a scene to life: "The smell of cakes at missionary teas"; "hair white as skate." He is least successful when he tackles abstract themes: his language becomes flaccid and slides towards, or into, worn out "poetic diction."

In "Small Fortune," a poem about the little pleasures which add up to content-ment, he says "Turnpike trusts / Grew fat upon the twopenny toll." It is with such unpretentious but not to be despised currency that Mr. Williams buys our respect.

– Fleur Adcock

WILLIAMS, Hugo. British. Born in Windsor, Berkshire, 20 February 1942; son of the actor and playwright Hugh Williams. Educated at Eton College, 1955–60. Married Hermine Demoriane in 1965; has one child. Staff Writer, *Telegraph Magazine*, London, 1965; Assistant Editor, *London Magazine*, 1966–70. Recipient: Eric Gregory Award, 1966; Arts Council bursary, 1966; Cholmondeley Award, 1971. Address: 3 Raleigh Street, London W.1, England.

PUBLICATIONS

Verse

Symptoms of Loss: Poems. London and New York, Oxford University Press, 1965.
Poems. London, The Review, 1969.
Sugar Daddy. London and New York, Oxford University Press, 1970.
Cherry Blossom. London, Poem-of-the-Month Club, 1972.
Some Sweet Day. London and New York, Oxford University Press, 1975.

Other

All the Time in the World (travel). London, Alan Ross, 1966; Philadelphia, Chilton, 1968.

Editor, *"London Magazine" Poems, 1961–1966.* London, Alan Ross, 1966.

*   *   *

Hugo Williams is an accomplished, exact poet, the themes of many of whose poems are related to his experience of travel. His work conveys the immediate impression of one who is committed to self-expression in verse – of one in whom self-discovery is an essentially poetic process. Occasionally, as in most of the longish "Driving on the A30," he can be prosy, sheerly and perhaps too cleverly descriptive; nor, in spite of his intelligence, is he really at his best when writing poetry that depends for its effect upon "thought." In certain respects, although not in others, his objectivity gives him something in common with those avant garde American poets who concentrate upon celebrating objects for their own sake, and who eschew metaphor; but their actual influence seems negligible. He is at his best when, somewhat in the style of a French "new" novelist, he simply records his perceptions, relying upon his juxtaposition of them – rather than upon his feelings about them – to make his communication. This is seen most perfectly in "The Butcher":

The butcher carves veal for two.
The cloudy, frail slices fall over his knife.

His face is hurt by the parting sinews
And he looks up with relief, laying it on the scales.

He is a rosy young man with white eyelashes
Like a bullock. He always serves me now.

I think he knows about my life. How we prefer
To eat in when it's cold. How someone

With a foreign accent can only cook veal.
He writes the price on the grease-proof packet

And hands it to me courteously. His smile
Is the official seal on my marriage.

Here a vague and, circumstantially, wholly unjustified sense of existential unease –
or, to put it in another way, an awareness of the violence contained in human
imperfection and of the transitory nature of love – is beautifully conveyed; the
poem is fastidiously non-"confessional," and combines happiness with the ghost of
foreboding just as they are so often combined in life. It is too early now to say
whether this gifted poet will fulfil his promise; "The Butcher" and some other
poems suggest that he is developing into a poet of considerable originality and,
possibly, power.

– Martin Seymour-Smith

WILLIAMS, John Stuart. British (Welsh). Born in Mountain Ash, Glamorgan, 13
August 1920. Educated at Mountain Ash County School; University College, Cardiff, B.A. (honours) in English literature, M.A. Married Sheelagh Williams in 1948;
has two sons. Formerly, English Master, Whitchurch Grammar School, Glamorgan.
Since 1956, Head of the Department of English and Drama, City of Cardiff College
of Education. Formerly, Composer: works performed in London, and broadcast by
the BBC. Member, English Section, Welsh Academy (Yr Academi Gymreig). Recipient: Welsh Arts Council prize, 1971. Address: 52 Dan-y-Coed Road, Cyncoed,
Cardiff, Wales.

PUBLICATIONS

Verse

Last Fall. London, Outposts Publications, 1962.
Green Rain. Llandybie, Carmarthenshire, Christopher Davies, 1967.
Dic Penderyn and Other Poems. Llandysul, Cardiganshire, Gomer, 1970.
Banna Strand. Llandysul, Cardiganshire, Gomer, 1975.

Other

> Editor, with Richard Milner, *Dragons and Daffodils.* Llandybie, Carmarthen-
> shire, Christopher Davies, 1960.
> Editor, with Meic Stephens, *The Lilting House: An Anthology of Anglo-Welsh
> Poetry, 1917–1967.* Llandybie, Carmarthenshire, Christopher Davies, and
> London, Dent, 1969.
> Editor, *Poems '69.* Llandysul, Cardiganshire, Gomer, 1969.

Manuscript Collection: National Library of Wales, Aberystwyth.

Critical Studies: in *Outposts* (London), Winter 1967; introduction by Roland
Mathias, to *Green Rain*, 1967; *An Introduction to Anglo-Welsh Literature* by Raymond Garlick, Cardiff, University of Wales Press, 1970.

John Stuart Williams comments:

I was born and brought up in a sceptically anglicised mining community which
had few problems about its identity; it was stubbornly Welsh, and had small faith in
easy solutions. It was a place of sharp contrasts; the open hill was a short step
from the coalpits in the centre of town and we were often reminded of death by the
colliery hooter signalling an accident underground. A sense of the ambiguity of
reality has remained with me and much of my work is an attempt to establish
footholds in place and time from which to explore this and the obliquity of our
personal and national myths. "Banna Strand," first published in *Decal Poetry
Review* is a recent example:

> In my raincoat pocket, a faded carnet de bal;
> the stillness of mist, a girl on horseback
> frightened by something other than the sea,
> watching, waiting;
> such a pretty little beach . . .
> Is it my business what they do,
> what answers may come with sudden gardens?
> I am not Control.
> Hoofs in the shallows,
> fear in shadows coursing along the wet sand,
> the sharp fountains of sprayed light . . .
> What do you see through your Ross?
> A misleading group, windblown hair
> falsely suggesting private warmth.
> Everything is coded, graffiti on old stone,
> on Banna strand or beside the midland sea.

After writing this I was disconcerted to find that Banna strand was where
Casement had landed in Ireland for the last fatal time.

It would be easy and misleading to isolate literary influences, as my first lessons
in rhythm came from Music and the cinema. From the first I learned that rhythm is
more subtle than traditional metric easily allows, and from the second I first
learned about montage and the inter-relation of images, something later confirmed
in conversations with the late John Grierson. The reading came later. The natural

order of words is important to me even when I write in more obviously traditional forms, for it is against this pattern that I try to work my variations. This sometimes misfires, for what is natural to me, a valleys Welshman, may be different from what seems so to others. The danger inherent in my subject-matter is compounded in this way. One man's *déja vu* is, in any case, sometimes another's boredom. But this is a risk I have to take:

> Listening to silence,
> I praise both light and darkness.

Finally, if it is of any interest, the contemporaries I most admire at the moment are, in English, George Amabile, and in Welsh, Euros Bowen.

*   *   *

John Stuart Williams's premier achievement is a long dramatic poem, "Dic Penderyn," originally written for radio, which won a Welsh Arts Council prize in 1971. It is the story of the Merthyr Riots of 1831, the conflict between the workers and ironmasters, the violence and reprisals, and the struggle of men for free and decent lives. Dic Penderyn himself was the figure at the centre of the trouble: he wounded a Highlander (one of the troops brought in to quell the riots) and was later hanged at Cardiff. In this impressive poem, Penderyn focuses most of the emotion, as he did in real life among the oppressed ironworkers. (There are also four narrators who impersonate characters in the story, plus several lyrics for a folk-singer.) Williams's treatment is what might be termed poetic documentary – accurate, clear, and ordered, with the dramatic tension mounting effectively to its climax. The poetry contributes sinewy and colourful language to the sweep of events, linking images of blood, metal, fire, and nature:

> And the fierce summer leaps in
> With torchlight red on broken glass.
> The throbbing pulse grows louder,
> Until the whole town drowns
> In the blind heat of a dull drum.

Williams's individual poems are usually short, neat impressionistic pieces, resembling attractive snapshots, with titles like "Gironde," "River Walk," or "Beach at Ifracombe." One criticism levelled at him is that these rather "gnomic" poems briefly interest and entertain, but are essentially inconsequential. Apart from "Dic Penderyn," Williams's craft may be a modest one, but it is also a true one, honestly attained. There is a place in literature, as in painting, for the miniature water-colour, even though the heavy guns of contemporary criticism would have us believe otherwise. This particular, largely unsentimental Welsh miniaturist has a good deal to offer in the way of fresh observation and disinterested understanding. He can often breathe life into the oldest stock scenes and the most ordinary, banal moments.

– John Tripp

WILLIAMS, Jonathan (Chamberlain).   American.   Born in Asheville, North Carolina, 8 March 1929. Educated at Princeton University, New Jersey, 1947–49; Institute of Design, Chicago, 1951; Atelier 17, New York; Black Mountain College. North Carolina, 1951–56. Conscientious Objector: served in the United States Army Medical Corps, 1952–54. Since 1951, Executive Director, The Jargon Society, Inc., publishers, Highlands, North Carolina. Scholar-in-Residence, Aspen Institute, Colorado, 1967–68, and Maryland Institute College of Art, Baltimore, 1968–69; Poet-in-Residence, University of Kansas, Lawrence, 1971. Recipient: Guggenheim Fellowship, 1957; Longview Foundation grant, 1960; National Endowment for the Arts grant, 1968, 1969, 1970, 1973. D.H.L.: Maryland Institute College of Art, 1969. Address: Highlands, North Carolina 28741, U.S.A.; or, Corn Close, Dentdale, Sedbergh, Yorkshire, England.

PUBLICATIONS

Verse

Garbage Litters the Iron Face of the Sun's Child.   San Francisco, Jargon, 1951.
Red Gray.   Black Mountain, North Carolina, Jargon, 1951.
Four Stoppages.   Stuttgart, Jargon, 1953.
The Empire Finals at Verona.   Highlands, North Carolina, Jargon, 1959.
Lord! Lord! Lord!   Highlands, North Carolina, Jargon, 1959.
Amen Huzza Selah.   Black Mountain, North Carolina, Jargon, 1960.
Elegies and Celebrations.   Highlands, North Carolina, Jargon, 1962.
In England's Green & (A Garland and a Clyster).   San Francisco, Auerhahn Press, 1962.
Emblems for the Little Dells and Nooks and Corners of Paradise.   London, Jargon, 1962.
The Macon County North Carolina Meshuga Sound Society, Jonathan Williams, Musical Director, Presents: Lullabies, Twisters, Gibbers, Drags (à la manière de M. Louis Moreau Gottschalk, late of the City of New Orleans).   London, Jargon, 1963.
Lines about Hills above Lakes.   Fort Lauderdale, Florida, Roman Books, 1964.
Petite Concrete Concrete Suite.   Detroit, Fenian Head Centre Press, 1965.
Four Jargonelles from the Herbalist's Notebook.   Cambridge, Massachusetts, Lowell, 1966.
Paean to Dvorak, Deemer and McClure.   San Francisco, Dave Haselwood, 1966.
Affilati Attrezzi Per I Giardini di Catullo (bilingual edition).   Milan, Lerici Editore, 1966.
Mahler Becomes Politics, Beisbol.   London, Marlborough Gallery, 1967.
50! Epiphytes, -taphs, -tomes, -grams, -thets! 50!   London, Poet and Printer, 1967.
A French 75!   San Francisco, Dave Haselwood, 1967.
Polycotyledonous Poems.   Stuttgart, Edition Hansjörg Mayer, 1967.
The Lucidities: Sixteen in Visionary Company.   London, Turret Books, 1967.
Sharp Tools for Catullan Gardens.   Bloomington, Indiana University Fine Arts Department, 1968.
Descant on Rawthey's Madrigal: Conversations with Basil Bunting.   Lexington, Kentucky, Gnomon Press, 1968.
Ripostes.   Stuttgart, Editions Domberger, 1969.
An Ear in Bartram's Tree: Selected Poems, 1957–67.   Chapel Hill, University of North Carolina Press, 1969; New York, New Directions, 1972.

On Arriving at the Same Age as Jack Benny. Urbana, Illinois, Finial Press, 1969.

Mahler. London, Cape Goliard Press, 1969.

Six Rusticated, Wall-Eyed Poems. Baltimore, Maryland Institute Press, 1969.

The New Architectural Monuments of Baltimore City. Baltimore, Maryland Institute Press, 1970.

The Apocryphal Oracular Yeah-Sayings of Mae West. Baltimore, Maryland Institute Press, 1970.

Strung Out with Elgar on a Hill. Urbana, Illinois, Finial Press, 1971.

Blues and Roots, Rue and Bluets: A Garland for the Appalachians. New York, Grossman, 1971.

The Loco Logodaedalist in Situ: Selected Poems 1968–70. London, Cape Goliard Press, 1971; New York, Grossman, 1972.

Epitaph, with Thomas Meyer. Dentdale, Yorkshire, privately printed, 1972.

Fruits Confits, with Thomas Meyer. Dentdale, Yorkshire, privately printed, 1972.

Pairidaeza. Highlands, North Carolina, Jargon, 1973.

Imaginary Postcards. London, Trigram Press, 1973.

Clipped Greens. Urbana, Illinois, Finial Press, 1973.

Much Further Out Than You Thought. New York, David Lewis, 1973.

Who Is Little Enis? Lexington, Kentucky, Gnomon Press, 1973.

Adventures with a Twelve-Inch Pianist Beyond the Blue Horizon. Paris, Editions Claude Bernard, 1974.

Elite Elate Poems. New York, Grossman, 1974.

Other

Editor, *Edward Dahlberg, A Tribute: Essays, Reminiscences, Correspondence, Tributes.* New York, David Lewis, 1970.

Manuscript Collection: Jargon Society Archives, University of North Carolina Library, Chapel Hill.

Critical Studies: introduction by Guy Davenport to *An Ear in Bartram's Tree: Selected Poems, 1957–67,* 1969, 1972; "The Sound of Our Speaking" by Robert Morgan, in *The Nation* (New York), 6 September 1971; by Herbert Leibowitz, in *The New York Times Book Review,* 21 November 1971; Raymond Gardner, in *The Guardian* (London), 3 July 1972; in *Vort 4* (Silver Spring, Maryland), 1973.

Jonathan Williams comments:

I am primarily a poet, but since we do not live for ourselves alone I have always assumed (since 1951) that the publishing of my poetic enthusiasms was part of the job. And the reading of poems aloud to audiences – which I have done approximately six hundred times from Vancouver to Wien.

I have been called a Black Mountain Poet, a Beat Poet, a Southern-Poetry-Today Poet, a Light Poet, an Informalist Poet, a Formalist Poet, a Concrete Poet, a Found-Object Poet, a Relentlessly and Tiresomely Avant-garde Poet. To my knowledge all I am is a poet, like anyone else. I write as I can.

The masters of delectation and precision are my mentors: Blake, Marvell, Buson,

Archilochos, Martial, Catullus, Dickinson, Ono no Komachi, Basho, and Whitman. From more immediate times: Pound, William Carlos Williams, Robinson Jeffers, Kenneth Patchen, Kenneth Rexroth, Charles Olson, Ian Hamilton Finlay, Stevie Smith, Basil Bunting, J. V. Cunningham . . . I use all the devices I know, all the tricks in Orpheus's black bag – if it is possible to move rocks and trees, it is just possible to keep ice from forming in other human hearts. Poems are passionate things to give courage to those who respond to their messages. I write for those who long for the saving grace of the language. I never write for Laodiceans. The gentle reader and I are going to go round and round. Richard of St. Victor teaches us that in art and in life there are more things to love than we could possibly have imagined. *Odi et amo*, said Catullus. I want Catullus in the poems, and Willie Mays and Thomas Jefferson and Charles Ives and Apollo and hill farmers and people who talk trash. The language is airy, earthy, Regency, witty, offensive, etc. – whatever it needs to be. This is your friendly Local, Ecological Logodaedalist talking.

*   *   *

Jonathan Williams has been an important force in poetry since the early 1950's, when he studied at Black Mountain College and founded The Jargon Society, whose publishing record is remarkable: Williams has always ignored fashion and thus Jargon may fairly claim many important "discoveries" – in the form of first books by poets who only later became attractive to the anthologists and commercial publishers.

Williams' own poetry has remained just as idiosyncratic as his publishing tastes, and by ignoring fashion he has created a body of work uniquely his own, dedicated he says to "those who long for the saving grace of the language." One fine description of his poetry comes from Guy Davenport: "Its weightlessness is that of thistledown and like the thistle it bites." He is commonly known as a "light" poet; such a description acknowledges his wit, but ignores the power his poems often carry. He is "light" also in the sense that his poems are only rarely personal, and to my knowledge never "confessional." Williams writes of what he sees and hears, and if his descriptions fail to convey his actual feelings, the body of his work suggests a man of impeccable tastes, deep intellect, and occasional, profound disgust for the homogenization of his country-folk and the Twentieth Century deathlock bureaucracy holds on poetry.

For Williams is the true ecologist, not only in his love for nature, but in his concern for saving the words of a people whose language is undergoing severe mutation. Thanks to television we live in an era when a phrase like "No way," invented on Madison Avenue before Christmas, can be in every home by New Year. Williams detests the cultural death of his country, and when he's not keeping his distance in Yorkshire, he wanders the Appalachian trail, listening and writing down what's left to save of originality. And he visits wherever an audience assembles to hear what he has written, called by Buckminster Fuller, "our Johnny Appleseed."

A major "form" for Williams, is the "found poem." Poems like this, usually direct quotes, require good memory or the willingness to produce a pencil at unseemly moments:

> I figured
> anything anybody
> could do a lot of I
> could do a little
> of
>
> mebby
>   – "Mrs. Sadie Grindstaff, Weaver &
>   Factotum Explains the Work-Principle
>   to the Modern World"
>
> your points is blue
> and your timing's
> a week off
>   – "Sam Creswell, Auto Mechanic"

The title of Williams' selected poems, *An Ear in Bartram's Tree*, suggests his principal technique – to listen and to watch and then to record as objectively as possible what he's observed. The confinement of an ear in that tree hints also that the poet isn't in a position to act on what he hears, except to write it down. But there are exceptions, especially in his early poems. "A Little Tumescence" is characteristic of Williams' joy with language, in spite of the greater sorrow it can convey:

> this time, I mean it:
> twice tonight!
>
>   (*omne animal*, always
>   The Hope
>
> *triste, triste*
> situation, such outrageous
> limitation,
> limp,
>
>   simply

Among Williams' recent books, *Blues and Roots, Rue and Bluets* stands out as one of the few volumes of poetry in print where the "illustrations" and the poetry merge; the photographs by Nicholas Dean augment the silent wisdon of the poet, who holds himself in reserve to favor the words of Uncle Iv and Aunt Creasy, and of Snuffy Smith, who says:

> More mouth on
> that woman
>
> than ass
> on a goose

The world of Jonathan Williams' poetry is the still unprocessed world and the quickly fading language that surrounds us. Recording it's a monumental task. We are lucky to have a poet with the energy and humor necessary for the job.

– Geof Hewitt

WILLIAMS, Miller. American. Born in Hoxie, Arkansas, 8 April 1930. Educated at Arkansas State College, Conway, B.S. in biology 1951; University of Arkansas, Fayetteville, M.S. in zoology 1952. Married to Rebecca Kelley; has three children. Formerly, taught biology at McNeese State College, Lake Charles, Louisiana, and Millsaps College, Jackson, Mississippi; Associate Professor of English, Loyola University, New Orleans, 1966–70; Fulbright Professor of American Studies, National University of Mexico, 1970. Associate Professor, 1971–73, and since 1973, Professor of English, University of Arkansas. Visiting Professor, University of Chile, Santiago, 1964. Editor, *New Orleans Review*, 1967–70. Recipient: Henry Bellaman Award, 1957; Bread Loaf Writers Conference Fellowship, 1961; Amy Lowell Traveling Scholarship, 1963; Arts Fund Award, 1973. Address: Department of English, University of Arkansas, Fayetteville, Arkansas 72701, U.S.A.

PUBLICATIONS

Verse

A Circle of Stone: Poems. Baton Rouge, Louisiana State University Press, 1964.
Recital (bilingual edition). Valparaiso, Chile, Ediciones Océano, 1964.
So Long at the Fair. New York, Dutton, 1968.
The Only World There Is. New York, Dutton, 1971.
Halfway From Hoxie: New and Selected Poems. New York, Dutton, 1973.

Other

19 Poetas de Hoy en los EEUU. Valparaiso, Chile, United States Information Agency, 1966.
The Poetry of John Crowe Ransom. New Brunswick, New Jersey, Rutgers University Press, 1972.

Editor, with John William Corrington, *Southern Writing in the Sixties: Fiction* and *Poetry.* Baton Rouge, Louisiana State University Press, 2 vols., 1966, 1967.
Editor, *Poems and Antipoems,* by Nicanor Parra. New York, New Directions, 1967; London, Cape, 1968.
Editor, *The Achievement of John Ciardi: A Comprehensive Selection of His Poems with a Critical Introduction.* Chicago, Scott Foresman, 1969.
Editor and Translator, *Emergency Poems,* by Nicanor Parra. New York, New Directions, 1972.
Editor, *Contemporary Poetry in America.* New York, Random House, 1973.

Manuscript Collection: Special Collections, University of Arkansas Library, Fayetteville.

Critical Study: "About Miller Williams" by James Whitehead, in *The Dickinson Review* (North Dakota), Spring 1973.

*　　　*　　　*

Miller Williams knows the meters and forms of traditional poetry and when he discovers that a poem wants to cover a strict line, he lets it.

Then sometimes he moves as a graceful trooper through the mine fields of free verse. He has a marvelous ear and an easy hand with natural metaphor. He writes inside a sophisticated Southern idiom that can pick and choose as the spirit and flesh of his experience decide.

More often than not his poems are a gathering of strategies. On the page there seems to be a casual typography, but after a careful reading we understand the balance between common diction and complicated rhetoric.

Williams is a trained biologist, an ex-stockcar driver, and a cormorant reader of liberal and socialist literature. He is a basically optimistic man who suspects the changes and weathers of our lives include devils and probably a congregation of strange gods.

Williams has written for Judas and about the wife of a Venezuelan revolutionary – he has celebrated open love and plain sex and the glory and torture of old-fashioned families: frogs, hubcaps, metaphysical conceits, Einsteinian physics, and country songs are comfortable together in his books.

Williams' poetry is passionate, understated, regional, and elegant – but it doesn't wink or guffaw or play bored.

Williams is satisfied to be alive and he renders an imagined landscape that is finally a synthesis of romantic reflection and classical order. His waltz is gutbucket and he manages a funky minuet. Finally he is an intellectual, after verse has played the necessary game, and after the body has claimed to enjoy its fine excess. As in these lines from four poems:

> Think that when he sees how Christ is killed
> he does the only thing he knows to do
>
> *
>
> In New York
> taxi drivers know everything
> except what I ask them
>
> *
>
> every hope getting out of hand
> slings us hopelessly outward one by one
> till all that kept us common is undone
>
> *
>
> about the bullfight
> which was in Monterrey:
> the horns were lobster's claws
> the balls were blue
> the sword was love in the matador's right hand

Do you understand?

Do you understand?

– James Whitehead

WILLY, Margaret (Elizabeth). British. Born in London, 25 October 1919. Educated at Beckenham County School for Girls; Goldsmiths' College, University of London (W. H. Hudson Memorial Prize, 1938; Gilchrist Medal, 1940), Diploma in

1699

English literature 1940. Served in the Women's Land Army, 1942–46. Publishers Copywriter, 1936–42. Lecturer, St. Marylebone Literary Institute, London, 1966–72. Since 1950, British Council Lecturer; since 1956, Lecturer, City Literary Institute, London; since 1959, Lecturer, Goldsmiths' College, University of London; since 1973, Lecturer, Morley College, London. Since 1954, Editor, *English*, London. Recipient: Rockefeller-Atlantic Award, 1946. Fellow, Royal Society of Literature. Address: 1 Brockmere, 43 Wray Park Road, Reigate, Surrey, England.

PUBLICATIONS

Verse

The Invisible Sun.   London, Chaterson, 1946.
Every Star a Tongue.   London, Heinemann, 1951.

Other

Life Was Their Cry (biographical studies of Chaucer, Traherne, Fielding and Browning).   London, Evans, 1950.
The South Hams.   London, Hale, 1955.
Three Metaphysical Poets: Richard Crashaw, Henry Vaughan, Thomas Traherne.   London, Longman, 1961.
English Diarists: Evelyn and Pepys.   London, Longman, 1963.
Three Women Diarists: Celia Fiennes, Dorothy Wordsworth, Katherine Mansfield.   London, Longman, 1964.
A Critical Commentary on Emily Brontë's "Wuthering Heights."   London, Macmillan, 1966.
A Critical Commentary on Browning's "Men and Women."   London, Macmillan, 1968.

Editor, *Two Plays of Goldsmith.*   London, Arnold, 1962.
Editor, *Poems of Today: Fifth Series.*   London, Macmillan, 1963.
Editor, *The Metaphysical Poets.*   London, Arnold, 1971.

Margaret Willy comments:

   Although my poems have often had a country background (perhaps partly because of having worked on the land during the war and lived since in the country, which I love in all its moods, seasons and weathers), they are seldom mere descriptive or atmospheric pieces or "straight" portraits of place. Natural background, imagery and analogies are usually employed to communicate some of my main themes. These include the creative processes of the poet and various aspects of his striving to shape experience into words and trap what is transitory into an illusion of permanence; love and war; problems of human identity and alienation, the enigma – and adventure – of death; and the struggles, paradoxes and rewards of religious experience.
   In connection with the last, the particular period in English poetry which most interests and which I suppose could be said to have influenced me, is that of the seventeenth-century metaphysical and mystical poets – Donne, Herbert, Vaughan

and Traherne. The poetry and personality of Emily Brontë and *Wuthering Heights* have also made a deep and lasting impact. She is the subject of several of my poems about writers (others include Chaucer, Traherne, Dorothy Wordsworth and Lilian Bowes Lyon). The personalities of living people, too, fascinate me; and some whose experience I have tried to explore in my poetry are those of a young countryman, an old farm labourer, a cathedral verger, a singer, children, a mother and a dying elderly lady.

My verse-forms are on the whole traditional, but I have attempted to use as great a variety of rhythm and verse-pattern as possible.

*   *   *

Better known as a critic and editor of *English*, Margaret Willy would think of herself primarily as a poet, and indeed it is her poetic perception that has enabled her to penetrate to the heart of her subjects when she has chosen to write about the work of Chaucer, Traherne, and Emily Brontë. That she has published only two volumes of poetry would suggest that the responsibilities of editing have tended to crowd out the poetry. Nevertheless, she is a poet of considerable talent and, despite the quality of her critical work, it is to be regretted that she has written little poetry since the publication of her *Every Star a Tongue*.

She has a wide range of subject material – from personal relationships, sketches and portraits of people living and dead, to aspects of the changing seasons in the country, religion, art, philosophy, and death – and has varied her tone and structure to the needs of her subjects. One notices how often she thinks of dying as returning to the embraces of a lover – "Close in her arms, to lie with her for ever"; "Lay down to join his old, first love, the earth"; "tugged back earth's lover, reluctant to let him go" – but only so far as countrymen are concerned. She has written many poems on religious themes ("Annunciation" and "Mary's Carol" are among her best), but her conception of religious experience goes far beyond the conventional applications. We are provided with a clue to her beliefs in the poem on Thomas Traherne – "It showed him God in water, bird and tree" – and another in "The Old Poet" – ". . . he peers as though to see / Truth in a petal." The poems in which she expresses her love of natural beauty are those in which her faith is most fittingly communicated.

Because she has been so absorbed in her critical studies, her poems on Chaucer, Traherne, Emily Brontë and Dorothy Wordsworth are as much derived from experience as those concerned with personal relationships which, incidentally, are bound up with her reactions to nature. There is, in fact, a constant interface between her subjects: her "nature" poems turn out to be analogies with art and poetry; her travel poems become portraits, and her portraits reflective poems; and poems such as "Tiger at the Zoo" and "Fairground Music" can be interpreted on several levels. It is difficult, therefore, to divide her work into neat categories and perhaps we ought not to attempt it, simply allowing the total complexity and richness of experience to overlap and interact. Certainly Margaret Willy's poetry has never been given the close attention it deserves.

– Howard Sergeant

WILSON, Keith. American. Born in Clovis, New Mexico, 26 December 1927. Educated at the United States Naval Academy, Annapolis, Maryland, B.A. 1950;

University of New Mexico, Albuquerque, M.A. 1956. Served as a Lieutenant in the
United States Navy during the Korean War. Married Heloise Wilson in 1958; has
five children. Instructor, University of Nevada, Reno, 1956–57; Technical Writer,
Sandia Corporation, Albuquerque, 1958–60; Instructor, University of Arizona, Tuc-
son, 1960–65. Since 1965, Associate Professor of English and Poet-in-Residence,
New Mexico State University, Las Cruces. Recipient: University of New Mexico
D. H. Lawrence Fellowship, 1972; P.E.N. American Center grant, 1972; Westhafer
Award, 1972; National Endowment for the Arts grant, 1974. Address: 1500 Locust,
Las Cruces, New Mexico 88001, U.S.A.

PUBLICATIONS

Verse

> *Sketches for a New Mexico Hill Town.*   Portland, Oregon, Wine Press, 1966.
> *The Old Car and Other Blackpoems.*   Sacramento, California, Grande Ronde
> Press, 1968.
> *II Sequences.*   Portland, Oregon, Wine Press, 1968.
> *Lion's Gate.*   New York, Grove Press, 1968.
> *Graves Registry and Other Poems.*   New York, Grove Press, 1969.
> *The Shadow of Our Bones.*   Portland, Oregon, Trask House Press, 1969.
> *Psalms for Various Voices.*   Las Cruces, New Mexico, Tolar Creek Syndicate,
> 1969.
> *Homestead.*   San Francisco, Kayak Books, 1970.
> *Rocks.*   Oshkosh, Wisconsin, Road Runner Press, 1970.
> *The Old Man and Others.*   Las Cruces, New Mexico State University Press,
> 1970.
> *MidWatch.*   Fremont, Michigan, Sumac Press, 1972.

Other

> Editor, *The Dance Book: An Anthology of Southwestern Poems.*   Portland, Ore-
> gon, Trask House Press, 1970.

Critical Study: by William Winthrop, in *New Mexican* (Santa Fe), 25 August 1968.

Keith Wilson comments:

I hold with (or to) a number of concepts of the New American Poetry.
Three major areas of concern: (1) New Mexico Southwest, (2) the Sea, (3)
Emotional Geography. I often use methods derived, in part at least, from Charles
Olson's Projective Verse – he, Robert Duncan and Robert Creeley have been large
influences on me, as have both William Carlos Williams and – from childhood –
Robert Burns.

*   *   *

Keith Wilson's poetry is informed by a strong sense of history: both the some-times violent history before his time in his own Southwest, and his own personal experience with violence as a naval officer during the Korean War. A collection central to the first of these preoccupations, tracing both his personal and historical awareness of the Southwest, is his fine book, *Homestead; Graves Registry* traces the Korean War experience, and *MidWatch* (or *Graves Registry*, Parts IV and V) extends his meditations on his war experience and man's attraction to violence through the Vietnam War. These poems face up to the most unpleasant aspects of human existence, and contain powerful images: fountains of flesh rising from bombings, faces blown away by a single bullet, a man who shoots a pregnant sow and feasts on her piglets. Wilson's poetry gains additional force from his willing-ness to strive toward an affirmation, and, beyond this, a way toward some better life, in the face of the horrendous evidence of past human history. As he says toward the end of *MidWatch:*

> Ghosts walk, here in the memory
> I have lived a thousand lives or more,
> so have you, and you, and you, but our brains
> are recent ones, we live in the ruins of castles
> and forget we built them.

It is this sense of our own complicity, whether through repetition or reincarna-tion, in past history, that makes his preoccupation with his own ancestral past and New Mexico's roots in the past valuable; it is not merely nostalgia, but rather a desire to learn from the past how to avoid bumping into it again in the future, how to let the new brain rise from the ruins of the old:

> It was the purpose of these poems to show
> the glories of war, sadnesses of peace.
>
> Replace them both.

These poems are ultimately heartening; Wilson brings a compassion rather than self righteous anger to human follies, a forgiveness that may help us to forgive ourselves. Perhaps even violence is better than nothingness, he reminds us, than not being able to relate to one another at all:

> I let him pass,
> bearing him no enmity – how
> quickly he is gone. We'll never
> be friends and he can't eat
> me. We're no use to each other.
> — from "Sidewinder"

— Duane Ackerson

WINGFIELD, Sheila. British. Born in Hampshire, 23 May 1906. Educated at Roedean School, Brighton, Sussex. Married the Honourable M. Wingfield, later Viscount Powerscourt, in 1932 (died, 1973); has one daughter and two sons. Lives in Switzerland. Address: c/o Barclays Bank Ltd., 8 West Halkin Street, London S.W.1, England.

PUBLICATIONS

Verse

> *Poems.* London, Cresset Press, 1938.
> *Beat Drum, Beat Heart.* London, Cresset Press, 1946.
> *A Cloud Across the Sun.* London, Cresset Press, 1949.
> *A Kite's Dinner: Poems 1938–1954.* London, Cresset Press, 1954.
> *The Leaves Darken.* London, Weidenfeld and Nicolson, 1964.

Other

> *Real People* (autobiography). London, Cresset Press, 1952.
> *Sun Too Fast* (as Sheila Powerscourt). London, Bles, 1974.

Sheila Wingfield comments:

My determination to be a poet was formed in the nursery. But my passion for poetry was an affair that had to be conducted in a hole-and-corner way. In youth, parental disapproval forced the study of literature to be a hidden occupation; after marriage, private and public commitments swallowed up most of my time. So it was impossible for me to get to know other practitioners of my generation or younger writers. Hence my unhappy ignorance about what was being done or hatched by contemporaries; I read them, but usually long after various "movements" had been established.

Though it grieved me to miss what I thought of as vital and fertilising contacts, this privacy may have been good for my work. In such an intellectual vacuum, I had to be myself.

Technically, I have tried to give each poem its own form, smell, rhythm and logic. And to employ as large a vocabulary as possible. Also to use the impact of consonants to gain certain effects.

As for subject-matter – the Irish and English countryside and country ways in general are so deeply rooted in me that I fancy much of this blows through my work. History, archaeology, folklore and the superb economy of the classical Greeks are other influences. These tendencies came together in forming my poetic outlook. This can be stated simply. What is personally felt must be fused with what is being, and has been, felt by *Others.* But always in terms of the factual. Nothing woolly or disembodied will do. The same goes for events (which are in fact emotions suffered throughout history and in many lands). Personal dislike for amorphous description is shown by the 2,000-line poem, *Beat Drum, Beat Heart,* which compares men at war with women in love, and men at peace with women out of love, and is in fact a lengthy psychological-philosophical piece without one philosophical expression and I fancy hardly an abstract noun in it. It attempts to sweep over whole cultures and peoples and histories – but invariably in terms of known or perhaps only suspected feelings, expressed in a way that makes such feelings recognisable by a great variety of human beings.

*   *   *

Sheila Wingfield's first book, *Poems,* contained work that was praised by Yeats and Walter de la Mare, and her later collections *A Cloud Across the Sun, A Kite's*

Dinner, and *The Leaves Darken* have all had their admirers. Yet her verse as a whole remains little known, and she is hardly ever represented in anthologies. This seems unfair, since despite some faults of poetic diction ("No longer, Muse, no longer shall I wait"), her poems are technically well-accomplished and sometimes memorable. The sections "Women in Love" and "Women at Peace" from her long poem *Beat Drum, Beat Heart* contain what is perhaps the best of her work, and it is observable that in them she writes rather more personally than is her usual custom, with a result that the rhythms are more natural and various. Elizabeth Jennings has drawn attention to her other virtues: "At her best she has a sense of the heraldic, the emblematic which can produce glittering lines. One should not forget either Miss Wingfield's detailed observation of natural objects. She never goes wrong when she writes about the countryside or about animals."

– Robert Nye

WITHEFORD, Hubert. New Zealander. Born in Wellington, 18 March 1921. Educated at Wellesley College, Wellington; Victoria University, Wellington, M.A. in history. Married to Noel Brooke; has one son. Staff Member, New Zealand Prime Minister's Office, 1939–45, and New Zealand War History Branch, 1945–53. Staff Member, 1954–67, and since 1968, Head of Overseas Section, Reference Division, Central Office of Information, London. Recipient: Jessie Mackay Prize, 1963. Address: 88 Roxborough Road, Harrow, Middlesex, England.

PUBLICATIONS

Verse

Shadow of the Flame: Poems 1942–47.   Auckland, Pelorus Press, 1949.
The Falcon Mask.   Christchurch, Pegasus Press, 1951.
The Lightning Makes a Difference: Poems.   Auckland, Paul's Book Arcade, and London, Brookside Press, 1962.
A Native, Perhaps Beautiful.   Christchurch, Caxton Press, 1967.

Hubert Witheford quotes from his introductory note to *A Native, Perhaps Beautiful:*

Many of the poems spring from sombre emotions. So far as I am concerned, other emotions yield themselves less readily to poetry, that is to transformation, that is to surprise. The great white whale who breaks the surface of my customary stupidities rises from a very dark place.

*   *   *

Hubert Witheford has carved a small niche for himself in New Zealand poetry not so much by the often too amorphous content of his poetry as by what a critic called his "singular precision in his continual whittling of language." Where he begins with something to say, an "idea," it seems, he tends to fail: such a poem as "Elegy in Orongoringo Valley," though gracefully written, seems too manufactured – as in its final stanza:

> Here and in exile and in lost anguish
> He found no frenzy to win him this wanton –
> In his full failure glistens the wild bush
> Too long remembered, too long forgotten.

This rather slack and artificial use of language contrasts strongly with such lines as:

> Each year my heart becomes more dry.

> Through nerveless fingers life like me
> In slow storm runs to the ground;
> Not distance nor insentience provides
> Cuirass against that mild fatality.

This is both subtle and precise, and the irony of "mild" is nicely and honestly placed. Witheford, however, is on the whole at his best in freer forms, where his rhythms are more confident and he does not feel obliged to be "poetical" in order to fit himself into a preconceived mould. Thus "Barbarossa" is one of his most adventurous and original poems, in which he uses rhyme as and when he wishes, and to good effect:

> . . . I sit down
> A stop to stories of the deaths of kings.
> I watch the telegraph
> Poles. A great hand plucks the strings.

> – Martin Seymour-Smith

WONG MAY.   Chinese (Singapore citizen).   Born in Chungking in 1944. Educated at the University of Singapore, B.A. in English literature 1965; University of Iowa, Iowa City (Writers Workshop Fellow, 1966–67), M.F.A. 1968. Married Michael Coey in 1973. Assistant Editor, United Business Publications, New York, 1968–69. Recipient: D.A.A.D. Fellowship, Berlin, 1972. Address: c/o Harcourt Brace Jovanovich Inc., 757 Fifth Avenue, New York, New York 10017, U.S.A.

PUBLICATIONS

Verse

A Bad Girl's Book of Animals.   New York, Harcourt Brace, 1969.
Reports.   New York, Harcourt Brace, 1972.
Wannsee Poems.   Berlin, Literarisches Colloquim, 1974.

Other

Translator, with H. C. Buch, *Der Einsturz der Lei-feng Pagoda*, by Lu Hsun. Hamburg, Rowohlt, 1973.

*   *   *

Wong May's poems are enticed out of single moments. She possesses a point of view, a comprehensive intelligence, and it is these rather than specific themes which engender the poetry. *A Bad Girl's Book of Animals* reveals a personality distinctive in its combination of whimsicality, adultness ("maturity" would be too pedestrian and misleading), innocence, charm, and sharp, ironic sympathy. As we can expect, her perceptions are unusual, though completely acceptable, proving their quality and reach in the life they uncover, the new focus they bring to well-tried subjects. In "Summer Guide," for instance, the encounter between two people generates a mistrust of body and mind, a conflict between the desire to be loved and a feeling of distaste at the prospect:

> I distrust, mistrust you equally:
> The whole field of sun-
> flowers charged, choked,
> can't stand themselves
> their earth electrified
>
> their sky steers away rapid
> west-west-wise. You distrust
> mistrust yourselves equally.

The uncertainty is made specific. Deceptively simple language is supported by shrewd organization. By repeating or splitting them, by varying their contexts, she characteristically exploits the associative powers of words, their delicate yet hard-hitting meanings: "I wish pain were / a thing like a tooth- / ache, sharpened / / Into a point" ("The Man Who Dies"). Lines are left open to form subsequent affinities, to allow development by expansion, or contrast or a shift in the direction of thought. It is a technique she employs extensively, especially in the first few poems of her collection. But craftsmanship has its temptations. At times the technical performance is overdone, as in "Without Qualms" and "Small Thing." The poems become mannered, seem to lack point and fail to rise above dexterous verbal manipulation which is there, one suspects, dutifully compensating for the feeble material.

A certain charm, an ability to express surprise, and a more open, less contrived power available in poems written before she left for the U.S.A. appear to have been refined out of her poetry. And they are an altogether regrettable loss.

But despite these reservations, her poetry is of considerable interest and includes some of the best poems written in Malaya or Singapore.

– Edwin Thumboo

WONG PHUI NAM. Malaysian. Born in Kuala Lumpur, 20 September 1935. Educated at the University of Singapore, B.A. Currently, Economist, Malaysian

Industrial Development Finance Berhad, Kuala Lumpur. Address: Malaysian Industrial Development Finance Berhad, 117 Jalan Ampang, Kuala Lumpur, Selanger, Malaysia.

PUBLICATIONS

Verse

How the Hills Are Distant.   Kuala Lumpur, Tenggara, 1968.

*   *   *

All of Wong Phui Nam's poetry deals with preparations for a kind of self-renewal. They take place in a luminous world just behind the senses, only tenuously related to the common processes of thought. Here a private drama is prosecuted with stoic fatality in anticipation of an expected disaster – or is it an epiphany?

> The flares strung out to the jetty's end
> burn for your death, burn for a sick consciousness,
> the wharves where the debris of old crates and wagons
> smoulders with its hurt, for the great ship
> crawling out across the water, towards the islands,
> towards the sky, as you leave these tides to beat upon
> estuaries new to this gathering dark.

The effort to make out whether the hoped-for conclusion is to be regarded as disaster or epiphany generates the tension in his work; it is the source of his concern to achieve an exactness in the presentation of "a private landscape" which has public significance.

Wong's poetry develops a visual intensity in explicating emotion in concrete metaphors. Especially in *How the Hills Are Distant* one cannot escape the impression of watching a skilfully edited film. A camera-eye picks out objects and scenes in a strange, almost unpeopled landscape, while gradually it is the observer's loneliness, his quiet terror, which impresses more than the things observed:

> About the empty market square
> we do not gather like agitated elders
> in expectation of a runner in with the news,
> the invaders held by the few at a narrow mountain pass,
> bearers of good news being no more of the fashion.
> You who would look for signs, or starve
> among a wilderness, of stone, there are only the boulders
> drowning in pits of worked out mining leases.
> From the main street of the town,
> see how the hills are distant, locked in their silences.

In Wong's more recent poems there is a decisive effort to people his desolate landscapes. As he has said, he wrote of people who "find themselves having to live by institutions and folkways which are not of their heritage, having to absorb the manners of languages not their own." In "Remembering Grandma" (*Tenggara,*

April 1968) objectivity of tone combines with allusive utterance in the portrayal of a Chinese grandmother contemplating her unlikely progeny:

> Baba [i.e. of mixed Chinese-Malay parentage] children
> animal and tartar,
> breaking out in a strange babble of tongues.

Wong puts to original use in his poetry the cultural minutiae which have made us in Malaysia / Singapore the polyglot community we are today. He achieves a precision of image while evoking an intangible air of decay and confusing change. The father portrayed in the concluding stanza of his poem is wholly defined by his Baby Austin 7, his Pitman manuals, his copy of *Robinson Crusoe*, and last but not least, his marriage to his wife's 14-year-old niece. When taken together, these details function also as an ironic portrait of a man culturally adrift.

What Wong is doing in Asian poetry in English is not dissimilar to what Robert Lowell is doing in America. There is the same rejection of the temptation (to which too many present-day poets have succumbed) to make poetic hay of bourgeois grievances, the same meticulous interest in oblique statement. Like Lowell, Wong holds unyieldingly to personal experience seen in a wide context as the principal factor of a poet's salvation; he is preoccupied with the obscure kinds of violence done to the individual by new societies everywhere.

– Lloyd Fernando

WOODCOCK, George. Canadian. Born in Winnipeg, Manitoba, 8 May 1912. Educated at Morley College, London. Married Ingeborg Linzer in 1949. Lecturer, University of Washington, Seattle, 1954–55; Lecturer, 1956–57, Assistant Professor, 1958–61, and Associate Professor of English, 1961–63, University of British Columbia, Vancouver. Editor, *Now*, London, 1940–47; Editorial Adviser, Porcupine Press, London, 1946–48, and Canadian Broadcasting Corporation *Anthology* programme, 1955–61; Advisory Editor, *Tamarack Review*, Toronto, 1956–60; Contributing Editor, *Arts Magazine*, New York, 1962–64. Since 1954, Contributing Editor, *Dissent*, New York; since 1959, Editor, *Canadian Literature*, Vancouver. Fellow, Royal Geographical Society. Recipient: Guggenheim Fellowship, 1951; Canadian Government Overseas Fellowship, 1957; Canada Council travel grant, 1961, 1963, 1965, 1968, Killam Fellowship, 1970, and Molson Prize, 1972; Governor-General's Award, for non-fiction, 1967; Canadian Centennial Medal, 1967; University of British Columbia Medal, for biography, 1972. LL.D.: University of Victoria, British Columbia; D.Litt.: Sir George Williams University, Montreal; University of Ottawa. Fellow, Royal Society of Canada. Address: 6429 McCleery Street, Vancouver 13, British Columbia, Canada.

PUBLICATIONS

Verse

The White Island. London, Fortune Press, 1940.
The Centre Cannot Hold. London, Routledge, 1943.

Imagine the South.   Pasadena, California, Untide Press, 1947.
Selected Poems.   Toronto, Clarke Irwin, 1967.

Plays

Maskerman (broadcast, 1960).   Published in *Prism* (Vancouver), Winter 1961.

Radio Plays: *Maskerman*, 1960; *The Island of Demons*, 1962; *The Benefactor*, 1963; *The Empire of Shadows*, 1964; *The Floor of the Night*, 1965; *The Brideship*, music by Robert Turner, 1967.

Other

New Life to the Land: Anarchist Proposals for Agriculture.   London, Freedom Press, 1942.
Railways and Society.   London, Freedom Press, 1943.
Anarchy or Chaos.   London, Freedom Press, 1944.
William Godwin: A Biographical Study.   London, Porcupine Press, and New York, Irving Ravin, 1946.
The Basis of Communal Living.   London, Freedom Press, 1947.
The Incomparable Aphra.   London, Boardman, 1948.
The Writer and Politics.   London, Porcupine Press, 1948.
The Paradox of Oscar Wilde.   London, Boardman, 1949; New York, Macmillan, 1950.
The Anarchist Prince: A Biographical Study of Peter Kropotkin, with Ivan Avakumovic.   London, Boardman, 1950.
Ravens and Prophets: An Account of Journeys in British Columbia, Alberta and Southern Alaska.   London, Wingate, 1952.
Pierce-Joseph Proudhon: A Biography.   New York, Macmillan, and London, Routledge, 1956.
To the City of the Dead: An Account of Travels in Mexico.   London, Faber, 1957.
Incas and Other Men: Travels in the Andes.   London, Faber, 1959.
Anarchism: A History of Libertarian Ideas and Movements.   New York, Meridian, 1962; London, Penguin, 1963.
Faces of India: A Travel Narrative.   London, Faber, 1964.
Civil Disobedience.   Toronto, Canadian Broadcasting Corporation, 1966.
The Greeks in India.   London, Faber, 1966.
Asia, Gods and Cities: Aden to Tokyo.   London, Faber, 1966.
The Crystal Spirit: A Study of George Orwell.   Boston, Little Brown, 1966; London, Cape, 1967.
Kerala: A Portrait of the Malabar Coast.   London, Faber, 1967.
The Doukhobors, with Ivan Avakumovic.   Toronto and London, Faber, and New York, Oxford University Press, 1968.
The Trade Union Movement and the Government: A Lecture.   Leicester, Leicester University Press, 1968.
The British in the Far East.   London, Weidenfeld and Nicolson, and New York, Atheneum, 1969.
Hugh MacLennan.   Toronto, Copp Clark, 1969.
Henry Walter Bates: Naturalist of the Amazons.   London, Faber, and New York, Barnes and Noble, 1969.
Odysseus Ever Returning: Essays on Canadian Writers and Writing.   Toronto, McClelland and Stewart, 1970.
The Hudson's Bay Company.   New York, Crowell Collier, 1970.

Canada and the Canadians. London, Faber, and Harrisburg, Pennsylvania, Stackpole Books, 1970; revised edition, Faber, 1973.

Mordecai Richler. Toronto, McClelland and Stewart, 1970.

Into Tibet: The Early British Explorers. London, Faber, and New York, Barnes and Noble, 1971.

Mohandas Gandhi. New York, Viking Press, 1971; as *Gandhi*, London, Fontana, 1972.

Dawn and the Darkest Hour: A Study of Aldous Huxley. London, Faber, and New York, Viking Press, 1972.

Herbert Read: The Stream and the Source. London, Faber, 1972.

The Rejection of Politics. Toronto, New Press, 1972.

Who Killed the British Empire? London, Cape, and New York, Quadrangle Books, 1974.

Editor, *A Hundred Years of Revolution: 1848 and After.* London, Porcupine Press, 1948; New York, Haskell House, 1974.

Editor, *The Letters of Charles Lamb.* London, Grey Walls Press, 1950.

Editor, *A Choice of Critics.* Toronto, Oxford University Press, 1966.

Editor, *Variations on the Human Theme.* Toronto, Ryerson Press, 1966.

Editor, *The Sixties: Canadian Writers and Writing of the Decade.* Vancouver, University of British Columbia Press, 1969.

Editor, *Malcolm Lowry: The Man and His Work.* Vancouver, University of British Columbia Press, 1971.

Editor, *Wyndham Lewis in Canada.* Vancouver, University of British Columbia Press, 1971.

Editor, *Typee: A Peep at Polynesian Life,* by Herman Melville. London, Penguin, 1972.

Editor, *Poets and Critics.* Toronto, Oxford University Press, 1974.

Editor, *Colony and Confederation.* Vancouver, University of British Columbia, 1974.

Critical Studies: *George Woodcock* by Peter Hughes, Toronto, McClelland and Stewart, 1974; *From Here to There: A Guide to Canadian Literature since 1960* by Frank Davey, Erin, Ontario, Press Porcépic, 1974.

George Woodcock comments:

In the 1960's I was more concerned with dramatic verse than other types of poetry. Recently I have returned to lyric poetry.

I think that, whatever he may spout about his verse, almost every poet has long lost sight of everything except the work as it stands and is not even the best man to talk about its more multiple meanings. I have often found that readers have found true things in my poems of which I have been at first unaware.

*   *   *

George Woodcock's history as a poet resembles that of several other writers in his age group. The poems he wrote just before and during the Second World War were based on a belief that revolutionary changes would take place in society. In this period Woodcock was associated with the Anarchist movement, and edited the influential radical literary magazine *Now* for some years after the War, before leaving England for Canada. In recent years he has written a valuable history of anarchism and a study of George Orwell, as well as several travel books.

Judged as a poet simply, he is very much a man of the thirties in the sense that his poetic style and social attitude could hardly have been nurtured in any other time. His best poems fall into two groups. The first, and more powerfully imaginative, deal with an invented scene or story in fabulous yet realistic terms. "The Island," rightly familiar from anthologies, is the finest of his poems of this kind. A group of men come to an island, and capture and torture an inhabitant in the attempt to make him tell some secret about hidden gold. Under the torture his joints burst, fire jets from the ruptures:

> There lay before us on the rigid rack
> Straw limbs and a horse's polished skull.
> Gulls mocked as walked away across the sea
> The man we hunted but could not keep or kill.

It is wrong to look for too precise a meaning in such poems. Their deliberate ambiguity increases rather than diminishes the effect of the vivid images and the direct narrative style.

These fables or parables are timeless. Woodcock's other characteristic kind of poem obtains an effect from its immediacy. He shows us much more clearly than most writers of his generation what it was like to be a particular kind of Left-wing intellectual in the years before and during the War. The titles are revealing: "Waterloo Bridge," "Sunday on Hampstead Heath," "Wartime Evening in Cambridge." The quality of the observation raises these poems above poetic journalism, and their firm anchoring in time and place ("the green Cam slithers beneath me, the yellow girl / Rubs my shoulder") make their concern for the future more than merely personal. In Woodcock's poetic vision there are only two human possibilities, either the extinction of a generation in war by death and the increasing suppression of freedom, the "daily evils undermining love," or the prospect of some eventual happiness on "a tamarisked and temperate shore" which is actually never reached in his poetry. Individual joy is seen as something lasting only an instant, and perhaps as itself a kind of illusion since one can be happy only by building personal walls against events outside: "And when the events attack, what walls shall stand?" The attitude produced poignant and charming poems, but when the war ended and this social structure remained unchanged except in minor details, Woodcock survived as writer and social commentator, but his poetic vision faded.

– Julian Symons

WOODS, John (Warren). American. Born in Martinsville, Indiana, 12 July 1926. Educated at Indiana University, Bloomington, B.S. 1949, M.A. 1955; University of Iowa, Iowa City. Served in the United States Air Force. Married Emily Newbury in 1951; has two sons. Assistant Professor, 1955–60, Associate Professor, 1961–64, and since 1965, Professor of English, Western Michigan University, Kalamazoo. Visiting Professor of English, University of California, Irvine, 1967–68. Recipient: Bread Loaf Writers Conference Robert Frost Fellowship, 1962; Yaddo Fellowship, 1963, 1964; Theodore Roethke Prize (*Poetry Northwest*, Seattle), 1968; National

Endowment for the Arts grant, 1969. Address: Department of English, Western Michigan University, Kalamazoo, Michigan 49001, U.S.A.

PUBLICATIONS

Verse

The Deaths at Paragon, Indiana.   Bloomington, Indiana University Press, 1955.
On the Morning of Color.   Bloomington, Indiana University Press, 1961.
The Cutting Edge.   Bloomington, Indiana University Press, 1966.
Keeping Out of Trouble.   Bloomington, Indiana University Press, 1968.
Turning to Look Back, Poems 1955–1970.   Bloomington, Indiana University Press, 1972.
The Knees of Widows.   Kalamazoo, Michigan, Westigan Review Press, 1972.
Voyages to the Inland Sea II: Essays and Poems, with Felix Pollack and James Hearst, edited by John Judson.   La Crosse, University of Wisconsin Center for Contemporary Poetry, 1972.
Alcohol.   Grand Rapids, Michigan, Pilot Press, 1973.
A Bone Flicker.   La Crosse, Wisconsin, Juniper Books, 1973.

Critical Studies: by Richard Hugo, in *Northwest Review* (Eugene, Oregon), 1967; David Etter, in *Chicago Review,* Winter 1972.

John Woods comments:

All that is important about my poetry to the general reader lies in the poetry itself. If, Dear General Reader, we might sit down together over a bottle, we might begin a friendship, an enemyship, a love affair, whatever. Until then, the great, whirling mass of particulars that make up You, and I, can only meet at the interface of my poems.

*   *   *

John Woods, a master of contemporary idiom, sets his poems in the twentieth century Midwest. Through three generations of Indiana farm folk, "between the two wars of father and son," he expresses human hopes and anxieties with an exceptional poetic sense of place and of time. Grandfather's recollection of genealogy is vague, yet certain:

> I don't know where we came from.
> So many graves stay open too long,
> so many girls lie back tonight
> trying to be secret rivers in the limestone.

Woods has discovered a language needing no support of learned notes for characters who "think back along their bones." Generations die back into the Indiana corn knowing, instinctively, that Adonis is violently stoned red before regeneration. Woods chooses apt items for his own totem:

> I shaped a man, my totem animal,
> from branches, murky soil, and pasture dung . . . .
> From a bird stoned red beneath an elm,
> I took a wing for tongue.

Woods, indeed, takes a wing for tongue. His language is lively, his imagery precise, and his rhythms range from the conversational tempo of the elegiac poems on life before death to a swift tumble of images in his wry, humorous asides on life's perplexities.

Turning to Look Back represents his poetic range amply. His first group, "The Deaths at Paragon," gathers elegiac poems on generation and death. Sophisticated love poems, both lithe and muscular, follow in "In Time of Apples." Poems of social commentary are gathered in "Red Telephones"; and formal lyrics, including a fine sestina, in "Barley Tongues."

Dave Etter, writing in the *Chicago Review* (1972), declares Woods "the best poet writing in America today." Etter is on solid ground.

– Edward Callan

WRIGHT, David (John Murray).   British.   Born in Johannesburg, South Africa, 23 February 1920. Educated at St. John's Preparatory School, Johannesburg, 1927; Northampton School for the Deaf, 1934–39; Oriel College, Oxford, 1939–42, B.A. 1942. Married Phillipa Reid in 1951. Staff Member, *Sunday Times*, London, 1942–47; Editor, with Tristram Hull, *Nimbus*, London, 1955–56; Editor, with Patrick Swift, *X* magazine, London, 1959–62. Recipient: Rockefeller-Atlantic Award, 1950; Guinness Award, 1958, 1960; Gregory Fellowship, University of Leeds, 1965–67. Address: c/o A. D. Peters Ltd., 10 Buckingham Street, Adelphi, London WC2N 6BU, England.

PUBLICATIONS

Verse

> *Poems.*   London, Editions Poetry, 1949.
> *Moral Stories.*   St. Ives, Cornwall, Latin Press, 1952.
> *Moral Stories.*   London, Derek Verschoyle, 1954.
> *Monologue of a Deaf Man.*   London, Deutsch, 1958.
> *Adam at Evening.*   London, Hodder and Stoughton, 1965.
> *Poems.*   Leeds, Leeds University, 1966.
> *Nerve Ends.*   London, Hodder and Stoughton, 1969.
> *Corgi Modern Poets in Focus 1,* with others, edited by Dannie Abse.   London, Corgi, 1971.
> *A South African Album.*   Cape Town, David Philip, 1975.

Other

Roy Campbell. London, Longman, 1960.
Algarve, with Patrick Swift. London, Barrie and Rockliff, 1965; revised edition, Barrie and Jenkins, 1971.
Minho and North Portugal: A Portrait and a Guide, with Patrick Swift. London, Barrie and Rockliff, 1968.
Deafness: A Personal Account. London, Allen Lane, and New York, Stein and Day, 1969.
Lisbon: A Portrait and a Guide, with Patrick Swift. London, Barrie and Jenkins, 1971.

Editor, with John Heath-Stubbs, *The Forsaken Garden: An Anthology of Poetry, 1824–1909.* London, Lehmann, 1950.
Editor, with John Heath-Stubbs, *The Faber Book of Twentieth Century Verse: An Anthology of Verse in Britain 1900–1950.* London, Faber, 1953; revised edition, 1965, 1975.
Editor, *The Mid-Century: English Poetry, 1940–60.* London, Penguin, 1965.
Editor, *Longer Contemporary Poems.* London, Penguin, 1966.
Editor, *The Penguin Book of English Romantic Verse.* London, Penguin, 1968.
Editor, *Recollections of the Lakes and the Lake Poets,* by Thomas de Quincey. London, Penguin, 1970.
Editor, *Records of Shelley, Byron, and the Author,* by Edward Trelawny. London, Penguin, 1973.

Translator, *Beowulf.* London, Penguin, 1957.
Translator, *The Canterbury Tales,* by Geoffrey Chaucer. London, Barrie and Rockliff, 1964; New York, Random House, 1965.

Critical Studies: by Dannie Abse, in *Corgi Modern Poets in Focus 1,* 1971; *Guide to Modern World Literature* by Martin Seymour-Smith, London, Wolfe, 1973.

David Wright comments:

> Love, death, liberty, and what we are all here for,
> Whether the date is November twenty-three or doomsday,
> Discussions of this kind, they somehow manage to ignore:
> Theirs is a message of purest frivolity.
>
> Affirming the unprovable, they have nothing to say
> But that the fine point of existence, the instant's span
> Between the void before and the void after, is really
> Valid (and what is the use of knowing this?). Again,
>
> They do not say anything but by analogy.

*　　　*　　　*

Though numbered among the South African exiles, David Wright seems not so much troubled as interested by his displacement. He says firmly that he was

> Born in a dominion to which he hoped not to go back
> Since predisposed to imagine white possibly black

But beyond this general acknowledgement, he is not much given to beating the air about the plight of his non-white fellow countrymen. One feels he has had to conserve much of his energy for overcoming his own plight of total deafness, getting through university and leading a very active existence in literary London. Yet a certain ironical recall of his early home produces some of his most attractive poetry. His dry-eyed memories are of "the legless kaffir on the Town Hall pavement," "a European tram bellowing down to Norwood," and "her lion-crouched woods and silver-hatted mountains." His even gaze respects the "last passion" in David Livingstone, the curiosity to find the source of the Nile:

> In which prayer dying, David Livingstone
> Passed, and those whom he could not save
> Carried his bones to Zanzibar and England,
> But kept his heart and innards in their proper grave.

And there is the cheerful balance of his portrait of Roy Campbell:

> My countryman, the poet, wears a Stetson;
> He can count his enemies, but not his friends.
> A retired soldier living in Kensington,
> Who limps along the Church Street to the Swan.

Indeed it is as a raconteur in verse that David Wright achieves some of his best and most pleasing effects, as in his three "Moral Stories," particularly the tale of the fisherman transformed to a god:

> His hair growing green as shallows, his colour
> Turned blue as out of soundings, flashing with scales:
> Divinity and ocean took him over.

The sea flows through much of David Wright's poetry, for which he himself offers the reason – that he was conceived on a liner "Sliding like a swan on a careless ocean." Liberty, the great requirement of poetry is as uneasy and uncertain as the sea, and possibly as treacherous. Security is a sort of gaol,

> With paper and pen, with a room, and with time to think,
> Everything, in fact, unnecessary to the Muse.

Ironically he salutes an Emperor Penguin that died in Regents Park:

> To die of a desire for freedom and bad weather. . . .

> – Anthony Delius

WRIGHT, James (Arlington). American. Born in Martin's Ferry, Ohio, 13 December 1927. Educated at Kenyon College, Gambier, Ohio, B.A.; University of Washington, Seattle, M.S., Ph.D. Married to Edith Anne Runk; has two sons. Has taught at the University of Minnesota, Minneapolis, and Macalaster College, St.

Paul, Minnesota. Since 1966, Instructor in English, Hunter College, New York. Recipient: Fulbright Scholarship, 1952; Eunice Teitjens Memorial Prize, 1955, and Oscar Blumenthal Prize, 1968 (*Poetry,* Chicago); Yale Series of Younger Poets award, 1957; National Institute of Arts and Letters grant, 1959; Guggenheim Fellowship, 1964; Brandeis University Creative Arts Award, 1970; Academy of American Poets Fellowship, 1971; Melville Cane Award, 1972; Pulitzer Prize, 1972. Lives in New York City.

PUBLICATIONS

Verse

The Green Wall.   New Haven, Connecticut, Yale University Press, 1957.
Saint Judas.   Middletown, Connecticut, Wesleyan University Press, 1959.
The Lion's Tail and Eyes: Poems Written Out of Laziness and Silence, with Robert Bly and William Duffy.   Madison, Minnesota, Sixties Press, 1962.
The Branch Will Not Break: Poems.   Middletown, Connecticut, Wesleyan University Press, and London, Longman, 1963.
Shall We Gather at the River.   Middletown, Connecticut, Wesleyan University Press, 1968; London, Rapp and Whiting, 1969.
Collected Poems.   Middletown, Connecticut, Wesleyan University Press, 1971.
Two Citizens.   New York, Farrar Straus, 1974.

Recording: *Today's Poets 3*, with others, Folkways.

Other

Translator, with Robert Bly, *Twenty Poems of Georg Trakl.*   Madison, Minnesota, Sixties Press, 1961.
Translator, with Robert Bly and John Knoepfle, *Twenty Poems of César Vallejo.*   Madison, Minnesota, Sixties Press, 1962.
Translator, *The Rider on the White Horse*, by Theodor Storm.   New York, New American Library, 1964.
Translator, with Robert Bly, *Twenty Poems of Pablo Neruda.*   Madison, Minnesota, Sixties Press, and London, Rapp and Whiting, 1968.
Translator, with Robert Bly and John Knoepfle, *Neruda and Vallejo: Selected Poems.*   Boston, Beacon Press, 1971.
Translator, *Wandering: Notes and Sketches*, by Hermann Hesse.   New York, Farrar Straus, and London, Cape, 1972.

James Wright Comments:

I have written about the things I am deeply concerned with – crickets outside my window, cold and hungry old men, ghosts in the twilight, horses in a field, a red-haired child in her mother's arms, a feeling of desolation in the fall, some cities I've known.

I try and say how I love my country and how I despise the way it is treated. I try and speak of the beauty and again of the ugliness in the lives of the poor and neglected.

I have changed the way I've written, when it seemed appropriate, and continue to do so.

                              *   *   *

James Wright's *Collected Poems* contains most of *The Green Wall*, and all of *Saint Judas*, *The Branch Will Not Break*, and *Shall We Gather at the River*, plus some translations and 33 new poems. This impressive volume, although it covers a poetic career of only 14 years, reveals a genuine experimenter, a poet who can, like Yeats, consciously transform himself. Thus we can speak already of Wright's "phases," and I think we can discern 3 distinct stages of development: the early rich and formal poems of the first two books; the spare and "deep-image" work of *Branch*; and the loose and pain-filled later poems. For these stages also reveal a strange and tragic curve of emotional development: Wright's concern for human suffering, which was never absent from his earlier work, and which seemed to have been temporarily balanced by the bright joy of so much of *Branch*, now reappears as an obsession without let or hindrance or (often) control in an avalanche of anguish and despair in *River* and "New Poems."

The Green Wall and *Saint Judas* are written largely in regular stanzas and literary language. The first is lush with the Dylan-Thomas-like ecstasy of a young poet discovering his medium and his powerful sensibility, and is notable for its hallucinatory sense of the seasons and their montagistic overlappings. In "Eleutheria," for example, after rhapsodically portraying an erotic experience in the glowing country of summer and autumn, he says:

> Lovers' location is the first to fade.
> They wander back in winter, but there is
> No comfortable grass to couch a dress.

Saint Judas is somewhat reminiscent, however, in its more rugged subjects and feelings, of Hardy, Robinson, Masters, and Frost. It deals in a stark and compassionate way with love and loss and death in the lives of a dramatic cast of characters. "At Thomas Hardy's Birthplace, 1953," is indicative, for Hardy "turned aside [from nature] and heard the human wail, / That other sound." Then there is a sequence of love poems treating painfully but movingly the loss and sorrow of a love that is failing. Finally, there is a section concerned with crime and violence, the innocent and the guilty – as, for example, in the Caryl Chessman and George Doty poems, "American Twilights" and "At the Executed Murderer's Grave." Here is more than abstract humanitarianism, for Wright sees that there is no absolute difference between the murderer and the rest of us, that the executioner is only doing coldly what his victim did out of madness or passion or grief.

No longer using conventional diction, regular stanzas, and straightforward structures, *The Branch* is given to open and direct lines, poems of varying lengths, and easy and natural language. Far surpassing his dogmatic master, Robert Bly, Wright builds his poems, in haiku fashion, on hard images which are juxtaposed in shocking combinations of experience, leaving the connections and transitions to be inferred by the reader. There is, correspondingly, a tendency to shift from the external dramatic world inward to the subjective world. "Autumn Begins in Martin's Ferry, Ohio," for example, although still in the objective mode of the preceding volume, implies universes of suppressed violence within as it portrays the erotic frustration of the parents of high school footballers, and concludes:

> Therefore,
> Their sons grow suicidally beautiful
> At the beginning of October,
> And gallop terribly against each other's bodies.

"Lying on a Hammock at William Duffy's Farm" gives the first 12 of its 13 lines to a literal description, marvelously bright, of a peaceful rural scene, and then concludes abruptly with: "I have wasted my life" – implying that this is the first time he has noticed these things so sharply, and that he has wasted his life up to now in not loafing and inviting his soul.

"Fear Is What Quickens Me," with its compressed and dramatic realization of civilization vs. eros, is another notable poem. As is "Today I Was So Happy, So I Made This Poem," which begins with the usual sharply-etched image – a squirrel seen in moonlight – and ends:

> An eagle rejoices in the oak trees of heaven,
> Crying
> *This is what I wanted.*

Finally, "A Blessing" is one of his best. The speaker and a friend see two loving Indian ponies in a pasture, who respond gently and happily to them. The speaker's left hand is being nuzzled by the slenderer pony, and he concludes:

> Suddenly I realize
> That if I stepped out of my body I would break
> Into blossom.

For sweetness and passion, for precision and surprise, this poem is very nearly perfect, and has justly won a place in many anthologies.

The emotional – and sometimes artistic – descent, however, is dizzying as we come to *Shall We Gather at the River* and the "New Poems." For unrelieved wretchedness, these pieces must be unmatched in contemporary poetry, and suggest that Wright is returning, after the brief high of *Branch*, to some old and fundamental unresolved despair. Surely the name itself of the 1968 volume suggests the Dead gathering by the Styx, and some of the titles are all-too-indicative of its contents and mood: "In Terror of Hospital Bills," "The Poor Washed Up by Chicago Winter," "Old Age Compensation," "Listening to the Mourners." But it is not until the "New Poems" that we actually touch what one hopes is the bottom of this agony:

> We are men.
> It doesn't even satisfy us
> To kill one another.
> We are a smear of obscenity. . . .
> I have no use for the human creature. . . .
> I am born one, out of an accidental hump of chemistry.
> I have no use.
>   – from "A Secret Gratitude"

Such hatred and self-hatred is the polarity, it seems to me, of his compassion for the unfortunate and his probing self-awareness, and the total context of the poem, which is about Edna Millay and Eugen Boissevain, and which does in fact have a rather positive ending, does not really integrate and transform the section from which the above lines were taken. It is not even a Swiftian revulsion from human life; it is, rather, a kind of self-indulgent, non-cathertic nausea.

A similar stylistic slackness is found in "Many of Our Waters":

> If you do not care one way or another about
> The preceding lines,
> Please do not go on listening
> On any account of mine.
> Please leave the poem.
> Thank you.

There is a strange desperation here, a kind of hysteria, which I hope presages Wright's transition to phase four:

> All this time I've been slicking into my own words
> The beautiful language of my friends.
> I have to use my own, now.
> That's why this scattering poem sounds the way it does.

He is ready for another transformation, and he seems bewildered:

> The kind of poetry I want to write is
> The poetry of a grown man.

May the Muse grant that he find it! And we can only hope that his capacity for frequent change is a sign of growth rather than of some basic instability. I do not think, however, that the poetry of a grown man is found by writing poorly, and then by acknowledging that one is writing poorly. Irony and self-awareness, even anti-poetry, require more than that. But when all is said and done, Wright is a genuinely passionate poet who does not withhold or spare himself, and his best work still makes him one of the most interesting and promising younger poets writing in the United States today.

– Norman Friedman

WRIGHT, Judith. Australian. Born in Armidale, New South Wales, 31 May 1915. Educated at New South Wales Correspondence School; New England Girls School, Armidale; University of Sydney, B.A. Married to J. P. McKinney (died); has one daughter. Worked as a secretary, clerk and statistician, 1938–49. Commonwealth Literary Fund Lecturer, Australia, 1949, 1962. Since 1967, Honours Tutor in English, University of Queensland, Brisbane. Guest Delegate, World Poetry Conference, Canada, 1967. Recipient: Grace Leven Prize, 1949, 1972; Commonwealth Literary Fund Fellowship, 1964; *Encyclopedia Britannica* Award, 1964. D.Litt.: University of Queensland, Brisbane, 1962; University of New England, Armidale, 1963. Lives in North Tamborine, Queensland.

PUBLICATIONS

Verse

The Moving Image: Poems. Melbourne, Meanjin Press, 1946.
Woman to Man. Sydney, Angus and Robertson, 1949.
The Gateway. Sydney, Angus and Robertson, 1953.
The Two Fires. Sydney, Angus and Robertson, 1955.
Birds: Poems. Sydney, Angus and Robertson, 1962.
(Poems), selected and introduced by the author. Sydney, Angus and Robertson, 1963.
Five Senses: Selected Poems. Sydney, Angus and Robertson, 1963.
City Sunrise. Brisbane, Shapcott Press, 1964.
The Other Half: Poems. Sydney, Angus and Robertson, 1966.
Poetry from Australia: Pergamon Poets 6, with Randolph Stow and William Hart-Smith, edited by Howard Sergeant. Oxford, Pergamon Press, 1969.
Collected Poems 1942–1970. Sydney, Angus and Robertson, 1971.
Alive: Poems. Sydney, Angus and Robertson, 1973.

Short Stories

The Nature of Love. Melbourne, Sun Books, 1966.

Other

The Generations of Men. Melbourne, Oxford University Press, 1959.
King of the Dingoes (juvenile). Melbourne, Oxford University Press, and London, Angus and Robertson, 1959.
Range the Mountains High (juvenile). London, Angus and Robertson, 1962.
Shaw Neilson (biography and selected verse). Sydney, Angus and Robertson, 1963.
Charles Harpur. Melbourne, Lansdowne Press, 1963.
The Day the Mountains Played (juvenile). London, Angus and Robertson, 1963.
Country Towns (juvenile). London, Oxford University Press, 1964.
Preoccupations in Australian Poetry. Melbourne and London, Oxford University Press, 1965.
The River and the Road (juvenile). Melbourne, Lansdowne Press, 1966; London, Angus and Robertson, 1967; revised edition, Lansdowne Press, 1971.
Henry Lawson. Melbourne, London, and New York, Oxford University Press, 1967.
Conservation as an Emerging Concept. Sydney, Australian Conservation Foundation, 1971.

Editor, *Australian Poetry 1948.* Sydney, Angus and Robertson, 1948.
Editor, *A Book of Australian Verse.* Melbourne and London, Oxford University Press, 1956; revised edition, 1968.
Editor, *New Land, New Language: An Anthology of Australian Verse.* Melbourne and London, Oxford University Press, 1957.
Editor, with A. K. Thomson, *The Poet's Pen.* Brisbane, Jacaranda Press, 1966.
Editor, *Witnesses of Spring: Unpublished Poems,* by Shaw Neilson. Sydney, Angus and Robertson, 1970.

Critical Studies: by F. Brissenden and others, in *Critical Essays on Judith Wright*, Brisbane, Jacaranda Press, 1968.

Judith Wright comments:

The background of my work lies in my main life concerns, as an Australian whose family on both sides were early comers to a country which was one of the last to be settled by the whites, and were from the beginning farmers and pastoralists. Brought up in a landscape once of extraordinary beauty, but despised by its settlers because of its unfamiliarity, I have I suppose been trying to expiate a deep sense of guilt over what we have done to the country, to its first inhabitants of all kinds, and are still and increasingly doing. This is one aspect of the sources of my work. I have never for long been an urban-dweller, and the images I use and also my methods no doubt reflect my ties to the landscape I live in. I tend to use "traditional" – i.e., biological – rhythms more than free or new forms, which I see as better adapted to urban living and urban tensions and problems.

Another strong influence on my work has been my relationship with my husband whose philosophical investigation of the sources and development of Western thought I shared in till his death. As a woman poet, the biological aspect of feminine experience has naturally been of importance in my work also. I expect my poetry is of a kind which no urban technological society will produce again, but I have tried to remain faithful to my own experience and outlook rather than engage in experimental verse for which it does not fit me.

*   *   *

Judith Wright is perhaps the best-known and the most widely-read Australian poet writing today and one of the few whose reputation extends outside Australia. She is a talented critic, has written a number of moving and capable short stories and a delightful history of her family's establishment as pioneers in Australia, *The Generations of Men*; but her strength lies in poetry. Within the range of her poetry what distinguishes her most is, first, her re-creation of the Australian landscape, especially of the New England district of New South Wales, its people, its history, and the way one influences the other, an intense evocation of the spirit of place; and, second, her poems dealing with the relations of men and women, women and their lovers, their husbands and their children. The high plains and harsh hill-country of New England is something that she is able to evoke because it is where she grew up, something that is inside her and not simply a landscape without:

> The hard inquiring wind strikes to the bone
> and whines division. Many roads meet here
> in me, the traveller and the ways I travel
> All the hills' gathered waters feed my seas
> Who am the swimmer and the mountain river;
> And the long slopes' concurrence is my flesh
> Who am the gazer and the land I stare on.

This has been something important for Australian poetry, in which until recently poets were much obsessed with the country itself but always as something they aimed at capturing in verse. Judith Wright has shown us all how to succeed by treating the scene as something within, something to start from and take for granted.

The other main aspect of her poetry is metaphysical: it aims at the spiritual mystery of human life and human relationships, the biological correspondences that lie beneath the merely personal relationships of men and women. In this respect her most outstanding achievement has been to speak for and establish the metaphysical poetic vision of a woman, as opposed to the predominant male vision that poetry presents, as in "Woman to Child":

> I wither and you break from me;
> Yet though you dance in living light,
> I am the earth, I am the root
> I am the stem that fed the fruit
> The link that joins you to the night.

Judith Wright's recent poetry has been much concerned with the native Australian birds, animals and plants, whose essence she presents in verse. Her concern with their preservation – she is a prime mover in the Wild Life Preservation Society – arises from and continues to feed this interest. Her *Preoccupations in Australian Poetry* is an interesting essay in the definition and assessment of the main characteristics that distinguish poetry in Australia.

– A. D. Hope

YATES, J. Michael. Canadian. Born in Fulton, Missouri, U.S.A., 10 April 1938. Educated at Westminster College, Fulton; University of Kansas City, Missouri (Poetry Prize, 1960), B.A. 1960, M.A. 1961; University of Michigan, Ann Arbor (Hopwood Award, for poetry, 1964, for drama, 1964). Promotional Director, Public Radio Corporation, Houston, 1961–62; Teaching Fellow, University of Michigan, 1962–63; Instructor in English and Creative Writing, Ohio University, Athens, 1964–65; Special Lecturer in Literature and Creative Writing, University of Alaska, Fairbanks, 1965–66; Associate Professor of Creative Writing, University of British Columbia, Vancouver, 1966–71; Visiting Professor of English, Universiry of Arkansas, Fayetteville, Fall 1972. Editor-in-Chief, 1966–67, and Poetry Editor, 1966–71, *Prism International*, and Member of the Editorial Board, Prism International Press, Mission, British Columbia, 1966–71; Founding Editor, with Andreas Schroeder, *Contemporary Literature in Translation*, Vancouver, 1968; Member of the Editorial Board, *Mundus Artium*, Athens, Ohio; General Editor, *Campus Canada*. Since 1971, President, Sono Nis Press, Vancouver. Recipient: International Broadcasting Award, 1961, 1962; Canada Council grant, 1968, 1969, 1971; *The Far Point* Contributor's Prize, 1970. Address: 33492 Cherry Street, Mission, British Columbia, Canada.

PUBLICATIONS

Verse

Spiral of Mirrors. Francestown, New Hampshire, Golden Quill Press, 1967.
Hunt in an Unmapped Interior and Other Poems. Francestown, New Hampshire, Golden Quill Press, 1967.

Canticle for Electronic Music. Victoria, British Columbia, Charles Morriss, 1967.
Parallax, with Bob Flick. Victoria, British Columbia, Charles Morriss, 1968.
The Great Bear Lake Meditations. Ottawa, Oberon Press, 1970.
Selected Poems. Ottawa, Oberon Press, 1972.

Plays

Subjunction (produced Fairbanks, 1965).
Night Freight (broadcast 1968; produced Toronto, 1972). Toronto, Playwrights Co-op, 1972.

Screenplay: *The Grand Edit*, 1966.

Radio Plays: *The Broadcaster*, 1968; *Theatre of War*, 1968; *The Calling*, 1968; *Night Freight*, 1968; *The Panel*, 1968.

Novel

Exploding. Vancouver, Sono Nis Press, 1972.

Short Stories

Man in the Glass Octopus. Vancouver, Sono Nis Press, 1968.

Other

The Abstract Beast (fiction and drama). Vancouver, Sono Nis Press, 1971.

Editor, with Andreas Schroeder, *Contemporary Poetry of British Columbia.* Vancouver, Sono Nis Press, 2 vols., 1970, 1972.
Editor, with Charles Lillard, *Volvox: Poetry from the Unofficial Languages of Canada in English Translation.* Vancouver, Sono Nis Press, 1971.
Editor, *Contemporary Fiction of British Columbia.* Vancouver, Sono Nis Press, 1971.

J. Michael Yates comments:

1. For me, an image is one of an infinite number of entrances into an arena where something ineffable is going on. If the thing I'm after were statable, probably it would be better said in expository prose. The issues most often taken up by good poetry usually require use of the silences between and behind words. For this mode of communication, metaphor, indirection are the best engines.

2. With each piece, I attempt to cause a structure, a system, of images whose parts belong dissonantly to a whole whose meaning cannot be stated. I mean Stravinsky's dissonance. In the *Poetics of Music*, he suggests that dissonance is only a transitional element; consonance must be achieved one way or another – either in the instrumentation or in the ear of the listener. The latter is my way – to give

the reader the "thing" I'm talking about, frame by frame, and ask him to project it inside him in the manner that most entertains him. Different and isolate as each of us is, it seems the only honesty.

3. Ideally, fifteen readers will make fifteen very different (and fifteen equally justifiable) poems from a piece I have written. As I'm different from you at any moment, I differ from myself through successive moments – even the most familiar things change with changes in the coordinates of consciousness and time. I couldn't possibly recreate the coordinates of consciousness that produced a given piece and thereby tell you what it means.

4. Ideally, a reader would come to a poem relaxed, with open consciousness, no preconceptions nor suspicions that the poem is a locked door and someone some-where – probably the treacherous bastard author – is hiding the key. The parts of a poem which persist inside a reader arrive there via personal correspondences. Exterior interpretations remain merely exterior. Belief in one's own associations is difficult, very difficult. But only those will translate the poem from "mine" to "yours."

5. Ideally, one would read a poem as if he were the first reader in history to read a poem – and as if no one on earth were reading a poem at that moment. Impossible. Necessary.

6. Ideally, I write as if no one has ever written a poem. As if no one is writing now. Ridiculous. Imperative.

7. "Understanding" is a sweet, vague Renaissance dream which never came true. According to me, poems are not to be understood, but responded to. Understanding promises universal truth. Naive. I'm a rare user and no pusher at all of either reality or its ism. I don't assume a "representative universe." As if one could come to an "understanding" about such things.

*   *   *

An overview of the work of J. Michael Yates is complicated by the diversity of forms in which he writes and by his marked experimentation, self-education, and maturation as a writer. This apologia notwithstanding, there are themes and images common to all Yates' output, from the early poems to the plays of *The Abstract Beast*. And common to all his work, too, is a certain self-consciousness, arising partly from the experimentation, but largely from a self-image of the "young man as Artist," an image which matures as surely as does his technique. In fact, there is a connection between these two observations, for Yates' self-image is not a pose, but, rather, a preoccupation with the notion that the ideas of the writer are his whole world and reality. This Lockean fascination with a state of being in which the mind becomes a substitute for the existent is seen perhaps most clearly in *Man in the Glass Octopus* but is prefigured in the early poems of *Hunt in an Unmapped Interior* (whose title suggests it) and continues into the endless series of lenses viewing lenses of the *Parallax* poems. It also prompts the recurrent images of animals eating animals, cameras filming cameras, and mirrors mirroring mirrors with which the poems are filled. As well, it explains the persona of the author/nar-rator as Adam naming Creation, which D. G. Jones has cited as a major theme of all Canadian writing and which in Yates' poems (notably *The Great Bear Lake Meditations*), is extended until the mind of Adam becomes the Mind of God, Itself an insubstantial mirror of Yates' own consciousness. And finally, it is embodied in the name of Yates' press, at once an *impressa* and a complication: Sono Nis – "the I is not."

Each of these concerns is introduced in *Hunt in an Unmapped Interior*, a collection of poems strongly reminiscent of Wallace Stevens, in which the short pieces are deft and incisive, the longer poems ruminative. *Canticle for Electronic Music* is disappointing after this auspicious first collection; again Yates has difficulty in sustaining the longer poem. *Great Bear Lake Meditations* is a more mature work, in which the Adam persona is accepted and in which Yates' love of words becomes congruent with his myth – if the poet's only reality is imaginative, then words become symbols of nothing other than aspects of his imagination. In *Parallax*, Yates gropes toward but fails to quite reach a further refinement in which if "words are better than talk . . . [then] silence [is] better than words." The poems attempt the visual, building upon camera imagery. But to create a "silent" poem without words is ultimately to produce a blank page and these poems, however compelling, are "at the verge of total desire that ends in the half-act."

In *The Abstract Beast*, Yates looks to other forms and modifies his poems into the prose they have always approached and into highly successful short radio plays (which would be less successful on stage). Perhaps realizing after *Man in the Glass Octopus* that the end-point of his self-preoccupation would be self-nihilism, Yates has tempered his myth; while it is still obvious it is less obsessive. The result is a collection that with the exception of some unfortunately reprinted, early pieces is as inventive as it is exciting. What thinness does arise in the stories and the sometimes disturbing inconclusiveness of the plays are most likely the result of another shift in development and hopefully will not continue into later work. Much more will be heard of J. Michael Yates.

– S. R. Gilbert

YOUNG, Al. American. Born in Ocean Springs, Mississippi, 31 May 1939. Educated at the University of Michigan, Ann Arbor (Co-Editor, *Generation* magazine), 1957–61; Stanford University, California (Wallace E. Stegner Creative Writing Fellow), 1966–67; University of California, Berkeley, A.B. in Spanish 1969. Married Arline June Belch in 1963; has one son. Free-lance Musician, 1958–64; Disk Jockey, KJAZ-FM, San Francisco, 1961–65; Instructor and Linguistic Consultant, San Francisco Neighborhood Youth Corps Writing Workshop, 1968–69; Writing Instructor, Teenage Workshop, San Francisco Museum of Art, 1968–69; Jones Lecturer in Creative Writing, Stanford University, 1969–74. Since 1966, Founding Editor, *Loveletter*, San Francisco; since 1972, Co-Editor, *Yardbird Reader*, Berkeley, California; Contributing Editor, since 1972, *Changes*, New York, and since 1973, *Umoja*, New Mexico. Recipient: National Endowment for the Arts grant, 1968, 1969; San Francisco Foundation Joseph Henry Jackson Award, 1969; Guggenheim Fellowship, 1974; National Endowment for the Arts grant, 1974. Agent: Lynn Nesbitt, International Famous Agency, 1301 Avenue of the Americas, New York, New York 10019. Address: 373 Oxford Street, Palo Alto, California 94306, U.S.A.

PUBLICATIONS

Verse

Dancing: Poems. New York, Corinth Books, 1969.
The Song Turning Back into Itself. New York, Holt Rinehart, 1971.
Some Recent Fiction. San Francisco, San Francisco Book Company, 1974.

Plays

Screenplays: *Nigger*, 1972; *Sparkle*, 1972.

Novels

Snakes. New York, Holt Rinehart, 1970; London, Sidgwick and Jackson, 1971.
Who Is Angelina? New York, Holt Rinehart, 1975.

Bibliography: in *New Black Voices*, edited by Abraham Chapman, New York, New American Library, 1972.

Critical Studies: "Reader's Report" by Martin Levin, in *The New York Times Book Review*, 17 May 1970; "Growing Up Black" by L. E. Sissman, in *The New Yorker*, 11 July 1970; "Jazzed Up," in the *Times Literary Supplement* (London), 30 July 1971; "Al Young's *Snakes*: Words to the Music" by Neil Schmitz, in *Paunch 35* (Buffalo), February 1972.

Al Young comments:

I see my poetry as being essentially autobiographical in subject matter and detail, characterized by a marked personal and lyrical mysticism as well as a concern with social and spiritual problems of contemporary man in a technological environment that grows hourly more impersonal and unreal. My favorite themes are those of love, the infinite changeability of the world as well as its eternal changelessness, and the kind of meaning (both private and universal) that flowers out of everyday life. My influences in general have been Black culture and popular speech (Southern rural and urban U.S.) and music in particular (jazz, Afro-American folk and popular music, the music of Charles Mingus and John Coltrane which defies categorization, Caribbean music of both English- and Spanish-speaking peoples); American Indian poetry and song; Hindu philosophy. Some poets I admire and have consciously learned from: Li Po, Nicolás Guillén, Rabindranath Tagore, the poetry of the *Bible*, Federico Garcia Lorca, Kenneth Patchen, Blaise Cendrars, early T. S. Eliot, Rimbaud, Brecht, LeRoi Jones, Mayakovsky, Denise Levertov, Leopold Senghor, Kenneth Rexroth, Cervantes, Diane Wakoski and Nicanor Parra.

Besides being as necessary as food, water, air, sunlight and sleep – poetry is my way of celebrating Spirit, in all of its infinite forms (charted and uncharted) as the central unifying force in Creation.

*   *   *

Al Young's impressionistic scenario "2 Takes from *Love in Los Angeles*" shows us how the surface culture of the contemporary center of mobile social life debases hope and feeling until "Love licks its lip / at no one." Young's poetic project, however, is not simply to document, nor even to protest. It is rather to discover in the world where loneliness is the shadow of human love, the means by which poetry might serve its traditional function of providing significance and fostering ecstasy.

He achieves a first step in poems of controlled autobiographical focus where accidental, specific details of ordinary life gain meaning by association. The sequence of a day's ordinary events – songs heard on the radio, food eaten for lunch and being cooked for dinner – becomes a love letter in "Dear Arl," and in "A Dance for Li Po" bringing home groceries stimulates reflection on the variety of good places the poet has been over the years. The move from present detail to past events is only a step, but for Young the crucial one, because it brings to his verse the power of memory to sustain meaning. Poems on Ma Rainey and on music heard in his youth acknowledge a mothering culture in the volume *Dancing*. Then, in *The Song Turning Back into Itself*, he converts memory into the principle of a fluid reality wherein the past influences the present and establishes among the variables of all the lived and future moments a continuity for an individual lifetime.

While memory is the mediation producing philosophical significance for Young, it is poetry itself, and its companion art of music, which dynamically embody the principle because of their intrinsic power of evocation and expression. The entire movement of Young's esthetic-philosophical project is contained in the seven part poem "The Song Turning Back into Itself." Here the images of circling in time and space lead into statement of the power of song to create new versions of love and loneliness while also organizing past experience of those states. There is, too, a Whitman-like sense of the capacity of poetry to generate identity through its expression of the spiritual basis of experience: "My soul / seeks your soul // Let us laugh / each at the other / & be friends." Appropriately the sequence concludes with a jazz inspired fly-away song in which the poet soars over rooftops alive and waking.

Analogy with Whitman might be extended, just as might Young's stress on the traditional purposes of poetry. Still, his work records the making of a specifically contemporary American poet. There is no mistaking that in the tone which permits him to call poetry a

> magic wafer you take
> into your mouth
> &
> swallow for dear life

– John M. Reilly

YOUNG, David (Pollock). American. Born in Davenport, Iowa, 14 December 1936. Educated at Carleton College, Northfield, Minnesota, B.A. 1958; Yale University, New Haven, Connecticut, M.A. 1959, Ph.D. 1965. Married Chloe Hamilton in 1963; has two children. Instructor, 1961–65, Assistant Professor, 1965–68, Associate Professor, 1969–73, and since 1973, Professor of English, Oberlin College, Ohio. Since 1969, Editor, *Field: Contemporary Poetry and Poetics*, Oberlin. Co-Owner, Triskelion Press, Oberlin. Recipient: Tane Award (*Massachusetts Review*, Amherst), 1965; National Endowment for the Arts grant, 1967; International Poetry Forum United States Award, 1968. Address: 220 Shipherd Circle, Oberlin, Ohio 44074, U.S.A.

PUBLICATIONS

Verse

> *Sweating Out the Winter: Poems.* Pittsburgh, University of Pittsburgh Press, 1969.
> *Six Poems from Wang Wei.* Oberlin, Ohio, Triskelion Press, 1969.
> *Thoughts of Chairman Mao.* Oberlin, Ohio, Triskelion Press, 1970.
> *Boxcars.* New York, Ecco Press, 1974.

Other

> *Something of Great Constancy: The Art of "A Midsummer Night's Dream."* New Haven, Connecticut, Yale University Press, 1966.
> *The Heart's Forest: A Study of Shakespeare's Pastoral Plays.* New Haven, Connecticut, Yale University Press, 1972.
>
> Editor, *Twentieth Century Interpretations of "Henry IV, Part Two": A Collection of Critical Essays.* New York, Prentice Hall, 1968.
>
> Translator, *Selected Poems*, by Eugenio Montale. New York, New Directions, 1965.

*   *   *

David Young's poetry has a strong sense of the American Midwest where he was born and now teaches; it is poetry of a flat land dreaming of quiet transformations, unsatisfied but calm:

> All to the south the dazed, hot landscape lies,
> Under its piled thunderheads,
> Dreaming of love and survival.

His poetry reminds one of the work of another Midwestern poet, William Stafford, in that it has a controlled skilfulness which makes itself unobtrusive. There is an essential modesty to their work. And, like Stafford, Young has a quality of faithfulness, of commitment to his own problematic existence; he does not, as so many Americans do, attempt to change his life by merely changing place, by running to New York or California. He faces the emptiness and solitude the land presents to him:

> A lonely country? . . .
> . . . What's this but
> Acceptable solitude? And who'd
> Trade it for any multitude?

Young's work is that of a man whose edges are gently blurring, who reaches quietly for something just outside of the room he lives in – a twilight poetry in which past and present, desire and "reality," lose their hard outlines, gliding in and out of one another.

Two of the most prominent influences on Young's writing are apparent in his excellent imitations of Stevens ("Putting It Mildly") and of Robert Bly ("Oh

Salmon-colored Edsel''), but he is not confined by any particular mode. His poems are sometimes humorous, often witty, and on some occasions even employ rhyme or meter. The mainstream of Young's poetry, though, is apparent in his ''The Small-Town Poets,'' a fine poem which seems a self-portrait of sorts. The small plane which appears there, as it does in many of his poems, is an apt emblem for his poetic imagination, looping easily, observing things from a certain height with nostalgia and delight, wit and good will.

– Lawrence Russ

YOUNG, Douglas (Cuthbert Colquhoun). Scottish. Born in Tayport, Fife, 5 June 1913. Educated at Merchiston Castle, Edinburgh; University of St. Andrews, M.A. 1934; New College, Oxford, 1934–38, M.A., D.Litt. Married Helena Gossaree Auchterlonie in 1943; has two daughters. Taught Greek and Latin at the University of Aberdeen, 1938–41, St. Andrews University, 1947–68, and University of Minnesota, Minneapolis, 1963–64; Professor of Classics, McMaster University, Hamilton, Ontario, 1968–70. Since 1970, Paddison Professor of Greek, University of North Carolina, Chapel Hill. Since 1947, Editor, with Maurice Lindsay, Saltire Modern Poets series, Edinburgh. Chairman, Scottish National Party, 1942–45; and Scottish P.E.N., 1957–60. Address: Makarsbield, Tayport, Fife, Scotland. *Died 24 October 1973.*

PUBLICATIONS

Verse

    Auntran Blads: An Outwale o Verses. Glasgow, Maclellan, 1943.
    A Braird o Thristles. Glasgow, Maclellan, 1947.
    Selected Poems. Edinburgh, Oliver and Boyd, 1950.

Plays

    The Puddocks, adaptation of a play by Aristophanes. Makarsbield, Fife, Douglas Young, 1957.
    The Burdies: A Comedy in Scots Verse, adaptation of a play by Aristophanes (produced Edinburgh, 1959). Makarsbield, Fife, Douglas Young, 1959.

Other

    Quislings in Scotland. Glasgow, Scottish Secretariat, 1942.
    The Free Minded Scot. Glasgow, Scottish Secretariat, 1942.
    William Wallace and This War. Glasgow, Scottish Secretariat, 1943.
    Facism for the Highlands? Gauleiter for Wales? (address). Glasgow, Scottish National Party, 1943.

An Appeal to Scots Honour. Glasgow, Scottish Secretariat, 1944.

British Invasion of Scottish Rights. Glasgow, Scottish Secretariat, 1944.

The Re-Colonisation of Scotland. Glasgow, Scottish Secretariat, 1946.

"Plastic Scots" and the Scottish Literary Tradition (address). Glasgow, privately printed, 1947.

The International Importance of Scottish Nationalism. Glasgow, Scottish Secretariat, 1947.

The Idea of a Scottish National Congress (lecture). Edinburgh, privately printed, 1948.

The Use of Scots for Prose (lecture). Greenock, Greenock Philosophical Society, 1949.

Labour Record on Scotland, 1945–1949 (address). Glasgow, Scottish Secretariat, 1949.

Chasing an Ancient Greek: Discursive Reminiscences of an European Journey. London, Hollis and Carter, 1950.

Romanisation in Scotland. Tayport, Fife, privately printed, 1956.

Edinburgh in the Age of Sir Walter Scott. Norman, University of Oklahoma Press, 1965.

Scots Burds and English Reviewers: A Case Study of Theatre Critics and Their Contradictions in Regard to the First International Festival Production by Edinburgh's Royal Lyceum Theatre Company, 1966. Edinburgh, M. Macdonald, 1966.

St. Andrews: Town and Gown, Royal and Ancient. London, Cassell, 1969.

Scotland. London, Cassell, 1971.

Editor, *Scottish Verse 1851–1951.* London, Nelson, 1952.

Editor, *Theognis.* Leipzig, Teubner, 1961.

Douglas Young comments:

I consider myself primarily a classical scholar and historian. Verse-translator of plays of Aeschylus and Euripides, for stage performances, and of Gaelic poetry, especially Sorley Maclean. I belong to the old-fashioned school that scans and usually rhymes. Otherwise a complete "loner."

Verse d'occasion, or "Poems for several occasions." Main influences Greek and Latin and the Scots tradition from Barbour to MacDiarmid.

I have been an intermittent, but sometimes quite accomplished, minor poet; and a few of my poems have become orally current among people in Scotland, so much so that they are occasionally quoted (even to me) as anonymous productions. I have never "tried to achieve" anything in verse. Verses occasionally come into my head, some of which I write down; but I have never bothered much about publishing them, so far.

*   *   *

Greek scholar, linguist, wit, Scottish nationalist, translator, anthologist – Douglas Young is a learned man of many parts who turned to poetry among other interests but did not feel the sense of dedication to it as an art of consuming importance. Nevertheless, despite his relatively meagre output, he has produced a handful of poems which have become anthology pieces, and has his place in the history of the Scottish Renascence literary movement. Most of his poems are in Scots, and although the best of them tend to use a fairly straightforward and traditional kind of Scots, others show his delighted rediscovery of the Scottish linguistic potential in Jamieson's dictionary, a book he describes in his poem "Thesaurus Paleo-Scoticus" as "a kist o ferlies" (a chest of marvels). His best-known poem, "Last Lauch," is a sardonic epigram on the grim tree that outlived the minister who said it would die. In "Dulce et Decorum . . ." he is equally sardonic about an imposing war memorial with a "muckle black angel" and blames the people of Fife for being "mair keen to pit out siller on daith nor on life." Death and childbirth are treated with insight and feeling in "The Shepherd's Dochter" and "For a Wife in Jizzen."

As translator, Young has shown his virtuosity in poems turned from Russian to German, English to French, and Scots to Greek, but his versions from the Gaelic of Sorley Maclean, in both Scots and English, are the most valuable. Remarkable in their ingenuity, though not received with universal approbation, were his Scots renderings of Aristophanes' *The Birds* and *The Frogs*.

– Edwin Morgan

YOUNG, Ian (George).   British; Canadian Landed Immigrant.   Born in London, 5 January 1945. Educated at Beal Grammar School, Ilford, Essex, 1957–63; Malvern Collegiate Institute, Toronto; Victoria College, University of Toronto, 1964–67, 1970. Associate Editor, *Acta Victoriana*, Toronto, 1966–67; Editor, *Cyclops*, Toronto, 1968, and *Eyeopener Poetry Supplement*, Toronto, 1968–69. Since 1969, Editor, *Catalyst*, and Manager, Catalyst Press, Scarborough, Ontario; since 1973, Book Editor, *Option*, Toronto; since 1974, Contributing Editor, *Gay Sunshine*, San Francisco. Press Secretary, 1969–71, and Chairman, 1972–73, University of Toronto Homophile Association. Recipient: Canada Council grant, 1969, 1974, bursary, 1972; Ontario Council for the Arts grant, 1970. Address: 315 Blantyre Avenue, Scarborough, Ontario M1N 2S6, Canada.

PUBLICATIONS

Verse

White Garland: 9 Poems for Richard.   Scarborough, Ontario, Cyclops, 1969.
Year of the Quiet Sun.   Toronto, House of Anansi, 1969.
Double Exposure.   Trumansburg, New York, New Books, 1970.
Cool Fire, with Richard Phelan.   Scarborough, Ontario, Catalyst, 1970.
Lions in the Stream, with Richard Phelan.   Scarborough, Ontario, Catalyst, 1971.
Some Green Moths.   Scarborough, Ontario, Catalyst, 1972.
Autumn Angels.   Toronto, Village Book Store, 1973.
Yuletide Story.   Scarborough, Ontario, Catalyst, 1973.

Other

The Male Homosexual in Literature: A Bibliography.   Metuchen, New Jersey, Scarecrow Press, 1975.

Editor, *The Male Muse: A Gay Anthology.* Trumansburg, New York, Crossing Press, 1973.

Translator, *Curieux d'Amour*, by Count Jacques d'Adelsward Ferson. London, Timothy d'Arch Smith, 1970.

Critical Studies: "The Younger Toronto Poets Add Up to Just One" by Andreas Schroeder, in *Vancouver Province*, 7 February 1969; by Debbie Young, in *The Carleton* (Ottawa), 6 February 1970; Bob Bossin, in *The Varsity* (Toronto), 6 February 1970; introduction by John Gill, to *Double Exposure*, 1970; Robert Peters, in *Gay Sunshine* (San Francisco) January-February 1973; "Ian Young's Verse Delights" by Jim Eggeling, in *The Advocate* (Los Angeles), 25 April 1973.

*   *   *

Ian Young is the Strato of contemporary poetry. Most recently he has published *The Male Muse*, an anthology of contemporary gay poetry that is the *Mousa Paidike* of its time. That there is a doctrinaire cast to Young's introduction to the anthology – "the growing impetus of the homophile/gay liberation movement" – is indicative of the weaknesses in that anthology, which nonetheless contains some very fine work by some surprising authors.

It is indicative too of a more general flaw in Young's own work – the tendency for obsession to override poetry. Only occasionally does one think of Cavafy – or better, Durrell's poem on Cavafy – the ironic distance and the tough-minded disdain for what Sir Thomas Browne called "the foolishest act that a man ever commits in his life."

But such disdain for the foolishness of the flesh is not fashionable at the moment, certainly not in Canadian poetry where a great deal of over-compensating for the 19th century is still in full voice. And one has, in fairness, to point to a fine descriptive ability and a delicious sensuality in Young's work:

> How I wanted him
> when he came
> into the room
> with a new blue kerchief
>
> when he knotted it
> round his neck
> like a noose of sky

But there is sometimes a sense of strain in his work – the necessary touches of fashionable surrealism or the laboured deference to haiku and the cults of karma and *om*. Here more than anywhere one feels the absence of a restraining versification where emotion might be recollected in a tranquility productive of better poetry. The "punk's hands" that he fears and celebrates are a paradigm of that wrestle in poetry which more often he needs to engage. For there is no doubt of his ability who is, in his own words, "hunter / hunted / and long sharp knife."

– D. D. C. Chambers

ZATURENSKA, Marya. American. Born in Kiev, Russia, 12 September 1902; emigrated to the United States in 1909, naturalized, 1912. Educated at Valparaiso University, Indiana, 1922–23; University of Wisconsin, Madison, 1923–25. Married the poet and critic Horace Gregory, *q.v.*, in 1925; has two children. Recipient: John Reed Memorial Award, 1922, Guarantor's Award, 1937, and Jacob Glatstein Memorial Award, 1973 (*Poetry*, Chicago); Shelley Memorial Award, 1935; Pulitzer Prize, 1938. Address: Closter Road, Palisades, Rockland County, New York 10964, U.S.A.

PUBLICATIONS

Verse

Threshold and Hearth. New York, Macmillan, 1934.
Cold Morning Sky. New York, Macmillan, 1937.
The Listening Landscape. New York, Macmillan, 1941.
The Golden Mirror. New York, Macmillan, 1944.
Selected Poems. New York, Grove Press, 1954.
Terraces of Light. New York, Grove Press, 1960.
Collected Poems. New York, Viking Press, 1965.
The Hidden Waterfalls. New York, Vanguard Press, 1974.

Other

A History of American Poetry, 1900–1940, with Horace Gregory. New York, Harcourt Brace, 1946.
Christina Rossetti: A Portrait with Background. New York, Macmillan, 1949.

Editor, with Horace Gregory, *The Mentor Book of Religious Verse.* New York, New American Library, 1957.
Editor, with Horace Gregory, *The Crystal Cabinet: An Invitation to Poetry.* New York, Holt Rinehart, 1962.
Editor, *The Collected Poems of Sara Teasdale.* New York, Macmillan, 1966.
Editor, with Horace Gregory, *The Silver Swan: Poems of Romance and Mystery.* New York, Holt Rinehart, 1966.
Editor, with Horace Gregory, *Selected Poems of Christina Rossetti.* New York, Macmillan, 1970.

Marya Zaturenska comments:

I am an independent. My style, my manner is my own. My poetry is traditional and lyrical with a music and a diction which I hope is my own.

*   *   *

The work of Marya Zaturenska is perhaps best understood by placing it in a poetic tradition she herself has spoken of, that is, the tradition of Christina Rossetti and Sara Teasdale. In style and subject matter, it was popular two generations ago, about the time that Ms. Zaturenska's second voume, *Cold Morning Sky*, received the Pulitzer Prize. Its chief characteristics are a regular metrical pattern, often quatrains, and generalized nature imagery, as in "Spring Morning":

> The arrowy gold whose winter span
> Of life was lost in wind and water
> Shed from the sky, to waters ran
> Casting new life upon the water.

Nature provides the background in the early poems for conventional reflections on the transitoriness of life and the changing seasons, in such representative poems as "The Scythe, The Spindle, and the Cypress Tree" and "The Runaway," both written in couplets.

The last four poems in her *Collected Poems* return somewhat to the earlier mood of melancholy and quiet reverie, particularly in "Metaphysics of Night" and "Homage to Christina Rossetti," as in the following stanza:

> For you the Sacred Muse revealed her illumined way
> And taught the simple heart, devout and true,
> How to praise God in fire-touched songs that pray
> Songs that Teresa heard, Siena's Catherine knew.

In the poems of the middle years, beginning with *The Golden Mirror*, the setting tends to be more dramatic. A tension emerges between speaker and subject, and the poems exhibit a strength and vigor quite different from the lyricism of the early poems. "The Recall of Eurydice," for example, describes the loss of Orpheus and of life on earth, as Eurydice returns to become, in Hell, "a nameless shade, among the nameless shades." In poems based on classic myths, as Louis Untermeyer has said, Marya Zaturenska brings "fresh life to mythological figures, not merely reanimating a legend, but creating a new and complex character." One can say the same about her poems on historical figures, such as "The Affliction of William Cowper," which skillfully conveys the anguish and despair of that distinguished poet's struggle with madness.

Ms. Zaturenska's poems with a contemporary setting are, on the whole, less successful, lacking usually a precision of language or a proper idiom to link subject and mood. The spiritual conflict that characterizes so much of contemporary life seems very distant from her later religious poems. They suggest that her strength as a poet lies with the subjects and sensibility of an earlier time, as in those poems published in *Poetry* magazine during the 1920's, while she was still an undergraduate – meditative poems, detached and serene.

– Michael True

ZIMMER, Paul J. American. Born in Canton, Ohio, 18 September 1934. Educated at Kent State University, Kent, Ohio, 1952–53, 1956–59, B.A. 1968. Married Suzanne Koklauner in 1959; has one daughter and one son. Macy's Book Department Manager, San Francisco, 1961–63; Manager, San Francisco News Company, 1963–65; Manager, U.C.L.A. Bookstore, Los Angeles, 1965–67. Poet-in-Residence,

Chico State College, California, Spring 1971. Since 1967, Assistant Director, University of Pittsburgh Press, and Editor, Pitt Poetry series. Recipient: Borestone Mountain Award, 1971; National Endowment for the Arts grant, 1974. Address: 5515 Hobart Street, Pittsburgh, Pennsylvania 15217, U.S.A.

PUBLICATIONS

Verse

A Seed on the Wind: Poems. San Francisco, privately printed, 1960.
The Ribs of Death. New York, October House, 1967.
The Republic of Many Voices. New York, October House, 1969.

Critical Studies: "Recent Poetry" by Hayden Carruth, in *Hudson Review* (New York), Summer 1968; "Recent Poetry" by Robert Boyers, in *Partisan Review* (New Brunswick, New Jersey), 1969; James Den Boer, in *Voyages* (Washington, D.C.), Spring 1970; "The Importance of Being Zimmer" by the author, in *American Poets in 1975*, edited by William Heyen, Indianapolis, Bobbs Merrill, 1975.

Paul Zimmer comments:

Because of early scholastic difficulties I was more or less forced to regard myself as a failure as a young person. Consequently when I began writing poetry I was not able to make poems about myself, not thinking myself important enough to write about. I began casting my voice into characters I had made up: Peregrine, Mordecai, Phineas, Alphonse, Wanda, Imbellis, Cecil, Willis, etc. I guess, in some ways, I was trying to make my own mythologies (create my own little world?). I look upon this period of my work as an apprenticeship for making the autobiographical-type poems I have been working on in recent years – the Zimmer poems. Of late the autobiographical work and the early cast-creating seem to be growing together into a kind of dialogue. Making poems is the best and most exhilarating thing I do. I still derive a great deal of energy from reading people like Yeats, Skelton, Garcia Lorca, Neruda, Roethke, Browning, Clare, Shakespeare, Chaucer, and many others.

*   *   *

Paul Zimmer is a protean poet whose personae are not so much depicted as created; we witness poet and subjects in process of becoming. A vivid verbal imagination projects the common, lonely, unwanted, neurotic, merely eccentric, and truly mad people of these poems into the elements which surround them and are soon to reclaim them in death, while inanimate objects assume the habits and attributes of human life. Zimmer makes the stock-in-trade of synaesthesia and personification his own by force of an original, often startling point-of-view: "One Vision. / Mine." *The Ribs of Death* not only shows this individual stamp on a wide variety of material but also demonstrates a poetic development. A deft, almost eighteenth-century irony characterizes the first poems. Lord Fluting dreams of an illusory America "where the buffalo turn / Broadside to the hunting horns," but discovers the horrors of a primitive country, and asks "Where are the teepees filled with gold?" The Colonies are infected with the sins and superstitions of the Old World; the "great new land" seemed "too full of sun / For ancient shadows," yet the darkness has become so deep that witches are needed to fill "the belly of some flame." The malaise lingers on, but in turning to more recent times, Zimmer becomes more personal in tone, particularly when speaking of his life and art. The once-Catholic poet is "projected into shapes," his province now catholic enough to gather the buckskinned pioneer, the football player, the oil driller, and the witty Handel with the dying Keats and seafaring Conrad under the title of Poet. He can portray death in the placid invalid and eager consumptive and read it in the quick demise of a snapping wave-tip and in the dullness of a blighted apple.

In *The Republic of Many Voices*, he aims again at a variety of subjects, linked now with a connecting theme of rebirth, growth, and death and with a self-conscious tone. But what was magical in the earlier volume tends to lose its charm through repetition. From his still-skewed angle of vision, people fascinate not as personalities so much as curiosities; after the first half-dozen and despite the variation, would-be originals give off a superficial glint, like other objects of a mechanical process. Alonzo is a snowflake, Rollo bears the ocean, Fritz strangles on the world, Carlos becomes the mountain he climbs. Invested with attributes of nature, certain personae have the power of fantastic hybrids. Gus's "guts ache with elm blight" as he "shaves his dewy chin of all its pixie moss." In the "Mordecai" poems Zimmer works several character transformations upon a Black man, but with typically liberal guilt calls the portraiture mere "egghead prattling." Enlarging his self-portrait, he presents telling sketches of home and school, marred, though, with sentimentality and adolescent peevishness (one poem wreaks vengeance upon an old teaching "nun"). Scenes of youthful adventure, close-calls, and lucky accidents shine more vividly, evoking crucial moments of emerging poetic insight. Tenderness and good-humor infuse tales of adolescent sexuality and love, though lines get clotted with excessive botanical metaphors. Despite his missteps, one is grateful he is willing to take chances. "I know I sing the birds / And bloom the flowers myself," he notes with confidence, and many of these poems give evidence to hope for further discoveries and growth.

– Joseph Parisi

ZINNES, Harriet. American. Born in Hyde Park, Massachusetts. Educated at Hunter College, New York, B.A. 1939; Brooklyn College, New York, M.A. 1944; New York University, Ph.D. 1953. Married Irving Zinnes in 1943; has one daughter and one son. Editor, Raritan Arsenal Publications Division, Metuchen, New Jersey, 1942–43; Associate Editor, *Harper's Bazaar*, New York, 1944–46; Tutor, Hunter College, 1946–49. Assistant Professor, 1949–53, and since 1962, Associate Professor of English, Queens College, City University of New York, Flushing. Director, Poetry and Fiction Workshop, University of Oklahoma, Norman, 1959–60; Lecturer, Rutgers University, New Brunswick, New Jersey, 1960–62; Art and Literary Critic, *The Weekly Tribune*, Geneva, Switzerland, 1968–69; Visiting Professor of American Literature, University of Geneva, Spring 1970. Since 1971, Editorial Staff Member, *Pictures on Exhibit*, New York; currently, Poetry Coordinator, Great Neck Public Library, Long Island, New York. Recipient: MacDowell Fellowship, 1972, 1973, 1974. Agent: Roberta Kent, W.B. Agency, 156 East 52nd Street, New York,

New York 10022. Address: Department of English, Queens College, Flushing, New York 11367, U.S.A.

Publications

Verse

Waiting and Other Poems.   Lanham, Maryland, Goosetree·Press, 1964.
An Eye for an I: Poems.   New York, Folder Editions, 1966.

Critical Study: by Robert Hazel, in *Masterplots: 1966 Annual*, edited by Frank N. Magill, New York, Salem Press, 1967.

Harriet Zinnes comments:

Ezra Pound is my chief influence – principally through his emphasis on a new music discovered through a spare and rigorous poetic line. He has also taught me that the one hard, stripped word is always better than the tired few. Robert Bly is my second influence. He taught me what I should always have known: that only through the exact vision, through the closely observed object will the true poem emerge – and that there must always be a detailed natural image or object in the poem. I feel that I have a hard, ironical approach to reality, and the reality I see is as much surreal as real. Painting, next to poetry, has always absorbed me. And now that I have written a volume of prose poems, I can see the poem itself opening up for me, evolving into – what new form?

*   *   *

Harriet Zinnes's poetry invites analogies to modern painting and sculpture. Many of her poems are verbal collages, collections of "found objects" (verse equivalents of Duchamp's "readymades"), the significance of whose juxtaposition depends, at least in part, upon the ingenuity of the reader. In the four-part "Electronic Music" she bows and points to Rauschenberg, splicing together the tapes and other electronic communications gear with the debris of a technological society. Others of her poetic constructs display the irony, wit, and seeming innocence of a Miro sculpture, where, again, the relevance of the configuration lies in the eye of the imaginative beholder. She notes: "(Nothing is far-fetched / that the mind seizes upon.)" She makes Dadaist games of the jumble of life. The persona exclaims: "What an antic traffic jam I am." Playful typography figures in "MEn" and "and the fruit," while drawings supplement other poems, for "Words are not enough / (as any poet knows)." Despite her considerable skill, she harbors a lingering distrust for the lexicon; she is dissatisfied with words "utilized until meaningless." After the first echo, "That word remembered / is death / a verbal corpse."

Nonetheless, she is seldom at a loss for the precise terms to fashion a spare and telling line, particularly when writing of city life. The urban child is engrossed in a gutter pool before his yardless house. In the park the persona views sparrows and ducks with affection and annoyance. A green leaf pushes its way into an artist's "acrylic garden." The twittering air conditioners in "Cityscape" must do for murmuring sea waves, and the stone birds on the mantlepiece have to stand in for living sea gulls. She captures the city-dweller at his classic recreation, the cocktail party, where one guest beckons: "Come find me as I whisper to my enemies." Another, insecure in the company of such sophisticates, lets her masks fall and asks in anguish: "Is it I? Is it I?" Zinnes also catches the rhythms of conversation in several segments of "Entropisms," a long prose poem made partly of snippets that seem cut from intellectual-artistic soirées, New York style. Along with the snatches of wit and aphorism, she lets mingle fragments both banal and arch. (She even allows Buckminster Fuller to parody himself.) Again as in *An Eye for an I*, she depicts existential moments; her selected short scenes and speeches jostle one another or make curious associations. "All things are not equal. Two substances and two other substances make all kinds of things." Let another "Entropism" serve as partial index to her art: "Hour after hour a fledgling word in space. Silence surrounds embodies sings *only when the word cuts it*."

– Joseph Parisi

ZUKOFSKY, Louis. American. Born in New York City, 23 January 1904. Educated at Columbia University, New York, M.A. 1924. Married Celia Thaew in 1939; has one son. Taught at the University of Wisconsin, Madison, 1930–31; Colgate University, Hamilton, New York, 1947; Polytechnic Institute of Brooklyn, New York, 1947–1966. Recipient: Longview Foundation Award, 1961; Union League Civic and Arts Foundation Prize, 1964, and Oscar Blumenthal Prize, 1966 (*Poetry*, Chicago); National Endowment for the Arts grant, 1966, 1968. Address: 240 Central Park South, New York, New York 10019, U.S.A.

PUBLICATIONS

Verse

First Half of "A" – 9. New York, privately printed, 1940.
55 Poems. Prairie City, Illinois, Press of J. A. Decker, 1941.
Anew: Poems. Prairie City, Illinois, Press of J. A. Decker, 1946.
Some Time/Short Poems. Highlands, North Carolina, Jargon, 1956.
Barely and Widely. New York, Celia Zukofsky, 1958.
"A" 1–12. Kyoto, Origin Press, 1959; London, Cape, 1966; New York, Doubleday, 1967.
16 Once Published. Edinburgh, Wild Hawthorn Press, 1962.
I's, Pronounced "Eyes." New York, Trobar Press, 1963.
After I's. Pittsburgh, Boxwood Press-Mother Press, 1964.
Found Objects 1962–1926. Georgetown, Kentucky, H. B. Chapin, 1964.
An Unearthing: A Poem. Cambridge, Massachusetts, privately printed, 1965.
Iyyob. London, Turret Books, 1965.
I Sent Thee Late. Cambridge, Massachusetts, privately printed, 1965.
Finally a Valentine. Stroud, Gloucestershire, Piccolo Press, 1965.
All: The Collected Short Poems, 1923–1958. New York, Norton, 1965; London, Cape, 1966.

All: The Collected Short Poems, 1956–1964.   New York, Norton, 1966; London, Cape, 1967.
"A" – 9.   Cologne, Hansjörg Mayer, 1966.
Little: A Fragment for Careenagers.   Los Angeles, Black Sparrow Press, 1967.
"A" – 14.   London, Turret Books, 1967.
"A" 13–21.   London, Cape, and New York, Doubleday, 1969.
The Gas Age: A Poem.   Newcastle upon Tyne, Ultima Thule Bookshops, 1969.
All: The Collected Shorter Poems, 1923–1964.   New York, Norton, 1971.
"A" – 24.   New York, Grossman, 1972.

Play

Arise, Arise.   New York, Grossman, 1973.

Short Stories

It Was.   Kyoto, Origin Press, 1961.
Ferdinand, Including It Was.   London, Cape, and New York, Grossman, 1968.
Little.   New York, Grossman, 1970.

Other

Le Style Apollinaire, with René Taupin.   Paris, 1934.
Bottom: On Shakespeare (criticism, poetry, and music).   Austin, Ark Press-University of Texas Press, 1963.
Prepositions: The Collected Critical Essays of Louis Zukofsky.   London, Rapp and Carroll, 1967; New York, Horizon Press, 1968.
Autobiography.   New York, Grossman, 1970.

Editor, *An "Objectivists" Anthology.*   New York and Le Beausset, France, To Publishers, 1932.
Editor, *A Test of Poetry.*   New York, Objectivist Press, 1948; London, Routledge, 1952.

Translator, with Celia Zukofsky, *Catullus: Fragmenta*, music by Paul Zukofsky.   London, Turret Books, 1969.
Translator, with Celia Zukofsky, *Catullus.*   London, Cape Goliard Press, and New York, Grossman, 1969.

Critical Studies: by Guy Davenport, in *Agenda* (London), Autumn-Winter 1970; Kenneth Cox, in *Agenda* (London), Autumn-Winter 1971.

*   *   *

In the modern world, few poets of Louis Zukofsky's importance have been required to work in such personal obscurity and neglect. As recently as 1962, his name was not mentioned in *The Reader's Encyclopaedia of American Literature*, the standard popular reference of its kind. Nor was the term "Objectivism." Yet today, thanks to the efforts of younger poets – particularly Denise Levertov, Cid Corman, and Henry Rago – virtually all Zukofsky's work is back in print, and his place in American poetry is both understood and assured.

Zukofsky began writing in the twenties, clearly influenced by such elder poets as Ezra Pound, William Carlos Williams, and H. D. In the thirties, responding to the rising influence in America of Eliot, Yeats, and the symbolist tradition generally, Zukofsky and several other poets, including George Oppen and Charles Reznikoff, established the "Objectivist" movement as a means of promulgating their belief in the primacy and inviolability both of the natural object in poetry and of poetry as a natural object. In some respects, it was a return to the principles of Imagism, but with a more elaborate philosophical grounding. At this time, Zukofsky edited *An "Objectivists" Anthology*, published in France, and a special Objectivist number of *Poetry*, the verse magazine published in Chicago; but they attracted relatively little notice, although today both are collectors' items. During the forties and fifties, the period dominated by Eliot, who in turn dominated the Southern Agrarian poets and the New Critics, little was heard of either Zukofsky or Objectivism.

Nevertheless, Zukofsky continued working. In 1927 he had begun his major poetic work, a sequence entitled simply *A*, which is still in progress. In a wide range of forms but staying close to the analogy of music, the poem ranges over many themes, especially the celebration of conjugal solidarity in the face of the dangers and discontents of modern civilization. Certainly, it is one of the finest tributes to marriage ever written. Zukofsky's wife and son, both of whom are musicans, are continuing figures in the poem, like recurring motifs in a symphony. For Zukofsky, in fact, the interdependence of music and poetry is so great that at times it seems as if only an accident has turned his specific impulse into words for a voice instead of notes for a violin. He has written:

> The lines of this new song are nothing
> But a tune making the nothing full. . . .

Clearly, this is a representation of his own working method, which extrapolates poetry from the particular musical qualities of words and images. Clearly, too, only a poet of remarkable sensitivity to the tonal qualities of speech could make it work.

Zukofsky does make it work, both in *A* and in his shorter poems, although some of the latter, in their finical sound-play, seem more like a musician's noodling than finished productions. At the same time, no one should mistake Zukofsky's lyricism for the kind of verse-making that is merely pretty or merely effective. On the contrary, his work has a chordal density that is Bach-like, not to say rock-like; and when it is, as often, informed by intense social indignation and humane concern, it takes on great richness and force. It is, whatever else, testimony to a striking, complex, vivid personality.

Translation and criticism are virtually the same as poetry in Zukofsky's creative endeavor. He and his wife, Celia Zukofsky, have done translations from Catullus, for example, which make the exploration of language a poetic feat equal to archaeology, and Zukofsky's critical writing, especially on Shakespeare, proceeds in the same personal, experimental way. All this material – poems, translations and prose – must be read together. It is integrated not only by the poet's undeviating esthetic objectives but by his use of the same methods and materials in everything he writes.

– Hayden Carruth

ZURNDORFER, Lotte. British. Born in Germany, in 1929. Educated at Watford Grammar School; St. Hugh's College, Oxford. Married; has two daughters. Currently, Lecturer in English, University of Helsinki. Address: Myotale 5, Mankans, Finland.

PUBLICATIONS

Verse

(Poems). Oxford, Fantasy Press, 1952.
Poems. London, Chatto and Windus-Hogarth Press, 1960.

Lotte Zurndorfer comments:

I am a midnight writer whose children wake at 6 a.m.

*   *   *

The poetry of Lotte Zurndorfer is so quiet that it is in danger of bowing itself out of recognition. She has published only one collection. Its themes are decorous, as can be seen from the titles of the better poems: "Peony," "Cathedral," "Autumn and a New Country," "Letter Poem." From this last one could quote:

> Snow falls; in France I see the long garden,
> The tall trees, poplar or plane-tree, the houses
> High and narrow; and so across the Norman
> Landscape is drawn this familiar
> Mnemonic for home: snowflakes fining in distance,
> And where I am it is soundless –
> The far yellowing has children calling, sirens
> From the river, traffic snoring. I think
> Of you and write you letters. . . .

The details are selected to suggest an uncomfortable sort of country – "*long* garden," "*tall* trees," houses "*high* and *narrow.*" There is a delicate play on the word "drawn" – the snow is drawn across the landscape like a familiar curtain concealing an unfamiliar set. It is also drawn as one might decorate a picture sent to a friend, to render a drawn-out terrain more comprehensible. In this way, a context is created for the unusual word, almost a conceit, "mnemonic." Such technique as this could be used to considerable effect. It may be no accident that one of Miss Zurndorfer's most striking poems to date is a translation of Baudelaire: "La Servante au grand coeur. . . ." Since her first language is German, perhaps her skill and sensitivity would be best employed in recreating poems of her own country in English. This, after all, is a great age of translation; the omens are propitious. At any rate, those who were impressed by her Fantasy Press pamphlet emanating from the Oxford of 1952 would be glad to see her poetic career resume after this pause of several years.

– Philip Hobsbaum

APPENDIX

BAXTER, James K(eir). New Zealander. Born in Dunedin, 29 June 1926, son of the author Archibald Baxter. Educated at Quaker schools in New Zealand and England; Otago University, Dunedin; Victoria University, Wellington, B.A. 1952. Married Jacqueline Sturm in 1948; two children. Worked as a labourer, journalist, school-teacher. Editor, *Numbers* magazine, Wellington, 1954–60. Spent 5 months in India studying school publications, 1958. Started commune in Jerusalem (a Maori community on the Wanganui River), 1969. Recipient: UNESCO grant, 1958; Robert Burns Fellowship, University of Otago, 1966, 1967. *Died 22 October 1972.*

PUBLICATIONS

Verse

    Beyond the Palisade: Poems. Christchurch, Caxton Press, 1944.
    Blow, Wind of Fruitfulness. Christchurch, Caxton Press, 1948.
    Hart Crane. Christchurch, Catspaw Press, 1948.
    Rapunzel: A Fantasia for Six Voices. Wellington, privately printed, 1948.
    Charm for Hilary. Christchurch, Catspaw Press, 1949.
    Poems Unpleasant, with Louis Johnson and Anton Vogt. Christchurch, Pegasus Press, 1952.
    The Fallen House: Poems. Christchurch, Caxton Press, 1953.
    Lament for Barney Flanagan. Wellington, privately printed, 1954.
    Traveller's Litany. Wellington, Handcraft Press, 1955.
    The Night Shift: Poems of Aspects of Love, with others. Wellington, Capricorn Press, 1957.
    The Iron Breadboard: Studies in New Zealand Writing (verse parodies). Wellington, Mermaid Press, 1957.
    In Fires of No Return: Poems. London and New York, Oxford University Press, 1958.
    Chosen Poems, 1958. Bombay, Konkan Institute of Arts and Sciences, 1958.
    Ballad of Calvary Street. Wellington, privately printed, 1960.
    Howrah Bridge and Other Poems. London and New York, Oxford University Press, 1961.
    Poems. Wellington, Teachers College, 1964.
    Pig Island Letters. London and New York, Oxford University Press, 1966.
    A Death Song for M. Mouldybroke. Christchurch, Caxton Press, 1967.
    A Small Ode on Mixed Flatting: Elicited by the Decision of the Otago University Authorities to Forbid This Practice among Students. Christchurch, Caxton Press, 1967.
    The Lion Skin: Poems. Dunedin, Bibliography Room, University of Otago, 1967.
    A Bucket of Blood for a Dollar: A Conversation Between Uncle Sam and the Rt. Hon. Keith Holyoake, Prime Minister of New Zealand. Christchurch, John Summers Bookshop, 1968.
    The Rock Woman: Selected Poems. London and New York, Oxford University Press, 1969.
    Ballad of the Stonegut Sugar Works. Auckland, privately printed, 1969.
    Jerusalem Sonnets: Poems for Colin Durning. Dunedin, Bibliography Room, University of Otago, 1970.
    The Junkies and the Fuzz. Wellington, Wai-te-ata Press, 1970.

Jerusalem Daybook (poetry and prose journal). Wellington, Price Milburn, 1971.
Jerusalem Blues (2). Wellington, Bottle Press, 1971.
Autumn Testament (poetry and prose journal). Wellington, Price Milburn, 1972.
Four God Songs. Wellington, Futuna Press, 1972.
Letter to Peter Olds. Dunedin, Caveman Press, 1972.
Runes. London and New York, Oxford University Press, 1973.

Plays

Jack Winter's Dream (broadcast, 1958).   Included in *The Wide Open Cage and Jack Winter's Dream*, 1959.
The Wide Open Cage (produced Wellington, 1959; New York, 1962).   Included in *The Wide Open Cage and Jack Winter's Dream*, 1959.
The Wide Open Cage and Jack Winter's Dream: Two Plays. Hastings, New Zealand, Capricorn Press, 1959.
The Spots of the Leopard (produced New York, 1963; Wellington, 1967).
The Band Rotunda (produced Dunedin, 1967).   Included in *The Devil and Mr. Mulcahy and The Band Rotunda*, 1971.
The Sore-Footed Man, based on *Philoctetes* by Euripides (produced Dunedin, 1967).   Included in *The Sore-Footed Man and The Temptations of Oedipus*, 1971.
The Bureaucrat (produced Dunedin, 1967).
The Devil and Mr. Mulcahy (produced Dunedin, 1967).   Included in *The Devil and Mr. Mulcahy and The Band Rotunda*, 1971.
Mr. O'Dwyer's Dancing Party (produced Dunedin, 1968).
The Day Flanagan Died (produced Dunedin, 1969).
The Temptations of Oedipus (produced Dunedin, 1970).   Included in *The Sore-Footed Man and The Temptations of Oedipus*, 1971.
The Devil and Mr. Mulcahy and The Band Rotunda. Auckland, Heinemann, 1971.
The Sore-Footed Man and The Temptations of Oedipus. Auckland, Heinemann, 1971.

Radio Play: *Jack Winter's Dream*, 1958.

Other

Recent Trends in New Zealand Poetry. Christchurch, Caxton Press, 1951.
The Fire and the Anvil: Notes on Modern Poetry. Wellington, New Zealand University Press, 1955; revised edition, New York, Cambridge University Press, 1960.
Oil (primary school bulletin). Wellington, School Publications, 1957.
The Coaster (primary school bulletin). Wellington, School Publications, 1959.
The Trawler (primary school bulletin). Wellington, School Publications, 1961.
New Zealand in Colour, photographs by Kenneth and Jean Bigwood. Wellington, Reed, 1961; London, Thames and Hudson, and Belmont, Massachusetts, Wellington Books, 1962.
The Old Earth Closet: A Tribute to Regional Poetry. Wellington, privately printed, 1965.
Aspects of Poetry in New Zealand. Christchurch, Caxton Press, 1967.

The Man on the Horse (lectures).   Dunedin, University of Otago Press, and
      London, Oxford University Press, 1967.
The Flowering Cross: Pastoral Articles.   Dunedin, New Zealand Tablet, 1969.
The Six Faces of Love: Lenten Lectures.   Wellington, Futuna Press, 1972.
A Walking Stick for an Old Man.   Wellington, CMW Print, 1972.

Critical Study: *The Poetry of James K. Baxter* by John E. Weir, Wellington,
Oxford University Press, 1970.

                              *   *   *

    James K. Baxter was the most compelling and colourful poet to appear in New
Zealand after the Second World War. His family background (radical-Scottish
farming on his father's side, Anglo-Scots university intellectual on his mother's)
helps to account for his peculiar blend of native Celtic eloquence and derived,
self-conscious literary influences. His first book of verse, published when he was
only eighteen, showed already a gift for phrase-making ("In this scarred country,
this cold threshold land/The mountains crouch like tigers"), a romantic fondness
for mythology, and strong undertones of social protest. His early student years in
Dunedin were wild enough to give him something of the reputation of an antipodean Dylan Thomas, but first-hand knowledge of life on the outcast fringes of a
small affluent society was to provide him with fertile subjects for later exploration
in verse and drama. He married a Maori fellow-student, moved to Wellington
(hailed as the "sterile whore of a thousand bureaucrats"), and worked at a number
of tough manual jobs before completing an arts degree and finding a niche – with
fellow-poets Alistair Campbell and Louis Johnson – in the School Publications
Branch of the Education Department. Two decisive actions of these middle years
were "going off the grog," and becoming a Roman Catholic. In 1966 he returned to
Dunedin as Robert Burns Fellow at Otago University, and later was engaged in
social work in that city.
    Baxter's current reputation has been won not merely by technical accomplish-
ment (like Burns he can sing both high and low, and turn a very racy ballad) but by
his power to make poetic speech relevant to the daily lives of ordinary people. The
poems in *Blow, Wind of Fruitfulness* have a strong regional colouring and often
record vividly the seascapes and mountain country of Otago; the main theme is
loss of innocence. *The Fallen House* shows a new interest in human motive and
character, under the influence of Thomas Hardy. The impulse towards dramatic
lyric is carried further in Baxter's first verse-collection to be published in England,
In Fires of No Return, which also includes a group of baroque, confessional
religious poems. Two later volumes show clearly the literary influence of Lawrence
Durrell and Robert Lowell. *Howrah Bridge* gathers up some effective earlier pieces
("The Morgue," "Wild Bees") along with a batch of travel poems written on a
UNESCO visit to India in 1958. *Pig Island Letters* is more relaxed and conversational in tone, but handles some of the old tensions of belief and choice with a new
sureness of structure and language – as in the last section of the title sequence,
"At Taieri Mouth," "The Hollow Place," "Tomcat."
    Baxter is in many ways a traditional neo-romantic poet whose strength lies in his
unforced warmth and candour, in the grave musical richness of his language at its
best, and in his wide sympathies as a man speaking to other men. His weaknesses,
equally clearly, arise from occasional diffuseness and too-resonant rhetorical
flourishes, something of an obsession with sex and original sin, and a perhaps
uncertain judgement of his own best work. He wrote vigorous if not very precise

literary criticism (*The Fire and the Anvil* and *The Man on the Horse*), and some admirable verse-parodies of contemporary New Zealand poets (*The Iron Breadboard*). Of the considerable body of plays – realistic, symbolist, expressionist, abstract – he had performed by experimental drama groups in New Zealand and abroad, several have now found their way into print. Though his work is undeniably uneven, its variety and vitality are always impressive. He wrote in 1965: "There is a spot in the arena to which the fighting bull returns (a different spot for each bull) and from which he comes out more assured and formidable. For me it was once the beaches of the place I grew up in; then the pub; and latterly perhaps the hour of death which one looks forward to. If this spot is correctly located one can generally go on writing" (*Recent Poetry in New Zealand*, edited by Charles Doyle, Auckland, Collins, 1965).

"What happens is either meaningless to me," Baxter claimed, "or else it is mythology." W. H. Oliver insists that "The Fall is the one myth in his poetry"; on another view, he can be seen to have attempted from the start to build up his own personal myth around his country, his family history, his wife, and a number of chosen figures, places, and attitudes of compulsive denial or acceptance. No one more successfully assimilated the authentic flavour of the New Zealand vernacular into poetic speech. In this sense, Baxter is a genuinely popular poet, who somehow succeeded in becoming bard, scapegoat, and moral censor to a not notably imaginative tribe.

—James Bertram

BERRYMAN, John. American. Born in McAlester, Oklahoma, 25 October 1914. Educated at South Kent School, Connecticut; Columbia University, New York, A.B. 1936 (Phi Beta Kappa); Clare College, Cambridge (Kellett Fellow, 1936–37; Oldham Shakespeare Scholar, 1937), B.A. 1938; Princeton University, New Jersey (Creative Writing Fellow), 1943–44. Married Eileen Patricia Mulligan in 1942 (marriage dissolved); Ann Levine (marriage dissolved); Kathleen Donahue; three children. Instructor in English, Wayne State University, Detroit, 1939 and Princeton University, 1940–43; Briggs-Copeland Instructor in English Composition, Harvard University, Cambridge, Massachusetts, 1945–49; Lecturer in English, University of Washington, Seattle, 1950; Elliston Lecturer in Poetry, University of Cincinnati, Ohio, 1951–52; Member of the English Department, rising to the rank of Professor, University of Minnesota, Minneapolis, 1954–72. Recipient: Rockefeller grant, 1944, 1946; *Kenyon Review*–Doubleday Award, for short story, 1945; Guarantors Prize, 1948, and Levinson Prize, 1950 (*Poetry*, Chicago); Shelley Memorial Award, 1949; National Institute of Arts and Letters grant, 1950; Hodder Fellowship, Princeton University, 1950; Guggenheim Fellowship, 1952; Harriet Monroe Award, 1957; *Partisan Review* Fellowship, 1957; Brandeis University Creative Arts Award, 1959; Loines Award, 1964; Pulitzer Prize, 1965; Academy of American Poets Fellowship, 1966; National Endowment for the Arts grant, 1967; Bollingen Prize, 1968; Emily Clark Balch Prize (*Virginia Quarterly Review*), 1968; National Book Award, 1969. D.Let.: Drake University, Des Moines, Iowa, 1971.

Member: National Institute of Arts and Letters; American Academy of Arts and Sciences; Academy of American Poets. *Died 7 January 1972.*

PUBLICATIONS

Verse

Five Young American Poets, with others. New York, New Directions, 1940.
Poems. New York, New Directions, 1942.
The Dispossessed: Poems. New York, Sloane, 1948.
Homage to Mistress Bradstreet. New York, Farrar Straus, 1956; as *Homage to Mistress Bradstreet and Other Poems*, London, Faber, 1959.
His Thought Made Pockets & the Plane Buckt. Pawlet, Vermont, Claude Fredericks, 1958.
77 Dream Songs. New York, Farrar Straus, and London, Faber, 1964.
Berryman's Sonnets. New York, Farrar Straus, 1967; London, Faber, 1968.
Short Poems. New York, Farrar Straus, 1967.
I Haved Moved to Dublin. . . . Dublin, Graduates Club, 1967.
His Toy, His Dream, His Rest: 308 Dream Songs. New York, Farrar Straus, 1968; London, Faber, 1969.
The Dream Songs. New York, Farrar Straus, 1969.
Love and Fame. New York, Farrar Straus, 1970; London, Faber, 1971; revised edition, Farrar Straus, 1972.
Selected Poems 1938–1968. London, Faber, 1972.
Delusions, Etc. New York, Farrar Straus, and London, Faber, 1972.

Novel

Recovery. New York, Farrar Straus, and London, Faber, 1973.

Other

Stephen Crane (biography). New York, Sloane, and London, Methuen, 1950.

Editor, with Ralph Ross and Allen Tate, *The Arts of Reading* (anthology). New York, Crowell, 1960.
Editor, *The Unfortunate Traveller; or, The Life of Jack Wilton*, by Thomas Nash. London, Putnam, 1960.

Bibliography: *John Berryman: A Checklist* by Richard J. Kelly, Metuchen, New Jersey, Scarecrow Press, 1972; *John Berryman: A Descriptive Bibliography* by Ernest C. Stefanik, Jr., Pittsburgh, University of Pittsburgh Press, 1972.

Critical Study: *John Berryman* by William J. Martz, Minneapolis, University of Minnesota Press, and London, Oxford University Press. 1969.

*   *   *

From the appearance of his "Twenty Poems" in the anthology *Five Young American Poets*, John Berryman was immediately recognized at the forefront of his talented generation, a group of poets including Robert Lowell, Delmore Schwartz, and Randall Jarrell. Most of Berryman's early poems and those in several subsequent volumes are reprinted in his *Short Poems*, but this part of his *oeuvre* – which might well represent another poet's life work – has been quite overshadowed by his three long sequences: *Homage to Mistress Bradstreet*, two volumes of his "dream songs," and *Berryman's Sonnets* (published in 1967 but written in the 1940's). In a period when most poets attempting works of magnitude have followed the examples of Yeats, Pound, and Eliot and abandoned commitment to a single strophic form, Berryman wrote long, intricate works in regular (though sometimes variably repeated) stanzas. The imposition of a formal order upon his wildly conflicting emotions and wide-ranging materials is among Berryman's most impressive accomplishments.

The *Sonnets* are strictly Petrarchan, the convention revived in a fashion both traditional and contemporary. This is the psychological analysis of a love affair, the purpose for which the sonnet form was first devised. Berryman's syncopated, frank, and quirky diction stamp these sonnets as his own. *Homage* successfully enacts an extended metaphysical conceit, that "Mistress Bradstreet," the Puritan poetess, is both the mistress, across the dead centuries, of the contemporary poet, and his alter ego. Like all of Berryman's work this poem is psychologically intense and complex; the voice begins as his own, then merges into Anne Bradstreet's: the verse is crabb'd allusive to details in her work, life, and readings. The tangible sense of her spitiual searchings and straitened self-fulfilment striates the knotty music of Berryman's lines. His participation in her life becomes a means of his imaginative discovery of America.

The complex texture, the intensity of vision, the willed idiosyncrasy of syntax and the confected diction of *Homage* all prefigure the verse in *77 Dream Songs* and *His Toy, His Dream, His Rest*. These later books comprise a single work in 385 sections, each arranged in three six-line stanzas, the lines varying greatly in length and stress, the stanzas in rhyme pattern. Here the conceit of "dream songs" gives the poet warrant for nondiscursive syntax and for the manipulation of several projected voices. One is a white man in black-face who speaks the dialect of the Negro in a minstrel show and is named Henry, or Pussy-cat. He is heard in meditation or in colloquy with a friend who calls him Mr. Bones. At other times we hear the poet's more normative voice.

These strategies – simple in conception, intricate in effect – make possible the exploration of, seemingly, any and every subject, a man's whole life and dream-life poured through his varied voices. The scope of the work suggests comparison to *The Cantos*, the differences as revealing as the parallels. Where Pound rooted his work in his historical imagination, Berryman reflects the inward self-preoccupation of a later generation whose sensibility reflects psychoanalytic experience. This is the generation which found Robert Lowell's *Life Studies* the key to its sufferings. Lowell, in that book rejecting history, myth and rhetoric, followed W. C. Williams in achieving the simple syntax of and immediacy of unpremeditated speech; but Berryman, who sometimes writes with analagous clarity, achieves his effects by counterpointing his several voices, natural, colloquial, literary, grand-mannered, demotic. Yet his dream songs share with *Life Studies* their confessional tone and air of uninhibited self-revelation. What comes through as a result of the complexity of tone and texture is a very uneven yet compelling image of modern man suffering, exulting, catching himself exulting and putting himself down, taking wry delight in the knowledge of his own small pleasures and larger failures. The reader is required to bear with many dry patches, much incoherenee, and he is obliged to learn a new language in order to let Berryman's dreamer, its sole speaker, converse with him:

Henry sats in de plane & was gay.
Careful Henry nothing said aloud
but where a Virgin out of cloud
to her Mountain dropt in light,
his thought made pockets & the plane buckt.
'Parm me, lady.' 'Orright.'

—77 Dream Songs, 5

The willed colloquiality produces comic effects. Elsewhere the tone is tender, wry, fierce, anguished. The minstrel master of demotic syntax is a persona of the same sensibility who swiped a memorable title, *His Toy, His Dream, His Rest,* from three compositions in *The Fitzwilliam Virginal Book* by Giles Farnaby (c. 1560–1600?). Berryman's archness, his wildly comic alternations between the emotionally freer, more libidinous life-style of his white-man-in-black-face and the self that can't escape the strictures of the external world; the primitive energy of his playfulness with language; and perhaps above all the sense of subversion against the rigidities of society given by the willed dream-life in which Berryman's voices mock and undermine and lash out against the pieties of the world they and he can manage to live in only, or best, in dreams: these effects of the dream songs on the reader make his long poem memorable. Its idiosyncrasies seem determined by its time; its delights may well prove to be lasting.

After *Dream Songs* Berryman published two further books of verse, *Love and Fame* and, posthumously, *Delusions, Etc.* In these his style underwent yet a further transformation; abandoning the involutions, elisions, and intensities of *Dream Songs,* he abandoned also the melange of voices and the 18-line verse unit; in their place, now writing in irregularly rhythmic quatrains, came a self-exploitative, determinedly prosaic style, as the poet re-imagined his student days at Columbia and Cambridge universities in the first of these books, and addressed Beethoven, Frost, and other great predecessors in the second. Both contain sequences of religious themes, as Berryman continued to search for his lost faith. Another posthumous work was his novel, *Recovery,* also autobiographical, an account of his struggle with alcoholism.

Berryman's *oeuvre* reflects his life-long effort to find or fuse a style equal to the terrible psychological pressures of his themes of self-revelation and self-discovery. It seems probable that *Homage to Mistress Bradstreet* and *Dream Songs* will be found the most enduring of his works; *Homage* is surely the best unified of his longer poems, though there are structural patterns and thematic continuities and refrains secreted in *Dream Songs* which, when identified, make that long series seem less a random miscellany, more an artistic construct. In any case its structure, based on the accumulation of discrete poems with violent changes of diction, tone, and persona, like Robert Lowell's *Notebook,* represents in its flux and exacerbation the fate of the long poem in America during the latter part of the present century.

—Daniel Hoffman

DAY LEWIS, C(ecil). Pseudonym: **Nicholas Blake.** Born in Ballintubber, Ireland, 27 April 1904. Educated at Sherborne School, Dorset; Wadham College, Oxford, M.A. Served as an Editor in the Ministry of Information, London, 1941–46. Married Mary King in 1928 (divorced, 1951); Jill Balcon in 1951: four children. Taught at Summerfields School, Oxford, 1927–28; Larchfield, Helensburgh,

1928–30; Cheltenham College, Gloucestershire, 1930–35; Professor of Poetry, Oxford University, 1951–56; Norton Professor of Poetry, Harvard University, Cambridge, Massachusetts, 1964–65. Clark Lecturer, 1946, and Sidgwick Lecturer, 1956, Cambridge University; Warton Lecturer, British Academy, London, 1951; Byron Lecturer, University of Nottingham, 1952; Chancellor Dunning Lecturer, Queen's University, Kingston, Ontario, 1954; Compton Lecturer, University of Hull, Yorkshire, 1968. Director of Chatto and Windus Ltd., publishers, London, 1954–72. Member of the Arts Council of Great Britain, 1962–67. Honorary Fellow, Wadham College, Oxford, 1968. D.Litt.: University of Exeter, 1965; University of Hull, 1969; Litt.D.: Trinity College, Dublin, 1968. Fellow, 1944, Vice-President, 1958, and Companion of Literature, 1964, Royal Society of Literature; Honorary Member, American Academy of Arts and Letters, 1966; Member, Irish Academy of Letters, 1968. C.B.E. (Commander, Order of the British Empire), 1950. Poet Laureate, 1968. *Died 22 May 1972.*

PUBLICATIONS

Verse

Beechen Vigil and Other Poems. London, Fortune Press, 1925.
Country Comets. London, Martin Hopkinson, 1928.
Transitional Poem. London, Hogarth Press, 1929.
From Feathers to Iron. London, Hogarth Press, 1931.
The Magnetic Mountain. London, Hogarth Press, 1933.
Collected Poems, 1929–1933. London, Hogarth Press, 1935; with *A Hope for Poetry*, New York, Random House, 1935.
A Time to Dance and Other Poems. London, Hogarth Press, 1935.
Noah and the Waters. London, Hogarth Press, 1936.
A Time to Dance, Noah and the Waters and Other Poems, with an Essay, Revolution in Writing. New York, Random House, 1936.
Overtures to Death and Other Poems. London, Cape, 1938.
Poems in Wartime. London, Cape, 1940.
Selected Poems. London, Hogarth Press, 1940.
Word over All. London, Cape, 1943; New York, Transatlantic, 1944.
(Poems). London, Eyre and Spottiswoode, 1943.
Short Is the Time: Poems, 1936–1943 (includes *Overtures to Death* and *Word over All*). New York, Oxford University Press, 1945.
Poems, 1943–1947. London, Cape, and New York, Oxford University Press, 1948.
Collected Poems, 1929–1936. London, Hogarth Press, 1948.
Selected Poems. London, Penguin, 1951; revised edition, 1957, 1969.
An Italian Visit. London, Cape, and New York, Harper, 1953.
Collected Poems. London, Cape-Hogarth Press, 1954.
Christmas Eve. London, Faber, 1954.
The Newborn: D.M.B., 29th April, 1957. London, Favil Press of Kensington, 1957.
Pegasus and Other Poems. London, Cape, 1957; New York, Harper, 1958.
The Gate and Other Poems. London, Cape, 1962.
Requiem for the Living. New York, Harper, 1964.
On Not Saying Anything. Cambridge, Massachusetts, privately printed, 1964.
A Marriage Song for Albert and Barbara. Cambridge, Massachusetts, privately printed, 1965.

The Room and Other Poems.   London, Cape, 1965.
C. Day Lewis: Selections from His Poetry,   edited   by   Patric
   Dickinson.   London, Chatto and Windus, 1967.
Selected Poems.   New York, Harper, 1967.
The Abbey That Refused to Die: A Poem.   County Mayo, Ireland, Ballintubber
   Abbey, 1967.
The Whispering Roots.   London, Cape, 1970; as *The Whispering Roots and
   Other Poems*, New York, Harper, 1970.
Going My Way.   London, Poem-of-the-Month Club, 1970.

Recording: *Poems*, Argo, 1974.

Novels

The Friendly Tree.   London, Cape, 1936; New York, Harper, 1937.
Starting Point.   London, Cape, 1937; New York, Harper, 1938.
Child of Misfortune.   London, Cape, 1939.

Novels (as Nicholas Blake)

A Question of Proof.   London, Collins, and New York, Harper, 1935.
Thou Shell of Death.   London, Collins, 1936; as *Shell of Death*, New York,
   Harper, 1936.
There's Trouble Brewing.   London, Collins, and New York, Harper, 1937.
The Beast Must Die.   London, Collins, and New York, Harper, 1938.
The Smiler with the Knife.   London, Collins, and New York, Harper, 1939.
Malice in Wonderland.   London, Collins, 1940; as *Summer Camp Mystery*,
   New York, Harper, 1940.
The Case of the Abominable Snowman.   London, Collins, 1941; as *Corpse in
   the Snowman*, New York, Harper, 1941. .
Minute for Murder.   London, Collins, 1947; New York, Harper, 1948.
Head of a Traveller.   London, Collins, and New York, Harper, 1949.
The Dreadful Hollow.   London, Collins, and New York, Harper, 1953.
The Whisper in the Gloom.   London, Collins, and New York, Harper, 1954.
A Tangled Web.   London, Collins, and New York, Harper, 1956.
End of Chapter.   London, Collins, and New York, Harper, 1957.
A Penknife in My Heart.   London, Collins, and New York, Harper, 1958.
The Widow's Cruise.   London, Collins, and New York, Harper, 1959.
The Worm of Death.   London, Collins, and New York, Harper, 1961.
The Deadly Joker.   London, Collins, 1963.
The Sad Variety.   London, Collins, and New York, Harper, 1964.
The Morning after Death.   London, Collins, and New York, Harper, 1966.
The Nicholas Blake Omnibus (includes *The Beast Must Die, A Tangled Web,
   A Penknife in My Heart*).   London, Collins, 1966.
The Private Wound.   London, Collins, and New York, Harper, 1968.

Other

Dick Willoughby (juvenile).   Oxford, Blackwell, 1933; New York, Random
   House, 1938.
A Hope for Poetry.   Oxford, Blackwell, 1934; with *Collected Poems*, New
   York, Random House, 1935.

Revolution in Writing. London, Hogarth Press, 1935; New York, Random House, 1936.

Imagination and Thinking, with L. Susan Stebbing. London, British Institute of Adult Education, 1936.

We're Not Going to Do Nothing: A Reply to Mr. Aldous Huxley's Pamphlet "What Are You Going to Do about It?" London, Left Review, 1936; Folcroft, Pennsylvania, Folcroft Editions, 1970.

Poetry for You: A Book for Boys and Girls on the Enjoyment of Poetry. Oxford, Blackwell, 1944; New York, Oxford University Press, 1947.

The Poetic Image. London, Cape, and New York, Oxford University Press, 1947.

Enjoying Poetry: A Reader's Guide. London, National Book League, 1947.

The Colloquial Element in English Poetry. Newcastle upon Tyne, Literary and Philosophical Society, 1947.

The Otterbury Incident (juvenile). London, Putnam, 1948; New York, Viking Press, 1949.

The Poet's Task. Oxford, Clarendon Press, 1951; Folcroft, Pennsylvania, Folcroft Editions, 1970.

The Grand Manner. Nottingham, University of Nottingham, 1962.

The Lyrical Poetry of Thomas Hardy. London, Oxford University Press, 1953; Folcroft, Pennsylvania, Folcroft Editions, 1970.

Notable Images of Virtue: Emily Brontë, George Meredith, W. B. Yeats. Toronto, Ryerson Press, 1954; Folcroft, Pennsylvania, Folcroft Editions, 1969.

The Poet's Way of Knowledge. Cambridge, University Press, 1957.

The Buried Day (autobiography). London, Chatto and Windus, and New York, Harper, 1960.

The Lyric Impulse. Cambridge, Massachusetts, Harvard University Press, and London, Chatto and Windus, 1965.

Thomas Hardy, with R. A. Scott-James. London, Longman, 1965.

A Need for Poetry? Hull, University of Hull, 1968.

On Translating Poetry: A Lecture. Abingdon-on-Thames, Berkshire, Abbey Press, 1970.

Editor, with W. H. Auden, *Oxford Poetry 1927.* Oxford, Blackwell, 1927.

Editor, with others, *A Writer in Arms,* by Ralph Fox. London, Lawrence and Wishart, 1937.

Editor, *The Mind in Chains: Socialism and the Cultural Revolution.* London, Muller, 1937; Folcroft, Pennsylvania, Folcroft Editions, 1972.

Editor, *The Echoing Green: An Anthology of Verse.* Oxford, Blackwell, 3 vols., 1937.

Editor, with Charles Fenby, *Anatomy of Oxford: An Anthology.* London, Cape, 1938.

Editor, with L. A. G. Strong, *A New Anthology of Modern Verse, 1920–1940.* London, Methuen, 1941.

Editor, with others, *Orion: Volume II* and *Volume III.* London, Nicholson and Watson, 1945, 1946.

Editor, *The Golden Treasury of the Best Songs and Lyrical Poems in the English Language,* by Francis Turner Palgrave. London, Collins, 1954.

Editor, with John Lehmann, *The Chatto Book of Modern Poetry, 1915–1955.* London, Chatto and Windus, 1956.

Editor, with Kathleen Nott and Thomas Blackburn, *New Poems 1957.* London, Joseph, 1957.

Editor, *A Book of English Lyrics.* London, Chatto and Windus, 1961; as
  English Lyric Poems, 1500–1900, New York, Appleton Century Crofts, 1961.
Editor, *The Collected Poems of Wilfred Owen.* London, Chatto and Windus,
  1964; revised edition, New York, New Directions, 1964.
Editor, *The Midnight Skaters: Poems for Young Readers,* by Edmund
  Blunden. London, Bodley Head, 1968.
Editor, *The Poems of Robert Browning.* Cambridge, Limited Editions Club,
  1969; New York, Heritage Press, 1971.
Editor, *A Choice of Keats's Verse.* London, Faber, 1971.
Editor, *Crabbe.* London, Penguin, 1973.

Translator, *The Georgics of Virgil.* London, Cape, 1940; New York, Oxford
  University Press, 1947.
Translator, *The Graveyard by the Sea,* by Paul Valéry. London, Secker and
  Warburg, 1947.
Translator, *The Aeneid of Virgil.* London, Hogarth Press, and New York,
  Oxford University Press, 1952.
Translator, *The Eclogues of Virgil.* London, Cape, 1963; with *The Georgics,*
  New York, Doubleday, 1964.
Translator, with Mátyás Sárközi, *The Tomtit in the Rain: Traditional Hun-
  garian Rhymes,* by Erzsi Gazdas. London, Chatto and Windus, 1971.

Bibliography: *C. Day Lewis, The Poet Laureate: A Bibliography* by Geoffrey
Handley-Taylor and Timothy d'Arch Smith, London and Chicago, St. James Press,
1968.

Manuscript Collections: New York Public Library; State University of New York
at Buffalo; British Museum, London; University of Liverpool.

Critical Studies: *C. Day Lewis* by Clifford Dyment, London, British Council–
National Book League, 1955, revised edition, 1963; *Stephen Spender, Louis
MacNeice, Cecil Day Lewis: A Critical Essay* by Derek Stanford, Grand Rapids,
Michigan, William B. Eerdmans, 1969.

*   *   *

"The selves who wrote these poems," C. Day Lewis said in surveying his work,
"are strangers to me"; and on another occasion he saw his poems as representing
"a series of fresh beginnings" rather than "a continuous line."
  It is true that Mr. Day Lewis's poetry changed with the times and with his
enlarging interests – giving it, incidentally, a welcome variety of subject – but the
reader, unbound by the writer's inevitable subjectivity, will readily recognise its
constancy of authorship and therefore its consequent "continuous line" of manner
and matter.
  This line is made up of two strands, one of lyricism and the other of introspection.
  Read in retrospect, one now sees that the lyrical verve of *Beechen Vigil* and
Country Comets — the two "extra-canonical" volumes of the twenties – was not
merely a youthful evanescence but the tentative first appearance of a peculiarly
musical poetic personality. The *tempi* of the music have altered as Mr. Day

Lewis's poetic personality has altered but, whether *presto con brio* as in the thirties or *andante con sensibilità* as in the sixties, the lyrical impetus is always prominent, giving his poems a melodic gracefulness and a prosodic subtlety that is not common in our time. The music has, however, always a modern sound, for even when Mr. Day Lewis conforms to an orthodox metrical form it is an orthodoxy transmitted through a twentieth-century sensibility; for the most part, however, he avails himself of most of the technical innovations at the service of the contemporary writer of verse, employing expertly such devices as speech rhythm, colloquial idiom, assonance, ellipsis, para-rhyme, and internal rhyme.

The other strand in the continuous line – introspection – was also understandably modified through the years, directed earlier to sociological ends and later to personal ones. Like a number of poets of his generation, Mr. Day Lewis in the nineteen-thirties was attracted to a socialist idealism as a therapy for society's maladies but found that for him adoption of the political and ethical ideologies involved presented difficulties. It was a problem of loyalties – of choosing between the values of the established but obsolescent order which had provided his culture and those of an emergent order which promised greater social justice but which threatened the existence of much in the old order thought admirable and which, therefore, menaced as well as enticed:

> I wished to commit myself to the irretrievable
> As a bee is committed to the bell, or a suicide
> Already half way from the parapet, to the river:
> But the river whisked away and the flower turned nasty.
> Or perhaps I was a coward.

The moral problem was complicated by an emotional one, a feeling – common to many intellectuals and artists of the period – of guilt at possessing privilege in a time of so much under-privilege:

> Morning brought tears and daisies, afternoon
> A tennis party. Athletic clergymen. Flannels –
> The uniform of a class, of a way of thinking,
> Or of not thinking: as I looked for a lost ball
> In the laurels, they smirched with pit-grime. . . .

A sincere writer always, Mr. Day Lewis, before being able with conviction to address himself to criticising the condition of society, felt it necessary to be assured of his qualifications for the task by making a preparatory enquiry into the condition of his own mind and heart. The result is *Transitional Poem*, a work in which ratiocinative precision and searching self-analysis are combined with much beauty of writing. Valuable as an insight into Mr. Day Lewis's uneasy temperament and affording clues to his later development, the poem is not a simple one, for thought and image are intricately interlocked; yet it succeeds in making metaphysical discussion exhilarating and has lucidity as an artistic communication of an individual predicament.

After the intensity of this poem, there comes a relaxation of tension in *From Feathers to Iron*. Whereas the former dealt with the relation of a man to society, the latter deals with the relation of a man to a woman, from its beginning in physical passion:

> Some say we walk out of Time altogether
> This way into a region where the primrose
> Shows an immortal dew, sun at meridian
> Stands up for ever and in scent the lime tree

to its fulfilment in the birth of a child:

> Come out in the sun, for a man is born today!

But, although on the whole a serene poem, social concern is not absent from it. The child has a double role in the story: it is an acquisition to the family and it is a future citizen with the power of decision:

> But born to essential dark,
> To an age that toes the line
> And never o'ersteps the mark.
> Take off your coat: grow lean:
> Suffer humiliation:
> Patrol the passes alone,
> And eat your iron ration.
> Else, wag as the world wags –
> One more mechanical jane
> Or gentleman in wax.

The change in emphasis, from political thought as soliloquy in *Transitional Poem* to political thought as homily in *From Feathers to Iron*, is attributable to the influence of W. H. Auden, whose leadership had an energising effect on the literary temper of the period and whose principle was that poetry should cease to look inward and should look outward. The effect of this doctrine on Mr. Day Lewis's work, the switch from the allusive to the direct, is particularly apparent in *The Magnetic Mountain*. This – like its predecessors a series of short poems united by a principal theme, a form which Mr. Day Lewis handles adroitly – is an outspoken advocacy, by means of satire, eloquence, and exhortation, of the need for a revolutionary change in society. Using the metaphor of a journey and abounding in apt railway imagery, the poem is an appeal to regard the present as past and move on to a better future.

Disquiet caused by aggressive Fascism and triumphing Nazism abroad, and by poverty and unemployment at home, contributed largely to the emotive origin of these volumes, as it does to *A Time to Dance*, the verse-play *Noah and the Waters* and *Overtures to Death*. In *A Time to Dance* and *Overtures to Death* this disquiet is made urgent by premonitions of war, providing the theme of lyrics which give moving personal utterance to the general fear. They also contain two tales – "Flight to Australia" and "The Nabara" – which must surely rank among the outstanding verse narratives in modern literature.

With the declaration of war in 1939 and opposition to Fascism and Nazism resolved from apostrophe into fact, there is a shift of object in Mr. Day Lewis's introspection. Hitherto it had been engaged with the individual as a responsible functionary in the community rather than with the individual for his own sake, but now private issues begin to take precedence over public. The influence of the activist W. H. Auden makes way for that of the contemplative Thomas Hardy. By examination of his own thoughts and feelings Mr. Day Lewis discovers a sympathy between them and those of his fellows, enriching his work with a sounder psychological perception and a more affectionate appreciation of human vagary than it had formerly. This new approach is to be noticed in the wartime poems included in *Word over All*, in which private soldiers are described not with an eye to their sociological significance but simply as *private* soldiers:

> I write this verse to record the men who have watched with me –
> Spot who is good at darts, Squibby at repartee,
> Mark and Cyril, the dead shots, Ralph with a ploughman's gait,
> Gibson, Harris and Long, old hands for the barricade. . . .

The trend from the ideological to the personal is continued in the reflective poems contained in *Poems 1943–1947*; and in *An Italian Visit* he comments with detachment on the sometimes intolerant and ingenuous, but ardent and hopeful evangelist of the political past:

> We who "flowered" in the Thirties
> Were an odd lot; sceptical yet susceptible,
> Dour though enthusiastic, horizon-addicts
> And future-fans, terribly apt to ask what
> Our all-very-fine sensations were in aid of.
> We did not, you will remember, come to coo.

This poem describes the travel impressions of three people who are, in fact, projections of the author himself, and it is to the exploration of the plurality of his character that his post-war volumes owe their satisfying deep and wide range of content. Having no longer to speak with the voice of the committed reformer, he found the freedom to speak with his own voice – or with, rather, the several voices of a composite personality, expressing the result of his self-scrutiny in *Pegasus*, *The Gate*, and *The Room*, variously as confession and reminiscence and, externalising what in his own nature is common to human nature, as character sketch, crime story, allegory, aphorism. Introspection, which began in the twenties with the self, then in the thirties became concerned with self and society, in recent years returned to the self; and in his own selfhood the poet discovered his kinship to the selfhood of others.

—Clifford Dyment

GARRIGUE, Jean. American. Born in Evansville, Indiana, 8 December 1914. Educated at the University of Chicago, B.A. 1937; University of Iowa, Iowa City, M.F.A. 1943. Edited a weekly newspaper for the U.S.O. during World War II. Instructor, Bard College, Annandale-on-Hudson, New York, 1951–52, Queens College, Flushing, New York, 1952–53, New School for Social Research, New York, 1955–56, and University of Connecticut, Storrs, 1960–61; Lecturer in Poetry, Smith College, Northampton, Massachusetts, 1965–66; Poet-in-Residence, University of Washington, Seattle, 1970. Poetry Editor, *The New Leader*, New York, 1965–72. Scholar, Radcliffe Institute for Independent Study, Cambridge, Massachusetts, 1968–70. Recipient: Rockefeller grant, 1954, 1966; Union League Civic and Arts Foundation prize (*Poetry*, Chicago), 1956; *Hudson Review* Fellowship, 1957; Longview Award, 1958; Guggenheim grant, 1960; National Institute of Arts and Letters grant, 1961; Lowell Mason Palmer Award, 1961; Emily Clark Balch Prize (*Virginia Quarterly Review*), 1966; Melville Cane Award, 1968. *Died 27 December 1972.*

PUBLICATIONS

Verse

Five Young American Poets, with others. New York, New Directions, 1944.
The Ego and the Centaur. New York, New Directions, 1947.

The Monument Rose: Poems. New York, Noonday Press, 1953.
A Water Walk by Villa d'Este. New York, St. Martin's Press, 1959; London, Macmillan, 1960.
Country Without Maps. New York, Macmillan, 1964.
New and Selected Poems. New York, Macmillan, 1967.
Studies for an Actress and Other Poems. New York, Macmillan, 1973.

Short Stories

The Animal Hotel. New York, Eakins Press, 1966.
Chartres and Prose Poems. New York, Eakins Press, 1971.

Other

Marianne Moore. Minneapolis, University of Minnesota Press, 1965; London, Oxford University Press, 1966.

Editor, *Translations by American Poets.* Athens, Ohio University Press, 1970.

*   *   *

Jean Garrigue published steadily for nearly three decades, and was one of the most productive of America's women poets, yet presumably because she did not make any of the fashionable shifts in style or outlook, she is not as well known as some who have done less – and less distinguished – work. She is a frankly romantic lyricist whose warmest responses are reserved for the lovely, and she can be elegant as well as rich, as in the following passage from "For the Fountains and Fountaineers of Villa d'Este" in *A Water Walk by Villa d'Este*;

> To tread the crests of the fountains,
> To walk on the foam of their flowers,
> Upthrust in a vertical climbing
> Spires of the falling and changing stuff
> In a ghost play of dance
> Creating beyond their climbing
> Caps of their vapor, a white turbulence
> Of that which so changes beyond them
> It is sur-foam, surf-combed,
> It is got by the mathematics of climbing –
> To reach by those aerobatics into white snows of the mounting –
> There to dissolve into
> What brings all the condensed fury of dews
> Back down into descending.

From time to time the poet appears to be overwhelmed by the beauty and impermanence of a subject, with the result that there is a temporary blurring. Often this is brought about by a risk taken, a plunge beneath surfaces, and the poet's ambition must be honored. Yet she can be direct as she need be, as in "Notes from Underground,'' one of the best of the shorter pieces in the above-mentioned volume:

> That's enough I said to the mourning dove
> Quite enough, now be quiet awhile.
> And enough, I said to the snuffling horse
> Beating the life out of the grass
> By treading one track in the field round and round.
>
> And enough, I said to the probing ant
> And the nibbling caterpillar,
> And you, oh thrush, who lift your voice
> Of watery joy twice over twice.
>
> Enough, you moles, you farmering worms,
> You groundhogs who spade and plough.
> Enough roots grappling, trees thrusting
> Vast systems of life tenaciously down.
>
> Hush, you crickets. Stop, you brook.
> You clouds sailing, you rain falling.
> Enough, birds, bulbs, enough, seeds, bones,
> For I am done with motion.

There is a high proportion of success in the poet's *Country Without Maps*, which contains the long piece "Pays Perdu," a consistently rewarding narrative which displays her talents to the full but which, because of the interspersed prose passages, is formally flawed. If such a poem indicates that she was not content with the easily arrived at, and best suggests the degree of her commitment to the complete life of poetry, it is perhaps inevitable that she should be most finished an artist in work that is centered in a more intimately felt world, one full of precious objects, gardens and animals. Whatever its subject or the limits of its ambition, Jean Garrigue brought to her poem a warmth of response and a complex sensibility.

—Lucien Stryk

HUGHES, (James) Langston. American. Born in Joplin, Missouri, 1 February 1902. Educated at Central High School, Cleveland, 1916–20; Columbia University, New York, 1921–22; Lincoln University, Pennsylvania (Witter Bynner Award, 1926), B.A. 1929. During World War II, Member of the Music and Writers war boards. Seaman, 1923–25; busboy, Wardman Park Hotel, Washington, D.C., 1925. Madrid Correspondent, Baltimore *Afro–American*, 1937; Columnist, Chicago *Defender*, 1943–67, and for New York *Post*, 1962–67. Founder of the Harlem Suitcase Theatre, New York, 1938, New Negro Theatre, Los Angeles, 1939, and Skyloft Players, Chicago, 1941. Visiting Professor in Creative Writing, Atlanta University, Georgia, 1947; Poet-in-Residence, University of Chicago Laboratory School, 1949. Recipient: *Opportunity* magazine prize, 1925; *Crisis* magazine prize, 1925; Harmon Gold Medal for literature, 1931; Rosenwald Fellowship, 1931, 1940; Guggenheim Fellowship, 1935; National Institute of Arts and letters grant, 1946;

Anisfield-Wolfe Award, 1953; Spingarn Medal, 1960. D.Litt.: Lincoln University, 1943; Howard University, Washington, D.C., 1963; Western Reserve University, Cleveland, 1964. Member, National Institute of Arts and Letters, 1961, and American Academy of Arts and Sciences. *Died 22 May 1967.*

PUBLICATIONS

Verse

The Weary Blues. New York and London, Knopf, 1926.
Fine Clothes to the Jew. New York and London, Knopf, 1927.
Dear Lovely Death. Amenia, New York, Troutbeck Press, 1931.
The Negro Mother and Other Dramatic Recitations. New York, Golden Stair Press, 1931.
The Dream Keeper and Other Poems. New York, Knopf, 1932.
Scottsboro Limited: Four Poems and a Play in Verse. New York, Golden Stair Press, 1932.
A New Song. New York, International Workers Order, 1938.
Shakespeare in Harlem. New York, Knopf, 1942.
Freedom's Plow. New York, Musette, 1943.
Jim Crow's Last Stand. New York, Negro Publication Society of America, 1943.
Lament for Dark Peoples and Other Poems, edited by H. Driessen. Amsterdam, H. von Krimpen, 1944.
Fields of Wonder. New York, Knopf, 1947.
One-Way Ticket. New York, Knopf, 1949.
Montage of a Dream Deferred. New York, Holt, 1951.
Selected Poems. New York, Knopf, 1959.
Ask Your Mama: 12 Moods for Jazz. New York, Knopf, 1961.
The Panther and the Lash: Poems of Our Times. New York, Knopf, 1967.
Don't You Turn Back: Poems, edited by Lee Bennett Hopkins. New York, Knopf, 1969.

Recordings: *Simple Speaks His Mind,* Folkways, 1952; *The Dream Keeper and Other Poems,* Folkways, 1955; *The Weary Blues and Other Poems,* MGM, 1958; *Did You Ever Hear the Blues?,* United Artists, 1959.

Plays

The Gold Piece, in *The Brownies' Book* (New York), July 1921.
Mulatto (produced New York, 1935; original version produced Cleveland, 1939). Included in *Five Plays,* 1963; in *Three Negro Plays,* London, Penguin, 1969.
Little Ham (produced Cleveland, 1935). Included in *Five Plays,* 1963.
Troubled Island (produced Cleveland, 1935; revised version, music by William Grant Still (produced New York, 1949). New York, Leeds Music Corporation, 1949.
When the Jack Hollers, with Arna Bontemps (produced Cleveland, 1936).
Joy to My Soul (produced Cleveland, 1937).

Soul Gone Home (produced Cleveland, 1937(?)).   Included in *Five Plays*, 1963.
Don't You Want to Be Free?, music by Carroll Tate (also director: produced New York, 1937). Published in *One Act Play Magazine* (New York), October 1938.
Front Porch (produced Cleveland, 1938).
The Sun Do Move (produced Chicago, 1942).
Pvt. Jim Crow (radio script), in *Negro Story* (Chicago), May-June 1945.
Booker T. Washington at Atlanta (broadcast, 1945). Published in *Radio Drama in Action*, edited by Eric Barnouw, New York, Farrar and Rinehart, 1945.
Street Scene (lyrics only), book by Elmer Rice, music by Kurt Weill (produced New York, 1947).   New York, Chappell, 1947.
The Barrier, music by Jan Meyerowitz (produced New York, 1950).
Just Around the Corner (lyrics only), book by Abby Mann and Bernard Drew, music by Joe Sherman (produced Ogunquit, Maine, 1951).
Simply Heavenly, music by David Martin (produced New York, 1957; London, 1958).   New York, Dramatists Play Service, 1959.
Esther, music by Jan Meyerowitz (produced Urbana, Illinois, 1957).
Shakespeare in Harlem, with James Weldon Johnson (produced New York, 1959).
Port Town, music by Jan Meyerowitz (produced Lenox, Massachusetts, 1960).
The Ballad of the Brown King, music by Margaret Bonds (produced New York, 1960).
Black Nativity (produced New York, 1961; England tour, 1962).
Gospel Glow (produced New York, 1962).
Tambourines to Glory, music by Jobe Huntley, based on novel by Hughes (produced New York, 1963).   Included in *Five Plays*, 1963.
Five Plays (includes *Mulatto, Soul Gone Home, Little Ham, Simply Heavenly, Tambourines to Glory*), edited by Webster Smalley.   Bloomington, Indiana University Press, 1963.
Jerico-Jim Crow (produced New York, 1963).
The Prodigal Son (produced New York, 1965).

Screenplay: *Way Down South*, with Clarence Muse, 1939.

Radio scripts: *Jubilee*, with Arna Bontemps, 1941; *Brothers*, 1942; *Freedom's Plow*, 1943; *John Henry Hammers It Out*, with Peter Lyons, 1943; *In the Service of My Country*, 1944; *The Man Who Went to War*, 1944 (UK); *Booker T. Washington at Atlanta*, 1945; *Swing Time at the Savoy*, with Noble Sissle, 1949.

Television scripts: *The Big Sea*, 1965; *It's a Mighty World*, 1965; *Strollin' Twenties*, 1966.

Recordings: *Street Scene*, Columbia; *Simply Heavenly*, Columbia; *Jerico-Jim Crow*, Folkways, 1964.

Novels

Not Without Laughter.   New York and London, Knopf, 1930.
Simple Speaks His Mind.   New York, Simon and Schuster, 1950; London, Gollancz, 1951.
Simple Takes a Wife.   New York, Simon and Schuster, 1953; London, Gollancz, 1954.

Simple Stakes a Claim. New York, Rinehart, 1957; London, Gollancz, 1958.
Tambourines to Glory. New York, Day, 1958; London, Gollancz, 1959.
The Best of Simple. New York, Hill and Wang, 1961.
Simple's Uncle Sam. New York, Hill and Wang, 1965.

Short Stories

The Ways of White Folks. New York, Knopf, and London, Allen and Unwin, 1934.
Laughing to Keep from Crying. New York, Holt, 1952.
Something in Common and Other Stories. New York, Hill and Wang, 1963.

Other

Popo and Fifina: Children of Haiti, with Arna Bontemps. New York, Macmillan, 1932.
The Big Sea: An Autobiography. New York, Knopf, 1940; London, Hutchinson, 1941.
The First Book of Negroes (juvenile). New York, Watts, 1952.
The First Book of Rhythms (Juvenile). New York, Watts, 1954; London, Edmund Ward, 1964.
Famous American Negroes (juvenile). New York, Dodd Mead, 1954.
The Sweet Flypaper of Life, with Roy DeCarava (on Harlem). New York, Simon and Schuster, 1955.
Famous Negro Music Makers (juvenile). New York, Dodd Mead, 1955.
The First Book of Jazz (juvenile). New York, Watts, 1955; revised edition, 1962; London, Mayflower, 1962.
A Pictorial History of the Negro in America, with Milton Meltzer. New York, Crown, 1956; revised edition, 1963.
I Wonder As I Wander: An Autobiographical Journey. New York, Rinehart, 1956.
The First Book of the West Indies (juvenile). New York, Watts, 1956; as· *The First Book of the Caribbean*, London, Edmund Ward, 1965.
The Langston Hughes Reader. New York, Braziller, 1958.
The First Book of Africa (juvenile). New York, Watts, 1960; London, Mayflower, 1961; revised edition, Watts, 1964.
Famous Negro Heroes of America (juvenile). New York, Dodd Mead, 1958.
Fight for Freedom: The Story of the NAACP. New York, Norton, 1962.
Black Magic: A Pictorial History of the Negro in American Entertainment, with Milton Meltzer. New York, Prentice Hall, 1967.
Black Misery. New York, P. S. Erikson, 1969.
Good Morning, Revolution: Uncollected Social Protest Writings, edited by Faith Berry. New York, L. Hill, 1973.

Editor, *Four Lincoln University Poets.* Lincoln, Pennsylvania, Lincoln University Herald, 1930.
Editor, with Arna Bontemps, *The Poetry of the Negro 1746–1949: An Anthology.* New York, Doubleday, 1949; revised edition, 1970.
Editor, with Waring Guney and Bruce M. Wright, *Lincoln University Poets.* New York, Fine Editions Press, 1954.
Editor, with Arna Bontemps, *The Book of Negro Folklore.* New York, Dodd Mead, 1959.

Editor, *An African Treasury: Articles, Essays, Stories, Poems by Black Africans.* New York, Crown, 1960; London, Gollancz, 1961.
Editor, *Poems from Black Africa.* Bloomington, Indiana University Press, 1963.
Editor, *New Negro Poets: USA.* Bloomington, Indiana University Press, 1964.
Editor, *The Book of Negro Humor.* New York, Dodd Mead, 1966.
Editor, *La poésie negro–américaine* (bilingual edition). Paris, Editions Seghers, 1966.
Editor, *Anthologie africaine et malgache.* Paris, Seghers, 1966.
Editor, The Best Short Stories by Negro Writers: An Anthology from 1899 to the Present. Boston, Little Brown, 1967.

Translator, with Mercer Cook, *Masters of the Dew,* by Jacques Roumain. New York, Reynal and Hitchcock, 1947.
Translator, with Ben Frederic Carruthers, *Cuba Libre,* by Nicolás Guillén. Los Angeles, Ward Ritchie Press, 1948.
Translator, *Gypsy Ballads,* by Federico García Lorca. Beloit, Wisconsin, Beloit College, 1951.
Translator, *Selected Poems of Gabriela Mistral.* Bloomington, Indiana University Press, 1957.

Bibliography: *A Bio-Bibliography of Langston Hughes, 1920–1967* by Donald C. Dickinson, Hamden, Connecticut, Shoe String Press, 1967.

Manuscript Collections: James Weldon Johnson Memorial Collection, Yale University, New Haven, Connecticut; State University of New York, Buffalo.

Critical Studies: *A Bio-Bibliography of Langston Hughes, 1902–1967* by Donald C. Dickinson, Hamden, Connecticut, Shoe String Press, 1967; *Langston Hughes* by James A. Emanuel, New York, Twayne, 1967; *Langston Hughes: A Biography* by Milton Meltzer, New York, Crowell, 1968; *Black Troubadour: Langston Hughes* by Charlemae Rollins, Chicago, Rand McNally, 1971; *Langston Hughes, Black Genius: A Critical Evaluation* edited by Therman B. O'Daniel, New York, Morrow, 1971; *A Concordance to the Poetry of Langston Hughes* by Stanley Schatt and Peter Mandelik, Detroit, Gale, 1974.

*   *   *

Who can fail to love Langston Hughes, a man whose open pleasure in humanity led him to visit nearly every inhabited spot on the globe, abide the ambivalence of people's behavior with understanding, taking their own small offenses with humor and large injustices done against them with proportionate ridicule, and through it all remain as much a son of Harlem as his character Jesse B. Simple, because "it's so full of Negroes"? He earned the recognition due him, but it will do us most of the honor to call him an American classic.

Hughes' verse brings together two of the healthiest strains of American culture. The first is that of Afro-American folk living, formally evidenced by the statement and response pattern, six line stanzas and dominant four accents of the blues, which Margaret Walker (*Phylon*, 1950) credits as the first significant introduction of Negro idiom into poetry since the time of Paul Dunbar; by the improvisational manner of sharp changes, variations, and shifty rhythms which Hughes made a poetic equivalent of be-bop in *Montage of a Dream Deferred*; and by the multiple voices – old and young, male and female, sad or briefly pleased – who speak Black English throughout the poems. The forms exist in Hughes' poetry for the same reason they do in popular life: because they functionally represent the attitudes and responses to living experience that distinguish the country folk and urban masses from assimilationist Negroes and bourgeois whites.

In seeking to reconcile literary art and folk life, Hughes was originally part of the generation of the Harlem Renaissance, the time of New Negroes infused with racial pride and seeking to gain equality in art as much as in society. Like his contemporaries, Hughes found in Africa, which he actually visited as well as imagined, the source of imagery for immediately felt needs of a man who lived and spoke the language of the New World (e.g., "Dream Variations" and "Danse Africaine"), and like them he, too, celebrated an exotic Harlem of the 1920's ("Jazzonia"). All the while, though, and increasingly so with the advent of the Great Depression, Hughes expressed the feelings of those who take life a day at a time with a mixture of resolution and despair, pain and laughter – those who sing the blues (e.g., "The Weary Blues," "Bound No'th Blues," "The Morning After," etc.).

Probably Langston Hughes is the most complete realist in American poetry. He writes of love betrayed, foolish children, romantically susceptible older folk, scandal, and shiftlessness; yet he neither thinks people behave as they do because they have been reduced to monstrous victims, nor betrays a concealed program for their uplift. Of course, he protests racial injustice, because it is self-evident that racial oppression amounts to a denial of the right to live, but even so he's going to live. Thus, the essay "My Adventures as a Social Poet" (*Phylon*, 1947), which tells of the enemies Hughes made among the narrow minded, is written with the same recognition of the troubles a black man encounters combined with high-spirited feeling about living as the poem about the potential suicide ("life Is Fine") who concludes:

> Though you may hear me holler,
> And you may see me cry –
> I'll be dogged, sweet baby,
> If you gonna see me die.
> > *Life is fine!*
> > *Fine as wine!*
> > *Life is fine!*

The second major strain in Hughes' poetry – strongly modified by the first – is the democratic tradition. The central motif of *Montage of a Dream Deferred* and the numerous references in other poems to dreams invoked or betrayed blend into a representation of the principle of mass unity. The unity is not entirely black. "Daybreak in Alabama" envisions a potential song of human communion as harmonious as the natural world. Like Whitman, whom he praises for minding each detail as he went seeking and finding ("Old Walt"), Hughes can adopt a generic national persona as in "Let America Be America Again," while a poem such as "Freedom's Plow" seems a good deal like a Sandburg rhapsody to ideals. Still and all Hughes is an Afro-American poet and a realist. The blacks' questioning in "Freedom Train" is more in his line. Democratic ideals are goals of social behavior, good ideas that are "true anyhow no matter how many/Liars use those words" ("In Explanation of Our Times"), but they do not have the supernal reality, attributed to them by philosophical idealists. As Simple says, democracy is just doing what ought to be done.

Perhaps in the end it is Hughes' personality, distilled through the being of the people in his writing, that best accounts for the affection his readers have for him.

If that is so, there is much to learn from the fact, for the outlook on life he expresses is the other side of the story of American civilization. It is an outlook that, because it does not produce goods or profits as ends in themselves, is a genuinely human way of living. Hughes, too, calls it soul.

—John M. Reilly

JARRELL, Randall. American. Born in Nashville, Tennessee, 6 May 1914. Educated at Vanderbilt University, Nashville, B.S. (Phi Beta Kappa) in psychology 1936, M.A. in English 1939. Served as a celestial navigation tower operator in the United States Army Air Corps, 1942–46. Married Mary Eloise von Schrader in 1952. Instructor in English, Kenyon College, Gambier, Ohio, 1937–39, University of Texas, Austin, 1939–42, and Sarah Lawrence College, Bronxville, New York, 1946–47; Associate Professor, 1947–58, and Professor of English, 1958–65, Women's College of the University of North Carolina (later, University of North Carolina at Greensboro). Lecturer, Salzburg Seminar in American Civilization, 1948; Visiting Fellow in Creative Writing, Princeton University, New Jersey, 1951–52; Fellow, Indiana School of Letters, Bloomington, Summer 1952; Visiting Professor of English, University of Illinois, Urbana, 1953; Elliston Lecturer, University of Cincinnatti, Ohio, 1958; Phi Beta Kappa Visiting Scholar, 1964–65. Acting Literary Editor, *The Nation*, New York, 1946–47; Poetry Critic, *Partisan Review*, New Brunswick, New Jersey, 1949–53, and *Yale Review*, New Haven, Connecticut, 1955–57; Member of the Editorial Board, *American Scholar*, Washington, D.C., 1957–65. Consultant in Poetry, Library of Congress, Washington, D.C., 1956–58. Recipient: *Southern Review* Prize, 1936; Jeanette Sewell Davis Prize, 1943, Levinson Prize, 1948, and Oscar Blumenthal Prize, 1951 (*Poetry*, Chicago); J. P. Bishop Memorial Literary Prize (*Sewanee Review*), 1946; Guggenheim Fellowship, 1946; National Institute of Arts and Letters grant, 1951; National Book Award, 1961; Oliver Max Gardner Award, University of North Carolina, 1962; American Association of University Women Juvenile Award, 1964; Ingram Merrill Award, 1965. D.H.L.: Bard College, Annandale-on-Hudson, New York, 1962. Member, National Institute of Arts and Letters; Chancellor, Academy of American Poets, 1956. *Died 14 October 1965.*

PUBLICATIONS

Verse

Five Young American Poets, with others. New York, New Directions, 1940.
Blood for a Stranger. New York, Harcourt Brace, 1942.
Little Friend, Little Friend. New York, Dial Press, 1945.
Losses. New York, Harcourt Brace, 1948.
The Seven-League Crutches. New York, Harcourt Brace, 1951.
Selected Poems. New York, Knopf, 1955; London, Faber, 1956.

Uncollected Poems. Cincinnati, Ohio, privately printed; 1958.

The Woman at the Washington Zoo: Poems and Translations. New York, Atheneum, 1960.

Selected Poems. New York, Atheneum, 1964.

The Lost World: New Poems. New York, Macmillan, 1965; London, Eyre and Spottiswoode, 1966.

The Complete Poems. New York, Farrar Straus, 1969; London, Faber, 1971.

The Achievement of Randall Jarrell: A Comprehensive Selection of His Poems with a Critical Introduction, by Frederick J. Hoffman. Chicago, Scott Foresman, 1970.

Jerome: The Biography of a Poem. New York, Grossman, 1971.

Play

The Three Sisters, adaptation of a play by Chekhov (produced New York, 1964). New York, Macmillan, 1969.

Novel

Pictures from an Institution: A Comedy. New York, Knopf, and London, Faber, 1954.

Other

Poetry and the Age (essays). New York, Knopf, 1953; London, Faber, 1955.

Poets, Critics, and Readers (address). Charlottesville, University of Virginia Press, 1959.

A Sad Heart at the Supermarket: Essays and Fables. New York, Atheneum, 1962; London, Eyre and Spottiswoode, 1965.

The Gingerbread Rabbit (juvenile). New York, Macmillan, and London, Collier Macmillan, 1964.

The Bat-Poet (juvenile). New York, Macmillan, 1964; London, Collier Macmillan, 1966.

The Animal Family (juvenile). New York, Pantheon, 1965; London, Hart Davis, 1967.

The Third Book of Criticism (essays). New York, Farrar Straus, 1969; London, Faber, 1974.

Editor, *The Anchor Book of Stories.* New York, Doubleday, 1958.

Editor, *The Best Short Stories of Rudyard Kipling.* New York, Doubleday, 1961.

Editor, *The English in England,* by Rudyard Kipling. New York, Doubleday, 1962.

Editor, *Six Russian Short Novels.* New York, Doubleday, 1963.

Editor, *The English in India: Short Stories in the Vernacular,* by Rudyard Kipling. Gloucester, Massachusetts, Peter Smith, 1970.

Translator, with Moses Hadas, *The Ghetto and the Jews of Rome,* by Ferdinand Gregorovius. New York, Schocken Books, 1948.

Translator, *The Rabbit Catcher and Other Fairy Tales of Ludwig Bechstein.* New York, Macmillan, and London, Macmillan, 1962.

Translator, *The Golden Bird and Other Fairy Tales by the Brothers Grimm.* New York, Macmillan, 1962.
Translator, *Snow White and the Seven Dwarfs: A Tale from the Brothers Grimm.* New York, Farrar Straus, 1972; London, Penguin, 1974.
Translator, *The Juniper Tree and Other Tales by the Brothers Grimm.* New York, Farrar Straus, 1973.
Translator, *Goethe's Faust: Part One.* New York, Farrar Straus, 1974.

Bibliography: *Randall Jarrell: A Bibliography* by Charles M. Adams, Chapel Hill, University of North Carolina Press, and London, Oxford University Press, 1958; supplement in *Analects I* (Greensboro, North Carolina), Spring 1961.

Manuscript Collections: Walter Clinton Jackson Library, University of North Carolina, Chapel Hill; Berg Collection, New York Public Library.

Critical Studies: *Randall Jarrell, 1914–1965* edited by Robert Lowell, Peter Taylor, and Robert Penn Warren, New York, Farrar Straus, 1967; *The Poetry of Randall Jarrell* by Suzanne Ferguson, Baton Rouge, Louisiana State University Press, 1971.

*   *   *

The sustained richness of Randall Jarrell's *Selected Poems* and of his last collection, *The Lost World,* tends to obscure the fact that despite his early technical sophistication, he matured slowly as a poet. The posthumous *Complete Poems* now includes all the verse (some dating from 1934) which Jarrell himself had wisely omitted from the 1955 selection – poems which suffer badly from Auden's influence and are further weakened, as Delmore Schwartz once observed, by a "thinness and abstractness of texture and reference." The poems in *Little Friend, Little Friend,* however, especially the frequently anthologized war pieces, are completely Jarrell's own and in retrospect explain his initially cryptic remark that all good poets are essentially war poets.
In a 1951 poem, "The Face," Jarrell's aging Princess (the Marschallin of Strauss and von Hofmannsthal) looks into her mirror and thinks:

> This is what happens to everyone.
> At first you get bigger, you know more,
> Then something goes wrong.
> You are, and you say: I am –
> And you were . . . I've been too long.
>
> I know there's no saying no,
> But just the same you say it. No.
> I'll point to myself and say: I'm not like this.
> I'm the same as always inside.
> – And even that's not so.
>
> I thought: If nothing happens . . .
> And nothing happened.
> Here I am.
>   But it's not *right.*
> If just living can do this,
> Living is more dangerous than anything:
>
> It is terrible to be alive.

The theme, stated here with untypical directness, is repeated with infinitely subtle variations in some of Jarrell's most moving later poems, "Seele im Raum," "Next Day," and "The Lost Children," and is in fact never more than just below the immediate surface of his best verse. The war which all men fight – and inevitably lose – is the war with time and an indifferent universe. Thinking sadly about a maimed veteran Jarrell asks:

> How can I care about you much, or pick you out
> From all the others other people loved
> And sent away to die for them! You are a ticket
> Someone bought and lost on, a stray animal:
> You have lost even the right to be condemned.
> I see you looking helplessly about, in histories,
> Bewildered with your terrible companions, Pain
> And Death and Empire: what have you understood, to die?
> Were you worth, soldier, all that people said
> To be spent so willingly? Surely your one theory, to live,
> Is nonsense to the practice of the centuries.

But of course Jarrell does care, intensely. The speaker in "The Survivor among Graves" realizes that everyone faces the same hopeless struggle:

> The haunters and the haunted, among graves
> Mirror each other sightlessly; in soundless
> Supplication, a last unheard
> Unison, reach to each other: *Say again,*
> Say the voices, *say again*
> *That life is – what it is not;*
> *That, somewhere, there is – something, something;*
> *That we are waiting; that we are waiting.*

"What life is not" is fulfillment, the sense of a justifying purpose for human life and suffering. The child of "90 North" reaches his fabled North Pole only to find:

> Here at the actual pole of my existence,
> Where all that I have done is meaningless,
> Where I die or live by accident alone –
>
> Where, living or dying, I am still alone;
> . . . .
> I see at last that all the knowledge
>
> I wrung from darkness – that the darkness flung me –
> Is worthless as ignorance: nothing comes from nothing,
> The darkness from the darkness. Pain comes from the darkness
> And we call it wisdom. It is pain.

It is poems such as these that confirm Robert Lowell's observation that with all his dazzling gifts, Jarrell was "the most heartbreaking English poet of his generation."

Just as the soldier serves as a basic metaphor for Jarrell, so too does the child, learning by his losses (and through his encounters with the *märchen*, those symbolic fairy tales for which Jarrell had an almost obsessive fascination), and the sensitive adult as well, experiencing great works of the imagination, whether in music, the visual arts, or literature. The import of the true work, as Jarrell states repeatedly throughout his poetry and criticism, is that of Rilke's archaic torso of

Apollo: *you must change your life* – you must grow, that is, into a new, more intense consciousness of being. Yet the imperative to change leads to the tragic paradox at the center of Jarrell's work. We change, by the pressure of experience, knowledge and increasing sensitivity, but there is no goal to achieve, no transcendence, no escape, finally, from a world in which it is "terrible to be alive." There is only stoicism, such consolation as knowing the worst can bring, and the compassionate realization that others too must suffer. Life is made bearable – perhaps bearable – by such knowledge and sympathy and in Jarrell's own case by the miraculous recapturing of childhood happiness. "I reach out to it empty handed," Jarrell wrote at the end, and:

> my hand comes back empty,
> And yet emptiness is traded for its emptiness,
> I have found that Lost World in the Lost and Found
> Columns whose grey illegible advertisements
> My soul has memorized world after world:
> LOST – NOTHING. STRAYED FROM NOWHERE. NO REWARD.
> I hold in my own hands, in happiness,
> Nothing: the nothing for which there's no reward.

The lost world of childhood no longer exists, is "nothing" now; and yet through memory (and by the art of fixing memory in the poem), the poet can hold his nothing in his hands, "in happiness." There is no reward beyond this: memory and art carry their own fulfillment for the poet and for his perceptive readers, who have lived vicariously through the superlative imaginative recreations which Jarrell presents in this final volume.

No brief thematic identification of Jarrell's concerns can begin to do justice to the embodied beauty of the poems themselves. Sweeping judgments are as dangerous as they are vulnerable, but among the poets who followed after the first great generation of modern American poets, Eliot, Stevens, Frost, and Pound, Jarrell may well be the most gifted and eloquent. His poetry is frequently demanding in its subtleties, but is difficult, finally, in the same sense that Jarrell had in mind when he observed that some of Frost's best poems are "hard to understand, but easy to love."

—Elmer Borklund

KAVANAGH, Patrick.   Irish.   Born in Inniskeen, 21 October 1904. Educated at Kednaminsha National School, 1910–16. Married Katherine Moloney in 1967. Farmer and shoemaker, Inniskeen, 1920–36. Lived in London and Dublin, 1936–42. Columnist ("City Commentary"), *Irish Press*, Dublin, 1942–44; Film Critic and Feature Writer, *The Standard*, Dublin, 1943–49; Editor, *Kavanagh's Weekly*, Dublin, 1952; Contributor, *Nimbus* magazine, London, 1954, and *The Farmer's Journal*, 1958–63 and *RTV-Guide* magazine, 1963–67, Dublin. Extra-Mural Lecturer, University College, Dublin, 1956–59. Recipient: A. E. Memorial Award, 1940; Arts Council of Great Britain Award, 1967. *Died 30 November 1967.*

PUBLICATIONS

Verse

Ploughman and Other Poems. London, Macmillan, 1936.
The Great Hunger. Dublin, Cuala Press, 1942.
A Soul for Sale: Poems. London, Macmillan, 1947.
Recent Poems. New York, The Peter Kavanagh Hand Press, 1958.
Come Dance with Kitty Stobling and Other Poems. London, Longman, 1960;
    Chester Springs, Pennsylvania, Dufour, 1964.
Collected Poems. London, MacGibbon and Kee, and New York, Devin
    Adair, 1964.
Complete Poems, edited by Peter Kavanagh. New York, The Peter Kavanagh
    Hand Press, 1972.

Recording: *Almost Everything,* Claddah, 1965.

Plays

Self Portrait (televised, 1962). Dublin, Dolmen Press, 1964.
Tarry Flynn (produced Dublin, 1966).

Television Feature: *Self Portrait,* 1962.

Novel

Tarry Flynn. London, Pilot Press, 1948; New York, Devin Adair, 1949.

Other

The Green Fool (autobiography). London, Joseph, 1938; New York, Harper,
    1939.
Collected Pruse. London, MacGibbon and Kee, 1967.
*Lapped Furrows: Correspondence, 1933–1967, Between Patrick and Peter
    Kavanagh, With Other Documents,* edited by Peter Kavanagh. New York,
    The Peter Kavanagh Hand Press, 1969.
November Haggard: Uncollected Prose and Verse of Patrick Kavanagh, edited
    by Peter Kavanagh. New York, The Peter Kavanagh Hand Press, 1971.

Bibliography: *Garden of the Golden Apples: A Bibliography of Patrick Kavanagh*
by Peter Kavanagh, New York, The Peter Kavanagh Hand Press, 1972.

Manuscript Collections: National Library of Ireland, Dublin; The Peter Kavanagh
Hand Press, New York.

*   *   *

I met Patrick Kavanagh just once. He told me that he was dying. He seemed
cheerful about it, pointing out that some Irish officials had awarded him a pension
when his incurable disease was confirmed. "Like a prize each year until I die," he

said. The prospect of cheating officialdom gave him one amusing reason for living – I am sure he had others, more serious. In fact he lived on for five years. I hope the prizes didn't stop.

I have just reread the reprint of his *Collected Poems* and realised what an excellent poet he is, much more various than memories of the early verse allowed for. This book runs from the lyrical simplicities about tinkers and blackbirds which he wrote while still scraping a living from a farm in Monaghan, through the long poem about Ireland which made his reputation and brought the police to his door ("The Great Hunger"), to the parish of gossip about matters of life and death which constitutes the later major verse.

Intuitive, epigrammatic, shrewd, Kavanagh is always the peasant, seeing how much he can get away with, returning again and again to a handful of themes perceived as underlying all creation. Here is a complete short poem which gives his authentic flavour, "Sanctity":

> To be a poet and not know the trade,
> To be a lover and repel all women;
> Twin ironies by which great saints are made,
> The agonising pincer-jaws of Heaven.

There is an arresting sentence in his early autobiography, *The Green Fool*, first published in 1938 but then withdrawn as a result of a libel action brought by Oliver St. John Gogarty. This runs: "I turned away from the door of Literature and continued my work among poetry, potatoes, and old boots." What is significant here is not the naive equation of "poetry and potatoes" with what is real, but the degree of ironic self-knowledge implicit in Kavanagh's quite consciously setting himself up as a peasant-poet, and declaring his intention of *working his way through* that chosen role. As C. H. Sisson has written, in his *English Poetry 1900–1950: An Assessment*: "He discovered that 'the Ireland thing' got in the way, and he aspired to free himself from it. Because he was an Irish peasant he wanted to rid himself of the *notion* of the Irish peasant." This, as Sisson concedes, Kavanagh achieved, especially in the outburst of poems which came towards the end of his life, where "his constant preoccupation is to see the world otherwise than through ideas."

Kavanagh possessed very considerable formal skill – he had obeyed Yeats's injunction that Irish poets should "learn their trade" and "sing whatever is well made," while discarding the Yeatsian robes of rhetoric and the magician's hat which so often go with this if it be misinterpreted as an invitation to the oracular. His sonnets, in particular, are an extraordinary extension of the form. Here is one of the best of them, "Canal Bank Walk," which dates from 1957:

> Leafy-with-love banks and the green waters of the canal
> Pouring Redemption for me, that I do
> The will of God, wallow in the habitual, the banal,
> Grow with nature again as before I grew.
> The bright stick trapped, the breeze adding a third
> Party to the couple kissing on an old seat,
> And a bird gathering materials for the nest for the Word
> Eloquently new and abandoned to its delirious beat.
> O unworn world enrapture me, encapture me in a web
> Of fabulous grass and eternal voices by a beech,
> Feed the gaping need of my senses, give me ad lib
> To pray unselfconsciously with overflowing speech
> For this soul needs to be honoured with a new dress woven
> From green and blue things and arguments that cannot be proven.

When he wished to catch the mind's movements in rhythms not far removed from those of common speech, Kavanagh was equally adept. The more I read in the posthumous *Collected Poems* the more convinced I become that his was a major voice, original and profound, and a voice which will still be heard when the louder voices of his more fashionable contemporaries have been long forgotten.

—Robert Nye

MacNEICE, (Frederick) Louis. British. Born in Belfast, Northern Ireland, 12 September 1907. Educated at Sherborne School; Marlborough College; Merton College, Oxford, 1926–30, B.A. (honours) in classics and philosophy 1930. Married Mary Ezra in 1930 (marriage dissolved, 1937): one son; the singer Hedli Anderson in 1942: one daughter. Lecturer in Classics, University of Birmingham, 1930–36; Lecturer in Greek, Bedford College, London, 1936–40; Visiting Lecturer in English, Cornell University, Ithaca, New York, 1940; Visiting Lecturer in Poetry and Drama, Sarah Lawrence College, Bronxville, New York, 1954–55. Feature Writer and Producer, BBC London, 1941–61. Director, British Council British Institute, Athens, 1950–51. Clark Lecturer, Cambridge University, 1963. Recipient: Harriet Monroe Memorial Prize (*Poetry*, Chicago), 1940; Premio d'Italia, for radio play, 1959. D.Litt.: Queen's University of Belfast, 1957. C.B.E. (Commander, Order of the British Empire), 1958. *Died 3 September 1963.*

PUBLICATIONS

Verse

>
> *Blind Fireworks: Poems.* London, Gollancz, 1929.
> *Poems.* London, Faber, 1935; New York, Random House, 1937.
> *Letters from Iceland,* with W. H. Auden. London, Faber, and New York, Random House, 1937.
> *The Earth Compels: Poems.* London, Faber, 1938.
> *Autumn Journal: A Poem.* London, Faber, and New York, Random House, 1939.
> *The Last Ditch.* Dublin, Cuala Press, 1940.
> *Selected Poems.* London, Faber, 1940.
> *Poems 1925–1940.* New York, Random House, 1940.
> *Plant and Phantom: Poems.* London, Faber, 1941.
> *Springboard: Poems 1941–1944.* London, Faber, 1944; New York, Random House, 1945.
> *Holes in the Sky: Poems 1944–1947.* London, Faber, 1948; New York, Random House, 1949.
> *Collected Poems 1925–1948.* London, Faber, 1949; New York, Oxford University Press, 1963.
> *Ten Burnt Offerings.* London, Faber, 1952; New York, Oxford University Press, 1953.

Autumn Sequel: A Rhetorical Poems in XXVI Cantos. London, Faber, 1954.
The Other Wing. London, Faber, 1954.
Visitations. London, Faber, 1957; New York, Oxford University Press, 1958.
Eighty-Five Poems, Selected by the Author. London, Faber, and New York, Oxford University Press, 1959.
Solstices. London, Faber, and New York, Oxford University Press, 1961.
The Burning Perch. London, Faber, and New York, Oxford University Press, 1963.
Selected Poems, edited by W. H. Auden. London, Faber, 1964.
The Collected Poems of Louis MacNeice, edited by E. R. Dodds. London, Faber, 1966; New York, Oxford University Press, 1967.

Recordings: *Louis MacNeice Reading His Own Poems*, Argo, 1961; *Louis MacNeice Reads from His Own Works*, Decca, 1966.

Plays

The Station Bell (produced Birmingham, 1935).
The Agamemnon, adaptation of the play by Aeschylus (produced London, 1936). London, Faber, 1936; New York, Harcourt Brace, 1937.
Out of the Picture (produced London, 1937). London, Faber, 1937; New York, Harcourt Brace, 1938.
Christopher Columbus: A Radio Play (broadcast, 1942). London, Faber, 1944.
Sunbeams in His Hat (broadcast, 1944). Included in *The Dark Tower and Other Radio Scripts*, 1947.
The Nosebag (broadcast, 1944). Included in *The Dark Tower and Other Radio Scripts*, 1947.
The March Hare Saga: The March Hare Resigns and *Salute to All Fools* (broadcast, 1945, 1946). Included in *The Dark Tower and Other Radio Scripts*, 1947.
The Dark Tower, music by Benjamin Britten (broadcast, 1946). Included in *The Dark Tower and Other Radio Scripts*, 1947.
Enter Caesar (broadcast, 1946). Included in *Persons from Porlock and Other Plays for Radio*, 1969.
The Dark Tower and Other Radio Scripts (includes *Sunbeams in His Hat, The March Hare Saga*). London, Faber, 1947.
Faust, Parts I and II (abridged version), adaptation of the play by Goethe (broadcast, 1949). London, Faber, 1951; New York, Oxford University Press, 1952.
Traitors in Our Way (produced Belfast, 1957).
East of the Sun and West of the Moon (broadcast, 1959). Included in *Persons from Porlock and Other Plays for Radio*, 1969.
They Met on Good Friday (broadcast, 1959). Included in *Persons from Porlock and Other Plays for Radio*, 1969.
The Administrator (broadcast, 1961). Included in *The Mad Islands and The Administrator*, 1964.
The Mad Islands (broadcast, 1962). Included in *The Mad Islands and The Administrator*, 1964.
The Mad Islands and The Administrator: Two Radio Plays. London, Faber, 1964.
Persons from Porlock (broadcast, 1963). Included in *Persons from Porlock and Other Plays for Radio*, 1969.

One for the Grave: A Modern Morality Play (produced Dublin, 1966). London, Faber, and New York, Oxford University Press, 1968.
Persons from Porlock and Other Plays for Radio (includes *Enter Caesar, East of the Sun and West of the Moon, They Met on Good Friday*). London, BBC Publications, 1969.

Screenplay: *The Conquest of Everest*, 1953.

Radio Plays and Features: *Word from America*, 1941; *Cook's Tour of the London Subways*, 1941; *The March of the 10,000*, 1941; *The Stones Cry Out* (series), 1941; *Freedom's Ferry*, 1941; *Dr. Chekhov*, 1941; *The Glory that Is Greece*, 1941; *Rogue's Gallery*, 1941; *Salute to the New Year*, 1941; *Vienna*, 1942; *Salutation to Greece*, 1942; *Calling All Fools*, 1942; *Salute to the U.S.S.R.*, 1942; *Alexander Nevsky*, 1942; *The Debate Continues*, 1942; *Black Gallery* (series), 1942; *The Undefeated of Yugoslavia*, 1942; *Britain to America*, 1942; *The United Nations: A Tribute*, 1942; *Halfway House*, 1942; *Salute to the U.S. Army*, 1942; *Christopher Columbus*, 1942; *Salute to Greece*, 1942; *Salute to the United Nations*, 1943; *Two Men and America*, 1943; *The Four Freedoms* (series), 1943; *Long Live Greece*, 1943; *Zero Hour*, 1943; *The Death of Byron*, 1943; *Sicily and Freedom*, 1943; *The Death of Marlowe*, 1943; *Independence Day*, 1943; *Four Years at War*, 1943; *Lauro de Bosis: The Story of My Death*, 1943; *The Spirit of Russia*, 1943; *The Fifth Freedom*, 1943; *Ring in the New*, 1943; *The Sacred Band*, 1944; *Sunbeams in His Hat*, 1944; *The Nosebag*, 1944; *This Breed of Men*, 1944; *D Day*, 1944; *He Had a Date*, 1944; *Why Be a Poet?*, 1944; *The Golden Ass*, 1944; *Cupid and Psyche*, 1944; *The Year in Review*, 1944; *A Roman Holiday*, 1945; *The March Hare Resigns*, 1945; *London Victorious*, 1945; *A Voice from Norway*, 1945; *The Dark Tower*, 1946; *Salute to All Fools'*, 1946; *Poetry Promenade* (series), 1946; *Enter Caesar*, 1946; *The Careerist*, 1946; *Agamemnon*, 1946; *Book of Verse* (series), 1946; *Aristophanes: Enemy of Cant*, 1946; *The Heartless Giant*, 1946; *The Death of Gunnar*, 1947; *The Burning of Njal*, 1947; *Portrait of Rome*, 1947; *"Autumn Journal": A Selection*, 1947; *India at First Sight*, 1948; *Portrait of Delhi*, 1948; *The Road to Independence*, 1948; *Pakistan*, 1948; *The Two Wicked Sisters*, 1948; *No Other Road*, 1948; *Trimalchio's Feast*, 1948; *The Queen of Air and Darkness*, 1949; *Louis MacNeice Reads His Poetry*, 1949; *Faust* (six parts), 1949; *Portrait of Athens*, 1951; *Burnt Offerings*, 1951; *In Search of Anoyia*, 1951; *Delphi: The Centre of the World*, 1952; *One Eye Wild*, 1952; *The Twelve Days of Christmas*, 1953; *Time Hath Brought Me Hither*, 1953; *Return to Atlantis*, 1953; *Where No Wounds Were*, 1954; *Prisoner's Progress*, 1954; *Autumn Sequel* (series), 1954; *Return to a School*, 1954; *The Waves*, 1955; *The Fullness of the Nile*, 1955; *The Star We Follow*, with Ritchie Calder, 1955; *Also among the Prophets*, 1956; *Bow Bells*, 1956; *Spires and Gantries*, 1956; *Carpe Diem*, 1956; *From Bard to Busker*, 1956; *Nuts in May*, 1957; *An Oxford Anthology*, 1957; *The Stones of Oxford*, 1957; *Border Ballads*, 1958; *All Fools' at Home*, 1958; *Health in Their Hands*, 1958; *New Poetry*, 1959; *Scrums and Dreams*, 1959; *Poems by Tennyson*, 1959; *They Met on Good Friday*, 1959; *Mosaic of Youth*, 1959; *East of the Sun and West of the Moon,* 1959; *The Odyssey* (series), with others, 1960; *The Administrator*, 1961; *Poems of Salvatore Quasimodo*, 1961; *Let's Go Yellow*, 1961; *The Mad Islands*, 1962; *Latin Poetry*, 1963; *New Poetry*, 1963; *Mediaeval Latin Poetry*, 1963; *Persons from Porlock*, 1963.

Novel

Roundabout Way (as Louis Malone). London and New York, Putnam, 1932. 1932.

Other

I Crossed the Minch (travel and verse).   London and New York, Longman, 1938.

Modern Poetry: A Personal Essay.   London and New York, Oxford University Press, 1938.

Zoo.   London, Joseph, 1938.

The Poetry of W. B. Yeats.   London and New York, Oxford University Press, 1941.

Meet the U.S. Army.   London, Board of Education–Ministry of Information, 1943.

The Penny That Rolled Away (juvenile).   New York, Putnam, 1954; as *The Sixpence That Rolled Away*, London, Faber, 1956.

Astrology, edited by Douglas Hill.   London, W. H. Allen-Aldus, and New York, Doubleday, 1964.

Varieties of Parable (The Clark Lectures).   Cambridge, University Press, 1965.

The Strings Are False: An Unfinished Autobiography, edited by E. R. Dodds.   London, Faber, 1965; New York, Oxford University Press, 1966.

Editor, with Stephen Spender, *Oxford Poetry 1929.*   Oxford, Blackwell, 1929.

Editor, with Bonamy Dobrée and Philip Larkin, *New Poems 1958: A P.E.N. Anthology.*   London, Joseph, 1958.

Bibliography: *A Bibliography of the Works of Louis MacNeice* by C. M. Armitage and Neil Clark, London, Kaye and Ward, 1973.

Manuscript Collections: University of Texas, Austin; Lockwood Memorial Library, State University of New York, Buffalo; Columbia University, New York; Berg Collection, New York Public Library.

Critical Studies: *Louis MacNeice* by John Press, London, Longman, 1965; *Louis MacNeice* by E. E. Smith, New York, Twayne, 1970; *Apollo's Blended Dream: A Study of the Poetry of Louis MacNeice* by William T. McKinnon, London, Oxford University Press, 1971; *The Poetry of Louis MacNeice* by D. B. Moore, Leicester, Leicester University Press, 1972.

*   *   *

Anthologists do not always choose happily from poets; but in the case of Louis MacNeice there has been a general consensus about one poem which does effectively give in miniature part of the essence of MacNeice – the lyric "Snow," written in January 1935. It is a poem that has been subjected to a good deal of solemn, footling, and irrelevant analysis: twelve lines of apparent simplicity have brought the exegetes out in force. It is a sensuous poem – sight, taste, touch and hearing overlap in it – and it is also a poem about apprehension, multiplicity and quiddity:

> World is crazier and more of it than we think,
> Incorrigibly plural. I peel and portion
> A tangerine and spit the pips and feel
> The drunkenness of things being various.

And behind or beyond this variousness is an unarticulated sense of menace, of the "otherness" of the world:

> There is more than glass between the snow and the huge roses.

"Snow" does all this, in a sense, lightly, teasingly, lyrically. And it is because MacNeice's tone was often apparently light that he tended, right from the beginning, with *Blind Fireworks* and *Poems*, to be classified – indeed, patronised – as a lightweight, a journalist in verse. Since his death in 1963, however, more and more he has come to seem the most interesting and impressive of the conventionally grouped "Thirties poets," next in stature to Auden and, like Auden, a poet who cannot be thought of as confined to one particular decade. His last two books, *Solstices* and *The Burning Perch*, contain poems as good as anything he wrote in the 1930's.

Important in MacNeice's personality was his feeling for his roots in Ireland, the strong memories of what he felt was in many ways an unhappy childhood, his training as a classical scholar, together with a delight in non-intellectual things (games, drink, food), and – most of all – the tug between the gregarious and genial man and the melancholy solitary. He seemed to write for his own voice – what I have described elsewhere as a "nasal, rather harsh voice, disdainful Oxford grafted onto strangled Ulster." This can be heard most characteristically in the recordings he made (several are available) of his poem "Bagpipe Music," another favourite in the anthologies.

Though he was an observant "social" poet, aware of what was going on in the larger world, his best poems draw on personal depths, and wholly lack that over-jaunty insouciance that mars some of his work with what he himself called "A twitter of inconsequent vitality." He went through a difficult period of about ten years (roughly, the mid-1940's until the mid-1950's), when he continued to be the prolific poet he always was but produced work which too often seemed to be both copious and strained. The work he had to do for the BBC, by which he was employed as a Features writer and producer for twenty years, may have had something to do with this, encouraging a tedious fluency and a hectic "public" manner that did not suit him. Examples of this are the mechanical triplets he churned out in *Autumn Sequel*, an "occasional" poem that almost entirely lacks the incisiveness of its predecessor, *Autumn Journal*: the latter is both a marvellously atmospheric verse-commentary and an acute piece of political, social and personal observation.

A key early poem is "Turf-stacks," which dates from 1932. In it, he looks nostalgically but without sentimentality at the simple – and also onerous – life of the Irish peasantry, and contrasts with it other men's need "of a fortress against ideas and against the/Shuddering insidious shock of the theory-vendors,/The little sardine men. . . ." The urge to escape, to keep one's privacy, is there, again, in "Memoranda for Horace," which dates from the last year of his life:

> . . . and yet today in London
> When all the loudspeakers bellow
> "Wolf repeat Wolf!" I can find asylum
> As you did, either in language
> Or laughter or with the tangles.

In the thirty years that lie between these two poems, there is a whole range of forms, subjects, incidents and enthusiasms in MacNeice; but the central personality is the same – wry, angular, watchful, a curious mixture of reticence and fluency, aware that nothing was simple or plain yet impatient with obfuscation and pretentiousness. MacNeice found his poetic voice, or voices, early; and he was always a thorough professional. Even when he is occasionally tedious or strained, his grip on form is impressive. His *Collected Poems,* finely edited by E. R. Dodds, is one of the most *enjoyable* books of modern times.

—Anthony Thwaite

O'HARA, Frank (Francis Russell O'Hara).   American.   Born in Baltimore, Maryland, 27 June 1926. Educated privately in piano and musical composition, 1933–43; at New England Conservatory of Music, Boston, 1946–50; Harvard University, Cambridge, Massachusetts, 1946–50, A.B. in English 1950; University of Michigan, Ann Arbor (Hopwood Award, 1951), M.A. 1951. Served in the United States Navy, 1944–46. Staff Member, 1951–54, and Fellowship Curator, 1955–64, Associate Curator, 1965, and Curator of the International Program, 1966, Museum of Modern Art, New York. Editorial Associate, *Art News* magazine, New York, 1954–56; Art Editor, *Kulchur Magazine,* New York, 1962–64. Collaborated in several poem-painting and poem-lithograph projects. Recipient: Ford Fellowship, for drama, 1956. *Died 25 July 1966.*

PUBLICATIONS

Verse

A City Winter and Other Poems.   New York, Tibor de Nagy Gallery, 1952.
Oranges.   New York, Tibor de Nagy Gallery, 1953.
Meditations in an Emergency.   Palma, Mallorca, M. Alcover, 1956; New York, Grove Press, and London, John Calder, 1957.
Hartigan and Rivers with O'Hara: An Exhibition of Pictures, with Poems. New York, Tibor de Nagy Gallery, 1959.
Second Avenue.   New York, Totem Press–Corinth Books, and London, Centaur Press, 1960.
Odes.   New York, Tiber Press, 1960.
Featuring Frank O'Hara.   Buffalo, New York, Audit/Poetry, 1964.
Lunch Poems.   San Francisco, City Lights Books, 1964.
Love Poems: Tentative Title.   New York, Tibor de Nagy Gallery, 1965.
In Memory of My Feelings: A Selection of Poems, edited by Bill Berkson.   New York, Museum of Modern Art, 1967.
Two Pieces.   London, Long Hair Books, 1969.
Odes.   New York, Poets Press, 1969.
The Collected Poems of Frank O'Hara, edited by Donald Allen.   New York, Knopf, 1971.
Selected Poems.   New York, Vintage, 1974.
Hymns of St. Bridget, with Bill Berkson.   New York, Boke Press, 1974.

Plays

Try! Try! (produced Cambridge, Massachusetts, 1951; revised version, New York, 1952).   Published in *Artists' Theatre,* edited by Herbert Machiz, New York, Grove Press, and London, Evergreen Books, 1960.

Change Your Bedding (produced Cambridge, Massachusetts, 1952).
Love's Labor: An Eclogue (produced New York, 1959). New York, Ameri-
can Theater for poets, 1964.
Awake in Spain (produced New York, 1960). New York, American Theater
for Poets, 1960.
The General Returns from One Place to Another (produced New York, 1964).

Screenplay: *The Last Clean Shirt.*

Other

Jackson Pollack. New York, Braziller, 1959.
A Frank O'Hara Miscellany. Bolinas, California, Grey Fox Press, 1974.
Art Chronicles 1954–1966. New York, Braziller, 1974.

Editor, *Robert Motherwell: A Catalogue with Selections from the Artist's
Writings.* New York, Museum of Modern Art, 1966.

Theatrical Activities:

Actor: **Play** – *Desire Caught by the Tail* by Pablo Picasso, New York, 1952.

*   *   *

F. S. C. Northrop speaks in *The Logic of the Sciences and the Humanities* of the
value of relentlessly generalizing a given verifiable scientific theory. This extends,
as he himself might point out, to the humanities, where the weakness of a
particular aesthetic may be seen by the relentless attempt to hypostasize it. In
much of so-called "New York School" work, the relentless derivatives of American surrealism, "abstract expressionism," pop, or what label you will, show
weaknesses of an art without the transcendental term, an art low, repetitive,
solopsistic. But in the great original, Frank O'Hara, one sees the intense first case,
with all its multifoliate strengths. While the few verse plays seem merely vapid
verse descendants of the early Auden-and-Isherwood collaborations, or the Auden
of "The Orators," the poetry of O'Hara speaks to us as a sensuous analogue of
Lorca.
   If the weakness of the "hardboiled empiricist," in Northrop's scheme, is that of
the impressionist, fresh but lacking in the theoretical or moral component, then the
charge of "frivolity," often hurled at O'Hara, can be understood. O'Hara's way
out of a mere "abstract impressionism" was to be converted early to a Paster-
nakian sense of "the revolutionary city." While the "pure facts" of his "I Do This
–I Do That" poems are now everyone's ineffable birthright, O'Hara's mature
strength lies in this continuous affirmation of liberty and possible liberations. His
personalism, randomnesses, spontaneities, hermeticisms, etc., must be interpreted
as Dr. Meyer Schapiro interpreted the paintings of Pollock: efforts in a hypocritical
age to maintain an integrity despite manufactured vocabularies.
   In some of the poems of Allen Ginsberg – a friend of O'Hara's – there is
adumbrated a romantic love of "experience and travel" and O'Hara's connection
to this was in his love for the purely inductive methods of empiricism. He was, in
this sense, as Kenneth Koch pointed out years ago, the most competent poet to

convey New York City in its pure factuality. If he has seemed a revolutionary poet without a revolution, he made of this lack a central and abiding metaphor.

Very early he mastered and modulated academic dictions into something tessellated, vivid, everyday. The early "To the Harbormaster," recited at his funeral by John Ashbery, remains one of the finest examples of his coherent laments. His later, discontinuous streams might seem the work of a mind unable to sustain a vehicle or tenor, but this early exemplum proves that he could.

His discontinuities were selected audaciously to break down false, glib, "silver" continuities (see in the by-now infamous Hall-Pack anthology of the 1950's) with a reliance on neo-Georgianism, neo-Yeatsism, "neo, neo, neo." O'Hara's disjunction was a betrayal of the norm, releasing the usual emotions of such a betrayal. Psychologism, naturalism, verismo, too, are betrayed, as they are in his flat, parodistic plays (one is reminded, too, of Koch's farces).

Where the political poems of the Latin American surrealists often seem purple and mismanaged, O'Hara was able to synthesize private and public dimensions through a *collagiste* method analogous to Robert Rauschenberg's. Influenced by Neruda, he is capable of the rhapsodical manner allied to a drab and touching quality of newspaperese.

While never as flat and plain as the prose parodies of John Ashbery, it is O'Hara's *collagiste* flatness, in juxtaposition to his glamours, camps, and *potestas* or bravura passages, which distinguish him from the Latin Americans of his generation – the witty prose of Borges being the exception here. While James Wright and Robert Bly were influenced by the Chinese poets of the Tang period, Rilke, Trakl, and the Latin American surrealists, O'Hara seemed best able to digest and enucleate all such influences but with no connotatively encrusted diction. And his parodies are explicit and sharp.

Behind his images of whimsy, his Firbankian modes, behind his nostalgias and manners, behind the "Chaucerian cheerfulness" that Vendler has evaluated, lies O'Hara's peculiarly revolutionary hedonism, shared by Koch, and which, in the love poems (see *Love Poems: Tentative Title*) result in poems of exquisite empathies in a time of crisis. The Keatsian obsession with pleasure is fundamental, but an elementary other is addressed, a Buberian need for a real "you" is resolved, and the poems seem as convincing as overheard telephone conversations. In his long "Ode to Michael Goldberg's Birth and Other Births," with its closing crescendo "and he shall be the wings of an extraordinary liberty,"one notes a sustained mode of examining one's self as an "other," as in the self-lacerating monologues of Ashbery. These sustained, self-lacerating, prose-ridden odes seem exemplary syntheses.

For many poets of his so-called "New York School" the problem lay in the aestheticization of the universe. This problem, comparable to the eroticization of the ego, with its concomitant dessications and addictions, was not a problem for O'Hara, who did not give in to a regressive narcissism. He found a proper relationship to things, and he speaks of this rapport in his great Mayakovskian "A True Account of Talking to the Sun at Fire Island." As with his friend LeRoi Jones, cultural psychopathology was adequately summoned, abused, and/or countermanded. His adequate vision of the city was not one of mere Whitmanesque joys; even in *Second Avenue*, the city is also an incubus, a spectre, like the cyst which grew larger than the host. In many poets influenced by O'Hara, the city and the facts of urbanity loom more solidly than the poets themselves. But this was not O'Hara's problem, though he is seen too often as thoughtless and exponentially dandified.

His poetry is filled with his resentments, and his rights to those resentments. While his coterie may have glamorized false collaborations (see the *Locus Solus* issue on Collaboration, edited by Koch) in direct ratio to its truer lack of relations, the best work of O'Hara is of a non-imperialistic ego, never engulfed or engulfing.

If his work seems capricious, it reminds us that, as Whitehead said, "exactness is a fake."

—David Shapiro

OKIGBO, Christopher (Ifenayichukwu). Nigerian. Born in Ojoto, Onitsha Province, in 1932. Educated at Umuahia Government College; University College, Ibadan, 1951–56, B.A. in classics, 1956. Served in the Biafran Defense Forces: killed in action, 1967. Married Sefi, daughter of the Attah of Igberra, in 1963: one daughter. Worked for the Nigerian Tobacco Company and the United Africa Company. Latin teacher, Fiditi Grammar School, 1959–60; Assistant Librarian, University of Nsukka, 1960–62; Cambridge University Press Nigerian Representative, 1962–66. *Died 1967.*

PUBLICATIONS

Verse

> *Heavensgate.* Ibadan, Mbari, 1962.
> *Limits.* Ibadan, Mbari, 1964.
> *Labyrinths, with Path of Thunder.* London, Heinemann, and New York, Africana, 1971.

Critical Study: *Christopher Okigbo: Creative Rhetoric* by Sunday O. Anonzie, London, Evans, 197fl.

*   *   *

The death of Christopher Okigbo, a rich and rarely attractive personality, in the 1967 war in Nigeria, was a tragic loss to African literature in English. He was one of the most promising of that group of poets of whom Wole Soyinka said, "they regroup images of Ezra Pound round the oil bean and the nude spear." Certainly the influence of Pound is evident in Okigbo's work, in the light, floating rhythms, in the abolition of transitions and connectives, in the cool, outlined imagery, and in the vast rag-bag of learning. Okigbo's poetry has an impressive intellectual content which seems to come from blending a Latin view of life with an African energy and feeling. His poetry brings the powerful oral tradition of Africa into the world of contemporary literary practice, and he manages with a considerable degree of

success to keep these two traditions and idioms in play without friction or
disharmony:

> The Stars have departed,
> the sky in monocle
> surveys the world under.
>
> The stars have departed,
> and I – where am I?
>
> Stretch, stretch, O antennae,
> to clutch at this hour,
>
> fulfilling each moment in a
> broken monody.

Okigbo was a peculiarly conscious poet, in the manner of Pound and Eliot, and
there are a remarkable number of oblique or half-suppressed references to the
work of other poets in his verse, just as there are many – too many, one often
thinks – private references in the manner of Auden. But there is unmistakably a
highly distinctive literary personality implicit in the poetry, together with a gift for
rhythmic variation and considerable metaphorical vivacity. He was brought up as a
Christian but still maintained a living relationship with his own village and its gods
and rituals, and in fact managed successfully to reconcile these two modes of
religious experience. Religious experience is a basic and constant theme of the
poetry. He accepts its presence and reality with a naturalness quite uncommon in
contemporary verse; and although he maintained in an interview in 1965 (*Journal of
Commonwealth Literature*, July 1970) that he saw the African writer as having no
particular function as teacher or preacher, except simply to be a writer, he takes a
decidedly sacred or priestly view of his own function as poet. In the opening
passage of *Heavensgate*, his first volume of poems, he wrote:

> Before you, mother Idoto,
>   naked I stand,
> before your watery presence,
>   a prodigal,
>
> leaning on an oilbean;
> lost in your legend . . .
>
> Under your power wait I on barefoot,
> Watchman for the watchword at
>   HEAVENSGATE:
>
> out of the depths my cry
> give ear and hearken.

In much of his poetry, and fairly explicitly in the late sequence, "Limits," he
attempts to identify, or at least to bring very closely together, religious experience
and poetic experience, as well as the processes of religious and poetic inspiration.
He saw each as the attempt to achieve a ritual integrity. It is clear that Okigbo had
not arrived at a clear or full articulation of his poetic theory, but all his practice
demonstrates that he had, in spite of a certain immaturity, a pure and impressive
talent. His talent gained in richness and point from his never suffering any feeling
of alienation from his own society or its past, from his supple virtuosity in
exploring the most varied sources of imagery, rhythm and illusion, and from his

never attempting to muffle the effect of poetry by importing into it other social or political ends.

—William Walsh

OLSON, Charles (John). American. Born in Worcester, Massachusetts, 27 December 1910. Educated at Wesleyan University, Middletown, Connecticut; Yale University, New Haven, Connecticut; Harvard University, Cambridge, Massachusetts, B.A. 1932, M.A. 1933. Taught at Clark University, Worcester, and Harvard University, 1936–39; Instructor and Rector, Black Mountain College, North Carolina, 1951–56. Recipient: Guggenheim grant (twice); Wenner-Gren Foundation grant, to study Mayan hieroglyphics, 1952; Oscar Blumenthal prize (*Poetry*, Chicago), 1965; National Endowment for the Arts grant, 1966, 1968. *Died 10 January 1970.*

PUBLICATIONS

Verse

> *Corrado Cagli March 31 Through April 19 1947.* New York, Knoedler, 1947.
> *Y & X.* Washington, D.C., Black Sun Press, 1948.
> *Letter for Melville 1951.* Black Mountain, North Carolina, privately printed, 1951.
> *This.* Black Mountain, North Carolina, Black Mountain College Graphics Workshop, 1952.
> *In Cold Hell, in Thicket.* Palma, Mallorca, Divers Press, 1953; San Francisco, Four Seasons Foundation, 1967.
> *The Maximus Poems 1–10.* Stuttgart, Jonathan Williams, 1953.
> *Ferrini and Others,* with others. Berlin, Gerhardt, 1955.
> *Anecdotes of the Late War.* Highlands, North Carolina, Jargon, 1955.
> *The Maximus Poems 11–22.* Stuttgart, Jonathan Williams, 1956.
> *O'Ryan 2 4 6 8 10.* San Francisco, White Rabbit Press, 1958; expanded edition as *O'Ryan 12345678910,* 1965.
> *Projective Verse.* New York, Totem Press, 1959.
> *The Maximus Poems.* New York, Jargon–Corinth Books, and London, Centaur Press, 1960.
> *The Distances: Poems.* New York, Grove Press, and London, Evergreen Books, 1960.
> *Maximus, From Dogtown I.* San Francisco, Auerhahn Press, 1961.
> *Signature to Petition on Ten Pound Island Asked of Me by Mr. Vincent Ferrini.* San Francisco, Oyez, 1964.
> *West.* London, Cape Goliard Press, 1966.
> *Charles Olson Reading at Berkeley,* edited by Zoe Brown. San Francisco, Coyote Books, 1966.
> *Before Your Very Eyes!,* with others. London, Cape Goliard Press, 1967.
> *The Maximus Poems, IV, V, VI.* London, Cape Goliard Press, and New York, Grossman, 1968.

Added to Making a Republic. Buffalo, New York, Institute of Further Studies, 1968.
Clear Shifting Water. Buffalo, New York, Institute of Further Studies, 1968.
That There Was a Woman in Gloucester, Massachusetts. Buffalo, New York, Institute of Further Studies, 1968.
Wholly Absorbed into My Own Conduits. Buffalo, New York, Institute of Further Studies, 1968.
Casual Mythology. San Francisco, Four Seasons Foundation, 1969.
Archaeologist of Morning: The Collected Poems Outside the Maximus Series. London, Cape Goliard Press, and New York, Grossman, 1970.
Maximus, to Himself. San Francisco, Spanish Main Press, 1970.
The Maximus Poems, Volume Three, edited by Charles Boer and George F. Butterick. New York, Grossman, 1975.

Short Story

Stocking Cap: A Story. San Francisco, Four Seasons Foundation, 1966.

Other

Call Me Ishmael: A Study of Melville. New York, Reynal and Hitchcock, 1947; London, Cape, 1967.
Apollonius of Tyana: A Dance, with Some Words, for Two Actors. Black Mountain, North Carolina, Black Mountain College, 1951.
Mayan Letters, edited by Robert Creeley. Palma, Mallorca, Divers Press, 1953; London, Cape, and New York, Grossman, 1968.
A Bibliography on America for Ed Dorn. San Francisco, Four Seasons Foundation, 1964.
Pleistocene Man: Letters from Charles Olson to John Clarke during October, 1965. Buffalo, New York, Institute of Further Studies, 1968.
Human Universe and Others Essays, edited by Donald Allen. San Francisco, Auerhahn Society, 1965.
Proprioception. San Francisco, Four Seasons Foundation, 1965.
Selected Writings, edited by Robert Creeley. New York, New Directions, 1966.
Letters for "Origin," 1950–1956, edited by Albert Glover. London, Cape Goliard Press, 1969.
The Special View of History, edited by Ann Charters. Berkeley, California, Oyez, 1970.
Poetry and Truth: The Beloit Lectures and Poems, edited by George F. Butterick. San Francisco, Four Seasons Foundation, 1971.
Additional Prose: A Bibliography on America, Proprioception, and Other Notes and Essays, edited by George F. Butterick. Bolinas, California, Four Seasons Foundation, 1974.
The Post Office: A Memoir to His Father. Bolinas, California, Grey Fox Press, 1974.

Bibliography: *A Bibliography of Works by Charles Olson* by George F. Butterick and Albert Glover, New York, Phoenix Bookshop, 1967.

*   *   *

Because Charles Olson has been considered the mentor of an entire school of poets – that growing out of the extremely interesting Black Mountain College group in the early Fifties – his readers have been as interested in knowing his doctrines as his poems. A typical (and reductive) summary of Olson's essay on Projective Verse is a claim by former Oxford Professor of Poetry Roy Fuller that Olson's Essay "conveniently contains its recipes and claims," chiefly "a number of exhortations to write good verse. . . . A poem is to concentrate on the syllable rather than, e.g., on metre and rhyme. The line must be kept from slowness, deadness, by being suspicious of description, of adjectives, of similes. The individual breath gives language its force, the force of speech, and in so far as the logical conventions of syntax hamper this force they must, in projective verse, go. The typewriter, because of its precision with spacing, is the personal and instantaneous recorder of the poet's work: with it he can indicate exactly the breath, the pauses, the suspension – even of syllables – and the juxtaposition – even of parts of phrases – he intends." Fuller then comments on Olson's sentimentality, perhaps failing to realize that sentimentality and dead seriousness often look alike. In his major work, *The Maximus Poems*, Olson not only demonstrated his theories, "found his measure," but also constructed a suitable vehicle for quite varied poems, both of his personal experience and of his reactions to the city of Gloucester, Massachusetts "where fishing continues/and my heart lies." Whether his poem's parallels and indebtedness to Pound's *Cantos* and Williams's *Paterson* really matters, I can't say; to me the poem justifies itself in individual songs:

> that which will last,
> that! o my people, where shall you find it, how, where, where shall you listen
> when all is become billboards, when, all, even silence, is spray-gunned?
> when even our bird, my roofs,
> cannot be heard
> when even you, when sound itself is neoned in?

Olson's domestic poems of everyday life are intense, whether he is cussing out the Melville society (his *Call Me Ishmael* is an important book, especially in tracing Melville's sources in Shakespeare), or commenting on his household:

> Or the plumbing,
> that it doesn't work, this I like, have even used paper clips
> as well as string to hold the ball up And flush it
> with my hand
> But that the car doesn't, that no moving thing moves
> without that song I'd void my ear of, the musickracket
> of all ownership. . . .

But Olson harks "back to an older polis,/who has this tie to a time when the port" was involved in a fabulous history. To me, these lines about John Smith and Miles Standish, about what fourteen men required as food and supplies in the winter of 1624/25, these asides on "the nature of the cargo" are not so interesting as the present, when Olson observes:

> love was
> Or ought to be,
> like an orange tree!
> (The way they do grow
> in that ex-sea soil,
> in that pumice dust only a fowl
> can scratch a living from).

His pictures achieve the vividness of a Hiroshige, or of netsuke:

> They should raise a monument
> to a fisherman crouched down
> behind a hogshead, protecting
> his dried fish.

Many of Olson's disciples prefer to concentrate on the philosophy in his work, and on his fairly systematic and interesting ideas, delivered in reaction to the classics, to Sumerians and Mayans, expounded in letters that have become a literature in themselves; they would be unhappy to find him characterized as a master of sketches, glimpses. But to me his best poems are humorous and domestic, rather than scholarly; his best work can be read without footnotes. Many who worship Olson, whose integrity as teacher and artist has inspired them, have perhaps overlooked his lines: "There is a limit/to what a car/will do." In concentrating on his seriousness they overlook the maker of netsuke; they neglect to admire the lightness, the humor, of the artist they've overlooked by turning him into a sage. This is, after all, the man who ate his own polishing cloth:

> Trouble
> with the car. And for a buck
> they gave me
> what I found myself
> eating! A polishing
> cloth. And I went right on
> eating it, it was that good.
> And thick, color
> orange & black, with a map – the billowing dress
> the big girl wears
> every so often.

In the time since his death, Olson has been more than ever venerated as a poet who inspired and taught such students as Robert Creeley and Hilda Morley, who continue to acknowledge his importance for their work. Many poets, including this one, felt a genuine grief for the loss of Charles Olson, and some of us much resented the vulgarity of the picture published in *The Antioch Review* of Charles Olson in his casket. A better memorial is in the work of his students and followers, in whom his words are "modified in the guts of the living."

—David Ray

PATCHEN, Kenneth. American. Born in Niles, Ohio, 13 December 1911. Educated at Warren High School, Ohio; the Experimental College, University of Wisconsin, Madison, 1928–29. Married Miriam Oikemus in 1934. Also an artist: one-man show of books, graphics, and paintings, Corcoran Gallery, Washington, D.C., 1969. Recipient: Guggenheim Fellowship, 1936; Shelley Memorial Award, 1954; National Endowment for the Arts Distinguished Service Grant, 1967. *Died 8 January 1972*

PUBLICATIONS

Verse

Before the Brave.   New York, Random House, 1936.

First Will and Testament.   New York, New Directions, 1939.

The Teeth of the Lion.   New York, New Directions, 1942.

The Dark Kingdom.   New York, Harriss and Givens, 1942.

Cloth of the Tempest.   New York and London, Harper, 1943.

An Astonished Eye Looks Out of the Air: Being Some Poems Old and New Against War and in Behalf of Life.   Waldport, Oregon, Untide Press, 1945.

Outlaw of the Lowest Planet, edited by David Gascoyne.   London, Grey Walls Press, 1946.

Selected Poems.   New York, New Directions, 1946; revised edition, 1958, 1964.

Pictures of Life and of Death.   New York, Padell, 1947.

They Keep Riding Down All the Time.   New York, Padell, 1947.

Panels for the Walls of Heaven.   Berkeley, California, Bern Porter, 1947.

Patchen: Man of Anger and Light, with A Letter to God by Kenneth Patchen, with Henry Miller.   New York, Padell, 1947.

Be Music, Night: Poem for Voice and Piano, music by David Leo Diamond.   New York, Carl Fischer, 1948.

CCCLXXIV Poems.   New York, Padell, 1948.

To Say If You Love Someone and Other Selected Love Poems.   Prairie City, Illinois, Decker Press, 1948.

Red Wine and Yellow Hair.   New York, New Directions, 1949.

Fables and Other Little Tales.   Karlsruhe, Germany, Jonathan Williams, 1953.

The Famous Boating Party and Other Poems in Prose.   New York, New Directions, 1954.

Orchards, Thrones and Caravans.   San Francisco, Print Workshop, 1955.

Glory Never Guesses: Being a Collection of 18 Poems with Decorations and Drawings.   San Francisco, privately printed, 1956.

A Surprise for the Bagpipe Player: A Collection of 18 Poems with Decorations and Drawings.   San Francisco, privately printed, 1956.

When We Were Here Together.   New York, New Directions, 1957.

Hurrah for Anything: Poems and Drawings.   Highlands, North Carolina, Jargon, 1957.

Two Poems for Christmas.   Palo Alto, California, privately printed, 1958.

Poem-scapes.   Highlands, North Carolina, Jargon, 1958.

Pomes Penyeach.   Seattle, privately printed, 1959.

Poems of Humor and Protest.   San Francisco, City Lights Books, 1960.

Because It Is: Poems and Drawings.   New York, New Directions, 1960.

A Poem for Christmas.   Palo Alto, California, privately printed, 1960.

The Love Poems of Kenneth Patchen.   San Francisco, City Lights Books, 1960; London, Scorpion Press, 1961.

Patchen Drawing-Poem.   Palo Alto, California, Patchen Cards, 1962.

Picture Poems.   Palo Alto, California, Patchen Cards, 1962.

Doubleheader.   New York, New Directions, 1966.

Hallelujah Anyway.   New York, New Directions, 1966.

Where Are the Other Rowboats?   Privately printed, 1966.

But Even So (includes drawings).   New York, New Directions, 1968.

Love and War Poems, edited by Dennis Gould.   Mickleover, Derby, Whisper and Shout, 1968.

Selected Poems.   London, Cape, 1968.

The Collected Poems of Kenneth Patchen. New York, New Directions, 1968.
Aflame and Afun of Walking Faces: Fables and Drawings. New York, New Directions, 1970.
There's Love All Day: Poems, edited by Dee Danner Barwick. Kansas City, Missouri, Hallmark Editions, 1970.
Wonderings. New York, New Directions, 1971.
In Quest of Candlelighters. New York, New Directions, 1972.

Recordings: *Kenneth Patchen Reads His Poetry with the Chamber Jazz Sextet,* Cadence, 1958; *Kenneth Patchen Reads Poetry with Jazz in Canada,* Folkways, 1959; *Kenneth Patchen Reads His Selected Poems,* Folkways, 1959; *Kenneth Patchen Reads His Love Poems,* Folkways, 1961.

Plays

Now You See It (Don't Look Now) (produced New York, 1966).

Radio Play: *City Wears a Slouch Hat,* 1942.

Novels

The Journal of Albion Moonlight. Privately printed, 1941.
The Memoirs of a Shy Pornographer: An Amusement. New York, New Directions, 1945; London, Grey Walls Press, 1948.
Sleepers Awake. New York, Padell, 1946.
See You in the Morning. New York, Padell, 1948; London, Grey Walls Press, 1949.

Other

Kenneth Patchen: Painter of Poems (exhibition catalogue). Baltimore, Garamond-Pridemark Press, 1969.
The Argument of Innocence: A Selection from the Pictureworks of Kenneth Patchen, edited by Peter Veres. San Francisco, Scrimshaw Press, 1975.

Bibliography: *Kenneth Patchen: A First Bibliography* by Gail Eaton, Denver, Swallow, 1948.

*   *   *

Kenneth Patchen was one of America's great poet-prophets. This range of his work holds the wildness of America's energy and all the horror implicit in her need for self-destruction. It continues the proud fury of Whitman's large vision of the U.S.A.

Patchen's work is a Bible torn out of America's heart. It is the prophet's urgent warning. It is a righteous refusal to accept the end of man.

Everything Patchen created reveals his effort to make sense of a people bent on destroying the human spirit and the planet man lives upon. Patchen warned man, hating, loving and smooth-talking man, for over a quarter of a century. Like all great poet-prophets, Patchen continued to forgive man. To bind the wounds and heal the maimed and mad victims of America's paradox.

It's all there in his work. In the many volumes of poetry. In his illuminated tracts and ikons: his talismanic wall-hangings warning Fear and Stupidity that Love is in town and well-armed. It's there in his blood-roaring apocalyptic novels, *The Journal of Albion Moonlight* and *Sleepers Awake*. The waterfall of those novels is balanced rightly with his two love novels: the naked *See You in the Morning* and *Memoirs of a Shy Pornographer*. It's there in the care and charm of his handbound, handpainted books. It's there in his voice reading his poems backed-up by the Chamber Jazz Sextet.

It's there in his work. The history of the American poet-myth.

During the Depression, Patchen wrote Blakean hymns to the Revolution of the Proletariat – which really didn't happen. (All revolts seem to change masks and the revolutionaries often wind-up looking suspiciously like the Enemy.) Patchen was hailed as one of the foremost young Proletarian Poets:

> O not the drill and brazen energy of singing.
> We shall reach a stand and cause for fighting.
> O we should be the hunter in the hall of eternity.
>
> —"The World Will Have Little Note,"
> in *Before the Brave*

But the workers didn't have time to read or use Patchen's poems.

During World War II he wrote passionate and furious words to fight back insane shadow-beasts bent on devouring earth. His songs insisted on man's great potential. They sang of love's imperative necessity. We must care, or we perish:

> And begin again.
> It would take little to be free.
> That no man live at the expense of another.
> Because no man can own what belongs to all.
> Because no man can kill what all must use.
> Because no man can lie when all are betrayed.
> Because no man can hate when all are hated.
>
> —"What Is the Beautiful," in *Cloth of the Tempest*

But soldiers need bullets and bombs, not poems. When man makes war his singing turns to screaming. The screams are louder than death. The screams are louder than the bombs, the bullets, or the poems.

It is a paradox. The center of man's need to create is his journey to Light. Yet, at the same time, and on the same road, man will refuse to listen to the message of Angels. In his desire to conquer earth and himself, man often re-routes God's messengers. This paradox is crucial to understanding the poet-myth in America:

> I never had any other desire so strong, and so like to covetousness, as that one which I have had always, that I might be master 'at last of a small house and a contenting woman, with moderate conveniences joined to them, and, living there and with her to love, dedicate the remainder of my life only to the culture of myself. . . .
>
> —"I Never Had Any Other Desire So Strong," in *First Will and Testament*

Patchen was the wounded Cupid of the American dream.

He lay on his back in dark pain. His spinal agony limited his mobility. He was cared for by his wife Miriam. She protected him and acted as his liaison to the outer world. She provided space and ease for him to work.

For over twenty years, Patchen was infirm. Doctors, operations, hospital expenses, pharmacological idiocy, combined with the basic needs of survival, drained him and wounded him, but did not crush him. This kind of torture-wheel, a strange space-station, rarely stops spinning around most poets. Often it blinds them. Thank God it rarely silences them.

Patchen's work has always sung to the youth. His work reveals and affirms their hopes and strength. His work has always spoken to men of spirit and passion. From the mid-30's to today, Patchen's intense and humane visions have inspired new generations of poets and writers. Like Blake and Whitman, his spiritual forefathers, Patchen's work lays the vital groundwork of man's future. His work continues the necessary stream of visionary art for our time and for Eternity.

—David Meltzer

PLATH, Sylvia. American. Born in Boston, Massachusetts, 27 October 1932. Educated at Smith College, Northampton, Massachusetts, B.A. (summa cum laude) in English 1955; Newnham College, Cambridge (Fulbright Scholar), 1955–57, M.A. 1957. Married Ted Hughes, *q.v.*, in 1956: one daughter and one son. Guest Editor, *Mademoiselle* magazine, New York, Summer 1953. Instructor in English, Smith College, 1957–58. Moved to England in 1959. Recipient: Bess Hokin Award (*Poetry*, Chicago), 1957; Yaddo Fellowship, 1959; Cheltenham Festival award, 1961; Saxon Fellowship, 1961. *Died 11 February 1963.*

PUBLICATIONS

Verse

A Winter Ship (published anonymously). Edinburgh, Tragara Press, 1960.
The Colossus and Other Poems. London, Heinemann, 1960; New York, Knopf, 1962; as The Colossus, Heinemann, 1967.
Ariel. London, Faber, 1965; New York, Harper, 1966.
Uncollected Poems. London, Turret Books, 1965.
Wreath for a Bridal. Frensham, Surrey, Sceptre Press, 1970.
Million Dollar Month. Frensham, Surrey, Sceptre Press, 1971.
Fiesta Melons: Poems. Exeter, Devon, Rougemont Press, 1971.
Crossing the Water, edited by Ted Hughes. London, Faber, 1971; as Crossing the Water: Transitional Poems, New York, Harper, 1971.
Crystal Gazer and Other Poems. London, Rainbow Press, 1971.
Lyonesse: Poems. London, Rainbow Press, 1971.
Winter Trees. London, Faber, 1971; New York, Harper, 1972.

Play

> *Three Women: A Monologue for Three Voices* (broadcast, 1962; produced New
> York and London, 1973).

> Radio Play: *Three Women*, 1962 (UK).

Novel

> *The Bell Jar* (as Victoria Lucas). London, Heinemann, 1963; as Sylvia Plath,
> London, Faber, 1966; with drawings, New York, Harper, 1971.

Short Stories

> *Penguin Modern Stories 2*, with others. London, Penguin, 1969.

Other

> *The Penguin Sylvia Plath.* London, Penguin, 1975.
> *Letters Home*, edited by Aurelia Plath. New York, Harper, 1975.

> Editor, *American Poetry Now: A Selection of the Best Poems by Modern
> American Writers.* London, Oxford University Press, 1961.

Bibliographies: by Mary Kinzie, Daniel Lynn Conrad, and Suzanne D. Kurman in
The Art of Sylvia Plath: A Symposium edited by Charles Newman, Bloomington,
Indiana University Press, and London, Faber, 1970; *A Chronological Checklist of
the Periodical Publications of Sylvia Plath* by Eric Homberger, Exeter, Devon,
University of Exeter American Arts Documentation Centre, 1970.

Critical Studies: *The Art of Sylvia: A Symposium* edited by Charles Newman,
Bloomington, Indiana University Press, and London, Faber, 1970; *A Closer Look
at "Ariel": A Memory of Sylvia Plath* by Nancy Hunter Steiner, New York,
Harpers Magazine Press, 1973, London, Faber, 1974; *Sylvia Plath* by Eileen M.
Aird, New York, Harper, 1973, Edinburgh, Oliver and Boyd, 1974; *Sylvia Plath:
Method and Madness* by Edward Butscher, New York, Seabury Press, 1975.

*　　　*　　　*

After her suicide in 1963, Sylvia Plath gained that kind of public notoriety that
seems inevitably reserved for just those artists who die voluntarily. She was 30
years old, the mother of two children. By 1965, *Ariel* was published, a book
consisting of poems, the dust jacket says, "Written in the last months of her life,
and often rushed out at the rate of two or three a day." There followed re-
publication of her first volume of poems, *The Colossus*, and of *The Bell Jar*, a
novel first published in England under the pseudonym Victoria Lucas. Within three

years of her death Sylvia Plath became the world's most widely-read contemporary suicide. Critics pointed to the suicideal hints within her beautifully crafted poems and implied that their authenticity derived somehow from the *fait accompli*.

In *The Bell Jar*, which recounts the author's experience as a prize-winning college writer who attempts suicide, Plath anticipated the grim humor of her own posthumous popularity. "Then I remembered that at medical school Buddy had won a prize for persuading the most relatives of dead people to have their dead ones cut up whether they needed it or not, in the interests of science." Following *Ariel*, a number of other poetry collections were issued, but her best work, and that indisputably finished by her own hand, is available in the three books mentioned here by title.

While it is inescapable that the grim humor of Plath's work reflects the personality of a suicide (as the writings of Professors reflect the personalities or professors) the actual life, the liveliness, the play within her writing is too often missed by readers whose attention is diverted by her death. At 30, Plath had developed her craft to a point far beyond what many poets ever reach. That she did so within the confines of motherhood and a shaky marriage suggests that like a citrus seed, poets progress fastest when squeezed. And her cry of desperate ordinariness reminds us that the universe of death may be far more intriguing to the genius than flower gardens and changing diapers. That the Woman's Movement had emerged some 15 years ago!

Sylvia Plath's poems are so personal that they often assume separate personae. "Daddy," a hateful love poem for a father whose early death she resents, blends the voice of a young girl with that of a hardened adult. Like much of her work, the poem has rhyme, established here with the repetition (more than 60 times in 80 lines!) of a single sound:

> You stand at the blackboard, daddy,
> In the picture I have of you,
> A cleft in your chin instead of your foot
> But no less a devil for that, no not
> Any less the black man who
>
> Bit my pretty red heart in two.
> I was ten when they buried you.
> At twenty I tried to die
> And get back, back, back to you.
> I thought even the bones would do.

The limerick quality within these verses, in contrast to the subject, reinforces the struggle between the poem's personae. The culmination of the struggle and the play is realized with the final lines, where the poem focuses on its own deepest bitterness:

> There's a stake in your fat black heart
> And the villagers never liked you.
> They are dancing and stamping on you.
> They always *knew* it was you.
> Daddy, daddy, you bastard, I'm through.

In "Cut," which describes slicing with the shears "My thumb instead of an onion," Plath takes the other road and celebrates pain so lightly that the slightness of her reaction becomes a part of the poem's substance. Again, the persona vibrates between at least two identities, that of gardener and that of cut thumb, which (pun intended) *becomes* the poet:

The balled
Pulp of your heart
Confronts its small
Mill of silence

How you jump –
Trepanned veteran,
Dirty girl,
Thumb stump.

—final lines of "Cut"

Plath's genius existed not so much in the uniqueness of her vision as in what she could do with that vision linguistically, how compact and almost orderly she could make it all, in opposition, always, to the pathos thus described. Here, finally, from *The Colossus*, is "Aftermath" in its entirety:

Compelled by calamity's magnet
They loiter and stare as if the house
Burnt-out were theirs, or as if they thought
Some scandal might any minute ooze
From a smoke-choked closet into light;
No deaths, no prodigious injuries
Glut these hunters after an old meat,
Blood-spoor of the austere tragedies.

Mother Medea in a green smock
Moves humbly as any housewife through
Her ruined apartments, taking stock
Of charred shoes, the sodden upholstery:
Cheated of the pyre and the rack,
The crowd sucks her last tear and turns away.

—Geof Hewitt

ROETHKE, Theodore (Huebner).   American.   Born in Saginaw, Michigan, 25 May 1908. Educated at John Moore School, 1913–21, and Arthur Hill High School, 1921–25, Saginaw; University of Michigan, Ann Arbor, 1925–29, B.A. 1929 (Phi Beta Kappa), M.A. 1936; Harvard University, Cambridge, Massachusetts, 1930–31. Married Beatrice O'Connell in 1953. Instructor in English, 1931–35, Director of Public Relations, 1934, and Varsity Tennis Coach, 1934–35, Lafayette College, Easton, Pennsylvania; Instructor in English, Michigan State University, East Lansing, Fall 1935; Instructor, 1936–40, Assistant Professor, 1940–43, and Associate Professor of English Composition, 1947, Pennsylvania State University, University Park; Instructor, Bennington College, Vermont, 1943–46; Associate Professor, 1947–48, Professor of English, 1948–62, and Honorary Poet-in-Residence, 1962–63, University of Washington, Seattle. Phi Beta Kappa Poet, College of William and Mary, Williamsburg, Virginia, 1956. Recipient: Yaddo fellowship, 1945; Guggenheim grant, 1945, 1950; Eunice Tietjens Memorial Prize, 1947, and Levinson Prize, 1951 (*Poetry*, Chicago); National Institute of Arts and Letters grant, 1952;

Fund for the Advancement of Education Fellowship, 1952; Ford grant, 1952, 1959; Pulitzer Prize, 1954; Fulbright Fellowship, 1955; Borestone Mountain Award, 1958; National Book Award, 1959, 1965; Bollingen Prize, 1959; Poetry Society of America Prize, 1962; Shelley Memorial Award, 1962. D.H.L.: University of Michigan, 1962. *Died 1 August 1963.*

PUBLICATIONS

Verse

> *Open House.* New York, Knopf, 1941.
> *The Lost Son and Other Poems.* New York, Doubleday, 1948; London, Lehmann, 1949.
> *Praise to the End!* New York, Doubleday, 1951.
> *The Waking: Poems 1933–1953.* New York, Doubleday, 1953.
> *Words for the Wind.* London, Secker and Warburg, 1957; New York, Doubleday, 1958.
> *The Exorcism.* San Francisco, Poems in Folio, 1957.
> *Sequence, Sometimes Metaphysical, Poems.* Iowa City, Stone Wall Press, 1963.
> *The Far Field.* New York, Doubleday, 1964; London, Faber, 1965.
> *Two Poems.* Privately printed, 1965.
> *The Achievement of Theodore Roethke: A Comprehensive Selection of His Poems, with a Critical Introduction,* edited by William J. Martz. Chicago, Scott Foresman, 1966.
> *Collected Poems.* New York, Doubleday, 1966; as *The Collected Poems of Theodore Roethke,* London, Faber, 1968.
> *Selected Poems,* edited by Beatrice Roethke. London, Faber, 1969.

> Recordings: *Words for the Wind,* Folkways; *The Light and Serious Side of Theodore Roethke,* Folkways; *Theodore Roethke Reading His Poetry,* Caedmon, 1972.

Other

> *I Am! Says the Lamb* (juvenile). New York, Doubleday, 1961.
> *Party at the Zoo* (juvenile). New York, Crowell-Collier, and London, Macmillan, 1963.
> *On the Poet and His Craft: Selected Prose of Theodore Roethke,* edited by Ralph J. Mills, Jr. Seattle and London, University of Washington Press, 1965.
> *Selected Letters,* edited by Ralph J. Mills, Jr. Seattle, University of Washington Press, 1968; London, Faber, 1970.
> *Straw for the Fire: From the Notebooks of Theodore Roethke, 1943–1963,* edited by David Wagoner. New York, Doubleday, 1972.
> *Dirty Dinky and Other Creatures: Poems for Children,* edited by Beatrice Roethke and Stephen Lushington. New York, Doubleday, 1973.

Bibliography: *Theodore Roethke: A Bibliography* by James R. McLeod, Kent, Ohio, Kent State University Press, 1973.

Critical Studies: *Theodore Roethke* by Ralph J. Mills, Jr., Minneapolis, University of Minnesota Press, and London, Oxford University Press, 1963; *Theodore Roethke: Essays on His Poetry* by Arnold S. Stein, Seattle, University of Washington Press, 1965; *Theodore Roethke: An Introduction to the Poetry* by Karl Malkoff, New York and London, Columbia University Press, 1966; *The Glass House: The Life of Theodore Roethke* by Allan Seager, New York, McGraw Hill, 1968; *Profile of Theodore Roethke* by William Heyen, Columbus, Ohio, Charles E. Merrill, 1971; *The Wild Prayer of Longing: Poetry and the Sacred* by Nathan A. Scott, New Haven, Connecticut, and London, Yale University Press, 1971; *A Concordance to the Poems of Theodore Roethke* by Gary Lane, Metuchen, New Jersey, Scarecrow Press, 1972; *Theodore Roethke's Dynamic Vision* by Richard Allen Blessing, Bloomington, Indiana University Press, 1974; *The Garden Master* by Rosemary Sullivan, Seattle, University of Washington Press, 1974.

*   *   *

Theodore Roethke was one of the most original of the post-war American poets. He was a nature poet, with all the particular concatenation of themes and images that word implies. His poetic ancestors, as he was fond of calling them, were the visionary poets: Blake, Wordsworth, Clare, Smart, and their American counterparts, Whitman, Emerson – poets who find in the metamorphic world of nature a direct language of being. But Roethke's vision of nature was eccentric. His great poetry begins in the private world of the greenhouses of his childhood. His father had been a florist in Michigan, owning what were at one time the largest greenhouses in the state. This was the kind of world that could shape a poet's imagination, since the greenhouse came to be a microcosmic image; in fact a universe, complete, exhaustive, with its own eschatology of heaven and hell, a moist artificial womb of growth. When Roethke reclaimed this world, his attention was riveted on growth, on the wilful tenacious struggle of plants into being in a drive against death: "I can hear, underground, that sucking and sobbing, / In my veins, in my bones I feel it"; in effect, in this artificial cell of forced growth, he sought to explore the essentially creative impulse compelling life. Later his natural realm would extend to swamps and boglands, those perfect mirrors of the turbulent psyche; to snails, slugs, snakes and frogs, the "small shapes, willow-shy" which in his work represent the extremity of instinctual life alien to the human condition. What overwhelms in this instinctive world is Roethke's capacity for empathic response, his ability to place himself within the life he contemplated in order to coincide with it, to achieve an experience of identity. There is something childlike, or better, primitive and animistic in his celebration of the intuitive capacity of the imagination which endears him to all readers. Yet as Stanley Kunitz remarked, Roethke could not be content with simply naming the things he loved, he was driven to converting them to symbols, that painful ritual.

He came into his own as a poet with the greenhouse sequence written between 1942 and 1946 when he discovered how to use the slimy world of botanic growth as an imagistic focus to embody private suffering and disorder. *The Lost Son* sequence, one of his greatest achievements as a poet, followed. These are dark poems of suffering and mental disorder composed in a surrealistic language which attempts to reproduce the psychic shorthand of the unconscious. They describe an interior journey into complete and terrifying self-absorption. Throughout his life Roethke suffered from periodic experiences of mental breakdown which he symbolized as the condition of the lost son. His private relationship to his father, who died when he was fifteen, became the model for his sense of an existential state of loss, one of those transformations that are the key to great art. What may have been a struggle for personal identity became a human struggle for spiritual identity: "a struggle out of the slime . . . a slow spiritual progress."

Roethke's regressive exploration of psychic extremity was very sophisticated, often indebted to Jung through Maud Bodkin, so that the concepts of collective unconscious, rebirth, integration, are essential to his poems. Through his harrowing experiences he became convinced of an *a priori* principle of being beyond intellect – a still center or soul, not an objective reality but a goal in an on-going process of spiritual ascent. In his later poems, which are almost neo-Elizabethan in their formal elegance, he is deeply interested in mysticism, that area of psychic experience so puzzling and yet so vital to modern sensibility. Yet there is no mystical piety in his work. The idea of soul is an emotional hypothesis built out of the sheerest force of will, an act of faith which had to be constantly renewed. In the end, he is a poet of life, of celebration: "Now I adore my life / With the Bird, the abiding Leaf, . . . For love, for Love's sake." One is drawn to the words of James Dickey for a final assessment of Roethke's work: "There is no poetry anywhere that is so valuably conscious of the human body . . . no poetry that can place the body in an *environment* – wind, seascape, greenhouse, forest, desert, mountainside, among animals or insects or stones – so vividly and evocatively, waking unheard of exchanges between the place and human responsiveness at its most creative. He more than any other is a poet of pure being."

—Rosemary Sullivan

SCHWARTZ, Delmore. American. Born in Brooklyn, New York, 8 December 1913. Educated at the University of Wisconsin, Madison, 1931; New York University (Editor, *Mosaic* magazine), 1933–35, B.A. in philosophy 1935; Harvard University, Cambridge, Massachusetts, 1935–37. Married Gertrude Buckman (marriage dissolved); Elizabeth Pollet in 1949. Briggs-Copeland Instructor in English Composition, 1940, Instructor in English, 1941–45, and Assistant Professor of English, 1946–47, Harvard University. Fellow, Kenyon School of English, Gambier, Ohio, Summer 1950; Visiting Professor at New York University, Indiana School of Letters, Bloomington, Princeton University, New Jersey, and University of Chicago. Editor, 1943–47, and Associate Editor, 1947–55, *Partisan Review*, New Brunswick, New Jersey; associated with *Perspectives* magazine, New York, 1952–53; Literary Consultant, New Directions, publishers, New York, 1952–53; Poetry Editor and Film Critic, *New Republic* magazine, Washington, D.C., 1955–57. Recipient: Guggenheim Fellowship, 1940; National Institute of Arts and Letters grant, 1953; *Kenyon Review* Fellowship, 1957; Levinson Prize (*Poetry*, Chicago), 1959; Bollingen Prize, 1960; Shelley Memorial Award, 1960. *Died 11 July 1966.*

PUBLICATIONS

Verse

In Dreams Begin Responsibilities (includes short story and play). New York, New Directions, 1938.

A Season in Hell (bilingual edition), by Arthur Rimbaud.   New York, New
   Directions, 1939.
Genesis: Book One (includes prose).   New York, New Directions, 1943.
Vaudeville for a Princess and Other Poems (includes prose).   New York, New
   Directions, 1950.
Summer Knowledge: New and Selected Poems, 1938–1958.   New York,
   Doubleday, 1959.

Play

Shenandoah; or, The Naming of the Child.   New York, New Directions, 1941.

Short Stories

The World Is a Wedding and Other Stories.   New York, New Directions,
   1948; London, Lehmann, 1949.
Successful Love and Other Stories.   New York, Corinth Books, 1961.

Other

*American Poetry at Mid-Century: Lectures Presented under the Auspices of the
   Gertrude Clarke Whittall Poetry and Literature Fund,* with John Crowe
   Ransom and John Hall Wheelock.   Washington, D.C., Library of Congress,
   1958.
The Selected Essays of Delmore Schwartz, edited by Donald A. Dike and
   David H. Zucker.   Chicago and London, University of Chicago Press, 1970.

Editor, *Syracuse Poems 1964.*   Syracuse, New York, Syracuse University
   Department of English, 1965.

Critical Study: *Delmore Schwartz* by Richard McDougall, New York, Twayne,
1974.

*   *   *

By design or unhappy accident, *Summer Knowledge,* which Delmore Schwartz
called a selective but nevertheless "representative" volume, contains all of the
verse which won him considerable acclaim during the thirties and early forties, as
well as the more problematic late poetry. The volume is intended to convey a
particular point of view, though it is hardly one which Schwartz' admirers might
have predicted: he moves, rather mysteriously, from a questioning kind of lyricism
to a more affirmative but much less convincing late manner.
   The early poems from *In Dreams Begin Responsibilities* are now brought together
under the heading "The Dream of Knowledge." The Virgilian refrain "Happy is he
who knows the causes of things" haunts the young poet. Knowledge, understanding, is the aim, the dream, the means of achieving responsible selfhood and the
remission of old pains. "This is the first of spectacles," asserts one of the
presiding spirits of *Genesis: Book One*:

> O this
> Consoles in the last illness all our pain:
> Gazing upon the old life's vaudeville,
> Viewing the motions of the struggling will,
> Seeking the causes of each fresh event. . . .

Schwartz' simple Freudianism demands first of all an "understanding" of his parents; thus throughout the self-indulgent stretches of *Genesis* (and the brief verse play, *Shenandoah*) he insists on tracing the forces which shaped the forces which then shaped him. (In all fairness it should be added that when Schwartz did discover a suitable form for his family chronicle he produced one of the finest of all American short "stories," the title piece of *In Dreams Begin Responsibilities*.)

But inevitably knowledge brings disillusionment:

> Well! The heart of man is known.
> It is a cactus bloom.

Soon enough there is the fear that all aspirations to knowledge in this world of appearances, "In the naked bed, in Plato's cave," may be futile. Each morning merely repeats

> the mystery of beginning
> again and again,
> while History is unforgiven.

The ultimate basis of true awareness is the recognition of mortality: "Decide that you are dying," a symbolic Father tells his equally symbolic Son: "act in that shadow . . . Your own self acts then, then you know." Yet "what can any actor know?" complains the shade of Socrates in another poem: only

> the contradiction in every act,
> the infinite task of the human heart.

This task requires not only self-knowledge but the responsibility to "love one another," as Schwartz concludes in "The Old Age of Faust." But the finest early poems are the least didactic, the simple lyrical expressions of doubt, sorrow and tentative hope. "The Ballad of the Children of the Czar," "Tired and Unhappy, You Think of Houses," "The Ballet of the Fifth Year"; the wistful funny poems, "The Heavy Bear Who Goes with Me" (the poet's body and its awkward demands) and "A Dog Named Ego, the Snowflakes as Kisses" – these and another half-dozen or so affecting short works are the poems which encouraged admirers to place Schwartz in the company of Jarrell, Lowell, Berryman, Wilbur, and Karl Shapiro.

The poems which alternate with the somewhat arch prose pieces of *Vaudeville for a Princess* are often strained, as if Schwartz were trying hard to live up to the hopes of his *Partisan Review* colleagues for a kind of big American Spender, a Keats who had read Marx and Freud. And the last poems, with very few exceptions (notably "Seurat's Sunday Afternoon along the Seine") are pretentious efforts in which Schwartz seems desperate to convince himself and his readers, by mere blunt assertion, that the natural world at its natural zenith (and our Laurentian "summer knowledge" of it), while admittedly incomplete, is enough. By this time Schwartz had lost the power to clothe his thought. The long lines are rhythmically slack and self-consciously vatic; the verse is too often "free" in the worst sense of that much-abused term. Those who remember Schwartz' best work from the thirties may understandably *want* to like these final gestures, but to make serious claims for them is to do a disservice to the relatively limited but genuine poetic talent which fashioned a handful of moving poems.

—Elmer Borklund

SINGER, Burns (James Hyman Singer). American. Born in New York City, 29 August 1928; emigrated to Scotland in 1932. Educated at schools in Glasgow, and Maud, Aberdeenshire; University of Glasgow, 1945, 1949–51: studied zoology. Married Marie Battle in 1956. Travelled in Europe, 1945–47. Research Assistant, Scottish Home Department Marine Laboratory, Aberdeen, 1951–55. Free-lance Writer and Reviewer, London, 1955–59, and Cambridge, 1959–64. Leverhulme Research Fellow, Marine Laboratory, Plymouth, Devon, 1964. *Died 8 September 1964.*

PUBLICATIONS

Verse

The Gentle Engineer. Rome, Botteghe Oscure, 1952.
Still and All: Poems. London, Secker and Warburg, 1957; Chester Springs, Pennsylvania, Dufour, 1959.
The Collected Poems of Burns Singer, edited by W. A. S. Keir. London, Secker and Warburg, 1970.

Other

Living Silver: An Impression of the British Fishing Industry. London, Secker and Warburg, 1957; Boston, Houghton Mifflin, 1958.

Editor and Translator, with Jerzy Peterkiewicz, Five Centuries of Polish Poetry, 1450–1950. London, Secker and Warburg, 1960; Chester Springs, Pennsylvania, Dufour, 1962.

Television documentary: *Between the Tides*, 1956.

*   *   *

The Collected Poems of Burns Singer, edited and introduced by W. A. S. Keir, and with a preface by Hugh MacDiarmid, was published in 1970. Singer himself died young, in 1964. The only collection of poems he published during his lifetime was *Still and All*. The *Collected* volume adds sixty-four poems to this. There are others that have so far escaped the net – for instance, "S.O.S. Lifescene."

Singer was one of a number of recent Scottish poets who have sought to master philosophy, in the technical sense, and reproduce it in their verse. The process of his poetry is speculative. Walter Keir has suggested that Wittgenstein may have had a bad influence on him, and certainly a self-conscious passion for ratiocination did little to help Singer in his quest for clarity, slowing down the movement of his mind on the page and involving him in a grinding debate with his subject-matter which makes for passages that achieve only a turgid 'kind of pre-poetry. In its concern with the difficulty of utterance, his verse has several points of contact with that of his friend W. S. Graham. The long argumentative poems which Hugh MacDiarmid was writing in the thirties and forties also left their mark upon Singer's style.

This poet's best work re-vivifies the uses of formal dialectic, however, and sounds a note which, while modern, harks back to the real master of its kind, John Donne:

> Gently, my darling, I will hurt by saying
> But the one word that it would hurt to silence.
> I smother it in every syntax, miming
> With different motions but a constant meaning
> Till strangers marvel at my way of living.

In these lines the utterance, though cooled by the need to be precise, has an urgency which Singer denies himself in over-intellectualised meditations upon linguistics such as "A Sort of Language," or unsuccessful escapes into surrealism as in "Respect." The beginning stanza of the title poem in *Still and All* may also be taken to represent him at his finest:

> I give my word on it. There is no way
> Other than this. There is no other way
> Of speaking. I am my name. I find my place
> Empty without a word, and my word is
> Given again. It is nothing less than all
> Given away again, and all still truly
> Returned on a belief. Believe me now.
> There is no other. There is no other way.

The reader is held by the conviction of the tone, and the honest subtlety of the argument. Plain words have been found for something hard to say. This is cerebral poetry, verse stripped of image, puritanical in its need to retreat from things seen or heard or smelt or felt into a world of the mind where the poet can be alone with his concentration upon the possibility of saying anything true, or of speaking at all. Yet for all its bareness and spareness, Singer's work exerts a fascination – "the fascination of what's difficult." It should also be noted that in such near-narrative poems as "The Transparent Prisoner" he found a partial way out of his solipsistic dilemmas.

—Robert Nye

SMITH, Stevie (Florence Margaret Smith).   British.   Born in Hull, Yorkshire, 20 September 1902. Educated at Palmers Green High School, London, and the North London Collegiate School for Girls. Secretary to Neville Pearson, Newnes Publishing Company, London, 1923–53. Occasional writer and broadcaster for the BBC.

Recipient: Cholmondeley Award, 1966; Queen's Gold Medal for Poetry, 1969. *Died 8 March 1971.*

PUBLICATIONS

Verse

A Good Time Was Had by All. London, Cape, 1937.
Tender Only to One: Poems and Drawings. London, Cape, 1938.
Mother, What Is a Man? Poems and Drawings. London, Cape, 1942.
Harold's Leap. London, Chapman and Hall, 1950.
Not Waving But Drowning: Poems. London, Deutsch, 1957.
Selected Poems. London, Longman, 1962; New York, New Directions, 1964.
The Frog Prince and Other Poems. London, Longman, 1966.
Penguin Modern Poets 8, with Edwin Brock and Geoffrey Hill. London, Penguin, 1966.
The Best Beast: Poems. New York, Knopf, 1969.
Francesca in Winter. London, Poem-of-the-Month Club, 1970.
Corgi Modern Poets in Focus 4, edited by Jeremy Robson. London, Corgi, 1971.
Two in One: Selected Poems and The Frog Prince and Other Poems. London, Longman, 1971.
Scorpion and Other Poems. London, Longman, 1972.
Collected Poems. London, Lane, 1974.

Recordings: *Reading Her Own Poems*, Listener, 1967; *Poems*, with Adrian Mitchell, Argo, 1974.

Novels

Novel on Yellow Paper; or, Work It Out for Yourself. London, Cape, 1936; New York, Morrow, 1937.
Over the Frontier. London, Cape, 1938.
The Holiday. London, Chapman and Hall, 1949.

Other

Some Are More Human than Others: Sketch-Book. London, Gaberbocchus, 1958.
Cats in Colour. London, Batsford, 1959; New York, Viking Press, 1960.

Editor, *T. S. Eliot: A Symposium for His 70th Birthday.* London, Hart Davis, 1958.
Editor, *The Batsford Book of Children's Verse.* London, Batsford, 1970; as *The Poet's Garden*, New York, Viking Press, 1970.

Critical Study: *Ivy and Stevie: Ivy Compton-Burnett and Stevie Smith: Conversations and Reflections* by Kay Dick, London, Duckworth, 1971.

*   *   *

Sometimes angular, grotesque and elusive, the note of Stevie Smith's verse remains quite unmistakable. Her manner was evolved gradually, without much fuss (the poems which appeared in *Granta* in the middle thirties already exemplify the style), and she grew no more prim or cautious with time. Fundamentally Stevie Smith's poems are exercises in brinksmanship. There is a calculated dottiness about much of her writing; her themes are often *grand guignol*, her structures those of planned bathetic overkill. She likes to adopt a gnomic Crazy Jane mode in which there seems to be an escape route to frivolity: then the poem slams shut, and we are left with melancholy, frustration, rage.

Like earlier masters of Comic and Curious Verse, she is adept at turning cheerful doggerel forms to strange or disturbing ends. A poem like "The Singing Cat" exploits the very predictability of rhyme and meter in the usual nonsense verse. She frequently chooses a quasi-ballad rhythm: "The Parklands" starts off as an allusion to (if not quite a parody of) the song "Clementine," and then modulates into an area of grave romantic mythology. Popular songs are guyed elsewhere; jarring rhymes in a poem such as "I Remember" lend an air of outrageous bravura to what could be languid whimsy in the Cummings manner.

Miss Smith satisfies perfectly the requirements for the ideal reader of poetry, as laid down by W. H. Auden. She delighted in riddles and spells, carried off intricate technical feats, and deployed subtle effects of lexical play, as in "Mr. Over" of the punning "*v*." Her bent was always towards fantasy and fable: "Come On, Come Back," for example, couched in a sort of SF allegory. Her poems are often anecdotal, and she made something of a speciality of cautionary tales which for me recall Wordsworth (rather than Blake, a comparison often proposed). She was not frightened to use the boldest personification, and a somewhat fey quality in her imagination is redeemed by the wit and energy of the language. Her themes are occasionally medieval, her cadences biblical, but the movement of the verse is live and elastic.

Stevie Smith worked through several personae (often employing a kind of paramusical chorus of disembodied "voices"). Her moods were many, from feeble protest to anguish and from nightmare states to pathos: she could also achieve a Thurberesque lunacy. She could take the bones of the clerihew form and imbue them with an almost hysterical sense of personal loss or religious abandonment. At her best, in "Not Waving, But Drowning," "The Wedding Photograph," or "In the Park," she was a most resourceful and striking writer. And even at her worst, she was never less than a highly individual and skilful poet.

—J. P. W. Rogers

THOMAS, Dylan (Marlais). Welsh. Born in Swansea, Glamorganshire, 27 October 1914. Educated at Swansea Grammar School. Worked with a documentary film unit during World War II. Married Caitlin Macnamara in 1936: two sons and one daughter. Reporter, *South Wales Daily Post*, Swansea, 1931–32. From 1933, Free-lance Writer. Visited the United States in 1950, 1952, 1953. Recipient: Oscar Blumenthal Prize, 1938, and Levinson Prize, 1945 (*Poetry*, Chicago); Foyle Poetry Prize, 1953. *Died 9 November 1953.*

PUBLICATIONS

Verse

18 Poems.   London, Sunday Referee–Parton Bookshop, 1934.
Twenty-Five Poems.   London, Dent, 1936.
The Map of Love: Verse and Prose.   London, Dent, 1939.
The World I Breathe (includes stories).   New York, New Directions, 1939.
New Poems.   New York, New Directions, 1943.
Deaths and Entrances: Poems.   London, Dent, 1946.
Twenty-Six Poems.   London, Dent, and New York, New Directions, 1950.
In Country Sleep and Other Poems.   New York, New Directions, 1952.
Collected Poems 1934–1952.   London, Dent, 1952; as The Collected Poems of
    Dylan Thomas, New York, New Directions, 1953.
Two Epigrams of Fealty.   London, privately printed, 1954.
Galsworthy and Gawsworth.   London, privately printed, 1954.
The Poems of Dylan Thomas, edited by Daniel Jones.   London, Dent, and
    New York, New Directions, 1971.

Recording: Dylan Thomas Reading His Complete Recorded Poetry, Caedmon,
1963.

Plays

Return Journey (broadcast, 1947).   Published in New Directions: Five One-Act
    Plays in the Modern Idiom, edited by Alan Durband, London, Hutchinson,
    1961.
The Doctor and the Devils, from the Story by Donald Taylor (film-
    script).   London, Dent, and New York, New Directions, 1953.
Under Milk Wood: A Play for Voices (produced New York, 1953; Edinburgh
    and London, 1956).   New York, New Directions, and London, Dent, 1954.
The Beach of Falesá (film-script).   New York, Stein and Day, 1963; London,
    Cape, 1964.
Twenty Years A-Growing: A Film Script from the Story by Maurice
    O'Sullivan.   London, Dent, 1964.
Me and My Bike: An Unfinished Film-Script.   New York, McGraw Hill, and
    London, Triton, 1965.
The Doctor and the Devils and other Scripts (includes Twenty Years A-Grow-
    ing, A Dream of Winter, The Londoner).   New York, New Directions, 1966.

Screenplays: New Towns for Old, 1942; Our Country, 1944; When We Build
Again, 1945; The Three Weird Sisters, with Louise Birt and David Evans, 1948;
No Room at the Inn, with Ivan Foxwell, 1948

Short Stories

Portrait of the Artist as a Young Dog.   London, Dent, and New York, New
    Directions, 1940.
A Prospect of the Sea and Other Stories and Prose Writings, edited by Daniel
    Jones.   London, Dent, 1955.
Adventures in the Skin Trade.   New York, New Directions, 1955; as Adven-
    tures in the Skin Trade and Other Stories, London, Putnam, 1955.

Rebecca's Daughters.   London, Triton, 1965; Boston, Little Brown, 1966.
Two Tales: Me and My Bike, and Rebecca's Daughters.   New York, Sphere,
   1968.
The Outing.   London, Dent, 1971.

Other

Selected Writings of Dylan Thomas, edited by John L. Sweeney.   New York,
   New Directions, 1946.
Quite Early One Morning: Broadcasts.   London, Dent, and New York, New
   Directions, 1954.
Conversations about Christmas.   New York, New Directions, 1954.
Letters to Vernon Watkins, edited by Vernon Watkins.   London, Dent-Faber,
   and New York, New Directions, 1957.
Miscellany: Poems, Stories, Broadcasts.   London, Dent, 1963.
The Colour of Saying: An Anthology of Verse Spoken by Dylan Thomas, edited
   by Ralph N. Maud and Aneirin Talfan Davies.   London, Dent, 1963; as
   Dylan Thomas's Choice: An Anthology of Verse Spoken by Dylan Thomas,
   New York, New Directions, 1964.
Selected   Letters   of   Dylan   Thomas,   edited   by   Constantine
   FitzGibbon.   London, Dent, 1966; New York, New Directions, 1967.
Miscellany Two: A Visit to Grandpa's and Other Stories and Poems.   London,
   Dent, 1966.
The Notebooks of Dylan Thomas, edited by Ralph N. Maud.   New York,
   New Directions, 1967; as *Poet in the Making: The Notebooks of Dylan
   Thomas,* London, Dent, 1968.
The Collected Prose of Dylan Thomas.   New York, New Directions, 1969.
Twelve More Letters.   London, Turret Books, 1970.
Selected Writings, edited by J. P. Harries.   London, Heinemann, 1970.
Early Prose Writings, edited by Walford Davies.   London, Dent, and New
   York, New Directions, 1971.
Living and Writing, edited by Christopher Capeman.   London, Dent, 1972.

Bibliographies: *Dylan Thomas: A Bibliography* by J. Alexander Rolph, London,
Dent, and New York, New Directions, 1956; *Dylan Thomas in Print* by Ralph
Maud and A. Glover, Pittsburgh, University of Pittsburgh Press, and London,
H. M. Snyder, 1970, including *Appendix, 1969–1971* by Walford Davies, London,
Dent, 1972.

Critical Studies (a selection): *The Poetry of Dylan Thomas* by Elder Olson,
Chicago, University of Chicago Press, 1954; *Dylan Thomas in America: An
Intimate Journal* by John Malcolm Brinnin, Boston, Little Brown, 1954; *A
Casebook on Dylan Thomas,* edited by John Malcolm Brinnin, London,
Heinemann, 1960; *A Reader's Guide to Dylan Thomas* by William York Tindall,
New York, Noonday Press, and London, Thames and Hudson, 1962; *Dylan: Druid
of the Broken Body* by Aneirin Talfan Davies, London, Dent, 1964, New York,
Barnes and Noble, 1966; *The Life of Dylan Thomas* by Constantine FitzGibbon,
London, Dent, and Boston, Little Brown, 1965; *Dylan Thomas: A Collection of
Critical Essays,* edited by C. B. Cox, New York, Prentice Hall, 1966; *A Concor-
dance to the Collected Poems of Dylan Thomas* by Robert Coleman Williams,
Lincoln, University of Nebraska Press, 1967; *Dylan Thomas: New Critical Essays,*
edited by Walford Davies, London, Dent, 1972.

*   *   *

Dylan Thomas's working life as a poet lasted a little over twenty years, but the most extraordinary thing about it was how much of the foundations were laid in a very short period towards the beginning. From 1931 to 1935, he drafted, and in many cases actually completed, most of his best poems. In other words, he had created something like the most significant Thomas *oeuvre* by the age of 21. There are later poems, of course, such as "Fern Hill" and "Do Not Go Gentle into That Good Night," that were not laid down at this early period, and which certainly stand among his best. But the poems he was writing in his late adolescence established his main themes and his recognisable manner.

The themes are simple – sex, birth, death, nostalgia for childhood – but they are worked on and worked over with incessant verbal complexity. His method of writing, to be seen fascinatingly in his work-sheets, shows a man constructing hermetic works of art with the concentration of a rapt, almost hypnotised, caddis-worm: words are listed for their sound-properties, their taste in the mouth so to speak, and then are glued on to the frail and tenuous body of prose "sense" underneath. Take, for the example, the first of the sonnets in the "Altarwise by Owl-Light" sequence, written in 1935. The first six lines run:

> Altarwise by owl-light in the half-way house
> The gentleman lay graveward with his furies;
> Abaddon in the hangnail cracked from Adam,
> And, from his fork, a dog among the fairies,
> The atlas-eater with a jaw for news,
> Bit out the mandrake with to-morrow's scream.

Much analysis has been devoted to the poems in this sequence, most of it ludicrous in its ponderous ingenuities; and certainly it would be difficult to give a prose summary, in all but the barest form, of what is going on. Yet there are poems that precede the sequence with a plainer rhetoric that is often very effective: "The Force That Through the Green Fuse Drives the Flower," for example, "And Death Shall Have No Dominion," and – a very early poem – "Out of the Sighs":

> Out of the sighs a little comes,
> But not of grief, for I have knocked down that
> Before the agony; the spirit grows,
> Forgets, and cries;
> A little comes, is tasted and found good. . . .

Periodically, and increasingly, Thomas went through barren patches, commemorated as early as September 1938, when he wrote:

> On no work of words now for three lean months in the bloody
> Belly of the rich year and the big purse of my body
> I bitterly take to task my poverty and craft. . . .

The exalted impasto technique of this craft was a difficult one to safeguard against the distractions of earning a living (he was almost always an indigent free-lance), friends and congenial parasites, drink, and a generally evasive way of life. It sometimes seems a wonder that he could write at all, so hedged about was he with self-destructive impulses and a mode of composition that began blindly, with difficulty, with almost purely verbal and rhythmical impulses, and which often seemed to be fighting its way out of a smothering sack, padlocked against reason and reasonableness.

But the fact is that he managed at least a dozen times (some readers would put the figure much higher than that) to triumph against all the odds and produce work which is unique in English: rich, resonant, with a musical quality that was ideally suited to his own reading at its best. (There are many recordings of Thomas reading his poems: the better ones, in my opinion, are not those which were made in public halls and auditoriums during his tours of the United States, when he was too often tempted to bellow even his quieter poems, but the studio recordings done for the BBC and other organisations, which have an inwardness and intimacy he could manage perfectly.) "The Hand That Signed the Paper," "After the Funeral," "Poem in October," "The Hunchback in the Park" – these are among Thomas's best poems, and among the best poems of the century. The technical contortions of some of the later pieces, such as "Vision and Prayer," "In Country Sleep," and the Prologue to the *Collected Poems*, can be put on one side when one considers the simple inevitability of another late poem, "Do Not Go Gentle into That Good Night." The Dylan Thomas "legend," the reminiscences and sycophantic memorialising, the considerable apparatus of pseudo-commentary that has grown up round the man and his work – all these should not stand between the reader (or listener) and the finest achievements of this narrow but intense, strange and often eloquent genius.

—Anthony Thwaite

WATKINS, Vernon (Phillips). Welsh. Born in Maesteg, Glamorganshire, 27 June 1906. Educated at Swansea Grammar School, Glamorganshire; Repton School, Yorkshire; Magdalene College, Cambridge, 1924–25: studied modern languages. Served in the Home Guard, 1939–41, and Royal Air Force, 1941–45. Married Gwendolyn Mary Davies in 1944: five children. Clerk, Lloyds Bank, Swansea, 1925–41, 1946–65. Visiting Lecturer in Modern Poetry, University of Washington, Seattle, 1964, 1967; Calouste Gulbenkian Fellow in Poetry, University College, Swansea, 1965–66. Recipient: Levinson Prize (*Poetry*, Chicago), 1953; Guinness Prize, 1957. D.Litt.: University of Wales, Cardiff, 1966. Fellow, Royal Society of Literature. *Died 8 October 1967.*

PUBLICATIONS

Verse

The Ballad of Mari Lwyd and Other Poems.   London, Faber, 1941.
The Lamp and the Veil: Poems.   London, Faber, 1945.
The Lady with the Unicorn: Poems.   London, Faber, 1948.
Selected Poems.   New York, New Directions, 1948.
The Death Bell: Poems and Ballads.   London, Faber, and New York, New
   Directions, 1954.
Cypress and Acacia.   London, Faber, 1959; New York, New Directions, 1960.

Affinities: Poems. London, Faber, 1962; New York, New Directions, 1963.
Selected Poems 1930–1960. London, Faber, and New York, New Directions, 1967.
Arrival in East Shelby. Privately printed, 1968.
Pergamon Poets 4, with Kathleen Raine, edited by Evan Owen. Oxford and New York, Pergamon Press, 1968.
Fidelities. London, Faber, 1968; New York, New Directions, 1969.
Vernon Watkins and Jon Silkin: Poems. London, Longman, 1969.
Uncollected Poems. London, Enitharmon Press, 1969.
Elegiac Sonnet (bilingual edition). Milan, M'Arte Edizioni, 1970.

Other

Editor, *Letters to Vernon Watkins*, by Dylan Thomas. London, Dent, and New York, New Directions, 1957.
Editor, *Landmarks and Voyages: Poetry Supplement.* London, Poetry Book Society, 1957.

Translator, *The North Sea*, by Heinrich Heine. London, Faber, and New York, New Directions, 1955.

Bibliography: *Two Swansea Poets: Dylan Thomas and Vernon Watkins*, Swansea, Swansea Public Libraries, 1969.

Manuscript Collection: British Museum, London.

Critical Study: *Vernon Watkins, 1906–1967* edited by Leslie Norris, London, Faber, 1970.

*   *   *

The poems of Vernon Watkins are of a sort so uncommon in our day that they deserve what almost amounts to a new set of critical tools for their evaluation, although their individuality may not be apparent at first reading. It is true that in an age predominantly visual in expression, his verse springs most often "from a musical source"; that although experimental forms are popular, he remained constant to traditional patterns – even if he was within them a great craftsman and a sure inventor; and that when critics insist on dealing with each lyric as a singular artefact, his work is inter-related to the extent that we can read it almost as one long poem. It is, however, his material that is most unusual: in a life dedicated to poetry, during which he published eight important collections, numerous translations, and left behind substantial unpublished work, his themes remained those which obsessed him as a young man, developing naturally in profundity and richness.

When he was twenty-two he experienced the extraordinary vision which was to shape the direction of his life and work. He saw, more clearly than the things of this world, the true nature of Time and Eternity. After "this revolution of sensibility" as he called it, he was never again able to write a poem dominated by time, nor to think of this world as in any way ruled by time. It took him some time to develop a language and a style which could deal with his "transfigured vision of the world"; he continued to read widely, as he did throughout his life, but he gained most help from Yeats, whose work remained a continuing inspiration to him, and just as valuably – if more briefly – from the example and friendship of Dylan Thomas.

Watkins believed that the true artist received his inspiration from a religious source, that inspiration was a religious experience in which the artist recognised the appearance and qualities of the eternal world, and that it was his responsibility to await such inspiration and then interpret it through the practice of his art. In this way, those of us who are not artists will be able to understand something of the nature of the real world, of which ours is a faulty shadow. Such a belief demonstrates Watkins's affinity with poets like Vaughan and Blake, as well as with Yeats – although Watkins himself believed that all true artists are such interpreters. His 1962 volume, *Affinities*, is an explicit statement of this belief: in it he calls for the support not only of the poets, but of dancers like Nijinsky, and painters such as Michaelangelo. So timeless a point of view meant that Watkins was quite unaware of fashion – his verse is neither fashionable nor unfashionable – but very much aware of the permanent virtues of his art.

His points of view accounts, too, for the recurring images to be found in his work, although they are less noticeable in his later poems. Such imagery tends always to stand for the defeat of time: I mean the fountain, which gives out water without stop, the foal, the violet, the hawthorn (or, as Watkins most frequently calls it, the "may"), and the sycamore. This last symbol, for example is used in the early poem "Sycamore," in which the long-living tree is compared with the brief life of man. The tree is not only itself long-lived, but is perpetuated through its highly fertile fruits, its wood is used to make musical instruments – and art is necessary for the understanding of true reality – and it was, moreover, the tree into which Zaccheus climbed to see Jesus pass through Jericho. This last point, barely touched on in "Sycamore," becomes the central issue in "Zaccheus in the Leaves", a poem from *The Lady with the Unicorn*. This reminds us that, for Watkins, the ability to see the truth, that faculty given only to true artists, was a religious gift; indeed, although there were true artists before the coming of Christ, it is only through the intervention of Christ that perfect inspiration is to be found. Thus, the vision of Zaccheus was a species of inspiration; he saw the eternal world because of the presence of Christ.

The poem which most clearly states this belief is, perhaps, "Music of Colours – White Blossom. . . ." Here the poet, having walked the cliffs above Swansea Bay and admired the white of the foam, retraces his footsteps the next day after a fall of snow, and sees the spray he had thought white no more than grey. He reflects that true whiteness does not exist in this world, not in white blossom, nor shell, nor snow, nor in "Marlowe's queen." Nor does it exist in myth, in the white swan's-down of "Web-footed Jupiter" as he descends to Leda, since the poets of other religions are not able to see as clearly as those inspired by Christ's truth. Indeed, the only true whiteness "must have been/When His eyes looked down and made the leper clean." And the position of the artist is that he can "know nothing of Earth or colour until I know I lack/Original white. . . ."

This is an important stage in Watkins's development, and was followed by his assumption of the personality of the early Welsh poet, Taliesin. In Welsh mytho-logy, Taliesin, as a small boy, accidentally swallowed the three magical drops of Inspiration, and saw Past, Future, and Present all at once. The attraction of such a persona for Watkins was very great. Here was a voice he could use to discharge his incredible responsibility to the rest of us, to speak boldly and simply of the nature of inspiration and of the truth of eternity. The Taliesin poems, most particularly "Taliesin and the Spring of Vision," are Watkins's clearest statements, in a personal sense, of his great themes. Later he found the work of Hölderlin of equal importance, and the work of the German poet enabled him to intensify and modify his personal vision, as we can see in Watkins's poem "The Childhood of Hölderlin."

Briefly, then, Watkins attacks the conventional idea of time on several fronts: through the inspiration given to true artists which enables the idea of eternity to be known, through personal love, which is akin to ideal love and may be all that some people can achieve, and through the practice of art (both the second and third of these attitudes can be found in "The Lady with the Unicorn," and other poems contain all three ideas). After his prolonged meditations on these themes in the Taliesin poems, the Hölderlin poems, and, indeed, all the poems in *Affinities*, it seems almost as if Watkins had decided to turn his attention to this world, for his posthumous volume *Fidelities* contains a number of poems new in the attention they pay to the visible and palpable detail of the physical world. In "The Guest," a remarkable poem from that collection, he makes our mortal world eternal, a miraculous demonstration for his belief in the power of art in lines so perfect they seem without art:

> The cliff's crossed path lay silvered with slug tracks
> Where webs of hanging raindrops caught the sun.
> A thrush with snail cocked sideways like an axe
> Knocked with quick beak to crack it on a stone. . . .

In these late poems Watkins had achieved the synthesis of the mortal and the eternal worlds, and the tragedy is that he died at the height of his powers. He was a wholly serious and dedicated poet, his concerns always those of absolute great poetry.

—Leslie Norris

EXPLANATORY NOTES
ON RECENT POETIC MOVEMENTS
AND
A SELECTION
of
POETRY ANTHOLOGIES SINCE 1960

Beats poets and fiction writers who emerged in the late 1940's and early 1950's in New York City, rejecting materialism and seeking a "beatific" alternative; often inspired by jazz and Eastern religions; Jack Kerouac's novel *On the Road* epitomizes the assumptions of the group as much as the poetry does; the writers were later associated with San Francisco and City Lights Books. See Gregory Corso, Lawrence Ferlinghetti, Allen Ginsberg, Thom Gunn, Michael McClure, Harold Norse. **Anthologies:** *Beat Scene*, 1960; *Beat Poets*, 1961; *Beatitude Anthology*, 1965.

Black Mountain Poets geographical "fix" for the poets influenced by Charles Olson's Projectivism; Black Mountain College, North Carolina, employed several poets on the faculty, including Olson as Rector; the poets were linked with Robert Creeley's *Black Mountain Review* and Cid Corman's *Origin* magazine. See David Bromige, Paul Carroll, Ed Dorn, Robert Duncan, Ronald Johnson, Denise Levertov, Joel Oppenheimer, John Weiners, Jonathan Williams, as well as Olson. **Anthology:** *The Gist of "Origin,"* 1973.

Concrete Poetry an international movement concerned with the appearance of verse on the page; a subsidiary unit centers on "sound" verse. See Earle Birney, Bill Bissett, Bob Cobbing, Ian Hamilton Finlay, Sylvester Houédard, Richard Kostelanetz, Edwin Morgan, bpNichol, Alan Riddell, Aram Saroyan, Mary Ellen Solt, Emmett Williams. **Anthologies:** *Anthology of Concrete Poetry*, 1967; *The Chicago Review Anthology of Concretism*, 1967; *Concrete Poetry*, 1967; *Concrete Poetry*, 1969; *The Cosmic Chef*, 1970; *Mindplay*, 1970.

Confessional Poets term of emphasis suggesting the use of very personal and private subject matter, with an association of painful experience and a struggle with madness. See John Berryman, Robert Lowell, Sylvia Plath, Anne Sexton, William Snodgrass.

Deep Imagism phrase locating the source of poetic imagination in intense subjective perception of the unconscious, as opposed to the more objective viewpoint of the Projectivists. See Robert Bly, George Economou, Jonathan Greene, Robert Kelly, Bill Knott, William Matthews, Bert Meyers, Jerome Rothenberg, Diane Wakoski, James Wright.

The Group a personal association of British poets, urging a more colloquial and socially aware verse than that associated with The Movement. See Martin Bell, Christopher Hampton, Geoffrey Hill, Philip Hobsbaum, Edward Lucie-Smith, George MacBeth, Adrian Mitchell, Peter Porter, Peter Redgrove, Anthony Thwaite. **Anthology:** *A Group Anthology*, 1963.

The Movement anthology-based grouping of poets, primarily placed together as a reaction against the Id-focused verse of the 1940's, and stressing intellectuality, compassion, and irony. See Kingsley Amis, Robert Conquest, D. J. Enright, Thom Gunn, Elizabeth Jennings, Philip Larkin, John Wain. **Anthologies:** *New Lines*, London, Macmillan, 1956, and *New Lines II*, 1963.

New Black Aesthetic a phrase suggesting a reliance on qualities specifically associated with Black life – an oral, colloquial rhetoric, a strong community consciousness – as opposed to the formal, tradition-oriented qualities usually associated with poetry. See Alvin Aubert, Lucille Clifton, Mari Evans, Nikki Giovanni, LeRoi Jones, Don L. Lee, Audre Lorde, Clarence Major, Dudley Randall, Ishmael Reed, Carolyn M. Rodgers, Sonia Sanchez, Margaret Walker. **Anthologies:** *Black Fire*, 1968; *Black Poetry*, 1969; *Understanding the New Black Poetry*, 1972.

New York Poets the diverse literary wing of a New York City-based arts movement of the 1960's and 1970's which also includes filmakers, photographers, actors, and painters; some of the most influential members, including Frank O'Hara, worked on *Art News* magazine, and much of the poetry reveals an interest in the techniques of modern painting; the verse is one development of Projectivism. See John Ashbery, Michael Benedikt, Bill Berkson, Joseph Ceravolo, Kenward Elmslie, Edward Field, Kenneth Koch, Frank O'Hara, Ron Padgett, James Schuyler, David Shapiro, Anne Waldman. **Anthology:** *An Anthology of New York Poets*, 1970.

Objectivism centering on the Objectivist Press (New York), an aesthetic movement linking the ideas of imagism with larger structural concerns, and influenced by William Carlos Williams and Ezra Pound. See George Oppen, Carl Rakosi, Charles Reznikoff, Eli Siegel, Louis Zukofsky. **Anthology:** *An "Objectivists" Anthology*, edited by Louis Zukofsky, New York, To Publishers, 1932.

Pop Poetry British group related to Beat poets in their association with music, especially jazz or pop, with declaimed or set lyrics, and with an emphasis on live performance. See Henry Graham, Adrian Henri, Michael Horovitz, Christopher Logue, Barry MacSweeney, Roger McGough, Jeff Nuttall. **Anthology:** *The Liverpool Scene*, 1967.

Projective Verse name given to verse written under the influence of Charles Olson's essay "Projective Verse" (1950), essentially an attempt to encourage verse in open forms, deriving in part from Objectivism, and becoming important to poets associated with the San Francisco Renaissance, the Beats, the Black Mountain Poets, and the New York Poets, *qq.v.* **Anthology:** *The New American Poetry*, 1960.

San Francisco Renaissance geographical term relating to, especially, those non-academic poets concerned with verse in open forms, and linked to the Beats and the Projective Verse writers. See James Broughton, Robert Duncan, William Everson, Andrew Hoyem, David Meltzer, Kenneth Patchen, Kenneth Rexroth, Gary Snyder. **Anthology:** *The San Francisco Poets*, 1971.

*   *   *

An African Treasury: Art, Essays, Stories, Poems, by Black Africans, edited by Langston Hughes. New York, Crown, 1960; London, Gollancz, 1961.

African Voices: An Anthology of Native African Writing, edited by Peggy Rutherfoord. New York, Vanguard Press, 1960.

African Writing Today, edited by Ezekiel Mphahlele. London, Penguin, 1967.

African–English Literature: A Short Survey and Anthology of Prose and Poetry, edited by Anne Tibble. London, Peter Owen, 1965.

Afro–American Literature: An Introduction, edited by Robert E. Hayden, David J. Burrows, and Frederick R. Lapides. New York, Harcourt Brace, 1971.

American Literary Anthology 1–3, various editors. New York, Farrar Straus, 1968; New York, Random House, 1969; New York, Viking Press, 1970.

American Negro Poetry, edited by Arna Bontemps. New York, Hill and Wang, 1963.

American Poems: A Contemporary Collection, edited by Jascha Kessler. Carbondale, Southern Illinois University Press, 1964.

American Poetry Now: A Selection of the Best Poems by Modern American Writers, edited by Sylvia Plath. London, Oxford University Press, 1961.

An Anthology of Commonwealth Verse, edited by Margaret J. O'Donnell. London, Blackie, 1963.

An Anthology of Concrete Poetry, edited by Emmett Williams. New York, Something Else Press, 1967.

An Anthology of Current Poetry.   New York, Grossman, 1967.

An Anthology of Free Verse, edited by James Reeves.   Oxford, Blackwell, 1968.

An Anthology of Malaysian Poetry in English.   Kuala Lumpur, University of Malaya Press, 1966.

Anthology of Modern Poetry, edited by John Wain.   London, Hutchinson, 1963.

An Anthology of Modern Verse, 1940–1960, edited by Elizabeth Jennings. London, Methuen, 1961.

An Anthology of New York Poets, edited by Ron Padgett and David Shapiro. New York, Random House, 1970.

An Anthology of Revolutionary Poetry.   New York, Smyrna Press, 1968.

An Anthology of Twentieth Century New Zealand Poetry, edited by Vincent O'Sullivan.   London, Oxford University Press, 1970.

An Anthology of Verse by American Negroes, edited by N. I. White and W. C. Jackson.   Durham, North Carolina, Moore, 1969.

Ardentia Verba, edited by Barbara Fischer.   Deer Park, Long Island, New York, Penman Publications, 1967.

Asian P.E.N. Anthology, edited by F. Sionil Jose.   Manila, Solidaridad Publishing House, 1966; New York, Taplinger, 1967.

Astronauts of Inner Space.   San Francisco, SPR Editions, 1966.

Australian Idiom: An Anthology of Contemporary Prose and Poetry, edited by H. P. Heseltine.   Melbourne, Cheshire, 1963; London, Angus and Robertson, 1964.

Australian Poetry 1960.   Sydney, Angus and Robertson, 1960. (Published annually)

Australian Poetry Now, edited by Thomas W. Shapcott.   Melbourne, Sun Books, 1970.

Australian Poets Speak, edited by Ian Mudie and Colin Thiele.   Adelaide, Rigby, 1961.

Australian Writing Today, edited by Charles Higham.   London, Penguin, 1968.

Beat Poets, edited by Gene Baro.   London, Vista Books, 1961.

The Beat Scene, edited by Elias Wilentz.   New York, Corinth Books, 1960.

Beatitude Anthology.   San Francisco, City Lights Books, 1965.

Best Poems of 1959: The Borestone Mountain Poetry Awards.   Palo Alto, California, Pacific Books – Stanford University Press, 1960. (Published annually)

Beyond the Blues: New Poems by American Negroes, edited by Rosey E. Pool. Aldington, Kent, Hand and Flower Press, 1962; Chester Springs, Pennsylvania, Dufour Editions, 1965.

Black Fire: An Anthology of Afro-American Writing, edited by LeRoi Jones and Larry Neal.   New York, Morrow, 1968.

Black Out Loud, edited by Arnold Adoff.   New York, Macmillan, 1970.

Black Poetry: A Supplement to Anthologies Which Exclude Black Poets, edited by Dudley Randall.   Detroit, Broadside Press, 1969.

The Black Poets: A New Anthology, edited by Dudley Randall. New York, Bantam, 1971.

Black Voices: An Anthology of Afro-American Literature, edited by Abraham Chapman. New York, New American Library, 1968.

The Blasted Pine: An Anthology of Satire, Invective and Disrespectful Verse, revised edition, edited by F. R. Scott and A. J. M. Smith. Toronto, Macmillan, 1967.

The Blue Guitar: A Selection of Modern Verse, edited by D. G. Rutledge and J. M. Bassett. Toronto, McClelland and Stewart, 1968.

A Book of African Verse, edited by John Reed and Clive Wake. London, Heinemann, 1964.

A Book of Australian Verse, revised edition, edited by Judith Wright. Melbourne and London, Oxford University Press, 1968.

Breaklight: The Poetry of the Caribbean, edited by Andrew Salkey. New York, Doubleday, 1972.

Breakthrough: Poetry in Britain During the Sixties, edited by R. B. Heath. London, Hamish Hamilton, 1970.

Breakthrough: A Treasury of Contemporary American-Jewish Literature, edited by Irving Malin and Irwin Stark. New York, McGraw Hill, 1964.

British Poetry since 1945, edited by Edward Lucie-Smith. London, Penguin, 1970.

A Broadside Treasury, edited by Gwendolyn Brooks. Detroit, Broadside Press, 1971.

Bunga Emas: An Anthology of Contemporary Malaysian Literature, 1930–1963, edited by T. Wignesan. London, Blond, and Kuala Lumpur, Raybooks, 1964.

Canada First: A Mare Usque ad Edmonton; New Canadian Poets, edited by Peter Anson. Toronto, House of Anansi, 1969.

A Canadian Anthology: Poems from the Fiddlehead, 1945–1959. Fredericton, New Brunswick, Fiddlehead, 1961.

A Canadian Folio. Santa Barbara, California, Unicorn Press, 1969.

Caribbean Literature: An Anthology, edited by G. R. Coulthard. London, University of London Press, 1966.

Caribbean Verse: An Anthology, edited by O. R. Dathorne. London, Heinemann, 1967.

Caribbean Voices 1 and 2: An Anthology of West Indian Poetry, edited by John Figueroa. London, Evans, 1966, 1970.

A Caterpillar Anthology: A Selection of Poetry and Prose from Caterpillar Magazine, edited by Clayton Eshleman. New York, Doubleday, 1971.

A Century of Canadian Literature, edited by H. G. Green and Guy Sylvestre. Toronto, Ryerson Press, 1967.

The Chicago Review Anthology of Concretism, edited by Eugene Wildman. Denver, Swallow, 1967.

Chief Modern Poets of England and America, revised edition, edited by Gerald D. Sanders and others. New York, Macmillan, 1962.

Children of Albion: Poetry of the Underground in Britain, edited by Michael Horovitz.   Harmondsworth, Middlesex, Penguin Books, 1969.

Civil Liberties and the Arts: Selections from "Twice-a-Year," 1938–1948, edited by William Wasserstrom.   Syracuse, New York, Syracuse University Press, 1964.

C'mon Everybody: Poetry of the Dance, edited by bpNichol.   London, Corgi, 1969.

The Colour of Saying: An Anthology of Verse Spoken by Dylan Thomas, edited by Ralph Maud and Aneirin Talfan Davies.   London, Dent, 1963; as *Dylan Thomas's Choice*, New York, New Directions, 1964.

Come to Power: Eleven Contemporary American Indian Poets, edited by Dick Lourie.   Trumansburg, New York, Crossing Press, 1974.

Commonwealth Poems of Today, edited by Howard Sergeant.   London, John Murray, 1967.

Concrete Poetry: An International Anthology, edited by Stephen Bann.   London, Alan Ross, 1967.

Concrete Poetry: A World View, edited by Mary Ellen Solt and Willis Barnstone.   Bloomington, Indiana University Press, 1969.

Contemporaries, edited by Jean Malley and Hale Tokay.   New York, Viking Press, 1972.

Contemporary: An Anthology of the Poetry of Our Times, 1940–1964, edited by A. A. Evans.   London, University of London Press, 1965.

Contemporary American Poetry, edited by Donald Hall.   London, Penguin, 1962, 1972.

Contemporary American Poetry, edited by H. Lincoln Foster.   New York, Macmillan, 1963.

Contemporary American Poetry, edited by Al Poulin, Jr.   Boston, Houghton Mifflin, 1971.

The Contemporary American Poets: American Poetry since 1940, edited by Mark Strand.   Cleveland, World, 1969.

Contemporary Scottish Verse, edited by Norman MacCaig and Alexander Scott.   London, Calder and Boyars, 1970.

A Controversy of Poets: An Anthology of Contemporary American Poetry, edited by Paris Leary and Robert Kelly.   New York, Doubleday, 1965.

The Cosmic Chef: An Evening of Concrete, edited by bpNichol.   Ottawa, Oberon Press, 1970.

A Country in the Mind: An Anthology of Stories and Poems, edited by Ray B. West, Jr.   Sausalito, California, Angel Island Publications, 1962.

The Dance Book: An Anthology of Southwestern Poems, edited by Keith Wilson.   Portland, Oregon, Trask House Press, 1970.

Dark Symphony: Negro Literature in America, edited by James A. Emanuel and Theodore Gross.   New York, Free Press, 1968.

Dawn and Dusk: Poems of Our Time, edited by Charles Causley.   Leicester, Brockhampton Press, 1962.

Decade: A Collection of Poems from the First Ten Years of the Wesleyan Writing Program, edited by Norman Pearson. Middletown, Connecticut, Wesleyan University Press, 1969.

Dices; or, Black Bones, edited by Adam David Miller. Boston, Houghton Mifflin, 1970.

The Distinctive Voice: Twentieth Century American Poetry, edited by William J. Martz. Chicago, Scott Foresman, 1966.

The Dolmen Anthology of Irish Writing, edited by John Montague. Dublin, Dolmen Press, and London, Oxford University Press, 1962.

The Doveglion Book of Philippine Poetry, edited by José Garcia Villa. Manila, Katha Editions, 1962.

Doves for the Seventies, edited by Peter Robins. London, Corgi, 1969.

Dragons and Daffodils: An Anthology of Verse, edited by John Stuart Williams and Richard Milner. Llandybie, Carmarthenshire, Christopher Davies, 1960; Chester Springs, Pennsylvania, Dufour, 1961.

Drum Beat, edited by L. Okala. Nairobi, East African Publishing House, 1967.

East of America: An Anthology of Cape Cod Poets. Chatham, Massachusetts, Chatham Press, 1969.

The East Side Scene: American Poetry 1960–1965, edited by Allen de Loach. Buffalo, New York, Buffalo University Press, 1968.

Eating the Menu: A Contemporary American Poetry 1970–1974, edited by Bruce Edward Taylor. Dubuque, Iowa, Kendall Hunt, 1974.

Eight by Eight, edited by Vincent Buckley. Brisbane, Jacaranda Press, 1963.

Eight Modern American Poets, edited by C. W. Gillan. London, Harrap, 1971.

XI Hunter Valley Poets + VII, edited by Norman Talbot. Newcastle, New South Wales, privately printed, 1966.

English Poems of the Twentieth Century, edited by Eli Mandel and Desmond Maxwell. Toronto, Macmillan, 1971.

English Poetry in Quebec, edited by John Glassco. Montreal, McGill University Press, 1965.

Equinox 1: An Anthology of New Writing from the Philippines, edited by F. Sionil Jose. Manila, Solidaridad Publishing House, 1965.

Evergreen Review Reader, 1957–1967: A Ten Year Anthology, edited by Barney Rosset. New York, Grove Press, 1968.

The Faber Book of Irish Verse, edited by John Montague. London, Faber, 1970.

The Faber Book of Modern Verse, revised edition, edited by Anne Ridler. London, Faber, 1960; revised edition, edited by Donald Hall, 1965.

The Faber Book of Twentieth Century Verse, revised edition, edited by John Heath-Stubbs and David Wright. London, Faber, 1965.

Festschrift for Marianne Moore's Seventy Seventh Birthday, edited by Thurairajah Tambimuttu. New York, Tambimuttu and Mass, 1965.

Fifteen Winds: A Selection of Modern Canadian Poems, edited by A. L. Purdy. Toronto, Ryerson Press, 1969.

50 Modern American and British Poets, 1920–1970, edited by Louis Untermeyer. New York, McKay, 1973.

The First Five Years: A Selection from the Tamarack Review, edited by Robert Weaver. Toronto, Oxford University Press, 1962.

The First Paperback Poets Anthology, edited by Roger McDonald. Brisbane, University of Queensland Press, 1974.

A First Reader of Contemporary American Poetry, edited by Patrick Gleeson. Columbus, Ohio, Merrill, 1969.

Flash Point: An Anthology of Modern Poetry, edited by Robert Shaw. Leeds, Arnold, 1964.

For Malcolm: Poems on the Life and Death of Malcolm X, edited by Dudley Randall and Margaret G. Burroughs. Detroit, Broadside Press, 1967.

45–60: An Anthology of English Poetry, 1945–1960, edited by Thomas Blackburn. London, Putnam, 1960.

Forty Women Poets of Canada, edited by Dorothy Livesay and Seymour Mayne. Montreal, Ingluvin, 1971.

Fourteen British and American Poets, edited by Rowland L. Collins. New York, Macmillan, 1964.

From the Ashes: Voices of Watts, edited by Budd Schulberg. New York, New American Library, 1967.

From the Belly of the Shark: A New Anthology of Native Americans: Poems by Chicanos, Eskimos, Hawaiians, Indians, Puerto Ricans in the U.S.A., with Related Poems by Others, edited by Walter Lowenfels. New York, Vintage, 1973.

From the Hungarian Revolution: A Collection of Poems, edited by David Ray. Ithaca, New York, Cornell University Press, 1966.

Frontier of Going: An Anthology of Space Poetry, edited by John Fairfax. London, Panther, 1969.

The Fugitive Poets: Modern Southern Poetry in Perspective, edited by William C. Pratt. New York, Dutton, 1965.

A Garland for Dylan Thomas, edited by George P. Firmage and Oscar Williams. New York, October House, 1963.

Garlands for Christmas, edited by Chad Walsh. New York, Macmillan, 1965.

Geiger, Geiger: An Anthology of Experimental Texts, edited by Maurizio Spatola. New York, Wittenborn, 2 vols., 1967, 1968.

Generation Now, edited by Raymond Souster and Richard Woollatt. Toronto, Longman, 1970.

Georgian Poetry, edited by James Reeves. London, Penguin, 1962.

Gift of Tongues: A Selection from the Work of Fourteen 20th Century Poets, edited by Thomas Blackburn. London, Nelson, 1967.

The Gist of "Origin": An Anthology, edited by Cid Corman. New York, Grossman, 1973.

The Golden Year: The Poetry Society of America Anthology, 1910–1960, edited by Melville Cane and others.   New York, Fine Editions Press, 1960.

Great Occasions: Readings for the Celebration of Birth, Coming-of-Age, Marriage, and Death, edited by Carl Seaberg.   Boston, Beacon Press, 1968.

A Group Anthology, edited by Edward Lucie-Smith and Philip Hobsbaum. London, Oxford University Press, 1963.

Guinness Book of Poetry, 1958–1959.   London, Putnam, 1960. (Published regularly)

The Happy Unicorns: The Poetry of the Under-25's, edited by Sally Purcell and Libby Purves.   London, Sidgwick and Jackson, 1971.

Heartland: Poems of the Midwest, edited by Lucien Stryk.   DeKalb, Northern Illinois University Press, 1967.

Hero's Way: Contemporary Poems in the Mythic Tradition, edited by J. A. Allen. New York, Prentice Hall, 1971.

Holding Your Eight Hands: A Book of Science Fiction Verse, edited by Edward Lucie-Smith.   New York, Doubleday, 1969; London, Rapp and Whiting, 1970.

The Hollins Poets, edited by Louis D. Rubin.   Charlottesville, University Press of Virginia, 1967.

The House That Jack Built: Poems for Shelter, edited by Brian Patten and Pat Krett.   London, Allen and Unwin, 1973.

The Hudson Review Anthology, edited by Frederick Morgan.   New York, Vintage, 1961.

The Human Voice: Women Poets of Canada Anthology.   Homestead, Florida, Olivant Press, 1967.

I Am the Darker Brother: An Anthology of Modern Poems by Negro Americans, edited by Arnold Adoff.   New York, Macmillan, 1968.

I Burn for England: An Anthology of the Poetry of World War 2, edited by Charles Hamblett.   London, Leslie Frewen, 1966.

Illinois Poets: A Selection, edited by E. Earle Stibitz.   Carbondale, Southern Illinois University Press, 1968.

The Imagist Poem: Modern Poetry in Miniature, edited by William C. Pratt. New York, Dutton, 1963.

In a Time of Revolution: Poems from Our Third World, edited by Walter Lowenfels.   New York, Random House, 1969.

Indian Poetry in English Today, edited by Pritish Nandy.   New Delhi, Sterling, 1973.

Indian Writing in English, edited by K. R. Srinivasa Iyengar.   New York, Taplinger-Asian Publications, 1962.

Inside Outer Space: New Poems of the Space Age, edited by Robert Vas Dias. New York, Doubleday, 1970.

It Is the Poem Singing into Your Eyes: Anthology of New Young Poets, edited by Arnold Adoff.   New York, Harper, 1971.

It's World That Makes the Love Go Round: Modern Poetry Selected from "Breakthru" International Poetry Magazine, edited by Ken Geering. London, Corgi, 1968.

Jazz Poems, edited by Anselm Hollo. London, Vista Books, 1963.

Jump Bad: A New Chicago Anthology, edited by Gwendolyn Brooks. Detroit, Broadside Press, 1971.

Kaleidoscope: Poems by American Negro Poets, edited by Robert E. Hayden. New York, Harcourt Brace, 1967.

The Kennedy Reader, edited by Jay David. Indianapolis, Bobbs Merrill, 1967.

Landfall Country: Work from "Landfall," 1947–1961, edited by Charles Brasch. Christchurch, Caxton Press, 1962.

Lean Out of the Window: An Anthology of Modern Poetry, edited by Sara Hannum and Gwendolyn E. Reed. New York, Atheneum, 1965.

Let There Be God: An Anthology of Modern Religious Poetry, edited by T. H. Parker and F. J. Teskey. Oxford, Religious Education Press, 1968.

The Lilting House: An Anthology of Anglo-Welsh Poetry, 1917–1967, edited by John Stuart Williams and Meic Stephens. London, Dent, and Llandybie, Carmarthenshire, Christopher Davies, 1969.

The Literature of Australia, edited by Geoffrey Dutton. Melbourne, Penguin Books, 1964; Baltimore, Penguin Books, 1965.

A Little Treasury of Modern Poetry, revised edition, edited by Oscar Williams. New York, Scribner, 1970.

Live Poetry, edited by Kathleen Koppell. New York, Holt Rinehart, 1971.

The Liverpool Scene, edited by Edward Lucie-Smith. London, Rapp and Carroll, 1967.

The Living Underground: An Anthology of Contemporary American Poetry, edited by Sam Cornish and Hugh Fox. East Lansing, Michigan, Ghost Dance Press, 1969.

Living Voices: An Anthology of Contemporary Verse, edited by Jon Silkin. London, Vista Books, 1960.

The London Bridge Book of Verse: Poems from 1900–1960, edited by N. L. Clay. London, Heinemann, 1962.

London Magazine Poems, 1961–1966, edited by Hugo Williams. London, Alan Ross, 1966.

Longer Contemporary Poems, edited by David Wright. London, Penguin, 1966.

Losers Weepers: Poems Found Practically Anywhere. San Francisco, Kayak Books, 1969.

Love Love Love: The New Love Poetry, edited by Pete Roche. London, Corgi, 1967.

Made in Canada: New Poems of the Seventies, edited by Raymond Souster and Douglas Lochhead. Ottawa, Oberon Press, 1970.

The Major Young Poets, edited by Al Lee. Cleveland, World, 1971.

The Male Muse: A Gay Anthology, edited by Ian Young. Trumansburg, New York, Crossing Press, 1973.

A Map of Modern English Verse, edited by John Press. London, Oxford University Press, 1969.

Mark in Time: Eighty Photographs and Poems, Usually Selected by the Poet, edited by Nick Harvey. San Francisco, Glide, 1971.

The Mentor Book of Irish Poetry, edited by Denis A. Garrity. New York, New American Library, 1965.

Messages: Poems from Ghana, edited by Kofi Awooner and George Adali-Morthy. London, Heinemann, 1970; New York, Humanities Press, 1971.

The Mid-Century: English Poetry 1940–1960, edited by David Wright. London, Penguin, 1965.

Midland: 25 Years of Poetry and Fiction Selected from the Writing Workshops of the State University of Iowa and *Midland II*, edited by Paul Engle and others. New York, Random House, 1961, 1970.

Midstream Reader, edited by Shlomo Katz. New York, Yoseloff, 1960.

Mindplay: An Anthology of British Concrete Poetry, edited by John J. Sharkey. London, Lorimer Films, 1970.

Mindscapes, edited by Richard Peck. New York, Delacorte Press, 1971.

Modern American Poetry, revised edition, edited by Louis Untermeyer. New York, Harcourt Brace, 1962, 1969.

Modern and Contemporary Afro-American Poetry, edited by Bernard Bell. Boston, Allyn and Bacon, 1972.

Modern Australian Poetry, edited by David Campbell. Melbourne, Sun Books, 1970.

Modern Australian Verse (Poetry in Australia II), edited by Douglas Stewart. Sydney, Angus and Robertson, 1964; Berkeley, University of California Press, 1965; revised edition, Angus and Robertson, 1971.

Modern Australian Writing, edited by Geoffrey Dutton. London, Fontana, 1966.

Modern British Poetry, revised edition, edited by Louis Untermeyer. New York, Harcourt Brace, 1962, 1969.

Modern Canadian Verse: In English and French, edited by A. J. M. Smith. Toronto, Oxford University Press, 1967.

Modern Folk Ballads, edited by Charles Causley. London, Studio Vista, 1966.

Modern Indian Poetry in English: The Writers Workshop Selection: An Anthology and a Credo, edited by P. Lal. Calcutta, Writers Workshop, 1969.

Modern Irish Poetry, edited by Derek Mahon. London, Sphere, 1972.

Modern Love Poems, edited by D. J. Klemer. New York, Doubleday, 1961.

Modern Love Poems, edited by John Smith. London, Studio Vista, 1966.

Modern Occasions: New Fiction, Poetry, Drama and Criticism by 21 Writers, edited by Philip Rahv. New York, Farrar Straus, 1966.

Modern Poems for the Commonwealth, edited by Maurice Woolman and John Spencer. London, Harrap, 1966.

Modern Poetry, revised edition, edited by Maynard Mack and others. New York, Prentice Hall, 1961.

Modern Poetry from Africa, edited by Ulli Beier and Gerald Moore. London, Penguin, 1963.

The Modern Poets: An American-British Anthology, edited by John Malcolm Brinnin and Bill Reed. New York, McGraw Hill, 1963, 1970.

Modern Religious Poems: A Contemporary Collection, edited by Jacob Trapp. New York, Harper, 1964.

Modern Religious Verse, edited by Timothy Beaumont. London, Studio Vista, 1966.

Modern Scottish Poetry: An Anthology of the Scottish Renaissance, revised edition, edited by Maurice Lindsay. London, Faber, 1966.

The Moderns: An Anthology of New Writing in America, edited by LeRoi Jones. New York, Corinth Books, 1963; London, MacGibbon and Kee, 1965.

Mountain Moving Day: Poems by Women, edited by Elaine Gill. Trumansburg, New York, Crossing Press, 1973.

Naked Poetry: Recent American Poetry in Open Forms, and *Naked Poetry 2*, edited by Stephen Berg and Robert Mezey. Indianapolis, Bobbs Merrill, 1969, 1974.

Natural Process: An Anthology of New Black Poets, edited by Theodore Wilente and Tom Weatherly, Jr. New York, Hill and Wang, 1970.

Negro Verse, edited by Anselm Hollo. London, Vista Books, 1964.

New American and Canadian Poetry, edited by John Gill. Boston, Beacon Press, 1971.

New American Poetry, edited by Richard Monaco. New York, McGraw Hill, 1973.

The New American Poetry, 1945–1960, edited by Donald M. Allen. New York, Grove Press, 1960.

The New American Poets. Chicago, Big Table Books, 1960.

New American Review 1, edited by Theodore Solotaroff. New York, New American Library, 1967. (Published regularly)

The New Black Poetry, edited by Clarence Major. New York, International Publishers, 1969.

New British Poets, edited by Michael Schmidt. Oxford, Carcanet Press, 1973.

New Choice, edited by John Anthony Colmer and Dorothy Colmer. Wellington, Reed, and Melbourne, Cheshire, 1967.

New Directions in Prose and Poetry 17, edited by James Laughlin. New York, New Directions, 1961. (Published regularly)

New Directions Reader, edited by Hayden Carruth and James Laughlin. New York, New Directions, 1964.

The New Generation of Poets. New York, Black Sun Press, 1969.

New Horizons, revised edition, edited by B. C. Diltz and R. J. McMaster. Toronto, McClelland and Stewart, 1965.

New Impulses in Australian Poetry, edited by Rodney Hall and Thomas W. Shapcott. Brisbane, University of Queensland Press, 1968.

New Indian Writing, edited by Howard McCord. San Francisco, City Lights Books, 1970.

New Irish Writing. Dublin, Dolmen Press, and London, Oxford University Press, 1970.

New Jazz Poets (recording and text), edited by Walter Lowenfels. Detroit, Broadside Press, 1967.

New Lines II, edited by Robert Conquest. London, Macmillan, 1963.

New Modern Poetry: British and American Poetry since World War II, edited by M. L. Rosenthal. New York, Macmillan, 1967.

New Negro Poets USA, edited by Langston Hughes. Bloomington, Indiana University Press, 1964.

New Poems 1960, A P.E.N. Anthology. London, Hutchinson, 1960. (Published annually)

The New Poetry, edited by A. Alvarez. London, Penguin, 1962, 1966.

New Poetry Anthology I and *II*, edited by Michael Anania. Chicago, Swallow Press, 1969, 1971.

New Poets, New Music, edited by John Schmittroth and John Mahoney. Cambridge, Massachusetts, Winthrop, 1970.

New Poets of England and America: Second Selection, edited by Donald Hall and Robert Pack. Cleveland, World, 1962.

New Poets of Ireland, edited by Donald Carroll. Denver, Alan Swallow, 1963.

New South African Writing 1, South African P.E.N. Centre. Cape Town, Purnell, 1964. (And later volumes)

New Voices of the Commonwealth, edited by Howard Sergeant. London, Evans, 1968.

New Wave Canada: The New Explosion in Canadian Poetry, edited by Raymond Souster. Toronto, Contact Press, 1966.

New World Writing 16. Philadelphia, Lippincott, 1960. (And later volumes)

New Writing from the Philippines: A Critique and an Anthology, edited by Leonard Casper. Syracuse, New York, Syracuse University Press, 1966.

New Writing in the Caribbean, edited by A. J. Seymour. Georgetown, Guyana, Government of Guyana, 1972.

The New Writing in the U.S.A., edited by Donald Allen and Robert Creeley. London, Penguin, 1967.

The New York Times Anthology. New York, Macmillan, 1970.

The New Yorker Book of Poems. New York, Viking Press, 1969.

New Zealand Farm and Station Verse, 1850–1950, edited by Airini Elizabeth Woodhouse. Christchurch, Whitcombe and Tombs, 1967.

New Zealand Poetry Yearbook, 1960. Christchurch, Pegasus Press, 1960. (Published annually)

Nine Black Poets, edited by Robert Baird Shuman.   Durham, North Carolina, Moore, 1968.

Nine Modern Poets, edited by E. L. Black.   London, Macmillan, 1966.

19 Necromancers from Now, edited by Ishmael Reed.   New York, Doubleday, 1970.

No More Masks: An Anthology of Poems by Women, edited by Florence Howe and Ellen Bass.   New York, Doubleday, 1973.

Northwest Poets, edited by James Bertolino.   Madison, Wisconsin, Quixote Press, 1968.

The Norton Anthology of Modern Poetry, edited by Richard Ellman and Robert O'Clair.   New York, Norton, 1973.

The Now Voices: The Poetry of the Present, edited by Angelo Carli and Theodore Kilman.   New York, Scribner, 1971.

Of Poem.   New Rochelle, New York, Elizabeth Press, 1966.

Of Poetry and Power: Poems Occasioned by the Presidency and by the Death of John F. Kennedy, edited by Erwin A. Glikes and Paul Schwaber.   New York, Basic Books, 1964.

Off the Shelf, edited by A. K. Thomson.   Brisbane, Jacaranda Press, 1960.

The Old Pals' Act, edited by Pete Brown.   London, Allison and Busby, 1970.

On City Streets: An Anthology of Poetry, edited by Nancy Larrick.   New York, M. Evans, 1968.

On Native Grounds: Australian Writing from Meanjin Quarterly, edited by C. B. Cristesen.   Sydney and London, Angus and Robertson, 1968.

Once Again, edited by J. F. Bory.   New York, New Directions, 1968.

100 American Poems of the Twentieth Century, edited by Lawrence Perrine and J. M. Reid.   New York, Harcourt Brace, 1966.

100 More Story Poems, edited by Elinor Parker.   New York, Crowell, 1960.

100 Postwar Poems: British and American, edited by M. L. Rosenthal.   New York, Macmillan, 1968.

One Hundred Years of Alaska Poetry, Poetry Society of Alaska.   Denver, Swallow, 1966.

Open Poetry, edited by Ronald Gross and George Quasha.   New York, Simon and Schuster, 1973.

Out of the War Shadow, edited by Denise Levertov.   New York, War Resisters League, 1967.

The Oxford Book of Canadian Verse: In English and French, edited by A. J. M. Smith.   Toronto, Oxford University Press, 1960, 1965.

The Oxford Book of Twentieth Century Verse, edited by Philip Larkin.   Oxford, Clarendon Press, 1973.

The Oxford Book of Scottish Verse, edited by John MacQueen and Tom Scott.   Oxford, Clarendon Press, 1966.

The Partisan Review Anthology, edited by William Philips and Philip Rahv.   New York, Holt Rinehart, 1962.

The Penguin Book of Australian Verse, edited by Harry Heseltine. London, Penguin, 1972.

The Penguin Book of Canadian Verse, revised edition, edited by Ralph Gustafson. London, Penguin, 1967, 1975.

The Penguin Book of Contemporary Verse, 1918–1960, edited by Kenneth Allott. London, Penguin, 1962.

The Penguin Book of Irish Verse, edited by Brendan Kennelly. London, Penguin, 1970.

The Penguin Book of Modern Verse Translation, edited by George Steiner. London, Penguin, 1966.

The Penguin Book of New Zealand Verse, edited by Allan Curnow. London, Penguin, 1960; revised edition, edited by Douglas Stewart, 1966.

The Penguin Book of Scottish Verse, edited by Tom Scott. London, Penguin, 1970.

The Penguin Book of South African Verse, edited by Jack Cope and Uys Krige. London, Penguin, 1968.

Poems Addressed to Hugh MacDiarmid, edited by Duncan Glen. Preston, Lancashire, Akros, 1967.

Poems from Black Africa, edited by Langston Hughes. Bloomington, Indiana University Press, 1963.

Poems from Poetry and Jazz in Concert: An Anthology, edited by Jeremy Robson. London, Souvenir Press, 1969.

Poems from the Virginia Quarterly Review, 1925–1967. Charlottesville, University Press of Virginia, 1969.

Poems Now, edited by Hettie Jones. New York, Kulchur Press, 1966.

Poems of Black Africa, edited by Wole Soyinka. London, Secker and Warburg, 1973.

Poems of Doubt and Belief: An Anthology of Modern Religious Poetry, edited by Tom Driver and Robert Pack. New York, Macmillan, 1964.

Poems of North Carolina, edited by Richard Walser. New York, Garret and Massie, 1963.

Poems of Our Moment, edited by John Hollander. New York, Pegasus, 1968.

Poems of Protest, edited by Robin Wright. London, Studio Vista, 1966.

Poems of Protest Old and New: A Selection of Poems, edited by Arnold Kenseth. New York, Macmillan, and London, Collier Macmillan, 1968.

Poems of This Century, edited by C. B. Cox and A. E. Dyson. London, Arnold, 1968.

Poems of Today: Fifth Series, edited by Margaret Willey. London, Macmillan, 1963.

Poems Southwest, edited by A. Wilbur Stevens. Prescott, Arizona, Prescott College Press, 1968.

Poetica Moderna, edited by Mordecai S. Rubin. University, Alabama, University of Alabama Press, 1966.

Poetry: The Golden Anniversary Issue, edited by Henry Rago.   Chicago, University of Chicago Press, 1967.

Poetry: Introduction 1.   London, Faber, 1969. (And later volumes)

Poetry in Rhodesia: 75 Years, edited by D. E. Borrell.   Salisbury, The College Press, 1968.

Poetry 1900–1965: An Anthology, edited by George MacBeth.   London, Longman-Faber, 1967.

The Poetry of Black America: Anthology of the Twentieth Century, edited by Arnold Adoff.   New York, Harper, 1973.

Poetry of Mid-Century, 1940–1960, edited by Milton Wilson.   Toronto, McClelland and Stewart, 1964.

Poetry of Our Time: An Introduction to 20th Century Poetry Including Modern Canadian Poetry, edited by Louis Dudek.   Toronto, Macmillan, 1965.

Poetry of the Committed Individual: A "Stand" Anthology of Poetry, edited by Jon Silkin.   London, Penguin-Gollancz, 1973.

Poetry of the Forties, edited by Robin Skelton.   London, Penguin, 1968.

The Poetry of the Negro, 1946–1970, edited by Langston Hughes and Arna Bontemps.   New York, Doubleday, 1970.

Poetry of the 1940's, edited by Howard Sergeant.   London, Longman, 1970.

Poetry of the 1930's: An Anthology, edited by Allan Rodway.   London, Longman, 1967.

Poetry of the 1920's: An Anthology, edited by Sydney Bolt.   London, Longman, 1967.

Poetry of the Scots, edited by Tom Scott.   Oxford, Pergamon Press, 1970.

Poetry of the Thirties, edited by Robin Skelton.   London, Penguin, 1964.

The Poetry of War, 1939–1945, edited by Ian Hamilton.   London, Alan Ross, 1965.

A Poetry Reading Against the Vietnam War, edited by David Ray and Robert Bly.   Madison, Minnesota, American Writers Against the Vietnam War, 1966.

Poetry Southeast, edited by Frank Steele.   Martin, Tennessee Poetry Journal, 1968.

Poets: Gallery Series/One, edited by Wallace Kirkland.   Chicago, Harper Square Press, 1967.

Poet's Choice, edited by Paul Engle and Joseph Langland.   New York, Dial Press, 1962.

Poets of Contemporary Canada, 1960–1970, edited by Eli Mandel.   Toronto, McClelland and Stewart, 1972.

Poets of North Carolina, edited by Richard G. Walser.   Chapel Hill, University of North Carolina Press, 1963.

Poets of Our Time, edited by F. E. S. Finn.   London, Murray, 1965.

Poets of the Confederation, edited by Malcolm M. Ross.   Toronto, McClelland and Stewart, 1967.

Poets of the Midwest, edited by J. R. LeMaster.   Appalachia, Virginia, Young Publications, 1966.

Poets of the Twenties: 100 Great Poems, edited by Chad Powers Smith. Port Washington, New York, McCutcheon, 1967.

Poets of Today: A New American Anthology, edited by Walter Lowenfels. New York, International Publishers, 1964.

Poets on Street Corners, edited by Olga Carlisle.   New York, Random House, 1969.

Political Poetry, edited by David Ignatow.   New York, Chelsea, 1960.

Port Chicago Poets: A New Voice in Anthology, edited by Don Arthur Torgersen.   Chicago, International MSS, 1966.

Possibilities of Poetry: An Anthology of American Contemporaries, edited by Richard Kostelanetz.   New York, Dell, 1969.

Present-Day English Poetry, edited by A. J. Kirkman.   London, Hart Davis, 1966.

Psyche: The Feminine Poetic Consciousness, edited by Barbara Segnitz and Carol Rainey.   New York, Dial Press, 1973.

Quickly Aging Here: Some Poets of the 1970's, edited by Geof Hewitt. New York, Doubleday, 1969.

Ramblers, Gamblers and Lovers: A Book of Poetry, edited by Lawrence Swinburne. New York, McGraw Hill, 1968.

Recent Poetry in New Zealand, edited by Charles Doyle.   Auckland, Collins, 1965.

Red Clay Reader 2, edited by Charleen Whisnant.   Charlotte, North Carolina, Southern Review-Red Clay Reader, 1965. (And later volumes)

Reflections on a Gift of Watermelon Pickle and Other Modern Verse, edited by Stephen Dunning, Edward Lueders, and High Smith.   Flint, Michigan, Lothrop, 1966.

Revolution of the Word: A New Gathering of American Avant-Garde Poetry, edited by Jerome Rothenberg.   New York, Seabury Press, 1974.

Rising Early: Story Poems and Ballads of the Twentieth Century, edited by Charles Causley.   Leicester, Brockhampton Press, 1964; as *Modern Ballads and Story Poems*, New York, Watts, 1965.

Rising Tide: Twentieth Century American Women Poets, edited by Laura Chester and Sharon Barba.   New York, Washington Square Press, 1973.

A Rock Against the Wind: Black Love Poems, edited by Lindsay Patterson. New York, Dodd Mead, 1974.

The San Francisco Poets, edited by David Meltzer.   New York, Ballantine, 1971.

The Scottish Literary Revival: An Anthology of Twentieth Century Poetry, edited by George Bruce.   London, Collier Macmillan, 1968.

Scottish Poetry One, edited by George Bruce and others.   Edinburgh, Edinburgh University Press, 1966. (Published annually)

The Second Century Anthologies of Verse, edited by Roberta Allison Charlesworth and Dennis Lee.   Toronto, Oxford University Press, 1967.

Seeds of Liberation, edited by Paul Goodman.   New York, Braziller, 1965.

A Selection of Contemporary Religious Poetry, edited by Samuel A. Hazo.   Glen Rock, New Jersey, Paulist Press, 1963.

Settling America: The Ethnic Expression of Fourteen Contemporary Poets, edited by David Kherdian.   New York, Macmillan, 1974.

Seven Modern Poets: An Anthology, edited by J. R. Osgerby.   London, Chatto and Windus, 1968.

Seven Poets, edited by Edwin Thumboo.   Kuala Lumpur, University of Malaya Press, 1969.

Shake the Kaleidoscope: A New Anthology of Modern Poetry, edited by Milton Klonsky.   New York, Pocket Books, 1973.

Shouts and Murmurs: A Selection from "The Observer," edited by C. Dunn.   London, Hodder and Stoughton, 1963.

The Sixties: An Anthology of Poetry of the 1960's, edited by F. E. S. Finn.   London, Murray, 1970.

The Smith Poets.   New York, The Smith, 1971.

Some Haystacks Don't Even Have Any Needle and Other Complete Modern Poems, edited by Stephen Dunning and others.   Flint, Michigan, Lothrop, 1969.

Soon One Morning: New Writings by American Negroes, 1940–1962, edited by Herbert Hill.   New York, Knopf, 1963; as *Black Voices: New Writings by American Negroes*, London, Elek, 1964.

Soulscript: An Anthology of New Black Poetry, edited by June Jordan.   New York, Doubleday, 1970.

Soundings: New Canadian Poets, edited by Jack Ludwig and Andy Wainwright.   Toronto, House of Anansi, 1970.

Sounds and Silences: Poetry for Now, edited by Richard Peck.   New York, Delacorte Press, 1970.

South African Writing Today, edited by Nadine Gordimer and Lionel Abrahams.   London, Penguin, 1967.

Southern Poetry Review: A Decade of Poetry.   Raleigh, North Carolina State University, 1969.

Southern Writing in the Sixties, edited by John William Corrington and Miller Williams.   Baton Rouge, Louisiana State University Press, 2 vols., 1967.

Stop and Listen: An Anthology of Thirteen Living Poets, edited by John Fairfax.   London, Longman, 1969.

Storm Warning: The New Canadian Poets, edited by A. L. Purdy.   Toronto, McClelland and Stewart, 1971.

T. O. Now: The Young Toronto Poets, edited by Dennis Lee.   Toronto, House of Anansi, 1968.

T. S. Eliot: Homage from India, edited by P. Lal.   Calcutta, Writers Workshop, 1965.

Technicians of the Sacred: A Range of Poetries from Africa, America, Asia and Oceania, edited by Jerome Rothenberg. New York, Doubleday, 1968.

Ten Anglo-Welsh Poets, edited by Sam Adams. Cheadle, Cheshire, Carcanet Press, 1974.

Ten Contemporary Poets, edited by Maurice Woolman. London, Harrap, 1963.

Ten Irish Poets, edited by James Simmons. Cheadle, Cheshire, Carcanet Press, 1974.

Ten Poets of Our Time, edited by James M. Charlton. London, Macmillan, 1966.

Ten Twentieth Century Poets, edited by William Stanley Bunnell. Bath, Somerset, Brodie, 1963.

Ten Years of Quest, edited by Abu Sayeed Ayyub and Amlan Datta. Bombay, Manaktala, and Edinburgh, Chambers, 1966.

The Terrible Rain: The War Poets, 1939–1945, edited by Brian Gardner. London, Methuen, 1966.

Thirteen American Poets, edited by Kirby Congdon. Preston, Lancashire, Akros, 1966.

31 New American Poets, edited by Ron Schreiber. New York, Hill and Wang, 1969.

This Day and Age: An Anthology of Modern Poetry in English, edited by Stanley Hewett. London, Arnold, 1960.

Thumbprints: An Anthology of Hitchhiking Poems, edited by Douglas Fetherling. Toronto, Peter Martin, 1969.

Today's Negro Voices: An Anthology of Young Negro Poets, edited by Beatrice Murphy. New York, Messner, 1970.

Today's Poets: American and British Poetry since the 1930's, edited by Chad Walsh. New York, Scribner, 1964.

Tunes on a Tin Whistle: Some Real-Life Poetry, edited by Alan Crang. Oxford, Pergamon Press, 1967.

Twelve American Poets, edited by Stephen E. Whicher and Lars Ahnebrink. New York, Oxford University Press, 1961.

Twelve Modern Scottish Poets, edited by Charles King. London, University of London Press, 1971.

Twelve Poets, 1950–1970, edited by Alexander Craig. Brisbane, Jacaranda Press, 1971.

12 Poets and 1 Painter, edited by Donald Allen. San Francisco, Four Seasons Foundation, 1964.

Twentieth-Century American Poetry, revised edition, edited by Conrad Aiken. New York, Modern Library, 1963.

Twentieth Century Love Poems, edited by C. B. Cox and A. E. Dyson. Hull, Yorkshire, Critical Quarterly, 1964.

Twentieth Century Love Poems, edited by John Smith. London, Studio Vista, 1969.

Twentieth Century Love Poetry, edited by S. Bolt. London, Hutchinson, 1969.

Twentieth Century Parody: American and British, edited by Buling Lowrey. New York, Harcourt Brace, 1960.

Twentieth Century Poetry, edited by Carol Marshall.   Boston, Houghton Mifflin, 1971.

23 Modern British Poets, edited by John Matthias.   Chicago, Swallow Press, 1971.

Understanding the New Black Poetry: Black Speech and Black Music as Poetic References, edited by Stephen Henderson.   New York, Morrow, 1972.

A Unicorn Folio.   Santa Barbara, California, Unicorn Press, 1969.

Up the Line to Death, edited by Brian Gardner.   London, Methuen, 1964.

Verse in Australia.   Adelaide, Australian Letters, 1960. (And later volumes)

Vibrations: Poems of Youth, edited by George Bowering.   Toronto, Gage, 1970.

The Vital Decade: 10 Years of Australian Art and Letters, edited by Geoffrey Dutton and Max Harris.   Melbourne, Sun Books, 1968.

The Voice of Black Africa, edited by Howard Sergeant.   Oxford, Pergamon Press, 1970.

The Voice of Poetry: An Anthology from 1930 to the Present Day, revised edition, edited by Hermann Peschmann.   London, Evans, 1969.

The Voice That Is Great Within Us: An Anthology of Contemporary American Poetry, edited by Hayden Carruth.   New York, Bantam, 1970.

War Poems, edited by Diane di Prima.   New York, Poets Press, 1968.

War Poetry: An Anthology, edited by D. L. Jones.   Oxford, Pergamon Press, 1968.

We Speak As Liberators: New Black Poets Speak, edited by Orde Coombs. New York, Dodd Mead, 1970.

Welsh Voices: An Anthology of New Poetry from Wales, edited by Bryn Griffiths.   London, Dent, 1967.

West African Verse: An Anthology, edited by Donatus Ibe Nwoga.   London, Longman, 1967.

West Coast Seen, edited by John Brown and others.   Vancouver, Talonbooks, 1969.

A Western Sampler: 9 Contemporary Poets.   Georgetown, California, Talisman Press, 1963.

Where Is Vietnam? American Poets Respond, edited by Walter Lowenfels and Nan Braymer.   New York, Doubleday, 1967.

Where Steel Winds Blow: An Anthology of Anti-War Poetry, edited by R. Cromie.   New York, McKay, 1969.

The Whispering Wind: Poetry by Young American Indians, edited by Terry Allen.   New York, Doubleday, 1972.

Without Adam: The Femina Anthology of Poetry, edited by Joan Murray Simpson. London, Femina Books, 1968.

The Women Poets in English: An Anthology, edited by Ann Stanford.   New York, McGraw Hill, 1972.

The Word Is Here: Poetry from Modern Africa, edited by Keorapetse Kgosit-sile. New York, Doubleday, 1973.

Words from the House of the Dead: An Anthology of Prison Writings from Soledad, edited by Joseph Bruchac and William Witherup. Greenfield Center, New York, Greenfield Review Press, 1971.

The World Anthology: Poems from the St. Mark's Poetry Project, and *Another World*, edited by Anne Waldman. Indianapolis, Bobbs Merrill, 1969, 1971.

Writers Workshop Miscellany. Calcutta, Writers Workshop, 1966.

Writing in England Today: The Last Fifteen Years, edited by Karl Miller. London, Penguin, 1968.

The Writing on the Wall: 108 American Poets of Protest, edited by Walter Lowenfels. New York, Doubleday, 1969.

You Better Believe It: Black Verse in English from Africa, The West Indies, and the United States, edited by Paul Breman. London, Penguin, 1973.

The Young American Poets, edited by Paul Carroll. Chicago, Follett, 1968.

The Young British Poets, edited by Jeremy Robson. London, Chatto and Windus, 1971.

Young Commonwealth Poets '65, edited by P. L. Brent. London, Heinemann, 1965.

NOTES ON ADVISERS
AND
CONTRIBUTORS

ABDUL MAJID BIN NABI BAKSH. Assistant Lecturer in English, University of Malaya, Kuala Lumpur. Author of *Critical History of the Filipino Novel in English.* **Essays:** Carlos A. Angeles, p. 33; Ricaredo Demetillo, p. 364; Edith Tiempo, p. 1545.

ACKERSON, Duane. Assistant Professor of English and Director of Creative Writing, Idaho State University, Pocatello; Editor, *The Dragonfly,* Pocatello. Verse pamphlets include *UA Flight to Chicago,* 1971, *Inventory,* 1971, *Old Movie House,* 1972, and *Weathering,* 1974. Fiction published in magazines and the anthology *Generation,* 1973. **Essays:** James Den Boer, p. 366; Russell Edson, p. 425; Vi Gale, p. 527; Geof Hewitt, p. 679; Robert Huff, p. 744; David Jaffin, p. 772; Chester Kallman, p. 809; John Knoepfle, p. 844; James Koller, p. 850; Tom McKeown, p. 1025; Richard Shelton, p. 1390; Adrien Stoutenburg, p. 1504; Keith Wilson, p. 1701.

ADCOCK, Fleur. See her entry on p. 19. **Essays:** Basil Dowling, p. 390; Bill Manhire, p. 989; George McWhirter, p. 1029; Dabney Stuart, p. 1515; Ian Wedde, p. 1645; Herbert Williams, p. 1689.

ALLEN, Donald. Associated with the Grove Press, since 1950; Editor, with Barney Rosset, of *The Evergreen Review,* 1957–59, and West Coast Editor since 1960; Owner, The Grey Fox Press, Bolinas, California. Editor, *Selected Poems of Lorca,* 1955; *The New American Poetry 1945–60,* 1960; *New American Story* (with Robert Creeley), 1965; *New Writing in the U.S.A.* (with Creeley), 1967; *The Collected Poems of Frank O'Hara,* 1970; *Poetics of the New American Poetry* (with Warren Tallman), 1973. Translator of *Four Plays* by Ionesco, 1958.

ANDRÉ, Michael. Editor of *Unmuzzled Ox* magazine, New York. Author of *Get Serious* (verse), 1973. Contributor to *Art News,* New York. **Essays:** Bill Bissett, p. 123; Robin Blaser, p. 130; Michael Brownstein, p. 193; Paul Carroll, p. 232; Kenward Elmslie, p. 432; Gene Fowler, p. 506; Walter Lowenfels, p. 942; bpNichol, p. 1113; Jeff Nuttall, p. 1128; James Schuyler, p. 1353.

AUGUSTINE, Jane. Adjunct Lecturer, John Jay College, City University of New York; Member of the Editorial Board, *Aphra,* a feminist literary quarterly. Poems published in little magazines. **Essays:** Richard Kostelanetz, p. 855; Rochelle Owens, p. 1157; Marge Piercy, p. 1186; Judith Johnson Sherwin, p. 1392; Mary Ellen Solt, p. 1457; Constance Urdang, p. 1585.

BAKER, Houston A., Jr. Professor of English, University of Virginia, Charlottesville. Taught at Yale University, New Haven, Connecticut, 1968–70. Author of *Long Black Song: Essays in Black American Literature and Culture,* 1972, and *Singers of Daybreak: Studies in Black American Literature,* 1974. Editor of *Black Literature in America,* 1971, and *Twentieth-Century Interpretations of "Native Son,"* 1972. **Essays:** James A. Emanuel, p. 434; Nikki Giovanni, p. 553; Carolyn M. Rodgers, p. 1293.

BAKER, Roger. Free-lance Writer. Author of *The Book of London,* 1968; *Drag: A History of Female Impersonation on the Stage,* 1968. Regular Book Reviewer for *The Times,* and *Books and Bookmen*; contributor to *Daily Telegraph Magazine, Queen, Harper's,* and *Illustrated London News.* **Essay:** Laurence Collinson, p. 273.

BEAVER, Bruce. See his entry on p. 63. **Essays:** Vincent Buckley, p. 206; Rosemary Dobson, p. 385; Geoffrey Dutton, p. 410; Gwen Harwood, p. 653; Geoffrey Lehmann, p. 888; Les A. Murray, p. 1095; Grace Perry, p. 1176; Hal Porter, p. 1202; Francis Webb, p. 1638.

BEETON, D. R. Professor of English, University of South Africa, Pretoria. Author of two radio series, *From Cape to Zambezi: A Survey of South African English Poetry* and *New Voices: Some Contemporary South African Poets and Their Work.* Co-Editor of *South Africa Poetry: A Critical Anthology,* 1966. Verse published in *The Penguin Book of South African Verse,* 1968, and in magazines. **Essay:** Sydney Clouts, p. 259.

BELL, Charles G. See his entry on p. 78. **Essay:** Galway Kinnell, p. 829.

BENESA, Leonidas V. Lecturer, Silliman University, Philippines. Editor, *Solidarity* and *Signatures* magazines. President of the Art Association of the Philippines. **Essay:** Emmanuel Torres, p. 1559.

BERGÉ, Carol. See her entry on p. 98. **Essays:** Isabella Stewart Gardner, p. 527; LeRoi Jones, p. 799; Michael McClure, p. 1008; Howard Moss, p. 1086.

BERGONZI, Bernard. Senior Lecturer in English, University of Warwick. Author of *Descartes and the Animals,* 1954; *The Early H. G. Wells,* 1961; *Heroes Twilight,* 1965; *The Situation of the Novel,* 1970; *T. S. Eliot,* 1971. Contributor to *The Observer, TLS,* and other periodicals. **Essays:** Robert Conquest, p. 288; Malcolm Cowley, p. 317; Gavin Ewart, p. 462; Colin Falck, p. 469; David Gascoyne, p. 536; Geoffrey Grigson, p. 592; Rayner Heppenstall, p. 674; John Holloway, p. 714; Richard Kell, p. 815; Norman MacCaig, p. 953; Nicholas Moore, p. 1072; Philip Oakes, p. 1133; Edgell Rickword, p. 1275; Philip Toynbee, p. 1562.

BERTRAM, James. Associate Professor of English, Victoria University of Wellington. Editor of *Phoenix,* 1932; associated with the founding of *Landfall,* 1946. Author of several books on China; Editor of *New Zealand Letters of Thomas Arnold the Younger,* 1966; contributor to *Student Guide to English Poetry,* 1969. **Essays:** Fleur Adcock, p. 19; Rewi Alley, p. 20; James K. Baxter, p. 1745; Alistair Campbell, p. 227; Ruth Dallas, p. 344; Owen Leeming, p. 887; Vincent O'Sullivan, p. 1155.

BIRNEY, Earle. See his entry on p. 118.

BLOOM, Harold. Professor of English, Yale University, New Haven, Connecticut. Author of several books on Blake and the Romantics; his most recent books are *Ringers in the Tower: Studies in the Romantic Tradition,* 1971, *Yeats,* 1972, and *The Anxiety of Influence: A Theory of Poetry,* 1973. **Essay:** John Hollander, p. 707.

BLY, Robert. See his entry on p. 139. **Essay:** Donald Hall, p. 617.

BODE, Carl. Professor of English, University of Maryland, College Park, since 1947. Author of two volumes of verse and several books on American culture, the most recent being *Antebellum Culture,* 1970, *Midcentury America: Life in the 1850's,* 1972, and *Mencken,* 1973, Editor of several volumes of Thoreau's writings, *The Young Rebel in American Literature,* 1959, and *Ralph Waldo Emerson,* 1968. **Essay:** Chad Walsh, p. 1618.

BORKLUND, Elmer. Associate Professor of English, Pennsylvania State University, University Park. Former Associate Editor, *The Chicago Review.* Articles and reviews published in *Modern Philology, Commentary, New York Herald Tribune Book Week, Journal of General Education;* literary entries in *The World Book Encyclopedia.* **Essays:** Charles G. Bell, p. 78; Randall Jarrell, p. 1766; James Michie, p. 1076; Frederick Morgan, p. 1080; Elder Olson, p. 1141; Delmore Schwartz, p. 1796; R. G. Vliet, p. 1598.

BOSTIC, Corrine. Part-time Faculty Member, Quinsigamond Community College, Worcester, Massachusetts; Radio Broadcaster, WTAG and WICN-FM. Author of *Requiem for Bluesville* (verse), 1970; *The Horns of Freedom* (play), 1971; *Blacks* (essay), 1972. Editor of *Message in Black*, 1971. **Essays:** Victor Hernández Cruz, p. 331; Calvin C. Hernton, p. 677.

BOYERS, Robert. Member of the English Department, Skidmore College, Saratoga Springs, New York; Editor of *Salmagundi* magazine. Author of *Contemporary Poetry in America*, 1975. Editor, with Michael London, *Robert Lowell: The Poet in His Time*, 1969. **Essays:** Ben Belitt, p. 75; Alan Dugan, p. 395; Irving Feldman, p. 475; Louise Glück, p. 563; John Logan, p. 928; David Wagoner, p. 1602; Richard Wilbur, p. 1676.

BRADISH, Gaynor F. Visiting Lecturer at the State University of New York at Albany. Head of the Playwrights' Unit, Actor's Studio, New York, 1962–63; Head of the Dunster Drama Workshop, Harvard University; first director of Department of Dramatic Literature at New York University, to 1968. Director of *Asylum* by Arthur Kopit, New York, 1963. Drama Advisor, Hill and Wang publishers, 1961–67. Author of Introduction to Kopit's *Oh Dad, Poor Dad . . .*, 1960. **Essays:** Kay Boyle, p. 159; M. L. Rosenthal, p. 1304; Thomas Whitbread, p. 1663.

BRATHWAITE, Edward. See his entry on p. 163. **Essays:** Martin Carter, p. 235; Frank Collymore, p. 275; Wilson Harris, p. 638; Anthony McNeill, p. 1027; A. J. Seymour, p. 1376.

BROWNJOHN, Alan. See his entry on p. 190. **Essays:** Allen Ginsberg, p. 549; Ian Hamilton, p. 628; Peter Porter, p. 1205; W. D. Snodgrass, p. 1452.

BRUCE, George. See his entry on p. 195. **Essays:** Tom Buchan, p. 201; Stewart Conn, p. 284; Helen B. Cruickshank, p. 330; Robin Fulton, p. 524; Duncan Glen, p. 559; Alastair Mackie, p. 963; Joseph Macleod, p. 971; Pete Morgan, p. 1082; Alistair Reid, p. 1262; Sydney Tremayne, p. 1564.

BRUCHAC, Joseph. Editor of *The Greenfield Review*, Greenfield Center, New York. Taught in Ghana, 1966–69. Author of the poetry pamphlets *Indian Mountain*, 1971, *The Buffalo in the Syracuse Zoo*, 1972, and *Great Meadow Words of Hearsay and Heresy*, 1973, and of *The Poetry of Pop*, 1974. Editor of *Words from the House of the Dead: Anthology of Prison Writings from Soledad* (with William Witherup), 1971. **Essays:** Chinua Achebe, p. 13; Syl Cheyney-Coker, p. 242; Michael Echeruo, p. 422; Taban lo Liyong, p. 923; John Okai, p. 1138; James Welch, p. 1650.

BURNS, Jim. See his entry on p. 220. **Essays:** Ray Bremser, p. 169; Michael Horovitz, p. 724; Barry MacSweeney, p. 979.

BYRD, Don. Member of the English Department, State University of New York, Albany. Verse and criticism published in periodicals. Currently completing a book on Charles Olson. **Essays:** Kenneth Irby, p. 763; Joanne Kyger, p. 864; Jackson Mac Low, p. 974.

CALLAN, Edward. Professor of English, Western Michigan University, Kalamazoo. Author of *W. H. Auden: Annotated Checklist*, 1958; *Albert Luthuli*, 1961; *Alan Paton*, 1968. Editor of *The Long View* by Alan Paton, 1968. Book reviews published in *Saturday Review*, and essays on Auden and Yeats published in periodicals. **Essay:** John Woods, p. 1712.

CAREW, Rivers. Editor of *The Dublin Magazine* since 1963. Author of *Figures Out of Mist* (with Timothy Brownlow), 1967. Verse published in *The Penguin Book of Irish Verse*, 1970, and in periodicals. **Essays:** Monk Gibbon, p. 543; Valentin Iremonger, p. 766; Michael Longley, p. 932; Richard Weber, p. 1643.

CARRUTH, Hayden. See his entry on p. 233. **Essays:** Carol Bergé, p. 98; Wendell Berry, p. 109; Philip Booth, p. 148; Robert Creeley, p. 322; Thomas Hornsby Ferrill, p. 479; Arthur Gregor, p. 586; Kenneth Koch, p. 848; James Laughlin, p.

876; James Merrill, p. 1037; W. S. Merwin, p. 1039; Adrienne Rich, p. 1270; Harvey Shapiro, p. 1385; Diane Wakoski, p. 1607; Louis Zukofsky, p. 1739.

CAUSLEY, Charles.   See his entry on p. 238. **Essay:** Jack Clemo, p. 255.

CHAMBERS, D. D. C.   Assistant Professor of English, Trinity College, Toronto. **Essays:** Leonard Cohen, p. 267; John Robert Colombo, p. 279; David Helwig, p. 667; George Jonas, p. 789; William Stafford, p. 1478; Ian Young, p. 1732.

CHARTERS, Samuel.   Poet, Critic, and Music Historian. His most recent books are *From a Swedish Notebook* (verse), *Some Poems/Poets* (critical studies), *Robert Johnson: A Life*, *The Songs*, and *The Legacy of the Blues*. **Essays:** James Broughton, p. 182; Larry Eigner, p. 427; Philip Lamantia, p. 868.

CHURCH, Richard.   Poet, Novelist, and Critic. His most recent volumes were *The Burning Bush* (verse), 1967, *Prince Albert* (novel), 1963, and *The Wonder of Words*, 1970. Died, 1972. **Essays:** Edmund Blunden, p. 134; Patric Dickinson, p. 378; Ruth Pitter, p. 1194; William Plomer, p. 1198.

CLARK, Alan.   Librarian since 1957, currently with the Royal Society Library, London; has conducted poetry courses at Braziers Park Adult College, Ipsden, Oxfordshire. Essay on Laura Riding published in *Stand*. **Essay:** Laura Riding, p. 1278.

CLARKE, Austin.   See his entry on p. 252. **Essays:** Seamus Heaney, p. 662; Pearce Hutchinson, p. 756; Brendan Kennelly, p. 823; Ewart Milne, p. 1056; Desmond O'Grady, p. 1136.

CLUYSENAAR, Anne.   See her entry on p. 261. **Essays:** Wayne Brown, p. 188; John Cotton, p. 312; Oswald Mtshali, p. 1089; Christopher Pilling, p. 1190; Michael Smith, p. 1440; Daniel Weissbort, p. 1649.

COHEN, Arthur A.   Author of *In the Days of Simon Stern* (novel), 1973, and *Osip Emilevich Mandelstam: An Essay in Antiphon*, 1974. **Essay:** David Shapiro, p. 1384.

COLOMBO, John Robert.   See his entry on p. 279. **Essays:** Patrick Anderson, p. 30; Margaret Atwood, p. 37; George Bowering, p. 154; Elizabeth Brewster, p. 171; Frederick Cogswell, p. 265; Ronald Everson, p. 457; Doug Fetherling, p. 481; Don Gutteridge, p. 613; Daryl Hine, p. 687; Harry Howith, p. 738; Lionel Kearns, p. 814; Dennis Lee, p. 882; Douglas LePan, p. 893; Gwendolyn MacEwen, p. 961; Eli Mandel, p. 987; Seymour Mayne, p. 1000; David McFadden, p. 1017; Glen Siebrasse, p. 1394; Miriam Waddington, p. 1600; Wilfred Watson, p. 1637.

COOKSON, William.   Editor of *Agenda*, London. **Essays:** Anne Beresford, p. 94; Peter Dale, p. 241; Peter Levi, p. 903; Tom Scott, p. 1362; Charles Tomlinson, p. 1554; Peter Whigham, p. 1659.

COOLEY, John R.   Assistant Professor of English, Western Michigan University, Kalamazoo. Essays on Thomas Hardy, Eudora Welty, and Stephen Crane published in periodicals. **Essays:** George Economou, p. 424; Leonard Nathan, p. 1104; Thomas Parkinson, p. 1168.

COONEY, Seamus.   Associate Professor of English, Western Michigan University, Kalamazoo. Editor of *By the Well of Living and Seeing: New and Selected Poems* by Charles Reznikoff, 1974. Author of essays on Byron, Scott, Lawrence, Binyon, and Austin Clarke. **Essays:** David Bromige, p. 178; Cid Corman, p. 302; Theodore Enslin, p. 447; Patricia Goedicke, p. 568; Jonathan Greene, p. 584; Jack Hirschman, p. 689; Ron Loewinsohn, p. 926; David Meltzer, p. 1033; Bert Meyers, p. 1042; F. D. Reeve, p. 1256; Stephen Stepanchev, p. 1491; Nancy Willard, p. 1681.

COTTON, John.   See his entry on p. 312. **Essays:** Alan Brownjohn, p. 190; Jim Burns, p. 220; Bob Cobbing, p. 262; David Holbrook, p. 701; Molly Holden, p. 704; Glyn Hughes, p. 746; B. S. Johnson, p. 780; James Kirkup, p. 836; Edward

Lucie-Smith, p. 945; John Mole, p. 1067; Sally Purcell, p. 1221; Peter Scupham, p. 1368; James Simmons, p. 1404; C. H. Sisson, p. 1417; Ted Walker, p. 1615.

DAMASHEK, Richard. Assistant Professor of Literature, Sangamon State University, Springfield, Illinois; Book Reviewer, *Books Abroad*, Norman, Oklahoma. Author of essays on Randall Jarrell and Ingmar Bergman. **Essays:** R. H. W. Dillard, p. 381; Paul Petrie, p. 1181; Ruth Whitman, p. 1669.

DAVIES, Aneirin Talfan. Head of Programmes, BBC, Wales. Author of *Dylan: Druid of the Broken Body*, 1965. Editor of *The Colour of Saying: An Anthology of Verse Spoken by Dylan Thomas*, 1963. **Essay:** David Jones, p. 793.

DELIUS, Anthony. See his entry on p. 362. **Essay:** David Wright, p. 1714.

DESY, Peter. Instructor in English, University of Akron, Ohio. Verse published in magazines and anthologies. **Essay:** Robert Vas Dias, p. 1592.

DEUTSCH, Babette. See her entry on p. 368. **Essays.** Elizabeth Bishop, p. 121; John Crowe Ransom, p. 1240.

DILLARD, R. H. W. See his entry on p. 381. **Essays:** George Garrett, p. 533; Julia Randall, p. 1236; David Slavitt, p. 1428.

DOEPKE, Dale. Member of the English Department, University of Akron, Ohio. Author of essays on 19th and 20th century American literature. **Essays:** Jane Cooper, p. 296; R. P. Dickey, p. 374.

DORSINVILLE, Max. Assistant Professor of English, McGill University, Montreal. Author of *Caliban Without Prospero: An Essay on Quebec and Black Literature*, 1974, and articles in *PMLA*, *Canadian Literature*, and *Livres et Auteurs Quebeçois*. **Essays:** Joan Finnigan, p. 493; Michael Gnarowski, p. 565.

DUDEK, Louis. See his entry on p. 393. **Essays:** D. G. Jones, p. 792; James Reaney, p. 1246.

DUNN, Douglas. See his entry on p. 403. **Essay:** Shirley Toulson, p. 1560.

DYMENT, Clifford. Poet and Free-Lance Writer. His last volume was *Collected Poems*, 1970. Died, 1971. **Essay:** C. Day Lewis, p. 1751.

EAGLETON, Terry. Faculty member, Jesus College, Cambridge. Author of *The New Left*, 1966, and *Shakespeare and Society*, 1967. **Essay:** Jon Silkin, p. 1397.

EMANUEL, James A. See his entry on p. 434.

EWART, Gavin. See his entry on p. 462. **Essay:** Harold Massingham, p. 993.

EZEKIEL, Nissim. See his entry on p. 464. **Essay:** Kamala Das, p. 351.

FERNANDO, Lloyd. Professor and Head of the English Department, University of Malaya, Kuala Lumpur; Co-Editor, *Tenggara* magazine, Kuala Lumpur. Editor of *Twenty-Two Malaysian Stories*, 1968. Compiler of annual bibliography of Malaysia-Singapore for *Journal of Commonwealth Literature*, Leeds. **Essay:** Wong Phui Nam, p. 1707.

FLETCHER, Ian. See his entry on p. 501. **Essays:** Terence Tiller, p. 1547; John Wain, p. 1604.

FRANCIS, Carol A. Instructor in English, Roosevelt University, Chicago. **Essay:** Louis Untermeyer, p. 1577.

FRASER, G. S. See his entry on p. 512. **Essays:** Samuel Beckett, p. 64; Ronald Bottrall, p. 152; Lawrence Durrell, p. 405; William Empson, p. 436; Philip Hobsbaum, p. 694; Kathleen Raine, p. 1226; I. A. Richards, p. 1271; Sacheverell Sitwell, p. 1419; Constantine Trypanis, p. 1568.

FRIEDMAN, Norman. Professor of English, Queens College, City University of New York. Author of *E. E. Cummings: The Art of His Poetry*, 1960; *Poetry: An Introduction to Its Form and Art* (with C. A. McLaughlin), 1961; *Logic, Rhetoric and Style* (with McLaughlin), 1963; *E. E. Cummings: The Growth of a Writer*, 1964; *Love and the Mortality of Freedom*, 1965. Editor of *E. E. Cummings: A Collection of Critical Essays*, 1972. Verse published in anthologies. **Essays:** John Ashbery, p. 34; Kenneth Burke, p. 216; Robert Francis, p. 510; Richard Howard, p. 730; Barbara Howes, p. 735; Vern Rutsala, p. 1327; Louis Simpson, p. 1408; James Wright, p. 1716.

FULTON, Robin. See his entry on p. 524. **Essays:** Anne Cluysenaar, p. 261; Elaine Feinstein, p. 473; James Fenton, p. 476; David Gill, p. 547; Daniel Huws, p. 758; Alan Riddell, p. 1277; Derick S. Thomson, p. 1541; Kenneth White, p. 1665.

GATES, Norman T. Associate Professor of English, Rider College, Trenton, New Jersey. Author of *The Poetry of Richard Aldington*, 1974. **Essays:** Francis Warner, p. 1623; James Whitehead, p. 1668.

GERMAIN, Edward B. Assistant Professor of English, Pomona College, Claremont, California. Editor of *Flag of Ecstasy: Selected Poems of Charles Henri Ford*, 1972, and a forthcoming anthology, *The Surrealist Poem in English*. **Essays:** Robert Dana, p. 345; Charles Henri Ford, p. 503; Ron Padgett, p. 1163; Edouard Roditi, p. 1294.

GILBERT, S. R. Instructor in Drama and Canadian Literature, Capilano College, North Vancouver. Author of the play *A Glass Darkly*, published in *Dialogue and Dialectic*, 1972. **Essays:** Stanley Cooperman, p. 298; Charles Doyle, p. 391; Phyllis Gotlieb, p. 572; J. Michael Yates, p. 1723.

GNAROWSKI, Michael. See his entry on p. 565. **Essays:** Milton Acorn, p. 16; Douglas Barbour, p. 56; Henry Beissel, p. 73; Dorothy Livesay, p. 919; John Newlove, p. 1112; David Wevill, p. 1653.

GREENBERG, Alvin. Professor of English, Macalester College, St. Paul. Author of several volumes of verse – *The Metaphysical Giraffe*, 1968, *The House of the Would-Be Gardener*, 1972, and *Dark Lands*, 1973 – and a novel, *Going Nowhere*, 1971. Former Editor of *Minnesota Review*. **Essay:** Margaret Randall, p. 1238.

GUNN, Thom. See his entry on p. 605. **Essay:** Gary Snyder, p. 1454.

GUSTAFSON, Ralph. See his entry on p. 608. **Essays:** Louis Dudek, p. 393; Robert Finch, p. 486; Michael Ondaatje, p. 1145; Raymond Souster, p. 1461.

HALL, Donald. See his entry on p. 617. **Essay:** Robert Lowell, p. 938.

HALL, Rodney. See his entry on p. 621. **Essays:** A. D. Hope, p. 721; Roger McDonald, p. 1013.

HARNETT, Ruth. Lecturer in English, Rhodes University, Grahamstown, South Africa. **Essays:** Guy Butler, p. 225; Anne Welsh, p. 1652.

HEATON, David M. Associate Professor of Comparative Literature, and Chairman of the Undergraduate English Program, Ohio University, Athens. Verse, verse translations, and articles on Ted Hughes and Alan Sillitoe published in periodicals. **Essays:** George P. Elliott, p. 430; Alan Stephens, p. 1492.

HEWITT, Geof. See his entry on p. 679. **Essays:** Léonie Adams, p. 17; Marvin Bell, p. 83; Michael Benedikt, p. 88; Richard Brautigan, p. 167; Peter Davison, p. 355; Bob Dylan, p. 412; Edward Field, p. 483; George Hitchcock, p. 691; Richard Hugo, p. 752; Ronald Johnson, p. 784; Robert Kelly, p. 817; Bill Knott, p. 846;

William Matthews, p. 998; George Oppen, p. 1147; Sylvia Plath, p. 1790; Muriel Rukeyser, p. 1321; Aram Saroyan, p. 1334; Gilbert Sorrentino, p. 1458; Robert Sward, p. 1519; James Tate, p. 1533; Theodore Weiss, p. 1647; Jonathan Williams, p. 1694.

HEYEN, William. Associate Professor of English, State University College, Brockport, New York. Author of *Depth of Field* (verse), 1970, and *Noise in the Trees: Poems and a Memoir*, 1974. Editor of *A Profile of Theodore Roethke*, 1971. **Essays:** Lucien Stryk, p. 1512; Hollis Summers, p. 1517; Lewis Turco, p. 1570.

HILL, Douglas. Free-lance Writer. Author of several books, including *John Keats*, 1968, *Regency London*, 1969, and *Magic and Superstition*, 1969. Verse published in periodicals and anthologies. **Essays:** Bernard Kops, p. 852; Jeremy Robson, p. 1288.

HOBSBAUM, Philip. See his entry on p. 694. **Essays:** Francis Berry, p. 106; Keith Bosley, p. 150; Stanley Cook, p. 293; Jeni Couzyn, p. 315; Frederick Grubb, p. 596; Christopher Levenson, p. 898; Derek Mahon, p. 983; Roy McFadden, p. 1016; Matthew Mead, p. 1030; Eric Millward, p. 1054; Paul Muldoon, p. 1092; Robert Nye, p. 1131; E. J. Scovell, p. 1365; John Tripp, p. 1566; Lotte Zurndorfer, p. 1742.

HOEFER, Jacqueline. Member of the English Department, San Francisco State College. Essays on Beckett and other modern writers published in periodicals. **Essay:** Katherine Hoskins, p. 725.

HOFFMAN, Daniel. See his entry on p. 697. **Essays:** A. R. Ammons, p. 27; John Berryman, p. 1748; Abbie Huston Evans, p. 453; William Meredith, p. 1035; William Jay Smith, p. 1446; Robert Penn Warren, p. 1633.

HOPE, A. D. See his entry on p. 721. **Essay:** Judith Wright, p. 1720.

HUDSON, Theodore R. Associate Professor of English, District of Columbia Teachers College. Author of *A LeRoi Jones (Amiri Baraka) Bibliography*, 1971, and *From LeRoi Jones to Amiri Baraka: The Literary Works*, 1973. Regular contributor to *Bibliographic Survey: The Negro in Print*. **Essays:** Lucille Clifton, p. 258; Don L. Lee, p. 883; Larry Neal, p. 1109; Sonia Sanchez, p. 1329; Margaret Walker, p. 1613.

JAMES, Charles L. Associate Professor of English, Swarthmore College, Pennsylvania. Author of *The Black Writer in America* (bibliography), 1969. Editor of *From the Roots: Short Stories by Black Americans*, 1970. Currently working on a study of Arna Bontemps. **Essays:** Michael S. Harper, p. 636; Etheridge Knight, p. 842; Donald Petersen, p. 1180; Ishmael Reed, p. 1254.

JAMES, Louis. Senior Lecturer in English and American Literature, University of Kent, Canterbury. Author of *The Islands in Between*, 1968. **Essay:** Derek Walcott, p. 1609.

JENNINGS, Elizabeth. See her entry on p. 775. **Essays:** Henry Reed, p. 1250; Michael Schmidt, p. 1347.

JONES, Eldred D. Professor of English, Fourah Bay College, University of Sierra Leone, Freetown. Author of *Othello's Countrymen: The Africans in English Renaissance Drama*, 1955, and *African Literature Today*, 1973. **Essays:** Lenrie Peters, p. 1178; Wole Soyinka, p. 1464.

JONES, Glyn. See his entry on p. 796. **Essays:** Leslie Norris, p. 1122; R. S. Thomas, p. 1539.

KEESING, Nancy. Free-lance Writer. Author of *Showground Sketch* (verse), 1968; *Douglas Stewart*, 1965, the children's novel *By Gravel and Gum*, 1963. Editor of

Australian Bush Ballads, 1955, and *Old Bush Songs*, 1957, both with Douglas Stewart, and *Australian Short Stories*, 1970. **Essays:** Douglas Stewart, p. 1499; Randolph Stow, p. 1507.

KENDLE, Burton.   Professor of English, Roosevelt University, Chicago. Articles on Lawrence, Chekhov, and John Cheever published in magazines. **Essays:** John William Corrington, p. 308; Paul Dehn, p. 359; Sandra Hochman, p. 696; Phyllis McGinley, p. 1018; Robert Pack, p. 1161; May Sarton, p. 1336; Muriel Spark, p. 1468; Peter Viereck, p. 1594; Rex Warner, p. 1624.

KENNELLY, Brendan.   See his entry on p. 823. **Essay:** Michael Hartnett, p. 649.

KINSELIA, Thomas.   See his entry on p. 833. **Essays:** Austin Clarke, p. 252; Richard Murphy, p. 1094.

KORGES, James.   Free-lance Writer. Author of *Erskine Caldwell*, 1969. Editor of *Critique: Studies in Modern Fiction*, 1962–70. **Essays:** Howard Baker, p. 52; Edgar Bowers, p. 156; Charles Gullans, p. 604; Vassar Miller, p. 1053; Paul Ramsay, p. 1232.

KOSTELANETZ, Richard.   See his entry on p. 855. **Essays:** Clark Coolidge, p. 295; Emmett Williams, p. 1684.

LINDBERG, Stanley W.   Assistant Professor of English, Ohio University, Athens; Editor, *The Ohio Review: A Journal of the Humanities*. **Essays:** Michael Casey, p. 237; R. A. D. Ford, p. 505.

LINDNER, Carl.   Member of the Humanistic Studies Division, University of Wisconsin – Parkside, Kenosha. **Essays:** Michael Anania, p. 29; Allen Planz, p. 1197; Knute Skinner, p. 1426.

LINDSAY, Maurice.   See his entry on p. 914. **Essays:** George Bruce, p. 195; Douglas Dunn, p. 403; Padraic Fallon, p. 470; G. S. Fraser, p. 512; Hugh MacDiarmid, p. 955; Alasdair Maclean, p. 965; Edwin Morgan, p. 1077; Sydney Goodsir Smith, p. 1442.

LUCIE-SMITH, Edward.   See his entry on p. 945. **Essays:** A. Alvarez, p. 23; Basil Bunting, p. 213; John Ciardi, p. 244; Barry Cole, p. 269; Tony Connor, p. 286; Kevin Crossley-Holland, p. 327; J. V. Cunningham, p. 333; Ruth Fainlight, p. 466; Lawrence Ferlinghetti, p. 477; Roy Fisher, p. 495; Karen Gershon, p. 538; Henry Graham, p. 574; Lee Harwood, p. 654; Hamish Henderson, p. 670; Adrian Henri, p. 672; Brian Jones, p. 791; Erica Jong, p. 802; X. J. Kennedy, p. 822; Christopher Logue, p. 930; Roger McGough, p. 1021; Christopher Middleton, p. 1048; Adrian Mitchell, p. 1060; John Frederick Nims, p. 1120; Harold Norse, p. 1124; Brian Patten, p. 1171; Tom Raworth, p. 1242; Peter Redgrove, p. 1248; Alan Rook, p. 1297; Eli Siegel, p. 1395; Alan Sillitoe, p. 1399; Anne Stevenson, p. 1498; D. M. Thomas, p. 1538; Rosemary Tonks, p. 1558; William Wantling, p. 1621.

LUSCHEI, Glenna.   Associated with the Solo Press and the Cosmep Women's Committee, San Luis Obispo, California. Author of *Back into My Body: Poems*, 1974. **Essays:** Alan Brilliant, p. 173; Teo Savory, p. 1340.

MacCAIG, Norman.   See his entry on p. 953. **Essays:** Laurie Lee, p. 885; Alexander Scott, p. 1357.

MACNAB, Roy.   See his entry on p. 976. **Essays:** R. N. Currey, p. 338; Anthony Delius, p. 362; F. T. Prince, p. 1209.

MALANGA, Gerard.   Poet, Actor, and Film-Maker. Currently, Acquisitions Editor, Freeway Press, Los Angeles. His most recent books of verse are *Incantations*, 1974, and *This Is Charles Olson Speaking*, 1975. **Essay:** Sam Cornish, p. 306.

MATHIAS, Roland. See his entry on p. 996. **Essays:** Dannie Abse, p. 11; Glyn Jones, p. 796.

MATTHEWS, William. See his entry on p. 998. **Essays:** Kenneth O. Hanson, p. 633; Dennis Schmitz, p. 1349; James Scully, p. 1366.

MATTHIAS, John. Member of the English Department, University of Notre Dame, Indiana. Author of *Bucyrus* (verse), 1971. **Essay:** Gael Turnbull, p. 1572.

MAYO, E. L. See his entry on p. 1002. **Essays:** James Bertolino, p. 111; Anselm Hollo, p. 709; Robert Mezey, p. 1043; David Ray, p. 1244.

McELROY, George. Lecturer at Indiana University Northwest, Gary. Writer for the University of Chicago Home Study Department's Great Books syllabus; author of a text on drama for the University of Wisconsin's Home Study Department. Regular Contributor to *Opera News*, for 20 years. **Essays:** D. K. Das, p. 349; Pritish Nandy, p. 1102.

MELTZER, David. See his entry on p. 1033. **Essays:** Asa Benveniste, p. 92; Bill Berkson, p. 100; John Brandi, p. 162; Diane di Prima, p. 383; Lenore Kandel, p. 810; Mary Norbert Körte, p. 854; Lewis MacAdams, p. 948; Kenneth Patchen, p. 1786; George Stanley, p. 1484; Lewis Warsh, p. 1633.

MILLS, Ralph J. Jr. Professor of English, University of Illinois at Chicago Circle. Author of books on Theodore Roethke, Richard Eberhart, Edith Sitwell, and Kathleen Raine, and of *Contemporary American Poetry*, 1965, *Creation's Very Self*, 1969, and *Cry of the Human: Essays on Contemporary American Poetry*, 1975. Editor of Roethke's prose and letters. **Essays:** Stephen Berg, p. 96; James Dickey, p. 371; Richard Eberhart, p. 418; H. R. Hays, p. 658; David Ignatow, p. 759; Stanley Kunitz, p. 861; Denise Levertov, p. 900; Laurence Lieberman, p. 911; Anne Sexton, p. 1373; Karl Shapiro, p. 1387.

MOKASHI-PUNEKAR, Shankar. See his entry on p. 1065. **Essay:** P. Lal, p. 865.

MOLESWORTH, Charles. Member of the English Department, Queens College, City University of New York. **Essays:** Joseph Ceravolo, p. 241; William Dickey, p. 376; William Oxley, p. 1159; William Pillin, p. 1188; Charles Simic, p. 1402; Ann Stanford, p. 1483.

MONTAGUE, John. See his entry on p. 1069. **Essays:** John Hewitt, p. 680; Thomas Kinsella, p. 833; Carolyn Kizer, p. 841.

MORGAN, Edwin. See his entry on p. 1077. **Essays:** D. M. Black, p. 126; Ian Hamilton Finlay, p. 490; Robert Garioch, p. 530; W. S. Graham, p. 575; Dom Sylvester Houédard, p. 727; Tom Leonard, p. 892; Liz Lochhead, p. 925; W. Price Turner, p. 1574; Douglas Young, p. 1730.

MORGAN, Gerald. Editor of *Poetry Wales*, Cardiff. Editor of *This Worlds of Wales: An Anthology of Anglo-Welsh Poetry from the 17th to the 20th Centuries*, 1969. **Essay:** Raymond Garlick, p. 531.

MOSER, Norman. Free-lance Writer and Editor. Author of *Open Season* (verse), 1970, and criticism published in periodicals. Editor of *Bay Window*, later *Bay Area Arts Review*, and *Transfer*, both in San Francisco, and *Illuminations*, Santa Fe. **Essay:** Charles Bukowski, p. 207.

MUKHERJEE, Meenakshi. Member of the English Department, Fergusson College, University of Poona, India. Author of *The Twice-Born Fiction* (on the Anglo-Indian novel), 1971. Translator of Bengali poetry into English. **Essays:** Zulfikar Ghose, p. 541; Paul Jacob, p. 769; Shankar Mokashi-Punekar, p. 1065; Monika Varma, p. 1590.

MURPHY, Rosalie. Editor of the 1970 edition of *Contemporary Poets of the English Language*. **Essay:** Reed Whittemore, p. 1671.

NAGARAJAN, S. Professor and Head of the Department of English, University of Poona, India. **Essays:** Nissim Ezekiel, p. 464; Dom Moraes, p. 1075; A. K. Ramanujan, p. 1230.

NELSON, Rudy. Assistant Professor of English, State University of New York, Albany. **Essay:** Edwin Honig, p. 716.

NEWLOVE, John. See his entry on p. 1112. **Essay:** Joseph Rosenblatt, p. 1302.

NORRIS, Leslie. See his entry on p. 1122. **Essay:** Vernon Watkins, p. 1806.

NYE, Robert. See his entry on p. 1131. **Essays:** Anthony Howell, p. 733; Patrick Kavanagh, p. 1770; Maurice Lindsay, p. 914; John Moat, p. 1064; Vladimir Nabokov, p. 1099; Basil Payne, p. 1174; Martin Seymour-Smith, p. 1379; Burns Singer, p. 1799; John Updike, p. 1583; Roderick Watson, p. 1636; Sheila Wingfield, p. 1703.

OXLEY, William. See his entry on p. 1159. **Essay:** Peter Russell, p. 1324.

PARIS, Jerry. Member of the English Department, State University of New York, Albany. **Essays:** Hilary Corke, p. 301; Judson Crews, p. 326; Judson Jerome, p. 778; Lyn Lifshin, p. 912.

PARISI, Joseph. Teacher in Chicago. **Essays:** Charles Boer, p. 142; William Burford, p. 215; Louis Coxe, p. 320; Maurice English, p. 442; Josephine Jacobsen, p. 770; William H. Matchett, p. 995; Louise Townsend Nicholl, p. 1117; Frederick Seidel, p. 1370; Paul Zimmer, p. 1735; Harriet Zinnes, p. 1737.

PARKER, Derek. Editor of *The Poetry Review*, London, since 1966. Author of many books, including *The Fall of Phaethon and Other Poems*, 1954, *Byron and His World*, 1968, *Astrology?*, 1970, and *John Donne and His World*, 1975. Editor of *Selected Letters of Edith Sitwell* (with John Lehmann), 1970. **Essays:** Gavin Bantock, p. 54; Alan Bold, p. 144; Leonard Clark, p. 248; Alex Comfort, p. 281; Gregory Corso, p. 310; Ronald Duncan, p. 400; Christopher Fry, p. 515; John Lehmann, p. 890; Norman Nicholson, p. 1118; A. L. Rowse, p. 1316; John Smith, p. 1436.

PEREIRA, E. Professor of English, University of South Africa, Pretoria. Editor of the anthology *The Poet's Circle*. Author of radio broadcasts and articles in periodicals and the *Dictionary of South African Biography*. **Essay:** Adèle Naudé, p. 1107.

PETERS, Lenrie. See his entry on p. 1178. **Essays:** John Pepper Clark, p. 247; Okot p'Bitek, p. 1175.

PETERSEN, Kirsten Holst. Member of the English Department (Commonwealth literature division), University of Aarhus, Denmark. **Essays:** Roy Macnab, p. 976; Harold Stewart, p. 1502.

PLOMER, William. See his entry on p. 1198. **Essay:** John Betjeman, p. 114.

PORTER, Peter. See his entry on p. 1205. **Essays:** Martin Bell, p. 81; Edwin Brock, p. 175; George MacBeth, p. 950; Anthony Thwaite, p. 1544.

PRESS, John. Area Officer, British Council, Oxford, since 1972. Author of two volumes of verse – *Uncertainties*, 1956, and *Guy Fawkes Night*, 1959 – and several critical books, including *Rule and Energy*, 1963, *A Map of English Verse*, 1969, *The Lengthening Shadows*, 1971, and *John Betjeman*, 1974. **Essays:** J. C. Hall, p. 620; Laurence Whistler, p. 1661.

RANDALL, Dudley. See his entry on p. 1234. **Essay:** Robert Hayden, p. 656.

RANDALL, Julia.   See her entry on p. 1236. **Essay:** Howard Nemerov, p. 1110.

RAVENSCROFT, Arthur.   Senior Lecturer in English Literature, University of Leeds; Founding Editor, *Journal of Commonwealth Literature,* Leeds. Author of *Chinua Achebe,* 1969. Translator, with C. K. Johnson, *Journal of Jan Van Riebeeck,* vol. 3, 1958.

RAY, David.   See his entry on p. 1244. **Essays:** Robert Bly, p. 139; Gwendolyn Brooks, p. 180; Elliott Coleman, p. 271; Ed Dorn, p. 387; Robert Duncan, p. 397; Horace Gregory, p. 588; Archibald MacLeish, p. 967; E. L. Mayo, p. 1002; Thomas McGrath, p. 1022; Josephine Miles, p. 1050; Charles Olson, p. 1783; Kenneth Rexroth, p. 1264; Charles Reznikoff, p. 1267; Stephen Spender, p. 1471.

REID, J. C.   Professor of English, University of Auckland. Author of *The Mind and Art of Coventry Patmore,* 1957; *Francis Thompson: Man and Poet,* 1959; *Thomas Hood,* 1963; *Bucks and Bruisers: Pierce Egan and Regency England,* 1971. Died, 1972. **Essays:** M. K. Joseph, p. 804; Kendrick Smithyman, p. 1450; Charles Spear, p. 1471; Hone Tuwhare, p. 1576.

REILLY, John M.   Associate Professor of English, State University of New York at Albany. Editor of *Twentieth Century Interpretations of "Invisible Man,"* 1970, and author of essays on Dos Passos, Richard Wright, Chester Himes, and radical writers of the thirties. **Essays:** Alvin Aubert, p. 39; Langston Hughes, p. 1760; Clarence Major, p. 985; Dudley Randall, p. 1234; Al Young, p. 1726.

RICKARDS, Colin.   Press Correspondent in Latin America and the Caribbean, for 12 years; now with Caribnews, London. Author of *Caribbean Power,* 1963, and *The Man from Devil's Island,* 1968. **Essay:** Louise Bennett, p. 90.

RODDICK, Alan.   See his entry on p. 1292. **Essays:** Sam Hunt, p. 755; Kevin Ireland, p. 765.

ROGERS, J. P. W.   Member of the Department of English, King's College, University of London. Former Editor of the *Cambridge Review.* Verse and articles published in periodicals and broadcast. **Essays:** Donald Davie, p. 353; Stevie Smith, p. 1800.

ROHLEHR, Gordon.   Member of the English Department, University of the West Indies, Port of Spain, Trinidad. **Essay:** Edward Brathwaite, p. 163.

RUSS, Lawrence.   Currently on a writing fellowship at the University of Massachusetts, Amherst. Verse published in magazines and anthologies. **Essays:** Henri Coulette, p. 314; Jim Harrison, p. 641; Milton Kessler, p. 826; Lou Lipsitz, p. 918; Jack Marshall, p. 992; William Pitt Root, p. 1298; David Young, p. 1728.

RUTHERFORD, Anna.   Head of the Commonwealth Literature division of the University of Aarhus, Denmark; Editor of *Commonwealth Newsletter,* and Chairman of the European branch of the Commonwealth Literature and Language Association. Books: *Commonwealth Short Stories,* 1971; *Commonwealth,* 1972. **Essays:** Nan McDonald, p. 1012; J. R. Rowland, p. 1314; Thomas W. Shapcott, p. 1381; Colin Thiele, p. 1536.

SCHROEDER, Andreas.   See his entry on p. 1351. **Essay:** Michael Bullock, p. 210.

SCOTT, Alexander.   See his entry on p. 1357. **Essays:** George Mackay Brown, p. 185; Donald Campbell, p. 230; Alan Jackson, p. 767; Ruthven Todd, p. 1551.

SERGEANT, Howard.   See his entry on p. 1372. **Essays:** Kofi Awooner, p. 50; Taner Baybars, p. 61; Martin Booth, p. 146; Kwesi Brew, p. 170; Dennis Brutus, p. 199; Marcus Cumberlege, p. 332; John Figueroa, p. 484; Robert Gittings, p. 555; Bryn Griffiths, p. 591; Harry Guest, p. 602; Christopher Hampton, p. 630; Keith

Harrison, p. 643; Douglas Livingstone, p. 922; Charles Madge, p. 981; Gabriel Okara, p. 1140; Betty Parvin, p. 1170; W. H. Petty, p. 1183; John Pudney, p. 1217; Paul Roche, p. 1289; Margaret Willy, p. 1699.

SEYMOUR-SMITH, Martin.　See his entry on p. 1379. **Essays:** Thomas Blackburn, p. 127; John Malcolm Brinnin, p. 173; George Buchanan, p. 204; Charles Edward Eaton, p. 414; Federico Espino, p. 451; John Fairfax, p. 467; Robert Fitzgerald, p. 497; Ian Fletcher, p. 501; John Fuller, p. 519; Denis Goacher, p. 566; Giles Gordon, p. 569; Robert Graves, p. 576; Tony Harrison, p. 644; Norman Hidden, p. 682; Charles Higham, p. 684; Andrew Hoyem, p. 740; Alejandrino Hufana, p. 742; Peter Jay, p. 774; P. J. Kavanagh, p. 812; Edward Lowbury, p. 936; James J. McAuley, p. 1006; Kathleen Nott, p. 1125; Tom Pickard, p. 1184; J. H. Prynne, p. 1214; James Reeves, p. 1258; Jon Stallworthy, p. 1481; John Tagliabue, p. 1524; Nathaniel Tarn, p. 1526; Ivan White, p. 1664; Hugo Williams, p. 1690; Hubert Witheford, p. 1705.

SHAPCOTT, Thomas W.　See his entry on p. 1381. **Essays:** Bruce Dawe, p. 357; Rodney Hall, p. 621; Evan Jones, p. 795; John Manifold, p. 990; Ronald McCuaig, p. 1011; Ian Mudie, p. 1090; Craig Powell, p. 1208; Roland Robinson, p. 1286; David Rowbotham, p. 1312; R. A. Simpson, p. 1412; Vivian Smith, p. 1445; Christopher Wallace-Crabbe, p. 1616.

SHAPIRO, David.　See his entry on p. 1384. **Essay:** Frank O'Hara, p. 1778.

SHUCARD, Alan R.　Assistant Professor of English, University of Wisconsin – Parkside, Kenosha. Author of *The Gorgon Bag*, 1970, and *The Louse on the Head of the Lord*, 1972. **Essays:** Mari Evans, p. 454; Kenneth Leslie, p. 897; Stanley Moss, p. 1088.

SILKIN, Jon.　See his entry on p. 1397. **Essays:** Gene Baro, p. 60; Michael Hamburger, p. 623; Ken Smith, p. 1438.

SIMPSON, Joan Murray.　Free-lance Writer. Author of two novels, *A Bracelet of Bright Hair*, 1961, and *Picaflor and the Viceroy*, 1966. Editor of *Without Adam: The Femina Anthology of Poetry*, 1968. **Essay:** Frances Bellerby, p. 85.

SKELTON, Robin.　See his entry on p. 1423. **Essay:** John Montague, p. 1069.

SMITH, A. J. M.　See his entry on p. 1430. **Essays:** Margaret Avison, p. 49; John Glassco, p. 557; Ralph Gustafson, p. 608; Irving Layton, p. 879; Jay Macpherson, p. 978; Alden Nowlan, p. 1127; F. R. Scott, p. 1359.

SMITHYMAN, Kendrick.　See his entry on p. 1450. **Essays:** Louis Johnson, p. 783; Keith Sinclair, p. 1413; C. K. Stead, p. 1488.

SPEARS, M. K.　Libby Shearn Moody Professor of English, Rice University, Houston. Author of *The Poetry of W. H. Auden*, 1963; *Hart Crane*, 1965; *Dionysus and the City: Modernism in Twentieth Century Poetry*, 1970; *Space Against Time in Modern American Poetry*, 1972. Editor of *Auden: A Collection of Critical Essays*, 1964. **Essay:** W. H. Auden, p. 41.

SQUIRES, Radcliffe.　See his entry on p. 1476. **Essays:** Brewster Ghiselin, p. 539; Allen Tate, p. 1529.

STAFFORD, William.　See his entry on p. 1478. **Essays:** William Everson, p. 458; John Haines, p. 615; May Swenson, p. 1522.

STAUFFER, Donald Barlow.　Associate Professor of English, State University of New York, Albany. Author of several articles on Poe, and *A Short History of American Poetry*, 1974. **Essay:** Stanley Burnshaw, p. 222.

STEAD, C. K.　See his entry on p. 1488. **Essays:** Allen Curnow, p. 335; Janet

Frame, p. 508; Denis Glover, p. 561; David Mitchell, p. 1063; Alan Roddick, p. 1292.

STERN, Carol Simpson. Chairman of the English Department, Roosevelt University, Chicago. Author of a forthcoming bibliography of the criticism of Arthur Symons and a book on Symons. **Essays:** Pauline Hanson, p. 634; Susan Musgrave, p. 1097; Kenneth Pitchford, p. 1191; Stephen Sandy, p. 1332.

STEVENS, Holly. Business Manager of *The Yale Review*, New Haven, Connecticut; Director of the Connecticut Poetry Circuit. Editor of *The Letters of Wallace Stevens*, 1966. **Essay:** Mark Strand, p. 1509.

STEVENS, Joan. Professor of English, Victoria University, Wellington. Author of *The New Zealand Novel 1860–1965*, 1966, and *New Zealand Short Stories: A Survey*, 1968, as well as numerous articles on the Brontës, Thackeray, and Dickens. **Essay:** Ruth Gilbert, p. 546.

STEVENSON, Anne. See her entry on p. 1498. **Essays:** Radcliffe Squires, p. 1476; Richard Tillinghast, p. 1550; Jean Valentine, p. 1587.

STEWART, Douglas. See his entry on p. 1499. **Essays:** John Blight, p. 132; David Campbell, p. 228; Robert D. FitzGerald, p. 499.

STRAND, Mark. See his entry on p. 1509. **Essay:** Donald Justice, p. 806.

STRYK, Lucien. See his entry on p. 1512. **Essays:** Hayden Carruth, p. 233; Donald Finkel, p. 488; Jean Garrigue, p. 1758; Philip Levine, p. 906; James Schevill, p. 1343; George Starbuck, p. 1486.

SULLIVAN, Rosemary. Assistant Professor, University of Victoria, British Columbia. Author of *The Garden Master* (a study of Theodore Roethke), 1974, and articles on Roethke, Robert Lowell, and Samuel Beckett published in *Canadian Literature* and other periodicals. **Essay:** Theodore Roethke, p.

SYLVESTER, William. Professor of English and Comparative Literature, State University of New York, Buffalo. Author of *Curses, Omens, Prayers* (verse), 1974. Translator of *Agamemnon*, 1972. **Essay:** Daniel Hoffman, p. 697.

SYMONS, Julian. Free-lance Writer. Poet, novelist, and critic. Most recent books include the novels *The Players and the Game*, 1972, and *The Plot Against Roger Rider*, 1973, the critical work *Bloody Murder*, 1972, and an edition of the essays and biographies of A. J. A. Symons. **Essays:** Roy Fuller, p. 521; Thom Gunn, p. 605; Alan Ross, p. 1306; George Woodcock, p. 1709.

TATE, Allen. See his entry on p. 1529.

TAYLOR, Henry. Associate Professor of English, The American University, Washington, D.C. Author of two volumes of verse, *The Horse Show at Midnight*, 1966, and *Breakings*, 1971. **Essays:** Samuel Hazo, p. 660; Robert Watson, p. 1634.

TAYLOR, Myron. Associate Professor of English, State University of New York, Albany. Articles on Shakespeare published in *The Christian Scholar*, *SEL*, and *Shakespeare Quarterly*. **Essay:** Daniel Berrigan, p. 101.

TERRY, Arthur. Professor of Spanish, The Queen's University, Belfast. Author of *Catalan Literature*, 1973. Editor of *An Anthology of Spanish Poetry 1500–1700*, 2 vols., 1965, 1968. **Essay:** Laurence Lerner, p. 895.

THOMSON, Derick S. See his entry on p. 1541. **Essay:** Iain Crichton Smith, p. 1433.

THUMBOO, Edwin. Lecturer in English, University of Singapore; Editor of *Poetry Singapore.* Author of *Rib of Earth* (verse), 1956. Editor, *Seven Poets*, 1969. **Essay:** Wong May, p. 1706.

THWAITE, Anthony. See his entry on p. 1544. **Essays:** Kingsley Amis, p. 24; George Barker, p. 57; Patricia Beer, p. 71; Charles Causley, p. 238; Ted Hughes, p. 749; Elizabeth Jennings, p. 775; Philip Larkin, p. 872; Louis MacNeice, p. 1773; Anne Ridler, p. 1284; Vernon Scannell, p. 1341; Dylan Thomas, p. 1802.

TIBBLE, Anne. Free-lance Writer. Author of *African Literature*, 1964; *The Story of English Literature*, 1970, and books on Helen Keller, Gertrude Bell, Gordon, and John Clare. Editor, with John Tibble, of *Selected Poems* by Clare, 1974. **Essay:** Howard Sergeant, p. 1372.

TOWNS, Saundra. Lecturer in English, Bernard Baruch College, City University of New York. Articles published in *Black World*, *Black Position*, and other periodicals; currently working on a study of Chester Himes. **Essays:** Keorapetse Kgositsile, p. 828; Audre Lorde, p. 935; Raymond R. Patterson, p. 1173.

TRIPP, John. See his entry on p. 1566. **Essays:** Anthony Conran, p. 290; Gloria Evans Davies, p. 455; Peter Gruffydd, p. 599; Jeremy Hooker, p. 719; Robert Morgan, p. 1083; John Ormond, p. 1153; A. G. Prys-Jones, p. 1215; Meic Stephens, p. 1494; Harri Webb, p. 1640; Gwyn Williams, p. 1686; John Stuart Williams, p. 1691.

TRUE, Michael. Associate Professor of English, Assumption College, Worcester, Massachusetts. Author of *Worcester Poets: With Notes Toward a Literary History*, 1971, and articles published in *Commonweal*, *The Critic*, and other periodicals. **Essays:** Barbara Guest, p. 600; Ramon Guthrie, p. 610; Maxine Kumin, p. 859; John L'Heureux, p. 909; Larry Rubin, p. 1319; L. E. Sissman, p. 1415; C. K. Williams, p. 1682; Marya Zaturenska, p. 1734.

TRYPANIS, Constantine. See his entry on p. 1568. **Essay:** Richmond Lattimore, p. 875.

TURNER, Roland. Free-lance Writer. Editor of *The Grants Register* and *The Writers Directory.* **Essay:** David Harsent, p. 647.

VAN DOMELEN, John. Member of the English Department, University of Northern Iowa, Cedar Falls. **Essay:** John Heath-Stubbs, p. 663.

VAN DOREN, Mark. Poet, Novelist, Critic, and Editor. His *Collected and New Poems* was published in 1963; *Collected Stories*, 3 vols., 1962–68; *Autobiography*, 1958. Died, 1972. **Essay:** Babette Deutsch, p. 368.

VAN SICKLE, Milton. Associate Editor, *Trace*, Hollywood, California. **Essay:** Gil Orlovitz, p. 1151.

VINSON, James. Editor of the Contemporary Writers of the English Language series. **Essays:** Mona Van Duyn, p. 1588; Anne Waldman, p. 1612.

WAKOSKI, Diane. See her entry on p. 1607. **Essays:** Clayton Eshleman, p. 449; Joel Oppenheimer, p. 1149; Carl Rakosi, p. 1229; Jerome Rothenberg, p. 1309; Armand Schwerner, p. 1355; Peter Wild, p. 1679.

WALSH, William. Head of the Department of Education, University of Leeds, Yorkshire. Author of *Use of Imagination*, 1958, *A Human Idiom*, 1964, *A Manifold Voice*, 1970, and books on Coleridge, R. K. Narayan, V. S. Naipaul, and D. J. Enright. **Essays:** D. J. Enright, p. 444; A. L. Hendriks, p. 671; Geoffrey Hill, p. 686; George Johnston, p. 787; Christopher Okigbo, p. 1781; Frederic Prokosch, p. 1211.

WARSH, Lewis. See his entry on p. 1633. **Essays:** Ted Berrigan, p. 104; Tom Clark, p. 251; Ed Sanders, p. 1330; Philip Whalen, p. 1655; John Wieners, p. 1673.

WHITEHEAD, James. See his entry on p. 1668. **Essay:** Miller Williams, p. 1698.

WILLIAMS, John Stuart. See his entry on p. 1691. **Essay:** Roland Mathias, p. 996.

WILSON, Joseph. Lecturer in Creative Writing, Anna Maria College, Paxton, Massachusetts. Verse published in little magazines. **Essays:** John Beecher, p. 68; Michael Dennis Browne, p. 188; Paul Engle, p. 439; Anthony Hecht, p. 666; Joseph Langland, p. 870; Ned O'Gorman, p. 1135; Raymond Roseliep, p. 1299; John Hall Wheelock, p. 1657.

WOODCOCK, George. See his entry on p. 1709. **Essays:** Earle Birney, p. 118; Roy Daniells, p. 347; P. K. Page, p. 1166; A. W. Purdy, p. 1223; Andreas Schroeder, p. 1351; Robin Skelton, p. 1423; A. J. M. Smith, p. 1430; Peter Stevens, p. 1496; Phyllis Webb, p. 1641.

WRIGHT, Judith. See her entry on p. 1720. **Essays:** William Hart-Smith, p. 651; James McAuley, p. 1004.

YABES, Leopoldo Y. Professor of English and Dean of the Graduate School, University of the Philippines, Quezon City; Editor of *Philippine Social Sciences and Humanities Review* since 1963. Author of many books, including *Philippine Literature in English 1898–1957*, 1958; *The Filipino Struggle for Intellectual Freedom and Other Essays on Philippine Life and Thought*, 1959; *In Larger Freedom*, 1961. **Essay:** José Garcia Villa, p. 1597.